MAJOR BRITISH POETS
OF THE
ROMANTIC PERIOD

MAJOR BRITISH
POETS
OF THE
ROMANTIC PERIOD

EDITED BY

William Heath

AMHERST COLLEGE

Macmillan Publishing Co., Inc.

NEW YORK

MACMILLAN PUBLISHING CO., INC.
866 Third Avenue, New York, New York 10022

COLLIER-MACMILLAN CANADA, LTD., Toronto, Ontario

Library of Congress catalog card number: 71–165242

Printing: 5 6 7 8 9   Year: 3 4 5 6 7

ISBN 0-02-352900-8

ACKNOWLEDGMENTS

The editor makes grateful acknowledgment to the publishers and editors for permission to reprint the following selections:

POEMS:

From *Poetical Sketches*; *Songs of Innocence*; *The Book of Thel*; *The French Revolution*; *The Marriage of Heaven and Hell*; From Blake's *Notebook*; *Visions of the Daughters of Albion*; *America a Prophecy*; *Songs of Experience*; *The* [First] *Book of Urizen*; From *The Four Zoas: Vala night the Ninth Being the Last Judgment*; From the Pickering Manuscript and the *Notebook*; *Milton a Poem in 2 books*; From *Jerusalem*. Prose: *An Island in the Moon*; Letters; *Annotations to Wordsworth's Poems*. All from *The Poetry and Prose of William Blake* by David V. Erdman, commentary by Harold Bloom. Copyright © 1965 by David V. Erdman and Harold Bloom. Reprinted by permission of Doubleday & Company, Inc.

"Home at Grasmere," from *Poetical Works of William Wordsworth*, edited by E. de Selincourt and Helen Darbishire. Copyright 1949 by Clarendon Press, Oxford. Reprinted by permission of the Clarendon Press, Oxford.

"The Ruined Cottage" from *The Music of Humanity* by Jonathan Wordsworth. Copyright © 1969 by Jonathan Wordsworth. Reprinted by permission of Harper & Row, Publishers, Inc., and A. D. Peters & Co., London.

S. T. Coleridge, "A Letter to ———" transcribed from the original in the Dove Cottage Library with permission of the Trustees of Dove Cottage, and previously printed in George Whalley *Coleridge and Sara Hutchinson and the Asra Poems* (London: Routledge & Kegan Paul; Toronto: University of Toronto Press, 1955), © George Whalley.

"Notes" from *The Notebooks of Samuel Taylor Coleridge*, edited by Kathleen Coburn, Bollingen Series L, volume I, Text: 1794–1804. Copyright © 1957 by Princeton University Press. Reprinted by permission of Princeton University Press.

"I will kneel at thine altar . . ."; "The Monarch's Funeral"; "To the Republicans of North America"; "To Harriet on Her Birthday, August 1, 1812"; "On Launching Some Bottles Filled with Knowledge into the Bristol Channel"; "To Harriet" ["Harriet, thy kiss . . ."] From *The Esdaile Notebook*, by Percy Bysshe Shelley, edited by Kenneth Neil Cameron. Copyright © 1964 by The Carl and Lily Pforzheimer Foundation, Inc. Reprinted by permission of Alfred A. Knopf, Inc.

"The Triumph of Life" from *Shelley's "The Triumph of Life,"* by Donald H. Reiman. Copyright © 1965 by the University of Illinois Press. Reprinted by permission of The University of Illinois Press.

John Keats, "'Tis the witching time . . ." and "Why did I laugh tonight? . . ." Reprinted by permission of the publishers from Hyder Edward Rollins, ed., *The Letters of John Keats, 1814–1821*. Cambridge, Mass.: Harvard University Press, Copyright, 1958, by the President and Fellows of Harvard College.

KEATS'S LETTERS:

To B. R. Haydon, 10, 11, May 1817; To Benjamin Bailey, 8 October 1817; To Benjamin Bailey, 22 November 1817; To George and Tom Keats, 22 December 1817; To J. H. Reynolds, 3 May 1818; To Benjamin Bailey, 18, 22 July 1818; To Richard Woodhouse, 27 October 1818; To George and Georgiana Keats, 14, 16, 21, 24, 31 October 1818; To George and Georgiana Keats, 14, 19 February, 3 (?), 12, 13, 17, 19 March, 15, 16, 21, 30 April, 3 May 1819; To J. H. Reynolds, 21 September 1819; To George and Georgiana Keats, 17, 18, 20, 21, 24, 25, 27 September 1819; To Fanny Brawne, 19 October 1819; To Fanny Brawne [#1], March (?) 1820; To Fanny Brawne [#2], March (?) 1820; To Fanny Brawne, 5 July (?) 1820; To Fanny Brawne, August (?) 1820; To Percy Bysshe Shelley, 16 August 1820; To Charles Brown, 30 November 1820. Reprinted by permission of the publishers from Hyder Edward Rollins, ed., *The Letters of John Keats, 1814–1821*. Cambridge, Mass.: Harvard University Press, Copyright, 1958, by the President and Fellows of Harvard College.

To George and Georgiana Keats, 17, 18, 20, 21, 24, 25, 27 September 1819. Reprinted by permission of The Pierpont Morgan Library.

To Fanny Brawne [#2], March (?) 1820. Reprinted by permission of Princeton University Press.

To Fanny Brawne, August (?) 1820, in Henry W. and Albert A. Berg Collection, The New York Public Library, Astor, Lenox and Tilden Foundations. Reprinted by permission of the New York Public Library.

PREFACE

THIS anthology tries to bring forward and illuminate the life, the reality, of the literature presented in it, and its success must be measured in terms of the extent to which the works it contains cease to be preserved moments of the past and become living events for the reader. The individual works of the six major British poets of the early nineteenth century are presented in the context of their origin in the imagination of each author rather than in their place in a historical system or thematic pattern. At times this policy has caused a violation of conventional notions of literary quality. For instance, a large number of Keats's early poems have been included because in their naive elaborateness they seem to offer a way to comprehend some of the energy of the prodigious imagination that later invested the odes or *The Fall of Hyperion*.

I have tried to construct an anthology in which the poets are allowed to speak without much interference. Apart from a brief account of each writer's career, his work is subjected only to such editorial interruption as seems necessary to make the sense of a poem clear. An editor can make an informed guess as to what the majority of readers generally will not know, but he cannot predict what any single reader will want to know to advance his understanding, partly because the relationship between information and understanding in the reading of poetry is so tenuous.

The introductions, headnotes, and to some extent the bibliographies and outlines of events represent one reader's guesses, compromises, and prejudices. The work of each of the six poets is presented as fully as possible within the limits set by the optimum size of this volume, with an attempt to indicate—sometimes at the cost of omitting conventionally important works—the range of a writer's interests and the complex modes of his imagination.

Some prose selections are included for each writer to illustrate ways by which the contexts of his poems can be enlarged. There are letters on literary subjects or the composition of poems by Blake, Wordsworth, Coleridge, Byron, and Keats; Coleridge and Byron are represented by notebook and journal entries where their imaginations can be seen composing the world for themselves (ostensibly) rather than for other readers; and there are major (and still influential) essays in literary criticism by Wordsworth, Coleridge, and Shelley. Keats's letters, because they are an astonishing record of the growth of a literary imagination, are represented extensively; and Blake's *An Island in the Moon*, his unfinished early prose satire, is reprinted because it offers particular insight into his use of wit rather than vision as another way of organizing his world. Of the six writers, only Coleridge suffers in being seen mainly as a writer of verse. This anthology could not begin to give adequate examples of his work as a critic of the drama, political theorist, philosopher, or journalist.

A NOTE ON THE SELECTION OF POEMS AND TEXTS

As in most editions designed for the general reader, this anthology reprints when possible the text of a poem that apparently received its author's final approval—usually the final version of a poem printed during the author's lifetime, or the edition that had his most careful supervision. (The many exceptions to this principle—posthumously published poems, for instance—are noted later in the discussion of selections from individual poets and in headnotes to individual poems.) As a consequence of this policy, neither the date of composition, appearing on the left after each poem, nor the date of first publication, appearing on the right, may coincide exactly with the particular text of the poem as printed here.

Although obvious printing errors in early editions of the poems have been corrected and seriously misleading forms have been emended, in most of the selections the author's original spelling and punctuation are retained. Arguments can be made for the appropriateness of a modernized text for a modern reader, but an editor then runs the risk of altering the rhythm, sense, or pronunciation of a poetic line by imposing his own standards of technical consistency upon it. Some early nineteenth-century spellings may appear odd ("gulph" for "gulf"), and few poets or their editors at the time bothered to be as consistent as our contemporaries in matters of spelling or grammar. However, the discrepancies are rarely frequent or flagrant enough to distract a reader, and the visual difference may usefully remind us—as it does with older poets—that, however congenial in spirit, these artists are not historically our contemporaries.

Clarity rather than consistency is the principle used in assigning titles: when a poet's own title is clear, or when an early editor's title is traditional, it is used; elsewhere first lines or opening words are used.

Editorial explanatory footnotes are numbered consecutively within a work and are separated from the rest of the text column by a decorative rule. Coleridge, Wordsworth, Byron, and Shelley all annotated their own poems, sometimes heavily, and their own notes are not separated from the poem texts by a rule. They are marked throughout by the traditional reference marks commonly used in the nineteenth century, asterisks, daggers, etc.

BLAKE. For the reasons given in the introduction to Blake, he is particularly difficult to represent in any anthology. Most of Blake's major works were "published" by him in the form of engravings, on which the text was written out by Blake in his own characteristic handwriting, intermingled with illustrations. The pages printed from these plates were then usually hand colored ("illuminated") by Blake himself. A text of these engraved poems that is not also a facsimile of their printed and illuminated pages is a compromise that translates a unique visual and verbal art form into a literary one. The works reprinted here in their verbal entirety are still nevertheless incomplete, as they are in all type-set editions, to the extent that in perfect estate they depend on more than words.

Blake's engraved works were not "published" in the usual sense. When he had a purchaser, he printed and colored for him a unique version, sometimes changing the text of poems or their order, and coloring the illustrations more or less elaborately as whim and price suggested. A full text for any one of the engraved poems, then, would include an account of all its known variations. The alternative, adopted here, is to supply an edited version that attempts to distill from all the texts an extrapolated version that probably corresponds to no one original printed copy. The date on the right following a poem indicates the point after which few important alterations were made, and it may not coincide with the date of publication in the conventional sense.

The texts in this selection of Blake's works follow those established by David B. Erdman in *The Poetry and Prose of William Blake* (New York, 1965). As Erdman points out in the introduction to his edition, Blake's process of engraving the plates himself for his poems meant that he alone of all poets had absolute and individual control over their form from conception to finished book. Yet, as Erdman says, no poet suffered more than he from nineteenth-century editors who insisted on clarifying, finishing, or improving his text. Erdman's texts, reprinted here, are an attempt to carry as faithfully as possible into conventional typography what appears etched on Blake's plates or written in his manuscripts. However difficult Blake's punctuation (or lack of it) may be to a modern reader used to having his eye and mind guided more directly and consistently, it seems undeniable that Blake wanted at least his engraved poems to be seen in this less familar way. The manuscript selections—the poems from the *Notebooks*, the last book of *The Four Zoas*, and *An Island in the Moon*—are all works-in-progress that Blake never brought to their intended final form, and they are so unfinished that heavy editing would have meant the extensive imposition of form (and thus meaning). This task has been left to the reader. It should be noted that the dates of composition of many of the manuscript poems are uncertain.

Of Blake's engraved prophetic works, the shorter ones are printed complete, but this was not practicable for *Jerusalem*, which is represented by its first chapter, rather than by a sample of its varying moments, in order to provide an introduction to the whole work rather than an implied substitute for it.

WORDSWORTH. The order used in reprinting Wordsworth's poems is usually chronological, in order of composition, but the text used is most frequently that which seems to have received Wordsworth's final approval—generally the six-volume Moxon edition of 1849–50 (the source for most modern editions, including the standard one edited by Ernest de Selincourt and Helen Darbishire in 1940–49 and revised in 1952–54). As de Selincourt has pointed out, Wordsworth was an unusually scrupulous editor, supervising the printings of his poems even in his seventies, a half-century after he had written many of them. The readings of the 1849–50 edition, then (except for misprints here corrected), can be assumed to have Wordsworth's final approval. This anthology, however, does *not* retain the thematic arrangement that Wordsworth himself gave to the collected editions of his poems and that is preserved by the de Selincourt edition.

Although an argument could be made for printing earlier versions and first editions in an anthology arranged chronologically, it would seem that to know which *poem* Wordsworth wrote first is information of general interset, but to know which *word* he used first is a matter for more specialized scholarship and does not justify reprinting an unfamiliar text. Moreover, unlike Byron, Shelley, and Keats, Wordsworth lived to oversee the repeated publication of his major poems over four and even five decades, and had much greater opportunity than they—who died young—to make several printed revisions.

Nevertheless, a few major exceptions to these principles have been made:

1. Wordsworth's contributions to the 1798 *Lyrical Ballads* are here presented as a unit, following the order and incorporating the text used in the first edition of that volume. The historical importance of this edition seems to justify its separation from similar poems composed at the same time but published in later editions. Indeed, a case could be made for the unity of *Lyrical Ballads* as a single work rather than an anthology of poems. Editorial notes and dates of composition have of course been added to the poems, and Coleridge's contributions to the volume have been omitted (they are all printed in the section on Coleridge).

2. "Ode: Intimations of Immortality" appears in this anthology among the poems of 1802 (rather than 1804 when it was probably completed) because its first four stanzas, which do date from the spring of 1802, have significant affinities with the other poems composed that spring.

3. Wordsworth's long poem on his own life, posthumously entitled *The Prelude*, exists in two distinct and relatively finished versions: one is the text finished by 1805, in thirteen books, "Addressed to S. T. Coleridge"; a second version in fourteen books, revised as of 1839 and set aside for publication after Wordsworth's death, is reprinted here. Although it has been argued that the 1805 text is livelier, less abstract, less conventionalized in literary form and religious doctrine, the later text is adopted here because it does represent the poet's subsequent reflections, and because the 1805 text is easily available in separate and parallel-text editions, where the question of comparative literary merit can be more easily explored.

4. Some liberty has been taken in ordering sonnets, so as to bring them together whenever chronology is not too flagrantly disregarded by doing so. Similarly, the three poems on the death of John Wordsworth appear together.

5. The text of *The Ruined Cottage* reprinted here is that recently edited by Jonathan Wordsworth from a manuscript that represents the poem as of about 1798, well before Wordsworth expanded and adapted it to be Book I of *The Excursion*. Similarly, *Home at Grasmere*, though not published in Wordsworth's lifetime in the form it has here, contains passages of exceptional literary and biographical interest. Both works in a sense are edited fragments rather than finished poems, and no attempt has been made to indicate cancellations or alternate readings that appear in the manuscripts.

COLERIDGE. Because the total amount of finished poetry Coleridge left is comparatively small, and because he wrote no long poem of the dimension of *Endymion* or *Don Juan* or *The Prelude*, choosing the important poems for an anthology of selected works is relatively easy. Editorial taste accounts for most omissions from among the minor pieces. The texts for the poems published by Coleridge himself, as in E. H. Coleridge's standard two-volume edition (1912), are those of the last edition published in the poet's lifetime, the 1834 Pickering edition. The original letter version of *Dejection* is that edited by George Whalley (1955) from the Dove Cottage manuscript, but the few other posthumously printed poems follow the texts given in the E. H. Coleridge edition.

BYRON. Variety as well as quality has been a particularly important consideration in selecting many of Byron's shorter poems, and some very early ones are included to illustrate Byron's shifting attitude toward himself as a poet as well as to indicate the range of his interests. The rarely reprinted satire on bluestockings called *The Blues* is, like *English Bards and Scotch Reviewers*, an amusing view of the cultural and social world toward which Byron expressed such ambivalent feelings. The values and limitations of *Childe Harold* are most fully seen in Canto III of that poem; and from Byron's greatest literary achievement, *Don Juan*, the first two cantos and the final (London) cantos are reprinted in full. Except for these two works, all poems are reprinted in full, and the cantos selected from these two poems are complete within themselves..

Texts of most of the poems are those appearing in the six-volume 1831 edition of *The Works of Lord Byron* published by Murray (the source as well of E. H. Coleridge's seven-volume edition of 1898–1904). Coleridge's edition, where possible, used texts supervised by Byron, or edited by Gifford, but gave the poems (except for those from *The Hours of Idleness*) uniform typography. This edition also published for the first time Canto XVII of *Don Juan* and first reproduced (posthumously) many of Byron's notes. Corrections to the text incorporated by E. H. Coleridge or noted by subsequent editors have been adopted without comment.

Don Juan has been treated somewhat differently. No consistent edition of the whole poem appeared in Byron's lifetime (three publishers were involved), and Byron's supervision (from Italy and Greece) cannot have been thorough. The text used here is based on the first editions, with their inconsistent typography and punctuation. (It is the basic text, too, of the variorum edition edited in 1957 by T. G. Steffan and W. W. Pratt.) However, obvious errors have been corrected, expurgated lines have been restored, the suppressed verse Dedication (first printed by Murray in 1833) and the unfinished Canto XVII (first published by Coleridge in 1903) are added in their respective places, and the unfinished prose preface (first published in 1901 in the Murray edition of Byron's prose edited by Prothero) is included in its manuscript, rather than its edited, form.

SHELLEY. Except for the passages from the rarely anthologized *Revolt of Islam*, all Shelley's poems here are complete. Some of the earliest poems appear in their fuller versions discovered in the *Esdaile Notebook* (published 1964), but most poems read as printed in the editions that appeared during Shelley's lifetime or in Mary Shelley's posthumous editions (1824, 1839) of her husband's work. As in Hutchinson's edition (1905), Shelley's punctuation is rarely emended, his capitals are retained (though sometimes regularized), and his spelling is made slightly more consistent when its erratic nature would be distracting. Errors in earlier editions of *Prometheus Unbound* pointed out by L. J. Zillman in his variorum text (1968) are here corrected. *The Triumph of Life*, left in very fragmentary state at Shelley's death, is given here in the manuscript version recently edited by D. H. Reiman (1965) rather than in the more "finished" and perhaps more familiar but less authentic version edited by Mrs. Shelley.

KEATS. The chronological order of these poems is that defined in C. L. Finney's *The Evolution of Keats's Poetry* (1936), but modified by later studies, such as W. J. Bate's *John Keats* (1963) and Miriam Allott's edition in the Longman Annotated Poets series (1970). The greatest omission from this selection is the last three books of *Endymion*. Some of Keats's early work, and much that is labeled "Trivia" by Garrod in his standard edition (1939, revised 1958), is included as evidence of the development of Keats's interests and the range of his wit.

For poems published in Keats's lifetime (in *Poems* in 1817, *Endymion* in 1818, and the *Lamia* volume in 1820), the first printed text is followed (with obvious corrections);for works first published posthumously in Milnes' *Literary Remains* (1848) or elsewhere, the readings of the most authoritative manuscripts have been re-reviewed, particularly for the poems written out by Keats in his letters, and their best readings adopted in the text. The text of *The Fall of Hyperion* is, of course, that of Woodhouse's transcript, there being neither an early printed version nor a surviving manuscript in Keats's own hand.

To achieve helpful as well as accurate physical presentation of the work of our poets, a special effort has been made in this anthology to print the poems of Coleridge, Wordsworth, Byron, and Shelley as the poets themselves set them out, with their own complete rubrics of dedications, introductions, advertisements, headnotes, epigraphs, arguments, and footnotes, and also with clear typographical distinction between such authorial apparatus and purely editorial comment. Keats's work, virtually devoid of apparatus, has presented no problem on this score. As already mentioned, Blake's is a different kind of problem, unique to itself.

Similarly, the page and column divisions in this book have been governed by respect for the structures of the poems themselves. It is no easy matter, on a page or column of necessarily fixed length, to maintain the integrity of a couplet, to avoid the breaking of a short stanza, or to achieve the breaking of long stanzas only in metrically sensible places. I call attention to the successful meeting of these and other vexing problems of page make-up not only because I believe the reader and the poets to be well served by the results in ease of understanding and in appearance of the poems but also to acknowledge with thanks the careful and innovative design work of Mr. Charles Farrell at Macmillan. He and my editors Mr. D. Anthony English and Miss Frances Long have collaborated to achieve an end that I hope will please others as it does me. We believe the poets, too, would appreciate fidelity to their styling.

The dates after each selection indicate, at the left, the approximate date or dates of composition and, at the right, the date of first publication, either in periodical or book form. A short general bibliography of recent works on more than one of the six writers, or on their period, appears at the end of the selections, immediately preceding the Index.

W. H.

CONTENTS

[xi]

WILLIAM WORDSWORTH
1770–1850

GEORGE GORDON, LORD BYRON
1788–1824

PERCY BYSSHE SHELLEY
1792–1822

CONTENTS [xix

INTRODUCTION

THE literature of any age can perform any number of functions. It can be a translucent medium through which we look at a part of the past, or it can be an opaque reflector by which we see ourselves. "The eye," says Brutus to Cassius in *Julius Caesar*, "sees not itself / But by reflection, by some other things." To call our own age as "revolutionary" as that period between 1780 and 1830 would require tedious, and not very satisfactory, definitions. What most matters is not the label, but whether an individual reader can see in the world of those writers—their concerns, their joys, fears, and excitements—anything that illuminates his own life and gives meaning to the span of time that separates him from them.

Certainly the six writers whose work appears in this volume saw themselves as living in an age of great and almost incomprehensible change. The French Revolution has subsequently been called the most significant event in Western history, and these writers—even at the time—would probably have agreed. "Bliss was it in that dawn to be alive, / But to be young was very Heaven!" wrote Wordsworth long after he had abandoned the hopes that sustained the bliss. And none of these writers, however much many of them regretted the decline of this extraordinary energy into factionalism and Napoleonic adventurism, ever denied his early enthusiasm. Almost anything seemed possible, as Wordsworth and Coleridge in 1798 set out in *Lyrical Ballads* to define literary standards based on the authentic speech of the freeborn man (a poet, they insisted, is a man speaking to men), rather than on the inherited consensus of the ages. Blake, whose first major prophecy called *The French Revolution* was never engraved in his lifetime, chose a more distant but equally symbolic revolution for *America* (1793). The shock of change was constantly before these writers, and they saw literature in part as a means for understanding, tapping, and finally shaping the energy released by the shock. Their unsympathetic critics, understandably, saw both in change and its literary proponents a serious threat to the world from which security and dependable expectation seemed to come. Marshall McLuhan has argued (in *The Gutenberg Galaxy* and *Understanding Media*) that poets and other artists first imaginatively project those changes in human consciousness which are only later articulated in abstract theory. Before the middle of the nineteenth century, in the virtual absence of social science (i.e., sociology, psychology, contemporary political theory), it was the task of poets and philosophers both to project and to record the changing consciousness and its vision of the world. Indeed, to Shelley, poets were the unacknowledged legislators of the world.

Much of the effort of these writers was, in fact, directed toward reconciling their sense of what the world might become if the energy of human potential were realized according to their hopes and visions, with the awareness that the meaning and value of this energy seemed to be changing in the unpredictable events taking place from moment to moment. Blake and Shelley, for instance, imagined patterns of consciousness and behavior drastically different from any of those by which men lived in a fallen world. Byron's Don Juan, on the other hand, is the protean figure who collects experience, not meaning; who seeks repetition rather than continuity. The absurd man, says Camus, in *The Myth of Sisyphus*, multiplies what he cannot unify. What Northrup Frye says of Blake and Wordsworth applies to some extent to the other four writers as well: they sought "the imaginative rediscovery of the immediate," and the "immediate" was a context that seemed to change from moment to moment. As Wordsworth warned in the Preface to *Lyrical Ballads*, the assault of novelty on one's consciousness posed a threat from which the responsible writer ought to try to protect him. Danger was in the pressure of urban living, and the acceleration of words:

> For a multitude of causes, unknown to former times, are now acting with a combined force to blunt the discriminating powers of the mind, and, unfitting it for all voluntary exertion, to reduce it to a state of almost savage torpor. The most effective of these causes are the great national events which are daily taking place, and the increasing accumulation of men in cities, where the uniformity of their occupations produces a craving for extraordinary incident, which the rapid communication of intelligence hourly gratifies.

Against the dangers of alienation and fragmentation of man and his consciousness stands the poet who "looks before and after":

> He is the rock of defence for human nature; an upholder and preserver, carrying everywhere with him relationship and love. In spite of difference of soil and climate, of language and manners, of laws and customs; in spite of things silently gone out of mind, and things violently destroyed; the poet binds together by passion and knowledge the vast empire of human society, as it is spread over the whole earth, and over all time.

As the literacy rate began to increase significantly for the first time since the reign of Elizabeth, more and more readers would find in print sources both of intellectual stimulation and of escape from thought. Nonconformist clergymen, for instance, were delighted that their congregations could increasingly do the individual biblical interpretation which was a main article of their faith, but they were equally suspicious of the other subjects to which a newly literate imagination could be lured: sexual license, political protest. Official or informal censorship of writers for political and moral ends became an important issue. Writers and their works were dangerous, and men were held strictly accountable for what they said: one of Keats's earliest poems was called "Written on the Day that Mr. Leigh Hunt Left Prison"; Shelley was expelled from Oxford for publishing and especially for publicizing *The Necessity of Atheism*; Blake was tried for sedition; Coleridge and Wordsworth were followed about the hills and valleys of Somerset by an incompetent informer who thought their conversations about Spinoza were derogatory references to him as the Spy Nosy; and Byron was kept out of England, if not driven out, by sexual scandal and gossip; but his words, and much of the money they brought him, went to the support of revolutionary and liberation movements in Italy and Greece that posed no threat to the British government. At no earlier time did a writer's language have this sort of unpredictable impact: raising questions about the role of art in education and society, about free speech itself—questions that have hardly been answered satisfactorily since.

MANY attempts have been made to define romanticism in England as something more than an arbitrary assemblage of works produced by writers within a chronological period. Most of these attempts become lamps at least as revealing about their own interior formulation as about the writers they were intended to illuminate. Writers are not often able, or willing, to see themselves as part of the "movement" to which subsequent historians have assigned them, nor are many historians content with the assignments and labels set out by their predecessors. "Romantic" is a label as good or as faulty as the functions the user puts it to. Here, and in the title of this anthology, it usually refers rather arbitrarily to those writers—now seen as prominent—who did the greater part of their major work between the time of the French Revolution (the Bastille fell in 1789) and the first Reform Bill (1832), which began the enlargement of the electorate in England to dimensions that could for the first time be called democratic. The period coincided with astonishing inventions in science and technology, discoveries in geography, developments in economic organization and influence, innovation in political theory and practice. But in the most general terms it was an age in which prominent writers were particularly conscious of their individual power of vision and imagination, of their (sometimes collective) wish to see these visions and perceptions broadcast throughout the land, but of their failure individually and collectively to gain the role and influence in society they thought they ought to have. A writer's confidence, as poet and often as politician and revolutionary, came from his willingness to think radically about Man, Society, and their relations to Nature and the larger environment. "Heroic" was a word that was and is used frequently, if at times desperately, for Keats's courage as he died, Wellington's performance at Waterloo (1815), and Nelson's at Trafalgar (1805). Byron's *Don Juan* begins with a plea for a real hero in an age that has produced so many counterfeit ones, and the poem itself asks of its characters (and its reader) heroism in behavior not words, a willingness to live without the name.

Occasions for hope, despair, and hope renewed occurred as frequently in public political and journalistic terms as they did in literary ones. Optimism for revolution gave way to despair at the terror; the enthusiasm for Napoleon led to disgust at his aggressions, then jubilation at his defeat. But victories like Waterloo were temporary and their effect often illusory. The defeat of Napoleon did not enable a new freedom for France, and for the economically oppressed English workingman it brought an even harsher lot than he had suffered during the war years. But if the "Peterloo" massacre (in 1819), in which a troop of mounted yeomanry in Manchester brutally ran down a crowd of protesting weavers, could be the source of satiric commentary on Waterloo, it was by such events that the working class, under duress, could found its consciousness of its mission, needs, and duties. Only politicians, not writers, could hope to remain tied to explicit and consistent policies and loyalties during such transformational events and moods.

UNQUESTIONABLY the world within which these poets wrote was about to become far less green and pleasant. Blake's "dark Satanic mills" were not based on an industrial reality he observed, but they soon could be. The great nature painters, like the poets, depended upon open canvasses, open landscapes, whether in Wordsworth's Grasmere or Constable's Flatford. The moment of vision for the early Wordsworth and Constable alike, took place at a definable position in the dimensions of space as well as of time. They attempted to see, unlimited by preconceptions based on literary or artistic conventions, what was before them. The interrelation of the self and the environment at such a moment was a visionary experience, to be related as directly as possible. External reality, for both, had a positive value, and could be used to enhance the life of its perceiver. The "efficacious spirit," says Wordsworth in *The Prelude*, that elevates our lives is found

> Among those passages of life that give
> Profoundest knowledge to what point, and how,
> The mind is lord and master—outward sense
> The obedient servant of her will. . . .

And one result is insight into a new world of contending realities,

> as ruled by those fixed laws
> Whence spiritual dignity originates,
> Which do both give it being and maintain
> A balance, an ennobling interchange
> Of action from without and from within;
> The excellence, pure function, and best power
> Both of the object seen, and eye that sees.

But everything seemed to conspire against such moments of vision and accommodation. Even the visual landscape itself was changing, in town and country, in ways that alienated men from their natural environment and from one another, and made such acts of artistic vision more difficult and yet perhaps more necessary. The Enclosure Acts, beginning in the eighteenth century, fractured the countryside by hedgerows and low walls, and cut men off from the land they had previously held and used in common. Cities, increasingly the centers of industrial activity, were soon to be linked and sooted by railroads. Constable once said, "I never saw an ugly thing in my life." Yet even to Wordsworth in 1802 the freak shows at London's Bartholomew Fair (described in *The Prelude*) are the "true epitome / Of what the mighty City is herself," a place where people live

> melted and reduced
> To one identity, by differences
> That have no law, no meaning, and no end—

With the advantage of hindsight modern critics and historians can begin to see in the early nineteenth century that estrangement between art and industry, man and environment, which led to the ugliness that D. H. Lawrence found most characteristic of England in the reign of Victoria:

It was ugliness which betrayed the spirit of man, in the nineteenth century. The great crime which the moneyed classes and promoters of industry committed in the palmy Victorian days was the condemning of the workers to ugliness, ugliness, ugliness: meanness and formless and ugly surroundings, ugly ideals, ugly religion, ugly hope, ugly love, ugly clothes, ugly furniture, ugly houses, ugly relationship between workers and employers. The human soul needs actual beauty even more than bread.

The elegance of Regency style in dress, furnishing, architecture—even in manners —was illusory. Its superficiality was less often noted by the poets than it ought to have been. Blake and (in his satires) Byron, who had little else in common, were almost alone among major poets in responding forcefully to the paradoxes and hypocrisies of the world, fulfilling partially the critical responsibility that Matthew Arnold later in the century assigned to all literary men. It is not surprising that Arnold's misgivings about the poets of the first half of his century were based on what he saw as their lack of general knowledge and their ineffectuality. It is perhaps unfair but certainly understandable to take the romantics to task for their failure to find a language of social and political criticism adequate to their theoretical radicalism. The Shelley of "The Sensitive Plant," the Byron of *The Giaour*, the Keats of *Endymion*, seemed to have as little to say explicitly on the subject of how man ought to live as did the most fantastic of the Gothic novelists, like Monk Lewis, or painters, like John Martin. The "visionary" landscape could be a transformation of a present scene, as in Constable or Turner, or it could be an entire replacement, as in the work of Martin, of Fuseli, or of Samuel Palmer. For these poets and painters, as for many of their successors, truth had become a fugitive and individual thing, to which the world of fact and industry was not often hospitable.

Although lines can be drawn and analogies made between these six British poets and the larger philosophical movement called European romanticism, such connections often seem arbitrary. Coleridge, to be sure, was an active student of modern European as well as ancient philosophy, and many of his ideas reached Wordsworth through their collaboration, but few of them at that time went further as abstractions. Other poets read foreign literary and philosophical works, but even though they met one another occasionally, and several actually collaborated, there seems to have been no attempt on the part of British poets to found a school or movement on the European model. Shelley and Byron, for instance, collaborated frequently in Italy, but the common concern was more likely to be political journalism (editing the *Liberal*) than philosophy. Mary Shelley wrote *Frankenstein*, indeed, as part of a contest in which both her husband and Byron were involved, but the event was more a parlor game than an instance of shared literary ambitions and assumptions. Keats seems seldom to have found literary conversation or advice as helpful as reflection on his own life, and Blake's letters show the unlikelihood of any other writer's intervening in his imagination.

Because these six writers so clearly wrote as individuals, and because each in different ways enacted the growing separation between the writer, his audience, and the sources of national power, it is difficult to specify their effect. It is easy to say that since Wordsworth, man has looked at his natural environment with new expectations, or that Wordsworth and Blake (with their successors) gave the child a significance as bearer of truth and destructible spirit that he might not otherwise have had. Since the extraordinary early deaths of Keats and Shelley, the artist and his career are perhaps seen as somehow more tenuous and fated. Undoubtedly the most popular figure at the time was Byron—when he heard the news, the young Tennyson went out and carved "Byron is dead" on a rock—but his influence on British art and intellectual history was probably least permanent. The most important effect any writer can have is to change in some way the consciousness of his readers, to alter the way they live and think about their lives, to become part of the unarticulated assumptions that underlie their behavior. To the extent that we share in the consciousness these writers altered, the less likely are we to be able to say what they mean. To know the influence on us of the English romantic poets is to feel the shock of familiarity in their very words— not in any account of their achievements.

William Blake

1757–1827

Perhaps because relatively few of Blake's letters survive, perhaps because his contemporaries understood him so uncertainly, few accounts of his life can be very thorough, and many of them perpetuate legends that now seem less than likely: that he and his wife greeted friends while sitting naked in their summer house, that Blake saved Thomas Paine by warning him of imminent arrest, that Blake fell in love with Mary Wollstonecraft, the wife of William Godwin and author of *A Vindication of the Rights of Woman*. No biographical accounts are less trustworthy than those attempting to describe an eccentric. It is clear from the poems that Blake was involved with the major political, social, and intellectual events (and often men) of his time; but it is also clear that his relation to those events was oblique. The one story about him that should be legendary, but is not, is the account he himself gives in letters of his arrest for sedition at Felpham and his acquittal at Chichester; the story is an example of this obliquity.

In a fit of rage Blake pushed out of his garden what he assumed to be a trespassing soldier. Perhaps through injured pride (there were a good many witnesses), the soldier accused Blake of making treasonous statements against the king and army in the process of expelling him. And in spite of the evidence of witnesses and Blake's own denial, the remarks the soldier repeated sound like authentic Blakean anger after it had passed through a vulgar and equally angry mind. According to John Scholfield, one Blake, a Miniature Painter, said

> . . . we (meaning the People of England) were like a Parcel of Children, that they would play with themselves till they got scalded and burnt, that the French Knew our Strength very well, and if Bonaparte should come he would be Master of Europe in an Hour's Time, that England might depend upon it, that when he set his Foot [on] English Ground that every Englishman would have his choice whether to have his Throat cut, or to join the French, and that he was a strong Man, and would certainly begin to cut Throats, and the strongest Man must conquer—that he damned the King of England—his country and his subjects, that his Soldiers were all bound for Slaves, and all his Poor People in general. . . .

If Blake offered any threat to the existing order of things, it obviously was not as an assailant of soldiers—everyone except Scholfield seems clearly to have recognized that. But Blake, alone, in his genuine fear for his own safety, seems to have realized that he could be seen as dangerous if anyone had understood him. He alone seems to recognize that the absurdity of the terms in which the case was being conducted did not mean that no case existed. As had happened so often before, and would happen again, his audience misunderstood in a way that preserved his freedom and disparaged his talent. The amiable eccentric who appears in the legends easily won his case because the radical artist never had occasion to appear in the courtroom.

Blake's career as poet and engraver was unsuccessfully (in his own time) devoted to creating a new audience that could see the world in his terms. But perhaps sensing that the demands were revolutionary, his audience reduced them to something that could be easily accommodated: the distortions of mystical eccentricity at best, the ravings of madness at worst. Yet from the beginning Blake insisted on the individuality of his own art and on the importance of a fundamentally reformed relation between artist and audience to promote it. He first saw his process of relief etching, by which most of his illuminated books between 1788 and 1822 were produced, as a technological device for producing a medium in which the artist and his reader would be brought together without the necessity of a publisher's intervention to reduce words to the impersonal medium of conventional print and a book to a commodity for the marketplace.

Although Blake, the modern social historian E. P. Thompson says, should not have been all that difficult for someone who had learned to read at the end of the eighteenth century with Bunyan's *Pilgrim's Progress* as his basic text, for a modern reader who has learned to distrust allegory, to expect complex ideas to be expressed by complex syntax, and to assume that the ability of language to convey rationality is its main virtue, the task is more difficult. The conventional reader is both the enemy of Blake's style and his justification for using it. His first aim, certainly as early as the *Songs of Innocence*, is not, like Conrad's, to make the reader see, but to make him re-see, to become as a little child so that he can relive and re-experience the directness of apprehension and feeling that his rational education has made less and less available. Let a reader first imagine the world inhabited by a child and re-create the simplicity of its dimensions (big, little, light, dark), the immediateness of its hopes and fears (to stay up late, to get lost), and its chaotic freedoms of time and space, where anything can happen next, and a new world lies just over the horizon or around the corner. From this point of view, the mode of the *Songs of Innocence* seems inevitable, and the adult characters who appear in the poems are only those who protect (and sometimes threaten) this freedom: nurses and shepherds, mothers and fathers. Most readers of the songs are not, of course, children. But to the extent that they are successful readers they re-enter imaginatively the world they once inhabited as children. Inevitably the effect is satirical, because a dimension of purer experience is set beside that of the everyday, and evaluation is encouraged. Several of the songs first appeared in Blake's unfinished satirical tale called (by later editors) *An Island in the Moon*, and there the songs rather suddenly interrupt the absurd goings-on of a salon of experimenters, philosophers, artists, social climbers, and purveyors of religious cant. Used in this way the songs implicitly demonstrate that fully expressed satire need not be nihilistic. But put together in a volume five years later, and combined after another five years with a collection called *Songs of Experience*, the poems acquire contexts that considerably alter their impact if not their meaning.

As a unit, the *Songs of Innocence* define a world as well as a feeling, a world in which one sort of experience is isolated (on the page and in the reader's feelings) from all those kinds of experience that usually accompany it. Of course it is therefore an incomplete world, not a substitute for the one the reader lives in, and the incompleteness is directly expressed by the experiences evoked in the poems that immediately followed this collection, as well as in the parallel *Songs of Experience*. In *The Book of Thel*, for instance, innocence is seen not as a state but as part of a process. Unlike the children who speak in the songs, Thel asks questions about who she is and what she will become, and is unsatisfied by the simple forms of acceptance she finds in the Vales of Har. Like a fairy-tale heroine, she has the privilege of leaving her sanctuary, her unborn state, and later returning to it if she wishes. To be born to life, she discovers with horror, is also to be condemned to frustration and death: living means experiencing the limitations imposed by other people ("the poison of a smile") and even by the body's anatomy ("a little curtain of flesh on the bed of our desire"). The voice that speaks with finality in this poem comes from the grave that is her birthplace, and provides not answers but new questions for which there are no answers. Thel escapes from self-hood and individuation by fleeing back to the security that existed before her birth and her humanity.

The mysteries Thel cannot bear are also, of course, questions for Blake—and presumably for his reader and more complex modes are necessary to contain them. In the world of becoming, words are not things, and an ambition is not the same as its fulfillment. Whether our language is the cause or effect of the way we see the world, its very nature depends on distinctions (between then and now, here and there, this and that) that Blake insisted on questioning. But the means for asking questions were part of that which he wished to examine: to use words to explore the nature of linguistic rationality is rather like trying to see one's own eye without a mirror. Unless there is some external position of detachment or reflection, nothing can be said.

For Blake, two things took the place of the mirror: the use of colored illuminations merged with an engraved text forces the reader to notice that the act of reading these poems at least includes looking *at* something, not absorbing it from an effectually disappearing medium such as print. And unexpected relations between words within the statements can force the reader to abandon, probably with some reluctance and uncertainty, his notions of rational and literary expectation. In *The Marriage of Heaven and Hell*, which Blake engraved in 1790, both devices for forcing a new kind of attention are used with energy and deliberation. The effect of the engraving (the process of which is also one of the subjects of the poem) has to be seen in an original or facsimile edition to be appreciated, but the literary method is explicit in the title as well as in every line: the narrative is dialectical and cyclical; the separate events and statements of which it is constructed are ironic in the sense that the orthodox ("angelic") meanings and interpretations are played against the imaginative ("diabolical") ones. At almost every point, then, the reader has to ask himself what he is "really" reading, and like Thel he discovers that to understand what he is told he must have a clear and committed sense of his own identity. Rigid orthodoxy and easy relativism are both made untenable, and the possibility of reading on demands an acceptance of Blake's contention that without contraries there is no progression. According to Blake, in political history, in Christian theology, in great works of literature such as *Paradise*

Lost, and finally in the nature of each individual, diabolical energy and restrictive convention, sin and virtue, chaos and order, innocence and experience, are in eternal combat with one another. If the nature of experience is dramatic, its meaning at any one moment is static, and only a unique artistic mode can accommodate both possibilities simultaneously. Most of the Proverbs of Hell, separately, are intended to shock anyone who takes conventional proverbs as serious forms of wisdom— "Sooner murder an infant in its cradle than nurse unacted desires"—yet they are responsible expressions of an attitude (that exuberant activity is preferable to deadness)—yet again, this attitude is defined as originating in Hell—yet, to complete the circle, Heaven and Hell are not absolutes but contrary states of the human soul. It is the continuously repeated inversions of standards that makes the total irony of *The Marriage of Heaven and Hell* more complex than it seems at any one moment.

In the later prophetic works, the difficulties are less often allowed for by the playing off of one attitude against another, as in the Proverbs or the *Songs of Experience*, and more frequently dramatized by the creation of mythological characters, their realms, and their relations with one another in ways that are not primarily social or historical or narrative but partake of all three. The *Visions of the Daughters of Albion* is relatively easy to follow because it is Blake's closest approach to a conventionally dramatic mode. An event occurs—Bromion's rape of Oothoon—and however odd the setting and language, a sense of a dramatic situation involving a violated girl, a rapist, and her jealous lover can help the reader through a series of set arguments about the relation between sexuality and identity. Oothoon's defense of particularity—of self, and moment, and desire—is itself marvelously particular, as Bromion's defense based on absolutes is appropriately abstract. As in a drama, their way of speaking re-creates what they are and what they feel—in Theotormon's lamentation, Oothoon's song of joy and freedom. Social customs, sexual behavior, scientific exploration are here in their own terms—and Oothoon especially, in her humanity, creates smaller human scenes (the loveless marriage, for instance) with a vitality that does more than just illustrate an argument. Here, more than anywhere else in Blake, characters are identifiable by their voices as well as their statements.

No mode, of course, could satisfy Blake for long, and he was just as suspicious of literary systems as of religious or philosophical ones. The *Songs of Experience* were bound together with their contraries in the *Songs of Innocence* in 1794, and thereafter the volumes were never issued separately, so that their existence too was deprived of finality. To be sure Blake came to rely increasingly on names for his characters—Orc for the revolutionary energy that opposes Urizen the restrictive lawgiver, and Los for the blacksmith-artist who frees and remolds law with energy and humanity. But the persistence of names and attitudes (the cyclical opposition of Orc and Urizen can be easily located even in the very early poems on the four seasons) never limits the range of the ways in which their relations can be recombined and reordered. Both *America* and "Night the Ninth" of *The Four Zoas* are prophetic poems about war and judgment and apocalypse; both derive from the Book of Revelation and northern mythologies; both are concerned with Orc, Albion, and Urizen. But the difference between them depends on more than the obvious historical analogue of the first work. Each demands from the reader a different order of response, a different way of getting from one line to the next.

Because so much depends on learning how to read Blake by moving progressively from work to work, explanations of what happens in the later prophecies, especially *Milton* and *Jerusalem*, are likely to seem to the beginning reader obscure, or irrelevant to what he needs to help him. The assistance of a critic or expositor can help him get under way with the easier and earlier poems, because a clear sense of what happens there, and how, is what he most needs to read the later works. But probably no other writer until Joyce was as insistent as Blake on educating his own readers and supplying them with texts to match their increasing competence. Blake offers a vision of experience as fulfilling as that of any major artist, but it is a mistake to suppose its imaginative rewards are available without an intensive form of self-education that requires time and knowledge and study as well as sympathy and openness to the unconventional. Analogies between Blake's ways of expanding consciousness and those provided by physiological and chemical means are misleading, because they emphasize the visual nature of particularity at the expense of Blake's equal insistence on intellectual effort. For him "antirational" is not a synonym for "easy." Even after 150 years few readers have given the later prophecies the sort of attention that raises them beyond exercises in explication or curiosities in the history of religious mythology.

The reader who is willing to give the sort of attention Blake demands is rewarded with a vision of imaginative human possibility comprehensive enough to include theology, history, politics, literature, and a mode of psychology that is astonishingly modern. Blake's promise, to the committed reader, is that he shall never again be as he was. Once understood, the relation between freedom and restriction, whether personal or public, becomes a means for individual enrichment. Love and joy are released, understood, made an integral part of wisdom and experience, for no prophet was ever less gloomy about final judgment than Blake. God, women, society—known rightly— are sources of the enhancement of feeling, and the end is a world in which everything that lives is holy. However hard he tries to terrify (in *London* for instance), the exultation of having brought a vision to life overcomes poet and sympathetic reader alike. Keats and Wordsworth, who found that the imagination exposed as well as liberated the self, might be pardoned for seeing in Blake more eccentricity than art. For all the complexity of its expression, Blake's sense of the world is finally permeated with an optimism that can seem almost childlike in its naïveté. Perhaps it is this quality of organized innocence that so threatened the canting and egotistical, and that denied so vehemently the value of established opinions in theology, politics, and human relationships. And no age has ever been more insistent on its established opinions (conservative or radical) than the early nineteenth century. If Blake's contemporaries kept finding answers that satisfied them, Blake insists that they had not even been asking the right questions. If everything is holy, an artist's mission is no less radical than to open the way, by whatever means, to the holiness in ourselves and in the world around us—to show us a world in a grain of sand and eternity in an hour.

OUTLINE OF EVENTS

1757	Nov. 28	Born in London, son of James (17?–1784) and Catherine (1722–1792) Blake of Broad (now Broadwick) Street, near Carnaby Market.
1762	Apr. 25	Catherine Sophia Boucher [Blake] born.
1767		Attends Pars Drawing School in the Strand.
1768–1769		Begins to write, presumably some of the poems later (1783) published in *Poetical Sketches*.
1772		Begins apprenticeship (to last seven years) with engraver Basire.
1774		Makes sketches at Westminster Abbey for Gough's *Sepulchral Monuments in Great Britain*.
1776–1777		Composes last of poems to appear in *Poetical Sketches*.
1779		Apprenticeship ends; he studies briefly at the Royal Academy; perhaps meets Sir Joshua Reynolds. Employed as engraver by J. Johnson, bookseller.
1780		Meets artists Stothard, Flaxman, Fuseli; exhibits at the Royal Academy.
1782	Aug. 18	Marries Catherine Boucher (1762–1831); moves to Green Street.
1783		*Poetical Sketches* published.
1784		Begins prose satire *An Island in the Moon* (which contains several of the *Songs of Innocence*); opens a print shop next door to family house in Broad Street.
1785		Gives up print shop; moves to Poland Street.
1788		First uses process of relief engraving.
1789		Finishes *Songs of Innocence* and *The Book of Thel*; probably begins *The French Revolution*.
1790		*The Marriage of Heaven and Hell*.
1791		*The French Revolution* is set up in type, but never published; moves to Lambeth.
1793		Finishes *Visions of the Daughters of Albion, America*.
1794		Finishes *Songs of Experience, Europe, The Book of Urizen*.
1795		*The Song of Los, The Book of Los, The Book of Ahania*.
1797		*The Four Zoas*.
1800		Moves (Sept.) to Felpham, near Chichester, Sussex.
1800–1803		At Felpham revises *Zoas*; probably begins *Milton* and *Jerusalem*.
1803	Aug.	Arrested for sedition after altercation with dragoon at Felpham.
	Sept.	Returns to London.
1804	Jan. 11	Acquitted at trial for sedition at Chichester. Begins engraving *Milton* (completed by 1809) and *Jerusalem* (completed 1820).
1807–1808		Makes designs for Milton's *Paradise Lost*.

1809	Writes long *Descriptive Catalogue* for exhibition of his work; by this date completes engraving of *Milton*.
1810	Publishes engravings of Chaucer's Canterbury pilgrims.
1811–1817	Little is known of Blake's activities during this period.
1818	Meets John Linnell, painter, who becomes his friend and patron.
1820	Finishes *Jerusalem*; begins illustrations for Virgil's *Pastorals*.
1822	Issues *The Ghost of Abel*, a dramatic poem dedicated to Byron, and his last work produced by relief engraving.
1825	Completes engravings for *Job*.
1826	Makes designs for Dante's *Divine Comedy* (for Linnell); meets S. T. Coleridge.
1827	Aug. 12 Blake dies.

SELECTED BIBLIOGRAPHY

EDITIONS AND BIBLIOGRAPHICAL INFORMATION

The Poetry and Prose of William Blake, ed. D. V. Erdman with commentary by H. Bloom (1965, rev. 1970).

The Complete Writings of William Blake, ed. G. Keynes (1957, rev. 1966, rev. 1969).

The Poems of William Blake ed. W. H. Stevenson and D. V. Erdman (1971).

The Prophetic Writings of William Blake, ed. D. J. Sloss and J. P. R. Wallis (2 vols., 1926).

Facsimile editions thus far published by the Trianon Press for the Blake Trust under the direction of Geoffrey Keynes include: *Jerusalem* (1952); *Songs of Innocence and of Experience* (1955); *The Book of Urizen* (1958); *Visions of the Daughters of Albion* (1959); *The Marriage of Heaven and Hell* (1960); *America* (1963); *The Book of Thel* (1965); *Milton* (1967).

The Notebook of William Blake, ed. G. Keynes (1935).

Letters of William Blake, ed. G. Keynes (1956; rev. 1968).

A Concordance to the Writings of William Blake, ed. D. V. Erdman (2 vols., 1967).

A Blake Bibliography: Annotated Lists of Works, Studies, and Blakeana, ed. G. E. Bentley, Jr., and M. K. Nurmi (1964).

"A Finding List of Reproductions of Blake's Art," *Blake Newsletter* III (1969), 24–41, 64–70.

BIOGRAPHICAL INFORMATION

A. GILCHRIST, *Life of William Blake* (1863; ed. by R. Todd, 1945).

A. SYMONS, *William Blake* (1907).

M. WILSON, *Life of William Blake* (1927; rev. 1948).

R. LISTER, *William Blake* (1968).

G. E. BENTLEY, JR., *Blake Records* (1969).

GENERAL CRITICISM

S. F. DAMON, *William Blake: His Philosophy and Symbols* (1924).

M. PLOWMAN, *An Introduction to the Study of Blake* (1927).

M. SCHORER, *William Blake: The Politics of Vision* (1946).

N. FRYE, *Fearful Symmetry* (1947).

J. MILES, "The Language of William Blake," *English Institute Essays* (1950).

H. M. MARGOLIOUTH, *William Blake* (1951).

D. V. ERDMAN, *Blake: Prophet Against Empire* (1954, rev. 1969).

R. F. GLECKNER, *The Piper and the Bard* (1959).

J. E. GRANT, ed., *Discussions of William Blake* (1961).

H. ADAMS, *William Blake: A Reading of the Shorter Poems* (1963).

H. BLOOM, *Blake's Apocalypse* (1963).

J. H. HAGSTRUM, *William Blake, Poet and Printer: An Introduction to the Illuminated Verse* (1964).

G. KEYNES, *William Blake: Poet, Printer, Prophet* (1964).

S. F. DAMON, *A Blake Dictionary* (1965).

N. FRYE, ed., *Blake: A Collection of Critical Essays* (1966).

J. HOLLOWAY, *Blake: The Lyric Poetry* (1968).

K. RAINE, *Blake and Tradition* (2 vols., 1968).

M. D. PALEY, ed., *Twentieth Century Interpretations of Songs of Innocence and of Experience* (1969).

D. V. ERDMAN and J. E. GRANT, eds., *Blake's Visionary Forms Dramatic* (1970).

J. O'NEILL, ed., *Critics on Blake* (1971).

M. D. PALEY, *Energy and the Imagination: A Study of the Development of Blake's Thought* (1971).

POEMS

FROM

POETICAL SKETCHES.

by W. B.

London: Printed in the Year MDCCLXXXIII.

———◦◦◦◦———

TO SPRING.

O thou, with dewy locks, who lookest down
Thro' the clear windows of the morning; turn
Thine angel eyes upon our western isle,
Which in full choir hails thy approach, O Spring!

The hills tell each other, and the list'ning
Vallies hear; all our longing eyes are turned
Up to thy bright pavillions: issue forth,
And let thy holy feet visit our clime.

Come o'er the eastern hills, and let our winds
Kiss thy perfumed garments; let us taste   10
Thy morn and evening breath; scatter thy pearls
Upon our love-sick land that mourns for thee.

O deck her forth with thy fair fingers; pour
Thy soft kisses on her bosom; and put
Thy golden crown upon her languish'd head,
Whose modest tresses were bound up for thee!

TO SUMMER.

O thou who passest thro' our vallies in
Thy strength, curb thy fierce steeds, allay the heat
That flames from their large nostrils! thou, O
      Summer,
Oft pitched'st here thy golden tent, and oft
Beneath our oaks hast slept, while we beheld
With joy, thy ruddy limbs and flourishing hair.

Beneath our thickest shades we oft have heard
Thy voice, when noon upon his fervid car
Rode o'er the deep of heaven; beside our springs
Sit down, and in our mossy vallies, on   10
Some bank beside a river clear, throw thy
Silk draperies off, and rush into the stream:
Our vallies love the Summer in his pride.

Our bards are fam'd who strike the silver wire:
Our youth[s] are bolder than the southern swains:
Our maidens fairer in the sprightly dance:
We lack not songs, nor instruments of joy,
Nor echoes sweet, nor waters clear as heaven,
Nor laurel wreaths against the sultry heat.

TO AUTUMN

O Autumn, laden with fruit, and stained
With the blood of the grape, pass not, but sit
Beneath my shady roof, there thou may'st rest,
And tune thy jolly voice to my fresh pipe;
And all the daughters of the year shall dance!
Sing now the lusty song of fruits and flowers.

"The narrow bud opens her beauties to
"The sun, and love runs in her thrilling veins;
"Blossoms hang round the brows of morning, and
"Flourish down the bright cheek of modest eve,   10
"Till clust'ring Summer breaks forth into singing,
"And feather'd clouds strew flowers round her head.

"The spirits of the air live on the smells
"Of fruit; and joy, with pinions light, roves round
"The gardens, or sits singing in the trees."
    Thus sang the jolly Autumn as he sat,
    Then rose, girded himself, and o'er the bleak
    Hills fled from our sight; but left his golden load.

TO WINTER.

O Winter! bar thine adamantine doors:
The north is thine; there hast thou built thy dark
Deep-founded habitation. Shake not thy roofs,
Nor bend thy pillars with thine iron car.

He hears me not, but o'er the yawning deep
Rides heavy; his storms are unchain'd; sheathed
In ribbed steel, I dare not lift mine eyes;
For he hath rear'd his sceptre o'er the world.

Lo! now the direful monster, whose skin clings
To his strong bones, strides o'er the groaning rocks:
He withers all in silence, and his hand   11
Unclothes the earth, and freezes up frail life.

He takes his seat upon the cliffs, the mariner
Cries in vain. Poor little wretch! that deal'st
With storms; till heaven smiles, and the monster
Is driv'n yelling to his caves beneath mount Hecla.[1]

---

[1] Volcano in Iceland.

TO THE EVENING STAR

Thou fair-hair'd angel of the evening,
Now, while the sun rests on the mountains, light
Thy bright torch of love; thy radiant crown
Put on, and smile upon our evening bed!
Smile on our loves; and, while thou drawest the
Blue curtains of the sky, scatter thy silver dew
On every flower that shuts its sweet eyes
In timely sleep. Let thy west wind sleep on
The lake; speak si[l]ence with thy glimmering eyes,
And wash the dusk with silver. Soon, full soon,   10
Dost thou withdraw; then the wolf rages wide,
And the lion glares thro' the dun forest:
The fleeces of our flocks are cover'd with
Thy sacred dew: protect them with thine influence.

SONG
["How sweet I roam'd . . ."]

How sweet I roam'd from field to field,
    And tasted all the summer's pride,
'Till I the prince of love beheld,
    Who in the sunny beams did glide!

He shew'd me lilies for my hair,
    And blushing roses for my brow;
He led me through his gardens fair,
    Where all his golden pleasures grow.

With sweet May dews my wings were wet,
    And Phoebus fir'd my vocal rage;   10
He caught me in his silken net,
    And shut me in his golden cage.

He loves to sit and hear me sing,
    Then, laughing, sports and plays with me;
Then stretches out my golden wing,
    And mocks my loss of liberty.

SONG
["My silks and fine array"]

My silks and fine array,
    My smiles and languish'd air,
By love are driv'n away;
    And mournful lean Despair
Brings me yew to deck my grave:
Such end true lovers have.

His face is fair as heav'n,
    When springing buds unfold;
O why to him was't giv'n,
    Whose heart is wintry cold?   10
His breast is love's all worship'd tomb,
Where all love's pilgrims come.

Bring me an axe and spade,
    Bring me a winding sheet;
When I my grave have made,
    Let winds and tempests beat:
Then down I'll lie, as cold as clay.
True love doth pass away!

SONG
["Love and harmony combine"]

Love and harmony combine,
And around our souls intwine,
While thy branches mix with mine,
And our roots together join.

Joys upon our branches sit,
Chirping loud, and singing sweet;
Like gentle streams beneath our feet
Innocence and virtue meet.

Thou the golden fruit dost bear,
I am clad in flowers fair;   10
Thy sweet boughs perfume the air,
And the turtle buildeth there.

There she sits and feeds her young,
Sweet I hear her mournful song;
And thy lovely leaves among,
There is love: I hear his tongue.

There his charming nest doth lay,
There he sleeps the night away;
There he sports along the day,
And doth among our branches play.   20

SONG
["I love the jocund dance"]

I love the jocund dance,
    The softly-breathing song,
Where innocent eyes do glance,
    And where lisps the maiden's tongue.

I love the laughing vale,
    I love the echoing hill,
Where mirth does never fail,
    And the jolly swain laughs his fill.

I love the pleasant cot,
    I love the innocent bow'r.   10
Where white and brown is our lot,
    Or fruit in the mid-day hour.

I love the oaken seat,
    Beneath the oaken tree,
Where all the old villagers meet,
    And laugh our sports to see.

I love our neighbours all,
    But, Kitty, I better love thee;
And love them I ever shall;
    But thou art all to me.   20

SONG
["Memory, hither come"]

Memory, hither come,
    And tune your merry notes;
And, while upon the wind,
    Your music floats,
I'll pore upon the stream,
Where sighing lovers dream,
And fish for fancies as they pass
Within the watery glass.

I'll drink of the clear stream,
    And hear the linnet's song;   10
And there I'll lie and dream
    The day along:
And, when night comes, I'll go
    To places fit for woe;
Walking along the darken'd valley,
    With silent Melancholy.

MAD SONG

The wild winds weep,
    And the night is a-cold;
Come hither, Sleep,
    And my griefs infold:

But lo! the morning peeps
   Over the eastern steeps,
And the rustling birds of dawn
   The earth do scorn.

Lo! to the vault
   Of paved heaven,   10
With sorrow fraught
   My notes are driven:
They strike the ear of night
   Make weep the eyes of day;
They make mad the roaring winds,
   And with tempests play.

Like a fiend in a cloud
   With howling woe,
After night I do croud,
   And with night will go;   20
I turn my back to the east,
From whence comforts have increas'd;
For light doth seize my brain
   With frantic pain.

SONG
["Fresh from the dewy hill . . ."]

Fresh from the dewy hill, the merry year
Smiles on my head, and mounts his flaming car;
Round my young brows the laurel wreathes a shade,
And rising glories beam around my head.

My feet are wing'd, while o'er the dewy lawn,
I meet my maiden, risen like the morn:
Oh bless those holy feet, like angels' feet;
Oh bless those limbs, beaming with heav'nly light!

Like as an angel glitt'ring in the sky,
In times of innocence, and holy joy;   10
The joyful shepherd stops his grateful song,
To hear the music of an angel's tongue.

So when she speaks, the voice of Heaven I hear
So when we walk, nothing impure comes near;
Each field seems Eden, and each calm retreat;
Each village seems the haunt of holy feet.

But that sweet village where my black-ey'd maid,
Closes her eyes in sleep beneath night's shade:
Whene'er I enter, more than mortal fire
Burns in my soul, and does my song inspire.   20   [1769-1778]

SONG
["When early morn walks forth . . ."]

When early morn walks forth in sober grey;
Then to my black ey'd maid I haste away,
When evening sits beneath her dusky bow'r,
And gently sighs away the silent hour;
The village bell alarms, away I go;
And the vale darkens at my pensive woe.

To that sweet village, where my black ey'd maid
Doth drop a tear beneath the silent shade,
I turn my eyes; and, pensive as I go,   9
Curse my black stars, and bless my pleasing woe.

Oft when the summer sleeps among the trees,
Whisp'ring faint murmurs to the scanty breeze,
I walk the village round; if at her side
A youth doth walk in stolen joy and pride,
I curse my stars in bitter grief and woe,
That made my love so high, and me so low.

O should she e'er prove false, his limbs I'd tear,
And throw all pity on the burning air;
I'd curse bright fortune for my mixed lot,
And then I'd die in peace, and be forgot.   20

TO THE MUSES

Whether on Ida's shady brow,
   Or in the chambers of the East,
The chambers of the sun, that now
   From antient melody have ceas'd;

Whether in Heav'n ye wander fair,
   Or the green corners of the earth,
Or the blue regions of the air,
   Where the melodious winds have birth;

Whether on chrystal rocks ye rove,
   Beneath the bosom of the sea   10
Wand'ring in many a coral grove,
   Fair Nine, forsaking Poetry!

How have you left the antient love
   That bards of old enjoy'd in you!
The languid strings do scarcely move!
   The sound is forc'd, the notes are few!

[1783]

SONGS OF INNOCENCE

Blake tried over twenty different ways of ordering these songs, and not one can be seen as final. The arrangement used here is the one that Blake used most often for the combined Songs of Innocence and of Experience, *published after 1794.*

SONGS of INNOCENCE

1789

The Author & Printer   W Blake

INTRODUCTION

Piping down the valleys wild
Piping songs of pleasant glee
On a cloud I saw a child.
And he laughing said to me.

Pipe a song about a Lamb;
So I piped with merry chear,
Piper pipe that song again—
So I piped, he wept to hear.

Drop thy pipe thy happy pipe
Sing thy songs of happy chear,   10
So I sung the same again
While he wept with joy to hear

Piper sit thee down and write
In a book that all may read—
So he vanish'd from my sight.
And I pluck'd a hollow reed.

And I made a rural pen,
And I stain'd the water clear,
And I wrote my happy songs
Every child may joy to hear   20

THE SHEPHERD.

How sweet is the Shepherds sweet lot,
From the morn to the evening he strays:
He shall follow his sheep all the day
And his tongue shall be filled with praise.

For he hears the lambs innocent call,
And he hears the ewes tender reply,
He is watchful while they are in peace,
For they know when their Shepherd is nigh.

THE ECCHOING GREEN

The Sun does arise,
And make happy the skies.
The merry bells ring
To welcome the Spring.
The sky-lark and thrush,
The birds of the bush,
Sing louder around,
To the bells chearful sound.
While our sports shall be seen
On the Ecchoing Green.   10

Old John with white hair
Does laugh away care,
Sitting under the oak,
Among the old folk,
They laugh at our play,
And soon they all say.
Such such were the joys.
When we all girls & boys,
In our youth-time were seen,
On the Ecchoing Green.   20

Till the little ones weary
No more can be merry
The sun does descend,
And our sports have an end:
Round the laps of their mothers,
Many sisters and brothers,
Like birds in their nest,
Are ready for rest;
And sport no more seen,
On the darkening Green.   30

THE LAMB

Little Lamb who made thee
    Dost thou know who made thee
Gave thee life & bid thee feed.
By the stream & e'or the mead;
Gave thee clothing of delight,
Softest clothing wooly bright;
Gave thee such a tender voice,
Making all the vales rejoice!
    Little Lamb who made thee
    Dost thou know who made thee   10

Little Lamb I'll tell thee,
    Little Lamb I'll tell thee!
He is called by thy name,
For he calls himself a Lamb:

He is meek & he is mild,
He became a little child:
I a child & thou a lamb,
We are called by his name.
    Little Lamb God bless thee.
    Little Lamb God bless thee.   20

THE LITTLE BLACK BOY.

My mother bore me in the southern wild,
And I am black, but O! my soul is white;
White as an angel is the English child:
But I am black as if bereav'd of light.

My mother taught me underneath a tree
And sitting down before the heat of day,
She took me on her lap and kissed me,
And pointing to the east began to say.

Look on the rising sun: there God does live
And gives his light, and gives his heat away.   10
And flowers and trees and beasts and men recieve
Comfort in morning joy in the noon day.

And we are put on earth a little space,
That we may learn to bear the beams of love,
And these black bodies and this sun-burnt face
Is but a cloud, and like a shady grove.

For when our souls have learn'd the heat to bear
The cloud will vanish we shall hear his voice.
Saying: come out from the grove my love & care,
And round my golden tent like lambs rejoice.   20

Thus did my mother say and kissed me,
And thus I say to little English boy.
When I from black and he from white cloud free,
And round the tent of God like lambs we joy:

Ill shade him from the heat till he can bear,
To lean in joy upon our fathers knee.
And then I'll stand and stroke his silver hair,
And be like him and he will then love me.

THE BLOSSOM.

    Merry Merry Sparrow
    Under leaves so green
    A happy Blossom
    Sees you swift as arrow
    Seek your cradle narrow
    Near my Bosom.

    Pretty Pretty Robin
    Under leaves so green
    A happy Blossom
    Hears you sobbing sobbing   10
    Pretty Pretty Robin
    Near my Bosom.

THE CHIMNEY SWEEPER

When my mother died I was very young,
And my father sold me while yet my tongue,
Could scarcely cry weep weep weep weep.
So your chimneys I sweep & in soot I sleep.

Theres little Tom Dacre, who cried when his head
That curl'd like a lambs back, was shav'd, so I said.
Hush Tom never mind it, for when your head's bare,
You know that the soot cannot spoil your white hair.

And so he was quiet, & that very night,
As Tom was a sleeping he had such a sight,   10
That thousands of sweepers Dick, Joe Ned & Jack
Were all of them lock'd up in coffins of black

And by came an Angel who had a bright key,
And he open'd the coffins & set them all free.
Then down a green plain leaping laughing they run
And wash in a river and shine in the Sun.

Then naked & white, all their bags left behind,
They rise upon clouds, and sport in the wind.
And the Angel told Tom if he'd be a good boy,
He'd have God for his father & never want joy.   20

And so Tom awoke and we rose in the dark
And got with our bags & our brushes to work.
Tho' the morning was cold, Tom was happy & warm,
So if all do their duty, they need not fear harm.

THE LITTLE BOY LOST

    Father, father, where are you going
    O do not walk so fast.
    Speak father, speak to your little boy
    Or else I shall be lost,

    The night was dark no father was there
    The child was wet with dew.
    The mire was deep, & the child did weep
    And away the vapour flew.

THE LITTLE BOY FOUND

The little boy lost in the lonely fen,
Led by the wand'ring light,
Began to cry, but God ever nigh,
Appeared like his father in white.

He kissed the child & by the hand led
And to his mother brought,
Who in sorrow pale, thro' the lonely dale
Her little boy weeping sought.

LAUGHING SONG,

When the green woods laugh, with the voice of joy
And the dimpling stream runs laughing by,
When the air does laugh with our merry wit,
And the green hill laughs with the noise of it.

When the meadows laugh with lively green
And the grasshopper laughs in the merry scene,
When Mary and Susan and Emily,
With their sweet round mouths sing Ha, Ha, He.

When the painted birds laugh in the shade
Where our table with cherries and nuts is spread 10
Come live & be merry and join with me,
To sing the sweet chorus of Ha, Ha, He.

A CRADLE SONG

Sweet dreams form a shade,
O'er my lovely infants head.
Sweet dreams of pleasant streams,
By happy silent moony beams.

Sweet sleep with soft down,
Weave thy brows an infant crown.
Sweet sleep Angel mild,
Hover o'er my happy child.

Sweet smiles in the night,
Hover over my delight.   10
Sweet smiles Mothers smiles
All the livelong night beguiles.

Sweet moans, dovelike sighs,
Chase not slumber from thy eyes.
Sweet moans, sweeter smiles,
All the dovelike moans beguiles.

Sleep sleep happy child.
All creation slept and smil'd.
Sleep sleep, happy sleep,
While o'er thee thy mother weep.   20

Sweet babe in thy face,
Holy image I can trace.
Sweet babe once like thee,
Thy maker lay and wept for me

Wept for me for thee for all,
When he was an infant small.
Thou his image ever see,
Heavenly face that smiles on thee.

Smiles on thee on me on all,
Who became an infant small,   30
Infant smiles are his own smiles.
Heaven & earth to peace beguiles.

THE DIVINE IMAGE.

To Mercy Pity Peace and Love,
All pray in their distress:
And to these virtues of delight
Return their thankfulness.

For Mercy Pity Peace and Love,
Is God our father dear:
And Mercy Pity Peace and Love,
Is Man his child and care.

For Mercy has a human heart
Pity, a human face: 10
And Love, the human form divine,
And Peace, the human dress.

Then every man of every clime,
That prays in his distress,
Prays to the human form divine
Love Mercy Pity Peace.

And all must love the human form,
In heathen, turk or jew.
Where Mercy, Love & Pity dwell
There God is dwelling too.   20

HOLY THURSDAY

On Ascension Day the children in London charity schools were taken (in uniform—e.g., red and green) to services in St. Paul's Cathedral.

HOLY THURSDAY

Twas on a Holy Thursday their innocent faces clean
The children walking two & two in red & blue & green
Grey headed beadles walkd before with wands as
    white as snow
Till into the high dome of Pauls they like Thames
    waters flow

O what a multitude they seemd these flowers of
    London town
Seated in companies they sit with radiance all their
    own
The hum of multitudes was there but multitudes of
    lambs
Thousands of little boys & girls raising their innocent
    hands

Now like a mighty wind they raise to heaven the voice
    of song
Or like harmonious thunderings the seats of heaven
    among   10
Beneath them sit the aged men wise guardians of the
    poor
Then cherish pity, lest you drive an angel from your
    door

NIGHT.

The sun descending in the west
The evening star does shine.
The birds are silent in their nest,
And I must seek for mine,
The moon like a flower,
In heavens high bower;
With silent delight,
Sits and smiles on the night.

Farewell green fields and happy groves,
Where flocks have took delight;   10
Where lambs have nibbled, silent moves
The feet of angels bright;
Unseen they pour blessing,
And joy without ceasing,
On each bud and blossom,
And each sleeping bosom.

They look in every thoughtless nest,
Where birds are coverd warm;
They visit caves of every beast,
To keep them all from harm;   20
If they see any weeping,
That should have been sleeping
They pour sleep on their head
And sit down by their bed.

When wolves and tygers howl for prey
They pitying stand and weep;
Seeking to drive their thirst away,
And keep them from the sheep.
But if they rush dreadful;
The angels most heedful,   30
Recieve each mild spirit,
New worlds to inherit.

And there the lions ruddy eyes,
Shall flow with tears of gold:
And pitying the tender cries,
And walking round the fold:
Saying: wrath by his meekness
And by his health, sickness,
Is driven away,
From our immortal day.   40

And now beside thee bleating lamb,
I can lie down and sleep;
Or think on him who bore thy name,
Graze after thee and weep.
For wash'd in lifes river,
My bright mane for ever,
Shall shine like the gold,
As I guard o'er the fold.

SPRING

Sound the Flute!
Now it's mute.
Birds delight
Day and Night.
Nightingale
In the dale
Lark in Sky
Merrily
Merrily Merrily to welcome in the Year

Little Boy   10
Full of joy.
Little Girl
Sweet and small,

Cock does crow
So do you.
Merry voice
Infant noise
Merrily Merrily to welcome in the Year

Little Lamb
Here I am,   20
Come and lick
My white neck.
Let me pull
Your soft Wool.
Let me kiss
Your soft face.
Merrily Merrily we welcome in the Year

NURSE'S SONG

When the voices of children are heard on the green
And laughing is heard on the hill,
My heart is at rest within my breast
An every thing else is still

Then come home my children, the sun is gone down
And the dews of night arise
Come come leave off play, and let us away
Till the morning appears in the skies

No no let us play, for it is yet day
And we cannot go to sleep   10
Besides in the sky, the little birds fly
And the hills are all coverd with sheep

Well well go & play till the light fades away
And then go home to bed
The little ones leaped & shouted & laugh'd
And all the hills ecchoed

INFANT JOY

I have no name
I am but two days old.—
What shall I call thee?
I happy am
Joy is my name,—
Sweet joy befall thee!

Pretty joy!
Sweet joy but two days old.
Sweet joy I call thee:
Thou dost smile.   10
I sing the while
Sweet joy befall thee.

A DREAM

Once a dream did weave a shade,
O'er my Angel-guarded bed,
That an Emmet lost it's way.
Where on grass methought I lay.

Troubled wilderd and folorn
Dark benighted travel-worn,
Over many a tangled spray
All heart-broke I heard her say.

O my children! do they cry
Do they hear their father sigh.   10
Now they look abroad to see,
Now return and weep for me.

Pitying I drop'd a tear:
But I saw a glow-worm near:
Who replied. What wailing wight
Calls the watchman of the night.

I am set to light the ground,
While the beetle goes his round:
Follow now the beetles hum,
Little wanderer hie thee home.   20

ON ANOTHERS SORROW

Can I see anothers woe,
And not be in sorrow too.
Can I see anothers grief,
And not seek for kind relief.

Can I see a falling tear,
And not feel my sorrows share,
Can a father see his child,
Weep, nor be with sorrow fill'd.

Can a mother sit and hear,
An infant groan an infant fear—   10
No no never can it be.
Never never can it be.

And can he who smiles on all
Hear the wren with sorrows small,
Hear the small birds grief & care
Hear the woes that infants bear—

And not sit beside the nest
Pouring pity in their breast,
And not sit the cradle near
Weeping tear on infants tear.   20

And not sit both night & day,
Wiping all our tears away.
O! no never can it be.
Never never can it be.

He doth give his joy to all.
He becomes an infant small.
He becomes a man of woe
He doth feel the sorrow too.

Think not, thou canst sigh a sigh,
And thy maker is not by.   30
Think not, thou canst weep a tear,
And thy maker is not near.

O! he gives to us his joy,
That our grief he may destroy
Till our grief is fled & gone
He doth sit by us and moan.

[1784–1789]   [1789]

THE BOOK of THEL

The Author & Printer Willm Blake, 1789.

—⊶⊙⊷—

[PLATE i]

THEL'S *Motto*,

Does the Eagle know what is in the pit?
Or wilt thou go ask the Mole:
Can Wisdom be put in a silver rod?
Or Love in a golden bowl?

[PLATE 1]

THEL

I

The daughters of Mne Seraphim [1] led round their
    sunny flocks,
All but the youngest. she in paleness sought the secret
    air.
To fade away like morning beauty from her mortal
    day:
Down by the river of Adona her soft voice is heard:
And thus her gentle lamentation falls like morning
    dew.

◇◇◇◇◇◇◇◇◇◇◇◇◇◇◇◇◇◇◇◇◇◇◇◇◇

[1] Perhaps Blake's error for "the Seraphim" (the highest order of angels). Thel, whose name suggests the Greek for "will" or "desire," is a preexistent inhabitant of the vales of Har, or innocence, analogous to the Garden of Adonis ("Adona") and to Eden.

O life of this our spring! why fades the lotus of the
    water?
Why fade these children of the spring? born but to
    smile & fall.
Ah! Thel is like a watry bow, and like a parting cloud,
Like a reflection in a glass. like shadows in the water.
Like dreams of infants. like a smile upon an infants
    face,   10
Like the doves voice, like transient day, like music in
    the air,
Ah! gentle may I lay me down, and gentle rest my
    head.
And gentle sleep the sleep of death. and gentle hear
    the voice
Of him that walketh in the garden in the evening time.

The Lilly of the valley breathing in the humble grass
Answer'd the lovely maid and said; I am a watry
    weed,
And I am very small, and love to dwell in lowly vales;
So weak, the gilded butterfly scarce perches on my
    head
Yet I am visited from heaven and he that smiles on all.
Walks in the valley. and each morn over me spreads
    his hand   20
Saying, rejoice thou humble grass, thou new-born lilly
    flower,
Thou gentle maid of silent valleys. and of modest
    brooks;
For thou shalt be clothed in light, and fed with
    morning manna:
Till summers heat melts thee beside the fountains and
    the springs
To flourish in eternal vales: then why should Thel
    complain,

[PLATE 2]

Why should the mistress of the vales of Har, utter a
    sigh.

She ceasd & smild in tears, then sat down in her silver
    shrine.

Thel answerd. O thou little virgin of the peaceful
    valley.
Giving to those that cannot crave, the voiceless, the
    o'ertired.
Thy breath doth nourish the innocent lamb, he smells
    thy milky garments,
He crops thy flowers. while thou sittest smiling in his
    face,
Wiping his mild and meekin mouth from all contagious
    taints.

Thy wine doth purify the golden honey, thy perfume,
Which thou dost scatter on every little blade of grass
    that springs
Revives the milked cow, & tames the fire-breathing
    steed.   10
But Thel is like a faint cloud kindled at the rising
    sun:
I vanish from my pearly throne, and who shall find
    my place.

Queen of the vales the Lilly answerd, ask the tender
    cloud,
And it shall tell thee why it glitters in the morning sky,
And why it scatters its bright beauty thro' the humid
    air.
Descend O little cloud & hover before the eyes of Thel.

The Cloud descended, and the Lilly bowd her modest
    head:
And went to mind her numerous charge among the
    verdant grass.

[PLATE 3]
              II

O little Cloud the virgin said, I charge thee tell to me,
Why thou complainest not when in one hour thou
    fade away:
Then we shall seek thee but not find; ah Thel is like to
    Thee.
I pass away. yet I complain, and no one hears my
    voice.

The Cloud then shew'd his golden head & his bright
    form emerg'd,
Hovering and glittering on the air before the face of
    Thel.

O virgin know'st thou not. our steeds drink of the
    golden springs
Where Luvah doth renew his horses: look'st thou on
    my youth,
And fearest thou because I vanish and am seen no
    more.
Nothing remains; O maid I tell thee, when I pass
    away,   10
It is to tenfold life, to love, to peace, and raptures
    holy:
Unseen descending, weigh my light wings upon
    balmy flowers;
And court the fair eyed dew. to take me to her shining
    tent;
The weeping virgin, trembling kneels before the risen
    sun,

Till we arise link'd in a golden band, and never part;
But walk united, bearing food to all our tender flowers
Dost thou O little Cloud? I fear that I am not like
    thee;
For I walk through the vales of Har. and smell the
    sweetest flowers;
But I feed not the little flowers: I hear the warbling
    birds,
But I feed not the warbling birds. they fly and seek
    their food;   20
But Thel delights in these no more because I fade
    away,
And all shall say, without a use this shining woman
    liv'd,
Or did she only live. to be at death the food of worms.

The Cloud reclind upon his airy throne and answer'd
    thus.

Then if thou art the food of worms. O virgin of the
    skies,
How great thy use. how great thy blessing; every thing
    that lives,
Lives not alone, nor for itself: fear not and I will call
The weak worm from its lowly bed, and thou shalt
    hear its voice.
Come forth worm of the silent valley, to thy pensive
    queen.

The helpless worm arose, and sat upon the Lillys leaf,
And the bright Cloud saild on, to find his partner in
    the vale.   31

[PLATE 4]
              III
Then Thel astonish'd view'd the Worm upon its dewy
    bed.

Art thou a Worm? image of weakness. art thou but a
    Worm?
I see thee like an infant wrapped in the Lillys leaf:
Ah weep not little voice, thou can'st not speak. but
    thou can'st weep;
Is this a Worm? I see thee lay helpless & naked:
    weeping,
And none to answer, none to cherish thee with mothers
    smiles.

The Clod of Clay heard the Worms voice, & raisd her
    pitying head;
She bow'd over the weeping infant, and her life
    exhal'd
In milky fondness, then on Thel she fix'd her humble
    eyes.   9

O beauty of the vales of Har. we live not for ourselves,
Thou seest me the meanest thing, and so I am indeed;
My bosom of itself is cold. and of itself is dark,

[PLATE 5]

But he that loves the lowly, pours his oil upon my
    head.
And kisses me, and binds his nuptial bands around
    my breast,
And says; Thou mother of my children, I have loved
    thee.
And I have given thee a crown that none can take away
But how this is sweet maid, I know not, and I cannot
    know,
I ponder, and I cannot ponder; yet I live and love.

The daughter of beauty wip'd her pitying tears with
    her white veil,
And said. Alas! I knew not this, and therefore did I
    weep:
That God would love a Worm I knew, and punish the
    evil foot
That wilful, bruis'd its helpless form: but that he
    cherish'd it   10
With milk and oil. I never knew; and therefore did I
    weep,
And I complaind in the mild air, because I fade away,
And lay me down in thy cold bed, and leave my
    shining lot.

Queen of the vales, the matron Clay answerd; I heard
    thy sighs.
And all thy moans flew o'er my roof. but I have call'd
    them down:
Wilt thou O Queen enter my house. 'tis given thee to
    enter,
And to return; fear nothing. enter with thy virgin feet.

[PLATE 6]

          IV

The eternal gates terrific porter lifted the northern
    bar:
Thel enter'd in & saw the secrets of the land unknown;
She saw the couches of the dead, & where the fibrous
    roots
Of every heart on earth infixes deep its restless twists:
A land of sorrows & of tears where never smile was
    seen.

She wanderd in the land of clouds thro' valleys dark,
    listning
Dolours & lamentations: waiting oft beside a dewy
    grave

She stood in silence. listning to the voices of the
    ground,
Till to her own grave plot she came, & there she sat
    down.
And heard this voice of sorrow breathed from the
    hollow pit.   10

Why cannot the Ear be closed to its own destruction?
Or the glistning Eye to the poison of a smile!
Why are Eyelids stord with arrows ready drawn,
Where a thousand fighting men in ambush lie?
Or an Eye of gifts & graces, show'ring fruits & coined
    gold!
Why a Tongue impress'd with honey from every
    wind?
Why an Ear, a whirlpool fierce to draw creations in?
Why a Nostril wide inhaling terror trembling &
    affright
Why a tender curb upon the youthful burning boy!
Why a little curtain of flesh on the bed of our desire?

The Virgin started from her seat, & with a shriek.   21
Fled back unhinderd till she came into the vales of
    Har
          The End

[1789]   [1789]

THE FRENCH REVOLUTION

This poem originally was to have seven books. Book I was set up in type and printed by Joseph Johnson in 1791, but it was never published; the remaining books, if written, did not survive. The characters of this poem are both real and symbolic. The dukes of Bourbon, Bretagne, and Burgundy are Blake's inventions. Henry IV (1553–1610) is invoked (as he was by some of Blake's French contemporaries) as the model of a Protestant and benevolent king. The Duke d'Orléans (Philippe Égalité), member of the Mountain (the Left), voted for the execution of the king. The others— Lafayette the soldier, Necker minister of finances (whose dismissal was the immediate cause of the storming of the Bastille), Target the jurist, Bailly the Mayor of Paris, Mirabeau orator and revolutionary leader, the Abbé Sieyès, Clermont-Tonnere, and the Duc D'Aumont—were mostly moderates who tried in one way and another to reconcile monarchy and revolution. Some, like Clermont and Bailly, later fell into disfavor and were executed; others, like Lafayette and Sieyès, retained their influence in postrevolutionary France.

THE
FRENCH REVOLUTION.
A POEM,
IN SEVEN BOOKS.
BOOK THE FIRST.

LONDON: Printed for J. Johnson, N° 72,
St Paul's Church-yard. MDCCXCI.
{Price One Shilling.}

———◦◉◦———

ADVERTISEMENT.

The remaining Books of this Poem are finished,
and will be published in their Order.

———◦◉◦———

THE FRENCH REVOLUTION

Book the First.

The dead brood over Europe, the cloud and vision
    descends over chearful France;
O cloud well appointed! Sick, sick: the Prince on his
    couch, wreath'd in dim
And appalling mist; his strong hand outstretch'd,
    from his shoulder down the bone
Runs aching cold into the scepter too heavy for mortal
    grasp. No more
To be swayed by visible hand, nor in cruelty bruise
    the mild flourishing mountains.

Sick the mountains, and all their vineyards weep, in
    the eyes of the kingly mourner;
Pale is the morning cloud in his visage. Rise, Necker:
    the ancient dawn calls us
To awake from slumbers of five thousand years. I
    awake, but my soul is in dreams;
From my window I see the old mountains of France,
    like aged men, fading away.

Troubled, leaning on Necker, descends the King, to
    his chamber of council; shady mountains   10
In fear, utter voices of thunder, the woods of France
    embosom the sound;
Clouds of wisdom prophetic reply, and roll over the
    palace roof heavy.
Forty men: each conversing with woes in the infinite
    shadows of his soul,
Like our ancient fathers in regions of twilight, walk,
    gathering round the King;
Again the loud voice of France cries to the morning,
    the morning prophecies to its clouds.

For the Commons convene in the Hall of the Nation.
    France shakes! And the heavens of France
Perplex'd vibrate round each careful countenance!
    Darkness of old times around them
Utters loud despair, shadowing Paris; her grey towers
    groan, and the Bastile trembles.
In its terrible towers the Governor stood, in dark fogs
    list'ning the horror;
A thousand his soldiers, old veterans of France,
    breathing red clouds of power and dominion,   20
Sudden seiz'd with howlings, despair, and black night,
    he stalk'd like a lion from tower
To tower, his howlings were heard in the Louvre;
    from court to court restless he dragg'd
His strong limbs; from court to court curs'd the fierce
    torment unquell'd,
Howling and giving the dark command; in his soul
    stood the purple plague,
Tugging his iron manacles, and piercing through the
    seven towers dark and sickly,
Panting over the prisoners like a wolf gorg'd; and the
    den nam'd Horror held a man
Chain'd hand and foot, round his neck an iron band,
    bound to the impregnable wall.
In his soul was the serpent coil'd round in his heart,
    hid from the light, as in a cleft rock;
And the man was confin'd for a writing prophetic: in
    the tower nam'd Darkness, was a man
Pinion'd down to the stone floor, his strong bones
    scarce cover'd with sinews; the iron rings   30

Were forg'd smaller as the flesh decay'd, a mask of
    iron on his face hid the lineaments
Of ancient Kings, and the frown of the eternal lion
    was hid from the oppressed earth.
In the tower named Bloody, a skeleton yellow
    remained in its chains on its couch
Of stone, once a man who refus'd to sign papers of
    abhorrence; the eternal worm
Crept in the skeleton. In the den nam'd Religion, a
    loathsome sick woman, bound down
To a bed of straw; the seven diseases of earth, like
    birds of prey, stood on the couch,
And fed on the body. She refus'd to be whore to the
    Minister, and with a knife smote him.
In the tower nam'd Order, an old man, whose white
    beard cover'd the stone floor like weeds
On margin of the sea, shrivel'd up by heat of day
    and cold of night; his den was short
And narrow as a grave dug for a child, with spiders
    webs wove, and with slime   40
Of ancient horrors cover'd, for snakes and scorpions
    are his companions; harmless they breathe
His sorrowful breath: he, by conscience urg'd, in the
    city of Paris rais'd a pulpit,
And taught wonders to darken'd souls. In the den
    nam'd Destiny a strong man sat,
His feet and hands cut off, and his eyes blinded; round
    his middle a chain and a band
Fasten'd into the wall; fancy gave him to see an image
    of despair in his den,
Eternally rushing round, like a man on his hands and
    knees, day and night without rest:
He was friend to the favourite. In the seventh tower,
    nam'd the tower of God, was a man
Mad, with chains loose, which he dragg'd up and
    down; fed with hopes year by year, he pined
For liberty; vain hopes: his reason decay'd, and the
    world of attraction in his bosom
Center'd, and the rushing of chaos overwhelm'd his
    dark soul. He was confin'd   50
For a letter of advice to a King, and his ravings in
    winds are heard over Versailles.

But the dens shook and trembled, the prisoners look
    up and assay to shout; they listen,
Then laugh in the dismal den, then are silent, and a
    light walks round the dark towers.
For the Commons convene in the Hall of the Nations;
    like spirits of fire in the beautiful
Porches of the Sun, to plant beauty in the desart
    craving abyss, they gleam
On the anxious city; all children new-born first behold
    them; tears are fled,

And they nestle in earth-breathing bosoms. So the
    city of Paris, their wives and children,
Look up to the morning Senate, and visions of sorrow
    leave pensive streets.

But heavy brow'd jealousies lower o'er the Louvre,
    and terrors of ancient Kings
Descend from the gloom and wander thro' the palace,
    and weep round the King and his Nobles.   60
While loud thunders roll, troubling the dead, Kings
    are sick throughout all the earth,
The voice ceas'd: the Nation sat: And the triple forg'd
    fetters of times were unloos'd.
The voice ceas'd: the Nation sat: but ancient darkness
    and trembling wander thro' the palace.

As in day of havock and routed battle, among thick
    shades of discontent,
On the soul-skirting mountains of sorrow cold waving:
    the Nobles fold round the King,
Each stern visage lock'd up as with strong bands of
    iron, each strong limb bound down as with
    marble,
In flames of red wrath burning, bound in astonishment
    a quarter of an hour.

Then the King glow'd: his Nobles fold round, like the
    sun of old time quench'd in clouds;
In their darkness the King stood, his heart flam'd, and
    utter'd a with'ring heat, and these words burst
    forth:

"The nerves of five thousand years ancestry tremble,
    shaking the heavens of France;   70
"Throbs of anguish beat on brazen war foreheads,
    they descend and look into their graves.

"I see thro' darkness, thro' clouds rolling round me,
    the spirits of ancient Kings
"Shivering over their bleached bones; round them
    their counsellors look up from the dust,
"Crying: 'Hide from the living! Our bonds and our
    prisoners shout in the open field,
"'Hide in the nether earth! Hide in the bones! Sit
    obscured in the hollow scull.
"'Our flesh is corrupted, and we [wear] away. We are
    not numbered among the living. Let us hide
"'In stones, among roots of trees. The prisoners have
    burst their dens,
"'Let us hide; let us hide in the dust; and plague and
    wrath and tempest shall cease.'"

He ceas'd, silent pond'ring, his brows folded heavy,
 his forehead was in affliction,
Like the central fire: from the window he saw his vast
 armies spread over the hills,   80
Breathing red fires from man to man, and from horse
 to horse; then his bosom
Expanded like starry heaven, he sat down: his Nobles
 took their ancient seats.

Then the ancientest Peer, Duke of Burgundy, rose
 from the Monarch's right hand, red as wines
From his mountains, an odor of war, like a ripe
 vineyard, rose from his garments,
And the chamber became as a clouded sky; o'er the
 council he stretch'd his red limbs,
Cloth'd in flames of crimson, as a ripe vineyard
 stretches over sheaves of corn,
The fierce Duke hung over the council; around him
 croud, weeping in his burning robe,
A bright cloud of infant souls; his words fall like
 purple autumn on the sheaves.

"Shall this marble built heaven become a clay
 cottage, this earth an oak stool, and these
 mowers
"From the Atlantic mountains, mow down all this
 great starry harvest of six thousand years? 90
"And shall Necker, the hind of Geneva, stretch out
 his crook'd sickle o'er fertile France,
"Till our purple and crimson is faded to russet, and
 the kingdoms of earth bound in sheaves,
"And the ancient forests of chivalry hewn, and the
 joys of the combat burnt for fuel;
"Till the power and dominion is rent from the pole,
 sword and scepter from sun and moon,
"The law and gospel from fire and air, and eternal
 reason and science
"From the deep and the solid, and man lay his faded
 head down on the rock
"Of eternity, where the eternal lion and eagle remain
 to devour?
"This to prevent, urg'd by cries in day, and prophetic
 dreams hovering in night,
"To enrich the lean earth that craves, furrow'd with
 plows; whose seed is departing from her;
"Thy Nobles have gather'd thy starry hosts round
 this rebellious city,   100
"To rouze up the ancient forests of Europe, with
 clarions of loud breathing war;
"To hear the horse neigh to the drum and trumpet,
 and the trumpet and war shout reply;
"Stretch the hand that beckons the eagles of heaven;
 they cry over Paris, and wait

"Till Fayette point his finger to Versailles; the eagles
 of heaven must have their prey."

He ceas'd, and burn'd silent, red clouds roll round
 Necker, a weeping is heard o'er the palace;
Like a dark cloud Necker paus'd, and like thunder on
 the just man's burial day he paus'd;
Silent sit the winds, silent the meadows, while the
 husbandman and woman of weakness
And bright children look after him into the grave, and
 water his clay with love,
Then turn towards pensive fields; so Necker paus'd,
 and his visage was cover'd with clouds.

The King lean'd on his mountains, then lifted his head
 and look'd on his armies, that shone 110
Through heaven, tinging morning with beams of
 blood, then turning to Burgundy troubled:
"Burgundy, thou wast born a lion! My soul is
 o'ergrown with distress
"For the Nobles of France, and dark mists roll round
 me and blot the writing of God
"Written in my bosom. Necker rise, leave the
 kingdom, thy life is surrounded with snares;
"We have call'd an Assembly, but not to destroy; we
 have given gifts, not to the weak;
"I hear rushing of muskets, and bright'ning of swords,
 and visages redd'ning with war,
"Frowning and looking up from brooding villages and
 every dark'ning city;
"Ancient wonders frown over the kingdom, and cries
 of women and babes are heard,
"And tempests of doubt roll around me, and fierce
 sorrows, because of the Nobles of France;
"Depart, answer not, for the tempest must fall, as in
 years that are passed away." 120

Dropping a tear the old man his place left, and when
 he was gone out
He set his face toward Geneva to flee, and the women
 and children of the city
Kneel'd round him and kissed his garments and wept;
 he stood a short space in the street,
Then fled; and the whole city knew he was fled to
 Geneva, and the Senate heard it.

But the Nobles burn'd wrathful at Necker's departure,
 and wreath'd their clouds and waters
In dismal volumes; as risen from beneath the
 Archbishop of Paris arose,
In the rushing of scales and hissing of flames and
 rolling of sulphurous smoke.

"Hearken, Monarch of France, to the terrors of
    heaven, and let thy soul drink of my counsel;
"Sleeping at midnight in my golden tower, the repose
    of the labours of men
"Wav'd its solemn cloud over my head. I awoke; a
    cold hand passed over my limbs, and behold
"An aged form, white as snow, hov'ring in mist,
    weeping in the uncertain light,   131
"Dim the form almost faded, tears fell down the shady
    cheeks; at his feet many cloth'd
"In white robes, strewn in air censers and harps,
    silent they lay prostrated;
"Beneath, in the awful void, myriads descending and
    weeping thro' dismal winds,
"Endless the shady train shiv'ring descended, from
    the gloom where the aged form wept.
"At length, trembling, the vision sighing, in a low
    voice, like the voice of the grasshopper
    whisper'd:
"'My groaning is heard in the abbeys, and God, so
    long worshipp'd, departs as a lamp
"'Without oil; for a curse is heard hoarse thro' the
    land, from a godless race
"'Descending to beasts; they look downward and
    labour and forget my holy law;
"'The sound of prayer fails from lips of flesh, and the
    holy hymn from thicken'd tongues: 140
"'For the bars of Chaos are burst; her millions
    prepare their fiery way
"'Thro' the orbed abode of the holy dead, to root up
    and pull down and remove,
"'And Nobles and Clergy shall fail from before me,
    and my cloud and vision be no more;
"'The mitre become black, the crown vanish, and the
    scepter and ivory staff
"'Of the ruler wither among bones of death; they
    shall consume from the thistly field,
"'And the sound of the bell, and voice of the sabbath,
    and singing of the holy choir,
"'Is turn'd into songs of the harlot in day, and cries
    of the virgin in night.
"'They shall drop at the plow and faint at the harrow,
    unredeem'd, unconfess'd, unpardon'd;
"'The priest rot in his surplice by the lawless lover,
    the holy beside the accursed,
"'The King, frowning in purple, beside the grey
    plowman, and their worms embrace together.'
"The voice ceas'd, a groan shook my chamber; I
    slept, for the cloud of repose returned,   151
"But morning dawn'd heavy upon me. I rose to bring
    my Prince heaven utter'd counsel.
"Hear my counsel, O King, and send forth thy
    Generals, the command of Heaven is upon thee;

"Then do thou command, O King, to shut up this
    Assembly in their final home;
"Let thy soldiers possess this city of rebels, that
    threaten to bathe their feet
"In the blood of Nobility; trampling the heart and
    the head; let the Bastile devour
"These rebellious seditious; seal them up, O
    Anointed, in everlasting chains."
He sat down, a damp cold pervaded the Nobles, and
    monsters of worlds unknown
Swam round them, watching to be delivered; When
    Aumont, whose chaos-born soul
Eternally wand'ring a Comet and swift-falling fire,
    pale enter'd the chamber;   160
Before the red Council he stood, like a man that
    returns from hollow graves.

"Awe surrounded, alone thro' the army a fear and a
    with'ring blight blown by the north;
"The Abbe de S[i]eyes from the Nation's Assembly.
    O Princes and Generals of France,
"Unquestioned, unhindered, awe-struck are the
    soldiers; a dark shadowy man in the form
"Of King Henry the Fourth walks before him in
    fires, the captains like men bound in chains
"Stood still as he pass'd, he is come to the Louvre,
    O King, with a message to thee;
"The strong soldiers tremble, the horses their manes
    bow, and the guards of thy palace are fled."

Up rose awful in his majestic beams Bourbon's strong
    Duke; his proud sword from his thigh
Drawn, he threw on the Earth! the Duke of Bretagne
    and the Earl of Borgogne
Rose inflam'd, to and fro in the chamber, like
    thunder-clouds ready to burst.   170

"What, damp all our fires, O spectre of Henry," said
    Bourbon; "and rend the flames
"From the head of our King! Rise, Monarch of
    France; command me, and I will lead
"This army of superstition at large, that the ardor of
    noble souls quenchless,
"May yet burn in France, nor our shoulders be
    plow'd with the furrows of poverty."

Then Orleans generous as mountains arose, and
    unfolded his robe, and put forth
His benevolent hand, looking on the Archbishop, who
    changed as pale as lead;
Would have risen but could not, his voice issued harsh
    grating; instead of words harsh hissings

Shook the chamber; he ceas'd abash'd. Then Orleans
    spoke, all was silent,
He breath'd on them, and said, "O princes of fire,
    whose flames are for growth not consuming,
"Fear not dreams, fear not visions, nor be you
    dismay'd with sorrows which flee at the
    morning;
"Can the fires of Nobility ever be quench'd, or the
    stars by a stormy night?   181
"Is the body diseas'd when the members are
    healthful? can the man be bound in sorrow
"Whose ev'ry function is fill'd with its fiery desire?
    can the soul whose brain and heart
"Cast their rivers in equal tides thro' the great
    Paradise, languish because the feet
"Hands, head, bosom, and parts of love, follow their
    high breathing joy?
"And can Nobles be bound when the people are free,
    or God weep when his children are happy?
"Have you never seen Fayette's forehead, or
    Mirabeau's eyes, or the shoulders of Target,
"Or Bailly the strong foot of France, or Clermont
    the terrible voice, and your robes
"Still retain their own crimson? mine never yet faded,
    for fire delights in its form.
"But go, merciless man! enter into the infinite
    labyrinth of another's brain   190
"Ere thou measure the circle that he shall run. Go,
    thou cold recluse, into the fires
"Of another's high flaming rich bosom, and return
    unconsum'd, and write laws.
"If thou canst not do this, doubt thy theories, learn
    to consider all men as thy equals,
"Thy brethren, and not as thy foot or thy hand, unless
    thou first fearest to hurt them."

The Monarch stood up, the strong Duke his sword
    to its golden scabbard return'd,
The Nobles sat round like clouds on the mountains,
    when the storm is passing away.
"Let the Nation's Ambassador come among Nobles,
    like incense of the valley."

Aumont went out and stood in the hollow porch, his
    ivory wand in his hand;
A cold orb of disdain revolv'd round him, and covered
    his soul with snows eternal.
Great Henry's soul shuddered, a whirlwind and fire
    tore furious from his angry bosom;   200
He indignant departed on horses of heav'n. Then the
    Abbe de S[i]eyes rais'd his feet
On the steps of the Louvre, like a voice of God
    following a storm, the Abbe follow'd

The pale fires of Aumont into the chamber, as a father
    that bows to his son;
Whose rich fields inheriting spread their old glory, so
    the voice of the people bowed
Before the ancient seat of the kingdom and mountains
    to be renewed.
"Hear, O Heavens of France, the voice of the people,
    arising from valley and hill;
"O'erclouded with power. Hear the voice of vallies,
    the voice of meek cities,
"Mourning oppressed on village and field, till the
    village and field is a waste.
"For the husbandman weeps at blights of the fife,
    and blasting of trumpets consume
"The souls of mild France; the pale mother nourishes
    her child to the deadly slaughter.   210
"When the heavens were seal'd with a stone, and the
    terrible sun clos'd in an orb, and the moon
"Rent from the nations, and each star appointed for
    watchers of night,
"The millions of spirits immortal were bound in the
    ruins of sulphur heaven
"To wander inslav'd; black, deprest in dark
    ignorance, kept in awe with the whip,
"To worship terrors, bred from the blood of revenge
    and breath of desire,
"In beastial forms; or more terrible men, till the
    dawn of our peaceful morning,
"Till dawn, till morning, till the breaking of clouds,
    and swelling of winds, and the universal voice,
"Till man raise his darken'd limbs out of the caves of
    night, his eyes and his heart
"Expand: where is space! where O Sun is thy
    dwelling! where thy tent, O faint slumb'rous
    Moon.
"Then the valleys of France shall cry to the soldier,
    'throw down thy sword and musket,   220
"'And run and embrace the meek peasant.' Her
    Nobles shall hear and shall weep, and put off
"The red robe of terror, the crown of oppression, the
    shoes of contempt, and unbuckle
"The girdle of war from the desolate earth; then the
    Priest in his thund'rous cloud
"Shall weep, bending to earth embracing the valleys,
    and putting his hand to the plow,
"Shall say, 'No more I curse thee; but now I will
    bless thee: No more in deadly black
"'Devour thy labour; nor lift up a cloud in thy
    heavens, O laborious plow,
"'That the wild raging millions, that wander in
    forests, and howl in law blasted wastes,
"'Strength madden'd with slavery, honesty, bound
    in the dens of superstition,

"'May sing in the village, and shout in the harvest, and
  woo in pleasant gardens,
"'Their once savage loves, now beaming with
  knowledge, with gentle awe adorned;   230
"'And the saw, and the hammer, the chisel, the pencil,
  the pen, and the instruments
"'Of heavenly song sound in the wilds once forbidden,
  to teach the laborious plowman
"'And shepherd deliver'd from clouds of war, from
  pestilence, from night-fear, from murder,
"'From falling, from stifling, from hunger, from cold,
  from slander, discontent and sloth;
"'That walk in beasts and birds of night, driven back
  by the sandy desart
"'Like pestilent fogs round cities of men: and the
  happy earth sing in its course,
"'The mild peaceable nations be opened to
  heav'n, and men walk with their fathers in
  bliss.'
"Then hear the first voice of the morning: 'Depart,
  O clouds of night, and no more
"'Return; be withdrawn cloudy war, troops of
  warriors depart, nor around our peaceable
  city
"'Breathe fires, but ten miles from Paris, let all be
  peace, nor a soldier be seen!'"   240

He ended; the wind of contention arose and the clouds
  cast their shadows, the Princes
Like the mountains of France, whose aged trees utter
  an awful voice, and their branches
Are shatter'd, till gradual a murmur is heard
  descending into the valley,
Like a voice in the vineyards of Burgundy, when
  grapes are shaken on grass;
Like the low voice of the labouring man, instead of
  the shout of joy;
And the palace appear'd like a cloud driven abroad;
  blood ran down the ancient pillars,
Thro' the cloud a deep thunder, the Duke of
  Burgundy, delivers the King's command.

"Seest thou yonder dark castle, that moated around,
  keeps this city of Paris in awe.
"Go command yonder tower, saying, 'Bastile depart,
  and take thy shadowy course.
"'Overstep the dark river, thou terrible tower, and
  get thee up into the country ten miles.   250
"'And thou black southern prison, move along the
  dusky road to Versailles; there
"'Frown on the gardens', and if it obey and depart,
  then the King will disband

"This war-breathing army; but if it refuse, let the
  Nation's Assembly thence learn,
"That this army of terrors, that prison of horrors, are
  the bands of the murmuring kingdom."

Like the morning star arising above the black waves,
  when a shipwreck'd soul sighs for morning,
Thro' the ranks, silent, walk'd the Ambassador back
  to the Nation's Assembly, and told
The unwelcome message; silent they heard; then a
  thunder roll'd round loud and louder,
Like pillars of ancient halls, and ruins of times remote
  they sat.
Like a voice from the dim pillars Mirabeau rose; the
  thunders subsided away;
A rushing of wings around him was heard as he
  brighten'd, and cried out aloud,   260
"Where is the General of the Nation?" the walls
  re-echo'd: "Where is the General of the
  Nation?"

Sudden as the bullet wrapp'd in his fire, when brazen
  cannons rage in the field,
Fayette sprung from his seat saying, Ready! then
  bowing like clouds, man toward man, the
  Assembly
Like a council of ardors seated in clouds, bending
  over the cities of men,
And over the armies of strife, where their children
  are marshall'd together to battle;
They murmuring divide, while the wind sleeps
  beneath, and the numbers are counted in silence,
While they vote the removal of War, and the pestilence
  weighs his red wings in the sky.

So Fayette stood silent among the Assembly, and the
  votes were given and the numbers numb'red;
And the vote was, that Fayette should order the army
  to remove ten miles from Paris.

The aged sun rises appall'd from dark mountains, and
  gleams a dusky beam   270
On Fayette, but on the whole army a shadow, for a
  cloud on the eastern hills
Hover'd, and stretch'd across the city and across the
  army, and across the Louvre,
Like a flame of fire he stood before dark ranks, and
  before expecting captains
On pestilent vapours around him flow frequent
  spectres of religious men weeping
In winds driven out of the abbeys, their naked souls
  shiver in keen open air,

Driven out by the fiery cloud of Voltaire, and
    thund'rous rocks of Rousseau,
They dash like foam against the ridges of the army,
    uttering a faint feeble cry.

Gleams of fire streak the heavens, and of sulphur
    the earth, from Fayette as he lifted his
    hand;
But silent he stood, till all the officers rush round him
    like waves
Round the shore of France, in day of the British flag,
    when heavy cannons   280
Affright the coasts, and the peasant looks over the sea
    and wipes a tear;
Over his head the soul of Voltaire shone fiery, and
    over the army Rousseau his white cloud
Unfolded, on souls of war-living terrors silent list'ning
    toward Fayette,
His voice loud inspir'd by liberty, and by spirits of the
    dead, thus thunder'd.

"The Nation's Assembly command, that the Army
    remove ten miles from Paris;
"Nor a soldier be seen in road or in field, till the
    Nation command return."

Rushing along iron ranks glittering the officers each
    to his station
Depart, and the stern captain strokes his proud steed,
    and in front of his solid ranks
Waits the sound of trumpet; captains of foot stand
    each by his cloudy drum;
Then the drum beats, and the steely ranks move, and
    trumpets rejoice in the sky.   290
Dark cavalry like clouds fraught with thunder ascend
    on the hills, and bright infantry, rank
Behind rank, to the soul shaking drum and shrill fife
    along the roads glitter like fire.

The noise of trampling, the wind of trumpets, smote
    the palace walls with a blast.
Pale and cold sat the King in midst of his peers, and
    his noble heart sunk, and his pulses
Suspended their motion, a darkness crept over his
    eye-lids, and chill cold sweat
Sat round his brows faded in faint death, his peers
    pale like mountains of the dead,
Cover'd with dews of night, groaning, shaking forests
    and floods. The cold newt
And snake, and damp toad, on the kingly foot crawl,
    or croak on the awful knee,
Shedding their slime, in folds of the robe the crown'd
    adder builds and hisses

From stony brows; shaken the forests of France, sick
    the kings of the nations,   300
And the bottoms of the world were open'd, and the
    graves of arch-angels unseal'd;
The enormous dead, lift up their pale fires and look
    over the rocky cliffs.

A faint heat from their fires reviv'd the cold Louvre;
    the frozen blood reflow'd.
Awful up rose the king, him the peers follow'd, they
    saw the courts of the Palace
Forsaken, and Paris without a soldier, silent, for the
    noise was gone up
And follow'd the army, and the Senate in peace, sat
    beneath morning's beam.

END OF THE FIRST BOOK.

[1789?–1791]   [1913]

THE MARRIAGE OF HEAVEN AND HELL

Although A Song of Liberty *was probably composed well after*
The Marriage of Heaven and Hell *was finished, it appears at
the end of all nine surviving copies of that poem.*

THE *MARRIAGE* of HEAVEN and HELL

[PLATE 2]

The Argument.

Rintrah [1] roars & shakes his fires in the burdened air;
Hungry clouds swag on the deep

Once meek, and in a perilous path,
The just man kept his course along
The vale of death.
Roses are planted where thorns grow.
And on the barren heath
Sing the honey bees.

Then the perilous path was planted:
And a river, and a spring   10
On every cliff and tomb;
And on the bleached bones
Red clay brought forth.

[1] Blake's personification of visionary wrath, who prophesies
the coming of a redeemer (Blake).

Till the villain left the paths of ease,
To walk in perilous paths, and drive
The just man into barren climes.

Now the sneaking serpent walks
In mild humility.
And the just man rages in the wilds
Where lions roam.   20

Rintrah roars & shakes his fires in the burdend air;
Hungry clouds swag on the deep.

[PLATE 3]

As a new heaven is begun, and it is now thirty-three
years since its advent: the Eternal Hell revives. And
lo! Swedenborg[2] is the Angel sitting at the tomb; his
writings are the linen clothes folded up. Now is the
dominion of Edom, & the return of Adam into Para-
dise; see Isaiah xxxiv & XXXV Chap:

Without Contraries is no progression. Attraction
and Repulsion, Reason and Energy, Love and Hate,
are necessary to Human existence.

From these contraries spring what the religious call
Good & Evil. Good is the passive that obeys Reason[.]
Evil is the active springing from Energy.

Good is Heaven. Evil is Hell.

[PLATE 4]

The voice of the Devil

All Bibles or sacred codes. have been the causes of
the following Errors.

1. That Man has two real existing principles Viz: a
Body & a Soul.

2. That Energy. calld Evil. is alone from the Body.
& that Reason. calld Good. is alone from the Soul.

3. That God will torment Man in Eternity for
following his Energies. But the following Contraries
to these are True

1 Man has no Body distinct from his Soul for that
calld Body is a portion of Soul discernd by the five
Senses, the chief inlets of Soul in this age

2 Energy is the only life and is from the Body and
Reason is the bound or outward circumference of
Energy.

3 Energy is Eternal Delight

[PLATE 5]

Those who restrain desire, do so because theirs is
weak enough to be restrained; and the restrainer or
reason usurps its place & governs the unwilling.

---

[2] Emanuel Swedenborg (1688–1772), Swedish scientist,
theologian, and mystic, whose teachings fascinated Blake.

And being restraind it by degrees becomes passive
till it is only the shadow of desire.

The history of this is written in Paradise Lost. &
the Governor or Reason is call'd Messiah.

And the original Archangel or possessor of the
command of the heavenly host, is calld the Devil or
Satan and his children are call'd Sin & Death

But in the Book of Job Miltons Messiah is call'd
Satan.

For this history has been adopted by both parties

It indeed appear'd to Reason as if Desire was cast
out, but the Devils account is, that the Messi[PL 6]ah
fell. & formed a heaven of what he stole from the
Abyss

This is shewn in the Gospel, where he prays to the
Father to send the comforter or Desire that Reason
may have Ideas to build on, the Jehovah of the Bible
being no other than he, who dwells in flaming fire.
Know that after Christs death, he became Jehovah.

But in Milton; the Father is Destiny, the Son, a
Ratio of the five senses. & the Holy-ghost, Vacuum!

Note. The reason Milton wrote in fetters when he
wrote of Angels & God, and at liberty when of Devils
& Hell, is because he was a true Poet and of the Devils
party without knowing it

A Memorable Fancy.

As I was walking among the fires of hell, delighted
with the enjoyments of Genius; which to Angels look
like torment and insanity. I collected some of their
Proverbs: thinking that as the sayings used in a nation,
mark its character, so the Proverbs of Hell, shew the
nature of Infernal wisdom better than any description
of buildings or garments.

When I came home; on the abyss of the five senses,
where a flat sided steep frowns over the present world.
I saw a mighty Devil folded in black clouds, hovering
on the sides of the rock, with cor[PL 7]roding fires he
wrote the following sentence now percieved by the
minds of men, & read by them on earth.[3]

How do you know but ev'ry Bird that cuts the airy
way,

Is an immense world of delight, clos'd by your
senses five?

Proverbs of Hell.

In seed time learn, in harvest teach, in winter enjoy.

Drive your cart and your plow over the bones of the
dead.

The road of excess leads to the palace of wisdom.

---

[3] Refers also to Blake's method of relief printing using copper
plates and acid.

Prudence is a rich ugly old maid courted by
　　Incapacity.
He who desires but acts not, breeds pestilence.
The cut worm forgives the plow.
Dip him in the river who loves water.
A fool sees not the same tree that a wise man sees.
He whose face gives no light, shall never become a
　　star.
Eternity is in love with the productions of time.　　10
The busy bee has no time for sorrow.
The hours of folly are measur'd by the clock, but of
　　wisdom: no clock can measure.
All wholsom food is caught without a net or a trap.
Bring out number weight & measure in a year of
　　dearth.
No bird soars too high. if he soars with his own
　　wings.
A dead body. revenges not injuries.
The most sublime act is to set another before you.
If the fool would persist in his folly he would become
　　wise
Folly is the cloke of knavery.
Shame is Prides cloke.　　　　　　　　　　　20

[PLATE 8]

Prisons are built with stones of Law, Brothels with
　　bricks of Religion.
The pride of the peacock is the glory of God.
The lust of the goat is the bounty of God.
The wrath of the lion is the wisdom of God.
The nakedness of woman is the work of God.
Excess of sorrow laughs. Excess of joy weeps.
The roaring of lions, the howling of wolves, the raging
　　of the stormy sea, and the destructive sword. are
　　portions of eternity too great for the eye of man.
The fox condemns the trap, not himself.
Joys impregnate. Sorrows bring forth.
Let man wear the fell of the lion. woman the fleece of
　　the sheep.　　　　　　　　　　　　　　30
The bird a nest, the spider a web, man friendship.
The selfish smiling fool. & the sullen frowning fool.
　　shall be both thought wise. that they may be a
　　rod.
What is now proved was once, only imagin'd.
The rat, the mouse, the fox, the rabbet; watch the
　　roots, the lion, the tyger, the horse, the elephant,
　　watch the fruits.
The cistern contains: the fountain overflows.
One thought. fills immensity.
Always be ready to speak your mind, and a base man
　　will avoid you.
Every thing possible to be believ'd is an image of truth.
The eagle never lost so much time. as when he
　　submitted to learn of the crow.

[PLATE 9]
The fox provides for himself. but God provides for
　　the lion.　　　　　　　　　　　　　　40
Think in the morning, Act in the noon, Eat in the
　　evening, Sleep in the night.
He who has sufferd you to impose on him knows you.
As the plow follows words, so God rewards prayers.
The tygers of wrath are wiser than the horses of
　　instruction
Expect poison from the standing water.
You never know what is enough unless you know
　　what is more than enough.
Listen to the fools reproach! it is a kingly title!
The eyes of fire, the nostrils of air, the mouth of water,
　　the beard of earth.
The weak in courage is strong in cunning.
The apple tree never asks the beech how he shall
　　grow, nor the lion. the horse, how he shall take
　　his prey.　　　　　　　　　　　　　　50
The thankful reciever bears a plentiful harvest.
If others had not been foolish, we should be so.
The soul of sweet delight, can never be defil'd,
When thou seest an Eagle, thou seest a portion of
　　Genius. lift up thy head!
As the catterpiller chooses the fairest leaves to lay her
　　eggs on, so the priest lays his curse on the fairest
　　joys.
To create a little flower is the labour of ages.
Damn. braces: Bless relaxes.
The best wine is the oldest. the best water the newest.
Prayers plow not! Praises reap not!
Joys laugh not! Sorrows weep not!　　　　　60

[PLATE 10]
The head Sublime, the heart Pathos, the genitals
　　Beauty, the hands & feet Proportion.
As the air to a bird or the sea to a fish, so is contempt
　　to the contemptible.
The crow wish'd every thing was black, the owl, that
　　every thing was white.
Exuberance is Beauty.
If the lion was advise'd by the fox. he would be
　　cunning.
Improve[me]nt makes strait roads, but the crooked
　　roads without Improvement, are roads of Genius.
Sooner murder an infant in its cradle than nurse
　　unacted desires
Where man is not nature is barren.
Truth can never be told so as to be understood, and
　　not be believ'd.
　　　　　Enough! or Too much　　　　　70

[PLATE 11]
　　The ancient Poets animated all sensible objects with

Gods or Geniuses, calling them by the names and adorning them with the properties of woods, rivers, mountains, lakes, cities, nations, and whatever their enlarged & numerous senses could perceive.

And particularly they studied the genius of each city & country. placing it under its mental deity.

Till a system was formed, which some took advantage of & enslav'd the vulgar by attempting to realize or abstract the mental deities from their objects; thus began Priesthood.

Choosing forms of worship from poetic tales.

And at length they pronounced that the Gods had orderd such things.

Thus men forgot that All deities reside in the human breast.

[PLATE 12]

A Memorable Fancy.

The Prophets Isaiah and Ezekiel dined with me, and I asked them how they dared so roundly to assert. that God spake to them; and whether they did not think at the time, that they would be misunderstood, & so be the cause of imposition.

Isaiah answer'd. I saw no God, nor heard any, in a finite organical perception; but my senses discover'd the infinite in every thing, and as I was then perswaded, & remain confirm'd; that the voice of honest indignation is the voice of God, I cared not for consequences but wrote.

Then I asked: does a firm perswasion that a thing is so, make it so?

He replied. All poets believe that it does, & in ages of imagination this firm perswasion removed mountains; but many are not capable of a firm perswasion of any thing.

Then Ezekiel said. The philosophy of the east taught the first principles of human perception some nations held one principle for the origin & some another, we of Israel taught that the Poetic Genius (as you now call it) was the first principle and all the others merely derivative, which was the cause of our despising the Priests & Philosophers of other countries, and prophecying that all Gods [PL 13] would at last be proved to originate in ours & to be the tributaries of the Poetic Genius, it was this. that our great poet King David desired so fervently & invokes so patheticly, saying by this he conquers enemies & governs kingdoms; and we so loved our God. that we cursed in his name all the deities of surrounding nations, and asserted that they had rebelled; from these opinions the vulgar came to think that all nations would at last be subject to the jews.

This said he, like all firm perswasions, is come to pass, for all nations believe the jews code and worship the jews god, and what greater subjection can be

I heard this with some wonder, & must confess my own conviction. After dinner I ask'd Isaiah to favour the world with his lost works, he said none of equal value was lost. Ezekiel said the same of his.

I also asked Isaiah what made him go naked and barefoot three years? he answerd, the same that made our friend Diogenes the Grecian.

I then asked Ezekiel. why he eat dung, & lay so long on his right & left side? he answerd. the desire of raising other men into a perception of the infinite this the North American tribes practise. & is he honest who resists his genius or conscience. only for the sake of present ease or gratification?

[PLATE 14]

The ancient tradition that the world will be consumed in fire at the end of six thousand years is true. as I have heard from Hell.

For the cherub with his flaming sword is hereby commanded to leave his guard at tree of life, and when he does, the whole creation will be consumed, and appear infinite. and holy whereas it now appears finite & corrupt.

This will come to pass by an improvement of sensual enjoyment.

But first the notion that man has a body distinct from his soul, is to be expunged; this I shall do, by printing in the infernal method, by corrosives, which in Hell are salutary and medicinal, melting apparent surfaces away, and displaying the infinite which was hid.

If the doors of perception were cleansed every thing would appear to man as it is, infinite.

For man has closed himself up, till he sees all things thro' narrow chinks of his cavern.

[PLATE 15]

A Memorable Fancy

I was in a Printing house in Hell & saw the method in which knowledge is transmitted from generation to generation.

In the first chamber was a Dragon-Man, clearing away the rubbish from a caves mouth; within, a number of Dragons were hollowing the cave,

In the second chamber was a Viper folding round the rock & the cave, and others adorning it with gold silver and precious stones.

In the third chamber was an Eagle with wings and feathers of air, he caused the inside of the cave to be infinite, around were numbers of Eagle like men, who built palaces in the immense cliffs.

In the fourth chamber were Lions of flaming fire raging around & melting the metals into living fluids.

In the fifth chamber were Unnam'd forms, which cast the metals into the expanse.

There they were reciev'd by Men who occupied the sixth chamber, and took the forms of books & were arranged in libraries.

[PLATE 16]

The Giants who formed this world into its sensual existence and now seem to live in it in chains, are in truth. the causes of its life & the sources of all activity, but the chains are, the cunning of weak and tame minds. which have power to resist energy, according to the proverb, the weak in courage is strong in cunning.

Thus one portion of being, is the Prolific. the other, the Devouring: to the devourer it seems as if the producer was in his chains, but it is not so, he only takes portions of existence and fancies that the whole.

But the Prolific would cease to be Prolific unless the Devourer as a sea recieved the excess of his delights.

Some will say, Is not God alone the Prolific? I answer, God only Acts & Is, in existing beings or Men.

These two classes of men are always upon earth, & they should be enemies; whoever tries [PL 17] to reconcile them seeks to destroy existence.

Religion is an endeavour to reconcile the two.

Note. Jesus Christ did not wish to unite but to separate them, as in the Parable of sheep and goats! & he says I came not to send Peace but a Sword.

Messiah or Satan or Tempter was formerly thought to be one of the Antediluvians who are our Energies.

A Memorable Fancy

An Angel came to me and said   O pitiable foolish young man! O horrible! O dreadful state! consider the hot burning dungeon thou art preparing for thyself to all eternity, to which thou art going in such career.

I said, perhaps you will be willing to shew me my eternal lot & we will contemplate together upon it and see whether your lot or mine is most desirable

So he took me thro' a stable & thro' a church & down into the church vault at the end of which was a mill: thro' the mill we went, and came to a cave. down the winding cavern we groped our tedious way till a void boundless as a nether sky appeard beneath us. & we held by the roots of trees and hung over this immensity, but I said, if you please we will commit ourselves to this void, and see whether providence is

here also, if you will not I will? but he answerd, do not presume O young man but as we here remain behold thy lot which will soon appear when the darkness passes away

So I remaind with him sitting in the twisted [PL 18] root of an oak. he was suspended in a fungus which hung with the head downward into the deep;

By degrees we beheld the infinite Abyss, fiery as the smoke of a burning city; beneath us at an immense distance was the sun, black but shining[;] round it were fiery tracks on which revolv'd vast spiders, crawling after their prey; which flew or rather swum in the infinite deep, in the most terrific shapes of animals sprung from corruption. & the air was full of them, & seemd composed of them; these are Devils. and are called Powers of the air, I now asked my companion which was my eternal lot? he said, between the black & white spiders

But now, from between the black & white spiders a cloud and fire burst and rolled thro the deep   blackning all beneath, so that the nether deep grew black as a sea & rolled with a terrible noise: beneath us was nothing now to be seen but a black tempest, till looking east between the clouds & the waves, we saw a cataract of blood mixed with fire and not many stones throw from us appeard and sunk again the scaly fold of a monstrous serpent[.] at last the east, distant about three degrees appeard a fiery crest above the waves[.] slowly it reared like a ridge of golden rocks till we discoverd two globes of crimson fire, from which the sea fled away in clouds of smoke, and now we saw, it was the head of Leviathan, his forehead was divided into streaks of green & purple like those on a tygers forehead: soon we saw his mouth & red gills hang just above the raging foam tinging the black deep with beams of blood, advancing toward [PL 19] us with all the fury of a spiritual existence.

My friend the Angel climb'd up from his station into the mill; I remain'd alone, & then this appearance was no more, but I found myself sitting on a pleasant bank beside a river by moon light hearing a harper who sung to the harp, & his theme was, The man who never alters his opinion is like standing water, & breeds reptiles of the mind.

But I arose, and sought for the mill, & there I found my Angel, who surprised asked me, how I escaped?

I answerd. All that we saw was owing to your metaphysics: for when you ran away, I found myself on a bank by moonlight hearing a harper, But now we have seen my eternal lot, shall I shew you yours? he laughd at my proposal; but I by force suddenly caught him in my arms, & flew westerly thro' the night, till we were elevated above the earths shadow: then I flung myself with him directly into the body of the sun, here I clothed myself in white, & taking in my hand Swedenborgs volumes sunk from the glorious clime, and passed all the planets till we came to saturn, here I staid to rest & then leap'd into the void, between saturn & the fixed stars.

Here said I! is your lot, in this space, if space it may be calld, Soon we saw the stable and the church, & I took him to the altar and open'd the Bible, and lo! it was a deep pit, into which I descended driving the Angel before me, soon we saw seven houses of brick, one we enterd; in it were a [PL 20] number of monkeys, baboons, & all of that species chaind by the middle, grinning and snatching at one another, but witheld by the shortness of their chains: however I saw that they sometimes grew numerous, and then the weak were caught by the strong and with a grinning aspect, first coupled with & then devourd, by plucking off first one limb and then another till the body was left a helpless trunk. this after grinning & kissing it with seeming fondness they devourd too; and here & there I saw one savourily picking the flesh off of his own tail; as the stench terribly annoyd us both we went into the mill, & I in my hand brought the skeleton of a body, which in the mill was Aristotles Analytics.

So the Angel said: thy phantasy has imposed upon me & thou oughtest to be ashamed.

I answerd: we impose on one another, & it is but lost time to converse with you whose works are only Analytics

Opposition is true Friendship.

[PLATE 21]

I have always found that Angels have the vanity to speak of themselves as the only wise; this they do with a confident insolence sprouting from systematic reasoning;

Thus Swedenborg boasts that what he writes is new; tho' it is only the Contents or Index of already publish'd books

A man carried a monkey about for a shew, & because he was a little wiser than the monkey, grew vain, and conciev'd himself as much wiser than seven men. It is so with Swedenborg; he shews the folly of churches & exposes hypocrites, till he imagines that all are religious. & himself the single [PL 22] one on earth that ever broke a net.

Now hear a plain fact: Swedenborg has not written one new truth: Now hear another: he has written all the old falshoods.

And now hear the reason. He conversed with Angels who are all religious, & conversed not with Devils who

all hate religion, for he was incapable thro' his conceited notions.

Thus Swedenborgs writings are a recapitulation of all superficial opinions, and an analysis of the more sublime, but no further.

Have now another plain fact: Any man of mechanical talents may from the writings of Paracelsus or Jacob Behmen,[4] produce ten thousand volumes of equal value with Swedenborg's. and from those of Dante or Shakespear, an infinite number.

But when he has done this, let him not say that he knows better than his master, for he only holds a candle in sunshine.

A Memorable Fancy

Once I saw a Devil in a flame of fire. who arose before an Angel that sat on a cloud. and the Devil utterd these words.

The worship of God is. Honouring his gifts in other men each according to his genius. and loving the [PL 23] greatest men best, those who envy or calumniate great men hate God, for there is no other God.

The Angel hearing this became almost blue but mastering himself he grew yellow, & at last white pink & smiling, and then replied,

Thou Idolater, is not God One? & is not he visible in Jesus Christ? and has not Jesus Christ given his sanction to the law of ten commandments and are not all other men fools, sinners, & nothings?

The Devil answer'd; bray a fool in a morter with wheat. yet shall not his folly be beaten out of him: if Jesus Christ is the greatest man, you ought to love him in the greatest degree; now hear how he has given his sanction to the law of ten commandments: did he not mock at the sabbath, and so mock the sabbaths God? murder those who were murderd because of him? turn away the law from the woman taken in adultery? steal the labor of others to support him? bear false witness when he omitted making a defence before Pilate? covet when he pray'd for his disciples, and when he bid them shake off the dust of their feet against such as refused to lodge them? I tell you, no virtue can exist without breaking these ten commandments.'. Jesus was all virtue, and acted from im[PL 24]pulse. not from rules.

When he had so spoken: I beheld the Angel who stretched out his arms embracing the flame of fire & he was consumed and arose as Elijah.

Note. This Angel, who is now become a Devil, is my particular friend: we often read the Bible together

4 Paracelsus (1493?–1541), Swiss-German alchemist; Jakob Böhme (1575–1624), German theologian and mystic.

in its infernal or diabolical sense which the world shall have if they behave well

I have also: The Bible of Hell: which the world shall have whether they will or no.

One Law for the Lion & Ox is Oppression

[PLATE 25]

A Song of Liberty

1. The Eternal Female groand! it was heard over all the Earth:

2. Albions coast is sick silent; the American meadows faint!

3. Shadows of Prophecy shiver along by the lakes and the rivers and mutter across the ocean? France rend down thy dungeon;

4. Golden Spain burst the barriers of old Rome;

5. Cast thy keys O Rome into the deep down falling, even to eternity down falling,

6. And weep

7. In her trembling hands she took the new born terror howling:

8. On those infinite mountains of light now barr'd out by the atlantic sea, the new born fire stood before the starry king!

9. Flag'd with grey brow'd snows and thunderous visages the jealous wings wav'd over the deep.

10. The speary hand burned aloft, unbuckled was the shield, forth went the hand of jealousy among the flaming hair, and [PL 26] hurl'd the new born wonder thro' the starry night.

11. The fire, the fire, is falling!

12. Look up! look up! O citizen of London. enlarge thy countenance; O Jew, leave counting gold! return to thy oil and wine; O African! black African! (go. winged thought widen his forehead.)

13. The fiery limbs, the flaming hair, shot like the sinking sun into the western sea.

14. Wak'd from his eternal sleep, the hoary element roaring fled away:

15. Down rushd beating his wings in vain the jealous king; his grey brow'd councellors, thunderous warriors, curl'd veterans, among helms, and shields, and chariots[,] horses, elephants: banners, castles, slings and rocks,

16. Falling, rushing, ruining! buried in the ruins, on Urthona's dens.

17. All night beneath the ruins, then their sullen flames faded emerge round the gloomy king,

18. With thunder and fire: leading his starry hosts thro' the waste wilderness [PL 27] he promulgates his ten commands, glancing his beamy eyelids over the deep in dark dismay,

19. Where the son of fire in his eastern cloud, while the morning plumes her golden breast,

20. Spurning the clouds written with curses, stamps the stony law to dust, loosing the eternal horses from the dens of night, crying

Empire is no more! and now the lion & wolf shall cease.

Chorus

Let the Priests of the Raven of dawn, no longer in deadly black. with hoarse note curse the sons of joy. Nor his accepted breathren whom, tyrant, he calls free: lay the bound or build the roof. Nor pale religious letchery call that virginity, that wishes but acts not!

For every thing that lives is Holy

[1790–93]   [1793]

BLAKE'S NOTEBOOK

The poems in this section are taken from the notebook Blake used from 1793 to 1811 for working out poems, making sketches, jotting down notes. Although the book was used by editors and biographers such as D. G. Rossetti, Swinburne, and Yeats, the complete text of the poems in it was not published until 1905. Since many of the poems are extensively revised and often contain indecipherable lines, any printing of them requires either elaborate textual notes or unusual reliance on the speculations of editors. The second course is followed here, since a photographic reproduction of the Notebook is easily available.

FROM

BLAKE'S NOTEBOOK

"Never pain to tell . . ."

Never pain to tell thy love
Love that never told can be
For the gentle wind does move
Silently invisibly

I told my love I told my love
I told her all my heart
Trembling cold in ghastly fears
Ah she doth depart

Soon as she was gone from me
A traveller came by   10
Silently invisibly
O was no deny

"I feard the fury . . ."

I feard the fury of my wind
Would blight all blossoms fair & true
And my sun it shind & shind
And my wind it never blew

But a blossom fair or true
Was not found on any tree
For all blossoms grew & grew
Fruitless false tho fair to see

"I saw a chapel . . ."

I saw a chapel all of gold
That none did dare to enter in
And many weeping stood without
Weeping mourning worshipping

I saw a serpent rise between
The white pillars of the door
And he forcd & forcd & forcd
Down the golden hinges tore

And along the pavement sweet
Set with pearls & rubies bright   10
All his slimy length he drew
Till upon the altar white

Vomiting his poison out
On the bread & on the wine
So I turnd into a sty
And laid me down among the swine

"I laid me down . . ."

I laid me down upon a bank
Where love lay sleeping
I heard among the rushes dank
Weeping Weeping

Then I went to the heath & the wild
To the thistles & thorns of the waste
And they told me how they were beguild
Driven out & compeld to be chaste

I ASKED A THIEF

The text used here is that of the fair copy Blake signed and dated in 1796. The revised text of the Notebook copy is verbally identical.

"I asked a thief . . ."

I askéd a thief to steal me a peach
He turned up his eyes.
I ask'd a lithe lady to lie her down
Holy & meek she cries—

As soon as I went
An angel came.
He wink'd at the thief
And smil'd at the dame—

And without one word said
Had a peach from the tree
And still as a maid
Enjoy'd the lady.

"WHY SHOULD I CARE"

This is, perhaps, the earliest version of the poem that eventually appeared as London (*see below*) *in* Songs of Experience.

"Why should I care . . ."

Why should I care for the men of thames
Or the cheating waves of charterd streams
Or shrink at the little blasts of fear
That the hireling blows into my ear

Tho born on the cheating banks of Thames
Tho his waters bathed my infant limbs
The Ohio shall wash his stains from me
I was born a slave but I go to be free

"Silent Silent Night"

Silent Silent Night
Quench the holy light
Of thy torches bright

For possessd of Day
Thousand spirits stray
That sweet joys betray

Why should joys be sweet
Used with deceit
Nor with sorrows meet

But an honest joy   10
Does itself destroy
For a harlot coy

TO NOBODADDY

Why art thou silent & invisible
Father of Jealousy
Why dost thou hide thyself in clouds
From every searching Eye

Why darkness & obscurity
In all thy words & laws
That none dare eat the fruit but from
The wily serpents jaws
Or is it because Secrecy
gains females loud applause   10

THE FAIRY

Come hither my sparrows
My little arrows
If a tear or a smile
Will a man beguile
If an amorous delay
Clouds a sunshiny day
If the step of a foot
Smites the heart to its root
Tis the marriage ring
Makes each fairy a king   10

So a fairy sung
From the leaves I sprung
He leapd from the spray
To flee away
But in my hat caught
He soon shall be taught
Let him laugh let him cry
Hes my butterfly
For I've pulld out the Sting
Of the marriage ring   20

MOTTO TO THE SONGS OF INNOCENCE & OF EXPERIENCE

The Good are attracted by Mens perceptions
    And Think not for themselves
        Till Experience teaches them to catch
    And to cage the Fairies & Elves

And then the Knave begins to snarl
And the Hypocrite to howl
And all his good Friends shew their private ends
And the Eagle is known from the Owl

SEVERAL QUESTIONS ANSWERED
The Notebook arrangement suggests that Blake intended these stanzas to form a group; they appear in a variety of orders, combinations, and texts. Perhaps they should be regarded as a series of aphorisms from which a poem might have been made.

SEVERAL QUESTIONS ANSWERED

Eternity

He who binds to himself a joy
Does the winged life destroy
But he who kisses the joy as it flies
Lives in Eternitys sun rise

The look of love alarms
Because 'tis filld with fire
But the look of soft deceit
Shall Win the lovers hire

Soft deceit & Idleness
These are Beauties sweetest dress   10

What is it men in women do require
The lineaments of Gratified Desire
What is it women do in men require
The lineaments of Gratified Desire

An ancient Proverb

Remove away that blackning church
Remove away that marriage hearse
Remove away that————[1]of blood
Youll quite remove the ancient curse

LET THE BROTHELS OF PARIS BE OPENED
The following lines are taken from a section of Blake's notebook that deletions, revisions and reordering make particularly difficult to decipher. In his edition of Blake D. V. Erdman suggests that Blake began with the idea of the brothels, then conceived of a poem presenting three symbolic figures, as in The Visions of the Daughters of Albion. *Says Erdman, "Most of [Blake's] energy on these two manuscript pages, once the Fayette-King-Queen idea has grown out of the "Brothels" poem, is expended on arranging and rearranging a few simple rhetorical questions around the central frozen image of a moment of betrayal located at the storm center of the French Revolution." The text printed here is a compromise, neither entirely an editor's conjecture nor a complete transcription of all the words in the manuscript. But the main lines, though abandoned by Blake, seemed of sufficient*

[1] Where the dash now stands Blake wrote first "place," and then "man." Erdman suggests that Blake may have wished to avoid writing the word "palace." See *London* above.

interest to be reproduced. Both Erdman's textual notes and Keynes's conjectural "finishing" of the poem in the Oxford edition should be consulted.

"Let the brothels of Paris be opened"

Let the Brothels of Paris be opened
With many an alluring dance
To awake the Physicians thro the city
Said the beautiful Queen of France

Then old Nobodaddy aloft
Farted & belchd & coughd
And said I love hanging & drawing & quartering
Every bit as well as war & slaughtering

Then he swore a great & solemn Oath
To kill the people I am loth   10
But If they rebel they must go to hell
They shall have a Priest & a passing bell

The King awoke on his couch of gold
As soon as he heard these tidings told
Arise & come both fife & drum
And the ~~Famine~~[1] shall eat both crust & crumb

The Queen of France just touchd this Globe
And the Pestilence darted from her robe
But our good Queen quite grows to the ground
And a great many suckers grow all around   20

Who will exchange his own fire side[2]
For the stone of anothers door
Who will exchange his wheaten loaf
For the links of a dungeon floor

Fayette[3] beheld the King & Queen
In curses & iron bound
But mute Fayette wept tear for tear
And guarded them around

[1] Blake struck out this word but failed to substitute any other.
[2] Although these stanzas are clearly related to those above and are usually printed as part of the same poem, their separation in the manuscript is quite definite. One cancelled stanza from this section reads:

> Fayette Fayette thourt bought & sold
> And sold is thy happy morrow
> Thou gavest the tears of Pity away
> In exchange for the tears of sorrow

[3] Marquis de Lafayette (1757–1834), soldier, statesman, aristocratic friend of the American and French Revolutions, who protected as long as possible the lives of Louis XVI and Marie Antoinette. Blake made the name republican by omitting the first two letters. See also *The French Revolution*, p. 26 above, and Coleridge's sonnet to him, p. 434 below.

O who would smile on the wintry seas
& Pity the stormy roar   30
Or who will exchange his new born child
For the dog at the wintry door

WHEN KLOPSTOCK ENGLAND DEFIED
Friedrich Gottlieb Klopstock (1724–1803), often considered by his English contemporaries the German Milton, argued that the coarse tone of English writers precluded their achieving poetic grandeur. This scatalogical version of divine inspiration is Blake's equally defiant reply. Erdman suggests that the poem Blake anticipates writing is The Four Zoas (Vala), and dates these lines c. 1797–99; Keynes links them to those above on Lafayette and dates them c. 1793.

"When Klopstock England defied"

When Klopstock England defied
Uprose terrible Blake in his pride
For old Nobodaddy aloft
Farted & Belchd & coughd
Then swore a great oath that made heavn quake
And calld aloud to English Blake
Blake was giving his body ease
At Lambeth beneath the poplar trees
From his seat then started he
And turnd himself round three times three   10
The Moon at that sight blushd scarlet red
The stars threw down their cups & fled
And all the devils that were in hell
Answered with a ninefold yell
Klopstock felt the intripled turn
And all his bowels began to churn
And his bowels turned round three times three
And lockd in his soul with a ninefold key
That from his body it neer could be parted
Till to the last trumpet it was farted   20
Then again old Nobodaddy swore
He neer had seen such a thing before
Since Noah was shut in the ark
Since Eve first chose her hell fire spark
Since twas the fashion to go naked
Since the old anything was created
And so feeling he begd him to turn again
And ease poor Klopstocks nine fold pain
From pity then he redend round
And the Spell removed unwound   30
If Blake could do this when he rose up from
    shite
What might he not do if he sat down to write

[1793 ff.]   [1863, 1905, etc.]

[END OF SELECTIONS FROM THE NOTEBOOK]

VISIONS OF THE DAUGHTERS OF ALBION
Blake invented most of the names for his characters in this poem: Oothoon perhaps taken from Oithona in Ossian; Bromion from the Greek for "thundering" and perhaps "stinking"; Theotormon more clearly "tormented by God." Urizen, who appears here for the first time in Blake's poetry, may get his name either from the Greek for "horizon" or from the pun on Your Reason. Although characters, scenes, and themes from Blake's other prophecies occur frequently here, and although allusions to contemporary history are deliberate and complex (see Erdman, Prophet Against Empire), nevertheless the universal dramatic situation and language make this the most easily accessible of the prophecies.

VISIONS of the
Daughters of Albion

The Eye sees more than the Heart knows.

Printed by Will:ᵐ Blake: 1793.

[PLATE iii]

The Argument

I loved Theotormon
And I was not ashamed
I trembled in my virgin fears
And I hid in Leutha's vale!

I plucked Leutha's flower,
And I rose up from the vale;
But the terrible thunders tore
My virgin mantle in twain.

[PLATE 1]

Visions

ENSLAV'D, the Daughters of Albion weep: a
   trembling lamentation
Upon their mountains; in their valleys. sighs toward
   America.

For the soft soul of America, Oothoon wanderd in woe,
Along the vales of Leutha seeking flowers to comfort
   her;
And thus she spoke to the bright Marygold of Leutha's
   vale
  Art thou a flower! art thou a nymph! I see thee now
   a flower;
  Now a nymph! I dare not pluck thee from thy dewy
   bed?

The Golden nymph replied; pluck thou my flower
   Oothoon the mild
Another flower shall spring, because the soul of
   sweet delight
Can never pass away. she ceas'd & closd her golden
   shrine.   10

Then Oothoon pluck'd the flower saying, I pluck thee
   from thy bed
Sweet flower. and put thee here to glow between my
   breasts
And thus I turn my face to where my whole soul seeks.

Over the waves she went in wing'd exulting swift
   delight;
And over Theotormons reign, took her impetuous
   course.

Bromion rent her with his thunders. on his stormy
   bed
Lay the faint maid, and soon her woes appalld his
   thunders hoarse

Bromion spoke. behold this harlot here on Bromions
   bed,
And let the jealous dolphins sport around the lovely
   maid;
Thy soft American plains are mine, and mine thy
   north & south: 20
Stampt with my signet are the swarthy children of the
   sun:
They are obedient, they resist not, they obey the
   scourge:
Their daughters worship terrors and obey the violent:

[PLATE 2]

Now thou maist marry Bromions harlot, and protect
   the child
Of Bromions rage, that Oothoon shall put forth in
   nine moons time

Then storms rent Theotormons limbs; he rolld his
   waves around.
And folded his black jealous waters round the
   adulterate pair
Bound back to back in Bromions caves terror &
   meekness dwell

At entrance Theotormon sits wearing the threshold
   hard
With secret tears; beneath him sound like waves on a
   desart shore

The voice of slaves beneath the sun, and children
    bought with money.
That shiver in religious caves beneath the burning
    fires
Of lust, that belch incessant from the summits of the
    earth   10

Oothoon weeps not: she cannot weep! her tears are
    locked up;
But she can howl incessant writhing her soft snowy
    limbs.
And calling Theotormons Eagles to prey upon her
    flesh.

I call with holy voice! kings of the sounding air,
Rend away this defiled bosom that I may reflect.
The image of Theotormon on my pure transparent
    breast.

The Eagles at her call descend & rend their bleeding
    prey;
Theotormon severely smiles. her soul reflects the
    smile;
As the clear spring mudded with feet of beasts grows
    pure & smiles.

The Daughters of Albion hear her woes. & eccho back
    her sighs.   20
Why does my Theotormon sit weeping upon the
    threshold;
And Oothoon hovers by his side, perswading him in
    vain:
I cry arise O Theotormon for the village dog
Barks at the breaking day. the nightingale has done
    lamenting.
The lark does rustle in the ripe corn, and the Eagle
    returns
From nightly prey, and lifts his golden beak to the
    pure east;
Shaking the dust from his immortal pinions to
    awake
The sun that sleeps too long. Arise my Theotormon
    I am pure.
Because the night is gone that clos'd me in its deadly
    black.
They told me that the night & day were all that I
    could see;   30
They told me that I had five senses to inclose me up.
And they inclos'd my infinite brain into a narrow
    circle.
And sunk my heart into the Abyss, a red round globe
    hot burning
Till all from life I was obliterated and erased.

Instead of morn arises a bright shadow, like an
    eye
In the eastern cloud: instead of night a sickly charnel
    house;
That Theotormon hears me not! to him the night and
    morn
Are both alike: a night of sighs, a morning of fresh
    tears;

[PLATE 3]
And none but Bromion can hear my lamentations.

With what sense is it that the chicken shuns the
    ravenous hawk?
With what sense does the tame pigeon measure out
    the expanse?
With what sense does the bee form cells? have not
    the mouse & frog
Eyes and ears and sense of touch? yet are their
    habitations.
And their pursuits, as different as their forms and as
    their joys:
Ask the wild ass why he refuses burdens: and the
    meek camel
Why he loves man: is it because of eye ear mouth or
    skin
Or breathing nostrils? No. for these the wolf and
    tyger have.
Ask the blind worm the secrets of the grave, and why
    her spires   10
Love to curl round the bones of death; and ask the
    rav'nous snake
Where she gets poison: & the wing'd eagle why he
    loves the sun
And then tell me the thoughts of man, that have been
    hid of old.

Silent I hover all the night, and all day could be
    silent.
If Theotormon once would turn his loved eyes
    upon me;
How can I be defild when I reflect thy image pure?
Sweetest the fruit that the worm feeds on. & the soul
    prey'd on by woe
The new wash'd lamb ting'd with the village smoke
    & the bright swan
By the red earth of our immortal river: I bathe my
    wings.
And I am white and pure to hover round
    Theotormons breast.   20

Then Theotormon broke his silence. and he
    answered.

Tell me what is the night or day to one o'erflowd
    with woe?
Tell me what is a thought? & of what substance is it
    made?
Tell me what is a joy? & in what gardens do joys
    grow?
And in what rivers swim the sorrows? and upon
    what mountains

[PLATE 4]

Wave shadows of discontent? and in what houses
    dwell the wretched
Drunken with woe forgotten, and shut up from cold
    despair.

Tell me where dwell the thoughts forgotten till thou
    call them forth
Tell me where dwell the joys of old! & where the
    ancient loves?
And when will they renew again & the night of
    oblivion past?
That I might traverse times & spaces far remote and
    bring
Comforts into a present sorrow and a night of pain
Where goest thou O thought? to what remote land is
    thy flight?
If thou returnest to the present moment of affliction
Wilt thou bring comforts on thy wings. and dews
    and honey and balm;   10
Or poison from the desart wilds, from the eyes of the
    envier.

Then Bromion said: and shook the cavern with his
    lamentation

Thou knowest that the ancient trees seen by thine
    eyes have fruit;
But knowest thou that trees and fruits flourish upon
    the earth
To gratify senses unknown? trees beasts and birds
    unknown:
Unknown, not unpercievd, spread in the infinite
    microscope,
In places yet unvisited by the voyager. and in worlds
Over another kind of seas, and in atmospheres
    unknown:
Ah! are there other wars, beside the wars of sword
    and fire!
And are there other sorrows, beside the sorrows of
    poverty!   20
And are there other joys, beside the joys of riches
    and ease?
And is there not one law for both the lion and the ox?

And is there not eternal fire, and eternal chains?
To bind the phantoms of existence from eternal life?

Then Oothoon waited silent all the day. and all the
    night,

[PLATE 5]

But when the morn arose, her lamentation renewd,
The Daughters of Albion hear her woes, & eccho
    back her sighs.

O Urizen! Creator of men! mistaken Demon of
    heaven:
Thy joys are tears! thy labour vain, to form men to
    thine image.
How can one joy absorb another? are not different
    joys
Holy, eternal, infinite! and each joy is a Love.

Does not the great mouth laugh at a gift? & the narrow
    eyelids mock
At the labour that is above payment, and wilt thou
    take the ape
For thy councellor? or the dog, for a schoolmaster to
    thy children?
Does he who contemns poverty, and he who turns
    with abhorrence   10
From usury: feel the same passion or are they moved
    alike?
How can the giver of gifts experience the delights of
    the merchant?
How the industrious citizen the pains of the
    husbandman.
How different far the fat fed hireling with hollow
    drum;
Who buys whole corn fields into wastes, and sings
    upon the heath:
How different their eye and ear! how different the
    world to them!
With what sense does the parson claim the labour of
    the farmer?
What are his nets & gins & traps. & how does he
    surround him
With cold floods of abstraction, and with forests of
    solitude,
To build him castles and high spires. where kings &
    priests may dwell.   20
Till she who burns with youth. and knows no fixed
    lot; is bound
In spells of law to one she loaths: and must she drag
    the chain
Of life, in weary lust! must chilling murderous
    thoughts. obscure

The clear heaven of her eternal spring? to bear the
  wintry rage
Of a harsh terror driv'n to madness, bound to hold a
  rod
Over her shrinking shoulders all the day; & all the
  night
To turn the wheel of false desire: and longings that
  wake her womb
To the abhorred birth of cherubs in the human
  form
That live a pestilence & die a meteor & are no more.
Till the child dwell with one he hates. and do the
  deed he loaths   30
And the impure scourge force his seed into its
  unripe birth
E'er yet his eyelids can behold the arrows of the day.

Does the whale worship at thy footsteps as the
  hungry dog?
Or does he scent the mountain prey, because his
  nostrils wide
Draw in the ocean? does his eye discern the flying
  cloud
As the ravens eye? or does he measure the expanse
  like the vulture?
Does the still spider view the cliffs where eagles
  hide their young?
Or does the fly rejoice. because the harvest is brought
  in?
Does not the eagle scorn the earth & despise the
  treasures beneath?
But the mole knoweth what is there, & the worm
  shall tell it thee.   40
Does not the worm erect a pillar in the mouldering
  church yard?

[PLATE 6]
And a palace of eternity in the jaws of the hungry
  grave
Over his porch these words are written. Take thy
  bliss O Man!
And sweet shall be thy taste & sweet thy infant joys
  renew!

Infancy, fearless, lustful, happy! nestling for delight
In laps of pleasure; Innocence! honest, open,
  seeking
The vigorous joys of morning light; open to virgin
  bliss,
Who taught thee modesty, subtil modesty! child of
  night & sleep
When thou awakest. wilt thou dissemble all thy
  secret joys

Or wert thou not, awake when all this mystery was
  disclos'd!
Then com'st thou forth a modest virgin knowing to
  dissemble   10
With nets found under thy night pillow, to catch
  virgin joy,
And brand it with the name of whore; & sell it in the
  night,
In silence. ev'n without a whisper, and in seeming
  sleep:
Religious dreams and holy vespers, light thy smoky
  fires:
Once were thy fires lighted by the eyes of honest
  morn
And does my Theotormon seek this hypocrite
  modesty!
This knowing, artful, secret, fearful, cautious,
  trembling hypocrite.
Then is Oothoon a whore indeed! and all the virgin
  joys
Of life are harlots: and Theotormon is a sick mans
  dream
And Oothoon is the crafty slave of selfish holiness. 20
But Oothoon is not so, a virgin fill'd with virgin
  fancies
Open to joy and to delight where ever beauty appears
If in the morning sun I find it: there my eyes are
  fix'd

[PLATE 7]
In happy copulation; if in evening mild. wearied
  with work;
Sit on a bank and draw the pleasures of this free born
  joy.

    The moment of desire! the moment of desire!
      The virgin
That pines for man; shall awaken her womb to
  enormous joys
In the secret shadows of her chamber; the youth
  shut up from
The lustful joy. shall forget to generate. & create an
  amorous image
In the shadows of his curtains and in the folds of his
  silent pillow.
Are not these the places of religion? the rewards of
  continence?
The self enjoyings of self denial? Why dost thou seek
  religion?
Is it because acts are not lovely, that thou seekest
  solitude,   10
Where the horrible darkness is impressed with
  reflections of desire.

Father of Jealousy. be thou accursed from the earth!

Why hast thou taught my Theotormon this accursed
   thing?

Till beauty fades from off my shoulders darken'd and
   cast out,

A solitary shadow wailing on the margin of non-
   entity.

I cry, Love! Love! Love! happy happy Love! free as
   the mountain wind!

Can that be Love, that drinks another as a sponge
   drinks water?

That clouds with jealousy his nights, with weepings
   all the day:

To spin a web of age around him. grey and hoary!
   dark!

Till his eyes sicken at the fruit that hangs before his
   sight.   20

Such is self-love that envies all! a creeping skeleton

With lamplike eyes watching around the frozen
   marriage bed.

But silken nets and traps of adamant will Oothoon
   spread,

And catch for thee girls of mild silver, or of furious
   gold;

I'll lie beside thee on a bank & view their wanton
   play

In lovely copulation bliss on bliss with Theotormon:

Red as the rosy morning, lustful as the first born
   beam,

Oothoon shall view his dear delight, nor e'er with
   jealous cloud

Come in the heaven of generous love; nor selfish
   blightings bring.

Does the sun walk in glorious raiment. on the secret
   floor   30

[PLATE 8]

Where the cold miser spreads his gold? or does the
   bright cloud drop

On his stone threshold? does his eye behold the beam
   that brings

Expansion to the eye of pity? or will he bind himself

Beside the ox to thy hard furrow? does not that mild
   beam blot

The bat, the owl, the glowing tyger, and the king of
   night.

The sea fowl takes the wintry blast. for a cov'ring to
   her limbs:

And the wild snake, the pestilence to adorn him with
   gems & gold.

And trees. & birds. & beasts. & men. behold their
   eternal joy.

Arise you little glancing wings, and sing your infant
   joy!

Arise and drink your bliss, for every thing that lives
   is holy!   10

Thus every morning wails Oothoon. but Theotormon
   sits

Upon the margind ocean conversing with shadows
   dire.

The Daughters of Albion hear her woes, & eccho
   back her sighs.

                    The End

[1793]   [1793]

AMERICA A PROPHECY

The text of two of the three canceled plates of America *is
provided at the end of the poem (plate a is a version of plate 3).
Plate b was probably intended to follow plate 3 (and replace
part of plate 4); Plate c apparently was to have come between
different versions of plates 8 and 9. No attempt is made here to
indicate the extensive changes made in these canceled plates.*

AMERICA a PROPHECY

LAMBETH

Printed by William Blake in the year 1793

[PLATE 1]

PRELUDIUM

The shadowy daughter of Urthona stood before red
   Orc.[1]

When fourteen suns had faintly journey'd o'er his
   dark abode;

His food she brought in iron baskets, his drink in
   cups of iron;

Crown'd with a helmet & dark hair the nameless
   female stood;

[1] Urthona (perhaps a pun on Earth-Owner), like Los, appar-
ently personifies the imaginative faculty of man; Orc (from the
Lat. *orcus* = hell) is the fiery spirit of revolutionary energy, and
in many of Blake's poems is the antagonist to Urizen, the paterna-
listic god of rationality and repressive control, who appears here
in plate 8.

A quiver with its burning stores, a bow like that of
    night,
When pestilence is shot from heaven; no other arms
    she need:
Invulnerable tho' naked, save where clouds roll
    round her loins,
Their awful folds in the dark air; silent she stood as
    night;
For never from her iron tongue could voice or sound
    arise;
But dumb till that dread day when Orc assay'd his
    fierce embrace.   10
Dark virgin; said the hairy youth, thy father stern
    abhorr'd;
Rivets my tenfold chains while still on high my spirit
    soars;
Sometimes an eagle screaming in the sky, sometimes
    a lion,
Stalking upon the mountains, & sometimes a whale I
    lash
The raging fathomless abyss, anon a serpent folding
Around the pillars of Urthona, and round thy dark
    limbs,
On the Canadian wilds I fold, feeble my spirit folds.
For chaind beneath I rend these caverns; when thou
    bringest food
I howl my joy! and my red eyes seek to behold thy
    face
In vain! these clouds roll to & fro, & hide thee from
    my sight.   20

[PLATE 2]
Silent as despairing love, and strong as jealousy,
The hairy shoulders rend the links, free are the wrists
    of fire;
Round the terrific loins he siez'd the panting
    struggling womb;
It joy'd: she put aside her clouds & smiled her first-
    born smile;
As when a black cloud shews its light'nings to the
    silent deep.

Soon as she saw the terrible boy then burst the virgin
    cry.

I know thee, I have found thee, & I will not let thee
    go;
Thou art the image of God who dwells in darkness of
    Africa;
And thou art fall'n to give me life in regions of dark
    death.
On my American plains I feel the struggling
    afflictions   10

Endur'd by roots that writhe their arms into the
    nether deep:
I see a serpent in Canada, who courts me to his love;
In Mexico an Eagle, and a Lion in Peru;
I see a Whale in the South-sea, drinking my soul
    away.
O what limb rending pains I feel. thy fire & my frost
Mingle in howling pains, in furrows by thy lightnings
    rent;
This is eternal death; and this the torment long
    foretold.

The stern Bard ceas'd, asham'd of his own song;
    enrag'd he swung
His harp aloft sounding, then dash'd its shining
    frame against
A ruin'd pillar in glittring fragments; silent he
    turn'd away,   20
And wander'd down the vales of Kent in sick & drear
    lamentings.

[PLATE 3]

A PROPHECY

The Guardian Prince of Albion[2] burns in his
    nightly tent,
Sullen fires across the Atlantic glow to America's
    shore:
Piercing the souls of warlike men, who rise in silent
    night,
Washington, Franklin, Paine & Warren, Gates,
    Hancock & Green;[3]
Meet on the coast glowing with blood from Albions
    fiery Prince.

Washington spoke; Friends of America look over the
    Atlantic sea;
A bended bow is lifted in heaven, & a heavy iron
    chain
Descends link by link from Albions cliffs across the
    sea to bind
Brothers & sons of America, till our faces pale and
    yellow;
Hands deprest, voices weak, eyes downcast, hands
    work-bruis'd,
Feet bleeding on the sultry sands, and the furrows of
    the whip
Descend to generations that in future times forget.—

    [2] George III of England.
    [3] Joseph Warren, Horatio Gates, and Nathaniel Greene were
all American generals during the Revolution, the military
counterparts of statesmen or thinkers like Benjamin Franklin,
John Hancock, and Tom Paine.

The strong voice ceas'd; for a terrible blast swept
    over the heaving sea;
The eastern cloud rent; on his cliffs stood Albions
    wrathful Prince
A dragon form clashing his scales at midnight he
    arose,
And flam'd red meteors round the land of Albion
    beneath[.]
His voice, his locks, his awful shoulders, and his
    glowing eyes,

[PLATE 4]

Appear to the Americans upon the cloudy night.

Solemn heave the Atlantic waves between the gloomy
    nations,
Swelling, belching from its deeps red clouds &
    raging Fires!
Albion is sick! America faints! enrag'd the Zenith
    grew.
As human blood shooting its veins all round the orbed
    heaven
Red rose the clouds from the Atlantic in vast wheels
    of blood
And in the red clouds rose a Wonder o'er the Atlantic
    sea;
Intense! naked! a Human fire fierce glowing, as the
    wedge
Of iron heated in the furnace; his terrible limbs were
    fire
With myriads of cloudy terrors banners dark &
    towers   10
Surrounded; heat but not light went thro' the murky
    atmosphere
The King of England looking westward trembles at
    the vision

[PLATE 5]

Albions Angel stood beside the Stone of night, [4] and
    saw
The terror like a comet, or more like the planet red
That once inclos'd the terrible wandering comets in
    its sphere.
Then Mars thou wast our center, & the planets three
    flew round
Thy crimson disk; so e'er the Sun was rent from thy
    red sphere;
The Spectre glowd his horrid length staining the
    temple long
With beams of blood; & thus a voice came forth,
    and shook the temple

---

[4] Moses' tablet containing the Ten Commandments.

[PLATE 6]

The morning comes, the night decays, the watchmen
    leave their stations;
The grave is burst, the spices shed, the linen wrapped
    up;
The bones of death, the cov'ring clay, the sinews
    shrunk & dry'd.
Reviving shake, inspiring move, breathing!
    awakening!
Spring like redeemed captives when their bonds &
    bars are burst;
Let the slave grinding at the mill, run out into the
    field:
Let him look up into the heavens & laugh in the
    bright air;
Let the inchained soul shut up in darkness and in
    sighing,
Whose face has never seen a smile in thirty weary
    years;
Rise and look out, his chains are loose, his dungeon
    doors are open.   10
And let his wife and children return from the
    opressors scourge;
They look behind at every step & believe it is a dream.
Singing. The Sun has left his blackness, & has found
    a fresher morning
And the fair Moon rejoices in the clear & cloudless
    night;
For Empire is no more, and now the Lion & Wolf
    shall cease.

[PLATE 7]

In thunders ends the voice. Then Albions Angel
    wrathful burnt
Beside the Stone of Night; and like the Eternal
    Lions howl
In famine & war, reply'd. Art thou not Orc; who
    serpent-form'd
Stands at the gate of Enitharmon [5] to devour her
    children;
Blasphemous Demon, Antichrist, hater of Dignities;
Lover of wild rebellion, and transgresser of Gods Law;
Why dost thou come to Angels eyes in this terrific
    form?

[PLATE 8]

The terror answerd: I am Orc, wreath'd round the
    accursed tree:
The times are ended; shadows pass the morning
    gins to break;

---

[5] The mother of Orc, Enitharmon here represents nature.
See also Chap. VI and Chap. VII, The [First] Book of Urizen,
below.

The fiery joy, that Urizen perverted to ten
    commands,
What night he led the starry hosts thro' the wide
    wilderness:
That stony law I stamp to dust: and scatter religion
    abroad
To the four winds as a torn book, & none shall
    gather the leaves;
But they shall rot on desart sands, & consume in
    bottomless deeps;
To make the desarts blossom, & the deeps shrink to
    their fountains,
And to renew the fiery joy, and burst the stony roof.
That pale religious letchery, seeking Virginity,   10
May find it in a harlot, and in coarse-clad honesty
The undefil'd tho' ravish'd in her cradle night and
    morn:
For every thing that lives is holy, life delights in life;
Because the soul of sweet delight can never be
    defil'd.
Fires inwrap the earthly globe, yet man is not
    consumed;
Amidst the lustful fires he walks: his feet become like
    brass,
His knees and thighs like silver, & his breast and
    head like gold.

[PLATE 9]

Sound! sound! my loud war-trumpets & alarm my
    Thirteen Angels![6]
Loud howls the eternal Wolf! the eternal Lion
    lashes his tail!
America is darkned; and my punishing Demons
    terrified
Crouch howling before their caverns deep like skins
    dry'd in the wind.
They cannot smite the wheat, nor quench the fatness
    of the earth.
They cannot smite with sorrows, nor subdue the
    plow and spade.
They cannot wall the city, nor moat round the castle
    of princes.
They cannot bring the stubbed oak to overgrow the
    hills.
For terrible men stand on the shores, & in their
    robes I see
Children take shelter from the lightnings, there
    stands Washington   10
And Paine and Warren with their foreheads reard
    toward the east
But clouds obscure my aged sight. A vision from
    afar!

‹›

[6] I.e., the American colonies.

Sound! sound! my loud war-trumpets & alarm my
    thirteen Angels:
Ah vision from afar! Ah rebel form that rent the
    ancient
Heavens; Eternal Viper self-renew'd, rolling in
    clouds
I see thee in thick clouds and darkness on America's
    shore.
Writhing in pangs of abhorred birth; red flames the
    crest rebellious
And eyes of death; the harlot womb oft opened in
    vain
Heaves in enormous circles, now the times are
    return'd upon thee,
Devourer of thy parent, now thy unutterable torment
    renews.   20
Sound! sound! my loud war trumpets & alarm my
    thirteen Angels!
Ah terrible birth! a young one bursting! where is the
    weeping mouth?
And where the mothers milk? instead those ever-
    hissing jaws
And parched lips drop with fresh gore; now roll
    thou in the clouds
Thy mother lays her length outstretch'd upon the
    shore beneath.
Sound! sound! my loud war-trumpets & alarm my
    thirteen Angels!
Loud howls the eternal Wolf: the eternal Lion
    lashes his tail!

[PLATE 10]

Thus wept the Angel voice & as he wept the terrible
    blasts
Of trumpets, blew a loud alarm across the Atlantic
    deep.
No trumpets answer; no reply of clarions or of fifes,
Silent the Colonies remain and refuse the loud alarm.

On those vast shady hills between America & Albions
    shore;
Now barr'd out by the Atlantic sea: call'd Atlantean
    hills:
Because from their bright summits you may pass to
    the Golden world
An ancient palace, archetype of mighty Emperies,
Rears its immortal pinnacles, built in the forest of
    God
By Ariston the king of beauty for his stolen bride,   10

Here on their magic seats the thirteen Angels sat
    perturb'd
For clouds from the Atlantic hover o'er the solemn
    roof.

[PLATE 11]

Fiery the Angels rose, & as they rose deep thunder
    roll'd
Around their shores: indignant burning with the
    fires of Orc
And Bostons Angel cried aloud as they flew thro'
    the dark night.

He cried: Why trembles honesty and like a
    murderer,
Why seeks he refuge from the frowns of his immortal
    station!
Must the generous tremble & leave his joy, to the
    idle: to the pestilence!
That mock him? who commanded this? what God?
    what Angel!
To keep the gen'rous from experience till the
    ungenerous
Are unrestraind performers of the energies of
    nature;   9
Till pity is become a trade, and generosity a science,
That men get rich by, & the sandy desart is giv'n to
    the strong
What God is he, writes laws of peace, & clothes him
    in a tempest
What pitying Angel lusts for tears, and fans himself
    with sighs
What crawling villain preaches abstinence & wraps
    himself
In fat of lambs? no more I follow, no more
    obedience pay.

[PLATE 12]

So cried he, rending off his robe & throwing down
    his scepter.
In sight of Albions Guardian, and all the thirteen
    Angels
Rent off their robes to the hungry wind, & threw
    their golden scepters
Down on the land of America. indignant they
    descended
Headlong from out their heav'nly heights, descending
    swift as fires
Over the land; naked & flaming are their lineaments
    seen
In the deep gloom, by Washington & Paine & Warren
    they stood
And the flame folded roaring fierce within the pitchy
    night
Before the Demon red, who burnt towards
    America,
In black smoke thunders and loud winds rejoicing
    in its terror   10

Breaking in smoky wreaths from the wild deep, &
    gath'ring thick
In flames as of a furnace on the land from North to
    South

[PLATE 13]

What time the thirteen Governors that England sent
    convene
In Bernards[7] house; the flames coverd the land, they
    rouze they cry
Shaking their mental chains they rush in fury to the
    sea
To quench their anguish; at the feet of Washington
    down fall'n
They grovel on the sand and writhing lie, while
    all
The British soldiers thro' the thirteen states sent up
    a howl
Of anguish: threw their swords & muskets to the
    earth & ran
From their encampments and dark castles seeking
    where to hide
From the grim flames; and from the visions of Orc:
    in sight
Of Albions Angel; who enrag'd his secret clouds
    open'd   10
From north to south, and burnt outstretchd on
    wings of wrath cov'ring
The eastern sky, spreading his awful wings across
    the heavens;
Beneath him roll'd his num'rous hosts, all Albions
    Angels camp'd
Darkend the Atlantic mountains & their trumpets
    shook the valleys
Arm'd with diseases of the earth to cast upon the
    Abyss,
Their numbers forty millions, must'ring in the
    eastern sky.

[PLATE 14]

In the flames stood & view'd the armies drawn out in
    the sky
Washington Franklin Paine & Warren Allen Gates
    & Lee:
And heard the voice of Albions Angel give the
    thunderous command:
His plagues obedient to his voice flew forth out of
    their clouds
Falling upon America, as a storm to cut them off
As a blight cuts the tender corn when it begins to
    appear.

---

7 Sir Francis Bernard, colonial governor of Massachusetts
from 1760 to 1769.

Dark is the heaven above, & cold & hard the earth
    beneath;
And as a plague wind fill'd with insects cuts off man
    & beast;
And as a sea o'erwhelms a land in the day of an
    earthquake:

Fury! rage! madness! in a wind swept through
    America   10
And the red flames of Orc that folded roaring fierce
    around
The angry shores, and the fierce rushing of
    th'inhabitants together:
The citizens of New-York close their books & lock
    their chests;
The mariners of Boston drop their anchors and
    unlade;
The scribe of Pensylvania casts his pen upon the
    earth;
The builder of Virginia throws his hammer down in
    fear.

Then had America been lost, o'erwhelm'd by the
    Atlantic,
And Earth had lost another portion of the infinite,
But all rush together in the night in wrath and raging
    fire
The red fires rag'd! the plagues recoil'd! then rolld
    they back with fury   20

[PLATE 15]
On Albions Angels; then the Pestilence began in
    streaks of red
Across the limbs of Albions Guardian, the spotted
    plague smote Bristols
And the Leprosy Londons Spirit, sickening all their
    bands;
The millions sent up a howl of anguish and threw
    off their hammerd mail,
And cast their swords & spears to earth, & stood a
    naked multitude.
Albions Guardian writhed in torment on the
    eastern sky
Pale quivring toward the brain his glimmering eyes,
    teeth chattering
Howling & shuddering his legs quivering; convuls'd
    each muscle & sinew
Sick'ning lay Londons Guardian, and the ancient
    miter'd York
Their heads on snowy hills, their ensigns sick'ning
    in the sky   10
The plagues creep on the burning winds driven by
    flames of Orc,

And by the fierce Americans rushing together in the
    night
Driven o'er the Guardians of Ireland and Scotland
    and Wales
They spotted with plagues forsook the frontiers &
    their banners seard
With fires of hell, deform their ancient heavens with
    shame & woe.
Hid in his caves the Bard of Albion[8] felt the enormous
    plagues.
And a cowl of flesh grew o'er his head & scales on his
    back & ribs;
And rough with black scales all his Angels fright
    their ancient heavens
The doors of marriage are open, and the Priests in
    rustling scales
Rush into reptile coverts, hiding from the fires of
    Orc,   20
That play around the golden roofs in wreaths of fierce
    desire,
Leaving the females naked and glowing with the
    lusts of youth

For the female spirits of the dead pining in bonds of
    religion;
Run from their fetters reddening, & in long drawn
    arches sitting:
They feel the nerves of youth renew, and desires of
    ancient times,
Over their pale limbs as a vine when the tender
    grape appears

[PLATE 16]
Over the hills, the vales, the cities, rage the red
    flames fierce;
The Heavens melted from north to south; and
    Urizen who sat
Above all heavens in thunders wrap'd, emerg'd his
    leprous head
From out his holy shrine, his tears in deluge piteous
Falling into the deep sublime! flag'd with grey-
    brow'd snows
And thunderous visages, his jealous wings wav'd
    over the deep;
Weeping in dismal howling woe he dark descended
    howling
Around the smitten bands, clothed in tears &
    trembling shudd'ring cold.
His stored snows he poured forth, and his icy
    magazines
He open'd on the deep, and on the Atlantic sea white
    shiv'ring.   10

⬦⬦⬦⬦⬦⬦⬦⬦⬦⬦⬦⬦⬦⬦⬦⬦⬦⬦⬦⬦⬦⬦⬦⬦⬦⬦⬦⬦⬦⬦

[8] William Whitehead, poet laureate until 1785.

Leprous his limbs, all over white, and hoary was his
    visage.
Weeping in dismal howlings before the stern
    Americans
Hiding the Demon red with clouds & cold mists
    from the earth;
Till Angels & weak men twelve years should govern
    o'er the strong:
And then their end should come, when France
    reciev'd the Demons light.

Stiff shudderings shook the heav'nly thrones! France
    Spain & Italy,
In terror view'd the bands of Albion, and the
    ancient Guardians
Fainting upon the elements, smitten with their own
    plagues
They show advance to shut the five gates of their
    law-built heaven
Filled with blasting fancies and with mildews of
    despair   20
With fierce disease and lust, unable to stem the fires
    of Orc;
But the five gates were consum'd, & their bolts and
    hinges melted
And the fierce flames burnt round the heavens, &
    round the abodes of men
                    FINIS

[1793]   [1793]

[Canceled Plates]

[PLATE b]

Reveal the dragon thro' the human; coursing swift
    as fire
To the close hall of counsel, where his Angel form
    renews.

In a sweet vale shelter'd with cedars, that eternal
    stretch
Their unmov'd branches, stood the hall; built when
    the moon shot forth,
In that dread night when Urizen call'd the stars
    round his feet;
Then burst the center from its orb, and found a
    place beneath;
And Earth conglob'd, in narrow room, roll'd round
    its sulphur Sun.
To this deep valley situated by the flowing Thames;
Where George the third holds council. & his Lords
    & Commons meet:
Shut out from mortal sight the Angel came; the vale
    was dark   10

With clouds of smoke from the Atlantic, that in
    volumes roll'd
Between the mountains, dismal visions mope around
    the house.

On chairs of iron, canopied with mystic ornaments
Of life by magic power condens'd; infernal forms
    art-bound
The council sat; all rose before the aged apparition;
His snowy beard that streams like lambent flames
    down his wide breast
Wetting with tears, & his white garments cast a
    wintry light.

Then as arm'd clouds arise terrific round the
    northern drum;
The world is silent at the flapping of the folding
    banners;
So still terrors rent the house: as when the solemn
    globe   20
Launch'd to the unknown shore, while Sotha held
    the northern helm,
Till to that void it came & fell; so the dark house
    was rent,
The valley mov'd beneath; its shining pillars split
    in twain,
And its roofs crack across down falling on th'Angelic
    seats.

[PLATE c (as revised)]

[*Then Albions Angel rose*] resolv'd to the cove of
    armoury:
His shield that bound twelve demons & their cities
    in its orb,
He took down from its trembling pillar; from its
    cavern deep,
His helm was brought by Londons Guardian, & his
    thirsty spear
By the wise spirit of Londons river: silent stood the
    King breathing damp mists:
And on his aged limbs they clasp'd the armour of
    terrible gold.
Infinite Londons awful spires cast a dreadful cold
Even on rational things beneath, and from the
    palace walls
Around Saint James's chill & heavy, even to the city
    gate.
On the vast stone whose name is Truth he stood, his
    cloudy shield   10

Smote with his scepter, the scale bound orb loud
    howld; th' ancie[nt] pillar
Trembling sunk, an earthquake roll'd along the
    mossy pile.

In glittring armour, swift as winds; intelligent as
    clouds;
Four winged heralds mount the furious blasts &
    blow their trumps
Gold, silver, brass & iron clangors clamoring rend
    the shores.
Like white clouds rising from the deeps, his fifty-two
    armies
From the four cliffs of Albion rise, mustering around
    their Prince;
Angels of cities and of parishes and villages and
    families,
In armour as the nerves of wisdom, each his station
    holds.   19
In opposition dire, a warlike cloud the myriads
    stood
In the red air before the Demon; [*seen even by mortal
    men:*
*Who call it Fancy, or shut the gates of sense & in their
    chambers,*
Sleep like the dead.] But like a constellation ris'n
    and blazing
Over the rugged ocean; so the Angels of Albion
    hung
a frowning shadow, like an aged King in arms of
    gold,
Who wept over a den, in which his only son
    outstretch'd
By rebels hands was slain; his white beard wav'd in
    the wild wind.

On mountains & cliffs of snow the awful apparition
    hover'd;
And like the voices of religious dead, heard in the
    mountains:
When holy zeal scents the sweet valleys of ripe virgin
    bliss;   30
Such was the hollow voice that o'er America
    lamented.
[*c.*1793]   [1925]

SONGS of EXPERIENCE
1794
The Author & Printer W Blake

———◦⊝◦———

INTRODUCTION.

Hear the voice of the Bard!
Who Present, Past, & Future sees
Whose ears have heard,
The Holy Word,
That walk'd among the ancient trees.

Calling the lapsed Soul
And weeping in the evening dew;
That might controll,
The starry pole;
And fallen fallen light renew!   10

O Earth O Earth return!
Arise from out the dewy grass;
Night is worn,
And the morn
Rises from the slumberous mass.

Turn away no more:
Why wilt thou turn away
The starry floor
The watry shore
Is giv'n thee till the break of day.   20

EARTH'S ANSWER

Earth rais'd up her head,
From the darkness dread & drear.
Her light fled:
Stony dread!
And her locks cover'd with grey despair.

Prison'd on watry shore
Starry Jealousy does keep my den
Cold and hoar
Weeping o'er
I hear the Father of the ancient men   10

Selfish father of men
Cruel jealous selfish fear
Can delight
Chain'd in night
The virgins of youth and morning bear.

Does spring hide its joy
When buds and blossoms grow?
Does the sower?
Sow by night?
Or the plowman in darkness plow?   20

Break this heavy chain,
That does freeze my bones around
Selfish! vain,
Eternal bane!
That free Love with bondage bound.

THE CLOD & THE PEBBLE

Love seeketh not Itself to please,
Nor for itself hath any care;
But for another gives its ease,
And builds a Heaven in Hells despair.

So sang a little Clod of Clay,
Trodden with the cattles feet:
But a Pebble of the brook,
Warbled out these metres meet.

Love seeketh only Self to please,
To bind another to its delight;   10
Joys in anothers loss of ease,
And builds a Hell in Heavens despite.

HOLY THURSDAY

Is this a holy thing to see,
In a rich and fruitful land,
Babes reducd to misery,
Fed with cold and usurous hand?

Is that trembling cry a song?
Can it be a song of joy?
And so many children poor?
It is a land of poverty!

And their sun does never shine.
And their fields are bleak & bare.   10
And their ways are fill'd with thorns.
It is eternal winter there.

For where-e'er the sun does shine,
And where-e'er the rain does fall:
Babe can never hunger there,
Nor poverty the mind appall.

THE LITTLE GIRL LOST

In futurity
I prophetic see,
That the earth from sleep,
(Grave the sentence deep)

Shall arise and seek
For her maker meek:
And the desart wild
Become a garden mild.

In the southern clime,
Where the summers prime,   10
Never fades away;
Lovely Lyca lay.

Seven summers old
Lovely Lyca told,
She had wanderd long,
Hearing wild birds song.

Sweet sleep come to me
Underneath this tree;
Do father, mother weep.—
"Where can Lyca sleep".   20

Lost in desart wild
Is your little child.
How can Lyca sleep,
If her mother weep.

If her heart does ake,
Then let Lyca wake;
If my mother sleep,
Lyca shall not weep.

Frowning frowning night,
O'er this desart bright,   30
Let thy moon arise,
While I close my eyes.

Sleeping Lyca lay;
While the beasts of prey,
Come from caverns deep,
View'd the maid asleep

The kingly lion stood
And the virgin view'd,
Then he gambold round
O'er the hallowd ground: 40

Leopards, tygers play,
Round her as she lay;
While the lion old,
Bow'd his mane of gold.

And her bosom lick,
And upon her neck,
From his eyes of flame,
Ruby tears there came;

While the lioness,
Loos'd her slender dress,   50
And naked they convey'd
To caves the sleeping maid.

THE LITTLE GIRL FOUND

All the night in woe
Lyca's parents go:
Over vallies deep,
While the desarts weep.

Tired and woe-begone,
Hoarse with making moan:
Arm in arm seven days,
They trac'd the desart ways.

Seven nights they sleep,
Among shadows deep: 10
And dream they see their child
Starv'd in desart wild.

Pale thro pathless ways
The fancied image strays,
Famish'd, weeping, weak
With hollow piteous shriek

Rising from unrest,
The trembling woman prest,
With feet of weary woe;
She could no further go.   20

In his arms he bore,
Her arm'd with sorrow sore;
Till before their way,
A couching lion lay.

Turning back was vain,
Soon his heavy mane,
Bore them to the ground;
Then he stalk'd around,

Smelling to his prey.
But their fears allay,   30
When he licks their hands;
And silent by them stands.

They look upon his eyes
Fill'd with deep surprise:
And wondering behold,
A spirit arm'd in gold.

On his head a crown
On his shoulders down,
Flow'd his golden hair.
Gone was all their care.   40

Follow me he said,
Weep not for the maid;
In my palace deep,
Lyca lies asleep.

Then they followed,
Where the vision led:
And saw their sleeping child,
Among tygers wild.

To this day they dwell
In a lonely dell   50
Nor fear the wolvish howl,
Nor the lions growl.

THE CHIMNEY SWEEPER

A little black thing among the snow:
Crying weep, weep, in notes of woe!
Where are thy father & mother? say?
They are both gone up to the church to pray.

Because I was happy upon the heath,
And smil'd among the winters snow:
They clothed me in the clothes of death,
And taught me to sing the notes of woe.

And because I am happy, & dance & sing,
They think they have done me no injury: 10
And are gone to praise God & his Priest & King
Who make up a heaven of our misery.

NURSES SONG

When the voices of children, are heard on the green
And whisprings are in the dale:
The days of my youth rise fresh in my mind,
My face turns green and pale.

Then come home my children, the sun is gone down
And the dews of night arise
Your spring & your day, are wasted in play
And your winter and night in disguise.

THE SICK ROSE

O Rose thou art sick.
The invisible worm,
That flies in the night
In the howling storm:

Has found out thy bed
Of crimson joy:
And his dark secret love
Does thy life destroy.

THE FLY.

Little Fly
Thy summers play,
My thoughtless hand
Has brush'd away.

Am not I
A fly like thee?
Or art not thou
A man like me?

For I dance
And drink & sing;   10
Till some blind hand
Shall brush my wing.

If thought is life
And strength & breath;
And the want
Of thought is death;

Then am I
A happy fly,
If I live,
Or if I die.   20

THE ANGEL

I Dreamt a Dream! what can it mean?
And that I was a maiden Queen:
Guarded by an Angel mild;
Witless woe, was ne'er beguil'd!

And I wept both night and day
And he wip'd my tears away
And I wept both day and night
And hid from him my hearts delight

So he took his wings and fled:
Then the morn blush'd rosy red: 10
I dried my tears & armd my fears,
With ten thousand shields and spears.

Soon my Angel came again:
I was arm'd, he came in vain:
For the time of youth was fled
And grey hairs were on my head.

THE TYGER

Tyger Tyger, burning bright,
In the forests of the night;
What immortal hand or eye,
Could frame thy fearful symmetry?

In what distant deeps or skies
Burnt the fire of thine eyes!
On what wings dare he aspire?
What the hand, dare sieze the fire?

And what shoulder, & what art,
Could twist the sinews of thy heart? 10
And when thy heart began to beat,
What dread hand? & what dread feet?

What the hammer? what the chain,
In what furnace was thy brain?
What the anvil? what dread grasp,
Dare its deadly terrors clasp?

When the stars threw down their spears
And water'd heaven with their tears:
Did he smile his work to see?
Did he who made the Lamb make thee? 20

Tyger, Tyger burning bright,
In the forests of the night:
What immortal hand or eye,
Dare frame thy fearful symmetry?

MY PRETTY ROSE TREE

A flower was offerd to me;
Such a flower as May never bore.
But I said I've a Pretty Rose-tree,
And I passed the sweet flower o'er.

Then I went to my Pretty Rose-tree;
To tend her by day and by night.
But my Rose turnd away with jealousy:
And her thorns were my only delight.

AH! SUN-FLOWER

Ah Sun-flower! weary of time,
Who countest the steps of the Sun:
Seeking after that sweet golden clime
Where the travellers journey is done.

Where the Youth pined away with desire,
And the pale Virgin shrouded in snow:
Arise from their graves and aspire,
Where my Sun-flower wishes to go.

THE LILLY

The modest Rose puts forth a thorn:
The humble Sheep, a threatning horn:
While the Lilly white, shall in Love delight,
Nor a thorn nor a threat stain her beauty bright

THE GARDEN OF LOVE

I went to the Garden of Love,
And saw what I never had seen:
A Chapel was built in the midst,
Where I used to play on the green.

And the gates of this Chapel were shut,
And Thou shalt not. writ over the door;
So I turn'd to the Garden of Love,
That so many sweet flowers bore,

And I saw it was filled with graves,
And tomb-stones where flowers should be: 10
And Priests in black gowns, were walking their
     rounds,
And binding with briars, my joys & desires.

THE LITTLE VAGABOND

Dear Mother, dear Mother, the Church is cold.
But the Ale-house is healthy & pleasant & warm;
Besides I can tell where I am use'd well,
Such usage in heaven will never do well.

But if at the Church they would give us some Ale.
And a pleasant fire, our souls to regale;
We'd sing and we'd pray, all the live-long day;
Nor ever once wish from the Church to stray,

Then the Parson might preach & drink & sing.
And we'd be as happy as birds in the spring: 10
And modest dame Lurch, who is always at Church,
Wou'ld not have bandy children nor fasting nor birch.

And God like a father rejoicing to see,
His children as pleasant and happy as he:
Would have no more quarrel with the Devil or the
     Barrel
But kiss him & give him both drink and apparel.

———

LONDON

For a probable early version of London *see* "Why should I
care. . . ." *In an intermediate version the poem appears in the
Notebook with* "dirty" *rather than* "charter'd" *in the first two
lines,* "see" *rather than* "mark" *in the third,* "german-forged
links" *rather than* "mind-forg'd manacles," *and other more
obvious alternatives. The fourth stanza, which appears to be an
addition, was rewritten at least four times.*

———

LONDON

I wander thro' each charter'd street,
Near where the charter'd Thames does flow.
And mark in every face I meet
Marks of weakness, marks of woe.

In every cry of every Man,
In every Infants cry of fear,
In every voice: in every ban,
The mind-forg'd manacles I hear

How the Chimney-sweepers cry
Every blackning Church appalls,   10
And the hapless Soldiers sigh,
Runs in blood down Palace walls

But most thro' midnight streets I hear
How the youthful Harlots curse
Blasts the new-born Infants tear
And blights with plagues the Marriage hearse

THE HUMAN ABSTRACT.

Pity would be no more,
If we did not make somebody Poor:
And Mercy no more could be,
If all were as happy as we;

And mutual fear brings peace;
Till the selfish loves increase.
Then Cruelty knits a snare,
And spreads his baits with care.

He sits down with holy fears,
And waters the ground with tears: 10
Then Humility takes its root
Underneath his foot.

Soon spreads the dismal shade
Of Mystery over his head;
And the Catterpiller and Fly,
Feed on the Mystery.

And it bears the fruit of Deceit,
Ruddy and sweet to eat;
And the Raven his nest has made
In its thickest shade.   20

The Gods of the earth and sea,
Sought thro' Nature to find this Tree
But their search was all in vain:
There grows one in the Human Brain

INFANT SORROW

My mother groand! my father wept.
Into the dangerous world I leapt:
Helpless, naked, piping loud;
Like a fiend hid in a cloud.

Struggling in my fathers hands:
Striving against my swadling bands:
Bound and weary I thought best
To sulk upon my mothers breast.

A POISON TREE.

I was angry with my friend;
I told my wrath, my wrath did end.
I was angry with my foe:
I told it not, my wrath did grow.

And I waterd it in fears,
Night & morning with my tears:
And I sunned it with smiles,
And with soft deceitful wiles.

And it grew both day and night.
Till it bore an apple bright.   10
And my foe beheld it shine.
And he knew that it was mine.

And into my garden stole,
When the night had veild the pole;
In the morning glad I see;
My foe outstretchd beneath the tree.

A LITTLE BOY LOST

Nought loves another as itself
Nor venerates another so.
Nor is it possible to Thought
A greater than itself to know:

And Father, how can I love you,
Or any of my brothers more?
I love you like the little bird
That picks up crumbs around the door.

The Priest sat by and heard the child.
In trembling zeal he siez'd his hair: 10
He led him by his little coat:
And all admir'd the Priestly care.

And standing on the altar high,
Lo what a fiend is here! said he:
One who sets reason up for judge
Of our most holy Mystery.

The weeping child could not be heard.
The weeping parents wept in vain:
They strip'd him to his little shirt.
And bound him in an iron chain.   20

And burn'd him in a holy place,
Where many had been burn'd before:
The weeping parents wept in vain.
Are such things done on Albions shore.

A LITTLE GIRL LOST

Children of the future Age,
Reading this indignant page:
Know that in a former time,
Love! sweet Love! was thought a crime.

In the Age of Gold,
Free from winters cold:
Youth and maiden bright,
To the holy light,
Naked in the sunny beams delight.

Once a youthful pair   10
Fill'd with softest care:
Met in garden bright,
Where the holy light,
Had just removd the curtains of the night.

There in rising day,
On the grass they play:
Parents were afar:
Strangers came not near:
And the maiden soon forgot her fear.

Tired with kisses sweet   20
They agree to meet,
When the silent sleep
Waves o'er heavens deep;
And the weary tired wanderers weep.

To her father white
Came the maiden bright:
But his loving look,
Like the holy book,
All her tender limbs with terror shook.

Ona! pale and weak!
To thy father speak:
O the trembling fear!
O the dismal care!
That shakes the blossoms of my hoary hair

TO TIRZAH

To Tirzah *does not appear in the three earliest versions of*
Songs of Experience, *and probably was not added until after
1800. Tirzah, representing here nature's bondage of man, also
appears in* The Four Zoas *and* Jerusalem.

TO TIRZAH

Whate'er is Born of Mortal Birth,
Must be consumed with the Earth
To rise from Generation free;
Then what have I to do with thee?

The Sexes sprung from Shame & Pride
Blow'd in the morn: in evening died
But Mercy changd Death into Sleep;
The Sexes rose to work & weep.

Thou Mother of my Mortal part
With cruelty didst mould my Heart,   10
And with false self-decieving tears,
Didst bind my Nostrils Eyes & Ears.

Didst close my Tongue in senseless clay
And me to Mortal Life betray:
The Death of Jesus set me free,
Then what have I to do with thee?

THE SCHOOL BOY

I love to rise in a summer morn,
When the birds sing on every tree;
The distant huntsman winds his horn,
And the sky-lark sings with me.
O! what sweet company.

But to go to school in a summer morn
O! it drives all joy away;
Under a cruel eye outworn,
The little ones spend the day,
In sighing and dismay.   10

Ah! then at times I drooping sit,
And spend many an anxious hour.
Nor in my book can I take delight,
Nor sit in learnings bower,
Worn thro' with the dreary shower

How can the bird that is born for joy,
Sit in a cage and sing.
How can a child when fears annoy,
But droop his tender wing,
And forget his youthful spring.   20

O! father & mother, if buds are nip'd,
And blossoms blown away,
And if the tender plants are strip'd
Of their joy in the springing day,
By sorrow and cares dismay,

How shall the summer arise in joy
Or the summer fruits appear
Or how shall we gather what griefs destroy
Or bless the mellowing year,
When the blasts of winter appear.

THE VOICE OF THE ANCIENT BARD.

Youth of delight come hither:
And see the opening morn,
Image of truth new born
Doubt is fled & clouds of reason
Dark disputes & artful teazing.
Folly is an endless maze,
Tangled roots perplex her ways,
How many have fallen there!
They stumble all night over bones of the dead;
And feel they know not what but care;   10
And wish to lead others when they should be led.

[c.1789–1794]   [1794–1801]

[END OF SONGS OF EXPERIENCE]

A DIVINE IMAGE

*Blake etched a plate of this poem, but never included it among
the* Songs of Experience. *However, it is found with two sets
of prints that were made from the plates after Blake's death.*

A DIVINE IMAGE

Cruelty has a Human Heart
And Jealousy a Human Face
Terror, the Human Form Divine
And Secrecy, the Human Dress

The Human Dress, is forged Iron
The Human Form, a fiery Forge.
The Human Face, a Furnace seal'd
The Human Heart, its hungry Gorge.

[c.1794]   [After 1827]

THE [FIRST] BOOK OF URIZEN

*All except the latest of the seven surviving copies of this work
are called* The First Book of Urizen; *probably the Book
of Ahania, which followed it, was originally conceived as
the* Second Book of Urizen. *For identification of Urizen
and Orc see footnote to plate 1, line 1, in* America a Proph-
ecy *and headnote to* Visions of the Daughters of Albion,
above.

THE [*FIRST*] BOOK of URIZEN

LAMBETH. Printed by Will Blake 1794

PRELUDIUM TO THE [*FIRST*] BOOK OF URIZEN

Of the primeval Priests assum'd power,
When Eternals spurn'd back his religion;
And gave him a place in the north,
Obscure, shadowy, void, solitary.

Eternals I hear your call gladly,
Dictate swift winged words, & fear not
To unfold your dark visions of torment.

[PLATE 3]

Chap: I

1. Lo, a shadow of horror is risen
In Eternity! Unknown, unprolific!
Self-closd, all-repelling: what Demon
Hath form'd this abominable void
This soul-shudd'ring vacuum?—Some
        said
"It is Urizen", But unknown, abstracted
Brooding secret, the dark power hid.

2. Times on times he divided, & measur'd
Space by space in his ninefold darkness
Unseen, unknown! changes appeard   10
In his desolate mountains rifted furious
By the black winds of perturbation

3. For he strove in battles dire
In unseen conflictions with shapes
Bred from his forsaken wilderness,
Of beast, bird, fish, serpent & element
Combustion, blast, vapour and cloud.

4. Dark revolving in silent activity:
Unseen in tormenting passions;
An activity unknown and horrible;   20
A self-contemplating shadow,
In enormous labours occupied

5. But Eternals beheld his vast forests
Age on ages he lay, clos'd, unknown,
Brooding shut in the deep; all avoid
The petrific abominable chaos

6. His cold horrors silent, dark Urizen
Prepar'd: his ten thousands of thunders
Rang'd in gloom'd array stretch out across
The dread world, & the rolling of wheels   30
As of swelling seas, sound in his clouds
In his hills of stor'd snows, in his mountains
Of hail & ice; voices of terror,
Are heard, like thunders of autumn,
When the cloud blazes over the harvests

Chap: II.

1. Earth was not: nor globes of attraction
The will of the Immortal expanded
Or contracted his all flexible senses.
Death was not, but eternal life sprung

2. The sound of a trumpet the heavens   40
Awoke & vast clouds of blood roll'd
Round the dim rocks of Urizen, so nam'd
That solitary one in Immensity

3. Shrill the trumpet: & myriads of
        Eternity,
[PLATE 4]
Muster around the bleak desarts
Now fill'd with clouds, darkness & waters
That roll'd perplex'd labring & utter'd
Words articulate, bursting in thunders
That roll'd on the tops of his mountains

4. From the depths of dark solitude. From
The eternal abode in my holiness,
Hidden set apart in my stern counsels
Reserv'd for the days of futurity,
I have sought for a joy without pain,   10
For a solid without fluctuation
Why will you die O Eternals?
Why live in unquenchable burnings?

5. First I fought with the fire; consum'd
Inwards, into a deep world within:
A void immense, wild dark & deep,
Where nothing was; Natures wide womb[.]
And self balanc'd stretch'd o'er the void
I alone, even I! the winds merciless
Bound; but condensing, in torrents   20
They fall & fall; strong I repell'd
The vast waves, & arose on the waters
A wide world of solid obstruction

6. Here alone I in books formd of metals
Have written the secrets of wisdom
The secrets of dark contemplation
By fightings and conflicts dire,
With terrible monsters Sin-bred:
Which the bosoms of all inhabit;
Seven deadly Sins of the soul.   30

7. Lo! I unfold my darkness: and on
This rock, place with strong hand the Book
Of eternal brass, written in my solitude.

8. Laws of peace, of love, of unity:
Of pity, compassion, forgiveness.
Let each chuse one habitation:
His ancient infinite mansion:
One command, one joy, one desire,
One curse, one weight, one measure
One King, one God, one Law.   40

Chap: III.

1. The voice ended, they saw his pale visage
Emerge from the darkness; his hand
On the rock of eternity unclasping
The Book of brass. Rage siez'd the strong

2. Rage, fury, intense indignation
In cataracts of fire blood & gall
In whirlwinds of sulphurous smoke:
And enormous forms of energy;
All the seven deadly sins of the soul
[PLATE 5]
In living creations appear'd
In the flames of eternal fury.

3. Sund'ring, dark'ning, thund'ring!
Rent away with a terrible crash
Eternity roll'd wide apart
Wide asunder rolling
Mountainous all around

Departing; departing, departing:
Leaving ruinous fragments of life
Hanging frowning cliffs & all between   10
An ocean of voidness unfathomable.

4. The roaring fires ran o'er the heav'ns
In whirlwinds & cataracts of blood
And o'er the dark desarts of Urizen
Fires pour thro' the void on all sides
On Urizens self-begotten armies.

5. But no light from the fires. all was darkness
In the flames of Eternal fury

6. In fierce anguish & quenchless flames
To the desarts and rocks He ran raging   20
To hide, but He cold not: combining
He dug mountains & hills in vast strength,
He piled them in incessant labour,
In howlings & pangs & fierce madness
Long periods in burning fires labouring
Till hoary, and age-broke, and aged,
In despair and the shadows of death.

7. And a roof, vast petrific around,
On all sides He fram'd: like a womb;
Where thousands of rivers in veins   30
Of blood pour down the mountains to cool
The eternal fires beating without
From Eternals; & like a black globe
View'd by sons of Eternity, standing
On the shore of the infinite ocean
Like a human heart strugling & beating
The vast world of Urizen appear'd.

8. And Los[1] round the dark globe of Urizen,
Kept watch for Eternals to confine,
The obscure separation alone;   40
For Eternity stood wide apart,
[PLATE 6]
As the stars are apart from the earth

9. Los wept howling around the dark Demon:
And cursing his lot; for in anguish,
Urizen was rent from his side;
And a fathomless void for his feet;
And intense fires for his dwelling.

10. But Urizen laid in a stony sleep
Unorganiz'd, rent from Eternity

---

[1] Here, as often, appearing as a blacksmith, Los embodies human creative energy and imagination.

11. The Eternals said: What is this? Death[.]
Urizen is a clod of clay.   10

[PLATE 7]

12: Los howld in a dismal stupor,
Groaning! gnashing! groaning!
Till the wrenching apart was healed

13: But the wrenching of Urizen heal'd not
Cold, featureless, flesh or clay,
Rifted with direful changes
He lay in a dreamless night

14: Till Los rouz'd his fires, affrighted
At the formless unmeasurable death.

[PLATE 8]

Chap: IV:[a]

1: Los smitten with astonishment
Frightend at the hurtling bones

2: And at the surging sulphureous
Perturbed Immortal mad raging

3: In whirlwinds & pitch & nitre
Round the furious limbs of Los

4: And Los formed nets & gins
And threw the nets round about

5: He watch'd in shuddring fear
The dark changes & bound every
    change   10
With rivets of iron & brass;

6. And these were the changes of Urizen.

[PLATE 10]

Chap: IV.[b]

1. Ages on ages roll'd over him!
In stony sleep ages roll'd over him!
Like a dark waste stretching chang'able
By earthquakes riv'n, belching sullen fires
On ages roll'd ages in ghastly
Sick torment; around him in whirlwinds
Of darkness the eternal Prophet howl'd
Beating still on his rivets of iron
Pouring sodor of iron; dividing
The horrible night into watches.   10

2. And Urizen (so his eternal name)
His prolific delight obscurd more & more
In dark secresy hiding in surgeing
Sulphureous fluid his phantasies.
The Eternal Prophet heavd the dark bellows,
And turn'd restless the tongs; and the
    hammer
Incessant beat; forging chains new & new
Num'bring with links. hours, days & years

3. The eternal mind bounded began to roll
Eddies of wrath ceaseless round & round,   20
And the sulphureous foam surgeing thick
Settled, a lake, bright, & shining clear:
White as the snow on the mountains cold.

4. Forgetfulness, dumbness, necessity!
In chains of the mind locked up,
Like fetters of ice shrinking together
Disorganiz'd, rent from Eternity,
Los beat on his fetters of iron;
And heated his furnaces & pour'd
Iron sodor and sodor of brass   30

5. Restless turnd the immortal inchain'd
Heaving dolorous! anguish'd! unbearable
Till a roof shaggy wild inclos'd
In an orb, his fountain of thought.

6. In a horrible dreamful slumber;
Like the linked infernal chain;
A vast Spine writh'd in torment
Upon the winds; shooting pain'd
Ribs, like a bending cavern
And bones of solidness, froze   40
Over all his nerves of joy.
And a first Age passed over,
And a state of dismal woe.

[PLATE 11]

7. From the caverns of his jointed Spine,
Down sunk with fright a red
Round globe hot burning deep
Deep down into the Abyss:
Panting: Conglobing, Trembling
Shooting out ten thousand branches
Around his solid bones.
And a second Age passed over,
And a state of dismal woe.

8. In harrowing fear rolling round;   10
His nervous brain shot branches
Round the branches of his heart.

On high into two little orbs
And fixed in two little caves
Hiding carefully from the wind,
His Eyes beheld the deep,
And a third Age passed over:
And a state of dismal woe.

9. The pangs of hope began,
In heavy pain striving, struggling.   20
Two Ears in close volutions.
From beneath his orbs of vision
Shot spiring out and petrified
As they grew. And a fourth Age passed
And a state of dismal woe.

10. In ghastly torment sick;
Hanging upon the wind;
[PLATE 13]
Two Nostrils bent down to the deep.
And a fifth Age passed over;
And a state of dismal woe.

11. In ghastly torment sick;
Within his ribs bloated round,
A craving Hungry Cavern;
Thence arose his channeld Throat,
And like a red flame a Tongue.
Of thirst & of hunger appeard.
And a sixth Age passed over: 10
And a state of dismal woe.

12. Enraged & stifled with torment
He threw his right Arm to the north
His left Arm to the south
Shooting out in anguish deep,
And his Feet stampd the nether Abyss
In trembling & howling & dismay.
And a seventh Age passed over:
And a state of dismal woe.

Chap: V.

1. In terrors Los shrunk from his task: 20
His great hammer fell from his hand:
His fires beheld, and sickening,
Hid their strong limbs in smoke.
For with noises ruinous loud;
With hurtlings & clashings & groans
The Immortal endur'd his chains,
Tho' bound in a deadly sleep.

2. All the myriads of Eternity:
All the wisdom & joy of life:
Roll like a sea around him,   30
Except what his little orbs
Of sight by degrees unfold.

3. And now his eternal life
Like a dream was obliterated

4. Shudd'ring, the Eternal Prophet smote
With a stroke, from his north to south region
The bellows & hammer are silent now
A nerveless silence, his prophetic voice
Siez'd; a cold solitude & dark void
The Eternal Prophet & Urizen clos'd   40

5. Ages on ages rolld over them
Cut off from life & light frozen
Into horrible forms of deformity
Los suffer'd his fires to decay
Then he look'd back with anxious desire
But the space undivided by existence
Struck horror into his soul.

6. Los wept obscur'd with mourning:
His bosom earthquak'd with sighs;
He saw Urizen deadly black,   50
In his chains bound, & Pity began,

7. In anguish dividing & dividing
For pity divides the soul
In pangs eternity on eternity
Life in cataracts pourd down his cliffs
The void shrunk the lymph into Nerves
Wand'ring wide on the bosom of night
And left a round globe of blood
Trembling upon the Void
[PLATE 15]
Thus the Eternal Prophet was divided
Before the death-image of Urizen
For in changeable clouds and darkness
In a winterly night beneath,
The Abyss of Los stretch'd immense:
And now seen now obscur'd, to the eyes
Of Eternals the visions remote
Of the dark seperation appear'd.
As glasses discover Worlds
In the endless Abyss of space,   10
So the expanding eyes of Immortals
Beheld the dark visions of Los,
And the globe of life blood trembling.

[PLATE 18]
8. The globe of life blood trembled
Branching out into roots;
Fibrous, writhing upon the winds;
Fibres of blood, milk and tears;
In pangs, eternity on eternity.
At length in tears & cries imbodied
A female form trembling and pale
Waves before his deathy face

9. All Eternity shudderd at sight
Of the first female now separate   10
Pale as a cloud of snow
Waving before the face of Los

10. Wonder, awe, fear, astonishment,
Petrify the eternal myriads;
At the first female form now separate
[PLATE 19]
They call'd her Pity, and fled

11. "Spread a Tent, with strong curtains around
        them
"Let cords & stakes bind in the Void
    That Eternals may no more behold them"

12. They began to weave curtains of darkness
They erected large pillars round the Void
With golden hooks fastend in the pillars
With infinite labour the Eternals
A woof wove, and called it Science

Chap: VI.

1. But Los saw the Female & pitied   10
He embrac'd her, she wept, she refus'd
In perverse and cruel delight
She fled from his arms, yet he followd

2. Eternity shudder'd when they saw,
Man begetting his likeness,
On his own divided image.

3. A time passed over, the Eternals
Began to erect the tent;
When Enitharmon, sick,
Felt a Worm within her womb.   20

4. Yet helpless it lay like a Worm
In the trembling womb
To be moulded into existence

5. All day the worm lay on her bosom
All night within her womb
The worm lay till it grew to a serpent
With dolorous hissings & poisons
Round Enitharmons loins folding,

6. Coild within Enitharmons womb
The serpent grew casting its scales,   30
With sharp pangs the hissings began
To change to a grating cry,
Many sorrows and dismal throes
Many forms of fish, bird & beast,
Brought forth an Infant form
Where was a worm before.

7. The Eternals their tent finished
Alarm'd with these gloomy visions
When Enitharmon groaning
Produc'd a man Child to the light.   40

8. A shriek ran thro' Eternity:
And a paralytic stroke;
At the birth of the Human shadow.

9. Delving earth in his resistless way;
Howling, the Child with fierce flames
Issu'd from Enitharmon.

10. The Eternals, closed the tent:
They beat down the stakes the cords
[PLATE 20]
Stretch'd for a work of eternity;
No more Los beheld Eternity.

11. In his hands he siez'd the infant
He bathed him in springs of sorrow
He gave him to Enitharmon.

Chap. VII.

1. They named the child Orc, he grew
Fed with milk of Enitharmon

2. Los awoke her; O sorrow & pain!
A tight'ning girdle grew,
Around his bosom. In sobbings   10
He burst the girdle in twain,
But still another girdle
Oppressd his bosom, In sobbings
Again he burst it. Again
Another girdle succeeds
The girdle was form'd by day;
By night was burst in twain.

3. These falling down on the rock
Into an iron Chain
In each other link by link lock'd   20

4. They took Orc to the top of a mountain.
O how Enitharmon wept!
They chain'd his young limbs to the rock
With the Chain of Jealousy
Beneath Urizens deathful shadow

5. The dead heard the voice of the child
And began to awake from sleep
All things. heard the voice of the child
And began to awake to life.

6. And Urizen craving with hunger   30
Stung with the odours of Nature
Explor'd his dens around

7. He form'd a line & a plummet
To divide the Abyss beneath.
He form'd a dividing rule:

8. He formed scales to weigh;
He formed massy weights;
He formed a brazen quadrant;
He formed golden compasses
And began to explore the Abyss   40
And he planted a garden of fruits

9. But Los encircled Enitharmon
With fires of Prophecy
From the sight of Urizen & Orc.

10. And she bore an enormous race

Chap. VIII.

1. Urizen explor'd his dens
Mountain, moor, & wilderness,
With a globe of fire lighting his journey
A fearful journey, annoy'd
By cruel enormities: forms   50
[PLATE 23]
Of life on his forsaken mountains

2. And his world teemd vast enormities
Frightning; faithless; fawning
Portions of life; similitudes
Of a foot, or a hand, or a head
Or a heart, or an eye, they swam mischevous
Dread terrors! delighting in blood

3. Most Urizen sicken'd to see
His eternal creations appear
Sons & daughters of sorrow on mountains   10
Weeping! wailing! first Thiriel appear'd
Astonish'd at his own existence
Like a man from a cloud born, & Utha
From the waters emerging, laments!
Grodna rent the deep earth howling
Amaz'd! his heavens immense cracks
Like the ground parch'd with heat; then
  Fuzon
Flam'd out! first begotten, last born.[2]
All his eternal sons in like manner
His daughters from green herbs & cattle   20
From monsters, & worms of the pit.

4. He in darkness clos'd, view'd all his race
And his soul sicken'd! he curs'd
Both sons & daughters; for he saw
That no flesh nor spirit could keep
His iron laws one moment.

5. For he saw that life liv'd upon death
[PLATE 25]
 The Ox in the slaughter house moans
The Dog at the wintry door
And he wept, & he called it Pity
And his tears flowed down on the winds

6. Cold he wander'd on high, over their cities
In weeping & pain & woe!
And where-ever he wanderd in sorrows
Upon the aged heavens
A cold shadow follow'd behind him
Like a spiders web, moist, cold, & dim   10
Drawing out from his sorrowing soul
The dungeon-like heaven dividing
Where ever the footsteps of Urizen
Walk'd over the cities in sorrow.

7. Till a Web dark & cold, throughout all
The tormented element stretch'd
From the sorrows of Urizens soul
And the Web is a Female in embrio.
None could break the Web, no wings of fire.

8. So twisted the cords, & so knotted   20
The meshes: twisted like to the human brain

9. And all calld it, The Net of Religion.

◇◇◇◇◇◇◇◇◇◇◇◇◇◇◇◇◇◇◇◇◇◇◇◇◇◇◇◇◇◇◇

[2] Thiriel, Utha, Grodna, and Fuzon are Blake's names for the
four elements: air, water, earth, and fire.

Chap: IX.

1. Then the Inhabitants of those Cities:
Felt their Nerves change into Marrow
And hardening Bones began
In swift diseases and torments,
In throbbings & shootings & grindings
Thro' all the coasts; till weaken'd
The Senses inward rush'd shrinking,
Beneath the dark net of infection.   30

2. Till the shrunken eyes clouded over
Discernd not the woven hipocrisy
But the streaky slime in their heavens
Brought together by narrowing perceptions
Appeard transparent air; for their eyes
Grew small like the eyes of a man
And in reptile forms shrinking together
Of seven feet stature they remain

3. Six days they. shrunk up from existence
And on the seventh day they rested   40
And they bless'd the seventh day, in sick hope:
And forgot their eternal life

4. And their thirty cities divided
In form of a human heart
No more could they rise at will
In the infinite void, but bound down
To earth by their narrowing perceptions
[PLATE 28]
They lived a period of years
Then left a noisom body
To the jaws of devouring darkness

5. And their children wept, & built
Tombs in the desolate places,
And form'd laws of prudence, and call'd them
The eternal laws of God

6. And the thirty cities remaind
Surrounded by salt floods, now call'd
Africa: its name was then Egypt.   10

7. The remaining sons of Urizen
Beheld their brethren shrink together
Beneath the Net of Urizen;
Perswasion was in vain;
For the ears of the inhabitants
Were wither'd, & deafen'd, & cold.
And their eyes could not discern,
Their brethren of other cities.

8. So Fuzon call'd all together
The remaining children of Urizen: 20
And they left the pendulous earth:
They called it Egypt, & left it.[3]

9. And the salt ocean rolled englob'd

The End of the [*first*] book of Urizen

[1794]   [1794]

THE FOUR ZOAS

The Four Zoas was never engraved by Blake (except for some passages later used in Milton *and* Jerusalem). *The manuscript was extensively altered over a long period of time. This is the last of the nine "Nights" into which the poem is divided. For identifications of characters, see notes to earlier poems —*Visions of the Daughters of Albion, America a Prophecy, *and* The [First] Book of Urizen. *The* Zoas *(from "the four beasts full of eyes before and behind" of Revelation) are the four dark powers or elements of man (Albion), now separated as a consequence of his fallen state. Their names are Urizen, Tharmas, Luvah, and Urthona.*

F R O M

THE FOUR ZOAS

VALA

Night the Ninth

Being The Last Judgment

And Los & Enitharmon builded Jerusalem weeping
Over the Sepulcher & over the Crucified body
Which to their Phantom Eyes appear'd still in the
Sepulcher
But Jesus stood beside them in the Spirit Separating
Their Spirit from their body. Terrified at Non
Existence
For such they deemd the death of the body. Los his
vegetable hands
Outstretchd his right hand branching out in fibrous
Strength
Siezd the Sun. His left hand like dark roots coverd the
Moon
And tore them down cracking the heavens across from
immense to immense
Then fell the fires of Eternity with loud & shrill   10

³ The exodus of the Israelites from Egypt, led by Moses.

Sound of Loud Trumpet thundering along from
heaven to heaven
A mighty sound articulate Awake ye dead &
come
To Judgment from the four winds Awake & Come
away
Folding like scrolls of the Enormous volume of
Heaven & Earth
With thunderous noise & dreadful shakings rocking
to & fro
The heavens are shaken & the Earth removed from
its place
The foundations of the Eternal hills discoverd
The thrones of Kings are shaken they have lost their
robes & crowns
The poor smite their opressors they awake up to the
harvest
The naked warriors rush together down to the sea
shore   20
Trembling before the multitudes of slaves now set at
liberty
They are become like wintry flocks like forests
stripd of leaves
The opressed pursue like the wind there is no room
for escape
The Spectre of Enitharmon let loose on the troubled
deep
Waild shrill in the confusion & the Spectre of
Urthona
Recievd her in the darkning South their bodies lost
they stood
Trembling & weak a faint embrace a fierce desire as
when
Two shadows mingle on a wall they wail & shadowy
tears
Fell down & shadowy forms of joy mixd with despair
& grief
Their bodies buried in the ruins of the Universe   30
Mingled with the confusion. Who shall call them
from the Grave

Rahab & Tirzah[1] wail aloud in the wild flames they
give up themselves to Consummation

The books of Urizen unroll with dreadful noise the
folding Serpent
Of Orc began to Consume in fierce raving fire his
fierce flames

¹ Rahab (a biblical name) is for Blake sometimes codified Moral Virtue, sometimes a form of the Church, sometimes the Whore of Babylon, but usually symbolic of political and spiritual tyranny. Tirzah similarly represents nature's bondage of man. In *Jerusalem* together they form Vala, the counterpart of Luvah, and the fallen form of Jerusalem.

Issud on all sides gathring strength in animating
  volumes
Roaming abroad on all the winds raging intense
  reddening
Into resistless pillars of fire rolling round & round
  gathering
Strength from the Earths consumd & heavens & all
  hidden abysses
Wherever the Eagle has Explord or Lion or Tyger
  trod
Or where the Comets of the night or stars of asterial
  day   40
Have shot their arrows or long beamed spears in
  wrath & fury

And all the while the trumpet sounds from the
  clotted gore & from the hollow den
Start forth the trembling millions into flames of
  mental fire
Bathing their limbs in the bright visions of Eternity

Then like the doves from pillars of Smoke the
  trembling families
Of women & children throughout every nation under
  heaven
Cling round the men in bands of twenties & of fifties
  pale
As snow that falls around a leafless tree upon the
  green
Their opressors are falln they have Stricken them
  they awake to life
Yet pale the just man stands erect & looking up to
  heavn   50
Trembling & strucken by the Universal stroke the
  trees unroot
The rocks groan horrible & run about. The mountains
  &
Their rivers cry with a dismal cry   the cattle gather
  together
Lowing they kneel before the heavens. the wild
  beasts of the forests
Tremble the Lion shuddering asks the Leopard.
  Feelest thou
The dread I feel unknown before My voice refuses
  to roar
And in weak moans I speak to thee This night
Before the mornings dawn the Eagle calld the
  Vulture
The Raven calld the hawk I heard them from my
  forests black
Saying Let us go up far for soon I smell upon the
  wind   60
A terror coming from the South. The Eagle & Hawk
  fled away

At dawn & Eer the sun arose the raven & Vulture
  followd
Let us flee also to the north. They fled. The Sons of
  Men
Saw them depart in dismal droves. The trumpet
  sounded loud
And all the Sons of Eternity Descended into
  Beulah[2]
In the fierce flames the limbs of Mystery lay
  consuming with howling
And deep despair. Rattling go up the flames around
  the Synagogue
Of Satan   Loud the Serpent Orc ragd thro his twenty
  Seven
Folds. The tree of Mystery went up in folding flames
Blood issud out in mighty volumes pouring in
  whirlpools fierce   70
From out the flood gates of the Sky The Gates are
  burst down pour
The torrents black upon the Earth the blood pours
  down incessant
Kings in their palaces lie drownd Shepherds their
  flocks their tents
Roll down the mountains in black torrents Cities
  Villages
High spires & Castles drownd in the black deluge
  Shoal on Shoal
Float the dead carcases of Men & Beasts driven to &
  fro on waves
Of foaming blood beneath the black incessant Sky
  till all
Mysterys tyrants are cut off & not one left on Earth

And when all Tyranny was cut off from the face of
  Earth
Around the Dragon form of Urizen & round his
  stony form   80
The flames rolling intense thro the wide Universe
Began to Enter the Holy City   Entring the dismal
  clouds
In furrowd lightnings break their way the wild
  flames whirring up
The Bloody Deluge living flames winged with
  intellect
And Reason round the Earth they march in order
  flame by flame
From the clotted gore & from the hollow den
Start forth the trembling millions into flames of
  mental fire
Bathing their Limbs in the bright visions of Eternity

◇◇◇◇◇◇◇◇◇◇◇◇◇◇◇◇◇◇◇◇◇◇◇◇◇◇◇◇◇◇◇◇

[2] Beulah (also an Old Testament word) for Blake is a realm or
condition of innocent and passive affection, rather than passionate
or imaginative love.

Beyond this Universal Confusion beyond the remotest
    Pole
Where their vortexes begin to operate there stands 90
A Horrible rock far in the South it was forsaken when
Urizen gave the horses of Light into the hands of
    Luvah [3]
On this rock lay the faded head of the Eternal Man
Enwrapped round with weeds of death cold in sorrow
    & woe
He lifts the blue lamps of his Eyes & cries with
    heavenly voice
Bowing his head over the consuming Universe he
    cried

O weakness & O weariness O war within my
    members
My sons exiled from my breast pass to & fro before
    me
My birds are silent on my hills flocks die beneath my
    branches
My tents are fallen my trumpets & the sweet sounds
    of my harp   100
Is silent on my clouded hills that belch forth storms
    & fires
My milk of cows & honey of bees & fruit of golden
    harvest
Are gatherd in the scorching heat & in the driving
    rain
My robe is turned to confusion & my bright gold to
    stones
Where once I sat   I weary walk in misery & pain
For from within my witherd breast grown narrow
    with my woes
The Corn is turnd to thistles & the apples into
    poison
The birds of song to murderous crows My joys to
    bitter groans
The voices of children in my tents to cries of helpless
    infants
And all exiled from the face of light & shine of
    morning   110
In this dark world a narrow house I wander up &
    down
I hear Mystery howling in these flames of
    Consummation
When shall the Man of future times become as in
    days of old
O weary life why sit I here & give up all my powers
To indolence to the night of death when indolence &
    mourning

Sit hovring over my dark threshold. tho I arise look
    out
And scorn the war within my members yet my heart
    is weak
And my head faint Yet will I look again unto the
    morning
Whence is this sound of rage of Men drinking each
    others blood
Drunk with the smoking gore & red but not with
    nourishing wine   120

The Eternal Man sat on the Rocks & cried with
    awful voice

O Prince of Light where art thou   I behold thee not
    as once
In those Eternal fields in clouds of morning stepping
    forth
With harps & songs where bright Ahania [4] sang
    before thy face
And all thy sons & daughters gatherd round my
    ample table
See you not all this wracking furious confusion
Come forth from slumbers of thy cold abstraction
    come forth
Arise to Eternal births shake off thy cold repose
Schoolmaster of souls great opposer of change arise
That the Eternal worlds may see thy face in peace &
    joy   130
That thou dread form of Certainty maist sit in town
    & village
While little children play around thy feet in gentle
    awe
Fearing thy frown loving thy smile O Urizen Prince
    of light

He calld the deep buried his voice & answer none
    returnd

Then wrath burst round the Eternal Man was wrath
    again he cried
Arise O stony form of death O dragon of the Deeps
Lie down before my feet O Dragon let Urizen arise
O how couldst thou deform those beautiful
    proportions
Of life & person for as the Person so is his life
    proportiond
Let Luvah rage in the dark deep even to
    Consummation   140
For if thou feedest not his rage it will subside in
    peace

---

[3] Luvah is a Zoa, the unfallen manifestation of Orc, represent-
ing undeveloped sexuality, one of the inner principles of emo-
tion. His name may come from " lover."

[4] Urizen's female counterpart.

But if thou darest obstinate refuse my stern behest
Thy crown & scepter I will sieze & regulate all my
    members
In stern severity & cast thee out into the indefinite
Where nothing lives, there to wander. & if thou
    returnst weary
Weeping at the threshold of Existence I will steel
    my heart
Against thee to Eternity & never recieve thee more
Thy self destroying beast formd Science shall be
    thy eternal lot
My anger against thee is greater than against this
    Luvah
For war is energy Enslavd but thy religion   150
The first author of this war & the distracting of
    honest minds
Into confused perturbation & strife & honour &
    pride
Is a deceit so detestable that I will cast thee out
If thou repentest not & leave thee as a rotten branch
    to be burnd
With Mystery the Harlot & with Satan for Ever &
    Ever
Error can never be redeemd in all Eternity
But Sin Even Rahab is redeemd in blood & fury &
    jealousy
That line of blood that stretchd across the windows
    of the morning
Redeemd from Errors power. Wake thou dragon of
    the deeps
Urizen wept in the dark deep anxious his Scaly
    form   160
To reassume the human & he wept in the dark deep

Saying O that I had never drank the wine nor eat the
    bread
Of dark mortality nor cast my view into futurity nor
    turnd
My back darkning the present clouding with a
    cloud
And building arches high & cities turrets & towers
    & domes
Whose smoke destroyd the pleasant garden & whose
    running Kennels
Chokd the bright rivers burdning with my Ships the
    angry deep
Thro Chaos seeking for delight & in spaces remote
Seeking the Eternal which is always present to the
    wise
Seeking for pleasure which unsought falls round the
    infants path   170
And on the fleeces of mild flocks who neither care
    nor labour
But I the labourer of ages whose unwearied hands

Are thus deformd with hardness with the sword
    & with the spear
And with the Chisel & the mallet I whose labours
    vast
Order the nations separating family by family
Alone enjoy not   I alone in misery supreme
Ungratified give all my joy unto this Luvah & Vala
Then Go O dark futurity I will cast thee forth from
    these
Heavens of my brain nor will I look upon futurity
    more   179
I cast futurity away & turn my back upon that void
Which I have made for lo futurity is in this moment
Let Orc consume let Tharmas rage let dark Urthona
    give [5]
All strength to Los & Enitharmon & let Los self
    cursd
Rend down this fabric as a wall ruind & family extinct
Rage Orc Rage Tharmas Urizen no longer curbs
    your rage

So Urizen spoke he shook his snows from off his
    Shoulders & arose
As on a Pyramid of mist his white robes scattering
The fleecy white renewd he shook his aged mantles
    off
Into the fires Then glorious bright Exulting in his
    joy   189
He sounding rose into the heavens in naked majesty
In radiant Youth. when Lo like garlands in the
    Eastern sky
When vocal may comes dancing from the East
Ahania came
Exulting in her flight as when a bubble rises up
On to the surface of a lake. Ahania rose in joy
Excess of Joy is worse than grief—her heart beat
    high her blood
Burst its bright Vessels She fell down dead at the
    feet of Urizen
Outstretchd a Smiling corse they buried her in a
    silent cave
Urizen dropt a tear the Eternal Man Darkend with
    sorrow

The three daughters of Urizen guard Ahanias Death
    couch
Rising from the confusion in tears & howlings &
    despair   200
Calling upon their fathers Name upon their Rivers
    dark

[5] Representing instinctual unity, Tharmas is the first of the
Zoas to fall. Urthona, whose fallen name is Los, represents imag-
inative power.

And the Eternal Man Said Hear my words O Prince
    of Light
Behold Jerusalem in whose bosom the Lamb of God
Is seen tho slain before her Gates he self renewd
    remains
Eternal & I thro him awake from deaths dark vale
The times revolve the time is coming when all these
    delights
Shall be renewd & all these Elements that now
    consume
Shall reflourish. Then bright Ahania shall awake
    from death
A glorious Vision to thine Eyes a Self renewing
    Vision
The spring. the summer to be thine then sleep the
    wintry days   210
In silken garments spun by her own hands against
    her funeral
The winter thou shalt plow & lay thy stores into thy
    barns
Expecting to recieve Ahania in the spring with joy
Immortal thou. Regenerate She & all the lovely Sex
From her shall learn obedience & prepare for a
    wintry grave
That spring may see them rise in tenfold joy &
    sweet delight
Thus shall the male & female live the life of Eternity
Because the Lamb of God Creates himself a bride &
    wife
That we his Children evermore may live in Jerusalem
Which now descendeth out of heaven a City yet a
    Woman   220
Mother of myriads redeemd & born in her spiritual
    palaces
By a New Spiritual birth Regenerated from Death

Urizen said. I have Erred & my Error remains with me
What Chain encompasses in what Lock is the river of
    light confind
That issues forth in the morning by measure & the
    evening by carefulness
Where shall we take our stand to view the infinite &
    unbounded
Or where are human feet for Lo our eyes are in the
    heavens

He ceasd for rivn link from link the bursting Universe
    explodes
All things reversd flew from their centers rattling
    bones
To bones Join, shaking convulsd the shivering clay
    breathes   230
Each speck of dust to the Earths center nestles round
    & round

In pangs of an Eternal Birth in torment & awe &
    fear
All spirits deceasd let loose from reptile prisons
    come in shoals
Wild furies from the tygers brain & from the lions
    Eyes
And from the ox & ass come moping terrors. from
    the Eagle
And raven numerous as the leaves of autumn   every
    species
Flock to the trumpet muttring over the sides of the
    grave & crying
In the fierce wind round heaving rocks & mountains
    filld with groans
On rifted rocks suspended in the air by inward fires
Many a woful company & many on clouds & waters
Fathers & friends Mothers & Infants Kings &
    Warriors   241
Priests & chaind Captives met together in a horrible
    fear
And every one of the dead appears as he had livd
    before
And all the marks remain of the slaves scourge &
    tyrants Crown
And of the Priests oergorged Abdomen & of the
    merchants thin
Sinewy deception & of the warriors ou[t]braving &
    thoughtlessness
In lineaments too extended & in bones too strait &
    long

They shew their wounds they accuse they sieze the
    opressor howlings began
On the golden palace Songs & joy on the desart the
    Cold babe
Stands in the furious air he cries the children of six
    thousand years   250
Who died in infancy rage furious a mighty multitude
    rage furious
Naked & pale standing on the expecting air to be
    deliverd
Rend limb from limb the Warrior & the tyrant
    reuniting in pain
The furious wind still rends around they flee in
    sluggish effort

They beg they intreat in vain now they Listend not
    to intreaty
They view the flames red rolling on thro the wide
    universe
From the dark jaws of death beneath & desolate
    shores remote
These covering Vaults of heaven & these trembling
    globes of Earth

One Planet calls to another & one star enquires of
    another
What flames are these coming from the South what
    noise what dreadful rout   260
As of a battle in the heavens hark heard you not the
    trumpet
As of fierce battle While they spoke the flames come
    on intense roaring

They see him whom they have piercd they wail
    because of him
They magnify themselves no more against Jerusalem
    Nor
Against her little ones the innocent accused before
    the Judges
Shines with immortal Glory trembling the Judge
    springs from his throne
Hiding his face in the dust beneath the prisoners feet
    & saying
Brother of Jesus what have I done intreat thy lord
    for me
Perhaps I may be forgiven While he speaks the
    flames roll on

And after the flames appears the Cloud of the Son of
    Man   270
Descending from Jerusalem with power and great
    Glory
All nations look up to the Cloud & behold him who
    was Crucified

The Prisoner answers you scourgd my father to
    death before my face
While I stood bound with cords & heavy chains.
    your hipocrisy
Shall now avail you nought. So speaking he dashd
    him with his foot

The Cloud is Blood dazling upon the heavens & in
    the cloud
Above upon its volumes is beheld a throne & a
    pavement
Of precious stones. surrounded by twenty four
    venerable patriarchs
And these again surrounded by four Wonders of the
    Almighty
Incomprehensible. pervading all amidst & round
    about   280
Fourfold each in the other reflected they are named
    Life's in Eternity
Four Starry Universes going forward from Eternity
    to Eternity

And the Falln Man who was arisen upon the Rock of
    Ages
Beheld the Vision of God & he arose up from the
    Rock
And Urizen arose up with him walking thro the
    flames
To meet the Lord coming to Judgment but the flames
    repelld them
Still to the Rock in vain they strove to Enter the
    Consummation
Together for the Redeemd Man could not enter the
    Consummation

Then siezd the Sons of Urizen the Plow they polishd
    it
From rust of ages all its ornaments of Gold & silver
    & ivory   290
Reshone across the field immense where all the
    nations
Darkend like Mould in the divided fallows where the
    weed
Triumphs in its own destruction they took down the
    harness
From the blue walls of heaven starry jingling
    ornamented
With beautiful art the study of angels the
    workmanship of Demons
When Heaven & Hell in Emulation strove in sports
    of Glory

The noise of rural work resounded thro the heavens
    of heavens
The horse[s] neigh from the battle the wild bulls
    from the sultry waste
The tygers from the forests & the lions from the
    sandy desarts
They Sing they sieze the instruments of harmony
    they throw away   300
The spear the bow the gun the mortar they level the
    fortifications
They beat the iron engines of destruction into wedges
They give them to Urthonas Sons ringing the
    hammers sound
In dens of death to forge the spade the mattock &
    the ax
The heavy roller to break the clods to pass over the
    nations

The Sons of Urizen Shout Their father rose The
    Eternal horses
Harnessd They calld to Urizen the heavens moved at
    their call

The limbs of Urizen shone with ardor. He laid his
   ha[n]d on the Plow
Thro dismal darkness drave the Plow of ages over
   Cities
And all their Villages over Mountains & all their
   Vallies   310
Over the graves & caverns of the dead   Over the
   Planets
And over the void Spaces over Sun & moon & star
   & constellation

Then Urizen commanded & they brought the Seed
   of Men
The trembling souls of All the Dead stood before
   Urizen
Weak wailing in the troubled air East west & north
   & south
He turnd the horses loose & laid his Plow in the
   northern corner
Of the wide Universal field. then Stepd forth into the
   immense

Then he began to sow the seed he girded round his
   loins
With a bright girdle & his skirt filld with immortal
   souls
Howling & Wailing fly the souls from Urizens
   strong hand   320

For from the hand of Urizen the myriads fall like stars
Into their own appointed places driven back by the
   winds
The naked warriors rush together down to the sea
   shores
They are become like wintry flocks like forests stripd
   of leaves
The Kings & Princes of the Earth cry with a feeble
   cry
Driven on the unproducing sands & on the hardend
   rocks
And all the while the flames of Orc follow the
   ventrous feet
Of Urizen & all the while the Trump of Tharmas
   sounds
Weeping & wailing fly the souls from Urizens strong
   hand
The daughters of Urizen stand with Cups & measures
   of foaming wine   330
Immense upon the heavens with bread & delicate
   repasts

Then follows the golden harrow in the midst of
   Mental fires

To ravishing melody of flutes & harps & softest voice
The seed is harrowd in while flames heat the black
   mould & cause
The human harvest to begin Towards the south
   first sprang
The myriads & in silent fear they look out from their
   graves

Then Urizen sits down to rest & all his wearied Sons
Take their repose on beds they drink they sing they
   view the flames
Of Orc in joy they view the human harvest springing
   up
A time they give to sweet repose till all the harvest is
   ripe   340

And Lo like the harvest Moon Ahania cast off her
   death clothes
She folded them up in care in silence & her brightning
   limbs
Bathd in the clear spring of the rock then from her
   darksom cave
Issud in majesty divine   Urizen rose up from his
   couch
On wings of tenfold joy clapping his hands his feet
   his radiant wings
In the immense as when the Sun dances upon the
   mountains
A shout of jubilee in lovely notes responds from
   daughter to daughter
From son to Son as if the Stars beaming innumerable
Thro night should sing soft warbling filling Earth
   & heaven
And bright Ahania took her seat by Urizen in songs
   & joy   350

The Eternal Man also sat down upon the Couches
   of Beulah
Sorrowful that he could not put off his new risen
   body
In mental flames the flames refusd they drove him
   back to Beulah
His body was redeemd to be permanent thro the
   Mercy Divine
And now fierce Orc had quite consumd himself in
   Mental flames
Expending all his energy against the fuel of fire
The Regenerate Man stoopd his head over the
   Universe & in
His holy hands recievd the flaming Demon &
   Demoness of Smoke
And gave them to Urizens hands the Immortal
   frownd Saying

Luvah & Vala [6] henceforth you are Servants obey &
   live   360
You shall forget your former state return & Love in
   peace
Into your place the place of seed not in the brain or
   heart
If Gods combine against Man Setting their Dominion
   above
The Human form Divine. Thrown down from their
   high Station
In the Eternal heavens of Human Imagination:
   buried beneath
In dark oblivion with incessant pangs ages on ages
In Enmity & war first weakend then in stern
   repentance
They must renew their brightness & their disorganizd
   functions
Again reorganize till they resume the image of the
   human
Cooperating in the bliss of Man obeying his Will   370
Servants to the infinite & Eternal of the Human form

Luvah & Vala descended & enterd the Gates of Dark
   Urthona
And walkd from the hands of Urizen in the shadows
   of Valas Garden
Where the impressions of Despair & Hope for ever
   vegetate
In flowers in fruits in fishes birds & beasts & clouds
   & waters
The land of doubts & shadows sweet delusions
   unformd hopes
They saw no more the terrible confusion of the
   wracking universe
They heard not saw not felt not all the terrible
   confusion
For in their orbed senses within closd up they
   wanderd at will
And those upon the Couches viewd them in the
   dreams of Beulah   380
As they reposd from the terrible wide universal
   harvest
Invisible Luvah in bright clouds hoverd over Valas
   head
And thus their ancient golden age renewd for Luvah
   spoke
With voice mild from his golden Cloud upon the
   breath of morning

◇◇◇◇◇◇◇◇◇◇◇◇◇◇◇◇◇◇◇◇◇◇◇◇◇◇◇◇

[6] Vala, the seducer of Albion, here joins Luvah in a rebirth
into innocence. With the consumption of Orc, they now act as
eternal forms.

Come forth O Vala from the grass & from the silent
   Dew
Rise from the dews of death for the Eternal Man is
   Risen

She rises among flowers & looks toward the Eastern
   clearness
She walks yea runs her feet are wingd on the tops of
   the bending grass
Her garments rejoice in the vocal wind & her hair
   glistens with dew
She answered thus Whose voice is this in the voice
   of the nourishing air   390
In the spirit of the morning awaking the Soul from
   its grassy bed
Where dost thou dwell for it is thee I seek & but for
   thee
I must have slept Eternally nor have felt the dew of
   thy morning
Look how the opening dawn advances with vocal
   harmony
Look how the beams foreshew the rising of some
   glorious power
The sun is thine he goeth forth in his majestic
   brightness
O thou creating voice that callest & who shall answer
   thee

Where dost thou flee O fair one where dost thou
   seek thy happy place

To yonder brightness there I haste for sure I came
   from thence
Or I must have slept eternally nor have felt the dew
   of morning   400

Eternally thou must have slept nor have felt the
   morning dew
But for yon nourishing sun tis that by which thou
   art arisen
The birds adore the sun the beasts rise up & play in
   his beams
And every flower & every leaf rejoices in his light
Then O thou fair one sit thee down for thou art as the
   grass
Thou risest in the dew of morning & at night art
   folded up

Alas am I but as a flower then will I sit me down
Then will I weep then Ill complain & sigh for
   immortality
And chide my maker thee O Sun that raisedst me to
   fall

So saying she sat down & wept beneath the apple
 trees   410

O be thou blotted out thou Sun that raisedst me to
 trouble
That gavest me a heart to crave & raisedst me thy
 phantom
To feel thy heat & see thy light & wander here alone
Hopeless if I am like the grass & so shall pass away

Rise sluggish Soul why sitst thou here why dost thou
 sit & weep
Yon Sun shall wax old & decay but thou shalt ever
 flourish
The fruit shall ripen & fall down & the flowers
 consume away
But thou shalt still survive arise O dry thy dewy
 tears

Hah! Shall I still survive whence came that sweet
 & comforting voice
And whence that voice of sorrow O sun thou art
 nothing now to me   420
Go on thy course rejoicing & let us both rejoice
 together
I walk among his flocks & hear the bleating of his
 lambs
O that I could behold his face & follow his pure feet
I walk by the footsteps of his flocks come hither
 tender flocks
Can you converse with a pure Soul that seeketh for
 her maker
You answer not then am I set your mistress in this
 garden
Ill watch you & attend your footsteps you are not
 like the birds
That sing & fly in the bright air but you do lick my
 feet
And let me touch your wooly backs follow me as I
 sing
For in my bosom a new song arises to my Lord 430
Rise up O Sun most glorious minister & light of day
Flow on ye gentle airs & bear the voice of my
 rejoicing
Wave freshly clear waters flowing around the tender
 grass
And thou sweet smelling ground put forth thy life
 in fruits & flowers
Follow me O my flocks & hear me sing my rapturous
 Song
I will cause my voice to be heard on the clouds that
 glitter in the sun
I will call & who shall answer me I will sing who
 shall reply

For from my pleasant hills behold the living living
 springs
Running among my green pastures delighting
 among my trees   439
I am not here alone my flocks you are my brethren
And you birds that sing & adorn the sky you are my
 sisters
I sing & you reply to my Song I rejoice & you are
 glad
Follow me O my flocks we will now descend into the
 valley
O how delicious are the grapes flourishing in the
 Sun
How clear the spring of the rock running among the
 golden sand
How cool the breezes of the vally & the arms of the
 branching trees
Cover us from the Sun come & let us sit in the
 Shade
My Luvah here hath placd me in a Sweet & pleasant
 Land
And given me fruits & pleasant waters & warm hills
 & cool valleys
Here will I build myself a house & here Ill call on
 his name   450
Here Ill return when I am weary & take my pleasant
 rest

So spoke the Sinless Soul & laid her head on the
 downy fleece
Of a curld Ram who stretchd himself in sleep beside
 his mistress
And soft sleep fell upon her eyelids in the silent noon
 of day

Then Luvah passed by & saw the sinless Soul
And said Let a pleasant house arise to be the dwelling
 place
Of this immortal Spirit growing in lower Paradise

He spoke & pillars were builded & walls as white as
 ivory
The grass she slept upon was pavd with pavement as
 of pearl   459
Beneath her rose a downy bed & a cieling coverd all

Vala awoke. When in the pleasant gates of sleep I
 enterd
I saw my Luvah like a spirit stand in the bright air
Round him stood spirits like me who reard me a
 bright house
And here I see thee house remain in my most pleasant
 world

My Luvah smild I kneeled down he laid his hand on
    my head
And when he laid his hand upon me from the gates
    of sleep I came
Into this bodily house to tend my flocks in my
    pleasant garden

So saying she arose & walked round her beautiful
    house
And then from her white door she lookd to see her
    bleating lambs
But her flocks were gone up from beneath the trees
    into the hills   470

I see the hand that leadeth me doth also lead my
    flocks
She went up to her flocks & turned oft to see her
    shining house
She stopd to drink of the clear spring & eat the grapes
    & apples
She bore the fruits in her lap she gatherd flowers for
    her bosom
She called to her flocks saying follow me o my
    flocks

They followd her to the silent vally beneath the
    spreading trees
And on the rivers margin she ungirded her golden
    girdle
She stood in the river & viewd herself within the
    watry glass
And her bright hair was wet with the waters She
    rose up from the river
And as she rose her Eyes were opend to the world of
    waters   480
She saw Tharmas sitting upon the rocks beside the
    wavy sea
He strokd the water from his beard & mournd faint
    thro the summer vales

And Vala stood on the rocks of Tharmas & heard his
    mournful voice

O Enion[7] my weary head is in the bed of death
For weeds of death have wrapd around my limbs in
    the hoary deeps
I sit in the place of shells & mourn & thou art closd
    in clouds
When will the time of Clouds be past & the dismal
    night of Tharmas

⬦⬦⬦⬦⬦⬦⬦⬦⬦⬦⬦⬦⬦⬦⬦⬦⬦⬦⬦⬦⬦⬦⬦⬦⬦

7 The maternal emanation of Tharmas—see note to line 182,
p. 70.

Arise O Enion Arise & smile upon my head
As thou dost smile upon the barren mountains and
    they rejoice
When wilt thou smile on Tharmas O thou bringer
    of golden day   490
Arise O Enion arise for Lo I have calmd my seas

So saying his faint head he laid upon the Oozy rock
And darkness coverd all the deep the light of Enion
    faded
Like a fa[i]nt flame quivering upon the surface of the
    darkness

Then Vala lifted up her hands to heaven to call on
    Enion
She calld but none could answer her & the Eccho
    of her voice returnd

Where is the voice of God that calld me from the
    silent dew
Where is the Lord of Vala dost thou hide in clefts of
    the rock
Why shouldst thou hide thyself from Vala from the
    soul that wanders desolate
She ceas'd & light beamd round her like the glory of
    the morning   500
And She arose out of the river & girded on her golden
    girdle

And now her feet step on the grassy bosom of the
    ground
Among her flocks & she turnd her eyes toward her
    pleasant house
And saw in the door way beneath the trees two little
    children playing
She drew near to her house & her flocks followd her
    footsteps
The Children clung around her knees she embracd
    them & wept over them

Thou little Boy art Tharmas & thou bright Girl Enion
How are ye thus renewd & brought into the Gardens
    of Vala

She embracd them in tears. till the sun descended
    the western hills
And then she enterd her bright house leading her
    mighty children   510
And when night came the flocks laid round the house
    beneath the trees
She laid the Children on the beds which she saw
    prepared in the house
Then last herself laid down & closd her Eyelids in soft
    slumbers

And in the morning when the Sun arose in the crystal
  sky
Vala awoke & calld the children from their gentle
  slumbers

Awake O Enion awake & let thine innocent Eyes
Enlighten all the Crystal house of Vala awake awake
Awake Tharmas awake awake thou child of dewy
  tears
Open the orbs of thy blue eyes & smile upon my
  gardens

The Children woke & smild on Vala. she kneeld by
  the golden couch   520
She presd them to her bosom & her pearly tears
  dropd down
O my sweet Children Enion let Tharmas kiss thy
  Cheek
Why dost thou turn thyself away from his sweet
  watry eyes
Tharmas henceforth in Valas bosom thou shalt
  find sweet peace
O bless the lovely eyes of Tharmas & the Eyes of
  Enion

They rose they went out wandring sometimes together
  sometimes alone
Why weepest thou Tharmas Child of tears in the
  bright house of joy
Doth Enion avoid the sight of thy blue heavenly
  Eyes
And dost thou wander with my lambs & wet their
  innocent faces
With thy bright tears because the steps of Enion are
  in the gardens   530
Arise sweet boy & let us follow the path of Enion

So saying they went down into the garden among the
  fruits
And Enion sang among the flowers that grew among
  the trees
And Vala said Go Tharmas weep not Go to Enion
He said O Vala I am sick & all this garden of
  Pleasure
Swims like a dream before my eyes but the sweet
  smelling fruit
Revives me to new deaths I fade even like a water lilly
In the suns heat till in the night on the couch of
  Enion
I drink new life & feel the breath of sleeping Enion
But in the morning she arises to avoid my Eyes   540
Then my loins fade & in the house I sit me down &
  weep

Chear up thy Countenance bright boy & go to Enion
Tell her that Vala waits her in the shadows of her
  garden

He went with timid steps & Enion like the ruddy
  morn
When infant spring appears in swelling buds &
  opening flowers
Behind her Veil withdraws so Enion turnd her modest
  head

But Tharmas spoke Vala seeks thee sweet Enion in
  the shades
Follow the steps of Tharmas, O thou brightness of
  the gardens
He took her hand reluctant she followd in infant
  doubts

Thus in Eternal Childhood straying among Valas
  flocks   550
In infant sorrow & joy alternate Enion & Tharmas
  playd
Round Vala in the Gardens of Vala & by her rivers
  margin
They are the shadows of Tharmas & of Enion in
  Valas world

And the sleepers who rested from their harvest work
  beheld these visions
Thus were the sleepers entertaind upon the Couches
  of Beulah

When Luvah & Vala were closd up in their world of
  shadowy forms
Darkness was all beneath the heavens only a little light
Such as glows out from sleeping spirits appeard in
  the deeps beneath
As when the wind sweeps over a Corn field the noise
  of souls
Thro all the immense borne down by Clouds swagging
  in autumnal heat   560
Muttering along from heaven to heaven hoarse roll
  the human forms
Beneath thick clouds dreadful lightnings burst &
  thunders roll
Down pour the torrent Floods of heaven on all the
  human harvest
Then Urizen sitting at his repose on beds in the
  bright South
Cried Times are Ended he Exulted he arose in joy
  he exulted
He pourd his light & all his Sons & daughters pourd
  their light

To exhale the spirits of Luvah & Vala thro the
    atmosphere
And Luvah & Vala saw the Light their spirits were
    Exhald
In all their ancient innocence the floods depart the
    clouds   569
Dissipate or sink into the Seas of Tharmas   Luvah
    sat
Above on the bright heavens in peace. the Spirits of
    Men beneath
Cried out to be deliverd & the Spirit of Luvah wept
Over the human harvest & over Vala the sweet
    wanderer
In pain the human harvest wavd in horrible groans
    of woe
The Universal Groan went up the Eternal Man was
    Darkend

Then Urizen arose & took his Sickle in his hand
There is a brazen sickle & a scythe of iron hid
Deep in the South guarded by a few solitary stars
This sickle Urizen took the scythe his sons embracd
And went forth & began to reap & all his joyful sons
Reapd the wide Universe & bound in Sheaves a
    wondrous harvest   581
They took them into the wide barns with loud
    rejoicings & triumph
Of flute & harp & drum & trumpet horn & clarion

The feast was spread in the bright South & the
    Regenerate Man
Sat at the feast rejoicing & the wine of Eternity
Was servd round by the flames of Luvah all Day &
    all the Night
And when Morning began to dawn upon the distant
    hills
a whirlwind rose up in the Center & in the Whirlwind
    a shriek
And in the Shriek a rattling of bones & in the rattling
    of bones
A dolorous groan & from the dolorous groan in
    tears   590
Rose Enion like a gentle light & Enion spoke saying

O Dreams of Death the human form dissolving
    companied
By beasts & worms & creeping things & darkness &
    despair
The clouds fall off from my wet brow the dust from
    my cold limbs
Into the Sea of Tharmas Soon renewd a Golden
    Moth
I shall cast off my death clothes & Embrace Tharmas
    again

For Lo the winter melted away upon the distant
    hills
And all the black mould sings. She speaks to her
    infant race her milk
Descends down on the sand. the thirsty sand drinks
    & rejoices
Wondering to behold the Emmet the Grasshopper the
    jointed worm   600
The roots shoot thick thro the solid rocks bursting
    their way
They cry out in joys of existence. the broad stems
Rear on the mountains stem after stem the scaly
    newt creeps
From the stone & the armed fly springs from the
    rocky crevice
The spider. The bat burst from the hardend slime
    crying
To one another What are we & whence is our joy &
    delight
Lo the little moss begins to spring & the tender
    weed
Creeps round our secret nest. Flocks brighten the
    Mountains
Herds throng up the Valley wild beasts fill the forests

Joy thrilld thro all the Furious form of Tharmas
    humanizing   610
Mild he Embracd her whom he sought he raisd her
    thro the heavens
Sounding his trumpet to awake the dead on high he
    soard
Over the ruind worlds the smoking tomb of the
    Eternal Prophet
The Eternal Man arose He welcomd them to the
    Feast
The feast was spread in the bright South & the
    Eternal Man
Sat at the feast rejoicing & the wine of Eternity
Was servd round by the flames of Luvah all day &
    all the night

And Many Eternal Men sat at the golden feast to see
The female form now separate They shudderd at the
    horrible thing
Not born for the sport and amusement of Man but
    born to drink up all his powers   620
They wept to see their shadows they said to one
    another this is Sin
This is the Generative world they rememberd the
    Days of old

And One of the Eternals spoke All was silent at the
    feast

Man is a Worm wearied with joy he seeks the caves
    of sleep
Among the Flowers of Beulah in his Selfish cold
    repose
Forsaking Brotherhood & Universal love in selfish
    clay
Folding the pure wings of his mind seeking the
    places dark
Abstracted from the roots of Science then inclosd
    around
In walls of Gold we cast him like a Seed into the
    Earth
Till times & spaces have passd over him duly every
    morn   630
We visit him covering with a Veil the immortal seed
With windows from the inclement sky we cover him
    & with walls
And hearths protect the Selfish terror till divided all
In families we see our shadows born.
    & thence we know   Ephesians
That Man subsists by Brotherhood &   iii c.
    Universal Love   10 v
We fall on one another necks more
    closely we embrace
Not for ourselves but for the Eternal family we live
Man liveth not by Self alone but in his brothers face
Each shall behold the Eternal Father & love & joy
    abound

So spoke the Eternal at the Feast they embracd the
    New born Man   640
Calling him Brother image of the Eternal Father.
    they sat down
At the immortal tables sounding loud their
    instruments of joy
Calling the Morning into Beulah the Eternal Man
    rejoicd

When Morning dawnd The Eternals rose to labour
    at the Vintage
Beneath they saw their sons & daughters wondering
    inconceivable
At the dark myriads in Shadows in the worlds
    beneath

The morning dawnd Urizen rose & in his hand the
    Flail
Sounds on the Floor heard terrible by all beneath
    the heavens
Dismal loud redounding the nether floor shakes with
    the sound
And all Nations were threshed out & the stars
    threshd from their husks   650

Then Tharmas took the Winnowing fan the
    winnowing wind furious
Above veerd round by the violent whirlwind driven
    west & south
Tossed the Nations like Chaff into the seas of Tharmas

O Mystery Fierce Tharmas cries Behold thy end is
    come
Art thou she that made the nations drunk with the
    cup of Religion
Go down ye Kings & Councillors & Giant Warriors
Go down into the depths go down & hide yourselves
    beneath
Go down with horse & Chariots & Trumpets of
    hoarse war

Lo how the Pomp of Mystery goes down into the
    Caves
Her great men howl & throw the dust & rend their
    hoary hair   660
Her delicate women & children shriek upon the
    bitter wind
Spoild of their beauty their hair rent & their skin
    shriveld up
Lo darkness covers the long pomp of banners on the
    wind
And black horses & armed men & miserable bound
    captives
Where shall the graves recieve them all & where shall
    be their place
And who shall mourn for Mystery who never loosd
    her Captives

Let the slave grinding at the mill run out into the
    field
Let him look up into the heavens & laugh in the
    bright air
Let the inchaind soul shut up in darkness & in
    sighing
Whose face has never seen a smile in thirty weary
    years   670
Rise & look out his chains are loose his dungeon
    doors are open
And let his wife & children return from the opressors
    scourge

They look behind at every step & believe it is a dream
Are these the Slaves that groand along the streets of
    Mystery
Where are your bonds & task masters are these the
    prisoners
Where are your chains where are your tears why do
    you look around

If you are thirsty there is the river go bathe your
    parched limbs
The good of all the Land is before you for Mystery is
    no more
Then All the Slaves from every Earth in the wide
    Universe
Sing a New Song drowning confusion in its happy
    notes   680
While the flail of Urizen sounded loud & the
    winnowing wind of Tharmas
So loud so clear in the wide heavens & the song that
    they sung was this
Composed by an African Black from the little Earth
    of Sotha

Aha Aha how came I here so soon in my sweet
    native land
How came I here Methinks I am as I was in my
    youth
When in my fathers house I sat & heard his chearing
    voice
Methinks I see his flocks & herds & feel my limbs
    renewd
And Lo my Brethren in their tents & their little ones
    around them

The song arose to the Golden feast the Eternal Man
    rejoicd
Then the Eternal Man said Luvah the Vintage is
    ripe arise   690
The sons of Urizen shall gather the vintage with
    sharp hooks
And all thy sons O Luvah bear away the families of
    Earth
I hear the flail of Urizen his barns are full no roo[m]
Remains & in the Vineyards stand the abounding
    sheaves beneath
The falling Grapes that odorous burst upon the
    winds. Arise
My flocks & herds trample the Corn my cattle browze
    upon
The ripe Clusters The shepherds shout for Luvah
    prince of Love
Let the Bulls of Luvah tread the Corn & draw the
    loaded waggon
Into the Barn while children glean the Ears around
    the door
Then shall they lift their innocent hands & stroke his
    furious nose   700
And he shall lick the little girls white neck & on her
    head
Scatter the perfume of his breath while from his
    mountains high

The lion of terror shall come down & bending his
    bright mane
And couching at their side shall eat from the curld
    boys white lap
His golden food and in the evening sleep before the
    Door

Attempting to be more than Man We become less
    said Luvah
As he arose from the bright feast drunk with the
    wine of ages
His crown of thorns fell from his head he hung his
    living Lyre
Behind the seat of the Eternal Man & took his
    way
Sounding the Song of Los descending to the
    Vineyards bright   710
His sons arising from the feast with golden baskets
    follow
A fiery train as when the Sun sings in the ripe
    vineyards
Then Luvah stood before the wine press all his
    fiery sons
Brought up the loaded Waggons with shoutings
    ramping tygers play
In the jingling traces furious lions sound the song of
    joy
To the golden wheels circling upon the pavement of
    heaven & all
The Villages of Luvah ring the golden tiles of the
    villages
Reply to violins & tabors to the pipe flute lyre &
    cymbal
Then fell the Legions of Mystery in maddning
    confusion
Down Down thro the immense with outcry fury &
    despair   720
Into the wine presses of Luvah howling fell the
    Clusters
Of human families thro the deep. the wine presses
    were filld
The blood of life flowd plentiful Odors of life
    arose
All round the heavenly arches & the Odors rose
    singing this song
O terrible wine presses of Luvah O caverns of the
    Grave
How lovely the delights of those risen again from
    death
O trembling joy excess of joy is like Excess of grief

So sang the Human Odors round the wine presses of
    Luvah

But in the Wine presses is wailing terror &
    despair
Forsaken of their Elements they vanish & are no
    more   730
No more but a desire of Being a distracted ravening
    desire
Desiring like the hungry worm & like the gaping
    grave
They plunge into the Elements the Elements cast
    them forth
Or else consume their shadowy semblance Yet they
    obstinate
Tho pained to distraction Cry O let us Exist for
This dreadful Non Existence is worse than pains of
    Eternal Birth
Eternal Death who can Endure. let us consume in
    fires
In waters stifling or in air corroding or in earth shut
    up
The Pangs of Eternal birth are better than the
    Pangs of Eternal Death

How red the sons & daughters of Luvah how they
    tread the Grapes   740
Laughing & shouting drunk with odors many fall
    oerwearied
Drownd in the wine is many a youth & maiden those
    around
Lay them on skins of tygers or the spotted Leopard or
    wild Ass
Till they revive or bury them in cool Grots making
    lamentation

But in the Wine Presses the Human Grapes Sing not
    nor dance
They howl & writhe in shoals of torment in fierce
    flames consuming
In chains of iron & in dungeons circled with ceaseless
    fires
In pits & dens & shades of death in shapes of torment
    & woe
The Plates the Screws and Racks & Saws & cords &
    fires & floods
The cruel joy of Luvahs daughters lacerating with
    knives   750
And whip[s] their Victims & the deadly sports of
    Luvahs sons

Timbrels & Violins sport round the Wine Presses
    The little Seed
The Sportive root the Earthworm the small beetle
    the wise Emmet

Dance round the Wine Presses of Luvah. the
    Centipede is there
The ground Spider with many Eyes the Mole
    clothed in Velvet
The Earwig armd the tender maggot emblem of
    Immortality
The Slow Slug the grasshopper that sings & laughs
    & drinks
The winter comes he folds his slender bones without
    a murmur
There is the Nettle that stings with soft down &
    there
The indignant Thistle whose bitterness is bred in
    his milk   760
And who lives on the contempt of his neighbour
    there all the idle weeds
That creep about the obscure places shew their
    various limbs
Naked in all their beauty dancing round the Wine
    Presses
They Dance around the Dying & they Drink the
    howl & groan
They catch the Shrieks in cups of gold they hand
    them to one another
These are the sports of love & these the sweet delights
    of amorous play
Tears of the grapes the death sweat of the Cluster the
    last sigh
Of the mild youth who listens to the luring songs of
    Luvah

The Eternal Man darkend with Sorrow & a wintry
    mantle
Coverd the Hills   He said O Tharmas rise & O
    Urthona   770

Then Tharmas & Urthona rose from the Golden
    feast satiated
With Mirth & Joy Urthona limping from his fall on
    Tharmas leand
In his right hand his hammer Tharmas held his
    Shepherds crook
Beset with gold gold were the ornaments formd by
    sons of Urizen

Then Enion & Ahania & Vala & the wife of Dark
    Urthona
Rose from the feast in joy ascending to their Golden
    Looms
There the wingd shuttle Sang the spindle & the
    distaff & the Reel
Rang sweet the praise of industry. Thro all the
    golden rooms

Heaven rang with winged Exultation   All beneath
    howld loud
With tenfold rout & desolation roard the Chasms
    beneath   780
Where the wide woof flowd down & where the
    Nation are gatherd together

Tharmas went down to the Wine presses & beheld
    the sons & daughters
Of Luvah quite exhausted with the Labour & quite
    filld
With new wine. that they began to torment one
    another and to tread
The weak. Luvah & Vala slept on the floor
    o'erwearied

Urthona calld his Sons around him Tharmas calld
    his sons
Numrous. they took the wine they separated the
    Lees
And Luvah was put for dung on the ground by the
    Sons of Tharmas & Urthona
They formed heavens of sweetest wo[o]d[s] of gold
    & silver & ivory
Of glass & precious stones They loaded all the
    waggons of heaven   790
And took away the wine of ages with solemn songs
    & joy

Luvah & Vala woke & all the sons & daughters of
    Luvah
Awoke they wept to one another & they reascended
To the Eternal Man in woe he cast them wailing into
The world of shadows thro the air till winter is over
    & gone

But the Human Wine stood wondering in all their
    delightful Expanses
The Elements subside the heavens rolld on with
    vocal harmony

Then Los who is Urthona rose in all his regenerate
    power
The Sea that rolld & foamd with darkness & the
    the shadows of death
Vomited out & gave up all the floods lift up their
    hands   800
Singing & shouting to the Man they bow their hoary
    heads
And murmuring in their channels flow & circle
    round his feet
Then Dark Urthona took the Corn out of the Stores
    of Urizen

He ground it in his rumbling Mills Terrible the
    distress
Of all the Nations of Earth ground in the Mills of
    Urthona
In his hand Tharmas takes the Storms, he turns the
    whirlwind Loose
Upon the wheels the stormy seas howl at his dread
    command
And Eddying fierce rejoice in the fierce agitation of
    the wheels
Of Dark Urthona Thunders Earthquakes Fires
    Water floods
Rejoice to one another loud their voices shake the
    Abyss   810
Their dread forms tending the dire mills The grey
    hoar frost was there
And his pale wife the aged Snow they watch over the
    fires
They build the Ovens of Urthona Nature in darkness
    groans
And Men are bound to sullen contemplations in the
    night
Restless they turn on beds of sorrow. in their inmost
    brain
Feeling the crushing Wheels they rise they write the
    bitter words
Of Stern Philosophy & knead the bread of knowledge
    with tears & groans

Such are the works of Dark Urthona Tharmas sifted
    the corn
Urthona made the Bread of Ages & he placed it
In golden & in silver baskets in heavens of precious
    stone   820
And then took his repose in Winter in the night of
    Time

The Sun has left his blackness & has found a fresher
    morning
And the mild moon rejoices in the clear & cloudless
    night
And Man walks forth from midst of the fires the evil
    is all consumd
His eyes behold the Angelic spheres arising night &
    day
The stars consumd like a lamp blown out & in their
    stead behold
The Expanding Eyes of Man behold the depths of
    wondrous worlds

One Earth one sea beneath nor Erring Globes wander
    but Stars
Of fire rise up nightly from the Ocean & one Sun

Each morning like a New born Man issues with songs
    & Joy   830
Calling the Plowman to his Labour & the Shepherd
    to his rest
He walks upon the Eternal Mountains raising his
    heavenly voice
Conversing with the Animal forms of wisdom night
    & day
That risen from the Sea of fire renewd walk oer the
    Earth

For Tharmas brought his flocks upon the hills & in
    the Vales
Around the Eternal Mans bright tent the little
    Children play
Among the wooly flocks The hammer of Urthona
    sounds
In the deep caves beneath his limbs renewd his
    Lions roar
Around the Furnaces & in Evening sport upon the
    plains
They raise their faces from the Earth conversing with
    the Man   840

How is it we have walkd thro fires & yet are not
    consumd
How is it that all things are changd even as in ancient
    times
The Sun arises from his dewy bed & the fresh airs
Play in his smiling beams giving the seeds of life to
    grow
And the fresh Earth beams forth ten thousand
    thousand springs of life
Urthona is arisen in his strength no longer now
Divided from Enitharmon no longer the Spectre Los
Where is the Spectre of Prophecy where the delusive
    Phantom
Departed & Urthona rises from the ruinous walls
In all his ancient strength to form the golden
    armour of science   850
For intellectual War   The war of swords departed
    now
The dark Religions are departed & sweet Science
    reigns

End of The Dream

[1795–1804]   [1893, correctly 1925]

FROM THE PICKERING MANUSCRIPT
AND THE NOTEBOOK
*This group of poems from the Notebook and from a fair-copy
manuscript called the Pickering MS were probably composed in
1800–1803, largely at Felpham.*

FROM THE PICKERING MANUSCRIPT AND THE NOTEBOOK

"Mock on Mock on . . ."[1]

Mock on Mock on Voltaire Rousseau
Mock on Mock on tis all in vain
You throw the sand against the wind
And the wind blows it back again

And every sand becomes a Gem
Reflected in the beams divine
Blown back they blind the mocking Eye
But still in Israels paths they shine

The Atoms of Democritus
And Newtons Particles of light   10
Are sands upon the Red sea shore
Where Israels tents do shine so bright

THE SMILE

There is a Smile of Love
And there is a Smile of Deceit
And there is a Smile of Smiles
In which these two Smiles meet

And there is a Frown of Hate
And there is a Frown of disdain
And there is a Frown of Frowns
Which you strive to forget in vain

For it sticks in the Hearts deep Core
And it sticks in the deep Back bone   10
And no Smile that ever was smild
But only one Smile alone

That betwixt the Cradle & Grave
It only once Smild can be
But when it once is Smild
Theres an end to all Misery

---

[1] From the Notebook. The remaining poems in this group are
found in the Pickering Manuscript.

THE GOLDEN NET

Three Virgins at the break of day
Whither young Man whither away
Alas for woe! alas for woe!
They cry & tears for ever flow
The one was Clothd in flames of fire
The other Clothd in iron wire
The other Clothd in tears & sighs
Dazling bright before my Eyes
They bore a Net of Golden twine
To hang upon the Branches fine   10
Pitying I wept to see the woe
That Love & Beauty undergo
To be consumd in burning Fires
And in ungratified desires
And in tears clothd Night & day
Melted all my Soul away
When they saw my Tears a Smile
That did Heaven itself beguile
Bore the Golden Net aloft
As on downy Pinions soft   20
Over the Morning of my day
Underneath the Net I stray
Now intreating Burning Fire
Now intreating Iron Wire
Now intreating Tears & Sighs
O when will the morning rise

THE MENTAL TRAVELLER

I traveld thro' a Land of Men
A Land of Men & Women too
And heard & saw such dreadful things
As cold Earth wanderers never knew

For there the Babe is born in joy
That was begotten in dire woe
Just as we Reap in joy the fruit
Which we in bitter tears did sow

And if the Babe is born a Boy
He's given to a Woman Old   10
Who nails him down upon a rock
Catches his shrieks in cups of gold

She binds iron thorns around his head
She pierces both his hands & feet
She cuts his heart out at his side
To make it feel both cold & heat

Her fingers number every Nerve
Just as a Miser counts his gold
She lives upon his shrieks & cries
And she grows young as he grows old   20

Till he becomes a bleeding youth
And she becomes a Virgin bright
Then he rends up his Manacles
And binds her down for his delight

He plants himself in all her Nerves
Just as a Husbandman his mould
And she becomes his dwelling place
And Garden fruitful seventy fold

An aged Shadow soon he fades
Wandring round an Earthly Cot   30
Full filled all with gems & gold
Which he by industry had got

And these are the gems of the Human Soul
The rubies & pearls of a lovesick eye
The countless gold of the akeing heart
The martyrs groan & the lovers sigh

They are his meat they are his drink
He feeds the Beggar & the Poor
And the wayfaring Traveller
For ever open is his door   40

His grief is their eternal joy
They make the roofs & walls to ring
Till from the fire on the hearth
A little Female Babe does spring

And she is all of solid fire
And gems & gold that none his hand
Dares stretch to touch her Baby form
Or wrap her in his swaddling-band

But She comes to the Man she loves
If young or old or rich or poor   50
They soon drive out the aged Host
A Beggar at anothers door

He wanders weeping far away
Untill some other take him in
Oft blind & age-bent sore distrest
Untill he can a Maiden win

And to allay his freezing Age
The Poor Man takes her in his arms
The Cottage fades before his sight
The Garden & its lovely Charms   60

The Guests are scatterd thro' the land
For the Eye altering alters all
The Senses roll themselves in fear
And the flat Earth becomes a Ball

The Stars Sun Moon all shrink away
A desart vast without a bound
And nothing left to eat or drink
And a dark desart all around

The honey of her Infant lips
The bread & wine of her sweet smile   70
The wild game of her roving Eye
Does him to Infancy beguile

For as he eats & drinks he grows
Younger & younger every day
And on the desart wild they both
Wander in terror & dismay

Like the wild Stag she flees away
Her fear plants many a thicket wild
While he pursues her night & day
By various arts of Love beguild   80

By various arts of Love & Hate
Till the wide desart planted oer
With Labyrinths of wayward Love
Where roams the Lion Wolf & Boar

Till he becomes a wayward Babe
And she a weeping Woman Old
Then many a Lover wanders here
The Sun & Stars are nearer rolld

The trees bring forth sweet Extacy
To all who in the desart roam   90
Till many a City there is Built
And many a pleasant Shepherds home

But when they find the frowning Babe
Terror strikes thro the region wide
They cry the Babe the Babe is Born
And flee away on Every side

For who dare touch the frowning form
His arm is witherd to its root
Lions Boars Wolves all howling flee
And every Tree does shed its fruit   100

And none can touch that frowning form
Except it be a Woman Old
She nails him down upon the Rock
And all is done as I have told

MARY

Although this poem is popularly supposed to have been addressed to Mary Wollstonecraft, wife of William Godwin and author of A Vindication of the Rights of Woman, *the connection is entirely conjectural.*

MARY

Sweet Mary the first time she ever was there
Came into the Ball room among the Fair
The young Men & Maidens around her throng
And these are the words upon every tongue

An Angel is here from the heavenly Climes
Or again does return the Golden times
Her eyes outshine every brilliant ray
She opens her lips tis the Month of May

Mary moves in soft beauty & conscious delight
To augment with sweet smiles all the joys of the
    Night   10
Nor once blushes to own to the rest of the Fair
That sweet Love & Beauty are worthy our care

In the Morning the Villagers rose with delight
And repeated with pleasure the joys of the night
And Mary arose among Friends to be free
But no Friend from henceforward thou Mary shalt
    see

Some said she was proud some calld her a whore
And some when she passed by shut to the door
A damp cold came oer her her blushes all fled
Her lillies & roses are blighted & shed   20

O why was I born with a different Face
Why was I not born like this Envious Race
Why did Heaven adorn me with bountiful hand
And then set me down in an envious Land

To be weak as a Lamb & smooth as a dove
And not to raise Envy is calld Christian Love
But if you raise Envy your Merits to blame
For planting such spite in the weak & the tame

I will humble my Beauty I will not dress fine
I will keep from the Ball & my Eyes shall not shine   30
And if any Girls Lover forsakes her for me
I'll refuse him my hand & from Envy be free

She went out in Morning attird plain & neat
Proud Marys gone Mad said the Child in the Street
She went out in Morning in plain neat attire
And came home in Evening bespatterd with mire

She trembled & wept sitting on the Bed side
She forgot it was Night & she trembled & cried
She forgot it was Night she forgot it was Morn
Her soft Memory imprinted with Faces of Scorn　　40

With Faces of Scorn & with Eyes of disdain
Like foul Fiends inhabiting Marys mild Brain
She remembers no Face like the Human Divine
All Faces have Envy sweet Mary but thine

And thine is a Face of sweet Love in Despair
And thine is a Face of mild sorrow & care
And thine is a Face of wild terror & fear
That shall never be quiet till laid on its bier

THE CRYSTAL CABINET

The Maiden caught me in the Wild
Where I was dancing merrily
She put me into her Cabinet
And Lockd me up with a golden Key

This Cabinet is formd of Gold
And Pearl & Crystal shining bright
And within it opens into a World
And a little lovely Moony Night

Another England there I saw
Another London with its Tower　　10
Another Thames & other Hills
And another pleasant Surrey Bower

Another Maiden like herself
Translucent lovely shining clear
Threefold each in the other closd
O what a pleasant trembling fear

O what a smile a threefold Smile
Filld me that like a flame I burnd
I bent to Kiss the lovely Maid
And found a Threefold Kiss returnd　　20

I strove to sieze the inmost Form
With ardor fierce & hands of flame
But burst the Crystal Cabinet
And like a Weeping Babe became

A weeping Babe upon the wild
And Weeping Woman pale reclind
And in the outward air again
I filld with woes the passing Wind

AUGURIES OF INNOCENCE

To see a World in a Grain of Sand
And a Heaven in a Wild Flower
Hold Infinity in the palm of your hand
And Eternity in an hour
A Robin Red breast in a Cage
Puts all Heaven in a Rage
A dove house filld with doves & Pigeons
Shudders Hell thro all its regions
A dog starvd at his Masters Gate
Predicts the ruin of the State　　10
A Horse misusd upon the Road
Calls to Heaven for Human blood
Each outcry of the hunted Hare
A fibre from the Brain does tear
A Skylark wounded in the wing
A Cherubim does cease to sing
The Game Cock clipd & armd for fight
Does the Rising Sun affright
Every Wolfs & Lions howl
Raises from Hell a Human Soul　　20
The wild deer wandring here & there
Keeps the Human Soul from Care
The Lamb misusd breeds Public strife
And yet forgives the Butchers Knife
The Bat that flits at close of Eve
Has left the Brain that wont Believe
The Owl that calls upon the Night
Speaks the Unbelievers fright
He who shall hurt the little Wren
Shall never be belovd by Men　　30
He who the Ox to wrath has movd
Shall never be by Woman lovd
The wanton Boy that kills the Fly
Shall feel the Spiders enmity
He who torments the Chafers sprite
Weaves a Bower in endless Night
The Catterpiller on the Leaf
Repeats to thee thy Mothers grief
Kill not the Moth nor Butterfly
For the Last Judgment draweth nigh　　40
He who shall train the Horse to War
Shall never pass the Polar Bar
The Beggers Dog & Widows Cat
Feed them & thou wilt grow fat
The Gnat that sings his Summers song
Poison gets from Slanders tongue
The poison of the Snake & Newt
Is the sweat of Envys Foot
The Poison of the Honey Bee
Is the Artists Jealousy　　50
The Princes Robes & Beggars Rags
Are Toadstools on the Misers Bags

A truth thats told with bad intent
Beats all the Lies you can invent
It is right it should be so
Man was made for Joy & Woe
And when this we rightly know
Thro the World we safely go
Joy & Woe are woven fine
A Clothing for the Soul divine   60
Under every grief & pine
Runs a joy with silken twine
The Babe is more than swadling Bands
Throughout all these Human Lands
Tools were made & Born were hands
Every Farmer Understands
Every Tear from Every Eye
Becomes a Babe in Eternity
This is caught by Females bright
And returnd to its own delight   70
The Bleat the Bark Bellow & Roar
Are Waves that Beat on Heavens Shore
The Babe that weeps the Rod beneath
Writes Revenge in realms of death
The Beggars Rags fluttering in Air
Does to Rags the Heavens tear
The soldier armd with Sword & Gun
Palsied strikes the Summers Sun
The poor Mans Farthing is worth more
Than all the Gold on Africs Shore   80
One Mite wrung from the Labrers hands
Shall buy & sell the Misers Lands
Or if protected from on high
Does that whole Nation sell & buy
He who mocks the Infants Faith
Shall be mock'd in Age & Death
He who shall teach the Child to Doubt
The rotting Grave shall neer get out
He who respects the Infants faith
Triumphs over Hell & Death   90
The Childs Toys & the Old Mans Reasons
Are the Fruits of the Two seasons
The Questioner who sits so sly
Shall never know how to Reply
He who replies to words of Doubt
Doth put the Light of Knowledge out
The Strongest Poison ever known
Came from Caesars Laurel Crown
Nought can deform the Human Race
Like to the Armours iron brace   100
When Gold & Gems adorn the Plow
To peaceful Arts shall Envy Bow
A Riddle or the Crickets Cry
Is to Doubt a fit Reply
The Emmets Inch & Eagles Mile
Make Lame Philosophy to smile

He who Doubts from what he sees
Will neer Believe do what you Please
If the Sun & Moon should doubt
Theyd immediately Go out   110
To be in a Passion you Good may do
But no Good if a Passion is in you
The Whore & Gambler by the State
Licencd build that Nations Fate
The Harlots cry from Street to Street
Shall weave Old Englands winding Sheet
The Winners Shout the Losers Curse
Dance before dead Englands Hearse
Every Night & every Morn
Some to Misery are Born   120
Every Morn & every Night
Some are Born to sweet delight
Some are Born to sweet delight
Some are Born to Endless Night
We are led to Believe a Lie
When we see not Thro the Eye
Which was Born in a Night to perish in a Night
When the Soul Slept in Beams of Light
God Appears & God is Light
To those poor Souls who dwell in Night   130
But does a Human Form Display
To those who Dwell in Realms of day

[1800–1803]   [1863, correctly 1905]

MILTON

John Milton's Paradise Regained *(rather than* Paradise Lost*) seems to be Blake's starting point here, but his attachment is to Milton as a poet and a prophet, not as a traditional Christian believer. Like Milton's Jesus, Blake celebrates Hebrew scripture rather than Greek literature as the imaginative model for man, and he goes on to condemn his predecessors and contemporaries for giving homage to the classical tradition. Many of the central characters and key terms have appeared in earlier prophecies, but important new characters (or characters seen in new ways) include Palamabron (sometimes Blake, or the redeemed Moses), his female counterpart Elynittria, Albion the Eternal Man (from other poems including* The Four Zoas*), and Milton's emanation Ololon, whose sixfold form ("she" is sometimes "they") allows her to represent lost human potential, or the river of life in Eden, or Milton's three daughters and three wives. The changing relation between Blake's Milton and Ololon is one of the central dramatic events of the poem. Realms of existence here include Beulah (see* The Four Zoas*, footnote to line 65), Ulro (the hell of single vision and abstraction), and Golgonooza, the city of art. Except for Milton and Ololon, most of the main characters, places, and situations reappear in Jerusalem. No brief account of the poem's action can clarify much in either of the major prophecies, and new readers may wish to turn almost immediately to such helpful resources as Bloom's* Blake's Apocalypse*, Erdman's* Prophet Against Empire*, and Damon's* Blake Dictionary*. The familiar hymn in the Preface has become the anthem of the British Labour Party, though the "mills" in line 8 are those of the gods rather than of industry.*

MILTON

a Poem in 2 Books

The Author & Printer W Blake 1804

To Justify the Ways of God to Men

❖

[PLATE 1]

PREFACE.

The Stolen and Perverted Writings of Homer & Ovid: of Plato & Cicero. which all Men ought to contemn: are set up by artifice against the Sublime of the Bible. but when the New Age is at leisure to Pronounce: all will be set right: & those Grand Works of the more ancient & consciously & professedly Inspired Men, will hold their proper rank, & the Daughters of Memory shall become the Daughters of Inspiration. Shakspeare & Milton were both curbd by the general malady & infection from the silly Greek & Latin slaves of the Sword.

Rouze up O Young Men of the New Age! set your foreheads against the ignorant Hirelings! For we have Hirelings in the Camp, the Court & the University: who would if they could, for ever depress Mental & prolong Corporeal War. Painters! on you I call! Sculptors! Architects! Suffer not the fash[i]onable Fools to depress your powers by the prices they pretend to give for contemptible works or the expensive advertizing boasts that they make of such works; believe Christ & his Apostles that there is a Class of Men whose whole delight in in Destroying. We do not want either Greek or Roman Models if we are but just & true to our own Imaginations, those Worlds of Eternity in which we shall live for ever; in Jesus our Lord.

> And did those feet in ancient time.
> Walk upon Englands mountains green:
> And was the holy Lamb of God,
> On Englands pleasant pastures seen!
>
> And did the Countenance Divine,
> Shine forth upon our clouded hills?
> And was Jerusalem builded here,
> Among these dark Satanic Mills?
>
> Bring me my Bow of burning gold:
> Bring me my Arrows of desire: 10
> Bring me my Spear: O clouds unfold!
> Bring me my Chariot of fire!
>
> I will not cease from Mental Fight,
> Nor shall my Sword sleep in my hand:
> Till we have built Jerusalem,
> In Englands green & pleasant Land.

Would to God that all the Lords people were Prophets.
Numbers XI. ch 29 v.

❖

[PLATE 2]

MILTON

Book the First

Daughters of Beulah! Muses who inspire the Poets
    Song
Record the journey of immortal Milton thro' your
    Realms
Of terror & mild moony lustre, in soft sexual
    delusions
Of varied beauty, to delight the wanderer and repose
His burning thirst & freezing hunger! Come into my
    hand
By your mild power; descending down the Nerves
    of my right arm

From out the Portals of my Brain, where by your ministry
The Eternal Great Humanity Divine. planted his Paradise,
And in it caus'd the Spectres of the Dead to take sweet forms
In likeness of himself. Tell also of the False Tongue! vegetated   10
Beneath your land of shadows: of its sacrifices. and
Its offerings; even till Jesus, the image of the Invisible God
Became its prey; a curse, an offering. and an atonement,
For Death Eternal in the heavens of Albion, & before the Gates
Of Jerusalem his Emanation, in the heavens beneath Beulah

Say first! what mov'd Milton, who walkd about in Eternity
One hundred years, pondring the intricate mazes of Providence
Unhappy tho in heav'n, he obey'd, he murmur'd not. he was silent
Viewing his Sixfold Emanation scatter'd thro' the deep
In torment! To go into the deep her to redeem & himself perish?   20
What cause at length mov'd Milton to this unexampled deed?
A Bards prophetic Song! for sitting at eternal tables,
Terrific among the Sons of Albion in chorus solemn & loud
A Bard broke forth! all sat attentive to the awful man.

Mark well my words! they are of your eternal salvation:

Three Classes are Created by the Hammer of Los, & Woven

[PLATE 3]

By Enitharmons Looms when Albion was slain upon his Mountains
And in his Tent, thro envy of Living Form, even of the Divine Vision
And of the sports of Wisdom in the Human Imagination
Which is the Divine Body of the Lord Jesus. blessed for ever.
Mark well my words. they are of your eternal salvation!

Urizen lay in darkness & solitude, in chains of the mind lock'd up
Los siezd his Hammer & Tongs; he labourd at his resolute Anvil
Among indefinite Druid rocks[1] & snows of doubt & reasoning.

Refusing all Definite Form, the Abstract Horror roofd. stony hard   9
And a first Age passed over & a State of dismal woe!

Down sunk with fright a red round Globe hot burning. deep
Deep down into the Abyss. panting: conglobing: trembling
And a second Age passed over & a State of dismal woe.

Rolling round into two little Orbs & closed in two little Caves
The Eyes beheld the Abyss: lest bones of solidness freeze over all
And a third Age passed over & a State of dismal woe.

From beneath his Orbs of Vision, Two Ears in close volutions
Shot spiring out in the deep darkness & petrified as they grew
And a fourth Age passed over & a State of dismal woe.

Hanging upon the wind, Two Nostrils bent down into the Deep   20
And a fifth Age passed over & a State of dismal woe.

In ghastly torment sick, a Tongue of hunger & thirst flamed out
And a sixth Age passed over & a State of dismal woe.

Enraged & stifled without & within: in terror & woe, he threw his
Right Arm to the north, his left Arm to the south, & his Feet
Stampd the nether Abyss in trembling & howling & dismay
And a seventh Age passed over & a State of dismal woe.

Terrified Los stood in the Abyss & his immortal limbs
Grew deadly pale; he became what he beheld: for a red

---

[1] Ancient British priests, presumed builders of Stonehenge, who practiced a "natural" (and therefore for Blake, false) religion based on superstition and reason rather than imagination.

Round Globe sunk down from his Bosom into the
    Deep in pangs   30
He hoverd over it trembling & weeping. suspended
    it shook
The nether Abyss in tremblings. he wept over it, he
    cherish'd it
In deadly sickening pain: till separated into a Female
    pale
As the cloud that brings the snow: all the while from
    his Back
A blue fluid exuded in Sinews hardening in the
    Abyss
Till it separated into a Male Form howling in
    Jealousy

Within labouring. beholding Without: from
    Particulars to Generals
Subduing his Spectre, they Builded the Looms of
    Generation
They Builded Great Golgonooza Times on Times
    Ages on Ages
First Orc was Born then the Shadowy Female: then
    All Los's Family   40
At last Enitharmon brought forth Satan Refusing
    Form, in vain
The Miller of Eternity made subservient to the Great
    Harvest
That he may go to his own Place Prince of the Starry
    Wheels

[PLATE 4]

Beneath the Plow of Rintrah & the Harrow of the
    Almighty
In the hands of Palamabron. Where the Starry Mills
    of Satan
Are built beneath the Earth & Waters of the Mundane
    Shell
Here the Three Classes of Men take their Sexual
    texture[.] Woven
The Sexual is Threefold: the Human is Fourfold.

If you account it Wisdom when you are angry to be
    silent, and
Not to shew it: I do not account that Wisdom but
    Folly.
Every Mans Wisdom is peculiar to his own
    Individ[u]ality
O Satan my youngest born, art thou not Prince of the
    Starry Hosts
And of the Wheels of Heaven, to turn the Mills day
    & night?   10
Art thou not Newtons Pantocrator weaving the
    Woof of Locke[?]

To Mortals thy Mills seem every thing & the Harrow
    of Shaddai [2]
A scheme of Human conduct invisible & incompre-
    hensible[.]
Get to thy Labours at the Mills & leave me to my
    wrath.

Satan was going to reply, but Los roll'd his loud
    thunders.

Anger me not! thou canst not drive the Harrow in
    pitys paths.
Thy Work is Eternal Death, with Mills & Ovens &
    Cauldrons.
Trouble me no more. thou canst not have Eternal Life

So Los spoke! Satan trembling obeyd weeping along
    the way.
Mark well my words, they are of your eternal
    Salvation   20

Between South Molton Street & Stratford Place:
    Calvarys foot [3]
Where the Victims were preparing for Sacrifice their
    Cherubim
Around their loins pourd forth their arrows & their
    bosoms beam
With all colours of precious stones, & their inmost
    palaces
Resounded with preparation of animals wild & tame
(Mark well my words! Corporeal Friends are Spiritual
    Enemies)
Mocking Druidical Mathematical Proportion of
    Length Bredth Highth
Displaying Naked Beauty! with Flute & Harp & Song

[PLATE 5]

Palamabron with the fiery Harrow in morning
    returning
From breathing fields. Satan fainted beneath the
    artillery
Christ took on Sin in the Virgins Womb, & put it off
    on the Cross

---

[2] "Pantocrator," Sir Isaac Newton's word for a cosmic copy-maker, is here a Satanic creator of a rationalistic world based on the principles of Newton and John Locke. The harrow of Shaddai (the Hebrew Almighty) belongs to true imaginers like Blake (Los, Palamabron), but has been stolen by deists and copy-makers (presumably including Blake's patron William Hayley).

[3] Tyburn, London's public gallows and therefore Calvary's foot, was near Blake's residence in S. Moulton Street (Marble Arch is now located at Tyburn). This site, presumably the secret location of London's Stone (pl. 6 below), is the center from which Blake imagines all of London and its suburbs (Blackheath, Highgate, etc.), all Britain (Caithness to Dover), and finally all the world radiating outward. This combination of geography with spiritual, political, and personal history is an even more dominant mode in *Jerusalem*.

All pitied the piteous & was wrath with the wrathful
   & Los heard it.

And this is the manner of the Daughters of Albion
   in their beauty
Every one is threefold in Head & Heart & Reins, &
   every one
Has three Gates into the Three Heavens of Beulah
   which shine
Translucent in their Foreheads & their Bosoms &
   their Loins
Surrounded with fires unapproachable: but whom
   they please
They take up into their Heavens in intoxicating
   delight   10
For the Elect cannot be Redeemd, but Created
   continually
By Offering & Atonement in the crue[l]ties of Moral
   Law
Hence the three Classes of Men take their fix'd
   destinations
They are the Two Contraries & the Reasoning
   Negative.

While the Females prepare the Victims. the Males at
   Furnaces
And Anvils dance the dance of tears & pain: loud
   lightnings
Lash on their limbs as they turn the whirlwinds loose
   upon
The Furnaces, lamenting around the Anvils & this
   their Song[:]

Ah weak & wide astray! Ah shut in narrow doleful
   form
Creeping in reptile flesh upon the bosom of the
   ground   20
The Eye of Man a little narrow orb closd up & dark
Scarcely beholding the great light conversing with
   the Void
The Ear, a little shell in small volutions shutting out
All melodies & comprehending only Discord and
   Harmony
The Tongue a little moisture fills, a little food it
   cloys
A little sound it utters & its cries are faintly heard
Then brings forth Moral Virtue the cruel Virgin
   Babylon

Can such an Eye judge of the stars? & looking thro
   its tubes
Measure the sunny rays that point their spears on
   Udanadan

Can such an Ear filld with the vapours of the
   yawning pit.   30
Judge of the pure melodious harp struck by a hand
   divine?
Can such closed Nostrils feel a joy? or tell of autumn
   fruits
When grapes & figs burst their covering to the joyful
   air
Can such a Tongue boast of the living waters? or take
   in
Ought but the Vegetable Ratio & loathe the faint
   delight
Can such gross Lips percieve? alas! folded within
   themselves
They touch not ought but pallid turn & tremble at
   every wind

Thus they sing Creating the Three Classes among
   Druid Rocks
Charles calls on Milton for Atonement. Cromwell is
   ready
James calls for fires in Golgonooza. for heaps of
   smoking ruins   40
In the night of prosperity and wantonness which he
   himself Created
Among the Daughters of Albion among the Rocks of
   the Druids
When Satan fainted beneath the arrows of Elynittria
And Mathematic Proportion was subdued by Living
   Proportion

[PLATE 6]
From Golgonooza the spiritual Four-fold London
   eternal
In immense labours & sorrows, ever building, ever
   falling,
Thro Albions four Forests which overspread all the
   Earth,
From London Stone to Blackheath east: to Hounslow
   west:
To Finchley north: to Norwood south: and the
   weights
Of Enitharmons Loom play lulling cadences on the
   winds of Albion
From Caithness in the north, to Lizard-point &
   Dover in the south

Loud sounds the Hammer of Los, & loud his
   Bellows is heard
Before London to Hampsteads breadths & Highgates
   heights To
Stratford & old Bow: & across to the Gardens of
   Kensington   10

On Tyburns Brook: loud groans Thames beneath the
    iron Forge
Of Rintrah & Palamabron of Theotorm[on] &
    Bromion, to forge the instruments
Of Harvest: the Plow & Harrow to pass over the
    Nations

The Surrey hills glow like the clinkers of the furnace:
    Lambeths Vale
Where Jerusalems foundations began; where they
    were laid in ruins
Where they were laid in ruins from every Nation &
    Oak Groves rooted
Dark gleams before the Furnace-mouth a heap of
    burning ashes
When shall Jerusalem return & overspread all the
    Nations
Return: return to Lambeths Vale O building of
    human souls
Thence stony Druid Temples overspread the Island
    white   20
And thence from Jerusalems ruins.. from her walls of
    salvation
And praise: thro the whole Earth were reard from
    Ireland
To Mexico & Peru west, & east to China & Japan;
    till Babel
The Spectre of Albion frownd over the Nations in
    glory & war
All things begin & end in Albions ancient Druid
    rocky shore
But now the Starry Heavens are fled from the mighty
    limbs of Albion

Loud sounds the Hammer of Los, loud turn the
    Wheels of Enitharmon
Her Looms vibrate with soft affections, weaving the
    Web of Life
Out from the ashes of the Dead; Los lifts his iron
    Ladles
With molten ore: he heaves the iron cliffs in his
    rattling chains   30
From Hyde Park to the Alms-houses of Mile-end &
    old Bow
Here the Three Classes of Mortal Men take their fixd
    destinations
And hence they overspread the Nations of the whole
    Earth & hence
The Web of Life is woven; & the tender sinews of
    life created
And the Three Classes of Men regulated by Los's
    Hammer

[PLATE 7]
The first, The Elect from before the foundation of
    the World:
The second, The Redeem'd. The Third, The
    Reprobate & form'd
To destruction from the mothers womb: follow with
    me my plow!

Of the first class was Satan: with incomparable
    mildness;
His primitive tyrannical attempts on Los: with most
    endearing love
He soft intreated Los to give to him Palamabrons
    station;
For Palamabron returnd with labour wearied every
    evening
Palamabron oft refus'd; and as often Satan offer'd
His service till by repeated offers and repeated
    intreaties
Los gave to him the Harrow of the Almighty; alas
    blamable   10
Palamabron. fear'd to be angry lest Satan should
    accuse him of
Ingratitude, & Los believe the accusation thro
    Satans extreme
Mildness. Satan labour'd all day. it was a thousand
    years
In the evening returning terrified overlabourd &
    astonish'd
Embrac'd soft with a brothers tears Palamabron, who
    also wept

Mark well my words! they are of your eternal salva-
    tion

Next morning Palamabron rose: the horses of the
    Harrow
Were maddend with tormenting fury, & the servants
    of the Harrow
The Gnomes, accus'd Satan, with indignation fury
    and fire.
Then Palamabron reddening like the Moon in an
    eclipse,   20
Spoke saying, You know Satans mildness and his
    self-imposition,
Seeming a brother, being a tyrant, even thinking
    himself a brother
While he is murdering the just; prophetic I behold
His future course thro' darkness and despair to
    eternal death
But we must not be tyrants also! he hath assum'd
    my place

For one whole day, under pretence of pity and love
    to me:
My horses hath he maddend! and my fellow servants
    injur'd:
How should he[,] he[,] know the duties of another?
    O foolish forbearance
Would I had told Los, all my heart! but patience O
    my friends,
All may be well: silent remain, while I call Los and
    Satan.   30

Loud as the wind of Beulah that unroots the rocks &
    hills
Palamabron call'd! and Los & Satan came before him
And Palamabron shew'd the horses & the servants.
    Satan wept,
And mildly cursing Palamabron, him accus'd of crimes
Himself had wrought. Los trembled; Satans
    blandishments almost
Perswaded the Prophet of Eternity that Palamabron
Was Satans enemy, & that the Gnomes being
    Palamabron's friends
Were leagued together against Satan thro' ancient
    enmity.
What could Los do? how could he judge, when
    Satans self, believ'd
That he had not oppres'd the horses of the Harrow,
    nor the servants.   40

So Los said, Henceforth Palamabron, let each his
    own station
Keep: nor in pity false, nor in officious brotherhood,
    where
None needs, be active. Mean time Palamabrons
    horses.
Rag'd with thick flames redundant, & the Harrow
    maddend with fury.
Trembling Palamabron stood, the strongest of
    Demons trembled:
Curbing his living creatures; many of the strongest
    Gnomes,
They bit in their wild fury, who also madden'd like
    wildest beasts

Mark well my words; they are of your eternal salvation

[PLATE 8]
Mean while wept Satan before Los, accusing
    Palamabron;
Himself exculpating with mildest speech. for himself
    believ'd
That he had not opress'd nor injur'd the refractory
    servants.

But Satan returning to his Mills (for Palamabron
    had serv'd
The Mills of Satan as the easier task) found all
    confusion
And back return'd to Los, not fill'd with vengeance
    but with tears,
Himself convinc'd of Palamabrons turpitude. Los
    beheld
The servants of the Mills drunken with wine and
    dancing wild
With shouts and Palamabrons songs, rending the
    forests green
With ecchoing confusion, tho' the Sun was risen on
    high.   10

Then Los took off his left sandal placing it on his head,
Signal of solemn mourning: when the servants of the
    Mills
Beheld the signal they in silence stood, tho' drunk
    with wine.
Los wept! But Rintrah also came, and Enitharmon on
His arm lean'd tremblingly observing all these things

And Los said. Ye Genii of the Mills! the Sun is on high
Your labours call you! Palamabron is also in sad
    dilemma.
His horses are mad! his Harrow confounded! his
    companions enrag'd.
Mine is the fault! I should have remember'd that
    pity divides the soul
And man, unmans: follow with me my Plow. this
    mournful day   20
Must be a blank in Nature: follow with me, and
    tomorrow again
Resume your labours, & this day shall be a mournful
    day

Wildly they follow'd Los and Rintrah, & the Mills
    were silent
They mourn'd all day, this mournful day of Satan
    & Palamabron:
And all the Elect & all the Redeem'd mourn'd one
    toward another
Upon the mountains of Albion among the cliffs of
    the Dead.

They Plow'd in tears! incessant pourd Jehovahs
    rain, & Molechs [4]
Thick fires contending with the rain, thunder'd
    above rolling

---

[4] Moloch (Molech) is the Ammonite fire-god to whom pagans
and sometimes Hebrews sacrificed their first-born sons. See also
Jerusalem, plate 15, line 34.

Terrible over their heads; Satan wept over
    Palamabron
Theotormon & Bromion contended on the side of
    Satan   30
Pitying his youth and beauty; trembling at eternal
    death:
Michael contended against Satan in the rolling
    thunder
Thulloh the friend of Satan also reprovd him; faint
    their reproof.

But Rintrah who is of the reprobate: of those form'd
    to destruction
In indignation. for Satans soft dissimulation of
    friendship!
Flam'd above all the plowed furrows, angry red and
    furious,
Till Michael sat down in the furrow weary dissolv'd
    in tears[.]
Satan who drave the team beside him, stood angry
    & red
He smote Thulloh & slew him, & he stood terrible
    over Michael
Urging him to arise: he wept! Enitharmon saw his
    tears   40
But Los hid Thulloh from her sight, lest she should
    die of grief
She wept: she trembled! she kissed Satan; she wept
    over Michael
She form'd a Space for Satan & Michael & for the
    poor infected[.]
Trembling she wept over the Space, & clos'd it
    with a tender Moon .

Los secret buried Thulloh, weeping disconsolate
    over the moony Space
But Palamabron called down a Great Solemn
    Assembly,
That he who will not defend Truth, may be compelled
    to
Defend a Lie, that he may be snared & caught & taken

[PLATE 9]
And all Eden descended into Palamabrons tent
Among Albions Druids & Bards, in the caves beneath
    Albions
Death Couch, in the caverns of death, in the corner
    of the Atlantic.
And in the midst of the Great Assembly Palamabron
    pray'd:
O God, protect me from my friends, that they have
    not power over me
Thou hast giv'n me power to protect myself from
    my bitterest enemies.

Mark well my words, they are of your eternal
    salvation

Then rose the Two Witnesses, Rintrah &
    Palamabron:
And Palamabron appeal'd to all Eden, and recievd
Judgment: and Lo! it fell on Rintrah and his rage: 10
Which now flam'd high & furious in Satan against
    Palamabron
Till it became a proverb in Eden. Satan is among the
    Reprobate.

Los in his wrath curs'd heaven & earth, he rent up
    Nations,
Standing on Albions rocks among high-reard Druid
    temples
Which reach the stars of heaven & stretch from pole
    to pole.
He displacd continents, the oceans fled before his
    face
He alter'd the poles of the world, east, west & north
    & south
But he clos'd up Enitharmon from the sight of all
    these things

For Satan flaming with Rintrahs fury hidden beneath
    his own mildness
Accus'd Palamabron before the Assembly of
    ingratitude! of malice: 20
He created Seven deadly Sins drawing out his
    infernal scroll,
Of Moral laws and cruel punishments upon the
    clouds of Jehovah
To pervert the Divine voice in its entrance to the
    earth
With thunder of war & trumpets sound, with armies of
    disease
Punishments & deaths musterd & number'd;
    Saying I am God alone
There is no other! let all obey my principles of moral
    individuality
I have brought them from the uppermost innermost
    recesses
Of my Eternal Mind, transgressors I will rend off
    for ever,
As now I rend this accursed Family from my
    covering.

Thus Satan rag'd amidst the Assembly! and his
    bosom grew   30
Opake against the Divine Vision: the paved terraces
    of
His bosom inwards shone with fires, but the stones
    becoming opake!

Hid him from sight, in an extreme blackness and
 darkness,
And there a World of deeper Ulro was open'd, in
 the midst
Of the Asembly. In Satans bosom a vast unfathomable
 Abyss.

Astonishment held the Assembly in an awful silence:
 and tears
Fell down as dews of night, & a loud solemn universal
 groan
Was utter'd from the east & from the west & from
 the south
And from the north; and Satan stood opake
 immeasurable
Covering the east with solid blackness, round his
 hidden heart,   40
With thunders utterd from his hidden wheels:
 accusing loud
The Divine Mercy, for protecting Palamabron in his
 tent.

Rintrah rear'd up walls of rocks and pour'd rivers &
 moats
Of fire round the walls: columns of fire guard around
Between Satan and Palamabron in the terrible
 darkness.

And Satan not having the Science of Wrath, but only
 of Pity:
Rent them asunder, and wrath was left to wrath, &
 pity to pity.
He sunk down a dreadful Death, unlike the slumbers
 of Beulah

The Separation was terrible: the Dead was repos'd
 on his Couch
Beneath the Couch of Albion, on the seven
 mou[n]tains of Rome   50
In the whole place of the Covering Cherub, Rome
 Babylon & Tyre.
His Spectre raging furious descended into its Space

[PLATE 10]
Then Los & Enitharmon knew that Satan is Urizen
Drawn down by Orc & the Shadowy Female into
 Generation
Oft Enitharmon enterd weeping into the Space,
 there appearing
An aged Woman raving along the Streets (the Space
 is named
Canaan) then she returnd to Los weary frighted as
 from dreams

The nature of a Female Space is this: it shrinks the
 Organs
Of Life till they become Finite & Itself seems
 Infinite
And Satan vibrated in the immensity of the Space!
 Limited
To those without but Infinite to those within: it fell
 down and
Became Canaan: closing Los from Eternity in Albions
 Cliffs   10
A mighty Fiend against the Divine Humanity
 mustring to War

Satan! Ah me! is gone to his own place, said Los!
 their God
I will not worship in their Churches, nor King in their
 Theatres
Elynittria! whence is this Jealousy running along the
 mountains
British Women were not Jealous when Greek &
 Roman were Jealous
Every thing in Eternity shines by its own Internal
 light: but thou
Darkenest every Internal light with the arrows of thy
 quiver
Bound up in the horns of Jealousy to a deadly fading
 Moon
And Ocalythron binds the Sun into a Jealous Globe
That every thing is fixd Opake without Internal
 light   20

So Los lamented over Satan, who triumphant divided
 the Nations

[PLATE 11]
He set his face against Jerusalem to destroy the Eon
 of Albion

But Los hid Enitharmon from the sight of all these
 things,
Upon the Thames whose lulling harmony repos'd
 her soul:
Where Beulah lovely terminates in rocky Albion:
Terminating in Hyde Park, on Tyburns awful brook.

And the Mills of Satan were separated into a moony
 Space
Among the rocks of Albions Temples, and Satans
 Druid sons
Offer the Human Victims throughout all the Earth,
 and Albions
Dread Tomb immortal on his Rock, overshadowd the
 whole Earth:

Where Satan making to himself Laws from his own
    identity.   10
Compell'd others to serve him in moral gratitude &
    submission
Being call'd God: setting himself above all that is
    called God.
And all the Spectres of the Dead calling themselves
    Sons of God
In his Synagogues worship Satan under the
    Unutterable Name

And it was enquir'd: Why in a Great Solemn
    Assembly
The Innocent should be condemn'd for the Guilty?
    Then an Eternal rose

Saying. If the Guilty should be condemn'd, he must
    be an Eternal Death
And one must die for another throughout all
    Eternity.
Satan is fall'n from his station & never can be
    redeem'd
But must be new Created continually moment by
    moment   20
And therefore the Class of Satan shall be calld the
    Elect, & those
Of Rintrah. the Reprobate, & those of Palamabron
    the Redeem'd
For he is redeem'd from Satans Law, the wrath
    falling on Rintrah,
And therefore Palamabron dared not to call a solemn
    Assembly
Till Satan had assum'd Rintrahs wrath in the day of
    mourning
In a feminine delusion of false pride self-deciev'd.

So spake the Eternal and confirm'd it with a
    thunderous oath.

But when Leutha (a Daughter of Beulah) beheld
    Satans condemnation
She down descended into the midst of the Great
    Solemn Assembly
Offering herself a Ransom for Satan, taking on her,
    his Sin.   30

Mark well my words. they are of your eternal
    salvation!

And Leutha stood glowing with varying colours
    immortal, heart-piercing
And lovely: & her moth-like elegance shone over the
    Assembly

At length standing upon the golden floor of
    Palamabron
She spake: I am the Author of this Sin! by my
    suggestion
My Parent power Satan has committed this
    transgression.
I loved Palamabron & I sought to approach his Tent,
But beautiful Elynittria with her silver arrows
    repelld me.

[PLATE 12]

For her light is terrible to me. I fade before her
    immortal beauty.
O wherefore doth a Dragon-form forth issue from
    my limbs
To sieze her new born son? Ah me! the wretched
    Leutha!
This to prevent, entering the doors of Satans brain
    night after night
Like sweet perfumes I stupified the masculine
    perceptions
And kept only the feminine awake. hence rose his soft
Delusory love to Palamabron: admiration join'd with
    envy
Cupidity unconquerable! my fault, when at noon of
    day
The Horses of Palamabron call'd for rest and
    pleasant death:
I sprang out of the breast of Satan, over the Harrow
    beaming   10
In all my beauty! that I might unloose the flaming
    steeds
As Elynittria use'd to do; but too well those living
    creatures
Knew that I was not Elynittria, and they brake the
    traces[.]
But me, the servants of the Harrow saw not: but as a
    bow
Of varying colours on the hills; terribly rag'd the
    horses.
Satan astonishd, and with power above his own
    controll
Compell'd the Gnomes to curb the horses, & to
    throw banks of sand
Around the fiery flaming Harrow in labyrinthine
    forms.
And brooks between to intersect the meadows in
    their course.
The Harrow cast thick flames: Jehovah thunderd
    above: 20
Chaos & ancient night fled from beneath the fiery
    Harrow:
The Harrow cast thick flames & orb'd us round in
    concave fires

A Hell of our own making. see, its flames still
  gird me round[.]
Jehovah thunder'd above! Satan in pride of heart
Drove the fierce Harrow among the constellations
  of Jehovah
Drawing a third part in the fires as stubble north &
  south
To devour Albion and Jerusalem the Emanation of
  Albion
Driving the Harrow in Pitys paths. 'twas then,
  with our dark fires
Which now gird round us (O eternal torment) I
  form'd the Serpent
Of precious stones & gold turn'd poisons on the
  sultry wastes   30
The Gnomes in all that day spar'd not; they curs'd
  Satan bitterly.
To do unkind things in kindness! with power armd,
  to say
The most irritating things in the midst of tears and
  love
These are the stings of the Serpent! thus did we by
  them; till thus
They in return retaliated, and the Living Creatures
  maddend.
The Gnomes labourd. I weeping hid in Satans
  inmost brain;
But when the Gnomes refus'd to labour more, with
  blandishments
I came forth from the head of Satan! back the
  Gnomes recoil'd.
And call'd me Sin, and for a sign portentous held me.
  Soon
Day sunk and Palamabron return'd, trembling I hid
  myself   40
In Satans inmost Palace of his nervous fine wrought
  Brain:
For Elynittria met Satan with all her singing
  women.
Terrific in their joy & pouring wine of wildest power
They gave Satan their wine: indignant at the burning
  wrath.
Wild with prophetic fury his former life became like
  a dream
Cloth'd in the Serpents folds, in selfish holiness
  demanding purity
Being most impure, self-condemn'd to eternal tears,
  he drove
Me from his inmost Brain & the doors clos'd with
  thunders sound
O Divine Vision who didst create the Female: to
  repose
The Sleepers of Beulah: pity the repentant Leutha.
  My   50

[PLATE 13]

Sick Couch bears the dark shades of Eternal Death
  infolding
The Spectre of Satan. he furious refuses to repose in
  sleep.
I humbly bow in all my Sin before the Throne
  Divine.
Not so the Sick-one; Alas what shall be done him to
  restore?
Who calls the Individual Law, Holy; and despises the
  Saviour.
Glorying to involve Albions Body in fires of eternal
  War—

Now Leutha ceas'd: tears flow'd: but the Divine
  Pity supported her.

All is my fault! We are the Spectre of Luvah the
  murderer
Of Albion: O Vala! O Luvah! O Albion! O lovely
  Jerusalem
The Sin was begun in Eternity, and will not rest to
  Eternity   10
Till two Eternitys meet together, Ah! lost! lost! lost!
  for ever!

So Leutha spoke. But when she saw that Enitharmon
  had
Created a New Space to protect Satan from
  punishment;
She fled to Enitharmons Tent & hid herself. Loud
  raging
Thunderd the Assembly dark & clouded, and they
  ratify'd
The kind decision of Enitharmon & gave a Time to
  the Space,
Even Six Thousand years; and sent Lucifer for its
  Guard.
But Lucifer refus'd to die & in pride he forsook his
  charge
And they elected Molech, and when Molech was
  impatient
The Divine hand found the Two Limits: first of
  Opacity, then of Contraction   20
Opacity was named Satan, Contraction was named
  Adam.
Triple Elohim came: Elohim wearied fainted: they
  elected Shaddai.
Shaddai angry, Pahad descended: Pahad terrified,
  they sent Jehovah 5

---

5 Blake assigns his seven cycles (Eyes) of history to Lucifer,
Moloch, Elohim, Shaddai, Pahad, Jehovah (these last four
Hebrew names for God), and finally Jesus.

And Jehovah was leprous; loud he call'd, stretching
　　　his hand to Eternity
For then the Body of Death was perfected in hypocritic
　　　holiness,
Around the Lamb, a Female Tabernacle woven in
　　　Cathedrons Looms
He died as a Reprobate. he was Punish'd as a
　　　Transgressor!
Glory! Glory! Glory! to the Holy Lamb of God
I touch the heavens as an instrument to glorify the
　　　Lord!

The Elect shall meet the Redeem'd. on Albions rocks
　　　they shall meet　　　　　　　　　　　　　　30
Astonish'd at the Transgressor, in him beholding the
　　　Saviour.
And the Elect shall say to the Redeemd. We behold
　　　it is of Divine
Mercy alone! of Free Gift and Election that we live.
Our Virtues & Cruel Goodnesses, have deserv'd
　　　Eternal Death.
Thus they weep upon the fatal Brook of Albions River.

But Elynittria met Leutha in the place where she was
　　　hidden.
And threw aside her arrows, and laid down her
　　　sounding Bow;
She sooth'd her with soft words & brought her to
　　　Palamabrons bed
In moments new created for delusion, interwoven
　　　round about,
In dreams she bore the shadowy Spectre of Sleep, &
　　　namd him Death.　　　　　　　　　　　　　40
In dreams she bore Rahab the mother of Tirzah &
　　　her sisters
In Lambeths vales; in Cambridge & in Oxford,
　　　places of Thought
Intricate labyrinths of Times and Spaces unknown,
　　　that Leutha lived
In Palamabrons Tent, and Oothoon was her charming
　　　guard.

The Bard ceas'd. All consider'd and a loud resounding
　　　murmur
Continu'd round the Halls; and much they questiond
　　　the immortal
Loud-voicd Bard. and many condemn'd the high
　　　tone'd Song
Saying Pity and Love are too venerable for the
　　　imputation
Of Guilt. Others said. If it is true! if the acts have
　　　been perform'd
Let the Bard himself witness. Where hadst thou this
　　　terrible Song　　　　　　　　　　　　　　50

The Bard replied. I am Inspired! I know it is Truth!
　　　for I Sing

[PLATE 14]

According to the inspiration of the Poetic Genius
Who is the eternal all-protecting Divine Humanity
To whom be Glory & Power & Dominion Evermore
　　　Amen

Then there was great murmuring in the Heavens of
　　　Albion
Concerning Generation & the Vegetative power &
　　　concerning
The Lamb the Saviour: Albion trembled to Italy
　　　Greece & Egypt
To Tartary & Hindostan & China & to Great America
Shaking the roots & fast foundations of the Earth in
　　　doubtfulness
The loud voic'd Bard terrify'd took refuge in
　　　Miltons bosom

Then Milton rose up from the heavens of Albion
　　　ardorous!　　　　　　　　　　　　　　　10
The whole Assembly wept prophetic, seeing in
　　　Miltons face
And in his lineaments divine the shades of Death &
　　　Ulro
He took off the robe of the promise, & ungirded
　　　himself from the oath of God

And Milton said, I go to Eternal Death! The Nations
　　　still
Follow after the detestable Gods of Priam; in pomp
Of warlike selfhood, contradicting and blaspheming.
When will the Resurrection come; to deliver the
　　　sleeping body
From corruptibility: O when Lord Jesus wilt thou
　　　come?
Tarry no longer; for my soul lies at the gates of death.
I will arise and look forth for the morning of the
　　　grave.　　　　　　　　　　　　　　　　20
I will go down to the sepulcher to see if morning
　　　breaks!
I will go down to self annihilation and eternal death,
Lest the Last Judgment come & find me unannihilate
And I be siez'd & giv'n into the hands of my own
　　　Selfhood.
The Lamb of God is seen thro' mists & shadows,
　　　hov'ring
Over the sepulchers in clouds of Jehovah & winds of
　　　Elohim
A disk of blood, distant; & heav'ns & earth's roll
　　　dark between

What do I here before the Judgment? without my
    Emanation?
With the daughters of memory, & not with the
    daughters of inspiration[?]   29
I in my Selfhood am that Satan: I am that Evil One!
He is my Spectre! in my obedience to loose him from
    my Hells
To claim the Hells, my Furnaces, I go to Eternal
    Death.
And Milton said. I go to Eternal Death! Eternity
    shudder'd
For he took the outside course, among the graves of
    the dead
A mournful shade. Eternity shudderd at the image of
    eternal death

Then on the verge of Beulah he beheld his own
    Shadow;
A mournful form double; hermaphroditic: male &
    female
In one wonderful body. and he enterd into it
In direful pain for the dread shadow, twenty-seven-
    fold
Reachd to the depths of dirast Hell, & thence to
    Albions land: 40
Which is this earth of vegetation on which now I write.

The Seven Angels of the Presence wept over Miltons
    Shadow!

[PLATE 15]

As when a man dreams, he reflects not that his body
    sleeps,
Else he would wake; so seem'd he entering his
    Shadow: but
With him the Spirits of the Seven Angels of the
    Presence
Entering; they gave him still perceptions of his
    Sleeping Body;
Which now arose and walk'd with them in Eden, as
    an Eighth
Image Divine tho' darken'd; and tho walking as one
    walks
In sleep; and the Seven comforted and supported him.

Like as a Polypus that vegetates beneath the deep!
They saw his Shadow vegetated underneath the
    Couch
Of death: for when he enterd into his Shadow:
    Himself: 10
His real and immortal Self: was as appeard to those
Who dwell in immortality, as One sleeping on a couch
Of gold; and those in immortality gave forth their
    Emanations

Like Females of sweet beauty, to guard round him &
    to feed
His lips with food of Eden in his cold and dim repose!
But to himself he seemd a wanderer lost in dreary
    night.

Onwards his Shadow kept its course among the
    Spectres; call'd
Satan, but swift as lightning passing them, startled
    the shades
Of Hell beheld him in a trail of light as of a comet
That travels into Chaos: so Milton went guarded
    within.   20

The nature of infinity is this: That every thing has its
Own Vortex; and when once a traveller thro' Eternity
Has passd that Vortex, he percieves it roll backward
    behind
His path, into a globe itself infolding; like a sun:
Or like a moon, or like a universe of starry majesty,
While he keeps onwards in his wondrous journey on
    the earth
Or like a human form, a friend with whom he livd
    benevolent.
As the eye of man views both the east & west
    encompassing
Its vortex; and the north & south, with all their starry
    host;
Also the rising sun & setting moon he views
    surrounding   30
His corn-fields and his valleys of five hundred acres
    square.
Thus is the earth one infinite plane, and not as
    apparent
To the weak traveller confin'd beneath the moony
    shade.
Thus is the heaven a vortex passd already, and the
    earth
A vortex not yet pass'd by the traveller thro' Eternity.

First Milton saw Albion upon the Rock of Ages,
Deadly pale outstretchd and snowy cold, storm
    coverd;
A Giant form of perfect beauty outstretchd on the
    rock
In solemn death: the Sea of Time & Space thunderd
    aloud
Against the rock, which was inwrapped with the
    weeds of death   40
Hovering over the cold bosom, in its vortex Milton
    bent down
To the bosom of death, what was underneath soon
    seemd above.

A cloudy heaven mingled with stormy seas in loudest
    ruin;
But as a wintry globe descends precipitant thro'
    Beulah bursting,
With thunders loud, and terrible: so Miltons shadow
    fell,
Precipitant loud thundring into the Sea of Time &
    Space.

Then first I saw him in the Zenith as a falling star,
Descending perpendicular, swift as the swallow or
    swift;
And on my left foot falling on the tarsus, enterd
    there;
But from my left foot a black cloud redounding
    spread over Europe.   50

Then Milton knew that the Three Heavens of Beulah
    were beheld
By him on earth in his bright pilgrimage of sixty
    years

[PLATE 16   Full-page design.]
[PLATE 17]
In those three females whom his Wives, & those three
    whom his Daughters
Had represented and containd, that they might be
    resum'd
By giving up of Selfhood: & they distant view'd his
    journey
In their eternal spheres, now Human, tho' their
    Bodies remain clos'd
In the dark Ulro till the Judgment: also Milton knew;
    they and
Himself was Human, tho' now wandering thro
    Death's Vale
In conflict with those Female forms, which in blood
    & jealousy
Surrounded him, dividing & uniting without end or
    number.

He saw the Cruelties of Ulro, and he wrote them
    down
In iron tablets: and his Wives & Daughters names
    were these   10
Rahab and Tirzah, & Milcah & Malah & Noah &
    Hoglah.
They sat rang'd round him as the rocks of Horeb
    round the land
Of Canaan: and they wrote in thunder smoke and fire
His dictate; and his body was the Rock Sinai; that
    body,
Which was on earth born to corruption: & the six
    Females

Are Hor & Peor & Bashan & Abarim & Lebanon &
    Hermon
Seven rocky masses terrible in the Desarts of Midian.

But Miltons Human Shadow continu'd journeying
    above
The rocky masses of The Mundane Shell; in the
    Lands
Of Edom & Aram & Moab & Midian & Amalek.[6]

The Mundane Shell, is a vast Concave Earth: an
    immense
Hardend shadow of all things upon our Vegetated
    Earth
Enlarg'd into dimension & deform'd into indefinite
    space,
In Twenty-seven Heavens and all their Hells; with
    Chaos
And Ancient Night; & Purgatory. It is a cavernous
    Earth
Of labyrinthine intricacy, twenty-seven folds of
    opakeness
And finishes where the lark mounts; here Milton
    journeyed
In that Region call'd Midian, among the Rocks of
    Horeb[.]
For travellers from Eternity. pass outward to Satan's
    seat,   29
But travellers to Eternity. pass inward to Golgonooza.

Los the Vehicular terror beheld him, & divine
    Enitharmon
Call'd all her daughters, Saying. Surely to unloose
    my bond
Is this Man come! Satan shall be unloosd upon
    Albion

Los heard in terror Enitharmons words: in fibrous
    strength
His limbs shot forth like roots of trees against the
    forward path
Of Miltons journey. Urizen beheld the immortal
    Man,

[PLATE 18]
And Tharmas Demon of the Waters, & Orc, who is
    Luvah

The Shadowy Female seeing Milton, howl'd in her
    lamentation
Over the Deeps outstretching her Twenty seven
    Heavens over Albion

---

[6] Most of these are the names of nations or mountains in and
around Canaan.

And thus the Shadowy Female howls in articulate
howlings

I will lament over Milton in the lamentations of the
afflicted
My Garments shall be woven of sighs & heart
broken lamentations
The misery of unhappy Families shall be drawn
out into its border
Wrought with the needle with dire sufferings poverty
pain & woe
Along the rocky Island & thence throughout the
whole Earth
There shall be the sick Father & his starving Family! there   10
The Prisoner in the stone Dungeon & the Slave at the
Mill
I will have Writings written all over it in Human
Words
That every Infant that is born upon the Earth shall
read
And get by rote as a hard task of a life of sixty
years
I will have Kings inwoven upon it & Councellors &
Mighty Men
The Famine shall clasp it together with buckles &
Clasps
And the Pestilence shall be its fringe & the War its
girdle
To divide into Rahab & Tirzah that Milton may come
to our tents
For I will put on the Human Form & take the Image
of God
Even Pity & Humanity but my Clothing shall be
Cruelty   20
And I will put on Holiness as a breastplate & as a
helmet
And all my ornaments shall be of the gold of broken
hearts
And the precious stones of anxiety & care & despera-
tion & death
And repentance for sin & sorrow & punishment &
fear
To defend me from thy terrors O Orc! my only
beloved!

Orc answerd. Take not the Human Form O loveliest.
Take not
Terror upon thee! Behold how I am & tremble lest
thou also
Consume in my Consummation; but thou maist take
a Form
Female & lovely, that cannot consume in Mans
consummation

Wherefore dost thou Create & Weave this Satan for
a Covering[?]   30
When thou attemptest to put on the Human Form,
my wrath
Burns to the top of heaven against thee in Jealousy
& Fear.
Then I rend thee asunder, then I howl over thy clay
& ashes
When wilt thou put on the Female Form as in times
of old
With a Garment of Pity & Compassion like the
Garment of God
His garments are long sufferings for the Children of
Men
Jerusalem is his Garment & not thy Covering Cherub
O lovely
Shadow of my delight who wanderest seeking for the
prey.

So spoke Orc when Oothoon & Leutha hoverd over
his Couch
Of fire in interchange of Beauty & Perfection in the
darkness   40
Opening interiorly into Jerusalem & Babylon shining
glorious
In the Shadowy Females bosom. Jealous her darkness
grew:
Howlings filld all the desolate places in accusations of
Sin
In Female beauty shining in the unformd void &
Orc in vain
Stretch'd out his hands of fire, & wooed: they triumph
in his pain

Thus darkend the Shadowy Female tenfold & Orc
tenfold
Glowd on his rocky Couch against the darkness:
loud thunders
Told of the enormous conflict[.] Earthquake beneath:
around;
Rent the Immortal Females, limb from limb & joint
from joint
And moved the fast foundations of the Earth to wake
the Dead   50

Urizen emerged from his Rocky Form & from his
Snows,

[PLATE 19]

And he also darkend his brows: freezing dark rocks
between
The footsteps. and infixing deep the feet in marble
beds:

That Milton labourd with his journey, & his feet
    bled sore
Upon the clay now changd to marble; also Urizen
    rose,
And met him on the shores of Arnon; & by the
    streams of the brooks

Silent they met, and silent strove among the streams,
    of Arnon
Even to Mahanaim, when with cold hand Urizen
    stoop'd down
And took up water from the river Jordan; pouring on
To Miltons brain the icy fluid from his broad cold
    palm.
But Milton took of the red clay of Succoth, moulding
    it with care   10
Between his palms; and filling up the furrows of
    many years
Beginning at the feet of Urizen, and on the bones
Creating new flesh on the Demon cold, and building
    him,
As with new clay a Human form in the Valley of Beth
    Peor.

Four Universes round the Mundane Egg remain
    Chaotic
One to the North, named Urthona: One to the South,
    named Urizen:
One to the East, named Luvah: One to the West,
    named Tharmas
They are the Four Zoa's that stood around the
    Throne Divine!
But when Luvah assum'd the World of Urizen to the
    South:
And Albion was slain upon his mountains, & in his
    tent;   20
All fell towards the Center in dire ruin, sinking down.
And in the South remains a burning fire; in the East
    a void.
In the West, a world of raging waters; in the North
    a solid,
Unfathomable! without end. But in the midst of
    these,
Is built eternally the Universe of Los and
    Enitharmon:
Towards which Milton went, but Urizen oppos'd his
    path.

The Man and Demon strove many periods. Rahab
    beheld
Standing on Carmel; Rahab and Tirzah trembled to
    behold

The enormous strife. one giving life, the other giving
    death
To his adversary. and they sent forth all their sons
    & daughters   30
In all their beauty to entice Milton across the river,

The Twofold form Hermaphroditic: and the
    Double-sexed;
The Female-male & the Male-female, self-dividing
    stood
Before him in their beauty, & in cruelties of holiness!
Shining in darkness, glorious upon the deeps of
    Entuthon.

Saying. Come thou to Ephraim! behold the Kings
    of Canaan!
The beautiful Amalekites, behold the fires of youth
Bound with the Chain of Jealousy by Los &
    Enitharmon;
The banks of Cam: cold learnings streams: Londons
    dark-frowning towers,
Lament upon the winds of Europe in Rephaims
    Vale.   40
Because Ahania rent apart into a desolate night,
Laments! & Enion wanders like a weeping inarticulate
    voice
And Vala labours for her bread & water among the
    Furnaces
Therefore bright Tirzah triumphs: putting on all
    beauty.
And all perfection, in her cruel sports among the
    Victims,
Come bring with thee Jerusalem with songs on the
    Grecian Lyre!
In Natural Religion! in experiments on Men,
Let her be Offerd up to Holiness! Tirzah numbers
    her;
She numbers with her fingers every fibre ere it grow;
Where is the Lamb of God? where is the promise of
    his coming?   50
Her shadowy Sisters form the bones, even the bones
    of Horeb:
Around the marrow! and the orbed scull around the
    brain!
His Images are born for War! for Sacrifice to Tirzah!
To Natural Religion! to Tirzah the Daughter of
    Rahab the Holy!
She ties the knot of nervous fibres, into a white brain!
She ties the knot of bloody veins, into a red hot heart!
Within her bosom Albion lies embalmd, never to
    awake
Hand is become a rock! Sinai & Horeb, is Hyle &
    Coban:

Scofield is bound in iron armour before Reubens
    Gate! [7]
She ties the knot of milky seed into two lovely
    Heavens   60

[PLATE 20]
Two yet but one: each in the other sweet reflected!
    these
Are our Three Heavens beneath the shades of
    Beulah, land of rest!
Come then to Ephraim & Manasseh O beloved-one!
Come to my ivory palaces O beloved of thy mother!
And let us bind thee in the bands of War & be thou
    King
Of Canaan and reign in Hazor where the Twelve
    Tribes meet.

So spoke they as in one voice! Silent Milton stood
    before
The darkend Urizen; as the sculptor silent stands
    before
His forming image; he walks round it patient
    labouring.
Thus Milton stood forming bright Urizen, while his
    Mortal part   10
Sat frozen in the rock of Horeb: and his Redeemed
    portion,
Thus form'd the Clay of Urizen; but within that
    portion
His real Human walkd above in power and majesty
Tho darkend; and the Seven Angels of the Presence
    attended him.

O how can I with my gross tongue that cleaveth to the
    dust,
Tell of the Four-fold Man, in starry numbers fitly
    orderd
Or how can I with my cold hand of clay! But thou O
    Lord
Do with me as thou wilt! for I am nothing, and vanity.
If thou chuse to elect a worm, it shall remove the
    mountains.
For that portion namd the Elect: the Spectrous body
    of Milton: 20
Redounding from my left foot into Los's Mundane
    space,
Brooded over his Body in Horeb against the
    Resurrection

[7] Several of the Sons of Albion, more prominent in *Jerusalem*, bear names alluding to Blake's contemporaries, including Scholfield (Schofield), the soldier who accused him of seditious utterances at Felpham.

Preparing it for the Great Consummation; red the
    Cherub on Sinai
Glow'd; but in terrors folded round his clouds of
    blood.

Now Albions sleeping Humanity began to turn upon
    his Couch;
Feeling the electric flame of Miltons awful precipitate
    descent.
Seest thou the little winged fly, smaller than a grain
    of sand?
It has a heart like thee; a brain open to heaven & hell,
Withinside wondrous & expansive; its gates are not
    clos'd,
I hope thine are not: hence it clothes itself in rich
    array;   30
Hence thou art cloth'd with human beauty O thou
    mortal man.
Seek not thy heavenly father then beyond the skies:
There Chaos dwells & ancient Night & Og & Anak
    old: [8]
For every human heart has gates of brass & bars of
    adamant,
Which few dare unbar because dread Og & Anak
    guard the gates
Terrific! and each mortal brain is walld and moated
    round
Within: and Og & Anak watch here; here is the Seat
Of Satan in its Webs; for in brain and heart and
    loins
Gates open behind Satans Seat to the City of
    Golgonooza
Which is the spiritual fourfold London, in the loins
    of Albion.   40

Thus Milton fell thro Albions heart, travelling outside
    of Humanity
Beyond the Stars in Chaos in Caverns of the
    Mundane Shell.

But many of the Eternals rose up from eternal tables
Drunk with the Spirit, burning round the Couch of
    death they stood
Looking down into Beulah: wrathful, fill'd with rage!
They rend the heavens round the Watchers in a
    fiery circle:
And round the Shadowy Eighth: the Eight close up
    the Couch
Into a tabernacle, and flee with cries down to the
    Deeps:

[8] Og and Anak (Old Testament names) are giants attempting to frustrate the search for the Promised Land.

Where Los opens his three wide gates, surrounded by
 raging fires!
They soon find their own place & join the Watchers
 of the Ulro.   50

Los saw them and a cold pale horror coverd o'er his
 limbs
Pondering he knew that Rintrah & Palamabron might
 depart:
Even as Reuben & as Gad; gave up himself to tears.
He sat down on his anvil-stock; and leand upon the
 trough.
Looking into the black water, mingling it with tears.

At last when desperation almost tore his heart in
 twain
He recollected an old Prophecy in Eden recorded,
And often sung to the loud harp at the immortal
 feasts
That Milton of the Land of Albion should up ascend
Forwards from Ulro from the Vale of Felpham; and
 set free   60
Orc from his Chain of Jealousy, he started at the
 thought

[PLATE 21]

And down descended into Udan-Adan; it was
 night;
And Satan sat sleeping upon his Couch in Udan-
 Adan:
His Spectre slept, his Shadow woke; when one sleeps
 th'other wakes.

But Milton entering my Foot; I saw in the nether
Regions of the Imagination; also all men on Earth,
And all in Heaven, saw in the nether regions of the
 Imagination
In Ulro beneath Beulah, the vast breach of Miltons
 descent.
But I knew not that it was Milton, for man cannot
 know
What passes in his members till periods of Space &
 Time
Reveal the secrets of Eternity: for more extensive 10
Than any other earthly things, are Mans earthly
 lineaments

And all this Vegetable World appeard on my left
 Foot,
As a bright sandal formd immortal of precious stones
 & gold:
I stooped down & bound it on to walk forward thro'
 Eternity.

There is in Eden a sweet River, of milk & liquid pearl.
Namd Ololon; on whose mild banks dwelt those who
 Milton drove
Down into Ulro: and they wept in long resounding
 song
For seven days of eternity, and the rivers living banks
The mountains wail'd! & every plant that grew, in
 solemn sighs lamented.

When Luvahs bulls each morning drag the sulphur
 Sun out of the Deep   20
Harnessd with starry harness black & shining kept by
 black slaves
That work all night at the starry harness, Strong and
 vigorous
They drag the unwilling Orb: at this time all the
 Family
Of Eden heard the lamentation, and Providence began.
But when the clarions of day sounded they drownd
 the lamentations
And when night came all was silent in Ololon: & all
 refusd to lament
In the still night fearing lest they should others molest.

Seven mornings Los heard them, as the poor bird
 within the shell
Hears its impatient parent bird; and Enitharmon
 heard them:
But saw them not, for the blue Mundane Shell
 inclos'd them in.   30

And they lamented that they had in wrath & fury &
 fire
Driven Milton into the Ulro; for now they knew too
 late
That it was Milton the Awakener: they had not heard
 the Bard,
Whose song calld Milton to the attempt; and Los
 heard these laments.
He heard them call in prayer all the Divine Family;
And he beheld the Cloud of Milton stretching over
 Europe.

But all the Family Divine collected as Four Suns
In the Four Points of heaven East, West & North &
 South,
Enlarging and enlarging till their Disks approachd
 each other;
And when they touch'd closed together Southward
 in One Sun   40
Over Ololon: and as One Man, who weeps over his
 brother,
In a dark tomb, so all the Family Divine. wept over
 Ololon.

Saying. Milton goes to Eternal Death! so saying, they
     groan'd in spirit
And were troubled! and again the Divine Family
     groaned in spirit!

And Ololon said, Let us descend also, and let us give
Ourselves to death in Ulro among the Transgressors.
Is Virtue a Punisher? O no! how is this wondrous
     thing:
This World beneath, unseen before: this refuge from
     the wars
Of Great Eternity! unnatural refuge! unknown by us
     till now!
Or are these the pangs of repentance? let us enter into
     them   50

Then the Divine Family said. Six Thousand Years
     are now
Accomplish'd in this World of Sorrow; Miltons
     Angel knew
The Universal Dictate; and you also feel this Dictate.
And now you know this World of Sorrow, and feel
     Pity. Obey
The Dictate! Watch over this World, and with your
     brooding wings,
Renew it to Eternal Life: Lo! I am with you alway
But you cannot renew Milton he goes to Eternal Death

So spake the Family Divine as One Man even Jesus
Uniting in One with Ololon & the appearance of One
     Man.
Jesus the Saviour appeard coming in the Clouds of
     Ololon!   60

[PLATE 22]
Tho driven away with the Seven Starry Ones into the
     Ulro
Yet the Divine Vision remains Every-where For-ever.
     Amen.
And Ololon lamented for Milton with a great
     lamentation.

While Los heard indistinct in fear, what time I bound
     my sandals
On; to walk forward thro' Eternity, Los descended
     to me:
And Los behind me stood; a terrible flaming Sun:
     just close
Behind my back; I turned round in terror, and
     behold.
Los stood in that fierce glowing fire; & he also stoop'd
     down
And bound my sandals on in Udan-Adan; trembling
     I stood   9

Exceedingly with fear & terror, standing in the Vale
Of Lambeth: but he kissed me, and wishd me health.
And I became One Man with him arising in my
     strength:
Twas too late now to recede. Los had enterd into my
     soul:
His terrors now posses'd me whole! I arose in fury
     & strength.

I am that Shadowy Prophet who Six Thousand Years
     ago
Fell from my station in the Eternal bosom. Six
     Thousand Years
Are finishd. I return! both Time & Space obey my
     will.
I in Six Thousand Years walk up and down: for not
     one Moment
Of Time is lost, nor one Event of Space unpermanent.
But all remain: every fabric of Six Thousand Years 20
Remains permanent: tho' on the Earth where Satan
Fell, and was cut off all things vanish & are seen no
     more
They vanish not from me & mine, we guard them
     first & last[.]
The generations of men run on in the tide of Time
But leave their destind lineaments permanent for
     ever & ever.

So spoke Los as we went along to his supreme abode

Rintrah and Palamabron met us at the Gate of
     Golgonooza
Clouded with discontent. & brooding in their minds
     terrible things

They said. O Father most beloved! O merciful
     Parent!
Pitying and permitting evil, tho strong & mighty to
     destroy.   30
Whence is this Shadow terrible? wherefore dost thou
     refuse
To throw him into the Furnaces! knowest thou not
     that he
Will unchain Orc? & let loose Satan, Og, Sihon &
     Anak,
Upon the Body of Albion? for this he is come!
     behold it written
Upon his fibrous left Foot black! most dismal to our
     eyes
The Shadowy Female shudders thro' heaven in
     torment inexpressible!
And all the Daughters of Los prophetic wail: yet in
     deceit,

They weave a new Religion from new Jealousy of
    Theotormon!
Miltons Religion is the cause: there is no end to
    destruction!
Seeing the Churches at their Period in terror &
    despair: 40
Rahab created Voltaire; Tirzah created Rousseau;
Asserting the Self-righteousness against the Universal
    Saviour,
Mocking the Confessors & Martyrs, claiming
    Self-righteousness;
With cruel Virtue: making War upon the Lambs
    Redeemed;
To perpetuate War & Glory. to perpetuate the Laws
    of Sin:
They perverted Swedenborgs Visions in Beulah &
    in Ulro;
To destroy Jerusalem as a Harlot & her Sons as
    Reprobates;
To raise up Mystery the Virgin Harlot Mother of
    War,
Babylon the Great, the Abomination of Desolation!
O Swedenborg! strongest of men, the Samson shorn
    by the Churches!   50
Shewing the Transgresors in Hell, the proud Warriors
    in Heaven:
Heaven as a Punisher & Hell as One under
    Punishment:
With Laws from Plato & his Greeks to renew the
    Trojan Gods,
In Albion; & to deny the value of the Saviours
    blood.
But then I rais'd up Whitefield, Palamabron raisd up
    Westley,
And these are the cries of the Churches before the two
    Witnesses[']
Faith in God the dear Saviour who took on the likeness
    of men:
Becoming obedient to death, even the death of the
    Cross
The Witnesses lie dead in the Street of the Great City
No Faith is in all the Earth: the Book of God is
    trodden under Foot: 60
He sent his two Servants Whitefield & Westley [9]
    were they Prophets
Or were they Idiots or Madmen? shew us Miracles!

[PLATE 23]

Can you have greater Miracles than these? Men who
    devote
Their lifes whole comfort to intire scorn & injury &
    death

Awake thou sleeper on the Rock of Eternity Albion
    awake
The trumpet of Judgment hath twice sounded: all
    Nations are awake
But thou art still heavy and dull: Awake Albion
    awake!
Lo Orc arises on the Atlantic. Lo his blood and fire
Glow on Americas shore: Albion turns upon his
    Couch
He listens to the sounds of War, astonishd and
    confounded:
He weeps into the Atlantic deep, yet still in dismal
    dreams
Unwakend! and the Covering Cherub advances
    from the East:,   10
How long shall we lay dead in the Street of the great
    City
How long beneath the Covering Cherub give our
    Emanations
Milton will utterly consume us & thee our beloved
    Father[.]
He hath enterd into the Covering Cherub, becoming
    one with
Albions dread Sons, Hand, Hyle & Coban surround
    him as
A girdle; Gwendolen & Conwenna [10] as a garment
    women
Of War & Religion; let us descend & bring him
    chained
To Bowlahoola O father most beloved! O mild
    Parent!
Cruel in thy mildness, pitying and permitting evil
Tho strong and mighty to destroy, O Los our
    beloved Father!   20

Like the black storm, coming out of Chaos, beyond
    the stars:
It issues thro the dark & intricate caves of the
    Mundane Shell
Passing the planetary visions, & the well adorned
    Firmament
The Sun rolls into Chaos & the stars into the
    Desarts;
And then the storms become visible, audible &
    terrible,
Covering the light of day, & rolling down upon the
    mountains,
Deluge all the country round. Such is a vision of Los;
When Rintrah & Palamabron spoke; and such his
    stormy face
Appeard, as does the face of heaven, when coverd
    with thick storms

---

[9] George Whitefield and John Wesley in the eighteenth
century founded English Methodism.

[10] Gwendolen and Conwenna are the youngest and oldest of
the twelve daughters of Albion.

Pitying and loving tho in frowns of terrible
    perturbation   30
But Los dispersd the clouds even as the strong winds
    of Jehovah.
And Los thus spoke. O noble Sons, be patient yet a
    little[.]
I have embracd the falling Death, he is become One
    with me
O Sons we live not by wrath. by mercy alone we live!
I recollect an old Prophecy in Eden recorded in gold;
    and oft
Sung to the harp: That Milton of the land of Albion
Should up ascend forward from Felphams Vale &
    break the Chain
Of Jealousy from all its roots; be patient therefore
    O my Sons
These lovely Females form sweet night and silence
    and secret
Obscurities to hide from Satans Watch-Fiends.
    Human loves   40
And graces; lest they write them in their Books, & in
    the Scroll
Of mortal life, to condemn the accused: who at Satans
    Bar
Tremble in Spectrous Bodies continually day and
    night
While on the Earth they live in sorrowful Vegetations
O when shall we tread our Wine-presses in heaven;
    and Reap
Our wheat with shoutings of joy, and leave the Earth
    in peace
Remember how Calvin and Luther in fury premature
Sow'd War and stern division between Papists &
    Protestants
Let it not be so now! O go not forth in Martyrdoms
    & Wars
We were plac'd here by the Universal Brotherhood
    & Mercy   50
With powers fitted to circumscribe this dark Satanic
    death
And that the Seven Eyes of God may have space for
    Redemption.
But how this is as yet we know not, and we cannot
    know;
Till Albion is arisen; then patient wait a little while,
Six Thousand years are passd away the end approaches
    fast;
This mighty one is come from Eden, he is of the Elect,
Who died from Earth & he is returnd before the
    Judgment. This thing
Was never known that one of the holy dead should
    willing return
Then patient wait a little while till the Last Vintage is
    over:

Till we have quenchd the Sun of Salah in the Lake of
    Udan Adan   60
O my dear Sons! leave not your Father, as your
    brethren left me[.]
Twelve Sons successive fled away in that thousand
    years of sorrow

[PLATE 24]

Of Palamabrons Harrow, & of Rintrahs wrath &
    fury:
Reuben & Manazzoth & Gad & Simeon & Levi,
And Ephraim & Judah were Generated, because
They left me, wandering with Tirzah: Enitharmon
    wept
One thousand years, and all the Earth was in a watry
    deluge
We calld him Menassheh because of the Generations
    of Tirzah
Because of Satan: & the Seven Eyes of God
    continually
Guard round them, but I the Fourth Zoa am also set
The Watchman of Eternity, the Three are not! & I
    am preserved   9
Still my four mighty ones are left to me in Golgonooza
Still Rintrah fierce, and Palamabron mild & piteous
Theotormon filld with care, Bromion loving Science
You O my Sons still guard round Los. O wander not
    & leave me
Rintrah, thou well rememberest when Amalek &
    Canaan
Fled with their Sister Moab into that abhorred Void
They became Nations in our sight beneath the hands
    of Tirzah.
And Palamabron thou rememberest when Joseph an
    infant;
Stolen from his nurses cradle wrapd in needle-work
Of emblematic texture, was sold to the Amalekite,
Who carried him down into Egypt where Ephraim &
    Menassheh   20
Gatherd my Sons together in the Sands of Midian
And if you also flee away and leave your Fathers side,
Following Milton into Ulro, altho your power is
    great
Surely you also shall become poor mortal vegetations
Beneath the Moon of Ulro: pity then your Fathers
    tears[.]
When Jesus raisd Lazarus from the Grave I stood &
    saw
Lazarus who is the Vehicular Body of Albion the
    Redeemd
Arise into the Covering Cherub who is the Spectre of
    Albion
By martyrdoms to suffer: to watch over the Sleeping
    Body.

Upon his Rock beneath his Tomb. I saw the Covering
Cherub   30
Divide Four-fold into Four Churches when Lazarus
arose
Paul, Constantine, Charlemaine, Luther; behold they
stand before us
Stretchd over Europe & Asia. come O Sons, come,
come away
Arise O Sons give all your strength against Eternal
Death
Lest we are vegetated, for Cathedrons Looms weave
only Death
A Web of Death: & were it not for Bowlahoola &
Allamanda[11]
No Human Form but only a Fibrous Vegetation
A Polypus of soft affections without Thought or
Vision
Must tremble in the Heavens & Earths thro all the
Ulro space[.]
Throw all the Vegetated Mortals into Bowlahoola   40
But as to this Elected Form who is returnd again
He is the Signal that the Last Vintage now approaches
Nor Vegetation may go on till all the Earth is reapd

So Los spoke. Furious they descended to Bowlahoola
& Allamanda
Indignant. unconvincd by Los's arguments &
thun[d]ers rolling
They saw that wrath now swayd and now pity absorbd
him
As it was, so it remaind & no hope of an end.

Bowlahoola is namd Law. by mortals, Tharmas
founded it:
Because of Satan, before Luban in the City of
Golgonooza.
But Golgonooza is namd Art & Manufacture by
mortal men.   50

In Bowlahoola Los's Anvils stand & his Furnaces
rage;
Thundering the Hammers beat & the Bellows blow
loud
Living self moving mourning lamenting & howling
incessantly
Bowlahoola thro all its porches feels tho' too fast
founded
Its pillars & porticoes to tremble at the force
Of mortal or immortal arm: and softly lilling flutes
Accordant with the horrid labours make sweet
melody

---

[11] Bowlahoola and Allamanda, digestion and circulation, are
the physical bases of existence in this elaborate anthropomorphic
model.

The Bellows are the Animal Lungs: the Hammers
the Animal Heart
The Furnaces the Stomach for digestion. terrible
their fury
Thousands & thousands labour. thousands play on
instruments   60
Stringed or fluted to ameliorate the sorrows of
slavery
Loud sport the dancers in the dance of death,
rejoicing in carnage
The hard dentant Hammers are lulld by the flutes lula
lula
The bellowing Furnaces['] blare by the long sounding
clarion
The double drum drowns howls & groans, the shrill
fife. shrieks & cries:
The crooked horn mellows the hoarse raving serpent,
terrible but harmonious
Bowlahoola is the Stomach in every individual man.

Los is by mortals nam'd Time Enitharmon is nam'd
Space
But they depict him bald & aged who is in eternal
youth
All powerful and his locks flourish like the brows of
morning   70
He is the Spirit of Prophecy the ever apparent
Elias
Time is the mercy of Eternity; without Times
swiftness
Which is the swiftest of all things: all were eternal
torment:
All the Gods of the Kingdoms of Earth labour in
Los's Halls.
Every one is a fallen Son of the Spirit of Prophecy
He is the Fourth Zoa, that stood arou[n]d the Throne
Divine.

[PLATE 25]
Loud shout the Sons of Luvah, at the Wine-presses
as Los descended
With Rintrah & Palamabron in his fires of resistless
fury.

The Wine-press on the Rhine groans loud, but all its
central beams
Act more terrific in the central Cities of the Nations
Where Human Thought is crushd beneath the iron
hand of Power.
There Los puts all into the Press, the Opressor & the
Opressed
Together, ripe for the Harvest & Vintage & ready for
the Loom.

They sang at the Vintage. This is the Last Vintage! & Seed

Shall no more be sown upon Earth, till all the Vintage is over

And all gatherd in, till the Plow has passd over the Nations   10

And the Harrow & heavy thundering Roller upon the mountains

And loud the Souls howl round the Porches of Golgonooza

Crying O God deliver us to the Heavens or to the Earths,

That we may preach righteousness & punish the sinner with death.

But Los refused, till all the Vintage of Earth was gatherd in.

And Los stood & cried to the Labourers of the Vintage in voice of awe.

Fellow Labourers! The Great Vintage & Harvest is now upon Earth

The whole extent of the Globe is explored: Every scatterd Atom

Of Human Intellect now is flocking to the sound of the Trumpet

All the Wisdom which was hidden in caves & dens, from ancient   20

Time; is now sought out from Animal & Vegetable & Mineral

The Awakener is come. outstretchd over Europe! the Vision of God is fulfilled

The Ancient Man upon the Rock of Albion Awakes,

He listens to the sounds of War astonishd & ashamed;

He sees his Children mock at Faith and deny Providence

Therefore you must bind the Sheaves not by Nations or Families

You shall bind them in Three Classes; according to their Classes

So shall you bind them.. Separating What has been Mixed

Since Men began to be Wove into Nations by Rahab & Tirzah

Since Albions Death & Satans Cutting-off from our awful Fields;   30

When under pretence to benevolence the Elect Subdud All

From the Foundation of the World. The Elect is one Class: You

Shall bind them separate: they cannot Believe in Eternal Life

Except by Miracle & a New Birth. The other two Classes;

The Reprobate who never cease to Believe, and the Redeemd,

Who live in doubts & fears perpetually tormented by the Elect

These you shall bind in a twin-bundle for the Consummation—

But the Elect must be saved [from] fires of Eternal Death,

To be formed into the Churches of Beulah that they destroy not the Earth

For in every Nation & every Family the Three Classes are born   40

And in every Species of Earth, Metal, Tree, Fish, Bird & Beast.

We form the Mundane Egg, that Spectres coming by fury or amity,

All is the same, & every one remains in his own energy[.]

Go forth Reapers with rejoicing. you sowed in tears

But the time of your refreshing cometh, only a little moment

Still abstain from pleasure & rest in the labours of eternity

And you shall Reap the whole Earth from Pole to Pole! from Sea to Sea

Begin[n]ing at Jerusalems Inner Court, Lambeth ruin'd and given

To the detestable Gods of Priam, to Apollo: and at the Asylum

Given to Hercules, who labour in Tirzahs Looms for bread   50

Who set Pleasure against Duty: who Create Olympic crowns

To make Learning a burden & the work of the Holy Spirit: Strife.

T[o] Thor & cruel Odin who first reard the Polar Caves

Lambeth mourns calling Jerusalem. she weeps & looks abroad

For the Lords coming, that Jerusalem may overspread all Nations[.]

Crave not for the mortal & perishing delights, but leave them

To the weak, and pity the weak as your infant care; Break not

Forth in your wrath lest you also are vegetated by Tirzah

Wait till the Judgement is past, till the Creation is consumed

And then rush forward with me into the glorious spiritual   60

Vegetation; the Supper of the Lamb & his Bride; and
    the
Awaking of Albion our friend and ancient companion.

So Los spoke. But lightnings of discontent broke on
    all sides round
And murmurs of thunder rolling heavy long & loud
    over the mountains
While Los calld his Sons around him to the Harvest
    & the Vintage.

Thou seest the Constellations in the deep & wondrous
    Night
They rise in order and continue their immortal
    courses
Upon the mountains & in vales with harp & heavenly
    song
With flute & clarion; with cups & measures filld
    with foaming wine.
Glittring the streams reflect the Vision of beatitude, 70
And the calm Ocean joys beneath & smooths his
    awful waves!

[PLATE 26]

These are the Sons of Los, & these the Labourers of
    the Vintage
Thou seest the gorgeous clothed Flies that dance &
    sport in summer
Upon the sunny brooks & meadows: every one the
    dance
Knows in its intricate mazes of delight artful·to weave:
Each one to sound his instruments of music in the
    dance,
To touch each other & recede; to cross & change &
    return
These are the Children of Los; thou seest the Trees
    on mountains
The wind blows heavy, loud they thunder thro' the
    darksom sky
Uttering prophecies & speaking instructive words to
    the sons
Of men: These are the Sons of Los! These the Visions
    of Eternity   10
But we see only as it were the hem of their garments
When with our vegetable eyes we view these
    wond'rous Visions

There are Two Gates thro which all Souls descend.
    One Southward
From Dover Cliff to Lizard Point. the other toward
    the North
Caithness & rocky Durness, Pentland & John Groats
    House.

The Souls descending to the Body, wail on the right
    hand
Of Los; & those deliverd from the Body, on the left
    hand
For Los against the east his force continually bends
Along the Valleys of Middlesex from Hounslow to
    Blackheath
Lest those Three Heavens of Beulah should the
    Creation destroy   20
And lest they should descend before the north &
    south Gates
Groaning with pity, he among the wailing Souls
    laments.

And these the Labours of the Sons of Los in
    Allamanda:
And in the City of Golgonooza: & in Luban: & around
The Lake of Udan-Adan, in the Forests of Entuthon
    Benython
Where Souls incessant wail, being piteous Passions
    & Desires
With neither lineament nor form but like to watry
    clouds
The Passions & Desires descend upon the hungry
    winds
For such alone Sleepers remain meer passion &
    appetite;
The Sons of Los clothe them & feed & provide houses
    & fields   30

And every Generated Body in its inward form,
Is a garden of delight & a building of magnificence,
Built by the Sons of Los in Bowlahoola & Allamanda
And the herbs & flowers & furniture & beds &
    chambers
Continually woven in the Looms of Enitharmons
    Daughters
In bright Cathedrons golden Dome with care & love
    & tears[.]
For the various Classes of Men are all markd out
    determinate
In Bowlahoola; & as the Spectres choose their
    affinities
So they are born on Earth, & every Class is
    determinate
But not by Natural but by Spiritual power alone.
    Because   40
The Natural power continually seeks & tends to
    Destruction
Ending in Death: which would of itself be Eternal
    Death
And all are Class'd by Spiritual, & not by Natural
    power.

And every Natural Effect has a Spiritual Cause, and
Not
A Natural: for a Natural Cause only seems, it is a
Delusion
Of Ulro: & a ratio of the perishing Vegetable Memory.

[PLATE 27]
But the Wine-press of Los is eastward of Golgonooza,
before the Seat
Of Satan. Luvah laid the foundation & Urizen
finish'd it in howling woe.
How red the sons & daughters of Luvah! here they
tread the grapes.
Laughing & shouting drunk with odours many fall
oerwearied
Drownd in the wine is many a youth & maiden: those
around
Lay them on skins of Tygers & of the spotted Leopard
& the Wild Ass
Till they revive, or bury them in cool grots, making
lamentation.

This Wine-press is call'd War on Earth, it is the
Printing-Press
Of Los; and here he lays his words in order above the
mortal brain
As cogs are formd in a wheel to turn the cogs of the
adverse wheel.   10

Timbrels & violins sport round the Wine-presses; the
little Seed;
The sportive Root, the Earth-worm, the gold Beetle;
the wise Emmet;
Dance round the Wine-presses of Luvah: the
Centipede is there:
The ground Spider with many eyes: the Mole clothed
in velvet
The ambitious Spider in his sullen web; the lucky
golden Spinner;
The Earwig armd: the tender Maggot emblem of
immortality:
The Flea: Louse: Bug: the Tape-Worm: all the
Armies of Disease:
Visible or invisible to the slothful vegetating Man.
The slow Slug: the Grasshopper that sings & laughs
& drinks:
Winter comes, he folds his slender bones without a
murmur.   20
The cruel Scorpion is there: the Gnat: Wasp: Hornet
& the Honey Bee:
The Toad & venomous Newt; the Serpent clothd in
gems & gold:

They throw off their gorgeous raiment: they rejoice
with loud jubilee
Around the Wine-presses of Luvah, naked & drunk
with wine.

There is the Nettle that stings with soft down; and
there
The indignant Thistle: whose bitterness is bred in
his milk:
Who feeds on contempt of his neighbour: there all the
idle Weeds
That creep around the obscure places, shew their
various limbs.
Naked in all their beauty dancing round the Wine-
presses.

But in the Wine-presses the Human grapes sing not,
nor dance   30
They howl & writhe in shoals of torment; in fierce
flames consuming,
In chains of iron & in dungeons circled with ceaseless
fires.
In pits & dens & shades of death: in shapes of
torment & woe.
The plates & screws & wracks & saws & cords & fires
& cisterns
The cruel joys of Luvahs Daughters lacerating with
knives
And whips their Victims & the deadly sport of
Luvahs Sons.

They dance around the dying, & they drink the howl
& groan
They catch the shrieks in cups of gold, they hand them
to one another:
These are the sports of love, & these the sweet
delights of amorous play
Tears of the grape, the death sweat of the cluster the
last sigh   40
Of the mild youth who listens to the lureing songs of
Luvah

But Allamanda calld on Earth Commerce, is the
Cultivated land
Around the City of Golgonooza in the Forests of
Entuthon:
Here the Sons of Los labour against Death Eternal;
through all
The Twenty-seven Heavens of Beulah in Ulro, Seat
of Satan,
Which is the False Tongue beneath Beulah: it is the
Sense of Touch:

The Plow goes forth in tempests & lightnings & the
    Harrow cruel
In blights of the east; the heavy Roller follows in
    howlings of woe.

Urizens sons here labour also; & here are seen the
    Mills
Of Theotormon, on the verge of the Lake of Udan-
    Adan: 50
These are the starry voids of night & the depths &
    caverns of earth
These Mills are oceans, clouds & waters ungovernable
    in their fury
Here are the stars created & the seeds of all things
    planted
And here the Sun & Moon receive their fixed
    destinations

But in Eternity the Four Arts: Poetry, Painting,
    Music,
And Architecture which is Science: are the Four
    Faces of Man.
Not so in Time & Space: there Three are shut out,
    and only
Science remains thro Mercy: & by means of Science,
    the Three
Become apparent in Time & Space, in the Three
    Professions
Poetry in Religion: Music, Law: Painting, in Physic
    & Surgery: 60
That Man may live upon Earth till the time of his
    awaking,
And from these Three, Science derives every
    Occupation of Men.
And Science is divided into Bowlahoola & Allamanda

[PLATE 28]
Some Sons of Los surround the Passions with
    porches of iron & silver
Creating form & beauty around the dark regions of
    sorrow,
Giving to airy nothing a name and a habitation
Delightful! with bounds to the Infinite putting off
    the Indefinite
Into most holy forms of Thought: (such is the power
    of inspiration)
They labour incessant; with many tears & afflictions:
Creating the beautiful House for the piteous sufferer.

Others; Cabinets richly fabricate of gold & ivory;
For Doubts & fears unform'd & wretched &
    melancholy
The little weeping Spectre stands on the threshold of
    Death   10

Eternal; and sometimes two Spectres like lamps
    quivering
And often malignant they combat (heart-breaking
    sorrowful & piteous)
Antamon takes them into his beautiful flexible
    hands,
As the Sower takes the seed, or as the Artist his clay
Or fine wax, to mould artful a model for golden
    ornaments.
The soft hands of Antamon draw the indelible line:
Form immortal with golden pen; such as the Spectre
    admiring
Puts on the sweet form; then smiles Antamon bright
    thro his windows
The Daughters of beauty look up from their Loom
    & prepare.
The integument soft for its clothing with joy &
    delight.   20

But Theotormon & Sotha stand in the Gate of Luban
    anxious
Their numbers are seven million & seven thousand &
    seven hundred
They contend with the weak Spectres, they fabricate
    soothing forms
The Spectre refuses. he seeks cruelty. they create the
    crested Cock
Terrified the Spectre screams & rushes in fear into
    their Net
Of kindness & compassion & is born a weeping terror.
Or they create the Lion & Tyger in compassionate
    thunderings[.]
Howling the Spectres flee: they take refuge in Human
    lineaments.

The Sons of Ozoth within the Optic Nerve stand
    fiery glowing   29
And the number of his Sons is eight millions &
    eight.
They give delights to the man unknown; artificial
    riches
They give to scorn, & their posessors to trouble &
    sorrow & care,
Shutting the sun. & moon. & stars. & trees. & clouds.
    & waters.
And hills. out from the Optic Nerve & hardening it
    into a bone
Opake. and like the black pebble on the enraged
    beach.
While the poor indigent is like the diamond which tho
    cloth'd
In rugged covering in the mine, is open all within
And in his hallowd center holds the heavens of bright
    eternity

Ozoth here builds walls of rocks against the surging
    sea
And timbers crampt with iron cramps bar in the joys
    of life   40
From fell destruction in the Spectrous cunning or
    rage. He Creates
The speckled Newt, the Spider & Beetle, the Rat &
    Mouse,
The Badger & Fox: they worship before his feet in
    trembling fear.

But others of the Sons of Los build Moments &
    Minutes & Hours
And Days & Months & Years & Ages & Periods;
    wondrous buildings
And every Moment has a Couch of gold for soft
    repose,
(A Moment equals a pulsation of the artery)
And between every two Moments stands a Daughter
    of Beulah
To feed the Sleepers on their Couches with maternal
    care.
And every Minute has an azure Tent with silken
    Veils.   50
And every Hour has a bright golden Gate carved with
    skill.
And every Day & Night, has Walls of brass & Gates
    of adamant,
Shining like precious stones & ornamented with
    appropriate signs:
And every Month, a silver paved Terrace builded
    high:
And every Year, invulnerable Barriers with high
    Towers.
And every Age is Moated deep with Bridges of silver
    & gold:
And every Seven Ages is Incircled with a Flaming
    Fire.
Now seven Ages is amounting to Two Hundred
    Years
Each has its Guard. each Moment Minute Hour Day
    Month & Year.
All are the work of Fairy hands of the Four Elements
The Guard are Angels of Providence on duty   60
    evermore
Every Time less than a pulsation of the artery
Is equal in its period & value to Six Thousand Years.

[PLATE 29]
For in this Period the Poets Work is Done: and all the
    Great
Events of Time start forth & are concievd in such a
    Period
Within a Moment: a Pulsation of the Artery.

The Sky is an immortal Tent built by the Sons of Los
And every Space that a Man views around his
    dwelling-place:
Standing on his own roof, or in his garden on a mount
Of twenty-five cubits in height, such space is his
    Universe;
And on its verge the Sun rises & sets. the Clouds bow
To meet the flat Earth & the Sea in such an orderd
    Space:
The Starry heavens reach no further but here bend
    and set   10
On all sides & the two Poles turn on their valves of
    gold:
And if he move his dwelling-place, his heavens also
    move.
Wher'eer he goes & all his neighbourhood bewail his
    loss:
Such are the Spaces called Earth & such its dimension:
As to that false appearance which appears to the
    reasoner,
As of a Globe rolling thro Voidness, it is a delusion of
    Ulro
The Microscope knows not of this nor the Telescope.
    they alter
The ratio of the Spectators Organs but leave Objects
    untouchd
For every Space larger than a red Globule of Mans
    blood.
Is visionary: and is created by the Hammer of Los   20
And every Space smaller than a Globule of Mans
    blood. opens
Into Eternity of which this vegetable Earth is but a
    shadow:
The red Globule is the unwearied Sun by Los created
To measure Time and Space to mortal Men. every
    morning.
Bowlahoola & Allamanda are placed on each side
Of that Pulsation & that Globule, terrible their power.

But Rintrah & Palamabron govern over Day & Night
In Allamanda & Entuthon Benython where Souls wail:
Where Orc incessant howls burning in fires of
    Eternal Youth,
Within the vegetated mortal Nerves; for every Man
    born is joined   30
Within into One mighty Polypus, and this Polypus
    is Orc.

But in the Optic vegetative Nerves Sleep was
    transformed
To Death in old time by Satan the father of Sin &
    Death
And Satan is the Spectre of Orc & Orc is the generate
    Luvah

But in the Nerves of the Nostrils, Accident being
    formed
Into Substance & Principle, by the cruelties of
    Demonstration
It became Opake & Indefinite; but the Divine
    Saviour,
Formed it into a Solid by Los's Mathematic power.
He named the Opake Satan: he named the Solid
    Adam

And in the Nerves of the Ear, (for the Nerves of the
    Tongue are closed)   40
On Albions Rock Los stands creating the glorious
    Sun each morning
And when unwearied in the evening he creates the
    Moon
Death to delude, who all in terror at their splendor
    leaves
His prey while Los appoints, & Rintrah & Palamabron
    guide
The Souls clear from the Rock of Death, that Death
    himself may wake
In his appointed season when the ends of heaven
    meet.

Then Los conducts the Spirits to be Vegetated, into
Great Golgonooza, free from the four iron pillars of
    Satans Throne
(Temperance, Prudence, Justice, Fortitude, the four
    pillars of tyranny)
That Satans Watch-Fiends touch them not before
    they Vegetate.   50

But Enitharmon and her Daughters take the pleasant
    charge.
To give them to their lovely heavens till the Great
    Judgment Day
Such is their lovely charge. But Rahab & Tirzah
    pervert
Their mild influences, therefore the Seven Eyes of
    God walk round
The Three Heavens of Ulro, where Tirzah & her
    Sisters
Weave the black Woof of Death upon Entuthon
    Benython
In the Vale of Surrey where Horeb terminates in
    Rephaim
The stamping feet of Zelophehads Daughters are
    coverd with Human gore
Upon the treddles of the Loom: they sing to the
    winged shuttle:
The River rises above his banks to wash the Woof: 60
He takes it in his arms: he passes it in strength thro
    his current

The veil of human miseries is woven over the Ocean
From the Atlantic to the Great South Sea, the
    Erythrean.

Such is the World of Los the labour of six thousand
    years.
Thus Nature is a Vision of the Science of the Elohim

End of the First Book.

====

The lines above the title to Book the Second of Milton *are
engraved in reversed (mirror) writing as part of the title design for
Book 2.*

====

[PLATE 30]
    How Wide the Gulf & Unpassable! between
    Simplicity & Insipidity Contraries are
    Positive A Negation is not a Contrary

Book the Second.

There is a place where Contrarieties are equally True
This place is called Beulah, It is a pleasant lovely
    Shadow
Where no dispute can come. Because of those who
    Sleep.
Into this place the Sons & Daughters of Ololon
    descended
With solemn mourning, into Beulahs moony shades
    & hills
Weeping for Milton: mute wonder held the Daughters
    of Beulah
Enrapturd with affection sweet and mild benevolence

Beulah is evermore Created around Eternity;
    appearing
To the Inhabitants of Eden, around them on all sides.
But Beulah to its Inhabitants appears within each
    district   10
As the beloved infant in his mothers bosom round
    incircled
With arms of love & pity & sweet compassion. But to
The Sons of Eden the moony habitations of Beulah,
Are from Great Eternity a mild & pleasant Rest.

And it is thus Created. Lo the Eternal Great
    Humanity
To whom be Glory & Dominion Evermore Amen
Walks among all his awful Family seen in every face
As the breath of the Almighty. such are the words of
    man to man
In the great Wars of Eternity, in fury of Poetic
    Inspiration,
To build the Universe stupendous: Mental forms
    Creating   20

But the Emanations trembled exceedingly, nor could
    they
Live, because the life of Man was too exceeding
    unbounded
His joy became terrible to them, they trembled & wept
Crying with one voice. Give us a habitation & a place
In which we may be hidden under the shadow of
    wings
For if we who are but for a time, & who pass away in
    winter
Behold these wonders of Eternity we shall consume
But you O our Fathers & Brothers, remain in Eternity
But grant us a Temporal Habitation. do you speak
To us; we will obey your words as you obey Jesus   30
The Eternal who is blessed for ever & ever. Amen

So spake the lovely Emanations; & there appeard a
    pleasant
Mild Shadow above: beneath: & on all sides round,

[PLATE 31]
Into this pleasant Shadow all the weak & weary
Like Women & Children were taken away as on
    wings
Of dovelike softness, & shadowy habitations prepared
    for them
But every Man returnd & went still going forward
    thro'
The Bosom of the Father in Eternity on Eternity
Neither did any lack or fall into Error without
A Shadow to repose in all the Days of happy Eternity

Into this pleasant Shadow Beulah, all Ololon
    descended
And when the Daughters of Beulah heard the
    lamentation
All Beulah wept, for they saw the Lord coming in the
    Clouds.   10
And the Shadows of Beulah terminate in rocky
    Albion.

And all Nations wept in affliction Family by Family
Germany wept towards France & Italy: England
    wept & trembled
Towards America: India rose up from his golden
    bed:
As one awakend in the night: they saw the Lord
    coming
In the Clouds of Ololon with Power & Great Glory!

And all the Living Creatures of the Four Elements,
    wail'd
With bitter wailing: these in the aggregate are named
    Satan

And Rahab: they know not of Regeneration, but only
    of Generation
The Fairies, Nymphs, Gnomes & Genii of the Four
    Elements   20
Unforgiving & unalterable: these cannot be
    Regenerated
But must be Created, for they know only of
    Generation
These are the Gods of the Kingdoms of the Earth: in
    contrarious
And cruel opposition: Element against Element,
    opposed in War
Not Mental, as the Wars of Eternity, but a Corporeal
    Strife
In Los's Halls continual labouring in the Furnaces
    of Golgonooza
Orc howls on the Atlantic: Enitharmon trembles: All
    Beulah weeps

Thou hearest the Nightingale begin the Song of
    Spring;
The Lark sitting upon his earthy bed: just as the
    morn
Appears; listens silent; then springing from the
    waving Corn-field! loud   30
He leads the Choir of Day! trill, trill, trill, trill,
Mounting upon the wings of light into the Great
    Expanse:
Reecchoing against the lovely blue & shining heavenly
    Shell:
His little throat labours with inspiration; every feather
On throat & breast & wings vibrates with the
    effluence Divine
All Nature listens silent to him & the awful Sun
Stands still upon the Mountain looking on this little
    Bird
With eyes of soft humility, & wonder love & awe.
Then loud from their green covert all the Birds begin
    their Song
The Thrush, the Linnet & the Goldfinch, Robin &
    the Wren   40
Awake the Sun from his sweet reverie upon the
    Mountain:
The Nightingale again assays his song, & thro the day,
And thro the night warbles luxuriant; every Bird of
    Song
Attending his loud harmony with admiration & love.
This is a Vision of the lamentation of Beulah over
    Ololon!

Thou percievest the Flowers put forth their precious
    Odours!
And none can tell how from so small a center comes
    such sweets

Forgetting that within that Center Eternity expands
Its ever during doors, that Og & Anak fiercely
  guard[.]
First eer the morning breaks joy opens in the flowery
  bosoms   50
Joy even to tears, which the Sun rising dries; first the
  Wild Thyme
And Meadow-sweet downy & soft waving among the
  reeds.
Light springing on the air lead the sweet Dance: they
  wake
The Honeysuckle sleeping on the Oak: the flaunting
  beauty
Revels along upon the wind; the White-thorn lovely
  May
Opens her many lovely eyes: listening the Rose still
  sleeps
None dare to wake her. soon she bursts her crimson
  curtaind bed
And comes forth in the majesty of beauty; every
  Flower:
The Pink, the Jessamine, the Wall-flower, the
  Carnation
The Jonquil, the mild Lilly opes her heavens! every
  Tree,   60
And Flower & Herb soon fill the air with an
  innumerable Dance
Yet all in order sweet & lovely, Men are sick with
  Love!
Such is a Vision of the lamentation of Beulah over
  Ololon

[PLATE 32]

And Milton oft sat up on the Couch of Death & oft
  conversed
In vision & dream beatific with the Seven Angels of
  the Presence

I have turned my back upon these Heavens builded
  on cruelty
My Spectre still wandering thro' them follows my
  Emanation
He hunts her footsteps thro' the snow & the wintry
  hail & rain
The idiot Reasoner laughs at the Man of
  Imagination
And from laughter proceeds to murder by
  undervaluing calumny

Then Hillel who is Lucifer replied over the Couch of
  Death
And thus the Seven Angels instructed him & thus
  they converse.

We are not Individuals but States: Combinations of
  Individuals   10
We were Angels of the Divine Presence: & were
  Druids in Annandale
Compelld to combine into Form by Satan, the Spectre
  of Albion,
Who made himself a God &, destroyed the Human
  Form Divine.
But the Divine Humanity & Mercy gave   כדבים
  us a Human Form   as multitudes
Because we were combind in Freedom &   Vox Populi[12]
  holy Brotherhood
While those combind by Satans Tyranny first in the
  blood of War
And Sacrifice &, next, in Chains of imprisonment:
  are Shapeless Rocks
Retaining only Satans Mathematic Holiness, Length:
  Bredth & Highth
Calling the Human Imagination: which is the Divine
  Vision & Fruition
In which Man liveth eternally: madness & blasphemy,
  against   20
Its own Qualities, which are Servants of Humanity,
  not Gods or Lords[.]
Distinguish therefore States from Individuals in
  those States.
States Change: but Individual Identities never
  change nor cease:
You cannot go to Eternal Death in that which can
  never Die.
Satan & Adam are States Created into Twenty-seven
  Churches
And thou O Milton art a State about to be Created
Called Eternal Annihilation that none but the Living
  shall
Dare to enter: & they shall enter triumphant over
  Death
And Hell & the Grave: States that are not, but ah!
  Seem to be.

Judge then of thy Own Self: thy Eternal Lineaments
  explore   30
What is Eternal & what Changeable? & what
  Annihilable!
The Imagination is not a State: it is the Human
  Existence itself
Affection or Love becomes a State, when divided
  from Imagination
The Memory is a State always, & the Reason is a
  State
Created to be Annihilated & a new Ratio Created

---

[12] The Hebrew for "multitudes" precedes the English; Vox
Populi = the voice of the people.

Whatever can be Created can be Annihilated Forms cannot
The Oak is cut down by the Ax, the Lamb falls by the Knife
But their Forms Eternal Exist, For-ever. Amen Halle[l]ujah

Thus they converse with the Dead watching round the Couch of Death.
For God himself enters Death's Door always with those that enter   40
And lays down in the Grave with them, in Visions of Eternity
Till they awake & see Jesus & the Linen Clothes lying
That the Females had Woven for them, & the Gates of their Fathers House

[PLATE 33]
And the Divine Voice was heard in the Songs of Beulah Saying

When I first Married you, I gave you all my whole Soul
I thought that you would love my loves & joy in my delights
Seeking for pleasures in my pleasures O Daughter of Babylon
Then thou wast lovely, mild & gentle. now thou art terrible
In jealousy & unlovely in my sight, because thou hast cruelly
Cut off my loves in fury till I have no love left for thee
Thy love depends on him thou lovest & on his dear loves
Depend thy pleasures which thou hast cut off by jealousy
Therefore I shew my Jealousy & set before you Death.   10
Behold Milton descended to Redeem the Female Shade
From Death Eternal; such your lot, to be continually Redeem'd
By death & misery of those you love & by Annihilation
When the Sixfold Female percieves that Milton annihilates
Himself: that seeing all his loves by her cut off: he leaves
Her also: intirely abstracting himself from Female loves
She shall relent in fear of death: She shall begin to give
Her maidens to her husband: delighting in his delight
And then & then alone begins the happy Female joy
As it is done in Beulah, & thou O Virgin Babylon Mother of Whoredoms   20

Shalt bring Jerusalem in thine arms in the night watches; and
No longer turning her a wandering Harlot in the streets
Shalt give her into the arms of God your Lord & Husband.

Such are the Songs of Beulah in the Lamentations of Ololon

[PLATE 34]
And all the Songs of Beulah sounded comfortable notes
To comfort Ololons lamentation, for they said[:]
Are you the Fiery Circle that late drove in fury & fire
The Eight Immortal Starry-Ones down into Ulro dark
Rending the Heavens of Beulah with your thunders & lightnings
And can you thus lament & can you pity & forgive?
Is terror changd to pity O wonder of Eternity!

And the Four States of Humanity in its Repose,
Were shewed them. First of Beulah a most pleasant Sleep
On Couches soft, with mild music, tended by Flowers of Beulah   10
Sweet Female forms, winged or floating in the air spontaneous
The Second State is Alla & the third State Al-Ulro;
But the Fourth State is dreadful; it is named Or-Ulro:
The First State is in the Head, the Second is in the Heart:
The Third in the Loins & Seminal Vessels & the Fourth
In the Stomach & Intestines terrible, deadly, unutterable
And he whose Gates are opend in those Regions of his Body
Can from those Gates view all these wondrous Imaginations

But Ololon sought the Or-Ulro & its fiery Gates
And the Couches of the Martyrs: & many Daughters of Beulah   20
Accompany them down to the Ulro with soft melodious tears
A long journey & dark thro Chaos in the track of Miltons course
To where the Contraries of Beulah War beneath Negations Banner

Then view'd from Miltons Track they see the Ulro: a vast Polypus
Of living fibres down into the Sea of Time & Space growing

A self-devouring monstrous Human Death Twenty-
    seven fold[.]
Within it sit Five Females & the nameless Shadowy
    Mother
Spinning it from her bowels with songs of amorous
    delight
And melting cadences that lure the Sleepers of Beulah
    down
The River Storge (which is Arnon) into the Dead
    Sea: 30
Around this Polypus Los continual builds the
    Mundane Shell

Four Universes round the Universe of Los remain
    Chaotic
Four intersecting Globes, & the Egg form'd World
    of Los
In midst; stretching from Zenith to Nadir, in midst of
    Chaos[.]
One of these Ruind Universes is to the North named
    Urthona
One to the South this was the glorious World of
    Urizen
One to the East, of Luvah: One to the West; of
    Tharmas.
But when Luvah assumed the World of Urizen in the
    South
All fell towards the Center sinking downward in dire
    Ruin

Here in these Chaoses the Sons of Ololon took their
    abode   40
In Chasms of the Mundane Shell which open on all
    sides round!
Southward & by the East within the Breach of
    Miltons descent
To watch the time, pitying & gentle to awaken
    Urizen
They stood in a dark land of death of fiery corroding
    waters
Where lie in evil death the Four Immortals pale and
    cold
And the Eternal Man, even Albion, upon the Rock of
    Ages[.]
Seeing Miltons Shadow, some Daughters of Beulah
    trembling
Returnd, but Ololon remaind before the Gates of the
    Dead

And Ololon looked down into the Heavens of Ulro
    in fear
They said. How are the Wars of man which in Great
    Eternity   50

Appear around, in the External Spheres of Visionary
    Life
Here renderd Deadly within the Life & Interior
    Vision
How are the Beasts & Birds & Fishes, & Plants &
    Minerals
Here fixd into a frozen bulk subject to decay &
    death[?]
Those Visions of Human Life & Shadows of Wisdom
    & Knowledge

[PLATE 35]
Are here frozen to unexpansive deadly destroying
    terrors[.]
And War & Hunting: the Two Fountains of the River
    of Life
Are become Fountains of bitter Death & of corroding
    Hell
Till Brotherhood is changd into a Curse & a
    Flattery
By Differences between Ideas, that Ideas themselves,
    (which are
The Divine Members) may be slain in offerings for
    sin
O dreadful Loom of Death! O piteous Female forms
    compelld
To weave the Woof of Death, On Camberwell
    Tirzahs Courts
Malahs on Blackheath, Rahab & Noah. dwell on
    Windsors heights
Where once the Cherubs of Jerusalem spread to
    Lambeths Vale   10
Milcahs Pillars shine from Harrow to Hampstead
    where Hoglah
On Highgates heights magnificent Weaves over
    trembling Thames
To Shooters Hill and thence to Blackheath the dark
    Woof! Loud
Loud roll the Weights & Spindles over the whole
    Earth let down
On all sides round to the Four Quarters of the World,
    eastward on
Europe to Euphrates & Hindu, to Nile & back in
    Clouds
Of Death across the Atlantic to America North &
    South

So spake Ololon in reminiscence astonishd, but they
Could not behold Golgonooza without passing the
    Polypus
A wondrous journey not passable by Immortal feet, &
    none   20
But the Divine Saviour can pass it without
    annihilation.

For Golgonooza cannot be seen till having passd the
    Polypus
It is viewed on all sides round by a Four-fold Vision
Or till you become Mortal & Vegetable in Sexuality
Then you behold its mighty Spires & Domes of
    ivory & gold

And Ololon examined all the Couches of the Dead.
Even of Los & Enitharmon & all the Sons of Albion
And his Four Zoas terrified & on the verge of Death
In midst of these was Miltons Couch, & when they
    saw Eight
Immortal Starry-Ones, guarding the Couch in
    flaming fires   30
They thunderous utterd all a universal groan falling
    down
Prostrate before the Starry Eight asking with tears
    forgiveness
Confessing their crime with humiliation and sorrow.

O how the Starry Eight rejoic'd to see Ololon
    descended!
And now that a wide road was open to Eternity,
By Ololons descent thro Beulah to Los & Enitharmon.

For mighty were the multitudes of Ololon, vast the
    extent
Of their great sway, reaching from Ulro to Eternity
Surrounding the Mundane Shell outside in its
    Caverns
And through Beulah. and all silent forbore to
    contend   40
With Ololon for they saw the Lord in the Clouds of
    Ololon

There is a Moment in each Day that Satan cannot
    find
Nor can his Watch Fiends find it, but the Industrious
    find
This Moment & it multiply. & when it once is found
It renovates every Moment of the Day if rightly
    placed[.]
In this Moment Ololon descended to Los &
    Enitharmon
Unseen beyond the Mundane Shell Southward in
    Miltons track

Just in this Moment when the morning odours rise
    abroad
And first from the Wild Thyme, stands a Fountain
    in a rock
Of crystal flowing into two Streams, one flows thro
    Golgonooza   50

And thro Beulah to Eden beneath Los's western Wall
The other flows thro the Aerial Void & all the
    Churches
Meeting again in Golgonooza beyond Satans Seat

The Wild Thyme is Los's Messenger to Eden, a
    mighty Demon
Terrible deadly & poisonous his presence in Ulro
    dark
Therefore he appears only a small Root creeping in
    grass
Covering over the Rock of Odours his bright purple
    mantle
Beside the Fount above the Larks nest in Golgonooza
Luvah slept here in death & here is Luvahs empty
    Tomb
Ololon sat beside this Fountain on the Rock of
    Odours.   60

Just at the place to where the Lark mounts, is a
    Crystal Gate
It is the enterance of the First Heaven named
    Luther: for
The Lark is Los's Messenger thro the Twenty-seven
    Churches
That the Seven Eyes of God who walk even to Satans
    Seat
Thro all the Twenty-seven Heavens may not slumber
    nor sleep
But the Larks Nest is at the Gate of Los, at the
    eastern
Gate of wide Golgonooza & the Lark is Los's
    Messenger

[PLATE 36]
When on the highest lift of his light pinions he arrives
At that bright Gate, another Lark meets him & back
    to back
They touch their pinions tip tip: and each descend
To their respective Earths & there all night consult
    with Angels
Of Providence & with the Eyes of God all night in
    slumbers
Inspired: & at the dawn of day send out another Lark
Into another Heaven to carry news upon his wings
Thus are the Messengers dispatchd till they reach the
    Earth again
In the East Gate of Golgonooza, & the Twenty-eighth
    bright
Lark. met the Female Ololon descending into my
    Garden   10
Thus it appears to Mortal eyes & those of the Ulro
    Heavens
But not thus to Immortals, the Lark is a mighty Angel.

For Ololon step'd into the Polypus within the
    Mundane Shell
They could not step into Vegetable Worlds without
    becoming
The enemies of Humanity except in a Female Form
And as One Female, Ololon and all its mighty Hosts
Appear'd: a Virgin of twelve years nor time nor
    space was
To the perception of the Virgin Ololon but as the
Flash of lightning but more quick the Virgin in my
    Garden
Before my Cottage stood, for the Satanic Space is
    delusion   20

For when Los joind with me he took me in his firy
    whirlwind
My Vegetated portion was hurried from Lambeths
    shades
He set me down in Felphams Vale & prepard a
    beautiful
Cottage for me that in three years I might write all
    these Visions
To display Natures cruel holiness: the deceits of
    Natural Religion[.]
Walking in my Cottage Garden, sudden I beheld
The Virgin Ololon & address'd her as a Daughter of
    Beulah

Virgin of Providence fear not to enter into my Cottage
What is thy message to thy friend? What am I now to
    do   29
Is it again to plunge into deeper affliction? behold me
Ready to obey, but pity thou my Shadow of Delight
Enter my Cottage, comfort her, for she is sick with
    fatigue

[PLATE 37]

The Virgin answerd. Knowest thou of Milton who
    descended
Driven from Eternity; him I seek! terrified at my Act
In Great Eternity which thou knowest! I come him to
    seek

So Ololon utterd in words distinct the anxious
    thought
Mild was the voice, but more distinct than any
    earthly
That Miltons Shadow heard & condensing all his
    Fibres
Into a strength impregnable of majesty & beauty
    infinite
I saw he was the Covering Cherub & within him
    Satan

And Raha[b], in an outside which is fallacious!
    within
Beyond the outline of Identity, in the Selfhood
    deadly   10
And he appeard the Wicker Man of Scandinavia in
    whom
Jerusalems children consume in flames among the
    Stars

Descending down into my Garden, a Human Wonder
    of God
Reaching from heaven to earth a Cloud & Human
    Form
I beheld Milton with astonishment & in him beheld
The Monstrous Churches of Beulah, the Gods of
    Ulro dark
Twelve monstrous dishumanizd terrors Synagogues
    of Satan.
A Double Twelve & Thrice Nine: such their divisions.

And these their Names & their Places within the
    Mundane Shell

In Tyre & Sidon I saw Baal & Ashtaroth. In Moab
    Chemosh   20
In Ammon, Molech: loud his Furnaces rage among
    the Wheels
Of Og, & pealing loud the cries of the Victims of Fire!
And pale his Priestesses infolded in Veils of Pestilence,
    border'd
With War; Woven in Looms of Tyre & Sidon by
    beautiful Ashtaroth.
In Palestine Dagon, Sea Monster! worshipd o'er the
    Sea.
Thammuz in Lebanon & Rimmon in Damascus
    curtaind
Osiris: Isis: Orus: in Egypt: dark their Tabernacles
    on Nile
Floating with solemn songs, & on the Lakes of
    Egypt nightly
With pomp, even till morning break & Osiris appear
    in the sky
But Belial of Sodom & Gomorrha, obscure Demon of
    Bribes   30
And secret Assasinations, not worshipd nor adord;
    but
With the finger on the lips & the back turnd to the
    light
And Saturn Jove & Rhea of the Isles of the Sea
    remote
These Twelve Gods. are the Twelve Spectre Sons of
    the Druid Albion[13]

---

[13] The same false gods are similarly cataloged by Milton in
Book I of *Paradise Lost*.

And these the names of the Twenty-seven Heavens
    & their Churches
Adam, Seth, Enos, Cainan, Mahalaleel, Jared,
    Enoch,
Methuselah, Lamech: these are Giants mighty
    Hermaphroditic
Noah, Shem, Arphaxad, Cainan the second, Salah,
    Heber,
Peleg, Reu, Serug, Nahor, Terah, these are the
    Female-Males   39
A Male within a Female hid as in an Ark &
    Curtains,
Abraham, Moses, Solomon, Paul, Constantine,
    Charlemaine
Luther, these seven are the Male-Females, the
    Dragon Forms
Religion hid in War, a Dragon red & hidden
    Harlot

All these are seen in Miltons Shadow who is the
    Covering Cherub
The Spectre of Albion in which the Spectre of Luvah
    inhabits
In the Newtonian Voids between the Substances of
    Creation

For the Chaotic Voids outside of the Stars are
    measured by
The Stars, which are the boundaries of Kingdoms,
    Provinces
And Empires of Chaos invisible to the Vegetable Man
The Kingdom of Og. is in Orion: Sihon is in
    Ophiucus   50
Og has Twenty-seven Districts; Sihons Districts
    Twenty-one
From Star to Star, Mountains & Valleys, terrible
    dimension
Stretchd out, compose the Mundane Shell, a mighty
    Incrustation
Of Forty-eight deformed Human Wonders of the
    Almighty
With Caverns whose remotest bottoms meet again
    beyond
The Mundane Shell in Golgonooza, but the Fires of
    Los, rage
In the remotest bottoms of the Caves, that none can
    pass
Into Eternity that way, but all descend to Los
To Bowlahoola & Allamanda & to Entuthon
    Benython

The Heavens are the Cherub, the Twelve Gods are
    Satan   60

[PLATE 38]
And the Forty-eight Starry Regions are Cities of the
    Levites
The Heads of the Great Polypus, Four-fold twelve
    enormity
In mighty & mysterious comingling enemy with
    enemy
Woven by Urizen into Sexes from his mantle of
    years[.]
And Milton collecting all his fibres into impregnable
    strength
Descended down a Paved work of all kinds of
    precious stones
Out from the eastern sky; descending down into my
    Cottage
Garden: clothed in black, severe & silent he
    descended.

The Spectre of Satan stood upon the roaring sea &
    beheld
Milton within his sleeping Humanity! trembling &
    shuddring   10
He stood upon the waves a Twenty-seven-fold
    mighty Demon
Gorgeous & beautiful: loud roll his thunders against
    Milton
Loud Satan thunderd, loud & dark upon mild
    Felpham shore
Not daring to touch one fibre he howld round upon
    the Sea.

I also stood in Satans bosom & beheld its desolations!
A ruind Man: a ruind building of God not made with
    hands;
Its plains of burning sand, its mountains of marble
    terrible:
Its pits & declivities flowing with molten ore &
    fountains
Of pitch & nitre: its ruind palaces & cities & mighty
    works;
Its furnaces of affliction in which his Angels &
    Emanations   20
Labour with blackend visages among its stupendous
    ruins
Arches & pyramids & porches colonades & domes:
In which dwells Mystery Babylon, here is her secret
    place
From hence she comes forth on the Churches in
    delight
Here is her Cup filld with its poisons, in these horrid
    vales
And here her scarlet Veil woven in pestilence & war:
Here is Jerusalem bound in chains, in the Dens of
    Babylon

In the Eastern porch of Satans Universe Milton
    stood & said

Satan! my Spectre! I know my power thee to
    annihilate
And be a greater in thy place, & be thy Tabernacle 30
A covering for thee to do thy will, till one greater
    comes
And smites me as I smote thee & becomes my
    covering.
Such are the Laws of thy false Heavns! but Laws of
    Eternity
Are not such: know thou: I come to Self Annihilation
Such are the Laws of Eternity that each shall
    mutually
Annihilate himself for others good, as I for thee[.]
Thy purpose & the purpose of thy Priests & of thy
    Churches
Is to impress on men the fear of death; to teach
Trembling & fear, terror, constriction; abject
    selfishness
Mine is to teach Men to despise death & to go on 40
In fearless majesty annihilating Self, laughing to
    scorn
Thy Laws & terrors, shaking down thy Synagogues
    as webs
I come to discover before Heavn & Hell the Self
    righteousness
In all its Hypocritic turpitude, opening to every eye
These wonders of Satans holiness shewing to the
    Earth
The Idol Virtues of the Natural Heart, & Satans Seat
Explore in all its Selfish Natural Virtue & put off
In Self annihilation all that is not of God alone:
To put off Self & all I have ever & ever Amen

Satan heard! Coming in a cloud, with trumpets &
    flaming fire,   50
Saying I am God the judge of all, the living & the
    dead
Fall therefore down & worship me. submit thy
    supreme
Dictate, to my eternal Will & to my dictate bow
I hold the Balances of Right & Just & mine the Sword
Seven Angels bear my Name & in those Seven I
    appear
But I alone am God & I alone in Heavn & Earth
Of all that live dare utter this, others tremble & bow

[PLATE 39]
Till All Things become One Great Satan, in Holiness
Oppos'd to Mercy, and the Divine Delusion Jesus be
    no more

Suddenly around Milton on my Path, the Starry
    Seven
Burnd terrible! my Path became a solid fire, as bright
As the clear Sun & Milton silent came down on my
    Path.
And there went forth from the Starry limbs of the
    Seven: Forms
Human; with Trumpets innumerable, sounding
    articulate
As the Seven spake; and they stood in a mighty
    Column of Fire
Surrounding Felphams Vale, reaching to the
    Mundane Shell, Saying

Awake Albion awake! reclaim thy Reasoning Spectre.
    Subdue   10
Him to the Divine Mercy, Cast him down into the
    Lake
Of Los, that ever burneth with fire, ever & ever Amen!
Let the Four Zoa's awake from Slumbers of Six
    Thousand Years

Then loud the Furnaces of Los were heard! & seen as
    Seven Heavens
Stretching from south to north over the mountains of
    Albion

Satan heard; trembling round his Body, he incircled it
He trembled with exceeding great trembling &
    astonishment
Howling in his Spectre round his Body hungring to
    devour
But fearing for the pain for if he touches a Vital,
His torment is unendurable: therefore he cannot
    devour: 20
But howls round it as a lion round his prey
    continually.
Loud Satan thunderd, loud & dark upon mild
    Felphams Shore
Coming in a Cloud with Trumpets & with Fiery Flame
An awful Form eastward from midst of a bright
    Paved-work
Of precious stones by Cherubim surrounded: so
    permitted
(Lest he should fall apart in his Eternal Death) to
    imitate
The Eternal Great Humanity Divine surrounded by
His Cherubim & Seraphim in ever happy Eternity
Beneath sat Chaos: Sin on his right hand Death on
    his left
And Ancient Night spread over all the heavn his
    Mantle of Laws   30
He trembled with exceeding great trembling &
    astonishment

Then Albion rose up in the Night of Beulah on his
    Couch
Of dread repose seen by the visionary eye; his face is
    toward
The east, toward Jerusalems Gates: groaning he sat
    above
His rocks. London & Bath & Legions & Edinburgh
Are the four pillars of his Throne; his left foot near
    London
Covers the shades of Tyburn: his instep from
    Windsor
To Primrose Hill stretching to Highgate & Holloway
London is between his knees: its basements fourfold
His right foot stretches to the sea on Dover cliffs, his
    heel   40
On Canterburys ruins; his right hand covers lofty
    Wales
His left Scotland; his bosom girt with gold involves
York, Edinburgh, Durham & Carlisle & on the front
Bath, Oxford, Cambridge Norwich; his right elbow
Leans on the Rocks of Erins Land, Ireland ancient
    nation[.]
His head bends over London: he sees his embodied
    Spectre
Trembling before him with exceeding great trembling
    & fear
He views Jerusalem & Babylon, his tears flow down
He movd his right foot to Cornwall, his left to the
    Rocks of Bognor
He strove to rise to walk into the Deep. but strength
    failing   50
Forbad & down with dreadful groans he sunk upon
    his Couch
In moony Beulah. Los his strong Guard walks round
    beneath the Moon

Urizen faints in terror striving among the Brooks of
    Arnon
With Miltons Spirit: as the Plowman or Artificer or
    Shepherd
While in the labours of his Calling sends his Thought
    abroad
To labour in the ocean or in the starry heaven. So
    Milton
Labourd in Chasms of the Mundane Shell, tho here
    before
My Cottage midst the Starry Seven, where the Virgin
    Ololon
Stood trembling in the Porch: loud Satan thunder'd
    on the stormy Sea
Circling Albions Cliffs in which the Four-fold World
    resides   60
Tho seen in fallacy outside: a fallacy of Satans
    Churches

[PLATE 40]
Before Ololon Milton stood & percievd the Eternal
    Form
Of that mild Vision; wondrous were their acts by me
    unknown
Except remotely; and I heard Ololon say to Milton

I see thee strive upon the Brooks of Arnon. there a
    dread
And awful Man I see, oercoverd with the mantle of
    years.
I behold Los & Urizen. I behold Orc & Tharmas;
The Four Zoa's of Albion & thy Spirit with them
    striving
In Self annihilation giving thy life to thy enemies
Are those who contemn Religion & seek to annihilate
    it
Become in their Femin[in]e portions the causes &
    promoters   10
Of these Religions, how is this thing? this Newtonian
    Phantasm
This Voltaire & Rousseau: this Hume & Gibbon &
    Bolingbroke[14]
This Natural Religion! this impossible absurdity
Is Ololon the cause of this? O where shall I hide my
    face
These tears fall for the little-ones: the Children of
    Jerusalem
Lest they be annihilated in thy annihilation.

No sooner she had spoke but Rahab Babylon
    appeard
Eastward upon the Paved work across Europe &
    Asia
Glorious as the midday Sun in Satans bosom glowing
A Female hidden in a Male, Religion hidden in War
Namd Moral Virtue; cruel two-fold Monster shining
    bright   21
A Dragon red & hidden Harlot which John in Patmos
    saw

And all beneath the Nations innumerable of Ulro
Appeard, the Seven Kingdoms of Canaan & Five
    Baalim
Of Philistea. into Twelve divided, calld after the
    Names
Of Israel: as they are in Eden. Mountain. River &
    Plain
City & sandy Desart intermingled beyond mortal ken

---

[14] These eighteenth-century English and French scientists,
historians, essayists, and philosophers, according to Blake, teach
the false "natural" religion of deism, which attempts to reconcile
faith to reason.

But turning toward Ololon in terrible majesty
    Milton
Replied. Obey thou the Words of the Inspired Man
All that can be annihilated must be annihilated   30
That the Children of Jerusalem may be saved from
    slavery
There is a Negation, & there is a Contrary
The Negation must be destroyd to redeem the
    Contraries
The Negation is the Spectre; the Reasoning Power in
    Man
This is a false Body: an Incrustation over my
    Immortal
Spirit; a Selfhood, which must be put off &
    annihilated alway
To cleanse the Face of my Spirit by Self-examination.

[PLATE 41]

To bathe in the Waters of Life; to wash off the Not
    Human
I come in Self-annihilation & the grandeur of
    Inspiration
To cast off Rational Demonstration by Faith in the
    Saviour
To cast off the rotten rags of Memory by Inspiration
To cast off Bacon, Locke & Newton from Albions
    covering
To take off his filthy garments, & clothe him with
    Imagination
To cast aside from Poetry, all that is not Inspiration
That it no longer shall dare to mock with the aspersion
    of Madness
Cast on the Inspired, by the tame high finisher of
    paltry Blots,
Indefinite, or paltry Rhymes; or paltry Harmonies. 10
Who creeps into State Government like a catterpiller
    to destroy
To cast off the idiot Questioner who is always
    questioning,
But never capable of answering; who sits with a sly
    grin
Silent plotting when to question, like a thief in a cave;
Who publishes doubt & calls it knowledge; whose
    Science is Despair,
Whose pretence to knowledge is Envy, whose whole
    Science is
To destroy the wisdom of ages to gratify ravenous
    Envy;
That rages round him like a Wolf day & night
    without rest
He smiles with condescension; he talks of
    Benevolence & Virtue
And those who act with Benevolence & Virtue, they
    murder time on time   20

These are the destroyers of Jerusalem, these are the
    murderers
Of Jesus, who deny the Faith & mock at Eternal Life!
Who pretend to Poetry that they may destroy
    Imagination;
By imitation of Natures Images drawn from
    Remembrance
These are the Sexual Garments, the Abomination of
    Desolation
Hiding the Human Lineaments as with an Ark &
    Curtains
Which Jesus rent: & now shall wholly purge away
    with Fire
Till Generation is swallowd up in Regeneration.

Then trembled the Virgin Ololon & replyd in clouds
    of despair

Is this our Femin[in]e Portion the Six-fold Miltonic
    Female   30
Terribly this Portion trembles before thee O awful
    Man
Altho' our Human Power can sustain the severe
    contentions
Of Friendship, our Sexual cannot: but flies into the
    Ulro.
Hence arose all our terrors in Eternity! & now
    remembrance
Returns upon us! are we Contraries O Milton, Thou
    & I
O Immortal! how were we led to War the Wars of
    Death
Is this the Void Outside of Existence, which if
    enter'd into

[PLATE 42]

Becomes a Womb? & is this the Death Couch of
    Albion
Thou goest to Eternal Death & all must go with thee

So saying, the Virgin divided Six-fold & with a shriek
Dolorous that ran thro all Creation a Double Six-fold
    Wonder!
Away from Ololon she divided & fled into the depths
Of Miltons Shadow as a Dove upon the stormy Sea.

Then as a Moony Ark Ololon descended to Felphams
    Vale
In clouds of blood, in streams of gore, with dreadful
    thunderings
Into the Fires of Intellect that rejoic'd in Felphams
    Vale
Around the Starry Eight: with one accord the Starry
    Eight became   10

One Man Jesus the Saviour. wonderful! round his
    limbs
The Clouds of Ololon folded as a Garment dipped in
    blood
Written within & without in woven letters: & the
    Writing
Is the Divine Revelation in the Litteral expression:
A Garment of War, I heard it namd the Woof of Six
    Thousand Years

And I beheld the Twenty-four Cities of Albion
Arise upon their Thrones to Judge the Nations of the
    Earth
And the Immortal Four in whom the Twenty-four
    appear Four-fold
Arose around Albions body: Jesus wept & walked
    forth
From Felphams Vale clothed in Clouds of blood, to
    enter into   20
Albions Bosom, the bosom of death & the Four
    surrounded him
In the Column of Fire in Felphams Vale; then to
    their mouths the Four
Applied their Four Trumpets & them sounded to the
    Four winds

Terror struck in the Vale I stood at that immortal
    sound
My bones trembled. I fell outstretchd upon the path
A moment, & my Soul returnd into its mortal state
To Resurrection & Judgment in the Vegetable Body
And my sweet Shadow of Delight stood trembling by
    my side

Immediately the Lark mounted with a loud trill from
    Felphams Vale
And the Wild Thyme from Wimbletons green &
    impurpled Hills   30
And Los & Enitharmon rose over the Hills of Surrey
Their clouds roll over London with a south wind, soft
    Oothoon
Pants in the Vales of Lambeth weeping oer her
    Human Harvest
Los listens to the Cry of the Poor Man: his Cloud
Over London in volume terrific, low bended in anger.

Rintrah & Palamabron view the Human Harvest
    beneath
Their Wine-presses & Barns stand open; the Ovens
    are prepar'd
The Waggons ready: terrific Lions & Tygers sport &
    play
All Animals upon the Earth, are prepard in all their
    strength

[PLATE 43]
To go forth to the Great Harvest & Vintage of the
    Nations

Finis

[1804–1808]   [1808, 1815]

JERUSALEM

The selection from the latest and longest of the prophetic books,
Jerusalem, *includes all of Chapter I (there are four chapters in
all) and the section called "To the Jews" that intervenes
between Chapters I and II. The whole poem is about four times
the length of this selection. The information in brackets describes
the arrangement of the lines on Blake's original plates, or indicates
restored deletions.*

*Most of the characters and terms in this poem have appeared in
earlier prophecies, especially* The Four Zoas *and* Milton, *and
they are not separately identified here.* Milton *can be considered
Blake's personal epic, celebrating the creative imagination located
within one consciousness, named for a poet both historically real
and spiritually ideal.* Jerusalem, *as a corollary epic, celebrates
universal rather than individual imagination and is named
appropriately for a city that is both real and ideal. In the first
chapter, reprinted here, the fallen Albion confronts the blacksmith-
creator Los. The preface "To the Public" is Blake's argument
for what he hopes the poem will do, rather than what it is about.*

*The epigraph in Greek, "Jesus [was] alone," is most likely
taken from the Gospel story of the Transfiguration: John,
Peter, and James, with Jesus, experience a vision in which
Elias (representing prophecy) and Moses (law) appear, and a
voice out of a cloud says: "This is my beloved son: hear him."
Suddenly the astonished disciples discover that only Jesus is
present. The "last words" of Christ referred to in the canceled
Greek of "To the Public" are those of Jesus at the Ascension:
"All power is given unto me in heaven and earth"* (Matt.
28:18).

F R O M

JERUSALEM
The Emanation of The Giant Albion

1804 Printed by W. Blake S^th Molton S^t.

⊰∘⊙∘⊱

[PLATE 1]

[FRONTISPIECE]

[ABOVE THE ARCHWAY:]

There is a Void, outside of Existence, which if enterd
    into
Englobes itself & becomes a Womb, such was Albions
    Couch
A pleasant Shadow of Repose calld Albions lovely
    Land

His Sublime & Pathos become Two Rocks fixd in the
     Earth
His Reason, his Spectrous Power, covers them above[.]
Jerusalem his Emanation is a Stone laying beneath[.]
O [*Albion behold Pitying*] behold the Vision of Albion

[ON RIGHT SIDE OF ARCHWAY:]

Half Friendship is the bitterest Enmity said Los
As he enterd the Door of Death for Albions sake
     Inspired
The long sufferings of God are not for ever there is a
     Judgment   10

[ON LEFT SIDE, IN REVERSED WRITING:]

Every Thing has its Vermin O Spectre of the Sleeping
     Dead!

———◦◖◉◗◦———

[PLATE 3]

SHEEP   GOATS

TO THE PUBLIC

After my three years slumber on the banks of the
Ocean, I again display my Giant forms to the Public:
My former Giants & Fairies having reciev'd the
highest reward possible: the [*love*] and [*friendship*]
of those with whom to be connected, is to be [*blessed:*]
I cannot doubt that this more consolidated & extended
Work, will be as kindly recieved

     The Enthusiasm of the following Poem, the Author
hopes [*no Reader will think presumptuousness or
arroganc*[*e*] *when he is reminded that the Ancients
entrusted their love to their Writing, to the full as
Enthusiastically as I have who Acknowledge mine for
my Saviour and Lord, for they were wholly absorb'd
in their Gods.*] I also hope the Reader will be with
me, wholly One in Jesus our Lord, who is the God
[*of Fire*] and Lord [*of Love*] to whom the Ancients
look'd and saw his day afar off, with trembling &
amazement.

     The Spirit of Jesus is continual forgiveness of Sin:
he who waits to be righteous before he enters into
the Saviours kingdom, the Divine Body; will never
enter there. I am perhaps the most sinful of men! I
pretend not to holiness! yet I pretend to love, to see,
to converse with daily, as man with man, & the more
to have an interest in the Friend of Sinners. Therefore
[*Dear*] Reader, [*forgive*] what you do not approve, &
[*love*] me for this energetic exertion of my talent.

          Reader! [*lover*] of books! [*lover*] of heaven,
     And of that God from whom [*all books are given,*]
     Who in mysterious Sinais awful cave
     To Man the wond'rous art of writing gave,

Again he speaks in thunder and in fire!
Thunder of Thought, & flames of fierce desire:
Even from the depths of Hell his voice I hear,
Within the unfathomd caverns of my Ear.
Therefore I print; nor vain my types shall be:
Heaven, Earth & Hell, henceforth shall live in
     harmony   10

          Of the Measure, in which
               the following Poem is written

     We who dwell on Earth can do nothing of our-
selves, every thing is conducted by Spirits, no less
than Digestion or Sleep. [*to Note the last words of
Jesus*, Εδοθη μοι πασα εξουσια εν ουρανω και επι
γης]
     When this Verse was first dictated to me I consid-
er'd a Monotonous Cadence like that used by Milton
& Shakspeare & all writers of English Blank Verse,
derived from the modern bondage of Rhyming; to be
a necessary and indispensible part of Verse. But I
soon found that in the mouth of a true Orator such
monotony was not only awkward, but as much a
bondage as rhyme itself. I therefore have produced
a variety in every line, both of cadences & number of
syllables. Every word and every letter is studied and
put into its fit place: the terrific numbers are reserved
for the terrific parts—the mild & gentle, for the mild
& gentle parts, and the prosaic, for inferior parts:
all are necessary to each other. Poetry Fetter'd,
Fetters the Human Race! Nations are Destroy'd, or
Flourish, in proportion as Their Poetry Painting
and Music, are Destroy'd or Flourish! The Primeval
State of Man, was Wisdom, Art, and Science.

———◦◖◉◗◦———

[PLATE 4]

Μονος ὁ Ιεσους

Jerusalem

Chap: 1

     Of the Sleep of Ulro! and of the passage through
Eternal Death! and of the awaking to Eternal Life.

This theme calls me in sleep night after night, &
     ev'ry morn
Awakes me at sun-rise, then I see the Saviour over me
Spreading his beams of love, & dictating the words of
     this mild song.

Awake! awake O sleeper of the land of shadows,
    wake! expand!
I am in you and you in me, mutual in love divine:
Fibres of love from man to man thro Albions pleasant
    land.
In all the dark Atlantic vale down from the hills of
    Surrey
A black water accumulates, return Albion! return!   10
Thy brethren call thee, and thy fathers, and thy
    sons,
Thy nurses and thy mothers, thy sisters and thy
    daughters
Weep at thy souls disease, and the Divine Vision is
    darkend:
Thy Emanation that was wont to play before thy
    face,
Beaming forth with her daughters into the Divine
    bosom [*Where ! !*]
Where hast thou hidden thy Emanation lovely
    Jerusalem
From the vision and fruition of the Holy-one?
I am not a God afar off, I am a brother and friend;
Within your bosoms I reside, and you reside in me:
Lo! we are One; forgiving all Evil; Not seeking
    recompense!   20
Ye are my members O ye sleepers of Beulah, land of
    shades!

But the perturbed Man away turns down the valleys
    dark;
[*Saying. We are not One: we are Many, thou most
    simulative*]
Phantom of the over heated brain! shadow of
    immortality!
Seeking to keep my soul a victim to thy Love! which
    binds
Man the enemy of man into deceitful friendships:
Jerusalem is not! her daughters are indefinite:
By demonstration, man alone can live, and not by
    faith.
My mountains are my own, and I will keep them to
    myself:
The Malvern and the Cheviot, the Wolds Plinlimmon
    & Snowdon   30
Are mine. here will I build my Laws of Moral
    Virtue!
Humanity shall be no more: but war & princedom &
    victory!

So spoke Albion in jealous fears, hiding his Emanation
Upon the Thames and Medway, rivers of Beulah:
    dissembling
His jealousy before the throne divine, darkening,
    cold!

[PLATE 5]

The banks of the Thames are clouded! the ancient
    porches of Albion are
Darken'd! they are drawn thro' unbounded space,
    scatter'd upon
The Void in incoherent despair! Cambridge &
    Oxford & London,
Are driven among the starry Wheels, rent away and
    dissipated,
In Chasms & Abysses of sorrow, enlarg'd without
    dimension, terrible[.]
Albions mountains run with blood, the cries of war &
    of tumult
Resound into the unbounded night, every Human
    perfection
Of mountain & river & city, are small & wither'd &
    darken'd
Cam is a little stream! Ely is almost swallowd up!
Lincoln & Norwich stand trembling on the brink of
    Udan-Adan!   10
Wales and Scotland shrink themselves to the west
    and to the north!
Mourning for fear of the warriors in the Vale of
    Entuthon-Benython
Jerusalem is scatterd abroad like a cloud of smoke
    thro' non-entity:
Moab & Ammon & Amalek & Canaan & Egypt &
    Aram
Recieve her little-ones for sacrifices and the delights
    of cruelty

Trembling I sit day and night, my friends are
    astonish'd at me.
Yet they forgive my wanderings, I rest not from my
    great task!
To open the Eternal Worlds, to open the immortal
    Eyes
Of Man inwards into the Worlds of Thought: into
    Eternity
Ever expanding in the Bosom of God. the Human
    Imagination   20
O Saviour pour upon me thy Spirit of meekness &
    love:
Annihilate the Selfhood in me, be thou all my
    life!
Guide thou my hand which trembles exceedingly
    upon the rock of ages,
While I write of the building of Golgonooza, & of
    the terrors of Entuthon:
Of Hand & Hyle & Coban, of Kwantok, Peachey,
    Brereton, Slayd & Hutton:
Of the terrible sons & daughters of Albion. and their
    Generations.

Scofield! Kox, Kotope and Bowen,[1] revolve most
    mightily upon
The Furnace of Los: before the eastern gate bending
    their fury.
They war, to destroy the Furnaces, to desolate
    Golgonooza:
And to devour the Sleeping Humanity of Albion in
    rage & hunger.   30
They revolve into the Furnaces Southward & are
    driven forth Northward
Divided into Male and Female forms time after time.
From these Twelve all the Families of England
    spread abroad.

The Male is a Furnace of beryll; the Female is a
    golden Loom;
I behold them and their rushing fires overwhelm my
    Soul,
In Londons darkness; and my tears fall day and night,
Upon the Emanations of Albions Sons! the Daughters
    of Albion
Names anciently rememberd, but now contemn'd as
    fictions!
Although in every bosom they controll our Vegetative
    powers.

These are united into Tirzah and her Sisters, on
    Mount Gilead,   40
Cambel & Gwendolen & Conwenna & Cordella &
    Ignoge.
And these united into Rahab in the Covering Cherub
    on Euphrates
Gwiniverra & Gwinefred, & Gonorill & Sabrina
    beautiful,
Estrild, Mehetabel & Ragan, lovely Daughters of
    Albion,
They are the beautiful Emanations of the Twelve
    Sons of Albion

The Starry Wheels revolv'd heavily over the
    Furnaces;
Drawing Jerusalem in anguish of maternal love,
Eastward a pillar of a cloud with Vala upon the
    mountains
Howling in pain, redounding from the arms of
    Beulahs Daughters,   49
Out from the Furnaces of Los above the head of Los.
A pillar of smoke writhing afar into Non-Entity,
    redounding

Till the cloud reaches afar outstretch'd among the
    Starry Wheels
Which revolve heavily in the mighty Void above the
    Furnaces

O what avail the loves & tears of Beulahs lovely
    Daughters
They hold the Immortal Form in gentle bands &
    tender tears
But all within is open'd into the deeps of Entuthon
    Benython
A dark and unknown night, indefinite, unmeasurable,
    without end.
Abstract Philosophy warring in enmity against
    Imagination
(Which is the Divine Body of the Lord Jesus. blessed
    for ever).
And there Jerusalem wanders with Vala upon the
    mountains,   60
Attracted by the revolutions of those Wheels the
    Cloud of smoke
Immense, and Jerusalem & Vala weeping in the
    Cloud
Wander away into the Chaotic Void, lamenting with
    her Shadow
Among the Daughters of Albion, among the Starry
    Wheels;
Lamenting for her children, for the sons & daughters
    of Albion

Los heard her lamentations in the deeps afar! his
    tears fall
Incessant before the Furnaces, and his Emanation
    divided in pain,
Eastward toward the Starry Wheels. But Westward,
    a black Horror,

[PLATE 6]

His spectre[2] driv'n by the Starry Wheels of Albions
    sons, black and
Opake divided from his back; he labours and he
    mourns!

For as his Emanation divided, his Spectre also
    divided
In terror of those starry wheels: and the Spectre
    stood over Los
Howling in pain: a blackning Shadow, blackning
    dark & opake

---

[1] Except for the first three, whose names have the complex etymology of Blake's inventions (e.g., Coban = Bacon, Hyle = Hayley, and the Greek word for "matter"), most of the sons of Albion are persons associated with Blake's trial for sedition, including the accusing soldiers, witnesses, and judges.

[2] As an Emanation is what is loved and created separate from the self, potentially containing an enriching relationship with it, so a Spectre is an unseparated abstraction, inside the self, which frustrates and denies the power of the imagination.

Cursing the terrible Los: bitterly cursing him for his
  friendship
To Albion, suggesting murderous thoughts against
  Albion.

Los rag'd and stamp'd the earth in his might &
  terrible wrath!
He stood and stampd the earth! then he threw down
  his hammer in rage &
In fury: then he sat down and wept, terrified! Then
  arose   10
And chaunted his song, labouring with the tongs and
  hammer:
But still the Spectre divided, and still his pain
  increas'd!
In pain the Spectre divided: in pain of hunger and
  thirst:
To devour Los's Human Perfection, but when he
  saw that Los

[PLATE 7]
Was living: panting like a frighted wolf, and howling
He stood over the Immortal, in the solitude and
  darkness:
Upon the darkning Thames, across the whole Island
  westward.
A horrible Shadow of Death, among the Furnaces:
  beneath
The pillar of folding smoke; and he sought by other
  means,
To lure Los: by tears, by arguments of science & by
  terrors:
Terrors in every Nerve, by spasms & extended pains:
While Los answer'd unterrified to the opake
  blackening Fiend

And thus the Spectre spoke: Wilt thou still go on to
  destruction?
Till thy life is all taken away by this deceitful
  Friendship?   10
He drinks thee up like water! like wine he pours thee
Into his tuns: thy Daughters are trodden in his
  vintage
He makes thy Sons the trampling of his bulls, they
  are plow'd
And harrowd for his profit, lo! thy stolen Emanation
Is his garden of pleasure! all the Spectres of his Sons
  mock thee
Look how they scorn thy once admired palaces! now
  in ruins
Because of Albion! because of deceit and friendship!
  For Lo!
Hand has peopled Babel & Nineveh: Hyle, Ashur &
  Aram:

Cobans son is Nimrod: his son Cush is adjoind to
  Aram,
By the Daughter of Babel, in a woven mantle of
  pestilence & war.   20
They put forth their spectrous cloudy sails; which
  drive their immense
Constellations over the deadly deeps of indefinite
  Udan-Adan[.]
Kox is the Father of Shem & Ham & Japheth, he is
  the Noah
Of the Flood of Udan-Adan. Hut'n is the Father of
  the Seven
From Enoch to Adam; Schofield is Adam who was
  New-
Created in Edom. I saw it indignant, & thou art not
  moved!
This has divided thee in sunder: and wilt thou still
  forgive?
O! thou seest not what I see! what is done in the
  Furnaces.
Listen, I will tell thee what is done in moments to
  thee unknown:
Luvah was cast into the Furnaces of affliction and
  sealed,   30
And Vala fed in cruel delight, the Furnaces with fire:
Stern Urizen beheld; urgd by necessity to keep
The evil day afar, and if perchance with iron power
He might avert his own despair: in woe & fear he saw
Vala incircle round the Furnaces where Luvah was
  clos'd:
With joy she heard his howlings, & forgot he was her
  Luvah,
With whom she liv'd in bliss in times of innocence &
  youth!
Vala comes from the Furnace in a cloud, but wretched
  Luvah
Is howling in the Furnaces, in flames among Albions
  Spectres,
To prepare the Spectre of Albion to reign over thee
  O Los,   40
Forming the Spectres of Albion according to his
  rage:
To prepare the Spectre sons of Adam, who is Scofield:
  the Ninth
Of Albions sons, & the father of all his brethren in the
  Shadowy
Generation. Cambel & Gwendolen wove webs of war
  & of
Religion, to involve all Albions sons, and when they
  had
Involv'd Eight; their webs roll'd outwards into
  darkness
And Scofield the Ninth remain on the outside of the
  Eight

And Kox, Kotope, & Bowen, One in him, a Fourfold
　　Wonder
Involv'd the Eight: Such are the Generations of the
　　Giant Albion,
To separate a Law of Sin, to punish thee in thy
　　members.　　　　　　　　　　　　　　　　50

Los answer'd. Altho' I know not this! I know far
　　worse than this:
I know that Albion hath divided me, and that thou O
　　my Spectre,
Hast just cause to be irritated: but look stedfastly
　　upon me:
Comfort thyself in my strength the time will arrive,
When all Albions injuries shall cease, and when we
　　shall
Embrace him tenfold bright, rising from his tomb in
　　immortality.
They have divided themselves by Wrath. they must
　　be united by
Pity: let us therefore take example & warning O my
　　Spectre,
O that I could abstain from wrath! O that the Lamb
Of God would look upon me and pity me in my fury.
In anguish of regeneration! in terrors of self
　　annihilation:　　　　　　　　　　　　　　　61
Pity must join together those whom wrath has torn in
　　sunder,
And the Religion of Generation which was meant for
　　the destruction
Of Jerusalem, become her covering, till the time of
　　the End.
O holy Generation [*Image*] of regeneration!
O point of mutual forgiveness between Enemies!
Birthplace of the Lamb of God incomprehensible!
The Dead despise & scorn thee, & cast thee out as
　　accursed:
Seeing the Lamb of God in thy gardens & thy palaces:
Where they desire to place the Abomination of
　　Desolation.　　　　　　　　　　　　　　　70
Hand sits before his furnace: scorn of others &
　　furious pride!
Freeze round him to bars of steel & to iron rocks
　　beneath
His feet: indignant self-righteousness like whirlwinds
　　of the north!

[PLATE 8]
Rose up against me thundering from the Brook of
　　Albions River
From Ranelagh & Strumbolo, from Cromwells
　　gardens & Chelsea ³

◇◇◇◇◇◇◇◇◇◇◇◇◇◇◇◇◇◇◇◇◇◇◇◇◇◇◇◇◇◇◇◇◇◇◇◇

³ Areas in London along the Thames, including the hospital
for pensioned veterans still located in Chelsea.

The place of wounded Soldiers. but when he saw my
　　Mace
Whirld round from heaven to earth, trembling he sat:
　　his cold
Poisons rose up: & his sweet deceits coverd them all
　　over
With a tender cloud. As thou art now; such was he O
　　Spectre
I know thy deceit & thy revenges, and unless thou
　　desist
I will certainly create an eternal Hell for thee.
　　Listen!
Be attentive! be obedient! Lo the Furnaces are
　　ready to recieve thee.
I will break thee into shivers! & melt thee in the
　　furnaces of death;　　　　　　　　　　　　10
I will cast thee into forms of abhorrence & torment if
　　thou
Desist not from thine own will, & obey not my stern
　　command!
I am closd up from my children: my Emanation is
　　dividing
And thou my Spectre art divided against me. But
　　mark
I will compell thee to assist me in my terrible labours.
　　To beat
These hypocritic Selfhoods on the Anvils of bitter
　　Death
I am inspired: I act not for myself: for Albions
　　sake
I now am what I am: a horror and an astonishment
Shuddring the heavens to look upon me: Behold
　　what cruelties
Are practised in Babel & Shinar, & have approachd
　　to Zions Hill　　　　　　　　　　　　　　20

While Los spoke, the terrible Spectre fell shuddring
　　before him
Watching his time with glowing eyes to leap upon his
　　prey[.]
Los opend the Furnaces in fear. the Spectre saw to
　　Babel & Shinar
Across all Europe & Asia. he saw the tortures of the
　　Victims.
He saw now from the ou[t]side what he before saw
　　& felt from within
He saw that Los was the sole, uncontrolld Lord of
　　the Furnaces
Groaning he kneeld before Los's iron-shod feet on
　　London Stone,
Hungring & thirsting for Los's life yet pretending
　　obedience.
While Los pursud his speech in threat'nings loud &
　　fierce.

Thou art my Pride & Self-righteousness: I have
   found thee out: 30
Thou art reveald before me in all thy magnitude &
   power
The Uncircumcised pretences to Chastity must be cut
   in sunder!
Thy holy wrath & deep deceit cannot avail against me
Nor shalt thou ever assume the triple-form of Albions
   Spectre
For I am one of the living: dare not to mock my
   inspired fury
If thou wast cast forth from my life! if I was dead
   upon the mountains
Thou mightest be pitied & lovd: but now I am
   living; unless
Thou abstain ravening I will create an eternal Hell
   for thee.
Take thou this Hammer & in patience heave the
   thundering Bellows
Take thou these Tongs: strike thou alternate with
   me: labour obedient[.]   40
Hand & Hyle & Kohan: Skofeld, Kox & Kotope,
   labour mightily[.]
In the Wars of Babel & Shinar, all their Emanations
   were
Condensd. Hand has absorbd all his Brethren in his
   might
All the infant Loves & Graces were lost, for the
   mighty Hand

[PLATE 9]
Condens'd his Emanations into hard opake
   substances;
And his infant thoughts & desires, into cold, dark,
   cliffs of death.
His hammer of gold he siezd; and his anvil of
   adamant.
He siez'd the bars of condens'd thoughts, to forge
   them:
Into the sword of war: into the bow and arrow:
Into the thundering cannon and into the murdering
   gun[.]
I saw the limbs form'd for exercise, contemn'd: &
   the beauty of
Eternity, look'd upon as deformity & loveliness as a
   dry tree:
I saw disease forming a Body of Death around the
   Lamb
Of God, to destroy Jerusalem, & to devour the body
   of Albion   10
By war and stratagem to win the labour of the
   husbandman:
Awkwardness arm'd in steel: folly in a helmet of
   gold:

Weakness with horns & talons: ignorance with a
   rav'ning beak!
Every Emanative joy forbidden as a Crime:
And the Emanations buried alive in the earth with
   pomp of religion:
Inspiration deny'd; Genius forbidden by laws of
   punishment!
I saw terrified; I took the sighs & tears, & bitter
   groans:
I lifted them into my Furnaces; to form the spiritual
   sword.
That lays open the hidden heart: I drew forth the
   pang
Of sorrow red hot: I workd it on my resolute anvil: 20
I heated it in the flames of Hand, & Hyle, & Coban
Nine times; Gwendolen & Cambel & Gwineverra
Are melted into the gold, the silver, the liquid ruby,
The crysolite, the topaz, the jacinth, & every precious
   stone.
Loud roar my Furnaces and loud my hammer is
   heard:
I labour day and night, I behold the soft affections.
Condense beneath my hammer into forms of cruelty
But still I labour in hope, tho' still my tears flow
   down.
That he who will not defend Truth, may be compelld
   to defend
A Lie: that he may be snared and caught and snared
   and taken   30
That Enthusiasm and Life may not cease: arise
   Spectre arise!

Thus they contended among the Furnaces with
   groans & tears;
Groaning the Spectre heavd the bellows, obeying
   Los's frowns;
Till the Spaces of Erin were perfected in the
   furnaces
Of affliction, and Los drew them forth, compelling
   the harsh Spectre.

[PLATE 10]
Into the Furnaces & into the valleys of the Anvils of
   Death
And into the mountains of the Anvils & of the heavy
   Hammers
Till he should bring the Sons & Daughters of
   Jerusalem to be
The Sons & Daughters of Los that he might protect
   them from
Albions dread Spectres; storming, loud, thunderous
   & mighty
The Bellows & the Hammers move compell'd by
   Los's hand.

And this is the manner of the Sons of Albion in their
      strength
They take the Two Contraries which are calld
      Qualities, with which
Every Substance is clothed, they name them Good
      & Evil
From them they make an Abstract, which is a
      Negation   10
Not only of the Substance from which it is derived
A murderer of its own Body: but also a murderer
Of every Divine Member: it is the Reasoning Power
An Abstract objecting power, that Negatives every
      thing
This is the Spectre of Man: the Holy Reasoning
      Power
And in its Holiness is closed the Abomination of
      Desolation

Therefore Los stands in London building Golgonooza
Compelling his Spectre to labours mighty; trembling
      in fear
The Spectre weeps, but Los unmovd by tears or
      threats remains

I must Create a System, or be enslav'd by another
      Mans   20
I will not Reason & Compare: my business is to
      Create

So Los, in fury & strength: in indignation & burning
      wrath
Shuddring the Spectre howls. his howlings terrify the
      night
He stamps around the Anvil, beating blows of stern
      despair
He curses Heaven & Earth, Day & Night & Sun &
      Moon
He curses Forest Spring & River, Desart & sandy
      Waste
Cities & Nations, Families & Peoples, Tongues &
      Laws
Driven to desperation by Los's terrors & threatning
      fears

Los cries, Obey my voice & never deviate from my
      will   29
And I will be merciful to thee: be thou invisible to all
To whom I make thee invisible, but chief to my own
      Children
O Spectre of Urthona: Reason not against their dear
      approach
Nor them obstruct with thy temptations of doubt &
      despair[.]

O Shame O strong & mighty Shame I break thy
      brazen fetters
If thou refuse, thy present torments will seem southern
      breezes
To what thou shalt endure if thou obey not my great
      will.

The Spectre answer'd. Art thou not ashamd of those
      thy Sins
That thou callest thy Children? lo the Law of God
      commands
That they be offered upon his Altar: O cruelty &
      torment
For thine are also mine! I have kept silent hitherto, 40
Concerning my chief delight: but thou hast broken
      silence
Now I will speak my mind! Where is my lovely
      Enitharmon
O thou my enemy, where is my Great Sin? She is also
      thine
I said: now is my grief at worst: incapable of being
Surpassed: but every moment it accumulates more &
      more
It continues accumulating to eternity! the joys of God
      advance
For he is Righteous: he is not a Being of Pity &
      Compassion
He cannot feel Distress: he feeds on Sacrifice &
      Offering:
Delighting in cries & tears & clothed in holiness &
      solitude
But my griefs advance also, for ever & ever without
      end   50
O that I could cease to be! Despair! I am Despair
Created to be the great example of horror & agony:
      also my
Prayer is vain I called for compassion: compassion
      mockd[,]
Mercy & pity threw the grave stone over me & with
      lead
And iron, bound it over me for ever: Life lives on my
Consuming: & the Almighty hath made me his
      Contrary
To be all evil, all reversed & for ever dead: knowing
And seeing life, yet living not; how can I then
      behold
And not tremble; how can I be beheld & not abhorrd

So spoke the Spectre shuddring, & dark tears ran
      down his shadowy face   60
Which Los wiped off, but comfort none could give!
      or beam of hope
Yet ceasd he not from labouring at the roarings of his
      Forge

With iron & brass Building Golgonooza in great
contendings
Till his Sons & Daughters came forth from the
Furnaces
At the sublime Labours for Los. compelld the invisible
Spectre

[PLATE 11]

To labours mighty, with vast strength, with his
mighty chains,
In pulsations of time, & extensions of space, like Urns
of Beulah
With great labour upon his anvils[;] & in his ladles
the Ore
He lifted, pouring it into the clay ground prepar'd
with art;
Striving with Systems to deliver Individuals from
those Systems;
That whenever any Spectre began to devour the
Dead,
He might feel the pain as if a man gnawd his own
tender nerves.

Then Erin came forth from the Furnaces, & all the
Daughters of Beulah
Came from the Furnaces, by Los's mighty power for
Jerusalems
Sake: walking up and down among the Spaces of
Erin: 10
And the Sons and Daughters of Los came forth in
perfection lovely!
And the Spaces of Erin reach'd from the starry
heighth, to the starry depth.

Los wept with exceeding joy & all wept with joy
together!
They feard they never more should see their Father,
who
Was built in from Eternity, in the Cliffs of Albion.

But when the joy of meeting was exhausted in loving
embrace;
Again they lament. O what shall we do for lovely
Jerusalem?
To protect the Emanations of Albions mighty ones
from cruelty?
Sabrina & Ignoge begin to sharpen their beamy spears
Of light and love: their little children stand with
arrows of gold: 20
Ragan is wholly cruel Scofield is bound in iron
armour!
He is like a mandrake in the earth before Reubens
gate:

He shoots beneath Jerusalems walls to undermine
her foundations!
Vala is but thy Shadow, O thou loveliest among
women!
A shadow animated by thy tears O mournful
Jerusalem!

[PLATE 12]

Why wilt thou give to her a Body whose life is but a
Shade?
Her joy and love, a shade: a shade of sweet repose:
But animated and vegetated, she is a devouring
worm:
What shall we do for thee O lovely mild Jerusalem?

And Los said. I behold the finger of God in terrors!
Albion is dead! his Emanation is divided from him!
But I am living! yet I feel my Emanation also
dividing
Such thing was never known! O pity me, thou all-
piteous-one!
What shall I do! or how exist, divided from
Enitharmon?
Yet why despair! I saw the finger of God go forth   10
Upon my Furnaces, from within the Wheels of
Albions Sons:
Fixing their Systems, permanent: by mathematic
power
Giving a body to Falshood that it may be cast off for
ever.
With Demonstrative Science piercing Apollyon with
his own bow!
God is within, & without! he is even in the depths of
Hell!

Such were the lamentations of the Labourers in the
Furnaces!
And they appeard within & without incircling on both
sides
The Starry Wheels of Albions Sons, with Spaces for
Jerusalem:
And for Vala the shadow of Jerusalem: the ever
mourning shade: 19
On both sides, within & without beaming gloriously!

Terrified at the sublime Wonder, Los stood before
his Furnaces.
And they stood around, terrified with admiration at
Erins Spaces
For the Spaces reachd from the starry heighth, to the
starry depth;
And they builded Golgonooza: terrible eternal
labour!

What are those golden builders doing? where was the
    burying-place
Of soft Ethinthus? near Tyburns fatal Tree? is that
Mild Zions hills most ancient promontory; near
    mournful
Ever weeping Paddington? is that Calvary and
    Golgotha?
Becoming a building of pity and compassion? Lo!
The stones are pity, and the bricks, well wrought
    affections: 30
Enameld with love & kindness, & the tiles engraven
    gold
Labour of merciful hands: the beams & rafters are
    forgiveness:
The mortar & cement of the work, tears of honesty:
    the nails,
And the screws & iron braces, are well wrought
    blandishments,
And well contrived words, firm fixing, never forgotten,
Always comforting the remembrance: the floors,
    humility,
The cielings, devotion: the hearths, thanksgiving:
Prepare the furniture O Lambeth in thy pitying
    looms![4]
The curtains, woven tears & sighs, wrought into
    lovely forms
For comfort. there the secret furniture of Jerusalems
    chamber   40
Is wrought: Lambeth! the Bride the Lambs Wife
    loveth thee:
Thou art one with her & knowest not of self in thy
    supreme joy.
Go on, builders in hope: tho Jerusalem wanders far
    away,
Without the gate of Los: among the dark Satanic
    wheels.

Fourfold the Sons of Los in their divisions: and
    fourfold,
The great City of Golgonooza: fourfold toward the
    north
And toward the south fourfold, & fourfold toward the
    east & west
Each within other toward the four points: that
    toward
Eden, and that toward the World of Generation,
And that toward Beulah, and that toward Ulro: 50
Ulro is the space of the terrible starry wheels of
    Albions sons:

4 Lambeth, the borough of south London where Blake lived
while first conceiving his myth as well as the site of the palace of
the Archbishop of Canterbury, here also seems to be used for its
punning association with Christ as the Lamb.

But that toward Eden is walled up, till time of
    renovation:
Yet it is perfect in its building, ornaments & perfection.

And the Four Points are thus beheld in Great Eternity
West, the Circumference: South, the Zenith: North,
The Nadir: East, the Center, unapproachable for
    ever.
These are the four Faces towards the Four Worlds of
    Humanity
In every Man. Ezekiel saw them by Chebars flood.[5]
And the Eyes are the South, and the Nostrils are the
    East.   59
And the Tongue is the West, and the Ear is the North.
And the North Gate of Golgonooza toward
    Generation;
Has four sculpturd Bulls terrible before the Gate of
    iron.
And iron, the Bulls: and that which looks toward
    Ulro,
Clay bak'd & enamel'd, eternal glowing as four
    furnaces:
Turning upon the Wheels of Albions sons with
    enormous power.
And that toward Beulah four, gold, silver, brass, &
    iron:

[PLATE 13]
And that toward Eden, four, form'd of gold, silver,
    brass, & iron.

The South, a golden Gate, has four Lions terrible,
    living!
That toward Generation, four, of iron carv'd
    wondrous:
That toward Ulro, four, clay bak'd, laborious
    workmanship
That toward Eden, four; immortal gold, silver, brass &
    iron.

The Western Gate fourfold, is closd: having four
    Cherubim
Its guards, living, the work of elemental hands,
    laborious task!
Like Men, hermaphroditic, each winged with eight
    wings
That towards Generation, iron; that toward Beulah,
    stone;
That toward Ulro, clay: that toward Eden, metals.   10
But all clos'd up till the last day, when the graves shall
    yield their dead

5 The vision here and in the succeeding lines relies on the
prophecies in Revelation and in Ezekiel.

The Eastern Gate, fourfold: terrible & deadly its
  ornaments:
Taking their forms from the Wheels of Albions sons;
  as cogs
Are formd in a wheel, to fit the cogs of the adverse
  wheel.

That toward Eden, eternal ice, frozen in seven folds
Of forms of death: and that toward Beulah, stone:
The seven diseases of the earth are carved terrible.
And that toward Ulro, forms of war: seven
  enormities:
And that toward Generation, seven generative forms.

And every part of the City is fourfold; & every
  inhabitant, fourfold.   20
And every pot & vessel & garment & utensil of the
  houses,
And every house, fourfold; but the third Gate in
  every one
Is closd as with a threefold curtain of ivory & fine
  linen & ermine.
And Luban stands in middle of the City. a moat of
  fire,
Surrounds Luban, Los's Palace & the golden
  Looms of Cathedron.

And sixty-four thousand Genii, guard the Eastern
  Gate:
And sixty-four thousand Gnomes, guard the
  Northern Gate:
And sixty-four thousand Nymphs, guard the Western
  Gate:
And sixty-four thousand Fairies, guard the Southern
  Gate:

Around Golgonooza lies the land of death eternal; a
  Land   30
Of pain and misery and despair and ever brooding
  melancholy:
In all the Twenty-seven Heavens, numberd from
  Adam to Luther;
From the blue Mundane Shell, reaching to the
  Vegetative Earth.

The Vegetative Universe, opens like a flower from
  the Earths center:
In which is Eternity. It expands in Stars to the
  Mundane Shell
And there it meets Eternity again, both within and
  without,
And the abstract Voids between the Stars are the
  Satanic Wheels.

There is the Cave; the Rock; the Tree; the Lake of
  Udan Adan;
The Forest, and the Marsh, and the Pits of bitumen
  deadly:
The Rocks of solid fire: the Ice valleys: the Plains   40
Of burning sand: the rivers, cataract & Lakes of Fire:
The Islands of the fiery Lakes: the Trees of Malice:
  Revenge:
And black Anxiety; and the Cities of the Salamandrine
  men:[6]
(But whatever is visible to the Generated Man,
Is a Creation of mercy & love, from the Satanic Void.)
The land of darkness flamed but no light, & no repose:
The land of snows of trembling, & of iron hail
  incessant:
The land of earthquakes: and the land of woven
  labyrinths:
The land of snares & traps & wheels & pit-falls & dire
  mills:
The Voids, the Solids, & the land of clouds & regions
  of waters: 50
With their inhabitants: in the Twenty-seven Heavens
  beneath Beulah:
Self-righteousnesses conglomerating against the
  Divine Vision:
A Concave Earth wondrous, Chasmal, Abyssal,
  Incoherent!
Forming the Mundane Shell: above; beneath: on all
  sides surrounding
Golgonooza: Los walks round the walls night and day.

He views the City of Golgonooza, & its smaller Cities:
The Looms & Mills & Prisons & Work-houses of Og
  & Anak:
The Amalekite: the Canaanite: the Moabite: the
  Egyptian:
And all that has existed in the space of six thousand
  years:
Permanent, & not lost not lost nor vanishd, & every
  little act,   60
Word, work, & wish, that has existed, all remaining
  still
In those Churches ever consuming & ever building
  by the Spectres
Of all the inhabitants of Earth wailing to be Created:
Shadowy to those who dwell not in them, meer
  possibilities:
But to those who enter into them they seem the only
  substances
For every thing exists & not one sigh nor smile nor
  tear,

---

[6] An allusion to the mythical salamander who could live in
fire, here used to refer to all men condemned to live in Ulro,
Blake's hell.

[PLATE 14]

One hair nor particle of dust, not one can pass away.

He views the Cherub at the Tree of Life, also the
    Serpent,
Orc the first born coild in the south: the Dragon
    Urizen:
Tharmas the Vegetated Tongue even the Devouring
    Tongue:
A threefold region, a false brain: a false heart:
And false bowels: altogether composing the False
    Tongue,
Beneath Beulah: as a watry flame revolving every way
And as dark roots and stems: a Forest of affliction,
    growing
In seas of sorrow. Los also views the Four Females:
Ahania, and Enion, and Vala, and Enitharmon lovely.
And from them all the lovely beaming Daughters of
    Albion,   11
Ahania & Enion & Vala, are three evanescent shades:
Enitharmon is a vegetated mortal Wife of Los:
His Emanation, yet his Wife till the sleep of Death is
    past.

Such are the Buildings of Los! & such are the Woofs
    of Enitharmon!

And Los beheld his Sons, and he beheld his
    Daughters:
Every one a translucent Wonder: a Universe within,
Increasing inwards, into length and breadth, and
    heighth:
Starry & glorious: and they every one in their bright
    loins:
Have a beautiful golden gate which opens into the
    vegetative world: 20
And every one a gate of rubies & all sorts of precious
    stones
In their translucent hearts, which opens into the
    vegetative world:
And every one a gate of iron dreadful and wonderful,
In their translucent heads, which opens into the
    vegetative world
And every one has the three regions Childhood:
    Manhood: & Age:
But the gate of the tongue: the western gate in them
    is clos'd,
Having a wall builded against it: and thereby the gates
Eastward & Southward & Northward, are incircled
    with flaming fires.
And the North is Breadth, the South is Heighth &
    Depth:
The East is Inwards: & the West is Outwards every
    way.   30

And Los beheld the mild Emanation Jerusalem
    eastward bending
Her revolutions toward the Starry Wheels in maternal
    anguish
Like a pale cloud arising from the arms of Beulahs
    Daughters:
In Entuthon Benythons deep Vales beneath
    Golgonooza.

[PLATE 15]

And Hand & Hyle rooted into Jerusalem by a fibre
Of strong revenge & Skofeld Vegetated by Reubens
    Gate
In every Nation of the Earth till the Twelve Sons of
    Albion
Enrooted into every Nation: a mighty Polypus
    growing
From Albion over the whole Earth: such is my awful
    Vision.

I see the Four-fold Man. The Humanity in deadly
    sleep
And its fallen Emanation. The Spectre & its cruel
    Shadow.
I see the Past, Present & Future, existing all at once
Before me; O Divine Spirit sustain me on thy wings!
That I may awake Albion from his long & cold repose
For Bacon & Newton sheathd in dismal steel, their
    terrors hang   11
Like iron scourges over Albion, Reasonings like vast
    Serpents
Infold around my limbs, bruising my minute
    articulations

I turn my eyes to the Schools & Universities of Europe
And there behold the Loom of Locke whose Woof
    rages dire
Washd by the Water-wheels of Newton. black the cloth
In heavy wreathes folds over every Nation; cruel
    Works
Of many Wheels I view, wheel without wheel, with
    cogs tyrannic
Moving by compulsion each other: not as those in
    Eden: which
Wheel within Wheel in freedom revolve in harmony
    & peace.   20

I see in deadly fear in London Los raging round his
    Anvil
Of death: forming an Ax of gold: the Four Sons of Los
Stand round him cutting the Fibres from Albions hills
That Albions Sons may roll apart over the Nations
While Reuben enroots his brethren in the narrow
    Canaanite

From the Limit Noah to the Limit Abram in whose
    Loins
Reuben in his Twelve-fold majesty & beauty shall
    take refuge
As Abraham flees from Chaldea shaking his goary
    locks
But first Albion must sleep, divided from the Nations

I see Albion sitting upon his Rock in the first Winter
And thence I see the Chaos of Satan & the World of
    Adam   31
When the Divine Hand went forth on Albion in the
    mid Winter
And at the place of Death when Albion sat in Eternal
    Death
Among the Furnaces of Los in the Valley of the Son
    of Hinnom [7]

[PLATE 16]
Hampstead Highgate Finchley Hendon Muswell
    hill: [8] rage loud
Before Bromions iron Tongs & glowing Poker
    reddening fierce
Hertfordshire glows with fierce Vegetation! in the
    Forests
The Oak frowns terrible, the Beech & Ash & Elm
    enroot
Among the Spiritual fires; loud the Corn fields
    thunder along
The Soldiers fife; the Harlots shriek; the Virgins
    dismal groan
The Parents fear: the Brothers jealousy: the Sisters
    curse
Beneath the Storms of Theotormon[;] & the
    thundring Bellows
Heaves in the hand of Palamabron who in Londons
    darkness
Before the Anvil, watches the bellowing flames:
    thundering   10
The Hammer loud rages in Rintrahs strong grasp
    swinging loud
Round from heaven to earth down falling with heavy
    blow
Dead on the Anvil, where the red hot wedge groans in
    pain
He quenches it in the black trough of his Forge:
    Londons River
Feeds the dread Forge, trembling & shuddering along
    the Valleys

⋅⋅⋅⋅⋅⋅⋅⋅⋅⋅⋅⋅⋅⋅⋅⋅⋅⋅⋅

[7] In the valley of the Son of Hinnom (later Ge-Hinnom, then
Gehenna) was Tophet, where children were burned in sacrifice
to Moloch (see Jeremiah).
[8] All suburbs north of London.

Humber & Trent roll dreadful before the Seventh
    Furnace
And Tweed & Tyne anxious give up their Souls for
    Albions sake
Lincolnshire Derbyshire Nottinghamshire
    Leicestershire
From Oxfordshire to Norfolk on the Lake of Udan
    Adan   19
Labour within the Furnaces, walking among the Fires
With Ladles huge & iron Pokers over the Island
    white.

Scotland pours out his Sons to labour at the Furnaces
Wales gives his Daughters to the Looms; England:
    nursing Mothers
Gives to the Children of Albion & to the Children of
    Jerusalem.
From the blue Mundane Shell even to the Earth of
    Vegetation
Throughout the whole Creation which groans to be
    deliverd
Albion groans in the deep slumbers of Death upon his
    Rock.

Here Los fixed down the Fifty-two Counties of
    England & Wales
The Thirty-six of Scotland, & the Thirty-four of
    Ireland
With mighty power, when they fled out at Jerusalems
    Gates   30
Away from the Conflict of Luvah & Urizen, fixing the
    Gates
In the Twelve Counties of Wales & thence Gates
    looking every way
To the Four Points: conduct to England & Scotland
    & Ireland
And thence to all the Kingdoms & Nations &
    Families of the Earth[.]
The Gate of Reuben in Carmarthenshire: the Gate of
    Simeon in
Cardiganshire: & the Gate of Levi in
    Montgomeryshire
The Gate of Judah Merionethshire: the Gate of Dan
    Flintshire
The Gate of Napthali, Radnorshire: the Gate of Gad
    Pembrokeshire
The Gate of Asher, Carnarvonshire the Gate of
    Issachar Brecknokshire
The Gate of Zebulun, Anglesea & Sodor. so is
    Wales divided.   40
The Gate of Joseph, Denbighshire: the Gate of
    Benjamin Glamorganshire
For the protection of the Twelve Emanations of
    Albions Sons

And the Forty Counties of England are thus divided
    in the Gates
Of Reuben Norfolk, Suffolk, Essex. Simeon Lincoln,
    York Lancashire
Levi. Middlesex Kent Surrey. Judah Somerset
    Glouster Wiltshire.
Dan. Cornwal Devon Dorset, Napthali. Warwick
    Leicester Worcester
Gad. Oxford Bucks Harford. Asher, Sussex
    Hampshire Berkshire
Issachar, Northampton Rutland Nottgham. Zebulun
    Bedford Huntgn Camb
Joseph Stafford Shrops Heref. Benjamin, Derby
    Cheshire Monmouth;
And Cumberland Northumberland Westmoreland
    & Durham are   50
Divided in the Gates of Reuben, Dan & Joseph

And the Thirty-six Counties of Scotland, divided in
    the Gates
Of Reuben Kincard Haddntn Forfar, Simeon Ayr
    Argyll Banff
Levi Edinburh Roxbro Ross. Judah, Abrdeen Berwik
    Dumfries
Dan Bute Caitnes Clakmanan. Napthali Nairn
    Invernes Linlithgo
Gad Peebles Perth Renfru. Asher Sutherlan Sterling
    Wigtoun
Issachar Selkirk Dumbartn Glasgo. Zebulun Orkney
    Shetland Skye
Joseph Elgin Lanerk Kinros. Benjamin Kromarty
    Murra Kirkubriht
Governing all by the sweet delights of secret amorous
    glances
In Enitharmons Halls builded by Los & his mighty
    Children⁹   60

All things acted on Earth are seen in the bright
    Sculptures of
Los's Halls & every Age renews its powers from these
    Works
With every pathetic story possible to happen from
    Hate or
Wayward Love & every sorrow & distress is carved
    here
Every Affinity of Parents Marriages & Friendships
    are here
In all their various combinations wrought with
    wondrous Art
All that can happen to Man in his pilgrimage of
    seventy years

⬦⬦⬦⬦⬦⬦⬦⬦⬦⬦⬦⬦⬦⬦⬦⬦⬦⬦⬦⬦⬦⬦

⁹ All of the 122 counties of England, Scotland, and Ireland are
assigned to corresponding Israelite tribes.

Such is the Divine Written Law of Horeb & Sinai:
And such the Holy Gospel of Mount Olivet &
    Calvary:

[PLATE 17]
His Spectre divides & Los in fury compells it to
    divide:
To labour in the fire, in the water, in the earth, in the
    air,
To follow the Daughters of Albion as the hound
    follows the scent
Of the wild inhabitant of the forest, to drive them
    from his own:
To make a way for the Children of Los to come from
    the Furnaces
But Los himself against Albions Sons his fury bends,
    for he
Dare not approach the Daughters openly lest he be
    consumed
In the fires of their beauty & perfection & be
    Vegetated beneath
Their Looms, in a Generation of death & resurrection
    to forgetfulness
They wooe Los continually to subdue his strength:
    he continually   10
Shews them his Spectre: sending him abroad over the
    four points of heaven
In the fierce desires of beauty & in the tortures of
    repulse! He is
The Spectre of the Living pursuing the Emanations
    of the Dead.
Shuddring they flee: they hide in the Druid Temples
    in cold chastity:
Subdued by the Spectre of the Living & terrified by
    undisguisd desire.

For Los said: Tho my Spectre is divided: as I am a
    Living Man
I must compell him to obey me wholly: that
    Enitharmon may not
Be lost: & lest he should devour Enitharmon: Ah me!
Piteous image of my soft desires & loves: O
    Enitharmon!
I will compell my Spectre to obey: I will restore to
    thee thy Children.   20
No one bruises or starves himself to make himself fit
    for labour!

Tormented with sweet desire for these beauties of
    Albion
They would never love my power if they did not seek
    to destroy
Enitharmon: Vala would never have sought & loved
    Albion

If she had not sought to destroy Jerusalem; such is
    that false
And Generating Love: a pretence of love to destroy
    love:
Cruel hipocrisy unlike the lovely delusions of Beulah:
And cruel forms, unlike the merciful forms of Beulahs
    Night

They know not why they love nor wherefore they
    sicken & die
Calling that Holy Love: which is Envy Revenge &
    Cruelty   30
Which separated the stars from the mountains: the
    mountains from Man
And left Man, a little grovelling Root, outside of
    Himself.
Negations are not Contraries: Contraries mutually
    Exist:
But Negations Exist Not: Exceptions & Objections
    & Unbeliefs
Exist not: nor shall they ever be Organized for ever &
    ever:
If thou separate from me, thou art a Negation: a meer
Reasoning & Derogation from me, an Objecting &
    cruel Spite
And Malice & Envy: but my Emanation, Alas! will
    become
My Contrary: O thou Negation, I will continually
    compell   39
Thee to be invisible to any but whom I please, &
    when
And where & how I please, and never! never! shalt
    thou be Organized
But as a distorted & reversed Reflexion in the
    Darkness
And in the Non Entity: nor shall that which is above
Ever descend into thee: but thou shalt be a Non
    Entity for ever
And if any enter into thee, thou shalt be an
    Unquenchable Fire
And he shall be a never dying Worm, mutually
    tormented by
Those that thou tormentest, a Hell & Despair for ever
    & ever.

So Los in secret with himself communed &
    Enitharmon heard
In her darkness & was comforted: yet still she divided
    away
In gnawing pain from Los's bosom in the deadly
    Night;   50
First as a red Globe of blood trembling beneath his
    bosom[.]

Suspended over her he hung: he infolded her in his
    garments
Of wool: he hid her from the Spectre, in shame &
    confusion of
Face; in terrors & pains of Hell & Eternal Death, the
Trembling Globe shot forth Self-living & Los howld
    over it:
Feeding it with his groans & tears day & night
    without ceasing:
And the Spectrous Darkness from his back divided
    in temptations,
And in grinding agonies in threats! stiflings! &
    direful strugglings.

Go thou to Skofield: ask him if he is Bath or if he is
    Canterbury [10]
Tell him to be no more dubious: demand explicit
    words   60
Tell him: I will dash him into shivers, where & at
    what time
I please: tell Hand & Skofield they are my ministers
    of evil
To those I hate: for I can hate also as well as they!

[PLATE 18]
From every-one of the Four Regions of Human
    Majesty,
There is an Outside spread Without, & an Outside
    spread Within
Beyond the Outline of Identity both ways, which
    meet in One:
An orbed Void of doubt, despair, hunger, & thirst &
    sorrow.
Here the Twelve Sons of Albion, join'd in dark
    Assembly,
Jealous of Jerusalems children, asham'd of her
    little-ones
(For Vala produc'd the Bodies. Jerusalem gave the
    Souls)
Became as Three Immense Wheels, turning upon
    one-another
Into Non-Entity, and their thunders hoarse appall
    the Dead
To murder their own Souls, to build a Kingdom
    among the Dead[:]   10

Cast! Cast ye Jerusalem forth! The Shadow of
    delusions!
The Harlot daughter! Mother of pity and
    dishonourable forgiveness
Our Father Albions sin and shame! But father now
    no more!

[10] I.e., ask if his power to repress life comes from his associa-
tion with the Established Church.

Nor sons! nor hateful peace & love, nor soft
    complacencies
With transgressors meeting in brotherhood around
    the table,
Or in the porch or garden. No more the sinful
    delights
Of age and youth and boy and girl and animal and
    herb,
And river and mountain, and city & village, and
    house & family.
Beneath the Oak & Palm, beneath the Vine and
    Fig-tree.
In self-denial!—But War and deadly contention,
    Between   20
Father and Son, and light and love! All bold asperities
Of Haters met in deadly strife, rending the house &
    garden
The unforgiving porches, the tables of enmity, and
    beds
And chambers of trembling & suspition, hatreds of age
    & youth
And boy & girl, & animal & herb, & river & mountain
And city & village, and house & family. That the
    Perfect,
May live in glory, redeem'd by Sacrifice of the Lamb
And of his children, before sinful Jerusalem. To build
Babylon the City of Vala, the Goddess Virgin-
    Mother.
She is our Mother! Nature! Jerusalem is our
    Harlot-Sister   30
Return'd with Children of pollution, to defile our
    House,
With Sin and Shame. Cast! Cast her into the Potters
    field.
Her little-ones, She must slay upon our Altars: and
    her aged
Parents must be carried into captivity, to redeem her
    Soul
To be for a Shame & a Curse, and to be our Slaves for
    ever

So cry Hand & Hyle the eldest of the fathers of
    Albions
Little-ones; to destroy the Divine Saviour; the Friend
    of Sinners,
Building Castles in desolated places, and strong
    Fortifications.
Soon Hand mightily devour'd & absorb'd Albions
    Twelve Sons.
Out from his bosom a mighty Polypus, vegetating in
    darkness,   40
And Hyle & Coban were his two chosen ones, for
    Emissaries
In War: forth from his bosom they went and return'd.

Like Wheels from a great Wheel reflected in the Deep
Hoarse turn'd the Starry Wheels, rending a way in
    Albions Loins
Beyond the Night of Beulah. In a dark & unknown
    Night,
Outstretch'd his Giant beauty on the ground in pain
    & tears:

[PLATE 19]
His Children exil'd from his breast pass to and fro
    before him
His birds are silent on his hills, flocks die beneath his
    branches
His tents are fall'n! his trumpets, and the sweet sound
    of his harp
Are silent on his clouded hills, that belch forth storms
    & fire.
His milk of Cows, & honey of Bees, & fruit of golden
    harvest,
Is gather'd in the scorching heat, & in the driving
    rain:
Where once he sat he weary walks in misery and pain:
His Giant beauty and perfection fallen into dust:
Till from within his witherd breast grown narrow
    with his woes:
The corn is turn'd to thistles & the apples into
    poison: 10
The birds of song to murderous crows, his joys to
    bitter groans!
 * The voices of children in his tents, to cries of helpless
    infants!
And self-exiled from the face of light & shine of
    morning,
In the dark world a narrow house! he wanders up and
    down,
Seeking for rest and finding none! and hidden far
    within,
His Eon weeping in the cold and desolated Earth.

All his Affections now appear withoutside: all his
    Sons,
Hand, Hyle & Coban, Guantok, Peachey, Brereton,
    Slayd & Hutton,
Scofeld, Kox, Kotope & Bowen; his Twelve Sons:
    Satanic Mill!
Who are the Spectres of the Twentyfour, each
    Double-form'd: 20
Revolve upon his mountains groaning in pain:
    beneath
The dark incessant sky, seeking for rest and finding
    none: ·
Raging against their Human natures, ravning to
    gormandize
The Human majesty and beauty of the Twentyfour.

Condensing them into solid rocks and with cruelty
    and abhorrence
Suspition & revenge, & the seven diseases of the Soul
Settled around Albion and around Luvah in his
    secret cloud[.]
Willing the Friends endur'd, for Albions sake, and for
Jerusalem his Emanation shut within his bosom;
Which hardend against them more and more; as he
    builded onwards   30
On the Gulph of Death in self-righteousness, that
    roll'd
Before his awful feet, in pride of virtue for victory:
And Los was roofd in from Eternity in Albions Cliffs
Which stand upon the ends of Beulah, and
    withoutside, all
Appear'd a rocky form against the Divine Humanity.

Albions Circumference was clos'd: his Center began
    darkning
Into the Night of Beulah, and the Moon of Beulah
    rose
Clouded with storms: Los his strong Guard walkd
    round beneath the Moon
And Albion fled inward among the currents of his
    rivers.

He found Jerusalem upon the River of his City soft
    respos'd   40
In the arms of Vala, assimilating in one with Vala
The Lilly of Havilah: and they sang soft thro'
    Lambeths vales,
In a sweet moony night & silence that they had
    created
With a blue sky spread over with wings and a mild
    moon,
Dividing & uniting into many female forms:
    Jerusalem
Trembling! then in one comingling in eternal tears,
Sighing to melt his Giant beauty, on the moony river.

[PLATE 20]
But when they saw Albion fall'n upon mild Lambeths
    vale:
Astonish'd! Terrified! they hover'd over his Giant
    limbs.
Then thus Jerusalem spoke, while Vala wove the
    veil of tears:
Weeping in pleadings of Love, in the web of despair.

Wherefore hast thou shut me into the winter of human
    life
And clos'd up the sweet regions of youth and virgin
    innocence:

Where we live, forgetting error, not pondering on evil:
Among my lambs & brooks of water, among my
    warbling birds:
Where we delight in innocence before the face of the
    Lamb:
Going in and out before him in his love and sweet
    affection.   10

Vala replied weeping & trembling, hiding in her veil.

When winter rends the hungry family and the snow
    falls:
Upon the ways of men hiding the paths of man and
    beast,
Then mourns the wanderer: then he repents his
    wanderings & eyes
The distant forest; then the slave groans in the
    dungeon of stone.
The captive in the mill of the stranger, sold for scanty
    hire.
They view their former life: they number moments
    over and over;
Stringing them on their remembrance as on a thread
    of sorrow.
Thou art my sister and my daughter! thy shame is
    mine also!   19
Ask me not of my griefs! thou knowest all my griefs.

Jerusalem answer'd with soft tears over the valleys.

O Vala what is Sin? that thou shudderest and weepest
At sight of thy once lov'd Jerusalem! What is Sin
    but a little
Error & fault that is soon forgiven; but mercy is not a
    Sin
Nor pity nor love nor kind forgiveness! O! if I have
    Sinned
Forgive & pity me! O! unfold thy Veil in mercy &
    love!
Slay not my little ones, beloved Virgin daughter of
    Babylon
Slay not my infant loves & graces, beautiful daughter
    of Moab
I cannot put off the human form I strive but strive in
    vain
When Albion rent thy beautiful net of gold and silver
    twine;   30
Thou hadst woven it with art, thou hadst caught me
    in the bands
Of love; thou refusedst to let me go: Albion beheld
    thy beauty
Beautiful thro' our Love's comeliness, beautiful thro'
    pity.

The Veil shone with thy brightness in the eyes of
    Albion,
Because it inclosd·pity & love; because we lov'd
    one-another!
Albion lov'd thee! he rent thy Veil! he embrac'd thee!
    he lov'd thee!
Astonish'd at his beauty & perfection, thou forgavest
    his furious love:
I redounded from Albions bosom in my virgin
    loveliness.
The Lamb of God receiv'd me in his arms he smil'd
    upon us: 39
He made me his Bride & Wife: he gave thee to Albion
Then was a time of love: O why is it passed away!

Then Albion broke silence and with groans reply'd

[PLATE 21]
O Vala! O Jerusalem! do you delight in my groans
You O lovely forms, you have prepared my
    death-cup:
The disease of Shame covers me from head to feet: I
    have no hope
Every boil upon my body is a separate & deadly Sin.[11]
Doubt first assailed me, then Shame took possession
    of me
Shame divides Families. Shame hath divided Albion
    in sunder!
First fled my Sons, & then my Daughters, then my
    Wild Animations
My Cattle next, last ev'n the Dog of my Gate. the
    Forests fled
The Corn-fields, & the breathing Gardens outside
    separated
The Sea; the Stars: the Sun: the Moon: drivn forth
    by my disease   10
All is Eternal Death unless you can weave a chaste
Body over an unchaste Mind! Vala! O that thou
    wert pure!
That the deep wound of Sin might be clos'd up with
    the Needle,
And with the Loom: to cover Gwendolen & Ragan
    with costly Robes
Of Natural Virtue[,] for their Spiritual forms without
    a Veil
Wither in Luvahs Sepulcher. I thrust him from my
    presence
And all my Children followd his loud howlings into
    the Deep.
Jerusalem! dissembler Jerusalem! I look into thy
    bosom:

I discover thy secret places: Cordella! I behold
Thee whom I thought pure as the heavens in
    innocence & fear: 20
Thy Tabernacle taken down, thy secret Cherubim
    disclosed
Art thou broken? Ah me Sabrina, running by my
    side:
In childhood what wert thou? unutterable anguish!
    Conwenna
Thy cradled infancy is most piteous. O hide, O hide!
Their secret gardens were made paths to the traveller:
I knew not of their secret loves with those I hated most,
Nor that their every thought was Sin & secret
    appetite[.]
Hyle sees in fear, he howls in fury over them, Hand
    sees
In jealous fear: in stern accusation with cruel stripes
He drives them thro' the Streets of Babylon before
    my face: 30
Because they taught Luvah to rise into my clouded
    heavens
Battersea and Chelsea mourn for Cambel &
    Gwendolen!
Hackney and Holloway sicken for Estrild & Ignoge!
Because the Peak, Malvern & Cheviot Reason in
    Cruelty
Penmaenmawr & Dhinas-bran Demonstrate in
    Unbelief
Manchester & Liverpool are in tortures of Doubt &
    Despair
Malden & Colchester Demonstrate: I hear my
    Childrens voices
I see their piteous faces gleam out upon the cruel
    winds
From Lincoln & Norwich, from Edinburgh &
    Monmouth:[12]
I see them distant from my bosom scourgd along the
    roads   40
Then lost in clouds; I hear their tender voices! clouds
    divide
I see them die beneath the whips of the Captains!
    they are taken
In solemn pomp into Chaldea across the bredths of
    Europe
Six months they lie embalmd in silent death:
    worshipped
Carried in Arks of Oak before the armies in the spring
Bursting their Arks they rise again to life: they play
    before
The Armies: I hear their loud cymbals & their deadly
    cries

---

[11] The parallel plights of Albion and Job, implicit throughout
the chapter, are here made explicit.

[12] Albion mourns his daughters in terms of the geography of
London boroughs, England, and Wales.

Are the Dead cruel? are those who are infolded in
    moral Law
Revengeful? O that Death & Annihilation were the
    same!

Then Vala answerd spreading her scarlet Veil over
    Albion   50

[PLATE 22]

Albion thy fear has made me tremble; thy terrors
    have surrounded me
Thy Sons have naild me on the Gates piercing my
    hands & feet:
Till Skofields Nimrod the mighty Huntsman Jehovah
    came,[13]
With Cush his Son & took me down. He in a golden
    Ark,
Bears me before his Armies tho my shadow hovers here
The flesh of multitudes fed & nourisd me in my
    childhood
My morn & evening food were prepard in Battles of
    Men
Great is the cry of the Hounds of Nimrod along the
    Valley
Of Vision, they scent the odor of War in the Valley of
    Vision.
All Love is lost! terror succeeds & Hatred instead of
    Love   10
And stern demands of Right & Duty instead of
    Liberty
Once thou wast to me the loveliest Son of heaven; but
    now
Where shall I hide from thy dread countenance &
    searching eyes
I have looked into the secret Soul of him I loved
And in the dark recesses found Sin & can never return.

Albion again utterd his voice beneath the silent Moon

I brought Love into light of day to pride in chaste
    beauty
I brought Love into light & fancied Innocence is no
    more

Then spoke Jerusalem O Albion! my Father Albion
Why wilt thou number every little fibre of my Soul
Spreading them out before the Sun like stalks of flax
    to dry?   21
The Infant Joy is beautiful, but its anatomy
Horrible ghast & deadly! nought shalt thou find in it
But dark despair & everlasting brooding melancholy!

◇◇◇◇◇◇◇◇◇◇◇◇◇◇◇◇◇◇◇

[13] In Vala's version of a warlike religion, Noah's great grand-
son Nimrod (" the mighty hunter ") is Jehovah.

Then Albion turnd his face toward Jerusalem & spoke

Hide thou Jerusalem in impalpable voidness, not to be
Touched by the hand nor seen with the eye: O
    Jerusalem
Would thou wert not & that thy place might never be
    found
But come O Vala with knife & cup: drain my blood
To the last drop! then hide me in thy Scarlet
    Tabernacle   30
For I see Luvah whom I slew. I behold him in my
    Spectre
As I behold Jerusalem in thee O Vala dark and cold

Jerusalem then stretchd her hand toward the Moon &
    spoke

Why should Punishment Weave the Veil with Iron
    Wheels of War
When Forgiveness might it Weave with Wings of
    Cherubim

Loud groand Albion from mountain to mountain &
    replied

[PLATE 23]
Jerusalem! Jerusalem! deluding shadow of Albion!
Daughter of my phantasy! unlawful pleasure!
    Albions curse!
I came here with intention to annihilate thee! But
My soul is melted away, inwoven within the Veil
Hast thou again knitted the Veil of Vala, which I for
    thee
Pitying rent in ancient times. I see it whole and more
Perfect, and shining with beauty! But thou! O
    wretched Father!

Jerusalem reply'd, like a voice heard from a sepulcher:
Father! once piteous! Is Pity a Sin? Embalm'd in
    Vala's bosom
In an Eternal Death for Albions sake, our best
    beloved.   10
Thou art my Father & my Brother: Why hast thou
    hidden me,
Remote from the divine Vision: my Lord and Saviour.

Trembling stood Albion at her words in jealous dark
    despair:
He felt that Love and Pity are the same; a soft
    repose!
Inward complacency of Soul: a Self-annihilation!
I have erred! I am ashamed! and will never return
    more:

I have taught my children sacrifices of cruelty:
 what shall I answer?
I will hide it from Eternals! I will give myself for my
 Children!
Which way soever I turn, I behold Humanity and Pity!

He recoil'd: he rush'd outwards; he bore the Veil
 whole away   20
His fires redound from his Dragon Altars in Errors
 returning.
He drew the Veil of Moral Virtue, woven for Cruel
 Laws,
And cast it into the Atlantic Deep, to catch the Souls
 of the Dead.
He stood between the Palm tree & the Oak of weeping
Which stand upon the edge of Beulah; and there
 Albion sunk
Down in sick pallid languor! These were his last
 words, relapsing!
Hoarse from his rocks, from caverns of Derbyshire &
 Wales
And Scotland, utter'd from the Circumference into
 Eternity.

Blasphemous Sons of Feminine delusion! God in the
 dreary Void
Dwells from Eternity, wide separated from the
 Human Soul   30
But thou deluding Image by whom imbu'd the Veil I
 rent
Lo here is Valas Veil whole, for a Law, a Terror & a
 Curse!
And therefore God takes vengeance on me: from my
 clay-cold bosom
My children wander trembling victims of his Moral
 Justice.
His snows fall on me and cover me, while in the Veil
 I fold
My dying limbs. Therefore O Manhood, if thou art
 aught
But a meer Phantasy, hear dying Albions Curse!
May God who dwells in this dark Ulro & voidness,
 vengeance take,
And draw thee down into this Abyss of sorrow and
 torture,
Like me thy Victim. O that Death & Annihilation
 were the same!   40

[PLATE 24]
What have I said? What have I done? O all-powerful
 Human Words!
You recoil back upon me in the blood of the Lamb
 slain in his Children.

Two bleeding Contraries equally true, are his
 Witnesses against me
We reared mighty Stones: we danced naked around
 them:
Thinking to bring Love into light of day, to
 Jerusalems shame:
Displaying our Giant limbs to all the winds of
 heaven! Sudden
Shame siezd us, we could not look on one-another for
 abhorrence: the Blue
Of our immortal Veins & all their Hosts fled from our
 Limbs,
And wanderd distant in a dismal Night clouded &
 dark:
The Sun fled from the Britons forehead: the Moon
 from his mighty loins: 10
Scandinavia fled with all his mountains filld with
 groans.

O what is Life & what is Man. O what is Death?
 Wherefore
Are you my Children, natives in the Grave to where I
 go
Or are you born to feed the hungry ravenings of
 Destruction
To be the sport of Accident! to waste in Wrath &
 Love, a weary
Life, in brooding cares & anxious labours, that prove
 but chaff.
O Jerusalem Jerusalem I have forsaken thy
 Courts
Thy Pillars of ivory & gold: thy Curtains of silk &
 fine
Linen: thy Pavements of precious stones: thy Walls
 of pearl
And gold, thy Gates of Thanksgiving thy Windows of
 Praise: 20
Thy Clouds of Blessing; thy Cherubims of Tender-
 mercy
Stretching their Wings sublime over the Little-ones
 Of Albion[.]
O Human Imagination O Divine Body I have
 Crucified
I have turned my back upon thee into the Wastes of
 Moral Law:
There Babylon is builded in the Waste, founded in
 Human desolation.
O Babylon thy Watchman stands over thee in the
 night
Thy severe Judge all the day long proves thee O
 Babylon
With provings of destruction, with giving thee thy
 hearts desire.

But Albion is cast forth to the Potter his Children to
    the Builders
To build Babylon because they have forsaken
    Jerusalem   30
The Walls of Babylon are Souls of Men: her Gates
    the Groans
Of Nations: her Towers are the Miseries of once
    happy Families.
Her Streets are paved with Destruction, her Houses
    built with Death
Her Palaces with Hell & the Grave; her Synagogues
    with Torments
Of ever-hardening Despair squared & polishd with
    cruel skill
Yet thou wast lovely as the summer cloud upon my
    hills
When Jerusalem was thy hearts desire in times of
    youth & love.
Thy Sons came to Jerusalem with gifts, she sent them
    away
With blessings on their hands & on their feet,
    blessings of gold,
And pearl & diamond: thy Daughters sang in her
    Courts: 40
They came up to Jerusalem; they walked before
    Albion
In the Exchanges of London every Nation walkd
And London walkd in every Nation mutual in love &
    harmony
Albion coverd the whole Earth, England encompassd
    the Nations,
Mutual each within others bosom in Visions of
    Regeneration;
Jerusalem coverd the Atlantic Mountains & the
    Erythrean,
From bright Japan & China to Hesperia France &
    England.
Mount Zion lifted his head in every Nation under
    heaven:
And the Mount of Olives was beheld over the whole
    Earth:
The footsteps of the Lamb of God were there: but
    now no more   50
No more shall I behold him, he is closd in Luvahs
    Sepulcher.
Yet why these smitings of Luvah, the gentlest mildest
    Zoa?
If God was Merciful this could not be: O Lamb of
    God
Thou art a delusion and Jerusalem is my Sin! O my
    Children
I have educated you in the crucifying cruelties of
    Demonstration

Till you have assum'd the Providence of God &
    slain your Father
Dost thou appear before me who liest dead in Luvahs
    Sepulcher
Dost thou forgive me! thou who wast Dead & art
    Alive?
Look not so merciful upon me O thou Slain Lamb of
    God
I die! I die in thy arms tho Hope is banishd from me.
Thundring the Veil rushes from his hand Vegetating
    Knot by   61
Knot, Day by Day, Night by Night; loud roll the
    indignant Atlantic
Waves & the Erythrean, turning up the bottoms of the
    Deeps

[PLATE 25]

And there was heard a great lamenting in Beulah: all
    the Regions
Of Beulah were moved as the tender bowels are
    moved: & they said:

Why did you take Vengeance O ye Sons of the
    mighty Albion?
Planting these Oaken Groves: Erecting these Dragon
    Temples
Injury the Lord heals but Vengeance cannot be
    healed:
As the Sons of Albion have done to Luvah: so they
    have in him
Done to the Divine Lord & Saviour, who suffers with
    those that suffer:
For not one sparrow can suffer, & the whole Universe
    not suffer also,
In all its Regions, & its Father & Saviour not pity and
    weep.
But Vengeance is the destroyer of Grace &
    Repentance in the bosom   10
Of the Injurer: in which the Divine Lamb is cruelly
    slain:
Descend O Lamb of God & take away the imputation
    of Sin
By the Creation of States & the deliverance of
    Individuals Evermore Amen

Thus wept they in Beulah over the Four Regions of
    Albion
But many doubted & despaird & imputed Sin &
    Righteousness
To Individuals & not to States, and these Slept in
    Ulro.[14]

---

[14] At this point Albion accepts his fallen state, and is in the
condition announced at the opening of the poem.

[PLATE 26]

SUCH VISIONS HAVE APPEARD TO ME
AS I MY ORDERD RACE HAVE RUN
JERUSALEM IS NAMED LIBERTY
AMONG THE SONS OF ALBION

[PLATE 27]

To the JEWS.

Jerusalem the Emanation of the Giant Albion! Can
it be? Is it a Truth that the Learned have explored?
Was Britain the Primitive Seat of the Patriarchal
Religion? It if is true: my title-page is also True, that
Jerusalem was & is the Emanation of the Giant
Albion. It is True, and cannot be controverted. Ye
are united O ye Inhabitants of Earth in One Religion.
The Religion of Jesus: the most Ancient, the Eternal:
& the Everlasting Gospel—The Wicked will turn it
to Wickedness, the Righteous to Righteousness.
Amen! Huzza! Selah![15]
"All things Begin & End in Albions Ancient
Druid Rocky Shore."

Your Ancestors derived their origin from Abraham,
Heber, Shem, and Noah, who were Druids: as the
Druid Temples (which are the Patriarchal Pillars &
Oak Groves) over the whole Earth witness to this
day.
You have a tradition, that Man anciently contain'd
in his mighty limbs all things in Heaven & Earth:
this you received from the Druids. "But now the
Starry Heavens are fled from the mighty limbs of
Albion"

Albion was the Parent of the Druids; & in his
Chaotic State of Sleep[,] Satan & Adam & the whole
World was Created by the Elohim.[16]

The fields from Islington to Marybone,
To Primrose Hill and Saint Johns Wood:
    Were builded over with pillars of gold,
And there Jerusalems pillars stood.

    Her Little-ones ran on the fields
The Lamb of God among them seen
    And fair Jerusalem his Bride:
Among the little meadows green.

Pancrass & Kentish-town repose
Among her golden pillars high: 10
    Among her golden arches which
Shine upon the starry sky.

    The Jews-harp-house & the Green Man;
The Ponds where Boys to bathe delight:
    The fields of Cows by Willans farm:
Shine in Jerusalems pleasant sight.

    She walks upon our meadows green:
The Lamb of God walks by her side:
    And every English Child is seen,
Children of Jesus & his Bride,   20

    Forgiving trespasses and sins
Lest Babylon with cruel Og,
    With Moral & Self-righteous Law
Should Crucify in Satans Synagogue!

    What are those golden Builders doing
Near mournful ever-weeping Paddington
    Standing above that mighty Ruin
Where Satan the first victory won.

    Where Albion slept beneath the Fatal Tree
And the Druids golden Knife,   30
    Rioted in human gore,
In Offerings of Human Life

    They groan'd aloud on London Stone
They groan'd aloud on Tyburns Brook
    Albion gave his deadly groan,
And all the Atlantic Mountains shook

    Albions Spectre from his Loins
Tore forth in all the pomp of War!
    Satan his name: in flames of fire
He stretch'd his Druid Pillars far.   40

    Jerusalem fell from Lambeth's Vale,
Down thro Poplar & Old Bow;
    Thro Malden & acros the Sea,
In War & howling death & woe.

    The Rhine was red with human blood:
The Danube rolld a purple tide:
    On the Euphrates Satan stood:
And over Asia stretch'd his pride.

    He witherd up sweet Zions Hill,
From every Nation of the Earth: 50
    He witherd up Jerusalems Gates,
And in a dark Land gave her birth.

---

[15] Apparently a direction to the reader, of uncertain signi-
ficance, found frequently in the Psalms.
[16] A Hebrew word (plural) used frequently for God in many
books of the Old Testament. Blake here fictionalizes or distorts
many of the traditional myths he cites in urging the Jews to
assert their destiny. But in the lyric that follows he brings
together events in contemporary Europe with those of his own
London childhood.

He witherd up the Human Form,
By laws of sacrifice for sin:
Till it became a Mortal Worm:
But O! translucent all within.

The Divine Vision still was seen
Still was the Human Form, Divine
Weeping in weak & mortal clay
O Jesus still the Form was thine.   60

And thine the Human Face & thine
The Human Hands & Feet & Breath
Entering thro' the Gates of Birth
And passing thro' the Gates of Death

And O thou Lamb of God, whom I
Slew in my dark self-righteous pride:
Art thou return'd to Albions Land!
And is Jerusalem thy Bride?

Come to my arms & never more
Depart; but dwell for ever here: 70
Create my Spirit to thy Love:
Subdue my Spectre to thy Fear.

Spectre of Albion! warlike Fiend!
In clouds of blood & ruin roll'd:
I here reclaim thee as my own
My Selfhood! Satan! armd in gold.

Is this thy soft Family-Love
Thy cruel Patriarchal pride
Planting thy Family alone,
Destroying all the World beside.   80

A mans worst enemies are those
Of his own house & family;
And he who makes his law a curse,
By his own law shall surely die.

In my Exchanges every Land
Shall walk, & mine in every Land,
Mutual shall build Jerusalem:
Both heart in heart & hand in hand.

If Humility is Christianity; you O Jews are the true Christians; If your tradition that Man contained in his Limbs, all Animals, is True & they were separated from him by cruel Sacrifices: and when compulsory cruel Sacrifices had brought Humanity into a Feminine Tabernacle, in the loins of Abraham & David: the Lamb of God, the Saviour became apparent on Earth as the Prophets had foretold? The Return of Israel is a Return to Mental Sacrifice & War. Take up the Cross O Israel & follow Jesus.

[1804-20]   [1820]

PROSE

AN ISLAND IN THE MOON
The title An Island in the Moon *was given by editiors to this fragmentary satire ("burlesque novel," G. Keynes calls it). Although some names are punning inventions (Gittipin), most of the characters presumably are based on Blake's contemporaries, and a few can be identified with some certainty: e.g., "Inflammable Gas" is Joseph Priestley, the discoverer of oxygen. Blake appears as Quid the Cynic. Obviously, this satire provided the context for some of the* Songs of Innocence.

AN ISLAND IN THE MOON

[Chapter 1]

In the Moon, is a certain Island near by a mighty continent, which small island seems to have some affinity to England. & what is more extraordinary the people are so much alike & their language so much the same that you would think you was among your friends. in this Island dwells three Philosophers Suction, the Epicurean, Quid the Cynic, & Sipsop, the Pythagorean I call them by the names of these sects tho the sects are not ever mentioned there as being quite out of date however the things still remain, and the vanities are the same. the three Philosophers sat together thinking of nothing. in comes—Etruscan Column the Antiquarian & after an abundance of Enquiries to no purpose sat himself down & described something that nobody listend to so they were employd when Mrs Gimblet came in [? *tipsy*] the corners of her mouth seemd I dont know how, but very odd as if she hoped you had not an ill opinion of her. to be sure we are all poor creatures. well she seated &

[*listened*] seemed to listen with great attention while the Antiquarian seemd to be talking of virtuous cats, but it was not so. she was thinking of the shape of her eyes & mouth & he was thinking, of his eternal fame the three Philosophers at this time were each endeavouring to conceal his laughter, (not at them but) at his own imaginations, this was the situation of this improving company, when in a great hurry, Inflammable Gass the Wind finder enterd. they seemd to rise & salute each other

Etruscan Column & Inflammable Gass fixd their eyes on each other, their tongues went in question & answer, but their thoughts were otherwise employd

I don't like his eyes said Etruscan Column. he's a foolish puppy said Inflammable Gass, smiling on him. the 3 Philosophers [⟨*the*⟩ ? *older*] the Cynic smiling the Epicurean seeming [*not*] studying the flame of the candle & the Pythagorean playing with the cat, listend with open mouths to the edifying discourses.

Sir said the Antiquarian I have seen these works & I do affirm that they are no such thing. they seem to me to be the most wretched paltry flimsy Stuff that ever— What d'ye say What dye say said Inflammable Gass, why why I wish I could see you write so. Sir said the Antiquarian, according to my opinion the author is an errant blockhead.—Your reason Your reason said Inflammable Gass—why why I think it very abominable to call a man a blockhead that you know nothing of.—Reason Sir said the Antiquarian I'll give you an example for your reason As I was walking along the street I saw a ⟨vast⟩ number of swallows on the [*top of an house*] rails of an old Gothic square they seemd to be going on their passage, as Pliny says as I was looking up, a little outré fellow pulling me by the sleeve cries pray Sir who do all they belong to. I turnd my self about with great [P 2] contempt. Said I, Go along you fool.—Fool said he who do you call fool I only askd you a civil question —[*here the*] I had a great mind to have thrashd the fellow only he was bigger than I—here Etruscan column left off—Inflammable Gass, recollecting himself Indeed I donot think the man was a fool for he seems to me to have been desirous of enquiring into the works of nature—Ha Ha Ha said the Pythagorean. it was reechod by Inflammable Gass to overthrow the argument—Etruscan Column then star[t]ing up & clenching both his fists was prepared to give a formal answer to the company But Ob[t]use Angle, entering the room having made a gentle bow, proceeded to empty his pockets of a vast number of papers, turned about & sat down wiped his [*head*] ⟨face⟩ with his pocket handkerchief & shutting his eyes began to scratch his head—well gentlemen said he what is the

cause of strife the Cynic answerd. they are only quarreling about Voltaire—Yes said the Epicurean & having a bit of fun with him. And said the Pythagorean endeavoring to incorporate their souls with their bodies

Obtuse Angle giving a grin said Voltaire understood nothing of the Mathematics and a man must be a fool ifaith not to understand the Mathematics

Inflammable Gass turning round hastily in his chair said Mathematics he found out a number of Queries in Philosophy. Obtuse Angle shutting his eyes & saying that he always understood better when he shut his eyes ⟨said⟩ In the first place it is of no use for a man to make Queries but to solve them, for a man may be a fool & make Queries but a man must have good sound sense to solve them. a query & an answer are as different as a strait line & a crooked one. secondly I, I, I. aye Secondly, Voltaire's a fool, says the Epicurean—Pooh says the Mathematician scratching his head with double violence, it is not worth Quarreling about.—The Antiquarian here got up—& hemming twice to shew the strength of his Lungs, said but my good Sir, Voltaire was immersed in matter, & seems to have understood very little but what he saw before his eyes, like the Animal upon the Pythagoreans lap always playing with its own tail. Ha Ha Ha said Inflammable Gass he was the Glory of France—I have got a bottle of air that would spread a Plague. here the Antiquarian shrugged up his shoulders & was silent while Inflammable Gass talkd for half an hour

When Steelyard ⟨the lawyer⟩ coming in stalking— with an act of parliament in his hand said that it was a shameful thing that acts of parliament should be in a free state, it had so engrossed his mind that he did not salute the company

Mrs Gimblet drew her mouth downwards

Chap 2^d

Tilly Lally the Siptippidist Aradobo, the dean of Morocco, Miss Gittipin Mrs Nannicantipot, ⟨Mrs Sigtagatist⟩ Gibble Gabble the wife of Inflammable Gass—& Little Scopprell enterd the room

(If I have not presented you with every character in the piece call me ass—)

Chap 3^d

In the Moon as Phebus stood over his oriental Gardening O ay come Ill sing you a song said the Cynic. the trumpeter shit in his hat said the Epicurean & clapt it on his head said the Pythagorean

Ill begin again said the Cynic

    Little Phebus came strutting in
    With his fat belly & his round chin
    What is it you would please to have
    Ho Ho
    I wont let it go at only so & so

Mrs Gimblet lookd as if they meant her. Tilly Lally laught like a Cherry clapper. Aradobo askd who was Phebus Sir. Obtuse Angle answerd, quickly, He was the God of Physic, Painting Perspective Geometry Geography Astronomy, Cookery, Chymistry [*Conjunctives*] Mechanics, Tactics Pathology Phraseology Theolog[y] Mythology Astrology Osteology, Somatology in short every art & science adorn'd him as beads round his neck. here Aradobo lookd Astonishd & askd if he understood Engraving—Obtuse Angle Answerd indeed he did.—Well said the other he was as great as Chatterton.[1] Tilly Lally turnd round to Obtuse Angle & askd who it was that was as great as Chatterton. Hay, how should I know Answered Obtuse Angle who was It Aradobo. why sir said he the Gentleman that the song was about. Ah said Tilly Lally I did not hear it. what was it Obtuse Angle. Pooh said he Nonsense. Mhm said Tilly Lally—it was Phebus said the Epicurean Ah that was the Gentleman said Aradobo. Pray Sir said Tilly Lally who was Phebus. Obtuse Angle answered the heathens in the old ages usd to have Gods that they worshipd & they usd to sacrifice to them you have read about that in the bible. Ah said Aradobo I thought I had read of Phebus in the Bible.—Aradobo you should always think before you speak said Obtuse Angle— Ha Ha Ha he means Pharaoh said Tilly Lally—I am ashamd of you making [P 4] use of the names in the Bible said M^{rs}. Sigtagatist. Ill tell you what Mrs Sinagain I dont think theres any harm in it, said Tilly Lally—No said Inflammable Gass. I have got a camera obscura at home what was it you was talking about. Law said Tilly Lally what has that to do with Pharoah—. Pho nonsense hang Pharoh & all his host said the Pythagorean sing away Quid—

Then the Cynic sung

    Honour & Genius is all I ask
    And I ask the Gods no more
      No more No more ⎱ the three Philosophers
      No more No more ⎰ bear chorus

Here Aradobo suckd his under lip

---
[1] Thomas Chatterton (1752–1770), British poet whose suicide at the age of seventeen made him, for Wordsworth and Keats among others, the model of unappreciated talent. See Blake's *Annotations to Wordsworth's Poems*, below.

Chap 4

Hang names said the Pythagorean whats Pharoh better than Phebus or Phebus than Pharoh. hang them both said the Cynic Dont be prophane said Mrs Sigtagatist. Why said Mrs Nannicantipot I dont think its prophane to say hang Pharoh. ah said Mrs Sinagain, I'm sure you ought to hold your tongue, for you never say any thing about the scriptures, & you hinder your husband from going to church—Ha Ha said Inflammable Gass what dont you like to go to church. no said Mrs Nannicantipot I think a person may be as good at home. If I had not a place of profit that forces me to go to church said Inflammable Gass Id see the parsons all hangd a parcel of lying—O said Mrs Sigtagatist if it was not for churches & chapels I should not have livd so long—there was I up in a Morning at four o clock when I was a Girl. I would run like the dickins till I was all in a heat. I would stand till I was ready to sink into the earth. ah Mr Huffcap would kick the bottom of the Pulpit out, with Passion, would tear off the sleeve of his Gown, & set his wig on fire & throw it at the people hed cry & stamp & kick & sweat and all for the good of their souls.—Im sure he must be a wicked villain said Mre Nannicantipot a passionate wretch. If I was a man Id wait at the bottom of the pulpit stairs & knock him down & run away.—You would You Ignorant jade I wish I could see you hit any of the ministers. you deserve to have your ears boxed you do.—Im sure this is not religion answers the [P 5] other—Then Mr Inflammable Gass ran & shovd his head into the fire & set his [*head*] hair all in a flame & ran about the room—No No he did not I was only making a fool of you

Chap 5

Obtuse Angle Scopprell Aradobo & Tilly Lally are all met in Obtuse Angles study—

Pray said Aradobo is Chatterton a Mathematician. No said Obtuse Angle how can you be so foolish as to think he was. Oh I did not think he was I only askd said Aradobo. How could you think he was not, & ask if he was said Obtuse Angle.—Oh no Sir I did think he was before you told me but afterwards I thought he was not

Obtuse Angle said in the first place you thought he was & then afterwards when I said he was not you thought he was not. why I know that—Oh no sir I thought that he was not but I askd to know whether he was.—How can that be said Obtuse Angle how could you ask & think that he was not—why said he. It came into my head that he was not—Why then said

Obtuse Angle you said that he was. Did I say so Law I did not think I said that—Did not he said Obtuse Angle   Yes said Scopprell. But I meant said Aradobo I I I cant think Law Sir I wish youd tell me, how it is

Then Obtuse Angle put his chin in his hand & said whenever you think you must always think for your-self—How Sir said Aradobo, whenever I think I must think myself I think I do—In the first place said he with a grin—Poo Poo said Obtuse Angle dont be a fool—

Then Tilly Lally took up a Quadrant & askd. [*what is this gim crank for*]. Is not this a sun dial. Yes said Scopprell but its broke—at this moment the three Philosophers enterd and lowring darkness hoverd oer th assembly.

Come said the Epicurean lets have some rum & water & hang the mathematics come Aradobo say some thing then Aradobo began In the first place I think I think in the first place that Chatterton was clever at Fissic Follogy, Pistinology, Aridology, Arography, Transmography Phizography, Hogamy HAtomy, & hall that but in the first place he eat wery little wickly that is he slept very little which he brought into a consumsion, & what was that that he took Fissic or somethink & so died

So all the people in the book enterd into the room & they could not talk any more to the present purpose

Chap 6

Then all went home & left the Philosophers. then Suction Askd if Pindar was not a better Poet than Ghiotto was a Painter

Plutarch[2] has not the life of Ghiotto said Sipsop no said Quid to be sure he was an Italian. well said Sunction that is not any proof. Plutarch was a nasty ignorant puppy said Quid I hate your sneaking rascals. theres Aradobo in [*twen*[ty]] ten or twelve years will be a far superior genius. Ah, said the Pythagorean Aradobo will make a very clever fellow. why said Quid I think that [*a*] ⟨any⟩ natural fool would make a clever fellow if he was properly brought up—Ah hang your reasoning said the Epicurean I hate reason-ing I do every thing by my feelings—

Ah said Sipsop, I only wish Jack [*Hunter*] Tearguts[3] had had the cutting of Plutarch he understands anatomy better than any of the Ancients hell plunge his knife up to the hilt in a single drive and thrust his fist in, and all in the space of a Quarter of an hour. he

does not mind their crying—tho they cry ever so hell Swear at them & keep them down with his fist & tell them that hell scrape their bones if they dont lay still & be quiet—What the devil should the people in the hospital that have it done for nothing, make such a piece of work for

Hang that said Suction let us have a Song
The [*Sipsop sang*] the Cynic sang

> When old corruption first begun
> Adornd in yellow vest
> He committed on flesh a whoredom
> O what a wicked beast
>
> 2
>
> From them a callow babe did spring
> And old corruption smild
> To think his race should never end
> For now he had a child
>
> 3
>
> He calld him Surgery & fed
> The babe with his own milk   10
> For flesh & he could neer agree
> She would not let him suck
>
> 4
>
> And this he always kept in mind
> And formd a crooked knife
> And ran about with bloody hands
> To seek his mothers life
>
> 5
>
> And as he ran to seek his mother
> He met with a dead woman
> He fell in love & married her
> A deed which is not common   20
>
> 6
>
> She soon grew pregnant & brought forth
> Scurvy & spotted fever
> The father grind & skipt about
> And said I'm made for ever
>
> 7
>
> For now I have procurd these imps
> Ill try experiments
> With that he tied poor scurvy down
> & stopt up all its vents
>
> 8
>
> And when the child began to swell
> He shouted out aloud   30
> Ive found the dropsy out & soon
> Shall do the world more good

---

[2] Plutarch (A.D. *c.* 46–*c.* 120) could have included Pindar (*c.* 522–*c.* 443 B.C.) in his *Lives* except that Pindar was Greek, but he could hardly have written about Giotto (*c.* 1266–1337), even though he was Italian.

[3] John Hunter (Tearguts) was an anatomist and surgeon at St. George's Hospital, London, when this was written.

9

He took up fever by the neck
And cut out all its spots
And thro the holes which he had made
He first discoverd guts

Ah said Sipsop you think we are rascals & we think
you are rascals. I do as I chuse   what is it to any body
what I do   I am always unhappy too. when I think of
Surgery—I dont know   I do it because I like it. My
father does what he likes & so do I. I think some how
Ill leave it off   There was a woman having her cancer
cut & she shriekd so, that I was quite sick

Chap 7

Good night said Sipsop, Good night said the other
two then Quid & Suction were left alone. then said
Quid I think that Homer is bombast & Shakespeare is
too wild & Milton has no feelings they might be easily
outdone   Chatterton never writ those poems. a parcel
of fools going to Bristol—if I was to go Id find it out
in a minute. but Ive found it out already—If I dont
knock them all up next year in the Exhibition Ill be
hangd said Suction. hang Philosophy I would not
give a farthing for it do all by your feelings and never
think at all about it. Im hangd if I dont get up to
morrow morning by four o clock & work Sir Joshua—
Before ten years are at an end said Quid how I will
work these poor milk [P 8] sop devils, an ignorant pack
of wretches

So they went to bed

Chap 8

Steelyard the Lawgiver, sitting at his table taking
extracts from Herveys Meditations among the tombs
& Youngs Night thoughts.[4] [*This is unfair . . .*] He is
not able to hurt me (said he) more than making me
Constable or taking away the parish business. Hah!

[*O what a scene is here what a disguise*]
My crop of corn is but a field of tares

Says Jerome happiness is not for us poor crawling
reptiles of the earth   Talk of happiness & happiness
its no such thing—every person has a something

Hear then the pride & knowledge of a Sailor
His sprit sail fore sail main sail & his mizen
A poor frail man god wot I know none frailer
I know no greater sinner than John Taylor

If I had only myself to care for I'd soon make Double
Elephant look foolish, & Filligree work I hope shall
live to see—

The wreck of matter & the crush of worlds
as Younge says

Obtuse Angle enterd the Room. What news Mr
Steelyard—I am Reading Theron & Aspasio, said he.
Obtuse Angle took up the books one by one   I dont
find it here said he. Oh no said the other it was the
meditations. Obtuse Angle took up the book & read
till the other was quite tir'd out

Then S[c]opprell & Miss Gittipin, coming in Scop-
prell took up a book & read the following passage.

An Easy of [*Human*] ⟨Huming⟩ Understanding by
John Lookye[5] Gent

John Locke said Obtuse Angle. O ay Lock said
Scopprell.

Now here said Miss Gittipin I never saw such com-
pany in my life. you are always talking of your books
I like to be where we talk.—you had better take a
walk, that we may have some pleasure I am sure I
never see any pleasure. theres Double Elephants Girls
they have their own way, & theres Miss Filligree work
she goes out in her coaches & her footman & her
maids & Stormonts & Balloon hats & a pair of Gloves
every day & the sorrows of Werter & Robinsons & the
Queen of Frances Puss colour & my Cousin Gibble
Gabble says that I am like nobody else   I might as
well be in a nunnery   There they go in Post chaises &
Stages to Vauxhall & Ranelagh   And I hardly know
what a coach is, except when I go to [P 9] Mr Jacko's[6]
he knows what riding is & his wife is the most agree-
able woman you hardly know she has a tongue in her
head   and he is the funniest fellow, & I do believe
he'll go in partnership with his master. & they have
black servants lodge at their house   I never saw such
a place in my life   he says he has Six & twenty rooms
in his house, and I believe it & he is not such a liar as

---

4 James Hervey's *Meditations Among the Tombs* (1746–1947)
and Edward Young's *Night Thoughts* (1742–1745) (which later
Blake illustrated) were highly popular reflections on death and
immortality. The form of *The Four Zoas* is probably influenced
by Young's poem. Hervey also wrote *Theron and Aspasio, or a
Series of Letters and Dialogues on the Most Important Subjects* (see
below).

5 I.e., John Locke (1632–1704), author of *An Essay on the
Human Understanding*.
6 Vauxhall and Ranelagh were fashionable London pleasure
spots, as Goethe's *The Sorrows of Werther* was at the time a
fashionable novel to be seen reading. Mister Jacko was a perfor-
ming monkey; "Perdita" Robinson, the mistress of George IV
when he was Prince, was known for her clothes and later her
memoirs.

Quid thinks he is. [*but he is always Envying*] Poo Poo
hold your tongue, said the Lawgiver. this quite pro-
vokd Miss Gittipin to interrupt her in her favourite
topic & she proceeded to use every Provoking speech
that ever she could, & he bore it ⟨more⟩ like a Saint
than a Lawgiver and with great Solemnity he ad-
dressd the company in these words

They call women the weakest vessel but I think they
are the strongest A girl has always more tongue than
a boy   I have seen a little brat no higher than a nettle
& she had as much tongue as a city clark but a boy
would be such a fool not have any thing to say and if
any body askd him a question he would put his head
into a hole & hide it. I am sure I take but little pleasure
you have as much pleasure as I have. there I stand &
bear every fools insult. if I had only myself to care for,
I'd wring off their noses

To this Scopprell answerd, I think the Ladies dis-
courses Mr Steelyard are some of them more im-
proving than any book. that is the way I have got
some of my knowledge

Then said Miss Gittipin, Mr Scopprell do you
know the song of Phebe and Jellicoe—no Miss said
Scopprell—then she repeated these verses while
Steelyard walkd about the room

> Phebe drest like beauties Queen
> Jellicoe in faint peagreen
> Sitting all beneath a grot
> Where the little lambkins trot
>
> Maidens dancing   loves a sporting
> All the country folks a courting
> Susan Johnny Bet & Joe
> Lightly tripping on a row
>
> Happy people who can be
> In happiness compard with ye   10
> The Pilgrim with his crook & hat
> Sees your happiness compleat

A charming Song indeed miss said Scopprell [*That
was all for*] here they receivd a summons for a merry
making at the Philosophers house

Chap 9

I say this evening [*we'd*] ⟨we'll⟩ all get drunk. I say
dash, an Anthem   an Anthem, said Suction

> Lo the Bat with Leathern wing
> Winking & blinking
> Winking & blinking
> Winking & blinking
> Like Doctor Johnson

Quid——O ho Said Doctor Johnson
          To Scipio Africanus [7]
          If you dont own me a Philosopher
          Ill kick your Roman Anus

Suction——A ha To Doctor Johnson   10
          Said Scipio Africanus
          Lift up my Roman Petticoat
          And kiss my Roman Anus

And the Cellar goes down with a Step (Grand
Chorus

Ho Ho Ho Ho Ho Ho Ho Hooooo my poooooor
siiides   I I should die if I was to live here said
Scopprell Ho Ho Ho Ho Ho

1st Vo   Want Matches
2d Vo   Yes Yes Yes
1   Vo   Want Matches
2d Vo   No————————

1st Vo   Want Matches
2d Vo   Yes Yes Yes
1st Vo   Want Matches
2d Vo   No————————

Here was Great confusion & disorder   Aradobo
said that the boys in the street sing something very
pritty & funny [*about London O no*] about Matches
Then Mrs Nannicantipot sung

> I cry my matches as far as Guild hall
> God bless the duke & his aldermen all

Then sung Scopprell

> I ask the Gods no more
>   no more no more

Then Said Suction   come Mr Lawgiver your song
and the Lawgiver sung

> As I walked forth one may morning
> To see the fields so pleasant & so gay
> O there did I spy a young maiden sweet
>
> Among the Violets that smell so sweet
>   Smell so sweet
>   Smell so sweet
> Among the Violets that smell so sweet

---

[7] Scipio Africanus, the Roman general who defeated Hannibal,
is an unlikely companion for Samuel Johnson.

Hang your Violets heres your Rum & water
[*sweeter*] O ay said Tilly Lally. Joe Bradley & I was
going along one day in the Sugar house   Joe Bradley
saw   for he had but one eye   saw a treacle jar   So
he goes of his blind side & dips his hand up to the
shoulder in treacle. here lick lick lick said he   Ha Ha
Ha Ha Ha   For he had but one eye   Ha Ha Ha Ho
then sung Scopprell

> And I ask the Gods no more
> no more no more
> no more no more

Miss Gittipin said he you sing like a harpsichord.
let your bounty descend to our fair ears and favour us
with a fine song
⟨then she sung⟩

> This frog he would a wooing ride
> Kitty alone   Kitty alone
> This frog he would a wooing ride
> Kitty alone & I
> Sing cock I cary Kitty alone
> Kitty alone   Kitty alone
> Cock I cary Kitty alone
> Kitty alone & I

Charming truly elegant said Scopprell

> And I ask the gods no more

Hang your Serious Songs, said Sipsop   & he sung
as follows

> Fa ra so bo ro
> Fa ra bo ra
> Sa ba ra ra ba rare roro
> Sa ra ra ra bo ro ro ro
> Radara
> Sarapodo no flo ro

Hang Italian songs   lets have English said Quid
[*Sing a Mathematical Song Obtuse Angle then he sung*]
⟨English Genius for ever   here I go⟩

> Hail Matrimony made of Love
> To thy wide gates how great a drove
> On purpose to be yok'd do come
> Widows & maids & Youths also
> That lightly trip on beauty's toe
> Or sit on beauty's bum

> Hail fingerfooted lovely Creatures
> The females of our human Natures
> Formed to suckle all Mankind
> Tis you that come in time of need   10
> Without you we shoud never Breed
> Or any Comfort find

> For if a Damsel's blind or lame
> Or Nature's hand has crooked her frame
> Or if she's deaf or is wall eyed
> Yet if her heart is well inclined
> Some tender lover she shall find
> That panteth for a Bride

> The universal Poultice this
> To cure whatever is amiss   20
> In damsel or in Widow gay
> It makes them smile it makes them skip
> Like Birds just cured of the pip
> They chirp & hop away

> Then come ye Maidens come ye Swains
> Come & be eased of all your pains
> In Matrimony's Golden cage—

I [*None of*] Go & be hanged said Scopprel how can
you have the face to make game of Matrimony [*What
you skipping flea how dare ye? Ill dash you through your
chair says the Cynic This Quid (cries out Miss
Gittipin) always spoils good company in this manner &
its a shame*]
Then Quid calld upon Obtuse Angle for a Song &
he wiping his face & looking on the corner of the
cieling Sang

> To be or not to be
> Of great capacity
> Like Sir Isaac Newton
> Or Locke or Doctor South
> Or Sherlock upon death
> Id rather be Sutton [8]

> For he did build a house
> For aged men & youth
> With walls of brick & stone
> He furnishd it within   10
> With whatever he could win
> And all his own

---

[8] Robert South and William Sherlock were late seventeenth-
century clergymen engaged in a controversy about the latter's
Practical Discourse Concerning Death (1689). Thomas Sutton
(1532–1611), philanthropist, founder of Charterhouse School.

He drew out of the Stocks
His money in a box
And sent his servant
To Green the Bricklayer
And to the Carpenter
He was so fervent

The chimneys were three score
The windows many more   20
And for convenience
He sinks & gutters made
And all the way he pavd
To hinder pestilence

Was not this a good man
Whose life was but a span
Whose name was Sutton

As Locke or Doctor South
Or Sherlock upon Death
Or Sir Isaac Newton   30

The Lawgiver was very attentive & begd to have it
sung over again & again till the company were tired &
insisted on the Lawgiver singing a song himself which
he readily complied with

This city & this country has brought forth many
    mayors
To sit in state & give forth laws out of their old oak
    chairs
With face as brown as any nut with drinking of
    strong ale
Good English hospitality O then it did not fail

With scarlet gowns & broad gold lace would make a
    yeoman sweat
With stockings rolld above their knees & shoes as
    black as jet
With eating beef & drinking beer O they were stout
    & hale
Good English hospitality O then it did not fail

Thus sitting at the table wide the Mayor &
    Aldermen
Were fit to give law to the city each eat as much
    as ten   10
The hungry poor enterd the hall to eat good beef &
    ale
Good English hospitality O then it did not fail

Here they gave a shout & the company broke up

Chap 10

Thus these happy Islanders spent their time but
felicity does not last long, for being met at the house of
Inflammable Gass the wind-finder, the following
affairs happend.

Come Flammable said Gibble Gabble & lets enjoy
ourselves   bring the Puppets. Hay Hay, said he, you
sho, why ya ya, how can you be so foolish.—Ha Ha
Ha she calls the experiments puppets   Then he went
up stairs & loaded the maid, with glasses, & brass
tubes, & magic pictures

Here ladies & gentlemen said he Ill shew you a louse
[*climing*] or a flea or a butterfly or a cock chafer the
blade bone of a tittle back   no no heres a bottle of wind
that I look up in the bog house. o dear   o dear   the
waters got into the sliders. look here Gibble Gabble—
lend me your handkerchief, Tilly Lally   Tilly Lally
took out his handkerchief which smeard the glass
worse than ever. then he screwd it on then he took the
sliders & then he set up the glasses for the Ladies to
view the pictures   thus he was employd & quite out
of breath

While Tilly Lally & Scopprell were pumping at the
air pump Smack went the glass—. Hang said Tilly
Lally. Inflammable Gass turnd short round & threw
down the table & Glasses & Pictures, & broke the
bottles of wind & let out the Pestilence. He saw the
Pestilence fly out of the bottle & cried out [P 14] while
he ran out of the room, come out come out   we are
putrified, we are corrupted, our lungs are destroyd
with the Flogiston   this will spread a plague all thro'
the Island   he was down stairs the very first   on the
back of him came all the others in a heap

So they need not bidding go

Chap 11

Another merry meeting at the house of Steelyard
the Lawgiver

After Supper Steelyard & Obtuse Angle had pumpd
Inflammable Gass quite dry. they playd at forfeits &
tryd every method to get good humour. said Miss
Gittipin pray Mr Obtuse Angle sing us a song   then
he sung

Upon a holy thursday their innocent faces clean
The children walking two & two in grey & blue &
    green
Grey headed beadles walkd before with wands as
    white as snow
Till into the high dome of Pauls they like thames
    waters flow

O what a multitude they seemed, these flowers of
    London town
Seated in companies they sit with radiance all their
    own
The hum of multitudes were there but multitudes of
    lambs
Thousands of little girls & boys riasing their
    innocent hands

Then like a mighty wind they raise to heavn the
    voice of song
Or like harmonious thunderings the seats of heavn
    among   10
Beneath them sit the revrend men the guardians of
    the poor
Then cherish pity lest you drive an angel from your
    door [9]

After this they all sat silent for a quarter of an hour
[& Mrs Sigtagatist] ⟨& Mʳˢ Nannicantipot⟩ said it
puts me in Mind of my [grand] mothers song

When the tongues of children are heard on the
    green
And laughing is heard on the hill
My heart is at rest within my breast
And every thing else is still

Then come home my children the sun is gone down
And the dews of night arise
Come Come leave off play & let us away
Till the morning appears in the skies

No No let us play for it is yet day
And we cannot go to sleep
Besides in the Sky the little birds fly   10
And the meadows are coverd with Sheep

Well Well go & play till the light fades away
And then go home to bed
The little ones leaped & shouted & laughd
And all the hills ecchoed

Then [Miss Gittipin] [Tilly Lally sung] [Quid] sung
⟨Quid⟩

O father father where are you going
O do not walk so fast
O speak father speak to your little boy
Or else I shall be lost

<hr>

[9] This and the two verses following are early versions of
some of the Songs of Innocence.

The night it was dark & no father was there
And the child was wet with dew
The mire was deep & the child did weep
And away the vapour flew

Here nobody could sing any longer, till Tilly Lally
pluckd up a spirit & he sung.

O I say you Joe
Throw us the ball
Ive a good mind to go
And leave you all
I never saw saw such a bowler
To bowl the ball in a tansey
And to clean it with my handkercher
Without saying a word

That Bills a foolish fellow
He has given me a black eye   10
He does not know how to handle a bat
Any more than a dog or a cat
He has knockd down the wicket
And broke the stumps
And runs without shoes to save his pumps

Here a laugh began and Miss Gittipin sung

Leave O leave [me] to my sorrows
Here Ill sit & fade away
Till Im nothing but a spirit
And I lose this form of clay
Then if chance along this forest
Any walk in pathless ways
Thro the gloom he'll see my shadow
Hear my voice upon the Breeze

The Lawgiver all the while sat delighted to see them
in such a serious humour Mʳ Scopprell said he you
must be acquainted with a great many songs. O dear
sir Ho Ho Ho I am no singer I must beg of one of
these tender hearted ladies to sing for me—they all
declined & he was forced to sing himself

Theres Doctor Clash
And Signior Falalasole
O they sweep in the cash
Into their purse hole
Fa me la sol   La me fa Sol

Great A little A
Bouncing B
Play away   Play away
Your out of the key
Fa me la sol   La me fa sol   10

Musicians should have
A pair of very good ears
And Long fingers & thumbs
And not like clumsy bears
Fa me la sol   La me fa sol

Gentlemen Gentlemen
Rap Rap Rap
Fiddle Fiddle Fiddle
Clap Clap Clap
Fa me la sol   La me fa sol   20

Hm said the Lawgiver, funny enough lets have
handels waterpiece then Sipsop sung

A crowned king,
On a white horse sitting
With his trumpets sounding
And Banners flying
Thro the clouds of smoke he makes his way
And the shout of his thousands fills his heart with
    rejoicing & victory
And the shout of his thousands fills his heart with
    rejoicing & victory
Victory Victory—twas William the prince of Orange

[Here a leaf or more is missing]

them Illuminating the Manuscript—Ay said she that
would be excellent. Then said he I would have all the
writing Engraved instead of Printed & at every other
leaf a high finishd print all in three Volumes folio, &
sell them a hundred pounds a piece. they would Print
off two thousand   then said she whoever will not have
them will be ignorant fools & will not deserve to live
Dont you think I have something of the Goats face
says he. Very like a Goats face—she answerd—I
think your face said he is like that noble beast the
Tyger—Oh I was at Mrs Sicknakens & I was speaking
of my abilities but their nasty hearts poor devils are
eat up with envy—they envy me my abilities & all the
Women envy your abilities   my dear   they hate
people who are of higher abil[it]ies than their nasty
filthy [Souls] Selves but do you outface them & then
Strangers will see you have an opinion—now I think
we should do as much good as we can when were are at
Mr Femality's   do yo[u] snap & take me up—and I
will fall into such a passion Ill hollow and stamp &
frighten all the People there & show them what truth
is—at this Instant Obtuse Angle came in   Oh I am
glad you are come said quid

[c. 1784]   [1907, correctly 1925]

LETTERS

[TO] REVd DR TRUSLER, ENGLEFIELD
GREEN, EGHAM, SURREY[1]

13 Hercules Buildings, Lambeth, August, 23, 1799
Revd Sir
    I really am sorry that you are falln out with the
Spiritual World Especially if I should have to answer
for it I feel very sorry that your Ideas & Mine on
Moral Painting differ so much as to have made you
angry with my method of Study. If I am wrong I am
wrong in good company. I had hoped your plan com-
prehended All Species of this Art & Especially that
you would not regret that Species which gives
Existence to Every other. namely Visions of Eternity
You say that I want somebody to Elucidate my Ideas.
But you ought to know that What is Grand is neces-
sarily obscure to Weak men. That which can be made
Explicit to the Idiot is not worth my care. The wisest
of the Ancients considerd what is not too Explicit as
the fittest for Instruction because it rouzes the
faculties to act. I name Moses Solomon Esop Homer
Plato
    But as you have favord me with your remarks on my
Design permit me in return to defend it against a mis-
taken one, which is. That I have supposed Ma-
levolence without a Cause.—Is not Merit in one a
Cause of Envy in another & Serenity & Happiness
& Beauty a Cause of Malevolence. But Want of
Money & the Distress of A Thief can never be
alledged as the Cause of his Thievery. for many
honest people endure greater hard ships with Forti-
tude We must therefore seek the Cause elsewhere
than in want of Money for that is the Miser passion,
not the Thiefs
    I have therefore proved your Reasonings Ill pro-
portiond which you can never prove my figures to be.
They are those of Michael Angelo Rafael & the
Antique & of the best living Models. I percieve that
your Eye[s] is perverted by Caricature Prints, which
ought not to abound so much as they do. Fun I love
but too much Fun is of all things the most loathsom.
Mirth is better than Fun & Happiness is better than
Mirth—I feel that a Man may be happy in This
World. And I know that This World Is a World of
Imagination & Vision I see Every thing I paint In This
World, but Every body does not see alike. To the

---

[1] Dr. John Trusler (1735–1820), clergyman, medical student,
and author of *Hogarth Moralized*, with whom Blake negotiated
about illustrating a book.

Eyes of a Miser a Guinea is more beautiful than the Sun & a bag worn with the use of Money has more beautiful proportions than a Vine filled with Grapes. The tree which moves some to tears of joy is in the Eyes of others only a Green thing that stands in the way. Some See Nature all Ridicule & Deformity & by these I shall not regulate my proportions, & Some Scarce see Nature at all But to the Eyes of the Man of Imagination Nature is Imagination itself. As a man is So he Sees. As the Eye is formed such are its Powers You certainly Mistake when you say that the Visions of Fancy are not to be found in This World. To Me This World is all One continued Vision of Fancy or Imagination & I feel Flatterd when I am told So. What is it sets Homer Virgil & Milton in so high a rank of Art. Why is the Bible more Entertaining & Instructive than any other book. Is it not because they are addressed to the Imagination which is Spiritual Sensation & but mediately to the Understanding or Reason Such is True Painting and such ⟨was⟩ alone valued by the Greeks & the best modern Artists. Consider what Lord Bacon says "Sense sends over to Imagination before Reason have judged & Reason sends over to Imagination before the Decree can be acted." See Advancem^t of Learning Part 2 P 47 of first Edition

But I am happy to find a Great Majority of Fellow Mortals who can Elucidate My Visions & Particularly they have been Elucidated by Children who have taken a greater delight in contemplating my Pictures than I even hoped. Neither Youth nor Childhood is Folly or Incapacity Some Children are Fools & so are some Old Men. But There is vast Majority on the side of Imagination or Spiritual Sensation

To Engrave after another Painter is infinitely more laborious than to Engrave ones own Inventions. And of the Size you require my price has been Thirty Guineas & I cannot afford to do it for less. I had Twelve for the Head I sent you as a Specimen, but after my own designs I could do at least Six times the quantity of labour in the same time which will account for the difference of price as also that Chalk Engraving is at least six times as laborious as Aqua tinta. I have no objection to Engraving after another Artist. Engraving is the profession I was apprenticed to, & should never have attempted to live by any thing else If orders had not come in for my Designs & Paintings, which I have the pleasure to tell you are Increasing Every Day. Thus If I am a Painter it is not to be attributed to Seeking after. But I am contented whether I live by Painting or Engraving

I am Revd Sir Your very obedient servant

WILLIAM BLAKE

[To] Mr BUTTS, G$_R$ MARLBOROUGH S$_T$, LONDON[1]

Felpham August 16. 1803

Dear Sir

I send 7 Drawings which I hope will please you. this I believe about balances our account—Our return to London draws on apace. our Expectation of meeting again with you is one of our greatest pleasures. Pray tell me how your Eyes do. I never sit down to work but I think of you & feel anxious for the sight of that friend whose Eyes have done me so much good— I omitted (very unaccountably) to copy out in my last Letter that passage in my rough sketch which related to your kindness in offering to Exhibit my 2 last Pictures in the Gallery in Berners Street it was in these Words. "I sincerely thank you for your kind offer of Exhibiting my 2 Pictures. the trouble you take on my account I trust will be recompensed to you by him who Seeth in Secret. if you should find it convenient to do so it will be gratefully rememberd by me among the other numerous kindnesses I have recievd from you"—

I go on with the remaining Subjects which you gave me commission to Execute for you but shall not be able to send any more before my return tho perhaps I may bring some with me finishd. I am at Present in a Bustle to defend myself against a very unwarrantable warrant from a Justice of Peace in Chichester. which was taken out against me by a Private in Captn Leathes's troop of 1st or Royal Dragoons for an assault & Seditious words. The wretched Man has terribly Perjurd himself as has his Comrade for as to Sedition not one Word relating to the King or Government was spoken by either him or me. His Enmity arises from my having turned him out of my Garden into which he was invited as an assistant by a Gardener at work therein, without my knowledge that he was so invited. I desired him as politely as was possible to go out of the Garden, he made me an impertinent answer I insisted on his leaving the Garden he refused I still persisted in desiring his departure he then threatend to knock out my Eyes with many abominable imprecations & with some contempt for my Person it affronted my foolish Pride I therefore took him by the Elbows & pushed him before me till I had got him out. there I intended to have left him. but he turning about put himself into a Posture of Defiance threatening & swearing at me. I perhaps foolishly & perhaps not, stepped out at the

---

[1] Thomas Butts (d. 1845), a friend and the most faithful purchaser of Blake's work.

Gate & putting aside his blows took him again by the Elbows & keeping his back to me pushed him forwards down the road about fifty yards he all the while endeavouring to turn round & strike me & raging & cursing which drew out several neighbours. at length when I had got him to where he was Quartered. which was very quickly done. we were met at the Gate by the Master of the house. The Fox Inn. (who is the proprietor of my Cottage) & his wife & Daughter. & the Mans Comrade. & several other people My Landlord compelld the Soldiers to go in doors after many abusive threats against me & my wife from the two Soldiers but not one word of threat on account of Sedition was utterd at that time. This method of Revenge was Plann'd beween them after they had got together into the Stable. This is the whole outline. I have for witnesses. The Gardener who is Hostler at the Fox & who Evidences that to his knowledge no word of the remotest tendency to Government or Sedition was utterd,—Our next door Neighbour a Millers wife who saw me turn him before me down the road & saw & heard all that happend at the Gate of the Inn who Evidences that no Expression of threatening on account of Sedition was utterd in the heat of their fury by either of the Dragoons. this was the womans own remark & does high honour to her good sense as she observes that whenever a quarrel happens the offence is always repeated. The Landlord of the Inn & His Wife & daughter will Evidence the Same & will evidently prove the Comrade perjurd who swore that he heard me ⟨while⟩ at the Gate utter Seditious words & D— the K— without which perjury I could not have been committed & I had no witness with me before the Justices who could combat his assertion as the Gardener remain in my Garden all the while & he was the only person I thought necessary to take with me. I have been before a Bench of Justices at Chichester this morning. but they as the Lawyer who wrote down the Accusation told me in private are compelld by the Military to suffer a prosecution to be enterd into altho they must know & it is manifest that the whole is a Fabricated Perjury. I have been forced to find Bail. Mr Hayley was kind enough to come forwards & Mr Seagrave Printer at Chichester. Mr H. in 100£ & Mr S. in 50£ & myself am bound in 100£ for my appearance at the Quarter Sessions which is after Michaelmass. So I shall have the Satisfaction to see my friends in Town before this Contemptible business comes on I say Contemptible for it must be manifest to every one that the whole accusation is a wilful Perjury. Thus you see my dear Friend that I cannot leave this place without some adventure, it has struck a consternation thro all the Villages round. Every Man is now afraid of speaking to or looking at a

Soldier. for the peaceable Villagers have always been forward in expressing their kindness for us & they express their sorrow at our departure as soon as they hear of it Every one here is my Evidence for Peace & Good Neighbourhood & yet such is the present state of things this foolish accusation must be tried in Public. Well I am content I murmur not & doubt not that I shall recieve Justice & am only sorry for the trouble & expense. I have heard that my Accuser is a disgraced Sergeant his name is John Scholfield. perhaps it will be in your power to learn somewhat about the Man I am very ignorant of what I am requesting of you. I only suggest what I know you will be kind enough to Excuse if you can learn nothing about him & what I as well know if it is possible you will be kind enough to do in this matter

Dear Sir This perhaps was sufferd to Clear up some doubts & to give opportunity to those whom I doubted to clear themselves of all imputation. If a Man offends me ignorantly & not designedly surely I ought to consider him with favour & affection. Perhaps the simplicity of myself is the origin of all offences committed against me. If I have found this I shall have learned a most valuable thing well worth three years perseverance. I have found it! It is certain! that a too passive manner. inconsistent with my active physiognomy had done me much mischief I must now express to you my conviction that all is come from the spiritual World for Good & not for Evil.

Give me your advice in my perilous adventure. burn what I have peevishly written about any friend. I have been very much degraded & injuriously treated. but if it all arise from my own fault I ought to blame myself

O why was I born with a different face
Why was I not born like the rest of my race
When I look each one starts! when I speak I offend
Then I'm silent & passive & lose every Friend

Then my verse I dishonour. My pictures despise
My person degrade & my temper chastise
And the pen is my terror. the pencil my shame
All my Talents I bury, and dead is my Fame

I am either too low or too highly prizd
When Elate I am Envy'd, When Meek I'm despis'd

This is but too just a Picture of my Present state I pray God to keep you & all men from it & to deliver me in his own good time. Pray write to me & tell me how you & your family Enjoy health.   My much terrified Wife joins me in love to you & Mrs Butts & all your family. I again take the liberty to beg of you to cause the Enclosd Letter to be delivered to my Brother & remain Sincerely & Affectionately Yours

WILLIAM BLAKE

BLAKE'S MEMORANDUM IN REFUTATION OF THE INFORMATION AND COMPLAINT OF JOHN SCOLFIELD, A PRIVATE SOLDIER, &C.

[August 1803]

The Soldier has been heard to say repeatedly, that he did not know how the Quarrel began, which he would not say if such seditious words were spoken.—

Mrs. Haynes Evidences, that she saw me turn him down the Road, & all the while we were at the Stable Door, and that not one word of charge against me was uttered, either relating to Sedition or any thing else; all he did was swearing and threatening.—

Mr. Hosier heard him say that he would be revenged, and would have me hanged if he could! He spoke this the Day after my turning him out of the Garden. Hosier says he is ready to give Evidence of this, if necessary.—

The Soldier's Comrade swore before the Magistrates, while I was present. that he heard me utter seditious words, at the Stable Door, and in particular. said, that he heard me D—n the K—g. Now I have all the Persons who were present at the Stable Door to witness that no Word relating to Seditious Subjects was uttered, either by one party or the other, and they are ready, on their Oaths, to say that I did not utter such Words.—

Mrs. Haynes says very sensibly, that she never heard People quarrel, but they always charged each other with the Offence, and repeated it to those around, therefore as the Soldier charged not me with Seditious Words at that Time, neither did his Comrade, the whole Charge must have been fabricated in the Stable afterwards.—

If we prove the Comrade perjured who swore that he heard me D—n the K—g, I believe the whole Charge falls to the Ground.

Mr. Cosens, owner of the Mill at Felpham, was passing by in the Road, and saw me and the Soldier and William standing near each other; he heard nothing, but says we certainly were not quarrelling.—

The whole Distance that William could be at any Time of the Conversation between me and the Soldier (supposing such Conversation to have existed) is only 12 Yards, & W— says that he was backwards and forwards in the Garden. It was still Day, there was no Wind stirring.

William says on his Oath, that the first Words that he heard me speak to the Soldier were ordering him out of the Garden; the truth is, I did not speak to the Soldier till then, & my ordering him out of the Garden was occasioned by his [P 2] saying something that I thought insulting.

The Time that I & the Soldier were together in the Garden, was not sufficient for me to have uttered the Things that he alledged.

The Soldier said to Mrs. Grinder, that it would be right to have my House searched, as I might have plans of the Country which I intended to send to the Enemy; he called me a Military Painter; I suppose mistaking the Words Miniature Painter, which he might have heard me called. I think that this proves, his having come into the Garden, with some bad Intention, or at least with a prejudiced Mind.

It is necessary to learn the Names of all that were present at the Stable Door, that we may not have any Witnesses brought against us, that were not there.

All the Persons present at the Stable Door were, Mrs. Grinder and her Daughter, all the Time; Mrs. Haynes & her Daughter all the Time; Mr. Grinder, part of the Time; Mr. Hayley's Gardener part of the Time.—Mrs. Haynes was present from my turning him out at my Gate, all the rest of the Time—What passed in the Garden, there is no Person but William & the Soldier, & myself can know.

There was not any body in Grinder's Tap-room, but an Old Man, named Jones, who (Mrs. Grinder says) did not come out—He is the same Man who lately hurt his Hand, & wears it in a sling—

The Soldier after he and his Comrade came together into the Tap-room, threatened to knock William's Eyes out (this was his often repeated Threat to me and to my Wife) because W— refused to go with him to Chichester, and swear against me. William said that he would not take a false Oath, for that he heard me say nothing of the Kind (i.e. Sedition) Mr. Grinder then reproved the Soldier for threatening William, and Mr Grinder said, that W— should not go, because of those Threats, especially as he was sure that no Seditious Words were Spoken.—

[P 3] William's timidity in giving his Evidence before the Magistrates, and his fear of uttering a Falsehood upon Oath, proves him to be an honest Man, & is to me an host of Strength. I am certain that if I had not turned the Soldier out of my Garden, I never should have been free from his Impertinence & Intrusion.

Mr. Hayley's Gardener came past at the Time of the Contention at the Stable Door, & going to the

Comrade said to hin, Is your Comrade drunk?—a Proof that he thought the Soldier abusive, & in an Intoxication of Mind.

If such a Perjury as this can take effect, any Villain in future may come & drag me and my Wife out of our House, & beat us in the Garden, or use us as he please, or is able, & afterwards go and swear our Lives away.

Is it not in the Power of any Thief who enters a Man's Dwelling, & robs him, or misuses his Wife or Children, to go & swear as this Man has sworn.

[To] George Cumberland Esqre
Culver Street Bristol[1]

N 3 Fountain Court Strand 12 April 1827
Dear Cumberland

I have been very near the Gates of Death & have returned very weak & an Old Man feeble & tottering, but not in Spirit & Life not in The Real Man The Imagination which Liveth for Ever. In that I am stronger & stronger as this Foolish Body decays. I thank you for the Pains you have taken with Poor Job. I know too well that a great majority of Englishmen are fond of The Indefinite which they Measure by Newtons Doctrine of the Fluxions of an Atom, A Thing that does not Exist. These are Politicians & think that Republican Art is Inimical to their Atom. For a Line or lineament is not formed by Chance a Line is a Line in its Minutest Sub-division[s] Strait or Crooked It is Itself & Not Intermeasurable with or by any Thing Else Such is Job but since the French Revolution Englishmen are all Intermeasurable One by Another Certainly a happy state of Agreement to which I for One do not Agree. God keep me from the Divinity of Yes & No too The Yea Nay Creeping Jesus from supposing Up & Down to be the same Thing as all Experimentalists must suppose

You are desirous I know to dispose of some of my Works & to make ⟨them⟩ Please. I am obliged to you & to all who do so But having none remaining of all that I had Printed I cannot Print more Except at a great loss for at the time I printed those things I had a whole House to range in now I am shut up in a Corner therefore am forced to ask a Price for them that I scarce expect to get from a Stranger. I am now Printing a Set of the Songs of Innocence & Experience for a Friend at Ten Guineas which I cannot do under Six Months consistent with my other Work, so that I have little hope of doing any more of such things. the Last Work I produced is a Poem Entitled Jerusalem the Emanation of the Giant Albion, but

find that to Print it will Cost my Time the amount of Twenty Guineas One I have Finishd It contains 100 Plates but it is not likely that I shall get a Customer for it

As you wish me to send you a list with the Prices of these things they are as follows

	£	s	d
America	6.	6.	0
Europe	6.	6.	0
Visions &c°	5.	5.	0
Thel	3.	3.	0
Songs of Inn. & Exp.	10.	10.	0
Urizen	6.	6.	0

The Little Card I will do as soon as Possible but when you Consider that I have been reduced to a Skeleton from which I am slowly recovering you will I hope have Patience with me.

Flaxman is Gone & we must All soon follow every one to his Own Eternal House Leaving the Delusive Goddess Nature & her Laws to get into Freedom from all Law of the Members into The Mind in which every one is King & Priest in his own House God Send it so on Earth as it is in Heaven
I am Dear Sir Yours Affectionately
WILLIAM BLAKE

ANNOTATIONS TO WORDSWORTH'S "POEMS"
These notes are written in the two-volume, 1815 edition of Wordsworth's Poems. The passages in smaller type are Wordsworth's words upon which Blake is commenting.

ANNOTATIONS TO WORDSWORTH'S *POEMS*

Titles marked "X" in pencil in the table of Contents are: Lucy Gray, We Are Seven, The Blind Highland Boy, The Brothers, Strange Fits of Passion, I met Louisa, Ruth, Michael..., Laodamia, To the Daisy, To the small Celandine, To the Cuckoo, A Night Piece, Yew Trees, She was a Phantom, I wandered lonely, Reverie of Poor Susan, Yarrow Unvisited, Yarrow Visited, Resolution and Independence, The Thorn, Hartleap Well, Tintern Abbey, Character of a Happy Warrior, Rob Roy's Grave, Expostulation and Reply, The Tables Turned, Ode to Duty, Miscellaneous Sonnets, Sonnets Dedicated to Liberty, The Old Cumberland Beggar, Ode—Intimations, &c.

PREFACE

[PAGE viii]   The powers requisite for the production of poetry are, first, those of observation and description, . . . whether the

---

¹ George Cumberland (b. 1754), an engraver, had known Blake for nearly thirty years.

things depicted be actually present to the senses, or have a place only in the memory. . . . 2ndly, Sensibility, . . .

One Power alone makes a Poet.—Imagination The Divine Vision

[PAGE 1] Poems Referring to the Period of Childhood

I see in Wordsworth the Natural Man rising up against the Spiritual Man Continually & then he is No Poet but a Heathen Philospher at Enmity against all true Poetry or Inspiration

[PAGE 3] And I could wish my days to be
Bound each to each by natural piety.

There is no such Thing as Natural Piety Because The Natural Man is at Enmity with God

[PAGE 43] To H.C. Six Years Old

This is all in the highest degree Imaginative & equal to any Poet but not Superior I cannot think that Real Poets have any competition None are greatest in the Kingdom of Heaven it is so in Poetry

[PAGE 44] Influence of Natural Objects
In calling forth and strengthening the Imagination
in Boyhood and early Youth.

Natural Objects always did & now do Weaken deaden & obliterate Imagination in Me Wordsworth must know that what he Writes Valuable is Not to be found in Nature Read Michael Angelos Sonnet vol 2 p. 179

[PAGE 341] Essay, Supplementary to the Preface.

I do not know who wrote these Prefaces they are very mischievous & direct contrary to Wordsworths own Practise

[PAGE 364] From what I saw with my own eyes, I knew that the imagery was spurious. In nature everything is distinct, yet nothing defined into absolute independent singleness. In Macpherson's work, it is exactly the reverse; everything (that is not stolen) is in this manner defined, insulated, dislocated, deadened,—yet nothing distinct. It will always be so when words are substituted for things. . . . Yet, much as these pretended treasures of antiquity have been admired, . . .

I Believe both Macpherson & Chatterton, that what they say is Ancient, Is so

[PAGE 365] . . . no Author in the least distinguished, has ventured formally to imitate them—except the Boy, Chatterton, on their first appearance.

I own myself an admirer of Ossian equally with any other Poet whatever Rowley & Chatterton also

[PAGE 375, final paragraph] . . . if [the Writer] were not persuaded that the Contents of these Volumes . . . evinced something of the "Vision and the Faculty divine," . . . he would not, if a wish could do it, save them from immediate destruction.

It appears to me as if the last Paragraph beginning With "Is it the result" Was writ by another hand & mind from the rest of these Prefaces. Perhaps they are the opinions of a Portrait or Landscape Painter Imagination is the Divine Vision not of The World nor of Man nor from Man as. he is a Natural Man but only as he is a Spiritual Man Imagination has nothing to do with Memory.

[1826]   [1880, correctly 1927]

William Wordsworth

1770–1850

THERE is a story told in Dorothy Wordsworth's account of their trip to Scotland in 1803 and in Christopher Wordsworth's *Memoirs* that Wordsworth, encountering a steam engine during a walk with Coleridge, turned to his companion and made some observation to the effect that it was "scarcely possible to divest oneself of the impression on seeing it that it had life and volition." "Yes," replied Coleridge, "it is a great giant with one idea." It would have been characteristic of Coleridge, and of his attitude toward Wordsworth, if his comment were meant also to refer to the man beside him. Other contemporaries of Wordsworth went out of their way to comment on the homely, powerful nobility of his features, the harsh guttural burr of his northern accent, and his manner in society of "insulating [himself] from worldly cares" by withdrawing into a role self-sustaining and oblivious of other roles.

Indeed a great giant with one idea, almost incapable of irony, Wordsworth must often have found Coleridge's sensibility exceedingly restless, and can hardly have comprehended Keats's fevered attempt to bring order to his imagination by risking, daring, breaking, fusing letters, poems, people. If Keats's poems did not exist, a reader of his letters could conceive of their tone and impact, if not of their achievement. But a reader of Wordsworth's letters sees, instead of a poet, a man moving comfortably, almost smugly, from domestic figure (husband, brother, lover all use the same language) to public monument—Poet Laureate, distributor of stamps, guide to the Lakes—apparently without looking back to consider possibilities or alternatives. "Carrying onward from childhood to the grave, in a state of serene happiness" is the way De Quincey put it, at least ten years before Wordsworth died.

But the poems do suggest the price at which such dedication and later serenity were bought, and share in the energy that went into sustaining the purpose and achieving the success. In publishing *Lyrical Ballads* Wordsworth (at 28) and Coleridge (at 26) announced a revolution in literary technique that implied a new sense of the place of man as well as literature in the world. Neither poet had much public reason to claim such attention. Kept from his inheritance by Lord Lonsdale, prevented by the outbreak of war with France in 1793 from returning to Orléans to marry Annette Vallon and join the daughter she bore him, living in Somerset with his sister Dorothy so that he could be near Coleridge, Wordsworth in 1798 had neither career nor prospects. His only available resources were literary talent and an enormous ambition to change the hearts of men. The tone of the brief Advertisement prefixed to the 1798 *Lyrical Ballads* varies from apology to presumption. The poems are "experiments," yet the reader is warned to cast aside all the expectations aroused by the word "poetry," to judge these works not with literary standards but with moral and psychological ones: "they should ask themselves if [this book] contains a natural delineation of human passions, human characters, and human incidents." Their enemies, Wordsworth and Coleridge insist, are the reader's "pre-established codes of decision," and the potential victim is not this volume, or any form of literature, but "our own pleasure," which we lose if we have no willingness to ask more of poetry than we have.

Probably no volume of poetry has ever insisted more bluntly on its significant newness, or had less apparent chance of effecting such a dramatic change in taste and perception. For the most part Wordsworth's contributions are unassertive and impersonal in manner. The reader is often invited to say "how true" or "how sad" but rarely to feel that he ought to change the way he defines his life and the manner in which he lives it. An early reader such as Charles Burney, who reviewed the volume for the *Monthly Review*, did not pretend to cast aside his expectations for poetry, and found the collection gloomy, moving, far too unsophisticated. But like many subsequent readers he was puzzled by Wordsworth's final contribution to the volume, finished only a few days before it was sent to the printer and Wordsworth left for Germany with his sister and Coleridge: *Lines Composed a Few Miles Above Tintern Abbey*. This intensely autobiographical poem asks that its reader make a new effort of attention, for the power, homeliness, serenity that people found in the man Wordsworth are here explicitly announced as the proper goals of all individual imaginations. By saying simply at the opening of the poem "I am here," the poet (and the sympathetic reader) allows himself to be led into a reconsideration of his place, time, purpose, self. And the act of self-definition takes place—as usual with Wordsworth—at the edge of oblivion. One false answer, one failure of confidence, and the world as well as the self disappear into abstraction—or, from the reader's point of view, the logic of the argument becomes nonsense. Indeed it is with a sense of relief as well as achievement that the speaker in this poem turns at the end, in an apparently uninhabited universe, to find and recognize and bless his sister. She is at least a tangible alternative to his abstract talk about Nature and the "sense sublime of something far more deeply interfused." The pattern of this poem is one that recurs again and again, in *The Excursion, The Prelude*, the Immortality Ode, and *Resolution and Independence*. Given a world that is by turns beautiful, hostile, sublimely indifferent, the poet must confront, as Thoreau was to say of himself years later, the essential facts of life. Critical readers of *Tintern Abbey*, pointing out inconsistencies of vocabulary, rhetorical tricks (the subtle shift from "I" to "we"), and the change in mode from lyric to dramatic, have found more paradoxes in the poem than Wordsworth at the time seems to have been willing to acknowledge. When Keats, two decades later, was exploring the problem of an imagination that exposes to ruin what it seeks to save, he used Wordsworth's poem as his example of that state of mind in which "we see not the balance of good and evil" and find ourselves surrounded by doors "all dark—all leading to dark passages." (See Keats's letter of May 3, 1818, to Reynolds.) Even Burney, in his review of the volume, worried that the poem was anti-intellectual, because it seemed to deny the role of education and culture on which it depended.

The existence of sources and analogues for many of Wordsworth's characteristic poems suggests that his interests were not entirely unique, but statements of self-assurance qualified by yearnings for permanence emerge persistently enough in his work of the following decade to invite the reader's interest in the particular biographical circumstances of the author. And the enormous achievement of *The Prelude*—the first fully analytical autobiography in English prose or verse—totally removes any temptation to see Wordsworth as the nearly anonymous author of traditional poems.

The poems in *Lyrical Ballads* were the tentative early definitions of a career Wordsworth created without the assistance of society, church, court, or marketplace. Except for Coleridge and his own sister, he worked alone at a time when a literary career was still very much a social activity. Wordsworth's first thirty years were lived in the eighteenth century, and he must have known many people who assumed (as did Saint-Évremond) that "The State of a Solitary Person, is a state of Violence. ... What distinction is there between Death and Retirement, between Solitude and the Grave? To live then as Man, 'tis necessary to converse with Men."* In "Home at Grasmere," the section of the largely unwritten great philosophical poem to be called *The Recluse* (to which all *The Prelude* was merely prologue) that Wordsworth began in 1800, he admits that the satisfactions of self-sufficiency are limited, and tries to reconcile the urge toward retirement with the equally forceful demands of worldly ambition. To retire, after his education and his experience in France, is to enter the serenity of the grave. But only from a confrontation with this sort of solitude can authentic achievement come. The temptations of absolute silence and oblivion, on the one side, and an immersion in a world of books and deeds and conversation, on the other, are never distant from these poems written before the end of 1802. The will to give up, and the will to fulfill ambitions in the world of letters, have to be reconciled in terms that Wordsworth could not find and so had to create—as the tension between beauty and fear is reconciled in *The Prelude*, sometimes by lyric or drama or narrative, and too often by simple abstract rhetoric. The immense value Wordsworth assigned to these earlier poems in his own life made him a poor critic of his own work, as Coleridge so often pointed out. His language was not for him simply a mode of expression; it was the medium through which he created and justified a life. However often he seems to be addressing mankind, his concern in the earlier poems is almost unremittingly with himself, or the kindred spirits in future ages who would make up a society located in the dimension of time rather than of place. There is almost constantly present a Wordsworth who defines a self through a poetic struggle with the things and beings of his world, and often a Wordsworth who tries to speak, in the full voice of the self he found, to the "vast empire of human society as it is spread over the whole earth, and over all time." The dual purpose, almost paradoxical, is symbolized by *The Prelude* itself: a poem composed to justify the claim that he was capable of writing poetry that would bind together this vast empire, it is addressed to only one man. It is not surprising that Wordsworth's first readers were alienated by his presumption, or that much later ones were flattered by his attention.

* *Works*, I (1700), 311–12, as quoted by Herbert Davis in *Jonathan Swift, Essays on His Satire and Other Studies* (1964), p. 262.

To assign a date to the apparent change in Wordsworth's style, to account for a decline in achievement if not ability, has become a critical commonplace. Arguments for causes and dates can be confusingly persuasive. But it is clear that the cohesive concern with self that links so many of the poems from 1798 to 1802 disappears. Except for the several poems occasioned by the loss of his brother John at sea in 1805, most of the later poems are easily seen as separate works, occasioned independently by an event, sight, separable moment of experience. Wordsworth's sudden interest in the sonnet in the summer of 1802 may reflect greater confidence in poetry as formal public speech. Although the sonnets written during and after his visit to Annette at Calais that August can almost be made to narrate a shift of the poet's attention from domestic to political events, they appear to arise from moments separable from one another, and are far less explicitly involved (than *Resolution and Independence*, for instance) with the ongoing preoccupations of the poet with his own life. By 1805, *The Prelude* had been substantially finished (though it was frequently revised and never published during the next forty-five years), and *The Excursion* has rarely rewarded its readers with an excitement of discovery that would compensate for the duration of attention it demands.

The calm assurance and relative impersonality of much of the later poetry suggest that Wordsworth's revolutionary literary ideals did sustain him but not the life of his poems, and a modern reader's impatience with many of these poems perhaps indicates that he taught us all too well to demand that poetry offer not just reassurance but "new compositions of feeling." It is the poet's responsibility, he says in 1802, "to render [the reader's] feelings more sane, pure, permanent, in short more consonant to nature, that is, to eternal nature, and the great moving spirit of things." When Wordsworth's voice begins to pall—as it does at times even in *The Prelude*— it is because he has urged us so often to expect so much, to recognize that the rectification of our feelings requires all the art, energy, courage, and genius that imagination and its language can provide. One critic has said that the test of a good Wordsworth poem is whether it can be read effectively aloud, and that the best lines simply contain more feeling than the human voice is capable of incorporating. Many of the late poems can be read aloud all too easily.

If Wordsworth was indeed a great giant with one idea, critics since Coleridge have tried to stand outside the assumptions Wordsworth has given us all as readers in order to say what that idea was. By insisting on the importance of *Resolution and Independence* Wordsworth himself has implied that a right reading of that poem is essential to an understanding of what he has to say elsewhere. And the best general gloss of the poem's statement remains the passage in Coleridge's "Theory of Life" where (without mentioning Wordsworth) he presents man with "the whole world in counterpoint to him," man and nature, separated; almost, man against nature. Yet, Coleridge says, a man also contains a whole world inside himself; although he arrives on earth naked and helpless, he is also potentially sovereign. To accommodate to his own existence he must be resigned to the real world, be sympathetic with the rest of mankind, be aware of the intercommunion with nature—and at the same time he must insist through genius and originality on his independence and individuality. The fully authentic man knows that "Life itself is not a *thing* . . . but an *act* and *process.*" In this poem both the leech gatherer and the speaker find their being, their "stay secure," in reconciling independent act and impersonal process through individuation—that is, they use what they see around them, in rather different ways, to create what they become. The one idea of the great giant is, then, the source of its life and volition.

Few writers have required more of their readers than Wordsworth does: a willingness to be bored, constant attention to a voice that speaks repeatedly of itself (the "egotistical sublime," Keats called it). Yet fewer poets still have offered their readers so much in return: a reassuring sense of dignity, importance, responsibility. John Stuart Mill was neither the first nor last nonliterary figure to find a kind of therapy in reading Wordsworth. The revolution that began in 1798 has so successfully changed our expectations about the subjects and effects appropriate to poetry that it now takes an effort of the imagination to hear new sounds in these poems, and to recognize that the feelings they express were indeed new to literature. Wordsworth seems so often to be saying what we already know, that the familiarity of the statement can prevent our discovering that we did not know it before he wrote, that we now do not know it well enough, and that it can be rediscovered and relived with careful rereading. When the best poems are read with the right sort of imaginative attention, the world that Wordsworth creates becomes a constantly exciting and mysterious place.

OUTLINE OF EVENTS

1770	Apr. 7	Born at Cockermouth (Cumberland), son of John Wordsworth (1741–1783) and Ann Cookson Wordsworth (1748–1778), brother of Richard (1768–1816), Dorothy (1771–1855), John (1772–1805), Christopher (1774–1846).
	Aug. 16	Mary Hutchinson (m. 1802) born.
1776	Apr.–Oct.	Enrolls at Gilbank's School (Cockermouth); later probably attends infant school at Penrith (1776–1777).
1778	Mar.	Mother dies at Penrith. Dorothy goes to live with cousin at Halifax. [See *Prelude*, V, 256 ff.]
1779	May	Enters Hawkshead Free Grammar School as boarder (where he stays, except for vacations, until 1787). [See *Prelude*, II.]
	June	Discovers clothes of drowned man beside Esthwaite Lake. [See *Prelude*, V, 426.]
1783	Dec.	Father dies at Cockermouth.
1784	Autumn	Composes first verses.
1785	June	Composes earliest surviving verses (on bicentenary of Hawkshead School).
1787	Mar.	Publishes first poem, *Sonnet ... Miss Helen Maria Williams*, in *European Magazine*.
	May	Wordsworth family decides to sue Sir James Lowther (later

		Lord Lonsdale) for wages owed to John Wordsworth, Sr. (unsettled until 1802).
	Oct.	Enters St. John's College, Cambridge. [See *Prelude*, III.]
	Dec.	First (brief) visit to London.
1788	Summer	Begins *An Evening Walk*.
1789	Winter	Richard Wordsworth enters London law office.
	July 14	Attack on Bastille.
1790	July–Oct.	On walking tour with Robert Jones in France, Germany, Switzerland, Italy (in August at Monastery of Grande Chartreuse, Mont Blanc, Simplon Pass). [See *Prelude*, VI, 321 ff.]
1791	Jan.	Qualifies for B.A.; goes to London.
	May–Aug.	In Wales with Jones. [See *Prelude*, XIV, 1–205.]
	Nov.	Returns to France. [See *Prelude*, IX–XI.]
	Dec.	Stays at Blois and Orléans; meets Annette Vallon. Begins *Descriptive Sketches*.
1792	Jan.–Oct.	At Blois and Orléans.
	Sept. 22	French Republic declared.
	Nov. or Dec.	Returns to London. [See *Prelude*, esp. X]
	Dec. 15	Anne-Caroline (d. 1862) born to Annette Vallon and William Wordsworth.
1793	Jan.–June	In London.
	Jan. 29	*An Evening Walk* and *Descriptive Sketches* published in London.
	Feb. 1	France declares war on England.
	July–Sept.	Goes to Isle of Wight, Salisbury Plain, North Wales (via Tintern Abbey).
	Oct.	Returns (uncertain) to France.
1794	Feb. (?earlier)–May	With Dorothy at Halifax, Whitehaven, Keswick.
	July 28	Death of Robespierre. [See *Prelude*, X, 481–603.]
1795	Jan.	Calvert dies, leaving legacy to Wordsworth.
	Feb.–Aug.	In London; seeing Godwin frequently.
	Aug.	Goes to Bristol; meets Southey, later S. T. Coleridge.
	Sept.	Moves with Dorothy to Racedown Lodge, Dorset (until July 1797). [See *Prelude*, I, 1–54.]
1796	Summer (to 1797)	Works on tragedy *The Borderers*.
1797	June	S. T. Coleridge visits Wordsworths at Racedown.
	July	Wordsworth and Dorothy visit S. T. Coleridge at Nether Stowey (Somerset); they see Alfoxden and move there July 16 (to stay until June 1798).
	Aug.	S. T. Coleridge, Wordsworth, and others investigated as potential saboteurs by government spy.
	Nov.	During walking tour Wordsworth and Coleridge plan *The Rime of the Ancient Mariner* and a volume of lyrical ballads.

1798	Jan. 20	Dorothy Wordsworth begins journal.
	Jan.–Mar.	Plans *Recluse*; works on *The Ruined Cottage*.
	Mar.–May	Composes many of original *Lyrical Ballads*, including *The Idiot Boy*, *We Are Seven*, *Goody Blake*.
	May 20	Hazlitt visits Coleridge and Wordsworth.
	Late June–early July	Wordsworth and Dorothy leave Alfoxden for Bristol.
	July 10–13	Wordsworth and Dorothy walk to Tintern Abbey and Wye valley. Wordsworth composes *Tintern Abbey* at this time.
	Aug.	Travels with Dorothy to London (via Oxford).
	Sept.	*Lyrical Ballads* appears (anonymously, though not yet officially published). Sails with Dorothy and Coleridge from Yarmouth to Hamburg.
	Oct. 6	William and Dorothy arrive in Goslar, Saxony.
	Oct.–Mar. (1799)	In Goslar composes (among others) *Ruth*, *Lucy Gray*, Matthew poems, part of *Prelude*.
1799	Mar.–Apr.	Travels with Dorothy in Germany.
	Apr.–May	Returns to England with Dorothy.
	May–Dec.	With Dorothy at Sockburn-on-Tees.
	Oct.	Coleridge arrives at Sockburn.
	Oct.–Nov.	With Coleridge on walking tour in north of England, including Lake District.
	Dec.	William and Dorothy move to Dove Cottage, Grasmere (Westmorland).
1800		During the year, Coleridge, John Wordsworth, and Mary Hutchinson visit Dove Cottage.
	Feb.	Composes *The Brothers*.
	Oct.–Dec.	Composes *Michael*.
1801		At Dove Cottage except for summer visit to Scotland.
	Jan.	*Lyrical Ballads* (2nd ed., 2 vols.) published.
	Dec.	Works at translations from Chaucer.
1802	Jan.–July	At Dove Cottage. Writes 39 poems during the year.
	Mar.	Composes *To a Butterfly*, "*My heart leaps up*," *Ode: Intimations of Immortality* (first four stanzas).
	Apr.	Composes *Written in March*, *Foresight*, "*Among all lovely things*." Coleridge writes first version of *Dejection: An Ode*.
	May	Death of Lord Lonsdale, whose successor agrees (in 1803) to pay salary owed to John Wordsworth, Sr., to his children. William composes *To a Skylark*, *A Farewell*, "*I grieved for Buonaparté*," *Resolution and Independence* (finished in July).
	July	William and Dorothy leave Grasmere for London and Calais.
	Aug.	William and Dorothy visit Annette Vallon and William's daughter Caroline at Calais. Composes at least nine sonnets.

	Sept.	William and Dorothy return to London. Wordsworth composes more sonnets. [See *Prelude*, VII, 649 ff.]
	Oct. 4	Marries Mary Hutchinson at Brompton, Yorkshire. Returns to Grasmere with Dorothy and Mary.
1803		At Dove Cottage.
	June 18	Son John born.
	Aug.	Sets out on tour of Scotland with Dorothy and Coleridge.
	Oct.	William and Dorothy return to Grasmere.
	Nov.	Composes *Yarrow Unvisited, To a Highland Girl*, and others.
1804		At Dove Cottage.
	Jan., Feb., Apr.	Writes most of Books III, IV, V, VI, and IX of *Prelude*.
	Feb.	Composes *Ode to Duty*.
	Apr. 2	S. T. Coleridge leaves for Malta.
	Aug. 16	Dora Wordsworth born.
	Oct.–Dec.	Writes most of Books VII, VIII, and X of *Prelude*.
1805		At Dove Cottage.
	Feb. 5	Brother John drowned in wreck of *Earl of Abergavenny*. (See poems *Elegaic Verses: In Memory of My Brother, John Wordsworth; To the Daisy; Elegaic Stanzas: Suggested by a Picture of Peele Castle, in a Storm, Painted by Sir John Beaumont;* letter to Richard Wordsworth, 11 February, 1805.)
	Apr.–May	Finishes first version of *Prelude*.
	June	Writes *Stepping Westward*.
	Nov.	Composes *The Solitary Reaper*.
1806	Jan.–Apr.	At Dove Cottage.
	Apr.–May	In London.
	June 16	Son Thomas born.
	July	Composes *Elegaic Stanzas . . . Peele Castle*.
	Aug.	S. T. Coleridge returns to England from Malta.
	Oct.	Wordsworths move to farmhouse at Coleorton lent by Sir George Beaumont.
1807	Jan.–Apr.	At Coleorton.
	Apr.	Visits London; returns to Coleorton with W. Scott.
	May	*Poems in Two Volumes* published.
	Aug.	Wordsworths return to Dove Cottage.
	Oct.	Begins *White Doe of Rylstone*.
	Nov.	De Quincey visits Dove Cottage.
1808	Jan.–June	At Dove Cottage.
	Feb.	Finishes *White Doe*.
	June	Wordsworths move to Allan Bank, Grasmere.
	Sept. 6	Daughter Catherine born.

	Sept.	Coleridge and De Quincey join household at Allan Bank.
	Nov.–Dec.	Writes tract on Convention of Cintra.
1809		At Allan Bank.
	June	Coleridge begins publication of *The Friend*.
	Nov.	De Quincey moves into Dove Cottage.
1810		At Allan Bank.
	Feb.	Publishes *Essay on Epitaphs* in *The Friend*.
	May 12	Son William born.
	Oct.	Becomes estranged from Coleridge.
1811	Jan.–May	At Allan Bank.
	May	Wordsworths move to the Rectory, Grasmere.
1812		At Rectory.
	May	Visits London; is partially reconciled with Coleridge.
	June 4	Death of daughter Catherine.
	Dec. 1	Death of son Thomas.
1813	Jan.–May	At Rectory.
	Mar.	Appointed Distributor of Stamps for Westmorland.
	May	Wordsworths move to Rydal Mount (where they live until his death in 1850).
1814	July	On tour in Scotland.
	Aug.	*Excursion* published.
1815	Mar.	Collected poems published.
1817	Dec.	Keats and Wordsworth meet in London at B. R. Haydon's.
1819	Jan.	Appointed Justice of the Peace for Westmorland.
	Apr.	*Peter Bell* published.
	May	*The Waggoner* published.
1820	May	*River Duddon* published.
	July–Nov.	Tours Switzerland, northern Italy, France with Mary and Dorothy.
1821		Death of Keats.
1822	Feb.–Mar.	*Memorials of a Tour on the Continent* and *Ecclesiastical Sonnets* published.
		Death of Shelley.
1823	May–June	On tour through the Netherlands.
1824		Death of Byron.
1827		Five-volume edition of poems published.
1828	June	Tours the Rhine with daughter Dora.
1829	Aug.–Sept.	On carriage tour of Ireland.
1834		Death of Coleridge.
1837		Six-volume edition of poems published.
	Mar.–Aug.	With H. Crabb Robinson on tour in France and Italy.

1839		Receives degree of D.C.L. from Oxford.
1843	Apr.	Becomes Poet Laureate on death of Southey.
1847	July 9	Death of Dora Wordsworth (Quillinan).
1850	Apr. 23	Wordsworth dies at Rydal Mount.
	July	*Prelude* published posthumously.

SELECTED BIBLIOGRAPHY

BIBLIOGRAPHIES

J. V. LOGAN, *Wordsworthian Criticism: A Guide and Bibliography* (1947).
E. F. HEALEY and D. H. STAM, *Wordsworthian Criticism, 1945–64* (1965).

EDITIONS

The Poetical Works of William Wordsworth, ed. E. de Selincourt and H.
  Darbishire (5 vols., 1940–1949, 1952–1954).
The Prelude ed. de Selincourt and Darbishire (1959).
The Prelude, A Parallel Text, ed. J. C. Maxwell (1971).
The Prose Works of William Wordsworth, ed. A. Grosart (3 vols., 1876).
The Literary Criticism of William Wordsworth, ed. P. M. Zall (1966).
The Letters of William and Dorothy Wordsworth, ed. E. de Selincourt (6 vols.,
  1935–1939); now being revised by C. L. Shaver, M. Moorman, and A. G.
  Hill (1967+).

BIOGRAPHICAL INFORMATION

The Journals of Dorothy Wordsworth, ed. E. de Selincourt (2 vols., 1941); ed.
  M. Moorman (1971).
CHRISTOPHER WORDSWORTH, *Memoirs of William Wordsworth* (2 vols.,
  1851).
G. M. HARPER, *William Wordsworth* (2 vols., 1916; rev. and abridged, 1929).
M. MOORMAN, *William Wordsworth* (2 vols., 1959–1965).
M. B. REED, *Wordsworth: The Chronology of the Early Years, 1770–1799*
  (1966).
T. W. THOMPSON, *Wordsworth's Hawkeshead*, ed. R. Woof (1970).

GENERAL CRITICISM

S. T. COLERIDGE, *Biographia Literaria* (1817).
F. R. LEAVIS, "Wordsworth," *Revaluations* (1936).
J. SMITH, "Wordsworth: A Preliminary Survey," *Scrutiny* (1938).
H. DARBISHIRE, *The Poet Wordsworth* (1950).
F. W. BATESON, *Wordsworth: A Re-interpretation* (1954, rev. 1956).
J. JONES, *The Egotistical Sublime* (1954).
D. FERRY, *The Limits of Mortality* (1959).
C. C. CLARKE, *Romantic Paradox* (1962).
J. DAVIS, ed., *Discussions of Wordsworth* (1964).
G. HARTMAN, *Wordsworth's Poetry, 1787–1814* (1964).
D. PERKINS, *Wordsworth and the Poetry of Sincerity* (1964).
C. WOODRING, *Wordsworth* (1965).
A. KING, *Wordsworth and the Artist's Vision: An Essay in Interpretation* (1966).
J. SCOGGINS, *Imagination and Fancy: Complementary Modes in the Poetry of
  Wordsworth* (1967).

M. Drabble, *Wordsworth* (1969).

G. Durant, *William Wordsworth* (1969).

J. Heffernan, *Wordsworth's Theory of Poetry: The Transforming Imagination* (1969).

W. J. B. Owen, *Wordsworth as Critic* (1969).

A. W. Thomson, ed., *Wordsworth's Mind and Art* (1969).

J. Wordsworth, *The Music of Humanity* (1969).

W. Heath, *Wordsworth and Coleridge: A Study of Their Literary Relations in 1801–2* (1970).

S. Prickett, *Coleridge and Wordsworth: The Poetry of Growth* (1970).

J. Wordsworth, ed., *Bicentenary Wordsworth Studies* (1970).

DISCUSSIONS OF PARTICULAR WORKS

The Prelude

R. D. Havens, *The Mind of a Poet* (2 vols., 1941).

A. F. Potts, *Wordsworth's Prelude: A Study of Its Literary Form* (1953).

J. P. Bishop, "Wordsworth and the 'Spots of Time,'" *ELH* (1959).

H. Lindenberger, *On Wordsworth's Prelude* (1963).

R. J. Onorato, *The Character of the Poet: Wordsworth in The Prelude* (1971).

Other Poems

L. Trilling, "Wordsworth's 'Ode: Intimations of Immortality,'" *The Liberal Imagination* (1950).

W. W. Robson, "Resolution and Independence," *Selected Criticism* (1967).

POEMS

AN EVENING WALK

In notes later dictated to Isabella Fenwick, Wordsworth explains that this poem, addressed to his sister Dorothy, was written during his first two vacations from Cambridge, and that the country-side and occasions are idealized ("a proof of my unwillingness to submit the poetic spirit to the claims of fact and real circumstance").

AN EVENING WALK.

An Epistle; in Verse.
Addressed to a Young Lady,
from the Lakes of the
North of England.

Argument

General Sketch of the Lakes—Author's Regret of his Youth passed amongst them—Short description of Noon—Cascade Scene—Noontide Retreat—Precipice and Sloping Lights—Face of Nature as the Sun declines— Mountain Farm, and the Cock—Slate Quarry—Sunset— Superstition of the Country, connected with that Moment —Swans—Female Beggar—Twilight Objects—Twilight Sounds—Western Lights—Spirits—Night—Moonlight— Hope—Night Sounds—Conclusion.

Far from my dearest friend, 'tis mine to rove
Thro bare grey dell, high wood, and pastoral cove;
His wizard course where hoary Derwent takes
Thro' craggs, and forest glooms, and opening lakes,
Staying his silent waves, to hear the roar
That stuns the tremulous cliffs of high Lodore:
Where silver rocks the savage prospect chear
Of giant yews that frown on Rydale's mere;
Where peace to Grasmere's lonely island leads,
To willowy hedgerows, and to emerald meads;   10
Leads to her bridge, rude church, and cottag'd
        grounds,
Her rocky sheepwalks, and her woodland bounds;
Where, bosom'd deep, the shy Winander* peeps
'Mid clust'ring isles, and holly-sprinkl'd steeps;

* These lines are only applicable to the middle part of that lake.

Where twilight glens endear my Esthwaite's shore,
And memory of departed pleasures, more.

Fair scenes! with other eyes, than once, I gaze,
The ever-varying charm your round displays,
Than when, erewhile, I taught, "a happy child,"
The echoes of your rocks my carols wild: 20
Then did no ebb of chearfulness demand
Sad tides of joy from Melancholy's hand;
In youth's wild eye the livelong day was bright,
The sun at morning, and the stars of night,
Alike, when first the vales the bittern fills
Or the first woodcocks* roam'd the moonlight hills.

Return Delights! with whom my road begun,
When Life rear'd laughing up her morning sun;
When Transport kiss'd away my april tear,
"Rocking as in a dream the tedious year;"   30
When link'd with thoughtless Mirth I cours'd the
        plain,
And hope itself was all I knew of pain.
For then, ev'n then, the little heart would beat
At times, while young Content forsook her seat,
And wild Impatience, panting upward, show'd
Where tipp'd with gold the mountain-summits
        glow'd.
Alas! the idle tale of man is found
Depicted in the dial's moral round;
With Hope Reflexion blends her social rays
To gild the total tablet of his days;   40
Yet still, the sport of some malignant Pow'r,
He knows but from its shade the present hour.
While, Memory at my side, I wander here,
Starts at the simplest sight th' unbidden tear,
A form discover'd at the well-known seat,
A spot, that angles at the riv'let's feet,
The cot the ray of morning trav'ling nigh,
And sail that glides the well-known alders by.
But why, ungrateful, dwell on idle pain?
To shew her yet some joys to me remain,   50
Say, will my friend, with soft affection's ear,
The history of a poet's ev'ning hear?
When, in the south, the wan noon brooding still,
Breath'd a pale steam around the glaring hill,
And shades of deep embattl'd clouds were seen
Spotting the northern cliffs with lights between;
Gazing the tempting shades to them deny'd,
When stood the shorten'd herds amid the tide,
Where, from the barren wall's unshelter'd end,
Long rails into the shallow lake extend;   60

* In the beginning of winter, these mountains, in the moon-
light nights, are covered with immense quantities of woodcocks;
which, in the dark nights, retire into the woods.

When schoolboys stretch'd their length upon the
        green
And round the humming elm, a glimmering scene!
In the brown park, in flocks, the troubl'd deer
Shook the still twinkling tail and glancing ear;
When horses in the wall-girt intake† stood,
Unshaded, eying far below, the flood,
Crouded behind the swain, in mute distress,
With forward neck the closing gate to press;
And long, with wistful gaze, his walk survey'd
Till dipp'd his pathway in the river shade;   70
—Then Quiet led me up the huddling rill,
Bright'ning with water-breaks the sombrous gill‡;
To where, while thick above the branches close,
In dark-brown bason its wild waves repose,
Inverted shrubs, and moss of darkest green,
Cling from the rocks, with pale wood-weeds between;
Save that, atop, the subtle sunbeams shine,
On wither'd briars that o'er the craggs recline;
Sole light admitted here, a small cascade,
Illumes with sparkling foam the twilight shade.   80
Beyond, along the visto of the brook,
Where antique roots its bustling path o'erlook,
The eye reposes on a secret bridge§
Half grey, half shagg'd with ivy to its ridge.
—Sweet rill, farewel! To-morrow's noon again,
Shall hide me wooing long thy wildwood strain;
But now the sun has gain'd his western road,
And eve's mild hour invites my steps abroad.

While, near the midway cliff, the silver'd kite
In many a whistling circle wheels her flight;   90
Slant wat'ry lights, from parting clouds a-pace,
Travel along the precipice's base;
Chearing its naked waste of scatter'd stone
By lychens grey, and scanty moss o'er-grown,
Where scarce the foxglove peeps, and thistle's beard,
And desert stone-chat, all day long, is heard.

How pleasant, as the yellowing sun declines,
And with long rays and shades the landscape shines;
To mark the birches' stems all golden light,
That lit the dark slant woods with silvery white!   100
The willows weeping trees, that twinkling hoar,
Glanc'd oft upturn'd along the breezy shore,
Low bending o'er the colour'd water, fold
Their moveless boughs and leaves like threads of
        gold;

† The word *intake* is local, and signifies a mountain-inclosure.
‡ Gill is also, I believe, a term confined to this country.
Glen, gill, and dingle, have the same meaning.
§ The reader, who has made the tour of this country, will
recognize in this description the features which characterize the
lower waterfall in the gardens of Rydale.

The skiffs with naked masts at anchor laid,
Before the boat-house peeping thro' the shade;
Th'unwearied glance of woodman's echo'd stroke;
And curling from the trees the cottage smoke.

Their pannier'd train a groupe of potters goad,
Winding from side to side up the steep road;   110
The peasant from yon cliff of fearful edge
Shot, down the headlong pathway darts his sledge;
Bright beams the lonely mountain horse illume,
Feeding 'mid purple heath, "green rings*," and
    broom;
While the sharp slope the slacken'd team confounds,
Downward† the pond'rous timber-wain resounds;
Beside their sheltering cross‡ of wall, the flock
Feeds on in light, nor thinks of winter's shock;
In foamy breaks the rill, with merry song,
Dash'd down the rough rock, lightly leaps along;   120
From lonesome chapel at the mountain's feet,
Three humble bells their rustic chime repeat;
Sounds from the water-side the hammer'd boat;
And blasted quarry thunders heard remote.

Ev'n here, amid the sweep of endless woods,
Blue pomp of lakes, high cliffs, and falling floods,
Not undelightful are the simplest charms
Found by the verdant door of mountain farms.

Sweetly§ ferocious round his native walks,
Gaz'd by his sister-wives, the monarch stalks;
Spur-clad his nervous feet, and firm his tread,
A crest of purple tops his warrior head.
Bright sparks his black and haggard eye-ball hurls
Afar, his tail he closes and unfurls;
Whose state, like pine-trees, waving to and fro,
Droops, and o'er canopies his regal brow,
On tiptoe rear'd he blows his clarion throat,
Threaten'd by faintly answering farms remote.

Bright'ning the cliffs between where sombrous
    pine,
And yew-trees o'er the silver rocks recline,   140
I love to mark the quarry's moving trains,
Dwarf pannier'd steeds, and men, and numerous
    wains:

How busy the enormous hive within,
While Echo dallies with the various din!
Some, hardly heard their chissel's clinking sound,
Toil, small as pigmies, in the gulph profound;
Some, dim between th' aereal cliffs descry'd,
O'erwalk the viewless plank from side to side;
These by the pale-blue rocks that ceaseless ring
Glad from their airy baskets hang and sing.   150

Hung o'er a cloud, above the steep that rears
It's edge all flame, the broad'ning sun appears;
A long blue bar it's ægis orb divides,
And breaks the spreading of it's golden tides;
And now it touches on the purple steep
That flings his shadow on the pictur'd deep.
Cross the calm lakes blue shades the cliffs aspire,
With tow'rs and woods a "prospect all on fire;"
The coves and secret hollows thro' a ray
Of fainter gold a purple gleam betray;   160
The gilded turf arrays in richer green
Each speck of lawn the broken rocks between;
Deep yellow beams the scatter'd boles illume,
Far in the level forest's central gloom;
Waving his hat, the shepherd in the vale
Directs his winding dog the cliffs to scale,
That, barking busy 'mid the glittering rocks,
Hunts, where he points, the intercepted flocks;
Where oaks o'erhang the road the radiance shoots
On tawny earth, wild weeds, and twisted roots;   170
The Druid‖ stones their lighted fane unfold
And all the babbling brooks are liquid gold;
Sunk¶ to a curve, the day-star lessens still,
Gives one bright glance, and sinks behind the hill.

In these lone vales, if aught of faith may claim,
Thin silver hairs, and ancient hamlet fame;
When up the hills, as now, retreats the light,
Strange apparitions mock the village sight.

A desperate form appears, that spurs his steed,
Along the midway cliffs with violent speed;   180
Unhurt pursues his lengthen'd flight, while all
Attend, at every stretch, his headlong fall.
Anon, in order mounts a gorgeous show
Of horsemen shadows winding to and fro;
And now the van is gilt with evening's beam
The rear thro' iron brown betrays a sullen gleam;

---

   * "Vivid rings of green." GREENWOOD'S Poem on Shooting.
   † "Down the rough slope the pond'rous waggon rings."
BEATTIE.
   ‡ These rude structures, to protect the flocks, are frequent
in this country: the traveller may recollect one in Withburne,
another upon Whinlatter.
   § "Dolcemente feroce."—TASSO.
   In this description of the cock, I remembered a spirited one
of the same animal in l'Agriculture, ou Les Géorgiques Fran-
çoises of M. Rossuet.

   ‖ Not far from Broughton is a Druid monument, of which I
do not recollect that any tour descriptive of this country makes
mention. Perhaps this poem may fall into the hands of some
curious traveller, who may thank me for informing him, that
up the Duddon, the river which forms the æstuary at Broughton,
may be found some of the most romantic scenery of these
mountains.
   ¶ From Thomson: see Scott's Critical Essays.

Lost* gradual o'er the heights in pomp they go,
While silent stands th' admiring vale below;
Till, but the lonely beacon all is fled,
That tips with eve's last gleam his spiry head.   190

Now while the solemn evening Shadows sail,
On red slow-waving pinions down the vale,
And, fronting the bright west in stronger lines,
The oak its dark'ning boughs and foliage twines,
I love beside the flowing lake to stray,
Where winds the road along the secret bay;
By rills that tumble down the woody steeps,
And run in transport to the dimpling deeps;
Along the "wild meand'ring" shore to view,
Obsequious Grace the winding swan pursue.   200
He swells his lifted chest, and backward flings
His bridling neck between his tow'ring wings;
Stately, and burning in his pride, divides
And glorying looks around, the silent tides:
On as he floats, the silver'd waters glow.
Proud of the varying arch and moveless form of snow.
While tender Cares and mild domestic Loves,
With furtive watch pursue her as she moves;
The female with a meeker charm succeeds,
And her brown little ones around her leads,   210
Nibbling the water lilies as they pass,
Or playing wanton with the floating grass:
She in a mother's care, her beauty's pride
Forgets, unweary'd watching every side,
She calls them near, and with affection sweet
Alternately relieves their weary feet;
Alternately† they mount her back, and rest
Close by her mantling wings' embraces prest.

Long may ye roam these hermit waves that sleep,
In birch besprinkl'd cliffs embosom'd deep;   220
These fairy holms untrodden, still, and green,
Whose shades protect the hidden wave serene;
Whence fragrance scents the water's desart gale,
The violet, and the lily‡ of the vale;
Where, tho' her far-off twilight ditty steal,
They not the trip of harmless milkmaid feel.

Yon tuft conceals your home, your cottage bow'r,
Fresh water rushes strew the verdant floor;
Long grass and willows form the woven wall,
And swings above the roof the poplar tall.   230
Thence issuing oft, unwieldly as ye stalk,
Ye crush with broad black feet your flow'ry walk;

* See a description of an appearance of this kind in Clark's "Survey of the Lakes", accompanied with vouchers of its veracity that may amuse the reader.
† This is a fact of which I have been an eyewitness.
‡ The lily of the valley is found in great abundance in the smaller islands of Winandermere.

Safe from your door ye hear at breezy morn,
The hound, the horse's tread, and mellow horn;
At peace inverted your lithe necks ye lave,
With the green bottom strewing o'er the wave;
No ruder sound your desart haunts invades,
Than waters dashing wild, or rocking shades.
Ye ne'er, like hapless human wanderers, throw
Your young on winter's winding sheet of snow.   240
Fair swan! by all a mother's joys caress'd,
Haply some wretch has ey'd, and call'd thee bless'd;
Who faint, and beat by summer's breathless ray,
Hath dragg'd her babes along this weary way;
While arrowy fire extorting feverish groans,
Shot stinging through her stark o'er-labour'd bones.
—With backward gaze, lock'd joints, and step of pain,
Her seat scarce left, she strives, alas! in vain,
To teach their limbs along the burning road
A few short steps to totter with their load,   250
Shakes her numb arm that slumbers with its weight,
And eyes through tears the mountain's shadeless height;
And bids her soldier come her woes to share,
Asleep on Bunker's charnel hill afar;
For hope's deserted well why wistful look?
Chok'd is the pathway, and the pitcher broke.

I see her now, deny'd to lay her head,
On cold blue nights, in hut or straw-built shed;
Turn to a silent smile their sleepy cry,
By pointing to a shooting star on high: 260
I hear, while in the forest depth he sees,
The Moon's fix'd gaze between the opening trees,
In broken sounds her elder grief demand,
And skyward lift, like one that prays, his hand,
If, in that country, where he dwells afar,
His father views that good, that kindly star;
—Ah me! all light is mute amid the gloom,
The interlunar cavern of the tomb.
—When low-hung clouds each star of summer hide,
And fireless are the valleys far and wide,   270
Where the brook brawls along the painful road,
Dark with bat haunted ashes stretching broad,
The distant clock forgot, and chilling dew,
Pleas'd thro' the dusk their breaking smiles to view,
Oft has she taught them on her lap to play
Delighted, with the glow-worm's harmless ray
Toss'd light from hand to hand; while on the ground
Small circles of green radiance gleam around.

Oh! when the bitter showers her path assail,
And roars between the hills the torrent gale,   280
—No more her breath can thaw their fingers cold,
Their frozen arms her neck no more can fold;

Scarce heard, their chattering lips her shoulder
          chill,
And her cold back their colder bosoms thrill;
All blind she wilders o'er the lightless heath,
Led by Fear's cold wet hand, and dogg'd by Death;
Death, as she turns her neck the kiss to seek,
Breaks off the dreadful kiss with angry shriek.
Snatch'd from her shoulder with despairing moan,
She clasps them at that dim-seen roofless
          stone—   290
"Now ruthless Tempest launch thy deadliest dart!
Fall fires—but let us perish heart to heart."
Weak roof a cow'ring form two babes to shield,
And faint the fire a dying heart can yield;
Press the sad kiss, fond mother! vainly fears
Thy flooded cheek to wet them with its tears;
Soon shall the Light'ning hold before thy head
His torch, and shew them slumbering in their bed,
No tears can chill them, and no bosom warms,
Thy breast their death-bed, coffin'd in thine
          arms.

Sweet are the sounds that mingle from afar,   301
Heard by calm lakes, as peeps the folding star,
Where the duck dabbles 'mid the rustling sedge,
And feeding pike starts from the water's edge,
Or the swan stirs the reeds, his neck and bill
Wetting, that drip upon the water still;
And heron, as resounds the trodden shore,
Shoots upward, darting his long neck before.
While, by the scene compos'd, the breast subsides,
Nought wakens or disturbs it's tranquil tides;   310
Nought but the char that for the may-fly leaps,
And breaks the mirror of the circling deeps;
Or clock, that blind against the wanderer born,
Drops at his feet, and stills his droning horn.
—The whistling swain that plods his ringing way
Where the slow waggon winds along the bay;
The sugh* of swallow flocks that twittering sweep,
The solemn curfew swinging long and deep;
The talking boat that moves with pensive sound,
Or drops his anchor down with plunge profound;
Of boys that bathe remote the faint uproar,   321
And restless piper wearying out the shore;
These all to swell the village murmurs blend,
That soften'd from the water-head descend.
While in sweet cadence rising small and still
The far-off minstrels of the haunted hill,
As the last bleating of the fold expires,
Tune in the mountain dells their water lyres.

* 'Sugh,' a Scotch word, expressive, as Mr. Gilpin explains
it, of the sound of the motion of a stick through the air, or of the
wind passing through the trees. See Burns' Cotter's Saturday
Night.

Now with religious awe the farewell light
Blends with the solemn colouring of the night;   330
'Mid groves of clouds that crest the mountain's brow,
And round the West's proud lodge their shadows
          throw,
Like Una† shining on her gloomy way,
The half seen form of Twilight roams astray;
Thence, from three paly loopholes mild and small,
Slow lights upon the lake's still bosom fall,
Beyond the mountain's giant reach that hides
In deep determin'd gloom his subject tides.
—'Mid the dark steeps repose the shadowy streams,
As touch'd with dawning moonlight's hoary gleams,
Long streaks of fairy light the wave illume   341
With bordering lines of intervening gloom,
Soft o'er the surface creep the lustres pale
Tracking with silvering path the changeful gale.
—'Tis restless magic all; at once the bright
Breaks on the shade, the shade upon the light,
Fair Spirits are abroad; in sportive chase
Brushing with lucid wands the water's face,
While music stealing round the glimmering deeps
Charms the tall circle of th' enchanted steeps.   350
—As thro' th' astonish'd woods the notes ascend,
The mountain streams their rising song suspend;
Below Eve's listening Star the sheep walk stills
It's drowsy tinklings on th' attentive hills;
The milkmaid stops her ballad, and her pail
Stays it's low murmur in th' unbreathing vale;
No night-duck clamours for his wilder'd mate,
Aw'd, while below the Genii hold their state.
—The pomp is fled, and mute the wondrous strains,
No wrack of all the pageant scene remains,   360
So‡ vanish those fair Shadows, human joys,
But Death alone their vain regret destroys.
Unheeded Night has overcome the vales,
On the dark earth the baffl'd vision fails,
If peep between the clouds a star on high,
There turns for glad repose the weary eye;
The latest lingerer of the forest train,
The lone black fir, forsakes the faded plain;
Last evening sight, the cottage smoke no more,
Lost in the deepen'd darkness, glimmers hoar;   370
High towering from the sullen dark-brown mere,
Like a black wall, the mountain steeps appear,
Thence red from different heights with restless gleam
Small cottage lights across the water stream,

† Alluding to this passage of Spenser—
                    "Her angel face
        As the great eye of Heaven shined bright,
        And made a sunshine in that shady place."
                              [The Færie Queene.]
‡ "So break those glittering shadows, human joys." Young.
                        [Edward Young's Night Thoughts.]

Nought else of man or life remains behind
To call from other worlds the wilder'd mind,
Till pours the wakeful bird her solemn strains
Heard* by the night-calm of the wat'ry plains.
—No purple prospects now the mind employ
Glowing in golden sunset tints of joy,   380
But o'er the sooth'd accordant heart we feel
A sympathetic twilight slowly steal,
And ever, as we fondly muse, we find
The soft gloom deep'ning on the tranquil mind.
Stay! pensive, sadly-pleasing visions, stay!
Ah no! as fades the vale, they fade away.
Yet still the tender, vacant gloom remains,
Still the cold cheek its shuddering tear retains.

   The bird, with fading light who ceas'd to thread
Silent the hedge or steaming rivulet's bed,   390
From his grey re-appearing tower shall soon
Salute with boding note the rising moon,
Frosting with hoary light the pearly ground,
And pouring deeper blue to Æther's bound;
Rejoic'd her solemn pomp of clouds to fold
In robes of azure, fleecy white, and gold,
While rose and poppy, as the glow-worm fades,
Checquer with paler red the thicket shades.
   Now o'er the eastern hill, where Darkness broods
O'er all its vanish'd dells, and lawns, and woods   400
Where but a mass of shade the sight can trace,
She lifts in silence up her lovely face;
Above the gloomy valley flings her light,
Far to the western slopes with hamlets white;
And gives, where woods the chequer'd upland
    strew,
To the green corn of summer autumn's hue.
   Thus Hope, first pouring from her blessed horn
Her dawn, far lovelier than the Moon's own morn;
'Till higher mounted, strives in vain to chear
The weary hills, impervious, black'ning near;   410
—Yet does she still, undaunted, throw the while
On darling spots remote her tempting smile.
—Ev'n now she decks for me a distant scene,
(For dark and broad the gulph of time between)
Gilding that cottage with her fondest ray,
(Sole bourn, sole wish, sole object of my way;
How fair it's lawn and silvery woods appear!
How sweet it's streamlet murmurs in mine ear!)
Where we, my friend, to golden days shall rise,
'Till our small share of hardly-paining sighs   420
(For sighs will ever trouble human breath)
Creep hush'd into the tranquil breast of Death.
   But now the clear-bright Moon her zenith gains,
And rimy without speck extend the plains;

  * 'Charming the night calm with her powerful song'. A line
of one of our older poets.

The deepest dell the mountain's breast displays,
Scarce hides a shadow from her searching rays;
From the dark-blue "faint silvery threads" divide
The hills, while gleams below the azure tide;
The scene is waken'd, yet its peace unbroke,
By silver'd wreaths of quiet charcoal smoke,   430
That, o'er the ruins of the fallen wood,
Steal down the hills, and spread along the flood.
   The song of mountain streams unheard by day,
Now hardly heard, beguiles my homeward way.
All air is, as the sleeping water, still,
List'ning th' aëreal music of the hill,
Broke only by the slow clock tolling deep,
Or shout that wakes the ferry-man from sleep,
Soon follow'd by his hollow-parting oar,
And echo'd hoof approaching the far shore;   440
Sound of clos'd gate, across the water born,
Hurrying the feeding hare thro' rustling corn;
The tremulous sob of the complaining owl;
And at long intervals the mill-dog's howl;
The distant forge's swinging thump profound;
Or yell in the deep woods of lonely hound.

[1787–89]   [1793]

LYRICAL BALLADS

*The following nineteen poems are Wordsworth's contributions
to* Lyrical Ballads; *they appear here in the same order as in the
1798 edition. All of Coleridge's contributions to the volume—
the first and most famous being "The Rime of the Ancyent
Marinere"—are here omitted.*

LYRICAL BALLADS,

WITH

A FEW OTHER POEMS.

ADVERTISEMENT

I T is the honourable characteristic of Poetry that its
materials are to be found in every subject which can
interest the human mind. The evidence of this fact
is to be sought, not in the writings of Critics, but in
those of Poets themselves.

The majority of the following poems are to be
considered as experiments. They were written chiefly
with a view to ascertain how far the language of
conversation in the middle and lower classes of
society is adapted to the purposes of poetic pleasure.
Readers accustomed to the gaudiness and inane
phraseology of many modern writers, if they persist
in reading this book to its conclusion, will perhaps
frequently have to struggle with feelings of strange-
ness and aukwardness: they will look round for
poetry, and will be induced to enquire by what
species of courtesy these attempts can be permitted to
assume that title. It is desirable that such readers, for
their own sakes, should not suffer the solitary word
Poetry, a word of very disputed meaning, to stand in
the way of their gratification; but that, while they
are perusing this book, they should ask themselves
if it contains a natural delineation of human passions,
human characters, and human incidents; and if the
answer be favourable to the author's wishes, that
they should consent to be pleased in spite of that
most dreadful enemy to our pleasures, our own pre-
established codes of decision.

Readers of superior judgment may disapprove of
the style in which many of these pieces are executed
it must be expected that many lines and phrases will
not exactly suit their taste. It will perhaps appear to
them, that wishing to avoid the prevalent fault of the
day, the author has sometimes descended too low,
and that many of his expressions are too familiar, and
not of sufficient dignity. It is apprehended, that the
more conversant the reader is with our elder writers,
and with those in modern times who have been the
most successful in painting manners and passions, the
fewer complaints of this kind will he have to make.

An accurate taste in poetry, and in all the other arts,
Sir Joshua Reynolds has observed, is an acquired
talent, which can only be produced by severe thought,
and a long continued intercourse with the best
models of composition. This is mentioned not with
so ridiculous a purpose as to prevent the most
inexperienced reader from judging for himself; but
merely to temper the rashness of decision, and to
suggest that if poetry be a subject on which much
time has not been bestowed, the judgment may be
erroneous, and that in many cases it necessarily will
be so.

The tale of Goody Blake and Harry Gill is founded
on a well-authenticated fact which happened in
Warwickshire. Of the other poems in the collection,
it may be proper to say that they are either absolute
inventions of the author, or facts which took place
within his personal observation or that of his friends.
The poem of the Thorn, as the reader will soon
discover, is not supposed to be spoken in the author's
own person: the character of the loquacious narrator
will sufficiently shew itself in the course of the story.
The Rime of the Ancyent Marinere was professedly
written in imitation of the *style*, as well as of the
spirit of the elder poets; but with a few exceptions,
the Author believes that the language adopted in it has
been equally intelligible for these three last centuries.
The lines entitled Expostulation and Reply, and those
which follow, arose out of conversation with a friend
who was somewhat unreasonably attached to modern
books of moral philosophy.

LINES

LEFT UPON A SEAT IN A · YEW-TREE WHICH
STANDS NEAR THE LAKE OF ESTHWAITE, ON
A DESOLATE PART OF THE SHORE, YET
COMMANDING A BEAUTIFUL PROSPECT

—N A Y, Traveller! rest. This lonely yew-tree stands
Far from all human dwelling: what if here
No sparkling rivulet spread the verdant herb;
What if these barren boughs the bee not loves;
Yet, if the wind breathe soft, the curling waves,
That break against the shore, shall lull thy mind
By one soft impulse saved from vacancy.

Who he was
That piled these stones, and with the mossy sod
First covered o'er, and taught this aged tree,   10

Now wild, to bend its arms in circling shade,
I well remember.—He was one who own'd
No common soul. In youth, by genius nurs'd,
And big with lofty views, he to the world
Went forth, pure in his heart, against the taint
Of dissolute tongues, 'gainst jealousy, and hate,
And scorn, against all enemies prepared,
All but neglect: and so, his spirit damped
At once, with rash disdain he turned away,
And with the food of pride sustained his soul   20
In solitude.—Stranger! these gloomy boughs
Had charms for him; and here he loved to sit,
His only visitants a straggling sheep,
The stone-chat, or the glancing sand-piper;
And on these barren rocks, with juniper,
And heath, and thistle, thinly sprinkled o'er,
Fixing his downward eye, he many an hour
A morbid pleasure nourished, tracing here
An emblem of his own unfruitful life:
And lifting up his head, he then would gaze   30
On the more distant scene; how lovely 'tis
Thou seest, and he would gaze till it became
Far lovelier, and his heart could not sustain
The beauty still more beauteous. Nor, that time,
Would he forget those beings, to whose minds,
Warm from the labours of benevolence,
The world, and man himself, appeared a scene
Of kindred loveliness: then he would sigh
With mournful joy, to think that others felt
What he must never feel: and so, lost man!   40
On visionary views would fancy feed,
Till his eye streamed with tears. In this deep vale
He died, this seat his only monument.

If thou be one whose heart the holy forms
Of young imagination have kept pure,
Stranger! henceforth be warned; and know, that
      pride,
Howe'er disguised in its own majesty,
Is littleness; that he, who feels contempt
For any living thing, hath faculties
Which he has never used; that thought with him   50
Is in its infancy. The man, whose eye
Is ever on himself, doth look on one,
The least of nature's works, one who might move
The wise man to that scorn which wisdom holds
Unlawful, ever. O, be wiser thou!
Instructed that true knowledge leads to love,
True dignity abides with him alone
Who, in the silent hour of inward thought,
Can still suspect, and still revere himself,
In lowliness of heart.   60

[1795–97]

THE FEMALE VAGRANT

By Derwent's side my Father's cottage stood,
(The Woman thus her artless story told)
One field, a flock, and what the neighbouring flood
Supplied, to him were more than mines of gold.
Light was my sleep; my days in transport roll'd:
With thoughtless joy I stretch'd along the shore
My father's nets, or watched, when from the fold
High o'er the cliffs I led my fleecy store,
A dizzy depth below! his boat and twinkling oar.

My father was a good and pious man,   10
An honest man by honest parents bred,
And I believe that, soon as I began
To lisp, he made me kneel beside my bed,
And in his hearing there my prayers I said:
And afterwards, by my good father taught,
I read, and loved the books in which I read;
For books in every neighbouring house I sought,
And nothing to my mind a sweeter pleasure brought.

Can I forget what charms did once adorn
My garden, stored with pease, and mint, and thyme,
And rose and lilly for the sabbath morn?   21
The sabbath bells, and their delightful chime;
The gambols and wild freaks at shearing time;
My hen's rich nest through long grass scarce espied;
The cowslip-gathering at May's dewy prime;
The swans, that, when I sought the water-side,
From far to meet me came, spreading their snowy
      pride.

The staff I yet remember which upbore
The bending body of my active sire;
His seat beneath the honeyed sycamore   30
When the bees hummed, and chair by winter fire;
When market-morning came, the neat attire
With which, though bent on haste, myself I deck'd;
My watchful dog, whose starts of furious ire,
When stranger passed, so often I have check'd;
The red-breast known for years, which at my
      casement peck'd.

The suns of twenty summers danced along,–
Ah! little marked, how fast they rolled away:
Then rose a mansion proud our woods among,
And cottage after cottage owned its sway,   40
No joy to see a neighbouring house, or stray
Through pastures not his own, the master took;
My Father dared his greedy wish gainsay;
He loved his old hereditary nook,
And ill could I the thought of such sad parting brook.

But, when he had refused the proffered gold,
To cruel injuries he became a prey,
Sore traversed in whate'er he bought and sold.
His troubles grew upon him day by day,
Till all his substance fell into decay.   50
His little range of water was denied,*
All but the bed where his old body lay,
All, all was seized, and weeping, side by side,
We sought a home where we uninjured might abide.

Can I forget that miserable hour,
When from the last hill-top, my sire surveyed,
Peering above the trees, the steeple tower,
That on his marriage-day sweet music made?
Till then he hoped his bones might there be laid,
Close by my mother in their native bowers: 60
Bidding me trust in God, he stood and prayed,–
I could not pray:—through tears that fell in showers,
Glimmer'd our dear-loved home, alas! no longer
      ours!

There was a youth whom I had loved so long,
That when I loved him not I cannot say.
'Mid the green mountains many and many a song
We two had sung, like little birds in May.
When we began to tire of childish play
We seemed still more and more to prize each other:
We talked of marriage and our marriage day;   70
And I in truth did love him like a brother,
For never could I hope to meet with such another.

His father said, that to a distant town
He must repair, to ply the artist's trade.
What tears of bitter grief till then unknown!
What tender vows our last sad kiss delayed!
To him we turned:—we had no other aid.
Like one revived, upon his neck I wept,
And her whom he had loved in joy, he said
He well could love in grief: his faith he kept;   80
And in a quiet home once more my father slept.

Four years each day with daily bread was blest,
By constant toil and constant prayer supplied.
Three lovely infants lay upon my breast;
And often, viewing their sweet smiles, I sighed,
And knew not why. My happy father died
When sad distress reduced the children's meal:
Thrice happy! that from him the grave did hide
The empty loom, cold hearth, and silent wheel,
And tears that flowed for ills which patience could
      not heal.   90

* Several of the Lakes in the north of England are let out
to different Fishermen, in parcels marked out by imaginary
lines drawn from rock to rock.

'Twas a hard change, an evil time was come;
We had no hope, and no relief could gain.
But soon, with proud parade, the noisy drum
Beat round, to sweep the streets of want and pain.
My husband's arms now only served to strain
Me and his children hungering in his view:
In such dismay my prayers and tears were vain:
To join those miserable men he flew;
And now to the sea-coast, with numbers more, we
      drew.

There foul neglect for months and months we bore,
Nor yet the crowded fleet its anchor stirred.   101
Green fields before us and our native shore,
By fever, from polluted air incurred,
Ravage was made, for which no knell was heard.
Fondly we wished, and wished away, nor knew,
'Mid that long sickness, and those hopes deferr'd,
That happier days we never more must view:
The parting signal streamed, at last the land
      withdrew,

But from delay the summer calms were past.
On as we drove, the equinoctial deep   110
Ran mountains-high before the howling blast.
We gazed with terror on the gloomy sleep
Of them that perished in the whirlwind's sweep,
Untaught that soon such anguish must ensue,
Our hopes such harvest of affliction reap,
That we the mercy of the waves should rue.
We reached the western world, a poor, devoted crew.

Oh! dreadful price of being to resign
All that is dear *in* being! better far
In Want's most lonely cave till death to pine,   120
Unseen, unheard, unwatched by any star;
Or in the streets and walks where proud men are,
Better our dying bodies to obtrude,
Than dog-like, wading at the heels of war,
Protract a curst existence, with the brood
That lap (their very nourishment!) their brother's
      blood.

The pains and plagues that on our heads came
      down,
Disease and famine, agony and fear,
In wood or wilderness, in camp or town,
It would thy brain unsettle even to hear.   130
All perished—all, in one remorseless year,
Husband and children! one by one, by sword
And ravenous plague, all perished: every tear
Dried up, despairing, desolate, on board
A British ship I waked, as from a trance restored.

Peaceful as some immeasurable plain
By the first beams of dawning light impress'd,
In the calm sunshine slept the glittering main.
The very ocean has its hour of rest,
That comes not to the human mourner's breast.   140
Remote from man, and storms of mortal care,
A heavenly silence did the waves invest;
I looked and looked along the silent air,
Until it seemed to bring a joy to my despair.

Ah! how unlike those late terrific sleeps!
And groans, that rage of racking famine spoke,
Where looks inhuman dwelt on festering heaps!
The breathing pestilence that rose like smoke!
The shriek that from the distant battle broke!
The mine's dire earthquake, and the pallid host   150
Driven by the bomb's incessant thunder-stroke
To loathsome vaults, where heart-sick anguish
    toss'd,
Hope died, and fear itself in agony was lost!

Yet does that burst of woe congeal my frame,
When the dark streets appeared to heave and gape,
While like a sea the storming army came,
And Fire from Hell reared his gigantic shape,
And Murder, by the ghastly gleam, and Rape
Seized their joint prey, the mother and the child!   159
But from these crazing thoughts my brain, escape!
—For weeks the balmy air breathed soft and mild,
And on the gliding vessel Heaven and Ocean
    smiled.

Some mighty gulph of separation past,
I seemed transported to another world:—
A thought resigned with pain, when from the mast
The impatient mariner the sail unfurl'd,
And whistling, called the wind that hardly curled
The silent sea. From the sweet thoughts of home,
And from all hope I was forever hurled.
For me—farthest from earthly port to roam   170
Was best, could I but shun the spot where man might
    come.

And oft, robb'd of my perfect mind, I thought
At last my feet a resting-place had found:
Here will I weep in peace, (so fancy wrought,)
Roaming the illimitable waters round;
Here watch, of every human friend disowned,
All day, my ready tomb the ocean-flood—
To break my dream the vessel reached its bound:
And homeless near a thousand homes I stood,
And near a thousand tables pined, and wanted
    food.

By grief enfeebled was I turned adrift,   181
Helpless as sailor cast on desart rock;
Nor morsel to my mouth that day did lift,
Nor dared my hand at any door to knock.
I lay, where with his drowsy mates, the cock
From the cross timber of an out-house hung;
How dismal tolled, that night, the city clock!
At morn my sick heart hunger scarcely stung,
Nor to the beggar's language could I frame my
    tongue.

So passed another day, and so the third: 190
Then did I try, in vain, the crowd's resort,
In deep despair by frightful wishes stirr'd,
Near the sea-side I reached a ruined fort:
There, pains which nature could no more support,
With blindness linked, did on my vitals fall;
Dizzy my brain, with interruption short
Of hideous sense; I sunk, nor step could crawl,
And thence was borne away to neighbouring hospital.

Recovery came with food: but still, my brain
Was weak, nor of the past had memory.   200
I heard my neighbours, in their beds, complain
Of many things which never troubled me;
Of feet still bustling round with busy glee,
Of looks where common kindness had no part,
Of service done with careless cruelty,
Fretting the fever round the languid heart,
And groans, which, as they said, would make a dead
    man start.

These things just served to stir the torpid sense,
Nor pain nor pity in my bosom raised.
Memory, though slow, returned with strength; and
    thence   210
Dismissed, again on open day I gazed,
At houses, men, and common light, amazed.
The lanes I sought, and as the sun retired,
Came, where beneath the trees a faggot blazed;
The wild brood saw me weep, my fate enquired,
And gave me food, and rest, more welcome, more
    desired.

My heart is touched to think that men like these,
The rude earth's tenants, were my first relief:
How kindly did they paint their vagrant ease!
And their long holiday that feared not grief,   220
For all belonged to all, and each was chief.
No plough their sinews strained; on grating road
No wain they drove, and yet, the yellow sheaf
In every vale for their delight was stowed:
For them, in nature's meads, the milky udder
    flowed.

Semblance, with straw and panniered ass, they
    made
Of potters wandering on from door to door:
But life of happier sort to me pourtrayed,
And other joys my fancy to allure;
The bag-pipe dinning on the midnight moor   230
In barn uplighted, and companions boon
Well met from far with revelry secure,
In depth of forest glade, when jocund June
Rolled fast along the sky his warm and genial moon.

But ill it suited me, in journey dark
O'er moor and mountain, midnight theft to hatch;
To charm the surly house-dog's faithful bark,
Or hang on tiptoe at the lifted latch;
The gloomy lantern, and the dim blue match,
The black disguise, the warning whistle shrill,   240
And ear still busy on its nightly watch,
Were not for me, brought up in nothing ill;
Besides, on griefs so fresh my thoughts were brooding
    still.

What could I do, unaided and unblest?
Poor Father! gone was every friend of thine:
And kindred of dead husband are at best
Small help, and, after marriage such as mine,
With little kindness would to me incline.
Ill was I then for toil or service fit:
With tears whose course no effort could confine,   250
By high-way side forgetful would I sit
Whole hours, my idle arms in moping sorrow knit.

I lived upon the mercy of the fields,
And oft of cruelty the sky accused;
On hazard, or what general bounty yields,
Now coldly given, now utterly refused.
The fields I for my bed have often used:
But, what afflicts my peace with keenest ruth
Is, that I have my inner self abused,
Foregone the home delight of constant truth,   260
And clear and open soul, so prized in fearless
    youth.

Three years a wanderer, often have I view'd,
In tears, the sun towards that country tend
Where my poor heart lost all its fortitude:
And now across this moor my steps I bend—
Oh! tell me whither—for no earthy friend
Have I.—She ceased, and weeping turned away,
As if because her tale was at an end
She wept;—because she had no more to say
Of that perpetual weight which on her spirit lay.   270

[1793 +]

GOODY BLAKE, AND HARRY GILL,

A TRUE STORY

OH! what's the matter? what's the matter?
What is't that ails young Harry Gill?
That evermore his teeth they chatter,
Chatter, chatter, chatter still.
Of waistcoats Harry has no lack,
Good duffle grey, and flannel fine;
He has a blanket on his back,
And coats enough to smother nine.

In March, December, and in July,
'Tis all the same with Harry Gill;   10
The neighbours tell, and tell you truly,
His teeth they chatter, chatter still.
At night, at morning, and at noon,
'Tis all the same with Harry Gill;
Beneath the sun, beneath the moon,
His teeth they chatter, chatter still.

Young Harry was a lusty drover,
And who so stout of limb as he?
His cheeks were red as ruddy clover,
His voice was like the voice of three.   20
Auld Goody Blake was old and poor,
Ill fed she was, and thinly clad;
And any man who pass'd her door,
Might see how poor a hut she had.

All day she spun in her poor dwelling,
And then her three hours' work at night!
Alas! 'twas hardly worth the telling,
It would not pay for candle-light.
—This woman dwelt in Dorsetshire,
Her hut was on a cold hill-side,   30
And in that country coals are dear,
For they come far by wind and tide.

By the same fire to boil their pottage,
Two poor old dames, as I have known,
Will often live in one small cottage,
But she, poor woman, dwelt alone.
'Twas well enough when summer came,
The long, warm, lightsome summer-day,
Then at her door the *canty* [1] dame
Would sit, as any linnet gay.   40

But when the ice our streams did fetter,
Oh! then how her old bones would shake!
You would have said, if you had met her,
'Twas a hard time for Goody Blake.

---

[1] Dialect; merry. W.'s italics.

Her evenings then were dull and dead;
Sad case it was, as you may think,
For very cold to go to bed,
And then for cold not sleep a wink.

Oh joy for her! when e'er in winter
The winds at night had made a rout,   50
And scatter'd many a lusty splinter,
And many a rotten bough about.
Yet never had she, well or sick,
As every man who knew her says,
A pile before-hand, wood or stick,
Enough to warm her for three days.

Now, when the frost was past enduring,
And made her poor old bones to ache,
Could any thing be more alluring,
Than an old hedge to Goody Blake?   60
And now and then, it must be said,
When her old bones were cold and chill,
She left her fire, or left her bed,
To seek the hedge of Harry Gill.

Now Harry he had long suspected
This trespass of old Goody Blake,
And vow'd that she should be detected,
And he on her would vengeance take.
And oft from his warm fire he'd go,
And to the fields his road would take,   70
And there, at night, in frost and snow,
He watch'd to seize old Goody Blake.

And once, behind a rick of barley,
Thus looking out did Harry stand;
The moon was full and shining clearly,
And crisp with frost the stubble-land.
—He hears a noise—he's all awake—
Again?—on tip-toe down the hill
He softly creeps—'Tis Goody Blake,
She's at the hedge of Harry Gill.   80

Right glad was he when he beheld her:
Stick after stick did Goody pull,
He stood behind a bush of elder,
Till she had filled her apron full.
When with her load she turned about,
The bye-road back again to take,
He started forward with a shout,
And sprang upon poor Goody Blake.

And fiercely by the arm he took her,
And by the arm he held her fast,   90
And fiercely by the arm he shook her,
And cried, "I've caught you then at last!"

Then Goody, who had nothing said,
Her bundle from her lap let fall;
And kneeling on the sticks, she pray'd
To God that is the judge of all.

She pray'd, her wither'd hand uprearing,
While Harry held her by the arm—
"God! who art never out of hearing,
"O may he never more be warm!"   100
The cold, cold moon above her head,
Thus on her knees did Goody pray,
Young Harry heard what she had said,
And icy-cold he turned away.

He went complaining all the morrow
That he was cold and very chill:
His face was gloom, his heart was sorrow,
Alas! that day for Harry Gill!
That day he wore a riding-coat,
But not a whit the warmer he: 110
Another was on Thursday brought,
And ere the Sabbath he had three.

'Twas all in vain, a useless matter,
And blankets were about him pinn'd;
Yet still his jaws and teeth they clatter,
Like a loose casement in the wind.
And Harry's flesh it fell away;
And all who see him say 'tis plain,
That, live as long as live he may,
He never will be warm again.   120

No word to any man he utters,
A-bed or up, to young or old;
But ever to himself he mutters,
"Poor Harry Gill is very cold."
A-bed or up, by night or day;
His teeth they chatter, chatter still.
Now think, ye farmers all, I pray,
Of Goody Blake and Harry Gill.

[1798]

LINES

WRITTEN AT A SMALL DISTANCE FROM MY
HOUSE, AND SENT BY MY LITTLE BOY TO THE
PERSON TO WHOM THEY ARE ADDRESSED

IT IS the first mild day of March:
Each minute sweeter than before,
The red-breast sings from the tall larch
That stands beside our door.

There is a blessing in the air,
Which seems a sense of joy to yield
To the bare trees, and mountains bare,
And grass in the green field.

My Sister! ('tis a wish of mine)
Now that our morning meal is done,   10
Make haste, your morning task resign;
Come forth and feel the sun.

Edward will come with you, and pray,
Put on with speed your woodland dress,
And bring no book, for this one day
We'll give to idleness.

No joyless forms shall regulate
Our living Calendar:
We from to-day, my friend, will date
The opening of the year.   20

Love, now an universal birth,
From heart to heart is stealing,
From earth to man, from man to earth,
—It is the hour of feeling.

One moment now may give us more
Than fifty years of reason;
Our minds shall drink at every pore
The spirit of the season.

Some silent laws our hearts may make,
Which they shall long obey;   30
We for the year to come may take
Our temper from to-day.

And from the blessed power that rolls
About, below, above;
We'll frame the measure of our souls,
They shall be tuned to love.

Then come, my sister! come, I pray,
With speed put on your woodland dress,
And bring no book; for this one day
We'll give to idleness.   40

[1798]

SIMON LEE,

THE OLD HUNTSMAN, WITH AN INCIDENT
IN WHICH HE WAS CONCERNED

IN the sweet shire of Cardigan,
Not far from pleasant Ivor-hall,
An old man dwells, a little man,
I've heard he once was tall.

Of years he has upon his back,
No doubt, a burthen weighty;
He says he is three score and ten,
But others say he's eighty.

A long blue livery-coat has he,
That's fair behind, and fair before;   10
Yet, meet him where you will, you see
At once that he is poor.
Full five and twenty years he lived
A running huntsman merry;
And, though he has but one eye left,
His cheek is like a cherry.

No man like him the horn could sound,
And no man was so full of glee;
To say the least, four counties round
Had heard of Simon Lee;   20
His master's dead, and no one now
Dwells in the hall of Ivor;
Men, dogs, and horses, all are dead;
He is the sole survivor.

His hunting feats have him bereft
Of his right eye, as you may see:
And then, what limbs those feats have left
To poor old Simon Lee!
He has no son, he has no child,
His wife, an aged woman,   30
Lives with him, near the waterfall,
Upon the village common.

And he is lean and he is sick,
His little body's half awry
His ancles they are swoln and thick
His legs are thin and dry.
When he was young he little knew
Of husbandry or tillage;
And now he's forced to work, though weak,
—The weakest in the village.   40

He all the country could outrun,
Could leave both man and horse behind;
And often, ere the race was done,
He reeled and was stone-blind.
And still there's something in the world
At which his heart rejoices;
For when the chiming hounds are out,
He dearly loves their voices!

Old Ruth works out of doors with him,
And does what Simon cannot do;   50
For she, not over stout of limb,
Is stouter of the two.

And though you with your utmost skill
From labour could not wean them,
Alas! 'tis very little, all
Which they can do between them.

Beside their moss-grown hut of clay,
Not twenty paces from the door,
A scrap of land they have, but they
Are poorest of the poor.   60
This scrap of land he from the heath
Enclosed when he was stronger;
But what avails the land to them,
Which they can till no longer?

Few months of life has he in store,
As he to you will tell,
For still, the more he works, the more
His poor old ancles swell.
My gentle reader, I perceive
How patiently you've waited,   70
And I'm afraid that you expect
Some tale will be related.

O reader! had you in your mind
Such stores as silent thought can bring,
O gentle reader! you would find
A tale in every thing.
What more I have to say is short,
I hope you'll kindly take it;
It is no tale; but should you think,
Perhaps a tale you'll make it.   80

One summer-day I chanced to see
This old man doing all he could
About the root of an old tree,
A stump of rotten wood.
The mattock totter'd in his hand;
So vain was his endeavour
That at the root of the old tree
He might have worked for ever.

"You're overtasked, good Simon Lee,
Give me your tool" to him I said;   90
And at the word right gladly he
Received my proffer'd aid.
I struck, and with a single blow
The tangled root I sever'd,
At which the poor old man so long
And vainly had endeavour'd.

The tears into his eyes were brought,
And thanks and praises seemed to run
So fast out of his heart, I thought
They never would have done.   100

—I've heard of hearts unkind, kind deeds
With coldness still returning.
Alas! the gratitude of men
Has oftner left me mourning.

[1798]

ANECDOTE FOR FATHERS

" *This was suggested in front of Alfoxden. The Boy was a son
of my friend, Basil Montagu, who had been two or three years
under our care. The name of Kilve is from a village on the
Bristol Channel, about a mile from Alfoxden; and the name of
Liswyn Farm was taken from a beautiful spot on the Wye.*"
[*Wordsworth to Isabella Fenwick*]

ANECDOTE FOR FATHERS,

SHEWING HOW THE ART OF LYING MAY BE TAUGHT

I HAVE a boy of five years old,
His face is fair and fresh to see;
His limbs are cast in beauty's mould,
And dearly he loves me.
One morn we stroll'd on our dry walk,
Our quiet house all full in view,
And held such intermitted talk
As we are wont to do.

My thoughts on former pleasures ran;
I thought of Kilve's delightful shore,   10
My pleasant home, when spring began,
A long, long year before.

A day it was when I could bear
To think, and think, and think again;
With so much happiness to spare,
I could not feel a pain.

My boy was by my side, so slim
And graceful in his rustic dress!
And oftentimes I talked to him,
In very idleness.   20

The young lambs ran a pretty race;
The morning sun shone bright and warm;
"Kilve," said I, "was a pleasant place,
"And so is Liswyn farm.

"My little boy, which like you more,"
I said and took him by the arm—
"Our home by Kilve's delightful shore,
"Or here at Liswyn farm?"

"And tell me, had you rather be,"
I said and held him by the arm,   30
"At Kilve's smooth shore by the green sea,
"Or here at Liswyn farm?"

In careless mood he looked at me,
While still I held him by the arm,
And said, "At Kilve I'd rather be
"Than here at Liswyn farm."

"Now, little Edward, say why so;
My little Edward, tell me why;"
"I cannot tell, I do not know."
"Why this is strange," said I.   40

"For, here are woods and green-hills warm;
"There surely must some reason be
"Why you would change sweet Liswyn farm
"For Kilve by the green sea."

At this, my boy, so fair and slim,
Hung down his head, nor made reply;
And five times did I say to him,
"Why? Edward, tell me why?"

His head he raised—there was in sight,
It caught his eye, he saw it plain—   50
Upon the house-top, glittering bright,
A broad and gilded vane.

Then did the boy his tongue unlock,
And thus to me he made reply;
"At Kilve there was no weather-cock,
"And that's the reason why."

Oh dearest, dearest boy! my heart
For better lore would seldom yearn,
Could I but teach the hundredth part
Of what from thee I learn.   60

[1798]

WE ARE SEVEN

"I composed it while walking in the grove at Alfoxden. My friends will not deem it too trifling to relate that while walking to and fro I composed the last stanza first, having begun with the last line. When it was all but finished, I came in and recited it to Mr. Coleridge and my sister, and said, 'A prefatory stanza must be added, and I should sit down to our little tea-meal with greater pleasure if my task were finished.' I mentioned in substance what I wished to be expressed, and Coleridge immediately threw off the stanza thus:—

'A little child, dear brother Jem,'—

I objected to the rhyme, 'dear brother Jem,' as being ludicrous, but we all enjoyed the joke of hitching-in our friend, James T[obin]'s

name, who was familiarly called Jem. He was the brother of the dramatist, and this reminds me of an anecdote which it may be worth while here to notice. The said Jem got a sight of the Lyrical Ballads as it was going through the press at Bristol, during which time I was residing in that city. One evening he came to me with a grave face, and said, 'Wordsworth, I have seen the volume that Coleridge and you are about to publish. There is one poem in it which I earnestly entreat you to cancel, for, if published, it will make you everlastingly ridiculous.' I answered that I felt much obliged by the interest he took in my good name as a writer, and begged to know what was the unfortunate piece he alluded to. He said, 'It is called We Are Seven.' —'Nay,' said I, 'that shall take its chance, however,' and he left me in despair." [Wordsworth to Isabella Fenwick]

WE ARE SEVEN

A SIMPLE child, dear brother Jim,
That lightly draws its breath,
And feels its life in every limb,
What should it know of death?

I met a little cottage girl,
She was eight years old, she said;
Her hair was thick with many a curl
That cluster'd round her head.

She had a rustic, woodland air,
And she was wildly clad;   10
Her eyes were fair, and very fair,
—Her beauty made me glad.

"Sisters and brothers, little maid,
"How many may you be?"
"How many? seven in all," she said,
And wondering looked at me.

"And where are they, I pray you tell?"
She answered, "Seven are we,
"And two of us at Conway dwell,
"And two are gone to sea.   20

"Two of us in the church-yard lie,
"My sister and my brother,
"And in the church-yard cottage, I
"Dwell near them with my mother."

"You say that two at Conway dwell,
"And two are gone to sea,
"Yet you are seven; I pray you tell
"Sweet Maid, how this may be?"

Then did the little Maid reply,
"Seven boys and girls are we;   30
"Two of us in the church-yard lie,
"Beneath the church-yard tree."

"You run about, my little maid,
"Your limbs they are alive;
"If two are in the church-yard laid,
"Then ye are only five."

"Their graves are green, they may be seen,"
　The little Maid replied,
"Twelve steps or more from my mother's door,
"And they are side by side.　　　　　40

"My stockings there I often knit,
"My 'kerchief there I hem;
"And there upon the ground I sit—
"I sit and sing to them.

"And often after sunset, Sir,
"When it is light and fair,
"I take my little porringer,
"And eat my supper there.

"The first that died was little Jane;
"In bed she moaning lay,　　　　　50
"Till God released her of her pain,
"And then she went away.

"So in the church-yard she was laid,
"And all the summer dry,
"Together round her grave we played,
"My brother John and I.

"And when the ground was white with snow,
"And I could run and slide,
"My brother John was forced to go,
"And he lies by her side."　　　　60

"How many are you then," said I,
"If they two are in Heaven?"
　The little Maiden did reply,
"O Master! we are seven."

"But they are dead; those two are dead!
"Their spirits are in heaven!"
　'Twas throwing words away; for still
　The little Maid would have her will,
　And said, "Nay, we are seven!"

[1798]

LINES
WRITTEN IN EARLY SPRING

I HEARD a thousand blended notes,
While in a grove I sate reclined,
In that sweet mood when pleasant thoughts
Bring sad thoughts to the mind.

To her fair works did nature link
The human soul that through me ran;
And much it griev'd my heart to think
What man has made of man.

Through primrose-tufts, in that sweet bower,
The periwinkle trail'd its wreathes;　　　10
And 'tis my faith that every flower
Enjoys the air it breathes.

The birds around me hopp'd and play'd:
Their thoughts I cannot measure,
But the least motion which they made,
It seem'd a thrill of pleasure.

The budding twigs spread out their fan,
To catch the breezy air;
And I must think, do all I can,
That there was pleasure there.　　　　20

If I these thoughts may not prevent,
If such be of my creed the plan,
Have I not reason to lament
What man has made of man?

[1798]

THE THORN

This poem, defended in the Advertisement above, was one that Wordsworth felt repeatedly called upon to explain. Coleridge objected to some of its lines, Byron mocked them (see his Preface to Don Juan).
　Although Wordsworth told Isabella Fenwick later that the poem began in his wish to make permanent the impressiveness of a thorn tree seen suddenly in a storm, he was also interested in the creation of a character who (he says in the 1800–1805 note) has become "credulous and talkative from indolence." He wished, he said, to "exhibit some of the general laws by which superstition acts upon the mind. Superstitious men are almost always men of slow faculties and deep feelings: their minds are not loose but adhesive; they have a reasonable share of imagination, by which word I mean the faculty which produces impressive effects out of simple elements; but they are utterly destitute of fancy, the power by which pleasure and surprise are excited by sudden varieties and by accumulated imagery. . . ."

THE THORN

I

THERE is a thorn; it looks so old,
In truth you'd find it hard to say,
How it could ever have been young,
It looks so old and grey.
Not higher than a two-years' child,
It stands erect this aged thorn;

No leaves it has, no thorny points;
It is a mass of knotted joints,
A wretched thing forlorn.
It stands erect, and like a stone   10
With lichens it is overgrown.

II

Like rock or stone, it is o'ergrown
With lichens to the very top,
And hung with heavy tufts of moss,
A melancholy crop:
Up from the earth these mosses creep,
And this poor thorn they clasp it round
So close, you'd say that they were bent
With plain and manifest intent,
To drag it to the ground;   20
And all had joined in one endeavour
To bury this poor thorn for ever.

III

High on a mountain's highest ridge,
Where oft the stormy winter gale
Cuts like a scythe, while through the clouds
It sweeps from vale to vale;
Not five yards from the mountain-path,
This thorn you on your left espy;
And to the left, three yards beyond,
You see a little muddy pond   30
Of water, never dry;
I've measured it from side to side:
'Tis three feet long, and two feet wide.

IV

And close beside this aged thorn,
There is a fresh and lovely sight,
A beauteous heap, a hill of moss,
Just half a foot in height.
All lovely colours there you see,
All colours that were ever seen,
And mossy network too is there,   40
As if by hand of lady fair
The work had woven been,
And cups, the darlings of the eye
So deep is their vermilion dye.

V

Ah me! what lovely tints are there!
Of olive-green and scarlet bright,
In spikes, in branches, and in stars,
Green, red, and pearly white.
This heap of earth o'ergrown with moss
Which close beside the thorn you see,   50

So fresh in all its beauteous dyes,
Is like an infant's grave in size
As like as like can be:
But never, never any where,
An infant's grave was half so fair.

VI

Now would you see this aged thorn,
This pond and beauteous hill of moss,
You must take care and chuse your time
The mountain when to cross.
For oft there sits, between the heap   60
That's like an infant's grave in size,
And that same pond of which I spoke,
A woman in a scarlet cloak,
And to herself she cries,
"Oh misery! oh misery!
"Oh woe is me! oh misery!"

VII

At all times of the day and night
This wretched woman thither goes,
And she is known to every star,
And every wind that blows;   70
And there beside the thorn she sits
When the blue day-light's in the skies,
And when the whirlwind's on the hill,
Or frosty air is keen and still,
And to herself she cries,
"Oh misery! oh misery!
"Oh woe is me! oh misery!"

VIII

"Now wherefore thus, by day and night,
"In rain, in tempest, and in snow,
"Thus to the dreary mountain-top   80
"Does this poor woman go?
"And why sits she beside the thorn
"When the blue day-light's in the sky,
"Or when the whirlwind's on the hill,
"Or frosty air is keen and still,
"And wherefore does she cry?—
"Oh wherefore? wherefore? tell me why
"Does she repeat that doleful cry?"

IX

I cannot tell; I wish I could;
For the true reason no one knows,   90
But if you'd gladly view the spot,
The spot to which she goes;
The heap that's like an infant's grave,
The pond—and thorn, so old and grey,

Pass by her door—'tis seldom shut—
And if you see her in her hut,
Then to the spot away!—
I never heard of such as dare
Approach the spot when she is there.

X

"But wherefore to the mountain-top   100
"Can this unhappy woman go,
"Whatever star is in the skies,
"Whatever wind may blow?"
  Nay rack your brain—'tis all in vain,
I'll tell you every thing I know;
But to the thorn, and to the pond
Which is a little step beyond,
I wish that you would go:
Perhaps when you are at the place
You something of her tale may trace.   110

XI

I'll give you the best help I can:
Before you up the mountain go,
Up to the dreary mountain-top,
I'll tell you all I know.
'Tis now some two and twenty years,
Since she (her name is Martha Ray)
Gave with a maiden's true good will
Her company to Stephen Hill;
And she was blithe and gay,
And she was happy, happy still   120
Whene'er she thought of Stephen Hill.

XII

And they had fix'd the wedding-day,
The morning that must wed them both;
But Stephen to another maid
Had sworn another oath;
And with this other maid to church
Unthinking Stephen went—
Poor Martha! on that woful day
A cruel, cruel fire, they say,
Into her bones was sent: 130
It dried her body like a cinder,
And almost turn'd her brain to tinder.

XIII

They say, full six months after this,
While yet the summer-leaves were green,
She to the mountain-top would go,
And there was often seen.
'Tis said, a child was in her womb,
As now to any eye was plain;

She was with child, and she was mad,
Yet often she was sober sad   140
From her exceeding pain.
Oh me! ten thousand times I'd rather
That he had died, that cruel father!

XIV

Sad case for such a brain to hold
Communion with a stirring child!
Sad case, as you may think, for one
Who had a brain so wild!
Last Christmas when we talked of this,
Old Farmer Simpson did maintain,
That in her womb the infant wrought   150
About its mother's heart, and brought
Her senses back again:
And when at last her time drew near,
Her looks were calm, her senses clear.

XV

No more I know, I wish I did,
And I would tell it all to you;
For what became of this poor child
There's none that ever knew:
And if a child was born or no,
There's no one that could ever tell;   160
And if 'twas born alive or dead,
There's no one knows, as I have said,
But some remember well,
That Martha Ray about this time
Would up the mountain often climb.

XVI

And all that winter, when at night
The wind blew from the mountain-peak,
'Twas worth your while, though in the dark,
The church-yard path to seek:
For many a time and oft were heard   170
Cries coming from the mountain-head,
Some plainly living voices were,
And others, I've heard many swear,
Were voices of the dead:
I cannot think, whate'er they say,
They had to do with Martha Ray.

XVII

But that she goes to this old thorn,
The thorn which I've described to you,
And there sits in a scarlet cloak,
I will be sworn is true.   180
For one day with my telescope,
To view the ocean wide and bright,

When to this country first I came,
Ere I had heard of Martha's name,
I climbed the mountain's height:
A storm came on, and I could see
No object higher than my knee.

XVIII

'Twas mist and rain, and storm and rain,
No screen, no fence could I discover,
And then the wind! in faith, it was   190
A wind full ten times over.
I looked around, I thought I saw
A jutting crag, and off I ran,
Head-foremost, through the driving rain,
The shelter of the crag to gain,
And, as I am a man,
Instead of jutting crag, I found
A woman seated on the ground.

XIX

I did not speak—I saw her face,
Her face it was enough for me;   200
I turned about and heard her cry,
"O misery! O misery!"
And there she sits, until the moon
Through half the clear blue sky will go,
And when the little breezes make
The waters of the pond to shake,
As all the country know,
She shudders and you hear her cry,
"Oh misery! oh misery!

XX

"But what's the thorn? and what's the pond?
"And what's the hill of moss to her?   211
"And what's the creeping breeze that comes
"The little pond to stir?"
I cannot tell; but some will say
She hanged her baby on the tree,
Some say she drowned it in the pond,
Which is a little step beyond,
But all and each agree,
The little babe was buried there,
Beneath that hill of moss so fair.   220

XXI

I've heard the scarlet moss is red
With drops of that poor infant's blood;
But kill a new-born infant thus!
I do not think she could.
Some say, if to the pond you go,
And fix on it a steady view,
The shadow of a babe you trace,
A baby and a baby's face,
And that it looks at you;

Whene'er you look on it, 'tis plain   230
The baby looks at you again.

XXII

And some had sworn an oath that she
Should be to public justice brought;
And for the little infant's bones
With spades they would have sought.
But then the beauteous hill of moss
Before their eyes began to stir;
And for full fifty yards around,
The grass it shook upon the ground;
But all do still aver   240
The little babe is buried there,
Beneath that hill of moss so fair.

XXIII

I cannot tell how this may be,
But plain it is, the thorn is bound
With heavy tufts of moss, that strive
To drag it to the ground.
And this I know, full many a time,
When she was on the mountain high,
By day, and in the silent night,
When all the stars shone clear and bright,
That I have heard her cry,   251
"Oh misery! oh misery!
"O woe is me! oh misery!"

[1798]

THE LAST OF THE FLOCK

IN DISTANT countries I have been
And yet I have not often seen
A healthy man, a man full grown
Weep in the public roads alone.
But such a one, on English ground,
And in the broad high-way, I met;
Along the broad high-way he came,
His cheeks with tears were wet.
Sturdy he seemed, though he was sad;
And in his arms a lamb he had.   10

He saw me, and he turned aside,
As if he wished himself to hide:
Then with his coat he made essay
To wipe those briny tears away.
I follow'd him, and said, "My friend
"What ails you? wherefore weep you so?"
—"Shame on me, Sir! this lusty lamb,
He makes my tears to flow.
To-day I fetched him from the rock;
He is the last of all my flock.   20

When I was young, a single man,
And after youthful follies ran,
Though little given to care and thought,
Yet, so it was, a ewe I bought;
And other sheep from her I raised,
As healthy sheep as you might see,
And then I married, and was rich
As I could wish to be;
Of sheep I number'd a full score,
And every year encreas'd my store.   30

Year after year my stock it grew,
And from this one, this single ewe,
Full fifty comely sheep I raised,
As sweet a flock as ever grazed!
Upon the mountain did they feed;
They throve, and we at home did thrive.
—This lusty lamb of all my store
Is all that is alive:
And now I care not if we die,
And perish all of poverty.   40

Ten children, Sir! had I to feed,
Hard labour in a time of need!
My pride was tamed, and in our grief
I of the parish ask'd relief.
They said I was a wealthy man;
My sheep upon the mountain fed,
And it was fit that thence I took
Whereof to buy us bread:"
"Do this; how can we give to you,"
They cried, "what to the poor is due?"   50

I sold a sheep as they had said,
And bought my little children bread,
And they were healthy with their food;
For me it never did me good.
A woeful time it was for me,
To see the end of all my gains,
The pretty flock which I had reared
With all my care and pains,
To see it melt like snow away!
For me it was a woeful day.   60

Another still! and still another!
A little lamb, and then its mother!
It was a vein that never stopp'd,
Like blood-drops from my heart they
          dropp'd.
Till thirty were not left alive
They dwindled, dwindled, one by one,
And I may say that many a time
I wished they all were gone:
They dwindled one by one away;
For me it was a woeful day.   70

To wicked deeds I was inclined,
And wicked fancies cross'd my mind,
And every man I chanc'd to see,
I thought he knew some ill of me.
No peace, no comfort could I find,
No ease, within doors or without,
And crazily, and wearily,
I went my work about.
Oft-times I thought to run away;
For me it was a woeful day.   80

Sir! 'twas a precious flock to me,
As dear as my own children be;
For daily with my growing store
I loved my children more and more.
Alas! it was an evil time;
God cursed me in my sore distress,
I prayed, yet every day I thought
I loved my children less;
And every week, and every day,
My flock, it seemed to melt away.   90

They dwindled, Sir, sad sight to see!
From ten to five, from five to three,
A lamb, a weather, and a ewe;
And then at last, from three to two;
And of my fifty, yesterday
I had but only one,
And here it lies upon my arm,
Alas! and I have none;
To-day I fetched it from the rock
It is the last of all my flock."   100

[1798]

THE MAD MOTHER

HER eyes are wild, her head is bare,
The sun has burnt her coal-black hair,
Her eye-brows have a rusty stain,
And she came far from over the main.
She has a baby on her arm,
Or else she were alone;
And underneath the hay-stack warm,
And on the green-wood stone,
She talked and sung the woods among;
And it was in the English tongue.   10

"Sweet babe! they say that I am mad,
But nay, my heart is far too glad;
And I am happy when I sing
Full many a sad and doleful thing:

Then, lovely baby, do not fear!
I pray thee have no fear of me,
But, safe as in a cradle, here
My lovely baby! thou shalt be,
To thee I know too much I owe;
I cannot work thee any woe.   20

A fire was once within my brain;
And in my head a dull, dull pain;
And fiendish faces one, two, three,
Hung at my breasts, and pulled at me.
But then there came a sight of joy;
It came at once to do me good;
I waked, and saw my little boy,
My little boy of flesh and blood;
Oh joy for me that sight to see!
For he was here, and only he.   30

Suck, little babe, oh suck again!
It cools my blood; it cools my brain;
Thy lips I feel them, baby! they
Draw from my heart the pain away.
Oh! press me with thy little hand;
It loosens something at my chest;
About that tight and deadly band
I feel thy little fingers press'd.
The breeze I see is in the tree;
It comes to cool my babe and me.   40

Oh! love me, love me, little boy!
Thou art thy mother's only joy;
And do not dread the waves below,
When o'er the sea-rock's edge we go;
The high crag cannot work me harm,
Nor leaping torrents when they howl;
The babe I carry on my arm,
He saves for me my precious soul;
Then happy lie, for blest am I;
Without me my sweet babe would die.   50

Then do not fear, my boy! for thee
Bold as a lion I will be;
And I will always be thy guide,
Through hollow snows and rivers wide
I'll build an Indian bower; I know
The leaves that make the softest bed:
And if from me thou wilt not go,
But still be true 'till I am dead,
My pretty thing! then thou shalt sing,
As merry as the birds in spring.   60

Thy father cares not for my breast,
'Tis thine, sweet baby, there to rest:
'Tis all thine own! and if its hue
Be changed, that was so fair to view,

'Tis fair enough for thee, my dove!
My beauty, little child, is flown;
But thou wilt live with me in love,
And what if my poor cheek be brown?
'Tis well for me; thou canst not see
How pale and wan it else would be.   70

Dread not their taunts, my little life!
I am thy father's wedded wife;
And underneath the spreading tree
We two will live in honesty.
If his sweet boy he could forsake,
With me he never would have stay'd:
From him no harm my babe can take,
But he, poor man! is wretched made,
And every day we two will pray
For him that's gone and far away.   80

I'll teach my boy the sweetest things;
I'll teach him how the owlet sings.
My little babe! thy lips are still,
And thou hast almost suck'd thy fill.
—Where art thou gone my own dear child?
What wicked looks are those I see?
Alas! alas! that look so wild,
It never, never came from me:
If thou art mad, my pretty lad,
Then I must be for ever sad.   90

Oh! smile on me, my little lamb!
For I thy own dear mother am.
My love for thee has well been tried:
I've sought thy father far and wide.
I know the poisons of the shade,
I know the earth-nuts fit for food;
Then, pretty dear, be not afraid;
We'll find thy father in the wood.
Now laugh and be gay, to the woods away!
And there, my babe; we'll live for aye.   100

[1798]

THE IDIOT BOY

" The last stanza . . . was the foundation of the whole. The words were reported to me by my dear friend, Thomas Poole; but I have since heard the same repeated of other Idiots. Let me add that this long poem was composed in the groves of Alfoxden, almost extempore; not a word, I believe, being corrected, though one stanza was omitted. I mention this in gratitude to those happy moments, for, in truth, I never wrote anything with so much glee." [Wordsworth to Isabella Fenwick]

THE IDIOT BOY

'Tis eight o'clock,—a clear March night,
The moon is up—the sky is blue,
The owlet in the moonlight air,
He shouts from nobody knows where;
He lengthens out his lonely shout,
Haloo! halloo! a long halloo!

—Why bustle thus about your door,
What means this bustle, Betty Foy?
Why are you in this mighty fret?
And why on horseback have you set   10
Him whom you love, your idiot boy?

Beneath the moon that shines so bright,
Till she is tired, let Betty Foy
With girt and stirrup fiddle-faddle;
But wherefore set upon a saddle
Him whom she loves, her idiot boy?

There's scarce a soul that's out of bed;
Good Betty! put him down again;
His lips with joy they burr at you,
But, Betty! what has he to do   20
With stirrup, saddle, or with rein?

The world will say 'tis very idle,
Bethink you of the time of night;
There's not a mother, no not one,
But when she hears what you have done,
Oh! Betty she'll be in a fright.

But Betty's bent on her intent,
For her good neighbour, Susan Gale,
Old Susan, she who dwells alone,
Is sick, and makes a piteous moan,   30
As if her very life would fail.

There's not a house within a mile,
No hand to help them in distress:
Old Susan lies a bed in pain,
And sorely puzzled are the twain,
For what she ails they cannot guess.

And Betty's husband's at the wood,
Where by the week he doth abide,
A woodman in the distant vale;
There's none to help poor Susan Gale,   40
What must be done? what will betide?

And Betty from the lane has fetched
Her pony, that is mild and good,
Whether he be in joy or pain,
Feeding at will along the lane,
Or bringing faggots from the wood.

And he is all in travelling trim,
And by the moonlight, Betty Foy
Has up upon the saddle set,
The like was never heard of yet,   50
Him whom she loves, her idiot boy.

And he must post without delay
Across the bridge that's in the dale,
And by the church, and o'er the down,
To bring a doctor from the town,
Or she will die, old Susan Gale.

There is no need of boot or spur,
There is no need of whip or wand,
For Johnny has his holly-bough,
And with a hurly-burly now   60
He shakes the green bough in his hand.

And Betty o'er and o'er has told
The boy who is her best delight,
Both what to follow, what to shun,
What do, and what to leave undone,
How turn to left, and how to right.

And Betty's most especial charge,
Was, "Johnny! Johnny! mind that you
"Come home again, nor stop at all,
"Come home again, whate'er befal,   70
"My Johnny do, I pray you do."

To this did Johnny answer make,
Both with his head, and with his hand,
And proudly shook the bridle too,
And then! his words were not a few,
Which Betty well could understand.

And now that Johnny is just going,
Though Betty's in a mighty flurry,
She gently pats the pony's side,
On which her idiot boy must ride,   80
And seems no longer in a hurry.

But when the pony moved his legs,
Oh! then for the poor idiot boy!
For joy he cannot hold the bridle,
For joy his head and heels are idle,
He's idle all for very joy.

And while the pony moves his legs,
In Johnny's left-hand you may see,
The green bough's motionless and dead;
The moon that shines above his head   90
Is not more still and mute than he.

His heart it was so full of glee,
That till full fifty yards were gone,
He quite forgot his holly whip,
And all his skill in horsemanship,
Oh! happy, happy, happy John.

And Betty's standing at the door,
And Betty's face with joy o'erflows,
Proud of herself, and proud of him
She sees him in his travelling trim;   100
How quietly her Johnny goes.

The silence of her idiot boy,
What hopes it sends to Betty's heart!
He's at the guide-post–he turns right,
She watches till he's out of sight,
And Betty will not then depart.

Burr, burr—now Johnny's lips they burr,
As loud as any mill, or near it,
Meek as a lamb the pony moves,
And Johnny makes the noise he loves,   110
And Betty listens, glad to hear it.

Away she hies to Susan Gale:
And Johnny's in a merry tune,
The owlets hoot, the owlets curr,
And Johnny's lips they burr, burr, burr,
And on he goes beneath the moon.

His steed and he right well agree,
For of this pony there's a rumour,
That should he lose his eyes and ears,
And should he live a thousand years,   120
He never will be out of humour.

But then he is a horse that thinks!
And when he thinks his pace is slack;
Now, though he knows poor Johnny well,
Yet for his life he cannot tell
What he has got upon his back.

So through the moonlight lanes they go,
And far into the moonlight dale,
And by the church, and o'er the down,
To bring a doctor from the town,   130
To comfort poor old Susan Gale.

And Betty, now at Susan's side,
Is in the middle of her story,
What comfort Johnny soon will bring,
With many a most diverting thing,
Of Johnny's wit and Johnny's glory.

And Betty's still at Susan's side:
By this time she's not quite so flurried;
Demure with porringer and plate
She sits, as if in Susan's fate   140
Her life and soul were buried.

But Betty, poor good woman! she,
You plainly in her face may read it,
Could lend out of that moment's store
Five years of happiness or more,
To any that might need it.

But yet I guess that now and then
With Betty all was not so well,
And to the road she turns her ears,
And thence full many a sound she hears,   150
Which she to Susan will not tell.

Poor Susan moans, poor Susan groans,
"As sure as there's a moon in heaven,"
Cries Betty, "he'll be back again;
"They'll both be here, 'tis almost ten,
"They'll both be here before eleven."

Poor Susan moans, poor Susan groans,
The clock gives warning for eleven;
'Tis on the stroke—"If Johnny's near,"
Quoth Betty "he will soon be here,   160
"As sure as there's a moon in heaven."

The clock is on the stroke of twelve,
And Johnny is not yet in sight,
The moon's in heaven, as Betty sees,
But Betty is not quite at ease;
And Susan has a dreadful night.

And Betty, half an hour ago,
On Johnny vile reflections cast;
"A little idle sauntering thing!"
With other names, an endless string,   170
But now that time is gone and past.

And Betty's drooping at the heart,
That happy time all past and gone,
"How can it be he is so late?
"The doctor he has made him wait,
"Susan! they'll both be here anon."

And Susan's growing worse and worse,
And Betty's in a sad quandary;
And then there's nobody to say
If she must go or she must stay: 180
—She's in a sad quandary.

The clock is on the stroke of one;
But neither Doctor nor his guide
Appear along the moonlight road,
There's neither horse nor man abroad,
And Betty's still at Susan's side.

And Susan she begins to fear
Of sad mischances not a few,
That Johnny may perhaps be drown'd,
Or lost perhaps, and never found;   190
Which they must both for ever rue.

She prefaced half a hint of this
With, "God forbid it should be true!"
At the first word that Susan said
Cried Betty, rising from the bed,
"Susan, I'd gladly stay with you.

"I must be gone, I must away,
"Consider, Johnny's but half-wise;
"Susan, we must take care of him,
"If he is hurt in life or limb"—   200
"Oh God forbid!" poor Susan cries.

"What can I do?" says Betty, going,
"What can I do to ease your pain?
"Good Susan tell me, and I'll stay;
"I fear you're in a dreadful way,
"But I shall soon be back again."

"Good Betty go, good Betty go,
"There's nothing that can ease my pain."
Then off she hies, but with a prayer
That God poor Susan's life would spare,   210
Till she comes back again.

So, through the moonlight lane she goes,
And far into the moonlight dale;
And how she ran, and how she walked,
And all that to herself she talked,
Would surely be a tedious tale.

In high and low, above, below,
In great and small, in round and square,
In tree and tower was Johnny seen,
In bush and brake, in black and green,   220
'Twas Johnny, Johnny, every where.

She's past the bridge that's in the dale,
And now the thought torments her sore,
Johnny perhaps his horse forsook,
To hunt the moon that's in the brook,
And never will be heard of more.

And now she's high upon the down,
Alone amid a prospect wide;
There's neither Johnny nor his horse,
Among the fern or in the gorse;   230
There's neither doctor nor his guide.

"Oh saints! what is become of him?
"Perhaps he's climbed into an oak,
"Where he will stay till he is dead;
"Or sadly he has been misled,
"And joined the wandering gypsey-folk.

"Or him that wicked pony's carried
"To the dark cave, the goblins' hall,
"Or in the castle he's pursuing,
"Among the ghosts, his own undoing;   240
"Or playing with the waterfall."

At poor old Susan then she railed,
While to the town she posts away;
"If Susan had not been so ill,
"Alas! I should have had him still,
"My Johnny, till my dying day."

Poor Betty! in this sad distemper,
The doctor's self would hardly spare,
Unworthy things she talked and wild,
Even he, of cattle the most mild,   250
The pony had his share.

And now she's got into the town,
And to the doctor's door she hies;
'Tis silence all on every side;
The town so long, the town so wide,
Is silent as the skies.

And now she's at the doctor's door,
She lifts the knocker, rap, rap, rap,
The doctor at the casement shews,
His glimmering eyes that peep and doze;   260
And one hand rubs his old night-cap.

"Oh Doctor! Doctor! where's my Johnny?"
"I'm here, what is't you want with me?"
"Oh Sir! you know I'm Betty Foy,
"And I have lost my poor dear boy,
"You know him—him you often see;

"He's not so wise as some folks be."
"The devil take his wisdom!" said
  The Doctor, looking somewhat grim,
"What, woman! should I know of him?"   270
  And, grumbling, he went back to bed.

"O woe is me! O woe is me!
"Here will I die; here will I die;
"I thought to find my Johnny here,
"But he is neither far nor near,
"Oh! what a wretched mother I!"

She stops, she stands, she looks about,
Which way to turn she cannot tell.
Poor Betty! it would ease her pain
If she had heart to knock again;   280
—The clock strikes three—a dismal knell!

Then up along the town she hies,
No wonder if her senses fail,
This piteous news so much it shock'd her,
She quite forgot to send the Doctor,
To comfort poor old Susan Gale.

And now she's high upon the down,
  And she can see a mile of road,
"Oh cruel! I'm almost three-score;
"Such night as this was ne'er before,   290
"There's not a single soul abroad."

She listens, but she cannot hear
The foot of horse, the voice of man;
The streams with softest sound are flowing,
The grass you almost hear it growing,
You hear it now if e'er you can.

The owlets through the long blue night
Are shouting to each other still:
Fond lovers, yet not quite hob nob,
They lengthen out the tremulous sob,   300
That echoes far from hill to hill.

Poor Betty now has lost all hope,
Her thoughts are bent on deadly sin;
A green-grown pond she just has pass'd,
And from the brink she hurries fast,
Lest she should drown herself therein.

And now she sits her down and weeps;
  Such tears she never shed before;
"Oh dear, dear pony! my sweet joy!
"Oh carry back my idiot boy!   310
"And we will ne'er o'erload thee more."

A thought is come into her head;
"The pony he is mild and good,
"And we have always used him well;
"Perhaps he's gone along the dell,
"And carried Johnny to the wood."

Then up she springs as if on wings;
She thinks no more of deadly sin;
If Betty fifty ponds should see,
The last of all her thoughts would be,   320
To drown herself therein.

Oh reader! now that I might tell
What Johnny and his horse are doing!
What they've been doing all this time,
Oh could I put it into rhyme,
A most delightful tale pursuing!

Perhaps, and no unlikely thought!
He with his pony now doth roam
The cliffs and peaks so high that are,
To lay his hands upon a star,   330
And in his pocket bring it home.

Perhaps he's turned himself about,
His face unto his horse's tail,
And still and mute, in wonder lost,
All like a silent horseman-ghost,
He travels on along the vale.

And now, perhaps, he's hunting sheep,
A fierce and dreadful hunter he!
Yon valley, that's so trim and green,
In five months' time, should he be seen,   340
A desart wilderness will be.

Perhaps, with head and heels on fire,
And like the very soul of evil,
He's galloping away, away,
And so he'll gallop on for aye,
The bane of all that dread the devil.

I to the muses have been bound,
These fourteen years, by strong indentures;
Oh gentle muses! let me tell
But half of what to him befel,   350
For sure he met with strange adventures.

Oh gentle muses! is this kind?
Why will ye thus my suit repel?
Why of your further aid bereave me?
And can ye thus unfriended leave me?
Ye muses! whom I love so well.

Who's yon, that, near the waterfall,
Which thunders down with headlong force,
Beneath the moon, yet shining fair,
As careless as if nothing were,   360
Sits upright on a feeding horse?

Unto his horse, that's feeding free,
He seems, I think, the rein to give;
Of moon or stars he takes no heed;
Of such we in romances read,
—'Tis Johnny! Johnny! as I live.

And that's the very pony too.
Where is she, where is Betty Foy?
She hardly can sustain her fears;
The roaring water-fall she hears,   370
And cannot find her idiot boy.

Your pony's worth his weight in gold,
Then calm your terrors, Betty Foy!
She's coming from among the trees,
And now, all full in view, she sees
Him whom she loves, her idiot boy.

And Betty sees the pony too:
Why stand you thus Good Betty Foy?
It is no goblin, 'tis no ghost,
'Tis he whom you so long have lost,   380
He whom you love, your idiot boy.

She looks again—her arms are up—
She screams—she cannot move for joy;
She darts as with a torrent's force,
She almost has o'erturned the horse,
And fast she holds her idiot boy.

And Johnny burrs and laughs aloud,
Whether in cunning or in joy,
I cannot tell; but while he laughs,
Betty a drunken pleasure quaffs,   390
To hear again her idiot boy.

And now she's at the pony's tail,
And now she's at the pony's head,
On that side now, and now on this,
And almost stifled with her bliss,
A few sad tears does Betty shed.

She kisses o'er and o'er again,
Him whom she loves, her idiot boy,
She's happy here, she's happy there,
She is uneasy every where;   400
Her limbs are all alive with joy.

She pats the pony, where or when
She knows not, happy Betty Foy!
The little pony glad may be,
But he is milder far than she,
You hardly can perceive his joy.

"Oh! Johnny, never mind the Doctor;
"You've done your best, and that is all"
She took the reins, when this was said,
And gently turned the pony's head   410
From the loud water-fall.

By this the stars were almost gone,
The moon was setting on the hill,
So pale you scarcely looked at her:
The little birds began to stir,
Though yet their tongues were still.

The pony, Betty, and her boy,
Wind slowly through the woody dale:
And who is she, be-times abroad,
That hobbles up the steep rough road?   420
Who is it, but old Susan Gale?

Long Susan lay deep lost in thought,
And many dreadful fears beset her,
Both for her messenger and nurse;
And as her mind grew worse and worse,
Her body it grew better.

She turned, she toss'd herself in bed,
On all sides doubts and terrors met her;
Point after point did she discuss;
And while her mind was fighting thus,   430
Her body still grew better.

"Alas! what is become of them?
"These fears can never be endured,
"I'll to the wood."—The word scarce said,
Did Susan rise up from her bed,
As if by magic cured.

Away she posts up hill and down,
And to the wood at length is come,
She spies her friends, she shouts a greeting;
Oh me! it is a merry meeting,   440
As ever was in Christendom.

The owls have hardly sung their last,
While our four travellers homeward wend;
The owls have hooted all night long,
And with the owls began my song,
And with the owls must end.

For while they all were travelling home,
Cried Betty, "Tell us Johnny, do,
"Where all this long night you have been,
"What you have heard, what you have seen,
"And Johnny, mind you tell us true."   451

Now Johnny all night long had heard
The owls in tuneful concert strive;
No doubt too he the moon had seen;
For in the moonlight he had been
From eight o'clock till five.

And thus to Betty's question, he
Made answer, like a traveller bold,
(His very words I give to you,)
"The cocks did crow to-whoo, to-whoo,   460
"And the sun did shine so cold."
—Thus answered Johnny in his glory,
And that was all his travel's story.

[1798]

LINES

WRITTEN NEAR RICHMOND, UPON THE THAMES, AT EVENING

How rich the wave, in front, imprest
With evening-twilight's summer hues,
While, facing thus the crimson west,
The boat her silent path pursues!
And see how dark the backward stream!
A little moment past, so smiling!
And still, perhaps, with faithless gleam,
Some other loiterer beguiling.

Such views the youthful bard allure,
But, heedless of the following gloom,   10
He deems their colours shall endure
'Till peace go with him to the tomb.
—And let him nurse his fond deceit,

And what if he must die in sorrow!
Who would not cherish dreams so sweet,
Though grief and pain may come to-morrow?

Glide gently, thus for ever glide,
O Thames! that other bards may see,
As lovely visions by thy side
As now, fair river! come to me.   20

Oh glide, fair stream! for ever so;
They quiet soul on all bestowing,
'Till all our minds for ever flow,
As thy deep waters now are flowing.

Vain thought! yet be as now thou art,
That in thy waters may be seen
The image of a poet's heart,
How bright, how solemn, how serene!
Such heart did once the poet bless,
Who, pouring here a *later ditty,   30
Could find no refuge from distress,
But in the milder grief of pity.

Remembrance! as we glide along,
For him suspend the dashing oar,
And pray that never child of Song
May know his freezing sorrows more.
How calm! how still! the only sound,
The dripping of the oar suspended!
—The evening darkness gathers round
By virtue's holiest powers attended.   40

[1788–97]

EXPOSTULATION AND REPLY

"Why William, on that old grey stone,
"Thus for the length of half a day,
"Why William, sit you thus alone,
"And dream your time away?

"Where are your books? that light bequeath'd
"To beings else forlorn and blind!
"Up! Up! and drink the spirit breath'd
"From dead men to their kind.

"You look round on your mother earth,
"As if she for no purpose bore you;   10
"As if you were her first-born birth,
"And none had lived before you!"

One morning thus, by Esthwaite lake,
When life was sweet I knew not why,
To me my good friend Matthew spake,
And thus I made reply.

* Collins's Ode on the death of Thomson, the last written, I believe, of the poems which were published during his lifetime. This Ode is also alluded to in the next stanza.[1]

◇◇◇◇◇◇◇◇◇◇◇◇◇◇◇◇◇◇◇◇◇◇◇◇◇◇◇◇◇◇◇◇◇◇

[1] Wordsworth refers to the poem in which William Collins (1721–1759) commemorates the death of James Thomson (1700–1748), author of *The Seasons* and other poems celebrating nature, at Richmond a half-century earlier.

"The eye it cannot chuse but see,
"We cannot bid the ear be still;
"Our bodies feel, where'er they be,
"Against, or with our will.   20

"Nor less I deem that there are powers,
"Which of themselves our minds impress,
"That we can feed this mind of ours,
"In a wise passiveness.

"Think you, mid all this mighty sum
"Of things for ever speaking,
"That nothing of itself will come,
"But we must still be seeking?

"—Then ask not wherefore, here, alone,
"Conversing as I may,   30
"I sit upon this old grey stone,
"And dream my time away."

[1798]

THE TABLES TURNED;

AN EVENING SCENE, ON THE
SAME SUBJECT

Up! up! my friend, and clear your looks,
Why all this toil and trouble?
Up! up! my friend, and quit your books,
Or surely you'll grow double.

The sun above the mountain's head,
A freshening lustre mellow,
Through all the long green fields has spread,
His first sweet evening yellow.

Books! 'tis a dull and endless strife,
Come, hear the woodland linnet,   10
How sweet his music; on my life
There's more of wisdom in it.

And hark! how blithe the throstle sings!
And he is no mean preacher;
Come forth into the light of things,
Let Nature be your teacher.

She has a world of ready wealth,
Our minds and hearts to bless—
Spontaneous wisdom breathed by health,
Truth breathed by chearfulness.   20

One impulse from a vernal wood
May teach you more of man;
Of moral evil and of good,
Than all the sages can.

Sweet is the lore which nature brings;
Our meddling intellect
Misshapes the beauteous forms of things;
—We murder to dissect.

Enough of science and of art;
Close up these barren leaves;   30
Come forth, and bring with you a heart
That watches and receives.

[1798]

OLD MAN TRAVELLING;

ANIMAL TRANQUILLITY AND DECAY,
A SKETCH

                    The little hedge-row birds,
That peck along the road, regard him not.
He travels on, and in his face, his step,
His gait, is one expression; every limb,
His look and bending figure, all bespeak
A man who does not move with pain, but moves
With thought—He is insensibly subdued
To settled quiet: he is one by whom
All effort seems forgotten, one to whom
Long patience has such mild composure given,   10
That patience now doth seem a thing, of which
He hath no need. He is by nature led
To peace so perfect, that the young behold
With envy, what the old man hardly feels.
—I asked him whither he was bound, and what
The object of his journey; he replied
"Sir! I am going many miles to take
"A last leave of my son, a mariner,
"Who from a sea-fight has been brought to Falmouth,
And there is dying in an hospital."   20

[1797–98]

THE COMPLAINT OF A
FORSAKEN INDIAN WOMAN

[*When a Northern Indian, from sickness, is unable to continue
his journey with his companions; he is left behind, covered over
with Deer-skins, and is supplied with water, food, and
fuel if the situation of the place will afford it. He is informed
of the track which his companions intend to pursue, and if he*

is unable to follow, or overtake them, he perishes alone in the Desart; unless he should have the good fortune to fall in with some other Tribes of Indians. It is unnecessary to add that the females are equally, or still more, exposed to the same fate. See that very interesting work, Hearne's Journey from Hudson's Bay to the Northern Ocean. When the Northern Lights, as the same writer informs us, vary their position in the air, they make a rustling and a crackling noise. This circumstance is alluded to in the first stanza of the following poem.]

BEFORE I see another day,
Oh let my body die away!
In sleep I heard the northern gleams;
The stars they were among my dreams;
In sleep did I behold the skies,
I saw the crackling flashes drive;
And yet they are upon my eyes,
And yet I am alive.
Before I see another day,
Oh let my body die away!   10

My fire is dead: it knew no pain;
Yet is it dead, and I remain.
All stiff with ice the ashes lie;
And they are dead, and I will die.
When I was well, I wished to live,
For clothes, for warmth, for food, and fire;
But they to me no joy can give,
No pleasure now, and no desire.
Then here contented will I lie;
Alone I cannot fear to die.   20

Alas! you might have dragged me on
Another day, a single one!
Too soon despair o'er me prevailed;
Too soon my heartless spirit failed;
When you were gone my limbs were stronger,
And Oh how grievously I rue,
That, afterwards, a little longer,
My friends, I did not follow you!
For strong and without pain I lay,
My friends, when you were gone away.   30

My child! they gave thee to another,
A woman who was not thy mother.
When from my arms my babe they took,
On me how strangely did he look!
Through his whole body something ran,
A most strange something did I see;
—As if he strove to be a man,
That he might pull the sledge for me.
And then he stretched his arms, how wild
Oh mercy! like a little child.   40

My little joy! my little pride!
In two days more I must have died.
Then do not weep and grieve for me;
I feel I must have died with thee.
Oh wind that o'er my head art flying,
The way my friends their course did bend,
I should not feel the pain of dying,
Could I with thee a message send.
Too soon, my friends, you went away;
For I had many things to say.   50

I'll follow you across the snow,
You travel heavily and slow:
In spite of all my weary pain,
I'll look upon your tents again.
My fire is dead, and snowy white
The water which beside it stood;
The wolf has come to me to-night,
And he has stolen away my food.
For ever left alone am I,
Then wherefore should I fear to die?   60

My journey will be shortly run,
I shall not see another sun,
I cannot lift my limbs to know
If they have any life or no.
My poor forsaken child! if I
For once could have thee close to me,
With happy heart I then would die,
And my last thoughts would happy be.
I feel my body die away,
I shall not see another day.   70

[1798]

THE CONVICT

THE glory of evening was spread through the west;
    —On the slope of a mountain I stood,
While the joy that precedes the calm season of rest
    Rang loud through the meadow and wood.

"And must we then part from a dwelling so fair?"
    In the pain of my spirit I said,
And with a deep sadness I turned, to repair
    To the cell where the convict is laid.

The thick-ribbed walls that o'ershadow the gate
    Resound; and the dungeons unfold: 10
I pause; and at length, through the glimmering grate,
    That outcast of pity behold.

His black matted head on his shoulder is bent,
    And deep is the sigh of his breath,
And with stedfast dejection his eyes are intent
    On the fetters that link him to death.

'Tis sorrow enough on that visage to gaze,
    That body dismiss'd from his care;
Yet my fancy has pierced to his heart, and pourtrays
    More terrible images there.   20

His bones are consumed, and his life-blood is dried,
    With wishes the past to undo;
And his crime, through the pains that o'erwhelm him,
        descried,
    Still blackens and grows on his view.

When from the dark synod, or blood-reeking field,
    To his chamber the monarch is led,
All soothers of sense their soft virtue shall yield,
    And quietness pillow his head.

But if grief, self-consumed, in oblivion would doze,
    And conscience her tortures appease,   30
'Mid tumult and uproar this man must repose;
    In the comfortless vault of disease.

When his fetters at night have so press'd on his
        limbs,
    That the weight can no longer be borne,
If, while a half-slumber his memory bedims,
    The wretch on his pallet should turn,

While the jail-mastiff howls at the dull clanking chain,
    From the roots of his hair there shall start
A thousand sharp punctures of cold-sweating pain,
    And terror shall leap at his heart.   40

But now he half-raises his deep-sunken eye,
    And the motion unsettles a tear;
The silence of sorrow it seems to supply,
    And asks of me why I am here.

"Poor victim! no idle intruder has stood
    "With o'erweening complacence our state to
        compare,
"But one, whose first wish is the wish to be good,
    "Is come as a brother thy sorrows to share.

"At thy name though compassion her nature resign,
    "Though in virtue's proud mouth thy report be a
        stain,   50
"My care, if the arm of the mighty were mine,
    "Would plant thee where yet thou might'st
        blossom again."

[1793-98]

TINTERN ABBEY

"No poem of mine was composed under circumstances more
pleasant for me to remember than this. I began it upon leaving
Tintern, after crossing the Wye, and concluded it just as I was
entering Bristol in the evening, after a ramble of four or five days,
with my Sister. Not a line of it was altered and not any part of it
written down till I reached Bristol." [Wordsworth to Isabella
Fenwick]

LINES
WRITTEN A FEW MILES ABOVE TINTERN ABBEY,
ON REVISITING THE BANKS OF THE
WYE DURING A TOUR,
July 13, 1798

FIVE years have passed; five summers, with the
        length
Of five long winters! and again I hear
These waters, rolling from their mountain-springs
With a sweet inland murmur.—Once again
Do I behold these steep and lofty cliffs,
Which on a wild secluded scene impress
Thoughts of more deep seclusion; and connect
The landscape with the quiet of the sky.
The day is come when I again repose
Here, under this dark sycamore, and view   10
These plots of cottage-ground, these orchard-tufts,
Which, at this season, with their unripe fruits,
Among the woods and copses lose themselves,
Nor, with their green and simple hue, disturb
The wild green landscape. Once again I see
These hedge-rows, hardly hedge-rows, little lines
Of sportive wood run wild; these pastoral farms
Green to the very door; and wreathes of smoke
Sent up, in silence, from among the trees,
With some uncertain notice, as might seem,   20
Of vagrant dwellers in the houseless woods,
Or of some hermit's cave, where by his fire
The hermit sits alone.

                            Though absent long,
These forms of beauty have not been to me,
As is a landscape to a blind man's eye:
But oft, in lonely rooms, and mid the din
Of towns and cities, I have owed to them,
In hours of weariness, sensations sweet,
Felt in the blood, and felt along the heart,
And passing even into my purer mind   30
With tranquil restoration:—feelings too
Of unremembered pleasure; such, perhaps,
As may have had no trivial influence
On that best portion of a good man's life;

His little, nameless, unremembered acts
Of kindness and of love. Nor less, I trust,
To them I may have owed another gift,
Of aspect more sublime; that blessed mood,
In which the burthen of the mystery,
In which the heavy and the weary weight   40
Of all this unintelligible world
Is lighten'd:—that serene and blessed mood,
In which the affections gently lead us on,
Until, the breath of this corporeal frame,
And even the motion of our human blood
Almost suspended, we are laid asleep
In body, and become a living soul:
While with an eye made quiet by the power
Of harmony, and the deep power of joy,
We see into the life of things.

     If this   50
Be but a vain belief, yet, oh! how oft,
In darkness, and amid the many shapes
Of joyless day-light; when the fretful stir
Unprofitable, and the fever of the world,
Have hung upon the beatings of my heart,
How oft, in spirit, have I turned to thee
O sylvan Wye! Thou wanderer through the woods,
How often has my spirit turned to thee!

And now, with gleams of half-extinguish'd thought,
With many recognitions dim and faint,   60
And somewhat of a sad perplexity,
The picture of the mind revives again:
While here I stand, not only with the sense
Of present pleasure, but with pleasing thoughts
That in this moment there is life and food
For future years. And so I dare to hope
Though changed, no doubt, from what I was, when
  first
I came among these hills; when like a roe
I bounded o'er the mountains, by the sides
Of the deep rivers, and the lonely streams,   70
Wherever nature led; more like a man
Flying from something that he dreads, than one
Who sought the thing he loved. For nature then
(The coarser pleasures of my boyish days,
And their glad animal movements all gone by,)
To me was all in all.—I cannot paint
What then I was. The sounding cataract
Haunted me like a passion: the tall rock,
The mountain, and the deep and gloomy wood,
Their colours and their forms, were then to me   80
An appetite: a feeling and a love,
That had no need of a remoter charm,
By thought supplied, or any interest
Unborrow'd from the eye.—That time is past,

And all its aching joys are now no more,
And all its dizzy raptures. Not for this
Faint I, nor mourn nor murmur: other gifts
Have followed, for such loss, I would believe,
Abundant recompence. For I have learned
To look on nature, not as in the hour   90
Of thoughtless youth, but hearing oftentimes
The still, sad music of humanity,
Not harsh nor grating, though of ample power
To chasten and subdue. And I have felt
A presence that disturbs me with the joy
Of elevated thoughts; a sense sublime
Of something far more deeply interfused,
Whose dwelling is the light of setting suns,
And the round ocean, and the living air,
And the blue sky, and in the mind of man,   100
A motion and a spirit, that impels
All thinking things, all objects of all thought,
And rolls through all things. Therefore am I still
A lover of the meadows and the woods,
And mountains; and of all that we behold
From this green earth; of all the mighty world
Of eye and ear, both what they half-create,*
And what perceive; well pleased to recognize
In nature and the language of the sense,
The anchor of my purest thoughts, the nurse,   110
The guide, the guardian of my heart, and soul
Of all my moral being.

     Nor, perchance,
If I were not thus taught, should I the more
Suffer my genial spirits to decay:
For thou art with me, here, upon the banks
Of this fair river; thou, my dearest Friend,
My dear, dear Friend, and in thy voice I catch
The language of my former heart, and read
My former pleasures in the shooting lights
Of thy wild eyes. Oh! yet a little while   120
May I behold in thee what I was once,
My dear, dear Sister! And this prayer I make,
Knowing that Nature never did betray
The heart that loved her; 'tis her privilege,
Through all the years of this our life, to lead
From joy to joy: for she can so inform
The mind that is within us, so impress
With quietness and beauty, and so feed
With lofty thoughts, that neither evil tongues,
Rash judgments, nor the sneers of selfish men,   130
Nor greetings where no kindness is, nor all

 * This line has a close resemblance to an admirable line of
Young, the exact expression of which I cannot recollect.[1]

♦♦♦♦♦♦♦♦♦♦♦♦♦♦♦♦♦

[1] Wordsworth has in mind Edward Young's *Night Thoughts*,
VI, 427.

The dreary intercourse of daily life,
Shall e'er prevail against us, or disturb
Our chearful faith that all which we behold
Is full of blessings. Therefore let the moon
Shine on thee in thy solitary walk;
And let the misty mountain winds be free
To blow against thee: and in after years,
When these wild ecstasies shall be matured
Into a sober pleasure, when thy mind   140
Shall be a mansion for all lovely forms,
Thy memory be as a dwelling-place
For all sweet sounds and harmonies; Oh! then,
If solitude, or fear, or pain, or grief,
Should be thy portion, with what healing thoughts
Of tender joy wilt thou remember me,
And these my exhortations! Nor, perchance,
If I should be, where I no more can hear
Thy voice, nor catch from thy wild eyes these gleams
Of past existence, wilt thou then forget   150
That on the banks of this delightful stream
We stood together; and that I, so long
A worshipper of Nature, hither came,
Unwearied in that service: rather say
With warmer love, oh! with far deeper zeal
Of holier love. Nor wilt thou then forget,
That after many wanderings, many years
Of absence, these steep woods and lofty cliffs,
And this green pastoral landscape, were to me
More dear, both for themselves, and for thy sake.   160

[1798]   [1798]

[END OF THE POEMS FROM
LYRICAL BALLADS]

THE RUINED COTTAGE

The Ruined Cottage went through a number of revisions and recopyings before it was finally incorporated in Book I of The Excursion. *This text is an edited version of MS. D, copied by Dorothy Wordsworth probably in 1799. Although never published by Wordsworth in this form, it is the closest he came to composing a compact, finished poem focussing on the story of Margaret, in which the character of the Pedlar is clearly subordinate.*

THE RUINED COTTAGE

FIRST PART

'TWAS Summer and the sun was mounted high.
Along the south the uplands feebly glared
Through a pale stream, and all the northern downs,
In clearer air ascending, shewed far off

Their surfaces with shadows dappled o'er
Of deep embattled clouds. Far as the sight
Could reach those many shadows lay in spots
Determined and unmoved, with steady beams
Of clear and pleasant sunshine interposed—
Pleasant to him who on the soft cool moss   10
Extends his careless limbs beside the root
Of some huge oak whose aged branches make
A twilight of their own, a dewy shade
Where the wren warbles while the dreaming man,
Half-conscious of that soothing melody,
With side-long eye looks out upon the scene,
By those impending branches made more soft,
More soft and distant.

                                    Other lot was mine.
Across a bare wide Common I had toiled
With languid feet which by the slipp'ry ground   20
Were baffled still, and when I stretched myself
On the brown earth my limbs from very heat
Could find no rest, nor my weak arm disperse
The insect host which gathered round my face
And joined their murmurs to the tedious noise
Of seeds of bursting gorse that crackled round.
I rose and turned towards a group of trees
Which midway in that level stood alone;
And thither come at length, beneath a shade
Of clustering elems that sprang from the same root   30
I found a ruined house, four naked walls
That stared upon each other. I looked round
And near the door I saw an aged Man,
Alone and stretched upon the cottage bench,
An iron-pointed staff lay at his side.
With instantanious joy I recognized
That pride of nature and of lowly life,
The venerable Armytage, a friend
As dear to me as is the setting sun.
                            Two days before   40
We had been fellow-travellers. I knew
That he was in this neighbourhood, and now
Delighted found him here in the cool shade.
He lay, his pack of rustic merchandize
Pillowing his head. I guess he had no thought
Of his way-wandering life. His eyes were shut,
The shadows of the breezy elms above
Dappled his face. With thirsty heat oppressed
At length I hailed him, glad to see his hat
Bedewed with water-drops, as if the brim   50
Had newly scooped a running stream. He rose
And pointing to a sun-flower, bade me climb
The [   ] wall where that same gaudy flower
Looked out upon the road.

It was a plot
Of garden-ground now wild, its matted weeds
Marked with the steps of those whom as they passed,
The goose-berry trees that shot in long lank slips,
Or currants hanging from their leafless stems
In scanty strings, had tempted to o'erleap
The broken wall. Within that cheerless spot,   60
Where two tall hedgerows of thick alder boughs
Joined in a damp cold nook, I found a well
Half-covered up with willow-flowers and grass.
I slaked my thirst and to the shady bench
Returned, and while I stood unbonneted
To catch the motion of the cooler air
The old Man said, "I see around me here
Things which you cannot see. We die, my Friend,
Nor we alone, but that which each man loved
And prized in his peculiar nook of earth   70
Dies with him, or is changed, and very soon
Even of the good is no memorial left.
The Poets, in their elegies and songs
Lamenting the departed, call the groves,
They call upon the hills and streams to mourn,
And senseless rocks—nor idly, for they speak
In these their invocations with a voice
Obedient to the strong creative power
Of human passion. Sympathies there are
More tranquil, yet perhaps of kindred birth,   80
That steal upon the meditative mind
And grow with thought. Beside yon spring I stood,
And eyed its waters till we seemed to feel
One sadness, they and I. For them a bond
Of brotherhood is broken; time has been
When every day the touch of human hand
Disturbed their stillness, and they ministered
To human comfort. When I stooped to drink
A spider's web hung to the water's edge,
And on the wet and slimy foot-stone lay   90
The useless fragment of a wooden bowl.
It moved my very heart.

           The day has been
When I could never pass this road but she
Who lived within these walls, when I appeared,
A daughter's welcome gave me, and I loved her
As my own child. Oh Sir, the good die first,
And they whose hearts are dry as summer dust
Burn to the socket. Many a passenger
Has blessed poor Margaret for her gentle looks
When she upheld the cool refreshment drawn   100
From that forsaken spring, and no one came
But he was welcome, no one went away
But that it seemed she loved him. She is dead,
The worm is on her cheek, and this poor hut,

Stripped of its outward garb of houshold flowers,
Of rose and sweet-briar, offers to the wind
A cold bare wall whose earthy top is tricked
With weeds and the rank spear-grass. She is dead,
And nettles rot and adders sun themselves
Where we have sate together while she nursed   110
Her infant at her breast. The unshod Colt,
The wandring heifer and the Potter's ass,
Find shelter now within the chimney-wall
Where I have seen her evening hearth-stone blaze
And through the window spread upon the road
Its chearful light. You will forgive me, Sir,
But often on this cottage do I muse
As on a picture, till my wiser mind
Sinks, yielding to the foolishness of grief.

She had a husband, an industrious man,   120
Sober and steady. I have heard her say
That he was up and busy at his loom
In summer ere the mower's scythe had swept
The dewy grass, and in the early spring
Ere the last star had vanished. They who passed
At evening, from behind the garden-fence
Might hear his busy spade, which he would ply
After his daily work till the day-light
Was gone, and every leaf and flower were lost
In the dark hedges. So they passed their days   130
In peace and comfort, and two pretty babes
Were their best hope next to the God in Heaven.

You may remember, now some ten years gone,
Two blighting seasons when the fields were left
With half a harvest. It pleased heaven to add
A worse affliction in the plague of war,
A happy land was stricken to the heart,
'Twas a sad time of sorrow and distress.
A wanderer among the cottages,
I with my pack of winter raiment saw   140
The hardships of that season. Many rich
Sunk down as in a dream among the poor,
And of the poor did many cease to be,
And their place knew them not. Meanwhile, abridged
Of daily comforts, gladly reconciled
To numerous self-denials, Margaret
Went struggling on through those calamitous years
With chearful hope. But ere the second autumn
A fever seized her husband. In disease
He lingered long, and when his strength returned   150
He found the little he had stored to meet
The hour of accident, or crippling age,
Was all consumed. As I have said, 'twas now
A time of trouble: shoals of artizans

Were from their daily labor turned away
To hang for bread on parish charity,
They and their wives and children, happier far
Could they have lived as do the little birds
That peck along the hedges, or the kite
That makes her dwelling in the mountain rocks.   160
Ill fared it now with Robert, he who dwelt
In this poor cottage. At his door he stood
And whistled many a snatch of merry tunes
That had no mirth in them, or with his knife
Carved uncouth figures on the heads of sticks,
Then idly sought about through every nook
Of house or garden any casual task
Of use or ornament, and with a strange
Amusing but uneasy novelty
He blended where he might the various tasks   170
Of summer, autumn, winter, and of spring.
But this endured not, his good-humour soon
Became a weight in which no pleasure was,
And poverty brought on a petted mood
And a sore temper. Day by day he drooped,
And he would leave his home, and to the town
Without an errand would he turn his steps,
Or wander here and there among the fields.
One while he would speak lightly of his babes
And with a cruel tongue, at other times   180
He played with them wild freaks of merriment,
And 'twas a piteous thing to see the looks
Of the poor innocent children. 'Every smile',
Said Margaret to me here beneath these trees,
'Made my heart bleed.'"

                    At this the old Man paused,
And looking up to those enormous elms
He said, "'Tis now the hour of deepest noon.
At this still season of repose and peace,
This hour when all things which are not at rest
Are chearful, while this multitude of flies   190
Fills all the air with happy melody,
Why should a tear be in an old man's eye?
Why should we thus with an untoward mind,
And in the weakness of humanity,
From natural wisdom turn our hearts away,
To natural comfort shut our eyes and ears,
And, feeding on disquiet, thus disturb
The calm of Nature with our restless thoughts?"

              END OF THE FIRST PART

SECOND PART

HE spake with somewhat of a solemn tone,
But when he ended there was in his face   200
Such easy chearfulness, a look so mild,
That for a little time it stole away
All recollection, and that simple tale
Passed from my mind like a forgotten sound.
A while on trivial things we held discourse,
To me soon tasteless. In my own despite
I thought of that poor woman as of one
Whom I had known and loved. He had rehearsed
Her homely tale with such familiar power,
With such an active countenance, an eye   210
So busy, that the things of which he spake
Seemed present, and, attention now relaxed,
There was a heartfelt chillness in my veins.
I rose, and turning from that breezy shade
Went out into the open air, and stood
To drink the comfort of the warmer sun.
Long time I had not stayed ere, looking round
Upon that tranquil ruin, I returned
And begged of the old man that for my sake
He would resume his story.   220
                    He replied,
"It were a wantonness, and would demand
Severe reproof, if we were men whose hearts
Could hold vain dalliance with the misery
Even of the dead, contented thence to draw
A momentary pleasure, never marked
By reason, barren of all future good.
But we have known that there is often found
In mournful thoughts, and always might be found,
A power to virtue friendly; were't not so
I am a dreamer among men, indeed   230
An idle dreamer. 'Tis a common tale
By moving accidents uncharactered,
A tale of silent suffering, hardly clothed
In bodily form, and to the grosser sense
But ill adapted, scarcely palpable
To him who does not think. But at your bidding
I will proceed.

              While thus it fared with them
To whom this cottage till that hapless year
Had been a blessed home, it was my chance
To travel in a country far remote;   240
And glad I was when, halting by yon gate
That leads from the green lane, again I saw
These lofty elm-trees. Long I did not rest:
With many pleasant thoughts I cheered my way
O'er the flat common. At the door arrived,
I knocked, and when I entered, with the hope

Of usual greeting, Margaret looked at me
A little while, then turned her head away
Speechless, and sitting down upon a chair
Wept bitterly. I wist not what to do,   250
Or how to speak to her. Poor wretch, at last
She rose from off her seat, and then, oh Sir,
I cannot tell how she pronounced my name.
With fervent love, and with a face of grief
Unutterably helpless, and a look
That seemed to cling upon me, she enquired
If I had seen her husband. As she spake
A strange surprize and fear came to my heart,
Nor had I power to answer ere she told
That he had disappeared—just two months gone.   260
He left his house: two wretched days had passed,
And on the third by the first break of light,
Within her casement full in view she saw
A purse of gold. 'I trembled at the sight',
Said Margaret, 'for I knew it was his hand
That placed it there. And on that very day
By one, a stranger, from my husband sent,
The tidings came that he had joined a troop
Of soldiers going to a distant land.
He left me thus. Poor Man, he had not heart   270
To take a farewell of me, and he feared
That I should follow with my babes, and sink
Beneath the misery of a soldier's life.'

This tale did Margaret tell with many tears,
And when she ended I had little power
To give her comfort, and was glad to take
Such words of hope from her own mouth as served
To cheer us both. But long we had not talked
Ere we built up a pile of better thoughts,
And with a brighter eye she looked around,   280
As if she had been shedding tears of joy.
We parted. It was then the early spring:
I left her busy with her garden tools,
And well remember, o'er that fence she looked,
And, while I paced along the foot-way path,
Called out and sent a blessing after me,
With tender chearfulness, and with a voice
That seemed the very sound of happy thoughts.

    I roved o'er many a hill and many a dale
With this my weary load, in heat and cold,   290
Through many a wood and many an open ground,
In sunshine or in shade, in wet or fair,
Now blithe, now drooping, as it might befal;
My best companions now the driving winds
And now the 'trotting brooks' and whispering trees,
And now the music of my own sad steps,
With many a short-lived thought that passed between
And disappeared.

                    I came this way again
Towards the wane of summer, when the wheat
Was yellow, and the soft and bladed grass   300
Sprang up afresh and o'er the hay-field spread
Its tender green. When I had reached the door
I found that she was absent. In the shade,
Where we now sit, I waited her return.
Her cottage in its outward look appeared
As chearful as before, in any shew
Of neatness little changed, but that I thought
The honeysuckle crowded round the door,
And from the wall hung down in heavier tufts.
And knots of worthless stone-crop started out   310
Along the window's edge, and grew like weeds
Against the lower panes. I turned aside
And strolled into her garden. It was changed.
The unprofitable bindweed spread his bells
From side to side, and with unwieldy wreaths
Had dragged the rose from its sustaining wall
And bent it down to earth. The border tufts,
Daisy, and thrift, and lowly camomile,
And thyme, had straggled out into the paths
Which they were used to deck.   320

                    Ere this an hour
Was wasted. Back I turned my restless steps,
And as I walked before the door it chanced
A stranger passed, and guessing whom I sought,
He said that she was used to ramble far.
The sun was sinking in the west, and now
I sate with sad impatience. From within
Her solitary infant cried aloud.
The spot though fair seemed very desolate,
The longer I remained more desolate;
And looking round I saw the corner-stones,   330
Till then unmarked, on either side the door
With dull red stains discoloured, and stuck o'er
With tufts and hairs of wool, as if the sheep
That feed upon the commons thither came
Familiarly, and found a couching-place
Even at her threshold.

                    The house-clock struck eight:
I turned and saw her distant a few steps.
Her face was pale and thin, her figure too
Was changed. As she unlocked the door she said,
'It grieves me you have waited here so long,   340
But in good truth I've wandered much of late,
And sometimes, to my shame I speak, have need
Of my best prayers to bring me back again.'
While on the board she spread our evening meal,
She told me she had lost her elder child,
That he for months had been a serving-boy,

Apprenticed by the parish. 'I perceive
You look at me, and you have cause. Today
I have been travelling far, and many days
About the fields I wander, knowing this   350
Only, that what I seek I cannot find.
And so I waste my time: for I am changed,
And to myself', said she, 'have done much wrong,
And to this helpless infant. I have slept
Weeping, and weeping I have waked. My tears
Have flowed as if my body were not such
As others are, and I could never die.
But I am now in mind and in my heart
More easy, and I hope', said she, 'that heaven
Will give me patience to endure the things   360
Which I behold at home.'

                    It would have grieved
Your very soul to see her. Sir, I feel
The story linger in my heart. I fear
'Tis long and tedious, but my spirit clings
To that poor woman. So familiarly
Do I perceive her manner and her look
And presence, and so deeply do I feel
Her goodness, that not seldom in my walks
A momentary trance comes over me,
And to myself I seem to muse on one   370
By sorrow laid asleep or borne away,
A human being destined to awake
To human life, or something very near
To human life, when he shall come again
For whom she suffered. Sir, it would have grieved
Your very soul to see her: evermore
Her eye-lids drooped, her eyes were downward cast,
And when she at her table gave me food
She did not look at me. Her voice was low,
Her body was subdued. In every act   380
Pertaining to her house-affairs appeared
The careless stillness which a thinking mind
Gives to an idle matter. Still she sighed,
But yet no motion of the breast was seen,
No heaving of the heart. While by the fire
We sate together, sighs came on my ear,
I knew not how, and hardly whence they came.
I took my staff, and when I kissed her babe
The tears stood in her eyes. I left her then
With the best hope and comfort I could give: 390
She thanked me for my will, but for my hope
It seemed she did not thank me.
                                        I returned
And took my rounds along this road again
Ere on its sunny bank the primrose flower
Had chronicled the earliest day of spring.
I found her sad and drooping. She had learned

No tidings of her husband; if he lived,
She knew not that he lived; if he were dead,
She knew not he was dead. She seemed the same
In person or appearance, but her house   400
Bespoke a sleepy hand of negligence.
The floor was neither dry nor neat, the hearth
Was comfortless,
The windows too were dim, and her few books,
Which one upon the other heretofore
Had been piled up against the corner-panes
In seemly order, now with straggling leaves
Lay scattered here and there, open or shut,
As they had chanced to fall. Her infant babe
Had from its mother caught the trick of grief,   410
And sighed among its playthings. Once again
I turned towards the garden-gate, and saw
More plainly still that poverty and grief
Were now come nearer to her. The earth was hard,
With weeds defaced and knots of withered grass;
No ridges there appeared of clear black mould,
No winter greenness. Of her herbs and flowers
It seemed the better part were gnawed away
Or trampled on the earth. A chain of straw,
Which had been twisted round the tender stem   420
Of a young apple-tree, lay at its root;
The bark was nibbled round by truant sheep.
Margaret stood near, her infant in her arms,
And, seeing that my eye was on the tree,
She said, 'I fear it will be dead and gone
Ere Robert come again.'

                    Towards the house
Together we returned, and she inquired
If I had any hope. But for her Babe,
And for her little friendless Boy, she said,
She had no wish to live—that she must die   430
Of sorrow. Yet I saw the idle loom
Still in its place. His sunday garments hung
Upon the self-same nail, his very staff
Stood undisturbed behind the door. And when
I passed this way beaten by Autumn winds,
She told me that her little babe was dead,
And she was left alone. That very time,
I yet remember, through the miry lane
She walked with me a mile, when the bare trees
Trickled with foggy damps, and in such sort   440
That any heart had ached to hear her, begged
That wheresoe'er I went I still would ask
For him whom she had lost. We parted then,
Our final parting; for from that time forth
Did many seasons pass ere I returned
Into this tract again.

Five tedious years
She lingered in unquiet widowhood,
A wife and widow. Needs must it have been
A sore heart-wasting. I have heard, my friend,
That in that broken arbour she would sit   450
The idle length of half a sabbath day;
There, where you see the toadstool's lazy head;
And when a dog passed by she still would quit
The shade and look abroad. On this old Bench
For hours she sate, and evermore her eye
Was busy in the distance, shaping things
Which made her heart beat quick. Seest thou that
    path?—
The green-sward now has broken its grey line—
There to and fro she paced through many a day
Of the warm summer, from a belt of flax   460
That girt her waist, spinning the long-drawn thread
With backward steps. Yet ever as there passed
A man whose garments shewed the Soldier's red,
Or crippled Mendicant in Sailor's garb,
The little child who sate to turn the wheel
Ceased from his toil, and she, with faltering voice,
Expecting still to learn her husband's fate,
Made many a fond inquiry; and when they
Whose presence gave no comfort, were gone by,
Her heart was still more sad. And by yon gate,   470
Which bars the traveller's road, she often stood,
And when a stranger horseman came, the latch
Would lift, and in his face look wistfully,
Most happy if from aught discovered there
Of tender feeling she might dare repeat
The same sad question.   Meanwhile her poor hut
Sunk to decay; for he was gone, whose hand
At the first nippings of October frost
Closed up each chink, and with fresh bands of straw
Chequered the green-grown thatch. And so she lived
Through the long winter, reckless and alone,   481
Till this reft house, by frost, and thaw, and rain,
Was sapped; and when she slept, the nightly damps
Did chill her breast, and in the stormy day
Her tattered clothes were ruffled by the wind
Even at the side of her own fire. Yet still
She loved this wretched spot, nor would for worlds
Have parted hence; and still that length of road,
And this rude bench, one torturing hope endeared,
Fast rooted at her heart. And here, my friend,   490
In sickness she remained; and here she died,
Last human tenant of these ruined walls."

The old Man ceased: he saw that I was moved.
From that low Bench rising instinctively,
I turned aside in weakness, nor had power
To thank him for the tale which he had told.
I stood, and leaning o'er the garden gate
Reviewed that Woman's suff'rings; and it seemed
To comfort me while with a brother's love
I blessed her in the impotence of grief.   500
At length towards the cottage I returned
Fondly, and traced with milder interest,
That secret spirit of humanity
Which, 'mid the calm oblivious tendencies
Of nature, 'mid her plants, her weeds and flowers,
And silent overgrowings, still survived.
The old man seeing this resumed, and said,
"My Friend, enough to sorrow have you given,
The purposes of wisdom ask no more:
Be wise and chearful, and no longer read   510
The forms of things with an unworthy eye.
She sleeps in the calm earth, and peace is here.
I well remember that those very plumes,
Those weeds, and the high spear-grass on that wall,
By mist and silent rain-drops silvered o'er,
As once I passed, did to my mind convey
So still an image of tranquility,
So calm and still, and looked so beautiful
Amid the uneasy thoughts which filled my mind,
That what we feel of sorrow and despair   520
From ruin and from change, and all the grief
The passing shews of being leave behind,
Appeared an idle dream that could not live
Where meditation was. I turned away,
And walked along my road in happiness."

He ceased. By this the sun declining shot
A slant and mellow radiance, which began
To fall upon us where beneath the trees
We sate on that low bench. And now we felt,
Admonished thus, the sweet hour coming on: 530
A linnet warbled from those lofty elms,
A thrush sang aloud, and other melodies
At distance heard, peopled the milder air.
The old man rose and hoisted up his load.
Together casting then a farewell look
Upon those silent walls, we left the shade;
And, ere the stars were visible, attained
A rustic inn, our evening resting-place.

THE END

[1797 ff.]   [1969]

THE REVERIE OF POOR SUSAN

At the corner of Wood Street, when daylight appears,
Hangs a Thrush that sings loud, it has sung for three
    years:
Poor Susan has passed by the spot, and has heard
In the silence of morning the song of the Bird.

'Tis a note of enchantment; what ails her? She sees
A mountain ascending, a vision of trees;
Bright volumes of vapour through Lothbury glide,
And a river flows on through the vale of Cheapside.[1]

Green pastures she views in the midst of the dale,
Down which she so often has tripped with her pail; 10
And a single small cottage, a nest like a dove's,
The one only dwelling on earth that she loves.

She looks, and her heart is in heaven: but they fade,
The mist and the river, the hill and the shade:
The stream will not flow, and the hill will not rise,
And the colours have all passed away from her eyes!

[1797]   [1800]

THE OLD CUMBERLAND BEGGAR

The class of Beggars, to which the Old Man here described
belongs, will probably soon be extinct. It consisted of poor,
and, mostly, old and infirm persons, who confined them-
selves to a stated round in their neighbourhood, and had
certain fixed days, on which, at different houses, they
regularly received alms, sometimes in money, but mostly
in provisions.

I saw an aged Beggar in my walk;
And he was seated, by the highway side,
On a low structure of rude masonry
Built at the foot of a huge hill, that they
Who lead their horses down the steep rough road
May thence remount at ease. The aged Man
Had placed his staff across the broad smooth stone
That overlays the pile; and, from a bag
All white with flour, the dole of village dames,
He drew his scraps and fragments, one by one; 10
And scanned them with a fixed and serious look
Of idle computation. In the sun,
Upon the second step of that small pile,
Surrounded by those wild unpeopled hills,
He sat, and ate his food in solitude:
And ever, scattered from his palsied hand,
That, still attempting to prevent the waste,

---

[1] All three street names refer to commercial districts of east London.

Was baffled still, the crumbs in little showers
Fell on the ground; and the small mountain birds,
Not venturing yet to peck their destined meal, 20
Approached within the length of half his staff.

Him from my childhood have I known; and then
He was so old, he seems not older now;
He travels on, a solitary Man,
So helpless in appearance, that for him
The sauntering Horseman throws not with a slack
And careless hand his alms upon the ground,
But stops,—that he may safely lodge the coin
Within the old Man's hat; nor quits him so,
But still, when he has given his horse the rein, 30
Watches the aged Beggar with a look
Sidelong, and half-reverted. She who tends
The toll-gate, when in summer at her door
She turns her wheel, if on the road she sees
The aged Beggar coming, quits her work,
And lifts the latch for him that he may pass.
The post-boy, when his rattling wheels o'ertake
The aged Beggar in the woody lane,
Shouts to him from behind; and, if thus warned
The old man does not change his course, the boy 40
Turns with less noisy wheels to the roadside,
And passes gently by, without a curse
Upon his lips or anger at his heart.

He travels on, a solitary Man;
His age has no companion. On the ground
His eyes are turned, and, as he moves along,
They move along the ground; and, evermore,
Instead of common and habitual sight
Of fields with rural works, of hill and dale,
And the blue sky, one little span of earth 50
Is all his prospect. Thus, from day to day.
Bow-bent, his eyes for ever on the ground,
He plies his weary journey; seeing still,
And seldom knowing that he sees, some straw,
Some scattered leaf, or marks which, in one track,
The nails of cart or chariot-wheel have left
Impressed on the white road,—in the same line,
At distance still the same. Poor Traveller!
His staff trails with him; scarcely do his feet
Disturb the summer dust; he is so still 60
In look and motion, that the cottage curs,
Ere he has passed the door, will turn away,
Weary of barking at him. Boys and girls,
The vacant and the busy, maids and youths,
The urchins newly breeched—all pass him by:
Him even the slow-paced waggon leaves behind.

But deem not this Man useless—Statesmen! ye
Who are so restless in your wisdom, ye

Who have a broom still ready in your hands
To rid the world of nuisances; ye proud,   70
Heart-swoln, while in your pride ye contemplate
Your talents, power, or wisdom, deem him not
A burthen of the earth! 'Tis Nature's law
That none, the meanest of created things,
Of forms created the most vile and brute,
The dullest or most noxious, should exist
Divorced from good—a spirit and pulse of good,
A life and soul, to every mode of being
Inseparably linked. Then be assured
That least of all can aught—that ever owned   80
The heaven-regarding eye and front sublime
Which man is born to—sink, howe'er depressed,
So low as to be scorned without a sin;
Without offence to God cast out of view;
Like the dry remnant of a garden-flower
Whose seeds are shed, or as an implement
Worn out and worthless. While from door to door,
This old Man creeps, the villagers in him
Behold a record which together binds
Past deeds and offices of charity   90
Else unremembered, and so keeps alive
The kindly mood in hearts which lapse of years,
And that half-wisdom half-experience gives,
Make slow to feel, and by sure steps resign
To selfishness and cold oblivious cares.
Among the farms and solitary huts,
Hamlets and thinly-scattered villages,
Where'er the aged Beggar takes his rounds,
The mild necessity of use compels
To acts of love; and habit does the work   100
Of reason; yet prepares that after-joy
Which reason cherishes. And thus the soul,
By that sweet taste of pleasure unpursued,
Doth find herself insensibly disposed
To virtue and true goodness. Some there are,
By their good works exalted, lofty minds,
And meditative, authors of delight
And happiness, which to the end of time
Will live, and spread, and kindle: even such minds
In childhood, from this solitary Being,   110
Or from like wanderer, haply have received
(A thing more precious far than all that books
Or the solicitudes of love can do!)
That first mild touch of sympathy and thought,
In which they found their kindred with a world
Where want and sorrow were. The easy man
Who sits at his own door,—and, like the pear
That overhangs his head from the green wall,
Feeds in the sunshine; the robust and young,
The prosperous and unthinking, they who live   120
Sheltered, and flourish in a little grove
Of their own kindred;—all behold in him

A silent monitor, which on their minds
Must needs impress a transitory thought
Of self-congratulation, to the heart
Of each recalling his peculiar boons,
His charters and exemptions; and, perchance,
Though he to no one give the fortitude
And circumspection needful to preserve
His present blessings, and to husband up   130
The respite of the season, he, at least,
And 'tis no vulgar service, makes them felt.

      Yet further.———Many, I believe, there are
Who live a life of virtuous decency,
Men who can hear the Decalogue and feel
No self-reproach; who of the moral law
Established in the land where they abide
Are strict observers; and not negligent
In acts of love to those with whom they dwell,
Their kindred, and the children of their blood.   140
Praise be to such, and to their slumbers peace!
—But of the poor man ask, the abject poor;
Go, and demand of him, if there be here
In this cold abstinence from evil deeds,
And these inevitable charities,
Wherewith to satisfy the human soul?
No—man is dear to man; the poorest poor
Long for some moments in a weary life
When they can know and feel that they have been,
Themselves, the fathers and the dealers-out   150
Of some small blessings; have been kind to such
As needed kindness, for this single cause,
That we have all of us one human heart.
—Such pleasure is to one kind Being known,
My neighbour, when with punctual care, each week,
Duly as Friday comes, though pressed herself
By her own wants, she from her store of meal
Takes one unsparing handful for the scrip
Of this old Mendicant, and, from her door
Returning with exhilarated heart,   160
Sits by her fire, and builds her hope in heaven.

      Then let him pass, a blessing on his head!
And while in that vast solitude to which
The tide of things has borne him, he appears
To breathe and live but for himself alone,
Unblamed, uninjured, let him bear about
The good which the benignant law of Heaven
Has hung around him: and, while life is his,
Still let him prompt the unlettered villagers
To tender offices and pensive thoughts.   170
—Then let him pass, a blessing on his head!
And, long as he can wander, let him breathe
The freshness of the valleys; let his blood

Struggle with frosty air and winter snows;
And let the chartered wind that sweeps the heath
Beat his grey locks against his withered face.
Reverence the hope whose vital anxiousness
Gives the last human interest to his heart.
May never HOUSE, misnamed of INDUSTRY,[1]
Make him a captive!—for that pent-up din,   180
Those life-consuming sounds that clog the air,
Be his the natural silence of old age!
Let him be free of mountain solitudes;
And have around him, whether heard or not,
The pleasant melody of woodland birds.
Few are his pleasures: if his eyes have now
Been doomed so long to settle upon earth
That not without some effort they behold
The countenance of the horizontal sun,
Rising or setting, let the light at least   190
Find a free entrance to their languid orbs,
And let him, *where* and *when* he will, sit down
Beneath the trees, or on a grassy bank
Of highway side, and with the little birds
Share his chance-gathered meal; and, finally,
As in the eye of Nature he has lived,
So in the eye of Nature let him die!

[1797]   [1800]

―――――
―――――

NUTTING

"*Written in Germany; intended as part of a poem on my own
life, [I.e., The Prelude], but struck out as not being wanted
there.*" [*Wordsworth to Isabella Fenwick*]

―――――
―――――

NUTTING

―――――――――IT seems a day
(I speak of one from many singled out)
One of those heavenly days that cannot die;
When, in the eagerness of boyish hope,
I left our cottage-threshold, sallying forth
With a huge wallet o'er my shoulders slung,
A nutting-crook in hand; and turned my steps
Tow'rd some far-distant wood, a Figure quaint,
Tricked out in proud disguise of cast-off weeds
Which for that service had been husbanded,   10
By exhortation of my frugal Dame[2]—
Motley accoutrement, of power to smile
At thorns, and brakes, and brambles,—and, in truth,
More ragged than need was! O'er path-less rocks,
Through beds of matted fern, and tangled thickets,

Forcing my way, I came to one dear nook
Unvisited, where not a broken bough
Drooped with its withered leaves, ungracious sign
Of devastation; but the hazels rose
Tall and erect, with tempting clusters hung,   20
A virgin scene!—A little while I stood,
Breathing with such suppression of the heart
As joy delights in; and, with wise restraint
Voluptuous, fearless of a rival, eyed
The banquet;—or beneath the trees I sate
Among the flowers, and with the flowers I played;
A temper known to those who, after long
And weary expectation, have been blest
With sudden happiness beyond all hope.
Perhaps it was a bower beneath whose leaves   30
The violets of five seasons re-appear
And fade, unseen by any human eye;
Where fairy water-breaks do murmur on
For ever; and I saw the sparkling foam,
And—with my cheek on one of those green stones
That, fleeced with moss, under the shady trees,
Lay round me, scattered like a flock of sheep—
I heard the murmur and the murmuring sound,
In that sweet mood, when pleasure loves to pay
Tribute to ease; and, of its joy secure,   40
The heart luxuriates with indifferent things,
Wasting its kindliness on stocks and stones,
And on the vacant air. Then up I rose,
And dragged to earth both branch and bough, with
   crash
And merciless ravage: and the shady nook
Of hazels, and the green and mossy bower,
Deformed and sullied, patiently gave up
Their quiet being: and, unless I now
Confound my present feelings with the past,
Ere from the mutilated bower I turned   50
Exulting, rich beyond the wealth of kings,
I felt a sense of pain when I beheld
The silent trees, and saw the intruding sky.—
Then, dearest Maiden, move along these shades
In gentleness of heart; with gentle hand
Touch—for there is a spirit in the woods.

[1798]   [1800]

―――――――――――――――――――――

[1] I.e., a euphemism for the poor house. See also Wordsworth's
letter to C. J. Fox, 14 January 1801.
[2] Wordsworth's teacher, Anne Tyson.

PETER BELL

In his notes to Isabella Fenwick, Wordsworth said that Peter Bell *was "founded upon an anecdote, which I read in a newspaper, of an ass being found hanging his head over a canal in a wretched posture. Upon examination a dead body was found in the water and proved to be the body of its master. . . ."*

Robert Southey, to whom the poem was dedicated when finally published in 1819, was poet laureate (the target of Byron's The Vision of Judgment*) and Coleridge's brother-in-law. See also Shelley's* Peter Bell the Third, *below.*

PETER BELL
A TALE

"What's in a *Name?*"

*   *   *   *   *

"Brutus will start a Spirit as soon as Cæsar!"

TO
ROBERT SOUTHEY, Esq., P.L., etc., etc.

MY DEAR FRIEND,

The Tale of Peter Bell, which I now introduce to your notice, and to that of the Public, has, in its Manuscript state, nearly survived its *minority:*—for it first saw the light in the summer of 1798. During this long interval, pains have been taken at different times to make the production less unworthy of a favourable reception; or, rather, to fit it for filling *permanently* a station, however humble, in the Literature of our Country. This has, indeed, been the aim of all my endeavours in Poetry, which, you know, have been sufficiently laborious to prove that I deem the Art not lightly to be approached; and that the attainment of excellence in it may laudably be made the principal object of intellectual pursuit by any man, who, with reasonable consideration of circumstances, has faith in his own impulses.

The Poem of Peter Bell, as the Prologue will show, was composed under a belief that the Imagination not only does not require for its exercise the intervention of supernatural agency, but that, though such agency be excluded, the faculty may be called forth as imperiously, and for kindred results of pleasure, by incidents within the compass of poetic probability, in the humblest departments of daily life. Since that Prologue was written, *you* have exhibited most splendid effects of judicious daring in the opposite and usual course. Let this acknowledgment make my peace with the lovers of the supernatural; and I am

persuaded it will be admitted that to you, as a Master in that province of the art, the following Tale, whether from contrast or congruity, is not an unappropriate offering. Accept it, then, as a public testimony of affectionate admiration from one with whose name yours has been often coupled (to use your own words) for evil and for good; and believe me to be, with earnest wishes that life and health may be granted you to complete the many important works in which you are engaged, and with high respect,

Most faithfully yours,

WILLIAM WORDSWORTH.

RYDAL MOUNT,
April 7, 1819.

PROLOGUE

THERE'S something in a flying horse,
There's something in a huge balloon;
But through the clouds I'll never float
Until I have a little Boat,
Shaped like the crescent-moon.

And now I *have* a little Boat,
In shape a very crescent-moon:
Fast through the clouds my Boat can sail;
But if perchance your faith should fail,
Look up—and you shall see me soon!   10

The woods, my Friends, are round you roaring,
Rocking and roaring like a sea;
The noise of danger's in your ears,
And ye have all a thousand fears
Both for my little Boat and me!

Meanwhile untroubled I admire
The pointed horns of my canoe;
And, did not pity touch my breast,
To see how ye are all distrest,
Till my ribs ached, I'd laugh at you!   20

Away we go, my Boat and I—
Frail man ne'er sate in such another;
Whether among the winds we strive,
Or deep into the clouds we dive,
Each is contented with the other.

Away we go—and what care we
For treasons, tumults, and for wars?
We are as calm in our delight
As is the crescent-moon so bright
Among the scattered stars.   30

Up goes my Boat among the stars
Through many a breathless field of light,
Through many a long blue field of ether,
Leaving ten thousand stars beneath her:
Up goes my little Boat so bright!

The Crab, the Scorpion, and the Bull—
We pry among them all; have shot
High o'er the red-haired race of Mars,
Covered from top to toe with scars;
Such company I like it not!   40

The towns in Saturn are decayed,
And melancholy Spectres throng them;—
The Pleiads, that appear to kiss
Each other in the vast abyss,
With joy I sail among them.

Swift Mercury resounds with mirth,
Great Jove is full of stately bowers;
But these, and all that they contain,
What are they to that tiny grain,
That little Earth of ours?   50

Then back to Earth, the dear green Earth:—
Whole ages if I here should roam,
The world for my remarks and me
Would not a whit the better be;
I've left my heart at home.

See! there she is, the matchless Earth!
There spreads the famed Pacific Ocean!
Old Andes thrusts yon craggy spear
Through the grey clouds; the Alps are here,
Like waters in commotion!   60

Yon tawny slip is Libya's sands;
That silver thread the river Dnieper;
And look, where clothed in brightest green
Is a sweet Isle, of isles the Queen;
Ye fairies, from all evil keep her!

And see the town where I was born!
Around those happy fields we span
In boyish gambols;—I was lost
Where I have been, but on this coast
I feel I am a man.   70

Never did fifty things at once
Appear so lovely, never, never;—
How tunefully the forests ring!
To hear the earth's soft murmuring
Thus could I hang for ever!

"Shame on you!" cried my little Boat,
"Was ever such a homesick Loon,
Within a living Boat to sit,
And make no better use of it;
A Boat twin-sister of the crescent-moon!   80

"Ne'er in the breast of full-grown Poet
Fluttered so faint a heart before;—
Was it the music of the spheres
That overpowered your mortal ears?
—Such din shall trouble them no more.

"These nether precincts do not lack
Charms of their own;—then come with me;
I want a comrade, and for you
There's nothing that I would not do;
Nought is there that you shall not see.   90

"Haste! and above Siberian snows
We'll sport amid the boreal morning;
Will mingle with her lustres gliding
Among the stars, the stars now hiding,
And now the stars adorning.

"I know the secrets of a land
Where human foot did never stray;
Fair is that land as evening skies,
And cool, though in the depth it lies
Of burning Africa.   100

"Or we'll into the realm of Faery,
Among the lovely shades of things;
The shadowy forms of mountains bare,
And streams, and bowers, and ladies fair,
The shades of palaces and kings!

"Or, if you thirst with hardy zeal
Less quiet regions to explore,
Prompt voyage shall to you reveal
How earth and heaven are taught to feel
The might of magic lore!"   110

"My little vagrant Form of light,
My gay and beautiful Canoe,
Well have you played your friendly part;
As kindly take what from my heart
Experience forces—then adieu!

"Temptation lurks among your words;
But, while these pleasures you're pursuing
Without impediment or let,
No wonder if you quite forget
What on the earth is doing.   120

"There was a time when all mankind
　Did listen with a faith sincere
　To tuneful tongues in mystery versed;
　Then Poets fearlessly rehearsed
　The wonders of a wild career.

"Go—(but the world's a sleepy world,
　And 'tis, I fear, an age too late)
　Take with you some ambitious Youth!
　For, restless Wanderer! I, in truth,
　Am all unfit to be your mate.   130

"Long have I loved what I behold,
　The night that calms, the day that cheers;
　The common growth of mother-earth
　Suffices me—her tears, her mirth,
　Her humblest mirth and tears.

"The dragon's wing, the magic ring,
　I shall not covet for my dower,
　If I along that lowly way
　With sympathetic heart may stray,
　And with a soul of power.   140

"These given, what more need I desire
　To stir, to soothe, or elevate?
　What nobler marvels than the mind
　May in life's daily prospect find,
　May find or there create?

"A potent wand doth Sorrow wield;
　What spell so strong as guilty Fear!
　Repentance is a tender Sprite;
　If aught on earth have heavenly might,
　'Tis lodged within her silent tear.   150

"But grant my wishes,—let us now
　Descend from this ethereal height;
　Then take thy way, adventurous Skiff,
　More daring far than Hippogriff,
　And by thy own delight!

"To the stone-table in my garden,
　Loved haunt of many a summer hour,
　The Squire is come: his daughter Bess
　Beside him in the cool recess
　Sits blooming like a flower.   160

"With these are many more convened;
　They know not I have been so far;—
　I see them there, in number nine,
　Beneath the spreading Weymouth-pine!
　I see them—there they are!

"There sits the Vicar and his Dame;
　And there my good friend, Stephen Otter;
　And, ere the light of evening fail,
　To them I must relate the Tale
　Of Peter Bell the Potter."   170

Off flew the Boat—away she flees,
Spurning her freight with indignation!
And I, as well as I was able,
On two poor legs, toward my stone-table
Limped on with sore vexation.

"O, here he is!" cried little Bess—
　She saw me at the garden-door;
"We've waited anxiously and long,"
　They cried, and all around me throng,
　Full nine of them or more!   180

"Reproach me not—your fears be still—
　Be thankful we again have met;—
　Resume, my Friends! within the shade
　Your seats, and quickly shall be paid
　The well-remembered debt."

I spake with faltering voice, like one
Not wholly rescued from the pale
Of a wild dream, or worse illusion;
But straight, to cover my confusion,
Began the promised Tale.   190

PART FIRST

ALL by the moonlight river-side
　Groaned the poor Beast—alas! in vain;
　The staff was raised to loftier height,
　And the blows fell with heavier weight
　As Peter struck—and struck again.

"Hold!" cried the Squire, "against the rules
　Of common sense you're surely sinning;
　This leap is for us all too bold;
　Who Peter was, let that be told,
　And start from the beginning."   200

——"A Potter,* Sir, he was by trade,"
　Said I, becoming quite collected;
"And wheresoever he appeared,
　Full twenty times was Peter feared
　For once that Peter was respected.

　* In the dialect of the North, a hawker of earthenware is thus
designated.

"He, two-and-thirty years or more,
    Had been a wild and woodland rover;
    Had heard the Atlantic surges roar
    On farthest Cornwall's rocky shore,
    And trod the cliffs of Dover.   210

"And he had seen Caernarvon's towers,
    And well he knew the spire of Sarum;
    And he had been where Lincoln bell
    Flings o'er the fen that ponderous knell—
    A far-renowned alarum.

"At Doncaster, at York, and Leeds,
    And merry Carlisle had he been;
    And all along the Lowlands fair,
    All through the bonny shire of Ayr;
    And far as Aberdeen.   220

"And he had been at Inverness;
    And Peter, by the mountain-rills,
    Had danced his round with Highland lasses;
    And he had lain beside his asses
    On lofty Cheviot Hills:

"And he had trudged through Yorkshire dales,
    Among the rocks and winding *scars;*
    Where deep and low the hamlets lie
    Beneath their little patch of sky
    And little lot of stars: 230

"And all along the indented coast,
    Bespattered with the salt-sea foam;
    Where'er a knot of houses lay
    On headland, or in hollow bay;—
    Sure never man like him did roam!

"As well might Peter, in the Fleet,
    Have been fast bound, a begging debtor;—
    He travelled here, he travelled there;—
    But not the value of a hair
    Was heart or head the better.   240

"He roved among the vales and streams,
    In the green wood and hollow dell;
    They were his dwellings night and day,—
    But nature ne'er could find the way
    Into the heart of Peter Bell.

"In vain, through every changeful year,
    Did Nature lead him as before;
    A primrose by a river's brim
    A yellow primrose was to him,
    And it was nothing more.   250

"Small change it made in Peter's heart
    To see his gentle panniered train
    With more than vernal pleasure feeding,
    Where'er the tender grass was leading
    Its earliest green along the lane.

"In vain, through water, earth, and air,
    The soul of happy sound was spread,
    When Peter on some April morn,
    Beneath the broom or budding thorn,
    Made the warm earth his lazy bed.   260

"At noon, when, by the forest's edge
    He lay beneath the branches high,
    The soft blue sky did never melt
    Into his heart; he never felt
    The witchery of the soft blue sky!

"On a fair prospect some have looked
    And felt, as I have heard them say,
    As if the moving time had been
    A thing as steadfast as the scene
    On which they gazed themselves away.   270

"Within the breast of Peter Bell
    These silent raptures found no place;
    He was a Carl as wild and rude
    As ever hue-and-cry pursued,
    As ever ran a felon's race.

"Of all that lead a lawless life,
    Of all that love their lawless lives,
    In city or in village small,
    He was the wildest far of all;—
    He had a dozen wedded wives.   280

"Nay, start not!—wedded wives—and twelve!
    But how one wife could e'er come near him,
    In simple truth I cannot tell;
    For, be it said of Peter Bell,
    To see him was to fear him.

"Though Nature could not touch his heart
    By lovely forms, and silent weather,
    And tender sounds, yet you might see
    At once that Peter Bell and she
    Had often been together.   290

"A savage wildness round him hung
    As of a dweller out of doors;
    In his whole figure and his mien
    A savage character was seen
    Of mountains and of dreary moors.

"To all the unshaped half-human thoughts
  Which solitary Nature feeds
  'Mid summer storms or winter's ice,
  Had Peter joined whatever vice
  The cruel city breeds.   300

"His face was keen as is the wind
  That cuts along the hawthorn-fence;
  Of courage you saw little there,
  But, in its stead, a medley air
  Of cunning and of impudence.

"He had a dark and sidelong walk,
  And long and slouching was his gait;
  Beneath his looks so bare and bold,
  You might perceive, his spirit cold
  Was playing with some inward bait.   310

"His forehead wrinkled was and furred;
  A work, one half of which was done
  By thinking of his 'whens' and 'hows';
  And half, by knitting of his brows
  Beneath the glaring sun.

"There was a hardness in his cheek,
  There was a hardness in his eye,
  As if the man had fixed his face,
  In many a solitary place,
  Against the wind and open sky!"   320

ONE NIGHT, (and now, my little Bess!
  We've reached at last the promised Tale;)
  One beautiful November night,
  When the full moon was shining bright
  Upon the rapid river Swale,

Along the river's winding banks
  Peter was travelling all alone;—
  Whether to buy or sell, or led
  By pleasure running in his head,
  To me was never known.   330

He trudged along through copse and brake
  He trudged along o'er hill and dale;
  Nor for the moon cared he a tittle,
  And for the stars he cared as little,
  And for the murmuring river Swale.

But, chancing to espy a path
  That promised to cut short the way;
  As many a wiser man hath done,
  He left a trusty guide for one
  That might his steps betray.   340

To a thick wood he soon is brought
  Where cheerily his course he weaves,
  And whistling loud may yet be heard,
  Though often buried like a bird
  Darkling, among the boughs and leaves.

But quickly Peter's mood is changed,
  And on he drives with cheeks that burn
  In downright fury and in wrath;—
  There's little sign the treacherous path
  Will to the road return!   350

The path grows dim, and dimmer still;
  Now up, now down, the Rover wends,
  With all the sail that he can carry,
  Till brought to a deserted quarry—
  And there the pathway ends.

He paused—for shadows of strange shape,
  Massy and black, before him lay;
  But through the dark, and through the cold,
  And through the yawning fissures old,
  Did Peter boldly press his way   360

Right through the quarry;—and behold
  A scene of soft and lovely hue!
  Where blue and grey, and tender green,
  Together make as sweet a scene
  As ever human eye did view.

Beneath the clear blue sky he saw
  A little field of meadow ground;
  But field or meadow name it not;
  Call it of earth a small green plot,
  With rocks encompassed round.   370

The Swale flowed under the grey rocks,
  But he flowed quiet and unseen:—
  You need a strong and stormy gale
  To bring the noise of the Swale
  To that green spot, so calm and green!

And is there no one dwelling here,
  No hermit with his beads and glass?
  And does no little cottage look
  Upon this soft and fertile nook?
  Does no one live near this green grass?   380

Across the deep and quiet spot
  Is Peter driving through the grass—
  And now has reached the skirting trees;
  When, turning round his head, he sees
  A solitary Ass.

"A prize!" cries Peter—but he first
Must spy about him far and near:
There's not a single house in sight,
No woodman's hut, no cottage light—
Peter, you need not fear!

There's nothing to be seen but woods,
And rocks that spread a hoary gleam,
And this one Beast, that from the bed
Of the green meadow hangs his head
Over the silent stream.

His head is with a halter bound;
The halter seizing, Peter leapt
Upon the Creature's back, and plied
With ready heels his shaggy side;
But still the Ass his station kept.   400

Then Peter gave a sudden jerk,
A jerk that from a dungeon-floor
Would have pulled up an iron ring;
But still the heavy-headed Thing
Stood just as he had stood before!

Quoth Peter, leaping from his seat,
"There is some plot against me laid;"
Once more the little meadow-ground
And all the hoary cliffs around
He cautiously surveyed.   410

All, all is silent—rocks and woods,
All still and silent—far and near!
Only the Ass, with motion dull,
Upon the pivot of his skull
Turns round his long left ear.

Thought Peter, What can mean all this?
Some ugly witchcraft must be here!
—Once more the Ass, with motion dull,
Upon the pivot of his skull
Turned round his long left ear.   420

Suspicion ripened into dread;
Yet, with deliberate action slow,
His staff high-raising, in the pride
Of skill, upon the sounding hide
He dealt a sturdy blow.

The poor Ass staggered with the shock;
And then, as if to take his ease,
In quiet uncomplaining mood,
Upon the spot where he had stood,
Dropped gently down upon his knees;   430

As gently on his side he fell;
And by the river's brink did lie;
And, while he lay like one that mourned,
The patient Beast on Peter turned
His shining hazel eye.

'Twas but one mild, reproachful look,
A look more tender than severe;
And straight in sorrow, not in dread,
He turned the eye-ball in his head
Towards the smooth river deep and clear.   440

Upon the Beast the sapling rings;
His lank sides heaved, his limbs they stirred;
He gave a groan, and then another,
Of that which went before the brother,
And then he gave a third.

All by the moonlight river side
He gave three miserable groans;
And not till now hath Peter seen
How gaunt the Creature is,—how lean
And sharp his staring bones!   450

With legs stretched out and stiff he lay:—
No word of kind commiseration
Fell at the sight from Peter's tongue;
With hard contempt his heart was wrung,
With hatred and vexation.

The meagre beast lay still as death;
And Peter's lips with fury quiver;
Quoth he, "You little mulish dog,
I'll fling your carcass like a log
Head-foremost down the river!"   460

An impious oath confirmed the threat—
Whereat from the earth on which he lay
To all the echoes, south and north,
And east and west, the Ass sent forth
A long and clamorous bray!

This outcry, on the heart of Peter,
Seems like a note of joy to strike,—
Joy at the heart of Peter knocks;
But in the echo of the rocks
Was something Peter did not like.   470

Whether to cheer his coward breast,
Or that he could not break the chain,
In this serene and solemn hour,
Twined round him by demoniac power,
To the blind work he turned again.

Among the rocks and winding crags;
Among the mountains far away;
Once more the Ass did lengthen out
More ruefully a deep-drawn shout,
The hard dry see-saw of his horrible bray!   480

What is there now in Peter's heart!
Or whence the might of this strange sound?
The moon uneasy looked and dimmer,
The broad blue heavens appeared to glimmer,
And the rocks staggered all around—

From Peter's hand the sapling dropped!
Threat has he none to execute;
"If any one should come and see
That I am here, they'll think," quoth he,
"I'm helping this poor dying brute."   490

He scans the Ass from limb to limb,
And ventures now to uplift his eyes;
More steady looks the moon, and clear,
More like themselves the rocks appear
And touch more quiet skies.

His scorn returns—his hate revives;
He stoops the Ass's neck to seize
With malice—that again takes flight;
For in the pool a startling sight
Meets him, among the inverted trees.   500

Is it the moon's distorted face?
The ghost-like image of a cloud?
Is it a gallows there portrayed?
Is Peter of himself afraid?
Is it a coffin,—or a shroud?

A grisly idol hewn in stone?
Or imp from witch's lap let fall?
Perhaps a ring of shining fairies?
Such as pursue their feared vagaries
In sylvan bower, or haunted hall?   510

Is it a fiend that to a stake
Of fire his desperate self is tethering?
Or stubborn spirit doomed to yell
In solitary ward or cell,
Ten thousand miles from all his brethren? [1]

<hr />

[1] In the 1819 edition only followed a stanza (used by Shelley as
the epigraph to *Peter Bell the Third*):

> Is it a party in a parlour?
> Cramm'd just as they on earth were cramm'd—
> Some sipping punch, some sipping tea,
> But, as you by their faces see,
> All silent and all damn'd!

Never did pulse so quickly throb,
And never heart so loudly panted;
He looks, he cannot choose but look;
Like some one reading in a book—
A book that is enchanted.   520

Ah, well-a-day for Peter Bell!
He will be turned to iron soon,
Meet Statue for the court of Fear!
His hat is up—and every hair
Bristles, and whitens in the moon!

He looks, he ponders, looks again;
He sees a motion—hears a groan;
His eyes will burst—his heart will break—
He gives a loud and frightful shriek,
And back he falls, as if his life were flown!   530

PART SECOND

WE left our Hero in a trance,
Beneath the alders, near the river;
The Ass is by the river-side,
And, where the feeble breezes glide,
Upon the stream the moonbeams quiver.

A happy respite! but at length
He feels the glimmering of the moon;
Wakes with glazed eye, and feebly sighing—
To sink, perhaps, where he is lying,
Into a second swoon!   540

He lifts his head, he sees his staff;
He touches—'tis to him a treasure!
Faint recollection seems to tell
That he is yet where mortals dwell—
A thought received with languid pleasure!

His head upon his elbow propped,
Becoming less and less perplexed,
Sky-ward he looks—to rock and wood—
And then—upon the glassy flood
His wandering eye is fixed.   550

Thought he, that is the face of one
In his last sleep securely bound!
So toward the stream his head he bent,
And downward thrust his staff, intent
The river's depth to sound.

Now—like a tempest-shattered bark,
That overwhelmed and prostrate lies,
And in a moment to the verge
Is lifted of a foaming surge—
Full suddenly the Ass doth rise!   560

His staring bones all shake with joy,
And close by Peter's side he stands:
While Peter o'er the river bends,
The little Ass his neck extends,
And fondly licks his hands.

Such life is in the Ass's eyes,
Such life is in his limbs and ears;
That Peter Bell, if he had been
The veriest coward ever seen,
Must now have thrown aside his fears.   570

The Ass looks on—and to his work
Is Peter quietly resigned;
He touches here—he touches there—
And now among the dead man's hair
His sapling Peter has entwined.

He pulls—and looks—and pulls again.
And he whom the poor Ass had lost,
The man who had been four days dead,
Head-foremost from the river's bed
Uprises like a ghost!   580

And Peter draws him to dry land;
And through the brain of Peter pass
Some poignant twitches, fast and faster;
"No doubt," quoth he, "he is the Master
Of this poor miserable Ass!"

The meagre shadow that looks on—
What would he now? what is he doing?
His sudden fit of joy is flown,—
He on his knees hath laid him down,
As if he were his grief renewing;   590

But no—that Peter on his back
Must mount, he shows well as he can:
Thought Peter then, come weal or woe,
I'll do what he would have me do,
In pity to this poor drowned man.

With that resolve he boldly mounts
Upon the pleased and thankful Ass;
And then, without a moment's stay,
That earnest Creature turned away,
Leaving the body on the grass.   600

Intent upon his faithful watch,
The Beast four days and nights had past;
A sweeter meadow ne'er was seen,
And there the Ass four days had been,
Nor ever once did break his fast:

Yet firm his step, and stout his heart;
The mead is crossed—the quarry's mouth
Is reached; but there the trusty guide
Into a thicket turns aside,
And deftly ambles towards the south.   610

When hark a burst of doleful sound!
And Peter honestly might say,
The like came never to his ears,
Though he has been, full thirty years,
A rover—night and day!

'Tis not a plover of the moors,
'Tis not a bittern of the fen;
Nor can it be a barking fox,
Nor night-bird chambered in the rocks,
Nor wild-cat in a woody glen!   620

The Ass is startled—and stops short
Right in the middle of the thicket;
And Peter, wont to whistle loud
Whether alone or in a crowd,
Is silent as a silent cricket.

What ails you now, my little Bess?
Well may you tremble and look grave!
This cry—that rings along the wood,
This cry—that floats adown the flood,
Comes from the entrance of a cave: 630

I see a blooming Wood-boy there,
And if I had the power to say
How sorrowful the wanderer is,
Your heart would be as sad as his
Till you had kissed his tears away!

Grasping a hawthorn branch in hand,
All bright with berries ripe and red,
Into the cavern's mouth he peeps;
Thence back into the moonlight creeps;
Whom seeks he—whom?—the silent dead: 640

His father!—Him doth he require—
Him hath he sought with fruitless pains.
Among the rocks, behind the trees;
Now creeping on his hands and knees,
Now running o'er the open plains.

And hither is he come at last,
When he through such a day has gone,
By this dark cave to be distrest
Like a poor bird—her plundered nest
Hovering around with dolorous moan!   650

Of that intense and piercing cry
The listening Ass conjectures well;
Wild as it is, he there can read
Some intermingled notes that plead
With touches irresistible.

But Peter—when he saw the Ass
Not only stop but turn, and change
The cherished tenor of his pace
That lamentable cry to chase—
It wrought in him conviction strange;   660

A faith that, for the dead man's sake
And this poor slave who loved him well,
Vengeance upon his head will fall,
Some visitation worse than all
Which ever till this night befell.

Meanwhile the Ass to reach his home
Is striving stoutly as he may;
But, while he climbs the woody hill,
The cry grows weak—and weaker still;
And now at last it dies away.   670

So with his freight the Creature turns
Into a gloomy grove of beech,
Along the shade with footsteps true
Descending slowly, till the two
The open moonlight reach.

And there, along the narrow dell,
A fair smooth pathway you discern,
A length of green and open road—
As if it from a fountain flowed—
Winding away between the fern.   680

The rocks that tower on either side
Build up a wild fantastic scene;
Temples like those among the Hindoos,
And mosques, and spires, and abbey-windows,
And castles all with ivy green!

And while the Ass pursues his way
Along this solitary dell,
As pensively his steps advance,
The mosques and spires change countenance,
And look at Peter Bell!   690

That unintelligible cry
Hath left him high in preparation,—
Convinced that he, or soon or late,
This very night will meet his fate—
And so he sits in expectation!

The strenuous Animal hath clomb
With the green path; and now he wends
Where, shining like the smoothest sea,
In undisturbed immensity
A level plain extends.   700

But whence this faintly-rustling sound
By which the journeying pair are chased?
—A withered leaf is close behind,
Light plaything for the sportive wind
Upon that solitary waste.

When Peter spied the moving thing,
It only doubled his distress;
"Where there is not a bush or tree,
The very leaves they follow me—
So huge hath been my wickedness!"   710

To a close lane they now are come,
Where, as before, the enduring Ass
Moves on without a moment's stop,
Nor once turns round his head to crop
A bramble-leaf or blade of grass.

Between the hedges as they go,
The white dust sleeps upon the lane;
And Peter, ever and anon
Back-looking, sees, upon a stone,
Or in the dust, a crimson stain.   720

A stain—as of a drop of blood
By moonlight made more faint and wan;
Ha! why these sinkings of despair?
He knows not how the blood comes there—
And Peter is a wicked man.

At length he spies a bleeding wound,
Where he had struck the Ass's head;
He sees the blood, knows what it is,—
A glimpse of sudden joy was his,
But then it quickly fled;   730

Of him whom sudden death had seized
He thought,—of thee, O faithful Ass!
And once again those ghastly pains,
Shoot to and fro through heart and reins,
And through his brain like lightning pass.

PART THIRD

I'VE heard of one, a gentle Soul,
Though given to sadness and to gloom,
And for the fact will vouch,—one night
It chanced that by a taper's light
This man was reading in his room;   740

Bending, as you or I might bend
At night o'er any pious book,
When sudden blackness overspread
The snow-white page on which he read,
And made the good man round him look.

The chamber walls were dark all round,—
And to his book he turned again;
—The light had left the lonely taper,
And formed itself upon the paper
Into large letters—bright and plain!   750

The godly book was in his hand—
And on the page, more black than coal,
Appeared, set forth in strange array,
A *word*—which to his dying day
Perplexed the good man's gentle soul.

The ghostly word, thus plainly seen,
Did never from his lips depart;
But he hath said, poor gentle wight!
It brought full many a sin to light
Out of the bottom of his heart.   760

Dread Spirits! to confound the meek
Why wander from your course so far,
Disordering colour, form, and stature!
—Let good men feel the soul of nature,
And see things as they are.

Yet, potent Spirits! well I know,
How ye, that play with soul and sense,
Are not unused to trouble friends
Of goodness, for most gracious ends—
And this I speak in reverence!   770

But might I give advice to you,
Whom in my fear I love so well;
From men of pensive virtue go,
Dread Beings! and your empire show
On hearts like that of Peter Bell.

Your presence often have I felt
In darkness and the stormy night;
And with like force, if need there be,
Ye can put forth your agency
When earth is calm, and heaven is bright.   780

Then, coming from the wayward world,
That powerful world in which ye dwell,
Come, Spirits of the Mind! and try,
To-night, beneath the moonlight sky,
What may be done with Peter Bell!

—O, would that some more skilful voice
My further labour might prevent!
Kind Listeners, that around me sit,
I feel that I am all unfit
For such high argument.   790

—I've played, I've danced, with my narration;
I loitered long ere I began:
Ye waited then on my good pleasure;
Pour out indulgence still, in measure
As liberal as ye can!

Our Travellers, ye remember well,
Are thridding a sequestered lane;
And Peter many tricks is trying,
And many anodynes applying,
To ease his conscience of its pain.   800

By this his heart is lighter far;
And, finding that he can account
So snugly for that crimson stain,
His evil spirit up again
Does like an empty bucket mount.

And Peter is a deep logician
Who hath no lack of wit mercurial;
"Blood drops—leaves rustle—yet," quoth he,
"This poor man never, but for me,
Could have had Christian burial.   810

"And, say the best you can, 'tis plain,
That here has been some wicked dealing;
No doubt the devil in me wrought;
I'm not the man who could have thought
An Ass like this was worth the stealing!"

So from his pocket Peter takes
His shining horn tobacco-box;
And, in a light and careless way,
As men who with their purpose play,
Upon the lid he knocks.   820

Let them whose voice can stop the clouds,
Whose cunning eye can see the wind,
Tell to a curious world the cause
Why, making here a sudden pause,
The Ass turned round his head and *grinned*.

Appalling process! I have marked
The like on heath, in lonely wood;
And, verily, have seldom met
A spectacle more hideous—yet
It suited Peter's present mood.   830

And, grinning in his turn, his teeth
He in jocose defiance showed—
When, to upset his spiteful mirth,
A murmur, pent within the earth,
In the dead earth beneath the road,

Rolled audibly!—it swept along,
A muffled noise—a rumbling sound!—
'Twas by a troop of miners made,
Plying with gunpowder their trade,
Some twenty fathoms under ground.   840

Small cause of dire effect! for, surely,
If ever mortal, King or Cotter,
Believed that earth was charged to quake
And yawn for his unworthy sake,
'Twas Peter Bell the Potter.

But, as an oak in breathless air
Will stand though to the centre hewn;
Or as the weakest things, if frost
Have stiffened them, maintain their post;
So he, beneath the gazing moon!—   850

The Beast bestriding thus, he reached
A spot where, in a sheltering cove,
A little chapel stands alone,
With greenest ivy overgrown,
And tufted with an ivy grove;

Dying insensibly away
From human thoughts and purposes,
It seemed—wall, window, roof and tower—
To bow to some transforming power,
And blend with the surrounding trees.   860

As ruinous a place it was,
Thought Peter, in the shire of Fife
That served my turn, when following still
From land to land a reckless will
I married my sixth wife!

The unheeding Ass moves slowly on,
And now is passing by an inn
Brim-full of a carousing crew,
That make, with curses not a few
An uproar and a drunken din.   870

I cannot well express the thoughts
Which Peter in those noises found;—
A stifling power compressed his frame,
While-as a swimming darkness came
Over that dull and dreary sound.

For well did Peter know the sound;
The language of those drunken joys
To him, a jovial soul, I ween,
But a few hours ago, had been
A gladsome and a welcome noise.   880

Now, turned adrift into the past,
He finds no solace in his course;
Like planet-stricken men of yore,
He trembles, smitten to the core
By strong compunction and remorse.

But, more than all, his heart is stung
To think of one, almost a child;
A sweet and playful Highland girl,
As light and beauteous as a squirrel,
As beauteous and as wild!   890

Her dwelling was a lonely house,
A cottage in a heathy dell;
And she put on her gown of green,
And left her mother at sixteen,
And followed Peter Bell.

But many good and pious thoughts
Had she; and, in the kirk to pray,
Two long Scotch miles, through rain or snow,
To kirk she had been used to go,
Twice every Sabbath-day.   900

And, when she followed Peter Bell,
It was to lead an honest life;
For he, with tongue not used to falter,
Had pledged his troth before the altar
To love her as his wedded wife.

A mother's hope is hers;—but soon
She drooped and pined like one forlorn;
From Scripture she a name did borrow;
Benoni, or the child of sorrow,[2]
She called her babe unborn.   910

For she had learned how Peter lived,
And took it in most grievous part;
She to the very bone was worn,
And, ere that little child was born,
Died of a broken heart.

⬦⬦⬦⬦⬦⬦⬦⬦⬦⬦⬦⬦⬦⬦⬦⬦⬦⬦⬦⬦⬦⬦⬦⬦

[2] I.e., Benjamin, the child of whose birth Rachel died.

And now the Spirits of the Mind
Are busy with poor Peter Bell;
Upon the rights of visual sense
Usurping, with a prevalence
More terrible than magic spell.   920

Close by a brake of flowering furze
(Above it shivering aspens play)
He sees an unsubstantial creature,
His very self in form and feature,
Not four yards from the broad highway:

And stretched beneath the furze he sees
The Highland girl—it is no other;
And hears her crying as she cried,
The very moment that she died,
"My mother! oh my mother!"   930

The sweat pours down from Peter's face,
So grievous is his heart's contrition;
With agony his eye-balls ache
While he beholds by the furze-brake
This miserable vision!

Calm is the well-deserving brute,
His peace hath no offence betrayed;
But now, while down that slope he wends,
A voice to Peter's ear ascends,
Resounding from the woody glade: 940

The voice, though clamorous as a horn
Re-echoed by a naked rock,
Comes from that tabernacle—List!
Within, a fervent Methodist
Is preaching to no heedless flock!

"Repent! repent!" he cries aloud,
"While yet ye may find mercy;—strive
To love the Lord with all your might;
Turn to him, seek him day and night,
And save your souls alive!   950

"Repent! repent! though ye have gone,
Through paths of wickedness and woe,
After the Babylonian harlot;
And, though your sins be red as scarlet,
They shall be white as snow!"

Even as he passed the door, these words
Did plainly come to Peter's ears;
And they such joyful tidings were,
The joy was more than he could bear!—
He melted into tears.   960

Sweet tears of hope and tenderness!
And fast they fell, a plenteous shower!
His nerves, his sinews seemed to melt;
Through all his iron frame was felt
A gentle, a relaxing, power!

Each fibre of his frame was weak;
Weak all the animal within;
But, in its helplessness, grew mild
And gentle as an infant child,
An infant that has known no sin.   970

'Tis said, meek Beast! that, through Heaven's grace,
He not unmoved did notice now
The cross upon thy shoulder scored,
For lasting impress, by the Lord
To whom all human-kind shall bow;

Memorial of his touch—that day
When Jesus humbly deigned to ride,
Entering the proud Jerusalem,
By an immeasurable stream
Of shouting people deified!   980

Meanwhile the persevering Ass
Turned towards a gate that hung in view
Across a shady lane; his chest
Against the yielding gate he pressed
And quietly passed through.

And up the stony lane he goes;
No ghost more softly ever trod;
Among the stones and pebbles he
Sets down his hoofs inaudibly,
As if with felt his hoofs were shod.   990

Along the lane the trusty Ass
Went twice two hundred yards or more,
And no one could have guessed his aim,—
Till to a lonely house he came,
And stopped beside the door.

Thought Peter, 'tis the poor man's home!
He listens—not a sound is heard
Save from the trickling household rill;
But, stepping o'er the cottage-sill
Forthwith a little Girl appeared.   0

She to the Meeting-house was bound
In hopes some tidings there to gather:
No glimpse it is, no doubtful gleam;
She saw—and uttered with a scream,
"My father! here's my father!"

The very word was plainly heard,
Heard plainly by the wretched Mother—
Her joy was like a deep affright:
And forth she rushed into the light,
And saw it was another!   10

And, instantly, upon the earth,
Beneath the full moon shining bright,
Close to the Ass's feet she fell;
At the same moment Peter Bell
Dismounts in most unhappy plight.

As he beheld the Woman lie
Breathless and motionless, the mind
Of Peter sadly was confused;
But, though to such demands unused,
And helpless almost as the blind,   20

He raised her up; and while he held
Her body propped against his knee,
The Woman waked—and when she spied
The poor Ass standing by her side,
She moaned most bitterly.

"Oh! God be praised—my heart's at ease—
For he is dead—I know it well!"
—At this she wept a bitter flood;
And, in the best way that he could,
His tale did Peter tell.   30

He trembles—he is pale as death;
His voice is weak with perturbation;
He turns aside his head, he pauses;
Poor Peter from a thousand causes
Is crippled sore in his narration.

At length she learned how he espied
The Ass in that small meadow-ground;
And that her Husband now lay dead,
Beside that luckless river's bed
In which he had been drowned.   40

A piercing look the Widow cast
Upon the Beast that near her stands;
She sees 'tis he, that 'tis the same;
She calls the poor Ass by his name,
And wrings, and wrings her hands.

"O wretched loss—untimely stroke!
If he had died upon his bed!
He knew not one forewarning pain;
He never will come home again—
Is dead, for ever dead!"   50

Beside the Woman Peter stands;
His heart is opening more and more;
A holy sense pervades his mind;
He feels what he for human-kind
Has never felt before.

At length, by Peter's arm sustained,
The Woman rises from the ground—
"Oh, mercy! something must be done,
My little Rachel, you must run,—
Some willing neighbour must be found.   60

"Make haste—my little Rachel—do,
The first you meet with—bid him come,
Ask him to lend his horse to-night,
And this good Man, whom Heaven requite,
Will help to bring the body home."

Away goes Rachel weeping loud;—
An Infant, waked by her distress,
Makes in the house a piteous cry;
And Peter hears the Mother sigh,
"Seven are they, and all fatherless!"   70

And now is Peter taught to feel
That man's heart is a holy thing;
And Nature, through a world of death,
Breathes into him a second breath,
More searching than the breath of spring.

Upon a stone the Woman sits
In agony of silent grief—
From his own thoughts did Peter start;
He longs to press her to his heart,
From love that cannot find relief.   80

But roused, as if through every limb
Had past a sudden shock of dread,
The Mother o'er the threshold flies,
And up the cottage stairs she hies,
And on the pillow lays her burning head.

And Peter turns his steps aside
Into a shade of darksome trees,
Where he sits down, he knows not how,
With his hands pressed against his brow,
His elbows on his tremulous knees.   90

There, self-involved, does Peter sit
Until no sign of life he makes
As if his mind were sinking deep
Through years that have been long asleep!
The trance is passed away—he wakes:

He lifts his head—and sees the Ass
Yet standing in the clear moonshine;
"When shall I be as good as thou?
Oh! would, poor beast, that I had now
A heart but half as good as thine!"   100

But *He*—who deviously hath sought
His Father through the lonesome woods,
Hath sought, proclaiming to the ear
Of night his grief and sorrowful fear—
He comes, escaped from fields and floods;—

With weary pace is drawing nigh;
He sees the Ass—and nothing living
Had ever such a fit of joy
As hath this little orphan Boy,
For he has no misgiving!   110

Forth to the gentle Ass he springs,
And up about his neck he climbs;
In loving words he talks to him,
He kisses, kisses face and limb,—
He kisses him a thousand times!

This Peter sees, while in the shade
He stood beside the cottage-door;
And Peter Bell, the ruffian wild,
Sobs loud, he sobs even like a child,
"Oh! God, I can endure no more!"   120

—Here ends my Tale: for in a trice
Arrived a neighbour with his horse;
Peter went forth with him straightway;
And, with due care, ere break of day,
Together they brought back the Corse.

And many years did this poor Ass,
Whom once it was my luck to see
Cropping the shrubs of Leming-Lane,
Help by his labour to maintain
The Widow and her family.   130

And Peter Bell, who, till that night,
Had been the wildest of his clan,
Forsook his crimes, renounced his folly,
And, after ten months' melancholy,
Became a good and honest man.

[1798]   [1819]

THE LUCY POEMS

"She dwelt among the untrodden ways," "Strange fits of passion . . .," "A slumber did my spirit seal," "Three years she grew . . .," and "I travelled among unknown men," are often grouped by editors as "the Lucy Poems." Presumably they refer to a single woman, usually identified as William's sister Dorothy.

" She dwelt among the untrodden ways "

SHE dwelt among the untrodden ways
    Beside the springs of Dove,
A Maid whom there were none to praise
    And very few to love:

A violet by a mossy stone
    Half hidden from the eye!
—Fair as a star, when only one
    Is shining in the sky.

She lived unknown, and few could know
    When Lucy ceased to be;   10
But she is in her grave, and, oh,
    The difference to me!

[1799]   [1800]

"Strange fits of passion . . ."

STRANGE fits of passion have I known:
    And I will dare to tell,
But in the Lover's ear alone,
    What once to me befell.

When she I loved looked every day
    Fresh as a rose in June,
I to her cottage bent my way,
    Beneath an evening-moon.

Upon the moon I fixed my eye,
    All over the wide lea;   10
With quickening pace my horse drew nigh
    Those paths so dear to me.

And now we reached the orchard-plot;
    And, as we climbed the hill,
The sinking moon to Lucy's cot
    Came near, and nearer still.

In one of those sweet dreams I slept,
    Kind Nature's gentlest boon!
And all the while my eyes I kept
    On the descending moon.   20

My horse moved on; hoof after hoof
    He raised, and never stopped;
When down behind the cottage roof,
    At once, the bright moon dropped.

What fond and wayward thoughts will slide
Into a Lover's head!
"O mercy!" to myself I cried,
"If Lucy should be dead!"

[1799]   [1800]

"A slumber did my spirit seal"

A SLUMBER did my spirit seal;
  I had no human fears:
She seemed a thing that could not feel
  The touch of earthly years.

No motion has she now, no force;
  She neither hears nor sees;
Rolled round in earth's diurnal course,
  With rocks, and stones, and trees.

[1799]   [1800]

LUCY GRAY;

OR, SOLITUDE

OFT I had heard of Lucy Gray:
And, when I crossed the wild,
I chanced to see at break of day
The solitary child.

No mate, no comrade Lucy knew;
She dwelt on a wide moor,
—The sweetest thing that ever grew
Beside a human door!

You yet may spy the fawn at play,
The hare upon the green;   10
But the sweet face of Lucy Gray
Will never more be seen.

"To-night will be a stormy night—
You to the town must go;
And take a lantern, Child, to light
Your mother through the snow."

"That, Father! will I gladly do:
'Tis scarcely afternoon—
The minster-clock has just struck two,
And yonder is the moon!"   20

At this the Father raised his hook,
And snapped a faggot-band;
He plied his work;—and Lucy took
The lantern in her hand.

Not blither is the mountain roe:
With many a wanton stroke
Her feet disperse the powdery snow,
That rises up like smoke.

The storm came on before its time:
She wandered up and down;   30
And many a hill did Lucy climb:
But never reached the town.

The wretched parents all that night
Went shouting far and wide;
But there was neither sound nor sight
To serve them for a guide.

At day-break on a hill they stood
That overlooked the moor;
And thence they saw the bridge of wood,
A furlong from their door.   40

They wept—and, turning homeward, cried,
"In heaven we all shall meet;"
—When in the snow the mother spied
The print of Lucy's feet.

Then downwards from the steep hill's edge
They tracked the footmarks small;
And through the broken hawthorn hedge,
And by the long stone-wall;

And then an open field they crossed:
The marks were still the same;   50
They tracked them on, nor ever lost;
And to the bridge they came.

They followed from the snowy bank
Those footmarks, one by one,
Into the middle of the plank;
And further there were none!

—Yet some maintain that to this day
She is a living child;
That you may see sweet Lucy Gray
Upon the lonesome wild.   60

O'er rough and smooth she trips along,
And never looks behind;
And sings a solitary song
That whistles in the wind.

[1799]   [1800]

MATTHEW

In the School of ———[1] is a tablet, on which are inscribed, in gilt letters, the Names of the several persons who have been Schoolmasters there since the foundation of the School, with the time at which they entered upon and quitted their office. Opposite to one of those Names the Author wrote the following lines.

IF Nature, for a favourite child,
In thee hath tempered so her clay,
That every hour thy heart runs wild,
Yet never once doth go astray,

Read o'er these lines; and then review
This tablet, that thus humbly rears
In such diversity of hue
Its history of two hundred years.

—When through this little wreck of fame,
Cipher and syllable! thine eye   10
Has travelled down to Matthew's name,
Pause with no common sympathy.

And, if a sleeping tear should wake,
Then be it neither checked nor stayed:
For Matthew a request I make
Which for himself he had not made.

Poor Matthew, all his frolics o'er,
Is silent as a standing pool;
Far from the chimney's merry roar,
And murmur of the village school.   20

The sighs which Matthew heaved were sighs
Of one tired out with fun and madness;
The tears which came to Matthew's eyes
Were tears of light, the dew of gladness.

Yet, sometimes, when the secret cup
Of still and serious thought went round,
It seemed as if he drank it up—
He felt with spirit so profound.

—Thou soul of God's best earthly mould!
Thou happy Soul! and can it be   30
That these two words of glittering gold
Are all that must remain of thee?

[1799]   [1800]

◇◇◇◇◇◇◇◇◇◇◇◇◇◇◇◇◇◇◇◇◇◇◇◇◇◇◇◇◇◇◇◇◇◇

    [1] Hawkshead.

THE TWO APRIL MORNINGS

WE walked along, while bright and red
Uprose the morning sun;
And Matthew stopped, he looked, and said,
"The will of God be done!"

A village schoolmaster was he,
With hair of glittering grey;
As blithe a man as you could see
On a spring holiday.

And on that morning, through the grass,
And by the steaming rills,   10
We travelled merrily, to pass
A day among the hills.

"Our work," said I, "was well begun,
Then, from thy breast what thought,
Beneath so beautiful a sun,
So sad a sigh has brought?"

A second time did Matthew stop;
And fixing still his eye
Upon the eastern mountain-top,
To me he made reply: 20

"Yon cloud with that long purple cleft
Brings fresh into my mind
A day like this which I have left
Full thirty years behind.

"And just above yon slope of corn
Such colours, and no other,
Were in the sky, that April morn,
Of this the very brother.

"With rod and line I sued the sport
Which that sweet season gave,   30
And, to the churchyard come, stopped short
Beside my daughter's grave.

"Nine summers had she scarcely seen,
The pride of all the vale;
And then she sang;—she would have been
A very nightingale.

"Six feet in earth my Emma lay;
And yet I loved her more,
For so it seemed, than till that day
I' e'er had loved before.   40

"And, turning from her grave, I met,
  Beside the churchyard yew,
A blooming Girl, whose hair was wet
  With points of morning dew.

"A basket on her head she bare;
  Her brow was smooth and white:
To see a child so very fair,
  It was a pure delight!

"No fountain from its rocky cave
  E'er tripped with foot so free;   50
She seemed as happy as a wave
  That dances on the sea.

"There came from me a sigh of pain
  Which I could ill confine;
I looked at her, and looked again:
  And did not wish her mine!"

Matthew is in his grave, yet now,
  Methinks, I see him stand,
As at that moment, with a bough
  Of wilding in his hand.   60

[1799]   [1800]

THE FOUNTAIN

A CONVERSATION

WE talked with open heart, and tongue
  Affectionate and true,
A pair of friends, though I was young,
  And Matthew seventy-two.

We lay beneath a spreading oak,
  Beside a mossy seat;
And from the turf a fountain broke,
  And gurgled at our feet.

"Now, Matthew!" said I, "let us match
  This water's pleasant tune   10
With some old border-song, or catch
  That suits a summer's noon;

"Or of the church-clock and the chimes
  Sing here beneath the shade,
That half-mad thing of witty rhymes
  Which you last April made!"

In silence Matthew lay, and eyed
  The spring beneath the tree;
And thus the dear old Man replied,
  The grey-haired man of glee: 20

"No check, no stay, this Streamlet fears;
  How merrily it goes!
'Twill murmur on a thousand years,
  And flow as now it flows.

"And here, on this delightful day,
  I cannot choose but think
How oft, a vigorous man, I lay
  Beside this fountain's brink.

"My eyes are dim with childish tears,
  My heart is idly stirred,   30
For the same sound is in my ears
  Which in those days I heard.

"Thus fares it still in our decay:
  And yet the wiser mind
Mourns less for what age takes away
  Than what it leaves behind

"The blackbird amid leafy trees,
  The lark above the hill,
Let loose their carols when they please,
  Are quiet when they will.   40

"With Nature never do *they* wage
  A foolish strife; they see
A happy youth, and their old age
  Is beautiful and free:

"But we are pressed by heavy laws;
  And often, glad no more,
We wear a face of joy, because
  We have been glad of yore.

"If there be one who need bemoan
  His kindred laid in earth,   50
The household hearts that were his own;
  It is the man of mirth.

"My days, my Friend, are almost gone,
  My life has been approved,
And many love me! but by none
  Am I enough beloved."

"Now both himself and me he wrongs,
  The man who thus complains!
I live and sing my idle songs
  Upon these happy plains;   60

"And, Matthew, for thy children dead
I'll be a son to thee!"
At this he grasped my hand, and said,
"Alas! that cannot be."

We rose up from the fountain-side;
And down the smooth descent
Of the green sheep-track did we glide;
And through the wood we went;

And, ere we came to Leonard's rock,
He sang those witty rhymes   70
About the crazy old church-clock,
And the bewildered chimes.

[1799]   [1800]

A POET'S EPITAPH

ART thou a Statist [1] in the van
Of public conflicts trained and bred?
—First learn to love one living man;
Then may'st thou think upon the dead.

A Lawyer art thou?—draw not nigh!
Go, carry to some fitter place
The keenness of that practised eye,
The hardness of that sallow face.

Art thou a Man of purple cheer?
A rosy Man, right pump to see?   10
Approach; yet, Doctor, not too near,
This grave no cushion is for thee. [2]

Or art thou one of gallant pride,
A Soldier and no man of chaff?
Welcome!—but lay thy sword aside,
And lean upon a peasant's staff.

Physician art thou?—one, all eyes,
Philosopher!—a fingering slave,
One that would peep and botanize
Upon his mother's grave?   20

Wrapt closely in thy sensual fleece,
O turn aside,—and take, I pray,
That he below may rest in peace,
Thy ever-dwindling soul, away!

---

[1] In early versions, "Statesman."
[2] A clergyman.

A Moralist perchance appears;
Led, Heaven knows how! to this poor sod:
And he has neither eyes nor ears;
Himself his world, and his own God;

One to whose smooth-rubbed soul can cling
Nor form, nor feeling, great or small;   30
A reasoning, self-sufficing thing,
An intellectual All-in-all!

Shut close the door; press down the latch;
Sleep in thy intellectual crust;
Nor lose ten tickings of thy watch
Near this unprofitable dust.

But who is He, with modest looks
And clad in homely russet brown?
He murmurs near the running brooks
A music sweeter than their own.   40

He is retired as noontide dew,
Or fountain in a noon-day grove;
And you must love him, ere to you
He will seem worthy of your love.

The outward shows of sky and earth,
Of hill and valley, he has viewed;
And impulses of deeper birth
Have come to him in solitude.

In common things that round us lie
Some random truths he can impart,—   50
The harvest of a quiet eye
That broods and sleeps on his own heart.

But he is weak; both Man and Boy,
Hath been an idler in the land;
Contented if he might enjoy
The things which others understand.

—Come hither in thy hour of strength;
Come, weak as is a breaking wave!
Here stretch thy body at full length;
Or build thy house upon this grave.   60

[1799]   [1800]

RUTH

WHEN Ruth was left half desolate,
Her Father took another Mate;
And Ruth, not seven years old,
A slighted child, at her own will
Went wandering over dale and hill,
In thoughtless freedom, bold.

And she had made a pipe of straw,
And music from that pipe could draw
Like sounds of winds and floods;
Had built a bower upon the green,   10
As if she from her birth had been
An infant of the woods.

Beneath her father's roof, alone
She seemed to live; her thoughts her own;
Herself her own delight;
Pleased with herself, nor sad, nor gay;
And, passing thus the live-long day,
She grew to woman's height.

There came a Youth from Georgia's shore—
A military casque he wore,   20
With splendid feathers drest;
He brought them from the Cherokees;
The feathers nodded in the breeze,
And made a gallant crest.

From Indian blood you deem him sprung:
But no! he spake the English tongue,
And bore a soldier's name;
And, when America was free
From battle and from jeopardy,
He 'cross the ocean came.   30

With hues of genius on his cheek
In finest tones the Youth could speak:
—While he was yet a boy,
The moon, the glory of the sun,
And streams that murmur as they run,
Had been his dearest joy.

He was a lovely Youth! I guess
The panther in the wilderness
Was not so fair as he;
And, when he chose to sport and play,   40
No dolphin ever was so gay
Upon the tropic sea.

Among the Indians he had fought,
And with him many tales he brought
Of pleasure and of fear;
Such tales as told to any maid
By such a Youth, in the green shade,
Were perilous to hear.

He told of girls—a happy rout!
Who quit their fold with dance and shout,   50
Their pleasant Indian town,
To gather strawberries all day long;
Returning with a choral song
When daylight is gone down.

He spake of plants that hourly change
Their blossoms, through a boundless range
Of intermingling hues;
With budding, fading, faded flowers
They stand the wonder of the bowers
From morn to evening dews.   60

He told of the magnolia, spread
High as a cloud, high over head!
The cypress and her spire;
—Of flowers that with one scarlet gleam
Cover a hundred leagues, and seem
To set the hills on fire.

The Youth of green savannahs spake,
And many an endless, endless lake,
With all its fairy crowds
Of islands, that together lie   70
As quietly as spots of sky
Among the evening clouds.

"How pleasant," then he said, "it were
A fisher or a hunter there,
In sunshine or in shade
To wander with an easy mind;
And build a household fire, and find
A home in every glade!

"What days and what bright years! Ah me!
Our life were life indeed, with thee   80
So passed in quiet bliss,
And all the while," said he "to know
That we were in a world of woe,
On such an earth as this!"

And then he sometimes interwove
Fond thoughts about a father's love:
"For there," said he, "are spun
Around the heart such tender ties,
That our own children to our eyes
Are dearer than the sun.   90

"Sweet Ruth! and could you go with me
My helpmate in the woods to be,
Our shed at night to rear;
Or run, my own adopted bride,
A sylvan huntress at my side,
And drive the flying deer!

"Beloved Ruth!"—No more he said.
The wakeful Ruth at midnight shed
A solitary tear:
She thought again—and did agree   100
With him to sail across the sea,
And drive the flying deer.

"And now, as fitting is and right,
We in the church our faith will plight,
A husband and a wife."
Even so they did; and I may say
That to sweet Ruth that happy day
Was more than human life.

Through dream and vision did she sink,
Delighted all the while to think   110
That on those lonesome floods,
And green savannahs, she should share
His board with lawful joy, and bear
His name in the wild woods.

But, as you have before been told,
This Stripling, sportive, gay, and bold,
And, with his dancing crest,
So beautiful, through savage lands
Had roamed about, with vagrant bands
Of Indians in the West.   120

The wind, the tempest roaring high,
The tumult of a tropic sky,
Might well be dangerous food
For him, a Youth to whom was given
So much of earth—so much of heaven,
And such impetuous blood.

Whatever in those climes he found
Irregular in sight or sound
Did to his mind impart
A kindred impulse, seemed allied   130
To his own powers, and justified
The workings of his heart.

Nor less, to feed voluptuous thought,
The beauteous forms of nature wrought,
Fair trees and gorgeous flowers;
The breezes their own languor lent;
The stars had feelings, which they sent
Into those favored bowers.

Yet, in his worst pursuits, I ween
That sometimes there did intervene   140
Pure hopes of high intent:
For passions linked to forms so fair
And stately, needs must have their share
Of noble sentiment.

But ill he lived, much evil saw
With men to whom no better law
Nor better life was known;
Deliberately, and undeceived,
Those wild men's vices he received,
And gave them back his own.   150

His genius and his moral frame
Were thus impaired, and he became
The slave of low desires:
A Man who without self-control
Would seek what the degraded soul
Unworthily admires.

And yet he with no feigned delight
Had wooed the Maiden, day and night
Had loved her, night and morn:
What could he less than love a Maid   160
Whose heart with so much nature played?
So kind and so forlorn!

Sometimes, most earnestly, he said,
"O Ruth! I have been worse than dead;
False thoughts, thoughts bold and vain,
Encompassed me on every side
When I, in confidence and pride,
Had crossed the Atlantic main.

"Before me shone a glorious world—
Fresh as a banner bright, unfurled   170
To music suddenly:
I looked upon those hills and plains,
And seemed as if let loose from chains,
To live at liberty.

"No more of this; for now, by thee
Dear Ruth! more happily set free
With nobler zeal I burn;
My soul from darkness is released,
Like the whole sky when to the east
The morning doth return."   180

Full soon that better mind was gone:
No hope, no wish remained, not one,—
They stirred him now no more;
New objects did new pleasure give,
And once again he wished to live
As lawless as before.

Meanwhile, as thus with him it fared,
They for the voyage were prepared,
And went to the sea-shore,
But, when they thither came, the Youth   190
Deserted his poor Bride, and Ruth
Could never find him more.

God help thee, Ruth!—Such pains she had,
That she in half a year was mad,
And in a prison housed;
And there, with many a doleful song
Made of wild words, her cup of wrong
She fearfully caroused.

Yet sometimes milder hours she knew,
Nor wanted sun, nor rain, nor dew,   200
Nor pastimes of the May;
—They all were with her in her cell;
And a clear brook with cheerful knell
Did o'er the pebbles play.

When Ruth three seasons thus had lain,
There came a respite to her pain;
She from her prison fled;
But of the Vagrant none took thought;
And where it liked her best she sought
Her shelter and her bread.   210

Among the fields she breathed again:
The master-current of her brain
Ran permanent and free;
And, coming to the Banks of Tone,
There did she rest; and dwell alone
Under the greenwood tree.

The engines of her pain, the tools
That shaped her sorrow, rocks and pools,
And airs that gently stir
The vernal leaves—she loved them still;   220
Nor ever taxed them with the ill
Which had been done to her.

A Barn her *winter* bed supplies;
But, till the warmth of summer skies
And summer days is gone,
(And all do in this tale agree)
She sleeps beneath the greenwood tree,
And other home hath none.

An innocent life, yet far astray!
And Ruth will, long before her day,   230
Be broken down and old:
Sore aches she needs must have! but less
Of mind, than body's wretchedness,
From damp, and rain, and cold.

If she is prest by want of food,
She from her dwelling in the wood
Repairs to a road-side;
And there she begs at one steep place
Where up and down with easy pace
The horsemen-travellers ride.   240

That oaten pipe of hers is mute,
Or thrown away; but with a flute
Her loneliness she cheers:
This flute, made of a hemlock stalk,
At evening in his homeward walk
The Quantock woodman hears.

I, too, have passed her on the hills
Setting her little water-mills
By spouts and fountains wild—
Such small machinery as she turned   250
Ere she had wept, ere she had mourned,
A young and happy Child!

Farewell! and when thy days are told,
Ill-fated Ruth, in hallowed mould
Thy corpse shall buried be,
For thee a funeral bell shall ring,
And all the congregation sing
A Christian psalm for thee.

[1799]   [1800]

"Three years she grew . . ."

THREE years she grew in sun and shower,
Then Nature said, "A lovelier flower
On earth was never sown;
This Child I to myself will take;
She shall be mine, and I will make
A Lady of my own.

"Myself will to my darling be
Both law and impulse: and with me
The Girl, in rock and plain,
In earth and heaven, in glade, and bower,   10
Shall feel an overseeing power
To kindle or restrain.

"She shall be sportive as the fawn
That wild with glee across the lawn
Or up the mountain springs;
And her's shall be the breathing balm,
And her's the silence and the calm
Of mute insensate things.

"The floating clouds their state shall lend
To her; for her the willow bend;   20
Nor shall she fail to see
Even in the motions of the Storm
Grace that shall mould the Maiden's form
By silent sympathy.

"The stars of midnight shall be dear
To her; and she shall lean her ear
In many a secret place
Where rivulets dance their wayward round,
And beauty born of murmuring sound
Shall pass into her face.   30

"And vital feelings of delight
 Shall rear her form to stately height,
  Her virgin bosom swell;
 Such thoughts to Lucy I will give
 While she and I together live
  Here in this happy dell."

Thus Nature spake—The work was done—
 How soon my Lucy's race was run!
  She died, and left to me
 This heath, this calm, and quiet scene; 40
 The memory of what has been,
  And never more will be.

[1799]   [1800]

THE BROTHERS

"THESE Tourists, heaven preserve us! needs must live
A profitable life: some glance along,
Rapid and gay, as if the earth were air,
And they were butterflies to wheel about
Long as the summer lasted: some, as wise,
Perched on the forehead of a jutting crag,
Pencil in hand and book upon the knee,
Will look and scribble, scribble on and look,
Until a man might travel twelve stout miles,
Or reap an acre of his neighbour's corn. 10
But, for that moping Son of Idleness,
Why can he tarry *yonder*?—In our church-yard
Is neither epitaph nor monument,
Tombstone nor name—only the turf we tread
And a few natural graves."

      To Jane, his wife,
Thus spake the homely Priest of Ennerdale.[1]
It was a July evening; and he sate
Upon the long stone-seat beneath the eaves
Of his old cottage,—as it chanced, that day,
Employed in winter's work. Upon the stone 20
His wife sate near him, teasing matted wool,
While, from the twin cards toothed with glittering
  wire,
He fed the spindle of his youngest child,
Who, in the open air, with due accord
Of busy hands and back-and-forward steps,
Her large round wheel was turning. Towards the field
In which the Parish Chapel stood alone,
Girt round with a bare ring of mossy wall,
While half an hour went by, the Priest had sent
Many a long look of wonder: and at last, 30

---

[1] Like most of the names in this poem, this refers to a village
(and area) in the Lake District northwest of Grasmere.

Risen from his seat, beside the snow-white ridge
Of carded wool which the old man had piled
He laid his implements with gentle care,
Each in the other locked; and down the path,
That from his cottage to the church-yard led,
He took his way, impatient to accost
The Stranger, whom he saw still lingering there.

'Twas one well known to him in former days,
A Shepherd-lad; who ere his sixteenth year
Had left that calling, tempted to entrust 40
His expectations to the fickle winds
And perilous waters; with the mariners
A fellow-mariner;—and so had fared
Through twenty seasons; but he had been reared
Among the mountains, and he in his heart
Was half a shepherd on the stormy seas.
Oft in the piping shrouds had Leonard heard
The tones of waterfalls, and inland sounds
Of caves and trees;—and, when the regular wind
Between the tropics filled the steady sail, 50
And blew with the same breath through days and
  weeks,
Lengthening invisibly its weary line
Along the cloudless Main, he, in those hours
Of tiresome indolence, would often hang
Over the vessel's side, and gaze and gaze;
And, while the broad blue wave and sparkling foam
Flashed round him images and hues that wrought
In union with the employment of his heart,
He, thus by feverish passion overcome,
Even with the organs of his bodily eye, 60
Below him, in the bosom of the deep,
Saw mountains; saw the forms of sheep that grazed
On verdant hills—with dwellings among trees,
And shepherds clad in the same country grey
Which he himself had worn.*

      And now, at last
From perils manifold, with some small wealth
Acquired by traffic 'mid the Indian Isles,
To his paternal home he is returned,
With a determined purpose to resume
The life he had lived there; both for the sake 70
Of many darling pleasures, and the love
Which to an only brother he has borne
In all his hardships, since that happy time
When, whether it blew foul or fair, they two
Were brother-shepherds on their native hills.
—They were the last of all their race: and now,
When Leonard had approached his home, his heart

---

* This description of the Calenture is sketched from an im-
perfect recollection of an admirable one in prose, by Mr.
Gilbert, author of the *Hurricane*.

Failed in him; and, not venturing to enquire
Tidings of one so long and dearly loved,
He to the solitary church-yard turned;   80
That, as he knew in what particular spot
His family were laid, he thence might learn
If still his Brother lived, or to the file
Another grave was added.—He had found
Another grave,—near which a full half-hour
He had remained; but, as he gazed, there grew
Such a confusion in his memory,
That he began to doubt; and even to hope
That he had seen this heap of turf before,—
That it was not another grave; but one   90
He had forgotten. He had lost his path,
As up the vale, that afternoon, he walked
Through fields which once had been well known to
          him:
And oh what joy this recollection now
Sent to his heart! he lifted up his eyes,
And, looking round, imagined that he saw
Strange alteration wrought on every side
Among the woods and fields, and that the rocks,
And everlasting hills themselves were changed.   99

By this the Priest, who down the field had come,
Unseen by Leonard, at the church-yard gate
Stopped short,—and thence, at leisure, limb by limb
Perused him with a gay complacency.
Ay, thought the Vicar, smiling to himself,
'Tis one of those who needs must leave the path
Of the world's business to go wild alone:
His arms have a perpetual holiday;
The happy man will creep about the fields,
Following his fancies by the hour, to bring
Tears down his cheek, or solitary smiles   110
Into his face, until the setting sun
Write fool upon his forehead.—Planted thus
Beneath a shed that over-arched the gate
Of this rude church-yard, till the stars appeared
The good Man might have communed with himself,
But that the Stranger, who had left the grave,
Approached; he recognized the Priest at once,
And, after greetings interchanged, and given
By Leonard to the Vicar as to one
Unknown to him, this dialogue ensued.   120
    Leonard. You live, Sir, in these dales, a quiet life:
Your years make up one peaceful family;
And who would grieve and fret, if, welcome come
And welcome gone, they are so like each other,
They cannot be remembered? Scarce a funeral
Comes to this church-yard once in eighteen months;
And yet, some changes must take place among you:
And you, who dwell here, even among these rocks,
Can trace the finger of mortality,

And see, that with our three score years and ten   130
We are not all that perish.—I remember,
(For many years ago I passed this road)
There was a foot-way all along the fields
By the brook-side—'tis gone—and the dark cleft!
To me it does not seem to wear the face
Which then it had!
    Priest.   Nay, Sir, for aught I know,
That chasm is much the same—
    Leonard.   But, surely, yonder—
    Priest. Ay, there, indeed, your memory is a friend
That does not play you false.—On that tall pike
(It is the loneliest place of all these hills)   140
There were two springs which bubbled side by side
As if they had been made that they might be
Companions for each other: the huge crag
Was rent with lightning—one hath disappeared;
The other, left behind, is flowing still.
For accidents and changes such as these,
We want not store of them;—a waterspout
Will bring down half a mountain; what a feast
For folks that wander up and down like you,
To see an acre's breadth of that wide cliff   150
One roaring cataract! a sharp May-storm
Will come with loads of January snow,
And in one night send twenty score of sheep
To feed the ravens; or a shepherd dies
By some untoward death among the rocks:
The ice breaks up and sweeps away a bridge;
A wood is felled:—and then for our own homes!
A child is born or christened, a field ploughed,
A daughter sent to service, a web spun,
The old house-clock is decked with a new face;   160
And hence, so far from wanting facts or dates
To chronicle the time, we all have here
A pair of diaries,—one serving, Sir,
For the whole dale, and one for each fire-side—
Yours was a stranger's judgment: for historians,
Commend me to these valleys!
    Leonard.   Yet your Church-yard
Seems, if such freedom may be used with you,
To say that you are heedless of the past:
An orphan could not find his mother's grave:
Here's neither head nor foot-stone, plate of brass,   170
Cross-bones nor skull,—type of our earthly state
Nor emblem of our hopes: the dead man's home
Is but a fellow to that pasture-field
    Priest. Why, there, Sir, is a thought that's new to
          me!
The stone-cutters, 'tis true, might beg their bread
If every English church-yard were like ours;
Yet your conclusion wanders from the truth:
We have no need of names and epitaphs;
We talk about the dead by our fire-sides.

And then, for our immortal part! *we* want   180
No symbols, Sir, to tell us that plain tale:
The thought of death sits easy on the man
Who has been born and dies among the mountains.
    Leonard. Your Dalesmen, then, do in each other's
       thoughts
Possess a kind of second life: no doubt
You, Sir, could help me to the history
Of half these graves?
    Priest.   For eight-score winters past,
With what I've witnessed, and with what I've heard,
Perhaps I might; and, on a winter-evening,
If you were seated at my chimney's nook,   190
By turning o'er these hillocks one by one,
We two could travel, Sir, through a strange round;
Yet all in the broad highway of the world.
Now there's a grave—your foot is half upon it,—
It looks just like the rest; and yet that man
Died broken-hearted.
    Leonard.   'Tis a common case.
We'll take another: who is he that lies
Beneath yon ridge, the last of those three graves?
It touches on that piece of native rock
Left in the church-yard wall.
    Priest.   That's Walter Ewbank.
He had as white a head and fresh a cheek   201
As ever were produced by youth and age
Engendering in the blood of hale four-score.
Through five long generations had the heart
Of Walter's forefathers o'erflowed the bounds
Of their inheritance, that single cottage—
You see it yonder! and those few green fields.
They toiled and wrought, and still, from sire to son,
Each struggled, and each yielded as before
A little—yet a little,—and old Walter,   210
They left to him the family heart, and land
With other burthens than the crop it bore.
Year after year the old man still kept up
A cheerful mind,—and buffeted with bond,
Interest, and mortgages; at last he sank,
And went into his grave before his time.
Poor Walter! whether it was care that spurred him
God only knows, but to the very last
He had the lightest foot in Ennerdale:
His pace was never that of an old man: 220
I almost see him tripping down the path
With his two grandsons after him:—but you,
Unless our Landlord be your host to-night,
Have far to travel,—and on these rough paths
Even in the longest day of midsummer—
    Leonard. But those two Orphans!
    Priest.   Orphans!—Such they were—
Yet not while Walter lived:—for, though their parents
Lay buried side by side as now they lie,

The old man was a father to the boys,
Two fathers in one father: and if tears,   230
Shed when he talked of them where they were not,
And hauntings from the infirmity of love,
Are aught of what makes up a mother's heart,
This old Man, in the day of his old age,
Was half a mother to them.—If you weep, Sir,
To hear a stranger talking about strangers,
Heaven bless you when you are among your kindred!
Ay—you may turn that way—it is a grave
Which will bear looking at.
    Leonard.   These boys—I hope
They loved this good old Man?—
    Priest.   They did—and truly: 240
But that was what we almost overlooked,
They were such darlings of each other. Yes,
Though from the cradle they had lived with Walter,
The only kinsman near them, and though he
Inclined to both by reason of his age,
With a more fond, familiar, tenderness;
They, notwithstanding, had much love to spare,
And it all went into each other's hearts.
Leonard, the elder by just eighteen months,
Was two years taller: 'twas a joy to see,   250
To hear, to meet them!—From their house the school
Is distant three short miles, and in the time
Of storm and thaw, when every watercourse
And unbridged stream, such as you may have noticed
Crossing our roads at every hundred steps,
Was swoln into a noisy rivulet,
Would Leonard then, when elder boys remained
At home, go staggering through the slippery fords,
Bearing his brother on his back. I have seen him,
On windy days, in one of those stray brooks,   260
Ay, more than once I have seen him, mid-leg deep,
Their two books lying both on a dry stone,
Upon the hither side: and once I said,
As I remember, looking round these rocks
And hills on which we all of us were born,
That God who made the great book of the world
Would bless such piety—
    Leonard.   It may be then—
    Priest. Never did worthier lads break English bread;
The very brightest Sunday Autumn saw,
With all its mealy clusters of ripe nuts,   270
Could never keep those boys away from church,
Ot tempt them to an hour of sabbath breach.
Leonard and James! I warrant, every corner
Among these rocks, and every hollow place
That venturous foot could reach, to one or both
Was known as well as to the flowers that grow there.
Like roe-bucks they went bounding o'er the hills;
They played like two young ravens on the crags:
Then they could write, ay, and speak too, as well

As many of their betters—and for Leonard! 280
The very night before he went away,
In my own house I put into his hand
A Bible, and I'd wager house and field
That, it he be alive, he has it yet.
   Leonard. It seems, these Brothers have not lived to
     be
A comfort to each other—
   Priest.   That they might
Live to such end is what both old and young
In this our valley all of us have wished,
And what, for my part, I have often prayed:
But Leonard—
   Leonard. Then James still is left among you! 290
   Priest. 'Tis of the elder brother I am speaking:
They had an uncle;—he was at that time
A thriving man, and trafficked on the seas:
And, but for that same uncle, to this hour
Leonard had never handled rope or shroud:
For the boy loved the life which we lead here;
And though of unripe years, a stripling only,
His soul was knit to this his native soil.
But, as I said, old Walter was too weak
To strive with such a torrent; when he died, 300
The estate and house were sold; and all their sheep,
A pretty flock, and which, for aught I know,
Had clothed the Ewbanks for a thousand years:—
Well—all was gone, and they were destitute,
And Leonard, chiefly for his Brother's sake,
Resolved to try his fortune on the seas.
Twelve years are past since we had tidings from him.
If there were one among us who had heard
That Leonard Ewbank was come home again,
From the Great Gavel,* down by Leeza's banks, 310
And down the Enna, far as Egremont,
The day would be a joyous festival;
And those two bells of ours, which there you see—
Hanging in the open air—but, O good Sir!
This is sad talk—they'll never sound for him—
Living or dead.—When last we heard of him,
He was in slavery among the Moors
Upon the Barbary coast.—'Twas not a little
That would bring down his spirit; and no doubt,
Before it ended in his death, the Youth 320
Was sadly crossed.—Poor Leonard! when we parted,
He took me by the hand, and said to me,
If e'er he should grow rich, he would return,

* The Great Gavel, so called, I imagine, from its resemblance to the gable end of a house, is one of the highest of the Cumberland mountains. It stands at the head of the several vales of Ennerdale, Wastdale, and Borrowdale.
   The Leeza is a river which flows into the Lake of Ennerdale: on issuing from the Lake, it changes its name, and is called the End, Eyne, or Enna. It falls into the sea a little below Egremont.

To live in peace upon his father's land,
And lay his bones among us.
   Leonard.   If that day
Should come, 'twould needs be a glad day for him;
He would himself, no doubt, be happy then
As any that should meet him—
   Priest.   Happy! Sir—
   Leonard. You said his kindred all were in their
     graves,
And that he had one Brother—
   Priest.   That is but 330
A fellow-tale of sorrow. From his youth
James, though not sickly, yet was delicate;
And Leonard being always by his side
Had done so many offices about him,
That, though he was not of a timid nature,
Yet still the spirit of a mountain-boy
In him was somewhat checked; and, when his Brother
Was gone to sea, and he was left alone,
The little colour that he had was soon
Stolen from his cheek; he drooped, and pined, and
     pined— 340
   Leonard. But these are all the graves of full-grown
     men!
   Priest. Ay, Sir, that passed away: we took him to
     us;
He was the child of all the dale—he lived
Three months with one, and six months with another;
And wanted neither food, nor clothes, nor love:
And many, many happy days were his.
But, whether blithe or sad, 'tis my belief
His absent Brother still was at his heart.
And, when he dwelt beneath our roof, we found
(A practice till this time unknown to him) 350
That often, rising from his bed at night,
He in his sleep would walk about, and sleeping
He sought his brother Leonard.—You are moved!
Forgive me, Sir: before I spoke to you,
I judged you most unkindly.
   Leonard.   But this Youth,
How did he die at last?
   Priest.   One sweet May-morning,
(It will be twelve years since when Spring returns)
He had gone forth among the new-dropped lambs,
With two or three companions, whom their course
Of occupation led from height to height 360
Under a cloudless sun—till he, at length,
Through weariness, or, haply, to indulge
The humour of the moment, lagged behind.
You see yon precipice;—it wears the shape
Of a vast building made of many crags;
And in the midst is one particular rock
That rises like a column from the vale,
Whence by our shepherds it is called, THE PILLAR.

Upon its aëry summit crowned with heath,
The loiterer, not unnoticed by his comrades,   370
Lay stretched at ease; but, passing by the place
On their return, they found that he was gone.
No ill was feared; till one of them by chance
Entering, when evening was far spent, the house
Which at that time was James's home, there learned
That nobody had seen him all that day:
The morning came, and still he was unheard of:
The neighbours were alarmed, and to the brook
Some hastened; some ran to the lake: ere noon
They found him at the foot of that same rock   380
Dead, and with mangled limbs. The third day after
I buried him, poor Youth, and there he lies!
　　Leonard.   And that then *is* his grave!—Before his
　　　death
You say that he saw many happy years?
　　Priest, Ay, that he did—
　　Leonard.   And all went well with
　　　him?—
　　Priest. If he had one, the Youth had twenty homes.
　　Leonard. And you believe, then, that his mind was
　　　easy?—
　　Priest. Yes, long before he died, he found that
　　　time
Is a true friend to sorrow; and unless
His thoughts were turned on Leonard's luckless
　　　fortune,   390
He talked about him with a cheerful love.
　　Leonard. He could not come to an unhallowed
　　　end!
　　Priest. Nay, God forbid!—You recollect I
　　　mentioned
A habit which disquietude and grief
Had brought upon him; and we all conjectured
That, as the day was warm, he had lain down
On the soft heath,—and, waiting for his comrades,
He there had fallen asleep; that in his sleep
He to the margin of the precipice
Had walked, and from the summit had fallen head-
　　　long: 400
And so no doubt he perished. When the Youth
Fell, in his hand he must have grasp'd, we think,
His shepherd's staff; for on that Pillar of rock
It had been caught mid-way; and there for years
It hung;—and mouldered there.
　　　　　　　　　　　　　The Priest here ended—
The Stranger would have thanked him, but he felt
A gushing from his heart, that took away
The power of speech. Both left the spot in silence;
And Leonard, when they reached the church-yard
　　　gate,
As the Priest lifted up the latch, turned round,—   410
And, looking at the grave, he said, "My Brother!"

The Vicar did not hear the words: and now,
He pointed towards his dwelling-place, entreating
That Leonard would partake his homely fare:
The other thanked him with an earnest voice;
But added, that, the evening being calm,
He would pursue his journey. So they parted.

It was not long ere Leonard reached a grove
That overhung the road: he there stopped short,
And, sitting down beneath the trees, reviewed   420
All that the Priest had said: his early years
Were with him:—his long absence, cherished hopes,
And thoughts which had been his an hour before,
All pressed on him with such a weight, that now,
This vale, where he had been so happy, seemed
A place in which he could not bear to live:
So he relinquished all his purposes.
He travelled back to Egremont: and thence,
That night, he wrote a letter to the Priest,
Reminding him of what had passed between them;
And adding, with a hope to be forgiven,   431
That it was from the weakness of his heart
He had not dared to tell him who he was.
This done, he went on shipboard, and is now
A seaman, a grey-headed Mariner.

[1800]   [1800]

HOME AT GRASMERE

With Coleridge's encouragement, Wordsworth by 1798 began planning a long philosophical poem on "Man, Nature and Society" entitled The Recluse. *This plan was never fulfilled in its original terms, but from it came* The Prelude (*at first considered part of* The Recluse, *but later called "preparatory"*), *and later also* The Excursion. *All that remains of* The Recluse *itself are these 860 lines subtitled "Home at Grasmere," first published as a whole in 1888 after the poet's death—Wordsworth himself once used the last 107 lines in his Preface to* The Excursion *as a prospectus of what the whole* Recluse *would have been. The text of lines 754 ff. is that of the 1850 edition of* The Excursion.

The traditional date of "Home at Grasmere" is 1800. However, it has recently been argued that most of its composition occurred in 1806 rather than 1800. (See J. A. Finch, "On the Dating of Home at Grasmere: *A New Approach," in* Bicentenary Wordsworth Studies in Memory of John Alban Finch, *ed. Jonathan Wordsworth, 1970.) Because Professor Finch's essay is a posthumously published first draft of an introduction that does not fully consider alternate points of view, and because at least some work was probably done on the poem in 1800, the traditional date and order are retained here. However, as Jonathan Wordsworth points out in his Preface to the* Studies, *"it is certainly no longer possible to say that* Home at Grasmere *belongs wholly to 1800."*

"Home at Grasmere" contains some of Wordsworth's most explicit statements about his own literary ambitions and their relation to the home he and his sister Dorothy had established at Grasmere in 1799.

THE RECLUSE.

PART FIRST. BOOK FIRST.

HOME AT GRASMERE

ONCE to the verge of yon steep barrier came
A roving School-boy; what the Adventurer's age
Hath now escaped his memory—but the hour,
One of a golden summer holiday,
He well remembers, though the year be gone.
Alone and devious from afar he came;
And, with a sudden influx overpowered
At sight of this seclusion, he forgot
His haste, for hasty had his footseps been
As boyish his pursuits; and, sighing said, 10
"What happy fortune were it here to live!
And, if a thought of dying, if a thought
Of mortal separation, could intrude
With paradise before him, here to die!"
No Prophet was he, had not even a hope,
Scarcely a wish, but one bright pleasing thought,
A fancy in the heart of what might be
The lot of Others, never could be his.

The Station whence he look'd was soft and green,
Not giddy yet aerial, with a depth 20

Of Vale below, a height of hills above.
For rest of body, perfect was the Spot,
All that luxurious nature could desire,
But stirring to the Spirit; who could gaze
And not feel motions there? He thought of clouds
That sail on winds; of Breezes that delight
To play on water, or in endless chase
Pursue each other through the yielding plain
Of grass or corn, oever and through and through,
In billow after billow, evermore
Disporting. Nor unmindful was the Boy
Of sunbeams, shadows, butterfies and birds,
Of fluttering Sylphs, and softly-gliding Fays,
Genii, and winged Angels that are Lords
Without restraint of all which they behold.
The illusion strengthening as he gazed, he felt
That such unfettered liberty was his,
Such power and joy; but only for this end,
To flit from field to rock, from rock to field,
From shore to island, and from isle to shore, 40
From open ground to covert, from a bed
Of meadow-flowers into a tuft of wood;
From high to low, from low to high, yet still
Within the bound of this high Concave; here
Must be his Home, this Valley be his World.

Since that day forth the place to him—*to me*
(For I who live to register the truth
Was that same young and happy Being) became
As beautiful to thought, as it had been,
When present, to the bodily sense; a haunt 50
Of pure affections, shedding upon joy
A brighter joy; and through such damp and gloom
Of the gay mind, as ofttimes splenetic Youth
Mistakes for sorrow, darting beams of light
That no self-cherished sadness could withstand:
And now 'tis mine, perchance for life, dear Vale,
Beloved Grasmere (let the Wandering Streams
Take up, the cloud-capt hills repeat, the Name),
One of thy lowly Dwellings is my Home.

And was the cost so great? and could it seem 60
An act of courage, and the thing itself
A conquest? who must bear the blame? sage Man
Thy prudence, thy experience—thy desires,
Thy apprehensions—blush thou for them all.

Yes, the realities of life so cold,
So cowardly, so ready to betray,
So stinted in the measure of their grace
As we pronounce them, doing them much wrong,
Have been to me more bountiful than hope,
Less timid than desire—but that is passed. 70

On Nature's invitation do I come,
By Reason sanctioned—Can the choice mislead,
That made the calmest, fairest spot of earth,
With all its unappropriated good,
My own; and not mine only, for with me
Entrenched, say rather peacefully embowered,
Under yon Orchard, in yon humble Cot,
A younger Orphan of a Home extinct,
The only Daughter of my Parents, dwells.

Aye, think on that, my Heart, and cease to stir,   80
Pause upon that, and let the breathing frame
No longer breathe, but all be satisfied.
—Oh if such silence be not thanks to God
For what hath been bestowed, then where, where then
Shall gratitude find rest? Mine eyes did ne'er
Fix on a lovely object, nor my mind
Take pleasure in the midst of happy thoughts,
But either She whom now I have, who now
Divides with me this loved Abode, was there,
Or not far off. Where'er my footsteps turned,   90
Her Voice was like a hidden Bird that sang,
The thought of her was like a flash of light,
Or an *unseen* companionship, a breath,
Or fragrance independent of the wind.
In all my goings, in the new and old
Of all my meditations, and in this
Favorite of all, in this the most of all.
—What Being, therefore, since the birth of Man
Had ever more abundant cause to speak
Thanks, and if favours of the heavenly Muse   100
Make him more thankful, then to call on verse
To aid him, and in Song resound his joy.
The boon is absolute; surpassing grace
To me hath been vouchsafed; among the bowers
Of blissful Eden this was neither given,
Nor could be given, possession of the good
Which had been sighed for, ancient thought fulfilled
And dear Imaginations realized
Up to their highest measure, yea and more.

Embrace me then, ye Hills, and close me in,   110
Now in the clear and open day I feel
Your guardianship; I take it to my heart;
'Tis like the solemn shelter of the night.
But I would call thee beautiful, for mild
And soft, and gay, and beautiful thou art,
Dear Valley, having in thy face a smile
Though peaceful, full of gladness, Thou art pleased,
Pleased with thy crags, and woody steeps, thy Lake,
Its one green Island and its winding shores;
The multitude of little rocky hills,   120
Thy Church and Cottages of mountain stone
Clustered like stars some few, but single most,

And lurking dimly in their shy retreats,
Or glancing at each other chearful looks,
Like separated stars with clouds between.
What want we? have we not perpetual streams,
Warm woods, and sunny hills, and fresh green fields,
And mountains not less green, and flocks, and herds,
And thickets full of songsters, and the voice
Of lordly birds, an unexpected sound   130
Heard now and then from morn till latest eve,
Admonishing the man who walks below
Of solitude, and silence in the sky?
These have we, and a thousand nooks of earth
Have also these, but no where else is found,
No where (or is it fancy?) can be found
The one sensation that is here; 'tis here,
Here as it found its way into my heart
In childhood, here as it abides by day,
By night, here only; or in chosen minds   140
That take it with them hence, where'er they go.
'Tis, but I cannot name it, 'tis the sense
Of majesty, and beauty, and repose,
A blended holiness of earth and sky,
Something that makes this individual Spot,
This small Abiding-place of many Men,
A termination, and a last retreat,
A Centre, come from wheresoe'er you will,
A Whole without dependence or defect,
Made for itself; and happy in itself,   150
Perfect Contentment, Unity entire.

Bleak season was it, turbulent and bleak,
When hitherward we journeyed, side by side,
Through bursts of sunshine and through flying
    showers,
Paced the long Vales, how long they were, and yet
How fast that length of way was left behind,
Wensley's rich Vale and Sedbergh's naked heights.
The frosty wind, as if to make amends
For its keen breath, was aiding to our steps,
And drove us onward like two ships at sea,   160
Or like two Birds, companions in mid air,
Parted and re-united by the blast.
Stern was the face of Nature; we rejoiced
In that stern countenance, for our Souls thence drew
A feeling of their strength. The naked Trees,
The icy brooks, as on we passed, appeared
To question us. "Whence come ye? to what end?"
They seemed to say; "What would ye," said the
    shower,
"Wild Wanderers, whither through my dark
    domain?"
The sunbeam said, "be happy." When this Vale   170
We entered, bright and solemn was the sky
That faced us with a passionate welcoming,

And led us to our threshold. Daylight failed
Insensibly, and round us gently fell
Composing darkness, with a quiet load
Of full contentment, in a little Shed
Disturbed, uneasy in itself as seemed,
And wondering at its new inhabitants.
It loves us now, this Vale so beautiful
Begins to love us! By a sudden storm,   180
Two months unwearied of severest storm,
It put the temper of our minds to proof,
And found us faithful through the gloom, and heard
The Poet mutter his prelusive songs
With chearful heart, an unknown voice of joy,
Among the silence of the woods and hills;
Silent to any gladsomeness of sound
With all their Shepherds.
                          But the gates of Spring
Are opened; churlish Winter hath given leave
That she should entertain for this one day,   190
Perhaps for many genial days to come,
His guests, and make them jocund. They are pleased,
But most of all the Birds that haunt the flood,
With the mild summons; inmates though they be
Of Winter's household, they keep festival
This day, who drooped, or seemed to droop, so long;
They shew their pleasure, and shall I do less?
Happier of happy though I be, like them
I cannot take possession of the sky,
Mount with a thoughtless impulse, and wheel there,
One of a mighty multitude, whose way   201
Is a perpetual harmony and dance
Magnificent. Behold, how with a grace
Of ceaseless motion, that might scarcely seem
Inferior to angelical, they prolong
Their curious pastime, shaping in mid air,
And sometimes with ambitious wing that soars
High as the level of the mountain tops,
A circuit ampler than the lake beneath,
Their own domain;—but ever, while intent   210
On tracing and retracing that large round,
Their jubilant activity evolves
Hundreds of curves and circlets, to and fro,
Upwards and downwards, progress intricate
Yet unperplexed, as if one spirit swayed
Their indefatigable flight. 'Tis done—
Ten times and more, I fancied it had ceased;
But lo! the vanished company again
Ascending, they approach—I hear their wings
Faint, faint at first; and then an eager sound   220
Passed in a moment—and as faint again!
They tempt the sun to sport among their plumes;
Tempt the smooth water, or the gleaming ice,
To shew them a fair image,—'tis themselves,
Their own fair forms, upon the glimmering plain,

Painted more soft and fair as they descend,
Almost to touch;—then up again aloft,
Up with a sally, and a flash of speed,
As if they scorned both resting-place and rest!

    This day is a thanksgiving, 'tis a day   230
Of glad emotion and deep quietness;
Not upon me alone hath been bestowed,
Me rich in many onward-looking thoughts,
The penetrating bliss; oh surely these
Have felt it, not the happy Quires of Spring,
Her own peculiar family of love
That sport among green leaves, a blither train.

    But two are missing—two, a lonely pair
Of milk-white Swans, wherefore are they not seen
Partaking this day's pleasure? From afar   240
They came, to sojourn here in solitude,
Chusing this Valley, they who had the choice
Of the whole world. We saw them day by day,
Through those two months of unrelenting storm,
Conspicuous at the centre of the Lake,
Their safe retreat; we knew them well, I guess
That the whole Valley knew them; but to us
They were more dear than may be well believed,
Not only for their beauty, and their still
And placid way of life, and constant love   250
Inseparable, not for these alone,
But that their state so much resembled ours,
They having also chosen this abode;
They strangers, and we strangers; they a pair,
And we a solitary pair like them.
They should not have departed; many days
Did I look forth in vain, nor on the wing
Could see them, nor in that small open space
Of blue unfrozen water, where they lodged,
And lived so long in quiet, side by side.   260
Shall we behold them, consecrated friends,
Faithful Companions, yet another year
Surviving, they for us, and we for them,
And neither pair be broken? Nay perchance
It is too late already for such hope,
The Dalesmen may have aimed the deadly tube,
And parted them; or haply both are gone
One death, and that were mercy given to both.
Recall my song the ungenerous thought; forgive,
Thrice favoured Region, the conjecture harsh   270
Of such inhospitable penalty,
Inflicted upon confidence so pure.
Ah, if I wished to follow where the sight
Of all that is before my eyes, the voice
Which speaks from a presiding Spirit here,
Would lead me, I should whisper to myself;
They who are dwellers in this holy place

Must needs themselves be hallowed, they require
No benediction from the Stranger's lips,
For they are blest already. None would give   280
The greeting "peace be with you" unto them,
For peace they have, it cannot but be theirs,
And mercy, and forbearance. Nay—not these,
Their healing offices a pure good-will
Precludes, and charity beyond the bounds
Of charity—an overflowing love,
Not for the Creature only, but for all
That is around them, love for every thing
Which in this happy Region they behold!

Thus do we soothe ourselves, and when the thought
Is pass'd, we blame it not for having come.   291
What, if I floated down a pleasant stream,
And now am landed, and the motion gone,
Shall I reprove myself? Ah no, the stream
Is flowing, and will never cease to flow,
And I shall float upon that Stream again.
By such forgetfulness the Soul becomes,
Words cannot say, how beautiful; then hail,
Hail to the visible Presence, hail to thee,
Delightful Valley, habitation fair!   300
And to whatever else of outward form
Can give us inward help, can purify,
And elevate, and harmonise, and soothe,
And steal away, and for a while deceive
And lap in pleasing rest, and bear us on
Without desire in full complacency,
Contemplating perfection absolute
And entertained as in a placid sleep.

But not betrayed by tenderness of mind
That feared, or wholly overlook'd the truth,   310
Did we come hither, with romantic hope
To find, in midst of so much loveliness,
Love, perfect love; of so much majesty
A like majestic frame of mind in those
Who here abide, the persons like the place.
Not from such hope, or aught of such belief
Hath issued any portion of the joy
Which I have felt this day. An awful voice,
'Tis true, hath in my walks been often heard,
Sent from the mountains or the sheltered fields,   320
Shout after shout—reiterated whoop
In manner of a bird that takes delight
In answering to itself; or like a hound
Single at chase among the lonely woods,
His yell repeating; yet it was in truth
A human voice—a Spirit of coming night,
How solemn when the sky is dark, and earth
Not dark, nor yet enlightened, but by snow
Made visible, amid a noise of winds

And bleatings manifold of mountain sheep.   330
Which in that iteration recognize
Their summons, and are gathering round for food,
Devoured with keenness ere to grove or bank
Or rocky *bield* [1] with patience they retire.

That very voice, which, in some timid mood
Of superstitious fancy, might have seemed
Awful as ever stray Demoniac [2] uttered,
His steps to govern in the Wilderness;
Or as the Norman Curfew's [3] regular beat,
To hearths when first they darkened at the knell: 340
That Shepherd's voice, it may have reached mine ear
Debased and under profanation, made
The ready Organ of articulate sounds
From ribaldry, impiety, or wrath
Issuing when shame hath ceased to check the brawls
Of some abused Festivity—so be it.
I came not dreaming of unruffled life,
Untainted manners; born among the hills,
Bred also there, I wanted not a scale
To regulate my hopes. Pleased with the good,   350
I shrink not from the evil with disgust,
Or with immoderate pain. I look for Man,
The common Creature of the brotherhood,
Differing but little from the Man elsewhere,
For selfishness, and envy, and revenge,
Ill neighbourhood—pity that this should be—
Flattery and double-dealing, strife and wrong.

Yet is it something gained, it is in truth
A mighty gain, that Labour here preserves
His rosy face, a Servant only here   360
Of the fire-side, or of the open field,
A Freeman, therefore, sound and unimpaired;
That extreme penury is here unknown,
And cold and hunger's abject wretchedness,
Mortal to body, and the heaven-born mind;
That they who want, are not too great a weight
For those who can relieve. Here may the heart
Breathe in the air of fellow-suffering
Dreadless, as in a kind of fresher breeze
Of her own native element, the hand   370
Be ready and unwearied without plea
From tasks too frequent, or beyond its power
For languor, or indifference, or despair.
And as these lofty barriers break the force
Of winds, this deep Vale,—as it doth in part
Conceal us from the Storm,—so here abides

---

[1] North of England dialect: refuge, or shelter.
[2] Someone possessed by demons; insane.
[3] The use of the curfew as a form of political oppression was traditionally (but inaccurately) blamed on William the Conqueror. See Wordsworth's *Excursion*, VIII, 172.

A Power and a protection for the mind,
Dispensed indeed to other solitudes,
Favored by noble privilege like this,
Where kindred independence of estate   380
Is prevalent, where he who tills the field,
He, happy Man! is Master of the field,
And treads the mountains which his Fathers trod.

Not less than half-way up yon Mountain's side
Behold a dusky spot, a grove of Firs,
That seems still smaller than it is; this grove
Is haunted—by what ghost? a gentle Spirit
Of memory faithful to the call of love;
For, as reports the Dame, whose fire sends up
Yon curling smoke from the grey cot below,   390
The trees (her first-born Child being then a babe)
Were planted by her husband and herself,
That ranging o'er the high and houseless ground
Their sheep might neither want (from perilous storm
Of winter, nor from summer's sultry heat)
A friendly covert: "And they knew it well,"
Said she, "for thither as the trees grew up,
We to the patient creatures carried food
In times of heavy snow." She then began
In fond obedience to her private thoughts   400
To speak of her dead Husband: is there not
An art, a music, and a strain of words
That shall be life, the acknowledged voice of life,
Shall speak of what is done among the fields,
Done truly there, or felt, of solid good
And real evil, yet be sweet withal,
More grateful, more harmonious than the breath,
The idle breath of softest pipe attuned
To pastoral fancies? Is there such a stream,
Pure and unsullied, flowing from the heart   410
With motions of true dignity and grace?
Or must we seek that stream where Man is not?
Methinks I could repeat in tuneful verse,
Delicious as the gentlest breeze that sounds
Through that aerial fir-grove, could preserve
Some portion of its human history
As gathered from the Matron's lips, and tell
Of tears that have been shed at sight of it,
And moving dialogues between this Pair,
Who in their prime of wedlock, with joint hands 420
Did plant the grove, now flourishing, while they
No longer flourish, he entirely gone,
She withering in her loneliness. Be this
A task above my skill; the silent mind
Has her own treasures, and I think of these,
Love what I see, and honour humankind.

No, we are not alone, we do not stand,
My Sister, here misplaced and desolate,

Loving what no one cares for but ourselves;
We shall not scatter through the plains and rocks   430
Of this fair Vale, and o'er its spacious heights
Unprofitable kindliness, bestowed
On objects unaccustomed to the gifts
Of feeling, which were chearless and forlorn
But few weeks past, and would be so again
Were we not here; we do not tend a lamp
Whose lustre we alone participate,
Which shines dependent upon us alone,
Mortal though bright, a dying, dying flame.
Look where we will, some human heart has been   440
Before us with its offering; not a tree
Sprinkles these little pastures, but the same
Hath furnished matter for a thought; perchance
For some one serves as a familiar friend.
Joy spreads, and sorrow spreads; and this whole Vale,
Home of untutored Shepherds as it is,
Swarms with sensation, as with gleams of sunshine,
Shadows or breezes, scents or sounds. Nor deem
These feelings, though subservient more than ours
To every day's demand for daily bread,   450
And borrowing more their spirit, and their shape
From self-respecting interests, deem them not
Unworthy therefore, and unhallowed: no,
They lift the animal being, do themselves
By Nature's kind and ever-present aid
Refine the selfishness from which they spring,
Redeem by love the individual sense
Of anxiousness with which they are combined.
And thus it is that fitly they become
Associates in the joy of purest minds,   460
They blend therewith congenially: meanwhile,
Calmly they breathe their own undying life
Through this their mountain sanctuary; long,
Oh long may it remain inviolate,
Diffusing health and sober chearfulness,
And giving to the moments as they pass
Their little boons of animating thought
That sweeten labour, make it seen and felt
To be no arbitrary weight imposed,
But a glad function natural to Man.   470

Fair proof of this, Newcomer though I be,
Already have I gained. The inward frame
Though slowly opening, opens every day
With process not unlike to that which chears
A pensive Stranger, journeying at his leisure
Through some Helvetian dell, when low-hung mists
Break up, and are beginning to recede;
How pleased he is where thin and thinner grows
The veil, or where it parts at once, to spy
The dark pines thrusting forth their spiky heads;   480
To watch the spreading lawns with cattle grazed,

Then to be greeted by the scattered huts,
As they shine out; and *see* the streams whose murmur
Had soothed his ear while they were hidden: how
    pleased
To have about him, which way e'er he goes,
Something on every side concealed from view,
In every quarter something visible,
Half-seen or wholly, lost and found again,
Alternate progress and impediment,
And yet a growing prospect in the main.   490

   Such pleasure now is mine, albeit forced,
Herein less happy than the Traveller
To cast from time to time a painful look
Upon unwelcome things, which unawares
Reveal themselves; not therefore is my heart
Depressed, nor does it fear what is to come;
But confident, enriched at every glance.
The more I see the more delight my mind
Receives, or by reflexion can create.
Truth justifies herself, and as she dwells   500
With Hope, who would not follow where she
    leads?

   Nor let me pass unheeded other loves
Where no fear is, and humbler sympathies.
Already hath sprung up within my heart
A liking for the small grey horse that bears
The paralytic Man, and for the brute—
In Scripture sanctified—the patient brute,
On which the cripple, in the Quarry maim'd,
Rides to and fro: I know them and their ways.
The famous Sheep-dog, first in all the Vale,   510
Though yet to me a Stranger, will not be
A Stranger long; nor will the blind man's guide,
Meek and neglected thing, of no renown!
Soon will peep forth the primrose; ere it fades
Friends shall I have at dawn, blackbird and thrush
To rouse me, and a hundred Warblers more:
And if those Eagles to their ancient hold
Return, Helvellyn's Eagles! with the Pair
From my own door I shall be free to claim
Acquaintance, as they sweep from cloud to cloud.   520
The owl that gives the name to Owlet-Crag
Have I heard whooping, and he soon will be
A chosen one of my regards. See there
The heifer in yon little croft belongs
To one who holds it dear; with duteous care
She reared it, and in speaking of her charge
I heard her scatter some endearing words
Domestic, and in spirit motherly
She being herself a Mother, happy Beast
If the caresses of a human voice   530
Can make it so, and care of human hands.

And ye as happy under Nature's care,
Strangers to me, and all men, or at least
Strangers to all particular amity,
All intercourse of knowledge or of love
That parts the individual from his kind,
Whether in large communities ye keep
From year to year, not shunning Man's abode,
A settled residence, or be from far,
Wild creatures, and of many homes, that come   540
The gifts of winds, and whom the winds again
Take from us at your pleasure—yet shall ye
Not want, for this, your own subordinate place
In my affections. Witness the delight
With which erewhile I saw that multitude
Wheel through the sky, and see them now at rest,
Yet not at rest, upon the glassy lake.
They *cannot* rest, they gambol like young whelps;
Active as lambs, and overcome with joy
They try all frolic motions; flutter, plunge,   550
And beat the passive water with their wings.
Too distant are they for plain view, but lo!
Those little fountains, sparkling in the sun,
Betray their occupation, rising up,
First one and then another silver spout,
As one or other takes the fit of glee,
Fountains and spouts, yet somewhat in the guise
Of play-thing fire-works, that on festal nights
Sparkle about the feet of wanton boys.
—How vast the compass of this theatre,   560
Yet nothing to be seen but lovely pomp
And silent majesty; the birch-tree woods
Are hung with thousand thousand diamond drops
Of melted hoar-frost, every tiny knot
In the bare twigs, each little budding-place
Cased with its several bead, what myriads there
Upon one tree, while all the distant grove
That rises to the summit of the steep
Shows like a mountain built of silver light.
See yonder the same pageant, and again   570
Behold the universal imagery
Inverted, all its sun-bright features touched
As with the varnish, and the gloss of dreams;
Dreamlike the blending also of the whole
Harmonious landscape; all along the shore
The boundary lost, the line invisible
That parts the image from reality;
And the clear hills, as high as they ascend
Heavenward, so piercing deep the lake below.
Admonished of the days of love to come   580
The raven croaks, and fills the upper air
With a strange sound of genial harmony;
And in and all about that playful band,
Incapable although they be of rest,
And in their fashion very rioters,

There is a stillness, and they seem to make
Calm revelry in that their calm abode.
Them leaving to their joyous hours I pass,
Pass with a thought the life of the whole year
That is to come, the throng of woodland flowers,   590
And lillies that will dance upon the waves.

     Say boldly then that solitude is not
Where these things are: he truly is alone,
He of the multitude whose eyes are doomed
To hold a vacant commerce day by day
With objects wanting life, repelling love;
He by the vast Metropolis immured,
Where pity shrinks from unremitting calls,
Where numbers overwhelm humanity,
And neighbourhood serves rather to divide   600
Than to unite. What sighs more deep than his,
Whose nobler will hath long been sacrificed;
Who must inhabit, under a black sky,
A City where, if indifference to disgust
Yield not, to scorn, or sorrow, living Men
Are ofttimes to their fellow-men no more
Than to the Forest Hermit are the leaves
That hang aloft in myriads—nay, far less,
For they protect his walk from sun and shower,
Swell his devotion with their voice in storms,   610
And whisper while the stars twinkle among them
His lullaby. From crowded streets remote,
Far from the living and dead wilderness
Of the thronged World, Society is here
A true Community, a genuine frame
Of many into one incorporate.
That must be looked for here, paternal sway,
One household, under God, for high and low,
One family, and one mansion; to themselves
Appropriate, and divided from the world   620
As if it were a cave, a multitude
Human and brute, possessors undisturbed
Of this Recess, their legislative Hall,
Their Temple, and their glorious Dwelling-place.

     Dismissing therefore, all Arcadian dreams,
All golden fancies of the golden Age,
The bright array of shadowy thoughts from times
That were before all time, or are to be
Ere time expire, the pageantry that stirs
And will be stirring when our eyes are fixed   630
On lovely objects, and we wish to part
With all remembrance of a jarring world,
—Take we at once this one sufficient hope,
What need of more? that we shall neither droop,
Nor pine for want of pleasure in the life
Scattered about us, nor through dearth of aught
That keeps in health the insatiable mind;

That we shall have for knowledge and for love
Abundance; and that, feeling as we do
How goodly, how exceeding fair, how pure   640
From all reproach is yon ethereal vault,
And this deep Vale its earthly counterpart,
By which, and under which, we are enclosed
To breathe in peace, we shall moreover find
(If sound, and what we ought to be ourselves,
If rightly we observe and justly weigh)
The Inmates not unworthy of their home
The Dwellers of their Dwelling.
                              And if this
Were otherwise, we have within ourselves
Enough to fill the present day with joy,   650
And overspread the future years with hope,
Our beautiful and quiet home, enriched
Already with a Stranger whom we love
Deeply, a Stranger of our Father's House,
A never-resting Pilgrim of the Sea,
Who finds at last an hour to his content
Beneath our roof. And others whom we love
Will seek us also, Sisters of our hearts,
And One, like them, a Brother of our hearts,
Philosopher and Poet, in whose sight   660
These Mountains will rejoice with open joy.
—Such is our wealth; O Vale of Peace, we are
And must be, with God's will, a happy Band.

     Yet 'tis not to enjoy that we exist,
For that end only; something must be done.
I must not walk in unreproved delight
These narrow bounds, and think of nothing more,
No duty that looks further, and no care.
Each Being has his office, lowly some
And common, yet all worthy if fulfilled   670
With zeal, acknowledgment that with the gift
Keeps pace a harvest answering to the seed—
Of ill-advised Ambition and of Pride
I would stand clear, but yet to me I feel
That an internal brightness is vouchsafed
That must not die, that must not pass away.
Why does this inward lustre fondly seek,
And gladly blend with outward fellowship?
Why do *they* shine around me whom I love?
Why do they teach me, whom I thus revere?   680
Strange question, yet it answers not itself.
That humble Roof embowered among the trees,
That calm fire-side, it is not even in them,
Blest as they are, to furnish a reply
That satisfies and ends in perfect rest.
Possessions have I that are solely mine,
Something within which yet is shared by none,
Not even the nearest to me and most dear,
Something which power and effort may impart,

I would impart it, I would spread it wide,   690
Immortal in the world which is to come.
Forgive me if I add another claim,
And would not wholly perish even in this,
Lie down and be forgotten in the dust,
I and the modest Partners of my days
Making a silent company in death;
Love, Knowledge, all my manifold delights
All buried with me without monument
Or profit unto any but ourselves.
It must not be, if I, divinely taught,   700
Be privileged to speak as I have felt
Of what in man is human or divine.

While yet an innocent Little-one, with a heart
That doubtless wanted not its tender moods,
I breathed (for this I better recollect)
Among wild appetites and blind desires,
Motions of savage instinct my delight
And exaltation. Nothing at that time
So welcome, no temptation half so dear
As that which urged me to a daring feat.   710
Deep pools, tall trees, balck chasms, and dizzy crags,
And tottering towers; I loved to stand and read
Their looks forbidding, read and disobey,
Sometimes in act, and evermore in thought.
With impulses that scarcely were by these
Surpassed in strength, I heard of danger, met
Or sought with courage; enterprize forlorn
By one, sole keeper of his own intent,
Or by a resolute few who for the sake
Of glory, fronted multitudes in arms.   720
Yea to this hour I cannot read a tale
Of two brave Vessels matched in deadly fight,
And fighting to the death, but I am pleased
More than a wise man ought to be. I wish,
Fret, burn, and struggle, and in soul am there;
But me hath Nature tamed, and bade to seek
For other agitations, or be calm;
Hath dealt with me as with a turbulent Stream,
Some nursling of the mountains, whom she leads
Through quiet meadows, after he has learnt   730
His strength, and had his triumph and his joy,
His desperate course of tumult and of glee.
That which in stealth by Nature was performed
Hath Reason sanctioned. Her deliberate Voice
Hath said, "Be mild and cleave to gentle things,
Thy glory and thy happiness be there.
Nor fear, though thou confide in me, a want
Of aspirations that *have* been, of foes
To wrestle with, and victory to complete,
Bounds to be leapt, darkness to be explored,   740
All that inflamed thy infant heart, the love,
The longing, the contempt, the undaunted quest,

All shall survive—though changed their office, all
Shall live,—it is not in their power to die."

Then farewell to the Warrior's schemes, farewell
The forwardness of Soul which looks that way
Upon a less incitement than the cause
Of Liberty endangered, and farewell
That other hope, long mine, the hope to fill
The heroic trumpet with the Muse's breath!   750
Yet in this peaceful Vale we will not spend
Unheard-of days, though loving peaceful thoughts.
A voice shall speak, and what will be the Theme?

On Man, on Nature, and on Human Life,
Musing in solitude, I oft perceive
Fair trains of imagery before me rise,
Accompanied by feelings of delight
Pure, or with no unpleasing sadness mixed;
And I am conscious of affecting thoughts
And dear remembrances, whose presence soothes   760
Or elevates the Mind, intent to weigh
The good and evil of our mortal state.
—To these emotions, whencesoe'er they come,
Whether from breath of outward circumstance,
Or from the Soul—an impulse to herself—
I would give utterance in numerous verse.
Of Truth, of Grandeur, Beauty, Love, and Hope,
And melancholy Fear subdued by Faith;
Of blessèd consolations in distress;
Of moral strength, and intellectual Power;   770
Of joy in widest commonalty spread;
Of the individual Mind that keeps her own
Inviolate retirement, subject there
To Conscience only, and the law supreme
Of that Intelligence which governs all—
I sing:—"fit audience let me find though few!"
So prayed, more gaining than he asked, the Bard—
In holiest mood. Urania, I shall need
Thy guidance, or a greater Muse, if such
Descend to earth or dwell in highest heaven!   780
For I must tread on shadowy ground, must sink
Deep—and, aloft ascending, breathe in worlds
To which the heaven of heavens is but a veil.
All strength—all terror, single or in bands,
That ever was put forth in personal form—
Jehovah—with his thunder, and the choir
Of shouting Angels, and the empyreal thrones—
I pass them unalarmed. Not Chaos, not
The darkest pit of lowest Erebus,
Nor aught of blinder vacancy, scooped out   790
By help of dreams—can breed such fear and awe
As fall upon us often when we look
Into our Minds, into the Mind of Man—
My haunt, and the main region of my song

—Beauty—a living Presence of the earth,
Surpassing the most fair ideal Forms
Which craft of delicate Spirits hath composed
From earth's materials—waits upon my steps;
Pitches her tents before me as I move,
An hourly neighbour. Paradise, and groves   800
Elysian, Fortunate Fields—like those of old
Sought in the Atlantic Main—why should they be
A history only of departed things,
Or a mere fiction of what never was?
For the discerning intellect of Man,
When wedded to this goodly universe
In love and holy passion, shall find these
A simple produce of the common day.
—I, long before the blissful hour arrives,
Would chant, in lonely peace, the spousal verse   810
Of this great consummation:—and, by words
Which speak of nothing more than what we are,
Would I arouse the sensual from their sleep
Of Death, and win the vacant and the vain
To noble raptures; while my voice proclaims
How exquisitely the individual Mind
(And the progressive powers perhaps no less
Of the whole species) to the external World
Is fitted:—and how exquisitely, too—
Theme this but little heard of among men—   820
The external World is fitted to the Mind;
And the creation (by no lower name
Can it be called) which they with blended might
Accomplish:—this is our high argument.
—Such grateful haunts foregoing, if I oft
Must turn elsewhere—to travel near the tribes
And fellowships of men, and see ill sights
Of madding passions mutually inflamed;
Must hear Humanity in fields and groves
Pipe solitary anguish; or must hang   830
Brooding above the fierce confederate storm
Of sorrow, barricadoed evermore
Within the walls of cities—may these sounds
Have their authentic comment; that even these
Hearing, I be not downcast or forlorn!—
Descend, prophetic Spirit! that inspir'st
The human Soul of universal earth,
Dreaming on things to come; and dost possess
A metropolitan temple in the hearts
Of mighty Poets: upon me bestow   840
A gift of genuine insight; that my Song
With star-like virtue in its place may shine,
Shedding benignant influence, and secure,
Itself, from all malevolent effect
Of those mutations that extend their sway
Throughout the nether sphere!—And if with this
I mix more lowly matter; with the thing
Contemplated, describe the Mind and Man

Contemplating; and who, and what he was—
The transitory Being that beheld   850
The Vision; when and where, and how he lived;—
Be not this labour useless. If such theme
May sort with highest objects, then—dread Power!
Whose gracious favour is the primal source
Of all illumination,—may my Life
Express the image of a better time,
More wise desires, and simpler manners;—nurse
My Heart in genuine freedom; all pure thoughts
Be with me;—so shall thy unfailing love
Guide, and support, and cheer me to the end!   860

[1800–1806?]   [1888]

<hr>

*Joanna Hutchinson was the youngest sister of Mary Hutchinson,
whom Wordsworth married in 1802.*

<hr>

TO JOANNA

AMID the smoke of cities did you pass
The time of early youth; and there you learned,
From years of quiet industry, to love
The living Beings by your own fire-side,
With such a strong devotion, that your heart
Is slow to meet the sympathies of them
Who look upon the hills with tenderness,
And make dear friendships with the streams and groves.
Yet we, who are transgressors in this kind,
Dwelling retired in our simplicity   10
Among the woods and fields, we love you well,
Joanna! and I guess, since you have been
So distant from us now for two long years,
That you will gladly listen to discourse,
However trivial, if you thence be taught
That they, with whom you once were happy, talk
Familiarly of you and of old times.

   While I was seated, now some ten days past,
Beneath those lofty firs, that overtop
Their ancient neighbour, the old steeple-tower,   20
The Vicar from his gloomy house hard by
Came forth to greet me; and, when he had asked,
"How fares Joanna, that wild-hearted Maid!
And when will she return to us?" he paused;
And, after short exchange of village news,
He with grave looks demanded, for what cause,
Reviving obsolete idolatry,
I, like a Runic Priest, in characters
Of formidable size had chiselled out
Some uncouth name upon the native rock,   30
Above the Rotha, by the forest-side.

—Now, by those dear immunities of heart
Engendered between malice and true love,
I was not loth to be so catechised,
And this was my reply:—"As it befell,
One summer morning we had walked abroad
At break of day, Joanna and myself.
—'Twas that delightful season when the broom,
Full-flowered, and visible on every steep,
Along the copses runs in veins of gold.   40
Our pathway led us on to Rotha's banks;
And when we came in front of that tall rock
That eastward looks, I there stopped short—and stood
Tracing the lofty barrier with my eye
From base to summit; such delight I found
To note in shrub and tree, in stone and flower,
That intermixture of delicious hues,
Along so vast a surface, all at once,
In one impression, by connecting force
Of their own beauty, imaged in the heart.   50
—When I had gazed perhaps two minutes' space,
Joanna, looking in my eyes, beheld
That ravishment of mine, and laughed aloud.
The Rock, like something starting from a sleep,
Took up the Lady's voice, and laughed again;
That ancient Woman seated on Helm-crag
Was ready with her cavern; Hammar-scar,
And the tall Steep of Silver-how, sent forth
A noise of laughter; southern Loughrigg heard,
And Fairfield answered with a mountain tone;   60
Helvellyn far into the clear blue sky
Carried the Lady's voice,—old Skiddaw blew
His speaking-trumpet;—back out of the clouds
Of Glaramara southward came the voice;
And Kirkstone tossed it from his misty head.
—Now whether (said I to our cordial Friend,
Who in the hey-day of astonishment
Smiled in my face) this were in simple truth
A work accomplished by the brotherhood
Of Ancient mountains, or my ear was touched   70
With dreams and visionary impulses
To me alone imparted, sure I am
That there was a loud uproar in the hills.
And, while we both were listening, to my side
The fair Joanna drew, as if she wished
To shelter from some object of her fear.
—And hence, long afterwards, when eighteen moons
Were wasted, as I chanced to walk alone
Beneath this rock, at sunrise, on a calm
And silent morning, I sat down, and there,   80
In memory of affections old and true,
I chiselled out in those rude characters
Joanna's name deep in the living stone:—
And I, and all who dwell by my fireside,
Have called the lovely rock, JOANNA'S ROCK."

NOTE.—In Cumberland and Westmoreland are several Inscriptions, upon the native rock, which, from the wasting of time, and the rudeness of the workmanship, have been mistaken for Runic. They are without doubt Roman.

The Rotha, mentioned in this poem, is the River which, flowing through the lakes of Grasmere and Rydale, falls into Wynandermere. On Helm-crag, that impressive single mountain at the head of the Vale of Grasmere, is a rock which from most points of view bears a striking resemblance to an old Woman cowering. Close by this rock is one of those fissures or caverns, which in the language of the country are called dungeons. Most of the mountains here mentioned immediately surround the Vale of Grasmere; of the others, some are at a considerable distance, but they belong to the same cluster.

[1800]   [1800]

MICHAEL

"The Sheepfold, on which so much of the poem turns, remains, or rather the ruins of it. The character and circumstances of Luke were taken from a family to whom had belonged, many years before, the house we lived in at Town-end, along with some fields and woodlands on the eastern shore of Grasmere. The name of the Evening Star was not in fact given to this house, but to another on the same side of the valley, more to the north."
[*Wordsworth to Isabella Fenwick*]

MICHAEL:

A PASTORAL POEM

IF from the public way you turn your steps
Up the tumultuous brook of Green-head Ghyll,
You will suppose that with an upright path
Your feet must struggle; in such bold ascent
The pastoral mountains front you, face to face.
But, courage! for around that boisterous brook
The mountains have all opened out themselves,
And made a hidden valley of their own.
No habitation can be seen; but they
Who journey thither find themselves alone   10
With a few sheep, with rocks and stones, and kites
That overhead are sailing in the sky.
It is in truth an utter solitude;
Nor should I have made mention of this Dell
But for one object which you might pass by,
Might see and notice not. Beside the brook
Appears a straggling heap of unhewn stones!
And to that simple object appertains
A story—unenriched with strange events,
Yet not unfit, I deem, for the fireside,   20
Or for the summer shade. It was the first
Of those domestic tales that spake to me
Of Shepherds, dwellers in the valleys, men
Whom I already loved;—not verily
For their own sakes, but for the fields and hills
Where was their occupation and abode.

And hence this Tale, while I was yet a Boy
Careless of books, yet having felt the power
Of Nature, by the gentle agency
Of natural objects, led me on to feel   30
For passions that were not my own, and think
(At random and imperfectly indeed)
On man, the heart of man, and human life.
Therefore, although it be a history
Homely and rude, I will relate the same
For the delight of a few natural hearts;
And, with yet fonder feeling, for the sake
Of youthful Poets, who among these hills
Will be my second self when I am gone.

UPON the forest-side in Grasmere Vale   40
There dwelt a Shepherd, Michael was his name;
An old man, stout of heart, and strong of limb.
His bodily frame had been from youth to age
Of an unusual strength: his mind was keen,
Intense, and frugal, apt for all affairs,
And in his shepherd's calling he was prompt
And watchful more than ordinary men.
Hence had he learned the meaning of all winds,
Of blasts of every tone; and oftentimes,
When others heeded not, He heard the South   50
Make subterraneous music, like the noise
Of bagpipers on distant Highland hills.
The Shepherd, at such warning, of his flock
Bethought him, and he to himself would say,
"The winds are now devising work for me!"
And, truly, at all times, the storm, that drives
The traveller to a shelter, summoned him
Up to the mountains: he had been alone
Amid the heart of many thousand mists,
That came to him, and left him, on the heights.   60
So lived he till his eightieth year was past.
And grossly that man errs, who should suppose
That the green valleys, and the streams and
          rocks,
Were things indifferent to the Shepherd's thoughts.
Fields, where with cheerful spirits he had breathed
The common air; hills, which with vigorous step
He had so often climbed; which had impressed
So many incidents upon his mind
Of hardship, skill or courage, joy or fear;
Which, like a book, preserved the memory   70
Of the dumb animals, whom he had saved,
Had fed or sheltered, linking to such acts
The certainty of honourable gain;
Those fields, those hills—what could they less? had
          laid
Strong hold on his affections, were to him
A pleasurable feeling of blind love,
The pleasure which there is in life itself.

His days had not been passed in singleness.
His Helpmate was a comely matron, old—
Though younger than himself full twenty years.   80
She was a woman of a stirring life,
Whose heart was in her house: two wheels she had
Of antique form; this large, for spinning wool;
That small, for flax; and if one wheel had rest,
It was because the other was at work.
The Pair had but one inmate in their house,
An only Child, who had been born to them
When Michael, telling o'er his years, began
To deem that he was old,—in shepherd's phrase,
With one foot in the grave. This only Son,   90
With two brave sheep-dogs tried in many a storm,
The one of an inestimable worth,
Made all their household. I may truly say,
That they were as a proverb in the vale
For endless industry. When day was gone,
And from their occupations out of doors
The Son and Father were come home, even then,
Their labour did not cease; unless when all
Turned to the cleanly supper-board, and there,
Each with a mess of pottage and skimmed milk,   100
Sat round the basket piled with oaten cakes,
And their plain home-made cheese. Yet when the meal
Was ended, Luke (for so the Son was named)
And his old Father both betook themselves
To such convenient work as might employ
Their hands by the fire-side; perhaps to card
Wool for the Housewife's spindle, or repair
Some injury done to sickle, flail, or scythe,
Or other implement of house or field.

Down from the ceiling, by the chimney's edge,   110
That in our ancient uncouth country style
With huge and black projection overbrowed
Large space beneath, as duly as the light
Of day grew dim the Housewife hung a lamp;
An aged utensil, which had performed
Service beyond all others of its kind.
Early at evening did it burn—and late,
Surviving comrade of uncounted hours,
Which, going by from year to year, had found,
And left the couple neither gay perhaps   120
Nor cheerful, yet with objects and with hopes,
Living a life of eager industry.
And now, when Luke had reached his eighteenth year,
There by the light of this old lamp they sate,
Father and Son, while far into the night
The Housewife plied her own peculiar work,
Making the cottage through the silent hours
Murmur as with the sound of summer flies.
This light was famous in its neighbourhood,
And was a public symbol of the life   130

That thrifty Pair had lived, For, as it chanced,
Their cottage on a plot of rising ground
Stood single, with large prospect, north and south,
High into Easedale, up to Dunmail-Raise,
And westward to the village near the lake;
And from this constant light, so regular,
And so far seen, the House itself, by all
Who dwelt within the limits of the vale,
Both old and young, was named THE EVENING
   STAR.

Thus living on through such a length of years,   140
The Shepherd, if he loved himself, must needs
Have loved his Helpmate; but to Michael's heart
This son of his old age was yet more dear—
Less from instinctive tenderness, the same
Fond spirit that blindly works in the blood of all—
Than that a child, more than all other gifts
That earth can offer to declining man,
Brings hope with it, and forward-looking thoughts,
And stirrings of inquietude, when they
By tendency of nature needs must fail.   150
Exceeding was the love he bare to him,
His heart and his heart's joy! For often-times
Old Michael, while he was a babe in arms,
Had done him female service, not alone
For pastime and delight, as is the use
Of fathers, but with patient mind enforced
To acts of tenderness; and he had rocked
His cradle, as with a woman's gentle hand.

And in a later time, ere yet the Boy
Had put on boy's attire, did Michael love,   160
Albeit of a stern unbending mind,
To have the Young-one in his sight, when he
Wrought in the field, or on his shepherd's stool
Sate with a fettered sheep before him stretched
Under the large old oak, that near his door
Stood single, and, from matchless depth of shade,
Chosen for the Shearer's covert from the sun,
Thence in our rustic dialect was called
The CLIPPING TREE,* a name which yet it bears.
There, while they two were sitting in the shade,   170
With others round them, earnest all and blithe,
Would Michael exercise his heart with looks
Of fond correction and reproof bestowed
Upon the Child, if he disturbed the sheep
By catching at their legs, or with his shouts
Scared them, while they lay still beneath the shears.

And when by Heaven's good grace the boy grew up
A healthy Lad, and carried in his cheek

* Clipping is the word used in the North of England for
shearing.

Two steady roses that were five years old;
Then Michael from a winter coppice cut   180
With his own hand a sapling, which he hooped
With iron, making it throughout in all
Due requisites a perfect shepherd's staff,
And gave it to the Boy; wherewith equipt
He as a watchman oftentimes was placed
At gate or gap, to stem or turn the flock;
And, to his office prematurely called,
There stood the urchin, as you will divine,
Something between a hindrance and a help;
And for this cause not always, I believe,   190
Receiving from his Father hire of praise;
Though nought was left undone which staff, or voice,
Or looks, or threatening gestures, could perform.

But soon as Luke, full ten years old, could stand
Against the mountain blasts; and to the heights,
Not fearing toil, nor length of weary ways,
He with his Father daily went, and they
Were as companions, why should I relate
That objects which the Shepherd loved before
Were dearer now? that from the Boy there came   200
Feelings and emanations—things which were
Light to the sun and music to the wind;
And that the old Man's heart seemed born again?

Thus in his Father's sight the Boy grew up:
And now, when he had reached his eighteenth year,
He was his comfort and his daily hope.

While in this sort the simple household lived
From day to day, to Michael's ear there came
Distressful tidings. Long before the time
Of which I speak, the Shepherd had been bound   210
In surety for his brother's son, a man
Of an industrious life, and ample means;
But unforeseen misfortunes suddenly
Had prest upon him; and old Michael now
Was summoned to discharge the forfeiture,
A grievous penalty, but little less
Than half his substance. This unlooked-for claim,
At the first hearing, for a moment took
More hope out of his life than he supposed
That any old man ever could have lost.   220
As soon as he had armed himself with strength
To look his trouble in the face, it seemed
The Shepherd's sole resource to sell at once
A portion of his patrimonial fields.
Such was his first resolve; he thought again,
And his heart failed him. "Isabel," said he,
Two evenings after he had heard the news,
"I have been toiling more than seventy years,
And in the open sunshine of God's love

Have we all lived; yet if these fields of ours   230
Should pass into a stranger's hand, I think
That I could not lie quiet in my grave.
Our lot is a hard lot; the sun itself
Has scarcely been more diligent than I;
And I have lived to be a fool at last
To my own family. An evil man
That was, and made an evil choice, if he
Were false to us; and, if he were not false,
There are ten thousand to whom loss like this
Had been no sorrow. I forgive him;—but
'Twere better to be dumb than to talk thus.   240

"When I began, my purpose was to speak
Of remedies and of a cheerful hope.
Our Luke shall leave us, Isabel; the land
Shall not go from us, and it shall be free;
He shall possess it, free as is the wind
That passes over it. We have, thou know'st,
Another kinsman—he will be our friend
In this distress. He is a prosperous man,
Thriving in trade—and Luke to him shall go,   250
And with his kinsman's help and his own thrift
He quickly will repair this loss, and then
He may return to us. If here he stay,
What can be done? Where every one is poor,
What can be gained?"

        At this the old Man paused,
And Isabel sat silent, for her mind
Was busy, looking back into past times.
There's Richard Bateman, thought she to herself,
He was a parish-boy—at the church-door
They made a gathering for him, shillings, pence,   260
And halfpennies, wherewith the neighbours bought
A basket, which they filled with pedlar's wares;
And, with this basket on his arm, the lad
Went up to London, found a master there,
Who, out of many, chose the trusty boy
To go and overlook his merchandise
Beyond the seas; where he grew wondrous rich,
And left estates and monies to the poor,
And, at his birth-place, built a chapel floored
With marble, which he sent from foreign lands.   270
These thoughts, and many others of like sort,
Passed quickly through the mind of Isabel,
And her face brightened. The old Man was glad,
And thus resumed:—"Well, Isabel! this scheme
These two days has been meat and drink to me.
Far more than we have lost is left us yet.
—We have enough—I wish indeed that I
Were younger;—but this hope is a good hope.
Make ready Luke's best garments, of the best
Buy for him more, and let us send him forth   280

To-morrow, or the next day, or to-night:
—If he *could* go, the Boy should go to-night."

    Here Michael ceased, and to the fields went forth
With a light heart. The Housewife for five days
Was restless morn and night, and all day long
Wrought on with her best fingers to prepare
Things needful for the journey of her son.
But Isabel was glad when Sunday came
To stop her in her work: for, when she lay
By Michael's side, she through the last two nights 290
Heard him, how he was troubled in his sleep:
And when they rose at morning she could see
That all his hopes were gone. That day at noon
She said to Luke, while they two by themselves
Were sitting at the door, "Thou must not go:
We have no other Child but thee to lose,
None to remember—do not go away,
For if thou leave thy Father he will die."
The Youth made answer with a jocund voice;
And Isabel, when she had told her fears,   300
Recovered heart. That evening her best fare
Did she bring forth, and all together sat
Like happy people round a Christmas fire.

    With daylight Isabel resumed her work;
And all the ensuing week the house appeared
As cheerful as a grove in Spring: at length
The expected letter from their kinsman came,
With kind assurances that he would do
His utmost for the welfare of the Boy;
To which, requests were added, that forthwith   310
He might be sent to him. Ten times or more
The letter was read over; Isabel
Went forth to show it to the neighbours round;
Nor was there at that time on English land
A prouder heart than Luke's. When Isabel
Had to her house returned, the old Man said,
"He shall depart to-morrow." To this word
The Housewife answered, talking much of things
Which, if at such short notice he should go,
Would surely be forgotten. But at length   320
She gave consent, and Michael was at ease.

    Near the tumultuous brook of Green-head Ghyll,
In that deep valley, Michael had designed
To build a Sheep-fold;* and, before he heard

* It may be proper to inform some readers, that a sheep-fold
in these mountains is an unroofed building of stone walls, with
different divisions. It is generally placed by the side of a brook,
for the convenience of washing the sheep; but it is also useful as
a shelter for them, and as a place to drive them into, to enable
the shepherds conveniently to single out one or more for any
particular purpose.

The tidings of his melancholy loss,
For this same purpose he had gathered up
A heap of stones, which by the streamlet's edge
Lay thrown together, ready for the work.
With Luke that evening thitherward he walked:
And soon as they had reached the place he stopped,
And thus the old Man spake to him:—"My son,   331
To-morrow thou wilt leave me: with full heart
I look upon thee, for thou art the same
That wert a promise to me ere thy birth,
And all thy life hast been my daily joy.
I will relate to thee some little part
Of our two histories; 'twill do thee good
When thou art from me, even if I should touch
On things thou canst not know of.——After thou
First cam'st into the world—as oft befalls   340
To new-born infants—thou didst sleep away
Two days, and blessings from thy Father's tongue
Then fell upon thee. Day by day passed on,
And still I loved thee with increasing love.
Never to living ear came sweeter sounds
Than when I heard thee by our own fire-side
First uttering, without words, a natural tune;
While thou, a feeding babe, didst in thy joy
Sing at thy Mother's breast. Month followed month,
And in the open fields my life was passed   350
And on the mountains; else I think that thou
Hadst been brought up upon thy Father's knees.
But we are playmates, Luke: among these hills,
As well thou knowest, in us the old and young
Have played together, nor with me didst thou
Lack any pleasure which a boy can know."
Luke had a manly heart; but at these words
He sobbed aloud. The old Man grasped his hand,
And said, "Nay, do not take it so—I see
That these are things of which I need not speak.   360
—Even to the utmost I have been to thee
A kind and a good Father: and herein
I but repay a gift which I myself
Received at others' hands; for, though now old
Beyond the common life of man, I still
Remember them who loved me in my youth.
Both of them sleep together: here they lived,
As all their Forefathers had done; and when
At length their time was come, they were not loth
To give their bodies to the family mould.   370
I wished that thou should'st live the life they lived,
But 'tis a long time to look back, my Son,
And see so little gain from threescore years.
These fields were burthened when they came to me;
Till I was forty years of age, not more
Than half of my inheritance was mine.
I toiled and toiled; God blessed me in my work,
And till these three weeks past the land was free.

—It looks as if it never could endure
Another Master. Heaven forgive me, Luke,   380
If I judge ill for thee, but it seems good
That thou shouldst go."
                      At this the old Man paused;
Then, pointing to the stones near which they stood,
Thus, after a short silence, he resumed:
"This was a work for us; and now, my Son,
It is a work for me. But, lay one stone—
Here, lay it for me, Luke, with thine own hands.
Nay, Boy, be of good hope;—we both may live
To see a better day. At eighty-four
I still am strong and hale;—do thou thy part;   390
I will do mine.—I will begin again
With many tasks that were resigned to thee:
Up to the heights, and in among the storms,
Will I without thee go again, and do
All works which I was wont to do alone,
Before I knew thy face.—Heaven bless thee, Boy!
Thy heart these two weeks has been beating fast
With many hopes; it should be so—yes—yes—
I knew that thou couldst never have a wish
To leave me, Luke: thou hast been bound to me   400
Only by links of love: when thou art gone,
What will be left to us!—But I forget
My purposes. Lay now the corner-stone,
As I requested; and hereafter, Luke,
When thou art gone away, should evil men
Be thy companions, think of me, my Son,
And of this moment; hither turn thy thoughts,
And God will strengthen thee: amid all fear
And all temptation, Luke, I pray that thou
May'st bear in mind the life thy Fathers lived,   410
Who, being innocent, did for that cause
Bestir them in good deeds. Now, fare thee well—
When thou return'st thou in this place wilt see
A work which is not here: a covenant
'Twill be between us; but, whatever fate
Befall thee, I shall love thee to the last,
And bear thy memory with me to the grave."

   The Shepherd ended here; and Luke stooped down,
And, as his Father had requested, laid
The first stone of the Sheep-fold. At the sight   420
The old Man's grief broke from him; to his heart
He pressed his Son, he kissèd him and wept;
And to the house together they returned.
—Hushed was that House in peace, or seeming peace,
Ere the night fell:—with morrow's dawn the Boy
Began his journey, and when he had reached
The public way, he put on a bold face;
And all the neighbours, as he passed their doors,
Came forth with wishes and with farewell prayers,
That followed him till he was out of sight.   430

A good report did from their Kinsman come,
Of Luke and his well-doing: and the Boy
Wrote loving letters, full of wondrous news,
Which, as the Housewife phrased it, were throughout
"The prettiest letters that were ever seen."
Both parents read them with rejoicing hearts.
So, many months passed on: and once again
The Shepherd went about his daily work
With confident and cheerful thoughts; and now
Sometimes when he could find a leisure hour   440
He to that valley took his way, and there
Wrought at the Sheep-fold. Meantime Luke
     began
To slacken in his duty; and, at length,
He in the dissolute city gave himself
To evil courses: ignominy and shame
Fell on him, so that he was driven at last
To seek a hiding-place beyond the seas.

There is a comfort in the strength of love;
'Twill make a thing endurable, which else
Would overset the brain, or break the heart: 450
I have conversed with more than one who well
Remember the old Man, and what he was
Years after he had heard this heavy news.
His bodily frame had been from youth to age
Of an unusual strength. Among the rocks
He went, and still looked up to sun and cloud,
And listened to the wind; and, as before,
Performed all kinds of labour for his sheep,
And for the land, his small inheritance.
And to that hollow dell from time to time   460
Did he repair, to build the Fold of which
His flock had need. 'Tis not forgotten yet
The pity which was then in every heart
For the old Man—and 'tis believed by all
That many and many a day he thither went,
And never lifted up a single stone.

There, by the Sheep-fold, sometimes was he seen
Sitting alone, or with his faithful Dog,
Then old, beside him, lying at his feet.
The length of full seven years, from time to time   470
He at the building of this Sheep-fold wrought,
And left the work unfinished when he died.
Three years, or little more, did Isabel
Survive her Husband: at her death the estate
Was sold, and went into a stranger's hand.
The Cottage which was named the EVENING
     STAR
Is gone—the ploughshare has been through the
     ground
On which it stood; great changes have been wrought
In all the neighbourhood:—yet the oak is left

That grew beside their door; and the remains   480
Of the unfinished Sheep-fold may be seen
Beside the boisterous brook of Green-head Ghyll.

[1800]   [1800]

"Tis said, that some have died for love"

'Tis said, that some have died for love:
And here and there a church-yard grave is found
In the cold north's unhallowed ground,
Because the wretched man himself had slain,
His love was such a grievous pain.
And there is one whom I five years have known;
He dwells alone
Upon Helvellyn's side:
He loved—the pretty Barbara died;
And thus he makes his moan: 10
Three years had Barbara in her grave been laid
When thus his moan he made:

"Oh, move, thou Cottage, from behind that oak!
Or let the aged tree uprooted lie,
That in some other way yon smoke
May mount into the sky!
The clouds pass on; they from the heavens depart:
I look—the sky is empty space;
I know not what I trace;
But when I cease to look, my hand is on my heart.   20

"O! what a weight is in these shades! Ye leaves,
That murmur once so dear, when will it cease?
Your sound my heart of rest bereaves,
It robs my heart of peace.
Thou Thrush, that singest loud—and loud and free,
Into yon row of willows flit,
Upon that alder sit;
Or sing another song, or choose another tree.

"Roll back, sweet Rill! back to thy mountain-
     bounds,
And there for ever be thy waters chained!   30
For thou dost haunt the air with sounds
That cannot be sustained;
If still beneath that pine-tree's ragged bough
Headlong yon waterfall must come,
Oh let it then be dumb!
Be anything, sweet Rill, but that which thou art now.

"Thou Eglantine, so bright with sunny showers,
Proud as a rainbow spanning half the vale,
Thou one fair shrub, oh! shed thy flowers,
And stir not in the gale.   40

For thus to see thee nodding in the air,
To see thy arch thus stretch and bend,
Thus rise and thus descend,—
Disturbs me till the sight is more than I can bear."

The Man who makes this feverish complaint
Is one of giant stature, who could dance
Equipped from head to foot in iron mail.
Ah gentle Love! if ever thought was thine
To store up kindred hours for me, thy face
Turn from me, gentle Love! nor let me walk   50
Within the sound of Emma's [1] voice, nor know
Such happiness as I have known to-day.

[1800]   [1800]

"I travelled among unknown men"

I TRAVELLED among unknown men,
    In lands beyond the sea;
Nor, England! did I know till then
    What love I bore to thee.

'Tis past, that melancholy dream!
    Nor will I quit thy shore
A second time; for still I seem
    To love thee more and more.

Among thy mountains did I feel
    The joy of my desire;   10
And she I cherished turned her wheel
    Beside an English fire.

Thy mornings showed, thy nights concealed,
    The bowers where Lucy played;
And thine too is the last green field
    That Lucy's eyes surveyed.

[1801]   [1807]

THE AFFLICTION OF MARGARET

I

WHERE art thou, my beloved Son,
Where art thou, worse to me than dead?
Oh find me, prosperous or undone!
Or, if the grave be now thy bed,
Why am I ignorant of the same
That I may rest; and neither blame
Nor sorrow may attend thy name?

---

[1] Wordsworth frequently uses this name, or "Emmeline,"
to refer to his sister Dorothy. See, for example, *To a Butterfly* [I],
p. 256.

II

Seven years, alas! to have received
No tidings of an only child;
To have despaired, have hoped, believed,   10
And been for evermore beguiled;
Sometimes with thoughts of very bliss!
I catch at them, and then I miss;
Was ever darkness like to this?

III

He was among the prime in worth,
An object beauteous to behold;
Well born, well bred; I sent him forth
Ingenuous, innocent, and bold:
If things ensued that wanted grace,
As hath been said, they were not base;   20
And never blush was on my face.

IV

Ah! little doth the young-one dream,
When full of play and childish cares,
What power is in his wildest scream,
Heard by his mother unawares!
He knows it not, he cannot guess:
Years to a mother bring distress;
But do not make her love the less.

V

Neglect me! no, I suffered long
From that ill thought; and, being blind,   30
Said, "Pride shall help me in my wrong:
Kind mother have I been, as kind
As ever breathed:" and that is true;
I've wet my path with tears like dew,
Weeping for him when no one knew.

VI

My Son, if thou be humbled, poor,
Hopeless of honour and of gain,
Oh! do not dread thy mother's door;
Think not of me with grief and pain:
I now can see with better eyes;   40
And worldly grandeur I despise,
And fortune with her gifts and lies.

VII

Alas! the fowls of heaven have wings,
And blasts of heaven will aid their flight;
They mount—how short a voyage brings
The wanderers back to their delight!
Chains tie us down by land and sea;
And wishes, vain as mine, may be
All that is left to comfort thee.

VIII

Perhaps some dungeon hears thee groan,   50
Maimed, mangled by inhuman men;
Or thou upon a desert thrown
Inheritest the lion's den;
Or hast been summoned to the deep,
Thou, thou and all thy mates, to keep
An incommunicable sleep.

IX

I look for ghosts; but none will force
Their way to me: 'tis falsely said
That there was ever intercourse
Between the living and the dead;   60
For, surely, then I should have sight
Of him I wait for day and night,
With love and longings infinite.

X

My apprehensions come in crowds;
I dread the rustling of the grass;
The very shadows of the clouds
Have power to shake me as they pass:
I question things and do not find
One that will answer to my mind;
And all the world appears unkind.   70

XI

Beyond participation lie
My troubles, and beyond relief:
If any chance to heave a sigh,
They pity me, and not my grief.
Then come to me, my Son, or send
Some tidings that my woes may end;
I have no other earthly friend!

[1801]   [1807]

TO A YOUNG LADY

WHO HAD BEEN REPROACHED FOR TAKING LONG WALKS IN THE COUNTRY

DEAR Child of Nature, let them rail!
—There is a nest in a green dale,
A harbour and a hold;
Where thou, a Wife and Friend, shalt see
Thy own heart-stirring days, and be
A light to young and old.

There, healthy as a shepherd boy,
And treading among flowers of joy
Which at no season fade,

Thou, while thy babes around thee cling,   10
Shalt show us how divine a thing
A Woman may be made.

Thy thoughts and feelings shall not die,
Nor leave thee, when grey hairs are nigh,
A melancholy slave;
But an old age serene and bright,
And lovely as a Lapland night,
Shall lead thee to thy grave.

[1801?]   [1802]

———

ALICE FELL

"Mr. Graham said he wished Wm. had been with him the other day—he was riding in a post-chaise and he heard a strange cry that he could not understand, the sound continued, and he called to the chaise driver to stop. It was a little girl that was crying as if her heart would burst. She had got up behind the chaise, and her cloak had been caught by the wheel, and was jammed in, and it hung there. She was crying after it. Poor thing. Mr. Graham took her into the chaise, and the cloak was released from the wheel, but the child's misery did not cease, for her cloak was torn to rags; it had been a miserable cloak before, but she had no other, and it was the greatest sorrow that could befal her. Her name was Alice Fell. She had no parents, and belonged to the next Town. At the next Town, Mr. G. left money with some respectable people in the town, to buy her a new cloak." [Dorothy Wordsworth, Journals, February 16, 1802]

———

ALICE FELL;

OR, POVERTY

THE post-boy drove with fierce career,
For threatening clouds the moon had drowned;
When, as we hurried on, my ear
Was smitten with a startling sound.

As if the wind blew many ways,
I heard the sound,—and more and more;
It seemed to follow with the chaise,
And still I heard it as before.

At length I to the boy called out;
He stopped his horses at the word,   10
But neither cry, nor voice, nor shout,
Nor aught else like it, could be heard.

The boy then smacked his whip, and fast
The horses scampered through the rain;
But, hearing soon upon the blast
They cry, I bade him halt again.

Forthwith alighting on the ground,
"Whence comes," said I, "this piteous moan?"
And there a little Girl I found,
Sitting behind the chaise, alone.　　　　　20

"My cloak!" no other word she spake,
But loud and bitterly she wept,
As if her innocent heart would break;
And down from off her seat she leapt.

"What ails you, child?"—she sobbed, "Look here!"
I saw it in the wheel entangled,
A weather-beaten rag as e'er
From any garden scare-crow dangled.

There, twisted between nave and spoke,
It hung, nor could at once be freed;　　　　30
But our joint pains unloosed the cloak,
A miserable rag indeed!

"And whither are you going, child,
To-night along these lonesome ways?"
"To Durham," answered she, half wild—
"Then come with me into the chaise."

Insensible to all relief
Sat the poor girl, and forth did send
Sob after sob, as if her grief
Could never, never have an end.　　　　　40

"My child, in Durham do you dwell?"
She checked herself in her distress,
And said, "My name is Alice Fell;
I'm fatherless and motherless.

"And I to Durham, Sir, belong."
Again, as if the thought would choke
Her very heart, her grief grew strong;
And all was for her tattered cloak!

The chaise drove on; our journey's end
Was nigh; and, sitting by my side,　　　　50
As if she had lost her only friend
She wept, nor would be pacified.

Up to the tavern-door we post;
Of Alice and her grief I told;
And I gave money to the host,
To buy a new cloak for the old.

"And let it be of duffil grey,
As warm a cloak as man can sell!"
Proud creature was she the next day,
The little orphan, Alice Fell!　　　　　60

[1802]　　　　　　　　　　　　　　[1807]

TO A BUTTERFLY [I]

STAY near me—do not take thy flight!
A little longer stay in sight!
Much converse do I find in thee,
Historian of my infancy!
Float near me; do not yet depart!
Dead times revive in thee:
Thou bring'st, gay creature as thou art!
A solemn image to my heart,
My father's family!

Oh! pleasant, pleasant were the days,　　　10
The time, when, in our childish plays,
My sister Emmeline and I
Together chased the butterfly!
A very hunter did I rush
Upon the prey:—with leaps and springs
I followed on from brake to bush;
But she, God love her! feared to brush
The dust from off its wings.

[1802]　　　　　　　　　　　　　　[1807]

TO THE CUCKOO

O BLITHE New-comer! I have heard,
I hear thee and rejoice.
O Cuckoo! shall I call thee Bird,
Or but a wandering Voice?

While I am lying on the grass
Thy twofold shout I hear,
From hill to hill it seems to pass
At once far off, and near.

Though babbling only to the Vale,
Of sunshine and of flowers,　　　　　　10
Thou bringest unto me a tale
Of visionary hours.

Thrice welcome, darling of the Spring!
Even yet thou art to me
No bird, but an invisible thing,
A voice, a mystery;

The same whom in my schoolboy days
I listened to; that Cry
Which made me look a thousand ways
In bush, and tree, and sky.　　　　　　20

To seek thee did I often rove
Through woods and on the green;
And thou wert still a hope, a love;
Still longed for, never seen.

And I can listen to thee yet;
Can lie upon the plain
And listen, till I do beget
That golden time again.

O blessèd Bird! the earth we pace
Again appears to be   30
An unsubstantial, faery place;
That is fit home for Thee!

[1802]   [1807]

THE RAINBOW

In an earlier manuscript version this poem is entitled "Extempore," and the next to last line reads "I should wish that all my days may be." In her journal for March 26, 1802, Dorothy Wordsworth writes: "While I was getting into bed, he wrote The Rainbow!" See also the note on the following poem.

THE RAINBOW

My heart leaps up when I behold
    A rainbow in the sky:
So was it when my life began;
So is it now I am a man;
So be it when I shall grow old,
    Or let me die!
The Child is father of the Man;
And I could wish my days to be
Bound each to each by natural piety.

[1802]   [1807]

ODE: INTIMATIONS OF IMMORTALITY
This poem, though not completed until 1804, is included here because according to Dorothy Wordsworth's journal her brother wrote its first four stanzas at breakfast on March 27, 1802, the morning immediately after he had written The Rainbow. These first four stanzas, at least, have obvious connections with the poems of the spring of 1802, and with Coleridge's almost simultaneous composition of the first version of Dejection: An Ode.

ODE

INTIMATIONS OF IMMORTALITY
FROM RECOLLECTIONS OF
EARLY CHILDHOOD

The Child is father of the Man;
And I could wish my days to be
Bound each to each by natural piety.

I

THERE was a time when meadow, grove, and stream,
The earth, and every common sight,
        To me did seem
        Apparelled in celestial light,
The glory and the freshness of a dream.
It is not now as it hath been of yore;—
        Turn wheresoe'er I may,
        By night or day,
The things which I have seen I now can see no more.

II

        The Rainbow comes and goes,   10
        And lovely is the Rose,
        The Moon doth with delight
Look round her when the heavens are bare;
        Waters on a starry night
        Are beautiful and fair;
    The sunshine is a glorious birth;
    But yet I know, where'er I go,
That there hath past away a glory from the earth.

III

Now, while the birds thus sing a joyous song,
    And while the young lambs bound   20
        As to the tabor's sound,
To me alone there came a thought of grief:
A timely utterance gave that thought relief,
        And I again am strong:
The cataracts blow their trumpets from the steep;
No more shall grief of mine the season wrong;
I hear the Echoes through the mountains throng,
The Winds come to me from the fields of sleep,

And all the earth is gay;
Land and sea 30
Give themselves up to jollity,
And with the heart of May
Doth every Beast keep holiday;—
Thou Child of Joy,
Shout round me, let me hear thy shouts, thou happy
Shepherd-boy!

IV

Ye blessèd Creatures, I have heard the call
Ye to each other make; I see
The heavens laugh with you in your jubilee;
My heart is at your festival,
My head hath its coronal,
The fulness of your bliss, I feel—I feel it all. 40
Oh evil day! if I were sullen
While Earth herself is adorning,
This sweet May-morning,
And the Children are culling
On every side,
In a thousand valleys far and wide,
Fresh flowers; while the sun shines warm,
And the Babe leaps up on his Mother's arm:—
I hear, I hear, with joy I hear! 50
—But there's a Tree, of many, one,
A single Field which I have looked upon,
Both of them speak of something that is gone:
The Pansy at my feet
Doth the same tale repeat:
Whither is fled the visionary gleam?
Where is it now, the glory and the dream?

V

Our birth is but a sleep and a forgetting:
The Soul that rises with us, our life's Star,
Hath had elsewhere its setting, 60
And cometh from afar:
Not in entire forgetfulness,
And not in utter nakedness,
But trailing clouds of glory do we come
From God, who is our home:
Heaven lies about us in our infancy!
Shades of the prison-house begin to close
Upon the growing Boy,
But He
Beholds the light, and whence it flows, 70
He sees it in his joy;
The Youth, who daily farther from the east
Must travel, still is Nature's Priest,
And by the vision splendid
Is on his way attended;
At length the Man perceives it die away,
And fade into the light of common day.

VI

Earth fills her lap with pleasures of her own;
Yearnings she hath in her own natural kind,
And, even with something of a Mother's mind, 80
And no unworthy aim,
The homely Nurse doth all she can
To make her Foster-child, her Inmate Man,
Forget the glories he hath known,
And that imperial palace whence he came.

VII

Behold the Child [1] among his new-born blisses,
A six years' Darling of a pigmy size!
See, where 'mid work of his own hand he lies,
Fretted by sallies of his mother's kisses,
With light upon him from his father's eyes! 90
See, at his feet, some little plan or chart,
Some fragment from his dream of human life,
Shaped by himself with newly-learned art;
A wedding or a festival,
A mourning or a funeral;
And this hath now his heart,
And unto this he frames his song:
Then will he fit his tongue
To dialogues of business, love, or strife;
But it will not be long 100
Ere this be thrown aside,
And with new joy and pride
The little Actor cons another part;
Filling from time to time his "humorous stage"
With all the Persons, down to palsied Age,
That Life brings with her in her equipage;
As if his whole vocation
Were endless imitation.

VIII

Thou, whose exterior semblance doth belie
Thy Soul's immensity; 110
Thou best Philosopher, who yet dost keep
Thy heritage, thou Eye among the blind,
That, deaf and silent, read'st the eternal deep,
Haunted for every by the eternal mind,—
Mighty Prophet! Seer blest!
On whom those truths do rest,
Which we are toiling all our lives to find,
In darkness lost, the darkness of the grave;
Thou, over whom thy Immortality
Broods like the Day, a Master o'er a Slave, 120
A Presence which is not to be put by;
Thou little Child, yet glorious in the might
Of heaven-born freedom on thy being's height,

---

[1] Perhaps referring to Coleridge's son Hartley. See *To H. C.*,
p. 272.

Why with such earnest pains dost thou provoke
The years to bring the inevitable yoke,
Thus blindly with thy blessedness at strife?
Full soon thy Soul shall have her earthly freight,
And custom lie upon thee with a weight,
Heavy as frost, and deep almost as life!

IX

O joy! that in our embers   130
Is something that doth live,
That nature yet remembers
What was so fugitive!
The thought of our past years in me doth breed
Perpetual benediction: not indeed
For that which is most worthy to be blest;
Delight and liberty, the simple creed
Of Childhood, whether busy or at rest,
With new-fledged hope still fluttering in his breast:—
Not for these I raise   140
The song of thanks and praise;
But for those obstinate questionings
Of sense and outward things,
Fallings from us, vanishings;
Blank misgivings of a Creature
Moving about in worlds not realised,
High instincts before which our mortal Nature
Did tremble like a guilty Thing surprised:[2]
But for those first affections,
Those shadowy recollections,   150
Which, be they what they may,
Are yet the fountain light of all our day,
Are yet a master light of all our seeing;
Uphold us, cherish, and have power to make
Our noisy years seem moments in the being
Of the eternal Silence: truths that wake,
To perish never;
Which neither listlessness, nor mad endeavour,
Nor Man nor Boy,
Nor all that is at enmity with joy,   160
Can utterly abolish or destroy!
Hence in a season of calm weather
Though inland far we be,
Our Souls have sight of that immortal sea
Which brought us hither,
Can in a moment travel thither,
And see the Children sport upon the shore,
And hear the mighty waters rolling evermore.

X

Then sing, ye Birds, sing, sing a joyous song!
And let the young Lambs bound   170
As to the tabor's sound!

We in thought will join your throng,
Ye that pipe and ye that play,
Ye that through your hearts to-day
Feel the gladness of the May!
What though the radiance which was once so bright
Be now for ever taken from my sight,
Though nothing can bring back the hour
Of splendour in the grass, of glory in the flower;
We will grieve not, rather find   180
Strength in what remains behind;
In the primal sympathy
Which having been must ever be;
In the soothing thoughts that spring
Out of human suffering;
In the faith that looks through death,
In years that bring the philosophic mind.

XI

And O, ye Fountains, Meadows, Hills, and Groves,
Forebode not any severing of our loves!
Yet in my heart of hearts I feel your might;   190
I only have relinquished one delight
To live beneath your more habitual sway.
I love the Brooks which down their channels fret,
Even more than when I tripped lightly as they;
The innocent brightness of a new-born Day
Is lovely yet;
The Clouds that gather round the setting sun
Do take a sober colouring from an eye
That hath kept watch o'er man's mortality;
Another race hath been, and other palms are won. 200
Thanks to the human heart by which we live,
Thanks to its tenderness, its joys, and fears,
To me the meanest flower that blows can give
Thoughts that do often lie too deep for tears.

[1802–1804]   [1807]

---

[2] *Hamlet*, I, i, 48.

"THESE CHAIRS..."

This fragment and the one that follows it appear in a manuscript (MS. M) containing many of the poems that were published in 1807. In her journal for April 29, 1802, Dorothy Wordsworth tells how she and her brother went to John's Grove and there "lay in the trench under the fence—he with his eyes shut, and listening to the waterfalls and the Birds.... William heard me breathing and rustling now and then, but we both lay still, and unseen by one another; he thought that it would be as sweet thus to lie so in the grave, to hear the peaceful sounds of the earth, and just to know that our dear friends were near."

"I HAVE THOUGHTS..."

In the manuscript the second poem immediately follows, headed Half an hour afterwards. *However, Dorothy Wordsworth's reference to it in her journal for April 22, 1802, as "the poem: 'I have thoughts that are fed by the sun'" suggests that Wordsworth may have considered them as separate poems.*

"These chairs . . ."

THESE Chairs they have no words to utter,
No fire is in the grate to stir or flutter,
The ceiling and floor are mute as a stone,
My chamber is hush'd and still,
  And I am alone,
  Happy and alone.

Oh who would be afraid of life,
The passion the sorrow and the strife,
  When he may be   10
  Shelter'd so easily?
May lie in peace on his bed
Happy as they who are dead.

[1802]   [1947]

"I have thoughts . . ."

I HAVE thoughts that are fed by the sun.
  The things which I see
  Are welcome to me,
  Welcome every one:

I do not wish to lie
  Dead, dead,
Dead without any company;
  Here alone on my bed,
With thoughts that are fed by the Sun,
And hopes that are welcome every one, 10
  Happy am I.

O Life, there is about thee
A deep delicious peace,
I would not be without thee,
  Stay, oh stay!

Yet be thou ever as now,
Sweetness and breath with the quiet of death,
Be but thou ever as now,
    Peace, peace, peace.

[1802]   [1947]

THE GLOW-WORM

AMONG all lovely things my Love had been;
Had noted well the stars, all flowers that grew
About her home; but she had never seen
A Glow-worm, never one, and this I knew.

While riding near her home one stormy night
A single Glow-worm did I chance to espy;
I gave a fervent welcome to the sight,
And from my Horse I leapt; great joy had I.

Upon a leaf the Glow-worm did I lay,
To bear it with me through the stormy night: 10
And, as before, it shone without dismay;
Albeit putting forth a fainter light.

When to the Dwelling of my Love I came,
I went into the Orchard quietly;
And left the Glow-worm, blessing it by name,
 Laid safely by itself, beneath a Tree.

The whole next day, I hoped, and hoped with fear;
At night the Glow-worm shone beneath the Tree:
I led my Lucy to the spot, "Look here!"
Oh! joy it was for her, and joy for me! 20

[1802]   [1807]

WRITTEN IN MARCH

WHILE RESTING ON THE BRIDGE
AT THE FOOT OF BROTHER'S WATER

  THE Cock is crowing,
  The stream is flowing,
  The small birds twitter,
  The lake doth glitter,
The green field sleeps in the sun;
  The oldest and youngest
  Are at work with the strongest;
  The cattle are grazing,
  Their heads never raising;
There are forty feeding like one! 10

Like an army defeated
The snow hath retreated,
And now doth fare ill
On the top of the bare hill;
The Ploughboy is whooping—anon—anon:
There's joy in the mountains;
There's life in the fountains;
Small clouds are sailing,
Blue sky prevailing;
The rain is over and gone!   20

[1802]   [1807]

TO A BUTTERFLY [II]

I've watched you now a full half-hour,
Self-poised upon that yellow flower;
And, little Butterfly! indeed
I know not if you sleep or feed.
How motionless!—not frozen seas
More motionless! and then
What joy awaits you, when the breeze
Hath found you out among the trees,
And calls you forth again!

This plot of orchard-ground is ours;   10
My trees they are, my Sister's flowers;
Here rest your wings when they are weary;
Here lodge as in a sanctuary!
Come often to us, fear no wrong;
Sit near us on the bough!
We'll talk of sunshine and of song,
And summer days, when we were young;
Sweet childish days, that were as long
As twenty days are now.

[1802]   [1807]

TO THE SMALL CELANDINE*

Pansies, lilies, kingcups, daisies,
Let them live upon their praises;
Long as there's a sun that sets,
Primroses will have their glory;
Long as there are violets,
They will have a place in story:
There's a flower that shall be mine,
'Tis the little Celandine.

* Common Pilewort.

Eyes of some men travel far
For the finding of a star;   10
Up and down the heavens they go,
Men that keep a mighty rout!
I'm as great as they, I trow,
Since the day I found thee out,
Little Flower—I'll make a stir,
Like a sage astronomer.

Modest, yet withal an Elf
Bold, and lavish of thyself;
Since we needs must first have met
I have seen thee, high and low,   20
Thirty years or more, and yet
'Twas a face I did not know;
Thou hast now, go where I may,
Fifty greetings in a day.

Ere a leaf is on a bush,
In the time before the thrush
Has a thought about her nest,
Thou wilt come with half a call,
Spreading out thy glossy breast
Like a careless Prodigal;   30
Telling tales about the sun,
When we've little warmth, or none.

Poets, vain men in their mood!
Travel with the multitude:
Never heed them; I aver
That they all are wanton wooers;
But the thrifty cottager,
Who stirs little out of doors,
Joys to spy thee near her home;
Spring is coming, Thou art come!   40

Comfort have thou of thy merit,
Kindly, unassuming Spirit!
Careless of thy neighbourhood,
Thou dost show thy pleasant face
On the moor, and in the wood,
In the lane;—there's not a place,
Howsoever mean it be,
But 'tis good enough for thee.

Ill befall the yellow flowers,
Children of the flaring hours!   50
Buttercups, that will be seen,
Whether we will see or no;
Others, too, of lofty mien;
They have done as worldlings do,
Taken praise that should be thine,
Little, humble Celandine.

Prophet of delight and mirth,
Ill-requited upon earth;
Herald of a mighty band,
Of a joyous train ensuing,   60
Serving at my heart's command,
Tasks that are no tasks renewing,
I will sing, as doth behove,
Hymns in praise of what I love!

[1802]   [1807]

TO THE SAME FLOWER

PLEASURES newly found are sweet
When they lie about our feet:
February last, my heart
First at sight of thee was glad;
All unheard of as thou art,
Thou must needs, I think, have had,
Celandine! and long ago,
Praise of which I nothing know.

I have not a doubt but he,
Whosoe'er the man might be,   10
Who the first with pointed rays
(Workman worthy to be sainted)
Set the sign-board in a blaze,
When the rising sun he painted,
Took the fancy from a glance
At thy glittering countenance.

Soon as gentle breezes bring
News of winter's vanishing,
And the children build their bowers,
Sticking 'kerchief-plots of mould   20
All about with full-blown flowers,
Thick as sheep in shepherd's fold!
With the proudest thou art there,
Mantling in the tiny square.

Often have I sighed to measure
By myself a lonely pleasure,
Sighed to think I read a book
Only read, perhaps, by me;
Yet I long could overlook
Thy bright coronet and Thee,   30
And thy arch and wily ways,
And thy store of other praise.

Blithe of heart, from week to week
Thou dost play at hide-and-seek;
While the patient primrose sits
Like a beggar in the cold,

Thou, a flower of wiser wits,
Slip'st into they sheltering hold;
Liveliest of the vernal train
When ye all are out again.   40

Drawn by what peculiar spell,
By what charm of sight or smell,
Does the dim-eyed curious Bee,
Labouring for her waxen cells,
Fondly settle upon Thee
Prized above all buds and bells
Opening daily at thy side,
By the season multiplied?

Thou art not beyond the moon,
But a thing "beneath our shoon:"   50
Let the bold Discoverer thrid
In his bark the polar sea;
Rear who will a pyramid;
Praise it is enough for me,
If there be but three or four
Who will love my little Flower.

[1802]   [1807]

THE SPARROW'S NEST

BEHOLD, within the leafy shade,
    Those bright blue eggs together laid!
    On me the chance-discovered sight
Gleamed like a vision of delight.
I started—seeming to espy
The home and sheltered bed,
The Sparrow's dwelling, which, hard by
My Father's house, in wet or dry
My sister Emmeline and I
    Together visited.   10

She looked at it and seemed to fear it;
Dreading, tho' wishing, to be near it:
Such heart was in her, being then
A little Prattler among men.
The Blessing of my later years
Was with me when a boy:
She gave me eyes, she gave me ears;
And humble cares, and delicate fears;
A heart, the fountain of sweet tears;
    And love, and thought, and joy.   20

[1802]   [1807]

RESOLUTION AND INDEPENDENCE

"This old Man I met a few hundred yards from my cottage; and the account of him is taken from his own mouth. I was in the state of feeling described in the beginning of the poem, while crossing over Barton Fell from Mr. Clarkson's, at the foot of Ullswater, towards Askham. The image of the hare I then observed on the ridge of the Fell." [*Wordsworth to Isabella Fenwick*]

* * * * *

"N.B. When Wm. and I returned from accompanying Jones, we met an old man almost double. He had on a coat, thrown over his shoulders above his waist-coat and coat. Under this he carried a bundle, and had an apron on and a night-cap. His face was interesting. He had dark eyes and a long nose. John, who afterwards met him at Wythburn, took him for a Jew. He was of Scotch parents, but had been born in the army. He had had a wife, and 'a good woman, and it pleased God to bless us with ten children.' All these were dead but one, of whom he had not heard for many years, a sailor. His trade was to gather leeches, but now leeches are scarce, and he had not strength for it. He lived by begging, and was making his way to Carlisle, where he should buy a few godly books to sell. He said leeches were very scarce, partly owing to this dry season, but many years they have been scarce—he supposed it owing to their being much sought after, that they did not breed fast, and were of slow growth. Leeches were formerly 2s. 6d. [per] 100; they are now 30s. He had been hurt in driving a cart, his leg broke, his body driven over, his skull fractured. He felt no pain till he recovered from his first insensibility. It was then late in the evening, when the light was just going away." [*Dorothy Wordsworth*, Journals, Oct. 3, 1800]

RESOLUTION AND INDEPENDENCE

I

THERE was a roaring in the wind all night;
The rain came heavily and fell in floods;
But now the sun is rising calm and bright;
The birds are singing in the distant woods;
Over his own sweet voice the Stock-dove broods;
The Jay makes answer as the Magpie chatters;
And all the air is filled with pleasant noise of waters.

II

All things that love the sun are out of doors;
The sky rejoices in the morning's birth;
The grass is bright with rain-drops;—on the moors
The hare is running races in her mirth;   11
And with her feet she from the plashy earth
Raises a mist; that, glittering in the sun,
Runs with her all the way, wherever she doth run.

III

I was a Traveller then upon the moor;
I saw the hare that raced about with joy;
I heard the woods and distant waters roar;
Or heard them not, as happy as a boy:
The pleasant season did my heart employ:
My old remembrances went from me wholly;   20
And all the ways of men, so vain and melancholy.

IV

But, as it sometimes chanceth, from the might
Of joy in minds that can no further go,
As high as we have mounted in delight
In our dejection do we sink as low;
To me that morning did it happen so;
And fear and fancies thick upon me came;
Dim sadness—and blind thoughts, I knew not, nor
          could name.

V

I heard the sky-lark warbling in the sky;
And I bethought me of the playful hare: 30
Even such a happy Child of earth am I;
Even as these blissful creatures do I fare;
Far from the world I walk, and from all care;
But there may come another day to me—
Solitude, pain of heart, distress, and poverty.

VI

My whole life I have lived in pleasant thought,
As if life's business were a summer mood;
As if all needful things would come unsought
To genial faith, still rich in genial good;
But how can He expect that others should   40
Build for him, sow for him, and at his call
Love him, who for himself will take no heed at all?

VII

I thought of Chatterton,[1] the marvellous Boy,
The sleepless Soul that perished in his pride;
Of Him who walked in glory and in joy
Following his plough, along the mountain-side:
By our own spirits are we deified:
We Poets in our youth begin in gladness;
But thereof come in the end despondency and
          madness.

VIII

Now, whether it were by peculiar grace,   50
A leading from above, a something given,
Yet it befell that, in this lonely place,
When I with these untoward thoughts had striven,
Beside a pool bare to the eye of heaven
I saw a Man before me unawares:
The oldest man he seemed that ever wore grey
          hairs.

---

[1] Thomas Chatterton (1752–1770), whose suicide at seventeen made him a frequently invoked example of unfulfilled promise. Robert Burns is the poet cited in line 45. The association of talent and madness, and the malignant effect of neglect, was supported by medical authority at the time.

IX

As a huge stone is sometimes seen to lie
Couched on the bald top of an eminence;
Wonder to all who do the same espy,
By what means it could thither come, and whence; 60
So that it seems a thing endued with sense:
Like a sea-beast crawled forth, that on a shelf
Of rock or sand reposeth, there to sun itself;

X

Such seemed this Man, not all alive nor dead,
Nor all asleep—in his extreme old age:
His body was bent double, feet and head
Coming together in life's pilgrimage;
As if some dire constraint of pain, or rage
Of sickness felt by him in times long past,
A more than human weight upon his frame had cast.

XI

Himself he propped, limbs, body, and pale face, 71
Upon a long grey staff of shaven wood:
And, still as I drew near with gentle pace,
Upon the margin of that moorish flood
Motionless as a cloud the old Man stood,
That heareth not the loud winds when they call;
And moveth all together, if it move at all.

XII

At length, himself unsettling, he the pond
Stirred with his staff, and fixedly did look
Upon the muddy water, which he conned, 80
As if he had been reading in a book:
And now a stranger's privilege I took;
And, drawing to his side, to him did say,
"This morning gives us promise of a glorious day."

XIII

A gentle answer did the old Man make,
In courteous speech which forth he slowly drew:
And him with further words I thus bespake,
"What occupation do you there pursue?
This is a lonesome place for one like you."
Ere he replied, a flash of mild surprise 90
Broke from the sable orbs of his yet-vivid eyes.

XIV

His words came feebly, from a feeble chest,
But each in solemn order followed each,
With something of a lofty utterance drest—
Choice word and measured phrase, above the reach
Of ordinary men; a stately speech;
Such as grave Livers do in Scotland use,
Religious men, who give to God and man their dues.

XV

He told, that to these waters he had come
To gather leeches,[2] being old and poor: 100
Employment hazardous and wearisome!
And he had many hardships to endure:
From pond to pond he roamed, from moor to moor;
Housing, with God's good help, by choice or chance;
And in this way he gained an honest maintenance.

XVI

The old Man still stood talking by my side;
But now his voice to me was like a stream
Scarce heard; nor word from word could I divide;
And the whole body of the Man did seem
Like one whom I had met with in a dream; 110
Or like a man from some far region sent,
To give me human strength, by apt admonishment.

XVII

My former thoughts returned: the fear that kills;
And hope that is unwilling to be fed;
Cold, pain, and labour, and all fleshly ills;
And mighty Poets in their misery dead.
—Perplexed, and longing to be comforted,
My question eagerly did I renew,
"How is it that you live, and what is it you do?"

XVIII

He with a smile did then his words repeat; 120
And said that, gathering leeches, far and wide
He travelled; stirring thus about his feet
The waters of the pools where they abide.
"Once I could meet with them on every side;
But they have dwindled long by slow decay;
Yet still I persevere, and find them where I may."

XIX

While he was talking thus, the lonely place,
The old Man's shape, and speech—all troubled me:
In my mind's eye I seemed to see him pace
About the weary moors continually, 130
Wandering about alone and silently.
While I these thoughts within myself pursued,
He, having made a pause, the same discourse renewed.

XX

And soon with this he other matter blended,
Cheerfully uttered, with demeanour kind,
But stately in the main; and when he ended,
I could have laughed myself to scorn to find

---

[2] Leeches were frequently applied to patients by eighteenth-
and nineteenth-century doctors to reduce the quantity of blood.

In that decrepit Man so firm a mind.
"God," said I, "be my help and stay secure; 139
I'll think of the Leech-gatherer on the lonely moor!"

[1802]   [1807]

*Stanzas 1–4 are usually assumed to be Wordsworth's description
of himself; Stanzas 5–8, his description of Coleridge.*

STANZAS

WRITTEN IN MY POCKET-COPY OF THOMSON'S "CASTLE OF INDOLENCE"

WITHIN our happy Castle there dwelt One
Whom without blame I may not overlook;
For never sun on living creature shone
Who more devout enjoyment with us took:
Here on his hours he hung as on a book,
On his own time here would he float away,
As doth a fly upon a summer brook;
But go to-morrow, or belike to-day,
Seek for him,—he is fled; and whither none can say.

Thus often would he leave our peaceful home, 10
And find elsewhere his business or delight;
Out of our Valley's limits did he roam:
Full many a time, upon a stormy night,
His voice came to us from the neighbouring height:
Oft could we see him driving full in view
At mid-day when the sun was shining bright;
What ill was on him, what he had to do,
A mighty wonder bred among our quiet crew.

Ah! piteous sight it was to see this Man
When he came back to us, a withered flower,— 20
Or like a sinful creature, pale and wan.
Down would he sit; and without strength or power
Look at the common grass from hour to hour:
And oftentimes, how long I fear to say,
Where apple-trees in blossom made a bower,
Retired in that sunshiny shade he lay;
And, like a naked Indian, slept himself away.

Great wonder to our gentle tribe it was
Whenever from our Valley he withdrew;
For happier soul no living creature has 30
Than he had, being here the long day through.
Some thought he was a lover, and did woo:
Some thought far worse of him, and judged him wrong;
But verse was what he had been wedded to;
And his own mind did like a tempest strong
ome to him thus, and drove the weary Wight along.

With him there often walked in friendly guise,
Or lay upon the moss by brook or tree,
A noticeable Man with large grey eyes,
And a pale face that seemed undoubtedly 40
As if a blooming face it ought to be;
Heavy his low-hung lip did oft appear,
Deprest by weight of musing Phantasy;[1]
Profound his forehead was, though not severe;
Yet some did think that he had little business here:

Sweet heaven forefend! his was a lawful right;
Noisy he was, and gamesome as a boy;
His limbs would toss about him with delight,
Like branches when strong winds the trees annoy.
Nor lacked his calmer hours device or toy 50
To banish listlessness and irksome care;
He would have taught you how you might employ
Yourself; and many did to him repair,—
And certes not in vain; he had inventions rare.

Expedients, too, of simplest sort he tried:
Long blades of grass, plucked round him as he lay,
Made, to his ear attentively applied,
A pipe on which the wind would deftly play;
Glasses he had, that little things display,
The beetle panoplied in gems and gold, 60
A mailèd angel on a battle-day;
The mysteries that cups of flowers enfold,
And all the gorgeous sights which fairies do behold.

He would entice that other Man to hear
His music, and to view his imagery:
And, sooth, these two were each to the other dear:
No livelier love in such a place could be:
There did they dwell—from earthly labour free,
As happy spirits as were ever seen;
If but a bird, to keep them company, 70
Or butterfly sate down, they were, I ween,
As pleased as if the same had been a Maiden-queen.

[1802]   [1815]

"I grieved for Buonaparté . . ."

I GRIEVED for Buonaparté, with a vain
And an unthinking grief! The tenderest mood
Of that Man's mind—what can it be? what food
Fed his first hopes? what knowledge could *he* gain?

[1] Apparently out of deference to Coleridge, Wordsworth here
replaced a line that reads (in MS.): "A face divine of heaven-born
idiotcy."

'Tis not in battles that from youth we train
The Governor who must be wise and good,
And temper with the sternness of the brain
Thoughts motherly, and meek as womanhood.
Wisdom doth live with children round her knees:
Books, leisure, perfect freedom, and the talk   10
Man holds with week-day man in the hourly walk
Of the mind's business: these are the degrees
By which true Sway doth mount; this is the stalk
True Power doth grow on; and her rights are these.

[1802]   [1802]

A FAREWELL

Written shortly before Wordsworth and his sister left for France to visit Annette Vallon and Wordsworth's daughter Caroline, and then went to Yorkshire for Wordsworth's wedding to Mary Hutchinson (the "Her" in the last stanza).

A FAREWELL

FAREWELL, thou little Nook of mountain-ground,
Thou rocky corner in the lowest stair
Of that magnificent temple which doth bound
One side of our whole vale with grandeur rare;
Sweet garden-orchard, eminently fair,
The lovliest spot that man hath ever found,
Farewell!—we leave these to Heaven's peaceful care,
Thee, and the Cottage which thou dost surround.

Our boat is safely anchored by the shore,
And there will safely ride when we are gone;   10
The flowering shrubs that deck our humble door
Will prosper, though untended and alone:
Fields, goods, and far-off chattels we have none:
These narrow bounds contain our private store
Of things earth makes, and sun doth shine upon;
Here are they in our sight—we have no more.

Sunshine and shower be with you, bud and bell!
For two months now in vain we shall be sought;
We leave you here in solitude to dwell
With these our latest gifts of tender thought;   20
Thou, like the morning, in thy saffron coat,
Bright gowan, and marsh-marigold, farewell!
Whom from the borders of the Lake we brought,
And placed together near our rocky Well.

We go for One to whom ye will be dear;
And she will prize this Bower, this Indian shed,
Our own contrivance, Building without peer!
—A gentle Maid, whose heart is lowly bred,

Whose pleasures are in wild fields gatherèd,
With joyousness, and with a thoughtful cheer,   30
Will come to you; to you herself will wed;
And love the blessed life that we lead here.

Dear Spot! which we have watched with tender heed,
Bringing thee chosen plants and blossoms blown
Among the distant mountains, flower and weed,
Which thou hast taken to thee as thy own,
Making all kindness registered and known;
Thou for our sakes, though Nature's child indeed,
Fair in thyself and beautiful alone,
Hast taken gifts which thou dost little need.   40

And O most constant, yet most fickle Place,
That hast thy wayward moods, as thou dost show
To them who look not daily on thy face;
Who, being loved, in love no bounds dost know,
And say'st, when we forsake thee, "Let them go!"
Thou easy-hearted Thing, with thy wild race
Of weeds and flowers, till we return be slow,
And travel with the year at a soft pace.

Help us to tell Her tales of years gone by,
And this sweet spring, the best beloved and best;   50
Joy will be flown in its mortality;
Something must stay to tell us of the rest.
Here, thronged with primroses, the steep rock's breast
Glittered at evening like a starry sky;
And in this bush our sparrow built her nest,
Of which I sang one song that will not die.

O happy Garden! whose seclusion deep
Hath been so friendly to industrious hours;
And to soft slumbers, that did gently steep
Our spirits, carrying with them dreams of flowers,   60
And wild notes warbled among leafy bowers;
Two burning months let summer overleap,
And, coming back with Her who will be ours,
Into thy bosom we again shall creep.

[1802]   [1815]

"The sun has long been set"

THE sun has long been set,
   The stars are out by twos and threes,
The little birds are piping yet
   Among the bushes and trees;
There's a cuckoo, and one or two thrushes,
And a far-off wind that rushes,
And a sound of water that gushes,
And the cuckoo's sovereign cry

Fills all the hollow of the sky.
　Who would go "parading" 10
In London, and "masquerading,"
On such a night of June
With that beautiful soft half-moon,
And all these innocent blisses?
On such a night as this is!

[1802] [1807]

════

COMPOSED UPON WESTMINSTER BRIDGE

"On Thursday morning, [July] 29th, [1802] we arrived in London. Wm. left me at the Inn. I went to bed, etc. etc. After various troubles and disasters, we left London on Saturday morning at ½-past 5 or 6, the 31st of July. (I have forgot which.) We mounted the Dover Coach at Charing Cross. It was a beautiful morning. The City, St. Paul's, with the river and a multitude of little Boats, made a most beautiful sight as we crossed Westminster Bridge. The houses were not overhung by their cloud of smoke, and they were spread out endlessly, yet the sun shone so brightly, with such a fierce light, that there was even something like the purity of one of nature's own grand spectacles." [Dorothy Wordsworth, Journals]

════

SONNET

COMPOSED UPON WESTMINSTER BRIDGE, SEPTEMBER 3, 1802

EARTH has not anything to show more fair:
Dull would he be of soul who could pass by
A sight so touching in its majesty:
This City now doth, like a garment, wear
The beauty of the morning; silent, bare,
Ships, towers, domes, theatres, and temples lie
Open unto the fields, and to the sky;
All bright and glittering in the smokeless air.
Never did sun more beautifully steep
In his first splendour, valley, rock, or hill; 10
Ne'er saw I, never felt, a calm so deep!
The river glideth at his own sweet will:
Dear God! the very houses seem asleep;
And all that mighty heart is lying still!

[1802] [1807]

SONNET

["It is a beauteous evening . . ."]

IT is a beauteous evening, calm and free,
The holy time is quiet as a Nun
Breathless with adoration; the broad sun
Is sinking down in its tranquillity;

The gentleness of heaven broods o'er the Sea:
Listen! the mighty Being is awake,
And doth with his eternal motion make
A sound like thunder—everlastingly.
Dear Child![1] dear Girl! that walkest with me here,
If thou appear untouched by solemn thought, 10
Thy nature is not therefore less divine:
Thou liest in Abraham's bosom all the year;
And worshipp'st at the Temple's inner shrine,
God being with thee when we know it not.

[1802] [1807]

SONNET

COMPOSED BY THE SEA-SIDE, NEAR CALAIS, AUGUST, 1802

FAIR Star of evening, Splendour of the west,
Star of my Country!—on the horizon's brink
Thou hangest, stooping, as might seem, to sink
On England's bosom; yet well pleased to rest,
Meanwhile, and be to her a glorious crest
Conspicuous to the Nations. Thou, I think,
Shouldst be my Country's emblem; and shouldst
　wink,
Bright Star! with laughter on her banners, drest
In thy fresh beauty. There! that dusky spot
Beneath thee, that is England; there she lies. 10
Blessings be on you both! one hope, one lot,
One life, one glory!—I, with many a fear
For my dear Country, many heartfelt sighs,
Among men who do not love her, linger here.

[1802] [1807]

════

CALAIS, AUGUST 1802

During the brief Peace of Amiens in the spring of 1802, English tourists in great numbers visited France.

∴

════

SONNET

CALAIS, AUGUST, 1802

IS IT a reed that's shaken by the wind,
Or what is it that ye go forth to see?
Lords, lawyers, statesmen, squires of low degree,
Men known, and men unknown, sick, lame, and
　blind,

---

[1] The child is Wordsworth's daughter (by Annette Vallon), whom he was then visiting at Calais.

Post forward all, like creatures of one kind,
With first-fruit offerings crowd to bend the knee
In France, before the new-born Majesty.
'Tis ever thus. Ye men of prostrate mind,
A seemly reverence may be paid to power;
But that's a loyal virtue, never sown   10
In haste, nor springing with a transient shower:
When truth, when sense, when liberty were flown,
What hardship had it been to wait an hour?
Shame on you, feeble Heads, to slavery prone!

[1802]   [1803]

SONNET

COMPOSED NEAR CALAIS,
ON THE ROAD LEADING TO ARDRES,
AUGUST 7, 1802

JONES![1] as from Calais southward you and I
Went pacing side by side, this public Way
Streamed with the pomp of a too-credulous day.
When faith was pledged to new-born Liberty:
A homeless sound of joy was in the sky:
From hour to hour the antiquated Earth
Beat like the heart of Man: songs, garlands, mirth,
Banners, and happy faces, far and nigh!
And now, sole register that these things were,
Two solitary greetings have I heard,
"*Good morrow, Citizen!*" a hollow word,
As if a dead man spake it! Yet despair
Touches me not, though pensive as a bird
Whose vernal coverts winter hath laid bare.

[1802]   [1807]

SONNET

CALAIS, AUGUST 15, 1802

FESTIVALS have I seen that were not names:
This is young Buonaparté's natal day,
And his is henceforth an established sway—
Consul for life.[2] With worship France proclaims
Her approbation, and with pomps and games.
Heaven grant that other Cities may be gay!
Calais is not: and I have bent my way
To the sea-coast, noting that each man frames

His business as he likes. Far other show
My youth here witnessed, in a prouder time;   10
The senselessness of joy was then sublime!
Happy is he, who, caring not for Pope,
Consul, or King, can sound himself to know
The destiny of Man, and live in hope.

[1802]   [1803]

SONNET

ON THE EXTINCTION OF THE
VENETIAN REPUBLIC[3]

ONCE did She hold the gorgeous east in fee;
And was the safeguard of the west: the worth
Of Venice did not fall below her birth,
Venice, the eldest Child of Liberty.
She was a maiden City, bright and free;
No guile seduced, no force could violate;
And, when she took unto herself a Mate,
She must espouse the everlasting Sea.[4]
And what if she had seen those glories fade,
Those titles vanish, and that strength decay;   10
Yet shall some tribute of regret be paid
When her long life hath reached its final day:
Men are we, and must grieve when even the Shade
Of that which once was great, is passed away.

[1802]   [1807]

TO TOUSSAINT L'OUVERTURE
*Toussaint, called The Opener (L'Ouverture), was a former slave
who led a rebellion against the French in Haiti. In 1802 he was
imprisoned in Paris, where he died the following year.*

SONNET

TO TOUSSAINT L'OUVERTURE

TOUSSAINT, the most unhappy man of men!
Whether the whistling Rustic tend his plough
Within thy hearing, or thy head be now
Pillowed in some deep dungeon's earless den;—

---

[1] Robert Jones, Wordsworth's companion during the walking
tour of France in 1790.
[2] On August 15, 1802, Napoleon had himself declared Consul for life.

[3] In 1797, Napoleon ended the status of Venice as an independent republic.
[4] A reference to the annual ceremony in which the Doge celebrated the marriage of Venice and the sea by dropping a ring into the Adriatic.

O miserable Chieftain! where and when
Wilt thou find patience! Yet die not; do thou
Wear rather in thy bonds a cheerful brow:
Though fallen thyself, never to rise again,
Live, and take comfort. Thou hast left behind
Powers that will work for thee; air, earth, and skies;
There's not a breathing of the common wind   11
That will forget thee; thou hast great allies;
Thy friends are exultations, agonies,
And love, and man's unconquerable mind.

[1802]   [1803]

SONNET

SEPTEMBER 1, 1802

Among the capricious acts of tyranny that disgraced those
times, was the chasing of all Negroes from France by
decree of the government: we had a Fellow-passenger who
was one of the expelled.

WE had a female Passenger who came
From Calais with us, spotless in array,—
A white-robed Negro, like a lady gay,
Yet downcast as a woman fearing blame;
Meek, destitute, as seemed, of hope or aim
She sate, from notice turning not away,
But on all proffered intercourse did lay
A weight of languid speech, or to the same
No sign of answer made by word or face:
Yet still her eyes retained their tropic fire,   10
That, burning independent of the mind,
Joined with the lustre of her rich attire
To mock the Outcast—O ye Heavens, be kind!
And feel, thou Earth, for this afflicted Race!

[1802]   [1803]

SONNET

COMPOSED IN THE VALLEY NEAR DOVER,
ON THE DAY OF LANDING

HERE, on our native soil, we breathe once more.
The cock that crows, the smoke that curls, that sound
Of bells;—those boys who in yon meadow-ground
In white-sleeved shirts are playing; and the roar
Of the waves breaking on the chalky shore;—
All, all are English. Oft have I looked round
With joy in Kent's green vales; but never found
Myself so satisfied in heart before.

Europe is yet in bonds; but let that pass,
Thought for another moment. Thou art free,   10
My Country! and 'tis joy enough and pride
For one hour's perfect bliss, to tread the grass
Of England once again, and hear and see,
With such a dear Companion at my side.

[1802]   [1807]

SONNET

SEPTEMBER, 1802. NEAR DOVER

INLAND, within a hollow vale, I stood;
And saw, while sea was calm and air was clear,
The coast of France—the coast of France how near!
Drawn almost into frightful neighbourhood.
I shrank: for verily the barrier flood
Was like a lake, or river bright and fair,
A span of waters; yet what power is there!
What mightiness for evil and for good!
Even so doth God protect us if we be
Virtuous and wise. Winds blow, and waters roll,   10
Strength to the brave, and Power, and Deity;
Yet in themselves are nothing! One decree
Spake laws to *them*, and said that by the soul
Only, the Nations shall be great and free.

[1802]   [1807]

SONNET

WRITTEN IN LONDON, SEPTEMBER, 1802

O FRIEND! I know not which way I must look
For comfort, being, as I am, opprest,
To think that now our life is only drest
For show; mean handy-work of craftsman, cook,
Or groom!—We must run glittering like a brook
In the open sunshine, or we are unblest:
The wealthiest man among us is the best:
No grandeur now in nature or in book
Delights us. Rapine, avarice, expense,
This is idolatry; and these we adore: 10
Plain living and high thinking are no more:
The homely beauty of the good old cause
Is gone; our peace, our fearful innocence,
And pure religion breathing household laws.

[1802]   [1807]

SONNET

LONDON, 1802

MILTON! thou shouldst be living at this hour:
England hath need of thee: she is a fen
Of stagnant waters: altar, sword, and pen,
Fireside, the heroic wealth of hall and bower,
Have forfeited their ancient English dower
Of inward happiness. We are selfish men;
Oh! raise us up, return to us again;
And give us manners, virtue, freedom, power.
Thy soul was like a Star, and dwelt apart;
Thou hadst a voice whose sound was like the sea: 10
Pure as the naked heavens, majestic free,
So didst thou travel on life's common way,
In cheerful godliness; and yet thy heart
The lowliest duties on herself did lay.

[1802]　　　　　　　　　　　　　　　　　[1807]

SONNET

["Great men have been among us . . ."]

GREAT men have been among us; hands that penned
And tongues that uttered wisdom—better none:
The later Sidney, Marvel, Harrington,
Young Vane, and others who called Milton friend.[1]
These moralists could act and comprehend:
They knew how genuine glory was put on;
Taught us how rightfully a nation shone
In splendour: what strength was, that would not bend
But in magnanimous meekness. France, 'tis strange,
Hath brought forth no such souls as we had then.   10
Perpetual emptiness! unceasing change!
No single volume paramount, no code,
No master spirit, no determined road;
But equally a want of books and men!

[1802]　　　　　　　　　　　　　　　　　[1807]

SONNET

["It is not to be thought of . . ."]

IT IS not to be thought of that the Flood
Of British freedom, which, to the open sea
Of the world's praise, from dark antiquity
Hath flowed, "with pomp of waters, unwithstood,"

---

[1] All were seventeenth-century poets who, with Milton, supported the Puritans and the Commonwealth. Milton was Wordsworth's model of the writer who achieved a vital relation with the governing and destiny of his country.

Rouse though it be full often to a mood
Which spurns the check of salutary bands,
That this most famous Stream in bogs and
    sands
Should perish; and to evil and to good
Be lost for ever.   In our halls is hung
Armoury of the invincible Knights of old: 10
We must be free or die, who speak the tongue
That Shakespeare spake; the faith and morals hold
Which Milton held.—In every thing we are
    sprung
Of Earth's first blood, have titles manifold.

[1802]　　　　　　　　　　　　　　　　　[1803]

SONNET

["When I have borne in memory . . ."]

WHEN I have borne in memory what has tamed
Great Nations, how ennobling thoughts depart
When men change swords for ledgers, and desert
The student's bower for gold, some fears
    unnamed
I had, my Country!—am I to be blamed?
Now, when I think of thee, and what thou art,
Verily, in the bottom of my heart,
Of those unfilial fears I am ashamed.
For dearly must we prize thee; we who find
In thee a bulwark for the cause of men;   10
And I by my affection was beguiled:
What wonder if a Poet now and then,
Among the many movements of his mind,
Felt for thee as a lover or a child!

[1802]　　　　　　　　　　　　　　　　　[1803]

SONNET

TO THE MEN OF KENT. OCTOBER, 1803

VANGUARD of Liberty, ye men of Kent,
Ye children of a Soil that doth advance
Her haughty brow against the coast of France,
Now is the time to prove your hardiment![2]
To France be words of invitation sent!
They from their fields can see the countenance
Of your fierce war, may ken the glittering lance,
And hear you shouting forth your brave intent.

---

[2] After hostilities with France were resumed in 1803, the English feared invasion across the Channel into Kent.

Left single, in bold parley, ye, of yore,
Did from the Norman win a gallant wreath;   10
Confirmed the charters that were yours before;—
No parleying now. In Britain is one breath;
We all are with you now from shore to shore;—
Ye men of Kent, 'tis victory or death!

[1803]   [1807]

SONNET

["Nuns fret not . . ."]

NUNS fret not at their convent's narrow room;
And hermits are contented with their cells;
And students with their pensive citadels;
Maids at the wheel, the weaver at his loom,
Sit blithe and happy; bees that soar for bloom,
High as the highest Peak of Furness-fells,
Will murmur by the hour in foxglove bells:
In truth the prison, unto which we doom
Ourselves, no prison is: and hence for me,
In sundry moods, 'twas pastime to be bound   10
Within the Sonnet's scanty plot of ground;
Pleased if some Souls (for such there needs must be)
Who have felt the weight of too much liberty,
Should find brief solace there, as I have found.

[1803 ?]   [1807]

SONNET

TO SLEEP

O GENTLE Sleep! do they belong to thee,
These twinklings of oblivion? Thou dost love
To sit in meekness, like the brooding Dove,
A captive never wishing to be free.
This tiresome night, O Sleep! thou art to me
A Fly, that up and down himself doth shove
Upon a fretful rivulet, now above,
Now on the water vexed with mockery.
I have no pain that calls for patience, no;
Hence am I cross and peevish as a child: 10
Am pleased by fits to have thee for my foe,
Yet ever willing to be reconciled:
O gentle Creature! do not use me so,
But once and deeply let me be beguiled.

[1803 ?]   [1807]

PERSONAL TALK[1]

I

I AM not One who much or oft delight
To season my fireside with personal talk,—
Of friends, who live within an easy walk,
Or neighbours, daily, weekly, in my sight:
And, for my chance-acquaintance, ladies bright,
Sons, mothers, maidens withering on the stalk,
These all wear out of me, like Forms, with chalk
Painted on rich men's floors, for one feast-night.[2]
Better than such discourse doth silence long,
Long, barren silence, square with my desire;   10
To sit without emotion, hope, or aim,
In the loved presence of my cottage-fire,
And listen to the flapping of the flame,
Or kettle whispering its faint undersong.

II

"Yet life," you say, "is life; we have seen and see,
And with a living pleasure we describe;
And fits of sprightly malice do but bribe
The languid mind into activity.
Sound sense, and love itself, and mirth and glee
Are fostered by the comment and the gibe."   20
Even be it so: yet still among your tribe,
Our daily world's true Worldlings, rank not me!
Children are blest, and powerful; their world lies
More justly balanced; partly at their feet,
And part far from them:—sweetest melodies
Are those that are by distance made more sweet;
Whose mind is but the mind of his own eyes,
He is a Slave; the meanest we can meet!

III

Wings have we,—and as far as we can go
We may find pleasure: wilderness and wood,   30
Blank ocean and mere sky, support that mood
Which with the lofty sanctifies the low.
Dreams, books, are each a world; and books, we know,
Are a substantial world, both pure and good:
Round these, with tendrils strong as flesh and blood,
Our pastime and our happiness will grow.
There find I personal themes, a plenteous store,
Matter wherein right voluble I am,
To which I listen with a ready ear;
Two shall be named, pre-eminently dear,—   40
The gentle Lady married to the Moor;
And heavenly Una with her milk-white Lamb.[3]

---

[1] A set of sonnets.
[2] The decorations often used on floors for special occasions.
[3] These two lines refer to Desdemona's love for Othello in Shakespeare's play and Una's for the Lamb in Book I of Spenser's *Faerie Queene*.

IV

Nor can I not believe but that hereby
Great gains are mine; for thus I live remote
From evil-speaking; rancour, never sought,
Comes to me not; malignant truth, or lie.
Hence have I genial seasons, hence have I
Smooth passions, smooth discourse, and joyous
    thought:
And thus from day to day my little boat
Rocks in its harbour, lodging peaceably.   50
Blessings be with them—and eternal praise,
Who gave us nobler loves, and nobler cares—
The Poets, who on earth have made us heirs
Of truth and pure delight by heavenly lays!
Oh! might my name be numbered among theirs,
Then gladly would I end my mortal days.

18 02–1804]   [1807]

SONNET

["Where lies the Land ..."]

WHERE lies the Land to which yon Ship must go?
Fresh as a lark mounting at break of day,
Festively she puts forth in trim array;
Is she for tropic suns, or polar snow?
What boots the inquiry?—Neither friend nor foe
She cares for; let her travel where she may,
She finds familiar names, a beaten way
Ever before her, and a wind to blow.
Yet still I ask, what haven is her mark?
And, almost as it was when ships were rare,   10
(From time to time, like Pilgrims, here and there
Crossing the waters) doubt, and something dark,
Of the old Sea some reverential fear,
Is with me at thy farewell, joyous Bark!

[1803?]   [1807]

SONNET

["The world is too much with us ..."]

THE world is too much with us; late and soon,
Getting and spending, we lay waste our powers:
Little we see in Nature that is ours;
We have given our hearts away, a sordid boon!
This Sea that bares her bosom to the moon;
The winds that will be howling at all hours,
And are up-gathered now like sleeping flowers;
For this, for everything, we are out of tune;

It moves us not.—Great God! I'd rather be
A Pagan suckled in a creed outworn;   10
So might I, standing on this pleasant lea,
Have glimpses that would make me less forlorn;
Have sight of Proteus rising from the sea;
Or hear old Triton blow his wreathèd horn.[1]

[1803?]   [1807]

TO H. C.

*Coleridge's eldest son Hartley (1796–1849) is also the child of
the Immortality Ode and the infant of Coleridge's* Frost at Mid-
night. *As a child he spent many weeks living with the Words-
worths. Dismissed from a fellowship at Oxford for intemperance,
he lived most of his life in Grasmere as a poet and part-time
schoolteacher.*

TO H. C.

SIX YEARS OLD

O THOU! whose fancies from afar are brought;
Who of thy words dost make a mock apparel,
And fittest to unutterable thought
The breeze-like motion and the self-born carol;
Thou faery voyager! that dost float
In such clear water, that thy boat
May rather seem
To brood on air than on an earthly stream;
Suspended in a stream as clear as sky,
Where earth and heaven do make one imagery;   10
O blessèd vision! happy child!
Thou art so exquisitely wild,
I think of thee with many fears
For what may be thy lot in future years.

I thought of times when Pain might be thy guest,
Lord of thy house and hospitality;
And Grief, uneasy lover! never rest
But when she sate within the touch of thee.
O too industrious folly!
O vain and causeless melancholy!   20
Nature will either end thee quite;
Or, lengthening out thy season of delight,
Preserve for thee, by individual right,
A young lamb's heart among the full-grown flocks.
What hast thou to do with sorrow,
Or the injuries of to-morrow?
Thou art a dew-drop, which the morn brings forth,
Ill fitted to sustain unkindly shocks,

---

[1] Proteus and Triton are classical gods of the sea.

Or to be trailed along the soiling earth;
A gem that glitters while it lives,   30
And no forewarning gives;
But, at the touch of wrong, without a strife
Slips in a moment out of life.

[1802]   [1807]

TO A HIGHLAND GIRL
*This poem and the two that follow it, are associated with the tour
of Scotland that Wordsworth, his sister, and sometimes Coleridge,
made in 1803.*

TO A HIGHLAND GIRL,

AT INVERSNEYDE, UPON LOCH LOMOND

SWEET Highland Girl, a very shower
Of beauty is thy earthly dower!
Twice seven consenting years have shed
Their utmost bounty on thy head:
And these grey rocks; that household lawn;
Those trees, a veil just half withdrawn;
This fall of water that doth make
A murmur near the silent lake;
This little bay; a quiet road
That holds in shelter thy Abode—   10
In truth together do ye seem
Like something fashioned in a dream;
Such Forms as from their covert peep
When earthly cares are laid asleep!
But, O fair Creature! in the light
Of common day, so heavenly bright,
I bless Thee, Vision as thou art,
I bless thee with a human heart;
God shield thee to thy latest years!
Thee, neither know I, nor thy peers;   20
And yet my eyes are filled with tears.

With earnest feeling I shall pray
For thee when I am far away:
For never saw I mien, or face,
In which more plainly I could trace
Benignity and home-bred sense
Ripening in perfect innocence.
Here scattered, like a random seed,
Remote from men, Thou dost not need
The embarrassed look of shy distress,
And maidenly shamefacedness: 30
Thou wear'st upon thy forehead clear
The freedom of a Mountaineer:
A face with gladness overspread!
Soft smiles, by human kindness bred!

And seemliness complete, that sways
Thy courtesies, about thee plays;
With no restraint, but such as springs
From quick and eager visitings
Of thoughts that lie beyond the reach   40
Of thy few words of English speech:
A bondage sweetly brooked, a strife
That gives thy gestures grace and life!
So have I, not unmoved in mind,
Seen birds of tempest-loving kind—
Thus beating up against the wind.

What hand but would a garland cull
For thee who art so beautiful?
O happy pleasure! here to dwell
Beside thee in some heathy dell;   50
Adopt your homely ways, and dress,
A Shepherd, thou a Shepherdess!
But I could frame a wish for thee
More like a grave reality:
Thou art to me but as a wave
Of the wild sea; and I would have
Some claim upon thee, if I could,
Though but of common neighbourhood.
What joy to hear thee, and to see!
Thy elder Brother I would be,   60
Thy Father—anything to thee!

Now thanks to Heaven! that of its grace
Hath led me to this lonely place.
Joy have I had; and going hence
I bear away my recompense.
In spots like these it is we prize
Our Memory, feel that she hath eyes:
Then, why should I be loth to stir?
I feel this place was made for her;
To give new pleasure like the past,   70
Continued long as life shall last.
Nor am I loth, though pleased at heart,
Sweet Highland Girl! from thee to part;
For I, methinks, till I grow old,
As fair before me shall behold,
As I do now, the cabin small,
The lake, the bay, the waterfall;
And Thee, the Spirit of them all!

[1803]   [1807]

YARROW UNVISITED

See the various Poems the scene of which is laid upon the
banks of the Yarrow; in particular, the exquisite Ballad of
Hamilton beginning—

> "Busk ye, busk ye, my bonny, bonny Bride,
> Busk ye, busk ye, my winsome Marrow!" [1]

FROM Stirling castle we had seen
The mazy Forth unravelled;
Had trod the banks of Clyde, and Tay,
And with the Tweed had travelled;
And when we came to Clovenford,
Then said my "*winsome Marrow*,"
"Whate'er betide, we'll turn aside,
And see the Braes of Yarrow."

"Let Yarrow folk, *frae* Selkirk town,
Who have been buying, selling,   10
Go back to Yarrow, 'tis their own;
Each maiden to her dwelling!
On Yarrow's banks let herons feed,
Hares couch, and rabbits burrow!
But we will downward with the Tweed,
Nor turn aside to Yarrow.

"There's Galla Water, Leader Haughs,
Both lying right before us;
And Dryborough, where with chiming Tweed
The lintwhites sing in chorus;   20
There's pleasant Tiviot-dale, a land
Made blithe with plough and harrow:
Why throw away a needful day
To go in search of Yarrow?

"What's Yarrow but a river bare,
That glides the dark hills under?
There are a thousand such elsewhere
As worthy of your wonder."
—Strange words they seemed of slight and scorn;
My True-love sighed for sorrow;   30
And looked me in the face, to think
I thus could speak of Yarrow!

"Oh! green," said I, "are Yarrow's holms,
And sweet is Yarrow flowing!
Fair hangs the apple frae the rock,*
But we will leave it growing.
O'er hilly path, and open Strath,
We'll wander Scotland thorough;
But, though so near, we will not turn
Into the dale of Yarrow.   40

* See Hamilton's Ballad as above.

[1] Wordsworth quotes William Hamilton's *The Braes of Yarrow*.

"Let beeves and home-bred kine partake
The sweets of Burn-mill meadow;
The swan on still St. Mary's Lake
Float double, swan and shadow!
We will not see them; will not go,
To-day, nor yet to-morrow;
Enough if in our hearts we know
There's such a place as Yarrow.

"Be Yarrow stream unseen, unknown!
It must, or we shall rue it: 50
We have a vision of our own;
Ah! why should we undo it?
The treasured dreams of times long past,
We'll keep them, winsome Marrow!
For when we're there, although 'tis fair,
'Twill be another Yarrow!

"If Care with freezing years should come,
And wandering seem but folly,—
Should we be loth to stir from home,
And yet be melancholy;   60
Should life be dull, and spirits low,
'Twill soothe us in our sorrow,
That earth hath something yet to show,
The bonny holms of Yarrow!"

[1803]   [1807]

AT THE GRAVE OF BURNS, 1803

SEVEN YEARS AFTER HIS DEATH

I SHIVER, Spirit fierce and bold,
At thought of what I now behold:
As vapours breathed from dungeons cold
    Strike pleasure dead,
So sadness comes from out the mould
    Where Burns is laid.

And have I then thy bones so near,
And thou forbidden to appear?
As if it were thyself that's here
    I shrink with pain;   10
And both my wishes and my fear
    Alike are vain.

Off weight—nor press on weight!—away
Dark thoughts!—they came, but not to stay;
With chastened feelings would I pay
    The tribute due
To him, and aught that hides his clay
    From mortal view.

Fresh as the flower, whose modest worth
He sang, his genius "glinted" forth,   20
Rose like a star that touching earth,
    For so it seems,
Doth glorify its humble birth
    With matchless beams.

The piercing eye, the thoughtful brow,
The struggling heart, where be they now?—
Full soon the Aspirant of the plough,
    The prompt, the brave,
Slept, with the obscurest, in the low
    And silent grave.   30

I mourned with thousands, but as one
More deeply grieved, for He was gone
Whose light I hailed when first it shone,
    And showed my youth
How Verse may build a princely throne
    On humble truth.

Alas! where'er the current tends,
Regret pursues and with it blends,—
Huge Criffel's hoary top ascends
    By Skiddaw seen,—
Neighbours we were, and loving friends   40
    We might have been;

True friends though diversely inclined;
But heart with heart and mind with mind,
Where the main fibres are entwined,
    Through Nature's skill,
May even by contraries be joined
    More closely still.

The tear will start, and let it flow;
Thou "poor Inhabitant below,"   50
At this dread moment—even so—
    Might we together
Have sate and talked where gowans blow,
    Or on wild heather.

What treasures would have then been placed
Within my reach; of knowledge graced
By fancy what a rich repast!
    But why go on?—
Oh! spare to sweep, thou mournful blast,
    His grave grass-grown.   60

There, too, a Son, his joy and pride,
(Not three weeks past the Stripling died,)
Lies gathered to his Father's side,
    Soul-moving sight!
Yet one to which is not denied
    Some sad delight.

For *he* is safe, a quiet bed
Hath early found among the dead,
Harboured where none can be misled,
    Wronged, or distrest;   70
And surely here it may be said
    That such are blest.

And oh for Thee, by pitying grace
Checked oft-times in a devious race,
May He, who halloweth the place
    Where Man is laid,
Receive thy Spirit in the embrace
    For which it prayed!

Sighing I turned away; but ere
Night fell I heard, or seemed to hear,   80
Music that sorrow comes not near,
    A ritual hymn,
Chanted in love that casts out fear
    By Seraphim.

[1803?]   [1892]

ODE TO DUTY

"This Ode is on the model of Gray's Ode to Adversity, which is copied from Horace's Ode to Fortune." [Wordsworth to Isabella Fenwick]. *The epigraph, adapted from Seneca's Moral Epistles, reads: "Finally I am not consciously good, but trained by habit so that I am able not only to act rightly but unable to act other than rightly." The sixth stanza was omitted in editions after 1807.*

ODE TO DUTY

'Jam non consilio bonus, sed more eò perductus, ut non tantum rectè facere possim, sed nisi rectè facere non possim."

STERN Daughter of the Voice of God!
O Duty! if that name thou love
Who art a light to guide, a rod
To check the erring, and reprove;
Thou, who art victory and law
When empty terrors overawe;
From vain temptations dost set free;
    And calm'st the weary strife of frail humanity!

There are who ask not if thine eye
Be on them; who, in love and truth,   10
Where no misgiving is, rely
Upon the genial sense of youth;

Glad Hearts! without reproach or blot;
Who do thy work, and know it not:
Oh! if through confidence misplaced
They fail, thy saving arms, dread Power! around them
    cast.

Serene will be our days and bright,
And happy will our nature be,
When love is an unerring light,   .
And joy its own security.   20
And they a blissful course may hold
Even now, who, not unwisely bold,
Live in the spirit of this creed;
Yet seek thy firm support, according to their need.

I, loving freedom, and untried;
No sport of every random gust,
Yet being to myself a guide,
Too blindly have reposed my trust:
And oft, when in my heart was heard
Thy timely mandate, I deferred   30
The task, in smoother walks to stray;
But thee I now would serve more strictly, if I may.

Through no disturbance of my soul,
Or strong compunction in me wrought,
I supplicate for thy control;
But in the quietness of thought:
Me this unchartered freedom tires;
I feel the weight of chance-desires:
My hopes no more must change their name,
I long for a repose that ever is the same.   40

Yet not the less would I throughout
Still act according to the voice
Of my own wish; and feel past doubt
That my submissiveness was choice:
Not seeking in the school of pride
For "precepts over dignified",
Denial and restraint I prize
No farther than they breed a second Will more wise.

Stern Lawgiver! yet thou dost wear
The Godhead's most benignant grace;   50
Nor know we anything so fair
As is the smile upon thy face:
Flowers laugh before thee on their beds
And fragrance in thy footing treads;
Thou dost preserve the stars from wrong;
And the most ancient heavens, through Thee, are
    fresh and strong.

To humbler functions, awful Power!
I call thee: I myself commend
Unto thy guidance from this hour;
Oh, let my weakness have an end!   60
Give unto me, made lowly wise,
The spirit of self-sacrifice;
The confidence of reason give;
And in the light of truth thy Bondman let me live!

[1804]   [1807]

─────────

I WANDERED LONELY AS A CLOUD

*"When we were in the woods beyond Gowbarrow Park [on the
west side of Ullswater] we saw a few daffodils close to the water-
side. We fancied that the lake had floated the seeds ashore, and
that the little colony had so sprung up. But as we went along there
were more and yet more; and at last, under the boughs of trees, we
saw that there was a long belt of them along the shore, about the
breadth of a country turnpike road. I never saw daffodils so beauti-
ful. They grew among the mossy stones about and about them;
some rested their heads upon these stones as on a pillow for weari-
ness; and the rest tossed and reeled and danced, and seemed as if
they verily laughed with the wind, that blew upon them over the
lake; they looked so gay, ever glancing, ever changing. This wind
blew directly over the lake to them. There was here and there a
little knot, and a few stragglers a few yards higher up; but they
were so few as not to disturb the simplicity, unity, and life of that
one busy highway."* [Dorothy Wordsworth, Journals, April 15,
1802]

─────────

"I wandered lonely as a cloud"

I WANDERED lonely as a cloud
That floats on high o'er vales and hills,
When all at once I saw a crowd,
A host, of golden daffodils;
Beside the lake, beneath the trees,
Fluttering and dancing in the breeze.

Continuous as the stars that shine
And twinkle on the milky way,
They stretched in never-ending line
Along the margin of a bay: 10
Ten thousand saw I at a glance,
Tossing their heads in sprightly dance.

The waves beside them danced; but they
Out-did the sparkling waves in glee:
A poet could not but be gay,
In such a jocund company:
I gazed—and gazed—but little thought
What wealth the show to me had brought:

For oft, when on my couch I lie
In vacant or in pensive mood,   20
They flash upon that inward eye
Which is the bliss of solitude;
And then my heart with pleasure fills,
And dances with the daffodils.

[1804]   [1807]

"She was a Phantom of delight"

SHE was a Phantom of delight
When first she gleamed upon my sight;
A lovely Apparition, sent
To be a moment's ornament;
Her eyes as stars of Twilight fair;
Like Twilight's, too, her dusky hair;
But all things else about her drawn
From May-time and the cheerful Dawn;
A dancing Shape, an Image gay,
To haunt, to startle, and way-lay.   10

I saw her upon nearer view,
A Spirit, yet a Woman too!
Her household motions light and free,
And steps of virgin-liberty;
A countenance in which did meet
Sweet records, promises as sweet;
A Creature not too bright or good
For human nature's daily food;
For transient sorrows, simple wiles,
Praise, blame, love, kisses, tears, and smiles.   20

And now I see with eye serene
The very pulse of the machine;
A Being breathing thoughtful breath,
A Traveller between life and death;
The reason firm, the temperate will,
Endurance, foresight, strength, and skill;
A perfect Woman, nobly planned,
To warn, to comfort, and command;
And yet a Spirit still, and bright
With something of angelic light.   30

[1804]   [1807]

THE SMALL CELANDINE

THERE is a Flower, the lesser Celandine,
That shrinks, like many more, from cold and rain;
And, the first moment that the sun may shine,
Bright as the sun himself, 'tis out again!

When hailstones have been falling, swarm on swarm,
Or blasts the green field and the trees distrest,
Oft have I seen it muffled up from harm,
In close self-shelter, like a Thing at rest.

But lately, one rough day, this Flower I passed
And recognised it, though an altered form,   10
Now standing forth an offering to the blast,
And buffeted at will by rain and storm.

I stopped, and said with inly-muttered voice,
"It doth not love the shower, nor seek the cold:
This neither is its courage nor its choice,
But its necessity in being old.

"The sunshine may not cheer it, nor the dew;
It cannot help itself in its decay;
Stiff in its members, withered, changed of hue."
And, in my spleen, I smiled that it was grey.   20

To be a Prodigal's Favourite—then, worse truth,
A miser's Pensioner—behold our lot!
O Man, that from thy fair and shining youth
Age might but take the things Youth needed not!

[1804]   [1807]

THE PRELUDE

With astonishingly modern psychological insight, Wordsworth at the age of twenty-eight apparently decided that his sense of identity as a poet depended on a clear sense of his own past, of what Coleridge was later to call a continuity in his own self-consciousness. Those who, according to Coleridge, are "annihilated as to the past" are also "dead to the future, or seek for the proofs of it everywhere, only not (where alone they can be found) in themselves" (see Essay V in the General Introduction to The Friend*). The Prelude, which Wordsworth apparently began thinking of as an autobiography during the summer after the lonely winter he and Dorothy spent in Germany, is just such an attempt to make from fragments a continuity, to explain and justify and project a literary career that would be true to his origins and to his ambitions. Probably no autobiography in English had ever been so ambitious, and few subsequent ones have been as successful in achieving an openness to the range of human feeling and experience. Working intermittently but energetically for the next six years, by 1805 he had produced a poem of thirteen books, over 8000 lines, dedicated and addressed to Coleridge. Even before its completion in this form, Wordsworth decided that it would never be published during his lifetime unless he had also finished* The Recluse, *to which it was preparatory. But for the rest of his career, actively for the next thirty-five years at least, he revised and re-edited the work for posthumous publication, so that it finally appeared in July 1850, three months after the poet's death.*

Annotated editions of The Prelude, *in both versions, abound, the most thorough being that of Ernest de Selincourt, revised by Helen Darbishire (1959), in which facing pages allow easy comparison of the two texts. The most recent parallel text, with notes, is that edited by J. C. Maxwell in the Penguin English Poets series (1971). The text reprinted here generally follows the Moxon edition of 1850, which was based on a manuscript thoroughly reviewed by Wordsworth in 1839 and edited after the poet's death by his nephew, Christopher Wordsworth, and his son-in-law, Edward Quillinan. Some emendations and corrections suggested by de Selincourt and Maxwell have been incorporated without comment. Mary Wordsworth chose the title when the poem was published—during his lifetime it was usually referred to as "the poem to Coleridge" or "the poem on my own life."*

The outline of events in Wordsworth's life, pp. 167 ff., may prove helpful in establishing a chronological order for the episodes recounted in the poem.

THE PRELUDE

OR,

GROWTH OF A POET'S MIND

AN AUTOBIOGRAPHICAL POEM

BOOK FIRST

INTRODUCTION—CHILDHOOD
AND SCHOOL-TIME

O THERE is blessing in this gentle breeze,
A visitant that while he fans my cheek

Doth seem half-conscious of the joy he brings
From the green fields, and from yon azure sky.
Whate'er his mission, the soft breeze can come
To none more grateful than to me; escaped
From the vast city, where I long had pined
A discontented sojourner: now free,
Free as a bird to settle where I will.
What dwelling shall receive me? in what vale   10
Shall be my harbour? underneath what grove
Shall I take up my home? and what clear stream
Shall with its murmur lull me into rest?
The earth is all before me.[1] With a heart
Joyous, nor scared at its own liberty,
I look about; and should the chosen guide
Be nothing better than a wandering cloud,
I cannot miss my way. I breathe again!
Trances of thought and mountings of the mind
Come fast upon me: it is shaken off,   20
That burthen of my own unnatural self,
The heavy weight of many a weary day
Not mine, and such as were not made for me.
Long months of peace (if such bold word accord
With any promises of human life),
Long months of ease and undisturbed delight
Are mine in prospect; whither shall I turn,
By road or pathway, or through trackless field,
Up hill or down, or shall some floating thing
Upon the river point me out my course?   30

   Dear Liberty! Yet what would it avail
But for a gift that consecrates the joy?
For I, methought, while the sweet breath of heaven
Was blowing on my body, felt within
A correspondent breeze, that gently moved
With quickening virtue, but is now become
A tempest, a redundant energy,
Vexing its own creation. Thanks to both,
And their congenial powers, that, while they join
In breaking up a long-continued frost,   40
Bring with them vernal promises, the hope
Of active days urged on by flying hours,—
Days of sweet leisure, taxed with patient thought
Abstruse, nor wanting punctual service high,
Matins and vespers, of harmonious verse!

   Thus far, O Friend![2] did I, not used to make
A present joy the matter of a song,

---

[1] In the Preamble (through line 45), Wordsworth frequently alludes, as here (and as in *Home at Grasmere*), to Adam and Eve's situation in Milton's *Paradise Lost*. The liberating journey here has details both of Wordsworth's move from London to Racedown (Dorset) in 1795 and to his settling at Grasmere with his sister in 1799.

[2] The Friend, throughout, is S. T. Coleridge, to whom the poem is addressed.

Pour forth that day my soul in measured strains
That would not be forgotten, and are here
Recorded: to the open fields I told   50
A prophecy: poetic numbers came
Spontaneously to clothe in priestly robe
A renovated spirit singled out,
Such hope was mine, for holy services.
My own voice cheered me, and, far more, the mind's
Internal echo of the imperfect sound;
To both I listened, drawing from them both
A cheerful confidence in things to come.

       Content and not unwilling now to give
A respite to this passion, I paced on   60
With brisk and eager steps; and came, at length,
To a green shady place, where down I sate
Beneath a tree, slackening my thoughts by choice,
And settling into gentler happiness.
'Twas autumn, and a clear and placid day,
With warmth, as much as needed, from a sun
Two hours declined towards the west; a day
With silver clouds, and sunshine on the grass,
And in the sheltered and the sheltering grove
A perfect stillness. Many were the thoughts   70
Encouraged and dismissed, till choice was made
Of a known Vale, whither my feet should turn,
Nor rest till they had reached the very door
Of the one cottage which methought I saw.
No picture of mere memory ever looked
So fair; and while upon the fancied scene
I gazed with growing love, a higher power
Than Fancy gave assurance of some work
Of glory there forthwith to be begun,
Perhaps too there performed. Thus long I mused,   80
Nor e'er lost sight of what I mused upon,
Save where, amid the stately grove of oaks,
Now here, now there, an acorn, from its cup
Dislodged, through sere leaves rustled, or at once
To the bare earth dropped with a startling sound.
From that soft couch I rose not, till the sun
Had almost touched the horizon; casting then
A backward glance upon the curling cloud
Of city smoke, by distance ruralised;
Keen as a Truant or a Fugitive,   90
But as a Pilgrim resolute, I took,
Even with the chance equipment of that hour,
The road that pointed toward the chosen Vale.
It was a splendid evening, and my soul
Once more made trial of her strength, nor lacked
Æolian visitations; but the harp [3]

Was soon defrauded, and the banded host
Of harmony dispersed in straggling sounds,
And lastly utter silence! 'Be it so;
Why think of any thing but present good?'   100
So, like a home-bound laborer I pursued
My way beneath the mellowing sun, that shed
Mild influence; nor left in me one wish
Again to bend the Sabbath of that time
To a servile yoke. What need of many words?
A pleasant loitering journey, through three days
Continued, brought me to my hermitage.
I spare to tell of what ensued, the life
In common things—the endless store of things,
Rare, or at least so seeming, every day   110
Found all about me in one neighbourhood—
The self-congratulation, and, from morn
To night, unbroken cheerfulness serene.
But speedily an earnest longing rose
To brace myself to some determined aim,
Reading or thinking; either to lay up
New stores, or rescue from decay the old
By timely interference: and therewith
Came hopes still higher, that with outward life
I might endue some airy phantasies   120
That had been floating loose about for years,
And to such beings temperately deal forth
The many feelings that oppressed my heart.
That hope hath been discouraged; welcome light
Dawns from the east, but dawns to disappear
And mock me with a sky that ripens not
Into a steady morning: if my mind,
Remembering the bold promise of the past,
Would gladly grapple with some noble theme,
Vain is her wish; where'er she turns she finds   130
Impediments from day to day renewed.

       And now it would content me to yield up
Those lofty hopes awhile, for present gifts
Of humbler industry. But, O dear Friend!
The Poet, gentle creature as he is,
Hath, like the Lover, his unruly times;
His fits when he is neither sick nor well,
Though no distress be near him but his own
Unmanageable thoughts: his mind, best pleased
While she as duteous as the mother dove [4]   140
Sits brooding, lives not always to that end,
But like the innocent bird, hath goadings on
That drive her as in trouble through the groves;
With me is now such passion, to be blamed
No otherwise than as it lasts too long.

---

[3] An Aeolian (or wind) harp is a lute whose strings sound
randomly when the wind passes over them. It was a favorite
image for the imagination. See Coleridge's *The Eolian Harp*,
pp. 441–42.

[4] See *Paradise Lost*, I, 21: "Dove-like [God's power] satst
brooding on the vast Abyss."

When, as becomes a man who would prepare
For such an arduous work, I through myself
Make rigorous inquisition, the report
Is often cheering; for I neither seem
To lack that first great gift, the vital soul,   150
Nor general Truths, which are themselves a sort
Of Elements and Agents, Under-powers,
Subordinate helpers of the living mind:
Nor am I naked of external things,
Forms, images, nor numerous other aids
Of less regard, though won perhaps with toil
And needful to build up a Poet's praise.
Time, place, and manners do I seek, and these
Are found in plenteous store, but nowhere such
As may be singled out with steady choice;   160
No little band of yet remembered names
Whom I, in perfect confidence, might hope
To summon back from lonesome banishment,
And make them dwellers in the hearts of men
Now living, or to live in future years.
Sometimes the ambitious Power of choice, mistaking
Proud spring-tide swellings for a regular sea,
Will settle on some British theme, some old
Romantic tale by Milton left unsung;
More often turning to some gentle place   170
Within the groves of Chivalry, I pipe
To shepherd swains, or seated harp in hand,
Amid reposing knights by a river side
Or fountain, listen to the grave reports
Of dire enchantments faced and overcome
By the strong mind, and tales of warlike feats,
Where spear encountered spear, and sword with sword
Fought, as if conscious of the blazonry
That the shield bore, so glorious was the strife;
Whence inspiration for a song that winds   180
Through ever changing scenes of votive quest
Wrongs to redress, harmonious tribute paid
To patient courage and unblemished truth,
To firm devotion, zeal unquenchable,
And Christian meekness hallowing faithful loves.
Sometimes, more sternly moved, I would relate
How vanquished Mithridates northward passed,
And, hidden in the cloud of years, became
Odin, the Father of a race by whom
Perished the Roman Empire: how the friends   190
And followers of Sertorious,[5] out of Spain
Flying, found shelter in the Fortunate Isles,

And left their usages, their arts and laws,
To disappear by a slow gradual death,
To dwindle and to perish one by one,
Starved in those narrow bounds: but not the soul
Of Liberty, which fifteen hundred years
Survived, and, when the European came
With skill and power that might not be withstood,
Did, like a pestilence, maintain its hold   200
And wasted down by glorious death that race
Of natural heroes: or I would record
How, in tyrannic times, some high-souled man,
Unnamed among the chronicles of kings,
Suffered in silence for Truth's sake: or tell,
How that one Frenchman,[6] through continued force
Of meditation on the inhuman deeds
Of those who conquered first the Indian Isles,
Went single in his ministry across
The Ocean; not to comfort the oppressed,   210
But, like a thirsty wind, to roam about
Withering the Oppressor: how Gustavus[7] sought
Help at his need in Dalecarlia's mines;
How Wallace fought for Scotland; left the name
Of Wallace to be found, like a wild flower,
All over his dear Country; left the deeds
Of Wallace,[8] like a family of Ghosts,
To people the steep rocks and river banks,
Her natural sanctuaries, with a local soul
Of independence and stern liberty.   220
Sometimes it suits me better to invent
A tale from my own heart, more near akin
To my own passions and habitual thoughts;
Some variegated story, in the main
Lofty, but the unsubstantial structure melts
Before the very sun that brightens it,
Mist into air dissolving! Then a wish,
My best and favourite aspiration, mounts
With yearning toward some philosophic song
Of Truth that cherishes our daily life;   230
With meditations passionate from deep
Recesses in man's heart, immortal verse
Thoughtfully fitted to the Orphean lyre;
But from this awful burthen I full soon
Take refuge and beguile myself with trust
That mellower years will bring a riper mind
And clearer insight. Thus my days are past
In contradiction; with no skill to part
Vague longing, haply bred by want of power,
From paramount impulse not to be withstood,   240

---

[5] Mithridates (line 187), king of Pontus, defeated by Roman Pompey in 66 B.C. Odin, a legendary barbarian king, was imagined to have then fled north to Sweden, and there founded the Goths who later sacked Rome. Sertorius, a Roman general but Pompey's enemy, was assassinated in 72 B.C. His followers were believed to have fled to the Canary (Fortunate) Islands. Their descendants fought against Spanish domination in 1493, but were defeated by disease.

---

[6] Dominique de Gourges, who in 1567 avenged a Spanish massacre of Frenchmen in Florida.

[7] Gustavus I (1496–1560) freed Sweden from the Danes. His wartime refuge was Dalecarlia, the "cradle of Swedish liberty."

[8] Sir William Wallace defended Scotland against Edward I of England at the end of the thirteenth century. A Scottish legendary hero.

A timorous capacity from prudence,
From circumspection, infinite delay.
Humility and modest awe themselves
Betray me, serving often for a cloak
To a more subtle selfishness; that now
Locks every function up in blank reserve,
Now dupes me, trusting to an anxious eye
That with intrusive restlessness beats off
Simplicity and self-presented truth.
Ah! better far than this, to stray about   250
Voluptuously through fields and rural walks,
And ask no record of the hours, resigned
To vacant musing, unreproved neglect
Of all things, and deliberate holiday.
Far better never to have heard the name
Of zeal and just ambition, than to live
Baffled and plagued by a mind that every hour
Turns recreant to her task; takes heart again,
Then feels immediately some hollow thought
Hang like an interdict upon her hopes.   260
This is my lot; for either still I find
Some imperfection in the chosen theme,
Or see of absolute accomplishment
Much wanting, so much wanting, in myself,
That I recoil and droop, and seek repose
In listlessness from vain perplexity,
Unprofitably travelling toward the grave,
Like a false steward who hath much received
And renders nothing back.
                              Was it for this
That one, the fairest of all rivers,[9] loved   270
To blend his murmurs with my nurse's song,
And, from his alder shades and rocky falls,
And from his fords and shallows, sent a voice
That flowed along my dreams? For this, didst thou,
O Derwent! winding among grassy holms
Where I was looking on, a babe in arms,
Make ceaseless music that composed my thoughts
To more than infant softness, giving me
Amid the fretful dwellings of mankind
A foretaste, a dim earnest, of the calm   280
That Nature breathes among the hills and groves.
When he had left the mountains and received
On his smooth breast the shadow of those towers
That yet survive, a shattered monument
Of feudal sway, the bright blue river passed
Along the margin of our terrace walk;
A tempting playmate whom we dearly loved.
Oh, many a time have I, a five years' child,
In a small mill-race severed from his stream,
Made one long bathing of a summer's day;   290

Basked in the sun, and plunged and basked again
Alternate, all a summer's day, or scoured
The sandy fields, leaping through flowery groves
Of yellow ragwort; or when rock and hill,
The woods, and distant Skiddaw's lofty height,
Were bronzed with deepest radiance, stood alone
Beneath the sky, as if I had been born
On Indian plains, and from my mother's hut
Had run abroad in wantonness, to sport
A naked savage, in the thunder shower.   300

Fair seed-time had my soul, and I grew up
Fostered alike by beauty and by fear:
Much favoured in my birth-place, and no less
In that beloved Vale [10] to which erelong
We were transplanted—there were we let loose
For sports of wider range. Ere I had told
Ten birth-days, when among the mountain slopes
Frost, and the breath of frosty wind, had snapped
The last autumnal crocus, 'twas my joy
With store of springes o'er my shoulder hung   310
To range the open heights where woodcocks ran
Along the smooth green turf. Through half the night,
Scudding away from snare to snare, I plied
That anxious visitation;—moon and stars
Were shining o'er my head. I was alone,
And seemed to be a trouble to the peace
That dwelt among them. Sometimes it befel
In these night wanderings, that a strong desire
O'erpowered my better reason, and the bird
Which was the captive of another's toil   320
Became my prey; and when the deed was done
I heard among the solitary hills
Low breathings coming after me, and sounds
Of undistinguishable motion, steps
Almost as silent as the turf they trod.

Nor less when spring had warmed the cultured Vale,
Roved we as plunderers where the mother-bird
Had in high places built her lodge; though mean
Our object and inglorious, yet the end
Was not ignoble. Oh! when I have hung   330
Above the raven's nest, by knots of grass
And half-inch fissures in the slippery rock
But ill sustained, and almost (so it seemed)
Suspended by the blast that blew amain,
Shouldering the naked crag, oh, at that time
While on the perilous ridge I hung alone,
With what strange utterance did the loud dry wind
Blow through my ear! the sky seemed not a sky
Of earth—and with what motion moved the clouds!

---

[9] The Derwent and the Cocker join near Cockermouth, Wordsworth's Cumberland birthplace.

[10] Esthwaite, containing the village of Hawkshead where Wordsworth attended school for eight years.

Dust as we are, the immortal spirit grows   340
Like a harmony in music; there is a dark
Inscrutable workmanship that reconciles
Discordant elements, makes them cling together
In one society. How strange that all
The terrors, pains, and early miseries,
Regrets, vexations, lassitudes interfused
Within my mind, should e'er have borne a part,
And that a needful part, in making up
The calm existence that is mine when I
Am worthy of myself! Praise to the end!   350
Thanks to the means which Nature deigned to employ;
Whether her fearless visitings, or those
That came with soft alarm, like hurtless light
Opening the peaceful clouds; or she may use
Severer interventions, ministry
More palpable, as best might suit her aim.

One summer evening (led by her) I found
A little boat tied to a willow tree
Within a rocky cave, its usual home.
Straight I unloosed her chain, and stepping in   360
Pushed from the shore. It was an act of stealth
And troubled pleasure, nor without the voice
Of mountain-echoes did my boat move on;
Leaving behind her still, on either side,
Small circles glittering idly in the moon,
Until they melted all into one track
Of sparkling light. But now, like one who rows,
Proud of his skill, to reach a chosen point
With an unswerving line, I fixed my view
Upon the summit of a craggy ridge,   370
The horizon's utmost boundary, for above
Was nothing but the stars and the grey sky.
She was an elfin pinnace; lustily
I dipped my oars into the silent lake,
And, as I rose upon the stroke, my boat
Went heaving through the water like a swan;
When, from behind that craggy steep till then
The horizon's bound, a huge peak, black and huge,
As if with voluntary power instinct
Upreared its head. I struck and struck again,   380
And growing still in stature the grim shape
Towered up between me and the stars, and still,
For so it seemed, with purpose of its own
And measured motion like a living thing,
Strode after me. With trembling oars I turned,
And through the silent water stole my way
Back to the covert of the willow tree;
There in her mooring-place I left my bark,—
And through the meadows homeward went, in grave
And serious mood; but after I had seen   390
That spectacle, for many days, my brain
Worked with a dim and undetermined sense

Of unknown modes of being; o'er my thoughts
There hung a darkness, call it solitude
Or blank desertion. No familiar shapes
Remained, no pleasant images of trees,
Of sea or sky, no colours of green fields;
But huge and mighty forms, that do not live
Like living men, moved slowly through the mind
By day, and were a trouble to my dreams.   400

Wisdom and Spirit of the universe!
Thou Soul that art the eternity of thought,
That givest to forms and images a breath
And everlasting motion, not in vain
By day or star-light thus from my first dawn
Of childhood didst thou intertwine for me
The passions that build up our human soul;
Not with the mean and vulgar works of man,
But with high objects, with enduring things—
With life and nature, purifying thus   410
The elements of feeling and of thought,
And sanctifying, by such discipline,
Both pain and fear, until we recognise
A grandeur in the beatings of the heart.
Nor was this fellowship vouchsafed to me
With stinted kindness. In November days,
When vapours rolling down the valley made
A lonely scene more lonesome, among woods
At noon, and 'mid the calm of summer nights,
When, by the margin of the trembling lake,   420
Beneath the gloomy hills homeward I went
In solitude, such intercourse was mine;
Mine was it in the fields both day and night,
And by the waters, all the summer long.

And in the frosty season, when the sun
Was set, and visible for many a mile
The cottage windows blazed through twilight gloom,
I heeded not their summons: happy time
It was indeed for all of us—for me
It was a time of rapture! Clear and loud   430
The village clock tolled six,—I wheeled about,
Proud and exulting like an untired horse
That cares not for his home. All shod with steel,
We hissed along the polished ice in games
Confederate, imitative of the chase
And woodland pleasures,—the resounding horn,
The pack loud chiming, and the hunted hare.
So through the darkness and the cold we flew,
And not a voice was idle; with the din
Smitten, the precipices rang aloud;   440
The leafless trees and every icy crag
Tinkled like iron; while far distant hills
Into the tumult sent an alien sound
Of melancholy not unnoticed, while the stars

Eastward were sparkling clear, and in the west
The orange sky of evening died away.
Not seldom from the uproar I retired
Into a silent bay, or sportively
Glanced sideway, leaving the tumultuous throng,
To cut across the reflex of a star   450
That fled, and, flying still before me, gleamed
Upon the glassy plain; and oftentimes,
When we had given our bodies to the wind,
And all the shadowy banks on either side
Came sweeping through the darkness, spinning still
The rapid line of motion, then at once
Have I, reclining back upon my heels,
Stopped short; yet still the solitary cliffs
Wheeled by me—even as if the earth had rolled
With visible motion her diurnal round!   460
Behind me did they stretch in solemn train,
Feebler and feebler, and I stood and watched
Till all was tranquil as a dreamless sleep.

Ye Presences of Nature in the sky
And on the earth! Ye Visions of the hills!
And Souls of lonely places! can I think
A vulgar hope was yours when ye employed
Such ministry, when ye through many a year
Haunting me thus among my boyish sports,
On caves and trees, upon the woods and hills,   470
Impressed upon all forms the characters
Of danger or desire; and thus did make
The surface of the universal earth
With triumph and delight, with hope and fear,
Work like a sea?
                Not uselessly employed,
Might I pursue this theme through every change
Of exercise and play, to which the year
Did summon us in his delightful round.

We were a noisy crew; the sun in heaven
Beheld not vales more beautiful than ours;   480
Nor saw a band in happiness and joy
Richer, or worthier of the ground they trod.
I could record with no reluctant voice
The woods of autumn, and their hazel bowers
With milk-white clusters hung; the rod and line,
True symbol of hope's foolishness, whose strong
And unreproved enchantment led us on
By rocks and pools shut out from every star,
All the green summer, to forlorn cascades
Among the windings hid of mountain brook   490
—Unfading recollections! at this hour
The heart is almost mine with which I felt,
From some hill-top on sunny afternoons,
The paper kite high among fleecy clouds
Pull at her rein like an impetuous courser;

Or, from the meadows sent on gusty days,
Beheld her breast the wind, then suddenly
Dashed headlong, and rejected by the storm.

Ye lowly cottages wherein we dwelt,
A ministration of your own was yours;   500
Can I forget you, being as you were
So beautiful among the pleasant fields
In which ye stood? or can I here forget
The plain and seemly countenance with which
Ye dealt out your plain comforts? Yet had ye
Delights and exultations of your own.
Eager and never weary we pursued
Our home-amusements by the warm peat-fire
At evening, when with pencil, and smooth slate
In square divisions parcelled out and all   510
With crosses and with cyphers scribbled o'er,
We schemed and puzzled, head opposed to head
In strife too humble to be named in verse:[11]
Or round the naked table, snow-white deal,
Cherry or maple, sate in close array,
And to the combat, Loo or Whist, led on
A thick-ribbed army; not, as in the world,
Neglected and ungratefully thrown by
Even for the very service they had wrought,
But husbanded through many a long campaign.   520
Uncouth assemblage was it, where no few
Had changed their functions; some, plebeian cards
Which Fate, beyond the promise of their birth,
Had dignified, and called to represent
The persons of departed potentates.
Oh, with what echoes on the board they fell!
Ironic diamonds,—clubs, hearts, diamonds, spades,
A congregation piteously akin!
Cheap matter offered they to boyish wit,
Those sooty knaves, precipitated down   530
With scoffs and taunts, like Vulcan out of heaven:
The paramount ace, a moon in her eclipse,
Queens gleaming through their splendour's last
        decay,
And monarchs surly at the wrongs sustained
By royal visages. Meanwhile abroad
Incessant rain was falling, or the frost
Raged bitterly, with keen and silent tooth;
And, interrupting oft that eager game,
From under Esthwaite's splitting fields of ice
The pent-up air, struggling to free itself,   540
Gave out to meadow grounds and hills a loud
Protracted yelling, like the noise of wolves
Howling in troops along the Bothnic Main.

---

[11] The first game is ticktacktoe; the others are card games. The mock-heroic description echoes that of Pope's *Rape of the Lock*, III, 25–100.

Nor, sedulous as I have been to trace
How Nature by extrinsic passion first
Peopled the mind with forms sublime or fair,
And made me love them, may I here omit
How other pleasures have been mine, and joys
Of subtler origin; how I have felt,
Not seldom even in that tempestuous time,   550
Those hallowed and pure motions of the sense
Which seem, in their simplicity, to own
An intellectual charm; that calm delight
Which, if I err not, surely must belong
To those first-born affinities that fit
Our new existence to existing things,
And, in our dawn of being, constitute
The bond of union between life and joy.

Yes, I remember when the changeful earth,
And twice five summers on my mind had stamped
The faces of the moving year, even then   561
I held unconscious intercourse with beauty
Old as creation, drinking in a pure
Organic pleasure from the silver wreaths
Of curling mist, or from the level plain
Of waters coloured by impending clouds.

The sands of Westmoreland, the creeks and bays
Of Cumbria's rocky limits, they can tell
How, when the Sea threw off his evening shade,
And to the shepherd's hut on distant hills   570
Sent welcome notice of the rising moon,
How I have stood, to fancies such as these
A stranger, linking with the spectacle
No conscious memory of a kindred sight,
And bringing with me no peculiar sense
Of quietness or peace; yet have I stood,
Even while mine eye hath moved o'er many a league
Of shining water, gathering as it seemed
Through every hair-breadth in that field of light
New pleasure like a bee among the flowers.   580

Thus oft amid those fits of vulgar joy
Which, through all seasons, on a child's pursuits
Are prompt attendants, 'mid that giddy bliss
Which, like a tempest, works along the blood
And is forgotten; even then I felt
Gleams like the flashing of a shield;—the earth
And common face of Nature spake to me
Rememberable things; sometimes, 'tis true,
By chance collisions and quaint accidents
(Like those ill-sorted unions, work supposed   590
Of evil-minded fairies), yet not vain
Nor profitless, if happy they impressed
Collateral objects and appearances,
Albeit lifeless then, and doomed to sleep

Until maturer seasons called them forth
To impregnate and to elevate the mind.
—And if the vulgar joy by its own weight
Wearied itself out of the memory,
The scenes which were a witness of that joy
Remained in their substantial lineaments   600
Depicted on the brain, and to the eye
Were visible, a daily sight; and thus
By the impressive discipline of fear,
By pleasure and repeated happiness,
So frequently repeated, and by force
Of obscure feelings representative
Of things forgotten, these same scenes so bright,
So beautiful, so majestic in themselves,
Though yet the day was distant, did become
Habitually dear, and all their forms   610
And changeful colours by invisible links
Were fastened to the affections.
                    I began
My story early—not misled, I trust,
By an infirmity of love for days
Disowned by memory—ere the birth of spring
Planting my snowdrops among winter snows:
Nor will it seem to thee, O Friend! so prompt
In sympathy, that I have lengthened out
With fond and feeble tongue a tedious tale.
Meanwhile, my hope has been, that I might fetch   620
Invogorating thoughts from former years;
Might fix the wavering balance of my mind,
And haply meet reproaches too, whose power
May spur me on, in manhood now mature,
To honourable toil. Yet should these hopes
Prove vain, and thus should neither I be taught
To understand myself, nor thou to know
With better knowledge how the heart was framed
Of him thou lovest; need I dread from thee
Harsh judgments, if the song be loth to quit   630
Those recollected hours that have the charm
Of visionary things, those lovely forms
And sweet sensations that throw back our life,
And almost make remotest infancy
A visible scene, on which the sun is shining?

One end at least hath been attained; my mind
Hath been revived, and if this genial mood
Desert me not, forthwith shall be brought down
Through later years the story of my life.
The road lies plain before me;—'tis a theme   640
Single and of determined bounds; and hence
I choose it rather at this time, than work
Of ampler or more varied argument,
Where I might be discomfited and lost:
And certain hopes are with me, that to thee
This labour will be welcome, honoured Friend!

BOOK SECOND

SCHOOL-TIME—(CONTINUED)

THUS far, O Friend! have we, though leaving much
Unvisited, endeavoured to retrace
The simple ways in which my childhood walked;
Those chiefly that first led me to the love
Of rivers, woods, and fields. The passion yet
Was in its birth, sustained as might befal
By nourishment that came unsought; for still
From week to week, from month to month, we lived
A round of tumult. Duly were our games
Prolonged in summer till the day-light failed: 10
No chair remained before the doors; the bench
And threshold steps were empty; fast asleep
The labourer, and the old man who had sate
A later lingerer; yet the revelry
Continued and the loud uproar: at last,
When all the ground was dark, and twinkling stars
Edged the black clouds, home and to bed we went,
Feverish with weary joints and beating minds.
Ah! is there one who ever has been young,
Nor needs a warning voice to tame the pride   20
Of intellect and virtue's self-esteem?
One is there, though the wisest and the best
Of all mankind, who covets not at times
Union that cannot be;—who would not give,
If so he might, to duty and to truth
The eagerness of infantine desire?
A tranquillising spirit presses now
On my corporeal frame, so wide appears
The vacancy between me and those days
Which yet have such self-presence in my mind,   30
That, musing on them, often do I seem
Two consciousnesses, conscious of myself
And of some other Being. A rude mass
Of native rock, left midway in the square
Of our small market village, was the goal
Or centre of these sports; and when, returned
After long absence, thither I repaired,
Gone was the old grey stone, and in its place
A smart Assembly-room usurped the ground
That had been ours. There let the fiddle scream,   40
And be ye happy! Yet, my Friends! I know
That more than one of you will think with me
Of those soft starry nights, and that old Dame
From whom the stone was named, who there had sate,
And watched her table with its huckster's wares
Assiduous, through the length of sixty years.

We ran a boisterous course; the year span round
With giddy motion. But the time approached
That brought with it a regular desire
For calmer pleasures, when the winning forms   50

Of Nature were collaterally attached
To every scheme of holiday delight
And every boyish sport, less grateful else
And languidly pursued.
                              When summer came,
Our pastime was, on bright half-holidays,
To sweep along the plain of Windermere
With rival oars; and the selected bourne
Was now an Island musical with birds
That sang and ceased not; now a Sister Isle
Beneath the oak's umbrageous covert, sown   60
With lilies of the valley like a field;
And now a third small Island, where survived
In solitude the ruins of a shrine
Once to Our Lady dedicate, and served
Daily with chaunted rites. In such a race
So ended, disappointment could be none,
Uneasiness, or pain, or jealousy:
We rested in the shade, all pleased alike,
Conquered and conqueror. Thus the pride of strength,
And the vain-glory of superior skill,   70
Were tempered; thus was gradually produced
A quiet independence of the heart;
And to my Friend who knows me I may add,
Fearless of blame, that hence for future days
Ensued a diffidence and modesty,
And I was taught to feel, perhaps too much,
The self-sufficing power of Solitude.

    Our daily meals were frugal, Sabine fare!
More than we wished we knew the blessing then
Of vigorous hunger—hence corporeal strength   80
Unsapped by delicate viands; for, exclude
A little weekly stipend, and we lived
Through three divisions of the quartered year
In penniless poverty. But now to school
From the half-yearly holidays returned,
We came with weightier purses, that sufficed
To furnish treats more costly than the Dame
Of the old grey stone, from her scant board, supplied.
Hence rustic dinners on the cool green ground,
Or in the woods, or by a river side   90
Or shady fountain, while among the leaves
Soft airs were stirring, and the mid-day sun
Unfelt shone brightly round us in our joy.
Nor is my aim neglected if I tell
How sometimes, in the length of those half-years,
We from our funds drew largely;—proud to curb,
And eager to spur on, the galloping steed;
And with the cautious inn-keeper, whose stud
Supplied our want, we haply might employ
Sly subterfuge, if the adventure's bound   100
Were distant: some famed temple where of yore
The Druids worshipped, or the antique walls

Of that large abbey, where within the Vale
Of Nightshade, to St. Mary's honour built,
Stands yet a mouldering pile with fractured arch,
Belfry, and images, and living trees,
A holy scene![1] Along the smooth green turf
Our horses grazed. To more than inland peace
Left by the west wind sweeping overhead
From a tumultuous ocean, trees and towers   110
In that sequestered valley may be seen,
Both silent and both motionless alike;
Such the deep shelter that is there, and such
The safeguard for repose and quietness.

   Our steeds remounted and the summons given,
With whip and spur we through the chauntry flew
In uncouth race, and left the cross-legged knight,
And the stone-abbot, and that single wren
Which one day sang so sweetly in the nave
Of the old church, that—though from recent showers
The earth was comfortless, and touched by faint   121
Internal breezes, sobbings of the place
And respirations, from the roofless walls
The shuddering ivy dripped large drops—yet still
So sweetly 'mid the gloom the invisible bird
Sang to herself, that there I could have made
My dwelling-place, and lived for ever there
To hear such music. Through the walls we flew
And down the valley, and, a circuit made   129
In wantonness of heart, through rough and smooth
We scampered homewards. Oh, ye rocks and streams,
And that still spirit shed from evening air!
Even in this joyous time I sometimes felt
Your presence, when with slackened step we breathed
Along the sides of the steep hills, or when
Lighted by gleams of moonlight from the sea
We beat with thundering hoofs the level sand.

   Midway on long Winander's eastern shore,
Within the crescent of a pleasant bay,
A tavern[2] stood; no homely-featured house,   140
Primeval like its neighbouring cottages,
But 'twas a splendid place, the door beset
With chaises, grooms, and liveries, and within
Decanters, glasses, and the blood-red wine.
In ancient times, or ere the Hall was built
On the large island, had this dwelling been
More worthy of a poet's love, a hut
Proud of its one bright fire and sycamore shade.
But—though the rhymes were gone that once inscribed
The threshold, and large golden characters,   150

<hr/>

[1] Furness Abbey, twenty miles southwest of Hawkshead.
[2] The White Lion at Bowness on Lake Windermere (Winander). The Hall (below) was a circular house built in 1770 on Belle Isle.

Spread o'er the spangled sign-board, had dislodged
The old Lion and usurped his place, in slight
And mockery of the rustic painter's hand—
Yet, to this hour, the spot to me is dear
With all its foolish pomp. The garden lay
Upon a slope surmounted by the plain
Of a small bowling-green; beneath us stood
A grove, with gleams of water through the trees
And over the tree-tops; nor did we want
Refreshment, strawberries and mellow cream.   160
There, while through half an afternoon we played
On the smooth platform, whether skill prevailed
Or happy blunder triumphed, bursts of glee
Made all the mountains ring. But, ere night-fall,
When in our pinnace we returned at leisure
Over the shadowy lake, and to the beach
Of some small island steered our course with one,
The Minstrel of the Troop, and left him there,
And rowed off gently, while he blew his flute
Alone upon the rock—oh, then, the calm   170
And dead still water lay upon my mind
Even with a weight of pleasure, and the sky,
Never before so beautiful, sank down
Into my heart, and held me like a dream!
Thus were my sympathies enlarged, and thus
Daily the common range of visible things
Grew dear to me: already I began
To love the sun; a boy I loved the sun,
Not as I since have loved him, as a pledge
And surety of our earthly life, a light   180
Which we behold and feel we are alive;
Nor for his bounty to so many worlds—
But for this cause, that I had seen him lay
His beauty on the morning hills, had seen
The western mountain touch his setting orb,
In many a thoughtless hour, when, from excess
Of happiness, my blood appeared to flow
For its own pleasure, and I breathed with joy.
And, from like feelings, humble though intense,
To patriotic and domestic love   190
Analogous, the moon to me was dear;
For I would dream away my purposes,
Standing to gaze upon her while she hung
Midway between the hills, as if she knew
No other region, but belonged to thee,
Yea, appertained by a peculiar right
To thee and thy grey huts, thou one dear Vale!

   Those incidental charms which first attached
My heart to rural objects, day by day
Grew weaker, and I hasten on to tell   200
How Nature, intervenient till this time
And secondary, now at length was sought
For her own sake. But who shall parcel out

His intellect by geometric rules,
Split like a province into round and square?
Who knows the individual hour in which
His habits were first sown, even as a seed?
Who that shall point as with a wand and say
'This portion of the river of my mind
Came from yon fountain?' Thou, my Friend! art one
More deeply read in thy own thoughts; to thee   211
Science appears but what in truth she is,
Not as our glory and our absolute boast,
But as a succedaneum,³ and a prop
To our infirmity. No officious slave
Art thou of that false secondary power
By which we multiply distinctions, then
Deem that our puny boundaries are things
That we perceive, and not that we have made.
To thee, unblinded by these formal arts,   220
The unity of all hath been revealed,
And thou wilt doubt, with me less aptly skilled
Than many are to range the faculties
In scale and order, class the cabinet
Of their sensations, and in voluble phrase
Run through the history and birth of each
As of a single independent thing.
Hard task, vain hope, to analyse the mind,
If each most obvious and particular thought,
Not in a mystical and idle sense,   230
But in the words of Reason deeply weighed,
Hath no beginning.
                    Blest the infant Babe,
(For with my best conjecture I would trace
Our Being's earthly progress,) blest the Babe,
Nursed in his Mother's arms, who sinks to sleep
Rocked on his Mother's breast; who with his soul
Drinks in the feelings of his Mother's eye!
For him, in one dear Presence, there exists
A virtue which irradiates and exalts
Objects through widest intercourse of sense.   240
No outcast he, bewildered and depressed:
Along his infant veins are interfused
The gravitation and the filial bond
Of nature that connect him with the world.
Is there a flower, to which he points with hand
Too weak to gather it, already love
Drawn from love's purest earthly fount for him
Hath beautified that flower; already shades
Of pity cast from inward tenderness
Do fall around him upon aught that bears   250
Unsightly marks of violence or harm.
Emphatically such a Being lives,
Frail creature as he is, helpless as frail,
An inmate of this active universe.

³ Substitute.

For feeling has to him imparted power
That through the growing faculties of sense
Doth like an agent of the one great Mind
Create, creator and receiver both,
Working but in alliance with the works
Which it beholds.—Such, verily, is the first   260
Poetic spirit of our human life,
By uniform control of after years,
In most, abated or suppressed; in some,
Through every change of growth and of decay,
Pre-eminent till death.
                    From early days,
Beginning not long after that first time
In which, a Babe, by intercourse of touch
I held mute dialogues with my Mother's heart,
I have endeavoured to display the means
Whereby this infant sensibility,   270
Great birthright of our being, was in me
Augmented and sustained. Yet is a path
More difficult before me; and I fear
That in its broken windings we shall need
The chamois' sinews, and the eagle's wing:
For now a trouble came into my mind
From unknown causes. I was left alone
Seeking the visible world, nor knowing why.
The props of my affections were removed,
And yet the building stood, as if sustained   280
By its own spirit! All that I beheld
Was dear, and hence to finer influxes
The mind lay open, to a more exact
And close communion. Many are our joys
In youth, but oh! what happiness to live
When every hour brings palpable access
Of knowledge, when all knowledge is delight,
And sorrow is not there! The seasons came,
And every season wheresoe'er I moved
Unfolded transitory qualities,   290
Which, but for this most watchful power of love,
Had been neglected; left a register
Of permanent relations, else unknown.
Hence life, and change, and beauty, solitude
More active even than 'best society'—
Society made sweet as solitude
By silent inobtrusive sympathies,
And gentle agitations of the mind
From manifold distinctions, difference   299
Perceived in things, where, to the unwatchful eye,
No difference is, and hence, from the same source,
Sublimer joy; for I would walk alone,
Under the quiet stars, and at that time
Have felt whate'er there is of power in sound
To breathe an elevated mood, by form
Or image unprofaned; and I would stand,
If the night blackened with a coming storm,

Beneath some rock, listening to notes that are
The ghostly language of the ancient earth,
Or make their dim abode in distant winds.   310
Thence did I drink the visionary power;
And deem not profitless those fleeting moods
Of shadowy exultation: not for this,
That they are kindred to our purer mind
And intellectual life; but that the soul,
Remembering how she felt, but what she felt
Remembering not, retains an obscure sense
Of possible sublimity, whereto
With growing faculties she doth aspire,
With faculties still growing, feeling still   320
That whatsoever point they gain, they yet
Have something to pursue.
                        And not alone
'Mid gloom and tumult, but no less 'mid fair
And tranquil scenes, that universal power
And fitness in the latent qualities
And essences of things, by which the mind
Is moved with feelings of delight, to me
Came strengthened with a superadded soul,
A virtue not its own. My morning walks
Were early;—oft before the hours of school   330
I travelled round our little lake, five miles
Of pleasant wandering. Happy time! more dear
For this, that one was by my side, a Friend,[4]
Then passionately loved; with heart how full
Would he peruse these lines! For many years
Have since flowed in between us, and, our minds
Both silent to each other, at this time
We live as if those hours had never been.
Nor seldom did I lift our cottage latch
Far earlier, and ere one smoke-wreath had risen   340
From human dwelling, or the thrush, high-perched,
Piped to the woods his shrill reveillé, sate
Alone upon some jutting eminence,
At the first gleam of dawn-light, when the Vale,
Yet slumbering, lay in utter solitude.
How shall I seek the origin? where find
Faith in the marvellous things which then I felt?
Oft in these moments such a holy calm
Would overspread my soul, that bodily eyes
Were utterly forgotten, and what I saw   350
Appeared like something in myself, a dream,
A prospect in the mind.
                        'Twere long to tell
What spring and autumn, what the winter snows,
And what the summer shade, what day and night,
Evening and morning, sleep and waking, thought
From sources inexhaustible, poured forth

◇◇◇◇◇◇◇◇◇◇◇◇◇◇◇◇◇◇◇◇◇◇◇◇◇◇◇
   [4] The late Rev. John Fleming of Rayrigg, Windermere.
[Note in 1850 edition.]

To feed the spirit of religious love
In which I walked with Nature. But let this
Be not forgotten, that I still retained
My first creative sensibility;   360
That by the regular action of the world
My soul was unsubdued. A plastic power
Abode with me; a forming hand, at times
Rebellious, acting in a devious mood;
A local spirit of his own, at war
With general tendency, but, for the most,
Subservient strictly to external things
With which it communed. An auxiliar light
Came from my mind, which on the setting sun
Bestowed new splendour; the melodious birds,   370
The fluttering breezes, fountains that ran on
Murmuring so sweetly in themselves, obeyed
A like dominion, and the midnight storm
Grew darker in the presence of my eye:
Hence my obeisance, my devotion hence,
And hence my transport.
                        Nor should this, perchance,
Pass unrecorded, that I still had loved
The exercise and produce of a toil,
Than analytic industry to me
More pleasing, and whose character I deem   380
Is more poetic as resembling more
Creative agency. The song would speak
Of that interminable building reared
By observation of affinities
In objects where no brotherhood exists
To passive minds. My seventeenth year was come;
And, whether from this habit rooted now
So deeply in my mind, or from excess
In the great social principle of life
Coercing all things into sympathy,   390
To unorganic natures were transferred
My own enjoyments; or the power of truth
Coming in revelation, did converse
With things that really are; I, at this time,
Saw blessings spread around me like a sea.
Thus while the days flew by, and years passed on,
From Nature and her overflowing soul,
I had received so much, that all my thoughts
Were steeped in feeling; I was only then
Contented, when with bliss ineffable   400
I felt the sentiment of Being spread
O'er all that moves and all that seemeth still;
O'er all that, lost beyond the reach of thought
And human knowledge, to the human eye
Invisible, yet liveth to the heart;
O'er all that leaps and runs, and shouts and sings,
Or beats the gladsome air; o'er all that glides
Beneath the wave, yea, in the wave itself,
And mighty depth of waters. Wonder not

If high the transport, great the joy I felt,   410
Communing in this sort through earth and heaven
With every form of creature, as it looked
Towards the Uncreated with a countenance
Of adoration, with an eye of love.
One song they sang, and it was audible,
Most audible, then, when the fleshly ear,
O'ercome by humblest prelude of that strain,
Forgot her functions, and slept undisturbed.

    If this be error, and another faith
Find easier access to the pious mind,   420
Yet were I grossly destitute of all
Those human sentiments that make this earth
So dear, if I should fail with grateful voice
To speak of you, ye mountains, and ye lakes
And sounding cataracts, ye mists and winds
That dwell among the hills were I was born.
If in my youth I have been pure in heart,
If, mingling with the world, I am content
With my own modest pleasures, and have lived
With God and Nature communing, removed   430
From little enmities and low desires,
The gift is yours; if in these times of fear,[5]
This melancholy waste of hopes o'erthrown,
If, 'mid indifference and apathy,
And wicked exultation when good men
On every side fall off, we know not how,
To selfishness, disguised in gentle names
Of peace and quiet and domestic love,
Yet mingled not unwillingly with sneers
On visionary minds; if, in this time   440
Of dereliction and dismay, I yet
Despair not of our nature, but retain
A more than Roman confidence, a faith
That fails not, in all sorrow my support,
The blessing of my life; the gift is yours,
Ye winds and sounding cataracts! 'tis yours,
Ye mountains! thine, O Nature! Thou hast fed
My lofty speculations; and in thee,
For this uneasy heart of ours, I find
A never-failing principle of joy   450
And purest passion.
             Thou, my Friend! wert reared
In the great city, 'mid far other scenes;[6]
But we, by different roads, at length have gained

The self-same bourne. And for this cause to thee
I speak, unapprehensive of contempt,
The insinuated scoff of coward tongues,
And all that silent language which so oft
In conversation between man and man
Blots from the human countenance all trace
Of beauty and of love. For thou hast sought   460
The truth in solitude, and, since the days
That gave thee liberty, full long desired
To serve in Nature's temple, thou hast been
The most assiduous of her ministers;
In many things my brother, chiefly here
In this our deep devotion.
                  Fare thee well!
Health and the quiet of a healthful mind
Attend thee! seeking oft the haunts of men,
And yet more often living with thyself,
And for thyself, so haply shall thy days   470
Be many, and a blessing to mankind.

BOOK THIRD

RESIDENCE AT CAMBRIDGE

IT WAS a dreary morning when the wheels
Rolled over a wide plain o'erhung with clouds,
And nothing cheered our way till first we saw
The long-roofed chapel of King's College lift
Turrets and pinnacles in answering files,
Extended high above a dusky grove.

    Advancing, we espied upon the road
A student clothed in gown and tasselled cap,
Striding along as if o'ertasked by Time,
Or covetous of exercise and air;   10
He passed—nor was I master of my eyes
Till he was left an arrow's flight behind.
As near and nearer to the spot we drew,
It seemed to suck us in with an eddy's force.
Onward we drove beneath the Castle; caught,
While crossing Magdalene Bridge, a glimpse of
    Cam;
And at the *Hoop* alighted, famous Inn.
    My spirit was up, my thoughts were full of hope;
Some friends I had, acquaintances who there
Seemed friends, poor simple school-boys, now hung
    round   20
With honour and importance: in a world
Of welcome faces up and down I roved;
Questions, directions, warnings and advice,
Flowed in upon me, from all sides; fresh day
Of pride and pleasure! to myself I seemed

---

[5] In 1799 Coleridge suggested to Wordsworth that he write
a poem addressed "to those, who, in consequence of the complete
failure of the French Revolution, have thrown up all hopes of the
amelioration of mankind, and are sinking into an almost epi-
curean selfishness, disguising the same under the soft titles of
domestic attachment and contempt for visionary *philosophes*."
(Cited by de Selincourt.)

[6] Coleridge attended school at Christ's Hospital, London. See
his *Frost at Midnight*, p. 464.

A man of business and expense, and went
From shop to shop about my own affairs,
To Tutor or to Tailor, as befel,
From street to street with loose and careless mind.

I was the Dreamer, they the Dream; I roamed   30
Delighted through the motley spectacle;
Gowns grave, or gaudy, doctors, students, streets,
Courts, cloisters, flocks of churches, gateways, towers:
Migration strange for a stripling of the hills,
A northern villager.
                    As if the change
Had waited on some Fairy's wand, at once
Behold me rich in monies, and attired
In splendid garb, with hose of silk, and hair
Powdered like rimy trees, when frost is keen.
My lordly dressing-gown, I pass it by,   40
With other signs of manhood that supplied
The lack of beard.—The weeks went roundly on,
With invitations, suppers, wine and fruit,
Smooth housekeeping within, and all without
Liberal, and suiting gentleman's array.

The Evangelist St. John,[1] my patron was:
Three Gothic courts are his, and in the first
Was my abiding-place, a nook obscure;
Right underneath, the College kitchens made
A humming sound, less tuneable than bees,   50
But hardly less industrious; with shrill notes
Of sharp command and scolding intermixed.
Near me hung Trinity's loquacious clock,
Who never let the quarters, night or day,
Slip by him unproclaimed, and told the hours
Twice over with a male and female voice.
Her pealing organ was my neighbour too;
And from my pillow, looking forth by light
Of moon or favouring stars, I could behold
The antechapel where the statue stood   60
Of Newton with his prism and silent face,
The marble index of a mind for ever
Voyaging through strange seas of Thought, alone.[2]

Of College labours, of the Lecturer's room
All studded round, as thick as chairs could stand,
With loyal students faithful to their books,
Half-and-half idlers, hardy recusants,
And honest dunces—of important days,
Examinations, when the man was weighed
As in a balance! of excessive hopes,   70
Tremblings withal and commendable fears,

––

[1] I.e., he was a student at St. John's College.
[2] A statue of Sir Isaac Newton stands in the antechapel of
Trinity College, next to St. John's.

Small jealousies, and triumphs good or bad,
Let others that know more speak as they know.
Such glory was but little sought by me,
And little won. Yet from the first crude days
Of settling time in this untried abode,
I was disturbed at times by prudent thoughts,
Wishing to hope without a hope, some fears
About my future worldly maintenance,
And, more than all, a strangeness in the mind,   80
A feeling that I was not for that hour,
Nor for that place. But wherefore be cast down?
For (not to speak of Reason and her pure
Reflective acts to fix the moral law
Deep in the conscience, nor of Christian Hope,
Bowing her head before her sister Faith
As one far mightier), hither I had come,
Bear witness Truth, endowed with holy powers
And faculties, whether to work or feel.
Oft when the dazzling show no longer new   90
Had ceased to dazzle, ofttimes did I quit
My comrades, leave the crowd, buildings and groves,
And as I paced alone the level fields
Far from those lovely sights and sounds sublime
With which I had been conversant, the mind
Drooped not; but there into herself returning,
With prompt rebound seemed fresh as heretofore.
At least I more distinctly recognized
Her native instincts: let me dare to speak
A higher language, say that now I felt   100
What independent solaces were mine,
To mitigate the injurious sway of place
Or circumstance, how far soever changed
In youth, or *to* be changed in manhood's prime;
Or for the few who shall be called to look
On the long shadows in our evening years,
Ordained precursors to the night of death.
As if awakened, summoned, roused, constrained,
I looked for universal things; perused
The common countenance of earth and sky: 110
Earth, nowhere unembellished by some trace
Of that first Paradise whence man was driven;
And sky, whose beauty and bounty are expressed
By the proud name she bears—the name of Heaven.
I called on both to teach me what they might;
Or turning the mind in upon herself
Pored, watched, expected, listened, spread my
          thoughts
And spread them with a wider creeping; felt
Incumbencies more awful, visitings
Of the Upholder of the tranquil soul,   120
That tolerates the indignities of Time,
And, from the centre of Eternity
All finite motions overruling, lives
In glory immutable. But peace! enough

Here to record that I was mounting now
To such community with highest truth—
A track pursuing, not untrod before,
From strict analogies by thought supplied
Or consciousnesses not to be subdued.
To every natural form, rock, fruit or flower,   130
Even the loose stones that cover the high-way,
I gave a moral life: I saw them feel,
Or linked them to some feeling: the great mass
Lay bedded in a quickening soul, and all
That I beheld respired with inward meaning.
Add that whate'er of Terror or of Love
Or Beauty, Nature's daily face put on
From transitory passion, unto this
I was as sensitive as waters are
To the sky's influence in a kindred mood   140
Of passion; was obedient as a lute
That waits upon the touches of the wind.
Unknown, unthought of, yet I was most rich—
I had a world about me—'twas my own;
I made it, for it only lived to me,
And to the God who sees into the heart.
Such sympathies, though rarely, were betrayed
By outward gestures and by visible looks:
Some called it madness—so indeed it was,
If child-like fruitfulness in passing joy,   150
If steady moods of thoughtfulness matured
To inspiration, sort with such a name;
If prophecy be madness; if things viewed
By poets in old time, and higher up
By the first men, earth's first inhabitants,
May in these tutored days no more be seen
With undisordered sight. But leaving this,
It was no madness, for the bodily eye
Amid my strongest workings evermore
Was searching out the lines of difference   160
As they lie hid in all external forms,
Near or remote, minute or vast, an eye
Which from a tree, a stone, a withered leaf,
To the broad ocean and the azure heavens
Spangled with kindred multitudes of stars,
Could find no surface where its power might sleep;
Which spake perpetual logic to my soul,
And by an unrelenting agency
Did bind my feelings even as in a chain.

    And here, O Friend! have I retraced my life   170
Up to an eminence, and told a tale
Of matters which not falsely may be called
The glory of my youth. Of genius, power,
Creation and divinity itself
I have been speaking, for my theme has been
What passed within me. Not of outward things
Done visibly for other minds, words, signs,

Symbols or actions, but of my own heart
Have I been speaking, and my youthful mind.
O Heavens! how awful is the might of souls,   180
And what they do within themselves while yet
The yoke of earth is new to them, the world
Nothing but a wild field where they were sown.
This is, in truth, heroic argument,
This genuine prowess, which I wished to touch
With hand however weak, but in the main
It lies far hidden from the reach of words.
Points have we all of us within our souls
Where all stand single; this I feel, and make
Breathings for incommunicable powers;   190
But is not each a memory to himself?
And, therefore, now that we must quit this theme,
I am not heartless, for there's not a man
That lives who hath not known his god-like hours,
And feels not what an empire we inherit
As natural beings in the strength of Nature.

    No more: for now into a populous plain
We must descend. A Traveller I am,
Whose tale is only of himself; even so,
So be it, if the pure of heart be prompt   200
To follow, and if thou, my honoured Friend!
Who in these thoughts art ever at my side,
Support, as heretofore, my fainting steps.

    It hath been told, that when the first delight
That flashed upon me from this novel show
Had failed, the mind returned into herself;
Yet true it is, that I had made a change
In climate, and my nature's outward coat
Changed also slowly and insensibly.
Full oft the quiet and exalted thoughts   210
Of loneliness gave way to empty noise
And superficial pastimes; now and then
Forced labour, and more frequently forced hopes;
And, worst of all, a treasonable growth
Of indecisive judgments, that impaired
And shook the mind's simplicity.—And yet
This was a gladsome time. Could I behold—
Who, less insensible than sodden clay
In a sea-river's bed at ebb of tide,
Could have beheld,—with undelighted heart,   220
So many happy youths, so wide and fair
A congregation in its budding-time
Of health, and hope, and beauty, all at once
So many divers samples from the growth
Of life's sweet season—could have seen unmoved
That miscellaneous garland of wild flowers
Decking the matron temples of a place
So famous through the world? To me, at least,
It was a goodly prospect: for, in sooth,

Though I had learnt betimes to stand unpropped,
And independent musings pleased me so   231
That spells seemed on me when I was alone,
Yet could I only cleave to solitude
In lonely places; if a throng was near
That way I leaned by nature; for my heart
Was social, and loved idleness and joy.

   Not seeking those who might participate
My deeper pleasures (nay, I had not once,
Though not unused to mutter lonesome songs,
Even with myself divided such delight,   240
Or looked that way for aught that might be
        clothed
In human language), easily I passed
From the remembrances of better things,
And slipped into the ordinary works
Of careless youth, unburthened, unalarmed.
Caverns there were within my mind which sun
Could never penetrate, yet did there not
Want store of leafy *arbours* where the light
Might enter in at will. Companionships,
Friendships, acquaintances, were welcome all.   250
We sauntered, played, or rioted; we talked
Unprofitable talk at morning hours;
Drifted about along the streets and walks,
Read lazily in trivial books, went forth
To gallop through the country in blind zeal
Of senseless horsemanship, or on the breast
Of Cam sailed boisterously, and let the stars
Come forth, perhaps without one quiet thought.

   Such was the tenor of the second act
In this new life. Imagination slept,   260
And yet not utterly. I could not print
Ground where the grass had yielded to the steps
Of generations of illustrious men,
Unmoved. I could not always lightly pass
Through the same gateways, sleep where they had
        slept,
Wake where they waked, range that inclosure old,
That garden of great intellects, undisturbed.
Place also by the side of this dark sense
Of noble feeling, that those spiritual men,
Even the great Newton's own ethereal self,   270
Seemed humbled in these precincts thence to be
The more endeared. Their several memories
        here
(Even like their persons in their portraits clothed
With the accustomed garb of daily life)
Put on a lowly and a touching grace
Of more distinct humanity, that left
All genuine admiration unimpaired.

   Beside the pleasant Mill of Trompington [3]
I laughed with Chaucer, in the hawthorn shade
Heard him, while birds were warbling, tell his tales
Of amorous passion. And that gentle Bard,   281
Chosen by the Muses for their Page of State—
Sweet Spenser, moving through his clouded heaven
With the moon's beauty and the moon's soft pace,
I called him Brother, Englishman, and Friend! [4]
Yea, our blind Poet, who, in his later day,
Stood almost single; uttering odious truth—
Darkness before, and danger's voice behind,
Soul awful—if the earth has ever lodged
An awful soul—I seemed to see him here   290
Familiarly, and in his scholar's dress
Bounding before me, yet a stripling youth—
A boy, no better, with his rosy cheeks
Angelical, keen eye, courageous look,
And conscious step of purity and pride.
Among the band of my compeers was one
Whom chance had stationed in the very room
Honoured by Milton's name. O temperate Bard!
Be it confest that, for the first time, seated
Within thy innocent lodge and oratory,   300
One of a festive circle, I poured out
Libations, to thy memory drank, till pride
And gratitude grew dizzy in a brain
Never excited by the fumes of wine
Before that hour, or since. Then, forth I ran
From the assembly; through a length of streets,
Ran, ostrich-like to reach our chapel door
In not a desperate or opprobrious time,
Albeit long after the importunate bell
Had stopped, with wearisome Cassandra voice   310
No longer haunting the dark winter night.
Call back, O Friend! a moment to thy mind
The place itself and fashion of the rites.
With careless ostentation shouldering up
My surplice, through the inferior throng I clove
Of the plain Burghers, who in audience stood
On the last skirts of their permitted ground,
Under the pealing organ. Empty thoughts!
I am ashamed of them: and that great Bard,
And thou, O Friend! who in thy ample mind   320
Hast placed me high above my best deserts,
Ye will forgive the weakness of that hour,
In some of its unworthy vanities,
Brother to many more.
                        In this mixed sort
The months passed on, remissly, not given up
To wilful alienation from the right,

----

[3] Chaucer's *Reeve's Tale* is set at Trumpington, two miles
south of Cambridge.
[4] Spenser (at Pembroke) and Milton (Christ's) had both been
Cambridge students.

Or walks of open scandal, but in vague
And loose indifference, easy likings, aims
Of a low pitch—duty and zeal dismissed,
Yet Nature, or a happy course of things   330
Not doing in their stead the needful work.
The memory languidly revolved, the heart
Reposed in noontide rest, the inner pulse
Of contemplation almost failed to beat.
Such life might not inaptly be compared
To a floating island, an amphibious spot
Unsound, of spongy texture, yet withal
Not wanting a fair face of water weeds
And pleasant flowers. The thirst of living praise,
Fit reverence for the glorious Dead, the sight   340
Of those long vistas, sacred catacombs,
Where mighty *minds* lie visibly entombed,
Have often stirred the heart of youth, and bred
A fervent love of rigorous discipline.—
Alas! such high emotion touched not me.
Look was there none within these walls to shame
My easy spirits, and discountenance
Their light composure, far less to instil
A calm resolve of mind, firmly addressed
To puissant efforts. Nor was this the blame   350
Of others but my own; I should, in truth,
As far as doth concern my single self,
Misdeem most widely, lodging it elsewhere:
For I, bred up 'mid Nature's luxuries,
Was a spoiled child, and rambling like the wind,
As I had done in daily intercourse
With those crystalline rivers, solemn heights,
And mountains; ranging like a fowl of the air,
I was ill-tutored for captivity;
To quit my pleasure, and, from month to month,   360
Take up a station calmly on the perch
Of sedentary peace. Those lovely forms
Had also left less space within my mind,
Which, wrought upon instinctively, had found
A freshness in those objects of her love,
A winning power, beyond all other power.
Not that I slighted books,—that were to lack
All sense,—but other passions in me ruled,
Passions more fervent, making me less prompt
To in-door study than was wise or well,   370
Or suited to those years. Yet I, though used
In magisterial liberty to rove,
Culling such flowers of learning as might tempt
A random choice, could shadow forth a place
(If now I yield not to a flattering dream)
Whose studious aspect should have bent me down
To instantaneous service; should at once
Have made me pay to science and to arts,
And written lore, acknowledged my liege lord,
A homage frankly offered up, like that   380

Which I had paid to Nature. Toil and pains
In this recess, by thoughtful Fancy built,
Should spread from heart to heart; and stately groves,
Majestic edifices, should not want
A corresponding dignity within.
The congregating temper that pervades
Our unripe years, not wasted, should be taught
To minister to works of high attempt—
Works which the enthusiast would perform with love.
Youth should be awed, religiously possessed   390
With a conviction of the power that waits
On knowledge, when sincerely sought and prized
For its own sake, on glory and on praise
If but by labour won, and fit to endure.
The passing day should learn to put aside
Her trappings here, should strip them off abashed
Before antiquity and stedfast truth
And strong book-mindedness; and over all
A healthy sound simplicity should reign,
A seemly plainness, name it what you will,   400
Republican or pious.
                              If these thoughts
Are a gratuitous emblazonry
That mocks the recreant age *we* live in, then
Be Folly and False-seeming free to affect
Whatever formal gait of discipline
Shall raise them highest in their own esteem—
Let them parade among the Schools at will,
But spare the House of God. Was ever known
The witless shepherd who persists to drive
A flock that thirsts not to a pool disliked?   410
A weight must surely hang on days begun
And ended with such mockery. Be wise,
Ye Presidents and Deans, and, till the spirit
Of ancient times revive, and youth be trained
At home in pious service, to your bells
Give seasonable rest, for 'tis a sound
Hollow as ever vexed the tranquil air;
And your officious doings bring disgrace
On the plain steeples of our English Church,
Whose worship, 'mid remotest village trees,   420
Suffers for this. Even Science, too, at hand
In daily sight of this irreverence,
Is smitten thence with an unnatural taint,
Loses her just authority, falls beneath
Collateral suspicion, else unknown.
This truth escaped me not, and I confess,
That having 'mid my native hills given loose
To a schoolboy's vision, I had raised a pile
Upon the basis of the coming time,
That fell in ruins round me. Oh, what joy   430
To see a sanctuary for our country's youth
Informed with such a spirit as might be
Its own protection; a primeval grove,

Where, though the shades with cheerfulness were
    filled,
Nor indigent of songs warbled from crowds
In under-coverts, yet the countenance
Of the whole place should bear a stamp of awe;
A habitation sober and demure
For ruminating creatures; a domain
For quiet things to wander in; a haunt   440
In which the heron should delight to feed
By the shy rivers, and the pelican
Upon the cypress spire in lonely thought
Might sit and sun himself.—Alas! Alas!
In vain for such solemnity I looked;
Mine eyes were crossed by butterflies, ears vexed
By chattering popinjays; the inner heart
Seemed trivial, and the impresses without
Of a too gaudy region.
               Different sight
Those venerable Doctors saw of old,   450
When all who dwelt within these famous walls
Led in abstemiousness a studious life;
When, in forlorn and naked chambers cooped
And crowded, o'er the ponderous books they hung
Like caterpillars eating out their way
In silence, or with keen devouring noise
Not to be tracked or fathered. Princes then
At matins froze, and couched at curfew-time,
Trained up through piety and zeal to prize
Spare diet, patient labour, and plain weeds.   460
O seat of Arts! renowned throughout the world!
Far different service in those homely days
The Muses' modest nurslings underwent
From their first childhood: in that glorious time
When Learning, like a stranger come from far,
Sounding through Christian lands her trumpet,
    roused
Peasant and king; when boys and youths, the growth
Of ragged villages and crazy huts,
Forsook their homes, and, errant in the quest
Of Patron, famous school or friendly nook,   470
Where, pensioned, they in shelter might sit down,
From town to town and through wide scattered realms
Journeyed with ponderous folios in their hands;
And often, starting from some covert place,
Saluted the chance comer on the road,
Crying, 'An obolus, a penny give
To a poor scholar!'⁵—when illustrious men,
Lovers of truth, by penury constrained,
Bucer, Erasmus, or Melancthon, read

⁵ A reference to Belisarius, the Byzantine who was said to
have begged in Constantinople after he was blinded. Bucer,
Erasmus, and Melancthon were European scholars in the early
sixteenth century. Bucer taught Greek at Cambridge; Erasmus
taught at Oxford and Cambridge (briefly).

Before the doors or windows of their cells   480
By moonshine through mere lack of taper light.

But peace to vain regrets! We see but darkly
Even when we look behind us, and best things
Are not so pure by nature that they needs
Must keep to all, as fondly all believe,
Their highest promise. If the mariner
When at reluctant distance he hath passed
Some tempting island, could but know the ills
That must have fallen upon him had he brought
His bark to land upon the wished-for shore,   490
Good cause would oft be his to thank the surf
Whose white belt scared him thence, or wind that blew
Inexorably adverse: for myself
I grieve not; happy is the gownèd youth,
Who only misses what I missed, who falls
No lower than I fell.
               I did not love,
Judging not ill perhaps, the timid course
Of our scholastic studies; could have wished
To see the river flow with ampler range
And freer pace; but more, far more, I grieved   500
To see displayed among an eager few,
Who in the field of contest persevered,
Passions unworthy of youth's generous heart
And mounting spirit, pitiably repaid,
When so disturbed, whatever palms are won.
From these I turned to travel with the shoal
Of more unthinking natures, easy minds
And pillowy; yet not wanting love that makes
The day pass lightly on, when foresight sleeps,
And wisdom and the pledges interchanged   510
With our own inner being are forgot.

Yet was this deep vacation not given up
To utter waste. Hitherto I had stood
In my own mind remote from social life,
(At least from what we commonly so name,)
Like a lone shepherd on a promontory
Who lacking occupation looks far forth
Into the boundless sea, and rather makes
Than finds what he beholds. And sure it is,
That this first transit from the smooth delights   520
And wild outlandish walks of simple youth
To something that resembled an approach
Towards human business, to a privileged world
Within a world, a midway residence
With all its intervenient imagery,
Did better suit my visionary mind,
Far better, than to have been bolted forth,
Thrust out abruptly into Fortune's way
Among the conflicts of substantial life;
By a more just gradation did lead on   530

To higher things; more naturally matured,
For permanent possession, better fruits,
Whether of truth or virtue, to ensue.
In serious mood, but oftener, I confess,
With playful zest of fancy did we note
(How could we less?) the manners and the ways
Of those who lived distinguished by the badge
Of good or ill report; or those with whom
By frame of Academic discipline
We were perforce connected, men whose sway   540
And known authority of office served
To set our minds on edge, and did no more.
Nor wanted we rich pastime of this kind,
Found everywhere, but chiefly in the ring
Of the grave Elders, men unscoured, grotesque
In character, tricked out like aged trees
Which through the lapse of their infirmity
Give ready place to any random seed
That chooses to be reared upon their trunks.

Here on my view, confronting vividly   550
Those shepherd swains whom I had lately left,
Appeared a different aspect of old age;
How different! yet both distinctly marked,
Objects embossed to catch the general eye,
Or portraitures for special use designed,
As some might seem, so aptly do they serve
To illustrate Nature's book of rudiments—
That book upheld as with maternal care
When she would enter on her tender scheme
Of teaching comprehension with delight,   560
And mingling playful with pathetic thoughts.

The surfaces of artificial life
And manners finely wrought, the delicate race
Of colours, lurking, gleaming up and down
Through that state arras woven with silk and gold;
This wily interchange of snaky hues,
Willingly or unwillingly revealed,
I neither knew nor cared for; and as such
Were wanting here, I took what might be found
Of less elaborate fabric. At this day   570
I smile, in many a mountain solitude
Conjuring up scenes as obsolete in freaks
Of character, in points of wit as broad,
As aught by wooden images performed
For entertainment of the gaping crowd
At wake or fair. And oftentimes do flit
Remembrances before me of old men—
Old humourists, who have been long in their
     graves,
And having almost in my mind put off
Their human names, have into phantoms passed   580
Of texture midway between life and books.

I play the loiterer: 'tis enough to note
That here in dwarf proportions were expressed
The limbs of the great world; its eager strifes
Collaterally pourtrayed, as in mock fight,
A tournament of blows, some hardly dealt
Though short of mortal combat; and whate'er
Might in this pageant be supposed to hit
An artless rustic's notice, this way less,
More that way, was not wasted upon me—   590
And yet the spectacle may well demand
A more substantial name, no mimic show,
Itself a living part of a live whole,
A creek in the vast sea; for, all degrees
And shapes of spurious fame and short-lived
     praise
Here sate in state, and fed with daily alms
Retainers won away from solid good;
And here was Labour, his own bond-slave;
     Hope,
That never set the pains against the prize;
Idleness halting with his weary clog,   600
And poor misguided Shame, and witless Fear,
And simple Pleasure foraging for Death;
Honour misplaced, and Dignity astray;
Feuds, factions, flatteries, enmity, and guile;
Murmuring submission, and bald government,
(The idol weak as the idolator,)
And Decency and Custom starving Truth,
And blind Authority beating with his staff
The child that might have led him; Emptiness
Followed as of good omen, and meek Worth   610
Left to herself unheard of and unknown.

Of these and other kindred notices
I cannot say what portion is in truth
The naked recollection of that time,
And what may rather have been called to life
By after-meditation. But delight
That, in an easy temper lulled asleep,
Is still with Innocence its own reward,
This was not wanting. Carelessly I roamed
As through a wide museum from whose stores   620
A casual rarity is singled out
And has its brief perusal, then gives way
To others, all supplanted in their turn;
Till 'mid this crowded neighbourhood of things
That are by nature most unneighbourly,
The head turns round and cannot right itself;
And though an aching and a barren sense
Of gay confusion still be uppermost,
With few wise longings and but little love,
Yet to the memory something cleaves at last,   630
Whence profit may be drawn in times to
     come.

Thus in submissive idleness, my Friend!
The labouring time of autumn, winter, spring,
Eight months! rolled pleasingly away; the ninth
Came and returned me to my native hills.

BOOK FOURTH
SUMMER VACATION

BRIGHT was the summer's noon when quickening
    steps
Followed each other till a dreary moor
Was crossed, a bare ridge clomb, upon whose top
Standing alone, as from a rampart's edge,
I overlooked the bed of Windermere,
Like a vast river, stretching in the sun.
With exultation, at my feet I saw
Lake, islands, promontories, gleaming bays,
A universe of Nature's fairest forms
Proudly revealed with instantaneous burst,   10
Magnificent, and beautiful, and gay.
I bounded down the hill shouting amain
For the old Ferryman; to the shout the rocks
Replied, and when the Charon[1] of the flood
Had staid his oars, and touched the jutting pier,
I did not step into the well-known boat
Without a cordial greeting. Thence with speed
Up the familiar hill I took my way
Towards that sweet Valley where I had been reared;
'Twas but a short hour's walk, ere veering round   20
I saw the snow-white church upon her hill
Sit like a thronèd Lady, sending out
A gracious look all over her domain.
Yon azure smoke betrays the lurking town;
With eager footsteps I advance and reach
The cottage threshold where my journey closed.
Glad welcome had I, with some tears, perhaps,
From my old Dame[2] so kind and motherly,
While she perused me with a parent's pride.
The thoughts of gratitude shall fall like dew   30
Upon thy grave, good creature! While my heart
Can beat never will I forget thy name.
Heaven's blessing be upon thee where thou liest
After thy innocent and busy stir
In narrow cares, thy little daily growth
Of calm enjoyments, after eighty years,
And more than eighty, of untroubled life,
Childless, yet by the strangers to thy blood

---

[1] In Greek mythology, the boatman who ferried the dead
across the river Styx.
[2] Anne Tyson (1713–1796), with whom the Wordsworth
brothers lived when attending Hawkshead Free Grammar
School.

Honoured with little less than filial love.
What joy was mine to see thee once again,   40
Thee and thy dwelling, and a crowd of things
About its narrow precincts all beloved,
And many of them seeming yet my own!
Why should I speak of what a thousand hearts
Have felt, and every man alive can guess?
The rooms, the court, the garden were not left
Long unsaluted, nor the sunny seat
Round the stone table under the dark pine,
Friendly to studious or to festive hours;
Nor that unruly child of mountain birth,   50
The froward brook, who, soon as he was boxed
Within our garden, found himself at once,
As if by trick insidious and unkind,
Stripped of his voice and left to dimple down
(Without an effort and without a will)
A channel paved by man's officious care.
I looked at him and smiled, and smiled again,
And in the press of twenty thousand thoughts,
'Ha,' quoth I, 'pretty prisoner, are you there!'
Well might sarcastic Fancy then have whispered,   60
'An emblem here behold of thy own life;
In its late course of even days with all
Their smooth enthralment;' but the heart was full,
Too full for that reproach. My aged Dame
Walked proudly at my side: she guided me;
I willing, nay—nay, wishing to be led.
—The face of every neighbour whom I met
Was like a volume to me: some were hailed
Upon the road, some busy at their work,
Unceremonious greetings interchanged   70
With half the length of a long field between.
Among my schoolfellows I scattered round
Like recognitions, but with some constraint
Attended, doubtless, with a little pride,
But with more shame, for my habiliments,
The transformation wrought by gay attire.
Not less delighted did I take my place
At our domestic table: and, dear Friend!
In this endeavour simply to relate
A Poet's history, may I leave untold   80
The thankfulness with which I laid me down
In my accustomed bed, more welcome now
Perhaps than if it had been more desired
Or been more often thought of with regret;
That lowly bed whence I had heard the wind
Roar and the rain beat hard, where I so oft
Had laid awake on summer nights to watch
The moon in splendour couched among the leaves
Of a tall ash, that near our cottage stood;
Had watched her with fixed eyes while to and fro   90
In the dark summit of the waving tree
She rocked with every impulse of the breeze.

Among the favourites whom it pleased me well
To see again, was one by ancient right
Our inmate, a rough terrier of the hills;
By birth and call of nature pre-ordained
To hunt the badger and unearth the fox
Among the impervious crags, but having been
From youth our own adopted, he had passed
Into a gentler service. And when first   100
The boyish spirit flagged, and day by day
Along my veins I kindled with the stir,
The fermentation, and the vernal heat
Of poesy, affecting private shades
Like a sick Lover, then this dog was used
To watch me, an attendant and a friend,
Obsequious to my steps early and late,
Though often of such dilatory walk
Tired, and uneasy at the halts I made.
A hundred times when, roving high and low,   110
I have been harassed with the toil of verse,
Much pains and little progress, and at once
Some lovely Image in the song rose up
Full-formed, like Venus rising from the sea;
Then have I darted forwards to let loose
My hand upon his back with stormy joy,
Caressing him again and yet again.
And when at evening on the public way
I sauntered, like a river murmuring
And talking to itself when all things else   120
Are still, the creature trotted on before;
Such was his custom; but whene'er he met
A passenger approaching, he would turn
To give me timely notice, and straightway,
Grateful for that admonishment, I hushed
My voice, composed my gait, and, with the air
And mien of one whose thoughts are free, advanced
To give and take a greeting that might save
My name from piteous rumours, such as wait
On men suspected to be crazed in brain.   130

     Those walks well worthy to be prized and loved—
Regretted!—that word, too, was on my tongue,
But they were richly laden with all good,
And cannot be remembered but with thanks
And gratitude, and perfect joy of heart—
Those walks in all their freshness now came back
Like a returning Spring. When first I made
Once more the circuit of our little lake,
If ever happiness hath lodged with man,
That day consummate happiness was mine,   140
Wide-spreading, steady, calm, contemplative.
The sun was set, or setting, when I left
Our cottage door, and evening soon brought on
A sober hour, not winning or serene,
For cold and raw the air was, and untuned;

But as a face we love is sweetest then
When sorrow damps it, or whatever look
It chance to wear is sweetest if the heart
Have fulness in herself; even so with me
It fared that evening. Gently did my soul   150
Put off her veil, and, self-transmuted, stood
Naked, as in the presence of her God.
While on I walked, a comfort seemed to touch
A heart that had not been disconsolate:
Strength came where weakness was not known to be,
At least not felt; and restoration came
Like an intruder knocking at the door
Of unacknowledged weariness. I took
The balance, and with firm hand weighed myself.
—Of that external scene which round me lay,   160
Little, in this abstraction, did I see;
Remembered less; but I had inward hopes
And swellings of the spirit, was rapt and soothed,
Conversed with promises, had glimmering views
How life pervades the undecaying mind;
How the immortal soul with God-like power
Informs, creates, and thaws the deepest sleep
That time can lay upon her; how on earth,
Man, if he do but live within the light
Of high endeavours, daily spreads abroad   170
His being armed with strength that cannot fail.
Nor was there want of milder thoughts, of love,
Of innocence, and holiday repose;
And more than pastoral quiet, 'mid the stir
Of boldest projects, and a peaceful end
At last, or glorious, by endurance won.
Thus musing, in a wood I sate me down
Alone, continuing there to muse: the slopes
And heights meanwhile were slowly overspread
With darkness, and before a rippling breeze   180
The long lake lengthened out its hoary line,
And in the sheltered coppice where I sate,
Around me from among the hazel leaves,
Now here, now there, moved by the straggling wind,
Came ever and anon a breath-like sound,
Quick as the pantings of the faithful dog,
The off and on companion of my walk;
And such, at times, believing them to be,
I turned my head to look if he were there;
Then into solemn thought I passed once more.   190

     A freshness also found I at this time
In human Life, the daily life of those
Whose occupations really I loved;
The peaceful scene oft filled me with surprise
Changed like a garden in the heat of spring
After an eight-days' absence. For (to omit
The things which were the same and yet appeared
Far otherwise) amid this rural solitude,

A narrow Vale where each was known to all,
'Twas not indifferent to a youthful mind   200
To mark some sheltering bower or sunny nook,
Where an old man had used to sit alone,
Now vacant; pale-faced babes whom I had left
In arms, now rosy prattlers at the feet
Of a pleased grandame tottering up and down;
And growing girls whose beauty, filched away
With all its pleasant promises, was gone
To deck some slighted playmate's homely cheek.

   Yes, I had something of a subtler sense,
And often looking round was moved to smiles   210
Such as a delicate work of humour breeds;
I read, without design, the opinions, thoughts,
Of those plain-living people now observed
With clearer knowledge; with another eye
I saw the quiet woodman in the woods,
The shepherd roam the hills. With new delight,
This chiefly, did I note my grey-haired Dame;
Saw her go forth to church or other work
Of state, equipped in monumental trim;
Short velvet cloak, (her bonnet of the like),   220
A mantle such as Spanish Cavaliers
Wore in old time. Her smooth domestic life,
Affectionate without disquietude,
Her talk, her business, pleased me; and no less
Her clear though shallow stream of piety
That ran on Sabbath days a fresher course;
With thoughts unfelt till now I saw her read
Her Bible on hot Sunday afternoons,
And loved the book, when she had dropped asleep
And made of it a pillow for her head.   230

   Nor less do I remember to have felt,
Distinctly manifested at this time,
A human-heartedness about my love
For objects hitherto the absolute wealth
Of my own private being and no more:
Which I had loved, even as a blessed spirit
Or Angel, if he were to dwell on earth,
Might love in individual happiness.
But now there opened on me other thoughts
Of change, congratulation or regret,   240
A pensive feeling! It spread far and wide;
The trees, the mountains shared it, and the brooks,
The stars of Heaven, now seen in their old haunts—
White Sirius glittering o'er the southern crags,
Orion with his belt, and those fair Seven,[3]
Acquaintances of every little child,
And Jupiter, my own beloved star!
Whatever shadings of mortality,

------

[3] I.e., the Big Dipper.

Whatever imports from the world of death
Had come among these objects heretofore,   250
Were, in the main, of mood less tender: strong,
Deep, gloomy were they, and severe; the scatterings
Of awe or tremulous dread, that had given way
In later youth to yearnings of a love
Enthusiastic, to delight and hope.

   As one who hangs down-bending from the side
Of a slow-moving boat, upon the breast
Of a still water, solacing himself
With such discoveries as his eye can make
Beneath him in the bottom of the deep,   260
Sees many beauteous sights—weeds, fishes, flowers,
Grots, pebbles, roots of trees, and fancies more,
Yet often is perplexed and cannot part
The shadow from the substance, rocks and sky,
Mountains and clouds, reflected in the depth
Of the clear flood, from things which there abide
In their true dwelling; now is crossed by gleam
Of his own image, by a sun-beam now,
And wavering motions sent he knows not whence,
Impediments that make his task more sweet;   270
Such pleasant office have we long pursued
Incumbent o'er the surface of past time
With like success, nor often have appeared
Shapes fairer or less doubtfully discerned
Than these to which the Tale, indulgent Friend!
Would now direct thy notice. Yet in spite
Of pleasure won, and knowledge not withheld,
There was an inner falling off—I loved,
Loved deeply all that had been loved before,
More deeply even than ever: but a swarm   280
Of heady schemes jostling each other, gawds,
And feast and dance, and public revelry,
And sports and games (too grateful in themselves,
Yet in themselves less grateful, I believe,
Than as they were a badge glossy and fresh
Of manliness and freedom) all conspired
To lure my mind from firm habitual quest
Of feeding pleasures, to depress the zeal
And damp those daily yearnings which had once been
       mine—
A wild, unworldly-minded youth, given up   290
To his own eager thoughts. It would demand
Some skill, and longer time than may be spared,
To paint these vanities, and how they wrought
In haunts where they, till now, had been unknown.
It seemed the very garments that I wore
Preyed on my strength, and stopped the quiet stream
Of self-forgetfulness.
                         Yes, that heartless chase
Of trivial pleasures was a poor exchange
For books and nature at that early age.

'Tis true, some casual knowledge might be gained
Of character or life; but at that time,   301
Of manners put to school I took small note,
And all my deeper passions lay elsewhere.
Far better had it been to exalt the mind
By solitary study, to uphold
Intense desire through meditative peace;
And yet, for chastisement of these regrets,
The memory of one particular hour
Doth here rise up against me. 'Mid a throng
Of maids and youths, old men, and matrons staid,
A medley of all tempers, I had passed   311
The night in dancing, gaiety, and mirth,
With din of instruments and shuffling feet,
And glancing forms, and tapers glittering,
And unaimed prattle flying up and down;
Spirits upon the stretch, and here and there
Slight shocks of young love-liking interspersed,
Whose transient pleasure mounted to the head,
And tingled through the veins. Ere we retired,
The cock had crowed, and now the eastern sky   320
Was kindling, not unseen, from humble copse
And open field, through which the pathway wound,
And homeward led my steps. Magnificent
The morning rose, in memorable pomp,
Glorious as e'er I had beheld—in front,
The sea lay laughing at a distance; near,
The solid mountains shone, bright as the clouds,
Grain-tinctured, drenched in empyrean light;[4]
And in the meadows and the lower grounds
Was all the sweetness of a common dawn—   330
Dews, vapours, and the melody of birds,
And labourers going forth to till the fields.

   Ah! need I say, dear Friend! that to the brim
My heart was full; I made no vows, but vows
Were then made for me; bond unknown to me
Was given, that I should be, else sinning greatly,
A dedicated Spirit. On I walked
In thankful blessedness, which yet survives.

   Strange rendezvous my mind was at that time,
A parti-coloured show of grave and gay,   340
Solid and light, short-sighted and profound;
Of inconsiderate habits and sedate,
Consorting in one mansion unreproved.
The worth I knew of powers that I possessed,
Though slighted and too oft misused. Besides,
That summer, swarming as it did with thoughts
Transient and idle, lacked not intervals
When Folly from the frown of fleeting Time
Shrunk, and the mind experienced in herself

⁴ Grain-tinctured: clear red.

Conformity as just as that of old   350
To the end and written spirit of God's works,
Whether held forth in Nature or in Man,
Through pregnant vision, separate or conjoined.

   When from our better selves we have too long
Been parted by the hurrying world, and droop,
Sick of its business, of its pleasures tired,
How gracious, how benign, is Solitude;
How potent a mere image of her sway;
Most potent when impressed upon the mind
With an appropriate human centre—hermit,   360
Deep in the bosom of the wilderness;
Votary (in vast cathedral, where no foot
Is treading, where no other face is seen)
Kneeling at prayers; or watchman on the top
Of lighthouse, beaten by Atlantic waves;
Or as the soul of that great Power is met
Sometimes embodied on a public road,
When, for the night deserted, it assumes
A character of quiet more profound
Than pathless wastes.   370
                     Once, when those summer months
Were flown, and autumn brought its annual show
Of oars with oars contending, sails with sails,
Upon Winander's spacious breast, it chanced
That—after I had left a flower-decked room
(Whose in-door pastime, lighted up, survived
To a late hour), and spirits overwrought
Were making night do penance for a day
Spent in a round of strenuous idleness—
My homeward course led up a long ascent,
Where the road's watery surface, to the top   380
Of that sharp rising, glittered to the moon
And bore the semblance of another stream
Stealing with silent lapse to join the brook
That murmured in the vale. All else was still;
No living thing appeared in earth or air,
And, save the flowing water's peaceful voice,
Sound there was none—but, lo! an uncouth shape,
Shown by a sudden turning of the road,
So near that, slipping back into the shade
Of a thick hawthorn, I could mark him well,   390
Myself unseen. He was of stature tall,
A span above man's common measure tall,
Stiff, lank, and upright; a more meagre man
Was never seen before by night or day.
Long were his arms, pallid his hands; his mouth
Looked ghastly in the moonlight: from behind,
A mile-stone propped him; I could also ken
That he was clothed in military garb,
Though faded, yet entire. Companionless,
No dog attending, by no staff sustained,   400
He stood, and in his very dress appeared

A desolation, a simplicity,
To which the trappings of a gaudy world
Make a strange back-ground. From his lips, ere long,
Issued low muttered sounds, as if of pain
Or some uneasy thought; yet still his form
Kept the same awful steadiness—at his feet
His shadow lay, and moved not. From self-blame
Not wholly free, I watched him thus; at length
Subduing my heart's specious cowardice,   410
I left the shady nook where I had stood
And hailed him. Slowly from his resting-place
He rose, and with a lean and wasted arm
In measured gesture lifted to his head
Returned my salutation; then resumed
His station as before; and when I asked
His history, the veteran, in reply,
Was neither slow nor eager; but, unmoved,
And with a quiet uncomplaining voice,
A stately air of mild indifference,   420
He told in few plain words a soldier's tale—
That in the Tropic Islands he had served,
Whence he had landed scarcely three weeks past;
That on his landing he had been dismissed,
And now was travelling towards his native home.
This heard, I said, in pity, 'Come with me.'
He stooped, and straightway from the ground took up
An oaken staff by me yet unobserved—
A staff which must have dropt from his slack hand
And lay till now neglected in the grass.   430
Though weak his step and cautious, he appeared
To travel without pain, and I beheld,
With an astonishment but ill suppressed,
His ghastly figure moving at my side;
Nor could I, while we journeyed thus, forbear
To turn from present hardships to the past,
And speak of war, battle, and pestilence,
Sprinkling this talk with questions, better spared,
On what he might himself have seen or felt.
He all the while was in demeanour calm,   440
Concise in answer; solemn and sublime
He might have seemed, but that in all he said
There was a strange half-absence, as of one
Knowing too well the importance of his theme,
But feeling it no longer. Our discourse
Soon ended, and together on we passed
In silence through a wood gloomy and still.
Up-turning, then, along an open field,
We reached a cottage. At the door I knocked,
And earnestly to charitable care   450
Commended him as a poor friendless man,
Belated and by sickness overcome.
Assured that now the traveller would repose
In comfort, I entreated that henceforth

He would not linger in the public ways,
But ask for timely furtherance and help
Such as his state required. At this reproof,
With the same ghastly mildness in his look,
He said, 'My trust is in the God of Heaven,
And in the eye of him who passes me!'   460

   The cottage door was speedily unbarred,
And now the soldier touched his hat once more
With his lean hand, and in a faltering voice,
Whose tone bespake reviving interests
Till then unfelt, he thanked me; I returned
The farewell blessing of the patient man,
And so we parted. Back I cast a look,
And lingered near the door a little space,
Then sought with quiet heart my distant home.

BOOK FIFTH

BOOKS

WHEN Contemplation, like the night-calm felt
Through earth and sky, spreads widely, and sends
      deep
Into the soul its tranquillizing power,
Even then I sometimes grieve for thee, O Man,
Earth's paramount Creature! not so much for woes
That thou endurest; heavy though that weight be,
Cloud-like it mounts, or touched with light divine
Doth melt away; but for those palms achieved,
Through length of time, by patient exercise
Of study and hard thought; there, there, it is   10
That sadness finds its fuel. Hitherto,
In progress through this work, my mind hath looked
Upon the speaking face of earth and heaven
As her prime teacher, intercourse with man
Established by the sovereign Intellect,
Who through that bodily image hath diffused,
As might appear to the eye of fleeting time,
A deathless spirit. Thou also, man! hast wrought,
For commerce of thy nature with herself,
Things that aspire to unconquerable life;   20
And yet we feel—we cannot choose but feel—
That they must perish. Tremblings of the heart
It gives, to think that our immortal being
No more shall need such garments; and yet man,
As long as he shall be the child of earth,
Might almost 'weep to have' what he may lose,[1]
Nor be himself extinguished, but survive,
Abject, depressed, forlorn, disconsolate.

[1] Quoted from Shakespeare's Sonnet 64.

A thought is with me sometimes, and I say,—
Should the whole frame of earth by inward throes   30
Be wrenched, or fire come down from far to scorch
Her pleasant habitations, and dry up
Old Ocean, in his bed left singed and bare,
Yet would the living Presence still subsist
Victorious, and composure would ensue,
And kindlings like the morning—presage sure
Of day returning and of life revived.
But all the meditations of mankind,
Yea, all the adamantine holds of truth
By reason built, or passion, which itself   40
Is highest reason in a soul sublime;
The consecrated works of Bard and Sage,
Sensuous or intellectual, wrought by men,
Twin labourers and heirs of the same hopes;
Where would they be? Oh! why hath not the Mind
Some element to stamp her image on
In nature somewhat nearer to her own?
Why, gifted with such powers to send abroad
Her spirit, must it lodge in shrines so frail?

One day, when from my lips a like complaint   50
Had fallen in presence of a studious friend,
He with a smile made answer, that in truth
'Twas going far to seek disquietude;
But on the front of his reproof confessed
That he himself had oftentimes given way
To kindred hauntings. Whereupon I told,
That once in the stillness of a summer's noon,
While I was seated in a rocky cave
By the sea-side, perusing, so it chanced,
The famous history of the errant knight   60
Recorded by Cervantes, these same thoughts
Beset me, and to height unusual rose,
While listlessly I sate, and, having closed
The book, had turned my eyes toward the wide sea.
On poetry and geometric truth,
And their high privilege of lasting life,
From all internal injury exempt,
I mused, upon these chiefly: and at length,
My senses yielding to the sultry air,
Sleep seized me, and I passed into a dream.   70
I saw before me stretched a boundless plain
Of sandy wilderness, all black and void,
And as I looked around, distress and fear
Came creeping over me, when at my side,
Close at my side, an uncouth shape appeared
Upon a dromedary, mounted high.
He seemed an Arab of the Bedouin tribes:
A lance he bore, and underneath one arm
A stone, and in the opposite hand, a shell
Of a surpassing brightness. At the sight   80

Much I rejoiced, not doubting but a guide
Was present, one who with unerring skill
Would through the desert lead me; and while yet
I looked and looked, self-questioned what this freight
Which the new-comer carried through the waste
Could mean, the Arab told me that the stone
(To give it in the language of the dream)
Was 'Euclid's Elements;' and 'This,' said he,
'Is something of more worth;' and at the word
Stretched forth the shell, so beautiful in shape,   90
In colour so resplendent, with command
That I should hold it to my ear. I did so,
And heard that instant in an unknown tongue,
Which yet I understood, articulate sounds,
A loud prophetic blast of harmony;
An Ode, in passion uttered, which foretold
Destruction to the children of the earth
By deluge, now at hand. No sooner ceased
The song, than the Arab with calm look declared
That all would come to pass of which the voice   100
Had given forewarning, and that he himself
Was going then to bury those two books:
The one that held acquaintance with the stars,
And wedded soul to soul in purest bond
Of reason, undisturbed by space or time;
The other that was a god, yea many gods,
Had voices more than all the winds, with power
To exhilarate the spirit, and to soothe,
Through every clime, the heart of human kind.
While this was uttering, strange as it may seem,   110
I wondered not, although I plainly saw
The one to be a stone, the other a shell;
Nor doubted once but that they both were books,
Having a perfect faith in all that passed.
Far stronger, now, grew the desire I felt
To cleave unto this man; but when I prayed
To share his enterprise, he hurried on
Reckless of me: I followed, not unseen,
For oftentimes he cast a backward look,
Grasping his twofold treasure.—Lance in rest,   120
He rode, I keeping pace with him; and now
He, to my fancy, had become the knight
Whose tale Cervantes tells; yet not the knight,
But was an Arab of the desert too;
Of these was neither, and was both at once.
His countenance, meanwhile, grew more disturbed;
And, looking backwards when he looked, mine eyes
Saw, over half the wilderness diffused,
A bed of glittering light: I asked the cause:
'It is,' said he, 'the waters of the deep   130
Gathering upon us;' quickening then the pace
Of the unwieldly creature he bestrode,
He left me: I called after him aloud;

He heeded not; but, with his twofold charge
Still in his grasp, before me, full in view,
Went hurrying o'er the illimitable waste,
With the fleet waters of a drowning world
In chase of him; whereat I waked in terror,
And saw the sea before me, and the book,
In which I had been reading, at my side.   140

   Full often, taking from the world of sleep
This Arab phantom, which I thus beheld,
This semi-Quixote, I to him have given
A substance, fancied him a living man,
A gentle dweller in the desert, crazed
By love and feeling, and internal thought
Protracted among endless solitudes;
Have shaped him wandering upon this quest!
Nor have I pitied him; but rather felt
Reverence was due to a being thus employed;   150
And thought that, in the blind and awful lair
Of such a madness, reason did lie couched.
Enow there are on earth to take in charge
Their wives, their children, and their virgin loves,
Or whatsoever else the heart holds dear;
Enow to stir for these; yea, will I say,
Contemplating in soberness the approach
Of an event so dire, by signs in earth
Or heaven made manifest, that I could share
That maniac's fond anxiety, and go   160
Upon like errand. Oftentimes at least
Me hath such strong entrancement overcome,
When I have held a volume in my hand,
Poor earthly casket of immortal verse,
Shakespeare, or Milton, labourers divine!
   Great and benign, indeed, must be the power
Of living nature, which could thus so long
Detain me from the best of other guides
And dearest helpers, left unthanked, unpraised.
Even in the time of lisping infancy,   170
And later down, in prattling childhood, even
While I was travelling back among those days,
How could I ever play an ingrate's part?
Once more should I have made those bowers resound,
By intermingling strains of thankfulness
With their own thoughtless melodies; at least
It might have well beseemed me to repeat
Some simply fashioned tale, to tell again,
In slender accents of sweet verse, some tale
That did bewitch me then, and soothes me now.   180
O Friend! O Poet! brother of my soul,
Think not that I could pass along untouched
By these remembrances. Yet wherefore speak?
Why call upon a few weak words to say
What is already written in the hearts
Of all that breathe?—what in the path of all

Drops daily from the tongue of every child,
Wherever man is found? The trickling tear
Upon the cheek of listening Infancy
Proclaims it, and the insuperable look   190
That drinks as if it never could be full.

   That portion of my story I shall leave
There registered: whatever else of power
Or pleasure, sown or fostered thus, may be
Peculiar to myself, let that remain
Where still it works, though hidden from all search
Among the depths of time. Yet is it just
That here, in memory of all books which lay
Their sure foundations in the heart of man,
Whether by native prose, or numerous verse,   200
That in the name of all inspirèd souls,
From Homer the great Thunderer, from the voice
That roars along the bed of Jewish song,
And that more varied and elaborate,
Those tumpet-tones of harmony that shake
Our shores in England,—from those loftiest notes
Down to the low and wren-like warblings, made
For cottagers and spinners at the wheel,
And sun-burnt travellers resting their tired limbs,
Stretched under wayside hedge-rows, ballad tunes,
Food for the hungry ears of little ones,   211
And of old men who have survived their joys:
'Tis just that in behalf of these, the works,
And of the men that framed them, whether known,
Or sleeping nameless in their scattered graves,
That I should here assert their rights, attest
Their honours, and should, once for all, pronounce
Their benediction; speak of them as Powers
For ever to be hallowed; only less,
For what we are and what we may become,   220
Than Nature's self, which is the breath of God,
Or His pure Word by miracle revealed.

   Rarely and with reluctance would I stoop
To transitory themes; yet I rejoice,
And, by these thoughts admonished, will pour out
Thanks with uplifted heart, that I was reared
Safe from an evil which these days have laid
Upon the children of the land, a pest
That might have dried me up, body and soul.[2]
This verse is dedicate to Nature's self,   230
And things that teach as Nature teaches: then,
Oh! where had been the Man, the Poet where,
Where had we been, we two, beloved Friend!
If in the season of unperilous choice,
In lieu of wandering, as we did, through vales

---

[2] Educational theorists, disciples of Rousseau, wished to
replace fantasy and fairy tales with true and morally uplifting
literature in the education of children.

Rich with indigenous produce, open ground
Of Fancy, happy pastures ranged at will,
We had been followed, hourly watched, and noosed,
Each in his several melancholy walk
Stringed like a poor man's heifer at its feed,   240
Led through the lanes in forlorn servitude;
Or rather like a stallèd ox debarred
From touch of growing grass, that may not taste
A flower till it have yielded up its sweets
A prelibation to the mower's scythe.

Behold the parent hen amid her brood,
Though fledged and feathered, and well pleased to
       part
And straggle from her presence, still a brood,
And she herself from the maternal bond
Still undischarged; yet doth she little more   250
Than move with them in tenderness and love,
A centre to the circle which they make;
And now and then, alike from need of theirs
And call of her own natural appetites,
She scratches, ransacks up the earth for food,
Which they partake at pleasure. Early died [3]
My honoured Mother, she who was the heart
And hinge of all our learnings and our loves:
She left us destitute, and, as we might,
Trooping together. Little suits it me   260
To break upon the sabbath of her rest
With any thought that looks at others' blame;
Nor would I praise her but in perfect love.
Hence am I checked: but let me boldly say,
In gratitude, and for the sake of truth,
Unheard by her, that she, not falsely taught,
Fetching her goodness rather from times past,
Than shaping novelties for times to come,
Had no presumption, no such jealousy,
Nor did by habit of her thoughts mistrust   270
Our nature, but had virtual faith that He
Who fills the mother's breast with innocent milk,
Doth also for our nobler part provide,
Under His great correction and control,
As innocent instincts, and as innocent food;
Or draws for minds that are left free to trust
In the simplicities of opening life
Sweet honey out of spurned or dreaded weeds.
This was her creed, and therefore she was pure
From anxious fear of error or mishap,   280
And evil, overweeningly so called;
Was not puffed up by false unnatural hopes,
Nor selfish with unnecessary cares,
Nor with impatience from the season asked
More than its timely produce; rather loved

The hours for what they are, than from regard
Glanced on their promises in restless pride.
Such was she—not from faculties more strong
Than others have, but from the times, perhaps,
And spot in which she lived, and through a grace   290
Of modest meekness, simple-mindedness,
A heart that found benignity and hope,
Being itself benign.
              My drift I fear
Is scarcely obvious; but, that common sense
May try this modern system by its fruits,
Leave let me take to place before her sight
A specimen pourtrayed with faithful hand.
Full early trained to worship seemliness,
This model of a child is never known
To mix in quarrels; that were far beneath   300
Its dignity; with gifts he bubbles o'er
As generous as a fountain; selfishness
May not come near him, nor the little throng
Of flitting pleasures tempt him from his path;
The wandering beggars propagate his name,
Dumb creatures find him tender as a nun,
And natural or supernatural fear,
Unless it leap upon him in a dream,
Touches him not. To enhance the wonder, see
How arch his notices, how nice his sense   310
Of the ridiculous; nor blind is he
To the broad follies of the licensed world,
Yet innocent himself withal, though shrewd,
And can read lectures upon innocence;
A miracle of scientific lore,
Ships he can guide across the pathless sea,
And tell you all their cunning; he can read
The inside of the earth, and spell the stars;
He knows the policies of foreign lands;
Can string you names of districts, cities, towns,   320
The whole world over, tight as beads of dew
Upon a gossamer thread; he sifts, he weighs;
All things are put to question; he must live
Knowing that he grows wiser every day
Or else not live at all, and seeing too
Each little drop of wisdom as it falls
Into the dimpling cistern of his heart:
For this unnatural growth the trainer blame,
Pity the tree.—Poor human vanity,
Wert thou extinguished, little would be left   330
Which he could truly love; but how escape?
For, ever as a thought of purer birth
Rises to lead him toward a better clime,
Some intermeddler still is on the watch
To drive him back, and pound him, like a stray,
Within the pinfold of his own conceit.
Meanwhile old grandame earth is grieved to find
The playthings, which her love designed for him,

Unthought of: in their woodland beds the flowers
Weep, and the river sides are all forlorn.   340
Oh! give us once again the wishing cap
Of Fortunatus, and the invisible coat
Of Jack the Giant-killer, Robin Hood,
And Sabra in the forest with St. George!
The child, whose love is here, at least, doth reap
One precious gain, that he forgets himself.

These mighty workmen of our later age,
Who, with a broad highway, have overbridged
The froward chaos of futurity,
Tamed to their bidding; they who have the skill   350
To manage books, and things, and make them act
On infant minds as surely as the sun
Deals with a flower; the keepers of our time,
The guides and wardens of our faculties,
Sages who in their prescience would control
All accidents, and to the very road
Which they have fashioned would confine us down,
Like engines; when will their presumption learn,
That in the unreasoning progress of the world
A wiser spirit is at work for us,   360
A better eye than theirs, most prodigal
Of blessings, and most studious of our good,
Even in what seem our most unfruitful hours?

There was a Boy: ye knew him well, ye cliffs
And islands of Winander!—many a time
At evening, when the earliest stars began
To move along the edges of the hills,
Rising or setting, would he stand alone
Beneath the trees or by the glimmering lake,
And there, with fingers interwoven, both hands   370
Pressed closely palm to palm, and to his mouth
Uplifted, he, as through an instrument,
Blew mimic hootings to the silent owls,
That they might answer him; and they would shout
Across the watery vale, and shout again,
Responsive to his call, with quivering peals,
And long halloos and screams, and echoes loud,
Redoubled and redoubled, concourse wild
Of jocund din; and, when a lengthened pause
Of silence came and baffled his best skill,   380
Then sometimes, in that silence while he hung
Listening, a gentle shock of mild surprise
Has carried far into his heart the voice
Of mountain torrents; or the visible scene
Would enter unawares into his mind,
With all its solemn imagery, its rocks,
Its woods, and that uncertain heaven, received
Into the bosom of the steady lake.[4]

4 In the earliest versions, this story is related in the first person.

This Boy was taken from his mates, and died
In childhood, ere he was full twelve years old.   390
Fair is the spot, most beautiful the vale
Where he was born; the grassy churchyard hangs
Upon a slope above the village school,
And through that churchyard when my way has led
On summer evenings, I believe that there
A long half hour together I have stood
Mute, looking at the grave in which he lies!
Even now appears before the mind's clear eye
That self-same village church; I see her sit
(The thronèd Lady whom erewhile we hailed)   400
On her green hill, forgetful of this Boy
Who slumbers at her feet,—forgetful, too,
Of all her silent neighbourhood of graves,
And listening only to the gladsome sounds
That, from the rural school ascending, play
Beneath her and about her. May she long
Behold a race of young ones like to those
With whom I herded!—(easily, indeed,
We might have fed upon a fatter soil
Of arts and letters—but be that forgiven)—   410
A race of real children; not too wise,
Too learned, or too good; but wanton, fresh,
And bandied up and down by love and hate;
Not unresentful where self-justified;
Fierce, moody, patient, venturous, modest, shy;
Mad at their sports like withered leaves in winds;
Though doing wrong and suffering, and full oft
Bending beneath our life's mysterious weight
Of pain, and doubt, and fear, yet yielding not
In happiness to the happiest upon earth.   420
Simplicity in habit, truth in speech,
Be these the daily strengtheners of their minds;
May books and Nature be their early joy!
And knowledge, rightly honoured with that name—
Knowledge not purchased by the loss of power!

Well do I call to mind the very week
When I was first intrusted to the care
Of that sweet Valley; when its paths, its shores,
And brooks were like a dream of novelty
To my half-infant thoughts; that very week,   430
While I was roving up and down alone,
Seeking I knew not what, I chanced to cross
One of those open fields, which, shaped like ears,
Make green peninsulas on Esthwaite's Lake:
Twilight was coming on, yet through the gloom
Appeared distinctly on the opposite shore
A heap of garments, as if left by one
Who might have there been bathing. Long I watched,
But no one owned them; meanwhile the calm lake
Grew dark with all the shadows on its breast,   440
And, now and then, a fish up-leaping snapped

The breathless stillness. The succeeding day,
Those unclaimed garments telling a plain tale
Drew to the spot an anxious crowd; some looked
In passive expectation from the shore,
While from a boat others hung o'er the deep,
Sounding with grappling irons and long poles.
At last, the dead man, 'mid that beauteous scene
Of trees and hills and water, bolt upright
Rose, with his ghastly face, a spectre shape   450
Of terror; yet no soul-debasing fear,
Young as I was, a child not nine years old,
Possessed me, for my inner eye had seen
Such sights before, among the shining streams
Of faëry land, the forest of romance.
Their spirit hallowed the sad spectacle
With decoration of ideal grace;
A dignity, a smoothness, like the works
Of Grecian art, and purest poesy.

    A precious treasure had I long possessed,   460
A little yellow, canvas-covered book,
A slender abstract of the Arabian tales;
And, from companions in a new abode,
When first I learnt, that this dear prize of mine
Was but a block hewn from a mighty quarry—
That there were four large volumes, laden all
With kindred matter, 'twas to me, in truth,
A promise scarcely earthly. Instantly,
With one not richer than myself, I made
A covenant that each should lay aside   470
The moneys he possessed, and hoard up more,
Till our joint savings had amassed enough
To make this book our own. Through several months,
In spite of all temptation, we preserved
Religiously that vow; but firmness failed,
Nor were we ever masters of our wish.

    And when thereafter to my father's house
The holidays returned me, there to find
That golden store of books which I had left,
What joy was mine! How often in the course   480
Of those glad respites, though a soft west wind
Ruffled the waters to the angler's wish
For a whole day together, have I lain
Down by thy side, O Derwent! murmuring stream,
On the hot stones, and in the glaring sun,
And there have read, devouring as I read,
Defrauding the day's glory, desperate!
Till with a sudden bound of smart reproach,
Such as an idler deals with in his shame,
I to the sport betook myself again.   490

    A gracious spirit o'er this earth presides,
And o'er the heart of man: invisibly
It comes, to works of unreproved delight,
And tendency benign, directing those
Who care not, know not, think not what they do.
The tales that charm away the wakeful night
In Araby, romances; legends penned
For solace by dim light of monkish lamps;
Fictions for ladies, of their love, devised
By youthful squires; adventures endless, spun   500
By the dismantled warrior in old age,
Out of the bowels of those very schemes
In which his youth did first extravagate;
These spread like day, and something in the shape
Of these will live till man shall be no more.
Dumb yearnings, hidden appetites, are ours,
And *they must* have their food. Our childhood sits,
Our simple childhood, sits upon a throne
That hath more power than all the elements.
I guess not what this tells of Being past,   510
Nor what it augurs of the life to come;
But so it is, and, in that dubious hour,
That twilight when we first begin to see
This dawning earth, to recognise, expect,
And in the long probation that ensues,
The time of trial, ere we learn to live
In reconcilement with our stinted powers,
To endure this state of meagre vassalage;
Unwilling to forego, confess, submit,
Uneasy and unsettled, yoke-fellows   520
To custom, mettlesome, and not yet tamed
And humbled down; oh! then we feel, we feel,
We know where we have friends. Ye dreamers, then,
Forgers of daring tales! we bless you then,
Impostors, drivellers, dotards, as the ape
Philosophy will call you: *then* we feel
With what, and how great might ye are in league,
Who make our wish, our power, our thought a deed,
An empire, a possession,—ye whom time
And seasons serve; all Faculties,—to whom   530
Earth crouches, the elemenets are potter's clay,
Space like a heaven filled up with northern lights,
Here, nowhere, there, and everywhere at once.

    Relinquishing this lofty eminence
For ground, though humbler, not the less a tract
Of the same isthmus, which our spirits cross
In progress from their native continent
To earth and human life, the Song might dwell
On that delightful time of growing youth,
When craving for the marvellous gives way   540
To strengthening love for things that we have seen;
When sober truth and steady sympathies,
Offered to notice by less daring pens,
Take firmer hold of us, and words themselves
Move us with conscious pleasure.

　　　　　　　　　　I am sad
At thought of raptures now for ever flown;
Almost to tears I sometimes could be sad
To think of, to read over, many a page,
Poems withal of name, which at that time
Did never fail to entrance me, and are now　　550
Dead in my eyes, dead as a theatre
Fresh emptied of spectators. Twice five years
Or less I might have seen, when first my mind
With conscious pleasure opened to the charm
Of words in tuneful order, found them sweet
For their own *sakes*, a passion, and a power;
And phrases pleased me chosen for delight,
For pomp, or love. Oft, in the public roads
Yet unfrequented, while the morning light
Was yellowing the hill tops, I went abroad　　560
With a dear friend, and for the better part
Of two delightful hours we strolled along
By the still borders of the misty lake,
Repeating favourite verses with one voice,
Or conning more, as happy as the birds
That round us chaunted. Well might we be glad,
Lifted above the ground by airy fancies,
More bright than madness or the dreams of wine;
And, though full oft the objects of our love
Were false, and in their splendour overwrought,　570
Yet was there surely then no vulgar power ʾ
Working within us,—nothing less, in truth,
Than that most noble attribute of man,
Though yet untutored and inordinate,
That wish for something loftier, more adorned,
Than is the common aspect, daily garb,
Of human life. What wonder, then, if sounds
Of exultation echoed through the groves!
For, images, and sentiments, and words,
And everything encountered or pursued　　580
In that delicious world of poesy,
Kept holiday, a never-ending show,
With music, incense, festival, and flowers!

　　Here must we pause: this only let me add,
From heart-experience, and in humblest sense
Of modesty, that he, who in his youth
A daily wanderer among woods and fields
With living Nature hath been intimate,
Not only in that raw unpractised time
Is stirred to extasy, as others are,　　590
By glittering verse; but further, doth receive,
In measure only dealt out to himself,
Knowledge and increase of enduring joy
From the great Nature that exists in works
Of mighty Poets. Visionary power
Attends the motions of the viewless winds,
Embodied in the mystery of words:

There, darkness makes abode, and all the host
Of shadowy things work endless changes there,
As in a mansion like their proper home,　　600
Even forms and substances are circumfused
By that transparent veil with light divine,
And, through the turnings intricate of verse,
Present themselves as objects recognised,
In flashes, and with glory not their own.

　　Thus far a scanty record is deduced
Of what I owed to books in early life;
Their later influence yet remains untold;
But as this work was taking in my mind
Proportions that seemed larger than had first　610
Been meditated, I was indisposed
To any further progress at a time
When these acknowledgements were left unpaid.

BOOK SIXTH
CAMBRIDGE AND THE ALPS

THE leaves were fading when to Esthwaite's banks
And the simplicities of cottage life
I bade farewell; and, one among the youth
Who, summoned by that season, reunite
As scattered birds troop to the fowler's lure,
Went back to Granta's [1] cloisters, not so prompt
Or eager, though as gay and undepressed
In mind, as when I thence had taken flight
A few short months before. I turned my face
Without repining from the coves and heights　　10
Clothed in the sunshine of the withering fern;
Quitted, not loth, the mild magnificence
Of calmer lakes and louder streams; and you,
Frank-hearted maids of rocky Cumberland,
You and your not unwelcome days of mirth,
Relinquished, and your nights of revelry,
And in my own unlovely cell sate down
In lightsome mood—such privilege has youth
That cannot take long leave of pleasant thoughts.

　　The bonds of indolent society　　　　　20
Relaxing in their hold, henceforth I lived
More to myself. Two winters may be passed
Without a separate notice: many books
Were skimmed, devoured, or studiously perused,
But with no settled plan. I was detached
Internally from academic cares;
Yet independent study seemed a course

──────────────────────────
[1] I.e., Cambridge. Granta is an old name for the river Cam
above Cambridge.

Of hardy disobedience toward friends
And kindred, proud rebellion and unkind.
This spurious virtue, rather let it bear   30
A name it more deserves, this cowardice,
Gave treacherous sanction to that over-love
Of freedom which encouraged me to turn
From regulations even of my own
As from restraints and bonds. Yet who can tell—
Who knows what thus may have been gained, both
          then
And at a later season, or preserved;
What love of nature, what original strength
Of contemplation, what intuitive truths,
The deepest and the best, what keen research,   40
Unbiassed, unbewildered, and unawed?

    The Poet's soul was with me at that time;
Sweet meditations, the still overflow
Of present happiness, while future years
Lacked not anticipations, tender dreams,
No few of which have since been realised;
And some remain, hopes for my future life.
Four years and thirty, told this very week,[2]
Have I been now a sojourner on earth,
By sorrow not unsmitten; yet for me   50
Life's morning radiance hath not left the hills,
Her dew is on the flowers. Those were the days
Which also first emboldened me to trust
With firmness, hitherto but lightly touched
By such a daring thought, that I might leave
Some monument behind me which pure hearts
Should reverence. The instinctive humbleness,
Maintained even by the very name and thought
Of printed books and authorship, began
To melt away; and further, the dread awe   60
Of mighty names was softened down and seemed
Approachable, admitting fellowship
Of modest sympathy. Such aspect now,
Though not familiarly, my mind put on,
Content to observe, to admire, and to enjoy.

    All winter long, whenever free to choose,
Did I by night frequent the College groves
And tributary walks; the last, and oft
The only one, who had been lingering there
Through hours of silence, till the porter's bell, 70
A punctual follower on the stroke of nine,
Rang with its blunt unceremonious voice,
Inexorable summons! Lofty elms,
Inviting shades of opportune recess,
Bestowed composure on a neighbourhood

[2] April 1804. Presumably Wordsworth is referring to the
moment at which he is writing these lines. Most of Book VI was
composed in 1804.

Unpeaceful in itself. A single tree
With sinuous trunk, boughs exquisitely wreathed,
Grew there; an ash which Winter for himself
Decked as in pride, and with outlandish grace:
Up from the ground, and almost to the top,   80
The trunk and every master branch were green
With clustering ivy, and the lightsome twigs
And outer spray profusely tipped with seeds
That hung in yellow tassels, while the air
Stirred them, not voiceless. Often have I stood
Foot-bound uplooking at this lovely tree
Beneath a frosty moon. The hemisphere
Of magic fiction, verse of mine perchance
May never tread; but scarcely Spenser's self
Could have more tranquil visions in his youth,   90
Or could more bright appearances create
Of human forms with superhuman powers,
Than I beheld loitering on calm clear nights
Alone, beneath this fairy work of earth.
    On the vague reading of a truant youth
'Twere idle to descant. My inner judgment
Not seldom differed from my taste in books,
As if it appertained to another mind,
And yet the books which then I valued most
Are dearest to me *now*; for, having scanned,   100
Not heedlessly, the laws, and watched the forms
Of Nature, in that knowledge I possessed
A standard, often usefully applied,
Even when unconsciously, to things removed
From a familiar sympathy.—In fine,
I was a better judge of thoughts than words,
Misled in estimating words, not only
By common inexperience of youth,
But by the trade in classic niceties,
The dangerous craft of culling term and phrase   110
From languages that want the living voice
To carry meaning to the natural heart;
To tell us what is passion, what is truth,
What reason, what simplicity and sense.

Yet may we not entirely overlook
The pleasure gathered from the rudiments
Of geometric science. Though advanced
In these inquiries, with regret I speak,
No farther than the threshold, there I found
Both elevation and composed delight: 120
With Indian awe and wonder, ignorance pleased
With its own struggles, did I meditate
On the relation those abstractions bear
To Nature's laws, and by what process led,
Those immaterial agents bowed their heads
Duly to serve the mind of earth-born man;
From star to star, from kindred sphere to sphere,
From system on to system without end.

More frequently from the same source I drew
A pleasure quiet and profound, a sense   130
Of permanent and universal sway,
And paramount belief; there, recognised
A type, for finite natures, of the one
Supreme Existence, the surpassing life
Which—to the boundaries of space and time,
Of melancholy space and doleful time,
Superior, and incapable of change,
Nor touched by welterings of passion—is,
And hath the name of, God. Transcendent peace
And silence did await upon these thoughts   140
That were a frequent comfort to my youth.

'Tis told by one whom stormy waters threw,
With fellow-sufferers by the shipwreck spared,
Upon a desert coast, that having brought
To land a single volume, saved by chance,
A treatise of Geometry, he wont,
Although of food and clothing destitute,
And beyond common wretchedness depressed,
To part from company and take this book
(Then first a self-taught pupil in its truths)   150
To spots remote, and draw his diagrams
With a long staff upon the sand, and thus
Did oft beguile his sorrow, and almost
Forget his feeling: so (if like effect
From the same cause produced, 'mid outward
        things
So different, may rightly be compared),
So was it then with me, and so will be
With Poets ever. Mighty is the charm
Of those abstractions to a mind beset
With images, and haunted by herself,   160
And specially delightful unto me
Was that clear synthesis built up aloft
So gracefully; even then when it appeared
Not more than a mere plaything, or a toy
To sense embodied: not the thing it is
In verity, an independent world,
Created out of pure intelligence.

    Such dispositions then were mine unearned
By aught, I fear, of genuine desert—
Mine, through heaven's grace and inborn aptitudes.
And not to leave the story of that time   171
Imperfect, with these habits must be joined,
Moods melancholy, fits of spleen, that loved
A pensive sky, sad days, and piping winds,
The twilight more than dawn, autumn than spring;
A treasured and luxurious gloom of choice
And inclination mainly, and the mere
Redundancy of youth's contentedness.
—To time thus spent, add multitudes of hours

Pilfered away, by what the Bard who sang[3]   180
Of the Enchanter Indolence hath called
'Good-natured lounging,' and behold a map
Of my collegiate life—far less intense
Than duty called for, or, without regard
To duty, *might* have sprung up of itself
By change of accidents, or even, to speak
Without unkindness, in another place.
Yet why take refuge in that plea ?—the fault,
This I repeat, was mine; mine be the blame.

    In summer, making quest for works of art,   190
Or scenes renowned for beauty, I explored
That streamlet whose blue current works its way
Between romantic Dovedale's spiry rocks;
Pried into Yorkshire dales, or hidden tracts
Of my own native region, and was blest
Between these sundry wanderings with a joy
Above all joys, that seemed another morn
Risen on mid noon; blest with the presence,
        Friend!
Of that sole Sister, she who hath been long
Dear to thee also, thy true friend and mine,[4]   200
Now, after separation desolate,
Restored to me—such absence that she seemed
A gift then first bestowed. The varied banks
Of Emont, hitherto unnamed in song,
And that monastic castle,[5] mid tall trees,
Low-standing by the margin of the stream,
A mansion visited (as fame reports)
By Sidney, where, in sight of our Helvellyn,
Or stormy Cross-fell, snatches he might pen
Of his Arcadia, by fraternal love   210
Inspired;—that river and those mouldering
        towers
Have seen us side by side, when, having clomb
The darksome windings of a broken stair,
And crept along a ridge of fractured wall,
Not without trembling, we in safety looked
Forth, through some Gothic window's open space,
And gathered with one mind a rich reward
From the far-stretching landscape, by the light
Of morning beautified, or purple eve;
Or, not less pleased, lay on some turret's head,   220
Catching from tufts of grass and hare-bell flowers
Their faintest whisper to the passing breeze,
Given out while mid-day heat oppressed the plains.

    [3] James Thompson, *The Castle of Indolence* (1748).
    [4] Wordsworth's reunion with Dorothy (they were raised
separately after their mother's death) probably occurred in the
summer of 1787.
    [5] The legend that Sidney visited Brougham Castle while
writing his pastoral romance (*Arcadia*) was false. A later Countess
of Pembroke, not Sidney's sister, lived there.

Another maid [6] there was, who also shed
A gladness o'er that season, then to me,
By her exulting outside look of youth
And placid under-countenance, first endeared;
That other spirit, Coleridge! who is now
So near to us, that meek confiding heart,
So reverenced by us both. O'er paths and fields   230
In all that neighbourhood, through narrow lanes
Of eglantine, and through the shady woods
And o'er the Border Beacon, and the waste
Of naked pools, and common crags that lay
Exposed on the bare fell, were scattered love,
The spirit of pleasure, and youth's golden gleam.
O Friend! we had not seen thee at that time,
And yet a power is on me, and a strong
Confusion, and I seem to plant thee there.
Far art thou wandered now in search of health   240
And milder breezes,—melancholy lot!
But thou art with us, with us in the past,
The present, with us in the times to come.
There is no grief, no sorrow, no despair,
No languor, no dejection, no dismay,
No absence scarcely can there be, for those
Who love as we do. Speed thee well! divide
With us they pleasure; thy returning strength,
Receive it daily as a joy of ours;
Share with us thy fresh spirits, whether gift   250
Of gales Etesian [7] or of tender thoughts.

I, too, have been a wanderer; but, alas!
How different the fate of different men.
Though mutually unknown, yea nursed and reared
As if in several elements, we were framed
To bend at last to the same discipline,
Predestined, if two beings ever were,
To seek the same delights, and have one health,
One happiness. Throughout this narrative,
Else sooner ended, I have borne in mind   260
For whom it registers the birth, and marks the growth,
Of gentleness, simplicity, and truth,
And joyous loves, that hallow innocent days
Of peace and self-command. Of rivers, fields,
And groves I speak to thee, my Friend! to thee,
Who, yet a liveried schoolboy, in the depths [8]
Of the huge city, on the leaded roof
Of that wide edifice, thy school and home,
Wert used to lie and gaze upon the clouds
Moving in heaven; or, of that pleasure tired,   270
To shut thine eyes, and by internal light [9]

See trees, and meadows, and thy native stream,
Far distant, thus beheld from year to year
Of a long exile. Nor could I forget,
In this late portion of my argument,
That scarcely, as my term of pupilage
Ceased, had I left those academic bowers
When thou wert thither guided. From the heart
Of London, and from cloisters there, thou camest,
And didst sit down in temperance and peace,   280
A rigorous student. What a stormy course [10]
Then followed. Oh! it is a pang that calls
For utterance, to think what easy change
Of circumstances might to thee have spared
A world of pain, ripened a thousand hopes,
For ever withered. Through this retrospect
Of my collegiate life I still have had
Thy after-sojourn in the self-same place
Present before my eyes, have played with times
And accidents as children do with cards,   290
Or as a man, who, when his house is built,
A frame locked up in wood and stone, doth still,
As impotent fancy prompts, by his fireside,
Rebuild it to his liking. I have thought
Of thee, thy learning, gorgeous eloquence,
And all the strength and plumage of thy youth,
Thy subtle speculations, toils abstruse,
Among the schoolmen, and Platonic forms
Of wild ideal pageantry, shaped out
From things well-matched or ill, and words for things,
The self-created sustenance of a mind   301
Debarred from Nature's living images,
Compelled to be a life unto herself,
And unrelentingly possessed by thirst
Of greatness, love, and beauty. Not alone,
Ah! surely not in singleness of heart
Should I have seen the light of evening fade
From smooth Cam's silent waters: had we met,
Even at that early time, needs must I trust
In the belief, that my maturer age,   310
My calmer habits, and more steady voice,
Would with an influence benign have soothed,
Or chased away, the airy wretchedness
That battened on thy youth. But thou hast trod
A march of glory, which doth put to shame
These vain regrets; health suffers in thee, else
Such grief for thee would be the weakest thought
That ever harboured in the breast of man.

A passing word erewhile did lightly touch
On wanderings of my own, that now embraced   320
With livelier hope a region wider far.

---

[6] Mary Hutchinson, whom Wordsworth married in 1802.
[7] Mediterranean winds that recur annually. When Wordsworth was writing this, Coleridge had just gone to Malta.
[8] At Christ's Hospital, London.
[9] See Coleridge's *Sonnet to the River Otter*, below.

[10] In December 1793, Coleridge left Cambridge and enlisted in the Dragoons as Silas Tomkyn Comberbache. For other events, see the outline of Coleridge's life, below, and his own *Dejection*.

When the third summer freed us from restraint,
A youthful friend, he too a mountaineer,
Not slow to share my wishes, took his staff,
And sallying forth, we journeyed side by side,[11]
Bound to the distant Alps. A hardy slight
Did this unprecedented course imply
Of college studies and their set rewards;
Nor had, in truth, the scheme been formed by me
Without uneasy forethought of the pain,　　　330
The censures, and ill-omening of those
To whom my worldly interests were dear.
But Nature then was sovereign in my mind,
And mighty forms, seizing a youthful fancy,
Had given a charter to irregular hopes.
In any age of uneventful calm
Among the nations, surely would my heart
Have been possessed by similar desire;
But Europe at that time was thrilled with joy,
France standing on the top of golden hours,　　　340
And human nature seeming born again.

Lightly equipped, and but a few brief looks
Cast on the white cliffs of our native shore
From the receding vessel's deck, we chanced
To land at Calais on the very eve
Of that great federal day;[12] and there we saw,
In a mean city, and among a few,
How bright a face is worn when joy of one
Is joy for tens of millions. Southward thence
We held our way, direct through hamlets, towns,　　　350
Gaudy with reliques of that festival,
Flowers left to wither on triumphal arcs,
And window-garlands. On the public roads,
And, once, three days successively, through paths
By which our toilsome journey was abridged,
Among sequestered villages we walked
And found benevolence and blessedness
Spread like a fragrance everywhere, when spring
Hath left no corner of the land untouched:
Where elms for many and many a league in files　　　360
With their thin umbrage, on the stately roads
Of that great kingdom, rustled o'er our heads,
For ever near us as we paced along:
How sweet at such a time, with such delight
On every side, in prime of youthful strength,
To feed a Poet's tender melancholy
And fond conceit of sadness, with the sound
Of undulations varying as might please
The wind that swayed them; once, and more than
　　　once,

Unhoused beneath the evening star we saw　　　370
Dances of liberty, and, in late hours
Of darkness, dances in the open air
Deftly prolonged, though grey-haired lookers on
Might waste their breath in chiding.
　　　　　　　　　　　　　Under hills—
The vine-clad hills and slopes of Burgundy,
Upon the bosom of the gentle Saone
We glided forward with the flowing stream.
Swift Rhone! thou wert the *wings* on which we cut
A winding passage with majestic ease
Between thy lofty rocks. Enchanting show　　　380
Those woods and farms and orchards did present,
And single cottages and lurking towns,
Reach after reach, succession without end
Of deep and stately vales! A lonely pair
Of strangers, till day closed, we sailed along,
Clustered together with a merry crowd
Of those emancipated, a blithe host
Of travellers, chiefly delegates returning
From the great spousals newly solemnised
At their chief city, in the sight of Heaven.　　　390
Like bees they swarmed, gaudy and gay as bees;
Some vapoured in the unruliness of joy,
And with their swords flourished as if to fight
The saucy air. In this proud company
We landed—took with them our evening meal,
Guests welcome almost as the angels were
To Abraham of old. The supper done,
With flowing cups elate and happy thoughts
We rose at signal given, and formed a ring
And, hand in hand, danced round and round the
　　　board;　　　400
All hearts were open, every tongue was loud
With amity and glee; we bore a name
Honoured in France, the name of Englishmen,
And hospitably did they give us hail,
As their forerunners in a glorious course;
And round and round the board we danced again.
With these blithe friends our voyage we renewed
At early dawn. The monastery bells
Made a sweet jingling in our youthful ears;
The rapid river flowing without noise,　　　410
And each uprising or receding spire
Spake with a sense of peace, at intervals
Touching the heart amid the boisterous crew
By whom we were encompassed. Taking leave
Of this glad throng, foot-travellers side by side,
Measuring our steps in quiet, we pursued
Our journey, and ere twice the sun had set
Beheld the Convent of Chartreuse,[13] and there

---

[11] With Robert Jones, Wordsworth went on a continental walking tour in the summer of 1790.

[12] July 14, 1790, was the first anniversary of the fall of the Bastille, and the day when Louis XVI swore fidelity to the constitution.

[13] The monastery of the Grand Chartreuse (Carthusian Order), near Grenoble, was not actually occupied until 1792. St. Bruno founded the order in 1084.

Rested within an awful *solitude*:
Yes, for even then no other than a place   420
Of soul-affecting *solitude* appeared
That far-famed region, though our eyes had seen,
As toward the sacred mansion we advanced,
Arms flashing, and a military glare
Of riotous men commissioned to expel
The blameless inmates, and belike subvert
That frame of social being, which so long
Had bodied forth the ghostliness of things
In silence visible and perpetual calm.
—'Stay, stay your sacrilegious hands!'—The voice
Was Nature's, uttered from her Alpine throne;   431
I heard it then and seem to hear it now—
'Your impious work forbear, perish what may,
Let this one temple last, be this one spot
Of earth devoted to eternity!'
She ceased to speak, but while St. Bruno's pines
Waved their dark tops, not silent as they waved,
And while below, along their several beds,
Murmured the sister streams of Life and Death,[14]
Thus by conflicting passions pressed, my heart   440
Responded; 'Honour to the patriot's zeal!
Glory and hope to new-born Liberty!
Hail to the mighty projects of the time!
Discerning sword that Justice wields, do thou
Go forth and prosper; and, ye purging fires,
Up to the loftiest towers of Pride ascend,
Fanned by the breath of angry Providence.
But oh! if Past and Future be the wings
On whose support harmoniously conjoined
Moves the great spirit of human knowledge, spare
These courts of mystery, where a step advanced   451
Between the portals of the shadowy rocks
Leaves far behind life's treacherous vanities,
For penitential tears and trembling hopes
Exchanged—to equalise in God's pure sight
Monarch and peasant: be the house redeemed
With its unworldly votaries, for the sake
Of conquest over sense, hourly achieved
Through faith and meditative reason, resting
Upon the word of heaven-imparted truth,   460
Calmly triumphant; and for humbler claim
Of that imaginative impulse sent
From these majestic floods, yon shining cliffs,
The untransmuted shapes of many worlds,
Cerulean ether's pure inhabitants,
These forests unapproachable by death,
That shall endure as long as man endures,
To think, to hope, to worship, and to feel,
To struggle, to be lost within himself

---

[14] *Guiers vif* and *Guiers mort* meet in the valley below the Grande Chartreuse.

In trepidation, from the blank abyss   470
To look with bodily eyes, and be consoled.'
Not seldom since that moment have I wished
That thou, O Friend! the trouble or the calm
Hadst shared, when, from profane regards apart,
In sympathetic reverence we trod
The floors of those dim cloisters, till that hour,
From their foundation, strangers to the presence
Of unrestricted and unthinking man.
Abroad, how cheeringly the sunshine lay
Upon the open lawns! Vallombre's groves   480
Entering, we fed the soul with darkness; thence
Issued, and with uplifted eyes beheld,
In different quarters of the bending sky,
The cross of Jesus stand erect, as if
Hands of angelic powers had fixed it there,
Memorial reverenced by a thousand storms;
Yet then, from the undiscriminating sweep
And rage of one State-whirlwind, insecure.

'Tis not my present purpose to retrace
That variegated journey step by step.   490
A march it was of military speed,
And Earth did change her images and forms
Before us, fast as clouds are changed in heaven.
Day after day, up early and down late,
From hill to vale we dropped, from vale to hill
Mounted—from province on to province swept,
Keen hunters in a chase of fourteen weeks,
Eager as birds of prey, or as a ship
Upon the stretch, when winds are blowing fair:
Sweet coverts did we cross of pastoral life,   500
Enticing valleys, greeted them and left
Too soon, while yet the very flash and gleam
Of salutation were not passed away.
Oh! sorrow for the youth who could have seen
Unchastened, unsubdued, unawed, unraised
To patriarchal dignity of mind,
And pure simplicity of wish and will,
Those sanctified abodes of peaceful man,
Pleased (though to hardship born, and compassed
    round
With danger, varying as the seasons change),   510
Pleased with his daily task, or, if not pleased,
Contented, from the moment that the dawn
(Ah! surely not without attendant gleams
Of soul-illumination) calls him forth
To industry, by glistenings flung on rocks,
Whose evening shadows lead him to repose.

Well might a stranger look with bounding heart
Down on a green recess, the first I saw
Of those deep haunts, an aboriginal vale,
Quiet and lorded over and possessed   520

By naked huts, wood-built, and sown like tents
Or Indian cabins over the fresh lawns
And by the river side.
                    That very day,
From a bare ridge we also first beheld
Unveiled the summit of Mont Blanc, and grieved
To have a soulless image on the eye
That had usurped upon a living thought
That never more could be. The wondrous Vale
Of Chamouny stretched far below, and soon
With its dumb cataracts and streams of ice,   530
A motionless array of mighty waves,
Five rivers broad and vast, made rich amends,
And reconciled us to realities;[15]
There small birds warble from the leafy trees,
The eagle soars high in the element,
There doth the reaper bind the yellow sheaf,
The maiden spread the haycock in the sun,
While Winter like a well-tamed lion walks,
Descending from the mountain to make sport
Among the cottages by beds of flowers.   540

     Whate'er in this wide circuit we beheld,
Or heard, was fitted to our unripe state
Of intellect and heart. With such a book
Before our eyes, we could not choose but read
Lessons of genuine brotherhood, the plain
And universal reason of mankind,
The truths of young and old. Nor, side by side
Pacing, two social pilgrims, or alone
Each with his humour, could we fail to abound
In dreams and fictions, pensively composed: 550
Dejection taken up for pleasure's sake,
And gilded sympathies, the willow wreath,
And sober posies of funereal flowers,
Gathered among those solitudes sublime
From formal gardens of the lady Sorrow,
Did sweeten many a meditative hour.

     Yet still in me with those soft luxuries
Mixed something of stern mood, an under-thirst
Of vigour seldom utterly allayed.
And from that source how different a sadness   560
Would issue, let one incident make known.
When from the Vallais we had turned, and clomb
Along the Simplon's steep and rugged road,[16]
Following a band of muleteers, we reached
A halting-place, where all together took
Their noon-tide meal. Hastily rose our guide,
Leaving us at the board; awhile we lingered,

---

[15] See Coleridge's *Hymn Before Sunrise* and Shelley's *Mont Blanc*, below.
[16] The Simplon Pass, from Switzerland to Italy.

Then paced the beaten downward way that led
Right to a rough stream's edge, and there broke off;
The only track now visible was one   570
That from the torrent's further brink held forth
Conspicuous invitation to ascend
A lofty mountain. After brief delay
Crossing the unbridged stream, that road we took,
And clomb with eagerness, till anxious fears
Intruded, for we failed to overtake
Our comrades gone before. By fortunate chance,
While every moment added doubt to doubt,
A peasant met us, from whose mouth we learned
That to the spot which had perplexed us first   580
We must descend, and there should find the road,
Which in the stony channel of the stream
Lay a few steps, and then along its banks;
And, that our future course, all plain to sight,
Was downwards, with the current of that stream.
Loth to believe what we so grieved to hear,
For still we had hopes that pointed to the clouds,
We questioned him again, and yet again;
But every word that from the peasant's lips
Came in reply, translated by our feelings,   590
Ended in this,—*that we had crossed the Alps.*

     Imagination—here the Power so called
Through sad incompetence of human speech,
That awful Power rose from the mind's abyss
Like an unfathered vapour that enwraps,
At once, some lonely traveller. I was lost;
Halted without an effort to break through;
But to my conscious soul I now can say—
'I recognise thy glory:' in such strength
Of usurpation, when the light of sense   600
Goes out, but with a flash that has revealed
The invisible world, doth greatness make abode,
There harbours, whether we be young or old.
Our destiny, our being's heart and home,
Is with infinitude, and only there;
With hope it is, hope that can never die,
Effort, and expectation, and desire,
And something evermore about to be.
Under such banners militant, the soul
Seeks for no trophies, struggles for no spoils   610
That may attest her prowess, blest in thoughts
That are their own perfection and reward,
Strong in herself and in beatitude
That hides her, like the mighty flood of Nile
Poured from his fount of Abyssinian clouds
To fertilise the whole Egyptian plain.

     The melancholy slackening that ensued
Upon those tidings by the peasant given
Was soon dislodged. Downwards we hurried fast,

And, with the half-shaped road which we had missed,
Entered a narrow chasm. The brook and road   621
Were fellow-travellers in this gloomy strait,
And with them did we journey several hours
At a slow pace. The immeasurable height
Of woods decaying, never to be decayed,
The stationary blasts of waterfalls,
And in the narrow rent at every turn
Winds thwarting winds, bewildered and forlorn,
The torrents shooting from the clear blue sky,
The rocks that muttered close upon our ears,   630
Black drizzling crags that spake by the way-side
As if a voice were in them, the sick sight
And giddy prospect of the raving stream,
The unfettered clouds and region of the Heavens,
Tumult and peace, the darkness and the light—
Were all like workings of one mind, the features
Of the same face, blossoms upon one tree;
Characters of the great Apocalypse,
The types and symbols of Eternity,
Of first, and last, and midst, and without end.   640

That night our lodging was a house that stood
Alone within the valley, at a point
Where, tumbling from aloft, a torrent swelled
The rapid stream whose margin we had trod;
A dreary mansion, large beyond all need,
With high and spacious rooms, deafened and stunned
By noise of waters, making innocent sleep
Lie melancholy among weary bones.

Uprisen betimes, our journey we renewed,
Led by the stream, ere noon-day magnified   650
Into a lordly river, broad and deep,
Dimpling along in silent majesty,
With mountains for its neighbours, and in view
Of distant mountains and their snowy tops,
And thus proceeding to Locarno's Lake,[17]
Fit resting-place for such a visitant.
Locarno! spreading out in width like Heaven,
How dost thou cleave to the poetic heart,
Bask in the sunshine of the memory;
And Como! thou, a treasure whom the earth   660
Keeps to herself, confined as in a depth
Of Abyssinian privacy, I spake
Of thee, thy chestnut woods, and garden plots
Of Indian corn tended by dark-eyed maids;
Thy lofty steeps, and pathways roofed with vines,
Winding from house to house, from town to town,
Sole link that binds them to each other; walks,
League after league, and cloistral avenues,
Where silence dwells if music be not there:

[17] Lago Maggiore, northern Italy.

While yet a youth undisciplined in verse,   670
Through fond ambition of that hour, I strove
To chant your praise; nor can approach you now
Ungreeted by a more melodious Song,
Where tones of Nature smoothed by learned Art
May flow in lasting current. Like a breeze
Or sunbeam over your domain I passed
In motion without pause; but ye have left
Your beauty with me, a serene accord
Of forms and colours, passive, yet endowed
In their submissiveness with power as sweet   680
And gracious, almost might I dare to say,
As virtue is, or goodness; sweet as love,
Or the remembrance of a generous deed,
Or mildest visitations of pure thought,
When God, the giver of all joy, is thanked
Religiously, in silent blessedness;
Sweet as this last herself, for such it is.

With those delightful pathways we advanced,
For two days' space, in presence of the Lake,
That, stretching far among the Alps, assumed   690
A character more stern. The second night,
From sleep awakened, and misled by sound
Of the church clock telling the hours with strokes
Whose import then we had not learned, we rose
By moonlight, doubting not that day was nigh,
And that meanwhile, by no uncertain path,
Along the winding margin of the lake,
Led, as before, we should behold the scene
Hushed in profound repose. We left the town
Of Gravedona with this hope; but soon   700
Were lost, bewildered among woods immense,
And on a rock sate down, to wait for day.
An open place it was, and overlooked,
From high, the sullen water far beneath,
On which a dull red image of the moon
Lay bedded, changing oftentimes its form
Like an uneasy snake. From hour to hour
We sate and sate, wondering, as if the night
Had been ensnared by witchcraft. On the rock
At last we stretched our weary limbs for sleep,   710
But *could not* sleep, tormented by the stings
Of insects, which, with noise like that of noon,
Filled all the woods. The cry of unknown birds;
The mountains more by blackness visible
And their own size, than any outward light;
The breathless wilderness of clouds; the clock
That told, with unintelligible voice,
The widely parted hours; the noise of streams,
And sometimes rustling motions nigh at hand,
That did not leave us free from personal fear;   720
And, lastly, the withdrawing moon, that set
Before us, while she still was high in heaven;—

These were our food; and such a summer's night
Followed that pair of golden days that shed
On Como's Lake, and all that round it lay,
Their fairest, softest, happiest influence.

But here I must break off, and bid farewell
To days, each offering some new sight, or fraught
With some untried adventure, in a course
Prolonged till sprinklings of autumnal snow   730
Checked our unwearied steps. Let this alone
Be mentioned as a parting word, that not
In hollow exultation, dealing out
Hyperboles of praise comparative;
Not rich one moment to be poor for ever;
Not prostrate, overborne, as if the mind
Herself were nothing, a mere pensioner
On outward forms—did we in presence stand
Of that magnificent region. On the front
Of this whole Song is written that my heart   740
Must, in such Temple, needs have offered up
A different worship. Finally, whate'er
I saw, or heard, or felt, was but a stream
That flowed into a kindred stream; a gale,
Confederate with the current of the soul,
To speed my voyage; every sound or sight,
In its degree of power, administered
To grandeur or to tenderness,—to the one
Directly, but to tender thoughts by means
Less often instantaneous in effect;   750
Led me to these by paths that, in the main,
Were more circuitous, but not less sure
Duly to reach the point marked out by Heaven.

Oh, most belovèd Friend! a glorious time,
A happy time that was; triumphant looks
Were then the common language of all eyes;
As if awaked from sleep, the Nations hailed
Their great expectancy: the fife of war
Was then a spirit-stirring sound indeed,
A black-bird's whistle in a budding grove.   760
We left the Swiss exulting in the fate
Of their near neighbours; and, when shortening fast
Our pilgrimage, nor distant far from home,
We crossed the Brabant armies on the fret[18]
For battle in the cause of Liberty.
A stripling, scarcely of the household then
Of social life, I looked upon these things
As from a distance; heard, and saw, and felt,
Was touched, but with no intimate concern;
I seemed to move along them, as a bird   770
Moves through the air, or as a fish pursues

Its sport, or feeds in its proper element;
I wanted not that joy, I did not need
Such help; the ever-living universe,
Turn where I might, was opening out its glories,
And the independent spirit of pure youth
Called forth, at every season, new delights
Spread round my steps like sunshine o'er green fields.

BOOK SEVENTH
RESIDENCE IN LONDON

SIX changeful years have vanished since I first
Poured out (saluted by that quickening breeze
Which met me issuing from the City's walls)
A glad preamble to this Verse: I sang
Aloud, with fervour irresistible
Of short-lived transport, like a torrent bursting,
From a black thunder-cloud, down Scafell's side[1]
To rush and disappear. But soon broke forth
(So willed the Muse) a less impetuous stream,
That flowed awhile with unabating strength,   10
Then stopped for years; not audible again
Before last primrose-time. Belovèd Friend!
The assurance which then cheered some heavy
      thoughts
On thy departure to a foreign land[2]
Has failed; too slowly moves the promised work.
Through the whole summer have I been at rest,
Partly from voluntary holiday,
And part through outward hindrance. But I heard,
After the hour of sunset yester-even,
Sitting within doors between light and dark,   20
A choir of redbreasts gathered somewhere near
My threshold,—minstrels from the distant woods
Sent in on Winter's service, to announce,
With preparation artful and benign,
That the rough lord had left the surly North
On his accustomed journey. The delight,
Due to this timely notice, unawares
Smote me, and, listening, I in whispers said,
'Ye heartsome Choristers, ye and I will be
Associates, and, unscared by blustering winds,   30
Will chant together.' Thereafter, as the shades
Of twilight deepened, going forth, I spied
A glow-worm underneath a dusky plume
Or canopy of yet unwithered fern,
Clear-shining, like a hermit's taper seen
Through a thick forest. Silence touched me here
No less than sound had done before; the child

---

[18] Belgian republican armies preparing to protect their
country from Leopold's attempt to restore the monarchy.

[1] Highest mountain in England, eight miles west of Grasmere.
[2] Coleridge's voyage to Malta, 1804.

Of Summer, lingering, shining by herself,
The voiceless worm on the unfrequented hills,
Seemed sent on the same errand with the choir   40
Of Winter that had warbled at my door,
And the whole year breathed tenderness and love.

The last night's genial feeling overflowed
Upon this morning, and my favourite grove,
Tossing in sunshine its dark boughs aloft,
As if to make the strong wind visible,
Wakes in me agitations like its own,
A spirit friendly to the Poet's task,
Which we will now resume with lively hope,
Nor checked by aught of tamer argument   50
That lies before us, needful to be told.

Returned from that excursion,[3] soon I bade
Farewell for ever to the sheltered seats
Of gownèd students, quitted hall and bower,
And every comfort of that privileged ground,
Well pleased to pitch a vagrant tent among
The unfenced regions of society.

Yet undetermined to what course of life
I should adhere, and seeming to possess
A little space of intermediate time   60
At full command, to London first I turned,
In no disturbance of excessive hope,
By personal ambition unenslaved,
Frugal as there was need, and, though self-willed,
From dangerous passions free. Three years had flown
Since I had felt in heart and soul the shock
Of the huge town's first presence, and had paced
Her endless streets, a transient visitant:
Now, fixed amid that concourse of mankind
Where Pleasure whirls about incessantly,   70
And life and labour seem but one, I filled
An idler's place; an idler well content
To have a house (what matter for a home?)
That owned him; living cheerfully abroad
With unchecked fancy ever on the stir,
And all my young affections out of doors.

There was a time when whatsoe'er is feigned
Of airy palaces, and gardens built
By Genii of romance; or hath in grave
Authentic history been set forth of Rome,   80
Alcairo, Babylon, or Persepolis;
Or given upon report by pilgrim friars,
Of golden cities ten months' journey deep
Among Tartarian wilds—fell short, far short,

Of what my fond simplicity believed
And thought of London—held me by a chain
Less strong of wonder and obscure delight.
Whether the bolt of childhood's Fancy shot
For me beyond its ordinary mark,
'Twere vain to ask; but in our flock of boys   90
Was One, a cripple from his birth, whom chance
Summoned from school to London; fortunate
And envied traveller! When the Boy returned,
After short absence, curiously I scanned
His mien and person, nor was free, in sooth,
From disappointment, not to find some change
In look and air, from that new region brought,
As if from Fairy-land. Much I questioned him;
And every word he uttered, on my ears
Fell flatter than a cagèd parrot's note,   100
That answers unexpectedly awry,
And mocks the prompter's listening. Marvellous
            things
Had vanity (quick Spirit that appears
Almost as deeply seated and as strong
In a Child's heart as fear itself) conceived
For my enjoyment. Would that I could now
Recal what then I pictured to myself
Of mitred Prelates, Lords in ermine clad,
The King, and the King's Palace, and, not last,
Nor least, Heaven bless him! the renowned Lord
            Mayor: 110
Dreams not unlike to those which once begat
A change of purpose in young Whittington,
When he, a friendless and a drooping boy,
Sate on a stone, and heard the bells speak out
Articulate music. Above all, one thought
Baffled my understanding: how men lived
Even next-door neighbours, as we say, yet still
Strangers, nor knowing each the other's name.

O, wond'rous power of words, by simple faith
Licensed to take the meaning that we love!   120
Vauxhall and Ranelagh![4] I then had heard
Of your green groves, and wilderness of lamps
Dimming the stars, and fireworks magical,
And gorgeous ladies, under splendid domes,
Floating in dance, or warbling high in air
The songs of spirits! Nor had Fancy fed
With less delight upon that other class
Of marvels, broad-day wonders permanent:
The River proudly bridged; the dizzy top
And Whispering Gallery of St. Paul's; the tombs   130
Of Westminster; the Giants of Guildhall;[5]

---

[3] With Robert Jones, described in Book VI. In January 1791
Wordsworth took his degree from Cambridge.

[4] Pleasure gardens, an early and more dignified form of
amusement park.
[5] Wooden statues of Gog and Magog.

Bedlam,[6] and those carved maniacs at the gates,
Perpetually recumbent; Statues—man,
And the horse under him—in gilded pomp
Adorning flowery gardens, 'mid vast squares;
The Monument, and that Chamber of the Tower
Where England's sovereigns sit in long array,
Their steeds bestriding,—every mimic shape
Cased in the gleaming mail the monarch wore,
Whether for gorgeous tournament addressed,   140
Or life or death upon the battle-field.
Those bold imaginations in due time
Had vanished, leaving others in their stead:
And now I looked upon the living scene;
Familiarly perused it; oftentimes,
In spite of strongest disappointment, pleased
Through courteous self-submission, as a tax
Paid to the object by prescriptive right.

Rise up, thou monstrous ant-hill on the plain
Of a too busy world! Before me flow,   150
Thou endless stream of men and moving things!
Thy every-day appearance, as it strikes—
With wonder heightened, or sublimed by awe—
On strangers, of all ages; the quick dance
Of colours, lights, and forms; the deafening din;
The comers and the goers face to face,
Face after face; the string of dazzling wares,
Shop after shop, with symbols, blazoned names,
And all the tradesman's honours overhead:
Here, fronts of houses, like a title-page,   160
With letters huge inscribed from top to toe;
Stationed above the door, like guardian saints,
There, allegoric shapes, female or male,
Or physiognomies of real men,
Land-warriors, kings, or admirals of the sea,
Boyle,[7] Shakespeare, Newton, or the attractive head
Of some quack-doctor, famous in his day.

Meanwhile the roar continues, till at length,
Escaped as from an enemy, we turn
Abruptly into some sequestered nook,   170
Still as a sheltered place when winds blow loud!
At leisure, thence, through tracts of thin resort,
And sights and sounds that come at intervals,
We take our way. A raree-show is here,
With children gathered round; another street
Presents a company of dancing dogs,
Or dromedary, with an antic pair
Of monkeys on his back; a minstrel band

Of Savoyards;[8] or, single and alone,
An English ballad-singer. Private courts,   180
Gloomy as coffins, and unsightly lanes
Thrilled by some female vendor's scream, belike
The very shrillest of all London cries,
May then entangle our impatient steps;
Conducted through those labyrinths, unawares,
To privileged regions and inviolate,
Where from their airy lodges studious lawyers
Look out on waters, walks, and gardens green.

Thence back into the throng, until we reach,
Following the tide that slackens by degrees,   190
Some half-frequented scene, where wider streets
Bring straggling breezes of suburban air.
Here files of ballads dangle from dead walls;
Advertisements, of giant-size, from high
Press forward, in all colours, on the sight;
These, bold in conscious merit, lower down
That, fronted with a most imposing word,
Is, peradventure, one in masquerade.
As on the broadening causeway we advance,
Behold, turned upwards, a face hard and strong   200
In lineaments, and red with over-toil.
'Tis one encountered here and everywhere;
A travelling cripple, by the trunk cut short,
And stumping on his arms. In sailor's garb
Another lies at length, beside a range
Of well-formed characters, with chalk inscribed
Upon the smooth flat stones: the Nurse is here,
The Bachelor, that loves to sun himself,
The military Idler, and the Dame,   209
That field-ward takes her walk with decent steps.

Now homeward through the thickening hubbub,
          where
See, among less distinguishable shapes,
The begging scavenger, with hat in hand;
The Italian, as he thrids his way with care,
Steadying, far-seen, a frame of images
Upon his head; with basket at his breast
The Jew; the stately and slow-moving Turk,
With freight of slippers piled beneath his arm!

Enough;—the mighty concourse I surveyed
With no unthinking mind, well pleased to note   220
Among the crowd all specimens of man,
Through all the colours which the sun bestows,
And every character of form and face:
The Swede, the Russian; from the genial south,
The Frenchman and the Spaniard; from remote

---

[6] St. Mary of Bethlehem Hospital for the insane, which could
be toured for amusement. The tourist's London in this book
becomes increasingly macabre.
[7] Seventeenth-century English chemist.

[8] Natives of Savoy, between France and Italy, who became
wandering minstrels.

America, the Hunter-Indian; Moors,
Malays, Lascars, the Tartar, the Chinese,
And Negro Ladies in white muslin gowns.

At leisure, then, I viewed, from day to day,
The spectacles within doors,—birds and beasts   230
Of every nature, and strange plants convened
From every clime; and, next, those sights that ape
The absolute presence of reality,
Expressing, as in mirror, sea and land,
And what earth is, and what she has to shew.
I do not here allude to subtlest craft,
By means refined attaining purest ends,
But imitations, fondly made in plain
Confession of man's weakness and his loves.
Whether the Painter, whose ambitious skill   240
Submits to nothing less than taking in
A whole horizon's circuit, do with power,
Like that of angels or commissioned spirits,
Fix us upon some lofty pinnacle,
Or in a ship on waters, with a world
Of life, and life-like mockery beneath,
Above, behind, far stretching and before;
Or more mechanic artist represent
By scale exact, in model, wood or clay,
From blended colours also borrowing help,   250
Some miniature of famous spots or things,—
St. Peter's Church; or, more aspiring aim,
In microscopic vision, Rome herself;
Or, haply, some choice rural haunt,—the Falls
Of Tivoli; and, high upon that steep,
The Sibyl's mouldering Temple! every tree,
Villa, or cottage, lurking among rocks
Throughout the landscape; tuft, stone, scratch
      minute—
All that the traveller sees when he is there.[9]

Add to these exhibitions, mute and still,   260
Others of wider scope, where living men,
Music, and shifting pantomimic scenes,
Diversified the allurement. Need I fear
To mention by its name, as in degree
Lowest of these and humblest in attempt,
Yet richly graced with honours of her own,
Half-rural Sadler's Wells? [10] Though at that time
Intolerant, as is the way of youth
Unless itself be pleased, here more than once
Taking my seat, I saw (nor blush to add,   270
With ample recompense) giants and dwarfs,
Clowns, conjurors, posture-masters, harlequins,

Amid the uproar of the rabblement,
Perform their feats. Nor was it mean delight
To watch crude Nature work in untaught minds;
To note the laws and progress of belief;
Though obstinate on this way, yet on that
How willingly we travel, and how far!
To have, for instance, brought upon the scene
The champion, Jack the Giant-killer: Lo!   280
He dons his coat of darkness; on the stage
Walks, and achieves his wonders, from the eye
Of living Mortal covert, 'as the moon
Hid in her vacant interlunar cave.'
Delusion bold! and how can it be wrought?
The garb he wears is black as death, the word
'*Invisible*' flames forth upon his chest.

Here, too, were 'forms and pressures of the time,'
Rough, bold, as Grecian comedy displayed
When Art was young; dramas of living men,   290
And recent things yet warm with life; a sea-fight,
Shipwreck, or some domestic incident
Divulged by Truth and magnified by Fame,
Such as the daring brotherhood of late
Set forth, too serious theme for that light place—
I mean, O distant Friend! a story drawn
From our own ground,—the Maid of Buttermere,—
And how, unfaithful to a virtuous wife
Deserted and deceived, the spoiler came
And wooed the artless daughter of the hills,   300
And wedded her, in cruel mockery
Of love and marriage bonds. These words to thee
Must needs bring back the moment when we first,
Ere the broad world rang with the maiden's name,
Beheld her serving at the cottage inn,
Both stricken, as she entered or withdrew,
With admiration of her modest mien
And carriage, marked by unexampled grace.
Not unfamiliarly we since that time
Have seen her,—her discretion have observed,   310
Her just opinions, delicate reserve,
Her patience, and humility of mind
Unspoiled by commendation and the excess
Of public notice—an offensive light
To a meek spirit suffering inwardly.[11]

From this memorial tribute to my theme
I was returning, when, with sundry forms
Commingled—shapes which met me in the way

9 Panoramic scenes, full scale and miniature, were popular entertainments in the early nineteenth century.
10 The playhouse in then suburban Islington specialized in unsophisticated entertainment.

11 The sentimental story of the daughter of the innkeeper in Buttermere (northwest of Grasmere) who was seduced by a bigamist and forger named John Hatfield (later hanged) was popular as a newspaper tale and as a dramatic farce. Partly through the efforts of Wordsworth and Coleridge, the Maid of Buttermere became a standard figure in popular culture.

That we must tread—thy image rose again,
Maiden of Buttermere! She lives in peace   320
Upon the spot where she was born and reared;
Without contamination doth she live
In quietness, without anxiety:
Beside the mountain chapel, sleeps in earth
Her new-born infant, fearless as a lamb
That, thither driven from some unsheltered place,
Rests underneath the little rock-like pile
When storms are raging. Happy are they both—
Mother and child!—These feelings, in themselves
Trite, do yet scarcely seem so when I think   330
On those ingenuous moments of our youth
Ere we have learnt by use to slight the crimes
And sorrows of the world. Those simple days
Are now my theme; and, foremost of the scenes,
Which yet survive in memory, appears
One, at whose centre sate a lovely Boy,[12]
A sportive infant, who, for six months' space,
Not more, had been of age to deal about
Articulate prattle—Child as beautiful
As ever clung around a mother's neck,   340
Or father fondly gazed upon with pride.
There, too, conspicuous for stature tall
And large dark eyes, beside her infant stood
The mother; but, upon her cheeks diffused,
False tints too well accorded with the glare
From play-house lustres thrown without reserve
On every object near. The Boy had been
The pride and pleasure of all lookers-on
In whatsoever place, but seemed in this
A sort of alien scattered from the clouds.   350
Of lusty vigour, more than infantine
He was in limb, in cheek a summer rose
Just three parts blown—a cottage-child—if e'er,
By cottage-door, on breezy mountain side,
Or in some sheltering vale, was seen a babe
By Nature's gifts so favoured. Upon a board
Decked with refreshments had this child been placed,
His little stage in the vast theatre,
And there he sate surrounded with a throng
Of chance spectators, chiefly dissolute men   360
And shameless women, treated and caressed;
Ate, drank, and with the fruit and glasses played,
While oaths and laughter and indecent speech
Were rife about him as the songs of birds
Contending after showers. The mother now
Is fading out of memory, but I see
The lovely Boy as I beheld him then
Among the wretched and the falsely gay,
Like one of those who walked with hair unsinged

Amid the fiery furnace. Charms and spells   370
Muttered on black and spiteful instigation
Have stopped, as some believe, the kindliest growths.
Ah, with how different spirit might a prayer
Have been preferred, that this fair creature, checked
By special privilege of Nature's love,
Should in his childhood be detained for ever!
But with its universal freight the tide
Hath rolled along, and this bright innocent,
Mary! may now have lived till he could look
With envy on thy nameless babe that sleeps,   380
Beside the mountain chapel, undisturbed.

Four rapid years had scarcely then been told
Since, travelling southward from our pastoral hills,
I heard, and for the first time in my life,
The voice of woman utter blasphemy—
Saw woman as she is to open shame
Abandoned, and the pride of public vice;
I shuddered, for a barrier seemed at once
Thrown in, that from humanity divorced
Humanity, splitting the race of man   390
In twain, yet leaving the same outward form.
Distress of mind ensued upon the sight
And ardent meditation. Later years
Brought to such spectacle a milder sadness,
Feelings of pure commiseration, grief
For the individual and the overthrow
Of her soul's beauty; farther I was then
But seldom led, or wished to go; in truth
The sorrow of the passion stopped me there.

But let me now, less moved, in order take   400
Our argument. Enough is said to show
How casual incidents of real life,
Observed where pastime only had been sought,
Outweighed, or put to flight, the set events
And measured passions of the stage, albeit
By Siddons[13] trod in the fulness of her power.
Yet was the theatre my dear delight;
The very gilding, lamps and painted scrolls,
And all the mean upholstery of the place,
Wanted not animation, when the tide   410
Of pleasure ebbed but to return as fast
With the ever-shifting figures of the scene,
Solemn or gay: whether some beauteous dame
Advanced in radiance through a deep recess
Of thick entangled forest, like the moon
Opening the clouds; or sovereign king, announced
With flourishing trumpet, came in full-blown state

---

[12] The lovely Boy—not Mary's child but a London prostitute's —is an additional instance of innocence preserved amidst iniquity.

[13] Sarah Siddons (Mrs. Sarah Kemble) was the foremost British actress at the end of the eighteenth century. In 1791 she was 36 years old.

Of the world's greatness, winding round with train
Of courtiers, banners, and a length of guards;
Or captive led in abject weeds, and jingling   420
His slender manacles; or romping girl
Bounced, leapt, and pawed the air; or mumbling sire,
A scare-crow pattern of old age dressed up
In all the tatters of infirmity
All loosely put together, hobbled in,
Stumping upon a cane with which he smites,
From time to time, the solid boards, and makes them
Prate somewhat loudly of the whereabout
Of one so overloaded with his years.
But what of this! the laugh, the grin, grimace,   430
The antics striving to outstrip each other,
Were all received, the least of them not lost,
With an unmeasured welcome. Through the night,
Between the show, and many-headed mass
Of the spectators, and each several nook
Filled with its fray or brawl, how eagerly
And with what flashes, as it were, the mind
Turned this way—that way! sportive and alert
And watchful, as a kitten when at play,
While winds are eddying round her, among straws
And rustling leaves. Enchanting age and sweet!   441
Romantic almost, looked at through a space,
How small, of intervening years! For then,
Though surely no mean progress had been made
In meditations holy and sublime,
Yet something of a girlish child-like gloss
Of novelty survived for scenes like these;
Enjoyment haply handed down from times
When at a country-playhouse, some rude barn
Tricked out for that proud use, if I perchance   450
Caught, on a summer evening through a chink
In the old wall, an unexpected glimpse
Of daylight, the bare thought of where I was
Gladdened me more than if I had been led
Into a dazzling cavern of romance,
Crowded with Genii busy among works
Not to be looked at by the common sun.

    The matter that detains us now may seem,
To many, neither dignified enough
Nor arduous, yet will not be scorned by them,   460
Who, looking inward, have observed the ties
That bind the perishable hours of life
Each to the other, and the curious props
By which the world of memory and thought
Exists and is sustained. More lofty themes,
Such as at least do wear a prouder face,
Solicit our regard; but when I think
Of these, I feel the imaginative power
Languish within me; even then it slept,
When, pressed by tragic sufferings, the heart   470

Was more than full; amid my sobs and tears
It slept, even in the pregnant season of youth.
For though I was most passionately moved
And yielded to all changes of the scene
With an obsequious promptness, yet the storm
Passed not beyond the suburbs of the mind;
Save when realities of act and mien,
The incarnation of the spirits that move
In harmony amid the Poet's world,
Rose to ideal grandeur, or, called forth   480
By power of contrast, made me recognise,
As at a glance, the things which I had shaped,
And yet not shaped, had seen and scarcely seen,
When, having closed the mighty Shakspeare's page,
I mused, and thought, and felt, in solitude.

    Pass we from entertainments, that are such
Professedly, to others titled higher,
Yet, in the estimate of youth at least,
More near akin to those than names imply,—
I mean the brawls of lawyers in their courts   490
Before the ermined judge, or that great stage
Where senators, tongue-favoured men, perform,
Admired and envied! Oh! the beating heart,
When one among the prime of these rise up,—
One, of whose name from childhood we had heard
Familiarly, a household term, like those,
The Bedfords, Glosters, Salisburys, of old
Whom the fifth Harry talks of.[14] Silence! hush!
This is no trifler, no short-flighted wit,
No stammerer of a minute, painfully   500
Delivered. No! the Orator hath yoked
The Hours, like young Aurora, to his car:
Thrice welcome Presence! how can patience e'er
Grow weary of attending on a track
That kindles with such glory! All are charmed,
Astonished; like a hero in romance,
He winds away his never-ending horn;
Words follow words, sense seems to follow sense:
What memory and what logic! till the strain
Transcendent, superhuman, as it seemed,   510
Grows tedious even in a young man's ear.

    Genius of Burke![15] forgive the pen seduced
By specious wonders, and too slow to tell
Of what the ingenuous, what bewildered men,
Beginning to mistrust their boastful guides,
And wise men, willing to grow wiser, caught,

---

[14] See Shakespeare's *Henry V*, iv, iii, 51-55.
[15] Edmund Burke (1729–1797) was not praised thus lavishly by
Wordsworth until the text of 1820. Before then, the conservative
statesman's opinions would not have been so congenial. Burke's
condemnation of the revolution in France was early, consistent,
and uncompromising.

Rapt auditors! from thy most eloquent tongue—
Now mute, for ever mute in the cold grave.
I see him,—old, but vigorous in age,—
Stand like an oak whose stag-horn branches start   520
Out of its leafy brow, the more to awe
The younger brethren of the grove. But some—
While he forewarns, denounces, launches forth,
Against all systems built on abstract rights,
Keen ridicule; the majesty proclaims
Of Institutes and Laws, hallowed by time;
Declares the vital power of social ties
Endeared by Custom; and with high disdain,
Exploding upstart Theory, insists
Upon the allegiance to which men are born—   530
Some—say at once a froward multitude—
Murmur (for truth is hated, where not loved)
As the winds fret within the Æolian cave,
Galled by their monarch's chain. The times were
     big
With ominous change, which, night by night,
     provoked
Keen struggles, and black clouds of passion raised;
But memorable moments intervened,
When Wisdom, like the Goddess from Jove's brain,
Broke forth in armour of resplendent words,
Startling the Synod. Could a youth, and one   540
In ancient story versed, whose breast had heaved
Under the weight of classic eloquence,
Sit, see, and hear, unthankful, uninspired?

   Nor did the Pulpit's oratory fail
To achieve its higher triumph. Not unfelt
Were its admonishments, nor lightly heard
The awful truths delivered thence by tongues
Endowed with various power to search the soul;
Yet ostentation, domineering, oft
Poured forth harangues, how sadly out of place!—
There have I seen a comely bachelor,   551
Fresh from a toilette of two hours, ascend
His rostrum, with seraphic glance look up,
And, in a tone elaborately low
Beginning, lead his voice through many a maze
A minuet course; and, winding up his mouth,
From time to time, into an orifice
Most delicate, a lurking eyelet, small,
And only not invisible, again
Open it out, diffusing thence a smile   560
Of rapt irradiation, exquisite.
Meanwhile the Evangelists, Isaiah, Job,
Moses, and he who penned, the other day,
The Death of Abel, Shakspeare, and the Bard
Whose genius spangled o'er a gloomy theme
With fancies thick as his inspiring stars,
And Ossian (doubt not, 'tis the naked truth)

Summoned from streamy Morven [16]—each and all
Would, in their turns, lend ornaments and flowers
To entwine the crook of eloquence that helped   570
This pretty Shepherd, pride of all the plains,
To rule and guide his captivated flock.

   I glance but at a few conspicuous marks,
Leaving a thousand others, that, in hall,
Court, theatre, conventicle, or shop,
In public room or private, park or street,
Each fondly reared on his own pedestal,
Looked out for admiration. Folly, vice,
Extravagance in gesture, mien, and dress,
And all the strife of singularity,   580
Lies to the ear, and lies to every sense—
Of these, and of the living shapes they wear,
There is no end. Such candidates for regard,
Although well pleased to be where they were found,
I did not hunt after, nor greatly prize,
Nor made unto myself a secret boast
Of reading them with quick and curious eye;
But, as a common produce, things that are
To-day, to-morrow will be, took of them
Such willing note, as, on some errand bound   590
That asks not speed, a Traveller might bestow
On sea-shells that bestrew the sandy beach,
Or daisies swarming through the fields of June.

   But foolishness and madness in parade,
Though most at home in this their dear domain,
Are scattered everywhere, no rarities,
Even to the rudest novice of the Schools.
Me, rather, it employed, to note, and keep
In memory, those individual sights
Of courage, or integrity, or truth,   600
Or tenderness, which there, set off by foil,
Appeared more touching. One will I select;
A Father—for he bore that sacred name—
Him saw I, sitting in an open square,
Upon a corner-stone of that low wall,
Wherein were fixed the iron pales that fenced
A spacious grass-plot; there, in silence, sate
This One Man, with a sickly babe outstretched
Upon his knee, whom he had thither brought
For sunshine, and to breathe the fresher air.   610
Of those who passed, and me who looked at him,
He took no heed; but in his brawny arms
(The Artificer was to the elbow bare,

[16] Salomon Gessner in translation (*Der Tod Abels*—1758), and the Bard Edward Young (*Night Thoughts*—1742–1745) were extremely popular at the turn of the century. James Macpherson's "Ossianic" poems, falsely claimed as translations from third-century Gaelic, were still popular but suspected by more experienced readers.

And from his work this moment had been stolen)
He held the child, and, bending over it,
As if he were afraid both of the sun
And of the air, which he had come to seek,
Eyed the poor babe with love unutterable.

    As the black storm upon the mountain top
Sets off the sunbeam in the valley, so   620
That huge fermenting mass of human-kind
Serves as a solemn back-ground, or relief,
To single forms and objects, whence they draw,
For feeling and contemplative regard,
More than inherent liveliness and power.
How oft, amid those overflowing streets,
Have I gone forward with the crowd, and said
Unto myself, 'The face of every one
That passes by me is a mystery!'   629
Thus have I looked, nor ceased to look, oppressed
By thoughts of what and whither, when and how,
Until the shapes before my eyes became
A second-sight procession, such as glides
Over still mountains, or appears in dreams;
And once, far-travelled in such mood, beyond
The reach of common indication, lost
Amid the moving pageant, I was smitten
Abruptly, with the view (a sight not rare)
Of a blind Beggar, who, with upright face,
Stood, propped against a wall, upon his chest   640
Wearing a written paper, to explain
His story, whence he came, and who he was.
Caught by the spectacle my mind turned round
As with the might of waters; an apt type
This label seemed of the utmost we can know,
Both of ourselves and of the universe;
And, on the shape of that unmoving man,
His steadfast face and sightless eyes, I gazed,
As if admonished from another world.

Though reared upon the base of outward things,   650
Structures like these the excited spirit mainly
Builds for herself; scenes different there are,
Full-formed, that take, with small internal help,
Possession of the faculties,—the peace
That comes with night; the deep solemnity
Of nature's intermediate hours of rest,
When the great tide of human life stands still;
The business of the day to come, unborn,
Of that gone by, locked up, as in the grave;
The blended calmness of the heavens and earth,   660
Moonlight and stars, and empty streets, and sounds
Unfrequent as in deserts; at late hours
Of winter evenings, when unwholesome rains
Are falling hard, with people yet astir,
The feeble salutation from the voice

Of some unhappy woman, now and then
Heard as we pass, when no one looks about,
Nothing is listened to. But these, I fear,
Are falsely catalogued; things that are, are not,
As the mind answers to them, or the heart   670
Is prompt, or slow, to feel. What say you, then,
To times, when half the city shall break out
Full of one passion, vengeance, rage, or fear?
To execution, to a street on fire,
Mobs, riots, or rejoicings? From these sights
Take one,—that ancient festival, the Fair,[17]
Holden where martyrs suffered in past time,
And named of St. Bartholomew; there, see
A work completed to our hands, that lays,
If any spectacle on earth can do,   680
The whole creative powers of man asleep!—
For once, the Muse's help will we implore,
And she shall lodge us, wafted on her wings,
Above the press and danger of the crowd,
Upon some showman's platform. What a shock
For eyes and ears! what anarchy and din,
Barbarian and infernal,—a phantasma,
Monstrous in colour, motion, shape, sight, sound!
Below, the open space, through every nook
Of the wide area, twinkles, is alive   690
With heads; the midway region, and above,
Is thronged with staring pictures and huge scrolls,
Dumb proclamations of the Prodigies;
With chattering monkeys dangling from their poles,
And children whirling in their roundabouts;
With those that stretch the neck and strain the eyes,
And crack the voice in rivalship, the crowd
Inviting; with buffoons against buffoons
Grimacing, writhing, screaming,—him who grinds
The hurdy-gurdy, at the fiddle weaves,   700
Rattles the salt-box, thumps the kettle-drum,
And him who at the trumpet puffs his cheeks,
The silver-collared Negro with his timbrel,
Equestrians, tumblers, women, girls, and boys,
Blue-breeched, pink-vested, with high-towering
    plumes.
All moveables of wonder, from all parts,
Are here—Albinos, painted Indians, Dwarfs,
The Horse of knowledge, and the learned Pig,
The Stone-eater, the man that swallows fire,
Giants, Ventriloquists, the Invisible Girl,   710
The Bust that speaks and moves its goggling eyes,
The Wax-work, Clock-work, all the marvellous craft
Of modern Merlins, Wild Beasts, Puppet-shows,
All out-o'-the-way, far-fetched, perverted things,

---

17 Bartholomew Fair, which Wordsworth visited with Charles
and Mary Lamb in 1802, was an annual event in Smithfield,
London. The sideshows described below were typical entertain-
ment.

All freaks of nature, all Promethean [18] thoughts
Of man, his dullness, madness, and their feats
All jumbled up together, to compose
A Parliament of Monsters. Tents and Booths
Meanwhile, as if the whole were one vast mill,
Are vomiting, receiving on all sides,   720
Men, Women, three-years Children, Babes in arms.

   Oh, blank confusion! true epitome
Of what the mighty City is herself
To thousands upon thousands of her sons,
Living amid the same perpetual whirl
Of trivial objects, melted and reduced
To one identity, by differences
That have no law, no meaning, and no end—
Oppression, under which even highest minds
Must labour, whence the strongest are not free.   730
But though the picture weary out the eye,
By nature an unmanageable sight,
It is not wholly so to him who looks
In steadiness, who hath among least things
An under-sense of greatest; sees the parts
As parts, but with a feeling of the whole.
This, of all acquisitions first, awaits
On sundry and most widely different modes
Of education, nor with least delight
On that through which I passed. Attention springs,
And comprehensiveness and memory flow,   741
From early converse with the works of God
Among all regions; chiefly where appear
Most obviously simplicity and power.
Think, how the everlasting streams and woods,
Stretched and still stretching far and wide, exalt
The roving Indian. On his desert sands
What grandeur not unfelt, what pregnant show
Of beauty, meets the sun-burnt Arab's eye:
And, as the sea propels, from zone to zone,   750
Its currents; magnifies its shoals of life
Beyond all compass; spreads, and sends aloft
Armies of clouds,—even so, its powers and aspects
Shape for mankind, by principles as fixed,
The views and aspirations of the soul
To majesty. Like virtue have the forms
Perennial of the ancient hills; nor less
The changeful language of their countenances
Quickens the slumbering mind, and aids the thoughts,
However multitudinous, to move   760
With order and relation. This, if still,
As hitherto, in freedom I may speak,
Not violating any just restraint,
As may be hoped, of real modesty,—
This did I feel, in London's vast domain.

The Spirit of Nature was upon me there;
The soul of Beauty and enduring Life
Vouchsafed her inspiration, and diffused,
Through meagre lines and colours, and the press
Of self-destroying, transitory things,   770
Composure, and ennobling Harmony.

BOOK EIGHTH

RETROSPECT.—LOVE OF NATURE
LEADING TO LOVE OF MAN

WHAT sounds are those, Helvellyn,[1] that are heard
Up to thy summit, through the depth of air
Ascending, as if distance had the power
To make the sounds more audible? What crowd
Covers, or sprinkles o'er, yon village green?
Crowd seems it, solitary hill! to thee,
Though but a little family of men,
Shepherds and tillers of the ground—betimes
Assembled with their children and their wives,
And here and there a stranger interspersed.   10
They hold a rustic fair—a festival,
Such as, on this side now, and now on that,
Repeated through his tributary vales,
Helvellyn, in the silence of his rest,
Sees annually, if clouds towards either ocean
Blown from their favourite resting-place, or mists
Dissolved, have left him an unshrouded head.
Delightful day it is for all who dwell
In this secluded glen, and eagerly
They give it welcome. Long ere heat of noon,   20
From byre or field the kine were brought; the sheep
Are penned in cotes; the chaffering is begun.
The heifer lows, uneasy at the voice
Of a new master; bleat the flocks aloud.
Booths are there none; a stall or two is here;
A lame man or a blind, the one to beg,
The other to make music; hither, too,
From far, with basket, slung upon her arm,
Of hawker's wares—books, pictures, combs, and
    pins—
Some aged woman finds her way again,   30
Year after year, a punctual visitant!
There also stands a speech-maker by rote,
Pulling the strings of his boxed raree-show;
And in the lapse of many years may come
Prouder itinerant, mountebank, or he
Whose wonders in a covered wain lie hid.
But one there is, the loveliest of them all,
Some sweet lass of the valley, looking out

---

[18] In the manner of Prometheus, who stole fire from Zeus;
thus, bold, original, creative, and ambitious.

[1] A mountain halfway between Grasmere and Keswick.

For gains, and who that sees her would not buy?
Fruits of her father's orchard, are her wares, 40
And with the ruddy produce, she walks round
Among the crowd, half pleased with half ashamed
Of her new office, blushing restlessly.
The children now are rich, for the old to-day
Are generous as the young; and, if content
With looking on, some ancient wedded pair
Sit in the shade together, while they gaze,
'A cheerful smile unbends the wrinkled brow,
The days departed start again to life,
And all the scenes of childhood reappear, 50
Faint, but more tranquil, like the changing sun
To him who slept at noon and wakes at eve.'[2]
Thus gaiety and cheerfulness prevail,
Spreading from young to old, from old to young,
And no one seems to want his share.—Immense
Is the recess, the circumambient world
Magnificent, by which they are embraced:
They move about upon the soft green turf:
How little they, they and their doings, seem,
And all that they can further or obstruct! 60
Through utter weakness pitiably dear,
As tender infants are: and yet how great!
For all things serve them: them the morning light
Loves, as it glistens on the silent rocks;
And them the silent rocks, which now from high
Look down upon them; the reposing clouds;
The wild brooks prattling from invisible haunts;
And old Helvellyn, conscious of the stir
Which animates this day their calm abode.

With deep devotion, Nature, did I feel, 70
In that enormous City's turbulent world
Of men and things, what benefit I owed
To thee, and those domains of rural peace,
Where to the sense of beauty first my heart
Was opened; tract more exquisitely fair
Than that famed paradise of ten thousand trees,
Or Gehol's[3] matchless gardens, for delight
Of the Tartarian dynasty composed
(Beyond that mighty wall, not fabulous,
China's stupendous mound) by patient toil 80
Of myriads and boon nature's lavish help;
There, in a clime from widest empire chosen,
Fulfilling (could enchantment have done more?)
A sumptuous dream of flowery lawns, with domes
Of pleasure sprinkled over, shady dells
For eastern monasteries, sunny mounts

[2] In a note Wordsworth explains that these lines are quoted from his friend Joseph Cottle (1770–1853), a Bristol bookseller and publisher.
[3] A famous Chinese park and garden, described in contemporary travel literature.

With temples crested, bridges, gondolas,
Rocks, dens, and groves of foliage taught to melt
Into each other their obsequious hues,
Vanished and vanishing in subtle chase, 90
Too fine to be pursued; or standing forth
In no discordant opposition, strong
And gorgeous as the colours side by side
Bedded among rich plumes of tropic birds;
And mountains over all, embracing all;
And all the landscape endlessly enriched
With waters running, falling, or asleep.

But lovelier far than this, the paradise
Where I was reared; in Nature's primitive gifts
Favoured no less, and more to every sense 100
Delicious, seeing that the sun and sky,
The elements, and seasons as they change,
Do find a worthy fellow-labourer there—
Man free, man working for himself, with choice
Of time, and place, and object; by his wants,
His comforts, native occupations, cares,
Cheerfully led to individual ends
Or social, and still followed by a train
Unwooed, unthought-of-even—simplicity,
And beauty, and inevitable grace. 110

Yea, when a glimpse of those imperial bowers
Would to a child be transport over-great,
When but a half-hour's roam through such a place
Would leave behind a dance of images,
That shall break in upon his sleep for weeks;
Even then the common haunts of the green earth,
And ordinary interests of man,
Which they embosom, all without regard
As both may seem, are fastening on the heart
Insensibly, each with the other's help. 120
For me, when my affections first were led
From kindred, friends, and playmates, to partake
Love for the human creature's absolute self,
That noticeable kindliness of heart
Sprang out of fountains, there abounding most
Where sovereign Nature dictated the tasks
And occupations which her beauty adorned,
And Shepherds were the men that pleased me first;
Not such as Saturn ruled 'mid Latian wilds,
With arts and laws so tempered, that their lives 130
Left, even to us toiling in this late day,
A bright tradition of the golden age;
Not such as, 'mid Arcadian fastnesses
Sequestered, handed down among themselves
Felicity, in Grecian song renowned;
Nor such as, when an adverse fate had driven,
From house and home, the courtly band whose fortunes

Entered, with Shakespeare's genius, the wild woods
Of Arden, amid sunshine or in shade,
Culled the best fruits of Time's uncounted hours,
Ere Phoebe sighed for the false Ganymede;   141
Or there where Perdita and Florizel
Together danced, Queen of the feast, and King;
Nor such as Spenser fabled.[4] True it is,
That I had heard (what he perhaps had seen)
Of maids at sunrise bringing in from far
Their May-bush, and along the street in flocks
Parading with a song of taunting rhymes,
Aimed at the laggards slumbering within doors;
Had also heard, from those who yet remembered,   150
Tales of the May-pole dance, and wreaths that decked
Porch, door-way, or kirk-pillar; and of youths,
Each with his maid, before the sun was up,
By annual custom, issuing forth in troops,
To drink the waters of some sainted well,
And hang it round with garlands. Love survives;
But, for such purpose, flowers no longer grow:
The times, too sage, perhaps too proud, have dropped
These lighter graces; and the rural ways
And manners which my childhood looked upon   160
Were the unluxuriant produce of a life
Intent on little but substantial needs,
Yet rich in beauty, beauty that was felt.
But images of danger and distress,
Man suffering among awful Powers and Forms;
Of this I heard, and saw enough to make
Imagination restless; nor was free
Myself from frequent perils; nor were tales
Wanting,—the tragedies of former times,
Hazards and strange escapes, of which the rocks   170
Immutable and everflowing streams,
Where'er I roamed, were speaking monuments.

   Smooth life had flock and shepherd in old time,
Long springs and tepid waters, on the banks
Of delicate Galesus; and no less
Those scattered along Adria's myrtle shores:
Smooth life had herdsman, and his snow-white herd
To triumphs and to sacrificial rites
Devoted, on the inviolable stream
Of rich Clitumnus; and the goat-herd lived   180
As calmly, underneath the pleasant brows
Of cool Lucretilis,[5] where the pipe was heard
Of Pan, invisible God, thrilling the rocks
With tutelary music, from all harm
The fold protecting. I myself, mature
In manhood then, have seen a pastoral tract
Like one of these, where Fancy might run wild,

Though under skies less generous, less serene:
There, for her own delight had Nature framed
A pleasure-ground, diffused a fair expanse   190
Of level pasture, islanded with groves
And banked with woody risings; but the Plain
Endless, here opening widely out, and there
Shut up in lesser lakes or beds of lawn
And intricate recesses, creek or bay
Sheltered within a shelter, where at large
The shepherd strays, a rolling hut his home.
Thither he comes with spring-time, there abides
All summer, and at sunrise ye may hear
His flageolet to liquid notes of love   200
Attuned, or sprightly fife resounding far.
Nook is there none, nor tract of that vast space
Where passage opens, but the same shall have
In turn its visitant, telling there his hours
In unlaborious pleasure, with no task
More toilsome than to carve a beechen bowl
For spring or fountain, which the traveller finds,
When through the region he pursues at will
His devious course. A glimpse of such sweet life
I saw when, from the melancholy walls   210
Of Goslar,[6] once imperial, I renewed
My daily walk along that wide champaign,
That, reaching to her gates, spreads east and west,
And northwards, from beneath the mountainous verge
Of the Hercynian[7] forest. Yet, hail to you
Moors, mountains, headlands, and ye hollow vales,
Ye long deep channels for the Atlantic's voice,
Powers of my native region! Ye that seize
The heart with firmer grasp! Your snows and streams
Ungovernable, and your terrifying winds,   220
That howl so dismally for him who treads
Companionless your awful solitudes!
There, 'tis the shepherd's task the winter long
To wait upon the storms: of their approach
Sagacious, into sheltering coves he drives
His flock, and thither from the homestead bears
A toilsome burden up the craggy ways,
And deals it out, their regular nourishment
Strewn on the frozen snow. And when the spring
Looks out, and all the pastures dance with lambs,   230
And when the flock, with warmer weather, climbs
Higher and higher, him his office leads
To watch their goings, whatsoever track
The wanderers choose. For this he quits his home
At day-spring, and no sooner doth the sun
Begin to strike him with a fire-like heat,
Than he lies down upon some shining rock,

---

[4] The references are to the pastoral plays of Shakespeare and poems of Spenser.
[5] Wordsworth would have read of the rivers and mountains of Calabria in Virgil or Horace.

---

[6] The city in Germany (Saxony) where William and Dorothy spent the winter of 1798–1799.
[7] I.e., of the Harz mountains.

And breakfasts with his dog. When they have stolen,
As is their wont, a pittance from strict time,
For rest not needed or exchange of love,   240
Then from his couch he starts; and now his feet
Crush out a livelier fragrance from the flowers
Of lowly thyme, by Nature's skill enwrought
In the wild turf: the lingering dews of morn
Smoke round him, as from hill to hill he hies,
His staff portending like a hunter's spear,
Or by its aid leaping from crag to crag,
And o'er the brawling beds of unbridged streams.
Philosophy, methinks, at Fancy's call,
Might deign to follow him through what he does 250
Or sees in his day's march; himself he feels,
In those vast regions where his service lies,
A freeman, wedded to his life of hope
And hazard, and hard labour interchanged
With that majestic indolence so dear
To native man. A rambling school-boy, thus
I felt his presence in his own domain,
As of a lord and master, or a power,
Or genius, under Nature, under God,
Presiding; and severest solitude   260
Had more commanding looks when he was there.
When up the lonely brooks on rainy days
Angling I went, or trod the trackless hills
By mists bewildered, suddenly mine eyes
Have glanced upon him distant a few steps,
In size a giant, stalking through thick fog,
His sheep like Greenland bears;[8] or, as he stepped
Beyond the boundary line of some hill-shadow,
His form hath flashed upon me, glorified
By the deep radiance of the setting sun: 270
Or him have I descried in distant sky,
A solitary object and sublime,
Above all height! like an aerial cross
Stationed alone upon a spiry rock
Of the Chartreuse, for worship. Thus was man
Ennobled outwardly before my sight,
And thus my heart was early introduced
To an unconscious love and reverence
Of human nature; hence the human form
To me became an index of delight,   280
Of grace and honour, power and worthiness.
Meanwhile this creature—spiritual almost
As those of books, but more exalted far;
Far more of an imaginative form
Than the gay Corin of the groves, who lives
For his own fancies, or to dance by the hour,
In coronal, with Phyllis[9] in the midst—

----

[8] I.e., polar bears.
[9] Corin and Phyllis are common names for the lovers in
pastoral romances.

Was, for the purposes of kind, a man
With the most common; husband, father; learned,
Could teach, admonish; suffered with the rest 290
From vice and folly, wretchedness and fear;
Of this I little saw, cared less for it,
But something must have felt.
                              Call ye these
    appearances—
Which I beheld of shepherds in my youth,
This sanctity of Nature given to man—
A shadow, a delusion, ye who pore
On the dead letter, miss the spirit of things;
Whose truth is not a motion or a shape
Instinct with vital functions, but a block
Or waxen image which yourselves have made,   300
And ye adore! But blessed be the God
Of Nature and of Man that this was so;
That men before my inexperienced eyes
Did first present themselves thus purified,
Removed, and to a distance that was fit:
And so we all of us in some degree
Are led to knowledge, whencesoever led,
And howsoever; were it otherwise,
And we found evil fast as we find good
In our first years, or think that it is found, 310
How could the innocent heart bear up and live!
But doubly fortunate my lot; not here
Alone, that something of a better life
Perhaps was round me than it is the privilege
Of most to move in, but that first I looked
At Man through objects that were great or fair;
First communed with him by their help. And thus
Was founded a sure safeguard and defence
Against the weight of meanness, selfish cares,
Coarse manners, vulgar passions, that beat in 320
On all sides from the ordinary world
In which we traffic. Starting from this point
I had my face turned toward the truth, began
With an advantage furnished by that kind
Of prepossession, without which the soul
Receives no knowledge that can bring forth good,
No genuine insight ever comes to her.
From the restraint of over-watchful eyes
Preserved, I moved about, year after year,
Happy, and now most thankful that my walk   330
Was guarded from too early intercourse
With the deformities of crowded life,
And those ensuing laughters and contempts,
Self-pleasing, which, if we would wish to think
With a due reverence on earth's rightful lord,
Here placed to be the inheritor of heaven,
Will not permit us; but pursue the mind,
That to devotion willingly would rise,
Into the temple and the temple's heart.

Yet deem not, Friend! that human kind with me
Thus early took a place pre-eminent;   341
Nature herself was, at this unripe time,
But secondary to my own pursuits
And animal activities, and all
Their trivial pleasures; and when these had drooped
And gradually expired, and Nature, prized
For her own sake, became my joy, even then—
And upwards through late youth, until not less
Than two-and-twenty summers had been told—
Was Man in my affections and regards   350
Subordinate to her, her visible forms
And viewless agencies: a passion, she,
A rapture often, and immediate love
Ever at hand; he, only a delight
Occasional, an accidental grace,
His hour being not yet come. Far less had then
The inferior creatures, beast or bird, attuned
My spirit to that gentleness of love
(Though they had long been carefully observed),
Won from me those minute obeisances   360
Of tenderness, which I may number now
With my first blessings. Nevertheless, on these
The light of beauty did not fall in vain,
Or grandeur circumfuse them to no end.

But when that first poetic faculty
Of plain Imagination and severe,
No longer a mute influence of the soul,
Ventured, at some rash Muse's earnest call,
To try her strength among harmonious words;
And to book-notions and the rules of art   370
Did knowlingly conform itself; there came
Among the simple shapes of human life
A wilfulness of fancy and conceit;
And Nature and her objects beautified
These fictions, as in some sort, in their turn,
They burnished her. From touch of this new
        power
Nothing was safe: the elder-tree that grew
Beside the well-known charnel-house had then
A dismal look: the yew-tree had its ghost,
That took his station there for ornament: 380
The dignities of plain occurrence then
Were tasteless, and truth's golden mean, a point
Where no sufficient pleasure could be found.
Then, if a widow, staggering with the blow
Of her distress, was known to have turned her steps
To the cold grave in which her husband slept,
One night, or haply more than one, through pain
Or half-insensate impotence of mind,
The fact was caught at greedily, and there
She must be visitant the whole year through,
Wetting the turf with never-ending tears.   390

Through quaint obliquities I might pursue
These cravings; when the fox-glove, one by one,
Upwards through every stage of the tall stem,
Had shed beside the public way its bells,
And stood of all dismantled, save the last
Left at the tapering ladder's top, that seemed
To bend as doth a slender blade of grass
Tipped with a rain-drop, Fancy loved to seat,
Beneath the plant despoiled, but crested still   400
With this last relic, soon itself to fall,
Some vagrant mother, whose arch little ones,
All unconcerned by her dejected plight,
Laughed as with rival eagerness their hands
Gathered the purple cups that round them lay,
Strewing the turf's green slope.
                              A diamond light
(Whene'er the summer sun, declining, smote
A smooth rock wet with constant springs) was seen
Sparkling from out a copse-clad bank that rose
Fronting our cottage. Oft beside the hearth   410
Seated, with open door, often and long
Upon this restless lustre have I gazed,
That made my fancy restless as itself.
'Twas now for me a burnished silver shield
Suspended over a knight's tomb, who lay
Inglorious, buried in the dusky wood:
An entrance now into some magic cave
Or palace built by fairies of the rock;
Nor could I have been bribed to disenchant
The spectacle, by visiting the spot.   420
Thus wilful Fancy, in no hurtful mood,
Engrafted far-fetched shapes on feelings bred
By pure Imagination: busy Power
She was, and with her ready pupil turned
Instinctively to human passions, then
Least understood. Yet, 'mid the fervent swarm
Of these vagaries, with an eye so rich
As mine was through the bounty of a grand
And lovely region, I had forms distinct
To steady me: each airy thought revolved   430
Round a substantial centre, which at once
Incited it to motion, and controlled.
I did not pine like one in cities bred,
As was thy melancholy lot, dear Friend!
Great Spirit as thou art, in endless dreams
Of sickliness, disjoining, joining, things
Without the light of knowledge. Where the harm,
If, when the woodman languished with disease
Induced by sleeping nightly on the ground
Within his sod-built cabin, Indian-wise,   440
I called the pangs of disappointed love,
And all the sad etcetera of the wrong,
To help him to his grave. Meanwhile the man,
If not already from the woods retired

To die at home, was haply, as I knew,
Withering by slow degrees, 'mid gentle airs,
Birds, running streams, and hills so beautiful
On golden evenings, while the charcoal pile
Breathed up its smoke, an image of his ghost
Or spirit that full soon must take her flight.   450
Nor shall we not be tending towards that point
Of sound humanity to which our Tale
Leads, though by sinuous ways, if here I shew
How Fancy, in a season when she wove
Those slender cords, to guide the unconscious Boy
For the Man's sake, could feed at Nature's call
Some pensive musings which might well beseem
Maturer years.

        A grove there is whose boughs
Stretch from the western marge of Thurston-mere,[10]
With length of shade so thick, that whoso glides   460
Along the line of low-roofed water, moves
As in a cloister. Once—while, in that shade
Loitering, I watched the golden beams of light
Flung from the setting sun, as they reposed
In silent beauty on the naked ridge
Of a high eastern hill—thus flowed my thoughts
In a pure stream of words fresh from the heart;
Dear native Region, wheresoe'er shall close
My mortal course, there will I think on you;
Dying, will cast on you a backward look;   470
Even as this setting sun (albeit the Vale
Is no where touched by one memorial gleam)
Doth with the fond remains of his last power
Still linger, and a farewell lustre sheds
On the dear mountain-tops where first he rose.

    Enough of humble arguments; recal,
My Song! those high emotions which thy voice
Has heretofore made known; that bursting forth
Of sympathy, inspiring and inspired,
When everywhere a vital pulse was felt,   480
And all the several frames of things, like stars,
Through every magnitude distinguishable,
Shone mutually indebted, or half lost
Each in the other's blaze, a galaxy
Of life and glory. In the midst stood Man,
Outwardly, inwardly contemplated,
As, of all visible natures, crown, though born
Of dust, and kindred to the worm; a Being,
Both in perception and discernment, first
In every capability of rapture,   490
Through the divine effect of power and love;
As, more than anything we know, instinct
With godhead, and, by reason and by will,
Acknowledging dependency sublime.

<hr />

[10] Another name for Coniston water, west of Hawkshead.

Ere long, the lonely mountains left, I moved,
Begirt, from day to day, with temporal shapes
Of vice and folly thrust upon my view,
Objects of sport, and ridicule, and scorn,
Manners and characters discriminate,
And little bustling passions that eclipsed,   500
As well they might, the impersonated thought,
The idea, or abstraction of the kind.

    An idler among academic bowers,
Such was my new condition, as at large
Has been set forth; yet here the vulgar light
Of present, actual, superficial life,
Gleaming through colouring of other times,
Old usages and local privilege,
Was welcome, softened, if not solemnised.
This notwithstanding, being brought more near   510
To vice and guilt, forerunning wretchedness,
I trembled,—thought, at times, of human life
With an indefinite terror and dismay,
Such as the storms and angry elements
Had bred in me; but gloomier far, a dim
Analogy to uproar and misrule,
Disquiet, danger, and obscurity.

    It might be told (but whereof speak of things
Common to all?) that, seeing, I was led
Gravely to ponder—judging between good   520
And evil, not as for the mind's delight
But for her guidance—one who was to *act*,
As sometimes to the best of feeble means
I did, by human sympathy impelled:
And, through dislike and most offensive pain,
Was to the truth conducted; of this faith
Never forsaken, that, by acting well,
And understanding, I should learn to love
The end of life, and every thing we know.

    Grave Teacher, stern Preceptress! for at times
Thou canst put on an aspect most severe;   531
London, to thee I willingly return.
Erewhile my verse played idly with the flowers
Enwrought upon thy mantle; satisfied
With that amusement, and a simple look
Of child-like inquisition now and then
Cast upwards on thy countenance, to detect
Some inner meanings which might harbour there.
But how could I in mood so light indulge,
Keeping such fresh remembrance of the day,   540
When, having thridded the long labyrinth
Of the suburban villages, I first
Entered thy vast dominion? On the roof
Of an itinerant vehicle I sate,
With vulgar men about me, trivial forms

Of houses, pavement, streets, of men and things,—
Mean shapes on every side: but, at the instant,
When to myself it fairly might be said,
The threshold now is overpast, (how strange
That aught external to the living mind   550
Should have such mighty sway! yet so it was),
A weight of ages did at once descend
Upon my heart; no thought embodied, no
Distinct remembrances, but weight and power,—
Power growing under weight: alas! I feel
That I am trifling: 'twas a moment's pause,—
All that took place within me came and went
As in a moment; yet with Time it dwells,
And grateful memory, as a thing divine.

The curious traveller, who, from open day,   560
Hath passed with torches into some huge cave,
The Grotto of Antiparos, or the Den
In old time haunted by that Danish Witch,
Yordas; [11] he looks around and sees the vault
Widening on all sides; sees, or thinks he sees,
Erelong, the massy roof above his head,
That instantly unsettles and recedes,—
Substance and shadow, light and darkess, all
Commingled, making up a canopy
Of shapes and forms and tendencies to shape   570
That shift and vanish, change and interchange
Like spectres,—ferment silent and sublime!
That after a short space works less and less,
Till, every effort, every motion gone,
The scene before him stands in perfect view
Exposed, and lifeless as a written book!—
But let him pause awhile, and look again,
And a new quickening shall succeed, at first
Beginning timidly, then creeping fast,
Till the whole cave, so late a senseless mass,   580
Busies the eye with images and forms
Boldly assembled,—here is shadowed forth
From the projections, wrinkles, cavities,
A variegated landscape,—there the shape
Of some gigantic warrior clad in mail,
The ghostly semblance of a hooded monk,
Veiled nun, or pilgrim resting on his staff:
Strange congregation! yet not slow to meet
Eyes that perceive through minds that can inspire.

Even in such sort had I at first been moved,   590
Nor otherwise continued to be moved,
As I explored the vast metropolis,
Fount of my country's destiny and the world's;
That great emporium, chronicle at once

[11] The first is on an island in the Aegean, the second in York-
shire.

And burial-place of passions, and their home
Imperial, their chief living residence.

With strong sensations teeming as it did
Of past and present, such a place must needs
Have pleased me, seeking knowledge at that time
Far less than craving power; yet knowledge came,
Sought or unsought, and influxes of power   601
Came, of themselves, or at her call derived
In fits of kindliest apprehensiveness,
From all sides, when whate'er was in itself
Capacious found, or seemed to find, in me
A correspondent amplitude of mind;
Such is the strength and glory of our youth!
The human nature unto which I felt
That I belonged, and reverenced with love,
Was not a punctual presence, but a spirit   610
Diffused through time and space, with aid derived
Of evidence from monuments, erect,
Prostrate, or leaning towards their common rest
In earth, the widely scattered wreck sublime
Of vanished nations, or more clearly drawn
From books and what they picture and record.

'Tis true, the history of our native land,
With those of Greece compared and popular Rome,
And in our high-wrought modern narratives
Stript of their harmonising soul, the life   620
Of manners and familiar incidents,
Had never much delighted me. And less
Than other intellects had mine been used
To lean upon extrinsic circumstance
Of record or tradition; but a sense
Of what in the Great City had been done
And suffered, and was doing, suffering, still,
Weighed with me, could support the test of thought;
And, in despite of all that had gone by,
Or was departing never to return,   630
There I conversed with majesty and power
Like independent natures. Hence the place
Was thronged with impregnations like the Wilds
In which my early feelings had been nursed—
Bare hills and valleys, full of caverns, rocks,
And audible seclusions, dashing lakes,
Echoes and waterfalls, and pointed crags
That into music touch the passing wind.
Here then my young imagination found
No uncongenial element; could here   640
Among new objects serve or give command,
Even as the heart's occasions might require,
To forward reason's else too scrupulous march.
The effect was, still more elevated views
Of human nature. Neither vice nor guilt,
Debasement undergone by body or mind,

Nor all the misery forced upon my sight,
Misery not lightly passed, but sometimes scanned
Most feelingly, could overthrow my trust
In what we *may* become; induce belief   650
That I was ignorant, had been falsely taught,
A solitary, who with vain conceits
Had been inspired, and walked about in dreams.
From those sad scenes when meditation turned,
Lo! every thing that was indeed divine
Retained its purity inviolate,
Nay brighter shone, by this portentous gloom
Set off; such opposition as aroused
The mind of Adam, yet in Paradise   659
Though fallen from bliss, when in the East he saw
Darkness ere day's mid course, and morning light
More orient in the western cloud, that drew
O'er the blue firmament a radiant white,
Descending slow with something heavenly fraught.

Add also, that among the multitudes
Of that huge city, oftentimes was seen
Affectingly set forth, more than elsewhere
Is possible, the unity of man,
One spirit over ignorance and vice
Predominant, in good and evil hearts   670
One sense for moral judgments, as one eye
For the sun's light. The soul when smitten thus
By a sublime *idea*, whencesoe'er
Vouchsafed for union or communion, feeds
On the pure bliss, and takes her rest with God.

.Thus from a very early age, O Friend!
My thoughts by slow gradations had been drawn
To human-kind, and to the good and ill
Of human life: Nature had led me on;
And oft amid the 'busy hum' [12] I seemed   680
To travel independent of her help,
As if I had forgotten her; but no,
The world of human-kind outweighed not hers
In my habitual thoughts; the scale of love,
Though filling daily, still was light, compared
With that in which *her* mighty objects lay.

BOOK NINTH

RESIDENCE IN FRANCE

EVEN as a river,—partly (it might seem)
Yielding to old remembrances, and swayed
In part by fear to shape a way direct,
That would engulph him soon in the ravenous sea—

Turns, and will measure back his course, far back,
Seeking the very regions which he crossed
In his first outset; so have we, my Friend!
Turned and returned with intricate delay.
Or as a traveller, who has gained the brow
Of some aerial Down, while there he halts   10
For breathing-time, is tempted to review
The region left behind him; and, if aught
Deserving notice have escaped regard,
Or been regarded with too careless eye,
Strives, from that height, with one and yet one more
Last look, to make the best amends he may:
So have we lingered. Now we start afresh
With courage, and new hope risen on our toil.
Fair greetings to this shapeless eagerness,
Whene'er it comes! needful in work so long,   20
Thrice needful to the argument which now
Awaits us! Oh, how much unlike the past!

Free as a colt at pasture on the hill,
I ranged at large, through London's wide domain,
Month after month. Obscurely did I live,
Not seeking frequent intercourse with men,
By literature, or elegance, or rank,
Distinguished. Scarcely was a year thus spent
Ere I forsook the crowded solitude,
With less regret for its luxurious pomp,   30
And all the nicely-guarded shows of art,
Than for the humble book-stalls in the streets,
Exposed to eye and hand where'er I turned.

France lured me forth; the realm that I had crossed
So lately, journeying toward the snow-clad Alps.
But now, relinquishing the scrip and staff,
And all enjoyment which the summer sun
Sheds round the steps of those who meet the day
With motion constant as his own, I went
Prepared to sojourn in a pleasant town,   40
Washed by the current of the stately Loire. [1]

Through Paris lay my readiest course, and there
Sojourning a few days, I visited,
In haste, each spot of old or recent fame,
The latter chiefly; from the field of Mars
Down to the suburbs of St. Antony,
And from Mont Martyr southward to the Dome
of Geneviève. In both her clamorous Halls,
The National Synod and the Jacobins,
I saw the Revolutionary Power   50
Toss like a ship at anchor, rocked by storms;
The Arcades I traversed, in the Palace huge

---

[12] From Milton's *L'Allegro*.

[1] Orléans.

Of Orleans;[2] coasted round and round the line
Of Tavern, Brothel, Gaming-house, and Shop,
Great rendezvous of worst and best, the walk
Of all who had a purpose, or had not;
I stared and listened, with a stranger's ears,
To Hawkers and Haranguers, hubbub wild!
And hissing Factionists with ardent eyes,
In knots, or pairs, or single. Not a look   60
Hope takes, or Doubt or Fear are forced to wear,
But seemed there present; and I scanned them all,
Watched every gesture uncontrollable,
Of anger, and vexation, and despite,
All side by side, and struggling face to face,
With gaiety and dissolute idleness.

    Where silent zephyrs sported with the dust
Of the Bastille, I sate in the open sun,
And from the rubbish gathered up a stone,
And pocketed the relic, in the guise   70
Of an enthusiast; yet, in honest truth,
I looked for something that I could not find,
Affecting more emotion than I felt;
For 'tis most certain, that these various sights,
However potent their first shock, with me
Appeared to recompense the traveller's pains
Less than the painted Magdalene of Le Brun,[3]
A beauty exquisitely wrought, with hair
Dishevelled, gleaming eyes, and rueful cheek
Pale and bedropped with everflowing tears.   80

    But hence to my more permanent abode
I hasten; there, by novelties in speech,
Domestic manners, customs, gestures, looks,
And all the attire of ordinary life,
Attention was engrossed; and, thus amused,
I stood, 'mid those concussions, unconcerned,
Tranquil almost, and careless as a flower
Glassed in a green-house, or a parlour shrub
That spreads its leaves in unmolested peace,
While every bush and tree, the country through,   90
Is shaking to the roots: indifference this
Which may seem strange: but I was unprepared
With needful knowledge, had abruptly passed
Into a theatre, whose stage was filled
And busy with an action far advanced.
Like others, I had skimmed, and sometimes read
With care, the master pamphlets of the day;
Nor wanted such half-insight as grew wild
Upon that meagre soil, helped out by talk
And public news; but having never seen   100

A chronicle that might suffice to show
Whence the main organs of the public power
Had sprung, their transmigrations, when and how
Accomplished, giving thus unto events
A form and body; all things were to me
Loose and disjointed, and the affections left
Without a vital interest. At that time,
Moreover, the first storm was overblown,
And the strong hand of outward violence
Locked up in quiet. For myself, I fear   110
Now in connection with so great a theme
To speak (as I must be compelled to do)
Of one so unimportant; night by night
Did I frequent the formal haunts of men,
Whom, in the city, privilege of birth
Sequestered from the rest, societies
Polished in arts, and in punctilio versed;
Whence, and from deeper causes, all discourse
Of good and evil of the time was shunned
With scrupulous care; but these restrictions soon 120
Proved tedious, and I gradually withdrew
Into a noisier world, and thus ere long
Became a patriot;[4] and my heart was all
Given to the people, and my love was theirs.

    A band of military Officers,
Then stationed in the city,[5] were the chief
Of my associates: some of these wore swords
That had been seasoned in the wars, and all
Were men well-born; the chivalry of France.
In age and temper differing, they had yet   130
One spirit ruling in each heart; alike
(Save only one, hereafter to be named)[6]
Were bent upon undoing what was done:
This was their rest and only hope; therewith
No fear had they of bad becoming worse,
For worst to them was come; nor would have stirred,
Or deemed it worth a moment's thought to stir,
In any thing, save only as the act
Looked thitherward. One, reckoning by years,
Was in the prime of manhood, and erewhile   140
He had sate lord in many tender hearts;
Though heedless of such honours now, and changed:
His temper was quite mastered by the times,
And they had blighted him, had eaten away
The beauty of his person, doing wrong
Alike to body and to mind: his port,
Which once had been erect and open, now
Was stooping and contracted, and a face,
Endowed by Nature with her fairest gifts

---

[2] All of these areas and buildings of Paris had been directly involved in violent uprisings during recent months.

[3] Charles le Brun (1616–1690), court painter and general art director to Louis XIV.

[4] Used here in the sense of "republican."

[5] Blois, where Wordsworth went from Orléans.

[6] Michel Armand Beaupuy (1755–1796), noble sympathizer with the Revolution, soldier and philosopher.

Of symmetry and light and bloom, expressed,   150
As much as any that was ever seen,
A ravage out of season, made by thoughts
Unhealthy and vexatious. With the hour,
That from the press of Paris duly brought
Its freight of public news, the fever came,
A punctual visitant, to shake this man,
Disarmed his voice and fanned his yellow cheek
Into a thousand colours; while he read,
Or mused, his sword was haunted by his touch
Continually, like an uneasy place   160
In his own body. 'Twas in truth an hour
Of universal ferment; mildest men
Were agitated; and commotions, strife
Of passion and opinion, filled the walls
Of peaceful houses with unquiet sounds.
The soil of common life, was, at that time,
Too hot to tread upon. Oft said I then,
And not then only, 'What a mockery this
Of history, the past and that to come!
Now do I feel how all men are deceived,   170
Reading of nations and their works, in faith,
Faith given to vanity and emptiness;
Oh! laughter for the page that would reflect
To future times the face of what now is!'
The land all swarmed with passion, like a plain
Devoured by locusts,—Carra, Gorsas,[7]—add
A hundred other names, forgotten now,
Nor to be heard of more; yet, they were powers,
Like earthquakes, shocks repeated day by day,
And felt through every nook of town and field.   180

Such was the state of things. Meanwhile the chief
Of my associates stood prepared for flight
To augment the band of emigrants in arms
Upon the borders of the Rhine, and leagued
With foreign foes mustered for instant war.[8]
This was their undisguised intent, and they
Were waiting with the whole of their desires
The moment to depart.
                    An Englishman,
Born in a land whose very name appeared
To license some unruliness of mind;   190
A stranger, with youth's further privilege,
And the indulgence that a half-learnt speech
Wins from the courteous; I, who had been else
Shunned and not tolerated, freely lived
With these defenders of the Crown, and talked,

And heard their notions; nor did they disdain
The wish to bring me over to their cause.

But though untaught by thinking or by books
To reason well of polity or law,
And nice distinctions, then on every tongue,   200
Of natural rights and civil; and to acts
Of nations and their passing interests,
(If with unworldly ends and aims compared)
Almost indifferent, even the historian's tale
Prizing but little otherwise than I prized
Tales of the poets, as it made the heart
Beat high, and filled the fancy with fair forms,
Old heroes and their sufferings and their deeds;
Yet in the regal sceptre, and the pomp
Of orders and degrees, I nothing found   210
Then, or had ever, even in crudest youth,
That dazzled me, but rather what I mourned
And ill could brook, beholding that the best
Ruled not, and feeling that they ought to rule.

For, born in a poor district, and which yet
Retaineth more of ancient homeliness,
Than any other nook of English ground,
It was my fortune scarcely to have seen,
Through the whole tenor of my school-day time,
The face of one, who, whether boy or man,   220
Was vested with attention or respect
Through claims of wealth or blood; nor was it least
Of many benefits, in later years
Derived from academic institutes
And rules, that they held something up to view
Of a Republic, where all stood thus far
Upon equal ground; that we were brothers all
In honour, as in one community,
Scholars and gentlemen; where, furthermore,
Distinction lay open to all that came,   230
And wealth and titles were in less esteem
Than talents, worth, and prosperous industry.
Add unto this, subservience from the first
To presences of God's mysterious power
Made manifest in Nature's sovereignty,
And fellowship with venerable books,
To sanction the proud workings of the soul,
And mountain liberty. It could not be
But that one tutored thus should look with awe
Upon the faculties of man, receive   240
Gladly the highest promises, and hail,
As best, the government of equal rights
And individual worth. And hence, O Friend!
If at the first great outbreak I rejoiced
Less than might well befit my youth, the cause
In part lay here, that unto me the events
Seemed nothing out of nature's certain course,

---

[7] Jean Louis Carra and Antoine Joseph Gorsas, journalists, later guillotined.
[8] After the flight of Louis in June 1791, most of the army officers, even those earlier sympathetic to the Revolution, joined the Royalist army on the Rhine.

A gift that was rather come late than soon.
No wonder, then, if advocates like these,
Inflamed by passion, blind with prejudice,   250
And stung with injury, at this riper day,
Were impotent to make my hopes put on
The shape of theirs, my understanding bend
In honour to their honour: zeal, which yet
Had slumbered, now in opposition burst
Forth like a Polar summer: every word
They uttered was a dart, by counter-winds
Blown back upon themselves; their reason seemed
Confusion-stricken by a higher power
Than human understanding, their discourse   260
Maimed, spiritless; and, in their weakness strong,
I triumphed.
                    Meantime, day by day, the roads
Were crowded with the bravest youth of France,
And all the promptest of her spirits, linked
In gallant soldiership, and posting on
To meet the war upon her frontier bounds.
Yet at this very moment do tears start
Into mine eyes: I do not say I weep—
I wept not then,—but tears have dimmed my sight,
In memory of the farewells of that time,   270
Domestic severings, female fortitude
At dearest separation, patriot love
And self-devotion, and terrestrial hope,
Encouraged with a martyr's confidence;
Even files of strangers, merely seen but once,
And for a moment, men from far with sound
Of music, martial tunes, and banners spread,
Entering the city, here and there a face,
Or person singled out among the rest,
Yet still a stranger and beloved as such;   280
Even by these passing spectacles my heart
Was oftentimes uplifted, and they seemed
Arguments sent from Heaven to prove the cause
Good, pure, which no one could stand up against,
Who was not lost, abandoned, selfish, proud,
Mean, miserable, wilfully depraved,
Hater perverse of equity and truth.

   Among that band of Officers was one,[9]
Already hinted at, of other mould—
A patriot, thence rejected by the rest,   290
And with an oriental loathing spurned,
As of a different caste. A meeker man
Than this lived never, nor a more benign,
Meek though enthusiastic. Injuries
Made *him* more gracious, and his nature then
Did breathe its sweetness out most sensibly,
As aromatic flowers on Alpine turf,

   [9] Michel Beaupuy. See note to line 132, above.

When foot hath crushed them. He through the events
Of that great change wandered in perfect faith,
As through a book, an old romance, or tale   300
Of Fairy, or some dream of actions wrought
Behind the summer clouds. By birth he ranked
With the most noble, but unto the poor
Among mankind he was in service bound,
As by some tie invisible, oaths professed
To a religious order. Man he loved
As man; and, to the mean and the obscure,
And all the homely in their homely works,
Transferred a courtesy which had no air
Of condescension; but did rather seem   310
A passion and a gallantry, like that
Which he, a soldier, in his idler day
Had paid to woman: somewhat vain he was,
Or seemed so, yet it was not vanity,
But fondness, and a kind of radiant joy
Diffused around him, while he was intent
On works of love or freedom, or revolved
Complacently the progress of a cause,
Whereof he was a part: yet this was meek
And placid, and took nothing from the man   320
That was delightful. Oft in solitude
With him did I discourse about the end
Of civil government, and its wisest forms;
Of ancient loyalty, and chartered rights,
Custom and habit, novelty and change;
Of self-respect, and virtue in the few
For patrimonial honour set apart,
And ignorance in the labouring multitude.
For he, to all intolerance indisposed,
Balanced these contemplations in his mind;   330
And I, who at that time was scarcely dipped
Into the turmoil, bore a sounder judgment
Than later days allowed; carried about me,
With less alloy to its integrity,
The experience of past ages, as, through help
Of books and common life, it makes sure way
To youthful minds, by objects over near
Not pressed upon, nor dazzled or misled
By struggling with the crowd for present ends.

   But though not deaf, nor obstinate to find   340
Error without excuse upon the side
Of them who strove against us, more delight
We took, and let this freely be confessed,
In painting to ourselves the miseries
Of royal courts, and that voluptuous life
Unfeeling, where the man who is of soul
The meanest thrives the most; where dignity,
True personal dignity, abideth not;
A light, a cruel, and vain world cut off
From the natural inlets of just sentiment,   350

From lowly sympathy and chastening truth;
Where good and evil interchange their names,
And thirst for bloody spoils abroad is paired
With vice at home. We added dearest themes—
Man and his noble nature, as it is
The gift which God has placed within his power,
His blind desires and steady faculties
Capable of clear truth, the one to break
Bondage, the other to build liberty
On firm foundations, making social life,   360
Through knowledge spreading and imperishable,
As just in regulation, and as pure
As individual in the wise and good.

We summoned up the honourable deeds
Of ancient Story, thought of each bright spot,
That could be found in all recorded time,
Of truth preserved and error passed away;
Of single spirits that catch the flame from Heaven,
And how the multitudes of men will feed
And fan each other; thought of sects, how keen   370
They are to put the appropriate nature on,
Triumphant over every obstacle
Of custom, language, country, love, or hate,
And what they do and suffer for their creed;
How far they travel, and how long endure;
How quickly mighty Nations have been formed,
From least beginnings; how, together locked
By new opinions, scattered tribes have made
One body, spreading wide as clouds in heaven.
To aspirations then of our own minds   380
Did we appeal; and, finally, beheld
A living confirmation of the whole
Before us, in a people from the depth
Of shameful imbecility uprisen,
Fresh as the morning star. Elate we looked
Upon their virtues; saw, in rudest men,
Self-sacrifice the firmest; generous love,
And continence of mind, and sense of right,
Uppermost in the midst of fiercest strife.

Oh, sweet it is, in academic groves,   390
Or such retirement, Friend! as we have known
In the green dales beside our Rotha's stream,
Greta, or Derwent,[10] or some nameless rill,
To ruminate, with interchange of talk,
On rational liberty, and hope in man,
Justice and peace. But far more sweet such toil—
Toil, say I, for it leads to thoughts abstruse—
If nature then be standing on the brink
Of some great trial, and we hear the voice
Of one devoted,—one whom circumstance   400

Hath called upon to embody his deep sense
In action, give it outwardly a shape,
And that of benediction to the world.
Then doubt is not, and truth is more than truth,—
A hope it is, and a desire; a creed
Of zeal, by an authority Divine
Sanctioned, of danger, difficulty, or death.
Such conversation, under Attic shades,
Did Dion hold with Plato; ripened thus
For a Deliverer's glorious task,—and such   410
He, on that ministry already bound,
Held with Eudemus and Timonides,
Surrounded by adventurers in arms,
When these two vessels with their daring freight,
For the Sicilian Tyrant's overthrow,
Sailed from Zacynthus,—philosophic war,
Led by Philosophers.[11] With harder fate,
Though like ambition, such was he, O Friend!
Of whom I speak. So Beaupuis (let the name
Stand near the worthiest of Antiquity)   420
Fashioned his life; and many a long discourse,
With like persuasion honoured, we maintained:
He on his part, accoutred for the worst.
He perished fighting, in supreme command,
Upon the borders of the unhappy Loire,[12]
For liberty, against deluded men,
His fellow country-men; and yet most blessed
In this, that he the fate of later times
Lived not to see, nor what we now behold,
Who have as ardent hearts as he had then.   430

Along that very Loire, with festal mirth
Resounding at all hours, and innocent yet
Of civil slaughter, was our frequent walk;
Or in wide forests of continuous shade,
Lofty and over-arched, with open space
Beneath the trees, clear footing many a mile—
A solemn region. Oft amid those haunts,
From earnest dialogues I slipped in thought,
And let remembrance steal to other times,
When, o'er those interwoven roots, moss-clad,   440
And smooth as marble or a waveless sea,
Some Hermit, from his cell forth-strayed, might pace
In sylvan meditation undisturbed;
As on the pavement of a Gothic church
Walks a lone Monk, when service hath expired,
In peace and silence. But if e'er was heard,—
Heard, though unseen,—a devious traveller,
Retiring or approaching from afar

---

[10] The rivers of Grasmere, Keswick, and Cockermouth.

[11] Wordsworth alludes to Plutarch's account of the philosophers Dion, Eudemus, and Timonides who defeated Dionysius II of Syracuse in 357 B.C.
[12] Actually Beaupuy survived to fulfill a distinguished career as republican soldier until he was killed at Elz in 1796.

With speed and echoes loud of trampling hoofs
From the hard floor reverberated, then   450
It was Angelica [13] thundering through the woods
Upon her palfrey, or that gentle maid
Erminia, fugitive as fair as she.
Sometimes methought I saw a pair of knights
Joust underneath the trees, that as in storm
Rocked high above their heads; anon, the din
Of boisterous merriment, and music's roar,
In sudden proclamation, burst from haunt
Of Satyrs in some viewless glade, with dance
Rejoicing o'er a female in the midst,   460
A mortal beauty, their unhappy thrall.
The width of those huge forests, unto me
A novel scene, did often in this way
Master my fancy while I wandered on
With that revered companion. And sometimes—
When to a convent in a meadow green,
By a brook-side, we came, a roofless pile,
And not by reverential touch of Time
Dismantled, but by violence abrupt—
In spite of those heart-bracing colloquies,   470
In spite of real fervour, and of that
Less genuine and wrought up within myself—
I could not but bewail a wrong so harsh,
And for the Matin-bell to sound no more
Grieved, and the twilight taper, and the cross
High on the topmost pinnacle, a sign
(How welcome to the weary traveller's eyes!)
Of hospitality and peaceful rest.
And when the partner of those varied walks
Pointed upon occasion to the site   480
Of Romorentin, home of ancient kings,
To the imperial edifice of Blois,
Or to that rural castle, name now slipped
From my remembrance, where a lady lodged,
By the first Francis wooed, and bound to him
In chains of mutual passion, from the tower,
As a tradition of the country tells,
Practised to commune with her royal knight
By cressets and love-beacons, intercourse
'Twixt her high-seated residence and his   490
Far off at Chambord on the plain beneath; [14]
Even here, though less than with the peaceful house
Religious, 'mid those frequent monuments
Of Kings, their vices and their better deeds,
Imagination, potent to inflame
At times with virtuous wrath and noble scorn,
Did also often mitigate the force
Of civic prejudice, the bigotry,

◇◇◇◇◇◇◇◇◇◇◇◇◇◇◇◇◇◇◇◇◇◇◇◇◇◇◇◇

[13] The heroine of Ariosto's epic *Orlando Furioso*; Erminia (line 453) is the heroine of Tasso's *Gerusalemme Liberata*.
[14] All of these chateaux are associated with Francis I (1494–1547).

So call it, of a youthful patriot's mind;
And on these spots with many gleams I looked   500
Of chivalrous delight. Yet not the less,
Hatred of absolute rule, where will of one
Is law for all, and of that barren pride
In them who, by immunities unjust,
Between the sovereign and the people stand,
His helper and not theirs, laid stronger hold
Daily upon me, mixed with pity too
And love; for where hope is, there love will be
For the abject multitude. And when we chanced
One day to meet a hunger-bitten girl,   510
Who crept along fitting her languid gait
Unto a heifer's motion, by a cord
Tied to her arm, and picking thus from the lane
Its sustenance, while the girl with pallid hands
Was busy knitting in a heartless mood
Of solitude, and at the sight my friend
In agitation said, "'Tis against *that*
That we are fighting,' I with him believed
That a benignant spirit was abroad
Which might not be withstood, that poverty   520
Abject as this would in a little time
Be found no more, that we should see the earth
Unthwarted in her wish to recompense
The meek, the lowly, patient child of toil.
All institutes for ever blotted out
That legalised exclusion, empty pomp
Abolished, sensual state and cruel power,
Whether by edict of the one or few;
And finally, as sum and crown of all,
Should see the people having a strong hand   530
In framing their own laws; whence better days
To all mankind. But, these things set apart,
Was not this single confidence enough
To animate the mind that ever turned
A thought to human welfare? That henceforth
Captivity by mandate without law
Should cease; and open accusation lead
To sentence in the hearing of the world,
And open punishment, if not the air
Be free to breathe in, and the heart of man   540
Dread nothing. From this height I shall not stoop
To humbler matter that detained us oft
In thought or conversation, public acts,
And public persons, and emotions wrought
Within the breast, as ever-varying winds
Of record or report swept over us;
But I might here, instead, repeat a tale,
Told by my Patriot friend, of sad events,
That prove to what low depth had struck the roots,
How widely spread the boughs, of that old tree   550

Which, as a deadly mischief, and a foul
And black dishonour, France was weary of.[15]

Oh, happy time of youthful lovers, (thus
My story may begin). Oh, balmy time,
In which a love-knot, on a lady's brow,
Is fairer than the fairest star in Heaven!
So might—and with that prelude *did* begin
The record; and, in faithful verse, was given
The doleful sequel.
               But our little bark
On a strong river boldly hath been launched;   560
And from the driving current should we turn
To loiter wilfully within a creek,
Howe'er attractive, Fellow voyager!
Would'st thou not chide? Yet deem not my pains lost:
For Vaudracour and Julia (so were named
The ill-fated pair) in that plain tale will draw
Tears from the hearts of others, when their own
Shall beat no more. Thou, also, there mayst read,
At leisure, how the enamoured youth was driven,
By public power abased, to fatal crime,[16]   570
Nature's rebellion against monstrous law;
How, between heart and heart, oppression thrust
Her mandates, severing whom true love had joined,
Harassing both; until he sank and pressed
The couch his fate had made for him; supine,
Save when the stings of viperous remorse,
Trying their strength, enforced him to start up,
Aghast and prayerless. Into a deep wood
He fled, to shun the haunts of human kind;
There dwelt, weakened in spirit more and more;   580
Nor could the voice of Freedom, which through
    France
Full speedily resounded, public hope,
Or personal memory of his own worst wrongs,
Rouse him; but, hidden in those gloomy shades,
His days he wasted,—an imbecile mind.

BOOK TENTH

RESIDENCE IN FRANCE—CONTINUED

IT WAS a beautiful and silent day
That overspread the countenance of earth,
Then fading with unusual quietness,—

A day as beautiful as e'er was given
To soothe regret, though deepening what it soothed,
When by the gliding Loire I paused, and cast
Upon his rich domains, vineyard and tilth,
Green meadow-ground, and many-coloured woods,
Again, and yet again, a farewell look;
Then from the quiet of that scene passed on,   10
Bound to the fierce Metropolis.[1] From his throne
The King had fallen, and that invading host—
Presumptuous cloud, on whose black front was written
The tender mercies of the dismal wind
That bore it—on the plains of Liberty
Had burst innocuous. Say in bolder words,
They—who had come elate as eastern hunters
Banded beneath the Great Mogul, when he
Erewhile went forth from Agra or Lahore,
Rajahs and Omrahs in his train, intent   20
To drive their prey enclosed within a ring
Wide as a province, but, the signal given,
Before the point of the life-threatening spear
Narrowing itself by moments—they, rash men,
Had seen the anticipated quarry turned
Into avengers, from whose wrath they fled
In terror. Disappointment and dismay
Remained for all whose fancies had run wild
With evil expectations; confidence
And perfect triumph for the better cause.   30

The State, as if to stamp the final seal
On her security, and to the world
Show what she was, a high and fearless soul,
Exulting in defiance, or heart-stung
By sharp resentment, or belike to taunt
With spiteful gratitude the baffled League,
That had stirred up her slackening faculties
To a new transition, when the King was crushed,
Spared not the empty throne, and in proud haste
Assumed the body and venerable name   40
Of a Republic. Lamentable crimes,
'Tis true, had gone before this hour, dire work
Of massacre, in which the senseless sword
Was prayed to as a judge; but these were past,
Earth free from them for ever, as was thought,—
Ephemeral monsters, to be seen but once!
Things that could only show themselves and die.

Cheered with this hope, to Paris I returned,
And ranged, with ardour heretofore unfelt,

---

[15] The tale of Vaudracour and Julia was omitted from drafts of *The Prelude* after it had been published separately in 1820. Although far more dramatic and tragic than the events of his own affair with Annette Vallon, the story appears to have been included as a substitute for the story about himself Wordsworth could not tell.

[16] Vaudracour kills the man his father has sent to prevent his marrying Julia, who is pregnant with his child. The child dies, Julia enters a convent, Vaudracour becomes a recluse.

[1] Wordsworth returned to Paris in October 1792, on his way to England. The king had been desposed and imprisoned in August. The Royalists invaded on August 19, and during early September Marat, Danton, and Robespierre organized a retaliation in which 3,000 Royalist suspects were executed. The Republic was proclaimed September 22.

The spacious city, and in progress passed   50
The prison where the unhappy Monarch lay,
Associate with his children and his wife
In bondage; and the palace, lately stormed
With roar of cannon by a furious host.
I crossed the square (an empty area then!)
Of the Carrousel, where so late had lain
The dead, upon the dying heaped, and gazed
On this and other spots, as doth a man
Upon a volume whose contents he knows
Are memorable, but from him locked up,   60
Being written in a tongue he cannot read,
So that he questions the mute leaves with pain,
And half upbraids their silence. But that night
I felt most deeply in what world I was,
What ground I trod on, and what air I breathed.
High was my room and lonely, near the roof
Of a large mansion or hotel, a lodge
That would have pleased me in more quiet times;
Nor was it wholly without pleasure then.
With unextinguished taper I kept watch,   70
Reading at intervals; the fear gone by
Pressed on me almost like a fear to come.
I thought of those September massacres,
Divided from me by one little month,
Saw them and touched: the rest was conjured up
From tragic fictions or true history,
Remembrances and dim admonishments.
The horse is taught his manage, and no star
Of wildest course but treads back his own steps;
For the spent hurricane the air provides   80
As fierce a successor; the tide retreats
But to return out of its hiding-place
In the great deep; all things have second birth;
The earthquake is not satisfied at once;
And in this way I wrought upon myself,
Until I seemed to hear a voice that cried,
To the whole city, 'Sleep no more.'[2] The trance
Fled with the voice to which it had given birth;
But vainly comments of a calmer mind
Promised soft peace and sweet forgetfulness.   90
The place, all hushed and silent as it was,
Appeared unfit for the repose of night,
Defenceless as a wood where tigers roam.

With early morning towards the Palace-walk
Of Orleans eagerly I turned; as yet
The streets were still; not so those long Arcades;
There, 'mid a peal of ill-matched sounds and cries,
That greeted me on entering, I could hear
Shrill voices from the hawkers in the throng,
Bawling, 'Denunciation of the Crimes   100

[2] As Macbeth hears just after he has killed Duncan.

Of Maximilian Robespierre;' the hand,
Prompt as the voice, held forth a printed speech,
The same that had been recently pronounced,
When Robespierre, not ignorant for what mark
Some words of indirect reproof had been
Intended, rose in hardihood, and dared
The man who had an ill surmise of him
To bring his charge in openness; whereat,
When a dead pause ensued, and no one stirred,
In silence of all present, from his seat   110
Louvet walked single through the avenue,
And took his station in the Tribune, saying,
'I, Robespierre, accuse thee!' Well is known
The inglorious issue of that charge, and how
He, who had launched the startling thunderbolt,
The one bold man, whose voice the attack had
          sounded,
Was left without a follower to discharge
His perilous duty, and retire lamenting
That Heaven's best aid is wasted upon men
Who to themselves are false.[3]

                    But these are things   120
Of which I speak, only as they were storm
Or sunshine to my individual mind,
No further. Let me then relate that now—
In some sort seeing with my proper eyes
That Liberty, and Life, and Death would soon
To the remotest corners of the land
Lie in the arbitrement of those who ruled
The capital City; what was struggled for,
And by what combatants victory must be won;
The indecision on their part whose aim   130
Seemed best, and the straightforward path of those
Who in attack or in defence were strong
Through their impiety—my inmost soul
Was agitated; yea, I could almost
Have prayed that throughout earth upon all men,
By patient exercise of reason made
Worthy of liberty, all spirits filled
With zeal expanding in Truth's holy light,
The gift of tongues might fall, and power arrive
From the four quarters of the winds to do   140
For France, what without help she could not do,
A work of honour; think not that to this
I added, work of safety: from all doubt
Or trepidation for the end of things
Far was I, far as angels are from guilt.

Yet did I grieve, nor only grieved, but thought
Of opposition and of remedies:

[3] Robespierre answered the charges of the Girondist Louvet
by claiming innocence in the September massacres, and easily
regained his popularity. In Wordsworth's view, the Girondist
majority was idealistic but impotent.

An insignificant stranger and obscure,
And one, moreover, little graced with power
Of eloquence even in my native speech,   150
And all unfit for tumult or intrigue,
Yet would I at this time with willing heart
Have undertaken for a cause so great
Service however dangerous. I revolved,
How much the destiny of Man had still
Hung upon single persons; that there was,
Transcendent to all local patrimony,
One nature, as there is one sun in heaven;
That objects, even as they are great, thereby
Do come within the reach of humblest eyes;   160
That man is only weak through his mistrust
And want of hope where evidence divine
Proclaims to him that hope should be most
      sure;
Nor did the inexperience of my youth
Preclude conviction, that a spirit strong
In hope, and trained to noble aspirations,
A spirit thoroughly faithful to itself,
Is for Society's unreasoning herd
A domineering instinct, serves at once
For way and guide, a fluent receptacle   170
That gathers up each petty straggling rill
And vein of water, glad to be rolled on
In safe obedience; that a mind, whose rest
Is where it ought to be, in self-restraint,
In circumspection and simplicity,
Falls rarely in entire discomfiture
Below its aim, or meets with, from without,
A treachery that foils it or defeats;
And, lastly, if the means on human will,
Frail human will, dependent should betray   180
Him who too boldly trusted them, I felt
That 'mid the loud distractions of the world
A sovereign voice subsists within the soul,
Arbiter undisturbed of right and wrong,
Of life and death, in majesty severe
Enjoining, as may best promote the aims
Of truth and justice, either sacrifice,
From whatsoever region of our cares
Or our infirm affections Nature pleads,
Earnest and blind, against the stern decree.   190

     On the other side, I called to mind those truths
That are the common-places of the schools—
(A theme for boys, too hackneyed for their
      sires,)
Yet, with a revelation's liveliness,
In all their comprehensive bearings known
And visible to philosophers of old,
Men who, to business of the world untrained,
Lived in the shade; and to Harmodius known

And his compeer Aristogiton,[4] known
To Brutus—that tyrannic power is weak,   200
Hath neither gratitude, nor faith, nor love,
Nor the support of good or evil men
To trust in; that the godhead which is ours
Can never utterly be charmed or stilled;
That nothing hath a natural right to last
But equity and reason; that all else
Meets foes irreconcilable, and at best
Lives only by variety of disease.

     Well might my wishes be intense, my thoughts
Strong and perturbed, not doubting at that time   210
But that the virtue of one paramount mind
Would have abashed those impious crests—have
      quelled
Outrage and bloody power, and, in despite
Of what the People long had been and were
Through ignorance and false teaching, sadder proof
Of immaturity, and in the teeth
Of desperate opposition from without—
Have cleared a passage for just government,
And left a solid birthright to the State,
Redeemed, according to example given   220
By ancient lawgivers.
                      In this frame of mind,
Dragged by a chain of harsh necessity,
So seemed it,—now I thankfully acknowledge,
Forced by the gracious providence of Heaven,—
To England I returned, else (though assured
That I both was and must be of small weight,
No better than a landsman on the deck
Of a ship struggling with a hideous storm)
Doubtless, I should have then made common cause
With some who perished;[5] haply perished too,   230
A poor mistaken and bewildered offering,—
Should to the breast of Nature have gone back,
With all my resolutions, all my hopes,
A Poet only to myself, to men
Useless, and even, beloved Friend! a soul
To thee unknown!
                Twice had the trees let fall
Their leaves, as often Winter had put on
His hoary crown, since I had seen the surge
Beat against Albion's shore, since ear of mine
Had caught the accents of my native speech   240
Upon our native country's sacred ground.
A patriot of the world, how could I glide
Into communion with her sylvan shades,
Erewhile my tuneful haunt? It pleased me more

---

4 Harmodius and Aristogiton conspired against the king in the
Athens of the sixth century B.C. Both were executed, but remem-
bered as heroes.
5 Girondists like Brissot, who was guillotined in 1793.

To abide in the great City,[6] where I found
The general air still busy with the stir
Of that first memorable onset made
By a strong levy of humanity
Upon the traffickers in Negro blood;[7]
Effort which, though defeated, had recalled   250
To notice old forgotten principles,
And through the nation spread a novel heat
Of virtuous feeling. For myself, I own
That this particular strife had wanted power
To rivet my affections; nor did now
Its unsuccessful issue much excite
My sorrow; for I brought with me the faith
That, if France prospered, good men would not long
Pay fruitless worship to humanity,
And this most rotten branch of human shame,   260
Object, so seemed it, of superfluous pains,
Would fall together with its parent tree.
What, then, were my emotions, when in arms
Britain put forth her free-born strength in league,
Oh, pity and shame! with those confederate Powers![8]
Not in my single self alone I found,
But in the minds of all ingenuous youth,
Change and subversion from that hour. No shock
Given to my moral nature had I known
Down to that very moment; neither lapse   270
Nor turn of sentiment that might be named
A revolution, save at this one time;
All else was progress on the self-same path
On which, with a diversity of pace,
I had been travelling: this a stride at once
Into another region. As a light
And pliant harebell, swinging in the breeze
On some grey rock—its birth-place—so had I
Wantoned, fast rooted on the ancient tower
Of my beloved country, wishing not   280
A happier fortune than to wither there:
Now was I from that pleasant station torn
And tossed about in whirlwind. I rejoiced,
Yea, afterwards—truth most painful to record!—
Exulted, in the triumph of my soul,
When Englishmen by thousands were o'erthrown,[9]
Left without glory on the field, or driven,
Brave hearts! to shameful flight. It was a grief,—
Grief call it not, 'twas anything but that,—
A conflict of sensations without name,   290
Of which *he* only, who may love the sight
Of a village steeple, as I do, can judge,
When, in the congregation bending all

---

[6] London.
[7] Attempts to abolish the slave trade failed in 1788 and 1792.
The law passed in 1807.
[8] France and England went to war in February 1793.
[9] The Duke of York was defeated in September 1793.

To their great Father, prayers were offered up,
Or praises for our country's victories;
And, 'mid the simple worshippers, perchance
I only, like an uninvited guest
Whom no one owned, sate silent, shall I add,
Fed on the day of vengeance yet to come.

Oh! much have they to account for, who could tear,
By violence, at one decisive rent,   301
From the best youth in England their dear pride,
Their joy, in England; this, too, at a time
In which worst losses easily might wear
The best of names, when patriotic love
Did of itself in modesty give way,
Like the Precursor when the Deity
Is come Whose harbinger he was; a time
In which apostasy from ancient faith
Seemed but conversion to a higher creed;   310
Withal a season dangerous and wild,
A time when sage Experience would have snatched
Flowers out of any hedge-row to compose
A chaplet in contempt of his grey locks.

When the proud fleet that bears the red-cross flag
In that unworthy service was prepared
To mingle, I beheld the vessels lie,
A brood of gallant creatures, on the deep
I saw them in their rest, a sojourner
Through a whole month of calm and glassy days   320
In that delightful island which protects
Their place of convocation [10]—there I heard,
Each evening, pacing by the still sea-shore,
A monitory sound that never failed,—
The sunset cannon. While the orb went down
In the tranquillity of nature, came
That voice, ill requiem! seldom heard by me
Without a spirit overcast by dark
Imaginations, sense of woes to come,
Sorrow for human kind, and pain of heart.   330

In France, the men, who, for their desperate ends,
Had plucked up mercy by the roots, were glad
Of this new enemy. Tyrants, strong before
In wicked pleas, were strong as demons now;
And thus, on every side beset with foes,
The goaded land waxed mad; the crimes of few
Spread into madness of the many; blasts
From hell came sanctified like airs from heaven.
The sternness of the just, the faith of those
Who doubted not that Providence had times   340
Of vengeful retribution, theirs who throned
The human Understanding paramount

---

[10] The Isle of Wight, in July 1793.

And made of that their God, the hopes of men
Who were content to barter short-lived pangs
For a paradise of ages, the blind rage
Of insolent tempers, the light vanity
Of intermeddlers, steady purposes
Of the suspicious, slips of the indiscreet,
And all the accidents of life were pressed
Into one service, busy with one work.   350
The Senate stood aghast, her prudence quenched,
Her wisdom stifled, and her justice scared,
Her frenzy only active to extol
Past outrages, and shape the way for new,
Which no one dared to oppose or mitigate.

Domestic carnage now filled the whole year [11]
With feast-days; old men from the chimney-nook,
The maiden from the bosom of her love,
The mother from the cradle of her babe,
The warrior from the field—all perished, all—   360
Friends, enemies, of all parties, ages, ranks,
Head after head, and never heads enough
For those that bade them fall. They found their joy,
They made it, proudly eager as a child,
(If light desires of innocent little ones
May with such heinous appetites be compared),
Pleased in some open field to exercise
A toy that mimics with revolving wings
The motion of a wind-mill; though the air
Do of itself blow fresh, and make the vanes   370
Spin in his eyesight, *that* contents him not,
But, with the plaything at arm's length, he sets
His front against the blast, and runs amain,
That it may whirl the faster.
                              Amid the depth
Of those enormities, even thinking minds
Forgot, at seasons, whence they had their being;
Forgot that such a sound was ever heard
As Liberty upon earth: yet all beneath
Her innocent authority was wrought,
Nor could have been, without her blessed name.   380
The illustrious wife of Roland,[12] in the hour
Of her composure, felt that agony,
And gave it vent in her last words. O Friend!
It was a lamentable time for man,
Whether a hope had e'er been his or not;
A woful time for them whose hopes survived
The shock; most woful for those few who still
Were flattered, and had trust in human kind:

They had the deepest feeling of the grief.
Meanwhile the Invaders fared as they deserved: 390
The Herculean Commonwealth had put forth her
    arms,
And throttled with an infant godhead's might
The snakes about her cradle; that was well,
And as it should be; yet no cure for them
Whose souls were sick with pain of what would be
Hereafter brought in charge against mankind.
Most melancholy at that time, O Friend!
Were my day-thoughts,—my nights were miserable;
Through months, through years, long after the last
    beat
Of those atrocities, the hour of sleep   400
To me came rarely charged with natural gifts,
Such ghastly visions had I of despair
And tyranny, and implements of death;
And innocent victims sinking under fear,
And momentary hope, and worn-out prayer,
Each in his separate cell, or penned in crowds
For sacrifice, and struggling with forced mirth
And levity in dungeons, where the dust
Was laid with tears. Then suddenly the scene
Changed, and the unbroken dream entangled me   410
In long orations, which I strove to plead
Before unjust tribunals,—with a voice
Labouring, a brain confounded, and a sense,
Death-like, of treacherous desertion, felt
In the last place of refuge—my own soul.

When I began in youth's delightful prime
To yield myself to Nature, when that strong
And holy passion overcame me first,
Nor day nor night, evening or morn, was free
From its oppression. But, O Power Supreme!   420
Without Whose care this world would cease to breathe,
Who from the fountain of Thy grace dost fill
The veins that branch through every frame of life,
Making man what he is, creature divine,
In single or in social eminence,
Above the rest raised infinite ascents
When reason that enables him to be
Is not sequestered—what a change is here!
How different ritual for this after-worship,
What countenance to promote this second love!   430
The first was service paid to things which lie
Guarded within the bosom of Thy will.
Therefore to serve was high beatitude;
Tumult was therefore gladness, and the fear
Ennobling, venerable; sleep secure,
And waking thoughts more rich than happiest dreams.

But as the ancient Prophets, borne aloft
In vision, yet constrained by natural laws

---

11 The Reign of Terror, September 1793 to July 1794, began
with the execution of the Girondists and ended with the fall and
execution of Robespierre.
12 Girondist leader, her last words were "O Liberté, que de
crimes l'on commet en ton nom"—O liberty, what crimes are
committed in thy name. See Coleridge's note to *The Eolian Harp*,
p. 441.

With them to take a troubled human heart,
Wanted not consolations, nor a creed   440
Of reconcilement, then when they denounced,
On towns and cities, wallowing in the abyss
Of their offences, punishment to come;
Or saw, like other men, with bodily eyes,
Before them, in some desolated place,
The wrath consummate and the threat fulfilled;
So, with devout humility be it said,
So, did a portion of that spirit fall
On me uplifted from the vantage-ground
Of pity and sorrow to a state of being   450
That through the time's exceeding fierceness saw
Glimpses of retribution, terrible,
And in the order of sublime behests:
But, even if that were not, amid the awe
Of unintelligible chastisement,
Not only acquiescences of faith
Survived, but daring sympathies with power,
Motions not treacherous or profane, else why
Within the folds of no ungentle breast
Their dread vibration to this hour prolonged?   460
Wild blasts of music thus could find their way
Into the midst of turbulent events;
So that worst tempests might be listened to.
Then was the truth received into my heart,
That, under heaviest sorrow earth can bring,
If from the affliction somewhere do not grow
Honour which could not else have been, a faith,
An elevation and a sanctity,
If new strength be not given nor old restored,
The blame is ours, not Nature's. When a taunt   470
Was taken up by scoffers in their pride,
Saying, 'Behold the harvest that we reap
From popular government and equality,'
I clearly saw that neither these nor aught
Of wild belief engrafted on their names
By false philosophy had caused the woe,
But a terrific reservoir of guilt
And ignorance filled up from age to age,
That could no longer hold its loathsome charge,
But burst and spread in deluge through the land.   480

    And as the desert hath green spots, the sea
Small islands scattered amid stormy waves,
So *that* disastrous period did not want
Bright sprinklings of all human excellence,
To which the silver wands of saints in Heaven
Might point with rapturous joy. Yet not the less,
For those examples in no age surpassed
Of fortitude and energy and love,
And human nature faithful to herself
Under worst trials, was I driven to think   490
Of the glad times when first I traversed France

A youthful pilgrim; above all reviewed
That eventide, when under windows bright
With happy faces and with garlands hung,
And through a rainbow-arch that spanned the street,
Triumphal pomp for liberty confirmed,
I paced, a dear companion at my side,
The town of Arras,[13] whence with promise high
Issued, on delegation to sustain
Humanity and right, *that* Robespierre,   500
He who thereafter, and in how short time!
Wielded the sceptre of the Atheist crew.
When the calamity spread far and wide—
And this same city, that did then appear
To outrun the rest in exultation, groaned
Under the vengeance of her cruel son,
As Lear reproached the winds [14]—I could almost
Have quarrelled with that blameless spectacle
For lingering yet an image in my mind
To mock me under such a strange reverse.   510

    O Friend! few happier moments have been mine
Than that which told the downfall of this Tribe
So dreaded, so abhorred.[15] The day deserves
A separate record. Over the smooth sands
Of Leven's ample estuary lay
My journey, and beneath a genial sun,
With distant prospect among gleams of sky
And clouds, and intermingling mountain tops,
In one inseparable glory clad,
Creatures of one ethereal substance met   520
In consistory, like a diadem
Or crown of burning seraphs as they sit
In the empyrean. Underneath that pomp
Celestial, lay unseen the pastoral vales
Among whose happy fields I had grown up
From childhood. On the fulgent spectacle,
That neither passed away nor changed, I gazed
Enrapt; but brightest things are wont to draw
Sad opposites out of the inner heart,
As even their pensive influence drew from mine.   530
How could it otherwise? for not in vain
That very morning had I turned aside
To seek the ground where, 'mid a throng of graves,
An honoured teacher of my youth [16] was laid,
And on the stone were graven by his desire
Lines from the churchyard elegy of Gray.[17]

[13] Robespierre was born in Arras, which Wordsworth (and Jones) had first visited in 1790.
[14] See Shakespeare's *King Lear*, III, ii.
[15] Robespierre was tried and executed July 28, 1794.
[16] William Taylor, Hawkshead schoolmaster, died in 1786, and was buried in the graveyard at Cartmel Priory. Wordsworth said that his portraits in *Matthew, The Two April Mornings,* and *The Fountain* were based partly on Taylor.
[17] The last four lines of Thomas Gray's *Elegy Written in a Country Churchyard* (1751).

This faithful guide, speaking from his death-bed,
Added no farewell to his parting counsel,
But said to me, 'My head will soon lie low;'
And when I saw the turf that covered him,   540
After the lapse of full eight years, those words,
With sound of voice and countenance of the Man,
Came back upon me, so that some few tears
Fell from me in my own despite. But now
I thought, still traversing that widespread plain,
With tender pleasure of the verses graven
Upon his tombstone, whispering to myself:
He loved the Poets, and, if now alive,
Would have loved me, as one not destitute
Of promise, nor belying the kind hope   550
That he had formed, when I, at his command,
Began to spin, with toil, my earliest songs.

As I advanced, all that I saw or felt
Was gentleness and peace. Upon a small
And rocky island near, a fragment stood
(Itself like a sea rock) the low remains
(With shells encrusted, dark with briny weeds)
Of a dilapidated structure, once
A Romish chapel, where the vested priest
Said matins at the hour that suited those   560
Who crossed the sands with ebb of morning tide.
Not far from that still ruin all the plain
Lay spotted with a variegated crowd
Of vehicles and travellers, horse and foot,
Wading beneath the conduct of their guide
In loose procession through the shallow stream
Of inland waters; the great sea meanwhile
Heaved at safe distance, far retired. I paused,
Longing for skill to paint a scene so bright
And cheerful, but the foremost of the band   570
As he approached, no salutation given
In the familiar language of the day,
Cried, 'Robespierre is dead!'—nor was a doubt,
After strict question, left within my mind
That he and his supporters all were fallen.

Great was my transport, deep my gratitude
To everlasting Justice, by this fiat
Made manifest. 'Come now, ye golden times,'
Said I forth-pouring on those open sands
A hymn of triumph: 'as the morning comes   580
From out the bosom of the night, come ye:
Thus far our trust is verified; behold!
They who with clumsy desperation brought
A river of Blood, and preached that nothing else
Could cleanse the Augean stable, by the might
Of their own helper have been swept away;
Their madness stands declared and visible;
Elsewhere will safety now be sought, and earth

March firmly towards righteousness and peace.'—
Then schemes I framed more calmly, when and how
The madding factions might be tranquillised,   591
And how through hardships manifold and long
The glorious renovation would proceed.
Thus interrupted by uneasy bursts
Of exultation, I pursued my way
Along that very shore which I had skimmed
In former days, when—spurring from the Vale
Of Nightshade, and St. Mary's mouldering fane,
And the stone abbot, after circuit made
In wantonness of heart, a joyous band   600
Of school-boys hastening to their distant home
Along the margin of the moonlight sea—
We beat with thundering hoofs the level sand.[18]

BOOK ELEVENTH
FRANCE—CONCLUDED

FROM that time forth, Authority in France
Put on a milder face; Terror had ceased,
Yet every thing was wanting that might give
Courage to them who looked for good by light
Of rational Experience, for the shoots
And hopeful blossoms of a second spring:
Yet, in me, confidence was unimpaired;
The Senate's language, and the public acts
And measures of the Government, though both
Weak, and of heartless omen, had not power   10
To daunt me; in the People was my trust:
And, in the virtues which mine eyes had seen,
I knew that wound external could not take
Life from the young Republic; that new foes
Would only follow, in the path of shame,
Their brethren, and her triumphs be in the end
Great, universal, irresistible.
This intuition led me to confound
One victory with another, higher far,—
Triumphs of unambitious peace at home,   20
And noiseless fortitude. Beholding still
Resistance strong as heretofore, I thought
That what was in degree the same was likewise
The same in quality,—that, as the worse
Of the two spirits then at strife remained
Untired, the better, surely, would preserve
The heart that first had roused him. Youth maintains,
In all conditions of society,
Communion more direct and intimate
With Nature,—hence, ofttimes, with reason too—
Than age or manhood, even. To Nature, then,   31

---

[18] Furness Abbey, south of Hawkshead. See Book II, above.

Power had reverted: habit, custom, law,
Had left an interregnum's open space
For *her* to move about in, uncontrolled.[1]
Hence could I see how Babel-like their task,
Who, by the recent deluge stupified,
With their whole souls went culling from the day
Its petty promises, to build a tower
For their own safety; laughed with my compeers
At gravest heads, by enmity to France   40
Distempered, till they found, in every blast
Forced from the street-disturbing newsman's horn,
For her great cause record or prophecy
Of utter ruin. How might we believe
That wisdom could, in any shape, come near
Men clinging to delusions so insane?
And thus, experience proving that no few
Of our opinions had been just, we took
Like credit to ourselves where less was due,
And thought that other notions were as sound,   50
Yea, could not but be right, because we saw
That foolish men opposed them.
                              To a strain
More animated I might here give way,
And tell, since juvenile errors are my theme,
What in those days, through Britain, was performed
To turn *all* judgments out of their right course;
But this is passion over-near ourselves,
Reality too close and too intense,
And intermixed with something, in my mind,
Of scorn and condemnation personal,   60
That would profane the sanctity of verse.
Our Shepherds, this say merely, at that time
Acted, or seemed at least to act, like men
Thirsting to make the guardian crook of law
A tool of murder; they who ruled the State,
Though with such awful proof before their eyes
That he, who would sow death, reaps death, or worse,
And can reap nothing better, child-like longed
To imitate, not wise enough to avoid;
Or left (by mere timidity betrayed)   70
The plain straight road, for one no better chosen
Than if their wish had been to undermine
Justice, and make an end of Liberty.[2]

But from these bitter truths I must return
To my own history. It hath been told
That I was led to take an eager part
In arguments of civil polity,[3]

<hr>

[1] I.e., after the fall of Robespierre.
[2] Political trials in England were defended as a wartime neces-
sity. The Habeas Corpus Act was suspended, and several friends
of Wordsworth and Coleridge—either political reformers or
French sympathizers—were prosecuted.
[3] Wordsworth here begins to recount in political terms the
events of Books IX and X.

Abruptly, and indeed before my time:
I had approached, like other youths, the shield
Of human nature from the golden side,   80
And would have fought, even to the death, to attest
The quality of the metal which I saw.
What there is best in individual man,
Of wise in passion, and sublime in power,
Benevolent in small societies,
And great in large ones, I had oft revolved,
Felt deeply, but not thoroughly understood
By reason: nay, far from it; they were yet,
As cause was given me afterwards to learn,
Not proof against the injuries of the day;   90
Lodged only at the sanctuary's door,
Not safe within its bosom. Thus prepared,
And with such general insight into evil,
And of the bounds which sever it from good,
As books and common intercourse with life
Must needs have given—to the inexperienced mind,
When the world travels in a beaten road,
Guide faithful as is needed—I began
To meditate with ardour on the rule
And management of nations; what it is   100
And ought to be; and strove to learn how far
Their power or weakness, wealth or poverty,
Their happiness or misery depend
Upon their laws, and fashion of the State.

O pleasant exercise of hope and joy!
For mighty were the auxiliars which then stood
Upon our side, we who were strong in love!
Bliss was it in that dawn to be alive,
But to be young was very Heaven! O times,
In which the meagre, stale, forbidding ways   110
Of custom, law, and statute, took at once
The attraction of a country in romance!
When Reason seemed the most to assert her rights
When most intent on making of herself
A prime enchantress to assist the work,
Which then was going forward in her name!
Not favoured spots alone, but the whole Earth,
The beauty wore of promise—that which sets
(As at some moments might not be unfelt
Among the bowers of Paradise itself)   120
The budding rose above the rose full blown.
What temper at the prospect did not wake
To happiness unthought of? The inert
Were roused, and lively natures rapt away!
They who had fed their childhood upon dreams,
The play-fellows of fancy, who had made
All powers of swiftness, subtilty, and strength
Their ministers,—who in lordly wise had stirred
Among the grandest objects of the sense,
And dealt with whatsoever they found there   130

As if they had within some lurking right
To wield it;—they, too, who of gentle mood
Had watched all gentle motions, and to these
Had fitted their own thoughts, schemers more mild,
And in the region of their peaceful selves;—
Now was it that *both* found, the meek and lofty
Did both find helpers to their hearts' desire,
And stuff at hand, plastic as they could wish,—
Were called upon to exercise their skill,
Not in Utopia,—subterranean fields,—   140
Or some secreted island, Heaven knows where!
But in the very world, which is the world
Of all of us,—the place where, in the end,
We find our happiness, or not at all!

    Why should I not confess that Earth was then
To me, what an inheritance, new-fallen,
Seems, when the first time visited, to one
Who thither comes to find in it his home?
He walks about and looks upon the spot
With cordial transport, moulds it and remoulds,   150
And is half pleased with things that are amiss,
'Twill be such joy to see them disappear.

    An active partisan, I thus convoked
From every object pleasant circumstance
To suit my ends; I moved among mankind
With genial feelings still predominant;
When erring, erring on the better part,
And in the kinder spirit; placable,
Indulgent, as not uninformed that men
See as they have been taught—Antiquity   160
Gives right to error; and aware, no less,
That throwing off oppression must be work
As well of License as of Liberty;
And above all—for this was more than all—
Not caring if the wind did now and then
Blow keen upon an eminence that gave
Prospect so large into futurity;
In brief, a child of Nature, as at first,
Diffusing only those affections wider
That from the cradle had grown up with me,   170
And losing, in no other way than light
Is lost in light, the weak in the more strong.

    In the main outline, such it might be said
Was my condition, till with open war
Britain opposed the liberties of France.
This threw me first out of the pale of love;
Soured and corrupted, upwards to the source,
My sentiments; was not, as hitherto,
A swallowing up of lesser things in great,
But change of them into their contraries;   180
And thus a way was opened for mistakes

And false conclusions, in degree as gross,
In kind more dangerous. What had been a pride,
Was now a shame; my likings and my loves
Ran in new channels, leaving old ones dry;
And hence a blow that, in maturer age,
Would but have touched the judgment, struck more
    deep
Into sensations near the heart: meantime,
As from the first, wild theories were afloat,[4]
To whose pretensions, sedulously urged,   190
I had but lent a careless ear, assured
That time was ready to set all things right,
And that the multitude, so long oppressed,
Would be oppressed no more.
                   But when events
Brought less encouragement, and unto these
The immediate proof of principles no more
Could be entrusted, while the events themselves,
Worn out in greatness, stripped of novelty,
Less occupied the mind, and sentiments   199
Could through my understanding's natural growth
No longer keep their ground, by faith maintained
Of inward consciousness, and hope that laid
Her hand upon her object—evidence
Safer, of universal application, such
As could not be impeached, was sought elsewhere.

    But now, become oppressors in their turn,
Frenchmen had changed a war of self-defence
For one of conquest,[5] losing sight of all
Which they had struggled for: now mounted up,
Openly in the eye of earth and heaven,   210
The scale of liberty. I read her doom,
With anger vexed, with disappointment sore,
But not dismayed, nor taking to the shame
Of a false prophet. While resentment rose
Striving to hide, what nought could heal, the wounds
Of mortified presumption, I adhered
More firmly to old tenets, and, to prove
Their temper, strained them more; and thus, in heat
Of contest, did opinions every day
Grow into consequence, till round my mind   220
They clung, as if they were its life, nay more,
The very being of the immortal soul.

    This was the time, when, all things tending fast
To depravation, speculative schemes—
That promised to abstract the hopes of Man
Out of his feelings, to be fixed thenceforth
For ever in a purer element—

---

    [4] Presumably such books as William Godwin's *Political Justice* (1793) and the tracts of other reformers.
    [5] I.e., the French attacks on Spain, Italy, Holland, and Germany in 1794–1795.

Found ready welcome.[6] Tempting region *that*
For Zeal to enter and refresh herself,
Where passions had the privilege to work,   230
And never hear the sound of their own names.
But, speaking more in charity, the dream
Flattered the young, pleased with extremes, nor least
With that which makes our Reason's naked self
The object of its fervour. What delight!
How glorious! in self-knowledge and self-rule,
To look through all the frailties of the world,
And, with a resolute mastery shaking off
Infirmities of nature, time, and place,
Build social upon personal Liberty,   240
Which, to the blind restraints of general laws
Superior, magisterially adopts
One guide, the light of circumstances, flashed
Upon an independent intellect.
Thus expectation rose again; thus hope,
From her first ground expelled, grew proud once
        more.
Oft, as my thoughts were turned to human kind,
I scorned indifference; but, inflamed with thirst
Of a secure intelligence, and sick
Of other longing, I pursued what seemed   250
A more exalted nature; wished that Man
Should start out of his earthly, worm-like state,
And spread abroad the wings of Liberty,
Lord of himself, in undisturbed delight—
A noble aspiration! *yet* I feel
(Sustained by worthier as by wiser thoughts)
The aspiration, nor shall ever cease
To feel it;—but return we to our course.

    Enough, 'tis true—could such a plea excuse
Those aberrations—had the clamorous friends   260
Of ancient Institutions said and done
To bring disgrace upon their very names;
Disgrace, of which, custom and written law,
And sundry moral sentiments as props
Or emanations of those institutes,
Too justly bore a part. A veil had been
Uplifted; why deceive ourselves? in sooth,
'Twas even so; and sorrow for the man
Who either had not eyes wherewith to see,
Or, seeing, had forgotten! A strong shock   270
Was given to old opinions; all men's minds
Had felt its power, and mine was both let loose,
Let loose and goaded. After what hath been
Already said of patriotic love,
Suffice it here to add, that, somewhat stern
In temperament, withal a happy man,
And therefore bold to look on painful things,

<hr>

[6] See note to line 189.

Free likewise of the world, and thence more bold,
I summoned my best skill, and toiled, intent
To anatomise the frame of social life,   280
Yea, the whole body of society
Searched to its heart. Share with me, Friend! the wish
That some dramatic tale, endued with shapes
Livelier, and flinging out less guarded words
Than suit the work we fashion, might set forth
What then I learned, or think I learned, of truth,
And the errors into which I fell, betrayed
By present objects, and by reasonings false
From their beginnings, inasmuch as drawn
Out of a heart that had been turned aside   290
From Nature's way by outward accidents,
And which was thus confounded, more and more
Misguided, and misguiding. So I fared,
Dragging all precepts, judgments, maxims, creeds,
Like culprits to the bar; calling the mind,
Suspiciously, to establish in plain day
Her titles and her honours; now believing,
Now disbelieving; endlessly perplexed
With impulse, motive, right and wrong, the ground
Of obligation, what the rule and whence   300
The sanction; till, demanding formal *proof*,
And seeking it in every thing, I lost
All feeling of conviction, and, in fine,
Sick, wearied out with contrarieties,
Yielded up moral questions in despair.

    This was the crisis of that strong disease,
This the soul's last and lowest ebb; I drooped,
Deeming our blessed reason of least use
Where wanted most: 'The lordly attributes
Of will and choice,' I bitterly exclaimed,   310
'What are they but a mockery of a Being
Who hath in no concerns of his a test
Of good and evil; knows not what to fear
Or hope for, what to covet or to shun;
And who, if those could be discerned, would yet
Be little profited, would see, and ask
Where is the obligation to enforce?
And, to acknowledged law rebellious, still,
As selfish passion urged, would act amiss;
The dupe of folly, or the slave of crime.'   320

    Depressed, bewildered thus, I did not walk
With scoffers, seeking light and gay revenge
From indiscriminate laughter, nor sate down
In reconcilement with an utter waste
Of intellect; such sloth I could not brook,
(Too well I loved, in that my spring of life,
Pains-taking thoughts, and truth, their dear reward)
But turned to abstract science, and there sought
Work for the reasoning faculty enthroned

Where the disturbances of space and time— 330
Whether in matter's various properties
Inherent, or from human will and power
Derived—find no admission. Then it was—
Thanks to the bounteous Giver of all good!—
That the beloved Sister in whose sight
Those days were passed, now speaking in a voice
Of sudden admonition—like a brook
That did but *cross* a lonely road, and now
Is seen, heard, felt, and caught at every turn,
Companion never lost through many a league— 340
Maintained for me a saving intercourse
With my true self; for, though bedimmed and changed
Much, as it seemed, I was no further changed
Than as a clouded, and not a waning moon:
She whispered still that brightness would return,
She, in the midst of all, preserved me still
A Poet, made me seek beneath that name,
And that alone, my office upon earth;
And, lastly, as hereafter will be shown,
If willing audience fail not, Nature's self, 350
By all varieties of human love
Assisted, led me back through opening day
To those sweet counsels between head and heart
Whence grew that genuine knowledge, fraught with
    peace,
Which, through the later sinkings of this cause,
Hath still upheld me, and upholds me now
In the catastrophe (for so they dream,
And nothing less), when, finally to close
And rivet down all the gains of France, a Pope
Is summoned in, to crown an Emperor [7]— 360
This last opprobrium, when we see a people,
That once looked up in faith, as if to Heaven
For manna, take a lesson from the dog
Returning to his vomit; when the sun
That rose in splendour, was alive, and moved
In exultation with a living pomp
Of clouds—his glory's natural retinue—
Hath dropped all functions by the gods bestowed,
And, turned into a gewgaw, a machine,
Sets like an Opera phantom.
            Thus, O Friend! 370
Through times of honour and through times of shame
Descending, have I faithfully retraced
The perturbations of a youthful mind
Under a long-lived storm of great events—
A story destined for thy ear, who now,
Among the fallen of nations, dost abide
Where Etna, over hill and valley, casts
His shadow stretching towards Syracuse,

The city of Timoleon![8] Righteous Heaven!
How are the mighty prostrated! They first, 380
They first of all that breathe should have awaked
When the great voice was heard from out the tombs
Of ancient heroes. If I suffered grief
For ill-requited France, by many deemed
A trifler only in her proudest day;
Have been distressed to think of what she once
Promised, now is; a far more sober cause
Thine eyes must see of sorrow in a land,
To the reanimating influence lost
Of memory, to virtue lost and hope, 390
Though with the wreck of loftier years bestrewn.

    But indignation works where hope is not,
And thou, O Friend! wilt be refreshed. There is
One great society alone on earth:
The noble Living and the noble Dead.

    Thine be such converse strong and sanative,
A ladder for thy spirit to reascend
To health and joy and pure contentedness;
To me the grief confined, that thou art gone
From this last spot of earth, where Freedom now 400
Stands single in her only sanctuary;
A lonely wanderer art gone, by pain
Compelled and sickness, at this latter day,
This sorrowful reverse for all mankind.
I feel for thee, must utter what I feel:
The sympathies erewhile in part discharged,
Gather afresh, and will have vent again:
My own delights do scarcely seem to me
My own delights; the lordly Alps themselves,
Those rosy peaks, from which the Morning looks
Abroad on many nations, are no more 411
For me that image of pure gladsomeness
Which they were wont to be. Through kindred scenes,
For purpose, at a time, how different!
Thou tak'st thy way, carrying the heart and soul
That Nature gives to Poets, now by thought
Matured, and in the summer of their strength.
Oh! wrap him in your shades, ye giant woods,
On Etna's side; and thou, O flowery field
Of Enna! is there not some nook of thine, 420
From the first play-time of the infant world
Kept sacred to restorative delight,
When from afar invoked by anxious love?

    Child of the mountains, among shepherds reared,
Ere yet familiar with the classic page,

---

[7] Pope Pius VII officiated at the crowning of Napoleon as emperor in December 1804.

[8] Coleridge was in Sicily from August to November 1804; Timoleon is honored as the man who freed Syracuse from tyrants in the fourth century B.C.

I learnt to dream of Sicily; and lo,
The gloom, that, but a moment past, was deepened
At thy command, at her command gives way;
A pleasant promise, wafted from her shores,
Comes o'er my heart: in fancy I behold   430
Her seas yet smiling, her once happy vales;
Nor can my tongue give utterance to a name
Of note belonging to that honoured isle,
Philosopher or Bard, Empedocles,[9]
Or Archimedes, pure abstracted soul!
That doth not yield a solace to my grief:
And, O Theocritus, so far have some
Prevailed among the powers of heaven and earth,
By their endowments, good or great, that they
Have had, as thou reportest, miracles   440
Wrought for them in old time; yea, not unmoved,
When thinking on my own beloved friend,
I hear thee tell how bees with honey fed
Divine Comates, by his impious lord
Within a chest imprisoned; how they came
Laden from blooming grove or flowery field,
And fed him there, alive, month after month,
Because the goatherd, blessed man! had lips
Wet with the Muses' nectar.
                              Thus I soothe
The pensive moments by this calm fire-side,   450
And find a thousand bounteous images
To cheer the thoughts of those I love, and mine.
Our prayers have been accepted; thou wilt stand
On Etna's summit, above earth and sea,
Triumphant, winning from the invaded heavens
Thoughts without bound, magnificent designs,
Worthy of poets who attuned their harps
In wood or echoing cave, for discipline
Of heroes; or, in reverence to the gods,
'Mid temples, served by sapient priests, and choirs
Of virgins crowned with roses. Not in vain   461
Those temples, where they in their ruins yet
Survive for inspiration, shall attract
Thy solitary steps: and on the brink
Thou wilt recline of pastoral Arethuse;[10]
Or, if that fountain be in truth no more,
Then, near some other spring, which, by the name
Thou gratulatest, willingly deceived,
I see thee linger a glad votary,
And not a captive pining for his home.   470

---

9 Empedocles (c. 490–c. 430 B.C.), Greek philosopher, killed
himself by jumping into the crater of Mt. Etna. Archimedes
(287?–212 B.C.), the physicist, and Theocritus (fl. c. 270 B.C.), the
pastoral poet, were also associated with Sicily. Comates (line 444)
is a character in Theocritus' *Idylls*.
10 Fountain on the island of Ortygia in the bay of Syracuse.
See Shelley's *Arethusa*, p. 916.

BOOK TWELFTH

IMAGINATION AND TASTE,
HOW IMPAIRED AND RESTORED

LONG time have human ignorance and guilt
Detained us, on what spectacles of woe
Compelled to look, and inwardly oppressed
With sorrow, disappointment, vexing thoughts,
Confusion of the judgment, zeal decayed,
And, lastly, utter loss of hope itself
And things to hope for! Not with these began
Our song, and not with these our song must end.—
Ye motions of delight, that haunt the sides
Of the green hills; ye breezes and soft airs,   10
Whose subtle intercourse with breathing flowers,
Feelingly watched, might teach Man's haughty race
How without injury to take, to give
Without offence; ye who, as if to show
The wondrous influence of power gently used,
Bend the complying heads of lordly pines,
And, with a touch, shift the stupendous clouds
Through the whole compass of the sky; ye brooks,
Muttering along the stones, a busy noise
By day, a quiet sound in silent night;   20
Ye waves, that out of the great deep steal forth
In a calm hour to kiss the pebbly shore,
Not mute, and then retire, fearing no storm;
And you, ye groves, whose ministry it is
To interpose the covert of your shades,
Even as a sleep, between the heart of man
And outward troubles, between man himself,
Not seldom, and his own uneasy heart:
Oh! that I had a music and a voice
Harmonious as your own, that I might tell   30
What ye have done for me. The morning shines,
Nor heedeth Man's perverseness; Spring returns,—
I saw the Spring return, and could rejoice,
In common with the children of her love,
Piping on boughs, or sporting on fresh fields,
Or boldly seeking pleasure nearer heaven
On wings that navigate cerulean skies.
So neither were complacency, nor peace,
Nor tender yearnings, wanting for my good
Through these distracted times; in Nature still 40
Glorying, I found a counterpoise in her,
Which, when the spirit of evil reached its height,
Maintained for me a secret happiness.

   This narrative, my Friend! hath chiefly told
Of intellectual power, fostering love,
Dispensing truth, and, over men and things,
Where reason yet might hesitate, diffusing
Prophetic sympathies of genial faith:

So was I favoured—such my happy lot—
Until that natural graciousness of mind   50
Gave way to overpressure from the times
And their disastrous issues. What availed,
When spells forbade the voyager to land,
That fragrant notice of a pleasant shore
Wafted, at intervals, from many a bower
Of blissful gratitude and fearless love?
Dare I avow that wish was mine to see,
And hope that future times *would* surely see,
The man to come, parted, as by a gulph,
From him who had been; that I could no more   60
Trust the elevation which had made me one
With the great family that still survives
To illuminate the abyss of ages past,
Sage, warrior, patriot, hero; for it seemed
That their best virtues were not free from taint
Of something false and weak, that could not stand
The open eye of Reason. Then I said,
'Go to the Poets; they will speak to thee
More perfectly of purer creatures;—yet
If reason be nobility in man,   70
Can aught be more ignoble than the man
Whom they delight in, blinded as he is
By prejudice, the miserable slave
Of low ambition or distempered love?'

In such strange passion, if I may once more
Review the past, I warred against myself—
A bigot to a new idolatry—
Like a cowled monk who hath forsworn the world,
Zealously laboured to cut off my heart
From all the sources of her former strength;   80
And as, by simple waving of a wand,
The wizard instantaneously dissolves
Palace or grove, even so could I unsoul
As readily by syllogistic words
Those mysteries of being which have made,
And shall continue evermore to make,
Of the whole human race one brotherhood.

What wonder, then, if, to a mind so far
Perverted, even the visible Universe
Fell under the dominion of a taste   90
Less spiritual, with microscopic view
Was scanned, as I had scanned the moral world?

O Soul of Nature! excellent and fair!
That didst rejoice with me, with whom I, too,
Rejoiced through early youth, before the winds
And roaring waters, and in lights and shades
That marched and countermarched about the hills
In glorious apparition, Powers on whom

I daily waited, now all eye and now
All ear; but never long without the heart   100
Employed, and man's unfolding intellect:
O Soul of Nature! that, by laws divine
Sustained and governed, still dost overflow
With an impassioned life, what feeble ones
Walk on this earth! how feeble have I been
When thou wert in thy strength! Nor this through
        stroke
Of human suffering, such as justifies
Remissness and inaptitude of mind,
But through presumption; even in pleasure
        pleased
Unworthily, disliking here, and there   110
Liking, by rules of mimic art transferred
To things above all art; but more,—for this,
Although a strong infection of the age,
Was never much my habit—giving way
To a comparison of scene with scene,
Bent overmuch on superficial things,
Pampering myself with meagre novelties
Of colour and proportion; to the moods
Of time and season, to the moral power,
The affections and the spirit of the place,   120
Insensible. Nor only did the love
Of sitting thus in judgment interrupt
My deeper feelings, but another cause,
More subtle and less easily explained,
That almost seems inherent in the creature,
A twofold frame of body and of mind.
I speak in recollection of a time
When the bodily eye, in every stage of life
The most despotic of our senses, gained
Such strength in *me* as often held my mind   130
In absolute dominion. Gladly here,
Entering upon abstruser argument,
Could I endeavour to unfold the means
Which Nature studiously employs to thwart
This tyranny, summons all the senses each
To counteract the other, and themselves,
And makes them all, and the objects with which all
Are conversant, subservient in their turn
To the great ends of Liberty and Power.
But leave we this: enough that my delights   140
(Such as they were) were sought insatiably.
Vivid the transport, vivid though not profound;
I roamed from hill to hill, from rock to rock,
Still craving combinations of new forms,
New pleasure, wider empire for the sight,
Proud of her own endowments, and rejoiced
To lay the inner faculties asleep.
Amid the turns and counterturns, the strife
And various trials of our complex being,
As we grow up, such thraldom of that sense   150

Seems hard to shun. And yet I knew a maid,[1]
A young enthusiast, who escaped these bonds;
Her eye was not the mistress of her heart;
Far less did rules prescribed by passive taste,
Or barren intermeddling subtleties,
Perplex her mind; but, wise as women are
When genial circumstance hath favoured them,
She welcomed what was given, and craved no
    more;
Whate'er the scene presented to her view,
That was the best, to that she was attuned   160
By her benign simplicity of life,
And through a perfect happiness of soul,
Whose variegated feelings were in this
Sisters, that they were each some new delight.
Birds in the bower, and lambs in the green field,
Could they have known her, would have loved;
    methought
Her very presence such a sweetness breathed,
That flowers, and trees, and even the silent hills,
And every thing she looked on, should have had
An intimation how she bore herself   170
Towards them and to all creatures. God delights
In such a being; for her common thoughts
Are piety, her life is gratitude.

Even like this maid, before I was called forth
From the retirement of my native hills,
I loved whate'er I saw: nor lightly loved,
But most intensely; never dreamt of aught
More grand, more fair, more exquisitely framed
Than those few nooks to which my happy feet
Were limited. I had not at that time   180
Lived long enough, nor in the least survived
The first diviner influence of this world,
As it appears to unaccustomed eyes.
Worshipping then among the depth of things,
As piety ordained; could I submit
To measured admiration, or to aught
That should preclude humility and love?
I felt, observed, and pondered; did not judge,
Yea, never thought of judging; with the gift
Of all this glory filled and satisfied.   190
And afterwards, when through the gorgeous Alps
Roaming, I carried with me the same heart:
In truth, the degradation—howsoe'er
Induced, effect, in whatsoe'er degree,
Of custom that prepares a partial scale
In which the little oft outweighs the great;
Or any other cause that hath been named;
Or lastly, aggravated by the times

---

[1] Presumably Mary Hutchinson, whom Wordsworth had
married in 1802; but possibly his sister Dorothy.

And their impassioned sounds, which well might
    make
The milder minstrelsies of rural scenes   200
Inaudible—was transient; I had known
Too forcibly, too early in my life,
Visitings of imaginative power
For this to last: I shook the habit off
Entirely and for ever, and again
In Nature's presence stood, as now I stand,
A sensitive being, a *creative* soul.

There are in our existence spots of time,
That with distinct pre-eminence retain
A renovating virtue, whence, depressed   210
By false opinion and contentious thought,
Or aught of heavier or more deadly weight,
In trivial occupations, and the round
Of ordinary intercourse, our minds
Are nourished and invisibly repaired;
A virtue, by which pleasure is enhanced,
That penetrates, enables us to mount,
When high, more high, and lifts us up when fallen.
This efficacious spirit chiefly lurks
Among those passages of life that give   220
Profoundest knowledge to what point, and how,
The mind is lord and master—outward sense
The obedient servant of her will. Such moments
Are scattered everywhere, taking their date
From our first childhood. I remember well,
That once, while yet my inexperienced hand
Could scarcely hold a bridle, with proud hopes
I mounted, and we journeyed towards the hills:
An ancient servant of my father's house
Was with me, my encourager and guide: 230
We had not travelled long, ere some mischance
Disjoined me from my comrade; and, through fear
Dismounting, down the rough and stony moor
I led my horse, and, stumbling on, at length
Came to a bottom, where in former times
A murderer had been hung in iron chains.
The gibbet-mast had mouldered down, the bones
And iron case were gone; but on the turf,
Hard by, soon after that fell deed was wrought,
Some unknown hand had carved the murderer's
    name.   240
The monumental letters were inscribed
In times long past; but still, from year to year,
By superstition of the neighbourhood,
The grass is cleared away, and to this hour
The characters are fresh and visible:
A casual glance had shown them, and I fled,
Faltering and faint, and ignorant of the road:
Then, reascending the bare common, saw
A naked pool that lay beneath the hills,

The beacon on the summit, and, more near,   250
A girl, who bore a pitcher on her head,
And seemed with difficult steps to force her way
Against the blowing wind. It was, in truth,
An ordinary sight; but I should need
Colours and words that are unknown to man,
To paint the visionary dreariness
Which, while I looked all round for my lost guide,
Invested moorland waste, and naked pool,
The beacon crowning the lone eminence,
The female and her garments vexed and tossed   260
By the strong wind. When, in the blessed hours
Of early love, the loved one at my side,
I roamed, in daily presence of this scene,
Upon the naked pool and dreary crags,
And on the melancholy beacon fell
A spirit of pleasure and youth's golden gleam;
And think ye not with radiance more sublime
For these remembrances, and for the power
They had left behind? So feeling comes in aid
Of feeling, and diversity of strength   270
Attends us, if but once we have been strong.
Oh! mystery of man, from what a depth
Proceed thy honours. I am lost, but see
In simple childhood something of the base
On which thy greatness stands; but this I feel,
That from thyself it comes, that thou must give,
Else never canst receive. The days gone by
Return upon me almost from the dawn
Of life: the hiding-places of man's power
Open; I would approach them, but they close.   280
I see by glimpses now; when age comes on,
May scarcely see at all; and I would give,
While yet we may, as far as words can give,
Substance and life to what I feel, enshrining,
Such is my hope, the spirit of the Past
For future restoration.—Yet another
Of these memorials:—
                    One Christmas-time,[2]
On the glad eve of its dear holidays,
Feverish, and tired, and restless, I went forth
Into the fields, impatient for the sight   290
Of those led palfreys that should bear us home;
My brothers and myself. There rose a crag,
That, from the meeting-point of two highways
Ascending, overlooked them both, far stretched;
Thither, uncertain on which road to fix
My expectation, thither I repaired,
Scout-like, and gained the summit; 'twas a day
Tempestuous, dark, and wild, and on the grass
I sate half-sheltered by a naked wall;
Upon my right hand couched a single sheep,   300

_____
[2] 1783.

Upon my left a blasted hawthorn stood;
With those companions at my side, I sate,
Straining my eyes intensely, as the mist
Gave intermitting prospect of the copse
And plain beneath. Ere we to school returned
That dreary time, ere we had been ten days
Sojourners in my father's house, he died,
And I and my three brothers, orphans then,
Followed his body to the grave. The event,
With all the sorrow that it brought, appeared   310
A chastisement; and when I called to mind
That day so lately past, when from the crag
I looked in such anxiety of hope;
With trite reflections of morality,
Yet in the deepest passion, I bowed low
To God, Who thus corrected my desires;
And, afterwards, the wind and sleety rain,
And all the business of the elements,
The single sheep, and the one blasted tree,
And the bleak music of that old stone wall,   320
The noise of wood and water, and the mist
That on the line of each of those two roads
Advanced in such indisputable shapes;
All these were kindred spectacles and sounds
To which I oft repaired, and thence would drink,
As at a fountain; and on winter nights,
Down to this very time, when storm and rain
Beat on my roof, or, haply, at noon-day,
While in a grove I walk, whose lofty trees,
Laden with summer's thickest foliage, rock   330
In a strong wind, some working of the spirit,
Some inward agitations thence are brought,
Whate'er their office, whether to beguile
Thoughts over busy in the course they took,
Or animate an hour of vacant ease.

BOOK THIRTEENTH

IMAGINATION AND TASTE,
HOW IMPAIRED AND RESTORED—
CONCLUDED

FROM Nature doth emotion come, and moods
Of calmness equally are Nature's gift:
This is her glory; these two attributes
Are sister horns that constitute her strength.
Hence Genius, born to thrive by interchange
Of peace and excitation, finds in her
His best and purest friend; from her receives
That energy by which he seeks the truth,
From her that happy stillness of the mind
Which fits him to receive it when unsought.   10

Such benefit the humblest intellects
Partake of, each in their degree; 'tis mine
To speak, what I myself have known and felt;
Smooth task! for words find easy way, inspired
By gratitude, and confidence in truth.
Long time in search of knowledge did I range
The field of human life, in heart and mind
Benighted; but, the dawn beginning now
To re-appear, 'twas proved that not in vain
I had been taught to reverence a Power   20
That is the visible quality and shape
And image of right reason; that matures
Her processes by steadfast laws; gives birth
To no impatient or fallacious hopes,
No heat of passion or excessive zeal,
No vain conceits; provokes to no quick turns
Of self-applauding intellect; but trains
To meekness, and exalts by humble faith;
Holds up before the mind intoxicate
With present objects, and the busy dance   30
Of things that pass away, a temperate show
Of objects that endure; and by this course
Disposes her, when over-fondly set
On throwing off incumbrances, to seek
In man, and in the frame of social life,
Whate'er there is desirable and good
Of kindred permanence, unchanged in form
And function, or, through strict vicissitude
Of life and death, revolving. Above all
Were re-established now those watchful thoughts   40
Which, seeing little worthy or sublime
In what the Historian's pen so much delights
To blazon—power and energy detached
From moral purpose—early tutored me
To look with feelings of fraternal love
Upon the unassuming things that hold
A silent station in this beauteous world.

Thus moderated, thus composed, I found
Once more in Man an object of delight,
Of pure imagination, and of love;   50
And, as the horizon of my mind enlarged,
Again I took the intellectual eye
For my instructor, studious more to see
Great truths, than touch and handle little ones.
Knowledge was given accordingly; my trust
Became more firm in feelings that had stood
The test of such a trial; clearer far
My sense of excellence—of right and wrong:
The promise of the present time retired
Into its true proportion; sanguine schemes,   60
Ambitious projects, pleased me less; I sought
For present good in life's familiar face,
And built thereon my hopes of good to come.

With settling judgments now of what would last
And what would disappear; prepared to find
Presumption, folly, madness, in the men
Who thrust themselves upon the passive world
As Rulers of the world; to see in these,
Even when the public welfare is their aim,
Plans without thought, or built on theories   70
Vague and unsound; and having brought the books
Of modern statists to their proper test,
Life, human life, with all its sacred claims
Of sex and age, and heaven-descended rights,
Mortal, or those beyond the reach of death;
And having thus discerned how dire a thing
Is worshipped in that idol proudly named
'The Wealth of Nations,'[1] *where* alone that wealth
Is lodged, and how increased; and having gained
A more judicious knowledge of the worth   80
And dignity of individual man,
No composition of the brain, but man
Of whom we read, the man whom we behold
With our own eyes—I could not but inquire—
Not with less interest than heretofore,
But greater, though in spirit more subdued—
Why is this glorious creature to be found
One only in ten thousand? What one is,
Why may not millions be? What bars are thrown
By Nature in the way of such a hope?   90
Our animal appetites and daily wants,
Are these obstructions insurmountable?
If not, then others vanish into air.
'Inspect the basis of the social pile:
Inquire,' said I, 'how much of mental power
And genuine virtue they possess who live
By bodily toil, labour exceeding far
Their due proportion, under all the weight
Of that injustice which upon ourselves
Ourselves entail.' Such estimate to frame   100
I chiefly looked (what need to look beyond?)
Among the natural abodes of men,
Fields with their rural works; recalled to mind
My earliest notices; with these compared
The observations made in later youth,
And to that day continued.—For, the time
Had never been when throes of mighty Nations
And the world's tumult unto me could yield,
How far soe'er transported and possessed,
Full measure of content; but still I craved   110
An intermingling of distinct regards
And truths of individual sympathy
Nearer ourselves. Such often might be gleaned
From the great City, else it must have proved

---

[1] Adam Smith's arguments for free trade and economic
individualism had been published in 1776.

To me a heart-depressing wilderness;
But much was wanting: therefore did I turn
To you, ye pathways, and ye lonely roads;
Sought you enriched with everything I prized,
With human kindnesses and simple joys.

Oh! next to one dear state of bliss, vouchsafed   120
Alas! to few in this untoward world,
The bliss of walking daily in life's prime
Through field or forest with the maid we love,
While yet our hearts are young, while yet we breathe
Nothing but happiness, in some lone nook,
Deep vale, or any where, the home of both,
From which it would be misery to stir:
Oh! next to such enjoyment of our youth,
In my esteem, next to such dear delight,
Was that of wandering on from day to day   130
Where I could meditate in peace, and cull
Knowledge that step by step might lead me on
To wisdom; or, as lightsome as a bird
Wafted upon the wind from distant lands,
Sing notes of greeting to strange fields or groves,
Which lacked not voice to welcome me in turn:
And, when that pleasant toil had ceased to please,
Converse with men, where if we meet a face
We almost meet a friend, on naked heaths
With long long ways before, by cottage bench,   140
Or well-spring where the weary traveller rests.

Who doth not love to follow with his eye
The windings of a public way? the sight,
Familiar object as it is, hath wrought
On my imagination since the morn
Of childhood, when a disappearing line,
One daily present to my eyes, that crossed
The naked summit of a far-off hill
Beyond the limits that my feet had trod,
Was like an invitation into space   150
Boundless, or guide into eternity.
Yes, something of the grandeur which invests
The mariner who sails the roaring sea
Through storm and darkness, early in my mind
Surrounded, too, the wanderers of the earth;
Grandeur as much, and loveliness far more.
Awed have I been by strolling Bedlamites;[2]
From many other uncouth vagrants (passed
In fear) have walked with quicker step; but why
Take note of this? When I began to enquire,   160
To watch and question those I met, and speak
Without reserve to them, the lonely roads
Were open schools in which I daily read
With most delight the passions of mankind,

[2] Madmen; see note in Book VII, to line 132.

Whether by words, looks, sighs, or tears, revealed;
There saw into the depth of human souls,
Souls that appear to have no depth at all
To careless eyes. And—now convinced at heart
How little those formalities, to which
With overweening trust alone we give   170
The name of Education, have to do
With real feeling and just sense; how vain
A correspondence with the talking world
Proves to the most; and called to make good search
If man's estate, by doom of Nature yoked
With toil, be therefore yoked with ignorance;
If virtue is indeed so hard to rear,
And intellectual strength so rare a boon—
I prized such walks still more, for there I found
Hope to my hope, and to my pleasure peace   180
And steadiness, and healing and repose
To every angry passion. There I heard,
From mouths of men obscure and lowly, truths
Replete with honour; sounds in unison
With loftiest promises of good and fair.

There are who think that strong affection, love
Known by whatever name, is falsely deemed
A gift, to use a term which they would use,
Of vulgar nature; that its growth requires
Retirement, leisure, language purified   190
By manners studied and elaborate;
That whoso feels such passion in its strength
Must live within the very light and air
Of courteous usages refined by art.
True is it, where oppression worse than death
Salutes the being at his birth, where grace
Of culture hath been utterly unknown,
And poverty and labour in excess
From day to day pre-occupy the ground
Of the affections, and to Nature's self   200
Oppose a deeper nature; there, indeed,
Love cannot be; nor does it thrive with ease
Among the close and overcrowded haunts
Of cities, where the human heart is sick,
And the eye feeds it not, and cannot feed.
—Yes, in those wanderings deeply did I feel
How we mislead each other; above all,
How books mislead us, seeking their reward
From judgments of the wealthy Few, who see
By artificial lights; how they debase   210
The Many for the pleasure of those Few;
Effeminately level down the truth
To certain general notions, for the sake
Of being understood at once, or else
Through want of better knowledge in the heads
That framed them; flattering self-conceit with words,
That, while they most ambitiously set forth

Extrinsic differences, the outward marks
Whereby society has parted man
From man, neglect the universal heart.   220

   Here, calling up to mind what then I saw,
A youthful traveller, and see daily now
In the familiar circuit of my home,
Here might I pause, and bend in reverence
To Nature, and the power of human minds,
To men as they are men within themselves.
How oft high service is performed within,
When all the external man is rude in show,—
Not like a temple rich with pomp and gold,
But a mere mountain chapel, that protects   230
Its simple worshippers from sun and shower.
Of these, said I, shall be my song; of these,
If future years mature me for the task,
Will I record the praises, making verse
Deal boldly with substantial things; in truth
And sanctity of passion, speak of these,
That justice may be done, obeisance paid
Where it is due: thus haply shall I teach,
Inspire, through unadulterated ears
Pour rapture, tenderness, and hope,—my theme   240
No other than the very heart of man,
As found among the best of those who live,
Not unexalted by religious faith,
Nor uninformed by books, good books, though few,
In Nature's presence: thence may I select
Sorrow, that is not sorrow, but delight;
And miserable love, that is not pain
To hear of, for the glory that redounds
Therefrom to human kind, and what we are.
Be mine to follow with no timid step   250
Where knowledge leads me: it shall be my pride
That I have dared to tread this holy ground,
Speaking no dream, but things oracular;
Matter not lightly to be heard by those
Who to the letter of the outward promise
Do read the invisible soul; by men adroit
In speech, and for communion with the world
Accomplished; minds whose faculties are then
Most active when they are most eloquent,
And elevated most when most admired.   260
Men may be found of other mould than these,
Who are their own upholders, to themselves
Encouragement, and energy, and will,
Expressing liveliest thoughts in lively words
As native passion dictates. Others, too,
There are among the walks of homely life
Still higher, men for contemplation framed,
Shy, and unpractised in the strife of phrase;
Meek men, whose very souls perhaps would sink
Beneath them, summoned to such intercourse: 270

Theirs is the language of the heavens, the power,
The thought, the image, and the silent joy:
Words are but under-agents in their souls;
When they are grasping with their greatest strength,
They do not breathe among them: this I speak
In gratitude to God, Who feeds our hearts
For His own service; knoweth, loveth us,
When we are unregarded by the world.

   Also about this time did I receive
Convictions still more strong than heretofore,   280
Not only that the inner frame is good,
And graciously composed, but that, no less,
Nature for all conditions wants not power
To consecrate, if we have eyes to see,
The outside of her creatures, and to breathe
Grandeur upon the very humblest face
Of human life. I felt that the array
Of act and circumstance, and visible form,
Is mainly to the pleasure of the mind
What passion makes them; that meanwhile the forms
Of Nature have a passion in themselves,   291
That intermingles with those works of man
To which she summons him; although the works
Be mean, have nothing lofty of their own;
And that the Genius of the Poet hence
May boldly take his way among mankind
Wherever Nature leads; that he hath stood
By Nature's side among the men of old,
And so shall stand for ever. Dearest Friend!
If thou partake the animating faith   300
That Poets, even as Prophets, each with each
Connected in a mighty scheme of truth,
Have each his own peculiar faculty,
Heaven's gift, a sense that fits him to perceive
Objects unseen before, thou wilt not blame
The humblest of this band who dares to hope
That unto him hath also been vouchsafed
An insight that in some sort he possesses,
A privilege whereby a work of his,
Proceeding from a source of untaught things   310
Creative and enduring, may become
A power like one of Nature's. To a hope
Not less ambitious once among the wilds
Of Sarum's Plain,[3] my youthful spirit was raised;
There, as I ranged at will the pastoral downs
Trackless and smooth, or paced the bare white roads
Lengthening in solitude their dreary line,
Time with his retinue of ages fled
Backwards, nor checked his flight until I saw
Our dim ancestral Past in vision clear;   320

---

   [3] Salisbury Plain is the location of Stonehenge and other
ancient stone monuments of mysterious religious significance.

Saw multitudes of men, and, here and there,
A single Briton clothed in wolf-skin vest,
With shield and stone-axe, stride across the wold;
The voice of spears was heard, the rattling spear
Shaken by arms of mighty bone, in strength,
Long mouldered, of barbaric majesty.
I called on Darkness—but before the word
Was uttered, midnight darkness seemed to take
All objects from my sight; and lo! again
The Desert visible by dismal flames;   330
It is the sacrificial altar, fed
With living men—how deep the groans! the voice
Of those that crowd the giant wicker thrills
The monumental hillocks, and the pomp
Is for both worlds, the living and the dead.
At other moments (for through that wide waste
Three summer days I roamed) where'er the Plain
Was figured o'er with circles, lines, or mounds,
That yet survive, a work, as some divine,
Shaped by the Druids, so to represent   340
Their knowledge of the heavens, and image forth
The constellations; gently was I charmed
Into a waking dream, a reverie
That, with believing eyes, where'er I turned,
Beheld long-bearded teachers, with white wands
Uplifted, pointing to the starry sky,
Alternately, and plain below, while breath
Of music swayed their motions, and the waste
Rejoiced with them and me in those sweet sounds.

This for the past, and things that may be viewed
Or fancied in the obscurity of years   351
From monumental hints: and thou, O Friend!
Pleased with some unpremeditated strains
That served those wanderings to beguile, hast said
That then and there my mind had exercised
Upon the vulgar forms of present things,
The actual world of our familiar days,
Yet higher power; had caught from them a tone,
An image, and a character, by books
Not hitherto reflected. Call we this   360
A partial judgment—and yet why? for *then*
We were as strangers; and I may not speak
Thus wrongfully of verse, however rude,
Which on thy young imagination, trained
In the great City, broke like light from far.
Moreover, each man's Mind is to herself
Witness and judge; and I remember well
That in life's every-day appearances
I seemed about this time to gain clear sight
Of a new world—a world, too, that was fit   370
To be transmitted, and to other eyes
Made visible; as ruled by those fixed laws
Whence spiritual dignity originates,

Which do both give it being and maintain
A balance, an ennobling interchange
Of action from without and from within;
The excellence, pure function, and best power
Both of the object seen, and eye that sees.

BOOK FOURTEENTH
CONCLUSION

IN one of those excursions (may they ne'er
Fade from remembrance!) through the Northern
    tracts
Of Cambria ranging with a youthful friend,
I left Bethgelert's huts at couching-time,
And westward took my way, to see the sun
Rise from the top of Snowdon.[1] To the door
Of a rude cottage at the mountain's base
We came, and roused the shepherd who attends
The adventurous stranger's steps, a trusty guide;
Then, cheered by short refreshment, sallied forth.   10

It was a close, warm, breezeless summer night,
Wan, dull, and glaring, with a dripping fog
Low-hung and thick that covered all the sky;
But, undiscouraged, we began to climb
The mountain-side. The mist soon girt us round,
And, after ordinary travellers' talk
With our conductor, pensively we sank
Each into commerce with his private thoughts:
Thus did we breast the ascent, and by myself
Was nothing either seen or heard that checked   20
Those musings or diverted, save that once
The shepherd's lurcher, who, among the crags,
Had to his joy unearthed a hedgehog, teased
His coiled-up prey with barkings turbulent.
This small adventure, for even such it seemed
In that wild place and at the dead of night,
Being over and forgotten, on we wound
In silence as before. With forehead bent
Earthward, as if in opposition set
Against an enemy, I panted up   30
With eager pace, and no less eager thoughts.
Thus might we wear a midnight hour away,
Ascending at loose distance each from each,
And I, as chanced, the foremost of the band;
When at my feet the ground appeared to brighten,
And with a step or two seemed brighter still;
Nor was time given to ask or learn the cause,

[1] Snowdon is the highest mountain in Wales (Cambria).
Wordsworth and Robert Jones climbed it in the summer of
1791.

For instantly a light upon the turf
Fell like a flash, and lo! as I looked up,
The Moon hung naked in a firmament 40
Of azure without cloud, and at my feet
Rested a silent sea of hoary mist.
A hundred hills their dusky backs upheaved
All over this still ocean; and beyond,
Far, far beyond, the solid vapours stretched,
In headlands, tongues, and promontory shapes,
Into the main Atlantic, that appeared
To dwindle, and give up his majesty,
Usurped upon far as the sight could reach.
Not so the ethereal vault; encroachment none 50
Was there, nor loss; only the inferior stars
Had disappeared, or shed a fainter light
In the clear presence of the full-orbed Moon,
Who, from her sovereign elevation, gazed
Upon the billowy ocean, as it lay
All meek and silent, save that through a rift—
Not distant from the shore whereon we stood,
A fixed, abysmal, gloomy, breathing-place—
Mounted the roar of waters, torrents, streams
Innumerable, roaring with one voice! 60
Heard over earth and sea, and, in that hour,
For so it seemed, felt by the starry heavens.

When into air had partially dissolved
That vision, given to spirits of the night
And three chance human wanderers, in calm thought
Reflected, it appeared to me the type
Of a majestic intellect, its acts
And its possessions, what it has and craves,
What in itself it is, and would become.
There I beheld the emblem of a mind 70
That feeds upon infinity, that broods
Over the dark abyss, intent to hear
Its voices issuing forth to silent light
In one continuous stream; a mind sustained
By recognitions of transcendent power,
In sense conducting to ideal form,
In soul of more than mortal privilege.
One function, above all, of such a mind
Had Nature shadowed there, by putting forth,
'Mid circumstances awful and sublime, 80
That mutual domination which she loves
To exert upon the face of outward things,
So moulded, joined, abstracted, so endowed
With interchangeable supremacy,
That men, least sensitive, see, hear, perceive,
And cannot choose but feel. The power, which all
Acknowledge when thus moved, which Nature thus
To bodily sense exhibits, is the express
Resemblance of that glorious faculty
That higher minds bear with them as their own. 90

This is the very spirit in which they deal
With the whole compass of the universe:
They from their native selves can send abroad
Kindred mutations; for themselves create
A like existence; and, whene'er it dawns
Created for them, catch it, or are caught
By its inevitable mastery,
Like angels stopped upon the wing by sound
Of harmony from Heaven's remotest spheres.
Them the enduring and the transient both 100
Serve to exalt; they build up greatest things
From least suggestions; ever on the watch,
Willing to work and to be wrought upon,
They need not extraordinary calls
To rouse them; in a world of life they live,
By sensible impressions not enthralled,
But by their quickening impulse made more prompt
To hold fit converse with the spiritual world,
And with the generations of mankind
Spread over time, past, present, and to come, 110
Age after age, till Time shall be no more.
Such minds are truly from the Deity,
For they are Powers; and hence the highest bliss
That flesh can know is theirs—the consciousness
Of Whom they are, habitually infused
Through every image and through every thought,
And all affections by communion raised
From earth to heaven, from human to divine;
Hence endless occupation for the Soul,
Whether discursive or intuitive; 120
Hence cheerfulness for acts of daily life,
Emotions which best foresight need not fear,
Most worthy then of trust when most intense.
Hence, amid ills that vex and wrongs that crush
Our hearts—if here the words of Holy Writ
May with fit reverence be applied—that peace
Which passeth understanding, that repose
In moral judgments which from this pure source
Must come, or will by man be sought in vain.

Oh! who is he that hath his whole life long 130
Preserved, enlarged, this freedom in himself?
For this alone is genuine liberty:
Where is the favoured being who hath held
That course unchecked, unerring, and untired,
In one perpetual progress smooth and bright?—
A humbler destiny have we retraced,
And told of lapse and hesitating choice,
And backward wanderings along thorny ways:
Yet—compassed round by mountain solitudes,
Within whose solemn temple I received 140
My earliest visitations, careless then
Of what was given me; and which now I range,
A meditative, oft a suffering man—

Do I declare—in accents which, from truth
Deriving cheerful confidence, shall blend
Their modulation with these vocal streams—
That, whatsoever falls my better mind,
Revolving with the accidents of life,
May have sustained, that, howsoe'er misled,
Never did I, in quest of right and wrong,   150
Tamper with conscience from a private aim;
Nor was in any public hope the dupe
Of selfish passions; nor did ever yield
Wilfully to mean cares or low pursuits,
But shrunk with apprehensive jealousy
From every combination which might aid
The tendency, too potent in itself,
Of use and custom to bow down the soul
Under a growing weight of vulgar sense,
And substitute a universe of death   ·   160
For that which moves with light and life informed,
Actual, divine, and true. To fear and love,
To love as prime and chief, for there fear ends,
Be this ascribed; to early intercourse,
In presence of sublime or beautiful forms,
With the adverse principles of pain and joy—
Evil as one is rashly named by men
Who know not what they speak. By love subsists
All lasting grandeur, by pervading love;
That gone, we are as dust.—Behold the fields   170
In balmy spring-time full of rising flowers
And joyous creatures; see that pair, the lamb
And the lamb's mother, and their tender ways
Shall touch thee to the heart; thou callest this love,
And not inaptly so, for love it is,
Far as it carries thee. In some green bower
Rest, and be not alone, but have thou there
The One who is thy choice of all the world:
There linger, listening, gazing, with delight
Impassioned, but delight how pitiable!   180
Unless this love by a still higher love
Be hallowed, love that breathes not without awe;
Love that adores, but on the knees of prayer,
By heaven inspired; that frees from chains the soul,
Bearing, in union with the purest, best,
Of earth-born passions, on the wings of praise
A mutual tribute to the Almighty's Throne.

    This spiritual Love acts not nor can exist
Without Imagination, which, in truth,
Is but another name for absolute power   190
And clearest insight, amplitude of mind,
And Reason in her most exalted mood.
This faculty hath been the feeding source
Of our long labour: we have traced the stream
From the blind cavern whence is faintly heard
Its natal murmur; followed it to light

And open day; accompanied its course
Among the ways of Nature, for a time
Lost sight of it bewildered and engulphed:
Then given it greeting as it rose once more   200
In strength, reflecting from its placid breast
The works of man and face of human life;
And lastly, from its progress have we drawn
Faith in life endless, the sustaining thought
Of human Being, Eternity, and God.

    Imagination having been our theme,
So also hath that intellectual Love,
For they are each in each, and cannot stand
Dividually.—Here must thou be, O Man!
Power to thyself; no Helper has thou here;   210
Here keepest thou in singleness thy state:
No other can divide with thee this work:
No secondary hand can intervene
To fashion this ability; 'tis thine,
The prime and vital principle is thine
In the recesses of thy nature, far
From any reach of outward fellowship,
Else is not thine at all. But joy to him,
Oh, joy to him who here hath sown, hath laid
Here, the foundation of his future years!   220
For all that friendship, all that love can do,
All that a darling countenance can look
Or dear voice utter, to complete the man,
Perfect him, made imperfect in himself,
All shall be his: and he whose soul hath risen
Up to the height of feeling intellect
Shall want no humbler tenderness; his heart
Be tender as a nursing mother's heart;
Of female softness shall his life be full,
Of humble cares and delicate desires,   230
Mild interests and gentlest sympathies.

    Child of my parents! Sister of my soul!
Thanks in sincerest verse have been elsewhere
Poured out for all the early tenderness
Which I from thee imbibed: and 'tis most true
That later seasons owed to thee no less;
For, spite of thy sweet influence and the touch
Of kindred hands that opened out the springs
Of genial thought in childhood, and in spite
Of all that unassisted I had marked   240
In life or nature of those charms minute
That win their way into the heart by stealth,
Still to the very going-out of youth,
I too exclusively esteemed *that* love,
And sought *that* beauty, which, as Milton sings,[2]
Hath terror in it. Thou didst soften down

[2] *Paradise Lost*, IX, 489–91.

This over-sternness; but for thee, dear Friend!
My soul, too reckless of mild grace, had stood
In her original self too confident,
Retained too long a countenance severe;   250
A rock with torrents roaring, with the clouds
Familiar, and a favourite of the stars:
But thou didst plant its crevices with flowers,
Hang it with shrubs that twinkle in the breeze,
And teach the little birds to build their nests
And warble in its chambers. At a time
When Nature, destined to remain so long
Foremost in my affections, had fallen back
Into a second place, pleased to become
A handmaid to a nobler than herself,   260
When every day brought with it some new sense
Of exquisite regard for common things,
And all the earth was budding with these gifts
Of more refined humanity, thy breath,
Dear Sister! was a kind of gentler spring
That went before my steps. Thereafter came
One whom with thee friendship had early paired; [3]
She came, no more a phantom to adorn
A moment, but an inmate of the heart,
And yet a spirit, there for me enshrined   270
To penetrate the lofty and the low;
Even as one essence of pervading light
Shines in the brightest of ten thousand stars,
And the meek worm that feeds her lonely lamp
Couched in the dewy grass.
                        With such a theme,
Coleridge! with this my argument, of thee
Shall I be silent? O capacious Soul!
Placed on this earth to love and understand,
And from thy presence shed the light of love,
Shall I be mute, ere thou be spoken of?   280
Thy kindred influence to my heart of hearts
Did also find its way. Thus fear relaxed
Her overweening grasp; thus thoughts and things
In the self-haunting spirit learned to take
More rational proportions; mystery,
The incumbent mystery of sense and soul,
Of life and death, time and eternity,
Admitted more habitually a mild
Interposition—a serene delight
In closelier gathering cares, such as become   290
A human creature, howsoe'er endowed,
Poet, or destined for a humbler name;
And so the deep enthusiastic joy,
The rapture of the hallelujah sent
From all that breathes and is, was chastened, stemmed
And balanced by pathetic truth, by trust

<hr>

[3] Mary Hutchinson and Dorothy Wordsworth had been
friends during childhood.

In hopeful reason, leaning on the stay
Of Providence; and in reverence for duty,
Here, if need be, struggling with storms, and there
Strewing in peace life's humblest ground with
       herbs,
At every season green, sweet at all hours.   301

    And now, O Friend! this history is brought
To its appointed close: the discipline
And consummation of a Poet's mind,
In everything that stood most prominent,
Have faithfully been pictured; we have reached
The time (our guiding object from the first)
When we may, not presumptuously, I hope,
Suppose my powers so far confirmed, and such
My knowledge, as to make me capable   310
Of building up a Work that shall endure.
Yet much hath been omitted, as need was;
Of books how much! and even of the other wealth
That is collected among woods and fields,
Far more: for Nature's secondary grace
Hath hitherto been barely touched upon,
The charm more superficial that attends
Her works, as they present to Fancy's choice
Apt illustrations of the moral world,
Caught at a glance, or traced with curious pains.   320

    Finally, and above all, O Friend! (I speak
With due regret) how much is overlooked
In human nature and her subtle ways,
As studied first in our own hearts, and then
In life among the passions of mankind,
Varying their composition and their hue,
Where'er we move, under the diverse shapes
That individual character presents
To an attentive eye. For progress meet,
Along this intricate and difficult path,   330
Whate'er was wanting, something had I gained,
As one of many schoolfellows compelled,
In hardy independence, to stand up
Amid conflicting interests, and the shock
Of various tempers; to endure and note
What was not understood, though known to be;
Among the mysteries of love and hate,
Honour and shame, looking to right and left,
Unchecked by innocence too delicate,
And moral notions too intolerant,   340
Sympathies too contracted. Hence, when called
To take a station among men, the step
Was easier, the transition more secure,
More profitable also; for, the mind
Learns from such timely exercise to keep
In wholesome separation the two natures,
The one that feels, the other that observes.

Yet one word more of personal concern—
Since I withdrew unwillingly from France,
I led an undomestic wanderer's life,   350
In London chiefly harboured, whence I roamed,
Tarrying at will in many a pleasant spot
Of rural England's cultivated vales
Or Cambrian solitudes. A youth—(he bore
The name of Calvert—it shall live, if words
Of mine can give it life,) in firm belief
That by endowments not from me withheld
Good might be furthered—in his last decay
Withdrawing, and from kindred whom he loved,
A part of no redundant patrimony   360
By a bequest sufficient for my needs [4]
Enabled me to pause for choice, and walk
At large and unrestrained, nor damped too soon
By mortal cares. Himself no Poet, yet
Far less a common follower of the world,
He deemed that my pursuits and labours lay
Apart from all that leads to wealth, or even
A necessary maintenance insures,
Without some hazard to the finer sense;
He cleared a passage for me, and the stream   370
Flowed in the bent of Nature.
                   Having now
Told what best merits mention, further pains
Our present purpose seems not to require,
And I have other tasks. Recall to mind
The mood in which this labour was begun,
O Friend! The termination of my course
Is nearer now, much nearer; yet even then,
In that distraction and intense desire,
I said unto the life which I had lived,
Where art thou? Hear I not a voice from thee   380
Which 'tis reproach to hear? Anon I rose
As if on wings, and saw beneath me stretched
Vast prospect of the world which I had been
And was; and hence this Song, which like a lark
I have protracted, in the unwearied heavens
Singing, and often with more plaintive voice
To earth attempered and her deep-drawn sighs,
Yet centring all in love, and in the end
All gratulant, if rightly understood.

Whether to me shall be allotted life,   390
And, with life, power to accomplish aught of worth,
That will be deemed no insufficient plea
For having given this story of myself,
Is all uncertain: but, beloved Friend!
When, looking back, thou seest, in clearer view
Than any liveliest sight of yesterday,

That summer, under whose indulgent skies,
Upon smooth Quantock's airy ridge we roved
Unchecked, or loitered 'mid her sylvan coombs,
Thou in bewitching words, with happy heart,   400
Didst chaunt the vision of that Ancient Man,
The bright-eyed Mariner, and rueful woes
Didst utter of the Lady Christabel;
And I, associate with such labour, steeped
In soft forgetfulness the livelong hours,
Murmuring of him who, joyous hap, was found,
After the perils of his moonlight ride,
Near the loud waterfall; or her who sate
In misery near the miserable Thorn;   409
When thou dost to that summer turn thy thoughts, [5]
And hast before thee all which then we were,
To thee, in memory of that happiness,
It will be known, by thee at least, my Friend!
Felt, that the history of a Poet's mind
Is labour not unworthy of regard:
To thee the work shall justify itself.

The last and later portions of this gift
Have been prepared, not with the buoyant spirits
That were our daily portion when we first
Together wantoned in wild Poesy,   420
But, under pressure of a private grief, [6]
Keen and enduring, which the mind and heart,
That in this meditative history
Have been laid open, needs must make me feel
More deeply, yet enable me to bear
More firmly; and a comfort now hath risen
From hope that thou art near, and wilt be soon
Restored to us in renovated health;
When, after the first mingling of our tears,
'Mong other consolations, we may draw   430
Some pleasure from this offering of my love.

Oh! yet a few short years of useful life,
And all will be complete, thy race be run,
Thy monument of glory will be raised;
Then, though (too weak to tread the ways of truth)
This age fall back to old idolatry,
Though men return to servitude as fast
As the tide ebbs, to ignominy and shame
By nations sink together, we shall still   439
Find solace—knowing what we have learnt to know,
Rich in true happiness if allowed to be
Faithful alike in forwarding a day

---

[4] Raisley Calvert, who died in 1795, left Wordsworth a bequest of £900.

[5] Wordsworth refers to the summer of 1798 when he (at Alfoxden) was writing many of the *Lyrical Ballads* and Coleridge nearby in Nether Stowey was working on *The Rime of the Ancient Mariner* and *Christabel*.

[6] The drowning of Wordsworth's brother John in 1805. See *Elegiac Verses* and other poems following.

Of firmer trust, joint labourers in the work
(Should Providence such grace to us vouchsafe)
Of their deliverance, surely yet to come.
Prophets of Nature, we to them will speak
A lasting inspiration, sanctified
By reason, blest by faith: what we have loved,
Others will love, and we will teach them how;
Instruct them how the mind of man becomes   450
A thousand times more beautiful than the earth
On which he dwells, above this frame of things
(Which, 'mid all revolutions in the hopes
And fears of men, doth still remain unchanged)
In beauty exalted, as it is itself
Of quality and fabric more divine.

[1798–1805, 1828–39, etc.]   [1850]

ELEGIAC VERSES

IN MEMORY OF MY BROTHER, JOHN WORDSWORTH

Commander of the E. I. Company's ship, the Earl of
Abergavenny, in which he perished by calamitous ship-
wreck, Feb. 6th, 1805. Composed near the Mountain
track, that leads from Grasmere through Grisdale Hawes,
where it descends towards Patterdale.

I

THE Sheep-boy whistled loud, and lo!
That instant, startled by the shock,
The Buzzard mounted from the rock
Deliberate and slow:
Lord of the air, he took his flight;
Oh! could he on that woeful night
Have lent his wing, my Brother dear,
For one poor moment's space to Thee,
And all who struggled with the Sea,
When safety was so near.   10

II

Thus in the weakness of my heart
I spoke (but let that pang be still)
When rising from the rock at will,
I saw the Bird depart.
And let me calmly bless the Power
That meets me in this unknown Flower,
Affecting type of him I mourn!
With calmness suffer and believe,
And grieve, and know that I must grieve,
Not cheerless, though forlorn.   20

III

Here did we stop; and here looked round
While each into himself descends,
For that last thought of parting Friends
That is not to be found.
Hidden was Grasmere Vale from sight,
Our home and his, his heart's delight,
His quiet heart's selected home.
But time before him melts away,
And he hath feeling of a day
Of blessedness to come.   30

IV

Full soon in sorrow did I weep,
Taught that the mutual hope was dust,
In sorrow, but for higher trust,
How miserably deep!
All vanished in a single word,
A breath, a sound, and scarcely heard.

Sea—Ship—drowned—Shipwreck—so it came,
The meek, the brave, the good, was gone;
He who had been our living John
Was nothing but a name.   40

V

That was indeed a parting! oh,
Glad am I, glad that it is past;
For there were some on whom it cast
Unutterable woe.
But they as well as I have gains;—
From many a humble source, to pains
Like these, there comes a mild release;
Even here I feel it, even this Plant
Is in its beauty ministrant
To comfort and to peace.   50

VI

He would have loved thy modest grace,
Meek Flower! To Him I would have said,
"It grows upon its native bed
Beside our Parting-place;
There, cleaving to the ground, it lies
With multitude of purple eyes,
Spangling a cushion green like moss;
But we will see it, joyful tide!
Some day, to see it in its pride,
The mountain will we cross."   60

VII

—Brother and friend, if verse of mine
Have power to make thy virtues known,
Here let a monumental Stone
Stand—sacred as a Shrine;
And to the few who pass this way,
Traveller or Shepherd, let it say,
Long as these mighty rocks endure,—
Oh do not Thou too fondly brood,
Although deserving of all good,
On any earthly hope, however pure! *   70

[1805]   [1842]

TO THE DAISY

Sweet Flower! belike one day to have
A place upon thy Poet's grave,
I welcome thee once more:
But He, who was on land, at sea,
My Brother, too, in loving thee,
Although he loved more silently,
Sleeps by his native shore.

* The plant alluded to is the Moss Campion (Silene acaulis,
of Linnæus).

Ah! hopeful, hopeful was the day
When to that Ship he bent his way,
To govern and to guide: 10
His wish was gained: a little time
Would bring him back in manhood's prime
And free for life, these hills to climb,
With all his wants supplied.

And full of hope day followed day
While that stout Ship at anchor lay
Beside the shores of Wight;
The May had then made all things green;
And, floating there, in pomp serene,
That Ship was goodly to be seen,   20
His pride and his delight!

Yet then, when called ashore, he sought
The tender peace of rural thought:
In more than happy mood
To your abodes, bright daisy Flowers!
He then would steal at leisure hours,
And loved you glittering in your bowers,
A starry multitude.

But hark the word!—the ship is gone;—
Returns from her long course:—anon   30
Sets sail:—in season due,
Once more on English earth they stand:
But, when a third time from the land
They parted, sorrow was at hand
For Him and for his crew.

Ill-fated Vessel!—ghastly shock!
—At length delivered from the rock,
The deep she hath regained;
And through the stormy night they steer;
Labouring for life, in hope and fear,   40
To reach a safer shore—how near,
Yet not to be attained!

"Silence!" the brave Commander cried;
To that calm word a shriek replied,
It was the last death-shriek.
—A few (my soul oft sees that sight)
Survive upon the tall mast's height;
But one dear remnant of the night—
For Him in vain I seek.

Six weeks beneath the moving sea   50
He lay in slumber quietly;
Unforced by wind or wave
To quit the Ship for which he died,
(All claims of duty satisfied);
And there they found him at her side;
And bore him to the grave.

Vain service! yet not vainly done
For this, if other end were none,
That He, who had been cast
Upon a way of life unmeet   60
For such a gentle Soul and sweet,
Should find an undisturbed retreat
Near what he loved, at last—

That neighbourhood of grove and field
To Him a resting-place should yield,
A meek man and a brave!
The birds shall sing and ocean make
A mournful murmur for *his* sake;
And Thou, sweet Flower, shalt sleep and wake
Upon his senseless grave.   70

[1805]   [1815]

ELEGIAC STANZAS

See Wordsworth's headnote to Elegiac Verses, *above, and his
letter to Richard Wordsworth (February 11, 1805), below.
Peele Castle is on an island in Morecambe Bay, off the Furness
Peninsula in Lancashire. The painting of it done by Words-
worth's friend Sir George Beaumont was used (in line engraving
form) as the frontispiece in several editions of Wordsworth's
Poems.*

ELEGIAC STANZAS

SUGGESTED BY A PICTURE OF
PEELE CASTLE, IN A STORM,
PAINTED BY SIR GEORGE BEAUMONT

I WAS thy neighbour once, thou rugged Pile!
Four summer weeks I dwelt in sight of thee:
I saw thee every day; and all the while
Thy Form was sleeping on a glassy sea.

So pure the sky, so quiet was the air!
So like, so very like, was day to day!
Whene'er I looked, thy Image still was there;
It trembled, but it never passed away.

How perfect was the calm! it seemed no sleep;
No mood, which season takes away, or brings: 10
I could have fancied that the mighty Deep
Was even the gentlest of all gentle Things.

Ah! THEN, if mine had been the Painter's hand,
To express what then I saw; and add the gleam,
The light that never was, on sea or land,
The consecration, and the Poet's dream;

I would have planted thee, thou hoary Pile
Amid a world how different from this!
Beside a sea that could not cease to smile;
On tranquil land, beneath a sky of bliss.   20

Thou shouldst have seemed a treasure-house divine
Of peaceful years; a chronicle of heaven;—
Of all the sunbeams that did ever shine
The very sweetest had to thee been given.

A Picture had it been of lasting ease,
Elysian quiet, without toil or strife;
No motion but the moving tide, a breeze,
Or merely silent Nature's breathing life.

Such, in the fond illusion of my heart,
Such Picture would I at that time have made: 30
And seen the soul of truth in every part,
A stedfast peace that might not be betrayed.

So once it would have been,—'tis so no more;
I have submitted to a new control:
A power is gone, which nothing can restore;
A deep distress hath humanised my Soul.

Not for a moment could I now behold
A smiling sea, and be what I have been:
The feeling of my loss will ne'er be old;
This, which I know, I speak with mind serene.   40

Then, Beaumont, Friend! who would have been the
        Friend,
If he had lived, of Him whom I deplore,
This work of thine I blame not, but commend;
This sea in anger, and that dismal shore.

O 'tis a passionate Work!—yet wise and well,
Well chosen is the spirit that is here;
That Hulk which labours in the deadly swell,
This rueful sky, this pageantry of fear!

And this huge Castle, standing here sublime,
I love to see the look with which it braves,   50
Cased in the unfeeling armour of old time,
The lightning, the fierce wind, and trampling waves.

Farewell, farewell the heart that lives alone,
Housed in a dream, at distance from the Kind!
Such happiness, wherever it be known,
Is to be pitied; for 'tis surely blind.

But welcome fortitude, and patient cheer,
And frequent sights of what is to be borne!
Such sights, or worse, as are before me here.—
Not without hope we suffer and we mourn.   60

[1805]   [1807]

STEPPING WESTWARD

While my Fellow-traveller and I were walking by the side of Loch Ketterine, one fine evening after sunset, in our road to a Hut where, in the course of our Tour, we had been hospitably entertained some weeks before, we met, in one of the loneliest parts of that solitary region, two well-dressed Women, one of whom said to us, by way of greeting, "What, you are stepping westward?"

"*WHAT, you are stepping westward?*"—" *Yea.*"
—'Twould be a *wildish* destiny,
If we, who thus together roam
In a strange Land, and far from home,
Were in this place the guests of Chance:
Yet who would stop, or fear to advance,
Though home or shelter he had none,
With such a sky to lead him on?

The dewy ground was dark and cold;
Behind, all gloomy to behold;   10
And stepping westward seemed to be
A kind of *heavenly* destiny:
I liked the greeting; 'twas a sound
Of something without place or bound;
And seemed to give me spiritual right
To travel through that region bright.

The voice was soft, and she who spake
Was walking by her native lake:
The salutation had to me
The very sound of courtesy: 20
Its power was felt; and while my eye
Was fixed upon the glowing Sky,
The echo of the voice enwrought
A human sweetness with the thought
Of travelling through the world that lay
Before me in my endless way.

[1805]   [1807]

William and Dorothy Wordsworth explain in a note and in her Journals that the following poem was suggested by a sentence of Thomas Wilkinson (in a MS. later published as Tours to the British Mountains*):* "*Passed a female who was reaping alone: she sung in Erse as she bended over her sickle; the sweetest human voice I ever heard: her strains were tenderly melancholy, and felt delicious, long after they were heard no more.*"

THE SOLITARY REAPER

BEHOLD her, single in the field,
Yon solitary Highland Lass!
Reaping and singing by herself;
Stop here, or gently pass!
Alone she cuts and binds the grain,
And sings a melancholy strain;
O listen! for the Vale profound
Is overflowing with the sound.

No Nightingale did ever chaunt
More welcome notes to weary bands   10
Of travellers in some shady haunt,
Among Arabian sands:
A voice so thrilling ne'er was heard
In spring-time from the Cuckoo-bird,
Breaking the silence of the seas
Among the farthest Hebrides.

Will no one tell me what she sings?—
Perhaps the plaintive numbers flow
For old, unhappy, far-off things,
And battles long ago: 20
Or is it some more humble lay,
Familiar matter of to-day?
Some natural sorrow, loss, or pain,
That has been, and may be again?

Whate'er the theme, the Maiden sang
As if her song could have no ending;
I saw her singing at her work,
And o'er the sickle bending:—
I listened, motionless and still;
And, as I mounted up the hill,   30
The music in my heart I bore,
Long after it was heard no more.

[1805]   [1807]

CHARACTER OF THE HAPPY WARRIOR

See Wordsworth's note to Elegiac Verses in Memory of My Brother *and his letter to Richard Wordsworth, 11 February 1805.*

"*The course of the great war with the French naturally fixed one's attention upon the military character, and, to the honour of our country, there were many illustrious instances of the qualities that constitute its highest excellence. Lord Nelson carried most of the virtues that the trials he was exposed to in his department of the service necessarily call forth and sustain . . . I will add, that many elements of the character here pourtrayed were found in my brother John, who perished by shipwreck, as mentioned elsewhere.*" [*Wordsworth to Isabella Fenwick*]

CHARACTER OF THE
HAPPY WARRIOR

WHO is the happy Warrior? Who is he
That every man in arms should wish to be?
—It is the generous Spirit, who, when brought
Among the tasks of real life, hath wrought
Upon the plan that pleased his boyish thought:
Whose high endeavours are an inward light
That makes the path before him always bright:
Who, with a natural instinct to discern
What knowledge can perform, is diligent to learn;
Abides by this resolve, and stops not there,   10
But makes his moral being his prime care;
Who, doomed to go in company with Pain,
And Fear, and Bloodshed, miserable train!
Turns his necessity to glorious gain;
In face of these doth exercise a power
Which is our human nature's highest dower;
Controls them and subdues, transmutes, bereaves
Of their bad influence, and their good receives:
By objects which might force the soul to abate
Her feeling, rendered more compassionate;   20
Is placable—because occasions rise
So often that demand such sacrifice;
More skilful in self-knowledge, even more pure,
As tempted more; more able to endure,
As more exposed to suffering and distress;
Thence, also, more alive to tenderness.
—'Tis he whose law is reason; who depends
Upon that law as on the best of friends;
Whence, in a state where men are tempted still
To evil for a guard against worse ill,   30
And what in quality or act is best
Doth seldom on a right foundation rest,
He labours good on good to fix, and owes
To virtue every triumph that he knows:
—Who, if he rise to station of command,
Rises by open means; and there will stand
On honourable terms, or else retire,

And in himself possess his own desire;
Who comprehends his trust, and to the same
Keeps faithful with a singleness of aim;   40
And therefore does not stoop, nor lie in wait
For wealth, or honours, or for worldly state;
Whom they must follow; on whose head must fall,
Like showers of manna, if they come at all:
Whose powers shed round him in the common strife,
Or mild concerns of ordinary life,
A constant influence, a peculiar grace;
But who, if he be called upon to face
Some awful moment to which Heaven has joined
Great issues, good or bad for human kind,   50
Is happy as a Lover; and attired
With sudden brightness, like a Man inspired;
And, through the heat of conflict, keeps the law
In calmness made, and sees what he foresaw;
Or if an unexpected call succeed,
Come when it will, is equal to the need:
—He who, though thus endued as with a sense
And faculty for storm and turbulence,
Is yet a Soul whose master-bias leans
To homefelt pleasures and to gentle scenes;   60
Sweet images! which, whereso'er he be,
Are at his heart; and such fidelity
It is his darling passion to approve;
More brave for this, that he hath much to love:—
'Tis, finally, the man, who lifted high,
Conspicuous object in a Nation's eye,
Or left unthought-of in obscurity,—
Who, with a toward or untoward lot,
Prosperous or adverse, to his wish or not—
Plays, in the many games of life, that one   70
Where what he most doth value must be won:
Whom neither shape of danger can dismay,
Nor thought of tender happiness betray;
Who, not content that former worth stand fast,
Looks forward, persevering to the last,
From well to better, daily self-surpast:
Who, whether praise of him must walk the earth
For ever, and to noble deeds give birth,
Or he must fall, to sleep without his fame,
And leave a dead unprofitable name—   80
Finds comfort in himself and in his cause;
And, while the mortal mist is gathering, draws
His breath in confidence of Heaven's applause:
This is the happy Warrior; this is He
That every Man in arms should wish to be.

[1805-1806]   [1807]

SONNET

THOUGHT OF A BRITON ON THE SUBJUGATION OF SWITZERLAND[1]

Two Voices are there; one is of the sea,
One of the mountains; each a mighty Voice:
In both from age to age thou didst rejoice,
They were thy chosen music, Liberty!
There came a Tyrant, and with holy glee
Thou fought'st against him; but hast vainly striven:
Thou from thy Alpine holds at length art driven,
Where not a torrent murmurs heard by thee.
Of one deep bliss thine ear hath been bereft:
Then cleave, O cleave to that which still is left;   10
For, high-souled Maid, what sorrow would it be
That Mountain floods should thunder as before,
And Ocean bellow from his rocky shore,
And neither awful Voice be heard by thee!

[1806-1807]   [1807]

"Yes, it was the mountain Echo"

Yes, it was the mountain Echo,
Solitary, clear, profound,
Answering to the shouting Cuckoo,
Giving to her sound for sound!

Unsolicited reply
To a babbling wanderer sent;
Like her ordinary cry,
Like—but oh, how different!

Hears not also mortal Life?
Hear not we, unthinking Creatures!   10
Slaves of folly, love, or strife—
Voices of two different natures?

Have not *we* too?—yes, we have
Answers, and we know not whence;
Echoes from beyond the grave,
Recognised intelligence!

Such rebounds our inward ear
Catches sometimes from afar—
Listen, ponder, hold them dear;
For of God,—of God they are.   20

[1806]   [1807]

───────────────
[1] Switzerland had been under French control since 1802.

SONG AT THE FEAST OF BROUGHAM CASTLE
Henry Lord Clifford, a Lancastrian, was forced by Yorkists to hide out as a shepherd for twenty-four years until Henry VII restored him. The period is that of the War of the Roses (red for Lancaster, white for York), fought to settle the succession of the British monarchy. The castle also appears in The Prelude, *VI, 199 ff., and in* The White Doe of Rylstone, *lines 267–307.*

SONG AT THE FEAST OF BROUGHAM CASTLE

UPON THE RESTORATION OF LORD CLIFFORD, THE SHEPHERD, TO THE ESTATES AND HONOURS OF HIS ANCESTORS

High in the breathless Hall the Minstrel sate,
And Emont's murmur mingled with the Song.—
The words of ancient time I thus translate,
A festal strain that hath been silent long:—

"From town to town, from tower to tower,
  The red rose is a gladsome flower.
Her thirty years of winter past,
The red rose is revived at last;
She lifts her head for endless spring,
For everlasting blossoming: 10
Both roses flourish, red and white:
In love and sisterly delight
The two that were at strife and blended,
And all old troubles now are ended.—
Joy! joy to both! but most to her
Who is the flower of Lancaster!
Behold her how She smiles to-day
On this great throng, this bright array!
Fair greeting doth she send to all
From every corner of the hall;   20
But chiefly from above the board
Where sits in state our rightful Lord,
A Clifford to his own restored!

  "They came with banner, spear, and shield;
And it was proved in Bosworth-field.
Not long the Avenger was withstood—
Earth helped him with the cry of blood:
St. George was for us, and the might
Of blessed Angels crowned the right.
Loud voice the Land has uttered forth,   30
We loudest in the faithful north:
Our fields rejoice, our mountains ring,
Our streams proclaim a welcoming;
Our strong-abodes and castles see
The glory of their loyalty.

"How glad is Skipton at this hour—
Though lonely, a deserted Tower;
Knight, squire, and yeoman, page and groom:
We have them at the feast of Brough'm.
How glad Pendragon—though the sleep   40
Of years be on her!—She shall reap
A taste of this great pleasure, viewing
As in a dream her own renewing.
Rejoiced is Brough, right glad, I deem,
Beside her little humble stream;
And she that keepeth watch and ward
Her statelier Eden's course to guard;
They both are happy at this hour,
Though each is but a lonely Tower:—
But here is perfect joy and pride   50
For one fair House by Emont's side,
This day, distinguished without peer,
To see her Master and to cheer—
Him, and his Lady-mother dear!

      "Oh! it was a time forlorn
When the fatherless was born—
Give her wings that she may fly,
Or she sees her infant die!
Swords that are with slaughter wild
Hunt the Mother and the Child.   60
Who will take them from the light?
—Yonder is a man in sight—
Yonder is a house—but where?
No, they must not enter there.
To the caves, and to the brooks,
To the clouds of heaven she looks;
She is speechless, but her eyes
Pray in ghostly agonies.
Blissful Mary, Mother mild,
Maid and Mother undefiled,   70
Save a Mother and her Child!

      "Now Who is he that bounds with joy
On Carrock's side, a Shepherd-boy?
No thoughts hath he but thoughts that pass
Light as the wind along the grass.
Can this be He who hither came
In secret, like a smothered flame?
O'er whom such thankful tears were shed
For shelter, and a poor man's bread!
God loves the Child; and God hath willed   80
That those dear words should be fulfilled,
The Lady's words, when forced away
The last she to her Babe did say:
'My own, my own, thy Fellow-guest
I may not be; but rest thee, rest,
For lowly shepherd's life is best!'

      "Alas! when evil men are strong
No life is good, no pleasure long.
The Boy must part from Mosedale's groves,
And leave Blencathara's rugged coves,   90
And quit the flowers that summer brings
To Glenderamakin's lofty springs;
Must vanish, and his careless cheer
Be turned to heaviness and fear.
—Give Sir Lancelot Threlkeld praise!
Hear it, good man, old in days!
Thou tree of covert and of rest
For this young Bird that is distrest;
Among thy branches safe he lay,
And he was free to sport and play,   100
When falcons were abroad for prey.

      "A recreant harp, that sings of fear
And heaviness in Clifford's ear!
I said, when evil men are strong,
No life is good, no pleasure long,
A weak and cowardly untruth!
Our Clifford was a happy Youth,
And thankful through a weary time,
That brought him up to manhood's prime.
—Again he wanders forth at will,   110
And tends a flock from hill to hill:
His garb is humble; ne'er was seen
Such garb with such a noble mien;
Among the shepherd-grooms no mate
Hath he, a Child of strength and state!
Yet lacks not friends for simple glee,
Nor yet for higher sympathy.
To his side the fallow-deer
Came, and rested without fear;
The eagle, lord of land and sea,   120
Stooped down to pay him fealty;
And both the undying fish that swim
Through Bowscale-tarn did wait on him;
The pair were servants of his eye
In their immortality;
And glancing, gleaming, dark or bright,
Moved to and fro, for his delight.
He knew the rocks which Angels haunt
Upon the mountains visitant;
He hath kenned them taking wing: 130
And into caves where Faeries sing
He hath entered; and been told
By Voices how men lived of old.
Among the heavens his eye can see
The face of thing that is to be;
And, if that men report him right,
His tongue could whisper words of might.
—Now another day is come,
Fitter hope, and nobler doom;

He hath thrown aside his crook, 140
And hath buried deep his book;
Armour rusting in his halls
On the blood of Clifford calls;—
'Quell the Scot,' exclaims the Lance—
Bear me to the heart of France,
Is the longing of the Shield—
Tell thy name, thou trembling Field;
Field of death, where'er thou be,
Groan thou with our victory!
Happy day, and mighty hour, 150
When our Shepherd in his power,
Mailed and horsed, with lance and sword,
To his ancestors restored
Like a re-appearing Star,
Like a glory from afar,
First shall head the flock of war!"

Alas! the impassioned minstrel did not know
How, by Heaven's grace, this Clifford's heart was
       framed:
How he, long forced in humble walks to go,
Was softened into feeling, soothed, and tamed. 160

Love had he found in huts where poor men lie;
His daily teachers had been woods and rills,
The silence that is in the starry sky,
The sleep that is among the lonely hills.

In him the savage virtue of the Race,
Revenge, and all ferocious thoughts were dead:
Nor did he change; but kept in lofty place
The wisdom which adversity had bred.

Glad were the vales, and every cottage-hearth;
The Shepherd-lord was honoured more and more;
And, ages after he was laid in earth, 171
"The good Lord Clifford" was the name he bore.

[1807]   [1807]

Is it a mirror?—or the nether Sphere
Opening to view the abyss in which she feeds 10
Her own calm fires?—But list! a voice is near;
Great Pan himself low-whispering through the reeds,
"Be thankful, thou; for, if unholy deeds
Ravage the world, tranquillity is here!"

[1807]   [1819]

SONNET

COMPOSED BY THE SIDE OF GRASMERE LAKE

CLOUDS, lingering yet, extend in solid bars
Through the grey west; and lo! these waters, steeled
By breezeless air to smoothest polish, yield
A vivid repetition of the stars;
Jove, Venus, and the ruddy crest of Mars
Amid his fellows beauteously revealed
At happy distance from earth's groaning field,
Where ruthless mortals wage incessant wars.

THE WHITE DOE
OF RYLSTONE;

OR,

THE FATE OF THE NORTONS

⊷◦◉◦⊶

ADVERTISEMENT

DURING the Summer of 1807 I visited, for the
first time, the beautiful country that surrounds
Bolton Priory in Yorkshire; and the Poem of the
WHITE DOE, founded upon a Tradition con-
nected with that place, was composed at the close of
the same year.[1]

⊷◦◉◦⊶

DEDICATION

IN trellised shed with clustering roses gay,
And, MARY! oft beside our blazing fire,
When years of wedded life were as a day
Whose current answers to the heart's desire,
Did we together read in Spenser's Lay
How Una, sad of soul—in sad attire,
The gentle Una, of celestial birth,
To seek her Knight went wandering o'er the earth.

Ah, then, Belovèd! pleasing was the smart,
And the tear precious in compassion shed   10
For Her, who, pierced by sorrow's thrilling dart,
Did meekly bear the pang unmerited;
Meek as that emblem of her lowly heart
The milk-white Lamb which in a line she led,—
And faithful, loyal in her innocence,
Like the brave Lion slain in her defence.

---

[1] The Advertisement appeared in the original (separate)
edition of 1815; when Wordsworth reprinted the poem in the
collective edition of 1820, he replaced it with the following more
comprehensive headnote:

The Poem of the White Doe of Rylstone is founded on a
local tradition, and on the Ballad in Percy's Collection, entitled
"The Rising of the North." The tradition is as follows:—
'About this time,' not long after the Dissolution, 'a White Doe,'
say the aged people of the neighbourhood, 'long continued
to make a weekly pilgrimage from Rylstone over the fells of
Bolton, and was constantly found in the Abbey Church-yard
during divine service; after the close of which she returned
home as regularly as the rest of the congregation.'—Dr.
[Thomas Dunham] Whitaker's HISTORY [and Antiquities]
OF THE DEANERY OF CRAVEN [1805].—Rylstone was the
property and residence of the Nortons, distinguished in that
ill-advised and unfortunate Insurrection; which led me to
connect with this tradition the principal circumstances of their
fate, as recorded in the Ballad.

Notes could we hear as of a faery shell
Attuned to words with sacred wisdom fraught;
Free Fancy prized each specious miracle,
And all its finer inspiration caught;   20
Till in the bosom of our rustic Cell,
We by a lamentable change were taught
That "bliss with mortal Man may not abide:"
How nearly joy and sorrow are allied!

For us the stream of fiction ceased to flow,
For us the voice of melody was mute.
—But, as soft gales dissolve the dreary snow,
And give the timid herbage leave to shoot,
Heaven's breathing influence failed not to
          bestow
A timely promise of unlooked-for fruit,   30
Fair fruit of pleasure and serene content
From blossoms wild of fancies innocent.

It soothed us—it beguiled us—then, to hear
Once more of troubles wrought by magic spell;
And griefs whose aery motion comes not near
The pangs that tempt the Spirit to rebel:
Then, with mild Una in her sober cheer,
High over hill and low adown the dell
Again we wandered, willing to partake
All that she suffered for her dear Lord's sake.   40

Then, too, this Song *of mine* once more could
          please,
Where anguish, strange as dreams of restless sleep,
Is tempered and allayed by sympathies
Aloft ascending, and descending deep,
Even to the inferior Kinds; whom forest-trees
Protect from beating sunbeams, and the sweep
Of the sharp winds;—fair Creatures!—to whom
          Heaven
A calm and sinless life, with love, hath given.

This tragic Story cheered us; for it speaks
Of female patience winning firm repose;   50
And, of the recompense that conscience seeks,
A bright, encouraging, example shows;
Needful when o'er wide realms the tempest
          breaks,
Needful amid life's ordinary woes;—
Hence, not for them unfitted who would bless
A happy hour with holier happiness.

He serves the Muses erringly and ill,
Whose aim is pleasure light and fugitive:
O, that my mind were equal to fulfil
The comprehensive mandate which they give—   60

Vain aspiration of an earnest will!
Yet in this moral Strain a power may live,
Belovèd Wife! such solace to impart
As it hath yielded to thy tender heart.

RYDAL MOUNT, WESTMORELAND,
April 20, 1815.

——◦◉◦——

    "Action is transitory—a step, a blow,
    The motion of a muscle—this way or that—
    'Tis done; and in the after-vacancy
    We wonder at ourselves like men betrayed:
    Suffering is permanent, obscure and dark,
    And has the nature of infinity.
    Yet through that darkness (infinite though it seem
    And irremoveable) gracious openings lie,
    By which the soul—with patient steps of thought
    Now toiling, wafted now on wings of prayer—
    May pass in hope, and, though from mortal bonds
    Yet undelivered, rise with sure ascent
    Even to the fountain-head of peace divine."

    "They that deny a God destroy Man's nobility: for
certainly Man is of kinn to the Beast by his Body, and
if he be not of kinn to God by his Spirit, he is a base
ignoble Creature. It destroys likewise Magnanimity,
and the raising of humane Nature: for take an example
of a Dog, and mark what a generosity and courage he
will put on, when he finds himself maintained by a
Man, who to him is instead of a God, or Melior Natura.
Which courage is manifestly such, as that Creature
without that confidence of a better Nature than his
own could never attain. So Man, when he resteth and
assureth himself upon Divine protection and favour,
gathereth a force and faith which human Nature in
itself could not obtain."   LORD BACON.

——◦◉◦——

CANTO FIRST

FROM Bolton's old monastic tower
The bells ring loud with gladsome power;
The sun shines bright; the fields are gay
With people in their best array
Of stole and doublet, hood and scarf,
Along the banks of crystal Wharf,
Through the Vale retired and lowly,
Trooping to that summons holy.
And, up among the moorlands, see
What sprinklings of blithe company!   10
Of lasses and of shepherd grooms,
That down the steep hills force their way,
Like cattle through the budded brooms;
Path, or no path, what care they?
And thus in joyous mood they hie
To Bolton's mouldering Priory.

What would they there?—full fifty
    years
That sumptuous Pile, with all its peers,
Too harshly hath been doomed to taste
The bitterness of wrong and waste: 20
Its courts are ravaged; but the tower
Is standing with a voice of power,
That ancient voice which wont to call
To mass or some high festival;
And in the shattered fabric's heart
Remaineth one protected part;
A Chapel, like a wild-bird's nest,
Closely embowered and trimly drest;
And thither young and old repair,
This Sabbath-day, for praise and prayer.   30

    Fast the church-yard fills;—anon
Look again, and they all are gone;
The cluster round the porch, and the folk
Who sate in the shade of the Prior's Oak!
And scarcely have they disappeared
Ere the prelusive hymn is heard:—
With one consent the people rejoice,
Filling the church with a lofty voice!
They sing a service which they feel:
For 'tis the sunrise now of zeal;   40
Of a pure faith the vernal prime—
In great Eliza's golden time.

    A moment ends the fervent din,
And all is hushed, without and within;
For though the priest, more tranquilly,
Recites the holy liturgy,
The only voice which you can hear
Is the river murmuring near.
—When soft!—the dusky trees between,
And down the path through the open green,   50
Where is no living thing to be seen;
And through yon gateway, where is found,
Beneath the arch with ivy bound,
Free entrance to the church-yard ground—
Comes gliding in with lovely gleam,
Comes gliding in serene and slow,
Soft and silent as a dream,
A solitary Doe!
White she is as lily of June,
And beauteous as the silver moon   60
When out of sight the clouds are driven
And she is left alone in heaven;
Or like a ship some gentle day
In sunshine sailing far away,
A glittering ship, that hath the plain
Of ocean for her own domain.

Lie silent in your graves, ye dead!
Lie quiet in your church-yard bed!
Ye living, tend your holy cares;
Ye multitude, pursue your prayers;   70
And blame not me if my heart and sight
Are occupied with one delight!
'Tis a work for sabbath hours
If I with this bright Creature go:
Whether she be of forest bowers,
From the bowers of earth below;
Or a Spirit for one day given,
A pledge of grace from purest heaven.

What harmonious pensive changes
Wait upon her as she ranges   80
Round and through this Pile of state
Overthrown and desolate!
Now a step or two her way
Leads through space of open day,
Where the enamoured sunny light
Brightens her that was so bright;
Now doth a delicate shadow fall,
Falls upon her like a breath,
From some lofty arch or wall,
As she passes underneath: 90
Now some gloomy nook partakes
Of the glory that she makes,—
High-ribbed vault of stone, or cell,
With perfect cunning framed as well
Of stone, and ivy, and the spread
Of the elder's bushy head;
Some jealous and forbidding cell,
That doth the living stars repel,
And where no flower hath leave to dwell.

The presence of this wandering Doe   100
Fills many a damp obscure recess
With lustre of a saintly show;
And, reappearing, she no less
Sheds on the flowers that round her blow
A more than sunny liveliness.
But say, among these holy places,
Which thus assiduously she paces,
Comes she with a votary's task,
Rite to perform, or boon to ask?
Fair Pilgrim! harbours she a sense   110
Of sorrow, or of reverence?
Can she be grieved for quire or shrine,
Crushed as if by wrath divine?
For what survives of house where God
Was worshipped, or where Man abode;
For old magnificence undone;
Or for the gentler work begun
By Nature, softening and concealing,

And busy with a hand of healing?
Mourns she for lordly chamber's hearth   120
That to the sapling ash gives birth;
For dormitory's length laid bare
Where the wild rose blossoms fair;
Or altar, whence the cross was rent,
Now rich with mossy ornament?
—She sees a warrior carved in stone,
Among the thick weeds, stretched alone;
A warrior, with his shield of pride
Cleaving humbly to his side,
And hands in resignation prest,   130
Palm to palm, on his tranquil breast;
As little she regards the sight
As a common creature might:
If she be doomed to inward care,
Or service, it must lie elsewhere.
—But hers are eyes serenely bright,
And on she moves—with pace how
    light!
Nor spares to stoop her head, and taste
The dewy turf with flowers bestrown;
And thus she fares, until at last   140
Beside the ridge of a grassy grave
In quietness she lays her down;
Gentle as a weary wave
Sinks, when the summer breeze hath
    died,
Against an anchored vessel's side;
Even so, without distress, doth she
Lie down in peace, and lovingly.

The day is placid in its going,
To a lingering motion bound,
Like the crystal stream now flowing   150
With its softest summer sound:
So the balmy minutes pass,
While this radiant Creature lies
Couched upon the dewy grass,
Pensively with downcast eyes.
—But now again the people raise
With awful cheer a voice of praise;
It is the last, the parting song;
And from the temple forth they throng,
And quickly spread themselves abroad,   160
While each pursues his several road.
But some—a variegated band
Of middle-aged, and old, and young,
And little children by the hand
Upon their leading mothers hung—
With mute obeisance gladly paid
Turn towards the spot where, full in view,
The white Doe, to her service true,
Her sabbath couch has made.

It was a solitary mound; 170
Which two spears' length of level ground
Did from all other graves divide:
As if in some respect of pride;
Or melancholy's sickly mood,
Still shy of human neighbourhood;
Or guilt, that humbly would express
A penitential loneliness.

"Look, there she is, my Child! draw near;
She fears not, wherefore, should we fear?
She means no harm;"—but still the Boy, 180
To whom the words were softly said,
Hung back, and smiled, and blushed for joy,
A shame-faced blush of glowing red!
Again the Mother whispered low,
"Now you have seen the famous Doe;
From Rylstone she hath found her way
Over the hills this sabbath day;
Her work, whate'er it be, is done,
And she will depart when we are gone;
Thus doth she keep, from year to year, 190
Her sabbath morning, foul or fair."

Bright was the Creature, as in dreams
The Boy had seen her, yea, more bright;
But is she truly what she seems?
He asks with insecure delight,
Asks of himself, and doubts,—and still
The doubt returns against his will:
Though he, and all the standers-by,
Could tell a tragic history
Of facts divulged, wherein appear 200
Substantial motive, reason clear,
Why thus the milk-white Doe is found
Couchant beside that lonely mound;
And why she duly loves to pace
The circuit of this hallowed place.
Nor to the Child's enquiring mind
Is such perplexity confined:
For, spite of sober Truth that sees
A world of fixed remembrances
Which to this mystery belong, 210
If, undeceived, my skill can trace
The characters of every face,
There lack not strange delusion here,
Conjecture vague, and idle fear,
And superstitious fancies strong,
Which do the gentle Creature wrong.

That bearded, staff-supported Sire—
Who in his boyhood often fed
Full cheerily on convent-bread
And heard old tales by the convent-fire, 220

And to his grave will go with scars,
Relics of long and distant wars—
That Old Man, studious to expound
The spectacle, is mounting high
To days of dim antiquity;
When Lady Aäliza mourned
Her Son, and felt in her despair
The pang of unavailing prayer;
Her Son in Wharf's abysses drowned,
The noble Boy of Egremound. 230
From which affliction—when the grace
Of God had in her heart found place—
A pious structure, fair to see,
Rose up, this stately Priory!
The Lady's work;—but now laid low;
To the grief of her soul that doth come and go,
In the beautiful form of this innocent Doe;
Which, though seemingly doomed in its breast
  to sustain
A softened remembrance of sorrow and pain,
Is spotless, and holy, and gentle, and bright; 240
And glides o'er the earth like an angel of light.

Pass, pass who will, yon chantry door;
And, through the chink in the fractured floor
Look down, and see a griesly sight;
A vault where the bodies are buried upright!
There, face by face, and hand by hand,
The Claphams and Mauleverers stand;
And, in his place, among son and sire,
Is John de Clapham, that fierce Esquire,
A valiant man, and a name of dread 250
In the ruthless wars of the White and Red;
Who dragged Earl Pembroke from Banbury
  church
And smote off his head on the stones of the porch!
Look down among them, if you dare;
Oft does the White Doe loiter there,
Prying into the darksome rent;
Nor can it be with good intent:
So thinks that Dame of haughty air,
Who hath a Page her book to hold,
And wears a frontlet edged with gold. 260
Harsh thoughts with her high mood agree—
Who counts among her ancestry
Earl Pembroke, slain so impiously!

That slender Youth, a scholar pale,
From Oxford come to his native vale,
He also hath his own conceit:
It is, thinks he, the gracious Fairy,
Who loved the Shepherd-lord to meet [1]

---

[1] See *Song at the Feast of Brougham Castle*, p. 363.

In his wanderings solitary:
Wild notes she in his hearing sang,   270
A song of Nature's hidden powers;
That whistled like the wind, and rang
Among the rocks and holly bowers.
'Twas said that She all shapes could wear;
And oftentimes before him stood,
Amid the trees of some thick wood,
In semblance of a lady fair;
And taught him signs, and showed him sights,
In Craven's dens, on Cumbrian heights;
When under cloud of fear he lay,   280
A shepherd clad in homely grey;
Nor left him at his later day.
And hence, when he, with spear and shield,
Rode full of years to Flodden-field,
His eye could see the hidden spring,
And how the current was to flow;
The fatal end of Scotland's King,
And all that hopeless overthrow.
But not in wars did he delight,
This Clifford wished for worthier might;   290
Nor in broad pomp, or courtly state;
Him his own thoughts did elevate,—
Most happy in the shy recess
Of Barden's lowly quietness.
And choice of studious friends had he
Of Bolton's dear fraternity;
Who, standing on this old church tower,
In many a calm propitious hour,
Perused, with him, the starry sky;
Or, in their cells, with him did pry   300
For other lore,—by keen desire
Urged to close toil with chemic fire;
In quest belike of transmutations
Rich as the mine's most bright creations.
But they and their good works are fled,
And all is now disquieted—
And peace is none, for living or dead!

Ah, pensive Scholar, think not so,
But look again at the radiant Doe!
What quiet watch she seems to keep,   310
Alone, beside that grassy heap!
Why mention other thoughts unmeet
For vision so composed and sweet?
While stand the people in a ring,
Gazing, doubting, questioning;
Yea, many overcome in spite
Of recollections clear and bright;
Which yet do unto some impart
An undisturbed repose of heart.
And all the assembly own a law   320
Of orderly respect and awe;

But see—they vanish one by one,
And last, the Doe herself is gone.

Harp! we have been full long beguiled
By vague thoughts, lured by fancies wild;
To which, with no reluctant strings,
Thou hast attuned thy murmurings;
And now before this Pile we stand
In solitude, and utter peace:
But, Harp! thy murmurs may not cease—   330
A Spirit, with his angelic wings,
In soft and breeze-like visitings,
Has touched thee—and a Spirit's hand:
A voice is with us—a command
To chant, in strains of heavenly glory,
A tale of tears, a mortal story!

CANTO SECOND

THE Harp in lowliness obeyed;
And first we sang of the green-wood shade
And a solitary Maid;
Beginning, where the song must end,   340
With her, and with her sylvan Friend;
The Friend, who stood before her sight,
Her only unextinguished light;
Her last companion in a dearth
Of love, upon a hopeless earth.

For She it was—this Maid, who wrought
Meekly, with foreboding thought,
In vermeil colours and in gold
An unblest work; which, standing by,
Her Father did with joy behold,—   350
Exulting in its imagery;
A Banner, fashioned to fulfil
Too perfectly his headstrong will:
For on this Banner had her hand
Embroidered (such her Sire's command)
The sacred Cross; and figured there
The five dear wounds our Lord did bear;
Full soon to be uplifted high,
And float in rueful company!

It was the time when England's Queen   360
Twelve years had reigned, a Sovereign dread;
Nor yet the restless crown had been
Disturbed upon her virgin head;
But now the inly-working North
Was ripe to send its thousands forth,
A potent vassalage, to fight
In Percy's and in Neville's right,

Two Earls fast leagued in discontent,
Who gave their wishes open vent;
And boldly urged a general plea,   370
The rites of ancient piety
To be triumphantly restored,
By the stern justice of the sword![2]
And that same Banner on whose breast
The blameless Lady had exprest
Memorials chosen to give life
And sunshine to a dangerous strife;
That Banner, waiting for the Call,
Stood quietly in Rylstone-hall.

It came; and Francis Norton said,   380
"O Father! rise not in this fray—
The hairs are white upon your head;
Dear Father, hear me when I say
It is for you too late a day!
Bethink you of your own good name:
A just and gracious queen have we,
A pure religion, and the claim
Of peace on our humanity.—
'Tis meet that I endure your scorn;
I am your son, your eldest born;   390
But not for lordship or for land,
My Father, do I clasp your knees;
The Banner touch not, stay your hand,
This multitude of men disband,
And live at home in blameless ease;
For these my brethren's sake, for me;
And, most of all, for Emily!"

Tumultuous noises filled the hall;
And scarcely could the Father hear
That name—pronounced with a dying fall—
The name of his only Daughter dear,   401
As on the banner which stood near
He glanced a look of holy pride,
And his moist eyes were glorified;
Then did he seize the staff, and say:
"Thou, Richard, bear'st thy father's name,
Keep thou this ensign till the day
When I of thee require the same:
Thy place be on my better hand;—
And seven as true as thou, I see,   410
Will cleave to this good cause and me."
He spake, and eight brave sons straightway
All followed him, a gallant band!

Thus, with his sons, when forth he came
The sight was hailed with loud acclaim

And din of arms and minstrelsy,
From all his warlike tenantry,
All horsed and harnessed with him to ride,—
A voice to which the hills replied!

But Francis, in the vacant hall,   420
Stood silent under dreary weight,—
A phantasm, in which roof and wall
Shook, tottered, swam before his sight;
A phantasm like a dream of night!
Thus overwhelmed, and desolate,
He found his way to a postern-gate;
And, when he waked, his languid eye
Was on the calm and silent sky;
With air about him breathing sweet,
And earth's green grass beneath his feet;   430
Nor did he fail ere long to hear
A sound of military cheer,
Faint—but it reached that sheltered spot;
He heard, and it disturbed him not.

There stood he, leaning on a lance
Which he had grasped unknowingly,
Had blindly grasped in that strong trance,
That dimness of heart-agony;
There stood he, cleansed from the despair
And sorrow of his fruitless prayer.   440
The past he calmly hath reviewed:
But where will be the fortitude
Of this brave man, when he shall see
That Form beneath the spreading tree,
And know that it is Emily?

He saw her where in open view
She sate beneath the spreading yew—
Her head upon her lap, concealing
In solitude her bitter feeling:
"Might ever son *command* a sire,   450
The act were justified to-day."
This to himself—and to the Maid,
Whom now he had approached, he said—
"Gone are they,—they have their desire;
And I with thee one hour will stay,
To give thee comfort if I may."

She heard, but looked not up, nor spake;
And sorrow moved him to partake
Her silence; then his thoughts turned round,
And fervent words a passage found.   460

"Gone are they, bravely, though misled;
With a dear Father at their head!
The Sons obey a natural lord;
The Father had given solemn word

---

[2] A reference to the attempt in 1569 by the earls of North-
umberland and Westmorland to free Mary Queen of Scots and
restore Catholicism.

To noble Percy; and a force
Still stronger, bends him to his course.
This said, our tears to-day may fall
As at an innocent funeral.
In deep and awful channel runs
This sympathy of Sire and Sons;   470
Untried our Brothers have been loved
With heart by simple nature moved;
And now their faithfulness is proved:
For faithful we must call them, bearing
That soul of conscientious daring.
—There were they all in circle—there
Stood Richard, Ambrose, Christopher,
John with a sword that will not fail,
And Marmaduke in fearless mail,
And those bright Twins were side by side;   480
And there, by fresh hopes beautified,
Stood He, whose arm yet lacks the power
Of man, our youngest, fairest flower!
I, by the right of eldest born,
And in a second father's place,
Presumed to grapple with their scorn,
And meet their pity face to face;
Yea, trusting in God's holy aid,
I to my Father knelt and prayed;
And one, the pensive Marmaduke,   490
Methought, was yielding inwardly,
And would have laid his purpose by,
But for a glance of his Father's eye,
Which I myself could scarcely brook.

"Then be we, each and all, forgiven!
Thou, chiefly thou, my Sister dear,
Whose pangs are registered in heaven—
The stifled sigh, the hidden tear,
And smiles, that dared to take their place,
Meek filial smiles, upon thy face,   500
As that unhallowed Banner grew
Beneath a loving old Man's view.
Thy part is done—thy painful part;
Be thou then satisfied in heart!
A further, though far easier, task
Than thine hath been, my duties ask;
With theirs my efforts cannot blend,
I cannot for such cause contend;
Their aims I utterly forswear;
But I in body will be there.   510
Unarmed and naked will I go,
Be at their side, come weal or woe:
On kind occasions I may wait,
See, hear, obstruct, or mitigate.
Bare breast I take and an empty hand."*—

* See the Old Ballad, "The Rising of the North".

Therewith he threw away the lance,
Which he had grasped in that strong trance;
Spurned it, like something that would stand
Between him and the pure intent
Of love on which his soul was bent.   520

"For thee, for thee, is left the sense
Of trial past without offence
To God or man; such innocence,
Such consolation, and the excess
Of an unmerited distress;
In that thy very strength must lie.
—O Sister, I could prophesy!
The time is come that rings the knell
Of all we loved, and loved so well:
Hope nothing, if I thus may speak   530
To thee, a woman, and thence weak:
Hope nothing, I repeat; for we
Are doomed to perish utterly:
'Tis meet that thou with me divide
The thought while I am by thy side,
Acknowledging a grace in this,
A comfort in the dark abyss.
But look not for me when I am gone,
And be no farther wrought upon:
Farewell all wishes, all debate,   540
All prayers for this cause, or for that!
Weep, if that aid thee; but depend
Upon no help of outward friend;
Espouse thy doom at once, and cleave
To fortitude without reprieve.
For we must fall, both we and ours—
This Mansion and these pleasant bowers,
Walks, pools, and arbours, homestead, hall—
Our fate is theirs, will reach them all;
The young horse must forsake his manger,   550
And learn to glory in a Stranger;
The hawk forget his perch; the hound
Be parted from his ancient ground:
The blast will sweep us all away—
One desolation, one decay!
And even this Creature!" which words saying,
He pointed to a lovely Doe,
A few steps distant, feeding, straying;
Fair creature, and more white than snow!
"Even she will to her peaceful woods   560
Return, and to her murmuring floods,
And be in heart and soul the same
She was before she hither came;
Ere she had learned to love us all,
Herself beloved in Rylstone-hall.
—But thou, my Sister, doomed to be
The last leaf on a blasted tree;
If not in vain we breathed the breath

Together of a purer faith;
If hand in hand we have been led,   570
And thou, (O happy thought this day!)
Not seldom foremost in the way;
If on one thought our minds have fed,
And we have in one meaning read;
If, when at home our private weal
Hath suffered from the shock of zeal,
Together we have learned to prize
Forbearance and self-sacrifice;
If we like combatants have fared,
And for this issue been prepared;   580
If thou art beautiful, and youth
And thought endue thee with all truth—
Be strong;—be worthy of the grace
Of God, and fill thy destined place:
A Soul, by force of sorrows high,
Uplifted to the purest sky
Of undisturbed humanity!"

He ended,—or she heard no more;
He led her from the yew-tree shade,
And at the mansion's silent door,   590
He kissed the consecrated Maid;
And down the valley then pursued,
Alone, the armèd Multitude.

CANTO THIRD

Now joy for you who from the towers
Of Brancepeth look in doubt and fear,
Telling melancholy hours!
Proclaim it, let your Masters hear
That Norton with his band is near!
The watchmen from their station high
Pronounced the word,—and the Earls descry,
Well-pleased, the armèd Company   601
Marching down the banks of Were.

Said fearless Norton to the pair
Gone forth to greet him on the plain—
"This meeting, noble Lords! looks fair,
I bring with me a goodly train;
Their hearts are with you: hill and dale
Have helped us: Ure we crossed, and Swale,
And horse and harness followed—see
The best part of their Yeomanry!   610
—Stand forth, my Sons!—these eight are mine,
Whom to this service I commend;
Which way soe'er our fate incline,
These will be faithful to the end;
They are my all"—voice failed him here—
"My all save one, a Daughter dear!

Whom I have left, Love's mildest birth,
The meekest Child on this blessed earth.
I had—but these are by my side,
These Eight, and this is a day of pride!   620
The time is ripe. With festive din
Lo! how the people are flocking in,—
Like hungry fowl to the feeder's hand
When snow lies heavy upon the land."

He spake bare truth; for far and near
From every side came noisy swarms
Of Peasants in their homely gear;
And, mixed with these, to Brancepeth came
Grave Gentry of estate and name,
And Captains known for worth in arms;   630
And prayed the Earls in self-defence
To rise, and prove their innocence.—
"Rise, noble Earls, put forth your might
For holy Church, and the People's right!"

The Norton fixed, at this demand,
His eye upon Northumberland,
And said; "The Minds of Men will own
No loyal rest while England's Crown
Remains without an Heir, the bait
Of strife and factions desperate;   640
Who, paying deadly hate in kind
Through all things else, in this can find
A mutual hope, a common mind;
And plot, and pant to overwhelm
All ancient honour in the realm.
—Brave Earls! to whose heroic veins
Our noblest blood is given in trust,
To you a suffering State complains,
And ye must raise her from the dust.
With wishes of still bolder scope   650
On you we look, with dearest hope;
Even for our Altars—for the prize
In Heaven, of life that never dies;
For the old and holy Church we mourn,
And must in joy to her return.
Behold!"—and from his Son whose stand
Was on his right, from that guardian hand
He took the Banner, and unfurled
The precious folds—"behold," said he,
"The ransom of a sinful world;   660
Let this your preservation be;
The wounds of hands and feet and side,
And the sacred Cross on which Jesus died!
—This bring I from an ancient hearth,
These Records wrought in pledge of love
By hands of no ignoble birth,
A Maid o'er whom the blessed Dove
Vouchsafed in gentleness to brood

While she the holy work pursued."
"Uplift the Standard!" was the cry   670
From all the listeners that stood round,
"Plant it,—by this we live or die."
The Norton ceased not for that sound,
But said; "The prayer which ye have heard,
Much injured Earls! by these preferred,
Is offered to the Saints, the sigh
Of tens of thousands, secretly."
"Uplift it!" cried once more the Band,
And then a thoughtful pause ensued:
"Uplift it!" said Northumberland—   680
Whereat, from all the multitude
Who saw the Banner reared on high
In all its dread emblazonry,
A voice of uttermost joy brake out:
The transport was rolled down the river of Were,
And Durham, the time-honoured Durham, did
    hear,
And the towers of Saint Cuthbert were stirred
    by the shout!

    Now was the North in arms:—they shine
In warlike trim from Tweed to Tyne,
At Percy's voice: and Neville sees   690
His Followers gathering in from Tees,
From Were, and all the little rills
Concealed among the forkèd hills—
Seven hundred Knights, Retainers all
Of Neville, at their Master's call
Had sate together in Raby Hall!
Such strength that Earldom held of yore;
Nor wanted at this time rich store
Of well-appointed chivalry.
—Not loth the sleepy lance to wield,   700
And greet the old paternal shield,
They heard the summons;—and, furthermore,
Horsemen and Foot of each degree,
Unbound by pledge of fealty,
Appeared, with free and open hate
Of novelties in Church and State;
Knight, burgher, yeoman, and esquire,
And Romish priest, in priest's attire.
And thus, in arms, a zealous Band
Proceeding under joint command,   710
To Durham first their course they bear;
And in Saint Cuthbert's ancient seat
Sang mass,—and tore the book of prayer,—
And trod the bible beneath their feet.

    Thence marching southward smooth and free
"They mustered their host at Wetherby,
Full sixteen thousand fair to see;"*

* From the Old Ballad.

The Choicest Warriors of the North!
But none for beauty and for worth
Like those eight Sons—who, in a ring,   720
(Ripe men, or blooming in life's spring)
Each with a lance, erect and tall,
A falchion, and a buckler small,
Stood by their Sire, on Clifford-moor,
To guard the Standard which he bore.
On foot they girt their Father round;
And so will keep the appointed ground
Where'er their march: no steed will he
Henceforth bestride;—triumphantly
He stands upon the grassy sod,   730
Trusting himself to the earth, and God.
Rare sight to embolden and inspire!
Proud was the field of Sons and Sire;
Of him the most; and, sooth to say,
No shape of man in all the array
So graced the sunshine of that day.
The monumental pomp of age
Was with this goodly Personage;
A stature undepressed in size,
Unbent, which rather seemed to rise,   740
In open victory o'er the weight
Of seventy years, to loftier height;
Magnific limbs of withered state;
A face to fear and venerate;
Eyes dark and strong; and on his head
Bright locks of silver hair, thick spread,
Which a brown morion half-concealed,
Light as a hunter's of the field;
And thus, with girdle round his waist,
Whereon the Banner-staff might rest   750
At need, he stood, advancing high
The glittering, floating Pageantry.

    Who sees him?—thousands see, and One
With unparticipated gaze;
Who, 'mong those thousands, friend hath none,
And treads in solitary ways.
He, following wheresoe'er he might,
Hath watched the Banner from afar,
As shepherds watch a lonely star,
Or mariners the distant light   760
That guides them through a stormy night.
And now, upon a chosen plot
Of rising ground, yon heathy spot!
He takes alone his far-off stand,
With breast unmailed, unweaponed hand.
Bold is his aspect; but his eye
Is pregnant with anxiety,
While, like a tutelary Power,
He there stands fixed from hour to hour:
Yet sometimes in more humble guise   770

Upon the turf-clad height he lies
Stretched, herdsman-like, as if to bask
In sunshine were his only task,
Or by his mantle's help to find
A shelter from the nipping wind:
And thus, with short oblivion blest,
His weary spirits gather rest.
Again he lifts his eyes; and lo!
The pageant glancing to and fro;
And hope is wakened by the sight,   780
He thence may learn, ere fall of night,
Which way the tide is doomed to flow.

    To London were the Chieftains bent;
But what avails the bold intent?
A Royal army is gone forth
To quell the RISING OF THE NORTH;
They march with Dudley at their head,
And, in seven days' space, will to York be led!—
Can such a mighty Host be raised
Thus suddenly, and brought so near?   790
The Earls upon each other gazed,
And Neville's cheek grew pale with fear;
For, with a high and valiant name,
He bore a heart of timid frame;
And bold if both had been, yet they
"Against so many may not stay." *
Back therefore will they hie to seize
A strong Hold on the banks of Tees;
There wait a favourable hour,
Until Lord Dacre with his power   800
From Naworth come; and Howard's aid
Be with them openly displayed.

    While through the Host, from man to man,
A rumour of this purpose ran,
The Standard trusting to the care
Of him who heretofore did bear
That charge, impatient Norton sought
The Chieftains to unfold his thought,
And thus abruptly spake;—"We yield
(And can it be?) an unfought field!—   810
How oft has strength, the strength of heaven,
To few triumphantly been given!
Still do our very children boast
Of mitred Thurston—what a Host
He conquered!—Saw we not the Plain
(And flying shall behold again)
Where faith was proved?—while to battle moved
The Standard, on the Sacred Wain
That bore it, compassed round by a bold
Fraternity of Barons old;   820
And with those grey-haired champions stood,

* From the Old Ballad.

Under the saintly ensigns three,
The infant Heir of Mowbray's blood—
All confident of victory!—
Shall Percy blush, then, for his name?
Must Westmoreland be asked with shame
Whose were the numbers, where the loss,
In that other day of Neville's Cross?
When the Prior of Durham with holy hand
Raised, as the Vision gave command,   830
Saint Cuthbert's Relic—far and near
Kenned on the point of a lofty spear;
While the Monks prayed in Maiden's Bower
To God descending in his power.
Less would not at our need be due
To us, who war against the Untrue;—
The delegates of Heaven we rise,
Convoked the impious to chastise:
We, we, the sanctities of old
Would re-establish and uphold: 840
Be warned"—His zeal the Chiefs confounded,
But word was given, and the trumpet sounded:
Back through the melancholy Host
Went Norton, and resumed his post.
Alas! thought he, and have I borne
This Banner raised with joyful pride,
This hope of all posterity,
By those dread symbols sanctified;
Thus to become at once the scorn
Of babbling winds as they go by,   850
A spot of shame to the sun's bright eye,
To the light clouds a mockery!
—"Even these poor eight of mine would stem—"
Half to himself, and half to them
He spake—"would stem, or quell, a force
Ten times their number, man and horse;
This by their own unaided might,
Without their father in their sight,
Without the Cause for which they fight;
A Cause, which on a needful day   860
Would breed us thousands brave as they."
—So speaking, he his reverend head
Raised toward that Imagery once more:
But the familiar prospect shed
Despondency unfelt before:
A shock of intimations vain,
Dismay, and superstitious pain,
Fell on him, with the sudden thought
Of her by whom the work was wrought:—
Oh wherefore was her countenance bright   870
With love divine and gentle light?
She would not, could not, disobey,
But her Faith leaned another way.
Ill tears she wept; I saw them fall,
I overheard her as she spake

Sad words to that mute Animal,
The White Doe, in the hawthorn brake;
She steeped, but not for Jesu's sake,
This Cross in tears: by her, and One
Unworthier far we are undone—　　　　　880
Her recreant Brother—he prevailed
Over that tender Spirit—assailed
Too oft alas! by her whose head
In the cold grave hath long been laid:
She first, in reason's dawn beguiled
Her docile, unsuspecting Child:
Far back—far back my mind must go
To reach the well-spring of this woe!

While thus he brooded, music sweet
Of border tunes was played to cheer　　　890
The footsteps of a quick retreat;
But Norton lingered in the rear,
Stung with sharp thoughts; and, ere the last
From his distracted brain was cast,
Before his Father, Francis stood,
And spake in firm and earnest mood.

"Though here I bend a suppliant knee
In reverence, and unarmed, I bear
In your indignant thoughts my share;
Am grieved this backward march to see　　　900
So careless and disorderly.
I scorn your Chiefs—men who would lead,
And yet want courage at their need:
Then look at them with open eyes!
Deserve they further sacrifice?—
If—when they shrink, nor dare oppose
In open field their gathering foes,
(And fast, from this decisive day,
Yon multitude must melt away;)
If now I ask a grace not claimed　　　910
While ground was left for hope; unblamed
Be an endeavour that can do
No injury to them or you.
My Father! I would help to find
A place of shelter, till the rage
Of cruel men do like the wind
Exhaust itself and sink to rest;
Be Brother now to Brother joined!
Admit me in the equipage
Of your misfortunes, that at least,　　　920
Whatever fate remain behind,
I may bear witness in my breast
To your nobility of mind!"

"Thou Enemy, my bane and blight!
Oh! bold to fight the Coward's fight

Against all good"—but why declare,
At length, the issue of a prayer
Which love had prompted, yielding scope
Too free to one bright moment's hope?
Suffice it that the Son, who strove　　　930
With fruitless effort to allay
That passion, prudently gave way;
Nor did he turn aside to prove
His Brothers' wisdom or their love—
But calmly from the spot withdrew;
His best endeavours to renew,
Should e'er a kindlier time ensue.

CANTO FOURTH

'TIS night: in silence looking down,
The Moon from cloudless ether sees
A Camp, and a beleaguered Town,
And Castle like a stately crown
On the steep rocks of winding Tees;—
And southward far, with moor between,
Hill-top, and flood, and forest green,
The bright Moon sees that valley small
Where Rylstone's old sequestered Hall
A venerable image yields
Of quiet to the neighbouring fields;
While from one pillared chimney breathes
The smoke, and mounts in silver wreaths.　　　950
—The courts are hushed;—for timely sleep
The greyhounds to their kennel creep;
The peacock in the broad ash-tree
Aloft is roosted for the night,
He who in proud prosperity
Of colours manifold and bright
Walked round, affronting the daylight;
And higher still, above the bower
Where he is perched, from yon lone Tower
The hall-clock in the clear moonshine　　　960
With glittering finger points at nine.

Ah! who could think that sadness here
Hath any sway? or pain, or fear?
A soft and lulling sound is heard
Of streams inaudible by day;
The garden pool's dark surface, stirred
By the night insects in their play,
Breaks into dimples small and bright;
A thousand, thousand rings of light
That shape themselves and disappear　　　970
Almost as soon as seen:—and lo!
Not distant far, the milk-white Doe—
The same who quietly was feeding
On the green herb, and nothing heeding,

When Francis, uttering to the Maid
His last words in the yew-tree shade,
Involved whate'er by love was brought
Out of his heart, or crossed his thought,
Of chance presented to his eye,
In one sad sweep of destiny—   980
The same fair Creature, who hath found
Her way into forbidden ground;
Where now—within this spacious plot
For pleasure made, a goodly spot,
With lawns and beds of flowers, and shades
Of trellis-work in long arcades,
And cirque and crescent framed by wall
Of close-clipt foliage green and tall,
Converging walks, and fountains gay,
And terraces in trim array—   990
Beneath yon cypress spiring high,
With pine and cedar spreading wide
Their darksome boughs on either side,
In open moonlight doth she lie;
Happy as others of her kind,
That, far from human neighbourhood,
Range unrestricted as the wind,
Through park, or chase, or savage wood.

But see the consecrated Maid
Emerging from a cedar shade   0
To open moonshine, where the Doe
Beneath the cypress-spire is laid;
Like a patch of April snow—
Upon a bed of herbage green,
Lingering in a woody glade
Or behind a rocky screen—
Lonely relic! which, if seen
By the shepherd, is passed by
With an inattentive eye
Nor more regard doth She bestow   10
Upon the uncomplaining Doe
Now couched at ease, though oft this day
Not unperplexed nor free from pain,
When she had tried, and tried in vain,
Approaching in her gentle way,
To win some look of love, or gain
Encouragement to sport or play;
Attempts which still the heart-sick Maid
Rejected, or with slight repaid.

Yet Emily is soothed;—the breeze   20
Came fraught with kindly sympathies.
As she approached yon rustic Shed
Hung with late-flowering woodbine, spread
Along the walls and overhead,
The fragrance of the breathing flowers
Revived a memory of those hours

When here, in this remote alcove,
(While from the pendent woodbine came
Like odours, sweet as if the same)
A fondly-anxious Mother strove   30
To teach her salutary fears
And mysteries above her years.
Yes, she is soothed: an Image faint,
And yet not faint—a presence bright
Returns to her—that blessèd Saint
Who with mild looks and language mild
Instructed here her darling Child,
While yet a prattler on the knee,
To worship in simplicity
The invisible God, and take for guide   40
The faith reformed and purified.

    'Tis flown—the Vision, and the sense
Of that beguiling influence;
"But oh! thou Angel from above,
Mute Spirit of maternal love,
That stood'st before my eyes, more clear
Than ghosts are fabled to appear
Sent upon embassies of fear;
As thou thy presence hast to me
Vouchsafed, in radiant ministry   50
Descend on Francis; nor forbear
To greet him with a voice, and say;—
'If hope be a rejected stay,
Do thou, my christian Son, beware
Of that most lamentable snare,
The self-reliance of despair!'"

    Then from within the embowered retreat
Where she had found a grateful seat
Perturbed she issues. She will go!
Herself will follow to the war,   60
And clasp her Father's knees;—ah, no!
She meets the insuperable bar,
The injunction by her Brother laid;
His parting charge—but ill obeyed—
That interdicted all debate,
All prayer for this cause or for that;
All efforts that would turn aside
The headstrong current of their fate:
Her duty is to stand and wait; [3]
In resignation to abide   70
The shock, AND FINALLY SECURE
O'ER PAIN AND GRIEF A TRIUMPH PURE.
—She feels it, and her pangs are checked.
But now, as silently she paced
The turf, and thought by thought was chased,

---

[3] An allusion to Milton's sonnet *When I Consider How My Light Is Spent.*

Came One who, with sedate respect,
Approached, and, greeting her, thus spake;
"An old man's privilege I take:
Dark is the time—a woeful day!
Dear daughter of affliction, say   80
How can I serve you? point the way."

  "Rights have you, and may well be bold:
You with my Father have grown old
In friendship—strive—for his sake go—
Turn from us all the coming woe:
This would I beg; but on my mind
A passive stillness is enjoined.
On you, if room for mortal aid
Be left, is no restriction laid;
You not forbidden to recline   90
With hope upon the Will divine."

  "Hope," said the old Man, "must abide
With all of us, whate'er betide.
In Craven's Wilds is many a den,
To shelter persecuted men:
Far under ground is many a cave,
Where they might lie as in the grave,
Until this storm hath ceased to rave:
Or let them cross the River Tweed,
And be at once from peril freed!"   100

  "Ah tempt me not!" she faintly sighed;
"I will not counsel nor exhort,—
With my condition satisfied;
But you, at least, may make report
Of what befals;—be this your task
This may be done;— 'tis all I ask!"
  She spake—and from the Lady's sight
The Sire, unconscious of his age
Departed promptly as a Page
Bound on some errand of delight.   110
—The noble Francis—wise as brave,
Thought he, may want not skill to save.
With hopes in tenderness concealed,
Unarmed he followed to the field;
Him will I seek: the insurgent Powers
Are now besieging Barnard's Towers,—
"Grant that the Moon which shines this night
May guide them in a prudent flight!"
  But quick the turns of chance and change,
And knowledge has a narrow range;   120
Whence idle fears, and needless pain,
And wishes blind, and efforts vain.—
The Moon may shine, but cannot be
Their guide in flight—already she
Hath witnessed their captivity.
She saw the desperate assault

Upon that hostile castle made;—
But dark and dismal is the vault
Where Norton and his sons are laid!
Disastrous issue!—he had said   130
"This night yon faithless Towers must yield,
Or we for ever quit the field.
—Neville is utterly dismayed,
For promise fails of Howard's aid;
And Dacre to our call replies
That *he* is unprepared to rise.
My heart is sick;—this weary pause
Must needs be fatal to our cause.
The breach is open—on the wall,
This night,—the Banner shall be planted!"   140
—'Twas done: his Sons were with him—all;
They belt him round with hearts undaunted
And others follow;—Sire and Son
Leap down into the court;—"'Tis won"—
They shout aloud—but Heaven decreed
That with their joyful shout should close
The triumph of a desperate deed
Which struck with terror friends and foes!
The friend shrinks back—the foe recoils
From Norton and his filial band;   150
But they, now caught within the toils,
Against a thousand cannot stand;—
The foe from numbers courage drew,
And overpowered that gallant few.
"A rescue for the Standard!" cried
The Father from within the walls;
But, see, the sacred Standard falls!—
Confusion through the Camp spread wide:
Some fled; and some their fears detained:
But ere the Moon had sunk to rest   160
In her pale chambers of the west,
Of that rash levy nought remained.

CANTO FIFTH

HIGH on a point of rugged ground
Among the wastes of Rylstone Fell,
Above the loftiest ridge or mound
Where foresters or shepherds dwell,
An edifice of warlike frame
Stands single—Norton Tower its name—
It fronts all quarters, and looks round
O'er path and road, and plain and dell,   170
Dark moor, and gleam of pool and stream,
Upon a prospect without bound.

  The summit of this bold ascent—
Though bleak and bare, and seldom free
As Pendle-hill or Pennygent

From wind, or frost, or vapours wet—
Had often heard the sound of glee
When there the youthful Nortons met,
To practise games and archery:
How proud and happy they! the crowd   180
Of Lookers-on how pleased and proud!
And from the scorching noon-tide sun,
From showers, or when the prize was won,
They to the Tower withdrew, and there
Would mirth run round, with generous fare;
And the stern old Lord of Rylstone-hall
Was happiest, proudest, of them all!

But now, his Child, with anguish pale,
Upon the height walks to and fro;
'Tis well that she hath heard the tale,   190
Received the bitterness of woe:
For she *had* hoped, had hoped and feared,
Such rights did feeble nature claim;
And oft her steps had hither steered,
Though not unconscious of self-blame;
For she her brother's charge revered,
His farewell words; and by the same,
Yea, by her brother's very name,
Had, in her solitude, been cheered.

Beside the lonely watch-tower stood   200
That grey-haired Man of gentle blood,
Who with her Father had grown old
In friendship; rival hunters they,
And fellow warriors in their day;
To Rylstone he the tidings brought;
Then on this height the Maid had sought,
And, gently as he could, had told
The end of that dire Tragedy,
Which it had been his lot to see.

To him the Lady turned; "You said   210
That Francis lives, *he* is not dead?"

"Your noble brother hath been spared;
To take his life they have not dared;
On him and on his high endeavour
The light of praise shall shine for ever!
Nor did he (such Heaven's will) in vain
His solitary course maintain;
Not vainly struggled in the might
Of duty, seeing with clear sight;
He was their comfort to the last,   220
Their joy till every pang was past.

"I witnessed when to York they came—
What, Lady, if their feet were tied;
They might deserve a good Man's blame;

But marks of infamy and shame—
These were their triumph, these their pride;
Nor wanted 'mid the pressing crowd
Deep feeling, that found utterance loud,
'Lo, Francis comes,' there were who cried,
'A Prisoner once, but now set free!   230
'Tis well, for he the worst defied
Through force of natural piety;
He rose not in this quarrel, he,
For concord's sake and England's good,
Suit to his Brothers often made
With tears, and of his Father prayed—
And when he had in vain withstood
Their purpose—then did he divide,
He parted from them; but at their side
Now walks in unanimity.   240
Then peace to cruelty and scorn,
While to the prison they are borne,
Peace, peace to all indignity!'

"And so in Prison were they laid—
Oh hear me, hear me, gentle Maid,
For I am come with power to bless,
By scattering gleams, through your distress,
Of a redeeming happiness.
Me did a reverent pity move
And privilege of ancient love;   250
And, in your service, making bold,
Entrance I gained to that strong-hold.

"Your Father gave me cordial greeting;
But to his purposes, that burned
Within him, instantly returned:
He was commanding and entreating,
And said—'We need not stop, my Son!
Thoughts press, and time is hurrying on'—
And so to Francis he renewed
His words, more calmly thus pursued.   260

"'Might this our enterprise have sped,
Change wide and deep the Land had seen,
A renovation from the dead,
A spring-tide of immortal green:
The darksome altars would have blazed
Like stars when clouds are rolled away;
Salvation to all eyes that gazed,
Once more the Rood had been upraised
To spread its arms, and stand for aye.
Then, then—had I survived to see   270
New life in Bolton Priory;
The voice restored, the eye of Truth
Re-opened that inspired my youth;
To see her in her pomp arrayed—
This Banner (for such vow I made)

Should on the consecrated breast
Of that same Temple have found rest:
I would myself have hung it high,
Fit offering of glad victory!

   "'A shadow of such thought remains   280
To cheer this sad and pensive time;
A solemn fancy yet sustains
One feeble Being—bids me climb
Even to the last—one effort more
To attest my Faith, if not restore.

   "'Hear then,' said he, 'while I impart,
My Son, the last wish of my heart.
The Banner strive thou to regain;
And, if the endeavour prove not vain,
Bear it—to whom if not to thee   290
Shall I this lonely thought consign?—
Bear it to Bolton Priory,
And lay it on Saint Mary's shrine;
To wither in the sun and breeze
'Mid those decaying sanctities.
There let at least the gift be laid,
The testimony there displayed;
Bold proof that with no selfish aim,
But for lost Faith and Christ's dear name,
I helmeted a brow though white,   300
And took a place in all men's sight;
Yea, offered up this noble Brood,
This fair unrivalled Brotherhood,
And turned away from thee, my Son!
And left—but be the rest unsaid,
The name untouched, the tear unshed;—
My wish is known, and I have done:
Now promise, grant this one request,
This dying prayer, and be thou blest!'

   "Then Francis answered—'Trust thy Son,
For, with God's will, it shall be done!'—   311

   "The pledge obtained, the solemn word
Thus scarcely given, a noise was heard,
And Officers appeared in state
To lead the prisoners to their fate.
They rose, oh! wherefore should I fear
To tell, or, Lady, you to hear?
They rose—embraces none were given—
They stood like trees when earth and heaven
Are calm; they knew each other's worth,   320
And reverently the Band went forth.
They met, when they had reached the door,
One with profane and harsh intent
Placed there—that he might go before
And, with that rueful Banner borne

Aloft in sign of taunting scorn,
Conduct them to their punishment:
So cruel Sussex, unrestrained
By human feeling, had ordained.
The unhappy Banner Francis saw,   330
And, with a look of calm command
Inspiring universal awe,
He took it from the soldier's hand;
And all the people that stood round
Confirmed the deed in peace profound.
—High transport did the Father shed
Upon his Son—and they were led,
Led on, and yielded up their breath;
Together died, a happy death!—
But Francis, soon as he had braved   340
That insult, and the Banner saved,
Athwart the unresisting tide
Of the spectators occupied
In admiration or dismay,
Bore instantly his Charge away."

   These things, which thus had in the sight
And hearing passed of Him who stood
With Emily, on the Watch-tower height,
In Rylstone's woeful neighbourhood,
He told; and oftentimes with voice   350
Of power to comfort or rejoice;
For deepest sorrows that aspire,
Go high, no transport ever higher.
"Yes—God is rich in mercy," said
The old Man to the silent Maid,
"Yet, Lady! shines, through this black night,
One star of aspect heavenly bright;
Your brother lives—he lives—is come
Perhaps already to his home;
Then let us leave this dreary place."   360
She yielded, and with gentle pace,
Though without one uplifted look,
To Rylstone-hall her way she took.

CANTO SIXTH

WHY comes not Francis?—From the doleful
   City
He fled,—and, in his flight, could hear
The death-sounds of the Minster-bell:
That sullen stroke pronounced farewell
To Marmaduke, cut off from pity!
To Ambrose that! and then a knell
For him, the sweet half-opened Flower!   370
For all—all dying in one hour!
—Why comes not Francis? Thoughts of love
Should bear him to his Sister dear

With the fleet motion of a dove;
Yea, like a heavenly messenger
Of speediest wing, should he appear.
Why comes he not?—for westward fast
Along the plain of York he passed;
Reckless of what impels or leads,
Unchecked he hurries on;—nor heeds   380
The sorrow, through the Villages,
Spread by triumphant cruelties
Of vengeful military force,
And punishment without remorse.
He marked not, heard not, as he fled;
All but the suffering heart was dead
For him abandoned to blank awe,
To vacancy, and horror strong:
And the first object which he saw,
With conscious sight, as he swept along—   390
It was the Banner in his hand!
He felt—and made a sudden stand.

He looked about like one betrayed:
What hath he done? what promise made?
Oh weak, weak moment! to what end
Can such a vain oblation tend,
And he the Bearer?—Can he go
Carrying this instrument of woe,
And find, find anywhere, a right
To excuse him in his Country's sight?   400
No; will not all men deem the change
A downward course, perverse and strange?
Here is it;—but how? when? must she,
The unoffending Emily,
Again this piteous object see?

Such conflict long did he maintain,
Nor liberty nor rest could gain:
His own life into danger brought
By this sad burden—even that thought,
Exciting self-suspicion strong,   410
Swayed the brave man to his wrong.
And how—unless it were the sense
Of all-disposing Providence,
Its will unquestionably shown—
How has the Banner clung so fast
To a palsied, and unconscious hand;
Clung to the hand to which it passed
Without impediment? And why
But that Heaven's purpose might be known
Doth now no hindrance meet his eye,   420
No intervention, to withstand
Fulfilment of a Father's prayer
Breathed to a Son forgiven, and blest
When all resentments were at rest,
And life in death laid the heart bare?—

Then, like a spectre sweeping by,
Rushed through his mind the prophecy
Of utter desolation made
To Emily in the yew-tree shade:
He sighed, submitting will and power   430
To the stern embrace of that grasping hour.
"No choice is left, the deed is mine—
Dead are they, dead!—and I will go,
And, for their sakes, come weal or woe,
Will lay the Relic on the shrine."

So forward with a steady will
He went, and traversed plain and hill;
And up the vale of Wharf his way
Pursued;—and, at the dawn of day,
Attained a summit whence his eyes   440
Could see the Tower of Bolton rise.
There Francis for a moment's space
Made halt—but hard! a noise behind
Of horsemen at an eager pace!
He heard, and with misgiving mind.
—'Tis Sir George Bowes who leads the Band:
They come, by cruel Sussex sent;
Who, when the Nortons from the hand
Of death had drunk their punishment,
Bethought him, angry and ashamed,   450
How Francis, with the Banner claimed
As his own charge, had disappeared,
By all the standers-by revered.
His whole bold carriage (which had quelled
Thus far the Opposer, and repelled
All censure, enterprise so bright
That even bad men had vainly striven
Against that overcoming light)
Was then reviewed, and prompt word given,
That to what place soever fled   460
He should be seized, alive or dead.

The troop of horse have gained the height
Where Francis stood in open sight.
They hem him round—"Behold the proof,"
They cried, "the Ensign in his hand!
He did not arm, he walked aloof!
For why?—to save his Father's land;
Worst Traitor of them all is he,
A Traitor dark and cowardly!"

"I am no Traitor," Francis said,   470
"Though this unhappy freight I bear;
And must not part with. But beware;—
Err not, by hasty zeal misled,
Nor do a suffering Spirit wrong,
Whose self-reproaches are too strong!"
At this he from the beaten road

Retreated towards a brake of thorn,
That like a place of vantage showed;
And there stood bravely, though forlorn.
In self-defence with warlike brow　　　480
He stood,—nor weaponless was now;
He from a Soldier's hand had snatched
A spear,—and, so protected, watched
The Assailants, turning round and round;
But from behind with treacherous wound
A Spearman brought him to the ground.
The guardian lance, as Francis fell,
Dropped from him; but his other hand
The Banner clenched; till, from out the Band,
One, the most eager for the prize,　　　490
Rushed in; and—while, O grief to tell!
A glimmering sense still left, with eyes
Unclosed the noble Francis lay—
Seized it, as hunters seize their prey;
But not before the warm life-blood
Had tinged more deeply, as it flowed,
The wounds the broidered Banner showed,
Thy fatal work, O Maiden, innocent as good!

Proudly the Horsemen bore away
The Standard; and where Francis lay　　　500
There was he left alone, unwept,
And for two days unnoticed slept.
For at that time bewildering fear
Possessed the country, far and near;
But, on the third day, passing by
One of the Norton Tenantry
Espied the uncovered Corse; the Man
Shrunk as he recognised the face,
And to the nearest homesteads ran
And called the people to the place.　　　510
—How desolate is Rylstone-hall!
This was the instant thought of all;
And if the lonely Lady there
Should be; to her thy cannot bear
This weight of anguish and despair.
So, when upon sad thoughts had prest
Thoughts sadder still, they deemed it best
That, if the Priest should yield assent
And no one hinder their intent,
Then, they, for Christian pity's sake,　　　520
In holy ground a grave would make;
And straightway buried he should be
In the Church-yard of the Priory.

Apart, some little space, was made
The grave where Francis must be laid.
In no confusion or neglect
This did they,—but in pure respect
That he was born of gentle blood;

And that there was no neighbourhood
Of kindred for him in that ground:　　　530
So to the Church-yard they are bound,
Bearing the body on a bier;
And psalms they sing—a holy sound
That hill and vale with sadness hear.

But Emily hath raised her head,
And is again disquieted;
She must behold!—so many gone,
Where is the solitary One?
And forth from Rylstone-hall stepped she,—
To seek her Brother forth she went,　　　540
And tremblingly her course she bent
Toward Bolton's ruined Priory.
She comes, and in the vale hath heard
The funeral dirge;—she sees the knot
Of people, see them in one spot—
And darting like a wounded bird
She reached the grave, and with her breast
Upon the ground received the rest,—
The consummation, the whole ruth
And sorrow of this final truth!　　　550

CANTO SEVENTH

"Powers there are
That touch each other to the quick—in modes
Which the gross world no sense hath to perceive,
No soul to dream of."

THOU Spirit, whose angelic hand
Was to the harp a strong command,
Called the submissive strings to wake
In glory for this Maiden's sake,
Say, Spirit! whither hath she fled
To hide her poor afflicted head?
What mighty forest in its gloom
Enfolds her?—is a rifted tomb
Within the wilderness her seat?
Some island which the wild waves beat—　　　560
Is that the Sufferer's last retreat?
Or some aspiring rock, that shrouds
Its perilous front in mists and clouds?
High-climbing rock, low sunless dale,
Sea, desert, what do these avail?
Oh take her anguish and her fears
Into a deep recess of years!

'Tis done;—despoil and desolation
O'er Rylstone's fair domain have blown;
Pools, terraces, and walks are sown　　　570
With weeds; the bowers are overthrown,

Or have given way to slow mutation,
While, in their ancient habitation
The Norton name hath been unknown.
The lordly Mansion of its pride
Is stripped; the ravage hath spread wide
Through park and field, a perishing
That mocks the gladness of the Spring!
And, with this silent gloom agreeing,
Appears a joyless human Being,   580
Of aspect such as if the waste
Were under her dominion placed.
Upon a primrose bank, her throne
Of quietness, she sits alone;—
Among the ruins of a wood,
Erewhile a covert bright and green,
And where full many a brave tree stood,
That used to spread its boughs, and ring
With the sweet birds' carolling.
Behold her, like a virgin Queen,   590
Neglecting in imperial state
These outward images of fate,
And carrying inward a serene
And perfect sway, through many a thought
Of chance and change, that hath been brought
To the subjection of a holy,
Though stern and rigorous, melancholy!
The like authority, with grace
Of awfulness, is in her face,—
There hath she fixed it; yet it seems   600
To o'ershadow by no native right
That face, which cannot lose the gleams,
Lose utterly the tender gleams,
Of gentleness and meek delight,
And loving-kindness ever bright:
Such is her sovereign mien:—her dress
(A vest with woollen cincture tied,
A hood of mountain-wool undyed)
Is homely,—fashioned to express
A wandering Pilgrim's humbleness.   610

And she *hath* wandered, long and far,
Beneath the light of sun and star;
Hath roamed in trouble and in grief,
Driven forward like a withered leaf,
Yea, like a ship at random blown
To distant places and unknown.
But now she dares to seek a haven
Among her native wilds of Craven;—
Hath seen again her Father's roof,
And put her fortitude to proof;   620
The mighty sorrow hath been borne,
And she is thoroughly forlorn:
Her soul doth in itself stand fast,
Sustained by memory of the past

And strength of Reason; held above
The infirmities of mortal love;
Undaunted, lofty, calm, and stable,
And awfully impenetrable.

And so—beneath a mouldered tree,
A self-surviving leafless oak   630
By unregarded age from stroke
Of ravage saved—sate Emily.
There did she rest, with head reclined,
Herself most like a stately flower,
(Such have I seen) whom chance of birth
Hath separated from its kind,
To live and die in a shady bower,
Single on the gladsome earth.

When, with a noise like distant thunder,
A troop of deer came sweeping by;   640
And, suddenly, behold a wonder!
For One, among those rushing deer,
A single One, in mid career
Hath stopped, and fixed her large full eye
Upon the Lady Emily;
A Doe most beautiful, clear-white,
A radiant creature, silver-bright!

Thus checked, a little while it stayed;
A little thoughtful pause it made;
And then advanced with stealth-like pace,   650
Drew softly near her, and more near—
Looked round—but saw no cause for fear;
So to her feet the Creature came,
And laid its head upon her knee,
And looked into the Lady's face,
A look of pure benignity,
And fond unclouded memory.
It is, thought Emily, the same,
The very Doe of other years!—
The pleading look the Lady viewed,   660
And, by her gushing thoughts subdued,
She melted into tears—
A flood of tears that flowed apace
Upon the happy Creature's face.

Oh, moment ever blest! O Pair
Beloved of Heaven, Heaven's chosen care,
This was for you a precious greeting;
And may it prove a fruitful meeting!
Joined are they, and the sylvan Doe
Can she depart? can she forego   670
The Lady, once her playful peer,
And now her sainted Mistress dear?
And will not Emily receive
This lovely chronicler of things

Long past, delights and sorrowings?
Lone Sufferer! will not she believe
The promise in that speaking face;
And welcome, as a gift of grace,
The saddest thought the Creature brings?

That day, the first of a re-union					680
Which was to teem with high communion,
That day of balmy April weather,
They tarried in the wood together.
And when, ere fall of evening dew,
She from her sylvan haunt withdrew,
The White Doe tracked with faithful pace
The Lady to her dwelling-place;
That nook where, on paternal ground,
A habitation she had found,
The Master of whose humble board					690
Once owned her Father for his Lord;
A hut, by tufted trees defended,
Where Rylstone brook with Wharf is blended.

When Emily by morning light
Went forth, the Doe stood there in sight.
She shrunk:—with one frail shock of pain
Received and followed by a prayer,
She saw the Creature once again;
Shun will she not, she feels, will bear;—
But, wheresoever she looked round,					700
All now was trouble-haunted ground;
And therefore now she deems it good
Once more this restless neighbourhood
To leave.—Unwooed, yet unforbidden,
The White Doe followed up the vale,
Up to another cottage, hidden
In the deep fork of Amerdale;
And there may Emily restore
Herself, in spots unseen before.
—Why tell of mossy rock, or tree,					710
By lurking Dernbrook's pathless side,
Haunts of a strengthening amity
That calmed her, cheered, and fortified?
For she hath ventured now to read
Of time, and place, and thought, and deed—
Endless history that lies
In her silent Follower's eyes;
Who with a power like human reason
Discerns the favourable season,
Skilled to approach or to retire,—					720
From looks conceiving her desire;
From look, deportment, voice, or mien,
That vary to the heart within.
If she too passionately wreathed
Her arms, or over-deeply breathed,
Walked quick or slowly, every mood

In its degree was understood;
Then well may their accord be true,
And kindliest intercourse ensue.
—Oh! surely 'twas a gentle rousing					730
When she by sudden glimpse espied
The White Doe on the mountain browsing,
Or in the meadow wandered wide!
How pleased, when down the Straggler sank
Beside her, on some sunny bank!
How soothed, when in thick bower enclosed,
They, like a nested pair, reposed!
Fair Vision! when it crossed the Maid
Within some rocky cavern laid,
The dark cave's portal gliding by,					740
White as whitest cloud on high
Floating through the azure sky.
—What now is left for pain or fear?
That Presence, dearer and more dear,
While they, side by side, were straying,
And the shepherd's pipe was playing,
Did now a very gladness yield
At morning to the dewy field,
And with a deeper peace endued
The hour of moonlight solitude.					750

With her Companion, in such frame
Of mind, to Rylstone back she came;
And, ranging through the wasted groves,
Received the memory of old loves,
Undisturbed and undistrest,
Into a soul which now was blest
With a soft spring-day of holy,
Mild, and grateful, melancholy:
Not sunless gloom or unenlightened,
But by tender fancies brightened.					760

When the bells of Rylstone played
Their sabbath music—"𝕲𝖔𝖉 𝖚𝖘 𝖆𝖞𝖉𝖊!" [4]
That was the sound they seemed to speak;
Inscriptive legend which I ween
May on these holy bells be seen,
That legend and her Grandsire's name;
And oftentimes the Lady meek
Had in her childhood read the same;
Words which she slighted at that day;
But now, when such sad change was wrought,
And of that lonely name she thought,					771
The bells of Rylstone seemed to say,
While she sate listening in the shade,
With vocal music, "𝕲𝖔𝖉 𝖚𝖘 𝖆𝖞𝖉𝖊;"
And all the hills were glad to bear
Their part in this effectual prayer.

---

[4] The inscription on the bells of Rylstone Church.

Nor lacked she Reason's firmest power;
But with the White Doe at her side
Up would she climb to Norton Tower,
And thence look round her far and wide,   780
Her fate there measuring;—all is stilled,—
The weak One hath subdued her heart;
Behold the prophecy fulfilled,
Fulfilled, and she sustains her part!
But here her Brother's words have failed;
Here hath a milder doom prevailed;
That she, of him and all bereft,
Hath yet this faithful Partner left;
This one Associate that disproves
His words, remains for her, and loves.   790
If tears are shed, they do not fall
For loss of him—for one, or all;
Yet sometimes, sometimes doth she weep
Moved gently in her soul's soft sleep;
A few tears down her cheek descend
For this her last and living Friend.

Bless, tender Hearts, their mutual lot,
And bless for both this savage spot;
Which Emily doth sacred hold
For reasons dear and manifold—   800
Here hath she, here before her sight,
Close to the summit of this height,
The grassy rock-encircled Pound
In which the Creature first was found.
So beautiful the timid Thrall
(A spotless Youngling white as foam)
Her youngest Brother brought it home;
The youngest, then a lusty boy,
Bore it, or led, to Rylstone-hall
With heart brimful of pride and joy!   810

But most to Bolton's sacred Pile,
On favouring nights, she loved to go;
There ranged through cloister, court, and aisle,
Attended by the soft-paced Doe;
Nor feared she in the still moonshine
To look upon Saint Mary's shrine;
Nor on the lonely turf that showed
Where Francis slept in his last abode.
For that she came; there oft she sate
Forlorn, but not disconsolate: 820
And, when she from the abyss returned
Of thought, she neither shrunk nor mourned;
Was happy that she lived to greet
Her mute Companion as it lay
In love and pity at her feet;
How happy in its turn to meet
The recognition! the mild glance
Beamed from that gracious countenance;

Communication, like the ray
Of a new morning, to the nature   830
And prospects of the inferior Creature!

A mortal Song we sing, by dower
Encouraged of celestial power;
Power which the viewless Spirit shed
By whom we were first visited;
Whose voice we heard, whose hand and wings
Swept like a breeze the conscious strings,
When, left in solitude, erewhile
We stood before this ruined Pile,
And, quitting unsubstantial dreams,   840
Sang in this Presence kindred themes;
Distress and desolation spread
Through human hearts, and pleasure dead,—
Dead—but to live again on earth,
A second and yet nobler birth;
Dire overthrow, and yet how high
The re-ascent in sanctity!
From fair to fairer; day by day
A more divine and loftier way!
Even such this blessèd Pilgrim trod,   850
By sorrow lifted towards her God;
Uplifted to the purest sky
Of undisturbed mortality.
Her own thoughts loved she; and could bend
A dear look to her lowly Friend;
There stopped; her thirst was satisfied
With what this innocent spring supplied:
Her sanction inwardly she bore,
And stood apart from human cares:
But to the world returned no more,   860
Although with no unwilling mind
Help did she give at need, and joined
The Wharfdale peasants in their prayers.
At length, thus faintly, faintly tied
To earth, she was set free, and died.
Thy soul, exalted Emily,
Maid of the blasted family,
Rose to the God from whom it came!
—In Rylstone Church her mortal frame
Was buried by her Mother's side.   870

Most glorious sunset! and a ray
Survives—the twilight of this day—
In that fair Creature whom the fields
Support, and whom the forest shields;
Who, having filled a holy place,
Partakes, in her degree, Heaven's grace;
And bears a memory and a mind
Raised far above the law of kind;
Haunting the spots with lonely cheer
Which her dear Mistress once held dear: 880

Loves most what Emily loved most—
The enclosure of this church-yard ground;
Here wanders like a gliding ghost,
And every sabbath here is found;
Comes with the people when the bells
Are heard among the moorland dells,
Finds entrance through yon arch, where way
Lies open on the sabbath day;
Here walks amid the mournful waste
Of prostrate altars, shrines defaced,   890
And floors encumbered with rich show
Of fret-work imagery laid low;
Paces softly, or makes halt,
By fractured cell, or tomb, or vault;
By plate of monumental brass
Dim-gleaming among weeds and grass,
And sculptured Forms of Warriors brave:
But chiefly by that single grave,
That one sequestered hillock green,
The pensive visitant is seen.   900
There doth the gentle Creature lie
With those adversities unmoved;
Calm spectacle, by earth and sky
In their benignity approved!
And aye, methinks, this hoary Pile,
Subdued by outrage and decay,
Looks down upon her with a smile,
A gracious smile, that seems to say—
"Thou, thou art not a Child of Time,
But Daughter of the Eternal Prime!"   910

[1807–1808]   [1815]

CHARACTERISTICS OF A CHILD
"*Picture of my daughter Catherine, who died the year after.*"
[*Wordsworth to Isabella Fenwick*] See also "Surprised by
joy . . . ," p. 390.

CHARACTERISTICS OF A CHILD THREE YEARS OLD

LOVING she is, and tractable, though wild;
And Innocence hath privilege in her
To dignify arch looks and laughing eyes;
And feats of cunning; and the pretty round
Of traspasses, affected to provoke
Mock-chastisement and partnership in play.
And, as a faggot sparkles on the hearth,
Not less if unattended and alone
Than when both young and old sit gathered round
And take delight in its activity;   10
Even so this happy Creature of herself
Is all-sufficient; solitude to her
Is blithe society, who fills the air
With gladness and involuntary songs.
Light are her sallies as the tripping fawn's
Forth-startled from the fern where she lay couched;
Unthought-of, unexpected, as the stir
Of the soft breeze ruffling the meadow-flowers,
Or from before it chasing wantonly
The many-coloured images imprest   20
Upon the bosom of a placid lake.

[1811]   [1815]

SONNET

["The power of Armies . . ."]

THE power of Armies is a visible thing,
Formal, and circumscribed in time and space;
But who the limits of that power shall trace
Which a brave People into light can bring
Or hide, at will,—for freedom combating
By just revenge inflamed? No foot may chase,
No eye can follow, to a fatal place
That power, that spirit, whether on the wing
Like the strong wind, or sleeping like the wind
Within its awful caves.—From year to year   10
Springs this indigenous produce far and near;
No craft this subtle element can bind,
Rising like water from the soil, to find
In every nook a lip that it may cheer.

[1811]   [1815]

LAODAMIA

The suicide of Laodamia, wife of Protesilaus (the first Greek to die at Troy), was celebrated as an instance of wifely devotion. In his notes for Isabella Fenwick, however, Wordsworth says that " The incident of the trees growing and withering put the subject into my thoughts, and I wrote with the hope of giving it a loftier tone than, so far as I know, has been given to it by any of the Ancients who have treated of it. It cost me more trouble than almost anything of equal length I have ever written."

LAODAMIA

"WITH sacrifice before the rising morn
Vows have I made by fruitless hope inspired;
And from the infernal Gods, 'mid shades forlorn
Of night, my slaughtered Lord have I required;
Celestial pity I again implore;—
Restore him to my sight—great Jove, restore!"

So speaking, and by fervent love endowed
With faith, the Suppliant heavenward lifts her hands;
While, like the sun emerging from a cloud,
Her countenance brightens—and her eye expands;   10
Her bosom heaves and spreads, her stature grows;
And she expects the issue in repose.

O terror! what hath she perceived?—O joy!
What doth she look on?—whom doth she behold?
Her Hero slain upon the beach of Troy?
His vital presence? his corporeal mould?
It is—if sense deceive her not—'tis He!
And a God leads him, wingèd Mercury!

Mild Hermes[1] spake—and touched her with his wand
That calms all fear; "Such grace hath crowned thy
Laodamía! that at Jove's command   [prayer,
Thy Husband walks the paths of upper air: 22
He comes to tarry with thee three hours' space;
Accept the gift, behold him face to face!"

Forth sprang the impassioned Queen her Lord to
Again that consummation she essayed;   [clasp;
But unsubstantial Form eludes her grasp
As often as that eager grasp was made.
The Phantom parts—but parts to re-unite,
And re-assume his place before her sight.   30

"Protesiláus, lo! thy guide is gone!
Confirm, I pray, the vision with thy voice:
This is our palace,—yonder is thy throne;
Speak, and the floor thou tread'st on will rejoice.
Not to appal me have the gods bestowed
This precious boon; and blest a sad abode."

[1] Hermes is the Greek name for Mercury.

"Great Jove, Laodamía! doth not leave
His gifts imperfect:—Spectre though I be,
I am not sent to scare thee or deceive;
But in reward of thy fidelity.   40
And something also did my worth obtain;
For fearless virtue bringeth boundless gain.

"Thou knowest, the Delphic oracle foretold
That the first Greek who touched the Trojan strand
Should die; but me the threat could not withhold:
A generous cause a victim did demand;
And forth I leapt upon the sandy plain;
A self-devoted chief—by Hector slain."

"Supreme of Heroes—bravest, noblest, best!
Thy matchless courage I bewail no more,   50
Which then, when tens of thousands were deprest
By doubt, propelled thee to the fatal shore;
Thou found'st—and I forgive thee—here thou art—
A nobler counsellor than my poor heart.

"But thou, though capable of sternest deed,
Wert kind as resolute, and good as brave;
And he, whose power restores thee, hath decreed
Thou should'st elude the malice of the grave:
Redundant are thy locks, thy lips as fair
As when their breath enriched Thessalian air.   60

"No Spectre greets me,—no vain Shadow this;
Come, blooming Hero, place thee by my side!
Give, on this well-known couch, one nuptial kiss
To me, this day, a second time thy bride!"
Jove frowned in heaven: the conscious Parcæ[2] threw
Upon those roseate lips a Stygian hue.

"This visage tells thee that my doom is past:
Nor should the change be mourned, even if the joys
Of sense were able to return as fast
And surely as they vanish. Earth destroys   70
Those raptures duly—Erebus[3] disdains:
Calm pleasures there abide—majestic pains.

"Be taught, O faithful Consort, to control
Rebellious passion: for the Gods approve
The depth, and not the tumult, of the soul;
A fervent, not ungovernable, love.
Thy transports moderate; and meekly mourn
When I depart, for brief is my sojourn—"

[2] Goddesses of fate.
[3] The primeval darkness of the lower world.

"Ah wherefore?—Did not Hercules by force
Wrest from the guardian Monster of the tomb   80
Alcestis, a reanimated corse,
Given back to dwell on earth in vernal bloom?
Medea's spells dispersed the weight of years,
And Æson stood a youth 'mid youthful peers.

"The Gods to us are merciful—and they
Yet further may relent: for mightier far
Than strength of nerve and sinew, or the sway
Of magic potent over sun and star,   88
Is love, though oft to agony distrest,   [breast.
And though his favourite seat be feeble woman's

"But if thou goest, I follow—" "Peace!" he said,—
She looked upon him and was calmed and cheered;
The ghastly colour from his lips had fled;
In his deportment, shape, and mien, appeared
Elysian beauty, melancholy grace,
Brought from a pensive though a happy place.

He spake of love, such love as Spirits feel
In worlds whose course is equable and pure;
No fears to beat away—no strife to heal—
The past unsighed for, and the future sure;   100
Spake of heroic arts in graver mood
Revived, with finer harmony pursued;

Of all that is most beauteous—imaged there
In happier beauty; more pellucid streams,
An ampler ether, a diviner air,
And fields invested with purpureal gleams;
Climes which the sun, who sheds the brightest day
Earth knows, is all unworthy to survey.

Yet there the Soul shall enter which hath earned
That privilege by virtue.—"Ill," said he,   110
"The end of man's existence I discerned,
Who from ignoble games and revelry
Could draw, when we had parted, vain delight,
While tears were thy best pastime, day and night;

"And while my youthful peers before my eyes
(Each hero following his peculiar bent)
Prepared themselves for glorious enterprise
By martial sports,—or, seated in the tent,
Chieftains and kings in council were detained;
What time the fleet at Aulis lay enchained,   120

"The wished-for wind was given:—I then revolved
The oracle, upon the silent sea;
And, if no worthier led the way, resolved
That, of a thousand vessels, mine should be
The foremost prow in pressing to the strand,—
Mine the first blood that tinged the Trojan sand.

"Yet bitter, oft-times bitter, was the pang
When of thy loss I thought, belovèd Wife!
On thee too fondly did my memory hang,   129
And on the joys we shared in mortal life,—   [flowers;
The paths which we had trod—these fountains,
My new-planned cities, and unfinished towers.

"But should suspense permit the Foe to cry,
'Behold they tremble!—haughty their array,
Yet of their number no one dares to die?'
In soul I swept the indignity away:
Old frailties then recurred:—but lofty thought,
In act embodied, my deliverance wrought.

"And Thou, though strong in love, art all too weak
In reason, in self-government too slow;   140
I counsel thee by fortitude to seek
Our blest re-union in the shades below.
The invisible world with thee hath sympathised;
Be thy affections raised and solemnised.

"Learn, by a mortal yearning, to ascend—
Seeking a higher object. Love was given,
Encouraged, sanctioned, chiefly for that end;
For this the passion to excess was driven—
That self might be annulled: her bondage prove
The fetters of a dream opposed to love."—   150

Aloud she shrieked! for Hermes reappears!   [vain:
Round the dear Shade she would have clung—'tis
The hours are past—too brief had they been years;
And him no mortal effort can detain:
Swift, toward the realms that know not earthly day,
He through the portal takes his silent way,
And on the palace-floor a lifeless corse She lay.

Thus, all in vain exhorted and reproved,
She perished; and, as for a wilful crime,
By the just Gods whom no weak pity moved,   160
Was doomed to wear out her appointed time,
Apart from happy Ghosts, that gather flowers
Of blissful quiet 'mid unfading bowers.

—Yet tears to human suffering are due;
And mortal hopes defeated and o'erthrown
Are mourned by man, and not by man alone,
As fondly he believes.—Upon the side
Of Hellespont (such faith was entertained)
A knot of spiry trees for ages grew

From out the tomb of him for whom she died;   170
And ever, when such stature they had gained
That Ilium's [4] walls were subject to their view,
The trees' tall summits withered at the sight;
A constant interchange of growth and blight!*

[1814]   [1815]

YARROW VISITED

SEPTEMBER, 1814

AND is this—Yarrow?—*This* the Stream
Of which my fancy cherished,
So faithfully, a waking dream?
An image that hath perished!
O that some Minstrel's harp were near,
To utter notes of gladness,
And chase this silence from the air,
That fills my heart with sadness!

Yet why?—a silvery current flows
With uncontrolled meanderings;   10
Nor have these eyes by greener hills
Been soothed, in all my wanderings.
And, through her depths, Saint Mary's Lake
Is visibly delighted;
For not a feature of those hills
Is in the mirror slighted.

A blue sky bends o'er Yarrow vale,
Save where that pearly whiteness
Is round the rising sun diffused,
A tender hazy brightness;   20
Mild dawn of promise! that excludes
All profitless dejection;
Though not unwilling here to admit
A pensive recollection.

Where was it that the famous Flower
Of Yarrow Vale lay bleeding?
His bed perchance was yon smooth mound
On which the herd is feeding:

And haply from this crystal pool,
Now peaceful as the morning,   30
The Water-wraith ascended thrice—
And gave his doleful warning. [1]

Delicious is the Lay that sings
The haunts of happy Lovers,
The path that leads them to the grove,
The leafy grove that covers:
And Pity sanctifies the Verse
That paints, by strength of sorrow,
The unconquerable strength of love;
Bear witness, rueful Yarrow!   40

But thou, that didst appear so fair
To fond imagination,
Dost rival in the light of day
Her delicate creation:
Meek loveliness is round thee spread,
A softness still and holy;
The grace of forest charms decayed,
And pastoral melancholy.

That region left, the vale unfolds
Rich groves of lofty stature,   50
With Yarrow winding through the pomp
Of cultivated nature;
And, rising from those lofty groves,
Behold a Ruin hoary!
The shattered front of Newark's Towers,
Renowned in Border story. [2]

Fair scenes for childhood's opening bloom,
For sportive youth to stray in;
For manhood to enjoy his strength;
And age to wear away in!   60
Yon cottage seems a bower of bliss,
A covert for protection
Of tender thoughts, that nestle there—
The brood of chaste affection.

How sweet, on this autumnal day,
The wild-wood fruits to gather,
And on my True-love's forehead plant
A crest of blooming heather!
And what if I enwreathed my own!
'Twere no offence to reason;   70
The sober Hills thus deck their brows
To meet the wintry season.

---

* For the account of these long-lived trees, see Pliny's "Natural History", ib. xvi. cap. 44; and for the features in the character of Protesilaus, see the "Iphigenia in Aulis" of Euripides. Virgil places the Shade of Laodamia in a mournful region, among unhappy Lovers,

——His Laodamia
It Comes.——[5]

[4] Troy.
[5] *Aeneid*, VI, 440–49.

[1] Wordsworth here alludes to legends associated with the Yarrow in stories and ballads. See also *Yarrow Unvisited*, p. 274.
[2] Sir Walter Scott's *Lay of the Last Minstrel*.

I see—but not by sight alone,
Loved Yarrow, have I won thee;
A ray of fancy still survives—
Her sunshine plays upon thee!
Thy ever-youthful waters keep
A course of lively pleasure;
And gladsome notes my lips can breathe,
Accordant to the measure.   80

The vapours linger round the Heights,
They melt, and soon must vanish;
One hour is theirs, nor more is mine—
Sad thought, which I would banish,
But that I know, where'er I go,
Thy genuine image, Yarrow!
Will dwell with me—to heighten joy,
And cheer my mind in sorrow.

[1814]   [1815]

SONNET

"Thee" of line 3 is Catherine Wordsworth, who died in June 1812 at the age of three. See note to "Characteristics of a Child Three Years Old."

SONNET

["Surprised by joy . . ."]

SURPRISED by joy—impatient as the Wind
I turned to share the transport—Oh! with whom
But Thee, deep buried in the silent tomb,
That spot which no vicissitude can find?
Love, faithful love, recalled thee to my mind—
But how could I forget thee? Through what power,
Even for the least division of an hour,
Have I been so beguiled as to be blind
To my most grievous loss!—That thought's return
Was the worst pang that sorrow ever bore,   10
Save one, one only, when I stood forlorn,
Knowing my heart's best treasure was no more;
That neither present time, nor years unborn
Could to my sight that heavenly face restore.

[1814?]   [1815]

SONNET

["Even as a dragon's eye . . ."]

EVEN as a dragon's eye that feels the stress
Of a bedimming sleep, or as a lamp
'Sullenly glaring through sepulchral damp,
So burns yon Taper 'mid a black recess

Of mountains, silent, dreary, motionless:
The lake below reflects it not; the sky
Muffled in clouds, affords no company
To mitigate and cheer its loneliness.
Yet, round the body of that joyless Thing
Which sends so far its melancholy light,   10
Perhaps are seated in domestic ring
A gay society with faces bright,
Conversing, reading, laughing;—or they sing,
While hearts and voices in the song unite.

[1814?]   [1815]

Benjamin R. Haydon (1786–1846), painter, defender of the Elgin Marbles, diarist, was Keats's close friend. His painting Christ's Triumphant Entry into Jerusalem *contains the faces of Wordsworth, Keats, William Hazlitt, and Charles Lamb. See Keats's several poems to Haydon.*

SONNET

TO B. R. HAYDON

HIGH is our calling, Friend!—Creative Art
(Whether the instrument of words she use,
Or pencil pregnant with ethereal hues,)
Demands the service of a mind and heart,
Though sensitive, yet, in their weakest part,
Heroically fashioned—to infuse
Faith in the whispers of the lonely Muse,
While the whole world seems adverse to desert.
And, oh! when Nature sinks, as oft she may,
Through long-lived pressure of obscure distress,
Still to be strenuous for the bright reward,   11
And in the soul admit of no decay,
Brook no continuance of weak-mindedness—
Great is the glory, for the strife is hard!

[1815]   [1816]

THE PASS OF KIRKSTONE
Kirkstone Pass appears frequently in Dorothy Wordsworth's Journals. *It runs northeast from Ambleside, and was for the Wordsworths one of the most frequented routes from the Grasmere region to Penrith and the north.*

THE PASS OF KIRKSTONE

I

WITHIN the mind strong fancies work,
A deep delight the bosom thrills,
Oft as I pass along the fork
Of these fraternal hills:

Where, save the rugged road, we find
No appanage of human kind,
Nor hint of man; if stone or rock
Seem not his handy-work to mock
By something cognizably shaped;
Mockery—or model roughly hewn,   10
And left as if by earthquake strewn,
Or from the Flood escaped:
Altars for Druid service fit;
(But where no fire was ever lit,
Unless the glow-worm to the skies
Thence offer nightly sacrifice)
Wrinkled Egyptian monument;
Green moss-grown tower; or hoary tent;
Tents of a camp that never shall be raised—
On which four thousand years have gazed!   20

II

Ye ploughshares sparkling on the slopes!
Ye snow-white lambs that trip
Imprisoned 'mid the formal props
Of restless ownership!
Ye trees, that may to-morrow fall
To feed the insatiate Prodigal!
Lawns, houses, chattels, groves, and fields,
All that the fertile valley shields;
Wages of folly—baits of crime,
Of life's uneasy game the stake,   30
Playthings that keep the eyes awake
Of drowsy, dotard Time;—
O care! O guilt!—O vales and plains,
Here, 'mid his own unvexed domains,
A Genius dwells, that can subdue
At once all memory of You,—
Most potent when mists veil the sky,
Mists that distort and magnify,
While the coarse rushes, to the sweeping breeze,
Sigh forth their ancient melodies!   40

III

List to those shriller notes!—*that* march
Perchance was on the blast,
When, through this Height's inverted arch,
Rome's earliest legion passed!
—They saw, adventurously impelled,
And older eyes than theirs behold,
This block—and yon, whose church-like frame
Gives to this savage Pass its name.
Aspiring Road! that lov'st to hide
Thy daring in a vapoury bourn,   50
Not seldom may the hour return
When thou shalt be my guide:
And I (as all men may find cause,
When life is at a weary pause,

And they have panted up the hill
Of duty with reluctant will)
Be thankful, even though tired and faint,
For the rich bounties of constraint;
Whence oft invigorating transports flow
That choice lacked courage to bestow!   60

IV

My Soul was grateful for delight
That wore a threatening brow;
A veil is lifted—can she slight
The scene that opens now?
Though habitation none appear,
The greenness tells, man must be there;
The shelter—that the pérspective
Is of the clime in which we live;
Where Toil pursues his daily round;
Where Pity sheds sweet tears—and Love,   70
In woodbine bower or birchen grove,
Inflicts his tender wound.
—Who comes not hither ne'er shall know
How beautiful the world below;
Nor can he guess how lightly leaps
The brook adown the rocky steeps.
Farewell, thou desolate Domain!
Hope, pointing to the cultured plain,
Carols like a shepherd-boy;
And who is she?—Can that be Joy!   80
Who, with a sunbeam for her guide,
Smoothly skims the meadows wide;
While Faith, from yonder opening cloud,
To hill and vale proclaims aloud,
"Whate'er the weak may dread, the wicked dare,
Thy lot, O Man, is good, thy portion fair!"

[1817]   [1820]

THE RIVER DUDDON

*The river Duddon, to which Wordsworth addressed a series of
thirty-four sonnets, "rises upon Wrynose Fell, on the confines
of Westmorland, Cumberland, and Lancashire; and . . . enters
the Irish Sea. . . ."*

F R O M

THE RIVER DUDDON

I

NOT envying Latian shades—if yet they throw
A grateful coolness round that crystal Spring,
Blandusia, prattling as when long ago
The Sabine Bard was moved her praise to sing;

Careless of flowers that in perennial blow
Round the moist marge of Persian fountains cling;
Heedless of Alpine torrents thundering
Through ice-built arches radiant as heaven's bow;
I seek the birthplace of a native Stream.—
All hail, ye mountains! hail, thou morning light!   10
Better to breathe at large on this clear height
Than toil in needless sleep from dream to dream:
Pure flow the verse, pure, vigorous, free, and bright,
For Duddon, long-loved Duddon, is my theme!

II

CHILD of the clouds! remote from every taint
Of sordid industry thy lot is cast;
Thine are the honours of the lofty waste;
Nor seldom, when with heat the valleys faint,
Thy handmaid Frost with spangled tissue quaint
Thy cradle decks;—to chant thy birth, thou hast
No meaner Poet than the whistling Blast,
And Desolation is thy Patron-saint!
She guards thee, ruthless Power! who would not spare
Those mighty forests, once the bison's screen,   10
Where stalked the huge deer to his shaggy lair*
Through paths and alleys roofed with darkest green;
Thousands of years before the silent air
Was pierced by whizzing shaft of hunter keen!

XXXIV
AFTER-THOUGHT

I THOUGHT of Thee, my partner and my guide,
As being past away.—Vain sympathies!
For, backward, Duddon! as I cast my eyes,
I see what was, and is, and will abide;
Still glides the Stream, and shall for ever glide;
The Form remains, the Function never dies;
While we, the brave, the mighty, and the wise,
We Men, who in our morn of youth defied
The elements, must vanish;—be it so!
Enough, if something from our hands have power   10
To live, and act, and serve the future hour;
And if, as toward the silent tomb we go,
Through love, through hope, and faith's transcendent
      dower,
We feel that we are greater than we know.

[1806–20]   [1820]

[END OF SELECTION FROM
THE RIVER DUDDON]

* The deer alluded to is the Leigh, a gigantic species long since extinct.

SEPTEMBER, 1819

THE sylvan slopes with corn-clad fields
Are hung, as if with golden shields,
Bright trophies of the sun!
Like a fair sister of the sky,
Unruffled doth the blue lake lie,
The mountains looking on.

And, sooth to say, yon vocal grove,
Albeit uninspired by love,
By love untaught to ring,
May well afford to mortal ear   10
An impulse more profoundly dear
Than music of the Spring.

For *that* from turbulence and heat
Proceeds, from some uneasy seat
In nature's struggling frame,
Some region of impatient life:
And jealousy, and quivering strife,
Therein a portion claim.

This, this is holy;—while I hear
These vespers of another year,   20
This hymn of thanks and praise,
My spirit seems to mount above
The anxieties of human love,
And earth's precarious days.

But list!—though winter storms be nigh,
Unchecked is that soft harmony:
There lives Who can provide
For all His creatures; and in Him,
Even like the radiant Seraphim,
These choristers confide.   30

[1819]   [1820]

FROM
ECCLESIASTICAL SONNETS

I

INTRODUCTION

I, WHO accompanied with faithful pace
Cerulean Duddon from its cloud-fed spring,
And loved with spirit ruled by his to sing
Of mountain-quiet and boon nature's grace;
I, who essayed the nobler Stream to trace
Of Liberty, and smote the plausive string
Till the checked torrent, proudly triumphing,
Won for herself a lasting resting-place;

Now seek upon the heights of Time the source
Of a HOLY RIVER,[1] on whose banks are found   10
Sweet pastoral flowers, and laurels that have crowned
Full oft the unworthy brow of lawless force;
And, for delight of him who tracks its course,
Immortal amaranth and palms abound.

V

UNCERTAINTY

DARKNESS surrounds us; seeking, we are lost
On Snowdon's wilds,[2] amid Brigantian coves,
Or where the solitary shepherd roves
Along the plain of Sarum, by the ghost
Of Time and shadows of Tradition crost;
And where the boatman of the Western Isles
Slackens his course—to marks those holy piles
Which yet survive on bleak Iona's coast.[3]
Nor these, nor monuments of eldest name,
Nor Taliesin's unforgotten lays,   10
Nor characters of Greek or Roman fame,
To an unquestionable Source have led;
Enough—if eyes, that sought the fountain-head
In vain, upon the growing Rill may gaze.

XXXIV

MUTABILITY

FROM low to high doth dissolution climb,
And sink from high to low, along a scale
Of awful notes, whose concord shall not fail;
A musical but melancholy chime,
Which they can hear who meddle not with crime,
Nor avarice, nor over-anxious care.
Truth fails not; but her outward forms that bear
The longest date do melt like frosty rime,
That in the morning whitened hill and plain
And is no more; drop like the tower sublime   10
Of yesterday, which royally did wear
His crown of weeds, but could not even sustain
Some casual shout that broke the silent air,
Or the unimaginable touch of Time.

[1] A subtitle explains that these poems will describe the time "from the introduction of Christianity into Britain to the consummation of the Royal Dominion"—i.e., from the time of St. Paul's mission in the first century to Henry VIII's destruction of the monasteries in the sixteenth.
[2] See *The Prelude*, Book XIV, lines 1–10 and notes.
[3] Iona, off the coast of the Royal Scotland, was supposedly the center of Celtic Christianity, and Sarum (Salisbury) Plain, in England, has many early religious monuments in addition to Stonehenge. Taliesin was a sixth-century Welsh bard.

XLVII

CONCLUSION

WHY sleeps the future, as a snake enrolled,
Coil within coil, at noon-tide? For the WORD
Yields, if with unpresumptuous faith explored,
Power at whose touch the sluggard shall unfold
His drowsy rings. Look forth!—that Stream
     behold,
THAT STREAM upon whose bosom we have passed
Floating at ease while nations have effaced
Nations, and Death has gathered to his fold
Long lines of mighty Kings—look forth, my Soul!
(Nor in this vision be thou slow to trust)   10
The living Waters, less and less by guilt
Stained and polluted, brighten as they roll,
Till they have reached the eternal City—built
For the perfected Spirits of the just!

[1821]   [1822]

[END OF SELECTION FROM
ECCLESIASTICAL SONNETS]

SONNET
["Scorn not the Sonnet . . ."]

SCORN not the Sonnet; Critic, you have frowned,
Mindless of its just honours; with this key
Shakspeare unlocked his heart; the melody
Of this small lute gave ease to Petrarch's wound;
A thousand times this pipe did Tasso sound;
With it Camöens soothed an exile's grief;
The Sonnet glittered a gay myrtle leaf
Amid the cypress with which Dante crowned
His visionary brow: a glow-worm lamp,
It cheered mild Spenser, called from Faery-land   10
To struggle through dark ways; and, when a
     damp
Fell round the path of Milton, in his hand
The Thing became a trumpet; whence he blew
Soul-animating strains—alas, too few!

[?]   [1827]

TO A SKYLARK

ETHEREAL minstrel! pilgrim of the sky!
Dost thou despise the earth where cares abound?
Or, while the wings aspire, are heart and eye
Both with thy nest upon the dewy ground?
Thy nest which thou canst drop into at will,
Those quivering wings composed, that music still!

Leave to the nightingale her shady wood;
A privacy of glorious light is thine;
Whence thou dost pour upon the world a flood
Of harmony, with instinct more divine;					10
Type of the wise who soar, but never roam;
True to the kindred points of Heaven and Home!

[1825]						[1827]

SONNET

IN ALLUSION TO VARIOUS RECENT HISTORIES AND NOTICES OF THE FRENCH REVOLUTION

PORTENTOUS change when History can appear
As the cool Advocate of foul device;
Reckless audacity extol, and jeer
At consciences perplexed with scruples nice!
They who bewail not, must abhor, the sneer
Born of Conceit, Power's blind Idolater;
Or haply sprung from vaunting Cowardice
Betrayed by mockery of holy fear.
Hath it not long been said the wrath of Man
Works not the righteousness of God? Oh bend,			10
Bend, ye Perverse! to judgments from on High,
Laws that lay under Heaven's perpetual ban
All principles of action that transcend
The sacred limits of humanity.

[?]							[1842]

WRITTEN AFTER THE DEATH OF CHARLES LAMB
Wordsworth and Coleridge's friend, author of the "Elia" essays and some poetry, Lamb (1775–1834) was employed throughout his adult life as a clerk in the East India House. When Lamb was twenty-one his sister Mary, in a fit of insanity, stabbed their mother to death. Lamb never married, and devoted much of his life to the care of his sister, who was only occasionally mad. Lamb died in Edmonton on December 27, 1834. See also Coleridge's This Lime-tree Bower My Prison, *p. 446.*

WRITTEN AFTER THE DEATH OF CHARLES LAMB

To a good Man of most dear memory
This Stone is sacred. Here he lies apart
From the great city where he first drew breath,
Was reared and taught; and humbly earned his bread,
To the strict labours of the merchant's desk
By duty chained. Not seldom did those tasks
Tease, and the thought of time so spent depress,
His spirit, but the recompence was high;
Firm Independence, Bounty's rightful sire;

Affections, warm as sunshine, free as air;			10
And when the precious hours of leisure came,
Knowledge and wisdom, gained from converse sweet
With books, or while he ranged the crowded streets
With a keen eye, and overflowing heart:
So genius triumphed over seeming wrong,
And poured out truth in works by thoughtful love
Inspired—works potent over smiles and tears.
And as round mountain-tops the lightning plays,
Thus innocently sported, breaking forth
As from a cloud of some grave sympathy,			20
Humour and wild instinctive wit, and all
The vivid flashes of his spoken words.
From the most gentle creature nursed in fields
Had been derived the name he bore—a name,
Wherever Christian altars have been raised,
Hallowed to meekness and to innocence;
And if in him meekness at times gave way,
Provoked out of herself by troubles strange,
Many and strange, that hung about his life;
Still, at the centre of his being, lodged			30
A soul by resignation sanctified:
And if too often, self-reproached, he felt
That innocence belongs not to our kind,
A power that never ceased to abide in him,
Charity, 'mid the multitude of sins
That she can cover, left not his exposed
To an unforgiving judgment from just Heaven.
O, he was good, if e'er a good Man lived!

					*	*	*	*	*

From a reflecting mind and sorrowing heart
Those simple lines flowed with an earnest wish,		40
Thought but a doubting hope, that they might serve
Fitly to guard the precious dust of him
Whose virtues called them forth. That aim is missed;
For much that truth most urgently required
Had from a faltering pen been asked in vain:
Yet, haply, on the printed page received,
The imperfect record, there, may stand unblamed
As long as verse of mine shall breathe the air
Of memory, or see the light of love.
	Thou wert a scorner of the fields, my Friend,		50
But more in show than truth; and from the fields,
And from the mountains, to thy rural grave
Transported, my soothed spirit hovers o'er
Its green untrodden turf, and blowing flowers;
And taking up a voice shall speak (tho' still
Awed by the theme's peculiar sanctity
Which words less free presumed not even to touch)
Of that fraternal love, whose heaven-lit lamp
From infancy, through manhood, to the last
Of threescore years, and to thy latest hour,		60

Burned on with ever-strengthening light, enshrined
Within thy bosom.   "Wonderful" hath been
The love established between man and man,
"Passing the love of women;" and between
Man and his help-mate in fast wedlock joined
Through God, is raised a spirit and soul of love
Without whose blissful influence Paradise
Had been no Paradise; and earth were now
A waste where creatures bearing human form,
Direst of savage beasts, would roam in fear,   70
Joyless and comfortless. Our days glide on;
And let him grieve who cannot choose but grieve
That he hath been an Elm without his Vine,
And her bright dower of clustering charities,
That, round his trunk and branches, might have clung
Enriching and adorning. Unto thee,
Not so enriched, not so adorned, to thee
Was given (say rather thou of later birth
Wert given to her) a Sister—'tis a word
Timidly uttered, for she *lives*, the meek,   80
The self-restraining, and the ever-kind;
In whom thy reason and intelligent heart
Found—for all interests, hopes, and tender cares,
All softening, humanising, hallowing powers,
Whether withheld, or for her sake unsought—
More than sufficient recompense!
                                Her love
(What weakness prompts the voice to tell it here?)
Was as the love of mothers; and when years,
Lifting the boy to man's estate, had called
The long-protected to assume the part   90
Of a protector, the first filial tie
Was undissolved; and, in or out of sight,
Remained imperishably interwoven
With life itself. Thus, 'mid a shifting world,
Did they together testify of time
And season's difference—a double tree
With two collateral stems sprung from one root;
Such were they—such thro' life they *might* have been
In union, in partition only such;
Otherwise wrought the will of the Most High;   100
Yet, thro' all visitations and all trials,
Still they were faithful; like two vessels launched
From the same beach one ocean to explore
With mutual help, and sailing—to their league
True, as inexorable winds, or bars
Floating or fixed of polar ice, allow.

    But turn we rather, let my spirit turn
With thine, O silent and invisible Friend!
To those dear intervals, nor rare nor brief,
When reunited, and by choice withdrawn   110
From miscellaneous converse, ye were taught

That the remembrance of foregone distress,
And the worse fear of future ill (which oft
Doth hang around it, as a sickly child
Upon its mother) maybe be both alike
Disarmed of power to unsettle present good
So prized, and things inward and outward held
In such an even balance, that the heart
Acknowledges God's grace, his mercy feels,
And in its depth of gratitude is still.   120

    O gift divine of quiet sequestration!
The hermit, exercised in prayer and praise,
And feeling daily on the hope of heaven,
Is happy in his vow, and fondly cleaves
To life-long singleness; but happier far
Was to your souls, and, to the thoughts of others,
A thousand times more beautiful appeared,
Your dual loneliness. The sacred tie
Is broken; yet why grieve? for Time but holds
His moiety in trust, till Joy shall lead   130
To the blest world where parting is unknown.

[1835]   [1837]

EXTEMPORE EFFUSION

James Hogg, known as the Ettrick Shepherd, died November 21,
1835. In an 1837 note to the poem, Wordsworth appends a short
list of other literary figures of his generation who had recently
died, including Scott and Crabbe in 1832, Coleridge and Lamb
in 1834.

EXTEMPORE EFFUSION UPON THE DEATH OF JAMES HOGG

When first, descending from the moorlands,
I saw the Stream of Yarrow glide
Along a bare and open valley,
The Ettrick Shepherd was my guide.

When last along its banks I wandered,
Through groves that had begun to shed
Their golden leaves upon the pathways,
My steps the Border-minstrel led.

The mighty Minstrel breathes no longer,
'Mid mouldering ruins low he lies;   10
And death upon the braes of Yarrow,
Has closed the Shepherd-poet's eyes:

Nor has the rolling year twice measured,
From sign to sign, its stedfast course,
Since every mortal power of Coleridge
Was frozen at its marvellous source;

The rapt One, of the godlike forehead,
The heaven-eyed creature sleeps in earth:
And Lamb, the frolic and the gentle,
Has vanished from his lonely hearth.   20

Like clouds that rake the mountain-summits,
Or waves that own no curbing hand,
How fast has brother followed brother,
From sunshine to the sunless land!

Yet I, whose lids from infant slumber
Were earlier raised, remain to hear
A timid voice, that asks in whispers,
"Who next will drop and disappear?"

Our haughty life is crowned with darkness,
Like London with its own black wreath,   30
On which with thee, O Crabbe! forth-looking.
I gazed from Hampstead's breezy heath.

As if but yesterday departed,
Thou too art gone before; but why,
O'er ripe fruit, seasonably gathered,
Should frail survivors heave a sigh?

Mourn rather for that holy Spirit,[1]
Sweet as the spring, as ocean deep;
For Her who, ere her summer faded,
Has sunk into a breathless sleep.   40

No more of old romantic sorrows,
For slaughtered Youth or love-lorn Maid!
With sharper grief is Yarrow smitten,
And Ettrick mourns with her their Poet dead.

[1835]   [1835]

---

*When a proposal to extend the Kendal and Westmorland
Railway farther into the Lake District threatened to bring crowds
of tourists and their entertainments ("wrestling matches, horse
and boat races without number, and pot-houses and beer-shops"),
Wordsworth wrote letters—and this sonnet—in protest.*

SONNET

ON THE PROJECTED
KENDAL AND WINDERMERE RAILWAY

Is THEN no nook of English ground secure
From rash assault?* Schemes of retirement sown
In youth, and 'mid the busy world kept pure
As when their earliest flowers of hope were blown,
Must perish;—how can they this blight endure?
And must he too the ruthless change bemoan
Who scorns a false utilitarian lure
'Mid his paternal fields at random thrown?
Baffle the threat, bright Scene, from Orrest-head
Given to the pausing traveller's rapturous glance:
Plead for thy peace, thou beautiful romance   11
Of nature; and, if human hearts be dead,
Speak, passing winds; ye torrents, with your strong
And constant voice, protest against the wrong.

[1844]   [1844]

---

[1] Mrs. Felicia Hemans (1793–1835), a poet and critic, popular in America as well as in England.

* The degree and kind of attachment which many of the yeomanry feel to their small inheritances can scarcely be over-rated. Near the house of one of them stands a magnificent tree, which a neighbour of the owner advised him to fell for profit's sake. "Fell it!" exclaimed the yeoman, "I had rather fall on my knees and worship it." It happens, I believe, that the intended railway would pass through this little property, and I hope that an apology for the answer will not be thought necessary by one who enters into the strength of the feeling.

ODE ON THE INSTALLATION

*Written with the assistance of his nephew Bishop Christopher
Wordsworth, this official poem by the Poet Laureate is one of
Wordsworth's last works.*

*The first stanza alludes to the defeat of Napoleon, and his
banishment by the British to St. Helena in 1815; the second
stanza to the death of Princess Charlotte, presumed heiress to
the throne of her grandfather George III, at Claremont Hall
(Esher, Surrey) in 1817. The succession of the monarchy,
complicated by her death and by the marriages of the three royal
dukes in 1818, was clarified when Victoria was born to the Duke
of Kent in May 1819 (stanza III). Her future consort, Prince
Albert of Saxe-Coburg-Gotha, was born in Germany later in the
same year. The Chancellorship of Cambridge (and Oxford) is a
ceremonial rather than an administrative office. The chief
academic officer is the Vice Chancellor.*

ODE ON THE INSTALLATION OF HIS ROYAL HIGHNESS PRINCE ALBERT AS CHANCELLOR OF THE UNIVERSITY OF CAMBRIDGE, JULY, 1847

FOR thirst of power that Heaven disowns,
   For temples, towers, and thrones
Too long insulted by the Spoiler's shock,
   Indignant Europe cast
   Her stormy foe at last
To reap the whirlwind on a Libyan rock.
   War is passion's basest game
   Madly played to win a name:
Up starts some tyrant, Earth and Heaven to dare,
   The servile million bow;   10
But will the Lightning glance aside to spare
   The Despot's laurelled brow?

   War is mercy, glory, fame,
   Waged in Freedom's holy cause,
   Freedom, such as man may claim
   Under God's restraining laws.
   Such is Albion's fame and glory,
   Let rescued Europe tell the story.
But lo! what sudden cloud has darkened all
   The land as with a funeral pall?   20
The Rose of England suffers blight,
The Flower has drooped, the Isle's delight;
   Flower and bud together fall;
A Nation's hopes lie crushed in Claremont's desolate
   Hall.

Time a chequered mantle wears—
   Earth awakes from wintry sleep:
Again the Tree a blossom bears;
   Cease, Britannia, cease to weep!

Hark to the peals on this bright May-morn!
They tell that your future Queen is born.   30
   A Guardian Angel fluttered
   Above the babe, unseen;
   One word he softly uttered,
   It named the future Queen;
And a joyful cry through the Island rang,
As clear and bold as the trumpet's clang,
   As bland as the reed of peace:
   "VICTORIA be her name!"
For righteous triumphs are the base
Whereon Britannia rests her peaceful fame.   40

Time, in his mantle's sunniest fold
Uplifted in his arms the child,
And while the fearless infant smiled,
Her happier destiny foretold:—
   "Infancy, by Wisdom mild,
   Trained to health and artless beauty;
   Youth, by pleasure unbeguiled
   From the lore of lofty duty;
   Womanhood in pure renown,
   Seated on her lineal throne;   50
   Leaves of myrtle in her Crown,
   Fresh with lustre all their own.
   Love, the treasure worth possessing
   More than all the world beside,
   This shall be her choicest blessing,
   Oft to royal hearts denied."

That eve, the Star of Brunswick shone
   With steadfast ray benign
On Gotha's ducal roof, and on
   The softly flowing Leine,   60
Nor failed to gild the spires of Bonn,
   And glittered on the Rhine.
Old Camus, too, on that prophetic night
   Was conscious of the ray;
And his willows whispered in its light,
   Not to the Zephyr's sway,
But with a Delphic life, in sight
   Of this auspicious day—
This day, when Granta[1] hails her chosen Lord,
   And proud of her award,   70
   Confiding in that Star serene,
Welcomes the Consort of a happy Queen.

   Prince, in these collegiate bowers,
   Where science, leagued with holier truth,
   Guards the sacred heart of youth,
   Solemn monitors are ours.

---

[1] The river Cam; see *The Prelude*, Book III.

These reverend aisles, these hallowed towers,
Raised by many a hand august,
Are haunted by majestic Powers,
The Memories of the Wise and Just,　　　80
Who, faithful to a pious trust,
Here, in the Founder's Spirit sought
To mould and stamp the ore of thought
In that bold form and impress high
That best betoken patriot loyalty.
Not in vain those Sages taught,—
True disciples, good as great,
Have pondered here their country's weal,
Weighed the Future by the Past,
Learned how social frames may last,　　　90
And how a Land may rule its fate
By constancy inviolate,
Though worlds to their foundations reel
The sport of factious Hate or godless Zeal.

Albert, in thy race we cherish
A Nation's strength that will not perish
While England's sceptred Line

True to the King of Kings is found;
Like that wise ancestor of thine
Who threw the Saxon shield o'er Luther's life　　　100
When first, above the yells of bigot strife,
The trumpet of the Living Word
Assumed a voice of deep portentous sound,
From gladdened Elbe to startled Tiber heard.
What shield more sublime
E'er was blazoned or sung?
And the PRINCE whom we greet
From its Hero is sprung.
Resound, resound the strain
That hails him for our own!　　　110
Again, again, and yet again,
For the Church, the State, the Throne!
And that Presence fair and bright,
Ever blest wherever seen,
Who deigns to grace our festal rite,
The Pride of the Islands, VICTORIA THE
　　　QUEEN!

[1847]　　　　　　　　　　　　　　　　[1847]

PROSE

PREFACE TO LYRICAL BALLADS
The Preface was altered in each edition of Lyrical Ballads. *The text used here is substantially that of 1800, with some clarifications from later editions.*

PREFACE TO THE SECOND AND SUBSEQUENT EDITIONS OF "LYRICAL BALLADS"

THE first Volume of these Poems has already been submitted to general perusal. It was published, as an experiment, which, I hoped, might be of some use to ascertain, how far, by fitting to metrical arrangement a selection of the real language of men in a state of vivid sensation, that sort of pleasure and that quantity of pleasure may be imparted, which a Poet may rationally endeavour to impart.

I had formed no very inaccurate estimate of the probable effect of those Poems: I flattered myself that they who should be pleased with them would read them with more than common pleasure: and, on the other hand, I was well aware, that by those who should dislike them, they would be read with more than common dislike. The result has differed from my expectation in this only, that a greater number have been pleased than I ventured to hope I should please.

*　　*　　*　　*　　*

Several of my Friends are anxious for the success of these Poems, from a belief that, if the views with which they were composed were indeed realised, a class of Poetry would be produced, well adapted to interest mankind permanently, and not unimportant in the quality, and in the multiplicity of its moral relations: and on this account they have advised me to prefix a systematic defence of the theory upon which the Poems were written. But I was unwilling to undertake the task, knowing that on this occasion the Reader would look coldly upon my arguments, since I might be suspected of having been principally influenced by the selfish and foolish hope of *reasoning* him into an approbation of these particular Poems: and I was still more unwilling to undertake the task, because, adequately to display the opinions, and fully to enforce the arguments, would require a space wholly disproportionate to a preface. For, to treat the subject with the clearness and coherence of which it is susceptible, it would be necessary to give a full account of the present state of the public taste in this country, and to determine how far this taste is healthy or depraved; which, again, could not be determined, without pointing out in what manner language and the human mind act and re-act on each other, and without retracing the revolutions, not of literature alone, but likewise of society itself. I have therefore altogether declined to enter regularly upon this defence; yet I am sensible, that there would be something like impropriety in abruptly obtruding upon the Public, without a few words of introduction, Poems so materially different from those upon which general approbation is at present bestowed.

It is supposed, that by the act of writing in verse an Author makes a formal engagement that he will gratify certain known habits of association; that he not only thus apprises the Reader that certain classes of ideas and expressions will be found in his book, but that others will be carefully excluded. This exponent or symbol held forth by metrical language must in different eras of literature have excited very different expectations: for example, in the age of Catullus, Terence, and Lucretius, and that of Statius or Claudian; and in our own country, in the age of Shakspeare and Beaumont and Fletcher, and that of Donne and Cowley, or Dryden, or Pope. I will not take upon me to determine the exact import of the promise which, by the act of writing in verse, an Author in the present day makes to his reader: but it will undoubtedly appear to many persons that I have not fulfilled the terms of an engagement thus voluntarily contracted. They who have been accustomed to the gaudiness and inane phraseology of many modern writers, if they persist in reading this book to its conclusion, will, no doubt, frequently have to struggle with feelings of strangeness and awkwardness: they will look round for poetry, and will be induced to inquire by what species of courtesy these attempts can be permitted to assume that title. I hope therefore the reader will not censure me for attempting to state what I have proposed to myself to perform; and also (as far as the limits of a preface will permit) to explain some of the chief reasons which have determined me in the choice of my purpose: that at least he may be spared any unpleasant feeling of disappointment, and that I myself may be protected from one of the most dishonourable accusations which can be brought against an Author; namely, that of an indolence which prevents him from endeavouring to ascertain what is his duty, or, when his duty is ascertained, prevents him from performing it.

The principal object, then, proposed in these Poems was to choose incidents and situations from common life, and to relate or describe them, through-out, as far as was possible in a selection of language really used by men, and, at the same time, to throw over them a certain colouring of imagination, whereby ordinary things should be presented to the mind in an unusual aspect; and, further, and above all, to make these incidents and situations interesting by tracing in them, truly though not ostentatiously, the primary laws of our nature: chiefly, as far as regards the manner in which we associate ideas in a state of excitement. Humble and rustic life was generally chosen, because, in that condition, the essential passions of the heart find a better soil in which they can attain their maturity, are less under restraint, and speak a plainer and more emphatic language; because in that condition of life our elementary feelings co-exist in a state of greater simplicity, and consequently, may be more accurately contemplated, and more forcibly communicated; because the manners of rural life germinate from those elementary feelings, and, from the necessary character of rural occupations, are more easily comprehended, and are more durable; and, lastly, because in that condition the passions of men are incorporated with the beautiful and permanent forms of nature. The language, too, of these men has been adopted (purified indeed from what appear to be its real defects, from all lasting and rational causes of dislike or disgust) because such men hourly communicate with the best objects from which the best part of language is originally derived; and because, from their rank in society and the sameness and narrow circle of their intercourse, being less under the influence of social vanity, they convey their feelings and notions in simple and unelaborated expressions. Accordingly, such a language, arising out of repeated experience and regular feelings, is a more permanent, and a far more philosophical language, than that which is frequently substituted for it by Poets, who think that they are conferring honour upon themselves and their art, in proportion as they separate themselves from the sympathies of men, and indulge in arbitrary and capricious habits of expression, in order to furnish food for fickle tastes, and fickle appetites, of their own creation.*

I cannot, however, be insensible to the present outcry against the triviality and meanness, both of thought and language, which some of my contemporaries have occasionally introduced into their metrical compositions; and I acknowledge that this defect, where it exists, is more dishonourable to the Writer's own character than false refinement or arbitrary innovation, though I should contend at the

---

* It is worthwhile here to observe, that the affecting parts of Chaucer are almost always expressed in language pure and universally intelligible even to this day.

same time, that it is far less pernicious in the sum of its consequences. From such verses the Poems in these volumes will be found distinguished at least by one mark of difference, that each of them has a worthy *purpose*. Not that I always began to write with a distinct purpose formally conceived; but habits of meditation have, I trust, so prompted and regulated my feelings, that my descriptions of such objects as strongly excite those feelings, will be found to carry along with them a *purpose*. If this opinion be errone-ous, I can have little right to the name of a Poet. For all good poetry is the spontaneous overflow of power-ful feelings: and though this be true, Poems to which any value can be attached were never produced on any variety of subjects but by a man who, being possessed of more than usual organic sensibility, had also thought long and deeply. For our continued influxes of feeling are modified and directed by our thoughts, which are indeed the representatives of all our past feelings; and, as by contemplating the relation of these general representatives to each other, we discover what is really important to men, so, by the repetition and continuance of this act, our feelings will be connected with important subjects, till at length, if we be originally possessed of much sensibility, such habits of mind will be produced, that, by obeying blindly and mechanically the impulses of those habits, we shall describe objects, and utter sentiments, of such a nature, and in such connection with each other, that the understanding of the Reader must necessarily be in some degree enlightened, and his affections strengthened and purified.

It has been said that each of these poems has a purpose. Another circumstance must be mentioned which distinguishes these Poems from the popular Poetry of the day; it is this, that the feeling therein developed gives importance to the action and situa-tion, and not the action and situation to the feeling.

A sense of false modesty shall not prevent me from asserting, that the Reader's attention is pointed to this mark of distinction, far less for the sake of these particular Poems than from the general importance of the subject. The subject is indeed important! For the human mind is capable of being excited without the application of gross and violent stimulants; and he must have a very faint perception of its beauty and dignity who does not know this, and who does not further know, that one being is elevated above another, in proportion as he possesses this capability. It has therefore appeared to me, that to endeavour to produce or enlarge this capability is one of the best services in which, at any period, a Writer can be engaged; but this service, excellent at all times, is especially so at the present day. For a multitude of

causes, unknown to former times, are now acting with a combined force to blunt the discriminating powers of the mind, and, unfitting it for all voluntary exer-tion, to reduce it to a state of almost savage torpor. The most effective of these causes are the great national events which are daily taking place, and the increasing accumulation of men in cities, where the uniformity of their occupations produces a craving for extraordinary incident, which the rapid com-munication of intelligence hourly gratifies. To this tendency of life and manners the literature and theatrical exhibitions of the country have conformed themselves. The invaluable works of our elder writers, I had almost said the works of Shakspeare and Milton, are driven into neglect by frantic novels, sickly and stupid German Tragedies, and deluges of idle and extravagant stories in verse.[1]—When I think upon this degrading thirst after outrageous stimula-tion I am almost ashamed to have spoken of the feeble endeavour made in these volumes to counter-act it; and, reflecting upon the magnitude of the general evil, I should be oppressed with no dis-honourable melancholy, had I not a deep impression of certain inherent and indestructible qualities of the human mind, and likewise of certain powers in the great and permanent objects that act upon it, which are equally inherent and indestructible; and were there not added to this impression a belief, that the time is approaching when the evil will be systematic-ally opposed, by men of greater powers, and with far more distinguished success.

Having dwelt thus long on the subjects and aim of these Poems, I shall request the Reader's permission to apprise him of a few circumstances relating to their *style*, in order, among other reasons, that he may not censure me for not having performed what I never attempted. The Reader will find that personifications of abstract ideas rarely occur in these volumes; and are utterly rejected, as an ordinary device to elevate the style, and raise it above prose. My purpose was to imitate, and, as far as is possible, to adopt the very language of men; and assuredly such personifications do not make any natural or regular part of that language. They are, indeed, a figure of speech occasionally prompted by passion, and I have made use of them as such; but have endeavoured utterly to reject them as a mechanical device of style, or as a family language which Writers in metre seem to lay claim to by prescription. I have wished to keep the Reader in the company of flesh and blood, persuaded

---

[1] The popular arts included the novelistic combination of horror and eroticism called Gothic—e.g., M. G. Lewis's *The Monk*—and the plays of the German *Sturm und Drang*.

that by so doing I shall interest him. Others who pursue a different track will interest him likewise; I do not interfere with their claim, but wish to prefer a claim of my own. There will also be found in these volumes little of what is usually called poetic diction; as much pains has been taken to avoid it as is ordinarily taken to produce it; this has been done for the reason already alleged, to bring my language near to the language of men; and further, because the pleasure which I have proposed to myself to impart, is of a kind very different from that which is supposed by many persons to be the proper object of poetry. Without being culpably particular, I do not know how to give my Reader a more exact notion of the style in which it was my wish and intention to write, than by informing him that I have at all times endeavoured to look steadily at my subject; consequently, there is I hope in these Poems little falsehood of description, and my ideas are expressed in language fitted to their respective importance. Something must have been gained by this practice, as it is friendly to one property of all good poetry, namely, good sense: but it has necessarily cut me off from a large portion of phrases and figures of speech which from father to son have long been regarded as the common inheritance of Poets. I have also thought it expedient to restrict myself still further, having abstained from the use of many expressions, in themselves proper and beautiful, but which have been foolishly repeated by bad Poets, till such feelings of disgust are connected with them as it is scarcely possible by any art of association to overpower.

If in a poem there should be found a series of lines, or even a single line, in which the language, though naturally arranged, and according to the strict laws of metre, does not differ from that of prose, there is a numerous class of critics, who, when they stumble upon these prosaisms, as they call them, imagine that they have made a notable discovery, and exult over the Poet as over a man ignorant of his own profession. Now these men would establish a canon of criticism which the Reader will conclude he must utterly reject, if he wishes to be pleased with these volumes. And it would be a most easy task to prove to him, that not only the language of a large portion of every good poem, even of the most elevated character, must necessarily, except with reference to the metre, in no respect differ from that of good prose, but likewise that some of the most interesting parts of the best poems will be found to be strictly the language of prose when prose is well written. The truth of this assertion might be demonstrated by innumerable passages from almost all the poetical writings, even of Milton himself. To illustrate the subject in a general

manner, I will here adduce a short composition of Gray, who was at the head of those who, by their reasonings, have attempted to widen the space of separation betwixt Prose and Metrical composition, and was more than any other man curiously elaborate in the structure of his own poetic diction.

> "In vain to me the smiling mornings shine,
>   And reddening Phoebus lifts his golden fire:
> The birds in vain their amorous descant join,
>   Or cheerful fields resume their green attire.
> These ears, alas! for other notes repine;
>   *A different object do these eyes require;*
> *My lonely anguish melts no heart but mine;*
> *And in my breast the imperfect joys expire;*
> Yet morning smiles the busy race to cheer,
> And new-born pleasure brings to happier men;
> The fields to all their wonted tribute bear;
> To warm their little loves the birds complain.
> *I fruitless mourn to him that cannot hear,*
> *And weep the more because I weep in vain.*"[2]

It will easily be perceived, that the only part of this Sonnet which is of any value is the lines printed in Italics; it is equally obvious, that, except in the rhyme, and in the use of the single word "fruitless" for fruitlessly, which is so far a defect, the language of these lines does in no respect differ from that of prose.

By the foregoing quotation it has been shown that the language of Prose may yet be well adapted to Poetry; and it was previously asserted, that a large portion of the language of every good poem can in no respect differ from that of good Prose. We will go further. It may be safely affirmed, that there neither is, nor can be, any *essential* difference between the language of prose and metrical composition. We are fond of tracing the resemblance between Poetry and Painting, and, accordingly, we call them Sisters: but where shall we find bonds of connection sufficiently strict to typify the affinity betwixt metrical and prose composition? They both speak by and to the same organs; the bodies in which both of them are clothed may be said to be of the same substance, their affections are kindred, and almost identical, not necessarily differing even in degree; Poetry* sheds no

---

* I here use the word "Poetry" (though against my own judgment) as opposed to the word Prose, and synonymous with metrical composition. But much confusion has been introduced into criticism by this contradistinction of Poetry and Prose, instead of the more philosophical one of Poetry and Matter of Fact, or Science. The only strict antithesis to Prose is Metre; nor is this, in truth, a *strict* antithesis, because lines and passages of metre so naturally occur in writing prose, that it would be scarcely possible to avoid them, even were it desirable.

◇◇◇◇◇◇◇◇◇◇◇◇◇◇◇◇◇◇◇◇◇◇◇◇◇◇◇◇◇◇

[2] *Sonnet on the Death of Richard West* (by Thomas Gray).

tears "such as Angels weep", but natural and human tears; she can boast of no celestial ichor that distinguishes her vital juices from those of prose; the same human blood circulates through the veins of them both.

If it be affirmed that rhyme and metrical arrangement of themselves constitute a distinction which overturns what has just been said on the strict affinity of metrical language with that of prose, and paves the way for other artificial distinctions which the mind voluntarily admits, I answer that the language of such Poetry as is here recommended is, as far as is possible, a selection of the language really spoken by men; that this selection, wherever it is made with true taste and feeling, will of itself form a distinction far greater than would at first be imagined, and will entirely separate the composition from the vulgarity and meanness of ordinary life; and, if metre be super-added thereto, I believe that a dissimilitude will be produced altogether sufficient for the gratification of a rational mind. What other distinction would we have? Whence is it to come? And where is it to exist? Not, surely, where the Poet speaks through the mouths of his characters: it cannot be necessary here, either for elevation of style, or any of its supposed ornaments: for, if the Poet's subject be judiciously chosen, it will naturally, and upon fit occasion, lead him to passions the language of which, if selected truly and judiciously, must necessarily be dignified and variegated, and alive with metaphors and figures. I forbear to speak of an incongruity which would shock the intelligent Reader, should the Poet inter-weave any foreign splendour of his own with that which the passion naturally suggests: it is sufficient to say that such addition is unnecessary. And, surely, it is more probable that those passages, which with propriety abound with metaphors and figures, will have their due effect, if, upon other occasions where the passions are of a milder character, the style also be subdued and temperate.

But, as the pleasure which I hope to give by the Poems now presented to the Reader must depend entirely on just notions upon this subject, and, as it is in itself of high importance to our taste and moral feelings, I cannot content myself with these detached remarks. And if, in what I am about to say, it shall appear to some that my labour is unnecessary, and that I am like a man fighting a battle without enemies, such persons may be reminded, that, whatever be the language outwardly holden by men, a practical faith in the opinions which I am wishing to establish is almost unknown. If my conclusions are admitted, and carried as far as they must be carried if admitted at all, our judgments concerning the works of the greatest Poets both ancient and modern will be far different from what they are at present, both when we praise, and when we censure: and our moral feelings influencing and influenced by these judgments will, I believe, be corrected and purified.

Taking up the subject, then, upon general grounds, let me ask, what is meant by the word Poet? What is a Poet? To whom does he address himself? And what language is to be expected from him?—He is a man speaking to men: a man, it is true, endowed with more lively sensibility, more enthusiasm and tenderness, who has a greater knowledge of human nature, and a more comprehensive soul, than are supposed to be common among mankind; a man pleased with his own passions and volitions, and who rejoices more than other men in the spirit of life that is in him; delighting to contemplate similar volitions and passions as manifested in the goings-on of the Universe, and habitually impelled to create them where he does not find them. To these qualities he has added a disposition to be affected more than other men by absent things as if they were present; an ability of conjuring up in himself passions, which are indeed far from being the same as those produced by real events, yet (especially in those parts of the general sympathy which are pleasing and delightful) do more nearly resemble the passions produced by real events, than anything which, from the motions of their own minds merely, other men are accustomed to feel in themselves:—whence, and from practice, he has acquired a greater readiness and power in expressing what he thinks and feels, and especially those thoughts and feelings which, by his own choice, or from the structure of his own mind, arise in him without immediate external excitement.

But whatever portion of this faculty we may suppose even the greatest Poet to possess, there cannot be a doubt that the language which it will suggest to him must often, in liveliness and truth, fall short of that which is uttered by men in real life, under the actual pressure of those passions, certain shadows of which the Poet thus produces, or feels to be produced, in himself.

However exalted a notion we would wish to cherish of the character of a Poet, it is obvious, that while he describes and imitates passions, his employment is in some degree mechanical, compared with the freedom and power of real and substantial action and suffering. So that it will be the wish of the Poet to bring his feelings near to those of the persons whose feelings he describes, nay, for short spaces of time, perhaps, to let himself slip into an entire delusion, and even confound and identify his own feelings with theirs; modifying only the language which is thus suggested to him by a consideration that he describes for a particular purpose, that of giving pleasure. Here, then, he will apply the principle of selection which has been already insisted upon. He will depend upon this for removing what would otherwise be painful or disgusting in the passion; he will feel that there is no necessity to trick out or to elevate nature: and, the more industriously he applies this principle, the deeper will be his faith that no words, which *his* fancy or imagination can suggest, will be to be compared with those which are the emanations of reality and truth.

But it may be said by those who do not object to the general spirit of these remarks, that, as it is impossible for the Poet to produce upon all occasions language as exquisitely fitted for the passion as that which the real passion itself suggests, it is proper that he should consider himself as in the situation of a translator, who does not scruple to substitute excellencies of another kind for those which are unattainable by him; and endeavours occasionally to surpass his original, in order to make some amends for the general inferiority to which he feels that he must submit. But this would be to encourage idleness and unmanly despair. Further, it is the language of men who speak of what they do not understand; who talk of Poetry as of a matter of amusement and idle pleasure; who will converse with us as gravely about a *taste* for Poetry, as they express it, as if it were a thing as indifferent as a taste for rope-dancing, or Frontiniac or Sherry. Aristotle, I have been told, has said, that Poetry is the most philosophic of all writing: it is so: its object is truth, not individual and local, but general, and operative; not standing upon external testimony, but carried alive into the heart by passion; truth which is its own testimony, which gives competence and confidence to the tribunal to which it appeals, and receives them from the same tribunal. Poetry is the image of man and nature. The obstacles which stand in the way of the fidelity of the Biographer and Historian, and of their consequent utility, are incalculably greater than those which are to be encountered by the Poet who comprehends the dignity of his art. The Poet writes under one restriction only, namely, the necessity of giving immediate pleasure to a human Being possessed of that information which may be expected from him, not as a lawyer, a physician, a mariner, an astronomer, or a natural philosopher, but as a Man. Except this one restriction, there is no object standing between the Poet and the image of things; between this, and the Biographer and Historian, there are a thousand.

Nor let this necessity of producing immediate pleasure be considered as a degradation of the Poet's art. It is far otherwise. It is an acknowledgment of the beauty of the universe, an acknowledgment the more sincere, because not formal, but indirect; it is a task light and easy to him who looks at the world in the spirit of love: further, it is a homage paid to the native and naked dignity of man, to the grand elementary principle of pleasure, by which he knows, and feels, and lives, and moves. We have no sympathy but what is propagated by pleasure: I would not be misunderstood; but wherever we sympathise with pain, it will be found that the sympathy is produced and carried on by subtle combinations with pleasure. We have no knowledge, that is, no general principles drawn from the contemplation of particular facts, but what has been built up by pleasure, and exists in us by pleasure alone. The Man of science, the Chemist and Mathematician, whatever difficulties and disgusts they may have had to struggle with, know and feel this. However painful may be the objects with which the Anatomist's knowledge is connected, he feels that his knowledge is pleasure; and where he has no pleasure he has no knowledge. What then does the Poet? He considers man and the objects that surround him as acting and re-acting upon each other, so as to produce an infinite complexity of pain and pleasure; he considers man in his own nature and in his ordinary life as contemplating this with a certain quantity of immediate knowledge, with certain convictions, intuitions, and deductions, which from habit acquire the quality of intuitions; he considers him as looking upon this complex scene of ideas and sensations, and finding everywhere objects that immediately excite in him sympathies which, from the necessities of his nature, are accompanied by an overbalance of enjoyment.

To this knowledge which all men carry about with them, and to these sympathies in which, without any other discipline than that of our daily life, we are fitted to take delight, the Poet principally directs his attention. He considers man and nature as essentially adapted to each other, and the mind of man as naturally the mirror of the fairest and most interesting properties of nature. And thus the Poet, prompted by this feeling of pleasure, which accompanies him through the whole course of his studies, converses with general nature, with affections akin to those, which, through labour and length of time, the Man of science has raised up in himself, by conversing with those particular parts of nature which are the objects of his studies. The knowledge both of the Poet and the Man of science is pleasure; but the knowledge of the one cleaves to us as a necessary part of our existence, our natural and unalienable inheritance; the other is a personal and individual acquisition, slow to come to us, and by no habitual and direct sympathy connecting us with our fellow-beings. The Man of science seeks truth as a remote and unknown benefactor; he cherishes and loves it in his solitude: the Poet, singing a song in which all human beings join with him, rejoices in the presence of truth as our visible friend and hourly companion. Poetry is the breath and finer spirit of all knowledge; it is the impassioned expression which is in the countenance of all Science. Emphatically may it be said of the Poet, as Shakspeare hath said of man, "that he looks before and after." He is the rock of defence for human nature; an upholder and preserver, carrying everywhere with him relationship and love. In spite of difference of soil and climate, of language and manners, of laws and customs: in spite of things silently gone out of mind, and things violently destroyed; the Poet binds together by passion and knowledge the vast empire of human society, as it is spread over the whole earth, and over all time. The objects of the Poet's thoughts are everywhere; though the eyes and senses of man are, it is true, his favourite guides, yet he will follow wheresoever he can find an atmosphere of sensation in which to move his wings. Poetry is the first and last of all knowledge—it is as immortal as the heart of man. If the labours of Men of science should ever create any material revolution, direct or indirect, in our condition, and in the impressions which we habitually receive, the Poet will sleep then no more than at present; he will be ready to follow the steps of the Man of science, not only in those general indirect effects, but he will be at his side, carrying sensation into the midst of the objects of the science itself. The remotest discoveries of the Chemist, the Botanist, or Mineralogist, will be as proper objects of the Poet's art as any upon which it can be employed, if the time should ever come when these things shall be familiar to us, and the relations under which they are contemplated by the followers of these respective sciences shall be manifestly and palpably material to us as enjoying and suffering beings. If the time should ever come when what is now called science, thus familiarised to men, shall be ready to put on, as it were, a form of flesh and blood, the Poet will lend his divine spirit to aid the transfiguration, and will welcome the Being thus produced, as a dear and genuine inmate of the household of man.—It is not, then, to be supposed that any one, who holds that sublime notion of Poetry which I have attempted to convey, will break in upon the sanctity and truth of his pictures by transitory and accidental ornaments, and endeavour to excite admiration of himself by arts, the necessity of which must manifestly depend upon the assumed meanness of his subject.

What has been thus far said applies to Poetry in general; but especially to those parts of composition where the Poet speaks through the mouths of his characters; and upon this point it appears to authorise the conclusion that there are few persons of good sense, who would not allow that the dramatic parts of composition are defective, in proportion as they deviate from the real language of nature, and are coloured by a diction of the Poet's own, either peculiar to him as an individual Poet or belonging simply to Poets in general; to a body of men who, from the circumstance of their compositions being in metre, it is expected will employ a particular language.

It is not, then, in the dramatic parts of composition that we look for this distinction of language; but still it may be proper and necessary where the Poet speaks to us in his own person and character. To this I answer by referring the Reader to the description before given of a Poet. Among the qualities there enumerated as principally conducing to form a Poet, is implied nothing differing in kind from other men, but only in degree. The sum of what was said is, that the Poet is chiefly distinguished from other men by a greater promptness to think and feel without immediate external excitement, and a greater power in expressing such thoughts and feelings as are produced in him in that manner. But these passions and thoughts and feelings are the general passions and thoughts and feelings of men. And with what are they connected? Undoubtedly with our moral sentiments and animal sensations, and with the causes which excite these; with the operations of the elements, and the appearances of the visible universe; with storm and sunshine, with the revolutions of the seasons, with cold and heat, with loss of friends and kindred, with injuries and resentments, gratitude and hope, with fear and sorrow. These, and the like, are the sensations and objects which the Poet describes, as they are the sensations of other men, and the objects which interest them. The Poet thinks and feels in the spirit of human passions. How, then, can his language differ in any material degree from that of all other men who feel vividly and see clearly? It might be *proved* that it is impossible. But supposing that this were not the case, the Poet might then be allowed to use a peculiar language when expressing his feelings for his own gratification, or that of men like himself. But Poets do not write for Poets alone, but for men. Unless therefore we are advocates for that admiration which subsists upon ignorance, and that pleasure which arises from hearing what we do not understand, the Poet must descend from this supposed height; and, in order to excite rational sympathy, he must express himself as other men express themselves.

To this it may be added, that while he is only selecting from the real language of men, or, which amounts to the same thing, composing, accurately in the spirit of such selection, he is treading upon safe ground, and we know what we are to expect from him. Our feelings are the same with respect to metre; for, as it may be proper to remind the Reader, the distinction of metre is regular and uniform, and not, like that which is produced by what is usually called POETIC DICTION, arbitrary, and subject to infinite caprices upon which no calculation whatever can be made. In the one case, the Reader is utterly at the mercy of the Poet, respecting what imagery or diction he may choose to connect with the passion; whereas, in the other, the metre obeys certain laws, to which the Poet and Reader both willingly submit because they are certain, and because no interference is made by them with the passion, but such as the concurring testimony of ages has shown to heighten and improve the pleasure which co-exists with it.

It will now be proper to answer an obvious question, namely, Why, professing these opinions, have I written in verse? To this, in addition to such answer as is included in what has been already said, I reply, in the first place, Because, however I may have restricted myself, there is still left open to me what confessedly constitutes the most valuable object of all writing, whether in prose or verse; the great and universal passions of men, the most general and interesting of their occupations, and the entire world of nature before me—to supply endless combinations of forms and imagery. Now, supposing for a moment that whatever is interesting in these objects may be as vividly described in prose, why should I be con-demned for attempting to superadd to such description the charm which, by the consent of all nations, is acknowledged to exist in metrical language? To this, by such as are yet unconvinced it may be answered that a very small part of the pleasure given by Poetry depends upon the metre, and that it is injudicious to write in metre, unless it be accompanied with the other artificial distinctions of style with which metre is usually accompanied, and that, by such deviation, more will be lost from the shock which will thereby be given to the Reader's associations than will be counterbalanced by any pleasure which he can derive from the general power of numbers. In answer to those who still contend for the necessity of accom-panying metre with certain appropriate colours of style in order to the accomplishment of its appro-priate end, and who also, in my opinion, greatly underrate the power of metre in itself, it might, perhaps, as far as relates to these Volumes have been almost sufficient to observe, that poems are extant,

written upon more humble subjects, and in a still more naked and simple style, which have continued to give pleasure from generation to generation. Now, if nakedness and simplicity be a defect, the fact here mentioned affords a strong presumption that poems somewhat less naked and simple are capable of affording pleasure at the present day; and, what I wished *chiefly* to attempt, at present, was to justify myself for having written under the impression of this belief.

But various causes might be pointed out why, when the style is manly, and the subject of some importance, words metrically arranged will long continue to impart such a pleasure to mankind as he who proves the extent of that pleasure will be desirous to impart. The end of Poetry is to produce excitement in co-existence with an overbalance of pleasure; but, by the supposition, excitement is an unusual and irregular state of the mind; ideas and feelings do not, in that state, succeed each other in accustomed order. If the words, however, by which this excitement is produced be in themselves power-ful, or the images and feelings have an undue propor-tion of pain connected with them, there is some danger that the excitement may be carried beyond its proper bounds. Now the co-presence of something regular, something to which the mind has been accustomed in various moods and in a less excited state, cannot but have great efficacy in tempering and restraining the passion by an intertexture of ordinary feeling, and of feeling not strictly and necessarily connected with the passion. This is unquestionably true; and hence, though the opinion will at first appear paradoxical, from the tendency of metre to divest language, in a certain degree, of its reality, and thus to throw a sort of half-consciousness of unsubstantial existence over the whole composition, there can be little doubt but that more pathetic situations and sentiments, that is, those which have a greater proportion of pain connected with them, may be endured in metrical composition, especially in rhyme, than in prose. The metre of the old ballads is very artless; yet they contain many passages which would illustrate this opinion; and, I hope, if the following Poems be attentively perused, similar instances will be found in them. This opinion may be further illustrated by appealing to the Reader's own experience of the reluctance with which he comes to the re-perusal of the distressful parts of Clarissa Harlowe, or the Gamester;[3] while Shakspeare's writings, in the most pathetic scenes, never act upon

---

[3] A now-forgotten domestic tragedy, by Edward Moore, first performed in 1753 by David Garrick.

us, as pathetic, beyond the bounds of pleasure—an effect which, in a much greater degree than might at first be imagined is to be ascribed to small, but continual and regular impulses of pleasurable surprise from the metrical arrangement.—On the other hand (what it must be allowed will much more frequently happen) if the Poet's words should be incommensurate with the passion, and inadequate to raise the Reader to a height of desirable excitement, then, (unless the Poet's choice of his metre has been grossly injudicious) in the feelings of pleasure which the Reader has been accustomed to connect with metre in general, and in the feeling, whether cheerful or melancholy, which he has been accustomed to connect with that particular movement of metre, there will be found something which will greatly contribute to impart passion to the words, and to effect the complex end which the Poet proposes to himself.

If I had undertaken a SYSTEMATIC defence of the theory here maintained, it would have been my duty to develope the various causes upon which the pleasure received from metrical language depends. Among the chief of these causes is to be reckoned a principle which must be well known to those who have made any of the Arts the object of accurate reflection; namely, the pleasure which the mind derives from the perception of similitude in dissimilitude. This principle is the great spring of the activity of our minds, and their chief feeder. From this principle the direction of the sexual appetite, and all the passions connected with it, take their origin: it is the life of our ordinary conversation; and upon the accuracy with which similitude in dissimilitude, and dissimilitude in similitude are perceived, depend our taste and our moral feelings. It would not be a useless employment to apply this principle to the consideration of metre, and to show that metre is hence enabled to afford much pleasure, and to point out in what manner that pleasure is produced. But my limits will not permit me to enter upon this subject, and I must content myself with a general summary.

I have said that poetry is the spontaneous overflow of powerful feelings: it takes its origin from emotion recollected in tranquillity: the emotion is contemplated till, by a species of re-action, the tranquillity gradually disappears, and an emotion, kindred to that which was before the subject of contemplation, is gradually produced, and does itself actually exist in the mind. In this mood successful composition generally begins, and in a mood similar to this it is carried on; but the emotion, of whatever kind, and in whatever degree, from various causes, is qualified by various pleasures, so that in describing any passions whatsoever, which are voluntarily described, the mind will, upon the whole, be in a state of enjoyment. If Nature be thus cautious to preserve in a state of enjoyment a being so employed, the Poet ought to profit by the lesson held forth to him, and ought especially to take care, that, whatever passions he communicates to his Reader, those passions, if his Reader's mind be sound and vigorous, should always be accompanied with an overbalance of pleasure. Now the music of harmonious metrical language, the sense of difficulty overcome, and the blind association of pleasure which has been previously received from works of rhyme or metre of the same or similar construction, an indistinct perception perpetually renewed of language closely resembling that of real life, and yet, in the circumstance of metre, differing from it so widely—all these imperceptibly make up a complex feeling of delight, which is of the most important use in tempering the painful feeling always found intermingled with powerful descriptions of the deeper passions. This effect is always produced in pathetic and impassioned poetry; while, in lighter compositions, the ease and gracefulness with which the Poet manages his numbers are themselves confessedly a principal source of the gratification of the Reader. All that it is *necessary* to say, however, upon this subject, may be effected by affirming, what few persons will deny, that, of two descriptions, either of passions, manners, or characters, each of them equally well executed, the one in prose and the other in verse, the verse will be read a hundred times where the prose is read once.

Having thus explained a few of my reasons for writing in verse, and why I have chosen subjects from common life, and endeavoured to bring my language near to the real language of men, if I have been too minute in pleading my own cause, I have at the same time been treating a subject of general interest; and for this reason a few words shall be added with reference solely to these particular poems, and to some defects which will probably be found in them. I am sensible that my associations must have sometimes been particular instead of general, and that, consequently, giving to things a false importance, I may have sometimes written upon unworthy subjects; but I am less apprehensive on this account, than that my language may frequently have suffered from those arbitrary connections of feelings and ideas with particular words and phrases, from which no man can altogether protect himself. Hence I have no doubt, that, in some instances, feelings, even of the ludicrous, may be given to my Readers by expressions which appeared to me tender and pathetic. Such faulty expressions, were I convinced they were faulty at present, and that they must necessarily continue to be so, I would willingly take all reasonable pains to correct. But it is dangerous to make these alterations on the simple authority of a few individuals, or even of certain classes of men; for where the understanding of an Author is not convinced, or his feelings altered, this cannot be done without great injury to himself: for his own feelings are his stay and support; and, if he set them aside in one instance, he may be induced to repeat this act till his mind shall lose all confidence in itself, and become utterly debilitated. To this it may be added, that the critic ought never to forget that he is himself exposed to the same errors as the Poet, and, perhaps, in a much greater degree: for there can be no presumption in saying of most readers, that it is not probable they will be so well acquainted with the various stages of meaning through which words have passed, or with the fickleness or stability of the relations of particular ideas to each other; and, above all, since they are so much less interested in the subject, they may decide lightly and carelessly.

Long as the Reader has been detained, I hope he will permit me to caution him against a mode of false criticism which has been applied to Poetry, in which the language closely resembles that of life and nature. Such verses have been triumphed over in parodies, of which Dr. Johnson's stanza is a fair specimen:—

> "I put my hat upon my head
> And walked into the Strand,
> And there I met another man
> Whose hat was in his hand."

Immediately under these lines let us place one of the most justly-admired stanzas of the *Babes in the Wood*.

> "These pretty Babes with hand in hand
> Went wandering up and down;
> But never more they saw the Man
> Approaching from the Town."

In both these stanzas the words, and the order of the words, in no respect differ from the most unimpassioned conversation. There are words in both, for example, "the Strand", and "the Town", connected with none but the most familiar ideas; yet the one stanza we admit as admirable, and the other as a fair example of the superlatively contemptible. Whence arises this difference? Not from the metre, not from the language, not from the order of the words; but the *matter* expressed in Dr. Johnson's stanza is contemptible. The proper method of treating trivial and simple verses, to which Dr. Johnson's

stanza would be a fair parallelism, is not to say, this is a bad kind of poetry, or, this is not poetry; but, this wants sense; it is neither interesting in itself, nor can *lead* to anything interesting; the images neither originate in that sane state of feeling which arises out of thought, nor can excite thought or feeling in the Reader. This is the only sensible manner of dealing with such verses. Why trouble yourself about the species till you have previously decided upon the genus? Why take pains to prove that an ape is not a Newton, when it is self-evident that he is not a man?

One request I must make of my reader, which is, that in judging these Poems he would decide by his own feelings genuinely, and not by reflection upon what will probably be the judgment of others. How common is it to hear a person say, I myself do not object to this style of composition, or this or that expression, but, to such and such classes of people it will appear mean or ludicrous! This mode of criticism, so destructive of all sound unadulterated judgment, is almost universal: let the Reader then abide, independently, by his own feelings, and, if he finds himself affected, let him not suffer such conjectures to interfere with his pleasure.

If an Author, by any single composition, has impressed us with respect for his talents, it is useful to consider this as affording a presumption, that on other occasions where we have been displeased, he, nevertheless, may not have written ill or absurdly; and further, to give him so much credit for this one composition as may induce us to review what has displeased us, with more care than we should otherwise have bestowed upon it. This is not only an act of justice, but, in our decisions upon poetry especially, may conduce, in a high degree, to the improvement of our own taste; for an *accurate* taste in poetry and in all the other arts, as Sir Joshua Reynolds has observed, is an *acquired* talent, which can only be produced by thought and a long-continued intercourse with the best models of composition. This is mentioned, not with so ridiculous a purpose as to prevent the most inexperienced Reader from judging for himself, (I have already said that I wish him to judge for himself;) but merely to temper the rashness of decision, and to suggest, that, if Poetry be a subject on which much time has not been bestowed, the judgment may be erroneous; and that, in many cases, it necessarily will be so.

Nothing would, I know, have so effectually contributed to further the end which I have in view, as to have shown of what kind the pleasure is, and how that pleasure is produced, which is confessedly produced by metrical composition essentially different from that which I have here endeavoured to recommend:

for the Reader will say that he has been pleased by such composition; and what more can be done for him? The power of any art is limited; and he will suspect, that, if it be proposed to furnish him with new friends, that can be only upon condition of his abandoning his old friends. Besides, as I have said, the Reader is himself conscious of the pleasure which he has received from such composition, composition to which he has peculiarly attached the endearing name of Poetry; and all men feel an habitual gratitude, and something of an honourable bigotry, for the objects which have long continued to please them: we not only wish to be pleased, but to be pleased in that particular way in which we have been accustomed to be pleased. There is in these feelings enough to resist a host of arguments; and I should be the less able to combat them successfully, as I am willing to allow, that, in order entirely to enjoy the Poetry which I am recommending, it would be necessary to give up much of what is ordinarily enjoyed. But, would my limits have permitted me to point out how this pleasure is produced, many obstacles might have been removed, and the Reader assisted in perceiving that the powers of language are not so limited as he may suppose; and that it is possible for poetry to give other enjoyments, of a purer, more lasting, and more exquisite nature. This part of the subject has not been altogether neglected, but it has not been so much my present aim to prove, that the interest excited by some other kinds of poetry is less vivid, and less worthy of the nobler powers of the mind, as to offer reasons for presuming, that if my purpose were fulfilled, a species of poetry would be produced, which is genuine poetry; in its nature well adapted to interest mankind permanently, and likewise important in the multiplicity and quality of its moral relations.

From what has been said, and from a perusal of the Poems, the Reader will be able clearly to perceive the object which I had in view: he will determine how far it has been attained; and, what is a much more important question, whether it be worth attaining: and upon the decision of these two questions will rest my claim to the approbation of the Public.

UPON EPITAPHS.

From 'The Friend,' Feb. 22, 1810.

It needs scarcely be said, that an Epitaph presupposes a Monument, upon which it is to be engraven. Almost all Nations have wished that certain external signs should point out the places where their dead are interred. Among savage tribes unacquainted with letters this has mostly been done either by rude stones placed near the graves, or by mounds of earth raised over them. This custom proceeded obviously from a twofold desire; first, to guard the remains of the deceased from irreverent approach or from savage violation: and, secondly, to preserve their memory. 'Never any,' says Camden,[1] 'neglected burial but some savage nations; as the Bactrians,[2] which cast their dead to the dogs; some varlet philosophers, as Diogenes, who desired to be devoured of fishes; some dissolute courtiers, as Mæcenas, who was wont to say, Non tumulum curo; sepelit natura relictos.'

I'm careless of a grave:—Nature her dead will save.

As soon as nations had learned the use of letters, epitaphs were inscribed upon these monuments; in order that their intention might be more surely and adequately fulfilled. I have derived monuments and epitaphs from two sources of feeling: but these do in fact resolve themselves into one. The invention of epitaphs, Weever, in his *Discourse of Funeral Monuments*, says rightly, 'proceeded from the presage of fore-feeling of immortality, implanted in all men naturally, and is referred to the scholars of Linus the Theban poet, who flourished about the year of the world two thousand seven hundred; who first bewailed this Linus their Master, when he was slain, in doleful verses, then called of him Œlina, afterwards Epitaphia, for that they were first sung at burials, after engraved upon the sepulchres.'

And, verily, without the consciousness of a principle of immortality in the human soul, Man could never have had awakened in him the desire to live in the remembrance of his fellows: mere love, or the yearning of kind towards kind, could not have produced it. The dog or horse perishes in the field, or in the stall, by the side of his companions, and is incapable of anticipating the sorrow with which his surrounding associates shall bemoan his death, or pine for his loss; he cannot pre-conceive this regret, he can form no thought of it; and therefore cannot possibly have a desire to leave such regret or remembrance behind him. Add to the principle of love which exists in the inferior animals, the faculty of reason which exists in Man alone; will the conjunction of of these account for the desire? Doubtless it is a necessary consequence of this conjunction; yet not I think as a direct result, but only to be come at through an intermediate thought, viz. that of an intimation or assurance within us, that some part of our nature is imperishable. At least the precedence,

[1] William Camden, *Remaines Concerning Britain's Languages . . . Epitaph's* (1657).
[2] Inhabitants of ancient land in W. Asia.

in order of birth, of one feeling to the other, is unquestionable. If we look back upon the days of childhood, we shall find that the time is not in remembrance when, with respect to our own individual Being, the mind was without this assurance; whereas, the wish to be remembered by our friends or kindred after death, or even in absence, is, as we shall discover, a sensation that does not form itself till the *social* feelings have been developed, and the Reason has connected itself with a wide range of objects. Forlorn, and cut off from communication with the best part of his nature, must that man be, who should derive the sense of immortality, as it exists in the mind of a child, from the same unthinking gaiety or liveliness of animal spirits with which the lamb in the meadow, or any other irrational creature is endowed; who should ascribe it, in short, to blank ignorance in the child; to an inability arising from the imperfect state of his faculties to come, in any point of his being, into contact with a notion of death; or to an unreflecting acquiescence in what had been instilled into him! Has such an unfolder of the mysteries of nature, though he may have forgotten his former self, ever noticed the early, obstinate, and unappeasable inquisitiveness of children upon the subject of origination? This single fact proves outwardly the monstrousness of those suppositions: for, if we had no direct external testimony that the minds of very young children meditate feelingly upon death and immortality, these inquiries, which we all know they are perpetually making concerning the *whence*, do necessarily include correspondent habits of interrogation concerning the *whither*. Origin and tendency are notions inseparably co-relative. Never did a child stand by the side of a running stream, pondering within himself what power was the feeder of the perpetual current, from what never-wearied sources the body of water was supplied, but he must have been inevitably propelled to follow this question by another: 'Towards what abyss is it in progress? what receptacle can contain the mighty influx?' And the spirit of the answer must have been, though the word might be sea or ocean, accompanied perhaps with an image gathered from a map, or from the real object in nature—these might have been the *letter*, but the *spirit* of the answer must have been *as* inevitably,—a receptacle without bounds or dimensions;—nothing less than infinity. We may, then, be justified in asserting, that the sense of immortality, if not a co-existent and twin birth with Reason, is among the earliest of her offspring: and we may further assert, that from these conjoined, and under their countenance, the human affections are gradually formed and opened out. This is not the place to enter into the recesses of these investigations; but the subject requires me here to make a plain avowal, that, for my own part, it is to me inconceivable, that the sympathies of love towards each other, which grow with our growth, could ever attain any new strength, or even preserve the old, after we had received from the outward senses the impression of death, and were in the habit of having that impression daily renewed and its accompanying feeling brought home to ourselves, and to those we love; if the same were not counteracted by those communications with our internal Being, which are anterior to all these experiences, and with which revelation coincides, and has through that coincidence alone (for otherwise it could not possess it) a power to affect us. I confess, with me the conviction is absolute, that, if the impression and sense of death were not thus counterbalanced, such a hollowness would pervade the whole system of things, such a want of correspondence and consistency, a disproportion so astounding betwixt means and ends, that there could be no repose, no joy. Were we to grow up unfostered by this genial warmth, a frost would chill the spirit, so penetrating and powerful, that there could be no motions of the life of love; and infinitely less could we have any wish to be remembered after we had passed away from a world in which each man had moved about like a shadow.— If, then, in a creature endowed with the faculties of foresight and reason, the social affections could not have unfolded themselves uncountenanced by the faith that Man is an immortal being; and if, consequently, neither could the individual dying have had a desire to survive in the remembrance of his fellows, nor on their side could they have felt a wish to preserve for future times vestiges of the departed; it follows, as a final inference, that without the belief in immortality, wherein these several desires originate, neither monuments nor epitaphs, in affectionate or laudatory commemoration of the deceased, could have existed in the world.

Simonides,[3] it is related, upon landing in a strange country, found the corse of an unknown person lying by the sea-side; he buried it, and was honoured throughout Greece for the piety of that act. Another ancient Philosopher, chancing to fix his eyes upon a dead body, regarded the same with slight, if not with contempt; saying, 'See the shell of the flown bird!' But it is not to be supposed that the moral and tender-hearted Simonides was incapable of the lofty movements of thought, to which that other Sage gave way at the moment while his soul was intent only upon the indestructible being; nor, on the other hand, that he,

---

[3] Greek lyric poet (556?–468?).

in whose sight a lifeless human body was of no more value than the worthless shell from which the living fowl had departed, would not, in a different mood of mind, have been affected by those earthly considerations which had incited the philosophic Poet to the performance of that pious duty. And with regard to this latter we may be assured that, if he had been destitute of the capability of communing with the more exalted thoughts that appertain to human nature, he would have cared no more for the corse of the stranger than for the dead body of a seal or porpoise which might have been cast up by the waves. We respect the corporeal frame of Man, not merely because it is the habitation of a rational, but of an immortal Soul. Each of these Sages was in sympathy with the best feelings of our nature; feelings which, though they seem opposite to each other, have another and a finer connection than that of contrast.— It is a connection formed through the subtle process by which, both in the natural and the moral world, qualities pass insensibly into their contraries, and things revolve upon each other. As, in sailing upon the orb of this planet, a voyage towards the regions where the sun sets, conducts gradually to the quarter where we have been accustomed to behold it come forth at its rising; and, in like manner, a voyage towards the east, the birth-place in our imagination of the morning, leads finally to the quarter where the sun is last seen when he departs from our eyes; so the contemplative Soul, travelling in the direction of mortality, advances to the country of everlasting life; and, in like manner, may she continue to explore those cheerful tracts, till she is brought back, for her advantage and benefit, to the land of transitory things —of sorrow and of tears.

On a midway point, therefore, which commands the thoughts and feelings of the two Sages whom we have represented in contrast, does the Author of that species of composition, the laws of which it is our present purpose to explain, take his stand. Accordingly, recurring to the twofold desire of guarding the remains of the deceased and preserving their memory, it may be said that a sepulchral monument is a tribute to a man as a human being; and that an epitaph (in the ordinary meaning attached to the word) includes this general feeling and something more; and is a record to preserve the memory of the dead, as a tribute due to his individual worth, for a satisfaction to the sorrowing hearts of the survivors, and for the common benefit of the living: which record is to be accomplished, not in a general manner, but, where it can, in *close connection with the bodily remains of the deceased*: and these, it may be added, among the modern nations of Europe, are deposited within, or

contiguous to, their places of worship. In ancient times, as is well known, it was the custom to bury the dead beyond the walls of towns and cities; and among the Greeks and Romans they were frequently interred by the way-sides.

I could here pause with pleasure, and invite the Reader to indulge with me in contemplation of the advantages which must have attended such a practice. We might ruminate upon the beauty which the monuments, thus placed, must have borrowed from the surrounding images of nature—from the trees, the wild flowers, from a stream running perhaps within sight or hearing, from the beaten road stretching its weary length hard by. Many tender similitudes must these objects have presented to the mind of the traveller leaning upon one of the tombs, or reposing in the coolness of its shade, whether he had halted from weariness or in compliance with the invitation, 'Pause, Traveller!' so often found upon the monuments. And to its epitaph also must have been supplied strong appeals to visible appearances or immediate impressions, lively and affecting analogies of life as a journey—death as a sleep overcoming the tired wayfarer—of misfortune as a storm that falls suddenly upon him—of beauty as a flower that passeth away, or of innocent pleasure as one that may be gathered—of virtue that standeth firm as a rock against the beating waves;—of hope 'undermined insensibly like the poplar by the side of the river that has fed it,' or blasted in a moment like a pine-tree by the stroke of lightning upon the mountain-top—of admonitions and heart-stirring remembrances, like a refreshing breeze that comes without warning, or the taste of the waters of an unexpected fountain. These, and similar suggestions, must have given, formerly, to the language of the senseless stone a voice enforced and endeared by the benignity of that Nature with which it was in unison.—We, in modern times, have lost much of these advantages; and they are but in a small degree counterbalanced to the inhabitants of large towns and cities, by the custom of depositing the dead within, or contiguous to, their places of worship; however splendid or imposing may be the appearance of those edifices, or however interesting or salutary the recollections associated with them. Even were it not true that tombs lose their monitory virtue when thus obtruded upon the notice of men occupied with the cares of the world, and too often sullied and defiled by those cares, yet still, when death is in our thoughts, nothing can make amends for the want of the soothing influences of Nature, and for the absence of those types of renovation and decay, which the fields and woods offer to the notice of the serious and contemplative mind. To feel the force of this sentiment, let a man only compare in imagination the unsightly manner in which our monuments are crowded together in the busy, noisy, unclean, and almost grassless church-yard of a large town, with the still seclusion of a Turkish cemetery, in some remote place; and yet further sanctified by the grove of cypress in which it is embosomed. Thoughts in the same temper as these have already been expressed with true sensibility by an ingenuous Poet of the present day. The subject of his poem is 'All Saints Church, Derby:' he has been deploring the forbidding and unseemly appearance of its burial-ground, and uttering a wish, that in past times the practice had been adopted of interring the inhabitants of large towns in the country.—

> Then in some rural, calm, sequestered spot,
> Where healing Nature her benignant look
> Ne'er changes, save at that lorn season, when,
> With tresses drooping o'er her sable stole,
> She yearly mourns the mortal doom of man,
> Her noblest work, (so Israel's virgins erst,
> With annual moan upon the mountains wept
> Their fairest gone,) there in that rural scene,
> So placid, so congenial to the wish
> The Christian feels, of peaceful rest within
> The silent grave, I would have stayed:

> *   *   *   *   *

> —wandered forth, where the cold dew of heaven
> Lay on the humbler graves around, what time
> The pale moon gazed upon the turfy mounds,
> Pensive, as though like me, in lonely muse,
> Twere brooding on the dead inhumed beneath.
> There while with him, the holy man of Uz,
> O'er human destiny I sympathised,
> Counting the long, long periods prophecy
> Decrees to roll, ere the great day arrives
> Of resurrection, oft the blue-eyed Spring
> Had met me with her blossoms, as the Dove,
> Of old, returned with olive leaf, to cheer
> The Patriarch mournin go'er a world destroyed:
> And I would bless her visit; for to me
> 'Tis sweet to trace the consonance that links
> As one, the works of Nature and the word
> Of God.—   JOHN EDWARDS.

A village church-yard, lying as it does in the lap of Nature, may indeed be most favourably contrasted with that of a town of crowded population; and sepulture therein combines many of the best tendencies which belong to the mode practised by the Ancients, with others peculiar to itself. The sensations of pious cheerfulness, which attend the celebration of the sabbath-day in rural places, are profitably chastised by the sight of the graves of kindred and friends, gathered together in that general home towards which the thoughtful yet happy spectators themselves are journeying. Hence a parish-church, in the stillness of the country, is a visible centre of a community of the living and the dead; a point to which are habitually referred the nearest concerns of both.

As, then, both in cities and villages, the dead are deposited in close connection with our places of worship, with us the composition of an epitaph naturally turns, still more than among the nations of antiquity, upon the most serious and solemn affections of the human mind; upon departed worth—upon personal or social sorrow and admiration—upon religion, individual and social—upon time, and upon eternity. Accordingly, it suffices, in ordinary cases, to secure a composition of this kind from censure, that it contain nothing that shall shock or be inconsistent with this spirit. But, to entitle an epitaph to praise, more than this is necessary. It ought to contain some thought or feeling belonging to the mortal or immortal part of our nature touchingly expressed; and if that be done, however general or even trite the sentiment may be, every man of pure mind will read the words with pleasure and gratitude. A husband bewails a wife; a parent breathes a sigh of disappointed hope over a lost child; a son utters a sentiment of filial reverence for a departed father or mother; a friend perhaps inscribes an encomium recording the companionable qualities, or the solid virtues, of the tenant of the grave, whose departure has left a sadness upon his memory. This and a pious admonition to the living, and a humble expression of Christian confidence in immortality, is the language of a thousand church-yards; and it does not often happen that anything, in a greater degree discriminate or appropriate to the dead or to the living, is to be found in them. This want of discrimination has been ascribed by Dr. Johnson, in his Essay upon the epitaphs of Pope, to two causes; first, the scantiness of the objects of human praise; and, secondly, the want of variety in the characters of men; or, to use his own words, 'to the fact, that the greater part of mankind have no character at all.' Such language may be holden without blame among the generalities of common conversation; but does not become a critic and a moralist speaking seriously upon a serious subject. The objects of admiration in human nature are not scanty, but abundant: and every man has a character of his own, to the eye that has skill to perceive it. The real cause of the acknowledged want of discrimination in sepulchral memorials is this: That to analyse the characters of others, especially of those whom we love, is not a common or natural employment of men at any time. We are not anxious unerringly to understand the constitution of the minds of those who have soothed, who have cheered, who have supported us: with whom we have been long and daily pleased or delighted. The affections are their own justification. The light of love in our hearts is a satisfactory evidence that there is a body of worth in the minds of our friends or kindred, whence that light has proceeded. We shrink from the thought of placing their merits and defects to be weighed against each other in the nice balance of pure intellect; nor do we find much temptation to detect the shades by which a good quality or virtue is discriminated in them from an excellence known by the same general name as it exists in the mind of another; and, least of all, do we incline to these refinements when under the pressure of sorrow, admiration, or regret, or when actuated by any of those feelings which incite men to prolong the memory of their friends and kindred, by records placed in the bosom of the all-uniting and equalising receptacle of the dead.

The first requisite, then, in an Epitaph is, that it should speak, in a tone which shall sink into the heart, the general language of humanity as connected with the subject of death—the source from which an epitaph proceeds—of death, and of life. To be born and to die are the two points in which all men feel themselves to be in absolute coincidence. This general language may be uttered so strikingly as to entitle an epitaph to high praise; yet it cannot lay claim to the highest unless other excellencies be superadded. Passing through all intermediate steps, we will attempt to determine at once what these excellencies are, and wherein consists the perfection of this species of composition.—It will be found to lie in a due proportion of the common or universal feeling of humanity to sensations excited by a distinct and clear conception, conveyed to the reader's mind, of the individual, whose death is deplored and whose memory is to be preserved; at least of his character as, after death, it appeared to those who loved him and lament his loss. The general sympathy ought to be quickened, provoked, and diversified, by particular thoughts, actions, images,—circumstances of age, occupation, manner of life, prosperity which the deceased had known, or adversity to which he had been subject; and these ought to be bound together and solemnised into one harmony by the general sympathy. The two powers should temper, restrain, and exalt each other. The reader ought to know who and what the man was whom he is called upon to think of with interest. A distinct conception should be given (implicitly where it can, rather than explicitly) of the individual lamented.—But the writer of an epitaph is not an anatomist, who dissects the internal frame of the mind; he is not even a painter, who executes a portrait at leisure and in entire tranquillity; his delineation, we must remember, is performed by the side of the grave; and, what is more, the grave of one whom he loves and admires. What purity and brightness is that virtue clothed in, the image of which must no longer bless our living eyes! The character of a deceased friend or beloved kinsman is not seen, no—nor ought to be seen, otherwise than as a tree through a tender haze or a luminous mist, that spiritualises and beautifies it; that takes away, indeed, but only to the end that the parts which are not abstracted may appear more dignified and lovely; may impress and affect the more. Shall we say, then, that this is not truth, not a faithful image; and that, accordingly, the purposes of commemoration cannot be answered?—It *is* truth, and of the highest order; for, though doubtless things are not apparent which did exist; yet, the object being looked at through this medium, parts and proportions are brought into distinct view which before had been only imperfectly or unconsciously seen: it is truth hallowed by love—the joint offspring of the worth of the dead and the affections of the living! This may easily be brought to the test. Let one, whose eyes have been sharpened by personal hostility to discover what was amiss in the character of a good man, hear the tidings of his death, and what a change is wrought in a moment! Enmity melts away; and, as it disappears, unsightliness, disproportion, and deformity, vanish; and, through the influence of commiseration, a harmony of love and beauty succeeds. Bring such a man to the tombstone on which shall be inscribed an epitaph on his adversary, composed in the spirit which we have recommended. Would he turn from it as from an idle tale? No;—the thoughtful look, the sigh, and perhaps the involuntary tear, would testify that it had a sane, a generous, and good meaning; and that on the writer's mind had remained an impression which was a true abstract of the character of the deceased; that his gifts and graces were remembered in the simplicity in which they ought to be remembered. The composition and quality of the mind of a virtuous man, contemplated by the side of the grave where his body is mouldering, ought to appear, and be felt as something midway between what he was on earth walking about with his living frailties, and what he may be presumed to be as a spirit in heaven.

It suffices, therefore, that the trunk and the main branches of the worth of the deceased be boldly and unaffectedly represented. Any further detail, minutely and scrupulously pursued, especially if this be done with laborious and antithetic discriminations, must inevitably frustrate its own purpose; forcing the passing Spectator to this conclusion,—either that the dead did not possess the merits ascribed to him, or that they who have raised a monument to his memory, and must therefore be supposed to have been closely connected with him, were incapable of perceiving those merits; or at least during the act of composition had lost sight of them; for, the understanding having been so busy in its petty occupation, how could the heart of the mourner be other than cold? and in either of these cases, whether the fault be on the part of the buried person or the survivors, the memorial is unaffecting and profitless.

Much better is it to fall short in discrimination than to pursue it too far, or to labour it unfeelingly. For in no place are we so much disposed to dwell upon those points, of nature and condition, wherein all men resemble each other, as in the temple where the universal Father is worshipped, or by the side of the grave which gathers all human Beings to itself, and 'equalises the lofty and the low.' We suffer and we weep with the same heart; we love and are anxious for one another in one spirit; our hopes look to the same quarter; and the virtues by which we are all to be furthered and supported, as patience, meekness, good-will, justice, temperance, and temperate desires, are in an equal degree the concern of us all. Let an Epitaph, then, contain at least these acknowledgments to our common nature; nor let the sense of their importance be sacrificed to a balance of opposite qualities or minute distinctions in individual character; which if they do not, (as will for the most part be the case,) when examined, resolve themselves into a trick of words, will, even when they are true and just, for the most part be grievously out of place; for, as it is probable that few only have explored these intricacies of human nature, so can the tracing of them be interesting only to a few. But an epitaph is not a proud writing shut up for the studious: it is exposed to all—to the wise and the most ignorant; it is condescending, perspicuous, and lovingly solicits regard; its story and admonitions are brief, that the thoughtless, the busy, and indolent, may not be deterred, nor the impatient tired: the stooping old man cons the engraven record like a second horn-book;—the child is proud that he can read it;—and the stranger is introduced through its mediation to the company of a friend: it is concerning all, and for all:—in the church-yard it is open to the day; the sun looks down upon the stone, and the rains of heaven beat against it.

Yet, though the writer who would excite sympathy is bound in this case, more than in any other, to give proof that he himself has been moved, it is to be remembered, that to raise a monument is a sober and a reflective act; that the inscription which it bears is intended to be permanent, and for universal perusal; and that, for this reason, the thoughts and feelings expressed should be permanent also—liberated from that weakness and anguish of sorrow which is in nature transitory, and which with instinctive decency retires from notice. The passions should be subdued, the emotions controlled; strong, indeed, but nothing ungovernable or wholly involuntary. Seemliness requires this, and truth requires it also: for how can the narrator otherwise be trusted? Moreover, a grave is a tranquillising object: resignation in course of time springs up from it as naturally as the wild flowers, besprinkling the turf with which it may be covered, or gathering round the monument by which it is defended. The very form and substance of the monument which has received the inscription, and the appearance of the letters, testifying with what a slow and laborious hand they must have been engraven, might seem to reproach the author who had given way upon this occasion to transports of mind, or to quick turns of conflicting passion; though the same might constitute the life and beauty of a funeral oration or elegiac poem.

These sensations and judgments, acted upon perhaps unconsciously, have been one of the main causes why epitaphs so often personate the deceased, and represent him as speaking from his own tombstone. The departed Mortal is introduced telling you himself that his pains are gone; that a state of rest is come; and he conjures you to weep for him no longer. He admonishes with the voice of one experienced in the vanity of those affections which are confined to earthly objects, and gives a verdict like a superior Being, performing the office of a judge, who has no temptations to mislead him, and whose decision cannot but be dispassionate. Thus is death disarmed of its sting, and affliction unsubstantialised. By this tender fiction, the survivors bind themselves to a sedater sorrow, and employ the intervention of the imagination in order that the reason may speak her own language earlier than she would otherwise have been enabled to do. This shadowy interposition also harmoniously unites the two worlds of the living and the dead by their appropriate affections. And it may be observed, that here we have an additional proof of the propriety with which sepulchral inscriptions were referred to the consciousness of immortality as their primal source.

I do not speak with a wish to recommend that an epitaph should be cast in this mould preferably to the still more common one, in which what is said comes from the survivors directly; but rather to point out how natural those feelings are which have induced men, in all states and ranks of society, so frequently to adopt this mode. And this I have done chiefly in order that the laws, which ought to govern the composition of the other, may be better understood. This latter mode, namely, that in which the survivors speak in their own persons, seems to me upon the whole preferable: as it admits a wider range of notices; and, above all, because, excluding the fiction which is the groundwork of the other, it rests upon a more solid basis.

Enough has been said to convey our notion of a perfect epitaph; but it must be borne in mind that one is meant which will best answer the *general* ends of that species of composition. According to the course pointed out, the worth of private life, through all varieties of situation and character, will be most honourably and profitably preserved in memory. Nor would the model recommended less suit public men, in all instances save of those persons who by the greatness of their services in the employments of peace or war, or by the surpassing excellence of their works in art, literature, or science, have made themselves not only universally known, but have filled the heart of their country with everlasting gratitude. Yet I must here pause to correct myself. In describing the general tenor of thought which epitaphs ought to hold, I have omitted to say, that if it be the *actions* of a man, or even some *one* conspicuous or beneficial act of local or general utility, which have distinguished him, and excited a desire that he should be remembered, then, of course, ought the attention to be directed chiefly to those actions or that act: and such sentiments dwelt upon as naturally arise out of them or it. Having made this necessary distinction, I proceed.—The mighty benefactors of mankind, as they are not only known by the immediate survivors, but will continue to be known familiarly to latest posterity, do not stand in need of biographic sketches, in such a place; nor of delineations of character to individualise them. This is already done by their Works, in the memories of men. Their naked names, and a grand comprehensive sentiment of civic gratitude, patriotic love, or human admiration—or the utterance of some elementary principle most essential in the constitution of true virtue;—or a declaration touching that pious humility and self-abasement, which are ever most profound as minds are most susceptible of genuine exaltation—or an intuition, communicated in adequate words, of the sublimity of intellectual power;—these are the only tribute which can here be paid—the only offering that upon such an altar would not be unworthy.

What needs my Shakspeare for his honoured bones
The labour of an age in pilèd-stones,

Or that his hallowed reliques should be hid
Under a stary-pointing pyramid?
Dear Son of Memory, great Heir of Fame,
What need'st thou such weak witness of thy name?
Thou in our wonder and astonishment
Hast built thyself a livelong monument,
And so sepulchred, in such pomp dost lie,
That kings for such a tomb would wish to die.[4]

LETTERS

C. J. Fox (1749–1806), Whig statesman and orator, was one of the half-dozen prominent persons to whom Wordsworth sent presentation copies of the second edition of Lyrical Ballads.

TO CHARLES JAMES FOX

Grasmere, Westmoreland January 14th 1801
Sir,
It is not without much difficulty, that I have summoned the courage to request your acceptance of these Volumes. Should I express my real feelings, I am sure that I should seem to make a parade of diffidence and humility.

Several of the poems contained in these Volumes are written upon subjects, which are the common property of all Poets, and which, at some period of your life, must have been interesting to a man of your sensibility, and perhaps may still continue to be so. It would be highly gratifying to me to suppose that even in a single instance the manner in which I have treated these general topics should afford you any pleasure; but such a hope does not influence me upon the present occasion; in truth I do not feel it. Besides, I am convinced that there must be many things in this collection, which may impress you with an unfavorable idea of my intellectual powers. I do not say this with a wish to degrade myself; but I am sensible that this must be the case, from the different circles in which we have moved, and the different objects with which we have been conversant.

Being utterly unknown to you as I am, I am well aware, that if I am justified in writing to you at all, it is necessary, my letter should be short; but I have feelings within me which I hope will so far shew themselves in this letter, as to excuse the trespass

---

[4] John Milton, *On Shakespeare* (1630). Wordsworth omits lines 9–14.

which I am afraid I shall make. In common with the whole of the English people I have observed in your public character a constant predominance of sensibility of heart. Necessitated as you have been from your public situation to have much to do with men in bodies, and in classes, and accordingly to contemplate them in that relation, it has been your praise that you have not thereby been prevented from looking upon them as individuals, and that you have habitually left your heart open to be influenced by them in that capacity. This habit cannot but have made you dear to Poets; and I am sure that, if since your first entrance into public life there has been a single true poet living in England, he must have loved you.

But were I assured that I myself had a just claim to the title of a Poet, all the dignity being attached to the word which belongs to it, I do not think that I should have ventured for that reason to offer these volumes to you: at present it is solely on account of two poems in the second volume, the one entitled "The Brothers," and the other "Michael," that I have been emboldened to take this liberty.

It appears to me that the most calamitous effect, which has followed the measures which have lately been pursued in this country, is a rapid decay of the domestic affections among the lower orders of society. This effect the present Rulers of this country are not conscious of, or they disregard it. For many years past, the tendency of society amongst almost all the nations of Europe has been to produce it. But recently by the spreading of manufactures through every part of the country, by the heavy taxes upon postage, by workhouses, Houses of Industry, and the invention of Soup-shops &c. &c. superadded to the encreasing disproportion between the price of labour and that of the necessaries of life, the bonds of domestic feeling among the poor, as far as the influence of these things has extended, have been weakened, and in innumerable instances entirely destroyed. The evil would be the less to be regretted, if these institutions were regarded only as palliatives to a disease; but the vanity and pride of their promoters are so subtly interwoven with them, that they are deemed great discoveries and blessings to humanity. In the mean time parents are separated from their children, and children from their parents; the wife no longer prepares with her own hands a meal for her husband, the produce of his labour; there is little doing in his house in which his affections can be interested, and but little left in it which he can love. I have two neighbours, a man and his wife, both upwards of eighty years of age; they live alone; the husband has been confined to his bed many months and has never had, nor till within these few weeks has ever needed, any body to attend to

him but his wife. She has recently been seized with a lameness which has often prevented her from being able to carry him his food to his bed; the neighbours fetch water for her from the well, and do other kind offices for them both, but her infirmities encrease. She told my Servant two days ago that she was afraid they must both be boarded out among some other Poor of the parish (they have long been supported by the parish) but she said, it was hard, having kept house together so long, to come to this, and she was sure that "it would burst her heart." I mention this fact to shew how deeply the spirit of independence is, even yet, rooted in some parts of the country. These people could not express themselves in this way without an almost sublime conviction of the blessings of independent domestic life. If it is true, as I believe, that this spirit is rapidly disappearing, no greater curse can befal a land.

I earnestly entreat your pardon for having detained you so long. In the two Poems, "The Brothers" and "Michael" I have attempted to draw a picture of the domestic affections as I know they exist amongst a class of men who are now almost confined to the North of England. They are small independent *proprietors* of land here called statesmen, men of respectable education who daily labour on their own little properties. The domestic affections will always be strong amongst men who live in a country not crowded with population, if these men are placed above poverty. But if they are proprietors of small estates, which have descended to them from their ancestors, the power which these affections will acquire amongst such men is inconceivable by those who have only had an opportunity of observing hired labourers, farmers, and the manufacturing Poor. Their little tract of land serves as a kind of permanent rallying point for their domestic feelings, as a tablet upon which they are written which makes them objects of memory in a thousand instances when they would otherwise be forgotten. It is a fountain fitted to the nature of social man from which supplies of affection, as pure as his heart was intended for, are daily drawn. This class of men is rapidly disappearing. You, Sir, have a consciousness, upon which every good man will congratulate you, that the whole of your public conduct has in one way or other been directed to the preservation of this class of men, and those who hold similar situations. You have felt that the most sacred of all property is the property of the Poor. The two poems which I have mentioned were written with a view to shew that men who do not wear fine cloaths can feel deeply. "Pectus enim est quod disertos facit, et vis mentis. Ideoque imperitis quoque, si modo sint aliquo affectu concitati, verba non desunt." [1] The poems are faithful copies from nature; and I hope, whatever effect they may have upon you, you will at least be able to perceive that they may excite profitable sympathies in many kind and good hearts, and may in some small degree enlarge our feelings of reverence for our species, and our knowledge of human nature, by shewing that our best qualities are possessed by men whom we are too apt to consider, not with reference to the points in which they resemble us, but to those in which they manifestly differ from us. I thought, at a time when these feelings are sapped in so many ways that the two poems might co-operate, however feebly, with the illustrious efforts which you have made to stem this and other evils with which the country is labouring, and it is on this account alone that I have taken the liberty of thus addressing you.

Wishing earnestly that the time may come when the country may perceive what it has lost by neglecting your advice, and hoping that your latter days may be attended with health and comfort.

I remain, With the highest respect and admiration,
Your most obedient and humble Servt
W Wordsworth

John Wilson (1785–1854), later a critic and reviewer (under the name of "Christopher North"), and friend of Wordsworth, was seventeen when he wrote the letter answered here.

TO JOHN WILSON

[Grasmere, 7 June 1802]

My dear Sir,

Had it not been for a very amiable modesty you could not have imagined that your letter could give me any offence. It was on many accounts highly grateful to me. I was pleas'd to find that I had given so much pleasure to an ingenuous and able mind and I further considered the enjoyment which you had had from my poems as an earnest that others might be delighted with them in the same or a like manner. It is plain from your letter that the pleasure which I have given you has not been blind or unthinking you have studied the poems and prove that you have entered into the spirit of them. They have not given you a cheap or vulgar pleasure therefore I feel that you are entitled to my kindest thanks for having done some violence to your natural diffidence in the communication which you have made to me.

[1] The quotation is from Quintilian: "Eloquence comes from passion and strength of mind. The most uneducated men always have words if they are moved by some passion."

There is scarcely any part of your letter that does not deserve particular notice, but partly from a weakness in my stomach and digestion and partly from certain habits of mind I do not write any letters unless upon business not even to my dearest Friends. Except during absence from my own family I have not written five letters of friendship during the last five years. I have mentioned this in order that I may retain your good opinion should my letter be less minute than you are entitled to expect. You seem to be desirous of my opinion on the influence of natural objects in forming the character of nations. This cannot be understood without first considering their influence upon men in general first with reference to such subjects as are common to all countries: and next such as belong exclusively to any particular country or in a greater degree to it than to another. Now it is manifest that no human being can be so besotted and debased by oppression, penury or any other evil which unhumanizes man as to be utterly insensible to the colours, forms, or smell of flowers, the voices and motions of birds and beasts, the appearances of the sky and heavenly bodies, the genial warmth of a fine day, the terror and uncomfortableness of a storm, &c &c. How dead soever many full-grown men may outwardly seem to these things they all are more or less affected by them, and in childhood, in the first practice and exercise of their senses, they must have been not the nourishers merely, but often the fathers of their passions. There cannot be a doubt that in tracts of country where images of danger, melancholy, grandeur, or loveliness, softness, and ease prevail, that they will make themselves felt powerfully in forming the characters of the people, so as to produce a uniformity of national character, where the nation is small and is not made up of men who, inhabiting different soils, climates, &c by their civil usages, and relations materially interfere with each other. It was so formerly, no doubt, in the Highlands of Scotland but we cannot perhaps observe much of it in our own island at the present day, because, even in the most sequestered places, by manufactures, traffic, religion, Law, interchange of inhabitants &c distinctions are done away which would otherwise have been strong and obvious. This complex state of society does not, however, prevent the characters of individuals from frequently receiving a strong bias not merely from the impressions of general nature, but also from local objects and images. But it seems that to produce these effects in the degree in which we frequently find them to be produced there must be a peculiar sensibility of original organization combining with moral accidents, as is exhibited in *The Brothers* and in *Ruth*—I mean, to produce this in a marked degree not that I believe that any man was ever brought up in the country without loving it, especially in his better moments, or in a district of particular grandeur or beauty without feeling some stronger attachment to it on that account than he would otherwise have felt. I include, you will observe, in these considerations the influence of climate, changes in the atmosphere and elements and the labours and occupations which particular districts require.

You begin what you say upon the Idiot Boy with this observation, that nothing is a fit subject for poetry which does not please. But here follows a question, Does not please whom? Some have little knowledge of natural imagery of any kind, and, of course, little relish for it, some are disgusted with the very mention of the words pastoral poetry, sheep or shepherds, some cannot tolerate a poem with a ghost or any supernatural agency in it, others would shrink from an animated description of the pleasures of love, as from a thing carnal and libidinous some cannot bear to see delicate and refined feelings ascribed to men in low conditions of society, because their vanity and self-love tell them that these belong only to themselves and men like themselves in dress, station, and way of life: others are disgusted with the naked language of some of the most interesting passions of men, because either it is indelicate, or gross, or vulgar, as many fine ladies could not bear certain expressions in The Mad Mother and the Thorn, and, as in the instance of Adam Smith, who, we are told, could not endure the Ballad of Clym of the Clough, because the author had not written like a gentleman; then there are professional, local and national prejudices forevermore some take no interest in the description of a particular passion or quality, as love of solitariness, we will say, genial activity of fancy, love of nature, religion, and so forth, because they have little or nothing of it in themselves, and so on without end. I return then to the question, please whom? or what? I answer, human nature, as it has been and ever will be. But where are we to find the best measure of this? I answer, from within; by stripping our own hearts naked, and by looking out of ourselves towards men who lead the simplest lives most according to nature men who have never known false refinements, wayward and artificial desires, false criticisms, effeminate habits of thinking and feeling, or who, having known these things, have outgrown them. This latter class is the most to be depended upon, but it is very small in number. People in our rank in life are perpetually falling into one sad mistake, namely, that of supposing that human nature and the persons they associate with are one and the same thing. Whom do we generally associate with? Gentlemen, persons of fortune, professional men, ladies persons who can afford to buy or can easily procure books of half a guinea price, hot-pressed, and printed upon superfine paper. These persons are, it is true, a part of human nature, but we err lamentably if we suppose them to be fair representatives of the vast mass of human existence. And yet few ever consider books but with reference to their power of pleasing these persons and men of a higher rank few descend lower among cottages and fields and among children. A man must have done this habitually before his judgment upon the Idiot Boy would be in any way decisive with me. I *know* I have done this myself habitually; I wrote the poem with exceeding delight and pleasure, and whenever I read it I read it with pleasure. You have given me praise for having reflected faithfully in my poems the feelings of human nature I would fain hope that I have done so. But a great Poet ought to do more than this he ought to a certain degree to rectify men's feelings, to give them new compositions of feeling, to render their feelings more sane pure and permanent, in short, more consonant to nature, that is, to eternal nature, and the great moving spirit of things. He ought to travel before men occasionally as well as at their sides. I may illustrate this by a reference to natural objects. What false notions have prevailed from generation to generation as to the true character of the nightingale. As far as my Friend's Poem in the Lyrical Ballads,[1] is read it will contribute greatly to rectify these. You will recollect a passage in Cowper where, speaking of rural sounds, he says—

"and *even* the boding Owl
    That hails the rising moon has charms for me."[2]

Cowper was passionately fond of natural objects yet you see he mentions it as a marvellous thing that he could connect pleasure with the cry of the owl. In the same poem he speaks in the same manner of that beautiful plant, the gorse; making in some degree an amiable boast of his loving it, "*unsightly*" and unsmooth" as it is. There are many aversions of this kind, which, though they have some foundation in nature, have yet so slight a one, that though they may have prevailed hundreds of years, a philosopher will look upon them as accidents. So with respect to many moral feelings, either of love or dislike what excessive admiration was payed in former times to personal prowess and military success it is so with the latter even at the present day but surely not nearly so much

---

[1] Coleridge's *The Nightingale*. See p. 441.
[2] William Cowper, *The Task*, i, 205–206.

as heretofore. So with regard to birth, and innumerable other modes of sentiment, civil and religious. But you will be inclined to ask by this time how all this applies to the Idiot Boy.[3] To this I can only say that the loathing and disgust which many people have at the sight of an Idiot, is a feeling which, though having some foundation in human nature is not necessarily attached to it in any virtuous degree, but is owing, in a great measure to a false delicacy, and, if I may say it without rudeness, a certain want of comprehensiveness of thinking and feeling. Persons in the lower classes of society have little or nothing of this: if an Idiot is born in a poor man's house, it must be taken care of and cannot be boarded out, as it would be by gentlefolks, or sent to a public or private receptacle for such unfortunate beings. Poor people seeing frequently among their neighbours such objects, easily forget whatever there is of natural disgust about them, and have therefore a sane state, so that without pain or suffering they perform their duties towards them. I could with pleasure pursue this subject, but I must now strictly adopt the plan which I proposed to myself when I began to write this letter, namely, that of setting down a few hints or memorandums, which you will think of for my sake.

I have often applied to Idiots, in my own mind, that sublime expression of scripture that, "*their life is hidden with God.*" They are worshipped, probably from a feeling of this sort, in several parts of the East. Among the Alps where they are numerous, they are considered, I believe, as a blessing to the family to which they belong I have indeed often looked upon the conduct of fathers and mothers of the lower classes of society towards Idiots as the great triumph of the human heart. It is there that we see the strength, disinterestedness, and grandeur of love, nor have I ever been able to contemplate an object that calls out so many excellent and virtuous sentiments without finding it hallowed thereby and having something in me which bears down before it, like a deluge, every feeble sensation of disgust and aversion.

There are in my opinion, several important mistakes in the latter part of your letter which I could have wished to notice; but I find myself much fatigued. These refer both to the Boy and the Mother. I must content myself simply with observing that it is probable that the principle cause of your dislike to this particular poem lies in the *word* Idiot. If there had been any such word in our language, *to which we had attached passion*, as lack-wit, half-wit, witless &c I should have certainly employed it in

preference but there is no such word. Observe, (this is entirely in reference to this particular poem) my Idiot is not one of those who cannot articulate and such as are usually disgusting in their persons—

"Whether in cunning or in joy"
"And then his words were not a few" &c

and the last speech at the end of the poem. The Boy whom I had in my mind was, by no means disgusting in his appearance quite the contrary and I have known several with imperfect faculties who are handsome in their persons and features. There is one, at present, within a mile of my own house remarkably so, though there is something of a stare and vacancy in his countenance. A Friend of mine, knowing that some persons had a dislike to the poem such as you have expressed advised me to add a stanza describing the person of the Boy so as entirely to separate him in the imaginations of my Readers from that class of idiots who are disgusting in their persons, but the narration in the poem is so rapid and impassioned that I could not find a place in which to insert the stanza without checking the progress of it, and so leaving a deadness upon the feeling. This poem has, I know, frequently produced the same effect as it did upon you and your Friends but there are many people also to whom it affords exquisite delight, and who indeed, prefer it to any other of my Poems. This proves that the feelings there delineated are such as all men *may* sympathize with. This is enough for my purpose. It is not enough for me as a poet, to delineate merely such feelings as all men *do* sympathise with but, it is also highly desirable to add to these others, such as all men *may* sympathize with, and such as there is reason to believe they would be better and more moral beings if they did sympathize with.

I conclude with regret, because I have not said one half of what I intended to say: but I am sure you will deem my excuse sufficient when I inform you that my head aches violently, and I am, in other respects, unwell. I must, however, again give you my warmest thanks for your kind letter. I shall be happy to hear from you again and do not think it unreasonable that I should request a letter from you when I feel that the answer which I may make to it will not perhaps, be above three or four lines. This I mention to you with frankness, and you will not take it ill after what I have before said of my remissness in writing letters.

I am, dear Sir
With great Respect,
Yours sincerely W Wordsworth.

---

[3] See *Lyrical Ballads*, pp. 179ff.

This part of a long letter that William and Dorothy wrote to both Hutchinson sisters concerns a version of Resolution and Independence *(i.e.,* The Leech-gatherer*) that no longer survives. See also the discussion of Coleridge's* Dejection, *p. 482.*

TO SARAH HUTCHINSON

[Grasmere, 14 June 1802]

*   *   *   *   *

My dear Sara

I am exceedingly sorry that the latter part of the Leech-gatherer has displeased you, the more so because I cannot take to myself (that being the case) much pleasure or satisfaction in having pleased you in the former part. I will explain to you in prose my feeling in writing that Poem, and then you will be better able to judge whether the fault be mine or yours or partly both. I describe myself as having been exalted to the highest pitch of delight by the joyousness and beauty of Nature and then as depressed, even in the midst of those beautiful objects, to the lowest dejection and despair. A young Poet in the midst of the happiness of Nature is described as overwhelmed by the thought of the miserable reverses which have befallen the happiest of all men, viz Poets—I think of this till I am so deeply impressed by it, that I consider the manner in which I was rescued from my dejection and despair almost as an interposition of Providence. 'Now whether it was by peculiar grace A leading from above'. A person reading this Poem with feelings like mine will have been awed and controuled, expecting almost something spiritual or supernatural—What is brought forward? 'A lonely place, a Pond' 'by which an old man *was*, far from all house or home'—not stood, not sat, but '*was*'—the figure presented in the most naked simplicity possible. This feeling of spirituality or supernaturalness is again referred to as being strong in my mind in this passage —'*How came he here* thought I or what can he be doing?' I then describe him, whether ill or well is not for me to judge with perfect confidence, but this I can *confidently* affirm, that, though I believe God has given me a strong imagination, I cannot conceive a figure more impressive than that of an old Man like this, the survivor of a Wife and ten children, travelling alone among the mountains and all lonely places, carrying with him his own fortitude, and the necessities which an unjust state of society has entailed upon him. You say and Mary (that is you can say no more than that) the Poem is *very well* after the introduction of the old man; this is not true, if it is not more than very well it is very bad, there is no intermediate state. You speak of his speech as tedious: everything is tedious when one does not read with the feelings of the Author—'*The Thorn*' is tedious to hundreds; and so is the *Idiot Boy*[1] to hundreds. It is in the character of the old man to tell his story in a manner which an *impatient* reader must necessarily feel as tedious. But Good God! Such a figure, in such a place, a pious self-respecting, miserably infirm, and [ ] Old Man telling such a tale!

My dear Sara, it is not a matter of indifference whether you are pleased with this figure and his employment; it may be comparatively so, whether you are pleased or not with *this Poem*; but it is of the utmost importance that you should have had pleasure from contemplating the fortitude, independence, persevering spirit, and the general moral dignity of this old man's character. Your feelings upon the Mother, and the Boys with the Butterfly, were not indifferent: it was an affair of whole continents of moral sympathy. I will talk more with you on this when we meet—at present, farewell and Heaven for ever bless you!

W. W.

John Wordsworth, captain of the Abergavenny, *was drowned when the ship struck a rock off the English coast on February 5, 1805. About three hundred of the four hundred aboard were drowned. Richard Wordsworth, a lawyer in London, wrote the following letter to William to inform him of the loss:*

Staple Inn   7th Febry 1805.

My dear Brother,

It is with the most painful concern that I inform you of the Loss of the Ship Abergavenny, off Weymouth last night.

I am acquainted with but few of the particulars of this melancholy Event. I am told that a great number of Persons have perished, and that our Brother John is amongst that number. Mr Joseph Wordsworth is amongst those who have been saved. The Ship struck against a Rock, and went to the Bottom. You will impart this to Dorothy in the best manner you can, and remember me most affectly to her, and your wife, believe me yours most sincerely,

Rd Wordsworth.

William wrote the following reply to his brother. (On the death of John, see also the poems Elegiac Verses, To the Daisy, *and* Elegiac Stanzas.*)*

TO RICHARD WORDSWORTH

[Grasmere] Monday Evening 11th Febry —05
My dear Brother,

The lamentable news which your Letter brought

---

[1] Both are in *Lyrical Ballads*, pp. 179ff.

has now been known to us seven hours during which time I have done all in my power to alleviate the distress of poor Dorothy and my Wife. Mary and I were walking out when the Letter came: it was brought by Sarah Hutchinson who had come from Kendal where she was staying, to be of use in the house and to comfort us: so that I had no power of breaking the force of the shock to Dorothy or to Mary. They are both very ill. Dorothy especially, on whom this loss of her beloved Brother will long take deep hold. I shall do my best to console her; but John was very dear to me and my heart will never forget him. God rest his soul! When you can bear to write do inform us not generally but as minutely as possible of the manner of this catastrophe. It would comfort us in this lonely place, though at present nobody in the house but myself could bear to hear a word on the subject. It is indeed a great affliction to us!

God bless you my dear Brother; Dorothys and Marys best love. We wish you were with us. God keep the rest of us together! the set is now broken. Farewell.

Dear Brother
Wm Wordsworth.

Samuel Taylor Coleridge

1772–1834

"THE Poet is dead in me!" wrote Coleridge to William Godwin in 1801. The obituary was premature, and probably Coleridge himself did not take it too seriously. Certainly his friends had become as accustomed to his extravagant confessions of failure as to his prodigious plans for the future: writing dozens of books, emigrating to a warmer climate, even raising acorns commercially. But in one sense the statement to Godwin has Coleridge's characteristic insight. He was a man whose being comprised many vocations, only one of which was the writing of poetry. Literary critic, philosopher, theologian, political scientist, amateur chemist and physician— Coleridge's activities covered an enormous range of the social and physical sciences as well as the humanities. The quantity of major poetry he wrote during a literary career that lasted forty-six years is, compared to what Keats wrote in five years or Shelley in ten, relatively small. And most of it was written before he was thirty.

Constantly questioning the value of what he wrote, his place among the poets of his day, the role poetry ought to play in the life of the civilized man and the ideal society, he was himself the best example of what he called (in *The Friend*) the writer who must tune his harp "in the hearing of those, who are to understand its after harmonies; the foundation stones of his edifice must lie open to common view, or his friends will hesitate to trust themselves beneath his roof." Among his major poems, "Christabel" remained unfinished, "Dejection" exists in three distinctly different versions, even *The Rime of the Ancient Mariner* underwent fundamental changes between its first appearance in 1798 and its subsequent appearance in *Lyrical Ballads*.

Because their careers are so interdependent, it is impossible to say much about Coleridge without mentioning Wordsworth. Whether or not he was justified in claiming credit for the best of Wordsworth's literary criticism, it was undoubtedly Coleridge's influence that encouraged Wordsworth to discover and articulate a theory for his own poetry, and though many other causes can be found for the increasing lack of self-criticism in Wordsworth's poetry after 1802, his distance from Coleridge and Coleridge's own greater investment of time in works of the philosophical imagination are surely important ones.

But the later separation between Wordsworth and Coleridge is not nearly as significant as the extraordinary coincidence that two such talented poets should have happened to meet in 1795 and begin seven years of collaboration that was sometimes as formal as the joint plan for the *Ancient Mariner* (Wordsworth eventually gave up), but more often a matter of discussion and implicit competition. During the years they spent near each other in Somerset, then as fellow travelers to Germany, later separated only by the ten miles between Grasmere and Keswick in the Lake District, Wordsworth and Coleridge saw each other almost continuously, and corresponded faithfully (often through Wordsworth's sister Dorothy) when either was away. Between them, partly as a result of their deliberate cooperation, the two poets probably had a more radical effect on the way English poetry is written and literature read than anyone before or since. Whether or not they set out to do so, they succeeded in altering the literary consciousness of their generation and of those to follow. And thanks largely to the range of Coleridge's literary criticism, the terms for assessing and appreciating this change are as eloquent as anyone could wish. If we can talk glibly today of the literary imagination, it is Coleridge's careful definition of the assumptions we now share with him that enables us to do so.

Coleridge's despair at ever being the sort of poet he hoped to become was almost constant. Few writers have ever met more continuous frustration: his chronic illness and the addiction to opium resulting from his attempts to alleviate it; the collapse of his plans for founding a utopian colony on the banks of the Susquehanna River because of Robert Southey's "treachery"; the incompatibility of his wife and the hopelessness, as an alternative, of his love for Sara Hutchinson. Inevitably modern readers have felt, as Coleridge's own contemporaries did, that no man could possibly be so exceedingly unlucky. And Coleridge himself was all too ready to admit that much of his distress was of his own doing. The demands he made on his family and friends, and on himself, often had little relation to their ability or his own to satisfy them. All he did and wrote is but a tiny fraction of what he had planned, and our sense of Coleridge as a man of unfulfilled talents is largely a result of his insistence on making his plans and his dissatisfactions public knowledge. His friends were discreet. Without himself as his own publicist, probably no one would now know of his addiction to opium or of his love for Sara Hutchinson, and the contexts in which we now read *Kubla Khan* and *Dejection* would be very different.

As recent critics have argued, there is a surprisingly strong case to be made for regarding Coleridge the artist as a traditional poet who aspires more to the impersonal mode of eighteenth-century poetry than to the self-analytical poetry of his own period. Our sense of *Dejection*, for instance, is unquestionably distorted by what we know about the circumstances of its composition, and there can be few instances in the history of English literature where the successive drafts of a greatly altered poem, the writer's comments on them, and the immediate influence of other major poems (Wordsworth's *Immortality Ode* and *Resolution and Independence*) are fully available for study. Even a quick comparison of the two versions yields a useful insight into Coleridge's methods, strengths and weaknesses as a poet. As Coleridge and Wordsworth both confront the task of saying something about the diminished perceptions and feelings that have come with approaching middle age, Coleridge's first response was highly autobiographical: the letter in verse to Sara Hutchinson on April 4, 1802, is a painful, ostensibly unedited pouring-forth of the miseries of his marriage and the frustrations of his love. Rather than a love letter, it is an apology for his being unable to write a love letter, and a very particular man, with little criticism of his literary voice, addresses a very particular woman. A reader unfamiliar with its context is probably justified in feeling rather embarrassed, and may hesitate to intrude as a literary critic into this half of an exchange so obviously personal. But *Dejection: An Ode*, as it was published in the form of a tribute to Wordsworth on his wedding day (and Coleridge's own wedding anniversary), and especially as it was later revised for *Sybilline Leaves*, is a work drastically different from the letter from which it derived. The Ode is half as long, all but a few of its personal allusions have been transformed into vague and impersonal gestures toward an imaginary and public audience, its form is now clearly and uncompromisingly that of a Pindaric ode, and the poet's concern now is with the shaping spirit of imagination rather than the personal troubles that have caused failure of that spirit. The reader of this later poem may sometimes be puzzled about the way he is supposed to move from line to line (the omission of the personal "causes" have made their effects rather obscure), but he never doubts that he is reading a poem in a mode with a long and impersonal tradition, whether or not he is familiar with its classical origins.

If Coleridge wrote poetry in part as therapy, and if his ability to compose was only partly as dependent on the events of his intellectual and domestic life as he says it was, it is also true that to Coleridge (perhaps more than to Wordsworth) poetry was a craft. Although many of the most successful of his poems are in the very personal mode Coleridge invented and called "The Conversation Poem" (e.g., *This Lime-Tree Bower, Frost at Midnight, To William Wordsworth*), he also experimented radically with forms that appear more traditional: the medievalism of *The Ancient Mariner* (in its first version even its spelling was archaic), the gothicism of *Christabel*. *Kubla Khan*, which seems to strike many readers as enormously powerful for reasons that elude satisfactory explanation, puzzled its author as well. He always called it a "fragment" when it appeared in his works, not because (as with *Christabel*) there was more to add to it, but because the poem itself must have seemed an unresolved joining of several experiments: adapting Jacobean travel books, exploring the effect of opium dreams on the imagination, using an elaborate symbolism for a statement about kinds of poetry and modes of imagination. The amateur laboratory scientist was never far away when Coleridge wrote, and Coleridge himself acknowledged experimenting repeatedly with self-induced feelings. Science, private emotion, literary craft were interests that Coleridge tried to force together by will and imagination.

Except for the plays, Coleridge apparently never attempted the sort of extended work he kept urging upon Wordsworth; he is in fact the only one of the major romantic poets not to have tried a sustained work in verse. If the examples of Spenser and Milton seem to have convinced his contemporaries that a single long work dealing with an elevated subject was the foundation of a literary career, and that no man was a true poet unless he had epic ambitions, Coleridge was apparently unwilling to invest that much time and energy in one direction, one single trial of the powers of invention of the sort that Keats describes in recounting his struggles with *Endymion*. The form of *Biographia Literaria* illustrates Coleridge's insistence on particularity at the expense of any overall neat and efficient Plan, even when the subject was his own intellectual life. His letters, for all their interest, might suggest that Coleridge's self-pity would have created a permanent enclosure preventing most significant personal relations, but all the reports of his conversation—from Hazlitt through Keats to Carlyle—attest to the versatility of his mind, the volatility of his imagination. Obviously he was a writer who could say sincerely at one moment that the poet in him was dead, and next day (or next hour) begin writing poetry again with renewed optimism. Just for this reason his accounts of "failure" (as in *Dejection*) become misleading when such momentary responses are given the appearance of more than personal authority by the permanence of language and finally print. Of course he did fail to become a poet of single-minded dedication like Wordsworth (as he explains in *To William Wordsworth*), he failed to invest all of his energy in a Great Poem, he failed (as most of his contemporaries did) to find an audience as responsive as he ideally imagined one might be. But he never spoke often enough of his successes, whether out of decorous modesty or genuine self-deprecation. The poems themselves do that, if they are read as more than illustrations of Coleridge's lack of faith in art. It is standard modern psychology to assume that a neurotic personality is least fitted to judge itself, and standard modern literary theory to assume that in any case deficiencies of character or personality are not consequently deficiencies of art.

Although Coleridge was not as prolific as Wordsworth, after 1802, when one had written *Dejection* and the other *Resolution and Independence*, the poetry he did write had none of Wordsworth's laureate pretensions. For years Coleridge continued to work with the metrical experiments that characterized his earlier work, and his wit about his own art never faltered. But by the last part of his career Coleridge—ill, addicted, separated from his wife and under the constant care and supervision of the Gillmans in Highgate (from 1816)—devoted his still considerable energies to the task of understanding his world through prose rather than discovering it through poetry. The amount of writing in prose he did in his lifetime was enormous, so that some of it has never been published and much of it has not been republished since the mid-nineteenth century. The collected edition of Coleridge's work now being prepared by a large staff of editors will comprise well over twenty large volumes. The fact that no such collection has yet been made, and no complete biography of Coleridge has yet been written, is a tribute to a man whose complex interests have never found a successor capable of comprehending all of them. Those who have studied his work within the context of a single discipline—literary criticism, say, or political theory, or the history of science—find Coleridge's ideas startlingly modern and comprehensive enough to be the work of a major innovator had he given his time to that one field alone. Few of the major literary critics of this century have avoided at some time quoting his famous description (in Chapter XIV of *Biographia Literaria* below) of the power of the poetry as revealed in

> the balance or reconciliation of opposite or discordant qualities: of sameness, with difference; of the general, with the concrete; the idea, with the image; the individual, with the representative; the sense of novelty and freshness, with old and familiar objects; a more than usual state of emotion, with more than usual order; judgement ever awake and steady self-possession, with enthusiasm and feeling profound or vehement; and while it blends and harmonizes the natural and the artificial, still subordinates art to nature; the manner to the matter; and our admiration of the poet to our sympathy with the poetry.

Like Charles Darwin, Coleridge has been accused by some modern historians of gathering credit, perhaps unintentionally, for ideas that were current at the time.

Unquestionably Coleridge was often careless about acknowledging sources, especially when they were in a language like German with which few of his contemporary English readers would be familiar. But works like the *Biographia Literaria*, and the full texts of the Notebooks now being published, show that the mode of Coleridge's philosophical imagination, like that of his literary one, operated in ways that make the usual conventions of reading and evaluation less appropriate. Regardless of his unacknowledged debts, it is clear that Coleridge now (and to a large extent in his own lifetime) stands for and helps to define for readers of English the philosophical and literary assumptions that have come to characterize our own epoch.

If interest in the poet Coleridge seems today to be subordinated to an interest in the critic and philosopher, it should be remembered that Coleridge (with Wordsworth) was one of the first to insist that writing be seen as the complex expression of a man's total sensibility, and defined writing poetry as the occupation for the writer which ideally "brings the whole soul of man into activity, with the subordination of its faculties to each other, according to their relative worth and dignity."

OUTLINE OF EVENTS

1772	Oct. 21	Born at Ottery St. Mary, Devon, to the Rev. John and Mrs. Anne Bowden Coleridge, the youngest son of a large family.
1781	Oct.	Death of John Coleridge.
1782–1790		Attends school at Christ's Hospital, London (until 1791), where one of his fellow students is Charles Lamb. Facility in Latin and Greek, taste in literature, encouraged by Upper Master James Boyer. Admires sonnets of W. L. Bowles. Meets and falls in love with Mary Ann Evans of London. Swims the New River, Newington, catches cold, health permanently impaired.
1791	Jan.	Wins scholarship at Jesus College, Cambridge.
1793	Dec.	In debt, despairing of winning Mary Evans's love, enlists in 15th Light Dragoons as Silas Tomkyn Comberbache.
1794	Apr.	Returns to Cambridge after family and friends purchase his release from army.
	June	Meets Robert Southey during visit to Oxford; together they plan emigration to America and the founding of a utopian community based on "pantisocratic" principles.
	July	On walking tour of Wales with Southey; in Bristol becomes engaged to Sara Fricker, whose sister Edith will marry Southey. Several of the Fricker sisters, and their mother, back plan for emigration.
	Sept.	*Fall of Robespierre*, by S. T. Coleridge and Southey, published. Poetry begins to appear in *Morning Chronicle*.
	Dec.	Leaves Cambridge (without a degree).
1795		In Bristol. Gives lectures on politics published as *Conciones ad Populum*. Meets Wordsworth.
	Oct. 4	Marries Sara Fricker; they live in or near Bristol (until 1796).

1796 Mar.–May Edits and publishes the *Watchman*.

Sept. 19 (David) Hartley Coleridge born.

Dec. Coleridges move to Nether Stowey (Somerset). *Poems on Various Occasions* published.

1797 June *Poems by S. T. Coleridge, Second Edition* published.

July William and Dorothy Wordsworth move to Alfoxden, six miles from Nether Stowey.
During the year, Coleridge begins *Ancient Mariner* (at first in collaboration with Wordsworth); publishes poetry in the *Morning Post*; completes *Osorio* (rejected); begins *Christabel* and *Kubla Khan*.

1798 Preaches at Unitarian Chapel, Shrewsbury, but turns down pastorate. Given annuity by Thomas and Josiah Wedgwood.

May 14 Berkeley Coleridge born (d. February 10, 1799).

Sept. *Lyrical Ballads* by Wordsworth and Coleridge published; meets William Hazlitt.

Sept. 16 Leaves for Hamburg, Ratzeburg, Göttingen (at first with the Wordsworths).

1799 July Returns to England.

Oct. Visits Sockburn (meets Sara Hutchinson) and Lake District (with Wordsworth).

Nov. Returns to London; resumes contributions to the *Morning Post*; resumes friendship with Charles Lamb; meets William Godwin frequently.

1800 July Coleridges settle at Greta Hall, Keswick, 10 miles from Wordsworths at Grasmere.

Sept. 14 Derwent Coleridge born.

1801 During the year, suffers from ill health, domestic unhappiness. Plans emigration to Azores.

Nov. Goes to London to write for the *Morning Post*, etc.

1802 Mar. Returns to Keswick.

Apr. 4 Writes verse letter to Sara Hutchinson, later revised as *Dejection: An Ode*.

Aug. On walking trip in Cumberland and Westmorland. Writes *Hymn Before Sunrise*.

Oct. 4 Wordsworth and Mary Hutchinson married; *Dejection* published in the *Morning Post*.

Dec. Sara Coleridge born. Coleridge returns briefly to Keswick.

1803 Aug. Tours Scotland with William and Dorothy Wordsworth, but parts from them after two weeks.

1804 Apr. Leaves for Malta, Sicily.

1805 Jan. Becomes Acting Secretary to British governor in Malta (until August).

1806 Jan.–June In Italy.

Aug. Arrives in England ill, penniless, planning separation from wife.

1807	Jan.	Wordsworth reads *Prelude* to Coleridge, who writes *To William Wordsworth*.
	Nov.	In London; formally separated from wife.
1808		Lectures on poetry at Royal Institution, London (until June).
	Aug.	Settles at Allan Bank, Grasmere, with Wordsworths (until 1810).
1809	June	Begins publication of the *Friend* (until March 1810).
1810	Oct.	Returns to London.
1811	Nov.	Lectures on English poetry at Scot's Corporation Hall (until January 1812).
1812	Feb.–Mar.	Last visit to Keswick.
1812	Jan.	*Osorio*, renamed *Remorse*, produced at Drury Lane with assistance of Lord Byron.
	Oct.	Lectures at Bristol on Shakespeare, education (until November). Begins *Biographia Literaria* during year.
1815	Aug.	*Remorse* produced in Bristol.
1816	Apr.	Places himself under care of Dr. James Gillman of Highgate (North London), with whom he lives until his death (1834).
	June	*Christabel* published. *Statesman's Manual* published during year.
1817	July–Aug.	*Biographia Literaria, Sybylline Leaves* (collected poems) published. Revised, collected edition of *The Friend* published.
1818–1823		Gives public lectures on literature, philosophy, etc.
1819	Apr.	Briefly meets Keats at Highgate.
1824	Mar.	Elected Royal Associate of Royal Society of Literature (until 1831, when position was abolished).
1825		*Aids to Reflection* published.
1828		Three-volume edition of *Poems* published.
	Summer	Travels in Germany with the Wordsworths.
1830		*Constitution of Church and State* published.
1833		R. W. Emerson visits Coleridge.
	July	Composes epitaph.
1834	July 25	Coleridge dies at Highgate.

SELECTED BIBLIOGRAPHY

EDITIONS

NOTE: A collected edition of Coleridge's work in verse and prose—including letters, annotations, a definitive biography, and a comprehensive bibliography—is in preparation. Volumes, as they appear, will of course replace many of the editions listed below. Volumes published thus far include *The Friend* (1969), *Lectures 1795: On Politics and Religion* (1970), and *The Watchman* (1970).

The Complete Poetical Works of Samuel Taylor Coleridge, ed. E. H. Coleridge (2 vols., 1912). Includes the dramas in Vol. 2.

The Poems of Samuel Taylor Coleridge, ed. E. H. Coleridge (1912). A page-for-page reprint in smaller format of Vol. 1 of Coleridge's large edition. In 1967, its title became *Coleridge: Poetical Works*.

Biographia Literaria, ed. J. Shawcross (2 vols., 1907).

Political Tracts of Wordsworth, Coleridge and Shelley, ed. R. J. White (1953).

Confessions of an Inquiring Spirit, ed. H. St. J. Hart (1956).

Shakespearean Criticism, ed. T. M. Raysor (2 vols., 1930).

Miscellaneous Criticism, ed. T. M. Raysor (1936).

Coleridge on the Seventeenth Century, ed. R. F. Brinkley (1955).

The Statesman's Manual (1816).

Aids to Reflection (1825).

On the Constitution of Church and State (1832).

Essays on His Own Times, ed. Sara Coleridge (3 vols., 1850).

Specimens of the Table Talk of the Late Samuel Taylor Coleridge, ed. H. N. Coleridge (1836).

Philosophical Lectures of Samuel Taylor Coleridge: 1818–1819, ed. K. Coburn (1949).

Coleridge on Logic and Learning, ed. A. D. Snyder (1929).

Anima Poetae [selections from the *Notebooks*], ed. E. H. Coleridge (1895).

Notebooks, ed. K. Coburn (3 dbl. vols., 1957, 1961, 1971; others to follow).

Collected Letters of Samuel Taylor Coleridge, ed. E. L. Griggs (6 vols., 1956–1972).

Minnow Among Tritons [letters of Mrs. S. T. Coleridge], ed. S. Potter (1934).

BIOGRAPHY

J. D. CAMPBELL, *Samuel Taylor Coleridge* (1894).
E. K. CHAMBERS, *Samuel Taylor Coleridge* (1938).
L. HANSON, *The Life of S. T. Coleridge: The Early Years* [to 1800] (1938).
H. M. MARGOLIOUTH, *Wordsworth and Coleridge* (1953).

CRITICISM

J. L. LOWES, *The Road to Xanadu* (1927; rev. 1930).
J. H. MUIRHEAD, *Coleridge as Philosopher* (1930).
I. A. RICHARDS, *Coleridge on Imagination* (1934).
S. POTTER, *Coleridge and S. T. C.* (1935).
D. W. HARDING, "The Theme of 'The Ancient Mariner,'" *Scrutiny* (March 1941).
N. P. STALLKNECHT, *Strange Seas of Thought* (1945).
B. WILLEY, *Coleridge on Imagination and Fancy* (1946).
R. P. WARREN, Introduction to *Rime of the Ancient Mariner* (1946).
B. WILLEY, "Samuel Taylor Coleridge," *Nineteenth Century Studies* (1949).
H. HOUSE, *Coleridge* (1953).
E. SCHNEIDER, *Coleridge, Opium and Kubla Khan* (1953).
G. WHALLEY, *Coleridge and Sara Hutchinson and the 'Asra' Poems* (1955).
J. B. BEER, *Coleridge the Visionary* (1959).
J. COLMER, *Coleridge: Critic of Society* (1959).
M. SUTHER, *The Dark Night of Samuel Taylor Coleridge* (1960).
C. WOODRING, *Politics in the Poetry of Coleridge* (1961).
R. H. FOGLE, *The Idea of Coleridge's Criticism* (1962).
M. P. SCHULZ, *The Poetic Voices of Coleridge* (1965).
W. EMPSON, "The Ancient Mariner," *Critical Quarterly* (1964).

E. MARCOVITZ, "Bemoaning the Lost Dream: Coleridge's Kubla Khan and Addiction," *Intern. Journal of Psychoanalysis* (1964).

J. A. APPLEYARD, *Coleridge's Philosophy of Literature, 1791–1819* (1965).

M. SUTHER, *Visions of Xanadu* (1965).

G. WATSON, *Coleridge the Poet* (1966).

W. WALSH, *Coleridge: The Work and the Relevance* (1967).

G. YARLOTT, *Coleridge and the Abysinnian Maid* (1967).

W. J. BATE, *Coleridge* (1968).

J. D. BOULGER, ed., *Twentieth Century Interpretations of The Rime of the Ancient Mariner* (1969).

R. HAVEN, *Patterns of Consciousness: An Essay on Coleridge* (1969).

W. HEATH, *Wordsworth and Coleridge: A Study of Their Literary Relations in 1801–1802* (1970).

S. PRICKETT, *Coleridge and Wordsworth: The Poetry of Growth* (1970).

J. R. DE J. JACKSON, *Coleridge: The Critical Heritage* (1971).

B. WILLEY, *Samuel Taylor Coleridge* (1972).

POEMS

NIL PEJUS EST CAELIBE VITÂ[1]

I

WHAT pleasures shall he ever find?
What joys shall ever glad his heart?
Or who shall heal his wounded mind,
If tortur'd by Misfortune's smart?
Who Hymeneal bliss will never prove,
That more than friendship, friendship mix'd with
   love.

II

Then without child or tender wife,
To drive away each care, each sigh,
Lonely he treads the paths of life
A stranger to Affection's tye: 10
And when from Death he meets his final doom
No mourning wife with tears of love shall wet his
   tomb.

III

Tho' Fortune, Riches, Honours, Pow'r,
Had giv'n with every other toy,
Those gilded trifles of the hour,
Those painted nothings sure to cloy:
He dies forgot, his name no son shall bear
To shew the man so blest once breath'd the vital air.

[1787]   [1893]

---

[1] "There is nothing worse than a celibate life."

DESTRUCTION OF THE BASTILLE

The citizens of Paris stormed the Bastille and released its prisoners on July 14, 1789. Demolition of the building followed shortly thereafter. For a more extensive account of similar feelings of elation (and the disillusionment that followed them) see Books IX to XI of Wordsworth's Prelude *and Coleridge's* France: An Ode, *p. 465. Stanzas II and III have not survived.*

DESTRUCTION OF THE BASTILLE

I

HEARD'ST thou yon universal cry,
   And dost thou linger still on Gallia's shore?
Go, Tyranny! beneath some barbarous sky
   Thy terrors, lost and ruin'd power deplore!
      What tho' through many a groaning age
      Was felt thy keen suspicious rage,
      Yet Freedom rous'd by fierce Disdain
      Has wildly broke thy triple chain,
And like the storm which Earth's deep entrails hide,
At length has burst its way and spread the ruins wide.

   *   *   *   *   *

IV

In sighs their sickly breath was spent; each gleam   11
   Of Hope had ceas'd the long long day to cheer;
Or if delusive, in some flitting dream,
   It gave them to their friends and children dear—

Awaked by lordly Insult's sound
To all the doubled horrors round,
Oft shrunk they from Oppression's band
While Anguish rais'd the desperate hand
For silent death; or lost the mind's controll,
Thro' every burning vein would tides of Frenzy roll.

V

But cease, ye pitying bosoms, cease to bleed!   21
    Such scenes no more demand the tear humane;
I see, I see! glad Liberty succeed
    With every patriot virtue in her train!
        And mark yon peasant's raptur'd eyes;
        Secure he views his harvests rise;
        No fetter vile the mind shall know,
        And Eloquence shall fearless glow.
Yes! Liberty the soul of Life shall reign.
Shall throb in every pulse, shall flow thro' every vein!

VI

Shall France alone a Despot spurn?   31
    Shall she alone, O Freedom, boast thy care?
Lo, round thy standard Belgia's heroes burn,
    Tho' Power's blood-stain'd streamers fire the air,
        And wider yet thy influence spread,
        Nor e'er recline thy weary head,
        Till every land from pole to pole
        Shall boast one independent soul!
And still, as erst, let favour'd Britain be
First ever of the first and freest of the free!

[1789?]   [1834]

Thomas Chatterton (1752–1770), who killed himself at the
age of 17, was a conventional example of unfulfilled literary
talent and ambition. See Wordsworth's Resolution and
Independence and Keats's sonnet to Chatterton. This poem
appears in the book kept by James Boyer, headmaster of Christ's
Hospital, of his pupils' best work. The two-line epigraph is from
Thomas Gray's Elegy Written in a Country Churchyard,
slightly altered.

MONODY ON THE
DEATH OF CHATTERTON

Cold penury repress'd his noble rage,
And froze the genial current of his soul.

Now prompts the Muse poetic lays,
    And high my bosom beats with love of Praise!
But, Chatterton! methinks I hear thy name,
For cold my Fancy grows, and dead each Hope of
    Fame.

When Want and cold Neglect had chill'd thy
    soul,
Athirst for Death I see thee drench the bowl!
    Thy corpse of many a livid hue
    On the bare ground I view,
Whilst various passions all my mind engage;
    Now in my breast distended with a sigh,   10
    And now a flash of Rage
Darts through the tear, that glistens in my eye.

Is this the land of liberal Hearts!
Is this the land, where Genius ne'er in vain
Pour'd forth her soul-enchanting strain?
    Ah me! yet Butler 'gainst the bigot foe
        Well-skill'd to aim keen Humour's dart,
        Yet Butler felt Want's poignant sting;
        And Otway, Master of the Tragic art,
        Whom Pity's self had taught to sing,[1]   20
Sank beneath a load of Woe;
This ever can the generous Briton hear,
And starts not in his eye th' indignant Tear?
    Elate of Heart and confident of Fame,
From vales where Avon sports, the Minstrel
    came,
        Gay as the Poet hastes along
        He meditates the future song,
How Ælla battled with his country's foes,
        And whilst Fancy in the air
        Paints him many a vision fair   30
His eyes dance rapture and his bosom glows.
With generous joy he views th' ideal gold:
    He listens to many a Widow's prayers,
    And many an Orphan's thanks he hears;
        He soothes to peace the care-worn breast,
        He bids the Debtor's eyes know rest,
        And Liberty and Bliss behold:
And now he punishes the heart of steel,
And her own iron rod he makes Oppression feel.

Fated to heave sad Disappointment's sigh,   40
To feel the Hope now rais'd, and now deprest,
To feel the burnings of an injur'd breast,
    From all thy Fate's deep sorrow keen
    In vain, O Youth, I turn th' affrighted eye;
    For powerful Fancy evernigh
The hateful picture forces on my sight.
    There, Death of every dear delight,
    Frowns Poverty of Giant mien!
In vain I seek the charms of youthful grace,
Thy sunken eye, thy haggard cheeks it shews,   50

---

[1] Samuel Butler (1612–1680), author of Hudibras, is cited as an
example of the king's ingratitude; the dramatist Thomas Otway
(1652–1685) died young and in poverty, rejected by Elizabeth
Barry, the mistress of the Earl of Rochester.

The quick emotions struggling in the Face
　　Faint index of thy mental Throes,
When each strong Passion spurn'd controll,
And not a Friend was nigh to calm thy stormy soul.

Such was the sad and gloomy hour
When anguish'd Care of sullen brow
Prepared the Poison's death-cold power.
Already to thy lips was rais'd the bowl,
When filial Pity stood thee by,
Thy fixed eyes she bade thee roll   60
On scenes that well might melt thy soul—
Thy native cot she held to view,
Thy native cot, where Peace ere long
Had listen'd to thy evening song;
Thy sister's shrieks she bade thee hear,
And mark thy mother's thrilling tear,
She made thee feel her deep-drawn sigh,
And all her silent agony of Woe.

And from *thy* Fate shall such distress ensue?
Ah! dash the poison'd chalice from thy hand!   70
And thou had'st dash'd it at her soft command;
But that Despair and Indignation rose,
And told again the story of thy Woes,
Told the keen insult of th' unfeeling Heart,
The dread dependence on the low-born mind,
Told every Woe, for which thy breast might smart,
Neglect and grinning scorn and Want combin'd—
　　Recoiling back, thou sent'st the friend of Pain
To roll a tide of Death thro' every freezing vein.
　　　O Spirit blest!   80
　　Whether th' eternal Throne around,
　　Amidst the blaze of Cherubim,
　　Thou pourest forth the grateful hymn,
　　Or, soaring through the blest Domain,
　　Enraptur'st Angels with thy strain,—
　　Grant me, like thee, the lyre to sound,
　　Like thee, with fire divine to glow—
　　But ah! when rage the Waves of Woe,   88
　　　Grant me with firmer breast t'oppose their hate,
　　And soar beyond the storms with upright eye elate!

[1790]   [1893]

MONODY ON A TEA-KETTLE

O MUSE who sangest late another's pain,
To griefs domestic turn thy coal-black steed!
With slowest steps thy funeral steed must go,
Nodding his head in all the pomp of woe:
Wide scatter round each dark and deadly weed,
And let the melancholy dirge complain,
(Whilst Bats shall shriek and Dogs shall howling
　　run)
The tea-kettle is spoilt and Coleridge is undone!

Your cheerful songs, ye unseen crickets, cease!
Let songs of grief your alter'd minds engage!   10
For he who sang responsive to your lay,
What time the joyous bubbles 'gan to play,
The *sooty swain* has felt the fire's fierce rage;—
Yes, he is gone, and all my woes increase;
I heard the water issuing from the wound—
No more the Tea shall pour its fragrant steams
　　around!

O Goddess best belov'd! Delightful Tea!
　　With thee compar'd what yields the madd'ning
　　　Vine?
Sweet power! who know'st to spread the calm
　　delight,
And the pure joy prolong to midmost night!   20
Ah! must I all thy varied sweets resign?
Enfolded close in grief thy form I see;
No more wilt thou extend thy willing arms,
Receive the *fervent Jove*, and yield him all thy charms!

How sink the mighty low by Fate opprest!—
Perhaps, O Kettle! thou by scornful toe
Rude urg'd t' ignoble place with plaintive din,
May'st rust obscure midst heaps of vulgar tin;—
As if no joy had ever seiz'd my breast
When from thy spout the streams did arching
　　fly,—   30
As if, infus'd, thou ne'er hadst known t' inspire
All the warm raptures of poetic fire!

But hark! or do I fancy the glad voice—
'What tho' the swain did wondrous charms
　　disclose—
(Not such did Memnon's sister sable drest)
Take these bright arms with royal face imprest,
A better Kettle shall thy soul rejoice,
And with Oblivion's wings o'erspread thy woes!'
Thus Fairy Hope can soothe distress and toil;
On empty Trivets she bids fancied Kettles boil!   40

[1790]   [1834]

SONNET

TO THE RIVER OTTER

DEAR native Brook! wild Streamlet of the West!
How many various-fated years have past,
　　What happy and what mournful hours, since last
I skimm'd the smooth thin stone along thy breast,
Numbering its light leaps! yet so deep imprest
Sink the sweet scenes of childhood, that mine eyes
　　I never shut amid the sunny ray,

But straight with all their tints thy waters rise,
  Thy crossing plank, thy marge with willows grey,
And bedded sand that vein'd with various dyes   10
Gleam'd through thy bright transparence! On my
    way,
  Visions of Childhood! oft have ye beguil'd
Lone manhood's cares, yet waking fondest sighs:
  Ah! that once more I were a careless Child!

[1793?]   [1796]

TO FORTUNE

*Coleridge's first appearance in print was probably the publication
of this poem in the* Morning Chronicle *on November 7, 1793.*

TO FORTUNE

ON BUYING A TICKET IN THE IRISH LOTTERY

Composed during a walk to and from the Queen's Head,
Gray's Inn Lane, Holborn, and Hornsby's and Co.,
Cornhill.

PROMPTRESS of unnumber'd sighs,
O snatch that circling bandage from thine eyes!
O look and smile! No common prayer
Solicits, Fortune! thy propitious care!
For, not a silken son of dress,
I clink the gilded chains of *politesse*,
Nor ask thy boon what time I scheme
Unholy Pleasure's frail and feverish dream;
Nor yet my view life's *dazzle* blinds—
Pomp!—Grandeur! Power!—I give you to the
    winds!
Let the little bosom cold   11
Melt only at the sunbeam ray of gold—
My pale cheeks glow—the big drops start—
The rebel *Feeling* riots at my heart!
And if in lonely durance pent,
Thy poor mite mourn a brief imprisonment—
That mite at Sorrow's faintest sound
Leaps from its scrip with an elastic bound!
But oh! if ever song thine ear
Might soothe, O haste with fost'ring hand to rear 20
One Flower of Hope! At Love's behest,
Trembling, I plac'd it in my secret breast:
And thrice I've view'd the vernal gleam,
Since oft mine eye, with Joy's electric beam,
Illum'd it—and its sadder hue
Oft moisten'd with the Tear's ambrosial dew!
Poor wither'd floweret! on its head
Has dark Despair his sickly mildew shed!

But thou, O Fortune! canst relume
Its deaden'd tints—and thou with hardier bloom 30
May'st haply tinge its beauties pale,
And yield the unsunn'd stranger to the western gale!

[1793]   [1793]

TO A YOUNG LADY

WITH A POEM ON THE FRENCH REVOLUTION

MUCH on my early youth I love to dwell,
Ere yet I bade that friendly dome farewell,
Where first, beneath the echoing cloisters pale,
I heard of guilt and wonder'd at the tale!
Yet though the hours flew by on careless wing,
Full heavily of Sorrow would I sing.
Aye as the Star of Evening flung its beam
In broken radiance on the wavy stream,
My soul amid the pensive twilight gloom   9
Mourn'd with the breeze, O Lee Boo![1] o'er thy tomb.
Where'er I wander'd, Pity still was near,
Breath'd from the heart and glisten'd in the tear:
No knell that toll'd but fill'd my anxious eye,
And suffering Nature wept that *one* should die!

Thus to sad sympathies I sooth'd my breast,
Calm, as the rainbow in the weeping West:
When slumbering Freedom roused by high Disdain
With giant Fury burst her triple chain!
Fierce on her front the blasting Dog-star glow'd;
Her banners, like a midnight meteor, flow'd; 20
Amid the yelling of the storm-rent skies!
She came, and scatter'd battles from her eyes!
Then Exultation waked the patriot fire
And swept with wild hand the Tyrtaean[2] lyre:
Red from the Tyrant's wound I shook the lance,
And strode in joy the reeking plains of France!

Fallen is the Oppressor, friendless, ghastly, low,
And my heart aches, though Mercy struck the blow.
With wearied thought once more I seek the shade,
Where peaceful Virtue weaves the Myrtle braid. 30
And O! if Eyes whose holy glances roll,
Swift messengers, and eloquent of soul;
If Smiles more winning, and a gentler Mien
Than the love-wilder'd Maniac's brain hath seen

---

[1] The son of the prince of the Pelew (Palau) Islands in the
South Pacific, who emigrated to England, died of smallpox, and
is buried in Greenwich churchyard.
[2] Tyrtaeus was a lame Greek poet of the seventh century B.C.
credited with rousing the Spartans to bravery so successfully
that his poems became a central part of the education of Spartan
youth.

Shaping celestial forms in vacant air,
If these demand the empassion'd Poet's care—
If Mirth and soften'd Sense and Wit refined,
The blameless features of a lovely mind;
Then haply shall my trembling hand assign
No fading wreath to Beauty's saintly shrine.   40
Nor, Sara! thou these early flowers refuse—
Ne'er lurk'd the snake beneath their simple hues;
No purple bloom the Child of Nature brings
From Flattery's night-shade: as he feels he sings.

[1794]   [1796]

PANTISOCRACY

*Pantisocracy was the principle upon which, in 1794, Coleridge
and Southey among others planned to establish a utopian com-
munity on the banks of the Susquehanna River in Pennsylvania.
See also the next two poems following, and the letter to Southey,
p. 505*

PANTISOCRACY

No more my visionary soul shall dwell
On joys that were; no more endure to weigh
The shame and anguish of the evil day,
Wisely forgetful! O'er the ocean swell
Sublime of Hope, I seek the cottag'd dell
Where Virtue calm with careless step may stray,
And dancing to the moonlight roundelay,
The wizard Passions weave an holy spell.
Eyes that have ach'd with Sorrow! Ye shall weep
Tears of doubt-mingled joy, like theirs who start   10
From Precipices of distemper'd sleep,
On which the fierce-eyed Fiends their revels keep,
And see the rising Sun, and feel it dart
New rays of pleasance trembling to the heart.

[1794]   [1849

ON THE PROSPECT OF ESTABLISHING
A PANTISOCRACY IN AMERICA

WHILST pale Anxiety, corrosive Care,
The tear of Woe, the gloom of sad Despair,
    And deepen'd Anguish generous bosoms rend;—
Whilst patriot souls their country's fate lament;
Whilst mad with rage demoniac, foul intent,
    Embattled legions Despots vainly send
To arrest the immortal mind's expanding ray
    Of everlasting Truth;—I other climes
Where dawns, with hope serene, a brighter day
    Than e'er saw Albion in her happiest times,   10

With mental eye exulting now explore,
    And soon with kindred minds shall haste to enjoy
(Free from the ills which here our peace destroy)
Content and Bliss on Transatlantic shore.

[1795]   [1826]

TO A YOUNG ASS

ITS MOTHER BEING TETHERED NEAR IT

POOR little Foal of an oppressed race!
I love the languid patience of thy face:
And oft with gentle hand I give thee bread,
And clap thy ragged coat, and pat thy head.
But what thy dulled spirits hath dismay'd,
That never thou dost sport along the glade?
And (most unlike the nature of things young)
That earthward still thy moveless head is hung?
Do thy prophetic fears anticipate,
Meek Child of Misery! thy future fate?   10
The starving meal, and all the thousand aches
'Which patient Merit of the Unworthy takes'?
Or is thy sad heart thrill'd with filial pain
To see thy wretched mother's shorten'd chain?
And truly, very piteous is *her* lot—
Chain'd to a log within a narrow spot,
Where the close-eaten grass is scarcely seen,
While sweet around her waves the tempting green!

Poor Ass! thy master should have learnt to show
Pity—best taught by fellowship of Woe!   20
For much I fear me that *He* lives like thee,
Half famish'd in a land of Luxury!
How *askingly* its footsteps hither bend?
It seems to say, 'And have I then *one* friend?'
Innocent foal! thou poor despis'd forlorn!
I hail thee *Brother*—spite of the fool's scorn!
And fain would take thee with me, in the Dell
Of Peace and mild Equality to dwell,
Where Toil shall call the charmer Health his bride,
And Laughter tickle Plenty's ribless side!   30
How thou wouldst toss thy heels in gamesome play,
And frisk about, as lamb or kitten gay!
Yea! and more musically sweet to me
Thy dissonant harsh bray of joy would be,
Than warbled melodies that soothe to rest
The aching of pale Fashion's vacant breast!

[1794]   [1794]

FROM
SONNETS ON EMINENT CHARACTERS

BURKE[1]

As late I lay in Slumber's shadowy vale,
  With wetted cheek and in a mourner's guise,
  I saw the sainted form of FREEDOM rise:
She spake! not sadder moans the autumnal gale—

'Great Son of Genius! sweet to me thy name,
  Ere in an evil hour with alter'd voice
  Thou bad'st Oppression's hireling crew rejoice
Blasting with wizard spell my laurell'd fame.

'Yet never, BURKE! thou drank'st Corruption's
    bowl!*
  Thee stormy Pity and the cherish'd lure   10
  Of Pomp, and proud Precipitance of soul
Wilder'd with meteor fires. Ah Spirit pure!

'That Error's mist had left thy purged eye:
So might I clasp thee with a Mother's joy!'

*Yet never, BURKE! thou dran'kst Corruption's bowl!
When I composed this line, I had not read the following
paragraph in the *Cambridge Intelligencer* (of Saturday, November
21, 1795):—
'*When Mr. Burke first crossed over the House of Commons from
the Opposition to the Ministry, he received a pension of £1200 a
year charged on the Kings Privy Purse.* When he had completed
his labours, it was then a question what recompense his service
deserved. Mr. Burke, wanting a present supply of money, it was
thought that a pension of £2000 *per annum* for *forty years
certain*, would sell for eighteen years' purchase, and bring him
of course £36,000. But this pension must, by the very un-
fortunate act of which Mr. Burke was himself the author, have
come before Parliament. Instead of this Mr. Pitt suggested the
idea of a pension of £2000 a year for *three lives*, to be charged
on the King's Revenue of the West India 4 1/2 per cents. This
was tried at the market, but it was found that it would not
produce the £36,000 which were wanted. In consequence of
this a pension of £2500 per annum, *for three lives*, on the
4 1/2 West India Fund, the lives to be nominated by Mr. Burke,
that he may accommodate the purchasers is *finally* granted to
this disinterested patriot. He has thus retir'd from the trade of
politics, with pensions to the amount of £3700 a year.'

[1] Edmund Burke (1729–1797) championed the cause of the
American Revolution but rejected the arguments in favor of the
French Revolution.

PRIESTLEY[2]

THOUGH rous'd by that dark Vizir Riot rude
  Have driven our PRIESTLEY o'er the Ocean swell;
  Though Superstition and her wolfish brood
Bay his mild radiance, impotent and fell;

Calm in his halls of brightness he shall dwell!
  For lo! RELIGION at his strong behest
  Start with mild anger from the Papal spell,
And flings to Earth her tinsel-glittering vest,

Her mitred State and cumbrous Pomp unholy;
  And JUSTICE wakes to bid th' Oppressor wail   10
  Insulting aye the wrongs of patient Folly;
And from her dark retreat by Wisdom won

Meek NATURE slowly lifts her matron veil
To smile with fondness on her gazing Son!

LA FAYETTE[3]

As when far off the warbled strains are heard
  That soar on Morning's wing the vales among;
  Within his cage the imprison'd Matin Bird
Swells the full chorus with a generous song:

He bathes no pinion in the dewy light,
  No Father's joy, no Lover's bliss he shares,
  Yet still the rising radiance cheers his sight—
His fellows' Freedom soothes the Captive's cares!

Thou, FAYETTE! who didst wake with startling voice
  Life's better Sun from that long wintry night,   10
  Thus in thy Country's triumphs shalt rejoice
And mock with raptures high the Dungeon's might:

For lo! the Morning struggles into Day,
And Slavery's spectres shriek and vanish from the ray!

[1794]   [1794]

[2] Joseph Priestley (1733–1804), discoverer of oxygen, was
forced into exile in America because of his ardent republican
sentiments. The Pantisocrats (see notes to poems above) hoped to
settle near him in Pennsylvania.
[3] The Marquis de Lafayette, French hero of the American
Revolution and early supporter of the French Revolution, had
been imprisoned by the Austrians and Prussians.

W. L. Bowles (1762–1850) wrote a collection of sonnets (1789) that became one of Coleridge's earliest literary enthusiasms.

TO THE REV. W. L. BOWLES*

[FIRST VERSION]

MY heart has thank'd thee, BOWLES! for those soft
    strains,
    That, on the still air floating, tremblingly
    Wak'd in me Fancy, Love, and Sympathy!
For hence, not callous to a Brother's pains

Thro' Youth's gay prime and thornless paths I went;
    And, when the *darker* day of life began,
    And I did roam, a thought-bewilder'd man!
Thy kindred Lays an healing solace lent,

Each lonely pang with dreamy joys combin'd,   9
    And stole from vain REGRET her scorpion stings;
    While shadowy PLEASURE, with mysterious wings,
Brooded the wavy and tumultuous mind,

Like that great Spirit, who with plastic sweep
Mov'd on the darkness of the formless Deep!

[SECOND VERSION]

My heart has thank'd thee, BOWLES! for those soft
    strains
    Whose sadness soothes me, like the murmuring
    Of wild-bees in the sunny showers of spring!
For hence not callous to the mourner's pains

Through Youth's gay prime and thornless paths I
    went:
    And when the mightier Throes of mind began,
    And drove me forth, a thought-bewilder'd man,
Their mild and manliest melancholy lent

A mingled charm, such as the pang consign'd
    To slumber, though the big tear it renew'd;   10
    Bidding a strange mysterious PLEASURE brood
Over the wavy and tumultuous mind,

As the great SPIRIT erst with plastic sweep
Mov'd on the darkness of the unform'd deep.

[1794]   [1794, 1796]

RELIGIOUS MUSINGS

Although Coleridge may have finished a full draft of Religious Musings *in 1794, he was continually revising the text and his annotations until 1834. This text is substantially that of 1834. The dates in brackets at the ends of the notes indicate the editions in which they first appeared. Many of the original 1796 notes were replaced in 1797, and not all of the notes first added in 1797 were carried forward to the final edition of 1834.*

RELIGIOUS MUSINGS[1]

A DESULTORY POEM,
WRITTEN ON THE CHRISTMAS EVE OF 1794

THIS is the time, when most divine to hear,
The voice of Adoration rouses me,
As with a Cherub's trump: and high upborne,
Yea, mingling with the Choir, I seem to view
The vision of the heavenly multitude,
Who hymned the song of Peace o'er Bethlehem's
    fields!
Yet thou more bright than all the Angel-blaze,
That harbingered thy birth, Thou Man of Woes!
Despiséd Galilaean![2] For the Great
Invisible (by symbols only seen)   10
With a peculiar and surpassing light
Shines from the visage of the oppressed good man,
When heedless of himself the scourgéd saint
Mourns for the oppressor. Fair the vernal mead,
Fair the high grove, the sea, the sun, the stars;
True impress each of their creating Sire!
Yet nor high grove, nor many-colour'd mead,
Nor the green ocean with his thousand isles,
Nor the starred azure, nor the sovran sun,
E'er with such majesty of portraiture   20
Imaged the supreme beauty uncreate,
As thou, meek Saviour! at the fearful hour
When thy insulted anguish winged the prayer

---

[1] In the original edition of 1796, and those of 1797 and 1803, the poem was prefixed with an epigraph, which is an adaptation of lines in the First Book of Akenside's *Pleasures of the Imagination*:

> What tho' first
> In years unseason'd, I attun'd the lay
> To idle Passion and unreal Woe?
> Yet serious Truth her empire o'er my song
> Hath now asserted; Falsehood's evil brood,
> Vice and deceitful Pleasure, she at once
> Excluded, and my Fancy's careless toil
> Drew to the better cause!

This was followed by an Argument:

Introduction. Person of Christ. His prayer on the Cross. The process of his Doctrines on the mind of the Individual. Character of the Elect. Superstition. Digression to the present War. Origin and Uses of Government and Property. The present State of Society. The French Revolution. Millenium. Universal Redemption. Conclusion.

[2] Christ.

Harped by Archangels, when they sing of mercy!
Which when the Almighty heard from forth his
    throne
Diviner light filled Heaven with ecstasy!
Heaven's hymnings paused: and Hell her yawning
    mouth
Closed a brief moment.

             Lovely was the death
Of Him whose life was Love! Holy with power
He on the thought-benighted Sceptic beamed   30
Manifest Godhead, melting into day
What floating mists of dark idolatry
Broke and misshaped the omnipresent Sire:*
And first by Fear uncharmed the drowséd Soul.
Till of its nobler nature it 'gan feel
Dim recollections; and thence soared to Hope,
Strong to believe whate'er of mystic good
The Eternal dooms for His immortal sons.
From Hope and firmer Faith to perfect Love
Attracted and absorbed: and centered there   40
God only to behold, and know, and feel,
Till by exclusive consciousness of God
All self-annihilated it shall make†
God its Identity: God all in all!
We and our Father one!
             And blest are they,
Who in this fleshly World, the elect of Heaven,
Their strong eye darting through the deeds of men,
Adore with steadfast unpresuming gaze
Him Nature's essence, mind, and energy!
And gazing, trembling, patiently ascend   50
Treading beneath their feet all visible things
As steps, that upward to their Father's throne
Lead gradual—else nor glorified nor loved.
They nor contempt embosom nor revenge:
For they dare know of what may seem deform
The Supreme Fair sole operant: in whose sight
All things are pure, his strong controlling love
Alike from all educing perfect good.
Their's too celestial courage, inly armed—
Dwarfing Earth's giant brood, what time they muse
On their great Father, great beyond compare!   61
And marching onwards view high o'er their heads

His waving banners of Omnipotence.
Who the Creator love, created Might
Dread not: within their tents no Terrors walk.
For they are holy things before the Lord
Aye unprofaned, though Earth should league with
    Hell;
God's altar grasping with an eager hand
Fear, the wild-visag'd, pale, eye-starting wretch,
Sure-refug'd hears his hot pursuing fiends   70
Yell at vain distance. Soon refresh'd from Heaven
He calms the throb and tempest of his heart.
His countenance settles; a soft solemn bliss
Swims in his eye—his swimming eye uprais'd:
And Faith's whole armour glitters on his limbs!
And thus transfigured with a dreadless awe,
A solemn hush of soul, meek he beholds
All things of terrible seeming: yea, unmoved
Views e'en the immitigable ministers
That shower down vengeance on these latter   80
    days.
For kindling with intenser Deity
From the celestial Mercy-seat they come,
And at the renovating wells of Love
Have fill'd their vials with salutary wrath,‡
To sickly Nature more medicinal
Than what soft balm the weeping good man pours
Into the lone despoiléd traveller's wounds!

Thus from the Elect, regenerate through faith,
Pass the dark Passions and what thirsty cares§
Drink up the spirit, and the dim regards   90
Self-centre. Lo they vanish! or acquire
New names, new features—by supernal grace
Enrobed with Light, and naturalised in Heaven.
As when a shepherd on a vernal morn
Through some thick fog creeps timorous with slow
    foot,
Darkling he fixes on the immediate road
His downward eye: all else of fairest kind
Hid or deformed. But lo! the bursting Sun!
Touched by the enchantment of that sudden beam
Straight the black vapour melteth, and in globes   100
Of dewy glitter gems each plant and tree;
On every leaf, on every blade it hangs!
Dance glad the new-born intermingling rays,
And wide around the landscape streams with glory!

* Τὸ Νοητὸν διηρήκασιν εἰς πολλῶν Θεῶν ἰδιότητας. DAMAS. DE
MYST AEGYPT. [1797][3]
† See this demonstrated by Hartley, vol. 1, p. 114, and vol. 2,
p. 329. See it likewise proved and freed from the charge of
Mysticism, by Pistorius in his Notes and Additions to part
second of Hartley on Man. Addition the 18th, the 653rd page
of the third volume of Hartley, Octavo Edition. [1797].

~~~~~~

[3] "Men have split up the Intelligible One into the peculiar
attributes of Gods many." This is actually a comment on the
line as it began in the original edition of 1796, i.e., "Split and
mishap'd" etc.

‡ And I heard a great voice out of the Temple saying to the
seven Angels, pour out the vials of the wrath of God upon the
earth. Revelation. xvi. 1. [1796].
§ Our evil Passions, under the influence of Religion, become
innocent and may be made to animate our virtue—in the same
manner as the thick mist melted by the Sun, increases the light
which it had before excluded. In the preceding paragraph,
agreeably to this truth, we had allegorically narrated the trans-
figuration of Fear into holy Awe. [1797]

There is one Mind, one omnipresent Mind,
Omnific. His most holy name is Love.
Truth of subliming import! with the which
Who feeds and saturates his constant soul,
He from his small particular orbit flies
With blest outstarting! From himself he flies,   110
Stands in the sun, and with no partial gaze
Views all creation; and he loves it all,
And blesses it, and calls it very good!
This is indeed to dwell with the Most High!
Cherubs and rapture-trembling Seraphim
Can press no nearer to the Almighty's throne.
But that we roam unconscious, or with hearts
Unfeeling of our universal Sire,
And that in His vast family no Cain
Injures uninjured (in her best-aimed blow   120
Victorious Murder a blind Suicide)
Haply for this some younger Angel now
Looks down on Human Nature: and, behold!
A sea of blood bestrewed with wrecks, where mad
Embattling Interests on each other rush
With unhelmed rage!

                    'Tis the sublime of man,
Our noontide Majesty, to know ourselves
Parts and proportions of one wondrous whole!
This fraternises man, this constitutes
Our charities and bearings. But 'tis God   130
Diffused through all, that doth make all one whole;
This the worst superstition, him except
Aught to desire, Supreme Reality!*
The plenitude and permanence of bliss!
O Fiends of Superstition! not that oft
The erring Priest hath stained with brother's blood
Your grisly idols, not for this may wrath
Thunder against you from the Holy One!
But o'er some plain that steameth to the sun,   139
Peopled with Death; or where more hideous Trade
Loud-laughing packs his bales of human anguish;
I will raise up a mourning, O ye Fiends!
And curse your spells, that film the eye of Faith,
Hiding the present God; whose presence lost,
The moral world's cohesion, we become
An Anarchy of Spirits! Toy-bewitched,
Made blind by lusts, disherited of soul,
No common centre Man, no common sire

* If to make aught but the Supreme Reality the object of
final pursuit be Superstition; if the attributing of sublime
properties to things or persons, which those things or persons
neither do or can possess, be superstition; then Avarice and
Ambition are Superstitions: and he who wishes to estimate
the evils of Superstition, should transport himself, not to the
temple of the Mexican Deities, but to the plains of Flanders, or
the coast of Africa.—Such is the sentiment convey'd in this
and the subsequent lines. [1797]

Knoweth! A sordid solitary thing,
Mid countless brethren with a lonely heart   150
Through courts and cities the smooth savage
    roams
Feeling himself, his own low self the whole;
When he by sacred sympathy might make
The whole one Self! Self, that no alien knows!
Self, far diffused as Fancy's wing can travel!
Self, spreading still! Oblivious of its own,
Yet all of all possessing! This is Faith!
This the Messiah's destined victory!

But first offences needs must come! Even now†
(Black Hell laughs horrible—to hear the scoff!)   160
Thee to defend, meek Galilaean! Thee
And thy mild laws of Love unutterable,
Mistrust and Enmity have burst the bands
Of social peace: and listening Treachery lurks
With pious fraud to snare a brother's life;
And childless widows o'er the groaning land
Wail numberless; and orphans weep for bread!
Thee to defend, dear Saviour of Mankind!
Thee, Lamb of God! Thee, blameless Prince of
    Peace!
From all sides rush the thirsty brood of War!—   170
Austria, and that foul Woman of the North,
The lustful murderess of her wedded lord!
And he, connatural Mind!‡ whom (in their songs
So bards of elder time had haply feigned)
Some Fury fondled in her hate to man,
Bidding her serpent hair in mazy surge
Lick his young face, and at his mouth imbreathe
Horrible sympathy! And leagued with these
Each petty German princeling, nursed in gore!

† January 21st, 1794, in the debate on the Address to his
Majesty, on the speech from the Throne, the Earl of Guildford
moved an Amendment to the following effect:—'That the
House hoped his Majesty would seize the earliest opportunity
to conclude a peace with France,' &c. This motion was opposed
by the Duke of Portland, who 'considered the war to be merely
grounded on one principle—the preservation of the CHRISTIAN
RELIGION'. May 30th, 1794, the Duke of Bedford moved a
number of Resolutions, with a view to the Establishment of a
Peace with France. He was opposed (among others) by Lord
Abingdon in these remarkable words: 'The best road to Peace,
my Lords, is WAR! and WAR carried on in the same manner
in which we are taught to worship our CREATOR, namely with
all our souls, and with all our minds, and with all our hearts,
and with all our strength.' [1797]
‡ That Despot who received the wages of an hireling that he
might act the part of a swindler, and who skulked from his
impotent attacks on the liberties of France to perpetrate more
successful iniquity in the plains of *Poland.* [1796][4]

<><><><><><><><><><><><><><><><><><><><><><><>
[4] Coleridge apparently is referring to Frederick Wilhelm of
Prussia (1744–1797).

Soul-hardened barterers of human blood!*   180
Death's prime slave-merchants! Scorpion-whips of
    Fate!
Nor least in savagery of holy zeal,
Apt for the yoke, the race degenerate,
Whom Britain erst had blushed to call her sons!
Thee to defend the Moloch Priest prefers
The prayer of hate, and bellows to the herd,
That Deity, Accomplice Deity
In the fierce jealousy of wakened wrath
Will go forth with our armies and our fleets
To scatter the red ruin on their foes!   190
O blasphemy! to mingle fiendish deeds
With blessedness!

          Lord of unsleeping Love,†
From everlasting Thou! We shall not die.
These, even these, in mercy didst thou form,
Teachers of Good through Evil, by brief wrong
Making Truth lovely, and her future might
Magnetic o'er the fixed untrembling heart.

In the primeval age a dateless while
The vacant Shepherd wander'd with his flock,
Pitching his tent where'er the green grass waved.   200
But soon Imagination conjured up
An host of new desires: with busy aim,
Each for himself, Earth's eager children toiled.
So Property began, twy-streaming fount,
Whence Vice and Virtue flow, honey and gall.
Hence the soft couch, and many-coloured robe,
The timbrel, and arched dome and costly feast,
With all the inventive arts, that nursed the soul
To forms of beauty, and by sensual wants
Unsensualised the mind, which in the means   210
Learnt to forget the grossness of the end,
Best pleasured with its own activity.
And hence Disease that withers manhood's arm,
The daggered Envy, spirit-quenching Want,
Warriors, and Lords, and Priests—all the sore ills‡

* The Father of the present Prince of Hesse Cassell sup-
ported himself and his strumpets at Paris by the vast sums which
he received from the British Government during the American
War for the flesh of his subjects. [1796]

† Art thou not from everlasting, O Lord, mine Holy One?
We shall not die. O Lord! thou hast ordained them for judg-
ment, &c. Habakkuk i. 12. [1796]

‡ I deem that the teaching of the gospel for hire is wrong;
because it gives the teacher an improper bias in favour of
particular opinions on a subject where it is of the last impor-
tance that the mind should be perfectly unbiassed. Such is my
private opinion; but I mean not to censure all hired teachers,
many among whom I know, and venerate as the best and wisest
of men—God forbid that I should think of these, when I use
the word PRIEST, a name after which any other term of
abhorrence would appear an anti-climax. By a Priest I mean a

That vex and desolate our mortal life.
Wide-wasting ills! yet each the immediate source
Of mightier good. Their keen necessities
To ceaseless action goading human thought
Have made Earth's reasoning animal her Lord;   220
And the pale-featured Sage's trembling hand
Strong as an host of arméd Deities,
Such as the blind Ionian fabled erst.

From Avarice thus, from Luxury and War
Sprang heavenly Science; and from Science Freedom.
O'er waken'd realms Philosophers and Bards
Spread in concentric circles: they whose souls,
Conscious of their high dignities from God,
Brook not Wealth's rivalry! and they, who long
Enamoured with the charms of order, hate   230
The unseemly disproportion: and whoe'er
Turn with mild sorrow from the Victor's car
And the low puppetry of thrones, to muse
On that blest triumph, when the Patriot Sage[5]
Called the red lightnings from the o'er-rushing cloud
And dashed the beauteous terrors on the earth
Smiling majestic. Such a phalanx ne'er
Measured firm paces to the calming sound
Of Spartan flute! These on the fated day,
When, stung to rage by Pity, eloquent men   240
Have roused with pealing voice the unnumbered
    tribes
That toil and groan and bleed, hungry and blind—
These, hush'd awhile with patient eye serene,
Shall watch the mad careering of the storm;
Then o'er the wild and wavy chaos rush
And tame the outrageous mass, with plastic might
Moulding Confusion to such perfect forms,
As erst were wont,—bright visions of the day!—
To float before them, when, the summer noon,
Beneath some arched romantic rock reclined   250
They felt the sea-breeze lift their youthful locks;
Or in the month of blossoms, at mild eve,
Wandering with desultory feet inhaled
The wafted perfumes, and the flocks and woods
And many-tinted streams and setting sun
With all his gorgeous company of clouds
Ecstatic gazed! then homeward as they strayed
Cast the sad eye to earth, and inly mused
Why there was misery in a world so fair.

man who holding the scourge of power in his right hand and a
bible (translated by authority) in his left, doth necessarily cause
the bible and the scourge to be associated ideas, and so produces
that temper of mind which leads to Infidelity—Infidelity which
judging of Revelation by the doctrines and practices of estab-
lished Churches honors God by rejecting Christ. [1796]

[5] A reference to Benjamin Franklin's experiments with
lightning.

Ah! far removed from all that glads the sense,   260
From all that softens or ennobles Man,
The wretched Many! Bent beneath their loads
They gape at pageant Power, nor recognise
Their cots' transmuted plunder! From the tree
Of Knowledge, ere the vernal sap had risen
Rudely disbranchéd! Blessed Society!
Fitliest depictured by some sun-scorched waste,
Where oft majestic through the tainted noon
The Simoom sails, before whose purple pomp*
Who falls not prostrate dies! And where by night,   270
Fast by each precious fountain on green herbs
The lion crouches: or hyaena dips
Deep in the lucid stream his bloody jaws;
Or serpent plants his vast moon-glittering bulk,
Caught in whose monstrous twine Behemoth† yells,
His bones loud-crashing!

                    O ye numberless,
Whom foul Oppression's ruffian gluttony
Drives from Life's plenteous feast! O thou poor
        Wretch
Who nursed in darkness and made wild by want,
Roamest for prey, yea thy unnatural hand   280
Dost lift to deeds of blood! O pale-eyed form,
The victim of seduction, doomed to know
Polluted nights and days of blasphemy;
Who in loathed orgies with lewd wassailers
Must gaily laugh, while thy remembered Home
Gnaws like a viper at thy secret heart!
O agéd Women! ye who weekly catch
The morsel tossed by law-forced charity,
And die so slowly, that none call it murder!
O loathly suppliants! ye, that unreceived   290
Totter heart-broken from the closing gates
Of the full Lazar-house; or, gazing, stand,
Sick with despair! O ye to Glory's field

Forced or ensnared, who, as ye gasp in death,
Bleed with new wounds beneath the vulture's beak!
O thou poor widow, who in dreams dost view
Thy husband's mangled corse, and from short doze
Start'st with a shriek; or in thy half-thatched cot
Waked by the wintry night-storm, wet and cold
Cow'rst o'er thy screaming baby! Rest awhile   300
Children of Wretchedness! More groans must rise,
More blood must stream, or ere your wrongs be full.
Yet is the day of Retribution nigh:
The Lamb of God hath opened the fifth seal:‡
And upward rush on swiftest wing of fire
The innumerable multitude of wrongs
By man on man inflicted! Rest awhile,
Children of Wretchedness! The hour is nigh
And lo! the Great, the Rich, the Mighty Men,
The Kings and the Chief Captains of the World,   310
With all that fixed on high like stars of Heaven
Shot baleful influence, shall be cast to earth,
Vile and down-trodden, as the untimely fruit
Shook from the fig-tree by a sudden storm.
Even now the storm begins:§ each gentle name,
Faith and meek Piety, with fearful joy
Tremble far-off—for lo! the Giant Frenzy
Uprooting empires with his whirlwind arm
Mocketh high Heaven; burst hideous from the cell
Where the old Hag, unconquerable, huge,   320
Creation's eyeless drudge, black Ruin, sits
Nursing the impatient earthquake.
                        O return!
Pure Faith! meek Piety! The abhorréd Form‖

---

* At eleven o'clock, while we contemplated with great pleasure the rugged top of Chiggre, to which we were fast approaching, and where we were to solace ourselves with plenty of good water, IDRIS cried out with a loud voice, 'Fall upon your faces, for here is the Simoom'.⁶ I saw from the S.E. an haze come on, in colour like the purple part of the rainbow, but not so compressed or thick. It did not occupy twenty yards in breadth, and was about twelve feet high from the ground.— We all lay flat on the ground, as if dead, till IDRIS told us it was blown over. The meteor, or purple haze, which I saw, was indeed passed; but the light air that still blew was of heat to threaten suffocation. Bruce's *Travels*, vol. 4, p. 557. [1796]

† Behemoth, in Hebrew, signified wild beasts in general. Some believe it is the Elephant, some the Hippopotamus; some affirm it is the Wild Bull. Poetically, it designates any large Quadruped. [1797]

---

⁶ A violent, hot, dry, and suffocating wind laden with sand from the deserts of Asia and Africa.

---

‡ See the sixth chapter of the Revelation of St. John the Divine. And I looked and beheld a pale horse; and his name that sat on him was Death, and Hell followed with him. And power was given unto them over the FOURTH part of the Earth to kill with sword, and with hunger, and with pestilence, and with the beasts of the Earth.—And when he had opened the fifth seal, I saw under the altar the souls of them that were slain for the word of God, and for the testimony which they held; and white robes were given unto every one of them; and it was said unto them, that they should rest yet for a little season, until their fellow servants also, and their brethren that should be killed as they were should be fulfilled. And I beheld when he had opened the sixth seal, the stars of Heaven fell unto the Earth, even as a fig-tree casteth her untimely figs when she is shaken of a mighty wind: And the kings of the earth, and the great men, and the rich men, and the chief captains, &c. [1796]

§ This passage alludes to the French Revolution; and the subsequent paragraph to the downfall of Religious Establishments. I am convinced that the Babylon of the Apocalypse does not apply to Rome exclusively; but to the union of Religion with Power and Wealth, wherever it is found. [1797]

‖ And there came one of the seven Angels which had the seven vials, and talked with me, saying unto me, come hither! I will show unto thee the judgment of the great Whore, that sitteth upon many waters: with whom the kings of the earth have committed fornication, &c. Revelation of St. John the Divine, chapter the seventeenth. [1796]

Whose scarlet robe was stiff with earthly pomp,
Who drank iniquity in cups of gold,
Whose names were many and all blasphemous,
Hath met the horrible judgment! Whence that cry?
The mighty army of foul Spirits shrieked
Disherited of earth! For she hath fallen
On whose black front was written Mystery;   330
She that reeled heavily, whose wine was blood;
She that worked whoredom with the Daemon Power,
And from the dark embrace all evil things
Brought forth and nurtured: mitred Atheism!
And patient Folly who on bended knee
Gives back the steel that stabbed him; and pale Fear
Haunted by ghastlier shapings than surround
Moon-blasted Madness when he yells at midnight!
Return pure Faith! return meek Piety!
The kingdoms of the world are your's: each heart 340
Self-governed, the vast family of Love
Raised from the common earth by common toil
Enjoy the equal produce. Such delights
As float to earth, permitted visitants!
When in some hour of solemn jubilee
The massy gates of Paradise are thrown
Wide open, and forth come in fragments wild
Sweet echoes of unearthly melodies,
And odours snatched from beds of Amaranth,
And they, that from the crystal river of life   350
Spring up on freshened wing, ambrosial gales!
The favoured good man in his lonely walk
Perceives them, and his silent spirit drinks
Strange bliss which he shall recognise in heaven.
And such delights, such strange beatitudes
Seize on my young anticipating heart
When that blest future rushes on my view!
For in his own and in his Father's might
The Saviour comes! While as the Thousand Years*
Lead up their mystic dance, the Desert shouts!   360
Old Ocean claps his hands! The mighty Dead
Rise to new life, whoe'er from earliest time
With conscious zeal had urged Love's wondrous plan,
Coadjutors of God. To Milton's trump
The high groves of the renovated Earth
Unbosom their glad echoes: inly hushed,
Adoring Newton his serener eye
Raises to heaven: and he of mortal kind

Wisest, he† first who marked the ideal tribes
Up the fine fibres through the sentient brain.   370
Lo! Priestley there, patriot, and saint, and sage,
Him, full of years, from his loved native land
Statesmen blood-stained and priests idolatrous
By dark lies maddening the blind multitude
Drove with vain hate. Calm, pitying he retired,
And mused expectant on these promised years.

O Years! the blest pre-eminence of Saints!
Ye sweep athwart my gaze, so heavenly bright,
The wings that veil the adoring Seraphs' eyes,
What time they bend before the Jasper Throne‡   380
Reflect no lovelier hues! Yet ye depart,
And all beyond is darkness! Heights most strange,
Whence Fancy falls, fluttering her idle wing.
For who of woman born may paint the hour,
When seized in his mid course, the Sun shall wane
Making noon ghastly! Who of woman born
May image in the workings of his thought,
How the black-visaged, red-eyed Fiend outstretched§
Beneath the unsteady feet of Nature groans,
In feverous slumbers—destined then to wake,   390
When fiery whirlwinds thunder his dread name
And Angels shout, Destruction! How his arm
The last great Spirit lifting high in air
Shall swear by Him, the ever-living One,
Time is no more!

    Believe thou, O my soul,‖
Life is a vision shadowy of Truth;
And vice, and anguish, and the wormy grave,
Shapes of a dream! The veiling clouds retire,
And lo! the Throne of the redeeming God
Forth flashing unimaginable day   400
Wraps in one blaze earth, heaven, and deepest hell.

Contemplant Spirits! ye that hover o'er
With untired gaze the immeasurable fount
Ebullient with creative Deity!
And ye of plastic power, that interfused
Roll through the grosser and material mass

 † David Hartley.[7]
 ‡ Rev. chap. iv. v. 2 and 3.—And immediately I was in the
Spirit: and behold, a Throne was set in Heaven and one sat on
the Throne. And he that sat was to look upon like a jasper and a
sardine stone, &c. [1797]
 § The final Destruction impersonated. [1797]
 ‖ This paragraph is intelligible to those, who, like the
Author, believe and feel the sublime system of Berkley [sic];
and the doctrine of the final Happiness of all men. [1797]

 * The Millenium:—in which I suppose, that Man will
continue to enjoy the highest glory, of which his human nature
is capable.—That all who in past ages have endeavoured to
ameliorate the state of man will rise and enjoy the fruits and
flowers, the imperceptible seeds of which they had sown in
their former Life: and that the wicked will during the same
period, be suffering the remedies adapted to their several bad
habits. I suppose that this period will be followed by the passing
away of this Earth and by our entering the state of pure intellect;
when all Creation shall rest from its labours. [1797]

 [7] Hartley, whose book was cited above, was an eighteenth-
century philosopher and psychologist. Coleridge named his first
child after him.

In organizing surge! Holies of God!
(And what if Monads of the infinite mind?)
I haply journeying my immortal course
Shall sometime join your mystic choir! Till then   410
I discipline my young and novice thought
In ministeries of heart-stirring song,
And ye on Meditation's heaven-ward wing
Soaring aloft I breathe the empyreal air
Of Love, omnific, omnipresent Love,
Whose day-spring rises glorious in my soul
As the great Sun, when he his influence
Sheds on the frost-bound waters—The glad stream
Flows to the ray and warbles as it flows.

[1794 ff.]   [1796 ff.]

TO THE NIGHTINGALE

SISTER of love-lorn Poets, Philomel!
How many Bards in city garret pent,
While at their window they with downward eye
Mark the faint lamp-beam on the kennell'd mud,
And listen to the drowsy cry of Watchmen
(Those hoarse unfeather'd Nightingales of Time!),
How many wretched Bards address *thy* name,
And hers, the full-orb'd Queen that shines above.
But I *do* hear thee, and the high bough mark,
Within whose mild moon-mellow'd foliage hid   10
Thou warblest sad thy pity-pleading strains.
O! I have listen'd, till my working soul,
Waked by those strains to thousand phantasies,
Absorb'd hath ceas'd to listen! Therefore oft,
I hymn thy name: and with a proud delight
Oft will I tell thee, Minstrel of the Moon!
'Most musical, most melancholy' Bird!
That all thy soft diversities of tone,
Tho' sweeter far than the delicious airs
That vibrate from a white-arm'd Lady's harp,   20
What time the languishment of lonely love
Melts in her eye, and heaves her breast of snow,
Are not so sweet as is the voice of her,
My Sara—best beloved of human kind!
When breathing the pure soul of tenderness,
She thrills me with the Husband's promis'd name![1]

[1795]   [1796]

---

[1] Sara Fricker, whom Coleridge married in 1795, when he still
planned to emigrate with Robert Southey (who married Sara's
sister Edith) and establish a pantisocratic community. She is the
Sara addressed in the following poem too—but not the Sara (Asra)
of later poems such as *Dejection*.

THE EOLIAN HARP

*For other instances of the wind harp used as an image of poetic
creation and inspiration see Wordsworth's* Prelude, I, 96 (and
note), III, 141–42, *and Coleridge's* Dejection: An Ode, p. 486.
*Although the instrument was invented in 1650, its appropriateness
as a metaphor for defining the relation between poet, song, and
external inspiration was not used until the end of the eighteenth
century. See especially Shelley's* A Defence of Poetry, p. 975.
*The passiveness implicitly assigned to the poet's imagination in
such a scheme later caused Coleridge to reject this image. For a
full discussion of its place in literary theory, see Abrams,* The
Mirror and the Lamp, *esp. Chapter III.*

THE EOLIAN HARP
COMPOSED AT CLEVEDON, SOMERSETSHIRE

MY pensive Sara! thy soft cheek reclined
Thus on mine arm, most soothing sweet it is
To sit beside our Cot, our Cot o'ergrown
With white-flower'd Jasmin, and the broad-leav'd
    Myrtle,
(Meet emblems they of Innocence and Love!)
And watch the clouds, that late were rich with light,
Slow saddening round, and mark the star of eve
Serenely brilliant (such should Wisdom be)
Shine opposite! How exquisite the scents
Snatch'd from yon bean-field! and the world *so*
    hush'd!   10
The stilly murmur of the distant Sea
Tells us of silence.

            And that simplest Lute,
Placed length-ways in the clasping casement,
    hark!
How by the desultory breeze caress'd,
Like some coy maid half yielding to her lover,
It pours such sweet upbraiding, as must needs
Tempt to repeat the wrong! And now, its strings
Boldlier swept, the long sequacious notes
Over delicious surges sink and rise,
Such a soft floating witchery of sound   20
As twilight Elfins make, when they at eve
Voyage on gentle gales from Fairy-Land,
Where Melodies round honey-dropping flowers,
Footless and wild, like birds of Paradise,
Nor pause, nor perch, hovering on untam'd wing!
O! the one Life within us and abroad,
Which meets all motion and becomes its soul,
A light in sound, a sound-like power in light,
Rhythm in all thought, and joyance every where—
Methinks, it should have been impossible   30
Not to love all things in a world so fill'd;
Where the breeze warbles, and the mute still air
Is Music slumbering on her instrument.

And thus, my Love! as on the midway slope
Of yonder hill I stretch my limbs at noon,
Whilst through my half-clos'd eye-lids I behold
The sunbeams dance, like diamonds, on the main,
And tranquil muse upon tranquillity;
Full many a thought uncall'd and undetain'd,
And many idle flitting phantasies,   40
Traverse my indolent and passive brain,
As wild and various as the random gales
That swell and flutter on this subject Lute!

And what if all of animated nature
Be but organic Harps diversely fram'd,
That tremble into thought, as o'er them sweeps
Plastic and vast, one intellectual breeze,
At once the Soul of each, and God of all?

But thy more serious eye a mild reproof
Darts, O beloved Woman! nor such thoughts   50
Dim and unhallow'd dost thou not reject,
And biddest me walk humbly with my God.
Meek Daughter in the family of Christ!
Well hast thou said and holily disprais'd
These shapings of the unregenerate mind;
Bubbles that glitter as they rise and break
On vain Philosophy's aye-babbling spring.
For never guiltless may I speak of him,
The Incomprehensible! save when with awe
I praise him, and with Faith that inly *feels*;*   60
Who with his saving mercies healéd me,
A sinful and most miserable man,
Wilder'd and dark, and gave me to possess
Peace, and this Cot, and thee, heart-honour'd Maid!

[1795]   [1796]

* L'athée n'est point à mes yeux un faux esprit; je puis vivre
avec lui aussi bien et mieux qu'avec le dévot, car il raisonne
davantage, mais il lui manque un sens, et mon âme ne se fond
point entièrement avec la sienne: il est froid au spectacle le plus
ravissant, et il cherche un syllogisme lorsque je rends une
action de grâce. 'Appel à l'impartiale postérité' par la Citoyenne
Roland, troisième partie, p. 67.¹

¹ "The Atheist is not, in my eyes, a man of ill faith; I can live
with him as well, nay, better than with the devotee; for he
reasons more; but he is deficient in a certain sense, and his soul
does not keep pace with mine; he is unmoved at a spectacle the
most ravishing, and he hunts for a syllogysm, where I am
impressed with awe and admiration." The translation of Citizeness
Marie-Jeanne Roland's *An Appeal to Impartial Posterity* was
published by Joseph Johnson in 1795. See also Wordsworth's
Prelude, X, 381–83, and note.

REFLECTIONS ON HAVING
LEFT A PLACE OF RETIREMENT

LOW was our pretty Cot: our tallest Rose
Peep'd at the chamber-window. We could hear
At silent noon, and eve, and early morn,
The Sea's faint murmur. In the open air
Our Myrtles blossom'd; and across the porch
Thick Jasmins twined: the little landscape round
Was green and woody, and refresh'd the eye.
It was a spot which you might aptly call
The Valley of Seclusion! Once I saw
(Hallowing his Sabbath-day by quietness)   10
A wealthy son of Commerce saunter by,
Bristowa's¹ citizen: methought, it calm'd
His thirst of idle gold, and made him muse
With wiser feelings: for he paus'd, and look'd
With a pleas'd sadness, and gaz'd all around,
Then eyed our Cottage, and gaz'd round again,
And sigh'd, and said, it was a Blesséd Place.
And we *were* bless'd. Oft with patient ear
Long-listening to the viewless sky-lark's note
(Viewless, or haply for a moment seen   20
Gleaming on sunny wings) in whisper'd tones
I've said to my Belovéd, 'Such, sweet Girl!
The inobtrusive song of Happiness,
Unearthly minstrelsy! then only heard
When the Soul seeks to hear; when all is hush'd,
And the Heart listens!'

                              But the time, when first
From that low Dell, steep up the stony Mount
I climb'd with perilous toil and reach'd the top,
Oh! what a goodly scene! *Here* the bleak mount,   29
The bare bleak mountain speckled thin with sheep;
Grey clouds, that shadowing spot the sunny fields;
And river, now with bushy rocks o'er-brow'd,
Now winding bright and full, with naked banks;
And seats, and lawns, the Abbey and the wood,
And cots, and hamlets, and faint city-spire;
The Channel *there*, the Islands and white sails,
Dim coasts, and cloud-like hills, and shoreless
    Ocean—
It seem'd like Omnipresence! God, methought,
Had built him there a Temple: the whole World
Seem'd *imag'd* in its vast circumference: 40
No *wish* profan'd my overwhelméd heart.
Blest hour! It was a luxury,—to be!

Ah! quiet Dell! dear Cot, and Mount sublime!
I was constrain'd to quit you. Was it right,

¹ Bristol, the city nearest Clevedon, where the cottage was
located.

While my unnumber'd brethren toil'd and bled,
That I should dream away the entrusted hours
On rose-leaf beds, pampering the coward heart
With feelings all too delicate for use?
Sweet is the tear that from some Howard's[2] eye
Drops on the cheek of one he lifts from earth: 50
And he that works me good with unmov'd face,
Does it but half: he chills me while he aids,
My benefactor, not my brother man!
Yet even this, this cold beneficence
Praise, praise it, O my Soul! oft as thou scann'st
The sluggard Pity's vision-weaving tribe!
Who sigh for Wretchedness, yet shun the Wretched,
Nursing in some delicious solitude
Their slothful loves and dainty sympathies!
I therefore go, and join head, heart, and hand,   60
Active and firm, to fight the bloodless fight
Of Science, Freedom, and the Truth in Christ,

Yet oft when after honourable toil
Rests the tir'd mind, and waking loves to dream,
My spirit shall revisit thee, dear Cot!
Thy Jasmin and thy window-peeping Rose,
And Myrtles fearless of the mild sea-air.
And I shall sigh fond wishes—sweet Abode!
Ah!—had none greater! And that all had such!
It might be so—but the time is not yet.   70
Speed it, O Father! Let thy Kingdom come!

[1795]   [1796]

---

[2] John Howard (1726–1790), philanthropist and prison reformer.

ODE TO THE DEPARTING YEAR

Coleridge's notes to the following poem are taken from the edition of 1803, unless otherwise indicated. The epigraph from Agamemnon *by Aeschylus (added in 1797) is spoken by Cassandra, who was given the gift of prophecy but deprived of the power of convincing her hearers:*

"*Woe for me, woe! Again the agony—
Dread pain that sees the future all too well
With ghastly preludes whirls and racks my soul....
Nay, then, believe me not: what skills belief
Or disbelief? Fate works its will—and thou
Wilt see and say in truth, Her tale was true.*"

ODE TO THE DEPARTING YEAR*

'Ιού ἰού, ὦ ὦ κακά.
'Υπ' αὖ με δεινὸς ὀρθομαντείας πόνος
Στροβεῖ, ταράσσων φροιμίοις δυσφροιμίοις.

Τὸ μέλλον ἥξει. Καὶ σύ μ' ἐν τάχει παρὼν
"Αγαν ἀληθόμαντιν οἰκτείρας ἐρεῖς.

Aeschyl. *Agam.* 1173–75; 1199–1200.

ARGUMENT

THE Ode commences with an address to the Divine Providence that regulates into one vast harmony all the events of time, however calamitous some of them may appear to mortals. The second Strophe calls on men to suspend their private joys and sorrows, and devote them for a while to the cause of humane nature in general. The first Epode speaks of the Empress of Russia, who died of an apoplexy on the 17th of November 1796; having just concluded a subsidiary treaty with the Kings combined against France. The first and second Antistrophe describe the Image of the Departing Year, etc., as in a vision. The second Epode prophesies, in anguish of spirit, the downfall of this country.

I

SPIRIT who sweepest the wild Harp of Time!
   It is most hard, with an untroubled ear
   Thy dark inwoven harmonies to hear!
Yet, mine eye fix'd on Heaven's unchanging clime
Long had I listen'd, free from mortal fear,
   With inward stillness, and a bowéd mind;
   When lo! its folds far waving on the wind,
I saw the train of the Departing Year!
   Starting from my silent sadness
   Then with no unholy madness,   10
Ere yet the enter'd cloud foreclos'd my sight,
I rais'd the impetuous song, and solemnis'd his flight.

---

* This Ode was written on the 24th, 25th, and 26th days of December, 1795; and published separately on the last day of the year.

II*

Hither, from the recent tomb,
From the prison's direr gloom,
From Distemper's midnight anguish;
And thence, where Poverty doth waste and languish;
Or where, his two bright torches blending,
Love illumines Manhood's maze;
Or where o'er cradled infants bending,
Hope has fix'd her wishful gaze;   20
Hither, in perplexed dance,
Ye Woes! ye young-eyed Joys! advance!
By Time's wild harp, and by the hand
Whose indefatigable sweep
Raises its fateful strings from sleep,
I bid you haste, a mix'd tumultuous band!
From every private bower,
And each domestic hearth,
Haste for one solemn hour;
And with a loud and yet a louder voice,   30
O'er Nature struggling in portentous birth,
Weep and rejoice!
Still echoes the dread Name that o'er the earth†
Let slip the storm, and woke the brood of Hell:
And now advance in saintly Jubilee
Justice and Truth! They too have heard thy spell,
They too obey thy name, divinest Liberty!

III‡

I mark'd Ambition in his war-array!
I heard the mailéd Monarch's troublous cry—
'Ah! wherefore does the Northern Conqueress
stay!§   40

* The second Strophe calls on men to suspend their private Joys and Sorrows, and to devote their passions for a while to the cause of human Nature in general.
† The Name of Liberty, which at the commencement of the French Revolution was both the occasion and the pretext of unnumbered crimes and horrors.
‡ The first Epode refers to the late Empress of Russia [Catherine the Great], who died of apoplexy on the 17th of November, 1796, having just concluded a subsidiary treaty with the kings combined against France.
§ A subsidiary Treaty had been just concluded; and Russia was to have furnished more effectual aid than that of pious manifestoes to the Powers combined against France. I rejoice—not over the deceased Woman (I never dared figure the Russian Sovereign to my imagination under the dear and venerable Character of WOMAN—WOMAN, that complex term for Mother, Sister, Wife!) I rejoice, as at the disenshrining of Daemon! I rejoice, as at the extinction of the evil Principle impersonated. This very day, six years ago, the massacre of Ismail was perpetrated. THIRTY THOUSAND HUMAN BEINGS, MEN, WOMEN, AND CHILDREN, murdered in cold blood, for no other crime than that their garrison had defended the place with perseverance and bravery. Why should I recall the poisoning of her husband, her iniquities in Poland, or her late unmotivated attack on Persia, the desolating ambition of her public

Groans not her chariot on its onward way?'
Fly, mailéd Monarch, fly!
Stunn'd by Death's twice mortal mace,
No more on Murder's lurid face
The insatiate Hag shall gloat with drunken eye!
Manes[1] of the unnumber'd slain!
Ye that gasp'd on Warsaw's plain!
Ye that erst at Ismail's tower,
When human ruin choked the streams,
Fell in Conquest's glutted hour,   50
Mid women's shrieks and infants' screams!
Spirits of the uncoffin'd slain,
Sudden blasts of triumph swelling,
Oft, at night, in misty train,
Rush around her narrow dwelling!
The exterminating Fiend is fled—
(Foul her life, and dark her doom)
Mighty armies of the dead
Dance, like death-fires, round her tomb!
Then with prophetic song relate,   60
Each some Tyrant-Murderer's fate!

IV‖

Departing Year! 'twas on no earthly shore
My soul beheld thy Vision! Where alone,
Voiceless and stern, before the cloudy throne,
Aye Memory sits: thy robe inscrib'd with gore,
With many an unimaginable groan
Thou storied'st thy sad hours! Silence ensued,
Deep silence o'er the ethereal multitude,
Whose locks with wreaths, whose wreaths with glories shone.
Then, his eye wild ardours glancing,   70
From the choiréd gods advancing,
The Spirit of the Earth made reverence meet,
And stood up, beautiful, before the cloudy seat.

V

Throughout the blissful throng,
Hush'd were harp and song:
Till wheeling round the throne the Lampads[2] seven,
(The mystic Words of Heaven)

---

life, or the libidinous excesses of her private hours! I have no wish to qualify myself for the office of Historiographer to the King of Hell—! December, 23, 1796. [1796]
‖ The first Antistrophe describes the Image of the Departing Years as in a vision; and concludes with introducing the Planetary Angel of the Earth preparing to address the Supreme Being.

◇◇◇◇◇◇◇◇◇◇◇◇◇◇◇◇◇◇◇◇◇◇◇◇◇◇◇◇◇◇◇◇◇◇

[1] Roman name for the deified souls of the dead.
[2] The seven lamps (Rev. 4:5) in the vision of God and the Lamb.

Permissive signal make:
The fervent Spirit bow'd, then spread his wings and
    spake!
    'Thou in stormy blackness throning   80
    Love and uncreated Light,
  By the Earth's unsolaced groaning,
    Seize thy terrors, Arm of might!
  By Peace with proffer'd insult scared,
    Masked Hate and envying Scorn!
    By years of Havoc yet unborn!
And Hunger's bosom to the frost-winds bared!
    But chief by Afric's wrongs,
    Strange, horrible, and foul!
  By what deep guilt belongs   90
To the deaf Synod, 'full of gifts and lies!' *
By Wealth's insensate laugh! by Torture's howl!
    Avenger, rise!
For ever shall the thankless Island scowl,
  Her quiver full, and with unbroken bow?
Speak! from thy storm-black Heaven O speak aloud!
    And on the darkling foe
Open thine eye of fire from some uncertain cloud!
  O dart the flash! O rise and deal the blow!
The Past to thee, to thee the Future cries!   100
  Hark! how wide Nature joins her groans below!
    Rise, God of Nature! rise.'

VI†

The voice had ceas'd, the Vision fled;
Yet still I gasp'd and reel'd with dread.
And ever, when the dream of night
Renews the phantom to my sight,
Cold sweat-drops gather on my limbs;
  My ears throb hot; my eye-balls start;
My brain with horrid tumult swims;
  Wild is the tempest of my heart;   110
And my thick and struggling breath
Imitates the toil of death!
No stranger agony confounds
  The Soldier on the war-field spread,
When all foredone with toil and wounds,
  Death-like he dozes among heaps of dead!

* 'In Europe the smoking villages of Flanders and the putri-fied fields of La Vendée—from Africa the unnumbered victims of a detestable Slave-Trade. In Asia the desolated plains of Indostan, and the millions whom a rice-contracting Governor caused to perish. In America the recent enormities of the Scalp-merchants. The four quarters of the globe groan beneath the intolerable iniquity of the nation.' See 'Addresses to the People', p. 46. [1817].

† The poem concludes with prophecying in anguish of Spirit the Downfall of this Country.

(The strife is o'er, the day-light fled,
  And the night-wind clamours hoarse!
See! the starting wretch's head
  Lies pillow'd on a brother's corse!)   120

VII

Not yet enslaved, not wholly vile,
O Albion! O my mother Isle!
Thy valleys, fair as Eden's bowers,
Glitter green with sunny showers;
Thy grassy uplands' gentle swells
  Echo to the bleat of flocks;
(Those grassy hills, those glittering dells
  Proudly ramparted with rocks)
And Ocean mid his uproar wild
Speaks safety to his Island-child!   130
Hence for many a fearless age
Has social Quiet lov'd thy shore;
Nor ever proud Invader's rage
Or sack'd thy towers, or stain'd thy fields with gore.

VIII

Abandon'd of Heaven!‡ mad Avarice thy guide,
At cowardly distance, yet kindling with pride—
Mid thy herds and thy corn-fields secure thou hast
  stood,
And join'd the wild yelling of Famine and Blood!
The nations curse thee! They will eager wondering
  Shall hear Destruction, like a vulture, scream! 140
Strange-eyed Destruction! who with many a dream

‡ *'Disclaim'd of Heaven!'*—The Poet from having considered the peculiar advantages, which this country has enjoyed, passes in rapid transition to the uses, which we have made of these advantages. We have been preserved by our insular situation, from suffering the actual horrors of War ourselves and we have shewn our gratitude to Providence for this immunity by our eagerness to spread those horrors over nations less happily situated. In the midst of plenty and safety we have raised or joined the yell for famine and blood. Of the one hundred and seven last years, fifty have been years of War. Such wickedness cannot pass unpunished. We have been proud and confident in our alliances and our fleets—but God has prepared the canker-worm, and will smite the *gourds* of our pride. 'Art thou better than populous No, that was situate among the rivers, that had the waters round about it, whose rampart was the Sea? Ethiopia and Egypt were her strength and it was infinite: Put and Lubim were her helpers. Yet she was carried away, she went into captivity: and they cast lots for her honourable men, and all her great men were bound in chains. Thou also shalt be drunken: all thy strongholds shall be like fig trees with the first ripe figs; if they be shaken, they shall even fall into the mouth of the eater. Thou hast multiplied thy merchants above the stars of heaven. Thy crowned are as the locusts and thy captains as the great grasshoppers which camp in the hedges in the cool-day; but when the Sun ariseth they flee away, and their place is not known where they are. There is no healing of thy bruise; thy wound is grievous: all, that hear the report of thee, shall clap hands over thee: for upon whom hath not thy wickedness passed continually?'*Nahum*, chap. iii.

Of central fires through nether seas up-thundering
  Soothes her fierce solitude; yet as she lies
  By livid fount, or red volcanic stream,
  If ever to her lidless dragon-eyes,
    O Albion! thy predestin'd ruins rise,
The fiend-hag on her perilous couch doth leap,
Muttering distemper'd triumph in her charméd sleep.

IX

    Away, my soul, away!
    In vain, in vain the Birds of warning sing—
And hark! I hear the famish'd brood of prey   151
Flap their lank pennons on the groaning wind!
    Away, my soul, away!
    I unpartaking of the evil thing,
      With daily prayer and daily toil
      Soliciting for food my scanty soil,
    Have wail'd my country with a loud Lament.
Now I recentre my immortal mind
    In the deep Sabbath of meek self-content;
Cleans'd from the vaporous passions that bedim   160
God's Image, sister of the Seraphim.

[1796]   [1796]

THIS LIME-TREE BOWER MY PRISON

The friends Coleridge refers to in his headnote below were Charles Lamb and William and Dorothy Wordsworth; the accident was Sara Coleridge's spilling a pan of hot milk on her husband's foot. The "strange calamity" of line 32 is Mary Lamb's murder of her and Charles's mother. See note to Wordsworth's Written After the Death of Charles Lamb, *p. 394.*

THIS LIME-TREE BOWER MY PRISON

[ADDRESSED TO CHARLES LAMB, OF THE
INDIA HOUSE, LONDON]

In the June of 1797 some long-expected friends paid a visit to the author's cottage; and on the morning of their arrival, he met with an accident, which disabled him from walking during the whole time of their stay. One evening, when they had left him for a few hours, he composed the following lines in the garden-bower.

WELL, they are gone, and here must I remain,
This lime-tree bower my prison! I have lost
Beauties and feelings, such as would have been
Most sweet to my remembrance even when age
Had dimm'd mine eyes to blindness! They, mean-
    while,
Friends, whom I never more may meet again,
On springy heath, along the hill-top edge,
Wander in gladness, and wind down, perchance,

To that still roaring dell, of which I told;
The roaring dell, o'erwooded, narrow, deep,   10
And only speckled by the mid-day sun;
Where its slim trunk the ash from rock to rock
Flings arching like a bridge;—that branchless ash,
Unsunn'd and damp, whose few poor yellow leaves
Ne'er tremble in the gale, yet tremble still,
Fann'd by the water-fall! and there my friends
Behold the dark green file of long lank weeds,*
That all at once (a most fantastic sight!)
Still nod and drip beneath the dripping edge
Of the blue clay-stone.

                Now, my friends emerge   20
Beneath the wide wide Heaven—and view again
The many-steepled tract magnificent
Of hilly fields and meadows, and the sea,
With some fair bark, perhaps, whose sails light up
The slip of smooth clear blue betwixt two Isles
Of purple shadow! Yes! they wander on
In gladness all; but thou, methinks, most glad,
My gentle-hearted Charles! for thou hast pined
And hunger'd after Nature, many a year,
In the great City pent, winning thy way   30
With sad yet patient soul, through evil and pain
And strange calamity! Ah! slowly sink
Behind the western ridge, thou glorious Sun!
Shine in the slant beams of the sinking orb,
Ye purple heath-flowers! richlier burn, ye clouds!
Live in the yellow light, ye distant groves!
And kindle, thou blue Ocean! So my friend
Struck with deep joy may stand, as I have stood,
Silent with swimming sense; yea, gazing round
On the wide landscape, gaze till all doth seem   40
Less gross than bodily; and of such hues
As veil the Almighty Spirit, when yet he makes
Spirits perceive his presence.

                  A delight
Comes sudden on my heart, and I am glad
As I myself were there! Nor in this bower,
This little lime-tree bower, have I not mark'd
Much that has sooth'd me. Pale beneath the blaze
Hung the transparent foliage; and I watch'd
Some broad and sunny leaf, and lov'd to see
The shadow of the leaf and stem above   50
Dappling its sunshine! And that walnut-tree
Was richly ting'd and a deep radiance lay
Full on the ancient ivy, which usurps
Those fronting elms, and now, with blackest mass

* The *Asplenium Scolopendrium*, called in some countries the Adder's Tongue, in others the Hart's Tongue, but Withering gives the Adder's Tongue as the trivial name of the *Ophioglossum* only.

Makes their dark branches gleam a lighter hue
Through the late twilight; and though now the bat
Wheels silent by, and not a swallow twitters,
Yet still the solitary humble-bee
Sings in the bean-flower! Henceforth I shall know
That Nature ne'er deserts the wise and pure;   60
No plot so narrow, be but Nature there,
No waste so vacant, but may well employ
Each faculty of sense, and keep the heart
Awake to Love and Beauty! and sometimes
'Tis well to be bereft of promis'd good,
That we may lift the soul, and contemplate
With lively joy the joys we cannot share.
My gentle-hearted Charles! when the last rook
Beat its straight path along the dusky air
Homewards, I blest it! deeming its black wing   70
(Now a dim speck, now vanishing in light)
Had cross'd the mighty Orb's dilated glory,
While thou stood'st gazing; or, when all was still,
Flew creeking o'er thy head, and had a charm*
For thee, my gentle-hearted Charles, to whom
No sound is dissonant which tells of Life.

[1797]   [1800]

THE FOSTER-MOTHER'S TALE

A DRAMATIC FRAGMENT

Foster-Mother. I never saw the man whom you
    describe.
Maria. 'Tis strange! he spake of you familiarly
As mine and Albert's common Foster-mother.
Foster-Mother. Now blessings on the man,
    whoe'er he be,
That joined your names with mine! O my sweet lady,
As often as I think of those dear times
When you two little ones would stand at eve
On each side of my chair, and make me learn
All you had learnt in the day; and how to talk
In gentle phrase, then bid me sing to you—   10
'Tis more like heaven to come than what *has* been!
    Maria. O my dear Mother! this strange man has
    left me

* Some months after I had written this line, it gave me
pleasure to find that Bartram had observed the same circum-
stance of the Savanna Crane. 'When these Birds move their
wings in flight, their strokes are slow, moderate and regular;
and even when at a considerable distance or high above us, we
plainly hear the quill-feathers: their shafts and webs upon one
another creek as the joints or working of a vessel in a tempestu-
ous sea.'[1]

    [1] Coleridge quotes William Bartram's *Travels Through North
Carolina . . .*, 1791.

Troubled with wilder fancies, than the moon
Breeds in the love-sick maid who gazes at it,
Till lost in inward vision, with wet eye
She gazes idly!—But that entrance, Mother!
    Foster-Mother. Can no one hear? It is a perilous
    tale!
    Maria. No one.
    Foster-Mother. My husband's father told it me,
Poor old Leoni!—Angels rest his soul!
He was a woodman, and could fell and saw   20
With lusty arm. You know that huge round beam
Which props the hanging wall of the old Chapel?
Beneath that tree, while yet it was a tree,
He found a baby wrapt in mosses, lined
With thistle-beards, and such small locks of wool
As hang on brambles. Well, he brought him home,
And rear'd him at the then Lord Velez' cost.
And so the babe grew up a pretty boy,
A pretty boy, but most unteachable—
And never learnt a prayer, nor told a bead,   30
But knew the names of birds, and mock'd their notes,
And whistled, as he were a bird himself:
And all the autumn 'twas his only play
To get the seeds of wild flowers, and to plant them
With earth and water, on the stumps of trees.
A Friar, who gather'd simples in the wood,
A grey-haired man—he lov'd this little boy,
The boy lov'd him—and, when the Friar taught him,
He soon could write with the pen: and from that time,
Lived chiefly at the Convent or the Castle.   40
So he became a very learnéd youth.
But Oh! poor wretch!—he read, and read, and read,
Till his brain turn'd—and ere his twentieth year,
He had unlawful thoughts of many things:
And though he prayed, he never lov'd to pray
With holy men, nor in a holy place—
But yet his speech, it was so soft and sweet,
The late Lord Velez ne'er was wearied with him.
And once, as by the north side of the Chapel
They stood together, chain'd in deep discourse,   50
The earth heav'd under them with such a groan,
That the wall totter'd, and had well-nigh fallen
Right on their heads. My Lord was sorely frighten'd;
A fever seiz'd him, and he made confession
Of all the heretical and lawless talk
Which brought this judgment: so the youth was
    seiz'd
And cast into that hole. My husband's father
Sobb'd like a child—it almost broke his heart:
And once as he was working in the cellar,
He heard a voice distinctly; 'twas the youth's,   60
Who sung a doleful song about green fields,
How sweet it were on lake or wild savannah,
To hunt for food, and be a naked man,

And wander up and down at liberty.
He always doted on the youth, and now
His love grew desperate; and defying death,
He made that cunning entrance I describ'd:
And the young man escap'd.
   Maria.   'Tis a sweet tale:
Such as would lull a listening child to sleep,
His rosy face besoil'd with unwiped tears.—   70
And what became of him?
   Foster-Mother.   He went on shipboard
With those bold voyagers, who made discovery
Of golden lands. Leoni's younger brother
Went likewise, and when he return'd to Spain,
He told Leoni, that the poor mad youth,
Soon after they arriv'd in that new world,
In spite of his dissuasion, seiz'd a boat,
And all alone, set sail by silent moonlight
Up a great river, great as any sea,
And ne'er was heard of more: but 'tis suppos'd,   80
He liv'd and died among the savage men.

[1797]   [1798]

THE RIME OF THE ANCIENT MARINER

In a rather different version, including archaic spelling but without marginal glosses, this poem appeared in the 1798 Lyrical Ballads *(along with* The Foster-Mother's Tale *and* The Nightingale, *which was substituted at the last minute for* Lewti*). The final version, here printed, was first published in 1817.*

The motto from Burnet's Archaeologiae Philosophicae *(1692) has been translated as follows:*

I easily believe that there are more invisible than visible things in the universe. But who will explain their families, and the ranks, relationships, distinctions and functions of all of them? What do they do? Where do they live? The human mind has ever striven for this knowledge, but never attained it. However, I have no doubt that it is good to contemplate in one's mind, as in a picture, the image of a greater and better world. Otherwise, the mind, accustomed to the trivial details of daily life, may contract itself and subside into trivial thoughts. But meanwhile we must be vigilant in our search for truth, and observe moderation, so that we can distinguish the certain from the uncertain, day from night.

The Argument is reprinted from the 1798 edition; Coleridge omitted it in 1817.

THE RIME OF THE ANCIENT MARINER

IN SEVEN PARTS

Facile credo, plures esse Naturas invisibiles quam visibiles in rerum universitate. Sed horum omnium familiam quis nobis enarrabit? et gradus et cognationes et discrimina et singulorum munera? Quid agunt? quae loca habitant? Harum rerum notitiam semper ambivit ingenium humanum, nunquam attigit. Juvat, interea, non diffiteor, quandoque in animo, tanquam in tabula, majoris et melioris mundi imaginem contemplari: ne mens assuefacta hodiernae vitae minutiis se contrahat nimis, et tota subsidat in pusillas cogitationes. Sed veritati interea invigilandum est, modusque servandus, ut certa ab incertis, diem a nocte, distinguamus.—T. BURNET, *Archaeol. Phil.* p. 68.

ARGUMENT

How a Ship having passed the Line was driven by storms to the cold Country towards the South Pole; and how from thence she made her course to the tropical Latitude of the Great Pacific Ocean; and of the strange things that befell; and in what manner the Ancyent Marinere came back to his own Country.

PART I

An ancient Mariner meeteth three Gallants bidden to a wedding-feast, and detaineth one.

IT IS an ancient Mariner,
And he stoppeth one of three,
'By thy long grey beard and glittering eye,
Now wherefore stopp'st thou me?

The Bridegroom's doors are opened wide,
And I am next of kin;
The guests are met, the feast is set:
May'st hear the merry din.'

He holds him with his skinny hand,
'There was a ship,' quoth he.   10
'Hold off! unhand me, grey-beard loon!'
Eftsoons [1] his hand dropt he.

The Wedding-Guest is spellbound by the eye of the old sea-faring man, and constrained to hear his tale.

He holds him with his glittering eye—
The Wedding-Guest stood still,
And listens like a three years' child:
The Mariner hath his will.

The Wedding-Guest sat on a stone:
He cannot choose but hear;
And thus spake on that ancient man,
The bright-eyed Mariner.   20

'The ship was cheered, the harbour
Merrily did we drop   [cleared,
Below the kirk, below the hill,
Below the lighthouse top.

The Mariner tells how the ship sailed southward with a good wind and fair weather, till it reached the line.

The Sun came up upon the left,
Out of the sea came he!
And he shone bright, and on the right
Went down into the sea.

Higher and higher every day,
Till over the mast at noon—'   30
The Wedding-Guest here beat his breast,
For he heard the loud bassoon.

The Wedding-Guest heareth the bridal music; but the Mariner continueth his tale.

The bride hath paced into the hall,
Red as a rose is she;
Nodding their heads before her goes
The merry minstrelsy.

The Wedding-Guest he beat his breast,
Yet he cannot choose but hear;
And thus spake on that ancient man,
The bright-eyed Mariner.   40

The ship driven by a storm toward the south pole.

'And now the STORM-BLAST came, and
Was tyrannous and strong: [he
He struck with his o'ertaking wings,
And chased us south along.

With sloping masts and dipping prow,
As who pursued with yell and blow
Still treads the shadow of his foe,
And forward bends his head,
The ship drove fast, loud roared the blast,
And southward aye we fled.   50

And now there came both mist and snow,
And it grew wondrous cold:
And ice, mast-high, came floating by,
As green as emerald.

The land of ice, and of fearful sounds where no living thing was to be seen.

And through the drifts the snowy clifts
Did send a dismal sheen:
Nor shapes of men nor beasts we ken—
The ice was all between.

The ice was here, the ice was there,
The ice was all around: 60
It cracked and growled, and roared and
Like noises in a swound!   [howled,

Till a great sea-bird, called the Albatross, came through the snow-fog, and was received with great joy and hospitality.

At length, did cross an Albatross,
Thorough the fog it came;
As if it had been a Christian soul,
We hailed it in God's name.

It ate the food it ne'er had eat,
And round and round it flew.
The ice did split with a thunder-fit;
The helmsman steered us through!   70

And lo! the Albatross proveth a bird of good omen, and followeth the ship as it returned northward through fog and floating ice.

And a good south wind sprung up
The Albatross did follow.   [behind;
And every day, for food or play,
Came to the mariner's hollo!

In mist or cloud, on mast or shroud,
It perched for vespers nine;   [white,
Whiles all the night, through fog-smoke
Glimmered the white Moon-shine.'

The ancient Mariner inhospitably killeth the pious bird of good omen.

'God save thee, ancient Mariner!
From the fiends, that plague thee thus!—
Why look'st thou so?'—With my cross-
I shot the ALBATROSS.   [bow

---

[1] At once.

PART II

THE Sun now rose upon the right: [2]
Out of the sea came he,
Still hid in mist, and on the left
Went down into the sea.

And the good south wind still blew
But no sweet bird did follow,   [behind,
Nor any day for food or play
Came to the mariners' hollo!   90

His shipmates cry out against the ancient Mariner, for killing the bird of good luck.

And I had done a hellish thing,
And it would work 'em woe:
For all averred, I had killed the bird
That made the breeze to blow.
Ah wretch! said they, the bird to slay,
That made the breeze to blow!

But when the fog cleared off, they justify the same, and thus make themselves accomplices in the crime.

Nor dim nor red, like God's own head,
The glorious Sun uprist:
Then all averred, I had killed the bird
That brought the fog and mist.   100
'Twas right, said they, such birds to slay,
That bring the fog and mist.

The fair breeze continues; the ship enters the Pacific Ocean, and sails northward, even till it reaches the Line.

The fair breeze blew, the white foam flew,
The furrow followed free;
We were the first that ever burst
Into that silent sea.

The ship hath been suddenly becalmed.

Down dropt the breeze, the sails dropt
'Twas sad as sad could be;   [down,
And we did speak only to break
The silence of the sea!   110

All in a hot and copper sky,
The bloody Sun, at noon,
Right up above the mast did stand,
No bigger than the Moon.

Day after day, day after day,
We stuck, nor breath nor motion;
As idle as a painted ship
Upon a painted ocean.

And the Albatross begins to be avenged.

Water, water, every where,
And all the boards did shrink;   120
Water, water, every where,
Nor any drop to drink.

The very deep did rot: O Christ!
That ever this should be!
Yea, slimy things did crawl with legs
Upon the slimy sea.

About, about, in reel and rout
The death-fires danced at night; [3]
The water, like a witch's oils,
Burnt green, and blue and white.   130

A Spirit had followed them; one of the invisible inhabitants of this planet, neither departed souls nor angels;

And some in dreams assuréd were
Of the Spirit that plagued us so;
Nine fathom deep he had followed us
From the land of mist and snow.

concerning whom the learned Jew, Josephus, and the Platonic Constantinopolitan, Michael Psellus, may be consulted. They are very numerous, and there is no climate or element without one or more.

And every tongue, through utter drought,
Was withered at the root;
We could not speak, no more than if
We had been choked with soot.

The ship-mates, in their sore distress, would fain throw the whole guilt on the ancient Mariner:

Ah! well a-day! what evil looks
Had I from old and young!   140
Instead of the cross, the Albatross
About my neck was hung.

in sign whereof they hang the dead sea-bird round his neck.

PART III

THERE passed a weary time. Each throat
Was parched, and glazed each eye.
A weary time! a weary time!
How glazed each weary eye,

The ancient Mariner beholdeth a sign in the element afar off.

When looking westward, I beheld
A something in the sky.

At first it seemed a little speck,
And then it seemed a mist;   150
It moved and moved, and took at last
A certain shape, I wist. [4]

A speck, a mist, a shape, I wist!
And still it neared and neared:
As if it dodged a water-sprite,
It plunged and tacked and veered.

---

[2] Because the ship, having rounded Cape Horn, is now sailing north into the Pacific.

[3] St. Elmo's fire, static electricity in the rigging traditionally considered an ill omen.
[4] I knew.

At its nearer
approach, it
seemeth him
to be a ship;
and at a dear
ransom he
freeth his
speech from
the bonds of
thirst.

With throats unslaked, with black lips
We could nor laugh nor wail;   [baked,
Through utter drought all dumb we
I bit my arm, I sucked the blood,   [stood!
And cried, A sail! a sail!   161

A flash of
joy;

With throats unslaked, with black lips
Agape they heard me call: [baked,
Gramercy! they for joy did grin,
And all at once their breath drew in,
As they were drinking all.

And horror
follows. For
can it be a
ship that
comes on-
ward without
wind or tide?

See! see! (I cried) she tacks no more!
Hither to work us weal;
Without a breeze, without a tide,
She steadies with upright keel!   170

The western wave was all a-flame.
The day was well nigh done!
Almost upon the western wave
Rested the broad bright Sun;
When that strange shape drove suddenly
Betwixt us and the Sun.

It seemeth
him but the
skeleton of a
ship.

And straight the Sun was flecked with
(Heaven's Mother send us grace!)   [bars,
As if through a dungeon-grate he peered
With broad and burning face.   180

Alas! (thought I, and my heart beat loud)
How fast she nears and nears!
Are those *her* sails that glance in the Sun,
Like restless gossameres?

And its ribs
are seen as
bars on the
face of the
setting Sun.

The Spectre-
Woman and
her Death-
mate, and no
other on
board the
skeleton ship.

Are those *her* ribs through which the Sun
Did peer, as through a grate?
And is that Woman all her crew?
Is that a DEATH? and are there two?
Is DEATH that woman's mate?

Like vessel,
like crew!

Death and
Life-in-Death
have diced
for the ship's
crew, and she
(the latter)
winneth the
ancient
Mariner.

Her lips were red, *her* looks were free, 190
Her locks were yellow as gold:
Her skin was as white as leprosy,
The Night-mare LIFE-IN-DEATH was
Who thicks man's blood with cold.   [she,

The naked hulk alongside came,
And the twain were casting dice;
'The game is done! I've won! I've won!'
Quoth she, and whistles thrice.

No twilight
within the
courts of the
Sun.

The Sun's rim dips; the stars rush out:
At one stride comes the dark;   200
With far-heard whisper, o'er the sea,
Off shot the spectre-bark.

At the rising
of the Moon,

We listened and looked sideways up!
Fear at my heart, as at a cup,
My life-blood seemed to sip!
The stars were dim, and thick the night,
The steersman's face by his lamp
                              [gleamed white;
From the sails the dew did drip—
Till clomb above the eastern bar
The hornéd Moon, with one bright star
Within the nether tip.   211

One after
another,

One after one, by the star-dogged Moon,[5]
Too quick for groan or sigh,
Each turned his face with a ghastly pang,
And cursed me with his eye.

His shipmates
drop down
dead.

Four times fifty living men,
(And I heard no sigh nor groan)
With heavy thump, a lifeless lump,
They dropped down one by one.

But Life-in-
Death begins
her work on
the ancient
Mariner.

The souls did from their bodies fly,—
They fled to bliss or woe!   221
And every soul, it passed me by,
Like the whizz of my cross-bow!

PART IV

The
Wedding-
Guest
feareth
that a Spirit
is talking to
him;

'I FEAR thee, ancient Mariner!
I fear thy skinny hand!
And thou art long, and lank, and brown,
As is the ribbed sea-sand.*

I fear thee and thy glittering eye,
And thy skinny hand, so brown.'—

But the
ancient
Mariner
assureth him
of his bodily
life, and pro-
ceedeth to
relate his hor-
rible penance.

Fear not, fear not, thou Wedding-Guest!
This body dropt not down.   231

Alone, alone, all, all alone,
Alone on a wide wide sea!
And never a saint took pity on
My soul in agony.

* For the last two lines of this stanza, I am indebted to Mr.
WORDSWORTH. It was on a delightful walk from Nether
Stowey to Dulverton, with him and his sister, in the Autumn of
1797, that this Poem was planned, and in part composed.

[5] "It is a common superstition among sailors that something
evil is about to happen whenever a star dogs the moon."
[Coleridge, in a manuscript note.]

He despiseth the creatures of the calm,

The many men, so beautiful!
And they all dead did lie:
And a thousand thousand slimy things
Lived on; and so did I.

And envieth that _they_ should live, and so many lie dead.

I looked upon the rotting sea,　　　240
And drew my eyes away;
I looked upon the rotting deck,
And there the dead men lay.

I looked to heaven, and tried to pray;
But or ever a prayer had gusht,
A wicked whisper came, and made
My heart as dry as dust.

I closed my lids, and kept them close,
And the balls like pulses beat;　　　249
For the sky and the sea, and the sea and
Lay like a load on my weary eye, [the sky
And the dead were at my feet.

But the curse liveth for him in the eye of the dead men.

The cold sweat melted from their limbs,
Nor rot nor reek did they:
The look with which they looked on me
Had never passed away.

An orphan's curse would drag to hell
A spirit from on high;
But oh! more horrible than that
Is the curse in a dead man's eye!　　　260
Seven days, seven nights, I saw that
And yet I could not die.　　　[curse,

In his loneliness and fixedness he yearneth towards the journeying Moon, and the stars that still sojourn, yet still move onward; and every where the blue sky belongs to them, and is their appointed rest, and their native country and their own natural homes, which they enter unannounced, as lords that are certainly expected and yet there is a silent joy at their arrival.

The moving Moon went up the sky.
And no where did abide:
Softly she was going up,
And a star or two beside—

Her beams bemocked the sultry main,
Like April hoar-frost spread;
But where the ship's huge shadow lay,
The charmèd water burnt alway　　　270
A still and awful red.

By the light of the Moon he beholdeth God's creatures of the great calm.

Beyond the shadow of the ship,
I watched the water-snakes:
They moved in tracks of shining white,
And when they reared, the elfish light
Fell off in hoary flakes.

Within the shadow of the ship
I watched their rich attire:
Blue, glossy green, and velvet black,
They coiled and swam; and every track
Was a flash of golden fire.　　　280

Their beauty and their happiness.

O happy living things! no tongue
Their beauty might declare:
A spring of love gushed from my heart,
And I blessed them unaware:

He blesseth them in his heart.

Sure my kind saint took pity on me,
And I blessed them unaware.

The spell begins to break.

The self-same moment I could pray;
And from my neck so free
The Albatross fell off, and sank　　　290
Like lead into the sea.

PART V

Oh sleep! it is a gentle thing.
Beloved from pole to pole!
To Mary Queen the praise be given!
She sent the gentle sleep from Heaven,
That slid into my soul.

By grace of the holy Mother, the ancient Mariner is refreshed with rain.

The silly buckets on the deck,
That had so long remained,
I dreamt that they were filled with dew;
And when I awoke, it rained.　　　300

My lips were wet, my throat was cold.
My garments all were dank;
Sure I had drunken in my dreams,
And still my body drank.

I moved, and could not feel my limbs:
I was so light—almost
I thought that I had died in sleep,
And was a blessèd ghost.

He heareth sounds and seeth strange sights and commotions in the sky and the element.

And soon I heard a roaring wind:
It did not come anear;　　　310
But with its sound it shook the sails,
That were so thin and sere.

The upper air burst into life!
And a hundred fire-flags sheen,
To and fro they were hurried about!
And to and fro, and in and out,
The wan stars danced between.

And the coming wind did roar more loud,
And the sails did sigh like sedge;   319
And the rain poured down from one black
The Moon was at its edge.   [cloud;

The thick black cloud was cleft, and still
The Moon was at its side:
Like waters shot from some high crag,
The lightning fell with never a jag,
A river steep and wide.

The loud wind never reached the ship,
Yet now the ship moved on!
Beneath the lighting and the Moon
The dead men gave a groan.   330

They groaned, they stirred, they all up-
Nor spake, nor moved their eyes;   [rose,
It had been strange, even in a dream,
To have seen those dead men rise.

The helmsman steered, the ship moved
Yet never a breeze up-blew;   [on;
The mariners all 'gan work the ropes,
Where they were wont to do;   339
They raised their limbs like lifeless
We were a ghastly crew.   [tools—

The body of my brother's son
Stood by me, knee to knee:
The body and I pulled at one rope,
But he said nought to me.

'I fear thee, ancient Mariner!'
Be calm, thou Wedding-Guest!
'Twas not those souls that fled in pain,
Which to their corses came again,
But a troop of spirits blest:

For when it dawned—they dropped their
And clustered round the mast;   [arms,
Sweet sounds rose slowly through their
And from their bodies passed.   [mouths,

Around, around, flew each sweet sound,
Then darted to the Sun;
Slowly the sounds came back again,
Now mixed, now one by one.

Sometimes a-dropping from the sky
I heard the sky-lark sing;
Sometimes all little birds that are,   360
How they seemed to fill the sea and air
With their sweet jargoning!

And now 'twas like all instruments,
Now like a lonely flute;
And now it is an angel's song,
That makes the heavens be mute.

It ceased; yet still the sails made on
A pleasant noise till noon,
A noise like of a hidden brook
In the leafy month of June,   370
That to the sleeping woods all night
Singeth a quiet tune.

Till noon we quietly sailed on,
Yet never a breeze did breathe:
Slowly and smoothly went the ship,
Moved onward from beneath.

Under the keel nine fathom deep,
From the land of mist and snow,
The spirit slid: and it was he
That made the ship to go.   380
The sails at noon left off their tune,
And the ship stood still also.

The Sun, right up above the mast,
Had fixed her to the ocean:
But in a minute she 'gan stir,
With a short uneasy motion—
Backwards and forwards half her length
With a short uneasy motion.

Then like a pawing horse let go,
She made a sudden bound: 390
It flung the blood into my head,
And I fell down in a swound.

How long in that same fit I lay,
I have not to declare;
But ere my living life returned,
I heard and in my soul discerned
Two voices in the air.

'Is it he?' quoth one, 'Is this the man?
By him who died on cross,
With his cruel bow he laid full low   400
The harmless Albatross.

The spirit who bideth by himself
In the land of mist and snow,
He loved the bird that loved the man
Who shot him with his bow.'

The other was a softer voice,
As soft as honey-dew:
Quoth he, 'The man hath penance done,
And penance more will do.'

PART VI

FIRST VOICE

'But tell me, tell me! speak again,   410
Thy soft response renewing—
What makes that ship drive on so fast?
What is the ocean doing?'

SECOND VOICE

'Still as a slave before his lord,
The ocean hath no blast;
His great bright eye most silently
Up to the Moon is cast—

If he may know which way to go;
For she guides him smooth or grim.
See, brother, see! how graciously   420
She looketh down on him.'

FIRST VOICE

The Mariner hath been cast into a trance: for the angelic power causeth the vessel to drive northward faster than human life could endure.

'But why drives on that ship so fast,
Without or wave or wind?'

SECOND VOICE

'The air is cut away before,
And closes from behind.

Fly, brother, fly! more high, more high!
Or we shall be belated:
For slow and slow that ship will go,
When the Mariner's trance is abated.'

The supernatural motion is retarded; the Mariner awakes, and his penance begins anew.

I woke, and we were sailing on   430
As in a gentle weather:
'Twas night, calm night, the moon was [high;
The dead men stood together.

All stood together on the deck,
For a charnel-dungeon fitter:
All fixed on me their stony eyes,
That in the Moon did glitter.

The pang, the curse, with which they
Had never passed away: [died,
I could not draw my eyes from theirs,   440
Nor turn them up to pray.

The curse is finally expiated.

And now this spell was snapt: once more
I viewed the ocean green,
And looked far forth, yet little saw
Of what had else been seen—

Like one, that on a lonesome road
Doth walk in fear and dread,
And having once turned round walks on,
And turns no more his head;
Because he knows, a frightful fiend   450
Doth close behind him tread.

But soon there breathed a wind on me,
Nor sound nor motion made:
Its path was not upon the sea,
In ripple or in shade.

It raised my hair, it fanned my cheek
Like a meadow-gale of spring—
It mingled strangely with my fears,
Yet it felt like a welcoming.

Swiftly, swiftly flew the ship,   460
Yet she sailed softly too:
Sweetly, sweetly blew the breeze—
On me alone it blew.

And the ancient Mariner beholdeth his native country.

Oh! dream of joy! is this indeed
The light-house top I see?
Is this the hill? is this the kirk?
Is this mine own countree?

We drifted o'er the harbour-bar,
And I with sobs did pray—
O let me be awake, my God!   470
Or let me sleep alway.

The harbour-bay was clear as glass,
So smoothly it was strewn!
And on the bay the moonlight lay,
And the shadow of the Moon.

The rock shone bright, the kirk no less,
That stands above the rock:
The moonlight steeped in silentness
The steady weathercock.

The angelic spirits leave the dead bodies,

And the bay was white with silent light,
Till rising from the same,   480
Full many shapes, that shadows were,
In crimson colours came.

And appear
in their own
forms of light.

A little distance from the prow
Those crimson shadows were:
I turned my eyes upon the deck—
Oh, Christ! what saw I there!

Each corse lay flat, lifeless and flat,
And, by the holy rood![6]
A man all light, a seraph-man,   490
On every corse there stood.

This seraph-band, each waved his hand:
It was a heavenly sight!
They stood as signals to the land,
Each one a lovely light;

This seraph-band, each waved his hand,
No voice did they impart—
No voice; but oh! the silence sank
Like music on my heart.

But soon I heard the dash of oars,   500
I heard the Pilot's cheer;
My head was turned perforce away,
And I saw a boat appear.

The Pilot and the Pilot's boy,
I heard them coming fast:
Dear Lord in Heaven! it was a joy
The dead men could not blast.

I saw a third—I heard his voice:
It is the Hermit good!
He singeth loud his godly hymns   510
That he makes in the wood.
He'll shrieve my soul, he'll wash away
The Albatross's blood.

PART VII

The Hermit
of the Wood,

THIS Hermit good lives in that wood
Which slopes down to the sea.
How loudly his sweet voice he rears!
He loves to talk with marineres
That come from a far countree.

He kneels at morn, and noon, and eve—
He hath a cushion plump: 520
It is the moss that wholly hides
The rotted old oak-stump.

The skiff-boat neared: I heard them talk,
'Why, this is strange, I trow!
Where are those lights so many and fair,
That signal made but now?'

Approacheth
the ship with
wonder.

'Strange, by my faith!' the Hermit said—
'And they answered not our cheer!
The planks looked warped! and see those
How thin they are and sere!   [sails,
I never saw aught like to them,   531
Unless perchance it were

Brown skeletons of leaves that lag
My forest-brook along;
When the ivy-tod[7] is heavy with snow,
And the owlet whoops to the wolf below,
That eats the she-wolf's young.'

'Dear Lord! it hath a fiendish look—
(The Pilot made reply)
I am a-feared'—'Push on, push on!'   540
Said the Hermit cheerily.

The boat came closer to the ship,
But I nor spake nor stirred;
The boat came close beneath the ship,
And straight a sound was heard.

The ship
suddenly
sinketh.

Under the water it rumbled on,
Still louder and more dread:
It reached the ship, it split the bay;
The ship went down like lead.

The ancient
Mariner is
saved in the
Pilot's boat.

Stunned by that loud and dreadful sound,
Which sky and ocean smote,   551
Like one that hath been seven days
My body lay afloat;   [drowned
But swift as dreams, myself I found
Within the Pilot's boat.

Upon the whirl, where sank the ship,
The boat spun round and round;
And all was still, save that the hill
Was telling of the sound.

I moved my lips—the Pilot shrieked   560
And fell down in a fit;
The holy Hermit raised his eyes,
And prayed where he did sit.

I took the oars: the Pilot's boy,
Who now doth crazy go,
Laughed loud and long, and all the while
His eyes went to and fro.
'Ha! ha!' quoth he, 'full plain I see,
The Devil knows how to row.'

---

[6] Cross.

[7] Ivy-bush.

And now, all in my own countree,   570
I stood on the firm land!
The Hermit stepped forth from the boat,
And scarcely he could stand.

The ancient Mariner earnestly entreateth the Hermit to shrieve him; and the penance of life falls on him.

'O shrieve me, shrieve me, holy man!'[8]
The Hermit crossed his brow.
'Say quick,' quoth he, 'I bid thee say—
What manner of man art thou?'

Forthwith this frame of mine was
With a woful agony,   [wrenched
Which force me to begin my tale;   580
And then it left me free.

And ever and anon throughout his future life an agony constraineth him to travel from land to land;

Since then, at an uncertain hour,
That agony returns:
And till my ghastly tale is told,
This heart within me burns.

I pass, like night, from land to land;
I have strange power of speech;
That moment that his face I see,
I know the man that must hear me:
To him my tale I teach.   590

What loud uproar bursts from that door!
The wedding-guests are there:
But in the garden-bower the bride
And bride-maids singing are:
And hark the little vesper bell,
Which biddeth me to prayer!

O Wedding-Guest! this soul hath been
Alone on a wide wide sea:
So lonely 'twas, that God himself
Scarce seemed there to be.   600

O sweeter than the marriage-feast,
'Tis sweeter far to me,
To walk together to the kirk
With a goodly company!—

To walk together to the kirk,
And all together pray,
While each to his great Father bends,
Old men, and babes, and loving friends
And youths and maidens gay!

And to teach, by his own example, love and reverence to all things that God made and loveth.

Farewell, farewell! but this I tell   610
To thee, thou Wedding-Guest!
He prayeth well, who loveth well
Both man and bird and beast.

He prayeth best, who loveth best
All things both great and small;
For the dear God who loveth us,
He made and loveth all.

The Mariner, whose eye is bright,
Whose beard with age is hoar,
Is gone: and now the Wedding-Guest
Turned from the bridegroom's door.   621

He went like one that hath been stunned,
And is of sense forlorn:
A sadder and a wiser man,
He rose the morrow morn.

[1797–98; rev. 1815]   [1817]

CHRISTABEL

Christabel *was planned for the second (1800) edition of* Lyrical Ballads—*in 1821 Coleridge was still hoping to complete it. The Preface first appeared in 1816.*

CHRISTABEL

PREFACE

THE first part of the following poem was written in the year 1797, at Stowey, in the county of Somerset. The second part, after my return from Germany, in the year 1800, at Keswick, Cumberland. It is probable that if the poem had been finished at either of the former periods, or if even the first and second part had been published in the year 1800, the impression of its originality would have been much greater than I dare at present expect. But for this I have only my own indolence to blame. The dates are mentioned for the exclusive purpose of precluding charges of plagiarism or servile imitation from myself. For there is amongst us a set of critics, who seem to hold, that every possible thought and image is traditional; who have no notion that there are such things as fountains in the world, small as well as great; and who would therefore charitably derive every rill they behold flowing, from a perforation made in some other man's tank. I am confident, however, that as far as the present poem is concerned, the celebrated poets[1] whose writings I might be suspected of having imitated, either in particular passages, or in the tone and the spirit of the whole, would be among the first to

---

[8] He makes the sign of the cross on his forehead, and asks to have his confession heard (to be shriven) so that he may receive absolution.

[1] Sir Walter Scott and Lord Byron had both read or heard *Christabel* before publication.

vindicate me from the charge, and who, on any striking
coincidence, would permit me to address them in this
doggerel version of two monkish Latin hexameters.

> 'Tis mine and it is likewise yours;
> But an if this will not do;
> Let it be mine, good friend! for I
> Am the poorer of the two.

I have only to add that the metre of Christabel is not,
properly speaking, irregular, though it may seem so from
its being founded on a new principle: namely, that of
counting in each line the accents, not the syllables. Though
the latter may vary from seven to twelve, yet in each line
the accents will be found to be only four. Nevertheless,
this occasional variation in number of syllables is not
introduced wantonly, or for the mere ends of convenience,
but in correspondence with some transition in the nature
of the imagery or passion.

Part I

'Tis the middle of night by the castle clock,
And the owls have awakened the crowing cock;
Tu—whit!——Tu—whoo!
And hark, again! the crowing cock.
How drowsily it crew.

Sir Leoline, the Baron rich,
Hath a toothless mastiff bitch;
From her kennel beneath the rock
She maketh answers to the clock,
Four for the quarters, and twelve for the hour;   10
Ever and aye, by shine and shower,
Sixteen short howls, not over loud;
Some say, she sees my lady's shroud.

Is the night chilly and dark?
The night is chilly, but not dark.
The thin gray cloud is spread on high,
It covers but not hides the sky.
The moon is behind, and at the full;
And yet she looks both small and dull.
The night is chill, the cloud is gray: 20
'Tis a month before the month of May,
And the Spring comes slowly up this way.

The lovely lady, Christabel,
Whom her father loves so well,
What makes her in the wood so late,
A furlong from the castle gate?
She had dreams all yesternight
Of her own betrothéd knight;
And she in the midnight wood will pray
For the weal of her lover that's far away.   30

She stole along, she nothing spoke,
The sighs she heaved were soft and low,
And naught was green upon the oak
But moss and rarest misletoe:
She kneels beneath the huge oak tree,
And in silence prayeth she.

The lady sprang up suddenly,
The lovely lady, Christabel!
It moaned as near, as near can be,
But what it is she cannot tell.—   40
On the other side it seems to be,
Of the huge, broad-breasted, old oak tree.

The night is chill; the forest bare;
Is it the wind that moaneth bleak?
There is not wind enough in the air
To move away the ringlet curl
From the lovely lady's cheek—
There is not wind enough to twirl
The one red leaf, the last of its clan,
That dances as often as dance it can,   50
Hanging so light, and hanging so high,
On the topmost twig that looks up at the sky.

Hush, beating heart of Christabel!
Jesu, Maria, shield her well!
She folded her arms beneath her cloak,
And stole to the other side of the oak.
     What sees she there?

There she sees a damsel bright,
Drest in a silken robe of white,
That shadowy in the moonlight shone: 60
The neck that made that white robe wan,
Her stately neck, and arms were bare;
Her blue-veined feet unsandal'd were,
And wildly glittered here and there
The gems entangled in her hair.
I guess, 'twas frightful there to see
A lady so richly clad as she—
Beautiful exceedingly!

Mary mother, save me now!
(Said Christabel,) And who art thou?   70

The lady strange made answer meet,
And her voice was faint and sweet:—
Have pity on my sore distress,
I scarce can speak for weariness:
Stretch forth thy hand, and have no fear!
Said Christabel, How camest thou here?
And the lady, whose voice was faint and sweet,
Did thus pursue her answer meet:—

My sire is of a noble line,
And my name is Geraldine: 80
Five warriors seized me yestermorn,
Me, even me, a maid forlorn:
They choked my cries with force and fright,
And tied me on a palfrey white.
The palfrey was as fleet as wind,
And they rode furiously behind.

They spurred amain, their steeds were white:
And once we crossed the shade of night.
As sure as Heaven shall rescue me,
I have no thought what men they be;   90
Nor do I know how long it is
(For I have lain entranced I wis)
Since one, the tallest of the five,
Took me from the palfrey's back,
A weary woman, scarce alive.
Some muttered words his comrades spoke:
He placed me underneath this oak;
He swore they would return with haste;
Whither they went I cannot tell—
I thought I heard, some minutes past,   100
Sounds as of a castle bell.
Stretch forth thy hand (thus ended she),
And help a wretched maid to flee.

Then Christabel stretched forth her hand,
And comforted fair Geraldine:
O well, bright dame! may you command
The service of Sir Leoline;
And gladly our stout chivalry
Will he send forth and friends withal
To guide and guard you safe and free   110
Home to your noble father's hall.

She rose: and forth with steps they passed
That strove to be, and were not, fast.
Her gracious stars the lady blest,
And thus spake on sweet Christabel:
All our household are at rest,
The hall as silent as the cell;
Sir Leoline is weak in health,
And may not well awakened be,
But we will move as if in stealth,   120
And I beseech your courtesy,
This night, to share your couch with me.

They crossed the moat, and Christabel
Took the key that fitted well;
A little door she opened straight,
All in the middle of the gate;
The gate that was ironed within and without,
Where an army in battle array had marched out.

The lady sank, belike through pain,
And Christabel with might and main   130
Lifted her up, a weary weight,
Over the threshold of the gate:
Then the lady rose again,
And moved, as she were not in pain.

So free from danger, free from fear,
They crossed the court: right glad they were.
And Christabel devoutly cried
To the lady by her side,
Praise we the Virgin all divine
Who hath rescued thee from thy distress!   140
Alas, alas! said Geraldine,
I cannot speak for weariness.
So free from danger, free from fear,
They crossed the court: right glad they were.

Outside her kennel, the mastiff old
Lay fast asleep, in moonshine cold.
The mastiff old did not awake,
Yet she an angry moan did make!
And what can ail the mastiff bitch?
Never till now she uttered yell   150
Beneath the eye of Christabel.
Perhaps it is the owlet's scritch:
For what can ail the mastiff bitch?

They passed the hall, that echoes still,
Pass as lightly as you will!
The brands were flat, the brands were dying,
Amid their own white ashes lying;
But when the lady passed, there came
A tongue of light, a fit of flame;
And Christabel saw the lady's eye,   160
And nothing else saw she thereby,
Save the boss of the shield of Sir Leoline tall,
Which hung in a murky old niche in the wall.
O softly tread, said Christabel,
My father seldom sleepeth well.

Sweet Christabel her feet doth bare,
And jealous of the listening air
They steal their way from stair to stair,
Now in glimmer, and now in gloom,
And now they pass the Baron's room,   170
As still as death, with stifled breath!
And now have reached her chamber door;
And now doth Geraldine press down
The rushes of the chamber floor.

The moon shines dim in the open air,
And not a moonbeam enters here.
But they without its light can see

The chamber carved so curiously,
Carved with figures strange and sweet,
All made out of the carver's brain, 180
For a lady's chamber meet:
The lamp with twofold silver chain
Is fastened to an angel's feet.

The silver lamp burns dead and dim;
But Christabel the lamp will trim.
She trimmed the lamp, and made it bright,
And left it swinging to and fro,
While Geraldine, in wretched plight,
Sank down upon the floor below.

O weary lady, Geraldine, 190
I pray you, drink this cordial wine!
It is a wine of virtuous powers;
My mother made it of wild flowers.

And will your mother pity me,
Who am a maiden most forlorn?
Christabel answered—Woe is me!
She died the hour that I was born.
I have heard the grey-haired friar tell
How on her death-bed she did say,
That she should hear the castle-bell 200
Strike twelve upon my wedding-day.
O mother dear! that thou wert here!
I would, said Geraldine, she were!
But soon with altered voice, said she—
'Off, wandering mother! Peak and pine!
I have power to bid thee flee.'
Alas! what ails poor Geraldine?
Why stares she with unsettled eye?
Can she the bodiless dead espy?
And why with hollow voice cries she, 210
'Off, woman, off! this hour is mine—
Though thou her guardian spirit be,
Off, woman, off! 'tis given to me.'

Then Christabel knelt by the lady's side,
And raised to heaven her eyes so blue—
Alas! said she, this ghastly ride—
Dear lady! it hath wildered you!
The lady wiped her moist cold brow,
And faintly said, ' 'tis over now!'

Again the wild-flower wine she drank: 220
Her fair large eyes 'gan glitter bright,
And from the floor whereon she sank,
The lofty lady stood upright:
She was most beautiful to see,
Like a lady of a far countrée.

And thus the lofty lady spake—
'All they who live in the upper sky,
Do love you, holy Christabel!
And you love them, and for their sake
And for the good which me befel, 230
Even I in my degree will try,
Fair maiden, to requite you well.
But now unrobe yourself; for I
Must pray, ere yet in bed I lie.'

Quoth Christabel, So let it be!
And as the lady bade, did she.
Her gentle limbs did she undress,
And lay down in her loveliness.

But through her brain of weal and woe
So many thoughts moved to and fro, 240
That vain it were her lids to close;
So half-way from the bed she rose,
And on her elbow did recline
To look at the lady Geraldine.

Beneath the lamp the lady bowed,
And slowly rolled her eyes around;
Then drawing in her breath aloud,
Like one that shuddered, she unbound
The cincture from beneath her breast:
Her silken robe, and inner vest, 250
Dropt to her feet, and full in view,
Behold! her bosom and half her side——
A sight to dream of, not to tell!
O shield her! shield sweet Christabel!

Yet Geraldine nor speaks nor stirs;
Ah! what a stricken look was hers!
Deep from within she seems half-way
To lift some weight with sick assay,
And eyes the maid and seeks delay;
Then suddenly, as one defied, 260
Collects herself in scorn and pride,
And lay down by the Maiden's side!—
And in her arms the maid she took,
  Ah wel-a-day!
And with low voice and doleful look
These words did say:
'In the touch of this bosom there worketh a spell,
Which is lord of thy utterance, Christabel!
Thou knowest to-night, and wilt know to-morrow,
This mark of my shame, this seal of my sorrow; 270
  But vainly thou warrest,
   For this is alone in
  Thy power to declare
   That in the dim forest
  Thou heard'st a low moaning,

And found'st a bright lady, surpassingly fair;
And didst bring her home with thee in love and in
    charity,
To shield her and shelter her from the damp air.'

THE CONCLUSION TO PART I

It was a lovely sight to see
The lady Christabel, when she   280
Was praying at the old oak tree.
    Amid the jaggéd shadows
    Of mossy leafless boughs,
    Kneeling in the moonlight,
    To make her gentle vows;
Her slender palms together prest,
Heaving sometimes on her breast;
Her face resigned to bliss or bale—
Her face, oh call it fair not pale,
And both blue eyes more bright than clear,   290
Each about to have a tear.

With open eyes (ah woe is me!)
Asleep, and dreaming fearfully,
Fearfully dreaming, yet, I wis,
Dreaming that alone, which is—
O sorrow and shame! Can this be she,
The lady, who knelt at the old oak tree?
And lo! the worker of these harms,
That holds the maiden in her arms,
Seems to slumber still and mild,   300
As a mother with her child.

A star hath set, a star hath risen,
O Geraldine! since arms of thine
Have been the lovely lady's prison.
O Geraldine! one hour was thine—
Thou'st had thy will! By tairn and rill,
The night-birds all that hour were still.
But now they are jubilant anew,
From cliff and tower, tu—whoo! tu—whoo!
Tu—whoo! tu—whoo! from wood and fell!   310

And see! the lady Christabel
Gathers herself from out her trance;
Her limbs relax, her countenance
Grows sad and soft; the smooth thin lids
Close o'er her eyes; and tears she sheds—
Large tears that leave the lashes bright!
And oft the while she seems to smile
As infants at a sudden light!

Yea, she doth smile, and she doth weep,
Like a youthful hèrmitess,   320
Beauteous in a wilderness,
Who, praying always, prays in sleep.

And, if she move unquietly,
Perchance, 'tis but the blood so free
Comes back and tingles in her feet.
No doubt, she hath a vision sweet.
What if her guardian spirit 'twere,
Where if she knew her mother near?
But this she knows, in joys and woes,
That saints will aid if men will call: 330
For the blue sky bends over all!

PART II

Each matin bell, the Baron saith,
Knells us back to a world of death.
These words Sir Leoline first said,
When he rose and found his lady dead:
These words Sir Leoline will say
Many a morn to his dying day!

And hence the custom and law began
That still at dawn the sacristan,
Who duly pulls the heavy bell,   340
Five and forty beads must tell
Between each stroke—a warning knell,
Which not a soul can choose but hear
From Bratha Head to Wyndèrmere.

Saith Bracy the bard, So let it knell!
And let the drowsy sacristan
Still count as slowly as he can!
There is no lack of such, I ween,
As well fill up the space between.
In Langdale Pike and Witch's Lair,   350
And Dungeon-ghyll so foully rent,
With ropes of rock and bells of air
Three sinful sextons' ghosts are pent,
Who all give back, one after t'other,
The death-note to their living brother;
And oft too, by the knell offended,
Just as their one! two! three! is ended,
The devil mocks the doleful tale
With a merry peal from Borodale.

The air is still! through mist and cloud   360
That merry peal comes ringing loud;
And Geraldine shakes off her dread,
And rises lightly from the bed;
Puts on her silken vestments white,
And tricks her hair in lovely plight,
And nothing doubting of her spell
Awakens the lady Christabel.
'Sleep you, sweet lady Christabel?
I trust that you have rested well.'

And Christabel awoke and spied 370
The same who lay down by her side—
O rather say, the same whom she
Raised up beneath the old oak tree!
Nay, fairer yet! and yet more fair!
For she belike hath drunken deep
Of all the blessedness of sleep!
And while she spake, her looks, her air
Such gentle thankfulness declare,
That (so it seemed) her girded vests
Grew tight beneath her heaving breasts. 380
'Sure I have sinn'd!' said Christabel,
'Now heaven be praised if all be well!'
And in low faltering tones, yet sweet,
Did she the lofty lady greet
With such perplexity of mind
As dreams too lively leave behind.

So quickly she rose, and quickly arrayed
Her maiden limbs, and having prayed
That He, who on the cross did groan,
Might wash away her sins unknown, 390
She forthwith led fair Geraldine
To meet her sire, Sir Leoline.

The lovely maid and the lady tall
Are pacing both into the hall,
And pacing on through page and groom,
Enter the Baron's presence-room.

The Baron rose, and while he prest
His gentle daughter to his breast,
With cheerful wonder in his eyes
The lady Geraldine espies, 400
And gave such welcome to the same,
As might beseem so bright a dame!

But when he heard the lady's tale,
And when she told her father's name,
Why waxed Sir Leoline so pale,
Murmuring o'er the name again,
Lord Roland de Vaux of Tryermaine?

Alas! they had been friends in youth;
But whispering tongues can poison truth;
And constancy lives in realms above; 410
And life is thorny; and youth is vain;
And to be wroth with one we love
Doth work like madness in the brain.
And thus it chanced, as I divine,
With Roland and Sir Leoline.
Each spake words of high disdain
And insult to his heart's best brother:
They parted—ne'er to meet again!

But never either found another
To free the hollow heart from paining— 420
They stood aloof, the scars remaining,
Like cliffs which had been rent asunder;
A dreary sea now flows between;—
But neither heat, nor frost, nor thunder,
Shall wholly do away, I ween,
The marks of that which once hath been.

Sir Leoline, a moment's space,
Stood gazing on the damsel's face:
And the youthful Lord of Tryermaine
Came back upon his heart again. 430

O then the Baron forgot his age,
His noble heart swelled high with rage;
He swore by the wounds in Jesu's side
He would proclaim it far and wide,
With trump and solemn heraldry,
That they, who thus had wronged the dame,
Were base as spotted infamy!
'And if they dare deny the same,
My herald shall appoint a week,
And let the recreant traitors seek 440
My tourney court—that there and then
I may dislodge their reptile souls
From the bodies and forms of men!'
He spake: his eye in lightning rolls!
For the lady was ruthlessly seized; and he kenned
In the beautiful lady the child of his friend!

And now the tears were on his face,
And fondly in his arms he took
Fair Geraldine, who met the embrace,
Prolonging it with joyous look. 450
Which when she viewed, a vision fell
Upon the soul of Christabel,
The vision of fear, the touch and pain!
She shrunk and shuddered, and saw again—
(Ah, woe is me! Was it for thee,
Thou gentle maid! such sights to see?)

Again she saw that bosom old,
Again she felt that bosom cold,
And drew in her breath with a hissing sound:
Whereat the Knight turned wildly round, 460
And nothing saw, but his own sweet maid
With eyes upraised, as one that prayed.

The touch, the sight, had passed away,
And in its stead that vision blest,
Which comforted her after-rest
While in the lady's arms she lay,

Had put a rapture in her breast,
And on her lips and o'er her eyes
Spread smiles like light!
                              With new surprise,
'What ails then my belovéd child?'   470
The Baron said—His daughter mild
Made answer, 'All will yet be well!'
I ween, she had no power to tell
Aught else: so mighty was the spell.

Yet he, who saw this Geraldine,
Had deemed her sure a thing divine:
Such sorrow with such grace she blended,
As if she feared she had offended
Sweet Christabel, that gentle maid!
And with such lowly tones she prayed   480
She might be sent without delay
Home to her father's mansion.
                                      'Nay!
Nay, by my soul!' said Leoline!
'Ho! Bracy the bard, the charge be thine!
Go thou, with music sweet and loud,
And take two steeds with trappings proud,
And take the youth whom thou lov'st best
To bear thy harp, and learn thy song,
And clothe you both in solemn vest,
And over the mountains haste along,   490
Lest wandering folk, that are abroad,
Detain you on the valley road.

'And when he has crossed the Irthing flood,
My merry bard! he hastes, he hastes
Up Knorren Moor, through Halegarth Wood,
And reaches soon that castle good
Which stands and threatens Scotland's wastes.

'Bard Bracy! bard Bracy! your horses are fleet,
Ye must ride up the hall, your music so sweet,
More loud than your horse's echoing feet!   500
And loud and loud to Lord Roland call,
Thy daughter is safe in Langdale hall!
Thy beautiful daughter is safe and free—
Sir Leoline greets thee thus through me!
He bids thee come without delay
With all thy numerous array
And take thy lovely daughter home:
And he will meet thee on the way
With all his numerous array
White with their panting palfreys' foam: 510
And, by mine honour! I will say,
That I repent me of the day
When I spake words of fierce disdain

To Roland de Vaux of Tryermaine!—
—For since that evil hour hath flown,
Many a summer's sun hath shone;
Yet ne'er found I a friend again
Like Roland de Vaux of Tryermaine.'

The lady fell, and clasped his knees,
Her face upraised, her eyes o'erflowing;   520
And Bracy replied, with faltering voice,
His gracious Hail on all bestowing!—
'Thy words, thou sire of Christabel,
Are sweeter than my harp can tell;
Yet might I gain a boon of thee,
This day my journey should not be,
So strange a dream hath come to me,
That I had vowed with music loud
To clear yon wood from thing unblest,
Warned by a vision in my rest!   530
For in my sleep I saw that dove,
That gentle bird, whom thou dost love,
And call'st by thy own daughter's name—
Sir Leoline! I saw the same
Fluttering, and uttering fearful moan,
Among the green herbs in the forest alone.
Which when I saw and when I heard,
I wonder'd what might ail the bird;
For nothing near it could I see,
Save the grass and green herbs underneath the
          old tree.   540

'And in my dream methought I went
To search out what might there be found;
And what the sweet bird's trouble meant,
That thus lay fluttering on the ground.
I went and peered, and could descry
No cause for her distressful cry;
But yet for her dear lady's sake
I stooped, methought, the dove to take,
When lo! I saw a bright green snake
Coiled around its wings and neck.   550
Green as the herbs on which it couched,
Close by the dove's its head it crouched;
And with the dove it heaves and stirs,
Swelling its neck as she swelled hers!
I woke; it was the midnight hour,
The clock was echoing in the tower;
But though my slumber was gone by,
This dream it would not pass away—
It seems to live upon my eye!
And thence I vowed this self-same day   560
With music strong and saintly song
To wander through the forest bare,
Lest aught unholy loiter there.'

Thus Bracy said: the Baron, the while,
Half-listening heard him with a smile;
Then turned to Lady Geraldine,
His eyes made up of wonder and love;
And said in courtly accents fine,
'Sweet maid, Lord Roland's beauteous dove,
With arms more strong than harp or song,   570
Thy sire and I will crush the snake!'
He kissed her forehead as he spake,
And Geraldine in maiden wise
Casting down her large bright eyes,
With blushing cheek and courtesy fine
She turned her from Sir Leoline;
Softly gathering up her train,
That o'er her right arm fell again;
And folded her arms across her chest,
And couched her head upon her breast,   580
And looked askance at Christabel——
Jesu, Maria, shield her well!

A snake's small eye blinks dull and shy;
And the lady's eyes they shrunk in her head,
Each shrunk up to a serpent's eye,
And with somewhat of malice, and more of
         dread,
At Christabel she looked askance!—
One moment—and the sight was fled!
But Christabel in dizzy trance
Stumbling on the unsteady ground   590
Shuddered aloud, with a hissing sound;
And Geraldine again turned round,
And like a thing, that sought relief,
Full of wonder and full of grief,
She rolled her large bright eyes divine
Wildly on Sir Leoline.

The maid, alas! her thoughts are gone,
She nothing sees—no sight but one!
The maid, devoid of guile and sin,
I know not how, in fearful wise,   600
So deeply had she drunken in
That look, those shrunken serpent eyes,
That all her features were resigned
To this sole image in her mind:
And passively did imitate
That look of dull and treacherous hate!
And thus she stood, in dizzy trance,
Still picturing that look askance
With forced unconscious sympathy
Full before her father's view——   610
As far as such a look could be
In eyes so innocent and blue!

And when the trance was o'er, the maid
Paused awhile, and inly prayed:
Then falling at the Baron's feet,
'By my mother's soul do I entreat
That thou this woman send away!'
She said: and more she could not say:
For what she knew she could not tell,
O'er-mastered by the mighty spell.   620

Why is thy cheek so wan and wild,
Sir Leoline? Thy only child
Lies at thy feet, thy joy, thy pride,
So fair, so innocent, so mild;
The same, for whom thy lady died!
O by the pangs of her dear mother
Think thou no evil of thy child!
For her, and thee, and for no other,
She prayed the moment ere she died:
Prayed that the babe for whom she died,   630
Might prove her dear lord's joy and pride!
     That prayer her deadly pangs beguiled,
              Sir Leoline!
     And wouldst thou wrong thy only child,
              Her child and thine?

Within the Baron's heart and brain
If thoughts, like these, had any share,
They only swelled his rage and pain,
And did but work confusion there.
His heart was cleft with pain and rage,   640
His cheeks they quivered, his eyes were wild,
Dishonoured thus in his old age;
Dishonoured by his only child,
And all his hospitality
To the wronged daughter of his friend
By more than woman's jealousy
Brought thus to a disgraceful end—
He rolled his eye with stern regard
Upon the gentle minstrel bard,
And said in tones abrupt, austere—   650
'Why, Bracy! dost thou loiter here?
I bade thee hence!' The bard obeyed;
And turning from his own sweet maid,
The agéd knight, Sir Leoline,
Led forth the Lady Geraldine!

THE CONCLUSION TO PART II

A little child, a limber elf,
Singing, dancing to itself,
A fairy thing with red round cheeks,
That always finds, and never seeks,

Makes such a vision to the sight   660
As fills a father's eyes with light;
And pleasures flow in so thick and fast
Upon his heart, that he at last
Must needs express his love's excess
With words of unmeant bitterness.
Perhaps 'tis pretty to force together
Thoughts so all unlike each other;
To mutter and mock a broken charm,
To dally with wrong that does no harm.
Perhaps 'tis tender too and pretty   670
At each wild word to feel within
A sweet recoil of love and pity.
And what, if in a world of sin
(O sorrow and shame should this be true!)
Such giddiness of heart and brain
Comes seldom save from rage and pain,
So talks as it's most used to do.

[1797–1801]   [1816]

FROST AT MIDNIGHT

THE Frost performs its secret ministry,
Unhelped by any wind. The owlet's cry
Came loud—and hark, again! loud as before.
The inmates of my cottage, all at rest,
Have left me to that solitude, which suits
Abstruser musings: save that at my side
My cradled infant slumbers peacefully.
'Tis calm indeed! so calm, that it disturbs
And vexes meditation with its strange
And extreme silentness. Sea, hill, and wood,   10
This populous village! Sea, and hill, and wood,
With all the numberless goings-on of life,
Inaudible as dreams! the thin blue flame
Lies on my low-burnt fire, and quivers not;
Only that film,* which fluttered on the grate,
Still flutters there, the sole unquiet thing.
Methinks, its motion in this hush of nature
Gives it dim sympathies with me who live,
Making it a companionable form,
Whose puny flaps and freaks the idling Spirit   20
By its own moods interprets, every where
Echo or mirror seeking of itself,
And makes a toy of Thought.

                        But O! how oft,
How oft, at school, with most believing mind,
Presageful, have I gazed upon the bars,
To watch that fluttering stranger! and as oft
With unclosed lids, already had I dreamt

* In all parts of the kingdom these films are called *strangers*
and supposed to portend the arrival of some absent friend.

Of my sweet birth-place, and the old church-tower,
Whose bells, the poor man's only music, rang
From morn to evening, all the hot Fair-day,   30
So sweetly, that they stirred and haunted me
With a wild pleasure, falling on mine ear
Most like articulate sounds of things to come!
So gazed I, till the soothing things, I dreamt,
Lulled me to sleep, and sleep prolonged my dreams!
And so I brooded all the following morn,
Awed by the stern preceptor's face, mine eye
Fixed with mock study on my swimming book:
Save if the door half opened, and I snatched
A hasty glance, and still my heart leaped up,   40
For still I hoped to see the *stranger's* face,
Townsman, or aunt, or sister more beloved,
My play-mate when we both were clothed alike!

    Dear Babe,[1] that sleepest cradled by my side,
Whose gentle breathings, heard in this deep calm,
Fill up the interspersèd vacancies
And momentary pauses of the thought!
My babe so beautiful! it thrills my heart
With tender gladness, thus to look at thee,
And think that thou shalt learn far other lore,   50
And in far other scenes! For I was reared
In the great city, pent 'mid cloisters dim,
And saw nought lovely but the sky and stars.
But *thou*, my babe! shalt wander like a breeze
By lakes and sandy shores, beneath the crags
Of ancient mountain, and beneath the clouds,
Which image in their bulk both lakes and shores
And mountain crags: so shalt thou see and hear
The lovely shapes and sounds intelligible
Of that eternal language, which thy God   60
Utters, who from eternity doth teach
Himself in all, and all things in himself.
Great universal Teacher! he shall mould
Thy spirit, and by giving make it ask.

    Therefore all seasons shall be sweet to thee,
Whether the summer clothe the general earth
With greenness, or the redbreast sit and sing
Betwixt the tufts of snow on the bare branch
Of mossy apple-tree, while the nigh thatch
Smokes in the sun-thaw; whether the eave-drops fall
Heard only in the trances of the blast,   71
Or if the secret ministry of frost
Shall hang them up in silent icicles,
Quietly shining to the quiet Moon.

[1798]   [1798]

[1] His son Hartley Coleridge. See note to Wordsworth's *To
H. C.*, p. 272.

FRANCE: AN ODE

The event that provoked this poem was the French invasion of Switzerland. It is Coleridge's explicit attempt to separate the principles of the Revolution, which he admired, from the actions of France, which he deplored.

FRANCE: AN ODE

I

YE Clouds! that far above me float and pause,
  Whose pathless march no mortal may controul!
Ye Ocean-Waves! that, wheresoe'er ye roll,
Yield homage only to eternal laws!
Ye Woods! that listen to the night-birds singing,
  Midway the smooth and perilous slope reclined,
Save when your own imperious branches swinging,
  Have made a solemn music of the wind!
Where, like a man beloved of God,
Through glooms, which never woodman trod,   10
    How oft, pursuing fancies holy,
My moonlight way o'er flowering weeds I wound,
  Inspired, beyond the guess of folly,
By each rude shape and wild unconquerable sound!
O ye loud Waves! and O ye Forests high!
  And O ye Clouds that far above me soared!
Thou rising Sun! thou blue rejoicing Sky!
  Yea, every thing that is and will be free!
Bear witness for me, wheresoe'er ye be,
  With what deep worship I have still adored   20
    The spirit of divinest Liberty.

II

When France in wrath her giant-limbs upreared,
  And with that oath, which smote air, earth, and sea,
  Stamped her strong foot and said she would be free,
Bear witness for me, how I hoped and feared!
With what a joy my lofty gratulation
  Unawed I sang, amid a slavish band:
And when to whelm the disenchanted nation,
  Like fiends embattled by a wizard's wand,
    The Monarchs marched in evil day,   30
    And Britain joined the dire array;[1]
  Though dear her shores and circling ocean,
Though many friendships, many youthful loves
  Had swoln the patriot emotion
And flung a magic light o'er all her hills and groves;
Yet still my voice, unaltered, sang defeat
  To all that braved the tyrant-quelling lance,
And shame too long delayed and vain retreat!

---

[1] France declared war against Austria and Prussia in 1792; in 1793 England went to war with France.

For ne'er, O Liberty! with partial aim
I dimmed thy light or damped thy holy flame;   40
  But blessed the paeans of delivered France,
And hung my head and wept at Britain's name.

III

'And what,' I said 'though Blasphemy's loud scream
  With that sweet music of deliverance strove!
  Though all the fierce and drunken passions wove
A dance more wild than e'er was maniac's dream!
  Ye storms, that round the dawning East assembled,
The Sun was rising, though ye hid his light!'
  And when, to soothe my soul, that hoped and
    trembled,
The dissonance ceased, and all seemed calm and
    bright;   50
  When France her front deep-scarr'd and gory
  Concealed with clustering wreaths of glory;
    When, insupportably advancing,
  Her arm made mockery of the warrior's ramp;
    While timid looks of fury glancing,
  Domestic treason, crushed beneath her fatal stamp,
Writhed like a wounded dragon in his gore;
  Then I reproached my fears that would not flee;
'And soon,' I said, 'shall Wisdom teach her lore
In the low huts of them that toil and groan!   60
And, conquering by her happiness alone,
  Shall France compel the nations to be free,
Till Love and Joy look round, and call the Earth their
    own.'

IV

Forgive me, Freedom! O forgive those dreams!
  I hear thy voice, I hear thy loud lament,
  From bleak Helvetia's icy caverns sent—
I hear thy groans upon her blood-stained streams!
  Heroes, that for your peaceful country perished,
And ye that, fleeing, spot your mountain-snows
  With bleeding wounds; forgive me, that I
    cherished   70
One thought that ever blessed your cruel foes!
  To scatter rage, and traitorous guilt,
  Where Peace her jealous home had built;
    A patriot-race to disinherit
Of all that made their stormy wilds so dear;
    And with inexpiable spirit
To taint the bloodless freedom of the mountaineer—
  O France, that mockest Heaven, adulterous, blind,
    And patriot only in pernicious toils!
Are these thy boasts, Champion of human kind?   80
  To mix with Kings in the low lust of sway,
  Yell in the hunt, and share the murderous prey;
  To insult the shrine of Liberty with spoils
    From freemen torn; to tempt and to betray?

V

The Sensual and the Dark rebel in vain,
Slaves by their own compulsion! In mad game
They burst their manacles and wear the name
    Of Freedom, graven on a heavier chain!
O Liberty! with profitless endeavour
Have I pursued thee, many a weary hour;   90
    But thou nor swell'st the victor's strain, nor ever
Didst breathe thy soul in forms of human power.
    Alike from all, howe'er they praise thee,
    (Nor prayer, nor boastful name delays thee)
    Alike from Priestcraft's harpy minions,
    And factious Blasphemy's obscener slaves,
    Thou speedest on thy subtle pinions,
The guide of homeless winds, and playmate of the
        waves!
And there I felt thee!—on that sea-cliff's verge,
    Whose pines, scarce travelled by the breeze above,
Had made one murmur with the distant surge!   101
Yes, while I stood and gazed, my temples bare,
And shot my being through earth, sea, and air,
    Possessing all things with intensest love,
    O Liberty! my spirit felt thee there.

[1798]   [1798]

LEWTI

OR THE CIRCASSIAN LOVE-CHAUNT

AT midnight by the stream I roved,
To forget the form I loved.
Image of Lewti! from my mind
Depart; for Lewti is not kind.
The Moon was high, the moonlight gleam
    And the shadow of a star
Heaved upon Tamaha's stream;
    But the rock shone brighter far,
The rock half sheltered from my view
By pendent boughs of tressy yew.—   10
So shines my Lewti's forehead fair,
Gleaming through her sable hair.
Image of Lewti! from my mind
Depart; for Lewti is not kind.

I saw a cloud of palest hue,
    Onward to the moon it passed;
Still brighter and more bright it grew,
With floating colours not a few,
    Till it reached the moon at last:
Then the cloud was wholly bright,   20
With a rich and amber light!
And so with many a hope I seek,
    And with such joy I find my Lewti;

And even so my pale wan cheek
    Drinks in as deep a flush of beauty!
Nay, treacherous image! leave my mind,
If Lewti never will be kind.

The little cloud—it floats away,
    Away it goes; away so soon!
Alas! it has no power to stay: 30
Its hues are dim, its hues are grey—
    Away it passes from the moon!
How mournfully it seems to fly,
    Ever fading more and more,
To joyless regions of the sky—
    And now 'tis whiter than before!
As white as my poor cheek will be,
    When, Lewti! on my couch I lie,
A dying man for love of thee.
Nay, treacherous image! leave my
        mind—   40
And yet, thou didst not look unkind.

I saw a vapour in the sky,
Thin, and white, and very high;
I ne'er beheld so thin a cloud:
    Perhaps the breezes that can fly
    Now below and now above,
Have snatched aloft the lawny shroud
    Of Lady fair—that died for love.
For maids, as well as youths, have perished
From fruitless love too fondly
        cherished.   50
Nay, treacherous image! leave my mind—
For Lewti never will be kind.

Hush! my heedless feet from under
    Slip the crumbling banks for ever:
Like echoes to a distant thunder,
    They plunge into the gentle river.
The river-swans have heard my tread,
And startle from their reedy bed.
O beauteous birds! methinks ye measure
    Your movements to some heavenly
        tune!   60
O beauteous birds! 'tis such a pleasure
    To see you move beneath the moon,
I would it were your true delight
To sleep by day and wake all night.

I know the place where Lewti lies,
When silent night has closed her eyes:
    It is a breezy jasmine-bower,
The nightingale sings o'er her head:
    Voice of the Night! had I the power

That leafy labyrinth to thread,   70
And creep, like thee, with soundless tread,
I then might view her bosom white
Heaving lovely to my sight,
As these two swans together heave
On the gently-swelling wave.

Oh! that she saw me in a dream,
    And dreamt that I had died for care;
All pale and wasted I would seem,
    Yet fair withal, as spirits are!
I'd die indeed, if I might see   80
Her bosom heave, and heave for me!
Soothe, gentle image! soothe my mind!
To-morrow Lewti may be kind.

[1798]   [1798]

FEARS IN SOLITUDE

WRITTEN IN APRIL 1798, DURING THE
ALARM OF AN INVASION[1]

A GREEN and silent spot, amid the hills,
A small and silent dell! O'er stiller place
No singing sky-lark ever poised himself.
The hills are heathy, save that swelling slope,
Which hath a gay and gorgeous covering on,
All golden with the never-bloomless furze,
Which now blooms most profusely: but the dell,
Bathed by the mist, is fresh and delicate
As vernal corn-field, or the unripe flax,
When, through its half-transparent stalks, at eve,   10
The level sunshine glimmers with green light.
Oh! 'tis a quiet spirit-healing nook!
Which all, methinks, would love; but chiefly he,
The humble man, who, in his youthful years,
Knew just so much of folly, as had made
His early manhood more securely wise!
Here he might lie on fern or withered heath,
While from the singing lark (that sings unseen
The minstrelsy that solitude loves best),
And from the sun, and from the breezy air,   20
Sweet influences trembled o'er his frame;
And he, with many feelings, many thoughts,
Made up a meditative joy, and found
Religious meanings in the forms of Nature!
And so, his senses gradually wrapt
In a half sleep, he dreams of better worlds,
And dreaming hears thee still, O singing lark,
That singest like an angel in the clouds!

---

[1] A French invasion of Britain had been expected for some
months.

My God! it is a melancholy thing
For such a man, who would full fain preserve   30
His soul in calmness, yet perforce must feel
For all his human brethren—O my God!
It weighs upon the heart, that he must think
What uproar and what strife may now be stirring
This way or that way o'er these silent hills—
Invasion, and the thunder and the shout,
And all the crash of onset; fear and rage,
And undetermined conflict—even now,
Even now, perchance, and in his native isle:
Carnage and groans beneath this blessed sun!   40
We have offended, Oh! my countrymen!
We have offended very grievously,
And been most tyrannous. From east to west
A groan of accusation pierces Heaven!
The wretched plead against us; multitudes
Countless and vehement, the sons of God,
Our brethren! Like a cloud that travels on,
Steamed up from Cairo's swamps of pestilence,
Even so, my countrymen! have we gone forth
And borne to distant tribes slavery and pangs,   50
And, deadlier far, our vices, whose deep taint
With slow perdition murders the whole man,
His body and his soul! Meanwhile, at home,
All individual dignity and power
Engulfed in Courts, Committees, Institutions,
Associations and Societies,
A vain, speech-mouthing, speech-reporting Guild,
One Benefit-Club for mutual flattery,
We have drunk up, demure as at a grace,
Pollutions from the brimming cup of wealth;   60
Contemptuous of all honourable rule,
Yet bartering freedom and the poor man's life
For gold, as at a market! The sweet words
Of Christian promise, words that even yet
Might stem destruction, were they wisely preached,
Are muttered o'er by men, whose tones proclaim
How flat and wearisome they feel their trade:
Rank scoffers some, but most too indolent
To deem them falsehoods or to know their truth.
Oh! blasphemous! the Book of Life is made   70
A superstitious instrument, on which
We gabble o'er the oaths we mean to break;
For all must swear—all and in every place,
College and wharf, council and justice-court;
All, all must swear, the briber and the bribed,
Merchant and lawyer, senator and priest,
The rich, the poor, the old man and the young;
All, all make up one scheme of perjury,
That faith doth reel; the very name of God
Sounds like a juggler's charm; and, bold with joy,   80
Forth from his dark and lonely hiding-place,
(Portentous sight!) the owlet Atheism,

Sailing on obscene wings athwart the noon,
Drops his blue-fringed lids, and holds them close,
And hooting at the glorious sun in Heaven,
Cries out, 'Where is it?'

          Thankless too for peace,
(Peace long preserved by fleets and perilous seas)
Secure from actual warfare, we have loved
To swell the war-whoop, passionate for war!
Alas! for ages ignorant of all   90
Its ghastlier workings, (famine or blue plague,
Battle, or seige, or flight through wintry snows,)
We, this whole people, have been clamorous
For war and bloodshed; animating sports,
The which we pay for as a thing to talk of,
Spectators and not combatants! No guess
Anticipative of a wrong unfelt,
No speculation on contingency,
However dim and vague, too vague and dim
To yield a justifying cause; and forth,   100
(Stuffed out with big preamble, holy names,
And adjurations of the God in Heaven,)
We send our mandates for the certain death
Of thousands and ten thousands! Boys and girls,
And women, that would groan to see a child
Pull off an insect's leg, all read of war,
The best amusement for our morning meal!
The poor wretch, who has learnt his only prayers
From curses, who knows scarcely words enough
To ask a blessing from his Heavenly Father,   110
Becomes a fluent phraseman, absolute
And technical in victories and defeats,
And all our dainty terms for fratricide;
Terms which we trundle smoothly o'er our tongues
Like mere abstractions, empty sounds to which
We join no feeling and attach no form!
As if the soldier died without a wound;
As if the fibres of this godlike frame
Were gored without a pang; as if the wretch,
Who fell in battle, doing bloody deeds,   120
Passed off to Heaven, translated and not killed:
As though he had no wife to pine for him,
No God to judge him! Therefore, evil days
Are coming on us, O my countrymen!
And what if all-avenging Providence,
Strong and retributive, should make us know
The meaning of our words, force us to feel
The desolation and the agony
Of our fierce doings?

          Spare us yet awhile,
Father and God! O! spare us yet awhile!   130
Oh! let not English women drag their flight
Fainting beneath the burthen of their babes,

Of the sweet infants, that but yesterday
Laughed at the breast! Sons, brothers, husbands, all
Who ever gazed with fondness on the forms
Which grew up with you round the same fire-side,
And all who ever heard the sabbath-bells
Without the infidel's scorn, make yourselves pure!
Stand forth! be men! repel an impious foe,
Impious and false, a light yet cruel race,   140
Who laugh away all virtue, mingling mirth
With deeds of murder; and still promising
Freedom, themselves too sensual to be free,
Poison life's amities, and cheat the heart
Of faith and quiet hope, and all that soothes,
And all that lifts the spirit! Stand we forth;
Render them back upon the insulted ocean,
And let them toss as idly on its waves
As the vile sea-weed, which some mountain-blast
Swept from our shores! And oh! may we return   150
Not with a drunken triumph, but with fear,
Repenting of the wrongs with which we stung
So fierce a foe to frenzy!

          I have told,
O Britons! O my brethren! I have told
Most bitter truth, but without bitterness.
Nor deem my zeal or factious or mistimed;
For never can true courage dwell with them,
Who, playing tricks with conscience, dare not look
At their own vices. We have been too long
Dupes of a deep delusion! Some, belike,   160
Groaning with restless enmity, expect
All change from change of constituted power;
As if a Government had been a robe,
On which our vice and wretchedness were tagged
Like fancy-points and fringes, with the robe
Pulled off at pleasure. Fondly these attach
A radical causation to a few
Poor drudges of chastising Providence,
Who borrow all their hues and qualities
From our own folly and rank wickedness,   170
Which gave them birth and nursed them. Others,
     meanwhile,
Dote with a mad idolatry; and all
Who will not fall before their images,
And yield them worship, they are enemies
Even of their country!

          Such have I been deemed.—
But, O dear Britain! O my Mother Isle!
Needs must thou prove a name most dear and holy
To me, a son, a brother, and a friend,
A husband, and a father! who revere
All bonds of natural love, and find them all   180
Within the limits of thy rocky shores.
O native Britain! O my Mother Isle!

How shouldst thou prove aught else but dear and holy
To me, who from thy lakes and mountain-hills,
Thy clouds, thy quiet dales, thy rocks and seas,
Have drunk in all my intellectual life,
All sweet sensations, all ennobling thoughts,
All adoration of the God in nature,
All lovely and all honourable things,
Whatever makes this mortal spirit feel   190
The joy and greatness of its future being?
There lives nor form nor feeling in my soul
Unborrowed from my country! O divine
And beauteous island! thou hast been my sole
And most magnificent temple, in the which
I walk with awe, and sing my stately songs,
Loving the God that made me!—

                              May my fears,
My filial fears, be vain! and may the vaunts
And menace of the vengeful enemy
Pass like the gust, that roared and died away   200
In the distant tree: which heard, and only heard
In this low dell, bowed not the delicate grass.

    But now the gentle dew-fall sends abroad
The fruit-like perfume of the golden furze:
The light has left the summit of the hill,
Though still a sunny gleam lies beautiful,
Aslant the ivied beacon. Now farewell,
Farewell, awhile, O soft and silent spot!
On the green sheep-track, up the heathy hill,
Homeward I wind my way; and lo! recalled   210
From bodings that have well-nigh wearied me,
I find myself upon the brow, and pause
Startled! And after lonely sojourning
In such a quiet and surrounded nook,
This burst of prospect, here the shadowy main,
Dim-tinted, there the mighty majesty
Of that huge amphitheatre of rich
And elmy fields, seems like society—
Conversing with the mind, and giving it
A livelier impulse and a dance of thought!   220
And now, belovéd Stowey! I behold
Thy church-tower, and, methinks, the four huge elms
Clustering, which mark the mansion of my friend;
And close behind them, hidden from my view,
Is my own lowly cottage, where my babe
And my babe's mother dwell in peace! With light
And quickened footsteps thitherward I tend,
Remembering thee, O green and silent dell!
And grateful, that by nature's quietness
And solitary musings, all my heart   230
Is softened, and made worthy to indulge
Love, and the thoughts that yearn for human kind.

[1798]   [1798]

THE NIGHTINGALE

*In the Roman myth Tereus raped his sister-in-law Philomela
and cut out her tongue, but she managed to weave her accusation
into a robe. Then she and her sister, in revenge, tricked Tereus
into eating his own son. When Tereus was about to kill the
sisters, the gods changed him into a hawk, Philomela into a
nightingale, and her sister Procne into a swallow.*

THE NIGHTINGALE

A CONVERSATION POEM, APRIL, 1798

No cloud, no relique of the sunken day
Distinguishes the West, no long thin slip
Of sullen light, no obscure trembling hues.
Come, we will rest on this old mossy bridge!
You see the glimmer of the stream beneath,
But hear no murmuring: it flows silently,
O'er its soft bed of verdure. All is still,
A balmy night! and though the stars be dim,
Yet let us think upon the vernal showers
That gladden the green earth, and we shall find   10
A pleasure in the dimness of the stars.
And hark! the Nightingale begins its song,
'Most musical, most melancholy' bird![1]
A melancholy bird? Oh! idle thought!
In Nature there is nothing melancholy.
But some night-wandering man whose heart was
          pierced
With the remembrance of a grievous wrong,
Or slow distemper, or neglected love,
(And so, poor wretch! filled all things with himself,
And made all gentle sounds tell back the tale   20
Of his own sorrow) he, and such as he,
First named these notes a melancholy strain.
And many a poet echoes the conceit;
Poet who hath been building up the rhyme
When he had better far have stretched his limbs
Beside a brook in mossy forest-dell,
By sun or moon-light, to the influxes
Of shapes and sounds and shifting elements
Surrendering his whole spirit, of his song
And of his fame forgetful! so his fame   30
Should share in Nature's immortality,
A venerable thing! and so his song
Should make all Nature lovelier, and itself
Be loved like Nature! But 'twill not be so;
And youths and maidens most poetical,
Who lose the deepening twilights of the spring
In ball-rooms and hot theatres, they still
Full of meek sympathy must heave their sighs
O'er Philomela's pity-pleading strains.

[1] Quoted from Milton's *Il Penseroso.*

My Friend, and thou, our Sister![2] we have learnt   40
A different lore: we may not thus profane
Nature's sweet voices, always full of love
And joyance! 'Tis the merry Nightingale
That crowds, and hurries, and precipitates
With fast thick warble his delicious notes,
As he were fearful that an April night
Would be too short for him to utter forth
His love-chant, and disburthen his full soul
Of all its music!

        And I know a grove
Of large extent, hard by a castle huge,   50
Which the great lord inhabits not; and so
This grove is wild with tangling underwood,
And the trim walks are broken up, and grass,
Thin grass and king-cups grow within the paths.
But never elsewhere in one place I knew
So many nightingales; and far and near,
In wood and thicket, over the wide grove,
They answer and provoke each other's song,
With skirmish and capricious passagings,
And murmurs musical and swift jug jug,   60
And one low piping sound more sweet than all—
Stirring the air with such a harmony,
That should you close your eyes, you might almost
Forget it was not day! On moonlight bushes,
Whose dewy leaflets are but half-disclosed,
You may perchance behold them on the twigs,
Their bright, bright eyes, their eyes both bright and
    full,
Glistening, while many a glow-worm in the shade
Lights up her love-torch.

        A most gentle Maid,
Who dwelleth in her hospitable home   70
Hard by the castle, and at latest eve
(Even like a Lady vowed and dedicate
To something more than Nature in the grove)
Glides through the pathways; she knows all their
    notes,
That gentle Maid! and oft, a moment's space,
What time the moon was lost behind a cloud,
Hath heard a pause of silence; till the moon
Emerging, hath awakened earth and sky
With one sensation, and those wakeful birds
Have all burst forth in choral minstrelsy,   80
As if some sudden gale had swept at once
A hundred airy harps! And she hath watched
Many a nightingale perch giddily
On blossomy twig still swinging from the breeze,
And to that motion tune his wanton song
Like tipsy Joy that reels with tossing head.

Farewell, O Warbler! till to-morrow eve,
And you, my friends! farewell, a short farewell!
We have been loitering long and pleasantly,
And now for our dear homes.—That strain again!   90
Full fain it would delay me! My dear babe,
Who, capable of no articulate sound,
Mars all things with his imitative lisp,
How he would place his hand beside his ear,
His little hand, the small forefinger up,
And bid us listen! And I deem it wise
To make him Nature's play-mate. He knows well
The evening-star; and once, when he awoke
In most distressful mood (some inward pain
Had made up that strange thing, an infant's dream—
I hurried with him to our orchard-plot,   101
And he beheld the moon, and, hushed at once,
Suspends his sobs, and laughs most silently,
While his fair eyes, that swam with undropped tears,
Did glitter in the yellow moon-beam! Well!—
It is a father's tale: But if that Heaven
Should give me life, his childhood shall grow up
Familiar with these songs, that with the night
He may associate joy.—Once more, farewell,   109
Sweet Nightingale! once more, my friends! farewell.

[1798]   [1798]

THE WANDERINGS OF CAIN

In the story in Genesis, after he murders his brother Abel, Cain is sent off by God a "fugitive and a vagabond" who can no longer receive strength from the earth. Lest anyone kill Cain and end his misery God sets a mark upon him and warns that "whosoever slayeth Cain, vengeance shall be taken on him sevenfold." In the land of Nod, "east of Eden," Cain and his wife have a son Enoch (Enos), after whom Cain names and builds a city.

THE WANDERINGS OF CAIN

PREFATORY NOTE

A PROSE composition, one not in metre at least, seems *primâ facie* to require explanation or apology. It was written in the year 1798, near Nether Stowey, in Somersetshire, at which place (*sanctum et amabile nomen!*[1] rich by so many associations and recollections) the author had taken up his residence in order to enjoy the society and close neighbourhood of a dear and honoured friend, T. Poole, Esq. The work was to have been written in concert with another [Wordsworth], whose name is too venerable within the precincts of genius to be unnecessarily brought into connection with such a trifle, and who was then residing at a small distance from Nether Stowey. The title and subject were suggested by myself, who likewise drew

---

[2] William and Dorothy Wordsworth.

[1] "A name holy and lovable."

out the scheme and the contents for each of the three books or cantos, of which the work was to consist, and which, the reader is to be informed, was to have been finished in one night! My partner undertook the first canto: I the second: and which ever had *done first*, was to set about the third. Almost thirty years have passed by; yet at this moment I cannot without something more than a smile moot the question which of the two things was the more impracticable, for a mind so eminently original to compose another man's thoughts and fancies, or for a taste so austerely pure and simple to imitate the Death of Abel? Methinks I see his grand and noble countenance as at the moment when having despatched my own portion of the task at full finger-speed, I hastened to him with my manuscript—that look of humourous despondency fixed on his almost blank sheet of paper, and then its silent mock-piteous admission of failure struggling with the sense of the exceeding ridiculousness of the whole scheme—which broke up in a laugh: and the Ancient Mariner was written instead.

Years afterward, however, the draft of the plan and proposed incidents, and the portion executed, obtained favour in the eyes of more than one person, whose judgment on a poetic work could not but have weighed with me, even though no parental partiality had been thrown into the same scale, as a make-weight: and I determined on commencing anew, and composing the whole in stanzas, and made some progress in realising this intention, when adverse gales drove my bark off the 'Fortunate Isles' of the Muses: and then other and more momentous interests prompted a different voyage, to firmer anchorage and a securer port. I have in vain tried to recover the lines from the palimpsest tablet of my memory: and I can only offer the introductory stanza, which had been committed to writing for the purpose of procuring a friend's judgment on the metre, as a specimen:—

> Encinctured with a twine of leaves,
> That leafy twine his only dress!
> A lovely Boy was plucking fruits,
> By moonlight, in a wilderness.
> The moon was bright, the air was free,
> And fruits and flowers together grew
> On many a shrub and many a tree:
> And all put on a gentle hue,
> Hanging in the shadowy air
> Like a picture rich and rare.
> It was a climate where, they say,
> The night is more belov'd than day.
> But who that beauteous Boy beguil'd,
> That beauteous Boy to linger here?
> Alone, by night, a little child,
> In place so silent and so wild—
> Has he no friend, no loving mother near?

I have here given the birth, parentage, and premature decease of the 'Wanderings of Cain, a poem,'—intreating, however, my Readers, not to think so meanly of my judgment as to suppose that I either regard or offer it as any excuse for the publication of the following fragment (and

I may add, of one or two others in its neighbourhood) in its primitive crudity. But I should find still greater difficulty in forgiving myself were I to record pro *taedio publico*[2] a set of petty mishaps and annoyances which I myself wish to forget. I must be content therefore with assuring the friendly Reader, that the less he attributes its appearance to the Author's will, choice, or judgment, the nearer to the truth he will be.

S. T. COLERIDGE [1828].

CANTO II

'A LITTLE further, O my father, yet a little further, and we shall come into the open moonlight.' Their road was through a forest of fir-trees; at its entrance the trees stood at distances from each other, and the path was broad, and the moonlight and the moonlight shadows reposed upon it, and appeared quietly to inhabit that solitude. But soon the path winded and became narrow; the sun at high noon sometimes speckled, but never illumined it, and now it was dark as a cavern.   10

'It is dark, O my father!' said Enos, 'but the path under our feet is smooth and soft, and we shall soon come out into the open moonlight.'

'Lead on, my child!' said Cain; 'guide me, little child!' And the innocent little child clasped a finger of the hand which had murdered the righteous Abel, and he guided his father. 'The fir branches drip upon thee, my son.' 'Yea, pleasantly, father, for I ran fast and eagerly to bring thee the pitcher and the cake, and my body is not yet cool. How happy the squirrels   20 are that feed on these fir-trees! they leap from bough to bough, and the old squirrels play round their young ones in the nest. I clomb a tree yesterday at noon, O my father, that I might play with them, but they leaped away from the branches, even to the slender twigs did they leap, and in a moment I beheld them on another tree. Why, O my father, would they not play with me? I would be good to them as thou art good to me: and I groaned to them even as thou groanest when thou givest me to eat, and when thou   30 coverest me at evening, and as often as I stand at thy knee and thine eyes look at me?' Then Cain stopped, and stifling his groans he sank to the earth, and the child Enos stood in the darkness beside him.

And Cain lifted up his voice and cried bitterly, and said, 'The Mighty One that persecuteth me is on this side and on that; he pursueth my soul like the wind, like the sand-blast he passeth through me; he is around me even as the air! O that I might be utterly no more! I desire to die—yea, the things that   40 never had life, neither move they upon the earth—

---

[2] "for the boredom of the public."

behold! they seem precious to mine eyes. O that a man might live without the breath of his nostrils. So I might abide in darkness, and blackness, and an empty space! Yea, I would lie down, I would not rise, neither would I stir my limbs till I became as the rock in the den of the lion, on which the young lion resteth his head whilst he sleepeth. For the torrent that roareth far off hath a voice: and the clouds in heaven look terribly on me; the Mighty One who is against me   50 speaketh in the wind of the cedar grove; and in silence am I dried up.' Then Enos spake to his father, 'Arise, my father, arise, we are but a little way from the place where I found the cake and the pitcher.' And Cain said, 'How knowest thou!' and the child answered—'Behold the bare rocks are a few of thy strides distant from the forest; and while even now thou wert lifting up thy voice, I heard the echo.' Then the child took hold of his father, as if he would raise him: and Cain being faint and feeble rose slowly on his knees   60 and pressed himself against the trunk of a fir, and stood upright and followed the child.

The path was dark till within three strides' length of its termination, when it turned suddenly; the thick black trees formed a low arch, and the moonlight appeared for a moment like a dazzling portal. Enos ran before and stood in the open air; and when Cain, his father, emerged from the darkness, the child was affrighted. For the mighty limbs of Cain were wasted as by fire; his hair was as the matted curls on the   70 bison's forehead, and so glared his fierce and sullen eye beneath; and the black abundant locks on either side, a rank and tangled mass, were stained and scorched, as though the grasp of a burning iron hand had striven to rend them; and his countenance told in a strange and terrible language of agonies that had been, and were, and were still to continue to be.

The scene around was desolate; as far as the eye could reach it was desolate; the bare rocks faced each other, and left a long and wide interval of thin   80 white sand. You might wander on and look round and round, and peep into the crevices of the rocks and discover nothing that acknowledged the influence of the seasons. There was no spring, no summer, no autumn: and the winter's snow, that would have been lovely, fell not on these hot rocks and scorching sands. Never morning lark had poised himself over this desert; but the huge serpent often hissed there beneath the talons of the vulture, and the vulture screamed, his wings imprisoned within the coils   90 of the serpent. The pointed and shattered summits of the ridges of the rocks made a rude mimicry of human concerns, and seemed to prophecy mutely of things that then were not; steeples, and battlements, and ships with naked masts. As far from the wood as a boy might sling a pebble of the brook, there was one rock by itself at a small distance from the main ridge. It had been precipitated there perhaps by the groan which the Earth uttered when our first father fell. Before you approached, it appeared to lie flat on   100 the ground, but its base slanted from its point, and between its point and the sands a tall man might stand upright. It was here that Enos had found the pitcher and cake, and to this place he led his father. But ere they had reached the rock they beheld a human shape: his back was towards them, and they were advancing unperceived, when they heard him smite his breast and cry aloud, 'Woe is me! woe is me! I must never die again, and yet I am perishing with thirst and hunger.'   110

Pallid, as the reflection of the sheeted lightning on the heavy-sailing night-cloud, became the face of Cain; but the child Enos took hold of the shaggy skin, his father's robe, and raised his eyes to his father, and listening whispered, 'Ere yet I could speak, I am sure, O my father, that I heard that voice. Have not I often said that I remembered a sweet voice? O my father! this is it': and Cain trembled exceedingly. The voice was sweet indeed, but it was thin and querulous, like that of a feeble slave in misery,   120 who despairs altogether, yet can not refrain himself from weeping and lamentation. And, behold! Enos glided forward, and creeping softly round the base of the rock, stood before the stranger, and looked up into his face. And the Shape shrieked, and turned round, and Cain beheld him, that his limbs and his face were those of his brother Abel whom he had killed! And Cain stood like one who struggles in his sleep because of the exceeding terribleness of a dream.

Thus as he stood in silence and darkness of   130 soul, the Shape fell at his feet, and embraced his knees, and cried out with a bitter outcry, 'Thou eldest born of Adam, whom Eve, my mother, brought forth, cease to torment me! I was feeding my flocks in green pastures by the side of quiet rivers, and thou killedst me; and now I am in misery.' Then Cain closed his eyes, and hid them with his hands; and again he opened his eyes, and looked around him, and said to Enos, 'What beholdest thou? Didst thou hear a voice, my son?' 'Yes, my father, I beheld a man   140 in unclean garments, and he uttered a sweet voice, full of lamentation.' Then Cain raised up the Shape that was like Abel, and said:—'The Creator of our father, who had respect unto thee, and unto thy offering, wherefore hath he forsaken thee?' Then the Shape shrieked a second time, and rent his garment, and his naked skin was like the white sands beneath their feet; and he shrieked yet a third time, and threw himself on his face upon the sand that was black with

the shadow of the rock, and Cain and Enos sate 150
beside him; the child by his right hand, and Cain by
his left. They were all three under the rock, and
within the shadow. The Shape that was like Abel
raised himself up, and spake to the child, 'I know
where the cold waters are, but I may not drink, where-
fore didst thou then take away my pitcher?' But Cain
said, 'Didst thou not find favour in the sight of the
Lord thy God?' The Shape answered, 'The Lord is
God of the living only, the dead have another God.'
Then the child Enos lifted up his eyes and 160
prayed; but Cain rejoiced secretly in his heart.
'Wretched shall they be all the days of their mortal
life,' exclaimed the Shape, 'who sacrifice worthy and
acceptable sacrifices to the God of the dead; but after
death their toil ceaseth. Woe is me, for I was well
beloved by the God of the living, and cruel wert thou,
O my brother, who didst snatch me away from his
power and his dominion.' Having uttered these words,
he rose suddenly, and fled over the sands: and Cain
said in his heart, 'The curse of the Lord is on 170
me; but who is the God of the dead?' and he ran after
the Shape, and the Shape fled shrieking over the
sands, and the sands rose like white mists behind the
steps of Cain, but the feet of him that was like Abel
disturbed not the sands. He greatly outrun Cain, and
turning short, he wheeled round, and came again to
the rock where they had been sitting, and where Enos
still stood; and the child caught hold of his garment as
he passed by, and he fell upon the ground. And Cain
stopped, and beholding him not, said, 'he has 180
passed into the dark woods,' and he walked slowly
back to the rocks; and when he reached it the child
told him that he had caught hold of his garment as he
passed by, and that the man had fallen upon the
ground: and Cain once more sate beside him, and said,
'Abel my brother, I would lament for thee, but that
the spirit within me is withered, and burnt up with
extreme agony. Now, I pray thee, by thy flocks, and by
thy pastures, and by the quiet rivers which thou
lovedst, that thou tell me all that thou knowest. 190
Who is the God of the dead? where doth he make his
dwelling? what sacrifices are acceptable unto him? for
I have offered, but have not been received; I have
prayed, and have not been heard; and how can I be
afflicted more than I already am?' The Shape arose
and answered, 'O that thou hadst had pity on me as I
will have pity on thee. Follow me, Son of Adam! and
bring thy child with thee!'

And they three passed over the white sands between
the rocks, silent as the shadows. . 200

[1798]   [1828]

THE BALLAD OF THE DARK LADIÉ

A FRAGMENT

BENEATH yon birch with silver bark,
And boughs so pendulous and fair,
The brook falls scatter'd down the rock:
    And all is mossy there!

And there upon the moss she sits,
The Dark Ladié in silent pain;
The heavy tear is in her eye,
    And drops and swells again.

Three times she sends her little page
Up the castled mountain's breast,   10
If he might find the Knight that wears
    The Griffin for his crest.

The sun was sloping down the sky,
And she had linger'd there all day,
Counting moments, dreaming fears—
    Oh wherefore can he stay?

She hears a rustling o'er the brook,
She sees far off a swinging bough!
''Tis He! 'Tis my betrothéd Knight!
    Lord Falkland, it is Thou!'   20

She springs, she clasps him round the neck,
She sobs a thousand hopes and fears,
Her kisses glowing on his cheeks
    She quenches with her tears.

    *   *   *   *

'My friends with rude ungentle words
They scoff and bid me fly to thee!
O give me shelter in thy breast!
    O shield and shelter me!

'My Henry, I have given thee much,
I gave what I can ne'er recall,   30
I gave my heart, I gave my peace,
    O Heaven! I gave thee all.'

The Knight made answer to the Maid,
While to his heart he held her hand,
'Nine castles hath my noble sire,
    None statelier in the land.

'The fairest one shall be my love's,
The fairest castle of the nine!
Wait only till the stars peep out,
    The fairest shall be thine: 40

'Wait only till the hand of eve
Hath wholly closed yon western bars,
And through the dark we two will steal
Beneath the twinkling stars!'—

'The dark? the dark? No! not the dark?
The twinkling stars? How, Henry? How?'
O God! 'twas in the eye of noon
He pledged his sacred vow!

And in the eye of noon my love
Shall lead me from my mother's door,   50
Sweet boys and girls all clothed in white
Strewing flowers before:

But first the nodding minstrels go
With music meet for lordly bowers,
The children next in snow-white vests,
Strewing buds and flowers!

And then my love and I shall pace,
My jet black hair in pearly braids,
Between our comely bachelors
And blushing bridal maids.   60

*   *   *   *

[1798]   [1834]

KUBLA KHAN

*Kubla Khan, grandson of Ghengis Khan, founded the Mongol
dynasty in China in the thirteenth century. The passage from
Samuel Purchas,* Purchas His Pilgrimage *(1613), reads as
follows: "In Xamdu did Cublai Can build a stately Palace,
encompassing sixteene miles of plaine ground with a wall,
wherein are fertile Meddowes, pleasant springs, delightfull
Streames, and all sorts of beasts of chase and game, and in the
middest thereof a sumptuous house of pleasure, which may be
removed from place to place." In a manuscript note Coleridge
expanded his account, below, of the poem's composition by
adding: "This fragment with a good deal more, not recoverable,
composed, in a sort of reverie brought on by two grains of opium,
taken to check a dysentery, at a farmhouse between Porlock and
Linton, a quarter of a mile from Culbone Church, in the fall of the
year, 1797." The importance of drug-induced dreams in this and
other poems has been a subject of continuing controversy. See
E. Schneider,* Coleridge, Opium and "Kubla Khan" *(1953),
the essay by Marcovitz, and the book by Hayter (in General
Bibliography).*

KUBLA KHAN

OR, A VISON IN A DREAM. A FRAGMENT.

THE following fragment is here published at the request
of a poet of great and deserved celebrity,[1] and, as far as the

[1] Lord Byron.

Author's own opinions are concerned, rather as a psycho-
logical curiosity, than on the ground of any supposed *poetic*
merits.

In the summer of the year 1797 [1798], the Author, then
in ill health, had retired to a lonely farm-house between
Porlock and Linton, on the Exmoor confines of Somerset
and Devonshire. In consequence of a slight indisposition,
an anodyne had been prescribed, from the effects of 10
which he fell asleep in his chair at the moment that he was
reading the following sentence, or words of the same sub-
stance, in 'Purchas's Pilgrimage': 'Here the Khan Kubla
commanded a palace to be built, and a stately garden there-
unto. And thus ten miles of fertile ground were inclosed
with a wall.' The Author continued for about three hours
in a profound sleep, at least of the external senses, during
which time he has the most vivid confidence, that he could
not have composed less than from two to three hundred
lines; if that indeed can be called composition in 20
which all the images rose up before him as *things*, with a
parallel production of the correspondent expressions, with-
out any sensation or consciousness of effort. On awaking
he appeared to himself to have a distinct recollection of the
whole, and taking his pen, ink, and paper, instantly and
eagerly wrote down the lines that are here preserved. At
this moment he was unfortunately called out by a person on
business from Porlock, and detained by him above an hour,
and on his return to his room, found, to his no small sur-
prise and mortification, that though he still retained 30
some vague and dim recollection of the general purport of
the vision, yet, with the exception of some eight or ten
scattered lines and images, all the rest had passed away
like the images on the surface of a stream into which a
stone has been cast, but, alas! without the after restoration
of the latter!

Then all the charm
Is broken—all that phantom-world so fair
Vanishes, and a thousand circlets spread,
And each mis-shape['s] the other. Stay awhile, 40
Poor youth! who scarcely dar'st lift up thine eyes—
The stream will soon renew its smoothness, soon
The visions will return! And lo, he stays,
And soon the fragments dim of lovely forms
Come trembling back, unite, and now once more
The pool becomes a mirror.[2]

Yet from the still surviving recollections in his mind, the
Author has frequently purposed to finish for himself what
had been originally, as it were, given to him. Σαμερον αδιον
ασω[3]: but the to-morrow is yet to come. 50
As a contrast to this vision, I have annexed a fragment
of a very different character, describing with equal
fidelity the dream of pain and disease.

[2] Coleridge quotes his own poem *The Picture*; reprinted p. 489.
[3] Quoted from Theocritus: "Today I'll sing a sweeter song,"
later altered to read "tomorrow."

In Xanadu did Kubla Khan.
A stately pleasure-dome decree:
Where Alph, the sacred river, ran
Through caverns measureless to man
    Down to a sunless sea.
So twice five miles of fertile ground
With walls and towers were girdled round:
And there were gardens bright with sinuous rills,
Where blossomed many an incense-bearing tree;
And here were forests ancient as the hills,   10
Enfolding sunny spots of greenery.

But oh! that deep romantic chasm which slanted
Down the green hill athwart a cedarn cover!
A savage place! as holy and enchanted
As e'er beneath a waning moon was haunted
By woman wailing for her demon-lover!
And from this chasm, with ceaseless turmoil
    seething,
As if this earth in fast thick pants were breathing,
A mighty fountain momently was forced:
Amid whose swift half-intermitted burst   20
Huge fragments vaulted like rebounding hail,
Or chaffy grain beneath the thresher's flail:
And 'mid these dancing rocks at once and ever
It flung up momently the sacred river.
Five miles meandering with a mazy motion
Through wood and dale the sacred river ran,
Then reached the caverns measureless to man,
And sank in tumult to a lifeless ocean:
And 'mid this tumult Kubla heard from far
Ancestral voices prophesying war!   30
    The shadow of the dome of pleasure
    Floated midway on the waves;
    Where was heard the mingled measure
    From the fountain and the caves.
It was a miracle of rare device,
A sunny pleasure-dome with caves of ice!

    A damsel with a dulcimer
    In a vision once I saw:
    It was an Abyssinian maid,
    And on her dulcimer she played,   40
    Singing of Mount Abora.
    Could I revive within me
    Her symphony and song,
    To such a deep delight 'twould win me,
That with music loud and long,
I would build that dome in air,
That sunny dome! those caves of ice!
And all who heard should see them there,
And all should cry, Beware! Beware!
His flashing eyes, his floating hair!   50

Weave a circle round him thrice,
And close your eyes with holy dread,
For he on honey-dew hath fed,
And drunk the milk of Paradise.

[1798]   [1816]

RECANTATION

In one note to this poem (1798) Coleridge says: "The following amusing Tale gives a very humourous description of the French Revolution, which is represented as an Ox." In another note handwritten and partly illegible over a copy of the poem he wrote: "Written when fears were entertained of an invasion, and Mr. Sheridan and Mr. Tierney were absurdly represented as having recanted because to [the French Revolution?] in its origin they, [having been favourable changed their opinion when the Revolutionists became unfaithful to their principles?]"

RECANTATION
ILLUSTRATED IN THE STORY OF THE MAD OX

I

An Ox, long fed with musty hay,
    And work'd with yoke and chain,
Was turn'd out on an April day,
When fields are in their best array,
And growing grasses sparkle gay
    At once with Sun and rain.

II

The grass was fine, the Sun was bright—
    With truth I may aver it;
The ox was glad, as well he might,
Thought a green meadow no bad sight,   10
And frisk'd,—to shew his huge delight,
    Much like a beast of spirit.

III

'*Stop, neighbours, stop, why these alarms?
    The ox is only glad!*'
But still they pour from cots and farms—
'Halloo!' the parish is up in arms,
(A *hoaxing*-hunt has always charms)
    'Halloo! the ox is mad.'

IV

The frighted beast scamper'd about—
    Plunge! through the hedge he drove: 20
The mob pursue with hideous rout,
A bull-dog fastens on his snout;
'He gores the dog! his tongue hangs out!
    He's mad, he's mad, by Jove!'

V

'STOP, NEIGHBOURS, STOP!' aloud did call
　A sage of sober hue.
But all at once, on him they fall,
And women squeak and children squall,
'What? would you have him toss us all?
　And dam'me, who are you?'　　　　30

VI

Oh! hapless sage! his ears they stun,
　And curse him o'er and o'er!
'You bloody-minded dog! (cries one,)
To slit your windpipe were good fun,
'Od blast you for an *impious* son
　Of a Presbyterian wh—re!'

VII

'You'd have him gore the Parish-priest,
　And run against the altar!
You fiend!' the sage his warnings ceas'd,
And north and south, and west and east,　40
Halloo! they follow the poor beast,
　Mat, Dick, Tom, Bob and Walter.

VIII

Old Lewis ('twas his evil day),
　Stood trembling in his shoes;
The ox was his—what cou'd he say?
His legs were stiffen'd with dismay,
The ox ran o'er him mid the fray,
　And gave him his death's bruise.

IX

The frighted beast ran on—(but here,
　No tale, (tho' in print, more true is)　　50
My Muse stops short in mid career—
Nay, gentle Reader, do not sneer!
I cannot chuse but drop a tear,
　A tear for good old Lewis!)

X

The frighted beast ran through the town,
　All follow'd, boy and dad,
Bull-dog, parson, shopman, clown:
The publicans rush'd from the Crown,
'Halloo! hamstring him! cut him down!'
　THEY DROVE THE POOR OX MAD.　60

XI

Should you a Rat to madness tease
　Why ev'n a Rat may plague you:
There's no Philosopher but sees
That Rage and Fear are one disease—
Though that may burn, and this may freeze,
　They're both alike the Ague.

XII

And so this Ox, in frantic mood,
　Fac'd round like any Bull!
The mob turn'd tail, and he pursued,
Till they with heat and fright were stew'd,　70
And not a chick of all this brood
　But had his belly full!

XIII

Old Nick's astride the beast, 'tis clear!
　Old Nicholas, to a tittle!
But all agree he'd disappear,
Would but the Parson venture near,
And through his teeth,* right o'er the steer,
　Squirt out some fasting-spittle.

XIV

Achilles was a warrior fleet,
　The Trojans he could worry:　　　　80
Our Parson too was swift of feet,
But shew'd it chiefly in retreat:
The victor Ox scour'd down the street,
　The mob fled hurry-scurry.

XV

Through gardens, lanes and fields new-
　　plough'd,
　Through *his* hedge, and through *her* hedge,
He plung'd and toss'd and bellow'd loud—
Till in his madness he grew proud
To see this helter-skelter crowd
　That had more wrath than courage!　　90

XVI

Alas! to mend the breaches wide
　He made for these poor ninnies,
They all must work, whate'er betide,
Both days and months, and pay beside
(Sad news for Av'rice and for Pride),
　A *sight* of golden guineas!

* According to the superstition of the West-Countries, if you
meet the Devil, you may either cut him in half with a straw,
or force him to disappear by spitting over his horns.

XVII

But here once more to view did pop
   The man that kept his senses—
And now he cried,—'Stop, neighbours, stop!
The Ox is mad! I would not swop,   100
No! not a school-boy's farthing top
   For all the parish-fences.'

XVIII

'The Ox is mad! Ho! Dick, Bob, Mat!
   'What means this coward fuss?
Ho! stretch this rope across the plat—
'Twill trip him up—or if not that,
Why, dam'me! we must lay him flat—
   See! here's my blunderbuss.'

XIX

'A lying dog! just now he said
   The Ox was only glad—   110
Let's break his Presbyterian head!'
'Hush!' quoth the sage, 'you've been misled;
No quarrels now! let's all make head,
   YOU DROVE THE POOR OX MAD.'

XX

As thus I sat, in careless chat,
   With the morning's wet newspaper,
In eager haste, without his hat,
As blind and blund'ring as a bat,
In came that fierce Aristocrat,
   Our pursy woollen-draper.   120

XXI

And so my Muse per force drew bit;
   And in he rush'd and panted!
'Well, have you heard?' No, not a whit.
'What, *ha'nt* you heard?' Come, out with it!
'That Tierney votes for Mister PITT,
   And Sheridan's *recanted*!'

[1798]   [1798]

HEXAMETERS

William and Dorothea are Wordsworth and his sister Dorothy. This poem was sent to them in a letter during the winter they all spent in Germany.

HEXAMETERS

WILLIAM, my teacher, my friend! dear William and
   dear Dorothea!
Smooth out the folds of my letter, and place it on desk
   or on table;

Place it on table or desk; and your right hands loosely
   half-closing,*
Gently sustain them in air, and extending the digit
   didactic,
Rest it a moment on each of the forks of the five-
   forkéd left hand,
Twice on the breadth of the thumb, and once on the
   tip of each finger;
Read with a nod of the head in a humouring recitativo;
And, as I live, you will see my hexameters hopping
   before you.
This is a galloping measure; a hop, and a trot, and a
   gallop!

All my hexameters fly, like stags pursued by the stag-
   hounds,
Breathless and panting, and ready to drop, yet flying
   still onwards,†
I would full fain pull in my hard-mouthed runway
   hunter;
But our English Spondeans are clumsy yet impotent
   curb-reins;
And so to make him go slowly, no way left have I but
   to lame him.

William, my head and my heart! dear Poet that feelest
   and thinkest!
Dorothy, eager of soul, my most affectionate sister!
Many a mile, O! many a wearisome mile are ye
   distant,
Long, long comfortless roads, with no one eye that
   doth know us.
O! it is all too far to send you mockeries idle:
Yea, and I feel it not right! But O! my friends, my
   belovéd!   20
Feverish and wakeful I lie,—I am weary of feeling and
   thinking.
Every thought is worn *down*, I am weary yet cannot be
   vacant.
Five long hours have I tossed, rheumatic heats, dry
   and flushing,
Gnawing behind in my head, and wandering and
   throbbing about me,
Busy and tiresome, my friends, as the beat of the
   boding night-spider.‡

I forgot the beginning of the line:

. . . my eyes are a burthen,
Now unwillingly closed, now open and aching with
   darkness.

* False metre.
† 'Still flying onwards' were perhaps better.
‡ False metre.

O! what a life is the eye! what a strange and
    inscrutable essence!
Him that is utterly blind, nor glimpses the fire that
    warms him;
Him that never beheld the swelling breast of his
    mother;   30
Him that smiled in his gladness as a babe that smiles
    in its slumber;
Even for him it exists, it moves and stirs in its prison;
Lives with a separate life, and 'Is it a Spirit?' he
    murmurs:
'Sure it has thoughts of its own, and to see is only a
    language.'

*There was a great deal more, which I have forgotten.
. . . The last line which I wrote, I remember, and write it
for the truth of the sentiment, scarcely less true in com-
pany than in pain and solitude:—*

William, my head and my heart! dear William and
    dear Dorothea!
You have all in each other; but I am lonely, and want
    you!

[1798–99]   [1851]

THE HOMERIC HEXAMETER[1]
DESCRIBED AND EXEMPLIFIED

STRONGLY it bears us along in swelling and limitless
    billows,
Nothing before and nothing behind but the sky and
    the ocean.

[1799?]   [1834]

THE OVIDIAN ELEGIAC METRE
DESCRIBED AND EXEMPLIFIED

IN the hexemeter rises the fountain's silvery column;
In the pentameter aye falling in melody back.

[1799]   [1834]

---

[1] These two pairs of couplets are translated from Friedrich
Schiller:

DER EPISCHE HEXAMETER
Schwindelnd trägt er dich fort auf rastlos strömenden Wogen;
Hinter dir siehst du, du siehst vor dir nur Himmel und Meer.

DAS DISTICHON
Im Hexameter steigt des Springquells flüssige Säule;
Im Pentameter drauf fällt sie melodisch herab.

LINES
WRITTEN IN THE ALBUM AT ELBINGERODE,
IN THE HARTZ FOREST

I STOOD on Brocken's* sovran height, and saw
Woods crowding upon woods, hills over hills,
A surging scene, and only limited
By the blue distance. Heavily my way
Downward I dragged through fir groves evermore,
Where bright green moss heaves in sepulchral
    forms
Speckled with sunshine; and, but seldom heard,
The sweet bird's song became a hollow sound;
And the breeze, murmuring indivisibly,
Preserved its solemn murmur most distinct   10
From many a note of many a waterfall,
And the brook's chatter; 'mid whose islet-stones
The dingy kidling with its tinkling bell
Leaped frolicsome, or old romantic goat
Sat, his white beard slow waving. I moved on
In low and languid mood:† for I had found
That outward forms, the loftiest, still receive
Their finer influence from the Life within;—
Fair cyphers else: fair, but of import vague
Or unconcerning, where the heart not finds   20
History or prophecy of friend, or child,
Or gentle maid, our first and early love,
Or father, or the venerable name
Of our adoréd country! O thou Queen,
Thou delegated Deity of Earth,
O dear, dear England! how my longing eye
Turned westward, shaping in the steady clouds
Thy sands and high white cliffs!

                         My native Land!
Filled with the thought of thee this heart was proud,
Yea, mine eye swam with tears: that all the view   30
From sovran Brocken, woods and woody hills,
Floated away, like a departing dream,
Feeble and dim! Stranger, these impulses
Blame thou not lightly; nor will I profane,
With hasty judgment or injurious doubt,
That man's sublimer spirit, who can feel

---

* The highest Mountain in the Harz, and indeed in North
Germany.
†   ——WHEN I have gaz'd
    From some high eminence on goodly vales,
    And cots and villages embower'd below,
    The thought would rise that all to me was strange
    Amid the scenes so fair, nor one small spot
    Where my tired mind might rest and call it home.
                    Southey's *Hymn to the Penates.*

That God is everywhere! the God who framed
Mankind to be one mighty family,
Himself our Father, and the World our Home.

[1799]   [1799]

LOVE

ALL thoughts, all passions, all delights,
Whatever stirs this mortal frame,
All are but ministers of Love,
        And feed his sacred flame.

Oft in my waking dreams do I
Live o'er again that happy hour,
When midway on the mount I lay,
        Beside the ruined tower.

The moonshine, stealing o'er the scene
Had blended with the lights of eve;   10
And she was there, my hope, my joy,
        My own dear Genevieve!

She leant against the arméd man,
The statue of the arméd knight;
She stood and listened to my lay,
        Amid the lingering light.

Few sorrows hath she of her own,
My hope! my joy! my Genevieve!
She loves me best, whene'er I sing
        The songs that make her grieve.   20

I played a soft and doleful air,
I sang an old and moving story—
An old rude song, that suited well
        That ruin wild and hoary.

She listened with a flitting blush,
With downcast eyes and modest grace;
For well she knew, I could not choose
        But gaze upon her face.

I told her of the Knight that wore
Upon his shield a burning brand;   30
And that for ten long years he wooed
        The Lady of the Land.

I told her how he pined: and ah!
The deep, the low, the pleading tone
With which I sang another's love,
        Interpreted my own.

She listened with a flitting blush,
With downcast eyes, and modest grace;
And she forgave me, that I gazed
        Too fondly on her face!   40

But when I told the cruel scorn
That crazed that bold and lovely Knight,
And that he crossed the mountain-woods,
        Nor rested day nor night;

That sometimes from the savage den,
And sometimes from the darksome shade,
And sometimes starting up at once
        In green and sunny glade,—

There came and looked him in the face
An angel beautiful and bright;   50
And that he knew it was a Fiend,
        This miserable Knight!

And that unknowing what he did,
He leaped amid a murderous band,
And saved from outrage worse than death
        The Lady of the Land!

And how she wept, and clasped his knees;
And how she tended him in vain—
And ever strove to expiate
        The scorn that crazed his brain;—   60

And that she nursed him in a cave;
And how his madness went away,
When on the yellow forest-leaves
        A dying man he lay;—

His dying words—but when I reached
That tenderest strain of all the ditty,
My faultering voice and pausing harp
        Disturbed her soul with pity!

All impulses of soul and sense
Had thrilled my guileless Genevieve;   70
The music and the doleful tale,
        The rich and balmy eve;

And hopes, and fears that kindle hope,
An undistinguishable throng,
And gentle wishes long subdued,
        Subdued and cherished long!

She wept with pity and delight,
She blushed with love, and virgin-shame;
And like the murmur of a dream,
        I heard her breathe my name.   80

Her bosom heaved—she stepped aside,
As conscious of my look she stepped—
  Then suddenly, with timorous eye
    She fled to me and wept.

She half enclosed me with her arms,
She pressed me with a meek embrace;
  And bending back her head, looked up.
    And gazed upon my face.

'Twas partly love, and partly fear,
And partly 'twas a bashful art,   90
  That I might rather feel, than see,
    The swelling of her heart.

I calmed her fears, and she was calm,
And told her love with virgin pride;
  And so I won my Genevieve,
    My bright and beauteous Bride.

[1799]   [1799]

APOLOGIA PRO VITA SUA[1]

THE poet in his lone yet genial hour
Gives to his eyes a magnifying power:
Or rather he emancipates his eyes
From the black shapeless accidents of size—
In unctuous cones of kindling coal,
Or smoke upwreathing from the pipe's trim bole,
  His gifted ken can see
  Phantoms of sublimity.

[1800]   [1822]

_____

THE MAD MONK

*There has recently been some question about Coleridge's author-
ship of this poem, one argument being that it is merely his re-
working of an early Wordsworth poem, the other that it is instead
Coleridge's deliberate parody of Wordsworth's manner. The con-
troversy centers on the close resemblance between lines 9–20 and
the first stanza of Wordsworth's Immortality Ode, p. 257. See
S. M. Parrish and D. V. Erdman, "Who Wrote The Mad
Monk? A Debate," Bulletin of the New York Public
Library, LXIV (1960), 209–237.*

_____

THE MAD MONK

I HEARD a voice from Etna's[2] side;
  Where o'er a cavern's mouth
    That fronted to the south

◇◇◇◇◇◇◇◇◇◇◇◇◇◇◇◇◇◇◇◇◇◇◇◇◇◇◇◇◇◇◇◇◇◇◇◇

  [1] "Apology for His Life."
  [2] Mt. Etna, volcano in Sicily.

A chestnut spread its umbrage wide:
A hermit or a monk the man might be;
  But him I could not see:
And thus the music flow'd along,
In melody most like to old Sicilian song:

'There was a time when earth, and sea, and skies,
  The bright green vale, and forest's dark recess,   10
With all things, lay before mine eyes
  In steady loveliness:
But now I feel, on earth's uneasy scene,
  Such sorrows as will never cease;—
  I only ask for peace;
If I must live to know that such a time has been!'
A silence then ensued:
    Till from the cavern came
    A voice;—it was the same!
And thus, in mournful tone, its dreary plaint
  renew'd: 20

'Last night, as o'er the sloping turf I trod,
  The smooth green turf, to me a vision gave
Beneath mine eyes, the sod—
  The roof of Rosa's grave!

My heart has need with dreams like these to strive,
  For, when I woke, beneath mine eyes I found
  The plot of mossy ground,
On which we oft have sat when Rosa was alive.—
Why must the rock, and margin of the flood,
  Why must the hills so many flow'rets bear,   30
Whose colours to a *murder'd* maiden's blood,
  Such sad resemblance wear?—

'*I struck the wound,*—this hand of mine!
For Oh, thou maid divine,
  I lov'd to agony!
The youth whom thou call'd'st thine
  Did never love like me!

'Is it the stormy clouds above
  That flash'd so red a gleam?
  On yonder downward trickling stream?—   40
'Tis not the blood of her I love.—
The sun torments me from his western bed,
  Oh, let him cease for ever to diffuse
  Those crimson spectre hues!
Oh, let me lie in peace, and be for ever dead!'

Here ceas'd the voice. In deep dismay,
Down thro' the forest I pursu'd my way.

[1800]   [1800]

ODE TO TRANQUILLITY

TRANQUILLITY! thou better name
Than all the family of Fame!
Thou ne'er wilt leave my riper age
To low intrigue, or factious rage;
For oh! dear child of thoughtful Truth,
To thee I gave my early youth,
And left the bark, and blest the steadfast shore,
Ere yet the tempest rose and scared me with its roar.

Who late and lingering seeks thy shrine,
On him but seldom, Power divine,   10
Thy spirit rests! Satiety
And Sloth, poor counterfeits of thee,
Mock the tired worldling. Idle Hope
And dire Remembrance interlope,
To vex the feverish slumbers of the mind:
The bubble floats before, the spectre stalks behind.

But me thy gentle hand will lead
At morning through the accustomed mead;
And in the sultry summer's heat
Will build me up a mossy seat;   20
And when the gust of Autumn crowds,
And breaks the busy moonlight clouds,
Thou best the thought canst raise, the heart attune,
Light as the busy clouds, calm as the gliding moon.

The feeling heart, the searching soul,
To thee I dedicate the whole!
And while within myself I trace
The greatness of some future race,
Aloof with hermit-eye I scan
The present works of present man—   30
A wild and dream-like trade of blood and guile,
Too foolish for a tear, too wicked for a smile!

[1801]   [1801]

---

*"Asra" is Coleridge's transliteration of "Sara"—here, Sara
Hutchinson. See note to* Dejection, *p. 482.*

TO ASRA

ARE there two things, of all which men possess,
That are so like each other and so near,
As mutual Love seems like to Happiness?
Dear Asra, woman beyond utterance dear!
This Love which ever welling at my heart,
Now in its living fount doth heave and fall,
Now overflowing pours thro' every part

Of all my frame, and fills and changes all,
Like vernal waters springing up through snow,
This Love that seeming great beyond the power   10
Of growth, yet seemeth ever more to grow,
Could I transmute the whole to one rich Dower
Of Happy Life, and give it all to Thee,
Thy lot, methinks, were Heaven, thy age, Eternity!

[1801]   [1893]

AN ODE TO THE RAIN

*This ode was written at Wordsworth's cottage at Grasmere, when
Coleridge, William, and Dorothy were meeting for the first time
in several months.*

AN ODE TO THE RAIN

COMPOSED BEFORE DAYLIGHT, ON THE MORNING
APPOINTED FOR THE DEPARTURE OF A VERY
WORTHY, BUT NOT VERY PLEASANT VISITOR,
WHOM IT WAS FEARED THE RAIN MIGHT
DETAIN

I

I KNOW it is dark; and though I have lain,
Awake, as I guess, an hour or twain,
I have not once opened the lids of my eyes,
But I lie in the dark, as a blind man lies.
O Rain! that I lie listening to,
You're but a doleful sound at best:
I owe you little thanks, 'tis true,
For breaking thus my needful rest!
Yet if, as soon as it is light,
O Rain! you will but take your flight,   10
I'll neither rail, nor malice keep,
Though sick and sore for want of sleep.
But only now, for this one day,
Do go, dear Rain! do go away!

II

O Rain! with your dull two-fold sound,
The clash hard by, and the murmur all round!
You know, if you know aught, that we,
Both night and day, but ill agree:
For days and months, and almost years,
Have limped on through this vale of tears,   20
Since body of mine, and rainy weather,
Have lived on easy terms together.
Yet if, as soon as it is light,
O Rain! you will but take your flight,
Though you should come again to-morrow,
And bring with you both pain and sorrow;

Though stomach should sicken and knees
    should swell—
I'll nothing speak of you but well.
But only now for this one day,
Do go, dear Rain! do go away!   30

III

    Dear Rain! I ne'er refused to say
You're a good creature in your way;
Nay, I could write a book myself,
Would fit a parson's lower shelf,
Showing how very good you are.—
What then? sometimes it must be fair
And if sometimes, why not to-day?
Do go, dear Rain! do go away!

IV

    Dear Rain! if I've been cold and shy,
Take no offence! I'll tell you why.   40
A dear old Friend e'en now is here,
And with him came my sister dear;
After long absence now first met,
Long months by pain and grief beset—
We three dear friends! in truth, we groan
Impatiently to be alone.
We three, you mark! and not one more!
The strong wish makes my spirit sore.
We have so much to talk about,
So many sad things to let out;   50
So many tears in our eye-corners,
Sitting like little Jacky Horners—
In short, as soon as it is day,
Do go, dear Rain! do go away.

V

    And this I'll swear to you, dear Rain!
Whenever you shall come again,
Be you as dull as e'er you could
(And by the bye 'tis understood,
You're not so pleasant as you're good),
Yet, knowing well your worth and place,   60
I'll welcome you with cheerful face;
And though you stayed a week or more,
Were ten times duller than before;
Yet with kind heart, and right good will,
I'll sit and listen to you still;
Nor should you go away, dear Rain!
Uninvited to remain.
But only now, for this one day,
Do go, dear Rain! do go away.

[1801]   [1802]

DEJECTION: AN ODE

Coleridge's attachment to Sara Hutchinson began in 1799, and for many years it was his imaginative alternative to the domestic deprivations he felt he suffered in his marriage to Sara Coleridge. (See the selections from the Notebooks, *and the letters to Godwin and Wedgwood for 1801–1802, pp. 509–512.) The first version of the poem was written just after Coleridge had heard Wordsworth read the first four stanzas of the Immortality Ode, and Wordsworth in turn began working on Resolution and Independence shortly after hearing this letter. The second version of* Dejection—*addressed this time to Wordsworth—was published in the* Morning Post *on October 4, 1802: the day William married Mary Hutchinson, and Coleridge's own wedding anniversary. The third, and final, version was first published in* Sibylline Leaves (1817).

[FIRST VERSION]

A LETTER TO SARA HUTCHINSON

April 4, 1802.—Sunday Evening.

WELL! if the Bard was weatherwise, who made
The grand old Ballad of Sir Patrick Spence,
This Night, so tranquil now, will not go hence
Unrous'd by winds, that ply a busier trade
Than that, which moulds yon clouds in lazy flakes,
Or the dull sobbing Draft, that drones & rakes
Upon the Strings of this Eolian Lute,[1]
    Which better far were mute.
    For, lo! the New Moon, winter-bright!
And overspread with phantom Light,   10
(With swimming phantom Light o'erspread
But rimm'd & circled with a silver Thread)
I see the Old Moon in her Lap, foretelling
The coming-on of Rain & squally Blast—
O! Sara! that the Gust ev'n now were swelling,
And the slant Night-shower driving loud & fast!

A Grief without a pang, void, dark, & drear,
A stifling, drowsy, unimpassion'd Grief
That finds no natural Outlet, no Relief
In word, or sigh, or tear—   20
This, Sara! well thou know'st,
Is that sore Evil, which I dread the most,
And oft'nest suffer! In this heartless Mood,
To other thoughts by yonder Throstle woo'd,
That pipes within the Larch tree, not unseen,
(The Larch, which pushes out in tassels green
It's bundled Leafits) woo'd to mild Delights
By all the tender Sounds & gentle Sights
Of this sweet Primrose-month—& *vainly* woo'd[.]
O dearest Sara! in this heartless Mood   30

---

[1] See note to Coleridge's *The Eolian Harp,* p. 441.

All this long Eve, so balmy & serene,
Have I been gazing on the western Sky
And it's peculiar Tint of Yellow Green—
And still I gaze—& with how blank an eye!
And those thin Clouds above, in flakes & bars,
That give away their Motion to the Stars;
Those Stars, that glide behind them, or between,
Now sparkling, now bedimm'd, but always seen;
Yon crescent Moon, as fix'd as if it grew
In it's own cloudless, starless Lake of Blue—   40
A boat becalm'd! dear William's Sky Canoe!²
—I see them all, so excellently fair!
I see, not feel, how beautiful they are.

        My genial Spirits fail—
        And what can these avail
To lift the smoth'ring Weight from off my Breast?
        It were a vain Endeavor,
        Tho' I should gaze for ever
On that Green Light, which lingers in the West!
I may not hope from outward Forms to win   50
The Passion & the Life, whose Fountains are within!
These lifeless Shapes, around, below, Above,
        O what can they impart?
When even the gentle Thought, that thou, my Love!
        Art gazing now, like me,
        And see'st the Heaven, I see—
Sweet thought it is—yet feebly stirs my Heart!

        Feebly! O feebly!—Yet
        (I well remember it)
In my first Dawn of Youth that Fancy stole   60
With many secret Yearnings on my Soul.
At eve, sky-gazing in "ecstatic fit"
(Alas! for cloister'd in a city School
The Sky was all, I knew, of Beautiful)
At the barr'd window often did I sit,
And oft upon the leaded School-roof lay,
        And to myself would say—
There does not live the Man so stripp'd of good
        affections
As not to love to see a Maiden's quiet Eyes
Uprais'd, and linking on sweet Dreams by dim
        Connections   70
To Moon, or Evening Star, or glorious western
        Skies—
While yet a Boy, this Thought would so pursue me
That often it became a kind of Vision to me!

        Sweet Thought! and dear of old
        To Hearts of finer Mould!
Ten thousand times by Friends & Lovers blest!

---

² See Wordsworth's *Peter Bell*, p. 213.

        I spake with rash Despair,
        And ere I was aware,
The weight was somewhat lifted from my Breast!
O Sara! in the weather-fended Wood,   80
Thy lov'd haunt! where the Stock-doves coo at Noon,
        I guess, that thou hast stood
And watch'd yon Crescent, & it's ghost-like Moon.
And yet, far rather in my present Mood
I would, that thou'dst been sitting all this while
Upon the sod-built Seat of Camomile—
And tho' thy Robin may have ceas'd to sing,
Yet needs for *my* sake must thou love to hear
        The Bee-hive murmuring near,
        That ever-busy & most quiet Thing   90
Which I have heard at Midnight murmuring.

        I feel my spirit moved—
        And wheresoe'er thou be,
        O Sister! O Beloved!
        Those dear mild Eyes, that see
        Even now the Heaven, *I see*—
There is a Prayer in them! It is for *me*—
And I, dear Sara—*I* am blessing *thee*!

It was as calm as this, that happy night
When Mary,³ thou, & I together were,   100
The low decaying Fire our only Light,
And listen'd to the Stillness of the Air!
O that affectionate & blameless Maid,
Dear Mary! on her Lap my head she lay'd—
        Her Hand was on my Brow,
        Even as my own is now;
And on my Cheek I felt thy eye-lash play.
Such joy I had, that I may truly say,
My Spirit was awe-stricken with the Excess
And trance-like Depth of it's brief Happiness.   110

Ah fair Remembrances, that so revive
The Heart, & fill it with a living Power,
Where were they, Sara?—or did I not strive
To win them to me?—on the fretting Hour
Then when I wrote thee that complaining Scroll,
Which even to bodily Sickness bruis'd thy Soul!
And yet thou blam'st thyself alone! And yet
        Forbidd'st me all Regret!

And must I not regret, that I distress'd
Thee, best belov'd! who lovest me the best?   120
My better mind had fled, I know not whither,
For O! was this an Absent Friend's Employ
To send from far both Pain & Sorrow thither

---

³ Sara's sister Mary, whom Wordsworth was about to marry.

Where still his Blessings should have call'd down
    Joy!
I read thy guileless Letter o'er again—
I hear thee of thy blameless Self complain—
And only this I learn—& this, alas! I know—
That thou art weak & pale with Sickness, Grief &
    Pain—
    And *I*—*I* made thee so!

O for my own sake I regret perforce   130
Whatever turns thee, Sara! from the course
Of calm Well-being & a Heart at rest!
When thou, & with thee those, whom thou lov'st
    best,
Shall dwell together in one happy Home,
One House, the dear *abiding* Home of All,
I too will crown me with a Coronal—[4]
Nor shall this Heart in idle Wishes roam
    Morbidly soft!
No! let me trust, that I shall wear away
In no inglorious Toils the manly Day,   140
And only now & then, & not too oft,
Some dear & memorable Eve will bless
Dreaming of all your Loves & Quietness.

Be happy, & I need thee not in sight.
Peace in thy Heart, & Quiet in thy Dwelling,
Health in thy Limbs, & in thine Eyes the Light
Of Love, & Hope, & honorable Feeling—
Where e'er I am, I shall be well content!
Not near thee, haply shall be more content!
To all things I prefer the Permanent.   150
And better seems it for a Heart, like mine,
Always to *know*, then sometimes to behold,
    Their Happiness & thine—
For Change doth trouble me with pangs untold!
To see thee, hear thee, feel thee—then to part!
    Oh!—it weighs down the Heart!
To *visit* those, I love, as I love thee,
Mary, & William, & dear Dorothy,
It is but a temptation to repine—
The transientness is Poison in the Wine,   160
Eats out the pith of Joy, makes all Joy hollow,
All Pleasure a dim Dream of Pain to follow!
    My own peculiar Lot, my house-hold Life
It is, & will remain, Indifference or Strife—
While *ye* are *well* & *happy*, twould but wrong
    you
If I should fondly yearn to be among you—
Wherefore, O wherefore! should I wish to be
A wither'd branch upon a blossoming Tree?

⁴ See Wordsworth's Immortality Ode, stanza IV, p. 258.

But (let me say it! for I vainly strive
To beat away the Thought), but if thou pin'd,   170
Whate'er the Cause, in body or in mind,
I were the miserablest Man alive
To know it & be absent! Thy Delights
Far off, or near, alike I may partake—
But O! to mourn for thee, & to forsake
All power, all hope of giving comfort to thee—
To know that thou art weak & worn with pain,
And not to hear thee, Sara! not to view thee—
    Not sit beside thy Bed
    Not press thy aching Head,   180
    Not bring thee Health again—
    At least to hope, to try—
By this Voice, which thou lov'st, & by this earnest
    Eye—

Nay, wherefore did I let it haunt my Mind
    The dark distressful Dream!
I turn from it, & listen to the Wind
Which long has rav'd unnotic'd! What a Scream
Of agony by Torture lengthen'd out
That Lute sent forth! O thou wild Storm without!
Jagg'd Rock, or mountain Pond, or Blasted Tree,   190
Or Pine-Grove, Whither Woodman never clomb,
Or lonely House, long held the Witches' Home,
Methinks were fitter Instruments for Thee,
Mad Lutanist! that in this month of Showers,
Of dark brown Gardens, & of peeping Flowers,
Mak'st Devil's Yule, with worse than wintry
    Song
The Blossoms, Buds, and timorous Leaves
    among!
Thou Actor, perfect in all tragic Sounds!
Thou mighty Poet, even to frenzy bold!
    What tell'st thou now about?   200
'Tis of the Rushing of an Host in Rout—
And many Groans from men with smarting
    Wounds—
At once they groan with smart, and shudder with the
    Cold!
Tis hush'd! there is a Trance of deepest Silence,
Again! but all that Sound, as of a rushing Crow'd,
And Groans & tremulous Shudderings, all are over—
And it has other Sounds, and all less deep, less loud!
    A Tale of less Affright,
    And temper'd with Delight,
As William's Self had made the tender Lay   210
    'Tis of a little Child
    Upon a heathy Wild,
Not far from home—but it has lost it's way—
And now groans low in utter grief & fear—
And now screams loud, & hopes to make it's Mother
    hear!

'Tis Midnight! and small Thoughts have I of Sleep—
Full seldom may my Friend such Vigils keep—
O breathe She softly in her gentle Sleep!
Cover her, gentle Sleep! with wings of Healing.
And be this Tempest but a mountain Birth!　　　220
May all the Stars hang bright about her Dwelling,
Silent, as tho' they *watch'd* the sleeping Earth!
Healthful & light, my Darling! may'st thou rise
　　　With clear & chearful Eyes—
And of the same good Tidings to me send!
　　　For, oh! beloved Friend!
I am not the buoyant Thing, I was of yore—
When like an own Child, I to *Joy* belong'd;
For others mourning oft, myself oft sorely wrong'd,
Yet bearing all things then, as if I nothing bore!　　230

　　　Yes, dearest Sara, yes!
There *was* a time when tho' my path was rough,
The Joy within me dallied with Distress;
And all Misfortunes were but as the Stuff
Whence Fancy made me Dreams of Happiness:
For Hope grew round me, like the climbing Vine,
And Leaves & Fruitage, not my own, seem'd mine!
But now Ill Tidings bow me down to earth /
Nor care I, that they rob me of my Mirth /
　　　But oh! each Visitation　　　　　240
Suspends what Nature gave me at my Birth,
My shaping Spirit of Imagination!
I speak not now of those habitual Ills
That wear out Life, when two unequal Minds
Meet in one House, & two discordant Wills—
　　　This leaves me, where it finds,
Past cure, & past Complaint—a fate Austere
Too fix'd & hopeless to partake of Fear!

But thou, dear Sara! (dear indeed thou art,
My Comforter! A Heart within my Heart!)　　　250
Thou, & the Few, we love, tho' few ye be,
Make up a world of Hopes & Fears for me.
And if Affliction, or distemp'ring Pain,
Or wayward Chance befall you, I complain
Not that I mourn—O Friends, most dear! most true!
　　　Methinks to weep with you
Were better far than to rejoice alone—
But that my coarse domestic Life has known
No habits of heart-nursing Sympathy,
No Griefs but such as dull and deaden me,　　　260
No mutual mild Enjoyments of it's own,
No Hopes of its own Vintage, None, o! none—
Whence when I mourn'd for you, my Heart might
　　　borrow
Fair forms & living Motions for it's Sorrow.
For not to think of what I needs must feel,
But to be still & patient all I can;

And haply by abstruse Research to steal
From my own Nature all the Natural Man—
This was my sole Resource, my wisest plan!
And that, which suits a part, infects the whole,　　270
And now is almost grown the Temper of my Soul.

My little Children are a Joy, a Love,
　　　A good Gift from above!
But what is Bliss, that still calls up a Woe,
　　　And makes it doubly keen
Compelling me to *feel*, as well as KNOW,
What a most blessed Lot mine might have been.
Those little Angel Children (woe is me!)
There have been hours, when feeling how they bind
And pluck out the wing-feathers of my Mind,　　280
Turning my Error to Necessity,
I have half-wish'd, they never had been born!
That seldom! But sad Thoughts they always bring,
And like the Poet's Philomel, I sing
My Love-song, with my breast against a Thorn.[5]

With no unthankful Spirit I confess,
This clinging Grief too, in it's turn, awakes
That Love, and Father's Joy; but O! it makes
The Love the greater, & the Joy far less.
These Mountains too, these Vales, these Woods, these
　　　Lakes,　　　　　　290
Scenes full of Beauty & of Loftiness
Where all my Life I fondly hop'd to live—
I were sunk low indeed, did they *no* solace give;
But oft I seem to feel, & evermore I fear,
They are not to me now the Things, which once they
　　　were.

O Sara! we receive but what we give,
And in *our* Life alone does Nature live.
Our's is her wedding Garment, our's her Shroud—
And would we aught behold of higher Worth
Than that inanimate cold World allow'd　　　300
To the poor loveless ever-anxious Crowd,
Ah! from the Soul itself must issue forth
A Light, a Glory, and a luminous Cloud
　　　Enveloping the Earth!
And from the Soul itself must there be sent
A sweet & potent Voice, of it's own Birth,
Of all sweet Sounds the Life & Element.

O pure of Heart! thou need'st not ask of me
What this strong music in the Soul may be,
　　　What, & wherein it doth exist,　　　310
This Light, this Glory, this fair luminous Mist,

---

[5] The nightingale's song was popularly supposed to be caused
by self-inflicted pain. For the story of Philomela see note to
Coleridge's *The Nightingale*, p. 470.

This beautiful & beauty-making Power!
JOY, innocent Sara! Joy, that ne'er was given
Save to the Pure, & in their purest Hour,
JOY, Sara! is the Spirit & the Power,
That wedding Nature to us gives in Dower
    A new Earth and a new Heaven
Undreamt of by the Sensual & the Proud!
Joy is that strong Voice, Joy that luminous Cloud—
    We, we ourselves rejoice!   320
And thence flows all that charms or ear or sight,
All melodies the Echoes of that Voice,
All Colors a Suffusion of that Light.

Sister & Friend of my devoutest Choice!
Thou being innocent & full of love,
And nested with the Darlings of thy Love,
And feeling in thy Soul, Heart, Lips, & Arms
Even what the conjugal & mother Dove,
That borrows genial Warmth from those, she warms,
    Feels in the thrill'd wings, blessedly outspread—
Thou free'd awhile from Cares & human Dread   331
By the Immenseness of the Good & Fair,
    Which thou seest every where—
Thus, thus, should'st thou rejoice!
To thee would all Things live from Pole to Pole,
Their Life the Eddying of thy living Soul.
O dear! O Innocent! O full of Love!
A very Friend! A Sister of my Choice—
O dear, as Light & Impulse from above,
Thus may'st thou ever, evermore rejoice!   340
                S.T.C.

[1802]   [1937]

[SECOND VERSION]

    "Late, late yestreen I saw the new Moon
    "With the Old Moon in her arms;
    "And I fear, I fear, my Master dear,
    "We shall have a deadly storm."
        BALLAD OF SIR PATRICK SPENCE.

DEJECTION:

AN ODE, WRITTEN APRIL 4, 1802.

I

WELL! If the Bard was weather-wise, who made
    The grand Old ballad of SIR PATRICK SPENCE,
    This night, so tranquil now, will not go hence
Unrous'd by winds, that ply a busier trade
Than those, which mould yon cloud, in lazy flakes,
Or the dull sobbing draft, that drones and rakes
Upon the strings of this Œolian lute,
    Which better far were mute.

For lo! the New Moon, winter-bright!
And overspread with phantom light,   10
(With swimming phantom light o'erspread,
But rimm'd and circled by a silver thread)
I see the Old Moon in her lap, foretelling
    The coming on of rain and squally blast:
And O! that even now the gust were swelling,
    And the slant night-show'r driving loud and fast!
Those sounds which oft have rais'd me, while they
    aw'd,
And sent my soul abroad,
Might now perhaps their wonted impulse give,
Might startle this dull pain, and make it move and
    live!   20

II

A grief without a pang, void, dark, and drear,
    A stifled, drowsy, unimpassion'd grief,
    Which finds no nat'ral outlet, no relief,
In word, or sigh, or tear—
O EDMUND! in this wan and heartless mood,
To other thoughts by yonder throstle woo'd,
All this long eve, so balmy and serene,
    Have I been gazing on the Western sky,
And its peculiar tint of yellow-green:
    And still I gaze—and with how blank an eye!   30
And those thin clouds above, in flakes and bars,
That give away their motion to the stars;
Those stars, that glide behind them, or between,
Now sparkling, now bedimm'd, but always seen;
Yon crescent moon, as fix'd as if it grew,
In its own cloudless, starless lake of blue,
A boat becalm'd! a lovely sky-canoe!
I see them all so excellently fair—
I *see*, not *feel* how beautiful they are!

III

My genial spirits fail;   40
    And what can these avail,
To lift the smoth'ring weight from off my breast?
    It were a vain endeavour,
    Though I should gaze for ever
On that green light that lingers in the west:
I may not hope from outward forms to win
The passion and the life, whose fountains are within.

IV

O EDMUND! we receive but what we give,
And in *our* life alone does Nature live:
Ours is her wedding-garment, ours her shroud! 50
And would we aught behold, of higher worth,
Than that inanimate cold world, *allow'd*
To the poor loveless ever-anxious crowd,

Ah! from the soul itself must issue forth,
A light, a glory, a fair luminous cloud
Enveloping the earth—
And from the soul itself must there be sent
A sweet and potent voice, of its own birth,
Of all sweet sounds the life and element!
O pure of heart! Thou need'st not ask of me   60
What this strong music in the soul may be?
What, and wherein it doth exist,
This light, this glory, this fair luminous mist,
This beautiful and beauty-making pow'r?
   Joy, virtuous EDMUND! joy that ne'er was given,
Save to the pure, and in their purest hour,
Joy, EDMUND! is the spirit and the pow'r,
Which wedding Nature to us gives in dow'r,
   A new Earth and new Heaven,
Undream'd of by the sensual and the proud—
JOY is the sweet voice, JOY the luminous cloud—
   We, we ourselves rejoice!
And thence flows all that charms or ear or sight,
All melodies the echoes of that voice,
All colours a suffusion from that light.
              Yes, dearest EDMUND, yes!
There was a time that, tho' my path was rough,
   This joy within me dallied with distress,
And all misfortunes were but as the stuff
   Whence fancy made me dreams of happiness: 80
For hope grew round me, like the twining vine,
And fruits, and foliage, not my own, seem'd mine.
But now afflictions bow me down to earth:
Nor care I, that they rob me of my mirth,
   But oh! each visitation
Suspends what nature gave me at my birth,
My shaping spirit of imagination.

[The Sixth and Seventh Stanzas omitted.]
   *   *   *   *   *
   *   *   *   *   *
   *   *   *   *   *

VIII

O wherefore did I let it haunt my mind
   This dark distressful dream?
I turn from it, and listen to the wind   90
   Which long has rav'd unnotic'd. What a scream
Of agony, by torture, lengthen'd out,
That lute sent forth! O wind, that rav'st without,
   Bare crag, or mountain-tairn,* or blasted tree,
Or pine-grove, whither woodman never clomb,

* Tairn, a small lake, generally, if not always, applied to the lakes up in the mountains, and which are the feeders of those in the vallies. This address to the wind will not appear extravagant to those who have heard it at night, in a mountainous country.

Or lonely house, long held the witches' home,
   Methinks were fitter instruments for thee,
Mad Lutanist! who, in this month of show'rs,
Of dark-brown gardens, and of peeping flow'rs,
Mak'st devil's yule, with worse than wintry song,   100
The blossoms, buds, and tim'rous leaves among.
   Thou Actor, perfect in all tragic sounds!
Thou mighty Poet, ev'n to frenzy bold!
      What tell'st thou now about?
     'Tis of the rushing of a host in rout,
   With many groans of men, with smarting wounds—
At once they groan with pain, and shudder with the
     cold!
But hush! there is a pause of deepest silence!
   And all that noise, as of a rushing crowd,
With groans, and tremulous shudderings—all is over!
   It tells another tale, with sounds less deep and
     loud—   111
     A tale of less affright.
     And temper'd with delight,
As EDMUND'S self had fram'd the tender lay—
     'Tis of a little child,
     Upon a lonesome wild
Not far from home; but she hath lost her way—
And now moans low, in utter grief and fear;
And now screams loud, and hopes to make her mother
   hear!

IX

'Tis midnight, and small thoughts have I of sleep;
Full seldom may my friend such vigils keep!   121
Visit him, gentle Sleep, with wings of healing,
   And may this storm be but a mountain-birth,
May all the stars hang bright above his dwelling,
   Silent, as though they *watch'd* the sleeping Earth!
     With light heart may he rise,
     Gay fancy, cheerful eyes,
And sing his lofty song, and teach me to rejoice!
O EDMUND, friend of my devoutest choice,
O rais'd from anxious dread and busy care,   130
By the immenseness of the good and fair
   Which thou see'st everywhere,
Joy lifts thy spirit, joy attunes thy voice,
To thee do all things live from pole to pole,
Their life the eddying of thy living soul!
O simple spirit, guided from above,
O lofty Poet, full of life and love,
Brother and friend of my devoutest choice,
Thus may'st thou ever, evermore rejoice!
                 ΕΣΤΗΣΕ.

[1802]   [1802]

[FINAL VERSION]

DEJECTION: AN ODE

Late, late yestreen I saw the new Moon,
With the old Moon in her arms;
And I fear, I fear, my Master dear!
We shall have a deadly storm.
          Ballad of Sir Patrick Spence.

I

WELL! If the Bard was weather-wise, who made
    The grand old ballad of Sir Patrick Spence,
    This night, so tranquil now, will not go hence
Unroused by winds, that ply a busier trade
Than those which mould yon cloud in lazy flakes,
Or the dull sobbing draft, that moans and rakes
Upon the strings of this Æolian lute,
        Which better far were mute.
    For lo! the New-moon winter-bright!
    And overspread with phantom light,   10
    (With swimming phantom light o'erspread
    But rimmed and circled by a silver thread)
I see the old Moon in her lap, foretelling
    The coming-on of rain and squally blast.
And oh! that even now the gust were swelling,
    And the slant night-shower driving loud and fast!
Those sounds which oft have raised me, whilst they
        awed,
        And sent my soul abroad,
Might now perhaps their wonted impulse give,
Might startle this dull pain, and make it move and
        live!   20

II

A grief without a pang, void, dark, and drear,
    A stifled, drowsy, unimpassioned grief,
    Which finds no natural outlet, no relief,
        In word, or sigh, or tear—
O Lady! in this wan and heartless mood,
To other thoughts by yonder throstle woo'd,
    All this long eve, so balmy and serene,
Have I been gazing on the western sky,
    And its peculiar tint of yellow green:
And still I gaze—and with how blank an eye!   30
And those thin clouds above, in flakes and bars,
That give away their motion to the stars;
Those stars, that glide behind them or between,
Now sparkling, now bedimmed, but always seen:
Yon crescent Moon, as fixed as if it grew
In its own cloudless, starless lake of blue;
I see them all so excellently fair,
I see, not feel, how beautiful they are!

III

My genial spirits fail;
    And what can these avail   40
To lift the smothering weight from off my breast?
    It were a vain endeavour,
    Though I should gaze for ever
On that green light that lingers in the west:
I may not hope from outward forms to win
The passion and the life, whose fountains are within.

IV

O Lady! we receive but what we give,
And in our life alone does Nature live:
Ours is her wedding garment, ours her shroud!
    And would we aught behold, of higher worth,   50
Than that inanimate cold world allowed
To the poor loveless ever-anxious crowd,
    Ah! from the soul itself must issue forth
A light, a glory, a fair luminous cloud
        Enveloping the Earth—
And from the soul itself must there be sent
    A sweet and potent voice, of its own birth,
Of all sweet sounds the life and element!

V

O pure of heart! thou need'st not ask of me
What this strong music in the soul may be!   60
What, and wherein it doth exist,
This light, this glory, this fair luminous mist,
This beautiful and beauty-making power.
    Joy, virtuous Lady! Joy that ne'er was given,
Save to the pure, and in their purest hour,
Life, and Life's effluence, cloud at once and shower,
Joy, Lady! is the spirit and the power,
Which wedding Nature to us gives in dower
        A new Earth and new Heaven,
Undreamt of by the sensual and the proud—   70
Joy is the sweet voice, Joy the luminous cloud—
        We in ourselves rejoice!
And thence flows all that charms or ear or sight,
    All melodies the echoes of that voice,
All colours a suffusion from that light.

VI

There was a time when, though my path was rough,
    This joy within me dallied with distress,
And all misfortunes were but as the stuff
    Whence Fancy made me dreams of happiness:
For hope grew round me, like the twining vine,   80
And fruits, and foliage, not my own, seemed mine.
But now afflictions bow me down to earth:
Nor care I that they rob me of my mirth;
        But oh! each visitation

Suspends what nature gave me at my birth,
  My shaping spirit of Imagination.
For not to think of what I needs must feel,
  But to be still and patient, all I can;
And haply by abstruse research to steal
  From my own nature all the natural man—   90
  This was my sole resource, my only plan:
Till that which suits a part infects the whole,
And now is almost grown the habit of my soul.

VII

Hence, viper thoughts, that coil around my mind,
  Reality's dark dream!
I turn from you, and listen to the wind,
  Which long has raved unnoticed. What a scream
Of agony by torture lengthened out
That lute sent forth! Thou Wind, that rav'st without,
  Bare crag, or mountain-tairn,* or blasted tree,   100
Or pine-grove whither woodman never clomb,
Or lonely house, long held the witches' home,
  Methinks were fitter instruments for thee,
Mad Lutanist! who in this month of showers,
Of dark-brown gardens, and of peeping flowers,
Mak'st Devils' yule, with worse than wintry song,
The blossoms, buds, and timorous leaves among.
  Thou Actor, perfect in all tragic sounds!
Thou mighty Poet, e'en to frenzy bold!
    What tell'st thou now about?   110
    'Tis of the rushing of an host in rout,
With groans, of trampled men, with smarting
    wounds—
At once they groan with pain, and shudder with the
    cold!
But hush! there is a pause of deepest silence!
  And all that noise, as of a rushing crowd,
With groans, and tremulous shudderings—all is
    over—
  It tells another tale, with sounds less deep and loud!
    A tale of less affright,
    And tempered with delight,
As Otway's[1] self had framed the tender lay,—   120
    'Tis of a little child
    Upon a lonesome wild,
Not far from home, but she hath lost her way:
And now moans low in bitter grief and fear,
And now screams loud, and hopes to make her mother
    hear.

  * Tairn is a small lake, generally if not always applied to the
lakes up in the mountains and which are the feeders of those in
the valleys. This address to the wind, will not appear extravagant
to those who have heard it at night and in a mountainous
country.

  [1] Thomas Otway (1652–1685), dramatist. See note to *Monody
on the Death of Chatterton*, p. 430.

VIII

'Tis midnight, but small thoughts have I of sleep:
Full seldom may my friend such vigils keep!
Visit her, gentle Sleep! with wings of healing,
  And may this storm be but a mountain-birth,
May all the stars hang bright above her dwelling, 130
  Silent as though they watched the sleeping Earth!
    With light heart may she rise,
    Gay fancy, cheerful eyes,
  Joy lift her spirit, joy attune her voice;
To her may all things live, from pole to pole,
Their life the eddying of her living soul!
  O simple spirit, guided from above,
Dear Lady, friend devoutest of my choice,
Thus mayest thou ever, evermore rejoice.

[1802]   [1817]

THE PICTURE

OR THE LOVER'S RESOLUTION

THROUGH weeds and thorns, and matted
    underwood
I force my way; now climb, and now descend
O'er rocks, or bare or mossy, with wild foot
Crushing the purple whorts;* while oft unseen,
Hurrying along the drifted forest-leaves,
The scared snake rustles. Onward still I toil,
I know not, ask not whither! A new joy,
Lovely as light, sudden as summer gust,
And gladsome as the first-born of the spring,
Beckons me on, or follows from behind,   10
Playmate, or guide! The master-passion quelled,
I feel that I am free. With dun-red bark
The fir-trees, and the unfrequent slender oak,
Forth from this tangle wild of bush and brake
Soar up, and form a melancholy vault
High o'er me, murmuring like a distant sea.

Here Wisdom might resort, and here Remorse;
Here too the love-lorn man, who, sick in soul,
And of this busy human heart aweary,
Worships the spirit of unconscious life   20
In tree or wild-flower.—Gentle lunatic!
If so he might not wholly cease to be,
He would far rather not be that he is;
But would be something that he knows not of,
In winds or waters, or among the rocks!

  * *Vaccinium Myrtillus*, known by the different names of
Whorts, Whortleberries, Bilberries; and in the north of England
Blea-berries and Bloom-berries.

But hence, fond wretch! breathe not contagion
   here!
No myrtle-walks are these: these are no groves
Where Love dare loiter! If in sullen mood
He should stray hither, the low stumps shall gore
His dainty feet, the briar and the thorn   30
Make his plumes haggard. Like a wounded bird
Easily caught, ensnare him, O ye Nymphs,
Ye Oreads chaste, ye dusky Dryades!
And you, ye Earth-winds! you that make at morn
The dew-drops quiver on the spiders' webs!
You, O ye wingless Airs! that creep between
The rigid stems of heath and bitten furze,
Within whose scanty shade, at summer-noon,
The mother-sheep hath worn a hollow bed—
Ye, that now cool her fleece with dropless damp,   40
Now pant and murmur with her feeding lamb.
Chase, chase him, all ye Fays, and elfin Gnomes!
With prickles sharper than his darts bemock
His little Godship, making him perforce
Creep through a thorn-bush on yon hedgehog's back.

   This is my hour of triumph! I can now
With my own fancies play the merry fool,
And laugh away worse folly, being free.
Here will I seat myself, beside this old,
Hollow, and weedy oak, which ivy-twine   50
Clothes as with net-work: here will I couch my
   limbs,
Close by this river, in this silent shade,
As safe and sacred from the step of man
As an invisible world—unheard, unseen,
And listening only to the pebbly brook
That murmurs with a dead, yet tinkling sound;
Or to the bees, that in the neighbouring trunk
Make honey-hoards. The breeze, that visits me,
Was never Love's accomplice, never raised
The tendril ringlets from the maiden's brow,   60
And the blue, delicate veins above her cheek;
Ne'er played the wanton—never half disclosed
The maiden's snowy bosom, scattering thence
Eye-poisons for some love-distempered youth,
Who ne'er henceforth may see an aspen-grove
Shiver in sunshine, but his feeble heart
Shall flow away like a dissolving thing.

Sweet breeze! thou only, if I guess aright,
Liftest the feathers of the robin's breast,
That swells its little breast, so full of song,   70
Singing above me, on the mountain-ash.
And thou too, desert stream! no pool of thine,
Though clear as lake in latest summer-eve,
Did e'er reflect that stately virgin's robe,
The face, the form divine, the downcast look

Contemplative! Behold! her open palm
Presses her cheek and brow! her elbow rests
On the bare branch of half-uprooted tree,
That leans towards its mirror! Who erewhile
Had from her countenance turned, or looked by
   stealth,   80
(For Fear is true-love's cruel nurse), he now
With steadfast gaze and unoffending eye,
Worships the watery idol, dreaming hopes
Delicious to the soul, but fleeting, vain,
E'en as that phantom-world on which he gazed,
But not unheeded gazed: for see, ah! see,
The sportive tyrant with her left hand plucks
The heads of tall flowers that behind her grow,
Lychnis, and willow-herb, and fox-glove bells:
And suddenly, as one that toys with time,   90
Scatters them on the pool! Then all the charm
Is broken—all that phantom world so fair
Vanishes, and a thousand circlets spread,
And each mis-shape the other. Stay awhile,
Poor youth, who scarcely dar'st lift up thine eyes!
The stream will soon renew its smoothness, soon
The visions will return! And lo! he stays:
And soon the fragments dim of lovely forms
Come trembling back, unite, and now once more
The pool becomes a mirror; and behold   100
Each wildflower on the marge inverted there,
And there the half-uprooted tree—but where,
O where the virgin's snowy arm, that leaned
On its bare branch? He turns, and she is gone!
Homeward she steals through many a woodland
   maze
Which he shall seek in vain. Ill-fated youth!
Go, day by day, and waste thy manly prime
In mad love-yearning by the vacant brook,
Till sickly thoughts bewitch thine eyes, and thou
Behold'st her shadow still abiding there,   110
The Naiad of the mirror!
                      Not to thee,
O wild and desert stream! belongs this tale:
Gloomy and dark art thou—the crowded firs
Spire from thy shores, and stretch across thy bed,
Making thee doleful as a cavern-well:
Save when the shy king-fishers build their nest
On thy steep banks, no loves hast thou, wild stream!

   This be my chosen haunt—emancipate
From Passion's dreams, a freeman, and alone,
I rise and trace its devious course. O lead,   120
Lead me to deeper shades and lonelier glooms.
Lo! stealing through the canopy of firs,
How fair the sunshine spots that mossy rock,
Isle of the river, whose disparted waves
Dart off asunder with an angry sound,

How soon to re-unite! And see! they meet,
Each in the other lost and found: and see
Placeless, as spirits, one soft water-sun
Throbbing within them, heart at once and eye!
With its soft neighbourhood of filmy clouds,   130
The stains and shadings of forgotten tears,
Dimness o'erswum with lustre! Such the hour
Of deep enjoyment, following love's brief feuds;
And hark, the noise of a near waterfall!
I pass forth into light—I find myself
Beneath a weeping birch (most beautiful
Of forest trees, the Lady of the Woods),
Hard by the brink of a tall weedy rock
That overbrows the cataract. How bursts
The landscape on my sight! Two crescent hills   140
Fold in behind each other, and so make
A circular vale, and land-locked, as might seem,
With brook and bridge, and grey stone cottages,
Half hid by rocks and fruit-trees. At my feet,
The whortle-berries are bedewed with spray,
Dashed upwards by the furious waterfall.
How solemnly the pendent ivy-mass
Swings in its winnow: All the air is calm.
The smoke from cottage-chimneys, tinged with
     light,
Rises in columns; from this house alone,   150
Close by the water-fall, the column slants,
And feels its ceaseless breeze. But what is this?
That cottage, with its slanting chimney-smoke,
And close beside its porch a sleeping child,
His dear head pillowed on a sleeping dog—
One arm between its fore-legs, and the hand
Holds loosely its small handful of wild-flowers,
Unfilletted, and of unequal lengths.
A curious picture, with a master's haste
Sketched on a strip of pinky-silver skin,   160
Peeled from the birchen bark! Divinest maid!
Yon bark her canvas, and those purple berries
Her pencil! See, the juice is scarcely dried
On the fine skin! She has been newly here;
And lo! yon patch of heath has been her couch—
The pressure still remains! O blessèd couch!
For this may'st thou flower early, and the sun,
Slanting at eve, rest bright, and linger long
Upon thy purple bells! O Isabel!
Daughter of genius! stateliest of our maids!   170
More beautiful than whom Alcaeus wooed,
The Lesbian woman of immortal song!
O child of genius! stately, beautiful,
And full of love to all, save only me,
And not ungentle e'en to me! My heart,
Why beats it thus? Through yonder coppice-wood
Needs must the pathway turn, that leads straightway
On to her father's house. She is alone!

The night draws on—such ways are hard to hit—
And fit it is I should restore this sketch,   180
Dropt unawares, no doubt. Why should I yearn
To keep the relique? 'twill but idly feed
The passion that consumes me. Let me haste!
The picture in my hand which she has left;
She cannot blame me that I followed her:
And I may be her guide the long wood through.

[1802]   [1802]

HYMN BEFORE SUNRISE

*Some of the images and notions expressed in this poem are taken
from a twenty-line poem in German by Friederike Brun called
"Chamouni at Sunrise." De Quincey was the first to accuse
Coleridge of plagiarism for his unacknowledged use of the
German poem.*

HYMN BEFORE SUN-RISE,
IN THE VALE OF CHAMOUNI

BESIDES the Rivers, Arve and Arveiron, which have their
sources in the foot of Mont Blanc, five conspicuous
torrents rush down its sides; and within a few paces of the
Glaciers, the Gentiana Major grows in immense numbers,
with its 'flowers of loveliest blue.'

HAST thou a charm to stay the morning-star
In his steep course? So long he seems to pause
On thy bald awful head, O sovran BLANC,
The Arve and Arveiron at thy base
Rave ceaselessly; but thou, most awful Form!
Risest from forth thy silent sea of pines,
How silently! Around thee and above
Deep is the air and dark, substantial, black,
An ebon mass: methinks thou piercest it,
As with a wedge! But when I look again,   10
It is thine own calm home, thy crystal shrine,
Thy habitation from eternity!
O dread and silent Mount! I gazed upon thee,
Till thou, still present to the bodily sense,
Didst vanish from my thought: entranced in prayer
I worshipped the Invisible alone.

Yet, like some sweet beguiling melody,
So sweet, we know not we are listening to it,
Thou, the meanwhile, wast blending with my
     Thought,
Yea, with my Life and Life's own secret joy: 20
Till the dilating Soul, enrapt, transfused,
Into the mighty vision passing—there
As in her natural form, swelled vast to Heaven!

Awake, my soul! not only passive praise
Thou owest! not alone these swelling tears,
Mute thanks and secret ecstasy! Awake,
Voice of sweet song! Awake, my heart, awake!
Green vales and icy cliffs, all join my Hymn.

Thou first and chief, sole sovereign of the Vale!
O struggling with the darkness all the night,　　30
And visited all night by troops of stars,
Or when they climb the sky or when they sink:
Companion of the morning-star at dawn,
Thyself Earth's rosy star, and of the dawn
Co-herald: wake, O wake, and utter praise!
Who sank thy sunless pillars deep in Earth?
Who filled thy countenance with rosy light?
Who made thee parent of perpetual streams?

And you, ye five wild torrents fiercely glad!
Who called you forth from night and utter death,　40
From dark and icy caverns called you forth,
Down those precipitous, black, jaggéd rocks,
For ever shattered and the same for ever?
Who gave you your invulnerable life,
Your strength, your speed, your fury, and your joy,
Unceasing thunder and eternal foam?
And who commanded (and the silence came),
Here let the billows stiffen, and have rest?

Ye Ice-falls! ye that from the mountain's brow
Adown enormous ravines slope amain—　　50
Torrents, methinks, that heard a mighty voice,
And stopped at once amid their maddest plunge!
Motionless torrents! silent cataracts!
Who made you glorious as the Gates of Heaven
Beneath the keen full moon? Who bade the sun
Clothe you with rainbows? Who, with living flowers
Of loveliest blue, spread garlands at your feet?—
GOD! let the torrents, like a shout of nations,
Answer! and let the ice-plains echo, GOD!　　59
GOD! sing ye meadow-streams with gladsome voice!
Ye pine-groves, with your soft and soul-like sounds!
And they too have a voice, yon piles of snow,
And in their perilous fall shall thunder, GOD!

Ye living flowers that skirt the eternal frost!
Ye wild goats sporting round the eagle's nest!
Ye eagles, play-mates of the mountain-storm!
Ye lightnings, the dread arrows of the clouds!
Ye signs and wonders of the element!
Utter forth God, and fill the hills with praise!

Thou too, hoar Mount! with thy sky-pointing
　　peaks,　　　　　　　　　　　　　　70
Oft from whose feet the avalanche, unheard,

Shoots downward, glittering through the pure serene
Into the depth of clouds, that veil thy breast—
Thou too again, stupendous Mountain! thou
That as I raise my head, awhile bowed low
In adoration, upward from thy base
Slow travelling with dim eyes suffused with tears,
Solemnly seemest, like a vapoury cloud,
To rise before me—Rise, O ever rise,
Rise like a cloud of incense from the Earth!　　80
Thou kingly Spirit throned among the hills,
Thou dread ambassador from Earth to Heaven,
Great Hierarch! tell thou the silent sky,
And tell the stars, and tell yon rising sun
Earth, with her thousand voices, praises GOD.

[1802]　　　　　　　　　　　　　　　[1802]

INSCRIPTION FOR A
FOUNTAIN ON A HEATH

THIS Sycamore, oft musical with bees,—
Such tents the Patriarchs loved! O long unharmed
May all its agéd boughs o'er-canopy
The small round basin, which this jutting stone
Keeps pure from falling leaves! Long may the Spring,
Quietly as a sleeping infant's breath,
Send up cold waters to the traveller
With soft and even pulse! Nor ever cease
Yon tiny cone of sand its soundless dance,
Which at the bottom, like a Fairy's Page,　　10
As merry and no taller, dances still,
Nor wrinkles the smooth surface of the Fount.
Here Twilight is and Coolness: here is moss,
A soft seat, and a deep and ample shade.
Thou may'st toil far and find no second tree.
Drink, Pilgrim, here; Here rest! and if thy heart
Be innocent, here too shalt thou refresh
Thy spirit, listening to some gentle sound,
Or passing gale or hum of murmuring bees!

[1802]　　　　　　　　　　　　　　　[1802]

A DAY-DREAM

MY eyes make pictures, when they are shut:
　　I see a fountain, large and fair,
A willow and a ruined hut,
　　And thee, and me and Mary there.
O Mary! make thy gentle lap our pillow!
Bend o'er us, like a bower, my beautiful green willow![1]

---

[1] See the first version of *Dejection* ("A letter...") p. 483, lines 99–110.

A wild-rose roofs the ruined shed,
　　And that and summer well agree:
And lo! where Mary leans her head,
　　Two dear names carved upon the tree!   10
And Mary's tears, they are not tears of sorrow:
Our sister and our friend will both be here to-morrow.

'Twas day! but now few, large, and bright,
　　The stars are round the crescent moon!
And now it is a dark warm night,
　　The balmiest of the month of June!
A glow-worm fall'n, and on the marge remounting
Shines, and its shadow shines, fit stars for our sweet
　　fountain.

O ever—ever be thou blest!
　　For dearly, Asra! love I thee!   20
This brooding warmth across my breast,
　　This depth of tranquil bliss—ah, me!
Fount, tree and shed are gone, I know not whither,
But in one quiet room we three are still together.

The shadows dance upon the wall,
　　By the still dancing fire-flames made;
And now they slumber, moveless all!
　　And now they melt to one deep shade!
But not from me shall this mild darkness steal thee:
I dream thee with mine eyes, and at my heart I feel
　　thee!   30

Thine eyelash on my cheek doth play—
　　'Tis Mary's hand upon my brow!
But let me check this tender lay
　　Which none may hear but she and thou!
Like the still hive at quiet midnight humming,
Murmur it to yourselves, ye two beloved women!

[1802]   [1828]

THE DAY-DREAM

FROM AN EMIGRANT TO HIS ABSENT WIFE

If thou wert here, these tears were tears of light!
　　But from as sweet a vision did I start
As ever made these eyes grow idly bright!
　　And though I weep, yet still around my heart
A sweet and playful tenderness doth linger,
Touching my heart as with an infant's finger.

My mouth half open, like a witless man,
　　I saw our couch, I saw our quiet room,
　　Its shadows heaving by the fire-light gloom;
And o'er my lips a subtle feeling ran,   10

All o'er my lips a soft and breeze-like feeling—
I know not what—but had the same been stealing

Upon a sleeping mother's lips, I guess
　　It would have made the loving mother dream
That she was softly bending down to kiss
　　Her babe, that something more than babe did seem,
A floating presence of its darling father,
And yet its own dear baby self far rather!

Across my chest there lay a weight, so warm!
　　As if some bird had taken shelter there;   20
And lo! I seemed to see a woman's form—
　　Thine, Sara, thine? O joy, if thine it were!
I gazed with stifled breath, and feared to stir it,
　　No deeper trance e'er wrapt a yearning spirit!

And now, when I seemed sure thy face to see,
　　Thy own dear self in our own quiet home;
There came an elfish laugh, and wakened me:
　　'Twas Frederic, who behind my chair had clomb,
And with his bright eyes at my face was peeping.
I blessed him, tried to laugh, and fell a-weeping!   30

[1801–1802]   [1802]

THE PAINS OF SLEEP

Ere on my bed my limbs I lay,
It hath not been my use to pray
With moving lips or bended knees;
But silently, by slow degrees,
My spirit I to Love compose,
In humble trust mine eye-lids close,
With reverential resignation,
No wish conceived, no thought exprest,
Only a sense of supplication;
A sense o'er all my soul imprest   10
That I am weak, yet not unblest,
Since in me, round me, every where
Eternal Strength and Wisdom are.

But yester-night I prayed aloud
In anguish and in agony,
Up-starting from the fiendish crowd
Of shapes and thoughts that tortured me:
A lurid light, a trampling throng,
Sense of intolerable wrong,
And whom I scorned, those only strong!   20
Thirst of revenge, the powerless will
Still baffled, and yet burning still!
Desire with loathing strangely mixed
On wild or hateful objects fixed.

Fantastic passions! maddening brawl!
And shame and terror over all!
Deeds to be hid which were not hid,
Which all confused I could not know
Whether I suffered, or I did:
For all seemed guilt, remorse or woe,   30
My own or others still the same
Life-stifling fear, soul-stifling shame.

So two nights passed: the night's dismay
Saddened and stunned the coming day.
Sleep, the wide blessing, seemed to me
Distemper's worst calamity.
The third night, when my own loud scream
Had waked me from the fiendish dream,
O'ercome with sufferings strange and wild,
I wept as I had been a child;   40
And having thus by tears subdued
My anguish to a milder mood,
Such punishments, I said, were due
To natures deepliest stained with sin,—
For aye entempesting anew
The unfathomable hell within,
The horror of their deeds to view,
To know and loathe, yet wish and do!
Such griefs with such men well agree,
But wherefore, wherefore fall on me?   50
To be beloved is all I need,
And whom I love, I love indeed.

[1803]   [1816]

"The silence of a City . . ."

THE silence of a City, how awful at Midnight!
Mute as the battlements and crags and towers
That Fancy makes in the clouds, yea, as mute
As the moonlight that sleeps on the steady vanes.
(or)
The cell of a departed anchoret,[1]
His skeleton and flitting ghost are there,
Sole tenants—
And all the City silent as the Moon
That steeps in quiet light the steady vanes
Of her huge temples.

[1804-1805]   [1912]

PHANTOM

ALL look and likeness caught from earth,
All accident of kin and birth,
Had pass'd away. There was no trace
Of aught on that illumined face,
Uprais'd beneath the rifted stone
But of one spirit all her own;—
She, she herself, and only she,
Shone through her body visibly.

[1805]   [1834]

AD VILMUM AXIOLOGUM[1]

THIS be the meed, that thy song creates a thousand-
    fold echo!
Sweet as the warble of woods, that awakes at the gale
    of the morning!
List! the Hearts of the Pure, like caves in the ancient
    mountains
Deep, deep *in* the Bosom, and *from* the Bosom
    resound it,
Each with a different tone, complete or in musical
    fragments—
All have welcomed thy Voice, and receive and retain
    and prolong it!

This is the word of the Lord! it is spoken, and Beings
    Eternal
Live and are borne as an Infant; the Eternal begets the
    Immortal:
Love is the Spirit of Life, and Music the Life of the
    Spirit!

[1805?]   [1893]

WHAT IS LIFE?

RESEMBLES life what once was deem'd of light,
    Too ample in itself for human sight?
An absolute self—an element ungrounded—
All that we see, all colours of all shade
    By encroach of darkness made?—
Is very life by consciousness unbounded?
And all the thoughts, pains, joys of mortal breath,
A war-embrace of wrestling life and death?

[1805]   [1829]

---

[1] Anchorite, or hermit.

[1] Wordsworth himself made up this Latin form of his name.

SEPARATION

A SWORDED man whose trade is blood,
    In grief, in anger, and in fear,
Thro' jungle, swamp, and torrent flood,
    I seek the wealth you hold so dear!

The dazzling charm of outward form,
    The power of gold, the pride of birth,
Have taken Woman's heart by storm—
    Usurp'd the place of inward worth.

Is not true Love of higher price
    Than outward Form, though fair to see, 10
Wealth's glittering fairy-dome of ice,
    Or echo of proud ancestry?—

O! Asra, Asra! couldst thou see
    Into the bottom of my heart,
There's such a mine of Love for thee,
    As almost might supply desert!

(This separation is, alas!
    Too great a punishment to bear;
O! take my life, or let me pass
    That life, that happy life, with her!) 20

The perils, erst with steadfast eye
    Encounter'd, now I shrink to see—
Oh! I have heart enough to die—
    Not half enough to part from Thee!

[1805?]   [1834]

TO WILLIAM WORDSWORTH

The poem to which the subtitle refers is The Prelude, *which although unpublished until 1850 had been finished in a thirteen-book version, addressed to Coleridge, in 1805.*

TO WILLIAM WORDSWORTH

COMPOSED ON THE NIGHT
AFTER HIS RECITATION OF A POEM ON
THE GROWTH OF AN INDIVIDUAL MIND

FRIEND of the wise! and Teacher of the Good!
Into my heart have I received that Lay
More than historic, that prophetic Lay
Wherein (high theme by thee first sung aright)
Of the foundations and the building up
Of a Human Spirit thou hast dared to tell
What may be told, to the understanding mind

Revealable; and what within the mind
By vital breathings secret as the soul
Of vernal growth, oft quickens in the heart   10
Thoughts all too deep for words!—

                          Theme hard as high!
Of smiles spontaneous, and mysterious fears
(The first-born they of Reason and twin-birth),
Of tides obedient to external force,
And currents self-determined, as might seem,
Or by some inner Power; of moments awful,
Now in thy inner life, and now abroad,
When power streamed from thee, and thy soul
    received
The light reflected, as a light bestowed—
Of fancies fair, and milder hours of youth,   20
Hyblean [1] murmurs of poetic thought
Industrious in its joy, in vales and glens
Native or outland, lakes and famous hills!
Or on the lonely high-road, when the stars
Were rising; or by secret mountain-streams,
The guides and the companions of thy way!

Of more than Fancy, of the Social Sense
Distending wide, and man beloved as man,
Where France in all her towns lay vibrating
Like some becalméd bark beneath the burst   30
Of Heaven's immediate thunder, when no cloud
Is visible, or shadow on the main.
For thou wert there, thine own brows garlanded,
Amid the tremor of a realm aglow,
Amid a mighty nation jubilant,
When from the general heart of human kind
Hope sprang forth like a full-born Deity!
——Of that dear Hope afflicted and struck down,
So summoned homeward, thenceforth calm and sure
From the dread watch-tower of man's absolute self,
With light unwaning on her eyes, to look   41
Far on—herself a glory to behold,
The Angel of the vision! Then (last strain)
Of Duty, chosen Laws controlling choice,
Action and joy!—An Orphic [2] song indeed,
A song divine of high and passionate thoughts
To their own music chaunted!

                          O great Bard!
Ere yet that last strain dying awed the air,
With stedfast eye I viewed thee in the choir
Of ever-enduring men. The truly great   50
Have all one age, and from one visible space

---

[1] From Hybla, a Sicilian town noted for honey.
[2] From Orpheus, who in Greek mythology charmed Pluto into allowing him to try to lead his wife Eurydice out of Hades.

Shed influence! They, both in power and act,
Are permanent, and Time is not with them,
Save as it worketh for them, they in it.
Nor less a sacred Roll, than those of old,
And to be placed, as they, with gradual fame
Among the archives of mankind, thy work
Makes audible a linkéd lay of Truth,
Of Truth profound a sweet continuous lay,
Not learnt, but native, her own natural notes!   60
Ah! as I listened with a heart forlorn,
The pulses of my being beat anew:
And even as Life returns upon the drowned,
Life's joy rekindling roused a throng of pains—
Keen pangs of Love, awakening as a babe
Turbulent, with an outcry in the heart;
And fears self-willed, that shunned the eye of Hope;
And Hope that scarce would know itself from Fear;
Sense of past Youth, and Manhood come in vain,
And Genius given, and Knowledge won in vain;   70
And all which I had culled in wood-walks wild,
And all which patient toil had reared, and all,
Commune with thee had opened out—but flowers
Strewed on my corse, and borne upon my bier,
In the same coffin, for the self-same grave!

   That way no more! and ill beseems it me,
Who came a welcomer in herald's guise,
Singing of Glory, and Futurity,
To wander back on such unhealthful road,
Plucking the poisons of self-harm! And ill   80
Such intertwine beseems triumphal wreaths
Strew'd before thy advancing!

                         Nor do thou,
Sage Bard! impair the memory of that hour
Of thy communion with my nobler mind
By pity or grief, already felt too long!
Nor let my words import more blame than needs.
The tumult rose and ceased: for Peace is nigh
Where Wisdom's voice has found a listening heart.
Amid the howl of more than wintry storms,
The Halcyon [3] hears the voice of vernal hours   90
Already on the wing.

                    Eve following eve,
Dear tranquil time, when the sweet sense of Home
Is sweetest! moments for their own sake hailed
And more desired, more precious, for thy song,
In silence listening, like a devout child,
My soul lay passive, by thy various strain
Driven as in surges now beneath the stars,

⬦⬦⬦⬦⬦⬦⬦⬦⬦⬦⬦⬦⬦⬦⬦⬦⬦⬦⬦⬦⬦⬦⬦⬦⬦⬦⬦⬦⬦⬦⬦⬦
   [3] A mythical bird able to calm the sea and nest on it in winter.

With momentary stars of my own birth,
Fair constellated foam, still darting off
Into the darkness; now a tranquil sea,   100
Outspread and bright, yet swelling to the moon.

And when—O Friend! my comforter and guide!
Strong in thyself, and powerful to give strength!—
Thy long sustainéd Song finally closed,
And thy deep voice had ceased—yet thou thyself
Wert still before my eyes, and round us both
That happy vision of belovéd faces—
Scarce conscious, and yet conscious of its close
I sate, my being blended in one thought
(Thought was it? or aspiration? or resolve?)   110
Absorbed, yet hanging still upon the sound—
And when I rose, I found myself in prayer.

[1807]   [1817]

PSYCHE

THE butterfly the ancient Grecians made
The soul's fair emblem, and its only name—*
But of the soul, escaped the slavish trade
Of mortal life!—For in this earthly frame
Ours is the reptile's lot, much toil, much blame,
Manifold motions making little speed,
And to deform and kill the things whereon we feed.

[1808]   [1817]

Fragment: "Two wedded hearts . . ."

TWO wedded hearts, if ere were such,
Imprison'd in adjoining cells,
Across whose thin partition-wall
The builder left one narrow rent,
And where, most content in discontent,
A joy with itself at strife—
Die into an intenser life.

[1808]   [1893]

THE VISIONARY HOPE

SAD lot, to have no Hope! Though lowly kneeling
He fain would frame a prayer within his breast,
Would fain entreat for some sweet breath of healing,
That his sick body might have ease and rest;

⬦⬦⬦⬦⬦⬦⬦⬦⬦⬦⬦⬦⬦⬦⬦⬦⬦⬦⬦⬦⬦⬦⬦⬦⬦⬦⬦⬦⬦⬦⬦⬦
   * Psyche means both Butterfly and Soul.

He strove in vain! the dull sighs from his chest
Against his will the stifling load revealing,
Though Nature forced; though like some captive
    guest,
Some royal prisoner at his conqueror's feast,
An alien's restless mood but half concealing,
The sternness on his gentle brow confessed,   10
Sickness within and miserable feeling:
Though obscure pangs made curses of his dreams,
And dreaded sleep, each night repelled in vain,
Each night was scattered by its own loud screams:
Yet never could his heart command, though fain,
One deep full wish to be no more in pain.

   That Hope, which was his inward bliss and boast,
Which waned and died, yet ever near him stood,
Though changed in nature, wander where he would—
For Love's Despair is but Hope's pining Ghost!   20
For this one hope he makes his hourly moan,
He wishes and can wish for this alone!
Pierced, as with light from Heaven, before its gleams
(So the love-stricken visionary deems)
Disease would vanish, like a summer shower,
Whose dews fling sunshine from the noon-tide bower!
Or let it stay! yet this one Hope should give
Such strength that he would bless his pains and live.

[1810?]   [1834]

EPITAPH ON AN INFANT

ITS balmy lips the infant blest
Relaxing from its Mother's breast,
How sweet it heaves the happy sigh
Oh innocent satiety!

And such my Infant's latest sigh!
Oh tell, rude stone! the passer by,
That here the pretty babe doth lie,
Death sang to sleep with Lullaby.

[1811]   [1811]

TIME, REAL AND IMAGINARY
In a note Coleridge explains that by "imaginary Time" he means a schoolboy's living in daydreams that anticipate his next holiday.

TIME, REAL AND IMAGINARY
AN ALLEGORY

ON the wide level of a mountain's head,
(I knew not where, but 'twas some faery place)
Their pinions, ostrich-like, for sails out-spread,
Two lovely children run an endless race,
    A sister and a brother!
    This far outstripp'd the other;
  Yet ever runs she with reverted face,
  And looks and listens for the boy behind:
    For he, alas! is blind!
O'er rough and smooth with even step he passed,   10
And knows not whether he be first or last.

[1812?]   [1817]

HUMAN LIFE
ON THE DENIAL OF IMMORTALITY

IF dead, we cease to be; if total gloom
  Swallow up life's brief flash for aye, we fare
As summer-gusts, of sudden birth and doom,
  Whose sound and motion not alone declare,
But are their whole of being! If the breath
  Be Life itself, and not its task and tent,
If even a soul like Milton's can know death;
  O Man! thou vessel purposeless, unmeant,
Yet drone-hive strange of phantom purposes!
  Surplus of Nature's dread activity,   10
Which, as she gazed on some nigh-finished vase,
Retreating slow, with meditative pause,
  She formed with restless hands unconsciously.
Blank accident! nothing's anomaly!

   If rootless thus, thus substanceless thy state,
Go, weigh thy dreams, and be thy hopes, thy fears,
The counter-weights!—Thy laughter and thy tears
  Mean but themselves, each fittest to create
And to repay the other! Why rejoices
  Thy heart with hollow joy for hollow good?   20
  Why cowl thy face beneath the mourner's hood?
Why waste thy sighs, and thy lamenting voices,
  Image of Image, Ghost of Ghostly Elf,
That such a thing as thou feel'st warm or cold?

Yet what and whence thy gain, if thou withhold
  These costless shadows of thy shadowy self?
Be sad! be glad! be neither! seek, or shun!
Thou hast no reason why! Thou canst have none;
Thy being's being is contradiction.

[1815?]   [1817]

FAITH, HOPE, AND CHARITY

FROM THE ITALIAN OF GUARINI

FAITH

Let those whose low delights to Earth are given
  Chaunt forth their earthly Loves! but we
  Must make an holier minstrelsy,
And, heavenly-born, will sing the Things of Heaven.

CHARITY

But who for us the listening Heart shall gain?
  Inaudible as of the sphere
  Our music dies upon the ear,
Enchanted with the mortal Syren's strain.

HOPE

Yet let our choral songs abound!
  Th' inspiring Power, its living Source,   10
  May flow with them and give them force,
If, elsewhere all unheard, in Heaven they sound.

ALL

Aid thou our voice, Great Spirit! thou whose flame
  Kindled the Songster sweet of Israel,
  Who made so high to swell
Beyond a mortal strain thy glorious Name.

CHARITY AND FAITH

Though rapt to Heaven, our mission and our care
  Is still to sojourn on the Earth,
  To shape, to soothe, Man's second Birth,
And re-ascend to Heaven, Heaven's prodigal Heir! 20

CHARITY

What is Man's soul of Love deprived?

HOPE. FAITH

It like a Harp untunéd is,
That sounds, indeed, but sounds amiss.

CHARITY. HOPE

From holy Love all good gifts are derived.

FAITH

But 'tis time that every nation
Should hear how loftily we sing.

FAITH. HOPE. CHARITY

See, O World, see thy salvation!
Let the Heavens with praises ring.
Who would have a Throne above,
Let him hope, believe and love;
And whoso loves no earthly song,   30
But does for heavenly music long,
Faith, Hope, and Charity for him,
Shall sing like wingéd Cherubim.

[1815]   [1912]

LIMBO

*   *   *   *   *

The sole true Something—This! In Limbo's Den
It frightens Ghosts, as here Ghosts frighten men.
Thence cross'd unseiz'd—and shall some fated hour
Be pulveris'd by Demogorgon's [1] power,
And given as poison to annihilate souls—
Even now it shrinks them—they shrink in as Moles
(Nature's mute monks, live mandrakes of the ground)
Creep back from Light—then listen for its sound;—
See but to dread, and dread they know not why—
The natural alien of their negative eye.   10

'Tis a strange place, this Limbo!—not a Place,
Yet name it so;—where Time and weary Space
Fettered from flight, with night-mare sense of fleeing,
Strive for their last crepuscular half-being;—
Lank Space, and scytheless Time with branny hands
Barren and soundless as the measuring sands,
Not mark'd by flit of Shades,—unmeaning they
As moonlight on the dial of the day!
But that is lovely—looks like Human Time,—
An Old Man with a steady look sublime,   20
That stops his earthly task to watch the skies;
But he is blind—a Statue hath such eyes;—
Yet having moonward turn'd his face by chance,
Gazes the orb with moon-like countenance,
With scant white hairs, with foretop bald and high,
He gazes still,—his eyeless face all eye;—
As 'twere an organ full of silent sight,
His whole face seemeth to rejoice in light!
Lip touching lip, all moveless, bust and limb—
He seems to gaze at that which seems to gaze on him!

[1] In ancient mythology, the mysterious, infernal power or divinity. See Shelley's *Prometheus Unbound*, below.

No such sweet sights doth Limbo den immure,   31
Wall'd round, and made a spirit-jail secure,
By the mere horror of blank Naught-at-all,
Whose circumambience doth these ghosts enthral.
A lurid thought is growthless, dull Privation,
Yet that is but a Purgatory curse;
Hell knows a fear far worse,
A fear—a future state;—'tis positive Negation!

[1817]   [1893]

THE KNIGHT'S TOMB

WHERE is the grave of Sir Arthur O'Kellyn?
Where may the grave of that good man be?—
By the side of a spring, on the breast of Helvellyn,
Under the twigs of a young birch tree!
The oak that in summer was sweet to hear,
And rustled its leaves in the fall of the year,
And whistled and roared in the winter alone,
Is gone,—and the birch in its stead is grown.—
The Knight's bones are dust,
And his good sword rust;—   10
His soul is with the saints, I trust.

[1817?]   .   [1834]

ON DONNE'S POETRY

WITH Donne, whose muse on dromedary trots,
Wreathe iron pokers into true-love knots;
Rhyme's sturdy cripple, fancy's maze and clue,
Wit's forge and fire-blast, meaning's press and screw.

[1818?]   [1836]

TO NATURE

IT may indeed be phantasy, when I
    Essay to draw from all created things
    Deep, heartfelt, inward joy that closely clings;
And trace in leaves and flowers that round me lie
Lessons of love and earnest piety.
    So let it be; and if the wide world rings
    In mock of this belief, it brings
Nor fear, nor grief, nor vain perplexity.
So will I build my altar in the fields,
    And the blue sky my fretted dome shall be,   10
And the sweet fragrance that the wild flower yields
    Shall be the incense I will yield to Thee,
Thee only God! and thou shalt not despise
Even me, the priest of this poor sacrifice.

[1820?]   [1836]

YOUTH AND AGE

VERSE, a breeze mid blossoms straying,
Where Hope clung feeding, like a bee—
Both were mine! Life went a-maying
            With Nature, Hope, and Poesy,
                When I was young!

When I was young?—Ah, woful When!
Ah! for the change 'twixt Now and Then!
This breathing house not built with hands,
This body that does me grievous wrong,
O'er aery cliffs and glittering sands,   10
How lightly then it flashed along:—
Like those trim skiffs, unknown of yore,
On winding lakes and rivers wide,
That ask no aid of sail or oar,
That fear no spite of wind or tide!
Nought cared this body for wind or weather
When Youth and I lived in't together.

Flowers are lovely; Love is flower-like;
Friendship is a sheltering tree;
O! the joys, that came down shower-like,   20
Of Friendship, Love, and Liberty,
                Ere I was old!

Ere I was old? Ah woful Ere,
Which tells me, Youth's no longer here!
O Youth! for years so many and sweet,
'Tis known, that Thou and I were one,
I'll think it but a fond conceit—
It cannot be that Thou art gone!
Thy vesper-bell hath not yet toll'd:—
And thou wert aye a masker bold!   30
What strange disguise hast now put on,
To make believe, that thou art gone?
I see these locks in silvery slips,
This drooping gait, this altered size:
But Spring-tide blossoms on thy lips,
And tears take sunshine from thine eyes!
Life is but thought: so think I will
That Youth and I are house-mates still.

Dew-drops are the gems of morning,
But the tears of mournful eve!   40
Where no hope is, life's a warning
That only serves to make us grieve,
                When we are old:

That only serves to make us grieve
With oft and tedious taking-leave,

Like some poor nigh-related guest,
That may not rudely be dismist;
Yet hath outstay'd his welcome while,
And tells the jest without the smile.

[1823–32]   [1839]

WORK WITHOUT HOPE

LINES COMPOSED 21ST FEBRUARY 1825

ALL Nature seems at work. Slugs leave their lair—
The bees are stirring—birds are on the wing—
And Winter slumbering in the open air,
Wears on his smiling face a dream of Spring!
And I the while, the sole unbusy thing,
Nor honey make, nor pair, nor build, nor sing.

Yet well I ken the banks where amaranths blow,
Have traced the fount whence streams of nectar flow.
Bloom, O ye amaranths! bloom for whom ye may,
For me ye bloom not! Glide, rich streams, away!   10
With lips unbrightened, wreathless brow, I stroll:
And would you learn the spells that drowse my soul?
Work without Hope draws nectar in a sieve,
And Hope without an object cannot live.

[1825]   [1828]

A CHARACTER

A BIRD who for his other sins
Had liv'd amongst the Jacobins;[1]
Though like a kitten amid rats,
Or callow tit in nest of bats,
He much abhorr'd all democrats;
Yet nathless stood in ill report
Of wishing ill to Church and Court,
Tho' he'd nor claw, nor tooth, nor sting,
And learnt to pipe God save the King;
Tho' each day did new feathers bring,   10
All swore he had a leathern wing;
Nor polish'd wing, nor feather'd tail,
Nor down-clad thigh would aught avail;
And tho'—his tongue devoid of gall—
He civilly assur'd them all:—
'A bird am I of Phoebus[2] breed,
And on the sunflower cling and feed;
My name, good Sirs, is Thomas Tit!'
The bats would hail him Brother Cit,[3]

Or, at the furthest, cousin-german.   20
At length the matter to determine,
He publicly denounced the vermin;
He spared the mouse, he praised the owl;
But bats were neither flesh nor fowl.
Blood-sucker, vampire, harpy, goul,
Came in full clatter from his throat,
Till his old nest-mates chang'd their note
To hireling, traitor, and turncoat,—
A base apostate who had sold
His very teeth and claws for gold;—   30
And then his feathers!—sharp the jest—
No doubt he feather'd well his nest!
'A Tit indeed! aye, tit for tat—
With place and title, brother Bat,
We soon shall see how well he'll play
Count Goldfinch, or Sir Joseph Jay!'
    Alas, poor Bird! and ill-bestarr'd—
Or rather let us say, poor Bard!
And henceforth quit the allegoric,
With metaphor and simile,   40
For simple facts and style historic:—
Alas, poor Bard! no gold had he;
Behind another's team he stept,
And plough'd and sow'd, while others reapt;
The work was his, but theirs the glory,
Sic vos non vobis,[4] his whole story.
Besides, whate'er he wrote or said
Came from his heart as well as head;
And though he never left in lurch
His king, his country, or his church,   50
'Twas but to humour his own cynical
Contempt of doctrines Jacobinical;
To his own conscience only hearty,
'Twas but by chance he serv'd the party;—
The self-same things had said and writ,
Had Pitt been Fox, and Fox been Pitt;[5]
Content his own applause to win,
Would never dash thro' thick and thin,
And he can make, so say the wise,
No claim who makes no sacrifice;—   60
And bard still less:—what claim had he,
Who swore it vex'd his soul to see
So grand a cause, so proud a realm,
With Goose and Goody at the helm;
Who long ago had fall'n asunder
But for their rivals' baser blunder,
The coward whine and Frenchified
Slaver and slang of the other side?—

---

[1] The most militant of the French revolutionaries. Coleridge here writes about himself as the bird and bard.
[2] God of the Sun, and poetry, Apollo.
[3] Citizen.

[4] "Thus do you work, but not for yourself alone" (Vergil).
[5] As a parliamentary reporter at the turn of the century, Coleridge frequently heard debates between William Pitt, the Tory prime minister (1783–1801, 1804–1806) and his Whig opponent Charles James Fox.

Thus, his own whim his only bribe,
Our Bard pursued his old A. B. C.   70
Contented if he could subscribe
In fullest sense his name Ἐστηστε;[6]
('Tis Punic Greek for 'he hath stood!')
Whate'er the men, the cause was good;
And therefore with a right good will,
Poor fool, he fights their battles still.
Tush! squeak'd the Bats;—a mere bravado
To whitewash that base renegado;
'Tis plain unless you're blind or mad,
His conscience for the bays he barters;—   80
And true it is—as true as sad—
These circlets of green baize he had—
But then, alas! they were his garters!

  Ah! silly Bard, unfed, untended,
His lamp but glimmer'd in its socket;
He lived unhonour'd and unfriended
With scarce a penny in his pocket;—
Nay—tho' he hid it from the many—
With scarce a pocket for his penny!

[1825]   [1834]

THE TWO FOUNTS

STANZAS ADDRESSED TO A LADY ON HER
RECOVERY WITH UNBLEMISHED LOOKS, FROM
A SEVERE ATTACK OF PAIN

'TWAS my last waking thought, how it could be
That thou, sweet friend, such anguish should'st
   endure;
When straight from Dreamland came a Dwarf, and
   he
Could tell the cause, forsooth, and knew the cure.

Methought he fronted me with peering look
Fix'd on my heart; and read aloud in game
The loves and griefs therein, as from a book:
And uttered praise like one who wished to blame.

In every heart (quoth he) since Adam's sin
Two Founts there are, of Suffering and of Cheer!   10
That to let forth, and this to keep within!
But she, whose aspect I find imaged here,

Of Pleasure only will to all dispense,
That Fount alone unlock, by no distress
Choked or turned inward, but still issue thence
Unconquered cheer, persistent loveliness.

---

[6] I.e.. the Greek transliteration of "S.T.C." and Coleridge's
frequent signature in journals. See, e.g., the conclusion of second
version of *Dejection*, p. 487.

As on the driving cloud the shiny bow,
That gracious thing made up of tears and light,
Mid the wild rack and rain that slants below
Stands smiling forth, unmoved and freshly bright;   20

As though the spirits of all lovely flowers,
Inweaving each its wreath and dewy crown,
Or ere they sank to earth in vernal showers,
Had built a bridge to tempt the angels down.

Even so, Eliza! on that face of thine,
On that benignant face, whose look alone
(The soul's translucence thro' her crystal shrine!)
Has power to soothe all anguish but thine own,

A beauty hovers still, and ne'er takes wing,
But with a silent charm compels the stern   30
And tort'ring Genius of the bitter spring,
To shrink aback, and cower upon his urn.

Who then needs wonder, if (no outlet found
In passion, spleen, or strife) the Fount of Pain
O'erflowing beats against its lovely mound,
And in wild flashes shoots from heart to brain?

Sleep, and the Dwarf with that unsteady gleam
On his raised lip, that aped a critic smile,
Had passed: yet I, my sad thoughts to beguile,
Lay weaving on the tissue of my dream;   40

Till audibly at length I cried, as though
Thou hadst indeed been present to my eyes,
O sweet, sweet sufferer; if the case be so,
I pray thee, be less good, less sweet, less wise!

In every look a barbéd arrow send,
On those soft lips let scorn and anger live!
Do any thing, rather than thus, sweet friend!
Hoard for thyself the pain, thou wilt not give!

[1826]   [1827]

NE PLUS ULTRA

*The title usually means perfection—"beyond which there is
nothing." Here, however, Coleridge uses it in the sense of positive
negation.*

NE PLUS ULTRA

SOLE POSITIVE of Night!
Antipathist of Light!
Fate's only essence! primal scorpion rod—
The one permitted opposite of God!—

Condenséd blackness and abysmal storm
    Compacted to one sceptre
      Arms the Grasp enorm—
        The Intercepter—
The Substance that still casts the shadow Death!—
      The Dragon foul and fell—   10
        The unrevealable,
And hidden one, whose breath
Gives wind and fuel to the fires of Hell!
      Ah! sole despair
    Of both th' eternities in Heaven!
Sole interdict of all-bedewing prayer,
      The all-compassionate!
    Save to the Lampads Seven [1]
Reveal'd to none of all th' Angelic State,
      Save to the Lampads Seven,   20
    That watch the throne of Heaven!

[1826?]   [1834]

CONSTANCY TO AN IDEAL OBJECT

SINCE all that beat about in Nature's range,
Or veer or vanish; why should'st thou remain
The only constant in a world of change,
O yearning Thought! that liv'st but in the brain?
Call to the Hours, that in the distance play,
The faery people of the future day——
Fond Thought! not one of all that shining swarm
Will breathe on thee with life-enkindling breath,
Till when, like strangers shelt'ring from a storm,
Hope and Despair meet in the porch of Death!   10
Yet still thou haunt'st me; and though well I see,
She is not thou, and only thou art she,
Still, still as though some dear embodied Good,
Some living Love before my eyes there stood
With answering look a ready ear to lend,
I mourn to thee and say—'Ah! loveliest friend!
That this the meed of all my toils might be,
To have a home, an English home, and thee!'
Vain repetition! Home and Thou are one.
The peacefull'st cot, the moon shall shine upon,   20
Lulled by the thrush and wakened by the lark,
Without thee were but a becalméd bark,
Whose Helmsman on an ocean waste and wide
Sits mute and pale his mouldering helm beside.

And art thou nothing? Such thou art, as when
The woodman winding westward up the glen
At wintry dawn, where o'er the sheep-track's maze
The viewless snow-mist weaves a glist'ning haze,

Sees full before him, gliding without tread,
An image* with a glory round its head;   30
The enamoured rustic worships its fair hues,
Nor knows he makes the shadow, he pursues!

[1826?]   [1828]

COLOGNE

IN Köln, a town of monks and bones,
And pavements fanged with murderous stones,
And rags, and hags, and hideous wenches;
I counted two and seventy stenches,
All well defined, and several stinks!
Ye Nymphs that reign o'er sewers and sinks,
  The river Rhine, it is well known,
  Doth wash your city of Cologne;
But tell me, Nymphs, what power divine
Shall henceforth wash the river Rhine?†

[1828]   [1834]

PHANTOM OR FACT

A DIALOGUE IN VERSE

AUTHOR

A LOVELY form there sate beside my bed,
And such a feeding calm its presence shed,
A tender love so pure from earthly leaven,
That I unnethe [1] the fancy might control,
'Twas my own spirit newly come from heaven,
Wooing its gentle way into my soul!
But ah! the change—It had not stirr'd, and yet—
Alas! that change how fain would I forget!

---

   * This phenomenon, which the Author has himself experienced, and of which the reader may find a description in one of the earlier volumes of the *Manchester Philosophical Transactions*, is applied figuratively to the following passage in the *Aids to Reflection*:—
  'Pindar's fine remark respecting the different effects of Music, on different characters, holds equally true of Genius—as many as are not delighted by it are disturbed, perplexed, irritated. The beholder either recognizes it as a projected form of his own Being, that moves before him with a Glory round its head, or recoils from it as a Spectre.'—[Coleridge] *Aids to Reflection* [1825], p. 220.
  † As Necessity is the mother of Invention, and extremes beget each other, the facts above recorded may explain how this *ancient* town (which, alas! as sometimes happens with venison, *has been kept too long*), *came to be the birthplace of the most fragrant of spirituous fluids, the* EAU DE COLOGNE.

<hr/>

[1] The Seven Lamps of the vision in Rev. 4:5. See *Ode on the Departing Year*, above.

[1] With difficulty.

That shrinking back, like one that had mistook!
That weary, wandering, disavowing look!   10
'Twas all another, feature, look, and frame,
And still, methought, I knew, it was the same!

FRIEND

This riddling tale, to what does it belong?
Is't history? vision? or an idle song?
Or rather say at once, within what space
Of time this wild disastrous change took
    place?

AUTHOR

Call it a moment's work (and such it seems)
This tale's a fragment from the life of dreams;
But say, that years matur'd the silent strife,
And 'tis a record from the dream of life.   20

[1830?]   [1834]

DESIRE

WHERE true Love burns Desire is Love's pure
    flame;
It is the reflex of our earthly frame,
That takes its meaning from the nobler part,
And but translates the language of the heart.

[1830?]   [1834]

SELF-KNOWLEDGE

—E coelo descendit γνῶθι σεαυτόν—JUVENAL, xi. 27.[1]

Γνῶθι σεαυτόν!—and is this the prime
And heaven-sprung adage of the olden time!—
Say, canst thou make thyself?—Learn first that
    trade;—
Haply thou mayst know what thyself had made.
What hast thou, Man, that thou dar'st call thine
    own?—
What is there in thee, Man, that can be known?—
Dark fluxion, all unfixable by thought,
A phantom dim of past and future wrought,
Vain sister of the worm,—life, death, soul, clod—
Ignore thyself, and strive to know thy God!   10

[1832]   [1834]

[1] The statement from Juvenal reads: "And then descended from heaven, Know thyself." See Coleridge's letter to Godwin, p. 509.

LOVE'S APPARITION AND EVANISHMENT

AN ALLEGORIC ROMANCE

LIKE a lone Arab, old and blind,
Some caravan had left behind,
Who sits beside a ruin'd well,
    Where the shy sand-asps bask and swell;
And now he hangs his agéd head aslant,
And listens for a human sound—in vain!
And now the aid, which Heaven alone can grant,
Upturns his eyeless face from Heaven to gain;—
Even thus, in vacant mood, one sultry hour,
Resting my eye upon a drooping plant,   10
With brow low-bent, within my garden-bower,
I sate upon the couch of camomile;
And—whether 'twas a transient sleep, perchance,
Flitted across the idle brain, the while
I watch'd the sickly calm with aimless scope,
In my own heart; or that, indeed a trance,
Turn'd my eye inward—thee, O genial Hope,
Love's elder sister! thee did I behold,
Drest as a bridesmaid, but all pale and cold,
With roseless cheek, all pale and cold and dim,   20
    Lie lifeless at my feet!
And then came Love, a sylph in bridal trim,
    And stood beside my seat;
She bent, and kiss'd her sister's lips,
    As she was wont to do;—
Alas! 'twas but a chilling breath
Woke just enough of life in death
    To make Hope die anew.

L'ENVOY

In vain we supplicate the Powers above;
There is no resurrection for the Love   30
That, nursed in tenderest care, yet fades away
In the chill'd heart by gradual self-decay.

[1833]   [1834]

EPITAPH

STOP, Christian passer-by!—Stop, child of God,
And read with gentle breast. Beneath this sod
A poet lies, or that which once seem'd he.
O, lift one thought in prayer for S. T. C.;
That he who many a year with toil of breath
Found death in life, may here find life in death!
Mercy for praise—to be forgiven for fame
He ask'd, and hoped, through Christ. Do thou the
    same!

[9th November, 1833]   [1834]

PROSE

LETTERS

To George Coleridge

—Sunday night. Feb. [23,] 1794

My Brother would have heard from me long ere this, had I not been unwell—unwell indeed—I verily thought, that I was hastening to that quiet Bourne, Where grief is hush'd—And when my recovered Strength would have enabled me to have written to you, so utterly dejected were my Spirits, that my letter would have displayed such a hopelessness of all future Comfort, as would have approached to Ingratitude—

Pardon me, my more than brother—! if it be the sickly jealousy of a mind sore with 'self-contracted miseries'—but was your last letter written in the same tone of tenderness with your former! Ah me! what awaits me from within and without, after the first tumult of Pity shall have subsided—Well were it, if the consciousness of having merited it could arm my Heart for the patient endurance of it—.

Sweet in the sight of God and celestial Spirits are the tears of Penitence—the pearls of heaven—the Wine of Angels!—Such has been the Language of Divines—but Divines have exaggerated.—Repentance may bestow that tranquillity, which will enable man to pursue a course of undeviating harmlessness, but it can not restore to the mind that inward sense of Dignity, which is the parent of every kindling Energy! —I am not, what I was:—*Disgust*—I *feel*, as if it had— jaundiced all my Faculties.

I laugh almost like an insane person when I cast my eye backward on the prospect of my past two years— What a gloomy *Huddle* of eccentric Actions, and dim-discovered motives! To real Happiness I bade adieu from the moment, I received my first Tutor's Bill— since that time since that period my Mind has been irradiated by Bursts only of Sunshine—at all other times gloomy with clouds, or turbulent with tempests. Instead of manfully disclosing the disease, I concealed it with a shameful Cowardice of sensibility, till it cankered my very Heart.—I became a proverb to the University for Idleness—the time, which I should have bestowed on the academic studies, I employed in dreaming out wild Schemes of impossible extrication. It had been better for me, if my Imagination had been

less vivid—I could not with such facility have shoved aside Reflection! How many and how many hours have I stolen from the bitterness of Truth in these soul-enervating Reveries—in building magnificent Edifices of Happiness on some fleeting Shadow of Reality! My Affairs became more and more involved—I fled to Debauchery—fled from silent and solitary Anguish to all the uproar of senseless Mirth! Having, or imagining that I had, no *stock* of Happiness, to which I could look forwards, I seized the empty gratifications of the moment, and snatched at the Foam, as the Wave passed by me.——I feel a painful blush on my cheek, while I write it—but even for the Un. Scholarship, for which I affected to have read so severely, I did not read three days uninterruptedly—for the whole six weeks, that preceded the examination, I was almost constantly intoxicated! My Brother, you shudder as you read——

When the state of my affairs became known to you, and by your exertions, and my Brothers' generous Confidence a fair Road seemed open to extrication— Almighty God! What a sequel!——

I loitered away more money on the road, and in town than it was possible for me to justify to my Conscience—and when I returned to Cambridge a multitude of petty Embarrassments buzzed round me, like a Nest of Hornets—Embarrassments, which in my wild carelessness I had forgotten, and many of which I had contracted almost without knowing it—So small a sum remained, that I could not mock my Tutor with it—My Agitations were delirium—I formed a Party, dashed to London at eleven o'clock at night, and for three days lived in all the tempest of Pleasure— resolved on my return—but I will not shock your religious feelings—I again returned to Cambridge— staid a week—such a week! Where Vice has not annihilated Sensibility, there is little need of a Hell! On Sunday night I packed up a few things,—went off in the mail—staid about a week in a strange way, still looking forwards with a kind of recklessness to the dernier resort of misery—An accident of a very singular kind prevented me—and led me to adopt my present situation—where what I have suffered—but enough—may he, who in mercy dispenseth Anguish, be gracious to me!

Ulcera possessis alte suffusa medullis
Non leviore manu, ferro sanantur et igni,
Ne coeat frustra mox eruptura cicatrix—

Ad vivum penetrant flammae, quò funditus humor
Defluat, et vacuis corrupto sanguine venis
Exundet fons ille mali. Claud.[1]——

I received a letter from Tiverton on Thursday full of wisdom, and tenderness, and consolation—I answered it immediately—Let me have the comfort of hearing from you—I will write again to morrow night—

S. T. C.—

Robert Southey (1774–1843) became Poet Laureate in 1813, and was one of Byron's favorite targets. He married Edith Fricker, Sara's sister, and thus was Coleridge's brother-in-law. See the poems on Pantisocracy, p, 433.

TO ROBERT SOUTHEY

Sept—18th—[1794]   10 o clock Thursday Morning

Well, my dear Southey! I am at last arrived at Jesus.[2] My God! how tumultuous are the movements of my Heart—Since I quitted this room what and how important Events have been evolved! America! Southey! Miss Fricker!—Yes—Southey—you are right—Even Love is the creature of strong Motive—I certainly love her. I think of her incessantly & with unspeakable tenderness—with that inward melting away of Soul that symptomatizes it.

Pantisocracy—O I shall have such a scheme of it! My head, my heart are all alive—I have drawn up my arguments in battle array—they shall have the *Tactician* Excellence of the Mathematician with the Enthusiasm of the Poet—The Head shall be the Mass—the Heart the fiery Spirit, that fills, informs, and agitates the whole—Harwood!—Pish! I say nothing of him—

SHAD GOES WITH US. HE IS MY BROTHER!

I am longing to be with you—Make Edith my Sister—Surely, Southey! we shall be frendotatoi meta frendous. Most friendly where all are friends. She must therefore be more emphatically my Sister.

Brookes & Berdmore, as I suspected, have spread

---

[1] "When an ulcer has penetrated to the marrow of the bones the touch of a hand is useless, steel and fire must sane the place that the wound heal not on the surface, like any moment to re-open. The flame must penetrate to the quick to make a way for the foul humours to escape; in order that, once the veins are emptied of corrupted blood, the fountainhead of the evil may be dried up." From Claudian, *Against Eutropius*, translated by Maurice Platnauer (Loeb Classical Library).

[2] I.e., Jesus College, Cambridge.

my Opinions in mangled forms at Cambridge—Caldwell the most excellent, the most pantisocratic of Aristocrats, has been laughing at me—Up I arose terrible in Reasoning—he fled from me—because 'he could not answer for his own Sanity sitting so near a madman of Genius!' He told me, that the Strength of my Imagination had intoxicated my Reason—and that the acuteness of my Reason had given a directing Influence to my Imagination.—Four months ago the Remark would not have been more elegant than Just—. Now it is Nothing.—

I like your Sonnets exceedingly—the best of any I have yet seen.—tho' to the eye Fair is the extended Vale—should be   To the Eye   Tho' fair the extended Vale—I by no means disapprove of Discord introduced to produce *effect*—nor is my Ear so fastidious as to be angry with it where it could not have been avoided without weakening the Sense—But Discord for Discord's sake is rather too licentious.—

'Wild wind' has no other but alliterative beauty—it applies to a storm, not to the Autumnal Breeze that makes the trees rustle mournfully—Alter it to

That rustle to the sad wind moaning by.

''Twas a long way & tedious'—& the three last lines are marked Beauties—unlaboured Strains poured soothingly along from the feeling Simplicity of Heart.—The next Sonnet is altogether exquisite—the circumstance common yet new to Poetry—the moral accurate & full of Soul. '*I never saw*['] &c is most exquisite——I am almost ashamed to write the following—it is so inferior—Ashamed! No—Southey—God knows my heart—I am *delighted* to feel you superior to me in Genius as in Virtue.

No more my Visionary Soul shall dwell
On Joys, that were! No more endure to weigh
The Shame and Anguish of the evil Day,
Wisely forgetful! O'er the Ocean swell
Sublime of Hope I seek the cottag'd Dell,
Where Virtue calm with careless step may stray,
And dancing to the moonlight Roundelay
The Wizard Passions weave an holy Spell.
Eyes that have ach'd with Sorrow! ye shall weep
Tears of doubt-mingled Joy, like their's who start
From Precipices of distemper'd Sleep,
On which the fierce-eyed Fiends their Revels k[eep,]
And see the rising Sun, & feel it dart
New Rays of Pleasance trembling to the Heart.[3]

I have heard from Allen—and write the *third* Letter to him. Your's is the *second*.—Perhaps you would like two Sonnets I have written to my Sally.——

---

[3] Lines 1–8 were incorporated into *Monody on the Death of Chatterton*, p. 430.

When I have received an answer from Allen, I will tell you the contents of his first Letter.—

My Comp— to Heath——

I will write you a huge big Letter next week—at present I have to transact the Tragedy Business, to wait on the Master, to write to Mrs Southey, Lovell, &c &c—

God love you— &

S. T. Coleridge

Mary Ann Evans, whom Coleridge had known since he was ten and thought he loved, tried to dissuade him from his Pantisocratic plan. This letter is a final, desperate appeal for her sympathy. Within a year he had married Sara Fricker, who was enthusiastic about it.

TO MARY EVANS

[London.]   [Early November 1794]

Too long has my Heart been the torture house of Suspense. After infinite struggles of Irresolution I will at last dare to request of you, Mary! that you will communicate to me whether or no you are engaged to Mr ——. I conjure you not to consider this request as presumptuous Indelicacy. Upon mine Honor, I have made it with no other Design or Expectation than that of arming my fortitude by total hopelessness. Read this Letter with benevolence—and consign it to Oblivion.

For four years I have *endeavored* to smother a very ardent attachment—in what degree I have succeeded, you must know better than I can. With quick perceptions of moral Beauty it was impossible for me not to admire in you your sensibility regulated by Judgment, your Gaiety proceeding from a cheerful Heart acting on the stores of a strong Understanding. At first I voluntarily invited the recollection of these qualities into my mind—I made them the perpetual Object of my Reveries—yet I entertained no one Sentiment beyond that of the immediate Pleasure annexed to the thinking of You. At length it became an Habit. I awoke from the Delusion, and found that I had unwittingly harboured a Passion which I felt neither the power or the courage to subdue. My associations were irrevocably formed, and your Image was blended with every idea. I thought of you incessantly: yet that Spirit (if Spirit there be that condescends to record the lonely Beatings of my heart) that Spirit knows, that I thought of you with the purity of a Brother. Happy were I, had it been with no more than a Brother's ardor!

The Man of dependent fortunes while he fosters an attachment commits an act of Suicide on his happiness. I possessed no Establishment—my views were very distant—I saw, that you regarded me merely with the kindness of a Sister——What expectations *could* I form? I formed no expectations—I was ever resolving to subdue the disquieting Passion: still some inexplicable Suggestion palsied my Efforts, and I clung with desperate fondness to this Phantom of Love, it's mysterious Attractions and hopeless Prospects. It was a faint and rayless Hope! Yet It soothed my Solitude with many a delightful day-dream. It was a faint and rayless Hope! Yet I nursed it in my Bosom with an Agony of Affection, even as a Mother her sickly Infant.——

But these are the poisoned Luxuries of a diseased Fancy! Indulge, Mary! this my first, my last request— and restore me to *Reality*, however gloomy. Sad and full of heaviness will the Intelligence be—my heart will die within me—I shall receive it however with steadier resignation from yourself, than were it announced to me (haply on your marriage Day!) by a Stranger! Indulge my request—I will not disturb your Peace by even a *Look* of Discontent—still less will I offend your Ear by the Whine of selfish Sensibility. In a few months I shall enter at the Temple—and there seek forgetful Calmness—where only it can be found —in incessant and useful Activity.

Were you not possessed of a Mind and of a Heart above the usual Lot of Women I should not have written you sentiments, that would be unintelligible to three fourths of your Sex. But our Feelings are congenial, though your [our?] attachment is doomed not to be reciprocal. You will not deem so meanly of me as to believe that I shall regard Mr——with the jaundiced Eye of disappointed Passion. God forbid! He, whom you honor with your Affections, becomes sacred to me. I shall love him for *your* Sake—the time may perhaps come, when I shall be Philosopher enough—not to envy him for *his own*!

S. T. Coleridge.

I return to Cambridge tomorrow Morning.

*Thomas Poole (1765–1837) was Coleridge's neighbor in Nether
Stowey, and a lifelong friend. This and the following letter,
written a day later, suggest the enormous range of Coleridge's
interests.*

TO THOMAS POOLE

Monday Night [23 March 1801]
My dear Friend

I received your kind Letter of the 14th—I was
agreeably disappointed in finding that you had been
interested in the Letter respecting Locke—those
which follow are abundantly more entertaining &
important; but I have no one to transcribe them—
nay, three Letters are written which have not been
sent to Mr Wedgewood, because I have no one to
transcribe them for me—& I do not wish to be without
Copies— / of that Letter, which you have, I have no
Copy.—It is somewhat unpleasant to me, that Mr
Wedgewood has never answered my letter requesting
his opinion of the utility of such a work, nor acknow-
leged the receipt of the long Letter containing the
evidence that the whole of Locke's system, as far as it
was a system, & with the exclusion of those parts only
which have been given up as absurdities by his warm-
est admirers, pre-existed in the writings of Des Cartes,
in a far more pure, elegant, & delightful form.——Be
not afraid, that I shall join the party of the *Little-ists*—
I believe, that I shall delight you by the detection of
their artifices—Now Mr Locke was the founder of this
sect, himself a perfect Little-ist. My opinion is this—
that deep Thinking is attainable only by a man of deep
Feeling, and that all Truth is a species of Revelation.
The more I understand of Sir Isaac Newton's works,
the more boldly I dare utter to my own mind & there-
fore to *you*, that I believe the Souls of 500 Sir Isaac
Newtons would go to the making up of a Shakspere or
a Milton. But if it please the Almighty to grant me
health, hope, and a steady mind, (always the 3 clauses
of my hourly prayers) before my 30th year I will
thoroughly understand the whole of Newton's Works
—At present, I must content myself with endeavour-
ing to make myself entire master of his easier work,
that on Optics. I am exceedingly delighted with the
beauty & neatness of his experiments, & with the
accuracy of his *immediate* Deductions from them—but
the opinions founded on these Deductions, and indeed
his whole Theory is, I am persuaded, so exceedingly
superficial as without impropriety to be deemed false.
Newton was a mere materialist—*Mind* in his system
is always passive—a lazy Looker-on on an external
World. If the mind be not *passive*, if it be indeed made
in God's Image, & that too in the sublimest sense—

the Image of the *Creator*—there is ground for suspi-
cion, that any system built on the passiveness of the
mind must be false, as a system. / I need not observe,
My dear Friend, how unutterably silly & contemptible
these Opinions would be, if written to any but to
another Self. I assure you, solemnly assure you, that
you & Wordsworth are the only men on Earth to
whom I would have uttered a word on this subject—.
It is a rule, by which I hope to direct all my literary
efforts, to let my Opinions & my Proofs go together.
It is *insolent* to *differ* from the public *opinion* in
opinion, if it be only *opinion*. It is sticking up little *i by
itself i* against the whole alphabet. But one *word* with
meaning in it is worth the whole alphabet together—
such is a sound Argument, an incontrovertible Fact.—
O for a lodge in a Land, where human Life was an
end, to which Labor was only a Means, instead of
being, as it [is] here, a mere means of carrying on
Labor.—I am oppressed at times with a true heart-
gnawing melancholy when I contemplate the state of
my poor oppressed Country.—God knows, it is as
much as I can do to put meat & bread on my own
table; & hourly some poor starving wretch comes to
my door, to put in his claim for part of it.—It fills me
with indignation to hear the *croaking* accounts, which
the English Emigrants send home of America. The
society is so bad—the manners so vulgar—the servants
so insolent.—Why then do they not seek out one
another, & make a society—? It is arrant ingratitude
to talk so of a Land in which there is no Poverty but
as a consequence of absolute Idleness—and to talk of
it too with abuse comparatively with England, with a
place where the laborious Poor are dying with Grass
with[in] their Bellies!—It is idle to talk of the Seasons
—as if that country must not needs be miserably
misgoverned in which an unfavorable Season intro-
duces a famine. No! No! dear Poole! it is our pestilent
Commerce, our unnatural Crowding together of men
in Cities, & our Government by Rich Men, that are
bringing about the manifestations of offended Deity.
——I am assured, that such is the depravity of the
public mind, that no literary man can find bread in
England except by misemploying & debasing his
Talents—that nothing of real excellence would be
either felt or understood. The annuity, which I hold,
perhaps by a very precarious Tenure, will shortly
from the decreasing value of money become less than
one half of what it was when first allowed to me—If I
were allowed to retain it, I would go & settle near
Priestly,[1] in America / I shall, no doubt, get a certain
price for the two or three works, which I shall next
publish—; but I foresee, they will not sell—the Book-

---

[1] See Coleridge's sonnet to Priestley, above.

sellers finding this will treat me as an unsuccessful Author—i.e. they will employ me only as an anonymous Translator at a guinea a sheet—(I will write *across* my other writing in order to finish what I have to say.) I have no doubt, that I could make 500£ a year, if I liked. But then I must forego all desire of Truth and Excellence. I say, I would go to America, if Wordsworth would go with me, & we could persuade two or three Farmers of this Country who are exceedingly attached to us, to accompany us—I would go, if the difficulty of procuring sustenance in this Country remain in the state & degree, in which it is at present. Not on any romantic Scheme, but merely because Society has become a matter of great Indifference to me—I grow daily more & more attached to Solitude—but it is a matter of the utmost Importance to be removed from seeing and suffering *Want*.

God love you, my dear Friend!—

S. T. Coleridge.

To Thomas Poole

Keswick, Tuesday, March 24. 1801

My dearest Poole

The latter half of my yesterday's Letter was written in 'a wildly-wailing strain.' The truth is, I was horribly hypochondriacal. So many miserable Beings, that day, travelling with half-famished children, had levied contributions on us, that when I received the Newspaper, I could scarcely read the Debates; my heart swelled so within me at the brutal Ignorance & Hardheartedness of all Parties alike—Add to this, I was affected by a Rheumatism in the back part of my head—and Add to this too, that I was irritated by the necessity, I was under, of intermitting most important & hitherto successful Researches, in order to earn a trifle of ready money by scribbling for a Newspaper. Having given to my own conscience proof of the activity & industry of my nature I seemed to myself to be entitled to exert those powers & that industry in the way, I myself approved.—In that mood of mind nothing appeared to me so delightful as to live in a Land where Corn & Meat were in abundance—& my imagination pointed to no other place, than those inland parts of America where there is little communication with their foul Cities, & all the articles of *Life*, of course, to be had for a trifle.—But my Country is my Country; and I will never leave it, till I am starved out of it.—Do not mistake me, my dear Poole!—I am not alarmed for the present year. I know that what I shall have finished in two or three months will fetch a fair Price, & disembarrass me compleatly; but I foresee, that my works will not sell, & that the Book-

sellers finding this will have nothing to do with me, except as an anonymous Hack at starving Wages. The Country is divided into two Classes—one rioting & wallowing in the wantonness of wealth, the other struggling for the necessaries of Life.—The Booksellers feel this—Longman told me, that 'scarcely any, but Books of expence, sold well. Expensive Paper, & Ornaments &c were never layed out in vain. For the chief Buyers of Books were the Wealthy who bought them for Furniture.'—Now what can *I* write that could please the Taste of a Rich Man?—Dear Poole—a man may be so kindly tempered by nature, and so fortunately placed by unusual circumstances, as that for a while he shall, tho' rich, bear up against the anti-human Influences of Riches; but they will at last conquer him. It is necessary for the human Being in the present state of society to have felt the pressures of actual Hardships, in order to be a moral Being. Where these have been never & in no degree felt, our very deeds of Pity do to a certain point co-operate to deprave us. Consider for a moment the different Feelings with which a poor woman in a cottage gives a piece of Bread & a cup of warm Tea to another poor Woman travelling with a Babe at her Back, & the Feelings with which a Lady lets two pence drop from her Carriage Window, out of the envelope of perfumed Paper by which her Pocket is defended from the Pollution of Copper——the difference is endless. But all this is better for our fire side Conversation, than for an eight-penny Letter.

I have sent you two more Letters, & will send the Rest / all of which you must bring back with you when you come.—When you come, I shall beg you to bring me a *Present*—it is, three Prisms—they will cost you 8 shillings a piece.

Some time ago I mentioned to you a thought which had suggested itself to me, of making Acorns more serviceable. I am convinced that this is practicable simply by malting them.—There was a total failure of acorns in this country last year, or I would have tried it. But last week as I was turning up some ground in my garden, I found a few acorns just beginning to sprout—and I eat them—they were, as I had anticipated, perfectly *sweet* & fine-flavored, & wholly & absolutely without any of that particular & offensive Taste which Acorns, when crude, leave upon the Palate, & Throat.—I have no doubt that they would make both bread & beer, of an excellent taste & nutritious Quality.—It may be objected,—Suppose this—what gain?—They fatten pigs at present—. This is however inaccurately stated—Where there are large woods of Oak, a few Pigs may be fattened—but Acorns are so uncertain a Crop, that except in large woods Pigs can never be kept on that speculation—& in truth of the Acorns [drop]ped every year $\frac{9}{10}$ths are wasted. Secondly, Pigs fed with only acorns have a bad flavor / thirdly, *Pigs* are likewise & more regularly fatted with Potatoes & Barley-meal—& if the Objection, which I have stated, held good against the *humanization* of Acorns it would have held good against the introduction of Potatoes & Barley, as human Food—nay, it actually has been made in Germany & France against Potatoes.—What gain, said they?—they are already useful—we fatten our Pigs with them.——In this Country Oaks thrive uncommonly well, & in very bleak & rocky Places—and I have little doubt, that by extending & properly managing the Plantation of Oaks, there might be 20 Families maintained where now there is one——For Corn in this country is a most uncertain crop; but it so happens, that those very seasons which utterly destroy Corn produce an overflow of Acorns, & those Seasons, which are particularly favorable to Corn, prevent the Harvest of Acorns. Thus, the Summer before last all the Corn was spoilt, but there was a prodigious Crop of Acorns—last summer there was a fine Crop of excellent Corn in these Counties (which never want as much moisture as Corn needs) but no acorns.—If my hopes should be realized by my experiments, it would add another to the innumerable Instances of the Almighty's wisdom & Love—making the Valleys & the Mountains supply, each the Failure of the other. When the Mountains are struck with drouth, the Valleys give Corn—when the Valleys are rotted with rain, the Mountains yield Acorns.——The great objection at present to the Planting of Oaks is their slow Growth (the young wood which is weeded out not paying sufficient for the *Board & Lodging* of the wood destined for Timber) —But very young Trees bear a certain proportion of acorns——Oaks, I apprehend, draw, even more than other T[rees], their nourishment from the moisture &c of the air, for they thrive in dry soils alone; yet are most fruitful in wet seasons. It is worth trying whether the Oak would be injured if the Leaves were taken off after the Acorns have fallen / they make a food for Horses, Cows, & Sheep.—Should it be true, that the Oak is fructified by superficial Irrigation, what a delightful Thing it would be if in every Plot adjacent to Mountain Cottages stood half a dozen noble Oaks, & the little red apple-cheeked children in drouthy seasons were turning a small Fire engine into the air so as to fall on them! Merciful God! what a contrast to the employment of these dear Beings by a wheel or a machine in a hellish Cotton Factory!—'See! see! what a pretty Rainbow *I* have made!'—&c &c *Write to me*—I cannot express to you what a consolation, I receive from your Letters! S. T. C.

My Wife has a violent Cold—Derwent is quite well —& Hartley has the worms. Do not forget to ask Chester for Greenough's address.—Love to your dear Mother.—

The Farmers in these Northern Counties are getting rich. Their Crops last year were excellent; but the County itself is starving. If it were found, that Potatoes would bear Carriage as well as Grain, there would be no Food left in the County. It would all go to Liverpool and Manchester, &c.

William Godwin (1756–1836), political philosopher (Political Justice), *was at times a friend of and an influence on Wordsworth, Coleridge, and Shelley (who was also his son-in-law). The tragedy to which he refers is Godwin's* Abbas, King of Persia.

To William Godwin

Greta Hall, Keswick   Wednesday, March 25, 1801
Dear Godwin

I fear, your Tragedy will find me in a very unfit state of mind to sit in Judgement on it. I have been, during the last 3 months, undergoing a process of intellectual *exsiccation*. In my long Illness I had compelled into hours of Delight many a sleepless, painful hour of Darkness by chasing down metaphysical Game—and since then I have continued the Hunt, till I found myself unaware at the Root of Pure Mathematics—and up that tall smooth Tree, whose few poor Branches are all at it's very summit, am I climbing by pure adhesive strength of arms and thighs—still slipping down, still renewing my ascent. —You would not know me—! all sounds of similitude keep at such a distance from each other in my mind, that I have *forgotten* how to make a rhyme—I look at the Mountains (that visible God Almighty that looks in at all my windows) I look at the Mountains only for the Curves of their outlines; the Stars, as I behold them, form themselves into Triangles—and my hands are scarred with scratches from a Cat, whose back I was rubbing in the Dark in order to see whether the sparks from it were refrangible by a Prism. The Poet is dead in me—my imagination (or rather the Somewhat that had been imaginative) lies, like a Cold Snuff on the circular Rim of a Brass Candle-stick, without even a stink of Tallow to remind you that it was once cloathed & mitred with Flame. That is past by!—I was once a Volume of Gold Leaf, rising & riding on every breath of Fancy—but I have beaten myself back into weight & density, & now I sink in quicksilver, yea, remain squat and square on the earth amid the hurricane, that makes Oaks and Straws join in one Dance, fifty yards high in the Element.

However, I will do what I can—Taste & Feeling have I none, but what I have, give I unto thee.—— But I repeat, that I am unfit to decide on any but works of severe Logic.

I write now to beg, that, if you have not sent your Tragedy, you may remember to send Antonio with it, which I have not yet seen—& likewise my Campbell's Pleasures of Hope, which Wordsworth wishes to see.

Have you seen the second Volume of the Lyrical Ballads, & the Preface prefixed to the First?——I should judge of a man's Heart, and Intellect precisely according to the degree & intensity of the admiration, with which he read those poems——Perhaps, instead of Heart I should have said Taste, but when I think of The Brothers, of Ruth, and of Michael, I recur to the expression, & am enforced to say *Heart*. If I die, and the Booksellers will give you any thing for my Life, be sure to say—'Wordsworth descended on him, like the Γνῶθι σεαυτόν from Heaven;[1] by shewing to him what true Poetry was, he made him know, that he himself was no Poet.'

In your next Letter you will perhaps give me some hints respecting your prose Plans.—.

God bless you
& S. T. Coleridge

I have inoculated my youngest child, Derwent, with the Cowpox—he passed thro' it without any sickness. —I myself am the Slave of Rheumatism—indeed, tho' in a certain sense I *am recovered* from my Sickness, yet I have by no means *recovered* it. I congratulate you on the settlement of Davy[2] in London.—I hope, that his enchanting manners will not draw too many Idlers round him, to harrass & vex his mornings.—. . .

P.S.—What is a fair Price—what might an Author of reputation fairly ask from a Bookseller for one Edition, of a 1000 Copies, of a five Shilling Book?—

Thomas Wedgwood (1771–1805), heir of the pottery family, was a benefactor of both Wordsworth and Coleridge. In 1802 Coleridge expected to accompany him on a long trip abroad, but Wedgwood's deteriorating health prevented it.

To Thomas Wedgwood

Oct. 20, 1802. Greta Hall, Keswick

My dear Sir

This is my Birth-day, my thirtieth. It will not appear wonderful to you therefore, when I tell you

[1] "Know thyself." All the poems mentioned in this paragraph are Wordsworth's.
[2] Sir Humphry Davy (1778–1829), chemist and long-time friend of Coleridge.

that before the arrival of your Letter I had been thinking with a great weight of different feelings concerning you & your dear Brother. For I have good reason to believe, that I should not now have been alive, if in addition to other miseries I had had immediate poverty pressing upon me. I will never again remain silent so long. It has not been altogether Indolence or my habits of Procrastination which have kept me from writing, but an eager wish, I may truly say, a Thirst of Spirit to have something honorable to tell you of myself——at present, I must be content to tell you something cheerful. My Health is very much better. I am stronger in every respect: & am not injured by study or the act of sitting at my writing Desk. But my eyes suffer, if at any time I have been intemperate in the use of Candlelight.—This account supposes another, namely, that my mind is calmer & more at ease.—My dear Sir! when I was last with you at Stowey, my heart was often full, & I could scarcely keep from communicating to you the tale of my domestic distresses. But how could I add to your depression, when you were low? or how interrupt or cast a shade on your good spirits, that were so rare & so precious to you?—After my return to Keswick I was, if possible, more miserable than before. Scarce a day passed without such a scene of discord between me & Mrs Coleridge, as quite incapacitated me for any worthy exertion of my faculties by degrading me in my own estimation. I found my temper injured, & daily more so; the good & pleasurable Thoughts, which had been the support of my moral character, departed from my solitude—I determined to go abroad—but alas! the less I loved my wife, the more dear & necessary did my children seem to me. I found no comfort except in the driest speculations—in the ode to dejection, which you were pleased with, these Lines in the original followed the line—My shaping Spirit of Imagination.

For not to think of what I needs must feel,
But to be still and patient, all I can,
And haply by abstruse Research to steal
From my own Nature all the natural Man—
This was my sole resource, my only plan,
And that which suits a part infects the whole
And now is almost grown the Temper of my Soul.[1]—

I give you these Lines for the Truth & not for the Poetry—.—However about two months ago after a violent quarrel I was taken suddenly ill with spasms in my stomach—I expected to die—Mrs C. was, of course, shocked & frightened beyond measure—&

[1] See the versions of *Dejection*, pp. 482–489.

two days after, I being still very weak & pale as death, she threw herself upon me, & made a solemn promise of amendment—& she has kept her promise beyond any hope, I could have flattered myself with: and I have reason to believe, that two months of tranquillity, & the sight of my now not colourless & cheerful countenance, have really made her feel as a Wife ought to feel. If any woman wanted an exact & copious Recipe, 'How to make a Husband compleatly miserable', I could furnish her with one—with a Probatum est,[2] tacked to it.—Ill tempered Speeches sent after me when I went out of the House, ill-tempered Speeches on my return, my friends received with freezing looks, the least opposition or contradiction occasioning screams of passion, & the sentiments, which I held most base, ostentatiously avowed—all this added to the utter negation of all, which a Husband expects from a Wife—especially, living in retirement—& the consciousness, that I was myself growing a worse man / O dear Sir! no one can tell what I have suffered. I can say with strict truth, that the happiest half-hours, I have had, were when all of a sudden, as I have been sitting alone in my Study, I have burst into Tears.——But better days have arrived, & are still to come. I have had visitations of Hope, that I may yet be something of which those, who love me, may be proud.—I cannot write that without recalling dear Poole—I have heard twice—& written twice—& I fear, that by a strange fatality one of the Letters will have missed him.—Leslie[3] was here sometime ago. I was very much pleased with him.—And now I will tell you what I am doing. I dedicate three days in the week to the Morning Post / and shall hereafter write for the far greater part such things as will be of as permanent Interest, as any thing I can hope to write ——& you will shortly see a little Essay of mine justifying the writing in a Newspaper. My Comparison of the French with the Roman Empire was very favorably received.—The Poetry, which I have sent, has been merely the emptying out of my Desk. The Epigrams are wretched indeed; but they answered Stuart's[4] purpose better than better things—/. I ought not to have given any signature to them whatsoever / I never dreamt of acknowleging either them or the Ode to the Rain. As to feeble expressions & unpolished Lines—there is the Rub! Indeed, my dear Sir! I do value your opinion very highly—I should think your judgment on the sentiment, the imagery, the flow of a Poem decisive / at least, if it differed from my own, & after frequent consideration mine remained different—it would leave me at least perplexed. For you are a perfect electrometer in these things— / but in point of poetic Diction I am not so well s[atisf]ied that you do not require a certain *Aloofness* from [the la]nguage of real Life, which I think deadly to Poetry. Very shortly however, I shall present you from the Press with my opinions in full on the subject of Style both in prose & verse—& I am confident of one thing, that I shall convince you that I have thought much & patiently on the subject, & that I understand the whole strength of my Antagonists' Cause.—For I am now busy on the subject—& shall in a very few weeks go to the Press with a Volume on the Prose writings of Hall, Milton, & Taylor—& shall immediately follow it up with an Essay on the writings of Dr. Johnson, & Gibbon—. And in these two Volumes I flatter myself, that I shall present a fair History of English Prose.—If my life & health remain, & I do but write half as much and as regularly, as I have done during the last six weeks, these will be finished by January next—& I shall then put together my memorandum Book on the subject of poetry. In both I have sedulously endeavoured to state the Facts, & the Differences, clearly & acutely—& my reasons for the Preference of one style to another are secondary to this.—Of this be assured, that I will never give any thing to the world in propriâ personâ, in my own name, which I have not tormented with the File. I sometimes suspect, that my foul Copy would often appear to general Readers more polished, than my fair Copy—many of the feeble & colloquial Expressions have been industriously substituted for others, which struck me as artificial, & not standing the test—as being neither the language of passion nor distinct Conceptions.—Dear Sir! indulge me with looking still further on to my literary Life. I have since my twentieth year meditated an heroic poem on the Siege of Jerusalem by Titus—this is the Pride, & the Stronghold of my Hope. But I never think of it except in my best moods.—The work, to which I dedicate the ensuing years of my Life, is one which highly pleased Leslie in prospective / & my paper will not let me prattle to you about it.——I have written what you most wished me to write—all about myself—.—Our climate is inclement, & our Houses not as compact as they might be / but it is a stirring climate / & the worse the weather, the more unceasingly entertaining are my Study Windows—& the month, that is to come, is the Glory of the year with us. A very warm Bedroom I can promise you, & one that at the same time commands our finest Lake— & mountain-view. If Leslie could not go abroad with you, & I could in any way mould my manners & habits to suit you, I should of all things like to be your companion. Good nature, an affectionate Disposition, &

---

[2] "Tried and proven."
[3] Sir John Leslie (1766–1832), mathematician and philosopher.
[4] Daniel Stuart, editor of the *Morning Post* to which Coleridge contributed both prose and verse.

so thorough a sympathy with the nature of your complaint that I should feel no pain, not the most momentary, in being told by you what your feelings required, at the time in which they required it—this I should bring with me. But I need not say, that you may say to me—'you don't suit me', without inflicting the least mortification.—Of course, this Letter is for your Brother, as for you—but I shall write to him soon. God bless you, & S. T. Coleridge

Richard Sharp (1759–1835) was a businessman who promoted literary conversation, clubs, and pilgrimages.

TO RICHARD SHARP

King's Arms, Kendal. Jan. 15, 1804—Sunday
Morning

My dear Sir

I give you thanks—and, that I may make the best of so poor & unsubstantial a Return, permit me to say, that they are such Thanks, as only come from a Nature unworldly by Constitution and by Habit, and now rendered more than ever impressible by sudden Restoration—Resurrection I might say—from a long long sick bed. I had gone to Grasmere to take my Farewell of William Wordsworth, his Wife, and his sister—and thither your Letters followed me—O dear Sir! I am heart-sick and stomach-sick of speaking and writing concerning myself—nay, let me be proud, not my self—but concerning my miserable carcase—the Caterpillar Skin which, I believe, the Butterfly Elect is wriggling off, tho' with no small Labor and Agony. —I was at Grasmere a whole month—so ill, as that till the last week I was unable to read your letters— not that my inner Being was disturbed—on the contrary, it seemed more than usually serene and self-sufficing—but the exceeding Pain, of which I suffered every now and then, and the fearful Distresses of my sleep, had taken away from me the connecting Link of voluntary power, which continually combines that Part of us by which we know ourselves to be, with that outward Picture or Hieroglyphic, by which we hold communion with our Like—between the Vital and the Organic—or what Berkley,[1] I suppose, would call— Mind and it's sensuous Language. I had only just strength enough to smile gratefully on my kind Nurses, who tended me with Sister's and Mother's Love, and often, I well know, wept for me in their

sleep, and watched for me even in their Dreams. O dear Sir! it does a man's heart good, I will not say, to know such a Family, but even—to know, that there *is* such a Family. In spite of Wordsworth's occasional Fits of Hypochondriacal Uncomfortableness—from which more or less, and at longer or shorter Intervals, he has never been wholly free from his very Childhood —in spite of this hypochondriacal *Graft* in his Nature, as dear Wedgwood calls it, his is the happiest Family, I ever saw—and *were* it not in too great Sympathy with my Ill health—*were* I in good Health and their Neighbour—I verily believe, that the Cottage in Grasmere Vale would be a proud sight for Philosophy. It is with no idle feeling of Vanity that I speak of my Importance to them—that it is *I* rather than another, is almost an Accident; but being so very happy within themselves they are too good, not the more for that very reason to want a Friend and common Object of Love out of their Household.—I have met with several genuine Philologists, Philonoists, Phisiophilists, keen hunters after knowledge and Science; but Truth and Wisdom are higher names than these—and *revering* Davy,[2] I am half angry with him for doing that which would make me laugh in another man—I mean, for prostituting and profaning the name of Philosopher, great Philosopher, eminent Philosopher &c &c &c to every Fellow, who has made a lucky experiment, tho' the man should be frenchified to the Heart, and tho' the whole Seine with all it's filth & poison flows in his Veins and Arteries—Of our common Friends, my dear Sir! I flatter myself that you and I should agree in fixing on T. Wedgwood, and on Wordsworth, as genuine Philosophers—for I have often said (and no wonder, since not a day passes but the conviction of the truth of it is renewed in me and with the conviction the accompanying Esteem and Love) often have I said that T. Wedgwood's Faults impress me with Veneration for his moral and intellectual character more than almost any other Man's Virtues: for under circumstances like his, to have a Fault only in that Degree is I doubt not in the eye of God to possess a high Virtue. Who does not prize the Retreat of Moreau more than all the Straw-blaze of Bonaparte's Victories?—and then to make it (as Wedgwood really does) a sort of crime even to think of his Faults by so many Virtues retained, cultivated and preserved in growth & blossom, in a climate—where now the Gusts so rise and eddy, that deeply-rooted must *that* be which is not snatched up & made a play thing of by them;—and now 'the parching Air Burns frore.'[3]— Mr. Wordsworth does not excite that almost painfully

---

[1] George Berkeley (1685–1753), Irish bishop and philosopher, after whom Coleridge named his second child.

[2] See note to Coleridge's letter to Godwin, p. 509
[3] Milton's *Paradise Lost*, Bk. II, lines 594–95.

profound moral admiration, which the sense of the exceeding Difficulty of a given Virtue can alone call forth, & which therefore I feel exclusively toward T. Wedgwood; but on the other hand, he is an object to be contemplated with greater complacency—because he both deserves to be, and *is*, a happy man—and a happy man, not from natural Temperament—for therein lies his main obstacle—not by enjoyment of the good things of this world—for even to this Day from the first Dawn of his Manhood he has purchased Independence and Leisure for great & good pursuits by austere frugality and daily Self-denial—nor yet by an accidental confluence of amiable and happy-making Friends and Relatives, for every one near to his heart has been placed there by Choice and after Knowlege and Deliberation—but he is a happy man, because he is a Philosopher—because he knows the intrinsic value of the Different objects of human Pursuit, and regulates his Wishes in Subordination to that Knowlege—because he feels, and with a *practical* Faith, the Truth of that which you, more than once, my dear Sir, have with equal good sense & Kindness pressed upon me, that we can do but one thing well, & that therefore we must make a choice—he has made that choice from his early youth, has pursued & is pursuing it—and certainly no small part of his happiness is owing to this Unity of Interest, & that Homogeneity of character which is the natural consequence of it—& which that excellent man, the Poet Sotheby, noticed to me as the characteristic of Wordsworth. Wordsworth is a Poet, a most original Poet—he no more resembles Milton than Milton resembles Shakespere —no more resembles Shakespere than Shakespere resembles Milton—he is himself: and I dare affirm that he will hereafter be admitted as the first & greatest philosophical Poet—the only man who has effected a compleat and constant synthesis of Thought & Feeling and combined them with Poetic Forms, with the music of pleasurable passion and with Imagination or the *modifying* Power in that highest sense of the word in which I have ventured to oppose it to Fancy, or the *aggregating* power—in that sense in which it is a dim Analogue of Creation, not all that we can *believe* but all that we can *conceive* of creation. Wordsworth is a Poet, and I feel myself a better Poet, in knowing how to honour *him*, than in all my own poetic Compositions, all I have done or hope to do—and I prophesy immortality to his *Recluse*, as the first & finest philosophical Poem, if only it be (as it undoubtedly will be) a Faithful Transcript of his own most august & innocent Life, of his own habitual Feelings & Modes of seeing and hearing.—My dear Sir! I began a Letter with a heart, heaven knows! how full of gratitude toward you—and I have flown off into a whole-Letter-full respecting Wedgwood & Wordsworth. Was it that my Heart demanded an outlet for grateful Feelings—for a long *stream* of them—and that I felt it would be oppressive to you if I wrote to you of yourself half of what I wished to write? or was it that I knew I should be in Sympathy with you—& that few subjects are more pleasing to you than the Details of the merits of two men, whom, I am sure, you *esteem* equally with myself—tho' accidents have thrown me or rather Providence has placed me in a closer connection with them, both as confidential Friends, & the one as my Benefactor, & to whom I owe that my Bed of Sickness has not been in a House of Want, unless I had *bought* the contrary at the Price of my Conscience by becoming a Priest.—

I leave this place this afternoon having walked from Grasmere yesterday. I walked the 19 miles thro' mud & Drizzle, fog & stifling air, in four hours and 35 minutes—& was not in the least fatigued so that you may see that my sickness has not much weakened me —Indeed the Suddenness & seeming Perfectness of my Recovery is [are] really astonishing. In a single hour I have changed from a state that seemed next to Death, swoln Limbs, racking Teeth, & sick & convulsed stomach to a state of elastic Health—so that I have said—If I have been dreaming yet you, Wordsworth, have been awake. And Wordsworth has answered—I could not expect any one to believe it who had not seen it—These changes have always been produced by sudden changes of the weather—dry hot weather or dry frosty weather seem alike friendly to me, and my persuasion is strong as the Life within me that a year's residence in Madeira would renovate me. I shall spend two days in Liverpool—& hope to be in London, Coach & Coachmen permitting, on Friday Afternoon or Saturday at the furthest—And on this day week I look forward to the pleasure of thanking you personally—for I still hope to avail myself of your kind Introductions—I mean to wait in London till a good Vessel sails for Madeira, but of this when I see you—believe me my dear Sir,

With grateful & affectionate thanks

Your sincere Friend
S. T. Coleridge

FROM

NOTEBOOKS

1803 and 1799

[1575]

Print of the Darlington Ox, sprigged with Spots.—Viewed in all moods, consciously, uncons. semiconsc.—with vacant, with swimming eyes—made a Thing of Nature by the repeated action of the Feelings. O Heaven when I think how perishable Things, how imperishable Thoughts seem to be!—For what is Forgetfulness? Renew the state of affection or bodily Feeling, same or similar—sometimes dimly similar / and instantly the trains of forgotten Thought rise from their living catacombs!—Old men, & Infancy / and Opium, probably by its narcotic effect on the whole seminal organization, in a large Dose, or after long use, produces the same effect on the *visual, & passive* memory/. so far was written in my b.pocket[book] Nov. 25th 1799—Monday Afternoon, the Sun shining in upon the Print, in beautiful Lights—& I just about to take Leave of Mary—& having just before taken leave of Sara.—I did not then know Mary's & William's attachment /

　　　The lingering Bliss,
　The long entrancement of a True-love Kiss.
Nov. 24th—the Sunday—Conundrums & Puns & Stories & Laughter—with Jack Hutchinson—Stood up round the Fire, et Saræ manum a tergo longum in tempus prensabam, and tunc temporis, tunc primum, amor me levi spiculo, venenato, eheu! & insanabili, &c.
Oct. 22. 23. 24th. on the road in a post-chaise with poor Cottle / the modest men in conversation, the vain the envious in their closets, & on their pillows!—Oct. 27th, 1799. Is [. . . . .]

[1576]

Ten Kisses short as one, one long as twenty.

[1577]

Slanting Pillars of Light, like Ladders up to Heaven,

their base always a field of vivid green Sunshine /—This is Oct. 19. 1803. Wed. Morn. tomorrow my Birth Day, 31 years of age!—O me! my very heart dies!—This *year* has been one painful Dream / I have done nothing!—O for God's sake, let me whip & spur, so that Christmas may not pass without some thing having been done /—at all events to finish The Men & the Times, & to collect them & all my Newspaper Essays into one Volume / to collect all my poems, finishing the Vision of the Maid of Orleans, ~~one~~ & the Dark Ladie, & make a second Volume / & to finish Christabel.—I ought too, in common gratitude, to write out my two Tours, for Sally Wedgwood /

Oct. 19. 1803. The general Fast Day—and all hearts anxious concerning the Invasion.—A grey Day, windy—the vale, like a place in Faery, with the autumnal Colours, the orange, the red-brown, the crimson. the light yellow, the yet lingering Green, Beeches ~~all~~ & Birches, as they were blossoming Fire & Gold!—& the Sun in slanting pillars, or illuminated small parcels of mist, or single spots of softest greyish Light, now racing, now slowly gliding, now stationary /—the mountains cloudy—the Lake has been a mirror so very clear, that the water became almost invisible—& now it rolls in white Breakers, like a Sea; & the wind snatches up the water, & drifts it like Snow /—and now the Rain Storm pelts against my Study Window!—Ο Σαρα Σαρα why am I not happy! why have I not an unencumbered Heart! these beloved Books still before me, this noble Room, the very centre to which a whole world of beauty converges, the deep reservoir into which all these streams & currents of lovely Forms flow—my own mind so populous, so active, so full of noble schemes, so capable of realizing them / this heart so loving, so filled with noble affections—O Ασρα! wherefore am I not happy! why for years have I not enjoyed one pure & sincere pleasure!—one full Joy!—one genuine Delight, that rings sharp to the Beat of the Finger!—all cracked, & dull with base Alloy!—Di Boni! mihi vim et virtutem / vel tu, [. . . . . .], eheu! perdite amatio!

But still have said to the poetic Feeling when it has awak'd in the Heart—Go!—come tomorrow.—

A day of Storm / at dinner an explosion of Temper from the Sisters / a dead Sleep after Dinner / the Rhubarb had its usual enfeebling-narcotic effect / I slept again with dreams of sorrow & pain, tho' not of downright Fright & prostration / I was worsted but not conquered—in sorrows and in sadness & in sore & angry Struggles—but not trampled down / but this will all come again, if I do not take care.

Storm all night—the wind scourging & lashing the rain, with the pauses of self-wearying Violence that returns to its wild work as if maddened by the necessity of the Pause / I, half-dozing, list'ning to the same, not without solicitations of the poetic Feeling / for from I have written, Oct. 20. 1803, on Thursday Morning, 40 minutes past 2°clock.

[1578]

In the North every Brook, every Crag, almost every Field has a name / a proof of greater Independence & of a Society truer to Nature.

[1579]

All about Sockburn & indeed generally thro' the North Riding of Yorkshire & in Durham, Asses are counted so lucky that they are almost universally kept among Cows in Dairy Farms. If a man should buy a Horse of great Value he immediately purchases an Ass—for Luck! The Ass runs both with the Horse & with the Cows; especially with the Cows, as in calving they are more subject to accidents.—

[1580]

Sept. 11. 1799. I was with Southey at Lesley Cleve, and passed over a Bridge of Rocks, then a Bridge, the low stream running underneath, but in high swells the bed of a Torrent—& still in the Interstices of the Rocks lay the Foam of the Yester-night's Torrent.

[1581]

Sept. 12, at Dartmouth / observed the Moon thrusting thro' a thin Slip of white Cloud about half her own Breadth pushed with contracted Point, like the narrower end of the egg, then emerging recovered her shape above, & the under half entering the cloud contracted in the same manner.

[1582]

Thousand—from Thou + Sand?—or from Tassen, an old Suabian word = acervare.—Sept. 14 at Newton Bushel compared Southey in the Ann. Anthology[1] to a Salmon dressed with Shrimp Sauce. 1/2 a mile from Newton Bushel took this from a Garden Gate / Man Traps and Spring Guns till'd in this Garden.— Till = to prepare—put ready. Till, until—to till— all the same word.—And this is the whole account that I preserve of my interesting Tour in Devonshire with Southey—tho' we were at that interesting Bovy Waterfall—thro' that wild Dell of Ashes that leads to Ashburton, most like the approach to Matterdale from Keswick / to Dartington, Totness, Dartmouth / Dartmouth itself so very well worth describing.— N.B. Did I write to Wordsworth any Description— and of the man, near Totness, who took us two miles out of our way on a long Journey—as we thought to shew us a nearer way—but in reality only to shew us a field of 4 acres, for which a Farmer had given 40 years purchase / the rent being 2 £ per acre!—O how we laughed & cursed!—I have at this moment very

distinct visual impressions of this Tour (namely, Oct. 19. 1803) of Torbay—& the village of Paynton with the Castle—and I had the black Pocket-book.

[1583]

At Oct. 25th. I was with Cottle[2] in a Post Chaise at Easingwold—& suppose I left Bristol. Oct. 22. 1799 for my most important Journey to the North.— Governments gouge. Scotchmen returning to Scotland = stream flowing back to its fountain. at Tadcaster saw a most interesting Picture on the road—a flock of sheep, and perhaps 200 yards behind a sick Sheep with its head on the ground, a dog looking up at the little Boy's face—and the poor little sheep boy standing close by the sick Sheep, anxiously looking forward to the Flock—not knowing what to do! I never saw distressful Doubt so strongly painted.— Saw, that Day, some Sheep passing a Bank & leaping off it with their heads turned to the quarter from whence they leapt on the Bank, repeatedly came to it again—a true argumentum in circulo!—

[1584]

Taste for Paradox in my man of Roads—always preferred cold water in shaving—& turned the glass & looked steadily at its Back while shaving, &c &c.

BIOGRAPHIA LITERARIA

As Wordsworth's Prelude was an account of the growth of his own mind rather than a narrative of the events of his life, so Coleridge's autobiography is made up of "biographical sketches of my literary life and opinions." Chapters XIII and XIV, among the most theoretical, have been frequently cited as providing key ideas and terms for modern literary theory. Earlier chapters do offer some narrative accounts of Coleridge's activities, and several later ones very specifically concern themselves with Wordsworth's poems.

BIOGRAPHIA LITERARIA
(1817)

FROM

CHAPTER XIII

* * * * *

DES CARTES, speaking as a naturalist, and in imitation of Archimedes, said, give me matter and motion and I will construct you the universe. We must of course understand him to have meant: I will render the construction of the universe intelligible. In the same sense the transcendental philosopher says; grant

---

[1] *Annual Anthology.*

[2] Joseph Cottle (1770–1853), Bristol publisher, bookseller, and minor poet, an early friend of Wordsworth and Coleridge.

me a nature having two contrary forces, the one of which tends to expand infinitely, while the other strives to apprehend or *find* itself in this infinity, and I will cause the world of intelligences with the whole system of their representations to rise up before you. Every other science presupposes intelligence as already existing and complete: the philosopher contemplates it in its growth, and as it were represents its history to the mind from its birth to its maturity.

*   *   *   *   *

The IMAGINATION then, I consider either as primary, or secondary. The primary IMAGINATION I hold to be the living Power and prime Agent of all human Perception, and as a repetition in the finite mind of the eternal act of creation in the infinite I AM. The secondary Imagination I consider as an echo of the former, co-existing with the conscious will, yet still as identical with the primary in the *kind* of its agency, and differing only in *degree*, and in the *mode* of its operation. It dissolves, diffuses, dissipates, in order to re-create; or where this process is rendered impossible, yet still at all events it struggles to idealize and to unify. It is essentially *vital*, even as all objects (*as* objects) are essentially fixed and dead.

FANCY, on the contrary, has no other counters to play with, but fixities and definites. The Fancy is indeed no other than a mode of Memory emancipated from the order of time and space; while it is blended with, and modified by that empirical phenomenon of the will, which we express by the word CHOICE. But equally with the ordinary memory the Fancy must receive all its materials ready made from the law of association.

Whatever more than this, I shall think it fit to declare concerning the powers and privileges of the imagination in the present work, will be found in the critical essay on the uses of the Supernatural in poetry, and the principles that regulate its introduction: which the reader will find prefixed to the poem of 𝕿𝖍𝖊 𝕬𝖓𝖈𝖎𝖊𝖓𝖙 𝕸𝖆𝖗𝖎𝖓𝖊𝖗.

CHAPTER XIV

Occasion of the Lyrical Ballads, and the objects originally proposed—Preface to the second edition—The ensuing controversy, its causes and acrimony—Philosophic definitions of a poem and poetry with scholia.

DURING the first year that Mr. Wordsworth and I were neighbours, our conversations turned frequently on the two cardinal points of poetry, the power of exciting the sympathy of the reader by a faithful adherence to the truth of nature, and the power of giving the interest of novelty by the modifying colors of imagination. The sudden charm, which accidents of light and shade, which moon-light or sun-set diffused over a known and familiar landscape, appeared to represent the practicability of combining both. These are the poetry of nature. The thought suggested itself (to which of us I do not recollect) that a series of poems might be composed of two sorts. In the one, the incidents and agents were to be, in part at least, supernatural; and the excellence aimed at was to consist in the interesting of the affections by the dramatic truth of such emotions, as would naturally accompany such situations, supposing them real. And real in *this* sense they have been to every human being who, from whatever source of delusion, has at any time believed himself under supernatural agency. For the second class, subjects were to be chosen from ordinary life; the characters and incidents were to be such, as will be found in every village and its vicinity, where there is a meditative and feeling mind to seek after them, or to notice them, when they present themselves.

In this idea originated the plan of the "Lyrical Ballads"; in which it was agreed, that my endeavours should be directed to persons and characters supernatural, or at least romantic; yet so as to transfer from our inward nature a human interest and a semblance of truth sufficient to procure for these shadows of imagination that willing suspension of disbelief for the moment, which constitutes poetic faith. Mr. Wordsworth, on the other hand, was to propose to himself as his object, to give the charm of novelty to things of every day, and to excite a feeling analogous to the supernatural, by awakening the mind's attention from the lethargy of custom, and directing it to the loveliness and the wonders of the world before us; an inexhaustible treasure, but for which, in consequence of the film of familiarity and selfish solicitude we have eyes, yet see not, ears that hear not, and hearts that neither feel nor understand.

With this view I wrote "The Ancient Mariner," and was preparing among other poems, "The Dark Ladie," and the "Christabel," in which I should have more nearly realized my ideal, than I had done in my first attempt. But Mr. Wordsworth's industry had proved so much more successful, and the number of his poems so much greater, that my compositions, instead of forming a balance, appeared rather an interpolation of heterogeneous matter. Mr. Wordsworth added two or three poems written in his own character, in the impassioned, lofty, and sustained diction, which is characteristic of his genius. In this form the "Lyrical Ballads" were published; and were presented by him, as an *experiment*, whether subjects, which from their nature rejected the usual ornaments and extra-collo-quial style of poems in general, might not be so managed in the language of ordinary life as to produce the pleasureable interest, which it is the peculiar business of poetry to impart. To the second edition he added a preface of considerable length; in which, notwithstanding some passages of apparently a contrary import, he was understood to contend for the extension of this style to poetry of all kinds, and to reject as vicious and indefensible all phrases and forms of style that were not included in what he (unfortunately, I think, adopting an equivocal expression) called the language of *real* life. From this preface, prefixed to poems in which it was impossible to deny the presence of original genius, however mistaken its direction might be deemed, arose the whole long-continued controversy. For from the conjunction of perceived power with supposed heresy I explain the inveteracy and in some instances, I grieve to say, the acrimonious passions, with which the controversy has been conducted by the assailants.

Had Mr. Wordsworth's poems been the silly, the childish things, which they were for a long time described as being; had they been really distinguished from the compositions of other poets merely by meanness of language and inanity of thought; had they indeed contained nothing more than what is found in the parodies and pretended imitations of them; they must have sunk at once, a dead weight, into the slough of oblivion, and have dragged the preface along with them. But year after year increased the number of Mr. Wordsworth's admirers. They were found too not in the lower classes of the reading public, but chiefly among young men of strong sensibility and meditative minds; and their admiration (inflamed perhaps in some degree by opposition) was distinguished by its intensity, I might almost say, by its *religious* fervor. These facts, and the intellectual energy of the author, which was more or less consciously felt, where it was outwardly and even boisterously denied, meeting with sentiments of aversion to his opinions, and of alarm at their consequences, produced an eddy of criticism, which would of itself have borne up the poems by the violence, with which it whirled them round and round. With many parts of this preface, in the sense attributed to them, and which the words undoubtedly seem to authorize, I never concurred; but on the contrary objected to them as erroneous in principle, and as contradictory (in appearance at least) both to other parts of the same preface, and to the author's own practice in the greater number of the poems themselves. Mr. Wordsworth in his recent collection has, I find, degraded this prefatory disquisition to the end of his second volume, to be read or not at the reader's

choice. But he has not, as far as I can discover, announced any change in his poetic creed. At all events, considering it as the source of a controversy, in which I have been honored more than I deserve by the frequent conjunction of my name with his, I think it expedient to declare once for all, in what points I coincide with his opinions, and in what points I altogether differ. But in order to render myself intelligible I must previously, in as few words as possible, explain my ideas, first, of a POEM; and secondly, of POETRY itself, in *kind*, and in *essence*.

The office of philosophical *disquisition* consists in just *distinction*; while it is the privilege of the philosopher to preserve himself constantly aware, that distinction is not division. In order to obtain adequate notions of any truth, we must intellectually separate its distinguishable parts; and this is the technical *process* of philosophy. But having so done, we must then restore them in our conceptions to the unity, in which they actually co-exist; and this is the *result* of philosophy. A poem contains the same elements as a prose composition; the difference therefore must consist in a different object being proposed. According to the difference of the object will be the difference of the combination. It is possible, that the object may be merely to facilitate the recollection of any given facts or observations by artificial arrangement; and the composition will be a poem, merely because it is distinguished from prose by metre, or by rhyme, or by both conjointly. In this, the lowest sense, a man might attribute the name of a poem to the well-known enumeration of the days in the several months;

"Thirty days hath September,
April, June, and November," &c.

and others of the same class and purpose. And as a particular pleasure is found in anticipating the recurrence of sounds and quantities, all compositions that have this charm super-added, whatever be their contents, *may* be entitled poems.

So much for the superficial *form*. A difference of object and contents supplies an additional ground of distinction. The immediate purpose may be the communication of truths; either of truth absolute and demonstrable, as in works of science; or of facts experienced and recorded, as in history. Pleasure, and that of the highest and most permanent kind, may *result* from the *attainment* of the end; but it is not itself the immediate end. In other works the communication of pleasure may be the immediate purpose; and though truth, either moral or intellectual, ought to be the *ultimate* end, yet this will distinguish the character of the author, not the class to which the work belongs. Blest indeed is that state of society, in which the immediate purpose would be baffled by the perversion of the proper ultimate end; in which no charm of diction or imagery could exempt the Bathyllus even of an Anacreon, or the Alexis of Virgil, from disgust and aversion![1]

But the communication of pleasure may be the immediate object of a work not metrically composed; and that object may have been in a high degree attained, as in novels and romances. Would then the mere superaddition of metre, with or without rhyme, entitle *these* to the name of poems? The answer is, that nothing can permanently please, which does not contain in itself the reason why it is so, and not otherwise. If metre be superadded, all other parts must be made consonant with it. They must be such, as to justify the perpetual and distinct attention to each part, which an exact correspondent recurrence of accent and sound are calculated to excite. The final definition then, so deduced, may be thus worded. A poem is that species of composition, which is opposed to works of science, by proposing for its *immediate* object pleasure, not truth; and from all other species (having *this* object in common with it) it is discriminated by proposing to itself such delight from the *whole*, as is compatible with a distinct gratification from each component *part*.

Controversy is not seldom excited in consequence of the disputants attaching each a different meaning to the same word; and in few instances has this been more striking, than in disputes concerning the present subject. If a man chooses to call every composition a poem, which is rhyme, or measure, or both, I must leave his opinion uncontroverted. The distinction is at least competent to characterize the writer's intention. If it were subjoined, that the whole is likewise entertaining or affecting, as a tale, or as a series of interesting reflections, I of course admit this as another fit ingredient of a poem, and an additional merit. But if the definition sought for be that of a *legitimate* poem, I answer, it must be one, the parts of which mutually support and explain each other; all in their proportion harmonizing with, and supporting the purpose and known influences of metrical arrangement. The philosophic critics of all ages coincide with the ultimate judgement of all countries, in equally denying the praises of a just poem, on the one hand, to a series of striking lines or distiches, each of which, absorbing the whole attention of the reader to itself, disjoins it from its context, and makes it a separate whole, instead of an harmonizing part; and on the

other hand, to an unsustained composition, from which the reader collects rapidly the general result, unattracted by the component parts. The reader should be carried forward, not merely or chiefly by the mechanical impulse of curiosity, or by a restless desire to arrive at the final solution; but by the pleasureable activity of mind excited by the attractions of the journey itself. Like the motion of a serpent, which the Egyptians made the emblem of intellectual power; or like the path of sound through the air; at every step he pauses and half recedes, and from the retrogressive movement collects the force which again carries him onward. "Præcipitandus est *liber* spiritus," says Petronius Arbiter most happily.[2] The epithet, *liber*, here balances the preceding verb; and it is not easy to conceive more meaning condensed in fewer words.

But if this should be admitted as a satisfactory character of a poem, we have still to seek for a definition of poetry. The writings of PLATO, and Bishop TAYLOR, and the "Theoria Sacra" of BURNET,[3] furnish undeniable proofs that poetry of the highest kind may exist without metre, and even without the contra-distinguishing objects of a poem. The first chapter of Isaiah (indeed a very large portion of the whole book) is poetry in the most emphatic sense; yet it would be not less irrational than strange to assert, that pleasure, and not truth, was the immediate object of the prophet. In short, whatever *specific* import we attach to the word, poetry, there will be found involved in it, as a necessary consequence, that a poem of any length neither can be, or ought to be, all poetry. Yet if an harmonious whole is to be produced, the remaining parts must be preserved *in keeping* with the poetry; and this can be no otherwise effected than by such a studied selection and artificial arrangement, as will partake of *one*, though not a *peculiar* property of poetry. And this again can be no other than the property of exciting a more continuous and equal attention than the language of prose aims at, whether colloquial or written.

My own conclusions on the nature of poetry, in the strictest use of the word, have been in part anticipated in the preceding disquisition on the fancy and imagination. What is poetry? is so nearly the same question with, what is a poet? that the answer to the one is involved in the solution of the other. For it is a distinction resulting from the poetic genius itself, which

---

[1] Bathyllus and Alexis are beautiful young men celebrated by the Greek Anacreon and the Roman Vergil (second *Eclogue*), respectively.

[2] From Petronius' *Satyricon*: "the free spirit must be propelled onward."

[3] Jeremy Taylor (1613–1667) and Thomas Burnet (c. 1635–1715) were both bishops, philosophers, and theologians, as well as distinguished prose stylists. An example of Burnet's prose is prefaced to *The Rime of the Ancient Mariner*.

sustains and modifies the images, thoughts, and emotions of the poet's own mind.

The poet, described in *ideal* perfection, brings the whole soul of man into activity, with the subordination of its faculties to each other, according to their relative worth and dignity. He diffuses a tone and spirit of unity, that blends, and (as it were) *fuses*, each into each, by that synthetic and magical power, to which we have exclusively appropriated the name of imagination. This power, first put in action by the will and understanding, and retained under their irremissive, though gentle and unnoticed, controul (*laxis effertur habenis*) reveals itself in the balance or reconciliation of opposite or discordant qualities: of sameness, with difference; of the general, with the concrete; the idea, with the image; the individual, with the representative; the sense of novelty and freshness, with old and familiar objects; a more than usual state of emotion, with more than usual order; judgement ever awake and steady self-possession, with enthusiasm and feeling profound or vehement; and while it blends and harmonizes the natural and the artificial, still subordinates art to nature; the manner to the matter; and our admiration of the poet to our sympathy with the poetry. "Doubtless," as Sir John Davies observes of the soul (and his words may with slight alteration be applied, and even more appropriately, to the poetic IMAGINATION)

"Doubtless this could not be, but that she turns
    Bodies to spirit by sublimation strange,
As fire converts to fire the things it burns,
    As we our food into our nature change.

From their gross matter she abstracts their forms,
    And draws a kind of quintessence from things;
Which to her proper nature she transforms,
    To bear them light on her celestial wings.

Thus does she, when from individual states
    She doth abstract the universal kinds;
Which then re-clothed in divers names and fates
    Steal access through our senses to our minds." [4]

Finally, GOOD SENSE is the BODY of poetic genius, FANCY its DRAPERY, MOTION its LIFE, and IMAGINATION the SOUL that is everywhere, and in each; and forms all into one graceful and intelligent whole.

---

[4] From Davies's *Nosce Teipsum* (1599).

FROM

THE FRIEND

(1809-10)

ESSAY IV.
ON METHOD.

Ὁ δὲ μετὰ ταῦτα δίκαιόν ἐςι ποιεῖν, ἄκουε, ἵνα σοι καὶ ἀποκρίνωμαι ὃ σὺ ἐρωτᾷς, πῶς χρὴ ἔχειν ἐμὲ καὶ σὲ πρὸς ἀλλήλους. Εἰ μὲν ὅλως φιλοσοφίας καταπεφρόνηκας, ἐᾶν χαίρειν· εἰ δὲ παρ' ἑτέρου ἀκήκοας ἤ αὐτὸς βελτίονα εὔρηκας τῶν παρ' ἐμοί, ἐκεῖνα τίμα· εἰ δ' ἄρα τὰ παρ' ἡμῶν σοι ἀρέσκει, τιμητέον καὶ ἐμὲ μάλιςα.

Plato [1]

Hear then what are the terms on which you and I ought to stand toward each other. If you hold philosophy altogether in contempt, bid it farewell. Or if you have heard from any other person, or have yourself found out a better than mine, then give honour to that, which ever it be. But if the doctrine taught in these our works please you, then it is but just that you should honour me too in the same proportion.

WHAT is that which first strikes us, and strikes us at once, in a man of education, and which, among educated men, so instantly distinguishes the man of superior mind, that (as was observed with eminent propriety of the late Edmund Burke) "we cannot stand under the same arch-way during a shower of rain, without finding him out?" Not the weight or novelty of his remarks; not any unusual interest of facts communicated by him; for we may suppose both the one and the other precluded by the shortness of our intercourse, and the triviality of the subjects. The difference will be impressed and felt, though the conversation should be confined to the state of the weather or the pavement. Still less will it arise from any peculiarity in his words and phrases. For if he be, as we now assume, a well-educated man as well as a man of superior powers, he will not fail to follow the golden rule of Julius Cæsar, *insolens verbum, tanquam scopulum, evitare*. [2] Unless where new things necessitate new terms, he will avoid an unusual word as a rock. It must have been among the earliest lessons of his youth, that the breach of this precept, at all times hazardous, becomes ridiculous in the topics of ordinary conversation. There remains but one other point of distinction possible; and this must be, and in fact is, the true cause of the impression made on us. It is the unpremeditated and evidently habitual arrangement of his words, grounded on the habit of foreseeing,

---

[1] From the *Second Letter to Dion*.
[2] "Avoid the unusual word as you would a rock."

in each integral part, or (more plainly) in every sentence, the whole that he then intends to communicate. However irregular and desultory his talk, there is method in the fragments.

Listen, on the other hand, to an ignorant man, though perhaps shrewd and able in his particular calling, whether he be describing or relating. We immediately perceive, that his memory alone is called into action; and that the objects and events recur in the narration in the same order, and with the same accompaniments, however accidental or impertinent, in which they had first occurred to the narrator. The necessity of taking breath, the efforts of recollection, and the abrupt rectification of its failures, produce all his pauses; and with exception of the "and then," the "and there," and the still less significant, "and so," they constitute likewise all his connections.

Our discussion, however, is confined to method as employed in the formation of the understanding, and in the constructions of science and literature. It would indeed be superfluous to attempt a proof of its importance in the business and economy of active or domestic life. From the cotter's hearth or the workshop of the artizan to the palace or the arsenal, the first merit, that which admits neither substitute nor equivalent, is, that every thing be in its place. Where this charm is wanting, every other merit either loses its name, or becomes an additional ground of accusation and regret. Of one, by whom it is eminently possessed, we say proverbially, he is like clock-work. The resemblance extends beyond the point of regularity, and yet falls short of the truth. Both do, indeed, at once divide and announce the silent and otherwise indistinguishable lapse of time. But the man of methodical industry and honorable pursuits does more; he realizes its ideal divisions, and gives a character and individuality to its moments. If the idle are described as killing time, he may be justly said to call it into life and moral being, while he makes it the distinct object not only of the consciousness, but of the conscience. He organizes the hours, and gives them a soul; and that, the very essence of which is to fleet away, and evermore to have been, he takes up into his own permanence, and communicates to it the imperishableness of a spiritual nature. Of the *good and faithful servant*, whose energies, thus directed, are thus methodized, it is less truly affirmed, that he lives in time, than that time lives in him. His days, months, and years, as the stops and punctual marks in the records of duties performed, will survive the wreck of worlds, and remain extant when time itself shall be no more.

But as the importance of method in the duties of social life is incomparably greater, so are its practical elements proportionably obvious, and such as relate to the will far more than to the understanding. Henceforward, therefore, we contemplate its bearings on the latter.

The difference between the products of a well-disciplined and those of an uncultivated understanding, in relation to what we will now venture to call the science of method, is often and admirably exhibited by our great dramatist. I scarcely need refer my readers to the Clown's evidence, in the first scene of the second act of Measure for Measure, or to the Nurse in Romeo and Juliet. But not to leave the position, without an instance to illustrate it, I will take the easy-yielding Mrs. Quickly's relation of the circumstances of Sir John Falstaff's debt to her:—

FALSTAFF.　What is the gross sum that I owe thee?
HOST.　Marry, if thou wert an honest man, thyself and the money too. Thou didst swear to me upon a parcel-gilt goblet, sitting in my Dolphin chamber, at the round table, by a sea-coal fire, upon Wednesday in Whitsun week, when the prince broke thy head for liking his father to a singing-man of Windsor; thou didst swear to me then, as I was washing thy wound, to marry me and make me my lady thy wife. Canst thou deny it? Did not goodwife Keech, the butcher's wife, come in then and call me gossip Quickly?—coming in to borrow a mess of vinegar; telling us she had a good dish of prawns; whereby thou didst desire to eat some; whereby I told thee they were ill for a green wound, &c.*

And this, be it observed, is so far from being carried beyond the bounds of a fair imitation, that the poor soul's thoughts and sentences are more closely interlinked than the truth of nature would have required, but that the connections and sequence, which the habit of method can alone give, have in this instance a substitute in the fusion of passion. For the absence of method, which characterizes the uneducated, is occasioned by an habitual submission of the understanding to mere events and images as such, and independent of any power in the mind to classify or appropriate them. The general accompaniments of time and place are the only relations which persons of this class appear to regard in their statements. As this constitutes their leading feature, the contrary excellence, as distinguishing the well-educated man, must be referred to the contrary habit. Method, therefore, becomes natural to the mind which has been accustomed to contemplate not things only, or for their own sake alone, but likewise and chiefly the relations of things, either their relations to each other, or to the observer, or to the state and apprehension of the hearers. To enumerate and analyze these rela-

* *2 Henry IV*, II, i, 91 ff.

tions, with the conditions under which alone they are discoverable, is to teach the science of method.

The enviable results of this science, when knowledge has been ripened into those habits which at once secure and evince its possession, can scarcely be exhibited more forcibly as well as more pleasingly, than by contrasting with the former extract from Shakspeare the narration given by Hamlet to Horatio of the occurrences during his proposed transportation to England, and the events that interrupted his voyage:—

 HAM. Sir, in my heart there was a kind of fighting
That would not let me sleep: methought, I lay
Worse than the mutines in the bilboes. Rashly,
And praised be rashness for it——Let us know,
Our indiscretion sometimes serves us well,
When our deep plots do fail: and that should teach us,
There's a divinity that shapes our ends,
Rough-hew them how we will.
 HOR. That is most certain.
 HAM. Up from my cabin,
My sea-gown scarf'd about me, in the dark
Grop'd I to find them out; had my desire;
Finger'd their packet; and, in fine, withdrew
To my own room again: making so bold,
My fears forgetting manners, to unseal
Their grand commission; where I found, Horatio,
A royal knavery; an exact command—
Larded with many several sorts of reasons,
Importing Denmark's health, and England's too,
With, ho! such bugs and goblins in my life—
That on the supervise, no leisure bated,
No, not to stay the grinding of the axe,
My head should be struck off!
 HOR. Is't possible?
 HAM. Here's the commission;—read it at more
 leisure.*

Here the events, with the circumstances of time and place, are all stated with equal compression and rapidity, not one introduced which could have been omitted without injury to the intelligibility of the whole process. If any tendency is discoverable, as far as the mere facts are in question, it is the tendency to omission: and, accordingly, the reader will observe in the following quotation that the attention of the narrator is called back to one material circumstance, which he was hurrying by, by a direct question from the friend to whom the story is communicated, "How was this sealed?" But by a trait which is indeed peculiarly characteristic of Hamlet's mind, ever disposed to generalize, and meditative to excess (but which, with due abatement and reduction, is distinctive of every powerful and methodizing intellect), all

the digressions and enlargements consist of reflections, truths, and principles of general and permanent interest, either directly expressed or disguised in playful satire.

 ————————I sat me down;
Devis'd a new commission; wrote it fair.
I once did hold it, as our statists do,
A baseness to write fair, and laboured much
How to forget that learning; but, sir, now
It did me yeoman's service. Wilt thou know
The effect of what I wrote?
 HOR. Aye, good my lord.
 HAM. An earnest conjuration from the king,—
As England was his faithful tributary;
As love between them, like the palm, might flourish,
As peace should still her wheaten garland wear,
And stand a comma 'tween their amities,
And many such like ases of great charge—
That on the view and knowing of these contents,
Without debatement further, more or less,
He should the bearers put to sudden death,
No shriving time allowed.
 HOR. How was this seal'd?
 HAM. Why, even in that was heaven ordinant.
I had my father's signet in my purse,
Which was the model of that Danish seal:
Folded the writ up in the form of the other;
Subscribed it; gave't the impression; placed it safely,
The changeling never known. Now, the next day
Was our sea-fight; and what to this was sequent,
Thou know'st already.
 HOR. So Guildenstern and Rosencrantz go to't?
 HAM. Why, man, they did make love to this
 employment.
They are not near my conscience: their defeat
Doth by their own insinuation grow.
'Tis dangerous when the baser nature comes
Between the pass and fell incensed points
Of mighty opposites.†

It would, perhaps, be sufficient to remark of the preceding passage, in connection with the humorous specimen of narration,

 Fermenting o'er with frothy circumstance,

in Henry IV., that if, overlooking the different value of the matter in each, we considered the form alone, we should find both immethodical,—Hamlet from the excess, Mrs. Quickly from the want, of reflection and generalization; and that method, therefore, must result from the due mean or balance between our passive impressions and the mind's own re-action on the same. Whether this re-action do not suppose or imply a primary act positively originating in the mind

---

* Act V. sc. 2.

† Act V. sc. 2.

itself, and prior to the object in order of nature, though co-instantaneous with it in its manifestation, will be hereafter discussed. But I had a further purpose in thus contrasting these extracts from our myriad-minded bard, μυριονοῦς ἀνηρ. I wished to bring forward, each for itself, these two elements of method, or, to adopt an arithmetical term, its two main factors.

Instances of the want of generalization are of no rare occurrence in real life: and the narrations of Shakspeare's Hostess and the Tapster differ from those of the ignorant and unthinking in general by their superior humor, the poet's own gift and infusion, not by their want of method, which is not greater than we often meet with in that class, of which they are the dramatic representatives. Instances of the opposite fault, arising from the excess of generalization and reflection in minds of the opposite class, will, like the minds themselves, occur less frequently in the course of our own personal experience. Yet they will not have been wanting to our readers, nor will they have passed unobserved, though the great poet himself (ὁ τὴν ἑαυτοῦ ψυχὴν ὡσεi ὕλην τινα ἀσώματον μορφαῖς ποικιλαῖς μορφώσας*) has more conveniently supplied the illustrations. To complete, therefore, the purpose aforementioned, that of presenting each of the two components as separately as possible, I chose an instance in which, by the surplus of its own activity, Hamlet's mind disturbs the arrangement, of which that very activity had been the cause and impulse.

Thus exuberance of mind, on the one hand, interferes with the forms of method; but sterility of mind, on the other, wanting the spring and impulse to mental action, is wholly destructive of method itself. For in attending too exclusively to the relations which the past or passing events and objects bear to general truth, and the moods of his own thought, the most intelligent man is sometimes in danger of overlooking that other relation, in which they are likewise to be placed to the apprehension and sympathies of his hearers. His discourse appears like soliloquy intermixed with dialogue. But the uneducated and unreflecting talker overlooks all mental relations, both logical and psychological; and consequently precludes all method which is not purely accidental. Hence the nearer the things and incidents in time and place, the more distant, disjointed, and impertinent to each other, and to any common purpose, will they appear in his narration: and this from the want of a staple, or starting-post, in the narrator himself; from the absence of the leading thought, which, borrowing a phrase from the nomenclature of legislation, I may not inaptly call the initiative. On the contrary, where the habit of method is present and effective, things the most remote and diverse in time, place, and outward circumstance, are brought into mental contiguity and succession, the more striking as the less expected. But while I would impress the necessity of this habit, the illustrations adduced give proof that in undue preponderance, and when the prerogative of the mind is stretched into despotism, the discourse may degenerate into the grotesque or the fantastical.

With what a profound insight into the constitution of the human soul is this exhibited to us in the character of the Prince of Denmark, where flying from the sense of reality, and seeking a reprieve from the pressure of its duties in that ideal activity, the overbalance of which, with the consequent indisposition to action, is his disease, he compels the reluctant good sense of the high yet healthful-minded Horatio to follow him in his wayward meditation amid the graves!

HAM. To what base uses we may return, Horatio! Why may not imagination trace the noble dust of Alexander, till he find it stopping a bung-hole?

HOR. 'Twere to consider too curiously, to consider so.

HAM. No, 'faith, not a jot; but to follow him thither with modesty enough, and likelihood to lead it: As thus; Alexander died, Alexander was buried, Alexander returneth to dust; the dust is earth; of earth we make loam: And why of that loam whereto he was converted, might they not stop a beer-barrel?

    Imperious Cæsar, dead, and turn'd to clay,
    Might stop a hole to keep the wind away!†

But let it not escape our recollection, that when the objects thus connected are proportionate to the connecting energy, relatively to the real, or at least to the desirable sympathies, of mankind: it is from the same character that we derive the genial method in the famous soliloquy, "To be, or not to be"‡—which, admired as it is, and has been, has yet received only the first-fruits of the admiration due to it.

We have seen that from the confluence of innumerable impressions in each moment of time the mere passive memory must needs tend to confusion; a rule, the seeming exceptions to which (the thunder-bursts in Lear, for instance) are really confirmations of its truth. For, in many instances, the predominance of some mighty passion takes the place of the guiding thought and the result presents the method of nature, rather than the habit of the individual. For thought, imagination (and I may add, passion), are, in their

---

* He that moulded his own soul, as some incorporeal material, into various forms.—THEMISTIUS.

† Act V. sc. 1.
‡ Act III. sc. 1.

very essence, the first, connective, the latter co-aduna-
tive: and it has been shown, that if the excess lead to
method misapplied, and to connections of the mo-
ment, the absence, or marked deficiency, either pre-
cludes method altogether, both form and substance;
or (as the following extract will exemplify) retains the
outward form only.

> My liege and madam, to expostulate
> What majesty should be, what duty is,
> Why day is day, night night, and time is time,
> Were nothing but to waste night, day and time.
> Therefore—since brevity is the soul of wit,
> And tediousness the limbs and outward flourishes,—
> I will be brief. Your noble son is mad:
> Mad call I it; for to define true madness,
> What is't, but to be nothing else but mad!
> But let that go.
>   QUEEN. More matter with less art.
>   POL. Madam, I swear, I use no art at all.
> That he is mad, 'tis true: 'tis true, 'tis pity:
> And pity 'tis, 'tis true: a foolish figure;
> But farewell it, for I will use no art.
> Mad let us grant him then: and now remains,
> That we find out the cause of this effect,
> Or rather say the cause of this defect:
> For this effect defective comes by cause.
> Thus it remains, and the remainder thus
> Perpend.*

Does not the irresistible sense of the ludicrous in
this flourish of the soul-surviving body of old Polon-
ius's intellect, not less than in the endless confirma-
tions and most undeniable matters of fact, of Tapster

* Act II. sc. 2.

Pompey or the hostess of the tavern, prove to our
feelings, even before the word is found which presents
the truth to our understandings, that confusion and
formality are but the opposite poles of the same null-
point?

It is Shakspeare's peculiar excellence, that through-
out the whole of his splendid picture gallery (the
reader will excuse the acknowledged inadequacy of
this metaphor), we find individuality every where,
mere portrait no where. In all his various characters,
we still feel ourselves communing with the same
nature, which is every where present as the vegetable
sap in the branches, sprays, leaves, buds, blossoms,
and fruits, their shapes, tastes, and odours. Speaking
of the effect, that is, his works themselves, we may
define the excellence of their method as consisting in
that just proportion, that union and interpenetration,
of the universal and the particular, which must ever
pervade all works of decided genius and true science.
For method implies a progressive transition, and it is
the meaning of the word in the original language. The
Greek μέθοδος is literally a way or path of transit. Thus
we extol the Elements of Euclid, or Socrates' discourse
with the slave in the Menon of Plato, as methodical, a
term which no one who holds himself bound to think
or speak correctly, would apply to the alphabetical
order or arrangement of a common dictionary. But as
without continuous transition there can be no method,
so without a preconception there can be no transition
with continuity. The term, method, cannot therefore,
otherwise than by abuse, be applied to a mere dead
arrangement, containing in itself no principle of pro-
gression.

George Gordon, Lord Byron

1788–1824

INSISTING all the while that he was not really a poet, Byron became one of the most prolific and versatile of early nineteenth-century English writers. Continually treating his readers with indifference or contempt, he became one of the most popular writers in the history of English literature. The resource of detachment for Byron was not primarily a mode of teasing his readers or amusing himself. Acutely sensitive to the discrepancy between human aspiration and man's prospects for final significance in the world he inhabited, Byron always suggests that the comic mask he so often wears is a defense against the tragic nature of the world it looks upon. If like a Promethean hero he speaks repeatedly of extending infinitely the limits of human experience, the state he settles for is survival rather than victory. The world to Byron is a source of conflict not joy, and truces are rare and unsatisfactory. As a writer, and as a man, he was a formidable opponent, and his victims were often his admirers. His manner was so assertive, whether or not it was authentic, that few of his contemporaries (or readers) found indifference to him a possible response.

To put on a disguise, to play a role, can be a hostile act: if no one is taken in, the joke has failed. Yet it can also be an act necessary for survival, a means of keeping the real and vulnerable self protected and undiscovered. In its most direct form, Byron's role-playing can be seen in his relationships with other people. The morning after his marriage to Annabella Milbanke, lying in a bed turned crimson by the firelight passing through red curtains, Byron turned to his solemn blue-stocking bride and said, "Good God, I am surely in Hell!" Lady Byron was not amused by this nor by the year of more complex posing (and exposing) that followed it, which included her husband's breaking soda water bottles with a poker in the room under the one in which she was delivering their only child, and his flaunting before her of a passionate attachment to his half sister Augusta. Eventually Annabella decided he was mad or evil or perverted, and her refusal to return to him, with the gossip that accompanied it, made Byron decide to leave England forever at the age of twenty-eight. However much a victim he felt, Byron must also have known how inevitably the consequence followed upon his behavior.

Lady Byron's humorlessness—Byron liked to call her the Princess of Parallelograms —had more witnesses than Byron. The absence of a sense of humor is a defect difficult to forgive, although there is no particular moral value in its presence. So even if we assume that some jokes go too far, we also hesitate to draw the line that defines excess unless our most immediate interests are involved. In fact, we often discover our interests by recognizing that someone else has made fun of a value we prize. At some point another man's joke (or mockery) may cause our shock, anger, disgust or revulsion. And ideally (if we are dealing with art rather than burlesque) we are forced to reexamine our own values. Most art of the past cannot do this easily to a modern reader: topical satire at best remains amusing but is rarely shocking (as much Restoration drama is only amusing), or else modern terms and attitudes available to the reader allow him to place and contain the shock by "understanding" it, as with the work of the Marquis de Sade. We do not easily allow ourselves to be shocked, or exhilarated. Perhaps we know that defining the limit of our humor exposes us to the superiority of someone who refuses to stop there, who can mock one more solemnity, question one more assumption. The ability to provoke a committed response in someone else while preserving a means of detachment for himself characterizes Byron's art as a writer as well as his way of conducting relations with other people. To force a reader (or a wife) into declaring the limit of his tolerance leaves the poet free and the reader committed. Intensity of feeling is indeed created, and it remains under the control of its creator. This mode of behavior in Byron helps to account for the fascination, fear, and often hatred with which his contemporaries regarded him. "Mad—bad and dangerous to know" is the way Lady Caroline Lamb described him when she first met him in 1812, just after the publication of *Childe Harold* when Byron awoke to find himself famous. Within a few days she was his mistress, briefly.

But even five years earlier, when *Hours of Idleness* was published, provocation and escape were present in literary form. Many of the poems in the collection are adolescent love poems to his cousin Mary Chaworth (at twenty-five, however, Byron claimed that his only violent passionate attachment occurred when he was seven), and it is easy to imagine a naive poet publishing them in all seriousness, or a self-critical one suppressing them entirely. Obviously the poems are important to Byron because they are his, but this egocentricity must have been balanced by an objective awareness that they were not very good. So by the tone he takes toward his reader in the lengthy preface, Byron contrives to have the advantage of both attitudes. By turns apologetic and proud, he is deferential to and contemptuous of his reader. "The [poems'] merit, if they possess any, will be liberally allowed; their numerous faults, on the other hand, cannot expect that favour which has been denied to others of maturer years, decided character, and far greater ability." Denying his own originality ("but I have not been guilty of intentional plagiarism"), explaining that poetry is not his "primary vocation" (he writes "to divert the dull moments of indisposition or the monotony of a vacant hour"), he hopes this first and *final* self-indulgence will bring him "the not very magnificent prospect of ranking amongst 'the mob of gentlemen who write.'" And, though he denies its validity, he takes the trouble to quote Johnson's remark "That when a man of rank appeared in the character of an author, he deserved to have his merit handsomely allowed." He offers, in effect, every opportunity to a reader who wishes to praise him, and yet allows himself every excuse should a reader prove hostile. The reader is invited to indulge himself as deeply as he wishes, but the author apparently reserves every means imaginable to escape from commitment to what he has said. Here, for the first and last time, Byron is simply a trimmer.

Henry Peter Brougham in the *Edinburgh Review* takes advantage of the complexity of Byron's defenses in the Preface to go one step further. In reviewing the volume, he smoothly grants the privilege that Byron professes to waive (his rank is the only consideration "that induces us to give Lord Byron's poems a place in our review"), he finds that Byron's plea of youth merely emphasizes that such writing "happens in the life of nine men in ten who were educated in England," and finally ironically expresses his gratitude for *Hours of Idleness*: "Therefore, let us take what we get [since Byron has promised never to write again] and be thankful. What right have we poor devils to be nice? We are well off to have got so much from a man of this Lord's station. . . . Again, we say, let us be thankful; and, with honest Sancho, bid God bless the giver, nor look the gift horse in the mouth." [1]

Less protected than he thought he was, Byron was obviously shocked, a victim of his own game. His wrath at this review, finally objectified so vigorously in *English Bards and Scotch Reviewers*, was directed to defending his taste, his wit, his sophistication—not his ability as a sentimental poet. Perceptively Brougham had seen that it was the attitude of the Preface rather than the sentiments of the poems in which Byron had invested most of himself, and Brougham's review had the fortunate effect of forcing Byron to choose the weapon with which he was most proficient when he replied to the challenge. Not even Byron (later) claimed that the judgments of his contemporaries he expressed in *English Bards* were fair, or that the poem makes a consistent whole, or that it achieves anything like the satires of Pope on which it was modeled in admiration. But in its exuberant abuse of fellow poets and the conspiracy of reviewers that Byron suspected of perpetuating their success, the poem is a guide to Regency tastelessness. If, for reasons implicit in the history of culture, Byron cannot, like Pope, create or invoke a confident standard of Good Taste, he can instantly locate the occasional silliness of Wordsworth, or catalog in couplets the absurd apparatus of the fashionable world:

> Thus saith the *Preacher*: 'Nought beneath the sun
> Is new,' yet still from change to change we run.
> What varied wonders tempt us as they pass!
> The Cow-pox, Tractors, Calvinism, and Gas,
> In turns appear, to make the vulgar stare,
> Till the swoln bubble bursts—and all is air!
> Nor less new schools of Poetry arise,
> Where dull pretenders grapple for the prize:
> O'er Taste awhile these Pseudo-bards prevail;
> Each country Book-club bows the knee to Baal,
> And hurling lawful Genius from the throne,
> Erects a shrine and idol of its own;
> Some leaden calf—but whom it matters not,
> From soaring SOUTHEY, down to grovelling STOTT.

The love-sick adolescent who spoke in *Hours of Idleness* is replaced by the undergraduate wit—but a poet has also replaced a "gentleman who writes."

Having failed to protect himself in the Preface to *Hours of Idleness* by being simultaneously proud, contemptuous, and obsequious toward his work and his readers, Byron never again offered his work in this way as hostage for himself. If naive readers

---

[1] The review is reprinted in *Selected Prose and Poetry of the Romantic Period*, ed. G. R. Creeger and J. W. Reed, Jr. (1964).

too simply took *Childe Harold* as a serious self-portrait, Byron laughed at their gullibility while he enjoyed their admiration. The Byronic hero fascinated and excited him as much as it did his public, but he had the advantage of knowing when the pose was adopted or set aside, and how imitations of Wordsworth and Shelley (especially in Canto III) could bring him the satisfaction of at once being poetic and yet knowing that the poetic was only a part of himself. He, not Childe Harold, all too obviously enjoys the fact that extremes of feeling can be invoked, played upon, and then dismissed with words. The Satanic and the satiric, as Byron saw them, were parallel weapons of the writer's armory, alternative modes of creating and protecting the self while attacking the unexamined cant of others. Everything should be seen once with attention, said Byron of a public execution, and once seen it could be both a horror and a joke. If the reader shuddered or laughed, he and not Byron was committing himself to a single response.

The stance Byron adopts in *English Bards* is that of being the only honest man in a world of knaves too fallen even to challenge him: "I have been mostly in London," he says in his postscript to the second edition, "ready to answer for my transgressions and in daily expectation of sundry cartels; but alas! 'the age of chivalry is over' or in the vulgar tongue, there is no spirit now-a-days." This sense of the end—of honesty, chivalry, taste, bravery, and opportunity—pervades most of Byron's poetry. Had he lived at a different time, he says in his journal, or more candidly had he been a different man, anything might have been possible. But being himself, now, nothing is possible: ". . . *aut Caesar aut nihil* . . . to be the first man . . . the Washington or the Aristides—the leader in talent and truth—is next to the Divinity! Franklin, Penn, and next to these, either Brutus or Cassius—even Mirabeau—or St. Just. I shall never be anything, or rather always be nothing. The most I can hope is, that some will say, 'He might, perhaps, if he would.'"[2] Too self-critical to be nostalgic and too cynical to be satisfied with any disguise for very long, Byron as a writer went from one work to another daring his readers to believe what he could not—that virtue and honesty and intelligence are somewhere rewarded, that the power of a Napoleon could somehow be reconciled to the passion of a Rousseau, that freedom and judgment are not always at odds, and that a means could be found, however explosive, for fusing the boundless interior of man ("Soul—heart—mind—passions—feelings") with the illimitable exterior of the world he inhabits ("Sky—Mountains—River—Winds—Lake"): "As it is, I live and die unheard, / With a most voiceless thought, sheathing it as a sword." (*Childe Harold*, III, stanzas 96 and 97)

However disenchanted with the relation between language and belief, reality and dream, Byron was, or pretended to be, he was never voiceless or unheard. To reach the limits of expression, for this writer, is a chance to turn again to a new pose. In *Childe Harold III* he moves from the majestic but sheathed voice on the mountain tops to the bitter and self-pitying complaint of an abused husband and estranged father, at the end of the canto. Byron sought for his writing a form that would allow the mobility of feeling and apprehension full play, and for his life a style that would be heroic beyond criticism and mockery. He seemed to have found the first in *Don Juan*,

---

[2] See *Journal* for November 23, 1813, p. 764.

the other in the struggle of the Greeks against the Turks. Both ventures ended, typically, without being completed. If the Preface to *Hours of Idleness* was too transparently self-protective to be successful, the pose of *Don Juan* is an almost perfect tour de force in making sure that the author and the poem cannot be identified.

No feeling, no value, goes unquestioned by *Don Juan*, and no question is allowed an answer. No hero, no narrative, no style retains consistency, except the purely mechanical one of rhyme and meter. Terror and love and innocence are invoked, only to be mocked, but mockery is itself exposed as a superficial device. A narrator who says he can't find any heroes in the world implicitly nominates himself, but Byron persistently refuses to serve:

> The only two that in my recollection
>   Have sung of heaven and hell, or marriage, are
> Dante and Milton, and of both the affection
>   Was hapless in their nuptials, for some bar
> Of fault or temper ruin'd the connexion
>   (Such things, in fact, it don't ask much to mar);
> But Dante's Beatrice and Milton's Eve
> Were not drawn from their spouses, you conceive.
>   (III, 10)

Here pretending to make a literary statement at first (that marriage is not a possible subject for most poets), Byron enlarges it into a social and psychological joke about the extremity of feeling involved in marriage, and then disowns any serious intention by the colloquial cynicism of his language ("such things it don't ask much to mar"), and the sly hint of gossip at the end. In a stanza he has gone from talking of heaven and hell, Dante and Milton, down to a sneer about domestic life with Lady Byron—and leaves the reader no indication of what here, if anything, he is to take seriously.

Only in the London cantos (XI–XVI) of *Don Juan* does Byron come close to accepting responsibility for the extended view of a world that includes himself, and the virtue he commits himself to is what he calls elsewhere gentlemanliness, the antithesis of vulgarity. Gentlemanliness as it applies to writing (rather than social behavior), Byron says in a letter about Pope, cannot be defined, can only be known in examples, though it includes sporting with one's subject as a master rather than serving it as a slave, avoids pedantry, and like blackguardism (but not vulgarity) it includes wit, humor, and strong sense. And even at moments in the presentation of Lady Adeline in Canto XIV there is some sympathy that tempers the wit:

> Our gentle Adeline had one defect—
>   Her heart was vacant, though a splendid mansion;
> Her conduct had been perfectly correct,
>   As she had seen nought claiming its expansion.
> A wavering spirit may be easier wreck'd
>   Because 'tis frailer, doubtless, than a stanch one;
> But when the latter works its own undoing,
> Its inner crash is like an earthquake's ruin.

> She loved her lord, or thought so; but *that* love
>   Cost her an effort, which is a sad toil,
> The stone of Sysiphus, if once we move
>   Our feelings 'gainst the nature of the soil.
> She had nothing to complain of, or reprove,
>   No bickerings, no connubial turmoil:
> Their union was a model to behold,
> Serene and noble,—conjugal, but cold.

Compared to the tone of the stanza about Milton, Dante, and marriage, the attitude here is complex, subtle, sympathetic. For a moment, a few lines, Lady Adeline is a prototype for a George Eliot or Henry James heroine, the woman of imagination and sensibility locked in a marriage that the world finds ideal but that her heart cannot accept. Rarely does Byron extend such sympathy to anyone but himself, and even then self-pity often excludes this sort of complexity.

Perhaps it is significant that *Don Juan* was written just as the English novel was being seriously used for confronting social and psychological reality—in the same decade that Jane Austen wrote her major novels, well before Dickens and George Eliot. The novelist's ability to create characters in a fictitious social world, and yet maintain enough moral aloofness to put responsibility on the construction of the tale rather than the commentary of the artist, is one that Byron might have envied. Like Pope in the exuberance of his wit, Byron had little of the resourceful confidence in his own judgment or his own literary imagination on which Pope's satire depended. Had he found a literary form that allowed him more freedom from explicit comment, Byron might have written more, and more confidently. But English literature would have been deprived of the unique if desperate masterpiece, *Don Juan*, for the style of Byron's art, like that of his life, depended on a fundamental dissatisfaction with the conditions of existence that was close to comic self-contempt at some times, tragic at others.

OUTLINE OF EVENTS

1783		Augusta Byron [Leigh] born to Capt. John Byron and his first wife, Lady Carmarthen.
1788	Jan. 22	George Gordon Byron born to Captain Byron and his second wife, Catherine Byron, at 16 Holles Street, London.
1789		Byron and mother move to Aberdeen, Scotland.
1791	Aug. 2	Captain Byron (father) dies in France, leaving family impoverished.
1792	May 17	Anne Isabella Milbanke (later Lady Byron) born.
1794–1798		Attends grammar school, Aberdeen.
1798	May 19	Becomes sixth Baron Byron after death of his granduncle, William "the Wicked Lord" Byron. He and mother visit but do not live at Newstead Abbey.

1799–1800		Attends Dr. Glennie's academy, Dulwich (London).
1801–1805		Attends Harrow School.
1803	Summer	Meets and falls in love with Mary Chaworth of Annesley Hall, near Newstead.
1805	Oct.	Enters Trinity College, Cambridge.
1806		First volume of poems, *Fugitive Pieces*, is privately printed but suppressed by Byron. He spends a year away from Cambridge, at Southwell and London.
1807	Jan.	*Poems on Various Occasions* appears anonymously; in June it is published under Byron's name as *Hours of Idleness*.
	Spring	Returns to Cambridge; meets J. C. Hobhouse.
1808	Jan.	*Hours of Idleness* unfavorably reviewed in *Edinburgh Review*.
	July 4	Takes M.A. degree; leaves Cambridge for Newstead Abbey.
1809		Takes seat in House of Lords.
	Mar.	*English Bards and Scotch Reviewers* published.
	July	Byron and Hobhouse leave for tour of Spain, Portugal, Albania, etc.
	Oct.	Begins *Childe Harold*.
1810	Jan.–Mar.	In Athens; writes *Maid of Athens* and finishes first two cantos of *Childe Harold*.
	May	Visits Turkey; swims the Hellespont; returns to Athens.
1811	May	Leaves Athens for England via Malta.
	July	Arrives in England.
	Aug. 1	Mother dies at Newstead.
	Nov.	Meets Lord Holland, Tom Moore, Samuel Rogers.
1812	Feb. 27	In maiden speech in House of Lords opposes Frame-breaking bill; defends textile laborers of Nottingham.
	Mar.	*Childe Harold I* and *II* published by John Murray; subsequently Byron meets Sheridan, Southey, Leigh Hunt, Mme. de Staël, "Monk" Lewis, Anne Isabella (Annabella) Milbanke; love affairs with Lady Caroline Lamb and Lady Oxford.
1813	Mar.	Augusta Leigh, half sister, visits Byron. *Giaour* and *Bride of Abydos* published.
1814	Sept. 15	Engagement to Annabella Milbanke (who had rejected Byron in 1812) announced.
1815	Jan. 2	Byron and Annabella married at Seaham; live at Piccadilly Terrace, London. Meets Scott; *Hebrew Melodies* published; active in management of Drury Lane Theatre.
	Dec. 10	Augusta Ada born to Lord and Lady Byron.
1816	Jan.	Lady Byron leaves London; later suggests a separation.
	Apr.	Begins affair with Claire Clairmont.

	Apr. 25	Sails for Belgium, en route to Switzerland, leaving England for last time.
	May	Meets Shelley at Geneva; renews affair with Claire Clairmont.
	August 29	Shelleys and Claire Clairmont leave for England.
	Nov.	Byron moves to Venice. *Childe Harold III* published.
	Dec.	*Prisoner of Chillon* published.
1817	Jan.	Allegra, daughter of Byron and Claire Clairmont, born.
	June	*Manfred* published; *Childe Harold IV* and *Beppo* completed.
	Nov.	Byron sells Newstead Abbey.
1818	Feb.	*Beppo* published.
	Apr.	*Childe Harold IV* published; Shelleys, Claire, Allegra return from England; live in Venice.
	July	*Don Juan* begun (Canto I finished in September).
1819	Apr.	Byron forms liaison with Teresa Guiccioli, daughter of Count Gamba of Ravenna.
	July	*Don Juan I* and *II* published.
1820		Byron moves to Guiccioli palace in Ravenna, involved in revolutionary activities of Gamba family (against Austria).
1821		Allegra placed in convent at Bagnacavallo. *Don Juan III, IV, V*; *Mario Faliero, Sardanapalus, Two Foscari, Cain* published.
	Nov.	Byron and Teresa and exiled Gambas move to Pisa, are joined by Shelleys; Byron meets Greek leader Mavrocordato.
1822	Apr. 20	Allegra dies in a convent near Ravenna.
	June	Leigh Hunt arrives to establish the *Liberal* with Byron and Shelley.
	July 8	Shelley drowned off Viareggio. *Vision of Judgment* published.
	Sept.	Byron moves to Genoa with Gambas.
1823		*The Blues, Don Juan VI–XIV* published.
	Spring	Byron elected to London Greek Committee.
	July 16	Leaves for Greece.
	Aug.–Dec.	Joins revolutionary forces in western Greece; by December is in Missolonghi.
1824	Jan.–Mar.	Organizes corps of soldiers; plans offensive against Turks.
	Mar.	*Don Juan XV* and *XVI* published.
	Apr. 9	Falls ill.
	Apr. 19	Byron dies of fever at Missolonghi.
	July 16	Buried at Hucknall, near Newstead Abbey.
1851	Oct. 18	Augusta Byron Leigh dies.
1852	Nov. 29	Augusta Ada Byron [Lady Lovelace] dies.
1860	May 16	Lady Byron dies.
1873	Mar.	Teresa Guiccioli [Lady de Boissy] dies.

SELECTED BIBLIOGRAPHY

BIBLIOGRAPHIES AND CONCORDANCES

A Bibliography of the Writings in Verse and Prose of George Gordon Noel, Baron Byron, by T. J. Wise (2 vols., 1932–1933).

L. A. MARCHAND, "Recent Byron Scholarship," *Essays in Literary History*, ed. R. Kirk and C. F. Main (1960).

A Concordance to the Poetry of Byron, ed. I. Young (1965).

A Concordance to Byron's Don Juan, ed. C. W. Hagelman and R. J. Barnes (1967).

EDITIONS

The Works of Lord Byron, Poetry, ed. E. H. Coleridge (7 vols., 1898–1904).

The Works of Lord Byron, Prose, ed. R. E. Prothero (6 vols., 1898–1901).

Don Juan: A Variorum Edition, ed. T. G. Steffan and W. W. Pratt (4 vols., 1957).

Don Juan, ed. T. G. Steffan and W. W. Pratt (1972) [Penguin English Poets series].

Lord Byron's Cain: Twelve Essays and a Text with Variants and Annotations, ed. T. G. Steffan (1969).

BIOGRAPHY

L. A. MARCHAND, *Byron: A Biography* (3 vols., 1957).

D. L. MOORE, *The Late Lord Byron* (1961).

L. A. MARCHAND, *Byron: A Portrait* (1970).

R. GREBANIER, *The Uninhibited Byron: An Account of his Sexual Confusion* (1971).

E. S. LOVELL, Jr., ed., *His Very Self and Voice* (1954).

E. S. LOVELL, Jr., ed., *Thomas Medwin: Conversations of Lord Byron* (1966).

M. ELWIN, *Lord Byron's Wife* (1962).

P. GUNN, *My Dearest Augusta: A Biography of Augusta Leigh* (1968).

GENERAL CRITICISM

W. S. CALVERT, *Byron: Romantic Paradox* (1935).

F. R. LEAVIS, "Byron's Satire," *Revaluation* (1936).

E. F. BOYD, *Don Juan: A Critical Study* (1945).

T. S. ELIOT, "Byron," *On Poetry and Poets* (1957).

W. W. ROBSON, *Byron as Poet* (1959).

G. M. RIDENOUR, *The Style of Don Juan* (1960).

P. WEST, *Byron and the Spoiler's Art* (1960).

A. RUTHERFORD, *Byron: A Critical Study* (1961).

W. H. MARSHALL, *The Structure of Byron's Major Poems* (1962).

P. WEST, ed., *Byron: A Collection of Critical Essays* (1963).

G. M. RIDENOUR, "The Mode of Byron's *Don Juan*," *PMLA* (1964).

A. KERNAN, "Don Juan," *The Plot of Satire* (1965).

L. A. MARCHAND, *Byron's Poetry: A Critical Introduction* (1965).

W. H. AUDEN, "Byron: The Making of a Comic Poet," *New York Review* (Aug. 18, 1966).

R. GLECKNER, *Byron and the Ruins of Paradise* (1967).

W. P. ELLEDGE, *Byron and the Dynamics of Metaphor* (1968).

J. J. McGANN, *Fiery Dust: Byron's Poetic Development* (1968).

E. E. BOSTETTER, ed., *Twentieth Century Interpretations of Don Juan* (1969).

M. G. COOKE, *The Blind Man Traces the Circle: On the Patterns and Philosophy of Byron's Poetry* (1969).

D. PARKER, *Byron and His World* (1969).

P. G. TRUEBLOOD, *Lord Byron* (1969).

A. RUTHERFORD, *Byron: The Critical Heritage* (1970).

POEMS

FROM

HOURS OF IDLENESS

ON THE DEATH OF A YOUNG LADY, COUSIN TO THE AUTHOR, AND VERY DEAR TO HIM.*

1.

HUSH'D are the winds, and still the evening gloom,
 Not e'en a zephyr wanders through the grove,
Whilst I return to view my Margaret's tomb,
 And scatter flowers on the dust I love.

2.

Within this narrow cell reclines her clay,
 That clay, where once such animation beam'd;
The King of Terrors seiz'd her as his prey;
 Not worth, nor beauty, have her life redeem'd.

3.

Oh! could that King of Terrors pity feel,
 Or Heaven reverse the dread decree of fate,
Not here the mourner would his grief reveal,
 Not here the Muse her virtues would relate.

4.

But wherefore weep? Her matchless spirit soars
 Beyond where splendid shines the orb of day;
And weeping angels lead her to those bowers,
 Where endless pleasures virtuous deeds repay.

5.

And shall presumptuous mortals Heaven arraign!
 And, madly, Godlike Providence accuse!
Ah! no, far fly from me attempts so vain;—
 I'll ne'er submission to my God refuse.

6.

Yet is remembrance of those virtues dear,
 Yet fresh the memory of that beauteous face;
Still they call forth my warm affection's tear,
 Still in my heart retain their wonted place.

[1802]   [1806]

* The author claims the indulgence of the reader more for this piece than, perhaps, any other in the collection; but as it was written at an earlier period than the rest (being composed at the age of fourteen), and his first essay, he preferred submitting it to the indulgence of his friends in its present state, to making either addition or alteration.

ON LEAVING NEWSTEAD ABBEY.

Why dost thou build the hall, Son of the winged days? Thou lookest from thy tower to-day: yet a few years, and the blast of the desart comes: it howls in thy empty court.—OSSIAN.

1.

THROUGH thy battlements, Newstead, the hollow
 winds whistle:
 Thou, the hall of my Fathers, art gone to decay;
In thy once smiling garden, the hemlock and thistle
 Have choak'd up the rose, which late bloom'd in the
  way.

2.

Of the mail-cover'd Barons, who, proudly, to battle,
 Led their vassals from Europe to Palestine's plain,
The escutcheon and shield, which with ev'ry blast
  rattle,
 Are the only sad vestiges now that remain.

3.

No more doth old Robert, with harp-stringing
 numbers,
 Raise a flame, in the breast, for the war-laurell'd
  wreath;
Near Askalon's towers, John of Horistan slumbers,
 Unnerv'd is the hand of his minstrel, by death.

4.

Paul and Hubert too sleep in the valley of Cressy;
 For the safety of Edward and England they fell:
My Fathers! the tears of your country redress ye;
 How you fought! how you died! still her annals can
  tell.

5.

On Marston,† with Rupert,‡ 'gainst traitors
 contending,
 Four brothers enrich'd, with their blood, the bleak
  field;
For the rights of a monarch their country defending,
 Till death their attachment to royalty seal'd.

† The battle of Marston Moor, where the adherents of Charles I were defeated.
‡ Son of the Elector Palatine and related to Charles I. He afterwards commanded the Fleet in the reign of Charles II.

6.

Shades of heroes, farewell! your descendant departing
  From the seat of his ancestors, bids you adieu!
Abroad, or at home, your remembrance imparting
  New courage, he'll think upon glory and you.

7.

Though a tear dim his eye at this sad separation,
  'Tis nature, not fear, that excites his regret;
Far distant he goes, with the same emulation,
  The fame of his Fathers he ne'er can forget.

8.

That fame, and that memory, still will he cherish;
  He vows that he ne'er will disgrace your renown:
Like you will he live, or like you will he perish;
  When decay'd, may he mingle his dust with your
    own!

[1803]   [1806]

TO CAROLINE. [I]

1.

THINK'ST thou I saw thy beauteous eyes,
  Suffus'd in tears, implore to stay;
And heard *unmov'd* thy plenteous sighs,
  Which said far more than words can say?

2.

Though keen the grief *thy* tears exprest,
  When love and hope lay *both* o'erthrown;
Yet still, my girl, *this* bleeding breast
  Throbb'd, with deep sorrow, as *thine own.*

3.

But, when our cheeks with anguish glow'd,
  When *thy* sweet lips were join'd to mine;
The tears that from *my* eyelids flow'd
  Were lost in those which fell from *thine.*

4.

Thou could'st not feel my burning cheek,
  Thy gushing tears had quench'd its flame,
And, as thy tongue essay'd to speak,
  In *sighs alone* it breath'd my name.

5.

And yet, my girl, weep in vain,
  In vain our fate in sighs deplore;
Remembrance only can remain,
  But *that*, will make us weep the more.

6.

Again, thou best belov'd, adieu!
  Ah! if thou canst, o'ercome regret,
Nor let thy mind past joys review,
  Our only *hope* is, to *forget!*

[1805]   [1806]

TO CAROLINE. [II]

1.

OH! when shall the grave hide for ever my sorrow?
  Oh! when shall my soul wing her flight from this
    clay?
The present is hell! and the coming to-morrow
  But brings, with new torture, the curse of to-day.

2.

From my eye flows no tear, from my lips flow no
    curses,
  I blast not the fiends who have hurl'd me from bliss;
For poor is the soul which, bewailing, rehearses
  Its querulous grief, when in anguish like this—

3.

Was my eye, 'stead of tears, with red fury flakes
    bright'ning,
  Would my lips breathe a flame which no stream
    could assuage,
On our foes should my glance launch in vengeance its
    lightning,
  With transport my tongue give a loose to its rage.

4.

But now tears and curses, alike unavailing,
  Would add to the souls of our tyrants delight;
Could they view us our sad separation bewailing,
  Their merciless hearts would rejoice at the sight.

5.

Yet, still, though we bend with a feign'd resignation,
  Life beams not for us with one ray that can cheer;
Love and Hope upon earth bring no more consolation,
  In the grave is our hope, for in life is our fear.

6.

Oh! when, my ador'd, in the tomb will they place me,
  Since, in life, love and friendship for ever are fled?
If again in the mansion of death I embrace thee,
  Perhaps they will leave unmolested—the dead.

[1805]   [1806]

ON THE DEATH OF MR. FOX

William Pitt (1759–1806) was Tory prime minister from 1783 to 1801, 1804 to 1806. Charles James Fox (1749–1806) was his constant opponent during his first ministry. After Pitt's death in January 1806, Fox opposed the motion for giving him public honors. Fox died the same year.

ON THE DEATH OF MR. FOX,

THE FOLLOWING ILLIBERAL IMPROMPTU
APPEARED IN THE "MORNING POST."

"OUR Nation's foes lament on *Fox's* death,
But bless the hour, when PITT resign'd his breath:
These feelings wide, let Sense and Truth unclue,
We give the palm, where Justice points its due."

TO WHICH THE AUTHOR OF THESE PIECES
SENT THE FOLLOWING REPLY FOR
INSERTION IN THE "MORNING CHRONICLE."

OH, factious viper! whose envenom'd tooth
Would mangle, still, the dead, perverting truth;
What, though our "nation's foes" lament the fate,
With generous feeling, of the good and great;
Shall dastard tongues essay to blast the name
Of him, whose meed exists in endless fame?
When PITT expir'd in plenitude of power,
Though ill success obscur'd his dying hour,
Pity her dewy wings before him spread,
For noble spirits "war not with the dead:"   10
His friends in tears, a last sad requiem gave,
As all his errors slumber'd in the grave;
He sunk, an Atlas bending 'neath the weight
Of cares o'erwhelming our conflicting state.
When, lo! a Hercules, in FOX, appear'd,
Who for a time the ruin'd fabric rear'd:
He, too, is fall'n, who Britain's loss supplied,
With him, our fast reviving hopes have died;
Not one great people, only, raise his urn,
All Europe's far-extended regions mourn.   20
"These feelings wide, let Sense and Truth unclue,
To give the palm where Justice points its due;"
Yet, let not canker'd Calumny assail,
Or round her statesman wind her gloomy veil.
FOX! o'er whose corse a mourning world must weep,
Whose dear remains in honour'd marble sleep;
For whom, at last, e'en hostile nations groan,
While friends and foes, alike, his talents own.—
FOX! shall, in Britain's future annals, shine,
Nor e'en to PITT, the patriot's *palm* resign;   30
Which Envy, wearing Candour's sacred mask,
For PITT, and PITT alone, has dar'd to ask.

[1806]   [1806]

LINES ADDRESSED TO A YOUNG LADY.

AS THE AUTHOR WAS DISCHARGING HIS PIS-
TOLS IN A GARDEN, TWO LADIES PASSING
NEAR THE SPOT WERE ALARMED BY THE
SOUND OF A BULLET HISSING NEAR THEM,
TO ONE OF WHOM THE FOLLOWING STANZAS
WERE ADDRESSED THE NEXT MORNING.

1.

DOUBTLESS, sweet girl! the hissing lead,
    Wafting destruction o'er thy charms
And hurtling o'er thy lovely head,*
    Has fill'd that breast with fond alarms.

2.

Surely some envious Demon's force,
    Vex'd to behold such beauty here,
Impell'd the bullet's viewless course,
    Diverted from its first career.

3.

Yes! in that nearly fatal hour,
    The ball obey'd some hell-born guide;
But Heaven, with interposing power,
    In pity turn'd the death aside.

4.

Yet, as perchance one trembling tear
    Upon that thrilling bosom fell;
Which *I*, th' unconscious cause of fear,
    Extracted from its glistening cell;—

5.

Say, what dire penance can atone
    For such an outrage, done to thee?
Arraign'd before thy beauty's throne,
    What punishment wilt thou decree?

6.

Might I perform the Judge's part,
    The sentence I should scarce deplore;
It only would restore a heart,
    Which but belong'd to *thee* before.

7.

The least atonement I can make
    Is to become no longer free;
Henceforth, I breathe but for thy sake,
    Thou shalt be *all in all* to me.

* This word is used by Gray in his poem to the Fatal
Sisters:—

    "Iron-sleet of arrowy shower
    Hurtles in the darken'd air."

8.

But thou, perhaps, may'st now reject
　　Such expiation of my guilt;
Come then—some other mode elect?
　　Let it be death—or what thou wilt.

9.

Choose, then, relentless! and I swear
　　Nought shall thy dread decree prevent;
Yet hold—one little word forbear!
　　Let it be aught but *banishment*.

[?]　　　　　　　　　　　　　　　　[1806]

THE FIRST KISS OF LOVE.

'Α βάρβῖτος δὲ χορδαῖς
'Ερωτα μοῦνον ἠχεῖ
ANACREON[1]

1.

AWAY with your fictions of flimsy romance,
　　Those tissues of falsehood which Folly has wove;
Give me the mild beam of the soul-breathing glance,
　　Or the rapture which dwells on the first kiss of love.

2.

Ye rhymers, whose bosoms with fantasy glow,
　　Whose pastoral passions are made for the grove;
From what blest inspiration your sonnets would flow,
　　Could you ever have tasted the first kiss of love.

3.

If Apollo should e'er his assistance refuse,
　　Or the Nine be dispos'd from your service to rove,
Invoke them no more, bid adieu to the Muse,
　　And try the effect, of the first kiss of love.

4.

I hate you, ye cold compositions of art,
　　Though prudes may condemn me, and bigots
　　　　reprove;
I court the effusions that spring from the heart,
　　Which throbs, with delight, to the first kiss of love.

5.

Your shepherds, your flocks, those fantastical themes,
　　Perhaps may amuse, yet they never can move:
Arcadia displays but a region of dreams;
　　What are visions like these, to the first kiss of love?

6.

Oh! cease to affirm that man, since his birth,
　　From Adam, till now, has with wretchedness strove;
Some portion of Paradise still is on earth,
　　And Eden revives, in the first kiss of love.

⬦⬦⬦⬦⬦⬦⬦⬦⬦⬦⬦⬦⬦⬦⬦⬦⬦⬦⬦⬦⬦⬦⬦
[1] Ode I: But the strings of the lute sound only of love.

7.

When age chills the blood, when our pleasures are
　　　　past—
　　For years fleet away with the wings of the dove—
The dearest remembrance will still be the last,
　　Our sweetest memorial, the first kiss of love.

[1806]　　　　　　　　　　　　　　　[1807]

LINES WRITTEN BENEATH AN ELM IN THE CHURCHYARD OF HARROW.*

SPOT of my youth! whose hoary branches sigh,
Swept by the breeze that fans thy cloudless sky;
Where now alone I muse, who oft have trod,
With those I loved, thy soft and verdant sod;
With those who, scatter'd far, perchance deplore,
Like me, the happy scenes they knew before:
Oh! as I trace again thy winding hill,
Mine eyes admire, my heart adores thee still,
Thou drooping Elm! beneath whose boughs I lay,
And frequent mus'd the twilight hours away;　　10
Where, as they once were wont, my limbs recline,
But, ah! without the thoughts which then were mine:
How do thy branches, moaning to the blast,
Invite the bosom to recall the past,
And seem to whisper, as they gently swell,
"Take, while thou canst, a lingering, last farewell!"

　　When Fate shall chill, at length, this fever'd breast,
And calm its cares and passions into rest,
Oft have I thought, 'twould soothe my dying hour,—
If aught may soothe, when Life resigns her power,—
To know some humbler grave, some narrow cell,　　21
Would hide my bosom where it lov'd to dwell;
With this fond dream, methinks 'twere sweet to die—
And here it linger'd, here my heart might lie;
Here might I sleep where all my hopes arose,
Scene of my youth, and couch of my repose;
For ever stretch'd beneath this mantling shade,
Press'd by the turf where once my childhood play'd;
Wrapt by the soil that veils the spot I lov'd,
Mix'd with the earth o'er which my footsteps mov'd;
Blest by the tongues that charm'd my youthful ear,
Mourn'd by the few my soul acknowledged here;
Deplor'd by those in early days allied,　　33
And unremember'd by the world beside.

[1807]　　　　　　　　　　　　　　　[1808]

[END OF SELECTIONS FROM
HOURS OF IDLENESS]

* "And I said, O that I had wings like a dove, for then I would fly away, and be at rest."—Psalm lv. 6. This verse also constitutes a part of the most beautiful anthem in our language.

The allusions in this poem are thoroughly annotated in Vol. I of the E. H. Coleridge edition of Byron's Works (1898). Some of Byron's notes omitted from or altered in Coleridge's edition are here (and elsewhere) restored.

ENGLISH BARDS,

AND

SCOTCH REVIEWERS;

A SATIRE.

"I had rather be a kitten, and cry, mew!
Than one of these same metre ballad-mongers."
                                    SHAKESPEARE.

"Such shameless Bards we have; and yet 'tis true,
There are as mad, abandon'd Critics, too."
                                    POPE.

PREFACE.

*A*LL my friends, learned and unlearned, have urged me not to publish this Satire with my name. If I were to be "turned from the career of my humour by quibbles quick, and paper bullets of the brain," I should have complied with their counsel. But I am not to be terrified by abuse, or bullied by reviewers, with or without arms. I can safely say that I have attacked none personally, who did not commence on the offensive. An Author's works are public property: he who purchases may judge, and publish his opinion if he pleases; and the Authors I have endeavoured to commemorate may do by me as I have done by them. I dare say they will succeed better in condemning my scribblings, than in mending their own. But my object is not to prove that I can write well, but, if possible, to make others write better.

As the Poem has met with far more success than I expected, I have endeavoured in this Edition to make some additions and alterations, to render it more worthy of public perusal.

In the First Edition of this Satire, published anonymously, fourteen lines on the subject of Bowles's Pope were written by, and inserted at the request of, an ingenious friend of mine,* who has now in the press a volume of Poetry. In the present Edition they are erased, and some of my own substituted in their stead; my only reason for this being that which I conceive would operate with any other person in the same manner,—a determination not to publish with my name any production, which was not entirely and exclusively my own composition.

  * John Cam Hobhouse.

With regard to the real talents of many of the poetical persons whose performances are mentioned or alluded to in the following pages, it is presumed by the Author that there can be little differences of opinion in the Public at large; though, like other sectaries, each has his separate tabernacle of proselytes, by whom his abilities are overrated, his faults overlooked, and his metrical canons received without scruple and without consideration. But the unquestionable possession of considerable genius by several of the writers here censured renders their mental prostitution more to be regretted. Imbecility may be pitied, or, at worst, laughed at and forgotten; perverted powers demand the most decided reprehension. No one can wish more than the Author that some known and able writer had undertaken their exposure; but Mr. Gifford [1] has devoted himself to Massinger, and, in the absence of the regular physician, a country practitioner may, in cases of absolute necessity, be allowed to prescribe his nostrum to prevent the extension of so deplorable an epidemic, provided there be no quackery in his treatment of the malady. A caustic is here offered; as it is to be feared nothing short of actual cautery can recover the numerous patients afflicted with the present prevalent and distressing* rabies *for rhyming.—As to the Edinburgh Reviewers, it would indeed require an Hercules to crush the Hydra; but if the Author succeeds in merely "bruising one of the heads of the serpent," though his own hand should suffer in the encounter, he will be amply satisfied.*

STILL* must I hear?—shall hoarse FITZGERALD
        bawl
His creaking couplets in a tavern hall,
And I not sing, lest, haply, Scotch Reviews
Should dub me scribbler, and denounce my *Muse?*
Prepare for rhyme—I'll publish, right or wrong:
Fools are my theme, let Satire be my song.

Oh! Nature's noblest gift—my grey goose-quill!
Slave of my thoughts, obedient to my will,

  * IMITATION
    "Semper ego auditor tantum? nunquamne reponam.
    Vexatus toties rauci Theseide Codri?"
                          JUVENAL, *Satire I.* i. 1

Mr. Fitzgerald, facetiously termed by Cobbett the "Small Beer Poet," inflicts his annual tribute of verse on the Literary Fund: not content with writing, he spouts in person, after the company have imbibed a reasonable quantity of bad port, to enable them to sustain the operation.

  [1] William Gifford (1756–1826), first editor of the *Quarterly Review*; Thomas Fitzgerald (1759–1829) in line 1 below was a minor poet of public events.

Torn from thy parent bird to form a pen,
That mighty instrument of little men!   10
The pen! foredoomed to aid the mental throes
Of brains that labour, big with Verse or Prose;
Though Nymphs forsake, and Critics may deride,
The Lover's solace, and the Author's pride.
What Wits! what Poets dost thou daily raise!
How frequent is thy use, how small thy praise!
Condemned at length to be forgotten quite,
With all the pages which 'twas thine to write.
But thou, at least, mine own especial pen!
Once laid aside, but now assumed again,   20
Our task complete, like Hamet's* shall be free;
Though spurned by others, yet beloved by me:
Then let us soar to-day; no common theme,
No Eastern vision, no distempered dream
Inspires—our path, though full of thorns, is plain;
Smooth be the verse, and easy be the strain.

When Vice triumphant holds her sov'reign sway,
Obey'd by all who nought beside obey;
When Folly, frequent harbinger of crime,
Bedecks her cap with bells of every Clime;   30
When knaves and fools combined o'er all prevail,
And weigh their Justice in a Golden Scale,
E'en then the boldest start from public sneers,
Afraid of Shame, unknown to other fears,
More darkly sin, by Satire kept in awe,
And shrink from Ridicule, though not from Law.

Such is the force of Wit! but not belong
To me the arrows of satiric song;
The royal vices of our age demand
A keener weapon, and a mightier hand.   40
Still there are follies, e'en for me to chase,
And yield at least amusement in the race:
Laugh when I laugh, I seek no other fame,
The cry is up, and scribblers are my game:
Speed, Pegasus!—ye strains of great and small,
Ode! Epic! Elegy!—have at you all!
I, too, can scrawl, and once upon a time
I poured along the town a flood of rhyme,
A schoolboy freak, unworthy praise or blame;
I printed—older children do the same.   50
'Tis pleasant, sure, to see one's name in print;
A Book's a Book, altho' there's nothing in't.
Not that a Title's sounding charm can save
Or scrawl or scribbler from an equal grave:

This LAMB[2] must own, since his patrician name
Failed to preserve the spurious Farce from shame.*
No matter, GEORGE continues still to write,†
Tho' now the name is veiled from public sight.
Moved by the great example, I pursue
The self-same road, but make my own review: 60
Not seek great JEFFREY'S,[3] yet like him will be
Self-constituted Judge of Poesy.

A man must serve his time to every trade
Save Censure—Critics all are ready made.
Take hackneyed jokes from MILLER,[4] got by rote,
With just enough of learning to misquote;
A man well skilled to find, or forge a fault;
A turn for punning—call it Attic salt;
To JEFFREY go, be silent and discreet,
His pay is just ten sterling pounds per sheet: 70
Fear not to lie, 'twill seem a *sharper* hit;
Shrink not from blasphemy, 'twill pass for wit;
Care not for feeling—pass your proper jest,
And stand a Critic, hated yet caress'd.

And shall we own such judgment? no—as soon
Seek roses in December—ice in June;
Hope constancy in wind, or corn in chaff,
Believe a woman or an epitaph,
Or any other thing that's false, before
You trust in Critics, who themselves are sore;   80
Or yield one single thought to be misled
By JEFFREY'S heart, or LAMB'S Bœotian head.‡
To these young tyrants, by themselves misplaced,
Combined usurpers on the Throne of Taste;
To these, when Authors bend in humble awe,
And hail their voice as Truth, their word as Law;
While these are Censors, 'twould be sin to spare; §
While such are Critics, why should I forbear?
But yet, so near all modern worthies run,
'Tis doubtful whom to seek, or whom to shun;   90
Nor know we when to spare, or where to strike,
Our Bards and Censors are so much alike.

* This ingenuous youth is mentioned more particularly, with his production, in another place. (*Vide post*, l. 516.)
† In the *Edinburgh Review*.
‡ Messrs. Jeffrey and Lamb are the alpha and omega, the first and last of the *Edinburgh Review*: the others are mentioned hereafter.
§ IMITATION
　　"Stulta est Clementia, cum tot ubique
　　　—— occuras perituræ parcere chartæ."
　　　　　　　JUVENAL, *Sat. I.* ll. 17–18.

[2] George Lamb (1784–1834), Lady Byron's first cousin, a minor playwright and essayist.
[3] Francis Jeffrey (1773–1850), founder and editor of the *Edinburgh Review*.
[4] Joe Miller (1684–1738), an actor to whom the first anthology of jokes is traditionally attributed.

* Cid Hamet Benengeli promises repose to his pen, in the last chapter of *Don Quixote*. Oh! that our voluminous gentry would follow the example of Cid Hamet Benengeli!

Then should you ask me,* why I venture o'er
The path which POPE and GIFFORD trod before;
If not yet sickened, you can still proceed;
Go on; my rhyme will tell you as you read.
"But hold!" exclaims a friend,—"here's some
　　　neglect:
This—that—and t'other line seem incorrect."
What then? the self-same blunder Pope has got,
And careless Dryden—"Aye, but Pye⁵ has not:"—
Indeed!—'tis granted, faith!—but what care I?　　101
Better to err with POPE, than shine with PYE.

Time was, ere yet in these degenerate days
Ignoble themes obtained mistaken praise,
When Sense and Wit with Poesy allied,
No fabled Graces, flourished side by side,
From the same fount their inspiration drew,
And, reared by Taste, bloomed fairer as they grew.
Then, in this happy Isle, a POPE's pure strain
Sought the rapt soul to charm, nor sought in vain;
A polished nation's praise aspired to claim,　　111
And raised the people's, as the poet's fame.
Like him great DRYDEN poured the tide of song,
In stream less smooth, indeed, yet doubly strong.
Then CONGREVE's scenes could cheer, or OTWAY's
　　melt;⁶
For Nature then an English audience felt—
But why these names, or greater still, retrace,
When all to feebler Bards resign their place?
Yet to such times our lingering looks are cast,
When taste and reason with those times are past.　　120
Now look around, and turn each trifling page,
Survey the precious works that please the age;
This truth at least let Satire's self allow,
No dearth of Bards can be complained of now.
The loaded Press beneath her labour groans,
And Printers' devils shake their weary bones;
While SOUTHEY's⁷ Epics cram the creaking shelves,
And LITTLE's⁸ Lyrics shine in hot-pressed twelves.
Thus saith the *Preacher:* "Nought beneath the sun
Is new,"† yet still from change to change we run.

* IMITATION
　　"Cur tamen hoc potius libeat decurrere campo,
　　　Per quem magnus equos Auruncæ flexit, alumnus,
　　　Si vacat, et placidi rationem admittitis, edam."
　　　　　　　　　　　　　　JUVENAL, *Sat. I.* ll. 19–21.
† Eccles. chapter i. verse 9.

⋄⋄⋄⋄⋄⋄⋄⋄⋄⋄⋄⋄⋄⋄⋄⋄⋄⋄⋄⋄⋄⋄⋄⋄⋄⋄

⁵ Henry James Pye (1745–1813), Poet Laureate from 1790 to
1813, succeeded by Robert Southey. See also first stanza of the
Dedication to *Don Juan,* p. 651.
⁶ John Dryden (1631–1700), William Congreve (1670–1729),
Thomas Otway (1652–1685).
⁷ Robert Southey (1774–1843), Poet Laureate from 1813 to
1843, Coleridge's brother-in-law, target of *A Vision of Judgment.*
⁸ Thomas Moore (1779–1852) published his first poems under
the name of Thomas Little (1801).

What varied wonders tempt us as they pass!　　131
The Cow-pox, Tractors, Galvanism, and Gas,
In turns appear, to make the vulgar stare,
Till the swoln bubble bursts—and all is air!
Nor less new schools of Poetry arise,
Where dull pretenders grapple for the prize:
O'er Taste awhile these Pseudo-bards prevail;
Each country Book-club bows the knee to Baal,
And, hurling lawful Genius from the throne,
Erects a shrine and idol of its own;　　140
Some leaden calf—but whom it matters not,
From soaring SOUTHEY, down to groveling STOTT.*

Behold! in various throngs the scribbling crew,
For notice eager, pass in long review:
Each spurs his jaded Pegasus apace,
And Rhyme and Blank maintain an equal race;
Sonnets on sonnets crowd, and ode on ode;
And Tales of Terror jostle on the road;
Immeasurable measures move along;
For simpering Folly loves a varied song,　　150
To strange, mysterious Dulness still the friend,
Admires the strain she cannot comprehend.
Thus Lays of Minstrels†—may they be the last!—
On half-strung harps whine mournful to the blast.

* Stott, better known in the *Morning Post* by the name of
Hafiz. This personage is at present the most profound explorer
of the bathos. I remember, when the reigning family left
Portugal, a special Ode of Master Stott's beginning thus:—
(*Stott loquitur quod Hibernia*)—

　　"Princely offspring of Braganza,
　　　Erin greets thee with a stanza," etc.

Also a Sonnet to Rats, well worthy of the subject and a most
thundering Ode, commencing as follows:—

　　"Oh! for a Lay! loud as the surge
　　　That lashes Lapland's sounding shore."

Lord have mercy on us! the "Lay of the Last Minstrel" was
nothing to this.
† See the "Lay of the Last Minstrel," *passim.* Never was any
plan so incongruous and absurd as the groundwork of this
production. The entrance of Thunder and Lightning prologuis-
ing to Bayes' tragedy,⁹ unfortunately takes away the merit of
originality from the dialogue between Messieurs the Spirits of
Flood and Fell in the first canto. Then we have the amiable
William of Deloraine, "a stark moss-trooper," videlicet, a happy
compound of poacher, sheep-stealer, and highwayman. The
propriety of his magical lady's injunction not to read can only be
equalled by his candid acknowledgment of his independence of
the trammels of spelling, although, to use his own elegant
phrase, "'twas his neckverse at Harribee," *i.e.* the gallows.
　　The biography of Gilpin Horner, and the marvellous pedes-
trian page who travelled twice as fast as his master's horse,
without the aid of seven-leagued boots, are *chefs d'œuvre* in the
improvement of taste. For incident we have the invisible, but by

⋄⋄⋄⋄⋄⋄⋄⋄⋄⋄⋄⋄⋄⋄⋄⋄⋄⋄⋄⋄⋄⋄⋄⋄⋄⋄

⁹ In the parody drama, attacking Dryden, *The Rehearsal,* by
George Villiers, Duke of Buckingham (1628–1687) and others.

While mountain spirits prate to river sprites,
That dames may listen to the sound at nights;
And goblin brats, of Gilpin Horner's brood
Decoy young Border-nobles through the wood,
And skip at every step, Lord knows how high,
And frighten foolish babes, the Lord knows why;
While high-born ladies in their magic cell,   161
Forbidding Knights to read who cannot spell,
Despatch a courier to a wizard's grave,
And fight with honest men to shield a knave.

Next view in state, proud prancing on his roan,
The golden-crested haughty Marmion,
Now forging scrolls, now foremost in the fight,
Not quite a Felon, yet but half a Knight,
The gibbet or the field prepared to grace;
A mighty mixture of the great and base.   170
And think'st thou, SCOTT! by vain conceit perchance,
On public taste to foist thy stale romance,
Though MURRAY with his MILLER may combine
To yield thy muse just half-a-crown per line?
No! when the sons of song descend to trade,
Their bays are sear, their former laurels fade,
Let such forego the poet's sacred name,
Who rack their brains for lucre, not for fame:
Still for stern Mammon may they toil in vain!
And sadly gaze on Gold they cannot gain!   180
Such be their meed, such still the just reward
Of prostituted Muse and hireling bard!
For this we spurn Apollo's venal son,
And bid a long "good night to Marmion."*

These are the themes that claim our plaudits now;
These are the Bards to whom the Muse must bow;
While MILTON, DRYDEN, POPE, alike forgot,
Resign their hallowed Bays to WALTER SCOTT.

The time has been, when yet the Muse was young,
When HOMER swept the lyre, and MARO sung,   190
An Epic scarce ten centuries could claim,
While awe-struck nations hailed the magic name:

The work of each immortal Bard appears
The single wonder of a thousand years.*
Empires have mouldered from the face of earth,
Tongues have expired with those who gave them birth,
Without the glory such a strain can give,
As even in ruin bids the language live.
Not so with us, though minor Bards, content,
On one great work a life of labour spent: 200
With eagle pinion soaring to the skies,
Behold the Ballad-monger SOUTHEY rise!
To him let CAMOËNS, MILTON, TASSO yield,
Whose annual strains, like armies, take the field.
First in the ranks see Joan of Arc advance,
The scourge of England and the boast of France!
Though burnt by wicked BEDFORD for a witch,
Behold her statue placed in Glory's niche;
Her fetters burst, and just released from prison,
A virgin Phœnix from her ashes risen.   210
Next see tremedous Thalaba come on,†
Arabia's monstrous, wild, and wond'rous son;
Domdaniel's dread destroyer, who o'erthrew
More mad magicians than the world e'er knew.
Immortal Hero! all thy foes o'ercome,
For ever reign—the rival of Tom Thumb![10]

Since startled Metre fled before they face,
Well wert thou doomed the last of all thy race!
Well might triumphant Genii bear thee hence,
Illustrious conqueror of common sense!   220
Now, last and greatest, Madoc spreads his sails,
Cacique in Mexico,[11] and Prince in Wales;
Tells us strange tales, as other travellers do,
More old than Mandeville's, and not so true.
Oh, SOUTHEY! SOUTHEY!‡ cease thy varied song!
A bard may chaunt too often and too long:

---

no means sparing box on the ear bestowed on the page, and the entrance of a Knight and Charger into the castle, under the very natural disguise of a wain of hay. Marmion, the hero of the latter romance, is exactly what William of Deloraine would have been, had he been able to read and write. The poem was manufactured for Messrs. CONSTABLE, MURRAY, and MILLER, worshipful Booksellers, in consideration of the receipt of a sum of money; and truly, considering the inspiration, it is a very creditable production. If Mr. SCOTT will write for hire, let him do his best for his paymasters, but not disgrace his genius, which is undoubtedly great, by a repetition of Black-Letter Ballad imitations.

* "Good night to Marmion"—the pathetic and also prophetic exclamation of Henry Blount, Esquire, on the death of honest Marmion.

* As the *Odyssey* is so closely connected with the story of the *Iliad*, they may almost be classed as one grand historical poem. In alluding to Milton and Tasso, we consider the *Paradise Lost* and *Gerusalemme Liberata* as their standard efforts; since neither the *Jerusalem Conquered* of the Italian, nor the *Paradise Regained* of the English bard, obtained a proportionate celebrity to their former poems. Query: Which of Mr. Southey's will survive?

† *Thalaba*, Mr. SOUTHEY'S second poem, is written in open defiance of precedent and poetry. Mr. S. wished to produce something novel, and succeeded to a miracle. *Joan of Arc* was marvellous enough, but *Thalaba* was one of those poems "which," in the words of PORSON, "will be read when Homer and Virgil are forgotten, but—*not till then*."

‡ We beg Mr. Southey's pardon: "Madoc disdains the degraded title of Epic." See his Preface. Why is Epic degraded: and by whom? Certainly the late Romaunts of Masters Cottle,

[10] The hero of Henry Fielding's farce, *The Tragedy of Tragedies or the Life and Death of Tom Thumb the Great* (1730).

[11] Southey's *Madoc* is divided into "Madoc in Wales" and "Madoc in Atzlan." A "cacique" is a native chief of the West Indies.

As thou art strong in verse, in mercy, spare!
A fourth, alas! were more than we could bear.
But if, in spite of all the world can say,
Thou still wilt verseward plod thy weary way;   230
If still in Berkeley-Ballads most uncivil,
Thou wilt devote old women to the devil,*
The babe unborn they dread intent may rue:
"God help thee," SOUTHEY,† and they readers too.

Next comes the dull disciple of thy school,
That mild apostate from poetic rule,
The simple WORDSWORTH, framer of a lay
As soft as evening in his favourite May,
Who warns his friend "to shake off toil and trouble,
And quit his books, for fear of growing double;" ‡ 240
Who, both by precept and example, shows
That prose is verse, and verse is merely prose;
Convincing all, by demonstration plain,
Poetic souls delight in prose insane;
And Christmas stories tortured into rhyme
Contain the essence of the true sublime.
Thus, when he tells the tale of Betty Foy,
The idiot mother of "an idiot Boy;"
A moon-struck, silly lad, who lost his way,
And, like his bard, confounded night with day; § 250
So close on each pathetic part he dwells,
And each adventure so sublimely tells,
That all who view the "idiot in his glory"
Conceive the Bard the hero of the story.

Laureat Pye, Ogilvy, Hole, and gentle Mistress Cowley, have
not exalted the Epic Muse; but, as Mr. SOUTHEY'S poem
"disdains the appellation," allow us to ask—has he substituted
anything better in its stead? or must he be content to rival Sir
RICHARD BLACKMORE in the quantity as well as quality of his
verse?

* See *The Old Woman of Berkeley*, a ballad by Mr. Southey,
wherein an aged gentlewoman is carried away by Beelzebub on
a "high trotting horse."

† The last line, "God help thee," is an evident plagiarism
from the *Anti-Jacobin* to Mr. Southey, on his Dactylics:—

"God help thee, silly one!"
                    Poetry of the Anti-Jacobin, p. 23.
‡ *Lyrical Ballads*, p. 4.—"The Tables Turned," Stanza 1.

"Up, up, my friend, and clear your looks,
     Why all this toil and trouble?
Up, up, my friend, and quit your books,
     Or surely you'll grow double."

§ Mr. W. in his preface labours hard to prove that prose and
verse are much the same, and certainly his precepts and practice
are strictly conformable:—

"And thus to Betty's questions he
     Made answer, like a traveller bold.
'The cock did crow, to-whoo, to-whoo,
     And the sun did shine so cold.'"
                    Lyrical Ballads, p. 129.

Shall gentle COLERIDGE pass unnoticed here,
To turgid ode and tumid stanza dear?
Though themes of innocence amuse him best,
Yet still Obscurity's a welcome guest.
If Inspiration should her aid refuse
To him who takes a Pixy for a muse,*   260
Yet none in lofty numbers can surpass
The bard who soars to elegize an ass:
So well the subject suits his noble mind,
He brays, the Laureate of the long-eared kind.

Oh! wonder-working LEWIS! [12] Monk, or Bard,
Who fain would make Parnassus a church-yard!
Lo! wreaths of yew, not laurel, bind thy brow,
Thy Muse a Sprite, Apollo's sexton thou!
Whether on ancient tombs thou tak'st thy stand,
By gibb'ring spectres hailed, thy kindred band;   270
Or tracest chaste descriptions on thy page,
To please the females of our modest age;
All hail, M.P.!† from whose infernal brain
Thin-sheeted phantoms glide, a grisly train;
At whose command "grim women" throng in crowds,
And kings of fire, of water, and of clouds,
With "small grey men,"—"wild yagers," and what
     not,
To crown with honour thee and WALTER SCOTT:
Again, all hail! if tales like thine may please,
St. Luke alone can vanquish the disease: 280
Even Satan's self with thee might dread to dwell,
And in thy skull discern a deeper Hell.

Who in soft guise, surrounded by a choir
Of virgins melting, not to Vesta's fire,
With sparkling eyes, and cheek by passion flushed
Strikes his wild lyre, whilst listening dames are
     hushed?
'Tis LITTLE! young Catullus of his day,
As sweet, but as immoral, in his Lay!
Grieved to condemn, the Muse must still be just,
Nor spare melodious advocates of lust.   290
Pure is the flame which o'er her altar burns;
From grosser incense with disgust she turns
Yet kind to youth, this expiation o'er,
She bids thee "mend thy line, and sin no more."

---

* COLERIDGE'S *Poems*, p. 11, "Songs of the Pixies," *i.e.*
Devonshire Fairies; p. 42, we have "Lines to a Young Lady;"
and, p. 52, "Lines to a Young Ass."

† "For every one knows little Matt's an M.P." See a poem
to Mr. Lewis, in *The Statesman*, supposed to be written by
Mr. Jekyll.

◇◇◇◇◇◇◇◇◇◇◇◇◇◇◇◇◇◇◇◇◇◇◇◇◇◇◇◇◇◇◇◇◇◇◇◇

[12] Matthew Gregory ["Monk"] Lewis (1775–1818), author
of *Ambrosio, or the Monk* (1795), *Tales of Wonder* (1801), and other
Gothic novels and ballads.

For thee, translator of the tinsel song,
To whom such glittering ornaments belong,
Hibernian STRANGFORD! with thine eyes of blue,*
And boasted locks of red or auburn hue,
Whose plaintive strain each love-sick Miss admires,
And o'er harmonious fustian half expires,   300
Learn, if thou canst, to yield thine author's sense,
Nor vend thy sonnets on a false pretence.
Think'st thou to gain they verse a higher place,
By dressing Camoëns† in a suit of lace?
Mend, STRANGFORD! mend thy morals and thy
          taste;
Be warm, but pure; be amorous, but be chaste:
Cease to decieve; thy pilfered harp restore,
Nor teach the Lusian Bard to copy MOORE.

Behold—Ye Tarts!—one moment spare the text!—
HAYLEY's last work, and worst—until his next;   310
Whether he spin poor couplets into plays,
Or damn the dead with purgatorial praise,‡
His style in youth or age is still the same,
For ever feeble and for ever tame.
Triumphant first see "Temper's Triumphs" shine!
At least I'm sure they triumphed over mine.
Of "Music's Triumphs," all who read may swear
That luckless Music never triumph'd there. §

Moravians, rise! bestow some meet reward
On dull devotion—Lo! the Sabbath Bard,   320
Sepulchral GRAHAME, pours his notes sublime
In mangled prose, nor e'en aspires to rhyme;
Breaks into blank the Gospel of St. Luke, ‖
And boldly pilfers from the Pentateuch;
And, undisturbed by conscientious qualms,
Perverts the Prophets, and purloins the Psalms.

Hail, Sympathy! thy soft idea brings
A thousand visions of a thousand things,
And shows, still whimpering thro' threescore of years,
The maudlin prince of mournful sonneteers.   330
And art thou not their prince, harmonious Bowles![15]
Thou first, great oracle of tender souls?
Whether thou sing'st with equal ease, and grief,
The fall of empires, or a yellow leaf;
Whether they muse most lamentably tells
What merry sounds proceed from Oxford bells,*
Or, still in bells delighting, finds a friend
In every chime that jingled from Ostend;
Ah! how much juster were thy Muse's hap,
If to thy bells thou would'st but add a cap!   340
Delightful BOWLES! still blessing and still blest,
All love thy strain, but children like it best.
'Tis thine, with gentle LITTLE's moral song,
To soothe the mania of the amorous throng!
With thee our nursery damsels shed their tears,
Ere Miss as yet completes her infant years:
But in her teens thy whining powers are vain;
She quits poor BOWLES for LITTLE's purer strain.
Now to soft themes thou scornest to confine
The lofty numbers of a harp like thine;   350
"Awake a louder and a loftier strain,"†
Such as none heard before, or will again!
Where all discoveries jumbled from the flood,
Since first the leaky ark reposed in mud,
By more or less, are sung in every book,
From Captain Noah down to Captain Cook.
Nor this alone—but, pausing on the road,
The Bard sighs forth a gentle episode,‡
And gravely tells—attend, each beauteous Miss!—
When first Madeira trembled to a kiss.   360
Bowles! in thy memory let this precept dwell,
Stick to thy Sonnets, Man!—at least they sell.
But if some new-born whim, or larger bribe,
Prompt thy crude brain, and claim thee for a scribe:

---

* The reader, who may wish for an explanation of this, may refer to "Strangford's Camoëns," p. 127, note to p. 56, or to the last page of the *Edinburgh Review* of Strangford's Camoëns.

† It is also to be remarked, that the things given to the public as poems of Camoëns are no more to be found in the original Portuguese, than in the Song of Solomon.

‡ See his various Biographies of defunct Painters, etc.[13]

§ Hayley's two most notorious verse productions are *Triumphs of Temper* and *The Triumph of Music.* He has also written much Comedy in rhyme, Epistles, etc., etc. As he is rather an elegant writer of notes and biography, let us recommend POPE's advice to WYCHERLEY to Mr. H.'s consideration, viz., "to convert poetry into prose," which may be easily done by taking away the final syllable of each couplet.

‖ Mr. Grahame[14] has poured forth two volumes of Cant, under the name of *Sabbath Walks* and *Biblical Pictures.*

---

[13] William Hayley (1745–1820) was Blake's patron.
[14] James Grahame (1765–1811), a lawyer who later took Holy Orders.

* See Bowles's "Sonnet to Oxford" and "Stanzas on hearing the Bells of Ostend."

† "Awake a louder," etc., is the first line in BOWLES's *Spirit of Discovery:* a very spirited and pretty dwarf Epic. Among other exquisite lines we have the following:—

——"A kiss
Stole on the list'ning silence, never yet
Here heard; they trembled even as if the power, etc. etc.

That is, the woods of Madeira trembled to a kiss; very much astonished, as well they might be, at such a phenomenon.

‡ The episode above alluded to is the story of "Robert à Machin" and "Anna d'Arfet," a pair of constant lovers, who performed the kiss above mentioned, that startled the woods of Madeira.

---

[15] William Lisle Bowles (1768–1850), sonneteer, greatly admired by Coleridge, but particularly criticized by Byron for his edition of Pope (see esp. ll. 367–84).

If 'chance some bard, though once by dunces feared,
Now, prone in dust, can only be revered;
If Pope, whose fame and genius, from the first,
Have foiled the best of critics, needs the worst,
Do thou essay: each fault, each failing scan;
The first of poets was, alas! but man.   370
Rake from each ancient dunghill ev'ry pearl,
Consult Lord Fanny, and confide in CURLL;*
Let all the scandals of a former age
Perch on thy pen, and flutter o'er thy page;
Affect a candour which thou canst not feel,
Clothe envy in a garb of honest zeal;
Write, as if St. John's soul could still inspire,
And do from hate what MALLET† did for hire.
Oh! hadst thou lived in that congenial time,
To rave with DENNIS, and with RALPH to rhyme;‡
Thronged with the rest around his living head,   381
Not raised thy hoof against the lion dead,
A meet reward had crowned thy glorious gains,
And linked thee to the Dunciad for thy pains. §

Another Epic! Who inflicts again
More books of blank upon the sons of men?
Bœotian COTTLE, rich Bristowa's boast,
Imports old stories from the Cambrian coast,
And sends his goods to market—all alive!
Lines forty thousand, Cantos twenty-five!   390
Fresh fish from Hippocrene! who'll buy? who'll buy?
The precious bargain's cheap—in faith, not I.
Your turtle-feeder's verse must needs be flat,
Though Bristol bloat him with the verdant fat;
If Commerce fills the purse, she clogs the brain,
And AMOS COTTLE strikes the Lyre in vain.
In him an author's luckless lot behold!
Condemned to make the books which once he sold.
Oh, AMOS COTTLE!—Phœbus! what a name
To fill the speaking-trump of future fame!—   400
Oh, AMOS COTTLE! for a moment think
What meagre profits spring from pen and ink!
When thus devoted to poetic dreams,
Who will peruse thy prostituted reams?

* CURLL is one of the Heroes of the *Dunciad*, and was a bookseller. Lord Fanny is the poetical name of Lord HERVEY, author of *Lines to the Imitator of Horace*.

† Lord BOLINGBROKE hired MALLET to traduce POPE after his decease, because the poet had retained some copies of a work by Lord Bolingbroke—the "Patriot King,"—which that splendid, but malignant genius had ordered to be destroyed.

‡ Dennis the critic, and Ralph the rhymester:—

"Silence, ye Wolves! while Ralph to Cynthia howls,
  Making Night hideous: answer him, ye owls!"
                                              DUNCIAD

§ See Bowles's late edition of Pope's works, for which he received three hundred pounds. Thus Mr. B. has experienced how much easier it is to profit by the reputation of another, than to elevate his own.

Oh! pen perverted! paper misapplied!
Had COTTLE* still adorned the counter's side,
Bent o'er the desk, or, born to useful toils,
Been taught to make the paper which he soils,
Ploughed, delved, or plied the oar with lusty limb,
He had not sung of Wales, nor I of him.   410

As Sisyphus against the infernal steep
Rolls the huge rock whose motions ne'er may sleep,
So up thy hill, ambrosial Richmond! heaves
Dull MAURICE† all his granite weight of leaves:
Smooth, solid monuments of mental pain!
The petrifactions of a plodding brain,
That, ere they reach the top, fall lumbering back
      again.

With broken lyre and cheek serenely pale,
Lo! sad Alcæus wanders down the vale;
Though fair they rose, and might have bloomed at
      last,   420
His hopes have perished by the northern blast:
Nipped in the bud by Caledonian gales,
His blossoms wither as the blast prevails!
O'er his lost works let *classic* SHEFFIELD weep;
May no rude hand disturb their early sleep!‡

Yet say! why should the Bard, at once, resign
His claim to favour from the sacred Nine?
For ever startled by the mingled howl
Of Northern Wolves, that still in darkness prowl;
A coward Brood, which mangle as they prey,   430
By hellish instinct, all that cross their way;
Aged or young, the living or the dead,
No mercy find—these harpies must be fed.

* Mr. Cottle, Amos, Joseph, I don't know which, but one or both, once sellers of books they did not write, and now writers of books they do not sell, have published a pair of Epics—*Alfred* (poor Alfred! Pye has been at him too!)—*Alfred* and the *Fall of Cambria*.[16]

† Mr. Maurice[17] hath manufactured the component part of a ponderous quarto, upon the beauties of "Richmond Hill," and the like:—it also takes in a charming view of Turnham Green, Hammersmith, Brentford, Old and New, and the parts adjacent.

‡ Poor MONTGOMERY, though praised by every English Review, has been bitterly reviled by the *Edinburgh*. After all, the Bard of Sheffield is a man of considerable genius. His *Wanderer of Switzerland* is worth a thousand *Lyrical Ballads*, and at least fifty *Degraded Epics*.[18]

⟡⟡⟡⟡⟡⟡⟡⟡⟡⟡⟡⟡⟡⟡⟡⟡⟡⟡⟡⟡⟡⟡⟡⟡⟡⟡⟡

[16] Amos and Joseph Cottle were Bristol ("Bristowa") booksellers, minor poets, and—especially Joseph—early supporters of Wordsworth and Coleridge.

[17] The Rev. Thomas Maurice (1754–1824), assistant keeper of MSS at the British Museum.

[18] James Montgomery (1771–1854) was attacked by the *Edinburgh Review* in 1807.

Why do the injured unresisting yield
The calm possession of their native field?
Why tamely thus before their fangs retreat,
Nor hunt the blood-hounds back to Arthur's Seat?*

Health to immortal JEFFREY! once, in name,
England could boast a judge almost the same;
In soul so like, so merciful, yet just,   440
Some think that Satan has resigned his trust,
And given the Spirit to the world again,
To sentence Letters, as he sentenced men.
With hand less mighty, but with heart as black,
With voice as willing to decree the rack;
Bred in the Courts betimes, though all that law
As yet hath taught him is to find a flaw,—
Since well instructed in the patriot school
To rail at party, though a party tool—
Who knows? if chance his patrons should restore   450
Back to the sway they forfeited before,
His scribbling toils some recompense may meet,
And raise this Daniel to the Judgment-Seat.
Let JEFFREY's shade indulge the pious hope,
And greeting thus, present him with a rope:
"Heir to my virtues! man of equal mind!
Skilled to condemn as to traduce mankind,
This cord receive! for thee reserved with care,
To wield in judgment, and at length to wear."

Health to great JEFFREY! Heaven preserve his life,
To flourish on the fertile shores of Fife,   461
And guard it sacred in its future wars,
Since authors sometimes seek the field of Mars!
Can none remember that eventful day,
That ever-glorious, almost fatal fray,
When LITTLE's leadless pistol met his eye,†
And Bow-street Myrmidons stood laughing by?
Oh, day disastrous! on her firm-set rock,
Dunedin's castle felt a secret shock;
Dark rolled the sympathetic waves of Forth,   470
Low groaned the startled whirlwinds of the north;

TWEED ruffled half his waves to form a tear,
The other half pursued his calm career;*
ARTHUR's steep summit nodded to its base,
The surly Tolbooth scarcely kept her place.
The Tolbooth felt—for marble sometimes can,
On such occasions, feel as much as man—
The Tolbooth felt defrauded of his charms,
If JEFFREY died, except within her arms:†
Nay last, not least, on that portentous morn,   480
The sixteenth story, where himself was born,
His patrimonial garret, fell to ground,
And pale Edina shuddered at the sound:
Strewed were the streets around with milk-white
      reams,
Flowed all the Canongate with inky streams;
This of his candour seemed the sable dew,
That of his valour showed the bloodless hue;
And all with justice deemed the two combined
The mingled emblems of his mighty mind.
But Caledonia's goddess hovered o'er   490
The field, and saved him from the wrath of Moore;
From either pistol snatched the vengeful lead,
And straight restored it to her favourite's head;
That head, with greater than magnetic power,
Caught it, as Danäe caught the golden shower,
And, though the thickening dross will scarce refine,
Augments its ore, and is itself a mine.
"My son," she cried, "ne'er thirst for gore again,
Resign the pistol and resume the pen;
O'er politics and poesy preside,   500
Boast of thy country, and Britannia's guide!
For long as Albion's heedless sons submit,
Or Scottish taste decides on English wit,
So long shall last thine unmolested reign,
Nor any dare to take thy name in vain.
Behold, a chosen band shall aid thy plan,
And own thee chieftain of the critic clan.
First in the oat-fed phalanx shall be seen
The travelled Thane, Athenian Aberdeen.‡
HERBERT shall wield THOR's hammer,§ and
      sometimes   510
In gratitude, thou'lt praise his rugged rhymes.

* Arthur's Seat; the hill which overhangs Edinburgh.
† In 1806, Messrs. Jeffrey and Moore met at Chalk Farm.
The duel was prevented by the interference of the Magistracy;
and on examination, the balls of the pistols were found to have
evaporated. This incident gave occasion to much waggery in the
daily prints.
I am informed that Mr. Moore published at the time a dis-
avowal of the statements in the newspapers, as far as regarded
himself; and, in justice to him, I mention this circumstance. As
I never heard of it before, I cannot state the particulars, and was
only made acquainted with the fact very lately. November 4,
1811.[19]

[19] The second paragraph of the note was added in the Fifth
Edition. As a matter of fact, it was Jeffrey's pistol that was found
to be without a ball.

* The Tweed here behaved with proper decorum; it would
have been highly reprehensible in the English half of the river
to have shown the smallest symptom of apprehension.
† This display of sympathy on the part of the Tolbooth (the
principal prison in Edinburgh), which truly seems to have been
most affected on this occasion, is much to be commended. It
was to be apprehended, that the many unhappy criminals
executed in the front might have rendered the Edifice more
callous. She is said to be of the softer sex, because her delicacy
of feeling on this day was truly feminine, though, like most
feminine impulses, perhaps a little selfish.
‡ His Lordship has been much abroad, is a member of the
Athenian Society, and reviewer of Gell's *Topography of Troy*.
§ Mr. Herbert is a translator of Icelandic and other poetry.

Smug SYDNEY* too thy bitter page shall seek,
And classic HALLAM,† much renowed for Greek;
SCOTT may perchance his name and influence lend,
And paltry PILLANS‡ shall traduce his friend;
While gay Thalia's luckless votary, LAMB,§
Damned like the Devil—Devil-like will damn.
Known be thy name! unbounded be thy sway!
Thy HOLLAND's banquets shall each toil repay!
While grateful Britain yields the praise she owes　520
To HOLLAND's hirelings and to Learning's foes.
Yet mark one caution ere thy next Review
Spread its light wings of Saffron and of Blue,
Beware lest blundering BROUGHAM‖ destroy the
　　sale,
Turn Beef to Bannocks, Cauliflowers to Kail."

One of the principal pieces is a *Song on the Recovery of Thor's Hammer*: the translation is a pleasant chant in the vulgar tongue, and endeth thus:—

> "Instead of money and rings, I wot,
> The hammer's bruises were her lot.
> Thus Odin's son his hammer got."

　* The Rev. SYDNEY SMITH,[20] the reputed Author of *Peter Plymley's Letters*, and sundry criticisms.
　† Mr. HALLAM[21] reviewed PAYNE KNIGHT's "Taste," and was exceedingly severe on some Greek verses therein. It was not discovered that the lines were Pindar's till the press rendered it impossible to cancel the critique, which still stands an everlasting monument of Hallam's ingenuity.[22]—The said Hallam is incensed because he is falsely accused, seeing that he never dineth at Holland House. If this be true, I am sorry—not for having said so, but on his account, as I understand his Lordship's feasts are preferable to his compositions. If he did not review Lord HOLLAND's performance, I am glad; because it must have been painful to read, and irksome to praise it. If Mr. HALLAM will tell me who did review it, the real name shall find a place in the text; provided, nevertheless, the said name be of two orthodox musical syllables, and will come into the verse; till then, HALLAM must stand for want of a better.
　‡ Pillans is a tutor at Eton.[23]
　§ The Honourable G. Lambe reviewed "BERESFORD's Miseries," and is moreover Author of a farce enacted with much applause at the Priory, Stanmore; and damned with great expedition at the late theatre, Covent Garden. It was entitled *Whistle for It*.
　‖ Mr. Brougham, in No. XXV. of the *Edinburgh Review*, throughout the article concerning Don Pedro de Cevallos, has displayed more politics than policy; many of the worthy burgesses of Edinburgh being so incensed at the infamous principles it evinces, as to have withdrawn their subscriptions. It seems that Mr. Brougham is not a Pict, as I supposed, but a Borderer, and his name is pronounced Broom, from Trent to Tay:—so be it.

---

　[20] Smith (1771–1845) was canon of St. Paul's, a celebrated wit, and a founder of the *Edinburgh Review*.
　[21] Henry Hallam (1777–1859), historian.
　[22] The remainder of this note was added in the Second Edition.
　[23] James Pillans (1778–1864), Professor of Humanity in the University, Edinburgh.

Thus having said, the kilted Goddess kist
Her son, and vanished in a Scottish mist.

　Then prosper, JEFFREY! pertest of the train*
Whom Scotland pampers with her fiery grain!
Whatever blessing waits a genuine Scot,　　　530
In double portion swells thy glorious lot;
For thee Edina culls her evening sweets,
And showers their odours on thy candid sheets,
Whose Hue and Fragrance to thy work adhere—
This scents its pages, and that gilds its rear.†
Lo! blushing Itch, coy nymph, enamoured grown,
Forsakes the rest, and cleaves to thee alone,
And, too unjust to other Pictish men,
Enjoys thy person, and inspires thy pen!

　Illustrious HOLLAND! hard would be his lot,　540
His hirelings mentioned, and himself forgot!
HOLLAND, with HENRY PETTY[24] at his back,
The whipper-in and huntsman of the pack.
Blest be the banquets spread at Holland House,
Where Scotchmen feed, and Critics may carouse!
Long, long beneath that hospitable roof
Shall Grub-street dine, while duns are kept aloof.
See honest HALLAM lay aside his fork,
Resume his pen, review his Lordship's work,
And, grateful for the dainties on his plate,　　550
Declare his landlord can at least translate!‡
Dunedin! view thy children with delight,
They write for food—and feed because they write:
And lest, when heated with the unusual grape,
Some glowing thoughts should to the press escape,
And tinge with red the female reader's cheek,
My lady skims the cream of each critique;
Breathes o'er the page her purity of soul,
Reforms each error, and refines the whole.§

---

　* I ought to apologise to the worthy Deities for introducing a new Goddess with short petticoats to their notice: but, alas! what was to be done? I could not say Caledonia's Genius, it being well known there is no genius to be found from Clackmannan to Caithness; yet without supernatural agency, how was Jeffrey to be saved? The national "Kelpies" are too unpoetical, and the "Brownies" and "gude neighbours" (spirits of a good disposition) refused to extricate him. A Goddess, therefore has been called for the purpose; and great ought to be the gratitude of Jeffrey, seeing it is the only communication he ever held, or is likely to hold, with anything heavenly.
　† See the colour of the back binding of the *Edinburgh Review*.
　‡ Lord Holland has translated some specimens of Lope de Vega, inserted in his life of the author. Both are bepraised by his *disinterested* guests.
　§ Certain it is her ladyship is suspected of having displayed

---

　[24] Lord Holland (1773–1840) and his kinsman Henry Petty (1780–1863) are here made ringleaders for the Whigs and Edinburgh Reviewers who met at Holland House.

Now to the Drama turn—Oh! motley sight! 560
What precious scenes the wondering eyes invite:
Puns, and a Prince within a barrel pent,*
And Dibdin's nonsense yield complete content.
Though now, thank Heaven! the Rosciomania's o'er.[25]
And full-grown actors are endured once more;
Yet what avail their vain attempts to please,
While British critics suffer scenes like these;
While REYNOLDS vents his "*dammes!*" "poohs!"
      and "zounds!"†
And common-place and common sense confounds?
While KENNEY'S "World"—ah! where is
      KENNEY'S wit?—   570
Tires the sad gallery, lulls the listless Pit;
And BEAUMONT'S pilfered Caratach affords
A tragedy complete in all but words? ‡
Who but must mourn, while these are all the rage
The degradation of our vaunted stage?
Heavens! is all sense of shame and talent gone?
Have we no living Bard of merit?—none?
Awake, GEORGE COLMAN! CUMBERLAND,
      awake![27]
Ring the alarum bell! let folly quake!
Oh! SHERIDAN! if aught can move thy pen,   580
Let Comedy assume her throne again;
Abjure the mummery of German schools;
Leave new Pizarros to translating fools;
Give, as thy last memorial to the age,
One classic drama, and reform the stage.
Gods! o'er those boards shall Folly rear her head,
Where GARRICK trod, and SIDDONS lives to
      tread? [28]
On those shall Farce display buffoonery's mask,
And HOOK conceal his heroes in a cask?

Shall sapient managers new scenes produce   590
From CHERRY, SKEFFINGTON,* and Mother
      GOOSE?
While SHAKESPEARE, OTWAY, MASSINGER, forgot,
On stalls must moulder, or in closets rot?
Lo! with what pomp the daily prints proclaim
The rival candidates for Attic fame!
In grim array though LEWIS' spectres rise,
Still SKEFFINGTON and GOOSE divide the prize.
And sure *great* Skeffington must claim our praise,
For skirtless coats and skeletons of plays
Renowned alike; whose genius ne'er confines   600
Her flight to garnish Greenwood's gay designs;†
Nor sleeps with "Sleeping Beauties," but anon
In five facetious acts comes thundering on.
While poor John Bull, bewildered with the scene,
Stares, wondering what the devil it can mean;
But as some hands applaud, a venal few!
Rather than sleep, why John applauds it too.

Such are we now. Ah! wherefore should we turn
To what our fathers were, unless to mourn?
Degenerate Britons! are ye dead to shame,   610
Or, kind to dulness, do you fear to blame?
Well may the nobles of our present race
Watch each distortion of a NALDI'S face;
Well may they smile on Italy's buffoons,
And worship CATALANI'S pantaloons,‡
Since their own Drama yields no fairer trace
Of wit than puns, of humour than grimace.

Then let Ausonia, skill'd in every art
To soften manners, but corrupt the heart,
Pour her exotic follies o'er the town,   620
To sanction Vice, and hunt Decorum down:
Let wedded strumpets languish o'er DESHAYES,[31]
And bless the promise which his form displays;

---

her matchless wit in the *Edinburgh Review*. However that may
be, we know from good authority, that the manuscripts are sub-
mitted to her perusal—no doubt, for correction.

* In the melo-drama of *Tekeli*, that heroic prince is clapt into
a barrel on the stage; a new asylum for distressed heroes.

† All these are favourite expressions of Mr. Reynolds and
prominent in his comedies, living and defunct.

‡ Mr. T. Sheridan, the new Manager of Drury Lane theatre,
stripped the Tragedy of *Bonduca* of the dialogue, and exhibited
the scenes as the spectacle of *Caractacus*. Was this worthy of his
sire ? or of himself ? [26]

* Mr. [now Sir Lumley] Skeffington is the illustrious author
of *The Sleeping Beauty ;* and some comedies, particularly *Maids
and Bachelors : Baccalaurii baculo magis quam lauro digni.*[29]

† Mr. Greenwood is, we believe, scene-painter to Drury
Lane theatre—as such, Mr. Skeffington is much indebted to him.

‡ Naldi and Catalani require little notice; for the visage of
the one, and the salary of the other, will enable us long to
recollect these amusing vagabonds. Besides, we are still black
and blue from the squeeze on the first night of the lady's
appearance in trousers.[30]

---

[25] William Betty (1791–1874), "the Young Roscius," was an
exceedingly popular actor. Reynolds and Kenney (below) are
minor playwrights.
[26] Thomas Sheridan (1775–1817), the son of Richard Brinsley
Sheridan, the most famous of eighteenth-century dramatists.
[27] George Colman (1762–1836) and Richard Cumberland
(1732–1811), playwrights.
[28] David Garrick retired as an actor in 1776; Mrs. Sarah
Siddons not until 1812.

[29] Lumley St. George Skeffington (1768–1850), playwright
and dandy. Andrew Cherry (1762–1812), mentioned in the same
line, was an actor.
[30] Guiseppe Naldi (1770–1820) and Angelica Catalani (c. 1785–
1849) were opera singers who came to England from Italy
("Ausonia" in line 618). Catalani was one of the most famous
sopranos of the age.
[31] Deshayes was ballet-master at the King's Theatre; Gayton,
Presle, Angiolini, Collini (lines 624–30) were dancers there.

While Gayton bounds before th' enraptured looks
Of hoary Marquises, and stripling Dukes:
Let high-born lechers eye the lively Presle
Twirl her light limbs, that spurn the needless veil;
Let Angiolini bare her breast of snow,
Wave the white arm, and point the pliant toe;
Collini trill her love-inspiring song,   630
Strain her fair neck, and charm the listening throng!
Whet not your scythe, Suppressors of our Vice!
Reforming Saints! too delicately nice!
By whose decrees, our sinful souls to save,
No Sunday tankards foam, no barbers shave;
And beer undrawn, and beards unmown, display
Your holy reverence for the Sabbath-day.

    Or hail at once the patron and the pile
Of vice and folly, Greville and Argyle!*
Where yon proud palace, Fashion's hallow'd fane,
Spreads wide her portals for the motley train,   641
Behold the new Petronius† of the day,
Our arbiter of pleasure and of play!
There the hired eunuch, the Hesperian choir,
The melting lute, the soft lascivious lyre,
The song from Italy, the step from France,
The midnight orgy, and the mazy dance,
The smile of beauty, and the flush of wine,
For fops, fools, gamesters, knaves, and Lords
        combine:
Each to his humour—Comus all allows;   650
Champaign, dice, music, or your neighbour's spouse.
Talk not to us, ye starving sons of trade!
Of piteous ruin, which oursevles have made;
In Plenty's sunshine Fortune's minions bask,
Nor think of Poverty, except "en masque,"
When for the night some lately titled ass
Appears the beggar which his grandsire was,
The curtain dropped, the gay Burletta o'er,
The audience take their turn upon the floor:

    * To prevent any blunder, such as mistaking a street for a
man, I beg leave to state, that it is the institution, and not the
Duke of that name, which is here alluded to.
    A gentleman, with whom I am slightly acquainted, lost in the
Argyle Rooms several thousand pounds at Backgammon. It is
but justice to the manager in this instance to say, that some
degree of disapprobation was manifested: but why are the im-
plements of gaming allowed in a place devoted to the society of
both sexes? A pleasant thing for the wives and daughters of
those who are blessed or cursed with such connections, to hear
the Billiard-Balls rattling in one room, and the dice in another!
That this is the case I myself can testify, as a late unworthy
member of an Institution which materially affects the morals of
the higher orders, while the lower may not even move to the
sound of a tabor and fiddle, without a chance of indictment for
riotous behaviour.
    † Petronius, "Arbiter elegantarium" to Nero "and a very
pretty fellow in his day," as Mr. Congreve's "Old Bachelor"
saith of Hannibal.

Now round the room the circling dow'gers sweep,
Now in loose waltz the thin-clad daughters leap;   661
The first in lengthened line majestic swim,
The last display the free unfettered limb!
Those for Hibernia's lusty sons repair
With art the charms which Nature could not spare;
These after husbands wing their eager flight,
Nor leave much mystery for the nuptial night.

    Oh! blest retreats of infamy and ease,
Where, all forgotten but the power to please,
Each maid may give a loose to genial thought,   670
Each swain may teach new systems, or be taught:
There the blithe youngster, just returned from Spain,
Cuts the light pack, or calls the rattling main;
The jovial Caster's set, and seven's the Nick,[32]
Or—done!—a thousand on the coming trick!
If, mad with loss, existence 'gins to tire,
And all your hope or wish is to expire,
Here's POWELL'S pistol ready for your life,
And, kinder still, two PAGETS for your wife:
Fit consummation of an earthly race   680
Begun in folly, ended in disgrace,
While none but menials o'er the bed of death,
Wash thy red wounds, or watch thy wavering breath;
Traduced by liars, and forgot by all,
The mangled victim of a drunken brawl,
To live like CLODIUS, and like FALKLAND fall.*[33]

    Truth! rouse some genuine Bard, and guide his
        hand
To drive this pestilence from out the land.
E'en I—least thinking of a thoughtless throng,
Just skilled to know the right and choose the wrong,
Freed at that age when Reason's shield is lost,   691
To fight my course through Passion's countless host,
Whom every path of Pleasure's flow'ry way
Has lured in turn, and all have led astray—
E'en I must raise my voice, e'en I must feel
Such scenes, such men, destroy the public weal:

    * I knew the late Lord Falkland well. On Sunday night I
beheld him presiding at his own table, in all the honest pride of
hospitality; on Wednesday morning, at three o'clock, I saw
stretched before me all that remained of courage, feeling, and a
host of passions. He was a gallant and successful officer: his
faults were the faults of a sailor—as such, Britons will forgive
them. He died like a brave man in a better cause; for had he
fallen in like manner on the deck of the frigate to which he was
just appointed, his last moments would have been held up by
his countrymen as an example to succeeding heroes.

[32] Terms from dicing.
[33] In March 1807, A. Powell killed Viscount Falkland in a
duel over an insult delivered at a coffeehouse; Clodius intrigued
with Cæsar's wife, Pompeia.

Altho' some kind, censorious friend will say,
"What art thou better, meddling fool, than they?"
And every Brother Rake will smile to see
That miracle, a Moralist in me.   700
No matter—when some Bard in virtue strong,
Gifford perchance, shall raise the chastening song,
Then sleep my pen for ever! and my voice
Be only heard to hail him, and rejoice,
Rejoice, and yield my feeble praise, though I
May feel the lash that Virtue must apply.

    As for the smaller fry, who swarm in shoals
From silly HAFIZ up to simple BOWLES,*
Why should we call them from their dark abode,
In Broad St. Giles's or Tottenham-Road?   710
Or (since some men of fashion nobly dare
To scrawl in verse) from Bond-street or the Square?
If things of Ton[34] their harmless lays indite,
Most wisely doomed to shun the public sight,
What harm? in spite of every critic elf,
Sir T. may read his stanzas to himself;
MILES ANDREWS[35] still his strength in couplets try,
And live in prologues, though his dramas die.
Lords too are Bards: such things at times befall,
And 'tis some praise in Peers to write at all.   720
Yet, did or Taste or Reason sway the times,
Ah! who would take their titles with their rhymes?
ROSCOMMON! SHEFFIELD! with your spirits fled,
No future laurels deck a noble head;
No Muse will cheer, with renovating smile,
The paralytic puling of CARLISLE.[36]
The puny schoolboy and his early lay
Men pardon, if his follies pass away;
But who forgives the Senior's ceaseless verse,
Whose hairs grow hoary as his rhymes grow worse?
What heterogeneous honours deck the Peer!   731
Lord, rhymester, petit-maître, pamphleteer!†

---

    * What would be the sentiments of the Persian Anacreon, HAFIZ, could he rise from his splendid sepulchre at Sheeraz (where he reposes with FERDOUSI and SADI, the Oriental Homer and Catullus), and behold his name assumed by one STOTT of DROMORE, the most impudent and execrable of literary poachers for the Daily Prints?

    † The Earl of Carlisle has lately published an eighteen-penny pamphlet on the state of the Stage, and offers his plan for building a new theatre. It is to be hoped his Lordship will be permitted to bring forward anything for the Stage—except his own tragedies.

    [34] Fashion, modishness.
    [35] Miles Peter Andrews (d. 1824), powder-mill owner and frequenter of playhouses, who wrote a play.
    [36] The Earl of Carlisle (1748–1825), Byron's kinsman, and one-time guardian, is compared unfavorably with the Earl of Roscommon and the Duke of Buckingham, both distinguished writers a century or so earlier.

So dull in youth, so drivelling in his age,
His scenes alone had damned our sinking stage;
But Managers for once cried, "Hold, enough!"
Nor drugged their audience with the tragic stuff.
Yet at their judgment let his Lordship laugh,
And case his volumes in congenial calf;
Yes! doff that covering, where Morocco shines,
And hang a calf-skin on those recreant lines.*   740

    With you, ye Druids! rich in native lead,
Who daily scribble for your daily bread:
With you I war not: GIFFORD'S heavy hand
Has crushed, without remorse, your numerous band.
On "All the Talents" vent your venal spleen;
Want is your plea, let Pity be your screen.
Let Monodies on Fox regale your crew,
And Melville's Mantle† prove a Blanket too!
One common Lethe waits each hapless Bard,
And, peace be with you! 'tis your best reward.   750
Such damning fame; as Dunciads only give
Could bid your lines beyond a morning live;
But now at once your fleeting labours close,
With names of greater note in blest repose.
Far be't from me unkindly to upbraid
The lovely ROSA'S prose in masquerade,
Whose strains, the faithful echoes of her mind,
Leave wondering comprehension far behind.‡
Though Crusca's bards no more our journals fill,
Some stragglers skirmish round the columns still;   760
Last of the howling host which once was Bell's,
Matilda snivels yet, and Hafiz yells;
And Merry's[37] metaphors appear anew,
Chained to the signature of O. P. Q.§

    When some brisk youth,[38] the tenant of a stall,
Employs a pen less pointed than his awl,
Leaves his snug shop, forsakes his store of shoes,
St. Crispin quits, and cobbles for the Muse,

---

    *   "Doff that lion's hide,
   And hang a calf-skin on those recreant limbs."
                 SHAKESPEARE, *King John*
Lord Carlisle's works, most resplendently bound, form a conspicuous ornament to his book-shelves:—
    "The rest is all but leather and prunella."
    † "Melville's Mantle," a parody on *Elijah's Mantle*, a poem.
    ‡ This lovely little Jessica, the daughter of the noted Jew King, seems to be a follower of the Della Crusca school and has published two volumes of very respectable absurdities in rhyme, as times go; besides sundry novels in the style of the first edition of *The Monk*.
    § These are the signatures of various worthies who figure in the poetical departments of the newspapers.

    [37] Robert Merry (1755–1798), leader of a group of minor poets who called themselves the Della Cruscans, which Gifford attacked in *The Baviad* (1794) and *The Mæviad* (1795).
    [38] Apparently, Joseph Blacket, a shoemaker turned poet.

Heavens! how the vulgar stare! how crowds applaud!
How ladies read, and Literati laud!   770
If chance some wicked wag should pass his jest,
'Tis sheer ill-nature—don't the world know best?
Genius must guide when wits admire the rhyme,
And CAPEL LOFFT* declares 'tis quite sublime.
Hear, then, ye happy sons of needless trade!
Swains! quit the plough, resign the useless spade!
Lo! BURNS and BLOOMFIELD, nay, a greater far,
GIFFORD was born beneath an adverse star,
Forsook the labours of a servile state,
Stemmed the rude storm, and triumphed over Fate:
Then why no more? If Phœbus smiled on you,   781
BLOOMFIELD! why not on brother Nathan too?†
Him too the Mania, not the Muse, has seized;
Not inspiration, but a mind diseased:
And now no Boor can seek his last abode,
No common be inclosed without an ode.
Oh! since increased refinement deigns to smile
On Britain's sons, and bless our genial Isle,
Let Poesy go forth, pervade the whole,
Alike the rustic, and mechanic soul!   790
Ye tuneful cobblers! still your notes prolong,
Compose at once a slipper and a song;
So shall the fair your handywork peruse,
Your sonnets sure shall please—perhaps your shoes.
May Moorland weavers boast Pindaric skill,
And tailors' lays be longer than their bill!
While punctual beaux reward the grateful notes,
And pay for poems—when they pay for coats.

   To the famed throng now paid the tribute due,‡
Neglected Genius! let me turn to you.   800
Come forth, oh CAMPBELL! give thy talents scope;
Who dares aspire if thou must cease to hope?
And thou, melodious ROGERS! rise at last,
Recall the pleasing memory of the past;§

Arise! let blest remembrance still inspire,
And strike to wonted tones thy hallowed lyre;
Restore Apollo to his vacant throne,
Assert thy country's honour and thine own.
What! must deserted Poesy still weep
Where her last hopes with pious COWPER sleep?
Unless, perchance, from his cold bier she turns,   811
To deck the turf that wraps her minstrel, BURNS!
No! though contempt hath marked the spurious
         brood,
The race who rhyme from folly, or for food,
Yet still some genuine sons 'tis hers to boast,
Who, least affecting, still affect the most:
Feel as they write, and write but as they feel—
Bear witness GIFFORD,* SOTHEBY,† MACNEIL.‡

   "Why slumbers GIFFORD?" once was asked in
         vain;
Why slumbers GIFFORD? let us ask again.§   820
Are there no follies for his pen to purge?
Are there no fools whose backs demand the scourge?
Are there no sins for Satire's Bard to greet?
Stalks not gigantic Vice in every street?
Shall Peers or Princes tread pollution's path,
And 'scape alike the Laws and Muse's wrath?
Nor blaze with guilty glare through future time,
Eternal beacons of consummate crime?
Arouse thee, GIFFORD! be thy promise claimed,
Make bad men better, or at least ashamed.   830

Unhappy WHITE!‖ while life was in its spring,
And thy young Muse just waved her joyous wing,
The Spoiler swept that soaring Lyre away,
Which else had sounded an immortal lay.

---

   * Capel Lofft, Esq., the Mæcenas of shoemakers, and Preface-writer-General to distressed versemen; a kind of gratis Accoucheur to those who wish to be devliered of rhyme, but do not know how to bring it forth.
   † See Nathaniel Bloomfield's ode, elegy, or whatever he or any one else chooses to call it, on the enclosures of "Honington Green."[39]
   ‡ Vide *Recollections of a Weaver in the Moorlands of Staffordshire.*[40]
   § It would be superfluous to recall to the mind of the reader the authors of *The Pleasures of Memory* and *The Pleasures of Hope,* the most beautiful didactic poems in our language, if we except Pope's *Essay on Man*: but so many poetasters have started up, that even the names of Campbell and Rogers are become strange.

<>--<>--<>--<>--<>--<>--<>--<>--<>--<>

   [39] Lofft was a patron to Robert Bloomfield, whose brother was a shoemaker.
   [40] Byron recalled the title inexactly. The author was T. Bakewell, who also wrote *A Domestic Guide to Insanity,* 1805.

   * GIFFORD, author of the *Baviad* and *Mæviad,* the first satires of the day, and translator of Juvenal.
   † SOTHEBY, translator of WIELAND'S *Oberon* and Virgil's *Georgics,* and author of *Saul,* an epic poem.[41]
   ‡ MACNEIL, whose poems are deservedly popular, particularly "SCOTLAND's Scaith," and the "Waes of War," of which ten thousand copies were sold in one month.[42]
   § Mr. GIFFORD promised publicly that the *Baviad* and *Mæviad* should not be his last original works: let him remember, "Mox in reluctantes dracones."
   ‖ Henry Kirke White died at Cambridge, in October 1806, in consequence of too much exertion in the pursuit of studies that would have matured a mind which disease and poverty could not impair, and which Death itself destroyed rather than subdued. His poems abound in such beauties as must impress the reader with the liveliest regret that so short a period was alotted to talents, which would have dignified even the sacred functions he was destined to assume.

<>--<>--<>--<>--<>--<>--<>--<>--<>--<>

   [41] William Sotheby (1757–1833), litterateur and literary patron.
   [42] Hector Macneil (1746–1816), minor poet.

Oh! what a noble heart was here undone,
When Science' self destroyed her favourite son!
Yes, she too much indulged thy fond pursuit,
She sowed the seeds, but Death has reaped the
 fruit.
'Twas thine own Genius gave the final blow,
And helped to plant the wound that laid thee low:
So the struck Eagle, stretched upon the plain,   841
No more through rolling clouds to soar again,
Viewed his own feather on the fatal dart,
And winged the shaft that quivered in his heart;
Keen were his pangs, but keener far to feel
He nursed the pinion which impelled the steel;
While the same plumage that had warmed his nest
Drank the last life-drop of his bleeding breast.

There be who say, in these enlightened days,
That splendid lies are all the poet's praise;   850
That strained Invention, ever on the wing,
Alone impels the modern Bard to sing:
'Tis true, that all who rhyme—nay, all who write,
Shrink from that fatal word to Genius—Trite;
Yet Truth sometimes will lend her noblest fires,
And decorate the verse herself inspires:
This fact in Virtue's name let CRABBE [43] attest;
Though Nature's sternest Painter, yet the best.

And here let SHEE* and Genius find a place,
Whose pen and pencil yield an equal grace;   860
To guide whose hand the sister Arts combine,
And trace the Poet's or the Painter's line;
Whose magic touch can bid the canvas glow,
Or pour the easy rhyme's harmonious flow;
While honours, doubly merited, attend
The Poet's rival, but the Painter's friend.

Blest is the man who dares approach the bower
Where dwelt the Muses at their natal hour;
Whose steps have pressed, whose eye has marked
 afar,
The clime that nursed the sons of song and war,   870
The scenes which Glory still must hover o'er,
Her place of birth, her own Achaian shore.
But doubly blest is he whose heart expands
With hallowed feelings for those classic lands;
Who rends the veil of ages long gone by,
And views their remnants with a poet's eye!

WRIGHT!* 'twas thy happy lot at once to view
Those shores of glory, and to sing them too;
And sure no common Muse inspired thy pen
To hail the land of Gods and Godlike men.   880

And you, associate Bards!† who snatched to light
Those gems too long withheld from modern sight;
Whose mingling taste combined to cull the wreath
While Attic flowers Aonian odours breathe,
And all their renovated fragrance flung,
To grace the beauties of your native tongue;
Now let those minds, that nobly could transfuse
The glorious Spirit of the Grecian Muse,
Though soft the echo, scorn a borrowed tone:
Resign Achaia's lyre, and strike your own.   890

Let these, or such as these, with just applause,
Restore the Muse's violated laws;
But not in flimsy DARWIN'S [46] pompous chime,
That mighty master of unmeaning rhyme,
Whose gilded cymbals, more adorned than clear,
The eye delighted, but fatigued the ear,
In show the simple lyre could once surpass,
But now, worn down, appear in native brass;
While all his train of hovering sylphs around
Evaporate in similes and sound: 900
Him let them shun, with him let tinsel die:
False glare attracts, but more offends the eye.‡

Yet let them not to vulgar WORDSWORTH stoop,
The meanest object of the lowly group,
Whose verse, of all but childish prattle void,
Seems blessed harmony to LAMB and LLOYD:§
Let them—but hold, my Muse, nor dare to teach
A strain far, far beyond thy humble reach:

* Mr. Wright, late Consul-General for the Seven Islands, is author of a very beautiful poem, just published: it is entitled *Horæ Ionicæ*, and is descriptive of the isles and the adjacent coast of Greece.
 † The translators of the Anthology have since published separate poems, which evince genius that only requires opportunity to attain eminence. [45]
 ‡ The neglect of *The Botanic Garden* is some proof of returning taste. The scenery is its sole recommendation.
 § Messrs. Lamb and Lloyd, the most ignoble followers of Southey and Co. [47]

 45 Byron refers to *Translations Chiefly from the Greek Anthology* (1806) by the Rev. Robert Bland (1779–1825) and others.
 46 Erasmus Darwin (1731–1802), poet and naturalist, was the grandfather of Charles Darwin.
 47 I.e., Charles Lamb and Charles Lloyd (1725–1839), once Coleridge's protégé, a poet and novelist. On Lamb, see the notes, above, to Coleridge's *This Lime-Tree Bower My Prison*, p. 446, and Wordsworth's *Written on the Death of Charles Lamb*, p. 394. Lamb and Southey's names were coupled in a line in the *Anti-Jacobin*, recalled by Byron, as advocates of French socialism.

* Mr. Shee, author of *Rhymes on Art* and *Elements of Art*. [44]

 43 George Crabbe (1754–1832), author of *The Village*, etc.
 44 Sir Martin Archer Shee (1770–1850) was president of the Royal Academy from 1830 to 1845.

The native genius with their being given   909
Will point the path, and peal their notes to heaven.

   And thou, too, SCOTT!* resign to minstrels rude
The wilder Slogan of a Border feud:
Let others spin their meagre lines for hire;
Enough for Genius, if itself inspire!
Let SOUTHEY sing, altho' his teeming muse,
Prolific every spring, be too profuse;
Let simple WORDSWORTH chime his childish verse,
And brother COLERIDGE lull the babe at nurse;
Let Spectre-mongering LEWIS aim, at most,
To rouse the Galleries, or to raise a ghost;   920
Let MOORE still sigh; let STRANGFORD steal from
   MOORE,
And swear that CAMOËNS sang such notes of yore;
Let HAYLEY hobble on, MONTGOMERY rave,
And godly GRAHAME chant a stupid stave;
Let sonneteering BOWLES his strains refine,
And whine and whimper to the fourteenth line;
Let STOTT, CARLISLE,† MATILDA, and the rest
Of Grub Street, and of Grosvenor Place the best,

  * By the bye, I hope that in Mr. Scott's next poem, his hero or heroine will be less addicted to "Grammarye," and more to Grammar, than the Lady of the Lay and her Bravo, William of Deloraine.

  † It may be asked, why I have censured the Earl of Carlisle, my guardian and relative, to whom I dedicated a volume of puerile poems a few years ago?—The guardianship was nominal, at least as far as I have been able to discover; the relationship I cannot help, and am very sorry for it; but as his Lordship seemed to forget it on a very essential occasion to me, I shall not burden my memory with the recollection. I do not think that personal differences sanction the unjust condemnation of a brother scribbler; but I see no reason why they should not as a preventive, when the author, noble or ignoble, has for a series of years, beguiled a "discerning public" (as the advertisements have it) with divers reams of most orthodox, imperial nonsense. Besides, I do not step aside to vituperate the earl: no—his works come fairly in review with those of other Patrician Literati. If, before I escaped from my teens, I said anything in favour of his Lordship's paper books, it was in the way of dutiful dedication, and more from the advice of others than my own judgment, and I seize the first opportunity of pronouncing my sincere recantation. I have heard that some persons conceive me to be under obligations to Lord CARLISLE: if so, I shall be most particularly happy to learn what they are, and where conferred, that they may be duly appreciated and publicly acknowledged. What I have humbly advanced as an opinion on his printed things, I am prepared to support, if necessary, by quotations from Elegies, Eulogies, Odes, Episodes, and certain facetious and dainty tragedies bearing his name and mark:—

    "What can ennoble knaves, or *fools*, or cowards?
    Alas! not all the blood of all the Howards."

So says Pope. Amen! [48]

◇◇◇◇◇◇◇◇◇◇◇◇◇◇◇◇◇◇◇◇◇◇◇◇◇◇◇◇◇◇◇◇◇

[48] In 1816 Byron wrote numerous comments in the margins of a copy of the poem; his second thought on the above footnote reads, "Much too savage, whatever the foundation might be."

Scrawl on, 'till death release us from the strain,
Or Common Sense assert her rights again;   930
But Thou,[49] with powers that mock the aid of praise,
Should'st leave to humbler Bards ignoble lays:
Thy country's voice, the voice of all the Nine,
Demand a hallowed harp—that harp is thine.
Say! will not Caledonia's annals yield
The glorious record of some nobler field,
Than the vile foray of a plundering clan,
Whose proudest deeds disgrace the name of man?
Or Marmion's acts of darkness, fitter food
For SHERWOOD'S outlaw tales of ROBIN HOOD?
Scotland! still proudly claim thy native Bard,   941
And be thy praise his first, his best reward!
Yet not with thee alone his name should live,
But own the vast renown a world can give;
Be known, perchance, when Albion is no more,
And tell the tale of what she was before;
To future times her faded fame recall,
And save her glory, though his country fall.

   Yet what avails the sanguine Poet's hope,
To conquer ages, and with time to cope?   950
New eras spread their wings, new nations rise,
And other Victors* fill th' applauding skies;
A few brief generations fleet along,
Whose sons forget the Poet and his song:
E'en now, what once-loved Minstrels scarce may
   claim
The transient mention of a dubious name!
When Fame's loud trump hath blown its noblest blast,
Though long the sound, the echo sleeps at last;
And glory, like the Phœnix midst her fires,
Exhales her odours, blazes, and expires.   960

   Shall hoary Granta[50] call her sable sons,
Expert in science, more expert at puns?
Shall these approach the Muse? ah, no! she flies,
Even from the tempting ore of Seaton's prize;
Though Printers condescend the press to soil
With rhyme by HOARE, and epic blank by HOYLE:[51]
Not him whose page, if still upheld by whist,
Requires no sacred theme to bid us list.†

  * Tollere humo, victorque virum volitare per ora.—VIRGIL.

  † The *Games of Hoyle*, well known to the votaries of Whist, Chess, etc., are not to be superseded by the vagaries of his poetical namesake, whose poem comprised, as expressly stated in the advertisement, all the "Plagues of Egypt."

◇◇◇◇◇◇◇◇◇◇◇◇◇◇◇◇◇◇◇◇◇◇◇◇◇◇◇◇◇◇◇◇◇

[49] Sir Walter Scott.
[50] The River Cam, Cambridge.
[51] Hoare and Hoyle were winners of the Seatonian prize at Cambridge.

Ye! who in Granta's honours would surpass,
Must mount her Pegasus, a full-grown ass;   970
A foal well worthy of her ancient Dam,
Whose Helicon is duller than her Cam.

There CLARKE,* still striving piteously "to
    please,"
Forgetting doggerel leads not to degrees,
A would-be satirist, a hired Buffoon,
A monthly scribbler of some low Lampoon,
Condemned to drudge, the meanest of the mean,
And furbish falsehoods for a magazine,
Devotes to scandal his congenial mind;
Himself a living libel on mankind.   980

Oh! dark asylum of a Vandal race!†
At once the boast of learning, and disgrace!
So lost to Phœbus, that nor Hodgson's ‡ verse
Can make thee better, nor poor Hewson's§ worse.
But where fair Isis rolls her purer wave,
The partial Muse delighted loves to lave;

* This person, who has lately betrayed the most rabid symp-
toms of confirmed authorship, is writer of a poem denominated
The Art of Pleasing, as "Lucus a non lucendo," containing little
pleasantry, and less poetry. He also acts as monthly stipendiary
and collector of calumnies for the *Satirist*. If this unfortunate
young man would exchange the magazines for the mathematics,
and endeavour to take a decent degree in his university, it
might eventually prove more serviceable than the present salary.
    Note.—An unfortunate young person of Emanuel College,
Cambridge, ycleped Hewson Clarke, has lately manifested the
most rabid symptoms of confirmed Authorship. His Disorder
commenced some years ago, and the *Newcastle Herald* teemed
with his precocious essays, to the great edification of the Bur-
gesses of Newcastle, Morpeth, and the parts adjacent even unto
Berwick upon Tweed. These have been abundantly scurrilous
upon the [town] of Newcastle, his native spot, Mr. Mathias and
Anacreon Moore. What these men had done to offend Mr.
Hewson Clarke is not known, but surely the town in whose
markets he had sold meat and in whose weekly journal he had
written prose deserved better treatment. Mr. H. C. should
recollect the proverb "'tis a villainous bird that defiles his own
nest." He now writes in the *Satirist*. We recommend the young
man to abandon the magazines for mathematics, and to believe
that a high degree at Cambridge will be more advantageous, as
well as profitable in the end, than his present precarious
gleanings.
    † "Into Cambridgeshire the Emperor Probus transported a
considerable body of Vandals."—Gibbon's *Decline and Fall*,
ii. 83. There is no reason to doubt the truth of this assertion; the
breed is still in high perfection.
    ‡ This gentleman's name requires no praise: the man who in
translation displays unquestionable genius may be well ex-
pected to excel in original composition, of which, it is to be
hoped, we shall soon see a splendid specimen.[52]
    § Hewson Clarke, *Esq.*, as it is written.

[52] Francis Hodgson (1781–1852) was Byron's close friend.

On her green banks a greener wreath she wove,
To crown the Bards that haunt her classic grove;
Where RICHARDS wakes a genuine poet's fires,
And modern Britons glory in their Sires.*   990

For me, who, thus unasked, have dared to tell
My country, what her sons should know too well,
Zeal for her honour bade me here engage
The host of idiots that infest her age;
No just applause her honoured name shall lose,
As first in freedom, dearest to the Muse.
Oh! would thy bards but emulate thy fame,
And rise more worthy, Albion, of thy name!
What Athens was in science, Rome in power,
What Tyre appeared in her meridian hour,   o
'Tis thine at once, fair Albion! to have been—
Earth's chief Dictatress, Ocean's lovely Queen:
But Rome decayed, and Athens strewed the plain,
And Tyre's proud piers lie shattered in the main;
Like these, thy strength may sink, in ruin hurled,
And Britain fall, the bulwark of the world.
But let me cease, and dread Cassandra's fate,
With warning ever scoffed at, till too late;
To themes less lofty still my lay confine,
And urge thy Bards to gain a name like thine.   10

Then, hapless Britain! be thy rulers blest,
The senate's oracles, the people's jest!
Still hear thy motley orators dispense
The flowers of rhetoric, though not of sense,
While CANNING'S colleagues hate him for his wit,
And old dame PORTLAND† fills the place of PITT.

Yet once again, adieu! ere this the sail
That wafts me hence is shivering in the gale;
And Afric's coast and Calpe's adverse height,
And Stamboul's [55] minarets must greet my sight: 20
Thence shall I stray through Beauty's native clime,‡
Where Kaff§ is clad in rocks, and crowned with
    snows sublime.

* The *Aboriginal Britons*, an excellent poem by Richards.[53]
    † A friend of mine being asked, why his Grace of Portland
was likened to an old woman? replied, "he supposed it was
because he was past bearing." His Grace is now gathered to
his grandmothers, where he sleeps as sound as ever; but even
his sleep was better than his colleagues' waking. 1811.[54]
    ‡ Georgia.
    § Mount Caucasus.

[53] The Rev. George Richards (1769–1835), Fellow of Oriel
College, Cambridge.
[54] The Duke of Portland became prime minister after the
death of William Pitt in 1806. George Canning (1770–1827) was
foreign secretary.
[55] Calpe (line above) is Gibraltar; Stamboul is Instanbul
(Constantinople).

But should I back return, no tempting press
Shall drag my Journal from the desk's recess;
Let coxcombs, printing as they come from far,
Snatch his own wreath of Ridicule from Carr;
Let ABERDEEN and ELGIN* still pursue
The shade of fame through regions of Virtù;
Waste useless thousands on their Phidian freaks,
Misshapen monuments and maimed antiques;   30
And make their grand saloons a general mart
For all the mutilated blocks of art:
Of Dardan tours let Dilettanti tell,
I leave topography to rapid GELL;†
And, quite content, no more shall interpose
To stun the public ear—at least with Prose.

   Thus far I've held my undisturbed career,
Prepared for rancour, steeled 'gainst selfish fear;
This thing of rhyme I ne'er disdained to own—
Though not obtrusive, yet not quite unknown: 40
My voice was heard again, though not so loud,
My page, though nameless, never disavowed;
And now at once I tear the veil away:—
Cheer on the pack! the Quarry stands at bay,
Unscared by all the din of MELBOURNE house,
By LAMB's resentment, or by HOLLAND's spouse,
By JEFFREY's harmless pistol, HALLAM's rage,
Edina's brawny sons and brimstone page.
Our men in buckram shall have blows enough,
And feel they too are "penetrable stuff:"   50
And though I hope not hence unscathed to go,
Who conquers me shall find a stubborn foe.
The time hath been, when no harsh sound would fall
From lips that now may seem imbued with gall;
Nor fools nor follies tempt me to despise
The meanest thing that crawled beneath my eyes:

But now, so callous grown, so changed since youth,
I've learned to think, and sternly speak the truth;
Learned to deride the critic's starch decree,
And break him on the wheel he meant for me;   60
To spurn the rod a scribbler bids me kiss,
Nor care if courts and crowds applaud or hiss:
Nay more, though all my rival rhymesters frown,
I too can hunt a Poetaster down;
And, armed in proof, the gauntlet cast at once
To Scotch marauder, and to Southern dunce.
Thus much I've dared; if my incondite lay
Hath wronged these righteous times, let others say:
This, let the world, which knows not how to spare,
Yet rarely blames unjustly, now declare.   70

[1807-1808]   [1809]

---

   * Lord Elgin would fain persuade us that all the figures, with
and without noses, in his stoneshop, are the work of Phidias.
"Credat Judæus!"[56]
   † Mr. Gell's *Topography of Troy and Ithaca* cannot fail to
ensure the approbation of every man possessed of classical taste,
as well for the information Mr. Gell conveys to the mind of the
reader, as for the ability and research the respective works
display.[57]

◇◇◇◇◇◇◇◇◇◇◇◇◇◇◇◇◇◇◇◇◇◇◇◇◇◇◇◇◇◇◇◇◇

   [56] Lord Elgin was then transferring the marbles from the
Parthenon to the British Museum (see Keats's poems on the Elgin
marbles, p. 1054). The Earl of Aberdeen had written a criticism
of Sir William Gell's *Topography of Troy* in the *Edinburgh Review*.
   [57] Byron's changing opinions of Gell are amusingly reflected
in the different adjectives that stood at various times before his
name. In the manuscript this was "coxcombe," but as the first
edition was going through press Byron changed it to "classic."
Having in 1811 visited the site of Troy himself, he changed it
again to "rapid," and added a note:

   Rapid, indeed! He topographised and typographised King
   Priam's dominions in three days! I called him 'classic' before I
   saw the Troad, but since have learned better than to tack to
   his name what don't belong to it.

LINES INSCRIBED UPON A CUP FORMED FROM A SKULL.

1.

START not—nor deem my spirit fled:
  In me behold the only skull,
From which, unlike a living head,
  Whatever flows is never dull.

2.

I lived, I loved, I quaff'd, like thee:
  I died: let earth my bones resign;
Fill up—thou canst not injure me;
  The worm hath fouler lips than thine.

3.

Better to hold the sparkling grape,
  Than nurse the earth-worm's slimy brood;
And circle in the goblet's shape
  The drink of Gods, than reptile's food.

4.

Where once my wit, perchance, hath shone,
  In aid of others' let me shine;
And when, alas! our brains are gone,
  What nobler substitute than wine?

5.

Quaff while thou canst: another race,
  When thou and thine, like me, are sped,
May rescue thee from earth's embrace,
  And rhyme and revel with the dead.

6.

Why not? since through life's little day
  Our heads such sad effects produce;
Redeem'd from worms and wasting clay,
  This chance is theirs, to be of use.

[1808]   [1814]

———

This monument and its inscription can still be seen in the garden of Newstead Abbey. The dog's grave is supposed to have been intentionally located as close as possible to the site of the altar of the original Abbey.

———

INSCRIPTION ON THE MONUMENT OF A NEWFOUNDLAND DOG.

WHEN some proud son of man returns to earth,
Unknown to glory, but upheld by birth,
The sculptor's art exhausts the pomp of woe
And storied urns record who rest below:
When all is done, upon the tomb is seen,
Not what he was, but what he should have been:
But the poor dog, in life the firmest friend,
The first to welcome, foremost to defend,
Whose honest heart is still his master's own,
Who labours, fights, lives, breathes for him alone,   10
Unhonour'd falls, unnoticed all his worth—
Denied in heaven the soul he held on earth:
While Man, vain insect! hopes to be forgiven,
And claims himself a sole exclusive Heaven.
Oh Man! thou feeble tenant of an hour,
Debased by slavery, or corrupt by power,
Who knows thee well must quit thee with disgust,
Degraded mass of animated dust!
Thy love is lust, thy friendship all a cheat,
Thy smiles hypocrisy, thy words deceit!   20
By nature vile, ennobled but by name,
Each kindred brute might bid thee blush for shame.
Ye! who perchance behold this simple urn,
Pass on—it honours none you wish to mourn:
To mark a Friend's remains these stones arise;
I never knew but one,—and here he lies.

[1808]   [1809]

STANZAS TO A LADY, ON LEAVING ENGLAND

'TIS done—and shivering in the gale
The bark unfurls her snowy sail;
And whistling o'er the bending mast,
Loud sings on high the fresh'ning blast;
And I must from this land be gone,
Because I cannot love but one.

But could I be what I have been,
And could I see what I have seen—
Could I repose upon the breast
Which once my warmest wishes blest—   10
I should not seek another zone
Because I cannot love but one.

'Tis long since I beheld that eye
Which gave me bliss or misery;
And I have striven, but in vain,
Never to think of it again:
For though I fly from Albion,
I still can only love but one.

As some lone bird, without a mate,
My weary heart is desolate;   20
I look around, and cannot trace
One friendly smile or welcome face,
And ev'n in crowds am still alone,
Because I cannot love but one.

And I will cross the whitening foam,
And I will seek a foreign home;
Till I forget a false fair face,
I ne'er shall find a resting-place;
My own dark thoughts I cannot shun,
But ever love, and love but one.   30

The poorest, veriest wretch on earth
Still finds some hospitable hearth,
Where friendship's or love's softer glow
May smile in joy or soothe in woe;
But friend or leman I have none.
Because I cannot love but one.

I go—but wheresoe'er I flee
There's not an eye will weep for me;
There's not a kind congenial heart,
Where I can claim the meanest part;   40
Nor thou, who hast my hopes undone,
Wilt sigh, although I love but one.

To think of every early scene,
Of what we are, and what we've been,
Would whelm some softer hearts with woe—
But mine, alas! has stood the blow:
Yet still beats on as it begun,
And never truly loves but one.

And who that dear loved one may be,
Is not for vulgar eyes to see;   50
And why that early love was cross'd,
Thou know'st the best, I feel the most:
But few that dwell beneath the sun
Have loved so long, and loved but one.

I've tried another's fetters too,
With charms perchance as fair to view;
And I would fain have loved as well,
But some unconquerable spell
Forbade my bleeding breast to own
A kindred care for aught but one.   60

'Twould soothe to take one lingering view,
And bless thee in my last adieu;
Yet wish I not those eyes to weep
For him that wanders o'er the deep;
His home, his hope, his youth are gone,
Yet still he loves, and loves but one.

[1809]   [1809]

LINES TO MR. HODGSON

Francis Hodgson (1781–1852) met Byron at Cambridge, and was his constant correspondent during this first trip abroad. He later became a clergyman, and Provost of Eton.

LINES TO MR. HODGSON.

WRITTEN ON BOARD THE LISBON PACKET.

I.

HUZZA! Hodgson, we are going,
    Our embargo's off at last;
Favourable breezes blowing
    Bend the canvas o'er the mast.
From aloft the signal's streaming,
    Hark! the farewell gun is fired;
Women screeching, tars blaspheming,
    Tell us that our time's expired.
        Here's a rascal
        Come to task all,
    Prying from the Custom-house;
        Trunks unpacking
        Cases cracking,
    Not a corner for a mouse
'Scapes unsearched amid the racket,
Ere we sail on board the Packet.

2.

Now our boatmen quit their mooring,
    And all hands must ply the oar;
Baggage from the quay is lowering,
    We're impatient, push from shore.
"Have a care! that case holds liquor—
    Stop the boat—I'm sick—oh Lord!"
"Sick, Ma'am, damme, you'll be sicker,
    Ere you've been an hour on board."
        Thus are screaming
        Men and women,
    Gemmen, ladies, servants, Jacks;
        Here entangling,
        All are wrangling,
    Stuck together close as wax.—
Such the general noise and racket,
Ere we reach the Lisbon Packet.

3.

Now we've reached her, lo! the Captain,
    Gallant Kidd, commands the crew;
Passengers their berths are clapt in,
    Some to grumble, some to spew.

"Hey day! call you that a cabin?
　Why 't is hardly three feet square:
Not enough to stow Queen Mab in—
　Who the deuce can harbour there?"
　　　　"Who, sir? plenty—
　　　　Nobles twenty
　Did at once my vessel fill."—
　　　　"Did they? Jesus,
　　　　How you squeeze us!
　Would to God they did so still:
Then I'd 'scape the heat and racket
Of the good ship, Lisbon Packet."

4.

Fletcher! Murray! Bob! where are you?
　Stretched along the deck like logs—
Bear a hand, you jolly tar, you!
　Here's a rope's end for the dogs.
Hobhouse muttering fearful curses,
　As the hatchway down he rolls,
Now his breakfast, now his verses,
　Vomits forth—and damns our souls.
　　　　"Here's a stanza
　　　　On Braganza—
　Help!"—"A couplet?"—"No, a cup
　　　　Of warm water—"
　　　　"What's the matter?"
　"Zounds! my liver's coming up;
I shall not survive the racket
Of this brutal Lisbon Packet."

5.

Now at length we're off for Turkey,
　Lord knows when we shall come back!
Breezes foul and tempests murky
　May unship us in a crack.
But, since Life at most a jest is,
　As philosophers allow,
Still to laugh by far the best is,
　Then laugh on—as I do now.
　　　　Laugh at all things,
　　　　Great and small things,
　Sick or well, at sea or shore;
　　　　While we're quaffing,
　　　　Let's have laughing—
　Who the devil cares for more?—
Some good wine! and who would lack it,
Ev'n on board the Lisbon Packet?

[1809]　　　　　　　　　　　　　[1830]

WRITTEN AFTER SWIMMING FROM SESTOS TO ABYDOS.*

1.

IF, in the month of dark December,
　Leander, who was nightly wont
(What maid will not the tale remember?)
　To cross thy stream, broad Hellespont!

2.

If, when the wintry tempest roared,
　He sped to Hero, nothing loth,
And thus of old thy current poured,
　Fair Venus! how I pity both!

3.

For *me*, degenerate modern wretch,
　Though in the genial month of May,
My dripping limbs I faintly stretch,
　And think I've done a feat to-day.

4.

But since he crossed the rapid tide,
　According to the doubtful story,
To woo,—and—Lord knows what beside,
　And swam for Love, as I for Glory;

* On the 3rd of May, 1810, while the *Salsette* (Captain Bathurst) was lying in the Dardanelles, Lieutenant Ekenhead, of that frigate, and the writer of these rhymes, swam from the European shore to the Asiatic—by the by, from Abydos to Sestos would have been more correct. The whole distance from the place whence we started to our landing on the other side, including the length we were carried by the current, was computed by those on board the frigate at upwards of four English miles, though the actual breadth is barely one. The rapidity of the current is such that no boat can row directly across, and it may, in some measure, be estimated from the circumstance of the whole instance being accomplished by one of the parties in an hour and five, and by the other in an hour and ten minutes. The water was extremely cold, from the melting of the mountain snows. About three weeks before, in April, we had made an attempt; but having ridden all the way from the Troad the same morning, and the water being of an icy chillness, we found it necessary to postpone the completion till the frigate anchored below the castles; when we swam the straits as just stated, entering a considerable way above the European, and landing below the Asiatic, fort. [Le] Chevalier says that a young Jew swam the same distance for his mistress; and Olivier mentions its having been done by a Neapolitan; but our consul, Tarragona, remembered neither of these circumstances, and tried to dissuade us from the attempt. A number of the *Salsette's* crew were known to have accomplished a greater distance; and the only thing that surprised me was that, as doubts had been entertained of the truth of Leander's story, no traveller had ever endeavoured to ascertain its practicability.[1]

◇◇◇◇◇◇◇◇◇◇◇◇◇◇◇◇◇◇◇◇◇◇◇◇◇◇◇◇◇◇

[1] See also *Don Juan*, II, 105.

5.

'Twere hard to say who fared the best:
    Sad mortals! thus the Gods still plague you!
He lost his labour, I my jest:
    For he was drowned, and I've the ague.

[1810]   [1812]

4.

Maid of Athens! I am gone:
Think of me, sweet! when alone.
Though I fly to Istambol,‡
Athens holds my heart and soul:
Can I cease to love thee? No!
Ζώη μοῦ, σᾶς ἀγαπῶ.

[1810]   [1812]

MAID OF ATHENS, ERE WE PART.[1]

Ζώη μοῦ, σᾶς ἀγαπῶ.

1.

MAID of Athens, ere we part,
Give, oh give me back my heart!
Or, since that has left my breast,
Keep it now, and take the rest!
Hear my vow before I go,
Ζώη μοῦ, σᾶς ἀγαπῶ.*

2.

By those tresses unconfined,
Wooed by each Ægean wind;
By those lids whose jetty fringe
Kiss thy soft cheeks' blooming tinge;
By those wild eyes like the roe,
Ζώη μοῦ, σᾶς ἀγαπῶ.

3.

By that lip I long to taste;
By that zone-encircled waist;
By all the token-flowers † that tell
What words can never speak so well;
By love's alternate joy and woe,
Ζώη μοῦ, σᾶς ἀγαπῶ.

* *Zoë mou, sas agapo*, or Ζώη μοῦ, σᾶς ἀγαπῶ, Romaic expression of tenderness: if I translate it, I shall affront the gentlemen, as it may seem that I supposed they could not; and if I do not, I may affront the ladies. For fear of any misconstruction on the part of the latter, I shall do so, begging pardon of the learned. It means, "My life, I love you!" which sounds very prettily in all languages, and is as much in fashion in Greece at this day as, Juvenal tells us, the two first words were amongst the Roman ladies, whose erotic expressions were all Hellenised.

† In the East (where ladies are not taught to write, lest they should scribble assignations), flowers, cinders, pebbles, etc., convey the sentiments of the parties, by that universal deputy of Mercury—an old woman. A cinder says "I burn for thee," a bunch of flowers tied with hair, "Take me and fly;" but a pebble declares—what nothing else can.

[1] Text, punctuation and notes are those of the edition of 1823.   ‡ Constantinople.

THE GIAOUR:

A FRAGMENT OF A TURKISH TALE.

"One fatal remembrance—one sorrow that throws
Its bleak shade alike o'er our joys and our woes—
To which Life nothing darker nor brighter can bring,
For which joy hath no balm—and affliction no sting."
MOORE.

TO

SAMUEL ROGERS, ESQ.

AS A SLIGHT BUT MOST SINCERE TOKEN
OF ADMIRATION OF HIS GENIUS,
RESPECT FOR HIS CHARACTER,
AND GRATITUDE FOR HIS FRIENDSHIP,

THIS PRODUCTION IS INSCRIBED

BY HIS OBLIGED
AND AFFECTIONATE SERVANT,
BYRON.

LONDON, *May*, 1813.

ADVERTISEMENT.

THE tale which these disjointed fragments present, is founded upon circumstances now less common in the East than formerly; either because the ladies are more circumspect than in the "olden time," or because the Christians have better fortune, or less enterprise. The story, when entire, contained the adventures of a female slave, who was thrown, in the Mussulman manner, into the sea for infidelity, and avenged by a young Venetian, her lover, at the time the Seven Islands were possessed by the Republic of Venice, and soon after the Arnauts were beaten back from the Morea, which they had ravaged for some time subsequent to the Russian invasion. The desertion of the Mainotes, on being refused the plunder of Misitra, led to the abandonment of that enterprise, and to the desolation of the Morea, during which the cruelty exercised on all sides was unparalleled even in the annals of the faithful.

THE GIAOUR.

No breath of air to break the wave
That rolls below the Athenian's grave,
That tomb* which, gleaming o'er the cliff,
First greets the homeward-veering skiff
High o'er the land he saved in vain;
When shall such Hero live again?

* * * * *

Fair clime! where every season smiles
Benignant o'er those blessed isles,
Which, seen from far Colonna's height,
Make glad the heart that hails the sight,   10
And lend to loneliness delight.
There mildly dimpling, Ocean's cheek
Reflects the tints of many a peak
Caught by the laughing tides that lave
These Edens of the eastern wave:
And if at times a transient breeze
Break the blue crystal of the seas,
Or sweep one blossom from the trees,
How welcome is each gentle air
That wakes and wafts the odours there!   20
For there the Rose, o'er crag or vale,
Sultana of the Nightingale,†
      The maid for whom his melody,
      His thousand songs are heard on high,
Blooms blushing to her lover's tale:
His queen, the garden queen, his Rose,
Unbent by winds, unchilled by snows,
Far from the winters of the west,
By every breeze and season blest,
Returns the sweets by Nature given   30
In softest incense back to Heaven;
And grateful yields that smiling sky
Her fairest hue and fragrant sigh.
And many a summer flower is there,
And many a shade that Love might share,
And many a grotto, meant for rest,
That holds the pirate for a guest;
Whose bark in sheltering cove below
Lurks for the passing peaceful prow,

---

* A tomb above the rocks on the promontory, by some supposed the sepulchre of Themistocles.[1]
† The attachment of the nightingale to the rose is a well-known Persian fable. If I mistake not, the "Bulbul of a thousand tales" is one of his appellations.

[1] He was the Athenian leader of the fifth century B.C., later exiled.

Till the gay mariner's guitar *   40
Is heard, and seen the Evening Star;
Then stealing with the muffled oar,
Far shaded by the rocky shore,
Rush the night-prowlers on the prey,
And turn to groans his roundelay.
Strange—that where Nature loved to trace,
As if for Gods, a dwelling place,
And every charm and grace hath mixed
Within the Paradise she fixed,
There man, enamoured of distress,   50
Should mar it into wilderness,
And trample, brute-like, o'er each flower
That tasks not one laborious hour;
Nor claims the culture of his hand
To bloom along the fairy land,
But springs as to preclude his care,
And sweetly woos him—but to spare!
Strange—that where all is Peace beside,
There Passion riots in her pride,
And Lust and Rapine wildly reign   60
To darken o'er the fair domain.
It is as though the Fiends prevailed
Against the Seraphs they assailed,
And, fixed on heavenly thrones, should dwell
The freed inheritors of Hell;
So soft the scene, so formed for joy,
So curst the tyrants that destroy!

    He who hath bent him o'er the dead
Ere the first day of Death is fled,
The first dark day of Nothingness,   70
The last of Danger and Distress,
(Before Decay's effacing fingers
Have swept the lines where Beauty lingers,)
And marked the mild angelic air,
The rapture of Repose that's there,
The fixed yet tender traits that streak
The languor of the placid cheek,
And—but for that sad shrouded eye,
    That fires not, wins not, weeps not, now,
    And but for that chill, changeless brow,   80
Where cold Obstruction's apathy †
Appals the gazing mourner's heart,
As if to him it could impart
The doom he dreads, yet dwells upon;
Yes, but for these and these alone,
Some moments, aye, one treacherous hour,
He still might doubt the Tyrant's power;

So fair, so calm, so softly sealed,
The first, last look by Death revealed!‡
Such is the aspect of this shore;   90
'Tis Greece, but living Greece no more!
So coldly sweet, so deadly fair,
We start, for Soul is wanting there.
Hers is the loveliness in death,
That parts not quite with parting breath;
But beauty with that fearful bloom,
That hue which haunts it to the tomb,
Expression's last receding ray,
A gilded Halo hovering round decay,
The farewell beam of Feeling past away!   100
Spark of that flame, perchance of heavenly birth,
Which gleams, but warms no more its cherished earth!

    Clime of the unforgotten brave!
Whose land from plain to mountain-cave
Was Freedom's home or Glory's grave!
Shrine of the mighty! can it be,
That this is all remains of thee?
Approach, thou craven crouching slave:
    Say, is not this Thermopylæ?
These waters blue that round you lave,—   110
    Oh servile offspring of the free—
Pronounce what sea, what shore is this?
The gulf, the rock of Salamis!
These scenes, their story not unknown,
Arise, and make again your own;
Snatch from the ashes of your Sires
The embers of their former fires;
And he who in the strife expires
Will add to theirs a name of fear
That Tyranny shall quake to hear,   120
And leave his sons a hope, a fame,
They too will rather die than shame:
For Freedom's battle once begun,
Bequeathed by bleeding Sire to Son,
Though baffled oft is ever won.
Bear witness, Greece, thy living page!
Attest it many a deathless age!
While Kings, in dusty darkness hid,
Have left a nameless pyramid,
Thy Heroes, though the general doom   130
Hath swept the column from their tomb,

* The guitar is the constant amusement of the Greek sailor
by night; with a steady fair wind, and during a calm, it is
accompanied always by the voice, and often by dancing.
†   "Ay, but to die and go we know not where,
        To lie in cold obstruction?"
        Measure for Measure, Act III, Sc. 2.

‡ I trust that few of my readers have ever had an opportunity
of witnessing what is here attempted in description; but those
who have will probably retain a painful remembrance of that
singular beauty which pervades, with few exceptions, the features
of the dead, a few hours, and but for a few hours, after "the
spirit is not there." It is to be remarked in cases of violent death
by gun-shot wounds, the expression is always that of languor,
whatever the natural energy of the sufferer's character; but in
death from a stab the countenance preserves its traits of feeling
or ferocity, and the mind its bias, to the last.

A mightier monument command,
The mountains of their native land!
There points thy Muse to stranger's eye
The graves of those that cannot die!
'Twere long to tell, and sad to trace,
Each step from Splendour to Disgrace;
Enough—no foreign foe could quell
Thy soul, till from itself it fell;
Yes! Self-abasement paved the way   140
To villain-bonds and despot sway.

What can he tell who treads thy shore?
    No legend of thine olden time,
No theme on which the Muse might soar
High as thine own in days of yore,
    When man was worthy of thy clime.
The hearts within thy valleys bred,
The fiery souls that might have led
    Thy sons to deeds sublime,
Now crawl from cradle to the Grave,   150
Slaves—nay, the bondsmen of a Slave,*
    And callous, save to crime;
Stained with each evil that pollutes
Mankind, where least above the brutes;
Without even savage virtue blest,
Without one free or valiant breast,
Still to the neighbouring ports they waft
Proverbial wiles, and ancient craft;
In this the subtle Greek is found,
For this, and this alone, renowned.   160
In vain might Liberty invoke
The spirit to its bondage broke
Or raise the neck that courts the yoke:
No more her sorrows I bewail,
Yet this will be a mournful tale,
And they who listen may believe,
Who heard it first had cause to grieve.

    *   *   *   *   *

Far, dark, along the blue sea glancing,
The shadows of the rocks advancing
Start on the fisher's eye like boat   170
Of island-pirate or Mainote;
And fearful for his light caïque,
He shuns the near but doubtful creek:
Though worn and weary with his toil,
And cumbered with his scaly spoil,
Slowly, yet strongly, plies the oar,
Till Port Leone's safer shore

Receives him by the lovely light
That best becomes an Eastern night.

    *   *   *   *   *

Who thundering comes on blackest steed,[2]   180
With slackened bit and hoof of speed?
Beneath the clattering iron's sound
The caverned Echoes wake around
In lash for lash, and bound for bound;
The foam that streaks the courser's side
Seems gathered from the Ocean-tide:
Though weary waves are sunk to rest,
There's none within his rider's breast;
And though to-morrow's tempest lower,
'Tis calmer than thy heart, young Giaour![†]   190
I know thee not, I loathe thy race,
But in thy lineaments I trace
What Time shall strengthen, not efface:
Though young and pale, that sallow front
Is scathed by fiery Passion's brunt;
Though bent on earth thine evil eye,
As meteor-like thou glidest by,
Right well I view and deem thee one
Whom Othman's sons should slay or shun.

On—on he hastened, and he drew   200
My gaze of wonder as he flew:
Though like a Demon of the night
He passed, and vanished from my sight,
His aspect and his air impressed
A troubled memory on my breast,
And long upon my startled ear
Rung his dark courser's hoofs of fear.

† Infidel [3]

---

[2] "The reciter of the tale is a Turkish fisherman, who has been employed during the day in the gulf of Ægina, and in the evening, apprehensive of the Mainote pirates who infest the coast of Attica, lands with his boat on the harbour of Port Leone, the ancient Piræus. He becomes the eye-witness of nearly all the incidents in the story and in one of them is a principal agent. It is to his feelings, and particularly to his religious prejudices that we are indebted for some of the most forcible and splendid parts of the poem."—Note by George Agar Ellis, 1797–1823.

[3] "In Dr. Clarke's *Travels* [*in Europe, Asia, Africa*, 1810–24.], this word, which means *Infidel*, is always written according to its English pronunciation, *Djour*. Lord Byron adopted the Italian spelling usual among the Franks of the Levant."—Note to Edition 1832.

"The pronunciation of the word depends on its origin. If it is associated with the Arabic *jawr*, a "deviating" or "erring," the initial consonant would be soft, but if with the Persian *gawr*, or *guebre*, "a fire-worshipper," the word should be pronounced *Gow-er*—as Gower Street has come to be pronounced. It is to be remarked that to the present day the Nestorians of Urumiah are contemned as *Gy-ours* (the G hard), by their Mohammedan countrymen.—(From information kindly supplied by Mr. A. G. Ellis, of the Oriental Printed Books and MSS. Department, British Museum.)"—Note by E. H. Coleridge, 1900.

---

* Athens is the property of the Kislar Aga (the slave of the Seraglio and guardian of the women), who appoints the Waywode. A pander and eunuch—these are not polite, yet true appellations—now *governs* the *governor* of Athens!

He spurs his steed; he nears the steep,
That, jutting, shadows o'er the deep;
He winds around; he hurries by; 210
The rock relieves him from mine eye;
For, well I ween, unwelcome he
Whose glance is fixed on those that flee;
And not a star but shines too bright
On him who takes such timeless flight.
He wound along; but ere he passed
One glance he snatched, as if his last,
A moment checked his wheeling steed,
A moment breathed him from his speed,
A moment on his stirrup stood— 220
Why looks he o'er the olive wood?
The Crescent glimmers on the hill,
The Mosque's high lamps are quivering still
Though too remote for sound to wake
In echoes of the far tophaike,*
The flashes of each joyous peal
Are seen to prove the Moslem's zeal.
To-night, set Rhamazani's sun;
To-night, the Bairam feast's begun;
To-night—but who and what art thou 230
Of foreign garb and fearful brow?
And what are these to thine or thee,
That thou shouldst either pause or flee?

He stood—some dread was on his face,
Soon Hatred settled in its place:
It rose not with the reddening flush
Of transient Anger's hasty blush,
But pale as marble o'er the tomb,
Whose ghastly whiteness aids its gloom.
His brow was bent, his eye was glazed; 240
He raised his arm, and fiercely raised,
And sternly shook his hand on high,
As doubting to return or fly;
Impatient of his flight delayed,
Here loud his raven charger neighed—
Down glanced that hand, and grasped his blade;
That sound had burst his waking dream,
As Slumber starts at owlet's scream.
The spur hath lanced his courser's sides;
Away—away—for life he rides: 250

Swift as the hurled on high jerreed†
Springs to the touch his startled steed;
The rock is doubled, and the shore
Shakes with the clattering tramp no more;
The crag is won, no more is seen
His Christian crest and haughty mien.
'Twas but an instant he restrained
That fiery barb so sternly reined;
'Twas but a moment that he stood,
Then sped as if by Death pursued; 260
But in that instant o'er his soul
Winters of Memory seemed to roll,
And gather in that drop of time
A life of pain, an age of crime.
O'er him who loves, or hates, or fears,
Such moment pours the grief of years:
What felt *he* then, at once opprest
By all that most distracts the breast?
That pause, which pondered o'er his fate,
Oh, who its dreary length shall date! 270
Though in Time's record nearly nought,
It was Eternity to Thought!
For infinite as boundless space
The thought that Conscience must embrace,
Which in itself can comprehend
Woe without name, or hope, or end.

The hour is past, the Giaour is gone;
And did he fly or fall alone?
Woe to that hour he came or went!
The curse for Hassan's sin was sent 280
To turn a palace to a tomb;
He came, he went, like the Simoom,‡
That harbinger of Fate and gloom,
Beneath whose widely-wasting breath
The very cypress droops to death—
Dark tree, still sad when others' grief is fled,
The only constant mourner o'er the dead!

The steed is vanished from the stall;
No serf is seen in Hassan's hall;
The lonely Spider's thin gray pall 290
Waves slowly widening o'er the wall;
The Bat builds in his Haram bower,
And in the fortress of his power

---

* "Tophaike," musket.—The Bairam is announced by the cannon at sunset: the illumination of the Mosques, and the firing of all kinds of small arms, loaded with *ball*, proclaim it during the night.⁴

◇◇◇◇◇◇◇◇◇◇◇◇◇◇◇◇◇◇◇◇◇◇◇◇◇◇◇◇◇◇◇◇◇◇◇◇

⁴ Bairam is the Moslem Easter, a three-day festival.

† Jerreed, or Djerrid, a blunted Turkish javelin, which is darted from horseback with great force and precision. It is a favourite exercise of the Mussulmans; but I know not if it can be called a *manly* one, since the most expert in the art are the Black Eunuchs of Constantinople. I think, next to these, a Mamlouk at Smyrna was the most skilful that came within my observation.

‡ The blast of the desert, fatal to everything living, and often alluded to in eastern poetry.

The Owl usurps the beacon-tower;
The wild-dog howls o'er the fountain's brim,
With baffled thirst, and famine, grim;
For the stream has shrunk from its marble bed,
Where the weeds and the desolate dust are spread.
'Twas sweet of yore to see it play 300
And chase the sultriness of day,
As springing high the silver dew
In whirls fantastically flew,
And flung luxurious coolness round
The air, and verdure o'er the ground.
'Twas sweet, when cloudless stars were bright,
To view the wave of watery light,
And hear its melody by night.
And oft had Hassan's Childhood played
Around the verge of that cascade;
And oft upon his mother's breast 310
That sound had harmonized his rest;
And oft had Hassan's Youth along
Its bank been soothed by Beauty's song;
And softer seemed each melting tone
Of Music mingled with its own.
But ne'er shall Hassan's Age repose
Along the brink at Twilight's close:
The stream that filled that font is fled—
The blood that warmed his heart is shed!
And here no more shall human voice 320
Be heard to rage, regret, rejoice.
The last sad note that swelled the gale
Was woman's wildest funeral wail:
That quenched in silence, all is still,
But the lattice that flaps when the wind is shrill:
Though raves the gust, and floods the rain,
No hand shall close its clasp again.
On desert sands 'twere joy to scan
The rudest steps of fellow man,
So here the very voice of Grief 330
Might wake an Echo like relief—
At least 'twould say, "All are not gone;
There lingers Life, though but in one"—
For many a gilded chamber's there,
Which Solitude might well forbear;
Within that dome as yet Decay
Hath slowly worked her cankering way—
But gloom is gathered o'er the gate,
Nor there the Fakir's self will wait;
Nor there will wandering Dervise stay, 340
For Bounty cheers not his delay;
Nor there will weary stranger halt
To bless the sacred "bread and salt."*
Alike must Wealth and Poverty

Pass heedless and unheeded by,
For Courtesy and Pity died
With Hassan on the mountain side.
His roof, that refuge unto men,
Is Desolation's hungry den.
The guest flies the hall, and the vassal from labour,
Since his turban was cleft by the infidel's sabre!† 351

* * * * *

I hear the sound of coming feet,
But not a voice mine ear to greet;
More near—each turban I can scan,
And silver-sheathèd ataghan;‡
The foremost of the band is seen
An Emir by his garb of green:§
"Ho! who art thou?—this low salam ‖
Replies of Moslem faith I am.
The burthen ye so gently bear, 360
Seems one that claims your utmost care,
And, doubtless, holds some precious freight—
My humble bark would gladly wait."

"Thou speakest sooth: thy skiff unmoor,
And waft us from the silent shore;
Nay, leave the sail still furled, and ply
The nearest oar that's scattered by,
And midway to those rocks where sleep
The channelled waters dark and deep.
Rest from your task—so—bravely done, 370
Our course has been right swiftly run;
Yet 'tis the longest voyage, I trow,
That one of— * * *

* * * * *"

Sullen it plunged, and slowly sank,
The calm wave rippled to the bank;
I watched it as it sank, methought
Some motion from the current caught

---

† I need hardly observe, that Charity and Hospitality are the first duties enjoined by Mahomet; and to say truth, very generally practised by his disciples. The first praise that can be bestowed on a chief is a panegyric on his bounty; the next, on his valour.

‡ The ataghan, a long dagger worn with pistols in the belt, in a metal scabbard, generally of silver; and, among the wealthier, gilt, or of gold.

§ Green is the privileged colour of the prophet's numerous pretended descendants; with them, as here, faith (the family inheritance) is supposed to supersede the necessity of good words: they are the worst of a very indifferent brood.

‖ "Salam aleikoum! aleikoum salam!" peace be with you; be with you peace—the salutation reserved for the faithful:— to a Christian, "Urlarula!" a good journey; or "saban hiresem, saban serula," good morn, good even; and sometimes, "may your end be happy!" are the usual salutes.

---

* To partake of food, to break bread and salt with your host, insures the safety of the guest; even though an enemy, his person from that moment is sacred.

Bestirred it more,—'twas but the beam
That checkered o'er the living stream:
I gazed, till vanishing from view,　　　　　　380
Like lessening pebble it withdrew;
Still less and less, a speck of white
That gemmed the tide, then mocked the sight;
And all its hidden secrets sleep,
Known but to Genii of the deep,
Which, trembling in their coral caves,
They dare not whisper to the waves.

　　　*　　　*　　　*　　　*　　　*

　As rising on its purple wing
The insect-queen* of Eastern spring,
O'er emerald meadows of Kashmeer　　　　390
Invites the young pursuer near,
And leads him on from flower to flower
A weary chase and wasted hour,
Then leaves him, as it soars on high,
With panting heart and tearful eye:
So Beauty lures the full-grown child,
With hue as bright, and wing as wild:
A chase of idle hopes and fears,
Begun in folly, closed in tears.
If won, to equal ills betrayed,　　　　　　400
Woe waits the insect and the maid;
A life of pain, the loss of peace;
From infant's play, and man's caprice:
The lovely toy so fiercely sought
Hath lost its charm by being caught,
For every touch that wooed its stay
Hath brushed its brightest hues away,
Till charm, and hue, and beauty gone,
'Tis left to fly or fall alone.
With wounded wing, or bleeding breast,　　410
Ah! where shall either victim rest?
Can this with faded pinion soar
From rose to tulip as before?
Or Beauty, blighted in an hour,
Find joy within her broken bower?
No: gayer insects fluttering by
Ne'er droop the wing o'er those that die,
And lovelier things have mercy shown
To every failing but their own,
And every woe a tear can claim　　　　　　420
Except an erring Sister's shame.

　　　*　　　*　　　*　　　*　　　*

The Mind, that broods o'er guilty woes,
　Is like the Scorpion girt by fire;
In circle narrowing as it glows,

The flames around their captive close,
Till inly searched by thousand throes,
　And maddening in her ire,
One sad and sole relief she knows—
The sting she nourished for her foes,
Whose venom never yet was vain,　　　　　430
Gives but one pang, and cures all pain,
And darts into her desperate brain:
So do the dark in soul expire,
Or live like Scorpion girt by fire;†
So writhes the mind Remorse hath riven,
Unfit for earth, undoomed for heaven,
Darkness above, despair beneath,
Around it flame, within it death!

　　*　　　*　　　*　　　*　　　*

　Black Hassan from the Haram flies,
Nor bends on woman's form his eyes;　　　440
The unwonted chase each hour employs,
Yet shares he not the hunter's joys.
Not thus was Hassan wont to fly
When Leila dwelt in his Serai.
Doth Leila there no longer dwell?
That tale can only Hassan tell:
Strange rumours in our city say
Upon that eve she fled away
When Rhamazan's‡ last sun was set,
And flashing from each Minaret　　　　　450
Millions of lamps proclaimed the feast
Of Bairam through the boundless East.
'Twas then she went as to the bath,
Which Hassan vainly searched in wrath;
For she was flown her master's rage
In likeness of a Georgian page,
And far beyond the Moslem's power
Had wronged him with the faithless Giaour.
Somewhat of this had Hassan deemed;
But still so fond, so fair she seemed,　　460
Too well he trusted to the slave
Whose treachery deserved a grave:
And on that eve had gone to Mosque,
And thence to feast in his Kiosk.
Such is the tale his Nubians tell,
Who did not watch their charge too well;

---

　† Alluding to the dubious suicide of the scorpion, so placed for experiment by gentle philosophers. Some maintain that the position of the sting, when turned toward the head, is merely a convulsive movement; but others have actually brought in the verdict "Felo de se." The scorpions are surely interested in a speedy decision of the question; as, if once fairly established as insect Catos, they will probably be allowed to live as long as they think proper, without being martyred for the sake of an hypothesis.
　‡ The cannon at sunset close the Rhamazan.

---

　* The blue-winged butterfly of Kashmeer, the most rare and beautiful of the species.

But others say, that on that night,
By pale Phingari's* trembling light,
The Giaour upon his jet-black steed
Was seen, but seen alone to speed   470
With bloody spur along the shore,
Nor maid nor page behind him bore.

*   *   *   *   *

Her eye's dark charm 'twere vain to tell,
But gaze on that of the Gazelle,
It will assist thy fancy well;
As large, as languishingly dark,
But Soul beamed forth in every spark
That darted from beneath the lid,
Bright as the jewel of Giamschid.†
Yea, *Soul*, and should our prophet say   480
That form was nought but breathing clay,
By Alla! I would answer nay;
Though on Al-Sirat's‡ arch I stood,
Which totters o'er the fiery flood,
With Paradise within my view,
And all his Houris beckoning through.
Oh! who young Leila's glance could read
And keep that portion of his creed
Which saith that woman is but dust,
A soulless toy for tyrant's lust?§   490
On her might Muftis gaze, and own
That through her eye the Immortal shone;
On her fair cheek's unfading hue
The young pomegranate's‖ blossoms strew
Their bloom in blushes ever new;

Her hair in hyacinthine flow,**
When left to roll its folds below,
As midst her handmaids in the hall
She stood superior to them all,
Hath swept the marble where her feet   500
Gleamed whiter than the mountain sleet
Ere from the cloud that gave it birth
It fell, and caught one stain of earth.
The cygnet nobly walks the water;
So moved on earth Circassia's daughter,
The loveliest bird of Franguestan!††
As rears her crest the ruffled Swan,
    And spurns the wave with wings of pride,
When pass the steps of stranger man
    Along the banks that bound her tide;   510
Thus rose fair Leila's white neck:—
Thus armed with beauty would she check
Intrusion's glance, till Folly's gaze
Shrunk from the charms it meant to praise.
Thus high and graceful was her gait;
Her heart as tender to her mate;
Her mate—stern Hassan, who was he?
Alas! that name was not for thee!

*   *   *   *   *

Stern Hassan hath a journey ta'en
With twenty vassals in his train,   520
Each armed, as best becomes a man,
With arquebuss and ataghan;
The chief before, as decked for war,
Bears in his belt the scimitar
Stained with the best of Arnaut blood,
When in the pass the rebels stood,
And few returned to tell the tale
Of what befell in Parne's vale.
The pistols which his girdle bore
Were those that once a Pasha wore,   530
Which still, though gemmed and bossed with gold,
Even robbers tremble to behold.
'Tis said he goes to woo a bride
More true than her who left his side;
The faithless slave that broke her bower,
And—worse than faithless—for a Giaour!

*   *   *   *   *

The sun's last rays are on the hill,
And sparkle in the fountain rill,
Whose welcome waters, cool and clear,
Draw blessings from the mountaineer: 540

---

* Phingari, the moon.

† The celebrated fabulous ruby of Sultan Giamschid, the Embellisher of Istakhar; from its splendour named Schebgerag, "the torch of night;" also "the cup of the sun," &. In the first edition, "Giamschid" was written as a word of three syllables, so D'Herbelot has it; but I am told Richardson reduces it to a dissyllable, and writes "Jamshid." I have left in the text the orthography of the one with the pronunciation of the other.

‡ Al-Sirat, the bridge of breadth narrower than the thread of a famished spider, and sharper than the edge of a sword, over which the Mussulmans must *skate* into Paradise, to which it is the only entrance; but this is not the worst, the river beneath being hell itself, into which, as may be expected, the unskilful and tender of foot contrive to tumble with a "facilis descensus Averni," not very pleasing in prospect to the next passenger. There is a shorter cut downwards for the Jews and Christians.

§ A vulgar error: the Koran allots at least a third of Paradise to well-behaved women; but by far the greater number of Mussulmans interpret the text their own way, and exclude their moieties from heaven. Being enemies to Platonics, they cannot discern "any fitness of things" in the souls of the other sex, conceiving them to be superseded by the Houris.

‖ An oriental simile, which may, perhaps, though fairly stolen, be deemed "plus Arabe qu'en Arabie."

** Hyacinthine, in Arabic "Sunbul;" as common a thought in the eastern poets as it was among the Greeks.

†† "Franguestan," Circassia.[5]

---

[5] See also Coleridge's *Lewti*, p. 467.

Here may the loitering merchant Greek
Find that repose 'twere vain to seek
In cities lodged too near his lord,
And trembling for his secret hoard—
Here may he rest where none can see,
In crowds a slave, in deserts free;
And with forbidden wine may stain
The bowl a Moslem must not drain

*   *   *   *   *

The foremost Tartar's in the gap
Conspicuous by his yellow cap;   550
The rest in lengthening line the while
Wind slowly through the long defile:
Above, the mountain rears a peak,
Where vultures whet the thirsty beak,
And theirs may be a feast to-night,
Shall tempt them down ere morrow's light;
Beneath, a river's wintry stream
Has shrunk before the summer beam,
And left a channel bleak and bare,
Save shrubs that spring to perish there: 560
Each side the midway path there lay
Small broken crags of granite gray,
By time, or mountain lightning, riven
From summits clad in mists of heaven;
For where is he that hath beheld
The peak of Liakura[6] unveiled?

*   *   *   *   *

They reach the grove of pine at last;
"Bismillah!* now the peril's past;
For yonder view the opening plain,
And there we'll prick our steeds amain:"   570
The Chaius spake, and as he said,
A bullet whistled o'er his head;
The foremost Tartar bites the ground!
  Scarce had they time to check the rein,
Swift from their steeds the riders bound;
  But three shall never mount again:
Unseen the foes that gave the wound,
  The dying ask revenge in vain.
With steel unsheathed, and carbine bent,
Some o'er their courser's harness leant,   580
  Half sheltered by the steed;
Some fly beneath the nearest rock,
And there await the coming shock,
  Nor tamely stand to bleed
Beneath the shaft of foes unseen,
Who dare not quit their craggy screen.

* Bismillah—"In the name of God;" the commencement of
all the chapters of the Koran but one, and of prayer and thanks-
giving.

◇◇◇◇◇◇◇◇◇◇◇◇◇◇◇◇◇◇◇◇◇◇◇◇◇◇◇◇◇◇

[6] Parnassus.

Stern Hassan only from his horse
Disdains to light, and keeps his course,
Till fiery flashes in the van
Proclaim too sure the robber-clan   590
Have well secured the only way
Could now avail the promised prey;
Then curled his very beard† with ire,
And glared his eye with fiercer fire;
"Though far and near the bullets hiss,
I've scaped a bloodier hour than this."
And now the foe their covert quit,
And call his vassals to submit;
But Hassan's frown and furious word
Are dreaded more than hostile sword,   600
Nor of his little band a man
Resigned carbine or ataghan,
Nor raised the craven cry, Amaun!‡
In fuller sight, more near and near,
The lately ambushed foes appear,
And, issuing from the grove, advance
Some who on battle-charger prance.
Who leads them on with foreign brand
Far flashing in his red right hand?
"'Tis he! 'tis he! I know him now;   610
I know him by his pallid brow;
I know him by the evil eye§
That aids his envious treachery;
I know him by his jet-black barb;
Though now arrayed in Arnaut garb,
Apostate from his own vile faith,
It shall not save him from the death:
'Tis he! well met in any hour,
Lost Leila's love—accursed Giaour!"

As rolls the river into Ocean,   620
In sable torrent wildly streaming;
  As the sea-tide's opposing motion,
In azure column proudly gleaming,
Beats back the current many a rood,
In curling foam and mingling flood,
While eddying whirl, and breaking wave,
Rouse by the blast of winter, rave;

† A phenomenon not uncommon with an angry Mussulman.
In 1809 the Captain Pacha's whiskers at a diplomatic audience
were no less lively with indignation than a tiger cat's, to the
horror of all the dragomans; the portentous mustachios twisted,
they stood erect of their own accord, and were expected every
moment to change their colour, but at last condescended to
subside, which, probably, saved more heads than they contained
hairs.

‡ "Amaun," quarter, pardon.

§ The "evil eye," a common superstition in the Levant, and
of which the imaginary effects are yet very singular on those who
conceive themselves affected.

Through sparkling spray, in thundering clash,
The lightnings of the waters flash
In awful whiteness o'er the shore,   630
That shines and shakes beneath the roar;
Thus—as the stream and Ocean greet,
With waves that madden as they meet—
Thus join the bands, whom mutual wrong,
And fate, and fury, drive along.
The bickering sabres' shivering jar;
    And pealing wide or ringing near
    Its echoes on the throbbing ear,
The deathshot hissing from afar;
The shock, the shout, the groan of war,   640
    Reverberate along the vale,
    More suited to the shepherd's tale:
Though few the numbers—theirs the strife,
That neither spares nor speaks for life!
Ah! fondly youthful hearts can press,
To seize and share the dear caress;
But Love itself could never pant
For all that Beauty sighs to grant
With half the fervour Hate bestows
Upon the last embrace of foes,   650
When grappling in the fight they fold
Those arms that ne'er shall lose their hold:
Friends meet to part; Love laughs at faith;
True foes, once met, are joined till death!

*   *   *   *   *

With sabre shivered to the hilt,
Yet dripping with the blood he spilt;
Yet strained within the severed hand
Which quivers round that faithless brand;
His turban far behind him rolled,
And cleft in twin its firmest fold;   660
His flowing robe by falchion torn,
And crimson as those clouds of morn
That, streaked with dusky red, portend
The day shall have a stormy end;
A stain on every bush that bore
A fragment of his palampore;*
His breast with wounds unnumbered riven,
His back to earth, his face to Heaven,
Fall'n Hassan lies—his unclosed eye
Yet lowering on his enemy,   670
As if the hour that sealed his fate
Surviving left his quenchless hate;
And o'er him bends that foe with brow
As dark as his that bled below.

*   *   *   *   *

"Yes, Leila sleeps beneath the wave,
But his shall be a redder grave;

* The flowered shawls generally worn by persons of rank.

Her spirit pointed well the steel
Which taught that felon heart to feel.
He called the Prophet, but his power
Was vain against the vengeful Giaour: 680
He called on Alla—but the word
Arose unheeded or unheard.
Thou Paynim fool! could Leila's prayer
Be passed, and thine accorded there?
I watched my time, I leagued with these,
The traitor in his turn to seize;
My wrath is wreaked, the deed is done,
And now I go—but go alone."

*   *   *   *   *
*   *   *   *   *

    The browsing camels' bells are tinkling:
His mother looked from her lattice high—   690
    She saw the dews of eve besprinkling
The pasture green beneath her eye,
    She saw the planets faintly twinkling:
"'Tis twilight—sure his train is nigh."
She could not rest in the garden-bower,
But gazed through the grate of his steepest tower.
"Why comes he not? his steeds are fleet,
Nor shrink they from the summer heat;
Why sends not the Bridegroom his promised gift?
Is his heart more cold, or his barb less swift?   700
Oh, false reproach! yon Tartar now
Has gained our nearest mountain's brow,
And warily the steep descends,
And now within the valley bends;
And he bears the gift at his saddle bow—
How could I deem his courser slow?
Right well my largess shall repay
His welcome speed, and weary way."

The Tartar lighted at the gate,
But scarce upheld his fainting weight: 710
His swarthy visage spake distress,
But this might be from weariness;
His garb with sanguine spots was dyed,
But these might be from his courser's side;
He drew the token from his vest—
Angel of Death! 'tis Hassan's cloven crest!
His calpac† rent—his caftan red—
"Lady, a fearful bride thy Son hath wed:
Me, not from mercy, did they spare,
But this empurpled pledge to bear.   720
Peace to the brave! whose blood is spilt:
Woe to the Giaour! for his the guilt."

*   *   *   *   *

† The "Calpac" is the solid cap or centre part of the head-dress; the shawl is wound round it, and forms the turban.

A Turban* carved in coarsest stone,
A Pillar with rank weeds o'ergrown,
Whereon can now be scarcely read
The Koran verse that mourns the dead,
Point out the spot where Hassan fell
A victim in that lonely dell.
There sleeps as true an Osmanlie
As e'er at Mecca bent the knee;   730
As ever scorned forbidden wine,
Or prayed with face towards the shrine,
In orisons resumed anew
At solemn sound of "Alla Hu!"†
Yet died he by a stranger's hand,
And stranger in his native land;
Yet died he as in arms he stood,
And unavenged, at least in blood.
But him the maids of Paradise
   Impatient to their halls invite,   740
And the dark heaven of Houris' eyes
  On him shall glance for ever bright;
They come—their kerchiefs green they wave,‡
And welcome with a kiss the brave!
Who falls in battle 'gainst a Giaour
Is worthiest an immortal bower.

    *   *   *   *   *

  But thou, false Infidel! shall writhe
Beneath avenging Monkir's§ scythe;
And from its torments 'scape alone
To wander round lost Eblis'‖ throne;   750
And fire unquenched, unquenchable,
Around, within, thy heart shall dwell;
Nor ear can hear nor tongue can tell
The tortures of that inward hell!

But first, on earth as Vampire** sent,
Thy corse shall from its tomb be rent:
Then ghastly haunt thy native place,
And suck the blood of all thy race;
There from thy daughter, sister, wife,
At midnight drain the stream of life;   760
Yet loathe the banquet which perforce
Must feed thy livid living corse:
Thy victims ere they yet expire
Shall know the demon for their sire,
As cursing thee, thou cursing them,
Thy flowers are withered on the stem.
But one that for thy crime must fall,
The youngest, most beloved of all,
Shall bless thee with a *father's* name—
That word shall wrap thy heart in flame!   770
Yet must thou end thy task, and mark
Her cheek's last tinge, her eye's last spark,
And the last glassy glance must view
Which freezes o'er its lifeless blue;
Then with unhallowed hand shalt tear
The tresses of her yellow hair,
Of which in life a lock when shorn
Affection's fondest pledge was worn,
But now is borne away by thee,
Memorial of thine agony!   780
Wet with thine own blest blood shall drip
Thy gnashing tooth and haggard lip;††
Then stalking to thy sullen grave,
Go—and with Gouls and Afrits rave;
Till these in horror shrink away
From Spectre more accursed than they!

    *   *   *   *   *

"How name ye yon lone Caloyer?
  His features I have scanned before
In mine own land: 'tis many a year,
  Since, dashing by the lonely shore,   790
I saw him urge as fleet a steed
As ever served a horseman's need.

---

* The turban, pillar, and inscriptive verse, decorate the tombs of the Osmanlies, whether in the cemetery or the wilderness. In the mountains you frequently pass similar mementos: and on enquiry you are informed that they record some victim of rebellion, plunder or revenge.

† "Alla Hu!" the concluding words of the Muezzin's call to prayer from the highest gallery on the exterior of the Minaret. On a still evening, when the Muezzin has a fine voice, which is frequently the case, the effect is solemn and beautiful beyond all the bells in Christendom.

‡ The following is part of a battle song of the Turks:—"I see—I see a dark-eyed girl of Paradise, and she waves a handkerchief, a kerchief of green; and cries aloud, "Come, kiss me, for I love thee," &.

§ Monkir and Nekir are the inquisitors of the dead, before whom the corpse undergoes a slight noviciate and preparatory training for damnation. If the answers are none of the clearest, he is hauled up with a scythe and thumped down with a red hot mace till properly seasoned, with a variety of subsidiary probations. The office of these angels is no sinecure; there are but two, and the number of orthodox deceased being in a small proportion to the remainder, their hands are always full.

‖ Eblis, the Oriental Prince of Darkness.

** The Vampire superstition is still general in the Levant. Honest Tournefort tells a long story, which Mr. Southey, in the notes on *Thalaba*, quotes about these "Vroucolochas," as he calls them. The Romaic term is "Vardoulacha." I recollect a whole family being terrified by the scream of a child, which they imagined must proceed from such a visitation. The Greeks never mention the word without horror. I find that "Broucolokas" is an old legitimate Hellenic appellation—at least is so applied to Arsenius, who, according to the Greeks, was after his death animated by the Devil.—The moderns, however, use the word I mention.

†† The freshness of the face, and the wetness of the lip with blood, are the never-failing signs of a Vampire. The stories told in Hungary and Greece of these foul feeders are singular, and some of them most *incredibly* attested.

But once I saw that face, yet then
It was so marked with inward pain,
I could not pass it by again;
It breathes the same dark spirit now,
As death were stamped upon his brow.

"'Tis twice three years at summer tide
    Since first among our freres he came;
And here it soothes him to abide   800
    For some dark deed he will not name.
But never at our Vesper prayer,
Nor e'er before Confession chair
Kneels he, nor recks he when arise
Incense or anthem to the skies,
But broods within his cell alone,
His faith and race alike unknown.
The sea from Paynim land he crost,
And here ascended from the coast;
Yet seems he not of Othman race,   810
But only Christian in his face:
I'd judge him some stray renegade,
Repentant of the change he made,
Save that he shuns our holy shrine,
Nor tastes the sacred bread and wine.
Great largess to these walls he brought,
And thus our Abbot's favour bought;
But were I Prior, not a day
Should brook such stranger's further stay,
Or pent within our penance cell   820
Should doom him there for aye to dwell.
Much in his visions mutters he
Of maiden whelmed beneath the sea;
Of sabres clashing, foemen flying,
Wrongs avenged, and Moslem dying.
On cliff he hath been known to stand,
And rave as to some bloody hand
Fresh severed from its parent limb,
Invisible to all but him,
Which beckons onward to his grave,   830
And lures to leap into the wave."

      *   *   *   *   *
      *   *   *   *   *

    Dark and unearthly is the scowl
That glares beneath his dusky cowl:
The flash of that dilating eye
Reveals too much of times gone by;
Though varying, indistinct its hue,
Oft with his glance the gazer rue,
For in it lurks that nameless spell,
Which speaks, itself unspeakable,
A spirit yet unquelled and high,   840
That claims and keeps ascendancy;
And like the bird whose pinions quake,
But cannot fly the gazing snake,

Will others quail beneath his look,
Nor 'scape the glance they scarce can brook.
From him the half-affrighted Friar
When met alone would fain retire,
As if that eye and bitter smile
Transferred to others fear and guile:
Not oft to smile descendeth he,   850
And when he doth 'tis sad to see
That he but mocks at Misery.
How that pale lip will curl and quiver!
Then fix once more as if for ever;
As if his sorrow or disdain
Forbade him e'er to smile again.
Well were it so—such ghastly mirth
From joyaunce ne'er derived its birth.
But sadder still it were to trace
What once were feelings in that face: 860
Time hath not yet the features fixed,
But brighter traits with evil mixed;
And there are hues not always faded,
Which speak a mind not all degraded
Even by the crimes through which it waded:
The common crowd but see the gloom
Of wayward deeds, and fitting doom;
The close observer can espy
A noble soul, and lineage high:
Alas! though both bestowed in vain,   870
Which Grief could change, and Guilt could stain,
It was no vulgar tenement
To which such lofty gifts were lent,
And still with little less than dread
On such the sight is riveted.
The roofless cot, decayed and rent,
    Will scarce delay the passer-by;
The tower by war or tempest bent,
While yet may frown one battlement,
    Demands and daunts the stranger's eye;   880
Each ivied arch, and pillar lone,
Pleads haughtily for glories gone!

"His floating robe around him folding,
    Slow sweeps he through the columned aisle;
With dread beheld, with gloom beholding
    The rites that sanctify the pile.
But when the anthem shakes the choir,
And kneel the monks, his steps retire;
By yonder lone and wavering torch
His aspect glares within the porch;   890
There will he pause till all is done—
And hear the prayer, but utter none.
See—by the half-illumined wall
His hood fly back, his dark hair fall,
That pale brow wildly wreathing round,
As if the Gorgon there had bound

The sablest of the serpent-braid
That o'er her fearful forehead strayed:
For he declines the convent oath,
And leaves those locks unhallowed growth,   900
But wears our garb in all beside;
And, not from piety but pride,
Gives wealth to walls that never heard
Of his one holy vow nor word.
Lo!—mark ye, as the harmony
Peals louder praises to the sky,
That livid cheek, that stony air
Of mixed defiance and despair!
Saint Francis, keep him from the shrine!
Else may we dread the wrath divine   910
Made manifest by awful sign.
If ever evil angel bore
The form of mortal, such he wore;
By all my hope of sins forgiven,
Such looks are not of earth nor heaven!"

To Love the softest hearts are prone,
But such can ne'er be all his own;
Too timid in his woes to share,
Too meek to meet, or brave despair;
And sterner hearts alone may feel   920
The wound that Time can never heal.
The rugged metal of the mine
Must burn before its surface shine,
But plunged within the furnace-flame,
It bends and melts—though still the same;
Then tempered to thy want, or will,
'Twill serve thee to defend or kill—
A breast-plate for thine hour of need,
Or blade to bid thy foeman bleed;
But if a dagger's form it bear,   930
Let those who shape its edge, beware!
Thus Passion's fire, and Woman's art,
Can turn and tame the sterner heart;
From these its form and tone are ta'en,
And what they make it, must remain,
But break—before it bend again.

     *   *   *   *   *
     *   *   *   *   *

If solitude succeed to grief,
Release from pain is slight relief;
The vacant bosom's wilderness
Might thank the pang that made it less.   940
We loathe what none are left to share:
Even bliss—'twere woe alone to bear;
The heart once left thus desolate
Must fly at last for ease—to hate.
It is as if the dead could feel
The icy worm around them steal,

And shudder, as the reptiles creep
To revel o'er their rotting sleep,
Without the power to scare away
The cold consumers of their clay!   950
It is as if the desert bird,*
    Whose beak unlocks her bosom's stream
    To still her famished nestlings' scream,
Nor mourns a life to them transferred,
Should rend her rash devoted breast,
And find them flown her empty nest.
The keenest pangs the wretched find
    Are rapture to the dreary void,
The leafless desert of the mind,
    The waste of feelings unemployed.   960
Who would be doomed to gaze upon
A sky without a cloud or sun?
Less hideous far the tempest's roar,
Than ne'er to grave the billows more—
Thrown, when the war of winds is o'er,
A lonely wreck on Fortune's shore,
'Mid sullen calm, and silent bay,
Unseen to drop by dull decay;—
Better to sink beneath the shock
Than moulder piecemeal on the rock!   970

     *   *   *   *   *

"Father! thy days have passed in peace,
    'Mid counted beads, and countless prayer;
To bid the sins of others cease,
    Thyself without a crime or care,
Save transient ills that all must bear,
Has been thy lot from youth to age;
And thou wilt bless thee from the rage
Of passions fierce and uncontrolled,
Such as thy penitents unfold,
Whose secret sins and sorrows rest   980
Within thy pure and pitying breast.
My days, though few, have passed below
In much of Joy, but more of Woe;
Yet still in hours of love or strife,
I've 'scaped the weariness of Life:
Now leagued with friends, now girt by foes,
I loathed the languor of repose.
Now nothing left to love or hate,
No more with hope or pride elate,
I'd rather be the thing that crawls   990
Most noxious o'er a dungeon's walls,
Than pass my dull, unvarying days,
Condemned to meditate and gaze.
Yet, lurks a wish within my breast
For rest—but not to feel 'tis rest.

* The pelican is, I believe, the bird so libelled, by the impu-
tation of feeding her chickens with her blood.

Soon shall my Fate that wish fulfil;
    And I shall sleep without the dream
Of what I was, and would be still,
    Dark as to thee my deeds may seem:
My memory now is but the tomb   0
Of joys long dead; my hope, their doom:
Though better to have died with those
Than bear a life of lingering woes.
My spirit shrunk not to sustain
The searching throes of ceaseless pain;
Nor sought the self-accorded grave
Of ancient fool and modern knave:
Yet death I have not feared to meet;
And in the field it had been sweet,
Had Danger wooed me on to move   10
The slave of Glory, not of Love.
I've braved it—not for Honour's boast;
I smile at laurels won or lost;
To such let others carve their way,
For high renown, or hireling pay:
But place again before my eyes
Aught that I deem a worthy prize—
The maid I love, the man I hate—
And I will hunt the steps of fate,
To save or slay, as these require,   20
Through rending steel, and rolling fire:
Nor needst thou doubt this speech from one
Who would but do—what he *hath* done.
Death is but what the haughty brave,
The weak must bear, the wretch must crave;
Then let life go to Him who gave:
I have not quailed to Danger's brow
When high and happy—need I *now*?

            *   *   *   *

"I loved her, Friar! nay, adored—
    But these are words that all can use—   30
I proved it more in deed than word;
There's blood upon that dinted sword,
    A stain its steel can never lose:
'Twas shed for her, who died for me,
    It warmed the heart of one abhorred:
Nay, start not—no—nor bend thy knee,
    Nor midst my sin such act record;
Thou wilt absolve me from the deed,
For he was hostile to thy creed!
The very name of Nazarene   40
Was wormwood to his Paynim spleen.
Ungrateful fool! since but for brands
Well wielded in some hardy hands,
And wounds by Galileans given—
The surest pass to Turkish heaven—
For him his Houris still might wait
Impatient at the Prophet's gate.

I loved her—Love will find its way
Through paths where wolves would fear to prey;
And if it dares enough, 'twere hard   50
If passion met not some reward—
No matter how, or where, or why,
I did not vainly seek, nor sigh:
Yet sometimes, with remorse, in vain
I wish she had not loved again.
She died—I dare not tell thee how;
But look—'tis written on my brow!
There read of Cain the curse and crime,
In characters unworn by Time:
Still, ere thou dost condemn me, pause;   60
Not mine the act, though I the cause.
Yet did he but what I had done
Had she been false to more than one.
Faithless to him—he gave the blow;
But true to me—I laid him low:
Howe'er deserved her doom might be,
Her treachery was truth to me;
To me she gave her heart, that all
Which Tyranny can ne'er enthrall;
And I, alas! too late to save!   70
Yet all I then could give, I gave—
'Twas some relief—our foe a grave.*

---

* This superstition of a second-hearing (for I never met with
downright second-sight in the East) fell once under my own
observation. On my third journey to Cape Colonna, early in
1811, as we passed through the defile that leads from the hamlet
between Keratia and Colonna, I observed Dervish Tahiri riding
rather out of the path, and leaning his head upon his hand, as if
in pain. I rode up and inquired. "We are in peril," he answered.
"What peril? We are not now in Albania, nor in the passes to
Ephesus, Messalunghi, or Lepanto; there are plenty of us, well
armed, and the Choriates have not courage to be thieves."—
"True, Affendi, but nevertheless the shot is ringing in my ears."
—"The shot. Not a tophaike has been fired this morning."—
"I hear it notwithstanding—Bom—Bom—as plainly as I hear
your voice."—"Psha!"—"As you please, Affendi; if it is written,
so will it be."—I left this quick-eared predestinarian, and rode
up to Basili, his Christian compatriot, whose ears, though not at
all prophetic, by no means relished the intelligence. We all
arrived at Colonna, remained some hours, and returned
leisurely, saying a variety of brilliant things, in more languages
than spoiled the building of Babel, upon the mistaken seer.
Romaic, Arnaout, Turkish, Italian, and English were all exer-
cised, in various conceits, upon the unfortunate Mussulman.
While we were contemplating the beautiful prospect, Dervish
was occupied about the columns. I thought he was deranged into
an antiquarian, and asked him if he had become a "*Palao—castro*"
man? "No," said he; "but these pillars will be useful in making
a stand;" and added other remarks which at least evinced his
own belief in his troublesome faculty of *forehearing*. On our
return to Athens we heard from Leoné (a prisoner set ashore
some days after) of the intended attack of the Mainotes, men-
tioned, with the cause of its not taking place, in the notes to
Childe Harold, Canto 2nd. I was at some pains to question the
man, and he described the dresses, arms, and marks of the
horses of our party so accurately, that, with other circumstances,

His death sits lightly; but her fate
Has made me—what thou well mayst hate.
   His doom was sealed—he knew it well,
Warned by the voice of stern Taheer,
Deep in whose darkly boding ear
The deathshot pealed of murder near,
   As filed the troop to where they fell!
He died too in the battle broil,   80
A time that heeds nor pain nor toil;
One cry to Mahomet for aid,
One prayer to Alla all he made:
He knew and crossed me in the fray—
I gazed upon him where he lay,
And watched his spirit ebb away:
Though pierced like pard by hunter's steel,
He felt not half that now I feel.
I searched, but vainly searched, to find
The workings of a wounded mind;   90
Each feature of that sullen corse
Betrayed his rage, but no remorse.
Oh, what had Vengeance given to trace
Despair upon his dying face!
The late repentance of that hour
When Penitence hath lost her power
To tear one terror from the grave,
And will not soothe, and cannot save.

          *   *   *   *   *

"The cold in clime are cold in blood,
   Their love can scarce deserve the name;   100
But mine was like the lava flood
   That boils in Ætna's breast of flame.
I cannot prate in puling strain
Of Ladye-love, and Beauty's chain:
If changing cheek, and scorching vein,
Lips taught to writhe, but not complain,
If bursting heart, and maddening brain,
And daring deed, and vengeful steel,
And all that I have felt, and feel,

we could not doubt of *his* having been in "villanous company"
and ourselves in a bad neighbourhood. Dervish became a sooth-
sayer for life, and I dare say is now hearing more musketry than
ever will be fired, to the great refreshment of the Arnaouts of
Berat and his native mountains.—I shall mention one trait more
of this singular race. In March, 1811, a remarkably stout and
active Arnaout came (I believe the fiftieth on the same errand)
to offer himself as an attendant, which was declined. "Well,
Affendi," quoth he, "may you live!—you would have found me
useful. I shall leave the town for the hills tomorrow; in the
winter I return, perhaps you will then receive me."—Dervish,
who was present, remarked as a thing of course, and of no conse-
quence, "in the meantime he will join the Klephtes" (robbers),
which was true to the letter. If not cut off, they come down in
the winter, and pass it unmolested in some town, where they are
often as well known as their exploits.

Betoken love—that love was mine,   110
And shown by many a bitter sign.
'Tis true, I could not whine nor sigh,
I knew but to obtain or die.
I die—but first I have possessed,
And come what may, I *have been* blessed.
Shall I the doom I sought upbraid?
No—reft of all, yet undismayed
But for the thought of Leila slain,
Give me the pleasure with the pain,
So would I live and love again.   120
I grieve, but not, my holy Guide!
For him who dies, but her who died:
She sleeps beneath the wandering wave—
Ah! had she but an earthly grave,
This breaking heart and throbbing head
Should seek and share her narrow bed.
She was a form of Life and Light,
That, seen, became a part of sight;
And rose, where'er I turned mine eye,
The Morning-star of Memory!   130

"Yes, Love indeed is light from heaven;
   A spark of that immortal fire
With angels shared, by Alla given,
   To lift from earth our low desire.
Devotion wafts the mind above,
But Heaven itself descends in Love;
A feeling from the Godhead caught,
To wean from self each sordid thought;
A ray of Him who formed the whole;
A Glory circling round the soul!   140
I grant *my* love imperfect, all
That mortals by the name miscall;
Then deem it evil, what thou wilt;
But say, oh say, *hers* was not Guilt!
She was my Life's unerring Light:
That quenched—what beam shall break my night?
Oh! would it shone to lead me still,
Although to death or deadliest ill!
Why marvel ye, if they who lose
   This present joy, this future hope,   150
   No more with Sorrow meekly cope;
In phrensy then their fate accuse;
In madness do those fearful deeds
   That seem to add but Guilt to Woe?
Alas! the breast that inly bleeds
   Hath nought to dread from outward blow:
Who falls from all he knows of bliss,
Cares little into what abyss.
Fierce as the gloomy vulture's now
   To thee, old man, my deeds appear: 160
I read abhorrence on thy brow,
   And this too was I born to bear!

'Tis true, that, like that bird of prey,
With havock have I marked my way:
But this was taught me by the dove,
To die—and know no second love.
This lesson yet hath man to learn,
Taught by the thing he dares to spurn:
The bird that sings within the brake,
The swan that swims upon the lake,   170
One mate, and one alone, will take.
And let the fool still prone to range,
And sneer on all who cannot change,
Partake his jest with boasting boys;
I envy not his varied joys,
But deem such feeble, heartless man,
Less than yon solitary swan;
Far, far beneath the shallow maid
He left believing and betrayed.
Such shame at least was never mine—   180
Leila! each thought was only thine!
My good, my guilt, my weal, my woe,
My hope on high—my all below.
Each holds no other like to thee,
Or, if it doth, in vain for me:
For worlds I dare not view the dame
Resembling thee, yet not the same.
The very crimes that mar my youth,
This bed of death—attest my truth!
'Tis all too late—thou wert, thou art   190
The cherished madness of my heart!

"And she was lost—and yet I breathed,
But not the breath of human life:
A serpent round my heart was wreathed,
And stung my every thought to strife.
Alike all time, abhorred all place,
Shuddering I shrank from Nature's face,
Where every hue that charmed before
The blackness of my bosom wore.
The rest thou dost already know,   200
And all my sins, and half my woe.
But talk no more of penitence;
Thou seest I soon shall part from hence:
And if thy holy tale were true,
The deed that's done canst *thou* undo?
Think me not thankless—but this grief
Looks not to priesthood for relief.*
My soul's estate in secret guess:
But wouldst thou pity more, say less.

When thou canst bid my Leila live,   210
Then will I sue thee to forgive;
Then plead my cause in that high place
Where purchased masses proffer grace.
Go, when the hunter's hand hath wrung
From forest-cave her shrieking young,
And calm the lonely lioness:
But soothe not—mock not *my* distress!

"In earlier days, and calmer hours,
When heart with heart delights to blend,
Where bloom my native valley's bowers,   220
I had—Ah! have I now?—a friend!
To him this pledge I charge thee send,
Memorial of a youthful vow;
I would remind him of my end:
Though souls absorbed like mine allow
Brief thought to distant Friendship's claim,
Yet dear to him my blighted name.
'Tis strange—he prophesied my doom,
And I have smiled—I then could smile—
When Prudence would his voice assume,   230
And warn—I recked not what—the while:
But now Remembrance whispers o'er
Those accents scarcely marked before.
Say—that his bodings came to pass,
And he will start to hear their truth,
And wish his words had not been sooth:
Tell him—unheeding as I was,
Through many a busy bitter scene
Of all our golden youth had been,
In pain, my faltering tongue had tried   240
To bless his memory—ere I died;
But Heaven in wrath would turn away,
If Guilt should for the guiltless pray.
I do not ask him not to blame,
Too gentle he to wound my name;
And what have I to do with Fame?
I do not ask him not to mourn,
Such cold request might sound like scorn;
And what than Friendship's manly tear
May better grace a brother's bier?   250
But bear this ring, his own of old,
And tell him—what thou dost behold!
The withered frame, the ruined mind,
The wrack by passion left behind,
A shrivelled scroll, a scattered leaf,
Seared by the autumn blast of Grief!

*   *   *   *   *

"Tell me no more of Fancy's gleam,
No, father, no, 'twas not a dream;
Alas! the dreamer first must sleep,
I only watched, and wished to weep;   260

---

* The monk's sermon is omitted. It seems to have had so little effect upon the patient, that it could have no hopes from the reader. It may be sufficient to say that it was of the customary length (as may be perceived from the interruptions and uneasiness of the patient), and was delivered in the usual tone of all orthodox preachers.

But could not, for my burning brow
Throbbed to the very brain as now:
I wished but for a single tear,
As something welcome, new, and dear:
I wished it then, I wish it still;
Despair is stronger than my will.
Waste not thine orison, despair
Is mightier than thy pious prayer:
I would not, if I might, be blest;
I want no Paradise, but rest.   270
'Twas then—I tell thee—father! then
I saw her; yes, she lived again;
And shining in her white symar*
As through yon pale gray cloud the star
Which now I gaze on, as on her,
Who looked and looks far lovelier;
Dimly I view its trembling spark;
To-morrow's night shall be more dark;
And I, before its rays appear,
That lifeless thing the living fear.   280
I wander—father! for my soul
Is fleeting towards the final goal.
I saw her—friar! and I rose
Forgetful of our former woes;
And rushing from my couch, I dart,
And clasp her to my desperate heart;
I clasp—what is it that I clasp?
No breathing form within my grasp,
No heart that beats reply to mine—
Yet, Leila! yet the form is thine!   290
And art thou, dearest, changed so much
As meet my eye, yet mock my touch?
Ah! were thy beauties e'er so cold,
I care not—so my arms enfold
The all they ever wished to hold.
Alas! around a shadow prest
They shrink upon my lonely breast;
Yet still 'tis there! In silence stands,
And beckons with beseeching hands!
With braided hair, and bright-black eye—   300
I knew 'twas false—she could not die!
But *he* is dead! within the dell
I saw him buried where he fell;
He comes not—for he cannot break
From earth;—why then art *thou* awake?
They told me wild waves rolled above
The face I view—the form I love;
They told me—'twas a hideous tale!—
I'd tell it, but my tongue would fail:
If true, and from thine ocean-cave   310
Thou com'st to claim a calmer grave,

Oh! pass thy dewy fingers o'er
This brow that then will burn no more;
Or place them on my hopeless heart:
But, Shape or Shade! whate'er thou art,
In mercy ne'er again depart!
Or farther with thee bear my soul
Than winds can waft or waters roll!

*   *   *   *   *

"Such is my name, and such my tale.
    Confessor! to thy secret ear   320
I breathe the sorrows I bewail,
    And thank thee for the generous tear
This glazing eye could never shed.
Then lay me with the humblest dead,
And, save the cross above my head,
Be neither name nor emblem spread,
By prying stranger to be read,
Or stay the passing pilgrim's tread."†
He passed—nor of his name and race
He left a token or a trace,   330
Save what the Father must not say
Who shrived him on his dying day:
This broken tale was all we knew
Of her he loved, or him he slew.

[1813]   [1813]

† The circumstance to which the above story relates was not
very uncommon in Turkey. A few years ago the wife of Muchtar
Pacha complained to his father of his son's supposed infidelity;
he asked with whom, and she had the barbarity to give in a list
of the twenty handsomest women in Yanina. They were seized,
fastened up in sacks, and drowned in the lake the same night!
One of the guards who was present informed me that not one of
the victims uttered a cry, or showed a symptom of terror at so
sudden a "wrench from all we know, from all we love." The
fate of Phrosine, the fairest of this sacrifice, is the subject of
many a Romaic and Arnaout ditty. The story in the text is one
told of a young Venetian many years ago, and now nearly for-
gotten. I heard it by accident recited by one of the coffee-house
story-tellers who abound in the Levant, and sing or recite their
narratives. The additions and interpolations by the translator
will be easily distinguished from the rest, by the want of Eastern
imagery; and I regret that my memory has retained so few
fragments of the original. For the contents of some of the notes
I am indebted partly to D'Herbelot, and partly to that most
Eastern, and, as Mr. Weber justly entitles it, "sublime tale," the
"Caliph Vathek." I do not know from what source the author of
that singular volume may have drawn his materials; some of his
incidents are to be found in the *Bibliothèque Orientale;* but for
correctness of costume, beauty of description, and power of
imagination, it far surpasses all European imitations, and bears
such marks of originality that those who have visited the East
will find some difficulty in believing it to be more than a trans-
lation. As an Eastern tale, even Rasselas must bow before it; his
"Happy Valley" will not bear a comparison with the "Hall of
Eblis."

* "Symar,"—Shroud.

ODE TO
NAPOLEON BUONAPARTE.

"Expende Annibalem:—quot libras in duce summo
  Invenies ?"
        JUVENAL, *Sat.* x. [1]

"The Emperor Nepos was acknowledged by the
Senate, by the *Italians*, and by the Provincials of *Gaul;*
his moral virtues, and military talents, were loudly cele-
brated; and those who derived any private benefit
from his government announced in prophetic strains
the restoration of public felicity. * * By this shame-
ful abdication, he protracted his life a few years, in
a very ambiguous state, between an Emperor and an
Exile, till——"—Gibbon's *Decline and Fall*, vol. vi,
p. 220

I.

'TIS done—but yesterday a King!
  And armed with Kings to strive—
And now thou art a nameless thing:
  So abject—yet alive!
Is this the man of thousand thrones,
Who strewed our earth with hostile bones,
  And can he thus survive?
Since he, miscalled the Morning Star,
Nor man nor fiend hath fallen so far.

II.

Ill-minded man! why scourge thy kind
  Who bowed so low the knee?
By gazing on thyself grown blind,
  Thou taught'st the rest to see.
With might unquestioned,—power to save,—
Thine only gift hath been the grave
  To those that worshipped thee;
Nor till thy fall could mortals guess
Ambition's less than littleness!

III.

Thanks for that lesson—it will teach
  To after-warriors more
Than high Philosophy can preach,
  And vainly preached before.
That spell upon the minds of men
Breaks never to unite again,
  That led them to adore
Those Pagod things of sabre-sway,
With fronts of brass, and feet of clay.

IV.

The triumph, and the vanity,
  The rapture of the strife—*
The earthquake-voice of Victory,
  To thee the breath of life;
The sword, the sceptre, and that sway
Which man seemed made but to obey,
  Wherewith renown was rife—
All quelled!—Dark Spirit! what must be
The madness of thy memory!

V.

The Desolator desolate!
  The Victor overthrown!
The Arbiter of others' fate
  A Suppliant for his own!
Is it some yet imperial hope
That with such change can calmly cope?
  Or dread of death alone?
To die a Prince—or live a slave—
Thy choice is most ignobly brave!

VI.

He who of old would rend the oak,
  Dreamed not of the rebound;†
Chained by the trunk he vainly broke—
  Alone—how looked he round?
Thou, in the sternness of thy strength,
An equal deed hast done at length,
  And darker fate hast found:
He fell, the forest prowlers' prey;
But thou must eat thy heart away!

VII.

The Roman,‡ when his burning heart
  Was slaked with blood of Rome,
Threw down the dagger—dared depart,
  In savage grandeur, home.—
He dared depart in utter scorn
Of men that such a yoke had borne,
  Yet left him such a doom!
His only glory was that hour
Of self-upheld abandoned power.

* "Certaminis *gaudia*"—the expression of Attila in his
harangue to his army, previous to the battle of Chalons, given
in Cassiodorus.
  † Milo. [2]   ‡ Sylla.[3]

---

[1] "Produce the urn that Hannibal contains
  And weigh the mighty dust which yet remains;
  AND IS THIS ALL!"
        JUVENAL, *Satires*, X, 147, trans. Gifford,
literally: "Weigh Hannibal. How many pounds do you find in
the greatest leader?"

[2] Milo of Crotona (sixth century B.C.?), who was caught by a
tree he was trying to split, and devoured by wolves.
[3] Lucius Cornelius Sulla (138–78 B.C.), Roman General.

VIII.

The Spaniard,[4] when the lust of sway
   Had lost its quickening spell,
Cast crowns for rosaries away,
   An empire for a cell;
A strict accountant of his beads,
A subtle disputant on creeds,
   His dotage trifled well:
Yet better had he neither known
A bigot's shrine, nor despot's throne.

IX.

But thou—from thy reluctant hand
   The thunderbolt is wrung—
Too late thou leav'st the high command
   To which thy weakness clung;
All Evil Spirit as thou art,
It is enough to grieve the heart
   To see thine own unstrung;
To think that God's fair world hath been
The footstool of a thing so mean;

X.

And Earth hath spilt her blood for him,
   Who thus can hoard his own!
And Monarchs bowed the trembling limb,
   And thanked him for a throne!
Fair Freedom! we may hold thee dear,
When thus thy mightiest foes their fear
   In humblest guise have shown.
Oh! ne'er may tyrant leave behind
A brighter name to lure mankind!

XI.

Thine evil deeds are writ in gore,
   Nor written thus in vain—
Thy triumphs tell of fame no more,
   Or deepen every stain:
If thou hadst died as Honour dies,
Some new Napoleon might arise,
   To shame the world again—
But who would soar the solar height,
To set in such a starless night?

XII.

Weigh'd in the balance, hero dust
   Is vile as vulgar clay;
Thy scales, Mortality! are just
   To all that pass away:
But yet methought the living great
Some higher sparks should animate,
   To dazzle and dismay:
Nor deem'd Contempt could thus make mirth
Of these, the Conquerors of the earth.

XIII.

And she, proud Austria's mournful flower,
   Thy still imperial bride;[5]
How bears her breast the torturing hour?
   Still clings she to thy side?
Must she too bend, must she too share
Thy late repentance, long despair,
   Thou throneless Homicide?
If still she loves thee, hoard that gem,—
'Tis worth thy vanished diadem!

XIV.

Then haste thee to thy sullen Isle,
   And gaze upon the sea;
That element may meet thy smile—
   It ne'er was ruled by thee!
Or trace with thine all idle hand
In loitering mood upon the sand
   That Earth is now as free!
That Corinth's pedagogue hath now
Transferred his by-word to thy brow.[6]

XV.

Thou Timour! in his captive's cage*
What thoughts will there be thine,
While brooding in thy prisoned rage?
   But one—"The world *was* mine!"
Unless, like he of Babylon,[8]
All sense is with thy sceptre gone,
   Life will not long confine
That spirit poured so widely forth—
So long obeyed—so little worth!

XVI.

Or, like the thief of fire from heaven,†
   Wilt thou withstand the shock?
And share with him, the unforgiven,
   His vulture and his rock!
Foredoomed by God—by man accurst,
And that last act, though not thy worst,
   The very Fiend's arch mock;‡
He in his fall preserved his pride,
And, if a mortal, had as proudly died!

* The cage of Bajazet, by order of Tamerlane.[7]
† Prometheus.
‡   ——"The very fiend's arch mock—
    To lip a wanton, and suppose her chaste."
                  SHAKESPEARE.

[5] Napoleon's second wife, Marie Louise (1791–1847), who later married the Count de Neipper, the Austrian ambassador.
[6] Dionysius the Younger, banished from Syracuse, went to Corinth and opened a school (344 B.C.).
[7] After the battle of Angora, 1402.
[8] Nebuchadnezzar II, who was reputed to have become a werewolf.

[4] Charles V (1500–1558), who retired to a monastery.

XVII.

There was a day—there was an hour,
   While earth was Gaul's—Gaul thine—
When that immeasurable power
   Unsated to resign
Had been an act of purer fame
Than gathers round Marengo's [9] name
   And gilded thy decline,
Through the long twilight of all time,
Despite some passing clouds of crime.

XVIII.

But thou forsooth must be a King
   And don the purple vest,
As if that foolish robe could wring
   Remembrance from thy breast.
Where is that faded garment? where
The gewgaws thou wert fond to wear,
   The star, the string, the crest?
Vain froward child of Empire! say,
Are all thy playthings snatched away?

XIX.

Where may the wearied eye repose
   When gazing on the Great;
Where neither guilty glows,
   Nor despicable state?
Yes—One—the first—the last—the best—
The Cincinnatus [10] of the West,
   Whom Envy dared not hate,
Bequeathed the name of Washington,
To make man blush there was but one!

[1814]   [1814]

SHE WALKS IN BEAUTY.

I.

SHE walks in Beauty, like the night
   Of cloudless climes and starry skies;
And all that's best of dark and bright
   Meet in her aspect and her eyes:
Thus mellowed to that tender light
   Which Heaven to gaudy day denies.

II.

One shade the more, one ray the less,
   Had half impaired the nameless grace
Which waves in every raven tress,
   Or softly lightens o'er her face;
Where thoughts serenely sweet express,
   How pure, how dear their dwelling-place.

III.

And on that cheek, and o'er that brow,
   So soft, so calm, yet eloquent,
The smiles that win, the tints that glow,
   But tell of days in goodness spent,
A mind at peace with all below,
   A heart whose love is innocent!

[1814]   [1815]

FARE THEE WELL.

"Alas! they had been friends in youth;
   But whispering tongues can poison truth:
And Constancy lives in realms above;
   And Life is thorny; and youth is vain:
And to be wroth with one we love,
   Doth work like madness in the brain:

   *   *   *   *   *

But never either found another
   To free the hollow heart from paining—
They stood aloof, the scars remaining,
   Like cliffs which had been rent asunder;
A dreary sea now flows between,
   But neither heat, nor frost, nor thunder,
Shall wholly do away, I ween,
   The marks of that which once hath been."
          COLERIDGE'S *Christabel.*

FARE thee well! and if for ever,
   Still for ever, fare *thee* well:
Even though unforgiving, never
   'Gainst thee shall my heart rebel.
Would that breast were bared before thee
   Where thy head so oft hath lain,
While that placid sleep came o'er thee
   Which thou ne'er canst know again:
Would that breast, by thee glanced over,
   Every inmost thought could show!   10
Then thou would'st at last discover
   'Twas not well to spurn it so.
Though the world for this commend thee—
   Though it smile upon the blow,
Even its praises must offend thee,
   Founded on another's woe:

---

9 On June 14, 1800, Napoleon defeated the Austrians at this village in northern Italy.
10 Roman general of the fifth century B.C., often cited for his simple virtue.

Though my many faults defaced me,
  Could no other arm be found,
Than the one which once embraced me,
  To inflict a cureless wound? 20
Yet, oh yet, thyself deceive not—
  Love may sink by slow decay,
But by sudden wrench, believe not
  Hearts can thus be torn away:
Still thine own its life retaineth—
  Still must mine, though bleeding, beat;
And the undying thought which paineth
  Is—that we no more may meet.
These are words of deeper sorrow
  Than the wail above the dead; 30
Both shall live—but every morrow
  Wake us from a widowed bed.
And when thou would'st solace gather—
  When our child's first accents flow[1]—
Wilt thou teach her to say "Father!"
  Though his care she must forego?
When her little hands shall press thee—
  When her lip to thine is pressed—
Think of him whose prayer shall bless thee—
  Think of him thy love *had* blessed! 40
Should her lineaments resemble
  Those thou never more may'st see,
Then thy heart will softly tremble
  With a pulse yet true to me.
All my faults perchance thou knowest—
  All my madness—none can know;
All my hopes—where'er thou goest—
  Wither—yet with *thee* they go.
Every feeling hath been shaken;
  Pride—which not a world could bow— 50
Bows to thee—by thee forsaken,
  Even my soul forsakes me now.
But 'tis done—all words are idle—
  Words from me are vainer still;
But the thoughts we cannot bridle
  Force their way without the will.
Fare thee well! thus disunited—
  Torn from every nearer tie—
Seared in heart—and lone—and blighted—
  More than this I scarce can die. 60

[1816]   [1816]

---

[1] Augusta Ada, born 1815.

CHILDE HAROLD'S PILGRIMAGE

In Cantos I and II, written in 1809–1810, the melancholy and disillusioned pilgrim visits Portugal, Spain, and Greece in search of an ideal happiness. In Canto IV, after the events that follow in the Canto below, the imaginary pilgrim is abandoned, and the poet speaks directly in his celebration of Italy. Augusta Ada Byron, who is addressed in the first stanza and in the last four, was only one month old when Lady Byron left her husband early in 1816. Byron never saw his daughter again.

  The notes reprinted here are those Byron added to the edition of 1816.

FROM

CHILDE HAROLD'S PILGRIMAGE.

CANTO THE THIRD.

"Afin que cette application vous forçât à penser à autre chose. Il n'y a en vérité de remède que celui-la et le temps."—*Lettres du Roi de Prusse et de M. D'Alembert.*[1]

I.

Is thy face like thy mother's, my fair child!
  ADA! sole daughter of my house and heart?
When last I saw thy young blue eyes they smiled,
And then we parted,—not as now we part,
But with a hope.—
        Awaking with a start,
The waters heave around me; and on high
The winds lift up their voices: I depart,
Whither I know not; but the hour's gone by,
When Albion's lessening shores could grieve or glad
  mine eye.

II.

Once more upon the waters! yet once more!
  And the waves bound beneath me as a steed
That knows his rider. Welcome to their roar!
Swift be their guidance, wheresoe'er it lead!
Though the strained mast should quiver as a reed,
And the rent canvass fluttering strew the gale,
Still must I on; for I am as a weed,
Flung from the rock, on Ocean's foam, to sail
Where'er the surge may sweep, the tempest's breath
  prevail.

---

[1] "In order that this application [of your attention] force you to think of something else. Truly, as a remedy there is only that, and time." The advice of Frederick II of Prussia to Jean d'Alembert, the eighteenth-century philosopher who had lost a close friend.

III.

In my youth's summer I did sing of One,[2]
  The wandering outlaw of his own dark mind;
  Again I seize the theme, then but begun,
  And bear it with me, as the rushing wind
  Bears the cloud onwards: in that Tale I find
  The furrows of long thought, and dried-up tears,
  Which, ebbing, leave a sterile track behind,
  O'er which all heavily the journeying years
Plod the last sands of life,—where not a flower appears.

IV.

Since my young days of passion—joy, or pain—
  Perchance my heart and harp have lost a string—
  And both may jar: it may be, that in vain
  I would essay as I have sung to sing:
  Yet, though a dreary strain, to this I cling;
  So that it wean me from the weary dream
  Of selfish grief or gladness—so it fling
  Forgetfulness around me—it shall seem
To me, though to none else, a not ungrateful theme.

V.

He, who grown agèd in this world of woe,
  In deeds, not years, piercing the depths of life,
  So that no wonder waits him—nor below
  Can Love or Sorrow, Fame, Ambition, Strife,
  Cut to his heart again with the keen knife
  Of silent, sharp endurance—he can tell
  Why Thought seeks refuge in lone caves, yet rife
  With airy images, and shapes which dwell
Still unimpaired, though old, in the Soul's haunted
    cell.

VI.

'Tis to create, and in creating live
  A being more intense that we endow
  With form our fancy, gaining as we give
  The life we image, even as I do now—
  What am I? Nothing: but not so art thou,
  Soul of my thought! with whom I traverse earth,
  Invisible but gazing, as I glow
  Mixed with thy spirit, blended with thy birth,
And feeling still with thee in my crushed feelings'
    dearth.

VII.

Yet must I think less wildly:—I *have* thought
  Too long and darkly, till my brain became,
  In its own eddy boiling and o'erwrought,
  A whirling gulf of phantasy and flame:

² I.e., the Childe Harold of the two earlier cantos.

And thus, untaught in youth my heart to tame,
  My springs of life were poisoned. 'Tis too late!
  Yet am I changed; though still enough the same
  In strength to bear what Time can not abate,
And feed on bitter fruits without accusing Fate.

VIII.

Something too much of this:—but now 'tis past,
  And the spell closes with its silent seal—
  Long absent HAROLD re-appears at last;
  He of the breast which fain no more would feel,
  Wrung with the wounds which kill not, but ne'er
  Yet Time, who changes all, had altered him   [heal;
  In soul and aspect as in age: years steal
  Fire from the mind as vigour from the limb;
And Life's enchanted cup but sparkles near the brim.

IX.

His had been quaffed too quickly, and he found
  The dregs were wormwood; but he filled again,
  And from a purer fount, on holier ground,
  And deemed its spring perpetual—but in vain!
  Still round him clung invisibly a chain
  Which galled for ever, fettering though unseen,
  And heavy though it clanked not; worn with pain,
  Which pined although it spoke not, and grew keen,
Entering with every step he took through many a
    scene.

X.

Secure in guarded coldness, he had mixed
  Again in fancied safety with his kind,
  And deemed his spirit now so firmly fixed
  And sheathed with an invulnerable mind,
  That, if no joy, no sorrow lurked behind;
  And he, as one, might 'midst the many stand
  Unheeded, searching through the crowd to find
  Fit speculation—such as in strange land
He found in wonder-works of God and Nature's hand.

XI.

But who can view the ripened rose, nor seek
  To wear it? who can curiously behold
  The smoothness and the sheen of Beauty's cheek,
  Nor feel the heart can never all grow old?
  Who can contemplate Fame through clouds unfold
  The star which rises o'er her steep, nor climb?
  Harold, once more within the vortex, rolled
  On with the giddy circle, chasing Time,
Yet with a nobler aim than in his Youth's fond prime.

XII.

But soon he knew himself the most unfit
  Of men to herd with Man, with whom he held
  Little in common; untaught to submit
  His thoughts to others, though his soul was quelled

In youth by his own thoughts; still uncompelled,
He would not yield dominion of his mind
To Spirits against whom his own rebelled,
Proud though in desolation—which could find
A life within itself, to breathe without mankind.

XIII.

Where rose the mountains, there to him were friends;
Where rolled the ocean, thereon was his home;
Where a blue sky, and glowing clime, extends,
He had the passion and the power to roam;
The desert, forest, cavern, breaker's foam,
Were unto him companionship; they spake
A mutual language, clearer than the tome
Of his land's tongue, which he would oft forsake
For Nature's pages glassed by sunbeams on the lake.

XIV.

Like the Chaldean,[3] he could watch the stars,
Till he had peopled them with beings bright
As their own beams; and earth, and earth-born jars,
And human frailties, were forgotten quite:
Could he have kept his spirit to that flight
He had been happy; but this clay will sink
Its spark immortal, envying it the light
To which it mounts, as if to break the link
That keeps us from yon heaven which woos us to its
    brink.

XV.

But in Man's dwellings he became a thing
Restless and worn, and stern and wearisome,
Drooped as a wild-born falcon with clipt wing,
To whom the boundless air alone were home:
Then came his fit again, which to o'ercome,
As eagerly the barred-up bird will beat
His breast and beak against his wiry dome
Till the blood tinge his plumage—so the heat
Of his impeded Soul would through his bosom eat.

XVI.

Self-exiled Harold wanders forth again,
With nought of Hope left—but with less of gloom;
The very knowledge that he lived in vain,
That all was over on this side the tomb,
Had made Despair a smilingness assume,   [wreck
Which, though 'twere wild,—as on the plundered
When mariners would madly meet their doom
With draughts intemperate on the sinking deck,—
Did yet inspire a cheer, which he forbore to check.

[3] Ancient Babylonians, to whom occult powers were often ascribed.

XVII.

Stop!—for thy tread is on an Empire's dust!
An Earthquake's spoil is sepulchred below!
Is the spot marked with no colossal bust?
Nor column trophied for triumphal show?
None; but *the moral's truth* tells simpler so.—
As the ground was before, thus let it be;—
How that red rain hath made the harvest grow!
And is this all the world has gained by thee,
Thou first and last of Fields![4] king-making Victory?

XVIII.

And Harold stands upon this place of skulls,
The grave of France, the deadly Waterloo!
How in an hour the Power which gave annuls
Its gifts, transferring fame as fleeting too!—
In "pride of place" here last the Eagle flew,*
Then tore with bloody talon the rent plain,
Pierced by the shaft of banded nations through;
Ambition's life and labours all were vain—
He wears the shattered links of the World's broken
    chain.

XIX.

Fit retribution! Gaul may champ the bit
And foam in fetters;—but is Earth more free?
Did nations combat to make *One* submit?
Or league to teach all Kings true Sovereignty?
What! shall reviving Thraldom again be
The patched-up Idol of enlightened days?
Shall we, who struck the Lion down, shall we
Pay the Wolf homage? proffering lowly gaze
And servile knees to Thrones? No! *prove* before ye
    praise!

XX.

If not, o'er one fallen Despot boast no more!
In vain fair cheeks were furrowed with hot tears
For Europe's flowers long rooted up before
The trampler of her vineyards; in vain, years
Of death, depopulation, bondage, fears,
Have all been borne, and broken by the accord
Of roused-up millions: all that most endears
Glory, is when the myrtle wreathes a Sword,
Such as Harmodius [5] drew on Athens' tyrant Lord.†

* "Pride of place" is a term of falconry, and means the highest pitch of flight. See Macbeth, &c.:—

    "An eagle towering in his pride of place,
        Was by a mousing Owl hawked at and killed."

† See the famous song on Harmodius and Aristogiton. The best English translation is in Bland's Anthology, by Mr. Denman:—

    "With myrtle my sword will I wreathe," &c.

[4] Waterloo, where Wellington and von Blücher defeated Napoleon in June 1815.
[5] One of the assassins of Hipparchus, in Athens of the sixth century B.C.

XXI.

There was a sound of revelry by night,
  And Belgium's Capital had gathered then
  Her Beauty and her Chivalry—and bright
  The lamps shone o'er fair women and brave men;
  A thousand hearts beat happily; and when
  Music arose with its voluptuous swell,
  Soft eyes looked love to eyes which spake again,
  And all went merry as a marriage bell;*
But hush! hark! a deep sound strikes like a rising knell!

XXII.

Did ye not hear it?—No—'twas but the Wind,
  Or the car rattling o'er the stony street;
  On with the dance! let joy be unconfined;
  No sleep till morn, when Youth and Pleasure meet
  To chase the glowing Hours with flying feet—
  But hark!—that heavy sound breaks in once more,
  As if the clouds its echo would repeat;
  And nearer—clearer—deadlier than before!
Arm! Arm! it is—it is—the cannon's opening roar!

XXIII.

Within a windowed niche of that high hall
  Sate Brunswick's fated Chieftain;[7] he did hear
  That sound the first amidst the festival,
  And caught its tone with Death's prophetic ear;
  And when they smiled because he deemed it near,
  His heart more truly knew that peal too well
  Which stretched his father on a bloody bier,
  And roused the vengeance blood alone could quell;
He rushed into the field, and, foremost fighting, fell.

XXIV.

Ah! then and there was hurrying to and fro—
  And gathering tears, and tremblings of distress,
  And cheeks all pale, which but an hour ago
  Blushed at the praise of their own loveliness—
  And there were sudden partings, such as press
  The life from out young hearts, and choking sighs
  Which ne'er might be repeated; who could guess
  If ever more should meet those mutual eyes,
Since upon night so sweet such awful morn could rise!

XXV.

And there was mounting in hot haste—the steed,
  The mustering squadron, and the clattering car,
  Went pouring forward with impetuous speed,
  And swiftly forming in the ranks of war—

---

* On the night previous to the action, it is said that a ball was given at Brussels.[6]

6 The ball given by the Duchess of Richmond on June 14, 1815, is a central event in Thackeray's *Vanity Fair* as well.
7 The Duke of Brunswick was one of the first nobles to be killed in the battle.

And the deep thunder peal on peal afar;
  And near, the beat of the alarming drum
  Roused up the soldier ere the Morning Star;
  While thronged the citizens with terror dumb,
Or whispering, with white lips—"The foe! They
  come! they come!"

XXVI.

And wild and high the "Cameron's Gathering" rose!
  The war-note of Lochiel, which Albyn's hills
  Have heard, and heard, too, have her Saxon foes:—
  How in the noon of night that pibroch thrills,
  Savage and shrill! But with the breath which fills
  Their mountain-pipe, so fill the mountaineers
  With the fierce native daring which instils
  The stirring memory of a thousand years,
And Evan's—Donald's fame rings in each clansman's
  ears!†

XXVII.

And Ardennes waves above them her green leaves,‡
  Dewy with Nature's tear-drops, as they pass—
  Grieving, if aught inanimate e'er grieves,
  Over the unreturning brave,—alas!
  Ere evening to be trodden like the grass
  Which now beneath them, but above shall grow
  In its next verdure, when this fiery mass
  Of living Valour, rolling on the foe
And burning with high Hope, shall moulder cold and
  low.

XXVIII.

Last noon beheld them full of lusty life;—
  Last eve in Beauty's circle proudly gay;
  The Midnight brought the signal-sound of strife,
  The Morn the marshalling in arms,—the Day
  Battle's magnificently-stern array!
  The thunder-clouds close o'er it, which when rent
  The earth is covered thick with other clay
  Which her own clay shall cover, heaped and pent,
Rider and horse,—friend,—foe,—in one red burial
  blent!

---

† Sir Evan Cameron, and his descendant Donald, the "gentle Lochiel" of the "forty-five."[8]

‡ The wood of Soignies is supposed to be a remanant of the "forest of Ardennes," famous in Boiardo's Orlando, and immortal in Shakespeare's "As You Like It." It is also celebrated in Tacitus as being the spot of successful defence by the Germans against the Roman encroachments.—I have ventured to adopt the name connected with nobler associations than those of mere slaughter.

8 John Cameron, son of Donald, greatgrandson of Evan, was one of a series of the clan's chieftains to fight in a major battle. John was killed at Waterloo.

XXIX.

Their praise is hymned by loftier harps than mine;
   Yet one I would select from that proud throng,
   Partly because they blend me with his line,
   And partly that I did his Sire some wrong,
   And partly that bright names will hallow song;[9]
   And his was of the bravest, and when showered
   The death-bolts deadliest the thinned files along,
   Even where the thickest of War's tempest lowered,
They reached no nobler breast than thine, young,
   gallant Howard!

XXX.

There have been tears and breaking hearts for thee,
   And mine were nothing, had I such to give;
   But when I stood beneath the fresh green tree,
   Which living waves where thou didst cease to live,
   And saw around me the wide field revive
   With fruits and fertile promise, and the Spring
   Come forth her work of gladness to contrive,
   With all her reckless birds upon the wing,
I turned from all she brought to those she could not
   bring.*

XXXI.

I turned to thee, to thousands, of whom each
   And one as all a ghastly gap did make
   In his own kind and kindred, whom to teach
   Forgetfulness were mercy for their sake;

* My guide from Mount St. Jean over the field seemed intelligent and accurate. The place where Major Howard fell was not far from two tall and solitary trees (there was a third cut down, or shivered in the battle), which stand a few yards from each other at a pathway's side. Beneath these he died and was buried. The body has since been removed to England. A small hollow for the present marks where it lay, but will probably soon be effaced; the plough has been upon it, and the grain is. After pointing out the different spots where Picton and other gallant men had perished, the guide said, "Here Major Howard lay: I was near him when wounded." I told him my relationship, and he seemed then still more anxious to point out the particular spot and circumstances. The place is one of the most marked in the field, from the peculiarity of the two trees above mentioned. I went on horseback twice over the field, comparing it with my recollection of similar scenes. As a plain, Waterloo seems marked out for the scene of some great action, though this may be mere imagination: I have viewed with attention those of Platea, Troy, Mantinea, Leuctra, Chæronea, and Marathon: and the field around Mount St. Jean and Hougoumont appears to want little but a better cause, and that undefinable but impressive halo which the lapse of ages throws around a celebrated spot, to vie in interest with any or all of these, except, perhaps, the last mentioned.

<hr />

[9] The reference is to Major Frederick Howard, killed at Waterloo, whose father, the Earl of Carlisle, Byron's guardian, was attacked in *English Bards and Scotch Reviewers*, p. 549.

The Archangel's trump, not Glory's, must awake
Those whom they thirst for; though the sound of
   May for a moment soothe, it cannot slake   [Fame
   The fever of vain longing, and the name
So honoured but assumes a stronger, bitterer claim.

XXXII.

They mourn, but smile at length—and, smiling,
   The tree will wither long before it fall;   [mourn:
   The hull drives on, though mast and sail be torn;
   The roof-tree sinks, but moulders on the hall
   In massy hoariness; the ruined wall
   Stands when its wind-worn battlements are gone;
   The bars survive the captive they enthral;   [sun;
   The day drags through though storms keep out the
And thus the heart will break, yet brokenly live on:

XXXIII.

Even as a broken Mirror, which the glass
   In every fragment multiplies—and makes
   A thousand images of one that was,
   The same—and still the more, the more it breaks;
   And thus the heart will do which not forsakes,
   Living in shattered guise; and still, and cold,
   And bloodless, with its sleepless sorrow aches,
   Yet withers on till all without is old,
Showing no visible sign, for such things are untold.

XXXIV.

There is a very life in our despair,
   Vitality of poison,—a quick root
   Which feeds these deadly branches; for it were
   As nothing did we die; but Life will suit
   Itself to Sorrow's most detested fruit,
   Like to the apples on the Dead Sea's shore,†
   All ashes to the taste: Did man compute
   Existence by enjoyment, and count o'er
Such hours 'gainst years of life,—say, would he name
   threescore?

XXXV.

The Psalmist numbered out the years of man:
   They are enough; and if thy tale be *true*,
   Thou, who didst grudge him even that fleeting span,
   More than enough, thou fatal Waterloo!
   Millions of tongues record thee, and anew
   Their children's lips shall echo them, and say—
   "Here, where the sword united nations drew,
   Our countrymen were warring on that day!"
And this is much—and all—which will not pass away.

† The (fabled) apples on the brink of the lake Asphaltes were said to be fair without, and within, ashes. Vide Tacitus, Histor. l. 5.7.

XXXVI.

There sunk the greatest, nor the worst of men,
  Whose Spirit, antithetically mixed,
One moment of the mightiest, and again
  On little objects with like firmness fixed;
  Extreme in all things! hadst thou been betwixt,
Thy throne had still been thine, or never been;
  For Daring made thy rise as fall: thou seek'st
Even now to re-assume the imperial mien,
And shake again the world, the Thunderer of the
    scene![10]

XXXVII.

Conqueror and Captive of the Earth art thou!
  She trembles at thee still, and thy wild name
Was ne'er more bruited in men's minds than now
  That thou art nothing, save the jest of Fame,
  Who wooed thee once, thy Vassal, and became
The flatterer of thy fierceness—till thou wert
  A God unto thyself; nor less the same
To the astounded kingdoms all inert,
Who deemed thee for a time whate'er thou didst
    assert.

XXXVIII.

Oh, more or less than man—in high or low—
  Battling with nations, flying from the field;
Now making monarchs' necks thy footstool, now
  More than thy meanest soldier taught to yield;
  An Empire thou couldst crush, command, rebuild,
But govern not thy pettiest passion, nor,
  However deeply in men's spirits skilled,
Look through thine own, nor curb the lust of War,
Nor learn that tempted Fate will leave the loftiest
    Star.

XXXIX.

Yet well thy soul hath brooked the turning tide
  With that untaught innate philosophy,
Which, be it Wisdom, Coldness, or deep Pride,
  Is gall and wormwood to an enemy.
  When the whole host of hatred stood hard by,
To watch and mock thee shrinking, thou hast
  With a sedate and all-enduring eye;—   [smiled
When Fortune fled her spoiled and favorite child,
He stood unbowed beneath the ills upon him piled.

XL.

Sager than in thy fortunes; for in them
  Ambition steeled thee on too far to show
That just habitual scorn, which could contemn
  Men and their thoughts; 'twas wise to feel, not so

To wear it ever on thy lip and brow,
  And spurn the instruments thou wert to use
Till they were turned unto thine overthrow:
  'Tis but a worthless world to win or lose;
So hath it proved to thee, and all such lot who choose.

XLI.

If, like a tower upon a headlong rock,
  Thou hadst been made to stand or fall alone,
  Such scorn of man had helped to brave the shock;
But men's thoughts were the steps which paved thy
  Their admiration thy best weapon shone;   [throne,
  The part of Philip's son was thine,[11] not then
  (Unless aside thy Purple had been thrown)
Like stern Diogenes to mock at men—
For sceptred Cynics Earth were far too wide a den.*

XLII.

But Quiet to quick bosoms is a Hell,
  And *there* hath been thy bane; there is a fire
  And motion of the Soul which will not dwell
In its own narrow being, but aspire
  Beyond the fitting medium of desire;
  And, but once kindled, quenchless evermore,
Preys upon high adventure, nor can tire
  Of aught but rest; a fever at the core,
Fatal to him who bears, to all who ever bore.

XLIII.

This makes the madmen who have made men mad
  By their contagion; Conquerors and Kings,
  Founders of sects and systems, to whom add
Sophists, Bards, Statesmen, all unquiet things
  Which stir too strongly the soul's secret springs,
  And are themselves the fools to those they fool;
Envied, yet how unenviable! what stings
  Are theirs! One breast laid open were a school
Which would unteach Mankind the lust to shine or
    rule:

* The great error of Napoleon, "if we have writ our annals true," was a continued obtrusion on mankind of his want of all community of feeling for or with them; perhaps more offensive to human vanity than the active cruelty of more trembling and suspicious tyranny. Such were his speeches to public assemblies as well as individuals; and the single expression which he is said to have used on returning to Paris after the Russian winter had destroyed his army, rubbing his hands over a fire, "This is pleasanter than Moscow," would probably alienate more favour from his cause than the destruction and reverses which led to the remark.

[11] Alexander the Great, son of Philip of Macedon, conquered and ruled Greece, Egypt, and the Persian Empire in the fourth century B.C.

[10] Napoleon, who in 1815 was banished by the British to the island of St. Helena.

XLIV.

Their breath is agitation, and their life
    A storm whereon they ride, to sink at last,
    And yet so nursed and bigoted to strife,
    That should their days, surviving perils past,
    Melt to calm twilight, they feel overcast
    With sorrow and supineness, and so die;
    Even as a flame unfed, which runs to waste
    With its own flickering, or a sword laid by,
Which eats into itself, and rusts ingloriously.

XLV.

He who ascends to mountain-tops, shall find
    The loftiest peaks most wrapt in clouds and snow;
    He who surpasses or subdues mankind,
    Must look down on the hate of those below.
    Though high *above* the Sun of Glory glow,
    And far *beneath* the Earth and Ocean spread,
    Round him are icy rocks, and loudly blow
    Contending tempests on his naked head,
And thus reward the toils which to those summits led.

XLVI.

Away with these! true Wisdom's world will be
    Within its own creation, or in thine,
    Maternal Nature! for who teems like thee,
    Thus on the banks of thy majestic Rhine?
    There Harold gazes on a work divine,
    A blending of all beauties; streams and dells,
    Fruit, foliage, crag, wood, cornfield, mountain, vine,
    And chiefless castles breathing stern farewells
From gray but leafy walls, where Ruin greenly dwells.

XLVII.

And there they stand, as stands a lofty mind,
    Worn, but unstooping to the baser crowd,
    All tenantless, save to the crannying Wind,
    Or holding dark communion with the Cloud
    There was a day when they were young and proud;
    Banners on high, and battles [12] passed below;
    But they who fought are in a bloody shroud,
    And those which waved are shredless dust ere now,
And the bleak battlements shall bear no future blow.

XLVIII.

Beneath these battlements, within those walls,
    Power dwelt amidst her passions; in proud state
    Each robber chief upheld his arméd halls,
    Doing his evil will, nor less elate

---

[12] Battalions.

Than mightier heroes of a longer date.
    What want these outlaws conquerors should have*
    But History's purchased page to call them great?
    A wider space—an ornamented grave?
Their hopes were not less warm, their souls were full
    as brave.

XLIX.

In their baronial feuds and single fields,
    What deeds of prowess unrecorded died!
    And Love, which lent a blazon to their shields,
    With emblems well devised by amorous pride,
    Through all the mail of iron hearts would glide;
    But still their flame was fierceness, and drew on
    Keen contest and destruction near allied,
    And many a tower for some fair mischief won,
Saw the discoloured Rhine beneath its ruin run.

L.

But Thou, exulting and abounding river!
    Making thy waves a blessing as they flow
    Through banks whose beauty would endure for ever
    Could man but leave thy bright creation so,
    Nor its fair promise from the surface mow
    With the sharp scythe of conflict,—then to see
    Thy valley of sweet waters, were to know
    Earth paved like Heaven—and to seem such to me,
Even now what wants thy stream?—that it should
    Lethe be.

LI.

A thousand battles have assailed thy banks,
    But these and half their fame have passed away,
    And Slaughter heaped on high his weltering ranks:
    Their very graves are gone, and what are they?
    Thy tide washed down the blood of yesterday,
    And all was stainless, and on thy clear stream
    Glassed, with its dancing light, the sunny ray;
    But o'er the blacken'd memory's blighting dream
Thy waves would vainly roll, all sweeping as they
    seem.

LII.

Thus Harold inly said, and passed along,
    Yet not insensible to all which here
    Awoke the jocund birds to early song
    In glens which might have made even exile dear:
    Though on his brow were graven lines austere,
    And tranquil sternness, which had ta'en the place
    Of feelings fiercer far but less severe—
    Joy was not always absent from his face,
But o'er it in such scenes would steal with transient
    trace.

> * "What wants that knave
>   That a king should have?"

was King James's question on meeting Johnny Armstrong and
his followers in full accoutrements.—See the Ballad.

LIII.

Nor was all Love shut from him, though his days
　　Of Passion had consumed themselves to dust.
　　It is in vain that we would coldly gaze
　　On such as smile upon us; the heart must
　　Leap kindly back to kindness, though Disgust
　　Hath weaned it from all worldlings: thus he felt,
　　For there was soft Remembrance, and sweet Trust
In one fond breast, to which his own would melt,
And in its tenderer hour on that his bosom dwelt.[13]

LIV.

And he had learned to love,—I know not why,
　　For this in such as him seems strange of mood,—
　　The helpless looks of blooming Infancy,
　　Even in its earliest nurture; what subdued,
　　To change like this, a mind so far imbued
　　With scorn of man, it little boots to know;
　　But thus it was; and though in solitude
Small power the nipped affections have to grow,
In him this glowed when all beside had ceased to glow.

LV.

And there was one soft breast, as hath been said,
　　Which unto his was bound by stronger ties
　　Than the church links withal; and—though unwed,
　　That love was pure—and, far above disguise,
　　Had stood the test of mortal enmities
　　Still undivided, and cemented more
　　By peril, dreaded most in female eyes;
But this was firm, and from a foreign shore
Well to that heart might his these absent greetings
　　pour!

I.

The castled Crag of Drachenfels*
　　Frowns o'er the wide and winding Rhine,
　　Whose breast of waters broadly swells
　　Between the banks which bear the vine,
　　And hills all rich with blossomed trees,
　　And fields which promise corn and wine,
　　And scattered cities crowning these,
　　Whose far white walls along them shine,
　　Have strewed a scene, which I should see
　　With double joy wert *thou* with me.

* The castle of Drachenfels stands on the highest summit of
"the Seven Mountains," over the Rhine banks; it is in ruins, and
connected with some singular traditions. It is the first in view
of the road from Bonn, but on the opposite side of the river;[14]
on this bank, nearly facing it, are the remains of another, called
the Jew's Castle, and a large cross, commemorative of the
murder of a chief by his brother. The number of castles and
cities along the course of the Rhine on both sides is very great,
and their situations remarkably beautiful.

[13] Apparently a reference to Byron's half sister Augusta Leigh.
See his journal-letter to her, p. 767.
[14] It is on the right bank between Remagen and Bonn.

2.

And peasant girls, with deep blue eyes,
　　And hands which offer early flowers,
　　Walk smiling o'er this Paradise;
　　Above, the frequent feudal towers
　　Through green leaves lift their walls of gray;
　　And many a rock which steeply lowers,
　　And noble arch in proud decay,
　　Look o'er this vale of vintage-bowers;
　　But one thing want these banks of Rhine,—
　　Thy gentle hand to clasp in mine!

3.

I send the lilies given to me—
　　Though long before thy hand they touch,
　　I know that they must withered be,
　　But yet reject them not as such;
　　For I have cherished them as dear,
　　Because they yet may meet thine eye,
　　And guide thy soul to mine even here,
　　When thou behold'st them drooping nigh,
　　And know'st them gathered by the Rhine,
　　And offered from my heart to thine!

4.

The river nobly foams and flows—
　　The charm of this enchanted ground,
　　And all its thousand turns disclose
　　Some fresher beauty varying round:
　　The haughtiest breast its wish might bound
　　Through life to dwell delighted here;
　　Nor could on earth a spot be found
　　To Nature and to me so dear—
　　Could thy dear eyes in following mine
　　Still sweeten more these banks of Rhine!

LVI.

By Coblentz, on a rise of gentle ground,
　　There is a small and simple Pyramid,
　　Crowning the summit of the verdant mound;
　　Beneath its base are Heroes' ashes hid—
　　Our enemy's—but let not that forbid
　　Honour to Marceau![15] o'er whose early tomb
　　Tears, big tears, gushed from the rough soldier's
　　Lamenting and yet envying such a doom,　　[lid,
Falling for France, whose rights he battled to resume.

LVII.

Brief, brave, and glorious was his young career,—
　　His mourners were two hosts, his friends and foes;
　　And fitly may the stranger lingering here
　　Pray for his gallant Spirit's bright repose;—

[15] General Francois Marceau, of the French Republican
Army, killed on the Rhine in 1796, near the fortress of Ehren-
breitstein.

For he was Freedom's Champion, one of those,
  The few in number, who had not o'erstept
  The charter to chastise which she bestows
  On such as wield her weapons; he had kept
The whiteness of his soul—and thus men o'er him
    wept. *

LVIII.

Here Ehrenbreitstein, with her shattered wall†
  Black with the miner's blast, upon her height
  Yet shows of what she was, when shell and ball
  Rebounding idly on her strength did light:—
A Tower of Victory! from whence the flight
  Of baffled foes was watched along the plain:
  But Peace destroyed what War could never blight,
  And laid those proud roofs bare to Summer's rain—
On which the iron shower for years had poured in vain.

LIX.

Adieu to thee, fair Rhine! How long delighted
  The stranger fain would linger on his way!
  Thine is a scene alike where souls united
  Or lonely Contemplation thus might stray;
And could the ceaseless vultures cease to prey
  On self-condemning bosoms, it were here,
  Where Nature, nor too sombre nor too gay,
  Wild but not rude, awful yet not austere,
Is to the mellow Earth as Autumn to the year.

* The monument of the young and lamented General Marceau (killed by a rifle-ball at Alterkirchen on the last day of the fourth year of the French republic) still remains as described.

The inscriptions on his monument are rather too long, and not required: his name was enough; France adored, and her enemies admired; both wept over him.—His funeral was attended by the generals and detachments from both armies. In the same grave General Hoche is interred, a gallant man also in every sense of the word; but though he distinguished himself greatly in battle, *he* had not the good fortune to die there: his death was attended by suspicions of poison.

A separate monument (not over his body, which is buried by Marceau's) is raised for him near Andernach, opposite to which one of his most memorable exploits was performed, in throwing a bridge to an island on the Rhine. The shape and style are different from that of Marceau's, and the inscription more simple and pleasing:—"The Army of the Sambre and Meuse / to its Commander-in-Chief / Hoche."

This is all, and as it should be. Hoche was esteemed among the first of France's earlier generals, before Buonaparte monopolised her triumphs. He was the destined commander of the invading army of Ireland.

† Ehrenbreitstein, *i.e.* "the broad Stone of Honour," one of the strongest fortresses in Europe, was dismantled and blown up by the French at the truce of Leoben.—It had been, and could only be, reduced by famine or treachery. It yielded to the former, aided by surprise. After having seen the fortifications of Gibraltar and Malta, it did not much strike by comparison; but the situation is commanding. General Marceau besieged it in vain for some time, and I slept in a room where I was shown a window at which he is said to have been standing observing the progress of the siege by moonlight, when a ball struck immediately below it.

LX.

Adieu to thee again! a vain adieu!
  There can be no farewell to scene like thine;
  The mind is coloured by thy every hue;
  And if reluctantly the eyes resign
  Their cherished gaze upon thee, lovely Rhine!
'Tis with the thankful glance of parting praise;
  More mighty spots may rise—more glaring shine,
  But none unite in one attaching maze
The brilliant, fair, and soft,—the glories of old days,

LXI.

The negligently grand, the fruitful bloom
  Of coming ripeness, the white city's sheen,
  The rolling stream, the precipice's gloom,
  The forest's growth, and Gothic walls between,—
  The wild rocks shaped, as they had turrets been,
In mockery of man's art; and these withal
  A race of faces happy as the scene,
  Whose fertile bounties here extend to all,
Still springing o'er thy banks, though Empires near
    them fall.

LXII.

But these recede. Above me are the Alps,
  The Palaces of Nature, whose vast walls
  Have pinnacled in clouds their snowy scalps,
  And throned Eternity in icy halls
  Of cold Sublimity, where forms and falls
The Avalanche—the thunderbolt of snow!
  All that expands the spirit, yet appals,
  Gather around these summits, as to show
How Earth may pierce to Heaven, yet leave vain man
    below.

LXIII.

But ere these matchless heights I dare to scan,
  There is a spot should not be passed in vain,—
  Morat! the proud, the patriot field![16] where man
  May gaze on ghastly trophies of the slain,
  Nor blush for those who conquered on that plain;
Here Burgundy bequeathed his tombless host,
  A bony heap, through ages to remain,
  Themselves their monument;—the Stygian coast
Unsepulchred they roamed, and shrieked each
    wandering ghost.‡

‡ The chapel is destroyed, and the pyramid of bones diminished to a small number by the Burgundian legion in the service of France; who anxiously effaced this record of their ancestors' less successful invasions. A few still remain, notwithstanding the pains taken by the Burgundians for ages (all who passed that way removing a bone to their own country), and the less

[16] In 1476 the Swiss defeated the Burgundians under Charles the Rash here, and that battle—like Marathon (fifth century B.C.) but unlike Waterloo and Cannae (third century B.C.)—was a significant victory in a righteous cause.

LXIV.

While Waterloo with Cannæ's carnage vies,
   Morat and Marathon twin names shall stand;
   They were true Glory's stainless victories,
   Won by the unambitious heart and hand
   Of a proud, brotherly, and civic band,
   All unbought champions in no princely cause
   Of vice-entailed Corruption; they no land
   Doomed to bewail the blasphemy of laws
Making King's rights divine, by some Draconic [17]
   clause.

LXV.

By a lone wall a lonelier column rears
   A gray and grief-worn aspect of old days;
   'Tis the last remnant of the wreck of years,
   And looks as with the wild-bewildered gaze
   Of one to stone converted by amaze,
   Yet still with consciousness; and there it stands
   Making a marvel that it not decays,
   When the coeval pride of human hands,
Levelled Aventicum—hath strewed her subject
   lands. *

LXVI.

And there—oh! sweet and sacred be the name!—
   Julia—the daughter—the devoted—gave
   Her youth to Heaven; her heart, beneath a claim
   Nearest to Heaven's, broke o'er a father's grave.
   Justice is sworn 'gainst tears, and hers would crave
   The life she lived in—but the Judge was just—
   And then she died on him she could not save.
   Their tomb was simple, and without a bust,
And held within their urn one mind—one heart—one
   dust. †

LXVII.

But these are deeds which should not pass away,
   And names that must not wither, though the Earth
   Forgets her empires with a just decay,
   The enslavers and the enslaved—their death and
   The high, the mountain-majesty of Worth   [birth;
   Should be—and shall, survivor of its owe,
   And from its immortality, look forth
   In the sun's face, like yonder Alpine snow, ‡
Imperishably pure beyond all things below.

LXVIII.

Lake Leman woos me with its crystal face,
   The mirror where the stars and mountains view
   The stillness of their aspect in each trace
   Its clear depth yields of their far height and hue:
   There is too much of Man here, to look through
   With a fit mind the might which I behold;
   But soon in me shall Loneliness renew
   Thoughts hid, but not less cherished than of old,
Ere mingling with the herd had penned me in their
   fold.

LXIX.

To fly from, need not be to hate, mankind:
   All are not fit with them to stir and toil,
   Nor is it discontent to keep the mind
   Deep in its fountain, lest it overboil
   In the hot throng, where we become the spoil
   Of our infection, till too late and long
   We may deplore and struggle with the coil,
   In wretched interchange of wrong for wrong
Midst a contentious world, striving where none are
   strong.

LXX.

There, in a moment, we may plunge our years
   In fatal penitence, and in the blight
   Of our own Soul turn all our blood to tears,
   And colour things to come with hues of Night;
   The race of life becomes a hopeless flight
   To those that walk in darkness: on the sea
   The boldest steer but where their ports invite—
   But there are wanderers o'er Eternity
Whose bark drives on and on, and anchored ne'er
   shall be.

---

justifiable larcenies of the Swiss postilions, who carried them off to sell for knife-handles; a purpose for which the whiteness imbibed by the bleaching of years had rendered them in great request. Of these relics I ventured to bring away as much as may have made a quarter of a hero, for which the sole excuse is, that if I had not, the next passer-by might have perverted them to worse uses than the careful preservation which I intend for them.

   * Aventicum (near Morat) was the Roman capital of Helvitia, where Avenches now stands.

   † Julia Alpinula, a young Aventian priestess, died soon after a vain endeavour to save her father, condemned to death as a traitor by Aulus Cæcina. Her epitaph was discovered many years ago;—it is thus:— / Julia Alpinula / Hic jaceo. / Infelicis patris, infelix proles / Deæ Aventiæ Sacerdos / Exorare patris necem non potui / Male mori in fatis ille erat / Vixi annos XXIII / —I know of no human composition so affecting as this, nor a history of deeper interest. These are the names and actions which ought not to perish, and to which we turn with a true and healthy tenderness, from the wretched and glittering detail of a confused mass of conquests and battles, with which the mind is

roused for a time to a false and feverish sympathy, from whence it recurs at length with all the nausea consequent on such intoxication. [18]

   ‡ This is written in the eye of Mont Blanc (June 3d, 1816) which even at this distance dazzles mine. (July 20th.) I this day observed for some time the distinct reflection of Mont Blanc and Mont Argentiere in the calm of the lake, which I was crossing in my boat; the distance of these mountains from their mirror is 60 miles.

   [17] After the Athenian Draco; used for a law of unusual harshness.

   [18] The inscription quoted by Byron is actually a sixteenth-century forgery.

LXXI.

Is it not better, then, to be alone,
　　And love Earth only for its earthly sake?
　　By the blue rushing of the arrowy Rhone,*
　　Or the pure bosom of its nursing Lake,[19]
　　Which feeds it as a mother who doth make
　　A fair but froward infant her own care,
　　Kissing its cries away as these awake;—
　　Is it not better thus our lives to wear,
Than join the crushing crowd, doomed to inflict or
　　bear?

LXXII.

I live not in myself, but I become
　　Portion of that around me; and to me
　　High mountains are a feeling, but the hum
　　Of human cities torture: I can see
　　Nothing to loathe in Nature, save to be
　　A link reluctant in a fleshly chain,
　　Classed among creatures, when the soul can flee,
　　And with the sky—the peak—the heaving plain
Of Ocean, or the stars, mingle—and not in vain.

LXXIII.

And thus I am absorbed, and this is life:—
　　I look upon the peopled desert past,
　　As on a place of agony and strife,
　　Where, for some sin, to Sorrow I was cast,
　　To act and suffer, but remount at last
　　With a fresh pinion; which I feel to spring,
　　Though young, yet waxing vigorous as the Blast
　　Which it would cope with, on delighted wing,
Spurning the clay-cold bonds which round our being
　　cling.

LXXIV.

And when, at length, the mind shall be all free
　　From what it hates in this degraded form,
　　Reft of its carnal life, save what shall be
　　Existent happier in the fly and worm,—
　　When Elements to Elements conform,
　　And dust is as it should be, shall I not
　　Feel all I see less dazzling but more warm?
　　The bodiless thought? the Spirit of each spot?
Of which, even now, I share at times the immortal lot?

LXXV.

Are not the mountains, waves, and skies, a part
　　Of me and of my Soul, as I of them?
　　Is not the love of these deep in my heart
　　With a pure passion? should I not contemn

All objects, if compared with these? and stem
　　A tide of suffering, rather than forego
　　Such feelings for the hard and worldly phlegm
　　Of those whose eyes are only turned below,
Gazing upon the ground, with thoughts which dare
　　not glow?

LXXVI.

But this is not my theme; and I return
　　To that which is immediate, and require
　　Those who find contemplation in the urn,
　　To look on One, whose dust was once all fire,—
　　A native of the land where I respire
　　The clear air for a while—a passing guest,
　　Where he became a being,—whose desire
　　Was to be glorious; 'twas a foolish quest,
The which to gain and keep, he sacrificed all rest.

LXXVII.

Here the self-torturing sophist, wild Rousseau,[20]
　　The apostle of Affliction, he who threw
　　Enchantment over Passion, and from Woe
　　Wrung overwhelming eloquence, first drew
　　The breath which made him wretched; yet he knew
　　How to make Madness beautiful, and cast
　　O'er erring deeds and thoughts, a heavenly hue
　　Of words, like sunbeams, dazzling as they past
The eyes, which o'er them shed tears feelingly and
　　fast.

LXXVIII.

His love was Passion's essence—as a tree
　　On fire by lightning; with ethereal flame
　　Kindled he was, and blasted; for to be
　　Thus, and enamoured, were in him the same.
　　But his was not the love of living dame,
　　Nor of the dead who rise upon our dreams,
　　But of ideal Beauty, which became
　　In him existence, and o'erflowing teems
Along his burning page, distempered though it seems.

LXXIX.

This breathed itself to life in Julie,[21] *this*
　　Invested her with all that's wild and sweet;
　　This hallowed, too, the memorable kiss†
　　Which every morn his fevered lip would greet,

† This refers to the account in his "Confessions" of his
passion for the Comtesse d'Houdetot (the mistress of St.
Lambert) and his long walk every morning for the sake of the
single kiss which was the common salutation of French acquain-
tance.—Rousseau's description of his feelings on this occasion

* The colour of the Rhone at Geneva is *blue*, to a depth of
tint which I have never seen equalled in water, salt or fresh,
except in the Mediterranean and Archipelago.

[19] Geneva.

[20] The French novelist and philosopher Jean Jacques Rousseau
(1712–1778), born at Geneva, is used by Byron as the counter-
point to Napoleon throughout this part of Canto III. His work is
also seen as part of the inspiration for the Revolution.
[21] Rousseau's *Julie: ou, la Nouvelle Héloïse* (1761).

From hers, who but with friendship his would
    meet;
But to that gentle touch, through brain and breast
Flashed the thrilled Spirit's love-devouring heat;
In that absorbing sigh perchance more blest
Than vulgar minds may be with all they seek possest.

LXXX.

His life was one long war with self-sought foes,
    Or friends by him self-banished; for his mind
    Had grown Suspicion's sanctuary, and chose,
    For its own cruel sacrifice, the kind,
    'Gainst whom he raged with fury strange and blind.
    But he was phrensied,—wherefore, who may know?
    Since cause might be which Skill could never find;
    But he was phrensied by disease or woe,
To that worst pitch of all, which wears a reasoning
    show.

LXXXI.

For then he was inspired, and from him came,
    As from the Pythian's mystic cave of yore,[22]
    Those oracles which set the world in flame,
    Nor ceased to burn till kingdoms were no more:
    Did he not this for France? which lay before
    Bowed to the inborn tyranny of years?
    Broken and trembling to the yoke she bore,
    Till by the voice of him and his compeers,
Roused up to too much wrath which follows o'ergrown
    fears?

LXXXII.

They made themselves a fearful monument!
    The wreck of old opinions—things which grew,
    Breathed from the birth of Time: the veil they rent,
    And what behind it lay, all earth shall view.
    But good with ill they also overthrew,
    Leaving but ruins, wherewith to rebuild
    Upon the same foundation, and renew   [refilled,
    Dungeons and thrones, which the same hour
As heretofore, because Ambition was self-willed.

LXXXIII.

But this will not endure, nor be endured!
    Mankind have felt their strength, and made it felt.
    They might have used it better, but, allured
    By their new vigour, sternly have they dealt

On one another; Pity ceased to melt
    With her once natural charities. But they,
    Who in Oppression's darkness caved had dwelt,
    They were not eagles, nourished with the day;
What marvel then, at times, if they mistook their
    prey?

LXXXIV.

What deep wounds ever closed without a scar?
    The heart's bleed longest, and but heal to wear
    That which disfigures it; and they who war
    With their own hopes, and have been vanquished,
    Silence, but not submission: in his lair   [bear
    Fixed Passion holds his breath, until the hour
    Which shall atone for years; none need despair:
    It came—it cometh—and will come,—the power
To punish or forgive—in *one* we shall be slower.

LXXXV.

Clear, placid Leman! thy contrasted lake,
    With the wild world I dwelt in, is a thing
    Which warns me, with its stillness, to forsake
    Earth's troubled waters for a purer spring.
    This quiet sail is as a noiseless wing
    To waft me from distraction; once I loved
    Torn Ocean's roar, but thy soft murmuring
    Sounds sweet as if a Sister's voice reproved,
That I with stern delights should e'er have been so
    moved.

LXXXVI.

It is the hush of night, and all between
    Thy margin and the mountains, dusk, yet clear,
    Mellowed and mingling, yet distinctly seen,
    Save darkened Jura,[23] whose capt heights appear
    Precipitously steep; and drawing near,
    There breathes a living fragrance from the shore,
    Of flowers yet fresh with childhood; on the ear
    Drops the light drip of the suspended oar,
Or chirps the grasshopper one good-night carol more.

LXXXVII.

He is an evening reveller, who makes
    His life an infancy, and sings his fill;
    At intervals, some bird from out the brakes
    Starts into voice a moment, then is still.
    There seems a floating whisper on the hill,
    But that is fancy—for the Starlight dews
    All silently their tears of Love instil,
    Weeping themselves away, till they infuse
Deep into Nature's breast the spirit of her hues.

---

may be considered as the most passionate, yet not impure,
description and expression of love that ever kindled into words;
which, after all, must be felt, from their very force, to be inade-
quate to the delineation; a painting can give no sufficient idea
of the ocean.

[22] The home of the oracles in the temple of Apollo at Delphi.

[23] A mountain range extending two hundred miles along the French-Swiss border.

LXXXVIII.

Ye Stars! which are the poetry of Heaven!
  If in your bright leaves we would read the fate
  Of men and empires,—'tis to be forgiven,
  That in our aspirations to be great,
  Our destinies o'erleap their mortal state,
  And claim a kindred with you; for ye are
  A Beauty and a Mystery, and create
  In us such love and reverence from afar,
That Fortune,—Fame,—Power,—Life, have named
    themselves a Star.

LXXXIX.

All Heaven and Earth are still—though not in sleep,
  But breathless, as we grow when feeling most;
  And silent, as we stand in thoughts too deep:—
  All Heaven and Earth are still: From the high host
  Of stars, to the lulled lake and mountain-coast,
  All is concentered in a life intense,
  Where not a beam, nor air, nor leaf is lost,
  But hath a part of Being, and a sense
Of that which is of all Creator and Defence.

XC.

Then stirs the feeling infinite, so felt
  In solitude, where we are *least* alone;
  A truth, which through our being then doth melt,
  And purifies from self: it is a tone,
  The soul and source of Music, which makes known
  Eternal harmony, and sheds a charm
  Like to the fabled Cytherea's zone,[24]
  Binding all things with beauty;—'twould disarm
The spectre Death, had he substantial power to harm.

XCI.

Not vainly did the early Persian make
  His altar the high places, and the peak
  Of earth-o'ergazing mountains,* and thus take
  A fit and unwalled temple, there to seek

* It is to be recollected, that the most beautiful and impressive doctrines of the divine Founder of Christianity were delivered, not in the *Temple*, but on the *Mount*.

To waive the question of devotion, and turn to human eloquence,—the most effectual and splendid specimens were not pronounced within walls. Demosthenes addressed the public and popular assemblies. Cicero spoke in the forum. That this added to their effect on the mind of both orator and hearers, may be conceived from the difference between what we read of the emotions then and there produced, and those we ourselves experience in the perusal in the closet. It is one thing to read the Iliad at Sigæum and on the tumuli, or by the springs with Mount Ida above, and the plain and rivers and Archipelago

[24] The girdle of Venus (Cytheria) gave its wearer irresistible attraction.

The Spirit, in whose honour shrines are weak
Upreared of human hands. Come, and compare
Columns and idol-dwellings—Goth or Greek—
With Nature's realms of worship, earth and air—
Nor fix on fond abodes to circumscribe thy prayer!

XCII.

The sky is changed!—and such a change!† Oh Night,
  And Storm, and Darkness, ye are wondrous strong,
  Yet lovely in your strength, as is the light
  Of a dark eye in Woman! Far along,
  From peak to peak, the rattling crags among
  Leaps the live thunder! Not from one lone cloud,
  But every mountain now hath found a tongue,
  And Jura answers, through her misty shroud,
Back to the joyous Alps, who call to her aloud!

XCIII.

And this is in the Night:—Most glorious Night!
  Thou wert not sent for slumber! let me be
  A sharer in thy fierce and far delight,—
  A portion of the tempest and of thee!
  How the lit lake shines, a phosphoric sea,
  And the big rain comes dancing to the earth!
  And now again 'tis black,—and now, the glee
  Of the loud hills shakes with its mountain-mirth,
As if they did rejoice o'er a young Earthquake's birth.

around you; and another to trim your taper over it in a snug library—*this* I know.

Were the early and rapid progress of what is called Methodism to be attributed to any cause beyond the enthusiasm excited by its vehement faith and doctrines (the truth or error of which I presume neither to canvass nor to question) I should venture to ascribe it to the practice of preaching in the *fields*, and the unstudied and extemporaneous effusions of its teachers. The Mussulmans, whose erroneous devotion (at least in the lower orders) is most sincere, and therefore impressive, are accustomed to repeat their prescribed orisons and prayers, wherever they may be, at the stated hours—of course frequently in the open air, kneeling upon a light mat (which they carry for the purpose of a bed or cushion as required); the ceremony lasts some minutes, during which they are totally absorbed, and only living in their supplication: nothing can disturb them. On me the simple and entire sincerity of these men, and the spirit which appeared to be within and upon them, made a far greater impression than any general rite which was ever performed in places of worship, of which I have seen those of almost every persuasion under the sun; including most of our own sectaries, and the Greek, the Catholic, the Armenian, the Lutheran, the Jewish, and the Mahometan. Many of the negroes, of whom there are numbers in the Turkish empire, are idolaters, and have free exercise of their belief and its rites; some of these I had a distant view of at Patras; and, from what I could make out of them, they appeared to be of a truly Pagan description, and not very agreeable to a spectator.

† The thunder-storms to which these lines refer occurred on the 13th of June, 1816, at midnight. I have seen among the Acroceraunian mountains of Chimari several more terrible, but none more beautiful.

XCIV.

Now, where the swift Rhone cleaves his way between
  Heights which appear as lovers who have parted
  In hate, whose mining depths so intervene,
  That they can meet no more, though broken-
    hearted:
  Though in their souls, which thus each other
  Love was the very root of the fond rage [thwarted,
  Which blighted their life's bloom, and then
  Itself expired, but leaving them an age [departed:—
Of years all winters,—war within themselves to wage:

XCV.

Now, where the quick Rhone thus hath cleft his way,
  The mightiest of the storms hath ta'en his stand:
  For here, not one, but many, make their play,
  And fling their thunder-bolts from hand to hand,
  Flashing and cast around: of all the band,
  The brightest through these parted hills hath forked
  His lightnings,—as if he did understand,
  That in such gaps as Desolation worked,
There the hot shaft should blast whatever therein
  lurked.

XCVI.

Sky—Mountains—River—Winds—Lake—
  Lightnings! ye!
  With night, and clouds, and thunder—and a Soul
  To make these felt and feeling, well may be
  Things that have made me watchful; the far roll
  Of your departing voices, is the knoll
  Of what in me is sleepless,—if I rest.
  But where of ye, O Tempests! is the goal?
  Are ye like those within the human breast?
Or do ye find, at length, like eagles, some high nest?

XCVII.

Could I embody and unbosom now
  That which is most within me,—could I wreak
  My thoughts upon expression, and thus throw
  Soul—heart—mind—passions—feelings—strong or
  All that I would have sought, and all I seek, [weak—
  Bear, know, feel—and yet breathe—into *one* word,
  And that one word were Lightning, I would speak;
  But as it is, I live and die unheard,
With a most voiceless thought, sheathing it as a sword.

XCVIII.

The Moon is up again, the dewy Morn,
  With breath all incense, and with cheek all bloom—
  Laughing the clouds away with playful scorn,
  And living as if earth contained no tomb,—

And glowing into day: we may resume
  The march of our existence: and thus I,
  Still on thy shores, fair Leman! may find room
  And food for meditation, nor pass by
Much, that may give us pause, if pondered fittingly.

XCIX.

Clarens! sweet Clarens birthplace of deep Love! [25]
  Thine air is the young breath of passionate Thought;
  Thy trees take root in Love; the snows above,
  The very Glaciers have his colours caught,
  And Sun-set into rose-hues sees them wrought*
  By rays which sleep there lovingly: the rocks,
  The permanent crags, tell here of Love, who sought
  In them a refuge from the worldly shocks,
Which stir and sting the Soul with Hope that woos,
  then mocks.

* Rousseau's Héloïse, Lettre 17, Part 4, note. "Ces montagnes sont si hautes qu'une demi-heure après le soleil couche, leurs sommets sont éclairés de ses rayons; dont le rouge forme sur ces cimes blanches *une belle couleur de rose*, qu'on aperçoit de fort loin."—This applies more particularly to the heights over Meillerie.—"J'allai à Vevay loger à la Clef, et pendant deux jours que j'y restai sans voir personne, je pris pour cette ville un amour qui m'a suivi dans tous mes voyages, et qui m'y a fait établir enfin les héros de mon roman. Je dirais volontiers à ceux qui ont du goût et qui sort sensibles: Allez à Vevay—visitez le pays, examinez les sites, promenez-vous sur le lac, et dites si la nature n'a pas fait ce beau pays pour une Julie, pour une Claire, et pour un St. Preux; mais ne les y cherchez pas."—Les Confessions, livre iv. p. 306, Lyons, ed. 1796.

In July, 1816, I made a voyage round the Lake of Geneva: and, as far as my own observations have led me in a not uninterested nor inattentive survey of all the scenes most celebrated by Rousseau in his "Héloïse," I can safely say, that in this there is no exaggeration. It would be difficult to see Clarens (with the scenes around it, Vevay, Chillon, Bôveret, St. Gingo, Meillerie, Evian, and the entrances of the Rhone) without being forcibly struck with its peculiar adaptation to the persons and events with which it has been peopled. But this is not all; the feeling with which all around Clarens, and the opposite rocks of Meillerie, is invested, is of a still higher and more comprehensive order than the mere sympathy with individual passion; it is a sense of the existence of love in its most extended and sublime capacity, and of our own participation of its good and of its glory: it is the great principle of the universe, which is there more condensed, but not less manifested; and of which, though knowing ourselves a part, we lose our individuality, and mingle in the beauty of the whole.

If Rousseau had never written, nor lived, the same associations would not less have belonged to such scenes. He has added to the interest of his works by their adoption; he has shown his sense of their beauty by the selection; but they have done that for him which no human being could do for them.

I had the fortune (good or evil as it might be) to sail from Meillerie (where we landed for some time) to St. Gingo during a lake storm, which added to the magnificence of all around, although occasionally accompanied by danger to the boat, which was small and overloaded. It was over this very part of the lake

[25] *Julie: ou, La Nouvelle Héloïse*, Rousseau's novel, is set here.

C.

Clarens! by heavenly feet thy paths are trod,—
　Undying Love's, who here ascends a throne
　To which the steps are mountains; where the God
　Is a pervading Life and Light,—so shown
　Not on those summits solely, nor alone
　In the still cave and forest; o'er the flower
　His eye is sparkling, and his breath hath blown,
　His soft and summer breath, whose tender power
Passes the strength of storms in their most desolate
　hour.

CI.

All things are here of *Him;* from the black pines,
　Which are his shade on high, and the loud roar
　Of torrents, where he listeneth, to the vines
　Which slope his green path downward to the shore,
　Where the bowed Waters meet him, and adore,
　Kissing his feet with murmurs; and the Wood,
　The covert of old trees, with trunks all hoar,
　But light leaves, young as joy, stands where it stood,
Offering to him, and his, a populous solitude.

CII.

A populous solitude of bees and birds,
　And fairy-formed and many-coloured things,
　Who worship him with notes more sweet than
　And innocently open their glad wings, 　　[words,
　Fearless and full of life: the gush of springs,
　And fall of lofty fountains, and the bend
　Of stirring branches, and the bud which brings
　The swiftest thought of Beauty, here extend
Mingling—and made by Love—unto one mighty end.

---

that Rousseau has driven the boat of St. Preux and Madame
Wolmar to Meillerie for shelter during a tempest.

　On gaining the shore at St. Gingo, I found that the wind had
been sufficiently strong to blow down some fine old chestnut
trees on the lower part of the mountains. On the opposite
height of Clarens is a Chateau. The hills are covered with
vineyards, and interspersed with some small but beautiful
woods; one of these was named the "Bosquet de Julie;" and it
is remarkable that, though long ago cut down by the brutal
selfishness of the monks of St. Bernard (to whom the land
appertained), that the ground might be enclosed into a vineyard
for the miserable drones of an execrable superstition, the in-
habitants of Clarens still point out the spot where its trees
stood, calling it by the name which consecrated and survived
them. Rousseau has not been particularly fortunate in the
preservation of the "local habitations" he has given to "airy
nothings." The Prior of Great St. Bernard has cut down some
of his woods for the sake of a few casks of wine, and Buonaparte
has levelled part of the rocks of Meillerie in improving the road
to the Simplon. The road is an excellent one; but I cannot quite
agree with a remark which I heard made, that "La route vaut
mieux que les souvenirs."

CIII.

He who hath loved not, here would learn that lore,
　And make his heart a spirit; he who knows
　That tender mystery, will love the more;
　For this is Love's recess, where vain men's woes,
　And the world's waste, have driven him far from
　For 'tis his nature to advance or die; 　　[those,
　He stands not still, but or decays, or grows
　Into a boundless blessing, which may vie
With the immortal lights, in its eternity!

CIV.

'Twas not for fiction chose Rousseau this spot,
　Peopling it with affections; but he found
　It was the scene which Passion must allot
　To the Mind's purified beings; 'twas the ground
　Where early Love his Psyche's zone unbound,
　And hallowed it with loveliness: 'tis lone,
　And wonderful, and deep, and hath a sound,
　And sense, and sight of sweetness; here the Rhone
Hath spread himself a couch, the Alps have reared a
　throne.

CV.

Lausanne! and Ferney! ye have been the abodes
　Of Names which unto you bequeathed a name;*
　Mortals, who sought and found, by dangerous
　A path to perpetuity of Fame: 　　[roads,
　They were gigantic minds, and their steep aim
　Was, Titan-like, on daring doubts to pile 　　[flame
　Thoughts which should call down thunder, and the
　Of Heaven again assailed—if Heaven, the while,
On man and man's research could deign do more than
　smile.

CVI.

The one was fire and fickleness, a child
　Most mutable in wishes, but in mind
　A wit as various,—gay, grave, sage, or wild,—
　Historian, bard, philosopher, combined;
　He multiplied himself among mankind,
　The Proteus of their talents: But his own
　Breathed most in ridicule,—which, as the wind,
　Blew where it listed, laying all things prone,—
Now to o'erthrow a fool, and now to shake a throne.[26]

CVII.

The other, deep and slow, exhausting thought,
　And hiving wisdom with each studious year,
　In meditation dwelt—with learning wrought,
　And shaped his weapon with an edge severe,

* Voltaire and Gibbon.

◇◆

[26] Voltaire (1694–1778), poet, historian and satirist, lived at
Ferney at the end of his life.

Sapping a solemn creed with solemn sneer;
The lord of irony,—that master-spell,
Which stung his foes to wrath, which grew from
And doomed him to the zealot's ready Hell,   [fear
Which answers to all doubts so eloquently well.[27]

CVIII.

Yet, peace be with their ashes,—for by them,
If merited, the penalty is paid;
It is not ours to judge,—far less condemn;
The hour must come when such things shall be
Known unto all,—or hope and dread allayed   [made
By slumber, on one pillow, in the dust,
Which, thus much we are sure, must lie decayed;
And when it shall revive, as is our trust,
'Twill be to be forgiven—or suffer what is just.

CIX.

But let me quit Man's works, again to read
His Maker's, spread around me, and suspend
This page, which from my reveries I feed,
Until it seems prolonging without end.
The clouds above me to the white Alps tend,
And I must pierce them, and survey whate'er
May be permitted, as my steps I bend
To their most great and growing region, where
The earth to her embrace compels the powers of air.

CX.

Italia too! Italia! looking on thee,
Full flashes on the Soul the light of ages,
Since the fierce Carthaginian almost won thee,
To the last halo of the Chiefs and Sages
Who glorify thy consecrated pages;
Thou wert the throne and grave of empires;[28] still,
The fount at which the panting Mind assuages
Her thirst of knowledge, quaffing there her fill,
Flows from the eternal source of Rome's imperial hill.

CXI.

Thus far have I proceeded in a theme
Renewed with no kind auspices:—to feel
We are not what we have been, and to deem
We are not what we should be,—and to steel
The heart against itself; and to conceal,
With a proud caution, love, or hate, or aught,—
Passion or feeling, purpose, grief, or zeal,—
Which is the tyrant Spirit of our thought,
Is a stern task of soul:—No matter,—it is taught.

CXII.

And for these words, thus woven into song,
It may be that they are a harmless wile,—
The colouring of the scenes which fleet along,
Which I would seize, in passing, to beguile
My breast, or that of others, for a while.
Fame is the thirst of youth,—but I am not
So young as to regard men's frown or smile,
As loss or guerdon[29] of a glorious lot;—
I stood and stand alone,—remembered or forgot.

CXIII.

I have not loved the World, nor the World me;
I have not flattered its rank breath, nor bowed
To its idolatries a patient knee,
Nor coined my cheek to smiles,—nor cried aloud
In worship of an echo: in the crowd
They could not deem me one of such—I stood
Among them, but not of them—in a shroud   [could,
Of thoughts which were not their thoughts, and still
Had I not filed my mind, which thus itself subdued. *

CXIV.

I have not loved the World, nor the World me,—
But let us part fair foes; I do believe,
Though I have found them not, that there may be
Words which are things,— hopes which will not
And Virtues which are merciful, nor weave [deceive,
Snares for the failing; I would also deem
O'er others' griefs that some sincerely grieve—†
That two, or one, are almost what they seem,—
That Goodness is no name—and Happiness no dream.

CXV.

My daughter! with thy name this song begun!
My daughter! with thy name thus much shall
I see thee not—I hear thee not—but none   [end!—
Can be so wrapt in thee; Thou art the Friend
To whom the shadows of far years extend:
Albeit my brow thou never should'st behold,
My voice shall with thy future visions blend,
And reach into thy heart,—when mine is cold,—
A token and a tone, even from thy father's mould.

---

27 Edward Gibbon (1737–1794) completed Vol. 4 and wrote Vols. 5 and 6 of *The Decline and Fall of the Roman Empire* at Lausanne.
28 The Roman Empire engulfed some empires such as the Persian and Carthaginian, and in its dissolution gave rise to others such as the Gothic.

*   —"If it be thus,
For Banquo's issue have I *filed* my mind."—
                                                    MACBETH.
† It is said by Rochefoucault that "there is *always* something in the misfortunes of men's best friends not displeasing to them."

---

29 Reward.

CXVI.

To aid thy mind's developement,—to watch
  Thy dawn of little joys,—to sit and see
  Almost thy very growth,—to view thee catch
  Knowledge of objects,—wonders yet to thee!
  To hold thee lightly on a gentle knee,
  And print on thy soft cheek a parent's kiss,—
  This, it should seem, was not reserved for me—
  Yet this was in my nature:—as it is,
I know not what is there, yet something like to this.

CXVII.

Yet, though dull Hate as duty should be taught,
  I know that thou wilt love me: though my name
  Should be shut from thee, as a spell still fraught
  With desolation, and a broken claim: [same,
  Though the grave closed between us,—'twere the
  I know that thou wilt love me—though to drain
  My blood from out thy being were an aim,
  And an attainment,—all would be in vain,—
Still thou would'st love me, still that more than life
  retain.

CXVIII.

The child of Love! though born in bitterness,
  And nurtured in Convulsion! Of thy sire
  These were the elements,—and thine no less.
  As yet such are around thee,—but thy fire
  Shall be more tempered, and thy hope far higher!
  Sweet be thy cradled slumbers! O'er the sea
  And from the mountains where I now respire,
  Fain would I waft such blessing upon thee,
As—with a sigh—I deem thou might'st have been
  to me!

[1816]   [1816]

THE PRISONER OF CHILLON

*The speaker of the following poem was modeled on Francois
Bonivard, a sixteenth-century religious leader and defender of
Geneva, imprisoned by Duke Charles III of Savoy in the
dungeon at Chillon for six years. He was released by the
Bernese in 1836. A prefatory sonnet and long note on Bonivard
(in French) are here omitted.*

THE PRISONER OF CHILLON.

I.

My hair is grey, but not with years,
  Nor grew it white
  In a single night,*
As men's have grown from sudden fears:
My limbs are bowed, though not with toil,
  But rusted with a vile repose,
For they have been a dungeon's spoil,
  And mine has been the fate of those
To whom the goodly earth and air
Are banned, and barred—forbidden fare;   10
But this was for my father's faith
I suffered chains and courted death;
That father perished at the stake
For tenets he would not forsake;
And for the same his lineal race
In darkness found a dwelling place;
We were seven—who now are one,
  Six in youth, and one in age,
Finished as they had begun,
  Proud of Persecution's rage;   20
One in fire, and two in field,
Their belief with blood have sealed,
Dying as their father died,
For the God their foes denied;—
Three were in a dungeon cast,
Of whom this wreck is left the last.

II.

There are seven pillars of Gothic mould,
In Chillon's dungeons deep and old,
There are seven columns, massy and grey,
Dim with a dull imprisoned ray,   30
A sunbeam which hath lost its way,
And through the crevice and the cleft
Of the thick wall is fallen and left;
Creeping o'er the floor so damp,
Like a marsh's meteor lamp:
And in each pillar there is a ring,

* Ludovico Sforza and others.—The same is asserted of
Marie Antoinette's, the wife of Louis the Sixteenth, though not
in quite so short a period. Grief is said to have the same effect;
to such, and not to fear, this change in *her* was to be attributed.

And in each ring there is a chain;
That iron is a cankering thing,
  For in these limbs its teeth remain,
With marks that will not wear away,   40
Till I have done with this new day,
Which now is painful to these eyes,
Which have not seen the sun so rise
For years—I cannot count them o'er,
I lost their long and heavy score
When my last brother drooped and died,
And I lay living by his side.

III.

They chained us each to a column stone,
And we were three—yet, each alone;
We could not move a single pace,   50
We could not see each other's face,
But with that pale and livid light
That made us strangers in our sight:
And thus together—yet apart,
Fettered in hand, but joined in heart,
'Twas still some solace in the dearth
Of the pure elements of earth,
To hearken to each other's speech,
And each turn comforter to each
With some new hope, or legend old,   60
Or song heroically bold;
But even these at length grew cold.
Our voices took a dreary tone,
An echo of the dungeon stone,
    A grating sound, not full and free,
    As they of yore were wont to be:
    It might be fancy—but to me
They never sounded like our own.

IV.

I was the eldest of the three,
    And to uphold and cheer the rest   70
    I ought to do—and did my best—
And each did well in his degree.
    The youngest, whom my father loved,
Because our mother's brow was given
To him, with eyes as blue as heaven—
    For him my soul was sorely moved:
And truly might it be distressed
To see such bird in such a nest;
For he was beautiful as day—
    (When day was beautiful to me   80
    As to young eagles, being free)—
    A polar day, which will not see
A sunset till its summer's gone,
    Its sleepless summer of long light,
The snow-clad offspring of the sun:
    And thus he was as pure and bright,

And in his natural spirit gay,
With tears for nought but others' ills,
And then they flowed like mountain rills,
Unless he could assuage the woe   90
Which he abhorred to view below.

V.

The other was as pure of mind,
But formed to combat with his kind;
Strong in his frame, and of a mood
Which 'gainst the world in war had stood,
And perished in the foremost rank
    With joy:—but not in chains to pine:
His spirit withered with their clank,
    I saw it silently decline—
    And so perchance in sooth did mine: 100
But yet I forced it on to cheer
Those relics of a home so dear.
He was a hunter of the hills,
    Had followed there the deer and wolf;
    To him this dungeon was a gulf,
And fettered feet the worst of ills.

VI.

    Lake Leman lies by Chillon's walls:
A thousand feet in depth below
Its massy waters meet and flow;
Thus much the fathom-line was sent   110
From Chillon's snow-white battlement,*
    Which round about the wave inthralls:
A double dungeon wall and wave
Have made—and like a living grave.
Below the surface of the lake
The dark vault lies wherein we lay:
We heard it ripple night and day;
    Sounding o'er our heads it knocked;
And I have felt the winter's spray

---

  * The Château de Chillon is situated between Clarens and Villeneuve, which last is at one extremity of the Lake of Geneva. On its left are the entrances of the Rhone, and opposite are the heights of Meillerie and the range of Alps above Boveret and St. Gingo. Near it, on a hill behind, is a torrent: below it, washing its walls, the lake has been fathomed to the depth of 800 feet, French measure: within it are a range of dungeons, in which the early reformers, and subsequently prisoners of state, were confined. Across one of the vaults is a beam black with age, on which we were informed that the condemned were formerly executed. In the cells are seven pillars, or, rather, eight, one being half merged in the wall; In some of these are rings for the fetters and the fettered: in the pavement the steps of Bonnivard have left their traces. He was confined here several years. It is by this castle that Rousseau has fixed the catastrophe of his Héloïse, in the rescue of one of her children by Julie from the water; the shock of which, and the illness produced by the immersion, is the cause of her death. The château is large, and seen along the lake for a great distance. The walls are white.

Wash through the bars when winds were high
And wanton in the happy sky;   121
   And then the very rock hath rocked,
   And I have felt it shake, unshocked,
Because I could have smiled to see
The death that would have set me free.

VII.

I said my nearer brother pined,
I said his mighty heart declined,
He loathed and put away his food;
It was not that 'twas coarse and rude,
For we were used to hunter's fare,   130
And for the like had little care:
The milk drawn from the mountain goat
Was changed for water from the moat,
Our bread was such as captives' tears
Have moistened many a thousand years,
Since man first pent his fellow men
Like brutes within an iron den;
But what were these to us or him?
These wasted not his heart or limb;
My brother's soul was of that mould   140
Which in a palace had grown cold,
Had his free breathing been denied
The range of the steep mountain's side;
But why delay the truth?—he died.
I saw, and could not hold his head,
Nor reach his dying hand—nor dead,—
Though hard I strove, but strove in vain,
To rend and gnash my bonds in twain.
He died—and they unlocked his chain,
And scooped for him a shallow grave   150
Even from the cold earth of our cave.
I begged them, as a boon, to lay
His corse in dust whereon the day
Might shine—it was a foolish thought,
But then within my brain it wrought,
That even in death his freeborn breast
In such a dungeon could not rest.
I might have spared my idle prayer—
They coldly laughed—and laid him there:
The flat and turfless earth above   160
The being we so much did love;
His empty chain above it leant,
Such Murder's fitting monument!

VIII.

But he, the favourite and the flower,
Most cherished since his natal hour,
His mother's image in fair face,
The infant love of all his race,
His martyred father's dearest thought,
My latest care, for whom I sought

To hoard my life, that his might be   170
Less wretched now, and one day free;
He, too, who yet had held untired
A spirit natural or inspired—
He, too, was struck, and day by day
Was withered on the stalk away.
Oh, God! it is a fearful thing
To see the human soul take wing
In any shape, in any mood:
I've seen it rushing forth in blood,
I've seen it on the breaking ocean   180
Strive with a swoln convulsive motion,
I've seen the sick and ghastly bed
Of Sin delirious with its dread:
But these were horrors—this was woe
Unmixed with such—but sure and slow:
He faded, and so calm and meek,
So softly worn, so sweetly weak,
So tearless, yet so tender—kind,
And grieved for those he left behind;
With all the while a cheek whose bloom   190
Was as a mockery of the tomb,
Whose tints as gently sunk away
As a departing rainbow's ray;
An eye of most transparent light,
That almost made the dungeon bright;
And not a word of murmur—not
A groan o'er his untimely lot,—
A little talk of better days,
A little hope my own to raise,
For I was sunk in silence—lost   200
In this last loss, of all the most;
And then the sighs he would suppress
Of fainting Nature's feebleness,
More slowly drawn, grew less and less:
I listened, but I could not hear;
I called, for I was wild with fear;
I knew 'twas hopeless, but my dread
Would not be thus admonishéd;
I called, and thought I heard a sound—
I burst my chain with one strong bound,   210
And rushed to him:—I found him not,
I only stirred in this black spot,
I only lived, *I* only drew
The accursed breath of dungeon-dew;
The last, the sole, the dearest link
Between me and the eternal brink,
Which bound me to my failing race,
Was broken in this fatal place.
One on the earth, and one beneath—
My brothers—both had ceased to
    breathe: 220
I took that hand which lay so still,
Alas! my own was full as chill;

I had not strength to stir, or strive,
But felt that I was still alive—
A frantic feeling, when we know
That what we love shall ne'er be so.
    I know not why
    I could not die,
I had no earthly hope—but faith,
And that forbade a selfish death.   230

IX.

What next befell me then and there
    I know not well—I never knew—
First came the loss of light, and air,
    And then of darkness too:
I had no thought, no feeling—none—
Among the stones I stood a stone,
And was, scarce conscious what I wist,
As shrubless crags within the mist;
For all was blank, and bleak, and grey;
It was not night—it was not day;   240
It was not even the dungeon-light,
So hateful to my heavy sight,
But vacancy absorbing space,
And fixedness—without a place;
There were no stars—no earth—no time—
No check—no change—no good—no crime—
But silence, and a stirless breath
Which neither was of life nor death;
A sea of stagnant idleness,
Blind, boundless, mute, and motionless!   250

X.

A light broke in upon my brain,—
    It was the carol of a bird;
It ceased, and then it came again,
    The sweetest song ear ever heard,
And mine was thankful till my eyes
Ran over with the glad surprise,
And they that moment could not see
I was the mate of misery;
But then by dull degrees came back
My senses to their wonted track;   260
I saw the dungeon walls and floor
Close slowly round me as before,
I saw the glimmer of the sun
Creeping as it before had done,
But through the crevice where it came
That bird was perched, as fond and tame,
    And tamer than upon the tree;
A lovely bird, with azure wings,
And song that said a thousand things,
    And seemed to say them all for me!   270
I never saw its like before,
I ne'er shall see its likeness more:

It seemed like me to want a mate,
But was not half so desolate,
And it was come to love me when
None lived to love me so again,
And cheering from my dungeon's brink,
Had brought me back to feel and think.
I know not if it late were free,
    Or broke its cage to perch on mine,   280
But knowing well captivity,
    Sweet bird! I could not wish for thine!
Or if it were, in wingéd guise,
A visitant from Paradise;
For—Heaven forgive that thought! the while
Which made me both to weep and smile—
I sometimes deemed that it might be
My brother's soul come down to me;
But then at last away it flew,
And then 'twas mortal well I knew,   290
For he would never thus have flown—
And left me twice so doubly lone,—
Lone—as the corse within its shroud,
Lone—as a solitary cloud,
    A single cloud on a sunny day,
While all the rest of heaven is clear,
A frown upon the atmosphere,
That hath no business to appear
    When skies are blue, and earth is gay.

XI.

A kind of change came in my fate,   300
My keepers grew compassionate;
I know not what had made them so,
They were inured to sights of woe,
But so it was:—my broken chain
With links unfastened did remain,
And it was liberty to stride
Along my cell from side to side,
And up and down, and then athwart,
And tread it over every part;
And round the pillars one by one,   310
Returning where my walk begun,
Avoiding only, as I trod,
My brothers' graves without a sod;
For if I thought with heedless tread
My step profaned their lowly bed,
My breath came gaspingly and thick,
And my crushed heart felt blind and sick.

XII.

I made a footing in the wall,
    It was not therefrom to escape,
For I had buried one and all,   320
    Who loved me in a human shape;

And the whole earth would henceforth be
A wider prison unto me:
No child—no sire—no kin had I,
No partner in my misery;
I thought of this, and I was glad,
For thought of them had made me mad;
But I was curious to ascend
To my barred windows, and to bend
Once more, upon the mountains high,   330
The quiet of a loving eye.

XIII.

I saw them—and they were the same,
They were not changed like me in frame;
I saw their thousand years of snow
On high—their wide long lake below,
And the blue Rhone in fullest flow;
I heard the torrents leap and gush
O'er channelled rock and broken bush;
I saw the white-walled distant town,
And whiter sails go skimming down;   340
And then there was a little isle,*
Which in my very face did smile,
    The only one in view;
A small green isle, it seemed no more,
Scarce broader than my dungeon floor,
But in it there were three tall trees,
And o'er it blew the mountain breeze,
And by it there were waters flowing,
And on it there were young flowers growing,
    Of gentle breath and hue.   350
The fish swam by the castle wall,
And they seemed joyous each and all;
The eagle rode the rising blast,
Methought he never flew so fast
As then to me he seemed to fly;
And then new tears came in my eye,
And I felt troubled—and would fain
I had not left my recent chain;
And when I did descend again,
The darkness of my dim abode   360
Fell on me as a heavy load;
It was as is a new-dug grave,
Closing o'er one we sought to save,—
And yet my glance, too much opprest,
Had almost need of such a rest.

* Between the entrances of the Rhone and Villeneuve, not far from Chillon, is a very small island; the only one I could perceive in my voyage round and over the lake, within its circumference. It contains a few trees (I think not above three), and from its singleness and diminutive size has a peculiar effect upon the view.

XIV.

It might be months, or years, or days—
    I kept no count, I took no note—
I had no hope my eyes to raise,
    And clear them of their dreary mote;
At last men came to set me free;   370
    I asked not why, and recked not where;
It was at length the same to me,
Fettered or fetterless to be,
    I learned to love despair.
And thus when they appeared at last,
And all my bonds aside were cast,
These heavy walls to me had grown
A hermitage—and all my own!
And half I felt as they were come
To tear me from a second home: 380
With spiders I had friendship made,
And watched them in their sullen trade,
Had seen the mice by moonlight play,
And why should I feel less than they?
We were all inmates of one place,
And I, the monarch of each race,
Had power to kill—yet, strange to tell!
In quiet we had learned to dwell;
My very chains and I grew friends,
So much a long communion tends   390
To make us what we are:—even I
Regained my freedom with a sigh.

[1816]   [1816]

EPISTLE TO AUGUSTA

Although Byron never again saw his half sister Augusta Byron Leigh after his departure from England in 1816, their correspondence was a means by which Byron maintained a connection between his present and past life, and a source of information about his daughter and wife. In spite of Lady Byron's allegation that the incestuous relation between Byron and Augusta was the main reason for their separation, the two women wrote to each other frequently after Byron's departure. See Byron's journal-letter to her, p. 767.

EPISTLE TO AUGUSTA.

I.

MY Sister! my sweet Sister! if a name
Dearer and purer were, it should be thine.
Mountains and seas divide us, but I claim
No tears, but tenderness to answer mine:
Go where I will, to me thou art the same—
A loved regret which I would not resign,
There yet are two things in my destiny,—
A world to roam through, and a home with thee.

II.

The first were nothing—had I still the last,
It were the haven of my happiness;
But other claims and other ties thou hast,
And mine is not the wish to make them less.
A strange doom is thy father's son's, and past
Recalling, as it lies beyond redress;
Reversed for him our grandsire's fate of yore,—
He had no rest at sea, nor I on shore.

III.

If my inheritance of storms hath been
In other elements, and on the rocks
Of perils, overlooked or unforeseen,
I have sustained my share of worldly shocks,
The fault was mine; nor do I seek to screen
My errors with defensive paradox;
I have been cunning in mine overthrow,
The careful pilot of my proper woe.

IV.

Mine were my faults, and mine be their reward.
My whole life was a contest, since the day
That gave me being, gave me that which marred
The gift,—a fate, or will, that walked astray;
And I at times have found the struggle hard,
And thought of shaking off my bonds of clay:
But now I fain would for a time survive,
If but to see what next can well arrive.

V.

Kingdoms and Empires in my little day
I have outlived, and yet I am not old;
And when I look on this, the petty spray
Of my own years of trouble, which have rolled
Like a wild bay of breakers, melts away:
Something—I know not what—does still uphold
A spirit of slight patience;—not in vain,
Even for its own sake, do we purchase Pain.

VI.

Perhaps the workings of defiance stir
Within me—or, perhaps, a cold despair
Brought on when ills habitually recur,—
Perhaps a kinder clime, or purer air,
(For even to this may change of soul refer,
And with light armour we may learn to bear,)
Have taught me a strange quiet, which was not
The chief companion of a calmer lot.

VII.

I feel almost at times as I have felt
In happy childhood; trees, and flowers, and brooks,
Which do remember me of where I dwelt,
Ere my young mind was sacrified to books,
Come as of yore upon me, and can melt
My heart with recognition of their looks;
And even at moments I could think I see
Some living thing to love—but none like thee.

VIII.

Here are the Alpine landscapes which create
A fund for contemplation;—to admire
Is a brief feeling of a trivial date;
But something worthier do such scenes inspire:
Here to be lonely is not desolate,
For much I view which I could most desire,
And, above all, a Lake I can behold
Lovelier, not dearer, than our own of old.

IX.

Oh that thou wert but with me!—but I grow
The fool of my own wishes, and forget
The solitude which I have vaunted so
Has lost its praise in this but one regret;
There may be others which I less may show;—
I am not of the plaintive mood, and yet
I feel an ebb in my philosophy,
And the tide rising in my altered eye.

X.

I did remind thee of our own dear Lake,*
By the old Hall which may be mine no more.[1]
Leman's is fair; but think not I forsake
The sweet remembrance of a dearer shore:
Sad havoc Time must with my memory make,
Ere that or thou can fade these eyes before;
Though, like all things which I have loved, they are
Resigned for ever, or divided far.

XI.

The world is all before me; I but ask
Of Nature that with which she will comply—
It is but in her Summer's sun to bask,
To mingle with the quiet of her sky,
To see her gentle face without a mask,
And never gaze on it with apathy.
She was my early friend, and now shall be
My sister—till I look again on thee.

* The Lake of Newstead Abbey.

<><><><><><><><><><><><><><><><><><><><><><><>

[1] Byron was in the process of selling Newstead Abbey.

XII.

I can reduce all feelings but this one;
And that I would not;—for at length I see
Such scenes as those wherein my life begun—
The earliest—even the only paths for me—
Had I but sooner learnt the crowd to shun,
I had been better than I now can be;
The Passions which have torn me would have
      slept;
I had not suffered, and *thou* hadst not wept.

XIII.

With false Ambition what had I to do?
Little with Love, and least of all with Fame;
And yet they came unsought, and with me grew,
And made me all which they can make—a Name.
Yet this was not the end I did pursue;
Surely I once beheld a nobler aim.
But all is over—I am one the more
To baffled millions which have gone before.

XIV.

And for the future, this world's future may
From me demand but little of my care;
I have outlived myself by many a day;
Having survived so many things that were;
My years have been no slumber, but the prey
Of ceaseless vigils; for I had the share
Of life which might have filled a century,
Before its fourth in time had passed me by.

XV.

And for the remnant which may be to come
I am content; and for the past I feel
Not thankless,—for within the crowded sum
Of struggles, Happiness at times would steal,
And for the present, I would not benumb
My feelings farther.—Nor shall I conceal
That with all this I still can look around,
And worship Nature with a thought profound.

XVI.

For thee, my own sweet sister, in thy heart
I know myself secure, as thou in mine;
We were and are—I am, even as thou art—
Beings who ne'er each other can resign;
It is the same, together or apart,
From Life's commencement to its slow decline
We are entwined—let Death come slow or fast,
The tie which bound the first endures the last!

[1816]   [1830]

DARKNESS

I HAD a dream, which was not all a dream.
The bright sun was extinguished, and the stars
Did wander darkling in the eternal space,
Rayless, and pathless, and the icy Earth
Swung blind and blackening in the moonless air;
Morn came and went—and came, and brought no
      day,
And men forgot their passions in the dread
Of this their desolation; and all hearts
Were chilled into a selfish prayer for light:
And they did live by watchfires—and the thrones,   10
The palaces of crownéd kings—the huts,
The habitations of all things which dwell,
Were burnt for beacons; cities were consumed,
And men were gathered round their blazing homes
To look once more into each other's face;
Happy were those who dwelt within the eye
Of the volcanos, and their mountain-torch:
A fearful hope was all the world contained;
Forests were set on fire—but hour by hour
They fell and faded—and the crackling trunks   20
Extinguished with a crash—and all was black.
The brows of men by the despairing light
Wore an unearthly aspect, as by fits
The flashes fell upon them; some lay down
And hid their eyes and wept; and some did rest
Their chins upon their clenchéd hands, and smiled;
And others hurried to and fro, and fed
Their funeral piles with fuel, and looked up
With mad disquietude on the dull sky,
The pall of a past World; and then again   30
With curses cast them down upon the dust,
And gnashed their teeth and howled: the wild birds
      shrieked,
And, terrified, did flutter on the ground,
And flap their useless wings; the wildest brutes
Came tame and tremulous; and vipers crawled
And twined themselves among the multitude,
Hissing, but stingless—they were slain for food:
And War, which for a moment was no more,
Did glut himself again:—a meal was bought
With blood, and each sate sullenly apart   40
Gorging himself in gloom: no Love was left;
All earth was but one thought—and that was Death,
Immediate and inglorious; and the pang
Of famine fed upon all entrails—men
Died, and their bones were tombless as their flesh;
The meagre by the meagre were devoured,
Even dogs assailed their masters, all save one,
And he was faithful to a corse, and kept
The birds and beasts and famished men at bay,

Till hunger clung[1] them, or the dropping dead   50
Lured their lank jaws; himself sought out no food,
But with a piteous and perpetual moan,
And a quick desolate cry, licking the hand
Which answered not with a caress—he died.
The crowd was famished by degrees; but two
Of an enormous city did survive,
And they were enemies: they met beside
The dying embers of an altar-place
Where had been heaped a mass of holy things
For an unholy usage; they raked up,   60
And shivering scraped with their cold skeleton hands
The feeble ashes, and their feeble breath
Blew for a little life, and made a flame
Which was a mockery; then they lifted up
Their eyes as it grew lighter, and beheld
Each other's aspects—saw, and shrieked, and died—
Even of their mutual hideousness they died,
Unknowing who he was upon whose brow
Famine had written Fiend. The World was void,
The populous and the powerful was a lump,   70
Seasonless, herbless, treeless, manless, lifeless—
A lump of death—a chaos of hard clay.
The rivers, lakes, and ocean all stood still,
And nothing stirred within their silent depths;
Ships sailorless lay rotting on the sea,
And their masts fell down piecemeal: as they dropped
They slept on the abyss without a surge—
The waves were dead; the tides were in their grave,
The Moon, their mistress, had expired before;
The winds were withered in the stagnant air,   80
And the clouds perished; Darkness had no need
Of aid from them—She was the Universe.

[1816]   [1816]

PROMETHEUS

*To many poets of the early nineteenth century, the figure of the
Titan who stole fire from Mount Olympus and gave it to man was
a particularly attractive and symbolic one. See* Manfred, *p. 603,
and Shelley's* Prometheus Unbound, *p. 852.*

PROMETHEUS.

I.

TITAN! to whose immortal eyes
    The sufferings of mortality,
    Seen in their sad reality,
Were not as things that gods despise;

---

[1] Dialectical word: shrivelled, as of fruit.

What was thy pity's recompense?
A silent suffering, and intense;
The rock, the vulture, and the chain,
All that the proud can feel of pain,
The agony they do not show,
The suffocating sense of woe,   10
    Which speaks but in its loneliness,
And then is jealous lest the sky
Should have a listener, nor will sigh
    Until its voice is echoless.

II.

Titan! to thee the strife was given
    Between the suffering and the will,
    Which torture where they cannot kill;
And the inexorable Heaven,
And the deaf tyranny of Fate,
The ruling principle of Hate,   20
Which for its pleasure doth create
The things it may annihilate,
Refused thee even the boon to die:
The wretched gift Eternity
Was thine—and thou hast borne it well.
All that the Thunderer wrung from thee
Was but the menace which flung back
On him the torments of thy rack;
The fate thou didst so well foresee,
But would not to appease him tell;   30
And in thy Silence was his Sentence,
And in his Soul a vain repentance,
And evil dread so ill dissembled,
That in his hand the lightnings trembled.

III.

Thy Godlike crime was to be kind,
    To render with thy precepts less
    The sum of human wretchedness,
And strengthen Man with his own mind;
But baffled as thou wert from high,
Still in thy patient energy,   40
In the endurance, and repulse
    Of thine impenetrable Spirit,
Which Earth and Heaven could not convulse,
    A mighty lesson we inherit:
Thou art a symbol and a sign
    To Mortals of their fate and force;
Like thee, Man is in part divine,
    A troubled stream from a pure source;
And Man in portions can foresee
His own funereal destiny;   50
His wretchedness, and his resistance,
And his sad unallied existence:

To which his Spirit may oppose
Itself—an equal to all woes—
　　And a firm will, and a deep sense,
Which even in torture can descry
　　Its own concentered recompense,
Triumphant where it dares defy,
And making Death a Victory.

[1816]　　　　　　　　　　　　　　　　　[1816]

LINES ON HEARING THAT
LADY BYRON WAS ILL.

AND thou wert sad—yet I was not with thee;
　　And thou wert sick, and yet I was not near;
Methought that Joy and Health alone could be
　　Where I was *not*—and pain and sorrow here!
And is it thus?—it is as I foretold,
　　And shall be more so; for the mind recoils
Upon itself, and the wrecked heart lies cold,
　　While Heaviness collects the shattered spoils.
It is not in the storm nor in the strife
　　We feel benumbed, and wish to be no more,　　10
　　But in the after-silence on the shore,
When all is lost, except a little life.

I am too well avenged!—but 'twas my right;
　　Whate'er my sins might be, *thou* wert not sent
To be the Nemesis [1] who should requite—
　　Nor did Heaven choose so near an instrument.
Mercy is for the merciful!—if thou
　　Hast been of such, 'twill be accorded now.
Thy nights are banished from the realms of sleep:—
　　Yes! they may flatter thee, but thou shalt feel　　20
　　A hollow agony which will not heal,
For thou art pillowed on a curse too deep;
Thou hast sown in my sorrow, and must reap
　　The bitter harvest in a woe as real!
I have had many foes, but none like thee;
　　For 'gainst the rest myself I could defend,
　　And be avenged, or turn them into friend;
But thou in safe implacability
Hadst nought to dread—in thy own weakness
　　　　shielded,
And in my love, which hath but too much yielded,　　30
　　And spared, for thy sake, some I should not spare;
And thus upon the world—trust in thy truth,
And the wild fame of my ungoverned youth—
　　On things that were not, and on things that are—

<hr>

[1] Goddess of revenge.

Even upon such a basis hast thou built
A monument, whose cement hath been guilt!
　　The moral Clytemnestra [2] of thy lord,
　　And hewed down, with an unsuspected sword,
Fame, peace, and hope—and all the better life
　　Which, but for this cold treason of thy heart,　　40
Might still have risen from out the grave of strife,
　　And found a nobler duty than to part.
But of thy virtues didst thou make a vice,
　　Trafficking with them in a purpose cold,
　　For present anger, and for future gold—
And buying others' grief at any price.
And thus once entered into crooked ways,
The early truth, which was thy proper praise,
Did not still walk beside thee—but at times,
And with a breast unknowing its own crimes,　　50
Deceit, averments incompatible,
Equivocations, and the thoughts which dwell
　　In Janus-spirits [3]—the significant eye
Which learns to lie with silence—the pretext
Of prudence, with advantages annexed—
The acquiescence in all things which tend,
No matter how, to the desired end—
　　All found a place in thy philosophy.
The means were worthy, and the end is won—
I would not do by thee as thou has done!　　60

[1816]　　　　　　　　　　　　　　　　　[1832]

<hr>

SONG FOR THE LUDDITES

*Ned Ludd, a probably deranged weaver who broke stocking
frames in a fit of fury, gave his name to disaffected workers in
general, especially those who resisted mechanization in the textile
industry. Byron's first speech in the House of Lords (1812) was
in defense of frame-breakers.*

<hr>

SONG FOR THE LUDDITES.

I.

As the Liberty lads o'er the sea
Bought their freedom, and cheaply, with blood,
　　So we, boys, we
　　Will *die* fighting, or *live* free,
And down with all kings but King Ludd!

<hr>

[2] Wife of Agamemnon, who for her lover Aegisthos murdered
her husband when he returned from Troy.
[3] The god of gates and doorways, Janus was depicted facing
both ways.

2.

When the web that we weave is complete,
And the shuttle exchanged for the sword,
   We will fling the winding sheet
   O'er the despot at our feet,
And dye it deep in the gore he has poured.

3.

Though black as his heart its hue,
Since his veins are corrupted to mud,
   Yet this is the dew
   Which the tree shall renew
Of Liberty, planted by Ludd!

[1816]   [1830]

SO WE'LL GO NO MORE A-ROVING.

1.

So we'll go no more a-roving
   So late into the night,
Though the heart be still as loving,
   And the moon be still as bright.

2.

For the sword outwears its sheath,
   And the soul wears out the breast,
And the heart must pause to breathe,
   And Love itself have rest.

3.

Though the night was made for loving,
   And the day returns too soon,
Yet we'll go no more a-roving
   By the light of the moon.

[1817]   [1830]

MANFRED

Byron claimed to have been ignorant of Marlowe's Doctor Faustus when he wrote Manfred, and that his only acquaintance with the Faust legend was having heard a translation of a few verses of Goethe's drama. The actual inspiration, he said, was not literary at all, but the mountain peaks of the Alps where the events take place. Goethe, who reviewed it, was one of its most enthusiastic admirers.

MANFRED:

A DRAMATIC POEM.

"There are more things in heaven and earth, Horatio,
Than are dreamt of in your philosophy."[1]

ACT I.

SCENE I.—MANFRED *alone.*—*Scene, a Gothic
Gallery.*—*Time, Midnight.*

  Man. The lamp must be replenished, but even
    then
It will not burn so long as I must watch:
My slumbers—if I slumber—are not sleep,
But a continuance of enduring thought,
Which then I can resist not: in my heart
There is a vigil, and these eyes but close
To look within; and yet I live, and bear
The aspect and the form of breathing men.
But Grief should be the Instructor of the wise;
Sorrow is Knowledge: they who know the most   10
Must mourn the deepest o'er the fatal truth,
The Tree of Knowledge is not that of Life.
Philosophy and science, and the springs
Of Wonder, and the wisdom of the World,
I have essayed, and in my mind there is
A power to make these subject to itself—
But they avail not: I have done men good,
And I have met with good even among men—
But this availed not: I have had my foes,
And none have baffled, many fallen before me—   20
But this availed not:—Good—or evil—life—
Powers, passions—all I see in other beings,
Have been to me as rain unto the sands,
Since that all-nameless hour. I have no dread,
And feel the curse to have no natural fear,
Nor fluttering throb, that beats with hopes or wishes,
Or lurking love of something on the earth.

---

[1] *Hamlet*, Act I, Scene 5, lines 166–67.

Now to my task.—
    Mysterious Agency!
Ye Spirits of the unbounded Universe!
Whom I have sought in darkness and in light— 30
Ye, who do compass earth about, and dwell
In subtler essence—ye, to whom the tops
Of mountains inaccessible are haunts,
And Earth's and Ocean's caves familiar things—
I call upon ye by the written charm
Which gives me power upon you—Rise! Appear!
         [*A Pause.*
They come not yet.—Now by the voice of him
Who is the first among you—by this sign,
Which makes you tremble—by the claims of him
Who is undying,—Rise! Appear!—Appear! 40
         [*A pause.*
If it be so.—Spirits of Earth and Air,
Ye shall not so elude me! By a power,
Deeper than all yet urged, a tyrant-spell,
Which had its birthplace in a star condemned,
The burning wreck of a demolished world,
A wandering hell in the eternal Space;
By the strong curse which is upon my Soul,
The thought which is within me and around me,
I do compel ye to my will.—Appear!
[*A star is seen at the darker end of the gallery: it is*
 stationary; and a voice is heard singing.

FIRST SPIRIT.

 Mortal! to thy bidding bowed, 50
 From my mansion in the cloud,
 Which the breath of Twilight builds,
 And the Summer's sunset gilds
 With the azure and vermilion,
 Which is mixed for my pavilion;
 Though thy quest may be forbidden,
 On a star-beam I have ridden,
 To thine adjuration bowed:
 Mortal—be thy wish avowed!

Voice of the SECOND SPIRIT.

Mont Blanc is the Monarch of mountains; 60
 They crowned him long ago
On a throne of rocks, in a robe of clouds,
 With a Diadem of snow.
Around his waist are forests braced,
 The Avalanche in his hand;
But ere it fall, that thundering ball
 Must pause for my command.
The Glacier's cold and restless mass
 Moves onward day by day;
But I am he who bids it pass, 70
 Or with its ice delay.

I am the Spirit of the place,
 Could make the mountain bow
And quiver to his caverned base—
 And what with me would'st *Thou?*

Voice of the THIRD SPIRIT.

In the blue depth of the waters,
 Where the wave hath no strife,
Where the Wind is a stranger,
 And the Sea-snake hath life,
Where the Mermaid is decking 80
 Her green hair with shells,
Like the storm on the surface
 Came the sound of thy spells;
O'er my calm Hall of Coral
 The deep Echo rolled—
To the Spirit of Ocean
 Thy wishes unfold!

FOURTH SPIRIT.

Where the slumbering Earthquake
 Lies pillowed on fire,
And the lakes of bitumen 90
 Rise boilingly higher;
Where the roots of the Andes
 Strike deep in the earth,
As their summits to heaven
 Shoot soaringly forth;
I have quitted my birthplace,
 Thy bidding to bide—
Thy spell hath subdued me,
 Thy will be my guide!

FIFTH SPIRIT.

I am the Rider of the wind, 100
 The Stirrer of the storm;
The hurricane I left behind
 Is yet with lightning warm;
To speed to thee, o'er shore and sea
 I swept upon the blast:
The fleet I met sailed well—and yet
 'Twill sink ere night be past.

SIXTH SPIRIT.

My dwelling is the shadow of the Night,
Why doth thy magic torture me with light?

SEVENTH SPIRIT.

The Star which rules thy destiny 110
Was ruled, ere earth began, by me:
It was a World as fresh and fair
As e'er revolved round Sun in air;
Its course was free and regular,
Space bosomed not a lovelier star.

The Hour arrived—and it became
A wandering mass of shapeless flame,
A pathless Comet, and a curse,
The menace of the Universe;
Still rolling on with innate force,   120
Without a sphere, with a course,
A bright deformity on high,
The monster of the upper sky!
And Thou! beneath its influence born—
Thou worm! whom I obey and scorn—
Forced by a Power (which is not thine,
And lent thee but to make thee mine)
For this brief moment to descend,
Where these weak Spirits round thee bend
And parley with a thing like thee—   130
What would'st thou, Child of Clay! with me?

The SEVEN SPIRITS.

Earth—ocean—air—night—mountains—winds—
        thy Star,
Are at thy beck and bidding, Child of Clay!
Before thee at thy quest their Spirits are—
What would'st thou with us, Son of mortals—say?

Man. Forgetfulness——
First Spirit.   Of what—of whom—and
        why?
Man. Of that which is within me; read it there—
Ye know it—and I cannot utter it.
Spirit. We can but give thee that which we possess:
Ask of us subjects, sovereignty, the power   140
O'er earth—the whole, or portion—or a sign
Which shall control the elements, whereof
We are the dominators,—each and all,
These shall be thine.
Man.   Oblivion—self-oblivion!
Can ye not wring from out the hidden realms
Ye offer so profusely—what I ask?
Spirit. It is not in our essence, in our skill;
But—thou may'st die.
Man.   Will Death bestow it on me?
Spirit. We are immortal, and do not forget;
We are eternal; and to us the past   150
Is, as the future, present. Art thou answered?
Man. Ye mock me—but the Power which brought
        ye here
Hath made you mine. Slaves, scoff not at my will!
The Mind—the Spirit—the Promethean spark,
The lightning of my being, is as bright,
Pervading, and far darting as your own,
And shall not yield to yours, though cooped in clay!
Answer, or I will teach you what I am.
Spirit. We answer—as we answered; our reply
Is even in thine own words.

Man.   Why say ye so?   160
Spirit. If, as thou say'st, thine essence be as ours,
We have replied in telling thee, the thing
Mortals call death hath nought to do with us.
Man. I then have called ye from your realms in
        vain;
Ye cannot, or ye will not, aid me.
Spirit.   Say—
What we possess we offer; it is thine:
Bethink ere thou dismiss us; ask again;
Kingdom, and sway, and strength, and length of
        days—
Man. Accurséd! what have I to do with days?
They are too long already.—Hence—begone!   170
Spirit. Yet pause: being here, our will would do
        thee service;
Bethink thee, is there then no other gift
Which we can make not worthless in thine eyes?
Man. No, none: yet stay—one moment, ere we
        part,
I would behold ye face to face. I hear
Your voices, sweet and melancholy sounds,
As Music on the waters; and I see
The steady aspect of a clear large Star;
But nothing more. Approach me as ye are,
Or one—or all—in your accustomed forms.   180
Spirit. We have no forms, beyond the elements
Of which we are the mind and principle:
But choose a form—in that we will appear.
Man. I have no choice; there is no form on earth
Hideous or beautiful to me. Let him,
Who is most powerful of ye, take such aspect
As unto him may seem most fitting—Come!
Seventh Spirit (*appearing in the shape of a beautiful
        female figure*). Behold!
Man.   Oh God! if it be thus, and *thou*
Art not a madness and a mockery,
I yet might be most happy. I will clasp thee,   190
And we again will be——
                    [*The figure vanishes.*
                My heart is crushed!
                    [MANFRED *falls senseless.*

(*A voice is heard in the Incantation which follows.*)

When the Moon is on the wave,
    And the glow-worm in the grass,
And the meteor on the grave,
    And the wisp on the morass;
When the falling stars are shooting,
And the answered owls are hooting,
And the silent leaves are still
In the shadow of the hill,
Shall my soul be upon thine,   200
With a power and with a sign.

Though thy slumber may be deep,
Yet thy Spirit shall not sleep;
There are shades which will not vanish,
There are thoughts thou canst not banish;
By a Power to thee unknown,
Thou canst never be alone;
Thou art wrapt as with a shroud,
Thou art gathered in a cloud;
And for ever shalt thou dwell   210
In the spirit of this spell.

Though thou seest me not pass by,
Thou shalt feel me with thine eye
As a thing that, though unseen,
Must be near thee, and hath been;
And when in that secret dread
Thou hast turned around thy head,
Thou shalt marvel I am not
As thy shadow on the spot,
And the power which thou dost feel   220
Shall be what thou must conceal.

And a magic voice and verse
Hath baptized thee with a curse;
And a Spirit of the air
Hath begirt thee with a snare;
In the wind there is a voice
Shall forbid thee to rejoice;
And to thee shall Night deny
All the quiet of her sky;
And the day shall have a sun,   230
Which shall make thee wish it done.

From thy false tears I did distil
An essence which hath strength to kill;
From thy own heart I then did wring
The black blood in its blackest spring;
From thy own smile I snatched the snake,
For there it coiled as in a brake;
From thy own lip I drew the charm
Which gave all these their chiefest harm;
In proving every poison known,   240
I found the strongest was thine own.

By the cold breast and serpent smile,
By thy unfathomed gulfs of guile,
By that most seeming virtuous eye,
By thy shut soul's hypocrisy;
By the perfection of thine art
Which passed for human thine own heart;
By thy delight in others' pain,
And by thy brotherhood of Cain,
I call upon thee! and compel   250
Thyself to be thy proper Hell!

And on thy head I pour the vial
Which doth devote thee to this trial;
Nor to slumber, nor to die,
Shall be in thy destiny;
Though thy death shall still seem near
To thy wish, but as a fear;
Lo! the spell now works around thee,
And the clankless chain hath bound thee;
O'er thy heart and brain together   260
Hath the word been passed—now wither!

SCENE II.—*The Mountain of the Jungfrau.—Time,
Morning.*—MANFRED *alone upon the cliffs.*

  Man. The spirits I have raised abandon me,
The spells which I have studied baffle me,
The remedy I recked of tortured me;
I lean no more on superhuman aid;
It hath no power upon the past, and for
The future, till the past be gulfed in darkness,
It is not of my search.—My Mother Earth!
And thou fresh-breaking Day, and you, ye Mountains,
Why are ye beautiful? I cannot love ye.
And thou, the bright Eye of the Universe,   10
That openest over all, and unto all
Art a delight—thou shin'st not on my heart.
And you, ye crags, upon whose extreme edge
I stand, and on the torrent's brink beneath
Behold the tall pines dwindled as to shrubs
In dizziness of distance; when a leap,
A stir, a motion, even a breath, would bring
My breast upon its rocky bosom's bed
To rest for ever—wherefore do I pause?
I feel the impulse—yet I do not plunge;   20
I see the peril—yet do not recede;
And my brain reels—and yet my foot is firm:
There is a power upon me which withholds,
And makes it my fatality to live,—
If it be life to wear within myself
This barrenness of Spirit, and to be
My own Soul's sepulchre, for I have ceased
To justify my deeds unto myself—
The last infirmity of evil. Aye,
Thou winged and cloud-cleaving minister,   30
          [*An Eagle passes*
Whose happy flight is highest into heaven,
Well may'st thou swoop so near me—I should be
Thy prey, and gorge thine eaglets; thou art gone
Where the eye cannot follow thee; but thine
Yet pierces downward, onward, or above,
With a pervading vision.—Beautiful!
How beautiful is all this visible world!
How glorious in its action and itself!
But we, who name ourselves its sovereigns, we,

Half dust, half deity, alike unfit 40
To sink or soar, with our mixed essence make
A conflict of its elements, and breathe
The breath of degradation and of pride,
Contending with low wants and lofty will,
Till our Mortality predominates,
And men are—what they name not to themselves,
And trust not to each other. Hark! the note,

[*The Shepherd's pipe in the distance is heard.*

The natural music of the mountain reed—
For here the patriarchal days are not
A pastoral fable—pipes in the liberal air, 50
Mixed with the sweet bells of the sauntering herd;
My soul would drink those echoes. Oh, that I were
The viewless spirit of a lovely sound,
A living voice, a breathing harmony,
A bodiless enjoyment—born and dying
With the blest tone which made me!

Enter from below a CHAMOIS HUNTER.

Chamois Hunter. Even so
This way the Chamois leapt: her nimble feet
Have baffled me; my gains to-day will scarce
Repay my break-neck travail.—What is here?
Who seems not of my trade, and yet hath reached 60
A height which none even of our mountaineers,
Save our best hunters, may attain: his garb
Is goodly, his mien manly, and his air
Proud as a free-born peasant's, at this distance:
I will approach him nearer.

Man. (*not perceiving the other*). To be thus—
Grey-haired with anguish, like these blasted pines,
Wrecks of a single winter, barkless, branchless,
A blighted trunk upon a cursèd root,
Which but supplies a feeling to Decay—
And to be thus, eternally but thus, 70
Having been otherwise! Now furrowed o'er
With wrinkles, ploughed by moments, not by years
And hours, all tortured into ages—hours
Which I outlive!—Ye toppling crags of ice!
Ye Avalanches, whom a breath draws down
In moutainous o'erwhelming, come and crush me!
I hear ye momently above, beneath,
Crash with a frequent conflict; but ye pass,
And only fall on things that still would live;
On the young flourishing forest, or the hut 80
And hamlet of the harmless villager.

C. Hun. The mists begin to rise from up the valley;
I'll warn him to descend, or he may chance
To lose at once his way and life together.

Man. The mists boil up around the glaciers; clouds
Rise curling fast beneath me, white and sulphury,
Like foam from the roused ocean of deep Hell,
Whose every wave breaks on a living shore,

Heaped with the damned like pebbles.—I am giddy.

C. Hun. I must approach him cautiously; if near,
A sudden step will startle him, and he 91
Seems tottering already.

Man. Mountains have fallen,
Leaving a gap in the clouds, and with the shock
Rocking their Alpine brethren; filling up
The ripe green valleys with Destruction's splinters;
Damming the rivers with a sudden dash,
Which crushed the waters into mist, and made
Their fountains find another channel—thus,
Thus, in its old age, did Mount Rosenberg [1]—
Why stood I not beneath it?

C. Hun. Friend! have a care, 100
Your next step may be fatal!—for the love
Of Him who made you, stand not on that brink!

Man. (*not hearing him*). Such would have been for me
a fitting tomb;
My bones had then been quiet in their depth;
They had not then been strewn upon the rocks
For the wind's pastime—as thus—thus they shall
be—
In this one plunge.—Farewell, ye opening Heavens!
Look not upon me thus reproachfully—
You were not meant for me—Earth! take these atoms!

[*As* MANFRED *is in act to spring from the cliff, the*
CHAMOIS HUNTER *seizes and retains him*
with a sudden grasp.

C. Hun. Hold, madman!—though aweary of thy
life, 110
Stain not our pure vales with thy guilty blood:
Away with me——I will not quit my hold.

Man. I am most sick at heart——nay, grasp me
not—
I am all feebleness—the mountains whirl
Spinning around me——I grow blind——What art
thou?

C. Hun. I'll answer that anon.—Away with me——
The clouds grow thicker——there—now lean on
me—
Place your foot here—here, take this staff, and cling
A moment to that shrub—now give me your hand,
And hold fast by my girdle—softly—well— 120
The Chalet will be gained within an hour:
Come on, we'll quickly find a surer footing,
And something like a pathway, which the torrent
Hath washed since winter.—Come, 'tis bravely
done—
You should have been a hunter.—Follow me.

[*As they descend the rocks with difficulty, the scene*
closes.

⬦⬦⬦⬦⬦⬦⬦⬦⬦⬦⬦⬦⬦⬦⬦⬦⬦⬦⬦⬦⬦⬦⬦⬦⬦⬦⬦

[1] In 1806 a landslide on Rossberg buried four villages and
herds of cattle, killing over 450 people.

ACT II.

SCENE I.—*A Cottage among the Bernese Alps.—*
MANFRED *and the* CHAMOIS HUNTER.

C. Hun. No—no—yet pause—thou must not yet
    go forth:
Thy mind and body are alike unfit
To trust each other, for some hours, at least;
When thou art better, I will be thy guide—
But whither?
    Man.   It imports not: I do know
My route full well, and need no further guidance.
    C. Hun. Thy garb and gait bespeak thee of high
    lineage—
One of the many chiefs, whose castled crags
Look o'er the lower valleys—which of these
May call thee lord? I only know their portals;   10
My way of life leads me but rarely down
To bask by the huge hearths of those old halls,
Carousing with the vassals; but the paths,
Which step from out our mountains to their doors,
I know from childhood—which of these is thine?
    Man. No matter.
    C. Hun.   Well, Sir, pardon me the question,
And be of better cheer. Come, taste my wine;
'Tis of an ancient vintage; many a day
'T has thawed my veins among our glaciers, now
Let it do thus for thine—Come, pledge me fairly!   20
    Man. Away, away! there's blood upon the brim!
Will it then never—never sink in the earth?
    C. Hun. What dost thou mean? thy senses wander
    from thee.
    Man. I say 'tis blood—my blood! the pure warm
    stream
Which ran in the veins of my fathers, and in ours
When we were in our youth, and had one heart,
And loved each other as we should not love,
And this was shed: but still it rises up,
Colouring the clouds, that shut me out from Heaven,
Where thou art not—and I shall never be.   30
    C. Hun. Man of strange words, and some
    half-maddening sin,
Which makes thee people vacancy, whate'er
Thy dread and sufferance be, there's comfort yet—
The aid of holy men, and heavenly patience——
    Man. Patience—and patience! Hence—that word
    was made
For brutes of burthen, not for birds of prey!
Preach it to mortals of a dust like thine,—
I am not of thine order.
    C. Hun.   Thanks to Heaven!
I would not be of thine for the free fame
Of William Tell; but whatsoe'er thine ill,   40

It must be borne, and these wild starts are useless.
    Man. Do I not bear it?—Look on me—I live.
    C. Hun. This is convulsion, and no healthful life.
    Man. I tell thee, man! I have lived many years,
Many long years, but they are nothing now
To those which I must number: ages—ages—
Space and eternity—and consciousness,
With the fierce thirst of death—and still unslaked!
    C. Hun. Why on thy brow the seal of middle age
Hath scarce been set; I am thine elder far.   50
    Man. Think'st thou existence doth depend on
    time?
It doth; but actions are our epochs: mine
Have made my days and nights imperishable,
Endless, and all alike, as sands on the shore,
Innumerable atoms; and one desert,
Barren and cold, on which the wild waves break,
But nothing rests, save carcasses and wrecks,
Rocks, and the salt-surf weeds of bitterness.
    C. Hun. Alas! he's mad—but yet I must not leave
    him.
    Man. I would I were—for then the things I see   60
Would be but a distempered dream.
    C. Hun.   What is it
That thou dost see, or think thou look'st upon?
    Man. Myself, and thee—a peasant of the Alps—
Thy humble virtues, hospitable home,
And spirit patient, pious, proud, and free;
Thy self-respect, grafted on innocent thoughts;
Thy days of health, and nights of sleep; thy toils,
By danger dignified, yet guiltless; hopes
Of cheerful old age and a quiet grave,
With cross and garland over its green turf,   70
And thy grandchildren's love for epitaph!
This do I see—and then I look within—
It matters not—my Soul was scorched already!
    C. Hun. And would'st thou then exchange thy lot
    for mine?
    Man. No, friend! I would not wrong thee, nor
    exchange
My lot with living being: I can bear—
However wretchedly, 'tis still to bear—
In life what others could not brook to dream,
But perish in their slumber.
    C. Hun.   And with this—
This cautious feeling for another's pain,   80
Canst thou be black with evil?—say not so.
Can one of gentle thoughts have wreaked revenge
Upon his enemies?
    Man.   Oh! no, no, no!
My injuries came down on those who loved me—
On those whom I best loved: I never quelled
An enemy, save in my just defence—
But my embrace was fatal.

C. Hun. Heaven give thee rest!
And Penitence restore thee to thyself;
My prayers shall be for thee.
Man. I need them not,
But can endure thy pity. I depart— 90
'Tis time—farewell!—Here's gold, and thanks for
thee—
No words—it is thy due.—Follow me not—
I know my path—the mountain peril's past:
And once again I charge thee, follow not!
[_Exit_ MANFRED.

SCENE II.—_A lower Valley in the Alps.—
A Cataract._

Enter MANFRED.

It is not noon—the Sunbow's rays* still arch
The torrent with the many hues of heaven,
And roll the sheeted silver's waving column
O'er the crag's headlong perpendicular,
And fling its lines of foaming light along,
And to and fro, like the pale courser's tail,
The Giant steed, to be bestrode by Death,
As told in the Apocalypse.² No eyes
But mine now drink this sight of loveliness;
I should be sole in this sweet solitude, 10
And with the Spirit of the place divide
The homage of these waters.—I will call her.
[MANFRED _takes some of the water into the
palm of his hand and flings it into the air,
muttering the adjuration. After a pause, the
WITCH OF THE ALPS rises beneath the arch
of the sunbow of the torrent._
Beautiful Spirit! with thy hair of light,
And dazzling eyes of glory, in whose form
The charms of Earth's least mortal daughters grow
To an unearthly stature, in an essence
Of purer elements; while the hues of youth,—
Carnationed like a sleeping Infant's cheek,
Rocked by the beating of her mother's heart,
Or the rose tints, which Summer's twilight leaves 20
Upon the lofty Glacier's virgin snow,
The blush of earth embracing with her Heaven,—
Tinge thy celestial aspect, and make tame
The beauties of the Sunbow which bends o'er thee.
Beautiful Spirit! in thy calm clear brow,
Wherein is glassed serenity of Soul,
Which of itself shows immortality,

* The iris is formed by the rays of the sun over the lower
part of the Alpine torrents: it is exactly like a rainbow come down
to pay a visit, and so close that you may walk into it: this effect
lasts till noon.

◇◇◇◇◇◇◇◇◇◇◇◇◇◇◇◇◇◇◇◇◇◇◇◇◇◇◇◇◇◇◇◇◇◇◇◇

² In the Revelation of St. John.

I read that thou wilt pardon to a Son
Of Earth, whom the abstruser powers permit
At times to commune with them—if that he 30
Avail him of his spells—to call thee thus,
And gaze on thee a moment.
Witch. Son of Earth!
I know thee, and the Powers which give thee power!
I know thee for a man of many thoughts,
And deeds of good and ill, extreme in both,
Fatal and fated in thy sufferings.
I have expected this—what would'st thou with me?
Man. To look upon thy beauty—nothing further.
The face of the earth hath maddened me, and I
Take refuge in her mysteries, and pierce 40
To the abodes of those who govern her—
But they can nothing aid me. I have sought
From them what they could not bestow, and now
I search no further.
Witch. What could be the quest
Which is not in the power of the most powerful,
The rulers of the invisible?
Man. A boon;—
But why should I repeat it? 'twere in vain.
Witch. I know not that; let thy lips utter it.
Man. Well, though it torture me, 'tis but the same;
My pang shall find a voice. From my youth upwards
My Spirit walked not with the souls of men, 51
Nor looked upon the earth with human eyes;
The thirst of their ambition was not mine,
The aim of their existence was not mine;
My joys—my griefs—my passions—and my powers,
Made me a stranger; though I wore the form,
I had no sympathy with breathing flesh,
Nor midst the Creatures of Clay that girded me
Was there but One who——but of her anon.
I said with men, and with the thoughts of men, 60
I held but slight communion; but instead,
My joy was in the wilderness,—to breathe
The difficult air of the iced mountain's top,
Where the birds dare not build—nor insect's wing
Flit o'er the herbless granite; or to plunge
Into the torrent, and to roll along
On the swift whirl of the new-breaking wave
Of river-stream, or Ocean, in their flow.
In these my early strength exulted; or
To follow through the night the moving moon, 70
The stars and their development; or catch
The dazzling lightnings till my eyes grew dim;
Or to look, list'ning, on the scattered leaves,
While Autumn winds were at their evening song.
These were my pastimes, and to be alone;
For if the beings, of whom I was one,—
Hating to be so,—crossed me in my path,
I felt myself degraded back to them,

And was all clay again. And then I dived,
In my lone wanderings, to the caves of Death,   80
Searching its cause in its effect; and drew
From withered bones, and skulls, and heaped up dust,
Conclusions most forbidden. Then I passed
The nights of years in sciences untaught,
Save in the old-time; and with time and toil,
And terrible ordeal, and such penance
As in itself hath power upon the air,
And spirits that do compass air and earth,
Space, and the peopled Infinite, I made
Mine eyes familiar with Eternity,   90
Such as, before me, did the Magi, and
He who from out their fountain-dwellings raised
Eros and Anteros,* at Gadara,³
As I do thee;—and with my knowledge grew
The thirst of knowledge, and the power and joy
Of this most bright intelligence, until——
   Witch. Proceed.
   Man.   Oh! I but thus prolonged my
       words,
Boasting these idle attributes, because
As I approach the core of my heart's grief—
But—to my task. I have not named to thee   100
Father or mother, mistress, friend, or being,
With whom I wore the chain of human ties;
If I had such, they seemed not such to me—
Yet there was One——
   Witch.   Spare not thyself—proceed.
   Man. She was like me in lineaments—her eyes—
Her hair—her features—all, to the very tone
Even of her voice, they said were like to mine;
But softened all, and tempered into beauty:
She had the same lone thoughts and wanderings,
The quest of hidden knowledge, and a mind   110
To comprehend the Universe: nor these
Alone, but with them gentler powers than mine,
Pity, and smiles, and tears—which I had not;
And tenderness—but that I had for her;
Humility—and that I never had.
Her faults were mine—her virtues were her own—
I loved her, and destroyed her!
   Witch.   With thy hand?
   Man. Not with my hand, but heart, which broke
       her heart;
It gazed on mine, and withered. I have shed
Blood, but not hers—and yet her blood was shed;
I saw—and could not stanch it.   121
   Witch.   And for this—

* The philosopher Jamblicus. The story of the raising of
Eros and Anteros may be found in his life by Eunapius. It is
well told.

³ Gadara is a city of ancient Palestine.

A being of the race thou dost despise—
The order, which thine own would rise above,
Mingling with us and ours,—thou dost forego
The gifts of our great knowledge, and shrink'st back
To recreant mortality——Away!
   Man. Daughter of Air! I tell thee, since that hour—
But words are breath—look on me in my sleep,
Or watch my watchings—Come and sit by me!
My solitude is solitude no more,   130
But peopled with the Furies;—I have gnashed
My teeth in darkness till returning morn,
Then cursed myself till sunset;—I have prayed
For madness as a blessing—'tis denied me.
I have affronted Death—but in the war
Of elements the waters shrunk from me,
And fatal things passed harmless; the cold hand
Of an all-pitiless Demon held me back,
Back by a single hair, which would not break.
In Fantasy, Imagination, all   140
The affluence of my soul—which one day was
A Crœsus⁴ in creation—I plunged deep,
But, like an ebbing wave, it dashed me back
Into the gulf of my unfathomed thought.
I plunged amidst Mankind—Forgetfulness
I sought in all, save where 'tis to be found—
And that I have to learn—my Sciences,
My long pursued and superhuman art,
Is mortal here: I dwell in my despair—
And live—and live for ever.
   Witch.   It may be   150
That I can aid thee.
   Man.   To do this thy power
Must wake the dead, or lay me low with them.
Do so—in any shape—in any hour—
With any torture—so it be the last.
   Witch. That is not in my province; but if thou
Wilt swear obedience to my will, and do
My bidding, it may help thee to thy wishes.
   Man. I will not swear—Obey! and whom? the
       Spirits
Whose presence I command, and be the slave
Of those who served me—Never!
   Witch.   Is this all?   160
Hast thou no gentler answer?—Yet bethink thee,
And pause ere thou rejectest.
   Man.   I have said it.
   Witch. Enough! I may retire then—say!
   Man.   Retire!
       [*The* WITCH *disappears.*
   Man. (*alone*). We are the fools of Time and
       Terror: Days

⁴ Last king of Lydia (sixth century B.C.), of fabled wealth,
killed by the Persians.

Steal on us, and steal from us; yet we live,
Loathing our life, and dreading still to die.
In all the days of this detested yoke—
This vital weight upon the struggling heart,
Which sinks with sorrow, or beats quick with pain,
Or joy that ends in agony or faintness—   170
In all the days of past and future—for
In life there is no present—we can number
How few—how less than few—wherein the soul
Forbears to pant for death, and yet draws back
As from a stream in winter, though the chill
Be but a moment's. I have one resource
Still in my science—I can call the dead,
And ask them what it is we dread to be:
The sternest answer can but be the Grave,
And that is nothing: if they answer not——   180
The buried Prophet answered to the Hag
Of Endor;[5] and the Spartan Monarch drew
From the Byzantine maid's unsleeping spirit
An answer and his destiny—he slew
That which he loved, unknowing what he slew,
And died unpardoned—though he called in aid
The Phyxian Jove, and in Phigalia roused
The Arcadian Evocators to compel
The indignant shadow to depose her wrath,
Or fix her term of vengeance—she replied   190
In words of dubious import, but fulfilled.*
If I had never lived, that which I love
Had still been living; had I never loved,
That which I love would still be beautiful,
Happy and giving happiness. What is she?
What is she now?—a sufferer for my sins—
A thing I dare not think upon—or nothing.
Within few hours I shall not call in vain—
Yet in this hour I dread the thing I dare:
Until this hour I never shrunk to gaze   200
On spirit, good or evil—now I tremble,
And feel a strange cold thaw upon my heart.
But I can act even what I most abhor,
And champion human fears.—The night approaches.
                                              [*Exit.*

* The story of Pausanias, king of Sparta, (who commanded the Greeks at the battle of Platea, and afterwards perished for an attempt to betray the Lacedæmonians), and Cleonice, is told in Plutarch's life of Cimon; and in the Laconics of Pausanias the Sophist in his description of Greece.

[5] Saul ("the buried Prophet") received a prevision of his death from the Witch of Endor (and the spirit of Samuel) before the battle of Gilboa in the eleventh century B.C.

SCENE III.—*The summit of the Jungfrau Mountain.*

Enter FIRST DESTINY.

The Moon is rising broad, and round, and bright;
And here on snows, where never human foot
Of common mortal trod,[6] we nightly tread,
And leave no traces: o'er the savage sea,
The glassy ocean of the mountain ice,
We skim its rugged breakers, which put on
The aspect of a tumbling tempest's foam,
Frozen in a moment—a dead Whirlpool's image:
And this most steep fantastic pinnacle,
The fretwork of some earthquake—where the clouds
Pause to repose themselves in passing by—   11
Is sacred to our revels, or our vigils;
Here do I wait my sisters, on our way
To the Hall of Arimanes—for to-night
Is our great festival—'tis strange they come not.

A Voice without, singing.

The Captive Usurper,
    Hurled down from the throne,
Lay buried in torpor,
    Forgotten and lone;
I broke through his slumbers,   20
    I shivered his chain,
I leagued him with numbers—
    He's Tyrant again!
With the blood of a million he'll answer my care,
With a Nation's destruction—his flight and despair!

Second Voice, without.

The Ship sailed on, the Ship sailed fast,
But I left not a sail, and I left not a mast;
There is not a plank of the hull or the deck,
And there is not a wretch to lament o'er his wreck;
Save one, whom I held, as he swam, by the hair,   30
And he was a subject well worthy my care;
A traitor on land, and a pirate at sea—
But I saved him to wreak further havoc for me!

FIRST DESTINY, *answering.*

The City lies sleeping;
    The morn, to deplore it,
May dawn on it weeping:
    Sullenly, slowly,
The black plague flew o'er it—
    Thousands lie lowly;
Tens of thousands shall perish;   40
    The living shall fly from
The sick they should cherish;

[6] Actually the Jungfrau was first ascended in 1811.

But nothing can vanquish
　The touch that they die from.
　　Sorrow and anguish,
　And evil and dread,
　　Envelope a nation;
　The blest are the dead,
　Who see not the sight
　　Of their own desolation;　　　　　50
　This work of a night—
This wreck of a realm—this deed of my doing—
For ages I've done, and shall still be renewing!

Enter the SECOND and THIRD DESTINIES.

The Three.

　Our hands contain the hearts of men,
　　Our footsteps are their graves;
　We only give to take again
　　The Spirits of our slaves!

First Des.　Welcome!—Where's Nemesis?
Second Des.　　　　　　　　　At some
　　great work;
But what I know not, for my hands were full.
Third Des.　Behold she cometh.

Enter NEMESIS.[7]

First Des.　　　　　Say, where hast thou been?
My Sisters and thyself are slow to-night.　　61
　Nem.　I was detained repairing shattered thrones—
Marrying fools, restoring dynasties—
Avenging men upon their enemies,
And making them repent their own revenge;
Goading the wise to madness; from the dull
Shaping out oracles to rule the world
Afresh—for they were waxing out of date,
And mortals dared to ponder for themselves,
To weigh kings in the balance—and to speak　70
Of Freedom, the forbidden fruit.—Away!
We have outstayed the hour—mount we our clouds!
　　　　　　　　　　　　　　[*Exeunt.*

SCENE IV.—*The Hall of Arimanes.*[8]—*Arimanes on his Throne, a Globe of Fire, surrounded by the Spirits.*

Hymn of the SPIRITS.

Hail to our Master!—Prince of Earth and Air!
　Who walks the clouds and waters—in his hand
The sceptre of the Elements, which tear
　Themselves to chaos at his high command!
He breatheth—and a tempest shakes the sea;
　He speaketh—and the clouds reply in thunder;

<hr>

7 The Greek goddess of retributive justice.
8 The spirit of evil, the counter-creator.

He gazeth—from his glance the sunbeams flee;
　He moveth—Earthquakes rend the world asunder.
Beneath his footsteps the Volcanoes rise;
　His shadow is the Pestilence: his path　　　10
The comets herald through the crackling skies;
　And Planets turn to ashes at his wrath.
To him War offers daily sacrifice;
　To him Death pays his tribute; Life is his,
With all its Infinite of agonies—
　And his the Spirit of whatever is!

Enter the DESTINIES and NEMESIS.

First Des.　Glory to Arimanes! on the earth
His power increaseth—both my sisters did
His bidding, nor did I neglect my duty!
　Second Des.　Glory to Arimanes! we who bow　20
The necks of men, bow down before his throne!
　Third Des.　Glory to Arimanes! we await
His nod!
　Nem.　Sovereign of Sovereigns! we are thine,
And all that liveth, more or less, is ours,
And most things wholly so; still to increase
Our power, increasing thine, demands our care,
And we are vigilant. Thy late commands
Have been fulfilled to the utmost.

Enter MANFRED.

A Spirit.　　　　　　　　　What is here?
A mortal!—Thou most rash and fatal wretch,
Bow down and worship!
　Second Spirit.　　　　I do know the man—　30
A Magian of great power, and fearful skill!
　Third Spirit.　Bow down and worship, slave!—
　　What, know'st thou not
Thine and our Sovereign?—Tremble, and obey!
　All the Spirits.　Prostrate thyself, and thy
　　condemnéd clay,
Child of the Earth! or dread the worst.
　Man.　　　　　　　　　I know it;
And yet ye see I kneel not.
　Fourth Spirit.　　　　'Twill be taught thee.
　Man. 'Tis taught already;—many a night on the
　earth,
On the bare ground, have I bowed down my face,
And strewed my head with ashes; I have known
The fulness of humiliation—for　　　　　40
I sunk before my vain despair, and knelt
To my own desolation.
　Fifth Spirit.　　　Dost thou dare
Refuse to Arimanes on his throne
What the whole earth accords, beholding not
The terror of his Glory?—Crouch! I say.

Man. Bid *him* bow down to that which is above
     him,
The overruling Infinite—the Maker
Who made him not for worship—let him kneel,
And we will kneel together.
     The Spirits.   Crush the worm!
Tear him in pieces!—
     First Des.   Hence! Avaunt!—he's mine.
Prince of the Powers invisible! This man   51
Is of no common order, as his port
And presence here denote: his sufferings
Have been of an immortal nature—like
Our own; his knowledge, and his powers and will,
As far as is compatible with clay,
Which clogs the ethereal essence, have been such
As clay hath seldom borne; his aspirations
Have been beyond the dwellers of the earth,
And they have only taught him what we know—   60
That knowledge is not happiness, and science
But an exchange of ignorance for that
Which is another kind of ignorance.
This is not all—the passions, attributes
Of Earth and Heaven, from which no power, nor
     being,
Nor breath from the worm upwards is exempt,
Have pierced his heart; and in their consequence
Made him a thing—which—I who pity not,
Yet pardon those who pity. He is mine—
And thine it may be; be it so, or not—   70
No other Spirit in this region hath
A soul like his—or power upon his soul.
     Nem. What doth he here then?
     First Des.   Let *him* answer
     that.
     Man. Ye know what I have known; and without
     power
I could not be amongst ye: but there are
Powers deeper still beyond—I come in quest
Of such, to answer unto what I seek.
     Nem. What would'st thou?
     Man.   *Thou* canst not reply to
     me.
Call up the dead—my question is for them.
     Nem. Great Arimanes, doth thy will avouch   80
The wishes of this mortal?
     Ari.   Yea.
     Nem.   Whom wouldst thou
Uncharnel?
     Man. One without a tomb—call up
Astarte.[9]

◇◇◇◇◇◇◇◇◇◇◇◇◇◇◇◇◇◇◇◇◇◇◇◇◇◇◇◇◇◇◇◇◇◇◇◇

[9] From Astoreth, Phoenecian goddess of fertility and sexu-
ality, the bride and mother of Adonis.

NEMESIS.
     Shadow! or Spirit!
          Whatever thou art,
     Which still doth inherit
          The whole or a part
     Of the form of thy birth,
          Of the mould of thy clay,
     Which returned to the earth,   90
          Re-appear to the day!
     Bear what thou borest,
          The heart and the form,
     And the aspect thou worest
          Redeem from the worm.
     Appear!—Appear!—Appear!
     Who sent thee there requires thee here!
[*The Phantom of* ASTARTE *rises and stands in the
     midst.*
     Man. Can this be death? there's bloom upon her
     cheek;
But now I see it is no living hue,
But a strange hectic—like the unnatural red   100
Which Autumn plants upon the perished leaf.
It is the same! Oh, God! that I should dread
To look upon the same—Astarte!—No,
I cannot speak to her—but bid her speak—
Forgive me or condemn me.

NEMESIS.
     By the Power which hath broken
          The grave which enthralled thee,
     Speak to him who hath spoken,
          Or those who have called thee!
     Man.   She is silent,
And in that silence I am more than answered.   110
     Nem. My power extends no further. Prince of Air!
It rests with thee alone—command her voice.
     Ari. Spirit—obey this sceptre!
     Nem.   Silent still!
She is not of our order, but belongs
To the other powers. Mortal! thy quest is vain,
And we are baffled also.
     Man.   Hear me, hear me—
Astarte! my belovéd! speak to me:
I have so much endured—so much endure—
Look on me! the grave hath not changed thee more
Than I am changed for thee. Thou lovedst me   120
Too much, as I loved thee: we were not made
To torture thus each other—though it were
The deadliest sin to love as we have loved.
Say that thou loath'st me not—that I do bear
This punishment for both—that thou wilt be
One of the blesséd—and that I shall die;
For hitherto all hateful things conspire

To bind me in existence—in a life
Which makes me shrink from Immortality—
A future like the past. I cannot rest.   130
I know not what I ask, nor what I seek:
I feel but what thou art, and what I am;
And I would hear yet once before I perish
The voice which was my music—Speak to me!
For I have called on thee in the still night,
Startled the slumbering birds from the hushed
    boughs,
And woke the mountain wolves, and made the caves
Acquainted with thy vainly echoed name,
Which answered me—many things answered me—
Spirits and men—but thou wert silent all.   140
Yet speak to me! I have outwatched the stars,
And gazed o'er heaven in vain in search of thee.
Speak to me! I have wandered o'er the earth,
And never found thy likeness—Speak to me!
Look on the fiends around—they feel for me:
I fear them not, and feel for thee alone.
Speak to me! though it be in wrath;—but say—
I reck not what—but let me hear thee once—
This once—once more!
    Phantom of Astarte. Manfred!
    Man.   Say on, say on—
I live but in the sound—it is thy voice!   150
    Phan. Manfred! To-morrow ends thine earthly ills.
Farewell!
    Man. Yet one word more—am I forgiven?
    Phan. Farewell!
    Man.   Say, shall we meet again?
    Phan.   Farewell!
    Man. One word for mercy! Say thou lovest me.
    Phan. Manfred!
            [*The Spirit of* ASTARTE *disappears.*
    Nem.   She's gone, and will not be
        recalled:
Her words will be fulfilled. Return to the earth.
    A Spirit. He is convulsed—This is to be a mortal,
And seek the things beyond mortality.
    Another Spirit. Yet, see, he mastereth himself, and
        makes
His torture tributary to his will.   160
Had he been one of us, he would have made
An awful Spirit.
    Nem.   Hast thou further question
Of our great Sovereign, or his worshippers?
    Man. None.
    Nem.   Then for a time farewell.
    Man. We meet then! Where? On the earth?—
Even as thou wilt: and for the grace accorded
I now depart a debtor. Fare ye well!
                        [*Exit* MANFRED.
        (*Scene closes.*)

ACT III.

SCENE I.—*A Hall in the Castle of Manfred.*

MANFRED *and* HERMAN.

    Man. What is the hour?
    Her.   It wants but one till sunset,
And promises a lovely twilight.
    Man.   Say,
Are all things so disposed of in the tower
As I directed?
    Her.   All, my Lord, are ready:
Here is the key and casket.
    Man.   It is well:
Thou mayst retire.   [*Exit* HERMAN.
    Man. (*alone*). There is a calm upon me—
Inexplicable stillness! which till now
Did not belong to what I knew of life.
If that I did not know Philosophy
To be of all our vanities the motliest,   10
The merest word that ever fooled the ear
From out the schoolman's jargon, I should deem
The golden secret, the sought "Kalon," found,[10]
And seated in my soul. It will not last,
But it is well to have known it, though but once:
It hath enlarged my thoughts with a new sense,
And I within my tablets would note down
That there is such a feeling. Who is there?

Re-enter HERMAN.

    Her. My Lord, the Abbot of St. Maurice craves[11]
To greet your presence.

Enter the ABBOT OF ST. MAURICE

    Abbot.   Peace be with Count
        Manfred!   20
    Man. Thanks, holy father! welcome to these walls;
Thy presence honours them, and blesseth those
Who dwell within them.
    Abbot.   Would it were so, Count!—
But I would fain confer with thee alone.
    Man. Herman, retire.—What would my reverend
        guest?
    Abbot. Thus, without prelude:—Age and zeal—
        my office—
And good intent must plead my privilege;
Our near, though not acquainted neighbourhood,
May also be my herald. Rumours strange,
And of unholy nature, are abroad,   30
And busy with thy name—a noble name

---

[10] Beauty; the ultimate good.
[11] The Abbey of St. Maurice was founded in the Rhone Valley near Villeneuve in the fourth century.

For centuries: may he who bears it now
Transmit it unimpaired!
Man.   Proceed,—I listen.
Abbot. 'Tis said thou holdest converse with the
        things
Which are forbidden to the search of man;
That with the dwellers of the dark abodes,
The many evil and unheavenly spirits
Which walk the valley of the Shade of Death,
Thou communest. I know that with mankind,
Thy fellows in creation, thou dost rarely   40
Exchange thy thoughts, and that thy solitude
Is as an Anchorite's—were it but holy.
Man. And what are they who do avouch these
        things?
Abbot. My pious brethren—the scaréd peasantry—
Even thy own vassals—who do look on thee
With most unquiet eyes. Thy life's in peril!
Man. Take it.
Abbot.   I come to save, and not destroy:
I would not pry into thy secret soul;
But if these things be sooth, there still is time
For penitence and pity: reconcile thee   50
With the true church, and through the church to
        Heaven.
Man. I hear thee. This is my reply—whate'er
I may have been, or am, doth rest between
Heaven and myself—I shall not choose a mortal
To be my mediator—Have I sinned
Against your ordinances? prove and punish!
Abbot. My son! I did not speak of punishment,
But penitence and pardon;—with thyself
The choice of such remains—and for the last,
Our institutions and our strong belief   60
Have given me power to smooth the path from sin
To higher hope and better thoughts; the first
I leave to Heaven,—"Vengeance is mine alone!"
So saith the Lord, and with all humbleness
His servant echoes back the awful word.
Man. Old man! there is no power in holy men,
Nor charm in prayer, nor purifying form
Of penitence, nor outward look, nor fast,
Nor agony—nor, greater than all these,
The innate tortures of that deep Despair,   70
Which is Remorse without the fear of Hell,
But all in all sufficient to itself
Would make a hell of Heaven—can exorcise
From out the unbounded spirit the quick sense
Of its own sins—wrongs—sufferance—and revenge
Upon itself; there is no future pang
Can deal that justice on the self-condemned
He deals on his own soul.
Abbot.   All this is well;
For this will pass away, and be succeeded

By an auspicious hope, which shall look up   80
With calm assurance to that blessed place,
Which all who seek may win, whatever be
Their earthly errors, so they be atoned:
And the commencement of atonement is
The sense of its necessity. Say on—
And all our church can teach thee shall be taught;
And all we can absolve thee shall be pardoned.
Man. When Rome's sixth Emperor [12] was near his
        last,
The victim of a self-inflicted wound,
To shun the torments of a public death   90
From senates once his slaves, a certain soldier,
With show of loyal pity, would have stanched
The gushing throat with his officious robe;
The dying Roman thrust him back, and said—
Some empire still in his expiring glance—
"It is too late—is this fidelity?"
Abbot. And what of this?
Man.   I answer with the
        Roman—
"It is too late!"
Abbot.   It never can be so,
To reconcile thyself with thy own soul,
And thy own soul with Heaven. Hast thou no hope?
'Tis strange—even those who do despair above,   101
Yet shape themselves some fantasy on earth,
To which frail twig they cling, like drowning men.
Man. Aye—father! I have had those early visions,
And noble aspirations in my youth,
To make my own the mind of other men,
The enlightener of nations; and to rise
I knew not whither—it might be to fall;
But fall, even as the mountain-cataract,
Which having leapt from its more dazzling height, 110
Even in the foaming strength of its abyss,
(Which casts up misty columns that become
Clouds raining from the re-ascended skies,)
Lies low but mighty still.— But this is past,
My thoughts mistook themselves.
Abbot.   And wherefore so?
Man. I could not tame my nature down; for he
Must serve who fain would sway; and soothe, and sue,
And watch all time, and pry into all place,
And be a living Lie, who would become
A mighty thing amongst the mean—and such   120
The mass are; I disdained to mingle with
A herd, though to be leader—and of wolves.
The lion is alone, and so am I.
Abbot. And why not live and act with other men?
Man. Because my nature was averse from life;
And yet not cruel; for I would not make,

---

[12] Nero.

But find a desolation. Like the Wind,
The red-hot breath of the most lone Simoom,[13]
Which dwells but in the desert, and sweeps o'er
The barren sands which bear no shrubs to blast,　130
And revels o'er their wild and arid waves,
And seeketh not, so that it is not sought,
But being met is deadly,—such hath been
The course of my existence; but there came
Things in my path which are no more.
　　Abbot.　　　　　　　　　　Alas!
I 'gin to fear that thou art past all aid
From me and from my calling; yet so young,
I still would——
　　Man.　　　　　Look on me! there is an order
Of mortals on the earth, who do become
Old in their youth, and die ere middle age,　140
Without the violence of warlike death;
Some perishing of pleasure—some of study—
Some worn with toil, some of mere weariness,—
Some of disease—and some insanity—
And some of withered, or of broken hearts;
For this last is a malady which slays
More than are numbered in the lists of Fate,
Taking all shapes, and bearing many names.
Look upon me! for even of all these things
Have I partaken; and of all these things,　150
One were enough; then wonder not that I
Am what I am, but that I ever was,
Or having been, that I am still on earth.
　　Abbot. Yet, hear me still——
　　Man.　　　　　　　Old man! I do respect
Thine order, and revere thine years; I deem
Thy purpose pious, but it is in vain:
Think me not churlish; I would spare thyself,
Far more than me, in shunning at this time
All further colloquy—and so—farewell.
　　　　　　　　　　　[*Exit* MANFRED.
　　Abbot. This should have been a noble creature: he
Hath all the energy which would have made　161
A goodly frame of glorious elements,
Had they been wisely mingled; as it is,
It is an awful chaos—Light and Darkness—
And mind and dust—and passions and pure
　　thoughts
Mixed, and contending without end or order,—
All dormant or destructive. He will perish—
And yet he must not—I will try once more,
For such are worth redemption; and my duty
Is to dare all things for a righteous end.　170
I'll follow him—but cautiously, though surely.
　　　　　　　　　　　[*Exit* ABBOT.

◇◇◇◇◇◇◇◇◇◇◇◇◇◇◇◇◇◇◇◇◇◇◇◇◇◇

[13] The hot, dry wind of the African and Arabian deserts.
See also *The Giaour*, p. 562; and particularly Coleridge's *Religious
Musings*, p. 439, note *, quoting from Bruce's *Travels*.

SCENE II.—*Another Chamber.*

MANFRED *and* HERMAN.

　Her. My lord, you bade me wait on you at sunset:
He sinks behind the mountain.
　Man.　　　　　　　　Doth he so?
I will look on him.
　　　　[MANFRED *advances to the Window of the Hall.*
　　　　　Glorious Orb! the idol
Of early nature, and the vigorous race
Of undiseased mankind, the giant sons *
Of the embrace of Angels, with a sex
More beautiful than they, which did draw down
The erring Spirits who can ne'er return.—
Most glorious Orb! that wert a worship, ere
The mystery of thy making was revealed!　10
Thou earliest minister of the Almighty,
Which gladdened, on their mountain tops, the hearts
Of the Chaldean shepherds, till they poured
Themselves in orisons! Thou material God!
And representative of the Unknown—
Who chose thee for his shadow! Thou chief Star!
Centre of many stars! which mak'st our earth
Endurable, and temperest the hues
And hearts of all who walk within thy rays!
Sire of the seasons! Monarch of the climes,　20
And those who dwell in them! for near or far,
Our inborn spirits have a tint of thee
Even as our outward aspects;—thou dost rise,
And shine, and set in glory. Fare thee well!
I ne'er shall see thee more. As my first glance
Of love and wonder was for thee, then take
My latest look: thou wilt not beam on one
To whom the gifts of life and warmth have been
Of a more fatal nature. He is gone—
I follow.　　　　　　　　[*Exit* MANFRED.

SCENE III.—*The Mountains—The Castle of Man-
　　fred at some distance—A Terrace before a Tower.
　　—Time, Twilight.*

HERMAN, MANUEL, *and other dependants of*
　　　　　　MANFRED.

　Her. 'Tis strange enough! night after night, for
　　years,
He hath pursued long vigils in this tower,
Without a witness. I have been within it,—
So have we all been oft-times; but from it,

* "And it came to pass, that the *Sons of God* saw the
daughters of men, that they were fair," &c.—"There were giants
in the earth in those days; and also after that, when the *Sons of
God* came in unto the daughters of men, and they bare children
to them, the same became mighty men which were of old, men
of renown."—*Genesis*, ch. vi. verses 2 and 4.

Or its contents, it were impossible
To draw conclusions absolute, of aught
His studies tend to. To be sure, there is
One chamber where none enter: I would give
The fee of what I have to come these three years,
To pore upon its mysteries.
    Manuel.   'Twere dangerous;   10
Content thyself with what thou know'st already.
    Her. Ah! Manuel! thou art elderly and wise,
And couldst say much; thou hast dwelt within the
        castle—
How many years is't?
    Manuel.   Ere Count Manfred's birth,
I served his father, whom he nought resembles.
    Her. There be more sons in like predicament!
But wherein do they differ?
    Manuel.   I speak not
Of features or of form, but mind and habits;
Count Sigismund was proud, but gay and free,—
A warrior and a reveller; he dwelt not   20
With books and solitude, nor made the night
A gloomy vigil, but a festal time,
Merrier than day; he did not walk the rocks
And forests like a wolf, nor turn aside
From men and their delights.
    Her.   Beshrew the hour,
But those were jocund times! I would that such
Would visit the old walls again; they look
As if they had forgotten them.
    Manuel.   These walls
Must change their chieftain first. Oh! I have seen
Some strange things in them, Herman.
    Her.   Come, be
        friendly;   30
Relate me some to while away our watch:
I've heard thee darkly speak of an event
Which happened hereabouts, by this same tower.
    Manuel. That was a night indeed! I do remember
'Twas twilight, as it may be now, and such
Another evening:—yon red cloud, which rests
On Eigher's pinnacle,[14] so rested then,—
So like that it might be the same; the wind
Was faint and gusty, and the mountain snows
Began to glitter with the climbing moon;   40
Count Manfred was, as now, within his tower,—
How occupied, we knew not, but with him
The sole companion of his wanderings
And watchings—her, whom of all earthly things
That lived, the only thing he seemed to love,—
As he, indeed, by blood was bound to do,
The Lady Astarte, his——
               Hush! who comes here?

---

[14] A peak of the Bernese Alps.

Enter the ABBOT.

    Abbot. Where is your master?
    Her.   Yonder in the tower.
    Abbot. I must speak with him.
    Manuel.   'Tis impossible;
He is most private, and must not be thus   50
Intruded on.
    Abbot.   Upon myself I take
The forfeit of my fault, if fault there be—
But I must see him.
    Her.   Thou hast seen him once
This eve already.
    Abbot.   Herman! I command thee,
Knock, and apprize the Count of my approach.
    Her. We dare not.
    Abbot.   Then it seems I must be herald
Of my own purpose.
    Manuel.   Reverend father, stop—
I pray you pause.
    Abbot.   Why so?
    Manuel.   But step this way,
And I will tell you further.   [*Exeunt.*

SCENE IV.—*Interior of the Tower.*

MANFRED *alone.*

The stars are forth, the moon above the tops
Of the snow-shining mountains.—Beautiful!
I linger yet with Nature, for the Night
Hath been to me a more familiar face
Than that of man; and in her starry shade
Of dim and solitary loveliness,
I learned the language of another world.
I do remember me, that in my youth,
When I was wandering,—upon such a night
I stood within the Coliseum's wall,   10
'Midst the chief relics of almighty Rome;
The trees which grew along the broken arches
Waved dark in the blue midnight, and the stars
Shone through the rents of ruin; from afar
The watch-dog bayed beyond the Tiber; and
More near from out the Cæsars' palace came
The owl's long cry, and, interruptedly,
Of distant sentinels the fitful song
Begun and died upon the gentle wind.
Some cypresses beyond the time-worn breach   20
Appeared to skirt the horizon, yet they stood
Within a bowshot. Where the Cæsars dwelt,
And dwell the tuneless birds of night, amidst
A grove which springs through levelled battlements,
And twines its roots with the imperial hearths,
Ivy usurps the laurel's place of growth;
But the gladiators' bloody Circus stands,

A noble wreck in ruinous perfection,
While Cæsar's chambers, and the Augustan halls,
Grovel on earth in indistinct decay.—   30
And thou didst shine, thou rolling Moon, upon
All this, and cast a wide and tender light,
Which softened down the hoar austerity
Of rugged desolation, and filled up,
As 'twere anew, the gaps of centuries;
Leaving that beautiful which still was so,
And making that which was not—till the place
Became religion, and the heart ran o'er
With silent worship of the Great of old,—
The dead, but sceptred, Sovereigns, who still rule 40
Our spirits from their urns.
                           'Twas such a night!
'Tis strange that I recall it at this time;
But I have found our thoughts take wildest flight
Even at the moment when they should array
Themselves in pensive order.

                Enter the ABBOT.

  Abbot.   My good Lord!
I crave a second grace for this approach;
But yet let not my humble zeal offend
By its abruptness—all it hath of ill
Recoils on me; its good in the effect
May light upon your head—could I say *heart*— 50
Could I touch *that*, with words or prayers, I should
Recall a noble spirit which hath wandered,
But is not yet all lost.
  Man.   Thou know'st me not;
My days are numbered, and my deeds recorded:
Retire, or 'twill be dangerous—Away!
  Abbot. Thou dost not mean to menace me?
  Man.   Not I!
I simply tell thee peril is at hand,
And would preserve thee.
  Abbot.   What dost thou mean?
  Man.   Look there!
What dost thou see?
  Abbot.   Nothing.
  Man.   Look there, I say,
And steadfastly;—now tell me what thou seest? 60
  Abbot. That which should shake me,—but I fear it
        not:
I see a dusk and awful figure rise,
Like an infernal god, from out the earth;
His face wrapt in a mantle, and his form
Robed as with angry clouds: he stands between
Thyself and me—but I do fear him not.
  Man. Thou hast no cause—he shall not harm
        thee—but
His sight may shock thine old limbs into palsy.
I say to thee—Retire!

  Abbot.   And I reply—
Never—till I have battled with this fiend:—   70
What doth he here?
  Man.   Why—aye—what doth he here?
I did not send for him,—he is unbidden.
  Abbot. Alas! lost Mortal! what with guests like
        these
Hast thou to do? I tremble for thy sake:
Why dost he gaze on thee, and thou on him?
Ah! he unveils his aspect: on his brow
The thunder-scars are graven; from his eye
Glares forth the immortality of Hell—
Avaunt!—
  Man.   Pronounce—what is thy mission?
  Spirit.   Come!
  Abbot. What art thou, unknown being? answer!—
        speak!   80
  Spirit. The genius of this mortal.—Come! 'tis time.
  Man. I am prepared for all things, but deny
The Power which summons me. Who sent thee
        here?
  Spirit. Thou'lt know anon—Come! come!
  Man.   I have commanded
Things of an essence greater far than thine,
And striven with thy masters. Get thee hence!
  Spirit. Mortal! thine hour is come—Away! I say.
  Man. I knew, and know my hour is come, but not
To render up my soul to such as thee:
Away! I'll die as I have lived—alone.   90
  Spirit. Then I must summon up my brethren.—
        Rise!

                    [*Other Spirits rise up.*
  Abbot. Avaunt! ye evil ones!—Avaunt! I say,—
Ye have no power where Piety hath power,
And I do charge ye in the name—
  Spirit.   Old man!
We know ourselves, our mission, and thine order;
Waste not thy holy words on idle uses,
It were in vain: this man is forfeited.
Once more—I summon him—Away! Away!
  Man. I do defy ye,—though I feel my soul
Is ebbing from me, yet I do defy ye;   100
Nor will I hence, while I have earthly breath
To breathe my scorn upon ye—earthly strength
To wrestle, though with spirits; what ye take
Shall be ta'en limb by limb.
  Spirit.   Reluctant mortal!
Is this the Magian who would so pervade
The world invisible, and make himself
Almost our equal? Can it be that thou
Art thus in love with life? the very life
Which made thee wretched?
  Man.   Thou false fiend, thou
        liest!

My life is in its last hour,—*that* I know,   110
Nor would redeem a moment of that hour;
I do not combat against Death, but thee
And thy surrounding angels; my past power
Was purchased by no compact with thy crew,
But by superior science—penance, daring,
And length of watching, strength of mind, and skill
In knowledge of our Fathers—when the earth
Saw men and spirits walking side by side,
And gave ye no supremacy: I stand
Upon my strength—I do defy—deny—   120
Spurn back, and scorn ye!—
   Spirit.   But thy many crimes
Have made thee——
   Man.   What are they to such as thee?
Must crimes be punished but by other crimes,
And greater criminals?—Back to thy hell!
Thou hast no power upon me, *that* I feel;
Thou never shalt possess me, *that* I know:
What I have done is done; I bear within
A torture which could nothing gain from thine:
The Mind which is immortal makes itself
Requital for its good or evil thoughts,—   130
Is its own origin of ill and end—
And its own place and time: its innate sense,
When stripped of this mortality, derives
No colour from the fleeting things without,
But is absorbed in sufferance or in joy,
Born from the knowledge of its own desert.
Thou didst not tempt me, and thou couldst not tempt
   me;
I have not been thy dupe, nor am thy prey—
But was my own destroyer, and will be
My own hereafter.—Back, ye baffled fiends!   140
The hand of Death is on me—but not yours!
                [*The Demons disappear.*
   Abbot. Alas! how pale thou art—thy lips are
      white—
And thy breast heaves—and in thy gasping throat
The accents rattle: Give thy prayers to Heaven—
Pray—albeit but in thought,—but die not thus.
   Man. 'Tis over—my dull eyes can fix thee not;
But all things swim around me, and the earth
Heaves as it were beneath me. Fare thee well—
Give me thy hand.
   Abbot.   Cold—cold—even to the heart—
But yet one prayer—Alas! how fares it with thee?   150
   Man. Old man! 'tis not so difficult to die.
                [MANFRED *expires.*
   Abbot. He's gone—his soul hath ta'en its earthless
      flight;
Whither? I dread to think—but he is gone.

[1816–17]   [1817]

BEPPO:
A VENETIAN STORY.

   Rosalind. Farewell, Monsieur Traveller; Look, you lisp, and wear strange suits: disable all the benefits of your own country; be out of love with your Nativity, and almost chide God for making you that countenance you are; or I will scarce think you have swam in a *Gondola.*
        As You Like It, act iv. sc. 1.

        Annotation of the Commentators.

   That is, been at *Venice*, which was much visited by the young English gentlemen of those times, and was *then* what *Paris* is *now*—the seat of all dissoluteness.—S.A.[1]

I.

'TIS known, at least it should be, that throughout
   All countries of the Catholic persuasion,
Some weeks before Shrove Tuesday comes about,
   The People take their fill of recreation,
And buy repentance, ere they grow devout,
   However high their rank, or low their station,
With fiddling, feasting, dancing, drinking, masquing,
And other things which may be had for asking.

II.

The moment night with dusky mantle covers
   The skies (and the more duskily the better),
The Time less liked by husbands than by lovers
   Begins, and Prudery flings aside her fetter;
And Gaiety on restless tiptoe hovers,
   Giggling with all the gallants who beset her;
And there are songs and quavers, roaring, humming,
Guitars, and every other sort of strumming.

III.

And there are dresses splendid, but fantastical,
   Masks of all times and nations, Turks and Jews,
And harlequins and clowns, with feats gymnastical,
   Greeks, Romans, Yankee-doodles, and Hindoos;
All kinds of dress, except the ecclesiastical,
   All people, as their fancies hit, may choose,
But no one in these parts may quiz the Clergy,—
Therefore take heed, ye Freethinkers! I charge ye.

[1] Samuel Ayscough, editor of a Shakespeare in 1807.

IV.

You'd better walk about begirt with briars,
　　Instead of coat and smallclothes, than put on
A single stitch reflecting upon friars,
　　Although you swore it only was in fun;
They'd haul you o'er the coals, and stir the fires
　　Of Phlegethon [2] with every mother's son,
Nor say one mass to cool the cauldron's bubble
That boiled your bones, unless you paid them
　　　　double.

V.

But saving this, you may put on whate'er
　　You like by way of doublet, cape, or cloak,
Such as in Monmouth-street, or in Rag Fair,
　　Would rig you out in seriousness or joke;
And even in Italy such places are,
　　With prettier name in softer accents spoke,
For, bating Covent Garden, I can hit on
No place that's called "Piazza" in Great Britain.

VI.

This feast is named the Carnival, which being
　　Interpreted, implies "farewell to flesh:"
So called, because the name and thing agreeing,
　　Through Lent they live on fish both salt and fresh.
But why they usher Lent with so much glee in,
　　Is more than I can tell, although I guess
'Tis as we take a glass with friends at parting,
In the Stage-Coach or Packet, just at starting.

VII.

And thus they bid farewell to carnal dishes,
　　And solid meats, and highly spiced ragouts,
To live for forty days on ill-dressed fishes,
　　Because they have no sauces to their stews;
A thing which causes many "poohs" and "pishes,"
　　And several oaths (which would not suit the Muse),
From travellers accustomed from a boy
To eat their salmon, at the least, with soy;

VIII.

And therefore humbly I would recommend
　　"The curious in fish-sauce," before they cross
The sea, to bid their cook, or wife, or friend,
　　Walk or ride to the Strand, and buy in gross
(Or if set out beforehand, these may send
　　By any means least liable to loss),
Ketchup, Soy, Chili-vinegar, and Harvey,
Or, by the Lord! a Lent will well nigh starve ye;

IX.

That is to say, if your religion's Roman,
　　And you at Rome would do as Romans do,
According to the proverb,—although no man,
　　If foreign, is obliged to fast; and you,
If Protestant, or sickly, or a woman,
　　Would rather dine in sin on a ragout—
Dine and be d—d! I don't mean to be coarse,
But that's the penalty, to say no worse.

X.

Of all the places where the Carnival
　　Was most facetious in the days of yore,
For dance, and song, and serenade, and ball,
　　And Masque, and Mime, and Mystery, and more
Than I have time to tell now, or at all,
　　Venice the bell from every city bore,—
And at the moment when I fix my story,
That sea-born city was in all her glory.

XI.

They've pretty faces yet, those same Venetians,
　　Black eyes, arched brows, and sweet expressions
　　　　still;
Such as of old were copied from the Grecians,
　　In ancient arts by moderns mimicked ill;
And like so many Venuses of Titian's
　　(The best's at Florence—see it, if ye will,)
They look when leaning over the balcony,
Or stepped from out a picture by Giorgione, [3]

XII.

Whose tints are Truth and Beauty at their best;
　　And when you to Manfrini's palace go, [4]
That picture (howsoever fine the rest)
　　Is loveliest to my mind of all the show;
It may perhaps be also to *your* zest,
　　And that's the cause I rhyme upon it so:
'Tis but a portrait of his Son, and Wife,
And self; but *such* a Woman! Love in life!

XIII.

Love in full life and length, not love ideal,
　　No, nor ideal beauty, that fine name,
But something better still, so very real,
　　That the sweet Model must have been the same;
A thing that you would purchase, beg, or steal,
　　Wer't not impossible, besides a shame:
The face recalls some face, as 'twere with pain,
You once have seen, but ne'er will see again;

---

[3] Giorgio Barbarelli, "Giorgione" (1478–1511), Venetian painter.
[4] In Venice.

[2] Mythical river of fire in Hades.

XIV.

One of those forms which flit by us, when we
   Are young, and fix our eyes on every face;
And, oh! the Loveliness at times we see
   In momentary gliding, the soft grace,
The Youth, the Bloom, the Beauty which agree,
   In many a nameless being we retrace,
Whose course and home we knew not, nor shall know,
Like the lost Pleiad * seen no more below.

XV.

I said that like a picture by Giorgione
   Venetian women were, and so they *are*,
Particularly seen from a balcony,
   (For beauty's sometimes best set off afar)
And there, just like a heroine of Goldoni,[6]
   They peep from out the blind, or o'er the bar;
And truth to say, they're mostly very pretty,
And rather like to show it, more's the pity!

XVI.

For glances beget ogles, ogles sighs,
   Sighs wishes, wishes words, and words a letter,
Which flies on wings of light-heeled Mercuries,
   Who do such things because they know no better;
And then, God knows what mischief may arise,
   When Love links two young people in one fetter,
Vile assignations, and adulterous beds,
Elopements, broken vows, and hearts, and heads.

XVII.

Shakspeare described the sex in Desdemona
   As very fair, but yet suspect in fame,
And to this day from Venice to Verona
   Such matters may be probably the same,
Except that since those times was never known a
   Husband whom mere suspicion could inflame
To suffocate a wife no more than twenty,
Because she had a "Cavalier Servente."[7]

XVIII.

Their jealousy (if they are ever jealous)
   Is of a fair complexion altogether,
Not like that sooty devil of Othello's,
   Which smothers women in a bed of feather,
But worthier of these much more jolly fellows,
   When weary of the matrimonial tether
His head for such a wife no mortal bothers,
But takes at once another, or *another's*.

* "Quae *septem* dici, *sex* tamen esse solent."—Ovid.[5]

5 "Usually called seven, though only six in number."
6 Carlo Goldini (1707–1793), Italian dramatist.
7 The publicly acknowledged lover of a married woman.

XIX.

Didst ever see a Gondola? For fear
   You should not, I'll describe it you exactly:
'Tis a long covered boat that's common here,
   Carved at the prow, built lightly, but compactly,
Rowed by two rowers, each call'd "Gondolier,"
   It glides along the water looking blackly,
Just like a coffin clapt in a canoe,
Where none can make out what you say or do.

XX.

And up and down the long canals they go,
   And under the Rialto shoot along,
By night and day, all paces, swift or slow,
   And round the theatres, a sable throng,
They wait in their dusk livery of woe,—
   But not to them do woeful things belong,
For sometimes they contain a deal of fun,
Like mourning coaches when the funeral's done.

XXI.

But to my story.—'Twas some years ago,
   It may be thirty, forty, more or less,
The Carnival was at its height, and so
   Were all kinds of buffoonery and dress;
A certain lady went to see the show,
   Her real name I know not, nor can guess,
And so we'll call her Laura, if you please,
Because it slips into my verse with ease.

XXII.

She was not old, nor young, nor at the years
   Which certain people call a "*certain age*,"
Which yet the most uncertain age appears,
   Because I never heard, nor could engage
A person yet by prayers, or bribes, or tears,
   To name, define by speech, or write on page,
The period meant precisely by that word,—
Which surely is exceedingly absurd.

XXIII.

Laura was blooming still, had made the best
   Of Time, and Time returned the compliment,
And treated her genteelly, so that, dressed,
   She looked extremely well where'er she went;
A pretty woman is a welcome guest,
   And Laura's brow a frown had rarely bent;
Indeed, she shone all smiles, and seemed to flatter
Mankind with her black eyes for looking at her.

XXIV.

She was a married woman; 'tis convenient,
    Because in Christian countries 'tis a rule
To view their little slips with eyes more lenient;
    Whereas if single ladies play the fool,
(Unless within the period intervenient
    A well-timed wedding makes the scandal cool)
I don't know how they ever can get over it,
Except they manage never to discover it.

XXV.

Her husband sailed upon the Adriatic,
    And made some voyages, too, in other seas,
And when he lay in Quarantine for pratique [8]
    (A forty days' precaution 'gainst disease),
His wife would mount, at times, her highest attic,
    For thence she could discern the ship with ease:
He was a merchant trading to Aleppo,
His name Giuseppe, called more briefly, Beppo.*

XXVI.

He was a man as dusky as a Spaniard,
    Sunburnt with travel, yet a portly figure;
Though coloured, as it were, within a tanyard,
    He was a person both of sense and vigour—
A better seaman never yet did man yard;
    And she, although her manners showed no rigour,
Was deemed a woman of the strictest principle,
So much as to be thought almost invincible.

XXVII.

But several years elapsed since they had met;
    Some people thought the ship was lost, and some
That he had somehow blundered into debt,
    And did not like the thought of steering home;
And there were several offered any bet,
    Or that he would, or that he would not come;
For most men (till by losing rendered sager)
Will back their own opinions with a wager.

XXVIII.

'Tis said that their last parting was pathetic,
    As partings often are, or ought to be,
And their presentiment was quite prophetic,
    That they should never more each other see,
(A sort of morbid feeling, half poetic,
    Which I have known occur in two or three,)
When kneeling on the shore upon her sad knee
He left this Adriatic Ariadne. [9]

* Beppo is the *Joe* of the Italian *Joseph*.

[8] Clean bill of health after quarantine.
[9] Minos' daughter, who helped Theseus out of the labyrinth
of the Minotaur.

XXIX.

And Laura waited long, and wept a little,
    And thought of wearing weeds, as well she might;
She almost lost all appetite for victual,
    And could not sleep with ease alone at night;
She deemed the window-frames and shutters brittle
    Against a daring housebreaker or sprite,
And so she thought it prudent to connect her
With a vice-husband, *chiefly* to *protect her*.

XXX.

She chose, (and what is there they will not choose,
    If only you will but oppose their choice?)
Till Beppo should return from his long cruise,
    And bid once more her faithful heart rejoice,
A man some women like, and yet abuse—
    A Coxcomb was he by the public voice;
A Count of wealth, they said, as well as quality,
And in his pleasures of great liberality.

XXXI.

And then he was a Count, and then he knew
    Music, and dancing, fiddling, French and Tuscan;
The last not easy, be it known to you,
    For few Italians speak the right Etruscan.
He was a critic upon operas, too,
    And knew all niceties of sock and buskin; [10]
And no Venetian audience could endure a
Song, scene, or air, when he cried "seccatura!" [11]

XXXII.

His "bravo" was decisive, for that sound
    Hushed "Academie" sighed in silent awe;
The fiddlers trembled as he looked around,
    For fear of some false note's detected flaw;
The "Prima Donna's" tuneful heart would bound,
    Dreading the deep damnation of his "Bah!"
Soprano, Basso, even the Contra-Alto,
Wished him five fathom under the Rialto.

XXXIII.

He patronised the Improvisatori,
    Nay, could himself extemporise some stanzas,
Wrote rhymes, sang songs, could also tell a story,
    Sold pictures, and was skilful in the dance as
Italians can be, though in this their glory
    Must surely yield the palm to that which France
In short, he was a perfect Cavaliero,   [has;
And to his very valet seemed a hero.

[10] The traditional symbols of comedy and tragedy.
[11] "Boring."

XXXIV.

Then he was faithful too, as well as amorous;
  So that no sort of female could complain,
Although they're now and then a little clamorous,
  He never put the pretty souls in pain;
His heart was one of those which most enamour us,
  Wax to receive, and marble to retain:
He was a lover of the good old school,
Who still become more constant as they cool.

XXXV.

No wonder such accomplishments should turn
  A female head, however sage and steady—
With scarce a hope that Beppo could return,
  In law he was almost as good as dead, he
Nor sent, nor wrote, nor showed the least concern,
  And she had waited several years already:
And really if a man won't let us know
That he's alive, he's *dead*—or should be so.

XXXVI.

Besides, within the Alps, to every woman,
  (Although, God knows, it is a grievous sin,)
'Tis, I may say, permitted to have *two* men;
  I can't tell who first brought the custom in,
But "Cavalier Serventes" are quite common,
  And no one notices or cares a pin;
And we may call this (not to say the worst)
A *second* marriage which corrupts the *first*.

XXXVII.

The word was formerly a "Cicisbeo," [12]
  But *that* is now grown vulgar and indecent;
The Spaniards call the person a "*Cortejo*,"*
  For the same mode subsists in Spain, though recent;
In short it reaches from the Po to Teio,
  And may perhaps at last be o'er the sea sent:
But Heaven preserve Old England from such courses!
Or what becomes of damage and divorces?

XXXVIII.

However, I still think, with all due deference
  To the fair *single* part of the creation,
That married ladies should preserve the preference
  In *tête à tête* or general conversation—
And this I say without peculiar reference
  To England, France, or any other nation—
Because they know the world, and are at ease,
And being natural, naturally please.

* Cortejo is pronounced Corte*h*o, with an aspirate, according to the Arabesque guttural. It means what there is as yet no precise name for in England, though the practice is as common as in any tramontane country whatever.

[12] "Beautiful chick" inverted.

XXXIX.

'Tis true, your budding Miss is very charming,
  But shy and awkward at first coming out,
So much alarmed, that she is quite alarming,
  All Giggle, Blush; half Pertness, and half Pout;
And glancing at *Mamma*, for fear there's harm in
  What you, she, it, or they, may be about:
The Nursery still lisps out in all they utter—
Beside, they always smell of bread and butter.

XL.

But "Cavalier Servente" is the phrase
  Used in politest circles to express
This supernumerary slave, who stays
  Close to the lady as a part of dress,
Her word the only law which he obeys.
  His is no sinecure, as you may guess;
Coach, servants, gondola, he goes to call,
And carries fan and tippet, gloves and shawl.

XLI.

With all its sinful doings, I must say,
  That Italy's a pleasant place to me,
Who love to see the Sun shine every day,
  And vines (not nailed to walls) from tree to tree
Festooned, much like the back scene of a play,
  Or melodrame, which people flock to see,
When the first act is ended by a dance
In vineyards copied from the South of France.

XLII.

I like on Autumn evenings to ride out,
  Without being forced to bid my groom be sure
My cloak is round his middle strapped about,
  Because the skies are not the most secure;
I know too that, if stopped upon my route,
  Where the green alleys windingly allure,
Reeling with *grapes* red wagons choke the way,—
In England 'twould be dung, dust, or a dray.

XLIII.

I also like to dine on becaficas, [13]
  To see the Sun set, sure he'll rise to-morrow,
Not through a misty morning twinkling weak as
  A drunken man's dead eye in maudlin sorrow,
But with all Heaven t'himself; the day will break as
  Beauteous as cloudless, nor be forced to borrow
That sort of farthing candlelight which glimmers
Where reeking London's smoky cauldron simmers.

[13] Small songbirds ("fig-peckers") eaten in Italy as a delicacy.

XLIV.

I love the language, that soft bastard Latin,
    Which melts like kisses from a female mouth,
And sounds as if it should be writ on satin,
    With syllables which breathe of the sweet South,
And gentle liquids gliding all so pat in,
    That not a single accent seems uncouth,
Like our harsh northern whistling, grunting guttural,
Which we're obliged to hiss, and split, and sputter all.

XLV.

I like the women too (forgive my folly!),
    From the rich peasant cheek of ruddy bronze,
And large black eyes that flash on you a volley
    Of rays that say a thousand things at once,
To the high Dama's brow, more melancholy,
    But clear, and with a wild and liquid glance,
Heart on her lips, and soul within her eyes,
Soft as her clime, and sunny as her skies.

XLVI.

Eve of the land which still is Paradise!
    Italian Beauty didst thou not inspire
Raphael, who died in thy embrace,* and vies
    With all we know of Heaven, or can desire,
In what he hath bequeathed us?—in what guise,
    Though flashing from the fervour of the Lyre,
Would *words* describe thy past and present glow,
While yet Canova[14] can create below? †

XLVII.

"England! with all thy faults I love thee still," [15]
    I said at Calais, and have not forgot it;
I like to speak and lucubate my fill;
    I like the government (but that is not it);
I like the freedom of the press and quill;
    I like the Habeas Corpus (when we've got it);
I like a Parliamentary debate,
Particularly when 'tis not too late;

* For the received accounts of the cause of Raphael's death,
see his Lives.
    † (In talking thus, the writer, more especially
        Of women, would be understood to say,
    He speaks as a spectator, not officially,
        And always, reader, in a modest way;
    Perhaps, too, in no very great degree shall he
        Appear to have offended in this lay,
    Since, as all know, without the sex, our sonnets
        Would seem unfinish'd, like their untrimm'd bonnets.)
                    (Signed)   PRINTER'S DEVIL

[14] Raphael (Sanzio), Renaissance Italian painter and architect;
Antonio Canova, contemporary Italian sculptor.
[15] Quoted from Cowper's *The Task* (1784–91).

XLVIII.

I like the taxes, when they're not too many;
    I like a seacoal fire, when not too dear;
I like a beef-steak, too, as well as any;
    Have no objection to a pot of beer;
I like the weather,—when it is not rainy,
    That is, I like two months of every year.
And so God save the Regent, Church, and King!
Which means that I like all and every thing.

XLIX.

Our standing army, and disbanded seamen,
    Poor's rate, Reform, my own, the nation's debt,
Our little riots just to show we're free men,
    Our trifling bankruptcies in the Gazette,
Our cloudy climate, and our chilly women,
    All these I can forgive, and those forget,
And greatly venerate our recent glories,
And wish they were not owing to the Tories.

L.

But to my tale of Laura,—for I find
    Digression is a sin, that by degrees
Becomes exceeding tedious to my mind,
    And, therefore, may the reader too displease—
The gentle reader, who may wax unkind,
    And crying little for the Author's ease,
Insist on knowing what he means—a hard
And hapless situation for a Bard.

LI.

Oh! that I had the art of easy writing
    What should be easy reading! could I scale
Parnassus, where the Muses sit inditing
    Those pretty poems never known to fail,
How quickly would I print (the world delighting)
    A Grecian, Syrian, or *Assy*rian tale;
And sell you, mixed with western Sentimentalism,
Some samples of the *finest Orientalism.*

LII.

But I am but a nameless sort of person,
    (A broken Dandy lately on my travels)
And take for rhyme, to hook my rambling verse on,
    The first that Walker's Lexicon unravels,[16]
And when I can't find that, I put a worse on,
    Not caring as I ought for critics' cavils;
I've half a mind to tumble down to prose,
But verse is more in fashion—so here goes!

[16] John Walker, *Rhyming Dictionary* (1775).

LIII.

The Count and Laura made their new arrangement,
  Which lasted, as arrangements sometimes do,
For half a dozen years without estrangement;
  They had their little differences, too;
Those jealous whiffs, which never any change meant;
  In such affairs there probably are few
Who have not had this pouting sort of squabble,
From sinners of high station to the rabble.

LIV.

But, on the whole, they were a happy pair,
  As happy as unlawful love could make them;
The gentleman was fond, the lady fair,
  Their chains so slight, 'twas not worth while to
    break them:
The World beheld them with indulgent air;
  The pious only wished "the Devil take them!"
He took them not; he very often waits,
And leaves old sinners to be young ones' baits.

LV.

But they were young: Oh! what without our Youth
  Would Love be! What would Youth be without
    Love!
Youth lends its joy, and sweetness, vigour, truth,
  Heart, soul, and all that seems as from above;
But, languishing with years, it grows uncouth—
  One of few things Experience don't improve;
Which is, perhaps, the reason why old fellows
Are always so preposterously jealous.

LVI.

It was the Carnival, as I have said
  Some six and thirty stanzas back, and so
Laura the usual preparations made,
  Which you do when your mind's made up to go
To-night to Mrs. Boehm's masquerade,[17]
  Spectator, or Partaker in the show;
The only difference known between the cases
Is—*here*, we have six weeks of "varnished faces."

LVII.

Laura, when dressed, was (as I sang before)
  A pretty woman as was ever seen,
Fresh as the Angel o'er a new inn door,
  Or frontispiece of a new Magazine,
With all the fashions which the last month wore,
  Coloured, and silver paper leaved between
That and the title-page, for fear the Press
Should soil with parts of speech the parts of dress.

---

[17] A lavish party given in London in June 1817, and fully reported in the papers.

LVIII.

They went to the Ridotto; 'tis a hall
  Where People dance, and sup, and dance again;
Its proper name, perhaps, were a masqued ball,
  But that's of no importance to my strain;
'Tis (on a smaller scale) like our Vauxhall,
  Excepting that it can't be spoilt by rain;
The company is "mixed" (the phrase I quote is
As much as saying, they're below your notice);

LIX.

For a "mixed company" implies that, save
  Yourself and friends, and half a hundred more,
Whom you may bow to without looking grave,
  The rest are but a vulgar set, the Bore
Of public places, where they basely brave
  The fashionable stare of twenty score
Of well-bred persons, called "*The World;*" but I,
Although I know them, really don't know why.

LX.

This is the case in England; at least was
  During the dynasty of Dandies, now
Perchance succeeded by some other class
  Of imitated Imitators:—how
Irreparably soon decline, alas!
  The Demagogues of fashion: all below
Is frail; how easily the world is lost
By Love, or War, and, now and then,—by Frost!

LXI.

Crushed was Napoleon by the northern Thor,
  Who knocked his army down with icy hammer,
Stopped by the *Elements*—like a Whaler—or
  A blundering novice in his new French grammar;
Good cause had he to doubt the chance of war,
  And as for Fortune—but I dare not d—n her,
Because, were I to ponder to Infinity,
The more I should believe in her Divinity.

LXII.

She rules the present, past, and all to be yet,
  She gives us luck in lotteries, love, and marriage;
I cannot say that she's done much for me yet;
  Not that I mean her bounties to disparage,
We've not yet closed accounts, and we shall see yet
  How much she'll make amends for past miscarriage;
Meantime the Goddess I'll no more importune,
Unless to thank her when she's made my fortune.

LXIII.

To turn,—and to return;—the Devil take it!
　This story slips for ever through my fingers,
Because, just as the stanza likes to make it,
　It needs must be—and so it rather lingers;
This form of verse began, I can't well break it,
　But must keep time and tune like public singers;
But if I once get through my present measure,
I'll take another when I'm next at leisure.

LXIV.

They went to the Ridotto ('tis a place
　To which I mean to go myself to-morrow,
Just to divert my thoughts a little space
　Because I'm rather hippish, and may borrow
Some spirits, guessing at what kind of face
　May lurk beneath each mask; and as my sorrow
Slackens its pace sometimes, I'll make, or find,
Something shall leave it half an hour behind.)

LXV.

Now Laura moves along the joyous crowd,
　Smiles in her eyes, and simpers on her lips;
To some she whispers, others speaks aloud;
　To some she curtsies, and to some she dips,
Complains of warmth, and this complaint avowed,
　Her lover brings the lemonade, she sips;
She then surveys, condemns, but pities still
Her dearest friends for being dressed so ill.

LXVI.

One has false curls, another too much paint,
　A third—where did she buy that frightful turban?
A fourth's so pale she fears she's going to faint,
　A fifth's look's vulgar, dowdyish, and suburban,
A sixth's white silk has got a yellow taint,
　A seventh's thin muslin surely will be her bane,
And lo! an eighth appears,—"I'll see no more!"
For fear, like Banquo's kings, they reach a score.

LXVII.

Meantime, while she was thus at others gazing,
　Others were levelling their looks at her;
She heard the men's half-whispered mode of praising
　And, till 'twas done, determined not to stir;
The women only thought it quite amazing
　That, at her time of life, so many were
Admirers still,—but "Men are so debased,
Those brazen Creatures always suit their taste."

LXVIII.

For my part, now, I ne'er could understand
　Why naughty women—but I won't discuss
A thing which is a scandal to the land,
　I only don't see why it should be thus;
And if I were but in a gown and band,
　Just to entitle me to make a fuss,
I'd preach on this till Wilberforce and Romilly [18]
Should quote in their next speeches from my homily.

LXIX.

While Laura thus was seen, and seeing, smiling,
　Talking, she knew not why, and cared not what,
So that her female friends, with envy broiling,
　Beheld her airs, and triumph, and all that;
And well-dressed males still kept before her filing,
　And passing bowed and mingled with her chat;
More than the rest one person seemed to stare
With pertinacity that's rather rare.

LXX.

He was a Turk, the colour of mahogany;
　And Laura saw him, and at first was glad,
Because the Turks so much admire philogyny,
　Although their usage of their wives is sad;
'Tis said they use no better than a dog any
　Poor woman, whom they purchase like a pad:
They have a number, though they ne'er exhibit 'em,
Four wives by law, and concubines "ad libitum."

LXXI.

They lock them up, and veil, and guard them daily,
　They scarcely can behold their male relations,
So that their moments do not pass so gaily
　As is supposed the case with northern nations;
Confinement, too, must make them look quite palely;
　And as the Turks abhor long conversations,
Their days are either passed in doing nothing,
Or bathing, nursing, making love, and clothing.

LXXII.

They cannot read, and so don't lisp in criticism;
　Nor write, and so they don't affect the Muse;
Were never caught in epigram or witticism,
　Have no romances, sermons, plays, reviews,—
In Harams learning soon would make a pretty schism,
　But luckily these Beauties are no "Blues;"
No bustling *Botherby* [19] have they to show 'em
"That charming passage in the last new poem:"

---

[18] William Wilberforce (1759–1833) and Sir Samuel Romilly (1757–1818) were both reformers and famous orators.
[19] William Sotheby (1757–1833), poet and translator, praised in *English Bards*, had since lost Byron's favor. He is also presented as Botherby in *The Blues*, p. 630.

LXXIII.

No solemn, antique gentleman of rhyme,
　Who having angled all his life for Fame,
And getting but a nibble at a time,
　Still fussily keeps fishing on, the same
Small "Triton of the minnows," the sublime
　Of Mediocrity, the furious tame,
The Echo's echo, usher of the school
Of female wits, boy bards—in short, a fool!

LXXIV.

A stalking oracle of awful phrase,
　The approving "*Good!*" (by no means GOOD in
　　law)
Humming like flies around the newest blaze,
　The bluest of bluebottles you e'er saw,
Teasing with blame, excruciating with praise,
　Gorging the little fame he gets all raw,
Translating tongues he knows not even by letter,
And sweating plays so middling, bad were better.

LXXV.

One hates an author that's *all author*—fellows
　In foolscap uniforms turned up with ink,
So very anxious, clever, fine, and jealous,
　One don't know what to say to them, or think,
Unless to puff them with a pair of bellows;
　Of Coxcombry's worst coxcombs e'en the pink
Are preferable to these shreds of paper,
These unquenched snuffings of the midnight taper.

LXXVI.

Of these same we see several, and of others,
　Men of the world, who know the World like Men,
Scott, Rogers, Moore, and all the better brothers,
　Who think of something else besides the pen;
But for the children of the "Mighty Mother's,"
　The would-be wits, and can't-be gentlemen,
I leave them to their daily "tea is ready,"
Smug coterie, and literary lady.

LXXVII.

The poor dear Mussul*women* whom I mention
　Have none of these instructive pleasant people,
And *one* would seem to them a new invention,
　Unknown as bells within a Turkish steeple;
I think 'twould almost be worth while to pension
　(Though best-sown projects very often reap ill)
A missionary author—just to preach
Our Christian usage of the parts of speech.

LXXVIII.

No Chemistry for them unfolds her gases,
　No Metaphysics are let loose in lectures,
No Circulating Library amasses
　Religious novels, moral tales, and strictures
Upon the living manners, as they pass us;
　No Exhibition glares with annual pictures;
They stare not on the stars from out their attics,
Nor deal (thank God for that!) in Mathematics.

LXXIX.

Why I thank God for that is no great matter,
　I have my reasons, you no doubt suppose,
And as, perhaps, they would not highly flatter,
　I'll keep them for my life (to come) in prose;
I fear I have a little turn for Satire,
　And yet methinks the older that one grows
Inclines us more to laugh than scold, though Laughter
Leaves us so doubly serious shortly after.

LXXX.

Oh, Mirth and Innocence! Oh, Milk and Water!
　Ye happy mixtures of more happy days!
In these sad centuries of sin and slaughter,
　Abominable Man no more allays
His thirst with such pure beverage. No matter,
　I love you both, and both shall have my praise:
Oh, for old Saturn's reign of sugar-candy!—
Meantime I drink to your return in brandy.

LXXXI.

Our Laura's Turk still kept his eyes upon her,
　Less in the Mussulman than Christian way,
Which seems to say, "Madam, I do you honour,
　And while I please to stare, you'll please to stay."
Could staring win a woman, this had won her,
　But Laura could not thus be led astray;
She had stood fire too long and well, to boggle
Even at this Stranger's most outlandish ogle.

LXXXII.

The morning now was on the point of breaking,
　A turn of time at which I would advise
Ladies who have been dancing, or partaking
　In any other kind of exercise,
To make their preparations for forsaking
　The ball-room ere the Sun begins to rise,
Because when once the lamps and candles fail,
His blushes make them look a little pale.

LXXXIII.

I've seen some balls and revels in my time,
  And stayed them over for some silly reason, •
And then I looked (I hope it was no crime)
  To see what lady best stood out the season;
And though I've seen some thousands in their prime
  Lovely and pleasing, and who still may please on,
I never saw but one (the stars withdrawn)
Whose bloom could after dancing dare the Dawn.

LXXXIV.

The name of this Aurora I'll not mention,
  Although I might, for she was nought to me
More than that patent work of God's invention,
  A charming woman, whom we like to see;
But writing names would merit reprehension,
  Yet if you like to find out this fair *She*,
At the next London or Parisian ball
You still may mark her cheek, out-blooming all.

LXXXV.

Laura, who knew it would not do at all
  To meet the daylight after seven hours' sitting
Among three thousand people at a ball,
  To make her curtsey thought it right and fitting;
The Count was at her elbow with her shawl,
  And they the room were on the point of quitting,
When lo! those curséd Gondoliers had got
Just in the very place where they *should not*.

LXXXVI.

In this they're like our coachmen, and the cause
  Is much the same—the crowd, and pulling,
      hauling,
With blasphemies enough to break their jaws,
  They make a never intermitted bawling.
At home, our Bow-street gem'men keep the laws, [20]
  And here a sentry stands within your calling;
But for all that, there is a deal of swearing,
And nauseous words past mentioning or bearing.

LXXXVII.

The Count and Laura found their boat at last,
  And homeward floated o'er the silent tide,
Discussing all the dances gone and past;
  The dancers and their dresses, too, beside;
Some little scandals eke; but all aghast
  (As to their palace-stairs the rowers glide)
Sate Laura by the side of her adorer,
When lo! the Mussulman was there before her!

---

[20] The Bow Street Runners were an early version of the London police force.

LXXXVIII.

"Sir," said the Count, with brow exceeding grave,
  "Your unexpected presence here will make
It necessary for myself to crave
  Its import? But perhaps 'tis a mistake;
I hope it is so; and, at once to waive
  All compliment, I hope so for *your* sake;
You understand my meaning, or you *shall*."
"Sir," (quoth the Turk) "'tis no mistake at all:

LXXXIX.

"That Lady is *my wife!*" Much wonder paints
  The lady's changing cheek, as well it might;
But where an Englishwoman sometimes faints,
  Italian females don't do so outright;
They only call a little on their Saints,
  And then come to themselves, almost, or quite;
Which saves much hartshorn, salts, and sprinkling
      faces,
And cutting stays, as usual in such cases.

XC.

She said,—what could she say? Why, not a word;
  But the Count courteously invited in
The Stranger, much appeased by what he heard:
  "Such things, perhaps, we'd best discuss within,"
Said he; "don't let us make ourselves absurd
  In public, by a scene, nor raise a din,
For then the chief and only satisfaction
Will be much quizzing on the whole transaction."

XCI.

They entered, and for Coffee called—it came,
  A beverage for Turks and Christians both,
Although the way they make it's not the same.
  Now Laura, much recovered, or less loth
To speak, cries "Beppo! what's your pagan name?
  Bless me! your beard is of amazing growth!
And how came you to keep away so long?
Are you not sensible 'twas very wrong?

XCII.

"And are you *really*, *truly*, now a Turk?
  With any other women did you wive?
Is't true they use their fingers for a fork?
  Well, that's the prettiest Shawl—as I'm alive!
You'll give it me? They say you eat no pork.
  And how so many years did you contrive
To—Bless me! did I ever? No, I never
Saw a man grown so yellow! How's your liver?

XCIII.

"Beppo! that beard of yours becomes you not;
  It shall be shaved before you're a day older:
Why do you wear it? Oh! I had forgot—
  Pray don't you think the weather here is colder?
How do I look? You shan't stir from this spot
  In that queer dress, for fear that some beholder
Should find you out, and make the story known.
How short your hair is! Lord! how grey it's
    grown!"

XCIV.

What answer Beppo made to these demands
  Is more than I know. He was cast away
About where Troy stood once, and nothing stands;
  Became a slave of course, and for his pay
Had bread and bastinadoes, till some bands
  Of pirates landing in a neighbouring bay,
He joined the rogues and prospered, and became
A renegado of indifferent fame.

XCV.

But he grew rich, and with his riches grew so
  Keen the desire to see his home again,
He thought himself in duty bound to do so,
  And not be always thieving on the main;
Lonely he felt, at times, as Robin Crusoe,
  And so he hired a vessel come from Spain,
Bound for Corfu: she was a fine polacca,²¹
Manned with twelve hands, and laden with tobacco.

XCVI.

Himself, and much (heaven knows how gotten!) cash,
  He then embarked, with risk of life and limb,
And got clear off, although the attempt was rash;
  He said that *Providence* protected him—
For my part, I say nothing—lest we clash
  In our opinions:—well—the ship was trim,
Set sail, and kept her reckoning fairly on,
Except three days of calm when off Cape Bonn.²²

XCVII.

They reached the Island, he transferred his lading,
  And self and live stock to another bottom,
And passed for a true Turkey-merchant, trading
  With goods of various names—but I've forgot 'em.
However, he got off by this evading,
  Or else the people would perhaps have shot him;
And thus at Venice landed to reclaim
His wife, religion, house, and Christian name.

---

²¹ Three-masted sailing ship of the Mediterranean.
²² The northern point of Tunisia.

XCVIII.

His wife received, the Patriarch re-baptised him,
  (He made the Church a present, by the way;)
He then threw off the garments which disguised him,
  And borrowed the Count's smallclothes for a day:
His friends the more for his long absence prized him,
  Finding he'd wherewithal to make them gay,
With dinners, where he oft became the laugh of them,
For stories—but *I* don't believe the half of them.

XCIX.

Whate'er his youth had suffered, his old age
  With wealth and talking made him some amends;
Though Laura sometimes put him in a rage,
  I've heard the Count and he were always friends.
My pen is at the bottom of a page,
  Which being finished, here the story ends:
'Tis to be wished it had been sooner done,
But stories somehow lengthen when begun.

[1817]   [1818]

SONNET TO THE PRINCE REGENT

The lands and title of Lord Fitzgerald, who was one of the leaders of the United Irishmen in their rebellion in 1797–1798, were declared forfeit on his death (from wounds received in being captured) in 1798. The forfeiture was repealed in August 1819.

SONNET TO THE PRINCE REGENT.
ON THE REPEAL OF
LORD EDWARD FITZGERALD'S FORFEITURE.

TO BE the father of the fatherless,
  To stretch the hand from the throne's height, and
  His offspring, who expired in other days   [raise
To make thy Sire's sway by a kingdom less,—
This is to be a monarch, and repress
  Envy into unutterable praise.
  Dismiss thy guard, and trust thee to such traits,
For who would lift a hand, except to bless?
  Were it not easy, Sir, and is't not sweet
  To make thyself belovéd? and to be
Omnipotent by Mercy's means? for thus
  Thy Sovereignty would grow but more complete,
A despot thou, and yet thy people free,
  And by the heart—not hand—enslaving us.

[1819]   [1830]

EPITAPH FOR WILLIAM PITT.

  WITH Death doomed to grapple,
    Beneath this cold slab, he
  Who lied in the Chapel
    Now lies in the Abbey.

[1820]   [1830]

William Cobbett (1763–1835), radical farmer-journalist, rescued from obscurity in America the bones of the English and American revolutionary Tom Paine (1737–1809), and planned to have a monument built for them in England. Failing, he left the bones to his descendants, and eventually they disappeared.

EPIGRAM.

  IN digging up your bones, Tom Paine,
    Will. Cobbett has done well:
  You visit him on Earth again,
    He'll visit you in Hell.

  or—

  You come to him on Earth again
    He'll go with you to Hell!

[1820]   [1830]

JOHN KEATS.

WHO killed John Keats?
  "I," says the Quarterly,
    So savage and Tartarly;
  "'T was one of my feats."

Who shot the arrow?
  "The poet-priest Milman
    (So ready to kill man)
  "Or Southey, or Barrow." [1]

[1821]   [1830]

THE BLUES: A LITERARY ECLOGUE

This short skit—comparable in some ways to Blake's An Island in the Moon above—was written hastily, and Byron first intended it only as a joke, though he later printed it anonymously in the Liberal, which he, Shelley, and Hunt were editing in Italy.

Byron's references to women with intellectual (and social) pretensions are frequent and contemptuous—blues, blue-stockings, blue-bottles, he calls them. Although there was apparently a society of women so named in Renaissance Italy, the popular explanation of these cognate terms is that they were applied in England in the late eighteenth century to a group of women who resolved not to be shocked at Benjamin Stillingfleet's wearing blue worsted stockings at formal evening parties.

The identities of some of the personalities intended are quite transparent, but others are purely conjectural. The most likely identifications are:

WORDSWORDS *and* MOUTHY: *Wordsworth and Southey.*

BOTHERBY: *William Sotheby, a minor poet and dramatist, friend of Coleridge (see Beppo, LXXII, p. 626).*

LORD *and* LADY BLUEMONT: *Sir George and Lady Beaumont, friends and benefactors of the Wordsworths; Sir George was a landscape painter and founder of the National Gallery.*

MISS DIDDLE: *Lydia White, a wealthy Irish hostess.*

MISS LILAC: *Annabella Milbanke, before she was Lady Byron.*

SCAMP: *Probably William Hazlitt, the critic, lecturer, and essayist.*

SIR RICHARD *and* LADY BLUEBOTTLE: *Perhaps Lord and Lady Holland, at whose house in Kensington Byron had*

---

[1] The actual author of the review (*Quarterly Review*, April 1818) was John Wilson Croker. That the harsh criticism of *Endymion* hastened Keats's death was widely believed. See *Don Juan*, Canto Eleven, LX, p. 704, and Shelley's *Adonais*, p. 951.

*met most of the intellectual aristocracy after his sudden fame
with* Childe Harold.

INKEL: *Apparently Byron.*
TRACY: *Thomas Moore* (?).

THE BLUES:

A LITERARY ECLOGUE.

ECLOGUE THE FIRST.

London.—Before the Door of a Lecture Room.

Enter TRACY, *meeting* INKEL.

Ink. You're too late.
Tra.   Is it over?
Ink.   Nor will be this hour.
But the benches are crammed, like a garden in flower.
With the pride of our belles, who have made it the
     fashion;
So, instead of "beaux arts," we may say "la *belle*
     passion"
For learning, which lately has taken the lead in
The world, and set all the fine gentlemen reading.
     Tra. I know it too well, and have worn out my
     patience
With studying to study your new publications.
There's Vamp, Scamp, and Mouthy, and
     Wordswords and Co.
With their damnable——
     Ink.   Hold, my good friend, do
     you know   10
Whom you speak to?
     Tra.   Right well, boy, and so does
     "the Row:"
You're an author—a poet—
     Ink.   And think you that I
Can stand tamely in silence, to hear you decry
The Muses?
     Tra.   Excuse me: I meant no offence
To the Nine,[1] though the number who make some
     pretence
To their favours is such——but the subject to drop,
I am just piping hot from a publisher's shop,
(Next door to the pastry-cook's; so that when I
Cannot find the new volume I wanted to buy
On the bibliopole's shelves, it is only two paces,   20
As one finds every author in one of those places:)
Where I just had been skimming a charming critique,
So studded with wit, and so sprinkled with Greek!

---

[1] The Nine Muses.

Where your friend—you know who—has just got
     such a threshing,
That it is, as the phrase goes, extremely "*refreshing.*"[2]
What a beautiful word!
     Ink.   Very true; 'tis so soft
And so cooling—they use it a little too oft;
And the papers have got it at last—but no matter.
So they've cut up our friend then?
     Tra.   Not left him a
     tatter—
Not a rag of his present or past reputation,   30
Which they call a disgrace to the age, and the nation.
     Ink. I'm sorry to hear this! for friendship, you
     know——
Our poor friend!—but I thought it would terminate so.
Our friendship is such, I'll read nothing to shock it.
You don't happen to have the Review in your pocket?
     Tra. No; I left a round dozen of authors and others
(Very sorry, no doubt, since the cause is a brother's)
All scrambling and jostling, like so many imps,
And on fire with impatience to get the next glimpse.
     Ink. Let us join them.
     Tra.   What, won't you return to
     the lecture?   40
     Ink. Why the place is so crammed, there's not room
     for a spectre.
Besides, our friend Scamp is to-day so absurd—
     Tra. How can you know that till you hear him?
     Ink.   I heard
Quite enough; and, to tell you the truth, my retreat
Was from his vile nonsense, no less than the heat.
     Tra. I have had no great loss then?
     Ink.   Loss!—such a
     palaver!
I'd inoculate sooner my wife with the slaver
Of a dog when gone rabid, than listen two hours
To the torrent of trash which around him he pours,
Pumped up with such effort, disgorged with such
     labour,   50
That——come—do not make me speak ill of one's
     neighbour.
     Tra. I make you!
     Ink.   Yes, you! I said nothing until
You compelled me, by speaking the truth——
     Tra.   *To*
     speak ill!
Is that your deduction?
     Ink.   When speaking of Scamp ill,
I certainly *follow, not set* an example.
The fellow's a fool, an impostor, a zany.
     Tra. And the crowd of to-day shows that one fool
     makes many.

---

[2] Supposedly this as a term for literary appraisal was first
used by Jeffrey in the *Edinburgh Review.*

But we two will be wise.
 Ink.   Pray, then, let us retire.
 Tra. I would, but——
 Ink.   There must be attraction
 much higher
Than Scamp, or the Jew's harp he nicknames his
 lyre,   60
To call *you* to this hotbed.
 Tra.   I own it—'tis true—
A fair lady——
 Ink. A spinster?
 Tra.   Miss Lilac.
 Ink.   The Blue!
 Tra. The heiress! The angel!
 Ink.   The devil! why, man,
Pray get out of this hobble as fast as you can.
You wed with Miss Lilac! 'twould be your perdition:
She's a poet, a chymist, a mathematician.[3]
 Tra. I say she's an angel.
 Ink.   Say rather an *angle*.
If you and she marry, you'll certainly wrangle.
I say she's a Blue, man, as blue as the ether. 69
 Tra. And is that any cause for not coming together?
 Ink. Humph! I can't say I know any happy
 alliance
Which has lately sprung up from a wedlock with
 science.
She's so learnéd in all things, and fond of concerning
Herself in all matters connected with learning,
That——
 Tra. What?
 Ink.   I perhaps may as well hold my
 tongue;
But there's five hundred people can tell you you're
 wrong.
 Tra. You forget Lady Lilac's as rich as a Jew.
 Ink. Is it miss or the cash of mamma you pursue?
 Tra. Why, Jack, I'll be frank with you—something
 of both.
The girl's a fine girl.
 Ink.   And you feel nothing loth 80
To her good lady-mother's reversion; and yet
Her life is as good as your own, I will bet.
 Tra. Let her live, and as long as she likes; I
 demand
Nothing more than the heart of her daughter and
 hand.
 Ink. Why, that heart's in the inkstand—that hand
 on the pen.
 Tra. A propos—Will you write me a song now and
 then?

---

[3] Lady Byron (Annabella Milbanke) was both poet and mathematician, and of course an heiress.

 Ink. To what purpose?
 Tra.   You know, my dear friend,
 that in prose
My talent is decent, as far as it goes;
But in rhyme——
 Ink.   You're a terrible stick, to be sure.
 Tra. I own it; and yet, in these times, there's no
 lure   90
For the heart of the fair like a stanza or two;
And so, as I can't, will you furnish a few?
 Ink. In your name?
 Tra.   In my name. I will copy them
 out,
To slip into her hand at the very next rout.
 Ink. Are you so far advanced as to hazard this?
 Tra.   Why,
Do you think me subdued by a Blue-stocking's eye,
So far as to tremble to tell her in rhyme
What I've told her in prose, at the least, as sublime?
 Ink. As sublime! If it be so, no need of my Muse.
 Tra. But consider, dear Inkel, she's one of the
 "Blues."   100
 Ink. As sublime!—Mr. Tracy—I've nothing to
 say.
Stick to prose—As sublime!!—but I wish you good
 day.
 Tra. Nay, stay, my dear fellow—consider—I'm
 wrong;
I own it; but, prithee, compose me the song.
 Ink. As sublime!!
 Tra.   I but used the expression in
 haste.
 Ink. That may be, Mr. Tracy, but shows damned
 bad taste.
 Tra. I own it, I know it, acknowledge it—what
Can I say to you more?
 Ink.   I see what you'd be at:
You disparage my parts with insidious abuse,
Till you think you can turn them best to your own
 use.   110
 Tra. And is that not a sign I respect them?
 Ink.   Why
 that
To be sure makes a difference.
 Tra.   I know what is what:
And you, who're a man of the gay world, no less
Than a poet of t'other, may easily guess
That I never could mean, by a word, to offend
A genius like you, and, moreover, my friend.
 Ink. No doubt; you by this time should know what
 is due
To a man of——but come—let us shake hands.
 Tra.   You
 knew,

And you *know*, my dear fellow, how heartily I,
Whatever you publish, am ready to buy.   120
  Ink. That's my bookseller's business; I care not
    for sale;
Indeed the best poems at first rather fail.
There were Renegade's epics,[4] and Botherby's
    plays,
And my own grand romance——
  Tra.   Had its full share of
    praise.
I myself saw it puffed in the "Old Girl's Review."
  Ink. What Review?
  Tra.   'Tis the English "Journal de
    Trevoux;"[5]
A clerical work of our Jesuits at home.
Have you never yet seen it?
  Ink.   That pleasure's to come.
  Tra. Make haste then.
  Ink.   Why so?
  Tra.   I have heard people
    say   129
That it threatened to give up the *ghost* t'other day.
  Ink. Well, that is a sign of some *spirit*.
  Tra.   No doubt.
Shall you be at the Countess of Fiddlecome's rout?
  Ink. I've a card, and shall go: but at present, as
    soon
As friend Scamp shall be pleased to step down from
    the moon,
(Where he seems to be soaring in search of his wits),
And an interval grants from his lecturing fits,
I'm engaged to the Lady Bluebottle's collation,
To partake of a luncheon and learn'd conversation:
'Tis a sort of reunion for Scamp, on the days
Of his lecture, to treat him with cold tongue and
    praise.   140
And I own, for my own part, that 'tis not unpleasant.
Will you go? There's Miss Lilac will also be present.
  Tra. That "metal's attractive."[6]
  Ink.   No doubt—to the
    pocket.
  Tra. You should rather encourage my passion than
    shock it.
But let us proceed; for I think by the hum——
  Ink. Very true; let us go, then, before they can
    come,
Or else we'll be kept here an hour at their levee,
On the rack of cross questions, by all the blue bevy.
Hark! Zounds, they'll be on us; I know by the drone
Of old Botherby's spouting ex-cathedrâ tone.   150

<hr />

[4] A name applied to Southey.
[5] A French Jesuit, anti-Protestant review, which is here
compared to the *British* ("Old Girl's") *Review*.
[6] *Hamlet*, about Ophelia: III, ii, 112.

Aye! there he is at it. Poor Scamp! better join
Your friends, or he'll pay you back in your own coin.
  Tra. All fair; 'tis but lecture for lecture.
  Ink.   That's
    clear.
But for God's sake let's go, or the Bore will be here.
Come, come: nay, I'm off.
                          [*Exit* INKEL.
  Tra.   You are right, and I'll
    follow;
'Tis high time for a "*Sic me servavit Apollo*."
And yet we shall have the whole crew on our kibes,
Blues, dandies, and dowagers, and second-hand
    scribes,
All flocking to moisten their exquisite throttles
With a glass of Madeira at Lady Bluebottle's.   160
                          [*Exit* TRACY.

ECLOGUE THE SECOND.

An Apartment in the House of
LADY BLUEBOTTLE.—*A Table prepared.*

SIR RICHARD BLUEBOTTLE *solus*.

Was there ever a man who was married so sorry?
Like a fool, I must needs do the thing in a hurry.
My life is reversed, and my quiet destroyed;
My days, which once passed in so gentle a void,
Must now, every hour of the twelve, be employed;
The twelve, do I say?—of the whole twenty-four,
Is there one which I dare call my own any more?
What with driving and visiting, dancing and dining,
What with learning, and teaching, and scribbling,
    and shining,
In science and art, I'll be cursed if I know   10
Myself from my wife; for although we are two,
Yet she somehow contrives that all things shall be
    done
In a style which proclaims us eternally one.
But the thing of all things which distresses me more
Than the bills of the week (though they trouble me
    sore)
Is the numerous, humorous, backbiting crew
Of scribblers, wits, lecturers, white, black, and blue,
Who are brought to my house as an inn, to my cost—
For the bill here, it seems, is defrayed by the host—
No pleasure! no leisure! no thought for my pains,   20
But to hear a vile jargon which addles my brains;
A smatter and chatter, gleaned out of reviews,
By the rag, tag, and bobtail, of those they call
    "BLUES;"
A rabble who know not——But soft, here they come!
Would to God I were deaf! as I'm not, I'll be dumb.

Enter LADY BLUEBOTTLE, MISS LILAC, LADY
    BLUEMOUNT, MR. BOTHERBY, INKEL,
    TRACY, MISS MAZARINE, *and others, with*
    SCAMP *the Lecturer, etc., etc.*

  Lady Blueb. Ah! Sir Richard, good morning: I've
    brought you some friends.
  Sir Rich. (*bows, and afterwards aside*). If friends,
    they're the first.
  Lady Blueb.   But the luncheon attends.
I pray ye be seated "*sans cérémonie.*"
Mr. Scamp, you're fatigued; take your chair there,
    next me.   [*They all sit.*
  Sir Rich. (*aside*). If he does, his fatigue is to come.
  Lady Blueb.   Mr. Tracy—
Lady Bluemount—Miss Lilac—be pleased, pray, to
    place ye;   31
And you, Mr. Botherby—
  Both.   Oh, my dear Lady,
I obey.
  Lady Blueb. Mr. Inkel, I ought to upbraid ye:
You were not at the lecture.
  Ink.   Excuse me, I was;
But the heat forced me out in the best part—alas!
And when—
  Lady Blueb. To be sure it was broiling; but then
You have lost such a lecture!
  Both.   The best of the ten.
  Tra. How can you know that? there are two more.
  Both.   Because
I defy him to beat this day's wondrous applause.
The very walls shook.
  Ink.   Oh, if that be the test,   40
I allow our friend Scamp has this day done his best.
Miss Lilac, permit me to help you;—a wing?
  Miss Lil. No more, sir, I thank you. Who lectures
    next spring?
  Both. Dick Dunder.
  Ink.   That is, if he lives.
  Miss Lil.   And why
    not?
  Ink. No reason whatever, save that he's a sot.
Lady Bluemount! a glass of Madeira?
  Lady Bluem.   With pleasure.
  Ink. How does your friend Wordswords, that
    Windermere treasure?
Does he stick to his lakes, like the leeches he sings,[7]
And their gatherers, as Homer sung warriors and
    kings?
  Lady Bluem. He has just got a place.

  Ink.   As a footman?
  Lady Bluem.   For shame!
Nor profane with your sneers so poetic a name. 51
  Ink. Nay, I meant him no evil, but pitied his
    master;
For the poet of pedlers 'twere, sure, no disaster
To wear a new livery; the more, as 'tis not
The first time he has turned both his creed and his
    coat.
  Lady Bluem. For shame! I repeat. If Sir George
    could but hear——
  Lady Blueb. Never mind our friend Inkel; we all
    know, my dear,
'Tis his way.
  Sir Rich. But his place——
  Ink.   Is perhaps like friend
    Scamp's,
A lecturer's.
  Lady Bluem. Excuse me—'tis one in the
    "Stamps:"
He is made a collector.
  Tra.   Collector!
  Sir Rich.   How?
  Miss Lil.   What? 60
  Ink. I shall think of him oft when I buy a new hat:
There his works will appear——
  Lady Bluem.   Sir, they reach to the
    Ganges.
  Ink. I sha'n't go so far—I can have them at
    Grange's.*
  Lady Bluem. Oh fie!
  Miss Lil.   And for shame!
  Lady Bluem.   You're too bad.
  Both.   Very good!
  Lady Bluem. How good?
  Lady Blueb.   He means nought—'tis his phrase.
  Lady Bluem.   He
    grows rude.
  Lady Blueb. He means nothing; nay, ask him.
  Lady Bluem.   Pray,
    Sir! did you mean
What you say?
  Ink.   Never mind if he did; 'twill be seen
That whatever he means won't alloy what he says.
  Both. Sir!
  Ink.   Pray be content with your portion of
    praise;
'Twas in your defence.
  Both.   If you please, with submission
I can make out my own.
  Ink.   It would be your perdition. 71

---

[7] A reference to Wordsworth's *Resolution and Independence*
(p. 263) and (ll. 49–60) to his appointment as Distributor for
(tax) Stamps in Westmorland.

* Grange is or was a famous pastry cook and fruiterer in
Piccadilly.

While you live, my dear Botherby, never defend
Yourself or your works; but leave both to a friend.
Apropos—Is your play then accepted at last?
   Both. At last?
   Ink.   Why I thought—that's to say—there had
    passed
A few green-room whispers, which hinted,—you
    know
That the taste of the actors at best is so so.
   Both. Sir, the green-room's in rapture, and so's the
    Committee.
   Ink. Aye—yours are the plays for exciting our
    "pity
And fear," as the Greek says: for "purging the
    mind,"   80
I doubt if you'll leave us an equal behind.
   Both. I have written the prologue, and meant to
    have prayed
For a spice of your wit in an epilogue's aid.
   Ink. Well, time enough yet, when the play's to be
    played.
Is it cast yet?
   Both.   The actors are fighting for parts,
As is usual in that most litigious of arts.
   Lady Blueb. We'll all make a party, and go the
    first night.
   Tra. And you promised the epilogue, Inkel.
   Ink.   Not
    quite.
However, to save my friend Botherby trouble,
I'll do what I can, though my pains must be double.
   Tra. Why so?
   Ink.   To do justice to what goes before.   91
   Both. Sir, I'm happy to say, I've no fears on that
    score.
Your parts, Mr. Inkel, are——
   Ink.   Never mind *mine*;
Stick to those of your play, which is quite your own
    line.
   Lady Bluem. You're a fugitive writer, I think, sir,
    of rhymes?
   Ink. Yes, ma'am; and a fugitive reader sometimes.
On Wordswords, for instance, I seldom alight,
Or on Mouthey, his friend, without taking to flight.
   Lady Bluem. Sir, your taste is too common; but
    time and posterity
Will right these great men, and this age's severity   100
Become its reproach.
   Ink.   I've no sort of objection,
So I'm not of the party to take the infection.
   Lady Blueb. Perhaps you have doubts that they
    ever will *take*?
   Ink. Not at all; on the contrary, those of the lake
Have taken already, and still will continue

To take—what they can, from a groat to a guinea,
Of pension or place;—but the subject's a bore.
   Lady Bluem. Well, sir, the time's coming.
   Ink.   Scamp!
    don't you feel sore?
What say you to this?
   Scamp.   They have merit, I own;   109
Though their system's absurdity keeps it unknown.
   Ink. Then why not unearth it in one of your
    lectures?
   Scamp. It is only time past which comes under my
    strictures.
   Lady Blueb. Come, a truce with all tartness;—the
    joy of my heart
Is to see Nature's triumph o'er all that is art.
Wild Nature!—Grand Shakespeare!
   Both.   And down
    Aristotle!
   Lady Bluem. Sir George thinks exactly with Lady
    Bluebottle:
And my Lord Seventy-four, who protects our dear
    Bard,
And who gave him his place, has the greatest regard
For the poet, who, singing of pedlers and asses,
Has found out the way to dispense with Parnassus.
   Tra. And you, Scamp!—
   Scamp.   I needs must confess I'm
    embarrassed.   121
   Ink. Don't call upon Scamp, who's already so
    harassed
With old *schools*, and new *schools*, and no *schools*,
    and all *schools*.
   Tra. Well, one thing is certain, that *some* must be
    fools.
I should like to know who.
   Ink.   And I should not be sorry
To know who are *not*:—it would save us some worry.
   Lady Blueb. A truce with remark, and let nothing
    control
This "feast of our reason, and flow of the soul."
Oh! my dear Mr. Botherby! sympathise!—I
Now feel such a rapture, I'm ready to fly,   130
I feel so elastic—"*so buoyant—so buoyant!*"*
   Ink. Tracy! open the window.
   Tra.   I wish her much joy
    on't.
   Both. For God's sake, my Lady Bluebottle, check
    not
This gentle emotion, so seldom our lot
Upon earth. Give it way: 'tis an impulse which lifts
Our spirits from earth—the sublimest of gifts;

---

* Fact from life, with the *words*.

For which poor Prometheus was chained to his
　　mountain:
'Tis the source of all sentiment—feeling's true
　　fountain;
'Tis the Vision of Heaven upon Earth: 'tis the gas
Of the soul: 'tis the seizing of shades as they pass,　140
And making them substance: 'tis something divine:—
　　Ink. Shall I help you, my friend, to a little more
　　　　wine?
　　Both. I thank you: not any more, sir, till I dine.
　　Ink. Apropos—Do you dine with Sir Humphry [8]
　　　　to day?
　　Tra. I should think with *Duke* Humphry was more
　　　　in your way.
　　Ink. It might be of yore; but we authors now look
To the Knight, as a landlord, much more than the
　　Duke.
The truth is, each writer now quite at his ease is,
And (except with his publisher) dines where he
　　pleases.
But 'tis now nearly five, and I must to the Park.　150
　　Tra. And I'll take a turn with you there till 'tis dark.
And you, Scamp—
　　Scamp.　　　　Excuse me! I must to my notes,
For my lecture next week.
　　Ink.　　　　　　He must mind whom he
　　quotes
Out of "Elegant Extracts."
　　Lady Blueb.　　　　Well, now we break up;
But remember Miss Diddle invites us to sup.
　　Ink. Then at two hours past midnight we all meet
　　　　again,
For the sciences, sandwiches, hock, and champagne!
　　Tra. And the sweet lobster salad!
　　Both.　　　　　　　I honour that
　　meal;
For 'tis then that our feelings most genuinely—feel.
　　Ink. True; feeling is truest *then*, far beyond
　　　　question:　　　　　　　　　　　　　160
I wish to the gods 'twas the same with digestion!
　　Lady Blueb. Pshaw!—never mind that; for one
　　　　moment of feeling
Is worth—God knows what.
　　Ink.　　　　　　'Tis at least worth
　　concealing
For itself, or what follows—But here comes your
　　carriage.
　　Sir Rich. (*aside*). I wish all these people were
　　　　d——d with *my* marriage!　　　　[*Exeunt.*

[1821]　　　　　　　　　　　　　　　　[1823]

───────────────────────

[8] Sir Humphry Davy (1778–1829), chemist, president of the
Royal Society, once a friend of Coleridge (and Wordsworth).
He was knighted in 1812, made a baronet in 1819.

THE VISION OF JUDGMENT

*In 1821 Robert Southey, then Poet Laureate, published a
celebration of George III called* A Vision of Judgment, *with a
preface attacking the "Satanic School" of lascivious writers.
Taking this to be an attack on himself, Byron wrote* The Vision
as a satiric reply to A Vision.

*Quevedo was an early seventeenth-century prose satirist
(here "reborn"). Southey had written a radical drama called*
Wat Tyler *in 1798, which was published without his consent
and to his great embarrassment in 1817. The epigraph is from*
The Merchant of Venice (IV, i, 218, 336). *The wording of
Byron's notes is that of the edition of 1832.*

THE VISION OF
JUDGMENT

BY

QUEVEDO REDIVIVUS.

SUGGESTED BY THE COMPOSITION SO ENTITLED
BY THE AUTHOR OF "WAT TYLER."

"A Daniel come to judgment! yea, a Daniel!
I thank thee, Jew, for teaching me that word."

───────⊸⊙⊸───────

PREFACE.

IT hath been wisely said, that "One fool makes
many;" and it hath been poetically observed—

"[That] fools rush in where angels fear to tread." [1]

If Mr. Southey had not rushed in where he had
no business, and where he never was before, and
never will be again, the following poem would not
have been written. It is not impossible that it may be
as good as his own, seeing that it cannot, by any
species of stupidity, natural or acquired, be *worse*.
The gross flattery, the dull impudence, the renegado
intolerance, and impious cant, of the poem by the
author of "Wat Tyler," are something so stupendous
as to form the sublime of himself—containing the
quintessence of his own attributes.

So much for his poem—a word on his preface. In
this preface it has pleased the magnanimous Laureate
to draw the picture of a supposed "Satanic School,"
the which he doth recommend to the notice of the
legislature; thereby adding to his other laurels the
ambition of those of an informer. If there exists
anywhere, except in his imagination, such a School, is
he not sufficiently armed against it by his own intense

───────────────────────

[1] Pope, *Essay on Criticism*, line 625.

vanity? The truth is that there are certain writers whom Mr. S. imagines, like Scrub, to have "talked of *him*; for they laughed consumedly."[2]

I think I know enough of most of the writers to whom he is supposed to allude, to assert, that they, in their individual capacities, have done more good, in the charities of life, to their fellow-creatures, in any one year, than Mr. Southey has done harm to himself by his absurdities in his whole life; and this is saying a great deal. But I have a few questions to ask.

1stly, Is Mr. Southey the author of *Wat Tyler*?

2ndly, Was he not refused a remedy at law by the highest judge of his beloved England, because it was a blasphemous and seditious publication?

3rdly, Was he not entitled by William Smith, in full parliament, "a rancorous renegado?"

4thly, Is he not poet laureate, with his own lines on Martin the regicide staring him in the face?

And, 5thly, Putting the four preceding items together, with what conscience dare *he* call the attention of the laws to the publications of others, be they what they may?[3]

I say nothing of the cowardice of such a proceeding; its meanness speaks for itself; but I wish to touch upon the *motive*, which is neither more nor less than that Mr. S. has been laughed at a little in some recent publications, as he was of yore in the *Anti-jacobin*, by his present patrons. Hence all this "skimble scamble stuff" about "Satanic," and so forth. However, it is worthy of him—"*qualis ab incepto.*"

If there is anything obnoxious to the political opinions of a portion of the public in the following poem, they may thank Mr. Southey. He might have written hexameters, as he has written everything else, for aught that the writer cared—had they been upon another subject. But to attempt to canonise a monarch, who, whatever were his household virtues, was neither a successful nor a patriot king,—inasmuch as several years of his reign passed in war with America and Ireland, to say nothing of the aggression upon France—like all other exaggeration, necessarily begets opposition. In whatever manner he may be spoken of in this new *Vision*, his *public* career will not be more favourably transmitted by history. Of his private virtues (although a little expensive to the nation) there can be no doubt.

With regard to the supernatural personages treated

of, I can only say that I know as much about them, and (as an honest man) have a better right to talk of them than Robert Southey. I have also treated them more tolerantly. The way in which that poor insane creature, the Laureate, deals about his judgments in the next world, is like his own judgment in this. If it was not completely ludicrous, it would be something worse. I don't think that there is much more to say at present.

QUEVEDO REDIVIVUS.

P.S.—It is possible that some readers may object, in these objectionable times, to the freedom with which saints, angels, and spiritual persons discourse in this *Vision*. But, for precedents upon such points, I must refer him to Fielding's *Journey from this World to the next*, and to the Visions of myself, the said Quevedo, in Spanish or translated. The reader is also requested to observe, that no doctrinal tenets are insisted upon or discussed; that the person of the Deity is carefully withheld from sight, which is more than can be said for the Laureate, who hath thought proper to make him talk, not "like a school-divine," but like the unscholarlike Mr. Southey. The whole action passes on the outside of heaven; and Chaucer's *Wife of Bath*, Pulci's *Morgante Maggiore*, Swift's *Tale of a Tub*, and the other works above referred to, are cases in point of the freedom with which saints, etc., may be permitted to converse in works not intended to be serious.

Q. R.

*** Mr. Southey being, as he says, a good Christian and vindictive, threatens, I understand, a reply to this our answer. It is to be hoped that his visionary faculties will in the meantime have acquired a little more judgment, properly so called: otherwise he will get himself into new dilemmas. These apostate jacobins furnish rich rejoinders. Let him take a specimen. Mr. Southey laudeth grievously "one Mr. Landor,"[4] who cultivates much private renown in the shape of Latin verses; and not long ago, the poet laureate dedicated to him, it appeareth, one of his fugitive lyrics, upon the strength of a poem called "*Gebir*." Who could suppose, that in this same Gebir the aforesaid Savage Landor (for such is his grim cognomen) putteth into the infernal regions no less a person than the hero of his friend Mr. Southey's heaven,—yea, even George the Third! See also how personal Savage becometh, when he hath a mind.

[2] From George Farquhar, *The Beaux Stratagem* (1707).
[3] The charges against Southey are slightly distorted. The refusal of legal assistance in preventing subsequent publication of *Wat Tyler* in 1817 (after Southey's views had changed) were not based on its contents, William Smith *did*, however, attack him in the House of Commons in 1817. Another early Southey poem is about the cell of a regicide.

[4] Walter Savage Landor (1775–1864) had just published a volume of poems in Latin.

The following is his portrait of our late gracious sovereign:—

(Prince Gebir having descended into the infernal regions, the shades of his royal ancestors are, at his request, called up to his view; and he exclaims to his ghostly guide)—

"'Aroar, what wretch that nearest us? what wretch
Is that with eyebrows white and slanting brow?
Listen! him yonder who, bound down supine,
Shrinks yelling from that sword there, engine-hung;
He too amongst my ancestors! I hate
The despot, but the dastard I despise.
Was he our countryman?'
                              'Alas, O king!
Iberia bore him, but the breed accurst
Inclement winds blew blighting from north-east.'
'He was a warrior then, nor fear'd the gods?'
'Gebir, he feared the Demons, not the gods,
Though them indeed his daily face adored;
And was no warrior, yet the thousand lives
Squandered, as stones to exercise a sling,
And the tame cruelty and cold caprice—
Oh madness of mankind! addressed, adored!'"
                                        Gebir

I omit noticing some edifying Ithyphallics of Savagius, wishing to keep the proper veil over them, if his grave but somewhat indiscreet worshipper will suffer it; but certainly these teachers of "great moral lessons" are apt to be found in strange company.

———◦◉◦———

I.

SAINT PETER sat by the celestial gate:
   His keys were rusty, and the lock was dull,
So little trouble had been given of late;
   Not that the place by any means was full,
But since the Gallic era "eighty-eight" [5]
   The Devils had ta'en a longer, stronger pull,
And "a pull altogether," as they say
At sea—which drew most souls another way.

II.

The Angels all were singing out of tune,
   And hoarse with having little else to do,
Excepting to wind up the sun and moon,
   Or curb a runaway young star or two,
Or wild colt of a comet, which too soon
   Broke out of bounds o'er the ethereal blue,
Splitting some planet with its playful tail,
As boats are sometimes by a wanton whale.

---

[5] 1788, just before the French Revolution.

III.

The Guardian Seraphs had retired on high,
   Finding their charges past all care below;
Terrestrial business filled nought in the sky
   Save the Recording Angel's black bureau;
Who found, indeed, the facts to multiply
   With such rapidity of vice and woe,
That he had stripped off both his wings in quills,
And yet was in arrear of human ills.

IV.

His business so augmented of late years,
   That he was forced, against his will, no doubt,
(Just like those cherubs, earthly ministers,)
   For some resource to turn himself about,
And claim the help of his celestial peers,
   To aid him ere he should be quite worn out
By the increased demand for his remarks:
Six Angels and twelve Saints were named his clerks.

V.

This was a handsome board—at least for Heaven;
   And yet they had even then enough to do,
So many Conquerors' cars were daily driven,
   So many kingdoms fitted up anew;
Each day, too, slew its thousands six or seven,
   Till at the crowning carnage, Waterloo,
They threw their pens down in divine disgust—
The page was so besmeared with blood and dust.

VI.

This by the way; 'tis not mine to record
   What Angels shrink from: even the very Devil
On this occasion his own work abhorred,
   So surfeited with the infernal revel:
Though he himself had sharpened every sword,
   It almost quenched his innate thirst of evil.
(Here Satan's sole good work deserves insertion—
'Tis, that he has both Generals in reversion.) [6]

VII.

Let's skip a few short years of hollow peace,
   Which peopled earth no better, Hell as wont,
And Heaven none—they form the tyrant's lease,
   With nothing but new names subscribed upon 't;
'Twill one day finish: meantime they increase,
   "With seven heads and ten horns," and all in
      front, [7]
Like Saint John's foretold beast; but ours are born
Less formidable in the head than horn.

---

[6] Napoleon and the Duke of Wellington. Napoleon had just died (though Byron did not know it), but Wellington lived until 1852.

[7] See Rev. XIII.

VIII.

In the first year of Freedom's second dawn
   Died George the Third; although no tyrant, one
Who shielded tyrants, till each sense withdrawn
   Left him nor mental nor external sun:
A better farmer ne'er brushed dew from lawn,
   A worse king never left a realm undone![8]
He died—but left his subjects still behind,
One half as mad—and t'other no less blind.

IX.

He died! his death made no great stir on earth:
   His burial made some pomp; there was profusion
Of velvet—gilding—brass—and no great dearth
   Of aught but tears—save those shed by collusion:
For these things may be bought at their true worth;
   Of elegy there was the due infusion—
Bought also; and the torches, cloaks and banners,
Heralds, and relics of old Gothic manners,

X.

Formed a sepulchral melodrame. Of all
   The fools who flocked to swell or see the show,
Who cared about the corpse? The funeral
   Made the attraction, and the black the woe,
There throbbed not there a thought which pierced
     the pall;
   And when the gorgeous coffin was laid low,
It seemed the mockery of hell to fold
The rottenness of eighty years in gold.

XI.

So mix his body with the dust! It might
   Return to what it *must* far sooner, were
The natural compound left alone to fight
   Its way back into earth, and fire, and air;
But the unnatural balsams merely blight
   What Nature made him at his birth, as bare
As the mere million's base unmummied clay—
Yet all his spices but prolong decay.

XII.

He's dead—and upper earth with him has done;
   He's buried; save the undertaker's bill,
Or lapidary scrawl, the world is gone
   For him, unless he left a German will:[9]
But where's the proctor who will ask his son?
   In whom his qualities are reigning still,
Except that household virtue, most uncommon,
Of constancy to a bad, ugly woman.

---

[8] When George III died on January 29, 1820, he was blind and
insane. His son had been ruling as Prince Regent since 1811.
  [9] George II hid his father's will when he succeeded him.

XIII.

"God save the king!" It is a large economy
   In God to save the like; but if he will
Be saving, all the better; for not one am I
   Of those who think damnation better still:
I hardly know too if not quite alone am I
   In this small hope of bettering future ill
By circumscribing, with some slight restriction,
The eternity of Hell's hot jurisdiction.

XIV.

I know this is unpopular; I know
   'Tis blasphemous; I know one may be damned
For hoping no one else may e'er be so;
   I know my catechism; I know we're crammed
With the best doctrines till we quite o'erflow;
   I know that all save England's Church have
     shammed,
And that the other twice two hundred churches
And synagogues have made a *damned* bad purchase.

XV.

God help us all! God help me too! I am,
   God knows, as helpless as the Devil can wish,
And not a whit more difficult to damn,
   Than is to bring to land a late-hooked fish,
Or to the butcher to purvey the lamb;
   Not that I'm fit for such a noble dish,
As one day will be that immortal fry
Of almost every body born to die.

XVI.

Saint Peter sat by the celestial gate,
   And nodded o'er his keys: when, lo! there came
A wondrous noise he had not heard of late—
   A rushing sound of wind, and stream, and flame;
In short, a roar of things extremely great,
   Which would have made aught save a Saint
     exclaim;
But he, with first a start and then a wink,
Said, "There's another star gone out, I think!"

XVII.

But ere he could return to his repose,
   A Cherub flapped his right wing o'er his eyes—
At which Saint Peter yawned, and rubbed his nose:
   "Saint porter," said the angel, "prithee rise!"
Waving a goodly wing, which glowed, as glows
   An early peacock's tail, with heavenly dyes:
To which the saint replied, "Well, what's the matter?
"Is Lucifer come back with all this clatter?"

XVIII.

"No," quoth the Cherub: "George the Third is
         dead."
    "And who *is* George the Third?" replied the
         apostle:
"*What George? what Third?*" "The King of
         England," said
The angel. "Well! he won't find kings to jostle
Him on his way; but does he wear his head?
Because the last we saw here had a tustle,
And ne'er would have got into Heaven's good graces,
Had he not flung his head in all our faces.[10]

XIX.

"He was—if I remember—King of France;
    That head of his, which could not keep a crown
On earth, yet ventured in my face to advance
    A claim to those of martyrs—like my own:[11]
If I had my sword, as I had once
    When I cut ears off, I had cut him down;
But having but my *keys*, and not my brand,
I only knocked his head from out his hand.

XX.

"And then he set up such a headless howl,
    That all the Saints came out and took him in;
And there he sits by Saint Paul, cheek by jowl;
    That fellow Paul—the parvenù! The skin
Of Saint Bartholomew, which makes his cowl
    In heaven, and upon earth redeemed his sin,
So as to make a martyr, never sped
Better than did this weak and wooden head.[12]

XXI.

"But had it come up here upon its shoulders,
    There would have been a different tale to tell:
The fellow-feeling in the Saint's beholders
    Seems to have acted on them like a spell;
And so this very foolish head Heaven solders
    Back on its trunk: it may be very well,
And seems the custom here to overthrow
Whatever has been wisely done below."

XXII.

The Angel answered, "Peter! do not pout:
    The King who comes has head and all entire,
And never knew much what it was about—
    He did as doth the puppet—by its wire,

---

[10] Louis XVI of France, guillotined in 1793.
[11] St. Peter was supposed to have been martyred during the
reign of Nero (A.D. 67).
[12] St. Bartholomew was said to have been flayed before he was
beheaded.

And will be judged like all the rest, no doubt:
    My business and your own is not to inquire
Into such matters, but to mind our cue—
Which is to act as we are bid to do."

XXIII.

While thus they spake, the angelic caravan,
    Arriving like a rush of mighty wind,
Cleaving the fields of space, as doth the swan
    Some silver stream (say Ganges, Nile, or Inde,
Or Thames, or Tweed), and midst them an old
         man
    With an old soul, and both extremely blind,
Halted before the gate, and, in his shroud,
Seated their fellow-traveller on a cloud.

XXIV.

But bringing up the rear of this bright host
    A Spirit of a different aspect waved
His wings, like thunder-clouds above some coast
    Whose barren beach with frequent wrecks is
         paved;
His brow was like the deep when tempest-tossed;
    Fierce and unfathomable thoughts engraved
Eternal wrath on his immortal face,
And *where* he gazed a gloom pervaded space.

XXV.

As he drew near, he gazed upon the gate
    Ne'er to be entered more by him or Sin,
With such a glance of supernatural hate,
    As made Saint Peter wish himself within;
He pottered with his keys at a great rate,
    And sweated through his Apostolic skin:
Of course his perspiration was but ichor,
Or some such other spiritual liquor.

XXVI.

The very Cherubs huddled all together,
    Like birds when soars the falcon; and they felt
A tingling to the tip of every feather,
    And formed a circle like Orion's belt
Around their poor old charge; who scarce knew
         whither
    His guards had led him, though they gently dealt
With royal Manes (for by many stories,
And true, we learn the Angels all are Tories).

XXVII.

As things were in this posture, the gate flew
   Asunder, and the flashing of its hinges
Flung over space an universal hue
   Of many-coloured flame, until its tinges
Reached even our speck of earth, and made a new
   Aurora borealis spread its fringes
O'er the North Pole; the same seen, when ice-bound,
By Captain Parry's crew, in "Melville's Sound." [13]

XXVIII.

And from the gate thrown open issued beaming
   A beautiful and mighty Thing of Light,
Radiant with glory, like a banner streaming
   Victorious from some world-o'erthrowing fight:
My poor comparisons must needs be teeming
   With earthly likenesses, for here the night
Of clay obscures our best conceptions, saving
Johanna Southcote, or Bob Southey raving. [14]

XXIX.

'Twas the Archangel Michael: all men know
   The make of Angels and Archangels, since
There's scarce a scribbler has not one to show,
   From the fiends' leader to the Angels' Prince.
There also are some altar-pieces, though
   I really can't say that they much evince
One's inner notions of immortal spirits;
But let the connoisseurs explain *their* merits.

XXX.

Michael flew forth in glory and in good;
   A goodly work of him from whom all Glory
And Good arise; the portal past—he stood;
   Before him the young Cherubs and Saints hoary—
(I say *young*, begging to be understood
   By looks, not years; and should be very sorry
To state, they were not older than St. Peter,
But merely that they seemed a little sweeter).

XXXI.

The Cherubs and the Saints bowed down before
   That arch-angelic Hierarch, the first
Of Essences angelical who wore
   The aspect of a god; but this ne'er nursed
Pride in his heavenly bosom, in whose core
   No thought, save for his Maker's service, durst
Intrude, however glorified and high;
He knew him but the Viceroy of the sky.

[13] During Sir Edward Parry's search for a northwest passage,
1819–1820.
[14] Joanna Southcott (1750–1814), religious prophet, died
saying she would give birth to the new Messiah.

XXXII.

He and the sombre, silent Spirit met—
   They knew each other both for good and ill;
Such was their power, that neither could forget
   His former friend and future foe; but still
There was a high, immortal, proud regret
   In either's eye, as if 'twere less their will
Than destiny to make the eternal years
Their date of war, and their "Champ Clos" [15] the
      spheres.

XXXIII.

But here they were in neutral space: we know
   From Job, that Satan hath the power to pay
A heavenly visit thrice a-year or so;
   And that the "Sons of God," like those of clay,
Must keep him company; and we might show
   From the same book, in how polite a way
The dialogue is held between the Powers
Of Good and Evil—but 'twould take up hours.

XXXIV.

And this is not a theologic tract,
   To prove with Hebrew and with Arabic,
If Job be allegory or a fact,
   But a true narrative; and thus I pick
From out the whole but such and such an act
   As sets aside the slightest thought of trick.
'Tis every tittle true, beyond suspicion,
And accurate as any other vision.

XXXV.

The spirits were in neutral space, before
   The gate of Heaven; like eastern thresholds is [16]
The place where Death's grand cause is argued o'er,
   And souls despatched to that world or to this;
And therefore Michael and the other wore
   A civil aspect: though they did not kiss,
Yet still between his Darkness and his Brightness
There passed a mutual glance of great politeness.

XXXVI.

The Archangel bowed, not like a modern beau,
   But with a graceful oriental bend,
Pressing one radiant arm just where below
   The heart in good men is supposed to tend;
He turned as to an equal, not too low,
   But kindly; Satan met his ancient friend
With more hauteur, as might an old Castilian
Poor Noble meet a mushroom rich civilian.

[15] Tournament ground.
[16] In Near Eastern cities, gateways were used for deliberations,
audiences, etc.

XXXVII.

He merely bent his diabolic brow
    An instant; and then raising it, he stood
In act to assert his right or wrong, and show
    Cause why King George by no means could or
      should
Make out a case to be exempt from woe
    Eternal, more than other kings, endued
With better sense and hearts, whom History mentions,
Who long have "paved Hell with their good
      intentions." [17]

XXXVIII.

Michael began: "What wouldst thou with this man,
    Now dead, and brought before the Lord? What ill
Hath he wrought since his mortal race began,
    That thou canst claim him? Speak! and do thy will,
If it be just: if in this earthly span
    He hath been greatly failing to fulfil
His duties as a king and mortal, say,
And he is thine; if not—let him have way."

XXXIX.

"Michael!" replied the Prince of Air, "even here
    Before the gate of Him thou servest, must
I claim my subject: and will make appear
    That as he was my worshipper in dust,
So shall he be in spirit, although dear
    To thee and thine, because nor wine nor lust
Were of his weaknesses; yet on the throne
He reigned o'er millions to serve me alone.

XL.

"Look to *our* earth, or rather *mine*; it was,
    Once, more thy master's: but I triumph not
In this poor planet's conquest; nor, alas!
    Need he thou servest envy me my lot:
With all the myriads of bright worlds which pass
    In worship round him, he may have forgot
Yon weak creation of such paltry things:
I think few worth damnation save their kings,

XLI.

"And these but as a kind of quit-rent, to
    Assert my right as Lord: and even had
I such an inclination, 'twere (as you
    Well know) superfluous; they are grown so bad,
That Hell has nothing better left to do
    Than leave them to themselves: so much more mad
And evil by their own internal curse,
Heaven cannot make them better, nor I worse.

[17] Ascribed to Samuel Johnson in Boswell's *Life*.

XLII.

"Look to the earth, I said, and say again:
    When this old, blind, mad, helpless, weak, poor
      worm
Began in youth's first bloom and flush to reign,
    The world and he both wore a different form,
And much of earth and all the watery plain
    Of Ocean called him king: through many a storm
His isles had floated on the abyss of Time;
For the rough virtues chose them for their clime.

XLIII.

"He came to his sceptre young; he leaves it old: [18]
    Look to the state in which he found his realm,
And left it; and his annals too behold,
    How to a minion first he gave the helm; [19]
How grew upon his heart a thirst for gold,
    The beggar's vice, which can but overwhelm
The meanest hearts; and for the rest, but glance
Thine eye along America and France.

XLIV.

"'Tis true, he was a tool from first to last
    (I have the workmen safe); but as a tool
So let him be consumed. From out the past
    Of ages, since mankind have known the rule
Of monarchs—from the bloody rolls amassed
    Of Sin and Slaughter—from the Cæsars' school,
Take the worst pupil; and produce a reign
More drenched with gore, more cumbered with the
    slain.

XLV.

"He ever warred with freedom and the free:
    Nations as men, home subjects, foreign foes,
So that they uttered the word 'Liberty!'
    Found George the Third their first opponent.
      Whose
History was ever stained as his will be
    With national and individual woes?
I grant his household abstinence; I grant
His neutral virtues, which most monarchs want;

XLVI.

"I know he was a constant consort; own
    He was a decent sire, and middling lord.
All this is much, and most upon a throne;
    As temperance, if at Apicius' board, [20]

[18] George III was only twenty-two when he ascended the throne in 1760.
[19] John Stuart, Earl of Bute, prime minister 1762–1763.
[20] Roman epicure, contrasted with the hermit of the next line.

Is more than at an anchorite's supper shown.
   I grant him all the kindest can accord;
And this was well for him, but not for those
   Millions who found him what Oppression chose.

XLVII.

"The New World shook him off; the Old yet groans
   Beneath what he and his prepared, if not
Completed: he leaves heirs on many thrones
   To all his vices, without what begot
Compassion for him—his tame virtues; drones
   Who sleep, or despots who have now forgot
A lesson which shall be re-taught them, wake
Upon the thrones of earth; but let them quake!

XLVIII.

"Five millions of the primitive, who hold
   The faith which makes ye great on earth, implored
A *part* of that vast *all* they held of old,—
   Freedom to worship—not alone your Lord,
Michael, but you, and you, Saint Peter! Cold
   Must be your souls, if you have not abhorred
The foe to Catholic participation [21]
In all the license of a Christian nation.

XLIX.

"True! he allowed them to pray God; but as
   A consequence of prayer, refused the law
Which would have placed them upon the same base
   With those who did not hold the Saints in awe."
But here Saint Peter started from his place
   And cried, "You may the prisoner withdraw:
Ere Heaven shall ope her portals to this Guelph, [22]
While I am guard, may I be damned myself!

L.

"Sooner will I with Cerberus exchange
   My office (and *his* is no sinecure)
Than see this royal Bedlam-bigot range
   The azure fields of Heaven, of that be sure!"
"Saint!" replied Satan, "you do well to avenge
   The wrongs he made your satellites endure;
And if to this exchange you should be given,
I'll try to coax *our* Cerberus up to Heaven!" [23]

21 George III opposed Catholic Emancipation throughout his reign.
22 The Hanovers were the modern representatives of the German ducal family founded in the ninth century.
23 Cerberus is a three-headed, serpent-tailed dog, guardian of the gate of Hades; Bedlam, from St. Mary of Bethlehem asylum for the insane.

LI.

Here Michael interposed: "Good Saint! and Devil!
   Pray, not so fast; you both outrun discretion.
Saint Peter! you were wont to be more civil:
   Satan! excuse this warmth of his expression,
And condescension to the vulgar's level:
   Even Saints sometimes forget themselves in session.
Have you got more to say?"—"No."—"If you
     please,
I'll trouble you to call your witnesses."

LII.

Then Satan turned and waved his swarthy hand,
   Which stirred with its electric qualities
Clouds farther off than we can understand,
   Although we find him sometimes in our skies;
Infernal thunder shook both sea and land
   In all the planets—and Hell's batteries
Let off the artillery, which Milton mentions
As one of Satan's most sublime inventions. [24]

LIII.

This was a signal unto such damned souls
   As have the privilege of their damnation
Extended far beyond the mere controls
   Of worlds past, present, or to come; no station
Is theirs particularly in the rolls
   Of Hell assigned; but where their inclination
Or business carries them in search of game,
They may range freely—being damned the same.

LIV.

They are proud of this—as very well they may,
   It being a sort of knighthood, or gilt key
Stuck in their loins; or like to an "entré"
   Up the back stairs, or such free-masonry.
I borrow my comparisons from clay,
   Being clay myself. Let not those spirits be
Offended with such base low likenesses;
We know their posts are nobler far than these.

LV.

When the great signal ran from Heaven to Hell—
   About ten million times the distance reckoned
From our sun to its earth, as we can tell
   How much time it takes up, even to a second,
For every ray that travels to dispel
   The fogs of London, through which, dimly
     beaconed,
The weathercocks are gilt some thrice a year,
If that the *summer* is not too severe:

24 See Book VI of *Paradise Lost*.

LVI.

I say that I can tell—'twas half a minute;
  I know the solar beams take up more time
Ere, packed up for their journey, they begin it;
  But then their Telegraph is less sublime,[25]
And if they ran a race, they would not win it
  'Gainst Satan's couriers bound for their own clime.
The sun takes up some years for every ray
To reach its goal—the Devil not half a day.

LVII.

Upon the verge of space, about the size
  Of half-a-crown, a little speck appeared
(I've seen a something like it in the skies
  In the Ægean, ere a squall); it neared,
And, growing bigger, took another guise;
  Like an aërial ship it tacked, and steered,
Or *was* steered (I am doubtful of the grammar
Of the last phrase, which makes the stanza stammer;

LVIII.

But take your choice): and then it grew a cloud;
  And so it was—a cloud of witnesses.
But such a cloud! No land ere saw a crowd
  Of locusts numerous as the heavens saw these;
They shadowed with their myriads Space; their loud
  And varied cries were like those of wild geese,
(If nations may be likened to a goose),
And realised the phrase of "Hell broke loose."

LIX.

Here crashed a sturdy oath of stout John Bull,
  Who damned away his eyes as heretofore:
There Paddy brogued "By Jasus!"—"What's your
    wull?"
  The temperate Scot exclaimed: the French ghost
    swore
In certain terms I shan't translate in full,
  As the first coachman will; and 'midst the war,
The voice of Jonathan was heard to express,[26]
"*Our* President is going to war, I guess."

LX.

Besides there were the Spaniard, Dutch, and Dane;
  In short, an universal shoal of shades
From Otaheite's[27] isle to Salisbury Plain,
  Of all climes and professions, years and trades,

---

[25] Probably not an electric telegraph, but a semaphore system, is what Byron refers to here.
[26] "Brother Jonathan" was an early personification of America.
[27] Tahiti.

Ready to swear against the good king's reign,
  Bitter as clubs in cards are against spades:
All summoned by this grand "subpœna," to
Try if kings mayn't be damned like me or you.

LXI.

When Michael saw this host, he first grew pale,
  As Angels can; next, like Italian twilight,
He turned all colours—as a peacock's tail,
  Or sunset streaming through a Gothic skylight
In some old abbey, or a trout not stale,
  Or distant lightning on the horizon *by* night,
Or a fresh rainbow, or a grand review
Of thirty regiments in red, green, and blue.

LXII.

Then he addressed himself to Satan: "Why—
  My good old friend, for such I deem you, though
Our different parties make us fight so shy,
  I ne'er mistake you for a *personal* foe;
Our difference is *political*, and I
  Trust that, whatever may occur below,
You know my great respect for you: and this
Makes me regret whate'er you do amiss—

LXIII.

"Why, my dear Lucifer, would you abuse
  My call for witnesses? I did not mean
That you should half of Earth and Hell produce;
  'Tis even superfluous, since two honest, clean,
True testimonies are enough: we lose
  Our Time, nay, our Eternity, between
The accusation and defence: if we
Hear both, 'twill stretch our immortality."

LXIV.

Satan replied, "To me the matter is
  Indifferent, in a personal point of view:
I can have fifty better souls than this
  With far less trouble than we have gone through
Already; and I merely argued his
  Late Majesty of Britain's case with you
Upon a point of form: you may dispose
Of him; I've kings enough below, God knows!"

LXV.

Thus spoke the Demon (late called "multifaced"
  By multo-scribbling Southey). "Then we'll call
One or two persons of the myriads placed
  Around our congress, and dispense with all

The rest," quoth Michael: "Who may be so graced
   As to speak first? there's choice enough—who shall
It be?" Then Satan answered, "There are many;
But you may choose Jack Wilkes as well as any." [28]

LXVI.

A merry, cock-eyed, curious-looking Sprite
   Upon the instant started from the throng,
Dressed in a fashion now forgotten quite;
   For all the fashions of the flesh stick long
By people in the next world; where unite
   All the costumes since Adam's, right or wrong,
From Eve's fig-leaf down to the petticoat,
Almost as scanty, of days less remote.

LXVII.

The Spirit looked around upon the crowds
   Assembled, and exclaimed, "My friends of all
The spheres, we shall catch cold amongst these
     clouds;
   So let's to business: why this general call?
If those are freeholders I see in shrouds,
   And 'tis for an election that they bawl,
Behold a candidate with unturned coat!
Saint Peter, may I count upon your vote?"

LXVIII.

"Sir," replied Michael, "you mistake; these things
   Are of a former life, and what we do
Above is more august; to judge of kings
   Is the tribunal met: so now you know."
"Then I presume those gentlemen with wings,"
   Said Wilkes, "are Cherubs; and that soul below
Looks much like George the Third, but to my mind
A good deal older—bless me! is he blind?"

LXIX.

"He is what you behold him, and his doom
   Depends upon his deeds," the Angel said;
"If you have aught to arraign in him, the tomb
   Gives license to the humblest beggar's head
To lift itself against the loftiest."—"Some,"
   Said Wilkes, "don't wait to see them laid in lead,
For such a liberty—and I, for one,
Have told them what I thought beneath the sun."

LXX.

"*Above* the sun repeat, then, what thou hast
   To urge against him," said the Archangel. "Why,"
Replied the spirit, "since old scores are past,
   Must I turn evidence? In faith, not I.

Besides, I beat him hollow at the last,
   With all his Lords and Commons: in the sky
I don't like ripping up old stories, since
His conduct was but natural in a prince.

LXXI.

"Foolish, no doubt, and wicked, to oppress
   A poor unlucky devil without a shilling;
But then I blame the man himself much less
   Than Bute and Grafton, [29] and shall be unwilling
To see him punished here for their excess,
   Since they were both damned long ago, and still in
Their place below: for me, I have forgiven,
And vote his *habeas corpus* into Heaven."

LXXII.

"Wilkes," said the Devil, "I understand all this;
   You turned to half a courtier ere you died, [30]
And seem to think it would not be amiss
   To grow a whole one on the other side
Of Charon's ferry; you forget that *his*
   Reign is concluded; whatsoe'er betide,
He won't be sovereign more: you've lost your labour,
For at the best he will but be your neighbour.

LXXIII.

"However, I knew what to think of it,
   When I beheld you in your jesting way,
Flitting and whispering round about the spit
   Where Belial, upon duty for the day,
With Fox's lard was basting William Pitt, [31]
   His pupil; I knew what to think, I say:
That fellow even in Hell breeds farther ills;
I'll have him *gagged*—'twas one of his own Bills.

LXXIV.

"Call Junius!" From the crowd a shadow stalked, [32]
   And at the name there was a general squeeze,
So that the very ghosts no longer walked
   In comfort, at their own aërial ease,
But were all rammed, and jammed (but to be
     balked,
   As we shall see), and jostled hands and knees,
Like wind compressed and pent within a bladder,
Or like a human colic, which is sadder.

---

[28] John Wilkes (1727–1797), repeatedly elected to and expelled from the House of Commons, long-time enemy of George III, later (1774) Lord Mayor of London and Chamberlain of the City of London.

[29] The Duke of Grafton, prime minister from 1768 to 1770, was more sympathetic to Wilkes than Bute had been.

[30] In his later years Wilkes voted against the Whigs, and became more conciliatory toward the king.

[31] Pitt as prime minister and Fox as leader of the Whigs were frequent opponents at the turn of the century. See also Coleridge's *A Character*, p. 500. Pitt introduced the Treason and Sedition Bills, repressing freedom of press and speech, in 1795.

[32] *The Letters of Junius*, attacking the king and his ministry, appeared anonymously from 1769 to 1772. No author was ever discovered, though more than fifty were proposed.

LXXV.

The shadow came—a tall, thin, grey-haired figure,
　　That looked as it had been a shade on earth;
Quick in its motions, with an air of vigour,
　　But nought to mark its breeding or its birth;
Now it waxed little, then again grew bigger,
　　With now an air of gloom, or savage mirth;
But as you gazed upon its features, they
Changed every instant—to *what*, none could say.

LXXVI.

The more intently the ghosts gazed, the less
　　Could they distinguish whose the features were;
The Devil himself seemed puzzled even to guess;
　　They varied like a dream—now here, now there;
And several people swore from out the press,
　　They knew him perfectly; and one could swear
He was his father; upon which another
Was sure he was his mother's cousin's brother:

LXXVII.

Another, that he was a duke, or knight,
　　An orator, a lawyer, or a priest,
A nabob, a man-midwife; but the wight
　　Mysterious changed his countenance at least
As oft as they their minds: though in full sight
　　He stood, the puzzle only was increased;
The man was a phantasmagoria in
Himself—he was so volatile and thin.

LXXVIII.

The moment that you had pronounced him *one*,
　　Presto! his face changed, and he was another;
And when that change was hardly well put on,
　　It varied, till I don't think his own mother
(If that he had a mother) would her son
　　Have known, he shifted so from one to t'other;
Till guessing from a pleasure grew a task,
At this epistolary "Iron Mask." [33]

LXXIX.

For sometimes he like Cerberus would seem—
　　"Three gentlemen at once" (as sagely says
Good Mrs. Malaprop); [34] then you might deem
　　That he was not even *one*; now many rays
Were flashing round him; and now a thick steam
　　Hid him from sight—like fogs on London days:
Now Burke, now Tooke, he grew to people's fancies
And certes often like Sir Philip Francis. [35]

LXXX.

I've an hypothesis—'tis quite my own;
　　I never let it out till now, for fear
Of doing people harm about the throne,
　　And injuring some minister or peer,
On whom the stigma might perhaps be blown;
　　It is—my gentle public, lend thine ear!
'Tis, that what Junius we are wont to call,
Was *really—truly*—nobody at all.

LXXXI.

I don't see wherefore letters should not be
　　Written without hands, since we daily view
Them written without heads; and books, we see,
　　Are filled as well without the latter too:
And really till we fix on somebody
　　For certain sure to claim them as his due,
Their author, like the Niger's mouth, will bother [36]
The world to say if *there* be mouth or author.

LXXXII.

"And who and what art thou?" the Archangel said.
　　"For *that* you may consult my title-page," [37]
Replied this mighty shadow of a shade:
　　"If I have kept my secret half an age,
I scarce shall tell it now."—"Canst thou upbraid,"
　　Continued Michael, "George Rex, or allege
Aught further?" Junius answered, "You had better
First ask him for *his* answer to my letter:

LXXXIII.

"My charges upon record will outlast
　　The brass of both his epitaph and tomb."
"Repent'st thou not," said Michael, "of some past
　　Exaggeration? something which may doom
Thyself if false, as him if true? Thou wast
　　Too bitter—is it not so?—in thy gloom
Of passion?"—"Passion!" cried the phantom dim,
"I loved my country, and I hated him.

LXXXIV.

"What I have written, I have written: let
　　The rest be on his head or mine!" So spoke
Old "*Nominis Umbra*;" and while speaking yet,
　　Away he melted in celestial smoke.
Then Satan said to Michael, "Don't forget
　　To call George Washington, and John Horne
　　　Tooke,
And Franklin;"—but at this time there was heard
A cry for room, though not a phantom stirred.

---

[33] A mysterious prisoner who died in the Bastille in 1703, later discovered to have been an Italian count convicted of treason at the court of the Duke of Mantua.
[34] Mrs. Malaprop is a character in Sheridan's *The Rivals*.
[35] Edmund Burke and Horne Tooke are possible authors of *Junius*, but Sir Philip Francis (1740–1818) is the most likely.

[36] The mouth of the Niger River is divided into a confusing series of estuaries.
[37] Under the title appeared "Stat Nominis Umbra": a shadow in place of a name.

LXXXV.

At length with jostling, elbowing, and the aid
　Of Cherubim appointed to that post,
The devil Asmodeus [38] to the circle made
　His way, and looked as if his journey cost
Some trouble. When his burden down he laid,
　"What's this?" cried Michael; "why, 'tis not a
　　ghost?"
"I know it," quoth the Incubus; "but he
Shall be one, if you leave the affair to me.

LXXXVI.

"Confound the renegado! I have sprained
　My left wing, he's so heavy; one would think
Some of his works about his neck were chained.
　But to the point; while hovering o'er the brink
Of Skiddaw (where as usual it still rained),[39]
　I saw a taper, far below me, wink,
And stooping, caught this fellow at a libel—
No less on History—than the Holy Bible.

LXXXVII.

"The former is the Devil's scripture, and
　The latter yours, good Michael: so the affair
Belongs to all of us, you understand.
　I snatched him up just as you see him there,
And brought him off for sentence out of hand:
　I've scarcely been ten minutes in the air—
At least a quarter it can hardly be:
I dare say that his wife is still at tea."

LXXXVIII.

Here Satan said, "I know this man of old,
　And have expected him for some time here;
A sillier fellow you will scarce behold,
　Or more conceited in his petty sphere:
But surely it was not worth while to fold
　Such trash below your wing, Asmodeus dear:
We had the poor wretch safe (without being bored
With carriage) coming of his own accord.

LXXXIX.

"But since he's here, let's see what he has done."
　"Done!" cried Asmodeus, "he anticipates
The very business you are now upon,
　And scribbles as if head clerk to the Fates.
Who knows to what his ribaldry may run,
　When such an ass as this, like Balaam's, prates?"
"Let's hear," quoth Michael, "what he has to say:
You know we're bound to that in every way."

XC.

Now the bard, glad to get an audience, which
　By no means often was his case below,
Began to cough, and hawk, and hem, and pitch
　His voice into that awful note of woe
To all unhappy hearers within reach
　Of poets when the tide of rhyme's in flow;
But stuck fast with his first hexameter,
Not one of all whose gouty feet would stir.

XCI.

But ere the spavined dactyls could be spurred
　Into recitative, in great dismay
Both Cherubim and Seraphim were heard
　To murmur loudly through their long array;
And Michael rose ere he could get a word
　Of all his foundered verses under way,
And cried, "For God's sake stop, my friend! 'twere
　　best—
'*Non Di, non homines*'—you know the rest." [40]

XCII.

A general bustle spread throughout the throng,
　Which seemed to hold all verse in detestation;
The Angels had of course enough of song
　When upon service; and the generation
Of ghosts had heard too much in life, not long
　Before, to profit by a new occasion:
The Monarch, mute till then, exclaimed, "What!
　　what!
Pye [41] come again? No more—no more of that!"

XCIII.

The tumult grew; an universal cough
　Convulsed the skies, as during a debate,
When Castlereagh has been up long enough [42]
　(Before he was first minister of state,
I mean—the *slaves hear now*); some cried "Off, off!"
　As at a farce; till, grown quite desperate,
The Bard Saint Peter prayed to interpose
(Himself an author) only for his prose.

XCIV.

The varlet was not an ill-favoured knave;
　A good deal like a vulture in the face,
With a hook nose and a hawk's eye, which gave
　A smart and sharper-looking sort of grace

---

[38] Traditional evil spirit in Jewish demonology; an incubus is an evil spirit believed to have sexual intercourse with sleeping women.
[39] A mountain peak in the Lake District near Southey's home.
[40] "Neither gods nor men (have room for mediocre poets)," from Horace's *Ars Poetica.*
[41] Henry James Pye, Poet Laureate from 1790 to 1813, was Southey's predecessor. See *English Bards*, line 102, p. 540.
[42] Viscount Castlereagh was Foreign Secretary and Leader in the House of Commons from 1812 to 1827.

To his whole aspect, which, though rather grave,
  Was by no means so ugly as his case;
But that, indeed, was hopeless as can be,
  Quite a poetic felony "*de se*."[43]

XCV.

Then Michael blew his trump, and stilled the noise
  With one still greater, as is yet the mode
On earth besides; except some grumbling voice,
  Which now and then will make a slight inroad
Upon decorous silence, few will twice
  Lift up their lungs when fairly overcrowed;
And now the Bard could plead his own bad cause,
With all the attitudes of self-applause.

XCVI.

He said—(I only give the heads)—he said,
  He meant no harm in scribbling; 'twas his way
Upon all topics; 'twas, besides, his bread,
  Of which he buttered both sides; 'twould delay
Too long the assembly (he was pleased to dread),
  And take up rather more time than a day,
To name his works—he would but cite a few—
"Wat Tyler"—"Rhymes on Blenheim"—
    "Waterloo."

XCVII.

He had written praises of a Regicide;
  He had written praises of all kings whatever;
He had written for republics far and wide,
  And then against them bitterer than ever;
For pantisocracy he once had cried
  Aloud, a scheme less moral than 'twas clever;
Then grew a hearty anti-jacobin—
Had turned his coat—and would have turned his
    skin.[44]

XCVIII.

He had sung against all battles, and again
  In their high praise and glory; he had called
Reviewing "the ungentle craft," and then*
  Became as base a critic as e'er crawled—
Fed, paid, and pampered by the very men
  By whom his muse and morals had been mauled:
He had written much blank verse, and blanker prose,
And more of both than any body knows.

    * See "Life of Henry Kirk White."

---

[43] I.e., suicide.
[44] These are all references to works and events in Southey's life and career. He had been Coleridge's main collaborator in planning Pantisocracy. See notes to Coleridge, *Pantisocracy*, p. 433, and Coleridge's letter to Southey, p. 505.

XCIX.

He had written Wesley's life:—here turning round
  To Satan, "Sir, I'm ready to write yours,
In two octavo volumes, nicely bound,
  With notes and preface, all that most allures
The pious purchaser; and there's no ground
  For fear, for I can choose my own reviewers:
So let me have the proper documents,
That I may add you to my other saints."

C.

Satan bowed, and was silent. "Well, if you,
  With amiable modesty, decline
My offer, what says Michael? There are few
  Whose memoirs could be rendered more divine.
Mine is a pen of all work; not so new
  As it was once, but I would make you shine
Like your own trumpet. By the way, my own
Has more of brass in it, and is as well blown.

CI.

"But talking about trumpets, here's my 'Vision!'
  Now you shall judge, all people—yes—you shall
Judge with my judgment! and by my decision
  Be guided who shall enter heaven or fall.
I settle all these things by intuition,
  Times present, past, to come—Heaven—Hell—and
    all,
Like King Alfonso.† When I thus see double,
I save the Deity some worlds of trouble."

CII.

He ceased, and drew forth an MS.; and no
  Persuasion on the part of Devils, Saints,
Or Angels, now could stop the torrent; so
  He read the first three lines of the contents;
But at the fourth, the whole spiritual show
  Had vanished, with variety of scents,
Ambrosial and sulphureous, as they sprang,
Like lightning, off from his "melodious twang."‡

CIII.

Those grand heroics acted as a spell;
  The Angels stopped their ears and plied their
    pinions;
The Devils ran howling, deafened, down to Hell;
  The ghosts fled, gibbering, for their own
    dominions—

† Alfonso, speaking of the Ptolomean system, said, that "had he been consulted at the creation of the world, he would have spared the Maker some absurdities."
‡ See Aubrey's account of the apparition which disappeared "with a curious perfume, and a *most melodious twang*;" or see the "*Antiquary*," vol. i. p. 225.

(For 'tis not yet decided where they dwell,
   And I leave every man to his opinions);
Michael took refuge in his trump—but, lo!
His teeth were set on edge, he could not blow!

CIV.

Saint Peter, who has hitherto been known
   For an impetuous saint, upraised his keys,
And at the fifth line knocked the poet down;
   Who fell like Phaeton, but more at ease,
Into his lake, for there he did not drown;
   A different web being by the Destinies
Woven for the Laureate's final wreath, whene'er
Reform shall happen either here or there.

CV.

He first sank to the bottom—like his works,
   But soon rose to the surface—like himself;
For all corrupted things are buoyed like corks,*
   By their own rottenness, light as an elf,
Or wisp that flits o'er a morass: he lurks,
   It may be, still, like dull books on a shelf,
In his own den, to scrawl some "Life" or "Vision,"
As Welborn says—"the Devil turned precisian."[45]

CVI

As for the rest, to come to the conclusion
   Of this true dream, the telescope is gone
Which kept my optics free from all delusion,
   And showed me what I in my turn have shown;
All I saw farther, in the last confusion,
   Was, that King George slipped into Heaven for one;
And when the tumult dwindled to a calm,
I left him practising the hundredth psalm.

[1821]   [1822]

A consistent text of Don Juan *that expresses the intentions of its author does not exist. Byron was not a systematic editor of his own work, the cantos were printed in six separate volumes by two different publishers with varying editorial practices during a five-year period, and Byron himself probably never saw the first editions of the eleven cantos that were published after he left England. The following selection, which relies on the work of many editors and especially that done by Professors Steffan and Pratt for the Variorum* Don Juan, *attempts to preserve the readings of first editions where possible and clear. Notes ascribed to Byron are those which modern editors usually accept as authentic (most are from the edition of 1823), though some of the more fragmentary citations have been absorbed into editorial footnotes. The Preface to Cantos I and II is based on a rough draft never finished by Byron and unpublished until 1901 (some minor corrections have been made in it). The dedicatory stanzas were included in the manuscript for Cantos I and II that Byron gave his publisher, John Murray, but he directed Murray to omit them from the first publication of the poem.*

A brief synopsis of events in the cantos omitted from this selection appears between Cantos II and XI.

FROM

DON JUAN

"Difficile est proprie communia dicere."
Hor. *Epist. ad Pison*[1]

PREFACE

In a note or preface (I forget which) by Mr. W. Wordsworth to a poem the Subject of which as far as it is intelligible is the remorse of an unnatural mother for the destruction of a natural child—the courteous Reader is desired to extend his usual courtesy to far as to suppose that the narrative is narrated by "the Captain of a Merchantman or small trading vessel lately retired upon a small annuity to some inland town—&c., &c." I quote from memory but conceive the above to be the sense, as far as there is Sense, of the note or preface to the aforesaid poem—as far as it is a poem.[2]

The poem—or production, to which I allude, is that which begins with—"There is a thorn, it is so old"—and then the Poet informs all who are willing to be informed, that its age was such as to leave great difficulty in the conception of its ever having been young at all—which is as much as to say, either that it was Coeval with the Creator of all things, or that it had been *born old*, and was thus appropriately by

---

* A drowned body lies at the bottom till rotten; it then floats, as most people know.

[45] In Massinger's *A New Way to Pay Old Debts* (1633).

---

[1] From Horace's *Epistle to Pisones:* "'Tis no slight task to write on common things.
[2] See Wordsworth's *The Thorn*, p. 188.

antithesis devoted to the Commemoration of a child that died young. The pond near it is described, according to mensuration,

> I measured it from side to side:
> 'Tis three feet long, and two feet wide.

Let me be excused from being particular in the detail of such things, as this is the Sort of writing which has superseded and degraded Pope in the eyes of the discerning British Public; and this Man is the kind of Poet who, in the same manner that Joanna Southcote found many thousand people to take her Dropsy for God Almighty re-impregnated, has found some hundreds of persons to misbelieve in his insanities, and hold his art as a kind of poetical Emanuel Swedenborg—or Richard Brothers—a parson Tozer—half Enthusiast and half Imposter.[3]

This rustic Gongora and vulgar Marini[4] of his Country's taste has long abandoned a mind capable of better things to the production of such trash as may support the reveries which he would reduce into a System of prosaic raving that is to supersede all that hitherto by the best and wisest of our fathers has been deemed poetry, and for his success—and what mountebank will not find proselytes? (from Count Cagliostro to Madame Krudner)[5]—he may partly thank his absurdity—& partly his having lent his more downright and unmeasured prose to the aid of a political party which acknowledges its real weakness, though fenced with the whole armour of artificial Power and defended by all the ingenuity of purchased Talent, in liberally rewarding with praise & pay even the meanest of its advocates. Amongst these last in self-degradation, this Thraso of poetry has long been a Gnatho in Politics, and may be met in print at some booksellers and several trunkmakers, and in person at dinner at Lord Lonsdale's.[6]

The Reader who has acquiesced in Mr. W. Wordsworth's supposition that his "Misery oh Misery" is related by the "Captain of a small, &c.," is requested to suppose by a like exertion of Imagination that the following epic Narrative is told by a Spanish Gentleman in a village in the Sierra Morena in the road between Monasterio & Seville, sitting at the door of a Posada, with the Curate of the hamlet on his right hand, a Segar in his mouth, a Jug of Malaga, or perhaps "right Sherris," before him on a small table containing the relics of an Olla Podrida: the time, Sunset: at some distance, a groupe of black eyed peasantry are dancing to the sound of the flute of a Portuguese Servant belonging to two foreign travellers who have an hour ago dismounted from their horses to spend the night on their way to the Capital of Andalusia. Of these, one is attending to the story; and the other, having sauntered further, is watching the beautiful movements of a tall peasant Girl whose whole Soul is in her eyes & her heart in the dance, of which she is the Magnet to ten thousand feelings that vibrate with her Own. Not far off a knot of French prisoners are contending with each other at the grated lattice of their temporary confinement for a view of the twilight festival. The two foremost are a couple of hussars, one of whom has a bandage on his forehead yet stained with the blood of a Sabre cut received in the recent skirmish which deprived him of his lawless freedom: his eyes sparkle in unison and his fingers beat time against the bars of his prison to the sound of the Fandango which is fleeting before him.

Our friend the Story-teller, at some distance with a small elderly audience, is supposed to tell his story without being much moved by the musical hilarity at the other end of the village Green. The Reader is further requested to suppose him (to account for his knowledge of English) either an Englishman settled in Spain—or a Spaniard who had travelled in England—perhaps one of the Liberals who have subsequently been so liberally rewarded by Ferdinand of grateful memory—for his restoration.[7]

Having supposed as much of this as the utter impossibility of a such a supposition will admit, the reader is requested to extend his supposed power of supposing so far as to conceive, that the dedication to Mr. Southey & several stanzas of the poem itself are interpolated by the English Editor. He may also imagine various causes for the tenor of the dedication. It may be presumed to be the production of a present Whig who, after being bred a transubstantial Tory, apostatized in an unguarded moment and, incensed at having got nothing by the exchange, has, in utter envy of the better success of the Author of Walter Tyler,[8] vented his renegado rancour on that immaculate person, for whose future immortality & present purity we have the best authority in his own repeated assurances. Or it may be supposed the work of a rival

---

[3] See note to stanza XXVIII of *The Vision of Judgment*. Emmanuel Swedenborg (see notes to Blake's *Marriage of Heaven and Hell*), Richard Brothers, and Parson Tozer are other religious mystics or prophets of varying significance and reliability.

[4] Gongora and Marini are early-seventeenth century poets (Spanish and Italian) noted for their elaborate styles.

[5] Count Cagliostro was an eighteenth-century alchemist and impostor; Baroness von Krüdener (1764–1824) was a religious mystic influential in the court of Tsar Alexander I.

[6] Lord Lonsdale helped Wordsworth become Distributor of Stamps for Westmorland (see *The Blues*). Thraso (a braggart) and Gnatho (a parasite) are characters in Terence's *Eunuchus*.

[7] Ferdinand VII of Spain put down the liberals after Wellington helped him regain his throne.

[8] Robert Southey. See various notes to *The Vision of Judgment*, above.

poet, obscured, if not by the present ready popularity of Mr. Southey, yet by the Postobits he has granted upon Posterity & usurious self-applause in which he has anticipated, with some profusion perhaps, the opinion of future ages, who are always more enlightened than contemporaries—more especially in the eyes of those whose figure in their own times has been disproportioned to their deserts. What Mr. Southey's deserts are, no one knows better than Mr. Southey: all his latter writings have displayed the writhing of a weakly human creature conscious of owing its worldly elevation to its own debasement (like a man who has made a fortune by the Slave-trade, or the retired keeper of a Gaming house or Brothel), and struggling convulsively to deceive others without the power of lying to himself.

But to resume: the dedication may be further supposed to be produced by some one who may have a cause of aversion from the said Southey, for some personal reason—perhaps a gross calumny invented or circulated by this Pantisocratic apostle of Apostasy, who is sometimes as unguarded in his assertions as atrocious in his conjectures, and feels the cravings of his wretched Vanity disappointed in its nobler hopes, & reduced to prey upon such Snatches of fame as his contributions to the Quarterly Review, and to consequent praise with which a powerful Journal repays its assistants, can afford him, by the abuse of whosoever may be more consistent or more successful than himself, and the provincial gang of scribblers gathered round him.

[1818 ?]   [1901]

—————>∘◉∘<—————

FRAGMENT

ON THE BACK OF THE MS. OF CANTO I

I WOULD to Heaven that I were so much Clay—
  As I am blood—bone—marrow, passion—feeling—
Because at least the past were past away—
  And for the future—(but I write this reeling,
Having got drunk exceedingly today
  So that I seem to stand upon the ceiling)
I say—the future is a serious matter—
And so—for God's sake—Hock and Sodawater.

—————>∘◉∘<—————

DEDICATION

I

BOB SOUTHEY! You 're a poet—Poet-laureate,
  And representative of all the race,
Although 'tis true that you turned out a Tory at
  Last,—yours has lately been a common case—

And now, my Epic Renegade! what are ye at?
  With all the Lakers,[1] in and out of place?
A nest of tuneful persons, to my eye
Like "four and twenty Blackbirds in a pye;

II

"Which pye being opened they began to sing,"
  (This old song and new simile holds good),
"A dainty dish to set before the King,"
  Or Regent, who admires such kind of food;—
And Coleridge, too, has lately taken wing,
  But like a hawk encumber'd with his hood,—
Explaining metaphysics to the nation—
I wish he would explain his Explanation.[2]

III

You, Bob! are rather insolent, you know,
  At being disappointed in your wish
To supersede all warblers here below,
  And be the only Blackbird in the dish;
And then you overstrain yourself, or so,
  And tumble downward like the flying fish
Gasping on deck, because you soar too high, Bob,
And fall, for lack of moisture quite a-dry, Bob![3]

IV

And Wordsworth, in a rather long "Excursion,"
  (I think the quarto holds five hundred pages),
Has given a sample from the vasty version
  Of his new system to perplex the sages;
'T is poetry—at least by his assertion.
  And may appear so when the dog-star rages—
And he who understands it would be able
To add a story to the Tower of Babel.

V

You—Gentlemen! by dint of long seclusion
  From better company, have kept your own
At Keswick, and, through still continued fusion
  Of one another's minds, at last have grown
To deem as a most logical conclusion,
  That Poesy has wreaths for you alone:
There is a narrowness in such a notion,
Which makes me wish you'd change your lakes for
                                        [ocean.

◇◇◇◇◇◇◇◇◇◇◇◇◇◇◇◇◇◇◇◇◇◇◇◇◇◇◇◇◇◇

[1] Wordsworth, Coleridge, and Southey.
[2] *Biographia Literaria* (see above) had been published in 1817.
[3] A "dry bob" was regency slang for intercourse without emission, though it also refers to a light blow that does not break the skin.

VI

I would not imitate the petty thought,
  Nor coin my self-love to so base a vice,
For all the glory your conversation brought,
  Since gold alone should not have been its price.
You have your salary; was 't for that you wrought?
  And Wordsworth has his place in the Excise.*
You 're shabby fellows—true—but poets still,
And duly seated on the immortal hill.

VII

Your bays may hide the baldness of your brows—
  Perhaps some virtuous blushes;—let them go—
To you I envy neither fruit nor boughs—
  And for the fame you would engross below,
The field is universal, and allows
  Scope to all such as feel the inherent glow:
Scott, Rogers, Campbell, Moore, and Crabbe, will try
'Gainst you the question with posterity.

VIII

For me, who, wandering with pedestrian Muses,
  Contend not with you on the wingéd steed,
I wish your fate may yield ye, when she chooses,
  The fame you envy, and the skill you need;
And recollect a poet nothing loses
  In giving to his brethren their full meed
Of merit, and complaint of present days
Is not the certain path to future praise.

IX

He that reserves his laurels for posterity
  (Who does not often claim the bright reversion)
Has generally no great crop to spare it, he
  Being only injured by his own assertion;
And although here and there some glorious rarity
  Arise like Titan from the sea's immersion,
The major part of such appellants go
To—God knows where—for no one else can know.

X

If, fallen in evil days on evil tongues,
  Milton appeal'd to the Avenger, Time,[4]
If Time, the Avenger, execrates his wrongs,
  And makes the word "Miltonic" mean "*Sublime*,"

He deigned not to belie his soul in songs,
  Nor turn his very talent to a crime;
He did not loathe the Sire to laud the Son,
But closed the tyrant-hater he begun.

XI

Think'st thou, could he—the blind Old Man—arise
  Like Samuel from the grave, to freeze once more
The blood of monarchs with his prophecies,
  Or be alive again—again all hoar
With time and trials, and those helpless eyes,
  And heartless daughters—worn—and pale—and
Would *he* adore a sultan? *he* obey   [poor;†
The intellectual eunuch Castlereagh?‡

XII

Cold-blooded, smooth-faced, placid miscreant!
  Dabbling its sleek young hands in Erin's gore,
And thus for wider carnage taught to pant,
  Transferred to gorge upon a sister shore,
The vulgarest tool that Tyranny could want,
  With just enough of talent, and no more,
To lengthen fetters by another fix'd,
And offer poison long already mix'd.

XIII

An orator of such set trash of phrase
  Ineffably—legitimately vile,
That even its grossest flatterers dare not praise,
  Nor foes—all nations—condescend to smile,—
Nor even a sprightly blunder's spark can blaze
  From that Ixion grindstone's ceaseless toil,[6]
That turns and turns to give the world a notion
Of endless torments and perpetual motion.

† "Pale, but not cadaverous:"—Milton's two elder daughters are said to have robbed him of his books, besides cheating and plaguing him in the economy of his house, &c. &c. His feelings on such an outrage, both as a parent and a scholar, must have been singularly painful. Hayley compares him to Lear. See part third, Life of Milton, by W. Hayley (or Hailey, as spelt in the edition before me).

‡ "Would *he* subside into a hackney Laureate—
    A scribbling, self-sold, soul-hired, scorn'd Iscariot?"

I doubt if "Laureate" and "Iscariot" be good rhymes, but must say, as Ben Jonson did to Sylvester, who challenged him to rhyme with—

    "I, John Sylvester,
      Lay with your sister."

Jonson answered,—"I, Ben Jonson, lay with your wife." Sylvester answered,—"That is not rhyme."—"No," said Ben Jonson; "but it is *true*."[5]

* Wordsworth's place may be in the Customs—it is, I think, in that or the Excise—besides another at Lord Lonsdale's table, where this poetical charlatan and political parasite licks up the crumbs with a hardened alacrity; the converted Jacobin having long subsided into the clownish sycophant of the worst prejudices of the aristocracy.

4 *Paradise Lost*, VII, 25–6. Milton had opposed Charles I, supported Cromwell, and consistently rejected Charles II.

5 Lord Castlereagh, Tory prime minister from 1812 to 1822, appears also in *The Vision of Judgment*. He stopped the Irish Rebellion ("Erin's Gore"). See also Shelley's *Mask of Anarchy*, p. 886. The "Laureat-Iscariot" couplet is an alternative in Byron's MS. The references to Castlereagh were often omitted.

6 For disloyalty to Zeus, Xion was chained to a wheel.

XIV

A bungler even in its disgusting trade,
    And botching, patching, leaving still behind
Something of which its masters are afraid—
    States to be curbed, and thoughts to be confined,
    Conspiracy or Congress to be made—
    Cobbling at manacles for all mankind—
A tinkering slave-maker, who mends old chains,
With God and Man's abhorrence for its gains.

XV

If we may judge of matter by the mind,
    Emasculated to the marrow *It*
Hath but two objects, how to serve, and bind,
    Deeming the chain it wears even men may fit,
    Eutropius of its many masters,—blind*
    To worth as freedom, wisdom as to wit,
Fearless—because *no* feeling dwells in ice,
Its very courage stagnates to a vice. [7]

XVI

Where shall I turn me not to *view* its bonds,
    For I will never *feel* them?—Italy!
Thy late reviving Roman soul desponds
    Beneath the lie this State-thing breathed o'er thee—
    Thy clanking chain, and Erin's yet green wounds,
    Have voices—tongues to cry aloud for me.
Europe has slaves—allies—kings—armies still,
And Southey lives to sing them very ill.

XVII

Meantime—Sir Laureate—I proceed to dedicate,
    In honest simple verse, this song to you,
And, if in flattering strains I do not predicate,
    'Tis that I still retain my "buff and blue;" [8]
My politics as yet are all to educate:
    Apostasy's so fashionable, too,
To keep *one* creed's a task grown quite Herculean;
Is it not so, my Tory, ultra-Julian? †

Venice, Sept. 16, 1818

[1818]   [1833]

* For the character of Eutropius, the eunuch and minister at the court of Arcadius, see Gibbon.
† I allude not to our friend Landor's hero, the traitor Count Julian, but to Gibbon's hero, vulgarly yclept "The Apostate."

[7] At this point Byron's manuscript contained a footnote addressed to his publisher:

Mr. John Murray,—As publisher to the Admiralty and of various Government works, if the five stanzas concerning Castlereagh should risk your ears or the Navy List, you may omit them in the publication. . . .

Castlereagh committed suicide in 1822, and was therefore dead when Murray finally published the dedication. Murray left the five stanzas as written in the published text, but he omitted Byron's note.
[8] The colors of the Whig (opposition) party were buff and blue, as were the covers of the *Edinburgh Review*.

CANTO THE FIRST

I

I WANT a hero: an uncommon want,
    When every year and month sends forth a new one,
Till, after cloying the gazettes with cant,
    The age discovers he is not the true one;
Of such as these I should not care to vaunt,
    I'll therefore take our ancient friend Don Juan,
We all have seen him in the Pantomime
Sent to the Devil somewhat ere his time.

II

Vernon, the butcher Cumberland, Wolfe, Hawke,
    Prince Ferdinand, Granby, Burgoyne, Keppel,
Evil and good, have had their tithe of talk,   [Howe,
    And filled their sign-posts then, like Wellesley now;
Each in their turn like Banquo's monarchs stalk,
    Followers of fame, "nine farrow" of that sow:
France, too, had Buonaparté and Demourier
Recorded in the Moniteur and Courier. [1]

III

Barnave, Brissot, Condorcet, Mirabeau,
    Petion, Clootz, Danton, Marat, La Fayette,
Were French, and famous people, as we know;
    And there were others, scarce forgotten yet,
Joubert, Hoche, Marceau, Lannes, Dessaix, Moreau,
    With many of the military set,
Exceedingly remarkable at times,
But not at all adapted to my rhymes. [2]

IV

Nelson was once Britannia's god of war,
    And still should be so, but the tide is turn'd;
There's no more to be said of Trafalgar,
    'Tis with our hero quietly inurned;
Because the army's grown more popular,
    At which the naval people are concern'd;
Besides, the Prince is all for the land-service,
Forgetting Duncan, Nelson, Howe, and Jervis. [3]

[1] The list of British military and naval heroes ends with Wellington (Wellesley).
[2] The first list were men active in the Revolution; the second soldiers serving Napoleon.
[3] The men in stanza IV are the British heroes of the war against Napoleon.

V

Brave men were living before Agamemnon
   And since, exceeding valorous and sage,
A good deal like him too, though quite the same none;
   But then they shone not on the poet's page,
And so have been forgotten:—I condemn none,
   But can't find any in the present age
Fit for my poem (that is, for my new one);
So, as I said, I'll take my friend Don Juan.

VI

Most epic poets plunge *"in medias res"* [4]
   (Horace makes this the heroic turnpike road)
And then your hero tells, whene'er you please,
   What went before—by way of episode,
While seated after dinner at his ease,
   Beside his mistress in some soft abode,
Palace, or garden, paradise, or cavern,
Which serves the happy couple for a tavern.

VII

That is the usual method, but not mine—
   My way is to begin with the beginning;
The regularity of my design
   Forbids all wandering as the worst of sinning,
And therefore I shall open with a line
   (Although it cost me half an hour in spinning)
Narrating somewhat of Don Juan's father,
And also of his mother, if you'd rather.

VIII

In Seville was he born, a pleasant city,
   Famous for oranges and women—he
Who has not seen it will be much to pity,
   So says the proverb—and I quite agree;
Of all the Spanish towns is none more pretty,
   Cadiz perhaps—but that you soon may see:—
Don Juan's parents lived beside the river,
A noble stream, and called the Guadalquivir.

IX

His father's name was Jóse—*Don*, of course,
   A true Hidalgo, free from every stain
Of Moor or Hebrew blood, he traced his source
   Through the most Gothic gentleman of Spain;
A better cavalier ne'er mounted horse,
   Or, being mounted, e'er got down again,
Than Jóse, who begot our hero, who
Begot—but that's to come—Well, to renew:

X

His mother was a learned lady, famed
   For every branch of every science known—
In every christian language ever named,
   With virtues equall'd by her wit alone:
She made the cleverest people quite ashamed,
   And even the good with inward envy groan,
Finding themselves so very much exceeded,
In their own way by all the things that she did.

XI

Her memory was a mine: she knew by heart
   All Calderon and greater part of Lopé, [5]
So, that if any actor miss'd his part,
   She could have served him for the prompter's copy;
For her Feinagle's were a useless art,
   And he himself obliged to shut up shop—he
Could never make a memory so fine as
That which adorn'd the brain of Donna Inez.

XII

Her favourite science was the mathematical,
   Her noblest virtue was her magnanimity,
Her wit (she sometimes tried at wit) was Attic all,
   Her serious sayings darken'd to sublimity;
In short, in all things she was fairly what I call
   A prodigy—her morning dress was dimity,
Her evening silk, or, in the summer, muslin,
And other stuffs, with which I won't stay puzzling.

XIII

She knew the Latin—that is, "the Lord's prayer,"
   And Greek—the alphabet—I'm nearly sure;
She read some French romances here and there,
   Although her mode of speaking was not pure;
For native Spanish she had no great care,
   At least her conversation was obscure;
Her thoughts were theorems, her words a problem,
As if she deemed that mystery would ennoble 'em.

XIV

She liked the English and the Hebrew tongue,
   And said there was analogy between 'em;
She proved it somehow out of sacred song,
   But I must leave the proofs to those who 've seen
     'em;
But this I heard her say, and can't be wrong,
   And all may think which way their judgments lean
     'em,
"'T is strange—the Hebrew noun which means
The English always use to govern d—n."   ['I am,'

---

4 The epic poet is supposed to begin in the midst of his story
(Horace's *Ars Poetica*).

5 Calderon de la Barca and Lope de Vega are Spanish drama-
tists of the eighteenth century. Feinagle invented a memory
system popular in Byron's time.

XV

Some women use their tongues—she *looked* a lecture,
  Each eye a sermon, and her brow a homily,
An all-in-all-sufficient self-director,
  Like the lamented late Sir Samuel Romilly
The Law's expounder, and the State's corrector
  Whose suicide was almost an anomaly—
One sad example more, that "All is vanity,"—
(The jury brought their verdict in "Insanity!")[6]

XVI

In short, she was a walking calculation,
  Miss Edgeworth's novels stepping from their
Or Mrs. Trimmer's books on education,   [covers,
  Or "Cœlebs' Wife" set out in quest of lovers,
Morality's prim personification,
  In which not Envy's self a flaw discovers;
To others' share let "female errors fall,"
For she had not even one—the worst of all.[7]

XVII

Oh! she was perfect past all parallel—
  Of any modern female saint's comparison;
So far above the cunning powers of hell,
  Her guardian angel had given up his garrison;
Even her minutest motions went as well
  As those of the best time-piece made by Harrison.[8]
In virtues nothing earthly could surpass her
Save thine "incomparable oil," Macassar!*

XVIII

Perfect she was, but as perfection is
  Insipid in this naughty world of ours,
Where our first parents never learn'd to kiss
  Till they were exiled from their earlier bowers,
Where all was peace, and innocence, and bliss,
  (I wonder how they got through the twelve hours)
Don Jóse, like a lineal son of Eve,
Went plucking various fruit without her leave.

* "Description des *vertus incomparables* de l'Huile de Macassar."—See the Advertisement.[9]

[6] Romilly, political reformer, was Lady Byron's lawyer. He committed suicide in 1818.
[7] The moralistic writers are Maria Edgeworth (1767–1849), Sarah Trimmer (1741–1810), Hannah More (1745–1833). The quoted line is from Pope's *Rape of the Lock*, II, 17.
[8] John Harrison made maritime chronometers.
[9] A popular hair oil imported from Macassar. The antimacassar was created as a defense against its stains.

XIX

He was a mortal of the careless kind,
  With no great love for learning, or the learn'd,
Who chose to go where'er he had a mind,
  And never dream'd his lady was concern'd:
The world, as usual, wickedly inclined
  To see a kingdom or a house o'erturn'd,
Whisper'd he had a mistress, some said *two*,
But for domestic quarrels *one* will do.

XX

Now Donna Inez had, with all her merit,
  A great opinion of her own good qualities;
Neglect, indeed, requires a saint to bear it,
  And such, indeed, she was in her moralities;
But then she had a devil of a spirit,
  And sometimes mix'd up fancies with realities,
And let few opportunities escape
Of getting her liege lord into a scrape.

XXI

This was an easy matter with a man
  Oft in the wrong, and never on his guard;
And even the wisest, do the best they can,
  Have moments, hours, and days, so unprepared,
That you might "brain them with their lady's fan";
  And sometimes ladies hit exceeding hard,
And fans turn into falchions in fair hands,
And why and wherefore no one understands.

XXII

'T is pity learnéd virgins ever wed
  With persons of no sort of education,
Or gentlemen, who, though well-born and bred,
  Grow tired of scientific conversation:
I don't choose to say much upon this head,
  I'm a plain man, and in a single station,
But—Oh! ye lords of ladies intellectual,
Inform us truly, have they not hen-peck'd you all?

XXIII

Don Jóse and his lady quarrelled—*why*,
  Not any of the many could divine,
Though several thousand people chose to try,
  'T was surely no concern of theirs nor mine;
I loathe that low vice curiosity,
  But if there's anything in which I shine
'T is in arranging all my friends' affairs,
Not having, of my own, domestic cares.

XXIV

And so I interfered, and with the best
　　Intentions, but their treatment was not kind;
I think the foolish people were possess'd,
　　For neither of them could I ever find,
Although their porter afterwards confess'd—
　　But that 's no matter, and the worst 's behind,
For little Juan o'er me threw, down stairs,
A pail of housemaid's water unawares.

XXV

A little curly-headed, good-for-nothing,
　　And mischief-making monkey from his birth;
His parents ne'er agreed except in doting
　　Upon the most unquiet imp on earth;
Instead of quarrelling, had they been but both in
　　Their senses, they'd have sent young master forth
To school, or had him soundly whipp'd at home,
To teach him manners for the time to come.

XXVI

Don Jóse and the Donna Inez led
　　For some time an unhappy sort of life,
Wishing each other, not divorced, but dead;
　　They lived respectably as man and wife,
Their conduct was exceedingly well-bred,
　　And gave no outward signs of inward strife,
Until at length the smother'd fire broke out,
And put the business past all kind of doubt.

XXVII

For Inez call'd some druggists and physicians,
　　And tried to prove her loving lord was *mad*,
But as he had some lucid intermissions,
　　She next decided he was only *bad*; [10]
Yet when they ask'd her for her depositions,
　　No sort of explanation could be had,
Save that her duty both to man and God
Required this conduct—which seem'd very odd.

XXVIII

She kept a journal, where his faults were noted,
　　And open'd certain trunks of books and letters,
All which might, if occasion served, be quoted;
　　And then she had all Seville for abettors,
Besides her good old grandmother (who doted);
　　The hearers of her case became repeaters,
Then advocates, inquisitors, and judges,
Some for amusement, others for old grudges.

[10] In gaining a legal separation from her husband, Lady Byron tried to prove him insane, then immoral.

XXIX

And then this best and meekest woman bore
　　With such serenity her husband's woes,
Just as the Spartan ladies did of yore,
　　Who saw their spouses kill'd, and nobly chose
Never to say a word about them more—
　　Calmly she heard such calumny that rose,
And saw *his* agonies with such sublimity,
That all the world exclaim'd, "What magnanimity!"

XXX

No doubt, this patience, when the world is damning us,
　　Is philosophic in our former friends;
'T is also pleasant to be deem'd magnanimous,
　　The more so in obtaining our own ends;
And what the lawyers call a "*malus animus*" [11]
　　Conduct like this by no means comprehends:
Revenge in person's certainly no virtue,
But then 't is not *my* fault, if *others* hurt you.

XXXI

And if our quarrels should rip up old stories,
　　And help them with a lie or two additional,
I'm not to blame, as you well know, no more is
　　Any one else—they were become traditional;
Besides, their resurrection aids our glories
　　By contrast, which is what we just were wishing all:
And science profits by this resurrection—
Dead scandals form good subjects for dissection.

XXXII

Their friends had tried at reconciliation,
　　Then their relations, who made matters worse;
('T were hard to tell upon a like occasion
　　To whom it may be best to have recourse—
I can't say much for friend or yet relation):
　　The lawyers did their utmost for divorce,
But scarce a fee was paid on either side
Before, unluckily, Don Jóse died.

XXXIII

He died: and most unluckily, because,
　　According to all hints I could collect
From Counsel learnéd in those kinds of laws,
　　(Although their talk 's obscure and circumspect)
His death contrived to spoil a charming cause;
　　A thousand pities also with respect
To public feeling, which on this occasion
Was manifested in a great sensation.

[11] "Malice aforethought."

XXXIV

But ah! he died; and buried with him lay
  The public feeling and the lawyer's fees:
His house was sold, his servants sent away,
  A Jew took one of his two mistresses,
A priest the other—at least so they say:
  I asked the doctors after his disease,
He died of the slow fever called the tertian,
And left his widow to her own aversion.

XXXV

Yet Jóse was an honourable man,
  That I must say, who knew him very well;
Therefore his frailties I'll no further scan,
  Indeed there were not many more to tell:
And if his passions now and then outran
  Discretion, and were not so peaceable
As Numa's (who was also named Pompilius),[12]
He had been ill brought up, and was born bilious.

XXXVI

Whate'er might be his worthlessness or worth,
  Poor fellow! he had many things to wound him.
Let's own—since it can do no good on earth—
  It was a trying moment that which found him
Standing alone beside his desolate hearth,
  Where all his household gods lay shiver'd round
No choice was left his feelings or his pride   [him:
Save Death or Doctors' Commons—so he died.[13]

XXXVII

Dying intestate, Juan was sole heir
  To a chancery suit, and messuages,[14] and lands,
Which, with a long minority and care,
  Promised to turn out well in proper hands:
Inez became sole guardian, which was fair,
  And answer'd but to Nature's just demands;
An only son left with an only mother
Is brought up much more wisely than another.

XXXVIII

Sagest of women, even of widows, she
  Resolved that Juan should be quite a paragon,
And worthy of the noblest pedigree,
  (His Sire was of Castile, his Dam from Aragon).
Then for accomplishments of chivalry,
  In case our lord the king should go to war again,
He learn'd the arts of riding, fencing, gunnery,
And how to scale a fortress—or a nunnery.

XXXIX

But that which Donna Inez most desired,
  And saw into herself each day before all
The learned tutors whom for him she hired,
  Was, that his breeding should be strictly moral;
Much into all his studies she inquired,
  And so they were submitted first to her, all,
Arts, sciences, no branch was made a mystery
To Juan's eyes, excepting natural history.

XL

The languages, especially the dead,
  The sciences, and most of all the abstruse,
The arts, at least all such as could be said
  To be the most remote from common use,
In all these he was much and deeply read:
  But not a page of anything that's loose,
Or hints continuation of the species,
Was ever suffer'd, lest he should grow vicious.

XLI

His classic studies made a little puzzle,
  Because of filthy loves of gods and goddesses,
Who in the earlier ages raised a bustle,
  But never put on pantaloons or boddices;
His reverend tutors had at times a tussle,
  And for their Aeneids, Iliads, and Odysseys,
Were forced to make an odd sort of apology,
For Donna Inez dreaded the mythology.

XLII

Ovid's a rake, as half his verses show him,
  Anacreon's morals are a still worse sample,
Catullus scarcely has a decent poem,
  I don't think Sappho's Ode a good example,
Although Longinus tells us there is no hymn* [ample;
  Where the sublime soars forth on wings more
But Virgil's songs are pure, except that horrid one
Beginning with "*Formosum Pastor Corydon.*"[16]

XLIII

Lucretius' irreligion is too strong
  For early stomachs, to prove wholesome food;
I can't help thinking Juvenal was wrong,
  Although no doubt his real intent was good,

---

* See Longinus, Section 10, "ἵνα μὴ ἕν τι περὶ αὐτὴν πάθος φαίνηται, παθῶν δὲ σύνοδος."[15]

12 Numa was the legendary second King of Rome, successor to Romulus, whose reign was peaceful.

13 Doctors' Commons is the court with jurisdiction over divorce, as Chancery (stanza XXXVII) deals with inheritance.

14 Messuage: House and buildings.

15 *On the Sublime*: "The effect desired is that not one passion only should be seen in her, but a concourse of passions" (trans. W. Rhys Roberts, 1899).

16 The poem deals with the love of the shepherd Corydon for the boy Alexis. See also note to Coleridge's *Biographia Literaria*, p. 518.

For speaking out so plainly in his song,
  So much indeed as to be downright rude;
And then what proper person can be partial
To all those nauseous epigrams of Martial? [17]

XLIV

Juan was taught from out the best edition,
  Expurgated by learned men, who place,
Judiciously, from out the schoolboy's vision,
  The grosser parts; but fearful to deface
Too much their modest bard by this omission,
  And pitying sore his mutilated case,
They only add them in an appendix,*
Which saves, in fact, the trouble of an index;

XLV

For there we have them all at one fell swoop,
  Instead of being scatter'd through the pages;
They stand forth marshall'd in a handsome troop,
  To meet the ingenuous youth of future ages,
Till some less rigid editor shall stoop
  To call them back into their separate cages,
Instead of standing staring all together,
Like garden gods—and not so decent either.

XLVI

The Missal too (it was the family Missal)
  Was ornamented in a sort of way
Which ancient mass-books often are, and this all
  Kinds of grotesques illumined; and how they,
Who saw those figures on the margin kiss all,
  Could turn their optics to the text and pray
Is more than I know—but Don Juan's mother
Kept this herself, and gave her son another.

XLVII

Sermons he read, and lectures he endured,
  And homilies, and lives of all the saints;
To Jerome and to Chrysostom inured,
  He did not take such studies for restraints;
But how faith is acquired, and then insured,
  So well not one of the aforesaid paints
As Saint Augustine in his fine Confessions,
Which make the reader envy his transgressions.

* Fact! There is, or was, such an edition, with all the obnoxious epigrams of Martial placed by themselves at the end.

[17] Lucretius, *On the Nature of Things*; Juvenal's *Satires*; Martial's *Epigrams*.

XLVIII

This, too, was a seal'd book to little Juan—
  I can't but say that his mamma was right,
If such an education was the true one.
  She scarcely trusted him from out her sight;
Her maids were old, and if she took a new one,
  You might be sure she was a perfect fright;
She did this during even her husband's life—
I recommend as much to every wife.

XLIX

Young Juan wax'd in goodliness and grace;
  At six a charming child, and at eleven
With all the promise of as fine a face
  As e'er to man's maturer growth was given:
He studied steadily, and grew apace,
  And seem'd, at least, in the right road to heaven,
For half his days were pass'd at church, the other
Between his tutors, confessor, and mother.

L

At six, I said, he was a charming child,
  At twelve he was a fine, but quiet boy;
Although in infancy a little wild,'
  They tamed him down amongst them; to destroy
His natural spirit not in vain they toil'd,
  At least it seem'd so; and his mother's joy
Was to declare how sage, and still, and steady,
Her young philosopher was grown already.

LI

I had my doubts, perhaps I have them still,
  But what I say is neither here nor there:
I knew his father well, and have some skill
  In character—but it would not be fair
From sire to son to augur good or ill:
  He and his wife were an ill-sorted pair—
But scandal 's my aversion—I protest
Against all evil speaking, even in jest.

LII

For my part I say nothing—nothing—but
  This I will say—my reasons are my own—
That if I had an only son to put
  To school (as God be praised that I have none),
'T is not with Donna Inez I would shut
  Him up to learn his catechism alone,
No—no—I 'd send him out betimes to college,
For there it was I pick'd up my own knowledge.

LIII

For there one learns—'t is not for me to boast,
    Though I acquired—but I pass over *that*,
As well as all the Greek I since have lost:—
    I say that there's the place—but "*Verbum sat*," [18]
I think I pick'd up too, as well as most,
    Knowledge of matters—but no matter *what*—
I never married—but, I think, I know
That sons should not be educated so.

LIV

Young Juan now was sixteen years of age,
    Tall, handsome, slender, but well knit; he seem'd
Active, though not so sprightly, as a page;
    And everybody but his mother deem'd
Him almost man; but she flew in a rage
    And bit her lips (for else she might have scream'd),
If any said so, for to be precocious
Was in her eyes a thing the most atrocious.

LV

Amongst her numerous acquaintance, all
    Selected for discretion and devotion,
There was the Donna Julia, whom to call
    Pretty were but to give a feeble notion
Of many charms in her as natural
    As sweetness to the flower, or salt to ocean,
Her zone to Venus, or his bow to Cupid,
(But this last simile is trite and stupid.)

LVI

The darkness of her oriental eye
    Accorded with her Moorish origin;
(Her blood was not all Spanish; by the by,
    In Spain, you know, this is a sort of sin.)
When proud Grenada fell, and, forced to fly,
    Boabdil wept, [19] of Donna Julia's kin
Some went to Africa, some staid in Spain,
Her great great grandmamma chose to remain.

LVII

She married (I forget the pedigree)
    With an Hidalgo, who transmitted down
His blood less noble than such blood should be;
    At such alliances his sires would frown,
In that point so precise in each degree
    That they bred *in and in*, as might be shown,
Marrying their cousins—nay, their aunts and nieces,
Which always spoils the breed, if it increases.

LVIII

This heathenish cross restored the breed again,
    Ruin'd its blood, but much improved its flesh;
For, from a root the ugliest in Old Spain
    Sprung up a branch as beautiful as fresh;
The sons no more were short, the daughters plain:
    But there's a rumour which I fain would hush,
'T is said that Donna Julia's grandmamma
Produced her Don more heirs at love than law.

LIX

However this might be, the race went on
    Improving still through every generation,
Until it center'd in an only son,
    Who left an only daughter; my narration
May have suggested that this single one
    Could be but Julia (whom on this occasion
I shall have much to speak about), and she
Was married, charming, chaste, and twenty-three.

LX

Her eye (I'm very fond of handsome eyes)
    Was large and dark, suppressing half its fire
Until she spoke, then through its soft disguise
    Flash'd an expression more of pride than ire,
And love than either; and there would arise
    A something in them which was not desire,
But would have been, perhaps, but for the soul
Which struggled through and chasten'd down the
                      [whole.

LXI

Her glossy hair was cluster'd o'er a brow
    Bright with intelligence, and fair, and smooth;
Her eyebrow's shape was like the aërial bow,
    Her cheek all purple with the beam of youth,
Mounting, at times, to a transparent glow,
    As if her veins ran lightning; she, in sooth,
Possess'd an air and grace by no means common:
Her stature tall—I hate a dumpy woman.

LXII

Wedded she was some years, and to a man
    Of fifty, and such husbands are in plenty;
And yet, I think, instead of such a ONE
    'T were better to have TWO of five and twenty,
Especially in countries near the sun:
    And now I think on 't, "mi vien in mente," [20]
Ladies even of the most uneasy virtue
Prefer a spouse whose age is short of thirty.

---

[18] I.e., *verbum sat sapiendi*: "a word to the wise is sufficient."
[19] Washington Irving in his *Chronicle of the Conquest of Granada* describes the Moorish leader weeping as he leaves the city taken by Spain.

[20] "It comes to my mind."

LXIII

'T is a sad thing, I cannot choose but say,
　And all the fault of that indecent sun,
Who cannot leave alone our helpless clay,
　But will keep baking, broiling, burning on,
　That howsoever people fast and pray,
　The flesh is frail, and so the soul undone:
What men call gallantry, and gods adultery,
Is much more common where the climate's sultry.

LXIV

Happy the nations of the moral north!
　Where all is virtue, and the winter season
Sends sin, without a rag on, shivering forth
　('T was snow that brought St. Anthony to reason);*
Where juries cast up what a wife is worth
　By laying whate'er sum, in mulct, they please on
The lover, who must pay a handsome price,
Because it is a marketable vice.

LXV

Alfonso was the name of Julia's lord,
　A man well looking for his years, and who
Was neither much beloved nor yet abhorr'd;
　They lived together as most people do,
　Suffering each other's foibles by accord,
　And not exactly either *one* or *two*;
Yet he was jealous, though he did not show it,
For jealousy dislikes the world to know it.

LXVI

Julia was—yet I never could see why—
　With Donna Inez quite a favourite friend;
Between their tastes there was small sympathy,
　For not a line had Julia ever penn'd:
Some people whisper (but, no doubt, they lie,
　For malice still imputes some private end)
That Inez had, ere Don Alfonso's marriage,
Forgot with him her very prudent carriage;

LXVII

And that still keeping up the old connexion,
　Which time had lately render'd much more chaste,
She took his lady also in affection,
　And certainly this course was much the best:
She flatter'd Julia with her sage protection,
　And complimented Don Alfonso's taste;
And if she could not (who can?) silence scandal,
At least she left it a more slender handle.

* For the particulars of St. Anthony's recipe for hot blood in cold weather, see Mr Aban Butler's "Lives of the Saints." 21

21 Actually it was St. Francis of Assisi.

LXVIII

I can't tell whether Julia saw the affair
　With other people's eyes, or if her own
Discoveries made, but none could be aware
　Of this, at least no symptom e'er was shown;
Perhaps she did not know, or did not care,
　Indifferent from the first, or callous grown:
I'm really puzzled what to think or say,
She kept her counsel in so close a way.

LXIX

Juan she saw, and, as a pretty child,
　Caressed him often—such a thing might be
Quite innocently done, and harmless styled,
　When she had twenty years, and thirteen he;
But I am not so sure I should have smiled
　When he was sixteen, Julia twenty-three,
These few short years make wond'rous alterations,
Particularly amongst sun-burnt nations.

LXX

Whate'er the cause might be, they had become
　Changed; for the dame grew distant, the youth shy,
Their looks cast down, their greetings almost dumb.
　And much embarrassment in either eye;
There surely will be little doubt with some
　That Donna Julia knew the reason why,
But as for Juan, he had no more notion
Than he who never saw the sea of ocean.

LXXI

Yet Julia's very coldness still was kind,
　And tremulously gentle her small hand
Withdrew itself from his, but left behind
　A little pressure, thrilling, and so bland
And slight, so very slight, that to the mind
　'T was but a doubt; but ne'er magician's wand
Wrought change with all Armida's fairy art 22
Like what this light touch left on Juan's heart.

LXXII

And if she met him, though she smiled no more,
　She look'd a sadness sweeter than her smile,
As if her heart had deeper thoughts in store
　She must not own, but cherished more the while,
For that compression in its burning core;
　Even innocence itself has many a wile,
And will not dare to trust itself with truth,
And love is taught hypocrisy from youth.

22 The art of Armida in Tasso's *Jerusalem Delivered* leads Rinaldo to forget his vow.

LXXIII

But passion most dissembles yet betrays
    Even by its darkness; as the blackest sky
Foretells the heaviest tempest, it displays
    Its workings through the vainly guarded eye,
And in whatever aspect it arrays
    Itself, 't is still the same hypocrisy;
Coldness or anger, even disdain or hate,
Are masks it often wears, and still too late.

LXXIV

Then there were sighs, the deeper for suppression,
    And stolen glances, sweeter for the theft,
And burning blushes, though for no transgression,
    Tremblings when met, and restlessness when left;
All these are little preludes to possession,
    Of which young passion cannot be bereft,
And merely tend to show how greatly Love is
Embarrass'd at first starting with a novice.

LXXV

Poor Julia's heart was in an awkward state;
    She felt it going, and resolved to make
The noblest efforts for herself and mate,
    For honour's, pride's, religion's, virtue's sake:
Her resolutions were most truly great,
    And almost might have made a Tarquin quake; [23]
She pray'd the Virgin Mary for her grace,
As being the best judge of a lady's case.

LXXVI

She vow'd she never would see Juan more,
    And next day paid a visit to his mother,
And look'd extremely at the opening door,
    Which, by the Virgin's grace, let in another;
Grateful she was, and yet a little sore—
    Again it opens, it can be no other,
'T is surely Juan now—No! I'm afraid
That night the Virgin was no further pray'd.

LXXVII

She now determined that a virtuous woman
    Should rather face and overcome temptation,
That flight was base and dastardly, and no man
    Should ever give her heart the least sensation;
That is to say, a thought beyond the common
    Preference, that we must feel upon occasion,
For people who are pleasanter than others,
But then they only seem so many brothers.

---

[23] The Tarquins were noted for their brutal courage as leaders of Rome.

LXXVIII

And even if by chance—and who can tell?
    The devil 's so very sly—she should discover
That all within was not so very well,
    And, if still free, that such or such a lover
Might please perhaps, a virtuous wife can quell
    Such thoughts, and be the better when they're over;
And if the man should ask, 't is but denial:
I recommend young ladies to make trial.

LXXIX

And, then, there are such things as love divine,
    Bright and immaculate, unmix'd and pure,
Such as the angels think so very fine,
    And matrons, who would be no less secure,
Platonic, perfect, "just such love as mine":
    Thus Julia said—and thought so, to be sure,
And so I'd have her think, were I the man
On whom her reveries celestial ran.

LXXX

Such love is innocent, and may exist
    Between young persons without any danger.
A hand may first, and then a lip be kissed;
    For my part, to such doings I'm a stranger,
But *hear* these freedoms form the utmost list
    Of all o'er which such love may be a ranger:
If people go beyond, 't is quite a crime,
But not my fault—I tell them all in time.

LXXXI

Love, then, but love within its proper limits,
    Was Julia's innocent determination
In young Don Juan's favour, and to him its
    Exertion might be useful on occasion;
And, lighted at too pure a shrine to dim its
    Ethereal lustre, with what sweet persuasion
He might be taught, by love and her together—
I really don't know what, nor Julia either.

LXXXII

Fraught with this fine intention, and well fenced
    In mail of proof—her purity of soul,
She, for the future of her strength convinced,
    And that her honour was a rock, or mole,
Exceeding sagely from that hour dispensed
    With any kind of troublesome control;
But whether Julia to the task was equal
Is that which must be mention'd in the sequel.

LXXXIII

Her plan she deem'd both innocent and feasible,
  And, surely, with a stripling of sixteen
Not scandal's fangs could fix on much that 's seizable,
  Or if they did so, satisfied to mean   [peaceable—
Nothing but what was good, her breast was
  A quiet conscience makes one so serene!
Christians have burnt each other, quite persuaded
That all the Apostles would have done as they did.

LXXXIV

And if in the mean time her husband died,
  But heaven forbid that such a thought should cross
Her brain, though in a dream! (and then she sigh'd)
  Never could she survive that common loss;
But just suppose that moment should betide,
  I only say suppose it—*inter nos*:
(This should be *entre nous*, for Julia thought
In French, but then the rhyme would go for nought.)

LXXXV

I only say, suppose this supposition:
  Juan being then grown up to man's estate
Would fully suit a widow of condition,
  Even seven years hence it would not be too late;
And in the interim (to pursue this vision)
  The mischief, after all, could not be great,
For he would learn the rudiments of love,
I mean the seraph way of those above.

LXXXVI

So much for Julia. Now we'll turn to Juan.
  Poor little fellow! he had no idea
Of his own case, and never hit the true one;
  In feelings quick as Ovid's Miss Medea,[24]
He puzzled over what he found a new one,
  But not as yet imagined it could be a
Thing quite in course, and not at all alarming,
Which, with a little patience, might grow charming.

LXXXVII

Silent and pensive, idle, restless, slow,
  His home deserted for the lonely wood,
Tormented with a wound he could not know,
  His, like all deep grief, plunged in solitude:
I'm fond myself of solitude or so,
  But then, I beg it may be understood,
By solitude I mean a sultan's, not
A hermit's, with a haram for a grot.

LXXXVIII

"Oh Love! in such a wilderness as this,
  Where transport and security entwine,
Here is the empire of thy perfect bliss,
  And here thou art a God indeed divine."*
The bard I quote from does not sing amiss,
  With the exception of the second line,
For that same twining "transport and security"
Are twisted to a phrase of some obscurity.

LXXXIX

The poet meant, no doubt, and thus appeals
  To the good sense and senses of mankind,
The very thing which everybody feels,
  As all have found on trial, or may find,
That no one likes to be disturb'd at meals
  Or love.—I won't say more about "entwined"
Or "transport," as we knew all that before,
But beg "Security" will bolt the door.

XC

Young Juan wandered by the glassy brooks,
  Thinking unutterable things; he threw
Himself at length within the leafy nooks
  Where the wild branch of the cork forest grew;
There poets find materials for their books,
  And every now and then we read them through,
So that their plan and prosody are eligible,
Unless, like Wordsworth, they prove unintelligible.

XCI

He, Juan (and not Wordsworth) so pursued
  His self-communion with his own high soul,
Until his mighty heart, in its great mood,
  Had mitigated part, though not the whole
Of its disease; he did the best he could
  With things not very subject to control,
And turned, without perceiving his condition,
Like Coleridge, into a metaphysician.

XCII

He thought about himself, and the whole earth,
  Of man the wonderful, and of the stars,
And how the deuce they ever could have birth;
  And then he thought of earthquakes, and of wars,
How many miles the moon might have in girth,
  Of air-balloons, and of the many bars
To perfect knowledge of the boundless skies;
And then he thought of Donna Julia's eyes.

* Campbell's Gertrude of Wyoming (I think) the opening of
Canto II.; but quote from memory.[25]

---

[24] Ovid describes the sudden feeling for Jason that strikes
Medea in the *Metamorphoses*.

[25] Byron quotes Thomas Campbell's *Gertrude of Wyoming*
(1809), the tale of a girl raised by Indians in Wyoming, Penn-
sylvania.

XCIII

In thoughts like these true wisdom may discern
   Longings sublime, and aspirations high,
Which some are born with, but the most part learn
   To plague themselves withal, they know not why:
'T was strange that one so young should thus concern
   His brain about the action of the sky;
If *you* think 't was philosophy that this did,
I can't help thinking puberty assisted.

XCIV

He pored upon the leaves, and on the flowers,
   And heard a voice in all the winds; and then
He thought of wood-nymphs and immortal bowers,
   And how the goddesses came down to men:
He miss'd the pathway, he forgot the hours,
   And when he look'd upon his watch again,
He found how much old Time had been a winner—
He also found that he had lost his dinner.

XCV

Sometimes he turned to gaze upon his book,
   Boscan, or Garcilasso;—by the wind [26]
Even as the page is rustled while we look,
   So by the poesy of his own mind
Over the mystic leaf his soul was shook,
   As if 't were one whereon magicians bind
Their spells, and give them to the passing gale,
According to some good old woman's tale.

XCVI

Thus would he while his lonely hours away
   Dissatisfied, nor knowing what he wanted;
Nor glowing reverie, nor poet's lay,
   Could yield his spirit that for which it panted,
A bosom whereon he his head might lay,
   And hear the heart beat with the love it granted,
With—several other things, which I forget,
Or which, at least, I need not mention yet.

XCVII

Those lonely walks, and lengthening reveries,
   Could not escape the gentle Julia's eyes;
She saw that Juan was not at his ease;
   But that which chiefly may, and must surprise,
Is, that the Donna Inez did not tease
   Her only son with question or surmise;
Whether it was she did not see, or would not,
Or, like all very clever people, could not.

26 Both are sixteenth-century Spanish sonneteers.

XCVIII

This may seem strange, but yet 't is very common;
   For instance—gentlemen, whose ladies take
Leave to o'erstep the written rights of woman,
   And break the—Which commandment is't they
(I have forgot the number, and think no man   [break?
   Should rashly quote, for fear of a mistake;)
I say, when these same gentlemen are jealous,
They make some blunder, which their ladies tell us.

XCIX

A real husband always is suspicious,
   But still no less suspects in the wrong place,
Jealous of some one who had no such wishes,
   Or pandering blindly to his own disgrace,
By harbouring some dear friend extremely vicious;
   The last indeed 's infallibly the case:
And when the spouse and friend are gone off wholly,
He wonders at their vice, and not his folly.

C

Thus parents also are at times short-sighted:
   Though watchful as the lynx, they ne'er discover,
The while the wicked world beholds delighted,
   Young Hopeful's mistress, or Miss Fanny's lover,
Till some confounded escapade has blighted
   The plan of twenty years, and all is over;
And then the mother cries, the father swears,
And wonders why the devil he got heirs.

CI

But Inez was so anxious, and so clear
   Of sight, that I must think, on this occasion,
She had some other motive much more near
   For leaving Juan to this new temptation,
But what that motive was, I shan't say here;
   Perhaps to finish Juan's education,
Perhaps to open Don Alfonso's eyes,
In case he thought his wife too great a prize.

CII

It was upon a day, a summer's day;—
   Summer 's indeed a very dangerous season,
And so is spring about the end of May;
   The sun, no doubt, is the prevailing reason;
But whatsoe'er the cause is, one may say,
   And stand convicted of more truth than treason,
That there are months which nature grows more
      merry in,—
March has its hares, and May must have its heroine.

CIII

'T was on a summer's day—the sixth of June:
　　I like to be particular in dates,
Not only of the age, and year, but moon;
　　They are a sort of post-house, where the Fates
Change horses, making history change its tune,
　　Then spur away o'er empires and o'er states,
Leaving at last not much besides chronology,
Excepting the post-obits of theology.

CIV

'T was on the sixth of June, about the hour
　　Of half-past six—perhaps still nearer seven,
When Julia sate within as pretty a bower
　　As e'er held houri in that heathenish heaven
Described by Mahomet, and Anacreon Moore,[27]
　　To whom the lyre and laurels have been given,
With all the trophies of triumphant song—
He won them well, and may he wear them long!

CV

She sate, but not alone; I know not well
　　How this same interview had taken place,
And even if I knew, I should not tell—
　　People should hold their tongues in any case;
No matter how or why the thing befell,
　　But there were she and Juan, face to face—
When two such faces are so, 't would be wise,
But very difficult, to shut their eyes.

CVI

How beautiful she look'd! her conscious heart
　　Glow'd in her cheek, and yet she felt no wrong.
Oh Love! how perfect is thy mystic art,
　　Strengthening the weak, and trampling on the
How self-deceitful is the sagest part　　　　[strong,
　　Of mortals whom thy lure hath led along—
The precipice she stood on was immense,
So was her creed in her own innocence.

CVII

She thought of her own strength, and Juan's youth,
　　And of the folly of all prudish fears,
Victorious virtue, and domestic truth,
　　And then of Don Alfonso's fifty years:
I wish these last had not occurr'd, in sooth,
　　Because that number rarely much endears,
And through all climes, the snowy and the sunny,
Sounds ill in love, whate'er it may in money.

---

27 Thomas Moore's first book was a translation of the Greek
poet noted for his praise of love and wine. Byron's *Hours of
Idleness* was influenced by Moore.

CVIII

When people say, "I've told you *fifty* times,"
　　They mean to scold, and very often do;
When poets say, "I've written *fifty* rhymes,"
　　They make you dread that they'll recite them too;
In gangs of *fifty*, thieves commit their crimes;
　　At *fifty* love for love is rare, 't is true,
But then, no doubt, it equally as true is,
A good deal may be bought for *fifty* Louis.

CIX

Julia had honour, virtue, truth, and love,
　　For Don Alfonso; and she inly swore,
By all the vows below to powers above,
　　She never would disgrace the ring she wore,
Nor leave a wish which wisdom might reprove;
　　And while she ponder'd this, besides much more,
One hand on Juan's carelessly was thrown,
Quite by mistake—she thought it was her own;

CX

Unconsciously she lean'd upon the other,
　　Which play'd within the tangles of her hair;
And to contend with thoughts she could not smother,
　　She seem'd by the distraction of her air.
'T was surely very wrong in Juan's mother
　　To leave together this imprudent pair,
She who for many years had watch'd her son so—
I'm very certain *mine* would not have done so.

CXI

The hand which still held Juan's, by degrees
　　Gently, but palpably confirm'd its grasp,
As if it said, "detain me, if you please";
　　Yet there's no doubt she only meant to clasp
His fingers with a pure Platonic squeeze;
　　She would have shrunk as from a toad, or asp,
Had she imagined such a thing could rouse
A feeling dangerous to a prudent spouse.

CXII

I cannot know what Juan thought of this,
　　But what he did, is much what you would do;
His young lip thank'd it with a grateful kiss,
　　And then, abash'd at its own joy, withdrew
In deep despair, lest he had done amiss,
　　Love is so very timid when 't is new:
She blush'd, and frown'd not, but she strove to speak,
And held her tongue, her voice was grown so weak.

CXIII

The sun set, and up rose the yellow moon:
   The devil 's in the moon for mischief; they
Who called her CHASTE, methinks, began too soon
   Their nomenclature; there is not a day,
The longest, not the twenty-first of June,
   Sees half the business in a wicked way
On which three single hours of moonshine smile—
And then she looks so modest all the while.

CXIV

There is a dangerous silence in that hour,
   A stillness, which leaves room for the full soul
To open all itself, without the power
   Of calling wholly back its self-control;
The silver light which, hallowing tree and tower,
   Sheds beauty and deep softness o'er the whole,
Breathes also to the heart, and o'er it throws
A loving languor, which is not repose.

CXV

And Julia sate with Juan, half embraced
   And half retiring from the glowing arm,
Which trembled like the bosom where 't was placed;
   Yet still she must have thought there was no harm,
Or else 't were easy to withdraw her waist;
   But then the situation had its charm,
And then—God knows what next—I can't go on;
I'm almost sorry that I e'er begun.

CXVI

Oh Plato! Plato! you have paved the way,
   With your confounded fantasies, to more
Immoral conduct by the fancied sway
   Your system feigns o'er the controlless core
Of human hearts, than all the long array
   Of poets and romancers:—You 're a bore,
A charlatan, a coxcomb—and have been,
At best, no better than a go-between.

CXVII

And Julia's voice was lost, except in sighs,
   Until too late for useful conversation;
The tears were gushing from her gentle eyes,
   I wish, indeed, they had not had occasion;
But who, alas! can love, and then be wise?
   Not that remorse did not oppose temptation:
A little still she strove, and much repented,
And whispering "I will ne'er consent"—consented.

CXVIII

'T is said that Xerxes [28] offer'd a reward
   To those who could invent him a new pleasure:
Methinks the requisition's rather hard,
   And must have cost his majesty a treasure:
For my part, I'm a moderate-minded bard,
   Fond of a little love (which I call leisure);
I care not for new pleasures, as the old
Are quite enough for me, so they but hold.

CXIX

Oh Pleasure! you're indeed a pleasant thing,
   Although one must be damn'd for you, no doubt;
I make a resolution every spring
   Of reformation, ere the year run out,
But, somehow, this my vestal vow takes wing,
   Yet still, I trust, it may be kept throughout:
I 'm very sorry, very much ashamed,
And mean, next winter, to be quite reclaim'd.

CXX

Here my chaste Muse a liberty must take—
   Start not! still chaster reader—she 'll be nice hence-
Forward, and there is no great cause to quake;
   This liberty is a poetic licence,
Which some irregularity may make
   In the design, and as I have a high sense
Of Aristotle and the Rules, 't is fit
To beg his pardon when I err a bit.

CXXI

This licence is to hope the reader will
   Suppose from June the sixth (the fatal day,
Without whose epoch my poetic skill
   For want of facts would all be thrown away),
But keeping Julia and Don Juan still
   In sight, that several months have passed; we 'll say
'T was in November, but I'm not so sure
About the day—the era's more obscure.

CXXII

We'll talk of that anon.—'T is sweet to hear
   At midnight on the blue and moonlit deep
The song and oar of Adria's gondolier,
   By distance mellow'd, o'er the waters sweep;
'T is sweet to see the evening star appear;
   'T is sweet to listen as the nightwinds creep
From leaf to leaf; 't is sweet to view on high
The rainbow, based on ocean, span the sky.

---

[28] King of Persia who unsuccessfully invaded Greece in the fifth century B.C.

CXXIII

'T is sweet to hear the watchdog's honest bark
  Bay deep-mouth'd welcome as we draw near home;
'T is sweet to know there is an eye will mark
  Our coming, and look brighter when we come;
'T is sweet to be awaken'd by the lark,
  Or lull'd by falling waters; sweet the hum
Of bees, the voice of girls, the song of birds,
The lisp of children, and their earliest words.

CXXIV

Sweet is the vintage, when the showering grapes
  In Bacchanal profusion reel to earth
Purple and gushing: sweet are our escapes
  From civic revelry to rural mirth;
Sweet to the miser are his glittering heaps,
  Sweet to the father is his first-born's birth,
Sweet is revenge—especially to women,
Pillage to soldiers, prize-money to seamen.

CXXV

Sweet is a legacy, and passing sweet
  The unexpected death of some old lady,[29]
Or gentleman of seventy years complete,
  Who 've made "us youth" wait too—too long
For an estate, or cash, or country seat,   [already
  Still breaking, but with stamina so steady,
That all the Israelites are fit to mob its
Next owner for their double-damned post-obits.[30]

CXXVI

'T is sweet to win, no matter how, one's laurels,
  By blood or ink, 't is sweet to put an end
To strife; 't is sometimes sweet to have our quarrels,
  Particularly with a tiresome friend;
Sweet is old wine in bottles, ale in barrels;
  Dear is the helpless creature we defend
Against the world; and dear the schoolboy spot
We ne'er forget, though there we are forgot.

CXXVII

But sweeter still than this, than these, than all,
  Is first and passionate love—it stands alone,
Like Adam's recollection of his fall;
  The tree of knowledge has been pluck'd—all 's
And life yields nothing further to recall   [known—
  Worthy of this ambrosial sin, so shown,
No doubt in fable, as the unforgiven
Fire which Prometheus filch'd for us from heaven.

---

[29] Byron was candid in his disappointment at his mother-in-law's longevity.
[30] Debt incurred on the expectation of inheritance.

CXXVIII

Man 's a strange animal, and makes strange use
  Of his own nature, and the various arts,
And likes particularly to produce
  Some new experiment to show his parts;
This is the age of oddities let loose,
  Where different talents find their different marts;
You 'd best begin with truth, and when you 've lost
Labour, there 's a sure market for imposture.   [your

CXXIX

What opposite discoveries we have seen!
  (Signs of true genius, and of empty pockets.)
One makes new noses, one a guillotine,
  One breaks your bones, one sets them in their
But vaccination certainly has been   [sockets;
  A kind antithesis to Congreve's rockets,
With which the Doctor paid off an old pox,
By borrowing a new one from an ox.[31]

CXXX

Bread has been made (indifferent) from potatoes;
  And galvanism has set some corpses grinning,
But has not answer'd like the apparatus
  Of the Humane Society's beginning,
By which men are unsuffocated gratis:
  What wondrous new machines have late been
I said the small-pox has gone out of late;   [spinning!
Perhaps it may be follow'd by the great.[32]

CXXXI

'T is said the great came from America;
  Perhaps it may set out on its return,—
The population there so spreads, they say
  'T is grown high time to thin it in its turn,
With war, or plague, or famine, any way
  So that civilisation they may learn;
And which in ravage the more loathsome evil is—
Their real *lues*, or our pseudo-syphillis?

CXXXII

This is the patent age of new inventions
  For killing bodies, and for saving souls,
All propagated with the best intentions;
  Sir Humphrey Davy's lantern, by which coals
Are safely mined for in the mode he mentions,
  Tombuctoo travels, voyages to the Poles,
Are ways to benefit mankind, as true,
Perhaps, as shooting them at Waterloo.

---

[31] The inventions include Perkin's metallic tractors, "a cure for all disorders"; a new artillery rocket; cowpox inoculations against smallpox; and (in the next stanza) the use of electric shocks on corpses. Compare *English Bards*, lines 131–41.
[32] Great pox = syphillis.

CXXXIII

Man 's a phenomenon, one knows not what,
　　And wonderful beyond all wondrous measure;
'T is pity though, in this sublime world, that
　　Pleasure's a sin, and sometimes sin's a pleasure;
Few mortals know what end they would be at,
　　But whether glory, power, or love, or treasure,
The path is through perplexing ways, and when
The goal is gain'd, we die, you know—and then—

CXXXIV

What then?—I do not know, no more do you—
　　And so good night.—Return we to our story:
'T was in November, when fine days are few,
　　And the far mountains wax a little hoary,
And clap a white cape on their mantles blue;
　　And the sea dashes round the promontory,
And the loud breaker boils against the rock,
And sober suns must set at five o'clock.

CXXXV

'T was, as the watchmen say, a cloudy night;
　　No moon, no stars, the wind was low or loud
By gusts, and many a sparkling hearth was bright
　　With the piled wood, round which the family
　　　crowd;
There 's something cheerful in that sort of light,
　　Even as a summer sky's without a cloud:
I 'm fond of fire, and crickets, and all that,
A lobster salad, and champaigne, and chat.

CXXXVI

'T was midnight—Donna Julia was in bed,
　　Sleeping, most probably,—when at her door
Arose a clatter might awake the dead,
　　If they had never been awoke before,
And that they have been so we all have read,
　　And are to be so, at the least, once more—
The door was fasten'd, but with voice and fist
First knocks were heard, then "Madam—Madam—
　　　　　　　　　　　　　　　　　　[hist!

CXXXVII

"For God's sake, Madam—Madam—here's my
　　With more than half the city at his back—　[master,
Was ever heard of such a curst disaster!
　　'T is not my fault—I kept good watch—Alack!
Do pray undo the bolt a little faster—
　　They 're on the stair just now, and in a crack
Will all be here; perhaps he yet may fly—
Surely the window 's not so *very* high!"

CXXXVIII

By this time Don Alfonso was arrived,
　　With torches, friends, and servants in great number;
The major part of them had long been wived,
　　And therefore paused not to disturb the slumber
Of any wicked woman, who contrived
　　By stealth her husband's temples to encumber:
Examples of this kind are so contagious,
Were *one* not punished, *all* would be outrageous.

CXXXIX

I can't tell how, or why, or what suspicion
　　Could enter into Don Alfonso's head;
But for a cavalier of his condition
　　It surely was exceedingly ill-bred,
Without a word of previous admonition,
　　To hold a levee round his lady's bed,
And summon lackeys, arm'd with fire and sword,
To prove himself the thing he most abhorr'd.

CXL

Poor Donna Julia! starting as from sleep,
　　(Mind—that I do not say—she had not slept)
Began at once to scream, and yawn, and weep;
　　Her maid Antonia, who was an adept,
Contrived to fling the bed-clothes in a heap,
　　As if she had just now from out them crept:
I can't tell why she should take all this trouble
To prove her mistress had been sleeping double.

CXLI

But Julia mistress, and Antonia maid,
　　Appear'd like two poor harmless women, who
Of goblins, but still more of men afraid,
　　Had thought one man might be deterr'd by two,
And therefore side by side were gently laid,
　　Until the hours of absence should run through,
And truant husband should return, and say,
"My dear, I was the first who came away."

CXLII

Now Julia found at length a voice, and cried,
　　"In heaven's name, Don Alfonso, what d' ye mean?
Has madness seized you? would that I had died
　　Ere such a monster's victim I had been!
What may this midnight violence betide,
　　A sudden fit of drunkenness or spleen?
Dare you suspect me, whom the thought would kill?
Search, then, the room!" Alfonso said, "I will."

CXLIII

He search'd, *they* search'd, and rummaged every
    where,
  Closet and clothes'-press, chest and window-seat,
And found much linen, lace, and several pair
  Of stockings, slippers, brushes, combs, complete,
With other articles of ladies fair,
  To keep them beautiful, or leave them neat:
Arras they prick'd and curtains with their swords,
And wounded several shutters, and some boards.

CXLIV

Under the bed they search'd, and there they found—
  No matter what—it was not that they sought;
They open'd windows, gazing if the ground
  Had signs of footmarks, but the earth said nought;
And then they stared each others' faces round:
  'T is odd, not one of all these seekers thought,
And seems to me almost a sort of blunder,
Of looking *in* the bed as well as under.

CXLV

During this inquisition Julia's tongue
  Was not asleep—"Yes, search and search," she
"Insult on insult heap, and wrong on wrong!   [cried,
  It was for this that I became a bride!
For this in silence I have suffer'd long
  A husband like Alfonso at my side;
But now I 'll bear no more, nor here remain,
If there be law or lawyers in all Spain.

CXLVI

"Yes, Don Alfonso! husband now no more,
  If ever you indeed deserved the name,
Is 't worthy of your years?—you have threescore,
  Fifty, or sixty—it is all the same—
Is 't wise or fitting causeless to explore
  For facts against a virtuous woman's fame?
Ungrateful, perjured, barbarous Don Alfonso,
How dare you think your lady would go on so?

CXLVII

"Is it for this I have disdain'd to hold
  The common privileges of my sex?
That I have chosen a confessor so old
  And deaf, that any other it would vex,
And never once he has had cause to scold,
  But found my very innocence perplex
So much, he always doubted I was married—
How sorry you will be when I 've miscarried!

CXLVIII

"Was it for this that no Cortejo e'er*
  I yet have chosen from out the youth of Seville?
Is it for this I scarce went any where,
  Except to bull-fights, mass, play, rout, and revel?
Is it for this, whate'er my suitors were,
  I favour'd none—nay, was almost uncivil?
Is it for this that General Count O'Reilly,
Who took Algiers, declares I used him vilely?†

CXLIX

"Did not the Italian *Musico* Cazzani
  Sing at my heart six months at least in vain?
Did not his countryman, Count Corniani,
  Call me the only virtuous wife in Spain?
Were there not also Russians, English, many?
  The Count Strongstroganoff I put in pain,
And Lord Mount Coffeehouse, the Irish peer,
Who kill'd himself for love (with wine) last year.[35]

CL

"Have I not had two bishops at my feet?
  The Duke of Ichar, and Don Fernan Nunez;
And is it thus a faithful wife you treat?
  I wonder in what quarter now the moon is:
I praise your vast forbearance not to beat
  Me also, since the time so opportune is—
Oh, valiant man! with sword drawn and cock'd
Now, tell me, don't you cut a pretty figure?   [trigger,

CLI

"Was it for this you took your sudden journey,
  Under pretence of business indispensable
With that sublime of rascals your attorney,
  Whom I see standing there, and looking sensible
Of having play'd the fool? though both I spurn, he
  Deserves the worst, his conduct 's less defensible,
Because, no doubt, 't was for his dirty fee,
And not from any love to you nor me.

  * The Spanish "Cortejo" is much the same as the Italian
"Cavalier Servente."[33]

  † Donna Julia here made a mistake. Count O'Reilly did not
take Algiers—but Algiers very nearly took him: he and his army
and fleet retreated with great loss, and not much credit, from
before that city in the year 17—.[34]

[33] See note to stanza XVII of *Beppo*, p. 621.
[34] This was an expedition in 1745 by the Spanish General
Alexander O'Reilly, who had been born in Ireland.
[35] The names of course are invented (e.g., Corniani =
cuckolded; "cazzani," from cazzo = penis).

CLII

"If he comes here to take a deposition,
   By all means let the gentleman proceed;
You 've made the apartment in a fit condition:—
   There's pen and ink for you, sir, when you need—
Let everything be noted with precision,
   I would not you for nothing should be fee'd—
But, as my maid 's undrest, pray turn your spies out."
"Oh!" sobb'd Antonia, "I could tear their eyes out."

CLIII

"There is the closet, there the toilet, there
   The anti chamber—search them under, over;
There is the sofa, there the great arm-chair,
   The chimney—which would really hold a lover.
I wish to sleep, and beg you will take care
   And make no further noise, till you discover
The secret cavern of this lurking treasure—
And when 't is found, let me, too, have that pleasure.

CLIV

"And now, Hidalgo! now that you have thrown
   Doubt upon me, confusion over all,
Pray have the courtesy to make it known
   Who is the man you search for? how d' ye call
Him? what 's his lineage? let him but be shown—
   I hope he 's young and handsome—is he tall?
Tell me—and be assured, that since you stain
My honour thus, it shall not be in vain.

CLV

"At least, perhaps, he has not sixty years,
   At that age he would be too old for slaughter,
Or for so young a husband's jealous fears—
   (Antonia! let me have a glass of water.)
I am ashamed of having shed these tears,
   They are unworthy of my father's daughter;
My mother dream'd not in my natal hour,
That I should fall into a monster's power.

CLVI

"Perhaps 't is of Antonia you are jealous,
   You saw that she was sleeping by my side
When you broke in upon us with your fellows:
   Look where you please—we 've nothing, sir, to hide;
Only another time, I trust, you 'll tell us,
   Or for the sake of decency abide
A moment at the door, that we may be
Drest to receive so much good company.

CLVII

"And now, sir, I have done, and say no more;
   The little I have said may serve to show
The guileless heart in silence may grieve o'er
   The wrongs to whose exposure it is slow:—
I leave you to your conscience as before,
   'T will one day ask you *why* you used me so?
God grant you feel not then the bitterest grief!
Antonia! where's my pocket-handkerchief?"

CLVIII

She ceased, and turn'd upon her pillow; pale
   She lay, her dark eyes flashing through their tears,
Like skies that rain and lighten; as a veil,
   Waved and o'ershading her wan cheek, appears
Her streaming hair; the black curls strive, but fail,
   To hide the glossy shoulder, which uprears
Its snow through all;—her soft lips lie apart,
And louder than her breathing beats her heart.

CLIX

The Senhor Don Alfonso stood confused;
   Antonia bustled round the ransack'd room,
And, turning up her nose, with looks abused
   Her master, and his myrmidons, of whom
Not one, except the attorney, was amused;
   He, like Achates, faithful to the tomb,[36]
So there were quarrels, cared not for the cause,
Knowing they must be settled by the laws.

CLX

With prying snub-nose, and small eyes, he stood,
   Following Antonia's motions here and there,
With much suspicion in his attitude;
   For reputations he had little care;
So that a suit or action were made good,
   Small pity had he for the young and fair,
And ne'er believed in negatives, till these
Were proved by competent false witnesses.

CLXI

But Don Alfonso stood with downcast looks,
   And, truth to say, he made a foolish figure;
When, after searching in five hundred nooks,
   And treating a young wife with so much rigour,
He gain'd no point, except some self-rebukes,
   Added to those his lady with such vigour
Had pour'd upon him for the last half-hour,
Quick, thick, and heavy—as a thunder-shower.

---

36 In Vergil's *Aeneid*, Achates followed and served Aeneas from Troy to Rome.

CLXII

At first he tried to hammer an excuse,
   To which the sole reply were tears, and sobs,
And indications of hysterics, whose
   Prologue is always certain throes, and throbs,
Gasps, and whatever else the owners choose:—
   Alfonso saw his wife, and thought of Job's;
He saw too, in perspective, her relations,
And then he tried to muster all his patience.

CLXIII

He stood in act to speak, or rather stammer,
   But sage Antonia cut him short before
The anvil of his speech received the hammer,
   With "Pray, sir, leave the room, and say no more,
Or madam dies."—Alfonso muttered, "D—n her,"
   But nothing else, the time of words was o'er;
He cast a rueful look or two, and did,
He knew not wherefore, that which he was bid.

CLXIV

With him retired his "*posse comitatus*," [37]
   The attorney last, who linger'd near the door,
Reluctantly, still tarrying there as late as
   Antonia let him—not a little sore
At this most strange and unexplained "*hiatus*"
   In Don Alfonso's facts, which just now wore
An awkward look; as he revolved the case,
The door was fasten'd in his legal face.

CLXV

No sooner was it bolted, than—Oh shame!
   Oh sin! Oh sorrow! and Oh womankind!
How can you do such things and keep your fame,
   Unless this world, and t' other too, be blind?
Nothing so dear as an unfilch'd good name!
   But to proceed—for there is more behind:
With much heartfelt reluctance be it said,
Young Juan slipp'd, half-smother'd, from the bed.

CLXVI

He had been hid—I don't pretend to say
   How, nor can I indeed describe the where—
Young, slender, and pack'd easily, he lay,
   No doubt, in little compass, round or square;
But pity him I neither must nor may
   His suffocation by that pretty pair;
'T were better, sure, to die so, than be shut
With maudlin Clarence in his Malmsey butt. [38]

CLXVII

And, secondly, I pity not, because
   He had no business to commit a sin,
Forbid by heavenly, fined by human laws;—
   At least 't was rather early to begin,
But at sixteen the conscience rarely gnaws
   So much as when we call our old debts in
At sixty years, and draw the accompts of evil,
And find a deuced balance with the Devil.

CLXVIII

Of his position I can give no notion:
   'T is written in the Hebrew Chronicle, [39]
How the physicians, leaving pill and potion,
   Prescribed, by way of blister, a young belle,
When old King David's blood grew dull in motion,
   And that the medicine answer'd very well;
Perhaps 't was in a different way applied,
For David lived, but Juan nearly died.

CLXIX

What 's to be done? Alfonso will be back
   The moment he has sent his fools away.
Antonia's skill was put upon the rack,
   But no device could be brought into play—
And how to parry the renew'd attack?
   Besides, it wanted but few hours of day:
Antonia puzzled; Julia did not speak,
But press'd her bloodless lips to Juan's cheek.

CLXX

He turn'd his lip to hers, and with his hand
   Call'd back the tangles of her wandering hair;
Even then their love they could not all command,
   And half forgot their danger and despair:
Antonia's patience now was at a stand—
   "Come, come, 't is no time for fooling there,"
She whisper'd, in great wrath—"I must deposit
This pretty gentleman within the closet:

CLXXI

"Pray, keep your nonsense for some lucker night—
   Who can have put my master in this mood?
What will become on 't—I'm in such a fright,
   The devil 's in the urchin, and no good—
Is this a time for giggling? this a plight?
   Why, don't you know that it may end in blood?
You'll lose your life, and I shall lose my place,
My mistress all, for that half-girlish face.

---

[37] Power or force of the county.
[38] See Shakespeare's *Richard III*, I, iv.

[39] I Kings 1:1–3.

CLXXII

"Had it but been for a stout cavalier
  Of twenty-five or thirty—(Come, make haste)
But for a child, what piece of work is here!
  (I really, madam, wonder at your taste—
Come, sir, get in)—my master must be near:
  There, for the present, at the least he's fast,
And if we can but till the morning keep
Our counsel—(Juan, mind, you must not sleep.)"

CLXXIII

Now, Don Alfonso entering, but alone,
  Closed the oration of the trusty maid:
She loiter'd, and he told her to be gone,
  An order somewhat sullenly obey'd;
However, present remedy was none,
  And no great good seem'd answer'd if she staid:
Regarding both with slow and sidelong view,
She snuff'd the candle, curtsied, and withdrew.

CLXXIV

Alfonso paused a minute—then begun
  Some strange excuses for his late proceeding;
He would not justify what he had done,
  To say the best, it was extremely ill-breeding;
But there were ample reasons for it, none
  Of which he specified in this his pleading:
His speech was a fine sample, on the whole,
Of rhetoric, which the learned call "*rigmarole*."

CLXXV

Julia said nought; though all the while there rose
  A ready answer, which at once enables
A matron, who her husband's foible knows,
  By a few timely words to turn the tables,
Which, if it does not silence, still must pose,
  Even if it should comprise a pack of fables;
'T is to retort with firmness, and when he
Suspects with *one*, do you reproach with *three*.

CLXXVI

Julia, in fact, had tolerable grounds,
  Alfonso's loves with Inez were well known;
But whether 't was that one's own guilt confounds,
  But that can't be, as has been often shown,
A lady with apologies abounds;
  It might be that her silence sprang alone
From delicacy to Don Juan's ear,
To whom she knew his mother's fame was dear.

CLXXVII

There might be one more motive, which makes two,
  Alfonso ne'er to Juan had alluded,
Mention'd his jealousy, but never who
  Had been the happy lover, he concluded,
Conceal'd amongst his premises; 't is true,
  His mind the more o'er this its mystery brooded;
To speak of Inez now were, one may say,
Like throwing Juan in Alfonso's way.

CLXXVIII

A hint, in tender cases, is enough;
  Silence is best: besides, there is a *tact*
(That modern phrase appears to me sad stuff,
  But it will serve to keep my verse compact)
Which keeps, when push'd by questions rather rough,
  A lady always distant from the fact—
The charming creatures lie with such a grace,
There's nothing so becoming to the face.

CLXXIX

They blush, and we believe them; at least I
  Have always done so: 't is of no great use,
In any case, attempting a reply,
  For then their eloquence grows quite profuse;
And when at length they 're out of breath, they sigh,
  And cast their languid eyes down, and let loose
A tear or two, and then we make it up;
And then—and then—and then—sit down and sup.

CLXXX

Alfonso closed his speech, and begg'd her pardon,
  Which Julia half withheld, and then half granted,
And laid conditions, he thought, very hard on,
  Denying several little things he wanted:
He stood like Adam lingering near his garden,
  With useless penitence perplexed and haunted;
Beseeching she no further would refuse,
When, lo! he stumbled o'er a pair of shoes.

CLXXXI

A pair of shoes!—what then? not much, if they
  Are such as fit with lady's feet, but these
(No one can tell how much I grieve to say)
  Were masculine; to see them, and to seize,
Was but a moment's act.—Ah! Well-a-day!
  My teeth begin to chatter, my veins freeze—
Alfonso first examined well their fashion,
And then flew out into another passion.

CLXXXII

He left the room for his relinquish'd sword,
  And Julia instant to the closet flew.
"Fly, Juan, fly! for heaven's sake—not a word—
  The door is open—you may yet slip through
The passage you so often have explored—
  Here is the garden-key—Fly—fly—Adieu!
Haste—haste! I hear Alfonso's hurrying feet—
Day has not broke—there's no one in the street."

CLXXXIII

None can say that this was not good advice,
  The only mischief was, it came too late;
Of all experience 't is the usual price,
  A sort of income-tax laid on by fate:
Juan had reach'd the room-door in a trice,
  And might have done so by the garden-gate,
But met Alfonso in his dressing-gown,
Who threatened death—so Juan knock'd him down.

CLXXXIV

Dire was the scuffle, and out went the light,
  Antonia cried out "Rape!" and Julia "Fire!"
But not a servant stirr'd to aid the fight.
  Alfonso, pommell'd to his heart's desire,
Swore lustily he'd be revenged this night;
  And Juan, too, blasphemed an octave higher;
His blood was up: though young, he was a Tartar,
And not at all disposed to prove a martyr.

CLXXXV

Alfonso's sword had dropp'd ere he could draw it,
  And they continued battling hand to hand,
For Juan very luckily ne'er saw it;
  His temper not being under great command,
If at that moment, he had chanced to claw it,
  Alfonso's days had not been in the land
Much longer.—Think of husbands', lovers' lives!
And how ye may be doubly widows—wives!

CLXXXVI

Alfonso grappled to detain the foe,
  And Juan throttled him to get away,
And blood ('t was from the nose) began to flow;
  At last, as they more faintly wrestling lay,
Juan contrived to give an awkward blow,
  And then his only garment quite gave way;
He fled, like Joseph, leaving it; but there,
I doubt, all likeness ends between the pair.[40]

CLXXXVII

Lights came at length, and men, and maids, who found
  An awkward spectacle their eyes before;
Antonia in hysterics, Julia swoon'd,
  Alfonso leaning, breathless by the door;
Some half-torn drapery scatter'd on the ground,
  Some blood, and several footsteps, but no more:
Juan the gate gain'd, turn'd the key about,
And liking not the inside, lock'd the out.

CLXXXVIII

Here ends this canto.—Need I sing, or say,
  How Juan, naked, favour'd by the night,
Who favours what she should not, found his way,
  And reach'd his home in an unseemly plight?
The pleasant scandal which arose next day,
  The nine days' wonder which was brought to light,
And how Alfonso sued for a divorce,
Were in the English newspapers, of course.

CLXXXIX

If you would like to see the whole proceedings,
  The depositions, and the cause at full,
The names of all the witnesses, the pleadings
  Of counsel to nonsuit, or to annul,
There's more than one edition, and the readings
  Are various, but they none of them are dull:
The best is that in short-hand ta'en by Gurney,[41]
Who to Madrid on purpose made a journey.

CXC

But Donna Inez, to divert the train
  Of one of the most circulating scandals
That had for centuries been known in Spain,
  At least since the retirement of the Vandals,
First vow'd (and never had she vow'd in vain)
  To Virgin Mary several pounds of candles;
And then, by the advice of some old ladies,
She sent her son to be shipp'd off from Cadiz.

CXCI

She had resolved that he should travel through
  All European climes, by land or sea,
To mend his former morals, and get new,
  Especially in France and Italy,
(At least this is the thing most people do).
  Julia was sent into a convent; she
Grieved, but, perhaps, her feelings may be better
Shown in the following copy of her letter:

---

[40] In Gen. 39:12, Potiphar's wife tries but fails to seduce Joseph.

[41] A contemporary shorthand reporter for court trials and Parliament.

CXCII

"They tell me 't is decided you depart:
    'T is wise—'t is well, but not the less a pain;
I have no further claim on your young heart,
    Mine is the victim, and would be again;
To love too much has been the only art
    I used;—I write in haste, and if a stain
Be on this sheet, 't is not what it appears;
My eyeballs burn and throb, but have no tears.

CXCIII

"I loved, I love you, for this love have lost
    State, station, heaven, mankind's, my own esteem,
And yet can not regret what it hath cost,
    So dear is still the memory of that dream;
Yet, if I name my guilt, 't is not to boast,
    None can deem harshlier of me than I deem:
I trace this scrawl because I cannot rest—
I 've nothing to reproach, or to request.

CXCIV

"Man's love is of man's life a thing apart,
    'T is a woman's whole existence; [42] Man may range
The court, camp, church, the vessel, and the mart,
    Sword, gown, gain, glory offer, in exchange
Pride, fame, ambition, to fill up his heart,
    And few there are whom these can not estrange;
Men have all these resources, we but one.
To love again, and be again undone.

CXCV

"You will proceed in pleasure, and in pride,
    Beloved and loving many; all is o'er
For me on earth, except some years to hide
    My shame and sorrow deep in my heart's core:
These I could bear, but cannot cast aside
    The passion which still rages as before,
And so farewell—forgive me, love me—No,
That word is idle now—but let it go.

CXCVI

"My breast has been all weakness, is so yet;
    But still I think I can collect my mind;
My blood still rushes where my spirit 's set,
    As roll the waves before the settled wind;
My heart is feminine, nor can forget—
    To all, except one image, madly blind;
So shakes the needle, and so stands the pole,
As vibrates my fond heart to my fix'd soul.

CXCVII

"I have no more to say, but linger still,
    And dare not set my seal upon this sheet,
And yet I may as well the task fulfil,
    My misery can scarce be more complete:
I had not lived till now, could sorrow kill;
    Death shuns the wretch who fain the blow would
And I must even survive this last adieu,   [meet,
And bear with life, to love and pray for you!"

CXCVIII

This note was written upon gilt-edged paper
    With a neat little crow-quill, slight and new;
Her small white hand could hardly reach the taper,
    It trembled as magnetic needles do,
And yet she did not let one tear escape her;
    The seal a sun-flower; "*Elle vous suit partout*," [43]
The motto, cut upon a white cornelian;
The wax was superfine, its hue vermilion.

CXCIX

This was Don Juan's earliest scrape; but whether
    I shall proceed with his adventures is
Dependent on the public altogether;
    We 'll see, however, what they say to this,
Their favour in an author's caps 's a feather,
    And no great mischief 's done by their caprice;
And if their approbation we experience,
Perhaps they'll have some more about a year hence.

CC

My poem 's epic, and is meant to be
    Divided in twelve books; each book containing,
With love, and war, a heavy gale at sea,
    A list of ships, and captains, and kings reigning,
New characters; the episodes are three:
    A panoramic view of hell 's in training,
After the style of Virgil and of Homer,
So that my name of Epic 's no misnomer.

CCI

All these things will be specified in time,
    With strict regard to Aristotle's rules,
The *vade mecum* of the true sublime, [44]
    Which makes so many poets, and some fools;
Prose poets like blank-verse, I 'm fond of rhyme,
    Good workmen never quarrel with their tools;
I 've got new mythological machinery,
And very handsome supernatural scenery,

---

[42] The phrase is adapted from Mme. de Staël, who used a version of it in several contexts.

[43] "She follows you everywhere."

[44] Literally "go with me"; a guide.

CCII

There 's only one slight difference between
  Me and my epic brethren gone before,
And here the advantage is my own, I ween;
  (Not that I have not several merits more,
But this will more peculiarly be seen);
  They so embellish, that 't is quite a bore
Their labyrinth of fables to thread through,
Whereas this story 's actually true.

CCIII

If any person doubt it, I appeal
  To history, tradition, and to facts,
To newspapers, whose truth all know and feel,
  To plays in five, and operas in three acts;
All these confirm my statement a good deal,
  But that which more completely faith exacts
Is, that myself, and several now in Seville,
Saw Juan's last elopement with the devil.

CCIV

If ever I should condescend to prose,
  I 'll write poetical commandments, which
Shall supersede beyond all doubt all those
  That went before; in these I shall enrich
My text with many things that no one knows,
  And carry precept to the highest pitch:
I 'll call the work "Longinus o'er a Bottle,
Or, Every Poet his *own* Aristotle." [45]

CCV

Thou shalt believe in Milton, Dryden, Pope;
  Thou shalt not set up Wordsworth, Coleridge,
Because the first is crazed beyond all hope, [Southey;
  The second drunk, the third so quaint and mouthey:
With Crabbe it may be difficult to cope,
  And Campbell's Hippocrene is somewhat drouthy:
Thou shalt not steal from Samuel Rogers, nor
Commit—flirtation with the muse of Moore.

CCVI

Thou shalt not covet Mr. Sotheby's Muse,
  His Pegasus, nor any thing that 's his;
Thou shalt not bear false witness like "the Blues"—
  (There 's one, at least, is very fond of this);
Thou shalt not write, in short, but what I choose:
  This is true criticism, and you may kiss—
Exactly as you please, or not, the rod,
But if you don't, I'll lay it on, by G—d! [46]

---

45 Both Longinus and Aristotle wrote (in Latin and Greek)
advice to poets, with different critical assumptions.
46 Many of the writers satirized appear also in *The Blues*
(p. 630); Crabbe, Rogers, and Moore he consistently praised. See
W. H. Auden's up-dating of these stanzas in his *Under Which Lyre*.
The Blue who bore false witness is of course Lady Byron.

CCVII

If any person should presume to assert
  This story is not moral, first, I pray,
That they will not cry out before they 're hurt,
  Then that they 'll read it o'er again, and say
(But, doubtless, nobody will be so pert),
  That this is not a moral tale, though gay;
Besides, in canto twelfth, I mean to show
The very place where wicked people go.

CCVIII

If, after all, there should be some so blind
  To their own good this warning to despise,
Led by some tortuosity of mind,
  Not to believe my verse and their own eyes,
And cry that they "the moral cannot find,"
  I tell him, if a clergyman, he lies;
Should captains the remark or critics make,
They also lie too—under a mistake.

CCIX

The public approbation I expect,
  And beg they'll take my word about the moral,
Which I with their amusement will connect
  (So children cutting teeth receive a coral);
Meantime they 'll doubtless please to recollect
  My epical pretensions to the laurel:
For fear some prudish readers should grow skittish,
I've bribed my grandmother's review—the British.

CCX

I sent it in a letter to the editor,
  Who thanked me duly by return of post—
I 'm for a handsome article his creditor;
  Yet, if my gentle Muse he please to roast,
And break a promise after having made it her,
  Denying the receipt of what it cost,
And smear his page with gall instead of honey,
All I can say is—that he had the money.

CCXI

I think that with this holy new alliance
  I may ensure the public, and defy
All other magazines of art or science,
  Daily, or monthly, or three monthly; I
Have not essay'd to multiply their clients,
  Because they tell me 't were in vain to try,
And that the Edinburgh Review and Quarterly
Treat a dissenting author very martyrly.

CCXII

" Non ego hoc ferrem calidus juventâ
   Consule Planco," Horace said, and so [47]
Say I; by which quotation there is meant a
   Hint that some six or seven good years ago
(Long ere I dreamt of dating from the Brenta,
   I was most ready to return a blow,
And would not brook at all this sort of thing
In my hot youth—when George the Third was King.

CCXIII

But now at thirty years my hair is grey—
   (I wonder what it will be like at forty?
I thought of a peruke the other day)
   My heart is not much greener; and, in short, I
Have squander'd my whole summer while 't was May
   And feel no more the spirit to retort; I
Have spent my life, both interest and principal,
And deem not, what I deem'd, my soul invincible.

CCXIV

No more—no more—Oh! never more on me
   The freshness of the heart can fall like dew,
Which out of all the lovely things we see
   Extracts emotions beautiful and new,
Hived in our bosoms like the bag o' the bee.
   Think'st thou the honey with those objects grew?
Alas! 't was not in them, but in thy power
To double even the sweetness of a flower.

CCXV

No more—no more—Oh! never more, my heart,
   Canst thou be my sole world, my universe!
Once all in all, but now a thing apart,
   Thou canst not be my blessing or my curse:
The illusion 's gone for ever, and thou art
   Insensible, I trust, but none the worse,
And in thy stead I 've got a deal of judgment,
Though heaven knows how it ever found a lodgment.

CCXVI

My days of love are over; me no more*
   The charms of maid, wife, and still less of widow,
Can make the fool of which they made before,—
   In short, I must not lead the life I did do;

   *   "Me nec femina, nec puer*
     Jam, nec spes animi credula mutui,
        Nec certare juvat mero;
     Nec vincire novis tempora floribus."—HOR.[48]

The credulous hope of mutual minds is o'er,
   The copious use of claret is forbid too,
So for a good old-gentlemanly vice,
I think I must take up with avarice.

CCXVII

Ambition was my idol, which was broken
   Before the shrines of Sorrow and of Pleasure;
And the two last have left me many a token
   O'er which reflection may be made at leisure:
Now, like Friar Bacon's brazen head, I've spoken,[49]
   "Time is, Time was, Time 's past:"—a chymic
     treasure
Is glittering Youth, which I have spent betimes—
My heart in passion, and my head on rhymes.

CCXVIII

What is the end of fame? 't is but to fill
   A certain portion of uncertain paper:
Some liken it to climbing up a hill,
   Whose summit, like all hills, is lost in vapour;
For this men write, speak, preach, and heroes kill,
   And bards burn what they call their "midnight
To have, when the original is dust,   [taper,"
A name, a wretched picture and worse bust.

CCXIX

What are the hopes of man? Old Egypt's King
   Cheops erected the first pyramid
And largest, thinking it was just the thing
   To keep his memory whole, and mummy hid;
But somebody or other rummaging,
   Burglariously broke his coffin's lid:
Let not a monument give you or me hopes,
Since not a pinch of dust remains of Cheops.[50]

CCXX

But I being fond of true philosophy,
   Say very often to myself, "Alas!
All things that have been born were born to die,
   And flesh (which Death mows down to hay) is grass;
You've passed your youth not so unpleasantly,
   And if you had it o'er again—'t would pass—
So thank your stars that matters are no worse,
And read your Bible, sir, and mind your purse."

---

[47] "I should not have borne this in the heat of youth when Plancus was Consul," Horace, *Odes*, III, 14.

[48] The lines of Horace that Byron paraphrases in the stanza and quotes in the note are from the *Odes*, IV, 1: "Now I no longer delight in woman or boy, nor in the fond hopes of a congenial mind, in wine bouts, or in binding my brows with fresh flowers."

[49] The legendary Friar Bacon was said to have made such a head. See Green's play *Friar Bacon and Friar Bungay*, where the head speaks these lines.

[50] The tomb of Cheops in the Great Pyramid had just been opened and found empty. Byron may have read Shelley's *Ozymandias* (p. 810).

CCXXI

But for the present, gentle reader! and
   Still gentler purchaser! the bard—that's I—
Must, with permission, shake you by the hand,
   And so your humble servant, and goodbye!
We meet again, if we should understand
   Each other; and if not, I shall not try
Your patience further than by this short sample—
'T were well if others follow'd my example.

CCXXII

"Go, little Book, from this my solitude!
   I cast thee on the waters, go thy ways!
And if, as I believe, thy vein be good,
   The world will find thee after many days." [51]
When Southey 's read, and Wordsworth understood,
   I can't help putting in my claim to praise—
The four first rhymes are Southey's every line:
For God's sake, reader! take them not for mine.

[1818]   [1819]

CANTO THE SECOND

I

OH ye! who teach the ingenuous youth of nations,
   Holland, France, England, Germany, or Spain,
I pray ye flog them upon all occasions,
   It mends their morals, never mind the pain:
The best of mothers and of educations
   In Juan's case were not employed in vain,
Since in a way, that's rather of the oddest, he
Became divested of his native modesty.

II

Had he but been placed at a public school,
   In the third form, or even in the fourth,
His daily task had kept his fancy cool,
   At least, had he been nurtured in the north;
Spain may prove an exception to the rule,
   But then exceptions always prove its worth—
A lad of sixteen causing a divorce
Puzzled his tutors very much, of course.

III

I can't say that it puzzles me at all,
   If all things be consider'd: first, there was
His lady-mother, mathematical,
   A—never mind; his tutor, an old ass;
A pretty woman—(that's quite natural,
   Or else the thing had hardly come to pass);
A husband rather old, not much in unity
With his young wife—a time, and opportunity.

[51] The lines are quoted from Southey's *Epilogue to the Lady of the Laureate.*

IV

Well—well, the world must turn upon its axis,
   And all Mankind turn with it, heads or tails,
And live and die, make love and pay our taxes,
   And as the veering wind shifts, shift our sails;
The king commands us, and the doctor quacks us,
   The Priest instructs, and so our life exhales,
A little breath, love, wine, ambition, fame,
Fighting, devotion, dust,—perhaps a name.

V

I said, that Juan had been sent to Cadiz—
   A pretty town, I recollect it well—
'T is there the mart of the colonial trade is,
   (Or was, before Peru learned to rebel)
And such sweet girls—I mean, such graceful ladies,
   Their very walk would make your bosom swell;
I can't describe it, though so much it strike,
Nor liken it—I never saw the like:

VI

An Arab horse, a stately stag, a barb
   New broke, a camelopard, a gazelle,
No—none of these will do;—and then their garb!
   Their veil and petticoat—Alas! to dwell
Upon such things would very near absorb
   A canto—then their feet and ancles—well
Thank heaven I've got no metaphor quite ready,
(And so, my sober Muse—come, let's be steady—

VII

Chaste Muse!—(well, if you must, you must)—the
     veil
   Thrown back a moment with the glancing hand,
While the o'erpowering eye, that turns you pale,
   Flashes into the heart:—All sunny land
Of love! when I forget you, may I fail
   To—say my prayers—but never was there plann'd
A dress through which the eyes give such a volley,
Excepting the Venetian Fazzioli.*

VIII

But to our tale: the Donna Inez sent
   Her son to Cadiz only to embark;
To stay there had not answer'd her intent,
   But why?—we leave the reader in the dark—
'T was for a voyage the young man was meant,
   As if a Spanish ship were Noah's ark,
To wean him from the wickedness of earth,
And send him like a dove of promise forth.

* *Fazzioli*—literally, the little handkerchiefs—the veils most availing at St. Mark.[1]

[1] Required for covering the head on entering cathedrals.

IX

Don Juan bade his valet pack his things
   According to direction, then received
A lecture and some money: for four springs
   He was to travel; and though Inez grieved,
(As every kind of parting has its stings)
   She hoped he would improve—perhaps believed:
A letter, too, she gave (he never read it)
Of good advice—and two or three of credit.

X

In the mean time, to pass her hours away,
   Brave Inez now set up a Sunday school
For naughty children, who would rather play
   (Like truant rogues) the devil, or the fool;
Infants of three years old were taught that day,
   Dunces were whipped, or set upon a stool:
The great success of Juan's education
Spurr'd her to teach another generation.

XI

Juan embark'd—the ship got under way,
   The wind was fair, the water passing rough;
A devil of a sea rolls in that Bay,
   As I, who 've cross'd it oft, know well enough;
And, standing on the deck, the dashing spray
   Flies in one's face, and makes it weather-tough:
And there he stood to take, and take again,
His first—perhaps his last—farewell of Spain.

XII

I can't but say it is an awkward sight
   To see one's native land receding through
The growing waters; it unmans one quite,
   Especially when life is rather new:
I recollect Great Britain's coast looks white,
   But almost every other country's blue,
When gazing on them, mystified by distance,
We enter on our nautical existence.

XIII

So Juan stood, bewilder'd, on the deck:
   The wind sung, cordage strain'd, and sailors swore,
And the ship creak'd, the town became a speck,
   From which away so fair and fast they bore.
The best of remedies is a beef-steak
   Against sea-sickness; try it, sir, before
You sneer, and I assure you this is true,
For I have found it answer—so may you.

XIV

Don Juan stood, and, gazing from the stern,
   Beheld his native Spain receding far:
First partings form a lesson hard to learn,
   Even nations feel this when they go to war;
There is a sort of unexprest concern,
   A kind of shock that sets one's heart ajar,
At leaving even the most unpleasant people
And places, one keeps looking at the steeple.

XV

But Juan had got many things to leave,
   His mother, and a mistress, and no wife,
So that he had much better cause to grieve
   Than many persons more advanced in life;
And if we now and then a sigh must heave
   At quitting even those we quit in strife,
No doubt we weep for those the heart endears—
That is, till deeper griefs congeal our tears.

XVI

So Juan wept, as wept the captive Jews
   By Babel's waters, still remembering Sion:[2]
I 'd weep, but mine is not a weeping Muse,
   And such light griefs are not a thing to die on;
Young men should travel, if but to amuse
   Themselves; and the next time their servants tie on
Behind their carriages their new portmanteau,
Perhaps it may be lined with this my canto.[3]

XVII

And Juan wept, and much he sigh'd and thought,
While his salt tears dropp'd into the salt sea,
"Sweets to the sweet"; (I like so much to quote;
   You must excuse this extract, 't is where she,
The Queen of Denmark, for Ophelia brought
   Flowers to the grave); and, sobbing often, he
Reflected on his present situation,
And seriously resolved on reformation.

XVIII

"Farewell, my Spain! a long farewell!" he cried,
   "Perhaps I may revisit thee no more,
But die, as many an exiled heart hath died,
   Of its own thirst to see again thy shore:
Farewell, where Guadalquivir's waters glide!
   Farewell, my mother! and, since all is o'er,
Farewell, too, dearest Julia!"—(here he drew
Her letter out again, and read it through).

---

[2] Psalm 137.
[3] Unsold book pages were used to line trunks.

XIX

"And oh! if e'er I should forget, I swear—
  But that 's impossible, and cannot be—
Sooner shall this blue ocean melt to air,
  Sooner shall earth resolve itself to sea,
Than I resign thine image, Oh, my fair!
  Or think of any thing excepting thee;
A mind diseased no remedy can physic—"
(Here the ship gave a lurch, and he grew sea-sick.)

XX

"Sooner shall heaven kiss earth—"(here he fell sicker)
  "Oh Julia! what is every other woe?—
(For God's sake let me have a glass of liquor;
  Pedro, Battista, help me down below.)
Julia, my love!—(you rascal, Pedro, quicker)—
  Oh Julia!—(this curst vessel pitches so)—
Beloved Julia, hear me still beseeching!"
(Here he grew inarticulate with retching.)

XXI

He felt that chilling heaviness of heart,
  Or rather stomach, which, alas! attends,
Beyond the best apothecary's art,
  The loss of love, the treachery of friends,
Or death of those we dote on, when a part
  Of us dies with them as each fond hope ends:
No doubt he would have been much more pathetic,
But the sea acted as a strong emetic.

XXII

Love 's a capricious power; I 've known it hold
  Out through a fever caused by its own heat,
But be much puzzled by a cough and cold,
  And find a quinsy very hard to treat;
Against all noble maladies he 's bold,
  But vulgar illnesses don't like to meet,
Nor that a sneeze should interrupt his sigh,
Nor inflammation redden his blind eye.

XXIII

But worst of all is nausea, or a pain
  About the lower region of the bowels;
Love, who heroically breathes a vein,[4]
  Shrinks from the application of hot towels,
And purgatives are dangerous to his reign,
  Sea-sickness death: his love was perfect, how else
Could Juan's passion, while the billows roar,
Resist his stomach, ne'er at sea before?

---

[4] Byron apparently has in mind a story about a father who sucked his child's blood when it would not flow freely during a bleeding.

XXIV

The ship, call'd the most holy "Trinidada,"
  Was steering duly for the port Leghorn;
For there the Spanish family Moncada
  Were settled long ere Juan's sire was born:
They were relations, and for them he had a
  Letter of introduction, which the morn
Of his departure had been sent him by
His Spanish friends for those in Italy.

XXV

His suite consisted of three servants and
  A tutor, the licentiate Pedrillo,
Who several languages did understand,
  But now lay sick and speechless on his pillow,
And, rocking in his hammock, long'd for land,
  His headache being increased by every billow;
And the waves oozing through the port-hole made
His birth a little damp, and him afraid.

XXVI

'T was not without some reason, for the wind
  Increased at night, until it blew a gale;
And though 't was not much to a naval mind,
  Some landsmen would have look'd a little pale,
For sailors are, in fact, a different kind:
  At sunset they began to take in sail,
For the sky show'd it would come on to blow,
And carry away, perhaps, a mast or so.[5]

XXVII

At one o'clock the wind with sudden shift
  Threw the ship right into the trough of the sea,
Which struck her aft, and made an awkward rift,
  Started the stern-post, also shatter'd the
Whole of her stern-frame, and, ere she could lift
  Herself from out her present jeopardy
The rudder tore away: 't was time to sound
The pumps, and there were four feet water found.

XXVIII

One gang of people instantly was put
  Upon the pumps, and the remainder set
To get up part of the cargo, and what not,
  But they could not come at the leak as yet;
At last they did get at it really, but
  Still their salvation was an even bet:
The water rushed through in a way quite puzzling,
While they thrust sheets, shirts, jackets, bales of
[muslin,

---

[5] Almost all the details are taken from Sir John Graham Dalyell's *Shipwrecks and Disasters at Sea* (1812).

XXIX

Into the opening; but all such ingredients
  Would have been vain, and they must have gone
Despite of all their efforts and expedients,   [down,
  But for the pumps: I'm glad to make them known
To all the brother tars who may have need hence,
  For fifty tons of water were upthrown
By them per hour, and they had all been undone
But for the maker, Mr. Mann, of London.

XXX

As day advanced the weather seem'd to abate,
  And then the leak they reckon'd to reduce,
And keep the ship afloat, though three feet yet
  Kept two hand and one chain-pump still in use.
The wind blew fresh again: as it grew late
  A squall came on, and while some guns broke loose,
A gust—which all descriptive power transcends—
Laid with one blast the ship on her beam ends.

XXXI

There she lay, motionless, and seem'd upset;
  The water left the hold, and wash'd the decks,
And made a scene men do not soon forget;
  For they remember battles, fires, and wrecks,
Or any other thing that brings regret,
  Or breaks their hopes, or hearts, or heads, or necks;
Thus drownings are much talk'd of by the divers
And swimmers who may chance to be survivors.

XXXII

Immediately the masts were cut away,
  Both main and mizen; first the mizen went,
The main-mast follow'd: but the ship still lay
  Like a mere log, and baffled our intent.
Foremast and bowsprit were cut down, and they
  Eased her at last (although we never meant
To part with all till every hope was blighted),
And then with violence the old ship righted.

XXXIII

It may be easily supposed, while this
  Was going on, some people were unquiet,
That passengers would find it much amiss
  To lose their lives as well as spoil their diet;
That even the able seaman, deeming his
  Days nearly o'er, might be disposed to riot,
As upon such occasions tars will ask
For grog, and sometimes drink rum from the cask.

XXXIV

There's nought, no doubt; so much the spirit calms
  As rum and true religion: thus it was,
Some plunder'd, some drank spirits, some sung psalms,
  The high wind made the treble, and as bass
The hoarse harsh waves kept time; fright cured the
    qualms
  Of all the luckless landsmen's sea-sick maws:
Strange sounds of wailing, blasphemy, devotion,
Clamour'd in chorus to the roaring ocean.

XXXV

Perhaps more mischief had been done, but for
  Our Juan, who, with sense beyond his years,
Got to the spirit-room, and stood before
  It with a pair of pistols; and their fears,
As if Death were more dreadful by his door
  Of fire than water, spite of oaths and tears,
Kept still aloof the crew, who, ere they sunk;
Thought it would be becoming to die drunk.

XXXVI

"Give us more grog," they cried, "for it will be
  All one an hour hence." Juan answered, "No!
'Tis true that death awaits both you and me,
  But let us die like men, not sink below
Like brutes":—and thus his dangerous post kept he,
  And none liked to anticipate the blow;
And even Pedrillo, his most reverend tutor,
Was for some rum a disappointed suitor.

XXXVII

The good old gentleman was quite aghast,
  And made a loud and pious lamentation;
Repented all his sins, and made a last
  Irrevocable vow of reformation;
Nothing should tempt him more (this peril past)
  To quit his academic occupation,
In cloisters of the classic Salamanca,
To follow Juan's wake like Sancho Panca.

XXXVIII

But now there came a flash of hope once more; [gone,
  Day broke, and the wind lull'd: the masts were
The leak increased; shoals round her, but no shore,
  The vessel swam, yet still she held her own.
They tried the pumps again, and though before
  Their desperate efforts seemed all useless grown,
A glimpse of sunshine set some hands to bale—
The stronger pumped, the weaker thrumm'd a sail.

XXXIX

Under the vessel's keel the sail was past,
    And for the moment it had some effect;
But with a leak, and not a stick of mast,
    Nor rag of canvas, what could they expect?
But still 't is best to struggle to the last,
    'T is never too late to be wholly wreck'd;
And though 't is true that man can only die once,
'T is not so pleasant in the Gulf of Lyons.

XL

There winds and waves had hurl'd them and from
Without their will, they carried them away;   [thence,
For they were forced with steering to dispense,
    And never had as yet a quiet day
On which they might repose, or even commence
    A jurymast or rudder, or could say
The ship would swim an hour, which, by good luck,
Still swam—though not exactly like a duck.

XLI

The wind, in fact, perhaps, was rather less,
    But the ship labour'd so, they scarce could hope
To weather out much longer; the distress
    Was also great with which they had to cope
For want of water, and their solid mess
    Was scant enough: in vain the telescope
Was used—nor sail nor shore appeared in sight,
Nought but the heavy sea, and coming night.

XLII

Again the weather threaten'd,—again blew
    A gale, and in the fore and after hold
Water appear'd; yet though the people knew
    All this, the most were patient, and some bold,
Until the chains and leathers were worn through
    Of all our pumps:—a wreck complete she roll'd,
At mercy of the waves, whose mercies are
Like human beings during civil war.

XLIII

Then came the carpenter, at last, with tears
    In his rough eyes, and told the captain, he
Could do no more: he was a man in years,
    And long had voyaged through many a stormy sea.
And if he wept at length they were not fears
    That made his eyelids as a woman's be,
But he, poor fellow, had a wife and children,
Two things for dying people quite bewildering.

XLIV

The ship was evidently settling now
    Fast by the head; and, all distinction gone,
Some went to prayers again, and made a vow
    Of candles to their saints—but there were none
To pay them with; and some look'd o'er the bow;
    Some hoisted out the boats; and there was one
That begged Pedrillo for an absolution,
Who told him to be damn'd—in his confusion.

XLV

Some lash'd them in their hammocks; some put on
    Their best clothes, as if going to a fair;
Some cursed the day on which they saw the sun,
    And gnash'd their teeth, and, howling, tore their
And others went on as they had begun,   [hair;
    Getting the boats out, being well aware
That a tight boat will live in a rough sea,
Unless with breakers close beneath her lee.

XLVI

The worst of all was, that in their condition,
    Having been several days in great distress,
'T was difficult to get out such provision
    As now might render their long suffering less:
Men, even when dying, dislike inanition;
    Their stock was damaged by the weather's stress:
Two casks of biscuit, and a keg of butter,
Were all that could be thrown into the cutter.

XLVII

But in the long-boat they contrived to stow
    Some pounds of bread, though injured by the wet;
Water, a twenty-gallon cask or so;
    Six flasks of wine; and they contrived to get
A portion of their beef up from below,
    And with a piece of pork, moreover, met,
But scarce enough to serve them for a luncheon—
Then there was rum, eight gallons in a puncheon.

XLVIII

The other boats, the yawl and pinnace, had
    Been stove in the beginning of the gale;
And the long-boat's condition was but bad,
    As there were but two blankets for a sail,
And one oar for a mast, which a young lad
    Threw in by good luck over the ship's rail;
And two boats could not hold, far less be stored,
To save one half the people then on board.

XLIX

'T was twilight, and the sunless day went down
  Over the waste of waters; like a veil,
Which, if withdrawn, would but disclose the frown
  Of one whose hate is masked but to assail,
Thus to their hopeless eyes the night was shown,
  And grimly darkled o'er the faces pale,
And the dim desolate deep: twelve days had Fear
Been their familiar, and now Death was here.

L

Some trial had been making at a raft,
  With little hope in such a rolling sea,
A sort of thing at which one would have laugh'd,
  If any laughter at such times could be,
Unless with people who too much have quaff'd,
  And have a kind of wild and horrid glee,
Half epileptical, and half hysterical:—
Their preservation would have been a miracle.

LI

At half-past eight o'clock, booms, hencoops, spars,
  And all things, for a chance, had been cast loose,
That still could keep afloat the struggling tars,
  For yet they strove, although of no great use:
There was no light in heaven but a few stars,
  The boats put off o'ercrowded with their crews;
She gave a heel, and then a lurch to port,
And, going down head foremost—sunk, in short.

LII

Then rose from sea to sky the wild farewell,
  Then shriek'd the timid, and stood still the brave,—
Then some leap'd overboard with dreadful yell,
  As eager to anticipate their grave;
And the sea yawn'd around her like a hell,
  And down she suck'd with her the whirling wave,
Like one who grapples with his enemy,
And strives to strangle him before he die.

LIII

And first one universal shriek there rush'd,
  Louder than the loud ocean, like a crash
Of echoing thunder; and then all was hush'd,
  Save the wild wind and the remorseless dash
Of billows; but at intervals there gush'd,
  Accompanied by a convulsive splash,
A solitary shriek, the bubbling cry
Of some strong swimmer in his agony.

LIV

The boats, as stated, had got off before,
  And in them crowded several of the crew;
And yet their present hope was hardly more
  Than what it had been, for so strong it blew
There was slight chance of reaching any shore;
  And then they were too many, though so few—
Nine in the cutter, thirty in the boat,
Were counted in them when they got afloat.

LV

All the rest perished; near two hundred souls
  Had left their bodies; and what's worse, alas!
When over Catholics the ocean rolls,
  They must wait several weeks before a mass
Takes off one peck of purgatorial coals,
  Because, till people know what's come to pass,
They won't lay out their money on the dead—
It costs three francs for every mass that's said.

LVI

Juan got into the long-boat, and there
  Contrived to help Pedrillo to a place;
It seem'd as if they had exchanged their care,
  For Juan wore the magisterial face
Which courage gives, while poor Pedrillo's pair
  Of eyes were crying for their owner's case:
Battista, though, (a name call'd shortly Tita),
Was lost by getting at some aqua-vita.

LVII

Pedro, his valet, too, he tried to save,
  But the same cause, conducive to his loss,
Left him so drunk, he jump'd into the wave,
  As o'er the cutter's edge he tried to cross,
And so he found a wine-and-watery grave;
  They could not rescue him although so close,
Because the sea ran higher every minute,
And for the boat—the crew kept crowding in it.

LVIII

A small old spaniel,—which had been Don Jóse's,
  His father's, whom he loved, as ye may think,
For on such things the memory reposes
  With tenderness—stood howling on the brink,
Knowing, (dogs have such intellectual noses!)
  No doubt, the vessel was about to sink;
And Juan caught him up, and ere he stepped
Off threw him in, then after him he leap'd.

LIX

He also stuff'd his money where he could
  About his person, and Pedrillo's too,
Who let him do, in fact, whate'er he would,
  Not knowing what himself to say, or do,
As every rising wave his dread renew'd;
  But Juan, trusting they might still get through,
And deeming there were remedies for any ill,
Thus re-embark'd his tutor and his spaniel.

LX

'T was a rough night, and blew so stiffly yet,
  That the sail was becalm'd between the seas,
Though on the wave's high top too much to set,
  They dared not take it in for all the breeze;
Each sea curl'd o'er the stern, and kept them wet,
  And made them bale without a moment's ease,
So that themselves as well as hopes were damp'd,
And the poor little cutter quickly swamp'd.

LXI

Nine souls more went in her: the long-boat still
  Kept above water, with an oar for mast,
Two blankets stitched together, answering ill
  Instead of sail, were to the oar made fast:
Though every wave roll'd menacing to fill,
  And present peril all before surpass'd,
They grieved for those who perish'd with the cutter,
And also for the biscuit-casks and butter.

LXII

The sun rose red and fiery, a sure sign
  Of the continuance of the gale: to run
Before the sea until it should grow fine,
  Was all that for the present could be done:
A few tea-spoonfuls of their rum and wine
  Were served out to the people, who begun
To faint, and damaged bread wet through the bags,
And most of them had little clothes but rags.

LXIII

They counted thirty, crowded in a space
  Which left scarce room for motion or exertion;
They did their best to modify their case, [immersion,
  One half sate up, though numb'd with the
While t' other half were laid down in their place,
  At watch and watch; thus, shivering like the tertian
Ague in its cold fit, they fill'd their boat,
With nothing but the sky for a great coat.

LXIV

'T is very certain the desire of life
  Prolongs it: this is obvious to physicians,
When patients, neither plagued with friends nor wife,
  Survive through very desperate conditions,
Because they still can hope, nor shines the knife
  Nor shears of Atropos [6] before their visions:
Despair of all recovery spoils longevity,
And makes men's miseries of alarming brevity.

LXV

'T is said that persons living on annuities
  Are longer lived than others,—God knows why,
Unless to plague the grantors,—yet so true it is,
  That some, I really think, *do* never die:
Of any creditors the worst a Jew it is,
  And *that 's* their mode of furnishing supply:
In my young days they lent me cash that way,
Which I found very troublesome to pay.

LXVI

'T is thus with people in an open boat,
  They live upon the love of life, and bear
More than can be believed, or even thought,
  And stand like rocks the tempest's wear and tear;
And hardship still has been the sailor's lot,
  Since Noah's ark went cruising here and there;
She had a curious crew as well as cargo,
Like the first old Greek privateer, the Argo. [7]

LXVII

But man is a carnivorous production,
  And must have meals, at least one meal a day;
He cannot live, like woodcocks, upon suction,
  But, like the shark and tiger, must have prey;
Although his anatomical construction
  Bears vegetables, in a grumbling way,
Your labouring people think, beyond all question,
Beef, veal, and mutton, better for digestion.

LXVIII

And thus it was with this our hapless crew;
  For on the third day there came on a calm,
And though at first their strength it might renew,
  And lying on their weariness like balm,
Lulled them like turtles sleeping on the blue
  Of ocean, when they woke they felt a qualm,
And fell all ravenously on their provision,
Instead of hoarding it with due precision.

---

6 One of the three Fates who cut the thread of life.
7 Used by Jason in seeking the Golden Fleece.

LXIX

The consequence was easily foreseen—
　　They ate up all they had, and drank their wine,
In spite of all remonstrances, and then
　　On what, in fact, next day were they to dine?
They hoped the wind would rise, these foolish men!
　　And carry them to shore; these hopes were fine,
But as they had but one oar, and that brittle,
It would have been more wise to save their victual.

LXX

The fourth day came, but not a breath of air,
　　And Ocean slumber'd like an unwean'd child:
The fifth day, and their boat lay floating there,
　　The sea and sky were blue, and clear, and mild—
With their one oar (I wish they had had a pair)
　　What could they do? and hunger's rage grew wild:
So Juan's spaniel, spite of his entreating,
Was kill'd, and portion'd out for present eating.

LXXI

On the sixth day they fed upon his hide,
　　And Juan, who had still refused, because
The creature was his father's dog that died,
　　Now feeling all the vulture in his jaws,
With some remorse received (though first denied)
　　As a great favour one of the fore-paws,
Which he divided with Pedrillo, who
Devour'd it, longing for the other too.

LXXII

The seventh day, and no wind—the burning sun
　　Blister'd and scorch'd, and, stagnant on the sea,
They lay like carcasses; and hope was none,
　　Save in the breeze that came not; savagely
They glared upon each other—all was done,
　　Water, and wine, and food,—and you might see
The longings of the cannibal arise
(Although they spoke not) in their wolfish eyes.

LXXIII

At length one whisper'd his companion, who
　　Whisper'd another, and thus it went round,
And then into a hoarser murmur grew,
　　An ominous, and wild, and desperate sound;
And when his comrade's thought each sufferer knew,
　　'T was but his own, suppress'd till now, he found:
And out they spoke of lots for flesh and blood,
And who should die to be his fellow's food.

LXXIV

But ere they came to this, they that day shared
　　Some leathern caps, and what remain'd of shoes;
And then they looked around them, and despaired,
　　And none to be the sacrifice would choose;
At length the lots were torn up, and prepared,
　　But of materials that much shock the Muse—
Having no paper, for the want of better,
They took by force from Juan Julia's letter.

LXXV

The lots were made, and mark'd, and mix'd, and
　　In silent horror, and their distribution　　[handed,
Lull'd even the savage hunger which demanded,
　　Like the Promethean vulture, this pollution;
None in particular had sought or plann'd it,
　　'T was nature gnaw'd them to this resolution,
By which none were permitted to be neuter—
And the lot fell on Juan's luckless tutor.

LXXVI

He but requested to be bled to death:
　　The surgeon had his instruments, and bled
Pedrillo, and so gently ebb'd his breath,
　　You hardly could perceive when he was dead.
He died as born, a Catholic in faith,
　　Like most in the belief in which they 're bred,
And first a little crucifix he kiss'd,
And then held out his jugular and wrist.

LXXVII

The surgeon, as there was no other fee,
　　Had his first choice of morsels for his pains;
But being thirstiest at the moment, he
　　Preferr'd a draught from the fast-flowing veins:
Part was divided, part thrown in the sea,
　　And such things as the entrails and the brains
Regaled two sharks, who followed o'er the billow—
The sailors ate the rest of poor Pedrillo.

LXXVIII

The sailors ate him, all save three or four,
　　Who were not quite so fond of animal food;
To these was added Juan, who, before
　　Refusing his own spaniel, hardly could
Feel now his appetite increased much more;
　　'T was not to be expected that he should,
Even in extremity of their disaster,
Dine with them on his pastor and his master.

LXXIX

'T was better that he did not; for, in fact,
    The consequence was awful in the extreme:
For they, who were most ravenous in the act,
    Went raging mad—Lord! how they did blaspheme!
And foam and roll, with strange convulsions rack'd,
    Drinking salt-water like a mountain-stream,
Tearing, and grinning, howling, screeching, swearing,
And, with hyaena-laughter, died despairing.

LXXX

Their numbers were much thinn'd by this infliction,
    And all the rest were thin enough, heaven knows;
And some of them had lost their recollection,
    Happier than they who still perceived their woes;
But others ponder'd on a new dissection,
    As if not warn'd sufficiently by those
Who had already perish'd, suffering madly,
For having used their appetites so sadly.

LXXXI

And next they thought upon the master's mate,
    As fattest; but he saved himself, because,
Besides being much averse from such a fate,
    There were some other reasons; the first was,
He had been rather indisposed of late,
    And that which chiefly proved his saving clause,
Was a small present made to him at Cadiz,
By general subscription of the ladies.

LXXXII

Of poor Pedrillo something still remain'd,
    But was used sparingly,—some were afraid,
And others still their appetites constrain'd,
    Or but at times a little supper made;
All except Juan, who throughout abstain'd,
    Chewing a piece of bamboo, and some lead:
At length they caught two boobies, and a noddy,[8]
And then they left off eating the dead body.

LXXXIII

And if Pedrillo's fate should shocking be,
    Remember Ugolino condescends
To eat the head of his arch-enemy
    The moment after he politely ends
His tale; if foes be food in hell, at sea
    'T is surely fair to dine upon our friends,
When shipwreck's short allowance grows too scanty,
Without being much more horrible than Dante.[9]

---

[8] Sea birds.
[9] In the *Inferno*, Ugolino leaves off gnawing the skull of his enemy long enough to tell his tale.

LXXXIV

And the same night there fell a shower of rain,   [earth
    For which their mouths gaped, like the cracks of
When dried to summer dust; till taught by pain,
    Men really know not what good water 's worth;
If you had been in Turkey or in Spain,
    Or with a famish'd boat's-crew had your birth,
Or in the desert heard the camel's bell,
You 'd wish yourself where Truth is—in a well.

LXXXV

It poured down torrents, but they were no richer
    Until they found a ragged piece of sheet,
Which served them as a sort of spongy pitcher,
    And when they deem'd its moisture was complete,
They wrung it out, and though a thirsty ditcher
    Might not have thought the scanty draught so sweet
As a full pot of porter, to their thinking
They ne'er till now had known the joys of drinking.

LXXXVI

And their baked lips, with many a bloody crack,
    Suck'd in the moisture, which like nectar stream'd;
Their throats were ovens, their swoln tongues were
        black,
    As the rich man's in hell, who vainly scream'd
To beg the beggar, who could not rain back
    A drop of dew, when every drop had seem'd
To taste of heaven—If this be true, indeed,
Some Christians have a comfortable creed.

LXXXVII

There were two fathers in this ghastly crew,
    And with them their two sons, of whom the one
Was more robust and hardy to the view,
    But he died early; and when he was gone,
His nearest messmate told his sire, who threw
    One glance on him, and said, "Heaven's will be
I can do nothing," and he saw him thrown   [done!
Into the deep without a tear or groan.

LXXXVIII

The other father had a weaklier child,
    Of a soft cheek, and aspect delicate;
But the boy bore up long, and with a mild
    And patient spirit held aloof his fate;
Little he said, and now and then he smiled,
    As if to win a part from off the weight
He saw increasing on his father's heart,
With the deep deadly thought, that they must part.

LXXXIX

And o'er him bent his sire, and never raised
  His eyes from off his face, but wiped the foam
From his pale lips, and ever on him gazed,   [come,
  And when the wished-for shower at length was
And the boy's eyes, which the dull film half glazed,
  Brighten'd, and for a moment seem'd to roam,
He squeezed from out a rag some drops of rain
Into his dying child's mouth—but in vain.

XC

The boy expired—the father held the clay,
  And look'd upon it long, and when at last
Death left no doubt, and the dead burthen lay
  Stiff on his heart, and pulse and hope were past,
He watch'd it wistfully, until away
  'T was borne by the rude wave wherein 't was cast;
Then he himself sunk down all dumb and shivering,
And gave no sign of life, save his limbs quivering.

XCI

Now overhead a rainbow, bursting through
  The scattering clouds, shone, spanning the dark sea,
Resting its bright base on the quivering blue;
  And all within its arch appear'd to be
Clearer than that without, and its wide hue
  Wax'd broad and waving, like a banner free,
Then changed like to a bow that's bent, and then
Forsook the dim eyes of these shipwreck'd men.

XCII

It changed, of course; a heavenly cameleon,
  The airy child of vapour and the sun,
Brought forth in purple, cradled in vermilion,
  Baptized in molten gold, and swathed in dun,
Glittering like crescents o'er a Turk's pavilion,
  And blending every colour into one,
Just like a black eye in a recent scuffle
(For sometimes we must box without the muffle).

XCIII

Our shipwreck'd seamen thought it a good omen—
  It is as well to think so, now and then;
'T was an old custom of the Greek and Roman,
  And may become of great advantage when
Folks are discouraged; and most surely no men
  Had greater need to nerve themselves again
Than these, and so this rainbow looked like hope—
Quite a celestial kaleidoscope.

XCIV

About this time a beautiful white bird,
  Webfooted, not unlike a dove in size
And plumage, (probably it might have err'd
  Upon its course), pass'd oft before their eyes,
And tried to perch, although it saw and heard
  The men within the boat, and in this guise
It came and went, and flutter'd round them till
Night fell:—this seem'd a better omen still.

XCV

But in this case I also must remark,
  'T was well this bird of promise did not perch,
Because the tackle of our shatter'd bark
  Was not so safe for roosting as a church;
And had it been the dove from Noah's ark,
  Returning there from her successful search,
Which in their way that moment chanced to fall
They would have eat her, olive-branch and all.

XCVI

With twilight it again come on to blow,
  But now with violence; the stars shone out,
The boat made way; yet now they were so low,
  They knew not where or what they were about;
Some fancied they saw land, and some said "No!"
  The frequent fog-banks gave them cause to doubt—
Some swore that they heard breakers, others guns,
And all mistook about the latter once.

XCVII

As morning broke, the light wind died away,
  When he who had the watch sung out and swore,
If 't was not land that rose with the sun's ray,
  He wish'd that land he never might see more;
And the rest rubbed their eyes and saw a bay,
  Or thought they saw, and shaped their course for
For shore it was, and gradually grew   [shore;
Distinct, and high, and palpable to view.

XCVIII

And then of these some part burst into tears,
  And others, looking with a stupid stare,
Could not yet separate their hopes from fears,
  And seem'd as if they had no further care;
While a few pray'd—(the first time for some years)—
  And at the bottom of the boat three were
Asleep; they shook them by the hand and head,
And tried to awaken them, but found them dead.

XCIX

The day before, fast sleeping on the water,
  They found a turtle of the hawk's-bill kind,
And by good fortune gliding softly, caught her,
  Which yielded a day's life, and to their mind
Proved even still a more nutritious matter,
  Because it left encouragement behind:
They thought that in such perils, more than chance
Had sent them this for their deliverance.

C

The land appear'd a high and rocky coast,
  And higher grew the mountains as they drew,
Set by a current, toward it: they were lost
  In various conjectures, for none knew
To what part of the earth they had been tost,
  So changeable had been the winds that blew;
Some thought it was Mount Aetna, some the highlands
Of Candia, Cyprus, Rhodes, or other islands.

CI

Meantime the current, with a rising gale,
  Still set them onwards to the welcome shore,
Like Charon's bark of spectres, dull and pale:
  Their living freight was now reduced to four,
And three dead, whom their strength could not avail
  To heave into the deep with those before,
Though the two sharks still follow'd them, and dash'd
The spray into their faces as they splash'd.

CII

Famine, despair, cold, thirst, and heat, had done
  Their work on them by turns, and thinn'd them to
Such things a mother had not known her son
  Amidst the skeletons of that gaunt crew;
By night chill'd, by day scorch'd, thus one by one
  They perish'd, until wither'd to these few,
But chiefly by a species of self-slaughter,
In washing down Pedrillo with salt water.

CIII

As they drew nigh the land, which now was seen
  Unequal in its aspect here and there,
They felt the freshness of its growing green,
  That waved in forest-tops, and smooth'd the air,
And fell upon their glazed eyes like a screen
  From glistening waves, and skies so hot and bare—
Lovely seem'd any object that should sweep
Away the vast, salt, dread, eternal deep.

CIV

The shore look'd wild, without a trace of man,
  And girt by formidable waves; but they
Were mad for land, and thus their course they ran,
  Though right ahead the roaring breakers lay:
A reef between them also now began
  To show its boiling surf and bounding spray,
But finding no place for their landing better,
They ran the boat for shore, and overset her.

CV

But in his native stream, the Guadalquivir,
  Juan to lave his youthful limbs was wont;
And having learnt to swim in that sweet river,
  Had often turn'd the art to some account:
A better swimmer you could scarce see ever,
  He could, perhaps, have pass'd the Hellespont,
As once (a feat on which ourselves we prided)
Leander, Mr. Ekenhead, and I did.[10]

CVI

So here, though faint, emaciated, and stark,
  He buoy'd his boyish limbs, and strove to ply
With the quick wave, and gain, ere it was dark,
  The beach which lay before him, high and dry:
The greatest danger here was from a shark,
  That carried off his neighbour by the thigh;
As for the other two, they could not swim,
So nobody arrived on shore but him.

CVII

Nor yet had he arrived but for the oar,
  Which, providentially for him, was wash'd
Just as his feeble arms could strike no more,
  And the hard wave o'erwhelm'd him as 't was
Within his grasp; he clung to it, and sore   [dash'd
  The waters beat while he thereto was lash'd;
At last, with swimming, wading, scrambling, he
Roll'd on the beach, half-senseless, from the sea:

CVIII

There, breathless, with his digging nails he clung
  Fast to the sand, lest the returning wave,
From whose reluctant roar his life he wrung,
  Should suck him back to her insatiate grave:
And there he lay, full length, where he was flung,
  Before the entrance of a cliff-worn cave,
With just enough of life to feel its pain,
And deem that it was saved, perhaps, in vain.

---

[10] See Byron's *Written After Swimming from Sestos to Abydos*,
p. 557.

CIX

With slow and staggering effort he arose,
　But sunk again upon his bleeding knee
And quivering hand; and then he look'd for those
　Who long had been his mates upon the sea,
But none of them appear'd to share his woes,
　Save one, a corpse from out the famish'd three,
Who died two days before, and now had found
An unknown barren beach for burial ground.

CX

And as he gazed, his dizzy brain spun fast,
　And down he sunk; and as he sunk, the sand
Swam round and round, and all his senses pass'd:
　He fell upon his side, and his stretch'd hand
Droop'd dripping on the oar (their jury-mast)
　And, like a wither'd lily, on the land
His slender frame and pallid aspect lay,
As fair a thing as e'er was formed of clay.

CXI

How long in his damp trance young Juan lay
　He knew not, for the earth was gone for him,
And Time had nothing more of night nor day
　For his congealing blood, and senses dim;
And how this heavy faintness pass'd away
　He knew not, till each painful pulse and limb,
And tingling vein, seem'd throbbing back to life,
For Death, though vanquish'd, still retired with strife.

CXII

His eyes he open'd, shut, again unclosed,
　For all was doubt and dizziness; he thought
He still was in the boat, and had but dozed,
　And felt again with his despair o'erwrought,
And wish'd it death in which he had reposed,
　And then once more his feelings back were brought,
And slowly by his swimming eyes was seen
A lovely female face of seventeen.

CXIII

'T was bending close o'er his, and the small mouth
　Seem'd almost prying into his for breath;
And chafing him, the soft warm hand of youth
　Recall'd his answering spirits back from death:
And, bathing his chill temples, tried to soothe
　Each pulse to animation, till beneath
Its gentle touch and trembling care, a sigh
To these kind efforts made a low reply.

CXIV

Then was the cordial pour'd, and mantle flung
　Around his scarce-clad limbs; and the fair arm
Raised higher the faint head which o'er it hung;
　And her transparent cheek, all pure and warm,
Pillow'd his death-like forehead; then she wrung
　His dewy curls, long drench'd by every storm;
And watch'd with eagerness each throb that drew
A sigh from his heaved bosom—and hers, too.

CXV

And lifting him with care into the cave,
　The gentle girl, and her attendant,—one
Young, yet her elder, and of brows less grave,
　And more robust of figure,—then begun
To kindle fire, and as the new flames gave
　Light to the rocks that roof'd them, which the sun
Had never seen, the maid, or whatsoe'er
She was, appear'd, distinct, and tall, and fair.

CXVI

Her brow was overhung with coins of gold,
　That sparkled o'er the auburn of her hair,
Her clustering hair, whose longer locks were roll'd
　In braids behind; and though her stature were
Even of the highest for a female mould,
　They nearly reach'd her heel; and in her air
There was a something which bespoke command,
As one who was a lady in the land.

CXVII

Her hair, I said, was auburn; but her eyes
　Were black as death, their lashes the same hue,
Of downcast length, in whose silk shadow lies
　Deepest attraction, for when to the view
Forth from its raven fringe the full glance flies,
　Ne'er with such force the swiftest arrow flew;
'T is as the snake late coil'd, who pours his length,
And hurls at once his venom and his strength.

CXVIII

Her brow was white and low, her cheek's pure dye
　Like twilight rosy still with the set sun;
Short upper lip—sweet lips! that make us sigh
　Ever to have seen such; for she was one
Fit for the model of a statuary,
　(A race of mere impostors, when all's done—
I 've seen much finer women, ripe and real,
Than all the nonsense of their stone ideal).

CXIX

I 'll tell you why I say so, for 't is just
　One should not rail without a decent cause:
There was an Irish lady, to whose bust
　I ne'er saw justice done, and yet she was
A frequent model; and if e'er she must
　Yield to stern Time and Nature's wrinkling laws,
They will destroy a face which mortal thought
Ne'er compass'd, nor less mortal chisel wrought.

CXX

And such was she, the lady of the cave:
　Her dress was very different from the Spanish,
Simpler, and yet of colours not so grave;
　For, as you know, the Spanish women banish
Bright hues when out of doors, and yet, while wave
　Around them (what I hope will never vanish)
The basquina and the mantilla, they [11]
Seem at the same time mystical and gay.

CXXI

But with our damsel this was not the case:
　Her dress was many-colour'd, finely spun;
Her locks curl'd negligently round her face,
　But through them gold and gems profusely shone:
Her girdle sparkled, and the richest lace
　Flow'd in her veil, and many a precious stone
Flash'd on her little hand; but, what was shocking,
Her small snow feet had slippers, but no stocking.

CXXII

The other female's dress was not unlike,
　But of inferior materials; she
Had not so many ornaments to strike,
　Her hair had silver only, bound to be
Her dowry; and her veil, in form alike,
　Was coarser; and her air, though firm, less free;
Her hair was thicker, but less long; her eyes
As black, but quicker, and of smaller size.

CXXIII

And these two tended him, and cheer'd him both
　With food and raiment, and those soft attentions,
Which are (as I must own) of female growth,
　And have ten thousand delicate inventions:
They made a most superior mess of broth,
　A thing which poesy but seldom mentions,
But the best dish that e'er was cook'd since Homer's
Achilles order'd dinner for new comers. [12]

---

[11] The basquiña is an outer skirt, the mantilla a shawl.
[12] A meal prepared for the Greek ambassadors: *Iliad,* IX.

CXXIV

I'll tell you who they were, this female pair,
　Lest they should seem princesses in disguise;
Besides, I hate all mystery, and that air
　Of clap-trap, which your recent poets prize;
And so, in short, the girls they really were
　They shall appear before your curious eyes,
Mistress and maid; the first was only daughter
Of an old man, who lived upon the water.

CXXV

A fisherman he had been in his youth,
　And still a sort of fisherman was he;
But other speculations were, in sooth,
　Added to his connexion with the sea,
Perhaps not so respectable, in truth:
　A little smuggling, and some piracy,
Left him, at last, the sole of many masters
Of an ill-gotten million of piastres.

CXXVI

A fisher, therefore, was he,—though of men,
　Like Peter the Apostle,—and he fished
For wandering merchant-vessels, now and then,
　And sometimes caught as many as he wish'd;
The cargoes he confiscated, and gain
　He sought in the slave-market too, and dish'd
Full many a morsel for that Turkish trade,
By which, no doubt, a good deal may be made.

CXXVII

He was a Greek, and on his isle had built
　(One of the wild and smaller Cyclades)
A very handsome house from out his guilt,
　And there he lived exceedingly at ease;
Heaven knows what cash he got, or blood he spilt,
　A sad old fellow was he, if you please;
But this I know, it was a spacious building,
Full of barbaric carving, paint, and gilding.

CXXVIII

He had an only daughter, called Haidée,
　The greatest heiress of the Eastern Isles;
Besides, so very beautiful was she,
　Her dowry was as nothing to her smiles:
Still in her teens, and like a lovely tree
　She grew to womanhood, and between whiles
Rejected several suitors, just to learn
How to accept a better in his turn.

CXXIX

And walking out upon the beach, below
   The cliff, towards sunset, on that day she found,
Insensible,—not dead, but nearly so,—
   Don Juan, almost famish'd, and half drown'd;
But being naked, she was shock'd, you know,
   Yet deem'd herself in common pity bound,
As far as in her lay, "to take him in,
A stranger" dying, with so white a skin.[13]

CXXX

But taking him into her father's house
   Was not exactly the best way to save,
But like conveying to the cat the mouse,
   Or people in a trance into their grave;
Because the good old man had so much "νοῦς,"[14]
   Unlike the honest Arab thieves so brave,
He would have hospitably cured the stranger,
And sold him instantly when out of danger.

CXXXI

And therefore, with her maid, she thought it best
   (A virgin always on her maid relies)
To place him in the cave for present rest:
   And when, at last, he open'd his black eyes,
Their charity increased about their guest;
   And their compassion grew to such a size,
It open'd half the turnpike-gates to heaven—
(St. Paul says 't is the toll which must be given).

CXXXII

They made a fire, but such a fire as they
   Upon the moment could contrive with such
Materials as were cast up round the bay,
   Some broken planks, and oars, that to the touch
Were nearly tinder, since so long they lay
   A mast was almost crumbled to a crutch;
But, by God's grace, here wrecks were in such plenty,
That there was fuel to have furnish'd twenty.

CXXXIII

He had a bed of furs, and a pelisse,
   For Haidée stripp'd her sables off to make
His couch; and, that he might be more at ease,
   And warm, in case by chance he should awake,
They also gave a petticoat apiece,
   She and her maid, and promised by day-break
To pay him a fresh visit, with a dish
For breakfast, of eggs, coffee, bread, and fish.

CXXXIV

And thus they left him to his lone repose:
   Juan slept like a top, or like the dead,
Who sleep at last, perhaps, (God only knows)
   Just for the present; and in his lull'd head
Not even a vision of his former woes
   Throbb'd in accursed dreams, which sometimes
Unwelcome visions of our former years,   [spread
Till the eye, cheated, opens thick with tears.

CXXXV

Young Juan slept all dreamless:—but the maid,
   Who smooth'd his pillow, as she left the den
Look'd back upon him, and a moment staid,
   And turn'd, believing that he call'd again.
He slumber'd; yet she thought, at least she said,
   (The heart will slip even as the tongue and pen)
He had pronounced her name—but she forgot
That at this moment Juan knew it not.

CXXXVI

And pensive to her father's house she went,
   Enjoining silence strict to Zoe, who
Better than her knew what, in fact, she meant,
   She being wiser by a year or two:
A year or two 's an age when rightly spent,
   And Zoe spent hers, as most women do,
In gaining all that useful sort of knowledge
Which is acquired in nature's good old college.

CXXVII

The morn broke, and found Juan slumbering still
   Fast in his cave, and nothing clash'd upon
His rest; the rushing of the neighbouring rill,
   And the young beams of the excluded sun,
Troubled him not, and he might sleep his fill;
   And need he had of slumber yet, for none
Had suffer'd more—his hardships were comparative
To those related in my grand-dad's Narrative.[15]

CXXXVIII

Not so Haidée; she sadly toss'd and tumbled,
   And started from her sleep, and, turning o'er,
Dream'd of a thousand wrecks, o'er which she
     stumbled,
   And handsome corpses strew'd upon the shore;
And woke her maid so early that she grumbled,
   And call'd her father's old slaves up, who swore
In several oaths—Armenian, Turk, and Greek,—
They knew not what to think of such a freak.

---

[13] The quotation is from Matthew 25:35, paraphrased.
[14] Sense, mind, spirit.

[15] *A Narrative of the Honourable John Byron*, etc. (1768): he was shipwrecked in Patagonia.

CXXXIX

But up she got, and up she made them get,
  With some pretence about the sun, that makes
Sweet skies just when he rises, or is set;
  And 't is, no doubt, a sight to see when breaks
Bright Phœbus, while the mountains still are wet
  With mist, and every bird with him awakes,
And night is flung off like a mourning suit
Worn for a husband, or some other brute.

CXL

I say, the sun is a most glorious sight,
  I 've seen him rise full oft, indeed of late
I have sat up on purpose all the night,
  Which hastens, as physicians say, one's fate;
And so all ye, who would be in the right
  In health and purse, begin your day to date
From day-break, and when coffin'd at fourscore,
Engrave upon the plate, you rose at four.

CXLI

And Haidée met the morning face to face;
  Her own was freshest, though a feverish flush
Had dyed it with the headlong blood, whose race
  From heart to cheek is curb'd into a blush,
Like to a torrent which a mountain's base,
  That overpowers some alpine river's rush,
Checks to a lake, whose waves in circles spread;
Or the Red Sea—but the sea is not red.

CXLII

And down the cliff the island virgin came,
  And near the cave her quick light footsteps drew,
While the sun smiled on her with his first flame,
  And young Aurora kiss'd her lips with dew,
Taking her for a sister; just the same
  Mistake you would have made on seeing the two,
Although the mortal, quite as fresh and fair,
Had all the advantage too of not being air.

CXLIII

And when into the cavern Haidée stepp'd
  All timidly, yet rapidly, she saw
That like an infant Juan sweetly slept;
  And then she stopp'd, and stood as if in awe,
(For sleep is awful) and on tiptoe crept
  And wrapt him closer, lest the air, too raw,
Should reach his blood, then o'er him still as death
Bent, with hush'd lips, that drank his scarce-drawn
                                                [breath.

CXLIV

And thus like to an angel o'er the dying
  Who die in righteousness, she lean'd; and there
All tranquilly the shipwreck'd boy was lying,
  As o'er him lay the calm and stirless air:
But Zoe the meantime some eggs was frying,
  Since, after all, no doubt the youthful pair
Must breakfast, and betimes—lest they should ask it,
She drew out her provision from the basket.

CXLV

She knew that the best feelings must have victual,
  And that a shipwreck'd youth would hungry be;
Besides, being less in love, she yawn'd a little,
  And felt her veins chill'd by the neighbouring sea;
And so, she cook'd their breakfast to a tittle;
  I can't say that she gave them any tea,
But there were eggs, fruit, coffee, bread, fish, honey,
With Scio wine,—and all for love, not money.

CXLVI

And Zoe, when the eggs were ready, and
  The coffee made, would fain have waken'd Juan;
But Haidée stopped her with her quick small hand,
  And without a word, a sign her finger drew on
Her lip, which Zoe needs must understand;
  And, the first breakfast spoilt, prepared a new one,
Because her mistress would not let her break
That sleep which seem'd as it would ne'er awake.

CXLVII

For still he lay, and on his thin worn cheek
  A purple hectic play'd like dying day
On the snow-tops of distant hills; the streak
  Of sufferance yet upon his forehead lay,   [weak;
Where the blue veins look'd shadowy, shrunk, and
  And his black curls were dewy with the spray,
Which weigh'd upon them yet, all damp and salt,
Mix'd with the stony vapours of the vault.

CXLVIII

And she bent o'er him, and he lay beneath,
  Hush'd as the babe upon its mother's breast,
Dropp'd as the willow when no winds can breathe,
  Lull'd like the depth of ocean when at rest,
Fair as the crowning rose of the whole wreath,
  Soft as the callow cygnet in its nest;
In short, he was a very pretty fellow,
Although his woes had turn'd him rather yellow.

CXLIX

He woke and gazed, and would have slept again,
  But the fair face which met his eye forbade
Those eyes to close, though weariness and pain
  Had further sleep a further pleasure made:
For woman's face was never form'd in vain
  For Juan, so that even when he pray'd
He turned from grisly saints, and martyrs hairy,
To the sweet portraits of the Virgin Mary.

CL

And thus upon his elbow he arose,
  And looked upon the lady, in whose cheek
The pale contended with the purple rose,
  As with an effort she began to speak;
Her eyes were eloquent, her words would pose,
  Although she told him, in good modern Greek,
With an Ionian accent, low and sweet,
That he was faint, and must not talk, but eat.

CLI

Now Juan could not understand a word,
  Being no Grecian; but he had an ear,
And her voice was the warble of a bird,
  So soft, so sweet, so delicately clear,
That finer, simpler music ne'er was heard;
  The sort of sound we echo with a tear,
Without knowing why—an overpowering tone,
Whence Melody descends as from a throne.

CLII

And Juan gazed as one who is awoke
  By a distant organ, doubting if he be
Not yet a dreamer, till the spell is broke
  By the watchman, or some such reality,
Or by one's early valet's cursed knock;
  At least it is a heavy sound to me,
Who like a morning slumber—for the night
Shows stars and women in a better light.

CLIII

And Juan, too, was help'd out from his dream,
  Or sleep, or whatsoe'er it was, by feeling
A most prodigious appetite: the steam
  Of Zoe's cookery no doubt was stealing
Upon his senses, and the kindling beam
  Of the new fire, which Zoe kept up, kneeling,
To stir her viands, made him quite awake
And long for food, but chiefly a beef-steak.

CLIV

But beef is rare within these oxless isles;
  Goat's flesh there is, no doubt, and kid, and mutton,
And, when a holiday upon them smiles,
  A joint upon their barbarous spits they put on:
But this occurs but seldom, between whiles,
  For some of these are rocks with scarce a hut on,
Others are fair and fertile, among which
This, though not large, was one of the most rich.

CLV

I say that beef is rare, and can't help thinking
  That the old fable of the Minotaur—
From which our modern morals, rightly shrinking,
  Condemn the royal lady's taste who wore
A cow's shape for a mask—was only (sinking
  The allegory) a mere type, no more,
That Pasiphae promoted breeding cattle,[16]
To make the Cretans bloodier in battle.

CLVI

For we all know that English people are
  Fed upon beef—I won't say much of beer,
Because 't is liquor only, and being far
  From this my subject, has no business here;
We know, too, they are very fond of war,
  A pleasure—like all pleasures—rather dear;
So were the Cretans—from which I infer,
That beef and battles both were owing to her.

CLVII

But to resume. The languid Juan raised
  His head upon his elbow, and he saw
A sight on which he had not lately gazed,
  As all his latter meals had been quite raw,
Three or four things, for which the Lord he praised,
  And, feeling still the famish'd vulture gnaw,
He fell upon whate'er was offer'd, like
A priest, a shark, an alderman, or pike.

CLVIII

He ate, and he was well supplied; and she,
  Who watch'd him like a mother, would have fed
Him past all bounds, because she smiled to see
  Such appetite in one she had deem'd dead:
But Zoe, being older than Haidée,
  Knew (by tradition, for she ne'er had read)
That famish'd people must be slowly nurst,
And fed by spoonfuls, else they always burst.

---

16 By the bull given her husband Minos of Crete, she gave birth to the Minotaur. See also Shelley's *Oedipus Tyrannus*, p. 931.

CLIX

And so she took the liberty to state,
    Rather by deeds than words, because the case
Was urgent, that the gentleman, whose fate
    Had made her mistress quit her bed to trace
The sea-shore at this hour, must leave his plate,
    Unless he wish'd to die upon the place—
She snatch'd it, and refused another morsel,
Saying, he had gorged enough to make a horse ill.

CLX

Next they—he being naked, save a tatter'd
    Pair of scarce decent trowsers—went to work,
And in the fire his recent rags they scatter'd,
    And dress'd him, for the present, like a Turk,
Or Greek—that is, although it not much matter'd,
    Omitting turban, slippers, pistols, dirk,—
They furnish'd him, entire, except some stitches,
With a clean shirt, and very spacious breeches.

CLXI

And then fair Haidée tried her tongue at speaking,
    But not a word could Juan comprehend,
Although he listened so that the young Greek in
    Her earnestness would ne'er have made an end;
And, as he interrupted not, went eking
    Her speech out to her protégé and friend,
Till pausing at the last her breath to take,
She saw he did not understand Romaic.[17]

CLXII

And then she had recourse to nods, and signs,
    And smiles, and sparkles of the speaking eye,
And read (the only book she could) the lines
    Of his fair face, and found, by sympathy,
The answer eloquent, where the soul shines
    And darts in one quick glance a long reply;
And thus in every look she saw exprest
A world of words, and things at which she guess'd.

CLXIII

And now, by dint of fingers and of eyes,
    And words repeated after her, he took
A lesson in her tongue; but by surmise,
    No doubt, less of her language than her look:
As he who studies fervently the skies
    Turns oftener to the stars than to his book,
Thus Juan learned his alpha beta better
From Haidée's glance than any graven letter.

<><><><><><><><><><><><><><><><><><><><><><><><><>
[17] I.e., modern Greek.

CLXIV

'T is pleasing to be school'd in a strange tongue
    By female lips and eyes—that is, I mean,
When both the teacher and the taught are young,
    As was the case, at least, where I have been; [wrong
They smile so when one 's right, and when one 's
    They smile still more, and then there intervene
Pressure of hands, perhaps even a chaste kiss;—
I learn'd the little that I know by this:

CLXV

That is, some words of Spanish, Turk, and Greek,
    Italian not at all, having no teachers;
Much English I cannot pretend to speak,
    Learning that language chiefly from its preachers,
Barrow, South, Tillotson, whom every week
    I study, also Blair, the highest reachers
Of eloquence in piety and prose—
I hate your poets, so read none of those.

CLXVI

As for the ladies, I have nought to say,
    A wanderer from the British world of fashion,
Where I, like other "dogs, have had my day,"
    Like other men too, may have had my passion—
But that, like other things, has pass'd away,
    And all her fools whom I *could* lay the lash on:
Foes, friends, men, women, now are nought to me
But dreams of what has been, no more to be.

CLXVII

Return we to Don Juan. He begun
    To hear new words, and to repeat them; but
Some feelings, universal as the sun,
    Were such as could not in his breast be shut
More than within the bosom of a nun:
    He was in love,—as you would be, no doubt,
With a young benefactress—so was she,
Just in the way we very often see.

CLXVIII

And every day by day-break—rather early
    For Juan, who was somewhat fond of rest—
She came into the cave, but it was merely
    To see her bird reposing in his nest;
And she would softly stir his locks so curly,
    Without disturbing her yet slumbering guest,
Breathing all gently o'er his cheek and mouth,
As o'er a bed of roses the sweet south.

CLXIX

And every morn his colour freshlier came,
    And every day helped on his convalescence;
'T was well, because health in the human frame
    Is pleasant, besides being true love's essence,
For health and idleness to passion's flame
    Are oil and gunpowder; and some good lessons
Are also learnt from Ceres and from Bacchus,
Without whom Venus will not long attack us.[18]

CLXX

While Venus fills the heart (without heart really
    Love, though good always, is not quite so good)
Ceres presents a plate of vermicelli,—
    For love must be sustain'd like flesh and blood,—
While Bacchus pours out wine, or hands a jelly:
    Eggs, oysters too, are amatory food;
But who is their purveyor from above
Heaven knows,—it may be Neptune, Pan, or Jove.

CLXXI

When Juan woke he found some good things ready,
    A bath, a breakfast, and the finest eyes
That ever made a youthful heart less steady,
    Besides her maid's, as pretty for their size;
But I have spoken of all this already—
    A repetition 's tiresome and unwise,—
Well—Juan, after bathing in the sea,
Came always back to coffee and Haidée.

CLXXII

Both were so young, and one so innocent,
    That bathing pass'd for nothing; Juan seem'd
To her, as 't were, the kind of being sent,
    Of whom these two years she had nightly dream'd,
A something to be loved, a creature meant
    To be her happiness, and whom she deem'd
To render happy; all who joy would win
Must share it,—Happiness was born a twin.

CLXXIII

It was such pleasure to behold him, such
    Enlargement of existence to partake
Nature with him, to thrill beneath his touch,
    To watch him slumbering, and to see him wake:
To live with him for ever were too much;
    But then the thought of parting made her quake:
He was her own, her ocean-treasure, cast
Like a rich wreck—her first love, and her last.

CLXXIV

And thus a moon roll'd on, and fair Haidée
    Paid daily visits to her boy, and took
Such plentiful precautions, that still he
    Remain'd unknown within his craggy nook;
At last her father's prows put out to sea,
    For certain merchantmen upon the look,
Not as of yore to carry off an Io,[19]
But three Ragusan vessels, bound for Scio.

CLXXV

Then came her freedom, for she had no mother,
    So that, her father being at sea, she was
Free as a married woman, or such other
    Female, as where she likes may freely pass,
Without even the incumbrance of a brother,
    The freest she that ever gazed on glass:
I speak of christian lands in this comparison,
Where wives, at least, are seldom kept in garrison.

CLXXVI

Now she prolong'd her visits and her talk
    (For they must talk), and he had learnt to say
So much as to propose to take a walk,—
    For little had he wander'd since the day
On which, like a young flower snapp'd from the stalk,
    Drooping and dewy on the beach he lay,—
And thus they walk'd out in the afternoon,
And saw the sun set opposite the moon.

CLXXVII

It was a wild and breaker-beaten coast,
    With cliffs above, and a broad sandy shore,
Guarded by shoals and rocks as by an host,
    With here and there a creek, whose aspect wore
A better welcome to the tempest-tost;
    And rarely ceased the haughty billow's roar,
Save on the dead long summer days, which make
The outstretch'd ocean glitter like a lake.

CLXXVIII

And the small ripple spilt upon the beach
    Scarcely o'erpass'd the cream of your champaigne,
When o'er the brim the sparkling bumpers reach,
    That spring-dew of the spirit! the heart's rain!
Few things surpass old wine; and they may preach
    Who please,—the more because they preach in
        vain,—
Let us have wine and woman, mirth and laughter,
Sermons and soda water the day after.

---

[18] The goddesses of food and wine are here seen as hand-maidens to the goddess of love.

[19] Herodotus tells of Io being carried off by Phoenecian merchants. This abduction is in the Adriatic near the coast of Yugoslavia.

CLXXIX

Man, being reasonable, must get drunk;
    The best of life is but intoxication:
Glory, the grape, love, gold, in these are sunk
    The hopes of all men, and of every nation;
Without their sap, how branchless were the trunk
    Of life's strange tree, so fruitful on occasion:
But to return,—Get very drunk, and when
You wake with head-ache, you shall see what then.

CLXXX

Ring for your valet—bid him quickly bring
    Some hock and soda-water, then you 'll know
A pleasure worthy Xerxes the great king;
    For not the blest sherbet, sublimed with snow,
Nor the first sparkle of the desert-spring,
    Nor Burgundy in all its sunset glow,
After long travel, ennui, love, or slaughter,
Vie with that draught of hock and soda-water!

CLXXXI

The coast—I think it was the coast that I
    Was just describing—Yes, it *was* the coast—
Lay at this period quiet as the sky,
    The sands untumbled, the blue waves untost,
And all was stillness, save the sea-bird's cry,
    And dolphin's leap, and the little billow crost
By some low rock or shelve, that made it fret
Against the boundary it scarcely wet.

CLXXXII

And forth they wander'd, her sire being gone,
    As I have said, upon an expedition;
And mother, brother, guardian, she had none,
    Save Zoe, who although with due precision
She waited on her lady with the sun,
    Thought daily service was her only mission,
Bringing warm water, wreathing her long tresses,
And asking now and then for cast-off dresses.

CLXXXIII

It was the cooling hour, just when the rounded
    Red sun sinks down behind the azure hill,
Which then seems as if the whole earth it bounded,
    Circling all nature, hush'd, and dim, and still,
With the far mountain-crescent half surrounded
    On one side, and the deep sea calm and chill
Upon the other, and the rosy sky
With one star sparkling through it like an eye.

CLXXXIV

And thus they wander'd forth, and hand in hand,
    Over the shining pebbles and the shells,
Glided along the smooth and harden'd sand,
    And in the worn and wild receptacles
Work'd by the storms, yet work'd as it were plann'd—
    In hollow halls, with sparry roofs and cells,
They turn'd to rest; and, each clasp'd by an arm,
Yields to the deep twilight's purple charm.

CLXXXV

They look'd up to the sky, whose floating glow
    Spread like a rosy ocean, vast and bright;
They gazed upon the glittering sea below,
    Whence the broad moon rose circling into sight;
They heard the wave's splash, and the wind so low,
    And saw each other's dark eyes darting light
Into each other—and, beholding this,
Their lips drew near, and clung into a kiss;

CLXXXVI

A long, long kiss, a kiss of youth, and love,
    And beauty, all concentrating like rays
Into one focus, kindled from above;
    Such kisses as belong to early days,
Where heart, and soul, and sense, in concert move,
    And the blood 's lava, and the pulse a blaze,
Each kiss a heart-quake,—for a kiss's strength,
I think, it must be reckon'd by its length.

CLXXXVII

By length I mean duration; theirs endured   [reckon'd,
    Heaven knows how long—no doubt they never
And if they had, they could not have secured
    The sum of their sensations to a second:
They had not spoken, but they felt allured,
    As if their souls and lips each other beckon'd,
Which, being join'd, like swarming bees they clung—
Their hearts the flowers from whence the honey
                             [sprung.

CLXXXVIII

They were alone, but not alone as they
    Who shut in chambers think it loneliness;
The silent ocean, and the starlight bay,
    The twilight glow, which momently grew less,
The voiceless sands, and dropping caves, that lay
    Around them, made them to each other press,
As if there were no life beneath the sky
Save theirs, and that their life could never die.

CLXXXIX

They fear'd no eyes nor ears on that lone beach;
  They felt no terrors from the night, they were
All in all to each other: though their speech
  Was broken words, they *thought* a language there,—
And all the burning tongues the passions teach
  Found in one sigh the best interpreter
Of nature's oracle—first love,—that all
Which Eve has left her daughters since her fall.

CXC

Haidée spoke not of scruples, ask'd no vows,
  Nor offer'd any; she had never heard
Of plight and promises to be a spouse,
  Or perils by a loving maid incurr'd;
She was all which pure ignorance allows,
  And flew to her young mate like a young bird;
And, never having dreamt of falsehood, she
Had not one word to say of constancy.

CXCI

She loved, and was belovéd—she adored,
  And she was worshipp'd after nature's fashion—
Their intense souls, into each other pour'd,
  If souls could die, had perish'd in that passion,—
But by degrees their senses were restored,
  Again to be o'ercome, again to dash on;
And, beating 'gainst *his* bosom, Haidée's heart
Felt as if never more to beat apart.

CXCII

Alas! they were so young, so beautiful,
  So lonely, loving, helpless, and the hour
Was that in which the heart is always full,
  And, having o'er itself no further power,
Prompts deeds eternity can not annul,
  But pays off moments in an endless shower
Of hell-fire—all prepared for people giving
Pleasure or pain to one another living.

CXCIII

Alas! for Juan and Haidée! they were
  So loving and so lovely—till then never,
Excepting our first parents, such a pair
  Had run the risk of being damn'd for ever:
And Haidée, being devout as well as fair,
  Had, doubtless, heard about the Stygian river,
And hell and purgatory—but forgot
Just in the very crisis she should not.

CXCIV

They look upon each other, and their eyes
  Gleam in the moonlight; and her white arm clasps
Round Juan's head, and his around her lies
  Half buried in the tresses which it grasps;
She sits upon his knee, and drinks his sighs,
  He hers, until they end in broken gasps;
And thus they form a group that's quite antique,
Half naked, loving, natural, and Greek.

CXCV

And when those deep and burning moments pass'd,
  And Juan sunk to sleep within her arms,
She slept not, but all tenderly, though fast,
  Sustain'd his head upon her bosom's charms;
And now and then her eye to heaven is cast,
  And then on the pale cheek her breast now warms,
Pillow'd on her o'erflowing heart, which pants
With all it granted, and with all it grants.

CXCVI

An infant when it gazes on a light,
  A child the moment when it drains the breast,
A devotee when soars the Host in sight,
  An Arab with a stranger for a guest,
A sailor when the prize has struck in fight,
  A miser filling his most hoarded chest,
Feel rapture; but not such true joy are reaping
As they who watch o'er what they love while sleeping.

CXCVII

For there it lies so tranquil, so beloved,
  All that it hath of life with us is living;
So gentle, stirless, helpless, and unmoved,
  And all unconscious of the joy 't is giving;
All it hath felt, inflicted, pass'd, and proved,
  Hush'd into depths beyond the watcher's diving:
There lies the thing we love with all its errors
And all its charms, like death without its terrors.

CXCVIII

The lady watch'd her lover—and that hour
  Of Love's, and Night's, and Ocean's solitude,
O'erflow'd her soul with their united power;
  Amidst the barren sand and rocks so rude
She and her wave-worn love had made their bower,
  Where nought upon their passion could intrude,
And all the stars that crowded the blue space
Saw nothing happier than her glowing face.

CXCIX

Alas! the love of women! it is known
   To be a lovely and a fearful thing;
For all of theirs upon that die is thrown,
   And if 't is lost, life hath no more to bring
To them but mockeries of the past alone,
   And their revenge is as the tiger's spring,
Deadly, and quick, and crushing; yet, as real
Torture is theirs, what they inflict they feel.

CC

They are right; for man, to man so oft unjust,
   Is always so to women: one sole bond
Awaits them, treachery is all their trust;
   Taught to conceal, their bursting hearts despond
Over their idol, till some wealthier lust
   Buys them in marriage—and what rests beyond?
A thankless husband, next, a faithless lover,
Then dressing, nursing, praying, and all's over.

CCI

Some take a lover, some take drams or prayers,
   Some mind their household, others dissipation,
Some run away, and but exchange their cares,
   Losing the advantage of a virtuous station;
Few changes e'er can better their affairs,
   Theirs being an unnatural situation,
From the dull palace to the dirty hovel:
Some play the devil, and then write a novel.[20]

CCII

Haidée was Nature's bride, and knew not this;
   Haidée was Passion's child, born where the sun
Showers triple light, and scorches even the kiss
   Of his gazelle-eyed daughters; she was one
Made but to love, to feel that she was his
   Who was her chosen: what was said or done
Elsewhere was nothing. She had nought to fear,
Hope, care, nor love, beyond, her heart beat *here*.

CCIII

And oh! that quickening of the heart, that beat!
   How much it costs us! yet each rising throb
Is in its cause as its effect so sweet,
   That Wisdom, ever on the watch to rob
Joy of its alchymy, and to repeat
   Fine truths; even Conscience, too, has a tough job
To make us understand each good old maxim,
So good—I wonder Castlereagh don't tax 'em.

CCIV

And now 't was done—on the lone shore were plighted
   Their hearts; the stars, their nuptial torches, shed
Beauty upon the beautiful they lighted:
   Ocean their witness, and the cave their bed,
By their own feelings hallow'd and united,
   Their priest was Solitude, and they were wed:
And they were happy, for to their young eyes
Each was an angel, and earth paradise.

CCV

Oh, Love! of whom great Caesar was the suitor,
   Titus the master, Antony the slave,
Horace, Catullus, scholars, Ovid tutor,
   Sappho the sage blue-stocking, in whose grave
All those may leap who rather would be neuter—
   (Leucadia's rock still overlooks the wave),
Oh, Love! thou art the very god of evil,
For, after all, we cannot call thee devil.[21]

CCVI

Thou mak'st the chaste connubial state precarious,
   And jestest with the brows of mightiest men:
Caesar and Pompey, Mahomet, Belisarius;
   Have much employed the muse of history's pen:
Their lives and fortunes were extremely various,
   Such worthies Time will never see again;
Yet to these four in three things the same luck holds,
They all were heroes, conquerors, and cuckolds.

CCVII

Thou mak'st philosophers; there 's Epicurus
   And Aristippus, a material crew!
Who to immoral courses would allure us
   By theories quite practicable too;
If only from the devil they would insure us,
   How pleasant were the maxim (not quite new),
"Eat, drink, and love, what can the rest avail us?"
So said the royal sage Sardanapalus.[22]

CCVIII

But Juan! had he quite forgotten Julia?
   And should he have forgotten her so soon?
I can't but say it seems to me most truly a
   Perplexing question; but, no doubt, the moon
Does these things for us, and whenever newly a
   Strong palpitation rises, 't is her boon,
Else how the devil is it that fresh features
Have such a charm for us poor human creatures?

---

20 Byron's one-time mistress Lady Caroline Lamb used one of his letters in her novel *Glenarvon* (1816).

21 The Roman emperor Titus overcame his love for Berenice, but not Antony his for Cleopatra. Horace and Catullus have many love lyrics, Ovid an *Art of Love*. Sappho of Lesbos supposedly leapt from the Leucadian rocks because of unrequited love for a boatman.

22 Epicurus and Aristippus both preached forms of hedonism. Sardanapalus was an obscure Syrian king, about whom Byron wrote a tragedy in 1821.

CCIX

I hate inconstancy—I loathe, detest,
  Abhor, condemn, abjure the mortal made
Of such quicksilver clay that in his breast
  No permanent foundation can be laid;
Love, constant love, has been my constant guest,
  And yet last night, being at a masquerade,
I saw the prettiest creature, fresh from Milan,
Which gave me some sensations like a villain.

CCX

But soon Philosophy came to my aid,
  And whisper'd, "Think of every sacred tie!"
"I will, my dear Philosophy!" I said,
  "But then her teeth, and then, Oh heaven! her eye!
I 'll just inquire if she be wife or maid,
  Or neither—out of curiosity."
"Stop!" cried Philosophy, with air so Grecian,
(Though she was masqued then as a fair Venetian;)

CCXI

"Stop!" so I stopp'd.—But to return: that which
  Men call inconstancy is nothing more
Than admiration due where nature's rich
  Profusion with young beauty covers o'er
Some favour'd object; and as in the niche
  A lovely statue we almost adore,
This sort of adoration of the real
Is but a heightening of the "beau ideal."

CCXII

'T is the perception of the beautiful,
  A fine extension of the faculties,
Platonic, universal, wonderful,
  Drawn from the stars, and filter'd through the skies,
Without which life would be extremely dull;
  In short, it is the use of our own eyes,
With one or two small senses added, just
To hint that flesh is formed of fiery dust.

CCXIII

Yet 't is a painful feeling, and unwilling,
  For surely if we always could perceive
In the same object graces quite as killing
  As when she rose upon us like an Eve,
'T would save us many a heart-ache, many a shilling,
  (For we must get them any-how, or grieve),
Whereas if one sole lady pleased for ever,
How pleasant for the heart, as well as liver!

CCXIV

The heart is like the sky, a part of heaven,
  But changes night and day too, like the sky;
Now o'er it clouds and thunder must be driven,
  And darkness and destruction as on high:
But when it hath been scorch'd, and pierced, and riven,
  Its storms expire in water-drops; the eye
Pours forth at last the heart's-blood turn'd to tears,
Which make the English climate of our years.

CCXV

The liver is the lazaret of bile,
  But very rarely executes its function,
For the first passion stays there such a while,
  That all the rest creep in and form a junction,
Like knots of vipers on a dunghill's soil,
  Rage, fear, hate, jealousy, revenge, compunction,
So that all mischiefs spring up from this entrail,
Like earthquakes from the hidden fire call'd "central."

CCXVI

In the mean time, without proceeding more
  In this anatomy, I 've finish'd now
Two hundred and odd stanzas as before,
  That being about the number I 'll allow
Each canto of the twelve, or twenty-four;
  And, laying down my pen, I make my bow,
Leaving Don Juan and Haidée to plead
For them and theirs with all who deign to read.

[1818–19]   [1819]

[*After the events described in Canto II, Lambro separates the lovers, Haidée dies, and Juan is sold to Turks as a slave. Here he meets an English adventurer named Johnson who has fought for the Russians and has been captured by the Turks. Both are sold to a Sultan whose Sultana, Gulbayez, falls in love with Juan but is rejected by him. Disguised as "Juanna," Juan spends an interlude with the Sultan's harem.*

Finally escaping from the Sultan, Juan and Johnson join the Russian army at the siege of Ismail, and as a reward for his bravery Juan is sent to St. Petersburg, where he becomes a courtier and favorite of Catherine the Great. When a mysterious illness makes him less satisfactory as a lover for the Empress, Juan is sent on a diplomatic mission to England. He is accompanied by his ward Leila, the orphan girl he rescued at the battle of Ismail in Canto VII].

CANTO THE ELEVENTH

I

WHEN Bishop Berkeley said "there was no matter," [1]
  And proved it—'t was no matter what he said:
They say his system 't is in vain to batter,
  Too subtle for the airiest human head;

---
[1] His *On the Principles of Human Knowledge* (1734) insisted that "matter" could only be an "idea."

And yet who can believe it! I would shatter
  Gladly all matters down to stone or lead,
Or adamant, to find the World a spirit,
And wear my head, denying that I wear it.

II

What a sublime discovery 't was to make the
  Universe universal Egotism!
That all 's ideal—*all ourselves*: I 'll stake the
  World (be it what you will) that *that 's* no Schism.
Oh Doubt!—if thou be'st Doubt, for which some take
  thee,
  But which I doubt extremely—thou sole prism
Of the Truth's rays, spoil not my draught of spirit!
Heaven's brandy,—though our brain can hardly bear
                                      [it.

III

For ever and anon comes Indigestion
  (Not the most "dainty Ariel")[2] and perplexes
Our soarings with another sort of question:
  And that which after all my spirit vexes,
Is, that I find no spot where man can rest eye on,
  Without confusion of the sorts and sexes,
Of beings, stars, and this unriddled wonder,
The World, which at the worst 's a glorious blunder—

IV

If it be chance; or if it be according
  To the Old Text, still better:—lest it should
Turn out so, we 'll say nothing 'gainst the wording,
  As several people think such hazards rude:
They 're right; our days are too brief for affording
  Space to dispute what *no one* ever could
Decide, and *every body one day* will
Know very clearly—or at least lie still.

V

And therefore will I leave off metaphysical
  Discussion, which is neither here nor there:
If I agree that what is, is; then this I call
  Being quite perspicuous and extremely fair.
The truth is, I 've grown lately rather phthisical:[3]
  I don't know what the reason is—the air
Perhaps; but as I suffer from the shocks
Of illness, I grow much more orthodox.

---

[2] In Shakespeare's *Tempest*.
[3] Asthmatic.

VI

The first attack at once proved the Divinity;
  (But *that* I never doubted, nor the Devil);
The next, the Virgin's mystical virginity;
  The third, the usual Origin of Evil;
The fourth at once established the whole Trinity
  On so uncontrovertible a level,
That I devoutly wished the three were four,
On purpose to believe so much the more.

VII

To our theme.—The man who has stood on the
  And looked down over Attica; or he [Acropolis,
Who has sailed where picturesque Constantinople is,
  Or seen Tombuctoo, or hath taken tea
In small-eyed China's crockery-ware metropolis,
  Or sat amidst the bricks of Nineveh,
May not think much of London's first appearance—
But ask him what he thinks of it a year hence?

VIII

Don Juan had got out on Shooter's Hill;
  Sunset the time, the place the same declivity
Which looks along that vale of good and ill
  Where London streets ferment in full activity;
While every thing around was calm and still,
  Except the creak of wheels, which on their pivot he
Heard,—and that bee-like, bubbling, busy hum
Of cities, that boil over with their scum:—

IX

I say, Don Juan, wrapt in contemplation,
  Walked on behind his carriage, o'er the summit,
And lost in wonder of so great a nation,
  Gave way to 't, since he could not overcome it.
"And here," he cried, "is Freedom's chosen station;
  Here peals the people's voice nor can entomb it
Racks, prisons, inquisitions; resurrection
Awaits it, each new meeting or election.

X

"Here are chaste wives, pure lives; here people pay
  But what they please; and if that things be dear,
'T is only that they love to throw away
  Their cash, to show how much they have a-year.
Here laws are all inviolate; none lay
  Traps for the traveller; every highway 's clear:
Here"—he was interrupted by a knife,
With "Damn your eyes! your money or your life!"

XI

These freeborn sounds proceeded from four pads,
  In ambush laid, who had perceived him loiter
Behind his carriage; and, like handy lads,
  Had seized the lucky hour to reconnoitre,
In which the heedless gentleman who gads
  Upon the road, unless he prove a fighter,
May find himself within that Isle of riches
Exposed to lose his life as well as breeches.

XII

Juan, who did not understand a word
  Of English, save their shibboleth, "God damn!"
And even that he had so rarely heard,
  He sometimes thought 't was only their "Salam,"
Or "God be with you!"—and 't is not absurd
  To think so; for half English as I am
(To my misfortune) never can I say
I heard them wish "God with you," save that way;—

XIII

Juan yet quickly understood their gesture,
  And being somewhat choleric and sudden,
Drew forth a pocket pistol from his vesture,
  And fired it into one assailant's pudding—
Who fell, as rolls an ox o'er in his pasture,
  And roared out, as he writhed his native mud in,
Unto his nearest follower or henchman,
"Oh Jack! I 'm floored by that ere bloody
                                         [Frenchman!"

XIV

On which Jack and his train set off at speed,
  And Juan's suite, late scattered at a distance,
Came up, all marvelling at such a deed,
  And offering, as usual, late assistance.
Juan, who saw the Moon's late minion [4] bleed
  As if his veins would pour out his existence,
Stood calling out for bandages and lint,
And wished he had been less hasty with his flint.

XV

"Perhaps," thought he, "it is the country's Wont
  To welcome foreigners in this way: now
I recollect some innkeepers who don't
  Differ, except in robbing with a bow,
In lieu of a bare blade and brazen front.
  But what is to be done? I can't allow
The fellow to lie groaning on the road:
So take him up; I'll help you with the load."

<hr>
[4] Falstaff's euphemism for thieves in Shakespeare's *1 Henry IV*.

XVI

But ere they could perform this pious duty,
  The dying man cried, "Hold! I 've got my gruel!
Oh! for a glass of *max*! [5] We've missed our booty—
  Let me die where I am!" And as the fuel
Of life shrunk in his heart, and thick and sooty
  The drops fell from his death-wound, and he drew
His breath,—he from his swelling throat untied   [ill
A kerchief, crying, "Give Sal that!"—and died.

XVII

The cravat stained with bloody drops fell down
  Before Don Juan's feet: he could not tell
Exactly why it was before him thrown,
  Nor what the meaning of the man's farewell.
Poor Tom was once a kiddy [6] upon town,
  A thorough varmint, and a *real* swell,
Full flash, all fancy, until fairly diddled,
His pockets first and then his body riddled.

XVIII

Don Juan, having done the best he could
  In all the circumstances of the case,
As soon as "Crowner's quest" allowed, pursued
  His travels to the capital apace;—
Esteeming it a little hard he should
  In twelve hours' time, and very little space,
Have been obliged to slay a freeborn native
In self-defence:—this made him meditative.

XIX

He from the world had cut off a great man,
  Who in his time had made heroic bustle.
Who in a row like Tom could lead the van,
  Booze in the ken, or at the spellken hustle?
Who queer a flat? Who (spite of Bow-street's ban)
  On the high toby-spice so flash the muzzle?
Who on a lark with black-eyed Sal (his blowing),
So prime, so swell, so nutty, and so knowing? *

<hr>
* The advance of science and of language has rendered it unnecessary to translate the above good and true English, spoken in its original purity by the select mobility and their patrons. The following is a stanza of a song which was very popular, at least in my early days:—

> On the high toby-spice flash the muzzle,
>   In spite of each gallows old scout;
> If you at the spellken can't hustle,
>   You'll be hobbled in making a clout.

<hr>
[5] Gin.
[6] A kiddy = a flashily dressed thief; a swell = any well-dressed person; flash = the affecting of a habit or manner in order to be noticed.

XX

But Tom 's no more—and so no more of Tom.
  Heroes must die; and by God's blessing 't is
Not long before the most of them go home.—
  Hail! Thamis, hail! Upon thy verge it is
That Juan's chariot, rolling like a drum
  In thunder, holds the way it can't well miss,
Through Kennington and all the other "tons,"
Which make us wish ourselves in town at once;—

XXI

Through Groves, so called as being void of trees,
  (Like *lucus* from *no* light); through prospects
      named
Mount Pleasant, as containing nought to please,
  Nor much to climb; through little boxes framed
Of bricks, to let the dust in at your ease,
  With "To be let," upon their doors proclaimed;
Through "Rows" most modestly called "Paradise,"
Which Eve might quit without much sacrifice;—

XXII

Through coaches, drays, choked turnpikes, and a
  Of wheels, and roar of voices, and confusion; [whirl
Here taverns wooing to a pint of "purl,"
  There mails fast flying off like a delusion;
There barber's blocks with periwigs in curl
  In windows; here the lamplighter's infusion
Slowly distilled into the glimmering glass,
(For in those days we had not got to gas):—8

XXIII

Through this, and much, and more, is the approach
  Of travellers to mighty Babylon:
Whether they come by horse, or chaise, or coach,
  With slight exceptions, all the ways seem one.
I could say more, but do not choose to encroach
  Upon the guide-book's privilege. The Sun
Had set some time, and night was on the ridge
Of twilight, as the party crossed the bridge.

        Then your Blowing will wax gallows haughty,
          When she hears of your scaly mistake,
        She'll surely turn snitch for the forty,
          That her Jack may be regular weight.

If there be any Gemman so ignorant as to require a traduction,
I refer him to my old friend and corporeal pastor and master,
John Jackson, Esq., Professor of Pugilism; who I trust still
retains the strength and symmetry of his model of a form,
together with his good humour, and athletic as well as mental
accomplishments.7

---

  7 Ken = house of thieves; spellken = playhouse; queer a
flat = put something over on a fool; high tobey-spice = robbery
on horseback; flash the muzzle = swagger; blowing = a
thief's whore; nutty = strongly inclined.
  8 Gas lighting came to London in 1812.

XXIV

That's rather fine, the gentle sound of Thamis—
  Who vindicates a moment too his stream—
Though hardly heard through multifarious
    "damme's:"
  The lamps of Westminster's more regular gleam,
The breadth of pavement, and yon shrine where
  A spectral resident—whose pallid beam   [Fame is
In shape of moonshine hovers o'er the pile—
Make this a sacred part of Albion's Isle.

XXV

The Druids' groves are gone—so much the better:
  Stone-Henge is not—but what the devil is it?—
But Bedlam still exists with its sage fetter,
  That madmen may not bite you on a visit;
The Bench too seats or suits full many a debtor;
  The Mansion House too (though some people
To me appears a stiff yet grand erection;   [quiz it)
But then the Abbey 's worth the whole collection.

XXVI

The line of lights too up to Charing Cross,
  Pall Mall, and so forth, have a coruscation
Like gold as in comparison to dross,
  Matched with the Continent's illumination,
Whose cities Night by no means deigns to gloss:
  The French were not yet a lamp-lighting nation,
And when they grew so—on their new-found lanthorn,
Instead of wicks, they made a wicked man turn.9

XXVII

A row of gentlemen along the streets
  Suspended, may illuminate mankind,
As also bonfires made of country seats;10
  But the old way is best for the purblind:
The other looks like phosphorus on sheets,
  A sort of Ignis-fatuus to the mind,
Which, though 't is certain to perplex and frighten,
Must burn more mildly ere it can enlighten.

XXVIII

But London 's so well lit, that if Diogenes
  Could recommence to hunt his *honest man*,
And found him not amidst the various progenies
  Of this enormous city's spreading span,
'T were not for want of lamps to aid his dodging his
  Yet undiscovered treasure. What *I* can,
I've done to find the same throughout life's journey,
But see the world is only one attorney.

---

  9 During the Revolution, lampposts were used for hanging.
  10 Burnings and protests were common during the Napoleonic
wars and the subsequent economic unrest. An *ignis fatuus* (line 6),
will-o'-the-wisp, is a phosphorescent light found over swampy
land.

XXIX

Over the stones still rattling, up Pall Mall,
    Through crowds and carriages, but waxing thinner
As thundered knockers broke the long-sealed spell
    Of doors 'gainst duns, and to an early dinner
Admitted a small party as night fell,—
    Don Juan, our young diplomatic sinner,
Pursued his path, and drove past some Hotels,
St. James's Palace, and St. James's "Hells."*

XXX

They reached the hotel: forth streamed from the
    A tide of well-clad waiters, and around   [front door
The mob stood, and as usual several score
    Of those pedestrian Paphians who abound
In decent London when the daylight's o'er;
    Commodious but immoral, they are found
Useful, like Malthus, in promoting marriage.[11]—
But Juan now is stepping from his carriage

XXXI

Into one of the sweetest of hotels,
    Especially for foreigners—and mostly
For those whom favour or whom fortune swells,
    And cannot find a bill's small items costly.
There many an envoy either dwelt or dwells,
    (The den of many a diplomatic lost lie),
Until to some conspicuous square they pass,
And blazon o'er the door their names in brass.

XXXII

Juan, whose was a delicate commission,
    Private, though publicly important, bore
No title to point out with due precision
    The exact affair on which he was sent o'er.
'T was merely known that on a secret mission
    A foreigner of rank had graced our shore,
Young, handsome, and accomplished, who was said
(In whispers) to have turned his Sovereign's head.

XXXIII

Some rumour also of some strange adventures
    Had gone before him, and his wars and loves;
And as romantic heads are pretty painters,
    And, above all, an Englishwoman's roves

* "Hells," gaming-houses. What their number may now
be, in this life, I know not. Before I was of age I knew them
pretty accurately, both "gold" and "silver." I was once nearly
called out by an acquaintance because, when he asked me where
I thought that his soul would be found hereafter, I answered,
"In Silver Hell."

[11] In his *Essay on the Principles of Population* (1798) he urged
fewer marriages as a curb on population growth. Paphians (in
line 4 above) are whores.

Into the excursive, breaking the indentures
    Of sober reason, wheresoe'er it moves,
He found himself extremely in the fashion,
Which serves our thinking people for a passion.

XXXIV

I don't mean that they are passionless, but quite
    The contrary; but then 't is in the head;
Yet as the consequences are as bright
    As if they acted with the heart instead,
What after all can signify the site
    Of ladies' lucubrations? So they lead
In safety to the place for which you start,
What matters if the road be head or heart?

XXXV

Juan presented in the proper place,
    To proper placemen, every Russ credential;
And was received with all the due grimace,
    By those who govern in the mood potential;
Who, seeing a handsome stripling with smooth face,
    Thought (what in state affairs is most essential)
That they as easily might *do* the youngster,
As hawks may pounce upon a woodland songster.

XXXVI

They erred, as aged men will do; but by
    And by we 'll talk of that; and if we don't,
'T will be because our notion is not high
    Of politicians and their double front,
Who live by lies, yet dare not boldly lie:
    Now what I love in women is, they won't
Or can't do otherwise than lie, but do it
So well, the very truth seems falsehood to it.

XXXVII

And, after all, what is a lie? 'T is but
    The truth in masquerade; and I defy
Historians, heroes, lawyers, priests to put
    A fact without some leaven of a lie.
The very shadow of true Truth would shut
    Up annals, revelations, poesy,
And prophecy—except it should be dated
Some years before the incidents related.

XXXVIII

Praised be all liars and all lies! Who now
    Can tax my mild Muse with misanthropy?
She rings the World's "Te Deum," and her brow
    Blushes for those who will not:—but to sigh

Is idle; let us like most others bow,
    Kiss hands, feet, any part of Majesty,
After the good example of "Green Erin,"[12]
Whose Shamrock now seems rather worse for wearing.

XXXIX

Don Juan was presented, and his dress
    And mien excited general admiration—
I don't know which was more admired or less:
    One monstrous diamond drew much observation,
Which Catherine in a moment of "*ivresse*"[13]
    (In love or brandy's fervent fermentation)
Bestowed upon him, as the public learned;
And, to say truth, it had been fairly earned.

XL

Besides the Ministers and underlings,
    Who must be courteous to the accredited
Diplomatists of rather wavering kings,
    Until their royal riddle 's fully read,
The very clerks,—those somewhat dirty springs
    Of office, or the House of Office, fed
By foul corruption into streams,—even they
Were hardly rude enough to earn their pay:

XLI

And insolence no doubt is what they are
    Employed for, since it is their daily labour,
In the dear offices of peace or war;
    And should you doubt, pray ask of your next
When for a passport, or some other bar   [neighbour,
    To freedom, he applied (a grief and a bore),
If he found not this spawn of tax-born riches,
Like lap-dogs, the least civil sons of b——s.

XLII

But Juan was received with much
    "*empressement*":[14]—
    These phrases of refinement I must borrow
From our next neighbours' land, where, like a
        chessman,
    There is a move set down for joy or sorrow,
Not only in mere talking, but the press. Man
    In islands is, it seems, downright and thorough,
More than on continents—as if the Sea
(See Billingsgate) made even the tongue more free.

---

[12] George IV was given an extremely cordial welcome in Ireland in 1820.
[13] Intoxication.
[14] Attention.

XLIII

And yet the British "Damme" 's rather Attic:[15]
    Your Continental oaths are but incontinent,
And turn on things which no Aristocratic
    Spirit would name, and therefore even I won't
This subject quote; as it would be schismatic   [anent
    In politesse, and have a sound affronting in 't:—
But "Damme" 's quite ethereal, though too daring—
Platonic blasphemy, the soul of swearing.

XLIV

For downright rudeness, ye may stay at home;
    For true or false politeness (and scarce *that
Now*) you may cross the blue deep and white foam—
    The first the emblem (rarely though) of what
You leave behind—the next of much you come
    To meet. However, 't is no time to chat
On general topics: poems must confine
Themselves to Unity, like this of mine.

XLV

In the Great World,—which, being interpreted
    Meaneth the West or worst end of a city,
And about twice two thousand people bred
    By no means to be very wise or witty,
But to sit up while others lie in bed,
    And look down on the universe with pity,—
Juan, as an inveterate Patrician,
Was well received by persons of condition.

XLVI

He was a bachelor, which is a matter
    Of import both to Virgin and to Bride
The former's hymeneal hopes to flatter;
    And (should she not hold fast by love or pride)
'T is also of some moment to the latter:
    A rib 's a thorn in a wed Gallant's side,
Requires decorum, and is apt to double
The horrid sin—and what's still worse, the trouble.

XLVII

But Juan was a bachelor—of arts,
    And parts, and hearts: he danced and sung, and had
An air as sentimental as Mozart's
    Softest of melodies; and could be sad
Or cheerful, without any "flaws or starts,"
    Just at the proper time; and though a lad,
Had seen the world—which is a curious sight,
And very much unlike what people write.

---

[15] Simple, pure, direct in style. Billingsgate fishmarket (Stanza XLII) gave its name to a form of swearing.

XLVIII

Fair virgins blushed upon him; wedded dames
  Bloomed also in less transitory hues;
For both commodities dwell by the Thames,
  The painting and the painted; youth, ceruse,
Against his heart preferred their usual claims,
  Such as no gentleman can quite refuse:
Daughters admired his dress, and pious mothers
Inquired his income, and if he had brothers.

XLIX

The milliners who furnish "drapery Misses"*
  Throughout the season, upon speculation
Of payment ere the honeymoon's last kisses
  Have waned into a crescent's coruscation,
Thought such an opportunity as this is,
  Of a rich foreigner's initiation,
Not to be overlooked,—and gave such credit,
That future bridegrooms swore, and sighed, and paid
                                              [it.

L

The Blues, that tender tribe, who sigh o'er sonnets,
  And with the pages of the last Review
Line the interior of their heads or bonnets,[16]
  Advanced in all their azure's highest hue:
They talked bad French of Spanish, and upon its
  Late authors asked him for a hint or two;
And which was softest, Russian or Castilian?
And whether in his travels he saw Ilion?

LI

Juan, who was a little superficial,
  And not in literature a great Drawcansir,[17]
Examined by this learned and especial
  Jury of matrons, scarce knew what to answer:

* "*Drapery Misses*."—This term is probably any thing
now but a *mystery*. It was however almost so to me when I first
returned from the East in 1811-1812. It means a pretty, a
highborn, a fashionable young female, well instructed by her
friends, and furnished by her milliner with a wardrobe upon
credit, to be repaid, when *married*, by the *husband*. The riddle
was first read to me by a young and pretty heiress, on my
praising the "drapery" of an "*untochered*" but "pretty vir-
ginities" (like Mrs. Anne Page) of the *then* day, which has now
been some years yesterday:—she assured me that the thing
was common in London; and as her own thousands, and
blooming looks, and rich simplicity of array, put any suspicion
in her own case out of the question, I confess I gave some credit
to the allegation. If necessary, authorities might be cited, in
which case I could quote both "drapery" and the wearers.
Let us hope, however, that it is now obsolete.

16 Waste paper was used for stuffing hats.
17 A braggart in the Duke of Buckingham's *Rehearsal* (1671).

His duties warlike, loving or official,
  His steady application as a dancer,
Had kept him from the brink of Hippocrene,
  Which now he found was blue instead of green.

LII

However, he replied at hazard, with
  A modest confidence and calm assurance,
Which lent his learned lucubrations pith,
  And passed for arguments of good endurance.
That prodigy, Miss Araminta Smith,
  (Who at sixteen translated "Hercules Furens"[18]
Into as furious English) with her best look,
Set down his sayings in her common-place book.

LIII

Juan knew several languages—as well
  He might—and brought them up with skill, in time
To save his fame with each accomplished belle,
  Who still regretted that he did not rhyme.
There wanted but this requisite to swell
  His qualities (with them) into sublime:
Lady Fitz-Frisky, and Miss Maevia Mannish,
Both longed extremely to be sung in Spanish.

LIV

However, he did pretty well, and was
  Admitted as an aspirant to all
The Coteries, and, as in Banquo's glass,[19]
  At great assemblies or in parties small,
He saw ten thousand living authors pass,
  That being about their average numeral;
Also the eighty "greatest living poets,"
As every paltry magazine can show *it's*.

LV

In twice five years the "greatest living poet,"
  Like to the champion in the fisty ring,
Is called on to support his claim, or show it,
  Although 't is an imaginary thing.
Even I—albeit I'm sure I did not know it,
  Nor sought of foolscap subjects to be king,—
Was reckoned, a considerable time,
The grand Napoleon of the realms of rhyme.

LVI

But Juan was my Moscow, and Faliero
  My Leipsic, and my Mont Saint Jean seems Cain:
"La Belle Alliance" of dunces down at zero,
  Now that the Lion's fall'n, may rise again:

18 *Furious Hercules* was by the Roman dramatist Seneca. No
Araminta Smith seems to have existed.
19 See *Macbeth*, IV, i.

But I will fall at least as fell my hero;
  Nor reign at all, or as a *monarch* reign;
Or to some lonely isle of Jailers go,
With turncoat Southey for my turnkey Lowe.[20]

LVII

Sir Walter reigned before me; Moore and Campbell
  Before and after; but now grown more holy,
The Muses upon Sion's hill must ramble,
  With poets almost clergymen, or wholly;
And Pegasus has a psalmodic amble
  Beneath the very Reverend Rowley Powley,[21]
Who shoes the glorious animal with stilts,
A modern Ancient Pistol—"by these hilts!"

LVIII

Still he excels that artificial hard
  Labourer in the same vineyard, though the vine
Yields him but vinegar for his reward,—
  That neutralised dull Dorus of the Nine;
That swarthy Sporus, neither man nor bard;
  That ox of verse, who *ploughs* for every line:—
Cambyses' roaring Romans beat at least
The howling Hebrews of Cybele's priest.—[22]

LIX

Then there 's my gentle Euphues; who, they say,
  Sets up for being a sort of *moral me*;[23]
He 'll find it rather difficult some day
  To turn out both, or either, it may be.
Some persons think that Coleridge hath the sway;
  And Wordsworth has supporters, two or three;
And that deep-mouthed Boeotian, "Savage Landor,"
Has taken for a swan rogue Southey's gander.

LX

John Keats, who was killed off by one critique,
  Just as he really promised something great,
If not intelligible,—without Greek
  Contrived to talk about the Gods of late,

Much as they might have been supposed to speak.
  Poor fellow! His was an untoward fate:—
'T is strange the mind, that very fiery particle,*
Should let itself be snuffed out by an Article.[24]

LXI

The list grows long of live and dead pretenders
  To that which none will gain—or none will know
The Conqueror at least; who, ere time renders
  His last award, will have the long grass grow
Above his burnt-out brain, and sapless cinders.
  If I might augur, I should rate but low
Their chances;—they're too numerous, like the thirty
Mock tyrants, when Rome's annals waxed but dirty.

LXII

This is the literary *lower* Empire,
  Where the Praetorian bands take up the matter;—
A "dreadful trade," like his who "gathers samphire,"[25]
  The insolent soldiery to soothe and flatter,
With the same feelings as you 'd coax a vampire.
  Now, were I once at home, and in good satire,
I 'd try conclusions with those Janizaries,
And show them *what* an intellectual war is.

LXIII

I think I know a trick or two, would turn
  Their flanks;—but it is hardly worth my while
With such small gear to give myself concern:
  Indeed I 've not the necessary bile;
My natural temper 's really aught but stern,
  And even my Muse's worst reproof 's a smile;
And then she drops a brief and modern curtsy,
And glides away, assured she never hurts ye.

LXIV

My Juan, whom I left in deadly peril
  Amongst live poets and blue ladies, passed
With some small profit through that field so sterile.
  Being tired in time and neither least nor last
Left it before he had been treated very ill;
  And henceforth found himself more gaily classed
Amongst the higher spirits of the day,
The sun's true son, no vapour, but a ray.

* "Divinæ particulum auræ."

[20] Byron describes the course of his career in terms of Napoleon's battles (and defeats). Lowe was governor of St. Helena while Napoleon was exiled there.
[21] The Reverend George Croly wrote *Paris in 1815*, an imitation of *Childe Harold*.
[22] This stanza is an elaborate attack on Henry Hart Milman (1791–1868), whom Byron suspected of trying to persuade John Murray to suspend publication of *Don Juan*. He also suspected him of attacking Keats in the *Quarterly Review* (April 1818).
[23] Barry Cornwall's *Diego de Montilla* had been compared to *Don Juan*.
[24] Shelley (see the Preface to *Adonais*, p. 951) helped to make the legend that the *Review* had killed Keats. Byron's Latin phrase—"particle of the divine breath"—is quoted from Horace's *Satires* (ii, 2, 79).
[25] *King Lear*, IV, vi, 15–16.

LXV

His morns he passed in business—which dissected,
   Was, like all business, a laborious nothing,
That leads to lassitude, the most infected
   And Centaur-Nessus garb of mortal clothing,[26]
And on our sofas makes us lie dejected,
   And talk in tender horrors of our loathing
All kinds of toil, save for our country's good—
Which grows no better, though 't is time it should.

LXVI

His afternoons he passed in visits, luncheons,
   Lounging, and boxing; and the twilight hour
In riding round those vegetable puncheons
   Called "Parks," where there is neither fruit nor
Enough to gratify a bee's slight munchings;   [flower
   But after all it is the only "bower,"
(In Moore's phrase) where the fashionable fair
Can form a slight acquaintance with fresh air.

LXVII

Then dress, then dinner, then awakes the world! [roar
   Then glare the lamps, then whirl the wheels, then
Through street and square fast flashing chariots, hurled
   Like harnessed meteors; then along the floor
Chalk mimics painting: then festoons are twirled;
   Then roll the brazen thunders of the door,
Which opens to the thousand happy few
An earthly Paradise of "Or Mulu."[27]

LXVIII

There stands the noble Hostess, nor shall sink
   With the three-thousandth curtsy; there the Waltz,
The only dance which teaches girls to think,
   Makes one in love even with its very faults.
Saloon, room, hall o'erflow beyond their brink,
   And long the latest of arrivals halts,
'Midst royal dukes and dames condemned to climb,
And gain an inch of staircase at a time.

LXIX

Thrice happy he, who, after a survey
   Of the good company, can win a corner,
A door that 's *in*, or boudoir *out* of the way,
   Where he may fix himself like small "Jack Horner,"
And let the Babel round run as it may,
   And look on as a mourner, or a scorner,
Or an approver, or a mere spectator,
Yawning a little as the night grows later.

---

[26] Deianira sent Hercules the poisoned tunic of the Centaur Nessus, which killed him.

[27] Ormolu, or gilded bronze, decorations for furniture were widely used in the early nineteenth century. Ballroom floors were frequently decorated with chalk pictures for special occasions (lines 4–5).

LXX

But this won't do, save by and by; and he
   Who, like Don Juan, takes an active share,
Must steer with care through all that glittering sea
   Of gems and plumes, and pearls and silks, to where
He deems it is his proper place to be;
   Dissolving in the waltz to some soft air,
Or proudlier prancing with mercurial skill
Where Science marshals forth her own quadrille.

LXXI

Or, if he dance not, but hath higher views
   Upon an heiress or his neighbour's bride,
Let him take care that that which he pursues
   Is not at once too palpably descried.
Full many an eager gentleman oft rues
   His haste: impatience is a blundering guide
Amongst a people famous for reflection,
Who like to play the fool with circumspection.

LXXII

But, if you can contrive, get next at supper;
   Or, if forestalled, get opposite and ogle:—
Oh, ye ambrosial moments! always upper
   In mind, a sort of sentimental bogle,*
Which sits for ever upon Memory's crupper,
   The ghost of vanished pleasures once in vogue! Ill
Can tender souls relate the rise and fall
Of hopes and fears which shake a single ball.

LXXIII

But these precautionary hints can touch
   Only the common run, who must pursue,
And watch, and ward; whose plans a word too much
   Or little overturns; and not the few
Or many (for the number 's sometimes such)
   Whom a good mien, especially if new,
Or fame, or name, for wit, war, sense, or nonsense,
Permits whate'er they please, or *did* not long since.

LXXIV

Our hero, as a hero, young and handsome,
   Noble, rich, celebrated, and a stranger,
Like other slaves of course must pay his ransom
   Before he can escape from so much danger
As will environ a conspicuous man. Some
   Talk about poetry, and "rack and manger,"[28]
And ugliness, disease, as toil and trouble,—
I wish they knew the life of a young noble.

---

* Scotch for goblin.

[28] Like "rack and ruin."

LXXV

They are young, but know not youth—it is
    anticipated;
  Handsome but wasted, rich without a sou;
Their vigour in a thousand arms is dissipated;
  Their cash comes *from*, their wealth goes *to* a Jew;
Both senates see their nightly votes participated
  Between the tyrant's and the tribunes' crew;
And having voted, dined, drunk, gamed, and whored,
The family vault receives another lord.

LXXVI

"Where is the world?" cries Young, "at *eighty*?"
    "Where
  The world in which a man was born?" Alas!
Where is the world of *eight* years past? *'T was there*—
  I look for it—'t is gone, a Globe of Glass!
Cracked, shivered, vanished, scarcely gazed on, ere
  A silent change dissolves the glittering mass.
Statesmen, chiefs, orators, queens, patriots, kings,
And dandies, all are gone on the wind's wings.

LXXVII

Where is Napoleon the Grand? God knows:
  Where little Castlereagh? The devil can tell:
Where Grattan, Curran, Sheridan, all those
  Who bound the bar or senate in their spell?
Where is the unhappy Queen, with all her woes?
  And where the Daughter, whom the Isles loved
    well?
Where are those martyred Saints the Five per Cents?
And where—oh where the devil are the Rents!

LXXVIII

Where 's Brummell? Dished. Where 's Long Pole
    Wellesley? Diddled.
  Where 's Whitbread? Romilly? Where 's George
    the Third?
Where is his will? (That's not so soon unriddled.)
  And where is "Fum" the Fourth, our "royal
    bird"?
Gone down, it seems, to Scotland to be fiddled
  Unto by Sawney's violin, we have heard.
"Caw me, caw thee"—for six months hath been
    hatching
This scene of royal itch and loyal scratching.

LXXIX

Where is Lord This? And where my Lady That?
  The Honourable Mistresses and Misses?
Some laid aside like an old opera hat,
  Married, unmarried, and remarried: (this is

An evolution oft performed of late).
  Where are the Dublin shouts—and London hisses?
Where are the Grenvilles? Turned as usual. Where
My friends the Whigs? Exactly where they were.

LXXX

Where are the Lady Carolines and Franceses?
  Divorced or doing thereanent. Ye annals
So brilliant, where the list of routs and dances is,—
  Thou Morning Post, sole record of the pannels
Broken in carriages, and all the phantasies [channels?
  Of fashion,—say what streams now fill those
Some die, some fly, some languish on the Continent,
Because the times have hardly left them *one* tenant.[29]

LXXXI

Some who once set their caps at cautious Dukes,
  Have taken up at length with younger brothers:
Some heiresses have bit at sharper's hooks:
  Some maids have been made wives, some merely
Others have lost their fresh and fairy looks: [mothers;
  In short, the list of alterations bothers:
There 's little strange in this, but something strange is
The unusual quickness of these common changes.

LXXXII

Talk not of seventy years as age; in seven
  I have seen more changes, down from monarchs to
The humblest individuals under heaven,
  Than might suffice a moderate century through.
I knew that nought was lasting, but now even
  Change grows too changeable, without being new:
Nought 's permanent among the human race,
Except the Whigs *not* getting into place.

LXXXIII

I have seen Napoleon, who seemed quite a Jupiter,
  Shrink to a Saturn. I have seen a Duke
(No matter which) turn politician stupider,
  If that can well be, than his wooden look.
But it is time that I should hoist my "blue Peter,"[30]
  And sail for a new theme:—I have seen—and shook
To see it—the King hissed, and then carest;
But don't pretend to settle which was best.

⟡⟡⟡⟡⟡⟡⟡⟡⟡⟡⟡⟡⟡

[29] This list in Stanzas LXXVII–LXXX of things and persons
gone includes Beau Brummell and the Duke of Wellington's
Nephew (Long Pole Wellesley) who were bankrupt; Samuel
Whitbread and Sir Samuel Romilly, who had killed themselves;
the divorced Queen Caroline and Princess Charlotte, once heir
apparent, who had died; Byron's ex-mistress Lady Caroline Lamb
and friend Lady Frances Wedderburn Webster, who were
estranged from their husbands.
[30] The flag announcing a ship's sailing.

LXXXIV

I have seen the landholders without a rap—
    I have seen Joanna Southcote—I have seen
The House of Commons turned to a tax-trap—
    I have seen that sad affair of the late Queen [31]—
I have seen crowns worn instead of a fool's-cap—
    I have seen a Congress doing all that 's mean—
I have seen some nations like o'erloaded asses
Kick off their burthens—meaning the high classes.

LXXXV

I have seen small poets, and great prosers, and
    Interminable—*not eternal*—speakers—
I have seen the Funds at war with house and land—
    I have seen the Country Gentlemen turn squeakers—
I have seen the people ridden o'er like sand [32]
    By slaves on horseback—I have seen malt liquors
Exchanged for "thin potations" by John Bull—
I have seen John half detect himself a fool.—

LXXXVI

But "Carpe diem," Juan, "Carpe, carpe!"
    To-morrow sees another race as gay
And transient, and devoured by the same harpy.
    "Life's a poor player,"—then "play out the play,
Ye villains!" and above all keep a sharp eye
    Much less on what you do than what you say:
Be hypocritical, be cautious, be
Not what you *seem*, but always what you *see*.

LXXXVII

But how shall I relate in other Cantos
    Of what befell our hero in the land,
Which 't is the common cry and lie to vaunt as
    A moral country? But I hold my hand—
For I disdain to write an Atalantis; [33]
    But 't is as well at once to understand,
You are *not* a moral people, and you know it
Without the aid of too sincere a poet.

LXXXVIII

What Juan saw and underwent, shall be
    My topic, with of course the due restriction
Which is required by proper courtesy;
    And recollect the work is only fiction,
And that I sing of neither mine nor me,
    Though every scribe, in some slight turn of diction,
Will hint allusions never *meant*. Ne'er doubt
This—when I speak, I *don't hint*, but *speak out*.

---

[31] Queen Caroline was tried for infidelity in 1820; for Joanna Southcote (line 2) see note, p. 641.
[32] Probably a reference to the "Peterloo" Massacre in Manchester in 1819. See Shelley's *Mask of Anarchy*, p. 886.
[33] A fictionalized memoir of the early eighteenth century.

LXXXIX

Whether he married with the third or fourth
    Offspring of some sage, husband-hunting Countess,
Or whether with some virgin of more worth
    (I mean in Fortune's matrimonial bounties),
He took to regularly peopling Earth,
    Of which your lawful awful wedlock fount is,—
Or whether he was taken in for damages,
For being too excursive in his homages,—

XC

Is yet within the unread events of time.
    Thus far, go forth, thou Lay, which I will back
Against the same given quantity of rhyme,
    For being as much the subject of attack
As ever yet was any work sublime,
    By those who love to say that white is black.
So much the better!—I may stand alone,
But would not change my free thoughts for a throne.

[1822–23]   [1823]

CANTO THE TWELFTH

I

Of all the barbarous Middle Ages, that
    Which is most barbarous is the middle age
Of man! it is—I really scarce know what;
    But when we hover between fool and sage,
And don't know justly what we would be at,—
    A period something like a printed page,
Black letter upon foolscap, while our hair
Grows grizzled, and we are not what we were,—

II

Too old for youth,—too young, at thirty-five,
    To herd with boys, or hoard with good
I wonder people should be left alive;   [threescore,—
    But since they are, that epoch is a bore:
Love lingers still, although 't were late to wive:
    And as for other love, the illusion 's o'er;
And Money, that most pure imagination,
Gleams only through the dawn of its creation.

III

Oh Gold! Why call we misers miserable?
    Theirs is the pleasure that can never pall;
Theirs is the best bower-anchor, the chain cable
    Which hold fast other pleasures great and small.
Ye who but see the saving man at table,
    And scorn his temperate board, as none at all,
And wonder how the wealthy can be sparing,
Know not what visions spring from each
                                    [cheese-paring.

IV

Love or lust makes man sick, and wine much sicker;
   Ambition rends, and gaming gains a loss;
But making money, slowly first, then quicker,
   And adding still a little through each cross
(Which *will* come over things) beats love or liquor,
   The gamester's counter, or the statesman's *dross*.
Oh Gold! I still prefer thee unto paper,
Which makes bank credit like a bark of vapour.

V

Who hold the balance of the world? Who reign
   O'er Congress, whether royalist or liberal?
Who rouse the shirtless patriots of Spain?
   (That make old Europe's journals squeak and
      gibber all.)
Who keep the world, both old and new, in pain
   Or pleasure? Who make politics run glibber all?
The shade of Bonaparte's noble daring?—
Jew Rothschild, and his fellow Christian, Baring.[1]

VI

Those, and the truly liberal Lafitte,
   Are the true lords of Euope. Every loan
Is not a merely speculative hit,
   But seats a nation or upsets a throne.
Republics also get involved a bit;
   Columbia's stock hath holders not unknown
On 'Change; and even thy silver soil, Peru,
Must get itself discounted by a Jew.

VII

Why call the miser miserable? as
   I said before: the frugal life is his,
Which in a saint or cynic ever was
   The theme of praise: a hermit would not miss
Canonization for the self-same cause,
   And wherefore blame gaunt Wealth's austerities?
Because, you 'll say, nought calls for such a trial;—
Then there 's more merit in his self-denial.

VIII

He is your only poet;—passion, pure
   And sparkling on from heap to heap, displays,
Possessed, the ore, of which *mere hopes* allure
   Nations athwart the deep: the golden rays
Flash up in ingots from the mine obscure:
   On him the diamond pours its brilliant blaze,
While the mild emerald's beam shades down the dyes
Of other stones, to soothe the miser's eyes.

[1] The shirtless Spanish patriots were those of the revolt of
1820; Nathan Rothschild and Alexander Baring headed London
banks, Jacques Lafitte (Stanza VI) a Paris one. Largebanks had been
supporting revolutions in South America in the hope of replacing
Spain's commercial interests with their own.

IX

The lands on either side are his: the ship
   From Ceylon, Inde, or far Cathay, unloads
For him the fragrant produce of each trip;
   Beneath his cars of Ceres groan the roads,
And the vine blushes like Aurora's lip;
   His very cellars might be kings' abodes;
While he, despising every sensual call,
Commands—the intellectual lord of all.

X

Perhaps he hath great projects in his mind,
   To build a college, or to found a race,
A hospital, a church,—and leave behind
   Some dome surmounted by his meagre face:
Perhaps he fain would liberate mankind
   Even with the very ore which makes them base;
Perhaps he would be wealthiest of his nation,
Or revel in the joys of calculation.

XI

But whether all, or each, or none of these
   May be the hoarder's principle of action,
The fool will call such mania a disease:—
   What is his *own*? Go—look at each transaction,
Wars, revels, loves—do these bring men more ease
   Than the mere plodding through each "vulgar
      fraction"?[2]
Or do they benefit mankind? Lean Miser!
Let spendthrifts' heirs inquire of yours—who 's wiser?

XII

How beauteous are rouleaus! how charming chests
   Containing ingots, bags of dollars, coins
(Not of old Victors, all whose heads and crests
   Weigh not the thin ore where their visage shines,
But) of fine unclipt gold, where dully rests
   Some likeness, which the glittering cirque confines,
Of modern, reigning, sterling, stupid stamp:—
Yes! ready money *is* Aladdin's lamp.

XIII

"Love rules the camp, the court, the grove,—for
     Love
   Is Heaven, and Heaven is Love":—so sings the
Which it were rather difficult to prove   [bard;
   (A thing with poetry in general hard).
Perhaps there may be something in "the grove,"
   At least it rhymes to "Love"; but I 'm prepared
To doubt (no less than Landlords of their rental)
If "courts" and "camps" be quite so sentimental.

[2] Common as opposed to decimal fractions.

XIV

But if Love don't, *Cash* does, and Cash alone:
   Cash rules the grove, and fells it too besides;
Without cash, camps were thin, and courts were none;
   Without cash, Malthus tells you, "take no brides."
So Cash rules Love the ruler, on his own
   High ground, as Virgin Cynthia sways the tides;
And as for "Heaven being Love," why not say honey
Is wax? Heaven is not Love, 't is Matrimony.

XV

Is not all Love prohibited whatever,
   Excepting marriage? which is love, no doubt
After a sort; but somehow people never
   With the same thought the two words have helped
Love may exist *with* marriage, and *should* ever,   [out.
   And marriage also may exist without;
But love *sans* banns is both a sin and shame,
And ought to go by quite another name.

XVI

Now if the "court" and "camp" and "grove" be not
   Recruited all with constant married men,
Who never coveted their neighbour's lot,
   I say *that* line's a lapsus of the pen;—
Strange too in my "buon camerado" Scott,
   So celebrated for his morals, when
My Jeffrey held him up as an example [3]
To me;—of whom these morals are a sample.

XVII

Well, if I don't succeed, I *have* succeeded,
   And that's enough; succeeded in my youth,
The only time when much success is needed:
   And my success produced what I in sooth
Cared most about; it need not now be pleaded—
   Whate'er it was, 'twas mine: I've paid, in truth,
Of late, the penalty of such success,
But have not learned to wish it any less.

XVIII

That suit in Chancery,—which some persons plead [4]
   In an appeal to the unborn, whom they,
In the faith of their procreative creed,
   Baptize Posterity, or future clay,—
To me seems but a dubious kind of reed
   To lean on for support in any way;
Since odds are that Posterity will know
No more of them, than they of her, I trow.

XIX

Why, I 'm Posterity—and so are you;
   And whom do we remember? Not a hundred.
Were every memory written down all true,
   The tenth or twentieth name would be but
     blundered:
Even Plutarch's lives have but picked out a few,
   And 'gainst those few your annalists have
And Mitford in the nineteenth century* [thundered;
Gives, with Greek truth, the good old Greek the lie.

XX

Good People all, of every degree,
   Ye gentle readers and ungentle writers,
In this twelfth Canto 't is my wish to be
   As serious as if I had for inditers
Malthus and Wilberforce:—the last set free
   The Negroes, and is worth a million fighters;
While Wellington has but enslaved the whites,
And Malthus does the thing 'gainst which he writes. [5]

XXI

I 'm serious—so are all men upon paper;
   And why should I not form my speculation,
And hold up to the sun my little taper?
   Mankind just now seem wrapt in meditation
On Constitutions and Steam-boats of vapour;
   While sages write against all procreation,
Unless a man can calculate his means
Of feeding brats the moment his wife weans.

XXII

That 's noble! That 's romantic! For my part,
   I think that "Philo-genitiveness" is [6]—
(Now here 's a word quite after my own heart,
   Though there 's a shorter a good deal than this,
If that politeness set it not apart;
   But I 'm resolved to say nought that 's amiss)—
I say, methinks that "Philo-gentiveness"
Might meet from men a little more forgiveness.

* See Mitford's *Greece*. "Græcia *Verax*." His great pleasure consists in praising tyrants, abusing Plutarch, spelling oddly, and writing quaintly; and what is strange after all, *his* is the best Modern History of Greece in any language, and he is perhaps the best of all modern historians whatsoever. Having named his sins, it is but fair to state his virtues—learning, labour, research, wrath, and partiality. I call the latter virtues in a writer, because they make him write in earnest.

[3] In the *Edinburgh Review*, 1822.
[4] Byron's publisher had attempted to stop a pirated edition of *Cain*.

[5] There was a legend that Malthus had eleven children; actually there were only three. Wilberforce was active in attempting to supress slavery.
[6] Byron's coinage for the "love of procreation."

XXIII

And now to business. Oh my gentle Juan!
   Thou art in London—in that pleasant place,
Where every kind of mischief's daily brewing,
   Which can await warm youth in its wild race.
'T is true that thy career is not a new one;
   Thou art no novice in the headlong chase
Of early life; but this is a new land
Which foreigners can never understand.

XXIV

What with a small diversity of climate,
   Of hot or cold, mercurial or sedate,
I could send forth my mandate like a primate
   Upon the rest of Europe's social state;
But thou art the most difficult to rhyme at,
   Great Britain, which the Muse may penetrate:
All countries have their "Lions," but in thee
There is but one superb menagerie.

XXV

But I am sick of politics. Begin,
   "*Paulo Majora.*" [7] Juan, undecided
Amongst the paths of being "taken in,"
   Above the ice had like a skater glided:
When tired of play, he flirted without sin
   With some of those fair creatures who have prided
Themselves on innocent tantalization,
And hate all vice except its reputation.

XXVI

But these are few, and in the end they make
   Some devilish escapade or stir, which shows
That even the purest people may mistake
   Their way through Virtue's primrose paths of
And then men stare, as if a new ass spake   [snows;
   To Balaam, and from tongue to ear o'erflows [8]
Quick silver Small Talk, ending (if you note it)
With the kind world's Amen!—"Who would have
                [thought it?"

XXVII

The little Leila, with her orient eyes,
   And tactiturn Asiatic disposition,
(Which saw all Western things with small surprise,
   To the surprise of people of condition,
Who think that novelties are butterflies
   To be pursued as food for inanition,)
Her charming figure and romantic history
Became a kind of fashionable mystery.

   7 "Let us turn to matters of greater weight."
   8 Num. 22:21.

XXVIII

The women much divided—as is usual
   Amongst the sex in little things or great.
Think not, fair creatures, that I mean to abuse you
   I have always liked you better than I state: [all—
Since I 've grown moral, still I must accuse you all
   Of being apt to talk at a great rate;
And now there was a general sensation
Amongst you, about Leila's education.

XXIX

In one point only were you settled—and
   You had reason;—'t was that a young Child of
As beautiful as her own native land,   [Grace,
   And far away, the last bud of her race,
Howe'er our friend Don Juan might command
   Himself for five, four, three, or two years' space,
Would be much better taught beneath the eye
Of Peeresses whose follies had run dry.

XXX

So first there was a generous emulation,
   And then there was a general competition,
To undertake the orphan's education.
   As Juan was a person of condition,
It had been an affront on this occasion
   To talk of a subscription or petition;
But sixteen dowagers, ten unwed she sages
Whose tale belongs to "Hallam's Middle Ages,"

XXXI

And one or two sad, separate wives, without
   A fruit to bloom upon their withering bough,
Begged to bring *up* the little girl, and "*out*,"—
   For that 's the phrase that settles all things now,
Meaning a virgin's first blush at a rout,
   And all her points as thorough-bred to show:
And I assure you, that like virgin honey
Tastes their first season (mostly if they have money).

XXXII

How all the needy honourable misters,
   Each out-at-elbow peer, or desperate dandy,
The watchful mothers, and the careful sisters
   (Who, by the by, when clever, are more handy
At making matches, where "'t is gold that glisters,"
   Than their *he* relatives) like flies o'er candy
Buzz round "*the* Fortune" with their busy battery,
To turn her head with waltzing and with flattery!

XXXIII

Each aunt, each cousin hath her speculation;
　Nay, married dames will now and then discover
Such pure disinterestedness of passion,
　I 've known them court an heiress for their lover.
"Tantaene!" [9] Such the virtues of high station!
　Even in the hopeful Isle, whose outlet 's "Dover":
While the poor rich wretch, object of these cares,
Has cause to wish her sire had had male heirs.

XXXIV

Some are soon bagged, and some reject three dozen.
　'T is fine to see them scattering refusals
And wish dismay o'er every angry cousin
　(Friends of the party) who begin accusals,
Such as—"Unless Miss (Blank) meant to have chosen
　Poor Frederick, why did she accord perusals
To his billets? *Why* waltz with him? Why, I pray,
Look *yes* last night, and yet say *no* to-day?"

XXXV

"Why?—Why?—Besides, Fred. really was *attached*;
　'T was not her fortune—he has enough without:
The time will come she 'll wish that she had snatched
　So good an opportunity, no doubt:—
But the old marchioness some plan had hatched,
　As I 'll tell Aurea at to-morrow's rout:
And after all poor Frederick may do better—
Pray did you see her answer to his letter?"

XXXVI

Smart uniforms and sparkling coronets
　Are spurned in turn, until her turn arrives,
After male loss of time, and hearts, and bets
　Upon the sweepstakes for substantial wives:
And when at last the pretty creature gets
　Some gentleman who fights, or writes, or drives,
It soothes the awkward squad of the rejected,
To find how very badly she selected.

XXXVII

For sometimes they accept some long pursuer,
　Worn out with importunity; or fall
(But here perhaps the instances are fewer)
　To the lot of him who scarce pursued at all.
A hazy widower turned of forty 's sure *
　(If 't is not vain examples to recall)
To draw a high prize: now, howe'er he got her, I
See nought more strange in this than 't other lottery.

* This line may puzzle the commentators more than the present generation.

[9] An allusion to a line in Vergil's *Aeneid*: "Can there be such fierce anger in heavenly spirits?"

XXXVIII

I, for my part—(one "modern instance" more,
　"True 't is a pity, pity 't is, 't is true")
Was chosen from out an amatory score,
　Albeit my years were less discreet than few;
But though I also had reformed before
　Those became one who soon were to be two,
I 'll not gainsay the generous public's voice,
That the young lady made a monstrous choice.

XXXIX

Oh, pardon me disgression—or at least
　Peruse! 'T is always with a moral end
That I dissert, like Grace before a feast:
　For like an aged aunt, or tiresome friend,
A rigid guardian, or a zealous priest,
　My Muse by exhortation means to mend
All people, at all times and in most places;
Which puts my Pegasus to these grave paces.

XL

But now I 'm going to be immoral; now
　I mean to show things really as they are,
Not as they ought to be: for I avow,
　That till we see what 's what in fact, we 're far
From much improvement with that virtuous plough
　Which skims the surface, leaving scarce a scar
Upon the black loam long manured by Vice,
Only to keep its corn at the old price.

XLI

But first of little Leila we 'll dispose,
　For like a day-dawn she was young and pure,
Or, like the old comparison of snows,
　Which are more pure than pleasant to be sure.
Like many people every body knows,
　Don Juan was delighted to secure
A goodly guardian for his infant charge,
Who might not profit much by being at large.

XLII

Besides, he had found out he was no tutor:
　(I wish that others would find out the same)
And rather wished in such things to stand neuter,
　For silly wards will bring their guardians blame:
So when he saw each ancient dame a suitor
　To make his little wild Asiatic tame,
Consulting "the Society for Vice
Suppression," Lady Pinchbeck was his choice.

XLIII

Olden she was—but had been very young;
   Virtuous she was—and had been, I believe:
Although the world has such an evil tongue
   That—but my chaster ear will not receive
An echo of a syllable that 's wrong:
   In fact, there 's nothing makes me so much grieve
As that abominable tittle-tattle,
Which is the cud eschewed by human cattle.

XLIV

Moreover I 've remarked (and I was once
   A slight observer in a modest way)
And so may every one except a dunce,
   That ladies in their youth a little gay,
Besides their knowledge of the world, and sense
   Of the sad consequence of going astray,
Are wiser in their warnings 'gainst the woe
Which the mere passionless can never know.

XLV

While the harsh Prude indemnifies her virtue
   By railing at the unknown and envied passion,
Seeking far less to save you than to hurt you,
   Or, what 's still worse, to put you out of fashion,—
The kinder veteran with calm words will court you,
   Entreating you to pause before you dash on;
Expounding and illustrating the riddle
Of epic Love's beginning, end, and middle.

XLVI

Now whether it be thus, or that they are stricter,
   As better knowing why they should be so,
I think you 'll find from many a family picture,
   That daughters of such mothers as may know
The world by experience rather than by lecture,
   Turn out much better for the Smithfield Show
Of vestals brought into the marriage mart,
Than those bred up by prudes without a heart.

XLVII

I said that Lady Pinchbeck had been talked about—
   As who has not, if female, young, and pretty?
But now no more the ghost of Scandal stalked about;
   She merely was deemed amiable and witty,
And several of her best bons-mots were hawked about;
   Then she was given to charity and pity,
And passed (at least the latter years of life)
For being a most exemplary wife.

XLVIII

High in high circles, gentle in her own,
   She was the mild reprover of the young,
Whenever—which means every day—they 'd shown
   An awkward inclination to go wrong.
The quantity of good she did 's unknown,
   Or at least would lengthen out my song:—
In brief, the little orphan of the East
Had raised an interest in her which increased.

XLIX

Juan too was a sort of favourite with her,
   Because she thought him a good heart at bottom,
A little spoiled, but not so altogether;
   Which was a wonder, if you think who got him,
And how he had been tossed, he scarce knew whither:
   Though this might ruin others, it did *not* him,
At least entirely—for he had seen too many
Changes in youth, to be surprised at any.

L

And these vicissitudes tell best in youth;
   For when they happen at a riper age,
People are apt to blame the Fates, forsooth,
   And wonder Providence is not more sage.
Adversity is the first path to truth:
   He who hath proved war, storm, or woman's rage,
Whether his winters be eighteen or eighty,
Hath won the experience which is deemed so weighty.

LI

How far it profits is another matter.—
   Our hero gladly saw his little charge
Safe with a lady, whose last grown-up daughter
   Being long married, and thus set at large,
Had left all the accomplishments she taught her
   To be transmitted, like the Lord Mayor's barge,
To the next comer; or—as it will tell
More Muse-like—say like Cytherea's shell. [10]

LII

I call such things transmission; for there is
   A floating balance of accomplishment
Which forms a pedigree from Miss to Miss,
   According as their minds or backs are bent.
Some waltz; some draw; some fathom the abyss
   Of metaphysics; others are content
With music; the most moderate shine as wits,
While others have a genius turned for fits.

[10] The shell on which Venus was said to have come from the sea at Cythera.

LIII

But whether fits, or wits, or harpsichords,
　　Theology, Fine Arts, or finer stays
May be the baits for gentlemen or lords
　　With regular descent, in these our days
The last year to the new transfers its hoards;
　　New vestals claim men's eyes with the same praise
Of "elegant" *et cetera*, in fresh batches—
All matchless creatures and yet bent on matches.

LIV

But now I will begin my poem.—'Tis
　　Perhaps a little strange, if not quite new,
That from the first of Cantos up to this
　　I 've not begun what we have to go through.
These first twelve books are merely flourishes,
　　Preludios, trying just a string or two
Upon my lyre, or making the pegs sure;
And when so, you shall have the overture.

LV

My Muses do not care a pinch of rosin
　　About what 's called success, or not succeeding:
Such thoughts are quite below the strain they have
　　　　chosen;
　　'T is a "great moral lesson" they are reading.
I thought, at setting off, about two dozen
　　Cantos would do; but at Apollo's pleading,
If that my Pegasus should not be foundered,
I think to canter gently through a hundred.

LVI

Don Juan saw that microcosm on stilts,
　　Yclept the Great World; for it is the least,
Although the highest: but as swords have hilts
　　By which their power of mischief is encreased,
When Man in battle or in quarrel tilts,
　　Thus the low world, north, south, or west, or east,
Must still obey the high—which is their handle,
Their moon, their sun, their gas, their farthing candle.

LVII

He had many friends who had many wives, and was
　　Well looked upon by both, to that extent
Of friendship which you may accept or pass,
　　It does nor good nor harm; being merely meant
To keep the wheels going of the higher class,
　　And draw them nightly when a ticket 's sent;
And what with masquerades, and fêtes, and balls,
For the first season such a life scarce palls.

LVIII

A young unmarried man, with a good name
　　And fortune, has an awkward part to play;
For good society is but a game,
　　"The royal game of Goose," as I may say,
Where every body has some separate aim,
　　An end to answer, or a plan to lay—
The single ladies wishing to be double,
The married ones to save the virgins trouble.

LIX

I don't mean this as general, but particular
　　Examples may be found of such pursuits:
Though several also keep their perpendicular
　　Like poplars, with good principles for roots;
Yet many have a method more *reticular*—
　　"Fishers for men," like Sirens with soft lutes:[11]
For talk six times with the same single lady,
And you may get the wedding dresses ready.

LX

Perhaps you 'll have a letter from the mother,
　　To say her daughter's feelings are trepanned;
Perhaps you 'll have a visit from the brother,
　　All strut and stays and whiskers, to demand
What "your intentions are"?—One way or other
　　It seems the virgin's heart expects your hand;
And between pity for her case and yours,
You 'll add to Matrimony's list of cures.

LXI

I 've known a dozen weddings made even *thus*,
　　And some of them high names: I have also known
Young men who—though they hated to discuss
　　Pretensions which they never dreamed to have
Yet neither frightened by a female fuss, 　　[shown—
　　Nor by mustachios moved, were let alone,
And lived, as did the broken-hearted fair,
In happier plight than if they formed a pair.

LXII

There 's also nightly, to the uninitiated,
　　A peril—not indeed like love or marriage,
But not the less for this to be depreciated:
　　It is— I meant and mean not to disparage
The show of virtue even in the vitiated—
　　It adds an outward grace unto their carriage—
But to denounce the amphibious sort of harlot,
"*Couleur de rose*," who 's neither white nor scarlet.

〰〰〰〰〰〰〰〰〰〰〰〰〰〰〰〰〰〰

11 Christ is of course the original "Fisher for men."

LXIII

Such is your cold coquette, who can't say "No,"
  And won't say "Yes," and keeps you on the off-ing
On a lee-shore, till it begins to blow—
  Then sees your heart wrecked, with an inward
This works a world of sentimental woe,   [scoffing.
  And sends new Werters yearly to their coffin;[12]
But yet is merely innocent flirtation,
Not quite adultery, but adulteration.

LXIV

"Ye gods, I grow a talker!" Let us prate.
  The next of perils, though I place it *sternest*,
Is when, without regard to "Church or State,"
  A wife makes or takes love in upright earnest.
Abroad, such things decide few women's fate—
  (Such, early traveller! is the truth thou learnest)—
But in Old England, when a young bride errs,
Poor thing! Eve's was a trifling case to her's.

LXV

For 't is a low, newspaper, humdrum, lawsuit
  Country, where a young couple of the same ages
Can't form a friendship, but the world o'erawes it.
  Then there 's the vulgar trick of those d—d
    damages!
A verdict—grievous foe to those who cause it!—
  Forms a sad climax to romantic homages;
Besides those soothing speeches of the pleaders,
And evidences which regale all readers!

LXVI

But they who blunder thus are raw beginners;
  A little genial sprinkling of hypocrisy
Has saved the fame of thousand splendid sinners,
  The loveliest Oligarchs of our Gynocrasy,[13]
You may see such at all the balls and dinners,
  Among the proudest of our Aristocracy,
So gentle, charming, charitable, chaste—
And all by having *tact* as well as taste.

LXVII

Juan, who did not stand in the predicament
  Of a mere novice, had one safeguard more;
For he was sick—no, 't was not the word *sick* I
    meant—
  But he had seen so much good love before,
That he was not in heart so very weak;—I meant
  But thus much, and no sneer against the shore
Of white cliffs, white necks, blue eyes, bluer stockings,
Tithes, taxes, duns, and doors with double knockings.

[12] In Goethe's *The Sorrows of Young Werther*, the hero kills himself.
[13] Gyneocracy: a government of women.

LXVIII

But coming young from lands and scenes romantic,
  Where lives not lawsuits must be risked for
    Passion,
And Passion's self must have a spice of frantic,
  Into a country where 't is half a fashion,
Seemed to him half commercial, half pedantic,
  Howe'er he might esteem this moral nation;
Besides (alas! his taste—forgive and pity!)
At first he did not think the women pretty.

LXIX

I say at *first*—for he found out at *last*,
  But by degrees, that they were fairer far
Than the more glowing dames whose lot is cast
  Beneath the influence of the Eastern Star.
A further proof we should not judge in haste;
  Yet inexperience could not be his bar
To taste:—the truth is, if men would confess,
That novelties *please* less than they *impress*.

LXX

Though travelled, I have never had the luck to
  Trace up those shuffling negroes, Nile or Niger,
To that impracticable place Timbuctoo,
  Where Geography finds no one to oblige her
With such a chart as may be safely stuck to—
  For Europe ploughs in Afric like "*bos piger*":[14]
But if I *had been* at Timbuctoo, there
No doubt I should be told that black is fair.

LXXI

It is. I will not swear that black is white;
  But I suspect in fact that white is black,
And the whole matter rests upon eye-sight.
  Ask a blind man, the best judge. You 'll attack
Perhaps this new position—but I 'm right;
  Or if I 'm wrong, I 'll not be ta'en aback:—
He hath no morn nor night, but all is dark
Within; and what seest thou? A dubious spark!

LXXII

But I 'm relapsing into metaphysics,
  That labyrinth, whose clue is of the same
Construction as your cures for hectic phthisics,
  Those bright moths fluttering round a dying
    flame:
And this reflection brings me to plain physics,
  And to the beauties of a foreign dame,
Compared with those of our pure pearls of price,
Those Polar summers, *all* sun, and some ice.

[14] "Lazy ox."

LXXIII

Or say they are like virtuous mermaids, whose
    Beginnings are fair faces, ends mere fishes;—
Not that there's not a quantity of those
    Who have a due respect for their own wishes.
Like Russians rushing from hot baths to snows*
    Are they, at bottom virtuous even when vicious:
They warm into a scrape, but keep of course,
As a reserve, a plunge into remorse.

LXXIV

But this has nought to do with their outsides.
    I said that Juan did not think them pretty
At the first blush; for a fair Briton hides
    Half her attractions—probably from pity—
And rather calmly into the heart glides,
    Than storms it as a foe would take a city;
But once *there* (if you doubt this, prithee try)
She keeps it for you like a true ally.

LXXV

She cannot step as does an Arab barb,[15]
    Or Andalusian girl from mass returning,
Nor wear as gracefully as Gauls her garb,
    Nor in her eye Ausonia's glance is burning;
Her voice, though sweet, is not so fit to warb-
    le those *bravuras* (which I still am learning
To like, though I have been seven years in Italy,
And have, or had, an ear that served me prettily);—

LXXVI

She cannot do these things, nor one or two
    Others, in that off-hand and dashing style
Which takes so much—to give the devil his due,—
    Nor is she quite so ready with her smile,
Nor settles all things in one interview,
    (A thing approved as saving time and toil);—
But though the soil may give you time and trouble,
Well cultivated, it will render double.

LXXVII

And if in fact she takes to a "*grande passion*,"
    It is a very serious thing indeed:
Nine times in ten 't is but caprice or fashion,
    Coquetry, or a wish to take the lead,
The pride of a mere child with a new sash on,
    Or wish to make a rival's bosom bleed;
But the *tenth* instance will be a Tornado,
For there's no saying what they will or may do.

* The Russians, as is well known, run out from their hot baths to plunge into the Neva; a pleasant practical antithesis, which it seems does them no harm.

[15] An Arabian horse from Barbary is an arab barb; Ausonia (line 4) is a classical name for Italy.

LXXVIII

The reason's obvious: if there's an éclat,
    They lose their caste at once, as do the Parias;
And when the delicacies of the law
    Have filled their papers with their comments [various,
Society, that china without flaw,
    (The hypocrite!) will banish them like Marius,[16]
To sit amidst the ruins of their guilt:
For Fame's a Carthage not so soon rebuilt.

LXXIX

Perhaps this is as it should be;—it is
    A comment on the Gospel's "Sin no more,
And be thy sins forgiven:"—but upon this
    I leave the Saints to settle their own score.
Abroad, though doubtless they do much amiss,
    An erring woman finds an opener door
For her return to Virtue—as they call
That Lady who should be at home to all.

LXXX

For me, I leave the matter where I find it,
    Knowing that such uneasy Virtue leads
People some ten times less in fact to mind it,
    And care but for discoveries and not deeds.
But as for Chastity, you'll never bind it
    By all the laws the strictest lawyer pleads,
But aggravate the crime you have not prevented,
By rendering desperate those who had else repented.

LXXXI

But Juan was no casuist, nor had pondered
    Upon the moral lessons of mankind:
Besides, he had not seen of several hundred
    A lady altogether to his mind.
A little "*blâsé*"—'t is not to be wondered
    At, that his heart had got a tougher rind:
And though not vainer from his past success,
No doubt his sensibilities were less.

LXXXII

He also had been busy seeing sights—
    The Parliament and all the other houses;
Had sat beneath the gallery at nights,
    To hear debates whose thunder *roused* (not *rouses*)
The world to gaze upon those northern lights,
    Which flashed as far as where the musk-bull
        browses;†
He had also stood at times behind the throne—
But Grey was not arrived, and Chatham gone.

† For a description and print of this inhabitant of the polar region and native country of the Aurorae Boreales, see Parry's Voyage in search of a North-West Passage.

[16] In exile from Rome, Marius went to Carthage, which he had once conquered.

LXXXIII

He saw however at the closing session,
    That noble sight, when *really* free the nation,
A king in constitutional possession
    Of such a throne as is the proudest station,
Though despots know it not—till the progression
    Of freedom shall complete their education.
'T is not mere splendour makes the show august
To eye or heart—it is the people's trust.

LXXXIV

There too he saw (whate'er he may be now)
    A Prince, the prince of princes at the time
With fascination in his very bow,
    And full of promise, as the spring of prime.
Though royalty was written on his brow,
    He had *then* the grace too, rare in every clime,
Of being, without alloy of fop or beau,
A finished gentleman from top to toe.[17]

LXXXV

And Juan was received, as hath been said,
    Into the best society: and there
Occurred what often happens, I'm afraid,
    However disciplined and *debonnaire*:—
The talent and good humour he displayed,
    Besides the marked distinction of his air,
Exposed him, as was natural, to temptation,
Even though himself avoided the occasion.

LXXXVI

But what, and where, with whom, and when, and why,
    Is not to be put hastily together;
And as my object is morality
    (Whatever people say) I don't know whether
I 'll leave a single reader's eyelid dry,
    But harrow up his feelings till they wither,
And hew out a huge monument of pathos,
As Phillip's son proposed to do with Athos.*

* A sculptor projected to hew Mount Athos into a statue of Alexander, with a city in one hand, and I believe a river in his pocket, with various other similar devices. But Alexander's gone, and Athos remains, I trust ere long to look over a nation of free men.[18]

‹•‹•‹•‹•‹•‹•‹•‹•‹•‹•‹•‹•‹•‹•‹•‹•‹•‹•‹•

[17] George IV, here seen as Prince Regent, was known for his knowledge of Greek and Latin poets and historians, his graceful manners, his great promise as a leader.
[18] In fact, Alexander (Philip's son) rejected the sculptor's proposal.

LXXXVII

Here the twelfth Canto of our introduction
    Ends. When the body of the book 's begun,
You 'll find it of a different construction
    From what some people say 't will be when done:
The plan at present's simply in concoction.
    I can't oblige you, reader! to read on;
That 's your affair, not mine: a real spirit
Should neither court neglect, nor dread to bear it.

LXXXVIII

And if my thunderbolt not always rattles,
    Remember, reader! you have had before
The worst of tempests and the best of battles
    That e'er were brewed from elements or gore,
Besides the most sublime of—Heaven knows what
    An Usurer could scarce expect much more—[else—
But my best Canto save one on Astronomy,
Will turn upon "Political Economy."

LXXXIX

That is your present theme for popularity:
    Now that the Public Hedge hath scarce a stake,
It grows an act of patriotic charity,
    To show the people the best way to break.
My plan (but I, if but for singularity,
    Reserve it) will be very sure to take.
Mean time read all the National-Debt sinkers,
And tell me what you think of your great thinkers.

[1823]   [1823]

CANTO THE THIRTEENTH

I

I NOW mean to be serious;—it is time,
    Since laughter now-a-days is deemed too serious;
A jest at Vice by Virtue 's called a crime,
    And critically held as deleterious:
Besides, the sad 's a source of the sublime,
    Although when long a little apt to weary us;
And therefore shall my lay soar high and solemn
As an old temple dwindled to a column.

II

The Lady Adeline Amundeville
    ('T is an old Norman name, and to be found
In pedigrees by those who wander still
    Along the last fields of that Gothic ground)—
Was high-born, wealthy by her father's will,
    And beauteous, even where beauties most abound,
In Britain—which, of course, true patriots find
The goodliest soil of Body and of Mind.

III

I 'll not gainsay them; it is not my cue;
  I'll leave them to their taste, no doubt the best;
An eye 's an eye, and whether black or blue,
  Is no great matter, so 't is in request:
'T is nonsense to dispute about a hue—
  The kindest may be taken as a test.
The fair sex should be always fair, and no man,
Till thirty, should perceive there 's a plain woman.

IV

And after that serene and somewhat dull
  Epoch, that awkward corner turned for days
More quiet, when our Moon 's no more at full,
  We may presume to criticize or praise;
Because Indifference begins to lull
  Our passions, and we walk in Wisdom's ways;
Also because the figure and the face
Hint, that 't is time to give the younger place.

V

I know that some would fain postpone this era,
  Reluctant as all placemen to resign
Their post; but theirs is merely a chimera,
  For they have passed life's equinoctial line:
But then they have their claret and madeira,
  To irrigate the dryness of decline;
And County Meetings, and the Parliament,
And debt, and what not, for their solace sent.

VI

And is there not Religion, and Reform,
  Peace, War, the taxes, and what 's called the
The struggle to be Pilots in a storm?   ["Nation"?
  The landed and the monied speculation?
The joys of mutual hate, to keep them warm,
  Instead of love, that mere hallucination?
Now hatred is by far the longest pleasure;
Men love in haste, but they detest at leisure.

VII

Rough Johnson, the great moralist, professed,
  Right honestly, "he liked an honest hater"—
The only truth that yet has been confest
  Within these latest thousand years or later.
Perhaps the fine old fellow spoke in jest:—
  For my part, I am but a mere spectator,
And gaze where'er the place or the hovel is,
Much in the mode of Goethe's Mephistopheles;

VIII

But neither love nor hate in much excess;
  Though 't was not once so. If I sneer sometimes,
It is because I cannot well do less,
  And now and then it also suits my rhymes.
I should be very willing to redress
  Men's wrongs, and rather check than punish crimes,
Had not Cervantes, in that too true tale
Of Quixote, shown how all such efforts fail.

IX

Of all tales 't is the saddest—and more sad,
  Because it makes us smile: his hero 's right,
And still pursues the right;—to curb the bad
  His only object, and 'gainst odds to fight,
His guerdon: 't is his virtue makes him mad!
  But his adventures form a sorry sight;—
A sorrier still is the great moral taught
By that real Epic unto all who have thought.

X

Redressing injury, revenging wrong,
  To aid the damsel and destroy the caitiff;
Opposing singly the united strong,
  From foreign yoke to free the helpless native:—
Alas! Must noblest views, like an old song,
  Be for mere Fancy's sport a theme creative?
A jest, a riddle, Fame through thin and thick sought?
And Socrates himself but Wisdom's Quixote?

XI

Cervantes smiled Spain's Chivalry away;
  A single laugh demolished the right arm
Of his own country;—seldom since that day
  Has Spain had heroes. While Romance could charm,
The world gave ground before her bright array;
  And therefore have his volumes done such harm,
That all their glory, as a composition,
Was dearly purchased by his land's perdition.

XII

I 'm "at my old Lunes"—digression, and forget [1]
  The lady Adeline Amundeville;
The fair most fatal Juan ever met,
  Although she was not evil, nor meant ill;
But Destiny and Passion spread the net,
  (Fate is a good excuse for our own will),
And caught them;—what do they *not* catch, methinks?
But I 'm not Oedipus, and life 's a Sphinx.

[1] Lunes are fits of madness.

XIII

I tell the tale as it is told, nor dare
   To venture a solution: "*Davus sum*!" [2]
And now I will proceed upon the pair.
   Sweet Adeline, amidst the gay world's hum,
Was the Queen-Bee, the glass of all that 's fair;
   Whose charms made all men speak, and women
The last 's a miracle, and such was reckoned,   [dumb.
And since that time there has not been a second.

XIV

Chaste was she, to detraction's desperation,
   And wedded unto one she had loved well;
A man known in the councils of the nation,
   Cool, and quite English; imperturbable,
Though apt to act with fire upon occasion;
   Proud of himself and her; the world could tell
Nought against either, and both seemed secure—
She in her virtue, he in his hauteur.

XV

It chanced some diplomatical relations,
   Arising out of business, often brought
Himself and Juan in their mutual stations
   Into close contact. Though reserved, nor caught
By specious seeming, Juan's youth, and patience,
   And talent, on his haughty spirit wrought,
And formed a basis of esteem, which ends
In making men what Courtesy calls friends.

XVI

And thus Lord Henry, who was cautious as
   Reserve and pride could make him, and full slow
In judging men—when once his judgment was
   Determined, right or wrong, on friend or foe,
Had all the pertinacity pride has,
   Which knows no ebb to its imperious flow,
And loves or hates, disdaining to be guided,
Because its own good pleasure hath decided.

XVII

His friendships therefore, and no less aversions,
   Though oft well founded, which confirmed but
His prepossessions, like the laws of Persians   [more
   And Medes, would ne'er revoke what went before.
His feelings had not those strange fits, like tertians,
   Of common likings, which make some deplore
What they should laugh at—the mere ague still
Of Men's regard, the fever or the chill.

XVIII

"'Tis not in mortals to command success:
   But *do you more*, Sempronius—*don't* deserve it"; [3]
And take my word, you won't have any less.
   Be wary, watch the time, and always serve it;
Give gently way, when there 's too great a press;
   And for your conscience, only learn to nerve it,—
For, like a racer or a boxer training,
'T will make, if proved, vast efforts without paining.

XIX

Lord Henry also liked to be superior,
   As most men do, the little or the great;
The very lowest find out an inferior,
   At least they think so, to exert their state
Upon: for there are very few things wearier
   Than solitary Pride's oppressive weight,
Which mortals generously would divide,
By bidding others carry while they ride.

XX

In birth, in rank, in fortune likewise equal,
   O'er Juan he could no distinction claim;
In years he had the advantage of time's sequel;
   And, as he thought, in country much the same—
Because bold Britons have a tongue and free quill,
   At which all modern nations vainly aim;
And the Lord Henry was a great debater,
So that few members kept the House up later.

XXI

These were advantages: and then he thought—
   It was his foible, but by no means sinister—
That few or none more than himself had caught
   Court mysteries, having been himself a minister:
He liked to teach that which he had been taught,
   And greatly shone whenever there had been a stir;
And reconciled all qualities which grace man,
Always a Patriot, and sometimes a Placeman.

XXII

He liked the gentle Spaniard for his gravity;
   He almost honoured him for his docility;
Because, though young, he acquiesced with suavity,
   Or contradicted but with proud humility.
He knew the world, and would not see depravity
   In faults which sometimes show the soil's fertility,
If that the weeds o'erlive not the first crop—
For then they are very difficult to stop.

---

[2] "I am Davus, not Oedipus" and therefore cannot solve the
riddle of the Sphinx (in Terence's *Andrea*).

---

[3] An allusion to Addison's *Cato*.

XXIII

And then he talked with him about Madrid,
   Constantinople, and such distant places;
Where people always did as they were bid,
   Or did what they should not with foreign graces.
Of coursers also spake they: Henry rid
   Well, like most Englishmen, and loved the races;
And Juan, like a true-born Andalusian,
Could back a horse, as despots ride a Russian.

XXIV

And thus acquaintance grew, at noble routs,
   And diplomatic dinners, or at other—
For Juan stood well both with Ins and Outs,
   As in Freemasonry a higher brother.
Upon his talent Henry had no doubts,
   His manner showed him sprung from a high
And all men like to show their hospitality   [mother;
To him whose breeding marches with his quality.

XXV

At Blank-Blank Square;—for we will break no
     squares[4]
   By naming streets: since men are so censorious,
And apt to sow an author's wheat with tares,
   Reaping allusions private and inglorious,
Where none were dreamt of, unto love's affairs,
   Which were, or are, or are to be notorious,
That therefore do I previously declare,
Lord Henry's mansion was in Blank-Blank Square.

XXVI

Also there bin another pious reason*
   For making squares and streets anonymous;
Which is, that there is scarce a single season
   Which doth not shake some very splendid house
With some slight heart-quake of domestic treason—
   A topic Scandal doth delight to rouse:
Such I might stumble over unawares,
Unless I knew the very chastest Squares.

XXVII

'T is true, I might have chosen Piccadilly,
   A place where peccadillos are unknown;
But I have motives, whether wise or silly,
   For letting that pure sanctuary alone.
Therefore I name not square, street, place, until I
   Find one where nothing naughty can be shown,
A vestal shrine of innocence of heart:
Such are—but I have lost the London Chart.

   *   With every thing that pretty *bin*,
          My lady sweet arise.—Shakspeare

   4 To "break a square" is to disrupt an order.

XXVIII

At Henry's mansion then, in Blank-Blank Square,
   Was Juan a *recherché*, welcome guest,
As many other noble Scions were;
   And some who had but talent for their crest;
Or wealth, which is a passport every where;
   Or even mere fashion, which indeed 's the best
Recommendation;—and to be well drest
Will very often supersede the rest.

XXIX

And since "there 's safety in a multitude
   Of counsellors," as Solomon has said,
Or some one for him, in some sage, grave mood;—
   Indeed we see the daily proof displayed
In Senates, at the Bar, in wordy feud,
   Where'er collective wisdom can parade,
Which is the only cause that we can guess
Of Britain's present wealth and happiness;—

XXX

But as "there 's safety grafted in the number
   Of Counsellors" for men,—thus for the sex
A large acquaintance lets not Virtue slumber;
   Or should it shake, the choice will more perplex—
Variety itself will more encumber.
   'Midst many rocks we guard more against wrecks;
And thus with women: howsoe'er it shocks some's
Self-love, there 's safety in a crowd of coxcombs.

XXXI

But Adeline had not the least occasion
   For such a shield, which leaves but little merit
To virtue proper, or good education.
   Her chief resource was in her own high spirit,
Which judged mankind at their due estimation;
   And for coquetry, she disdained to wear it:
Secure of admiration: its impression
Was faint, as of an every-day possession.

XXXII

To all she was polite without parade;
   To some she showed attention of that kind
Which flatters, but is flattery conveyed
   In such a sort as cannot leave behind
A trace unworthy either wife or maid;—
   A gentle, genial courtesy of mind,
To those who were or passed for meritorious,
Just to console sad Glory for being glorious;

XXXIII

Which is in all respects, save now and then,
    A dull and desolate appendage. Gaze
Upon the Shades of those distinguished men,
    Who were or are the puppet-shows of praise,
The praise of persecution. Gaze again
    On the most favoured; and amidst the blaze
Of sunset halos o'er the laurel-browed,
What can ye recognise?—A gilded cloud.

XXXIV

There also was of course in Adeline
    That calm Patrician polish in the address,
Which ne'er can pass the equinoctial line
    Of anything which Nature would express;
Just as a Mandarin finds nothing fine,—
    At least his manner suffers not to guess,
That any thing he views can greatly please.
Perhaps we have borrowed this from the Chinese—

XXXV

Perhaps from Horace: his "*Nil admirari*" [5]
    Was what he called the "Art of Happiness";
An art on which the artists greatly vary,
    And have not yet attained to much success.
However, 't is expedient to be wary:
    Indifference *certes* don't produce distress;
And rash Enthusiasm in good society
Were nothing but a moral Inebriety.

XXXVI

But Adeline was not indifferent: for
    (*Now* for a common place!) beneath the snow,
As a Volcano holds the lava more
    Within—*et cætera*. Shall I go on?—No!
I hate to hunt down a tired metaphor:
    So let the often used volcano go.
Poor thing! How frequently, by me and others,
It hath been stirred up till its smoke quite smothers.

XXXVII

I 'll have another figure in a trice:—
    What say you to a bottle of champagne?
Frozen into a very vinous ice,
    Which leaves few drops of that immortal rain,
Yet in the very centre, past all price,
    About a liquid glassful will remain;
And this is stronger than the strongest grape
Could e'er express in its expanded shape:

XXXVIII

'T is the whole spirit brought to a quintessence;
    And thus the chilliest aspects may concentre
A hidden nectar under a cold presence.
    And such are many—though I only meant her
From whom I now deduce these moral lessons,
    On which the Muse has always sought to enter :—
And your cold people are beyond all price,
When once you have broken their confounded ice.

XXXIX

But after all they are a North-West Passage
    Unto the glowing India of the soul;
And as the good ships sent upon that message
    Have not exactly ascertained the Pole
(Though Parry's efforts look a lucky presage) [6]
    Thus gentlemen may run upon a shoal;
For if the Pole 's not open, but all frost,
(A chance still) 't is a voyage or vessel lost.

XL

And young beginners may as well commence
    With quiet cruizing o'er the ocean woman;
While those who are not beginners, should have sense
    Enough to make for port, ere Time shall summon
With his grey signal flag; and the past tense,
    The dreary "*Fuimus*" of all things human, [7]
Must be declined, while life's thin thread 's spun out
Between the gaping heir and gnawing gout.

XLI

But Heaven must be diverted: its diversion
    Is sometimes truculent—but never mind:
The world upon the whole is worth the assertion
    (If but for comfort) that all things are kind:
And that same devilish doctrine of the Persian,
    Of the two Principles, but leaves behind [8]
As many doubts as any other doctrine
Has ever puzzled Faith withal, or yoked her in.

XLII

The English winter—ending in July,
    To recommence in August—now was done.
'T is the postilion's Paradise: wheels fly;
    On roads, East, South, North, West, there is a run.
But for post horses who finds sympathy?
    Man's pity 's for himself, or for his son,
Always premising that said son at college
Has not contracted much more debt than knowledge.

---

[5] "Admire nothing."

[6] Sir William Parry (1790–1855), admiral and explorer, sought a northwest passage.

[7] "We have been."

[8] The creative and destructive forces (of Zoroastrianism). See *Manfred*, p. 603ff.

XLIII

The London winter 's ended in July—
  Sometimes a little later. I don't err
In this: whatever other blunders lie
  Upon my shoulders, here I must aver
My Muse a glass of Weatherology;
  For Parliament is our Barometer:
Let Radicals its other acts attack,
Its sessions form our only almanack.

XLIV

When its quicksilver 's down at zero,—lo!
  Coach, chariot, luggage, baggage, equipage!
Wheels whirl from Carlton palace to Soho,
  And happiest they who horses can engage;
The turnpikes glow with dust; and Rotten Row
  Sleeps from the chivalry of this bright age;
And tradesmen, with long bills and longer faces,
Sigh—as the postboys fasten on the traces.

XLV

They and their bills, "Arcadians both," are left*
  To the Greek Kalends of another session.[9]
Alas! to them of ready cash bereft,
  What hope remains? Of *hope* the full possession,
Or generous draft, conceded as a gift,
  At a long date—till they can get a fresh one,—
Hawked about at a discount, small or large;—
Also the solace of an overcharge.

XLVI

But these are trifles. Downward flies my Lord,
  Nodding beside my Lady in his carriage.
Away! away! "Fresh horses!" are the word,
  And changed as quickly as hearts after marriage;
The obsequious landlord hath the change restored;
  The postboys have no reason to disparage
Their fee; but ere the watered wheels may hiss hence,
The ostler pleads for a small reminiscence.

XLVII

'T is granted; and the valet mounts the dickey—
  That gentleman of lords and gentlemen;
Also my Lady's gentlewoman, tricky,
  Tricked out, but modest more than poet's pen
Can paint, "*Cosi Viaggino i Ricchi!*"[10]
  (Excuse a foreign slipslop now and then,
If but to show I 've travell'd; and what 's travel,
Unless it teaches one to quote and cavil?)

* "Arcades ambo."

[9] The Roman "kalends" do not appear in the Greek calendar; hence, "never."
[10] "Thus the rich travel."

XLVIII

The London winter and the country summer
  Were well nigh over. 'T is perhaps a pity,
When Nature wears the gown that doth become her,
  To lose those best months in a sweaty city,
And wait until the nightingale grows dumber,
  Listening debates not very wise or witty,
Ere patriots their true *country* can remember;—
But there 's no shooting (save grouse) till September.

XLIX

I 've done with my tirade. The world was gone;
  The twice two thousand, for whom earth was made,
Were vanished to be what they call alone,—
  That is, with thirty servants for parade,
As many guests or more; before whom groan
  As many covers, duly, daily laid.
Let none accuse Old England's hospitality—
Its quantity is but condensed to quality.

L

Lord Henry and the Lady Adeline
  Departed, like the rest of their compeers,
The peerage, to a mansion very fine;
  The Gothic Babel of a thousand years.
None than themselves could boast a longer line,
  Where Time through heroes and through beauties steers;
And oaks, as olden as their pedigree,
Told of their sires, a tomb in every tree.

LI

A paragraph in every paper told
  Of their departure: such is modern fame:
'T is pity that it takes no further hold
  Than an advertisement, or much the same;
When, ere the ink be dry, the sound grows cold.
  The Morning Post was foremost to proclaim—
"Departure, for his country seat, to-day,
Lord H. Amundeville and Lady A.

LII

"We understand the splendid host intends
  To entertain, this autumn, a select
And numerous party of his noble friends;
  'Midst whom we have heard, from sources quite correct,
The Duke of D— the shooting season spends,
  With many more by rank and fashion decked;
Also a foreigner of high condition,
The Envoy of the secret Russian mission."

LIII

And thus we see—who doubts the Morning Post?
   (Whose articles are like the "Thirty-nine,"[11]
Which those most swear to who believe them most)—
   Our gay Russ Spaniard was ordained to shine,
Decked by the rays reflected from his host,
   With those who, Pope says, "greatly daring dine."
'T is odd, but true,—last war the News abounded
More with these dinners than the killed or
                    [wounded;—

LIV

As thus: "On Thursday there was a grand dinner;
   Present, Lords A. B. C."—Earls, dukes, by name
Announced with no less pomp than victory's winner:
   Then underneath, and in the very same
Column: Date, "Falmouth. There has lately been here
   The Slap-Dash regiment, so well known to fame;
Whose loss in the late action we regret:
The vacancies are filled up—see Gazette."

LV

To Norman Abbey whirled the noble pair,—[12]
   An old, old monastery once, and now
Still older mansion, of a rich and rare
   Mixed Gothic, such as Artists all allow
Few specimens yet left us can compare
   Withal: it lies perhaps a little low,
Because the monks preferred a hill behind,
To shelter their devotion from the wind.

LVI

It stood embosom'd in a happy valley,
   Crown'd by high woodlands, where the Druid oak
Stood like Caractacus in act to rally[13]   [stroke;
   His host, with broad arms 'gainst the thunder-
And from beneath his boughs were seen to sally
   The dappled foresters—as day awoke,
The branching stag swept down with all his herd,
To quaff a brook which murmured like a bird.

LVII

Before the mansion lay a lucid lake,
   Broad as transparent, deep, and freshly fed
By a river, which its soften'd way did take
   In currents through the calmer water spread
Around: the wildfowl nestled in the brake
   And sedges, brooding in their liquid bed:
The woods sloped downwards to its brink, and stood
With their green faces fix'd upon the flood.

11 The thirty-nine statements subscribed to by those who take orders in the Church of England.
12 Most of the details in the following stanzas come from Byron's Newstead Abbey.
13 Caradoc, British king of the first century of the Christian era, who withstood the Romans for nine years.

LVIII

Its outlet dash'd into a deep cascade,
   Sparkling with foam, until again subsiding
Its shriller echoes—like an infant made
   Quiet—sank into softer ripples, gliding
Into a rivulet; and thus allay'd
   Pursued its course, now gleaming, and now hiding
Its windings through the woods; now clear, now blue,
According as the skies their shadows threw.

LIX

A glorious remnant of the Gothic pile,
   (While yet the church was Rome's) stood half apart
In a grand Arch, which once screened many an aisle.
   These last had disappear'd—a loss to Art:
The first yet frowned superbly o'er the soil,
   And kindled feelings in the roughest heart,
Which mourn'd the power of time's or tempest's
In gazing on that venerable Arch.   [march,

LX

Within a niche, nigh to its pinnacle,
   Twelve Saints had once stood sanctified in stone;
But these had fallen, not when the friars fell,
   But in the war which struck Charles from his throne,
When each house was a fortalice—as tell
   The annals of full many a line undone,—
The gallant Cavaliers, who fought in vain
For those who knew not to resign or reign.

LXI

But in a higher niche, alone, but crown'd,
   The Virgin-Mother of the God-born child,
With her son in her blesséd arms, look'd round,
   Spared by some chance when all beside was spoil'd;
She made the earth below seem holy ground.
   This may be superstition, weak or wild,
But even the faintest relics of a shrine
Of any worship, wake some thoughts divine.

LXII

A mighty window, hollow in the centre,
   Shorn of its glass of thousand colourings,
Through which the deepen'd glories once could enter,
   Streaming from off the sun like seraph's wings,
Now yawns all desolate: now loud, now fainter,
   The gale sweeps through its fretwork, and oft sings
The owl his anthem, where the silenced quire
Lie with their hallelujahs quench'd like fire.

LXIII

But in the noontide of the Moon, and when
   The wind is winged from one point of heaven,
There moans a strange unearthly sound, which then
   Is musical—a dying accent driven
Through the huge Arch, which soars and sinks again.
   Some deem it but the distant echo given
Back to the Night wind by the waterfall,
And harmonized by the old choral wall:

LXIV

Others, that some original shape, or form
   Shaped by decay perchance, hath given the power
(Though less than that of Memnon's statue, warm
   In Egypt's rays, to harp at a fixed hour) [14]
To this grey ruin, with a voice to charm.
   Sad, but serene, it sweeps o'er tree or tower;
The cause I know not, nor can solve; but such
The fact:—I 've heard it,—once perhaps too much.

LXV

Amidst the court a Gothic fountain play'd,
   Symmetrical, but deck'd with carvings quaint—
Strange faces, like to men in masquerade,
   And here perhaps a monster, there a Saint:
The spring gush'd through grim mouths, of granite
   And sparkled into basins, where it spent   [made,
Its little torrent in a thousand bubbles,
Like man's vain glory, and his vainer troubles.

LXVI

The mansion's self was vast and venerable,
   With more of the monastic than has been
Elsewhere preserved: the cloisters still were stable,
   The cells too and refectory, I ween:
An exquisite small chapel had been able,
   Still unimpair'd, to decorate the scene;
The rest had been reform'd, replaced, or sunk,
And spoke more of the baron than the monk.

LXVII

Huge halls, long galleries, spacious chambers, joined
   By no quite lawful marriage of the Arts,
Might shock a Connoisseur; but when combined,
   Form'd a whole which, irregular in parts,
Yet left a grand impression on the mind,
   At least of those whose eyes are in their hearts.
We gaze upon a Giant for his stature,
Nor judge at first if all be true to Nature.

[14] Herodotus tells of such an Egyptian statue.

LXVIII

Steel Barons, molten the next generation
   To silken rows of gay and garter'd Earls,
Glanced from the walls in goodly preservation:
   And Lady Marys blooming into girls,
With fair long locks, had also kept their station:
   And Countesses mature in robes and pearls:
Also some beauties of Sir Peter Lely,
Whose drapery hints we may admire them freely.

LXIX

Judges in very formidable ermine
   Were there, with brows that did not much invite
The accused to think their Lordships would determine
   His cause by leaning much from might to right:
Bishops, who had not left a single sermon;
   Attornies-General, awful to the sight,
As hinting more (unless our judgments warp us)
Of the "Star Chamber" than of "Habeas Corpus." [15]

LXX

Generals, some all in armour, of the old
   And iron time, ere Lead had ta'en the lead;
Others in wigs of Marlborough's martial fold,
   Huger than twelve of our degenerate breed:
Lordlings with staves of white, or keys of gold:
   Nimrods, whose canvas scarce contain'd the steed;
And here and there some stern high Patriot stood,
Who could not get the place for which he sued.

LXXI

But ever and anon, to soothe your vision,
   Fatigued with these hereditary glories,
There rose a Carlo Dolce or a Titian,
   Or wilder group of savage Salvatore's: *
Here danced Albano's boys, and here the sea shone
   In Vernet's ocean lights; and there the stories
Of martyrs awed, as Spagnoletto tainted
His brush with all the blood of all the sainted.

LXXII

Here sweetly spread a landscape of Lorraine;
   There Rembrandt made his darkness equal light,
Or gloomy Caravaggio's gloomier stain
   Bronzed o'er some lean and stoic Anchorite:—
But, lo! a Teniers woos, and not in vain,
   Your eyes to revel in a livelier sight:
His bell-mouthed goblet makes me feel quite Danish†
Or Dutch with thirst—What, ho! a flask of Rhenish.

* Salvator Rosa.
† If I err not, "Your Dane" is one of Iago's Catalogue of Nations "exquisite in their drinking."

[15] The Star Chamber was a court designed to try in secret people thought to be a menace to public safety; it is the direct denial of the right of *habeas corpus*.

LXXIII

Oh, reader! if that thou canst read,—and know,
 'T is not enough to spell, or even to read,
To constitute a reader; there must go
 Virtues of which both you and I have need.
Firstly, begin with the beginning—(though
 That clause is hard); and secondly, proceed;
Thirdly, commence not with the end—or, sinning
In this sort, end at least with the beginning.

LXXIV

But, reader, thou hast patient been of late,
 While I, without remorse of rhyme, or fear,
Have built and laid out ground at such a rate,
 Dan Phoebus takes me for an auctioneer.
That Poets were so from their earliest date,
 By Homer's "Catalogue of Ships," is clear;
But a mere modern must be moderate—
I spare you then the furniture and plate.

LXXV

The mellow Autumn came, and with it came
 The promised party, to enjoy its sweets.
The corn is cut, the manor full of game;
 The pointer ranges, and the sportsman beats
In russet jacket:—lynx-like is his aim,
 Full grows his bag, and wonder*ful* his feats.
Ah, nutbrown Partridges! Ah, brilliant Pheasants!
And ah, ye Poachers!—'Tis no sport for peasants.

LXXVI

An English autumn, though it hath no vines,
 Blushing with Bacchant coronals along
The paths, o'er which the far festoon entwines
 The red grape in the sunny lands of song,
Hath yet a purchased choice of choicest wines;
 The Claret light, and the Madeira strong.
If Britain mourn her bleakness, we can tell her
The very best of vineyards is the cellar.

LXXVII

Then, if she hath not that serene decline
 Which makes the Southern Autumn's day appear
As if 't would to a second spring resign
 The season, rather than to winter drear,—
Of in-door comforts still she hath a mine,—
 The sea-coal fires, the earliest of the year;
Without doors too she may compete in mellow,
As what is lost in green is gained in yellow.

LXXVIII

And for the effeminate *villeggiatura* [16]—
 Rife with more horns than hounds—she hath the
So animated that it might allure a   [chase,
 Saint from his beads to join the jocund race:
Even Nimrod's self might leave the plains of Dura,*
 And wear the Melton jacket for a space:—
If she hath no wild boars, she hath a tame
Preserve of Bores, who ought to be made game.

LXXIX

The noble guests, assembled at the Abbey,
 Consisted of—we give the sex the pas—
The Duchess of Fitz-Fulke; the Countess Crabbey;
 The Ladies Scilly, Busey;—Miss Eclat,
Miss Bombazeen, Miss Mackstay, Miss O'Tabbey,
 And Mrs. Rabbi, the rich banker's squaw;
Also the honourable Mrs. Sleep,
Who look'd a white lamb, yet was a black sheep:

LXXX

With other Countesses of Blank—but rank;
 At once the "lie" and the "*élite*" of crowds;
Who pass like water filtered in a tank,
 All purged and pious from their native clouds;
Or paper turned to money by the Bank:
 No matter how or why, the passport shrouds
The "*passée*" and the passed; for good society
Is no less famed for tolerance than piety:

LXXXI

That is, up to a certain point; which point
 Forms the most difficult in punctuation.
Appearances appear to form the joint
 On which it hinges in a higher station;
And so that no explosion cry "Aroint
 Thee, Witch!" or each Medea has her Jason;
Or (to the point with Horace and with Pulci)
"*Omne tulit punctum*, quae *miscuit utile dulci.*" [17]

LXXXII

I can't exactly trace their rule of right,
 Which hath a little leaning to a lottery.
I 've seen a virtuous woman put down quite
 By the mere combination of a Coterie;

* In Assyria.

◇—◇—◇—◇—◇—◇—◇—◇—◇—◇—◇—◇—◇—◇—◇—◇—◇

[16] A sojourn in the country (during the hot season). Nimrod (line 5) was a king of Babylon. A Melton jacket (line 6) was worn for hunting.
[17] Horace, *Epist. ad Pisones:* "Those gain all votes who mix the pleasant with the profitable."

Also a So-So Matron boldly fight
    Her way back to the world by dint of plottery,
And shine the very *Siria* of the spheres,*
Escaping with a few slight, scarless sneers.

LXXXIII

I have seen more than I 'll say:—but we will see
    How our *villeggiatura* will get on.
The party might consist of thirty-three
    Of highest caste—the Brahmins of the ton.
I have named a few, not foremost in degree,
    But ta'en at hazard as the rhyme may run.
By way of sprinkling, scatter'd amongst these,
There also were some Irish absentees.

LXXXIV

There was Parolles too, the legal bully,[19]
    Who limits all his battles to the bar
And senate: when invited elsewhere, truly,
    He shows more appetite for words than war.
There was the young bard Rackrhyme, who had newly
    Come out and glimmer'd as a six-weeks' star.
There was Lord Pyrrho too, the great freethinker;
And Sir John Pottledeep, the mighty drinker.

LXXXV

There was the Duke of Dash, who was a—duke,
    "Aye, every inch a" duke; there were twelve peers
Like Charlemagne's—and all such peers in look
    And intellect, that neither eyes nor ears
For commoners had ever them mistook.
    There were the six Miss Rawbolds—pretty dears!
All song and sentiment; whose hearts were set
Less on a convent than a coronet.

LXXXVI

There were four Honourable Misters, whose
    Honour was more before their names than after;
There was the preux Chevalier de la Ruse,
    Whom France and Fortune lately deign'd to waft
Whose chiefly harmless talent was to amuse;   [here,
    But the clubs found it rather serious laughter,
Because—such was his magic power to please—
The dice seem'd charm'd too with his repartees.

* Siria, *i.e.*, bitch star.[18]

<hr />

[18] Not the dog-star (Sirius).
[19] Henry Brougham, whom Byron objected to as a political coward for his behavior in Parliament and as a meddler for his siding with Lady Byron. He did not know he had also written the anonymous review of *Hours of Idleness* (see Introduction, pp. 526–27).

LXXXVII

There was Dick Dubious the metaphysician,
    Who loved philosophy and a good dinner;
Angle, the *soi-disant* mathematician;
    Sir Henry Silvercup, the great race-winner.
There was the Reverend Rodomont Precisian,
    Who did not hate so much the sin as sinner:
And Lord Augustus Fitz-Plantagenet,
Good at all things, but better at a bet.

LXXXVIII

There was Jack Jargon the gigantic guardsman;
    And General Fireface, famous in the field,
A great tactician, and no less a swordsman,
    Who ate, last war, more Yankees than he kill'd.
There was the waggish Welsh Judge, Jefferies
    Hardsman,
    In his grave office so completely skill'd,
That when a culprit came for condemnation,
He had his Judge's joke for consolation.

LXXXIX

Good company 's a chess-board—there are kings,
    Queens, bishops, knights, rooks, pawns; the world 's
    a game;
Save that the puppets pull at their own strings;
    Methinks gay Punch hath something of the same.
My Muse, the butterfly hath but her wings,
    Not stings, and flits through ether without aim,
Alighting rarely:—were she but a hornet,
Perhaps there might be vices which would mourn it.

XC

I had forgotten—but must not forget—
    An Orator, the latest of the session,
Who had deliver'd well a very set
    Smooth speech, his first and maidenly transgression
Upon debate: the papers echoed yet
    With his *début*, which made a strong impression,
And rank'd with what is every day display'd—
"The best first speech that ever yet was made."

XCI

Proud of his "Hear hims!" proud too of his vote
    And lost virginity of oratory,
Proud of his learning (just enough to quote)
    He revell'd in his Ciceronian glory:
With memory excellent to get by rote,
    With wit to hatch a pun or tell a story,
Graced with some merit and with more effrontery,
"His Country's pride," he came down to the country.

XCII

There also were two wits by acclamation,
  Longbow from Ireland, Strongbow from the
Both lawyers and both men of education;   [Tweed,
  But Strongbow's wit was of more polish'd breed:
Longbow was rich in an imagination,
  As beautiful and bounding as a steed,
But sometimes stumbling over a potatoe,—
While Strongbow's best things might have come from
                                              [Cato.

XCIII

Strongbow was like a new-tuned harpsichord;
  But Longbow wild as an Aeolian harp,[20]
With which the winds of heaven can claim accord,
  And make a music, whether flat or sharp.
Of Strongbow's talk you would not change a word;
  At Longbow's phrases you might sometimes carp:
Both wits—one born so, and the other bred,
This by his heart—his rival by his head.

XCIV

If all these seem an heterogeneous mass
  To be assembled at a country seat,
Yet think, a specimen of every class
  Is better than a humdrum *tête-à-tête*.
The days of Comedy are gone, alas!
  When Congreve's fool could vie with Moliere's *bête*:
Society is smooth'd to that excess,
That manners hardly differ more than dress.

XCV

Our ridicules are kept in the back-ground—
  Ridiculous enough, but also dull;
Professions too are no more to be found
  Professional; and there is nought to cull
Of folly's fruit; for, though your folls abound,
  They're barren and not worth the pains to pull.
Society is now one polish'd horde,
Formed of two mighty tribes, the *Bores* and *Bored*.

XCVI

But from being farmers, we turn gleaners, gleaning
  The scanty but right-well thrashed ears of truth;
And, gentle reader! when you gather meaning,
  You may be Boaz, and I—modest Ruth.
Further I'd quote, but Scripture intervening
  Forbids. A great impression in my youth
Was made by Mrs. Adams, where she cries,
"That Scriptures out of church are blasphemies." *

* "Mrs. Adams answered Mr. Adams, that it was blasphe-
mous to talk of Scripture out of church." This dogma was
broached to her husband—the best Christian in any book.—
See Joseph Andrews, in the last chapters.

〜〜〜〜〜〜〜〜〜〜〜〜〜〜〜〜〜〜〜〜〜〜〜〜〜
[20] See headnote to Coleridge's *Eolian Harp*, p. 441.

XCVII

But what we can we glean in this vile age
  Of chaff, although our gleanings be not grist.
I must not quite omit the talking sage,
  Kit-Cat, the famous conversationist,
Who, in his common-place book, had a page
  Prepared each morn for evenings. "List, oh list!"—
"Alas, poor Ghost!"—What unexpected woes
Await those who have studied their *bons mots*!

XCVIII

Firstly, they must allure the conversation,
  By many windings to their clever clinch;
And secondly, must let slip no occasion,
  Nor *bate* (abate) their hearers of an *inch*,
But take an ell—and make a great sensation,
  If possible; and thirdly, never flinch
When some smart talker puts them to the test,
But seize the last word, which no doubt's the best.

XCIX

Lord Henry and his lady were the hosts;
  The party we have touch'd on were the guests.
Their table was a board to tempt even ghosts
  To pass the Styx for more substantial feasts.
I will not dwell upon ragoûts or roasts,
  Albeit all human history attests
That happiness for Man—the hungry sinner!—
Since Eve ate apples, much depends on dinner.

C

Witness the lands which "flowed with milk and
  Held out unto the hungry Israelites: [honey,"
To this we have added since, the love of money,
  The only sort of pleasure which requites.
Youth fades, and leaves our days no longer sunny;
  We tire of Mistresses and Parasites;
But oh, Ambroisial Cash! Ah! who would lose thee?
When we no more can use, or even abuse thee!

CI

The gentlemen got up betimes to shoot,
  Or hunt: the young, because they liked the sport—
The first thing boys like, after play and fruit;
  The middle-aged, to make the day more short;
For *ennui* is a growth of English root,
  Though nameless in our language:—we retort
The fact for words, and let the French translate
That awful yawn which sleep can not abate.

CII

The elderly walked through the library,
    And tumbled books, or criticized the pictures,
Or sauntered through the gardens piteously,
    And made upon the hot-house several strictures,
Or rode a nag, which trotted not too high,
    Or on the morning papers read their lectures,
Or on the watch their longing eyes would fix,
Longing at sixty for the hour of six.

CIII

But none were "*gêné*" [21] the great hour of union
    Was rung by dinner's knell; till then all were
Masters of their own time—or in communion,
    Or solitary, as they chose to bear
The hours, which how to pass is but to few known.
    Each rose up at his own, and had to spare
What time he chose for dress, and broke his fast
When, where, and how he chose for that repast.

CIV

The ladies—some rouged, some a little pale—
    Met the morn as they might. If fine, they rode,
Or walked; if foul, they read, or told a tale,
    Sung, or rehearsed the last dance from abroad;
Discussed the fashion which might next prevail,
    And settled bonnets by the newest code,
Or cramm'd twelve sheets into one little letter,
To make each correspondent a new debtor.

CV

For some had absent lovers, all had friends;
    The earth has nothing like a She epistle,
And hardly heaven—because it never ends.
    I love the mystery of a female missal,
Which, like a creed, ne'er says all it intends,
    But full of cunning as Ulysses' whistle,
When he allured poor Dolon:—you had better [22]
Take care what you reply to such a letter.

CVI

Then there were billiards; cards, too, but *no* dice;—
    Save in the Clubs no man of honour plays;—
Boats when 't was water, skaiting when 't was ice,
    And the hard frost destroy'd the scenting days:
And angling too, that solitary vice,
    Whatever Izaak Walton sings or says:
The quaint, old, cruel coxcomb, in his gullet
Should have a hook, and a small trout to pull it.*

* It would have taught him humanity at least. This senti-
mental savage, whom it is a mode to quote (amongst the nove-
lists) to show their sympathy for innocent sports and old songs,

[21] Constrained.
[22] A Trojan spy, tricked by Ulysses.

CVII

With evening came the banquet and the wine;
    The *conversazione*; the duet
Attuned by voices more or less divine,
    (My heart or head aches with the memory yet).
The four Miss Rawbolds in a glee would shine;
    But the two youngest loved more to be set
Down to the harp—because to music's charms
They added graceful necks, white hands and arms.

CVIII

Sometimes a dance (though rarely on field days,
    For then the gentlemen were rather tired)
Display'd some sylph-like figures in its maze:
    Then there was small-talk ready when required;
Flirtation—but decorous; the mere praise
    Of charms that should or should not be admired.
The hunters fought their fox-hunt o'er again,
And then retreated soberly—at ten.

CIX

The politicians, in a nook apart,
    Discuss'd the world, and settled all the spheres;
The wits watched every loophole for their art,
    To introduce a *bon mot* head and ears;
Small is the rest of those who would be smart,
    A moment's good thing may have cost them years
Before they find an hour to introduce it,
And then, even *then*, some bore may make them lose it.

CX

But all was gentle and aristocratic
    In this our party; polish'd, smooth and cold,
As Phidian forms cut out of marble Attic.
    There now are no 'Squire Westerns as of old;
And our Sophias are not so emphatic,
    But fair as then, or fairer to behold.
We have no accomplish'd blackguards, like Tom
But gentlemen in stays, as stiff as stones.   [Jones,

teaches how to sew up frogs, and break their legs by way of
experiment, in addition to the art of angling, the cruellest, the
coldest, and the stupidest of pretended sports. They may talk
about the beauties of nature, but the angler merely thinks of
his dish of fish; he has no leisure to take his eyes from off the
streams, and a single *bite* is worth to him more than all the
scenery around. Besides, some fish bite best on a rainy day. The
whale, the shark, and the tunny fishery have somewhat of noble
and perilous in them; even net fishing, trawling, &c. are more
humane and useful—but angling! No angler can be a good man.

    "One of the best men I ever knew;—as humane, delicate-
minded, generous, and excellent a creature as any in the world,
was an angler: true he angled with painted flies, and would
have been incapable of the extravagances of I. Walton."

    The above addition was made by a friend in reading over the
MS.—"*Audi alteram partem*"—I leave it to counterbalance my
own observation.

CXI

They separated at an early hour;
  That is, ere midnight—which is London's noon:
But in the country ladies seek their bower
  A little earlier than the waning Moon.
Peace to the slumbers of each folded flower—
  May the rose call back its true colours soon!
Good hours of fair cheeks are the fairest tinters,
And lower the price of rouge—at least some winters.

[1823]   [1823]

CANTO THE FOURTEENTH

I

IF from great Nature's or our own abyss
  Of thought, we could but snatch a certainty,
Perhaps mankind might find the path they miss—
  But then 't would spoil much good philosophy.
One system eats another up, and this
  Much as old Saturn ate his progeny;
For when his pious consort gave him stones
In lieu of sons, of these he made no bones.

II

But System doth reverse the Titan's breakfast,
  And eats her parents, albeit the digestion
Is difficult. Pray tell me, can you make fast,
  After due search, your faith to any question?
Look back o'er ages, ere unto the stake fast
  You bind yourself, and call some mode the best one.
Nothing more true than *not* to trust your senses;
And yet what are your other evidences?

III

For me, I know nought; nothing I deny,
  Admit, reject, contemn; and what know *you*,
Except perhaps that you were born to die?
  And both may after all turn out untrue.
An age may come, Font of Eternity,
  When nothing shall be either old or new.
Death, so call'd, is a thing which makes men weep,
And yet a third of life is pass'd in sleep.

IV

A sleep without dreams, after a rough day
  Of toil, is what we covet most; and yet
How clay shrinks back from more quiescent clay!
  The very Suicide that pays his debt
At once without instalments (an old way
  Of paying debts, which creditors regret)
Lets out impatiently his rushing breath,
Less from disgust of life than dread of death.

V

'T is round him, near him, here, there, every
    where;
  And there 's a courage which grows out of fear,
Perhaps of all most desperate, which will dare
  The worst to *know* it:—when the mountains rear
Their peaks beneath your human foot, and there
  You look down o'er the precipice, and drear
The gulf or rock yawns,—you can't gaze a minute,
Without an awful wish to plunge within it.

VI

'T is true, you don't—but, pale and struck with terror,
  Retire: but look into your past impression!
And you will find, though shuddering at the mirror
  Of your own thoughts, in all their self confession,
The lurking bias, be it truth or error,
  To the *unknown*; a secret prepossession,
To plunge with all your fears—but where? You know
And that 's the reason why you do—or do not.   [not,

VII

But what 's this to the purpose? you will say.
  Gent. Reader, nothing; a mere speculation,
For which my sole excuse is—'t is my way,
  Sometimes *with* and sometimes without occasion
I write what 's uppermost, without delay;
  This narrative is not meant for narration,
But a mere airy and fantastic basis,
To build up common things with common places.

VIII

You know, or don't know, that great Bacon saith,
  "Fling up a straw, 't will show the way the wind
    blows;"
And such a straw, borne on by human breath,
  Is Poesy, according as the mind glows;
A paper kite which flies 'twixt life and death,
  A shadow which the onward Soul behind throws:
And mine 's a bubble, not blown up for praise,
But just to play with, as an infant plays.

IX

The world is all before me, or behind;
  For I have seen a portion of that same,
And quite enough for me to keep in mind;—
  Of passions too, I have proved enough to blame,
To the great pleasure of our friends, mankind,
  Who like to mix some slight alloy with fame:
For I was rather famous in my time,
Until I fairly knock'd it up with rhyme.

X

I have brought this world about my ears, and eke
　　The other; that 's to say, the Clergy—who
Upon my head have bid their thunders break
　　In pious libels by no means a few.
And yet I can't help scribbling once a week,
　　Tiring old readers, nor discovering new.
In youth I wrote, because my mind was full,
And now because I feel it growing dull.

XI

But "why then publish?"—There are no rewards
　　Of fame or profit, when the world grows weary.
I ask in turn,—why do you play at cards?
　　Why drink? Why read?—To make some hour less
It occupies me to turn back regards　　　[dreary.
　　On what I 've seen or ponder'd, sad or cheery;
And what I write I cast upon the stream,
To swim or sink—I have had at least my dream.

XII

I think that were I *certain* of success,
　　I hardly could compose another line:
So long I 've battled either more or less,
　　That no defeat can drive me from the Nine.
This feeling 't is not easy to express,
　　And yet 't is not affected, I opine.
In play, there are two pleasures for your choosing—
The one is winning, and the other losing.

XIII

Besides, my Muse by no means deals in fiction:
　　She gathers a repertory of facts,
Of course with some reserve and slight restriction,
　　But mostly sings of human things and acts—
And that 's one cause she meets with contradiction;
　　For too much truth, at first sight, ne'er attracts;
And were her object only what 's call'd glory,
With more ease too she 'd tell a different story.

XIV

Love, war, a tempest—surely there 's variety;
　　Also a seasoning slight of lucubration;
A bird's-eye view too of that wild, Society;
　　A slight glance thrown on men of every station.
If you have nought else, here 's at least satiety
　　Both in performance and in preparation;
And though these lines should only line portmanteaus,
Trade will be all the better for these Cantos.

XV

The portion of this world which I at present
　　Have taken up to fill the following sermon,
Is one of which there 's no description recent:
　　The reason why, is easy to determine:
Although it seems both prominent and pleasant,
　　There is a sameness in its gems and ermine,
A dull and family likeness through all ages,
Of no great promise for poetic pages.

XVI

With much to excite, there 's little to exalt;
　　Nothing that speaks to all men and all times;
A sort of varnish over every fault;
　　A kind of common-place, even in their crimes;
Factitious passions, wit without much salt,
　　A want of that true nature which sublimes
Whate'er it shows with truth; a smooth monotony
Of character, in those at least who have got any.

XVII

Sometimes indeed, like soldiers off parade
　　They break their ranks and gladly leave the drill;
But then the roll-call draws them back afraid,
　　And they must be or seem what they were: still
Doubtless it is a brilliant masquerade;
　　But when of the first sight you have had your fill,
It palls—at least it did so upon me,
This Paradise of Pleasure and *Ennui*.

XVIII

When we have made our love, and gamed our gaming,
　　Drest, voted, shone, and, may be, something more;
With dandies dined; heard senators declaiming;
　　Seen beauties brought to market by the score;
Sad rakes to sadder husbands chastely taming;
　　There 's little left but to be bored or bore.
Witness those "*ci-devant jeunes hommes*" who stem
The stream, nor leave the world which leaveth them.

XIX

'T is said—indeed a general complaint—
　　That no one has succeeded in describing
The *Monde*, exactly as they ought to paint.
　　Some say, that Authors only snatch, by bribing
The porter, some slight scandals strange and quaint,
　　To furnish matter for their moral gibing;
And that their books have but one style in common—
My lady's prattle, filter'd through her woman.

XX

But this can't well be true, just now; for writers
　Are grown of the *Beau Monde* a part potential:
I 've seen them balance even the scale with fighters,
　Especially when young, for that's essential.
Why do their sketches fail them as inditers
　Of what they deem themselves most
　　consequential—
The *real* portrait of the highest tribe?
'T is that, in fact, there's little to describe.

XXI

" *Haud ignara loquor*;" these are *Nugæ*, "*quarum
　Pars* parva *fui*," but still Art and part.
Now I could much more easily sketch a harem,
　A battle, wreck, or history of the heart,
Than these things; and besides, I wish to spare 'em,
　For reasons which I choose to keep apart.
" *Vetabo Cereris sacrum qui vulgaret*"—
Which means that vulgar people must not share it.[1]

XXII

And therefore what I throw off is ideal—
　Lower'd, leaven'd, like a history of Freemasons;
Which bears the same relation to the real,
　As Captain Parry's voyage may do to Jason's.
The grand Arcanum 's not for men to see all;
　My music has some mystic diapasons;
And there is much which could not be appreciated
In any manner by the uninitiated.

XXIII

Alas! Worlds fall—and Woman, since she fell'd
　The World (as, since that history, less polite
Than true, hath been a creed so strictly held)
　Has not yet given up the practice quite.
Poor Thing of Usages! Coerc'd, compell'd,
　Victim when wrong, and martyr oft when right,
Condemn'd to child-bed, as men for their sins
Have shaving too entailed upon their chins,—

XXIV

A daily plague, which in the aggregate
　May average on the whole with parturition.
But as to women, who can penetrate
　The real sufferings of their she condition?
Man's very sympathy with their estate
　Has much of selfishness and more suspicion.
Their love, their virtue, beauty, education,
But form good housekeepers, to breed a nation.

[1] The first quotation is from Vergil's *Aeneid*, the second from Horace's *Odes*: "I speak by no means unknowingly of things in which I bore a small part" (altered from "large part.") The second: "I shall forbid him who has divulged the secrets of Ceres." "Nugæ" are jokes.

XXV

All this were very well, and can't be better;
　But even this is difficult, Heaven knows,
So many troubles from her birth beset her,
　Such small distinction between friends and foes,
The gilding wears so soon from off her fetter,
　That—but ask any woman if she 'd choose
(Take her at thirty, that is) to have been
Female or male? a schoolboy or a Queen?

XXVI

"Petticoat Influence" is a great reproach,
　Which even those who obey would fain be thought
To fly from, as from hungry pikes a roach;
　But since beneath it upon earth we are brought
By various joltings of life's hackney coach,
　I for one venerate a petticoat—
A garment of a mystical sublimity,
No matter whether russet, silk, or dimity.

XXVII

Much I respect, and much I have adored,
　In my young days, that chaste and goodly veil,
Which holds a treasure, like a Miser's hoard,
　And more attracts by all it doth conceal—
A golden scabbard on a Damasque sword,
　A loving letter with a mystic seal,
A cure for grief—for what can ever rankle
Before a petticoat and a peeping ancle?

XXVIII

And when upon a silent, sullen day,
　With a Sirocco, for example, blowing,
When even the sea looks dim with all its spray,
　And sulkily the river's ripple 's flowing,
And the sky shows that very ancient gray,
　The sober, sad antithesis to glowing,—
'T is pleasant, if *then* any thing is pleasant,
To catch a glimpse even of a pretty peasant.

XXIX

We left our heroes and our heroines
　In that fair clime which don't depend on climate,
Quite independent of the Zodiac's signs,
　Though certainly more difficult to rhyme at,
Because the sun and stars, and aught that shines,
　Mountains, and all we can be most sublime at,
Are there oft dull and dreary as a *dun*—
Whether a sky's or tradesman's, is all one.

XXX

An in-door life is less poetical;
  And out of door hath showers, and mists, and sleet,
With which I could not brew a pastoral
  But be it as it may, a bard must meet
All difficulties, whether great or small,
  To spoil his undertaking or complete,
And work away like spirit upon matter,
Embarrass'd somewhat both with fire and water.

XXXI

Juan—in this respect at least like saints—
  Was all things unto people of all sorts,
And lived contentedly, without complaints,
  In camps, in ships, in cottages, or courts—
Born with that happy soul which seldom faints,
  And mingling modestly in toils or sports.
He likewise could be most things to all women,
Without the coxcombry of certain *She* Men.

XXXII

A fox-hunt to a foreigner is strange;
  'T is also subject to the double danger
Of tumbling first, and having in exchange
  Some pleasant jesting at the awkward stranger:
But Juan had been early taught to range
  The wilds, as doth an Arab turn'd Avenger,
So that his horse, or charger, hunter, hack,
Knew that he had a rider on his back.

XXXIII

And now in this new field, with some applause,
  He clear'd hedge, ditch, and double post, and rail,
And never *craned*,* and made but few "*faux pas*,"
  And only fretted when the scent 'gan fail.
He broke, 't is true, some statutes of the laws
  Of hunting—for the sagest youth is frail;
Rode o'er the hounds, it may be, now and then,
And once o'er several Country Gentlemen.

* *Craning.*—"*To crane*" is, or was, an expression used to denote a Gentleman's stretching out his neck over a hedge, "to look before he leaped":—a pause in his "vaulting ambition," which in the field doth occasion some delay and execration in those who may be immediately behind the equestrian sceptic. "Sir, if you don't choose to take the lead let me"—was a phrase which generally sent the aspirant on again; and to good purpose: for though "the horse and rider" might fall, they made a gap, through which, and over him and his steed, the field might follow.

XXXIV

But on the whole, to general admiration,
  He acquitted both himself and horse: the 'squires
Marvell'd at merit of another nation;
  The boors cried "Dang it! who 'd have thought
The Nestors of the sporting generation [it?"—Sires,
  Swore praises, and recall'd their former fires;
The Huntsman's self relented to a grin,
And rated him almost a whipper-in.

XXXV

Such were his trophies;—not of spear and shield,
  But leaps, and bursts, and sometimes fox's brushes;
Yet I must own,—although in this I yield
  To patriot sympathy a Briton's blushes,—
He thought at heart like courtly Chesterfield,
  Who, after a long chase o'er hills, dales, bushes,
And what not, though he rode beyond all price,
Asked next day, "If men ever hunted *twice*?"†

XXXVI

He also had a quality uncommon
  To early risers after a long chase,
Who wake in winter ere the cock can summon
  December's drowsy day to his dull race,—
A quality agreeable to woman,
  When her soft, liquid words run on apace,
Who likes a listener, whether Saint or Sinner,—
He did not fall asleep just after dinner.

XXXVII

But, light and airy, stood on the alert,
  And shone in the best part of dialogue,
By humouring always what they might assert,
  And listening to the topics most in vogue;
Now grave, now gay, but never dull or pert;
  And smiling but in secret—cunning rogue!
He ne'er presumed to make an error clearer;—
In short, there never was a better hearer.

XXXVIII

And then he danced;—all foreigners excel
  The serious Angles in the eloquence
Of pantomime;—he danced, I say, right well,
  With emphasis, and also with good sense—
A thing in footing indispensable:
  He danced without theatrical pretence,
Not like a ballet-master in the van
Of his drill'd nymphs, but like a gentleman.

† See his Letters to his Son.

XXXIX

Chaste were his steps, each kept within due bound,
　　And Elegance was sprinkled o'er his figure;
Like swift Camilla, he scarce skimm'd the ground,[2]
　　And rather held in than put forth his vigour;
And then he had an ear for music's sound,
　　Which might defy a Crotchet Critic's rigour.
Such classic *pas—sans* flaws—set off our hero,
He glanced like a personified Bolero;

XL

Or like a flying Hour before Aurora,
　　In Guido's famous fresco, which alone
Is worth a tour to Rome, although no more a
　　Remnant were there of the old world's sole throne.
The "*tout ensemble*" of his movements wore a
　　Grace of the soft Ideal, seldom shown,
And ne'er to be described; for to the dolour
Of bards and prosers, words are void of colour.

XLI

No marvel then he was a favourite;
　　A full-grown Cupid, very much admired;
A little spoilt, but by no means so quite;
　　At least he kept his vanity retired.
Such was his tact, he could alike delight
　　The chaste, and those who are not so much inspired.
The Duchess of Fitz-Fulke, who loved "*tracasserie*,"
Began to treat him with some small "*agaçerie*."[3]

XLII

She was a fine and somewhat full-blown blonde,
　　Desirable, distinguish'd, celebrated
For several winters in the grand, *grand Monde*.
　　I'd rather not say what might be related
Of her exploits, for this were ticklish ground;
　　Besides there might be falsehood in what's stated:
Her late performance had been a dead set
At Lord Augustus Fitz-Plantagenet.

XLIII

This noble personage began to look
　　A little black upon this new flirtation;
But such small licences must lovers brook,
　　Mere freedoms of the female corporation.
Woe to the man who ventures a rebuke!
　　'T will but precipitate a situation
Extremely disagreeable, but common
To calculators when they count on woman.

2 A servant of Diana, she was known for her swiftness.
3 *Tracasserie* = mischief-making; *agaçerie* = flirtatiousness.

XLIV

The circle smil'd, then whisper'd, and then sneer'd;
　　The misses bridled, and the matrons frown'd;
Some hoped things might not turn out as they fear'd;
　　Some would not deem such women could be found;
Some ne'er believed one half of what they heard;
　　Some look'd perplex'd, and others look'd profound:
And several pitied with sincere regret
Poor Lord Augustus Fitz-Plantagenet.

XLV

But what is odd, none ever named the Duke,
　　Who, one might think, was something in the affair:
True, he was absent, and, 't was rumour'd, took
　　But small concern about the when, or where,
Or what his consort did: if he could brook
　　Her gaieties, none had a right to stare:
Theirs was that best of unions, past all doubt,
Which never meets, and therefore can't fall out.

XLVI

But, oh that I should ever pen so sad a line!
　　Fired with an abstract love of virtue, she,
My Dian of the Ephesians, Lady Adeline,
　　Began to think the Duchess' conduct free;
Regretting much that she had chosen so bad a line,
　　And waxing chiller in her courtesy,
Looked grave and pale to see her friend's fragility,
For which most friends reserve their sensibility.

XLVII

There's nought in this bad world like sympathy:
　　'T is so becoming to the soul and face;
Sets to soft music the harmonious sigh,
　　And robes sweet Friendship in a Brussels lace.
Without a friend, what were humanity,
　　To hunt our errors up with a good grace?
Consoling us with—"Would you had thought
　　　　twice!
Ah! if you had but follow'd my advice!"

XLVIII

O Job! you had two friends: one's quite enough,
　　Especially when we are ill at ease;
They are but bad pilots when the weather's rough,
　　Doctors less famous for their cures than fees.
Let no man grumble when his friends fall off,
　　As they will do like leaves at the first breeze:
When your affairs come round, one way or t' other,
Go to the coffee-house, and take another.*

* In Swift's or Horace Walpole's letters I think it is mentioned, that somebody regretting the loss of a friend, was answered by an universal Pylades: "When I lose one, I go to the Saint James's Coffee-house, and take another."

XLIX

But this is not my maxim: had it been,
   Some heart-aches had been spared me: yet I
I would not be a tortoise in his screen   [care not—
   Of stubborn shell, which waves and weather wear
'T is better on the whole to have felt and seen   [not:
   That which humanity may bear, or bear not:
'T will teach discernment to the sensitive,
And not to pour their ocean in a sieve.

L

Of all the horrid, hideous notes of woe,
   Sadder than owl-songs or the midnight blast,
Is that portentous phrase, "I told you so,"
   Utter'd by friends, those prophets of the past,
Who, 'stead of saying what you now should do,
   Own they foresaw that you would fall at last,
And solace your slight lapse 'gainst *bonos mores*,[4]
With a long memorandum of old stories.

LI

The Lady Adeline's serene severity
   Was not confined to feeling for her friend,
Whose fame she rather doubted with posterity,
   Unless her habits should begin to mend:
But Juan also shared in her austerity,
   But mix'd with pity, pure as e'er was penn'd:
His inexperience moved her gentle ruth,
And (as her junior by six weeks) his youth.

LII

These forty days' advantage of her years—
   And hers were those which can face calculation,
Boldly referring to the list of peers
   And noble births, nor dread the enumeration—
Gave her a right to have maternal fears
   For a young gentleman's fit education,
Though she was far from that leap year, whose leap,
In female dates, strikes Time all of a heap.

LIII

This may be fixed at somewhere before thirty—
   Say seven-and-twenty; for I never knew
The strictest in chronology and virtue
   Advance beyond, while they could pass for new.

I recollect having heard an anecdote of the same kind. Sir W. D. was a great gamester. Coming in one day to the club of which he was a member, he was observed to look melancholy. "What is the matter, Sir William?" cried Hare of facetious memory "Ah!" replied Sir W. "I have just *lost* poor Lady D." "*Lost!* What at—*Quinze or Hazard?*" was the consolatory rejoinder of the querist.

4 Good conduct.

O Time! Why dost not pause? Thy scythe, so dirty
   With rust, should surely cease to hack and hew.
Reset it; shave more smoothly, also slower,
   If but to keep thy credit as a mower.

LIV

But Adeline was far from that ripe age,
   Whose ripeness is but bitter at the best:
'T was rather her experience made her sage,
   For she had seen the world, and stood its test,
As I have said in—I forget what page;
   My Muse despises reference, as you have guess'd
By this time;—but strike six from seven-and-twenty,
And you will find her sum of years in plenty.

LV

At sixteen she came out; presented, vaunted,
   She put all coronets into commotion:
At seventeen too the world was still enchanted
   With the new Venus of their brilliant ocean:
At eighteen, though below her feet still panted
   A hecatomb of suitors with devotion,
She had consented to create again
That Adam, called "The Happiest of Men."

LVI

Since then she had sparkled through three glowing
      winters,
   Admired, adored; but also so correct,
That she had puzzled all the acutest hinters,
   Without the apparel of being circumspect:
They could not even glean the slightest splinters
   From off the marble, which had no defect.
She had also snatched a moment since her marriage
To bear a son and heir—and one miscarriage.

LVII

Fondly the wheeling fire-flies flew around her,
   Those little glitterers of the London night;
But none of these possess'd a sting to wound her—
   She was a pitch beyond a coxcomb's flight.
Perhaps she wish'd an aspirant profounder;
   But whatso'er she wished, she acted right;
And whether coldness, pride, or virtue dignify
A Woman, so she 's good, what does it signify?

LVIII

I hate a motive, like a lingering bottle
   Which with the landlord makes too long a stand,
Leaving all claretless the unmoistened throttle,
   Especially with politics on hand;

I hate it, as I hate a drove of cattle,
　　Who whirl the dust as Simooms whirl the sand;
I hate it as I hate an argument,
　　A Laureate's ode, or servile Peer's "Content."

LIX

'T is sad to hack into the roots of things,
　　They are so much intertwisted with the earth;
So that the branch a goodly verdure flings,
　　I reck not if an acorn gave it birth.
To trace all actions to their secret springs
　　Would make indeed some melancholy mirth;
But this is not at present my concern,
And I refer you to wise Oxenstiern.*

LX

With the kind view of saving an *éclat*,
　　Both to the Duchess and diplomatist,
The Lady Adeline, as soon 's she saw
　　That Juan was unlikely to resist—
(For foreigners don't know that a *faux pas*
　　In England ranks quite on a different list
From those of other lands unblest with Juries,
Whose verdict for such sin a certain cure is);—

LXI

The Lady Adeline resolved to take
　　Such measures as she thought might best impede
The farther progress of this sad mistake.
　　She thought with some simplicity indeed;
But innocence is bold even at the stake,
　　And simple in the world, and doth not need
Nor use those palisades by dames erected,
Whose virtue lies in never being detected.

LXII

It was not that she fear'd the very worst:
　　His Grace was an enduring, married man,
And was not likely all at once to burst
　　Into a scene, and swell the clients' clan
Of Doctors' Commons; but she dreaded first
　　The magic of her Grace's talisman,
And next a quarrel (as he seemed to fret)
With Lord Augustus Fitz-Plantagenet.

* The famous Chancellor Oxenstiern said to his son, on the
latter expressing his surprise upon the great effects arising from
petty causes in the presumed mystery of politics: "You see by
this, my son, with how little wisdom the kingdoms of the world
are governed."[5]

◇◇◇◇◇◇◇◇◇◇◇◇◇◇◇◇◇◇◇◇◇◇◇◇◇◇◇◇◇◇

[5] Count Axel Oxenstiern (1583–1654) was prime minister of
Sweden.

LXIII

Her Grace, too, passed for being an Intrigante,
　　And somewhat *méchante*[6] in her amorous sphere;
One of those pretty, precious plagues, which haunt
　　A lover with caprices soft and dear,
That like to *make* a quarrel, when they can't
　　Find one, each day of the delightful year;
Bewitching, torturing, as they freeze or glow,
And—what is worst of all—won't let you go;

LXIV

The sort of thing to turn a young man's head,
　　Or make a Werter of him in the end.[7]
No wonder then a purer soul should dread
　　This sort of chaste *liaison* for a friend;
It were much better to be wed or dead,
　　Than wear a heart a woman loves to rend.
'T is best to pause, and think, ere you rush on,
If that a "*bonne fortune*" be really "*bonne*."

LXV

And first, in the o'erflowing of her heart,
　　Which really knew or thought it knew no guile,
She called her husband now and then apart,
　　And bade him counsel Juan. With a smile
Lord Henry heard her plans of artless art
　　To wean Don Juan from the Siren's wile;
And answered, like a Statesman or a Prophet,
In such guise that she could make nothing of it.

LXVI

Firstly, he said, "he never interfered
　　In any-body's business but the king's":
Next, that "he never judged from what appear'd,
　　Without strong reason, of those sort of things":
Thirdly, that "Juan had more brain than beard,
　　And was not to be held in leading strings";
And fourthly, what need hardly be said twice,
"That good but rarely came from good advice."

LXVII

And, therefore, doubtless to approve the truth
　　Of the last axiom, he advised his spouse
To leave the parties to themselves, forsooth,
　　At least as far as *bienséance* allows:[8]
That time would temper Juan's faults of youth;
　　That young men rarely made monastic vows;
That opposition only more attaches—
But here a messenger brought in dispatches:

◇◇◇◇◇◇◇◇◇◇◇◇◇◇◇◇◇◇◇◇◇◇◇◇◇◇◇◇◇◇

[6] Mischievous.
[7] See note to Canto Twelve, LXIII, above.
[8] Propriety.

LXVIII

And being of the Council called "the Privy,"
　　Lord Henry walked into his Cabinet,
To furnish matter for some future Livy
　　To tell how he reduced the nation's debt;
And if their full contents I do not give ye,
　　It is because I do not know them yet;
But I shall add them in a brief appendix,
To come between mine epic and its index.

LXIX

But ere he went, he added a slight hint,
　　Another gentle common-place or two,
Such as are coined in Conversation's mint,
　　And pass, for want of better, though not new:
Then broke his packet, to see what was in 't,
　　And having casually glanced it through,
Retired: and, as he went out, calmly kissed her,
Less like a young wife than an aged sister.

LXX

He was a cold, good, honourable man,
　　Proud of his birth, and proud of every thing;
A goodly spirit for a state divan,
　　A figure fit to walk before a king;
Tall, stately, form'd to lead the courtly van
　　On birth-days, glorious with a star and string;
The very model of a Chamberlain—
And such I mean to make him when I reign.

LXXI

But there was something wanting on the whole—
　　I don't know what, and therefore cannot tell—
Which pretty women—the sweet souls!—call *Soul*.
　　Certes it was not body; he was well
Proportion'd, as a poplar or a pole,
　　A handsome man, that human miracle;
And in each circumstance of love or war
Had still preserved his perpendicular.

LXXII

Still there was something wanting, as I 've said—
　　That undefinable "*Je ne sçais quoi*,"
Which, for what I know, may of yore have led
　　To Homer's Iliad, since it drew to Troy
The Greek Eve, Helen, from the Spartan's bed;
　　Though on the whole, no doubt, the Dardan boy [9]
Was much inferior to King Menelaus;—
But thus it is some women will betray us.

<hr>

[9] Paris.

LXXIII

There is an awkward thing which much perplexes,
　　Unless like wise Tiresias we had proved
By turns the difference of the several sexes; [10]
　　Neither can show quite *how* they would be loved.
The sensual for a short time but connects us—
　　The sentimental boasts to be unmoved;
But both together form a kind of centaur,
Upon whose back 't is better not to venture.

LXXIV

A something all-sufficient for the *heart*
　　Is that for which the Sex are always seeking;
But how to fill up that same vacant part?
　　There lies the rub—and this they are but weak in.
Frail mariners afloat without a chart,　　[breaking;
　　They run before the wind through high seas
And when they have made the shore through ev'ry
'T is odd, or odds, it may turn out a rock.　　[shock,

LXXV

There is a flower called "Love in Idleness,"
　　For which see Shakspeare's ever blooming
I will not make his great description less,　　[garden;—
　　And beg his British Godship's humble pardon,
If in my extremity of rhyme's distress,
　　I touch a single leaf where he is warden;—
But though the flower is different, with the French
Or Swiss Rousseau, cry "*Voilà la Pervenche!*"*

LXXVI

Eureka! I have found it! What I mean
　　To say is, not that Love is Idleness,
But that in Love such Idleness has been
　　An accessory, as I have cause to guess.
Hard labour 's an indifferent go-between;
　　Your men of business are not apt to express
Much passion, since the merchant-ship, the Argo,
Conveyed Medea as her Supercargo.

LXXVII

"*Beatus ille procul!*" from "*negotiis*,"
　　Saith Horace;† the great little poet 's wrong;
His other maxim, "*Noscitur a sociis*,"
　　Is much more to the purpose of his song;

* See "La Nouvelle Heloïse." [11]
† Hor. Epod. Od. ii. [12]

<hr>

[10] Tiresias was transformed into a woman and back again. See Ovid's *Metamorphoses*.
[11] "There is the periwinkle." An allusion to an event in the *Confessions*.
[12] Horace, *Odes*: "Blest is he who is free from business." The other, not Horace's: "One is known by the company he keeps."

Though even that were sometimes too ferocious,
  Unless good company be kept too long;
But, in his teeth, whate'er their state or station,
  Thrice happy they who *have* an occupation!

LXXVIII

Adam exchanged his Paradise for ploughing,
  Eve made up millinery with fig leaves—
The earliest knowledge from the tree so knowing,
  As far as I know, that the Church receives:
And since that time it need not cost much showing,
  That many of the ills o'er which man grieves,
And still more women, spring from not employing
Some hours to make the remnant worth enjoying.

LXXIX

And hence high life is oft a dreary void,
  A rack of pleasures, where we must invent
A something wherewithal to be annoyed.
  Bards may sing what they please about *Content*;
Contented, when translated, means but cloyed;
  And hence arise the woes of sentiment,
Blue-devils, and Blue-stockings, and Romances
Reduced to practice, and perform'd like dances.

LXXX

I do declare, upon an affidavit,
  Romances, I ne'er read like those I have seen;
Nor, if unto the world I ever gave it,
  Would some believe that such a tale had been:
But such intent I never had, nor have it;
  Some truths are better kept behind a screen,
Especially when they would look like lies;
I therefore deal in generalities.

LXXXI

"An oyster may be crossed in Love"—and why?
  Because he mopeth idly in his shell,
And heaves a lonely subterraqueous sigh,
  Much as a monk may do within his cell:
And *à propos* of monks, their piety
  With sloth hath found it difficult to dwell;
Those vegetables of the Catholic creed
Are apt exceedingly to run to seed.

LXXXII

O Wilberforce! thou man of black renown,[13]
  Whose merit none enough can sing or say,
Thou hast struck one immense Colossus down,
  Thou moral Washington of Africa!

But there's another little thing, I own,
  Which you should perpetrate some summer's day,
And set the other half of earth to rights:
You have freed the *blacks*—now pray shut up the
                [whites.

LXXXIII

Shut up the bald-coot bully Alexander![14]
  Ship off the Holy Three to Senegal;   [gander,"
Teach them that "sauce for goose is sauce for
  And ask them how *they* like to be in thrall?
Shut up each high heroic Salamander,
  Who eats fire gratis (since the pay's but small);
Shut up—no, *not* the King, but the Pavilion,
Or else 't will cost us all another million.

LXXXIV

Shut up the world at large, let Bedlam out;
  And you will be perhaps surprised to find
All things pursue exactly the same route,
  As now with those of *soi-disant* sound mind.
This I could prove beyond a single doubt,
  Were there a jot of sense among mankind;
But till that point *d'appui* is found, alas![15]
Like Archimedes, I leave earth as 't was.

LXXXV

Our gentle Adeline had one defect—
  Her heart was vacant, though a splendid mansion;
Her conduct had been perfectly correct,
  As she had seen nought claiming its expansion.
A wavering spirit may be easier wreck'd,
  Because 't is frailer, doubtless, than a stanch one;
But when the latter works its own undoing,
Its inner crash is like an Earthquake's ruin.

LXXXVI

She loved her lord, or thought so; but *that* love
  Cost her an effort, which is a sad toil,
The stone of Sisyphus, if once we move
  Our feelings 'gainst the nature of the soil.
She had nothing to complain of, or reprove,
  No bickerings, no connubial turmoil:
Their union was a model to behold,
Serene and noble,—conjugal, but cold.

---

13 William Wilberforce worked for twenty years in Parliament to pass a bill to abolish the slave trade. Slavery was not abolished in the colonies until 1833, though the trade was ended in 1807.

14 Alexander of Russia was bald; the Holy Three (below) are the rulers of Russia, Prussia, and Austria; George IV (lines 7–8) was finishing the Pavilion at Brighton.
15 *Point d'appui*: fulcrum.

LXXXVII

There was no great disparity of years,
  Though much in temper; but they never clash'd:
They moved like stars united in their spheres,
  Or like the Rhone by Leman's waters wash'd,
Where mingled and yet separate appears
  The river from the lake, all bluely dash'd
Through the serene and placid glassy deep,
Which fain would lull its river-child to sleep.

LXXXVIII

Now when she once had ta'en an interest
  In any thing, however she might flatter
Herself that her intentions were the best—
  Intense intentions are a dangerous matter:
Impressions were much stronger than she guess'd,
  And gather'd as they run like growing water
Upon her mind; the more so, as her breast
Was not at first too readily impress'd.

LXXXIX

But when it was, she had that lurking demon
  Of double nature, and thus doubly named—
Firmness yclept in heroes, kings, and seamen,
  That is, when they succeed; but greatly blamed
As *obstinacy*, both in men and women,
  Whene'er their triumph pales, or star is tamed:—
And 't will perplex the casuist in morality
To fix the due bounds of this dangerous quality.

XC

Had Buonaparte won at Waterloo,
  It had been firmness; now 't is pertinacity:
Must the event decide between the two?
  I leave it to your people of sagacity
To draw the line between the false and true,
  If such can e'er be drawn by man's capacity:
My business is with Lady Adeline,
Who in her way too was a heroine.

XCI

She knew not her own heart; then how should I?
  I think not she was *then* in love with Juan:
If so, she would have had the strength to fly
  The wild sensation, unto her a new one:
She merely felt a common sympathy
  (I will not say it was a false or true one)
In him, because she thought he was in danger—
Her husband's friend, her own, young, and a stranger.

XCII

She was, or thought she was, his friend—and this
  Without the farce of Friendship, or romance
Of Platonism, which leads so oft amiss
  Ladies who have studied friendship but in France
Or Germany, where people *purely* kiss.
  To thus much Adeline would not advance;
But of such friendship as man's may to man be
She was as capable as woman can be.

XCIII

No doubt the secret influence of the sex
  Will there, as also in the ties of blood,
An innocent predominance annex,
  And tune the concord to a finer mood.
If free from passion, which all friendship checks.
  And your true feelings fully understood,
No friend like to a woman earth discovers,
So that you have not been nor will be lovers.

XCIV

Love bears within its breast the very germ
  Of change; and how should this be otherwise?
That violent things more quickly find a term
  Is shown through nature's whole analogies;
And how should the most fierce of all be firm?
  Would you have endless lightning in the skies?
Methinks Love's very title says enough:
How should "the *tender* Passion" e'er be *tough*?

XCV

Alas! by all experience, seldom yet
  (I merely quote what I have heard from many)
Had lovers not some reason to regret
  The passion which made Solomon a Zany.
I 've also seen some wives (not to forget
  The marriage state, the best or worst of any)
Who were the very paragons of wives,
Yet made the misery of at least two lives.

XCVI

I 've also seen some female *friends* ('t is odd,
  But true—as, if expedient, I could prove)
That faithful were through thick and thin, abroad,
  At home, far more than ever yet was Love—
Who did not quit me when Oppression trod
  Upon me; whom no scandal could remove;
Who fought, and fight, in absence, too, my battles,
Despite the snake Society's loud rattles.

XCVII

Whether Don Juan and chaste Adeline
   Grew friends in this or any other sense,
Will be discuss'd hereafter, I opine:
   At present I am glad of a pretence
To leave them hovering, as the effect is fine,
   And keeps the atrocious reader in *suspense*;
The surest way for ladies and for books
To bait their tender or their tenter hooks.

XCVIII

Whether they rode, or walk'd, or studied Spanish,
   To read Don Quixote in the original,
A pleasure before which all others vanish;
   Whether their talk was of the kind call'd "small,"
Or serious, are the topics I must banish
   To the next Canto; where perhaps I shall
Say something to the purpose, and display
Considerable talent in my way.

XCIX

Above all, I beg all men to forbear
   Anticipating aught about the matter:
They 'll only make mistakes about the fair,
   And Juan too, especially the latter.
And I shall take a much more serious air
   Than I have yet done, in this Epic Satire.
It is not clear that Adeline and Juan
Will fall; but if they do, 't will be their ruin.

C

But great things spring from little:—Would you
   That in our youth, as dangerous a passion   [think,
As e'er brought man and woman to the brink
   Of ruin, rose from such a slight occasion,
As few would ever dream could form the link
   Of such a sentimental situation?
You 'll never guess, I 'll bet you millions, milliards—
It all sprung from a harmless game at billiards.[16]

CI

'T is strange,—but true; for Truth is always strange—
   Stranger than Fiction: if it could be told,
How much would novels gain by the exchange!
   How differently the world would men behold!
How oft would vice and virtue places change!
   The new world would be nothing to the old,
If some Columbus of the moral seas
Would show mankind their soul's Antipodes.

CII

What "Antres vast and deserts idle," then [17]
   Would be discover'd in the human soul!
What Icebergs in the hearts of mighty men,
   What Self-love in the centre as their Pole!
What Anthropophagi in nine of ten
   Of those who hold the kingdoms in controul!
Were things but only call'd by their right name,
Caesar himself would be ashamed of Fame.

[1823]   [1823]

CANTO THE FIFTEENTH

I

AH!—What should follow slips from my reflection:
   Whatever follows ne'ertheless may be
As àpropos of hope or retrospection,
   As though the lurking thought had follow'd free.
All present life is but an Interjection,
   An "Oh!" or "Ah!" of joy or misery,
Or a "Ha! ha!" or "Bah!"—a yawn, or "Pooh!"
Of which perhaps the latter is most true.

II

But, more or less, the whole 's a syncopé
   Or a singultus—emblems of Emotion, [1]
The grand Antithesis to great Ennui,
   Wherewith we break our bubbles on the ocean,
That Watery Outline of Eternity,
   Or miniature at least, as is my notion,
Which ministers unto the soul's delight,
In seeing matters which are out of sight.

III

But all are better than the sigh supprest,
   Corroding in the cavern of the heart,
Making the countenance a masque of rest
   And turning human nature to an art.
Few men dare show their thoughts of worst or best;
   Dissimulation always sets apart
A corner for herself; and, therefore Fiction
Is that which passes with least contradiction.

IV

Ah! who can tell? Or rather, who can not
   Remember, without telling, passion's errors?
The drainer of oblivion, even the sot,
   Hath got blue devils for his morning mirrors:
What though on Lethe's stream he seem to float,
   He cannot sink his tremours or his terrors;
The ruby glass that shakes within his hand
Leaves a sad sediment of Time's worst sand.

---

[16] Byron in a letter to Lady Melbourne describes his flirtation with Lady Frances Webster over a billiard table.

[17] From *Othello*, I, iii, 140.
[1] Syncopé = swoon; singultus = a sob.

V

And as for Love—O Love!—We will proceed.
  The Lady Adeline Amundeville,
A pretty name as one would wish to read,
  Must perch harmonious on my tuneful quill.
There's music in the sighing of a reed;
  There's music in the gushing of a rill;
There's music in all things, if men had ears:
Their Earth is but an echo of the spheres.

VI

The Lady Adeline, right honourable,
  And honour'd, ran a risk of growing less so;
For few of the soft sex are very stable
  In their resolves—alas! that I should say so;
They differ as wine differs from its label,
  When once decanted;—I presume to guess so,
But will not swear: yet both upon occasion,
Till old, may undergo adulteration.

VII

But Adeline was of the purest vintage,
  The unmingled essence of the grape; and yet
Bright as a new Napoleon from its mintage,
  Or glorious as a diamond richly set;
A page where Time should hesitate to print age,
  And for which Nature might forego her debt—
Sole creditor whose process doth involve in 't
The luck of finding every body solvent.

VIII

O Death! thou dunnest of all duns! thou daily
  Knockest at doors, at first with modest tap,
Like a meek tradesman when approaching palely
  Some splendid debtor he would take by sap:
But oft denied, as patience 'gins to fail, he
  Advances with exasperated rap,
And (if let in) insists, in terms unhandsome,
On ready money or a draft on Ransom. [2]

IX

Whate'er thou takest, spare awhile poor Beauty!
  She is so rare, and thou hast so much prey.
What though she now and then may slip from duty,
  The more 's the reason why you ought to stay.
Gaunt Gourmand! with whole nations for your booty,
  You should be civil in a modest way:
Suppress then some slight feminine diseases,
And take as many heroes as Heaven pleases.

[2] Byron's banker.

X

Fair Adeline, the more ingenuous
  Where she was interested (as was said),
Because she was not apt, like some of us,
  To like too readily, or too high bred
To show it—(points we need not now discuss)—
  Would give up artlessly both heart and head
Unto such feelings as seem'd innocent,
For objects worthy of the sentiment.

XI

Some parts of Juan's history, which Rumour,
  That live Gazette, had scatter'd to disfigure,
She had heard; but women hear with more good
  Such aberrations than we men of rigour: [humour
Besides, his conduct, since in England, grew more
  Strict, and his mind assumed a manlier vigour:
Because he had, like Alcibiades, [3]
The art of living in all climes with ease.

XII

His manner was perhaps the more seductive,
  Because he ne'er seem'd anxious to seduce;
Nothing affected, studied, or constructive
  Of coxcombry or conquest; no abuse
Of his attractions marr'd the fair perspective,
  To indicate a Cupidon broke loose,
And seem to say, "resist us if you can"—
Which makes a dandy while it spoils a man.

XIII

They are wrong—that 's not the way to set about it;
  As, if they told the truth, could well be shown.
But right or wrong, Don Juan was without it;
  In fact, his manner was his own alone:
Sincere he was—at least you could not doubt it,
  In listening merely to his voice's tone.
The Devil hath not in all his quiver's choice
An arrow for the heart like a sweet voice.

XIV

By Nature soft, his whole address held off
  Suspicion: though not timid, his regard
Was such as rather seem'd to keep aloof,
  To shield himself, than put you on your guard:
Perhaps 't was hardly quite assured enough,
  But Modesty 's at times its own reward
Like Virtue; and the absence of pretension
Will go much further than there 's need to mention.

[3] Plutarch ascribes this ability to Alcibiades, the Athenian general who was Socrates' protégé.

XV

Serene, accomplish'd, cheerful but not loud;
   Insinuating without insinuation;
Observant of the foibles of the crowd,
   Yet ne'er betraying this in conversation;
Proud with the proud, yet courteously proud,
   So as to make them feel he knew his station
And theirs:—without a struggle for priority,
He neither brooked nor claimed superiority.

XVI

That is, with men: with women he was what
   They pleased to make or take him for; and their
Imagination's quite enough for that:
   So that the outline's tolerably fair,
They fill the canvass up—and "verbum sat."
   If once their phantasies be brought to bear
Upon an object, whether sad or playful,
They can transfigure brighter than a Raphael.

XVII

Adeline, no deep judge of character,
   Was apt to add a colouring from her own.
'T is thus the good will amiably err,
   And eke the wise, as has been often shown.
Experience is the chief philosopher,
   But saddest when his science is well known:
And persecuted sages teach the schools
Their folly in forgetting there are fools.

XVIII

Was it not so, great Locke? and greater Bacon?
   Great Socrates? And thou Diviner still,*
Whose lot it is by man to be mistaken,
   And thy pure creed made sanction of all ill?
Redeeming worlds to be by bigots shaken,
   How was thy toil rewarded? We might fill
Volumes with similar sad illustrations,
But leave them to the conscience of the nations.

* As it is necessary in these times to avoid ambiguity, I say, that I mean, by "Diviner still," CHRIST. If ever God was Man—or Man God—he was *both*. I never arraigned his creed, but the use—or abuse—made of it. Mr. Canning one day quoted Christianity to sanction Negro Slavery, and Mr. Wilberforce had little to say in reply. And was Christ crucified, that black men might be scourged? If so, he had better been born a Mulatto, to give both colours an equal chance of freedom, or at least salvation.[4]

4 See Canto Fourteen, Stanza LXXXII, and note.

XIX

I perch upon an humbler promontory,
   Amidst life's infinite variety:
With no great care for what is nicknamed glory,
   But speculating as I cast mine eye
On what may suit or may not suit my story,
   And never straining hard to versify,
I rattle on exactly as I 'd talk
With any body in a ride or walk.

XX

I don't know that there may be much ability
   Shown in this sort of desultory rhyme;
But there 's a conversational facility,
   Which may round off an hour upon a time.
Of this I 'm sure at least, there 's no servility
   In mine irregularity of chime,
Which rings what 's uppermost of new or hoary,
Just as I feel the "Improvvisatore."

XXI

"Omnia vult *belle* Matho dicere—dic aliquando
   Et *bene*, dic *neutrum*, dic aliquando *male*." [5]
The first is rather more than mortal can do;
   The second may be sadly done or gaily;
The third is still more difficult to stand to;
   The fourth we hear, and see, and say too, daily:
The whole together is what I could wish
To serve in this conundrum of a dish.

XXII

A modest hope—but modesty 's my forte,
   And pride my feeble:—let us ramble on.
I meant to make this poem very short,
   But now I can't tell where it may not run.
No doubt, if I had wish'd to pay my court
   To critics, or to hail the *setting* sun
Of tyranny of all kinds, my concision
Were more;—but I was born for opposition.

XXIII

But then 't is mostly on the weaker side:
   So that I verily believe if they
Who now are basking in their full-blown pride
   Were shaken down, and "dogs had had their day,"
Though at the first I might perchance deride
   Their tumble, I should turn the other way,
And wax an Ultra-royalist in loyalty,
Because I hate even democratic royalty.

5 From Martial's *Epigrams:*

   "Thou finely wouldst say all? Say something well:
   Say something ill, if thou wouldst hear the bell."

XXIV

I think I should have made a decent spouse,
   If I had never proved the soft condition;
I think I should have made monastic vows,
   But for my own peculiar superstition:
'Gainst rhyme I never should have knocked my brows,
   Nor broken my own head, nor that of Priscian,[6]
Nor worn the motley mantle of a poet,
If some one had not told me to forego it.[7]

XXV

But "laissez aller"—knights and dames I sing,
   Such as the times may furnish. 'T is a flight
Which seems at first to need no lofty wing,
   Plumed by Longinus or the Stagyrite:[8]
The difficulty lies in colouring
   (Keeping the due proportions still in sight)
With Nature manners which are artificial,
And rend'ring general that which is especial.

XXVI

The difference is, that in the days of old
   Men made the manners; manners now make men—
Pinned like a flock, and fleeced too in their fold,
   At least nine, and a ninth beside of ten.
Now this at all events must render cold
   Your writers, who must either draw again
Days better drawn before, or else assume
The present, with their common-place costume.

XXVII

We 'll do our best to make the best on 't:—March!
   March, my Muse! If you cannot fly, yet flutter;
And when you may not be sublime, be arch,
   Or starch, as are the edicts statesmen utter.
We surely may find something worth research:
   Columbus found a new world in a cutter,
Or brigantine, or pink, of no great tonnage,
While yet America was in her non-age.

XXVIII

When Adeline, in all her growing sense
   Of Juan's merits and his situation,
Felt on the whole an interest intense,—
   Partly perhaps because a fresh sensation,
Or that he had an air of innocence,
   Which is for Innocence a sad temptation,—
As women hate half measures, on the whole,
She 'gan to ponder how to save his soul.

6 Roman grammarian.
7 See discussion of the review of *Hours of Idleness* in Introduction, pp. 526–27.
8 Longinus and Aristotle (the Stagyrite) both gave principles for literary composition.

XXIX

She had a good opinion of advice,
   Like all who give and eke receive it gratis,
For which small thanks are still the market price,
   Even where the article at highest rate is:
She thought upon the subject twice or thrice,
   And morally decided, the best state is
For morals, marriage; and this question carried,
She seriously advised him to get married.

XXX

Juan replied, with all becoming deference,
   He had a predilection for that tie;
But that, at present, with immediate reference
   To his own circumstances, there might lie
Some difficulties, as in his own preference,
   Or that of her to whom he might apply:
That still he'd wed with such or such a lady,
If that they were not married all already.

XXXI

Next to the making matches for herself,
   And daughters, brothers, sisters, kith or kin,
Arranging them like books on the same shelf,
   There 's nothing women love to dabble in
More (like a stock-holder in growing pelf)
   Than match-making in general: 't is no sin
Certes, but a preventative, and therefore
That is, no doubt, the only reason wherefore.

XXXII

But never yet (except of course a miss
   Unwed, or mistress never to be wed,
Or wed already, who object to this)
   Was there chaste dame who had not in her head
Some drama of the marriage unities,
   Observed as strictly both at board and bed,
As those of Aristotle, though sometimes
They turn out melodrames or pantomimes.

XXXIII

They generally have some only son,
   Some heir to a large property, some friend
Of an old family, some gay Sir John,
   Or grave Lord George, with whom perhaps might
A line, and leave posterity undone,   [end
   Unless a marriage was applied to mend
The prospect and their morals: and besides,
They have at hand a blooming glut of brides.

XXXIV

From these they will be careful to select,
　For this an heiress, and for that a beauty;
For one, a songstress who hath no defect,
　For t' other one who promises much duty;
For this a lady no one can reject,
　Whose sole accomplishments were quite a booty;
A second for her excellent connections;
A third, because there can be no objections.

XXXV

When Rapp the Harmonist embargoed Marriage*
　In his harmonious settlement—(which flourishes
Strangely enough as yet without miscarriage,
　Because it breeds no more mouths than it nourishes,
Without those sad expenses which disparage
　What Nature naturally most encourages)—
Why called he "Harmony" a state sans wedlock?
Now here have got the preacher at a dead lock.

XXXVI

Because he either meant to sneer at harmony
　Or marriage, by divorcing them thus oddly.
But whether reverend Rapp learn'd this in Germany
　Or no, 't is said his sect is rich and godly,
Pious and pure, beyond what I can term any
　Of ours, although they propagate more broadly.
My objection 's to his title, not his ritual,
Although I wonder how it grew habitual.

XXXVII

But Rapp is the reverse of zealous matrons,
　Who favour, malgré Malthus, generation—
Professors of that genial art, and patrons
　Of all the modest part of propagation,
Which after all at such a desperate rate runs,
　That half its produce tends to emigration,
That sad result of passions and potatoes—
Two weeds which pose our economic Catos.

* This extraordinary and flourishing German colony in America does not entirely exclude matrimony, as the "Shakers" do; but lays such restrictions upon it as prevent more than a certain quantum of births within a certain number of years; which births (as Mr. Hulme observes) generally arrive "in a little flock like those of a farmer's lambs, all within the same month perhaps." These Harmonists (so called from the name of their settlement) are represented as a remarkably flourishing, pious, and quiet people. See the various recent writers on America.[9]

[9] George Rapp and his followers settled Harmony and Economy, Pennsylvania, in the early nineteenth century.

XXXVIII

Had Adeline read Malthus? I can't tell;
　I wish she had: his book 's the eleventh
　　commandment,
Which says, "Thou shall not marry," unless *well*:
　This he (as far as I can understand) meant.
'T is not my purpose on his views to dwell,
　Nor canvass what "so eminent a hand" meant; *
But certes it conducts to lives ascetic,
Or turning marriage into arithmetic.

XXXIX

But Adeline, who probably presumed
　That Juan had enough of maintenance,
Or *separate* maintenance, in case 't was doom'd—
　As on the whole it is an even chance
That bridegrooms, after they are fairly *groom'd*,
　May retrograde a little in the dance
Of marriage—(which might form a painter's fame,
Like Holbein's "Dance of Death"—but 't is the
　　　　　　　　　　　　　　　　　　[same);—

XL

But Adeline determined Juan's wedding
　In her own mind, and that's enough for woman.
But then, with whom? There was the sage Miss
　　Reading,
　　Miss Raw, Miss Flaw, Miss Showman, and Miss
　　Knowman,
And the two fair co-heiresses Giltbedding.
　She deemed his merits something more than
All these were unobjectionable matches,　[common:
And might go on, if well wound up, like watches.

XLI

There was Miss Millpond,[10] smooth as summer's sea,
　That usual paragon, an only daughter,
Who seem'd the cream of equanimity,
　Till skimm'd—and then there was some milk and
With a slight shade of Blue, too, it might be,　[water,
　Beneath the surface; but what did it matter?
Love 's riotous, but marriage should have quiet,
And being consumptive, live on a milk diet.

XLII

And then there was the Miss Audacia Shoestring,
　A dashing demoiselle of good estate,
Whose heart was fix'd upon a star or bluestring;
　But whether English Dukes grew rare of late,

* Jacob Tonson, according to Mr. Pope, was accustomed to call his writers "able pens"—"persons of honour," and especially "eminent hands." Vide Correspondence, &c. &c.

[10] Lady Byron's maiden name was Milbanke.

Or that she had not harp'd upon the true string,
  By which such sirens can attract our great,
She took up with some foreign younger brother,
A Russ or Turk—the one 's as good as t' other.

XLIII

And then there was—but why should I go on,
  Unless the ladies should go off?—there was
Indeed a certain fair and fairy one,
  Of the best class, and better than her class,—
Aurora Raby, a young star who shone
  O'er life, too sweet an image for such glass,
A lovely being, scarcely form'd or moulded,
A Rose with all its sweetest leaves yet folded;

XLIV

Rich, noble, but an orphan; left an only
  Child to the care of guardians good and kind;
But still her aspect had an air so lonely!
  Blood is not water; and where shall we find
Feelings of youth like those which overthrown lie
  By death, when we are left, alas! behind,
To feel, in friendless palaces, a home
Is wanting, and our best ties in the tomb?

XLV

Early in years, and yet more infantine
  In figure, she had something of sublime
In eyes which sadly shone, as seraphs' shine.
  All youth—but with an aspect beyond time;
Radiant and grave—as pitying man's decline;
  Mournful—but mournful of another's crime,
She look'd as if she sat by Eden's door,
And grieved for those who could return no more.

XLVI

She was a Catholic, too, sincere, austere,
  As far as her own gentle heart allow'd,
And deem'd that fallen worship far more dear
  Perhaps because 't was fallen: her sires were proud
Of deeds and days when they had fill'd the ear
  Of nations, and had never bent or bow'd
To novel power; and as she was the last,
She held their old faith and old feelings fast.

XLVII

She gazed upon a world she scarcely knew,
  As seeking not to know it; silent, lone,
As grows a flower, thus quietly she grew,
  And kept her heart serene within its zone.

There was awe in the homage which she drew;
  Her spirit seem'd as seated on a throne
Apart from the surrounding world, and strong
In its own strength—most strange in one so young!

XLVIII

Now it so happen'd, in the catalogue
  Of Adeline, Aurora was omitted,
Although her birth and wealth had given her vogue
  Beyond the charmers we have already cited;
Her beauty also seem'd to form no clog
  Against her being mention'd as well fitted,
By many virtues, to be worth the trouble
Of single gentlemen who would be double.

XLIX

And this omission, like that of the bust
  Of Brutus at the pageant of Tiberius,
Made Juan wonder, as no doubt he must.
  This he express'd half smiling and half serious;
When Adeline replied with some disgust,
  And with an air, to say the least, imperious,
She marvell'd "what he saw in such a baby
As that prim, silent, cold Aurora Raby?"

L

Juan rejoined—"She was a Catholic,
  And therefore fittest, as of his persuasion;
Since he was sure his mother would fall sick,
  And the Pope thunder excommunication,
If—" But here Adeline, who seem'd to pique
  Herself extremely on the inoculation
Of others with her own opinions, stated—
As usual—the same reason which she late did.

LI

And wherefore not? A reasonable reason,
  If good, is none the worse for repetition;
If bad, the best way 's certainly to teaze on,
  And amplify: you lose much by concision,
Whereas insisting in or out of season
  Convinces all men, even a politician;
Or—what is just the same—it wearies out.
So the end 's gain'd, what signifies the route?

LII

Why Adeline had this slight prejudice—
  For prejudice it was—against a creature
As pure as sanctity itself from vice,
  With all the added charm of form and feature,

For me appears a question far too nice,
　Since Adeline was liberal by Nature;
But Nature 's Nature, and has more caprices
Than I have time, or will, to take to pieces.

LIII

Perhaps she did not like the quiet way
　With which Aurora on those baubles look'd,
Which charm most people in their earlier day:
　For there are few things by Mankind less brook'd,
And womankind too, if we so may say,
　Than finding thus their genius stand rebuked,
Like "Anthony's by Caesar," by the few
Who look upon them as they ought to do.

LIV

It was not envy—Adeline had none;
　Her place was far beyond it, and her mind.
It was not scorn—which could not light on one
　Whose greatest *fault* was leaving few to find:
It was not jealousy, I think: but shun
　Following the "ignes fatui" of mankind.
It was not—but 't is easier far, alas!
To say what it was not, than what it was.

LV

Little Aurora deem'd she was the theme
　Of such discussion. She was there a guest;
A beauteous ripple of the brilliant stream
　Of rank and youth, though purer than the rest,
Which flow'd on for a moment in the beam
　Time sheds a moment o'er each sparkling crest.
Had she known this, she would have calmly smiled—
She had so much, or little, of the child

LVI

The dashing and proud air of Adeline
　Imposed not upon her; she saw her blaze
Much as she would have seen a glowworm shine,
　Then turn'd unto the stars for loftier rays.
Juan was something she could not divine,
　Being no Sibyl in the new world's ways;
Yet she was nothing dazzled by the meteor,
Because she did not pin her faith on feature.

LVII

His fame too,—for he had that kind of fame
　Which sometimes plays the deuce with
　　womankind,
A heterogeneous mass of glorious blame,
　Half virtues and whole vices being combined;

Faults which attract because they are not tame;
　Follies trick'd out so brightly that they blind:—
These seals upon her wax made no impression,
Such was her coldness or her self-possession.

LVIII

Juan knew nought of such a character—
　High, yet resembling not his lost Haidée;
Yet each was radiant in her proper sphere:
　The Island girl, bred up by the lone sea,
More warm, as lovely, and not less sincere,
　Was Nature's all: Aurora could not be,
Nor would be thus;—the difference in them
Was such as lies between a flower and gem.

LIX

Having wound up with this sublime comparison,
　Methinks we may proceed upon our narrative,
And, as my friend Scott says, "I sound my
　　Warison;" 11
　Scott, the superlative of my comparative—
Scott, who can paint your Christian knight or Saracen,
　Serf, Lord, Man, with such skill as none would
　　share it, if
There had not been one Shakespeare and Voltaire,
Of one or both of whom he seems the heir.

LX

I say, in my slight way I may proceed
　To play upon the surface of Humanity.
I write the world, nor care if the world read,
　At least for this I cannot spare its vanity.
My Muse hath bred, and still perhaps may breed
　More foes by this same scroll: when I began it, I
Thought that it might turn out so—*now* I *know* it,
But still I am, or was, a pretty poet.

LXI

The conference or congress (for it ended
　As congresses of late do) of the Lady
Adeline and Don Juan rather blended
　Some acids with the sweets—for she was heady;
But, ere the matter could be marr'd or mended,
　The silvery bell rang, not for "dinner ready,"
But for that hour, called *half-hour*, given to dress,
Though ladies' robes seem scant enough for less.

LXII

Great things were now to be achieved at table,
　With massy plate for armour, knives and forks
For weapons; but what Muse since Homer's able
　(His feasts are not the worst part of his works)

11 War cry.

To draw up in array a single day-bill
  Of modern dinners? where more mystery lurks,
In soups or sauces, or a sole ragoût,
  Than witches, b—ches, or physicians brew.

LXIII

There was a goodly "soupe à la *bonne femme*,"
  Though God knows whence it came from; there
A turbot for relief of those who cram,   [was too
  Relieved with dindon à la Périgeux;
There also was—the sinner that I am!
  How shall I get this gourmand stanza through?—
Soupe à la Beauveau, whose relief was Dory,
Relieved itself by pork, for greater glory.

LXIV

But I must crowd all into one grand mess
  Or mass; for should I stretch into detail,
My Muse would run much more into excess,
  Than when some squeamish people deem her frail;
But though a "bonne vivante," I must confess
  Her stomach's not her peccant part: this tale
However doth require some slight refection,
Just to relieve her spirits from dejection.

LXV

Fowls à la Condé, slices eke of salmon,
  With sauces Génevoises, and haunch of venison;
Wines too, which might again have slain young
      Ammon—[12]
  A man like whom I hope we shan't see many soon;
They also set a glazed Westphalian ham on,
  Whereon Apicius would bestow his benison;
And then there was Champagne with foaming whirls,
As white as Cleopatra's melted pearls.

LXVI

Then there was God knows what "à l'Allemande,"
  "A l'Espagnole," "timballe," and "Salpicon"—
With things I can't withstand or understand,
  Though swallow'd with much zest upon the whole;
And "entremets" to piddle with at hand,
  Gently to lull down the subsiding soul;
While great Lucullus' *Robe triumphal* muffles—
(*There's fame*)—young Partridge 'fillets, deck'd with
          [truffles.*

* A dish "à la Lucullus." This hero, who conquered the East, has left his more extended celebrity to the transplantation of cherries (which he first brought into Europe), and the nomenclature of some very good dishes;—and I am not sure that (barring indigestion) he has not done more service to mankind by his cookery than by his conquests. A cherry-tree may weigh against a bloody laurel: besides, he has contrived to earn celebrity from both.

[12] Alexander the Great. Apicius (below) was a famous Roman glutton.

LXVII

What are the *fillets* on the victor's brow
  To these? They are rags or dust. Where is the arch
Which nodded to the nation's spoils below?
  Where the triumphal chariots' haughty march?
Gone to where Victories must like dinners go.
  Farther I shall not follow the research:
But oh! ye modern heroes with your cartridges,
When will your names lend lustre e'en to partridges?

LXVIII

Those truffles too are no bad accessaries,
  Followed by "Petits puits d'Amour"—a dish
Of which perhaps the cookery rather varies,
  So every one may dress it to his wish,
According to the best of dictionaries,
  Which encyclopedize both flesh and fish;
But even, sans "confitures," it no less true is,
There's pretty picking in those "petits puits."*

LXIX

The mind is lost in mighty contemplation
  Of intellect expanded on two courses;
And indigestion's grand multiplication
  Requires arithmetic beyond my forces.
Who would suppose, from Adam's simple ration,
  That cookery could have called forth such
As form a science and a nomenclature   [resources,
From out the commonest demands of nature?

LXX

The glasses jingled, and the palates tingled;
  The diners of celebrity dined well;
The ladies with more moderation mingled
  In the feast, pecking less than I can tell;
Also the younger men too: for a springald
  Can't like ripe age in gourmandise excel,
But thinks less of good eating than the whisper
(When seated next him) of some pretty lisper.

LXXI

Alas! I must leave undescribed the gibier,
  The salmi, the consommé, the purée,
All which I use to make my rhymes run glibber
  Than could roast beef in our rough John Bull way:
I must not introduce even a spare rib here,
  "Bubble and squeak" would spoil my liquid lay; [14]
But I have dined, and must forego, alas!
The chaste description even of a "Bécasse";

* "Petits puits d'amour garnis des confitures," a classical and well-known dish for part of the flank of a second course. [13]

[13] Cream puffs.
[14] Fried beef and cabbage. "Bécasse," below, is woodcock.

LXXII

And fruits, and ices, and all that art refines
  From nature for the service of the goût—
Taste or the *gout*,—pronounce it as inclines
  Your stomach! Ere you dine, the French will do;
But *after*, there are sometimes certain signs
  Which prove plain English truer of the two.
Hast ever *had* the *gout*? I have not had it—
But I may have, and you too, Reader, dread it.

LXXIII

The simple olives, best allies of wine,
  Must I pass over in my bill of fare?
I must, although a favourite "plat" of mine
  In Spain, and Lucca, Athens, every where:
On them and bread 't was oft my luck to dine,
  The grass my table-cloth, in open air,
On Sunium or Hymettus, like Diogenes,
Of whom half my philosophy the progeny is.[15]

LXXIV

Amidst this tumult of fish, flesh, and fowl,
  And vegetables, all in masquerade,
The guests were placed according to their roll,
  But various as the various meats display'd:
Don Juan sat next an "à l'Espagnole"—
  No damsel, but a dish, as hath been said;
But so far like a lady, that 't was drest
Superbly, and contained a world of zest.

LXXV

By some odd chance too he was placed between
  Aurora and the Lady Adeline—
A situation difficult, I ween,
  For man therein, with eyes and heart, to dine.
Also the conference which we have seen
  Was not such as to encourage him to shine;
For Adeline, addressing few words to him,
With two transcendant eyes seemed to look through
                                              [him.

LXXVI

I sometimes almost think that eyes have ears:
  This much is sure, that, out of earshot, things
Are somehow echoed to the pretty dears,
  Of which I can't tell whence their knowledge
Like that same mystic music of the spheres,   [springs.
  Which no one hears, so loudly though it rings.
'T is wonderful how oft the sex have heard
Long dialogues which pass'd without a word!

---

[15] Sunium (Colonna), and Hymettus are mountains in Greece;
Diogenes renounced all possessions.

LXXVII

Aurora sat with that indifference
  Which piques a preux Chevalier—as it ought:
Of all offences that 's the worst offence,
  Which seems to hint you are not worth a thought.
Now Juan, though no coxcomb in pretence,
  Was not exactly pleased to be so caught,
Like a good ship entangled among ice,
And after so much excellent advice.

LXXVIII

To his gay nothings, nothing was replied,
  Or something which was nothing, as urbanity
Required. Aurora scarcely look'd aside,
  Nor even smiled enough for any vanity.
The devil was in the girl! Could it be pride?
  Or modesty, or absence, or inanity?
Heaven knows! But Adeline's malicious eyes
Sparkled with her successful prophecies,

LXXIX

And look'd as much as if to say, "I said it;"—
  A kind of triumph I 'll not recommend,
Because it sometimes, as I have seen or read it,
  Both in the case of lover and of friend,
Will pique a gentleman, for his own credit,
  To bring what was a jest to a serious end:
For all men prophesy what *is* or *was*,
And hate those who won't let them come to pass.

LXXX

Juan was drawn thus into some attentions,
  Slight but select, and just enough to express,
To females of perspicuous comprehensions,
  That he would rather make them more than less.
Aurora at the last (so history mentions,
  Though probably much less a fact than guess)
So far relax'd her thoughts from their sweet prison,
As once or twice to smile, if not to listen.

LXXXI

From answering, she began to question: this
  With her was rare; and Adeline, who as yet
Thought her predictions went not much amiss,
  Began to dread she 'd thaw to a coquette—
So very difficult, they say, it is
  To keep extremes from meeting, when once set
In motion; but she here too much refined—
Aurora's spirit was not of that kind.

LXXXII

But Juan had a sort of winning way,
    A proud humility, if such there be,
Which show'd such deference to what females say,
    As if each charming word were a decree.
His tact, too, temper'd him from grave to gay,
    And taught him when to be reserved or free:
He had the art of drawing people out,
Without their seeing what he was about.

LXXXIII

Aurora, who in her indifference
    Confounded him in common with the crowd
Of flutterers, though she deemed he had more sense
    Than whispering foplings, or than witlings loud,—
Commenced (from such slight things will great
        commence)
    To feel that flattery which attracts the proud
Rather by deference than compliment,
And wins even by a delicate dissent.

LXXXIV

And then he had good looks;—that point was carried
    Nem. con. amongst the women, which I grieve
To say leads oft to *crim. con.* with the married[16]—
    A case which to the Juries we may leave,
Since with digressions we too long have tarried.
    Now though we know of old that looks deceive,
And always have done,—somehow these good looks
Make more impression than the best of books.

LXXXV

Aurora, who look'd more on books than faces,
    Was very young, although so very sage,
Admiring more Minerva than the Graces,
    Especially upon a printed page.
But Virtue's self, with all her tightest laces,
    Has not the natural stays of strict old age;
And Socrates, that model of all duty,
Own'd to a penchant, though discreet, for beauty.

LXXXVI

And girls of sixteen are thus far Socratic,
    But innocently so, as Socrates:
And really, if the Sage sublime and Attic
    At seventy years had phantasies like these,
Which Plato in his dialogues dramatic
    Has shown, I know not why they should displease
In virgins—always in a modest way,
Observe; for that with me 's a "sine quâ."*

* Subauditur "Non;" omitted for the sake of euphony.[17]

⬦⬦⬦⬦⬦⬦⬦⬦⬦⬦⬦⬦⬦⬦⬦⬦⬦⬦⬦⬦⬦⬦⬦

16 Legal terms: *Nem. con.* (nemine contradicenti) = no-one contradicting; *crim. con.* (criminal conversation) = adultery.
17 I.e., *sine quâ non* = essential condition.

LXXXVII

Also observe, that, like the great Lord Coke
    (See Littleton) whene'er I have expressed
Opinions two, which at first sight may look
    Twin opposites, the second is the best.
Perhaps I have a third too in a nook,
    Or none at all—which seems a sorry jest:
But if a writer should be quite consistent,
How could he possibly show things existent?

LXXXVIII

If people contradict themselves, can I
    Help contradicting them, and every body,
Even my veracious self?—But that 's a lie;
    I never did so, never will—how should I?
He who doubts all things nothing can deny;   [muddy,
    Truth's fountains may be clear—her streams are
And cut through such canals of contradiction,
That she must often navigate o'er fiction.

LXXXIX

Apologue, fable, poesy, and parable,
    Are false, but may be render'd also true,
By those who sow them in a land that 's arable:
    'T is wonderful what fable will not do!
'T is said it makes reality more bearable:
    But what 's reality? Who has its clue?
Philosophy? No; she too much rejects.
Religion? *Yes*; but which of all her sects?

XC

Some millions must be wrong, that 's pretty clear;
    Perhaps it may turn out that all were right.
God help us! Since we have need on our career
    To keep our holy beacons always bright,
'T is time that some new Prophet should appear,
    Or old indulge man with a second sight.
Opinions wear out in some thousand years,
Without a small refreshment from the spheres.

XCI

But here again, why will I thus entangle
    Myself with metaphysics? None can hate
So much as I do any kind of wrangle;
    And yet, such is my folly, or my fate,
I always knock my head against some angle
    About the present, past, or future state:
Yet I wish well to Trojan and to Tyrian,
For I was bred a moderate Presbyterian.

XCII

But though I am a temperate Theologian,
  And also meek as a Metaphysician,
Impartial between Tyrian and Trojan,
  As Eldon on a lunatic commission,—
In politics my duty is to show John
  Bull something of the lower world's condition.
It makes my blood boil like the springs of Hecla,*
To see men let these scoundrel Sovereigns break law.

XCIII

But politics, and policy, and piety,
  Are topics which I sometimes introduce,
Not only for the sake of their variety,
  But as subservient to a moral use;
Because my business is to *dress* society,
  And stuff with *sage* that very verdant goose.
And now, that we may furnish with some matter all
Tastes, we are going to try the supernatural.

XCIV

And now I will give up all argument;
  And positively henceforth no temptation
Shall "fool me to the top up of my bent";—[19]
  Yes, I 'll begin a thorough reformation.
Indeed, I never knew what people meant
  By deeming that my Muse's conversation
Was dangerous;—I think she is as harmless
As some who labour more and yet may charm less.

XCV

Grim reader! did you ever see a ghost?
  No; but you have heard—I understand—be dumb!
And don't regret the time you may have lost,
  For you have got that pleasure still to come:
And do not think I mean to sneer at most
  Of these things, or by ridicule benumb
That source of the sublime and the mysterious:—
For certain reasons, my belief is serious.

XCVI

Serious? You laugh;—you may: that will I not;
  My smiles must be sincere or not at all.
I say I do believe a haunted spot
  Exists—and where? That shall I not recall,

Because I 'd rather it should be forgot,
  "Shadows the soul of Richard" may appal.[20]
In short, upon the subject I 've some qualms very
Like those of the Philosopher of Malmsbury.†

XCVII

The night (I sing by night—sometimes an owl,
  And now and then a nightingale)—is dim,
And the loud shriek of sage Minerva's fowl
  Rattles around me her discordant hymn:
Old portraits from old walls upon me scowl—
  I wish to heaven they would not look so grim;
The dying embers dwindle in the grate—
I think too that I have sat up too late:

XCVIII

And therefore, though 't is by no means my way
  To rhyme at noon—when I have other things
To think of, if I ever think,—I say
  I feel some chilly midnight shudderings,
And prudently postpone, until mid-day,
  Treating a topic which alas but brings
Shadows;—but you must be in my condition
Before you learn to call this superstition.

XCIX

Between two worlds life hovers like a star,
  'Twixt night and morn, upon the horizon's verge:
How little do we know that which we are!
  How less what we may be! The eternal surge
Of time and tide rolls on, and bears afar
  Our bubbles; as the old burst, new emerge,
Lash'd from the foam of ages; while the graves
Of Empires heave but like some passing waves.

[1823]   [1824]

CANTO THE SIXTEENTH

I

THE antique Persians taught three useful things,
  To draw the bow, to ride, and speak the truth.
This was the mode of Cyrus, best of kings—
  A mode adopted since by modern youth.
Bows have they, generally with two strings;
  Horses they ride without remorse or ruth;
At speaking truth perhaps they are less clever,
But draw the long bow better now than ever.

---

* Hecla is a famous hot-spring in Iceland.[18]

[18] Usually now spelled Hekla, and actually a volcano; it is in S.W. Iceland.
[19] *Hamlet*, III, 2.

† Hobbes; who, doubting of his own soul, paid that compliment to the souls of other people as to decline their visits, of which he had some apprehension.

[20] Shakespeare's *Richard III*, V, iii, 217-20.

II

The cause of this effect, or this defect,—
    "For this effect defective comes by cause,"—[1]
Is what I have not leisure to inspect;
    But this I must say in my own applause,
Of all the Muses that I recollect,
    Whate'er may be her follies or her flaws
In some things, mine 's beyond all contradiction
The most sincere that ever dealt in fiction.

III

And as she treats all things, and ne'er retreats
    From anything, this Epic will contain
A wilderness of the most rare conceits,
    Which you might elsewhere hope to find in vain.
'T is true there be some bitters with the sweets,
    Yet mixed so slightly that you can't complain,
But wonder they so few are, since my tale is
"De rebus cunctis et quibûsdam aliis"[2]

IV

But of all truths which she has told, the most
    True is that which she is about to tell.
I said it was a story of a ghost—
    What then? I only know it so befell.
Have you explored the limits of the coast,
    Where all the dwellers of the earth must dwell?
'T is time to strike such puny doubters dumb as
The sceptics who would not believe Columbus.

V

Some people would impose now with authority,
    Turpin's or Monmouth Geoffry's Chronicle;[3]
Men whose historical superiority
    Is always greatest at a miracle.
But Saint Augustine has the great priority,
    Who bids all men believe the impossible,
Because 't is so. Who nibble, scribble, quibble, he
Quiets at once with "*quia* impossible."[4]

VI

And therefore, mortals, cavil not at all;
    Believe:—if 't is improbable, you *must*;
And if it is impossible, you *shall*:
    'T is always best to take things upon trust.
I do not speak profanely, to recall
    Those holier mysteries, which the wise and just
Receive as gospel, and which grow more rooted,
As all truths must, the more they are disputed.

VII

I merely mean to say what Johnson said,
    That in the course of some six thousand years,
All nations have believed that from the dead
    A visitant at intervals appears;
And what is strangest upon this strange head
    Is, that whatever bar the reason rears
'Gainst such belief, there 's something stronger still
In its behalf, let those deny who will.

VIII

The dinner and the soirée too were done,
    The supper too discussed, the dames admired,
The banqueteers had dropped off one by one—
    The song was silent, and the dance expired:
The last thin petticoats were vanished, gone
    Like fleecy clouds into the sky retired,
And nothing brighter gleamed through the saloon
Than dying tapers—and the peeping moon.

IX

The evaporation of a joyous day
    Is like the last glass of champagne, without
The foam which made its virgin bumper gay;
    Or like a system coupled with a doubt;
Or like a soda bottle when its spray
    Has sparkled and let half its spirit out;
Or like a billow left by storms behind,
Without the animation of the wind;

X

Or like an opiate which brings troubled rest,
    Or none; or like—like nothing that I know
Except itself;—such is the human breast;
    A thing, of which similitudes can show
No real likeness,—like the old Tyrian vest
    Dyed purple, none at present can tell how,
If from a shell-fish or from cochineal.*
So perish every tyrant's robe piece-meal!

XI

But next to dressing for a rout or ball,
    Undressing is a woe; our robe de chambre
May sit like that of Nessus and recall[5]
    Thoughts quite as yellow, but less clear than amber.
Titus exclaimed, "I 've lost a day!" Of all
    The nights and days most people can remember,
(I have had of both, some not to be disdained)
I wish they 'd state how many they have gained.

    * The composition of the old Tyrian purple, whether from a shell-fish or from cochineal, or from kermes, is still an article of dispute; and even its colour—some say purple, others scarlet: I say nothing.

---

[1] *Hamlet*, II, 2.
[2] "Concerning all things and some others."
[3] Medieval historians.
[4] Tertullian, not Augustine, asserts that Christ's resurrection is "certain because it is impossible."

[5] See note to Canto Eleven, Stanza LXV, p. 705.

XII

And Juan, on retiring for the night,
    Felt restless, and perplexed, and compromised;
He thought Aurora Raby's eyes more bright
    Than Adeline (such is advice) advised;
If he had known exactly his own plight,
    He probably would have philosophised;
A great resource to all, and ne'er denied
Till wanted; therefore Juan only sighed.

XIII

He sighed;—the next resource is the full moon,
    Where all sighs are deposited; and now
It happened luckily, the chaste orb shone
    As clear as such a climate will allow;
And Juan's mind was in the proper tone
    To hail her with the apostrophe—"Oh, Thou!"
Of amatory egotism the *Tuism*,
Which further to explain would be a truism.

XIV

But lover, poet, or astronomer,
    Shepherd, or swain, whoever may behold,
Feel some abstraction when they gaze on her:
    Great thoughts we catch from thence (besides a cold
Sometimes, unless my feelings rather err);
    Deep secrets to her rolling light are told;
The ocean's tides and mortal's brains she sways,
And also hearts, if there be truth in lays.

XV

Juan felt somewhat pensive, and disposed
    For contemplation rather than his pillow:
The Gothic chamber, where he was enclosed,
    Let in the rippling sound of the lake's billow,
With all the mystery by midnight caused:
    Below his window waved (of course) a willow;
And he stood gazing out on the cascade
That flashed and after darkened in the shade.

XVI

Upon his table or his toilet,—*which*
    Of these is not exactly ascertained—
(I state this, for I am cautious to a pitch
    Of nicety, where a fact is to be gained)
A lamp burned high, while he leant from a niche,
    Where many a gothic ornament remained,
In chiselled stone and painted glass, and all
That time has left our fathers of their Hall.

XVII

Then, as the night was clear though cold, he threw
    His chamber door wide open—and went forth
Into a gallery of a sombre hue,
    Long, furnished with old pictures of great worth,
Of knights and dames heroic and chaste too,
    As doubtless should be people of high birth.
But by dim lights the portraits of the dead
Have something ghastly, desolate, and dread.

XVIII

The forms of the grim knight and pictured saint
    Look living in the moon; and as you turn
Backward and forward to the echoes faint
    Of your own footsteps—voices from the urn
Appear to wake, and shadows wild and quaint
    Start from the frames which fence their aspects
As if to ask how you can dare to keep   [stern,
A vigil there, where all but death should sleep.

XIX

And the pale smile of Beauties in the grave,
    The charms of other days, in starlight gleams
Glimmer on high; their buried locks still wave
    Along the canvas; their eyes glance like dreams
On ours, or spars within some dusky cave,
    But death is imaged in their shadowy beams.
A picture is the past; even ere its frame
Be gilt, who sate hath ceased to be the same.

XX

As Juan mused on mutability,
    Or on his mistress—terms synonimous—
No sound except the echo of his sigh
    Or step ran sadly through that antique house,
When suddenly he heard, or thought so, nigh,
    A supernatural agent—or a mouse,
Whose little nibbling rustle will embarrass
Most people as it plays along the arras.

XXI

It was no mouse—but lo! a monk, arrayed
    In cowl and beads and dusky garb, appeared,
Now in the moonlight, and now lapsed in shade,
    With steps that trod as heavy, yet unheard;
His garments only a slight murmur made;
    He moved as shadowy as the sisters weird,
But slowly; and as he passed Juan by,
Glanced, without pausing, on him a bright eye.

XXII

Juan was petrified; he had heard a hint
    Of such a Spirit in these halls of old,
But thought, like most men, that there was nothing
    Beyond the rumour which such spots unfold,   [in 't
Coined from surviving superstition's mint,
    Which passes ghosts in currency like gold,
But rarely seen, like gold compared with paper.
And *did* he see this? or was it a vapour?

XXIII

Once, twice, thrice passed, repassed—the thing of air,
    Or earth beneath, or Heaven, or t' other place;
And Juan gazed upon it with a stare,
    Yet could not speak or move; but, on its base
As stands a statue, stood: he felt his hair
    Twine like a knot of snakes around his face;
He taxed his tongue for words, which were not
To ask the reverend person what he wanted.   [granted,

XXIV

The third time, after a still longer pause,
    The shadow passed away—but where? the hall
Was long, and thus far there was no great cause
    To think his vanishing unnatural:
Doors there were many, through which, by the laws
    Of physics, bodies whether short or tall
Might come or go; but Juan could not state
Through which the spectre seemed to evaporate.

XXV

He stood—how long he knew not, but it seemed
    An age,—expectant, powerless, with his eyes
Strained on the spot where first the figure gleamed;
    Then by degrees recalled his energies,
And would have passed the whole off as a dream,
    But could not wake; he was, he did surmise,
Waking already, and returned at length
Back to his chamber, shorn of half his strength.

XXVI

All there was as he left it: still his taper
    Burnt, and not *blue*, as modest tapers use,
Receiving sprites with sympathetic vapour;
    He rubbed his eyes, and they did not refuse
Their office: he took up an old newspaper;
    The paper was right easy to peruse;
He read an article the king attacking,
And a long eulogy of "Patent Blacking."

XXVII

This savoured of this world; but his hand shook;
    He shut his door, and after having read
A paragraph, I think about Horne Tooke,[6]
    Undrest, and rather slowly went to bed.
There couched all snugly on his pillow's nook.
    With what he had seen his phantasy he fed,
And thought it was no opiate, slumber crept
Upon him by degrees, and so he slept.

XXVIII

He woke betimes; and, as may be supposed,
    Pondered upon his visitant or vision,
And whether it ought not to be disclosed,
    At risk of being quizzed for superstition.
The more he thought, the more his mind was posed:
    In the mean time, his valet, whose precision
Was great, because his master brooked no less,
Knocked to inform him it was time to dress.

XXIX

He dressed; and like young people, he was wont
    To take some trouble with his toilet, but
This morning rather spent less time upon 't;
    Aside his very mirror soon was put;
His curls fell negligently o'er his front,
    His clothes were not curbed to their usual cut,
His very neckcloth's Gordian knot was tied
Almost an hair's breadth too much on one side.

XXX

And when he walked down into the saloon,
    He sate him pensive o'er a dish of tea,
Which he perhaps had not discovered soon,
    Had it not happened scalding hot to be,
Which made him have recourse unto his spoon;
    So much distrait he was, that all could see
That something was the matter—Adeline
The first—but *what* she could not well divine.

XXXI

She looked, and saw him pale, and turned as pale
    Herself; then hastily looked down, and muttered
Something, but what 's not stated in my tale.
    Lord Henry said, his muffin was ill buttered;
The Duchess of Fitz-Fulke played with her veil,
    And looked at Juan hard, but nothing uttered.
Aurora Raby, with her large dark eyes,
Surveyed him with a kind of calm surprise.

---

[6] John Horne Tooke (1736–1812), friend of Coleridge and of reform, appears in st. LXXXIV of *The Vision of Judgment*, p. 646.

XXXII

But seeing him all cold and silent still,
    And everybody wondering more or less,
Fair Adeline enquired, "If he were ill?"
    He started, and said, "Yes—no—rather—yes."
The family physician had great skill,
    And being present, now began to express
His readiness to feel his pulse and tell
The cause, but Juan said, "He was quite well."

XXXIII

"Quite well; yes; no."—These answers were
    mysterious,
    And yet his looks appeared to sanction both,
However they might savour of delirious;
    Something like illness of a sudden growth
Weighed on his spirit, though by no means serious.
    But for the rest, as he himself seemed loth
To state the case, it might be ta'en for granted
It was not the physician that he wanted.

XXXIV

Lord Henry, who had now discussed his chocolate,
    Also the muffin whereof he complained,
Said, Juan had not got his usual look elate,
    At which he marvelled, since it had not rained;
Then asked her Grace what news were of the Duke of
    late?
Her Grace replied, *his* Grace was rather pained
With some slight, light, hereditary twinges
Of gout, which rusts aristocratic hinges.

XXXV

Then Henry turned to Juan, and addressed
    A few words of condolence on his state:
"You look," quoth he, "as if you had had your rest
    Broke in upon by the Black Friar of late."
"What Friar?" said Juan; and he did his best
    To put the question with an air sedate,
Or careless; but the effort was not valid
To hinder him from growing still more pallid.

XXXVI

"Oh! have you never heard of the Black Friar?
    The Spirit of these walls?"—"In truth not I."
"Why Fame—but Fame you know 's sometimes a
    Tells an odd story, of which by the bye: [liar—
Whether with time the spectre has grown shyer,
    Or that our sires had a more gifted eye
For such sights, though the tale is half believed,
The Friar of late has not been oft perceived.

XXXVII

"The last time was—"—"I pray," said Adeline,—
    (Who watched the changes of Don Juan's brow,
And from its context thought she could divine
    Connections stronger than he chose to avow
With this same legend)—"if you but design
    To jest, you 'll choose some other theme just now,
Because the present tale has oft been told,
And is not much improved by growing old."

XXXVIII

"Jest!" quoth Milor; "Why, Adeline, you know
    That we ourselves—'t was in the Honey Moon—
Saw—" "Well, no matter, 't was so long ago;
    But, come, I 'll set your story to a tune."
Graceful as Dian when she draws her bow,
    She seized her harp, whose strings were kindled
As touched, and plaintively began to play   [soon
The air of "'T was a Friar of Orders Gray."

XXXIX

"But add the words," cried Henry, "which you made;
    For Adeline is half a poetess,"
Turning round to the rest, he smiling said.
    Of course the others could not but express
In courtesy their wish to see displayed
    By one *three* talents, for there were no less—
The voice, the words, the harper's skill, at once
Could hardly be united by a dunce.

XL

After some fascinating hesitation,—
    The charming of these charmers, who seem bound,
I can't tell why, to this dissimulation,—
    Fair Adeline, with eyes fixed on the ground
At first, then kindling into animation,
    Added her sweet voice to the lyric sound,
And sang with much simplicity,—a merit
Not the less precious, that we seldom hear it.

I

Beware! beware! of the Black Friar,
    Who sitteth by Norman stone,
For he mutters his prayer in the midnight air,
    And his mass of the days that are gone.
When the Lord of the Hill, Amundeville,
    Made Norman Church his prey,
And expelled the friars, one friar still
    Would not be driven away.

2

Though he came in his might, with King Henry's
    To turn church lands to lay,   [right,
With sword in hand, and torch to light
    Their walls, if they said nay,
A monk remained, unchased, unchained,
    And he did not seem formed of clay,
For he 's seen in the porch, and he 's seen in the
    Though he is not seen by day.   [church,

3

And whether for good, or whether for ill,
    It is not mine to say;
But still with the house of Amundeville
    He abideth night and day.
By the marriage bed of their lords, 't is said,
    He flits on the bridal eve;
And 't is held as faith, to their bed of death,
    He comes—but not to grieve.

4

When an heir is born, he is heard to mourn,
    And when aught is to befall
That ancient line, in the pale moonshine
    He walks from hall to hall.
His form you may trace, but not his face,
    'T is shadowed by his cowl;
But his eyes may be seen from the folds between,
    And they seem of a parted soul.

5

But beware! beware! of the Black Friar,
    He still retains his sway,
For he is yet the church's heir,
    Who ever may be the lay.
Amundeville is lord by day,
    But the monk is lord by night.
Nor wine nor wassail could raise a vassal
    To question that friar's right.

6

Say nought to him as he walks the hall,
    And he'll say nought to you;
He sweeps along in his dusky pall,
    As o'er the grass the dew.
Then Grammercy! for the Black Friar;
    Heaven sain him! fair or foul,
And whatsoe'er may be his prayer,
    Let ours be for his soul.

XLI

The lady's voice ceased, and the thrilling wires
    Died from the touch that kindled them to sound;
And the pause followed, which when song expires
    Pervades a moment those who listen round;
And then of course the circle much admires,
    Nor less applauds as in politeness bound,
The tones, the feeling, and the execution,
To the performer's diffident confusion.

XLII

Fair Adeline, though in a careless way,
    As if she rated such accomplishment
As the mere pastime of an idle day,
    Pursued an instant for her own content,
Would now and then as 't were *without* display,
    Yet *with* display in fact, at times relent
To such performances with haughty smile,
To show she *could*, if it were worth her while.

XLIII

Now this (but we will whisper it aside)
    Was—pardon the pedantic illustration—
Trampling on Plato's pride with greater pride,
    As did the Cynic on some like occasion;
Deeming the sage would be much mortified,
    Or thrown into a philosophic passion,
For a spoilt carpet—but the "Attic Bee"
Was much consoled by his own repartee.*

XLIV

Thus Adeline would throw into the shade,
    (By doing easily, whene'er she chose,
What dilettanti do with vast parade)
    Their sort of *half profession*; for it grows
To something like this when too oft displayed,
    And that it is so, every body knows,
Who have heard Miss That or This, or Lady T' other,
Show off—to please their company or mother.

XLV

Oh! the long evenings of duets and trios!
    The admirations and the speculations;
The "Mamma Mia's!" and the "Amor Mio's!"
    The "Tanti palpiti's" on such occasions:

* I think that it *was* a *carpet* on which Diogenes trod, with—
"Thus I trample on the pride of Plato!"—"With greater pride,"
as the other replied. But as *carpets*, are *meant* to be trodden
upon, my memory probably misgives me, and it might be a
robe, or tapestry, or a table-cloth, or some other expensive and
uncynical piece of furniture.

The "Lasciami's," and quavering "Addio's!"[7]
   Amongst our own most musical of nations;
With "Tu mi chamas's" from Portingale,
To soothe our ears, lest Italy should fail.*

XLVI

In Babylon's bravuras—as the home
   Heart-ballads of Green Erin or Grey Highlands,
That brings Lochaber back to eyes that roam
   O'er far Atlantic continents or islands,
The calentures of music which o'ercome
   All mountaineers with dreams that they are nigh
No more to be beheld but in such visions,—   [lands,
Was Adeline well versed, as compositions.

XLVII

She also had a twilight tinge of "*Blue*,"
   Could write rhymes, and compose more than she
Made epigrams occasionally too   [wrote,
   Upon her friends, as everybody ought.
But still from that sublimer azure hue,
   So much the present dye, she was remote,
Was weak enough to deem Pope a great poet,
And what was worse, was not ashamed to show it.

XLVIII

Aurora—since we are touching upon taste,
   Which now-a-days is the thermometer
By whose degrees all characters are classed—
   Was more Shakespearian, if I do not err.
The worlds beyond this world's perplexing waste
   Had more of her existence, for in her
There was a depth of feeling to embrace
Thoughts, boundless, deep, but silent too as Space.

* I remember that the mayoress of a provincial town, some-
what surfeited with a similar display from foreign parts, did
rather indecorously break through the applauses of an intelligent
audience—intelligent, I mean, as to music,—for the words,
besides being in recondite languages (it was some years before
the peace, ere all the world had travelled, and while I was a
collegian)—were sorely disguised by the performers;—this
mayoress, I say, broke out with, "Rot your Italianos! for my
part, I loves a simple ballat!" Rossini will go a good way to
bring most people to the same opinion, some day. Who would
imagine that he was to be the successor of Mozart? However, I
state this with diffidence, as a liege and loyal admirer of Italian
music in general, and of much of Rossini's: but we may say, as
the connoisseur did of painting, in The Vicar of Wakefield,
"that the picture would be better painted if the painter had
taken more pains."

[7] "Tanti palpiti" = heart throbs; "Lasciami" = allow me.
These were common phrases in popular songs.

XLIX

Not so her gracious, graceful, graceless Grace,
   The full-grown Hebe[8] of Fitz-Fulke, whose mind,
If she had any, was upon her face,
   And that was of a fascinating kind.
A little turn for mischief you might trace
   Also thereon,—but that 's not much; we find
Few females without some such gentle leaven,
For fear we should suppose us quite in heaven.

L

I have not heard she was at all poetic,
   Though once she was seen reading the "Bath
     Guide,"
And Hayley's "Triumphs," which she deemed
     pathetic,
   Because, she said, *her temper* had been tried
So much, the bard had really been prophetic
   Of what she had gone through with,—since a bride.
But of all verse, what most ensured her praise
Were sonnets to herself, or "Bouts rimés."[9]

LI

'T were difficult to say what was the object
   Of Adeline, in bringing this same lay
To bear on what appeared to her the subject
   Of Juan's nervous feelings on that day.
Perhaps she merely had the simple project
   To laugh him out of his supposed dismay;
Perhaps she might wish to confirm him in it,
Though why I cannot say—at least this minute.

LII

But so far the immediate effect
   Was to restore him to his self propriety,
A thing quite necessary to the elect,
   Who wish to take the tone of their society:
In which you cannot be too circumspect,
   Whether the mode be persiflage or piety,
But wear the newest mantle of hypocrisy,
On pain of much displeasing the Gynocrasy.[10]

LIII

And therefore Juan now began to rally
   His spirits, and without more explanation
To jest upon such themes in many a sally.
   Her Grace too also seized the same occasion,

[8] Goddess of youth.
[9] Christopher Anstey's *New Bath Guide* (1766) was a satirical
poem; William Hayley's *The Triumph of Temper* was a con-
temporary sentimental poem. *Bouts rimés* are rhymed endings for
which one writes the poem.
[10] Government by women.

With various similar remarks to tally,
　But wished for a still more detailed narration
Of this same mystic Friar's curious doings,
About the present family's deaths and wooings.

LIV

Of these few could say more than has been said;
　They passed as such things do, for superstition
With some, while others, who had more in dread
　The theme, half credited the strange tradition;
And much was talked on all sides on that head;
　But Juan, when cross-questioned on the vision,
Which some supposed (though he had not avowed it)
Had stirred him, answered in a way to cloud it.

LV

And then, the mid-day having worn to one,
　The company prepared to separate;
Some to their several pastimes, or to none,
　Some wondering 't was so early, some so late.
There was a goodly match too, to be run
　Between some greyhounds on my Lord's estate,
And a young race-horse of old pedigree,
Matched for the spring, whom several went to see.

LVI

There was a picture-dealer who had brought
　A special Titian, warranted original,
So precious that it was not to be bought,
　Though princes the possessor were besieging all—
The king himself had cheapened it, but thought
　The Civil List (he deigns to accept obliging all
His subjects by his gracious acceptation)
Too scanty, in these times of low taxation.

LVII

But as Lord Henry was a connoisseur,—
　The friend of artists, if not arts,—the owner,
With motives the most classical and pure,
　So that he would have been the very donor,
Rather than seller, had his wants been fewer,
　So much he deemed his patronage an honour,
Had brought the Capo d'opera,[11] not for sale,
But for his judgment,—never known to fail.

LVIII

There was a modern Goth, I mean a Gothic
　Bricklayer of Babel, called an architect,　[thick,
Brought to survey these grey walls which, though so
　Might have from time acquired some slight defect;

⬦⬦⬦⬦⬦⬦⬦⬦⬦⬦⬦⬦⬦⬦⬦⬦⬦⬦⬦⬦⬦⬦⬦⬦⬦⬦

11 Masterpiece.

Who, after rummaging the Abbey through thick
　And thin, produced a plan whereby to erect
New buildings of correctest conformation,
And throw down old, which he called *restoration*.

LIX

The cost would be a trifle—an "old song,"
　Set to some thousands ('t is the usual burden
Of that same tune, when people hum it long)—
　The price would speedily repay its worth in
An edifice no less sublime than strong,
　By which Lord Henry's good taste would go forth in
Its glory, through all ages shining sunny,
For Gothic daring shown in English money. *

LX

There were two lawyers busy on a mortgage
　Lord Henry wished to raise for a new purchase;
Also a lawsuit upon tenures burgage,[13]
　And one on tithes, which sure are Discord's torches,
Kindling Religion till she throws down *her* gage,
　"Untying" squires "to fight against the
　　churches";†
There was a prize ox, a prize pig, and ploughman,
For Henry was a sort of Sabine showman.

LXI

There were two poachers caught in a steel trap
　Ready for jail, their place of convalescence;
There was a country girl in a close cap
　And scarlet cloak (I hate the sight to see, since—
Since—since—in youth, I had the sad mishap—
　But luckily I have paid few parish fees since)
That scarlet cloak, alas! unclosed with Rigour,
Presents the problem of a double figure.

* "Ausu Romano aere Veneto" is the inscription (and well inscribed in this instance) on the sea walls between the Adriatic and Venice. The walls were a republican work of the Venetians; the inscription, I believe, Imperial; and inscribed by Napoleon the *First*. It is time to continue to him that title—there will be a second by and by, "Spes altera mundi," if he live; let him not defeat it like his father. But, in any case, he will be preferable to the Imbeciles. There is a glorious field for him, if he know how to cultivate it.[12]

†　　"Though ye *untie* the winds, and let them fight
　　　Against the churches."—*Macbeth*.

⬦⬦⬦⬦⬦⬦⬦⬦⬦⬦⬦⬦⬦⬦⬦⬦⬦⬦⬦⬦⬦⬦⬦⬦⬦⬦

12 Byron was referring to Napoleon, Duke of Reichstadt, who died at Vienna on 22 July 1832 at the age of 21. The Latin quotations are "Built with Roman Courage and Venetian money" and "the other hope of the world."
13 Tenure requiring yearly rent to the lord of the property.

LXII

A reel within a bottle is a mystery,
    One can't tell how it e'er got in or out;
Therefore the present piece of natural history,
    I leave to those who are fond of solving doubt;
And merely state, though not for the consistory,
    Lord Henry was a justice, and that Scout
The constable, beneath a warrant's banner,
Had bagged this poacher upon Nature's manor.

LXIII

Now Justices of Peace must judge all pieces
    Of mischief of all kinds, and keep the game
And morals of the country from caprices
    Of those who have not a licence for the same;
And of all things, excepting tithes and leases,
    Perhaps these are most difficult to tame:
Preserving partridges and pretty wenches
Are puzzles to the most precautious benches.

LXIV

The present culprit was extremely pale,
    Pale as if painted so; her cheek being red
By nature, as in higher dames less hale
    'T is white, at least when they just rise from bed.
Perhaps she was ashamed of seeming frail,
    Poor soul! for she was country born and bred,
And knew no better in her immorality
Than to wax white—for blushes are for quality.

LXV

Her black, bright, downcast, yet espiegle [14] eye,
    Had gathered a large tear into its corner,
Which the poor thing at times essayed to dry,
    For she was not a sentimental mourner,
Parading all her sensibility,
    Nor insolent enough to scorn the scorner,
But stood in trembling, patient tribulation,
To be called up for her examination.

LXVI

Of course these groups were scattered here and there,
    Not nigh the gay saloon of ladies gent.
The lawyers in the study; and in air
    The prize pig, ploughman, poachers; the men sent
From town, viz. architect and dealer, were
    Both busy (as a general in his tent
Writing dispatches) in their several stations,
Exulting in their brilliant lucubrations.

—◇—◇—◇—◇—◇—◇—◇—◇—◇—◇—◇—◇—◇—◇—◇—◇—◇—◇—

[14] Roguish.

LXVII

But this poor girl was left in the great hall,
    While Scout, the parish guardian of the frail,
Discussed (he hated beer yclept the "small")
    A mighty mug of *moral* double ale.
She waited until Justice could recall
    Its kind attentions to their proper pale,
To name a thing in nomenclature rather
Perplexing for most virgins—a child's father.

LXVIII

You see here was enough of occupation
    For the Lord Henry, linked with dogs and horses.
There was much hustle too and preparation
    Below stairs on the score of second courses,
Because, as suits their rank and situation,
    Those who in counties have great land resources,
Have "public days," when all men may carouse,
Though not exactly what's called "open house."

LXIX

But once a week or fortnight, *un*invited
    (Thus we translate a *general invitation*)
All country gentlemen, esquired or knighted,
    May drop in without cards, and take their station
At the full board, and sit alike delighted
    With fashionable wines and conversation;
And as the Isthmus of the grand connection,
Talk o'er themselves, the past and next election.

LXX

Lord Henry was a great electioneerer,
    Burrowing for boroughs like a rat or rabbit.
But county contests cost him rather dearer,
    Because the neighbouring Scotch Earl of Giftgabbit
Had English influence, in the self-same sphere here;
    His son, the Honourable Dick Dicedrabbit,
Was member for the "other Interest" (meaning
The same self-interest, with a different leaning).

LXXI

Courteous and cautious therefore in his county,
    He was all things to all men, and dispensed
To some civility, to others bounty,
    And promises to all—which last commenced
To gather to a somewhat large amount, he
    Not calculating how much they condensed;
But what with keeping some, and breaking others,
His word had the same value as another's.

LXXII

A friend to freedom and freeholders—yet
    No less a friend to government—he held,
That he exactly the just medium hit
    'Twixt place and patriotism—albeit compelled,
Such was his Sovereign's pleasure (though unfit,
    He added modestly, when rebels railed)
To hold some sinecures he wished abolished,
But that with them all law would be demolished.

LXXIII

He was "free to confess"—(whence comes this
        phrase?
    Is 't English? No—'tis only parliamentary)
That innovation's spirit now-a-days
    Had made more progress than for the last century.
He would not tread a factious path to praise,
    Though for the public weal disposed to venture
As for his place, he could but say this of it,   [high;
That the fatigue was greater than the profit.

LXXIV

Heaven, and his friends, knew that a private life
    Had ever been his sole and whole ambition;
But could he quit his king in times of strife,
    Which threatened the whole country with
        perdition?
When demagogues would with a butcher's knife
    Cut through and through (oh! damnable incision!)
The Gordian or the Geordi-an knot, whose strings
Have tied together Commons, Lords, and Kings.

LXXV

Sooner "come place into the civil list
    And champion him to the utmost—" he would
Till duly disappointed or dismissed: [keep it,
    Profit he cared not for, let others reap it;
But should the day come when place ceased to exist,
    The country would have far more cause to weep it:
For how could it go on? Explain who can!
He gloried in the name of Englishman.

LXXVI

He was as independent—aye, much more—
    Than those who were not paid for independence,
As common soldiers, or a common——Shore,
    Have in their several arts or parts ascendence
O'er the irregulars in lust or gore,
    Who do not give professional attendance.
Thus on the mob all statesmen are as eager
To prove their pride, as footmen to a beggar.

LXXVII

All this (save the last stanza) Henry said,
    And thought. I say no more—I've said too much;
For all of us have either heard or read—
    Off—or *upon* the hustings—some slight such
Hints from the independent heart or head
    Of the official candidate. I 'll touch
No more on this—the dinner-bell hath rung,
And grace is said; the grace I *should* have *sung*—

LXXVIII

But I'm too late, and therefore must make play.
    'T was a great banquet, such as Albion old
Was wont to boast—as if a glutton's tray
    Were something very glorious to behold.
But 't was a public feast and public day,—
    Quite full, right dull, guests hot, and dishes cold,
Great plenty, much formality, small cheer,
And every body out of their own sphere.

LXXIX

The squires familarly formal, and
    My lords and ladies proudly condescending;
The very servants puzzling how to hand   [bending
    Their plates—without it might be too much
From their high places by the sideboard's stand—
    Yet like their masters fearful of offending.
For any deviation from the graces
Might cost both man and master too—their *places*.

LXXX

There were some hunters bold, and coursers keen,
    Whose hounds ne'er erred, nor greyhounds
        deigned to lurch;
Some deadly shots too, Septembrizers,[15] seen
    Earliest to rise, and last to quit the search
Of the poor partridge through his stubble screen.
    There were some massy members of the church,
Takers of tithes, and makers of good matches,
And several who sung fewer psalms than catches.

LXXXI

There were some country wags too,—and, alas!
    Some exiles from the town, who had been driven
To gaze, instead of pavement, upon grass,
    And rise at nine in lieu of long eleven.
And lo! upon that day it came to pass,
    I sate next that o'erwhelming son of heaven,
The very powerful Parson, Peter Pith,[16]
The loudest wit I e'er was deafened with.

---

15 Hunters are compared to those who took part in the
September Massacres in Paris in 1792.
16 Sydney Smith, author of *Peter Plimley's Letters*, whom Byron
knew.

LXXXII

I knew him in his livelier London days,
  A brilliant diner out, though but a curate,
And not a joke he cut but earned its praise,
  Until preferment, coming at a sure rate,
(Oh, Providence! how wondrous are thy ways,
  Who would suppose thy gifts sometimes obdurate?)
Gave him, to lay the devil who looks o'er Lincoln,[17]
A fat fen vicarage, and nought to think on.

LXXXIII

His jokes were sermons, and his sermons jokes;
  But both were thrown away amongst the fens;
For wit hath no great friend in aguish folks.
  No longer ready ears and short-hand pens
Imbibed the gay bon'mot, or happy hoax:
  The poor priest was reduced to common sense,
Or to coarse efforts very loud and long,
To hammer a hoarse laugh from the thick throng.

LXXXIV

There *is* a difference, says the song, "between
  A beggar and a queen," or *was* (of late
The latter worse used of the two we've seen—
  But we'll say nothing of affairs of state)
A difference "'twixt a bishop and a dean,"
  A difference between crockery ware and plate,
As between English beef and Spartan broth—
And yet great heroes have been bred by both.

LXXXV

But of all nature's discrepancies, none
  Upon the whole is greater than the difference
Beheld between the country and the town,
  Of which the latter merits every preference
From those who have few resources of their own,
  And only think, or act, or feel with reference
To some small plan of interest or ambition—
Both which are limited to no condition.

LXXXVI

But "en avant!" The light loves languish o'er
  Long banquets and too many guests, although
A slight repast makes people love much more,
  Bacchus and Ceres being, as we know,
Even from our grammar upwards, friends of yore
  With vivifying Venus, who doth owe
To these the invention of champagne and truffles:
Temperance delights her, but long fasting ruffles.

[17] The gargoyle on St. Hugh's Chapel of Lincoln Cathedral.

LXXXVII

Dully past o'er the dinner of the day;
  And Juan took his place, he knew not where,
Confused, in the confusion, and distrait,
  And sitting as if nailed upon his chair:
Though knives and forks clanked round as in a fray,
  He seemed unconscious of all passing there,
Till some one, with a groan, exprest a wish
(Unheeded twice) to have a fin of fish.

LXXXVIII

On which, at the *third* asking of the banns,
  He started; and perceiving smiles around
Broadening to grins, he coloured more than once,
  And hastily—as nothing can confound
A wise man more than laughter from a dunce—
  Inflicted on the dish a deadly wound,
And with such hurry, that ere he could curb it,
He had paid his neighbour's prayer with half a turbot.

LXXXIX

This was no bad mistake, as it occurred,
  The supplicator being an amateur;
But others, who were left with scarce a third,
  Were angry—as they well might, to be sure,
They wondered how a young man so absurd
  Lord Henry at his table should endure;
And this, and his not knowing how much oats
Had fallen last market, cost his host three votes.

XC

They little knew, or might have sympathised,
  That he the night before had seen a ghost;
A prologue which but slightly harmonised
  With the substantial company engrossed
By Matter, and so much materialised,
  That one scarce knew at what to marvel most
Of two things—how (the question rather odd is)
Such bodies could have souls, or souls such bodies.

XCI

But what confused him more than smile or stare
  From all the 'squires and 'squiresses around,
Who wondered at the abstraction of his air,
  Especially as he had been renowned
For some vivacity among the fair,
  Even in the country circle's narrow bound—
(For little things upon my Lord's estate
Were good small-talk for others still less great)—

XCII

Was, that he caught Aurora's eye on his,
    And something like a smile upon her cheek.
Now this he really rather took amiss;
    In those who rarely smile, their smiles bespeak
A strong external motive; and in this
    Smile of Aurora's there was nought to pique
Or hope, or love, with any of the wiles
Which some pretend to trace in ladies' smiles.

XCIII

'T was a mere quiet smile of contemplation,
    Indicative of some surprise and pity;
And Juan grew carnation with vexation,
    Which was not very wise and still less witty,
Since he had gained at least her observation,
    A most important outwork of the city—
As Juan should have known, had not his senses
By last night's ghost been driven from their defences.

XCIV

But what was bad, she did not blush in turn,
    Nor seem embarrassed—quite the contrary;
Her aspect was as usual, still—*not* stern—
    And she withdrew, but cast not down, her eye,
Yet grew a little pale—with what? concern?
    I know not; but her colour ne'er was high—
Though sometimes faintly flushed—and always clear,
As deep seas in a Sunny Atmosphere.

XCV

But Adeline was occupied by fame
    This day; and watching, witching, condescending
To the consumers of fish, fowl, and game,
    And dignity with courtesy so blending,
As all must blend whose part it is to aim
    (Especially as the sixth year is ending)
At their lord's, son's, or similar connection's
Safe conduct through the rocks of re-elections.

XCVI

Though this was most expedient on the whole,
    And usual—Juan, when he cast a glance
On Adeline while playing her grand role,
    Which she went through as though it were a dance,
(Betraying only now and then her soul
    By a look scarce perceptibly askance
Of weariness or scorn) began to feel
Some doubt how much of Adeline was *real*;

XCVII

So well she acted, all and every part
    By turns—with that vivacious versatility,
Which many people take for want of heart.
    They err—'t is merely what is called mobility,*
A thing of temperament and not of art,
    Though seeming so, from its supposed facility;
And false—though true; for, surely they 're sincerest
Who are strongly acted on by what is nearest.

XCVIII

This makes your actors, artists, and romancers,
    Heroes sometimes, though seldom—sages never:
But speakers, bards, diplomatists, and dancers,
    Little that 's great, but much of what is clever;
Most orators, but very few financiers,
    Though all Exchequer Chancellors endeavour,
Of late years, to dispense with Cocker's rigours,[18]
And grow quite figurative with their figures.

XCIX

The poets of arithmetic are they
    Who, though they prove not two and two to be
Five, as they might do in a modest way,
    Have plainly made it out that four are three,
Judging by what they take, and what they pay.
    The Sinking Fund's unfathomable sea,
That most unliquidating liquid, leaves
The debt unsunk, yet sinks all it receives.[19]

C

While Adeline dispensed her airs and graces,
    The fair Fitz-Fulke seemed very much at ease;
Though too well bred to quiz men to their faces,
    Her laughing blue eyes with a glance could seize
The ridicules of people in all places—
    That honey of your fashionable bees—
And store it up for mischievous enjoyment;
And this at present was her kind employment.

* In French "mobilité." I am not sure that mobility is English, but it is expressive of a quality which rather belongs to other climates, though it is sometimes seen to a great extent in our own. It may be defined as an excessive susceptibility of immediate impressions—at the same time without *losing* the past: and is, though sometimes apparently useful to the possessor, a most painful and unhappy attribute.

[18] Cocker's *Arithmetic* (1677) was still the standard text.
[19] This scheme to reduce the national debt lost tens of millions of pounds in the hundred or so years of its operation.

CI

However, the day closed, as days must close;
  The evening also waned—and coffee came.
Each carriage was announced, and ladies rose,
  And curtseying off, as curtsies country dame,
Retired: with most unfashionable bows
  Their docile esquires also did the same,
Delighted with their dinner and their host,
But with the Lady Adeline the most.

CII

Some praised her beauty: others her great grace;
  The warmth of her politeness, whose sincerity
Was obvious in each feature of her face,
  Whose traits were radiant with the rays of verity.
Yes; *she* was truly worthy *her* high place!
  No one could envy her reserved prosperity;
And then her dress—what beautiful simplicity
Draperied her form with curious felicity!*

CIII

Meanwhile sweet Adeline deserved their praises,
  By an impartial indemnification
For all her past exertion and soft phrases,
  In a most edifying conversation,
Which turned upon their late guests' miens and faces,
  Their families, even to the last relation;
Their hideous wives, their horrid selves and dresses,
And truculent distortion of their tresses.

CIV

True, *she* said little—'t was the rest that broke
  Forth into universal epigram;
But then 't was to the purpose what she spoke:
  Like Addison's "faint praise," so wont to damn,
Her own but served to set off every joke,
  As music chimes in with a melodrame.
How sweet the task to shield an absent friend!
I ask but this of mine, to—*not* defend.

CV

There were but two exceptions to this keen
  Skirmish of wits o'er the departed; one,
Aurora, with her pure and placid mien;
  And Juan too, in general behind none
In gay remark on what he had heard or seen,
  Sate silent now, his usual spirits gone:
In vain he heard the others rail or rally,
He would not join them in a single sally.

* "Curiosa felicitas."—PETRONIUS ARBITER.

CVI

'T is true he saw Aurora look as though
  She approved his silence; she perhaps mistook
Its motive for that charity we owe
  But seldom pay the absent, nor would look
Further—it might or it might not be so.
  But Juan, sitting silent in his nook,
Observing little in his reverie,
Yet saw this much, which he was glad to see.

CVII

The ghost at least had done him this much good,
  In making him as silent as a ghost,
If in the circumstances which ensued
  He gained esteem where it was worth the most.
And certainly Aurora had renewed
  In him some feelings he had lately lost,
Or hardened; feelings which, perhaps ideal,
Are so divine, that I must deem them real:—

CVIII

The love of higher things and better days;
  The unbounded hope, and heavenly ignorance
Of what is called the world, and the world's ways;
  The moments when we gather from a glance
More joy than from all future pride or praise,
  Which kindle manhood, but can ne'er entrance
The heart in an existence of its own,
Of which another's bosom is the zone.

CIX

Who would not sigh Αι αι ταν Κυθερειαν!²⁰
  That *hath* a memory, or that *had* a heart?
Alas! *her* star must fade like that of Dian;
  Ray fades on ray, as years on years depart.
Anacreon only had the soul to tie an
  Unwithering myrtle round the unblunted dart
Of Eros; but though thou hast played us many tricks,
Still we respect thee, "Alma Venus Genetrix!" ²¹

CX

And full of sentiments, sublime as billows
  Heaving between this world and worlds beyond,
Don Juan, when the midnight hour of pillows
  Arrived, retired to his; but to despond
Rather than rest. Instead of poppies, willows
  Waved o'er his couch; he meditated, fond
Of those sweet bitter thoughts which banish sleep,
And make the wordling sneer, the youngling weep.

²⁰ "Woe, woe for Cytherea" from Bion's *Epitaph for Adonis.*
Dian's "star" is the moon.
²¹ An allusion to Lucretius, *On the Nature of Things*: "Mother
of Aeneas and his race, delight of men and gods, life-giving
Venus."

CXI

The night was as before: he was undrest,
    Saving his night gown, which is an undress;
Completely "sans culotte," and without vest;
    In short, he hardly could be clothed with less:
But apprehensive of his spectral guest,
    He sate, with feelings awkward to express
(By those who have not had such visitations)
Expectant of the ghost's fresh operations.

CXII

And not in vain he listened;—Hush! what 's that?
    I see—I see—Ah, no!—'t is not—yet 't is—
Ye powers! it is the—the—the—Pooh! the cat!
    The devil may take that stealthy pace of his!
So like a spiritual pit-a-pat,
    Or tiptoe of an amatory Miss,
Gliding the first time to a rendezvous,
And dreading the chaste echoes of her shoe.

CXIII

Again—what is 't? The wind? No, no,—this time
    It is the sable Friar as before,
With awful footsteps regular as rhyme,
    Or (as rhymes may be in these days) much more.
Again, through shadows of the night sublime,
    When deep sleep fell on men, and the world wore
The starry darkness round her like a girdle
Spangled with gems—the monk made his blood
                     [curdle.

CXIV

A noise like to wet fingers drawn on glass,*
    Which sets the teeth on edge; and a slight clatter
Like showers which on the midnight gusts will pass,
    Sounding like very supernatural water,
Came over Juan's ear, which throbbed, alas!
    For Immaterialism 's a serious matter;
So that even those whose faith is the most great
In Souls immortal, shun them tête-à-tête.

CXV

Were his eyes open?—Yes! and his mouth too.
    Surprise has this effect—to make one dumb,
Yet leave the gate which Eloquence slips through
    As wide as if a long speech were to come.
Nigh and more nigh the awful echoes drew,
    Tremendous to a mortal tympanum:
His eyes were open, and (as was before
Stated) his mouth. What opened next?—the door.

* See the account of the Ghost of the Uncle of Prince Charles of Saxony raised by Schroepfer—"Karl—Karl—was—walt wolt mich?"

CXVI

It opened with a most infernal creak,
    Like that of Hell. "Lasciate ogni speranza
Voich' entrate!" The hinge seemed to speak,[22]
    Dreadful as Dante's rhima, or this stanza;
Or—but all words upon such themes are weak;
    A single shade 's sufficient to entrance a
Hero—for what is substance to a Spirit?
Or how is 't *matter* trembles to come near it?

CXVII

The door flew wide, not swiftly,—but, as fly
    The sea-gulls, with a steady, sober flight—
And then swung back; nor close—but stood awry,
    Half letting in long shadows on the light,
Which still in Juan's candlesticks burned high,
    For he had two, both tolerably bright,
And in the doorway, darkening Darkness, stood
The sable Friar in his solemn hood.

CXVIII

Don Juan shook, as erst he had been shaken
    The night before; but being sick of shaking,
He first inclined to think he had been mistaken,
    And then to be ashamed of such mistaking;
His own internal ghost began to awaken
    Within him, and to quell his corporal quaking—
Hinting that soul and body on the whole
Were odds against a disembodied soul.

CXIX

And then his dread grew wrath, and his wrath fierce,
    And he arose, advanced—the shade retreated;
But Juan, eager now the truth to pierce,
    Followed, his veins no longer cold, but heated,
Resolved to thrust the mystery carte and tierce,
    At whatsoever risk of being defeated:
The ghost stopped, menaced, then retired, until
He reached the ancient wall, then stood stone still.

CXX

Juan put forth one arm—Eternal powers!
    It touched no soul, nor body, but the wall,
On which the moonbeams fell in silvery showers
    Checquered with all the tracery of the hall;
He shuddered, as no doubt the bravest cowers
    When he can't tell what 't is that doth appal.
How odd, a single hobgoblin's non-entity
Should cause more fear than a whole host's identity!*

*   "*Shadows* to-night
    Have struck more terror to the soul of Richard,
    Than can the *Substance* of ten thousand soldiers," &c.
                        see *Richard III.*

[22] "Abandon all hope, ye who enter here": Dante, *Inferno*, III, 9.

CXXI

But still the Shade remained: the blue eyes glared,
  And rather variably for stony death;
Yet one thing rather good the grave had spared,
  The ghost had a remarkably sweet breath:
A straggling curl showed he had been fair-haired;
  A red lip, with two rows of pearls beneath,
Gleamed forth, as through the casement's ivy shroud
The moon peeped, just escaped from a grey cloud.

CXXII

And Juan, puzzled, but still curious, thrust
  His other arm forth—Wonder upon wonder!
It pressed upon a hard but glowing bust,
  Which beat as if there was a warm heart under.
He found, as people on most trials must,
  That he had made at first a silly blunder,
And that in his confusion he had caught
Only the wall, instead of what he sought.

CXXIII

The ghost, if ghost it were, seemed a sweet soul
  As ever lurked beneath a holy hood:
A dimpled chin, a neck of ivory, stole
  Forth into something much like flesh and blood;
Back fell the sable frock and dreary cowl,
  And they revealed—alas! that e'er they should!
In full, voluptuous, but *not o'er*grown bulk,
The phantom of her frolic Grace—Fitz-Fulke!

[1823]   [1824]

CANTO THE SEVENTEENTH

I

THE world is full of orphans: firstly, those
  Who are so in the strict sense of the phrase;
But many a lonely tree the loftier grows
  Than others crowded in the Forest's maze—
The next are such as are not doomed to lose
  Their tender parents, in their budding days,
But, merely, their parental tenderness,
Which leaves them orphans of the heart no less.

II

The next are "*only* Children," as they are styled,
  Who grow up *Children* only, since the old saw
Pronounces that an "only"'s a spoilt child—
  But not to go too far, I hold it law,
That where their education, harsh or mild,
  Transgresses the great bounds of love or awe,
The sufferers—be 't in heart or intellect—
Whate'er the *cause*, are orphans in *effect*.

III

But to return unto the stricter rule—
  As far as words make rules—our common notion
Of orphan paints at once a parish school,
  A half-starved babe, a wreck upon Life's ocean,
A human (what the Italians nickname) "Mule"![1]
  A theme for Pity or some worse emotion;
Yet, if examined, it might be admitted
The wealthiest orphans are to be more pitied.

IV

Too soon they are parents to themselves: for what
  Are Tutors, Guardians, and so forth, compared
With Nature's genial Genitors? so that
  A child of Chancery, that Star-Chamber ward,
(I'll take the likeness I can first come at,)
  Is like—a duckling by Dame Partlett reared,
And frights—especially if 't is a daughter,
Th' old Hen—by running headlong to the water.

V

There is a common-place book argument,
  Which glibly glides from every vulgar tongue;
When any dare a new light to present,
  "If you are right; then everybody 's wrong!"
Suppose the converse of this precedent
  So often urged, so loudly and so long;
"If you are wrong, then everybody's right!"
Was ever everybody yet so quite?

VI

Therefore I would solicit free discussion
  Upon all points—no matter what, or whose—
Because as Ages upon Ages push on,
  The last is apt the former to accuse
Of pillowing its head on a pin-cushion,
  Heedless of pricks because it was obtuse:
What was a paradox becomes a truth or
A something like it—witness Luther!

VII

The Sacraments have been reduced to two,
  And Witches unto none, though somewhat late
Since burning agéd women (save a few—
  Not witches only b—ches—who create
Mischief in families, as some know or knew,
  Should still be singed, but slightly, let me state),
Has been declared an act of inurbanity,
Malgré Sir Matthew Hales's [2] great humanity.

[1] In a MS. note Byron says: "The Italians at least in some
parts of Italy call bastards and foundlings—'I Muli'—the
Mules—*why*—I cannot see, unless they mean to infer that the
offspring of Matrimony are Asses."
[2] A judge under Charles II who condemned two women to
death as witches in 1664.

VIII

Great Galileo was debarred the Sun,
   Because he fixed it; and, to stop his talking,
How Earth could round the solar orbit run,
   Found his own legs embargoed from mere walking:
The man was well-nigh dead, ere men begun
   To think his skull had not some need of caulking;
But now, it seems, he's right—his notion just:
No doubt a consolation to his dust.

IX

Pythagoras, Locke, Socrates—but pages
   Might be filled up, as vainly as before,
With the sad usage of all sorts of sages,
   Who in his life-time, each, was deemed a Bore!
The loftiest minds outrun their tardy ages: [more;
   This they must bear with and, perhaps, much
The wise man's sure when he no more can share it, he
Will have a firm Post Obit on posterity.

X

If such doom waits each intellectual Giant,
   We little people in our lesser way,
In Life's small rubs should surely be more pliant,
   And so for one will I—as well I may—
Would that I were less bilous—but, oh, fie on 't!
   Just as I make my mind up every day,
To be a "*totus, teres*,"[3] Stoic, Sage,
The wind shifts and I fly into a rage.

XI

Temperate I am—yet never had a temper;
   Modest I am—yet with some slight assurance;
Changeable too—yet somehow "*Idem semper*":[4]
   Patient—but not enamoured of endurance;
Cheerful—but, sometimes, rather apt to whimper:
   Mild—but at times a sort of "*Hercules furens*":[5]
So that I almost think that the same skin
For one without—has two or three within.

XII

Our Hero was, in Canto the Sixteenth,
   Left in a tender moonlight situation,
Such as enables Man to show his strength
   Moral or physical: on this occasion
Whether his virtue triumphed—or, at length,
   His vice—for he was of a kindling nation—
Is more than I shall venture to describe;—
Unless some Beauty with a kiss should bribe.

---

[3] "Wholly smooth," "even-tempered."
[4] "Always the same."
[5] Hercules was driven mad by Zeus' wife Hera out of jealousy; in one rage he killed his children, in another his friend.

XIII

I leave the thing a problem, like all things:—
   The morning came—and breakfast, tea and toast,
Of which most men partake, but no one sings.
   The company whose birth, wealth, worth, have cost
My trembling Lyre already several strings,
   Assembled with our hostess, and mine host;
The guests dropped in—the last but one, Her Grace,
The latest, Juan, with his virgin face.

XIV

Which best it is to encounter—Ghost, or none,
   'Twere difficult to say—but Juan looked
As if he had combated with more than one,
   Being wan and worn, with eyes that hardly brooked
The light, that through the Gothic windows shone:
   Her Grace, too, had a sort of air rebuked—
Seemed pale and shivered, as if she had kept
A vigil, or dreamt rather more than slept.

[1823]   [1903]

ON THIS DAY I COMPLETE MY THIRTY-SIXTH YEAR.

I.

'TIS time this heart should be unmoved,
   Since others it hath ceased to move:
Yet, though I cannot be beloved,
     Still let me love!

2.

My days are in the yellow leaf;
   The flowers and fruits of Love are gone;
The worm, the canker, and the grief
     Are mine alone!

3.

The fire that on my bosom preys
   Is lone as some Volcanic isle;
No torch is kindled at its blaze—
     A funeral pile.

4.

The hope, the fear, the jealous care,
   The exalted portion of the pain
And power of love, I cannot share,
     But wear the chain.

5.

But 't is not *thus*—and 't is not *here*—
    Such thoughts should shake my soul, nor *now*
Where Glory decks the hero's bier,
    Or binds his brow.

6.

The Sword, the Banner, and the Field,
    Glory and Greece, around me see!
The Spartan, borne upon his shield,
    Was not more free.

7.

Awake! (not Greece—she *is* awake!)
    Awake, my spirit! Think through *whom*
Thy life-blood tracks its parent lake,
    And then strike home!

8.

Tread those reviving passions down,
    Unworthy manhood!—unto thee
Indifferent should the smile or frown
    Of Beauty be.

9.

If thou regret'st thy youth, *why live?*
    The land of honourable death
Is here:—up to the Field, and give
    Away thy breath!

10.

Seek out—less often sought than found—
    A soldier's grave, for thee the best;
Then look around, and choose thy ground,
    And take thy Rest.

[1824]   [1824]

LOVE AND DEATH.

1.

I WATCHED thee when the foe was at our side,
    Ready to strike at him—or thee and me.
Were safety hopeless—rather than divide
    Aught with one loved save love and liberty.

2.

I watched thee on the breakers, when the rock
    Received our prow and all was storm and fear,
And bade thee cling to me through every shock;
    This arm would be thy bark, or breast thy bier.

3.

I watched thee when the fever glazed thine eyes,
    Yielding my couch and stretched me on the ground,
When overworn with watching, ne'er to rise
    From thence if thou an early grave hadst found.

4.

The earthquake came, and rocked the quivering wall,
    And men and nature reeled as if with wine.
Whom did I seek around the tottering hall?
    For thee. Whose safety first provide for? Thine.

5.

And when convulsive throes denied my breath
    The faintest utterance to my fading thought,
To thee—to thee—e'en in the gasp of death
    My spirit turned, oh! oftener than it ought.

6.

Thus much and more; and yet thou lov'st me not,
    And never wilt!   Love dwells not in our will.
Nor can I blame thee, though it be my lot
    To strongly, wrongly, vainly love thee still.

[1824]   [1887]

PROSE

F R O M

JOURNAL, 1813–14

[November 23, 1813]
... If I had any views in this country, they would probably be parliamentary. But I have no ambition; at least, if any, it would be *aut Cæsar aut nihil*.[1] My hopes are limited to the arrangement of my affairs, and settling either in Italy or the East (rather the last), and drinking deep of the languages and literature of both. Past events have unnerved me; and all I can now do is to make life an amusement, and look on while others play. After all, even the highest game of crowns and sceptres, what is it? *Vide* Napoleon's last twelve-month. It has completely upset my system of fatalism. I thought, if crushed, he would have fallen, when

---

[1] "Either Caesar or nothing."

fractus illabitur orbis,[2] and not have been pared away to gradual insignificance; that all this was not a mere *jeu* of the gods, but a prelude to greater changes and mightier events. But men never advance beyond a certain point; and here we are, retrograding, to the dull, stupid old system,—balance of Europe— poising straws upon kings' noses, instead of wringing them off! Give me a republic, or a despotism of one, rather than the mixed government of one, two, three. A republic!—look in the history of the Earth—Rome, Greece, Venice, France, Holland, America, our short (*eheu!*) Commonwealth, and compare it with what they did under masters. The Asiatics are not qualified to be republicans, but they have the liberty of demolishing despots, which is the next thing to it. To be the first man—not the Dictator—not the Sylla, but the Washington or the Aristides—the leader in talent and truth—is next to the Divinity! Franklin, Penn, and, next to these, either Brutus or Cassius— even Mirabeau—or St. Just. I shall never be any thing, or rather always be nothing. The most I can hope is, that some will say, "He might, perhaps, if he would."

Thursday, November 26. [1813]

Awoke a little feverish, but no headach—no dreams neither, thanks to stupor! Two letters; one from * * * *, the other from Lady Melbourne—both excellent in their respective styles. * * * *'s contained also a very pretty lyric on "concealed griefs;" if not her own, yet very like her. Why did she not say that the stanzas were, or were not, of her own composition? I do not know whether to wish them *hers* or not. I have no great esteem for poetical persons, particularly women; they have so much of the "ideal" in *practics*, as well as *ethics*.

I have been thinking lately a good deal of Mary Duff.[3] How very odd that I should have been so utterly, devotedly fond of that girl, at an age when I could neither feel passion, nor know the meaning of the word. And the effect! My mother used always to rally me about this childish amour; and, at last, many years after, when I was sixteen, she told me one day, "Oh, Byron, I have had a letter from Edinburgh, "from Miss Abercromby, and your old sweetheart "Mary Duff is married to a Mr. Co⁰." And what was my answer? I really cannot explain or account for my feelings at that moment; but they nearly threw me into convulsions, and alarmed my mother so much, that after I grew better, she generally avoided the

<hr>

[2] Horace, *Odes*, III, iii: "the world should fall shattered."
[3] Mary Duff (b. 1788) was a distant cousin, as was his third youthful love Mary Chaworth. Margaret Portus, the second, was a first cousin.

subject—to *me*—and contented herself with telling it to all her acquaintance. Now, what could this be? I had never seen her since her mother's *faux pas* at Aberdeen had been the cause of her removal to her grandmother's at Banff; we were both the merest children. I had and have been attached fifty times since that period; yet I recollect all we said to each other, all our caresses, her features, my restlessness, sleeplessness, my tormenting my mother's maid to write for me to her, which she at last did, to quiet me. Poor Nancy thought I was wild, and, as I could not write for myself, became my secretary. I remember, too, our walks, and the happiness of sitting by Mary, in the children's apartment, at their house not far from the Plain-stanes at Aberdeen, while her lesser sister Helen played with the doll, and we sat gravely making love, in our way.

How the deuce did all this occur so early? where could it originate? I certainly had no sexual ideas for years afterwards; and yet my misery, my love for that girl were so violent, that I sometimes doubt if I have ever been really attached since. Be that as it may, hearing of her marriage several years after was like a thunder-stroke—it nearly choked me—to the horror of my mother and the astonishment and almost incredulity of every body. And it is a phenomenon in my existence (for I was not eight years old) which has puzzled, and will puzzle me to the latest hour of it; and lately, I know not why, the *recollection* (*not* the attachment) has recurred as forcibly as ever. I wonder if she can have the least remembrance of it or me? or remember her pitying sister Helen for not having an admirer too? How very pretty is the perfect image of her in my memory—her brown, dark hair, and hazel eyes; her very dress! I should be quite grieved to see *her now*; the reality, however beautiful, would destroy, or at least confuse, the features of the lovely Peri which then existed in her, and still lives in my imagination, at the distance of more than sixteen years. I am now twenty-five and odd months. . . .

I think my mother told the circumstances (on my hearing of her marriage) to the Parkynses, and certainly to the Pigot family, and probably mentioned it in her answer to Miss A., who was well acquainted with my childish *penchant*, and had sent the news on purpose for *me*,—and thanks to her!

Next to the beginning, the conclusion has often occupied my reflections, in the way of investigation. That the facts are thus, others know as well as I, and my memory yet tells me so, in more than a whisper. But, the more I reflect, the more I am bewildered to assign any cause for this precocity of affection.

Lord Holland invited me to dinner to-day; but three days' dining would destroy me. So, without eating at all since yesterday, I went to my box at Covent Garden.

Saw * * * * looking very pretty, though quite a different style of beauty from the other two. She has the finest eyes in the world, out of which she pretends *not* to see, and the longest eyelashes I ever saw, since Leila's and Phannio's Moslem curtains of the light. She has much beauty,—just enough,—but is, I think, *méchante*.

I have been pondering on the miseries of separation, that—oh how seldom we see those we love! yet we live ages in moments, *when met*. The only thing that consoles me during absence is the reflection that no mental or personal estrangement, from ennui or disagreement, can take place; and when people meet hereafter, even though many changes may have taken place in the mean time, still, unless they are *tired* of each other, they are ready to reunite, and do not blame each other for the circumstances that severed them.

[November 27, 1813]

. . . Redde the *Edinburgh Review* of Rogers. He is ranked highly; but where he should be. There is a summary view of us all—*Moore* and *me* among the rest;[4] and both (the *first* justly) praised—though, by implication (justly again) placed beneath our memorable friend. Mackintosh is the writer, and also of the critique on the Stael. His grand essay on Burke, I hear, is for the next number. But I know nothing of the *Edinburgh*, or of any other *Review*, but from rumour; and I have long ceased; indeed, I could not, in justice, complain of any, even though I were to rate poetry, in general, and my rhymes in particular, more highly than I really do. To withdraw *myself* from *myself* (oh that cursed selfishness!) has ever been my sole, my entire, my sincere motive in scribbling at all; and publishing is also the continuance of the same object, by the action it affords to the mind, which else recoils upon itself. If I valued fame, I should flatter received opinions, which have gathered strength by time, and will yet wear longer than any living works to the contrary. But, for the soul of me, I cannot and will not give the lie to my own thoughts and doubts, come what may. If I am a fool, it is, at least, a doubting one; and I envy no one the certainty of his self-approved wisdom.

All are inclined to believe what they covet, from a lottery-ticket up to a passport to Paradise,—in which, from the description, I see nothing very tempting. My restlessness tells me I have something "within

"that passeth show." It is for Him, who made it, to prolong that spark of celestial fire which illuminates, yet burns, this frail tenement; but I see no such horror in a "dreamless sleep," and I have no conception of any existence which duration would not render tiresome. How else "fell the angels," even according to your creed? They were immortal, heavenly, and happy, as their *apostate Abdiel*[5] is now by his treachery. Time must decide; and eternity won't be the less agreeable or more horrible because one did not expect it. In the mean time, I am grateful for some good, and tolerably patient under certain evils—*grace à Dieu et mon bon tempérament*.

[December 13, 1813]

. . . one of the ablest men I know—a perfect Magliabecchi[6]—a devourer, a *Helluo* of books, and an observer of men,) has lent me a quantity of Burns's unpublished and never-to-be-published Letters. They are full of oaths and obscene songs. What an antithetical mind!—tenderness, roughness—delicacy, coarseness—sentiment, sensuality—soaring and grovelling, dirt and deity—all mixed up in that one compound of inspired clay!

It seems strange; a true voluptuary will never abandon his mind to the grossness of reality. It is by exalting the earthly, the material, the *physique* of our pleasures, by veiling these ideas, by forgetting them altogether, or, at least, never naming them hardly to one's self, that we alone can prevent them from disgusting.

[December 17, 18, 1813]

. . . Went to my box at Covent Garden to-night; and my delicacy felt a little shocked at seeing S * * *'s mistress (who, to my certain knowledge, was actually educated, from her birth, for her profession) sitting with her mother, "a three-piled b——d, b——d-Major to the army," in a private box opposite. I felt rather indignant; but, casting my eyes round the house, in the next box to me, and the next, and the next, were the most distinguished old and young Babylonians of quality;—so I burst out a laughing. It was really odd; Lady * * *divorced*—Lady * * and her daughter, Lady * *, both *divorceable*—Mrs. * *, in the next the *like*, and still nearer * * * * * *! What an assemblage to *me*, who know all their histories. It was as if the house had been divided between your public and your *understood* courtesans;—but the intriguantes much outnumbered the regular mercenaries. On the other side were only Pauline and *her*

4 Samuel Rogers, Thomas Moore, and Mme de Staël were all friends of Byron, as well as writers he admired.

5 *Paradise Lost*, V, 896.
6 Antonio Magliabecci (1633–1714), librarian to the Duke of Tuscany and famous collector.

mother, and, next box to her, three of inferior note. Now, where lay the difference between *her* and *mamma*, and Lady * * and daughter? except that the two last may enter Carleton[7] and any *other house*, and the two first are limited to the opera and b—— house. How I do delight in observing life as it really is!—and myself, after all, the worst of any. But no matter—I must avoid egotism, which, just now, would be no vanity.

I have lately written a wild, rambling, unfinished rhapsody, called "*The Devil's Drive*," the notion of which I took from Porson's "*Devil's Walk*."[8]

Sunday, February 27. [1814]

Here I am, alone, instead of dining at Lord H.'s, where I was asked,—but not inclined to go any where. Hobhouse says I am growing a *loup garou*,—a solitary hobgoblin. True;—"I am myself alone." The last week has been passed in reading—seeing plays—now and then visitors—sometimes yawning and sometimes sighing, but no writing,—save of letters. If I could always read, I should never feel the want of society. Do I regret it?—um!—"Man delights not me," and only one woman—at a time.

There is something to me very softening in the presence of a woman,—some strange influence, even if one is not in love with them—which I cannot at all account for, having no very high opinion of the sex. But yet,—I always feel in better humour with myself and every thing else, if there is a woman within ken. Even Mrs. Mule, my firelighter,—the most ancient and withered of her kind,—and (except to myself) not the best-tempered—always makes me laugh,—no difficult task when I am "i' the vein."

Heigho! I would I were in mine island!—I am not well; and yet I look in good health. At times, I fear, "I am not in my perfect mind;"—and yet my heart and head have stood many a crash, and what should ail them now? They prey upon themselves, and I am sick—sick—"Prithee, undo this button—why should "a cat, a rat, a dog have life—and *thou* no life at all?" Six-and-twenty years, as they call them, why, I might and should have been a Pasha by this time. "I 'gin to "be a-weary of the sun."[9]

Buonaparte is not yet beaten; but has rebutted Blucher, and repiqued Schwartzenburg. This it is to have a head. If he again wins, *Væ victis!*[10]

---

[7] The official residence of the Prince Regent, later George IV.
[8] Not by Porson, but by Coleridge and Southey, published 1799 as *The Devil's Thoughts*.
[9] The quotations in the three paragraphs are from *3 Henry VI* (V, vi), *Hamlet* (II, ii), *King Lear* (IV, vii), and *Macbeth* (V, v).
[10] Blücher at Nangis (February 17) and Prince Swartzenberg at Montereau (February 18).

F R O M

BYRON'S JOURNAL-LETTER TO AUGUSTA LEIGH, 1816

Sept. 18. [1816]

... Arrived the second time (1st time was by water) at Clarens, beautiful Clarens! Went to Chillon through Scenery worthy of I know not whom; went over the Castle of Chillon again. On our return met an English party in a carriage; a lady in it fast asleep!— fast asleep in the most anti-narcotic spot in the world —excellent! I remember, at Chamouni, in the very eyes of Mont Blanc, hearing another woman, English also, exclaim to her party "did you ever see any thing "more *rural?*"—as if it was Highgate, or Hampstead, or Brompton, or Hayes,—"*Rural!*" quotha!—Rocks, pines, torrents, Glaciers, Clouds, and Summits of eternal snow far above them—and "*Rural!*" I did not know the thus exclaiming fair one, but she was a very good kind of a woman.

Sept[r] 19th

At Clarens—the only book (except the Bible), a translation of "*Cecilia*" (Miss Burney's *Cecilia*); and the owner of the Cottage had also called her dog (a fat Pug ten years old, and hideous as *Tip*) after Cecilia's (or rather Delville's) dog, Fidde.

Rose at five: order the carriage round. Crossed the mountains to Montbovon on horseback, and on Mules, and, by dint of scrambling, on foot also; the whole route beautiful as a Dream, and now to me almost as indistinct. I am so tired; for though healthy, I have not the strength I possessed but a few years ago. At Mont Davant we breakfasted; afterwards, on a steep ascent dismounted, tumbled down, and cut a finger open; the baggage also got loose and fell down a ravine, till stopped by a large tree: swore; recovered baggage: horse tired and dropping; mounted Mule. At the approach of the summit of Dent Jamant dismounted again with H.[1] and all the party. Arrived at a lake in the very nipple of the bosom of the Mountain; left our quadrupeds with a Shepherd, and ascended further; came to some snow in patches, upon which my forehead's perspiration fell like rain, making the same dints as in a sieve: the chill of the wind and the snow turned me giddy, but I scrambled on and upwards. *H.* went to the highest *pinnacle*; I did not, but paused within a few yards (at an opening of the Cliff). In coming down, the Guide tumbled three times; I fell a laughing, and tumbled too—the descent luckily soft, though steep and slippery: H. also fell, but nobody hurt. The whole of the Mountain

---

[1] Byron's companion was his friend John Cam Hobhouse.

superb. A Shepherd on a very steep and high cliff playing upon his *pipe*; very different from *Arcadia*, (where I saw the pastors with a long Musquet instead of a Crook, and pistols in their Girdles). Our Swiss Shepherd's pipe was sweet, and his tune agreeable. Saw a cow strayed; am told that they often break their necks on and over the crags. Descended to Montbovon; pretty scraggy village, with a wild river and a wooden bridge. H. went to fish—caught one. Our carriage not come; our horses, mules, etc., knocked up; ourselves fatigued; but so much the better—I shall sleep.

The view from the highest points of to-day's journey comprized on one side the greatest part of Lake Leman; on the other, the valleys and mountains of the Canton of Fribourg, and an immense plain, with the Lakes of Neuchâtel and Morat, and all which the borders of these and of the Lake of Geneva inherit: we had both sides of the Jura before us in one point of view, with Alps in plenty. In passing a ravine, the Guide recommended strenuously a quickening of pace, as the Stones fall with great rapidity and occasional damage: the advice is excellent, but, like most good advice, impracticable, the road being so rough in this precise point, that neither mules, nor mankind, nor horses, can make any violent progress. Passed without fractures or menace thereof.

The music of the Cows' bells (for their wealth, like the Patriarchs', is cattle) in the pastures, (which reach to a height far above any mountains in Britain), and the Shepherds' shouting to us from crag to crag, and playing on their reeds where the steeps appeared almost inaccessible, with the surrounding scenery, realized all that I have ever heard or imagined of a pastoral existence:—much more so than Greece or Asia Minor, for there we are a little too much of the sabre and musquet order; and if there is a Crook in one hand, you are sure to see a gun in the other:—but this was pure and unmixed—solitary, savage, and patriarchal: the effect I cannot describe. As we went, they played the "Ranz des Vaches" and other airs, by way of farewell. I have lately repeopled my mind with Nature.

Sept.ʳ 22ᵈ

Left Thoun in a boat, which carried us the length of the lake in three hours. The lake small; but the banks fine: rocks down to the water's edge. Landed at Neuhause; passed Interlachen; entered upon a range of scenes beyond all description or previous conception. Passed a rock; inscription—2 brothers—one murdered the other; just the place for it. After a variety of windings came to an enormous rock. Girl with fruit—very pretty; blue eyes, good teeth, very

fair: long but good features—reminded me rather of F.ʸ. Bought some of her pears, and patted her upon the cheek; the expression of her face very mild, but good, and not at all coquettish. Arrived at the foot of the Mountain (the Yung frau, *i.e.* the Maiden); Glaciers; torrents; one of these torrents *nine hundred feet* in height of visible descent. Lodge at the Curate's. Set out to see the Valley; heard an Avalanche fall, like thunder; saw Glacier—enormous. Storm came on, thunder, lightning, hail; all in perfection, and beautiful. I was on horseback; Guide wanted to carry my cane; I was going to give it him, when I recollected that it was a Swordstick, and I thought the lightning might be attracted towards him; kept it myself; a good deal encumbered with it, and my cloak, as it was too heavy for a whip, and the horse was stupid, and stood still with every other peal. Got in, not very wet; the Cloak being staunch. H. wet through; H. took refuge in cottage; sent man, umbrella, and cloak (from the Curate's when I arrived) after him. Swiss Curate's house very good indeed,—much better than most English Vicarages. It is immediately opposite the torrent I spoke of. The torrent is in shape curving over the rock, like the *tail* of a white horse streaming in the wind, such as it might be conceived would be that of the "*pale* horse" on which *Death* is mounted in the Apocalypse.[2] It is neither mist nor water, but a something between both; it's immense height (nine hundred feet) gives it a wave, a curve, a spreading here, a condensation there, wonderful and indescribable. I think, upon the whole, that this day has been better than any of this present excursion.

[Sept 23]

... Arrived at the Grindenwald; dined, mounted again, and rode to the higher Glacier—twilight, but distinct—very fine Glacier, like *a frozen hurricane*. Starlight, beautiful, but a devil of a path! Never mind, got safe in; a little lightning; but the whole of the day as fine in point of weather as the day on which Paradise was made. Passed *whole woods of withered pines, all withered;* trunks stripped and barkless, branches lifeless; done by a single winter,—their appearance reminded me of me and my family.[3]

Sept.ʳ 29ᵗʰ

... In the weather for this tour (of 13 days), I have been very fortunate—fortunate in a companion (Mr. He.)—fortunate in our prospects, and exempt from even the little petty accidents and delays which often render journeys in a less wild country disappointing.

---

2 See *Manfred*, II, ii.
3 See *Manfred*, I, ii.

I was disposed to be pleased. I am a lover of Nature and an admirer of Beauty. I can bear fatigue and welcome privation, and have seen some of the noblest views in the world. But in all this—the recollections of bitterness, and more especially of recent and more home desolation, which must accompany me through life, have preyed upon me here; and neither the music of the Shepherd, the crashing of the Avalanche, nor the torrent, the mountain, the Glacier, the Forest, nor the Cloud, have for one moment lightened the weight upon my heart, nor enabled me to lose my own wretched identity in the majesty, and the power, and the Glory, around, above, and beneath me.

I am past reproaches; and there is a time for all things. I am past the wish of vengeance, and I know of none like for what I have suffered; but the hour will come, when what I feel must be felt, and the—but enough.

To you, dearest Augusta, I send, and *for* you I have kept this record of what I have seen and felt. Love me as you are beloved by me.

EXTRACTS FROM A DIARY: 1821

January 6, 1821.

Mist—thaw—slop—rain. No stirring out on horseback. Read Spence's *Anecdotes.* Pope a fine fellow—always thought him so. Corrected blunders in *nine* apophthegms of Bacon—all historical—and read Mitford's *Greece.* Wrote an epigram. Turned to a passage in Guinguené [1]—ditto in Lord Holland's *Lope de Vega.* [2] Wrote a note on *Don Juan.*

At eight went out to visit. Heard a little music—like music. Talked with Count Pietro G. of the Italian comedian Vestris, who is now at Rome—have seen him often act in Venice—a good actor—very. Somewhat of a mannerist; but excellent in broad comedy, as well as in the sentimental pathetic. He has made me frequently laugh and cry, neither of which is now a very easy matter—at least, for a player to produce in me.

Thought of the state of women under the ancient Greeks—convenient enough. Present state a remnant of the barbarism of the chivalric and feudal ages—artificial and unnatural. They ought to mind home—and be well fed and clothed—but not mixed in society. Well educated, too, in religion—but to read neither poetry nor politics—nothing but books of piety and cookery. Music—drawing—dancing—also a little gardening and ploughing now and then. I have seen them mending the roads in Epirus with good success. Why not, as well as haymaking and milking?

Came home, and read Mitford again, and played with my mastiff—gave him his supper. Made another reading to the epigram, but the turn the same. To-night at the theatre, there being a prince on his throne in the last scene of the comedy,—the audience laughed, and asked him for a *Constitution.* This shows the state of the public mind here, as well as the assassinations. It won't do. There must be a universal republic,—and there ought to be.

The crow is lame of a leg—wonder how it happened—some fool trod upon his toe, I suppose. The falcon pretty brisk—the cats large and noisy—the monkeys I have not looked to since the cold weather, as they suffer by being brought up. Horses must be gay—get a ride as soon as weather serves. Deuced muggy still—an Italian winter is a sad thing, but all the other seasons are charming.

What is the reason that I have been, all my lifetime, more or less *ennuyé?* and that, if any thing, I am rather less so now than I was at twenty, as far as my recollection serves? I do not know how to answer this, but presume that it is constitutional,—as well as the waking in low spirits, which I have invariably done for many years. Temperance and exercise, which I have practised at times, and for a long time together vigorously and violently, made little or no difference. Violent passions did;—when under their immediate influence—it is odd, but—I was in agitated, but *not* in depressed, spirits.

A dose of salts has the effect of a temporary inebriation, like light champagne, upon me. But wine and spirits make me sullen and savage to ferocity—silent, however, and retiring, and not quarrelsome, if not spoken to. Swimming also raises my spirits,—but in general they are low, and get daily lower. That is *hopeless;* for I do not think I am so much *ennuyé* as I was at nineteen. The proof is, that then I must game, or drink, or be in motion of some kind, or I was miserable. At present, I can mope in quietness; and like being alone better than any company—except the lady's whom I serve. But I feel a something, which makes me think that, if I ever reach near to old age, like Swift, "I shall die at top" first. Only I do not dread idiotism or madness so much as he did. On the contrary, I think some quieter stages of both must be preferable to much of what men think the possession of their senses.

---

[1] A contemporary French historian of Italian literature.
[2] A study of the life and works of the Spanish playwright, published 1817.

FROM

DETACHED THOUGHTS: 1821

13.

Whenever an American requests to see me (which is *not* unfrequently), I comply: 1^{stly}, because I respect a people who acquired their freedom by firmness without excess; and 2^{ndly}, because these trans-atlantic visits, "few and far between," make me feel as if talking with Posterity from the other side of the Styx. In a century or two, the new English and Spanish Atlantides will be masters of the old Countries in all probability, as Greece and Europe overcame their Mother Asia in the older, or earlier ages as they are called.

72.

When I first went up to College, it was a new and a heavy hearted scene for me. Firstly, I so much disliked leaving Harrow, that, though it was time (I being seventeen), it broke my very rest for the last quarter with counting the days that remained. I always *hated* Harrow till the last year and half, but then I liked it. Secondly, I wished to go to Oxford and not to Cambridge. Thirdly, I was so completely alone in this new world, that it half broke my Spirits. My companions were not unsocial, but the contrary—lively, hospitable, of rank, and fortune, and gay far beyond my gaiety. I mingled with, and dined and supped, etc., with them; but, I know not how, it was one of the deadliest and heaviest feelings of my life to feel that I was no longer a boy. From that moment I began to grow old in my own esteem; and in my esteem age is not estimable. I took my gradations in the vices with great promptitude, but they were not to my taste; for my early passions, though violent in the extreme, were concentrated, and hated division or spreading abroad. I could have left or lost the world with or for that which I loved; but, though my temperament was naturally burning, I could not share in the common place libertinism of the place and time without disgust. And yet this very disgust, and my heart thrown back upon itself, threw me into excesses perhaps more fatal than those from which I shrunk, as fixing upon me (at a time) the passions, which, spread amongst many, would have hurt only myself.

73.

People have wondered at the Melancholy which runs through my writings. Others have wondered at my personal gaiety; but I recollect once, after an hour, in which I had been sincerely and particularly gay, and rather brilliant, in company, my wife replying to me when I said (upon her remarking my high spirits) "and yet, Bell, I have been called and mis-called "Melancholy—you must have seen how falsely, "frequently." "No, B.," (she answered) "it is not "so: at *heart* you are the most melancholy of man- "kind, and often when apparently gayest."

74.

If I could explain at length the *real* causes which have contributed to increase this perhaps *natural* temperament of mine, this Melancholy which hath made me a bye-word, nobody would wonder; but this is impossible without doing much mischief. I do not know what other men's lives have been, but I cannot conceive anything more strange than some of the earlier parts of mine. I have written my memoirs, but omitted *all* the really *consequential* and *important* parts, from deference to the dead, to the living, and to those who must be both.

75.

I sometimes think that I should have written the *whole* as a *lesson*, but it might have proved a *lesson* to be *learnt* rather than *avoided;* for passion is a whirlpool, which is not to be viewed nearly without attraction from its Vortex.

76.

I must not go on with these reflections, or I shall be letting out some secret or other to paralyze posterity.

79.

My first dash into poetry was as early as 1800. It was the ebullition of a passion for my first Cousin Margaret Parker (daughter and grand-daughter of the two Admirals Parker), one of the most beautiful of evanescent beings. I have long forgotten the verses, but it would be difficult for me to forget her. Her dark eyes! her long eye-lashes! her completely Greek cast of face and figure! I was then about twelve—She rather older, perhaps a year. She died about a year or two afterwards, in consequence of a fall which injured her spine and induced consumption. Her Sister, Augusta (by some thought still more beautiful), died of the same malady; and it was indeed in attending her that Margaret met with the accident, which occasioned her own death. My Sister told me that, when she went to see her shortly before her death, upon accidentally mentioning my name, Margaret coloured through the paleness of mortality to the eyes, to the great astonishment of my Sister, who (residing with her Grandmother, Lady Holderness) saw at that time but little of me for family reasons, knew nothing of our attachment, nor could conceive why my name should affect her at such a time. I knew nothing of her illness (being at Harrow and in the country), till she was gone.

Some years after, I made an attempt at an Elegy. A very dull one. I do not recollect scarcely any thing equal to the *transparent* beauty of my cousin, or to the sweetness of her temper, during the short period of our intimacy. She looked as if she had been made out of a rainbow—all beauty and peace.

My passion had its usual effects upon me: I could not sleep, could not eat; I could not rest; and although I had reason to know that she loved me, it was the torture of my life to think of the time which must elapse before we could meet again—being usually about *twelve hours* of separation! But I was a fool then, and am not much wiser now.

80.

My passions were developed very early—so early, that few would believe me, if I were to state the period, and the facts which accompanied it. Perhaps this was one of the reasons which caused the anticipated melancholy of my thoughts—having anticipated life.

My earlier poems are the thoughts of one at least ten years older than the age at which they were written: I don't mean for their solidity, but their Experience. The two first Cantos of C^e H^d were completed at twenty two, and they were written as if by a man older than I shall probably ever be.

Percy Bysshe Shelley

1792–1822

MATTHEW ARNOLD tells this story: When Mrs. Shelley, after the poet's death, sought advice about a school for their son, she was advised to "send him somewhere where they will teach him to think for himself." Mrs. Shelley's objection was immediate: "Teach him to think for himself? Oh, my God, teach him rather to think like other people." The plea is poignant, coming from the daughter of two of England's most radical social and political reformers who had herself eloped at sixteen with Shelley and written *Frankenstein* at seventeen. Perhaps no one has ever known better than Mary Shelley what it is to live in a world apparently made up of people who think for themselves. Although some of Shelley's contemporaries tried to account for his eccentricities by ascribing them to the influence of others (beginning with his father, who blamed his friendship with Hogg for the profession of atheism that got him expelled during his second term at Oxford), it is clear enough that the "wildness" Shelley boasted of and others accused him of was self-generated. He simply did not think like other people, and was unusually fortunate (as Blake, for instance, was not) in finding people who shared this freedom from conventional patterns of thinking, acting, writing.

To locate this independence as a literary quality it is necessary to go no further than the *Ode to the West Wind*, where the subject of the poem may seem at odds with the interest of the poem. It is easy to illustrate an apparent inconsistency of metaphors here, and it is difficult to read without embarrassment "I fall upon the thorns of life— I bleed." If it is read as a conventional statement, as an instance of a man speaking to men, the poem may appear to invite ways of reading that cannot be sustained: a reader's attempt to make a clear and simple visual whole out of the intensely realized visual moments, for instance, is repeatedly frustrated. "Understanding" Shelley in the usual way here and elsewhere is very difficult, because the transition to another world or another way of using language is not developed, as it might be by Keats, in carefully dramatized steps away from the everyday world where most poetry readers initially live. Rather, the reader is asked to be indulgent, to waive his right to "understand" conventionally long enough to accept as Reality the imaginative vision and language of someone who neither thinks nor speaks entirely like other men, who distrusts language itself because it is logical and crude—unlike "thought" which, Shelley said,

can with difficulty visit the intricate and winding chambers which it inhabits. It is like a river whose rapid and perpetual stream flows outwards; like one in dread who speeds through the recesses of some haunted pile, and dares not look behind. The caverns of the mind are obscure, and shadowy; or pervaded with a lustre, beautifully bright indeed, but shining not beyond their portals.[1]

Most uses of language, in art as well as everyday intercourse, depend on an assumption, however tenuous or fictitious, that men basically do think alike, at least about those things that matter most. Shelley, however, begins by assuming that the area of experience that remains consciously unshared and intellectually unsharable is of foremost importance. If language works at all in expressing such private and unique experience, it works as enchantment rather than logic, and the poet has limited conscious control over the ways in which it works. To insist, as Shelley seems to, on the necessity of inspiration, after all, is to acknowledge one's own inadequacy as a deliberate creator and to deny much of the responsibility for what one writes. The poet is more a medium than a maker. And so the speaker in the *Ode to the West Wind* moves from being passive, then active, finally imperative as the west wind is incorporated within him. Similarly the reader is expected to be incorporated within and moved by the language of the poem in a context where words fuse rather than distinguish. Such fusions of poet and thing addressed, or reader and poem, are of course present in many other lyrics (*To a Skylark*, *Mont Blanc*, *The Cloud*) as well as in the longer, more complicated poems like *Epipsychidion* and *Prometheus Unbound*.

Just as the writer making these assumptions about language and experience has, or claims to have, diminished responsibility for what he says, it follows that the reader should not entirely be held to account for what he understands. For both, the first action—writing or reading—is separated as a *cause* from its consequence: expression, comprehension. It is easy to see how insisting on this division can lead to excuses for carelessness, laziness, or self-indulgence by the poet and his reader. As a man living in the world as well as an artist, Shelley has been repeatedly accused of moral and intellectual irresponsibility, and he himself was quick in retrospect to see the tragic events that surrounded him, like the deaths of three of his four children and the suicide of Harriet, as somehow his fault. But even in the absence of absolutes, Shelley also insisted on the possibility of virtue, generosity, love, unselfishness and freedom, and he saw it as the poet's obligation and privilege to promote these values. The destroying and preserving energy of the West Wind, finally, is to bring to mankind messages of liberation such as *A Philosophical View of Reform*; the poem prepares the way by re-creating the receptivity of the reader.

Power fascinated Shelley: power as it was resident in such experiences as contemplating Mont Blanc, and power as it could be harnessed for political and social regeneration. If anything was to bring together the active but abstract power felt in the goings-on of the universe and the particular but passive power of apprehension in the individual, it had to be the poet's imaginative act. Yet like many radicals he distrusted the discipline by which such a reconciliation might be brought about, whether it was the discipline of Christianity, or logic, or political leadership. In the everyday world, in the way other men think, the absolute cannot by definition be good, and power inevitably corrupts. Only by changing the terms of existence, changing the *way* men think as well as what they think, could any progress be made. Poems like *Prometheus*

---

[1] From *Speculations on Morals.*

Unbound and *Epipsychidion* aim at just such a transformation. Suppose—Shelley seems to say in the second of these—suppose popular mythology and songs were right and love *did* make the world go round, lovers lived another sort of existence, were transformed by their emotion. Then what would this world of love be like, what would it be like to make love within it, how would lovers behave as seen internally, in their own terms? In *The Eve of St. Agnes* Keats avoids committing himself to what happens in the world that Porphyro and Madeline create from their love by suddenly looking at it from the outside, seeing it disappear with them into the storm. But Shelley tries to confront this impossibility in its own terms—thinking for himself, and perhaps for Emilia Viviani:

> And day and night, aloof, from the high towers
> And terraces, the Earth and Ocean seem
> To sleep in one another's arms, and dream
> Of waves, flowers, clouds, woods, rocks, and all that we
> Read in their smiles, and call reality.

> * * * * * * * * *

> Meanwhile
> We two will rise, and sit, and walk together,
> Under the roof of blue Ionian weather,
> And wander in the meadows, or ascend
> The mossy mountains, where the blue heavens bend
> With lightest winds, to touch their paramour;
> Or linger, where the pebble-paven shore,
> Under the quick, faint kisses of the sea
> Trembles and sparkles as with ecstasy,—
> Possessing and possessed by all that is
> Within that calm circumference of bliss,
> And by each other, till to love and live
> Be one:— ...

No one can doubt Shelley's belief in the intensity of his own feelings. "I live ... for certain intoxicating moments," he wrote to Jane (Claire) Clairmont in 1821. But the reader, like Shelley, is inevitably perplexed by attempts to arrest their transience and give them permanent form. Again, in *Epipsychidion*:

> One life within two wills, one will beneath
> Two overshadowing minds, one life, one death,
> One Heaven, one Hell, one immortality,
> And one annihilation. Woe is me!
> The winged words on which my soul would pierce
> Into the height of love's rare Universe,
> Are chains of lead around its flight of fire—
> I pant, I sink, I tremble, I expire!

Elsewhere, appropriately, Shelley alludes to the attempt of Goethe's Faust to find that thing or experience for which he can say "Tarry awhile, thou art so beautiful," and most of what Shelley does give value to is in motion: flowing, blowing, diminishing, disappearing, invisible. The easy answer is for a poet to say that his poem gives the evanescent experience its permanent form, but form for Shelley is also dead. It is too facile for Shelley to say, for instance, that Keats lives on after his untimely death because his poems do: in *Adonais* Shelley dismisses this as a linguistic trick because anyone can in effect change death into life by changing letters around. If Keats is gone, so is the energy that went into the creation of the poems, however magnificent the postmortem effects. The most that can be done here is to recognize the paradox, and balance its totally ambiguous values:

> Life, like a dome of many-coloured glass,
> Stains the white radiance of Eternity,
> Until Death tramples it to fragments.—

For an agnostic and idealist, neither the dome nor the radiance is by itself enough, but taken together, as they inevitably exist in this world, they tend to negate each other.

With such contradictions always before him, it is perhaps surprising that Shelley wrote at all, and certainly it is his unusual intellectual courage that enabled him to write so often, with so much confidence. If the urbane narrator of *Julian and Maddalo* implies that silence is the safe and responsible approach to the inexpressible and the only alternative to a madman's ravings, a poem like *The Cloud*, written two years later, attempts to create a consciousness for something that is amorphous as well as inanimate, not by making it a metaphor for human life but by giving it its own life. The confident tone of such a poem seems to come from Shelley's assumption that in another sort of world such a transformation would be possible, and the fact that it can sound a bit silly is no more than an indication that we are not easily at home in such a world. A reader's charge that such a transformation is absurd is at least a useful indication of the limits of expression, and it was Shelley's fate (or choice) always to live in sight of the limits of what is possible.

No one knows what Shelley thought or said when he and Williams embarked in the *Don Juan* on July 8, 1822. Presumably they were warned about the risk of an approaching storm. And it seems unlikely that all the presentiments later remembered by his family and friends were invented after the event. His death may have been partly deliberate, partly an indifference to the consequence of a bold action: one sailor recounted afterwards seeing Shelley restrain Williams from taking down the sail that would destroy them. A year earlier he had completed his elegy for Keats with lines about himself that anticipate this situation:

> The breath whose might I have invoked in song
> Descends on me; my spirit's bark is driven,
> Far from the shore, far from the trembling throng
> Whose sails were never to the tempest given;
> The massy earth and sphered skies are riven!
> I am borne darkly, fearfully, afar;
> Whilst burning through the inmost veil of Heaven,
> The soul of Adonais, like a star,
> Beacons from the abode where the Eternal are.

When Shelley's body was found, his pocket contained a volume of Keats—open, with its covers turned back.

OUTLINE OF EVENTS

1791	Oct.	Timothy Shelley (1753–1844) and Elizabeth Pilfold (1763–18?) married at West Grinsted.
1792	Aug. 1	Percy Bysshe Shelley born at Field Place, near Horsham, Sussex.
1795		Harriet Westbrook (Shelley) born.
1797	Aug. 30	Mary Wollstonecraft Godwin (Shelley) born to Mary Wollstonecraft and William Godwin.
1798		Shelley is taught Latin by parson at Wornham.
1802		Attends Syon House Academy at Isleworth, near Brentford (until 1804).
1804	July 29	Enters Eton (until 1810).
1806	Mar. 15	John Shelley (brother) born.
1809		Falls in love with cousin, Harriet Grove, but they abandon plan to marry.
1810	Oct. 10	Enters University College, Oxford; meets Thomas Jefferson Hogg.
		Writes *Wandering Jew*, *Original Poetry of Victor and Cazire* (with sister Elizabeth), and two romances. Shelley is reading Godwin, Hume, Locke, Voltaire.
1811	Mar. 25	Shelley and Hogg expelled from Oxford for publishing *The Necessity of Atheism*, a pamphlet; they go to live in Poland Street, London. Shelley is alienated from his family.
	Apr. 18	Meets Harriet Westbrook.
	Aug.	Elopes to Edinburgh with Harriet Westbrook.
	Nov.–Dec.	Shelleys at Keswick (Cumberland); they meet Southey. Shelley initiates correspondence with William Godwin; receives annuity of £200 from father.
1812	Feb.	Shelleys leave for Ireland to work for political reform (until April).
		Writes *Address to the Irish People*.
	Apr.	Shelleys leave Dublin for Wales (until June), Lynmouth, Devon (until August), where Shelley is investigated for distributing seditious literature, and his servant is imprisoned.
	Sept.	Works for land reclamation project at Tremadoc, North Wales; arrested for debt.
	Oct.	Shelleys in London (until Nov. 13); they see Godwin constantly; meet Thomas Love Peacock.
	Nov.	Shelleys return to Tremadoc (until March). Shelley finishing *Queen Mab*.
1813	Mar.	Shelleys go to Dublin, Killarney, and London, where they remain until mid-July.

	May	*Queen Mab* privately printed, but not distributed except by Shelley to his friends.
	June 23	Daughter Ianthe (later Mrs. Esdaile, d. 1876) born.
		Shelleys meet the J. F. Newtons, Mrs. Boinville; they are temporarily converted to vegetarianism.
	July	Shelleys move to Brackness, Berkshire, to preserve friendship with Mrs. Boinville, perhaps also to avoid creditors; remain until October.
	Oct.	Shelleys travel to Edinburgh (by way of Lakes); remain until December.
	Dec.	Shelleys in London, Windsor, and then with Boinvilles at Bracknell (until June).
1814	Apr.	Harriet Shelley leaves her husband, temporarily.
	June	Shelley alone in London (until July 27); falls in love with Mary Godwin (then 16).
	July 14	Tells Harriet of his love for Mary, proposes to live with both of them; threatens and attempts suicide.
	July 28	Shelley, Mary, Jane (Claire) Clairmont (Mary's stepsister), leave for France, Switzerland, Germany, where they travel in poverty and discomfort.
	Sept. 13	Shelley, Mary, Claire return to London. Shelley, seeking money and avoiding creditors, lives in various lodgings.
	Nov. 30	Charles Shelley, son, born to Harriet.
1815	Jan. 5	Sir Bysshe Shelley, grandfather, dies, as an indirect result of which Shelley acquires an annuity of £1000, and is relieved of financial anxiety.
	Feb. 22	Child born to Shelley and Mary; dies two weeks later.
		Writes *Alastor*, sonnets about Wordsworth and Napoleon.
1816	Jan. 5	William born to Shelley and Mary.
	Feb.	*Alastor* published.
	May 3	Shelley and Mary leave for Geneva; they are joined by Claire Clairmont, who had recently become Byron's mistress.
	June–Sept.	At Coligny on Lake Leman, seeing Byron constantly. Mary writes *Frankenstein*; Shelley writes *Hymn to Intellectual Beauty*, later *Mont Blanc*.
	Sept.	Shelley and Mary return to England; live in Bath (until December).
	Oct. 9	Suicide of Fanny Imlay, Mary's half sister.
	Nov.	Visits Leigh Hunt at Hampstead; meets Keats, Hazlitt, etc.
	Dec. 10	Harriet Shelley's body found in Serpentine, Hyde Park, where she had apparently drowned herself at least a week earlier. Children Charles and Ianthe in custody of her sister Eliza.
	Dec. 30	Shelley and Mary Godwin married in London; they remain there until March.
1817	Jan. 12	Allegra, Claire Clairmont's daughter by Byron, born at Bath.
	Mar.	Shelleys move to Marlow. Shelley writing pamphlets for political reform; begins *Revolt of Islam* (finished in September).

	Sept. 2	Clara born to Mary and Shelley.
1818	Mar. 11	Shelleys, children, Claire Clairmont and daughter leave for Italy.
	Summer	At Bagni di Lucca for nine weeks, then they join Byron at Venice.
	Sept. 24	Death of Clara in Venice.
		Shelley begins *Prometheus Unbound*; writes *Lines Written Among the Euganean Hills*, *Julian and Maddalo*.
	Nov. 5	Shelleys leave for Naples, to stay until March.
		Shelley writes *Stanzas Written in Dejection*.
1819	Feb. 27	Has baptized as his own child Elena, born December 27 to unknown parents—possibly Claire Clairmont's child by Shelley.
	Mar.–May	In Rome. Finishes *Prometheus Unbound*; begins *Cenci*.
	June 7	William Shelley dies in Rome.
	June–Oct.	At or near Leghorn. *Cenci* rejected for production at Covent Garden. Shelley writes *Mask of Anarchy*, *Ode to the West Wind*.
	Oct.	Shelleys move to Florence (until January).
	Nov. 12	Percy Shelley born—only child by Mary to survive infancy.
		Shelley writes *Peter Bell III*, *England in 1819*, etc.
1820	Jan.–June	In Pisa. Writes *Ode to Liberty*, *To a Skylark*, *Sensitive Plant*, *Philosophical View of Reform* (finished); *Cenci* published.
	June 7	Death of adopted daughter Elena.
	June 15	Shelleys move to Leghorn to stay (until August) at Gisborne's (absent in England). Shelley writes *Letter to Maria Gisborne*.
	Aug.–Oct.	At Baths of Pisa. Shelley invites Keats to spend winter with them (he doesn't); writes *Witch of Atlas*, *Ode to Naples*, *Oedipus Tyrannus*.
	Oct. 22	Shelleys move back to Pisa (until May).
	Nov. 29	Shelley meets Emilia Viviani.
1821	Jan.	Friendship with Edward and Jane Williams begins.
	Feb.	Writes *Epipsychidion* for Emilia Viviani.
	Mar.	Writes *Defence of Poetry*.
	Apr. 16	Shelley and Williams almost drown in sailing accident between Leghorn and Pisa.
	May	Shelleys return to Baths of Pisa for summer.
	June–July	Completes *Adonais* (begun on hearing in April of Keats's death).
	Aug.	Goes to Ravenna to spend two weeks with Byron.
	Sept. 8	Emilia Viviani marries Luigi Bondi.
	Oct.	Shelleys move back to Pisa; Shelley writes *Hellas*.
	Nov. 1	Byron moves to Pisa.
1822	Jan.	Shelley, Williams, Trelawny plan boat to be used on bay of Lerici during summer. Shelley writes poems to Jane Williams.
	Apr. 20	Death of Allegra, daughter of Byron and Claire Clairmont.

Apr. 27   Shelleys, Williams, Trelawny move to Lerici for summer.

Shelley works on *Triumph of Life*.

July 1   Sails to Leghorn to meet Leigh Hunt, who has arrived to help Byron and Shelley start the *Liberal*; takes Hunt to Pisa to join Byron.

July 8   Shelley and Williams drowned when their *Don Juan* is destroyed in storm off Viareggio.

Aug. 13–14   Bodies of Shelley and Williams cremated on beach by Byron, Hunt, Trelawny.

1823   Jan. 21   Shelley's ashes buried in Protestant Cemetery, Rome, next to grave of son William Shelley, near Keats's grave.

1844   Death of Sir Timothy Shelley, father.

1851   Death of Mary Godwin Shelley, wife.

1889   Death of Sir Percy Shelley, son.

SELECTED BIBLIOGRAPHY

EDITIONS

The Complete Poetical Works of Percy Bysshe Shelley, ed. T. Hutchinson (1905; corrected G. M. Matthews, 1970).

The Complete Works of Percy Bysshe Shelley, ed. R. Ingpen and W. E. Peck (10 vols., 1926–1930).

Shelley's 'The Triumph of Life': A Critical Study, ed. D. H. Reiman (1965).

Shelley's 'Prometheus Unbound': The Text and the Drafts: Toward a Modern Definitive Edition, ed. L. J. Zillman (1968).

The Letters of Percy Bysshe Shelley, ed. F. L. Jones (2 vols., 1964).

Shelley's Prose, ed. D. L. Clark (1954).

The Esdaile Notebook, ed. K. C. Cameron (1964).

The Esdaile Poems, ed. N. Rogers (1966).

Shelley and His Circle, 1773–1822, ed. K. C. Cameron (vols. I-IV, 1961–1970).

BIOGRAPHIES

N. I. WHITE, *Shelley* (2 vols., 1940; rev. 1947); abridged as *Portrait of Shelley* (1945).

E. BLUNDEN, *Shelley* (1946).

J. O. FULLER, *Shelley: A Biography* (1968).

GENERAL CRITICISM

M. ARNOLD, "Shelley," *Essays in Criticism*, second series (1888).

C. BAKER, *Shelley's Major Poetry: The Fabric of a Vision* (1948).

K. C. CAMERON, *The Young Shelley: Genesis of a Radical* (1950).

D. DAVIE, "Shelley's Urbanity," *Purity of Diction in English Verse* (1952).

N. ROGERS, *Shelley at Work* (1956; rev. 1967).

H. BLOOM, *Shelley's Mythmaking* (1959).

E. WASSERMAN, *The Subtler Language* (1959).

M. WILSON, *Shelley's Later Poetry* (1959).

D. KING-HELE, *Shelley: His Thought and Work* (1960).

G. M. RIDENOUR, ed., *Shelley: A Collection of Critical Essays* (1965).

E. WASSERMAN, *Shelley's Prometheus Unbound: A Critical Reading* (1965).

S. REITER, *A Study of Shelley's Poetry* (1967).

J. S. CHERNAIK, "The Figure of the Poet in Shelley," *ELH* (1968).

R. B. WOODINGS, ed., *Shelley* (1968).

G. MacNIECE, *Shelley and the Revolutionary Idea* (1969).

D. H. REIMAN, *Percy Bysshe Shelley* (1969).

G. M. MATTHEWS, *Shelley* (1970).

J. W. WRIGHT, *Shelley's Myth of Metaphor* (1970).

E. R. WASSERMAN, *Shelley: A Critical Reading* (1971).

POEMS

THE ESDAILE NOTEBOOK

Most of Shelley's earliest poems—those written before 1814—survive only in a set of fair copies written out by Shelley into a small, bound notebook. This notebook was intended to be the setting copy for a printed edition, but the poems were rejected by the publisher and the edition did not materialize. Shelley subsequently gave the notebook to his first wife, Harriet, who transcribed several more of his poems (and one of her own) into it in 1814 and 1815. After her death in 1816, the notebook passed to Harriet's heirs, who successively owned it until 1962, when it was acquired by the Carl H. Pforzheimer Library. In 1964, the Library sponsored an edition of the notebook edited by K. C. Cameron, in which most of the poems were printed for the first time. The only previously published poems were six complete poems and various fragments of autobiographical interest which Shelley's biographer, Edward Dowden, had been permitted to print from the notebook in 1887. A handful of other poems appearing in the Notebook were also printed in the last century from other manuscript sources.

"I will kneel at thine altar ..."

I WILL kneel at thine altar, will crown thee with bays.
    Whether God, Love or Virtue thou art,
Thou shalt live ... aye! more long than these
        perishing lays
    Thou shalt live in this high-beating heart.
Dear love! from its life-strings thou never shall part,
    Tho' Prejudice clanking her chain,
    Tho' Interest groaning in gain,
May tell me thou closest to Heaven the door,
May tell me that thine is the way to be poor.

The victim of merciless tyranny's power   10
    May smile at his chains if with thee;
The most sense-enslaved loiterer in Passion's sweet
        bower
    Is a wretch if unhallowed by thee.
Thine, thine is the bond that alone binds the free.
    Can the free worship bondage? nay, more,
    What they feel not, believe not, adore—
What if felt, if believed, if existing must give
To thee to create, to eternize, to live—

For Religion more keen than the blasts of the North
    Darts its frost thro' the self-palsied soul;   20
Its slaves on the work of destruction go forth;
    The divinest emotions that roll
Submit—to the rod of its impious control.
    At the venemous blast of its breath,
    Love, concord, lies gasping in death,
Philanthropy utters a war-drowned cry
And selfishness, conquering, cries Victory!

Can we, then, thus tame, thus impassive behold
    That alone whence our life springs destroyed?
Shall Prejudice, Priestcraft, Opinion and Gold—   30
    Every passion with interest alloyed—
Where Love ought to reign, fill the desolate void?
    But the Avenger arises, the throne
    Of selfishness totters, its groan
Shakes the nations.—It falls, love seizes the sway;
The sceptre it bears unresisted away.

[1809]   [1964]

THE SOLITARY[1]

I

DAR'ST thou amid the varied multitude
    To live alone, an isolated thing?
    To see the busy beings round thee spring,
And care for none; in thy calm solitude,
A flower that scarce breathes in the desert rude
        To Zephyr's passing wing?

II

Not the swart Pariah in some Indian grove,
    Lone, lean, and hunted by his brother's hate,
    Hath drunk so deep the cup of bitter fate
As that poor wretch who cannot, cannot love: 10
He bears a load which nothing can remove,
        A killing, withering weight.

[1] Another text of this poem occurs in the Esdaile Notebook, differing only in details of punctuation and alignment.

III

He smiles—'tis sorrow's deadliest mockery;
  He speaks—the cold words flow not from his
    soul;
He acts like others, drains the genial bowl,—
Yet, yet he longs—although he fears—to die;
He pants to reach what yet he seems to fly,
  Dull life's extremest goal.

[1810]   [1870]

TO DEATH

DEATH, where is thy victory!
To triumph whilst I die,
To triumph whilst thine ebon wing
Infolds my shuddering soul,
O Death, where is thy sting?
Not when the tides of murder roll,
When Nations groan that Kings may bask in bliss,
Death, couldst thou boast a victory such as this?
    When in his hour
    Of pomp and power   10
Thy slave, the mightiest murderer, gave
    Mid nature's cries
    The sacrifice
Of myriads to glut the grave,
When sunk the tyrant, sensualism's slave,
Or Freedom's life-blood streamed upon thy shrine,
Stern despot, couldst thou boast a Victory such as
  mine?

To know, in dissolution's void,
That Earthly hopes and fears decay,
That every sense, but Love, destroyed,   20
Must perish with its kindred clay.
Perish ambition's crown!
Perish its sceptered sway!
From Death's pale front fade Pride's fastidious frown.
In death's damp vault the lurid fires decay
Which Envy lights at heaven-born virtue's beam
    That all the cares subside
    Which lurk beneath the tide
    Of life's unquiet stream. . . .
    Yes! this were Victory!   30
And on some rock whose dark form glooms the sky
To stretch these pale limbs when the soul is fled,
To baffle the lean passions of their prey,
To sleep within the chambers of the dead!—
Oh! not the Wretch around whose dazzling throne
His countless courtiers mock the words they say,
Triumphs, amid the bud of glory blown,
As I on Death's last pang and faint expiring groan.

Tremble, ye Kings whose luxury mocks the woe
That props thy column of unnatural state,   40
    Ye, the curses deep, tho' low,
    From misery's tortured breast that flow,
    Shall usher to your fate.—
Tremble, ye conquerors, at whose fell command
The War-fiend Riots o'er an happy land—
    Ye, desolation's gory throng
    Shall bear from victory along
    To Death's mysterious strand.
'Twere well that Vice no pain should know
    But every scene that memory gives   50
Tho' from the selfsame fount might flow
    The joy which Virtue aye receives . . .
It is the grave—no conqueror triumphs now;
    The wreathes of bay that bound his head
    Wither around his fleshless brow.
    Where is the mockery fled
    That fired the tyrant's gaze?
'Tis like the fitful glare that plays
On some dark-rolling thunder cloud,
    Plays whilst the thunders roar,   60
    But when the storm is past
    Fades like the warrior's name.
Death! in thy vault when Kings and peasants lie
Not power's stern rod or fame's most thrilling blasts
Can liberate thy captives from decay.
My triumph, their defeat; my joy, their shame!
Welcome then, peaceful Death, I'll sleep with thee—
Mine be thy quiet home, and thine my Victory.

[1810]   [1858, 1964]

THE MONARCH'S FUNERAL
AN ANTICIPATION[1]

THE glowing gloom of eventide
  Has quenched the sunbeam's latest glow
And lowers upon the woe and pride
  That blasts the city's peace below.

At such an hour how sad the sight,
  To mark a Monarch's funeral
When the dim shades of awful night
  Rest on the coffin's velvet pall;

To see the Gothic Arches shew
  A varied mass of light and shade,   10
While to the torches' crimson glow
  A vast cathedral is displayed;

---

[1] The Monarch whose death is anticipated here is George III
(who died in 1820).

To see with what a silence deep
    The thousands o'er this death scene brood
As tho' some wizard's charm did creep
    Upon the countless multitude;

To see this awful pomp of death
    For one frail mass of mouldering clay
When nobler men the tomb beneath
    Have sunk unwept, unseen away.   20

For who was he, the uncoffined slain,
    That fell in Erin's injured isle
Because his spirit dared disdain
    To light his country's funeral pile?

Shall he not ever live in lays
    The warmest that a Muse may sing
Whilst monumental marbles raise
    The fame of a departed King?

May not the Muse's darling theme
    Gather its glorious garland thence   30
Whilst some frail tombstone's Dotard dream
    Fades with a monarch's impotence!

—Yes, 'tis a scene of wondrous awe
    To see a coffined Monarch lay
That the wide grave's insatiate maw
    Be glutted with a regal prey!

Who *now* shall public councils guide?
    Who rack the poor on gold to dine?
Who waste the means of regal pride
    For which a million wretches pine?   40

It is a child of earthly breath,
    A being perishing as he,
Who throned in yonder pomp of death
    Hath now fulfilled his destiny.

Now dust to dust restore! . . . O Pride,
    Unmindful of thy fleeting power,
Whose empty confidence has vied
    With human life's most treacherous hour,

One moment feel that in the breast
    With regal crimes and troubles vext   50
The pampered Earthworms soon will rest,
    One moment feel . . . and die the next.

Yet deem not in the tomb's control
    The vital lamp of life can fail,
Deem not that e'er the Patriot's soul
    Is wasted by the withering gale.

The dross, which forms the *King*, is gone,
    And reproductive Earth supplies,
As senseless as the clay and stone
    In which the kindred body lies.   60

The soul which makes the *Man* doth soar
    And love alone survives to shed
All that its tide of bliss can pour
    Of Heaven upon the blessed dead.

So shall the Sun forever burn,
    So shall the midnight lightnings die,
And joy that glows at Nature's bourn
    Outlive terrestrial misery.

And will the crowd who silent stoop
    Around the lifeless Monarch's bier,   70
A mournful and dejected group,
    Breathe not one sigh, or shed one tear?

Ah! no. 'Tis wonder, 'tis not woe.
    Even royalists might groan to see
The *Father of the People* so
    Lost in the Sacred Majesty.

[1810]   [1964]

[LOVE]¹

Why is it said thou canst not live
    In a youthful breast and fair,
Since thou eternal life canst give,
    Canst bloom for ever there?
Since withering pain no power possessed,
    Nor age, to blanch thy vermeil hue,
Nor time's dread victor, death, confessed,
    Though bathed with his poison dew,
Still thou retain'st unchanging bloom,
Fixed tranquil, even in the tomb.   10
And oh! when on the blest, reviving,
    The day-star dawns of love,
Each energy of soul surviving
    More vivid, soars above,
Hast thou ne'er felt a rapturous thrill,
    Like June's warm breath, athwart thee fly,
O'er each idea then to steal,
    When other passions die?
Felt it in some wild noonday dream
When sitting by the lonely stream,   20

¹ The title is by Rosetti, the manuscript being untitled. This poem is not in the Esdaile Notebook.

Where Silence says, 'Mine is the dell';
   And not a murmur from the plain,
And not an echo from the fell,
   Disputes her silent reign.

[1811]   [1858]

TO THE REPUBLICANS OF NORTH AMERICA

BROTHERS! between you and me
   Whirlwinds sweep and billows roar,
Yet in spirit oft I see
   On the wild and winding shore
Freedom's bloodless banner wave,
Feel the pulses of the brave,
Unextinguished by the grave,
   See them drenched in sacred gore,
Catch the patriot's gasping breath
Murmuring Liberty in death.   10

Shout aloud! let every slave
   Crouching at corruption's throne
Start into a man, and brave
   Racks and chains without a groan!
Let the castle's heartless glow
And the hovel's vice and woe
Fade like gaudy flowers that blow,
   Weeds that peep and then are gone,
Whilst from misery's ashes risen
Love shall burst the Captive's prison.   20

Cotopaxi! bid the sound
   Thro' thy sister mountains ring
Till each valley smile around
   At the blissful welcoming.
And O! thou stern Ocean-deep,
Whose eternal billows sweep
Shores where thousands wake to weep
   Whilst they curse some villain King,
On the winds that fan thy breast
Bear thou news of freedom's rest.   30

Earth's remotest bounds shall start,
   Every despot's bloated cheek,
Pallid as his bloodless heart,
   Frenzy, woe and dread shall speak . . .
Blood may fertilize the tree
Of new bursting Liberty.
Let the guiltiness then be
   On the slaves that ruin wreak,
On the unnatural tyrant-brood
Slow to Peace and swift to blood.   40

Can the daystar dawn of love
   Where the flag of war unfurled
Floats with crimson stain above
   Such a desolated world . . .
Never! but to vengeance driven
When the patriot's spirit shriven
Seeks in deaths its native Heaven,
   Then to speechless horror hurled.
Widowed Earth may balm the bier
Of its memory with a tear.   50

[1812]   [1870, 1964]

SONNET

TO HARRIET ON HER BIRTHDAY

AUGUST 1, 1812

O thou, whose radiant eyes and beamy smile—
Yet even a sweeter somewhat indexing—
Have known full many an hour of mine to guile
Which else would only bitter memories bring,
O ever thus, thus! as on this natal day,
Tho' age's frost may blight those tender eyes,
Destroy that kindling cheek's transparent dyes
And those luxuriant tresses change to grey,
Ever as now with Love and Virtue's glow
May thy unwithering soul not cease to burn.   10
Still may thine heart with those pure thoughts o'erflow
Which force from mine such quick and warm return,
And I must love thee even more than this
Nor doubt that Thou and I part but to meet in bliss.

[1812]   [1964]

━━━━━

ON LAUNCHING SOME BOTTLES

In the summer of 1812, in Devon, Shelley frequently launched bottles containing his political pamphlets. Partly as a result of this activity, he was investigated for distributing seditious literature.

━━━━━

SONNET

ON LAUNCHING SOME BOTTLES
FILLED WITH KNOWLEDGE
INTO THE BRISTOL CHANNEL

VESSELS of Heavenly medicine! may the breeze,
Auspicious, waft your dark green forms to shore;
Safe may ye stern[1] the wide surrounding roar
Of the wild whirlwinds and the raging seas;

---

[1] To steer through.

And oh! if Liberty e'er deigned to stoop
From yonder lowly throne her crownless brow,
Sure she will breathe around your emerald group
The fairest breezes of her west that blow.
Yes! she will waft ye to some freeborn soul
Whose eyebeam, kindling as it meets your freight,   10
Her heaven-born flame on suffering Earth will light
Until Its radiance gleams from pole to pole
And tyrant-hearts with powerless envy burst
To see their night of ignorance dispersed.

[1812]   [1887, 1964]

TO HARRIET
["Harriet! thy kiss . . ."]

HARRIET! thy kiss to my soul is dear;
    At evil or pain I would never repine
If to every sigh and to every tear
    Were added a look and a kiss of thine.
Nor is it the look when it glances fire,
    Nor the kiss when bathed in the dew of delight,
Nor the throb of the heart when it pants desire
    From the shadows of eve to the morning light,

But the look when a lustre of joy-mingled woe
    Has faintly obscured all its bliss-beaming Heaven,
Such a lovely, benign and enrapturing glow   11
    As sunset can paint on the clouds of even,
And a kiss, which the languish of silent love,
    Tho' eloquent, faints with the toil of expressing
Yet so light, that thou canst not refuse, my dove!
    To add this one to the debt of caressing.

Harriet! adieu to all vice and care.
    Thy love is my Heaven, thy arms are my world;
While thy kiss and thy look to my soul remain dear
    I should smile tho' Earth from its base be hurled.
For a heart as pure and a mind as free   21
    As ever gave lover, to thee I give,
And all that I ask in return from thee
    Is to love like me and with me to live.

This heart that beats for thy love and bliss,
    Harriet! beats for its country too;
And it never would thrill with thy look or kiss
    If it dared to that country's cause be untrue.
Honor, and wealth and life it spurns,
    But thy love is a prize it is sure to gain,   30
And the heart that with love and virtue burns
    Will never repine at evil or pain.

[1812]   [1964]

ON LEAVING LONDON FOR WALES[1]

THOU miserable city! where the gloom
    Of penury mingles with the tyrant's pride,
And virtue bends in sorrow o'er the tomb
    Where Freedom's hope and Truth's high Courage
        died.
May floods and vales and mountains me divide
    From all the taints thy wretched walls contain,
That life's extremes in desolation wide
    No more heap horrors on my beating brain
Nor sting my shuddering heart to sympathy with
    pain.

With joy I breathe the last and full farewell   10
    That long has quivered on my burdened heart,
My natural sympathies to rapture swell
    As from its day thy cheerless glooms depart,
Nor all the glare thy gayest scenes impart
    Could lure one sigh, could steal one tear from me,
Or lull to languishment, the wakeful smart
    Which virtue feels for all 'tis forced to see,
Or quench the eternal flame of generous Liberty.

Hail to thee, Cambria, for the unfettered wind
    Which from thy wilds even now methinks I feel   20
Chasing the clouds that roll in wrath behind
    And tightening the soul's laxest nerves to steel!
True! Mountain Liberty alone may heal
    The pain which Custom's obduracies bring,
And he who dares in fancy even to steal
    One draught from Snowdon's ever-sacred spring
Blots out the unholiest rede of worldly witnessing.

And shall that soul to selfish peace resigned
    So soon forget the woe its fellows share?
Can Snowdon's Lethe from the freeborn mind   30
    So soon the page of injured penury tear?
Does this fine mass of human passion dare
    To sleep, unhonouring the patriot's fall,
Of life's sweet load in quietude to bear
    While millions famish even in Luxury's hall
And Tyranny high-raised stern lowers over all?

No, Cambria! never may thy matchless vales
    A heart so false to hope and virtue shield,
Nor ever may thy spirit-breathing gales
    Waft freshness to the slaves who dare to yield. 40
For me! . . . the weapon that I burn to wield
    I seek amid thy rocks to ruin hurled
That Reason's flag may over Freedom's field,
    Symbol of bloodless victory, wave unfurled—
A meteor-sign of love effulgent o'er the world.

[1] In the fall of 1812 Shelley and Harriet left London for
Tremadoc, North Wales, to work on a land reclamation project.

Hark to that shriek! my hand had almost clasped
  The dagger that my heart had cast away
When the pert slaves, whose wanton power had
    grasped
  All hope that springs beneath the eye of day,
Pass before memory's gaze in long array.   50
  The storm fleets by and calmer thoughts succeed,
Feelings once more mild reason's voice obey.
  Woe be the tyrants' and murderers' meed,
But Nature's wound alone should make their
    Conscience bleed.

Do thou, wild Cambria, calm each struggling thought;
  Cast thy sweet veil of rocks and woods between,
That by the soul to indignation wrought
  Mountains and dells be mingled with the scene.
Let me forever be what I have been,
  But not forever at my needy door   60
Let Misery linger, speechless, pale and lean.
  I am the friend of the unfriended poor;
Let me not madly stain their righteous cause in gore.

No more! the visions fade before my sight
  Which Fancy pictures in the waste of air
Like lovely dreams ere morning's chilling light,
  And sad realities alone are there.
Ah! neither woe nor fear nor pain can tear
  Their image from the tablet of my soul,
Nor the mad floods of Despotism where   70
  Lashed into desperate furiousness they roll,
Nor passion's soothing voice, nor interest's cold
    control.

[1812]   [1887, 1964]

EVENING

TO HARRIET

O THOU bright Sun! beneath the dark blue line
Of western distance that sublime descendest,
And, gleaming lovelier as thy beams decline,
Thy million hues to every vapour lendest,
And over cobweb lawn and grove and stream
Sheddest the liquid magic of thy light,
Till calm Earth, with the parting splendour bright,
Shews like the vision of a beauteous dream;
What gazer now with astronomic eye
Could coldly count the spots within thy sphere?   10
Such were thy lover, Harriet, could he fly
The thoughts of all that makes his passion dear,
And, turning senseless from thy warm caress,
Pick flaws in our close-woven happiness.

[1813]   [1887, 1964]

STANZAS.—APRIL, 1814[1]
["Away! the moor . . ."]

AWAY! the moor is dark beneath the moon,
  Rapid clouds have drank the last pale beam of even:
Away! the gathering winds will call the darkness soon,
  And profoundest midnight shroud the serene lights
    of heaven.

Pause not! The time is past! Every voice cries, Away!
  Tempt not with one last tear thy friend's ungentle
    mood:
Thy lover's eye, so glazed and cold, dares not entreat
    thy stay:
  Duty and dereliction guide thee back to solitude.

Away, away! to thy sad and silent home;
  Pour bitter tears on its desolated hearth;   10
Watch the dim shades as like ghosts they go and come,
  And complicate strange webs of melancholy mirth.

The leaves of wasted autumn woods shall float around
    thine head:
  The blooms of dewy spring shall gleam beneath thy
    feet:
But thy soul or this world must fade in the frost that
    binds the dead,
  Ere midnight's frown and morning's smile, ere thou
    and peace may meet.

The cloud shadows of midnight possess their own
    repose,
  For the weary winds are silent, or the moon is in the
    deep:
Some respite to its turbulence unresting ocean knows;
  Whatever moves, or toils, or grieves, hath its
    appointed sleep.   20

Thou in the grave shalt rest—yet till the phantoms
    flee
  Which that house and heath and garden made dear
    to thee erewhile,
Thy remembrance, and repentance, and deep
    musings, are not free
  From the music of two voices, and the light of one
    sweet smile.

[1814]   [1816]

---

[1] This poem is not included in the Esdaile Notebook.

TO HARRIETT[1]
["Thy look of love . . ."]

THY look of love has power to calm
  The stormiest passion of my Soul;
Thy gentle words are drops of balm
  In life's too bitter bowl.
No grief is mine but that alone
These choicest blessings I have known.

Harriett! if all who long to live
  In the warm sunshine of thine eye,
That price beyond all pain must give,—
  Beneath thy scorn to die;   10
Then hear thy chosen own, too late,
His heart most worthy of thy hate.

Be thou, then, one among mankind
  Whose heart is harder not for state—
Thou only, virtuous, gentle, kind,
  Amid a world of hate—
And by a slight endurance seal
A fellow being's lasting weal.

For pale with anguish in his cheek,
  His breath comes fast, his eyes are dim;   20
Thy name is struggling ere he speak;
  Weak is each trembling limb.
In mercy let him not endure
The misery of a fatal cure.

O, trust for once no erring guide!
  Bid the remorseless feeling flee;
'Tis malice, 'tis revenge, 'tis pride,
  'Tis any thing but thee.
O, deign a nobler pride to prove,
And pity if thou canst not love!

[1814]   [1887]

TO MARY WOLLSTONECRAFT GODWIN

In the early summer of 1814 Shelley, temporarily separated from his wife Harriet, met Mary Godwin, the sixteen-year-old daughter of the political theorist William Godwin and his wife Mary Wollstonecraft, the author of A Vindication of the Rights of Woman (*who had died giving birth to Mary*). *Shelley admired the work of both senior Godwins, and loved their daughter. He proposed to Harriet that he, she, and Mary live*

[1] This is one of the poems that Harriet transcribed into the Esdaile Notebook. "Harriett" with two t's was the legal spelling of her name, but both she and Shelley usually spelled it with one t.

together, but Harriet refused. In July Shelley, Mary, and Mary's half sister Claire Clairmont traveled together to the Continent. Harriet, pregnant, remained in England. Mary, now also pregnant, returned to England with Shelley in September.

TO MARY WOLLSTONECRAFT GODWIN

I

MINE eyes were dim with tears unshed;
  Yes, I was firm—thus wert not thou;—
My baffled looks did fear yet dread
  To meet your looks—I could not know
That anxiously they sought to shine
And longed to soothe and pity me.

II

To sit and curb the soul's mute rage
  Which preys upon itself alone;
To curse that life which is the cage
  Of fettered grief that dares not groan,   10
Hiding from many a careless eye
The scorned load of agony.

III

Whilst you alone, then not regarded,
  The faithful you alone should be,
To spend years thus, and be rewarded,
  As you, sweet love, requited me
When none were nigh—Oh I did wake
From torture for that moment's sake.

IV

Upon my heart your accents sweet
  Of peace and pity fell like dew   20
On flowers half dead;—thy lips did meet
  Mine tremblingly; thy dark eyes threw
Their soft persuasion on my brain,
Turning to bliss its wayward pain,
Charming away its dream of ——.[1]

V

We are not happy, sweet! our state
  Is strange and full of doubt and fear;
More need of words that ills abate;—
  Reserve or censure come not near
Our sacred friendship, lest there be   30
No solace left for you and me.

[1] Mrs. Shelley's text reads "pain" for the missing word. The stanza has an extra line.

VI

Gentle and good and mild thou art,
　　Nor can I live if thou appear
Aught but thyself, or turn thine heart
　　Away from me, or stoop to wear
The mask of scorn, although it be
To hide the love thou feel'st for me.

[1814]　　　　　　　　　　　　　　　　[1824, 1926]

TO ——
["O! There are spirits . . ."]
ΔΑΚΡΥΣΙ ΔΙΟΙΣΩ ΠΟΤΜΟΝ ΑΠΟΤΜΟΝ

OH! THERE are spirits of the air,
　　And genii of the evening breeze,
And gentle ghosts, with eyes as fair
　　As star-beams among twilight trees:—
Such lovely ministers to meet
Oft hast thou turned from men thy lonely feet.

With mountain winds, and babbling springs,
　　And moonlight seas, that are the voice
Of these inexplicable things,
　　Thou didst hold commune, and rejoice　　10
When they did answer thee; but they
Cast, like a worthless boon, thy love away.

And thou hast sought in starry eyes
　　Beams that were never meant for thine,
Another's wealth:—tame sacrifice
　　To a fond faith! still dost thou pine?
Still dost thou hope that greeting hands,
Voice, looks, or lips, may answer thy demands?

Ah! wherefore didst thou build thine hope
　　On the false earth's inconstancy?　　20
Did thine own mind afford no scope
　　Of love, or moving thoughts to thee?
That natural scenes or human smiles
Could steal the power to wind thee in their wiles.

Yes, all the faithless smiles are fled
　　Whose falsehood left thee broken-hearted;
The glory of the moon is dead;
　　Night's ghost and dreams have now departed;
Thine own soul still is true to thee,
But changed to a foul fiend through misery.　　30

[1815]

This fiend, whose ghastly presence ever
　　Beside thee like thy shadow hangs,
Dream not to chase;—the mad endeavour
　　Would scourge thee to severer pangs.
Be as thou art. Thy settled fate,
Dark as it is, all change would aggravate.

[1814]　　　　　　　　　　　　　　　　[1816]

MUTABILITY [I]

WE are as clouds that veil the midnight moon;
　　How restlessly they speed, and gleam, and quiver,
Streaking the darkness radiantly!—yet soon
　　Night closes round, and they are lost for ever:

Or like forgotten lyres, whose dissonant strings
　　Give various response to each varying blast,
To whose frail frame no second motion brings
　　One mood or modulation like the last.

We rest.—A dream has power to poison sleep;
　　We rise.—One wandering thought pollutes the day;
We feel, conceive or reason, laugh or weep;　　11
　　Embrace fond woe, or cast our cares away:

It is the same!—For, be it joy or sorrow,
　　The path of its departure still is free;
Man's yesterday may ne'er be like his morrow;
　　Nought may endure but Mutability.

[1814?]　　　　　　　　　　　　　　　　[1816]

[Sonnet]
TO WORDSWORTH

POET of Nature, thou hast wept to know
That things depart which never may return:
Childhood and youth, friendship and love's first glow,
Have fled like sweet dreams, leaving thee to mourn.
These common woes I feel. One loss is mine,
Which thou too feel'st; yet I alone deplore.
Thou wert as a lone star, whose light did shine
On some frail bark in winter's midnight roar:
Thou hast like to a rock-built refuge stood
Above the blind and battling multitude:　　10
In honoured poverty thy voice did weave
Songs consecrate to truth and liberty,—
Deserting these, thou leavest me to grieve,
Thus having been, that thou shouldst cease to be.

[1815]　　　　　　　　　　　　　　　　[1816]

[Sonnet]
FEELINGS OF A REPUBLICAN ON THE FALL OF BONAPARTE

I HATED thee, fallen tyrant! I did groan
To think that a most unambitious slave,
Like thou, shouldst dance and revel on the grave
Of Liberty. Thou mightst have built thy throne
Where it had stood even now: thou didst prefer
A frail and bloody pomp, which Time has swept
In fragments towards Oblivion. Massacre,
For this I prayed, would on thy sleep have crept,
Treason and Slavery, Rapine, Fear, and Lust,
And stifled thee, their minister. I know   10
Too late, since thou and France are in the dust,
That virtue owns a more eternal foe
Than Force or Fraud: old Custom, legal Crime,
And bloody Faith, the foulest birth of Time.

[1815]   [1816]

ALASTOR;
OR,
THE SPIRIT OF SOLITUDE.

PREFACE

THE poem entitled *Alastor* may be considered as allegorical of one of the most interesting situations of the human mind. It represents a youth of uncorrupted feelings and adventurous genius led forth by an imagination inflamed and purified through familiarity with all that is excellent and majestic, to the contemplation of the universe. He drinks deep of the fountains of knowledge, and is still insatiate. The magnificence and beauty of the external world sinks profoundly into the frame of his conceptions, and affords to their modifications a variety not to be exhausted. So long as it is possible for his desires to point towards objects thus infinite and unmeasured, he is joyous, and tranquil, and self-possessed. But the period arrives when these objects cease to suffice. His mind is at length suddenly awakened and thirsts for intercourse with an intelligence similar to itself. He images to himself the Being whom he loves. Conversant with speculations of the sublimest and most perfect natures, the vision in which he embodies his own imaginations unites all of wonderful, or wise, or beautiful, which the poet, the philosopher, or the lover could depicture. The intellectual faculties, the imagination, the functions of sense, have their respective requisitions on the sympathy of corresponding powers in other human beings. The Poet is represented as uniting these requisitions, and attaching them to a single image. He seeks in vain for a prototype of his conception. Blasted by his disappointment, he descends to an untimely grave.

The picture is not barren of instruction to actual men. The Poet's self-centred seclusion was avenged by the furies of an irresistible passion pursuing him to speedy ruin. But that Power which strikes the luminaries of the world with sudden darkness and extinction, by awakening them to too exquisite a perception of its influences, dooms to a slow and poisonous decay those meaner spirits that dare to abjure its dominion. Their destiny is more abject and inglorious as their delinquency is more contemptible and pernicious. They who, deluded by no generous error, instigated by no sacred thirst of doubtful knowledge, duped by no illustrious superstition, loving nothing on this earth, and cherishing no hopes beyond, yet keep aloof from sympathies with their kind, rejoicing neither in human joy nor mourning with human grief; these, and such as they, have their apportioned curse. They languish, because none feel with them their common nature. They are morally dead. They are neither friends, nor lovers, nor fathers, nor citizens of the world, nor benefactors of their country. Among those who attempt to exist without human sympathy, the pure and tender-hearted perish through the intensity and passion of their search after its communities, when the vacancy of their spirit suddenly makes itself felt. All else, selfish, blind, and torpid, are those unforeseeing multitudes who constitute, together with their own, the lasting misery and loneliness of the world. Those who love not their fellow-beings live unfruitful lives, and prepare for their old age a miserable grave.

> 'The good die first,
> And those whose hearts are dry as summer dust,
> Burn to the socket!'[1]

December 14, 1815.

<hr/>

Nondum amabam, et amare amabam, quaerebam quid amarem, amans amare.—*Confess. St. August.*[2]

EARTH, ocean, air, belovèd brotherhood!
If our great Mother has imbued my soul
With aught of natural piety to feel
Your love, and recompense the boon with mine;
If dewy morn, and odorous noon, and even,
With sunset and its gorgeous ministers,
And solemn midnight's tingling silentness;
If autumn's hollow sighs in the sere wood,
And winter robing with pure snow and crowns
Of starry ice the grey grass and bare boughs; 10
If spring's voluptuous pantings when she breathes
Her first sweet kisses, have been dear to me;
If no bright bird, insect, or gentle beast
I consciously have injured, but still loved
And cherished these my kindred; then forgive
This boast, belovèd brethren, and withdraw
No portion of your wonted favour now!

Mother of this unfathomable world!
Favour my solemn song, for I have loved
Thee ever, and thee only; I have watched 20
Thy shadow, and the darkness of thy steps,
And my heart ever gazes on the depth
Of thy deep mysteries. I have made my bed

<hr/>

[1] Wordsworth, *Excursion*, I, 519–21.
[2] "I loved not yet, and I loved to love; I sought for what I should love, loving love."—*Confessions* of St. Augustine, Book III.

In charnels and on coffins, where black death
Keeps record of the trophies won from thee,
Hoping to still these obstinate questionings
Of thee and thine, by forcing some lone ghost
Thy messenger, to render up the tale
Of what we are. In lone and silent hours,
When night makes a weird sound of its own stillness,
Like an inspired and desperate alchymist 31
Staking his very life on some dark hope,
Have I mixed awful talk and asking looks
With my most innocent love, until strange tears
Uniting with those breathless kisses, made
Such magic as compels the charmèd night
To render up thy charge: . . . and, though ne'er yet
Thou hast unveiled thy inmost sanctuary,
Enough from incommunicable dream,
And twilight phantasms, and deep noon-day thought,
Has shone within me, that serenely now 41
And moveless, as a long-forgotten 'lyre
Suspended in the solitary dome
Of some mysterious and deserted fane,
I wait thy breath, Great Parent, that my strain
May modulate with murmurs of the air,
And motions of the forests and the sea,
And voice of living beings, and woven hymns
Of night and day, and the deep heart of man.

There was a Poet whose untimely tomb 50
No human hands with pious reverence reared,
But the charmed eddies of autumnal winds
Built o'er his mouldering bones a pyramid
Of mouldering leaves in the waste wilderness:—
A lovely youth,—no mourning maiden decked
With weeping flowers, or votive cypress wreath,
The lone couch of his everlasting sleep:—
Gentle, and brave, and generous,—no lorn bard
Breathed o'er his dark fate one melodious sigh:
He lived, he died, he sung, in solitude. 60
Strangers have wept to hear his passionate notes,
And virgins, as unknown he passed, have pined
And wasted for fond love of his wild eyes.
The fire of those soft orbs has ceased to burn,
And Silence, too enamoured of that voice,
Locks its mute music in her rugged cell.

By solemn vision, and bright silver dream,
His infancy was nurtured. Every sight
And sound from the vast earth and ambient air,
Sent to his heart its choicest impulses. 70
The fountains of divine philosophy
Fled not his thirsting lips, and all of great,
Or good, or lovely, which the sacred past
In truth or fable consecrates, he felt
And knew. When early youth had passed, he left

His cold fireside and alienated home
To seek strange truths in undiscovered lands.
Many a wide waste and tangled wilderness
Has lured his fearless steps; and he has bought
With his sweet voice and eyes, from savage men,   80
His rest and food. Nature's most secret steps
He like her shadow has pursued, where'er
The red volcano overcanopies
Its fields of snow and pinnacles of ice
With burning smoke, or where bitumen lakes
On black bare pointed islets ever beat
With sluggish surge, or where the secret caves
Rugged and dark, winding among the springs
Of fire and poison, inaccessible
To avarice or pride, their starry domes   90
Of diamond and of gold expand above
Numberless and immeasurable halls,
Frequent with crystal column, and clear shrines
Of pearl, and thrones radiant with chrysolite.
Nor had that scene of ampler majesty
Than gems or gold, the varying roof of heaven
And the green earth lost in his heart its claims
To love and wonder; he would linger long
In lonesome vales, making the wild his home,
Until the doves and squirrels would partake   100
From this innocuous hand his bloodless food,
Lured by the gentle meaning of his looks,
And the wild antelope, that starts whene'er
The dry leaf rustles in the brake, suspend
Her timid steps to gaze upon a form
More graceful than her own.

                              His wandering step
Obedient to high thoughts, has visited
The awful ruins of the days of old:
Athens, and Tyre, and Balbec,[3] and the waste
Where stood Jerusalem, the fallen towers   110
Of Babylon, the eternal pyramids,
Memphis and Thebes, and whatsoe'er of strange
Sculptured on alabaster obelisk,
Or jasper tomb, or mutilated sphynx,
Dark Æthiopia in her desert hills
Conceals. Among the ruined temples there,
Stupendous columns, and wild images
Of more than man, where marble daemons watch
The Zodiac's brazen mystery,[4] and dead men
Hang their mute thoughts on the mute walls around,
He lingered, poring on memorials   121
Of the world's youth, through the long burning day
Gazed on those speechless shapes, nor, when the
       moon

---
[3] Ruined city in Damascus in Syria.
[4] The temple of Isis in Denderah, Egypt, has a Zodiac on its
ceiling.

Filled the mysterious halls with floating shades
Suspended he that task, but ever gazed
And gazed, till meaning on his vacant mind
Flashed like strong inspiration, and he saw
The thrilling secrets of the birth of time.

    Meanwhile an Arab maiden brought his food,
Her daily portion, from her father's tent,   130
And spread her matting for his couch, and stole
From duties and repose to tend his steps:—
Enamoured, yet not daring for deep awe
To speak her love:—and watched his nightly sleep,
Sleepless herself, to gaze upon his lips
Parted in slumber, whence the regular breath
Of innocent dreams arose: then, when red morn
Made paler the pale moon, to her cold home
Wildered, and wan, and panting, she returned.

    The Poet wandering on, through Arabie   140
And Persia, and the wild Carmanian waste,[5]
And o'er the aërial mountains which pour down
Indus and Oxus from their icy caves,
In joy and exultation held his way;
Till in the vale of Cashmire, far within
Its loneliest dell, where odorous plants entwine
Beneath the hollow rocks a natural bower,
Beside a sparkling rivulet he stretched
His languid limbs. A vision on his sleep
There came, a dream of hopes that never yet   150
Had flushed his cheek. He dreamed a veilèd maid
Sate near him, talking in low solemn tones.
Her voice was like the voice of his own soul
Heard in the calm of thought; its music long,
Like woven sounds of streams and breezes, held
His inmost sense suspended in its web
Of many-coloured woof and shifting hues.
Knowledge and truth and virtue were her theme,
And lofty hopes of divine liberty,
Thoughts the most dear to him, and poesy,   160
Herself a poet. Soon the solemn mood
Of her pure mind kindled through all her frame
A permeating fire: wild numbers then
She raised, with voice stifled in tremulous sobs
Subdued by its own pathos: her fair hands
Were bare alone, sweeping from some strange harp
Strange symphony, and in their branching veins
The eloquent blood told an ineffable tale.
The beating of her heart was heard to fill
The pauses of her music, and her breath   170
Tumultuously accorded with those fits
Of intermitted song. Sudden she rose,
As if her heart impatiently endured

Its bursting burthen: at the sound he turned,
And saw by the warm light of their own life
Her glowing limbs beneath the sinuous veil
Of woven wind, her outspread arms now bare,
Her dark locks floating in the breath of night,
Her beamy bending eyes, her parted lips
Outstretched, and pale, and quivering eagerly.   180
His strong heart sunk and sickened with excess
Of love. He reared his shuddering limbs and quelled
His gasping breath, and spread his arms to meet
Her panting bosom: . . . she drew back a while,
Then, yielding to the irresistible joy,
With frantic gesture and short breathless cry
Folded his frame in her dissolving arms.
Now blackness veiled his dizzy eyes, and night
Involved and swallowed up the vision; sleep,
Like a dark flood suspended in its course,   190
Rolled back its impulse on his vacant brain.

      Roused by the shock he started from his trance—
The cold white light of morning, the blue moon
Low in the west, the clear and garish hills,
The distinct valley and the vacant woods,
Spread round him where he stood. Whither have fled
The hues of heaven that canopied his bower
Of yesternight? The sounds that soothed his sleep,
The mystery and the majesty of Earth,
The joy, the exultation? His wan eyes   200
Gaze on the empty scene as vacantly
As ocean's moon looks on the moon in heaven.
The spirit of sweet human love has sent
A vision to the sleep of him who spurned
Her choicest gifts. He eagerly pursues
Beyond the realms of dream that fleeting shade;
He overleaps the bounds. Alas! Alas!
Were limbs, and breath, and being intertwined
Thus treacherously? Lost, lost, for ever lost,
In the wide pathless desert of dim sleep,   210
That beautiful shape! Does the dark gate of death
Conduct to thy mysterious paradise,
O Sleep? Does the bright arch of rainbow clouds,
And pendent mountains seen in the calm lake,
Lead only to a black and watery depth,
While death's blue vault, with loathliest vapours hung,
Where every shade which the foul grave exhales
Hides its dead eye from the detested day,
Conducts, O Sleep, to thy delightful realms?
This doubt with sudden tide flowed on his heart,   220
The insatiate hope which it awakened, stung
His brain even like despair.

                              While daylight held
The sky, the Poet kept mute conference
With his still soul. At night the passion came,

Like the fierce fiend of a distempered dream,
And shook him from his rest, and led him forth
Into the darkness.—As an eagle grasped
In folds of the green serpent, feels her breast
Burn with the poison, and precipitates
Through night and day, tempest, and calm, and cloud,
Frantic with dizzying anguish, her blind flight   231
O'er the wide aëry wilderness: thus driven
By the bright shadow of that lovely dream,
Beneath the cold glare of the desolate night,
Through tangled swamps and deep precipitous dells,
Startling with careless step the moonlight snake,
He fled. Red morning dawned upon his flight,
Shedding the mockery of its vital hues
Upon his cheek of death. He wandered on
Till vast Aornos seen from Petra's steep   240
Hung o'er the low horizon like a cloud;
Through Balk, and where the desolated tombs
Of Parthian kings scatter to every wind
Their wasting dust, wildly he wandered on,[6]
Day after day a weary waste of hours,
Bearing within his life the brooding care
That ever fed on its decaying flame.
And now his limbs were lean; his scattered hair
Sered by the autumn of strange suffering
Sung dirges in the wind; his listless hand   250
Hung like dead bone within its withered skin;
Life, and the lustre that consumed it, shone
As in a furnace burning secretly
From his dark eyes alone. The cottagers,
Who ministered with human charity
His human wants, beheld with wondering awe
Their fleeting visitant. The mountaineer,
Encountering on some dizzy precipice
That spectral form, deemed that the Spirit of wind
With lightning eyes, and eager breath, and feet   260
Disturbing not the drifted snow, had paused
In its career: the infant would conceal
His troubled visage in his mother's robe
In terror at the glare of those wild eyes,
To remember their strange light in many a dream
Of after-times; but youthful maidens, taught
By nature, would interpret half the woe
That wasted him, would call him with false names
Brother, and friend, would press his pallid hand
At parting, and watch, dim through tears, the path
Of his departure from their father's door.   271

      At length upon the lone Chorasmian shore [7]
He paused, a wide and melancholy waste
Of putrid marshes. A strong impulse urged

------

[6] Locations in Afghanistan, in ancient times Bactria, known as
Balkh in the Christian Era.
[7] In Turkestan, central Asia.

His steps to the sea-shore. A swan was there,
Beside a sluggish stream among the reeds.
It rose as he approached, and with strong wings
Scaling the upward sky, bent its bright course
High over the immeasurable main.
His eyes pursued its flight.—'Thou hast a home,   280
Beautiful bird; thou voyagest to thine home,
Where thy sweet mate will twine her downy neck
With thine, and welcome thy return with eyes
Bright in the lustre of their own fond joy.
And what am I that I should linger here,
With voice far sweeter than thy dying notes,
Spirit more vast than thine, frame more attuned
To beauty, wasting these surpassing powers
In the deaf air, to the blind earth, and heaven
That echoes not my thoughts?' A gloomy smile   290
Of desperate hope wrinkled his quivering lips.
For sleep, he knew, kept most relentlessly
Its precious charge, and silent death exposed,
Faithless perhaps as sleep, a shadowy lure,
With doubtful smile mocking its own strange charms.

Startled by his own thoughts he looked around.
There was no fair fiend near him, not a sight
Or sound of awe but in his own deep mind.
A little shallop floating near the shore
Caught the impatient wandering of his gaze.   300
It had been long abandoned, for its sides
Gaped wide with many a rift, and its frail joints
Swayed with the undulations of the tide.
A restless impulse urged him to embark
And meet lone Death on the drear ocean's waste;
For well he knew that mighty Shadow loves
The slimy caverns of the populous deep.

The day was fair and sunny, sea and sky
Drank its inspiring radiance, and the wind
Swept strongly from the shore, blackening the waves.
Following his eager soul, the wanderer   311
Leaped in the boat, he spread his cloak aloft
On the bare mast, and took his lonely seat,
And felt the boat speed o'er the tranquil sea
Like a torn cloud before the hurricane.

As one that in a silver vision floats
Obedient to the sweep of odorous winds
Upon resplendent clouds, so rapidly
Along the dark and ruffled waters fled
The straining boat.—A whirlwind swept it on,   320
With fierce gusts and precipitating force,
Through the white ridges of the chafèd sea.
The waves arose. Higher and higher still
Their fierce necks writhed beneath the tempest's
    scourge

Like serpents struggling in a vulture's grasp.
Calm and rejoicing in the fearful war
Of wave ruining on wave, and blast on blast
Descending, and black flood on whirlpool driven
With dark obliterating course, he sate:
As if their genii were the ministers   330
Appointed to conduct him to the light
Of those belovèd eyes, the Poet sate
Holding the steady helm. Evening came on,
The beams of sunset hung their rainbow hues
High 'mid the shifting domes of sheeted spray
That canopied his path o'er the waste deep;
Twilight, ascending slowly from the east,
Entwined in duskier wreaths her braided locks
O'er the fair front and radiant eyes of day;
Night followed, clad with stars. On every side   340
More horribly the multitudinous streams
Of ocean's mountainous waste to mutual war
Rushed in dark tumult thundering, as to mock
The calm and spangled sky. The little boat
Still fled before the storm; still fled, like foam
Down the steep cataract of a wintry river;
Now pausing on the edge of the riven wave;
Now leaving far behind the bursting mass
That fell, convulsing ocean: safely fled—
As if that frail and wasted human form,   350
Had been an elemental god.

At midnight
The moon arose: and lo! the ethereal cliffs
Of Caucasus, whose icy summits shone
Among the stars like sunlight, and around
Whose caverned base the whirlpools and the waves
Bursting and eddying irresistibly
Rage and resound for ever.—Who shall save?—
The boat fled on,—the boiling torrent drove,—
The crags closed round with black and jaggèd arms,
The shattered mountain overhung the sea,   361
And faster still, beyond all human speed,
Suspended on the sweep of the smooth wave,
The little boat was driven. A cavern there
Yawned, and amid its slant and winding depths
Ingulfed the rushing sea. The boat fled on
With unrelaxing speed.—'Vision and Love!'
The Poet cried aloud, 'I have beheld
The path of thy departure. Sleep and death
Shall not divide us long!'

The boat pursued
The windings of the cavern. Daylight shone   370
At length upon that gloomy river's flow;
Now, where the fiercest war among the waves
Is calm, on the unfathomable stream
The boat moved slowly. Where the mountain, riven,

Exposed those black depths to the azure sky,
Ere yet the flood's enormous volume fell
Even to the base of Caucasus, with sound
That shook the everlasting rocks, the mass
Filled with one whirlpool all that ample chasm;
Stair above stair the eddying waters rose,   380
Circling immeasurably fast, and laved
With alternating dash the gnarlèd roots
Of mighty trees, that stretched their giant arms
In darkness over it. I' the midst was left,
Reflecting, yet distorting every cloud,
A pool of treacherous and tremendous calm.
Seized by the sway of the ascending stream,
With dizzy swiftness, round, and round, and round,
Ridge after ridge the straining boat arose,
Till on the verge of the extremest curve,   390
Where, through an opening of the rocky bank,
The waters overflow, and a smooth spot
Of glassy quiet mid those battling tides
Is left, the boat paused shuddering.—Shall it sink
Down the abyss? Shall the reverting stress
Of that resistless gulf embosom it?
Now shall it fall?—A wandering stream of wind
Breathed from the west, has caught the expanded sail,
And, lo! with gentle motion, between banks
Of mossy slope, and on a placid stream,   400
Beneath a woven grove it sails, and, hark!
The ghastly torrent mingles its far roar,
With the breeze murmuring in the musical woods.
Where the embowering trees recede, and leave
A little space of green expanse, the cove
Is closed by meeting banks, whose yellow flowers
For ever gaze on their own drooping eyes,
Reflected in the crystal calm. The wave
Of the boat's motion marred their pensive task,
Which nought but vagrant bird, or wanton wind,   410
Or falling spear-grass, or their own decay
Had e'er disturbed before. The Poet longed
To deck with their bright hues his withered hair,
But on his heart its solitude returned,
And he forbore. Not the strong impulse hid
In those flushed cheeks, bent eyes, and shadowy
        frame
Had yet performed its ministry: it hung
Upon his life, as lightning in a cloud
Gleams, hovering ere it vanish, ere the floods
Of night close over it.

                The noonday sun   420
Now shone upon the forest, one vast mass
Of mingling shade, whose brown magnificence
A narrow vale embosoms. There, huge caves,
Scooped in the dark base of their aëry rocks
Mocking its moans, respond and roar for ever.

The meeting boughs and implicated leaves
Wove twilight o'er the Poet's path, as led
By love, or dream, or god, or mightier Death,
He sought in Nature's dearest haunt, some bank,
Her cradle, and his sepulchre. More dark   430
And dark the shades accumulate. The oak,
Expanding its immense and knotty arms,
Embraces the light beech. The pyramids
Of the tall cedar overarching, frame
Most solemn domes within, and far below,
Like clouds suspended in an emerald sky,
The ash and the acacia floating hang
Tremulous and pale. Like restless serpents, clothed
In rainbow and in fire, the parasites,
Starred with ten thousand blossoms, flow around   440
The grey trunks, and, as gamesome infants' eyes,
With gentle meanings, and most innocent wiles,
Fold their beams round the hearts of those that love,
These twine their tendrils with the wedded boughs
Uniting their close union; the woven leaves
Make net-work of the dark blue light of day,
And the night's noontide clearness, mutable
As shapes in the weird clouds. Soft mossy lawns
Beneath these canopies extend their swells,
Fragrant with perfumed herbs, and eyed with blooms
Minute yet beautiful. One darkest glen   451
Sends from its woods of musk-rose, twined with
        jasmine,
A soul-dissolving odour, to invite
To some more lovely mystery. Through the dell,
Silence and Twilight here, twin-sisters, keep
Their noonday watch, and sail among the shades,
Like vaporous shapes half seen; beyond, a well,
Dark, gleaming, and of most translucent wave,
Images all the woven boughs above,
And each depending leaf, and every speck   460
Of azure sky, darting between their chasms;
Nor aught else in the liquid mirror laves
Its portraiture, but some inconstant star
Between one foliaged lattice twinkling fair,
Or, painted bird, sleeping beneath the moon,
Or gorgeous insect floating motionless,
Unconscious of the day, ere yet his wings
Have spread their glories to the gaze of noon.

    Hither the Poet came. His eyes beheld
Their own wan light through the reflected lines   470
Of his thin hair, distinct in the dark depth
Of that still fountain; as the human heart,
Gazing in dreams over the gloomy grave,
Sees its own treacherous likeness there. He heard
The motion of the leaves, the grass that sprung
Startled and glanced and trembled even to feel
An unaccustomed presence, and the sound

Of the sweet brook that from the secret springs
Of that dark fountain rose. A Spirit [8] seemed
To stand beside him—clothed in no bright robes   480
Of shadowy silver or enshrining light,
Borrowed from aught the visible world affords
Of grace, or majesty, or mystery;—
But, undulating woods, and silent well,
And leaping rivulet, and evening gloom
Now deepening the dark shades, for speech assuming,
Held commune with him, as if he and it
Were all that was,—only . . . when his regard
Was raised by intense pensiveness, . . . two eyes,
Two starry eyes, hung in the gloom of thought,   490
And seemed with their serene and azure smiles
To beckon him.

Obedient to the light
That shone within his soul, he went, pursuing
The windings of the dell.—The rivulet
Wanton and wild, through many a green ravine
Beneath the forest flowed. Sometimes it fell
Among the moss with hollow harmony
Dark and profound. Now on the polished stones
It danced; like childhood laughing as it went:
Then, through the plain in tranquil wanderings crept,
Reflecting every herb and drooping bud   501
That overhung its quietness.—'O stream!
Whose source is inaccessibly profound,
Whither do thy mysterious waters tend?
Thou imagest my life. Thy darksome stillness,
Thy dazzling waves, thy loud and hollow gulfs,
Thy searchless fountain, and invisible course
Have each their type in me: and the wide sky,
And measureless ocean may declare as soon
What oozy cavern or what wandering cloud   510
Contains thy waters, as the universe
Tell where these living thoughts reside, when
    stretched
Upon thy flowers my bloodless limbs shall waste
I' the passing wind!'

Beside the grassy shore
Of the small stream he went: he did impress
On the green moss his tremulous step, that caught
Strong shuddering from his burning limbs. As one
Roused by some joyous madness from the couch
Of fever, he did move; yet, not like him,
Forgetful of the grave, where, when the flame   520
Of his frail exultation shall be spent,
He must descend. With rapid steps he went
Beneath the shade of trees, beside the flow
Of the wild babbling rivulet; and now

The forest's solemn canopies were changed
For the uniform and lightsome evening sky.
Grey rocks did peep from the spare moss, and
    stemmed
The struggling brook; tall spires of windlestrae [9]
Threw their thin shadows down the rugged slope,
And nought but gnarled roots of ancient pines [10]
Branchless and blasted, clenched with grasping roots
The unwilling soil. A gradual change was here,
Yet ghastly. For, as fast years flow away,
The smooth brow gathers, and the hair grows thin
And white, and where irradiate dewy eyes
Had shone, gleam stony orbs:—so from his steps
Bright flowers departed, and the beautiful shade
Of the green groves, with all their odorous winds
And musical motions. Calm, he still pursued
The stream, that with a larger volume now   540
Rolled through the labyrinthine dell; and there
Fretted a path through its descending curves
With its wintry speed. On every side now rose
Rocks, which, in unimaginable forms,
Lifted their black and barren pinnacles
In the light of evening, and, its precipice
Obscuring the ravine, disclosed above,
Mid toppling stones, black gulfs and yawning caves,
Whose windings gave ten thousand various tongues
To the loud stream. Lo! where the pass expands   550
Its stony jaws, the abrupt mountain breaks,
And seems, with its accumulated crags,
To overhang the world: for wide expand
Beneath the wan stars and descending moon
Islanded seas, blue mountains, mighty streams,
Dim tracts and vast, robed in the lustrous gloom
Of leaden-coloured even, and fiery hills
Mingling their flames with twilight, on the verge
Of the remote horizon. The near scene,
In naked and severe simplicity,   560
Made contrast with the universe. A pine,
Rock-rooted, stretched athwart the vacancy
Its swinging boughs, to each inconstant blast
Yielding one only response, at each pause
In most familiar cadence, with the howl
The thunder and the hiss of homeless streams
Mingling its solemn song, whilst the broad river,
Foaming and hurrying o'er its rugged path,
Fell into that immeasurable void
Scattering its waters to the passing winds.   570

Yet the grey precipice and solemn pine
And torrent, were not all;—one silent nook

---

[8] The alastor, or spirit of solitude.

[9] Coarse grass used for weaving.
[10] "Roots" is apparently an error for trunks, stumps, stems, or some similar one-syllable word.

Was there. Even on the edge of that vast mountain,
Upheld by knotty roots and fallen rocks,
It overlooked in its serenity
The dark earth, and the bending vault of stars.
It was a tranquil spot, that seemed to smile
Even in the lap of horror. Ivy clasped
The fissured stones with its entwining arms,
And did embower with leaves for ever green,   580
And berries dark, the smooth and even space
Of its inviolated floor, and here
The children of the autumnal whirlwind bore,
In wanton sport, those bright leaves, whose decay,
Red, yellow, or ethereally pale,
Rivals the pride of summer. 'Tis the haunt
Of every gentle wind, whose breath can teach
The wilds to love tranquillity. One step,
One human step alone, has ever broken
The stillness of its solitude:—one voice   590
Alone inspired its echoes;—even that voice
Which hither came, floating among the winds,
And led the loveliest among human forms
To make their wild haunts the depository
Of all the grace and beauty that endued
Its motions, render up its majesty,
Scatter its music on the unfeeling storm,
And to the damp leaves and blue cavern mould,
Nurses of rainbow flowers and branching moss,
Commit the colours of that varying cheek,   600
That snowy breast, those dark and drooping eyes.

     The dim and hornèd moon hung low, and poured
A sea of lustre on the horizon's verge
That overflowed its mountains. Yellow mist
Filled the unbounded atmosphere, and drank
Wan moonlight even to fulness: not a star
Shone, not a sound was heard; the very winds,
Danger's grim playmates, on that precipice
Slept, clasped in his embrace.—O, storm of death!
Whose sightless speed divides this sullen night: 610
And thou, colossal Skeleton, that, still
Guiding its irresistible career
In thy devastating omnipotence,
Art king of this frail world, from the red field
Of slaughter, from the reeking hospital,
The patriot's sacred couch, the snowy bed
Of innocence, the scaffold and the throne,
A mighty voice invokes thee. Ruin calls
His brother Death. A rare and regal prey
He hath prepared, prowling around the world;   620
Glutted with which thou mayst repose, and men
Go to their graves like flowers or creeping worms,
Nor ever more offer at thy dark shrine
The unheeded tribute of a broken heart.

     When on the threshold of the green recess
The wanderer's footsteps fell, he knew that death
Was on him. Yet a little, ere it fled,
Did he resign his high and holy soul
To images of the majestic past,
That paused within his passive being now,   630
Like winds that bear sweet music, when they breathe
Through some dim latticed chamber. He did place
His pale lean hand upon the rugged trunk
Of the old pine. Upon an ivied stone
Reclined his languid head, his limbs did rest,
Diffused and motionless, on the smooth brink
Of that obscurest chasm;—and thus he lay,
Surrendering to their final impulses
The hovering powers of life. Hope and despair,
The torturers, slept; no mortal pain or fear   640
Marred his repose, the influxes of sense,
And his own being unalloyed by pain,
Yet feebler and more feeble, calmly fed
The stream of thought, till he lay breathing there
At peace, and faintly smiling:—his last sight
Was the great moon, which o'er the western line
Of the wide world her mighty horn suspended,
With whose dun beams inwoven darkness seemed
To mingle. Now upon the jaggèd hills
It rests, and still as the divided frame   650
Of the vast meteor sunk, the Poet's blood,
That ever beat in mystic sympathy
With nature's ebb and flow, grew feebler still:
And when two lessening points of light alone
Gleamed through the darkness, the alternate gasp
Of his faint respiration scarce did stir
The stagnate night:—till the minutest ray
Was quenched, the pulse yet lingered in his heart.
It paused—it fluttered. But when heaven remained
Utterly black, the murky shades involved   660
An image, silent, cold, and motionless,
As their own voiceless earth and vacant air.
Even as a vapour fed with golden beams
That ministered on sunlight, ere the west
Eclipses it, was now that wondrous frame—
No sense, no motion, no divinity—
A fragile lute, on whose harmonious strings
The breath of heaven did wander—a bright stream
Once fed with many-voicèd waves—a dream
Of youth, which night and time have quenched for
     ever,   670
Still, dark, and dry, and unremembered now.

     O, for Medea's wondrous alchemy,[11]
Which wheresoe'er it fell made the earth gleam

---

[11] Skilled in witchcraft, she several times relied on her occult
powers to relieve a famine.

With bright flowers, and the wintry boughs exhale
From vernal blooms fresh fragrance! O, that God,
Profuse of poisons, would concede the chalice
Which but one living man has drained, who now,
Vessel of deathless wrath, a slave that feels
No proud exemption in the blighting curse
He bears, over the world wanders for ever,   680
Lone as incarnate death! [12] O, that the dream
Of dark magician in his visioned cave,
Raking the cinders of a crucible
For life and power, even when his feeble hand
Shakes in its last decay, were the true law
Of this so lovely world! But thou art fled
Like some frail exhalation; which the dawn
Robes in its golden beams,—ah! thou hast fled!
The brave, the gentle, and the beautiful,
The child of grace and genius. Heartless things   690
Are done and said i' the world, and many worms
And beasts and men live on, and mighty Earth
From sea and mountain, city and wilderness,
In vesper low or joyous orison,
Lifts still its solemn voice:—but thou art fled—
Thou canst no longer know or love the shapes
Of this phantasmal scene, who have to thee
Been purest ministers, who are, alas!
Now thou art not. Upon those pallid lips
So sweet even in their silence, on those eyes   700
That image sleep in death, upon that form
Yet safe from the worm's outrage, let no tear
Be shed—not even in thought. Nor, when those hues
Are gone, and those divinest lineaments,
Worn by the senseless wind, shall live alone
In the frail pauses of this simple strain,
Let not high verse, mourning the memory
Of that which is no more, or painting's woe
Or sculpture, speak in feeble imagery
Their own cold powers. Art and eloquence,   710
And all the shows o' the world are frail and vain
To weep a loss that turns their lights to shade.
It is a woe too 'deep for tears,' [13] when all
Is reft at once, when some surpassing Spirit,
Whose light adorned the world around it, leaves
Those who remain behind, not sobs or groans,
The passionate tumult of a clinging hope;
But pale despair and cold tranquillity,
Nature's vast frame, the web of human things,
Birth and the grave, that are not as they were.   720

[1815]   [1816]

[12] Ahasueras, the Wandering Jew, condemned to live home-
less until the Second Coming.
[13] See the last stanza of Wordsworth's Immortality Ode,
p. 259.

HYMN TO
INTELLECTUAL BEAUTY

I

THE awful shadow of some unseen Power
    Floats though unseen among us,—visiting
    This various world with as inconstant wing
As summer winds that creep from flower to flower,—
Like moonbeams that behind some piny mountain
        shower,
        It visits with inconstant glance
        Each human heart and countenance;
Like hues and harmonies of evening,—
        Like clouds in starlight widely spread,—
        Like memory of music fled,—   10
        Like aught that for its grace may be
Dear, and yet dearer for its mystery.

II

Spirit of BEAUTY, that dost consecrate
    With thine own hues all thou dost shine upon
    Of human thought or form,—where art thou gone?
Why dost thou pass away and leave our state,
This dim vast vale of tears, vacant and desolate?
        Ask why the sunlight not for ever
        Weaves rainbows o'er yon mountain-river,
Why aught should fail and fade that once is shown, 20
        Why fear and dream and death and birth
        Cast on the daylight of this earth
        Such gloom,—why man has such a scope
For love and hate, despondency and hope?

III

No voice from some sublimer world hath ever
    To sage or poet these responses given—
    Therefore the names of Demon, Ghost, and
        Heaven,
Remain the records of their vain endeavour,
Frail spells—whose uttered charm might not avail to
        sever,
        From all we hear and all we see,   30
        Doubt, chance, and mutability.
Thy light alone—like mist o'er mountains driven,
        Or music by the night wind sent
        Through strings of some still instrument,
        Or moonlight on a midnight stream,
Gives grace and truth to life's unquiet dream.

IV

Love, Hope, and Self-esteem, like clouds depart
    And come, for some uncertain moments lent.
    Man were immortal, and omnipotent,
Didst thou, unknown and awful as thou art,   40

Keep with thy glorious train firm state within his
    heart.
      Thou messenger of sympathies
      That wax and wane in lovers' eyes—
Thou—that to human thought art nourishment,
      Like darkness to a dying flame!
      Depart not as thy shadow came,
      Depart not—lest the grave should be,
Like life and fear, a dark reality.

V

While yet a boy I sought for ghosts, and sped   49
    Through many a listening chamber, cave and ruin,
    And starlight wood, with fearful steps pursuing
Hopes of high talk with the departed dead.
I called on poisonous names with which our youth is
    fed;
      I was not heard—I saw them not—
      When musing deeply on the lot
Of life, at that sweet time when winds are wooing
      All vital things that wake to bring
      News of birds and blossoming,—
      Sudden, thy shadow fell on me;
I shrieked, and clasped my hands in ecstasy!   60

VI

I vowed that I would dedicate my powers
    To thee and thine—have I not kept the vow?
    With beating heart and streaming eyes, even now
I call the phantoms of a thousand hours
Each from his voiceless grave: they have in visioned
      Of studious zeal or love's delight   [bowers
      Outwatched with me the envious night—
They know that never joy illumed my brow
      Unlinked with hope that thou wouldst free
      This world from its dark slavery,   70
      That thou—O awful LOVELINESS,
Wouldst give whate'er these words cannot express.

VII

The day becomes more solemn and serene
    When noon is past—there is a harmony
    In autumn, and a lustre in its sky,
Which through the summer is not heard or seen,
As if it could not be, as if it had not been!
      Thus let thy power, which like the truth
      Of nature on my passive youth
Descended, to my onward life supply   80
      Its calm—to one who worships thee,
      And every form containing thee,
      Whom, SPIRIT fair, thy spells did bind
To fear himself, and love all human kind.

[1816]   [1817]

MONT BLANC

*Mont Blanc, the highest mountain in the Alps, towers over the
valley of Chamounix, through which the river Arve flows,
meeting there the Rhone (see line 123). Coleridge's* Hymn
Before Sunrise in the Vale of Chamouni *(above) is nominally
located in the same spot, but Coleridge himself had not seen it
until after he had written the poem.*

MONT BLANC
LINES WRITTEN IN THE VALE OF CHAMOUNI

I

THE everlasting universe of things
Flows through the mind, and rolls its rapid waves,
Now dark—now glittering—now reflecting gloom—
Now lending splendour, where from secret springs
The source of human thought its tribute brings
Of waters,—with a sound but half its own,
Such as a feeble brook will oft assume
In the wild woods, among the mountains lone,
Where waterfalls around it leap for ever,
Where woods and winds contend, and a vast river   10
Over its rocks ceaselessly bursts and raves.

II

Thus thou, Ravine of Arve—dark, deep Ravine—
Thou many-coloured, many-voicèd vale,
Over whose pines, and crags, and caverns sail
Fast cloud-shadows and sunbeams: awful scene,
Where Power in likeness of the Arve comes down
From the ice-gulphs that gird his secret throne,
Bursting through these dark mountains like the flame
Of lightning through the tempest;—thou dost lie,
Thy giant brood of pines around thee clinging,   20
Children of elder time, in whose devotion
The chainless winds still come and ever came
To drink their odours, and their mighty swinging
To hear—an old and solemn harmony;
Thine earthly rainbows stretched across the sweep
Of the aethereal waterfall, whose veil
Robes some unsculptured image; the strange sleep
Which when the voices of the desert fail
Wraps all in its own deep eternity;—
Thy caverns echoing to the Arve's commotion,   30
A loud, lone sound no other sound can tame;
Thou art pervaded with that ceaseless motion,
Thou art the path of that unresting sound—
Dizzy Ravine! and when I gaze on thee
I seem as in a trance sublime and strange
To muse on my own separate fantasy,
My own, my human mind, which passively
Now renders and receives fast influencings,
Holding an unremitting interchange

With the clear universe of things around; 40
One legion of wild thoughts, whose wandering wings
Now float above thy darkness, and now rest
Where that or thou art no unbidden guest,
In the still cave of the witch Poesy,
Seeking among the shadows that pass by
Ghosts of all things that are, some shade of thee,
Some phantom, some faint image; till the breast
From which they fled recalls them, thou art there!

III

Some say that gleams of a remoter world
Visit the soul in sleep,—that death is slumber, 50
And that its shapes the busy thoughts outnumber
Of those who wake and live.—I look on high;
Has some unknown omnipotence unfurled
The veil of life and death? or do I lie
In dream, and does the mightier world of sleep
Spread far around and inaccessibly
Its circles? For the very spirit fails,
Driven like a homeless cloud from steep to steep
That vanishes among the viewless gales!
Far, far above, piercing the infinite sky, 60
Mont Blanc appears,—still, snowy, and serene—
Its subject mountains their unearthly forms
Pile around it, ice and rock; broad vales between
Of frozen floods, unfathomable deeps,
Blue as the overhanging heaven, that spread
And wind among the accumulated steeps;
A desert peopled by the storms alone,
Save when the eagle brings some hunter's bone,
And the wolf tracks her there—how hideously
Its shapes are heaped around! rude, bare, and high,
Ghastly, and scarred, and riven.—Is this the scene 71
Where the old Earthquake-daemon taught her young
Ruin? Were these their toys? or did a sea
Of fire envelop once this silent snow?
None can reply—all seems eternal now.
The wilderness has a mysterious tongue
Which teaches awful doubt, or faith so mild,
So solemn, so serene, that man may be,
But for such faith, with nature reconciled;
Thou hast a voice, great Mountain, to repeal 80
Large codes of fraud and woe; not understood
By all, but which the wise, and great, and good
Interpret, or make felt, or deeply feel.

IV

The fields, the lakes, the forests, and the streams,
Ocean, and all the living things that dwell
Within the daedal [1] earth; lightning, and rain,

---

[1] I.e., intricate, artful, as if shaped by Daedalus, the builder of the Labyrinth.

Earthquake, and fiery flood, and hurricane,
The torpor of the year when feeble dreams
Visit the hidden buds, or dreamless sleep
Holds every future leaf and flower;—the bound 90
With which from that detested trance they leap;
The works and ways of man, their death and birth,
And that of him and all that his may be;
All things that move and breathe with toil and sound
Are born and die; revolve, subside, and swell.
Power dwells apart in its tranquillity,
Remote, serene, and inaccessible:
And *this*, the naked countenance of earth,
On which I gaze, even these primæval mountains
Teach the adverting mind. The glaciers creep 100
Like snakes that watch their prey, from their far
        fountains,
Slow rolling on; there, many a precipice,
Frost and the Sun in scorn of mortal power
Have piled: dome, pyramid, and pinnacle,
A city of death, distinct with many a tower
And wall impregnable of beaming ice.
Yet not a city, but a flood of ruin
Is there, that from the boundaries of the sky
Rolls its perpetual stream; vast pines are strewing
Its destined path, or in the mangled soil 110
Branchless and shattered stand; the rocks, drawn
        down
From yon remotest waste, have overthrown
The limits of the dead and living world,
Never to be reclaimed. The dwelling-place
Of insects, beasts, and birds, becomes its spoil;
Their food and their retreat for ever gone,
So much of life and joy is lost. The race
Of man flies far in dread; his work and dwelling
Vanish, like smoke before the tempest's stream,
And their place is not known. Below, vast caves 120
Shine in the rushing torrents' restless gleam,
Which from those secret chasms in tumult welling
Meet in the vale, and one majestic River,
The breath and blood of distant lands, for ever
Rolls its loud waters to the ocean waves,
Breathes its swift vapours to the circling air.

V

Mont Blanc yet gleams on high;—the power is there,
The still and solemn power of many sights,
And many sounds, and much of life and death.
In the calm darkness of the moonless nights, 130
In the lone glare of day, the snows descend
Upon that Mountain; none beholds them there,
Nor when the flakes burn in the sinking sun,
Or the star-beams dart through them:—Winds
        contend
Silently there, and heap the snow with breath

Rapid and strong, but silently! Its home
The voiceless lightning in these solitudes
Keeps innocently, and like vapour broods
Over the snow. The secret Strength of things
Which governs thought, and to the infinite dome   140
Of Heaven is as a law, inhabits thee!
And what were thou, and earth, and stars, and sea,
If to the human mind's imaginings
Silence and solitude were vacancy?

[1816]   [1817]

TO ——— ["THE COLD EARTH SLEPT BELOW"]
One version of this poem was first published in Hunt's Literary
Pocket-Book *in 1823 under the heading, "November 1815."
Since the poem appears to refer to the suicide of Harriet Shelley
in the winter of 1816, most editors have assumed the poem was
deliberately misdated.*

TO ———
["The cold earth slept below"]

I

THE cold earth slept below,
    Above the cold sky shone;
And all around, with a chilling sound,
    From caves of ice and fields of snow,
    The wind of night like death did flow
        Under the sinking moon.

II

The wintry hedge was black,
    The brown grass was not seen,
The birds did rest in the dark thorn's breast,
    Whose roots, beside the pathway track,   10
    Bound hard the soil and many a crack
        The black frost made between.

III

Thine eyes glowed in the gleam
    Of the departing light;
As a starry beam on a deep dark stream
    Shines dimly, so the moon shone there,
    And it shone through the strings of thy tangled hair,
        Which shook in the blast of night.

IV

The moon made thy lips pale, beloved—
    The wind made thy bosom chill—   20
The air did shed on thy dear head
    Its frozen dew, and thou didst lie
    Where the bitter breath of the naked sky
        Might visit thee at will.

[1816]   [1823]

TO CONSTANTIA SINGING
*Presumably "Constantia" is Jane (Claire) Clairmont, Mary
Godwin's stepsister, Byron's mistress (she bore his daughter
Allegra), who lived with the Shelleys in Italy. This version of
the poem is from a notebook once owned by Claire Clairmont.
Mrs. Shelley published a quite different version in 1824. For
still another version, see J. Chernails, "Shelley's 'To Con-
stantia'," Times Literary Supplement, 6 Feb. 1969.*

TO CONSTANTIA SINGING

I

THY voice slow rising like a Spirit, lingers
    O'ershadowing it with soft and lulling wings,
The blood and life within thy snowy fingers
    Teach witchcraft to the instrumental strings.
—My brain is wild—my breath comes quick—
    The blood is listening in my frame,
And thronging shadows, fast and thick,
    Fall on my overflowing eyes;
My heart is quivering like a flame;
    As morning dew, that in the sunbeam dies,   10
    I am dissolved in these consuming exstasies.

II

I have no life, Constantia, but in thee
    Whilst, like the world-surrounding air, thy song
Flows on, and fills all things with melody:
    Now is thy voice a tempest swift and strong,
On which, as one in trance, upborne,
    Secure o'er rocks and waves I sweep,
Rejoicing, like a cloud of morn.
    Now 'tis the breath of summer's night,
Which, where the starry waters sleep,   20
    Round western isles, with incense-blossoms bright,
    Lingering, suspends my soul in its voluptuous
        flight.

III

A deep and breathless awe, like the swift change
    Of dreams unseen, but felt in youthful slumbers,
Wild, sweet, yet uncommunicably strange
    Thou breathest now in fast ascending numbers.
The cope of Heaven seems rent and cloven
    By the enchantment of thy strain,
And o'er my shoulders wings are woven
    To follow its sublime career   30
Beyond the mighty moons that wane
    Upon the verge of Nature's utmost sphere
    Till the world's shadowy walls are past and
        disappear.

IV

Cease cease—for such wild lessons madmen learn
  Long thus to sink—thus to be lost and die,
Perhaps is death indeed—Constantia turn!
  Yes! in thine eyes a power like light doth lie,
Even tho' the sounds, its voice that were
  Between thy lips, are laid to sleep—
Within thy breath, and on thy hair   40
Like odour, it is lingering yet—
  And from thy touch like fire doth leap.
  Even while I write, my burning cheeks are wet.
  Alas, that the torn heart can bleed, but not forget.

[1817]   [1824, 1926]

TO THE LORD CHANCELLOR

In 1817, after Harriet's suicide, the Lord Chancellor, the Earl of Eldon, issued a decree giving her family custody of Shelley's children by her.

TO THE LORD CHANCELLOR

I

THY country's curse is on thee, darkest crest
  Of that foul, knotted, many-headed worm,
Which rends our Mother's bosom—Priestly Pest!
  Masked Resurrection of a buried Form!

II

Thy country's curse is on thee! Justice sold,
  Truth trampled, Nature's landmarks overthrown,
And heaps of fraud-accumulated gold,
  Plead, loud as thunder, at Destruction's throne.

III

And, whilst that slow sure Angel which aye stands
  Watching the beck of Mutability,   10
Delays to execute her high commands
  And, though a nation weeps, spares thine and thee;

IV

Oh, let a father's curse be on thy soul,
  And let a daughter's hope be on thy tomb;
Be both, on thy grey head, a leaden cowl,
  To weigh thee down to thine approaching doom!

V

I curse thee by a parent's outraged love,
  By hopes long cherished and too lately lost,
By gentle feelings thou couldst never prove,
  By griefs which thy stern nature never crossed; 20

VI

By those infantine smiles of happy light,
  Which were a fire within a stranger's hearth,
Quenched even when kindled, in untimely night
  Hiding the promise of a lovely birth:

VII

By those unpractised accents of young speech,
  Which he who is a father thought to frame
To gentlest lore, such as the wisest teach—
  Thou strike the lyre of mind!—Oh, grief and shame!

VIII

By all the happy see in children's growth—
  That undeveloped flower of budding years— 30
Sweetness and sadness interwoven both,
  Source of the sweetest hopes and saddest fears—

IX

By all the days, under a hireling's care,
  Of dull constraint and bitter heaviness,—
O wretched ye if ever any were—
  Sadder than orphans, yet not fatherless!

X

By the false cant which on their innocent lips
  Must hang like poison on an opening bloom,
By the dark creeds which cover with eclipse
  Their pathway from the cradle to the tomb— 40

XI

By thy most impious Hell, and all its terror;
  By all the grief, the madness, and the guilt
Of thine impostures, which must be their error—
  That sand on which thy crumbling power is built—

XII

By thy complicity with lust and hate—
  Thy thirst for tears—thy hunger after gold—
The ready frauds which ever on thee wait—
  The servile arts in which thou hast grown old—

XIII

By thy most killing sneer, and by thy smile—
  By all the arts and snares of thy black den, 50
And—for thou canst outweep the crocodile—
  By thy false tears—those millstones braining men—

XIV

By all the hate which checks a father's love—
  By all the scorn which kills a father's care—
By those most impious hands which dared remove
  Nature's high bounds—by thee—and by despair—

XV

Yes, the despair which bids a father groan,
  And cry, "My children are no longer mine—
The blood within those veins may be mine own,
  But—Tyrant—their polluted souls are thine;—" 60

XVI

I curse thee—though I hate thee not.—O slave!
  If thou couldst quench the earth-consuming Hell
Of which thou art a daemon, on thy grave
  This curse should be a blessing. Fare thee well!

[1817]   [1839]

THE REVOLT OF ISLAM

The Revolt of Islam, Shelley's first attempt at a long (5000-line) epic with some mythological base, may have been written in competition with Keats (who at the same time was beginning Endymion). *Publication of the poem in its first form (called then* Laon and Cythna) *was refused because the lovers there are brother and sister. But Shelley changed only a few lines to enable its publication in 1818. The mythological content, especially in the first canto, is somewhat confusing, but the political and social intent of the poem is made very clear by the Preface: to renew the spirit of liberation that had lapsed into apathy after the Napoleonic wars. Shelley's father-in-law William Godwin obviously contributed to the political spirit of the poem, but a more important influence in making Cythna the more heroic and politically viable of the two figures was undoubtedly Mary Wollstonecraft's* A Vindication of the Rights of Woman (*see note to* To Mary Wollstonecraft Godwin *above*). *In its emphasis on the sexual, social, and political oppression of women, and in the explicit connection between women's place and slavery, the poem has some thematic parallels with Blake's* A Vision of the Daughters of Albion.*

In the first selection reprinted here Laon and Cythna first meet as children in Greece and declare their devotion to each other and to liberty. In Canto VIII (below), Cythna—who has been abducted for the Turkish tyrant's seraglio, led a revolution in Constantinople, and rescued Laon from a massacre—tells her lover of her rescue from a cavern in the sea by the crew of a slave ship. In later cantos Laon gives himself up as a human sacrifice to pagan priests, hoping thereby to free Cythna to go to America, but she dies with him in the Temple of the Spirit, where the war against tyranny is constantly renewed.

F R O M

THE REVOLT OF ISLAM

F R O M   T H E

PREFACE

. . . I have chosen a story of human passion in its most universal character, diversified with moving and romantic adventures, and appealing, in contempt of all artificial opinions or institutions, to the common sympathies of every human breast. I have made no attempt to recommend the motives which I would substitute for those at present governing mankind, by methodical and systematic argument. I would only awaken the feelings, so that the reader should see the beauty of true virtue, and be incited to those inquiries which have led to my moral and political creed, and that of some of the sublimest intellects in the world. The Poem therefore (with the exception of the first canto, which is purely introductory) is narrative, not didactic. It is a succession of pictures illustrating the growth and progress of individual mind aspiring after excellence, and devoted to the love of mankind; its influence in refining and making pure the most daring and uncommon impulses of the imagination, the understanding, and the senses; its impatience at 'all the oppressions which are done under the sun'; its tendency to awaken public hope, and to enlighten and improve mankind; the rapid effects of the application of that tendency; the awakening of an immense nation from their slavery and degradation to a true sense of moral dignity and freedom; the bloodless dethronement of their oppressors, and the unveiling of the religious frauds by which they had been deluded into submission; the tranquillity of successful patriotism, and the universal toleration and benevolence of true philanthropy; the treachery and barbarity of hired soldiers; vice not the object of punishment and hatred, but kindness and pity; the faithlessness of tyrants; the confederacy of the Rulers of the World, and the restoration of the expelled Dynasty by foreign arms; the massacre and extermination of the Patriots, and the victory of established power; the consequences of legitimate despotism,—civil war, famine, plague, superstition, and an utter extinction of the domestic affections; the judicial murder of the advocates of Liberty; the temporary triumph of oppression, that secure earnest of its final and inevitable fall; the transient nature of ignorance and error, and the eternity of genius and virtue. Such is the series of delineations of which the Poem consists. And, if the lofty passions with which it has been my scope to distinguish this story shall not excite in the reader a generous impulse, an ardent thirst for excellence, an interest profound and strong such as belongs to no meaner desires, let not the failure be imputed to a natural unfitness for human sympathy in these sublime and animating themes. It is the business of the Poet to communicate to others the pleasure and the enthusiasm arising out of those images and feelings in the vivid presence of which within his own mind consists at once his inspiration and his reward.

The panic which, like an epidemic transport, seized upon all classes of men during the excesses consequent upon the French Revolution, is gradually giving place to sanity. It has ceased to be believed that whole generations of mankind ought to consign themselves to a hopeless inheritance of ignorance and misery, because a nation of men who had been dupes and slaves for centuries were incapable of conducting themselves with the wisdom and tranquillity of freemen so soon as some of their fetters were partially loosened. That their conduct could not have been marked by any other characters than ferocity and thoughtlessness is the historical fact from which liberty derives all its recommendations, and falsehood the worst features of its deformity. There is a reflux in the tide of human things which bears the shipwrecked hopes of men into a secure haven after the storms are past. Methinks, those who now live have survived an age of despair.

The French Revolution may be considered as one of those manifestations of a general state of feeling among civilised mankind produced by a defect of correspondence between the knowledge existing in society and the improvement or gradual abolition of political institutions. The year 1788 may be assumed as the epoch of one of the most important crises produced by this feeling. The sympathies connected with that event extended to every bosom. The most generous and amiable natures were those which participated the most extensively in these sympathies. But such a degree of unmingled good was expected as it was impossible to realise. If the Revolution had been in every respect prosperous, then misrule and superstition would lose half their claims to our abhorrence, as fetters which the captive can unlock with the slightest motion of his fingers, and which do not eat with poisonous rust into the soul. The revulsion occasioned by the atrocities of the demagogues, and the re-establishment of successive tyrannies in France, was terrible, and felt in the remotest corner of the civilised world. Could they listen to the plea of reason who had groaned under the calamities of a social state according to the provisions of which one man riots in luxury whilst another famishes for want of bread? Can he who the day before was a trampled slave suddenly become liberal-minded, forbearing, and independent? This is the consequence of the habits of a state of society to be produced by resolute perseverance and indefatigable hope, and long-suffering and long-believing courage, and the systematic efforts of generations of men of intellect and virtue. Such is the lesson which experience teaches now. But, on the first reverses of hope in the progress of French liberty, the sanguine eagerness for good overleaped the solution of these questions, and for a time extinguished itself in the unexpectedness of their result. Thus, many of the most ardent and tender-hearted of the worshippers of public good have been morally ruined by what a partial glimpse of the events they deplored appeared to show as the melancholy desolation of all their cherished hopes. Hence gloom and misanthropy have become the characteristics of the age in which we live, the solace of a disappointment that unconsciously finds relief only in the wilful exaggeration of its own despair. . . .

FROM
CANTO II

XXX

FOR, before Cythna loved it, had my song
    Peopled with thoughts the boundless universe,
A mighty congregation, which were strong   930
    Where'er they trod the darkness to disperse
    The cloud of that unutterable curse
Which clings upon mankind:—all things became
    Slaves to my holy and heroic verse,
Earth, sea and sky, the planets, life and fame
And fate, or whate'er else binds the world's wondrous
    frame.

XXXI

And this beloved child thus felt the sway
    Of my conceptions, gathering like a cloud
The very wind on which it rolls away: 939
    Hers too were all my thoughts, ere yet, endowed
    With music and with light, their fountains flowed
In poesy; and her still and earnest face,
    Pallid with feelings which intensely glowed
Within, was turned on mine with speechless grace,
Watching the hopes which there her heart had learned
    to trace.

XXXII

In me, communion with this purest being
    Kindled intenser zeal, and made me wise
In knowledge, which, in hers mine own mind
    seeing,
    Left in the human world few mysteries:
    How without fear of evil or disguise   950
Was Cythna!—what a spirit strong and mild,
    Which death, or pain or peril could despise,
Yet melt in tenderness! what genius wild
Yet mighty, was enclosed within one simple child!

XXXIII

New lore was this—old age, with its gray hair,
    And wrinkled legends of unworthy things,
And icy sneers, is nought: it cannot dare
    To burst the chains which life for ever flings
    On the entangled soul's aspiring wings,
So is it cold and cruel, and is made   960
    The careless slave of that dark power which
    brings
Evil, like blight, on man, who, still betrayed
Laughs o'er the grave in which his living hopes are
    laid.

XXXIV

Nor are the strong and the severe to keep
    The empire of the world: thus Cythna taught
Even in the visions of her eloquent sleep,
    Unconscious of the power through which she
    wrought
    The woof of such intelligible thought,
As from the tranquil strength which cradled lay
    In her smile-peopled rest, my spirit sought   970
Why the deceiver and the slave has sway
O'er heralds so divine of truth's arising day.

XXXV

Within that fairest form, the female mind
    Untainted by the poison-clouds which rest
On the dark world, a sacred home did find:
    But else, from the wide earth's maternal breast,
    Victorious Evil, which had dispossessed
All native power, had those fair children torn,
    And made them slaves to soothe his vile unrest,
And minister to lust its joys forlorn,   980
Till they had learned to breathe the atmosphere of
    scorn.

XXXVI

This misery was but coldly felt, till she
    Became my only friend, who had endued
My purpose with a wider sympathy;
    Thus, Cythna mourned with me the servitude
    In which the half of humankind were mewed
Victims of lust and hate, the slaves of slaves,
    She mourned that grace and power were thrown
    as food
To the hyaena lust, who, among graves,
Over his loathèd meal, laughing in agony, raves.   990

XXXVII

And I, still gazing on that glorious child,
    Even as these thoughts flushed o'er her:—
    'Cythna sweet,
Well with the world art thou unreconciled;
    Never will peace and human nature meet
    Till free and equal man and woman greet
Domestic peace; and ere this power can make
    In human hearts its calm and holy seat,
This slavery must be broken'—as I spake,
From Cythna's eyes a light of exultation brake.

XXXVIII

She replied earnestly:—'It shall be mine,   1000
    This task, mine, Laon!—thou hast much to gain;
Nor wilt thou at poor Cythna's pride repine,
    If she should lead a happy female train

To meet thee over the rejoicing plain,
When myriads at thy call shall throng around
   The Golden City.'—Then the child did strain
My arm upon her tremulous heart, and wound
Her own about my neck, till some reply she found.

XXXIX

I smiled, and spake not.—'Wherefore dost thou
      smile
   At what I say? Laon, I am not weak   1011
And though my cheek might become pale the while,
   With thee, if thou desirest, will I seek
   Through their array of banded slaves to wreak
Ruin upon the tyrants. I had thought
   It was more hard to turn my unpractised cheek
To scorn and shame, and this beloved spot
And thee, O dearest friend, to leave and murmur not.

XL

'Whence came I what I am? Thou, Laon, knowest
   How a young child should thus undaunted be;
Methinks, it is a power which thou bestowest,   1020
   Through which I seek, by most resembling thee,
   So to become most good and great and free,
Yet far beyond this Ocean's utmost roar
   In towers and huts are many like to me,
Who, could they see thine eyes, or feel such lore
As I have learnt from them, like me would fear no
      more.

XLI

'Think'st thou that I shall speak unskilfully,
   And none will heed me? I remember now,
How once, a slave in tortures doomed to die,
   Was saved, because in accents sweet and low
   He sung a song his Judge loved long ago,   1031
As he was led to death.—All shall relent
   Who hear me—tears, as mine have flowed, shall
      flow
Hearts beat as mine now beats, with such intent
As renovates the world; a will omnipotent!

XLII

'Yes, I will tread Pride's golden palaces,
   Through Penury's roofless huts and squalid cells
Will I descend, where'er in abjectness
   Woman with some vile slave her tyrant dwells,
   There with the music of thine own sweet spells
Will disenchant the captives, and will pour   1041
   For the despairing, from the crystal wells
Of thy deep spirit, reason's might lore,
And power shall then abound, and hope arise once
      more.

XLIII

'Can man be free if woman be a slave?
   Chain one who lives, and breathes his boundless
      air,
To the corruption of a closèd grave!
Can they whose mates are beasts, condemned to bear
   Scorn, heavier far than toil or anguish, dare
To trample their oppressors? in their home   1050
   Among their babes, thou knowest a curse would
      wear
The shape of woman—hoary Crime would come
Behind, and Fraud rebuild religion's tottering dome.

XLIV

'I am a child:—I would not yet depart.
   When I go forth alone, bearing the lamp
Aloft which thou hast kindled in my heart,
   Millions of slaves from many a dungeon damp
   Shall leap in joy, as the benumbing cramp
Of ages leaves their limbs—no ill may harm
   Thy Cythna ever—truth its radiant stamp   1060
Has fixed, as an invulnerable charm
Upon her children's brow, dark Falsehood to disarm.

XLV

'Wait yet awhile for the appointed day—
   Thou wilt depart, and I with tears shall stand
Watching thy dim sail skirt the ocean gray;
   Amid the dwellers of this lonely land
   I shall remain alone—and they command
Shall then dissolve the world's unquiet trance,
   And, multitudinous as the desert sand
Borne on the storm, its millions shall advance,   1070
Thronging round thee, the light of their deliverance.

XLVI

'Then, like the forests of some pathless mountain,
   Which from remotest glens two warring winds
Involve in fire which not the loosened fountain
   Of broadest floods might quench, shall all the
      kinds
   Of evil, catch from our uniting minds
The spark which must consume them;—Cythna
      then
   Will have cast off the impotence that binds
Her childhood now, and through the paths of men
Will pass, as the charmed bird that haunts the
      serpent's den.   1080

XLVII

'We part!—O Laon, I must dare nor tremble
   To meet those looks no more!—Oh, heavy stroke!
Sweet brother of my soul! can I dissemble
   The agony of this thought?'—As thus she spoke

The gathered sobs her quivering accents broke,
And in my arms she hid her beating breast.
I remained still for tears—sudden she woke
As one awakes from sleep, and wildly pressed
My bosom, her whole frame impetuously possessed.

XLVIII

'We part to meet again—but yon blue waste,   1090
  Yon desert wide and deep holds no recess,
Within whose happy silence, thus embraced
  We might survive all ills in one caress:
  Nor doth the grave—I fear 'tis passionless—
Nor yon cold vacant Heaven:—we meet again
  Within the minds of men, whose lips shall bless
Our memory, and whose hopes its light retain
When these dissevered bones are trodden in the plain.'

XLIX

I could not speak, though she had ceased, for now
  The fountains of her feeling, swift and deep, 1100
Seemed to suspend the tumult of their flow;
  So we arose, and by the starlight steep
  Went homeward—neither did we speak nor weep,
But, pale, were calm with passion—thus subdued
  Like evening shades that o'er the mountains
    creep,
We moved towards our home; where, in this mood,
Each from the other sought refuge in solitude.

CANTO VIII

I

'I SATE beside the Steersman then, and gazing
  Upon the west, cried, "Spread the sails! Behold!
The sinking moon is like a watch-tower blazing
  Over the mountains yet;—the City of Gold 3202
  Yon Cape alone does from the sight withhold;
The stream is fleet—the north breathes steadily
  Beneath the stars, they tremble with the cold!
Ye cannot rest upon the dreary sea!—
Haste, haste to the warm home of happier destiny!"

II

'The Mariners obeyed—the Captain stood
  Aloof, and, whispering to the Pilot, said,
"Alas, alas! I fear we are pursued   3210
  By wicked ghosts: a Phantom of the Dead,
  The night before we sailed, came to my bed
In dream, like that!" The Pilot then replied,
  "It cannot be—she is a human Maid—
  Her low voice makes you weep—she is some bride,
Or daughter of high birth—she can be nought
    beside."

III

'We passed the islets, borne by wind and stream,
  And as we sailed, the Mariners came near
And thronged around to listen;—in the gleam
  Of the pale moon I stood, as one whom fear   3220
  May not attaint, and my calm voice did rear;
"Ye all are human—yon broad moon gives light
  To millions who the selfsame likeness wear,
Even while I speak—beneath this very night,
Their thoughts flow on like ours, in sadness or delight.

IV

'"What dream ye? Your own hands have built an
    home,
  Even for yourselves on a beloved shore:
For some, fond eyes are pining till they come,
  How they will greet him when his toils are o'er,
  And laughing babes rush from the well-known
    door!   3230
Is this your care? ye toil for your own good—
  Ye feel and think—has some immortal power
Such purposes? or in a human mood,
Dream ye some Power thus builds for man in solitude?

V

'"What is that Power? Ye mock yourselves, and
    give
  A human heart to what ye cannot know:
As if the cause of life could think and live!
  'Twere as if man's own works should feel, and
    show
  The hopes, and fears, and thoughts from which
    they flow,
And he be like to them! Lo! Plague is free   3240
  To waste, Blight, Poison, Earthquake, Hails and
    Snow,
Disease, and Want, and worse Necessity
Of hate and ill, and Pride, and Fear, and Tyranny!

VI

'"What is that Power? Some moon-struck sophist
    stood
  Watching the shade from his own soul upthrown
Fill Heaven and darken Earth, and in such mood
  The Form he saw and worshipped was his own,
  His likeness in the world's vast mirror shown;
And 'twere an innocent dream, but that a faith   3249
  Nursed by fear's dew of poison, grows thereon,
And that men say, that Power has chosen Death
On all who scorn its laws, to wreak immortal wrath.

VII

"'Men say that they themselves have heard and
    seen
    Or known from others who have known such
    things,
A Shade, a Form, which Earth and Heaven between
    Wields an invisible rod—that Priests and Kings,
    Custom, domestic sway, ay, all that brings
Man's freeborn soul beneath the oppressor's heel,
    Are his strong ministers, and that the stings 3259
Of death will make the wise his vengeance feel,
Though truth and virtue arm their hearts with tenfold
    steel.

VIII

"'And it is said, this Power will punish wrong;
    Yes, add despair to crime, and pain to pain!
And deepest hell, and deathless snakes among,
    Will bind the wretch on whom is fixed a stain,
    Which, like a plague, a burden, and a bane,
Clung to him while he lived;—for love and hate,
    Virtue and vice, they say are difference vain—
The will of strength is right—this human state
Tyrants, that they may rule, with lies thus desolate.

IX

"'Alas, what strength? Opinion is more frail 3271
    Than yon dim cloud now fading on the moon
Even while we gaze, though it awhile avail
    To hide the orb of truth—and every throne
    Of Earth or Heaven, though shadow, rests
    thereon,
One shape of many names:—for this ye plough
    The barren waves of ocean, hence each one
Is slave or tyrant; all betray and bow,
Command, or kill, or fear, or wreak, or suffer woe.

X

"'Its names are each a sign which maketh holy 3280
    All power—ay, the ghost, the dream, the shade
Of power—lust, falsehood, hate, and pride, and
    folly;
    The pattern whence all fraud and wrong is made,
    A law to which mankind has been betrayed;
And human love, is as the name well known
    Of a dear mother, whom the murderer laid
In bloody grave, and into darkness thrown,
Gathered her wildered babes around him as his own.

XI

"'O Love, who to the hearts of wandering men
    Art as the calm to Ocean's weary waves!   3290
Justice, or Truth, or Joy! those only can
    From slavery and religion's labyrinth caves

Guide us, as one clear star the seaman saves.
To give to all an equal share of good,
    To track the steps of Freedom, though through
    graves
She pass, to suffer all in patient mood,
To weep for crime, though stained with thy friend's
    dearest blood,

XII

"'To feel the peace of self-contentment's lot,
    To own all sympathies, and outrage none,
And in the inmost bowers of sense and thought,
    Until life's sunny day is quite gone down,   3301
    To sit and smile with Joy, or, not alone,
To kiss salt tears from the worn cheek of Woe;
    To live, as if to love and live were one,—
This is not faith or law, nor those who bow
To thrones on Heaven or Earth, such destiny may
    know.

XIII

"'But children near their parents tremble now,
    Because they must obey—one rules another,
And as one Power rules both high and low,
    So man is made the captive of his brother,   3310
    And Hate is throned on high with Fear her
    mother,
Above the Highest—and those fountain-cells,
    Whence love yet flowed when faith had choked
    all other,
Are darkened—Woman as the bond-slave dwells
Of man, a slave; and life is poisoned in its wells.

XIV

"'Man seeks for gold in mines, that he may weave
    A lasting chain for his own slavery;—
In fear and restless care that he may live
    He toils for others, who must ever be
    The joyless thralls of like captivity;   3320
He murders, for his chiefs delight in ruin;
    He builds the altar, that its idol's fee
May be his very blood; he is pursuing—
O, blind and willing wretch!—his own obscure
    undoing.

XV

"'Woman!—she is his slave, she has become
    A thing I weep to speak—the child of scorn,
The outcast of a desolated home;
    Falsehood, and fear, and toil, like waves have worn
    Channels upon her cheek, which smiles adorn,
As calm decks the false Ocean:—well ye know   3330
    What Woman is, for none of Woman born,
Can choose but drain the bitter dregs of woe,
Which ever from the oppressed to the oppressors flow.

XVI

'"This need not be; ye might arise, and will
    That gold should lose its power, and thrones their
        glory,
That love, which none may bind, be free to fill
    The world, like light; and evil faith, grown hoary
    With crime, be quenched and die.—Yon
        promontory
Even now eclipses the descending moon!—
    Dungeons and palaces are transitory—   3340
High temples fade like vapour—Man alone
Remains, whose will has power when all beside is
    gone.

XVII

'"Let all be free and equal!—From your hearts
    I feel an echo; through my inmost frame
Like sweetest sound, seeking its mate, it darts—
    Whence come ye, friends? Alas, I cannot name
    All that I read of sorrow, toil, and shame,
On your worn faces; as in legends old
    Which make immortal the disastrous fame
Of conquerors and impostors false and bold,   3350
The discord of your hearts, I in your looks behold.

XVIII

'"Whence come ye, friends? from pouring human
        blood
    Forth on the earth? Or bring ye steel and gold,
That Kings may dupe and slay the multitude?
    Or from the famished poor, pale, weak, and cold,
    Bear ye the earnings of their toil? Unfold!
Speak! Are your hands in slaughter's sanguine hue
    Stained freshly? have your hearts in guile grown old?
Know yourselves thus! ye shall be pure as dew,
And I will be a friend and sister unto you.   3360

XIX

'"Disguise it not—we have one human heart—
    All mortal thoughts confess a common home:
Blush not for what may to thyself impart
    Stains of inevitable crime: the doom
    Is this, which has, or may, or must become
Thine, and all humankind's. Ye are the spoil
    Which Time thus marks for the devouring tomb
Thou and thy thoughts and they, and all the toil
Wherewith ye twine the rings of life's perpetual coil.

XX

'"Disguise it not—ye blush for what ye hate,   3370
    And Enmity is sister unto Shame;
Look on your mind—it is the book of fate—
    Ah! it is dark with many a blazoned name

Of misery—all are mirrors of the same;
    But the dark fiend who with his iron pen
    Dipped in scorn's fiery poison, makes his fame
Enduring there, would o'er the heads of men
Pass harmless, if they scorned to make their hearts his
    den.

XXI

'"Yes, it is Hate—that shapeless fiendly thing
    Of many names, all evil, some divine,   3380
Whom self-contempt arms with a mortal sting;
    Which, when the heart its snaky folds entwine
    Is wasted quite, and when it doth repine
To gorge such bitter prey, on all beside
    It turns with ninefold rage, as with its twine
When Amphisbæna some fair bird has tied,
Soon o'er the putrid mass he threats on every side.

XXII

'"Reproach not thine own soul, but know thyself,
    Nor hate another's crime, nor loathe thine own.
It is the dark idolatry of self,   3390
    Which, when our thoughts and actions once are
        gone,
    Demands that man should weep, and bleed, and
        groan;
O vacant expiation! Be at rest.—
    The past is Death's, the future is thine own;
And love and joy can make the foulest breast
A paradise of flowers, where peace might build her
    nest.

XXIII

'"Speak thou! whence come ye?"—A Youth made
        reply:
    "Wearily, wearily o'er the boundless deep
We sail;—thou readest well the misery   3399
    Told in these faded eyes, but much doth sleep
    Within, which there the poor heart loves to keep,
Or dare not write on the dishonoured brow;
    Even from our childhood have we learned to
        steep
The bread of slavery in the tears of woe,
And never dreamed of hope or refuge until now.

XXIV

'"Yes—I must speak—my secret should have
        perished
    Even with the heart it wasted, as a brand
Fades in the dying flame whose life it cherished,
    But that no human bosom can withstand   3409
    Thee, wondrous Lady, and the mild command
Of thy keen eyes:—yes, we are wretched slaves,
    Who from their wonted loves and native land
Are reft, and bear o'er the dividing waves
The unregarded prey of calm and happy graves.

XXV

'"We drag afar from pastoral vales the fairest
    Among the daughters of those mountains lone,
We drag them there, where all things best and rarest
    Are stained and trampled:—years have come and
        gone
    Since, like the ship which bears me, I have known
No thought;—but now the eyes of one dear Maid
    On mine with light of mutual love have shone—
She is my life,—I am but as the shade   3422
Of her,—a smoke sent up from ashes, soon to fade.

XXVI

'"For she must perish in the Tyrant's hall—
    Alas, alas!"—He ceased, and by the sail
Sate cowering—but his sobs were heard by all,
    Ans still before the ocean and the gale
    The ship fled fast till the stars 'gan to fail,
And, round me gathered with mute countenance,
    The Seamen gazed, the Pilot, worn and pale 3430
With toil, the Captain with grey locks, whose glance
Met mine in restless awe—they stood as in a trance.

XXVII

'"Recede not! pause not now! Thou art grown old,
    But Hope will make thee young, for Hope and
        Youth
Are children of one mother, even Love—behold!
    The eternal stars gaze on us!—is the truth
    Within your soul? care for your own, or ruth
For others' sufferings? do ye thirst to bear
    A heart which not the serpent Custom's tooth
May violate?—Be free! and even here,   3440
Swear to be firm till death!" They cried "We swear!
    We swear!"

XXVIII

'The very darkness shook, as with a blast
    Of subterranean thunder, at the cry;
The hollow shore its thousand echoes cast
    Into the night, as if the sea, and sky,
    And earth, rejoiced with new-born liberty,
For in that name they swore! Bolts were undrawn,
    And on the deck, with unaccustomed eye
The captives gazing stood, and every one
Shrank as the inconstant torch upon her countenance
    shone.   3450

XXIX

'They were earth's purest children, young and fair,
    With eyes the shrines of unawakened thought,
And brows as bright as Spring or Morning, ere
    Dark time had there its evil legend wrought

In characters of cloud which wither not.—
    The change was like a dream to them; but soon
    They knew the glory of their altered lot,
In the bright wisdom of youth's breathless noon,
Sweet talk, and smiles, and sighs, all bosoms did
    attune.

XXX

'But one was mute, her cheeks and lips most fair,
    Changing their hue like lilies newly blown,   3461
Beneath a bright acacia's shadowy hair,
    Waved by the wind amid the sunny noon,
    Showed that her soul was quivering; and full
        soon
That Youth arose, and breathlessly did look
    On her and me, as for some speechless boon:
I smiled, and both their hands in mine I took,
And felt a soft delight from what their spirits shook.

[1817]   [1818]

A HATE-SONG

A HATER he came and sat by a ditch,
    And he took an old cracked lute;
And he sang a song which was more of a screech
    'Gainst a woman that was a brute.

[1817]   [1870]

LINES TO A CRITIC

I

HONEY from silk-worms who can gather,
    Or silk from the yellow bee?
The grass may grow in winter weather
    As soon as hate in me.

II

Hate men who cant, and men who pray,
    And men who rail like thee;
An equal passion to repay
    They are not coy like me.

III

Or seek some slave of power and gold,
    To be thy dear heart's mate;   10
Thy love will move that bigot cold
    Sooner than me, thy hate.

IV

A passion like the one I prove
Cannot divided be;
I hate thy want of truth and love—
How should I then hate thee?

[1817]   [1823]

[Sonnet]
OZYMANDIAS

I MET a traveller from an antique land
Who said: Two vast and trunkless legs of stone
Stand in the desert . . . Near them, on the sand,
Half sunk, a shattered visage lies, whose frown,
And wrinkled lip, and sneer of cold command,
Tell that its sculptor well those passions read
Which yet survive, stamped on these lifeless things,
The hand that mocked them, and the heart that fed:
And on the pedestal these words appear:
'My name is Ozymandias, king of kings: 10
Look on my works, ye Mighty, and despair!' [1]
Nothing beside remains. Round the decay
Of that colossal wreck, boundless and bare
The lone and level sands stretch far away.

[1817]   [1818]

---

[1] Ozymandias is a Greek name for the Egyptian king Rameses II. The historian Diodorus Siculas describes a funeral temple with inscribed lines much like these.

JULIAN AND MADDALO

A CONVERSATION

The meadows with fresh streams, the bees with thyme,
The goats with the green leaves of budding spring
Are saturated not—nor Love with tears.
                              VIRGIL'S *Gallus*.

———◦◦◦———

PREFACE

COUNT Maddalo [1] is a Venetian nobleman of ancient family and of great fortune, who, without mixing much in the society of his countrymen, resides chiefly at his magnificent palace in that city. He is a person of the most consummate genius, and capable, if he would direct his energies to such an end, of becoming the redeemer of his degraded country. But it is his weakness to be proud: he derives, from a comparison of his own extraordinary mind with the dwarfish intellects that surround him, an intense apprehension of the nothingness of human life. His passions and his powers are incomparably greater than those of other men; and, instead of the latter having been employed in curbing the former, they have mutually lent each other strength. His ambition preys upon itself, for want of objects which it can consider worthy of exertion. I say that Maddalo is proud, because I can find no other word to express the concentered and impatient feelings which consume him; but it is on his own hopes and affections only that he seems to trample, for in social life no human being can be more gentle, patient, and unassuming than Maddalo. He is cheerful, frank, and witty. His more serious conversation is a sort of intoxication; men are held by it as by a spell. He has travelled much; and there is an inexpressible charm in his relation of his adventures in different countries.

Julian is an Englishman of good family, passionately attached to those philosophical notions which assert the power of man over his own mind, and the immense improvements of which, by the extinction of certain moral superstitions, human society may be yet susceptible. Without concealing the evil in the world, he is for ever speculating how good may be made superior. He is a complete infidel, and a scoffer at all things reputed holy; and Maddalo takes a wicked pleasure in drawing out his taunts against religion. What Maddalo thinks on these matters is not exactly known. Julian, in spite of his heterodox opinions, is conjectured by his friends to possess some good

---

[1] Julian is intended to represent Shelley, Maddalo Byron.

qualities. How far this is possible the pious reader will determine. Julian is rather serious.

Of the Maniac I can give no information. He seems, by his own account, to have been disappointed in love. He was evidently a very cultivated and amiable person when in his right senses. His story, told at length, might be like many other stories of the same kind: the unconnected exclamations of his agony will perhaps be found a sufficient comment for the text of every heart.

───◦◦◎◦◦───

I RODE one evening with Count Maddalo
Upon the bank of land which breaks the flow
Of Adria towards Venice: a bare strand
Of hillocks, heaped from ever-shifting sand,
Matted with thistles and amphibious weeds,
Such as from earth's embrace the salt ooze breeds,
Is this; an uninhabited sea-side,
Which the lone fisher, when his nets are dried,
Abandons; and no other object breaks
The waste, but one dwarf tree and some few stakes   10
Broken and unrepaired, and the tide makes
A narrow space of level sand thereon,
Where 'twas our wont to ride while day went down.
This ride was my delight. I love all waste
And solitary places; where we taste
The pleasure of believing what we see
Is boundless, as we wish our souls to be:
And such was this wide ocean, and this shore
More barren than its billows; and yet more
Than all, with a remembered friend I love   20
To ride as then I rode;—for the winds drove
The living spray along the sunny air
Into our faces; the blue heavens were bare,
Stripped to their depths by the awakening north;
And, from the waves, sound like delight broke forth
Harmonising with solitude, and sent
Into our hearts aëreal merriment.
So, as we rode, we talked; and the swift thought,
Winging itself with laughter, lingered not,
But flew from brain to brain,—such glee was ours,   30
Charged with light memories of remembered hours,
None slow enough for sadness: till we came
Homeward, which always makes the spirit tame.
This day had been cheerful but cold, and now
The sun was sinking, and the wind also.
Our talk grew somewhat serious, as may be
Talk interrupted with such raillery
As mocks itself, because it cannot scorn
The thoughts it would extinguish:—'twas forlorn,
Yet pleasing, such as once, so poets tell,   40
The devils held within the dales of Hell

Concerning God, freewill and destiny:
Of all that earth has been or yet may be,
All that vain men imagine or believe,
Or hope can paint or suffering may achieve,
We descanted, and I (for ever still
Is it not wise to make the best of ill?)
Argued against despondency, but pride
Made my companion take the darker side.
The sense that he was greater than his kind   50
Had struck, methinks, his eagle spirit blind
By gazing on its own exceeding light.
Meanwhile the sun paused ere it should alight,
Over the horizon of the mountains;—Oh,
How beautiful is sunset, when the glow
Of Heaven descends upon a land like thee,
Thou Paradise of exiles, Italy!
Thy mountains, seas, and vineyards, and the towers
Of cities they encircle!—it was ours
To stand on thee, beholding it: and then,   60
Just where we had dismounted, the Count's men
Were waiting for us with the gondola.—
As those who pause on some delightful way
Though bent on pleasant pilgrimage, we stood
Looking upon the evening, and the flood
Which lay between the city and the shore,
Paved with the image of the sky . . . the hoar
And aëry Alps towards the North appeared
Through mist, an heaven-sustaining bulwark reared
Between the East and West; and half the sky   70
Was roofed with clouds of rich emblazonry
Dark purple at the zenith, which still grew
Down the steep West into a wondrous hue
Brighter than burning gold, even to the rent
Where the swift sun yet paused in his descent
Among the many-folded hills: they were
Those famous Euganean hills, which bear,
As seen from Lido thro' the harbour piles,
The likeness of a clump of peakèd isles—
And then—as if the Earth and Sea had been   80
Dissolved into one lake of fire, were seen
Those mountains towering as from waves of flame
Around the vaporous sun, from which there came
The inmost purple spirit of light, and made
Their very peaks transparent. 'Ere it fade,'
Said my companion, 'I will show you soon
A better station'—so, o'er the lagune
We glided; and from that funereal bark
I leaned, and saw the city, and could mark
How from their many isles, in evening's gleam,   90
Its temples and its palaces did seem
Like fabrics of enchantment piled to Heaven.
I was about to speak, when—'We are even
Now at the point I meant,' said Maddalo,
And bade the gondolieri cease to row.

'Look, Julian, on the west, and listen well
If you hear not a deep and heavy bell.'
I looked, and saw between us and the sun
A building on an island; such a one
As age to age might add, for uses vile,   100
A windowless, deformed and dreary pile;
And on the top an open tower, where hung
A bell, which in the radiance swayed and swung;
We could just hear its hoarse and iron tongue:
The broad sun sunk behind it, and it tolled
In strong and black relief.—'What we behold
Shall be the madhouse and its belfry tower,'
Said Maddalo, 'and ever at this hour
Those who may cross the water, hear that bell
Which calls the maniacs, each one from his cell,   110
To vespers.'—'As much skill as need to pray
In thanks or hope for their dark lot have they
To their stern maker,' I replied. 'O ho!
You talk as in years past,' said Maddalo.
''Tis strange men change not. You were ever still
Among Christ's flock a perilous infidel,
A wolf for the meek lambs—if you can't swim
Beware of Providence.' I looked on him,
But the gay smile had faded in his eye.
'And such,'—he cried, 'is our mortality,   120
And this must be the emblem and the sign
Of what should be eternal and divine!—
And like that black and dreary bell, the soul,
Hung in a heaven-illumined tower, must toll
Our thoughts and our desires to meet below
Round the rent heart and pray—as madmen do
For what? they know not,—till the night of death
As sunset that strange vision, severeth
Our memory from itself, and us from all
We sought and yet were baffled.' I recall   130
The sense of what he said, although I mar
The force of his expressions. The broad star
Of day meanwhile had sunk behind the hill,
And the black bell became invisible,
And the red tower looked gray, and all between
The churches, ships and palaces were seen
Huddled in gloom;—into the purple sea
The orange hues of heaven sunk silently.
We hardly spoke, and soon the gondola
Conveyed me to my lodging by the way.   140

    The following morn was rainy, cold and dim:
Ere Maddalo arose, I called on him,
And whilst I waited with his child I played;
A lovelier toy sweet Nature never made,
A serious, subtle, wild, yet gentle being,
Graceful without design and unforeseeing,
With eyes—Oh speak not of her eyes!—which seem
Twin mirrors of Italian Heaven, yet gleam

With such deep meaning, as we never see
But in the human countenance: with me   150
She was a special favourite: I had nursed
Her fine and feeble limbs when she came first
To this bleak world; and she yet seemed to know
On second sight her ancient playfellow,
Less changed than she was by six months or so;
For after her first shyness was worn out
We sate there, rolling billiard balls about,
When the Count entered. Salutations past—
'The word you spoke last night might well have cast
A darkness on my spirit—if I man be   161
The passive thing you say, I should not see
Much harm in the religions and old saws
(Tho' I may never own such leaden laws)
Which break a teachless nature to the yoke:
Mine is another faith'—thus much I spoke
And noting he replied not, added: 'See
This lovely child, blithe, innocent and free;
She spends a happy time with little care,
While we to such sick thoughts subjected are
As came on you last night—it is our will   170
That thus enchains us to permitted ill—
We might be otherwise—we might be all
We dream of happy, high, majestical.
Where is the love, beauty, and truth we seek
But in our mind? and if we were not weak
Should we be less in deed than in desire?'
'Ay, if we were not weak—and we aspire
How vainly to be strong!' said Maddalo:
'You talk Utopia.' 'It remains to know,'
I then rejoined, 'and those who try may find   180
How strong the chains are which our spirit bind;
Brittle perchance as straw . . . We are assured
Much may be conquered, much may be endured,
Of what degrades and crushes us. We know
That we have power over ourselves to do
And suffer—what, we know not till we try;
But something nobler than to live and die—
So taught those kings of old philosophy
Who reigned, before Religion made men blind;
And those who suffer with their suffering kind   190
Yet feel their faith, religion.'

                              'My dear friend,'
Said Maddalo, 'my judgement will not bend
To your opinion, though I think you might
Make such a system refutation-tight
As far as words go. I knew one like you
Who to this city came some months ago,
With whom I argued in this sort, and he
Is now gone mad,—and so he answered me,—
Poor fellow! but if you would like to go
We'll visit him, and his wild talk will show   200
How vain are such aspiring theories.'

'I hope to prove the induction otherwise,
And that a want of that true theory, still,
Which seeks a "soul of goodness" in things ill
Or in himself or others, has thus bowed
His being—there are some by nature proud,
Who patient in all else demand but this—
To love and be beloved with gentleness;
And being scorned, what wonder if they die
Some living death? this is not destiny   210
But man's own wilful ill.'

          As thus I spoke
Servants announced the gondola, and we
Through the fast-falling rain and high-wrought sea
Sailed to the island where the madhouse stands.
We disembarked. The clap of tortured hands,
Fierce yells and howlings and lamentings keen,
And laughter where complaint had merrier been,
Moans, shrieks, and curses, and blaspheming
    prayers
Accosted us. We climbed the oozy stairs
Into an old courtyard. I heard on high,   220
Then, fragments of most touching melody,
But looking up saw not the singer there—
Through the black bars in the tempestuous air
I saw, like weeds on a wrecked palace growing,
Long tangled locks flung wildly forth, and flowing,
Of those who on a sudden were beguiled
Into strange silence, and looked forth and smiled
Hearing sweet sounds.—Then I: 'Methinks there
    were
A cure of these with patience and kind care,
If music can thus move . . . but what is he   230
Whom we seek here?' 'Of his sad history
I know but this,' said Maddalo: 'he came
To Venice a dejected man, and fame
Said he was wealthy, or he had been so;
Some thought the loss of fortune wrought him woe;
But he was ever talking in such sort
As you do—far more sadly—he seemed hurt,
Even as a man with his peculiar wrong,
To hear but of the oppression of the strong,
Or those absurd deceits (I think with you   240
In some respects, you know) which carry through
The excellent impostors of this earth
When they outface detection—he had worth,
Poor fellow! but a humourist in his way'—
'Alas, what drove him mad?' 'I cannot say:
A lady came with him from France, and when
She left him and returned, he wandered then
About yon lonely isles of desert sand
Till he grew wild—he had no cash or land
Remaining,—the police had brought him here—   250
Some fancy took him and he would not bear

Removal; so I fitted up for him
Those rooms beside the sea, to please his whim,
And sent him busts and books and urns for flowers,
Which had adorned his life in happier hours,
And instruments of music—you may guess
A stranger could do little more or less
For one so gentle and unfortunate:
And those are his sweet strains which charm the
    weight
From madmen's chains, and make this Hell appear
A heaven of sacred silence, hushed to hear.'—   261
'Nay, this was kind of you—he had no claim,
As the world says'—'None—but the very same
Which I on all mankind were I as he
Fallen to such deep reverse;—his melody
Is interrupted—now we hear the din
Of madmen, shriek on shriek, again begin;
Let us now visit him; after this strain
He ever communes with himself again,
And sees nor hears not any.' Having said   270
These words we called the keeper, and he led
To an apartment opening on the sea—
There the poor wretch was sitting mournfully
Near a piano, his pale fingers twined
One with the other, and the ooze and wind
Rushed through an open casement, and did sway
His hair, and starred it with the brackish spray;
His head was leaning on a music book,
And he was muttering, and his lean limbs shook;
His lips were pressed against a folded leaf   280
In hue too beautiful for health, and grief
Smiled in their motions as they lay apart—
As one who wrought from his own fervid heart
The eloquence of passion, soon he raised
His sad meek face and eyes lustrous and glazed
And spoke—sometimes as one who wrote, and thought
His words might move some heart that heeded not,
If sent to distant lands: and then as one
Reproaching deeds never to be undone
With wondering self-compassion; then his speech
Was lost in grief, and then his words came each   291
Unmodulated, cold, expressionless,—
But that from one jarred accent you might guess
It was despair made them so uniform:
And all the while the loud and gusty storm
Hissed through the window, and we stood behind
Stealing his accents from the envious wind
Unseen. I yet remember what he said
Distinctly: such impression his words made.

    'Month after month,' he cried, 'to bear this load
And as a jade urged by the whip and goad   301
To drag life on, which like a heavy chain
Lengthens behind with many a link of pain!—

And not to speak my grief—O, not to dare
To give a human voice to my despair,
But live and move, and, wretched thing! smile on
As if I never went aside to groan,
And wear this mask of falsehood even to those
Who are most dear—not for my own repose—
Alas! no scorn or pain or hate could be   310
So heavy as that falsehood is to me—
But that I cannot bear more altered faces
Than needs must be, more changed and cold
 embraces,
More misery, disappointment, and mistrust
To own me for their father . . . Would the dust
Were covered in upon my body now!
That the life ceased to toil within my brow!
And then these thoughts would at the least be
 fled;
Let us not fear such pain can vex the dead.

'What Power delights to torture us? I know   320
That to myself I do not wholly owe
What now I suffer, though in part I may.
Alas! none strewed sweet flowers upon the way
Where wandering heedlessly, I met pale Pain
My shadow, which will leave me not again—
If I have erred, there was no joy in error,
But pain and insult and unrest and terror;
I have not as some do, bought penitence
With pleasure, and a dark yet sweet offence,
For then,—if love and tenderness and truth   330
Had overlived hope's momentary youth,
My creed should have redeemed me from repenting;
But loathèd scorn and outrage unrelenting
Met love excited by far other seeming
Until the end was gained . . . as one from dreaming
Of sweetest peace, I woke, and found my state
Such as it is.——

   'O Thou, my spirit's mate
Who, for thou art compassionate and wise,
Wouldst pity me from thy most gentle eyes
If this sad writing thou shouldst ever see—   340
My secret groans must be unheard by thee,
Thou wouldst weep tears bitter as blood to know
Thy lost friend's incommunicable woe.

'Ye few by whom my nature has been weighed
In friendship, let me not that name degrade
By placing on your hearts the secret load
Which crushes mine to dust. There is one road
To peace and that is truth, which follow ye!
Love sometimes leads astray to misery.
Yet think not though subdued—and I may well   350
Say that I am subdued—that the full Hell

Within me would infect the untainted breast
Of sacred nature with its own unrest;
As some perverted beings think to find
In scorn or hate a medicine for the mind
Which scorn or hate have wounded—O how vain!
The dagger heals not but may rend again . . .
Believe that I am ever still the same
In creed as in resolve, and what may tame
My heart, must leave the understanding free,   360
Or all would sink in this keen agony—
Nor dream that I will join the vulgar cry;
Or with my silence sanction tyranny;
Or seek a moment's shelter from my pain
In any madness which the world calls gain,
Ambition or revenge or thoughts as stern
As those which make me what I am; or turn
To avarice or misanthropy or lust . . .
Heap on me soon, O grave, thy welcome dust!
Till then the dungeon may demand its prey,   370
And Poverty and Shame may meet and say—
Halting beside me on the public way—
"That love-devoted youth is ours—let's sit
Beside him—he may live some six months yet."
Or the red scaffold, as our country bends,
May ask some willing victim, or ye friends
May fall under some sorrow which this heart
Or hand may share or vanquish or avert;
I am prepared—in truth with no proud joy—
To do or suffer aught, as when a boy   380
I did devote to justice and to love
My nature, worthless now! . . .

    'I must remove
A veil from my pent mind. 'Tis torn aside!
O, pallid as Death's dedicated bride,
Thou mockery which art sitting by my side,
Am I not wan like thee? at the grave's call
I haste, invited to thy wedding-ball
To greet the ghastly paramour, for whom
Thou hast deserted me . . . and made the tomb
Thy bridal bed . . . But I beside your feet   390
Will lie and watch ye from my winding sheet—
Thus . . . wide awake tho' dead . . . yet stay, O stay!
Go not so soon—I know not what I say—
Hear but my reasons . . . I am mad, I fear,
My fancy is o'erwrought . . . thou art not here . . .
Pale art thou, 'tis most true . . . but thou art gone,
Thy work is finished . . . I am left alone!—

. . . .

'Nay, was it I who wooed thee to this breast
Which, like a serpent, thou envenomest
As in repayment of the warmth it lent?   400
Didst thou not seek me for thine own content?

Did not thy love awaken mine? I thought
That thou wert she who said, "You kiss me not
Ever, I fear you do not love me now"—
In truth I loved even to my overthrow
Her, who would fain forget these words: but they
Cling to her mind, and cannot pass away.

.   .   .   .   .   .

'You say that I am proud—that when I speak
My lip is tortured with the wrongs which break
The spirit it expresses . . . Never one   410
Humbled himself before, as I have done!
Even the instinctive worm on which we tread
Turns, though it wound not—then with prostrate
     head
Sinks in the dust and writhes like me—and dies?
No: wears a living death of agonies!
As the slow shadows of the pointed grass
Mark the eternal periods, his pangs pass
Slow, ever-moving,—making moments be
As mine seem—each an immortality!

.   .   .   .   .   .

'That you had never seen me—never heard   420
My voice, and more than all had ne'er endured
The deep pollution of my loathed embrace—
That your eyes ne'er had lied love in my face—
That, like some maniac monk, I had torn out
The nerves of manhood by their bleeding root
With mine own quivering fingers, so that ne'er
Our hearts had for a moment mingled there
To disunite in horror—these were not
With thee, like some suppressed and hideous
     thought
Which flits athwart our musings, but can find   430
No rest within a pure and gentle mind . . .
Thou sealedst them with many a bare broad word,
And searedst my memory o'er them,—for I heard
And can forget not . . . they were ministered
One after one, those curses. Mix them up
Like self-destroying poisons in one cup,
And they will make one blessing which thou ne'er
Didst imprecate for, on me,——death.

.   .   .   .   .   .

                      'It were
A cruel punishment for one most cruel,
If such can love, to make that love the fuel   440
Of the mind's hell; hate, scorn, remorse, despair:
But *me*—whose heart a stranger's tear might wear
As water-drops the sandy fountain-stone,
Who loved and pitied all things, and could moan
For woes which others hear not, and could see
The absent with the glance of phantasy,

And with the poor and trampled sit and weep,
Following the captive to his dungeon deep;
Me—who am as a nerve o'er which do creep
The else unfelt oppressions of this earth,   450
And was to thee the flame upon thy hearth,
When all beside was cold—that thou on me
Shouldst rain these plagues of blistering agony—
Such curses are from lips once eloquent
With love's too partial praise—let none relent
Who intend deeds too dreadful for a name
Henceforth, if an example for the same
They seek . . . for thou on me lookedst so, and so—
And didst speak thus . . . and thus . . . I live to show
How much men bear and die not!

.   .   .   .   .   .

                   'Thou wilt tell, 460
With the grimace of hate, how horrible
It was to meet my love when thine grew less;
Thou wilt admire how I could e'er address
Such features to love's work . . . this taunt, though
     true,
(For indeed Nature nor in form nor hue
Bestowed on me her choicest workmanship)
Shall not be thy defence . . . for since thy lip
Met mine first, years long past, since thine eye kindled
With soft fire under mine, I have not dwindled
Nor changed in mind or body, or in aught   470
But as love changes what it loveth not
After long years and many trials.

                           'How vain
Are words! I thought never to speak again,
Not even in secret,—not to my own heart—
But from my lips the unwilling accents start,
And from my pen the words flow as I write,
Dazzling my eyes with scalding tears . . . my sight
Is dim to see that charactered in vain
On this unfeeling leaf which burns the brain
And eats into it . . . blotting all things fair   480
And wise and good which time had written there.

'Those who inflict must suffer, for they see
The work of their own hearts, and this must be
Our chastisement or recompense—O child!
I would that thine were like to be more mild
For both our wretched sakes . . . for thine the most
Who feelest already all that thou hast lost
Without the power to wish it thine again;
And as slow years pass, a funereal train
Each with the ghost of some lost hope or friend   490
Following it like its shadow, wilt thou bend
No thought on my dead memory?

.   .   .   .   .   .

'Alas, love!
Fear me not . . . against thee I would not move
A finger in despite. Do I not live
That thou mayst have less bitter cause to grieve?
I give thee tears for scorn and love for hate;
And that thy lot may be less desolate
Than his on whom thou tramplest, I refrain
From that sweet sleep which medicines all pain.
Then, when thou speakest of me, never say   500
"He could forgive not." Here I cast away
All human passions, all revenge, all pride;
I think, speak, act no ill; I do but hide
Under these words, like embers, every spark
Of that which has consumed me—quick and dark
The grave is yawning . . . as its roof shall cover
My limbs with dust and worms under and over
So let Oblivion hide this grief . . . the air
Closes upon my accents, as despair
Upon my heart—let death upon despair!'   510

He ceased, and overcome leant back awhile,
Then rising, with a melancholy smile
Went to a sofa, and lay down, and slept
A heavy sleep, and in his dreams he wept
And muttered some familiar name, and we
Wept without shame in his society.
I think I never was impressed so much;
The man who were not, must have lacked a touch
Of human nature . . . then we lingered not,
Although our argument was quite forgot,   520
But calling the attendants, went to dine
At Maddalo's; yet neither cheer nor wine
Could give us spirits, for we talked of him
And nothing else, till daylight made stars dim;
And we agreed his was some dreadful ill
Wrought on him boldly, yet unspeakable,
By a dear friend; some deadly change in love
Of one vowed deeply which he dreamed not of;
For whose sake he, it seemed, had fixed a blot
Of falsehood on his mind which flourished not   530
But in the light of all-beholding truth;
And having stamped this canker on his youth
She had abandoned him—and how much more
Might be his woe, we guessed not—he had store
Of friends and fortune once, as we could guess
From his nice habits and his gentleness;
These were now lost . . . it were a grief indeed
If he had changed one unsustaining reed
For all that such a man might else adorn.
The colours of his mind seemed yet unworn;   540
For the wild language of his grief was high,
Such as in measure were called poetry;
And I remember one remark which then
Maddalo made. He said: 'Most wretched men

Are cradled into poetry by wrong,
They learn in suffering what they teach in song.'

If I had been an unconnected man
I, from this moment, should have formed some plan
Never to leave sweet Venice,—for to me
It was delight to ride by the lone sea;   550
And then, the town is silent—one may write
Or read in gondolas by day or night,
Having the little brazen lamp alight,
Unseen, uninterrupted; books are there,
Pictures, and casts from all those statues fair
Which were twin-born with poetry, and all
We seek in towns, with little to recall
Regrets for the green country. I might sit
In Maddalo's great palace, and his wit
And subtle talk would cheer the winter night   560
And make me know myself, and the firelight
Would flash upon our faces, till the day
Might dawn and make me wonder at my stay:
But I had friends in London too: the chief
Attraction here, was that I sought relief
From the deep tenderness that maniac wrought
Within me—'twas perhaps an idle thought—
But I imagined that if day by day
I watched him, and but seldom went away,
And studied all the beatings of his heart   570
With zeal, as men study some stubborn art
For their own good, and could by patience find
An entrance to the caverns of his mind,
I might reclaim him from his dark estate:
In friendships I had been most fortunate—
Yet never saw I one whom I would call
More willingly my friend; and this was all
Accomplished not; such dreams of baseless good
Oft come and go in crowds or solitude
And leave no trace—but what I now designed   580
Made for long years impression on my mind.
The following morning, urged by my affairs,
I left bright Venice.

After many years
And many changes I returned; the name
Of Venice, and its aspect, was the same;
But Maddalo was travelling far away
Among the mountains of Armenia.
His dog was dead. His child had now become
A woman; such as it has been my doom
To meet with few,—a wonder of this earth,   590
Where there is little of transcendent worth,—
Like one of Shakespeare's women: kindly she,
And, with a manner beyond courtesy,
Received her father's friend; and when I asked
Of the lorn maniac, she her memory tasked,

And told as she had heard the mournful tale:
'That the poor sufferer's health began to fail
Two years from my departure, but that then
The lady who had left him, came again.
Her mien had been imperious, but she now   600
Looked meek—perhaps remorse had brought her low.
Her coming made him better, and they stayed
Together at my father's—for I played,
As I remember, with the lady's shawl—
I might be six years old—but after all
She left him' . . . 'Why, her heart must have been
          tough:
How did it end?' 'And was not this enough?
They met—they parted'—'Child, is there no more?'

'Something within that interval which bore
The stamp of *why* they parted, *how* they met: 610
Yet if thine agèd eyes disdain to wet
Those wrinkled cheeks with youth's remembered
          tears,
Ask me no more, but let the silent years
Be closed and cered over their memory
As yon mute marble where their corpses lie.'
I urged and questioned still, she told me how
All happened—but the cold world shall not know.

[1818]   [1824]

LINES WRITTEN AMONG THE
EUGANEAN HILLS

OCTOBER, 1818.

MANY a green isle needs must be
In the deep wide sea of Misery,
Or the mariner, worn and wan,
Never thus could voyage on—
Day and night, and night and day,
Drifting on his dreary way,
With the solid darkness black
Closing round his vessel's track;
Whilst above the sunless sky,
Big with clouds, hangs heavily,   10
And behind the tempest fleet
Hurries on with lightning feet,
Riving sail, and cord, and plank,
Till the ship has almost drank
Death from the o'er-brimming deep;
And sinks down, down, like that sleep
When the dreamer seems to be
Weltering through eternity;
And the dim low line before
Of a dark and distant shore   20

Still recedes, as ever still
Longing with divided will,
But no power to seek or shun,
He is ever drifted on
O'er the unreposing wave
To the haven of the grave.
What, if there no friends will greet;
What, if there no heart will meet
His with love's impatient beat;
Wander wheresoe'er he may,   30
Can he dream before that day
To find refuge from distress
In friendship's smile, in love's caress?
Then 'twill wreak him little woe
Whether such there be or no:
Senseless is the breast, and cold,
Which relenting love would fold;
Bloodless are the veins and chill
Which the pulse of pain did fill;
Every little living nerve   40
That from bitter words did swerve
Round the tortured lips and brow,
Are like sapless leaflets now
Frozen upon December's bough.

On the beach of a northern sea
Which tempests shake eternally,
As once the wretch there lay to sleep,
Lies a solitary heap,
One white skull and seven dry bones,
On the margin of the stones,   50
Where a few gray rushes stand,
Boundaries of the sea and land:
Nor is heard one voice of wail
But the sea-mews, as they sail
O'er the billows of the gale;
Or the whirlwind up and down
Howling, like a slaughtered town,
When a king in glory rides
Through the pomp of fratricides:
Those unburied bones around   60
There is many a mournful sound;
There is no lament for him,
Like a sunless vapour, dim,
Who once clothed with life and thought
What now moves nor murmurs not.

Ay, many flowering islands lie
In the waters of wide Agony:
To such a one this morn was led,
My bark by soft winds piloted:
'Mid the mountains Euganean   70
I stood listening to the paean

With which the legioned rooks did hail
The sun's uprise majestical;
Gathering round with wings all hoar,
Through the dewy mist they soar
Like gray shades, till the eastern heaven
Bursts, and then, as clouds of even,
Flecked with fire and azure, lie
In the unfathomable sky,
So their plumes of purple grain,   80
Starred with drops of golden rain,
Gleam above the sunlight woods,
As in silent multitudes
On the morning's fitful gale
Through the broken mist they sail,
And the vapours cloven and gleaming
Follow, down the dark steep streaming,
Till all is bright, and clear, and still,
Round the solitary hill.

Beneath is spread like a green sea   90
The waveless plain of Lombardy,
Bounded by the vaporous air,
Islanded by cities fair;
Underneath Day's azure eyes
Ocean's nursling, Venice lies,
A peopled labyrinth of walls,
Amphitrite's [1] destined halls,
Which her hoary sire now paves
With his blue and beaming waves.
Lo! the sun upsprings behind,   100
Broad, red, radiant, half-reclined
On the level quivering line
Of the waters crystalline;
And before that chasm of light,
As within a furnace bright,
Column, tower, and dome, and spire,
Shine like obelisks of fire,
Pointing with inconstant motion
From the altar of dark ocean
To the sapphire-tinted skies;   110
As the flames of sacrifice
From the marble shrines did rise,
As to pierce the dome of gold
Where Apollo spoke of old. [2]

Sun-girt City, thou hast been
Ocean's child, and then his queen;
Now is come a darker day, [3]
And thou soon must be his prey,

If the power that raised thee here
Hallow so thy watery bier.   120
A less drear ruin then than now,
With thy conquest-branded brow
Stooping to the slave of slaves
From thy throne, among the waves
Wilt thou be, when the sea-mew
Flies, as once before it flew,
O'er thine isles depopulate,
And all is in its ancient state,
Save where many a palace gate
With green sea-flowers overgrown   130
Like a rock of Ocean's own,
Topples o'er the abandoned sea
As the tides change sullenly.
The fisher on his watery way,
Wandering at the close of day,
Will spread his sail and seize his oar
Till he pass the gloomy shore,
Lest thy dead should, from their sleep
Bursting o'er the starlight deep,
Lead a rapid masque of death   140
O'er the waters of his path.

Those who alone thy towers behold
Quivering through aëreal gold,
As I now behold them here,
Would imagine not they were
Sepulchres, where human forms,
Like pollution-nourished worms,
To the corpse of greatness cling,
Murdered, and now mouldering:
But if Freedom should awake   150
In her omnipotence, and shake
From the Celtic Anarch's [4] hold
All the keys of dungeons cold,
Where a hundred cities lie
Chained like thee, ingloriously,
Thou and all thy sister band
Might adorn this sunny land,
Twining memories of old time
With new virtues more sublime;
If not, perish thou and they!—   160
Clouds which stain truth's rising day
By her sun consumed away—
Earth can spare ye: while like flowers,
In the waste of years and hours,
From your dust new nations spring
With more kindly blossoming.

Perish—let there only be
Floating o'er thy hearthless sea

---

[1] Wife of Neptune.
[2] The oracle at Delphi.
[3] Venice was under Austrian rule.

---

[4] The Austrian emperor's.

As the garment of thy sky
Clothes the world immortally,   170
One remembrance, more sublime
Than the tattered pall of time,
Which scarce hides thy visage wan;—
That a tempest-cleaving Swan 5
Of the songs of Albion,
Driven from his ancestral streams
By the might of evil dreams,
Found a nest in thee; and Ocean
Welcomed him with such emotion
That its joy grew his, and sprung   180
From his lips like music flung
O'er a mighty thunder-fit,
Chastening terror:—what though yet
Poesy's unfailing River,
Which through Albion winds forever
Lashing with melodious wave
Many a sacred Poet's grave,
Mourn its latest nursling fled?
What though thou with all thy dead
Scarce can for this fame repay   190
Aught thine own? oh, rather say
Though thy sins and slaveries foul
Overcloud a sunlike soul?
As the ghost of Homer clings
Round Scamander's wasting springs;
As divinest Shakespeare's might
Fills Avon and the world with light
Like omniscient power which he
Imaged 'mid mortality;
As the love from Petrarch's urn,   200
Yet amid yon hills doth burn,
A quenchless lamp by which the heart
Sees things unearthly;—so thou art,
Mighty spirit—so shall be
The City that did refuge thee.

Lo, the sun floats up the sky
Like thought-wingèd Liberty,
Till the universal light
Seems to level plain and height;
From the sea a mist has spread,   210
And the beams of morn lie dead
On the towers of Venice now,
Like its glory long ago.
By the skirts of that gray cloud
Many-domèd Padua proud
Stands, a peopled solitude,
'Mid the harvest-shining plain,
Where the peasant heaps his grain

In the garner of his foe,
And the milk-white oxen slow   220
With the purple vintage strain,
Heaped upon the creaking wain,
That the brutal Celt may swill
Drunken sleep with savage will;
And the sickle to the sword
Lies unchanged, though many a lord,
Like a weed whose shade is poison,
Overgrows this region's foison,
Sheaves of whom are ripe to come
To destruction's harvest-home: 230
Men must reap the things they sow,
Force from force must ever flow,
Or worse; but 'tis a bitter woe
That love or reason cannot change
The despot's rage, the slave's revenge.

Padua, thou within whose walls
Those mute guests at festivals,
Son and Mother, Death and Sin,
Played at dice for Ezzelin,
Till Death cried, 'I win, I win!' 6   240
And Sin cursed to lose the wager,
But Death promised, to assuage her,
That he would petition for
Her to be made Vice-Emperor,
When the destined years were o'er,
Over all between the Po
And the eastern Alpine snow,
Under the mighty Austrian.
Sin smiled so as Sin only can,
And since that time, ay, long before,   250
Both have ruled from shore to shore,—
That incestuous pair, who follow
Tyrants as the sun the swallow,
As Repentance follows Crime,
And as changes follow Time.

In thine halls the lamp of learning,7
Padua, now no more is burning;
Like a meteor, whose wild way
Is lost over the grave of day,
It gleams betrayed and to betray: 260
Once remotest nations came
To adore that sacred flame,
When it lit not many a hearth
On this cold and gloomy earth:
Now new fires from antique light
Spring beneath the wide world's might;

---

5 The rest of this section—through line 205—is about Byron.

6 See Coleridge's *Ancient Mariner*, ll. 195–98; Ezzelin III of Padua (1194–1259), a sadistic ruler and a suicide.

7 The University of Padua, famous in the Middle Ages.

But their spark lies dead in thee,
Trampled out by Tyranny.
As the Norway woodman quells,
In the depth of piny dells,   270
One light flame among the brakes,
While the boundless forest shakes,
And its mighty trunks are torn
By the fire thus lowly born:
The spark beneath his feet is dead,
He starts to see the flames it fed
Howling through the darkened sky
With a myriad tongues victoriously,
And sinks down in fear: so thou,
O Tyranny, beholdest now   280
Light around thee, and thou hearest
The loud flames ascend, and fearest:
Grovel on the earth; ay, hide
In the dust thy purple pride!
Noon descends around me now:
'Tis the noon of autumn's glow,
When a soft and purple mist
Like a vaporous amethyst,
Or an air-dissolvèd star
Mingling light and fragrance, far   290
From the curved horizon's bound
To the point of Heaven's profound,
Fills the overflowing sky;
And the plains that silent lie
Underneath, the leaves unsodden
Where the infant Frost has trodden
With his morning-wingèd feet,
Whose bright print is gleaming yet;
And the red and golden vines,
Piercing with their trellised lines   300
The rough, dark-skirted wilderness;
The dun and bladed grass no less,
Pointing from this hoary tower
In the windless air; the flower
Glimmering at my feet; the line
Of the olive-sandalled Apennine
In the south dimly islanded;
And the Alps, whose snows are spread
High between the clouds and sun;
And of living things each one;   310
And my spirit which so long
Darkened this swift stream of song,—
Interpenetrated lie
By the glory of the sky:
Be it love, light, harmony,
Odour, or the soul of all
Which from Heaven like dew doth fall,
Or the mind which feeds this verse
Peopling the lone universe.

Noon descends, and after noon   320
Autumn's evening meets me soon,
Leading the infantine moon,
And that one star, which to her
Almost seems to minister
Half the crimson light she brings
From the sunset's radiant springs:
And the soft dreams of the morn
(Which like wingèd winds had borne
To that silent isle, which lies
Mid remembered agonies,   330
The frail bark of this lone being) [8]
Pass, to other sufferers fleeing,
And its ancient pilot, Pain,
Sits beside the helm again.

Other flowering isles must be
In the sea of Life and Agony:
Other spirits float and flee
O'er that gulf: even now, perhaps,
On some rock the wild wave wraps,
With folded wings they waiting sit   340
For my bark, to pilot it
To some calm and blooming cove,
Where for me, and those I love,
May a windless bower be built,
Far from passion, pain, and guilt,
In a dell mid lawny hills,
Which the wild sea-murmur fills,
And soft sunshine, and the sound
Of old forests echoing round,
And the light and smell divine   350
Of all flowers that breathe and shine:
We may live so happy there,
That the Spirits of the Air,
Envying us, may even entice
To our healing Paradise
The polluting multitude;
But their rage would be subdued
By that clime divine and calm,
And the winds whose wings rain balm
On the uplifted soul, and leaves   360
Under which the bright sea heaves;
While each breathless interval
In their whisperings musical
The inspired soul supplies
With its own deep melodies,
And the love which heals all strife
Circling, like the breath of life,
All things in that sweet abode
With its own mild brotherhood:

[8] I.e., the poet.

They, not it, would change; and soon   370
Every sprite beneath the moon
Would repent its envy vain,
And the earth grow young again.

[1818]   [1819]

STANZAS,

WRITTEN IN DEJECTION, NEAR NAPLES

I

THE sun is warm, the sky is clear,
    The waves are dancing fast and bright,
Blue isles and snowy mountains wear
    The purple noon's transparent might,
    The breath of the moist air is light,
Around its unexpanded buds;
    Like many a voice of one delight,
    The winds, the birds, the ocean floods,
The City's voice itself, is soft like Solitude's.

II

I see the Deep's untrampled floor   10
    With green and purple sea-weeds strown;
I see the waves upon the shore,
    Like light dissolved in star-showers, thrown:
    I sit upon the sands alone,—
The lightning of the noon-tide ocean
    Is flashing round me, and a tone
    Arises from its measured motion,
How sweet! did any heart now share in my emotion.

III

Alas! I have nor hope nor health,
    Nor peace within nor calm around,   20
Nor that content surpassing wealth
    The sage in meditation found,
    And walked with inward glory crowned—
Nor fame, nor power, nor love, nor leisure.
    Others I see whom these surround—
    Smiling they live, and call life pleasure;—
To me that cup has been dealt in another measure.

IV

Yet now despair itself is mild,
    Even as the winds and waters are;
I could lie down like a tired child,   30
    And weep away the life of care
    Which I have borne, and yet must bear,
Till death like sleep might steal on me,
    And I might feel in the warm air
    My cheek grow cold, and hear the sea
Breathe o'er my dying brain its last monotony.

V

Some might lament that I were cold,
    As I, when this sweet day is gone,
Which my lost heart, too soon grown old,
    Insults with this untimely moan;   40
    They might lament—for I am one
Whom men love not,—and yet regret,
    Unlike this day, which, when the sun
    Shall on its stainless glory set,
Will linger, though enjoyed, like joy in memory yet.

[1818]   [1824]

FRAGMENT: TO BYRON

O MIGHTY mind, in whose deep stream this age
Shakes like a reed in the unheeding storm,
Why doest thou curb not thine own sacred rage?

[1818]   [1862]

SONNET
["Lift not the painted veil . . ."]

LIFT not the painted veil which those who live
Call Life: though unreal shapes be pictured there,
And it but mimic all we would believe
With colours idly spread,—behind, lurk Fear
And Hope, twin Destinies; who ever weave
Their shadows, o'er the chasm, sightless and drear.
I knew one who had lifted it—he sought,
For his lost heart was tender, things to love,
But found them not, alas! nor was there aught
The world contains, the which he could approve.   10
Through the unheeding many he did move,
A splendour among shadows, a bright blot
Upon this gloomy scene, a Spirit that strove
For truth, and like the Preacher found it not.

[1818]   [1824]

===

THE CENCI

Unlike Byron's Manfred, The Cenci *was written deliberately for stage presentation. But the play's concern with incest apparently caused its rejection by theaters, and it was never performed until 1886 (then privately, by the Shelley Society).*

===

THE CENCI.

A TRAGEDY,

IN FIVE ACTS.

❦

DEDICATION

TO

LEIGH HUNT, ESQ.

MY DEAR FRIEND,

I inscribe with your name, from a distant country, and after an absence whose months have seemed years, this the latest of my literary efforts.

Those writings which I have hitherto published, have been little else than visions which impersonate my own apprehensions of the beautiful and the just. I can also perceive in them the literary defects incidental to youth and impatience; they are dreams of what ought to be, or may be. The drama which I now present to you is a sad reality. I lay aside the presumptuous attitude of an instructor, and am content to paint, with such colours as my own heart furnishes, that which has been.

Had I known a person more highly endowed than yourself with all that it becomes a man to possess, I had solicited for this work the ornament of his name. One more gentle, honourable, innocent and brave; one of more exalted toleration for all who do and think evil, and yet himself more free from evil; one who knows better how to receive, and how to confer a benefit, though he must ever confer far more than he can receive; one of simpler, and, in the highest sense of the word, of purer life and manners, I never knew: and I had already been fortunate in friendships when your name was added to the list.

In that patient and irreconcilable enmity with domestic and political tyranny and imposture, which the tenor of your life has illustrated, and which, had I health and talents, should illustrate mine, let us, comforting each other in our task, live and die.

All happiness attend you!

Your affectionate friend,
PERCY B. SHELLEY.

ROME,
May 29, 1819.

❦

PREFACE

A MANUSCRIPT was communicated to me during my travels in Italy, which was copied from the archives of the Cenci Palace at Rome, and contains a detailed account of the horrors which ended in the extinction of one of the noblest and richest families of that city, during the pontificate of Clement VIII., in the year 1599. The story is, that an old man, having spent his life in debauchery and wickedness, conceived at length an implacable hatred towards his children; which showed itself towards one daughter under the form of an incestuous passion, aggravated by every circumstance of cruelty and violence. This daughter, after long and vain attempts to escape from what she considered a perpetual contamination both of body and mind, at length plotted with her mother-in-law [1] and brother to murder their common tyrant. The young maiden, who was urged to this tremendous deed by an impulse which overpowered its horror, was evidently a most gentle and amiable being, a creature formed to adorn and be admired, and thus violently thwarted from her nature by the necessity of circumstance and opinion. The deed was quickly discovered, and in spite of the most earnest prayers made to the Pope by the highest persons in Rome, the criminals were put to death. The old man had, during his life, repeatedly bought his pardon from the Pope for capital crimes of the most enormous and unspeakable kind, at the price of a hundred thousand crowns; the death therefore of his victims can scarcely be accounted for by the love of justice. The Pope, among other motives for severity, probably felt that whoever killed the Count Cenci deprived his treasury of a certain and copious source of revenue.* Such a story, if told so as to present to the reader all the feelings of those who once acted it, their hopes and fears, their confidences and misgivings, their various interests, passions, and opinions, acting upon and with each other, yet all conspiring to one tremendous end, would be as a light to make apparent some of the most dark and secret caverns of the human heart.

On my arrival at Rome, I found that the story of the Cenci was a subject not to be mentioned in Italian society without awakening a deep and breathless interest; and that the feelings of the company never failed to incline to a romantic pity for the wrongs, and a passionate exculpation of the horrible deed to which

---

* The Papal Government formerly took the most extraordinary precautions against the publicity of facts which offer so tragical a demonstration of its own wickedness and weakness; so that the communication of the MS. had become, until very lately, a matter of some difficulty.

[1] Stepmother—Shelley's error.

they urged her, who has been mingled two centuries with the common dust. All ranks of people knew the outlines of this history, and participated in the overwhelming interest which it seems to have the magic of exciting in the human heart. I had a copy of Guido's picture of Beatrice, which is preserved in the Colonna Palace, and my servant instantly recognized it as the portrait of *La Cenci*.

This national and universal interest which the story produces and has produced for two centuries, and among all ranks of people in a great City, where the imagination is kept for ever active and awake, first suggested to me the conception of its fitness for a dramatic purpose. In fact it is a tragedy which has already received, from its capacity of awakening and sustaining the sympathy of men, approbation and success. Nothing remained, as I imagined, but to clothe it to the apprehensions of my countrymen in such language and action as would bring it home to their hearts. The deepest and the sublimest tragic compositions, King Lear, and the two plays in which the tale of Ædipus is told, were stories which already existed in tradition, as matters of popular belief and interest, before Shakespeare and Sophocles made them familiar to the sympathy of all succeeding generations of mankind.

This story of the Cenci is indeed eminently fearful and monstrous: anything like a dry exhibition of it on the stage would be insupportable. The person who would treat such a subject must increase the ideal, and diminish the actual horror of the events, so that the pleasure which arises from the poetry which exists in these tempestuous sufferings and crimes, may mitigate the pain of the contemplation of the moral deformity from which they spring. There must also be nothing attempted to make the exhibition subservient to what is vulgarly termed a moral purpose. The highest moral purpose aimed at in the highest species of the drama, is the teaching the human heart, through its sympathies and antipathies, the knowledge of itself; in proportion to the possession of which knowledge, every human being is wise, just, sincere, tolerant, and kind. If dogmas can do more, it is well: but a drama is no fit place for the enforcement of them. Undoubtedly no person can be truly dishonoured by the act of another; and the fit return to make to the most enormous injuries is kindness and forbearance, and a resolution to convert the injurer from his dark passions by peace and love. Revenge, retaliation, atonement, are pernicious mistakes. If Beatrice had thought in this manner she would have been wiser and better; but she would never have been a tragic character: the few whom such an exhibition would have interested, could never have been sufficiently interested for a dramatic purpose, from the want of finding sympathy in their interest among the mass who surround them. It is in the restless and anatomising casuistry with which men seek the justification of Beatrice, yet feel that she has done what needs justification; it is in the superstitious horror with which they contemplate alike her wrongs and their revenge, that the dramatic character of what she did and suffered, consists.

I have endeavoured as nearly as possible to represent the characters as they probably were, and have sought to avoid the error of making them actuated by my own conceptions of right or wrong, false or true: thus under a thin veil converting names and actions of the sixteenth century into cold impersonations of my own mind. They are represented as Catholics, and as Catholics deeply tinged with religion. To a Protestant apprehension there will appear something unnatural in the earnest and perpetual sentiment of the relations between God and man which pervade the tragedy of the Cenci. It will especially be startled at the combination of an undoubting persuasion of the truth of the popular religion with a cool and determined perseverance in enormous guilt. But religion in Italy is not, as in Protestant countries, a cloak to be worn on particular days; or a passport which those who do not wish to be railed at carry with them to exhibit; or a gloomy passion for penetrating the impenetrable mysteries of our being, which terrifies its possessor at the darkness of the abyss to the brink of which it has conducted him. Religion coexists, as it were, in the mind of an Italian Catholic, with a faith in that of which all men have the most certain knowledge. It is interwoven with the whole fabric of life. It is adoration, faith, submission, penitence, blind admiration; not a rule for moral conduct. It has no necessary connexion with any one virtue. The most atrocious villain may be rigidly devout, and, without any shock to established faith, confess himself to be so. Religion pervades intensely the whole frame of society, and is, according to the temper of the mind which it inhabits, a passion, a persuasion, an excuse, a refuge; never a check. Cenci himself built a chapel in the court of his palace, and dedicated it to St. Thomas the Apostle, and established masses for the peace of his soul. Thus in the first scene of the fourth act Lucretia's design in exposing herself to the consequences of an expostulation with Cenci after having administered the opiate, was to induce him by a feigned tale to confess himself before death; this being esteemed by Catholics as essential to salvation; and she only relinquishes her purpose when she perceives that her perseverance would expose Beatrice to new outrages.

I have avoided with great care in writing this play the introduction of what is commonly called mere poetry, and I imagine there will scarcely be found a detached simile or a single isolated description, unless Beatrice's description of the chasm appointed for her father's murder should be judged to be of that nature.*

In a dramatic composition the imagery and the passion should interpenetrate one another, the former being reserved simply for the full development and illustration of the latter. Imagination is as the immortal God which should assume flesh for the redemption of mortal passion. It is thus that the most remote and the most familiar imagery may alike be fit for dramatic purposes when employed in the illustration of strong feeling, which raises what is low, and levels to the apprehension that which is lofty, casting over all the shadow of its own greatness. In other respects I have written more carelessly; that is, without an over-fastidious and learned choice of words. In this respect, I entirely agree with those modern critics who assert that in order to move men to true sympathy we must use the familiar language of men.[2] And that our great ancestors the ancient English poets are the writers, a study of whom might incite us to do that for our own age which they have done for theirs. But it must be the real language of men in general, and not that of any particular class to whose society the writer happens to belong. So much for what I have attempted; I need not be assured that success is a very different matter; particularly for one whose attention has but newly been awakened to the study of dramatic literature.

I endeavoured whilst at Rome to observe such monuments of this story as might be accessible to a stranger. The portrait of Beatrice at the Colonna Palace is admirable as a work of art: it was taken by Guido during her confinement in prison. But it is most interesting as a just representation of one of the loveliest specimens of the workmanship of Nature. There is a fixed and pale composure upon the features: she seems sad and stricken down in spirit, yet the despair thus expressed is lightened by the patience of gentleness. Her head is bound with folds of white drapery, from which the yellow strings of her golden hair escape, and fall about her neck. The moulding of her face is exquisitely delicate; the eye-brows are distinct and arched; the lips have that permanent meaning of imagination and sensibility which suffering has not repressed and which it seems as if death scarcely could extinguish. Her forehead is large and

clear; her eyes, which we are told were remarkable for their vivacity, are swollen with weeping and lustreless, but beautifully tender and serene. In the whole mien there is a simplicity and dignity which united with her exquisite loveliness and deep sorrow are inexpressibly pathetic. Beatrice Cenci appears to have been one of those rare persons in whom energy and gentleness dwell together without destroying one another: her nature was simple and profound. The crimes and miseries in which she was an actor and a sufferer are as the mask and the mantle in which circumstances clothed her for her impersonation on the scene of the world.

The Cenci Palace is of great extent; and, though in part modernized, there yet remains a vast and gloomy pile of feudal architecture in the same state as during the dreadful scenes which are the subject of this tragedy. The palace is situated in an obscure corner of Rome, near the quarter of the Jews, and from the upper windows you see the immense ruins of Mount Palatine half hidden under their profuse overgrowth of trees. There is a court in one part of the palace (perhaps that in which Cenci built the chapel to St. Thomas), supported by granite columns and adorned with antique friezes of fine workmanship, and built up according to the ancient Italian fashion, with balcony over balcony of open work. One of the gates of the palace, formed of immense stones, and leading through a passage dark and lofty, and opening into gloomy subterranean chambers, struck me particularly.

Of the Castle of Petrella, I could obtain no further information than that which is to be found in the manuscript.

———⊷◦⊜◦⊶———

DRAMATIS PERSONÆ.

COUNT FRANCESCO CENCI.
GIACOMO, ⎫
BERNARDO, ⎬ *his Sons.*
CARDINAL CAMILLO.
PRINCE COLONNA.
ORSINO, *a Prelate.*
SAVELLA, *the Pope's Legate.*
OLIMPIO, ⎫
MARZIO, ⎬ *Assassins.*
ANDREA, *Servant to* CENCI.

Nobles, Judges, Guards, Servants.

LUCRETIA, *Wife of* CENCI, *and step-mother of his children.*
BEATRICE, *his Daughter.*

---

* An idea in this speech was suggested by a most sublime passage in "El Purgatorio de San Patricio," of Calderon; the only plagiarism which I have intentionally committed in the whole piece.

‹◇◇◇◇◇◇◇◇◇◇◇◇◇◇◇◇◇◇◇◇◇◇◇◇◇◇◇›
[2] See Wordsworth's Preface to *Lyrical Ballads*, pp. 398–408.

The SCENE *lies principally in Rome, but changes during the Fourth Act to Petrella, a Castle among the Apulian Apennines.*

TIME.—During the Pontificate of Clement VIII.

—◦○◉○◦—

ACT I

SCENE I. *An Apartment in the* CENCI *Palace.*

Enter COUNT CENCI *and* CARDINAL CAMILLO.

Camillo. That matter of the murder is hushed up
If you consent to yield his Holiness
Your fief that lies beyond the Pincian gate.—
It needed all my interest in the conclave
To bend him to this point: he said that you
Bought perilous impunity with your gold;
That crimes like yours if once or twice compounded
Enriched the Church, and respited from hell
An erring soul which might repent and live;
But that the glory and the interest   10
Of the high throne he fills, little consist
With making it a daily mart of guilt
As manifold and hideous as the deeds
Which you scarce hide from men's revolted eyes.
Cenci. The third of my possessions—let it go!
Ay, I once heard the nephew of the Pope
Had sent his architect to view the ground,
Meaning to build a villa on my vines
The next time I compounded with his uncle:
I little thought he should outwit me so!   20
Henceforth no witness—not the lamp—shall see
That which the vassal threatened to divulge
Whose throat is choked with dust for his reward.
The deed he saw could not have rated higher
Than his most worthless life:—it angers me!
Respited me from Hell!—So may the Devil
Respite their souls from Heaven. No doubt Pope
     Clement,
And his most charitable nephews, pray
That the Apostle Peter and the Saints
Will grant for their sake that I long enjoy   30
Strength, wealth, and pride, and lust, and length of
     days
Wherein to act the deeds which are the stewards
Of their revenue.—But much yet remains
To which they show no title.
Camillo.   Oh, Count Cenci!
So much that thou mightst honourably live
And reconcile thyself with thine own heart
And with thy God, and with the offended world.
How hideously look deeds of lust and blood

Through those snow white and venerable hairs!—
Your children should be sitting round you now,   40
But that you fear to read upon their looks
The shame and misery you have written there.
Where is your wife? Where is your gentle daughter?
Methinks her sweet looks, which make all things else
Beauteous and glad, might kill the fiend within you.
Why is she barred from all society
But her own strange and uncomplaining wrongs?
Talk with me, Count,—you know I mean you well.
I stood beside your dark and fiery youth
Watching its bold and bad career, as men   50
Watch meteors, but it vanished not—I marked
Your desperate and remorseless manhood; now
Do I behold you in dishonoured age
Charged with a thousand unrepented crimes.
Yet I have ever hoped you would amend,
And in that hope have saved your life three times.
Cenci. For which Aldobrandino owes you now
My fief beyond the Pincian.—Cardinal,
One thing, I pray you, recollect henceforth,
And so we shall converse with less restraint.   60
A man you knew spoke of my wife and daughter—
He was accustomed to frequent my house;
So the next day *his* wife and daughter came
And asked if I had seen him; and I smiled:
I think they never saw him any more.
Camillo. Thou execrable man, beware!—
Cenci.   Of thee?
Nay this is idle:—We should know each other.
As to my character for what men call crime
Seeing I please my senses as I list,
And vindicate that right with force or guile,   70
It is a public matter, and I care not
If I discuss it with you. I may speak
Alike to you and my own conscious heart—
For you give out that you have half reformed me,
Therefore strong vanity will keep you silent
If fear should not; both will, I do not doubt.
All men delight in sensual luxury,
All men enjoy revenge; and most exult
Over the tortures they can never feel—
Flattering their secret peace with others' pain.   80
But I delight in nothing else. I love
The sight of agony, and the sense of joy,
When this shall be another's, and that mine.
And I have no remorse and little fear,
Which are, I think, the checks of other men.
This mood has grown upon me, until now
Any design my captious fancy makes
The picture of its wish, and it forms none
But such as men like you would start to know,
Is as my natural food and rest debarred   90
Until it be accomplished.

Camillo.   Art thou not
Most miserable?
   Cenci.   Why, miserable?—
No.—I am what your theologians call
Hardened;—which they must be in impudence,
So to revile a man's peculiar taste.
True, I was happier than I am, while yet
Manhood remained to act the thing I thought;
While lust was sweeter than revenge; and now
Invention palls:—Ay, we must all grow old—
And but that there yet remains a deed to act   100
Whose horror might make sharp an appetite
Duller than mine—I'd do—I know not what.
When I was young I thought of nothing else
But pleasure; and I fed on honey sweets:
Men, by St. Thomas! cannot live like bees,
And I grew tired:—yet, till I killed a foe,
And heard his groans, and heard his children's
   groans,
Knew I not what delight was else on earth,
Which now delights me little. I the rather
Look on such pangs as terror ill conceals,   110
The dry fixed eyeball; the pale quivering lip,
Which tell me that the spirit weeps within
Tears bitterer than the bloody sweat of Christ.
I rarely kill the body, which preserves,
Like a strong prison, the soul within my power,
Wherein I feed it with the breath of fear
For hourly pain.
   Camillo.   Hell's most abandoned fiend
Did never, in the drunkenness of guilt,
Speak to his heart as now you speak to me;
I thank my God that I believe you not.   120

          Enter ANDREA.

   Andrea. My Lord, a gentleman from Salamanca
Would speak with you.
   Cenci.   Bid him attend me in
The grand saloon.
                [*Exit* ANDREA
   Camillo.   Farewell; and I will pray
Almighty God that thy false, impious words
Tempt not his spirit to abandon thee.
                [*Exit* CAMILLO.
   Cenci. The third of my possessions! I must use
Close husbandry, or gold, the old man's sword,
Falls from my withered hand. But yesterday
There came an order from the Pope to make
Fourfold provision for my cursèd sons;   130
Whom I had sent from Rome to Salamanca,
Hoping some accident might cut them off;
And meaning if I could to starve them there.
I pray thee, God, send some quick death upon them!
Bernardo and my wife could not be worse

If dead and damned:—then, as to Beatrice—
          [*Looking around him suspiciously.*
I think they cannot hear me at that door;
What if they should? And yet I need not speak
Though the heart triumphs with itself in words.
O, thou most silent air, that shalt not hear   140
What now I think! Thou, pavement, which I tread
Towards her chamber,—let your echoes talk
Of my imperious step scorning surprise,
But not of my intent!—Andrea!

          Enter ANDREA.

   Andrea.   My lord?
   Cenci. Bid Beatrice attend me in her chamber
This evening:—no, at midnight and alone.
                   [*Exeunt.*

    SCENE II.   *A Garden of the Cenci Palace.*

  Enter BEATRICE *and* ORSINO, *as in conversation.*

   Beatrice. Pervert not truth,
Orsino. You remember where we held
That conversation;—nay, we see the spot
Even from this cypress;—two long years are past
Since, on an April midnight, underneath
The moonlight ruins of mount Palatine,
I did confess to you my secret mind.
   Orsino. You said you loved me then.
   Beatrice.   You are a
   Priest,
Speak to me not of love.
   Orsino.   I may obtain
The dispensation of the Pope to marry.   10
Because I am a Priest do you believe
Your image, as the hunter some struck deer,
Follows me not whether I wake or sleep?
   Beatrice. As I have said, speak to me not of love;
Had you a dispensation I have not;
Nor will I leave this home of misery
Whilst my poor Bernard, and that gentle lady
To whom I owe life, and these virtuous thoughts,
Must suffer what I still have strength to share.
Alas, Orsino! All the love that once   20
I felt for you, is turned to bitter pain.
Ours was a youthful contract, which you first
Broke, by assuming vows no Pope will loose.
And thus I love you still, but holily,
Even as a sister or a spirit might;
And so I swear a cold fidelity.
And it is well perhaps we shall not marry.
You have a sly, equivocating vein
That suits me not.—Ah, wretched that I am!
Where shall I turn? Even now you look on me   30
As you were not my friend, and as if you

Discovered that I thought so, with false smiles
Making my true suspicion seem your wrong.
Ah, no! forgive me; sorrow makes me seem
Sterner than else my nature might have been;
I have a weight of melancholy thoughts,
And they forbode,—but what can they forbode
Worse than I now endure?
    Orsino.   All will be well.
Is the petition yet prepared? You know
My zeal for all you wish, sweet Beatrice;   40
Doubt not but I will use my utmost skill
So that the Pope attend to your complaint.
    Beatrice. Your zeal for all I wish;—Ah me, you are
      cold!
Your utmost skill . . . speak but one word . . . (*aside*)
      Alas!
Weak and deserted creature that I am,
Here I stand bickering with my only friend!
                        [*To* ORSINO.
This night my father gives a sumptuous feast,
Orsino; he has heard some happy news
From Salamanca, from my brothers there,
And with this outward show of love he mocks   50
His inward hate. 'Tis bold hypocrisy,
For he would gladlier celebrate their deaths,
Which I have heard him pray for on his knees:
Great God! that such a father should be mine!
But there is mighty preparation made,
And all our kin, the Cenci, will be there,
And all the chief nobility of Rome.
And he has bidden me and my pale Mother
Attire ourselves in festival array.
Poor lady! She expects some happy change   60
In his dark spirit from this act; I none.
At supper I will give you the petition:
Till when—farewell.
    Orsino.   Farewell.
                     [*Exit* BEATRICE.
                  I know the Pope
Will ne'er absolve me from my priestly vow
But by absolving me from the revenue
Of many a wealthy see; and, Beatrice,
I think to win thee at an easier rate.
Nor shall he read her eloquent petition:
He might bestow her on some poor relation
Of his sixth cousin, as he did her sister,   70
And I should be debarred from all access.
Then as to what she suffers from her father,
In all this there is much exaggeration:—
Old men are testy and will have their way;
A man may stab his enemy, or his vassal,
And live a free life as to wine or women,
And with a peevish temper may return
To a dull home, and rate his wife and children;

Daughters and wives call this foul tyranny.
I shall be well content if on my conscience   80
There rest no heavier sin than what they suffer
From the devices of my love—a net
From which she shall escape not. Yet I fear
Her subtle mind, her awe-inspiring gaze,
Whose beams anatomize me nerve by nerve
And lay me bare, and make me blush to see
My hidden thoughts.—Ah, no! A friendless girl
Who clings to me, as to her only hope:—
I were a fool, not less than if a panther
Were panic-stricken by the antelope's eye,   90
It she escape me.
                      [*Exit.*

SCENE III.   *A Magnificent Hall in the Cenci Palace.*
                 A Banquet.

  Enter CENCI, LUCRETIA, BEATRICE, ORSINO,
         CAMILLO, NOBLES.

    Cenci. Welcome, my friends and kinsmen;
      welcome ye,
Princes and Cardinals, pillars of the church,
Whose presence honours our festivity.
I have too long lived like an anchorite,
And in my absence from your merry meetings
An evil word is gone abroad of me;
But I do hope that you, my noble friends,
When you have shared the entertainment here,
And heard the pious cause for which 'tis given,
And we have pledged a health or two together,   10
Will think me flesh and blood as well as you;
Sinful indeed, for Adam made all so,
But tender-hearted, meek and pitiful.
    First Guest. In truth, my Lord, you seem too light
      of heart,
Too sprightly and companionable a man,
To act the deeds that rumour pins on you.
                   [*To his Companion.*
I never saw such blithe and open cheer
In any eye!
    Second Guest. Some most desired event,
In which we all demand a common joy,
Has brought us hither; let us hear it, Count.   20
    Cenci. It is indeed a most desired event.
If, when a parent from a parent's heart
Lifts from this earth to the great Father of all
A prayer, both when he lays him down to sleep,
And when he rises up from dreaming it;
One supplication, one desire, one hope,
That he would grant a wish for his two sons,
Even all that he demands in their regard—
And suddenly beyond his dearest hope
It is accomplished, he should then rejoice,   30

And call his friends and kinsmen to a feast,
And task their love to grace his merriment,—
Then honour me thus far—for I am he.
    Beatrice (*to* LUCRETIA).—Great God! How
      horrible! Some dreadful ill
Must have befallen my brothers.
    Lucretia.   Fear not, Child,
He speaks too frankly.
    Beatrice.   Ah! My blood runs cold.
I fear that wicked laughter round his eye,
Which wrinkles up the skin even to the hair.
    Cenci. Here are the letters brought from Salamanca;
Beatrice, read them to your mother. God!   40
I thank thee! In one night didst thou perform,
By ways inscrutable, the thing I sought.
My disobedient and rebellious sons
Are dead!—Why, dead!—What means this change of
    cheer?
You hear me not, I tell you they are dead;
And they will need no food or raiment more:
The tapers that did light them the dark way
Are their last cost. The Pope, I think, will not
Expect I should maintain them in their coffins.
Rejoice with me—my heart is wondrous glad.   50
    [LUCRETIA *sinks, half fainting;*
            BEATRICE *supports her.*
    Beatrice. It is not true!—Dear lady, pray look up.
Had it been true, there is a God in Heaven,
He would not live to boast of such a boon.
Unnatural man, thou knowest that it is false.
    Cenci. Ay, as the word of God; whom here I call
To witness that I speak the sober truth;—
And whose most favouring Providence was shown
Even in the manner of their deaths. For Rocco
Was kneeling at the mass, with sixteen others,
When the church fell and crushed him to a mummy,
The rest escaped unhurt. Cristofano   61
Was stabbed in error by a jealous man,
Whilst she he loved was sleeping with his rival;
All in the self-same hour of the same night;
Which shows that Heaven has special care of me.
I beg those friends who love me, that they mark
The day a feast upon their calendars.
It was the twenty-seventh of December:
Ay, read the letters if you doubt my oath.
    [*The Assembly appears confused; several of*
            the guests rise.
    First Guest. Oh, horrible! I will depart—
    Second Guest.   And I.—
    Third Guest.   No, stay!
I do believe it is some jest; though faith!   71
'Tis mocking us somewhat too solemnly.
I think his son has married the Infanta,
Or found a mine of gold in El Dorado;

'Tis but to season some such news; stay, stay!
I see 'tis only raillery by his smile.
    Cenci (*filling a bowl of wine, and lifting it up*). Oh,
      thou bright wine whose purple splendour leaps
And bubbles gaily in this golden bowl
Under the lamplight, as my spirits do,
To hear the death of my accursèd sons!   80
Could I believe thou wert their mingled blood,
Then would I taste thee like a sacrament,
And pledge with thee the mighty Devil in Hell,
Who, if a father's curses, as men say,
Climb with swift wings after their children's souls,
And drag them from the very throne of Heaven,
Now triumphs in my triumph!—But thou art
Superfluous; I have drunken deep of joy,
And I will taste no other wine to-night.
Here, Andrea! Bear the bowl around.
    A Guest (*rising*).   Thou wretch!
Will none among this noble company   91
Check the abandoned villain?
    Camillo.   For God's sake
Let me dismiss the guests! You are insane,
Some ill will come of this.
    Second Guest.   Seize, silence him
    First Guest. I will!
    Third Guest.   And I!
    Cenci (*addressing those who rise with a threatening*
      gesture).   Who moves? Who
            speaks?
    [*turning to the Company*
            'tis nothing,
Enjoy yourselves.—Beware! For my revenge
Is as the sealed commission of a king
That kills, and none dare name the murderer.
    [*The Banquet is broken up; several of the*
            Guests are departing.
    Beatrice. I do entreat you, go not, noble guests;
What, although tyranny and impious hate   100
Stand sheltered by a father's hoary hair?
What, if 'tis he who clothed us in these limbs
Who tortures them, and triumphs? What, if we,
The desolate and the dead, were his own flesh,
His children and his wife, whom he is bound
To love and shelter? Shall we therefore find
No refuge in this merciless wide world?
O think what deep wrongs must have blotted out
First love, then reverence in a child's prone mind,
Till it thus vanquish shame and fear! O think!   110
I have borne much, and kissed the sacred hand
Which crushed us to the earth, and thought its stroke
Was perhaps some paternal chastisement!
Have excused much, doubted; and when no doubt
Remained, have sought by patience, love, and tears
To soften him, and when this could not be

I have knelt down through the long sleepless nights
And lifted up to God, the Father of all,
Passionate prayers: and when these were not heard
I have still borne,—until I meet you here,   120
Princes and kinsmen, at this hideous feast
Given at my brothers' deaths. Two yet remain,
His wife remains and I, whom if ye save not,
Ye may soon share such merriment again
As fathers make over their children's graves.
O Prince Colonna, thou art our near kinsman,
Cardinal, thou art the Pope's chamberlain,
Camillo, thou art chief justiciary,
Take us away!
    Cenci. (He has been conversing with CAMILLO
    during the first part of BEATRICE'S *speech; he*
    hears the conclusion, and now advances.)
              I hope my good friends here
Will think of their own daughters—or perhaps   130
Of their own throats—before they lend an ear
To this wild girl.
    Beatrice (not noticing the words of Cenci). Dare no
        one look on me?
None answer? Can one tyrant overbear
The sense of many best and wisest men?
Or is it that I sue not in some form
Of scrupulous law, that ye deny my suit?
O God! That I were buried with my brothers!
And that the flowers of this departed spring
Were fading on my grave! And that my father
Were celebrating now one feast for all!   140
    Camillo. A bitter wish for one so young and gentle;
Can we do nothing?
    Colonna.   Nothing that I see.
Count Cenci were a dangerous enemy:
Yet I would second any one.
    A Cardinal.   And I.
    Cenci. Retire to your chamber, insolent girl!
    Beatrice. Retire thou, impious man! Ay, hide
        thyself
Where never eye can look upon thee more!
Wouldst thou have honour and obedience
Who art a torturer? Father, never dream
Though thou mayst overbear this company,   150
But ill must come of ill.—Frown not on me!
Haste, hide thyself, lest with avenging looks
My brothers' ghosts should hunt thee from thy seat!
Cover thy face from every living eye,
And start if thou but hear a human step:
Seek out some dark and silent corner, there,
Bow thy white head before offended God,
And we will kneel around, and fervently
Pray that he pity both ourselves and thee.
    Cenci. My friends, I do lament this insane girl   160
Has spoilt the mirth of our festivity.

Good night, farewell; I will not make you longer
Spectators of our dull domestic quarrels.
Another time.—
          [*Exeunt all but* CENCI *and* BEATRICE.
          My brain is swimming round;
Give me a bowl of wine!   [*To* BEATRICE.
              Thou painted viper!
Beast that thou art! Fair and yet terrible!
I know a charm shall make thee meek and tame,
Now get thee from my sight!
              [*Exit* BEATRICE.
              Here, Andrea,
Fill up this goblet with Greek wine. I said
I would not drink this evening; but I must;   170
For, strange to say, I feel my spirits fail
With thinking what I have decreed to do.—
          [*Drinking the wine.*
Be thou the resolution of quick youth
Within my veins, and manhood's purpose stern,
And age's firm, cold, subtle villainy;
As if thou wert indeed my children's blood
Which I did thirst to drink! The charm works well;
It must be done; it shall be done, I swear!
                                    [*Exit.*

END OF THE FIRST ACT.

ACT II

SCENE I. *An Apartment in the Cenci Palace.*

Enter LUCRETIA *and* BERNARDO.

Lucretia. Weep not, my gentle boy; he struck but
    me
Who have borne deeper wrongs. In truth, if he
Had killed me, he had done a kinder deed.
O God, Almighty, do Thou look upon us,
We have no other friend but only Thee!
Yet weep not; though I love you as my own,
I am not your true mother.
    Bernardo.   O more, more,
Than ever mother was to any child,
That have you been to me! Had he not been
My father, do you think that I should weep?   10
    Lucretia. Alas! Poor boy, what else couldst thou
        have done?

Enter BEATRICE.

Beatrice (in a hurried voice). Did he pass this way?
    Have you seen him, brother?
Ah, no! that is his step upon the stairs;
'Tis nearer now; his hand is on the door;
Mother, if I to thee have ever been
A duteous child, now save me! Thou, great God,

Whose image upon earth a father is,
Dost Thou indeed abandon me? He comes;
The door is opening now; I see his face;
He frowns on others, but he smiles on me,   20
Even as he did after the feast last night.

Enter a Servant.

Almighty God, how merciful Thou art!
'Tis but Orsino's servant.—Well, what news?
    Servant. My master bids me say, the Holy Father
Has sent back your petition thus unopened.
                        [*Giving a paper.*
And he demands at what hour 'twere secure
To visit you again?
    Lucretia.   At the Ave Mary.
                        [*Exit Servant.*
So, daughter, our last hope has failed; Ah me!
How pale you look; you tremble, and you stand
Wrapped in some fixed and fearful meditation,   30
As if one thought were over strong for you:
Your eyes have a chill glare; O, dearest child!
Are you gone mad? If not, pray speak to me.
    Beatrice. You see I am not mad: I speak to you.
    Lucretia. You talked of something that your father
        did
After that dreadful feast? Could it be worse
Than when he smiled, and cried, 'My sons are
        dead!'
And every one looked in his neighbour's face
To see if others were as white as he?
At the first word he spoke I felt the blood   40
Rush to my heart, and fell into a trance;
And when it passed I sat all weak and wild;
Whilst you alone stood up, and with strong words
Checked his unnatural pride; and I could see
The devil was rebuked that lives in him.
Until this hour thus you have ever stood
Between us and your father's moody wrath
Like a protecting presence: your firm mind
Has been our only refuge and defence:
What can have thus subdued it? What can now   50
Have given you that cold melancholy look,
Succeeding to your unaccustomed fear?
    Beatrice. What is it that you say? I was just thinking
'Twere better not to struggle any more.
Men, like my father, have been dark and bloody,
Yet never—Oh! Before worse comes of it
'Twere wise to die: it ends in that at last.
    Lucretia. Oh, talk not so, dear child! Tell me at
        once
What did your father do or say to you?
He stayed not after that accursèd feast   60
One moment in your chamber.—Speak to me.
    Bernardo. Oh, sister, sister, prithee, speak to us!

Beatrice (*speaking very slowly with a forced calmness*).
    It was one word, Mother, one little word;
One look, one smile.   [*Wildly.*
                Oh! He has trampled me
Under his feet, and made the blood stream down
My pallid cheeks. And he has given us all
Ditch-water, and the fever-stricken flesh
Of buffaloes, and bade us eat or starve,
And we have eaten.—He has made me look
On my beloved Bernardo, when the rust   70
Of heavy chains has gangrened his sweet limbs,
And I have never yet despaired—but now!
What would I say?   [*Recovering herself.*
                Ah, no! 'tis nothing new.
The sufferings we all share have made me wild:
He only struck and cursed me as he passed;
He said, he looked, he did;—nothing at all
Beyond his wont, yet it disordered me.
Alas! I am forgetful of my duty,
I should preserve my senses for your sake.
    Lucretia. Nay, Beatrice; have courage, my sweet
        girl,   80
If any one despairs it should be I
Who loved him once, and now must live with him
Till God in pity call for him or me.
For you may, like your sister, find some husband,
And smile, years hence, with children round your
        knees;
Whilst I, then dead, and all this hideous coil
Shall be remembered only as a dream.
    Beatrice. Talk not to me, dear lady, of a husband.
Did you not nurse me when my mother died?
Did you not shield me and that dearest boy?   90
And had we any other friend but you
In infancy, with gentle words and looks,
To win our father not to murder us?
And shall I now desert you? May the ghost
Of my dead Mother plead against my soul
If I abandon her who filled the place
She left, with more, even, than a mother's love!
    Bernardo. And I am of my sister's mind. Indeed
I would not leave you in this wretchedness,
Even though the Pope should make me free to live
In some blithe place, like others of my age,   101
With sports, and delicate food, and the fresh air.
Oh, never think that I will leave you, Mother!
    Lucretia. My dear, dear children!

Enter CENCI, *suddenly.*

    Cenci.   What, Beatrice here!
Come hither!
                [*She shrinks back, and covers her face.*
            Nay, hide not your face, 'tis fair;
Look up! Why, yesternight you dared to look

With disobedient insolence upon me,
Bending a stern and an inquiring brow
On what I meant; whilst I then sought to hide
That which I came to tell you—but in vain.
    Beatrice (*wildly, staggering towards the door.*) O
      that the earth would gape! Hide me, O God!
    Cenci. Then it was I whose inarticulate words
Fell from my lips, and who with tottering steps
Fled from your presence, as you now from mine.
Stay, I command you—from this day and hour
Never again, I think, with fearless eye,
And brow superior, and unaltered cheek,
And that lip made for tenderness or scorn,
Shalt thou strike dumb the meanest of mankind;
Me least of all. Now get thee to thy chamber!   120
                        [*To* BERNARDO.
Thou too, loathed image of thy cursèd mother,
Thy milky, meek face makes me sick with hate!
           [*Exeunt* BEATRICE *and* BERNARDO.
    (*Aside*). So much has passed between us as must
      make
Me bold, her fearful.—'Tis an awful thing
To touch such mischief as I now conceive:
So men sit shivering on the dewy bank,
And try the chill stream with their feet; once in . . .
How the delighted spirit pants for joy!
    Lucretia (*advancing timidly towards him*). O
      husband! Pray forgive poor Beatrice.
She meant not any ill.
    Cenci.   Nor you perhaps?   130
Nor that young imp, whom you have taught by rote
Parricide with his alphabet? Nor Giacomo?
Nor those two most unnatural sons, who stirred
Enmity up against me with the Pope?
Whom in one night merciful God cut off:
Innocent lambs! They thought not any ill.
You were not here conspiring? You said nothing
Of how I might be dungeoned as a madman;
Or be condemned to death for some offence,
And you would be the witnesses?—This failing,   140
How just it were to hire assassins, or
Put sudden poison in my evening drink?
Or smother me when overcome by wine?
Seeing we had no other judge but God,
And He had sentenced me, and there were none
But you to be the executioners
Of His decree enregistered in Heaven?
Oh, no! You said not this?
    Lucretia.   So help me God,
I never thought the things you charge me with!
    Cenci. If you dare speak that wicked lie again   150
I'll kill you. What! It was not by your counsel
That Beatrice disturbed the feast last night?
You did not hope to stir some enemies

Against me, and escape, and laugh to scorn
What every nerve of you now trembles at?
You judged that men were bolder than they are;
Few dare to stand between their grave and me.
    Lucretia. Look not so dreadfully! By my salvation
I knew not aught that Beatrice designed;
Nor do I think she designed any thing   160
Until she heard you talk of her dead brothers.
    Cenci. Blaspheming liar! You are damned for this!
But I will take you where you may persuade
The stones you tread on to deliver you:
For men shall there be none but those who dare
All things—not question that which I command.
On Wednesday next I shall set out: you know
That savage rock, the Castle of Petrella:
'Tis safely walled, and moated round about:
Its dungeons underground, and its thick towers   170
Never told tales; though they have heard and seen
What might make dumb things speak.—Why do you
    linger?
Make speediest preparation for the journey!
                      [*Exit* LUCRETIA.
The all-beholding sun yet shines; I hear
A busy stir of men about the streets;
I see the bright sky through the window panes:
It is a garish, broad, and peering day;
Loud, light, suspicious, full of eyes and ears,
And every little corner, nook, and hole
Is penetrated with the insolent light.   180
Come darkness! Yet, what is the day to me?
And wherefore should I wish for night, who do
A deed which shall confound both night and day?
'Tis she shall grope through a bewildering mist
Of horror: if there be a sun in heaven
She shall not dare to look upon its beams;
Nor feel its warmth. Let her then wish for night;
The act I think shall soon extinguish all
For me: I bear a darker deadlier gloom
Than the earth's shade, or interlunar air,   190
Or constellations quenched in murkiest cloud,
In which I walk secure and unbeheld
Towards my purpose.—Would that it were done!
                           [*Exit.*

SCENE II.   *A Chamber in the Vatican.*

Enter CAMILLO *and* GIACOMO, *in conversation.*

    Camillo. There is an obsolete and doubtful law
By which you might obtain a bare provision
Of food and clothing—
    Giacomo.   Nothing more? Alas!
Bare must be the provision which strict law
Awards, and agèd, sullen avarice pays.
Why did my father not apprentice me

To some mechanic trade? I should have then
Been trained in no highborn necessities
Which I could meet not by my daily toil.
The eldest son of a rich nobleman   10
Is heir to all his incapacities;
He has wide wants, and narrow powers. If you,
Cardinal Camillo, were reduced at once
From thrice-driven beds of down, and delicate food,
An hundred servants, and six palaces,
To that which nature doth indeed require?—
   Camillo. Nay, there is reason in your plea; 'twere
    hard.
   Giacomo. 'Tis hard for a firm man to bear: but I
Have a dear wife, a lady of high birth,
Whose dowry in ill hour I lent my father   20
Without a bond or witness to the deed:
And children, who inherit her fine senses,
The fairest creatures in this breathing world;
And she and they reproach me not. Cardinal,
Do you not think the Pope would interpose
And stretch authority beyond the law?
   Camillo. Though your peculiar case is hard, I know
The Pope will not divert the course of law.
After that impious feast the other night
I spoke with him, and urged him then to check   30
Your father's cruel hand; he frowned and said,
'Children are disobedient, and they sting
Their fathers' hearts to madness and despair,
Requiting years of care with contumely.
I pity the Count Cenci from my heart;
His outraged love perhaps awakened hate,
And thus he is exasperated to ill.
In the great war between the old and young
I, who have white hairs and a tottering body,
Will keep at least blameless neutrality.'   40

Enter ORSINO.

You, my good Lord Orsino, heard those words.
   Orsino. What words?
   Giacomo.   Alas, repeat them not again!
There then is no redress for me, at least
None but that which I may achieve myself,
Since I am driven to the brink.—But, say,
My innocent sister and my only brother
Are dying underneath my father's eye.
The memorable torturers of this land,
Galeaz Visconti, Borgia, Ezzelin,
Never inflicted on their meanest slave   50
What these endure; shall they have no protection?
   Camillo. Why, if they would petition to the Pope
I see not how he could refuse it—yet
He holds it of most dangerous example
In aught to weaken the paternal power,
Being, as 'twere, the shadow of his own.

I pray you now excuse me. I have business
That will not bear delay.
               [*Exit* CAMILLO.
   Giacomo.   But you, Orsino,
Have the petition: wherefore not present it?
   Orsino. I have presented it, and backed it with   60
My earnest prayers, and urgent interest;
It was returned unanswered. I doubt not
But that the strange and execrable deeds
Alleged in it—in truth they might well baffle
Any belief—have turned the Pope's displeasure
Upon the accusers from the criminal:
So I should guess from what Camillo said.
   Giacomo. My friend, that palace-walking devil
    Gold
Has whispered silence to his Holiness:
And we are left, as scorpions ringed with fire.   70
What should we do but strike ourselves to death?
For he who is our murderous persecutor
Is shielded by a father's holy name,
Or I would—   [*Stops abruptly.*
   Orsino.   What? Fear not to speak your thought.
Words are but holy as the deeds they cover:
A priest who has forsworn the God he serves;
A judge who makes Truth weep at his decree;
A friend who should weave counsel, as I now,
But as the mantle of some selfish guile;
A father who is all a tyrant seems,   80
Were the profaner for his sacred name.
   Giacomo. Ask me not what I think; the unwilling
    brain
Feigns often what it would not; and we trust
Imagination with such phantasies
As the tongue dares not fashion into words,
Which have no words, their horror makes them dim
To the mind's eye.—My heart denies itself
To think what you demand.
   Orsino.   But a friend's bosom
Is as the inmost cave of our own mind
Where we sit shut from the wide gaze of day,   90
And from the all-communicating air.
You look what I suspected—
   Giacomo.   Spare me now!
I am as one lost in a midnight wood,
Who dares not ask some harmless passenger
The path across the wilderness, lest he,
As my thoughts are, should be—a murderer.
I know you are my friend, and all I dare
Speak to my soul that will I trust with thee.
But now my heart is heavy, and would take
Lone counsel from a night of sleepless care.   100
Pardon me, that I say farewell—farewell!
I would that to my own suspected self
I could address a word so full of peace.

Orsino. Farewell!—Be your thoughts better or
more bold.
                              [*Exit* GIACOMO.

I had disposed the Cardinal Camillo
To feed his hope with cold encouragement:
It fortunately serves my close designs
That 'tis a trick of this same family
To analyse their own and other minds.
Such self-anatomy shall teach the will   110
Dangerous secrets: for it tempts our powers,
Knowing what must be thought, and may be done,
Into the depth of darkest purposes:
So Cenci fell into the pit; even I,
Since Beatrice unveiled me to myself,
And made me shrink from what I cannot shun,
Show a poor figure to my own esteem,
To which I grow half reconciled. I'll do
As little mischief as I can; that thought
Shall fee the accuser conscience.   [*After a pause.*
                              Now what harm 120
If Cenci should be murdered?—Yet, if murdered,
Wherefore by me? And what if I could take
The profit, yet omit the sin and peril
In such an action? Of all earthly things
I fear a man whose blows outspeed his words;
And such is Cenci: and while Cenci lives
His daughter's dowry were a secret grave
If a priest wins her.—Oh, fair Beatrice!
Would that I loved thee not, or loving thee
Could but despise danger and gold and all   130
That frowns between my wish and its effect,
Or smiles beyond it! There is no escape . . .
Her bright form kneels beside me at the altar,
And follows me to the resort of men,
And fills my slumber with tumultuous dreams,
So when I wake my blood seems liquid fire;
And if I strike my damp and dizzy head
My hot palm scorches it: her very name,
But spoken by a stranger, makes my heart
Sicken and pant; and thus unprofitably   140
I clasp the phantom of unfelt delights
Till weak imagination half possesses
The self-created shadow. Yet much longer
Will I not nurse this life of feverous hours:
From the unravelled hopes of Giacomo
I must work out my own dear purposes.
I see, as from a tower, the end of all:
Her father dead; her brother bound to me
By a dark secret, surer than the grave;
Her mother scared and unexpostulating   150
From the dread manner of her wish achieved:
And she!—Once more take courage, my faint heart;
What dares a friendless maiden matched with thee?
I have such foresight as assures success:

Some unbeheld divinity doth ever,
When dread events are near, stir up men's minds
To black suggestions; and he prospers best,
Not who becomes the instrument of ill,
But who can flatter the dark spirit, that makes
Its empire and its prey of other hearts   160
Till it become his slave . . . as I will do.
                              [*Exit.*

END OF THE SECOND ACT.

ACT III

SCENE I.   *An Apartment in the Cenci Palace.*

LUCRETIA; *to her enter* BEATRICE.

Beatrice. (*She enters staggering, and speaks wildly.*)
    Reach me that handkerchief!—My brain is hurt;
My eyes are full of blood; just wipe them for me . . .
I see but indistinctly . . .
    Lucretia.   My sweet child,
You have no wound; 'tis only a cold dew
That starts from your dear brow . . . Alas! Alas!
What has befallen?
    Beatrice.   How comes this hair undone?
Its wandering strings must be what blind me so,
And yet I tied it fast.—O, horrible!
The pavement sinks under my feet! The walls
Spin round! I see a woman weeping there,   10
And standing calm and motionless, whilst I
Slide giddily as the world reels. . . . My God!
The beautiful blue heaven is flecked with blood;
The sunshine on the floor is black! The air
Is changed to vapours such as the dead breathe
In charnel pits! Pah! I am choked! There creeps
A clinging, black, contaminating mist
About me . . . 'tis substantial, heavy, thick,
I cannot pluck it from me, for it glues
My fingers and my limbs to one another,   20
And eats into my sinews, and dissolves
My flesh to a pollution, poisoning
The subtle, pure, and inmost spirit of life!
My God! I never knew what the mad felt
Before; for I am mad beyond all doubt!
                              [*More wildly.*
No, I am dead! These putrefying limbs
Shut round and sepulchre the panting soul
Which would burst forth into the wandering air!
                              [*A pause.*
What hideous thought was that I had even now?
'Tis gone; and yet its burthen remains here   30
O'er these dull eyes . . . upon this weary heart!
O, world! O, life! O, day! O, misery!

Lucretia. What ails thee, my poor child? She
    answers not:
Her spirit apprehends the sense of pain,
But not its cause; suffering has dried away
The source from which it sprung . . .
    Beatrice (franticly).   Like Parricide . . .
Misery has killed its father: yet its father
Never like mine . . . O, God! What thing am I?
    Lucretia. My dearest child, what has your father
        done?
    Beatrice (doubtfully). Who art thou, questioner?
        I have no father.   40
                                        [*Aside.*
She is the madhouse nurse who tends on me,
It is a piteous office.
                [*To* LUCRETIA, *in a slow, subdued voice.*
                Do you know
I thought I was that wretched Beatrice
Men speak of, whom her father sometimes hales
From hall to hall by the entangled hair;
At others, pens up naked in damp cells
Where scaly reptiles crawl, and starves her there,
Till she will eat strange flesh. This woful story
So did I overact in my sick dreams,
That I imagined . . . no, it cannot be!   50
Horrible things have been in this wide world,
Prodigious mixtures, and confusions strange
Of good and ill; and worse have been conceived
Than ever there was found a heart to do.
But never fancy imaged such a deed
As . . .   [*Pauses, suddenly recollecting herself.*
        Who art thou? Swear to me, ere I die
With fearful expectation, that indeed
Thou art not what thou seemest . . . Mother!
    Lucretia.   Oh!
My sweet child, know you . . .
    Beatrice.   Yet speak it not:
For then if this be truth, that other too   60
Must be a truth, a firm enduring truth,
Linked with each lasting circumstance of life,
Never to change, never to pass away.
Why so it is. This is the Cenci Palace;
Thou art Lucretia; I am Beatrice.
I have talked some wild words, but will no more.
Mother, come near me: from this point of time,
I am . . .   [*Her voice dies away faintly.*
    Lucretia. Alas! What has befallen thee, child?
What has thy father done?
    Beatrice.   What have I done?
Am I not innocent? Is it my crime   70
That one with white hair, and imperious brow,
Who tortured me from my forgotten years,
As parents only dare, should call himself
My father, yet should be!—Oh, what am I?

What name, what place, what memory shall be mine?
What retrospects, outliving even despair?
    Lucretia. He is a violent tyrant, surely, child:
We know that death alone can make us free;
His death or ours. But what can he have done
Of deadlier outrage or worse injury?   80
Thou art unlike thyself; thine eyes shoot forth
A wandering and strange spirit. Speak to me,
Unlock those pallid hands whose fingers twine
With one another.
    Beatrice.   'Tis the restless life
Tortured within them. If I try to speak
I shall go mad. Ay, something must be done;
What, yet I know not . . . something which shall make
The thing that I have suffered but a shadow
In the dread lightning which avenges it;
Brief, rapid, irreversible, destroying   90
The consequence of what it cannot cure.
Some such thing is to be endured or done:
When I know what, I shall be still and calm,
And never anything will move me more.
But now!—O blood, which art my father's blood,
Circling through these contaminated veins,
If thou, poured forth on the polluted earth,
Could wash away the crime, and punishment
By which I suffer . . . no, that cannot be!
Many might doubt there were a God above   100
Who sees and permits evil, and so die:
That faith no agony shall obscure in me.
    Lucretia. It must indeed have been some bitter
        wrong;
Yet what, I dare not guess. Oh, my lost child,
Hide not in proud impenetrable grief
Thy sufferings from my fear.
    Beatrice.   I hide them not.
What are the words which you would have me speak?
I, who can feign no image in my mind
Of that which has transformed me: I, whose thought
Is like a ghost shrouded and folded up   110
In its own formless horror: of all words,
That minister to mortal intercourse,
Which wouldst thou hear? For there is none to tell
My misery: if another ever knew
Aught like to it, she died as I will die,
And left it, as I must, without a name.
Death! Death! Our law and our religion call thee
A punishment and a reward . . . Oh, which
Have I deserved?
    Lucretia.   The peace of innocence;
Till in your season you be called to heaven.   120
Whate'er you may have suffered, you have done
No evil. Death must be the punishment
Of crime, or the reward of trampling down
The thorns which God has strewed upon the path

Which leads to immortality.
   Beatrice.   Ay, death . . .
The punishment of crime. I pray thee, God,
Let me not be bewildered while I judge.
If I must live day after day, and keep
These limbs, the unworthy temple of Thy spirit,
As a foul den from which what Thou abhorrest   130
May mock Thee, unavenged . . . it shall not be!
Self-murder . . . no, that might be no escape,
For Thy decree yawns like a Hell between
Our will and it:—O! In this mortal world
There is no vindication and no law
Which can adjudge and execute the doom
Of that through which I suffer.

Enter ORSINO.

(*She approaches him solemnly.*) Welcome, Friend!
I have to tell you that, since last we met,
I have endured a wrong so great and strange,
That neither life nor death can give me rest.   140
Ask me not what it is, for there are deeds
Which have no form, sufferings which have no tongue.
   Orsino. And what is he who has thus injured you?
   Beatrice. The man they call my father: a dread
    name.
   Orsino. It cannot be . . .
   Beatrice.   What it can be, or not,
Forbear to think. It is, and it has been;
Advise me how it shall not be again.
I thought to die; but a religious awe
Restrains me, and the dread lest death itself
Might be no refuge from the consciousness   150
Of what is yet unexpiated. Oh, speak!
   Orsino. Accuse him of the deed, and let the law
Avenge thee.
   Beatrice. Oh, ice-hearted counsellor!
If I could find a word that might make known
The crime of my destroyer; and that done,
My tongue should like a knife tear out the secret
Which cankers my heart's core; ay, lay all bare
So that my unpolluted fame should be
With vilest gossips a stale mouthèd story;
A mock, a byword, an astonishment:—   160
If this were done, which never shall be done,
Think of the offender's gold, his dreaded hate,
And the strange horror of the accuser's tale,
Baffling belief, and overpowering speech;
Scarce whispered, unimaginable, wrapped
In hideous hints . . . Oh, most assured redress!
   Orsino. You will endure it then?
   Beatrice.   Endure?—Orsino,
It seems your counsel is small profit.
             [*Turns from him, and speaks half to herself.*
             Ay,

All must be suddenly resolved and done.
What is this undistinguishable mist   170
Of thoughts, which rise, like shadow after shadow,
Darkening each other?
   Orsino.   Should the offender live?
Triumph in his misdeed? and make, by use,
His crime, whate'er it is, dreadful no doubt,
Thine element; until thou mayst become
Utterly lost; subdued even to the hue
Of that which thou permittest?
   Beatrice (*to herself*).   Mighty death!
Thou double-visaged shadow? Only judge!
Rightfullest arbiter!
             [*She retires absorbed in thought.*
   Lucretia.   If the lightning
Of God has e'er descended to avenge . . .   180
   Orsino. Blaspheme not! His high Providence
    commits
Its glory on this earth, and their own wrongs
Into the hands of men; if they neglect
To punish crime . . .
   Lucretia.   But if one, like this wretch,
Should mock, with gold, opinion, law, and power?
If there be no appeal to that which makes
The guiltiest tremble? If because our wrongs,
For that they are unnatural, strange, and monstrous,
Exceed all measure of belief? O God!
If, for the very reasons which should make   190
Redress most swift and sure, our injurer triumphs?
And we, the victims, bear worse punishment
Than that appointed for their torturer?
   Orsino.   Think not
But that there is redress where there is wrong,
So we be bold enough to seize it.
   Lucretia.   How?
If there were any way to make all sure,
I know not . . . but I think it might be good
To . . .
   Orsino. Why, his late outrage to Beatrice;
For it is such, as I but faintly guess,
As makes remorse dishonour, and leaves her   200
Only one duty, how she may avenge:
You, but one refuge from ills ill endured;
Me, but one counsel . . .
   Lucretia.   For we cannot hope
That aid, or retribution, or resource
Will arise thence, where every other one
Might find them with less need.
             [BEATRICE *advances.*
   Orsino.   Then . . .
   Beatrice.   Peace, Orsino!
And, honoured Lady, while I speak, I pray,
That you put off, as garments overworn,
Forbearance and respect, remorse and fear,

And all the fit restraints of daily life,   210
Which have been borne from childhood, but which
    now
Would be a mockery to my holier plea.
As I have said, I have endured a wrong,
Which, though it be expressionless, is such
As asks atonement; both for what is past,
And lest I be reserved, day after day,
To load with crimes an overburthened soul,
And be . . . what ye can dream not. I have prayed
To God, and I have talked with my own heart,
And have unravelled my entangled will,   220
And have at length determined what is right.
Art thou my friend, Orsino? False or true?
Pledge thy salvation ere I speak.
    Orsino.   I swear
To dedicate my cunning, and my strength,
My silence, and whatever else is mine,
To thy commands.
    Lucretia.   You think we should devise
His death?
    Beatrice. And execute what is devised,
And suddenly. We must be brief and bold.
    Orsino. And yet most cautious.
    Lucretia.   For the jealous laws
Would punish us with death and infamy   230
For that which it became themselves to do.
    Beatrice. Be cautious as ye may, but prompt.
    Orsino,
What are the means?
    Orsino.   I know two dull, fierce outlaws,
Who think man's spirit as a worm's, and they
Would trample out, for any slight caprice,
The meanest or the noblest life. This mood
Is marketable here in Rome. They sell
What we now want.
    Lucretia.   To-morrow before dawn,
Cenci will take us to that lonely rock,
Petrella, in the Apulian Apennines.   240
If he arrive there . . .
    Beatrice.   He must not arrive.
    Orsino. Will it be dark before you reach the tower?
    Lucretia. The sun will scarce be set.
    Beatrice.   But I remember
Two miles on this side of the fort, the road
Crosses a deep ravine; 'tis rough and narrow,
And winds with short turns down the precipice;
And in its depth there is a mighty rock,
Which has, from unimaginable years,
Sustained itself with terror and with toil
Over a gulf, and with the agony   250
With which it clings seems slowly coming down;
Even as a wretched soul hour after hour,
Clings to the mass of life; yet clinging, leans;

And leaning, makes more dark the dread abyss
In which it fears to fall: beneath this crag
Huge as despair, as if in weariness,
The melancholy mountain yawns . . . below,
You hear but see not an impetuous torrent
Raging among the caverns, and a bridge
Crosses the chasm; and high above there grow,   260
With intersecting trunks, from crag to crag,
Cedars, and yews, and pines; whose tangled hair
Is matted in one solid roof of shade
By the dark ivy's twine. At noonday here
'Tis twilight, and at sunset blackest night.
    Orsino. Before you reach that bridge make some
    excuse
For spurring on your mules, or loitering
Until . . .
    Beatrice. What sound is that?
    Lucretia. Hark! No, it cannot be a servant's step;
It must be Cenci, unexpectedly   270
Returned . . . Make some excuse for being here.
    Beatrice. (*To* ORSINO, *as she goes out.*) That step we
    hear approach must never pass
The bridge of which we spoke.
               [*Exeunt* LUCRETIA *and* BEATRICE.
    Orsino.   What shall I do?
Cenci must find me here, and I must bear
The imperious inquisition of his looks
As to what brought me hither: let me mask
Mine own in some inane and vacant smile.

Enter GIACOMO, *in a hurried manner.*

How! Have you ventured hither? Know you then
That Cenci is from home?
    Giacomo.   I sought him here;
And now must wait till he returns.
    Orsino.   Great God!   280
Weigh you the danger of this rashness?
    Giacomo.   Ay!
Does my destroyer know his danger? We
Are now no more, as once, parent and child,
But man to man; the oppressor to the oppressed;
The slanderer to the slandered; foe to foe:
He has cast Nature off, which was his shield,
And Nature casts him off, who is her shame;
And I spurn both. Is it a father's throat
Which I will shake, and say, I ask not gold;
I ask not happy years; nor memories   290
Of tranquil childhood; nor home-sheltered love;
Though all these hast thou torn from me, and more;
But only my fair fame; only one hoard
Of peace, which I thought hidden from thy hate,
Under the penury heaped on me by thee,
Or I will . . . God can understand and pardon,

Why should I speak with man?
   Orsino.   Be calm, dear friend.
   Giacomo. Well, I will calmly tell you what he did.
This old Francesco Cenci, as you know,
Borrowed the dowry of my wife from me,   300
And then denied the loan; and left me so
In poverty, the which I sought to mend
By holding a poor office in the state.
It had been promised to me, and already
I bought new clothing for my raggèd babes,
And my wife smiled; and my heart knew repose.
When Cenci's intercession, as I found,
Conferred this office on a wretch, whom thus
He paid for vilest service. I returned
With this ill news, and we sate sad together   310
Solacing our despondency with tears
Of such affection and unbroken faith
As temper life's worst bitterness; when he,
As he is wont, came to upbraid and curse,
Mocking our poverty, and telling us
Such was God's scourge for disobedient sons.
And then, that I might strike him dumb with shame,
I spoke of my wife's dowry; but he coined
A brief yet specious tale, how I had wasted
The sum in secret riot; and he saw   320
My wife was touched, and he went smiling forth.
And when I knew the impression he had made,
And felt my wife insult with silent scorn
My ardent truth, and look averse and cold,
I went forth too: but soon returned again;
Yet not so soon but that my wife had taught
My children her harsh thoughts, and they all cried,
'Give us clothes, father! Give us better food!
What you in one night squander were enough
For months!' I looked, and saw that home was hell.
And to that hell will I return no more   331
Until mine enemy has rendered up
Atonement, or, as he gave life to me
I will, reversing Nature's law . . .
   Orsino.   Trust me,
The compensation which thou seekest here
Will be denied.
   Giacomo.   Then . . . Are not my friend?
Did you not hint at the alternative,
Upon the brink of which you see I stand,
The other day when we conversed together?
My wrongs were then less. That word parricide,   340
Although I am resolved, haunts me like fear.
   Orsino. It must be fear itself, for the bare word
Is hollow mockery. Mark, how wisest God
Draws to one point the threads of a just doom,
So sanctifying it: what you devise
Is, as it were, accomplished.
   Giacomo.   Is he dead?

   Orsino. His grave is ready. Know that since we met
Cenci has done an outrage to his daughter.
   Giacomo. What outrage?
   Orsino.   That she speaks not, but
   you may
Conceive such half conjectures as I do,   350
From her fixed paleness, and the lofty grief
Of her stern brow bent on the idle air,
And her severe unmodulated voice,
Drowning both tenderness and dread; and last
From this; that whilst her step-mother and I,
Bewildered in our horror, talked together
With obscure hints; both self-misunderstood
And darkly guessing, stumbling, in our talk,
Over the truth, and yet to its revenge,
She interrupted us, and with a look   360
Which told before she spoke it, he must die: . . .
   Giacomo. It is enough. My doubts are well
   appeased;
There is a higher reason for the act
Than mine; there is a holier judge than me,
A more unblamed avenger. Beatrice,
Who in the gentleness of thy sweet youth
Hast never trodden on a worm, or bruised
A living flower, but thou hast pitied it
With needless tears! Fair sister, thou in whom
Men wondered how such loveliness and wisdom   370
Did not destroy each other! Is there made
Ravage of thee? O, heart, I ask no more
Justification! Shall I wait, Orsino,
Till he return, and stab him at the door?
   Orsino. Not so; some accident might interpose
To rescue him from what is now most sure;
And you are unprovided where to fly,
How to excuse or to conceal. Nay, listen:
All is contrived; success is so assured
That . . .

               Enter BEATRICE.

   Beatrice. 'Tis my brother's voice! You know me
   not?   380
   Giacomo. My sister, my lost sister!
   Beatrice.   Lost indeed!
I see Orsino has talked with you, and
That you conjecture things too horrible
To speak, yet far less than the truth. Now, stay not,
He might return: yet kiss me; I shall know
That then thou hast consented to his death.
Farewell, farewell! Let piety to God,
Brotherly love, justice and clemency,
And all things that make tender hardest hearts   389
Make thine hard, brother. Answer not . . . farewell.
                             [Exeunt severally.

SCENE II.   *A mean Apartment in* GIACOMO'S
                    House.

GIACOMO *alone.*

Giacomo. 'Tis midnight, and Orsino comes not yet.
          [*Thunder, and the sound of a storm.*
What! can the everlasting elements
Feel with a worm like man? If so, the shaft
Of mercy-wingèd lightning would not fall
On stones and trees. My wife and children sleep:
They are now living in unmeaning dreams:
But I must wake, still doubting if that deed
Be just which is most necessary. O,
Thou unreplenished lamp! whose narrow fire
Is shaken by the wind, and on whose edge   10
Devouring darkness hovers! Thou small flame,
Which, as a dying pulse rises and falls,
Still flickerest up and down, how very soon,
Did I not feed thee, wouldst thou fail and be
As thou hadst never been! So wastes and sinks
Even now, perhaps, the life that kindled mine:
But that no power can fill with vital oil
That broken lamp of flesh. Ha! 'tis the blood
Which fed these veins that ebbs till all is cold:
It is the form that moulded mine that sinks   20
Into the white and yellow spasms of death:
It is the soul by which mine was arrayed
In God's immortal likeness which now stands
Naked before Heaven's judgement seat!
                              [*A bell strikes.*
                              One! Two!
The hours crawl on; and when my hairs are white,
My son will then perhaps be waiting thus,
Tortured between just hate and vain remorse;
Chiding the tardy messenger of news
Like those which I expect. I almost wish
He be not dead, although my wrongs are great;   30
Yet . . . 'tis Orsino's step . . .

                    Enter ORSINO.

                              Speak!
Orsino.   I am come
To say he has escaped.
Giacomo.   Escaped!
Orsino.   And safe
Within Petrella. He passed by the spot
Appointed for the deed an hour too soon.
Giacomo. Are we the fools of such contingencies?
And do we waste in blind misgivings thus
The hours when we should act? Then wind and
          thunder,
Which seemed to howl his knell, is the loud laughter
With which Heaven mocks our weakness! I henceforth
Will ne'er repent of aught designed or done   40

But my repentance.
Orsino.   See, the lamp is out.
Giacomo. If no remorse is ours when the dim air
Has drank this innocent flame, why should be quail
When Cenci's life, that light by which ill spirits
See the worst deeds they prompt, shall sink for ever?
No, I am hardened.
Orsino.   Why, what need of this?
Who feared the pale intrusion of remorse
In a just deed? Although our first plan failed,
Doubt not but he will soon be laid to rest.
But light the lamp; let us not talk i' the dark.   50
    Giacomo (*lighting the lamp*). And yet once quenched
        I cannot thus relume
My father's life: do you not think his ghost
Might plead that argument with God?
Orsino.   Once again
You cannot now recall your sister's peace;
Your own extinguished years of youth and hope;
Nor your wife's bitter words; nor all the taunts
Which, from the prosperous, weak misfortune takes;
Nor your dead mother; nor . . .
Giacomo.   O, speak no more!
I am resolved, although this very hand
Must quench the life that animated it.   60
    Orsino. There is no need of that. Listen: you know
Olimpio, the castellan of Petrella
In old Colonna's time; him whom your father
Degraded from his post? And Marzio,
That desperate wretch, whom he deprived last year
Of a reward of blood, well earned and due?
    Giacomo. I know Olimpio; and they say he hated
Old Cenci, so, that in his silent rage
His lips grew white only to see him pass.
Of Marzio I know nothing.
Orsino.   Marzio's hate   70
Matches Olimpio's. I have sent these men,
But in your name, and as at your request,
To talk with Beatrice and Lucretia.
    Giacomo. Only to talk?
Orsino.   The moments which even now
Pass onward to to-morrow's midnight hour
May memorize their flight with death: ere then
They must have talked, and may perhaps have done,
And made an end . . .
Giacomo.   Listen! What sound is that?
    Orsino. The house-dog moans, and the beams
        crack: nought else.
    Giacomo. It is my wife complaining in her sleep:
I doubt not she is saying bitter things   81
Of me; and all my children round her dreaming
That I deny them sustenance.
Orsino.   Whilst he
Who truly took it from them, and who fills

Their hungry rest with bitterness, now sleeps
Lapped in bad pleasures, and triumphantly
Mocks thee in visions of successful hate
Too like the truth of day.
 Giacomo.   If e'er he wakes
Again, I will not trust to hireling hands . . .
 Orsino. Why, that were well. I must be gone;
  good-night.   90
When next we meet—may all be done!
 Giacomo.   And all
Forgotten: Oh, that I had never been!
             [*Exeunt.*

  END OF THE THIRD ACT.

ACT IV

SCENE I. *An Apartment in the Castle of Petrella.*

    Enter CENCI.

 Cenci. She comes not; yet I left her even now
Vanquished and faint. She knows the penalty
Of her delay: yet what if threats are vain?
Am I not now within Petrella's moat?
Or fear I still the eyes and ears of Rome?
Might I not drag her by the golden hair?
Stamp on her? Keep her sleepless till her brain
Be overworn? Tame her with chains and famine?
Less would suffice. Yet so to leave undone
What I most seek! No, 'tis her stubborn will   10
Which by its own consent shall stoop as low
As that which drags it down.

    Enter LUCRETIA.

       Thou loathèd wretch!
Hide thee from my abhorrence: fly, begone!
Yet stay! Bid Beatrice come hither.
 Lucretia.   Oh,
Husband! I pray for thine own wretched sake
Heed what thou dost. A man who walks like thee
Through crimes, and through the danger of his crimes,
Each hour may stumble o'er a sudden grave.
And thou art old; thy hairs are hoary gray;
As thou wouldst save thyself from death and hell,   20
Pity thy daughter; give her to some friend
In marriage: so that she may tempt thee not
To hatred, or worse thoughts, if worse there be.
 Cenci. What! like her sister who has found a home
To mock my hate from with prosperity?
Strange ruin shall destroy both her and thee
And all that yet remain. My death may be
Rapid, her destiny outspeeds it. Go,
Bid her come hither, and before my mood
Be changed, lest I should drag her by the hair.   30

 Lucretia. She sent me to thee, husband. At thy
  presence
She fell, as thou dost know, into a trance;
And in that trance she heard a voice which said,
'Cenci must die! Let him confess himself!
Even now the accusing Angel waits to hear
If God, to punish his enormous crimes,
Harden his dying heart!'
 Cenci.   Why—such things are . . .
No doubt divine revealings may be made.
'Tis plain I have been favoured from above,   39
For when I cursed my sons they died.—Ay . . . so . . .
As to the right or wrong, that's talk . . . repentance . . .
Repentance is an easy moment's work
And more depends on God than me. Well . . . well . . .
I must give up the greater point, which was
To poison and corrupt her soul.
   [*A pause;* LUCRETIA *approaches anxiously, and
     then shrinks back as he speaks.*
         One, two;
Ay . . . Rocco and Cristofano my curse
Strangled: and Giacomo, I think, will find
Life a worse Hell than that beyond the grave:
Beatrice shall, if there be skill in hate,
Die in despair, blaspheming: to Bernardo,   50
He is so innocent, I will bequeath
The memory of these deeds, and make his youth
The sepulchre of hope, where evil thoughts
Shall grow like weeds on a neglected tomb.
When all is done, out in the wide Campagna,
I will pile up my silver and my gold;
My costly robes, paintings and tapestries;
My parchments and all records of my wealth,
And make a bonfire in my joy, and leave
Of my possessions nothing but my name;   60
Which shall be an inheritance to strip
Its wearer bare as infamy. That done,
My soul, which is a scourge, will I resign
Into the hands of him who wielded it;
Be it for its own punishment or theirs,
He will not ask it of me till the lash
Be broken in its last and deepest wound;
Until its hate be all inflicted. Yet,
Lest death outspeed my purpose, let me make
Short work and sure . . .   [*Going.*
 Lucretia. (*Stops him.*) Oh, stay. It was a feint: 70
She had no vision, and she heard no voice.
I said it but to awe thee.
 Cenci.   That is well.
Vile palterer with the sacred truth of God,
Be thy soul choked with that blaspheming lie!
For Beatrice worse terrors are in store
To bend her to my will.
 Lucretia.   Oh! to what will?

What cruel sufferings more than she has known
Canst thou inflict?
   Cenci.   Andrea! Go call my daughter,
And if she comes not tell her that I come.
What sufferings? I will drag her, step by step,   80
Through infamies unheard of among men:
She shall stand shelterless in the broad noon
Of public scorn, for acts blazoned abroad,
One among which shall be ... What? Canst thou
    guess?
She shall become (for what she most abhors
Shall have a fascination to entrap
Her loathing will) to her own conscious self
All she appears to others; and when dead,
As she shall die unshrived and unforgiven,
A rebel to her father and her God,   90
Her corpse shall be abandoned to the hounds;
Her name shall be the terror of the earth;
Her spirit shall approach the throne of God
Plague-spotted with my curses. I will make
Body and soul a monstrous lump of ruin.

Enter ANDREA.

   Andrea. The Lady Beatrice ...
   Cenci.   Speak, pale slave! What
Said she?
   Andrea. My Lord, 'twas what she looked; she said:
'Go tell my father that I see the gulf
Of Hell between us two, which he may pass,
I will not.'
                   [*Exit* ANDREA.
   Cenci. Go thou quick, Lucretia,
Tell her to come; yet let her understand
Her coming is consent: and say, moreover,
That if she come not I will curse her.
                   [*Exit* LUCRETIA.
                 Ha!
With what but with a father's curse doth God
Panic-strike armèd victory, and make pale
Cities in their prosperity? The world's Father
Must grant a parent's prayer against his child,
Be he who asks even what men call me.
Will not the deaths of her rebellious brothers
Awe her before I speak? For I on them   110
Did imprecate quick ruin, and it came.

Enter LUCRETIA.

Well; what? Speak, wretch!
   Lucretia.   She said, 'I cannot come;
Go tell my father that I see a torrent
Of his own blood raging between us.'
   Cenci (*kneeling*).   God!
Hear me! If this most specious mass of flesh,
Which Thou hast made my daughter; this my blood,

This particle of my divided being;
Or rather, this my bane and my disease,
Whose sight infects and poisons me; this devil
Which sprung from me as from a hell, was meant   120
To aught good use; if her bright loveliness
Was kindled to illumine this dark world;
If nursed by Thy selectest dew of love
Such virtues blossom in her as should make
The peace of life, I pray Thee for my sake,
As Thou the common God and Father art
Of her, and me, and all; reverse that doom!
Earth, in the name of God, let her food be
Poison, until she be encrusted round
With leprous stains! Heaven, rain upon her head   130
The blistering drops of the Maremma's dew,
Till she be speckled like a toad; parch up
Those love-enkindled lips, warp those fine limbs
To loathèd lameness! All-beholding sun,
Strike in thine envy those life-darting eyes
With thine own blinding beams!
   Lucretia.   Peace! Peace!
For thine own sake unsay those dreadful words.
When high God grants He punishes such prayers.
   Cenci (*leaping up, and throwing his right hand
    towards Heaven*). He does His will, I mine!
    This in addition,
That if she have a child ...
   Lucretia.   Horrible thought!   140
   Cenci. That if she ever have a child; and thou,
Quick Nature! I adjure thee by thy God,
That thou be fruitful in her, and increase
And multiply, fulfilling his command,
And my deep imprecation! May it be
A hideous likeness of herself, that as
From a distorting mirror, she may see
Her image mixed with what she most abhors,
Smiling upon her from her nursing breast.
And that the child may from its infancy   150
Grow, day by day, more wicked and deformed,
Turning her mother's love to misery:
And that both she and it may live until
It shall repay her care and pain with hate,
Or what may else be more unnatural.
So he may hunt her through the clamorous scoffs
Of the loud world to a dishonoured grave.
Shall I revoke this curse? Go, bid her come,
Before my words are chronicled in Heaven.
                   [*Exit* LUCRETIA.
I do not feel as if I were a man,   160
But like a fiend appointed to chastise
The offences of some unremembered world.
My blood is running up and down my veins;
A fearful pleasure makes it prick and tingle:
I feel a giddy sickness of strange awe;

My heart is beating with an expectation
Of horrid joy.

Enter LUCRETIA.

        What? Speak!
    Lucretia.   She bids thee curse;
And if thy curses, as they cannot do,
Could kill her soul . . .
    Cenci.   She would not come. 'Tis well,
I can do both: first take what I demand,   170
And then extort concession. To thy chamber!
Fly ere I spurn thee: and beware this night
That thou cross not my footsteps. It were safer
To come between the tiger and his prey.
                        [*Exit* LUCRETIA.
It must be late; mine eyes grow weary dim
With unaccustomed heaviness of sleep.
Conscience! Oh, thou most insolent of lies!
They say that sleep, that healing dew of Heaven,
Steeps not in balm the foldings of the brain
Which thinks thee an impostor. I will go   180
First to belie thee with an hour of rest,
Which will be deep and calm, I feel: and then . . .
O, multitudinous Hell, the fiends will shake
Thine arches with the laughter of their joy!
There shall be lamentation heard in Heaven
As o'er an angel fallen; and upon Earth
All good shall droop and sicken, and ill things
Shall with a spirit of unnatural life
Stir and be quickened . . . even as I am now.
                        [*Exit.*

SCENE II.   *Before the Castle of Petrella.*

Enter BEATRICE *and* LUCRETIA *above on the*
                Ramparts.

    Beatrice. They come not yet.
    Lucretia.   'Tis scarce midnight.
    Beatrice   How slow
Behind the course of thought, even sick with speed,
Lags leaden-footed time!
    Lucretia.   The minutes pass . . .
If he should wake before the deed is done?
    Beatrice. O, mother! He must never wake again.
What thou hast said persuades me that our act
Will but dislodge a spirit of deep hell
Out of a human form.
    Lucretia.   'Tis true he spoke
Of death and judgement with strange confidence
For one so wicked; as a man believing   10
In God, yet recking not of good or ill.

And yet to die without confession! . . .
    Beatrice.   Oh!
Believe that Heaven is merciful and just,
And will not add our dread necessity
To the amount of his offences.

    Enter OLIMPIO *and* MARZIO, *below.*

    Lucretia.   See,
They come.
    Beatrice. All mortal things must hasten thus
To their dark end. Let us go down.
            [*Exeunt* LUCRETIA *and* BEATRICE *from above.*
    Olimpio. How feel you to this work?
    Marzio.   As one who thinks
A thousand crowns excellent market price
For an old murderer's life. Your cheeks are pale.   20
    Olimpio. It is the white reflection of your own,
Which you call pale.
    Marzio.   Is that their natural hue?
    Olimpio. Or 'tis my hate and the deferred desire
To wreak it, which extinguishes their blood.
    Marzio. You are inclined then to this business?
    Olimpio.   Ay.
If one should bribe me with a thousand crowns
To kill a serpent which had stung my child,
I could not be more willing.

    Enter BEATRICE *and* LUCRETIA, *below.*

                        Noble ladies!
    Beatrice. Are ye resolved?
    Olimpio.   Is he asleep?
    Marzio.   Is all
Quiet?
    Lucretia. I mixed an opiate with his drink: 30
He sleeps so soundly . . .
    Beatrice.   That his death will be
But as a change of sin-chastising dreams,
A dark continuance of the Hell within him,
Which God extinguish! But ye are resolved?
Ye know it is a high and holy deed?
    Olimpio. We are resolved.
    Marzio.   As to the how this act
Be warranted, it rests with you.
    Beatrice.   Well, follow!
    Olimpio. Hush! Hark! What noise is that?
    Marzio.   Ha! some
        one comes!
    Beatrice. Ye conscience-stricken cravens, rock to
        rest
Your baby hearts. It is the iron gate,   40
Which ye left open, swinging to the wind,
That enters whistling as in scorn. Come, follow!
And be your steps like mine, light, quick and bold.
                        [*Exeunt.*

SCENE III. *An Apartment in the Castle.*

Enter BEATRICE *and* LUCRETIA.

Lucretia. They are about it now.
Beatrice.   Nay, it is done.
Lucretia. I have not heard him groan.
Beatrice.   He will not groan.
Lucretia. What sound is that?
Beatrice.   List! 'tis the tread of feet
About his bed.
Lucretia.   My God!
If he be now a cold stiff corpse . . .
Beatrice.   O, fear not
What may be done, but what is left undone:
The act seals all.

Enter OLIMPIO *and* MARZIO.

                    Is it accomplished?
Marzio.   What?
Olimpio. Did you not call?
Beatrice.   When?
Olimpio.   Now.
Beatrice.   I ask if all
    is over?
Olimpio. We dare not kill an old and sleeping man;
His thin gray hair, his stern and reverend brow,   10
His veinèd hands crossed on his heaving breast,
And the calm innocent sleep in which he lay,
Quelled me. Indeed, indeed, I cannot do it.
    Marzio. But I was bolder; for I chid Olimpio,
And bade him bear his wrongs to his own grave
And leave me the reward. And now my knife
Touched the loose wrinkled throat, when the old man
Stirred in his sleep, and said, 'God! hear, O, hear,
A father's curse! What, art Thou not our Father?'
And then he laughed. I knew it was the ghost   20
Of my dead father speaking through his lips,
And could not kill him.
    Beatrice.   Miserable slaves!
Where, if ye dare not kill a sleeping man,
Found ye the boldness to return to me
With such a deed undone? Base palterers!
Cowards and traitors! Why, the very conscience
Which ye would sell for gold and for revenge
Is an equivocation: it sleeps over
A thousand daily acts disgracing men;
And when a deed where mercy insults Heaven . . .   30
Why do I talk?
            [*Snatching a dagger from one of them
                    and raising it.*
            Hadst thou a tongue to say,
'She murdered her own father!'—I must do it!

But never dream ye shall outlive him long!
    Olimpio. Stop, for God's sake!
    Marzio.   I will go back and
    kill him.
    Olimpio. Give me the weapon, we must do thy will.
    Beatrice. Take it! Depart! Return!
            [*Exeunt* OLIMPIO *and* MARZIO.
                    How pale thou art!
We do but that which 'twere a deadly crime
To leave undone.
    Lucretia.   Would it were done!
    Beatrice.   Even whilst
That doubt is passing through your mind, the world
Is conscious of a change. Darkness and Hell   40
Have swallowed up the vapour they sent forth
To blacken the sweet light of life. My breath
Comes, methinks, lighter, and the jellied blood
Runs freely through my veins. Hark!

Enter OLIMPIO *and* MARZIO.

                    He is . . .
    Olimpio.   Dead!
    Marzio. We strangled him that there might be no
    blood;
And then we threw his heavy corpse i' the garden
Under the balcony; 'twill seem it fell.
    Beatrice (*giving them a bag of coin*). Here, take this
    gold, and hasten to your homes.
And, Marzio, because thou wast only awed
By that which made me tremble, wear thou this!   50
            [*Clothes him in a rich mantle.*
It was the mantle which my grandfather
Wore in his high prosperity, and men
Envied his state: so may they envy thine.
Thou wert a weapon in the hand of God
To a just use. Live long and thrive! And, mark,
If thou has crimes, repent: this deed is none.
            [*A horn is sounded.*
    Lucretia. Hark, 'tis the castle horn; my God! it
    sounds
Like the last trump.
    Beatrice.   Some tedious guest is coming.
    Lucretia. The drawbridge is let down; there is a
    tramp
Of horses in the court; fly, hide yourselves!   60
            [*Exeunt* OLIMPIO *and* MARZIO.
    Beatrice. Let us retire to counterfeit deep rest;
I scarcely need to counterfeit it now:
The spirit which doth reign within these limbs
Seems strangely undisturbed. I could even sleep
Fearless and calm: all ill is surely past.
            [*Exeunt.*

SCENE IV.   *Another Apartment in the Castle.*

Enter on one side the LEGATE SAVELLA, *introduced by
a Servant, and on the other* LUCRETIA *and* BERNARDO.

Savella. Lady, my duty to his Holiness
Be my excuse that thus unseasonably
I break upon your rest. I must speak with
Count Cenci; doth he sleep?
 Lucretia (in a hurried and confused manner). I think
  he sleeps;
Yet wake him not, I pray, spare me awhile,
He is a wicked and a wrathful man;
Should he be roused out of his sleep to-night,
Which is, I know, a hell of angry dreams,
It were not well; indeed it were not well.
Wait till day break . . . *(aside)* O, I am deadly sick!   10
 Savella. I grieve thus to distress you, but the Count
Must answer charges of the gravest import,
And suddenly; such my commission is.
 Lucretia (with increased agitation). I dare not rouse
  him: I know none who dare . . .
'Twere perilous; . . . you might as safely waken
A serpent; or a corpse in which some fiend
Were laid to sleep.
 Savella.   Lady, my moments here
Are counted. I must rouse him from his sleep,
Since none else dare.
 Lucretia (aside). O, terror! O, despair!
(To BERNARDO.) Bernardo, conduct you the Lord
 Legate to   20
Your father's chamber.
     [*Exeunt* SAVELLA *and* BERNARDO.

     Enter BEATRICE.

 Beatrice.   'Tis a messenger
Come to arrest the culprit who now stands
Before the throne of unappealable God.
Both Earth and Heaven, consenting arbiters,
Acquit our deed.
 Lucretia. Oh, agony of fear!
Would that he yet might live! Even now I heard
The Legate's followers whisper as they passed
They had a warrant for his instant death.
All was prepared by unforbidden means
Which we must pay so dearly, having done. 30
Even now they search the tower, and find the body;
Now they suspect the truth; now they consult
Before they come to tax us with the fact;
O, horrible, 'tis all discovered!
 Beatrice.   Mother,
What is done wisely, is done well. Be bold
As thou art just. 'Tis like a truant child
To fear that others know what thou hast done,
Even from thine own strong consciousness, and thus

Write on unsteady eyes and altered cheeks
All thou wouldst hide. Be faithful to thyself, 40
And fear no other witness but thy fear.
For if, as cannot be, some circumstance
Should rise in accusation, we can blind
Suspicion with such cheap astonishment,
Or overbear it with such guiltless pride,
As murderers cannot feign. The deed is done,
And what may follow now regards not me.
I am as universal as the light;
Free as the earth-surrounding air; as firm
As the world's centre. Consequence, to me, 50
Is as the wind which strikes the solid rock
But it shakes it not.
     [*A cry within and tumult.*
 Voices.   Murder! Murder! Murder!

   Enter BERNARDO *and* SAVELLA.

Savella (to his followers). Go search the castle round;
  sound the alarm;
Look to the gates that none escape!
 Beatrice.   What now?
 Bernardo. I know not what to say . . . my father 's
  dead.
 Beatrice. How; dead! he only sleeps; you mistake,
  brother.
His sleep is very calm, very like death;
'Tis wonderful how well a tyrant sleeps.
He is not dead?
 Bernardo. Dead; murdered.
 Lucretia (with extreme agitation). Oh no, no,
He is not murdered though he may be dead; 60
I have alone the keys of those apartments.
 Savella. Ha! Is it so?
 Beatrice.   My Lord, I pray excuse us;
We will retire; my mother is not well:
She seems quite overcome with this strange horror.
    [*Exeunt* LUCRETIA *and* BEATRICE.
 Savella. Can you suspect who may have murdered
  him?
 Bernardo. I know not what to think.
 Savella.   Can you name any
Who had an interest in his death?
 Bernardo.   Alas!
I can name none who had not, and those most
Who most lament that such a deed is done;
My mother, and my sister, and myself. 70
 Savella. 'Tis strange! There were clear marks of
  violence.
I found the old man's body in the moonlight
Hanging beneath the window of his chamber,
Among the branches of a pine: he could not
Have fallen there, for all his limbs lay heaped
And effortless; 'tis true there was no blood . . .

Favour me, Sir; it much imports your house
That all should be made clear; to tell the ladies
That I request their presence.

                        [*Exit* BERNARDO.

      Enter GUARDS *bringing in* MARZIO.

  Guard.   We have one.
  Officer. My Lord, we found this ruffian and another
Lurking among the rocks; there is no doubt   81
But that they are the murderers of Count Cenci:
Each had a bag of coin; this fellow wore
A gold-inwoven robe, which shining bright
Under the dark rocks to the glimmering moon
Betrayed them to our notice: the other fell
Desperately fighting.
  Savella.   What does he confess?
  Officer. He keeps firm silence; but these lines
    found on him
May speak.
  Savella. Their language is at least sincere.

                          [*Reads*.

"*To the Lady Beatrice*.   90
   "*That the atonement of what my nature sickens
to conjecture may soon arrive, I send thee, at thy
brother's desire, those who will speak and do more
than I dare write. . . .*
              "*Thy devoted servant, Orsino*."

  Enter LUCRETIA, BEATRICE, *and* BERNARDO.

Knowest thou this writing, Lady?
  Beatrice.   No.
  Savella.   Nor thou?
  Lucretia. (*Her conduct throughout the scene is marked
    by extreme agitation*.) Where was it found? What
    is it? It should be
Orsino's hand! It speaks of that strange horror
Which never yet found utterance, but which made
Between that hapless child and her dead father
A gulf of obscure hatred.
  Savella.   Is it so?   100
Is it true, Lady, that thy father did
Such outrages as to awaken in thee
Unfilial hate?
  Beatrice.   Not hate, 'twas more than hate:
This is most true, yet wherefore question me?
  Savella. There is a deed demanding question done;
Thou hast a secret which will answer not.
  Beatrice. What sayest? My Lord, your words are
    bold and rash.
  Savella. I do arrest all present in the name
Of the Pope's Holiness. You must to Rome.   109
  Lucretia. O, not to Rome! Indeed we are not guilty.
  Beatrice. Guilty! Who dares talk of guilt? My Lord,
I am more innocent of parricide

Than is a child born fatherless . . . Dear mother,
Your gentleness and patience are no shield
For this keen-judging world, this two-edged lie,
Which seems, but is not. What! will human laws,
Rather will ye who are their ministers,
Bar all access to retribution first,
And then, when Heaven doth interpose to do
What ye neglect, arming familiar things   120
To the redress of an unwonted crime,
Make ye the victims who demanded it
Culprits? 'Tis ye are culprits! That poor wretch
Who stands so pale, and trembling, and amazed
If it be true he murdered Cenci, was
A sword in the right hand of justest God.
Wherefore should I have wielded it? Unless
The crimes which mortal tongue dare never name
God therefore scruples to avenge.
  Savella.   You own
That you desired his death?
  Beatrice.   It would have been 130
A crime no less than his, if for one moment
That fierce desire had faded in my heart.
'Tis true I did believe, and hope, and pray,
Ay, I even knew . . . for God is wise and just,
That some strange sudden death hung over him.
'Tis true that this did happen, and most true
There was no other rest for me on earth,
No other hope in Heaven . . . now what of this?
  Savella. Strange thoughts beget strange deeds;
    and here are both:
I judge thee not.
  Beatrice.   And yet, if you arrest me, 140
You are the judge and executioner
Of that which is the life of life: the breath
Of accusation kills an innocent name,
And leaves for lame acquittal the poor life
Which is a mask without it. 'Tis most false
That I am guilty of foul parricide;
Although I must rejoice, for justest cause,
That other hands have sent my father's soul
To ask the mercy he denied to me.
Now leave us free; stain not a noble house 150
With vague surmises of rejected crime;
Add to our sufferings and your own neglect
No heavier sum: let them have been enough:
Leave us the wreck we have.
  Savella.   I dare not, Lady.
I pray that you prepare yourselves for Rome:
There the Pope's further pleasure will be known.
  Lucretia. O, not to Rome! O, take us not to Rome!
  Beatrice. Why not to Rome, dear mother? There
    as here
Our innocence is as an armèd heel
To trample accusation. God is there   160

As here, and with His shadow ever clothes
The innocent, the injured and the weak;
And such are we. Cheer up, dear Lady, lean
On me; collect your wandering thoughts. My Lord,
As soon as you have taken some refreshment,
And had all such examinations made
Upon the spot, as may be necessary
To the full understanding of this matter,
We shall be ready. Mother; will you come?
 Lucretia. Ha! they will bind us to the rack, and
  wrest   170
Self-accusation from our agony!
Will Giacomo be there? Orsino? Marzio?
All present; all confronted; all demanding
Each from the other's countenance the thing
Which is in every heart! O, misery!
      [*She faints, and is borne out.*
 Savella. She faints: an ill appearance this.
 Beatrice,   My Lord,
She knows not yet the uses of the world.
She fears that power is as a beast which grasps
And loosens not: a snake whose look transmutes
All things to guilt which is its nutriment. 180
She cannot know how well the supine slaves
Of blind authority read the truth of things
When written on a brow of guilelessness:
She sees not yet triumphant Innocence
Stand at the judgement-seat of mortal man,
A judge and an accuser of the wrong
Which drags it there. Prepare yourself, my Lord;
Our suite will join yours in the court below.
          [*Exeunt.*

END OF THE FOURTH ACT.

ACT V

SCENE I. *An Appartment in* ORSINO'S *Palace.*

Enter ORSINO *and* GIACOMO.

 Giacomo. Do evil deeds thus quickly come to end?
O, that the vain remorse which must chastise
Crimes done, had but as loud a voice to warn
As its keen sting is mortal to avenge!
O, that the hour when present had cast off
The mantle of its mystery, and shown
The ghastly form with which it now returns
When its scared game is roused, cheering the hounds
Of conscience to their prey! Alas! Alas!
It was a wicked thought, a piteous deed, 10
To kill an old and hoary-headed father.
 Orsino. It has turned out unluckily, in truth.
 Giacomo. To violate the sacred doors of sleep;
To cheat kind Nature of the placid death
Which she prepares for overwearied age;

To drag from Heaven an unrepentant soul
Which might have quenched in reconciling prayers
A life of burning crimes . . .
 Orsino.   You cannot say
I urged you to the deed.
 Giacomo.   O, had I never
Found in thy smooth and ready countenance 20
The mirror of my darkest thoughts; hadst thou
Never with hints and questions made me look
Upon the monster of my thought, until
It grew familiar to desire . . .
 Orsino.   'Tis thus
Men cast the blame of their unprosperous acts
Upon the abettors of their own resolve;
Or anything but their weak, guilty selves.
And yet, confess the truth, it is the peril
In which you stand that gives you this pale sickness
Of penitence; confess 'tis fear disguised 30
From its own shame that takes the mantle now
Of thin remorse. What if we yet were safe?
 Giacomo. How can that be? Already Beatrice,
Lucretia and the murderer are in prison.
I doubt not officers are, whilst we speak,
Sent to arrest us.
 Orsino.   I have all prepared
For instant flight. We can escape even now,
So we take fleet occasion by the hair.
 Giacomo. Rather expire in tortures, as I may.
What! will you cast by self-accusing flight 40
Assured conviction upon Beatrice?
She, who alone in this unnatural work,
Stands like God's angel ministered upon
By fiends; avenging such a nameless wrong
As turns black parricide to piety;
Whilst we for basest ends . . . I fear, Orsino,
While I consider all your words and looks,
Comparing them with your proposal now,
That you must be a villain. For what end
Could you engage in such a perilous crime, 50
Training me on with hints, and signs, and smiles,
Even to this gulf? Thou art no liar? No,
Thou art a lie! Traitor and murderer!
Coward and slave! But, no, defend thyself;
          [*Drawing.*
Let the sword speak what the indignant tongue
Disdains to brand thee with.
 Orsino.   Put up your weapon.
Is it the desperation of your fear
Makes you thus rash and sudden with a friend,
Now ruined for your sake? If honest anger
Have moved you, know, that what I just proposed 60
Was but to try you. As for me, I think,
Thankless affection led me to this point,
From which, if my firm temper could repent,

I cannot now recede. Even whilst we speak
The ministers of justice wait below:
They grant me these brief moments. Now if you
Have any word of melancholy comfort
To speak to your pale wife, 'twere best to pass
Out at the postern, and avoid them so.
    Giacomo. O, generous friend! How canst thou
      pardon me?   70
Would that my life could purchase thine!
    Orsino.   That wish
Now comes a day too late. Haste; fare thee well!
Hear'st thou not steps along the corridor?
                         [*Exit* GIACOMO.
I'm sorry for it; but the guards are waiting
At his own gate, and such was my contrivance
That I might rid me both of him and them.
I thought to act a solemn comedy
Upon the painted scene of this new world,
And to attain my own peculiar ends
By some such plot of mingled good and ill   80
As others weave; but there arose a Power
Which grasped and snapped the threads of my device
And turned it to a net of ruin . . . Ha!
                       [*A shout is heard.*
Is that my name I hear proclaimed abroad?
But I will pass, wrapped in a vile disguise;
Rags on my back, and a false innocence
Upon my face, through the misdeeming crowd
Which judges by what seems. 'Tis easy then
For a new name and for a country new,
And a new life, fashioned on old desires,   90
To change the honours of abandoned Rome.
And these must be the masks of that within,
Which must remain unaltered . . . Oh, I fear
That what is past will never let me rest!
Why, when none else is conscious, but myself,
Of my misdeeds, should my own heart's contempt
Trouble me? Have I not the power to fly
My own reproaches? Shall I be the slave
Of . . . what? A word? which those of this false world
Employ against each other, not themselves;   100
As men wear daggers not for self-offence.
But if I am mistaken, where shall I
Find the disguise to hide me from myself,
As now I skulk from every other eye?
                            [*Exit.*

SCENE II.   *A Hall of Justice.*

CAMILLO, JUDGES, *&c., are discovered seated;*
    MARZIO *is led in.*

    First Judge. Accused, do you persist in your denial?
I ask you, are you innocent, or guilty?
I demand who were the participators

In your offence? Speak truth and the whole truth.
    Marzio. My God! I did not kill him; I know
      nothing;
Olimpio sold the robe to me from which
You would infer my guilt.
    Second Judge.   Away with him!
    First Judge. Dare you, with lips yet white from the
      rack's kiss
Speak false? Is it so soft a questioner,
That you would bandy lover's talk with it   10
Till it wind out your life and soul? Away!
    Marzio. Spare me! O, spare! I will confess.
    First Judge.   Then speak.
    Marzio. I strangled him in his sleep.
    First Judge.   Who urged
      you to it?
    Marzio. His own son Giacomo, and the young
      prelate
Orsino sent me to Petrella; there
The ladies Beatrice and Lucretia
Tempted me with a thousand crowns, and I
And my companion forthwith murdered him.
Now let me die.
    First Judge. This sounds as bad as truth. Guards,
      there,
Lead forth the prisoners!

    Enter LUCRETIA, BEATRICE, *and* GIACOMO,
                 guarded.

                      Look upon this man;   20
When did you see him last?
    Beatrice.   We never saw him.
    Marzio. You know me too well, Lady Beatrice.
    Beatrice. I know thee! How? where? when?
    Marzio.   You
      know 'twas I
Whom you did urge with menaces and bribes
To kill your father. When the thing was done
You clothed me in a robe of woven gold
And bade me thrive: how I have thriven, you see.
You, my Lord Giacomo, Lady Lucretia,
You know that what I speak is true.
          [BEATRICE *advances towards him; he covers*
                   his face, and shrinks back.
                           Oh, dart
The terrible resentment of those eyes   30
On the dead earth! Turn them away from me!
They wound: 'twas torture forced the truth. My
    Lords,
Having said this let me be led to death.
    Beatrice. Poor wretch, I pity thee: yet stay awhile.
    Camillo. Guards, lead him not away.
    Beatrice.   Cardinal
    Camillo,

You have a good repute for gentleness
And wisdom: can it be that you sit here
To countenance a wicked farce like this?
When some obscure and trembling slave is dragged
From sufferings which might shake the sternest heart
And bade to answer, not as he believes,   41
But as those may suspect or do desire
Whose questions thence suggest their own reply:
And that in peril of such hideous torments
As merciful God spares even the damned. Speak now
The thing you surely know, which is that you,
If your fine frame were stretched upon that wheel,
And you were told: 'Confess that you did poison
Your little nephew; that fair blue-eyed child
Who was the lodestar of your life:'—and though   50
All see, since his most swift and piteous death,
That day and night, and heaven and earth, and time,
And all the things hoped for or done therein
Are changed to you, through your exceeding grief,
Yet you would say, 'I confess anything:'
And beg from your tormentors, like that slave,
The refuge of dishonourable death.
I pray thee, Cardinal, that thou assert
My innocence.
     Camillo (*much moved*). What shall we think, my
          Lords?
Shame on these tears! I thought the heart was frozen
Which is their fountain. I would pledge my soul   61
That she is guiltless.
     Judge.   Yet she must be tortured.
     Camillo. I would as soon have tortured mine own
          nephew
(If he now lived he would be just her age;
His hair, too, was her colour, and his eyes
Like hers in shape, but blue and not so deep)
As that most perfect image of God's love
That ever came sorrowing upon the earth.
She is as pure as speechless infancy!
     Judge. Well, be her purity on your head, my Lord,
If you forbid the rack. His Holiness   71
Enjoined us to pursue this monstrous crime
By the severest forms of law; nay even
To stretch a point against the criminals.
The prisoners stand accused of parricide
Upon such evidence as justifies
Torture.
     Beatrice. What evidence? This man's?
     Judge.   Even so.
     Beatrice (*to* MARZIO). Come near. And who art
          thou thus chosen forth
Out of the multitude of living men
To kill the innocent?
     Marzio.   I am Marzio,   80
Thy father's vassal.

     Beatrice.   Fix thine eyes on mine;
Answer to what I ask.
                              [*Turning to the* JUDGES.
                    I prithee mark
His countenance: unlike bold calumny
Which sometimes dares not speak the thing it looks,
He dares not look the thing he speaks, but bends
His gaze on the blind earth.
(*To* MARZIO.)   What! wilt thou say
That I did murder my own father?
     Marzio.   Oh!
Spare me! My brain swims round . . . I cannot
          speak . . .
It was that horrid torture forced the truth.
Take me away! Let her not look on me!   90
I am a guilty miserable wretch;
I have said all I know; now, let me die!
     Beatrice. My Lords, if by my nature I had been
So stern, as to have planned the crime alleged,
Which your suspicions dictate to this slave,
And the rack makes him utter, do you think
I should have left this two-edged instrument
Of my misdeed; this man, this bloody knife
With my own name engraven on the heft,
Lying unsheathed amid a world of foes   100
For my own death? That with such horrible need
For deepest silence, I should have neglected
So trivial a precaution, as the making
His tomb the keeper of a secret written
On a thief's memory? What is his poor life?
What are a thousand lives? A parricide
Had trampled them like dust; and, see, he lives!
                              [*Turning to* MARZIO.
And thou . . .
     Marzio. Oh, spare me! Speak to me no more!
That stern yet piteous look, those solemn tones,
Wound worse than torture.
(*To the* JUDGES.)   I have told it all;   110
For pity's sake lead me away to death.
     Camillo. Guards, lead him nearer the Lady
          Beatrice,
He shrinks from her regard like autumn's leaf
From the keen breath of the serenest north.
     Beatrice. O thou who tremblest on the giddy verge
Of life and death, pause ere thou answerest me;
So mayst thou answer God with less dismay:
What evil have we done thee? I, alas!
Have lived but on this earth a few sad years,
And so my lot was ordered, that a father   120
First turned the moments of awakening life
To drops, each poisoning youth's sweet hope; and
          then
Stabbed with one blow my everlasting soul;
And my untainted fame; and even that peace

Which sleeps within the core of the heart's heart;
But the wound was not mortal; so my hate
Became the only worship I could lift
To our great father, who in pity and love,
Armed thee, as thou dost say, to cut him off;
And thus his wrong becomes my accusation;   130
And art thou the accuser? If thou hopest
Mercy in heaven, show justice upon earth:
Worse than a bloody hand is a hard heart.
If thou hast done murders, made thy life's path
Over the trampled laws of God and man,
Rush not before thy Judge, and say: 'My maker,
I have done this and more; for there was one
Who was most pure and innocent on earth;
And because she endured what never any
Guilty or innocent endured before: 140
Because her wrongs could not be told, not thought;
Because thy hand at length did rescue her;
I with my words killed her and all her kin.'
Think, I adjure you, what it is to slay
The reverence living in the minds of men
Towards our ancient house, and stainless fame!
Think what it is to strangle infant pity,
Cradled in the belief of guileless looks,
Till it become a crime to suffer. Think
What 'tis to blot with infamy and blood   150
All that which shows like innocence, and is,
Hear me, great God! I swear, most innocent,
So that the world lose all discrimination
Between the sly, fierce, wild regard of guilt,
And that which now compels thee to reply
To what I ask: Am I, or am I not
A parricide?
    Marzio.   Thou art not!
    Judge.   What is this?
    Marzio. I here declare those whom I did accuse
Are innocent. 'Tis I alone am guilty.
    Judge. Drag him away to torments; let them be
Subtle and long drawn out, to tear the folds   161
Of the heart's inmost cell. Unbind him not
Till he confess.
    Marzio.   Torture me as ye will:
A keener pang has wrung a higher truth
From my last breath. She is most innocent!
Bloodhounds, not men, glut yourselves well with me;
I will not give you that fine piece of nature
To rend and ruin.
                        [*Exit* MARZIO, *guarded.*
    Camillo.   What say ye now, my Lords?
    Judge. Let tortures strain the truth till it be white
As snow thrice sifted by the frozen wind.   170
    Camillo. Yet stained with blood.
    Judge (*to* BEATRICE).   Know you this
        paper, Lady?

Beatrice. Entrap me not with questions. Who
        stands here
As my accuser? Ha! wilt thou be he,
Who art my judge? Accuser, witness, judge,
What, all in one? Here is Orsino's name;
Where is Orsino? Let his eye meet mine.
What means this scrawl? Alas! ye know not what,
And therefore on the chance that it may be
Some evil, will ye kill us?

Enter an Officer.

    Officer.   Marzio's dead.
    Judge. What did he say?
    Officer.   Nothing. As soon as we
Had bound him on the wheel, he smiled on us,   181
As one who baffles a deep adversary;
And holding his breath, died.
    Judge.   There remains nothing
But to apply the question to those prisoners,
Who yet remain stubborn.
    Camillo.   I overrule
Further proceedings, and in the behalf
Of these most innocent and noble persons
Will use my interest with the Holy Father.
    Judge. Let the Pope's pleasure then be done.
        Meanwhile
Conduct these culprits each to separate cells;
And be the engines ready: for this night
If the Pope's resolution be as grave,
Pious, and just as once, I'll wring the truth
Out of those nerves and sinews, groan by groan.
                                        [*Exeunt.*

SCENE III.   *The Cell of a Prison.*

BEATRICE *is discovered asleep*
on a couch. Enter BERNARDO.

Bernardo. How gently slumber rests upon her face,
Like the last thoughts of some day sweetly spent
Closing in night and dreams, and so prolonged.
After such torments as she bore last night,
How light and soft her breathing comes. Ay me!
Methinks that I shall never sleep again.
But I must shake the heavenly dew of rest
From this sweet folded flower, thus . . . wake! awake!
What, sister, canst thou sleep?
    Beatrice (*awaking*).   I was just dreaming
That we were all in Paradise. Thou knowest   10
This cell seems like a kind of Paradise
After our father's presence.
    Bernardo.   Dear, dear sister,
Would that thy dream were not a dream! O God!

How shall I tell?
   Beatrice.   What wouldst thou tell, sweet
   brother?
   Bernardo. Look not so calm and happy, or even
   whilst
I stand considering what I have to say
My heart will break.
   Beatrice.   See now, thou mak'st me weep:
How very friendless thou wouldst be, dear child,
If I were dead. Say what thou hast to say.
   Bernardo. They have confessed; they could endure
   no more   20
The tortures . . .
   Beatrice.   Ha! What was there to confess?
They must have told some weak and wicked lie
To flatter their tormentors. Have they said
That they were guilty? O white innocence,
That thou shouldst wear the mask of guilt to hide
Thine awful and serenest countenance
From those who know thee not!

Enter JUDGE *with* LUCRETIA *and*
GIACOMO, *guarded.*

                            Ignoble hearts!
From some brief spasms of pain, which are at least
As mortal as the limbs through which they pass,
Are centuries of high splendour laid in dust?   30
And that eternal honour which should live
Sunlike, above the reek of mortal fame,
Changed to a mockery and a byword? What!
Will you give up these bodies to be dragged
At horses' heels, so that our hair should sweep
The footsteps of the vain and senseless crowd,
Who, that they may make our calamity
Their worship and their spectacle, will leave
The churches and the theatres as void
As their own hearts? Shall the light multitude   40
Fling, at their choice, curses or faded pity,
Sad funeral flowers to deck a living corpse,
Upon us as we pass to pass away,
And leave . . . what memory of our having been?
Infamy, blood, terror, despair? O thou,
Who wert a mother to the parentless,
Kill not thy child! Let not her wrongs kill thee!
Brother, lie down with me upon the rack,
And let us each be silent as a corpse;
It soon will be as soft as any grave.   50
'Tis but the falsehood it can wring from fear
Makes the rack cruel.
   Giacomo.   They will tear the truth
Even from thee at last, those cruel pains:
For pity's sake say thou art guilty now.
   Lucretia. Oh, speak the truth! Let us all quickly
   die;

And after death, God is our judge, not they;
He will have mercy on us.
   Bernardo.   If indeed
It can be true, say so, dear sister mine;
And then the Pope will surely pardon you,
And all be well.
   Judge.   Confess, or I will warp   60
Your limbs with such keen tortures . . .
   Beatrice.   Tortures! Turn
The rack henceforth into a spinning-wheel!
Torture your dog, that he may tell when last
He lapped the blood his master shed . . . not me!
My pangs are of the mind, and of the heart,
And of the soul; ay, of the inmost soul,
Which weeps within tears as of burning gall
To see, in this ill world where none are true,
My kindred false to their deserted selves.
And with considering all the wretched life   70
Which I have lived, and its now wretched end,
And the small justice shown by Heaven and Earth
To me or mine; and what a tyrant thou art,
And what slaves these; and what a world we make,
The oppressor and the oppressed . . . such pangs
   compel
My answer. What is it thou wouldst with me?
   Judge. Art thou not guilty of thy father's death?
   Beatrice. Or wilt thou rather tax high-judging God
That He permitted such an act as that
Which I have suffered, and which He beheld;   80
Made it unutterable, and took from it
All refuge, all revenge, all consequence,
But that which thou hast called my father's death?
Which is or is not what men call a crime,
Which either I have done, or have not done;
Say what ye will. I shall deny no more.
If ye desire it thus, thus let it be,
And so an end of all. Now do your will;
No other pains shall force another word.
   Judge. She is convicted, but has not confessed.   90
Be it enough. Until their final sentence
Let none have converse with them. You, young Lord,
Linger not here!
   Beatrice.   Oh, tear him not away!
   Judge. Guards, do your duty.
   Bernardo (*embracing* BEATRICE). Oh! would ye
   divide
Body from soul?
   Officer.   That is the headsman's business.
                 [*Exeunt all but* LUCRETIA, BEATRICE,
                             and GIACOMO.
   Giacomo. Have I confessed? Is it all over now?
No hope! No refuge! O weak, wicked tongue
Which hast destroyed me, would that thou hadst been
Cut out and thrown to dogs first! To have killed

My father first, and then betrayed my sister;   100
Ay, thee! the one thing innocent and pure
In this black guilty world, to that which I
So well deserve! My wife! my little ones!
Destitute, helpless, and I . . . Father! God!
Canst Thou forgive even the unforgiving,
When their full hearts break thus, thus! . . .
                              [*Covers his face and weeps.*
  Lucretia.   O my child!
To what a dreadful end are we all come!
Why did I yield? Why did I not sustain
Those torments? Oh, that I were all dissolved
Into these fast and unavailing tears,   110
Which flow and feel not!
  Beatrice.   What 'twas weak to do,
'Tis weaker to lament, once being done;
Take cheer! The God who knew my wrong, and made
Our speedy act the angel of His wrath,
Seems, and but seems, to have abandoned us.
Let us not think that we shall die for this.
Brother, sit near me; give me your firm hand,
You had a manly heart. Bear up! Bear up!
O dearest Lady, put your gentle head
Upon my lap, and try to sleep awhile: 120
Your eyes look pale, hollow and overworn,
With heaviness of watching and slow grief.
Come, I will sing you some low, sleepy tune,
Not cheerful, nor yet sad; some dull old thing,
Some outworn and unused monotony,
Such as our country gossips sing and spin,
Till they almost forget they live: lie down!
So, that will do. Have I forgot the words?
Faith! They are sadder than I thought they were.

SONG

    False friend, wilt thou smile or weep   130
    When my life is laid asleep?
    Little cares for a smile or a tear,
    The clay-cold corpse upon the bier!
        Farewell! Heigho!
        What is this whispers low?
    There is a snake in thy smile, my dear;
    And bitter poison within thy tear.

    Sweet sleep, were death like to thee,
    Or if thou couldst mortal be,
    I would close these eyes of pain;   140
    When to wake? Never again.
        O World! Farewell!
        Listen to the passing bell!
    It says, thou and I must part,
    With a light and a heavy heart.
             [*The scene closes.*

SCENE IV.   *A Hall of the Prison.*

Enter CAMILLO *and* BERNARDO.

  Camillo.   The Pope is stern; not to be moved or
    bent.
He looked as calm and keen as is the engine
Which tortures and which kills, exempt itself
From aught that it inflicts; a marble form,
A rite, a law, a custom: not a man.
He frowned, as if to frown had been the trick
Of his machinery, on the advocates
Presenting the defences, which he tore
And threw behind, muttering with hoarse, harsh
    voice:
'Which among ye defended their old father   10
Killed in his sleep?' Then to another: 'Thou
Dost this in virtue of thy place; 'tis well.'
He turned to me then, looking deprecation,
And said these three words, coldly: 'They must
    die.'
  Bernardo. And yet you left him not?
  Camillo.   I urged him
    still;
Pleading, as I could guess, the devilish wrong
Which prompted your unnatural parent's death.
And he replied: 'Paolo Santa Croce
Murdered his mother yester evening,
And he is fled. Parricide grows so rife   20
That soon, for some just cause no doubt, the young
Will strangle us all, dozing in our chairs.
Authority, and power, and hoary hair
Are grown crimes capital. You are my nephew,
You come to ask their pardon; stay a moment;
Here is their sentence; never see me more
Till, to the letter, it be all fulfilled.'
  Bernardo. O God, not so! I did believe indeed
That all you said was but sad preparation
For happy news. Oh, there are words and looks   30
To bend the sternest purpose! Once I knew them,
Now I forget them at my dearest need.
What think you if I seek him out, and bathe
His feet and robe with hot and bitter tears?
Importune him with prayers, vexing his brain
With my perpetual cries, until in rage
He strike me with his pastoral cross, and trample
Upon my prostrate head, so that my blood
May stain the senseless dust on which he treads,
And remorse waken mercy? I will do it!   40
Oh, wait till I return!
                [*Rushes out.*

  Camillo.   Alas! poor boy!
A wreck-devoted seaman thus might pray
To the deaf sea.

Enter LUCRETIA, BEATRICE, *and* GIACOMO, *guarded.*

Beatrice. I hardly dare to fear
That thou bring'st other news than a just pardon.
    Camillo. May God in heaven be less inexorable
To the Pope's prayers, than he has been to mine.
Here is the sentence and the warrant.
    Beatrice (*wildly*). O
My God! Can it be possible I have
To die so suddenly? So young to go
Under the obscure, cold, rotting, wormy ground!   50
To be nailed down into a narrow place;
To see no more sweet sunshine; hear no more
Blithe voice of living thing; muse not again
Upon familiar thoughts, sad, yet thus lost—
How fearful! to be nothing! Or to be . . .
What? Oh, where am I? Let me not go mad!
Sweet Heaven, forgive weak thoughts! If there
        should be
No God, no Heaven, no Earth in the void world;
The wide, gray, lampless, deep, unpeopled world!
If all things then should be . . . my father's spirit,   60
His eye, his voice, his touch surrounding me;
The atmosphere and breath of my dead life!
If sometimes, as a shape more like himself,
Even the form which tortured me on earth,
Masked in gray hairs and wrinkles, he should come
And wind me in his hellish arms, and fix
His eyes on mine, and drag me down, down, down!
For was he not alone omnipotent
On Earth, and ever present? Even though dead,
Does not his spirit live in all that breathe,   70
And work for me and mine still the same ruin,
Scorn, pain, despair? Who ever yet returned
To teach the laws of Death's untrodden realm?
Unjust perhaps as those which drive us now,
Oh, whither, whither?
    Lucretia. Trust in God's sweet love,
The tender promises of Christ: ere night,
Think, we shall be in Paradise.
    Beatrice. 'Tis past!
Whatever comes my heart shall sink no more.
And yet, I know not why, your words strike chill:
How tedious, false and cold seem all things. I   80
Have met with much injustice in this world;
No difference has been made by God or man,
Or any power moulding my wretched lot,
'Twixt good or evil, as regarded me.
I am cut off from the only world I know,
From light, and life, and love, in youth's sweet prime.
You do well telling me to trust in God,
I hope I do trust in Him. In whom else
Can any trust? And yet my heart is cold.

[*During the latter speeches* GIACOMO *has retired
    conversing with* CAMILLO, *who now goes out;*
    GIACOMO *advances.*

    Giacomo. Know you not, Mother . . . Sister, know
        you not?   90
Bernardo even now is gone to implore
The Pope to grant our pardon.
    Lucretia. Child, perhaps
It will be granted. We may all then live
To make these woes a tale for distant years:
Oh, what a thought! It gushes to my heart
Like the warm blood.
    Beatrice. Yet both will soon be cold.
Oh, trample out that thought! Worse than despair,
Worse than the bitterness of death, is hope:
It is the only ill which can find place
Upon the giddy, sharp and narrow hour   100
Tottering beneath us. Plead with the swift frost
That it should spare the eldest flower of spring:
Plead with awakening earthquake, o'er whose couch
Even now a city stands, strong, fair, and free;
Now stench and blackness yawn, like death. Oh, plead
With famine, or wind-walking Pestilence,
Blind lightning, or the deaf sea, not with man!
Cruel, cold, formal man; righteous in words,
In deeds a Cain. No, Mother, we must die:
Since such is the reward of innocent lives;   110
Such the alleviation of worst wrongs.
And whilst our murderers live, and hard, cold men,
Smiling and slow, walk through a world of tears
To death as to life's sleep; 'twere just the grave
Were some strange joy for us. Come, obscure Death,
And wind me in thine all-embracing arms!
Like a fond mother hide me in thy bosom,
And rock me to the sleep from which none wake.
Live ye, who live, subject to one another
As we were once, who now . . .

BERNARDO *rushes in.*

    Bernardo. Oh, horrible!   120
That tears, that looks, that hope poured forth in
        prayer,
Even till the heart is vacant and despairs,
Should all be vain! The ministers of death
Are waiting round the doors. I thought I saw
Blood on the face of one . . . What if 'twere fancy?
Soon the heart's blood of all I love on earth
Will sprinkle him, and he will wipe it off
As if 'twere only rain. O life! O world!
Cover me! let me be no more! To see
That perfect mirror of pure innocence   130
Wherein I gazed, and grew happy and good,
Shivered to dust! To see thee, Beatrice,
Who made all lovely thou didst look upon . . .

Thee, light of life . . . dead, dark! while I say, sister,
To hear I have no sister; and thou, Mother,
Whose love was as a bond to all our loves . . .
Dead! The sweet bond broken!

Enter CAMILLO *and* GUARDS.

                  They come! Let me
Kiss those warm lips before their crimson leaves
Are blighted . . . white . . . cold. Say farewell, before
Death chokes that gentle voice! Oh, let me hear   140
You speak!
   Beatrice. Farewell, my tender brother. Think
Of our sad fate with gentleness, as now:
And let mild, pitying thoughts lighten for thee
Thy sorrow's load. Err not in harsh despair,
But tears and patience. One thing more, my child:
For thine own sake be constant to the love
Thou bearest us; and to the faith that I,
Though wrapped in a strange cloud of crime and
      shame,
Lived ever holy and unstained. And though
Ill tongues shall wound me, and our common name
Be as a mark stamped on thine innocent brow   151
For men to point at as they pass, do thou
Forbear, and never think a thought unkind
Of those, who perhaps love thee in their graves.
So mayest thou die as I do; fear and pain
Being subdued. Farewell! Farewell! Farewell!
   Bernardo. I cannot say, farewell!
   Camillo   Oh, Lady
    Beatrice!
   Beatrice. Give yourself no unnecessary pain,
My dear Lord Cardinal. Here, Mother, tie
My girdle for me, and bind up this hair   160
In any simple knot; ay, that does well.
And yours I see is coming down. How often
Have we done this for one another; now
We shall not do it any more. My Lord,
We are quite ready. Well, 'tis very well.

THE END.

[1819]   [1820]

PROMETHEUS UNBOUND

Like Byron talking about Manfred, *Shelley claimed that the
sight of high mountains had as much importance to this work as
his classical sources. The evil spirit—the tyrant Jupiter—is as
much in the surroundings as in Prometheus' (or Shelley's) mind.
Love, Prometheus' sole resource in combating the villain, is a
combination of humanity and imagination, and involves the act
of perception.*

*Mrs. Shelley describes Shelley's use of myth in this poem as
follows:*

    *He followed certain classical authorities in figuring Saturn
as the good principle, Jupiter the usurping evil one, and
Prometheus as the regenerator, who, unable to bring mankind
back to primitive innocence, used knowledge as a weapon to
defeat evil, by leading mankind, beyond the state wherein they
are sinless through ignorance, to that in which they are virtuous
through wisdom. Jupiter punished the temerity of the Titan by
chaining him to a rock of Caucasus, and causing a vulture to devour
his still-renewed heart. There was a prophecy afloat in heaven
portending the fall of Jove, the secret of averting which was
known only to Prometheus; and the god offered freedom from
torture on condition of its being communicated to him. According
to the mythological story, this referred to the offspring of Thetis,
who was destined to be greater than his father. Prometheus at
last bought pardon for his crime of enriching mankind with his
gifts, by revealing the prophecy. Hercules killed the vulture,
and set him free; and Thetis was married to Peleus, the father
of Achilles.*

    *All the main characters except Demogorgon come from Aeschy-
lus'* Prometheus Bound. *Jupiter expresses a collective external
evil; Asia the essence of Nature (Panthea and Ione its lesser
aspects); and Demogorgon a sense of time and historical change
and process. By overcoming his own blinding passion for revenge,
Prometheus discovers the possibility of significant change. Harold
Bloom has said (in* The Visionary Company, *Chapter 5) that
if Blake could best envision the New Jerusalem, the quality of an
ideal city, Shelley offered the best advice on the arts of urbane
and moral behavior appropriate to such a place: ". . . it is Shel-
ley who has an instinctive sense of the manners of Blake's City."*

PROMETHEUS UNBOUND

A LYRICAL DRAMA

IN FOUR ACTS

Audisne Hæc, Amphiarae, Sub Terram abdite?[1]

PREFACE

THE Greek tragic writers, in selecting as their sub-
ject any portion of their national history or mytho-
logy, employed in their treatment of it a certain

---

[1] "Dost thou not hear, Amphiaraus, hidden beneath the
earth?" From Cicero, *Tusculan Disputations.*

arbitrary discretion. They by no means conceived themselves bound to adhere to the common interpretation or to imitate in story as in title their rivals and predecessors. Such a system would have amounted to a resignation of those claims to preference over their competitors which incited the composition. The Agamemnonian story was exhibited on the Athenian theatre with as many variations as dramas.

I have presumed to employ a similar licence. The 'Prometheus Unbound' of Æschylus supposed the reconciliation of Jupiter with his victim as the price of the disclosure of the danger threatened to his empire by the consummation of his marriage with Thetis. Thetis, according to this view of the subject, was given in marriage to Peleus, and Prometheus, by the permission of Jupiter, delivered from his captivity by Hercules. Had I framed my story on this model, I should have done no more than have attempted to restore the lost drama of Æschylus; an ambition, which, if my preference to this mode of treating the subject had incited me to cherish, the recollection of the high comparison such an attempt would challenge might well abate. But, in truth, I was averse from a catastrophe so feeble as that of reconciling the Champion with the Oppressor of mankind. The moral interest of the fable, which is so powerfully sustained by the sufferings and endurance of Prometheus, would be annihilated if we could conceive of him as unsaying his high language and quailing before his successful and perfidious adversary. The only imaginary being resembling in any degree Prometheus, is Satan; and Prometheus is, in my judgment, a more poetical character than Satan, because, in addition to courage, and majesty, and firm and patient opposition to omnipotent force, he is susceptible of being described as exempt from the taints of ambition, envy, revenge, and a desire for personal aggrandisement, which, in the Hero of Paradise Lost, interfere with the interest. The character of Satan engenders in the mind a pernicious casuistry which leads us to weigh his faults with his wrongs, and to excuse the former because the latter exceed all measure. In the minds of those who consider that magnificent fiction with a religious feeling it engenders something worse. But Prometheus is, as it were, the type of the highest perfection of moral and intellectual nature, impelled by the purest and the truest motives to the best and noblest ends.

This Poem was chiefly written upon the mountainous ruins of the Baths of Caracalla, among the flowery glades, and thickets of odoriferous blossoming trees, which are extended in ever winding labyrinths upon its immense platforms and dizzy arches suspended in the air. The bright blue sky of Rome, and the effect of the vigorous awakening spring in that divinest climate, and the new life with which it drenches the spirits even to intoxication, were the inspiration of this drama.

The imagery which I have employed will be found, in many instances, to have been drawn from the operations of the human mind, or from those external actions by which they are expressed. This is unusual in modern poetry, although Dante and Shakspeare are full of instances of the same kind: Dante indeed more than any other poet, and with greater success. But the Greek poets, as writers to whom no resource of awakening the sympathy of their contemporaries was unknown, were in the habitual use of this power; and it is the study of their works, (since a higher merit would probably be denied me,) to which I am willing that my readers should impute this singularity.

One word is due in candour to the degree in which the study of contemporary writings may have tinged my composition, for such has been a topic of censure with regard to poems far more popular, and indeed more deservedly popular, than mine. It is impossible that any one who inhabits the same age with such writers as those who stand in the foremost ranks of our own, can conscientiously assure himself that his language and tone of thought may not have been modified by the study of the productions of those extraordinary intellects. It is true, that, not the spirit of their genius, but the forms in which it has manifested itself, are due less to the peculiarities of their own minds than to the peculiarity of the moral and intellectual condition of the minds among which they have been produced. Thus a number of writers possess the form, whilst they want the spirit of those whom, it is alleged, they imitate; because the former is the endowment of the age in which they live, and the latter must be the uncommunicated lightning of their own mind.

The peculiar style of intense and comprehensive imagery which distinguishes the modern literature of England, has not been, as a general power, the product of the imitation of any particular writer. The mass of capabilities remains at every period materially the same; the circumstances which awaken it to action perpetually change. If England were divided into forty republics, each equal in population and extent to Athens, there is no reason to suppose but that, under institutions not more perfect than those of Athens, each would produce philosophers and poets equal to those who (if we except Shakspeare) have never been surpassed. We owe the great writers of the golden age of our literature to that fervid awakening of the public mind which shook to dust the oldest and most oppressive form of the Christian religion.

We owe Milton to the progress and development of the same spirit: the sacred Milton was, let it ever be remembered, a republican, and a bold inquirer into morals and religion. The great writers of our own age are, we have reason to suppose, the companions and forerunners of some unimagined change in our social condition, or the opinions which cement it. The cloud of mind is discharging its collected lightning, and the equilibrium between institutions and opinions is now restoring, or is about to be restored.

As to imitation, poetry is a mimetic art. It creates, but it creates by combination and representation. Poetical abstractions are beautiful and new, not because the portions of which they are composed had no previous existence in the mind of man or in nature, but because the whole produced by their combination has some intelligible and beautiful analogy with those sources of emotion and thought, and with the contemporary condition of them: one great poet is a masterpiece of nature which another not only ought to study but must study. He might as wisely and as easily determine that his mind should no longer be the mirror of all that is lovely in the visible universe, as exclude from his contemplation the beautiful which exists in the writings of a great contemporary. The pretence of doing it would be a presumption in any but the greatest; the effect, even in him, would be strained, unnatural, and ineffectual. A poet is the combined product of such internal powers as modify the nature of others; and of such external influences as excite and sustain these powers; he is not one, but both. Every man's mind is, in this respect, modified by all the objects of nature and art; by every word and every suggestion which he ever admitted to act upon his consciousness; it is the mirror upon which all forms are reflected, and in which they compose one form. Poets, not otherwise than philosophers, painters, sculptors, and musicians, are, in one sense, the creators, and, in another, the creations, of their age. From this subjection the loftiest do not escape. There is a similarity between Homer and Hesiod, between Æschylus and Euripides, between Virgil and Horace, between Dante and Petrarch, between Shakspeare and Fletcher, between Dryden and Pope; each has a generic resemblance under which their specific distinctions are arranged. If this similarity be the result of imitation, I am willing to confess that I have imitated.

Let this opportunity be conceded to me of acknowledging that I have, what a Scotch philosopher characteristically terms, 'a passion for reforming the world:' what passion incited him to write and publish his book, he omits to explain. For my part, I had rather be damned with Plato and Lord Bacon, than go to Heaven with Paley and Malthus.[2] But it is a mistake to suppose that I dedicate my poetical compositions solely to the direct enforcement of reform, or that I consider them in any degree as containing a reasoned system on the theory of human life. Didactic poetry is my abhorrence; nothing can be equally well expressed in prose that is not tedious and supererogatory in verse. My purpose has hitherto been simply to familiarize the highly refined imagination of the more select classes of poetical readers with beautiful idealisms of moral excellence; aware that until the mind can love, and admire, and trust, and hope, and endure, reasoned principles of moral conduct are seeds cast upon the highway of life which the unconscious passenger tramples into dust, although they would bear the harvest of his happiness. Should I live to accomplish what I purpose, that is, produce a systematical history of what appear to me to be the genuine elements of human society, let not the advocates of injustice and superstition flatter themselves that I should take Æschylus rather than Plato as my model.

The having spoken of myself with unaffected freedom will need little apology with the candid; and let the uncandid consider that they injure me less than their own hearts and minds by misrepresentation. Whatever talents a person may possess to amuse and instruct others, be they ever so inconsiderable, he is yet bound to exert them: if his attempt be ineffectual, let the punishment of an unaccomplished purpose have been sufficient; let none trouble themselves to heap the dust of oblivion upon his efforts; the pile they raise will betray his grave which might otherwise have been unknown.

DRAMATIS PERSONÆ.

PROMETHEUS.
DEMOGORGON.
JUPITER.
THE EARTH.
OCEAN.
APOLLO.
MERCURY.
HERCULES.
ASIA,
PANTHEA,   } *Oceanides.*
IONE,

---

[2] William Paley, who in the late eighteenth century argued for nature as a demonstration of the truth of Christianity; Robert Malthus (1766–1834), who predicted that rising population would defeat all attempts to improve man's physical well-being, and that war and disease are necessary checks on population.

THE PHANTASM OF JUPITER.
THE SPIRIT OF THE EARTH.
THE SPIRIT OF THE MOON.
SPIRITS OF THE HOURS.
SPIRITS. ECHOES. FAUNS.
FURIES.

—⟶∘⊙∘⟵—

ACT I

SCENE. *A Ravine of Icy Rocks in the Indian Cau-
casus.* PROMETHEUS *is discovered bound to the
Precipice.* PANTHEA *and* IONE *are seated at his feet.
Time, night. During the Scene, morning slowly
breaks.*

Prometheus. Monarch of Gods and Dæmons, and
    all Spirits
But One,[3] who throng those bright and rolling
    worlds,
Which Thou and I alone of living things
Behold with sleepless eyes! regard this Earth
Made multitudinous with thy slaves, whom thou
Requitest for knee-worship, prayer, and praise,
And toil, and hecatombs[4] of broken hearts,
With fear and self-contempt and barren hope.
Whilst me, who am thy foe, eyeless in hate,
Hast thou made reign and triumph, to thy scorn,   10
O'er mine own misery and thy vain revenge.
Three thousand years of sleep-unsheltered hours,
And moments aye divided by keen pangs
Till they seemed years, torture and solitude,
Scorn and despair,—these are mine empire.
More glorious far than that which thou surveyest
From thine unenvied throne, O, Mighty God!
Almighty, had I deigned to share the shame
Of thine ill tyranny, and hung not here
Nailed to this wall of eagle-baffling mountain,   20
Black, wintry, dead, unmeasured; without herb,
Insect, or beast, or shape or sound of life.
Ah me! alas, pain, pain ever, for ever!

No change, no pause, no hope! Yet I endure.
I ask the Earth, have not the mountains felt?
I ask yon Heaven, the all-beholding Sun,
Has it not seen? The Sea, in storm or calm,
Heaven's ever-changing Shadow, spread below,
Have its deaf waves not heard my agony?
Ah me! alas, pain, pain ever, for ever!   30

The crawling glaciers pierce me with the spears
Of their moon-freezing crystals, the bright chains
Eat with their burning cold into my bones.
Heaven's wingèd hound, polluting from thy lips
His beak in poison not his own, tears up
My heart,[5] and shapeless sights come wandering by,
The ghastly people of the realm of dream,
Mocking me: and the Earthquake-fiends are charged
To wrench the rivets from my quivering wounds
When the rocks split and close again behind: 40
While from their loud abysses howling throng
The genii of the storm, urging the rage
Of whirlwind, and afflict me with keen hail.
And yet to me welcome is day and night,
Whether one breaks the hoar frost of the morn,
Or starry, dim, and slow, the other climbs
The leaden-coloured east; for then they lead
The wingless, crawling hours, one among whom
—As some dark Priest hales the reluctant victim
Shall drag thee, cruel King, to kiss the blood   50
From these pale feet, which then might trample thee
If they disdained not such a prostrate slave.
Disdain! Ah no! I pity thee. What ruin
Will hunt thee undefended thro' the wide Heaven!
How will thy soul, cloven to its depth with terror,
Gape like a hell within! I speak in grief,
Not exultation, for I hate no more,
As then ere misery made me wise. The curse
Once breathed on thee I would recall. Ye Mountains,
Whose many-voicèd Echoes, through the mist   60
Of cataracts, flung the thunder of that spell!
Ye icy Springs, stagnant with wrinkling frost,
Which vibrated to hear me, and then crept
Shuddering thro' India! Thou serenest Air,
Thro' which the Sun walks burning without beams![6]
And ye swift Whirlwinds, who on poisèd wings
Hung mute and moveless o'er yon hushed abyss,
As thunder, louder than your own, made rock
The orbèd world! If then my words had power,
Though I am changed so that aught evil wish   70
Is dead within; although no memory be
Of what is hate, let them not lose it now!
What was that curse? for ye all heard me speak.

First Voice (from the Mountains).

Thrice three hundred thousand years
    O'er the Earthquake's couch we stood:
Oft, as men convulsed with fears,
    We trembled in our multitude.

---

[3] The Monarch addressed is Jupiter, the One is Prometheus himself.
[4] Huge sacrifice (literally, one hundred oxen).

[5] An eagle is sent daily to tear at Prometheus' entrails, and is kissed by Jupiter on its return.
[6] Shelley apparently believed rays would not be visible in the upper atmosphere.

Second Voice (*from the Springs*).

Thunderbolts had parched our water,
  We had been stained with bitter blood, 79
And had run mute, 'mid shrieks of slaughter,
  Thro' a city and a solitude.

Third Voice (*from the Air*).

I had clothed, since Earth uprose,
  Its wastes in colours not their own,
And oft had my serene repose
  Been cloven by many a rending groan.

Fourth Voice (*from the Whirlwinds*).

We had soared beneath these mountains
  Unresting ages; nor had thunder,
Nor yon volcano's flaming fountains,
  Nor any power above or under
  Ever made us mute with wonder.   90

First Voice.

But never bowed our snowy crest
As at the voice of thine unrest.

Second Voice.

Never such a sound before
To the Indian waves we bore.
A pilot asleep on the howling sea
Leaped up from the deck in agony,
And heard, and cried, 'Ah, woe is me!'
And died as mad as the wild waves be.

Third Voice.

By such dread words from Earth to Heaven
My still realm was never riven: 100
When its wound was closed, there stood
Darkness o'er the day like blood.

Fourth Voice.

And we shrank back: for dreams of ruin
To frozen caves our flight pursuing
Made us keep silence—thus—and thus—
Though silence is as hell to us.

The Earth. The tongueless Caverns of the craggy
    hills
Cried, 'Misery!' then; the hollow Heaven replied,
'Misery!' And the Ocean's purple waves,
Climbing the land, howled to the lashing winds, 110
And the pale nations heard it, 'Misery!'
    Prometheus. I hear a sound of voices: not the
        voice
Which I gave forth. Mother, thy sons and thou
Scorn him, without whose all-enduring will

Beneath the fierce omnipotence of Jove,
Both they and thou had vanished, like thin mist
Unrolled on the morning wind. Know ye not me,
The Titan? He who made his agony
The barrier to your else all-conquering foe?
Oh, rock-embosomed lawns, and snow-fed streams,
Now seen athwart frore vapours, deep below,   121
Through whose o'ershadowing woods I wandered
    once
With Asia, drinking life from her loved eyes
Why scorns the spirit which informs ye, now
To commune with me? me alone, who check'd,
As one who checks a fiend-drawn charioteer,
The falsehood and the force of him who reigns
Supreme, and with the groans of pining slaves
Fills your dim glens and liquid wildernesses:
Why answer ye not, still? Brethren!
    The Earth.   They dare not. 130
    Prometheus. Who dares? for I would hear that
        curse again.
Ha, what an awful whisper rises up!
'Tis scarce like sound: it tingles thro' the frame
As lightning tingles, hovering ere it strike.
Speak, Spirit! from thine inorganic voice
I only know that thou art moving near
And love. How cursed I him?
    The Earth.   How canst thou hear
Who knowest not the language of the dead?
    Prometheus. Thou art a living spirit; speak as they.
    The Earth. I dare not speak like life, lest Heaven's
        fell King
Should hear, and link me to some wheel of pain 140
More torturing than the one whereon I roll.
Subtle thou art and good, and tho' the Gods
Hear not this voice, yet thou art more than God,
Being wise and kind: earnestly hearken now.
    Prometheus. Obscurely thro' my brain, like
        shadows dim,
Sweep awful thoughts, rapid and thick. I feel
Faint, like one mingled in entwining love;
Yet 'tis not pleasure.
    The Earth.   No, thou canst not hear:
Thou art immortal, and this tongue is known   150
Only to those who die.
    Prometheus.   And what art thou,
O, melancholy Voice?
    The Earth.   I am the Earth,
Thy mother; she within whose stony veins,
To the last fibre of the loftiest tree
Whose thin leaves trembled in the frozen air,
Joy ran, as blood within a living frame,
When thou didst from her bosom, like a cloud
Of glory, arise, a spirit of keen joy!
And at thy voice her pining sons uplifted

Their prostrate brows from the polluting dust,   160
And our almighty Tyrant with fierce dread
Grew pale, until his thunder chained thee here.
Then, see those million worlds which burn and roll
Around us : their inhabitants beheld
My spherèd light wane in wide Heaven ; the sea
Was lifted by strange tempest, and new fire
From earthquake-rifted mountains of bright snow
Shook its portentous hair beneath Heaven's frown ;
Lightning and Inundation vexed the plains ;
Blue thistles bloomed in cities ; foodless toads   170
Within voluptuous chambers panting crawled :
When Plague had fallen on man, and beast, and worm,
And Famine ; and black blight on herb and tree ;
And in the corn, and vines, and meadow-grass,
Teemed ineradicable poisonous weeds
Draining their growth, for my wan breast was dry
With grief ; and the thin air, my breath, was stained
With the contagion of a mother's hate
Breathed on her child's destroyer ; ay, I heard
Thy curve, the which, if thou rememberest not,   180
Yet my innumerable seas and streams,
Mountains, and caves, and winds, and yon wide air,
And the inarticulate people of the dead,
Preserve, a treasured spell. We meditate
In secret joy and hope those dreadful words
But dare not speak them.
   Prometheus.   Venerable mother !
All else who live and suffer take from thee
Some comfort ; flowers, and fruits, and happy sounds,
And love, though fleeting ; these may not be mine.
But mine own words, I pray, deny me not.   190
  The Earth. They shall be told. Ere Babylon was
      dust,
The Magus Zoroaster,[7] my dead child,
Met his own image walking in the garden.
That apparition, sole of men, he saw.
For know there are two worlds of life and death :
One that which thou beholdest ; but the other
Is underneath the grave, where do inhabit
The shadows of all forms that think and live
Till death unite them and they part no more ;
Dreams and the light imaginings of men,   200
And all that faith creates or love desires,
Terrible, strange, sublime and beauteous shapes.
There thou art, and dost hang, a writhing shade,
'Mid whirlwind-peopled mountains ; all the gods
Are there, and all the powers of nameless worlds,
Vast, sceptred phantoms ; heroes, men, and beasts ;
And Demogorgon, a tremendous gloom ;
And he, the supreme Tyrant, on his throne
Of burning gold. Son, one of these shall utter

The curse which all remember. Call at will   210
Thine own ghost, or the ghost of Jupiter,
Hades or Typhon,[8] or what mightier Gods
From all-prolific Evil, since thy ruin
Have sprung, and trampled on my prostrate sons.
Ask, and they must reply : so the revenge
Of the Supreme may sweep thro' vacant shades,
As rainy wind thro' the abandoned gate
Of a fallen palace.
   Prometheus.   Mother, let not aught
Of that which may be evil, pass again
My lips, or those of aught resembling me.   220
Phantasm of Jupiter, arise, appear !

Ione.

My wings are folded o'er mine ears :
  My wings are crossèd o'er mine eyes :
Yet thro' their silver shade appears,
  And thro' their lulling plumes arise,
A Shape, a throng of sounds ;
  May it be no ill to thee
O thou of many wounds !
Near whom, for our sweet sister's sake,
Every thus we watch and wake.   230

Panthea.

The sound is of whirlwind underground,
  Earthquake, and fire, and mountains cloven ;
The shape is awful like the sound,
  Clothed in dark purple, star-inwoven.
A sceptre of pale gold
  To stay steps proud, o'er the slow cloud
His veinèd hand doth hold.
Cruel he looks, but calm and strong,
Like one who does, not suffers wrong.

Phantasm of Jupiter. Why have the secret powers
    of this strange world   240
Driven me, a frail and empty phantom, hither
On direst storms ? What unaccustomed sounds
Are hovering on my lips, unlike the voice
With which our pallid race hold ghastly talk
In darkness ? And, proud sufferer, who art thou ?
  Prometheus. Tremendous Image, as thou art must be
He whom thou shadowest forth. I am his foe,
The Titan. Speak the words which I would hear,
Although no thought inform thine empty voice.
  The Earth. Listen ! And though your echoes must
    be mute,   250
Gray mountains, and old woods, and haunted springs,
Prophetic caves, and isle-surrounding streams,

---

[7] The founder of the ancient Persian religion, about 1000 B.C.

[8] Hades is the name both of the underworld and its ruler, Pluto ; Typhon was a monster imprisoned by Jupiter.

Rejoice to hear what yet ye cannot speak.
   Phantasm. A spirit seizes me and speaks within:
It tears me as fire tears a thunder-cloud.
   Panthea. See, how he lifts his mighty looks, the
      Heaven
Darkens above.
   Ione.   He speaks! O shelter me!
   Prometheus. I see the curse on gestures proud and
      cold,
And looks of firm defiance, and calm hate,
And such despair as mocks itself with smiles,   260
Written as on a scroll: yet speak: Oh, speak!

Phantasm.

Fiend, I defy thee! with a calm, fixed mind,
   All that thou canst inflict I bid thee do;
Foul Tyrant both of Gods and Human-kind,
   One only being shalt thou not subdue.
Rain then thy plagues upon me here,
Ghastly disease, and frenzying fear;
And let alternate frost and fire
Eat into me, and be thine ire
Lightning, and cutting hail, and legioned forms 270
Of furies, driving by upon the wounding storms,

Aye, do thy worst. Thou art omnipotent.
   O'er all things but thyself I gave thee power,
And my own will. Be thy swift mischiefs sent
   To blast mankind, from yon ethereal tower.
Let thy malignant spirit move
In darkness over those I love:
On me and mine I imprecate
The utmost torture of thy hate;
And thus devote to sleepless agony,   280
This undeclining head while thou must reign on
   high.

But thou, who art the God and Lord: O, thou,
   Who fillest with thy soul this world of woe,
To whom all things of Earth and Heaven do bow
   In fear and worship: all-prevailing foe!
I curse thee! let a sufferer's curse
Clasp thee, his torturer, like remorse;
'Till thine Infinity shall be
A robe of envenomed agony;
And thine Omnipotence a crown of pain,   290
To cling like burning gold round thy dissolving
   brain.

Heap on thy soul, by virtue of this Curse,
   Ill deeds, then be thou damned, beholding
      good;
Both infinite as is the universe,
   And thou, and thy self-torturing solitude.

An awful image of calm power
Though now thou sittest, let the hour
Come, when thou must appear to be
That which thou art internally;
And after many a false and fruitless crime   300
Scorn track thy lagging fall thro' boundless space
   and time.

   Prometheus. Were these my words, O, Parent?
   The Earth.   They
      were thine.
   Prometheus. It doth repent me: words are quick
      and vain;
Grief for awhile is blind, and so was mine.
I wish no living thing to suffer pain.

The Earth.

Misery, Oh misery to me,
That Jove at length should vanquish thee.
Wail, howl aloud, Land and Sea,
The Earth's rent heart shall answer ye.
Howl, Spirits of the living and the dead,   310
Your refuge, your defence lies fallen and
   vanquishèd.

First Echo.

Lies fallen and vanquishèd!

Second Echo.

Fallen and vanquishèd!

Ione.

Fear not: 'tis but some passing spasm,
   The Titan is unvanquished still.
But see, where thro' the azure chasm
   Of yon forked and snowy hill
Trampling the slant winds on high
   With golden-sandalled feet, that glow
Under plumes of purple dye,   320
Like rose-ensanguined ivory,
   A Shape comes now,
Stretching on high from his right hand
A serpent-cinctured wand.

   Panthea. 'Tis Jove's world-wandering herald,
   Mercury.

Ione.

And who are those with hydra tresses
   And iron wings that climb the wind,
Whom the frowning God represses
   Like vapours steaming up behind,
Clanging loud, an endless crowd—   330

Panthea.

These are Jove's tempest-walking hounds,
Whom he gluts with groans and blood,
When charioted on sulphurous cloud
He bursts Heaven's bounds.

Ione.

Are they now led, from the thin dead
On new pangs to be fed?

Panthea.

The Titan looks as ever, firm, not proud.

First Fury. Ha! I scent life!
Second Fury.   Let me but look into his
    eyes!
Third Fury. The hope of torturing him smells like
    a heap
Of corpses, to a death-bird after battle.   340
First Fury. Darest thou delay, O Herald! take
    cheer, Hounds
Of Hell: what if the Son of Maia [9] soon
Should make us food and sport—who can please long
The Omnipotent?
Mercury.   Back to your towers of iron,
And gnash beside the streams of fire and wail
Your foodless teeth. Geryon, arise! and Gorgon,
Chimæra, and thou Sphinx, subtlest of fiends [10]
Who ministered to Thebes Heaven's poisoned wine,
Unnatural love, and more unnatural hate:
These shall perform your task.
First Fury.   Oh, mercy! mercy!
We die with our desire: drive us not back!   351
Mercury. Crouch then in silence.
                                   Awful Sufferer
To thee unwilling, most unwillingly
I come, by the great Father's will driven down,
To execute a doom of new revenge.
Alas! I pity thee, and hate myself
That I can do no more: aye from thy sight
Returning, for a season, heaven seems hell,
So thy worn form pursues me night and day,
Smiling reproach. Wise art thou, firm and good,   360
But vainly wouldst stand forth alone in strife
Against the Omnipotent; as yon clear lamps
That measure and divide the weary years
From which there is no refuge, long have taught
And long must teach. Even now thy Torturer arms
With the strange might of unimagined pains
The powers who scheme slow agonies in Hell,

And my commission is to lead them here,
Or what more subtle, foul, or savage fiends
People the abyss, and leave them to their task.   370
Be it not so! there is a secret known
To thee, and to none else of living things,
Which may transfer the sceptre of wide Heaven,
The fear of which perplexes the Supreme:
Clothe it in words, and bid it clasp his throne
In intercession; bend thy soul in prayer,
And like a suppliant in some gorgeous fane,
Let the will kneel within thy haughty heart:
For benefits and meek submission tame
The fiercest and the mightiest.
Prometheus.   Evil minds   380
Change good to their own nature. I gave all
He has; and in return he chains me here
Years, ages, night and day: whether the Sun
Split my parched skin, or in the moony night
The chrystal-wingèd snow cling round my hair:
Whilst my belovèd race is trampled down
By his thought-executing ministers.
Such is the tyrants' recompense: 'tis just:
He who is evil can receive no good;
And for a world bestowed, or a friend lost,   390
He can feel hate, fear, shame; not gratitude:
He but requites me for his own misdeed.
Kindness to such is keen reproach, which breaks
With bitter stings the light sleep of Revenge.
Submission, thou dost know I cannot try:
For what submission but that fatal word,
The death-seal of mankind's captivity,
Like the Sicilian's hair-suspended sword, [11]
Which trembles o'er his crown, would he accept,
Or could I yield? Which yet I will not yield.   400
Let others flatter Crime, where it sits throned
In brief Omnipotence: secure are they:
For Justice, when triumphant, will weep down
Pity, not punishment, on her own wrongs,
Too much avenged by those who err. I wait,
Enduring thus, the retributive hour
Which since we spake is even nearer now.
But hark, the hell-hounds clamour: fear delay:
Behold! Heaven lowers under thy Father's frown.
Mercury. Oh, that we might be spared: I to inflict
And thou to suffer! Once more answer me: 411
Thou knowest not the period of Jove's power?
Prometheus. I know but this, that it must come.
Mercury.   Alas!
Thou canst not count thy years to come of pain?

---

[9] Mercury, whose parents were Maia and Jupiter.
[10] These are all monsters known for their terrifying appearance.

[11] The king of Syracuse suspended a sword by a thread over the head of Damocles, to remind him how fragile was the happiness of kings.

Prometheus. They last while Jove must reign: nor
    more, nor less
Do I desire or fear.
    Mercury.   Yet pause, and plunge
Into Eternity, where recorded time,
Even all that we imagine, age on age,
Seems but a point, and the reluctant mind
Flags wearily in its unending flight,   420
Till it sink, dizzy, blind, lost, shelterless;
Perchance it has not numbered the slow years
Which thou must spend in torture, unreprieved?
    Prometheus. Perchance no thought can count them,
        yet they pass.
    Mercury. If thou might'st dwell among the Gods
        the while
Lapped in voluptuous joy?
    Prometheus.   I would not quit
This bleak ravine, these unrepentant pains.
    Mercury. Alas! I wonder at, yet pity thee.
    Prometheus. Pity the self-despising slaves of
        Heaven,
Not me, within whose mind sits peace serene,   430
As light in the sun, throned: how vain is talk!
Call up the fiends.
    Ione.   O, sister, look! White fire
Has cloven to the roots yon huge snow-loaded cedar;
How fearfully God's thunder howls behind!
    Mercury. I must obey his words and thine: alas!
Most heavily remorse hangs at my heart!
    Panthea. See where the child of Heaven, with
        wingèd feet,
Runs down the slanted sunlight of the dawn.
    Ione. Dear sister, close thy plumes over thine eyes
Lest thou behold and die: they come: they come   440
Blackening the birth of day with countless wings,
And hollow underneath, like death.
    First Fury.   Prometheus!
    Second Fury. Immortal Titan!
    Third Fury.   Champion of
        Heaven's slaves!
    Prometheus. He whom some dreadful voice invokes
        is here,
Prometheus, the chained Titan. Horrible forms,
What and who are ye? Never yet there came
Phantasms so foul thro' monster-teeming Hell
From the all-miscreative brain of Jove;
Whilst I behold such execrable shapes,
Methinks I grow like what I contemplate,   450
And laugh and stare in loathsome sympathy.
    First Fury. We are the ministers of pain, and fear,
And disappointment, and mistrust, and hate,
And clinging crime; and as lean dogs pursue
Thro' wood and lake some struck and sobbing fawn,
We track all things that weep, and bleed, and live,

When the great King betrays them to our will.
    Prometheus. Oh! many fearful natures in one name,
I know ye; and these lakes and echoes know
The darkness and the clangour of your wings.   460
But why more hideous than your loathèd selves
Gather ye up in legions from the deep?
    Second Fury. We knew not that: Sisters, rejoice,
        rejoice!
    Prometheus. Can aught exult in its deformity?
    Second Fury. The beauty of delight makes lovers
        glad,
Gazing on one another: so are we.
As from the rose which the pale priestess kneels
To gather for her festal crown of flowers
The aerial crimson falls, flushing her cheek,
So from our victim's destined agony   470
The shade which is our form invests us round,
Else we are shapeless as our mother Night.
    Prometheus. I laugh your power, and his who sent
        you here,
To lowest scorn. Pour forth the cup of pain.
    First Fury. Thou thinkest we will rend thee bone
        from bone,
And nerve from nerve, working like fire within?
    Prometheus. Pain is my element, as hate is thine;
Ye rend me now: I care not.
    Second Fury.   Dost imagine
We will but laugh into thy lidless eyes?
    Prometheus. I weigh not what ye do, but what ye
        suffer,   480
Being evil. Cruel was the power which called
You, or aught else so wretched, into light.
    Third Fury. Thou think'st we will live thro' thee,
        one by one,
Like animal life, and tho' we can obscure not
The soul which burns within, that we will dwell
Beside it, like a vain loud multitude
Vexing the self-content of wisest men:
That we will be dread thought beneath thy brain,
And foul desire round thine astonished heart,
And blood within thy labyrinthine veins   490
Crawling like agony?
    Prometheus.   Why, ye are thus now;
Yet am I king over myself, and rule
The torturing and conflicting throngs within,
As Jove rules you when Hell grows mutinous.

Chorus of Furies.

From the ends of the earth, from the ends of the earth,
Where the night has its grave and the morning its
        birth,
                Come, come, come!
Oh, ye who shake hills with the scream of your mirth,
When cities sink howling in ruin; and ye

Who with wingless footsteps trample the sea,   500
And close upon Shipwreck and Famine's track,
Sit chattering with joy on the foodless wreck;
        Come, come, come!
    Leave the bed, low, cold, and red,
    Strewed beneath a nation dead;
    Leave the hatred, as in ashes
      Fire is left for future burning:
    It will burst in bloodier flashes
      When ye stir it, soon returning:
    Leave the self-contempt implanted   510
    In young spirits, sense-enchanted,
      Misery's yet unkindled fuel:
    Leave Hell's secrets half unchanted
      To the maniac dreamer; cruel
    More than ye can be with hate
      Is he with fear.
          Come, come, come!
We are steaming up from Hell's wide gate
And we burthen the blasts of the atmosphere,
But vainly we toil till ye come here.   520

Ione. Sister, I hear the thunder of new wings.
Panthea. These solid mountains quiver with the
    sound
Even as the tremulous air: their shadows make
The space within my plumes more black than night.

First Fury.

Your call was as a wingèd car
Driven on whirlwinds fast and far;
It rapt us from red gulphs of war.

Second Fury.

From wide cities, famine-wasted;

Third Fury.

Groans half heard, and blood untasted;

Fourth Fury.

Kingly conclaves stern and cold,   530
Where blood with gold is bought and sold;

Fifth Fury.

From the furnace, white and hot,
In which—

A Fury.

    Speak not: whisper not:
I know all that ye would tell,
But to speak might break the spell
Which must bend the Invincible,
  The stern of thought;
He yet defies the deepest power of Hell.

A Fury.

Tear the veil!

Another Fury.
    It is torn.

Chorus.

        The pale stars of the morn
Shine on a misery, dire to be borne.   540
Dost thou faint, mighty Titan? We laugh thee to
    scorn.
Dost thou boast the clear knowledge thou waken'dst
    for man?
Then was kindled within him a thirst which outran
Those perishing waters; a thirst of fierce fever,
Hope, love, doubt, desire, which consume him for
    ever.
    One came forth of gentle worth [12]
    Smiling on the sanguine earth;
    His words outlived him, like swift poison
      Withering up truth, peace, and pity.
    Look! where round the wide horizon   550
      Many a million-peopled city
    Vomits smoke in the bright air.
Mark that outcry of despair!
    'Tis his mild and gentle ghost
      Wailing for the faith he kindled:
    Look again, the flames almost
      To a glow-worm's lamp have dwindled:
The survivors round the embers
  Gather in dread.
        Joy, joy, joy!   560
Past ages crowd on thee, but each one
    remembers,
And the future is dark, and the present is spread
Like a pillow of thorns for thy slumberless head.

Semichorus I.

Drops of bloody agony flow
From his white and quivering brow.
Grant a little respite now:
See a disenchanted nation [13]
Springs like day from desolation;
To truth its state is dedicate,
And Freedom leads it forth, her mate;   570
A legioned band of linkèd brothers
Whom Love calls children—

---

[12] Jesus.
[13] See Coleridge's *France, An Ode*, p. 465.

Semichorus II.

                'Tis another's:
See how kindred murder kin:
'Tis the vintage-time for death and sin:
Blood, like new wine, bubbles within:
    'Till Despair smothers
The struggling world, which slaves and tyrants
    win.
            [All the FURIES *vanish, except one.*
  Ione. Hark, sister! what a low yet dreadful groan
Quite unsuppressed is tearing up the heart
Of the good Titan, as storms tear the deep,   580
And beasts hear the sea moan in inland caves.
Darest thou observe how the fiends torture him?
  Panthea. Alas! I looked forth twice, but will no
    more.
  Ione. What didst thou see?
  Panthea.   A woeful sight: a youth
With patient looks nailed to a crucifix.
  Ione. What next?
  Panthea.   The heaven around, the earth
    below
Was peopled with thick shapes of human death,
All horrible, and wrought by human hands,
And some appeared the work of human hearts,
For men were slowly killed by frowns and smiles: 590
And other sights too foul to speak and live
Were wandering by. Let us not tempt worse fear
By looking forth: those groans are grief enough.
  Fury. Behold an emblem: those who do endure
Deep wrongs for man, and scorn, and chains, but
    heap
Thousandfold torment on themselves and him.
  Prometheus. Remit the anguish of that lighted
    stare;
Close those wan lips; let that thorn-wounded brow
Stream not with blood; it mingles with thy tears!
Fix, fix those tortured orbs in peace and death, 600
So thy sick throes shake not that crucifix,
So those pale fingers play not with thy gore.
O, horrible! Thy name I will not speak,
It hath become a curse. I see, I see
The wise, the mild, the lofty, and the just,
Whom thy slaves hate for being like to thee,
Some hunted by foul lies from their heart's home,
An early-chosen, late-lamented home;
As hooded ounces [14] cling to the driven hind;
Some linked to corpses in unwholesome cells: 610
Some—Hear I not the multitude laugh loud?—
Impaled in lingering fire: and mighty realms
Float by my feet, like sea-uprooted isles,

Whose sons are kneaded down in common blood
By the red light of their own burning homes.
  Fury. Blood thou canst see, and fire; and canst
    hear groans;
Worse things, unheard, unseen, remain behind.
  Prometheus. Worse?
  Fury.   In each human heart terror
    survives
The ravin it has gorged: the loftiest fear
All that they would disdain to think were true: 620
Hypocrisy and custom make their minds
The fanes [15] of many a worship, now outworn.
They dare not devise good for man's estate,
And yet they know not that they do not dare.
The good want power, but to weep barren tears.
The powerful goodness want: worse need for them.
The wise want love; and those who love want wisdom;
And all best things are thus confused to ill.
Many are strong and rich, and would be just,
But live among their suffering fellow-men 630
As if none felt: they know not what they do. [16]
  Prometheus. Thy words are like a cloud of wingèd
    snakes;
And yet I pity those they torture not.
  Fury. Thou pitiest them? I speak no more!
                         [Vanishes.
  Prometheus.   Ah woe!
Ah woe! Alas! pain, pain ever, for ever!
I close my tearless eyes, but see more clear
Thy works within my woe-illumèd mind,
Thou subtle tyrant! Peace is in the grave.
The grave hides all things beautiful and good:
I am a God and cannot find it there, 640
Nor would I seek it: for, though dread revenge,
This is defeat, fierce king, not victory.
The sights with which thou torturest gird my soul
With new endurance, till the hour arrives
When they shall be no types of things which are.
  Panthea. Alas! what sawest thou ?
  Prometheus.   There are
    two woes;
To speak, and to behold; thou spare me one.
Names are there, Nature's sacred watch-words, they
Were borne aloft in bright emblazonry;
The nations thronged around, and cried aloud, 650
As with one voice, Truth, liberty, and love!
Suddenly fierce confusion fell from heaven
Among them: there was strife, deceit, and fear:
Tyrants rushed in, and did divide the spoil.
This was the shadow of the truth I saw.

---

[15] Temples.
[16] An ironic allusion to Christ's words from the cross, Luke 23:34.

---

[14] Leopards or wildcats trained for hunting.

The Earth. I felt thy torture, son, with such mixed
   joy
As pain and virtue give. To cheer thy state
I bid ascend those subtle and fair spirits,
Whose homes are the dim caves of human thought,
And who inhabit, as birds wing the wind,   660
Its world-surrounding ether: they behold
Beyond that twilight realm, as in a glass,
The future: may they speak comfort to thee!
 Panthea. Look, sister, where a troop of spirits
   gather,
Like flocks of clouds in spring's delightful weather,
Thronging in the blue air!
 Ione.   And see! more come,
Like fountain-vapours when the winds are dumb,
That climb up the ravine in scattered lines.
And, hark? is it the music of the pines?
Is it the lake? Is it the waterfall?   670
 Panthea. 'Tis something sadder, sweeter far than
   all.

Chorus of Spirits.

From unremembered ages we
Gentle guides and guardians be
Of heaven-oppressed mortality;
And we breathe, and sicken not,
The atmosphere of human thought:
Be it dim, and dank, and gray,
Like a storm-extinguished day,
Travelled o'er by dying gleams;
 Be it bright as all between   680
Cloudless skies and windless streams,
 Silent, liquid, and serene;
As the birds within the wind,
 As the fish within the wave,
As the thoughts of man's own mind
 Float thro' all above the grave;
We make there our liquid lair,
Voyaging cloudlike and unpent
Thro' the boundless element:
Thence we bear the prophecy [17]   690
Which begins and ends in thee!

 Ione. More yet come, one by one: the air around
   them
Looks radiant as the air around a star.

First Spirit.

On a battle-trumpet's blast
I fled hither, fast, fast, fast,
'Mid the darkness upward cast.

---

[17] That revolution, self-sacrifice, wisdom, and poetry will persist and ultimately enable the triumph of love.

From the dust of creeds outworn,
From the tyrant's banner torn,
Gathering 'round me, onward borne,
There was mingled many a cry—   700
Freedom! Hope! Death! Victory!
Till they faded thro' the sky;
And one sound, above, around,
One sound beneath, around, above,
Was moving; 'twas the soul of love;
'Twas the hope, the prophecy,
Which begins and ends in thee.

Second Spirit.

A rainbow's arch stood on the sea,
Which rocked beneath, immoveably;
And the triumphant storm did flee,   710
Like a conqueror, swift and proud,
Between, with many a captive cloud,
A shapeless, dark and rapid crowd,
Each by lightning riven in half:
I heard the thunder hoarsely laugh:
Mighty fleets were strewn like chaff
And spread beneath a hell of death
O'er the white waters. I alit
On a great ship lightning-split,
And speeded hither on the sigh   720
Of one who gave an enemy
His plank, then plunged aside to die.

Third Spirit.

I sate beside a sage's bed,
And the lamp was burning red
Near the book where he had fed,
When a Dream with plumes of flame,
To his pillow hovering came,
And I knew it was the same
Which had kindled long ago
Pity, eloquence, and woe;   730
And the world awhile below
Wore the shade, its lustre made.
It has borne me here as fleet
As Desire's lightning feet:
I must ride it back ere morrow,
Or the sage will wake in sorrow.

Fourth Spirit.

On a poet's lips I slept
Dreaming like a love-adept
In the sound his breathing kept;
Nor seeks nor finds he mortal blisses,   740
But feeds on the aerial kisses
Of shapes that haunt thought's wildernesses.
He will watch from dawn to gloom
The lake-reflected sun illume

The yellow bees in the ivy-bloom,
Nor heed nor see, what things they be;
But from these create he can
Forms more real than living man,
Nurslings of immortality!
One of these awakened me,   750
And I sped to succour thee.

   Ione. Behold'st thou not two shapes from the east
    and west [18]
Come, as two doves to one belovèd nest,
Twin nurslings of the all-sustaining air
On swift still wings glide down the atmosphere?
And, hark! their sweet, sad voices! 'tis despair
Mingled with love and then dissolved in sound.
    Panthea. Canst thou speak, sister? all my words
     are drowned.
    Ione. Their beauty gives me voice. See how they
     float
On their sustaining wings of skiey grain,   760
Orange and azure deepening into gold:
Their soft smiles light the air like a star's fire.

       Chorus of Spirits.
Hast thou beheld the form of Love?

       Fifth Spirit.
             As over wide
    dominions
I sped, like some swift cloud that wings the wide
    air's wildernesses,
That planet-crested shape swept by on lightning-
    braided pinions,
Scattering the liquid joy of life from his ambrosial
    tresses:
His footsteps paved the world with light; but as I
    passed 'twas fading,
And hollow Ruin yawned behind: great sages
    bound in madness,
And headless patriots, and pale youths who perished,
    unupbraiding,
Gleamed in the night. I wandered o'er, till thou, O
    King of sadness,   770
Turned by thy smile the worst I saw to recollected
    gladness.

       Sixth Spirit.
Ah, sister! Desolation is a delicate thing:
    It walks not on the earth, it floats not on the air,
But treads with silent footstep, and fans with silent
    wing
    The tender hopes which in their hearts the best
    and gentlest bear;

---

[18] Hope and Despair.

Who, soothed to false repose by the fanning plumes
    above
    And the music-stirring motion of its soft and busy
    feet,
Dream visions of aërial joy, and call the monster,
    Love,
    And wake, and find the shadow Pain, as he whom
    now we greet.

       Chorus.
Tho' Ruin now Love's shadow be,   780
Following him, destroyingly,
   On Death's white and wingèd steed,
Which the fleetest cannot flee,
   Trampling down both flower and weed,
Man and beast, and foul and fair,
Like a tempest thro' the air;
Thou shalt quell this horseman grim,
Woundless though in heart or limb.

   Prometheus. Spirits! how know ye this shall be?

       Chorus.
In the atmosphere we breathe,   790
As buds grow red when the snow-storms flee,
   From Spring gathering up beneath,
Whose mild winds shake the elder brake,
And the wandering herdsmen know
That the white-thorn soon will blow:
    Wisdom, Justice, Love, and Peace,
   When they struggle to increase,
    Are to us as soft winds be
    To shepherd boys, the prophecy
    Which begins and ends in thee.   800

   Ione. Where are the Spirits fled?
   Panthea.   Only a sense
Remains of them, like the omnipotence
Of music, when the inspired voice and lute
Languish, ere yet the responses are mute,
Which thro' the deep and labyrinthine soul,
Like echoes thro' long caverns, wind and roll.
   Prometheus. How fair these airborn shapes! and yet
    I feel
Most vain all hope but love; and thou art far,
Asia! who, when my being overflowed,
Wert like a golden chalice to bright wine   810
Which else had sunk into the thirsty dust.
All things are still: alas! how heavily
This quiet morning weighs upon my heart;
Tho' I should dream I could even sleep with grief
If slumber were denied not. I would fain
Be what it is my destiny to be,
The saviour and the strength of suffering man,

Or sink into the original gulph of things:
There is no agony, and no solace left;
Earth can console, Heaven can torment no more. 820
    Panthea. Hast thou forgotten one who watches
        thee
The cold dark night, and never sleeps but when
The shadow of thy spirit falls on her?
    Prometheus. I said all hope was vain but love: thou
        lovest.
    Panthea. Deeply in truth; but the eastern star
        looks white,
And Asia waits in that far Indian vale,
The scene of her sad exile; rugged once
And desolate and frozen, like this ravine;
But now invested with fair flowers and herbs,
And haunted by sweet airs and sounds, which flow
Among the woods and waters, from the ether 831
Of her transforming presence, which would fade
If it were mingled not with thine. Farewell!

END OF THE FIRST ACT.

ACT II

SCENE I. *Morning. A lovely Vale in the Indian
Caucasus.* ASIA *alone.*

    Asia. From all the blasts of heaven thou hast
        descended:
Yes, like a spirit, like a thought, which makes
Unwonted tears throng to the horny eyes,
And beatings haunt the desolated heart,
Which should have learnt repose: thou hast
        descended
Cradled in tempests; thou dost wake, O Spring!
O child of many winds! As suddenly
Thou comest as the memory of a dream,
Which now is sad because it hath been sweet;
Like genius, or like joy which riseth up 10
As from the earth, clothing with golden clouds
The desert of our life.
This is the season, this the day, the hour;
At sunrise thou shouldst come, sweet sister mine,
Too long desired, too long delaying, come!
How like death-worms the wingless moments crawl!
The point of one white star is quivering still
Deep in the orange light of widening morn
Beyond the purple mountains: thro' a chasm
Of wind-divided mist the darker lake 20
Reflects it: now it wanes: it gleams again
As the waves fade, and as the burning threads
Of woven cloud unravel in pale air:
'Tis lost! and thro' yon peaks of cloudlike snow

The roseate sun-light quivers: hear I not
The Æolian music of her sea-green plumes
Winnowing the crimson dawn?

PANTHEA *enters.*

              I feel, I see
Those eyes which burn thro' smiles that fade in
    tears,
Like stars half quenched in mists of silver dew.
Belovèd and most beautiful, who wearest   30
The shadow of that soul by which I live,
How late thou art! the spherèd sun had climbed
The sea; my heart was sick with hope, before
The printless air felt thy belated plumes.
    Panthea. Pardon, great Sister! but my wings were
        faint
With the delight of a remembered dream,
As are the noontide plumes of summer winds
Satiate with sweet flowers. I was wont to sleep
Peacefully, and awake refreshed and calm
Before the sacred Titan's fall, and thy   40
Unhappy love, had made, thro' use and pity,
Both love and woe familiar to my heart
As they had grown to thine: erewhile I slept
Under the glaucous caverns of old Ocean
Within dim bowers of green and purple moss,
Our young Ione's soft and milky arms
Locked then, as now, behind my dark, moist hair,
While my shut eyes and cheek were pressed within
The folded depth of her life-breathing bosom:
But not as now, since I am made the wind   50
Which fails beneath the music that I bear
Of thy most wordless converse; since dissolved
Into the sense with which love talks, my rest
Was troubled and yet sweet; my waking hours
Too full of care and pain.
    Asia.   Lift up thine eyes,
And let me read thy dream.
    Panthea.   As I have said
With our sea-sister at his feet I slept.
The mountain mists, condensing at our voice
Under the moon, had spread their snowy flakes,
From the keen ice shielding our linkèd sleep.   60
Then two dreams came. One, I remember not.
But in the other his pale wound-worn limbs
Fell from Prometheus, and the azure night
Grew radiant with the glory of that form
Which lives unchanged within, and his voice fell
Like music which makes giddy the dim brain,
Faint with intoxication of keen joy:
'Sister of her whose footsteps pave the world
With loveliness—more fair than aught but her,
Whose shadow thou art—lift thine eyes on me.'   70
I lifted them: the overpowering light

Of that immortal shape was shadowed o'er
By love; which, from his soft and flowing limbs,
And passion-parted lips, and keen, faint eyes,
Steamed forth like vaporous fire; an atmosphere
Which wrapt me in its all-dissolving power,
As the warm ether of the morning sun
Wraps ere it drinks some cloud of wandering dew.
I saw not, heard not, moved not, only felt
His presence flow and mingle thro' my blood   80
Till it became his life, and his grew mine,
And I was thus absorb'd, until it past,
And like the vapours when the sun sinks down,
Gathering again in drops upon the pines,
And tremulous as they, in the deep night
My being was condensed; and as the rays
Of thought were slowly gathered, I could hear
His voice, whose accents lingered ere they died
Like footsteps of weak melody: thy name
Among the many sounds alone I heard   90
Of what might be articulate; tho' still
I listened through the night when sound was none.
Ione wakened then, and said to me:
'Canst thou divine what troubles me to night?
I always knew what I desired before,
Nor ever found delight to wish in vain.
But now I cannot tell thee what I seek;
I know not; something sweet, since it is sweet
Even to desire; it is thy sport, false sister;
Thou hast discovered some enchantment old,   100
Whose spells have stolen my spirit as I slept
And mingled it with thine: for when just now
We kissed, I felt within thy parted lips
The sweet air that sustained me, and the warmth
Of the life-blood, for loss of which I faint,
Quivered between our intertwining arms.'
I answered not, for the Eastern star grew pale,
But fled to thee.
    Asia.   Thou speakest, but thy words
Are as the air: I feel them not: Oh, lift
Thine eyes, that I may read his written soul!   110
    Panthea. I lift them tho' they droop beneath the
        load
Of that they would express: what canst thou see
But thine own fairest shadow imaged there?
    Asia. Thine eyes are like the deep, blue, boundless
        heaven
Contracted to two circles underneath
Their long, fine lashes; dark, far, measureless,
Orb within orb, and line thro' line inwoven.
    Panthea. Why lookest thou as if a spirit past?
    Asia. There is a change: beyond their inmost depth
I see a shade, a shape: 'tis He,[19] arrayed   120

In the soft light of his own smiles, which spread
Like radiance from the cloud-surrounded moon.
Prometheus, it is thine! depart not yet!
Say not those smiles that we shall meet again
Within that bright pavilion which their beams
Shall build on the waste world? The dream is told.
What shape is that between us? Its rude hair
Roughens the wind that lifts it, its regard
Is wild and quick, yet 'tis a thing of air
For thro' its grey robe gleams the golden dew   130
Whose stars the noon has quench'd not.
    Dream.   Follow!
        Follow!
    Panthea. It is mine other dream.
    Asia.   It disappears.
    Panthea. It passes now into my mind. Methought
As we sate here, the flower-infolding buds
Burst on yon lightning-blasted almond-tree,
When swift from the white Scythian wilderness
A wind swept forth wrinkling the Earth with frost:
I looked, and all the blossoms were blown down;
But on each leaf was stamped, as the blue bells
Of Hyacinth tell Apollo's written grief,[20]   140
O, FOLLOW, FOLLOW!
    Asia.   As you speak, your words
Fill, pause by pause, my own forgotten sleep
With shapes. Methought among the lawns together
We wandered, underneath the young gray dawn,
And multitudes of dense white fleecy clouds
Were wandering in thick flocks along the mountains
Shepherded by the slow, unwilling wind;
And the white dew on the new bladed grass,
Just piercing the dark earth, hung silently;
And there was more which I remember not: 150
But on the shadows of the morning clouds,
Athwart the purple mountain slope, was written
FOLLOW, O, FOLLOW! As they vanished by,
And on each herb, from which Heaven's dew had
        fallen,
The like was stamped, as with a withering fire,
A wind arose among the pines; it shook
The clinging music from their boughs, and then
Low, sweet, faint sounds, like the farewell of ghosts,
Were heard: OH, FOLLOW, FOLLOW, FOLLOW ME!
And then I said: 'Panthea, look on me.'   160
But in the depth of those belovèd eyes
Still I saw, FOLLOW, FOLLOW!
    Echo.   Follow, follow!
    Panthea. The crags, this clear spring morning,
        mock our voices

---

[19] Prometheus.

[20] The flower that sprung from the bloodstained ground when
Apollo accidentally killed Hyacinth bore on its leaves the word
"Ai" (woe).

As they were spirit-tongued.
Asia.   It is some being
Around the crags. What fine clear sounds! O, list!

Echoes (unseen).

Echoes we: listen!
    We cannot stay:
As dew-stars glisten
    Then fade away—
        Child of Ocean!   170

Asia. Hark! Spirits speak. The liquid responses
Of their aerial tongues yet sound.
Panthea.   I hear.

Echoes.

O, follow, follow,
    As our voice recedeth
Thro' the caverns hollow,
    Where the forest spreadeth;

(More distant.)

O, follow, follow!
    Thro' the caverns hollow,
As the song floats thou pursue,
Where the wild bee never flew,   180
Thro' the noon-tide darkness deep,
By the odour-breathing sleep
Of faint night flowers, and the waves
At the fountain-lighted caves,
While our music, wild and sweet,
Mocks thy gently falling feet,
        Child of Ocean!

Asia. Shall we pursue the sound? It grows more
        faint
And distant.
Panthea. List! the strain floats nearer now.

Echoes.

In the world unknown   190
    Sleeps a voice unspoken;
By thy step alone
    Can its rest be broken;
        Child of Ocean!

Asia. How the notes sink upon the ebbing wind!

Echoes.

O, follow, follow!
    Thro' the caverns hollow,
As the song floats thou pursue,
By the woodland noon-tide dew;

By the forests, lakes, and fountains   200
Thro' the many-folded mountains;
To the rents, and gulphs, and chasms,
Where the Earth reposed from spasms,
On the day when He and thou
Parted, to commingle now;
        Child of Ocean!

Asia. Come, sweet Panthea, link thy hand in mine,
And follow, ere the voices fade away.

SCENE II. *A Forest, intermingled with Rocks and
Caverns.* ASIA *and* PANTHEA *pass into it. Two
young Fauns are sitting on a Rock, listening.*

Semichorus I. of Spirits.

The path thro' which that lovely twain
    Have past, by cedar, pine, and yew.
    And each dark tree that ever grew,
    Is curtained out from Heaven's wide blue;
Nor sun, nor moon, nor wind, nor rain,
    Can pierce its interwoven bowers,
    Nor aught, save where some cloud of dew,
Drifted along the earth-creeping breeze,
Between the trunks of the hoar trees,
    Hangs each a pearl in the pale flowers   10
    Of the green laurel, blown anew;
And bends, and then fades silently,
One frail and fair anemone:
Or when some stars of many a one
That climbs and wanders thro' steep night,
Has found the cleft thro' which alone
Beams fall from high those depths upon
Ere it is borne away, away,
By the swift Heavens that cannot stay,
It scatters drops of golden light,   20
Like lines of rain that ne'er unite:
And the gloom divine is all around;
And underneath is the mossy ground.

Semichorus II.

There are voluptuous nightingales,
    Are awake thro' all the broad noon-day.
When one with bliss or sadness fails,
    And thro' the windless ivy-boughs,
    Sick with sweet love, droops dying away
On its mate's music-panting bosom;
Another from the swinging blossom,   30
    Watching to catch the languid close
    Of the last strain, then lifts on high
    The wings of the weak melody,
'Till some new strain of feeling bear
    The song, and all the woods are mute;
When there is heard thro' the dim air

The rush of wings, and rising there
  Like many a lake-surrounding flute,
Sounds overflow the listener's brain
So sweet, that joy is almost pain.   40

Semichorus I.

There those enchanted eddies play
  Of echoes, music-tongued, which draw,
  By Demogorgon's mighty law,
  With melting rapture, or sweet awe,
All spirits on that secret way;
  As inland boats are driven to Ocean
Down streams made strong with mountain-thaw:
    And first there comes a gentle sound
    To those in talk or slumber bound,
    And wakes the destined soft emotion,   50
Attracts, impels them: those who saw
    Say from the breathing earth behind
    There steams a plume-uplifting wind
Which drives them on their path, while they
    Believe their own swift wings and feet
The sweet desires within obey:
And so they float upon their way,
Until, still sweet, but loud and strong,
The storm of sound is driven along,
    Sucked up and hurrying as they fleet   60
    Behind, its gathering billows meet
And to the fatal mountain bear
Like clouds amid the yielding air.

First Faun. Canst thou imagine where those spirits
    live
Which make such delicate music in the woods?
We haunt within the least frequented caves
And closest coverts, and we know these wilds,
Yet never meet them, tho' we hear them oft:
Where may they hide themselves?
  Second Faun.   'Tis hard to tell:
I have heard those more skilled in spirits say,   70
The bubbles, which the enchantment of the sun
Sucks from the pale faint water-flowers that pave
The oozy bottom of clear lakes and pools,
Are the pavilions where such dwell and float
Under the green and golden atmosphere
Which noon-tide kindles thro' the woven leaves;
And when these burst, and the thin fiery air,
The which they breathed within those lucent domes,
Ascends to flow like meteors thro' the night,
They ride on them, and rein their headlong speed, 80
And bow their burning crests, and glide in fire
Under the waters of the earth again.
  First Faun. If such live thus, have others other lives,
Under pink blossoms or within the bells
Of meadow flowers, or folded violets deep,

Or on their dying odours, when they die,
Or in the sunlight of the spherèd dew?
  Second Faun. Aye, many more which we may well
    divine.
But, should we stay to speak, noontide would come,
And thwart Silenus find his goats undrawn,   90
And grudge to sing those wise and lovely songs
Of fate, and chance, and God, and Chaos old,
And Love, and the chained Titan's woful dooms,
And how he shall be loosed, and make the earth
One brotherhood: delightful strains which cheer
Our solitary twilights, and which charm
To silence the unenvying nightingales.

SCENE III.   *A Pinnacle of Rock among Mountains.*
ASIA *and* PANTHEA.

  Panthea. Hither the sound has borne us—to the
    realm
Of Demogorgon, and the mighty portal,
Like a volcano's meteor-breathing chasm,
Whence the oracular vapour is hurled up
Which lonely men drink wandering in their youth,
And call truth, virtue, love, genius, or joy,
That maddening wine of life, whose dregs they drain
To deep intoxication; and uplift,
Like Mænads who cry loud, Evoe! Evoe![21]
The voice which is contagion to the world.   10
  Asia. Fit throne for such a Power! Magnificent!
How glorious art thou, Earth! And if thou be
The shadow of some spirit lovelier still,
Though evil stain its work, and it should be
Like its creation, weak yet beautiful,
I could fall down and worship that and thee.
Even now my heart adoreth: Wonderful!
Look, sister, ere the vapour dim thy brain:
Beneath is a wide plain of billowy mist,
As a lake, paving in the morning sky,   20
With azure waves which burst in silver light,
Some Indian vale. Behold it, rolling on
Under the curdling winds, and islanding
The peak whereon we stand, midway, around,
Encinctured by the dark and blooming forests,
Dim twilight-lawns, and stream-illumined caves,
And wind-enchanted shapes of wandering mist;
And far on high the keen sky-cleaving mountains
From icy spires of sun-like radiance fling
The dawn, as lifted Ocean's dazzling spray,   30
From some Atlantic islet scattered up,
Spangles the wind with lamp-like water-drops.
The vale is girdled with their walls, a howl

---

[21] The nymphs who worship Bacchus, and tear to pieces those
who enter their orgies. See Euripides, *Bacchae.*

Of cataracts from their thaw-cloven ravines
Satiates the listening wind, continuous, vast,
Awful as silence. Hark! the rushing snow!
The sun-awakened avalanche! whose mass,
Thrice sifted by the storm, had gathered there
Flake after flake, in heaven-defying minds
As thought by thought is piled, till some great truth
Is loosened, and the nations echo round,   41
Shaken to their roots, as do the mountains now.
   Panthea. Look how the gusty sea of mist is breaking
In crimson foam, even at our feet! it rises
As Ocean at the enchantment of the moon
Round foodless men wrecked on some oozy isle.
   Asia. The fragments of the cloud are scattered up;
The wind that lifts them disentwines my hair;
Its billows now sweep o'er mine eyes; my brain
Grows dizzy; see'st thou shapes within the mist?   50
   Panthea. A countenance with beckoning smiles:
     there burns
An azure fire within its golden locks!
Another and another: hark! they speak!

Song of Spirits.

   To the deep, to the deep,
        Down, down!
   Through the shade of sleep,
   Through the cloudy strife
   Of Death and of Life;
   Through the veil and the bar
   Of things which seem and are   60
Even to the steps of the remotest throne,
        Down, down!

   While the sound whirls around,
        Down, down!
   As the fawn draws the hound,
   As the lightning the vapour,
   As a weak moth the taper;
   Death, despair; love, sorrow;
   Time both; to day, to morrow;
As steel obeys the spirit of the stone,   70
        Down, down.

   Through the gray, void abysm,
        Down, down!
   Where the air is no prism,[22]
   And the moon and stars are not,
   And the cavern-crags wear not
   The radiance of Heaven,
     Nor the gloom to Earth given,
Where there is one pervading, one alone,
        Down, down!   80

---

[22] Where the air does not separate light into colors.

   In the depth of the deep
        Down, down!
   Like veiled lightning asleep,
   Like the spark nursed in embers,
   The last look Love remembers,
   Like a diamond, which shines
   On the dark wealth of mines,
A spell is treasured but for thee alone.
        Down, down!

   We have bound thee, we guide thee;   90
        Down, down!
   With the bright form beside thee;
   Resist not the weakness,
   Such strength is in meekness
   That the Eternal, the Immortal,
   Must unloose through life's portal
The snake-like Doom coiled underneath his
   throne
        By that alone.

SCENE IV. *The Cave of* DEMOGORGON. ASIA *and*
PANTHEA.

   Panthea. What veilèd form sits on that ebon throne?
   Asia. The veil has fallen.
   Panthea.   I see a mighty darkness
Filling the seat of power, and rays of gloom
Dart round, as light from the meridian sun,
Ungazed upon and shapeless; neither limb,
Nor form, nor outline; yet we feel it is
A living Spirit.
   Demogorgon. Ask what thou wouldst know.
   Asia. What canst thou tell?
   Demogorgon.   All things thou dar'st
     demand.
   Asia. Who made the living world?
   Demogorgon.   God.
   Asia.   Who made
     all
That it contains? thought, passion, reason, will,   10
Imagination?
   Demogorgon. God: Almighty God.
   Asia. Who made that sense which, when the winds
     of spring
In rarest visitation, or the voice
Of one belovèd heard in youth alone,
Fills the faint eyes with falling tears which dim
The radiant looks of unbewailing flowers,
And leaves this peopled earth a solitude
When it returns no more?
   Demogorgon.   Merciful God.
   Asia. And who made terror, madness, crime,
     remorse,

Which from the links of the great chain of things, 　20
To every thought within the mind of man
Sway and drag heavily, and each one reels
Under the load towards the pit of death;
Abandoned hope, and love that turns to hate;
And self-contempt, bitterer to drink than blood;
Pain, whose unheeded and familiar speech
Is howling, and keen shrieks, day after day;
And Hell, or the sharp fear of Hell?
　　Demogorgon.　　　　　　　　　He reigns.
　　Asia. Utter his name: a world pining in pain
Asks but his name: curses shall drag him down. 　30
　　Demogorgon. He reigns.
　　Asia.　　　　　　　I feel, I know it: who?
　　Demogorgon.　　　　　　　　　He
　　reigns.
　　Asia. Who reigns? There was the Heaven and
　　Earth at first,
And Light and Love; then Saturn, from whose
　　throne [23]
Time fell, an envious shadow: such the state
Of the earth's primal spirits beneath his sway,
As the calm joy of flowers and living leaves
Before the wind or sun has withered them
And semivital worms; but he refused
The birthright of their being, knowledge, power,
The skill which wields the elements, the thought 　40
Which pierces this dim universe like light,
Self-empire, and the majesty of love;
For thirst of which they fainted. Then Prometheus
Gave wisdom, which is strength, to Jupiter,
And with this law alone, 'Let man be free,'
Clothed him with the dominion of wide Heaven.
To know nor faith, nor love, nor law; to be
Omnipotent but friendless is to reign;
And Jove now reigned; for on the race of man
First famine, and then toil, and then disease, 　50
Strife, wounds, and ghastly death unseen before,
Fell; and the unseasonable seasons drove
With alternating shafts of frost and fire,
Their shelterless, pale tribes to mountain caves:
And in their desert hearts fierce wants he sent,
And mad disquietudes, and shadows idle
Of unreal good, which levied mutual war,
So ruining the lair wherein they raged.
Prometheus saw, and waked the legioned hopes
Which sleep within folded Elysian flowers, 　60
Nepenthe, Moly, Amaranth, fadeless blooms, [24]
That they might hide with thin and rainbow wings
The shape of Death; and Love he sent to bind

The disunited tendrils of that vine
Which bears the wine of life, the human heart;
And he tamed fire which, like some beast of prey,
Most terrible, but lovely, played beneath
The frown of man; and tortured to his will
Iron and gold, the slaves and signs of power,
And gems and poisons, and all subtlest forms 　70
Hidden beneath the mountains and the waves.
He gave man speech, and speech created thought,
Which is the measure of the universe;
And Science struck the thrones of earth and heaven,
Which shook, but fell not; and the harmonious mind
Poured itself forth in all-prophetic song;
And music lifted up the listening spirit
Until it walked, exempt from mortal care,
Godlike, o'er the clear billows of sweet sound;
And human hands first mimicked and then mocked,
With moulded limbs more lovely than its own, 　81
The human form, till marble grew divine;
And mothers, gazing, drank the love men see
Reflected in their race, behold, and perish. [25]
He told the hidden power of herbs and springs,
And Disease drank and slept. Death grew like sleep.
He taught the implicated orbits woven
Of the wide-wandering stars; and how the sun
Changes his lair, and by what secret spell
The pale moon is transformed, when her broad
　　eye 　　　　　　　　　　　　　　　90
Gazes not on the interlunar sea:
He taught to rule, as life directs the limbs,
The tempest-wingèd chariots of the Ocean,
And the Celt knew the Indian. Cities then
Were built, and through their snow-like columns
　　flowed
The warm winds, and the azure æther shone,
And the blue sea and shadowy hills were seen.
Such, the alleviations of his state,
Prometheus gave to man, for which he hangs
Withering in destined pain: but who rains down 　100
Evil, the immedicable plague, which, while
Man looks on his creation like a God
And sees that it is glorious, drives him on
The wreck of his own will, the scorn of earth,
The outcast, the abandoned, the alone?
Not Jove: while yet his frown shook heaven, aye, when
His adversary from adamantine chains
Cursed him, he trembled like a slave. Declare
Who is his master? Is he too a slave?
　　Demogorgon. All spirits are enslaved which serve
　　things evil: 　　　　　　　　　　　110

---

[23] Saturn (in Greek, Cronos) was the king of the Titans.
[24] All are flowers to which miraculous powers were ascribed.

[25] Pregnant women would gaze at statues to give their children beauty great enough so that men seeing it would die of love.

Thou knowest if Jupiter be such or no.
 Asia. Whom calledst thou God?
 Demogorgon.   I spoke but as ye
  speak,
For Jove is the supreme of living things.
 Asia. Who is the master of the slave?
 Demogorgon.   If the abysm
Could vomit forth its secrets. . . . But a voice
Is wanting, the deep truth is imageless;
For what would it avail to bid thee gaze
On the revolving world? What to bid speak
Fate, Time, Occasion, Chance and Change? To these
All things are subject but eternal Love.   120
 Asia. So much I asked before, and my heart gave
The response thou hast given; and of such truths
Each to itself must be the oracle.
One more demand; and do thou answer me
As my own soul would answer, did it know
That which I ask. Prometheus shall arise
Henceforth the sun of this rejoicing world:
When shall the destined hour arrive?
 Demogorgon.   Behold!
 Asia. The rocks are cloven, and through the purple
  night
I see cars drawn by rainbow-wingèd steeds   130
Which trample the dim winds: in each there stands
A wild-eyed charioteer urging their flight.
Some look behind, as fiends pursued them there,
And yet I see no shapes but the keen stars:
Others, with burning eyes, lean forth, and drink
With eager lips the wind of their own speed,
As if the thing they loved fled on before,
And now, even now, they clasped it. Their bright
  locks
Stream like a comet's flashing hair: they all
Sweep onward.
 Demogorgon. These are the immortal Hours,   140
Of whom thou didst demand. One waits for thee.
 Asia. A spirit with a dreadful countenance
Checks its dark chariot by the craggy gulf.
Unlike thy brethren, ghastly charioteer,
Who art thou? Whither wouldst thou bear me? Speak!
 Spirit. I am the shadow of a destiny
More dread than is my aspect: ere yon planet
Has set, the darkness which ascends with me
Shall wrap in lasting night heaven's kingless throne.
 Asia. What meanest thou?
 Panthea.   That terrible shadow
  floats   150
Up from its throne, as may the lurid smoke
Of earthquake-ruined cities o'er the sea.
Lo! it ascends the car; the coursers fly
Terrified: watch its path among the stars

Blackening the night!
 Asia.   Thus I am answered: strange!
 Panthea. See, near the verge, another chariot stays;
An ivory shell inlaid with crimson fire,
Which comes and goes within its sculptured rim
Of delicate strange tracery; the young spirit
That guides it has the dove-like eyes of hope;   160
How its soft smiles attract the soul! as light
Lures wingèd insects thro' the lampless air.

      Spirit.

My coursers are fed with the lightning,
 They drink of the whirlwind's stream,
And when the red morning is brightning
 They bathe in the fresh sunbeam;
 They have strength for their swiftness I
  deem,
Then ascend with me, daughter of Ocean.
I desire: and their speed makes night kindle;
 I fear: they outstrip the Typhoon;   170
Ere the cloud piled on Atlas can dwindle
 We encircle the earth and the moon:
 We shall rest from long labours at noon:
Then ascend with me, daughter of Ocean.

SCENE V. *The Car pauses within a Cloud on the top
 of a snowy Mountain.* ASIA, PANTHEA, *and the*
 SPIRIT OF THE HOUR.

      Spirit.

On the brink of the night and the morning
 My coursers are wont to respire;
But the Earth has just whispered a warning
 That their flight must be swifter than fire:
 They shall drink the hot speed of desire!

 Asia. Thou breathest on their nostrils, but my
  breath
Would give them swifter speed.
 Spirit.   Alas! it could not.
 Panthea. Oh Spirit! pause, and tell whence is the .
  light
Which fills the cloud? the sun is yet unrisen.
 Spirit. The sun will rise not until noon. Apollo   10
Is held in heaven by wonder; and the light
Which fills this vapour, as the aerial hue
Of fountain-gazing roses fills the water,
Flows from thy mighty sister.
 Panthea.   Yes, I feel—
 Asia. What is it with thee, sister? Thou art pale.
 Panthea. How thou art changed! I dare not look
  on thee;
I feel but see thee not. I scarce endure

The radiance of thy beauty. Some good change
Is working in the elements, which suffer
Thy presence thus unveiled. The Nereids tell[26]   20
That on the day when the clear hyaline
Was cloven at thine uprise, and thou didst stand
Within a veinèd shell, which floated on
Over the calm floor of the crystal sea,
Among the Ægean isles, and by the shores
Which bear thy name; love, like the atmosphere
Of the sun's fire filling the living world,
Burst from thee, and illumined earth and heaven
And the deep ocean and the sunless caves
And all that dwells within them; till grief cast   30
Eclipse upon the soul from which it came:
Such art thou now; nor is it I alone,
Thy sister, thy companion, thine own chosen one,
But the whole world which seeks thy sympathy.
Hearest thou not sounds i' the air which speak the
        love
Of all articulate beings? Feelest thou not
The inanimate winds enamoured of thee? List!
                                        [*Music.*

    Asia. Thy words are sweeter than aught else but
        his
Whose echoes they are: yet all love is sweet,
Given or returned. Common as light is love,   40
And its familiar voice wearies not ever.
Like the wide heaven, the all-sustaining air,
It makes the reptile equal to the God:
They who inspire it most are fortunate,
As I am now; but those who feel it most
Are happier still, after long sufferings,
As I shall soon become.
    Panthea.   List! Spirits speak.

            Voice in the Air, singing.

    Life of Life! thy lips enkindle
        With their love the breath between them;
    And thy smiles before they dwindle   50
        Make the cold air fire; then screen them
    In those looks, where whoso gazes
    Faints, entangled in their mazes.

    Child of Light! thy limbs are burning
        Thro' the vest which seems to hide them;
    As the radiant lines of morning
        Thro' the clouds ere they divide them;
    And this atmosphere divinest
    Shrouds thee wheresoe'er thou shinest.

---

[26] Asia is here identified with Venus; hyaline ("like glass") =
the sea.

Fair are others; none beholds thee,   60
    But thy voice sounds low and tender
Like the fairest, for it folds thee
    From the sight, that liquid splendour,
And all feel, yet see thee never,
As I feel now, lost for ever!

Lamp of Earth! where'er thou movest
    Its dim shapes are clad with brightness
And the souls of whom thou lovest
    Walk upon the winds with lightness,
Till they fail, as I am failing,   70
Dizzy, lost, yet unbewailing!

                Asia.

    My soul is an enchanted boat,
    Which, like a sleeping swan, doth float
Upon the silver waves of thy sweet singing;
    And thine doth like an angel sit
    Beside the helm conducting it,
Whilst all the winds with melody are ringing.
    It seems to float ever, for ever,
    Upon that many-winding river,
    Between mountains, woods, abysses,   80
    A paradise of wildernesses!
Till, like one in slumber bound,
Borne to the ocean, I float down, around,
Into a sea profound, of ever-spreading sound:

    Meanwhile thy spirit lifts its pinions
    In music's most serene dominions;
Catching the winds that fan that happy heaven.
    And we sail on, away, afar,
    Without a course, without a star,
But, by the instinct of sweet music driven;   90
    Till through Elysian garden islets
    By thee, most beautiful of pilots,
    Where never mortal pinnace glided,
    The boat of my desire is guided:
Realms where the air we breathe is love,
Which in the winds and on the waves doth move,
Harmonizing this earth with what we feel above.

    We have pass'd Age's icy caves,
    And Manhood's dark and tossing waves,
And Youth's smooth ocean, smiling to betray:
    Beyond the glassy gulphs we flee   101
    Of shadow-peopled Infancy,
Through Death and Birth, to a diviner day;
    A paradise of vaulted bowers,
    Lit by downward-gazing flowers,

And watery paths that wind between
Wildernesses calm and green,
Peopled by shapes too bright to see,
And rest, having beheld; somewhat like thee;
Which walk upon the sea, and chaunt
    melodiously!   110

END OF THE SECOND ACT.

ACT III

SCENE I. *Heaven.* JUPITER *on his Throne;* THETIS
and the other Deities assembled.

Jupiter. Ye congregated powers of heaven, who
    share
The glory and the strength of him ye serve,
Rejoice! henceforth I am omnipotent.
All else had been subdued to me; alone
The soul of man, like unextinguished fire,
Yet burns towards heaven with fierce reproach, and
    doubt,
And lamentation, and reluctant prayer,
Hurling up insurrection, which might make
Our antique empire insecure, though built
On eldest faith, and hell's coeval, fear;   10
And tho' my curses thro' the pendulous air,
Like snow on herbless peaks, fall flake by flake,
And cling to it; tho' under my wrath's night
It climb the crags of life, step after step,
Which wound it, as ice wounds unsandalled feet,
It yet remains supreme o'er misery,
Aspiring, unrepressed, yet soon to fall:
Even now have I begotten a strange wonder,
That fatal child, the terror of the earth, [27]
Who waits but till the destined hour arrive,   20
Bearing from Demogorgon's vacant throne
The dreadful might of ever-living limbs
Which clothed that awful spirit unbeheld,
To redescend, and trample out the spark.
Pour forth heaven's wine, Idæan Ganymede, [28]
And let it fill the Dædal [29] cups like fire,
And from the flower-inwoven soil divine
Ye all-triumphant harmonies arise,
As dew from earth under the twilight stars:
Drink! be the nectar circling thro' your veins   30
The soul of joy, ye ever-living Gods,

---

[27] The son of Jupiter and Thetis, whom Jupiter expects to take
on the role of Demogorgon.
[28] Zeus took the boy from Mt. Ida to be cup-bearer for the
gods.
[29] As intricate as if made by Daedalus, the builder of the
Labyrinth.

Till exultation burst in one wide voice
Like music from Elysian winds.
                    And thou
Ascend beside me, veilèd in the light
Of the desire which makes thee one with me,
Thetis, bright image of eternity!
When thou didst cry, 'Insufferable might!
God! Spare me! I sustain not the quick flames,
The penetrating presence; all my being,
Like him whom the Numidian seps [30] did thaw   40
Into a dew with poison, is dissolved,
Sinking thro' its foundations:' even then
Two mighty spirits, mingling, made a third
Mightier than either, which, unbodied now,
Between us floats, felt, although unbeheld,
Waiting the incarnation, which ascends,
(Hear ye the thunder of the fiery wheels
Griding the winds?) from Demogorgon's throne.
Victory! victory! Feel'st thou not, O world,
The earthquake of his chariot thundering up   50
Olympus?

[*The Car of the* HOUR *arrives.* DEMOGORGON
descends, and moves towards the Throne of JUPITER.

    Awful shape, what art thou? Speak!
Demogorgon. Eternity. Demand no direr name.
Descend, and follow me down the abyss.
I am thy child, as thou wert Saturn's child;
Mightier than thee: and we must dwell together
Henceforth in darkness. Lift thy lightnings not.
The tyranny of heaven none may retain,
Or reassume, or hold, succeeding thee:
Yet if thou wilt, as 'tis the destiny
Of trodden worms to writhe till they are dead,   60
Put forth thy might.
    Jupiter.   Detested prodigy!
Even thus beneath the deep Titanian prisons
I trample thee! thou lingerest?
                    Mercy! mercy!
No pity, no release, no respite! Oh,
That thou wouldst make mine enemy my judge,
Even where he hangs, seared by my long revenge,
Oh Caucasus! he would not doom me thus.
Gentle, and just, and dreadless, is he not
The monarch of the world? What then art thou?
No refuge! no appeal!
                Sink with me then,   70
We two will sink on the wide waves of ruin,
Even as a vulture and a snake outspent
Drop, twisted in inextricable fight,
Into a shoreless sea. Let hell unlock
Its mounded oceans of tempestuous fire,

---

[30] Venomous serpent.

And whelm on them into the bottomless void
This desolated world, and thee, and me
The conqueror and the conquered, and the wreck
Of that for which they combated.
                       Ai! Ai![31]
The elements obey me not. I sink   80
Dizzily down, ever, for ever, down.
And, like a cloud, mine enemy above
Darkens my fall with victory! Ai, Ai!

SCENE II. *The Mouth of a great River in the Island
Atlantis.* OCEAN *is discovered reclining near the
Shore;* APOLLO *stands beside him.*

Ocean. He fell, thou sayest, beneath his conqueror's
    frown?
Apollo. Aye, when the strife was ended which made
    dim
The orb I rule, and shook the solid stars,
The terrors of his eye illumined heaven
With sanguine light, thro' the thick ragged skirts
Of the victorious darkness, as he fell:
Like the last glare of day's red agony,
Which, from a rent among the fiery clouds,
Burns far along the tempest-wrinkled deep.
Ocean. He sunk to the abyss? To the dark void? 10
Apollo. An eagle so caught in some bursting cloud
On Caucasus, his thunder-baffled wings
Entangled in the whirlwind, and his eyes
Which gazed on the undazzling sun, now blinded
By the white lightning, while the ponderous hail
Beats on his struggling form, which sinks at length
Prone, and the aerial ice clings over it.
Ocean. Henceforth the fields of Heaven-reflecting
    sea
Which are my realm, will heave, unstain'd with
    blood,
Beneath the uplifting winds, like plains of corn   20
Swayed by the summer air; my streams will flow
Round many-peopled continents, and round
Fortunate isles; and from their glassy thrones
Blue Proteus and his humid nymphs shall mark
The shadow of fair ships, as mortals see
The floating bark of the light laden moon
With that white star, its sightless pilot's crest,
Borne down the rapid sunset's ebbing sea;
Tracking their path no more by blood and groans,
And desolation, and the mingled voice   30
Of slavery and command; but by the light
Of wave-reflected flowers, and floating odours,
And music soft, and mild, free, gentle voices,
That sweetest music, such as spirits love.

[31] The Greek word for "Woe!"

Apollo. And I shall gaze not on the deeds which
    make
My mind obscure with sorrow, as eclipse
Darkens the sphere I guide; but list, I hear
The small, clear, silver lute of the young Spirit
That sits i' the morning star.
Ocean.   Thou must away;
Thy steeds will pause at even, till when farewell: 40
The loud deep calls me home even now to feed it
With azure calm out of the emerald urns
Which stand for ever full beside my throne.
Behold the Nereids under the green sea,
Their wavering limbs borne on the wind-like stream,
Their white arms lifted o'er their streaming hair
With garlands pied and starry sea-flower crowns,
Hastening to grace their mighty sister's joy.
               [*A sound of waves is heard.*
It is the unpastured sea hungering for calm.
Peace, monster; I come now. Farewell.
Apollo.   Farewell. 50

SCENE III. *Caucasus.* PROMETHEUS, HERCULES,
IONE, *the* EARTH, SPIRITS, ASIA, *and* PANTHEA,
borne in the Car with the SPIRIT OF THE HOUR.
HERCULES *unbinds* PROMETHEUS, *who descends.*

Hercules. Most glorious among spirits, thus doth
    strength
To wisdom, courage, and long-suffering love,
And thee, who art the form they animate,
Minister like a slave.
Prometheus.   Thy gentle words
Are sweeter even than freedom long desired
And long delayed.
               Asia, thou light of life,
Shadow of beauty unbeheld: and ye,
Fair sister nymphs, who made long years of pain
Sweet to remember, thro' your love and care:
Henceforth we will not part. There is a cave,   10
All overgrown with trailing odorous plants,
Which curtain out the day with leaves and flowers,
And paved with veinèd emerald, and a fountain
Leaps in the midst with an awakening sound.
From its curved roof the mountain's frozen tears
Like snow, or silver, or long diamond spires,
Hang downward, raining forth a doubtful light:
And there is heard the ever-moving air,
Whispering without from tree to tree, and birds,
And bees; and all around are mossy seats,   20
And the rough walls are clothed with long soft grass;
A simple dwelling, which shall be our own;
Where we will sit and talk of time and change,
As the world ebbs and flows, ourselves unchanged.
What can hide man from mutability?

And if ye sigh, then I will smile; and thou,
Ione, shalt chaunt fragments of sea-music,
Until I weep, when ye shall smile away
The tears she brought, which yet were sweet to shed.
We will entangle buds and flowers and beams   30
Which twinkle on the fountain's brim, and make
Strange combinations out of common things,
Like human babes in their brief innocence;
And we will search, with looks and words of love,
For hidden thoughts, each lovelier than the last,
Our unexhausted spirits; and like lutes
Touched by the skill of the enamoured wind,
Weave harmonies divine, yet ever new,
From difference sweet where discord cannot be;
And hither come, sped on the charmèd winds,   40
Which meet from all the points of heaven, as bees
From every flower aerial Enna feeds,
At their known island-homes in Himera,[32]
The echoes of the human world, which tell
Of the low voice of love, almost unheard,
And dove-eyed pity's murmured pain, and music,
Itself the echo of the heart, and all
That tempers or improves man's life, now free;
And lovely apparitions, dim at first,
Then radiant, as the mind, arising bright   50
From the embrace of beauty, whence the forms
Of which these are the phantoms, cast on them
The gathered rays which are reality,
Shall visit us, the progeny immortal
Of Painting, Sculpture, and rapt Poesy,
And arts, tho' unimagined, yet to be.
The wandering voices and the shadows these
Of all that man becomes, the mediators
Of that best worship love, by him and us
Given and returned; swift shapes and sounds, which
    grow   60
More fair and soft as man grows wise and kind,
And veil by veil, evil and error fall:
Such virtue has the cave and place around.
    [*Turning to the* SPIRIT OF THE HOUR.
For thee, fair Spirit, one toil remains. Ione,
Give her that curvèd shell, which Proteus old
Made Asia's nuptial boon, breathing within it
A voice to be accomplished, and which thou
Didst hide in grass under the hollow rock.
    Ione. Thou most desired Hour, more loved and
      lovely
Than all thy sisters, this is the mystic shell;   70
See the pale azure fading into silver
Lining it with a soft yet glowing light:
Looks it not like lulled music sleeping there?

    Spirit. It seems in truth the fairest shell of Ocean:
Its sound must be at once both sweet and strange.
    Prometheus. Go, borne over the cities of mankind
On whirlwind-footed coursers: once again
Outspeed the sun around the orbèd world;
And as thy chariot cleaves the kindling air,
Thou breathe into the many-folded shell,   80
Loosening its mighty music; it shall be
As thunder mingled with clear echoes: then
Return; and thou shalt dwell beside our cave.
And thou, O, Mother Earth!—
    The Earth.   I hear, I feel;
Thy lips are on me, and their touch runs down
Even to the adamantine central gloom
Along these marble nerves; 'tis life, 'tis joy,
And through my withered, old, and icy frame
The warmth of an immortal youth shoots down
Circling. Henceforth the many children fair   90
Folded in my sustaining arms; all plants,
And creeping forms, and insects rainbow-winged,
And birds, and beasts, and fish, and human shapes,
Which drew disease and pain from my wan bosom,
Draining the poison of despair, shall take
And interchange sweet nutriment; to me
Shall they become like sister-antelopes
By one fair dam, snow-white and swift as wind
Nursed among lilies near a brimming stream.
The dew-mists of my sunless sleep shall float   100
Under the stars like balm: night-folded flowers
Shall suck unwithering hues in their repose:
And men and beasts in happy dreams shall gather
Strength for the coming day, and all its joy:
And death shall be the last embrace of her[33]
Who takes the life she gave, even as a mother
Folding her child, says, 'Leave me not again.'
    Asia. Oh, mother! wherefore speak the name of
      death?
Cease they to love, and move, and breathe, and speak,
Who die?
    The Earth. It would avail not to reply: 110
Thou art immortal, and this tongue is known
But to the uncommunicating dead.
Death is the veil which those who live call life:
They sleep, and it is lifted: and meanwhile
In mild variety the seasons mild
With rainbow-skirted showers, and odorous winds,
And long blue meteors cleansing the dull night,
And the life-kindling shafts of the keen sun's
All-piercing bow, and the dew-mingled rain
Of the calm moonbeams, a soft influence mild,   120
Shall clothe the forests and the fields, ay, even
The crag-built deserts of the barren deep,

---

[32] Himera was a river town, Enna a hill town in ancient Sicily.

[33] The Earth.

With ever-living leaves, and fruits, and flowers.
And thou! There is a cavern where my spirit
Was panted forth in anguish whilst thy pain
Made my heart mad, and those who did inhale it
Became mad too, and built a temple there,
And spoke, and were oracular, and lured
The erring nations round to mutual war,
And faithless faith, such as Jove kept with thee;   130
Which breath now rises, as amongst tall weeds
A violet's exhalation, and it fills
With a serener light and crimson air
Intense, yet soft, the rocks and woods around;
It feeds the quick growth of the serpent vine,
And the dark linkèd ivy tangling wild,
And budding, blown, or odour-faded blooms
Which star the winds with points of coloured light,
As they rain thro' them, and bright golden globes
Of fruit, suspended in their own green heaven,   140
And thro' their veinèd leaves and amber stems
The flowers whose purple and translucid bowls
Stand ever mantling with aërial dew,
The drink of spirits: and it circles round,
Like the soft waving wings of noonday dreams,
Inspiring calm and happy thoughts, like mine,
Now thou art thus restored. This cave is thine.
Arise! Appear!
              [A SPIRIT *rises in the likeness of a winged child.*
              This is my torch-bearer;
Who let his lamp out in old time with gazing
On eyes from which he kindled it anew   150
With love, which is as fire, sweet daughter mine,
For such is that within thine own. Run, wayward,
And guide this company beyond the peak
Of Bacchic Nysa, Mænad-haunted mountain,[34]
And beyond Indus and its tribute rivers,
Trampling the torrent streams and glassy lakes
With feet unwet, unwearied, undelaying,
And up the green ravine, across the vale,
Beside the windless and crystalline pool,
Where ever lies, on unerasing waves,   160
The image of a temple, built above,
Distinct with column, arch, and architrave,
And palm-like capital, and over-wrought,
And populous with most living imagery,
Praxitelean shapes,[35] whose marble smiles
Fill the hushed air with everlasting love.
It is deserted now, but once it bore
Thy name, Prometheus; there the emulous youths
Bore to thy honour thro' the divine gloom
The lamp which was thine emblem; even as those   170
Who bear the untransmitted torch of hope

---

[34] The mountain in India where the Mænads nursed Bacchus.
[35] Praxiteles was a Greek sculptor of the fourth century B.C.

Into the grave, across the night of life,
As thou hast borne it most triumphantly
To this far goal of Time. Depart, farewell.
Beside that temple is the destined cave.

SCENE IV. *A Forest. In the Background a Cave.*
PROMETHEUS, ASIA, PANTHEA, IONE, *and the*
SPIRIT OF THE EARTH.

    Ione. Sister, it is not earthly: how it glides
Under the leaves! how on its head there burns
A light, like a green star, whose emerald beams
Are twined with its fair hair! how, as it moves,
The splendour drops in flakes upon the grass!
Knowest thou it?
    Panthea.   It is the delicate spirit
That guides the earth thro' heaven. From afar
The populous constellations call that light
The loveliest of the planets; and sometimes
It floats along the spray of the salt sea,   10
Or makes its chariot of a foggy cloud,
Or walks thro' fields or cities while men sleep,
Or o'er the mountain tops, or down the rivers,
Or thro' the green waste wilderness, as now,
Wondering at all it sees. Before Jove reigned
It loved our sister Asia, and it came
Each leisure hour to drink the liquid light
Out of her eyes, for which it said it thirsted
As one bit by a dipsas,[36] and with her
It made its childish confidence, and told her   20
All it had known or seen, for it saw much,
Yet idly reasoned what it saw; and called her,
For whence it sprung it knew not, nor do I,
Mother, dear mother.
    The Spirit of the Earth (running to ASIA). Mother,
              dearest mother;
May I then talk with thee as I was wont?
May I then hide my eyes in thy soft arms,
After thy looks have made them tired of joy?
May I then play beside thee the long noons,
When work is none in the bright silent air?
    Asia. I love thee, gentlest being, and henceforth   30
Can cherish thee unenvied: speak, I pray:
Thy simple talk once solaced, now delights.
    Spirit of the Earth. Mother, I am grown wiser,
              though a child
Cannot be wise like thee, within this day;
And happier too; happier and wiser both.
Thou knowest that toads, and snakes, and loathly
              worms,
And venomous and malicious beasts, and boughs
That bore ill berries in the woods, were ever

---

[36] Venomous serpent.

An hindrance to my walks o'er the green world:
And that, among the haunts of humankind,   40
Hard-featured men, or with proud, angry looks,
Or cold, staid gait, or false and hollow smiles,
Or the dull sneer of self-loved ignorance,
Or other such foul masks, with which ill thoughts
Hide that fair being whom we spirits call man;
And women too, ugliest of all things evil,
(Tho' fair, even in a world where thou art fair,
When good and kind, free and sincere like thee),
When false or frowning made me sick at heart
To pass them, tho' they slept, and I unseen.   50
Well, my path lately lay through a great city
Into the woody hills surrounding it:
A sentinel was sleeping at the gate:
When there was heard a sound, so loud, it shook
The towers amid the moonlight, yet more sweet
Than any voice but thine, sweetest of all;
A long, long sound, as it would never end:
And all the inhabitants leapt suddenly
Out of their rest, and gathered in the streets,
Looking in wonder up to Heaven, while yet   60
The music pealed along. I hid myself
Within a fountain in the public square,
Where I lay like the reflex of the moon
Seen in a wave under green leaves; and soon
Those ugly human shapes and visages
Of which I spoke as having wrought me pain,
Passed floating thro' the air, and fading still
Into the winds that scattered them; and those
From whom they passed seemed mild and lovely
        forms
After some foul disguise had fallen, and all   70
Were somewhat changed, and after brief surprise
And greetings of delighted wonder, all
Went to their sleep again: and when the dawn
Came, wouldst thou think that toads, and snakes, and
        efts,
Could e'er be beautiful? yet so they were,
And that with little change of shape or hue:
All things had put their evil nature off:
I cannot tell my joy, when o'er a lake
Upon a drooping bough with night-shade twined,
I saw two azure halcyons [37] clinging downward   80
And thinning one bright bunch of amber berries,
With quick long beaks, and in the deep there lay
Those lovely forms imaged as in a sky;
So, with my thoughts full of these happy changes,
We meet again, the happiest change of all.
    Asia. And never will we part, till thy chaste sister [38]

Who guides the frozen and inconstant moon
Will look on thy more warm and equal light
Till her heart thaw like flakes of April snow
And love thee.
    Spirit of the Earth. What; as Asia loves
        Prometheus?   90
    Asia. Peace, wanton, thou art yet not old enough.
Think ye by gazing on each other's eyes
To multiply your lovely selves, and fill
With spherèd fires the interlunar air?
    Spirit of the Earth. Nay, mother, while my sister
        trims her lamp
'Tis hard I should go darkling.
    Asia.   Listen; look!

                The SPIRIT OF THE HOUR *enters.*

    Prometheus. We feel what thou hast heard and
        seen: yet speak.
    Spirit of the Hour. Soon as the sound had ceased
        whose thunder filled
The abysses of the sky and the wide earth,
There was a change: the impalpable thin air   100
And the all-circling sunlight were transformed,
As if the sense of love dissolved in them
Had folded itself round the spherèd world.
My vision then grew clear, and I could see
Into the mysteries of the universe:
Dizzy as with delight I floated down,
Winnowing the lightsome air with languid plumes,
My coursers sought their birth-place in the sun,
Where they henceforth will live exempt from toil,
Pasturing flowers of vegetable fire.   110
And where my moonlike car will stand within
A temple, gazed upon by Phidian forms [39]
Of thee, and Asia, and the Earth, and me,
And you fair nymphs looking the love we feel;
In memory of the tidings it has borne;
Beneath a dome fretted with graven flowers,
Poised on twelve columns of resplendent stone,
And open to the bright and liquid sky.
Yoked to it by an amphisbaenic snake [40]
The likeness of those wingèd steeds will mock   120
The flight from which they find repose. Alas,
Whither has wandered now my partial tongue
When all remains untold which ye would hear?
As I have said I floated to the earth:
It was, as it is still, the pain of bliss
To move, to breathe, to be; I wandering went
Among the haunts and dwellings of mankind,
And first was disappointed not to see
Such mighty change as I had felt within

---

[37] Kingfishers (poetical). In fact, no kingfishers are vegetar-
ians, though some species feed on insects and reptiles instead of
fish. In Ovid, the halcyon is a symbol of love.
[38] Diana, goddess of the moon.

[39] Phidias, a Greek sculptor of the fifth century B.C.
[40] Serpent with a head at each end.

Expressed in outward things; but soon I looked,   130
And behold, thrones were kingless, and men walked
One with the other even as spirits do,
None fawned, none trampled; hate, disdain, or fear,
Self-love or self-contempt, on human brows
No more inscribed, as o'er the gate of hell,
'All hope abandon ye who enter here;'[41]
None frowned, none trembled, none with eager fear
Gazed on another's eye of cold command,
Until the subject of a tyrant's will
Became, worse fate, the abject of his own,   140
Which spurred him, like an outspent horse, to death.
None wrought his lips in truth-entangling lines
Which smiled the lie his tongue disdained to speak;
None, with firm sneer, trod out in his own heart
The sparks of love and hope till there remained
Those bitter ashes, a soul self-consumed,
And the wretch crept a vampire among men,
Infecting all with his own hideous ill;
None talked that common, false, cold, hollow talk
Which makes the heart deny the *yes* it breathes,   150
Yet question that unmeant hypocrisy
With such a self-mistrust as has no name.
And women, too, frank, beautiful, and kind
As the free heaven which rains fresh light and dew
On the wide earth, past; gentle radiant forms,
From custom's evil taint exempt and pure;
Speaking the wisdom once they could not think,
Looking emotions once they feared to feel,
And changed to all which once they dared not be,
Yet being now, made earth like heaven; nor pride,
Nor jealousy, nor envy, nor ill shame,   161
The bitterest of those drops of treasured gall,
Spoilt the sweet taste of the nepenthe, love.

Thrones, altars, judgement-seats, and prisons;
          wherein,
And beside which, by wretched men were borne
Sceptres, tiaras, swords, and chains, and tomes
Of reasoned wrong, glozed on by ignorance,
Were like those monstrous and barbaric shapes,
The ghosts of a no more remembered fame,
Which, from their unworn obelisks, look forth   170
In triumph o'er the palaces and tombs
Of those who were their conquerors: mouldering
          round
Those imaged to the pride of kings and priests,
A dark yet mighty faith, a power as wide
As is the world it wasted, and are now
But an astonishment; even so the tools
And emblems of its last captivity,
Amid the dwellings of the peopled earth,

---

[41] In Dante's *Inferno*, III, 9.

Stand, not o'erthrown, but unregarded now.
And those foul shapes, abhorred by god and man,
Which, under many a name and many a form   181
Strange, savage, ghastly, dark, and execrable,
Were Jupiter, the tyrant of the world;
And which the nations, panic-stricken, served
With blood, and hearts broken by long hope, and love
Dragged to his altars soiled and garlandless,
And slain amid men's unreclaiming tears,
Flattering the thing they feared, which fear was
          hate,
Frown, mouldering fast, o'er their abandoned shrines:
The painted veil, by those who were, called life,   190
Which mimicked, as with colours idly spread,
All men believed and hoped, is torn aside;
The loathsome mask has fallen, the man remains
Sceptreless, free, uncircumscribed, but man
Equal, unclassed, tribeless, and nationless,
Exempt from awe, worship, degree, the king
Over himself; just, gentle, wise: but man
Passionless; no, yet free from guilt or pain,
Which were, for his will made or suffered them,
Nor yet exempt, tho' ruling them like slaves,   200
From chance, and death, and mutability,
The clogs of that which else might oversoar
The loftiest star of unascended heaven,
Pinnacled dim in the intense inane.

END OF THE THIRD ACT.

ACT IV

SCENE.   *A Part of the Forest near the Cave of* PRO-
METHEUS. PANTHEA *and* IONE *are sleeping: they
awaken gradually during the first Song.*

Voice of unseen Spirits.

The pale stars are gone!
For the sun, their swift shepherd,
To their folds them compelling,
In the depths of the dawn,
Hastes, in meteor-eclipsing array, and they flee
          Beyond his blue dwelling,
          As fawns flee the leopard.
               But where are ye?

*A Train of dark Forms and Shadows passes by
          confusedly, singing.*

Here, oh, here:
We bear the bier   10
Of the Father of many a cancelled year
          Spectres we
          Of the dead Hours be,
We bear Time to his tomb in eternity.

Strew, oh, strew
Hair, not yew!
Wet the dusty pall with tears, not dew!
Be the faded flowers
Of Death's bare bowers
Spread on the corpse of the King of Hours!   20

Haste, oh, haste!
As shades are chased,
Trembling, by day, from heaven's blue waste.
We melt away,
Like dissolving spray,
From the children of a diviner day,
With the lullaby
Of winds that die
On the bosom of their own harmony!

                                        [*They vanish.*

Ione.

What dark forms were they?   30

Panthea.

The past Hours weak and gray,
With the spoil which their toil
Raked together
From the conquest but One could foil.

Ione.

Have they passed?

Panthea.

          They have passed;
They outspeeded the blast,
While 'tis said, they are fled:

Ione.

          Whither, oh, whither?

Panthea.

To the dark, to the past, to the dead.

Voice of unseen Spirits.

Bright clouds float in heaven,   40
Dew-stars gleam on earth,
Waves assemble on ocean,
They are gathered and driven
By the storm of delight, by the panic of glee!
They shake with emotion,
They dance in their mirth.
          But where are ye?

The pine boughs are singing
Old songs with new gladness,
The billows and fountains   50
Fresh music are flinging,
Like the notes of a spirit from land and from sea;
The storms mock the mountains
With the thunder of gladness.
          But where are ye?

Ione. What charioteers are these?
Panthea.   Where are their
          chariots?

Semichorus of Hours.

The voice of the Spirits of Air and of Earth
Have drawn back the figured curtain of sleep
Which covered our being and darkened our birth
In the deep.

A Voice.

In the deep?

Semichorus II.

          Oh, below the deep.   60

Semichorus I.

An hundred ages we had been kept
Cradled in visions of hate and care,
And each one who waked as his brother slept,
Found the truth—

Semichorus II.

Worse than his visions were!

Semichorus I.

We have heard the lute of Hope in sleep;
We have known the voice of Love in dreams,
We have felt the wand of Power, and leap—

Semichorus II.

As the billows leap in the morning beams!

Chorus.

Weave the dance on the floor of the breeze,
Pierce with song heaven's silent light,   70
Enchant the day that too swiftly flees,
To check its flight ere the cave of Night.

Once the hungry Hours were hounds
Which chased the day like a bleeding deer,
And it limped and stumbled with many wounds
Through the nightly dells of the desart year.

But now, oh weave the mystic measure
  Of music, and dance, and shapes of light,
Let the Hours, and the spirits of might and pleasure,
  Like the clouds and sunbeams, unite.

A Voice.

Unite! 80

Panthea. See, where the Spirits of the human
    mind
Wrapt in sweet sounds, as in bright veils, approach.

Chorus of Spirits.

  We join the throng
  Of the dance and the song,
By the whirlwind of gladness borne along;
  As the flying-fish leap
  From the Indian deep,
And mix with the sea-birds, half asleep.

Chorus of Hours.

Whence come ye, so wild and so fleet,
For sandals of lightning are on your feet,   90
And your wings are soft and swift as thought,
And your eyes are as love which is veilèd not?

Chorus of Spirits.

  We come from the mind
  Of human kind
Which was late so dusk, and obscene, and blind,
  Now 'tis an ocean
  Of clear emotion,
A heaven of serene and mighty motion.

  From that deep abyss
  Of wonder and bliss,   100
Whose caverns are crystal palaces;
  From those skiey towers
  Where Thought's crowned powers
Sit watching your dance, ye happy Hours!

  From the dim recesses
  Of woven caresses,
Where lovers catch ye by your loose tresses;
  From the azure isles,
  Where sweet Wisdom smiles,
Delaying your ships with her siren wiles.   110

  From the temples high
  Of Man's ear and eye,
Roofed over Sculpture and Poesy;
  From the murmurings
  Of the unsealed springs
Where Science bedews his Dædal wings.

  Years after years,
  Through blood, and tears,
And a thick hell of hatreds, and hopes, and fears;
  We waded and flew,   120
  And the islets were few
Where the bud-blighted flowers of happiness grew.

  Our feet now, every palm,
  Are sandalled with calm,
And the dew of our wings is a rain of balm;
  And, beyond our eyes,
  The human love lies
Which makes all it gazes on Paradise.

Chorus of Spirits and Hours.

  Then weave the web of the mystic measure;
From the depths of the sky and the ends of the earth,
  Come, swift Spirits of might and of pleasure,   131
Fill the dance and the music of mirth,
  As the waves of a thousand streams rush by
  To an ocean of splendour and harmony!

Chorus of Spirits.

  Our spoil is won,
  Our task is done,
We are free to dive, or soar, or run;
  Beyond and around,
  Or within the bound
Which clips the world with darkness round.   140

  We'll pass the eyes
  Of the starry skies
Into the hoar deep to colonize:
  Death, Chaos, and Night,
  From the sound of our flight,
Shall flee, like mist from a tempest's might.

  And Earth, Air, and Light,
  And the Spirit of Might,
Which drives round the stars in their fiery flight;
  And Love, Thought, and Breath,   150
  The powers that quell Death,
Wherever we soar shall assemble beneath.

  And our singing shall build
  In the void's loose field
A world for the Spirit of Wisdom to wield;
  We will take our plan
  From the new world of man,
And our work shall be called the Promethean.

Chorus of Hours.

Break the dance, and scatter the song;
  Let some depart, and some remain.   160

Semichorus I.

We, beyond heaven, are driven along:

Semichorus II.

Us the enchantments of earth retain:

Semichorus I.

Ceaseless, and rapid, and fierce, and free,
With the Spirits which build a new earth and sea,
And a heaven where yet heaven could never be.

Semichorus II.

Solemn, and slow, and serene, and bright,
Leading the Day and outspeeding the Night,
With the powers of a world of perfect light.

Semichorus I.

We whirl, singing loud, round the gathering sphere,
Till the trees, and the beasts, and the clouds appear
From its chaos made calm by love, not fear.   171

Semichorus II.

We encircle the ocean and mountains of earth,
And the happy forms of its death and birth
Change to the music of our sweet mirth.

Chorus of Hours and Spirits.

Break the dance, and scatter the song,
  Let some depart, and some remain,
Wherever we fly we lead along
In leashes, like starbeams, soft yet strong,
  The clouds that are heavy with love's sweet rain.

Panthea. Ha! they are gone!
Ione.   Yet feel you no delight
From the past sweetness?   181
  Panthea.   As the bare green hill
When some soft cloud vanishes into rain,
Laughs with a thousand drops of sunny water
To the unpavilioned sky!
  Ione.   Even whilst we speak
New notes arise. What is that awful sound?
  Panthea. 'Tis the deep music of the rolling world
Kindling within the strings of the waved air,
Æolian modulations.
  Ione.   Listen too,
How every pause is filled with under-notes,
Clear, silver, icy, keen, awakening tones,   190
Which pierce the sense, and live within the soul,
As the sharp stars pierce winter's crystal air
And gaze upon themselves within the sea.
  Panthea. But see where through two openings in
    the forest

Which hanging branches overcanopy,
And where two runnels of a rivulet,
Between the close moss violet-inwoven,
Have made their path of melody, like sisters
Who part with sighs that they may meet in smiles,
Turning their dear disunion to an isle   200
Of lovely grief, a wood of sweet sad thoughts;
Two visions of strange radiance float upon
The ocean-like enchantment of strong sound,
Which flows intenser, keener, deeper yet
Under the ground and through the windless air.
  Ione. I see a chariot like that thinnest boat,
In which the mother of the months is borne [42]
By ebbing light into her western cave,
When she upsprings from interlunar dreams,
O'er which is curved an orblike canopy   210
Of gentle darkness, and the hills and woods
Distinctly seen through that dusk airy veil,
Regard like shapes in an enchanter's glass;
Its wheels are solid clouds, azure and gold,
Such as the genii of the thunderstorm
Pile on the floor of the illumined sea
When the sun rushes under it; they roll
And move and grow as with an inward wind;
Within it sits a wingèd infant, white
Its countenance, like the whiteness of bright snow,
Its plumes are as feathers of sunny frost,   221
Its limbs gleam white, through the wind-flowing folds
Of its white robe, woof of ethereal pearl.
Its hair is white, the brightness of white light
Scattered in strings; yet its two eyes are heavens
Of liquid darkness, which the Deity
Within seems pouring, as a storm is poured
From jaggèd clouds, out of their arrowy lashes,
Tempering the cold and radiant air around,
With fire that is not brightness; in its hand   230
It sways a quivering moon-beam, from whose point
A guiding power directs the chariot's prow
Over its wheelèd clouds, which as they roll
Over the grass, and flowers, and waves, wake sounds,
Sweet as a singing rain of silver dew.
  Panthea. And from the other opening in the wood
Rushes, with loud and whirlwind harmony,
A sphere, which is as many thousand spheres,
Solid as chrystal, yet through all its mass
Flow, as through empty space, music and light: 240
Ten thousand orbs involving and involved,
Purple and azure, white, green, and golden,
Sphere within sphere; and every space between
Peopled with unimaginable shapes,
Such as ghosts dream dwell in the lampless deep,
Yet each inter-transpicuous, and they whirl

-----

42 Diana, goddess of the moon.

Over each other with a thousand motions,
Upon a thousand sightless axles spinning,
And with the force of self-destroying swiftness,
Intensely, slowly, solemnly roll on,   250
Kindling with mingled sounds, and many tones,
Intelligible words and music wild.
With mighty whirl the multitudinous orb
Grinds the bright brook into an azure mist
Of elemental subtlety, like light;
And the wild odour of the forest flowers,
The music of the living grass and air,
The emerald light of leaf-entangled beams
Round its intense yet self-conflicting speed,
Seem kneaded into one aerial mass   260
Which drowns the sense. Within the orb itself,
Pillowed upon its alabaster arms,
Like to a child o'erwearied with sweet toil,
On its own folded wings, and wavy hair,
The Spirit of the Earth is laid asleep,
And you can see its little lips are moving,
Amid the changing light of their own smiles,
Like one who talks of what he loves in dream.
    Ione. 'Tis only mocking the orb's harmony.
    Panthea. And from a star upon its forehead, shoot,
Like swords of azure fire, or golden spears   271
With tyrant-quelling myrtle overtwined,
Embleming heaven and earth united now,
Vast beams like spokes of some invisible wheel
Which whirl as the orb whirls, swifter than thought,
Filling the abyss with sun-like lightnings,
And perpendicular now, and now transverse,
Pierce the dark soil, and as they pierce and pass,
Make bare the secrets of the earth's deep heart;
Infinite mines of adamant and gold,   280
Valueless stones, and unimagined gems,
And caverns on crystalline columns poised
With vegetable silver overspread;
Wells of unfathomed fire, and water springs
Whence the great sea, even as a child is fed,
Whose vapours clothe earth's monarch mountain-tops
With kingly, ermine snow. The beams flash on
And make appear the melancholy ruins
Of cancelled cycles; anchors, beaks of ships;
Planks turned to marble; quivers, helms, and spears,
And gorgon-headed targes, and the wheels   291
Of scythèd chariots, and the emblazonry
Of trophies, standards, and armorial beasts,
Round which death laughed, sepulchred emblems
Of dead destruction, ruin within ruin!
The wrecks beside of many a city vast,
Whose population which the earth grew over
Was mortal, but not human; see, they lie
Their monstrous works, and uncouth skeletons,
Their statues, homes and fanes; prodigious shapes

Huddled in gray annihilation, split,   301
Jammed in the hard, black deep; and over these,
The anatomies of unknown wingèd things,
And fishes which were isles of living scale,
And serpents, bony chains, twisted around
The iron crags, or within heaps of dust
To which the tortuous strength of their last pangs
Had crushed the iron crags; and over these
The jaggèd alligator, and the might
Of earth-convulsing behemoth, which once   310
Were monarch beasts, and on the slimy shores,
And weed-overgrown continents of earth,
Increased and multiplied like summer worms
On an abandoned corpse, till the blue globe
Wrapped deluge round it like a cloak, and they
Yelled, gasped, and were abolished; or some God
Whose throne was in a comet, passed, and cried,
Be not! And like my words they were no more.

The Earth.

The joy, the triumph, the delight, the madness!
    The boundless, overflowing, bursting gladness,
The vaporous exultation not to be confined!   321
    Ha! ha! the animation of delight
    Which wraps me, like an atmosphere of light,
And bears me as a cloud is borne by its own wind.

The Moon.

Brother mine, calm wanderer,
    Happy globe of land and air,
Some Spirit is darted like a beam from thee,
    Which penetrates my frozen frame,
    And passes with the warmth of flame,
With love, and odour, and deep melody   330
        Through me, through me!

The Earth.

Ha! ha! the caverns of my hollow mountains,
    My cloven fire-crags, sound-exulting fountains
Laugh with a vast and inextinguishable laughter.
    The oceans, and the desarts, and the abysses,
    And the deep air's unmeasured wildernesses,
Answer from all their clouds and billows, echoing after.

They cry aloud as I do. Sceptred curse,[43]
    Who all our green and azure universe
Threatenedst to muffle round with black destruction,
        sending   340
    A solid cloud to rain hot thunder-stones,
    And splinter and knead down my children's bones,
All I bring forth, to one void mass battering and
        blending.

---

[43] I.e., Jupiter.

Until each crag-like tower, and storied column,
Palace, and obelisk, and temple solemn,
My imperial mountains crowned with cloud, and
  snow, and fire;
My sea-like forests, every blade and blossom
Which finds a grave or cradle in my bosom,
Were stamped by thy strong hate into a lifeless mire.

How art thou sunk, withdrawn, covered, drunk up
By thirsty nothing, as the brackish cup   351
Drained by a desart-troop, a little drop for all;
  And from beneath, around, within, above,
  Filling thy void annihilation, love
Burst in like light on caves cloven by the thunder-ball.

The Moon.

The snow upon my lifeless mountains
Is loosened into living fountains,
My solid oceans flow, and sing, and shine: 44
  A spirit from my heart bursts forth,
  It clothes with unexpected birth   360
My cold bare bosom: Oh! it must be thine
    On mine, on mine!

Gazing on thee I feel, I know
Green stalks burst forth, and bright flowers
  grow,
And living shapes upon my bosom move:
  Music is in the sea and air,
  Wingèd clouds soar here and there,
Dark with the rain new buds are dreaming of:
    'Tis love, all love!

The Earth.

It interpenetrates my granite mass,   370
  Through tangled roots and trodden clay doth pass
Into the utmost leaves and delicatest flowers;
  Upon the winds, among the clouds 'tis spread,
  It wakes a life in the forgotten dead,
They breathe a spirit up from their obscurest bowers.

And like a storm bursting its cloudy prison
  With thunder, and with whirlwind, has arisen
Out of the lampless caves of unimagined being:
  With earthquake shock and swiftness making shiver
  Thought's stagnant chaos, unremoved for ever,
Till hate, and fear, and pain, light-vanquished
  shadows, fleeing,   381

Leave Man, who was a manysided mirror,
  Which could distort to many a shape of error,
This true fair world of things, a sea reflecting
  love;
  Which over all his kind as the sun's heaven
  Gliding o'er ocean, smooth, serene, and even
Darting from starry depths radiance and life, doth
  move.

Leave man, even as a leprous child is left,
  Who follows a sick beast to some warm cleft
Of rocks, through which the might of healing springs
  is poured;   390
  Then when it wanders home with rosy smile,
  Unconscious, and its mother fears awhile
It is a spirit, then, weeps on her child restored.

Man, oh, not men! a chain of linkèd thought,
  Of love and might to be divided not,
Compelling the elements with adamantine stress;
  As the sun rules, even with a tyrant's gaze,
  The unquiet republic of the maze
Of planets, struggling fierce towards heaven's free
  wilderness.

Man, one harmonious soul of many a soul,   400
  Whose nature is its own divine control,
Where all things flow to all, as rivers to the sea;
  Familiar acts are beautiful through love;
  Labour, and pain, and grief, in life's green grove
Sport like tame beasts, none knew how gentle they
  could be!

His will, with all mean passions, bad delights,
  And selfish cares, its trembling satellites,
A spirit ill to guide, but mighty to obey,
  Is as a tempest-wingèd ship, whose helm
  Love rules, through waves which dare not
  overwhelm,   410
Forcing life's wildest shores to own its sovereign
  sway.

All things confess his strength. Through the cold
  mass
Of marble and of colour his dreams pass;
Bright threads whence mothers weave the robes their
  children wear;
  Language is a perpetual Orphic 45 song,
  Which rules with Dædal harmony a throng
Of thoughts and forms, which else senseless and
  shapeless were.

---

44 In Shelley's day, the moon was considered a frozen planet
of mountains and seas.

45 Like that of Orpheus, whose music could charm beasts,
storms, and trees; Dædal: see III, i, 26, p. 873.

The lightning is his slave; heaven's utmost deep
  Gives up her stars, and like a flock of sheep   419
They pass before his eye, are numbered, and roll on!
  The tempest is his steed, he strides the air;
  And the abyss shouts from her depth laid bare,
Heaven, hast thou secrets? Man unveils me; I have
    none.

The Moon.

  The shadow of white death has passed
  From my path in heaven at last,
A clinging shroud of solid frost and sleep;
    And through my newly-woven bowers,
    Wander happy paramours,
Less mighty, but as mild as those who keep
        Thy vales more deep.   430

The Earth.

As the dissolving warmth of dawn may fold
A half unfrozen dew-globe, green, and gold,
And crystalline, till it becomes a wingèd mist,
  And wanders up the vault of the blue day,
  Outlives the noon, and on the sun's last ray
Hangs o'er the sea, a fleece of fire and amethyst.

The Moon.

  Thou art folded, thou art lying
  In the light which is undying
Of thine own joy, and heaven's smile divine;
    All suns and constellations shower   440
    On thee a light, a life, a power
Which doth array thy sphere; thou pourest thine
        On mine, on mine!

The Earth.

I spin beneath my pyramid of night,[46]
  Which points into the heaven's dreaming
    delight,
Murmuring victorious joy in my enchanted sleep;
  As a youth lulled in love-dreams faintly sighing,
  Under the shadow of his beauty lying,
Which round his rest a watch of light and warmth
    doth keep.

The Moon.

  As in the soft and sweet eclipse,   450
  When soul meets soul on lovers' lips,
High hearts are calm, and brightest eyes are dull;
    So when thy shadow falls on me,
    Then am I mute and still, by thee
Covered; of thy love, Orb most beautiful,
        Full, oh, too full!

[46] Shadow cast by the earth; actually a cone.

  Thou art speeding round the sun
  Brightest world of many a one;
  Green and azure sphere which shinest
  With a light which is divinest   460
  Among all the lamps of Heaven
  To whom life and light is given;
  I, thy crystal paramour
  Borne beside thee by a power
  Like the polar Paradise,
  Magnet-like of lovers' eyes;
  I, a most enamoured maiden
  Whose weak brain is overladen
  With the pleasure of her love,
  Maniac-like around thee move   470
  Gazing, an insatiate bride,
  On thy form from every side
  Like a Mænad, round the cup
  Which Agave lifted up
  In the weird Cadmæan forest.[47]
  Brother, wheresoe'er thou soarest
  I must hurry, whirl and follow
  Through the heavens wide and hollow,
  Sheltered by the warm embrace
  Of thy soul from hungry space,   480
  Drinking from thy sense and sight
  Beauty, majesty, and might,
  As a lover or a chameleon
  Grows like what it looks upon,
  As a violet's gentle eye
  Gazes on the azure sky
Until its hue grows like what it beholds,
  As a gray and watery mist
  Glows like solid amethyst
Athwart the western mountain it enfolds,   490
    When the sunset sleeps
      Upon its snow—

The Earth.

  And the weak day weeps
    That it should be so.
Oh, gentle Moon, the voice of thy delight
Falls on me like thy clear and tender light
Soothing the seaman, borne the summer night,
    Through isles for ever calm;
Oh, gentle Moon, thy crystal accents pierce
The caverns of my pride's deep universe,   500
Charming the tiger joy, whose tramplings fierce
    Made wounds which need thy balm.

[47] Agave, the daughter of King Cadmus of Thebes, tore her son Pentheus to bits when he was caught watching a Dionysiac orgy. See also II, iii, 9, p. 868.

Panthea. I rise as from a bath of sparkling water,
A bath of azure light, among dark rocks,
Out of the stream of sound.
    Ione.   Ah me! sweet sister,
The stream of sound has ebbed away from us,
And you pretend to rise out of its wave,
Because your words fall like the clear, soft dew
Shaken from a bathing wood-nymph's limbs and
    hair.
    Panthea. Peace! peace! A mighty Power, which is
        as darkness,   510
Is rising out of Earth, and from the sky
Is showered like night, and from within the air
Bursts, like eclipse which had been gathered up
Into the pores of sunlight: the bright visions,
Wherein the singing spirits rode and shone,
Gleam like pale meteors through a watery night.
    Ione. There is a sense of words upon mine ear.
    Panthea. An universal sound like words: Oh,
        list!

Demogorgon.

Thou, Earth, calm empire of a happy soul,
    Sphere of divinest shapes and harmonies,   520
Beautiful orb! gathering as thou dost roll
    The love which paves thy path along the skies:

The Earth.

I hear: I am as a drop of dew that dies.

Demogorgon.

Thou, Moon, which gazest on the nightly Earth
    With wonder, as it gazes upon thee;
Whilst each to men, and beasts, and the swift
    birth
    Of birds, is beauty, love, calm, harmony:

The Moon.

I hear: I am a leaf shaken by thee!

Demogorgon.

Ye kings of suns and stars, Dæmons and Gods,
    Aetherial Dominations, who possess   530
Elysian, windless, fortunate abodes
    Beyond Heaven's constellated wilderness:

A Voice from above.

Our great Republic hears, we are blest, and bless.

Demogorgon.

Ye happy dead, whom beams of brightest verse
    Are clouds to hide, not colours to pourtray,
Whether your nature is that universe
    Which once ye saw and suffered—

A Voice from beneath.

              Or as they
Whom we have left, we change and pass away.

Demogorgon.

Ye elemental Genii, who have homes
    From man's high mind even to the central stone
Of sullen lead; from Heaven's star-fretted domes   541
    To the dull weed some sea-worm battens on:

A confused Voice.

We hear: thy words waken Oblivion.

Demogorgon.

Spirits, whose homes are flesh: ye beasts and birds,
    Ye worms, and fish; ye living leaves and buds;
Lightning and wind; and ye untameable herds,
    Meteors and mists, which throng air's solitudes:

A Voice.

Thy voice to us is wind among still woods.

Demogorgon.

Man, who wert once a despot and a slave;
    A dupe and a deceiver; a decay;   550
A traveller from the cradle to the grave
    Through the dim night of this immortal day:

All.

Speak: thy strong words may never pass away.

Demogorgon.

This is the day, which down the void abysm
At the Earth-born's [48] spell yawns for Heaven's
    despotism,
    And Conquest is dragged captive through the deep:
Love, from its awful throne of patient power
In the wise heart, from the last giddy hour
    Of dread endurance, from the slippery, steep,
And narrow verge of crag-like agony, springs   560
And folds over the world its healing wings.

Gentleness, Virtue, Wisdom, and Endurance,
These are the seals of that most firm assurance
    Which bars the pit over Destruction's strength;
And if, with infirm hand, Eternity,
Mother of many acts and hours, should free
    The serpent that would clasp her with his length; [49]
These are the spells by which to re-assume
An empire o'er the disentangled doom.

---

[48] Prometheus.
[49] I.e., the cycle may begin again.

To suffer woes which Hope thinks infinite;   570
To forgive wrongs darker than death or night;
  To defy Power, which seems omnipotent;
To love, and bear; to hope till Hope creates
From its own wreck the thing it contemplates;
  Neither to change, nor falter, nor repent;
This, like thy glory, Titan, is to be
Good, great and joyous, beautiful and free;
This is alone Life, Joy, Empire, and Victory.

[1818–19]   [1820]

THE MASK OF ANARCHY

In St. Peter's field, Manchester, on August 16, 1819, a mass meeting of thousands of dissatisfied workers and their families was brutally dispersed by yeoman cavalry, who killed a few people and injured hundreds. It has been popularly called the Peterloo Massacre, in ironic allusion to the English victory at Waterloo.

THE MASK OF ANARCHY

WRITTEN ON THE OCCASION OF THE MASSACRE AT MANCHESTER

I

As I lay asleep in Italy
There came a voice from over the Sea,
And with great power it forth led me
To walk in the visions of Poesy.

II

I met Murder on the way—
He had a mask like Castlereagh [1]—
Very smooth he looked, yet grim;
Seven blood-hounds followed him:

III

All were fat; and well they might
Be in admirable plight,   10
For one by one, and two by two,
He tossed them human hearts to chew,
Which from his wide cloak he drew.

IV

Next came Fraud, and he had on,
Like Eldon, an ermined gown; [2]
His big tears, for he wept well,
Turned to mill-stones as they fell;

V

And the little children, who
Round his feet played to and fro,
Thinking every tear a gem,   20
Had their brains knocked out by them.

VI

Clothed with the Bible, as with light,
And the shadows of the night,
Like Sidmouth, [3] next, Hypocrisy
On a crocodile rode by.

VII

And many more Destructions played
In this ghastly masquerade,
All disguised, even to the eyes,
Like Bishops, lawyers, peers, or spies.

VIII

Last came Anarchy: he rode   30
On a white horse splashed with blood;
He was pale even to the lips,
Like Death in the Apocalypse. [4]

IX

And he wore a kingly crown;
In his grasp a sceptre shone;
On his brow this mark I saw—
"I AM GOD, AND KING, AND LAW!"

X

With a pace stately and fast,
Over English land he past,
Trampling to a mire of blood   40
The adoring multitude.

XI

And a mighty troop around,
With their trampling shook the ground,
Waving each a bloody sword,
For the service of their Lord.

XII

And, with glorious triumph, they
Rode thro' England, proud and gay,
Drunk as with intoxication
Of the wine of desolation.

---

[1] Viscount Castlereagh, foreign secretary, also appears as Purganax in *Oedipus Tyrannus*, p. 933, and in Byron's dedication to *Don Juan*, p. 652. See also *To Sidmouth and Castlereagh*, p. 905.
[2] Lord Eldon, the lord chancellor, to whom Shelley addressed a poem in 1817 (p. 801). He also appears (as Dakry) in *Oedipus Tyrannus*.

---

[3] Tory Home Secretary.
[4] Rev. 6:8.

XIII

O'er fields and towns, from sea to sea,   50
Past the Pageant swift and free,
Tearing up, and trampling down;
Till they came to London town.

XIV

And each dweller, panic-stricken,
Felt his heart with terror sicken
Hearing the tempestuous cry
Of the triumph of Anarchy.

XV

For with pomp to meet him came,
Clothed in arms like blood and flame,
The hired murderers, who did sing,   60
"Thou art God, and Law, and King.

XVI

"We have waited, weak and lone
For thy coming, Mighty One!
Our purses are empty, our swords are cold.
Give us glory, and blood, and gold."

XVII

Lawyers and priests, a motley crowd,
To the earth their pale brows bowed,
Like a bad prayer not over loud,
Whispering—"Thou art Law and God!"

XVIII

Then all cried with one accord,   70
"Thou art King, and God, and Lord;
Anarchy, to thee we bow,
Be thy name made holy now!"

XIX

And Anarchy, the Skeleton,
Bowed and grinned to every one,
As well as if his education
Had cost ten millions to the nation.

XX

For he knew the Palaces
Of our Kings were nightly his;
His the sceptre, crown, and globe,   80
And the gold-inwoven robe.

XXI

So he sent his slaves before
To seize upon the Bank and Tower,
And was proceeding with intent
To meet his pensioned Parliament

XXII

When one fled past, a maniac maid,
And her name was Hope, she said:
But she looked more like Despair,
And she cried out in the air—

XXIII

"My father Time is weak and grey   90
With waiting for a better day;
See how idiot-like he stands,
Fumbling with his palsied hands!

XXIV

"He has had child after child,
And the dust of death is piled
Over every one but me—
Misery! oh, Misery!"

XXV

Then she lay down in the street,
Right before the horses' feet,
Expecting, with a patient eye,   100
Murder, Fraud, and Anarchy.

XXVI

When between her and her foes
A mist, a light, an image rose,
Small at first, and weak, and frail
Like the vapour of a vale:

XXVII

Till as clouds grow on the blast,
Like tower-crowned giants striding fast,
And glare with lightnings as they fly,
And speak in thunder to the sky,

XXVIII

It grew—a Shape arrayed in mail [5]   110
Brighter than the viper's scale,
And upborne on wings whose grain
Was as the light of sunny rain.

XXIX

On its helm, seen far away,
A planet, like the Morning's, lay;
And those plumes its light rained thro',
Like a shower of crimson dew.

⸻⸻⸻⸻⸻⸻⸻⸻⸻⸻

[5] Probably Liberty. "Grain" (line 112) is color.

XXX

With step as soft as wind it past
O'er the heads of men—so fast
That they knew the presence there,   120
And looked,—but all was empty air.

XXXI

As flowers beneath May's footsteps waken,
As stars from Night's loose hair are shaken,
As waves arise when loud winds call,
Thoughts sprung where'er that step did fall.

XXXII

And the prostrate multitude
Looked—and ankle-deep in blood,
Hope, that maiden most serene,
Was walking with a quiet mien:

XXXIII

And Anarchy, the ghastly birth,   130
Lay dead earth upon the earth;
The Horse of Death, tameless as wind
Fled, and with his hoofs did grind
To dust, the murderers thronged behind.

XXXIV

A rushing light of clouds and splendour,
A sense of awakening and yet tender
Was heard and felt—and at its close
These words of joy and fear arose

XXXV

As if their own indignant Earth
Which gave the sons of England birth   140
Had felt their blood upon her brow,
And shuddering with a mother's throe

XXXVI

Had turnèd every drop of blood
By which her face had been bedewed
To an accent unwithstood,—
As if her heart had cried aloud:

XXXVII

"Men of England, heirs of Glory,
Heroes of unwritten story,
Nurslings of one mighty Mother,
Hopes of her, and one another;   150

XXXVIII

"Rise like Lions after slumber
In unvanquishable number,
Shake your chains to earth like dew,
Which in sleep had fallen on you—
Ye are many—they are few.

XXXIX

"What is Freedom?—ye can tell
That which slavery is, too well—
For its very name has grown
To an echo of your own.

XL

"'Tis to work, and have such pay   160
As just keeps life from day to day
In your limbs as in a cell
For the tyrants' use to dwell:

XLI

"So that ye for them are made
Loom, and plough, and sword, and spade,
With or without your own will bent
To their defence and nourishment.

XLII

"'Tis to see your children weak
With their mothers pine and peak,
When the winter winds are bleak,—   170
They are dying whilst I speak.

XLIII

"'Tis to hunger for such diet
As the rich man in his riot
Casts to the fat dogs that lie
Surfeiting beneath his eye;

XLIV

"'Tis to let the Ghost of Gold [6]
Take from Toil a thousandfold
More than e'er its substance could
In the tyrannies of old:

XLV

"Paper coin—that forgery   180
Of the title deeds, which ye
Hold to something of the worth
Of the inheritance of Earth.

---

[6] I.e., paper money. See also *Peter Bell the Third*, III, v, p. 895.

XLVI

"'Tis to be a slave in soul
And to hold no strong controul
Over your own wills, but be
All that others make of ye.

XLVII

"And at length when ye complain
With a murmur weak and vain
'Tis to see the Tyrant's crew   190
Ride over your wives and you—
Blood is on the grass like dew.

XLVIII

"Then it is to feel revenge
Fiercely thirsting to exchange
Blood for blood—and wrong for wrong—
Do not thus when ye are strong.

XLIX

"Birds find rest, in narrow nest
When weary of their wingèd quest;
Beasts find fare, in woody lair
When storm and snow are in the air.   200

L

"Horses, oxen, have a home,
When from daily toil they come;
Household dogs, when the wind roars,
Find a home within warm doors.[7]

LI

"Asses, swine, have litter spread,
And with fitting food are fed;
All things have a home but one—
Thou, Oh, Englishman, hast none!

LII

"This is Slavery—savage men,
Or wild beasts within a den   210
Would endure not as ye do—
But such ills they never knew.

LIII

"What art thou, Freedom? O! could slaves
Answer from their living graves
This demand—tyrants would flee
Like a dream's dim imagery.

LIV

"Thou art not, as impostors say,
A shadow soon to pass away,
A superstition, and a name
Echoing from the cave of Fame.   220

LV

"For the labourer thou art bread,
And a comely table spread
From his daily labour come
To a neat and happy home.

LVI

"Thou art clothes, and fire, and food
For the trampled multitude—
No—in countries that are free
Such starvation cannot be
As in England now we see.

LVII

"To the rich thou art a check,   230
When his foot is on the neck
Of his victim, thou dost make
That he treads upon a snake.

LVIII

"Thou art Justice—ne'er for gold
May thy righteous laws be sold
As laws are in England—thou
Shield'st alike the high and low.

LIX

"Thou art Wisdom—Freemen never
Dream that God will damn for ever
All who think those things untrue,   240
Of which Priests make such ado.

LX

"Thou art Peace—never by thee
Would blood and treasure wasted be,
As tyrants wasted them, when all
Leagued to quench thy flame in Gaul.[8]

LXI

"What if English toil and blood
Was poured forth, even as a flood?
It availed,—Oh Liberty!
To dim—but not extinguish thee.

[7] This stanza does not appear in all editions or Mss.

[8] The alliance of Austria, Prussia, Holland, and England against France from 1792 on.

LXII

"Thou art Love—the rich have kist   250
    Thy feet, and like him following Christ
    Give their substance to the free
    And thro' the rough world follow thee.

LXIII

"Or turn their wealth to arms, and make
    War for thy belovèd sake
    On wealth, and war, and fraud—whence they
    Drew the power which is their prey.

LXIV

"Science, Poetry and Thought
    Are thy lamps; they make the lot
    Of the dwellers in a cot   260
    So serene, they curse it not.

LXV

"Spirit, Patience, Gentleness,
    All that can adorn and bless
    Art thou—let deeds, not words, express
    Thine exceeding loveliness.

LXVI

"Let a great Assembly be
    Of the fearless and the free
    On some spot of English ground
    Where the plains stretch wide around.

LXVII

"Let the blue sky overhead,   270
    The green earth on which ye tread,
    All that must eternal be
    Witness the solemnity.

LXVIII

"From the corners uttermost
    Of the bounds of English coast;
    From every hut, village and town
    Where those who live and suffer moan
    For others' misery or their own,

LXIX

"From the workhouse and the prison,
    Where pale as corpses newly risen,   280
    Women, children, young and old
    Groan for pain, and weep for cold—

LXX

"From the haunts of daily life
    Where is waged the daily strife
    With common wants and common cares
    Which sows the human heart with tares—

LXXI

"Lastly from the palaces
    Where the murmur of distress
    Echoes, like the distant sound
    Of a wind alive around   290

LXXII

"Those prison halls of wealth and fashion
    Where some few feel such compassion
    For those who groan, and toil, and wail
    As must make their brethren pale—

LXXIII

"Ye who suffer woes untold,
    Or to feel, or to behold
    Your lost country bought and sold
    With a price of blood and gold—

LXXIV

"Let a vast assembly be,
    And with great solemnity   300
    Declare with measured words that ye
    Are, as God has made ye, free—

LXXV

"Be your strong and simple words
    Keen to wound as sharpened swords,
    And wide as targes let them be,
    With their shade to cover ye.

LXXVI

"Let the tyrants pour around
    With a quick and startling sound,
    Like the loosening of a sea,
    Troops of armed emblazonry.   310

LXXVII

"Let the charged artillery drive,
    Till the dead air seems alive
    With the clash of clanging wheels,
    And the tramp of horses' heels.

LXXVIII

"Let the fixèd bayonet
    Gleam with sharp desire to wet
    Its bright point in English blood
    Looking keen as one for food.

LXXIX

"Let the horsemen's scimitars
Wheel and flash, like sphereless stars [9]   320
Thirsting to eclipse their burning
In a sea of death and mourning.

LXXX

"Stand ye calm and resolute,
Like a forest close and mute,
With folded arms, and looks which are
Weapons of an unvanquished war,

LXXXI

"And let Panic, who outspeeds
The career of armèd steeds
Pass, a disregarded shade
Thro' your phalanx undismayed.   330

LXXXII

"Let the laws of your own land,
Good or ill, between ye stand
Hand to hand, and foot to foot,
Arbiters of the dispute,

LXXXIII

"The old laws of England—they
Whose reverend heads with age are grey,
Children of a wiser day;
And whose solemn voice must be
Thine own echo—Liberty!

LXXXIV

"On those who first should violate   340
Such sacred heralds in their state
Rest the blood that must ensue,
And it will not rest on you.

LXXXV

"And if then the tyrants dare,
Let them ride among you there,
Slash, and stab, and maim, and hew,—
What they like, that let them do.

LXXXVI

"With folded arms and steady eyes,
And little fear, and less surprise
Look upon them as they slay   350
Till their rage has died away.

LXXXVII

"Then they will return with shame
To the place from which they came,
And the blood thus shed will speak
In hot blushes on their cheek.

LXXXVIII

"Every woman in the land
Will point at them as they stand—
They will hardly dare to greet
Their acquaintance in the street.

LXXXIX

"And the bold, true warriors   360
Who have hugged Danger in wars,
Will turn to those who would be free
Ashamed of such base company.

XC

"And that slaughter to the Nation
Shall steam up like inspiration,
Eloquent, oracular;
A volcano heard afar.

XCI

"And these words shall then become
Like oppression's thundered doom
Ringing thro' each heart and brain,   370
Heard again—again—again—

XCII

"Rise like Lions after slumber
In unvanquishable number—
Shake your chains to earth like dew
Which in sleep had fallen on you—
Ye are many—they are few."

[1819]   [1832]

---

[9] In ancient astronomy, each fixed star had its assigned sphere
within which it moved. A "sphereless star" may be a meteor.

PETER BELL THE THIRD

A parody and general criticism of Wordsworth (and Coleridge), this poem was written after John Hamilton Reynolds' parody Peter Bell, a Lyrical Ballad, *appeared almost simultaneously with Wordsworth's* Peter Bell, a Tale, *in April 1819. Both poems were reviewed in Leigh Hunt's* Examiner *in April and May, 1819.*

PETER BELL THE THIRD

BY

MICHING MALLECHO, ESQ.

Is it a party in a parlour,
Crammed just as they on earth were crammed,
Some sipping punch—some sipping tea;
But, as you by their faces see,
All silent, and all—damned!
　　　　Peter Bell, by W. WORDSWORTH.

OPHELIA.—What means this, my lord?
HAMLET.—Marry, this is Miching Mallecho; it means mischief.
　　　　　　　　　　　　SHAKSPEARE.

DEDICATION

TO THOMAS BROWN, ESQ.,
THE YOUNGER, H.F.[1]

DEAR TOM,

Allow me to request you to introduce Mr. Peter Bell to the respectable family of the Fudges; although he may fall short of those very considerable personages in the more active properties which characterise the Rat and the Apostate, I suspect that even you, their historian, will confess that he surpasses them in the more peculiarly legitimate qualification of intolerable dulness.

You know Mr. Examiner Hunt;[2] well—it was he who presented me to two of the Mr. Bells. My intimacy with the younger Mr. Bell naturally sprung from this introduction to his brothers. And in presenting him to you, I have the satisfaction of being able to assure you that he is considerably the dullest of the three.

There is this particular advantage in an acquaintance with any one of the Peter Bells, that if you know one Peter Bell, you know three Peter Bells; they are not one, but three; not three, but one. An awful mystery, which, after having caused torrents of blood, and having been hymned by groans enough to deafen the music of the spheres, is at length illustrated to the satisfaction of all parties in the theological world, by the nature of Mr. Peter Bell.

Peter is a polyhedric Peter, or a Peter with many sides. He changes colours like a cameleon, and his coat like a snake. He is a Proteus of a Peter. He was at first sublime, pathetic, impressive, profound; then dull; then prosy and dull; and now dull—O, so very dull! it is an ultra-legitimate dulness.

You will perceive that it is not necessary to consider Hell and the Devil as supernatural machinery. The whole scene of my epic is in "this world which is"—So Peter informed us before his conversion to *White Obi*——

—The world of all of us, *and where
We find our happiness, or not at all.*[3]

Let me observe that I have spent six or seven days in composing this sublime piece; the orb of my moon-like genius has made the fourth part of its revolution round the dull earth which you inhabit, driving you mad, while it has retained its calmness and its splendour, and I have been fitting this its last phase "to occupy a permanent station in the literature of my country."[4]

Your works, indeed, dear Tom, sell better; but mine are far superior. The public is no judge; posterity sets all to rights.

Allow me to observe that so much has been written of Peter Bell, that the present history can be considered only, like the Iliad, as a continuation of that series of cyclic poems, which have already been candidates for bestowing immortality upon, as the same time that they receive it from, his character and adventures. In this point of view I have violated no rule of syntax in beginning my composition with a conjunction; the full stop which closes the poem continued by me, being like the full stops at the end of the Iliad and Odyssey, a full stop of a very qualified import.

Hoping that the immortality which you have given to the Fudges, you will receive from them; and in the firm expectation, that when London shall be an habitation of bitterns, when St. Paul's and Westminster Abbey shall stand, shapeless and nameless ruins, in the midst of an unpeopled marsh; when the piers of Waterloo-Bridge shall become the nuclei of islets of reeds and osiers, and cast the jagged shadows of their

---

[1] This was a pseudonym of Thomas Moore; H. F. apparently means Historian of the Fudges (he wrote *The Fudge Family*).
[2] Leigh Hunt edited the weekly *Examiner* from 1808–1821.
[3] Wordsworth, *Prelude*, XI, 142 (also published in 1809 as *The French Revolution as it Appeared to Enthusiasts at Its Commencement*); *White Obi*: white magic(?).
[4] Shelley deliberately omits the phrase "however humble" which appears after "station" in Wordsworth's dedication of *Peter Bell* (see p. 213).

broken arches on the solitary stream, some trans-atlantic commentator will be weighing in the scales of some new and now unimagined system of criticism, the respective merits of the Bells and the Fudges, and their historians,

I remain, dear Tom,

Yours sincerely

MICHING MALLECHO.

December 1, 1819.

P.S.—Pray excuse the date of place; so soon as the profits of the publication come in, I mean to hire lodgings in a more respectable street.

———◦◦◦◦———

CONTENTS

———◦◦◦◦———

PROLOGUE

PETER BELLS, one, two and three,
O'er the wide world wandering be.—
First, the antenatal Peter,[5]
Wrapt in weeds of the same metre,
The so long predestined raiment
Clothed in which to walk his way meant
The second Peter; whose ambition
Is to link the proposition,
As the mean of two extremes—
(This was learnt from Aldric's themes)   10
Shielding from the guilt of schism
The orthodoxal syllogism;
The First Peter—he who was
Like the shadow in the glass
Of the second, yet unripe,
His substantial antitype.—
Then came Peter Bell the Second,[6]
Who henceforward must be reckoned
The body of a double soul,
And that portion of the whole   20

Without which the rest would seem
Ends of a disjointed dream.—
And the Third is he who has[7]
O'er the grave been forced to pass
To the other side, which is,—
Go and try else,—just like this.

Peter Bell the First was Peter
Smugger, milder, softer, neater,
Like the soul before it is
Born from *that* world into *this*.   30
The next Peter Bell was he,
Predevote, like you and me,
To good or evil as may come;
His was the severer doom,—
For he was an evil Cotter,
And a polygamic Potter.*
And the last is Peter Bell,
Damned since our first parents fell,
Damned eternally to Hell—
Surely he deserves it well!

———◦◦◦◦———

PART THE FIRST
DEATH

AND Peter Bell, when he had been
    With fresh-imported Hell-fire warmed,
Grew serious—from his dress and mien
'Twas very plainly to be seen
    Peter was quite reformed.

His eyes turned up, his mouth turned down;
    His accent caught a nasal twang;
He oiled his hair,† there might be heard
The grace of God in every word
    Which Peter said or sang.   10

---

* The oldest scholiasts read—

A dodecagamic Potter.

This is at once more descriptive and more megalophonous,—but the alliteration of the text had captivated the vulgar ear of the herd of later commentators.

    † To those who have not duly appreciated the distinction between *Whale* and *Russia* oil, this attribute might rather seem to belong to the Dandy than the Evangelic. The effect, when to the windward, is indeed so similar, that it requires a subtle naturalist to discriminate the animals. They belong, however, to distinct genera.

---

5 I.e., the version by Reynolds.
6 Wordsworth's poem.

7 Shelley's.

But Peter now grew old, and had
    An ill no doctor could unravel;
His torments almost drove him mad;—
Some said it was a fever bad—
    Some swore it was the gravel.

His holy friends then came about,
    And with long preaching and persuasion,
Convinced the patient that, without
The smallest shadow of a doubt,
    He was predestined to damnation.   20

They said—"Thy name is Peter Bell;
    Thy skin is of a brimstone hue;
Alive or dead—aye, sick or well—
The one God made to rhyme with hell;
    The other, I think, rhymes with you."

Then Peter set up such a yell!—
    The nurse, who with some water gruel
Was climbing up the stairs, as well
As her old legs could climb them—fell,
    And broke them both—the fall was cruel.   30

The Parson from the casement leapt
    Into the lake of Windermere—
And many an eel—though no adept
In God's right reason for it—kept
    Gnawing his kidneys half a year.

And all the rest rushed through the door,
    And tumbled over one another,
And broke their skulls.—Upon the floor
Meanwhile sat Peter Bell, and swore,
    And cursed his father and his mother;   40

And raved of God, and sin, and death,
    Blaspheming like an infidel;
And said, that with his clenchèd teeth,
He'd seize the earth from underneath,
    And drag it with him down to hell.

As he was speaking came a spasm,
    And wrenched his gnashing teeth asunder;
Like one who sees a strange phantasm
He lay,—there was a silent chasm
    Between his upper jaw and under.   50

And yellow death lay on his face;
    And a fixed smile that was not human
Told, as I understand the case,
That he was gone to the wrong place:—
    I heard all this from the old woman.

Then there came down from Langdale Pike [8]
    A cloud, with lightning, wind and hail;
It swept over the mountains like
An ocean,—and I heard it strike
    The woods and crags of Grasmere vale.   60

And I saw the black storm come
    Nearer, minute after minute;
Its thunder made the cataracts dumb;
With hiss, and clash, and hollow hum,
    It neared as if the Devil was in it.

The Devil *was* in it:—he had bought
    Peter for half-a-crown; and when
The storm which bore him vanished, nought
That in the house that storm had caught
    Was ever seen again.   70

The gaping neighbours came next day—
    They found all vanished from the shore:
The Bible, whence he used to pray,
Half scorched under a hen-coop lay;
    Smashed glass—and nothing more!

PART THE SECOND
THE DEVIL

THE DEVIL, I safely can aver,
    Has neither hoof, nor tail, nor sting;
Nor is he, as some sages swear,
A spirit, neither here nor there,
    In nothing—yet in everything.

He is—what we are; for sometimes
    The Devil is a gentleman;
At others a bard bartering rhymes
For sack; a statesman spinning crimes;
    A swindler, living as he can;   10

A thief, who cometh in the night,
    With whole boots and net pantaloons,
Like someone whom it were not right
To mention;—or the luckless wight,
    From whom he steals nine silver spoons.

But in this case he did appear
    Like a slop-merchant from Wapping,
And with smug face, and eye severe,
On every side did perk and peer
    Till he saw Peter dead or napping.   20

[8] A series of mountains to the southwest of Grasmere.

He had on an upper Benjamin [9]
  (For he was of the driving schism)
In the which he wrapt his skin
From the storm he travelled in,
  For fear of rheumatism.

He called the ghost out of the corse;—
  It was exceedingly like Peter,—
Only its voice was hollow and hoarse—
It had a queerish look of course—
  Its dress too was a little neater.   30

The Devil knew not his name and lot;
  Peter knew not that he was Bell:
Each had an upper stream of thought,
Which made all seem as it was not;
  Fitting itself to all things well.

Peter thought he had parents dear,
  Brothers, sisters, cousins, cronies,
In the fens of Lincolnshire;
He perhaps had found them there
  Had he gone and boldly shown his   40

Solemn phiz [10] in his own village;
  Where he thought oft when a boy
He'd clomb the orchard walls to pillage
The produce of his neighbour's tillage,
  With marvellous pride and joy.

And the Devil thought he had,
  'Mid the misery and confusion
Of an unjust war, just made
A fortune by the gainful trade
Of giving soldiers rations bad—   50
  The world is full of strange delusion;

That he had a mansion planned
  In a square like Grosvenor-square,
That he was aping fashion, and
That he now came to Westmorland
  To see what was romantic there.

And all this, though quite ideal,—
  Ready at a breath to vanish,—
Was a state not more unreal
Than the peace he could not feel,
  Or the care he could not banish.   60

After a little conversation,
  The Devil told Peter, if he chose,
He'd bring him to the world of fashion
By giving him a situation
  In his own service—and new clothes.

And Peter bowed, quite pleased and proud,
  And after waiting some few days
For a new livery—dirty yellow
Turned up with black—the wretched fellow   70
  Was bowled to Hell in the Devil's chaise.

PART THE THIRD
HELL

HELL is a city much like London—
  A populous and a smoky city;
There are all sorts of people undone,
And there is little or no fun done;
  Small justice shown, and still less pity.

There is a Castles, and a Canning,
  A Cobbett, and a Castlereagh; [11]
All sorts of caitiff corpses planning
All sorts of cozening for trepanning
  Corpses less corrupt than they.   10

There is a * * * , [12] who has lost
  His wits, or sold them, none knows which;
He walks about a double ghost,
And though as thin as Fraud almost—
  Ever grows more grim and rich.

There is a Chancery Court; a King;
  A manufacturing mob; a set
Of thieves who by themselves are sent
Similar thieves to represent;
  An army; and a public debt.   20

Which last is a scheme of paper money,
  And means—being interpreted—
"Bees, keep your wax—give us the honey,
And we will plant, while skies are sunny,
  Flowers, which in winter serve instead."

---

[9] A type of overcoat or greatcoat; perhaps from the coat of Joseph's younger brother.
[10] Face (from physiognomy).

[11] Castles was probably a government spy; George Canning was Foreign Secretary (1822–27); William Cobbett was a gentleman farmer and radical conservative journalist (author of *Rural Rides*) and social reformer; for Castlereagh, Canning's predecessor as Foreign Secretary, see *The Mask of Anarchy*, p. 886.
[12] This has been identified as Lord Eldon, the Lord Chancellor.

There is great talk of revolution—
  And a great chance of despotism—
German soldiers—camps—confusion—
Tumults—lotteries—rage—delusion—
  Gin—suicide—and methodism.   30

Taxes too, on wine and bread,
  And meat, and beer, and tea, and cheese,
From which those patriots pure are fed,
Who gorge before they reel to bed
  The tenfold essence of all these.

There are mincing women, mewing,
  (Like cats, who *amant miserè*,*)
Of their own virtue, and pursuing
Their gentler sisters to that ruin,
  Without which—what were chastity?†   40

Lawyers—judges—old hobnobbers
  Are there—bailiffs—chancellors—
Bishops—great and little robbers—
Rhymesters—pamphleteers—stock-jobbers—
  Men of glory in the wars,—

Things whose trade is, over ladies
  To lean, and flirt, and stare, and simper,
Till all that is divine in woman
Grows cruel, courteous, smooth, inhuman,
  Crucified 'twixt a smile and whimper.   50

Thrusting, toiling, wailing, moiling,
  Frowning, preaching—such a riot!
Each with never-ceasing labour,
Whilst he thinks he cheats his neighbour,
  Cheating his own heart of quiet.

And all these meet at levees;—
  Dinners convivial and political;—
Suppers of epic poets;—teas,
Where small talk dies in agonies;—
  Breakfasts professional and critical;—   60

Lunches and snacks so aldermanic
  That one would furnish forth ten dinners,
Where reigns a Cretan-tonguèd panic,
Lest news Russ, Dutch, or Alemannic [13]
  Should make some losers, and some winners;—

At conversazioni—balls—
  Conventicles—and drawing-rooms—
Courts of law—committees—calls
Of a morning—clubs—book-stalls—
  Churches—masquerades—and tombs.   70

And this is Hell—and in this smother
  All are damnable and damned;
Each one damning, damns the other;
They are damned by one another,
  By none other are they damned.

'Tis a lie to say, "God damns!"‡
  Where was Heaven's Attorney General
When they first gave out such flams?
Let there be an end of shams,
  They are mines of poisonous mineral.   80

Statesmen damn themselves to be
  Cursed; and lawyers damn their souls
To the auction of a fee;
Churchmen damn themselves to see
  God's sweet love in burning coals.

The rich are damned, beyond all cure,
  To taunt, and starve, and trample on
The weak and wretched; and the poor
Damn their broken hearts to endure
  Stripe on stripe, with groan on groan.   90

Sometimes the poor are damned indeed
  To take,—not means for being blest,—
But Cobbett's snuff, revenge; that weed
From which the worms that it doth feed
  Squeeze less than they before possessed.

And some few, like we know who,
  Damned—but God alone knows why—
To believe their minds are given
To make this ugly Hell a Heaven;
  In which faith they live and die.   100

---

* One of the attributes in Linnæus's description of the Cat. To a similar cause the caterwauling of more than one species of this genus is to be referred;—except, indeed, that the poor quadruped is compelled to quarrel with its own pleasures, whilst the biped is supposed only to quarrel with those of others.

† What would this husk and excuse for a virtue be without its kernel prostitution, or the kernel prostitution without this husk of a virtue? I wonder the women of the town do not form an association, like the Society for the Suppression of Vice, for the support of what may be called the "King, Church, and Constitution" of their order. But this subject is almost too horrible for a joke.

‡ This libel on our national oath, and this accusation of all our countrymen of being in the daily practice of solemnly as-severating the most enormous falsehood, I fear deserves the notice of a more active Attorney-General than that here alluded to.

[13] German.

Thus, as in a town, plague-stricken,
　　Each man be he sound or no
Must indifferently sicken;
As when day begins to thicken,
　　None knows a pigeon from a crow,—

So good and bad, sane and mad,
　　The oppressor and the oppressed;
Those who weep to see what others
Smile to inflict upon their brothers;
　　Lovers, haters, worst and best;　　　　110

All are damned—they breathe an air,
　　Thick, infected, joy-dispelling:
Each pursues what seems most fair,
Mining like moles, through mind, and there
Scoop palace-caverns vast, where Care
　　In thronèd state is ever dwelling.

PART THE FOURTH
SIN

Lo, Peter in Hell's Grosvenor-square,
　　A footman in the devil's service!
And the misjudging world would swear
That every man in service there
　　To virtue would prefer vice.

But Peter, though now damned, was not
　　What Peter was before damnation.
Men oftentimes prepare a lot
Which ere it finds them, is not what
　　Suits with their genuine station.　　　　10

All things that Peter saw and felt
　　Had a peculiar aspect to him;
And when they came within the belt
Of his own nature, seemed to melt,
　　Like cloud to cloud, into him.

And so the outward world uniting
　　To that within him, he became
Considerably uninviting
To those, who meditation slighting,
　　Were moulded in a different frame.　　　　20

And he scorned them, and they scorned him;
　　And he scorned all they did; and they
Did all that men of their own trim
Are wont to do to please their whim,
　　Drinking, lying, swearing, play.

Such were his fellow-servants; thus
　　His virtue, like our own, was built
Too much on that indignant fuss
Hypocrite Pride stirs up in us
　　To bully out another's guilt.　　　　30

He had a mind which was somehow
　　At once circumference and centre
Of all he might or feel or know;
Nothing went ever out, although
　　Something did ever enter.

He had as much imagination
　　As a pint-pot;—he never could
Fancy another situation,
From which to dart his contemplation,
　　Than that wherein he stood.　　　　40

Yet his was individual mind,
　　And new created all he saw
In a new manner, and refined
Those new creations, and combined
　　Them, by a master-spirit's law.

Thus—though unimaginative—
　　An apprehension clear, intense,
Of his mind's work, had made alive
The things it wrought on; I believe
　　Wakening a sort of thought in sense.　　　　50

But from the first 'twas Peter's drift
　　To be a kind of moral eunuch,
He touched the hem of Nature's shift,
Felt faint—and never dared uplift
　　The closest, all-concealing tunic.

She laughed the while, with an arch smile,
　　And kissed him with a sister's kiss,
And said—"My best Diogenes,
I love you well—but, if you please,
　　Tempt not again my deepest bliss.　　　　60

"'Tis you are cold—for I, not coy,
　　Yield love for love, frank, warm and true;
And Burns, a Scottish peasant boy—
His errors prove it—knew my joy
　　More, learnèd friend, than you.

" *Bocca bacciata non perde ventura*
   Anzi rinnuova come fa la luna:—[14]
So thought Boccaccio, whose sweet words might
      cure a
Male prude, like you, from what you now endure, a
   Low-tide in soul, like a stagnant laguna."   70

Then Peter rubbed his eyes severe,
   And smoothed his spacious forehead down,
With his broad palm;—'twixt love and fear,
He looked, as he no doubt felt, queer,
   And in his dream sate down.

The Devil was no uncommon creature;
   A leaden-witted thief—just huddled
Out of the dross and scum of nature;
A toad-like lump of limb and feature,
   With mind, and heart, and fancy muddled.   80

He was that heavy, dull, cold thing,
   The spirit of evil well may be:
A drone too base to have a sting;
Who gluts, and grimes his lazy wing,
   And calls lust, luxury.

Now he was quite the kind of wight
   Round whom collect, at a fixed æra,
Venison, turtle, hock, and claret,—
Good cheer—and those who come to share it—
   And best East Indian madeira;   90

It was his fancy to invite
   Men of science, wit, and learning,
Who came to lend each other light;
He proudly thought that his gold's might
   Had set those spirits burning.

And men of learning, science, wit,
   Considered him as you and I
Think of some rotten tree, and sit
Lounging and dining under it,
   Exposed to the wide sky.   100

And all the while, with loose fat smile,
   The willing wretch sat winking there,
Believing 'twas his power that made
That jovial scene—and that all paid
   Homage to his unnoticed chair.

<hr/>

[14] "The mouth that's kissed does not lose its charm, but rather
renews itself like the moon."

Though to be sure this place was Hell;
   He was the Devil—and all they—
What though the claret circled well,
And wit, like ocean, rose and fell?—
   Were damned eternally.   110

PART THE FIFTH
GRACE

AMONG the guests who often staid
   Till the Devil's petits-soupers,
A man there came, fair as a maid,[15]
And Peter noted what he said,
   Standing behind his master's chair.

He was a mighty poet—and
   A subtle-souled psychologist;
All things he seemed to understand,
Of old or new—of sea or land—
   But his own mind—which was a mist.   10

This was a man who might have turned
   Hell into Heaven—and so in gladness
A Heaven unto himself have earned;
But he in shadows undiscerned
   Trusted,—and damned himself to madness.

He spoke of poetry, and how
   "Divine it was—a light—a love—
A spirit which like wind doth blow
As it listeth, to and fro;
   A dew rained down from God above;   20

"A power which comes and goes like dream,
   And which none can ever trace—
Heaven's light on earth—Truth's brightest beam."
And when he ceased there lay the gleam
   Of those words upon his face.

Now Peter, when he heard such talk,
   Would, heedless of a broken pate,
Stand like a man asleep, or baulk
Some wishing guest of knife or fork,
   Or drop and break his master's plate.   30

At night he oft would start and wake
   Like a lover, and began
In a wild measure songs to make
On moor, and glen, and rocky lake,
   And on the heart of man—

<hr/>

[15] Coleridge.

And on the universal sky—
   And the wide earth's bosom green,—
And the sweet, strange mystery
Of what beyond these things may lie,
   And yet remain unseen.   40

For in his thought he visited
   The spots in which, ere dead and damned,
He his wayward life had led;
Yet knew not whence the thoughts were fed,
   Which thus his fancy crammed.

And these obscure remembrances
   Stirred such harmony in Peter,
That whensoever he should please,
He could speak of rocks and trees
   In poetic metre.   50

For though it was without a sense
   Of memory, yet he remembered well
Many a ditch and quick-set fence;
Of lakes he had intelligence,
   He knew something of heath and fell.

He had also dim recollections
   Of pedlars tramping on their rounds;
Milk-pans and pails; and odd collections
Of saws, and proverbs; and reflections
   Old parsons make in burying-grounds.   60

But Peter's verse was clear, and came
   Announcing from the frozen hearth
Of a cold age, that none might tame
The soul of that diviner flame
   It augured to the Earth:

Like gentle rains, on the dry plains,
   Making that green which late was grey,
Or like the sudden moon, that stains
Some gloomy chamber's window panes
   With a broad light like day.   70

For language was in Peter's hand,
   Like clay, while he was yet a potter;
And he made songs for all the land,
Sweet both to feel and understand,
   As pipkins late to mountain Cotter.

And Mr.——,[16] the bookseller,
   Gave twenty pounds for some;—then scorning
A footman's yellow coat to wear,
Peter, too proud of heart, I fear,
   Instantly gave the Devil warning.   80

Whereat the Devil took offence,
   And swore in his soul a great oath then,
"That for his damned impertinence,
He'd bring him to a proper sense
   Of what was due to gentlemen!"—

PART THE SIXTH
DAMNATION

O THAT mine enemy had written
   A book!"—cried Job:—a fearful curse;
If to the Arab, as the Briton,
'Twas galling to be critic-bitten:—
   The Devil to Peter wished no worse.

When Peter's next new book found vent,
   The Devil to all the first Reviews
A copy of it slily sent,
With five-pound note as compliment,
   And this short notice—"Pray abuse."   10

Then *seriatim*, month and quarter,
   Appeared such mad tirades.—One said—
"Peter seduced Mrs. Foy's daughter,[17]
Then drowned the mother in Ullswater,
   The last thing as he went to bed."

Another—"Let him shave his head!
   Where's Dr. Willis?—Or is he joking?
What does the rascal mean or hope,
No longer imitating Pope,
   In that barbarian Shakspeare poking?"   20

One more, "Is incest not enough?
   And must there be adultery too?
Grace after meat? Miscreant and Liar!
Thief! Blackguard! Scoundrel! Fool! Hell-fire
   Is twenty times too good for you.

---

[16] Joseph Cottle, the bookseller of Bristol, who published *Lyrical Ballads*.
[17] See Wordsworth's *Idiot Boy*, p. 194.

"By that last book of yours WE think
   You've double damned yourself to scorn;
We warned you whilst yet on the brink
You stood. From your black name will shrink
   The babe that is unborn."   30

All these Reviews the Devil made
   Up in a parcel, which he had
Safely to Peter's house conveyed.
For carriage, ten-pence Peter paid—
   Untied them—read them—went half mad.

"What!" cried he, "this is my reward
   For nights of thought, and days of toil?
Do poets, but to be abhorred
By men of whom they never heard,
   Consume their spirits' oil?   40

"What have I done to them?—and who
   Is Mrs. Foy? 'Tis very cruel
To speak of me and Betty so!
Adultery! God defend me! Oh!
   I've half a mind to fight a duel.

"Or," cried he, a grave look collecting,
   "Is it my genius, like the moon,
Sets those who stand her face inspecting,
That face within their brain reflecting,
   Like a crazed bell-chime, out of tune?"   50

For Peter did not know the town,
   But thought, as country readers do,
For half a guinea or a crown,
He bought oblivion or renown
   From God's own voice* in a review.

All Peter did on this occasion
   Was, writing some sad stuff in prose.
It is a dangerous invasion
When poets criticise; their station
   Is to delight, not pose.   60

The Devil then sent to Leipsic fair,
   For Born's translation of Kant's book;
A world of words, tail foremost, where
Right—wrong—false—true—and foul—and fair,
   As in a lottery-wheel are shook.

Five thousand crammed octavo pages
   Of German psychologics,—he
Who his *furor verborum* assuages
Thereon, deserves just seven months' wages
   More than will e'er be due to me.   70

I looked on them nine several days,
   And then I saw that they were bad;
A friend, too, spoke in their dispraise,—
He never read them;—with amaze
   I found Sir William Drummond had.

When the book came, the Devil sent
   It to P. Verbovale,† Esquire,
With a brief note of compliment,
By that night's Carlisle mail. It went,
   And set his soul on fire.   80

Fire, which *ex luce præbens fumum*,[20]
   Made him beyond the bottom see
Of truth's clear well—when I and you Ma'am,
Go, as we shall do, *subter humum*,
   We may know more than he.

Now Peter ran to seed in soul
   Into a walking paradox;
For he was neither part nor whole,
Nor good, nor bad—nor knave nor fool,
   —Among the woods and rocks   90

Furious he rode, where late he ran,
   Lashing and spurring his tame hobby;
Turned to a formal puritan,
A solemn and unsexual man,—
   He half believed *White Obi*.

This steed in vision he would ride,
   High trotting over nine-inch bridges,
With Flibbertigibbet, imp of pride,
Mocking and mowing by his side—
A mad-brained goblin for a guide—   100
   Over corn-fields, gates, and hedges.

† Quasi, *Qui valet verba* :—*i.e.* all the words which have been, are, or may be expended by, for, against, with, or on him. A sufficient proof of the utility of this history. Peter's progenitor who selected this name seems to have possessed a *pure anticipated cognition* of the nature and modesty of this ornament of his posterity.[19]

◇◇◇◇◇◇◇◇◇◇◇◇◇◇◇◇◇◇◇◇◇◇◇◇◇◇◇◇◇◇◇

[19] "Verbovale" is, literally, "Wordsworth."
[20] Literally, "from the light producing smoke"—see Horace's *Art of Poetry*, 143. The phrase in l. 84 means "below the earth."

* *Vox populi, vox dei.*[18] As Mr. Godwin truly observes of a more famous saying, *of some merit as a popular maxim, but totally destitute of philosophical accuracy.*

◇◇◇◇◇◇◇◇◇◇◇◇◇◇◇◇◇◇◇◇◇◇◇◇◇◇◇◇◇◇

[18] "The voice of the people is the voice of God."

After these ghastly rides, he came
   Home to his heart, and found from thence
Much stolen of its accustomed flame;
His thoughts grew weak, drowsy, and lame
   Of their intelligence.

To Peter's view, all seemed one hue;
   He was no whig, he was no tory;
No Deist and no Christian he;—
He got so subtle, that to be   110
   Nothing, was all his glory.

One single point in his belief
   From his organization sprung,
The heart-enrooted faith, the chief
Ear in his doctrines' blighted sheaf,
   That "happiness is wrong;"

So thought Calvin and Dominic;[21]
   So think their fierce successors, who
Even now would neither stint nor stick
Our flesh from off our bones to pick,   120
   If they might "do their do."

His morals thus were undermined:—
   The old Peter—the hard, old Potter—
Was born anew within his mind;
He grew dull, harsh, sly, unrefined,
   As when he tramped beside the Otter.*

In the death hues of agony
   Lambently flashing from a fish,
Now Peter felt amused to see
Shades like a rainbow's rise and flee,   130
   Mixed with a certain hungry wish.†

* A famous river in the new Atlantis of the Dynastophylic
Pantisocratists.[22]
† See the description of the beautiful colours produced dur-
ing the agonising death of a number of trout, in the fourth part
of a long poem in blank verse, published within a few years.[23]
That poem contains curious evidence of the gradual hardening of
a strong but circumscribed sensibility, of the perversion of a
penetrating but a panic-stricken understanding. The author
might have derived a lesson which he had probably forgotten
from these sweet and sublime verses.

   This lesson, Shepherd, let us two divide,
   Taught both by what she* shows and what conceals,
   Never to blend our pleasure or our pride
   With sorrow of the meanest thing that feels.

      * Nature.

[21] St. Dominic, founder of the Dominican order in the thir-
teenth century.
[22] See Coleridge's sonnet on Pantisocracy, p. 433. He was
born in Ottery St. Mary.
[23] See Wordsworth's The Excursion, VIII, ll. 568–71.

So in his Country's dying face
   He looked—and lovely as she lay,
Seeking in vain his last embrace,
Wailing her own abandoned case,
   With hardened sneer he turned away:

And coolly to his own soul said;—
   "Do you not think that we might make
A poem on her when she's dead:—
Or, no—a thought is in my head—   140
   Her shroud for a new sheet I'll take.

"My wife wants one.—Let who will bury
   This mangled corpse! And I and you,
My dearest Soul, will then make merry,
As the Prince Regent did with Sherry,—"
   "Aye—and at last desert me too."

And so his Soul would not be gay,
   But moaned within him; like a fawn
Moaning within a cave, it lay
Wounded and wasting, day by day,   150
   Till all its life of life was gone.

As troubled skies stain waters clear,
   The storm in Peter's heart and mind
Now made his verses dark and queer:
They were the ghosts of what they were,
   Shaking dim grave-clothes in the wind.

For he now raved enormous folly,
   Of Baptisms, Sunday-schools, and Graves,
'Twould make George Colman melancholy
To have heard him, like a male Molly,   160
   Chaunting those stupid staves.

Yet the Reviews, who heaped abuse
   On Peter while he wrote for freedom,
So soon as in his song they spy
The folly which soothes tyranny,
   Praise him, for those who feed 'em.

"He was a man, too great to scan;—
   A planet lost in truth's keen rays:—
His virtue, awful and prodigious;—
He was the most sublime, religious,   170
   Pure-minded Poet of these days."

As soon as he read that, cried Peter,
   "Eureka! I have found the way
To make a better thing of metre
Than e'er was made by living creature
   Up to this blessèd day."

Then Peter wrote odes to the Devil;—
  In one of which he meekly said:
"May Carnage and Slaughter,
Thy niece and thy daughter,[24]   180
May Rapine and Famine,
Thy gorge ever cramming,
  Glut thee with living and dead!

"May death and damnation,
  And consternation,
Flit up from hell with pure intent!
Slash them at Manchester,[25]
  Glasgow, Leeds and Chester;
Drench all with blood from Avon to Trent.

"Let thy body-guard yeomen   190
  Hew down babes and women,
And laugh with bold triumph till Heaven be rent.
When Moloch in Jewry,
  Munched children with fury,
It was thou, Devil, dining with pure intent."*

PART THE SEVENTH
DOUBLE DAMNATION

THE Devil now knew his proper cue.—
  Soon as he read the ode, he drove
To his friend Lord Mac Murderchouse's,
A man of interest in both houses,
  And said:—"For money or for love,

"Pray find some cure or sinecure;
  To feed from the superfluous taxes,
A friend of ours—a poet—fewer
Have fluttered tamer to the lure
  Than he." His lordship stands and racks his   10

---

* It is curious to observe how often extremes meet. Cobbett and Peter use the same language for a different purpose: Peter is indeed a sort of metrical Cobbett. Cobbett is, however, more mischievous than Peter, because he pollutes a holy and now unconquerable cause with the principles of legitimate murder; whilst the other only makes a bad one ridiculous and odious.

If either Peter or Cobbett should see this note, each will feel more indignation at being compared to the other than at any censure implied in the moral perversion laid to their charge.

◇◇◇◇◇◇◇◇◇◇◇◇◇◇◇◇

[24] Wordsworth's *Ode: 1815*, in the original version of which he wrote:

> But Thy [God's] most dreaded instrument,
> In working out a pure intent,
> Is Man—arrayed for mutual slaughter,
> —Yea, Carnage is thy daughter!

[25] Peterloo Massacre. See *The Mask of Anarchy*, p. 886.

Stupid brains, while one might count
  As many beads as he had boroughs,—
At length replies; from his mean front,
Like one who rubs out an account,
  Smoothing away the unmeaning furrows:

"It happens fortunately, dear Sir,
  I can. I hope I need require
No pledge from you, that he will stir
In our affairs;—like Oliver,[26]
  That he'll be worthy of his hire."   20

These words exchanged, the news sent off
  To Peter, home the Devil hied,—
Took to his bed! he had no cough,
No doctor,—meat and drink enough,—
  Yet that same night he died.

The Devil's corpse was leaded down;
  His decent heirs enjoyed his pelf,
Mourning-coaches, many a one,
Followed his hearse along the town:—
  Where was the devil himself?   30

When Peter heard of his promotion,
  His eyes grew like two stars for bliss:
There was a bow of sleek devotion,
Engendering in his back; each motion
  Seemed a Lord's shoe to kiss.

He hired a house, bought plate, and made
  A genteel drive up to his door,
With sifted gravel neatly laid,—
As if defying all who said,
  Peter was ever poor.   40

But a disease soon struck into
  The very life and soul of Peter—
He walked about—slept—had the hue
Of health upon his cheeks—and few
  Dug better—none a heartier eater.

And yet a strange and horrid curse
  Clung upon Peter, night and day,
Month after month the thing grew worse,
And deadlier than in this my verse,
  I can find strength to say.   50

◇◇◇◇◇◇◇◇◇◇◇◇◇◇◇◇◇◇◇◇◇◇◇◇

[26] Probably a government agent who provoked three demonstrators at Derby to break into violence. They were executed in 1817.

Peter was dull—he was at first
   Dull—O, so dull—so very dull!
Whether he talked, wrote, or rehearsed—
Still with this dulness was he cursed—
   Dull—beyond all conception—dull.

No one could read his books—no mortal,
   But a few natural friends, would hear him;
The parson came not near his portal;
His state was like that of the immortal
   Described by Swift—no man could bear him.   60

His sister, wife, and children yawned,
   With a long, slow, and drear ennui,
All human patience far beyond;
Their hopes of Heaven each would have pawned,
   Any where else to be.

But in his verse, and in his prose,
   The essence of his dulness was
Concentrated and compressed so close,
'Twould have made Guatimozin [27] doze
   On his red gridiron of brass.   70

A printer's boy, folding those pages,
   Fell slumbrously upon one side;
Like those famed seven who slept three ages.
To wakeful frenzy's vigil rages,
   As opiates, were the same applied.

Even the Reviewers who were hired
   To do the work of his reviewing,
With adamantine nerves, grew tired;—
Gaping and torpid they retired,
   To dream of what they should be doing.   80

And worse and worse, the drowsy curse
   Yawned in him, till it grew a pest—
A wide contagious atmosphere,
Creeping like cold through all things near;
   A power to infect and to infest.

His servant-maids and dogs grew dull;
   His kitten, late a sportive elf,
The woods and lakes, so beautiful,
Of dim stupidity were full,
   All grew dull as Peter's self.   90

[27] The son-in-law and successor of Montezuma, emperor of Aztec Mexico. He was tortured by Cortez.

The earth under his feet—the springs,
   Which lived within it a quick life,
The air, the winds of many wings,
That fan it with new murmurings,
   Were dead to their harmonious strife.

The birds and beasts within the wood,
   The insects, and each creeping thing,
Were now a silent multitude;
Love's work was left unwrought—no brood
   Near Peter's house took wing.   100

And every neighbouring cottager
   Stupidly yawned upon the other:
No jack-ass brayed; no little cur
Cocked up his ears;—no man would stir
   To save a dying mother.

Yet all from that charmed district went
   But some half-idiot and half-knave,
Who rather than pay any rent,
Would live with marvellous content,
   Over his father's grave.   110

No bailiff dared within that space,
   For fear of the dull charm, to enter;
A man would bear upon his face,
For fifteen months in any case,
   The yawn of such a venture.

Seven miles above—below—around—
   This pest of dulness holds its sway;
A ghastly life without a sound;
To Peter's soul the spell is bound—
   How should it ever pass away?   120

[1819]   [1839]

ODE TO THE WEST WIND*

I

O WILD West Wind, thou breath of Autumn's being,
Thou, from whose unseen presence the leaves dead
Are driven, like ghosts from an enchanter fleeing,

* This poem was conceived and chiefly written in a wood that skirts the Arno, near Florence, and on a day when that tempestuous wind, whose temperature is at once mild and animating, was collecting the vapours which pour down the autumnal rains. They began, as I foresaw, at sunset with a violent tempest of hail and rain, attended by the magnificent thunder and lightning peculiar to the Cisalpine regions.

The phenomenon alluded to at the conclusion of the third stanza is well known to naturalists. The vegetation at the bottom

Yellow, and black, and pale, and hectic red,
Pestilence-stricken multitudes: O thou,
Who chariotest to their dark wintry bed

The wingéd seeds, where they lie cold and low,
Each like a corpse within its grave, until
Thine azure sister of the Spring shall blow

Her clarion o'er the dreaming earth, and fill　　　10
(Driving sweet buds like flocks to feed in air)
With living hues and odours plain and hill:

Wild Spirit, which art moving everywhere;
Destroyer and preserver; hear, oh, hear!

II

Thou on whose stream, mid the steep sky's
　　　commotion,
Loose clouds like earth's decaying leaves are shed,
Shook from the tangled boughs of Heaven and Ocean,

Angels of rain and lightning: there are spread
On the blue surface of thine aëry surge,
Like the bright hair uplifted from the head　　　20

Of some fierce Maenad,[1] even from the dim verge
Of the horizon to the zenith's height,
The locks of the approaching storm. Thou dirge

Of the dying year, to which this closing night
Will be the dome of a vast sepulchre,
Vaulted with all thy congregated might

Of vapours, from whose solid atmosphere
Black rain, and fire, and hail will burst: oh, hear!

III

Thou who didst waken from his summer dreams
The blue Mediterranean, where he lay,　　　30
Lulled by the coil of his crystàlline streams,

Beside a pumice isle in Baiae's[2] bay,
And saw in sleep old palaces and towers
Quivering within the wave's intenser day,

All overgrown with azure moss and flowers
So sweet, the sense faints picturing them! Thou
For whose path the Atlantic's level powers

Cleave themselves into chasms, while far below
The sea-blooms and the oozy woods which wear
The sapless foliage of the ocean, know　　　40

Thy voice, and suddenly grow gray with fear,
And tremble and despoil themselves: oh, hear!

IV

If I were a dead leaf thou mightest bear;
If I were a swift cloud to fly with thee;
A wave to pant beneath thy power, and share

The impulse of thy strength, only less free
Than thou, O uncontrollable! If even
I were as in my boyhood, and could be

The comrade of thy wanderings over Heaven,
As then, when to outstrip thy skiey speed　　　50
Scarce seemed a vision; I would ne'er have striven

As thus with thee in prayer in my sore need.
Oh, lift me as a wave, a leaf, a cloud!
I fall upon the thorns of life! I bleed!

A heavy weight of hours has chained and bowed
One too like thee: tameless, and swift, and proud.

V

Make me thy lyre,[3] even as the forest is:
What if my leaves are falling like its own!
The tumult of thy mighty harmonies

Will take from both a deep, autumnal tone,　　　60
Sweet though in sadness. Be thou, Spirit fierce,
My spirit! Be thou me, impetuous one!

Drive my dead thoughts over the universe
Like withered leaves to quicken a new birth!
And, by the incantation of this verse,

Scatter, as from an unextinguished hearth
Ashes and sparks, my words among mankind!
Be through my lips to unawakened earth

The trumpet of a prophecy! O, Wind,
If Winter comes, can Spring be far behind?　　　70

[1819]　　　　　　　　　　　　　　　　　　[1820]

---

of the sea, of rivers, and of lakes, sympathizes with that of the
land in the change of seasons, and is consequently influenced by
the winds which announce it.

　1 One of the women belonging to the orgiastic cult of
Bacchus.
　2 West of Naples.

　3 The Aeolian, or wind, harp, which appears also in *A Defence
of Poetry*, p. 975, as well as in the works of Wordsworth and
Coleridge, p. 279, line 96, and p. 441.

SONG

TO THE MEN OF ENGLAND

I

MEN of England, wherefore plough
For the lords who lay ye low?
Wherefore weave with toil and care
The rich robes your tyrants wear?

II

Wherefore feed, and clothe, and save,
From the cradle to the grave,
Those ungrateful drones who would
Drain your sweat—nay, drink your blood?

III

Wherefore, Bees of England, forge
Many a weapon, chain, and scourge,   10
That these stingless drones may spoil
The forced produce of your toil?

IV

Have ye leisure, comfort, calm,
Shelter, food, love's gentle balm?
Or what is it ye buy so dear
With your pain and with your fear?

V

The seed ye sow, another reaps;
The wealth ye find, another keeps;
The robes ye weave, another wears;
The arms ye forge, another bears.   20

VI

Sow seed,—but let no tyrant reap;
Find wealth,—let no impostor heap;
Weave robes,—let not the idle wear;
Forge arms,—in your defence to bear.

VII

Shrink to your cellars, holes, and cells;
In halls ye deck another dwells.
Why shake the chains ye wrought? Ye see
The steel ye tempered glance on ye.

VIII

With plough and spade, and hoe and loom,
Trace your grave, and build your tomb,   30
And weave your winding-sheet, till fair
England be your sepulchre.

[1819]   [1839]

The figures satirized here are Sidmouth, Home Secretary, and Castlereagh, Foreign Secretary from 1812 to 1822, held responsible for the Peterloo Massacre. Both appear in The Mask of Anarchy *and in* Oedipus Tyrannus.

TO SIDMOUTH AND CASTLEREAGH

SIMILES FOR TWO POLITICAL CHARACTERS OF 1819

I

As from their ancestral oak
　Two empty ravens sound their clarion,
Yell by yell, and croak by croak,
When they scent the noonday smoke
　Of fresh human carrion:—

II

As two gibbering night-birds flit
　From their bowers of deadly yew,
Thro' the night to frighten it,
When the moon is in a fit,
　And the stars are none or few:—   10

III

As a shark and dog-fish wait
　Under an Atlantic isle,
For the Negro-ship, whose freight
Is the theme of their debate,
　Wrinkling their red gills the while—

IV

Are ye, two vultures sick for battle,
　Two scorpions under one wet stone,
Two bloodless wolves whose dry throats rattle,
Two crows perched on the murrained cattle,
　Two vipers tangled into one.   20

[1819]   [1832]

SONNET: ENGLAND IN 1819

AN old, mad, blind, despised, and dying king,[1]—
Princes, the dregs of their dull race, who flow
Through public scorn—mud from a muddy spring,—
Rulers who neither see, nor feel, nor know,
But leech-like to their fainting country cling,
Till they drop, blind in blood, without a blow,—
A people starved and stabbed in the untilled field,[2]—
An army, which liberticide and prey

---

[1] George III died in 1820.
[2] The Peterloo Massacre. See *The Mask of Anarchy*, p. 886.

Makes as a two-edged sword to all who wield—
Golden and sanguine laws which tempt and slay;   10
Religion Christless, Godless—a book sealed;
A Senate,—Time's worst statute [3] unrepealed,—
Are graves, from which a glorious Phantom may
Burst, to illumine our tempestuous day.

[1819]   [1839]

THE INDIAN SERENADE

I

I ARISE from dreams of thee
In the first sweet sleep of night,
When the winds are breathing low,
And the stars are burning bright:
I arise from dreams of thee,
And a spirit in my feet
Has led me—who knows how?
To thy chamber window—Sweet!

II

The wandering airs they faint
On the dark, the silent stream—   10
The Champak odours fail
Like sweet thoughts in a dream;
The nightingale's complaint—
It dies upon her heart;
As I must die on thine,
Oh, belovèd as thou art!

III

Oh lift me from the grass!
I die! I faint! I fail!
Let thy love in kisses rain
On my lips and eyelids pale.   20
My cheek is cold and white, alas!
My heart beats loud and fast;—
Oh! press it close to thine again,
Where it will break at last.

[1819]   [1822]

LOVE'S PHILOSOPHY

I

THE fountains mingle with the river
    And the rivers with the Ocean,
The winds of Heaven mix for ever
    With a sweet emotion;

Nothing in the world is single;
    All things by a law divine
In one another's being mingle—
    Why not I with thine?

II

See the mountains kiss high Heaven
    And the waves clasp one another;   10
No sister flower would be forgiven
    If it disdained its brother;
And the sunlight clasps the earth,
    And the moonbeams kiss the sea:
What are all these kissings worth
    If thou kiss not me?

[1819]   [1819]

══════
THE SENSITIVE PLANT
The leaves of one variety of mimosa, popularly called the Sensitive Plant, close up when they are touched.
══════

THE SENSITIVE PLANT

PART FIRST

A SENSITIVE Plant in a garden grew,
And the young winds fed it with silver dew,
And it opened its fan-like leaves to the light,
And closed them beneath the kisses of Night.

And the Spring arose on the garden fair,
Like the Spirit of Love felt everywhere;
And each flower and herb on Earth's dark breast
Rose from the dreams of its wintry rest.

But none ever trembled and panted with bliss
In the garden, the field, or the wilderness,   10
Like a doe in the noontide with love's sweet want,
As the companionless Sensitive Plant.

The snowdrop, and then the violet,
Arose from the ground with warm rain wet,
And their breath was mixed with fresh odour, sent
From the turf, like the voice and the instrument.

Then the pied wind-flowers [1] and the tulip tall,
And narcissi, the fairest among them all,
Who gaze on their eyes in the stream's recess,
Till they die of their own dear loveliness;   20

---

[3] George III was a constant opponent of Catholic Emancipation.

[1] Anemones.

And the Naiad-like lily of the vale,
Whom youth makes so fair and passion so pale
That the light of its tremulous bells is seen
Through their pavilions of tender green;

And the hyacinth purple, and white, and blue,
Which flung from its bells a sweet peal anew
Of music so delicate, soft, and intense,
It was felt like an odour within the sense;

And the rose like a nymph to the bath addressed,
Which unveiled the depth of her glowing breast,   30
Till, fold after fold, to the fainting air
The soul of her beauty and love lay bare:

And the wand-like lily, which lifted up,
As a Maenad, its moonlight-coloured cup,
Till the fiery star, which is its eye,
Gazed through clear dew on the tender sky;

And the jessamine faint, and the sweet tuberose,
The sweetest flower for scent that blows;
And all rare blossoms from every clime
Grew in that garden in perfect prime.   40

And on the stream whose inconstant bosom
Was pranked, under boughs of embowering blossom,
With golden and green light, slanting through
Their heaven of many a tangled hue,

Broad water-lilies lay tremulously,
And starry river-buds glimmered by,
And around them the soft stream did glide and dance
With a motion of sweet sound and radiance.

And the sinuous paths of lawn and of moss,
Which led through the garden along and across,   50
Some open at once to the sun and the breeze,
Some lost among bowers of blossoming trees,

Were all paved with daisies and delicate bells
As fair as the fabulous asphodels,[2]
And flow'rets which, drooping as day drooped too,
Fell into pavilions, white, purple, and blue,
To roof the glow-worm from the evening dew.

And from this undefilèd Paradise
The flowers (as an infant's awakening eyes
Smile on its mother, whose singing sweet   60
Can first lull, and at last must awaken it),

---

[2] A flower supposed to bloom forever in the Elysian Fields.

When Heaven's blithe winds had unfolded them,
As mine-lamps enkindle a hidden gem,
Shone smiling to Heaven, and every one
Shared joy in the light of the gentle sun;

For each one was interpenetrated
With the light and the odour its neighbour shed,
Like young lovers whom youth and love make dear
Wrapped and filled by their mutual atmosphere.

But the Sensitive Plant which could give small fruit 70
Of the love which it felt from the leaf to the root,
Received more than all, it loved more than ever,
Where none wanted but it, could belong to the giver,—

For the Sensitive Plant has no bright flower;
Radiance and odour are not its dower;
It loves, even like Love, its deep heart is full,
It desires what it has not, the Beautiful!

The light winds which from unsustaining wings
Shed the music of many murmurings;
The beams which dart from many a star   80
Of the flowers whose hues they bear afar;

The plumèd insects swift and free,
Like golden boats on a sunny sea,
Laden with light and odour, which pass
Over the gleam of the living grass;

The unseen clouds of the dew, which lie
Like fire in the flowers till the sun rides high,
Then wander like spirits among the spheres,
Each cloud faint with the fragrance it bears;

The quivering vapours of dim noontide,   90
Which like a sea o'er the warm earth glide,
In which every sound, and odour, and beam,
Move, as reeds in a single stream;

Each and all like ministering angels were
For the Sensitive Plant sweet joy to bear,
Whilst the lagging hours of the day went by
Like windless clouds o'er a tender sky.

And when evening descended from Heaven above,
And the Earth was all rest, and the air was all love,
And delight, though less bright, was far more deep,
And the day's veil fell from the world of sleep,   101

And the beasts, and the birds, and the insects were
In an ocean of dreams without a sound;   [drowned
Whose waves never mark, though they ever impress
The light sand which paves it, consciousness;

(Only overhead the sweet nightingale
Ever sang more sweet as the day might fail,
And snatches of its Elysian chant
Were mixed with the dreams of the Sensitive Plant);—

The Sensitive Plant was the earliest   110
Upgathered into the bosom of rest;
A sweet child weary of its delight,
The feeblest and yet the favourite,
Cradled within the embrace of Night.

PART SECOND

There was a Power in this sweet place,
An Eve in this Eden; a ruling Grace
Which to the flowers, did they waken or dream,
Was as God is to the starry scheme.

A Lady, the wonder of her kind,
Whose form was upborne by a lovely mind
Which, dilating, had moulded her mien and motion
Like a sea-flower unfolded beneath the ocean,

Tended the garden from morn to even:
And the meteors of that sublunar Heaven,   10
Like the lamps of the air when Night walks forth,
Laughed round her footsteps up from the Earth!

She had no companion of mortal race,
But her tremulous breath and her flushing face
Told, whilst the morn kissed the sleep from her eyes,
That her dreams were less slumber than Paradise:

As if some bright Spirit for her sweet sake
Had deserted Heaven while the stars were awake,
As if yet around her he lingering were,   19
Though the veil of daylight concealed him from her.

Her step seemed to pity the grass it pressed;
You might hear by the heaving of her breast,
That the coming and going of the wind
Brought pleasure there and left passion behind.

And wherever her aëry footstep trod,
Her trailing hair from the grassy sod
Erased its light vestige, with shadowy sweep,
Like a sunny storm o'er the dark green deep.

I doubt not the flowers of that garden sweet
Rejoiced in the sound of her gentle feet;   30
I doubt not they felt the spirit that came
From her glowing fingers through all their frame.

She sprinkled bright water from the stream
On those that were faint with the sunny beam;
And out of the cups of the heavy flowers
She emptied the rain of the thunder-showers.

She lifted their heads with her tender hands,
And sustained them with rods and osier-bands;
If the flowers had been her own infants, she
Could never have nursed them more tenderly.   40

And all killing insects and gnawing worms,
And things of obscene and unlovely forms,
She bore, in a basket of Indian woof,
Into the rough woods far aloof,—

In a basket, of grasses and wild-flowers full,
The freshest her gentle hands could pull
For the poor banished insects, whose intent,
Although they did ill, was innocent.

But the bee and the beamlike ephemeris   49
Whose path is the lightning's, and soft moths that kiss
The sweet lips of the flowers, and harm not, did she
Make her attendant angels be.

And many an antenatal tomb,
Where butterflies dream of the life to come,
She left clinging round the smooth and dark
Edge of the odorous cedar bark.

This fairest creature from earliest Spring
Thus moved through the garden ministering
All the sweet season of Summertide,
And ere the first leaf looked brown—she died!   60

PART THIRD

Three days the flowers of the garden fair,
Like stars when the moon is awakened, were,
Or the waves of Baiae, ere luminous
She floats up through the smoke of Vesuvius.

And on the fourth, the Sensitive Plant
Felt the sound of the funeral chant,
And the steps of the bearers, heavy and slow,
And the sobs of the mourners, deep and low;

The weary sound and the heavy breath,
And the silent motions of passing death,   10
And the smell, cold, oppressive, and dank,
Sent through the pores of the coffin-plank;

The dark grass, and the flowers among the grass,
Were bright with tears as the crowd did pass;
From their sighs the wind caught a mournful tone,
And sate in the pines, and gave groan for groan.

The garden, once fair, became cold and foul,
Like the corpse of her who had been its soul,
Which at first was lovely as if in sleep,
Then slowly changed, till it grew a heap   20
To make men tremble who never weep.

Swift Summer into the Autumn flowed,
And frost in the mist of the morning rode,
Though the noonday sun looked clear and bright,
Mocking the spoil of the secret night.

The rose-leaves, like flakes of crimson snow,
Paved the turf and the moss below.
The lilies were drooping, and white, and wan,
Like the head and the skin of a dying man.

And Indian plants, of scent and hue   30
The sweetest that ever were fed on dew,
Leaf by leaf, day after day,
Were massed into the common clay.

And the leaves, brown, yellow, and gray, and red,
And white with the whiteness of what is dead,
Like troops of ghosts on the dry wind passed;
Their whistling noise made the birds aghast.

And the gusty winds waked the wingèd seeds,
Out of their birthplace of ugly weeds,
Till they clung round many a sweet flower's stem,   40
Which rotted into the earth with them.

The water-blooms under the rivulet
Fell from the stalks on which they were set;
And the eddies drove them here and there,
As the winds did those of the upper air.

Then the rain came down, and the broken stalks
Were bent and tangled across the walks;
And the leafless network of parasite bowers
Massed into ruin; and all sweet flowers.

Between the time of the wind and the snow   50
All loathliest weeds began to grow,
Whose coarse leaves were splashed with many a speck,
Like the water-snake's belly and the toad's back.

And thistles, and nettles, and darnels rank,
And the dock, and henbane, and hemlock dank,
Stretched out its long and hollow shank,
And stifled the air till the dead wind stank.

And plants, at whose names the verse feels loath,
Filled the place with a monstrous undergrowth,
Prickly, and pulpous, and blistering, and blue,   60
Livid, and starred with a lurid dew.

And agarics, and fungi, with mildew and mould
Started like mist from the wet ground cold;
Pale, fleshy, as if the decaying dead
With a spirit of growth had been animated!

Spawn, weeds, and filth, a leprous scum,
Made the running rivulet thick and dumb,
And at its outlet flags huge as stakes
Dammed it up with roots knotted like water-snakes.

And hour by hour, when the air was still,   70
The vapours arose which have strength to kill;
At morn they were seen, at noon they were felt,
At night they were darkness no star could melt.

And unctuous meteors from spray to spray
Crept and flitted in broad noonday
Unseen; every branch on which they alit
By a venomous blight was burned and bit.

The Sensitive Plant, like one forbid,
Wept, and the tears within each lid
Of its folded leaves, which together grew,   80
Were changed to a blight of frozen glue.

For the leaves soon fell, and the branches soon
By the heavy axe of the blast were hewn;
The sap shrank to the root through every pore
As blood to a heart that will beat no more.

For Winter came: the wind was his whip:
One choppy finger was on his lip:
He had torn the cataracts from the hills
And they clanked at his girdle like manacles;

His breath was a chain which without a sound   90
The earth, and the air, and the water bound;
He came, fiercely driven, in his chariot-throne
By the tenfold blasts of the Arctic zone.

Then the weeds which were forms of living death
Fled from the frost to the earth beneath.
Their decay and sudden flight from frost
Was but like the vanishing of a ghost!

And under the roots of the Sensitive Plant
The moles and the dormice died for want:
The birds dropped stiff from the frozen air   100
And were caught in the branches naked and bare.

Firs there came down a thawing rain
And its dull drops froze on the boughs again;
Then there steamed up a freezing dew
Which to the drops of the thaw-rain grew;

And a northern whirlwind, wandering about
Like a wolf that had smelt a dead child out,
Shook the boughs thus laden, and heavy, and stiff,
And snapped them off with his rigid griff.

When Winter had gone and Spring came back   110
The Sensitive Plant was a leafless wreck;   [darnels,
But the mandrakes, and toadstools, and docks, and
Rose like the dead from their ruined charnels.

CONCLUSION

Whether the Sensitive Plant, or that
Which within its boughs like a Spirit sat,
Ere its outward form had known decay,
Now felt this change, I cannot say.

Whether that Lady's gentle mind,
No longer with the form combined
Which scattered love, as stars do light,   120
Found sadness, where it left delight,

I dare not guess; but in this life
Of error, ignorance, and strife,
Where nothing is, but all things seem,
And we the shadows of the dream,

It is a modest creed, and yet
Pleasant if one considers it,
To own that death itself must be,
Like all the rest, a mockery.

That garden sweet, that lady fair,   130
And all sweet shapes and odours there,
In truth have never passed away:
'Tis we, 'tis ours, are changed; not they.

For love, and beauty, and delight,
There is no death nor change: their might
Exceeds our organs, which endure
No light, being themselves obscure.

[1820]   [1820]

AN EXHORTATION

CHAMELEONS feed on light and air:
    Poets' food is love and fame:
If in this wide world of care
    Poets could but find the same
With as little toil as they,
    Would they ever change their hue
    As the light chameleons do,
Suiting it to every ray
        Twenty times a day?

Poets are on this cold earth,   10
    As chameleons might be,
Hidden from their early birth
    In a cave beneath the sea;
Where light is, chameleons change:
    Where love is not, poets do:
    Fame is love disguised: if few
Find either, never think it strange
        That poets range.

Yet dare not stain with wealth or power
    A poet's free and heavenly mind: 20
If bright chameleons should devour
    Any food but beams and wind,
They would grow as earthly soon
    As their brother lizards are.
    Children of a sunnier star,
Spirits from beyond the moon,
        O, refuse the boon!

[1820]

THE CLOUD

I

I BRING fresh showers for the thirsting flowers,
    From the seas and the streams;
I bear light shade for the leaves when laid
    In their noon-day dreams.
From my wings are shaken the dews that waken
    The sweets buds every one,
When rocked to rest on their mother's breast,
    As she dances about the sun.
I wield the flail of the lashing hail,
    And whiten the green plains under,   10
And then again I dissolve it in rain,
    And laugh as I pass in thunder.

II

I sift the snow on the mountains below,
   And their great pines groan aghast;
And all the night 'tis my pillow white,
   While I sleep in the arms of the blast.
Sublime on the towers of my skiey bowers,
   Lightning my pilot sits,
In a cavern under is fettered the thunder,
   It struggles and howls at fits;   20
Over earth and ocean, with gentle motion,
   This pilot is guiding me,
Lured by the love of the genii that move
   In the depths of the purple sea;
Over the rills, and the crags, and the hills,
   Over the lakes and the plains,
Wherever he dream, under mountain or stream,
   The Spirit he loves remains;
And I all the while bask in heaven's blue smile,
   Whilst he is dissolving in rains.   30

III

The sanguine Sunrise, with his meteor eyes,
   And his burning plumes outspread,
Leaps on the back of my sailing rack,
   When the morning star shines dead;
As on the jag of a mountain crag,
   Which an earthquake rocks and swings,
An eagle alit one moment may sit
   In the light of its golden wings.
And when sunset may breathe, from the lit sea
     beneath,
   Its ardours of rest and of love,   40
And the crimson pall of eve may fall
   From the depth of Heaven above,
With wings folded I rest, on mine airy nest,
   As still as a brooding dove.

IV

That orbèd maiden with white fire laden,
   Whom mortals call the Moon,
Glides glimmering o'er my fleece-like floor,
   By the midnight breezes strewn;
And wherever the beat of her unseen feet,
   Which only the angels hear,   50
May have broken the woof of my tent's thin roof,
   The stars peep behind her and peer;
And I laugh to see them whirl and flee,
   Like a swarm of golden bees,
When I widen the rent in my wind-built tent,
   Till the calm rivers, lakes, and seas,
Like strips of the sky fallen through me on high,
   Are each paved with the moon and these.

V

I bind the Sun's throne with a burning zone,
   And the Moon's with a girdle of pearl;   60
The volcanoes are dim, and the stars reel and swim,
   When the whirlwinds my banner unfurl.
From cape to cape, with a bridge-like shape,
   Over a torrent sea,
Sunbeam-proof, I hang like a roof,—
   The mountains its columns be.
The triumphal arch through which I march,
   With hurricane, fire, and snow,
When the Powers of the air are chained to my chair,
   Is the million-coloured bow;   70
The sphere-fire above its soft colours wove,
   While the moist Earth was laughing below.

VI

I am the daughter of Earth and Water,
   And the nursling of the Sky;
I pass through the pores of the ocean and shores;
   I change, but I cannot die.
For after the rain when with never a stain,
   The pavilion of Heaven is bare,
And the winds and sunbeams with their convex
     gleams,[1]
   Build up the blue dome of air,   80
I silently laugh at my own cenotaph,[2]
   And out of the caverns of rain,
Like a child from the womb, like a ghost from the
     tomb,
   I arise and unbuild it again.

[1820]   [1820]

TO A SKYLARK

HAIL to thee, blithe Spirit!
   Bird thou never wert,
That from Heaven, or near it,
   Pourest thy full heart
In profuse strains of unpremeditated art.

Higher still and higher
   From the earth thou springest
Like a cloud of fire;
   The blue deep thou wingest,   9
And singing still dost soar, and soaring ever singest.

---

[1] Refracted by the atmosphere.
[2] Monument for someone buried elsewhere.

In the golden lightning
    Of the sunken sun,
O'er which clouds are bright'ning,
    Thou dost float and run;
Like an unbodied joy whose race is just begun.

The pale purple even
    Melts around thy flight;
Like a star of Heaven,
    In the broad daylight
Thou art unseen, but yet I hear thy shrill delight,   20

Keen as are the arrows
    Of that silver sphere,
Whose intense lamp narrows
    In the white dawn clear,
Until we hardly see—we feel that it is there.

All the earth and air
    With thy voice is loud,
As, when night is bare,
    From one lonely cloud   [flowed.
The moon rains out her beams, and Heaven is over-

What thou art we know not;   31
    What is most like thee?
From rainbow clouds there flow not
    Drops so bright to see,
As from thy presence showers a rain of melody.

Like a poet hidden
    In the light of thought,
Singing hymns unbidden,
    Till the world is wrought
To sympathy with hopes and fears it heeded not: 40

Like a high-born maiden
    In a palace-tower,
Soothing her love-laden
    Soul in secret hour
With music sweet as love, which overflows her bower:

Like a glow-worm golden
    In a dell of dew,
Scattering unbeholden
    Its aërial hue   [view!
Among the flowers and grass, which screen it from the

Like a rose embowered   51
    In its own green leaves,
By warm winds deflowered,
    Till the scent it gives   [thieves:
Makes faint with too much sweet those heavy-winged

Sound of vernal showers
    On the twinkling grass,
Rain-awakened flowers,
    All that ever was
Joyous, and clear, and fresh, thy music doth surpass.

Teach us, Sprite or Bird,   61
    What sweet thoughts are thine:
I have never heard
    Praise of love or wine
That panted forth a flood of rapture so divine.

Chorus Hymeneal,
    Or triumphant chaunt,
Matched with thine would be all
    But an empty vaunt,
A thing wherein we feel there is some hidden want. 70

What objects are the fountains
    Of thy happy strain?
What fields, or waves, or mountains?
    What shapes of sky or plain?
What love of thine own kind? what ignorance of pain?

With thy clear keen joyance
    Languor cannot be:
Shadow of annoyance
    Never came near thee:
Thou lovest; but ne'er knew love's sad satiety.   80

Waking or asleep,
    Thou of death must deem
Things more true and deep
    Than we mortals dream,
Or how could thy notes flow in such a crystal stream?

We look before and after,
    And pine for what is not:
Our sincerest laughter
    With some pain is fraught;   [thought.
Our sweetest songs are those that tell of saddest

Yet if we could scorn   91
    Hate, and pride, and fear;
If we were things born
    Not to shed a tear,
I know not how thy joy we ever should come near.

Better than all measures
    Of delightful sound,
Better than all treasures
    That in books are found,
Thy skill to poet were, thou scorner of the ground!

Teach me half the gladness   101
  That thy brain must know,
Such harmonious madness
  From my lips would flow,
The world should listen then—as I am listening now.

[1820]   [1820]

ODE TO LIBERTY

After the end of French rule in 1814, Ferdinand VII regained the throne of Spain and established an absolutist regime. In 1820 a bloodless revolution forced him to free the press, abolish the Inquisition, and set up a form of democratic monarchy. This is Shelley's response to the first news of the rebellion, which he places in the context of the struggles for liberty in Athens, in Rome, in medieval Europe, and in Commonwealth England, and in America and in France at the end of the eighteenth century.

ODE TO LIBERTY

Yet, Freedom, yet, thy banner, torn but flying,
Streams like a thunder-storm against the wind.—BYRON.

I

A GLORIOUS people vibrated again
  The lightning of the nations: Liberty
From heart to heart, from tower to tower, o'er Spain,
  Scattering contagious fire into the sky,
Gleamed. My soul spurned the chains of its dismay,
    And in the rapid plumes of song
    Clothed itself, sublime and strong,
(As a young eagle soars the morning clouds among,)
  Hovering in verse o'er its accustomed prey;
    Till from its station in the Heaven of fame   10
  The Spirit's whirlwind rapped it, and the ray
  Of the remotest sphere of living flame
Which paves the void was from behind it flung,
  As foam from a ship's swiftness, when there came
A voice out of the deep: I will record the same.

II

The Sun and the serenest Moon sprang forth:
  The burning stars of the abyss were hurled
Into the depths of Heaven. The daedal earth,
  That island in the ocean of the world,
Hung in its cloud of all-sustaining air: 20
    But this divinest universe
    Was yet a chaos and a curse,
For thou wert not: but, power from worst producing
    worse,

The spirit of the beasts was kindled there,
  And of the birds, and of the watery forms,
And there was war among them, and despair
  Within them, raging without truce or terms:
The bosom of their violated nurse
  Groaned, for beasts warred on beasts, and worms
    on worms,
And men on men; each heart was as a hell of storms.

III

Man, the imperial shape, then multiplied   31
  His generations under the pavilion
Of the Sun's throne: palace and pyramid,
  Temple and prison, to many a swarming million
Were, as to mountain-wolves their raggèd caves.
    This human living multitude
    Was savage, cunning, blind, and rude,
For thou wert not; but o'er the populous solitude,
  Like one fierce cloud over a waste of waves,
    Hung Tyranny; beneath, sate deified   40
  The sister-pest, congregator of slaves,[1]
    Into the shadow of her pinions wide
Anarchs and priests, who feed on gold and blood
  Till with the stain their inmost souls are dyed,
  Drove the astonished herds of men from every side.

IV

The nodding promontories, and blue isles,
  And cloud-like mountains, and dividuous waves
Of Greece, basked glorious in the open smiles
  Of favouring Heaven: from their enchanted caves
Prophetic echoes flung dim melody.   50
    On the unapprehensive wild
    The vine, the corn, the olive mild,
Grew savage yet, to human use unreconciled;
  And, like unfolded flowers beneath the sea,
    Like the man's thought dark in the infant's brain,
  Like aught that is which wraps what is to be,
    Art's deathless dreams lay veiled by many a vein
Of Parian stone; and, yet a speechless child,
  Verse murmured, and Philosophy did strain
  Her lidless eyes for thee; when o'er the Aegean
    main   60

V

Athens arose: a city such as vision
  Builds from the purple crags and silver towers
Of battlemented cloud, as in derision
  Of kingliest masonry: the ocean-floors

---

[1] Perhaps Anarchy.

Pave it; the evening sky pavilions it;
    Its portals are inhabited
    By thunder-zonèd winds, each head
Within its cloudy wings with sun-fire garlanded,—
    A divine work! Athens, diviner yet,
     Gleamed with its crest of columns, on the will 70
    Of man, as on a mount of diamond, set;
     For thou wert, and thine all-creative skill
Peopled, with forms that mock the eternal dead
    In marble immortality, that hill
Which was thine earliest throne and latest oracle.

VI

Within the surface of Time's fleeting river
    Its wrinkled image lies, as then it lay
Immovably unquiet, and for ever
    It trembles, but it cannot pass away!
The voices of thy bards and sages thunder   80
     With an earth-awakening blast
     Through the caverns of the past:
(Religion veils her eyes; Oppression shrinks aghast:)
    A wingèd sound of joy, and love, and wonder,
     Which soars where Expectation never flew,
    Rending the veil of space and time asunder!
     One ocean feeds the clouds, and streams, and
      dew;
One Sun illumines Heaven; one Spirit vast
    With life and love makes chaos ever new,   89
    As Athens doth the world with thy delight renew.

VII

Then Rome was, and from thy deep bosom fairest,
    Like a wolf-cub from a Cadmaean Maenad,*
She drew the milk of greatness, though thy dearest
    From that Elysian food was yet unweanèd;
And many a deed of terrible uprightness
     By thy sweet love was sanctified;
     And in thy smile, and by thy side,
Saintly Camillus lived, and firm Atilius died.
    But when tears stained thy robe of vestal whiteness,
     And gold profaned thy Capitolian throne,   100
    Thou didst desert, with spirit-wingèd lightness,
     The senate of the tyrants: they sunk prone
Slaves of one tyrant: Palatinus sighed
    Faint echoes of Ionian song; that tone
    Thou didst delay to hear, lamenting to disown.[3]

* See the *Bacchae* of Euripides.[2]

<hr>

[2] The Maenads in the play suckled wolves.
[3] Camillus and Atilius were heroic and patriotic Roman
emperors; the Palatine Hill was where Virgil and Horace read
their poetry.

VIII

From what Hyrcanian glen or frozen hill,
    Or piny promontory of the Arctic main,
Or utmost islet inaccessible,
    Didst thou lament the ruin of thy reign,
Teaching the woods and waves, and desert rocks,   110
     And every Naiad's ice-cold urn,
     To talk in echoes sad and stern
Of that sublimest lore which man had dared unlearn?
    For neither didst thou watch the wizard flocks
     Of the Scald's dreams, nor haunt the Druid's
      sleep.
    What if the tears rained through thy shattered locks
     Were quickly dried? for thou didst groan, not
      weep,
When from its sea of death, to kill and burn,
    The Galilean serpent forth did creep,[4]
    And made thy world an undistinguishable heap. 120

IX

A thousand years the Earth cried, 'Where art thou?'
    And then the shadow of thy coming fell
On Saxon Alfred's olive-cinctured brow:
    And many a warrior-peopled citadel,
Like rocks which fire lifts out of the flat deep,
     Arose in sacred Italy,
     Frowning o'er the tempestuous sea
Of kings, and priests, and slaves, in tower-crowned
    majesty;
    That multitudinous anarchy did sweep
     And burst around their walls, like idle foam,   130
    Whilst from the human spirit's deepest deep
    Strange melody with love and awe struck dumb
Dissonant arms; and Art, which cannot die,
    With divine wand traced on our earthly home
    Fit imagery to pave Heaven's everlasting dome.

X

Thou huntress swifter than the Moon! thou terror
    Of the world's wolves! thou bearer of the quiver,
Whose sunlike shafts pierce tempest-wingèd Error
    As light may pierce the clouds when they dissever
In the calm regions of the orient day!   140
     Luther caught thy wakening glance;
     Like lightning, from his leaden lance
Reflected, it dissolved the visions of the trance

<hr>

[4] The medieval Christian Church.

In which, as in a tomb, the nations lay;
  And England's prophets hailed thee as their
      queen,
In songs whose music cannot pass away,
  Though it must flow forever: not unseen
Before the spirit-sighted countenance
  Of Milton didst thou pass, from the sad scene
  Beyond whose night he saw, with a dejected mien.[5]

XI

The eager hours and unreluctant years   151
  As on a dawn-illumined mountain stood,
Trampling to silence their loud hopes and fears,
  Darkening each other with their multitude,
And cried aloud, 'Liberty!' Indignation
    Answered Pity from her cave;
    Death grew pale within the grave,
And Desolation howled to the destroyer, Save!
  When like Heaven's Sun girt by the exhalation
    Of its own glorious light, thou didst arise,   160
  Chasing thy foes from nation unto nation
    Like shadows: as if day had cloven the skies
At dreaming midnight o'er the western wave,
  Men started, staggering with a glad surprise,
  Under the lightnings of thine unfamiliar eyes.

XII

Thou Heaven of earth! what spells could pall thee
      then
  In ominous eclipse? a thousand years
Bred from the slime of deep Oppression's den,
  Dyed all thy liquid light with blood and tears,
Till thy sweet stars could weep the stain away;   170
    How like Bacchanals of blood
    Round France, the ghastly vintage, stood
Destruction's sceptred slaves, and Folly's mitred
      brood!
  When one, like them, but mightier far than they,
    The Anarch of thine own bewildered powers,[6]
  Rose: armies mingled in obscure array,
    Like clouds with clouds, darkening the sacred
      bowers
Of serene Heaven. He, by the past pursued,
  Rests with those dead, but unforgotten hours,
  Whose ghosts scare victor kings in their ancestral
      towers.

XIII

England yet sleeps: was she not called of old?
  Spain calls her now, as with its thrilling thunder
Vesuvius wakens Aetna, and the cold
  Snow-crags by its reply are cloven in sunder:
O'er the lit waves every Aeolian isle
    From Pithecusa to Pelorus[7]
    Howls, and leaps, and glares in chorus:
They cry, 'Be dim; ye lamps of Heaven suspended
      o'er us!'
  Her chains are threads of gold, she need but smile
    And they dissolve; but Spain's were links of
      steel,   190
    Till bit to dust by virtue's keenest file.
    Twins of a single destiny! appeal
To the eternal years enthroned before us
  In the dim West; impress us from a seal,
  All ye have thought and done! Time cannot dare
      conceal.

XIV

Tomb of Arminius![8] render up thy dead
  Till, like a standard from a watch-tower's staff,
His soul may stream over the tyrant's head;
  Thy victory shall be his epitaph,
Wild Bacchanal of truth's mysterious wine,   200
    King-deluded Germany,
    His dead spirit lives in thee.
Why do we fear or hope? thou art already free!
  And thou, lost Paradise of this divine
    And glorious world! thou flowery wilderness!
  Thou island of eternity! thou shrine
    Where Desolation, clothed with loveliness,
Worships the thing thou wert! O Italy,
  Gather thy blood into thy heart; repress
  The beasts who make their dens thy sacred palaces.

XV

Oh, that the free would stamp the impious name   211
  Of K ING into the dust! or write it there,
So that this blot upon the page of fame
  Were as a serpent's path, which the light air
Erases, and the flat sands close behind!
    Ye the oracle have heard:
    Lift the victory-flashing sword,
And cut the snaky knots of this foul gordian word,

---

[5] Luther and Milton are both seen as Protestant reformers.
[6] Napoleon.

[7] Island in the Bay of Naples, and a cape in Sicily where the Spanish revolt was being initiated.
[8] German hero in the war of the Germanic tribes against Rome in the first century of the Christian era.

Which, weak itself as stubble, yet can bind
    Into a mass, irrefragably firm,   220
The axes and the rods which awe mankind;
    The sound has poison in it, 'tis the sperm
Of what makes life foul, cankerous, and abhorred;
    Disdain not thou, at thine appointed term,
    To set thine armèd heel on this reluctant worm.

XVI

Oh, that the wise from their bright minds would
    kindle
    Such lamps within the dome of this dim world,
That the pale name of PRIEST might shrink and
    dwindle
    Into the hell from which it first was hurled,
A scoff of impious pride from fiends impure;   230
    Till human thoughts might kneel alone,
        Each before the judgement-throne
Of its own aweless soul, or of the Power unknown!
    Oh, that the words which make the thoughts
        obscure
        From which they spring, as clouds of glimmering
        dew
    From a white lake blot Heaven's blue portraiture,
        Were stripped of their thin masks and various
        hue
And frowns and smiles and splendours not their own,
    Till in the nakedness of false and true
    They stand before their Lord, each to receive its
        due!   240

XVII

He who taught man to vanquish whatsoever
    Can be between the cradle and the grave
Crowned him the King of Life. Oh, vain endeavour!
    If on his own high will, a willing slave,
He had enthroned the oppression and the oppressor.
    What if earth can clothe and feed
        Amplest millions at their need,
And power in thought be as the tree within the seed?
    Or what if Art, an ardent intercessor,
        Driving on fiery wings to Nature's throne,   250
    Checks the great mother stooping to caress her,
        And cries: 'Give me, thy child, dominion
Over all height and depth'? if Life can breed
    New wants, and wealth from those who toil and
        groan
    Rend of thy gifts and hers a thousandfold for one!

XVIII

Come thou, but lead out of the inmost cave
Of man's deep spirit, as the morning-star
Beckons the Sun from the Eoan wave,
    Wisdom. I hear the pennons of her car

Self-moving, like cloud charioted by flame;   260
    Comes she not, and come ye not,
    Rulers of eternal thought,
To judge, with solemn truth, life's ill-apportioned lot?
    Blind Love, and equal Justice, and the Fame
    Of what has been, the Hope of what will be?
    O Liberty! if such could be thy name
    Wert thou disjoined from these, or they from
        thee:
If thine or theirs were treasures to be bought
    By blood or tears, have not the wise and free
    Wept tears, and blood like tears?—The solemn
    harmony   270

XIX

Paused, and the Spirit of that mighty singing
    To its abyss was suddenly withdrawn;
Then, as a wild swan, when sublimely winging
    Its path athwart the thunder-smoke of dawn,
Sinks headlong through the aëreal golden light
    On the heavy-sounding plain,
        When the bolt has pierced its brain;
As summer clouds dissolve, unburthened of their rain;
    As a far taper fades with fading night,
        As a brief insect dies with dying day,—   280
    My song, its pinions disarrayed of might,
        Drooped; o'er it closed the echoes far away
Of the great voice which did its flight sustain,
    As waves which lately paved his watery way
    Hiss round a drowner's head in their tempestuous
    play.

[1820]   [1820]

ARETHUSA

This lyric and the hymns of Apollo and Pan which follow were intended for dramas that Mary Shelley was writing. In Ovid's Metamorphoses *Arethusa is a nymph of Diana pursued under water by the river god Alpheus. Even after she has been changed into a fountain, Alpheus attempts to mingle his waters with hers, and Diana, the goddess of Chastity, helps her to escape by flowing underground to the island of Ortygia (on which Syracuse in Sicily is partly built). There, in a fountain, Alpheus finally joins her.*

ARETHUSA

I

ARETHUSA arose
From her couch of snows
In the Acroceraunian mountains,—
    From cloud and from crag,
    With many a jag,

Shepherding her bright fountains.
    She leapt down the rocks
    With her rainbow locks
Streaming among the streams;—
    Her steps paved with green   10
    The downward ravine
Which slopes to the western gleams;
    And gliding and springing,
    She went, ever singing,
In murmurs as soft as sleep;
    The Earth seemed to love her,
    And Heaven smiled above her,
As she lingered towards the deep.

II

    Then Alpheus bold,
    On his glacier cold,   20
With his trident the mountains strook;
    And opened a chasm
    In the rocks—with the spasm
All Erymanthus shook.[1]
    And the black south wind
    It unsealed behind
The urns of the silent snow,
    And earthquake and thunder
    Did rend in sunder
The bars of the springs below.   30
    And the beard and the hair
    Of the River-god were
Seen through the torrent's sweep,
    As he followed the light
    Of the fleet nymph's flight
To the brink of the Dorian deep.

III

    "Oh, save me! Oh, guide me!
    And bid the deep hide me,
For he grasps me now by the hair!"
    The loud Ocean heard,   40
    To its blue depth stirred,
And divided at her prayer;
    And under the water
    The Earth's white daughter
Fled like a sunny beam;
    Behind her descended
    Her billows, unblended
With the brackish Dorian stream:—
    Like a gloomy stain
    On the emerald main   50

Alpheus rushed behind,—
    As an eagle pursuing
    A dove to its ruin
Down the streams of the cloudy wind.

IV

    Under the bowers
    Where the Ocean Powers
Sit on their pearlèd thrones;
    Through the coral woods
    Of the weltering floods,
Over heaps of unvalued stones;   60
    Through the dim beams
    Which amid the streams
Weave a network of coloured light;
    And under the caves,
    Where the shadowy waves
Are as green as the forest's night:—
    Outspeeding the shark,
    And the sword-fish dark,
Under the Ocean's foam,
    And up through the rifts   70
    Of the mountain clifts
They passed to their Dorian home.

V

    And now from their fountains
    In Enna's mountains,
Down one vale where the morning basks,
    Like friends once parted
    Grown single-hearted,
They ply their watery tasks.
    At sunrise they leap
    From their cradles steep   80
In the cave of the shelving hill;
    At noon-tide they flow
    Through the woods below
And the meadows of asphodel;
    And at night they sleep
    In the rocking deep
Beneath the Ortygian shore;—
    Like spirits that lie
    In the azure sky
When they love but live no more.   90

[1820]   [1824]

---

[1] A mountain north of the river Alpheus.

HYMN OF APOLLO

I

THE sleepless Hours who watch me as I lie,
    Curtained with star-inwoven tapestries
From the broad moonlight of the sky,
    Fanning the busy dreams from my dim eyes,—
Waken me when their Mother, the gray Dawn,
Tells them that dreams and that the moon is gone.

II

Then I arise, and climbing Heaven's blue dome,
    I walk over the mountains and the waves,
Leaving my robe upon the ocean foam;
    My footsteps pave the clouds with fire; the caves   10
Are filled with my bright presence, and the air
Leaves the green earth to my embraces bare.

III

The sunbeams are my shafts, with which I kill
    Deceit, that loves the night and fears the day;
All men who do or even imagine ill
    Fly me, and from the glory of my ray
Good minds and open actions take new might,
Until diminished by the reign of Night.

IV

I feed the clouds, the rainbows and the flowers,
    With their æthereal colours; the moon's globe   20
And the pure stars in their eternal bowers
    Are cinctured with my power as with a robe;
Whatever lamps on Earth or Heaven may shine
Are portions of one power, which is mine.

V

I stand at noon upon the peak of Heaven,
    Then with unwilling steps I wander down
Into the clouds of the Atlantic even;
    For grief that I depart they weep and frown:
What look is more delightful than the smile
With which I soothe them from the western isle?   30

VI

I am the eye with which the Universe
    Beholds itself and knows it is divine;
All harmony of instrument or verse,
    All prophecy, all medicine is mine,
All light of art or nature;—to my song
Victory and praise in its own right belong.

[1820]   [1824]

HYMN OF PAN

I

FROM the forests and highlands
    We come, we come;
From the river-girt islands,
    Where loud waves are dumb
        Listening to my sweet pipings.
The wind in the reeds and the rushes,
    The bees on the bells of thyme,
The birds on the myrtle bushes,
    The cicale above in the lime,
And the lizards below in the grass,   10
Were silent as ever old Tmolus was,[1]
    Listening to my sweet pipings.

II

Liquid Peneus was flowing,
    And all dark Tempe lay
In Pelion's shadow, outgrowing[2]
    The light of the dying day,
        Speeded by my sweet pipings.
The Sileni, and Sylvans, and Fauns,[3]
    And the Nymphs of the woods and the
        waves,
To the edge of the moist river-lawns,
    And the brink of the dewy caves,   20
And all that did then attend and follow,
Were silent with love, as you now, Apollo,
    With envy of my sweet pipings.

---

[1] The god of Mount Tmolus will judge the competition.
[2] The river Penëus, the valley of Tempe, and Mount Pelion are all in Thessaly.
[3] Followers of Pan.

III

I sang of the dancing stars,
  I sang of the daedal Earth,
And of Heaven—and the giant wars,
  And Love, and Death, and Birth,—
    And then I changed my pipings,—
Singing how down the vale of Maenalus
  I pursued a maiden and clasped a reed.
Gods and men, we are all deluded thus!
  It breaks in our bosom and then we bleed:
All wept, as I think both ye now would,
If envy or age had not frozen your blood,
  At the sorrow of my sweet pipings.

[1820]   [1824]

LETTER TO MARIA GISBORNE

*In the summer of 1820, during the Gisbornes' absence on a trip to
England, the Shelleys lived at their house in Leghorn.*

LETTER

TO MARIA GISBORNE

LEGHORN, *July* 1, 1820.

THE spider spreads her webs, whether she be
In poet's tower, cellar, or barn, or tree;
The silk-worm in the dark green mulberry leaves
His winding sheet and cradle ever weaves;
So I, a thing whom moralists call worm,
Sit spinning still round this decaying form,
From the fine threads of rare and subtle thought—
No net of words in garish colours wrought
To catch the idle buzzers of the day—
But a soft cell, where when that fades away,   10
Memory may clothe in wings my living name
And feed it with the asphodels of fame,
Which in those hearts which must remember me
Grow, making love an immortality.

Whoever should behold me now, I wist,
Would think I were a mighty mechanist,[1]
Bent with sublime Archimedean art
To breathe a soul into the iron heart
Of some machine portentous, or strange gin,[2]
Which by the force of figured spells might win   20
Its way over the sea, and sport therein;
For round the walls are hung dread engines, such
As Vulcan never wrought for Jove to clutch

Ixion or the Titan:—or the quick
Wit of that man of God, St. Dominic,[3]
To convince Atheist, Turk, or Heretic,
Or those in philanthropic council met,[4]
Who thought to pay some interest for the debt
They owed to Jesus Christ for their salvation,
By giving a faint foretaste of damnation   30
To Shakespeare, Sidney, Spenser, and the rest
Who made our land an island of the blest,
When lamp-like Spain, who now relumes her fire
On Freedom's hearth, grew dim with Empire:[5]—
With thumbscrews, wheels, with tooth and spike and
    jag,
Which fishers found under the utmost crag
Of Cornwall and the storm-encompassed isles,
Where to the sky the rude sea rarely smiles
Unless in treacherous wrath, as on the morn
When the exulting elements in scorn,   40
Satiated with destroyed destruction, lay
Sleeping in beauty on their mangled prey,
As panthers sleep;—and other strange and dread
Magical forms the brick floor overspread,—
Proteus transformed to metal did not make
More figures, or more strange; nor did he take
Such shapes of unintelligible brass,
Or heap himself in such a horrid mass
Of tin and iron not to be understood;
And forms of unimaginable wood,   50
To puzzle Tubal Cain[6] and all his brood:
Great screws, and cones, and wheels, and groovèd
    blocks,
The elements of what will stand the shocks
Of wave and wind and time.—Upon the table
More knacks and quips there be than I am able
To catalogize in this verse of mine:—
A pretty bowl of wood—not full of wine,
But quicksilver; that dew which the gnomes drink
When at their subterranean toil they swink,
Pledging the demons of the earthquake, who   60
Reply to them in lava—cry halloo!
And call out to the cities o'er their head,—
Roofs, towers, and shrines, the dying and the dead,
Crash through the chinks of earth—and then all quaff
Another rouse, and hold their sides and laugh.
This quicksilver no gnome has drunk—within
The walnut bowl it lies, veinèd and thin,
In colour like the wake of light that stains
The Tuscan deep, when from the moist moon rains

---

[1] Mrs. Gisborne's son was an engineer.
[2] Engine.
[3] Vulcan is the god of metalworking; Ixion the king bound to a revolving wheel; the Titan is Prometheus; St. Dominic the founder of the Dominican Order of Monks.
[4] The council planning the Spanish expedition against England.
[5] See the *Ode to Liberty*, p. 913.
[6] In *Genesis*: the first metalworker.

The inmost shower of its white fire—the breeze   70
Is still—blue Heaven smiles over the pale seas.
And in this bowl of quicksilver—for I
Yield to the impulse of an infancy
Outlasting manhood—I have made to float
A rude idealism of a paper boat:—
A hollow screw with cogs—Henry will know
The thing I mean and laugh at me,—if so
He fears not I should do more mischief.—Next
Lie bills and calculations much perplexed,
With steam-boats, frigates, and machinery quaint   80
Traced over them in blue and yellow paint.
Then comes a range of mathematical
Instruments, for plans nautical and statical;
A heap of rosin, a queer broken glass
With ink in it;—a china cup that was
What it will never be again, I think,—
A thing from which sweet lips were wont to drink
The liquor doctors rail at—and which I
Will quaff in spite of them—and when we die
We'll toss up who died first of drinking tea,   90
And cry out,—'Heads or tails?' where'er we be.
Near that a dusty paint-box, some odd hooks,
A half-burnt match, an ivory block, three books,
Where conic sections, spherics, logarithms,
To great Laplace, from Saunderson and Sims,[7]
Lie heaped in their harmonious disarray
Of figures,—disentangle them who may.
Baron de Tott's Memoirs beside them lie,
And some odd volumes of old chemistry.
Near those a most inexplicable thing,   100
With lead in the middle—I'm conjecturing
How to make Henry understand; but no—
I'll leave, as Spenser says, with many mo,
This secret in the pregnant womb of time,
Too vast a matter for so weak a rhyme.

    And here like some weird Archimage sit I,
Plotting dark spells, and devilish enginery,
The self-impelling steam-wheels of the mind
Which pump up oaths from clergymen, and grind
The gentle spirit of our meek reviews   110
Into a powdery foam of salt abuse,
Ruffling the ocean of their self-content;—
I sit—and smile or sigh as is my bent,
But not for them—Libeccio[8] rushes round
With an inconstant and an idle sound,
I heed him more than them—the thunder-smoke
Is gathering on the mountains, like a cloak
Folded athwart their shoulders broad and bare;
The ripe corn under the undulating air

Undulates like an ocean;—and the vines   120
Are trembling wide in all their trellised lines—
The murmur of the awakening sea doth fill
The empty pauses of the blast;—the hill
Looks hoary through the white electric rain,
And from the glens beyond, in sullen strain,
The interrupted thunder howls; above
One chasm of Heaven smiles, like the eye of Love
On the unquiet world;—while such things are,
How could one worth your friendship heed the war
Of worms? the shriek of the world's carrion jays,   130
Their censure, or their wonder, or their praise?

    You are not here! the quaint witch Memory sees,
In vacant chairs, your absent images,
And points where once you sat, and now should be
But are not.—I demand if ever we
Shall meet as then we met;—and she replies,
Veiling in awe her second-sighted eyes;
'I know the past alone—but summon home
My sister Hope,—she speaks of all to come.'
But I, an old diviner, who knew well   140
Every false verse of that sweet oracle,
Turned to the sad enchantress once again,
And sought a respite from my gentle pain,
In citing every passage o'er and o'er
Of our communion—how on the sea-shore
We watched the ocean and the sky together,
Under the roof of blue Italian weather;
How I ran home through last year's thunder-storm,
And felt the transverse lightning linger warm
Upon my cheek—and how we often made   150
Feasts for each other, where good will outweighed
The frugal luxury of our country cheer,
As well it might, were it less firm and clear
Than ours must ever be;—and how we spun
A shroud of talk to hide us from the sun
Of this familiar life, which seems to be
But is not:—or is but quaint mockery
Of all we would believe, and sadly blame
The jarring and inexplicable frame
Of this wrong world:—and then anatomize   160
The purposes and thoughts of men whose eyes
Were closed in distant years;—or widely guess
The issue of the earth's great business,
When we shall be as we no longer are—
Like babbling gossips safe, who hear the war
Of winds, and sigh, but tremble not;—or how
You listened to some interrupted flow
Of visionary rhyme,—in joy and pain
Struck from the inmost fountains of my brain,
With little skill perhaps;—or how we sought   170
Those deepest wells of passion or of thought

---

[7] English and French mathematicians and astronomers.
[8] The southwest wind.

Wrought by wise poets in the waste of years,
Staining their sacred waters with our tears;
Quenching a thirst ever to be renewed!
Or how I, wisest lady!⁹ then endued
The language of a land which now is free,
And, winged with thoughts of truth and majesty,
Flits round the tyrant's sceptre like a cloud,
And bursts the peopled prisons, and cries aloud,
'My name is Legion!'—that majestic tongue   180
Which Calderon over the desert flung
Of ages and of nations; and which found
An echo in our hearts, and with the sound
Startled oblivion;—thou wert then to me
As is a nurse—when inarticulately
A child would talk as its grown parents do.
If living winds the rapid clouds pursue,
If hawks chase doves through the aethereal way,
Huntsmen the innocent deer, and beasts their prey,
Why should not we rouse with the spirit's blast   190
Out of the forest of the pathless past
These recollected pleasures?

                    You are now
In London, that great sea, whose ebb and flow
At once is deaf and loud, and on the shore
Vomits its wrecks, and still howls on for more.
Yet in its depth what treasures! You will see
That which was Godwin,—greater none than he
Though fallen—and fallen on evil times—to stand
Among the spirits of our age and land,
Before the dread tribunal of *to come*   200
The foremost,—while Rebuke cowers pale and dumb.
You will see Coleridge—he who sits obscure
In the exceeding lustre and the pure
Intense irradiation of a mind,
Which, with its own internal lightning blind,
Flags wearily through darkness and despair—
A cloud-encircled meteor of the air,
A hooded eagle among blinking owls.—
You will see Hunt—one of those happy souls
Which are the salt of the earth, and without whom   210
This world would smell like what it is—a tomb;
Who is, what others seem; his room no doubt
Is still adorned with many a cast from Shout,¹⁰
With graceful flowers tastefully placed about;
And coronals of bay from ribbons hung,
And brighter wreaths in neat disorder flung;
The gifts of the most learned among some dozens
Of female friends, sisters-in-law, and cousins.
And there is he with his eternal puns,
Which beat the dullest brain for smiles, like duns   220

Thundering for money at a poet's door;
Alas! it is no use to say, 'I'm poor!'
Or oft in graver mood, when he will look
Things wiser than were ever read in book,
Except in Shakespeare's wisest tenderness.—
You will see Hogg,—and I cannot express
His virtues,—though I know that they are great,
Because he locks, then barricades the gate
Within which they inhabit;—of his wit
And wisdom, you'll cry out when you are bit.   230
He is a pearl within an oyster shell,
One of the richest of the deep;—and there
Is English Peacock, with his mountain Fair,¹¹
Turned into a Flamingo;—that shy bird
That gleams i' the Indian air—have you not heard
When a man marries, dies, or turns Hindoo,
His best friends hear no more of him?—but you
Will see him, and will like him too, I hope,
With the milk-white Snowdonian Antelope
Matched with this cameleopard—his fine wit   240
Makes such a wound, the knife is lost in it;
A strain too learnèd for a shallow age,
Too wise for selfish bigots; let his page,
Which charms the chosen spirits of the time,
Fold itself up for the serener clime
Of years to come, and find its recompense
In that just expectation.—Wit and sense,
Virtue and human knowledge; all that might
Make this dull world a business of delight,
Are all combined in Horace Smith.¹²—And these,   250
With some exceptions, which I need not tease
Your patience by descanting on,—are all
You and I know in London.

                    I recall
My thoughts, and bid you look upon the night.
As water does a sponge, so the moonlight
Fills the void, hollow, universal air—
What see you?—unpavilioned Heaven is fair,
Whether the moon, into her chamber gone,
Leaves midnight to the golden stars, or wan
Climbs with diminished beams the azure steep;   260
Or whether clouds sail o'er the inverse deep,
Piloted by the many-wandering blast,
And the rare stars rush through them dim and fast:—
All this is beautiful in every land.—
But what see you beside?—a shabby stand
Of Hackney coaches—a brick house or wall
Fencing some lonely court, white with the scrawl

---

⁹ Maria Gisborne had been reading Spanish poems with Shelley. For events in Spain see the *Ode to Liberty*, p. 913.
¹⁰ London cast-maker.

¹¹ Thomas Love Peacock, the poet and novelist and close friend of Shelley, had just married a young woman from Wales, the Snowdonian Antelope of line 239.
¹² Smith (1779–1849) with his brother James wrote the volume of literary parodies called *Rejected Addresses* (1812).

Of our unhappy politics;—or worse—
A wretched woman reeling by, whose curse
Mixed with the watchman's, partner of her trade, 270
You must accept in place of serenade—
Or yellow-haired Pollonia murmuring
To Henry, some unutterable thing.[13]
I see a chaos of green leaves and fruit
Built round dark caverns, even to the root
Of the living stems that feed them—in whose bowers
There sleep in their dark dew the folded flowers;
Beyond, the surface of the unsickled corn
Trembles not in the slumbering air, and borne
In circles quaint, and ever-changing dance, 280
Like wingèd stars the fire-flies flash and glance,
Pale in the open moonshine, but each one
Under the dark trees seems a little sun,
A meteor tamed; a fixed star gone astray
From the silver regions of the milky way;—
Afar the Contadino's song is heard,
Rude, but made sweet by distance—and a bird
Which cannot be the Nightingale, and yet
I know none else that sings so sweet as it
At this late hour;—and then all is still— 290
Now—Italy or London, which you will!

Next winter you must pass with me; I'll have
My house by that time turned into a grave
Of dead despondence and low-thoughted care,
And all the dreams which our tormentors are;
Oh! that Hunt, Hogg, Peacock, and Smith were there,
With everything belonging to them fair!—
We will have books, Spanish, Italian, Greek;
And ask one week to make another week
As like his father, as I'm unlike mine, 300
Which is not his fault, as you may divine.
Though we eat little flesh and drink no wine,
Yet let's be merry: we'll have tea and toast;
Custards for supper, and an endless host
Of syllabubs and jellies and mince-pies,
And other such lady-like luxuries,—
Feasting on which we will philosophize!
And we'll have fires out of the Grand Duke's wood,
To thaw the six weeks' winter in our blood.
And then we'll talk;—what shall we talk about? 310
Oh! there are themes enough for many a bout
Of thought-entangled descant;—as to nerves—
With cones and parallelograms and curves
I've sworn to strangle them if once they dare
To bother me—when you are with me there.

And they shall never more sip laudanum,
From Helicon or Himeros;*—well, come,
And in despite of God and of the devil,
We'll make our friendly philosophic revel
Outlast the leafless time; till buds and flowers 320
Warn the obscure inevitable hours,
Sweet meeting by sad parting to renew;—
"To-morrow to fresh woods and pastures new."[15]

[1820]   [1824]

THE WITCH OF ATLAS

To Mary

(ON HER OBJECTING TO THE FOLLOWING POEM, UPON THE SCORE OF ITS CONTAINING NO HUMAN INTEREST)

I

How, my dear Mary,—are you critic-bitten,
    (For vipers kill, though dead) by some review,
That you condemn these verses I have written,
    Because they tell no story, false or true?
What, though no mice are caught by a young kitten,
    May it not leap and play as grown cats do,
Till its claws come? Prithee, for this one time,
Content thee with a visionary rhyme.

II

What hand would crush the silken-wingèd fly,
    The youngest of inconstant April's minions, 10
Because it cannot climb the purest sky,
    Where the swan sings, amid the sun's dominions?[1]
Not thine. Thou knowest 'tis its doom to die,
    When Day shall hide within her twilight pinions
The lucent eyes, and the eternal smile,
Serene as thine, which lent it life awhile.

III

To thy fair feet a wingèd Vision came,
    Whose date should have been longer than a day,
And o'er thy head did beat its wings for fame,
    And in thy sight its fading plumes display; 20
The watery bow burned in the evening flame,
    But the shower fell, the swift Sun went his way—
And that is dead.——O, let me not believe
That anything of mine is fit to live!

* Ἵμερος, from which the river Himera was named, is, with some slight shade of difference, a synonym of Love.[14]

---

[13] Mary Shelley had participated in a joke at the expense of Henry Reveley and the daughter of the Gisbornes' landlord, Apollonia Ricci.

[14] The Helicon is a mountain sacred to the Muses.
[15] This is the last line of Milton's *Lycidas*.
[1] Probably a reference to Byron. See *Lines Written Among the Euganean Hills*, p. 817.

IV

Wordsworth informs us he was nineteen years
   Considering and retouching Peter Bell;
Watering his laurels with the killing tears
   Of slow, dull care, so that their roots to Hell
Might pierce, and their wide branches blot the
      spheres
   Of Heaven, with dewy leaves and flowers; this well
May be, for Heaven and Earth conspire to foil   31
The over-busy gardener's blundering toil.

V

My Witch indeed is not so sweet a creature
   As Ruth or Lucy, whom his graceful praise
Clothes for our grandsons—but she matches Peter,
   Though he took nineteen years, and she three days
In dressing. Light the vest of flowing metre
   She wears; he, proud as dandy with his stays,
Has hung upon his wiry limbs a dress   39
Like King Lear's 'looped and windowed raggedness.'

VI

If you strip Peter, you will see a fellow
   Scorched by Hell's hyperequatorial climate
Into a kind of sulphureous yellow:
   A lean mark, hardly fit to fling a rhyme at;
In shape a Scaramouch, in hue Othello.
   If you unveil my Witch, no priests nor primate
Can shrive you of that sin,—if sin there be
In love, when it becomes idolatry.

THE WITCH OF ATLAS

I

BEFORE those cruel Twins, whom at one birth
   Incestuous Change bore to her father Time,   50
Error and Truth, had hunted from the Earth
   All those bright natures which adorned its prime,
And left us nothing to believe in, worth
   The pains of putting into learnèd rhyme,
A lady-witch there lived on Atlas' mountain
Within a cavern, by a secret fountain.

II

Her mother was one of the Atlantides:[2]
   The all-beholding Sun had ne'er beholden
In his wide voyage o'er continents and seas
   So fair a creature, as she lay enfolden   60

---

[2] The daughters of Atlas.

In the warm shadow of her loveliness;—
   He kissed her with his beams, and made all golden
The chamber of gray rock in which she lay—
She, in that dream of joy, dissolved away.

III

'Tis said, she first was changed into a vapour
   And then into a cloud, such clouds as flit,
Like splendour-wingèd moths about a taper,
   Round the red west when the sun dies in it:
And then into a meteor, such as caper
   On hill-tops when the moon is in a fit: 70
Then, into one of those mysterious stars
Which hide themselves between the Earth and Mars.

IV

Ten times the Mother of the Months had bent
   Her bow inside the folding-star,[3] and bidden
With that bright sign the billows to indent
   The sea-deserted sand—like children chidden,
At her command they ever came and went—
   Since in that cave a dewy splendour hidden
Took shape and motion: with the living form
Of this embodied Power, the cave grew warm.   80

V

A lovely lady garmented in light
   From her own beauty—deep her eyes, as are
Two openings of unfathomable night
   Seen through a Temple's cloven roof—her hair
Dark—the dim brain whirls dizzy with delight,
   Picturing her form; her soft smiles shone afar,
And her low voice was heard like love, and drew
All living things towards this wonder new.

VI

And first the spotted cameleopard came,
   And then the wise and fearless elephant;   90
Then the sly serpent, in the golden flame
   Of his own volumes intervolved;—all gaunt
And sanguine beasts her gentle looks made tame.
   They drank before her at her sacred fount;
And every beast of beating heart grew bold,
Such gentleness and power even to behold.

VII

The brinded lioness led forth her young,
   That she might teach them how they should forego
Their inborn thirst of death; the pard unstrung
   His sinews at her feet, and sought to know   100

---

[3] The evening star, when sheep are brought into the fold.

With looks whose motions spoke without a tongue
  How he might be as gentle as the doe.
The magic circle of her voice and eyes
All savage natures did imparadise.

VIII

And old Silenus, shaking a green stick
  Of lilies, and the wood-gods in a crew
Came, blithe, as in the olive copses thick
  Cicadae are, drunk with the noonday dew:
And Dryope and Faunus followed quick,
  Teasing the God to sing them something new;   110
Till in this cave they found the lady lone,
Sitting upon a seat of emerald stone.

IX

And universal Pan, 'tis said, was there,
  And though none saw him,—through the adamant
Of the deep mountains, through the trackless air,
  And through those livings spirits, like a want,
He passed out of his everlasting lair
  Where the quick heart of the great world doth pant,
And felt that wondrous lady all alone,—
And she felt him, upon her emerald throne.   120

X

And every nymph of stream and spreading tree,
  And every shepherdess of Ocean's flocks,
Who drives her white waves over the green sea,
  And Ocean with the brine on his gray locks,
And quaint Priapus [4] with his company,
  All came, much wondering how the enwombèd
    rocks
Could have brought forth so beautiful a birth;—
Her love subdued their wonder and their mirth.

XI

The herdsmen and the mountain maidens came,
  And the rude kings of pastoral Garamant—   130
Their spirits shook within them, as a flame
  Stirred by the air under a cavern gaunt:
Pigmies, and Polyphemes, by many a name,
  Centaurs, and Satyrs, and such shapes as haunt
Wet clefts,—and lumps neither alive nor dead,
Dog-headed, bosom-eyed,[5] and bird-footed.

XII

For she was beautiful—her beauty made
  The bright world dim, and everything beside
Seemed like the fleeting image of a shade:
  No thought of living spirit could abide,   140

---

[4] The God of procreation, personified as an erect phallus.
[5] Shelley once imagined this was the deformity of Geraldine in Coleridge's *Christabel* (I, 252–53), p. 459.

Which to her looks had ever been betrayed,
  On any object in the world so wide,
On any hope within the circling skies.
But on her form, and in her inmost eyes.

XIII

Which when the lady knew, she took her spindle
  And twined three threads of fleecy mist, and three
Long lines of light, such as the dawn may kindle
  The clouds and waves and mountains with; and she
As many star-beams, ere their lamps could dwindle
  In the belated moon, wound skilfully;   150
And with these threads a subtle veil she wove—
A shadow for the splendour of her love.

XIV

The deep recesses of her odorous dwelling
  Were stored with magic treasures—sounds of air,
Which had the power all spirits of compelling,
  Folded in cells of crystal silence there;
Such as we hear in youth, and think the feeling
  Will never die—yet ere we are aware,
The feeling and the sound are fled and gone,
And the regret they leave remains alone.   160

XV

And there lay Visions swift, and sweet, and quaint,
  Each in its thin sheath, like a chrysalis,
Some eager to burst forth, some weak and faint
  With the soft burthen of intensest bliss.
It was its work to bear to many a saint
  Whose heart adores the shrine which holiest is,
Even Love's:—and others white, green, gray, and
    black,
And of all shapes—and each was at her beck.

XVI

And odours in a kind of aviary
  Of ever-blooming Eden-trees she kept,   170
Clipped in a floating net, a love-sick Fairy
  Had woven from dew-beams while the moon yet
    slept;
As bats at the wired window of a dairy,
  They beat their vans; and each was an adept,
When loosed and missioned, making wings of winds,
To stir sweet thoughts or sad, in destined minds.

XVII

And liquors clear and sweet, whose healthful might
  Could medicine the sick soul to happy sleep,
And change eternal death into a night
  Of glorious dreams—or if eyes needs must weep,

Could make their tears all wonder and delight,   181
    She in her crystal vials did closely keep:
If men could drink of those clear vials, 'tis said
The living were not envied of the dead.

XVIII

Her cave was stored with scrolls of strange device,
    The works of some Saturnian Archimage,
Which taught the expiations at whose price
    Men from the Gods might win that happy age
Too lightly lost, redeeming native vice;   189
    And which might quench the Earth-consuming rage
Of gold and blood—till men should live and move
Harmonious as the sacred stars above;

XIX

And how all things that seem untameable,
    Not to be checked and not to be confined,
Obey the spells of Wisdom's wizard skill;
    Time, earth, and fire—the ocean and the wind,
And all their shapes—and man's imperial will;
    And other scrolls whose writings did unbind
The inmost lore of Love—let the profane
Tremble to ask what secrets they contain.   200

XX

And wondrous works of substances unknown,
    To which the enchantment of her father's power
Had changed those ragged blocks of savage stone,
    Were heaped in the recesses of her bower;
Carved lamps and chalices, and vials which shone
    In their own golden beams—each like a flower,
Out of whose depth a fire-fly shakes his light
Under a cypress in a starless night.

XXI

At first she lived alone in this wild home,
    And her own thoughts were each a minister,   210
Clothing themselves, or with the ocean foam,
    Or with the wind, or with the speed of fire,
To work whatever purposes might come
    Into her mind; such power her mighty Sire
Had girt them with, whether to fly or run,
Through all the regions which he shines upon.

XXII

The Ocean-nymphs and Hamadryades,
    Oreads and Naiads,[6] with long weedy locks,
Offered to do her bidding through the seas,
    Under the earth, and in the hollow rocks,   220

---

[6] Nymphs of the forests, mountains, and streams, respectively.

And far beneath the matted roots of trees,
    And in the gnarlèd heart of stubborn oaks,
So they might live for ever in the light
Of her sweet presence—each a satellite.

XXIII

"This may not be," the wizard maid replied;
    "The fountains where the Naiades bedew
Their shining hair, at length are drained and dried;
    The solid oaks forget their strength, and strew
Their latest leaf upon the mountains wide;
    The boundless ocean like a drop of dew   230
Will be consumed—the stubborn centre must
Be scattered, like a cloud of summer dust.

XXIV

"And ye with them will perish, one by one;—
    If I must sigh to think that this shall be,
If I must weep when the surviving Sun
    Shall smile on your decay—oh, ask not me
To love you till your little race is run;
    I cannot die as ye must—over me
Your leaves shall glance—the streams in which ye
      dwell   239
Shall be my paths henceforth, and so—farewell!"—

XXV

She spoke and wept:—the dark and azure well
    Sparkled beneath the shower of her bright tears,
And every little circlet where they fell
    Flung to the cavern-roof inconstant spheres
And intertangled lines of light:—a knell
    Of sobbing voices came upon her ears
From those departing Forms, o'er the serene
Of the white streams and of the forest green.

XXVI

All day the wizard lady sate aloof,
    Spelling out scrolls of dread antiquity,   250
Under the cavern's fountain-lighted roof;
    Or broidering the pictured poesy
Of some high tale upon her growing woof,
    Which the sweet splendour of her smiles could dye
In hues outshining heaven—and ever she
Added some grace to the wrought poesy.

XXVII

While on her hearth lay blazing many a piece
    Of sandal wood, rare gums, and cinnamon;
Men scarcely know how beautiful fire is—
    Each flame of it is as a precious stone   260

Dissolved in ever-moving light, and this
   Belongs to each and all who gaze upon.
The Witch beheld it not, for in her hand
She held a woof that dimmed the burning brand.

XXVIII

This lady never slept, but lay in trance
   All night within the fountain—as in sleep.
Its emerald crags glowed in her beauty's glance;
   Through the green splendour of the water deep
She saw the constellations reel and dance
   Like fire-flies—and withal did ever keep   270
The tenour of her contemplations calm,
With open eyes, closed feet, and folded plam.

XXIX

And when the whirlwinds and the clouds descended
   From the white pinnacles of that cold hill,
She passed at dewfall to a space extended,
   Where in a lawn of flowering asphodel
Amid a wood of pines and cedars blended,
   There yawned an inextinguishable well
Of crimson fire—full even to the brim,
And overflowing all the margin trim.   280

XXX

Within the which she lay when the fierce war
   Of wintry winds shook that innocuous liquor
In many a mimic moon and bearded star
   O'er woods and lawns;—the serpent heard it flicker
In sleep, and dreaming still, he crept afar—
   And when the windless snow descended thicker
Than autumn leaves, she watched it as it came
Melt on the surface of the level flame.

XXXI

She had a boat, which some say Vulcan wrought
   For Venus, as the chariot of her star;   290
But it was found too feeble to be fraught
   With all the ardours in that sphere which are,
And so she sold it, and Apollo bought
   And gave it to this daughter: from a car
Changed to the fairest and the lightest boat
Which ever upon mortal stream did float.

XXXII

And others say, that, when but three hours old,
   The first-born Love out of his cradle lept,
And clove dun Chaos with his wings of gold,
   And like a horticultural adept,   300

Stole a strange seed, and wrapped it up in mould,
   And sowed it in his mother's star,[7] and kept
Watering it all the summer with sweet dew,
And with his winds fanning it as it grew.

XXXIII

The plant grew strong and green, the snowy flower
   Fell, and the long and gourd-like fruit began
To turn the light and dew by inward power
   To its own substance; woven tracery ran
Of light firm texture, ribbed and branching, o'er
   The solid rind, like a leaf's veinèd fan—   310
Of which Love scooped this boat—and with soft
    motion
Piloted it round the circumfluous ocean.

XXXIV

This boat she moored upon her fount, and lit
   A living spirit within all its frame,
Breathing the soul of swiftness into it.
   Couched on the fountain like a panther tame,
One of the twain at Evan's[8] feet that sit—
   Or as on Vesta's sceptre a swift flame—
Or on blind Homer's heart a wingèd thought,—
In joyous expectation lay the boat.   320

XXXV

Then by strange art she kneaded fire and snow
   Together, tempering the repugnant mass
With liquid love—all things together grow
   Through which the harmony of love can pass;
And a fair Shape out of her hands did flow—
   A living Image, which did far surpass
In beauty that bright shape of vital stone
Which drew the heart out of Pygmalion.[9]

XXXVI

A sexless thing it was, and in its growth
   It seemed to have developed no defect   330
Of either sex, yet all the grace of both,—
   In gentleness and strength its limbs were decked;
The bosom swelled lightly with its full youth,
   The countenance was such as might select
Some artist that his skill should never die,
Imaging forth such perfect purity.

---

[7] Venus.
[8] Bacchus.
[9] The sculptor who fell in love with his statue, which then came to life.

XXXVII

From its smooth shoulders hung two rapid wings,
   Fit to have borne it to the seventh sphere,
Tipped with the speed of liquid lightenings,
   Dyed in the ardours of the atmosphere: 340
She led her creature to the boiling springs
   Where the light boat was moored, and said: "Sit
     here!"
And pointed to the prow, and took her seat
Beside the rudder, with opposing feet.

XXXVIII

And down the streams which clove those mountains
     vast,
   Around their inland islets, and amid
The panther-peopled forests, whose shade cast
   Darkness and odours, and a pleasure hid
In melancholy gloom, the pinnace passed;
   By many a star-surrounded pyramid   350
Of icy crag cleaving the purple sky,
And caverns yawning round unfathomably.

XXXIX

The silver noon into that winding dell,
   With slanted gleam athwart the forest tops,
Tempered like golden evening, feebly fell;
   A green and glowing light, like that which drops
From folded lilies in which glow-worms dwell,
   When Earth over her face Night's mantle wraps;
Between the severed mountains lay on high,
Over the stream, a narrow rift of sky.   360

XL

And ever as she went, the Image lay
   With folded wings and unawakened eyes;
And o'er its gentle countenance did play
   The busy dreams, as thick as summer flies,
Chasing the rapid smiles that would not stay,
   And drinking the warm tears, and the sweet sighs
Inhaling, which, with busy murmur vain,
They had aroused from that full heart and brain.

XLI

And ever down the prone vale, like a cloud
   Upon a stream of wind, the pinnace went: 370
Now lingering on the pools, in which abode
   The calm and darkness of the deep content
In which they paused; now o'er the shallow road
   Of white and dancing waters, all besprent
With sand and polished pebbles:—mortal boat
In such a shallow rapid could not float.

XLII

And down the earthquaking cataracts which shiver
   Their snow-like waters into golden air,
Or under chasms unfathomable ever
   Sepulchre them, till in their rage they tear   380
A subterranean portal for the river
   It fled—the circling sunbows did upbear
Its fall down the hoar precipice of spray,
Lighting it far upon its lampless way.

XLIII

And when the wizard lady would ascend
   The labyrinths of some many-winding vale,
Which to the inmost mountain upward tend—
   She called "Hermaphroditus!"[10]—and the pale
And heavy hue which slumber could extend
   Over its lips and eyes, as on the gale   390
A rapid shadow from a slope of grass,
Into the darkness of the stream did pass.

XLIV

And it unfurled its heaven-coloured pinions,
   With stars of fire spotting the steam below;
And from above into the Sun's dominions
   Flinging a glory, like the golden glow
In which Spring clothes her emerald-wingèd minions,
   All interwoven with fine feathery snow
And moonlight splendour of intensest rime,
With which frost paints the pines in winter time.   400

XLV

And then it winnowed the Elysian air
   Which ever hung about that lady bright,
With its aethereal vans—and speeding there,
   Like a star up the torrent of the night,
Or a swift eagle in the morning glare
   Breasting the whirlwind with impetuous flight,
The pinnace, oared by those enchanted wings,
Clove the fierce streams towards their upper springs.

XLVI

The water flashed, like sunlight by the prow
   Of a noon-wandering meteor flung to Heaven;   410
The still air seemed as if its waves did flow
   In tempest down the mountains; loosely driven
The lady's radiant hair streamed to and fro:
   Beneath, the billows having vainly striven
Indignant and impetuous, roared to feel
The swift and steady motion of the keel.

---

[10] In Ovid's *Metamorphoses*, the bisexual child of Hermes and
Aphrodite.

XLVII

Or, when the weary moon was in the wane,
   Or in the noon of interlunar night,
The lady-witch in visions could not chain
   Her spirit; but sailed forth under the light   420
Of shooting stars, and bade extend amain
   Its storm-outspeeding wings, the Hermaphrodite;
She to the Austral waters took her way,
Beyond the fabulous Thamondocana,[11]—

XLVIII

Where, like a meadow which no scythe has shaven,
   Which rain could never bend, or whirl-blast shake,
With the Antarctic constellations paven,
   Canopus and his crew, lay the Austral lake—
There she would build herself a windless haven
   Out of the clouds whose moving turrets make   430
The bastions of the storm, when through the sky
The spirits of the tempest thundered by:

XLIX

A haven beneath whose translucent floor
   The tremulous stars sparkled unfathomably,
And around which the solid vapours hoar,
   Based on the level waters, to the sky
Lifted their dreadful crags, and like a shore
   Of wintry mountains, inaccessibly
Hemmed in with rifts and precipices gray,
And hanging crags, many a cove and bay.   440

L

And whilst the outer lake beneath the lash
   Of the wind's scourge, foamed like a wounded
      thing,
And the incessant hail with stony clash
   Ploughed up the waters, and the flagging wing
Of the roused cormorant in the lightning flash
   Looked like the wreck of some wind-wandering
Fragment of inky thunder-smoke—this haven
Was as a gem to copy Heaven engraven,—

LI

On which that lady played her many pranks,
   Circling the image of a shooting star,   450
Even as a tiger on Hydaspes'[12] banks
   Outspeeds the antelopes which speediest are,
In her light boat; and many quips and cranks
   She played upon the water, till the car
Of the late moon, like a sick matron wan,
To journey from the misty east began.

LII

And then she called out of the hollow turrets
   Of those high clouds, white, golden and vermilion,
The armies of her ministering spirits—
   In mighty legions, million after million,   460
They came, each troop emblazoning its merits
   On meteor flags; and many a proud pavilion
Of the intertexture of the atmosphere
They pitched upon the plain of the calm mere.

LIII

They framed the imperial tent of their great Queen
   Of woven exhalations, underlaid
With lambent lightning-fire, as may be seen
   A dome of thin and open ivory inlaid
With crimson silk—cressets from the serene
   Hung there, and on the water for her tread   470
A tapestry of fleece-like mist was strewn,
Dyed in the beams of the ascending moon.

LIV

And on a throne o'erlaid with starlight, caught
   Upon those wandering isles of aëry dew,
Which highest shoals of mountain shipwreck not,
   She sate, and heard all that had happened new
Between the earth and moon, since they had brought
   The last intelligence—and now she grew
Pale as that moon, lost in the watery night—
And now she wept, and now she laughed outright. 480

LV

These were tame pleasures; she would often climb
   The steepest ladder of the crudded rack
Up to some beakèd cape of cloud sublime,
   And like Arion[13] on the dolphin's back
Ride singing through the shoreless air;—oft-time
   Following the serpent lightning's winding track,
She ran upon the platforms of the wind,
And laughed to hear the fire-balls roar behind.

LVI

And sometimes to those streams of upper air
   Which whirl the earth in its diurnal round,   490
She would ascend, and win the spirits there
   To let her join their chorus. Mortals found
That on those days the sky was calm and fair,
   And mystic snatches of harmonious sound
Wandered upon the earth where'er she passed,
And happy thoughts of hope, too sweet to last.

---

[11] Timbuctoo.
[12] Jhelum River in Pakistan.

[13] A poet saved by dolphins attracted by his music.

LVII

But her choice sport was, in the hours of sleep,
    To glide adown old Nilus, where he threads
Egypt and Aethiopia, from the steep
    Of utmost Axumè,[14] until he spreads,   500
Like a calm flock of silver-fleecèd sheep,
    His waters on the plain: and crested heads
Of cities and proud temples gleam amid,
And many a vapour-belted pyramid.

LVIII

By Moeris and the Mareotid lakes,[15]
    Strewn with faint blooms like bridal chamber floors,
Where naked boys bridling tame water-snakes,
    Or charioteering ghastly alligators,
Had left on the sweet waters mighty wakes
    Of those huge forms—within the brazen doors   510
Of the great Labyrinth slept both boy and beast,
Tired with the pomp of their Osirian feast.[16]

LIX

And where within the surface of the river
    The shadows of the massy temples lie,
And never are erased—but tremble ever
    Like things which every cloud can doom to die,
Through lotus-paven canals, and wheresoever
    The works of man pierced that serenest sky
With tombs, and towers, and fanes, 'twas her delight
To wander in the shadow of the night.   520

LX

With motion like the spirit of that wind
    Whose soft step deepens slumber, her light feet
Passed through the peopled haunts of humankind,
    Scattering sweet visions from her presence sweet,
Through fane, and palace-court, and labyrinth mined
    With many a dark and subterranean street
Under the Nile, through chambers high and deep
She passed, observing mortals in their sleep.

LXI

A pleasure sweet doubtless it was to see
    Mortals subdued in all the shapes of sleep.   530
Here lay two sister twins in infancy;
    There, a lone youth who in his dreams did weep;
Within, two lovers linkèd innocently
    In their loose locks which over both did creep
Like ivy from one stem;—and there lay calm
Old age with snow-bright hair and folded palm.

LXII

But other troubled forms of sleep she saw,
    Not to be mirrored in a holy song—
Distortions foul of supernatural awe,
    And pale imaginings of visioned wrong;   540
And all the code of Custom's lawless law
    Written upon the brows of old and young:
'This,' said the wizard maiden, 'is the strife
Which stirs the liquid surface of man's life.'

LXIII

And little did the sight disturb her soul.—
    We, the weak mariners of that wide lake
Where'er its shores extend or billows roll,
    Our course unpiloted and starless make
O'er its wild surface to an unknown goal:—
    But she in the calm depths her way could take,   550
Where in bright bowers immortal forms abide
Beneath the weltering of the restless tide.

LXIV

And she saw princes couched under the glow
    Of sunlike gems; and round each temple-court
In dormitories ranged, row after row,
    She saw the priests asleep—all of one sort—
For all were educated to be so.—
    The peasants in their huts, and in the port
The sailors she saw cradled on the waves,
And the dead lulled within their dreamless graves. 560

LXV

And all the forms in which those spirits lay
    Were to her sight like the diaphanous
Veils, in which those sweet ladies oft array
    Their delicate limbs, who would conceal from us
Only their scorn of all concealment: they
    Move in the light of their own beauty thus.
But these and all now lay with sleep upon them,
And little thought a Witch was looking on them.

LXVI

She, all those human figures breathing there,
    Beheld as living spirits—to her eyes   570
The naked beauty of the soul lay bare,
    And often through a rude and worn disguise
She saw the inner form most bright and fair—
    And then she had a charm of strange device,
Which, murmured on mute lips with tender tone,
Could make that spirit mingle with her own.

---

[14] Abyssinia.
[15] These are in the Nile delta, where a labyrinth was located.
[16] Osiris was the male fertility god.

LXVII

Alas! Aurora, what wouldst thou have given
      For such a charm when Tithon [17] became gray?
Or how much, Venus, of thy silver heaven
      Wouldst thou have yielded, ere Proserpina   580
Had half (oh! why not all?) the debt forgiven
      Which dear Adonis had been doomed to pay,
To any witch who would have taught you it?
The Heliad doth not know its value yet.

LXVIII

'Tis said in after times her spirit free
      Knew what love was, and felt itself alone—
But holy Dian could not chaster be
      Before she stooped to kiss Endymion,[18]
Than now this lady—like a sexless bee
      Tasting all blossoms, and confined to none,   590
Among those mortal forms, the wizard-maiden
Passed with an eye serene and heart unladen.

LXIX

To those she saw most beautiful, she gave
      Strange panacea in a crystal bowl:—
They drank in their deep sleep of that sweet wave,
      And lived thenceforward as if some control,
Mightier than life, were in them; and the grave
      Of such, when death oppressed the weary soul,
Was as a green and overarching bower
Lit by the gems of many a starry flower.   600

LXX

For on the night when they were buried, she
      Restored the embalmers' ruining, and shook
The light out of the funeral lamps, to be
      A mimic day within the deathy nook;
And she unwound the woven imagery
      Of second childhood's swaddling bands, and took
The coffin, its last cradle, from its niche,
And threw it with contempt into a ditch.

LXXI

And there the body lay, age after age,
      Mute, breathing, beating, warm, and undecaying,
Like one asleep in a green hermitage,   611
      With gentle smiles about its eyelids playing,
And living in its dreams beyond the rage
      Of death or life; while they were still arraying
In liveries ever new, the rapid, blind
And fleeting generations of mankind.

[17] Tithonus was given immortaility by Aurora, the goddess of dawn, but he neglected to ask for eternal youth; Venus gained six months a year on earth for Adonis from Proserpine. The Heliad (sun goddess), line 584, is the Witch of Atlas.
[18] See Keats's poem on the Moon's love for Endymion, p. 1026.

LXXII

And she would write strange dreams upon the brain
      Of those who were less beautiful, and make
All harsh and crooked purposes more vain
      Than in the desert is the serpent's wake   620
Which the sand covers—all his evil gain
      The miser in such dreams would rise and shake
Into a beggar's lap;—the lying scribe
Would his own lies betray without a bribe.

LXXIII

The priests would write an explanation full,
      Translating hieroglyphics into Greek,
How the God Apis really was a bull,
      And nothing more; and bid the herald stick
The same against the temple doors, and pull
      The old cant down; they licensed all to speak   630
Whate'er they thought of hawks, and cats, and geese,
By pastoral letters to each diocese.

LXXIV

The king would dress an ape up in his crown
      And robes, and seat him on his glorious seat,
And on the right hand of the sunlike throne
      Would place a gaudy mock-bird to repeat
The chatterings of the monkey.—Every one
      Of the prone courtiers crawled to kiss the feet
Of their great Emperor, when the morning came,
And kissed—alas, how many kiss the same!   640

LXXV

The soldiers dreamed that they were blacksmiths, and
      Walked out of quarters in somnambulism;
Round the red anvils you might see them stand
      Like Cyclopses in Vulcan's sooty abysm,
Beating their swords to ploughshares;—in a band
      The gaolers sent those of the liberal schism
Free through the streets of Memphis, much, I wis,
To the annoyance of king Amasis.[19]

LXXVI

And timid lovers who had been so coy,
      They hardly knew whether they loved or not,   650
Would rise out of their rest, and take sweet joy,
      To the fulfilment of their inmost thought;
And when next day the maiden and the boy
      Met one another, both, like sinners caught,
Blushed at the thing which each believed was done
Only in fancy—till the tenth moon shone;

[19] Egyptian king of the sixth century B.C.

LXXVII

And then the Witch would let them take no ill:
 Of many thousand schemes which lovers find,
The Witch found one,—and so they took their fill
 Of happiness in marriage warm and kind.   660
Friends who, by practice of some envious skill,
 Were torn apart—a wide wound, mind from
  mind!—
She did unite again with visions clear
Of deep affection and of truth sincere.

LXXVIII

These were the pranks she played among the cities
 Of mortal men, and what she did to Sprites
And Gods, entangling them in her sweet ditties
 To do her will, and show their subtle sleights,
I will declare another time; for it is
 A tale more fit for the weird winter nights   670
Than for these garish summer days, when we
Scarcely believe much more than we can see.

[1820]   [1824]

ŒDIPUS TYRANNUS

This is Shelley's response to the events surrounding George IV's attempts to free himself from the claims of his wife Queen Caroline, from whom he had been separated in 1796. Her position as Queen Consort was a matter of controversy until her trial for adultery in 1820 and her acquittal in 1821, She died shortly after her unsuccessful attempt to be present at George IV's coronation in 1821. Mrs. Shelley said that the poem was conceived on a day when Shelley, reading his Ode to Liberty *to a friend at the Baths of San Giuliano, was interrupted by the squealing of pigs outside their window. The Society for the Suppression of Vice had the poem withdrawn immediately after its publication.*

ŒDIPUS TYRANNUS;

OR,

SWELLFOOT the TYRANT.

A Tragedy.

IN TWO ACTS.

TRANSLATED FROM THE ORIGINAL DORIC.

————Choose Reform or civil-war,
When through thy streets, instead of hare with dogs,
A CONSORT-QUEEN shall hunt a KING with hogs,
Riding on the IONIAN MINOTAUR.

ADVERTISEMENT

THIS Tragedy is one of a triad, or system of three Plays, (an arrangement according to which the Greeks were accustomed to connect their Dramatic representations,) elucidating the wonderful and appalling fortunes of the SWELLFOOT dynasty. It was evidently written by some *learned Theban,* and, from its characteristic dulness, apparently before the duties on the importation of *Attic salt,*[1] had been repealed by the Bœotarchs. The tenderness with which he beats the PIGS proves him to have been a *sus Bœotiæ;* possibly *Epicuri de grege porcus;*[2] for, as the poet observes,

"A fellow feeling makes us wond'rous kind."

No liberty has been taken with the translation of this remarkable piece of antiquity, except the suppressing a seditious and blasphemous Chorus of the

---

[1] The ban on Athenian freedom of speech.
[2] A pig from the Epicurean sty.

Pigs and Bulls at the last act. The word Hoydipouse,[3] (or more properly Œdipus,) has been rendered literally SWELLFOOT, without its having been conceived necessary to determine whether a swelling of the hind or the fore feet of the Swinish Monarch is particularly indicated.

Should the remaining portions of this Tragedy be found, entitled, "*Swellfoot in Angaria,*" and "*Charite,*" the Translator might be tempted to give them to the reading Public.

——∘◎∘——

DRAMATIS PERSONÆ.

TYRANT SWELLFOOT, *King of Thebes.*
IONA TAURINA, *his Queen.*
MAMMON, *Arch-Priest of Famine.*
PURGANAX,
DAKRY,   }*Wizards, Ministers of* SWELLFOOT.
LAOCTONOS,
The GADFLY.
The LEECH.
The RAT.
The MINOTAUR.
MOSES, *the Sow-gelder.*
SOLOMON, *the Porkman.*
ZEPHANIAH, *Pig-Butcher.*
CHORUS *of the Swinish Multitude.*
Guards, Attendants, Priests, &c. &c.

SCENE.—*Thebes.*

——∘◎∘——

ACT I

SCENE I.   *A magnificent Temple, built of thigh-bones and death's-heads, and tiled with scalps. Over the Altar the statue of Famine, veiled; a number of Boars, Sows, and Sucking-pigs, crowned with thistle, shamrock, and oak, sitting on the steps, and clinging round the Altar of the Temple.*

Enter SWELLFOOT, *in his Royal robes, without perceiving the* Pigs.

Swellfoot.   Thou supreme Goddess! by whose power divine
These graceful limbs are clothed in proud array
          [*He contemplates himself with satisfaction.*
Of gold and purple, and this kingly paunch

Swells like a sail before a favouring breeze,
And these most sacred nether promontories
Lie satisfied with layers of fat; and these
Bœotian cheeks, like Egypt's pyramid,
(Nor with less toil were their foundations laid,*)
Sustain the cone of my untroubled brain,
That point, the emblem of a pointless nothing!   10
Thou to whom Kings and laurelled Emperors,
Radical-butchers, Paper-money-millers,
Bishops and deacons, and the entire army
Of those fat martyrs to the persecution
Of stifling turtle-soup, and brandy-devils,
Offer their secret vows! Thou plenteous Ceres
Of their Eleusis, hail![4]
     The Swine.   Eigh! eigh! eigh! eigh!
     Swellfoot.   Ha! what are ye,
Who, crowned with leaves devoted to the Furies,
Cling round this sacred shrine?   20
     Swine.   Aigh, aigh! aigh!
     Swellfoot.   What! ye that are
The very beasts that offered at her altar
With blood and groans, salt-cake, and fat, and
          inwards
Ever propitiate her reluctant will
When taxes are withheld?
     Swine.   Ugh! ugh! ugh!
     Swellfoot.   What! ye who grub
With filthy snouts my red potatoes up
In Allan's rushy bog? Who eat the oats
Up, from my cavalry in the Hebrides?[5]
Who swill the hog-wash soup my cooks digest   30
From bones, and rags, and scraps of shoe-leather,
Which should be given to cleaner Pigs than you?

The Swine.

Semichorus I.

The same, alas! the same;
Though only now the name
   Of Pig remains to me.

Semichorus II.

If 'twere your kingly will
Us wretched Swine to kill,
   What should we yield to thee?

---

* See *Universal History* for an account of the number of people who died, and the immense consumption of garlic by the wretched Egyptians, who made a sepulchre for the name as well as the bodies of their tyrants.

——◇◇◇◇——

[4] The Eleusian mysteries were celebrations of the goddess of grain (and abundance, fertility).

[5] I.e., the troops stationed in Ireland and Scotland.

---

[3] From *hoyt,* "to indulge in riotous mirth;" and πούς, or "foot."

Swellfoot. Why skin and bones, and some few
    hairs for mortar.

Chorus of Swine.

I have heard your Laureate [6] sing,   40
  That pity was a royal thing;
Under your mighty ancestors, we Pigs
  Were bless'd as nightingales on myrtle sprigs,
Or grasshoppers that live on noonday dew,
And sung, old annals tell, as sweetly too,
But now our sties are fallen in, we catch
  The murrain and the mange, the scab and itch;
Sometimes your royal dogs tear down our thatch,
  And then we seek the shelter of a ditch;
Hog-wash or grains, or ruta-baga, none   50
Has yet been ours since your reign begun.

First Sow

My Pigs, 'tis in vain to tug!

Second Sow

I could almost eat my litter!

First Pig

I suck, but no milk will come from the dug.

Second Pig

Our skin and our bones would be bitter.

The Boars

We fight for this rag of greasy rug,
Though a trough of wash would be fitter.

Semichorus.

Happier swine were they than we,
  Drowned in the Gadarean sea—
I wish that pity would drive out the devils   60
Which in your royal bosom hold their revels,
  And sink us in the waves of thy compassion!
Alas! the Pigs are an unhappy nation!
Now if your Majesty would have our bristles
  To bind your mortar with, or fill our colons
With rich blood, or make brawn out of our gristles,
  In policy—ask else your royal Solons—
You ought to give us hog-wash and clean straw,
And sties well thatched; besides, it is the law!

Swellfoot. This is sedition, and rank blasphemy!
Ho! there, my guards!   71

Enter a GUARD.

Guard.   Your sacred Majesty.
Swellfoot. Call in the Jews, Solomon the court
    porkman,[7]
Moses the sow-gelder, and Zephaniah
The hog-butcher.
Guard.   They are in waiting, Sire.

Enter SOLOMON, MOSES, *and* ZEPHANIAH.

Swellfoot. Out with your knife, old Moses, and spay
    those Sows,   75
    [*The* Pigs *run about in consternation.*
That load the earth with Pigs; cut close and deep.
Moral restraint I see has no effect,
Nor prostitution, nor our own example,
Starvation, typhus-fever, war, nor prison—
This was the art which the arch-priest of Famine   80
Hinted at in his charge to the Theban clergy—
Cut close and deep, good Moses.
Moses.   Let your Majesty
Keep the boars quiet, else—
Swellfoot.   Zephaniah, cut
That fat hog's throat, the brute seems overfed;
Seditious hunks! to whine for want of grains.
Zephaniah. Your sacred Majesty, he has the
    dropsy;—
We shall find pints of hydatids [8] in's liver,
He has not half an inch of wholesome fat
Upon his carious ribs—
Swellfoot.   'Tis all the same,
He'll serve instead of riot money, when   90
Our murmuring troops bivouac in Thebes' streets;
And January winds, after a day
Of butchering, will make them relish carrion.
Now, Solomon, I'll sell you in a lump
The whole kit of them.
Solomon.   Why, your Majesty,
I could not give——
Swellfoot.   Kill them out of the way,
That shall be price enough, and let me hear
Their everlasting grunts and whines no more!
    [*Exeunt, driving in the* SWINE.

Enter MAMMON, *the Arch-Priest; and*
PURGANAX,[9] *Chief of the Council of Wizards.*

Purganax. The future looks as black as death, a
    cloud,

---

[6] Robert Southey was Poet Laureate; see Byron's *The Vision of Judgment*, etc., p. 636.

[7] Followers of Malthus (*An Essay on the Principle of Population*), they employ the most direct way to keep the population from exceeding the food supply.
[8] Watery cysts, containing larvae of the tapeworm.
[9] Lord Castlereagh, Foreign Secretary. See *The Mask of Anarchy*, p. 886.

Dark as the frown of Hell, hangs over it—   100
The troops grow mutinous—the revenue fails—
There's something rotten in us—for the level
Of the State slopes, its very bases topple,
The boldest turn their backs upon themselves!
    Mammon. Why what's the matter, my dear fellow,
        now?
Do the troops mutiny?—decimate some regiments;
Does money fail?—come to my mint—coin paper,
Till gold be at a discount, and, ashamed
To show his bilious face, go purge himself,
In emulation of her vestal whiteness.   110
    Purganax. Oh, would that this were all! The
        oracle!!
    Mammon. Why it was I who spoke that oracle,
And whether I was dead drunk or inspired,
I cannot well remember; nor, in truth,
The oracle itself!
    Purganax.   The words went thus:—
"Bœotia, choose reform or civil war!
When through the streets, instead of hare with
        dogs,
A Consort Queen shall hunt a King with Hogs,
Riding on the Ionian Minotaur."[10]
    Mammon. Now if the oracle had ne'er foretold   120
This sad alternative, it must arrive,
Or not, and so it must now that it has,
And whether I was urg'd by grace divine,
Or Lesbian liquor to declare these words,
Which must, as all words must, be false or true;
It matters not: for the same Power made all,
Oracle, wine, and me and you—or none—
'Tis the same thing. If you knew as much
Of oracles as I do——
    Purganax.   You arch-priests
Believe in nothing; if you were to dream   130
Of a particular number in the Lottery,
You would not buy the ticket?
    Mammon.   Yet our tickets
Are seldom blanks. But what steps have you taken?
For prophecies when once they get abroad,
Like liars who tell the truth to serve their ends,
Or hypocrites who, from assuming virtue,
Do the same actions that the virtuous do,
Contrive their own fulfilment. This Iona—
Well—you know what the chaste Pasiphae did,
Wife to that most religious King of Crete,   140
And still how popular the tale is here;
And these dull Swine of Thebes boast their descent
From the free Minotaur. You know they still

Call themselves Bulls, though thus degenerate;
And every thing relating to a Bull
Is popular and respectable in Thebes.
Their arms are seven Bulls in a field gules,
They think their strength consists in eating beef,—
Now there were danger in the precedent
If Queen Iona—
    Purganax.   I have taken good care   150
That shall not be. I struck the crust o' the earth
With this enchanted rod, and Hell lay bare!
And from a cavern full of ugly shapes,
I chose a LEECH, a GADFLY, and a RAT.[11]
The gadfly was the same which Juno sent
To agitate Io* and which Ezechiel† mentions
That the Lord whistled for out of the mountains
Of utmost Ethiopia, to torment
Mesopotamian Babylon. The beast
Has a loud trumpet like the scarabee,[12]   160
His crookèd tail is barbed with many stings,
Each able to make a thousand wounds, and each
Immedicable; from his convex eyes
He sees fair things in many hideous shapes,
And trumpets all his falsehood to the world.
Like other beetles he is fed on dung—
He has eleven feet with which he crawls,
Trailing a blistering slime, and this foul beast
Has tracked Iona from the Theban limits,
From isle to isle, from city unto city,   170
Urging her flight from the far Chersonese
To fabulous Solyma, and the Ætnean Isle,
Ortygia, Melite, and Calypso's Rock,
And the swart tribes of Garamant and Fez,
Æolia and Elysium, and thy shores,
Parthenope, which now, alas! are free!
And through the fortunate Saturnian land,
Into the darkness of the West.
    Mammon.   But if
This Gadfly should drive Iona hither?
    Purganax. Gods! what an *if*! but there is my
        grey RAT;   180
So thin with want, he can crawl in and out
Of any narrow chink and filthy hole,
And he shall creep into her dressing-room,
And——
    Mammon. My dear friend, where are your wits?
        as if
She does not always toast a piece of cheese

* The *Prometheus Bound* of Æschylus.
† And the Lord whistled for the gadfly out of Æthiopia, and
for the bee out of Egypt. &c.—*Ezechiel.*

[10] Iona Taurina ("Joan Bull," wife of John Bull); her riding the
Minotaur is Shelley's allusion to George IV's possible attempt to
charge Queen Caroline with sexual irregularity. The Minotaur
was the offspring of Pasiphae and a white bull.

[11] Members of the Milan Commission, whose investigations of
Queen Caroline were delivered in a green bag (see lines 350 ff.).
[12] Scarab; beetle.

And bait the trap? and rats, when lean enough
To crawl through *such* chinks——
    Purganax.   But my LEECH—a
    leech
Fit to suck blood, with lubricous round rings,
Capaciously expatiative, which make
His little body like a red balloon,   190
As full of blood as that of hydrogen,
Sucked from men's hearts; insatiably he sucks
And clings and pulls—a horse-leech, whose deep
    maw
The plethoric King Swellfoot could not fill,
And who, till full, will cling for ever.
    Mammon.   This
For Queen Iona might suffice, and less;
But 'tis the Swinish multitude I fear,
And in that fear I have——
    Purganax.   Done what?
    Mammon.   Disinherited
My eldest son Chrysaor,[13] because he
Attended public meetings, and would always   200
Stand prating there of commerce, public faith,
Economy, and unadulterate coin,
And other topics, ultra-radical;
And have entailed my estate, called the Fool's
    Paradise,
And funds, in fairy-money, bonds, and bills,
Upon my accomplished daughter Banknotina,
And married her to the gallows.*
    Purganax.   A good match!
    Mammon. A high connexion, Purganax. The
    bridegroom
Is of a very ancient family
Of Hounslow Heath, Tyburn, and the New Drop,
And has great influence in both Houses;—Oh!   211
He makes the fondest husband; nay *too* fond,—
New married people should not kiss in public;
But the poor souls love one another so!
And then my little grandchildren, the gibbets,
Promising children as you ever saw,—
The young playing at hanging, the elder learning
How to hold radicals. They are well taught too,
For every gibbet says its catechism,
And reads a select chapter in the Bible   220
Before it goes to play.
           [*A most tremendous humming is heard.*
    Purganax.   Ha! what do I hear?

Enter the GADFLY.

    Mammon. Your Gadfly, as it seems, is tired of
    gadding.

Gadfly.

Hum! hum! hum!
From the lakes of the Alps, and the cold grey scalps
    Of the mountains, I come!
    Hum! hum! hum!
From Morocco and Fez, and the high palaces
    Of golden Byzantium;
From the temples divine of old Palestine,
    From Athens and Rome,   230
      With a ha! and a hum!
    I come! I come!

    All inn-doors and windows
      Were open to me;
    I saw all that sin does,
      Which lamps hardly see
That burn in the night by the curtained bed,—
The impudent lamps! for they blushed not red.
      Dinging and singing,
      From slumber I rung her,   240
Loud as the clank of an ironmonger!
      Hum! hum! hum!

    Far, far, far,
With the trump of my lips, and the sting at my hips,
    I drove her—afar!
    Far, far, far!
From city to city, abandoned of pity,
    A ship without needle or star;—
Homeless she past, like a cloud on the blast,
    Seeking peace, finding war;—   250
    She is here in her car,
    From afar, and afar;—
      Hum! hum!

I have stung her and wrung her,
    The venom is working;—
And if you had hung her
    With canting and quirking,
She could not be deader than she will be soon;—
I have driven her close to you, under the moon.
    Night and day, hum! hum! ha!   260
I have humm'd her and drumm'd her
From place to place, till at last I have dumbed her,
    Hum! hum! hum![14]

---

  * "If one should marry a gallows, and beget young gibbets,
I never saw one so prone."—*Cymbeline.*

[13] Traditionally the son of Medusa and Poseidon, born full-grown when Perseus beheaded Medusa.

[14] See *Prometheus Unbound*, I, ll. 503–20, p. 861.

Enter the LEECH *and the* RAT.

Leech.

I will suck
Blood or muck!
The disease of the state is a plethory,
Who so fit to reduce it as I?

Rat.

I'll slily seize and
Let the blood from her weasand,[15]—
Creeping through crevice, and chink, and cranny,　270
With my snaky tail, and my sides so scranny.

Purganax.

Aroint ye! thou unprofitable worm!
　　　　　　　　　　　　[*To the* LEECH.
And thou, dull beetle, get thee back to hell!
　　　　　　　　　　　　[*To the* GADFLY.
To sting the ghosts of Babylonian kings,
And the ox-headed Io——

Swine (within).

Ugh, ugh, ugh!
Hail! Iona the divine,
We will be no longer Swine,
But Bulls with horns and dewlaps.

Rat.

　　　　　　　　　　For,
You know, my lord, the Minotaur——　　280

Purganax (fiercely).

Be silent! get to hell! or I will call
The cat out of the kitchen. Well, Lord Mammon,
This is a pretty business.
　　　　　　　　　　[*Exit the* RAT.

Mammon.

　　　　　　I will go
And spell some scheme to make it ugly then.
　　　　　　　　　　　　[*Exit.*

Enter SWELLFOOT.

Swellfoot. She is returned! Taurina is in Thebes
When Swellfoot wishes that she were in hell!
Oh, Hymen! clothed in yellow jealousy,
And waving o'er the couch of wedded kings
The torch of discord with its fiery hair;
This is thy work, thou patron saint of queens!　290
Swellfoot is wived! though parted by the sea,
The very name of wife had conjugal rights;

Her cursed image ate, drank, slept with me,
And in the arms of Adiposa oft
Her memory has received a husband's——
　　　　[*A loud tumult, and cries of*
　　　　"Iona for ever!—No Swellfoot!"
Swellfoot.　　　　　　Hark!
How the Swine cry Iona Taurina;
I suffer the real presence; Purganax,
Off with her head!
Purganax.　　But I must first impannel
A jury of the Pigs.
Swellfoot.　　Pack them then.
Purganax. Or fattening some few in two separate
　　sties,　　　　　　　　　　300
And giving them clean straw, tying some bits
Of ribbon round their legs—giving their sows
Some tawdry lace, and bits of lustre glass,
And their young boars white and red rags, and tails
Of cows, and jay feathers, and sticking cauliflowers
Between the ears of the old ones; and when
They are persuaded, that by the inherent virtue
Of these things, they are all imperial Pigs,
Good Lord! they'd rip each other's bellies up,
Not to say, help us in destroying her.　　310
Swellfoot. This plan might be tried too;—where's
　　General Laoctonos?[16]

Enter LAOCTONOS *and* DAKRY.[17]

It is my royal pleasure
That you, Lord General, bring the head and body,
If separate it would please me better, hither
Of Queen Iona.
Laoctonos.　　That pleasure I well knew,
And made a charge with those battalions bold,
Called, from their dress and grin, the royal apes,
Upon the Swine, who, in a hollow square
Enclosed her, and received the first attack
Like so many rhinoceroses, and then　　320
Retreating in good order, with bare tusks
And wrinkled snouts presented to the foe,
Bore her in triumph to the public sty.
What is still worse, some Sows upon the ground
Have given the ape-guards apples, nuts, and gin,
And they all whisk their tails aloft, and cry,
"Long live Iona! down with Swellfoot!"
Purganax.　　　　　　Hark!
The Swine (without). Long live Iona! down with
　　Swellfoot!
Dakry.　　　I
Went to the garret of the swineherd's tower,
Which overlooks the sty, and made a long　　330

---

[15] Windpipe.

[16] Literally, "people-killer."
[17] Viscount Sidmouth, Home Secretary.

Harangue (all words) to the assembled Swine,
Of delicacy, mercy, judgment, law,
Morals, and precedents, and purity,
Adultery, destitution, and divorce,
Piety, faith, and state necessity,
And how I loved the Queen!—and then I wept,
With the pathos of my own eloquence,
And every tear turned to a mill-stone, which
Brained many a gaping Pig, and there was made
A slough of blood and brains upon the place,   340
Greased with the pounded bacon; round and round
The millstones rolled, ploughing the pavement up,
And hurling Sucking-Pigs into the air,
With dust and stones.——

Enter MAMMON.

   Mammon.   I wonder that grey wizards
Like you should be so beardless in their schemes;
It had been but a point of policy
To keep Iona and the Swine apart.
Divide and rule! but ye have made a junction
Between two parties who will govern you,
But for my art.—Behold this B A G ! it is   350
The poison B A G of that Green Spider huge,
On which our spies skulked in ovation through
The streets of Thebes, when they were paved with
    dead:
A bane so much the deadlier fills it now,
As calumny is worse than death,—for here
The Gadfly's venom, fifty times distilled,
Is mingled with the vomit of the Leech,
In due proportion, and black ratsbane, which
That very Rat, who, like the Pontic tyrant,[18]
Nurtures himself on poison, dare not touch;—   360
All is sealed up with the broad seal of Fraud,
Who is the Devil's Lord High Chancellor,
And over it the Primate of all Hell
Murmured this pious baptism:—"Be thou called
The GREEN BAG; and this power and grace
    be thine:
That thy contents, on whomsoever poured,
Turn innocence to guilt, and gentlest looks
To savage, foul, and fierce deformity.
Let all baptised by thy infernal dew
Be called adulterer, drunkard, liar, wretch!   370
No name left out which orthodoxy loves,
Court Journal or legitimate Review!—
Be they called tyrant, beast, fool, glutton, lover
Of other wives and husbands than their own—
The heaviest sin on this side of the Alps!
Wither they to a ghastly caricature

Of what was human!—let not man nor beast
Behold their face with unaverted eyes!
Or hear their names with ears that tingle not
With blood of indignation, rage, and shame!"—
This is a perilous liquor;—good my Lords.—   381
    [SWELLFOOT *approaches to touch the* GREEN BAG.
Beware! for God's sake, beware!—if you should
    break
The seal, and touch the fatal liquor——
   Purganax.   There,
Give it to me. I have been used to handle
All sorts of poisons. His dread majesty
Only desires to see the colour of it.
   Mammon. Now, with a little common sense, my
    Lords,
Only undoing all that has been done,
(Yet so as it may seem we but confirm it),
Our victory is assured. We must entice   390
Her Majesty from the sty, and make the Pigs
Believe that the contents of the GREEN BAG
Are the true test of guilt or innocence.
And that, if she be guilty, 'twill transform her
To manifest deformity like guilt.
If innocent, she will become transfigured
Into an angel, such as they say she is;
And they will see her flying through the air,
So bright that she will dim the noon-day sun;
Showering down blessings in the shape of comfits.
This, trust a priest, is just the sort of thing   401
Swine will believe. I'll wager you will see them
Climbing upon the thatch of their low sties,
With pieces of smoked glass, to watch her sail
Among the clouds, and some will hold the flaps
Of one another's ears between their teeth,
To catch the coming hail of comfits in.
You, Purganax, who have the gift o' the gab,
Make them a solemn speech to this effect:
I go to put in readiness the feast   410
Kept to the honour of our goddess Famine,
Where, for more glory, let the ceremony
Take place of the uglification of the Queen.
   Dakry (to *Swellfoot*)—I, as the keeper of your
    sacred conscience,
Humbly remind your Majesty that the care
Of your high office, as Man-milliner
To red Bellona, should not be deferred.
   Purganax. All part, in happier plight to meet
    again.
                                  [*Exeunt.*

---

[18] Mithridates, who took poison in small doses to make
himself immune.

ACT II

SCENE I.   *The Public Sty. The* Boars *in full Assembly.*

Enter PURGANAX.

Purganax.   Grant me your patience, Gentlemen
    and Boars,
Ye, by whose patience under public burthens
The glorious constitution of these styes
Subsists, and shall subsist. The Lean-Pig rates[19]
Grow with the growing populace of Swine,
The taxes, that true source of Piggishness
(How can I find a more appropriate term
To include religion, morals, peace, and plenty,
And all that fit Bœotia as a nation
To teach the other nations how to live?)   10
Increase with Piggishness itself; and still
Does the revenue, that great spring of all
The patronage, and pensions, and by-payments,
Which free-born Pigs regard with jealous eyes,
Diminish, till at length, by glorious steps,
All the land's produce will be merged in taxes,
And the revenue will amount to——nothing!
The failure of a foreign market for
Sausages, bristles, and blood-puddings,
And such home manufactures, is but partial;   20
And, that the population of the Pigs,
Instead of hog-wash, has been fed on straw
And water, is a fact which is—you know—
That is—it is a state-necessity—
Temporary, of course. Those impious Pigs,
Who, by frequent squeaks, have dared impugn
The settled Swellfoot system, or to make
Irreverent mockery of the genuflexions
Inculcated by the arch-priest, have been whipt
Into a loyal and an orthodox whine.[20]   30
Things being in this happy state, the Queen
Iona——

A loud cry from the Pigs.

    She is innocent! most innocent!
Purganax.   That is the very thing that I was
    saying,
Gentlemen Swine; the Queen Iona being
Most innocent, no doubt, returns to Thebes,
And the lean Sows and Boars collect about her,
Wishing to make her think that WE believe
(I mean those more substantial Pigs, who swill
Rich hog-wash, while the others mouth damp
    straw),

---

[19] The poor-rates.
[20] Censorship of the press.

That she is guilty; thus, the Lean-Pig faction   40
Seeks to obtain that hog-wash, which has been
Your immemorial right, and which I will
Maintain you in to the last drop of—
    A Boar (*interrupting him*).   What
Does any one accuse her of?
    Purganax.   Why, no one
Makes *any* positive accusation;—but
There were hints dropt, and so the privy wizards
Conceived that it became them to advise
His Majesty to investigate their truth;—
Not for his own sake; he could be content
To let his wife play any pranks she pleased,   50
If, by that sufferance, *he* could please the Pigs;
But then he fears the morals of the Swine,
The Sows especially, and what effect
It might produce upon the purity and
Religion of the rising generation
Of Sucking-Pigs, if it could be suspected
That Queen Iona—

                                  [*A pause.*

    First Boar.   Well, go on; we long
To hear what she can possibly have done.
    Purganax.   Why, it is hinted, that a certain Bull—
Thus much is *known*:—the milk-white Bulls that feed
Beside Clitumnus and the crystal lakes   61
Of the Cisalpine mountains, in fresh dews
Of lotus-grass and blossoming asphodel,
Sleeking their silken hair, and with sweet breath
Loading the morning winds until they faint
With living fragrance, are so beautiful!—
Well, *I* say nothing;—but Europa rode
On such a one from Asia into Crete,
And the enamoured sea grew calm beneath
His gliding beauty. And Pasiphæ,   70
Iona's grandmother,——but *she* is innocent!
And that both you and I, and all assert.
    First Boar. Most innocent!
    Purganax.   Behold this BAG; a
    bag—
    Second Boar. Oh! no GREEN BAGS!!
    Jealousy's eyes are green,
Scorpions are green, and water-snakes, and efts,
And verdigris, and—
    Purganax.   Honourable Swine,
In Piggish souls can prepossessions reign?
Allow me to remind you, grass is green—
All flesh is grass;—no bacon but is flesh—
Ye are but bacon. This divining BAG   80
(Which is not green, but only bacon colour)
Is filled with liquor, which if sprinkled o'er
A woman guilty of—we all know what—
Makes her so hideous, till she finds one blind,
She never can commit the like again.

If innocent, she will turn into an angel,
And rain down blessings in the shape of comfits
As she flies up to heaven. Now, my proposal
Is to convèrt her sacred Majesty
Into an angel, (as I am sure we shall do,)   90
By pouring on her head this mystic water.
                                   [*Showing the Bag.*
I know that she is innocent; I wish
Only to prove her so to all the world.
    First Boar. Excellent, just, and noble Purganax!
    Second Boar. How glorious it will be to see her
        Majesty
Flying above our heads, her petticoats
Streaming like—like—like—
    Third Boar.   Anything.
    Purganax.   Oh, no!
But like a standard of an admiral's ship,
Or like the banner of a conquering host,
Or like a cloud dyed in the dying day,   100
Unravelled on the blast from a white mountain;
Or like a meteor, or a war-steed's mane,
Or water-fall from a dizzy precipice
Scattered upon the wind.
    First Boar.   Or a cow's tail,—
    Second Boar. Or *anything*, as the learned Boar
        observed.
    Purganax. Gentlemen Boars, I move a resolution,
That her most sacred Majesty should be
Invited to attend the feast of Famine,
And to receive upon her chaste white body
Dews of Apotheosis from this BAG.   110
    [*A great confusion is heard of the* Pigs *out of
    Doors, which communicates itself to those
    within. During the first Strophe, the doors
    of the Sty are staved in, and a number of
    exceedingly lean* Pigs *and* Sows *and* Boars
    rush in.

                    Semichorus I.
No! Yes!

                    Semichorus II.
Yes! No!

                    Semichorus I.
A law!

                    Semichorus II.
A flaw!

                    Semichorus I.
Porkers, we shall lose our wash,
    Or must share it with the Lean Pigs!

                    First Boar.
Order! order! be not rash!
    Was there ever such a scene, Pigs!

            An old Sow (*rushing in*).
I never saw so fine a dash
    Since I first began to wean Pigs.   120

            Second Boar (*solemnly*).
The Queen will be an angel time enough.
    I vote, in form of an amendment, that
Purganax rub a little of that stuff
    Upon his face—

                    Purganax
[*His heart is seen to beat through his waistcoat.*
                    Gods! What would ye be at?

                Semichorus I.
Purganax has plainly shown a
    Cloven foot and jackdaw feather.

                Semichorus II.
I vote Swellfoot and Iona
    Try the magic test together;
Whenever royal spouses bicker,   130
    Both should try the magic liquor.

            An old Boar (*aside*).
A miserable state is that of Pigs,
For if their drivers would tear caps and wigs,
The Swine must bite each other's ear therefore.

            An old Sow (*aside*).
A wretched lot Jove has assigned to Swine,
Squabbling makes Pig-herds hungry, and they
        dine
On bacon, and whip Sucking-Pigs the more.

                    Chorus.
Hog-wash has been ta'en away:
    If the Bull-Queen is divested,
We shall be in every way   140
    Hunted, stript, exposed, molested;
Let us do whate'er we may,
    That she shall not be arrested.
QUEEN, we entrench you with walls of brawn,
    And palisades of tusks, sharp as a bayonet:

Place your most sacred person here. We pawn
    Our lives that none a finger dare to lay on it.
        Those who wrong you, wrong us;
        Those who hate you, hate us;

Those who sting you, sting us;   150
Those who bait you, bait us;
The *oracle* is now about to be
Fulfilled by circumvolving destiny;
Which says: "Thebes, choose *reform* or *civil war*,
    When through your streets, instead of hare with
        dogs,
    A CONSORT QUEEN shall hunt a KING with
        Hogs,
Riding upon the IONIAN MINOTAUR."

Enter IONA TAURINA.

Iona Taurina (*coming forward*).   Gentlemen Swine,
    and gentle Lady-pigs,
The tender heart of every Boar acquits
Their QUEEN, of any act incongruous   160
With native Piggishness, and she reposing
With confidence upon the grunting nation,
Has thrown herself, her cause, her life, her all,
Her innocence, into their Hoggish arms;
Nor has the expectation been deceived
Of finding shelter there. Yet know, great Boars,
(For such who ever lives among you finds you,
And so do I) the innocent are proud!
I have accepted your protection only
In compliment of your kind love and care,   170
Not for necessity. The innocent
Are safest there where trials and dangers wait;
Innocent Queens o'er white-hot plough-shares tread
Unsinged; and ladies, Erin's laureate sings it,*
Decked with rare gems, and beauty rarer still,
Walk'd from Killarney to the Giant's Causeway,
Through rebels, smugglers, troops of yeomanry,
White-boys, and Orange-boys, and constables,
Tithe-proctors, and excise people, uninjured!
Thus I!—   180
Lord PURGANAX, I do commit myself
Into your custody, and am prepared
To stand the test, whatever it may be!
    Purganax. This magnanimity in your sacred
        Majesty
Must please the Pigs. You cannot fail of being
A heavenly angel. Smoke your bits of glass,
Ye loyal Swine, or her transfiguration
Will blind your wondering eyes.
    An old Boar (*aside*).   Take care, my Lord,
They do not smoke you first.
    Purganax.   At the approaching feast
Of Famine, let the expiation be.   190
    Swine. Content! content!

---

* "Rich and rare were the gems she wore."—See Moore's
Irish Melodies.

Iona Taurina (*aside*).   I, most content of all,
Know that my foes even thus prepare their fall!
                                        [*Exeunt omnes.*

SCENE II.   *The interior of the Temple of* FAMINE.
    *The statue of the Goddess, a skeleton clothed in
    parti-coloured rags, seated upon a heap of
    skulls and loaves intermingled. A number of
    exceedingly fat Priests in black garments arrayed
    on each side, with marrow-bones and cleavers in
    their hands. A flourish of trumpets.*

Enter MAMMON *as Arch-priest,* SWELLFOOT,
    DAKRY, PURGANAX, LAOCTONOS, *followed by*
    IONA TAURINA *guarded. On the other side enter
    the* Swine.

Chorus of Priests.
*Accompanied by the Court Porkman
on marrow-bones and cleavers.*

Goddess bare, and gaunt, and pale,
Empress of the world, all hail!
What though Cretans old called thee
            City-crested Cybele?
We call thee FAMINE!
Goddess of fasts and feasts, starving and cramming;
Thro' thee, for emperors, kings, and priests and
        lords
Who rule by viziers, sceptres, bank-notes, words,
    The earth pours forth its plenteous fruits,
        Corn, wool, linen, flesh, and roots—   10
Those who consume these fruits thro' thee grow fat,
Those who produce these fruits through thee grow
        lean,
Whatever change takes place, oh, stick to that!
    And let things be as they have ever been;
    At least while we remain thy priests,
    And proclaim thy fasts and feasts!
Through thee the sacred SWELLFOOT dynasty
Is based upon a rock amid that sea
Whose waves are Swine—so let it ever be!

[SWELLFOOT, &c. *seat themselves at a table,
    magnificently covered at the upper end of the
    temple. Attendants pass over the stage with
    hog-wash in pails. A number of* Pigs, *exceedingly
    lean, follow them licking up the wash.*
    Mammon. I fear your sacred Majesty has lost   20
The appetite which you were used to have.
Allow me now to recommend this dish—
A simple kickshaw by your Persian cook,
Such as is served at the great King's second table.
The price and pains which its ingredients cost,
Might have maintained some dozen families

A winter or two—not more—so plain a dish
Could scarcely disagree.—
    Swellfoot.   After the trial,
And these fastidious Pigs are gone, perhaps
I may recover my lost appetite,—   30
I feel the gout flying about my stomach—
Give me a glass of Maraschino punch.
    Purganax (*filling his glass, and standing up*).   The
      glorious constitution of the Pigs!
    All. A toast! a toast! stand up, and three times
      three!
    Dakry. No heel-taps—darken day-lights!
    Laoctonos.   Claret,
      somehow,
Puts me in mind of blood, and blood of claret!
    Swellfoot. Laoctonos is fishing for a compliment,
But 'tis his due. Yes, you have drunk more wine,
And shed more blood, than any man in Thebes.
(*To Purganax*). For God's sake stop the grunting of
    those Pigs!   40
    Purganax. We dare not, Sire! 'tis Famine's
    privilege.

Chorus of Swine.

Hail to thee, hail to thee, Famine!
  Thy throne is on blood, and thy robe is of rags;
Thou devil which livest on damning;
  Saint of new churches, and cant, and GREEN
    BAGS;
    Till in pity and terror thou risest,
    Confounding the schemes of the wisest.
  When thou liftest thy skeleton form,
  When the loaves and the skulls roll about,
We will greet thee—the voice of a storm   50
    Would be lost in our terrible shout!

Then hail to thee, hail to thee, Famine!
  Hail to thee, Empress of Earth!
When thou risest, dividing possessions;
When thou risest, uprooting oppressions;
    In the pride of thy ghastly mirth.
Over palaces, temples, and graves,
We will rush as thy minister-slaves,
  Trampling behind in thy train,
Till all be made level again!   60

    Mammon. I hear a crackling of the giant bones
Of the dread image, and in the black pits
Which once were eyes, I see two livid flames.
These prodigies are oracular, and show
The presence of the unseen Deity.
Mighty events are hastening to their doom!
    Swellfoot. I only hear the lean and mutinous Swine
Grunting about the temple.

    Dakry.   In a crisis
Of such exceeding delicacy, I think
We ought to put Her Majesty, the QUEEN,   70
Upon her trial without delay.
    Mammon.   The BAG
Is here.
    Purganax. I have rehearsed the entire scene
With an ox-bladder and some ditch-water,
On Lady P——; it cannot fail.

                          [*Taking up the bag.*
                      Your Majesty (*to*
  SWELLFOOT)
In such a filthy business had better
Stand on one side, lest it should sprinkle you.
A spot or two on me would do no harm,
Nay, it might hide the blood, which the sad Genius
Of the Green Isle has fixed, as by a spell,   80
Upon my brow—which would stain all its seas,
But which those seas could never wash away!
    Iona Taurina. My Lord, I am ready—nay I am
    impatient
To undergo the test.

    [*A graceful figure in a semi-transparent veil passes
      unnoticed through the Temple; the word
      LIBERTY is seen through the veil, as if it were
      written in fire upon its forehead. Its words are
      almost drowned in the furious grunting of the
      Pigs, and the business of the trial. She kneels on
      the steps of the Altar, and speaks in tones at
      first faint and low, but which ever become louder
      and louder.*

    Mighty Empress! Death's white wife!
    Ghastly mother-in-law of Life!
    By the God who made thee such,
    By the magic of thy touch,
    By the starving and the cramming,
Of fasts and feasts!—by thy dread self, O Famine! 90
I charge thee! when thou wake the multitude,
Thou lead them not upon the paths of blood.
The earth did never mean her foison
For those who crown life's cup with poison
Of fanatic rage and meaningless revenge—
  But for those radiant spirits, who are still
The standard-bearers in the van of Change.
  Be they th' appointed stewards, to fill
The lap of Pain, and Toil, and Age!—
Remit, O Queen! thy accustom'd rage!   100
Be what thou art not! In voice faint and low
FREEDOM calls Famine,—her eternal foe,
To brief alliance, hollow truce.—Rise now!

    [*Whilst the veiled Figure has been chaunting this
      strophe,* MAMMON, DAKRY, LAOCTONOS,

and SWELLFOOT, *have surrounded* IONA TAURINA, *who, with her hands folded on her breast, and her eyes lifted to Heaven, stands, as with saint-like resignation, to wait the issue of the business, in perfect confidence of her innocence.* PURGANAX, *after unsealing the* GREEN BAG, *is gravely about to pour the liquor upon her head, when suddenly the whole expression of her figure and countenance changes; she snatches it from his hand with a loud laugh of triumph, and empties it over* SWELLFOOT *and his whole Court, who are instantly changed into a number of filthy and ugly animals, and rush out of the Temple. The image of* FAMINE *then arises with a tremendous sound, the* Pigs *begin scrambling for the loaves, and are tripped up by the skulls; all those who eat the loaves are turned into* Bulls, *and arrange themselves quietly behind the altar. The image of* FAMINE *sinks through a chasm in the earth, and a* MINOTAUR *rises.*

Minotaur. I am the Ionian Minotaur, the mightiest
Of all Europa's taurine progeny—
I am the old traditional Man-Bull;
And from my ancestors, having been Ionian,
I am called Ion, which, by interpretation,
Is JOHN; in plain Theban, that is to say,
My name's JOHN BULL; I am a famous hunter,
And can leap any gate in all Bœotia,   III
Even the palings of the royal park,
Or double ditch about the new enclosures;
And if your Majesty will deign to mount me,
At least till you have hunted down your game,
I will not throw you.

Iona Taurina. (*During this speech she has been putting on boots and spurs, and a hunting-cap, buckishly cocked on one side, and tucking up her hair, she leaps nimbly on his back.*) Hoa! hoa! tallyho! tallyho! ho! ho!

Come, let us hunt these ugly badgers down,[21]
These stinking foxes, these devouring otters,
These hares, these wolves, these anything but men.
Hey, for a whipper-in! my loyal Pigs,   121
Now let your noses be as keen as beagles',
Your steps as swift as greyhounds', and your cries
More dulcet and symphonius than the bells
Of village-towers, on sunshine holiday;
Wake all the dewy woods with jangling music.
Give them no law (are they not beasts of blood?)
But such as they gave you. Tallyho! ho!
Through forest, furze, and bog, and den, and desert,
Pursue the ugly beasts! tallyho! ho!   130

---

[21] Joan Bull, on the back of the Minotaur (Anarchy?) called John Bull, hunts down the peasants, who include the King and his court.

Full chorus of IONA *and the Swine.*

    Tallyho! tallyho!
Through rain, hail, and snow,
Through brake, gorse, and briar,
Through fen, flood, and mire,
    We go! we go!

    Tallyho! tallyho!
Through pond, ditch, and slough,
Wind them, and find them,
Like the Devil behind them,
    Tallyho! tallyho!

[*Exeunt, in full cry;* IONA *driving on the* SWINE, *with the empty* GREEN BAG.

THE END

[1820]   [1820]

THE TWO SPIRITS

AN ALLEGORY

[*Two genii stood before me in a dream*]

FIRST SPIRIT

O THOU, who plumed with strong desire
    Wouldst float above the earth, beware!
A Shadow tracks thy flight of fire—
        Night is coming!
Bright are the regions of the air,
And among the warmth and beams
    It was delight to wander there—
        Night is coming!

SECOND SPIRIT

The deathless stars are bright above;
    If I would cross the shade at night,   10
Within my heart is the lamp of love,
        And that is day!
And the moon will smile with gentle light
On my golden plumes where'er they move;
    The meteors will linger round my flight,
        And make night day.

FIRST SPIRIT

But if the whirlwinds of darkness waken
    Hail, and lightning, and stormy rain;
See, the bounds of the air are shaken—
        Night is coming!   20
    The red swift clouds of the hurricane
Yon declining sun have overtaken,
        The clash of the hail sweeps over the plain—
        Night is coming!

SECOND SPIRIT

I see the light, and I hear the sound;
　　I'll sail on the flood of the tempest dark,
With the calm within and the light around
　　　　Which makes night day:
　　And thou, when the gloom is deep and stark,
Look from thy dull earth, slumber-bound,　　　　　30
　　My moon-like flight thou then may'st mark
　　　　　On high, far away.

————————

Some say there is a precipice
　　Where one vast pine is frozen to ruin
O'er piles of snow and chasms of ice
　　　　Mid Alpine mountains;
　　And that the languid storm pursuing
That wingèd shape, for ever flies
　　Round those hoar branches, aye renewing
　　　　Its aëry fountains.　　　　　40

Some say when nights are dry and clear,
　　And the death-dews sleep on the morass,
Sweet whispers are heard by the traveller,
　　　　Which make night day:
　　And a silver shape like his early love doth pass
Upborne by her wild and glittering hair,
　　And when he awakes on the fragrant grass,
　　　　He finds night day.

[1820]　　　　　　　　　　　　　　　[1824]

TO THE MOON

I

Art thou pale for weariness
Of climbing heaven and gazing on the earth,
　　Wandering companionless
Among the stars that have a different birth,—
And ever changing, like a joyless eye
That finds no object worth its constancy?

II

Thou chosen sister of the Spirit,
That gazes on thee till in thee it pities . . .

[1820]　　　　　　　　　　　　　　　[1824]

LIBERTY

I

The fiery mountains answer each other;
　　Their thunderings are echoed from zone to zone;
The tempestuous oceans awake one another,
　　And the ice-rocks are shaken round Winter's
　　　　throne,
　　　　When the clarion of the Typhoon is blown.

II

From a single cloud the lightning flashes,
　　Whilst a thousand isles are illumined around;
Earthquake is trampling one city to ashes,
　　An hundred are shuddering and tottering; the
　　　　sound
　　　　Is bellowing underground.　　　　　10

III

But keener thy gaze than the lightning's glare,
　　And swifter thy step than the earthquake's tramp;
Thou deafenest the rage of the ocean; thy stare
　　Makes blind the volcanoes; the sun's bright lamp
　　　　To thine is a fen-fire damp.

IV

From billow and mountain and exhalation
　　The sunlight is darted through vapour and blast;
From spirit to spirit, from nation to nation,
　　From city to hamlet, thy dawning is cast,—
And tyrants and slaves are like shadows of night　　20
　　　　In the van of the morning light.

[1820]　　　　　　　　　　　　　　　[1824]

EPIPSYCHIDION

In December 1820 Shelley met and admired Emilia Viviani, who had been sent to a convent by her father. The Greek title is an invented word, meaning "soul out of my soul."

EPIPSYCHIDION:

VERSES ADDRESSED TO THE NOBLE

AND UNFORTUNATE LADY

EMILIA V——

NOW IMPRISONED IN THE CONVENT OF——

L'anima amante si slancia fuori del creato, e si crea nell' infinito un Mondo tutto per essa, diverso assai da questo oscuro e pauroso baratro.[1] HER OWN WORDS.

ADVERTISEMENT

THE writer of the following Lines died at Florence, as he was preparing for a voyage to one of the wildest of the Sporades,[2] which he had bought, and where he had fitted up the ruins of an old building, and where it was his hope to have realised a scheme of life, suited perhaps to that happier and better world of which he is now an inhabitant, but hardly practicable in this. His life was singular; less on account of the romantic vicissitudes which diversified it, than the ideal tinge which it received from his own character and feelings. The present Poem, like the *Vita Nuova* of Dante, is sufficiently intelligible to a certain class of readers without a matter-of-fact history of the circumstances to which it relates; and to a certain other class it must ever remain incomprehensible, from a defect of a common organ of perception for ideas of which it treats. Not but that *gran vergogna sarebbe a colui, che rimasse cosa sotto veste di figura, o di colore rettorico: e domandato non sapesse denudare le sue parole da cotal veste, in guisa che avessero verace intendimento.*[3]

The present poem appears to have been intended by the Writer as the dedication to some longer one.

---

[1] "The soul that loves throws itself ahead of all creation, and creates for itself in the infinite a world unto itself, very different from this obscure and frightful gulf."

[2] Islands in the Aegean Sea.

[3] From Dante's *Vita Nuova* (*A New Life*), the story of his love for Beatrice. "It would be disgraceful to make rhymes under the guise of metaphors or rhetorical coloring, and then when asked not know how to undress the words from such disguise and put them into a form in which they could be easily understood."

The stanza on the above page is almost a literal translation from Dante's famous Canzone

Voi, ch' intendendo, il terzo ciel movete, &c.[4]

The presumptuous application of the concluding lines to his own composition will raise a smile at the expense of my unfortunate friend: be it a smile not of contempt, but pity.

My Song, I fear that thou wilt find but few
Who fitly shall conceive thy reasoning,
Of such hard matter dost thou entertain;
Whence, if by misadventure, chance should bring
Thee to base company (as chance may do),
Quite unaware of what thou dost contain,
I prithee, comfort thy sweet self again,
My last delight! tell them that they are dull,
And bid them own that thou art beautiful.

EPIPSYCHIDION

SWEET Spirit! Sister of that orphan one,[5]
Whose empire is the name[6] thou weepest on,
In my heart's temple I suspend to thee
These votive wreaths of withered memory.

Poor captive bird! who, from thy narrow cage,
Pourest such music, that it might assuage
The ruggèd hearts of those who prisoned thee,
Were they not deaf to all sweet melody;
This song shall be thy rose: its petals pale
Are dead, indeed, my adored Nightingale!   10
But soft and fragrant is the faded blossom,
And it has no thorn left to wound thy bosom.

High, spirit-wingèd Heart! who dost for ever
Beat thine unfeeling bars with vain endeavour,
Till those bright plumes of thought, in which arrayed
It over-soared this low and worldly shade,
Lie shattered; and thy panting, wounded breast
Stains with dear blood its unmaternal nest!
I weep vain tears: blood would less bitter be,
Yet poured forth gladlier, could it profit thee.   20

---

[4] From Dante's *Convito*: "You who, intelligent, move the third heaven (of Venus)."

[5] Perhaps Mary Shelley, whose mother Mary Wollstonecraft died at her birth.

[6] Shelley.

Seraph of Heaven! too gentle to be human,
Veiling beneath that radiant form of Woman
All that is insupportable in thee
Of light, and love, and immortality!
Sweet Benediction in the eternal Curse!
Veiled Glory of this lampless Universe!
Thou Moon beyond the clouds! Thou living Form
Among the Dead! Thou Star above the Storm!
Thou Wonder, and thou Beauty, and thou Terror!
Thou Harmony of Nature's art! Thou Mirror   30
In whom, as in the splendour of the Sun,
All shapes look glorious which thou gazest on!
Ay, even the dim words which obscure thee now
Flash, lightning-like, with unaccustomed glow;
I pray thee that thou blot from this sad song
All of its much mortality and wrong,
With those clear drops, which start like sacred dew
From the twin lights thy sweet soul darkens through,
Weeping, till sorrow becomes ecstasy:
Then smile on it, so that it may not die.   40

I never thought before my death to see
Youth's vision thus made perfect. Emily,
I love thee; though the world by no thin name
Will hide that love from its unvalued shame.
Would we two had been twins of the same mother!
Or, that the name my heart lent to another
Could be a sister's bond for her and thee,
Blending two beams of one eternity! [7]
Yet were one lawful and the other true,
These names, though dear, could paint not, as is due,
How beyond refuge I am thine. Ah me!   51
I am not thine: I am a part of *thee*.

Sweet Lamp! my moth-like Muse has burned its
    wings;
Or, like a dying swan who soars and sings,
Young Love should teach Time, in his own gray
    style,
All that thou art. Art thou not void of guile,
A lovely soul formed to be blessed and bless?
A well of sealed and secret happiness,
Whose waters like blithe light and music are,
Vanquishing dissonance and gloom? A Star   60
Which moves not in the moving heavens, alone?
A Smile amid dark frowns? a gentle tone
Amid rude voices? a belovèd light?
A Solitude, a Refuge, a Delight?
A Lute, which those whom Love has taught to play
Make music on, to soothe the roughest day

[7] If Mary had been his sister and Emilia his wife; but neither
sister nor wife is an adequate name for her.

And lull fond Grief asleep? a buried treasure?
A cradle of young thoughts of wingless pleasure?
A violet-shrounded grave of Woe?—I measure
The world of fancies, seeking one like thee,   70
And find—alas! mine own infirmity.

She met me, Stranger, upon life's rough way,
And lured me towards sweet Death; as Night by Day,
Winter by Spring, or Sorrow by swift Hope,
Led into light, life, peace. An antelope,
In the suspended impulse of its lightness,
Were less aethereally light: the brightness
Of her divinest presence trembles through
Her limbs, as underneath a cloud of dew
Embodied in the windless heaven of June   80
Amid the splendour-wingèd stars, the Moon
Burns, inextinguishably beautiful:
And from her lips, as from a hyacinth full
Of honey-dew, a liquid murmur drops,
Killing the sense with passion; sweet as stops
Of planetary music heard in trance.
In her mild lights the starry spirits dance,
The sunbeams of those wells which ever leap
Under the lightnings of the soul—too deep
For the brief fathom-line of thought or sense.   90
The glory of her being, issuing thence,
Stains the dead, blank, cold air with a warm shade
Of unentangled intermixture, made
By Love, of light and motion: one intense
Diffusion, one serene Omnipresence,
Whose flowing outlines mingle in their flowing,
Around her cheeks and utmost fingers glowing
With the unintermitted blood, which there
Quivers, (as in a fleece of snow-like air
The crimson pulse of living morning quiver,)   100
Continuously prolonged, and ending never,
Till they are lost, and in that Beauty furled
Which penetrates and clasps and fills the world;
Scarce visible from extreme loveliness.
Warm fragrance seems to fall from her light dress
And her loose hair; and where some heavy tress
The air of her own speed has disentwined,
The sweetness seems to satiate the faint wind;
And in the soul a wild odour is felt,
Beyond the sense, like fiery dews that melt   110
Into the bosom of a frozen bud.—
See where she stands! a mortal shape indued
With love and life and light and deity,
And motion which may change but cannot die;
An image of some bright Eternity;
A shadow of some golden dream; a Splendour
Leaving the third sphere [8] pilotless; a tender

[8] Of Venus.

Reflection of the eternal Moon of Love
Under whose motions life's dull billows move;
A Metaphor of Spring and Youth and Morning;   120
A Vision like incarnate April, warning,
With smiles and tears, Frost the Anatomy [9]
Into his summer grave.
                        Ah, woe is me!
What have I dared? where am I lifted? how
Shall I descend, and perish not? I know
That Love makes all things equal: I have heard
By mine own heart this joyous truth averred:
The spirit of the worm beneath the sod
In love and worship, blends itself with God.

    Spouse! Sister! Angel! Pilot of the Fate   130
Whose course has been so starless! O too late
Belovèd! O too soon adored, by me!
For in the fields of Immortality
My spirit should at first have worshipped thine,
A divine presence in a place divine;
Or should have moved beside it on this earth,
A shadow of that substance, from its birth;
But not as now:—I love thee; yes, I feel
That on the fountain of my heart a seal
Is set, to keep its waters pure and bright   140
For thee, since in those *tears* thou hast delight.
We—are we not formed, as notes of music are,
For one another, though dissimilar;
Such difference without discord, as can make
Those sweetest sounds, in which all spirits shake
As trembling leaves in a continuous air?

    Thy wisdom speaks in me, and bids me dare
Beacon the rocks on which high hearts are wrecked.
I never was attached to that great sect,
Whose doctrine is, that each one should select   150
Out of the crowd a mistress or a friend,
And all the rest, though fair and wise, commend
To cold oblivion, though it is in the code
Of modern morals, and the beaten road
Which those poor slaves with weary footsteps tread,
Who travel to their home among the dead
By the broad highway of the world, and so
With one chained friend, perhaps a jealous foe,
The dreariest and the longest journey go.

    True Love in this differs from gold and clay,   160
That to divide is not to take away.
Love is like understanding, that grows bright,
Gazing on many truths; 'tis like thy light,
Imagination! which from earth and sky,
And from the depths of human fantasy,

◇◇◇◇◇◇◇◇◇◇◇◇◇◇◇◇◇◇◇◇◇◇◇◇◇◇◇◇◇◇◇

  [9] The skeleton of things.

As from a thousand prisms and mirrors, fills
The Universe with glorious beams, and kills
Error, the worm, with many a sun-like arrow
Of its reverberated lightning. Narrow
The heart that loves, the brain that contemplates,   170
The life that wears, the spirit that creates
One object, and one form, and builds thereby
A sepulchre for its eternity.

    Mind from its object differs most in this:
Evil from good; misery from happiness;
The baser from the nobler; the impure
And frail, from what is clear and must endure.
If you divide suffering and dross, you may
Diminish till it is consumed away;
If you divide pleasure and love and thought,   180
Each part exceeds the whole; and we know not
How much, while any yet remains unshared,
Of pleasure may be gained, of sorrow spared:
This truth is that deep well, whence sages draw
The unenvied light of hope; the eternal law
By which those live, to whom this world of life
Is as a garden ravaged, and whose strife
Tills for the promise of a later birth
The wilderness of this Elysian earth.

    There was a Being whom my spirit oft   190
Met on its visioned wanderings, far aloft,
In the clear golden prime of my youth's dawn,
Upon the fairy isles of sunny lawn,
Amid the enchanted mountains, and the caves
Of divine sleep, and on the air-like waves
Of wonder-level dream, whose tremulous floor
Paved her light steps;—on an imagined shore,
Under the gray beak of some promontory
She met me, robed in such exceeding glory,
That I beheld her not. In solitudes   200
Her voice came to me through the whispering woods,
And from the fountains, and the odours deep
Of flowers, which, like lips murmuring in their sleep
Of the sweet kisses which had lulled them there,
Breathed but of *her* to the enamoured air;
And from the breezes whether low or loud,
And from the rain of every passing cloud,
And from the singing of the summer-birds,
And from all sounds, all silence. In the words
Of antique verse and high romance,—in form,   210
Sound, colour—in whatever checks that Storm
Which with the shattered present chokes the past;
And in that best philosophy, whose taste
Makes this cold common hell, our life, a doom
As glorious as a fiery martyrdom;
Her Spirit was the harmony of truth.—

Then, from the caverns of my dreamy youth
I sprang, as one sandalled with plumes of fire,
And towards the lodestar of my one desire,
I flitted, like a dizzy moth, whose flight   220
Is as a dead leaf's in the owlet light,
When it would seek in Hesper's setting sphere
A radiant death, a fiery sepulchre,
As if it were a lamp of earthly flame.—
But She, whom prayers or tears then could not tame,
Passed, like a God throned on a wingèd planet,
Whose burning plumes to tenfold swiftness fan it,
Into the dreary cone of our life's shade;[10]
And as a man with mighty loss dismayed,   229
I would have followed, though the grave between
Yawned like a gulf whose spectres are unseen:
When a voice said:—'O thou of hearts the weakest,
The phantom is beside thee whom thou seekest.'
Then I—'Where?'—the world's echo answered
        'where?'
And in that silence, and in my despair,
I questioned every tongueless wind that flew
Over my tower of mourning, if it knew
Whither 'twas fled, this soul out of my soul;
And murmured names and spells which have control
Over the sightless tyrants of our fate;   240
But neither prayer nor verse could dissipate
The night which closed on her; nor uncreate
That world within this chaos, mine and me,
Of which she was the veiled Divinity,
The world I say of thoughts that worshipped her:
And therefore I went forth, with hope and fear
And every gentle passion sick to death,
Feeding my course with expectation's breath,
Into the wintry forest of our life;
And struggling through its error with vain strife,   250
And stumbling in my weakness and my haste,
And half bewildered by new forms, I passed,
Seeking among those untaught foresters
If I could find one form resembling hers,
In which she might have masked herself from me.
There,—One, whose voice was venomed melody
Sate by a well, under blue nightshade bowers;
The breath of her false mouth was like faint flowers,
Her touch was as electric poison,—flame
Out of her looks into my vitals came,   260
And from her living cheeks and bosom flew
A killing air, which pierced like honey-dew
Into the core of my green heart, and lay
Upon its leaves; until, as hair grown gray
O'er a young brow, they hid its unblown prime
With ruins of unseasonable time.

In many mortal forms I rashly sought
The shadow of that idol of my thought.
And some were fair—but beauty dies away:
Others were wise—but honeyed words betray: 270
And One was true—oh! why not true to me?
Then, as a hunted deer that could not flee,
I turned upon my thoughts, and stood at bay,
Wounded and weak and panting; the cold day
Trembled, for pity of my strife and pain.
When, like a noonday dawn, there shone again
Deliverance. One stood on my path who seemed
As like the glorious shape which I had dreamed
As is the Moon, whose changes ever run
Into themselves, to the eternal Sun;   280
The cold chaste Moon, the Queen of Heaven's
        bright isles,
Who makes all beautiful on which she smiles,
That wandering shrine of soft yet icy flame
Which ever is transformed, yet still the same,
And warms not but illumines. Young and fair
As the descended Spirit of that sphere,
She hid me, as the Moon may hide the night
From its own darkness, until all was bright
Between the Heaven and Earth of my calm mind,
And, as a cloud charioted by the wind,   290
She led me to a cave in that wild place,
And sate beside me, with her downward face
Illumining my slumbers, like the Moon
Waxing and waning o'er Endymion.
And I was laid asleep, spirit and limb,
And all my being became bright or dim
As the Moon's image in a summer sea,
According as she smiled or frowned on me;
And there I lay, within a chaste cold bed:
Alas, I then was nor alive nor dead:—   300
For at her silver voice came Death and Life,
Unmindful each of their accustomed strife,
Masked like twin babes, a sister and a brother,
The wandering hopes of one abandoned mother,
And through the cavern without wings they flew,
And cried 'Away, he is not of our crew.'
I wept, and though it be a dream, I weep.

What storms then shook the ocean of my sleep,
Blotting that Moon, whose pale and waning lips
Then shrank as in the sickness of eclipse;—   310
And how my soul was as a lampless sea,
And who was then its Tempest; and when She,
The Planet of that hour, was quenched, what frost
Crept o'er those waters, till from coast to coast
The moving billows of my being fell
Into a death of ice, immovable;—
And then—what earthquakes made it gape and split,
The white Moon smiling all the while on it,

These words conceal:—If not, each word would be
The key of staunchless tears. Weep not for me!   320

At length, into the obscure Forest came
The Vision I had sought through grief and shame.
Athwart that wintry wilderness of thorns
Flashed from her motion splendour like the Morn's,
And from her presence life was radiated
Through the gray earth and branches bare and dead;
So that her way was paved, and roofed above
With flowers as soft as thoughts of budding love;
And music from her respiration spread
Like light,—all other sounds were penetrated   330
By the small, still, sweet spirit of that sound,
So that the savage winds hung mute around;
And odours warm and fresh fell from her hair
Dissolving the dull cold in the frore air:
Soft as an Incarnation of the Sun,
When light is changed to love, this glorious One
Floated into the cavern where I lay,
And called my Spirit, and the dreaming clay
Was lifted by the thing that dreamed below
As smoke by fire, and in her beauty's glow   340
I stood, and felt the dawn of my long night
Was penetrating me with living light:
I knew it was the Vision veiled from me
So many years—that it was Emily.

Twin Spheres of light who rule this passive Earth,
This world of love, this *me*; and into birth
Awaken all its fruits and flowers, and dart
Magnetic might into its central heart;
And lift its billows and its mists, and guide
By everlasting laws, each wind and tide   350
To its fit cloud, and its appointed cave;
And lull its storms, each in the craggy grave
Which was its cradle, luring to faint bowers
The armies of the rainbow-wingèd showers;
And, as those married lights, which from the towers
Of Heaven look forth and fold the wandering globe
In liquid sleep and splendour, as a robe;
And all their many-mingled influence blend,
If equal, yet unlike, to one sweet end;—
So ye, bright regents, with alternate sway   360
Govern my sphere of being, night and day!
Thou, not disdaining even a borrowed might;
Thou, not eclipsing a remoter light;
And, through the shadow of the seasons three,
From Spring to Autumn's sere maturity,
Light it into the Winter of the tomb,
Where it may ripen to a brighter bloom.
Thou too, O Comet beautiful and fierce,
Who drew the heart of this frail Universe

Towards thine own; till, wrecked in that convulsion,
Alternating attraction and repulsion,   371
Thine went astray and that was rent in twain;
Oh, float into our azure heaven again!
Be there Love's folding-star at thy return;[11]
The living Sun will feed thee from its urn
Of golden fire; the Moon will veil her horn
In thy last smiles; adoring Even and Morn
Will worship thee with incense of calm breath
And lights and shadows; as the star of Death
And Birth is worshipped by those sisters wild   380
Called Hope and Fear—upon the heart are piled
Their offerings,—of this sacrifice divine
A World shall be the altar.

                        Lady mine,
Scorn not these flowers of thought, the fading birth
Which from its heart of hearts that plant puts forth
Whose fruit, made perfect by thy sunny eyes,
Will be as of the trees of Paradise.

    The day is come, and thou wilt fly with me.
To whatsoe'er of dull mortality
Is mine, remain a vestal sister still;   390
To the intense, the deep, the imperishable,
Not mine but me, henceforth be thou united
Even as a bride, delighting and delighted.
The hour is come:—the destined Star has risen
Which shall descend upon a vacant prison.
The walls are high, the gates are strong, thick set
The sentinels—but true Love never yet
Was thus constrained: it overleaps all fence:
Like lightning, with invisible violence
Piercing its continents; like Heaven's free breath,   400
Which he who grasps can hold not; liker Death,
Who rides upon a thought, and makes his way
Through temple, tower, and palace, and the array
Of arms: more strength has Love than he or they;
For it can burst his charnel, and make free
The limbs in chains, the heart in agony,
The soul in dust and chaos.

                        Emily,
A ship is floating in the harbour now,
A wind is hovering o'er the mountain's brow;
There is a path on the sea's azure floor,   410
No keel has ever ploughed that path before;
The halcyons[12] brood around the foamless isles;
The treacherous Ocean has forsworn its wiles;
The merry mariners are bold and free:
Say, my heart's sister, wilt thou sail with me?

[11] See *The Witch of Atlas*, l. 74, p. 923.
[12] Kingfishers. See note to *Prometheus Unbound*, III, iv, l. 80, p. 877.

Our bark is as an albatross, whose nest
Is a far Eden of the purple East;
And we between her wings will sit, while Night,
And Day, and Storm, and Calm, pursue their
    flight,
Our ministers, along the boundless Sea,   420
Treading each other's heels, unheededly.
It is an isle under Ionian skies,
Beautiful as a wreck of Paradise,
And, for the harbours are not safe and good,
This land would have remained a solitude
But for some pastoral people native there,
Who from the Elysian, clear, and golden air
Draw the last spirit of the age of gold,
Simple and spirited; innocent and bold.
The blue Aegean girds this chosen home,   430
With ever-changing sound and light and foam,
Kissing the sifted sands, and caverns hoar;
And all the winds wandering along the shore
Undulate with the undulating tide:
There are thick woods where sylvan forms abide;
And many a fountain, rivulet, and pond,
As clear as elemental diamond,
Or serene morning air; and far beyond,
The mossy tracks made by the goats and deer   439
(Which the rough shepherd treads but once a year)
Pierce into glades, caverns, and bowers, and halls
Built round with ivy, which the waterfalls
Illumining, with sound that never fails
Accompany the noonday nightingales;
And all the place is peopled with sweet airs;
The light clear element which the isle wears
Is heavy with the scent of lemon-flowers,
Which floats like mist laden with unseen showers,
And falls upon the eyelids like faint sleep;
And from the moss violets and jonquils peep,   450
And dart their arrowy odour through the brain
Till you might faint with that delicious pain.
And every motion, odour, beam, and tone,
With that deep music is in unison:
Which is a soul within the soul—they seem
Like echoes of an antenatal dream.—
It is an isle 'twixt Heaven, Air, Earth, and Sea,
Cradled, and hung in clear tranquillity;
Bright as that wandering Eden Lucifer,
Washed by the soft blue Oceans of young air.   460
It is a favoured place. Famine or Blight,
Pestilence, War and Earthquake, never light
Upon its mountain-peaks; blind vultures, they
Sail onward far upon their fatal way:
The wingèd storms, chanting their thunder-psalm
To other lands, leave azure chasms of calm
Over this isle, or weep themselves in dew,
From which its fields and woods ever renew

Their green and golden immortality.
And from the sea there rise, and from the sky   470
There fall, clear exhalations, soft and bright,
Veil after veil, each hiding some delight,
Which Sun or Moon or zephyr draw aside,
Till the isle's beauty, like a naked bride
Glowing at once with love and loveliness,
Blushes and trembles at its own excess:
Yet, like a buried lamp, a Soul no less
Burns in the heart of this delicious isle,
An atom of th' Eternal, whose own smile
Unfolds itself, and may be felt, not seen   480
O'er the gray rocks, blue waves, and forests green,
Filling their bare and void interstices.—
But the chief marvel of the wilderness
Is a lone dwelling, built by whom or how
None of the rustic island-people know:
'Tis not a tower of strength, though with its height
It overtops the woods; but, for delight,
Some wise and tender Ocean-King, ere crime
Had been invented, in the world's young prime,
Reared it, a wonder of that simple time,   490
An envy of the isles, a pleasure-house
Made sacred to his sister and his spouse.
It scarce seems now a wreck of human art,
But, as it were Titanic; in the heart
Of Earth having assumed its form, then grown
Out of the mountains, from the living stone,
Lifting itself in caverns light and high:
For all the antique and learnèd imagery
Has been erased, and in the place of it
The ivy and the wild-vine interknit   500
The volumes of their many-twining stems;
Parasite flowers illume with dewy gems
The lampless halls, and when they face, the sky
Peeps through their winter-woof of tracery
With moonlight patches, or star atoms keen,
Or fragments of the day's intense serene;—
Working mosaic on their Parian[13] floors.
And, day and night, aloof, from the high towers
And terraces, the Earth and Ocean seem
To sleep in one another's arms, and dream   510
Of waves, flowers, clouds, woods, rocks, and all that
    we
Read in their smiles, and call reality.

This isle and house are mine, and I have vowed
Thee to be lady of the solitude.—
And I have fitted up some chambers there
Looking towards the golden Eastern air,
And level with the living winds, which flow
Like waves above the living waves below.—

---

[13] Marble from the island of Paros.

I have sent books and music there, and all
Those instruments with which high Spirits call   520
The future from its cradle, and the past
Out of its grave, and make the present last
In thoughts and joys which sleep, but cannot die,
Folded within their own eternity.
Our simple life wants little, and true taste
Hires not the pale drudge Luxury, to waste
The scene it would adorn, and therefore still,
Nature with all her children haunts the hill.
The ring-dove, in the embowering ivy, yet
Keeps up her love-lament, and the owls flit   530
Round the evening tower, and the young stars
    glance
Between the quick bats in their twilight dance;
The spotted deer bask in the fresh moonlight
Before our gate, and the slow, silent night
Is measured by the pants of their calm sleep.
Be this our home in life, and when years heap
Their withered hours, like leaves, on our decay,
Let us become the overhanging day,
The living soul of this Elysian isle,
Conscious, inseparable, one. Meanwhile   540
We two will rise, and sit, and walk together,
Under the roof of blue Ionian weather,
And wander in the meadows, or ascend
The mossy mountains, where the blue heavens bend
With lightest winds, to touch their paramour;
Or linger, where the pebble-paven shore,
Under the quick, faint kisses of the sea
Trembles and sparkles as with ecstasy,—
Possessing and possessed by all that is
Within that calm circumference of bliss,   550
And by each other, till to love and live
Be one:—or, at the noontide hour, arrive
Where some old cavern hoar seems yet to keep
The moonlight of the expired night asleep,
Through which the awakened day can never peep;
A veil for our seclusion, close as night's,
Where secure sleep may kill thine innocent lights;
Sleep, the fresh dew of languid love, the rain
Whose drops quench kisses till they burn again.
And we will talk, until thought's melody   560
Become too sweet for utterance, and it die
In words, to live again in looks, which dart
With thrilling tone into the voiceless heart,
Harmonizing silence without a sound.
Our breath shall intermix, our bosoms bound,
And our veins beat together; and our lips
With other eloquence than words, eclipse
The soul that burns between them, and the wells
Which boil under our being's inmost cells,
The fountains of our deepest life, shall be   570
Confused in Passion's golden purity,

As mountain-springs under the morning sun.
We shall become the same, we shall be one
Spirit within two frames, oh! wherefore two?
One passion in twin-hearts, which grows and grew,
Till like two meteors of expanding flame,
Those spheres instinct with it become the same,
Touch, mingle, are transfigured; ever still
Burning, yet ever inconsumable:
In one another's substance finding food,   580
Like flames too pure and light and unimbued
To nourish their bright lives with baser prey,
Which point to Heaven and cannot pass away:
One hope within two wills, one will beneath
Two overshadowing minds, one life, one death,
One Heaven, one Hell, one immortality,
And one annihilation. Woe is me!
The wingèd words on which my soul would pierce
Into the height of Love's rare Universe,
Are chains of lead around its flight of fire—   590
I pant, I sink, I tremble, I expire!

———

Weak Verses, go, kneel at your Sovereign's feet,
And say:—'We are the masters of thy slave;
What wouldest thou with us and ours and thine?'
Then call your sisters from Oblivion's cave,
All singing loud: 'Love's very pain is sweet,
But its reward is in the world divine
Which, if not here, it builds beyond the grave.'
So shall ye live when I am there. Then haste
Over the hearts of men, until ye meet   600
Marina, Vanna, Primus,[14] and the rest,
And bid them love each other and be blessed:
And leave the troop which errs, and which reproves,
And come and be my guest,—for I am Love's.

[1821]   [1821]

———

[14] Shelley's names for Mary, Jane Williams, Edward Williams.

ADONAIS

The name "Adonais" explicitly alludes to the myth of Adonis, Venus's lover who was killed by a wild boar and who was allowed thereafter to spend half the year with Venus, the other half being spent in the underworld with Persephone, who had also fallen in love with him. Shelley's odd spelling of Adonis's name may be the result of early nineteenth-century attempts to identify him with the Hebrew Adonai as a god of fertility.

Shelley and others, among them Byron, ascribed the death of Keats to the effects on him of hostile comments about Endymion *by an anonymous reviewer in the* Quarterly Review *of April, 1818. The onset of tuberculosis, from which Keats actually died, was often linked to disappointment and frustrated love by early nineteenth-century physicians.*

ADONAIS

AN ELEGY ON THE DEATH OF

JOHN KEATS,

AUTHOR OF ENDYMION, HYPERION ETC.

Ἀστὴρ πρὶν μὲν ἔλαμπες ἐνι ζώοισιν Ἑῷος.
νῦν δε θανῶν λαμπεις Ἕσπερος ἐν φθιμένοις.
PLATO.[1]

—⤳⊙⊙⊙⤵—

PREFACE

Φάρμακον ἦλθε, βίων, ποτὶ σὸν στόμα, φάρμακον εἶδες·
Πῶς τευ τοῖς χείλεσσι ποτέδραμε, κοὐκ ἐγλυκάνθη;
Τίς δὲ βροτὸς τοσσοῦτον ἀνάμερος, ἢ κεράσαι τοι,
Ἢ δοῦναι λαλέοντι, τὸ φάρμακον; ἔκφυγεν ᾠδάν,
—MOSCHUS, EPITAPH. BION.[2]

IT is my intention to subjoin to the London edition of this poem a criticism upon the claims of its lamented object to be classed among the writers of the highest genius who have adorned our age. My known repugnance to the narrow principles of taste on which several of his earlier compositions were modelled prove at least that I am an impartial judge. I consider the fragment of *Hyperion* as second to nothing that was ever produced by a writer of the same years.

—◇—◇—◇—◇—◇—◇—◇—◇—◇—◇—◇—◇—◇—◇—

1   "Thou wert the morning star among the living,
        Ere thy fair light had fled;—
    Now, having died, thou art, as Hesperus, giving
        New splendour to the dead."
                            —[Shelley's translation]
The poem is ascribed to Plato in the Greek Anthology (*Anthologia Palatina*, vii, 670).
    2   "Poison came, Bion, to thy mouth—thou didst know poison. To such lips as thine did it come and it was not sweetened? What mortal so cruel that could mix poison for thee, or who could give thee venom that heard thy voice? Surely, he had no music in his soul."—[Moschus' *Epitaph for Bion*, trans. A. Lang]

John Keats died at Rome of a consumption, in his twenty-fourth year, on the — of ——— 1821,[3] and was buried in the romantic and lonely cemetery of the Protestants in that city, under the pyramid which is the tomb of Cestius, and the massy walls and towers, now mouldering and desolate, which formed the circuit of ancient Rome. The cemetery is an open space among the ruins covered in winter with violets and daisies. It might make one in love with death, to think that one should be buried in so sweet a place.

The genius of the lamented person to whose memory I have dedicated these unworthy verses was not less delicate and fragile than it was beautiful; and where cankerworms abound, what wonder, if its young flower was blighted in the bud? The savage criticism on his *Endymion*, which appeared in the *Quarterly Review*, produced the most violent effect on his susceptible mind; the agitation thus originated ended in the rupture of a blood-vessel in the lungs; a rapid consumption ensued, and the succeeding acknowledgments from more candid critics, of the true greatness of his powers, were ineffectual to heal the wound thus wantonly inflicted.

It may be well said that these wretched men know not what they do. They scatter their insults and their slanders without heed as to whether the poisoned shaft lights on a heart made callous by many blows or one like Keats's composed of more penetrable stuff. One of their associates is, to my knowledge, a most base and unprincipled calumniator. As to *Endymion*, was it a poem, whatever might be its defects, to be treated contemptuously by those who had celebrated with various degrees of complacency and panegyric, *Paris*, and *Woman*, and a *Syrian Tale*, and Mrs. Lefanu, and Mr. Barrett, and Mr. Howard Payne, and a long list of the illustrious obscure? Are these the men who in their venal good-nature presumed to draw a parallel between the Rev. Mr. Milman and Lord Byron? What gnat did they strain at here, after having swallowed all those camels? Against what woman taken in adultery dares the foremost of these literary prostitutes to cast his opprobrious stone? Miserable man! you, one of the meanest, have wantonly defaced one of the noblest specimens of the workmanship of God. Nor shall it be your excuse, that, murderer as you are, you have spoken daggers, but used none.

The circumstances of the closing scene of poor Keats's life were not made known to me until the *Elegy*

—◇—◇—◇—◇—◇—◇—◇—◇—◇—◇—◇—◇—◇—◇—

3 Actually his twenty-sixth year, on the twenty-third of February.

was ready for the press. I am given to understand that the wound which his sensitive spirit had received from the criticism of *Endymion* was exasperated at the bitter sense of unrequited benefits; the poor fellow seems to have been hooted from the stage of life, no less by those on whom he had wasted the promise of his genius, than those on whom he had lavished his fortune and his care. He was accompanied to Rome, and attended in his last illness by Mr. Severn, a young artist of the highest promise, who, I have been informed, "almost risked his own life, and sacrificed every prospect, to unwearied attendance upon his dying friend." Had I known these circumstances before the completion of my poem, I should have been tempted to add my feeble tribute of applause to the more solid recompense which the virtuous man finds in the recollection of his own motives. Mr. Severn can dispense with a reward from "such stuff as dreams are made of." His conduct is a golden augury of the success of his future career—may the unextinguished Spirit of his illustrious friend animate the creations of his pencil, and plead against Oblivion for his name!

ADONAIS

I

I WEEP for Adonais—he is dead!
O, weep for Adonais! though our tears
Thaw not the frost which binds so dear a head!
And thou, sad Hour, selected from all years
To mourn our loss, rouse thy obscure compeers,
And teach them thine own sorrow, say: 'With me
Died Adonais; till the Future dares
Forget the Past, his fate and fame shall be
An echo and a light unto eternity!'

II

Where wert thou mighty Mother,[4] when he lay, 10
When thy Son lay, pierced by the shaft which flies
In darkness? where was lorn Urania
When Adonais died? With veilèd eyes,
'Mid listening Echoes, in her Paradise
She sate, while one, with soft enamoured breath,
Rekindled all the fading melodies,
With which, like flowers that mock the corse
    beneath,
He had adorned and hid the coming bulk of Death.

---

[4] The Muse of astronomy, Urania, named in line 12.

III

Oh, weep for Adonais—he is dead!
Wake, melancholy Mother, wake and weep! 20
Yet wherefore? Quench within their burning bed
Thy fiery tears, and let thy loud heart keep
Like his, a mute and uncomplaining sleep;
For he is gone, where all things wise and fair
Descend;—oh, dream not that the amorous Deep
Will yet restore him to the vital air;
Death feeds on his mute voice, and laughs at our
    despair.

IV

Most musical of mourners, weep again!
Lament anew, Urania!—He died,
Who was the Sire of an immortal strain, 30
Blind, old, and lonely, when his country's pride,
The priest, the slave, and the liberticide,
Trampled and mocked with many a loathèd rite
Of lust and blood; he went, unterrified,
Into the gulf of death; but his clear Sprite
Yet reigns o'er earth; the third among the sons of
    light.[5]

V

Most musical of mourners, weep anew!
Not all to that bright station dared to climb;
And happier they their happiness who knew,
Whose tapers yet burn through that night of time
In which suns perished; others more sublime, 41
Struck by the envious wrath of man or god,
Have sunk, extinct in their refulgent prime;
And some yet live, treading the thorny road,
Which leads, through toil and hate, to Fame's serene
    abode.

VI

But now, thy youngest, dearest one, has perished—
The nursling of thy widowhood, who grew,
Like a pale flower by some sad maiden cherished,
And fed with true-love tears, instead of dew;
Most musical of mourners, weep anew! 50
Thy extreme hope, the loveliest and the last,
The bloom, whose petals nipped before they blew
Died on the promise of the fruit, is waste;
The broken lily lies—the storm is overpast.

VII

To that high Capital,[6] where kingly Death
Keeps his pale court in beauty and decay,
He came; and bought, with price of purest breath,
A grave among the eternal.—Come away!

---

[5] Milton, the third epic poet (after Homer and Dante).
[6] Rome.

Haste, while the vault of blue Italian day
Is yet his fitting charnel-roof! while still   60
He lies, as if in dewy sleep he lay;
Awake him not! surely he takes his fill
Of deep and liquid rest, forgetful of all ill.

VIII

He will awake no more, oh, never more!—
Within the twilight chamber spreads apace
The shadow of white Death, and at the door
Invisible Corruption waits to trace
His extreme way to her dim dwelling-place;
The eternal Hunger sits, but pity and awe
Soothe her pale rage, nor dares she to deface   70
So fair a prey, till darkness, and the law
Of change, shall o'er his sleep the mortal curtain draw.

IX

Oh, weep for Adonais!—The quick Dreams,
The passion-wingèd Ministers of thought,
Who were his flocks, whom near the living streams
Of his young spirit he fed, and whom he taught
The love which was its music, wander not,—
Wander no more, from kindling brain to brain,
But droop there, whence they sprung; and mourn
      their lot   79
Round the cold heart, where, after their sweet pain,
They ne'er will gather strength, or find a home again.

X

And one with trembling hands clasps his cold head,
And fans him with her moonlight wings, and cries;
'Our love, our hope, our sorrow, is not dead;
See, on the silken fringe of his faint eyes,
Like dew upon a sleeping flower, there lies
A tear some Dream has loosened from his brain.'
Lost Angel of a ruined Paradise!
She knew not 'twas her own; as with no stain
She faded, like a cloud which had outwept its rain.   90

XI

One from a lucid urn of starry dew
Washed his light limbs as if embalming them;
Another clipped her profuse locks, and threw
The wreath upon him, like an anadem,
Which frozen tears instead of pearls begem;
Another in her wilful grief would break
Her bow and wingèd reeds, as if to stem
A greater loss with one which was more weak;
And dull the barbèd fire against his frozen cheek.

XII

Another Splendour on his mouth alit,   100
That mouth, whence it was wont to draw the breath
Which gave it strength to pierce the guarded wit,
And pass into the panting heart beneath
With lightning and with music: the damp death
Quenched its caress upon his icy lips;
And, as a dying meteor stains a wreath
Of moonlight vapour, which the cold night clips,
It flushed through his pale limbs, and passed to its
      eclipse.

XIII

And others came . . . Desires and Adorations,
Wingèd Persuasions and veiled Destinies,   110
Splendours, and Glooms, and glimmering
      Incarnations
Of hopes and fears, and twilight Phantasies;
And Sorrow, with her family of Sighs,
And Pleasure, blind with tears, led by the gleam
Of her own dying smile instead of eyes,
Came in slow pomp;—the moving pomp might
      seem
Like pageantry of mist on an autumnal stream.

XIV

All he had loved, and moulded into thought,
From shape, and hue, and odour, and sweet sound,
Lamented Adonais. Morning sought   120
Her eastern watch-tower, and her hair unbound,
Wet with the tears which should adorn the ground,
Dimmed the aëreal eyes that kindle day;
Afar the melancholy thunder moaned,
Pale Ocean in unquiet slumber lay,
And the wild Winds flew round, sobbing in their
      dismay.

XV

Lost Echo sits amid the voiceless mountains,
And feeds her grief with his remembered lay,
And will no more reply to winds or fountains,
Or amorous birds perched on the young green
      spray,
Or herdsman's horn, or bell at closing day;
Since she can mimic not his lips, more dear   131
Than those for whose disdain she pined away
Into a shadow of all sounds:—a drear
Murmur, between their songs, is all the woodmen
      hear.

XVI

Grief made the young Spring wild, and she threw
      down
Her kindling buds, as if she Autumn were,
Or they dead leaves; since her delight is flown,
For whom should she have waked the sullen year?

To Phoebus was not Hyacinth so dear   140
Nor to himself Narcissus, as to both [7]
Thou, Adonais: wan they stand and sere
Amid the faint companions of their youth,
With dew all turned to tears; odour, to sighing ruth.

XVII

Thy spirit's sister, the lorn nightingale
Mourns not her mate with such melodious pain;
Not so the eagle, who like thee could scale
Heaven, and could nourish in the sun's domain
Her mighty youth with morning, doth complain,
Soaring and screaming round her empty nest,   150
As Albion wails for thee: the curse of Cain
Light on his head who pierced thy innocent breast,
And scared the angel soul that was its earthly guest!

XVIII

Ah, woe is me! Winter is come and gone,
But grief returns with the revolving year;
The airs and streams renew their joyous tone;
The ants, the bees, the swallows reappear;
Fresh leaves and flowers deck the dead Seasons'
The amorous birds now pair in every brake,   [bier;
And build their mossy homes in field and brere;
And the green lizard, and the golden snake,   161
Like unimprisoned flames, out of their trance awake.

XIX

Through wood and stream and field and hill and
    Ocean
A quickening life from the Earth's heart has burst
As it has ever done, with change and motion,
From the great morning of the world when first
God dawned on Chaos; in its stream immersed,
The lamps of Heaven flash with a softer light;
All baser things pant with life's sacred thirst;
Diffuse themselves; and spend in love's delight,
The beauty and the joy of their renewèd might.   171

XX

The leprous corpse, touched by this spirit tender,
Exhales itself in flowers of gentle breath;
Like incarnations of the stars, when splendour
Is changed to fragrance, they illumine death
And mock the merry worm that wakes beneath;
Nought we know, dies. Shall that alone which
Be as a sword consumed before the sheath   [knows
By sightless lightning?—the intense atom glows
A moment, then is quenched in a most cold repose.

---

7 Both Hyacinth, accidentally slain by Apollo (*Prometheus Unbound*, II, i, 140), and Narcissus, who fell in love with his own reflection and drowned, were changed into flowers.

XXI

Alas! that all we loved of him should be,   181
But for our grief, as if it had not been,
And grief itself be mortal! Woe is me!
Whence are we, and why are we? of what scene
The actors or spectators? Great and mean
Meet massed in death, who lends what life must
    borrow.
As long as skies are blue, and fields are green,
Evening must usher night, night urge the morrow,
Month follow month with woe, and year wake year to
    sorrow.

XXII

He will awake no more, oh, never more!   190
'Wake thou,' cried Misery, 'childless Mother, rise
Out of thy sleep, and slake, in thy heart's core,
A wound more fierce than his, with tears and sighs.'
And all the Dreams that watched Urania's eyes,
And all the Echoes whom their sister's song
Had held in holy silence, cried: 'Arise!'
Swift as a Thought by the snake Memory stung,
From her ambrosial rest the fading Splendour sprung.

XXIII

She rose like an autumnal Night, that springs
Out of the East, and follows wild and drear   200
The golden Day, which, on eternal wings,
Even as a ghost abandoning a bier,
Had left the Earth a corpse. Sorrow and fear
So struck, so roused, so rapt Urania;
So saddened round her like an atmosphere
Of stormy mist; so swept her on her way
Even to the mournful place where Adonais lay.

XXIV

Out of her secret Paradise she sped,
Through camps and cities rough with stone, and
    steel,
And human hearts, which to her aery tread   210
Yielding not, wounded the invisible
Palms of her tender feet where'er they fell:
And barbèd tongues, and thoughts more sharp than
    they,
Rent the soft Form they never could repel,
Whose sacred blood, like the young tears of May,
Paved with eternal flowers that undeserving way.

XXV

In the death-chamber for a moment Death,
Shamed by the presence of that living Might,
Blushed to annihilation, and the breath
Revisited those lips, and Life's pale light   220

Flashed through those limbs, so late her dear
    delight.
'Leave me not wild and drear and comfortless,
As silent lightning leaves the starless night!
Leave me not!' cried Urania: her distress
Roused Death: Death rose and smiled, and met her
    vain caress.

XXVI

'Stay yet awhile! speak to me once again;
Kiss me, so long but as a kiss may live;
And in my heartless breast and burning brain
That word, that kiss, shall all thoughts else survive,
With food of saddest memory kept alive,   230
Now thou art dead, as if it were a part
Of thee, my Adonais! I would give
All that I am to be as thou now art!
But I am chained to Time, and cannot thence depart!

XXVII

'O gentle child, beautiful as thou wert,
Why didst thou leave the trodden paths of men
Too soon, and with weak hands though mighty
    heart
Dare the unpastured dragon in his den?
Defenceless as thou wert, oh, where was then
Wisdom the mirrored shield, or scorn the spear?[8]
Or hadst thou waited the full cycle, when   241
Thy spirit should have filled its crescent sphere,
The monsters of life's waste had fled from thee like
    deer.

XXVIII

'The herded wolves, bold only to pursue;
The obscene ravens, clamorous o'er the dead;
The vultures to the conqueror's banner true
Who feed where Desolation first has fed,
And whose wings rain contagion;—how they fled,
When, like Apollo, from his golden bow
The Pythian of the age[9] one arrow sped   250
And smiled!—The spoilers tempt no second blow,
They fawn on the proud feet that spurn them lying
    low.

XXIX

'The sun comes forth, and many reptiles spawn;
He sets, and each ephemeral insect then
Is gathered into death without a dawn,
And the immortal stars awake again;
So is it in the world of living men:
A godlike mind soars forth, in its delight   258
Making earth bare and veiling heaven, and when
It sinks, the swarms that dimmed or shared its light
Leave to its kindred lamps the spirit's awful night.'

XXX

Thus ceased she: and the mountain shepherds
    came,
Their garlands sere, their magic mantles rent;
The Pilgrim of Eternity, whose fame
Over his living head like Heaven is bent,
An early but enduring monument,
Came, veiling all the lightnings of his song
In sorrow; from her wilds Ierne sent
The sweetest lyrist of her saddest wrong,
And Love taught Grief to fall like music from his
    tongue.   270

XXXI

Midst others of less note, came one frail Form,[10]
A phantom among men; companionless
As the last cloud of an expiring storm
Whose thunder is its knell; he, as I guess,
Had gazed on Nature's naked loveliness,
Actaeon-like, and now he fled astray[11]
With feeble steps o'er the world's wilderness,
And his own thoughts, along that rugged way,
Pursued, like raging hounds, their father and their
    prey.

XXXII

A pardlike Spirit beautiful and swift—   280
A Love in desolation masked;—a Power
Girt round with weakness;—it can scarce uplift
The weight of the superincumbent hour;
It is a dying lamp, a falling shower,
A breaking billow;—even whilst we speak
Is it not broken? On the withering flower
The killing sun smiles brightly: on a cheek
The life can burn in blood, even while the heart may
    break.

XXXIII

His head was bound with pansies overblown,
And faded violets, white, and pied, and blue;   290
And a light spear topped with a cypress cone,
Round whose rude shaft dark ivy-tresses grew
Yet dripping with the forest's noonday dew,
Vibrated, as the ever-beating heart
Shook the weak hand that grasped it; of that crew
He came the last, neglected and apart;
A herd-abandoned deer struck by the hunter's dart.

XXXIV

All stood aloof, and at his partial moan
Smiled through their tears; well knew that gentle
    band   300
Who in another's fate now wept his own,
As in the accents of an unknown land

---

[8] Perseus could kill Medusa only by looking at her reflection in his shield, because to look directly at her was fatal.

[9] Byron; the Pythian, literally, is Apollo.

[10] Shelley himself.

[11] Acteon, who saw Diana bathing naked, was turned into a stag and killed by his own dogs.

He sung new sorrow; sad Urania scanned
The Stranger's mien, and murmured: 'Who art
He answered not, but with a sudden hand   [thou?'
Made bare his branded and ensanguined brow,
Which was like Cain's or Christ's—oh! that it should
  be so![12]

XXXV

What softer voice is hushed over the dead?
Athwart what brow is that dark mantle thrown?
What form leans sadly o'er the white death-bed,
In mockery of monumental stone,   310
The heavy heart heaving without a moan?
If it be He,[13] who, gentlest of the wise,
Taught, soothed, loved, honoured the departed one,
Let me not vex, with inharmonious sighs,
The silence of that heart's accepted sacrifice.

XXXVI

Our Adonais has drunk poison—oh!
What deaf and viperous murderer could crown
Life's early cup with such a draught of woe?
The nameless worm would now itself disown:
It felt, yet could escape, the magic tone   320
Whose prelude held all envy, hate, and wrong,
But what was howling in one breast alone,
Silent with expectation of the song,
Whose master's hand is cold, whose silver lyre
  unstrung.

XXXVII

Live thou, whose infamy is not thy fame!
Live! fear no heavier chastisement from me,
Thou noteless blot on a remembered name!
But be thyself, and know thyself to be!
And ever at thy season be thou free
To spill the venom when thy fangs o'erflow;   330
Remorse and Self-contempt shall cling to thee;
Hot Shame shall burn upon thy secret brow,
And like a beaten hound tremble thou shalt—as now.

XXXVIII

Nor let us weep that our delight is fled
Far from these carrion kites that scream below;
He wakes or sleeps with the enduring dead;
Thou canst not soar where he is sitting now.[14]—
Dust to the dust! but the pure spirit shall flow
Back to the burning fountain whence it came,
A portion of the Eternal, which must glow   340
Through time and change, unquenchably the same,
Whilst thy cold embers choke the sordid hearth of
  shame.

---

[12] Though Cain (because he committed the first murder) was
the enemy of mankind and Christ the savior, both were outcasts.
[13] Leigh Hunt, who was an early influence on Keats, and later
coeditor (with Byron and Shelley) of the *Liberal*.
[14] I.e., the reviewer, the "nameless worm" of stanza XXXVI.

XXXIX

Peace, peace! he is not dead, he doth not sleep—
He hath awakened from the dream of life—
'Tis we, who lost in stormy visions, keep
With phantoms an unprofitable strife,
And in mad trance, strike with our spirit's knife
Invulnerable nothings.—*We* decay
Like corpses in a charnel; fear and grief
Convulse us and consume us day by day,   350
And cold hopes swarm like worms within our living
  clay.

XL

He has outsoared the shadow of our night;
Envy and calumny and hate and pain,
And that unrest which men miscall delight,
Can touch him not and torture not again;
From the contagion of the world's slow stain
He is secure, and now can never mourn
A heart grown cold, a head grown gray in vain;
Nor, when the spirit's self has ceased to burn,
With sparkless ashes load an unlamented urn.   360

XLI

He lives, he wakes—'tis Death is dead, not he;
Mourn not for Adonais.—Thou young Dawn,
Turn all thy dew to splendour, for from thee
The spirit thou lamentest is not gone;
Ye caverns and ye forests, cease to moan!
Cease, ye faint flowers and fountains, and thou Air,
Which like a mourning veil thy scarf hadst thrown
O'er the abandoned Earth, now leave it bare
Even to the joyous stars which smile on its despair!

XLII

He is made one with Nature: there is heard   370
His voice in all her music, from the moan
Of thunder, to the song of night's sweet bird;
He is a presence to be felt and known
In darkness and in light, from herb and stone,
Spreading itself where'er that Power may move
Which has withdrawn his being to its own;
Which wields the world with never-wearied love,
Sustains it from beneath, and kindles it above.

XLIII

He is a portion of the loveliness
Which once he made more lovely: he doth bear
His part, while the one Spirit's plastic stress   381
Sweeps through the dull dense world, compelling
All new successions to the forms they wear;   [there,
Torturing th' unwilling dross that checks its flight
To its own likeness, as each mass may bear;
And bursting in its beauty and its might
From trees and beasts and men into the Heaven's
  light.

XLIV

The splendours of the firmament of time
May be eclipsed, but are extinguished not;
Like stars to their appointed height they climb,   390
And death is a low mist which cannot blot
The brightness it may veil. When lofty thought
Lifts a young heart above its mortal lair,
And love and life contend in it, for what
Shall be its earthly doom, the dead live there
And move like winds of light on dark and stormy air.

XLV

The inheritors of unfulfilled renown
Rose from their thrones, built beyond mortal
    thought,
Far in the Unapparent. Chatterton
Rose pale,—his solemn agony had not   400
Yet faded from him; Sidney, as he fought
And as he fell and as he lived and loved
Sublimely mild, a Spirit without spot,
Arose; and Lucan, by his death approved:
Oblivion as they rose shrank like a thing reproved.[15]

XLVI

And many more, whose names on Earth are dark,
But whose transmitted effluence cannot die
So long as fire outlives the parent spark,
Rose, robed in dazzling immortality.
'Thou art become as one of us,' they cry,   410
'It was for thee yon kingless sphere has long
Swung blind in unascended majesty,
Silent alone amid an Heaven of Song.
Assume thy wingèd throne, thou Vesper of our
    throng!'

XLVII

Who mourns for Adonais? Oh, come forth,
Fond wretch! and know thyself and him aright.
Clasp with thy panting soul the pendulous Earth;
As from a centre, dart thy spirit's light
Beyond all worlds, until its spacious might
Satiate the void circumference: then shrink   420
Even to a point within our day and night;
And keep thy heart light lest it make thee sink
When hope has kindled hope, and lured thee to the
    brink.

XLVIII

Or go to Rome, which is the sepulchre,[16]
Oh, not of him, but of our joy: 'tis nought
That ages, empires, and religions there
Lie buried in the ravage they have wrought;
For such as he can lend,—they borrow not
Glory from those who made the world their prey;
And he is gathered to the kings of thought   430
Who waged contention with their time's decay,
And of the past are all that cannot pass away.

XLIX

Go thou to Rome,—at once the Paradise,
The grave, the city, and the wilderness;
And where its wrecks like shattered mountains rise,
And flowering weeds, and fragrant copses dress
The bones of Desolation's nakedness
Pass, till the spirit of the spot shall lead
Thy footsteps to a slope of green access
Where, like an infant's smile, over the dead   440
A light of laughing flowers along the grass is spread;

L

And gray walls moulder round, on which dull Time
Feeds, like slow fire upon a hoary brand;
And one keen pyramid with wedge sublime,[17]
Pavilioning the dust of him who planned
This refuge for his memory, doth stand
Like flame transformed to marble; and beneath,
A field is spread, on which a newer band
Have pitched in Heaven's smile their camp of
    death,
Welcoming him we lose with scarce extinguished
    breath.   450

LI

Here pause: these graves are all too young as yet
To have outgrown the sorrow which consigned
Its charge to each; and if the seal is set,
Here, on one fountain of a mourning mind,[18]
Break it not thou! too surely shalt thou find
Thine own well full, if thou returnest home,
Of tears and gall. From the world's bitter wind
Seek shelter in the shadow of the tomb.
What Adonais is, why fear we to become?

LII

The One remains, the many change and pass;   460
Heaven's light forever shines, Earth's shadows fly;
Life, like a dome of many-coloured glass,
Stains the white radiance of Eternity.

---

[15] Chatterton killed himself at seventeen (see Coleridge's poem, p. 430), the Roman poet Lucan at twenty-six; Sir Philip Sidney (1554–1586) died at thirty-two in battle in the war with Spain.

[16] Keats, who died in Rome, is buried in the Protestant cemetery there.

[17] The tomb of Caius Cestus, a Roman tribune.

[18] Shelley's son William, who died at the age of three and a half, was buried there in 1819.

Until Death tramples it to fragments.—Die,
If thou wouldst be with that which thou dost seek!
Follow where all is fled!—Rome's azure sky,
Flowers, ruins, statues, music, words, are weak
The glory they transfuse with fitting truth to speak.

LIII

Why linger, why turn back, why shrink, my Heart?
Thy hopes are gone before: from all things here
They have departed; thou shouldst now depart!
A light is passed from the revolving year,   472
And man, and woman; and what still is dear
Attracts to crush, repels to make thee wither.
The soft sky smiles,—the low wind whispers near:
'Tis Adonais calls! oh, hasten thither,
No more let Life divide what Death can join together.

LIV

That Light whose smile kindles the Universe,
That Beauty in which all things work and move,
That Benediction which the eclipsing Curse   480
Of birth can quench not, that sustaining Love
Which through the web of being blindly wove
By man and beast and earth and air and sea,
Burns bright or dim, as each are mirrors of
The fire for which all thirst; now beams on me,
Consuming the last clouds of cold mortality.

LV

The breath whose might I have invoked in song
Descends on me; my spirit's bark is driven,
Far from the shore, far from the trembling throng
Whose sails were never to the tempest given;   490
The massy earth and spherèd skies are riven!
I am borne darkly, fearfully, afar;
Whilst, burning through the inmost veil of Heaven,
The soul of Adonais, like a star,
Beacons from the abode where the Eternal are.

[1821]   [1821]

TO NIGHT

I

SWIFTLY walk over the western Wave,
          Spirit of Night!
Out of the misty eastern cave
Where, all the long and lone daylight,
Thou wovest dreams of joy and fear,
Which make thee terrible and dear,—
          Swift be thy flight!

[1821]

II

Wrap thy form in a mantle grey,
          Star-inwrought!
Blind with thine hair the eyes of Day,   10
Kiss her until she be wearied out,
Then wander o'er city, and sea, and land,
Touching all with thine opiate wand—
          Come, long-sought!

III

When I arose and saw the dawn,
          I sighed for thee;
When Light rode high, and the dew was gone,
And noon lay heavy on flower and tree,
And the weary Day turned to his rest,
Lingering like an unloved guest,   20
          I sighed for thee.

IV

Thy brother Death came, and cried,
          Wouldst thou me?
Thy sweet child Sleep, the filmy-eyed,
          Murmured like a noon-tide bee,
Shall I nestle near thy side?
Wouldst thou me?—And I replied,
          No, . . . not thee!

V

Death will come when thou art dead,
          Soon, too soon—   30
Sleep will come when thou art fled;
Of neither would I ask the boon
I ask of thee, belovèd Night—
Swift be thine approaching flight,
          Come soon, soon!

[1824]

TO ——

["Music, when soft voices die"]

MUSIC, when soft voices die,
Vibrates in the memory—
Odours, when sweet violets sicken,
Live within the sense they quicken.

Rose leaves, when the rose is dead,
Are heaped for the belovèd's bed;
And so thy thoughts, when thou art gone,
Love itself shall slumber on.

[1824]

SONG
["Rarely, rarely . . ."]

I

RARELY, rarely, comest thou,
  Spirit of Delight!
Wherefore hast thou left me now
  Many a day and night?
Many a weary night and day
'Tis since thou art fled away.

II

How shall ever one like me
  Win thee back again?
With the joyous and the free
  Thou wilt scoff at pain.   10
Spirit false! that hast forgot
All but those who need thee not.

III

As a lizard with the shade
  Of a trembling leaf,
Thou with sorrow art dismayed;
  Even the sighs of grief
Reproach thee, that thou art not near,
And reproach thou wilt not hear.

IV

Let me set my mournful ditty
  To a merry measure;—   20
Thou wilt never come for pity—
  Thou wilt come for pleasure;—
Pity then will cut away
Those cruel wings, and thou wilt stay—

V

I love all that thou lovest,
  Spirit of Delight!
The fresh Earth in new leaves drest,
  And the starry night,
Autumn evening, and the morn
When the golden mists are born.   30

VI

I love snow, and all the forms
  Of the radiant frost;
I love waves, and winds, and storms—
  Everything almost
Which is Nature's, and may be
Untainted by man's misery.

[1821]

VII

I love tranquil solitude,
  And such society
As is quiet, wise, and good;
  Between thee and me   40
What difference? but thou dost possess
The things I seek—not love them less.

VIII

I love Love—though he has wings,
  And like light can flee—
But, above all other things,
  Spirit, I love thee—
Thou art Love and Life! O come,
Make once more my heart thy home.

[1824]

MUTABILITY [II]

I

THE flower that smiles to-day
  To-morrow dies;
All that we wish to stay,
  Tempts and then flies.
What is this world's delight?
Lightning that mocks the night,
  Brief even as bright.

II

Virtue, how frail it is!
  Friendship how rare!
Love, how it sells poor bliss   10
  For proud despair!
But we, though soon they fall,
Survive their joy, and all
  Which ours we call.

III

Whilst skies are blue and bright,
  Whilst flowers are gay,
Whilst eyes that change ere night
  Make glad the day;
Whilst yet the calm hours creep,
Dream thou—and from thy sleep   20
  Then wake to weep.

[1824]

LINES

WRITTEN ON HEARING THE NEWS OF
THE DEATH OF NAPOLEON

WHAT! alive and so bold, O Earth?
  Art thou not overbold?
What! leapest thou forth as of old
  In the light of thy morning mirth,
The last of the flock of the starry fold?
Ha! leapest thou forth as of old?
Are not the limbs still when the ghost is fled,
And canst thou move, Napoleon being dead?

How! is not thy quick heart cold?
  What spark is alive on thy hearth?   10
How! is not *his* death-knell knolled?
  And livest *thou* still, Mother Earth?
Thou wert warming thy fingers old
O'er the embers covered and cold
Of that most fiery spirit, when it fled—
What, Mother, do you laugh now he is dead?

"Who has known of me of old," replied Earth,
  "Or who has my story told?
It is thou who art overbold."
  And the lightning of scorn laughed forth   20
As she sung, "to my bosom I fold
All my sons when their knell is knolled,
And so with living motion all are fed,
And the quick spring like weeds out of the dead.

"Still alive and still bold," shouted Earth,
  "I grow bolder, and still more bold.
The dead fill me ten thousandfold
  Fuller of speed, and splendour, and mirth;
I was cloudy, and sullen and cold,
Like a frozen chaos uprolled,   30
Till by the spirit of the mighty dead
My heart grew warm. I feed on whom I fed.

"Ay, alive and still bold," muttered Earth,
  "Napoleon's fierce spirit rolled,
In terror, and blood, and gold,
  A torrent of ruin to death from his birth.
Leave the millions who follow to mould
The metal before it be cold,   38
And weave into his shame, which like the dead
Shrouds me, the hopes that from his glory fled."

[1821]   [1822]

A LAMENT

I

O WORLD! O life! O time!
On whose last steps I climb,
  Trembling at that where I had stood before;
When will return the glory of your prime?
  No more—Oh, never more!

II

Out of the day and night
A joy has taken flight:
  Fresh spring, and summer, and winter hoar,
Move my faint heart with grief, but with delight
  No more—Oh, never more!   10

[1821]   [1824]

TO ——

["One word is too often profaned"]

I

ONE word is too often profaned
  For me to profane it,
One feeling too falsely disdained
  For thee to disdain it.
One hope is too like despair
  For prudence to smother,
And Pity from thee more dear
  Than that from another.

II

I can give not what men call love,
  But wilt thou accept not   10
The worship the heart lifts above
  And the Heavens reject not:
The desire of the moth for the star,
  Of the night for the morrow,
The devotion to something afar
  From the sphere of our sorrow?

[1821]   [1824]

TO ——

["When passion's trance . . ."]

I

WHEN passion's trance is overpast,
If tenderness and truth could last
Or live, whilst all wild feelings keep
Some mortal slumber, dark and deep,
I should not weep, I should not weep!

II

It were enough to feel, to see
Thy soft eyes gazing tenderly,
And dream the rest—and burn and be
The secret food of fires unseen,
Couldst thou but be as thou hast been.   10

III

After the slumber of the year
The woodland violets re-appear;
All things revive in field or grove,
And sky and sea; but two, which move,
And form all others, life and love.

[1821]   [1824]

EVENING

PONTE A MARE, PISA

I

THE sun is set; the swallows are asleep;
  The bats are flitting fast in the grey air;
The slow soft toads out of damp corners creep;
  And evening's breath, wandering here and there
Over the quivering surface of the stream,
Wakes not one ripple from its summer dream.

II

There are no dews on the dry grass to-night,
  Nor damp within the shadow of the trees;
The wind is intermitting, dry, and light;
  And in the inconstant motion of the breeze   10
The dust and straws are driven up and down,
And whirled about the pavement of the town.

III

Within the surface of the fleeting river
  The wrinkled image of the mountain lay,
Immovably unquiet, and forever
  It trembles, but it never fades away;
Go to the . . .
You, being changed, will find it then as now.

IV

The chasm in which the sun has sunk, is shut
  By darkest barriers of cinereous cloud,   20
Like mountain over mountain huddled—but
  Growing and moving upwards in a crowd,
And over it a space of watery blue,
Which the keen evening star is shining through.

[1821]   [1824]

SONNET TO BYRON

[I AM afraid these verses will not please you, but]
If I esteemed you less, Envy would kill
Pleasure, and leave to Wonder and Despair
The ministration of the thoughts that fill
The mind which, like a worm whose life may share
A portion of the unapproachable,
Marks your creations rise as fast and fair
As perfect worlds at the Creator's will.
But such is my regard that nor your power
To soar above the heights where others [climb],   10
Nor fame, that shadow of the unborn hour
Cast from the envious future on the time,
Moves one regret for his unhonoured name
Who dares these words:—the worm beneath the sod
May lift itself in homage of the God.

[1821]   [1832, 1870]

[Fragment]
ON KEATS

WHO DESIRED THAT ON HIS TOMB
SHOULD BE INSCRIBED—

"HERE lieth One whose name was writ on water!"
  But, ere the breath that could erase it blew,
Death, in remorse for that fell slaughter,
  Death, the immortalizing winter, flew
  Athwart the stream—and time's printless torrent
    grew
A scroll of crystal, blazoning the name
  Of Adonais!—

[1821]   [1839]

___

TO EDWARD WILLIAMS

The friendship between the Shelleys and Edward and Jane Williams began in Pisa at the beginning of 1821. In April, Shelley and Williams, a former army officer, almost drowned in a sailing accident; together they planned the building of the Don Juan *early in 1822, and Williams was drowned with Shelley in July. The poems to Jane are addressed to Mrs. Williams.*

___

TO EDWARD WILLIAMS

I

THE serpent [1] is shut out from Paradise.
  The wounded deer must seek the herb no more
    In which its heart's cure lies:
    The widowed dove must cease to haunt a bower

---
[1] Shelley's nickname was "The Snake."

Like that from which its mate with feignèd sighs
    Fled in the April hour.
    I too must seldom seek again
Near happy friends a mitigated pain.

II

Of hatred I am proud,—with scorn content;
    Indifference, that once hurt me, is now grown 10
    Itself indifferent;
    But, not to speak of love, pity alone
Can break a spirit already more than bent.
    The miserable one
    Turns the mind's poison into food,—
Its medicine is tears,—its evil, good.

III

Therefore, if now I see you seldomer,
    Dear friends, dear *friend!* know that I only fly
    Your looks, because they stir 19
    Griefs that should sleep, and hopes that cannot die.
The very comfort that they minister
    I scarce can bear, yet I,
    So deeply is the arrow gone,
Should quickly perish if it were withdrawn.

IV

When I return to my cold home, you ask
    Why I am not as I have ever been.
    You spoil me for the task
Of acting a forced part in life's dull scene,—
Of wearing on my brow the idle mask
    Of author, great or mean, 30
    In the world's carnival. I sought
Peace thus, and but in you I found it not.

V

Full half an hour, to-day, I tried my lot
    With various flowers, and every one still said,
    "She loves me—loves me not."
    And if this meant a vision long since fled—
If it meant fortune, fame, or peace of thought—
    If it meant,—but I dread
    To speak what you may know too well:
Still there was truth in the sad oracle. 40

VI

The crane o'er seas and forests seeks her home;
    No bird so wild but has its quiet nest
    When it no more would roam;
    The sleepless billows on the ocean's breast
Break like a bursting heart, and die in foam,
    And thus at length find rest:
    Doubtless there is a place of peace
Where *my* weak heart and all its throbs will cease.

VII

I asked her, yesterday, if she believed
    That I had resolution. One who *had* 50
    Would ne'er have thus relieved
    His heart with words,—but what his judgement
    bade
Would do, and leave the scorner unrelieved.
    These verses are too sad
    To send to you, but that I know,
Happy yourself, you feel another's woe.

[1822?]   [1834]

LINES

["When the lamp is shattered"]

I

WHEN the lamp is shattered,
The light in the dust lies dead—
    When the cloud is scattered,
The rainbow's glory is shed.
    When the lute is broken,
Sweet tones are remembered not;
    When the lips have spoken,
Loved accents are soon forgot.

II

    As music and splendour
Survive not the lamp and the lute, 10
    The heart's echoes render
No song when the spirit is mute:—
    No song but sad dirges,
Like the wind through a ruined cell,
    Or the mournful surges
That ring the dead seaman's knell.

III

    When hearts have once mingled,
Love first leaves the well-built nest;
    The weak one is singled
To endure what it once possesst. 20
    O, Love! who bewailest
The frailty of all things here,
    Why choose you the frailest
For your cradle, your home, and your bier?

IV

    Its passions will rock thee,
As the storms rock the ravens on high;
    Bright reason will mock thee,
Like the sun from a wintry sky.

From thy nest every rafter
Will rot, and thine eagle home   30
Leave thee naked to laughter,
When leaves fall and cold winds come.

[1822]   [1824]

TO JANE: THE INVITATION

BEST and brightest, come away,
Fairer far than this fair Day,
Which, like thee to those in sorrow,
Comes to bid a sweet good-morrow
To the rough year just awake
In its cradle on the brake.
The brightest hour of unborn Spring,
Through the winter wandering,
Found, it seems, the halcyon Morn,
To hoar February born;   10
Bending from Heaven, in azure mirth,
It kissed the forehead of the earth,
And smiled upon the silent sea,
And bade the frozen streams be free,
And waked to music all their fountains,
And breathed upon the frozen mountains,
And like a prophetess of May.
Strewed flowers upon the barren way,
Making the wintry world appear
Like one on whom thou smilest, dear.   20

Away, away, from men and towns,
To the wild wood and the downs—
To the silent wilderness
Where the soul need not repress
Its music lest it should not find
An echo in another's mind,
While the touch of Nature's art
Harmonizes heart to heart.
I leave this notice on my door
For each accustomed visitor:—   30
"I am gone into the fields
To take what this sweet hour yields;—
Reflection, you may come to-morrow,
Sit by the fireside with Sorrow.—
You with the unpaid bill, Despair,—
You, tiresome verse-reciter, Care,—
I will pay you in the grave,—
Death will listen to your stave.
Expectation too, be off!
To-day is for itself enough;   40
Hope, in pity mock not Woe
With smiles, nor follow where I go;

Long having lived on thy sweet food,
At length I find one moment's good
After long pain—with all your love,
This you never told me of."

Radiant Sister of the Day,
Awake! arise! and come away!
To the wild woods and the plains,
And the pools where winter rains   50
Image all their roof of leaves,
Where the pine its garland weaves
Of sapless green, and ivy dun,
Round stems that never kiss the sun,
Where the lawns and pastures be
And the sandhills of the sea;—
Where the melting hoar-frost wets
The daisy-star that never sets,
And wind-flowers and violets,
Which yet join not scent to hue,   60
Crown the pale year weak and new;
When the night is left behind
In the deep east, dun and blind,
And the blue noon is over us,
And the multitudinous
Billows murmur at our feet,
Where the earth and ocean meet,
And all things seem only one
In the universal sun.

[1822]   [1839]

TO JANE: THE RECOLLECTION

I

NOW the last day of many days,
All beautiful and bright as thou,
The loveliest and the last, is dead,
Rise, Memory, and write its praise!
Up!—to thy wonted work! come, trace
The epitaph of glory fled,
For now the Earth has changed its face,
A frown is on the Heaven's brow.

II

We wandered to the pine forest
That skirts the Ocean's foam,   10
The lightest wind was in its nest,
The tempest in its home.
The whispering waves were half asleep,
The clouds were gone to play,
And on the bosom of the deep
The smile of Heaven lay;

It seemed as if the hour were one
  Sent from beyond the skies,
Which scattered from above the sun
  A light of Paradise.   20

III

We paused amid the pines that stood
  The giants of the waste,
Tortured by storms to shapes as rude
  As serpents interlaced,
And soothed by every azure breath,
  That under Heaven is blown,
To harmonies and hues beneath,
  As tender as its own;
Now all the tree tops lay asleep,
  Like green waves on the sea,   30
As still as in the silent deep
  The ocean woods may be.

IV

How calm it was!—the silence there
  By such a chain was bound,
That even the busy wood-pecker
  Made stiller by her sound
The inviolable quietness;
  The breath of peace we drew
With its soft motion made not less
  The calm that round us grew.   40
There seemed from the remotest seat
  Of the white mountain waste,
To the soft flower beneath our feet,
  A magic circle traced,—
A spirit interfused around
  A thrilling silent life,—
To momentary peace it bound
  Our mortal nature's strife;—
And still I felt the centre of
  The magic circle there,   50
Was one fair form that filled with love
  The lifeless atmosphere.

V

We paused beside the pools that lie
  Under the forest bough,
Each seemed as 'twere a little sky
  Gulphed in a world below;
A firmament of purple light,
  Which in the dark earth lay,
More boundless than the depth of night,
  And purer than the day—   60
In which the lovely forests grew,
  As in the upper air,
More perfect both in shape and hue
  Than any spreading there.

There lay the glade and neighbouring lawn
  And through the dark green wood
The white sun twinkling like the dawn
  Out of a speckled cloud.
Sweet views, which in our world above
  Can never well be seen,   70
Were imaged by the water's love
  Of that fair forest green.
And all was interfused beneath
  With an Elsyian glow,
An atmosphere without a breath,
  A softer day below.
Like one beloved the scene had lent
  To the dark water's breast,
Its every leaf and lineament
  With more than truth exprest,   80
Until an envious wind crept by,
  Like an unwelcome thought,
Which from the mind's too faithful eye
  Blots one dear image out.
Though thou art ever fair and kind,
  The forests ever green,
Less oft is peace in Shelley's mind,
  Than calm in waters seen.

[1822]   [1824, 1839]

WITH A GUITAR, TO JANE

ARIEL to *MIRANDA*:[1]—Take
This slave of Music, for the sake
Of him who is the slave of thee,
And teach it all the harmony
In which thou canst, and only thou,
Make the delighted spirit glow,
Till joy denies itself again,
And, too intense, is turned to pain;
For by permission and command
Of thine own Prince Ferdinand,[2]   10
Poor Ariel sends this silent token
Of love that never can be spoken;
Your guardian spirit, Ariel, who,
From life to life, must still pursue
Your happiness; —for thus alone
Can Ariel ever find his own.
From Prospero's enchanted cell,
As the mighty verses tell,
To the throne of Naples, he
Lit you o'er the trackless sea,   20

---

[1] See Shakespeare's *Tempest*.
[2] Edward Williams.

Flitting on, your prow before,
Like a living meteor.
When you die, the silent Moon,
In her interlunar swoon,
Is not sadder in her cell
Than deserted Ariel.
When you live again on earth,
Like an unseen star of birth,
Ariel guides you o'er the sea
Of life from your nativity.   30
Many changes have been run
Since Ferdinand and you begun
Your course of love, and Ariel still
Has tracked your steps, and served your will;
Now, in humbler, happier lot,
This is all remembered not;
And now, alas! the poor sprite is
Imprisoned, for some fault of his,
In a body like a grave;—
From you, he only dares to crave,   40
For his service and his sorrow,
A smile to-day, a song to-morrow.

The artist who this idol wrought,
To echo all harmonious thought,
Felled a tree, while on the steep
The woods were in their winter sleep,
Rocked in that repose divine
On the wind-swept Apennine;
And dreaming, some of Autumn past,
And some of Spring approaching fast,   50
And some of April birds and showers,
And some of songs in July bowers,
And all of love;—and so this tree—,
O that such our death may be!— ·
Died in sleep, and felt no pain,
To live in happier form again:
From which, beneath Heaven's fairest star,
The artist wrought this loved Guitar,
And taught it justly to reply,
To all who question skilfully,   60
In language gentle as thine own;
Whispering in enamoured tone
Sweet oracles of woods and dells,
And summer winds in sylvan cells;
For it had learnt all harmonies
Of the plains and of the skies,
Of the forests and the mountains,
And the many-voicèd fountains;
The clearest echoes of the hills,
The softest notes of falling rills,   70
The melodies of birds and bees,
The murmuring of summer seas,

And pattering rain, and breathing dew,
And airs of evening; and it knew
That seldom-heard mysterious sound,
Which, driven on its diurnal round,
As it floats through boundless day,
Our world enkindles on its way.—
All this it knows, but will not tell
To those who cannot question well   80
The Spirit that inhabits it;
It talks according to the wit
Of its companions; and no more
Is heard than has been felt before,
By those who tempt it to betray
These secrets of an elder day:
But, sweetly as its answers will
Flatter hands of perfect skill,
It keeps its highest, holiest tone
For our belovèd Jane alone.   90

[1822]   [1832]

LINES WRITTEN IN THE
BAY OF LERICI

SHE left me at the silent time
When the moon had ceased to climb
The azure path of Heaven's steep,
 And like an albatross asleep,
Balanced on her wings of light,
Hovered in the purple night,
Ere she sought her ocean nest
In the chambers of the West.
She left me, and I stayed alone
Thinking over every tone   10
Which, though silent to the ear,
The enchanted heart could hear,
Like notes which die when born, but still
Haunt the echoes of the hill;
And feeling ever—Oh, too much!—
The soft vibration of her touch,
As if her gentle hand, even now
Lightly trembled on my brow;
And thus, although she absent were,
Memory gave me all of her   20
That even Fancy dares to claim:—
Her presence had made weak and tame
All passions, and I lived alone
In the time which is our own;
The past and future were forgot,
As they had been, and would be, not.
But soon, the guardian angel gone,
The dæmon reassumed his throne

In my faint heart. I dare not speak
My thoughts, but thus disturbed and weak　30
I sat, and saw the vessels glide
Over the ocean bright and wide
Like spirit-wingèd chariots sent
O'er some serenest element,
For ministrations strange and far,
As if to some Elysian star
Sailed for drink to medicine
Such sweet and bitter pain as mine.
And the wind that winged their flight
From the land came fresh and light,　40
And the scent of wingèd flowers,
And the coolness of the hours
Of dew, and sweet warmth left by day,
Were scattered o'er the twinkling bay,
And the fisher, with his lamp
And spear, about the low rocks damp
Crept, and struck the fish which came
To worship the delusive flame.
Too happy they, whose pleasure sought
Extinguishes all sense and thought　50
Of the regret that pleasure leaves,
Destroying life alone, not peace!

[1822]　　　　　　　　　　　　　[1862]

LINES

["We meet not as we parted"]

I

WE meet not as we parted,
　We feel more than all may see;
My bosom is heavy-hearted,
　And thine full of doubt for me:—
　One moment has bound the free.

II

That moment is gone for ever,
　Like lightning that flashed and died—
Like a snowflake upon the river—
　Like a sunbeam upon the tide,
　Which the dark shadows hide.　10

III

That moment from time was singled
　As the first of a life of pain;
The cup of its joy was mingled
　—Delusion too sweet though vain!
　Too sweet to be mine again.

IV

Sweet lips, could my heart have hidden
　That its life was crushed by you,
Ye would not have then forbidden
　The death which a heart so true
　Sought in your briny dew.　20

V

.　　　.　　　.　　　.　　　.

　　.　　　.　　　.　　　.

.　　　.　　　.　　　.　　　.

Methinks too little cost
For a moment so found, so lost!

[1822]　　　　　　　　　　　　　[1862]

The Triumph of Life, *left unfinished when Shelley died,
was edited by Mrs. Shelley, and others. The text here is based
on that of D. H. Reiman, and follows the unfinished manuscript
as closely as clarity allows. Some obvious corrections have been
made.*

THE TRIUMPH OF LIFE

SWIFT as a spirit hastening to his task
　Of glory & of good, the Sun sprang forth
Rejoicing in his splendour, & the mask

Of darkness fell from the awakened Earth.
　The smokeless altars of the mountain snows
　Flamed above crimson clouds, & at the birth

Of light, the Ocean's orison arose
　To which the birds tempered their matin lay.
All flowers in field or forest which unclose

Their trembling eyelids to the kiss of day,　10
Swinging their censers in the element,
　With orient incense lit by the new ray

Burned slow & inconsumably, & sent
　Their odorous sighs up to the smiling air,
And in succession due, did Continent,

Isle, Ocean, & all things that in them wear
The form & character of mortal mould
Rise as the Sun their father rose, to bear

Their portion of the toil which he of old
　Took as his own & then imposed on them;　20
But I, whom thoughts which must remain untold

Had kept as wakeful as the stars that gem
The cone of night, now they were laid asleep,
   Stretched my faint limbs beneath the hoary stem

Which an old chestnut flung athwart the steep
   Of a green Apennine: before me fled
The night; behind me rose the day; the Deep

Was at my feet, & Heaven above my head
When a strange trance over my fancy grew
   Which was not slumber, for the shade it spread   30

Was so transparent that the scene came through
   As clear as when a veil of light is drawn
O'er evening hills they glimmer; and I knew

That I had felt the freshness of that dawn,
Bathed in the same cold dew my brow & hair
   And sate as thus upon that slope of lawn

Under the self same bough, & heard as there
   The birds, the fountains & the Ocean hold
Sweet talk in music through the enamoured air.
   And then a Vision on my brain was rolled . . .   40

As in that trance of wondrous thought I lay
   This was the tenour of my waking dream.
Methought I sate beside a public way

Thick strewn with summer dust, & a great stream
Of people there was hurrying to & fro
   Numerous as gnats upon the evening gleam,

All hastening onward, yet none seemed to know
   Whither he went, or whence he came, or why
He made one of the multitude, yet so

Was borne amid the crowd as through the sky   50
One of the million leaves of summer's bier.—
   Old age & youth, manhood & infancy,

Mixed in one mighty torrent did appear,
   Some flying from the thing they feared & some
Seeking the object of another's fear,

And others as with steps towards the tomb
Pored on the trodden worms that crawled beneath,
   And others mournfully within the gloom

Of their own shadow walked, and called it death . . .
   And some fled from it as it were a ghost,   60
Half fainting in the affliction of vain breath.

But more with motions which each other crost
Pursued or shunned the shadows the clouds threw
   Or birds within the noonday ether lost,

Upon that path where flowers never grew;
   And weary with vain toil & faint for thirst
Heard not the fountains whose melodious dew

Out of their mossy cells forever burst
Nor felt the breeze which from the forest told
   Of grassy paths, & wood lawns interspersed   70

With overarching elms & caverns cold,
   And violet banks where sweet dreams brood, but
      they
Pursued their serious folly as of old. . . .

And as I gazed methought that in the way
The throng grew wilder, as the woods of June
   When the South wind shakes the extinguished day.

And a cold glare, intenser than the noon
   But icy cold, obscured with   [1]light
The Sun as he the stars. Like the young moon

When on the sunlit limits of the night   80
Her white shell trembles amid crimson air
   And whilst the sleeping tempest gathers might

Doth, as a herald of its coming, bear
   The ghost of her dead Mother, whose dim form
Bends in dark ether from her infant's chair,

So came a chariot on the silent storm
Of its own rushing splendour, and a Shape
   So sate within as one whom years deform

Beneath a dusky hood & double cape
   Crouching within the shadow of a tomb,   90
And o'er what seemed the head, a cloud like crape,

Was bent a dun & faint etherial gloom
Tempering the light; upon the chariot's beam
   A Janus-visaged Shadow did assume

The guidance of that wonder-winged team.
   The Shapes which drew it in thick lightnings
Were lost: I heard alone on the air's soft stream

The music of their ever moving wings.
All the four faces of that charioteer
   Had their eyes banded . . . little profit brings   100

Speed in the van & blindness in the rear,
   Nor then avail the beams that quench the Sun
Or that his banded eyes could pierce the sphere

---

[1] The word "blinding" appears in brackets in Mrs. Shelley's
edition, and is usually accepted as a conjectural word to fill out
the meter.

Of all that is, has been, or will be done.—
  So ill was the car guided, but it past
    With solemn speed majestically on . . .

The crowd gave way, & I arose aghast,
  Or seemed to rise, so mighty was the trance,
And saw like clouds upon the thunder blast

  The million with fierce song and maniac dance   110
Raging around; such seemed the jubilee
  As when to greet some conqueror's advance

Imperial Rome poured forth her living sea
  From senatehouse & prison & theatre
When Freedom left those who upon the free

  Had bound a yoke which soon they stooped to bear.
Nor wanted here the true similitude
  Of a triumphal pageant, for where'er

The chariot rolled a captive multitude
  Was driven; all those who had grown old in power
Or misery,—all who have their age subdued,   121

  By action or by suffering, and whose hour
Was drained to its last sand in weal or woe,
  So that the trunk survived both fruit & flower;

All those whose fame or infamy must grow
  Till the great winter lay the form & name
Of their own earth with them forever low,

  All but the sacred few who could not tame
Their spirits to the Conqueror, but as soon
  As they had touched the world with living flame

Fled back like eagles to their native noon,   131
  Or those who put aside the diadem
Of earthly thrones or gems, till the last one

  Were there;—for they of Athens & Jerusalem [2]
Were neither mid the mighty captives seen
  Nor mid the ribald crowd that followed them

Or fled before . . Now swift, fierce & obscene
  The wild dance maddens in the van, & those
Who lead it, fleet as shadows on the green,

  Outspeed the chariot & without repose   140
Mix with each other in tempestuous measure
  To savage music. . . . Wilder as it grows,

They, tortured by the agonizing pleasure,
  Convulsed & on the rapid whirlwinds spun
Of that fierce spirit, whose unholy leisure

[2] Socrates and Jesus.

Was soothed by mischief since the world begun,
  Throw back their heads & loose their streaming hair,
    And in their dance round her who dims the Sun

Maidens & youths fling their wild arms in air
  As their feet twinkle; they recede, and now   150
Bending within each other's atmosphere

  Kindle invisibly; and as they glow
Like moths by light attracted & repelled,
  Oft to new bright destruction come & go.

Till like two clouds into one vale impelled
  That shake the mountains when their lightnings
    mingle
And die in rain,—the fiery band which held

  Their natures, snaps . . . ere the shock cease to
    tingle
One falls and then another in the path
  Senseless, nor is the desolation single,   160

Yet ere I can say *where* the chariot hath
  Past over them; nor other trace I find
But as of foam after the Ocean's wrath

  Is spent upon the desert shore.—Behind,
Old men, and women foully disarrayed
  Shake their grey hair in the insulting wind,

Limp in the dance & strain with limbs decayed
  To reach the car of light which leaves them still
Farther behind & deeper in the shade.

  But not the less with impotence of will   170
They wheel, though ghastly shadows interpose
  Round them & round each other, and fulfill

Their work and to the dust whence they arose
  Sink & corruption veils them as they lie
And frost in these performs what fire in those.

  Struck to the heart by this sad pageantry,
Half to myself I said, "And what is this?
  Whose shape is that within the car? & why"—

I would have added—"is all here amiss?"
  But a voice answered . . "Life" . . . I turned &
    knew   180
(O Heaven have mercy on such wretchedness!)

  That what I thought was an old root which grew
To strange distortion out of the hill side
  Was indeed one of that deluded crew,

And that the grass which methought hung so wide
  And white, was but his thin discoloured hair.
And that the holes it vainly sought to hide

  Were or had been eyes.—"If thou canst forbear
To join the dance, which I had well forborne,"
  Said the grim Feature, of my thought aware,   190

"I will now tell that which to this deep scorn
  Led me & my companions, and relate
The progress of the pageant since the morn;

  "If thirst of knowledge doth not thus abate,
Follow it even to the night, but I
  Am weary" . . . Then like one who with the weight

Of his own words is staggered, wearily
  He paused, and ere he could resume, I cried,
"First who art thou?" . . . "Before thy memory

  "I feared, loved, hated, suffered, did, & died,   200
And if the spark with which Heaven lit my spirit
  Earth had with purer nutriment supplied

"Corruption would not now thus much inherit
  Of what was once Rousseau [3]—nor this disguise
Stained that within which still disdains to wear it.—

  "If I have been extinguished, yet there rise
A thousand beacons from the spark I bore."—
  "And who are those chained to the car?" "The
     Wise

"The great, the unforgotten: they who wore
  Mitres & helms & crowns, or wreaths of light,   210
Signs of thought's empire over thought; their lore

  "Taught them not this—to know themselves;
    their might
Could not repress the mutiny within,
  And for the morn of truth they feigned, deep night

"Caught them ere evening." "Who is he with chin
  Upon his breast and hands crost on his chain?"
"The Child of a fierce hour; he sought to win

  "The world, and lost all it did contain
Of greatness, in its hope destroyed; & more
  Of fame & peace than Virtue's self can gain   220

"Without the opportunity which bore
  Him on its eagle's pinion to the peak
From which a thousand climbers have before

"Fall'n as Napoleon fell."—I felt my cheek
  Alter to see the great form pass away
Whose grasp had left the giant world so weak

That every pigmy kicked it as it lay—
  And much I grieved to think how power & will
In opposition rule our mortal day—

  And why God made irreconcilable   230
Good & the means of good; and for despair
  I half disdained mine eye's desire to fill

With the spent vision of the times that were
  And scarce have ceased to be . . . "Dost thou
    behold,"
Said then my guide, "those spoilers spoiled, Voltaire,

"Frederic, & Kant, Catherine, & Leopold,
  Chained hoary anarch, demagogue & sage
Whose name the fresh world thinks already old—

"For in the battle Life & they did wage
  She remained conqueror—I was overcome   240
By my own heart alone, which neither age

  "Nor tears nor infamy nor now the tomb
Could temper to its object."—"Let them pass"—
  I cried—"the world & its mysterious doom

"Is not so much more glorious than it was
  That I desire to worship those who drew
New figures on its false & fragile glass

  "As the old faded."—"Figures ever new
Rise on the bubble, paint them how you may;
  We have but thrown, as those before us threw,   250

"Our shadows on it as it past away.
  But mark, how chained to the triumphal chair
The mighty phantoms of an elder day—

"All that is mortal of great Plato there
  Expiates the joy & woe his master [4] knew not;
That star that ruled his doom was far too fair—

"And Life, where long that flower of Heaven grew not,
  Conquered the heart by love which gold or pain
Or age or sloth or slavery could subdue not—

  "And near   walk the   twain,[5]   260
The tutor & his pupil,[6] whom Dominion
  Followed as tame as vulture in a chain.—

---

[3] Jean Jacques Rousseau (1712–1778), novelist, and social and political philosopher. See Byron's *Childe Harold, III*, pp. 588–89.

[4] Socrates.
[5] In the 1839 edition Mrs. Shelley added "him" to fill the first gap in this line, but she never attempted to fill the second one.
[6] Aristotle and Alexander the Great.

"The world was darkened beneath either pinion
  Of him whom from the flock of conquerors
Fame singled as her thunderbearing minion;

"The other long outlived both woes & wars,
Throned in new thoughts of men, and still had kept
  The jealous keys of truth's eternal doors

"If Bacon's[7] spirit   [8] had not leapt
  Like lightning out of darkness; he compelled   270
The Proteus[9] shape of Nature's as it slept

"To wake & to unbar the caves that held
The treasure of the secrets of its reign—
  See the great bards of old who inly quelled

"The passions which they sung, as by their strain
  May well be known: their living melody
Tempers its own contagion to the vein

  "Of those who are infected with it—I
Have suffered what I wrote, or viler pain!—

  "And so my words were seeds of misery—   280
Even as the deeds of others."—"Not as theirs,"
  I said—he pointed to a company

In which I recognized amid the heirs
  Of Caesar's crime[10] from him to Constantine,
The Anarchs old whose force & murderous snares

  Had founded many a sceptre bearing line
And spread the plague of blood & gold abroad,
  And Gregory[11] & John and men divine

Who rose like shadows between Man & god
  Till that eclipse, still hanging under Heaven,   290
Was worshipped by the world o'er which they strode

  For the true Sun it quenched.—"Their power was
     given
But to destroy," replied the leader—"I
  Am one of those who have created, even

"If it be but a world of agony."—
  "Whence camest thou & whither goest thou?
How did thy course begin," I said, "& why?

"Mine eyes are sick of this perpetual flow
Of people, & my heart of one sad thought.—
  Speak."—"Whence I came, partly I seem to
    know,   300

"And how & by what paths I have been brought
  To this dread pass, methinks even thou mayst
    guess
Why this should be my mind can compass not;

  "Whither the conqueror hurries me still less.
But follow thou, & from spectator turn
  Actor or victim in this wretchedness,

"And what thou wouldst be taught I then may learn
  From thee.—Now listen . . . In the April prime
When all the forest tops began to burn

  "With kindling green, touched by the azure clime
Of the young year, I found myself asleep   311
  Under a mountain which from unknown time

"Had yawned into a cavern high & deep,
  And from it came a gentle rivulet
Whose water like clear air in its calm sweep

  "Bent the soft grass & kept for ever wet
The stems of the sweet flowers, and filled the grove
  With sound which all who hear must needs forget

"All pleasure & all pain, all hate & love,
  Which they had known before that hour of rest:
A sleeping mother then would dream not of   321

  "The only child who died upon her breast
At eventide, a king would mourn no more
  The crown of which his brow was dispossest

"When the sun lingered o'er the Ocean floor
  To gild his rival's new prosperity.—
Thou wouldst forget thus vainly to deplore

  "Ills, which if ills, can find no cure from thee,
The thought of which no other sleep will quell
  Nor other music blot from memory—   330

"So sweet & deep is the oblivious spell.—
  Whether my life had been before that sleep
The Heaven which I imagine, or a Hell

  "Like this harsh world in which I wake to weep,
I know not. I arose & for a space
  The scene of woods & waters seemed to keep,

---

[7] Sir Francis Bacon (1561–1626), philosopher and essayist, regarded as the father of inductive reasoning and experimental science.

[8] Mrs. Shelley printed "eagle spirit" to fill the gap.

[9] Minor sea god, able to change shape and to predict the future.

[10] The dissolution of the Roman Empire.

[11] Pope Gregory the Great (sixth century A.D.).

"Though it was now broad day, a gentle trace
Of light diviner than the common Sun
Sheds on the common Earth, but all the place

"Was filled with many sounds woven into one   340
Oblivious melody, confusing sense
  Amid the gliding waves & shadows dun;

"And as I looked the bright omnipresence
Of morning through the orient cavern flowed,
And the Sun's image radiantly intense

"Burned on the waters of the well that glowed
Like gold, and threaded all the forest maze
  With winding paths of emerald fire—there stood

"Amid the sun, as he amid the blaze
Of his own glory, on the vibrating
Floor of the fountain, paved with flashing rays,

"A shape all light, which with one hand did fling
Dew on the earth, as if she were the Dawn
  Whose invisible rain forever seemed to sing

"A silver music on the mossy lawn,
  And still before her on the dusky grass
Iris [12] her many coloured scarf had drawn.—

"In her right hand she bore a crystal glass
Mantling with bright Nepenthe; [13]—the fierce
      splendour
Fell from her as she moved under the mass   360

"Of the deep cavern, & with palms so tender
  Their tread broke not the mirror of its billow,
Glided along the river, and did bend her

"Head under the dark boughs, till like a willow
Her fair hair swept the bosom of the stream
  That whispered with delight to be their pillow.—

"As one enamoured is upborne in dream
  O'er lily-paven lakes mid silver mist
To wondrous music, so this shape might seem

"Partly to tread the waves with feet which kist   370
The dancing foam, partly to glide along
  The airs that roughened the moist amethyst,

"Or the slant morning beams that fell among
  The trees, or the soft shadows of the trees;
And her feet ever to the ceaseless song

"Of leaves & winds & waves & birds & bees
And falling drops moved in a measure new
  Yet sweet, as on the summer evening breeze

"Up from the lake a shape of golden dew
  Between two rocks, athwart the rising moon,   380
Moves up the east, where eagle never flew.—

"And still her feet, no less than the sweet tune
To which they moved, seemed as they moved, to blot
  The thoughts of him who gazed on them, & soon

"All that was seemed as if it had been not,
  As if the gazer's mind was strewn beneath
Her feet like embers, & she, thought by thought,

"Trampled its fires into the dust of death,
As Day upon the threshold of the east
  Treads out the lamps of night, until the breath   390

"Of darkness reillumines even the least
  Of heaven's living eyes—like day she came,
Making the night a dream; and ere she ceased

"To move, as one between desire and shame
Suspended, I said—'If, as it doth seem,
  Thou comest from the realm without a name,

"'Into this valley of perpetual dream,
  Shew whence I came, and where I am, and why—
Pass not away upon the passing stream.'

"'Arise and quench thy thirst,' was her reply.   400
And as a shut lily, stricken by the wand
  Of dewy morning's vital alchemy,

"I rose; and, bending at her sweet command,
  Touched with faint lips the cup she raised,
And suddenly my brain became as sand

"Where the first wave had more than half erased
The track of deer on desert Labrador,
  Whilst the fierce wolf from which they fled amazed

"Leaves his stamp visibly upon the shore
  Until the second bursts—so on my sight   410
Burst a new Vision [14] never seen before.—

"And the fair shape waned in the coming light
As veil by veil the silent splendour drops
  From Lucifer, [15] amid the chrysolite

---

[12] Goddess of the rainbow.
[13] Drug causing forgetfulness.

[14] I.e., Life and the car.
[15] The morning star.

"Of sunrise ere it strike the mountain tops—
    And as the presence of that fairest planet
Although unseen is felt by one who hopes

    "That his day's path may end as he began it
In that star's smile, whose light is like the scent
    Of a jonquil when evening breezes fan it,   420

"Or the soft note in which his dear lament
    The Brescian shepherd breathes, or the caress
That turned his weary slumber to content.—

    "So knew I in that light's severe excess
The presence of that shape which on the stream
    Moved, as I moved along the wilderness,

"More dimly than a day appearing dream,
    The ghost of a forgotten form of sleep,
A light from Heaven whose half extinguished beam

    "Through the sick day in which we wake to weep
Glimmers, forever sought, forever lost.—   431
    So did that shape its obscure tenour keep

"Beside my path, as silent as a ghost;
    But the new Vision, and its cold bright car,
With savage music, stunning music, crost

    "The forest, and as if from some dread war
Triumphantly returning, the loud million
    Fiercely extolled the fortune of her star.—

"A moving arch of victory the vermilion
    And green & azure plumes of Iris had   440
Built high over her wind-winged pavilion,

    "And underneath aetherial glory clad
The wilderness, and far before her flew
    The tempest of the splendour which forbade

"Shadow to fall from leaf or stone;—the crew
    Seemed in that light like atomies that dance
Within a sunbeam.—Some upon the new

    "Embroidery of flowers that did enhance
The grassy vesture of the desart, played,
    Forgetful of the chariot's swift advance;   450

"Others stood gazing till within the shade
    Of the great mountain its light left them dim.—
Others outspeeded it, and others made

    "Circles around it like the clouds that swim
Round the high moon in a bright sea of air,
    And more did follow, with exulting hymn,

"The chariot & the captives fettered there,
    But all like bubbles on an eddying flood
Fell into the same track at last & were

    "Borne onward.—I among the multitude   460
Was swept; me sweetest flowers delayed not long,
    Me not the shadow nor the solitude,

"Me not the falling stream's Lethean song,
    Me, not the phantom of that early form
Which moved upon its motion,—but among

    "The thickest billows of the living storm
I plunged, and bared my bosom to the clime
    Of that cold light, whose airs too soon deform.—

"Before the chariot had begun to climb
    The opposing steep of that mysterious dell,   470
Behold a wonder worthy of the rhyme

    "Of him[16] whom from the lowest depths of Hell
Through every Paradise & through all glory
    Love led serene, & who returned to tell

"In words of hate & awe the wondrous story
    How all things are transfigured, except Love;
For deaf as is a sea which wrath makes hoary

    "The world can hear not the sweet notes that move
The sphere whose light is melody to lovers [17]—
    A wonder worthy of his rhyme—the grove   480

"Grew dense with shadows to its inmost covers,
    The earth was grey with phantoms, & the air
Was peopled with dim forms, as when there hovers

    "A flock of vampire-bats before the glare
Of the tropic sun, bringing ere evening
    Strange night upon some Indian isle,—thus

"Phantoms diffused around, & some did fling
    Shadows of shadows, yet unlike themselves,
Behind them, some like eaglets on the wing

    "Were lost in the white blaze, others like elves   490
Danced in a thousand unimagined shapes
    Upon the sunny streams & grassy shelves;

"And others sate chattering like restless apes
    On vulgar paws and voluble like fire.
Some made a cradle of the ermined capes

---

16 Dante.
17 I.e., Venus.

"Of kingly mantles, some upon the tiar
  Of pontiffs sate like vultures, others played
    Within the crown which girt with empire

"A baby's or an idiot's brow, & made
    Their nests in it; the old anatomies   500
Sate hatching their bare brood under the shade

  "Of demon wings, and laughed from their dead
      eyes
To reassume the delegated power
    Arrayed in which these worms did monarchize

"Who make this earth their charnel.—Others more
    Humble, like falcons sate upon the fist
Of common men, and round their heads did soar,

  "Or like small gnats & flies, as thick as mist
On evening marshes, thronged about the brow
    Of lawer, statesman, priest & theorist,   510

"And others like discoloured flakes of snow
    On fairest bosoms & the sunniest hair
Fell, and were melted by the youthful glow

"Which they extinguished; for like tears, they were
A veil to those from whose faint lids they rained
    In drops of sorrow.—I became aware

"Of whence those forms proceeded which thus
      stained
    The track in which we moved; after brief space
From every form the beauty slowly waned,

  "From every firmest limb & fairest face   520
The strength & freshness fell like dust, & left
    The action & the shape without the grace

"Of life; the marble brow of youth was cleft
    With care, and in the eyes where once hope shone
Desire like a lioness bereft

  "Of its last cub, glared ere it died; each one
Of that great crowd sent forth incessantly
    These shadows, numerous as the dead leaves
      blown

"In Autumn evening from a poplar tree—
    Each, like himself & like each other were,   530
At first, but soon distorted, seemed to be

  "Obscure clouds moulded by the casual air;
And of this stuff the car's creative ray
    Wrought all the busy phantoms that were there

"As the sun shapes the clouds—thus, on the way
    Mask after mask fell from the countenance
And form of all, and long before the day

  "Was old, the joy which waked like Heaven's
      glance
The sleepers in the oblivious valley, died,
    And some grew weary of the ghastly dance   540

"And fell, as I have fallen by the way side,
    Those soonest from whose forms most shadows
      past
And least of strength & beauty did abide."—

  "Then, what is Life?" I said . . . the cripple cast
His eye upon the car which now had rolled
    Onward, as if that look must be the last,

And answered. . . . "Happy those for whom the fold
    Of

[1822]   [1824, 1965]

PROSE

The Necessity of Atheism *was printed at Shelley's expense in February 1811, and went largely unnoticed until Shelley filled his Oxford bookseller's window with copies and sent copies, so he claimed, to every bishop in England and all the dignitaries at Oxford. He (and Hogg) were expelled within a few days. Much of the pamphlet was reprinted as a note to* Queen Mab.

THE NECESSITY OF ATHEISM.

Quod clarâ et perspicua demonstratione careat pro verò habere mens omnino nequit humana.
BACON de Augment. Scient.

ADVERTISEMENT

As a love of truth is the only motive which actuates the Author of this little tract, he earnestly entreats that those of his readers who may discover any deficiency in his reasoning, or may be in possession of proofs which his mind could never obtain, would offer them, together with their objections to the Public, as briefly, as methodically, as plainly as he has taken the liberty of doing. Thro' deficiency of proof,

An ATHEIST.

A CLOSE examination of the validity of the proofs adduced to support any proposition, has ever been allowed to be the only sure way of attaining truth, upon the advantages of which it is unnecessary to descant; our knowledge of the existence of a Deity is a subject of such importance that it cannot be too minutely investigated; in consequence of this conviction, we proceed briefly and impartially to examine the proofs which have been adduced. It is necessary first to consider the nature of Belief.

When a proposition is offered to the mind, it perceives the agreement or disagreement of the ideas of which it is composed. A perception of their agreement is termed belief, many obstacles frequently prevent this perception from being immediate, these the mind attempts to remove in order that the perception may be distinct. The mind is active in the investigation, in order to perfect the state of perception which is passive; the investigation being confused with the perception has induced many falsely to imagine that the mind is active in belief, that belief is an act of volition, in consequence of which it may be regulated by the mind; pursuing, continuing this

mistake they have attached a degree of criminality to disbelief of which in its nature it is incapable; it is equally so of merit.

The strength of belief like that of every other passion is in proportion to the degrees of excitement.

The degrees of excitement are three.

The senses are the sources of all knowledge to the mind, consequently their evidence claims the strongest assent.

The decision of the mind founded upon our own experience derived from these sources, claims the next degree.

The experience of others which addresses itself to the former one, occupies the lowest degree.—

Consequently no testimony can be admitted which is contrary to reason, reason is founded on the evidence of our senses.

Every proof may be referred to one of these three divisions; we are naturally led to consider what arguments we receive from each of them to convince us of the existence of a Deity.

1st. The evidence of the senses.—If the Deity should appear to us, if he should convince our senses of his existence; this revelation would necessarily command belief;—Those to whom the Deity has thus appeared, have the strongest possible conviction of his existence.

Reason claims the 2nd. place, it is urged that man knows that whatever is, must either have had a beginning or existed from all eternity, he also knows that whatever is not eternal must have had a cause.—Where this is applied to the existence of the universe, it is necessary to prove that it was created, until that is clearly demonstrated, we may reasonably suppose that it has endured from all eternity.—In a case where two propositions are diametrically opposite, the mind believes that which is less incomprehensible, it is easier to suppose that the Universe has existed from all eternity, than to conceive a being capable of creating it; if the mind sinks beneath the weight of one, is it an alleviation to increase the intolerability of the burden?—The other argument which is founded upon a man's knowledge of his own existence, stands thus. . . . A man knows not only he now is, but that there was a time when he did not exist, consequently there must have been a cause. . . . But what does this prove? we can only infer from effects causes exactly adequate to those effects; . . . But there certainly is a generative power which is effected by particular instruments; we cannot prove that it is inherent in these instruments, nor is the contrary hypothesis capable of demonstration; we admit that the generative power is incomprehensible, but to suppose that the same effect is produced by an eternal, omniscient, Almighty Being, leaves the cause in the obscurity, but renders it more incomprehensible.

The 3rd. and last degree of assent is claimed by Testimony . . . it is required that it should not be contrary to reason. . . . The testimony that the Deity convinces the senses of men of his existence can only be admitted by us, if our mind considers it less probable that these men should have been deceived, than that the Deity should have appeared to them . . . our reason can never admit the testimony of men, who not only declare that they were eye-witnesses of miracles but that the Deity was irrational, for he commanded that he should be believed, he proposed the highest rewards for faith, eternal punishments for disbelief . . . we can only command voluntary actions, belief is not an act of volition, the mind is even passive, from this it is evident that we have not sufficient testimony, or rather that testimony is insufficient to prove the being of a God, we have before shewn that it cannot be deduced from reason, . . . they who have been convinced by the evidence of the senses, they only can believe it.

From this it is evident that having no proofs from any of the three sources of conviction: the mind *cannot* believe the existence of a God, it is also evident that as belief is a passion of the mind, no degree of criminality can be attached to disbelief, they only are reprehensible who willingly neglect to remove the false medium thro' which their mind views the subject.

It is almost unnecessary to observe, that the general knowledge of the deficiency of such proof, cannot be prejudicial to society: Truth has always been found to promote the best interests of mankind. . . . Every reflecting mind must allow that there is no proof of the existence of a Deity.—Q.E.D.[1]

A DEFENCE OF POETRY

This is Shelley's reply to Thomas Love Peacock's The Four Ages of Poetry (1821), which pretended to argue that poetry had no value in civilized society; Mrs. Shelley eventually printed it in 1840.

A DEFENCE OF POETRY

ACCORDING to one mode of regarding those two classes of mental action, which are called reason and

imagination, the former may be considered as mind contemplating the relations borne by one thought to another, however produced; and the latter, as mind acting upon those thoughts so as to colour them with its own light, and composing from them, as from elements, other thoughts, each containing within itself the principle of its own integrity. The one is the τὸ ποιειν, or the principle of synthesis, and has for its objects those forms which are common to universal nature and existence itself; the other is the τὸ λογιζειν, or principle of analysis, and its action regards the relations of things, simply as relations; considering thoughts, not in their integral unity, but as the algebraical representations which conduct to certain general results. Reason is the enumeration of quantities already known; imagination is the perception of the value of those quantities, both separately and as a whole. Reason respects the differences, and imagination the similitudes of things. Reason is to imagination as the instrument to the agent, as the body to the spirit, as the shadow to the substance.

Poetry, in a general sense, may be defined to be "the expression of the imagination": and poetry is connate with the origin of man. Man is an instrument over which a series of external and internal impressions are driven, like the alternations of an ever-changing wind over an Æolian lyre,[1] which move it by their motion to ever-changing melody. But there is a principle within the human being, and perhaps within all sentient beings, which acts otherwise than in the lyre, and produces not melody, alone, but harmony, by an internal adjustment of the sounds or motions thus excited to the impressions which excite them. It is as if the lyre could accommodate its chords to the motions of that which strikes them, in a determined proportion of sound; even as the musician can accommodate his voice to the sound of the lyre. A child at play by itself will express its delight by its voice and motions; and every inflexion of tone and every gesture will bear exact relation to a corresponding antitype in the pleasurable impressions which awakened it; it will be the reflected image of that impression; and as the lyre trembles and sounds after the wind has died away, so the child seeks, by prolonging in its voice and motions the duration of the effect, to prolong also a consciousness of the cause. In relation to the objects which delight a child, these expressions are, what poetry is to higher objects. The savage (for the savage is to ages what the child is to years) expresses the emotions produced in him by surrounding objects in a similar manner; and

---

[1] *Quod erat demonstrandum:* "what was to have been proven" (and has been).

[1] See the note, p. 441, to Coleridge's *The Eolian Harp.*

language and gesture, together with plastic or pictorial imitation, become the image of the combined effect of those objects, and of his apprehension of them. Man in society, with all his passions and his pleasures, next becomes the object of the passions and pleasures of man; an additional class of emotions produces an augmented treasure of expressions; and language, gesture, and the imitative arts, become at once the representation and the medium, the pencil and the picture, the chisel and the statue, the chord and the harmony. The social sympathies, or those laws from which, as from its elements, society results, begin to develop themselves from the moment that two human beings coexist; the future is contained within the present, as the plant within the seed; and equality, diversity, unity, contrast, mutual dependence, become the principles alone capable of affording the motives according to which the will of a social being is determined to action, inasmuch as he is social; and constitute pleasure in sensation, virtue in sentiment, beauty in art, truth in reasoning, and love in the intercourse of kind. Hence men, even in the infancy of society, observe a certain order in their words and actions, distinct from that of the objects and the impressions represented by them, all expression being subject to the laws of that from which it proceeds. But let us dismiss those more general considerations which might involve an inquiry into the principles of society itself, and restrict our view to the manner in which the imagination is expressed upon its forms.

In the youth of the world, men dance and sing and imitate natural objects, observing in these actions, as in all others, a certain rhythm or order. And, although all men observe a similar, they observe not the same order, in the motions of the dance, in the melody of the song, in the combinations of language, in the series of their imitations of natural objects. For there is a certain order or rhythm belonging to each of these classes of mimetic representation, from which the hearer and the spectator receive an intenser and purer pleasure than from any other: the sense of an approximation to this order has been called taste by modern writers. Every man in the infancy of art, observes an order which approximates more or less closely to that from which this highest delight results: but the diversity is not sufficiently marked, as that its gradations should be sensible, except in those instances where the predominance of this faculty of approximation to the beautiful (for so we may be permitted to name the relation between this highest pleasure and its cause) is very great. Those in whom it exists in excess are poets, in the most universal sense of the word; and the pleasure resulting from the

manner in which they express the influence of society or nature upon their own minds, communicates itself to others, and gathers a sort of reduplication from that community. Their language is vitally metaphorical; that is, it marks the before unapprehended relations of things and perpetuates their apprehension, until the words which represent them, become, through time, signs for portions or classes of thoughts instead of pictures of integral thoughts; and then if no new poets should arise to create afresh the associations which have been thus disorganised, language will be dead to all the nobler purposes of human intercourse. These similitudes or relations are finely said by Lord Bacon to be "the same footsteps of nature impressed upon the various subjects of the world"*—and he considers the faculty which perceives them as the storehouse of axioms common to all knowledge. In the infancy of society every author is necessarily a poet, because language itself is poetry; and to be a poet is to apprehend the true and the beautiful, in a word, the good which exists in the relation, subsisting, first between existence and perception, and secondly between perception and expression. Every original language near to its source is in itself the chaos of a cyclic poem: the copiousness of lexicography and the distinctions of grammar are the works of a later age, and are merely the catalogue and the form of the creations of poetry.

But poets, or those who imagine and express this indestructible order, are not only the authors of language and of music, of the dance and architecture, and statuary, and painting; they are the institutors of laws, and the founders of civil society, and the inventors of the arts of life, and the teachers, who draw into a certain propinquity with the beautiful and the true, that partial apprehension of the agencies of the invisible world which is called religion. Hence all original religions are allegorical, or susceptible of allegory, and, like Janus, have a double face of false and true. Poets, according to the circumstances of the age and nation in which they appeared, were called, in the earlier epochs of the world, legislators, or prophets: a poet essentially comprises and unites both these characters. For he not only beholds intensely the present as it is, and discovers those laws according to which present things ought to be ordered, but he beholds the future in the present, and his thoughts are the germs of the flower and the fruit of latest time. Not that I assert poets to be prophets in the gross sense of the word, or that they can foretell the form as surely as they foreknow the spirit of events: such is the pretence of superstition, which would

* *De Augment. Scient.*, cap. I, Lib. iii.

make poetry an attribute of prophecy, rather than prophecy an attribute of poetry. A poet participates in the eternal, the infinite, and the one; as far as relates to his conceptions, time and place and number are not. The grammatical forms which express the moods of time, and the difference of persons, and the distinction of place, are convertible with respect to the highest poetry without injuring it as poetry; and the choruses of Æschylus, and the book of Job, and Dante's Paradise, would afford, more than any other writings, examples of this fact, if the limits of this essay did not forbid citation. The creations of sculpture, painting, and music, are illustrations still more decisive.

Language, colour, form, and religious and civil habits of action, are all the instruments and materials of poetry, they may be called poetry by that figure of speech which considers the effect as a synonyme of the cause. But poetry in a more restricted sense expresses those arrangements of language, and especially metrical language, which are created by that imperial faculty, whose throne is curtained within the invisible nature of man. And this springs from the nature itself of language, which is a more direct representation of the actions and passions of our internal being, and is susceptible of more various and delicate combinations, than colour, form, or motion, and is more plastic and obedient to the control of that faculty of which it is the creation. For language is arbitrarily produced by the imagination, and has relation to thoughts alone; but all other materials, instruments, and conditions of art, have relations among each other, which limit and interpose between conception and expression. The former is as a mirror which reflects, the latter as a cloud which enfeebles, the light of which both are mediums of communication. Hence the fame of sculptors, painters, and musicians, although the intrinsic powers of the great masters of these arts may yield in no degree to that of those who have employed language as the hieroglyphic of their thoughts, has never equalled that of poets in the restricted sense of the term; as two performers of equal skill will produce unequal effects from a guitar and a harp. The fame of legislators and founders of religions, so long as their institutions last, alone seems to exceed that of poets in the restricted sense; but it can scarcely be a question, whether, if we deduct the celebrity which their flattery of the gross opinions of the vulgar usually conciliates, together with that which belonged to them in their higher character of poets, any excess will remain.

We have thus circumscribed the meaning of the word Poetry within the limits of that art which is the most familiar and the most perfect expression of the faculty itself. It is necessary, however, to make the circle still narrower, and to determine the distinction between measured and unmeasured language; for the popular division into prose and verse is inadmissible in accurate philosophy.

Sounds as well as thoughts have relation both between each other and towards that which they represent, and a perception of the order of those relations has always been found connected with a perception of the order of those relations of thoughts. Hence the language of poets has ever affected a certain uniform and harmonious recurrence of sound, without which it were not poetry, and which is scarcely less indispensable to the communication of its action, than the words themselves, without reference to that peculiar order. Hence the vanity of translation; it were as wise to cast a violet into a crucible that you might discover the formal principle of its colour and odour, as seek to transfuse from one language into another the creations of a poet. The plant must spring again from its seed, or it will bear no flower— and this is the burthen of the curse of Babel.

An observation of the regular mode of the recurrence of this harmony in the language of poetical minds, together with its relation to music, produced metre, or a certain system of traditional forms of harmony of language. Yet it is by no means essential that a poet should accommodate his language to this traditional form, so that the harmony, which is its spirit, be observed. The practice is indeed convenient and popular, and to be preferred, especially in such composition as includes much form and action: but every great poet must inevitably innovate upon the example of his predecessors in the exact structure of his peculiar versification. The distinction between poets and prose writers is a vulgar error. The distinction between philosophers and poets has been anticipated. Plato was essentially a poet—the truth and splendour of his imagery, and the melody of his language, is the most intense that it is possible to conceive. He rejected the measure of the epic, dramatic, and lyrical forms, because he sought to kindle a harmony in thoughts divested of shape and action, and he forbore to invent any regular plan of rhythm which should include, under determinate forms, the varied pauses of his style. Cicero sought to imitate the cadence of his periods, but with little success. Lord Bacon was a poet.* His language has a sweet and majestic rhythm, which satisfies the sense, no less than the almost superhuman wisdom of his philosophy satisfies the intellect; it is a strain which

* See the *Filum Labyrinthi* and the *Essay on Death* particularly.

distends, and then bursts the circumference of the hearer's mind, and pours itself forth together with it into the universal element with which it has perpetual sympathy. All the authors of revolutions in opinion are not only necessarily poets as they are inventors, nor even as their words unveil the permanent analogy of things by images which participate in the life of truth; but as their periods are harmonious and rhythmical, and contain in themselves the elements of verse; being the echo of the eternal music. Nor are those supreme poets, who have employed traditional forms of rhythm on account of the form and action of their subjects, less capable of perceiving and teaching the truth of things, than those who have omitted that form. Shakspeare, Dante, and Milton (to confine ourselves to modern writers) are philosophers of the very loftiest power.

A poem is the image of life expressed in its eternal truth. There is this difference between a story and a poem, that a story is a catalogue of detached facts, which have no other bond of connexion than time, place, circumstance, cause and effect; the other is the creation of actions according to the unchangeable forms of human nature, as existing in the mind of the creator, which is itself the image of all other minds. The one is partial, and applies only to a definite period of time, and a certain combination of events which can never again recur; the other is universal, and contains within itself the germ of a relation to whatever motives or actions have place in the possible varieties of human nature. Time, which destroys the beauty and the use of the story of particular facts, stript of the poetry which should invest them, augments that of Poetry, and for ever develops new and wonderful applications of the eternal truth which it contains. Hence epitomes have been called the moths of just history; they eat out the poetry of it. The story of particular facts is as a mirror which obscures and distorts that which should be beautiful: Poetry is a mirror which makes beautiful that which is distorted.

The parts of a composition may be poetical, without the composition as a whole being a poem. A single sentence may be considered as a whole, though it be found in a series of unassimilated portions; a single word even may be a spark of inextinguishable thought. And thus all the great historians, Herodotus, Plutarch, Livy, were poets; and although the plan of these writers, especially that of Livy, restrained them from developing this faculty in its highest degree, they make copious and ample amends for their sub-jection, by filling all the interstices of their subjects with living images.

Having determined what is poetry, and who are poets, let us proceed to estimate its effects upon society.

Poetry is ever accompanied with pleasure: all spirits on which it falls open themselves to receive the wisdom which is mingled with its delight. In the infancy of the world, neither poets themselves nor their auditors are fully aware of the excellence of poetry: for it acts in a divine and unapprehended manner, beyond and above consciousness; and it is reserved for future generations to contemplate and measure the mighty cause and effect in all the strength and splendour of their union. Even in modern times, no living poet ever arrived at the fulness of his fame; the jury which sits in judgment upon a poet, belonging as he does to all time, must be composed of his peers: it must be impanneled by Time from the selectest of the wise of many generations. A Poet is a nightingale, who sits in darkness and sings to cheer its own solitude with sweet sounds; his auditors are as men entranced by the melody of an unseen musician, who feel that they are moved and softened, yet know not whence or why. The poems of Homer and his contemporaries were the delight of infant Greece; they were the elements of that social system which is the column upon which all succeeding civilization has reposed. Homer embodied the ideal perfection of his age in human character; nor can we doubt that those who read his verses were awakened to an ambition of becoming like to Achilles, Hector, and Ulysses: the truth and beauty of friendship, patriotism, and per-severing devotion to an object, were unveiled to the depths in these immortal creations: the sentiments of the auditors must have been refined and enlarged by a sympathy with such great and lovely impersona-tions, until from admiring they imitated, and from imitation they identified themselves with the objects of their admiration. Nor let it be objected, that these characters are remote from moral perfection, and that they can by no means be considered as edifying patterns for general imitation. Every epoch, under names more or less specious, has deified its peculiar errors; Revenge is the naked Idol of the worship of a semi-barbarous age; and Self-deceit is the veiled Image of unknown evil, before which luxury and satiety lie prostrate. But a poet considers the vices of his contemporaries as the temporary dress in which his creations must be arrayed, and which cover without concealing the eternal proportions of their beauty. An epic or dramatic personage is understood to wear them around his soul, as he may the antient armour or the modern uniform around his body; whilst it is easy to conceive a dress more graceful than either. The beauty of the internal nature cannot be so far concealed by its accidental vesture, but that the spirit of its form shall communicate itself to the very disguise, and indicate the shape it hides from the manner in which it is worn. A majestic form and graceful motions will express themselves through the most barbarous and tasteless costume. Few poets of the highest class have chosen to exhibit the beauty of their conceptions in its naked truth and splendour; and it is doubtful whether the alloy of costume, habit, &c., be not necessary to temper this planetary music for mortal ears.

The whole objection, however, of the immorality of poetry rests upon a misconception of the manner in which poetry acts to produce the moral improvement of man. Ethical science arranges the elements which poetry has created, and propounds schemes and proposes examples of civil and domestic life: nor is it for want of admirable doctrines that men hate, and despise, and censure, and deceive, and subjugate one another. But Poetry acts in another and diviner manner. It awakens and enlarges the mind itself by rendering it the receptacle of a thousand unapprehended combinations of thought. Poetry lifts the veil from the hidden beauty of the world, and makes familiar objects be as if they were not familiar; it reproduces all that it represents, and the impersonations clothed in its Elysian light stand thenceforward in the minds of those who have once contemplated them, as memorials of that gentle and exalted content which extends itself over all thoughts and actions with which it coexists. The great secret of morals is love; or a going out of our own nature, and an identification of ourselves with the beautiful which exists in thought, action, or person, not our own. A man, to be greatly good, must imagine intensely and comprehensively; he must put himself in the place of another and of many others; the pains and pleasures of his species must become his own. The great instrument of moral good is the imagination; and poetry administers to the effect by acting upon the cause. Poetry enlarges the circumference of the imagination by replenishing it with thoughts of ever new delight, which have the power of attracting and assimilating to their own nature all other thoughts, and which form new intervals and interstices whose void for ever craves fresh food. Poetry strengthens that faculty which is the organ of the moral nature of man, in the same manner as exercise strengthens a limb. A Poet therefore would do ill to embody his own conceptions of right and wrong, which are usually those of his place and time, in his poetical creations, which participate in neither. By this assumption of the inferior office of interpreting the effect, in which perhaps after all he might acquit himself but imperfectly, he would resign the glory in a participation in the cause. There was little danger that Homer, or any of the eternal Poets, should have so far misunderstood themselves as to have abdicated this throne of their widest dominion. Those in whom the poetical faculty, though great, is less intense, as Euripides, Lucan, Tasso, Spenser, have frequently affected a moral aim, and the effect of their poetry is diminished in exact proportion to the degree in which they compel us to advert to this purpose.

Homer and the cyclic poets were followed at a certain interval by the dramatic and lyrical Poets of Athens, who flourished contemporaneously with all that is most perfect in the kindred expressions of the poetical faculty; architecture, painting, music, the dance, sculpture, philosophy, and we may add, the forms of civil life. For although the scheme of Athenian society was deformed by many imperfections which the poetry existing in Chivalry and Christianity have erased from the habits and institutions of modern Europe; yet never at any other period has so much energy, beauty, and virtue, been developed; never was blind strength and stubborn form so disciplined and rendered subject to the will of man, or that will less repugnant to the dictates of the beautiful and the true, as during the century which preceded the death of Socrates.[2] Of no other epoch in the history of our species have we records and fragments stamped so visibly with the image of the divinity in man. But it is Poetry alone, in form, in action, or in language, which has rendered this epoch memorable above all others, and the storehouse of examples to everlasting time. For written poetry existed at that epoch simultaneously with the other arts, and it is an idle enquiry to demand which gave and which received the light, which all, as from a common focus, have scattered over the darkest periods of succeeding age. We know no more of cause and effect than a constant conjunction of events: Poetry is ever found to coexist with whatever other arts contribute to the happiness and perfection of man. I appeal to what has already been established to distinguish between the cause and the effect.

It was at the period here adverted to, that the Drama had its birth; and however a succeeding writer may have equalled or surpassed those few great specimens of the Athenian drama which have been preserved to us, it is indisputable that the art itself never was understood or practised according to the true philosophy of it, as at Athens. For the Athenians employed language, action, music, painting, the dance, and religious institutions, to produce a common effect in the representation of the loftiest

---

2 See *Ode to Liberty*, stanza V, p. 913.

idealisms of passion and of power; each division in the art was made perfect in its kind by artists of the most consummate skill, and was disciplined into a beautiful proportion and unity one towards another. On the modern stage a few only of the elements capable of expressing the image of the poet's conception are employed at once. We have tragedy without music and dancing; and music and dancing without the high impersonations of which they are the fit accompaniment, and both without religion and solemnity; religious institution has indeed been usually banished from the stage. Our system of divesting the actor's face of a mask, on which the many expressions appropriated to his dramatic character might be moulded into one permanent and unchanging expression, is favourable only to a partial and inharmonious effect; it is fit for nothing but a monologue, where all the attention may be directed to some great master of ideal mimicry. The modern practice of blending comedy with tragedy, though liable to great abuse in point of practice, is undoubtedly an extension of the dramatic circle; but the comedy should be as in King Lear, universal, ideal, and sublime. It is perhaps the intervention of this principle which determines the balance in favour of King Lear against the Œdipus Tyrannus or the Agamemnon, or, if you will the trilogies with which they are connected; unless the intense power of the choral poetry, especially that of the latter, should be considered as restoring the equilibrium. King Lear, if it can sustain this comparison, may be judged to be the most perfect specimen of the dramatic art existing in the world; in spite of the narrow conditions to which the poet was subjected by the ignorance of the philosophy of the drama which has prevailed in modern Europe. Calderon, in his religious Autos, has attempted to fulfil some of the high conditions of dramatic representation neglected by Shakspeare; such as the establishing a relation between the drama and religion, and the accommodating them to music and dancing; but he omits the observation of conditions still more important, and more is lost than gained by a substitution of the rigidly-defined and ever-repeated idealisms of a distorted superstition for the living impersonations of the truth of human passion.

But we digress.—The Author of the Four Ages of Poetry has prudently omitted to dispute on the effect of the Drama upon life and manners. For, if I know the Knight by the device of his shield, I have only to inscribe Philoctetes or Agamemnon or Othello upon mine to put to flight the giant sophisms which have enchanted him, as the mirror of intolerable light though on the arm of one of the weakest of the

Paladines could blind and scatter whole armies of necromancers and pagans. The connexion of scenic exhibitions with the improvement or corruption of the manners of men, has been universally recognised: in other words, the presence or absence of poetry in its most perfect and universal form, has been found to be connected with good and evil in conduct and habit. The corruption which has been imputed to the drama as an effect, begins, when the poetry employed in its constitution ends: I appeal to the history of manners whether the gradations of the growth of the one and the decline of the other have not corresponded with an exactness equal to any other example of moral cause and effect.

The drama at Athens, or wheresoever else it may have approached to its perfection, coexisted with the moral and intellectual greatness of the age. The tragedies of the Athenian poets are as mirrors in which the spectator beholds himself, under a thin disguise of circumstance, stript of all but that ideal perfection and energy which every one feels to be the internal type of all that he loves, admires, and would become. The imagination is enlarged by a sympathy with pains and passions so mighty, that they distend in their conception the capacity of that by which they are conceived; the good affections are strengthened by pity, indignation, terror and sorrow; and an exalted calm is prolonged from the satiety of this high exercise of them into the tumult of familiar life: even crime is disarmed of half its horror and all its contagion by being represented as the fatal consequence of the unfathomable agencies of nature; error is thus divested of its wilfulness; men can no longer cherish it as the creation of their choice. In a drama of the highest order there is little food for censure or hatred; it teaches rather self-knowledge and self-respect. Neither the eye nor the mind can see itself, unless reflected upon that which it resembles. The drama, so long as it continues to express poetry, is as a prismatic and many-sided mirror, which collects the brightest rays of human nature and divides and reproduces them from the simplicity of these elementary forms, and touches them with majesty and beauty, and multiplies all that it reflects, and endows it with the power of propagating its like wherever it may fall.

But in periods of the decay of social life, the drama sympathises with that decay. Tragedy becomes a cold imitation of the form of the great masterpieces of antiquity, divested of all harmonious accompaniment of the kindred arts; and often the very form misunderstood, or a weak attempt to teach certain doctrines, which the writer considers as moral truths; and which are usually no more than specious flatteries of some gross vice or weakness, with which the author, in common with his auditors, are infected. Hence what has been called the classical and domestic drama. Addison's "Cato" is a specimen of the one; and would it were not superfluous to cite examples of the other! To such purposes poetry cannot be made subservient. Poetry is a sword of lightning, ever unsheathed, which consumes the scabbard that would contain it. And thus we observe that all dramatic writings of this nature are unimaginative in a singular degree; they affect sentiment and passion, which, divested of imagination, are other names for caprice and appetite. The period in our own history of the grossest degradation of the drama is the reign of Charles II., when all forms in which poetry had been accustomed to be expressed became hymns to the triumph of kingly power over liberty and virtue. Milton stood alone illuminating an age unworthy of him. At such periods the calculating principle pervades all the forms of dramatic exhibition, and poetry ceases to be expressed upon them. Comedy loses its ideal universality: wit succeeds to humour; we laugh from self complacency and triumph, instead of pleasure; malignity, sarcasm and contempt, succeed to sympathetic merriment; we hardly laugh, but we smile. Obscenity, which is ever blasphemy against the divine beauty in life, becomes, from the very veil which it assumes, more active if less disgusting: it is a monster for which the corruption of society for ever brings forth new food, which it devours in secret.

The drama being that form under which a greater number of modes of expression of poetry are susceptible of being combined than any other, the connexion of poetry and social good is more observable in the drama than in whatever other form. And it is indisputable that the highest perfection of human society has ever corresponded with the highest dramatic excellence; and that the corruption or the extinction of the drama in a nation where it has once flourished, is a mark of a corruption of manners, and an extinction of the energies which sustain the soul of social life. But, as Machiavelli says of political institutions, that life may be preserved and renewed, if men should arise capable of bringing back the drama to its principles. And this is true with respect to poetry in its most extended sense; all language, institution and form, require not only to be produced but to be sustained: the office and character of a poet participates in the divine nature as regards providence, no less than as regards creation.

Civil war, the spoils of Asia, and the fatal predominance first of the Macedonian, and then of the Roman arms, were so many symbols of the extinction or suspension of the creative faculty in Greece. The bucolic writers, who found patronage under the lettered tyrants of Sicily and Egypt, were the latest representatives of its most glorious reign. Their poetry is intensely melodious; like the odour of the tuberose, it overcomes and sickens the spirit with excess of sweetness; whilst the poetry of the preceding age was as a meadow-gale of June, which mingles the fragrance of all the flowers of the field, and adds a quickening and harmonising spirit of its own which endows the sense with a power of sustaining its extreme delight. The bucolic and erotic delicacy in written poetry is correlative with that softness in statuary, music, and the kindred arts, and even in manners and institutions, which distinguished the epoch to which we now refer. Nor is it the poetical faculty itself, or any misapplication of it, to which this want of harmony is to be imputed. An equal sensibility to the influence of the senses and the affections is to be found in the writings of Homer and Sophocles: the former, especially, has clothed sensual and pathetic images with irresistible attractions. Their superiority over these succeeding writers consists in the presence of those thoughts which belong to the inner faculties of our nature, not in the absence of those which are connected with the external: their incomparable perfection consists in an harmony of the union of all. It is not what the erotic writers have, but what they have not, in which their imperfection consists. It is not inasmuch as they were Poets, but inasmuch as they were not Poets, that they can be considered with any plausibility as connected with the corruption of their age. Had that corruption availed so as to extinguish in them the sensibility to pleasure, passion, and natural scenery, which is imputed to them as an imperfection, the last triumph of evil would have been achieved. For the end of social corruption is to destroy all sensibility to pleasure; and, therefore, it is corruption. It begins at the imagination and the intellect as at the core, and distributes itself thence as a paralysing venom, through the affections into the very appetites, till all become a torpid mass in which sense hardly survives. At the approach of such a period, Poetry ever addresses itself to those faculties which are the last to be destroyed, and its voice is heard, like the footsteps of Astræa,[3] departing from the world. Poetry ever communicates all the pleasure which men are capable of receiving: it is ever still the light of life; the source of whatever of beautiful or generous or true can have place in an evil time. It will readily be confessed that those among the luxurious citizens of

---

[3] Goddess of justice.

Syracuse and Alexandria, who were delighted with the poems of Theocritus, were less cold, cruel, and sensual than the remnant of their tribe. But corruption must have utterly destroyed the fabric of human society before poetry can ever cease. The sacred links of that chain have never been entirely disjoined, which descending through the minds of many men is attached to those great minds, whence as from a magnet the invisible effluence is sent forth, which at once connects, animates and sustains the life of all. It is the faculty which contains within itself the seeds at once of its own and of social renovation. And let us not circumscribe the effects of the bucolic and erotic poetry within the limits of the sensibility of those to whom it was addressed. They may have perceived the beauty of those immortal compositions, simply as fragments and isolated portions: those who are more finely organised, or born in a happier age, may recognise them as episodes to that great poem, which all poets, like the co-operating thoughts of one great mind, have built up since the beginning of the world.

The same revolutions within a narrower sphere had place in antient Rome; but the actions and forms of its social life never seem to have been perfectly saturated with the poetical element. The Romans appear to have considered the Greeks as the selectest treasuries of the selectest forms of manners and of nature, and to have abstained from creating in measured language, sculpture, music, or architecture, any thing which might bear a particular relation to their own condition, whilst it might bear a general one to the universal constitution of the world. But we judge from partial evidence, and we judge perhaps partially. Ennius, Varro, Pacuvius, and Accius, all great poets, have been lost. Lucretius is in the highest, and Virgil in a very high sense, a creator. The chosen delicacy of the expressions of the latter, are as a mist of light which conceal from us the intense and exceeding truth of his conceptions of nature. Livy is instinct with poetry. Yet Horace, Catullus, Ovid, and generally the other great writers of the Virgilian age, saw man and nature in the mirror of Greece. The institutions also, and the religion of Rome, were less poetical than those of Greece, as the shadow is less vivid than the substance. Hence poetry in Rome, seemed to follow, rather than accompany, the perfection of political and domestic society. The true poetry of Rome lived in its institutions; for whatever of beautiful, true, and majestic, they contained, could have sprung only from the faculty which creates the order in which they consist. The life of Camillus, the death of Regulus; the expectation of the Senators, in their godlike state, of the victorious Gauls; the refusal

of the Republic to make peace with Hannibal, after the battle of Cannæ, were not the consequences of a refined calculation of the probable personal advantage to result from such a rhythm and order in the shews of life, to those who were at once the poets and the actors of these immortal dramas. The imagination beholding the beauty of this order, created it out of itself according to its own idea; the consequence was empire, and the reward ever-living fame. These things are not the less poetry, *quia carent vate sacro*.[4] They are the episodes of that cyclic poem written by Time upon the memories of men. The Past, like an inspired rhapsodist, fills the theatre of everlasting generations with their harmony.

At length the antient system of religion and manners had fulfilled the circle of its revolution. And the world would have fallen into utter anarchy and darkness, but that there were found poets among the authors of the Christian and Chivalric systems of manners and religion, who created forms of opinion and action never before conceived; which, copied into the imaginations of men, became as generals to the bewildered armies of their thoughts. It is foreign to the present purpose to touch upon the evil produced by these systems: except that we protest, on the ground of the principles already established, that no portion of it can be imputed to the poetry they contain.

It is probable that the astonishing poetry of Moses, Job, David, Solomon, and Isaiah, had produced a great effect upon the mind of Jesus and his disciples. The scattered fragments preserved to us by the biographers of this extraordinary person, are all instinct with the most vivid poetry. But his doctrines seem to have been quickly distorted. At a certain period after the prevalence of doctrines founded upon those promulgated by him, the three forms into which Plato had distributed the faculties of mind underwent a sort of apotheosis, and became the object of the worship of Europe. Here it is to be confessed that "Light seems to thicken," and

"The crow makes wing to the rooky wood,
Good things of day begin to droop and drowse,
And night's black agents to their preys do rouse."[5]

But mark how beautiful an order has sprung from the dust and blood of this fierce chaos! how the World, as from a resurrection, balancing itself on the golden wings of knowledge and of hope, has reassumed its yet unwearied flight into the Heaven of time. Listen to the music, unheard by outward ears, which is as a

---

4 Horace, *Odes*, IV: "because they lack a sacred poet."
5 Shakespeare, *Macbeth*, III, ii, 50–53 (slightly misquoted).

ceaseless and invisible wind, nourishing its ever-lasting course with strength and swiftness.

The poetry in the doctrines of Jesus Christ, and the mythology and institutions of the Celtic conquerors of the Roman empire, outlived the darkness and the convulsions connected with their growth and victory, and blended themselves into a new fabric of manners and opinion. It is an error to impute the ignorance of the dark ages to the Christian doctrines or the pre-dominance of the Celtic nations. Whatever of evil their agencies may have contained sprang from the extinction of the poetical principle, connected with the progress of despotism and superstition. Men, from causes too intricate to be here discussed, had become insensible and selfish: their own will had become feeble, and yet they were its slaves, and thence the slaves of the will of others: lust, fear, avarice, cruelty, and fraud, characterised a race amongst whom no one was to be found capable of *creating* in form, language, or institution. The moral anomalies of such a state of society are not justly to be charged upon any class of events immediately connected with them, and those events are most entitled to our approbation which could dissolve it most expeditiously. It is unfortunate for those who cannot distinguish words from thoughts, that many of these anomalies have been incorporated into our popular religion.

It was not until the eleventh century that the effects of the poetry of the Christian and Chivalric systems began to manifest themselves. The principle of equality had been discovered and applied by Plato in his Republic, as the theoretical rule of the mode in which the materials of pleasure and of power pro-duced by the common skill and labour of human beings ought to be distributed among them. The limitations of this rule were asserted by him to be determined only by the sensibility of each, or the utility to result to all. Plato, following the doctrines of Timæus and Pythagoras, taught also a moral and intellectual system of doctrine, comprehending at once the past, the present, and the future condition of man. Jesus Christ divulged the sacred and eternal truths contained in these views to mankind, and Christianity, in its abstract purity, became the exoteric expression of the esoteric doctrines of the poetry and wisdom of antiquity. The incorporation of the Celtic nations with the exhausted population of the south, impressed upon it the figure of the poetry existing in their mythology and institutions. The result was a sum of the action and reaction of all the causes included in it; for it may be assumed as a maxim that no nation or religion can supersede any other without incorporating into itself a portion of that which it supersedes. The abolition of personal and domestic slavery, and the emancipation of women from a great part of the degrading restraints of antiquity, were among the consequences of these events.

The abolition of personal slavery is the basis of the highest political hope that it can enter into the mind of man to conceive. The freedom of women pro-duced the poetry of sexual love. Love became a religion, the idols of whose worship were ever present. It was as if the statues of Apollo and the Muses had been endowed with life and motion, and had walked forth among their worshippers; so that earth became peopled by the inhabitants of a diviner world. The familiar appearance and proceedings of life became wonderful and heavenly; and a paradise was created as out of the wrecks of Eden. And as this creation itself is poetry, so its creators were poets; and language was the instrument of their art: "Galeotto fù il libro, e chi lo scrisse."[6] The Provençal Trou-veurs, or inventors, preceded Petrarch, whose verses are as spells, which unseal the inmost enchanted fountains of the delight which is in the grief of love. It is impossible to feel them without becoming a portion of that beauty which we contemplate: it were superfluous to explain how the gentleness and the elevation of mind connected with these sacred emotions can render men more amiable, and generous and wise, and lift them out of the dull vapours of the little world of self. Dante understood the secret things of love even more than Petrarch. His *Vita Nuova* is an inexhaustible fountain of purity of sentiment and language: it is the idealised history of that period, and those intervals of his life which were dedicated to love. His apotheosis of Beatrice in Paradise, and the gradations of his own love and her loveliness, by which as by steps he feigns himself to have ascended to the throne of the Supreme Cause, is the most glorious imagination of modern poetry. The acutest critics have justly reversed the judgment of the vulgar, and the order of the great acts of the "Divine Drama," in the measure of the admiration which they accord to the Hell, Purgatory, and Paradise. The latter is a perpetual hymn of everlasting Love. Love, which found a worthy poet in Plato alone of all the antients, has been celebrated by a chorus of the greatest writers of the renovated world; and the music has penetrated the caverns of society, and its echoes still drown the dissonance of arms and super-stition. At successive intervals, Ariosto, Tasso, Shakspeare, Spenser, Calderon, Rousseau, and the

---

6 "Galeotto was the book, and the one who wrote it." From Dante's *Inferno*, V, where Paolo and Francesca fall in love while reading a story of Gallehaut acting as go-between for Lancelot and Guinivere.

great writers of our own age, have celebrated the dominion of love, planting as it were trophies in the human mind of that sublimest victory over sensuality and force. The true relation borne to each other by the sexes into which human kind is distributed, has become less misunderstood; and if the error which confounded diversity with inequality of the powers of the two sexes has become partially recognised in the opinions and institutions of modern Europe, we owe this great benefit to the worship of which Chivalry was the law, and poets the prophets.

The poetry of Dante may be considered as the bridge thrown over the stream of time, which unites the modern and antient World. The distorted notions of invisible things which Dante and his rival Milton have idealised, are merely the mask and the mantle in which these great poets walk through eternity enveloped and disguised. It is a difficult question to determine how far they were conscious of the distinction which must have subsisted in their minds between their own creeds and that of the people. Dante at least appears to wish to mark the full extent of it by placing Riphæus, whom Virgil calls *justissimus unus*,[7] in Paradise, and observing a most heretical caprice in his distribution of rewards and punishments. And Milton's poem contains within itself a philosophical refutation of that system, of which, by a strange and natural antithesis, it has been a chief popular support. Nothing can exceed the energy and magnificence of the character of Satan as expressed in "Paradise Lost." It is a mistake to suppose that he could ever have been intended for the popular personification of evil. Implacable hate, patient cunning and a sleepless refinement of device to inflict the extremest anguish on an enemy, these things are evil; and, although venial in a slave, are not to be forgiven in a tyrant; although redeemed by much that ennobles his defeat in one subdued, are marked by all that dishonours his conquest in the victor. Milton's Devil as a moral being is as far superior to his God, as One who perseveres in some purpose which he has conceived to be excellent in spite of adversity and torture, is to One who in the cold security of undoubted triumph inflicts the most horrible revenge upon his enemy, not from any mistaken notion of inducing him to repent of a perseverance in enmity, but with the alleged design of exasperating him to deserve new torments. Milton has so far violated the popular creed (if this shall be judged to be a violation) as to have alleged no superiority of moral virtue to his God over his Devil. And this bold neglect of a direct

moral purpose is the most decisive proof of the supremacy of Milton's genius. He mingled as it were the elements of human nature as colours upon a single pallet, and arranged them in the composition of his great picture according to the laws of epic truth; that is, according to the laws of that principle by which a series of actions of the external universe and of intelligent and ethical beings is calculated to excite the sympathy of succeeding generations of mankind. The Divina Commedia and Paradise Lost have conferred upon modern mythology a systematic form; and when change and time shall have added one more superstition to the mass of those which have arisen and decayed upon the earth, commentators will be learnedly employed in elucidating the religion of ancestral Europe, only not utterly forgotten because it will have been stamped with the eternity of genius.

Homer was the first and Dante the second epic poet: that is, the second poet, the series of whose creations bore a defined and intelligible relation to the knowledge and sentiment and religion and political conditions of the age in which he lived, and of the ages which followed it: developing itself in correspondence with their development. For Lucretius had limed the wings of his swift spirit in the dregs of the sensible world;[8] and Virgil, with a modesty which ill became his genius, had affected the fame of an imitator, even whilst he created anew all that he copied; and none among the flock of Mock-birds, though their notes were sweet, Apollonius Rhodius, Quintus Calaber Smyrnetheus, Nonnus, Lucan, Statius, or Claudian,[9] have sought even to fulfil a single condition of epic truth. Milton was the third epic poet. For if the title of epic in its highest sense be refused to the Æneid, still less can it be conceded to the Orlando Furioso, the Gerusalemme Liberata, the Lusiad,[10] or the Fairy Queen.

Dante and Milton were both deeply penetrated with the antient religion of the civilized world; and its spirit exists in their poetry probably in the same proportion as its forms survived in the unreformed worship of modern Europe. The one preceded and the other followed the Reformation at almost equal intervals. Dante was the first religious reformer, and Luther surpassed him rather in the rudeness and acrimony, than in the boldness of his censures of papal usurpation. Dante was the first awakener of entranced Europe; he created a language, in itself music and persuasion, out of a chaos of inharmonious barbarisms. He was the congregator of those great

---

[7] Vergil called Riphæus "the most just of all the pagans" (*Aeneid*, II).

[8] In his *On The Nature of Things* Lucretius endorses an essentially materialist philosophy.

[9] The first three are Greek poets; the second three, Latin.

[10] Three sixteenth-century epics—two Italian, one Portuguese.

spirits who presided over the resurrection of learning; the Lucifer of that starry flock which in the thirteenth century shone forth from republican Italy, as from a heaven, into the darkness of the benighted world. His very words are instinct with spirit; each is as a spark, a burning atom of inextinguishable thought; and many yet lie covered in the ashes of their birth, and pregnant with a lightning which has yet found no conductor. All high poetry is infinite; it is as the first acorn, which contained all oaks potentially. Veil after veil may be undrawn, and the inmost naked beauty of the meaning never exposed. A great poem is a fountain for ever overflowing with the waters of wisdom and delight; and after one person and one age has exhausted all its divine effluence which their peculiar relations enable them to share, another and yet another succeeds, and new relations are ever developed, the source of an unforeseen and an unconceived delight.

The age immediately succeeding to that of Dante, Petrarch, and Boccaccio, was characterized by a revival of painting, sculpture, music, and architecture. Chaucer caught the sacred inspiration, and the superstructure of English literature is based upon the materials of Italian invention.

But let us not be betrayed from a defence into a critical history of Poetry and its influence on Society. Be it enough to have pointed out the effects of poets, in the large and true sense of the word, upon their own and all succeeding times, and to revert to the partial instances cited as illustrations of an opinion the reverse of that attempted to be established by the Author of the Four Ages of Poetry.

But poets have been challenged to resign the civic crown to reasoners and mechanists[11] on another plea. It is admitted that the exercise of the imagination is most delightful, but it is alleged, that that of reason is more useful. Let us examine as the grounds of this distinction, what is here meant by utility. Pleasure or good, in a general sense, is that which the consciousness of a sensitive and intelligent being seeks, and in which, when found, it acquiesces. There are two modes or degrees of pleasure, one durable, universal and permanent; the other transitory and particular. Utility may either express the means of producing the former or the latter. In the former sense, whatever strengthens and purifies the affections, enlarges the imagination, and adds spirit to sense, is useful. But the meaning in which the Author of the Four Ages of Poetry seems to have employed the word utility is the narrower one of banishing the importunity of the wants of our animal nature, the surrounding men with security of life, the dispersing the grosser delusions of superstition, and the conciliating such a degree of mutual forbearance among men as may consist with the motives of personal advantage.

Undoubtedly the promoters of utility, in this limited sense, have their appointed office in society. They follow the footsteps of poets, and copy the sketches of their creations into the book of common life. They make space, and give time. Their exertions are of the highest value, so long as they confine their administration of the concerns of the inferior powers of our nature within the limits due to the superior ones. But whilst the sceptic destroys gross superstitions, let him spare to deface, as some of the French writers have defaced, the eternal truths charactered upon the imaginations of men. Whilst the mechanist abridges, and the political economist combines, labour, let them beware that their speculations, for want of correspondence with those first principles which belong to the imagination, do not tend, as they have in modern England, to exasperate at once the extremes of luxury and want. They have exemplified the saying, "To him that hath, more shall be given; and from him that hath not, the little that he hath shall be taken away." The rich have become richer, and the poor have become poorer; and the vessel of the state is driven between the Scylla and Charybdis[12] of anarchy and despotism. Such are the effects which must ever flow from an unmitigated exercise of the calculating faculty.

It is difficult to define pleasure in its highest sense; the definition involving a number of apparent paradoxes. For, from an inexplicable defect of harmony in the constitution of human nature, the pain of the inferior is frequently connected with the pleasures of the superior portions of our being. Sorrow, terror, anguish, despair itself, are often the chosen expressions of an approximation to the highest good. Our sympathy in tragic fiction depends on this principle; tragedy delights by affording a shadow of the pleasure which exists in pain. This is the source also of the melancholy which is inseparable from the sweetest melody. The pleasure that is in sorrow is sweeter than the pleasure of pleasure itself. And hence the saying, "It is better to go to the house of mourning, than to the house of mirth."[13] Not that this highest species of pleasure is necessarily linked with pain. The delight of love and friendship, the ecstasy of the admiration of nature, the joy of the perception and still more of the creation of poetry is often wholly unalloyed.

---

[11] Mechanical engineers; inventors.

[12] The monster and the whirlpool guarding the straits between Italy and Sicily: *Odyssey*, Book XII.
[13] Eccles. 7:2.

The production and assurance of pleasure in this highest sense is true utility. Those who produce and preserve this pleasure are Poets or poetical philosophers.

The exertions of Locke, Hume, Gibbon, Voltaire, Rousseau,* and their disciples, in favour of oppressed and deluded humanity, are entitled to the gratitude of mankind. Yet it is easy to calculate the degree of moral and intellectual improvement which the world would have exhibited, had they never lived. A little more nonsense would have been talked for a century or two; and perhaps a few more men, women, and children, burnt as heretics. We might not at this moment have been congratulating each other on the abolition of the Inquisition in Spain.[14] But it exceeds all imagination to conceive what would have been the moral condition of the world if neither Dante, Petrarch, Boccaccio, Chaucer, Shakspeare, Calderon, Lord Bacon, nor Milton, had ever existed; if Raphael and Michael Angelo had never been born; if the Hebrew poetry had never been translated; if a revival of the study of Greek literature had never taken place; if no monuments of antient sculpture had been handed down to us; and if the poetry of the religion of the antient world had been extinguished together with its belief. The human mind could never, except by the intervention of these excitements, have been awakened to the invention of the grosser sciences, and that application of analytical reasoning to the aberrations of society, which it is now attempted to exalt over the direct expression of the inventive and creative faculty itself.

We have more moral, political and historical wisdom, than we know how to reduce into practice; we have more scientific and economical knowledge than can be accommodated to the just distribution of the produce which it multiplies. The poetry in these systems of thought, is concealed by the accumulation of facts and calculating processes. There is no want of knowledge respecting what is wisest and best in morals, government, and political economy, or at least, what is wiser and better than what men now practise and endure. But we let "*I dare not* wait upon *I would*, like the poor cat i' the adage."[15] We want the creative faculty to imagine that which we know; we want the generous impulse to act that which we imagine; we want the poetry of life: our calculations have outrun conception; we have eaten more than

we can digest. The cultivation of those sciences which have enlarged the limits of the empire of man over the external world, has, for want of the poetical faculty, proportionally circumscribed those of the internal world; and man, having enslaved the elements, remains himself a slave. To what but a cultivation of the mechanical arts in a degree disproportioned to the presence of the creative faculty, which is the basis of all knowledge, is to be attributed the abuse of all invention for abridging and combining labour, to the exasperation of the inequality of mankind? From what other cause has it arisen that these inventions which should have lightened, have added a weight to the curse imposed on Adam? Thus Poetry, and the principle of Self, of which Money is the visible incarnation, are the God and Mammon of the world.

The functions of the poetical faculty are twofold; by one it creates new materials for knowledge, and power and pleasure; by the other it engenders in the mind a desire to reproduce and arrange them according to a certain rhythm and order which may be called the beautiful and the good. The cultivation of poetry is never more to be desired than at periods when, from an excess of the selfish and calculating principle, the accumulation of the materials of external life exceed the quantity of the power of assimilating them to the internal laws of human nature. The body has then become too unwieldy for that which animates it.

Poetry is indeed something divine. It is at once the centre and circumference of knowledge; it is that which comprehends all science, and that to which all science must be referred. It is at the same time the root and blossom of all other systems of thought; it is that from which all spring, and that which adorns all; and that which, if blighted, denies the fruit and the seed, and withholds from the barren world the nourishment and the succession of the scions of the tree of life. It is the perfect and consummate surface and bloom of things; it is as the odour and the colour of the rose to the texture of the elements which compose it, as the form and the splendour of unfaded beauty to the secrets of anatomy and corruption. What were Virtue, Love, Patriotism, Friendship—what were the scenery of this beautiful Universe which we inhabit; what were our consolations on this side of the grave, and what were our aspirations beyond it, if Poetry did not ascend to bring light and fire from those eternal regions where the owl-winged faculty of calculation dare not ever soar? Poetry is not like reasoning, a power to be exerted according to the determination of the will. A man cannot say, "I will compose poetry." The

* I follow the classification adopted by the Author of the Four Ages of Poetry; but he was essentially a Poet. The others, even Voltaire, were mere reasoners.

◇◇

[14] In 1820; see *Letter to Maria Gisborne*, p. 919.
[15] *Macbeth*, I, vii, 44–5.

greatest poet even cannot say it: for the mind in creation is as a fading coal, which some invisible influence, like an inconstant wind, awakens to transitory brightness: this power arises from within, like the colour of a flower which fades and changes as it is developed, and the conscious portions of our natures are unprophetic either of its approach or its departure. Could this influence be durable in its original purity and force, it is impossible to predict the greatness of the results; but when composition begins, inspiration is already on the decline, and the most glorious poetry that has ever been communicated to the world is probably a feeble shadow of the original conception of the Poet. I appeal to the great poets of the present day, whether it be not an error to assert that the finest passages of poetry are produced by labour and study. The toil and the delay recommended by critics, can be justly interpreted to mean no more than a careful observation of the inspired moments, and an artificial connexion of the spaces between their suggestions by the intertexture of conventional expressions; a necessity only imposed by the limitedness of the poetical faculty itself. For Milton conceived the Paradise Lost as a whole before he executed it in portions. We have his own authority also for the Muse having "dictated" to him the "unpremeditated song," and let this be an answer to those who would allege the fifty-six various readings of the first line of the Orlando Furioso. Compositions so produced are to poetry what mosaic is to painting. This instinct and intuition of the poetical faculty is still more observable in the plastic and pictorial arts; a great statue or picture grows under the power of the artist as a child in the mother's womb; and the very mind which directs the hands in formation is incapable of accounting to itself for the origin, the gradations, or the media of the process.

Poetry is the record of the best and happiest moments of the happiest and best minds. We are aware of evanescent visitations of thought and feeling sometimes associated with place or person, sometimes regarding our own mind alone, and always arising unforeseen and departing unbidden, but elevating and delightful beyond all expression: so that even in the desire and the regret they leave, there cannot but be pleasure, participating as it does in the nature of its object. It is as it were the interpenetration of a diviner nature through our own; but its footsteps are like those of a wind over a sea, which the coming calm erases, and whose traces remain only, as on the wrinkled sand which paves it. These and corresponding conditions of being are experienced principally by those of the most delicate sensibility and the most enlarged imagination; and the state of mind produced by them is at war with every base desire. The enthusiasm of virtue, love, patriotism, and friendship, is essentially linked with these emotions; and whilst they last, self appears as what it is, an atom to a Universe. Poets are not only subject to these experiences as spirits of the most refined organisation, but they can colour all that they combine with the evanescent hues of this ethereal world; a word, or a trait in the representation of a scene or a passion, will touch the enchanted chord, and reanimate, in those who have ever experienced these emotions, the sleeping, the cold, the buried image of the past. Poetry thus makes immortal all that is best and most beautiful in the world; it arrests the vanishing apparitions which haunt the interlunations of life, and veiling them, or in language or in form, sends them forth among mankind, bearing sweet news of kindred joy to those with whom their sisters abide—abide, because there is no portal of expression from the caverns of the spirit which they inhabit into the universe of things. Poetry redeems from decay the visitations of the divinity in Man.

Poetry turns all things to loveliness; it exalts the beauty of that which is most beautiful, and it adds beauty to that which is most deformed; it marries exultation and horror, grief and pleasure, eternity and change; it subdues to union under its light yoke, all irreconcilable things. It transmutes all that it touches, and every form moving within the radiance of its presence is changed by wondrous sympathy to an incarnation of the spirit which it breathes; its secret alchemy turns to potable gold the poisonous waters which flow from death through life; it strips the veil of familiarity from the world, and lays bare the naked and sleeping beauty, which is the spirit of its forms.

All things exist as they are perceived; at least in relation to the percipient. "The mind is its own place, and of itself can make a Heaven of Hell, a Hell of Heaven." [16] But poetry defeats the curse which binds us to be subjected to the accident of surrounding impressions. And whether it spreads its own figured curtain, or withdraws life's dark veil from before the scene of things, it equally creates for us a being within our being. It makes us the inhabitants of a world to which the familiar world is a chaos. It reproduces the common Universe of which we are portions and percipients, and it purges from our inward sight the film of familiarity which obscures from us the wonder of our being. It compels us to feel that which we perceive, and to imagine that which we know. It creatures anew the universe, after it has been

---

[16] *Paradise Lost*, I, 254–55.

annihilated in our minds by the recurrence of impressions blunted by reiteration. It justifies that bold and true word of Tasso: *Non merita nome di creatore, se non Iddio ed il Poeta.*[17]

A poet, as he is the author to others of the highest wisdom, pleasure, virtue and glory, so he ought personally to be the happiest, the best, the wisest, and the most illustrious of men. As to his glory, let Time be challenged to declare whether the fame of any other institutor of human life be comparable to that of a poet. That he is the wisest, the happiest, and the best, inasmuch as he is a poet, is equally incontrovertible: the greatest Poets have been men of the most spotless virtue, of the most consummate prudence, and, if we could look into the interior of their lives, the most fortunate of men: and the exceptions, as they regard those who possessed the imaginative faculty in a high yet inferior degree, will be found on consideration to confirm rather than destroy the rule. Let us for a moment stoop to the arbitration of popular breath, and usurping and uniting in our own persons the incompatible characters of accuser, witness, judge and executioner, let us without trial, testimony, or form, determine that certain motives of those who are "there sitting where we dare not soar,"[18] are reprehensible. Let us assume that Homer was a drunkard, that Virgil was a flatterer, that Horace was a coward, that Tasso was a madman, that Lord Bacon was a peculator, that Raphael was a libertine, that Spenser was a poet laureate. It is inconsistent with this division of our subject to cite living poets, but Posterity has done ample justice to the great names now referred to. Their errors have been weighed and found to have been dust in the balance; if their sins were as scarlet, they are now white as snow: they have been washed in the blood of the mediator and the redeemer, Time. Observe in what a ludicrous chaos the imputations of real or fictitious crime have been confused in the contemporary calumnies against poetry and poets; consider how little is, as it appears—or appears, as it is; look to your own motives, and judge not, lest ye be judged.

Poetry, as has been said, in this respect differs from logic, that it is not subject to the controul of the active powers of the mind, and that its birth and recurrence has no necessary connexion with consciousness or will. It is presumptuous to determine that these are the necessary conditions of all mental causation, when mental effects are experienced insusceptible of being referred to them. The frequent recurrence of the poetical power, it is obvious to suppose, may produce in the mind an habit of order and harmony correlative with its own nature and with its effects upon other minds. But in the intervals of inspiration, and they may be frequent without being durable, a Poet becomes a man, and is abandoned to the sudden reflux of the influences under which others habitually live. But as he is more delicately organized than other men, and sensible to pain and pleasure, both his own and that of others, in a degree unknown to them, he will avoid the one and pursue the other with an ardour proportioned to this difference. And he renders himself obnoxious to calumny, when he neglects to observe the circumstances under which these objects of universal pursuit and flight have disguised themselves in one another's garments.

But there is nothing necessarily evil in this error, and thus cruelty, envy, revenge, avarice, and the passions purely evil, have never formed any portion of the popular imputations on the lives of poets.

I have thought it most favourable to the cause of truth to set down these remarks according to the order in which they were suggested to my mind, by a consideration of the subject itself, instead of following that of the treatise that excited me to make them public. Thus although devoid of the formality of a polemical reply; if the view they contain be just, they will be found to involve a refutation of the doctrines of the Four Ages of Poetry, so far at least as regards the first division of the subject. I can readily conjecture what should have moved the gall of the learned and intelligent author of that paper; I confess myself, like him, unwilling to be stunned by the Theseids of the hoarse Codri[19] of the day. Bavius and Mævius undoubtedly are, as they ever were, insufferable persons. But it belongs to a philosophical critic to distinguish rather than confound.

The first part of these remarks has related to Poetry in its elements and principles; and it has been shewn, as well as the narrow limits assigned them would permit, that what is called poetry, in a restricted sense, has a common source with all other forms of order and of beauty, according to which the materials of human life are susceptible of being arranged, and which is Poetry in an universal sense.

The second part[20] will have for its object an application of these principles to the present state of the cultivation of Poetry, and a defence of the attempt to idealize the modern forms of manners and opinions,

---

[17] "No one merits the name of creator, except God and the Poet."
[18] *Paradise Lost*, IV, 828–29.

[19] Juvenal attacked Codrus, said to have written a tragedy about Theseus; Bavius and Mævius, archetypal bad poets, were satirized in Vergil's *Eclogues*.
[20] Shelley never continued the essay.

and compel them into a subordination to the imaginative and creative faculty. For the literature of England, an energetic development of which has ever preceded or accompanied a great and free development of the national will, has arisen as it were from a new birth. In spite of the low-thoughted envy which would undervalue contemporary merit, our own will be a memorable age in intellectual achievements, and we live among such philosophers and poets as surpass beyond comparison any who have appeared since the last national struggle for civil and religious liberty. The most unfailing herald, companion, and follower of the awakening of a great people to work a beneficial change in opinion or institution, is Poetry. At such periods there is an accumulation of the power of communicating and receiving intense and impassioned conceptions respecting man and nature. The persons in whom this power resides, may often as far as regards many portions of their nature, have little apparent correspondence with that spirit of good of which they are the ministers. But even whilst they deny and abjure, they are yet compelled to serve, the Power which is seated upon the throne of their own soul. It is impossible to read the compositions of the most celebrated writers of the present day without being startled with the electric life which burns within their words. They measure the circumference and sound the depths of human nature with a comprehensive and all-penetrating spirit, and they are themselves perhaps the most sincerely astonished at its manifestations; for it is less their spirit than the spirit of the age. Poets are the hierophants of an unapprehended inspiration; the mirrors of the gigantic shadows which futurity casts upon the present; the words which express what they understand not; the trumpets which sing to battle, and feel not what they inspire; the influence which is moved not, but moves.[21] Poets are the unacknowleged legislators of the world.

---

[21] Aristotle called God the "Unmoved Mover" of the universe.

John Keats

1795–1821

IF IT is seen only in outline, the short life of John Keats at first appears uneventful. By the time they were twenty-five, or shortly thereafter, Wordsworth, Coleridge, Byron, and Shelley had attended either Oxford or Cambridge, had traveled extensively, had fathered children. Keats's experience, in contrast, was far more limited, and his literary education more a matter of chance than plan. In his relationships with people outside his family, he may appear diffident and even passive, his actions often seem to be responses to suggestions from friends or inspirations from a book he has chanced upon. In spite of living in London in the company of people with strongly committed views about society, politics, and religion, Keats seems to have had almost no abstract, programmatic interest in such subjects. The world he made for himself was, on the surface, very limited. But it was not as a consequence superficial. Rather, Keats's brief career was characterized by a chosen intensity and concentration of enormous talents and energies. André Maurois, biographer of both Shelley and Byron, says in *Aspects of Biography* that a great man often "reaches the point of literally 'playing' a part":

> that is to say, his personality loses something of that obscure complexity common to all men and acquires a unity which is not wholly artificial. A great man . . . finds himself modeled by the function he has to perform; unconsciously he aims at making his life a work of art, at becoming what the world would have him be; and so he acquires, not against his will, but in spite of himself and whatever may be his intrinsic worth, that statuesque quality which makes him a fine model for the artist.

A man of twenty-five who, fully aware of his impending death and heroically resisting it, ends his last letter by saying (to Brown), "I can scarcely bid you good-bye even in a letter. I always made an awkward bow," has indeed made his life a work of art, though it may be difficult to find a label for the unity he has created. Keats's poems and letters, taken together, give the lie to the appearance of uneventfulness—both were the means by which Keats reshaped the chaos and banality of the everyday into that rich intensity and astonishing order that exists beyond the ordinary round of dates, places, and people.

Few poets, especially at Keats's age, have ever been so articulate about the connections between their lives and their art. At twenty-one, in *Sleep and Poetry*, he projected for himself a literary career in terms that he would soon reject, but with an outline to which he was faithful. First there was to be a period of indulgence in luxury, "the fair / Visions of all places," seen from a bowery nook that yields refreshment and comfort, a sanctuary that enables one to "seize / Like a strong giant" the "events of this wide world." In being a protected spectator, he says, he would proudly discover at the shoulders of his spirit "Wings to find out immortality" so that he can eventually bid farewell to the self-indulgent joys of security, "pass them for a nobler life, / Where I may find the agonies, the strife / Of human hearts." Although he asked for ten years' apprenticeship in fantasy to prepare himself for such a heroic task, the writing of *Endymion* seems to have been more than enough, and even before that poem was finished his tone toward it and most of what it represented became mildly dismissive. Imagining he has been asked why he wrote such a long poem, he answers, "Do not the lovers of Poetry like to have a little Region to wander in where they may pick and choose, and in which the images are so numerous that many are forgotten and found new in a second Reading? . . . Besides a long Poem is a test of Invention which I take to be the Polar Star of Poetry. . . ."

A year and a half later, in a letter to J. H. Reynolds, Keats creates a new metaphor for his career when he compares himself (and Reynolds) to Wordsworth and says, thinking of *Tintern Abbey*, that if human life is "a large Mansion of Many Apartments" both poets have passed through "the infant or thoughtless Chamber" and the Chamber of Maiden-Thought where they were "intoxicated with the light and the atmosphere, . . . [saw] nothing but pleasant wonders, and [thought] of delaying there forever in delight." But the breathing there has also sharpened "one's vision into the heart and nature of Man," convinced "one's nerves that the world is full of Misery and Heartbreak, Pain, Sickness and oppression." As a result the chamber is darkened, doors on all sides are opened "all leading to dark passages—We see not the balance of good and evil. We are in a Mist." The present task, then, is the exploration of those passages, carrying forward the "burden of the Mystery." As in *Sleep and Poetry*, the way ahead is still necessarily vague, but the terms for the journey have radically altered. In that poem the present ideal was to "rest in silence, like two gems upcurled / In the recesses of a pearly shell" and the vision of the future if less luxurious was equally fantastic, with its chariot, steeds with shiny manes, and driver who writes with "such a hurrying glow." And the sense of "real things" in *Sleep and Poetry* was represented by a vague "muddy stream." At the end of the letter to Reynolds real things have become more explicit: "Moore's present to Hazlitt" and the blood spit by his dying brother Tom. The purpose of poetry, too, has subtly changed—no longer is it to be "a friend / To soothe the cares and lift the thoughts of man." Now, in May 1818, Keats sees poetry as a mode of exploration, and in later letters he will see it as the poet's means of creating his own identity and reconciling the paradox always implicit in the notion of consummation: the fact that an intense sense of present experience is necessary for fullness of feeling (whether religious, sexual, or aesthetic), but that a past before the experience and a future subsequent to it are equally necessary if the moment is to have the continuity on which meaning (and language) depends.

When at the end of 1816 Keats had hoped for ten years just to fulfill his apprenticeship as a poet of wonders, sensuous luxury, and escape, he had less than three years to write, four to live. As if he were aware of this foreshortening, the poems written during those subsequent three years show a rapidly accelerating intensity of concern with subject, style, purpose. Like the letters, they rarely dwell on, exhaust, or illustrate subjects. Rather, the poems are a way of exploring and discovering, and the poet seems to be barely finished before he rushes on to new dark passages and new styles with which to explore them. However often Keats expresses a delight in indolence, his literary sensibility was volatile. On March 25, 1818, at Teignmouth, Keats had just finished his rather disparaging preface to *Endymion* and sent to Reynolds a letter (reprinted below as *To J. H. Reynolds, Esq.*) largely in verse that is partly humorous doggerel, partly earnest discovery of a new and significant literary mode. Beginning with the absurd, inchoate images (shaped into amusing couplets) of a man falling asleep, he composes them gradually into a dream: first there is a vision of an enchanted castle, then a romantic fairly tale the frame of which is broken after thirty-five lines when a herdsman's story about what he has seen is not believed. Abruptly Keats steps back to comment on dreams and fantasy, deploring the fact that most dreams instead of providing a refuge "shadow our own soul's day-time / In the dark void of night." Unfortunately, he says, the imagination is not under the autonomous control of its possessor: "Things cannot to the will / Be settled, but they tease us out of thought," or perhaps "Imagination brought / Beyond its proper bound ... Cannot refer to any standard law / Of either earth or heaven." As a consequence the imagination that heightens the perception of beauty is simultaneously destructive: "It forces us in Summer skies to mourn, / It spoils the singing of the Nightingale."

He ends the verse epistle with another narrative, this time of his own experience: sitting on the Devon shore at evening he should have been satisfied with the beauty of the scene his eyes composed,

> but I saw
> Too far into the sea, where every maw
> The greater on the less feeds evermore—
> But I saw too distinct into the core
> Of an eternal fierce destruction.

Though he turns once again to make light of such "horrid" moods of the mind and to mock his own seriousness, this way of looking is one that Keats never subsequently relinquishes for long. Having once acknowledged that the destructive ferocity of a gentle robin ravening a worm is a smaller, equally terrible, version of the shark at savage prey, and that the smooth surface of all existence contains terror for the imaginative perceiver, he cannot forget it. He tells Reynolds that he will seek refuge from such awareness in new romance—the verse adaptation of Boccaccio's tale of Isabella and the pot of basil that he and Reynolds had discussed—and in less than a month he has finished it. But too honest to his own changing feelings to create another narrative in the mode of *Endymion*, Keats repeatedly breaks the tone of *Isabella* by looking too closely, for instance at the brothers who "turn'd an easy wheel" that made the ears of the Ceylon diver (who found their pearls) gush with blood and the seal on the cold ice "with piteous bark [lie] full of darts." Perhaps anyone could, looking at his shoes, imagine the horror of the slaughterhouse that produced their leather. But Keats here seems unable to stop looking and unable to

accept surfaces for more than a moment—his own imagination creates a reality far
more effecting to him than that of the tale he is adapting. His indignation is suddenly
aroused at what he has made, and his shrill protesting occupies several stanzas.
Only with an apostrophe to Boccaccio does he resume the narrative. Similar moments
occur repeatedly in the poem, with similarly awkward consequences for the narrative:

> Who hath not loiter'd in a green church-yard,
>   And let his spirit, like a demon-mole,
> Work through the clayey soil and gravel hard,
>   To see scull, coffin'd bones, and funeral stole;
> Pitying each form that hungry Death hath marr'd,
>   And filling it once more with human soul?
> Ah! this is holiday to what was felt
> When Isabella by Lorenzo knelt.

Not until the following winter, in *The Eve of St. Agnes*, did Keats find a mode that
could satisfactorily reconcile an interest in medieval narrative with a disposition to
see too far into and around his own creations, by making there the perception of
fantasy and reality the concern of the narrative itself. Before Porphyro and Madeline
flee into the storm, their world (and that of the reader) is turned inside out. And the
Odes, composed a year after *Isabella*, are the most direct confrontation of the
questions raised by the letter to Reynolds, even echoing its language. Is the nightin-
gale a vision or a waking dream? Is its singing spoiled by the perception of other
realities? Is the urn a sylvan historian or a cold pastoral, a moment of intense
experience or just a vase, and is its power to tease us out of thought its value or its
danger? An ode, unlike most narratives, can sustain such ambiguities—in which
both attitudes or experiences are real, and the existence of the poem itself shows how
contending realities can be sustained by composing them.

Of course no one changes his mind so simply and completely in writing a verse
epistle, least of all Keats, whose way of thinking is characterized by its contradictions
as well as its complexity. Any attempt to draw a line from the letter to Reynolds to the
Odes necessarily simplifies. Other very different and equally valid statements could
be made about the changes in Keats's versification, his shifting attitudes toward
fame and the public, his developing interest in drama, his increasing preoccupation
with the evanescence of experience and his sense of the failure of any sensuous
apprehension—of food, sexual pleasure, a season—to last. But all attempts to describe
the development of Keats's interests would probably share a sense of acceleration,
almost desperation, as though Keats knew very early that he must explore in a few
months the sort of questions to which most poets can devote decades. Wordsworth,
for instance, worked on *The Ruined Cottage* for fifteen years, off and on, until it
became Book I of *The Excursion*. *Peter Bell* lived for twenty years between conception
and publication, *The Prelude* for half a century. In contrast Keats worked away at
Hyperion, an epic narrative of the imaginative possibilities of life, from November
1818 until the following spring. When Keats reached the point at which Apollo
becomes a god, he abandoned the poem—perhaps because he could think of no more

he wanted to say as narrator of someone else's story. But less than five months later he returned to the questions that poem had raised, determined now to confront the significance of the poet's imagination in the first person, through a dream vision. But again he broke off as his invention was stopped by doubts so intense that any literary form he could imagine would distort them. The second try, *The Fall of Hyperion*, became a second fragment in Keats's impassioned search for role, style, belief, and vocation. Between the two versions he had written the great Odes, but they were finished and therefore finite statements of the paradoxes that both plagued and fascinated him. By looking upon the face of Moneta, Aileen Ward argues in her biography of Keats, Keats confronted directly the faces of fear and guilt and sexuality and death that haunt the poems and letters throughout his career. But in its definition of the poet's place among men, and in its style, the *Fall* is ambiguous, open-ended and impossible to fulfill explicitly. Nevertheless, the year framed by the two *Hyperions*, says Robert Gittings in *The Living Year*, "had been the greatest year of living growth of any English poet."

The popular speculation that had Keats lived he might have become a great dramatist, which arises in noticing Keats's fascination with Shakespeare and his humanistic approach to experience, gains credibility from the way in which Keats in the *Fall* exhausts one more style in his search for a mode responsive to his belief, congenial to his talents, and provocative to his ambitions. Because Keats had less confidence in conventional Christianity than Wordsworth and less sustained interest in myth-making than Shelley, drama would seem to have been the ideal mode in which to reconcile a growing interest in men and women (rather than Wonders) with his existential belief in the tragic nature of life. Like Wordsworth and Coleridge in 1802, Keats at the end of 1819 saw and was beginning to meet yet again the necessity for change—though the histories of Wordsworth and Coleridge also remind us that a final crucial change, whatever it means to the artist, is not necessarily conducive to great work.

Even before his deteriorating health forced silence on him, Keats knew he must choose between half-knowledge or none. Negative capability, which he praised in Shakespeare as the ability to exist "in uncertainties, mysteries, doubts, without any irritable reaching after fact and reason," was for him a matter of necessity (see his letter to his brothers in December 1817). From the fragments of articulated experience that most poets can look back on as the experiments of their youth, Keats had to construct a whole identity if he was to achieve his ambition to "be among the English poets at my death."

Keats's greatness depends in part on his having constructed so much out of what he did not have. His unsympathetic contemporaries—the reviewers who mocked the Cockney School—saw many of the same facts, with a very different emphasis, that Yeats did a century later:

> I see a school boy when I think of him
> With face and nose pressed to a sweetshop window
> For certainly he sank into his grave
> His senses and his heart unsatisfied

And made—being poor, ailing, and ignorant,
Shut out from all the luxury of the world,
The coarse bred son of livery stable keeper—
Luxuriant song.

And the song is luxuriant not only because of the beauty of its art. Few poets have ever shown so quickly such a range of ability, such an openness to the complexity of their own experience. However uneventful the facts of Keats's life, and however often he denied himself and was himself denied, this diminishment was the occasion for an intense struggle between imagination and the world which his art began to resolve almost as quickly as his illness ended it.

OUTLINE OF EVENTS

1794	Oct. 9	Thomas Keats (1774?–1804), head ostler and later manager of livery stable in Finsbury, north of London, marries Frances Jennings (1775–1810), daughter of the livery stable owner, at St. George's, Hanover Square.
1795	Oct. 31	Son John born.
1797	Feb. 28	Son George (1797–1841) born.
1799	Nov. 18	Son Tom (1799–1818) born.
1801	Apr. 28	Son Edward (1801–1805) born.
1803	June 3	Daughter Frances Mary (Fanny) [Llanos] (1803–1889) born.
		Keats, with George, later Tom, attends Clarke's School, Enfield (until 1811).
1804	Apr. 16	Father dies after riding accident.
	June 27	Mother marries William Rawlings. Keats children go to live with grandparents (John and Alice Jennings).
1805	Mar. 8	John Jennings dies. Family moves to Edmonton.
1810	Mar.	Keats's mother dies. Richard Abbey appointed guardian of four children.
1811	Summer	Keats leaves school; is apprenticed to Hammond, Edmonton surgeon.
1814		Writes *Imitation of Spenser, To Lord Byron, On Death*, etc.
	Dec.	Mrs. Jennings (grandmother) dies.
1815	Feb.	Keats writes sonnet on Leigh Hunt leaving prison; also *To Hope, Ode to Apollo*, etc.
	Oct.	Enters Guy's Hospital, London, as student; later dresser.
	Nov.	Writes *Epistle to G. F. Mathew, O Solitude*, etc.
1816	May	*O Solitude* published in *Examiner*.
	June	Writes "*To one who has been long in city pent*."
	July	Qualifies as apothecary, physician, surgeon.

	Aug.	Goes to Margate with brother Tom (until Sept.)
	Oct.	Takes lodgings with brothers in south London. Meets Leigh Hunt, B. R. Haydon, J. H. Reynolds. Writes *Chapman's Homer* sonnet.
	Nov.–Dec.	Writes sonnets to Haydon, *Sleep and Poetry*, "*I stood tiptoe.*"
	Dec.	Meets Shelley.
1817	Mar. 3	*Poems* published by C & D. Ollier.
	Mar. 25	By this date Keats has moved to Well Walk, Hampstead, with brothers.
	Apr. 15	Goes to Isle of Wight.
	Apr. 17	Writes *On the Sea.*
	Apr. 18	Begins to plan *Endymion.*
	Apr. 24	Goes to Margate; joined by brother Tom.
	June 10	Back in Hampstead.
	Sept. 3–Oct. 5	In Oxford with Benjamin Bailey.
	Nov. 28	Finishes first draft of *Endymion.*
	Dec. 16	Meets Wordsworth; sees him frequently in following weeks.
	Dec. 28	Haydon's dinner for Keats, Lamb, Wordsworth, etc.
1818	Jan. 3	Calls on Wordsworth and Sara Hutchinson.
	Jan. 20	Begins weekly attendance at Hazlitt's lectures.
	Jan. 22	Writes sonnet on rereading *King Lear.*
	Mar. 6–May 11	At Teignmouth, Devon, with brother Tom.
	Mar. 19	Writes Preface to *Endymion.*
	Mar. 25	Writes verse epistle to J. H. Reynolds; begins steady work on *Isabella.*
	April	*Endymion* published.
	April 27	Finishes *Isabella.*
	May 28(?)	George Keats marries Georgiana Wylie.
	June 22–Aug. 18	Goes to Liverpool, Lake District, Scotland, Ireland (briefly) with Charles Brown. George and Georgiana Keats sail for Philadelphia (later to Kentucky).
	Aug. 19–25	Keats suffers severe sore throat.
	Oct. 24	Meets Isabella Jones (first met at Hastings in spring of 1817).
	Nov. (perhaps earlier)	First meets Fanny Brawne (1800–1865).
	Nov. (to April 1819)	Works on *Hyperion.*
	Dec. 1	Brother Tom dies. Keats moved to Wentworth Place (Hampstead) with C. Brown.
1819	Jan. 18–Feb. 1	To Chichester, Bedhampton; writes *Eve of St. Agnes.*
	Apr. 11	Walks with S. T. Coleridge on Hampstead Heath.

	Apr. 21	Writes *La Belle Dame* (revised May 1820).
	May	Writes odes on Nightingale, Grecian Urn, Melancholy, Indolence.
	Aug. 12–Oct. 8	At Winchester with Brown (except for five-day visit to London in September).
	Sept. 19	Writes *To Autumn*.
	Oct. (or Nov.)	Formally engaged to Fanny Brawne.
	Oct. (Nov. or Dec.?)	*Bright Star* composed.
	Nov.	Works on *King Stephen*; writes "*I cry your mercy*."
	Dec.	*Otho* (Keats and Brown) accepted by Drury Lane.
1820	Feb. 3	Suffers severe hemorrhage.
	Feb. 13	Offers to break engagement to Fanny Brawne.
	June 23	Moves in with Leigh Hunts.
	July 1 (or 3)	*Lamia* volume published.
	Aug. 12	Returns to Hampstead to live with Brawnes.
	Aug. 16	Declines Shelley's invitation to join him in Italy.
	Sept. 13	Last meeting with Fanny Brawne.
	Sept. 18	Sails with Severn for Italy from Gravesend.
	Oct. 21	Arrives in Naples.
	Nov. 15	Keats and Severn take lodgings in Piazza di Spagna, Rome.
	Nov. 30	Last (surviving) letter to Charles Brown.
1821	Feb. 23	Keats dies at 11 p.m.
	Feb. 26	Buried in Protestant Cemetery, Rome.

SELECTED BIBLIOGRAPHY

BIBLIOGRAPHIES
Keats: A Bibliography and Reference Guide, ed. J. R. MacGillivray (1949).

EDITIONS
Poetical Works, ed. H. W. Garrod (1939, rev. 1958).
The Poems of Keats, ed. Miriam Allott (1970).
The Letters of John Keats, 1814–1821, ed. H. E. Rollins (2 vols., 1958).
The Keats Circle: Letters and Papers 1816–1878, ed. H. E. Rollins (2 vols., 1948; rev. 1965).

BIOGRAPHICAL INFORMATION
R. GITTINGS, *John Keats: The Living Year* (1954).
W. J. BATE, *John Keats* (1963).
A. WARD, *John Keats: The Making of a Poet* (1963).
R. GITTINGS, *John Keats* (1968).

GENERAL CRITICISM

M. R. RIDLEY, *Keats' Craftsmanship* (1933).

C. L. FINNEY, *The Evolution of Keats's Poetry* (2 vols., 1936).

F. R. LEAVIS, "Keats," *Revaluation* (1936).

H. M. MCLUHAN, "Aesthetic Pattern in Keats's Odes," *UTQ* (1943).

E. R. WASSERMAN, *The Finer Tone: Keats' Major Poems* (1953; rev. 1968).

L. TRILLING, "The Poet as Hero: Keats in His Letters," *The Opposing Self* (1955).

H. T. LYON, ed., *The Well-Read Urn* (1958).

W. J. BATE, ed., *Keats: A Collection of Critical Essays* (1964).

W. H. EVERT, *Aesthetic and Myth in the Poetry of Keats* (1965).

D. BUSH, *John Keats: His Life and Writings* (1966).

I. JACK, *Keats and the Mirror of Art* (1967).

R. MAYHEAD, *John Keats* (1967).

F. INGLIS, *Keats* (1968).

J. O'NEILL, ed., *Critics on Keats* (1968).

J. STILLINGER, ed., *Keats's Odes* (1968).

N. TALBOT, *The Major Poems of John Keats* (1968).

J. JONES, *John Keats's Dream of Truth* (1969).

A. DANZIG, ed., *Twentieth Century Interpretations of The Eve of St. Agnes* (1970).

M. DICKSTEN, *Keats and His Poetry: A Study in Development* (1971).

T. HILTON, *Keats and His World* (1971).

POEMS

IMITATION OF SPENSER

NOW Morning from her orient chamber came,
And her first footsteps touch'd a verdant hill;
Crowning its lawny crest with amber flame,
Silv'ring the untainted gushes of its rill;
Which, pure from mossy beds, did down distill,
And after parting beds of simple flowers,
By many streams a little lake did fill,
Which round its marge reflected woven bowers,
And, in its middle space, a sky that never lowers.

There the king-fisher saw his plumage bright   10
Vieing with fish of brilliant dye below;
Whose silkens fins, and golden scalès light
Cast upward, through the waves, a ruby glow:
There saw the swan his neck of arched snow,
And oar'd himself along with majesty;
Sparkled his jetty eyes; his feet did show
Beneath the waves like Afric's ebony,
And on his back a fay reclined voluptuously.

Ah! could I tell the wonders of an isle
That in that fairest lake had placed been,   20
I could e'en Dido of her grief[1] beguile;
Or rob from aged Lear his bitter teen:[2]
For sure so fair a place was never seen,
Of all that ever charm'd romantic eye:
It seem'd an emerald in the silver sheen
Of the bright waters; or as when on high,
Through clouds of fleecy white, laughs the cœrulean sky.

And all around it dipp'd luxuriously
Slopings of verdure through the glassy tide,
Which, as it were in gentle amity,   30
Rippled delighted up the flowery side;
As if to glean the ruddy tears, it tried,

---

[1] Aeneas has deserted her in favor of the city the gods have promised him.
[2] Sorrow.

Which fell profusely from the rose-tree stem!
Haply it was the workings of its pride,
In strife to throw upon the shore a gem
Outvieing all the buds in Flora's diadem.

[1814]   [1817]

ON PEACE

The occasion of the following poem was probably the end of the war with France in April 1814. In May, Louis XVIII returned to the throne, and Napoleon went to Elba.

[Sonnet]
ON PEACE

O PEACE! and dost thou with thy presence bless
    The dwellings of this war-surrounded Isle;
Soothing with placid brow our late distress,
    Making the triple kingdom brightly smile?
Joyful I hail thy presence; and I hail
    The sweet companions that await on thee;
Complete my joy—let not my first wish fail,
    Let the sweet mountain nymph thy favourite be,
With England's happiness proclaim Europa's Liberty.
O Europe! let not sceptred tyrants see   10
    That thou must shelter in thy former state;
Keep thy chains burst, and boldly say thou are free;
    Give thy kings law—leave not uncurbed the great;
    So with the honors past thou'lt win thy happier
        fate!

[1814?]   [1904]

[Sonnet]
TO LORD BYRON

BYRON! how sweetly sad thy melody!
    Attuning still the soul to tenderness,
    As if soft Pity, with unusual stress,
Had touch'd her plaintive lute, and thou, being by,
Hadst caught the tones, nor suffer'd them to die.
    O'ershading sorrow doth not make thee less
    Delightful: thou thy griefs dost dress
With a bright halo, shining beamily,
As when a cloud a golden moon doth veil,
    Its sides are ting'd with a resplendent glow,   10
Through the dark robe oft amber rays prevail,
    And like fair veins in sable marble flow;
Still warble, dying swan! still tell the tale,
    The enchanting tale, the tale of pleasing woe.

[1814]   [1848]

The occasion of this poem was the death of Keats's grandmother, Alice Jennings, in December 1814.

[Sonnet]
"As from the darkening gloom . . ."

AS from the darkening gloom a silver dove
    Upsoars, and darts into the Eastern light,
    On pinions that naught moves but pure delight,
So fled thy soul into the realms above,
Regions of peace and everlasting love;
    Where happy spirits, crown'd with circlets bright
    Of starry beam, and gloriously bedight,
Taste the high joy none but the blest can prove.
There thou or joinest the immortal quire
    In melodies that even Heaven fair   10
Fill with superior bliss, or, at desire
    Of the omnipotent Father, cleavest the air
On holy message sent—What pleasures higher?
    Wherefore does any grief our joy impair?

[1814]   [1876]

TO CHATTERTON

By killing himself in despair and poverty at the age of seventeen, Thomas Chatterton (1752–1770), the "marvelous boy" of Wordsworth's Resolution and Independence, became a conventional example of unfulfilled literary talent and unrequited ambition. Keats dedicated Endymion to his memory. See also Coleridge's Monody on the Death of Chatterton, p. 430.

[Sonnet]
TO CHATTERTON

O CHATTERTON! how very sad thy fate!
    Dear child of sorrow—son of misery!
    How soon the film of death obscur'd that eye,
Whence Genius wildly flash'd, and high debate.
How soon that voice, majestic and elate,
    Melted in dying numbers! Oh! how nigh
    Was night to thy fair morning. Thou didst die
A half-blown flow'ret which cold blasts amate.[1]
But this is past: thou art among the stars
    Of highest Heaven: to the rolling spheres   10
Thou sweetly singest: naught thy hymning mars,
    Above the ingrate world and human fears.
On earth the good man base detraction bars
    From thy fair name, and waters it with tears.

[1815]   [1848]

[1] "Destroy": an archaic word used by Chatterton.

Leigh Hunt (1784–1859), poet, essayist, editor, and political radical (he had been imprisoned for two years for calling the Prince Regent a "fat Adonis of fifty"), subsequently became a patron and mentor of Keats, a friend of Shelley and Byron as well.

[Sonnet]
WRITTEN ON THE DAY THAT MR. LEIGH HUNT LEFT PRISON

WHAT though, for showing truth to flatter'd state,
   Kind Hunt was shut in prison, yet has he,
   In his immortal spirit, been as free
As the sky-searching lark, and as elate.
Minion of grandeur! think you he did wait?
   Think you he nought but prison walls did see,
   Till, so unwilling, thou unturn'dst the key?
Ah, no! far happier, nobler was his fate!
In Spenser's halls he strayed, and bowers fair,
   Culling enchanted flowers; and he flew   10
With daring Milton through the fields of air:
   To regions of his own his genius true
Took happy flights. Who shall his fame impair
   When thou art dead, and all thy wretched crew?

[1815]   [1817]

TO HOPE

WHEN by my solitary hearth[1] I sit,
   And hateful thoughts enwrap my soul in gloom;
When no fair dreams before my "mind's eye" flit,
   And the bare heath of life presents no bloom;
     Sweet Hope, ethereal balm upon me shed,
     And wave thy silver pinions o'er my head.

Whene'er I wander, at the fall of night,
   Where woven boughs shut out the moon's bright
       ray,
Should sad Despondency my musings fright,
   And frown, to drive fair Cheerfulness away,   10
     Peep with the moon-beams through the leafy
       roof,
     And keep that fiend Despondence far aloof.

Should Disappointment, parent of Despair,
   Strive for her son to seize my careless heart;
When, like a cloud, he sits upon the air,
   Preparing on his spell-bound prey to dart:
     Chace him away, sweet Hope, with visage bright,
     And fright him as the morning frightens night!

Whene'er the fate of those I hold most dear[2]
   Tells to my fearful breast a tale of sorrow,   20
O bright-eyed Hope, my morbid fancy cheer;
   Let me awhile thy sweetest comforts borrow:
     Thy heaven-born radiance around me shed,
     And wave thy silver pinions o'er my head!

Should e'er unhappy love my bosom pain,
   From cruel parents, or relentless fair;
O let me think it is not quite in vain
   To sigh our sonnets to the midnight air!
     Sweet Hope, ethereal balm upon me shed,
     And wave thy silver pinions o'er my head!   30

In the long vista of the years to roll,
   Let me not see our country's honour fade:
O let me see our land retain her soul,
   Her pride, her freedom; and not freedom's shade.
     From thy bright eyes unusual brightness shed—
     Beneath thy pinions canopy my head!

Let me not see the patriot's high bequest,
   Great Liberty! how great in plain attire!
With the base purple of a court oppress'd,
   Bowing her head, and ready to expire: 40
     But let me see thee stoop from heaven on wings
     That fill the skies with silver glitterings!

And as, in sparkling majesty, a star
   Gilds the bright summit of some gloomy cloud;
Brightening the half-veil'd face of heaven afar:
   So, when dark thoughts my boding spirit shroud,
     Sweet Hope, celestial influence round me shed,
     Waving thy silver pinions o'er my head.

[1815]   [1817]

ODE TO APOLLO

IN thy western halls of gold
   When thou sittest in thy state,
Bards, that erst sublimely told
   Heroic deeds, and sang of fate,
With fervour seize their adamantine lyres,
Whose chords are solid rays, and twinkle radiant fires.

---

[1] In Edmonton, where he was apprenticed to the surgeon Thomas Hammond.

[2] His sister Fanny was living with her guardian Richard Abbey; George and Tom were working at Abbey's.

There Homer with his nervous [1] arms
    Strikes the twanging harp of war,
And even the western splendour warms,
    While the trumpets sound afar: 10
But, what creates the most intense surprise,
His soul looks out through renovated eyes.

Then, through thy Temple wide, melodious swells
    The sweet majestic tone of Maro's [2] lyre:
The soul delighted on each accent dwells,—
    Enraptured dwells,—not daring to respire,
The while he tells of grief around a funeral pyre.

'Tis awful silence then again;
    Expectant stand the spheres;
    Breathless the laurell'd peers,   20
Nor move, till ends the lofty strain,
Nor move till Milton's tuneful thunders cease,
And leave once more the ravish'd heavens in peace.

Thou biddest Shakspeare wave his hand,
    And quickly forward spring
The Passions—a terrific band—
    And each vibrates the string
That with its tyrant temper best accords,
While from their Master's lips pour forth the
        inspiring words.

A silver trumpet Spenser blows,   30
    And, as its martial notes to silence flee,
From a virgin chorus flows
    A hymn in praise of spotless Chastity. [3]
'Tis still! Wild warblings from the Æolian lyre [4]
Enchantment softly breathe, and tremblingly expire.

Next thy Tasso's [5] ardent numbers
    Float along the pleased air,
Calling youth from idle slumbers,
    Rousing them from Pleasure's lair:—
Then o'er the strings his fingers gently move,   40
And melt the soul to pity and to love.

But when *Thou* joinest with the Nine, [6]
    And all the powers of song combine,
    We listen here on earth:
The dying tones that fill the air,
And charm the ear of evening fair,
From thee, great God of Bards, receive their heavenly
        birth.

[1815]   [1848]

---

[1] Vigorous.
[2] Vergil (Publius Virgilius Maro).
[3] *Faerie Queene*, III.
[4] See note to Coleridge's *Eolian Harp*, p. 441.
[5] Author of the sixteenth-century Italian epic *Jerusalem Delivered*.
[6] Apollo and the Nine Muses.

[Three Sonnets on Woman]

[I]

WOMAN! when I behold thee flippant, vain,
    Inconstant, childish, proud, and full of fancies;
    Without that modest softening that enhances
The downcast eye, repentant of the pain
That its mild light creates to heal again:
    E'en then, elate, my spirit leaps, and prances,
    E'en then my soul with exultation dances
For that to love, so long, I've dormant lain:
But when I see thee meek, and kind, and tender,
    Heavens! how desperately do I adore   10
Thy winning graces;—to be thy defender
    I hotly burn—to be a Calidore—
A very Red Cross Knight—a stout Leander [1]—
    Might I be loved by thee like these of yore.

[II]

LIGHT feet, dark violet eyes, and parted hair;
    Soft dimpled hands, white neck, and creamy breast,
    Are things on which the dazzled senses rest
Till the fond, fixed eyes forget they stare.
From such fine pictures, heavens! I cannot dare
    To turn my admiration, though unpossess'd
    They be of what is worthy,—though not drest
In lovely modesty, and virtues rare.
Yet these I leave as thoughtless as a lark;
    These lures I straight forget,—e'en ere I dine,   10
Or thrice my palate moisten: but when I mark
    Such charms with mild intelligences shine,
My ear is open like a greedy shark,
    To catch the tunings of a voice divine.

[III]

AH! who can e'er forget so fair a being?
    Who can forget her half retiring sweets?
    God! she is like a milk-white lamb that bleats
For man's protection. Surely the All-seeing,
Who joys to see us with his gifts agreeing,
    Will never give him pinions, who intreats
    Such innocence to ruin,—who vilely cheats
A dove-like bosom. In truth there is no freeing
One's thoughts from such a beauty; when I hear
    A lay that once I saw her hand awake,   10
Her form seems floating palpable, and near;
    Had I e'er seen her from an arbour take
A dewy flower, oft would that hand appear,
    And o'er my eyes the trembling moisture shake.

[1815? 1816?]   [1817]

---

[1] Examples of devoted love: the first two in *The Faerie Queene*, Leander from the legend of his swimming the Hellespont to meet Hero.

TO SOME LADIES

WHAT though while the wonders of nature exploring,
  I cannot your light, mazy footsteps attend;
Nor listen to accents, that almost adoring,
  Bless Cynthia's face, the enthusiast's friend:[1]

Yet over the steep, whence the mountain stream
    rushes,
  With you, kindest friends, in idea I muse;
Mark the clear tumbling crystal, its passionate gushes,
  Its spray that the wild flower kindly bedews.

Why linger you so, the wild labyrinth strolling?
  Why breathless, unable your bliss to declare?   10
Ah! you list to the nightingale's tender condoling,
  Responsive to sylphs, in the moon beamy air.

'Tis morn, and the flowers with dew are yet drooping,
  I see you are treading the verge of the sea:
And now! ah, I see it—you just now are stooping
  To pick up the keep-sake intended for me.

If a cherub, on pinions of silver descending,
  Had bought me a gem from the fret-work of
    heaven;
And smiles with his star-cheering voice sweetly
    blending,
  The blessings of Tighe[2] had melodiously given;   20

It had not created a warmer emotion
  Than the present, fair nymphs, I was blest with
    from you,
Than the shell, from the bright golden sands of the
    ocean
  Which the emerald waves at your feet gladly threw.

For, indeed, 'tis a sweet and peculiar pleasure,
  (And blissful is he who such happiness finds,)
To possess but a sand in the hour of leisure,
  In elegant, pure, and aerial minds.

[1815]   [1817]

ON RECEIVING A CURIOUS SHELL,
AND A COPY OF VERSES,
FROM THE SAME LADIES

HAST thou from the caves of Golconda,[1] a gem
  Pure as the ice-drop that froze on the mountain?
Bright as the humming-bird's green diadem,
  When it flutters in sun-beams that shine through a
    fountain?

Hast thou a goblet for dark sparkling wine?
  That goblet right heavy, and massy, and gold?
And splendidly mark'd with the story divine
  Of Armida the fair, and Rinaldo the bold?[2]

Hast thou a steed with a mane richly flowing?
  Hast thou a sword that thine enemy's smart is?   10
Hast thou a trumpet rich melodies blowing?
  And wear'st thou the shield of the fam'd
    Britomartis?[3]

What is it that hangs from thy shoulder, so brave,
  Embroidered with many a spring-peering flower?
Is it a scarf that thy fair lady gave?
  And hastest thou now to that fair lady's bower?

Ah! courteous Sir Knight, with large joy thou art
    crown'd;
  Full many the glories that brighten thy youth!
I will tell thee my blisses, which richly abound
  In magical powers to bless, and to sooth.   20

On this scroll thou seest written in characters fair
  A sun-beamy tale of a wreath, and a chain;
And, warrior, it nurtures the property rare
  Of charming my mind from the trammels of pain.

This canopy mark: 'tis the work of a fay;
  Beneath its rich shade did King Oberon[4] languish,
When lovely Titania was far, far away,
  And cruelly left him to sorrow, and anguish.

There, oft would he bring from his soft sighing lute
  Wild strains to which, spell-bound, the nightingales
    listened;   30
The wondering spirits of heaven were mute,
  And tears 'mong the dewdrops of morning oft
    glistened.

[1] Hyderabad, in India, known for diamond mines.
[2] From Tasso's *Jerusalem Delivered* (1581).
[3] *The Faerie Queene*, Book III. She was originally a Cretan goddess of fishermen, sailors, and hunters.
[4] Titania and Oberon both appear as fairies in Shakespeare's *A Midsummer Night's Dream* as well as in the German poet Wieland's *Oberon*.

[1] The moon.
[2] Mary Tighe, a popular Irish poet of the early nineteenth century.

In this little dome, all those melodies strange,
    Soft, plaintive, and melting, for ever will sigh;
Nor e'er will the notes from their tenderness change;
    Nor e'er will the music of Oberon die.

So, when I am in a voluptuous vein,
    I pillow my head on the sweets of the rose,
And list to the tale of the wreath, and the chain,
    Till its echoes depart; then I sink to repose.   40

Adieu, valiant Eric![5] with joy thou art crown'd;
    Full many the glories that brighten thy youth,
I too have my blisses, which richly abound
    In magical powers, to bless and to sooth.

[1815]   [1817]

O SOLITUDE

Printed in Leigh Hunt's Examiner *in May 1816, this was
Keats's first published poem. Keats had moved to London to
study medicine.*

[Sonnet]
"O Solitude! . . ."

O SOLITUDE! if I must with thee dwell,
    Let it not be among the jumbled heap
    Of murky buildings; climb with me the steep,—
Nature's observatory—whence the dell,
Its flowery slopes, its river's crystal swell,
    May seem a span; let me thy vigils keep
    'Mongst boughs pavillion'd, where the deer's swift
        leap
Startles the wild bee from the fox-glove bell.
But though I'll gladly trace these scenes with thee,
    Yet the sweet converse of an innocent mind,   10
Whose words are images of thoughts refin'd,
    Is my soul's pleasure; and it sure must be
Almost the highest bliss of human-kind,
    When to thy haunts two kindred spirits flee.

[1815]   [1816]

---

*George Felton Mathew, a very minor poet, was one of Keats's
first literary friends (in 1816).*

[EPISTLE]
TO GEORGE FELTON MATHEW

SWEET are the pleasures that to verse belong,
And doubly sweet a brotherhood in song;
Nor can remembrance, Mathew! bring to view
A fate more pleasing, a delight more true
Than that in which the brother Poets joy'd,[1]
Who with combined powers, their wit employ'd
To raise a trophy to the drama's muses.
The thought of this great partnership diffuses
Over the genius-loving heart, a feeling
Of all that's high, and great, and good, and healing.   10

Too partial friend! fain would I follow thee
Past each horizon of fine poesy;
Fain would I echo back each pleasant note
As o'er Sicilian seas, clear anthems float
'Mong the light skimming gondolas far parted,
Just when the sun his farewell beam has darted:
But 'tis impossible; far different cares
Beckon me sternly from soft "Lydian airs",[2]
And hold my faculties so long in thrall,
That I am oft in doubt whether at all   20
I shall again see Phœbus in the morning:
Or flush'd Aurora in the roseate dawning!
Or a white Naiad in a rippling stream;
Or a rapt seraph in a moonlight beam;
Or again witness what with thee I've seen,
The dew by fairy feet swept from the green,
After a night of some quaint jubilee
Which every elf and fay had come to see:
When bright processions took their airy march
Beneath the curved moon's triumphal arch.   30

But might I now each passing moment give
To the coy muse, with me she would not live
In this dark city, nor would condescend
'Mid contradictions her delights to lend.
Should e'er the fine-eyed maid to me be kind,
Ah! surely it must be whene'er I find
Some flowery spot, sequester'd, wild, romantic,
That often must have seen a poet frantic;
Where oaks, that erst the Druid knew, are growing,
And flowers, the glory of one day, are blowing;   40

Where the dark-leav'd laburnum's drooping clusters
Reflect athwart the stream their yellow lustres,
And intertwined the cassia's[3] arms unite,
With its own drooping buds, but very white;
Where on one side are covert branches hung,
'Mong which the nightingales have always sung
In leafy quiet: where to pry, aloof,
Atween the pillars of the sylvan roof,
Would be to find where violet beds were nestling,
And where the bee with cowslip bells was wrestling. 50
There must be too a ruin dark, and gloomy,
To say "joy not too much in all that's bloomy."

Yet this is vain—U Mathew lend thy aid
To find a place where I may greet the maid—
Where we may soft humanity put on,
And sit, and rhyme and think on Chatterton;[4]
And that warm-hearted Shakespeare sent to meet him
Four laurell'd spirits, heaven-ward to intreat him.
With reverence would we speak of all the sages
Who have left streaks of light athwart their ages: 60
And thou shouldst moralize on Milton's blindness,
And mourn the fearful dearth of human kindness
To those who strove with the bright golden wing
Of genius, to flap away each sting
Thrown by the pitiless world. We next could tell
Of those who in the cause of freedom fell;
Of our own Alfred, of Helvetian Tell;[5]
Of him whose name to ev'ry heart's a solace,
High-minded and unbending William Wallace.
While to the rugged north our musing turns   70
We well might drop a tear for him, and Burns.

Felton! without incitements such as these,
How vain for me the niggard Muse to tease:
For thee, she will thy every dwelling grace,
And make "a sun-shine in a shady place:"
For thou wast once a flowret blooming wild,
Close to the source, bright, pure, and undefil'd,
Whence gush the streams of song: in happy hour
Came chaste Diana from her shady bower,
Just as the sun was from the east uprising;   80
And, as for him some gift she was devising,
Beheld thee, pluck'd thee, cast thee in the stream
To meet her glorious brother's greeting beam.
I marvel much that thou hast never told
How, from a flower, into a fish of gold

Apollo chang'd thee; how thou next didst seem
A black-eyed swan upon the widening stream;
And when thou first didst in that mirror trace
The placid features of a human face:
That thou hast never told thy travels strange,   90
And all the wonders of the mazy range
O'er pebbly crystal, and o'er golden sands;
Kissing thy daily food from Naiad's pearly hands.[6]

[November, 1815]   [1817]

"GIVE ME WOMEN..."
These lines, in Keats's handwriting, were found on the cover of a notebook kept by one of his fellow students at Guy's Hospital.

"Give me women . . ."

GIVE me women, wine and snuff
Until I cry out 'hold, enough!'
You may do so sans objection
Till the day of resurrection;
For bless my beard they aye shall be
My beloved Trinity.

[1815?]   [1915]

TO —— [MARY FROGLEY]
Earlier editors have assumed this poem was addressed to Keats's future sister-in-law, Georgiana Wylie. However it seems to have been sent to Mary Frogley, along with the poem that follows, as a valentine.

TO ——
[Mary Frogley]

HADST thou liv'd in days of old,
O what wonders had been told
Of thy lively countenance,
And thy humid eyes that dance
In the midst of their own brightness;
In the very fane of lightness.
Over which thine eyebrows, leaning,
Picture out each lovely meaning:
In a dainty bend they lie,
Like to streaks across the sky,   10
Or the feathers from a crow,
Fallen on a bed of snow.
Of thy dark hair that extends
Into many graceful bends:

---

[3] A shrub.
[4] See *To Chatterton*, p. 1000.
[5] King Alfred, the Saxon king, and William Tell. Like Wallace the Scot, below, they were all patriotic heroes of their respective countries. Burns is included apparently as a patriotic poet.

[6] The metamorphoses of Mathew are adapted from Ovid.

As the leaves of Hellebore [1]
Turn to whence they sprung before.
And behind each ample curl
Peeps the richness of a pearl.
Downward too flows many a tress
With a glossy waviness,   20
Full, and round like globes that rise
From the censer to the skies
Through sunny air. Add too, the sweetness
Of thy honied voice; the neatness
Of thine ankle lightly turn'd:
With those beauties, scarce discern'd,
Kept with such sweet privacy,
That they seldom meet the eye
Of the little loves that fly
Round about with eager pry.   30
Saving when, with freshening lave,
Thou dipp'st them in the taintless wave;
Like twin water lillies, born
In the coolness of the morn.
O, if thou hadst breathed then,
Now the Muses had been ten.
Couldst thou wish for lineage higher
Than twin sister of Thalia? [2]
At least for ever, evermore,
Will I call the Graces four.   40

Hadst thou liv'd when chivalry
Lifted up her lance on high,
Tell me what thou wouldst have been.
Ah! I see the silver sheen
Of thy broidered, floating vest
Cov'ring half thine ivory breast;
Which, O heavens! I should see,
But that cruel destiny
Has placed a golden cuirass there;
Keeping secret what is fair.   50
Like sunbeams in a cloudlet nested
Thy locks in knightly casque are rested:
O'er which bend four milky plumes
Like the gentle lilly's blooms
Springing from a costly vase.
See with what a stately pace
Comes thine alabaster steed;
Servant of heroic deed!
O'er his loins, his trappings glow
Like the northern lights on snow.   60
Mount his back! thy sword unsheath!
Sign of the enchanter's death;
Bane of every wicked spell;
Silencer of dragon's yell.

Alas! thou this wilt never do:
Thou art an enchantress too,
And wilt surely never spill
Blood of those whose eyes can kill.

[1816]   [1817]

[Sonnet]

TO ———

"Had I a man's fair form . . ."

HAD I a man's fair form, then might my sighs
    Be echoed swiftly through that ivory shell
    Thine ear, and find thy gentle heart; so well
Would passion arm me for the enterprize:
But ah! I am no knight whose foeman dies;
    No cuirass glistens on my bosom's swell;
    I am no happy shepherd of the dell
Whose lips have trembled with a maiden's eyes.
Yet must I dote upon thee,—call thee sweet,
    Sweeter by far than Hybla's honied roses   10
        When steep'd in dew rich to intoxication.
Ah! I will taste that dew, for me 'tis meet,
    And when the moon her pallid face discloses,
        I'll gather some by spells, and incantation.

[1816]   [1817]

SPECIMEN OF AN INDUCTION TO A POEM
*The longer poem to which this poem was to serve as "induction"
is the unfinished* Calidore, *which follows it.*

SPECIMEN OF AN INDUCTION
TO A POEM

LO! I must tell a tale of chivalry;
For large white plumes are dancing in mine eye.
Not like the formal crest of latter days:
But bending in a thousand graceful ways;
So graceful, that it seems no mortal hand,
Or e'en the touch of Archimago's wand, [1]
Could charm them into such an attitude.
We must think rather, that in playful mood,
Some mountain breeze had turned its chief delight,
To show this wonder of its gentle might.   10
Lo! I must tell a tale of chivalry;
For while I must, the lance points slantingly
Athwart the morning air: some lady sweet,
Who cannot feel for cold her tender feet,

---

[1] Christmas rose.
[2] Muse of festivals and comic poetry.

[1] The magician in *The Faerie Queene*, Book I.

From the worn top of some old battlement
Hails it with tears, her stout defender sent:
And from her own pure self no joy dissembling,
Wraps round her ample robe with happy trembling.
Sometimes, when the good Knight his rest would
    take,
It is reflected, clearly, in a lake,   20
With the young ashen boughs, 'gainst which it rests,
And th' half seen mossiness of linnets' nests.
Ah! shall I ever tell its cruelty,
When the fire flashes from a warrior's eye,
And his tremendous hand is grasping it,
And his dark brow for very wrath is knit?
Or when his spirit, with more calm intent,
Leaps to the honors of a tournament,
And makes the gazers round about the ring
Stare at the grandeur of the ballancing?   30
No, no! this is far off:—then how shall I
Revive the dying tones of minstrelsy,
Which linger yet about lone gothic arches,
In dark green ivy, and among wild larches?
How sing the splendour of the revelries,
When buts of wine are drunk off to the lees?
And that bright lance, against the fretted wall,
Beneath the shade of stately banneral,
Is slung with shining cuirass, sword, and shield?
Where ye may see a spur in bloody field.   40
Light-footed damsels move with gentle paces
Round the wide hall, and show their happy faces;
Or stand in courtly talk by fives and sevens:
Like those fair stars that twinkle in the heavens.
Yet must I tell a tale of chivalry:
Or wherefore comes that steed so proudly by?
Wherefore more proudly does the gentle knight
Rein in the swelling of his ample might?

Spenser! thy brows are arched, open, kind
And come like a clear sun-rise to my mind;   50
And always does my heart with pleasure dance,
When I think on thy noble countenance:
Where never yet was ought more earthly seen
Than the pure freshness of thy laurels green.
Therefore, great bard, I not so fearfully
Call on thy gentle spirit to hover nigh
My daring steps: or if thy tender care,
Thus startled unaware,
Be jealous that the foot of other wight
Should madly follow that bright path of light   60
Trac'd by thy lov'd Libertas[2]; he will speak,
And tell thee that my prayer is very meek;

That I will follow with due reverence,
And start with awe at mine own strange pretence.
Him thou wilt hear; so I will rest in hope
To see wide plains, fair trees and lawny slope:
The morn, the eve, the light, the shade, the flowers;
Clear streams, smooth lakes, and overlooking towers.

[1816]   [1817]

CALIDORE

Keats took the name of the following unfinished "tale of chivalry" from Book VI of Spenser's The Faerie Queene: *"The Legend of Sir Calidore, or, Of Courtesie." And Leigh Hunt's* The Story of Rimini *was clearly a model for its style.*

CALIDORE

A FRAGMENT

Young Calidore is paddling o'er the lake;
His healthful spirit eager and awake
To feel the beauty of a silent eve,
Which seem'd full loath this happy world to leave;
The light dwelt o'er the scene so lingeringly.
He bares his forehead to the cool blue sky,
And smiles at the far clearness all around,
Until his heart is well nigh over wound,
And turns for calmness to the pleasant green
Of easy slopes, and shadowy trees that lean   10
So elegantly o'er the waters' brim
And show their blossoms trim.
Scarce can his clear and nimble eye-sight follow
The freaks, and dartings of the black-wing'd swallow,
Delighting much, to see it half at rest,
Dip so refreshingly its wings, and breast
'Gainst the smooth surface, and to mark anon,
The widening circles into nothing gone.

And now the sharp keel of his little boat
Comes up with ripple, and with easy float,   20
And glides into a bed of water lillies:
Broad leav'd are they and their white canopies
Are upward turn'd to catch the heavens' dew.
Near to a little island's point they grew;
Whence Calidore might have the goodliest view
Of this sweet spot of earth. The bowery shore
Went off in gentle windings to the hoar
And light blue mountains: but no breathing man
With a warm heart, and eye prepared to scan
Nature's clear beauty, could pass lightly by   30
Objects that look'd out so invitingly
On either side. These, gentle Calidore
Greeted, as he had known them long before.

---

[2] Keats's name for Leigh Hunt. See *Written on the Day That Mr. Leigh Hunt Left Prison*, p. 1001.

The sidelong view of swelling leafiness,
Which the glad setting sun in gold doth dress;
Whence ever and anon the jay outsprings,
And scales upon the beauty of its wings.
The lonely turret, shatter'd, and outworn,
Stands venerably proud; too proud to mourn
Its long lost grandeur: fir trees grow around,   40
Aye dropping their hard fruit upon the ground.
The little chapel with the cross above
Upholding wreaths of ivy; the white dove,
That on the window spreads his feathers light,
And seems from purple clouds to wing its flight.
Green tufted islands casting their soft shades
Across the lake; sequester'd leafy glades,
That through the dimness of their twilight show
Large dock leaves, spiral foxgloves, or the glow
Of the wild cat's eyes,[1] or the silvery stems   50
Of delicate birch trees, or long grass which hems
A little brook. The youth had long been viewing
These pleasant things, and heaven was bedewing
The mountain flowers, when his glad senses caught
A trumpet's silver voice. Ah! it was fraught
With many joys for him: the warder's ken
Had found white coursers prancing in the glen:
Friends very dear to him he soon will see;
So pushes off his boat most eagerly,
And soon upon the lake he skims along,   60
Deaf to the nightingale's first under-song;
Nor minds he the white swans that dream so sweetly:
His spirit flies before him so completely.

And now he turns a jutting point of land,
Whence may be seen the castle gloomy, and grand:
Nor will a bee buzz round two swelling peaches,
Before the point of his light shallop [2] reaches
Those marble steps that through the water dip:
Now over them he goes with hasty trip,
And scarcely stays to ope the folding doors: 70
Anon he leaps along the oaken floors
Of halls and corridors.
Delicious sounds! those little bright-eyed things
That float about the air on azure wings,
Had been less heartfelt by him than the clang
Of clattering hoofs; into the court he sprang,
Just as two noble steeds, and palfreys twain,
Were slanting out their necks with loosened rein;
While from beneath the threat'ning portcullis
They brought their happy burthens. What a kiss,   80
What gentle squeeze he gave each lady's hand!
How tremblingly their delicate ancles spann'd!

Into how sweet a trance his soul was gone,
While whisperings of affection
Made him delay to let their tender feet
Come to the earth; with an incline so sweet
From their low palfreys o'er his neck they bent:
And whether there were tears of languishment,
Or that the evening dew had pearl'd their tresses,
He feels a moisture on his cheek, and blesses   90
With lips that tremble, and with glistening eye
All the soft luxury
That nestled in his arms. A dimpled hand,
Fair as some wonder out of fairy land,
Hung from his shoulder like the drooping flowers
Of whitest Cassia,[3] fresh from summer showers:
And this he fondled with his happy cheek
As if for joy he would no further seek;
When the kind voice of good Sir Clerimond
Came to his ear, like something from beyond   100
His present being: so he gently drew
His warm arms, thrilling now with pulses new,
From their sweet thrall, and forward gently bending,
Thank'd heaven that his joy was never ending;
While 'gainst his forehead he devoutly press'd
A hand heaven made to succour the distress'd;
A hand that from the world's bleak promontory
Had lifted Calidore for deeds of glory.

Amid the pages, and the torches' glare,
There stood a knight, patting the flowing hair   110
Of his proud horse's mane: he was withal
A man of elegance, and stature tall:
So that the waving of his plumes would be
High as the berries of a wild ash tree,
Or as the winged cap of Mercury.
His armour was so dexterously wrought
In shape, that sure no living man had thought
It hard, and heavy steel: but that indeed
It was some glorious form, some splendid weed,[4]
In which a spirit new come from the skies   120
Might live, and show itself to human eyes.
'Tis the far-fam'd, the brave Sir Gondibert,
Said the good man to Calidore alert;
While the young warrior with a step of grace
Came up,—a courtly smile upon his face,
And mailed hand held out, ready to greet
The large-eyed wonder, and ambitious heat
Of the aspiring boy; who as he led
Those smiling ladies, often turned his head
To admire the visor arched so gracefully   130
Over a knightly brow; while they went by

---

[1] Wild flowers.
[2] A light, open boat.

[3] Shrub.
[4] Dress.

The lamps that from the high-roof'd hall were pendent
And gave the steel a shining quite transcendent.

Soon in a pleasant chamber they are seated;
The sweet-lipp'd ladies have already greeted
All the green leaves that round the window clamber,
To show their purple stars, and bells of amber.
Sir Gondibert has doff'd his shining steel,
Gladdening in the free and airy feel
Of a light mantle; and while Clerimond   140
Is looking round about him with a fond
And placid eye, young Calidore is burning
To hear of knightly deeds, and gallant spurning
Of all unworthiness; and how the strong of arm
Kept off dismay, and terror, and alarm
From lovely woman: while brimful of this,
He gave each damsel's hand so warm a kiss,
And had such manly ardour in his eye,
That each at other look'd half staringly;
And then their features started into smiles   150
Sweet as blue heavens o'er enchanted isles.

Softly the breezes from the forest came,
Softly they blew aside the taper's flame;
Clear was the song from Philomel's⁵ far bower;
Grateful the incense from the lime-tree flower;
Mysterious, wild, the far heard trumpet's tone;
Lovely the moon in ether, all alone:
Sweet too the converse of these happy mortals,
As that of busy spirits when the portals
Are closing in the west; or that soft humming   160
We hear around when Hesperus is coming.⁶
Sweet be their sleep.* * * * * * * * *

[1816]   [1817]

[Sonnet]
"To one who has been long in city pent"

To one who has been long in city pent,
 'Tis very sweet to look into the fair
 And open face of heaven,—to breathe a prayer
Full in the smile of the blue firmament.
Who is more happy, when, with heart's content,
 Fatigued he sinks into some pleasant lair
 Of wavy grass, and reads a debonair
And gentle tale of love and languishment?

⁵ The nightingale.
⁶ The evening star.

Returning home at evening, with an ear
 Catching the notes of Philomel,¹—an eye   10
Watching the sailing cloudlet's bright career,
 He mourns that day so soon has glided by:
E'en like the passage of an angel's tear
 That falls through the clear ether silently.

[1816]   [1817]

TO A FRIEND WHO SENT ME SOME ROSES
The Friend in the following poem is Charles Wells, a schoolmate of Tom Keats and a friend of Hunt and Hazlitt. The occasion is apparently a minor quarrel. Wells later was denounced by Keats for hurrying Tom's death by playing on him a practical joke involving an assignation with a nonexistent young woman.

[Sonnet]
TO A FRIEND WHO SENT ME SOME ROSES

As late I rambled in the happy fields,
 What time the sky-lark shakes the tremulous dew
 From his lush clover covert;—when anew
Adventurous knights take up their dinted shields:
I saw the sweetest flower wild nature yields,
 A fresh-blown musk-rose; 'twas the first that threw
 Its sweets upon the summer: graceful it grew
As is the wand that queen Titania² wields.
And, as I feasted on its fragrancy,
 I thought the garden-rose it far excell'd: 10
But when, O Wells! thy roses came to me
 My sense with their deliciousness was spell'd:
Soft voices had they, that with tender plea
 Whisper'd of peace, and truth, and friendliness
  unquell'd.

[1816]   [1817]

[Sonnet]
"Oh! how I love . . ."

OH! how I love, on a fair summer's eve,
 When streams of light pour down the golden west,
 And on the balmy zephyrs tranquil rest
The silver clouds, far—far away to leave
All meaner thoughts, and take a sweet reprieve
 From little cares; to find, with easy quest,
 A fragrant wild, with Nature's beauty drest,
And there into delight my soul deceive.

¹ Nightingale. See note to Coleridge's *To the Nightingale*, p. 441.
² Queen of the fairies in *A Midsummer Night's Dream*.

There warm my breast with patriotic lore,
   Musing on Milton's fate—on Sydney's bier—[1]   10
     Till their stern forms before my mind arise:
Perhaps on the wing of Poesy upsoar,
   Full often dropping a delicious tear,
     When some melodious sorrow spells mine eyes.

[1816]   [1848]

[Sonnet]
TO MY BROTHER GEORGE

MANY the wonders I this day have seen:
   The sun, when first he kist away the tears
   That fill'd the eyes of morn;—the laurel'd peers
Who from the feathery gold of evening lean;—
The ocean with its vastness, its blue green,
   Its ships, its rocks, its caves, its hopes, its fears,—
   Its voice mysterious, which whoso hears
Must think on what will be, and what has been.
E'en now, dear George, while this for you I write,
   Cynthia is from her silken curtains peeping   10
So scantly, that it seems her bridal night,
   And she her half-discover'd revels keeping.
But what, without the social thought of thee,
Would be the wonders of the sky and sea?

[1816]   [1817]

[Epistle]
TO MY BROTHER GEORGE

FULL many a dreary hour have I past,
My brain bewilder'd, and my mind o'ercast
With heaviness; in seasons when I've thought
No spherey strains[2] by me could e'er be caught
From the blue dome, though I to dimness gaze
On the far depth where sheeted lightning plays;
Or, on the wavy grass outstretch'd supinely,
Pry 'mong the stars, to strive to think divinely:
That I should never hear Apollo's song,
Though feathery clouds were floating all along   10
The purple west, and, two bright streaks between,
The golden lyre itself were dimly seen:
That the still murmur of the honey bee
Would never teach a rural song to me:
That the bright glance from beauty's eyelids slanting
Would never make a lay of mine enchanting,

Or warm my breast with ardour to unfold
Some tale of love and arms in time of old.

But there are times, when those that love the bay,
Fly from all sorrowing far, far away;   20
A sudden glow comes on them, naught they see
In water, earth, or air, but poesy.
It has been said, dear George, and true I hold it,
(For knightly Spenser to Libertas told it,)
That when a Poet is in such a trance,
In air he sees white coursers paw, and prance,
Bestridden of gay knights, in gay apparel,
Who at each other tilt in playful quarrel,
And what we, ignorantly, sheet-lightning call,
Is the swift opening of their wide portal,   30
When the bright warder blows his trumpet clear,
Whose tones reach naught on earth but Poet's ear.
When these enchanted portals open wide,
And through the light the horsemen swiftly glide,
The Poet's eye can reach those golden halls,
And view the glory of their festivals:
Their ladies fair, that in the distance seem
Fit for the silv'ring of a seraph's dream;
Their rich brimm'd goblets, that incessant run
Like the bright spots that move about the sun;   40
And, when upheld, the wine from each bright jar
Pours with the lustre of a falling star.
Yet further off, are dimly seen their bowers,
Of which, no mortal eye can reach the flowers;
And 'tis right just, for well Apollo knows
'Twould make the Poet quarrel with the rose.
All that's reveal'd from that far seat of blisses,
Is, the clear fountains' interchanging kisses,
As gracefully descending, light and thin,
Like silver streaks across a dolphin's fin,   50
When he upswimmeth from the coral caves,
And sports with half his tail above the waves.

These wonders strange he sees, and many more,
Whose head is pregnant with poetic lore.
Should he upon an evening ramble fare
With forehead to the soothing breezes bare,
Would he naught see but the dark, silent blue
With all its diamonds trembling through and through?
Or the coy moon, when in the waviness
Of whitest clouds she does her beauty dress,   60
And staidly paces higher up, and higher,
Like a sweet nun in holy-day attire?
Ah, yes! much more would start into his sight—
The revelries, and mysteries of night:
And should I ever see them, I will tell you
Such tales as needs must with amazement spell you.

---

[1] Algernon Sidney (1622–1683) was a Whig hero of the Civil War. After the Restoration (1660) he went abroad, but returned to England in 1677, became embroiled in Whig plots, and was convicted and executed for treason.

[2] Music of the Spheres.

These are the living pleasures of the bard:
But richer far posterity's award.
What does he murmur with his latest breath,   69
While his proud eye looks through the film of death?
"What though I leave this dull, and earthly mould,
"Yet shall my spirit lofty converse hold
"With after times.—The patriot shall feel
"My stern alarum, and unsheath his steel;
"Or, in the senate thunder out my numbers
"To startle princes from their easy slumbers.
"The sage will mingle with each moral theme
"My happy thoughts sentudicious; he will teem
"With lofty periods when my verses fire him,
"And then I'll stoop from heaven to inspire him.   80
"Lays have I left of such a dear delight
"That maids will sing them on their bridal night.
"Gay villagers, upon a morn of May,
"When they have tired their gentle limbs with play,
"And form'd a snowy circle on the grass,
"And plac'd in midst of all that lovely lass
"Who chosen is their queen,—with her fine head
"Crowned with flowers purple, white, and red:
"For there the lily, and the musk-rose, sighing,
"Are emblems true of hapless lovers dying: 90
"Between her breasts, that never yet felt trouble,
"A bunch of violets full blown, and double,
"Serenely sleep:—she from a casket takes
"A little book,—and then a joy awakes
"About each youthful heart,—with stifled cries,
"And rubbing of white hands, and sparkling eyes:
"For she 's to read a tale of hopes, and fears;
"One that I foster'd in my youthful years:
"The pearls, that on each glist'ning circlet sleep,
"Gush ever and anon with silent creep,   100
"Lured by the innocent dimples. To sweet rest
"Shall the dear babe, upon its mother's breast,
"Be lull'd with songs of mine. Fair world, adieu!
"Thy dales, and hills, are fading from my view:
"Swiftly I mount, upon wide spreading pinions,
"Far from the narrow bounds of thy dominions.
"Full joy I feel, while thus I cleave the air,
"That my soft verse will charm thy daughters fair,
"And warm thy sons!" Ah, my dear friend and
    brother,
Could I, at once, my mad ambition smother,   110
For tasting joys like these, sure I should be
Happier, and dearer to society.
At times, 'tis true, I've felt relief from pain
When some bright thought has darted through my
    brain:
Through all that day I've felt a greater pleasure
Than if I'd brought to light a hidden treasure.
As to my sonnets, though none else should heed them,
I feel delighted, still, that you should read them.

Of late, too, I have had much calm enjoyment,   119
Stretch'd on the grass at my best lov'd employment
Of scribbling lines for you. These things I thought
While, in my face, the freshest breeze I caught.
E'en now I'm pillow'd on a bed of flowers
That crowns a lofty clift, which proudly towers
Above the ocean-waves. The stalks, and blades,
Chequer my tablet with their quivering shades.
On one side is a field of drooping oats,
Through which the poppies show their scarlet coats;
So pert and useless, that they bring to mind
The scarlet coats [3] that pester human-kind.   130
And on the other side, outspread, is seen
Ocean's blue mantle streak'd with purple, and green.
Now 'tis I see a canvass'd ship, and now
Mark the bright silver curling round her prow.
I see the lark down-dropping to his nest,
And the broad winged sea-gull never at rest;
For when no more he spreads his feathers free,
His breast is dancing on the restless sea.
Now I direct my eyes into the west,
Which at this moment is in sunbeams drest: 140
Why westward [4] turn? 'Twas but to say adieu!
'Twas but to kiss my hand, dear George, to you!

[1816]   [1817]

TO CHARLES COWDEN CLARKE

Clarke (1787–1877), son of the master of Keats's school at Enfield, encouraged Keats to write verse and introduced him to Leigh Hunt.

[Epistle]
TO CHARLES COWDEN CLARKE

OFT have you seen a swan superbly frowning,
And with proud breast his own white shadow
    crowning;
He slants his neck beneath the waters bright
So silently, it seems a beam of light
Come from the Galaxy: anon he sports,—
With outspread wings the Naiad Zephyr courts,
Or ruffles all the surface of the lake
In striving from its crystal face to take
Some diamond water drops, and them to treasure
In milky nest, and sip them off at leisure.   10
But not a moment can he there insure them,
Nor to such downy rest can he allure them;

---

[3] Soldiers.
[4] I.e., toward London, where George is while Keats is in Margate.

For down they rush as though they would be free,
And drop like hours into eternity.
Just like that bird am I in loss of time,
Whene'er I venture on the stream of rhyme;
With shatter'd boat, oar snapt, and canvass rent,
I slowly sail, scarce knowing my intent;
Still scooping up the water with my fingers,
In which a trembling diamond never lingers.   20

By this, friend Charles, you may full plainly see
Why I have never penn'd a line to thee:
Because my thoughts were never free, and clear,
And little fit to please a classic ear;
Because my wine was of too poor a savour
For one whose palate gladdens in the flavour
Of sparkling Helicon[1]:—small good it were
To take him to a desert rude, and bare,
Who had on Baiæ's shore reclin'd at ease,
While Tasso's page was floating in a breeze   30
That gave soft music from Armida's[2] bowers,
Mingled with fragrance from her rarest flowers:
Small good to one who had by Mulla's stream[3]
Fondled the maidens with the breasts of cream;
Who had beheld Belphœbe in a brook,
And lovely Una in a leafy nook,
And Archimago leaning o'er his book:
Who had of all that's sweet tasted, and seen,
From silv'ry ripple, up to beauty's queen;
From the sequester'd haunts of gay Titania,[4]   40
To the blue dwelling of divine Urania:[5]
One, who, of late, had ta'en sweet forest walks
With him who elegantly chats, and talks—
The wrong'd Libertas,[6]—who has told you stories
Of laurel chaplets, and Apollo's glories;
Of troops chivalrous prancing through a city,
And tearful ladies made for love, and pity:
With many else which I have never known.

Thus have I thought; and days on days have flown
Slowly, or rapidly—unwilling still   50
For you to try my dull, unlearned quill.
Nor should I now, but that I've known you long;
That you first taught me all the sweets of song;
The grand, the sweet, the terse, the free, the fine;
What swell'd with pathos, and what right divine:
Spenserian vowels that elope with ease,
And float along like birds o'er summer seas;

Miltonian storms, and more, Miltonian tenderness;
Michael in arms, and more, meek Eve's fair
      slenderness.
Who read for me the sonnet swelling loudly   60
Up to its climax and then dying proudly?
Who found for me the grandeur of the ode,
Growing, like Atlas, stronger from its load?
Who let me taste that more than cordial dram,
The sharp, the rapier-pointed epigram?
Shew'd me that epic was of all the king,
Round, vast, and spanning all like Saturn's ring?
You too upheld the veil from Clio's[7] beauty,
And pointed out the patriot's stern duty;
The might of Alfred, and the shaft of Tell;[8]   70
The hand of Brutus, that so grandly fell
Upon a tyrant's head.[9] Ah! had I never seen,
Or known your kindness, what might I have been?
What my enjoyments in my youthful years,
Bereft of all that now my life endears?
And can I e'er these benefits forget?
And can I e'er repay the friendly debt?
No, doubly no;—yet should these rhymings please,
I shall roll on the grass with two-fold ease:
For I have long time been my fancy feeding   80
With hopes that you would one day think the reading
Of my rough verses not an hour misspent;
Should it e'er be so, what a rich content!

Some weeks have pass'd since last I saw the spires
In lucent Thames reflected:—warm desires
To see the sun o'er peep the eastern dimness,
And morning shadows streaking into slimness
Across the lawny fields, and pebbly water;
To mark the time as they grow broad, and shorter;
To feel the air that plays about the hills,   90
And sips its freshness from the little rills;
To see high, golden corn wave in the light
When Cynthia smiles upon a summer's night,
And peers among the cloudlet's jet and white,
As though she were reclining in a bed
Of bean blossoms, in heaven freshly shed—
No sooner had I stepp'd into these pleasures
Than I began to think of rhymes and measures:
The air that floated by me seem'd to say
"Write! thou wilt never have a better day."   100
And so I did. When many lines I'd written,
Though with their grace I was not oversmitten,
Yet, as my hand was warm, I thought I'd better
Trust to my feelings, and write you a letter.
Such an attempt required an inspiration
Of peculiar sort,—a consummation;—

[1] The spring of Hippocrene, sacred to the Muses, next to the mountain Helicon.
[2] In Tasso's *Jerusalem Delivered*.
[3] Near Spenser's home in Ireland; the characters that follow appear in *The Faerie Queene*.
[4] Queen of the fairies.
[5] Muse of astronomy.
[6] Leigh Hunt.

[7] Muse of history.
[8] See *To George Felton Mathew*, p. 1004.
[9] I.e., the assassination of Julius Caesar.

Which, had I felt, these scribblings might have been
Verses from which the soul would never wean:
But many days have past since last my heart
Was warm'd luxuriously by divine Mozart;   110
By Arne delighted, or by Handel madden'd;[10]
Or by the song of Erin[11] pierc'd and sadden'd:
What time you were before the music sitting,
And the rich notes to each sensation fitting;
Since I have walk'd with you through shady lanes
That freshly terminate in open plains,
And revel'd in a chat that ceased not
When at night-fall among your books we got:
No, nor when supper came, nor after that,—
Nor when reluctantly I took my hat;   120
No, nor till cordially you shook my hand
Mid-way between our homes:—your accents bland
Still sounded in my ears, when I no more
Could hear your footsteps touch the grav'ly floor.
Sometimes I lost them, and then found again;
You chang'd the footpath for the grassy plain.
In those still moments I have wish'd you joys
That well you know to honour:—"Life's very toys
"With him," said I, "will take a pleasant charm;
"It cannot be that ought will work him harm."   130
These thoughts now come o'er me with all their
    might:—
Again I shake your hand,—friend Charles, good
    night.

[*September, 1816*]   [1817]

[Sonnet]
"How many bards . . ."

How many bards gild the lapses of time!
    A few of them have ever been the food
    Of my delighted fancy,—I could brood
Over their beauties, earthly, or sublime:
And often, when I sit me down to rhyme,
    These will in throngs before my mind intrude:
    But no confusion, no disturbance rude
Do they occasion; 'tis a pleasing chime.
So the unnumber'd sounds that evening store;   9
    The songs of birds—the whisp'ring of the leaves—
The voice of waters—the great bell that heaves
    With solemn sound,—and thousand others more,
That distance of recognizance bereaves,
    Make pleasing music, and not wild uproar.

[1816]   [1817]

<hr/>

[10] Clarke, a pianist, played the music of these three eighteenth-century composers frequently.
[11] Ireland (poetic).

ON FIRST LOOKING INTO CHAPMAN'S HOMER
Keats first read the translation of Homer by George Chapman (1559?–1634) in October 1816, and sent this sonnet to Clarke immediately afterward. Apparently much of the poem was composed as Keats walked from Clarke's to south London.

[Sonnet]
ON FIRST LOOKING INTO CHAPMAN'S HOMER

Much have I travell'd in the realms of gold,
    And many goodly states and kingdoms seen;
    Round many western islands have I been
Which bards in fealty[1] to Apollo hold.
Oft of one wide expanse had I been told
    That deep-brow'd Homer ruled as his demesne;
    Yet did I never breathe its pure serene
Till I heard Chapman speak out loud and bold:
Then felt I like some watcher of the skies
    When a new planet swims into his ken;[2]   10
Or like stout Cortez when with eagle eyes[3]
    He star'd at the Pacific—and all his men
Look'd at each other with a wild surmise—
    Silent, upon a peak in Darien.

[1816]   [1816]

"KEEN, FITFUL GUSTS..."
It was a five-mile walk from Leigh Hunt's cottage on Hampstead Heath to Keats's lodgings in south London. Apparently during his evening visit there they had discussed Milton's Lycidas *and Petrarch's poems to* Laura.

[Sonnet]
"Keen, fitful gusts . . ."

Keen, fitful gusts are whisp'ring here and there
    Among the bushes half leafless, and dry;
    The stars look very cold about the sky,
And I have many miles on foot to fare.
Yet feel I little of the cool bleak air,
    Or of the dead leaves rustling drearily,
    Or of those silver lamps that burn on high,
Or of the distance from home's pleasant lair:

<hr/>

[1] Poets are the vassals of Apollo, the god of the arts as well as the sun.
[2] F. W. Herschel discovered Uranus in 1781.
[3] Keats merges an account of Balboa seeing the Pacific from the isthmus of Darien with Cortez's first sight of Mexico City.

For I am brimfull of the friendliness
　　That in a little cottage I have found;　　10
Of fair-hair'd Milton's eloquent distress,
　　And all his love for gentle Lycid drown'd;
Of lovely Laura in her light green dress,
　　And faithful Petrarch gloriously crown'd.

[1816]   [1817]

This is your birth-day Tom, and I rejoice
　　That thus it passes smoothly, quietly.　　10
Many such eves of gently whisp'ring noise
　　May we together pass, and calmly try
What are this world's true joys,—ere the great voice,
　　From its fair face, shall bid our spirits fly.

[November 18, 1816]   [1817]

ADDRESSED TO HAYDON [I]

Keats met Benjamin Robert Haydon (1786–1846), painter and diarist, in 1816 at Leigh Hunt's. Haydon, who had energetically defended the British government's acquisition of the frieze of the Parthenon—the Elgin Marbles—included Keats (along with Wordsworth and other literary contemporaries) among the recognizable faces in his huge Christ's Triumphant Entry into Jerusalem (1820), which was intended to be a masterpiece and became instead a curiosity.

ADDRESSED TO HAYDON [II]

The three great spirits of the poem are Wordsworth, Leigh Hunt, and Haydon. Originally the next to last line read: "Of mighty Workings in a distant Mart?" but the last phrase was deliberately omitted on Haydon's advice.

[Sonnet]
ADDRESSED TO HAYDON [I]

HIGHMINDEDNESS, a jealousy for good,
　　A loving-kindness for the great man's fame,
　　Dwells here and there with people of no name,
In noisome alley, and in pathless wood:
And where we think the truth least understood,
　　Oft may be found a "singleness of aim",
　　That ought to frighten into hooded shame
A money-mong'ring, pitiable brood.
How glorious this affection for the cause
　　Of stedfast genius, toiling gallantly!　　10
What when a stout unbending champion awes
　　Envy, and Malice to their native sty?
Unnumber'd souls breathe out a still applause,
　　Proud to behold him in his country's eye.

[1816]   [1817]

[Sonnet]
ADDRESSED TO [HAYDON] [II]

GREAT spirits now on earth are sojourning;
　　He of the cloud, the cataract, the lake,
Who on Helvellyn's summit, wide awake,
Catches his freshness from Archangel's wing:
He of the rose, the violet, the spring,
　　The social smile, the chain for Freedom's sake:
　　And lo!—whose stedfastness would never take
A meaner sound than Raphael's whispering.
And other spirits there are standing apart
　　Upon the forehead of the age to come;　　10
These, these will give the world another heart,
　　And other pulses. Hear ye not the hum
Of mighty workings?——
　　Listen awhile ye nations, and be dumb.

[1816]   [1817]

[Sonnet]
TO MY BROTHERS

SMALL, busy flames play through the fresh laid coals,
　　And their faint cracklings o'er our silence creep
　　Like whispers of the household gods that keep
A gentle empire o'er fraternal souls.
And while, for rhymes, I search around the poles,
　　Your eyes are fix'd, as in poetic sleep,
　　Upon the lore so voluble and deep,
That aye at fall of night our care condoles.

[Sonnet]
TO G. A. W.
[Georgiana Wylie]

NYMPH of the downward smile, and sidelong glance,
　　In what diviner moments of the day
　　Art thou most lovely? When gone far astray
Into the labyrinths of sweet utterance?
Or when serenely wand'ring in a trance
　　Of sober thought? Or when starting away,
　　With careless robè, to meet the morning ray,
Thou spar'st the flowers in thy mazy dance?

Haply 'tis when thy ruby lips part sweetly,
  And so remain, because thou listenest: 10
But thou to please wert nurtured so completely
  That I can never tell what mood is best.
I shall as soon pronounce which Grace more neatly
  Trips it before Apollo than the rest.

[1816]   [1817]

[Sonnet]
TO KOSCIUSKO[1]

GOOD Koscuisko, thy great name alone
  Is a full harvest whence to reap high feeling;
  It comes upon us like the glorious pealing
Of the wide spheres—an everlasting tone.
And now it tells me, that in worlds unknown,
  The names of heroes, burst from clouds concealing,
  And change to harmonies, for ever stealing
Through cloudless blue, and round each silver throne.
It tells me too, that on a happy day,
  When some good spirit walks upon the earth,   10
  Thy name with Alfred's, and the great of yore
Gently commingling, gives tremendous birth
To a loud hymn, that sounds far, far away
  To where the great God lives for evermore.

[1816]   [1817]

[Sonnet]
"Happy is England . . ."

HAPPY is England! I could be content
  To see no other verdure than its own;
  To feel no other breezes than are blown
Through its tall woods with high romances blent:
Yet do I sometimes feel a languishment
  For skies Italian, and an inward groan
  To sit upon an Alp as on a throne,
And half forget what world of worlding meant.
Happy is England, sweet her artless daughters;
  Enough their simple loveliness for me,   10
    Enough their whitest arms in silence clinging:
  Yet do I often warmly burn to see
    Beauties of deeper glance, and hear their singing,
And float with them about the summer waters.

[1816]   [1817]

[1] Thaddeus Koscuisko (1746–1817) was a Polish patriot.

WRITTEN IN DISGUST

This poem, along with On The Grasshopper and Cricket, *and the sonnet on the Nile (perhaps others), was written as part of a series of exercises and literary contests (with time limits and set subjects) between Keats, Leigh Hunt, and sometimes others.*

[Sonnet]
WRITTEN IN DISGUST OF VULGAR SUPERSTITION

THE church bells toll a melancholy round,
  Calling the people to some other prayers,
  Some other gloominess, more dreadful cares,
More hearkening to the sermon's horrid sound.
Surely the mind of man is closely bound
  In some black spell; seeing that each one tears
  Himself from fireside joys, and Lydian airs,
And converse high of those with glory crown'd.
Still, still they toll, and I should feel a damp—
  A chill as from a tomb, did I not know   10
That they are going like an outburnt lamp;
  That 'tis their sighing, wailing ere they go
  Into oblivion;—that fresh flowers will grow,
And many glories of immortal stamp.

[1816]   [1876]

[Sonnet]
ON THE GRASSHOPPER AND CRICKET

THE poetry of earth is never dead:
  When all the birds are faint with the hot sun,
  And hide in cooling trees, a voice will run
From hedge to hedge about the new-mown mead;
That is the Grasshopper's—he takes the lead
  In summer luxury,—he has never done
  With his delights; for when tired out with fun
He rests at ease beneath some pleasant weed.
The poetry of earth is ceasing never:
  On a lone winter evening, when the frost   10
    Has wrought a silence, from the stove there shrills
The Cricket's song, in warmth increasing ever,
  And seems to one in drowsiness half lost,
    The Grasshopper's among some grassy hills.

[*December 30, 1816*]   [1817]

SLEEP AND POETRY

As I lay in my bed slepe full unmete
'Was unto me, but why that I ne might
'Rest I ne wist, for there n'as erthly wight
'[As I suppose] had more of hertis ese
'Than I, for I n'ad sicknesse nor disese.'
                                        CHAUCER.[1]

WHAT is more gentle than a wind in summer?
What is more soothing than the pretty hummer
That stays one moment in an open flower,
And buzzes cheerily from bower to bower?
What is more tranquil than a musk-rose blowing
In a green island, far from all men's knowing?
More heathful than the leafiness of dales?
More secret than a nest of nightingales?
More serene than Cordelia's countenance?
More full of visions than a high romance?   10
What, but thee, Sleep? Soft closer of our eyes!
Low murmurer of tender lullabies!
Light hoverer around our happy pillows!
Wreather of poppy buds, and weeping willows!
Silent entangler of a beauty's tresses!
Most happy listener! when the morning blesses
Thee for enlivening all the cheerful eyes
That glance so brightly at the new sun-rise.

But what is higher beyond thought than thee?
Fresher than berries of a mountain tree?   20
More strange, more beautiful, more smooth, more
          regal,
Than wings of swans, than doves, than dim-seen
          eagle?
What is it? And to what shall I compare it?
It has a glory, and nought else can share it:
The thought thereof is awful, sweet, and holy,
Chacing away all worldliness and folly;
Coming sometimes like fearful claps of thunder,
Or the low rumblings earth's regions under;
And sometimes like a gentle whispering
Of all the secrets of some wond'rous thing   30
That breathes about us in the vacant air;
So that we look around with prying stare,
Perhaps to see shapes of light, aerial lymning,
And catch soft floatings from a faint-heard hymning;
To see the laurel wreath, on high suspended,
That is to crown our name when life is ended.
Sometimes it gives a glory to the voice,
And from the heart up-springs 'Rejoice! rejoice!'

Sounds which will reach the Framer of all things,
And die away in ardent mutterings.   40

No one who once the glorious sun has seen,
And all the clouds, and felt his bosom clean
For his great Maker's presence, but must know
What 'tis I mean, and feel his being glow:
Therefore no insult will I give his spirit,
By telling what he sees from native merit.

O Poesy! for thee I hold my pen
That am not yet a glorious denizen
Of thy wide heaven—Should I rather kneel
Upon some mountain-top until I feel   50
A glowing splendour round about me hung,
And echo back the voice of thine own tongue?
O Poesy! for thee I grasp my pen
That am not yet a glorious denizen
Of thy wide heaven; yet, to my ardent prayer,
Yield from thy sanctuary some clear air,
Smoothed for intoxication by the breath
Of flowering bays, that I may die a death
Of luxury, and my young spirit follow
The morning sun-beams to the great Apollo   60
Like a fresh sacrifice; or, if I can bear
The o'erwhelming sweets, 'twill bring to me the fair
Visions of all places: a bowery nook
Will be elysium—an eternal book
Whence I may copy many a lovely saying
About the leaves, and flowers—about the playing
Of nymphs in woods, and fountains; and the shade
Keeping a silence round a sleeping maid;
And many a verse from so strange influence
That we must ever wonder how, and whence   70
It came. Also imaginings will hover
Round my fire-side, and haply there discover
Vistas of solemn beauty, where I'd wander
In happy silence, like the clear Meander[2]
Through its lone vales; and where I found a spot
Of awfuller shade, or an enchanted grot,
Or a green hill o'erspread with chequered dress
Of flowers, and fearful from its loveliness,
Write on my tablets all that was permitted,
All that was for our human senses fitted.   80
Then the events of this wide world I'd seize
Like a strong giant, and my spirit teaze
Till at its shoulders it should proudly see
Wings to find out an immortality.

Stop and consider! life is but a day;
A fragile dew-drop on its perilous way

---

[1] From *The Floure and the Leafe*, attributed erroneously to Chaucer in the early nineteenth century. See note to "*Written on a Blank Space at the End of Chaucer's Tale 'The Floure and the Lefe,*'" p. 1024.

[2] River in Asia famous in antiquity for its winding course.

From a tree's summit; a poor Indian's sleep
While his boat hastens to the monstrous steep
Of Montmorenci.³ Why so sad a moan?
Life is the rose's hope while yet unblown;   90
The reading of an ever-changing tale;
The light uplifting of a maiden's veil;
A pigeon tumbling in clear summer air;
A laughing school-boy, without grief or care,
Riding the springy branches of an elm.

O for ten years, that I may overwhelm
Myself in poesy; so I may do the deed
That my own soul has to itself decreed.
Then will I pass the countries that I see
In long perspective, and continually   100
Taste their pure fountains. First the realm I'll pass
Of Flora, and old Pan:⁴ sleep in the grass,
Feed upon apples red, and strawberries,
And choose each pleasure that my fancy sees;
Catch the white-handed nymphs in shady places,
To woo sweet kisses from averted faces,—
Play with their fingers, touch their shoulders white
Into a pretty shrinking with a bite
As hard as lips can make it: till agreed,
A lovely tale of human life we'll read.   110
And one will teach a tame dove how it best
May fan the cool air gently o'er my rest;
Another, bending o'er her nimble tread,
Will set a green robe floating round her head,
And still will dance with ever varied ease,
Smiling upon the flowers and the trees:
Another will entice me on, and on
Through almond blossoms and rich cinnamon;
Till in the bosom of a leafy world
We rest in silence, like two gems upcurl'd   120
In the recesses of a pearly shell.

And can I ever bid these joys farewell?
Yes, I must pass them for a nobler life,⁵
Where I may find the agonies, the strife
Of human hearts: for lo! I see afar,
O'er-sailing the blue cragginess, a car
And steeds with streamy manes—the charioteer
Looks out upon the winds with glorious fear:⁶
And now the numerous tramplings quiver lightly
Along a huge cloud's ridge; and now with sprightly
Wheel downward come they into fresher skies,   131
Tipt round with silver from the sun's bright eyes.

<hr />

³ Falls in Quebec.
⁴ Flora the goddess of flowers; Pan the god of nature.
⁵ For a later account of imaginative development, see the
letter to Reynolds of May 3, 1818, below.
⁶ Here, and previously, Keats probably has in mind engravings
of the French painter Nicolas Poussin (1594–1655) which he had
seen at Hunt's.

Still downward with capacious whirl they glide;
And now I see them on a green-hill's side
In breezy rest among the nodding stalks.
The charioteer with wond'rous gesture talks
To the trees and mountains; and there soon appear
Shapes of delight, of mystery, and fear,
Passing along before a dusky space
Made by some mighty oaks: as they would chase   140
Some ever-fleeting music on they sweep.
Lo! how they murmur, laugh, and smile, and weep:
Some with upholden hand and mouth severe;
Some with their faces muffled to the ear
Between their arms; some, clear in youthful bloom,
Go glad and smilingly athwart the gloom;
Some looking back, and some with upward gaze;
Yes, thousands in a thousand different ways
Flit onward—now a lovely wreath of girls
Dancing their sleek hair into tangled curls;   150
And now broad wings. Most awfully intent
The driver of those steeds is forward bent,
And seems to listen: O that I might know
All that he writes with such a hurrying glow.

The visions all are fled—the car is fled
Into the light of heaven, and in their stead
A sense of real things comes doubly strong,
And, like a muddy stream, would bear along
My soul to nothingness: but I will strive
Against all doubtings, and will keep alive   160
The thought of that same chariot, and the strange
Journey it went.

                 Is there so small a range
In the present strength of manhood, that the high
Imagination cannot freely fly
As she was wont of old? prepare her steeds,
Paw up against the light, and do strange deeds
Upon the clouds? Has she not shewn us all?
From the clear space of ether, to the small
Breath of new buds unfolding? From the meaning
Of Jove's large eye-brow, to the tender greening   170
Of April meadows? Here her altar shone,
E'en in this isle; and who could paragon
The fervid choir that lifted up a noise
Of harmony, to where it aye will poise
Its mighty self of convoluting sound,
Huge as a planet, and like that roll round,
Eternally around a dizzy void?
Ay, in those days the Muses were nigh cloy'd
With honors; nor had any other care
Than to sing out and sooth their wavy hair.   180

Could all this be forgotten? Yes, a schism
Nurtured by foppery and barbarism,

Made great Apollo blush for this his land.
Men were thought wise who could not understand
His glories: with a puling infant's force
They sway'd about upon a rocking horse,[7]
And thought it Pegasus. Ah dismal soul'd!
The winds of heaven blew, the ocean roll'd
Its gathering waves—ye felt it not. The blue
Bared its eternal bosom, and the dew   190
Of summer nights collected still to make
The morning precious: beauty was awake!
Why were ye not awake? But ye were dead
To things ye knew not of,—were closely wed
To musty laws lined out with wretched rule
And compass vile: so that ye taught a school
Of dolts to smooth, inlay, and clip, and fit,
Till, like the certain wands of Jacob's wit,[8]
Their verses tallied. Easy was the task:
A thousand handicraftsmen wore the mask   200
Of Poesy. Ill-fated, impious race!
That blasphemed the bright Lyrist[9] to his face,
And did not know it,—no, they went about,
Holding a poor, decrepid standard out
Mark'd with most flimsy mottos, and in large
The name of one Boileau![10]

                               O ye whose charge
It is to hover round our pleasant hills!
Whose congregated majesty so fills
My boundly reverence, that I cannot trace
Your hallowed names, in this unholy place,   210
So near those common folk; did not their shames
Affright you? Did our old lamenting Thames
Delight you? Did ye never cluster round
Delicious Avon, with a mournful sound,
And weep? Or did ye wholly bid adieu
To regions where no more the laurel grew?
Or did ye stay to give a welcoming
To some lone spirits who could proudly sing
Their youth away, and die? 'Twas even so:
But let me think away those times of woe: 220
Now 'tis a fairer season; ye have breathed
Rich benedictions o'er us; ye have wreathed
Fresh garlands: for sweet music has been heard
In many places;—some has been upstirr'd
From out its crystal dwelling in a lake,
By a swan's ebon bill; from a thick brake,
Nested and quiet in a valley mild,
Bubbles a pipe; fine sounds are floating wild
About the earth: happy are ye and glad.

These things are doubtless: yet in truth we've had   230
Strange thunders from the potency of song;
Mingled indeed with what is sweet and strong,
From majesty: but in clear truth the themes
Are ugly clubs, the Poets Polyphemes
Disturbing the grand sea.[11] A drainless shower
Of light is poesy; 'tis the supreme of power;
'Tis might half slumb'ring on its own right arm.
The very archings of her eye-lids charm
A thousand willing agents to obey,
And still she governs with the mildest sway: 240
But strength alone though of the Muses born
Is like a fallen angel: trees uptorn,
Darkness, and worms, and shrouds, and sepulchres
Delight it; for it feeds upon the burrs,
And thorns of life; forgetting the great end
Of poesy, that it should be a friend
To sooth the cares, and lift the thoughts of man.

    Yet I rejoice: a myrtle fairer than
E'er grew in Paphos,[12] from the bitter weeds
Lifts its sweet head into the air, and feeds   250
A silent space with ever sprouting green.
All tenderest birds there find a pleasant screen,
Creep through the shade with jaunty fluttering,
Nibble the little cupped flowers and sing.
Then let us clear away the choaking thorns
From round its gentle stem; let the young fawns,
Yeaned[13] in after times, when we are flown,
Find a fresh sward beneath it, overgrown
With simple flowers: let there nothing be
More boisterous than a lover's bended knee;   260
Nought more ungentle than the placid look
Of one who leans upon a closed book;
Nought more untranquil than the grassy slopes
Between two hills. All hail delightful hopes!
As she was wont, th' imagination
Into most lovely labyrinths will be gone,
And they shall be accounted poet kings
Who simply tell the most heart-easing things.
O may these joys be ripe before I die.

Will not some say that I presumptuously   270
Have spoken? that from hastening disgrace
'Twere better far to hide my foolish face?
That whining boyhood should with reverence bow
Ere the dread thunderbolt could reach? How!
If I do hide myself, it sure shall be
In the very fane, the light of Poesy:

---

[7] I.e., by abusing the rhymed couplet.
[8] In Gen. 30:27–43, Jacob tricks Laban by selective breeding using a variety of rods.
[9] Apollo.
[10] Nicolas Boileau (1636–1711), neo-classic French critic.

[11] Byron, perhaps Coleridge, are the poets Keats here compares to Polyphemus (the Cyclops) and his crude club.
[12] City in Cyprus.
[13] Borne.

If I do fall, at least I will be laid
Beneath the silence of a poplar shade;
And over me the grass shall be smooth shaven;
And there shall be a kind memorial graven.   280
But off Despondence! miserable bane!
They should not know thee, who athirst to gain
A noble end, are thirsty every hour.
What though I am not wealthy in the dower
Of spanning wisdom; though I do not know
The shiftings of the mighty winds that blow
Hither and thither all the changing thoughts
Of man: though no great minist'ring reason sorts
Out the dark mysteries of human souls
To clear conceiving: yet there ever rolls   290
A vast idea before me, and I glean
Therefrom my liberty; thence too I've seen
The end of aim of Poesy. 'Tis clear
As any thing most true; as that the year
Is made of the four seasons—manifest
As a large cross, some old cathedral's crest,
Lifted to the white clouds. Therefore should I
Be but the essence of deformity,
A coward, did my very eye-lids wink
At speaking out what I have dared to think.   300
Ah! rather let me like a madman run
Over some precipice; let the hot sun
Melt my Dedalian[14] wings, and drive me down
Convuls'd and headlong! Stay! an inward frown
Of conscience bids me be more calm awhile.
An ocean dim, sprinkled with many an isle,
Spreads awfully before me. How much toil!
How many days! what desperate turmoil!
Ere I can have explored its widenesses.
Ah, what a task! upon my bended knees,   310
I could unsay those—no, impossible!
Impossible!

        For sweet relief I'll dwell
On humbler thoughts, and let this strange assay
Begun in gentleness die so away.
E'en now all tumult from my bosom fades:
I turn full hearted to the friendly aids
That smooth the path of honour; brotherhood,
And friendliness the nurse of mutual good.
The hearty grasp that sends a pleasant sonnet
Into the brain ere one can think upon it;   320
The silence when some rhymes are coming out;
And when they're come, the very pleasant rout:
The message certain to be done to-morrow—
'Tis perhaps as well that it should be to borrow

Some precious book from out its snug retreat,
To cluster round it when we next shall meet.
Scarce can I scribble on; for lovely airs
Are fluttering round the room like doves in pairs;
Many delights of that glad day recalling,
When first my senses caught their tender falling.   330
And with these airs come forms of elegance
Stooping their shoulders o'er a horse's prance,
Careless, and grand—fingers soft and round
Parting luxuriant curls;—and the swift bound
Of Bacchus from his chariot, when his eye
Made Ariadne's cheek look blushingly.[15]
Thus I remember all the pleasant flow
Of words at opening a portfolio.

Things such as these are ever harbingers
To trains of peaceful images: the stirs   340
Of a swan's neck unseen among the rushes:
A linnet starting all about the bushes:
A butterfly, with golden wings broad parted,
Nestling a rose, convuls'd as though it smarted
With over pleasure—many, many more,[16]
Might I indulge at large in all my store
Of luxuries: yet I must not forget
Sleep, quiet with his poppy coronet:
For what there may be worthy in these rhymes
I partly owe to him—and thus: The chimes   350
Of friendly voices had just given place
To as sweet a silence, when I 'gan retrace
The pleasant day, upon a couch at ease.
It was a poet's house who keeps the keys
Of Pleasure's temple. Round about were hung
The glorious features of the bards who sung
In other ages—cold and sacred busts
Smiled at each other. Happy he who trusts
To clear Futurity his darling fame!
Then there were fauns and satyrs taking aim   360
At swelling apples with a frisky leap
And reaching fingers, 'mid a luscious heap
Of vine leaves. Then there rose to view a fane
Of liny marble, and thereto a train
Of nymphs approaching fairly o'er the sward:
One, loveliest, holding her white hand toward
The dazzling sun-rise: two sisters sweet
Bending their graceful figures till they meet
Over the trippings of a little child:
And some are hearing, eagerly, the wild   370
Thrilling liquidity of dewy piping.
See, in another picture, nymphs are wiping

---

[14] Dædalus and his son Icarus tried to escape from Crete by flying with wings of feathers secured by wax; Icarus fell into the sea and drowned when he flew so high that the sun melted his wings.

[15] Keats has in mind Titian's painting of Bacchus, the god of wine, arriving to console Ariadne after Theseus had abandoned her on Naxos.

[16] Paintings by Poussin, Claude, and Titian seem to be alluded to here.

Cherishingly Diana's timorous limbs;—
A fold of lawny mantle dabbling swims
At the bath's edge, and keeps a gentle motion
With the subsiding crystal: as when ocean
Heaves calmly its broad swelling smoothness o'er
Its rocky marge, and balances once more
The patient weeds; that now unshent by foam
Feel all about their undulating home.

Sappho's [17] meek head was there half smiling down
At nothing; just as though the earnest frown
Of over thinking had that moment góne
From off her brow, and left her all alone.

Great Alfred's too, with anxious, pitying eyes,
As if he always listened to the sighs
Of the goaded world; and Kosciusko's [18] worn
By horrid suffrance—mightily forlorn.

Petrarch, outstepping from the shady green,
Starts at the sight of Laura; [19] nor can wean   390
His eyes from her sweet face. Most happy they!
For over them was seen a free display
Of out-spread wings, and from between them shone
The face of Poesy: from off her throne
She overlook'd things that I scarce could tell.
The very sense of where I was might well
Keep Sleep aloof: but more than that there came
Thought after thought to nourish up the flame
Within my breast; so that the morning light
Surprised me even from a sleepless night;   400
And up I rose refresh'd, and glad, and gay,
Resolving to begin that very day
These lines; and howsoever they be done,
I leave them as a father does his son.

[1816]   [1817]

"I stood tip-toe . . ."

'Places of nestling green for Poets made.'
STORY OF RIMINI.[1]

I STOOD tip-toe upon a little hill,
The air was cooling, and so very still,
That the sweet buds which with a modest pride
Pull droopingly, in slanting curve aside,

Their scantly leaved, and finely tapering stems,
Had not yet lost those starry diadems
Caught from the early sobbing of the morn.
The clouds were pure and white as flocks new shorn,
And fresh from the clear brook; sweetly they slept
On the blue fields of heaven, and then there crept   10
A little noiseless noise among the leaves,
Born of the very sigh that silence heaves:
For not the faintest motion could be seen
Of all the shades that slanted o'er the green.
There was wide wand'ring for the greediest eye,
To peer about upon variety;
Far round the horizon's crystal air to skim,
And trace the dwindled edgings of its brim;
To picture out the quaint, and curious bending
Of a fresh woodland alley, never ending;   20
Or by the bowery clefts, and leafy shelves,
Guess where the jaunty streams refresh themselves.
I gazed awhile, and felt as light, and free
As though the fanning wings of Mercury [2]
Had played upon my heels: I was light-hearted,
And many pleasures to my vision started;
So I straightway began to pluck a posey
Of luxuries bright, milky, soft and rosy.

A bush of May flowers with the bees about them;
Ah, sure no tasteful nook would be without them;   30
And let a lush laburnum oversweep them,
And let long grass grow round the roots to keep them
Moist, cool and green; and shade the violets,
That they may bind the moss in leafy nets.

A filbert hedge with wild briar overtwined,
And clumps of woodbine taking the soft wind
Upon their summer thrones; there too should be
The frequent chequer of a youngling tree,
That with a score of light green brethren shoots
From the quaint mossiness of aged roots: 40
Round which is heard a spring-head of clear waters
Babbling so wildly of its lovely daughters
The spreading blue bells: it may haply mourn
That such fair clusters should be rudely torn
From their fresh beds, and scattered thoughtlessly
By infant hands, left on the path to die.

Open afresh your round of starry folds,
Ye ardent marigolds!
Dry up the moisture from your golden lids,
For great Apollo bids   50
That in these days your praises should be sung
On many harps, which he has lately strung;

---

[17] Lesbian poet of the seventh century B.C. who drowned herself by leaping into the sea.
[18] See sonnet *To Kosciusko*, p. 1015.
[19] See "Keen, fitful gusts . . .," p. 1013.
[1] By Leigh Hunt. See *On "The Story of Rimini"*, p. 1025.

---

[2] The messenger of the Gods, he had wings on cap and heels.

And when again your dewiness he kisses,
Tell him, I have you in my world of blisses:
So haply when I rove in some far vale,
His mighty voice may come upon the gale.

Here are sweet peas, on tip-toe for a flight:
With wings of gentle flush o'er delicate white,
And taper fingers catching at all things,
To bind them all about with tiny rings.   60

Linger awhile upon some bending planks
That lean against a streamlet's rushy banks,
And watch intently Nature's gentle doings:
They will be found softer than ring-dove's cooings.
How silent comes the water round that bend;
Not the minutest whisper does it send
To the o'erhanging sallows: blades of grass
Slowly across the chequer'd shadows pass.
Why, you might read two sonnets, ere they reach
To where the hurrying freshnesses aye preach   70
A natural sermon o'er their pebbly beds;
Where swarms of minnows show their little heads,
Staying their wavy bodies 'gainst the streams,
To taste the luxury of sunny beams
Temper'd with coolness. How they ever wrestle
With their own sweet delight, and ever nestle
Their silver bellies on the pebbly sand.
If you but scantily hold out the hand,
That very instant not one will remain;
But turn your eye, and they are there again.   80
The ripples seem right glad to reach those cresses,
And cool themselves among the em'rald tresses;
The while they cool themselves, they freshness give,
And moisture, that the bowery green may live:
So keeping up an interchange of favours,
Like good men in the truth of their behaviours.
Sometimes goldfinches one by one will drop
From low hung branches; little space they stop;
But sip, and twitter, and their feathers sleek;
Then off at once, as in a wanton freak: 90
Or perhaps, to show their black, and golden wings,
Pausing upon their yellow flutterings.
Were I in such a place, I sure should pray
That nought less sweet might call my thoughts away,
Than the soft rustle of a maiden's gown
Fanning away the dandelion's down;
Than the light music of her nimble toes
Patting against the sorrel as she goes.
How she would start, and blush, thus to be caught
Playing in all her innocence of thought.   100
O let me lead her gently o'er the brook,
Watch her half-smiling lips, and downward look;
O let me for one moment touch her wrist;
Let me one moment to her breathing list;

And as she leaves me may she often turn
Her fair eyes looking through her locks aubùrne.
What next? A tuft of evening primroses,
O'er which the mind may hover till it dozes;
O'er which it well might take a pleasant sleep,
But that 'tis ever startled by the leap   110
Of buds into ripe flowers; or by the flitting
Of diverse moths, that aye their rest are quitting;
Or by the moon lifting her silver rim
Above a cloud, and with a gradual swim
Coming into the blue with all her light.
O Maker of sweet poets, dear delight
Of this fair world, and all its gentle livers;
Spangler of clouds, halo of crystal rivers,
Mingler with leaves, and dew and tumbling streams,
Closer of lovely eyes to lovely dreams,   120
Lover of loneliness, and wandering,
Of upcast eye, and tender pondering!
Thee must I praise above all other glories
That smile us on to tell delightful stories.
For what has made the sage or poet write
But the fair paradise of Nature's light?
In the calm grandeur of a sober line,
We see the waving of the mountain pine;
And when a tale is beautifully staid,
We feel the safety of a hawthorn glade: 130
When it is moving on luxurious wings,
The soul is lost in pleasant smotherings:
Fair dewy roses brush against our faces,
And flowering laurels spring from diamond vases;
O'er head we see the jasmine and sweet briar,
And bloomy grapes laughing from green attire;
While at our feet, the voice of crystal bubbles
Charms us at once away from all our troubles:
So that we feel uplifted from the world,
Walking upon the white clouds wreath'd and curl'd.
So felt he, who first told, how Psyche went   141
On the smooth wind to realms of wonderment;
What Psyche felt, and Love, when their full lips
First touch'd; what amorous, and fondling nips
They gave each other's cheeks; with all their sighs,
And how they kist each other's tremulous eyes:
The silver lamp,—the ravishment,—the wonder—
The darkness,—loneliness,—the fearful thunder;
Their woes gone by, and both to heaven upflown,
To bow for gratitude before Jove's throne.[3]   150
So did he feel, who pull'd the boughs aside,
That we might look into a forest wide,
To catch a glimpse of Fawns, and Dryades
Coming with softest rustle through the trees;
And garlands woven of flowers wild, and sweet,
Upheld on ivory wrists, or sporting feet:

[3] See *Ode to Psyche*, p. 1077.

Telling us how fair, trembling Syrinx fled
Arcadian Pan, with such a fearful dread.[4]
Poor nymph,—poor Pan,—how he did weep to find,
Nought but a lovely sighing of the wind   160
Along the reedy stream; a half heard strain,
Full of sweet desolation—balmy pain.

What first inspired a bard of old to sing
Narcissus pining o'er the untainted spring?
In some delicious ramble, he had found
A little space, with boughs all woven round;
And in the midst of all, a clearer pool
Than e'er reflected in its pleasant cool
The blue sky here, and there, serenely peeping
Through tendril wreaths fantastically creeping.   170
And on the bank a lonely flower he spied,
A meek and forlorn flower, with naught of pride,
Drooping its beauty o'er the watery clearness,
To woo its own sad image into nearness:
Deaf to light Zephyrus it would not move;
But still would seem to droop, to pine, to love
So while the Poet stood in this sweet spot,
Some fainter gleamings o'er his fancy shot;
Nor was it long ere he had told the tale
Of young Narcissus, and sad Echo's bale.[5]   180
Where had he been, from whose warm head out-flew
That sweetest of all songs, that ever new,
That aye refreshing, pure deliciousness,
Coming ever to bless
The wanderer by moonlight? to him bringing
Shapes from the invisible world, unearthly singing
From out the middle air, from flowery nests,
And from the pillowy silkiness that rests
Full in the speculation of the stars.
Ah! surely he had burst our mortal bars;   190
Into some wond'rous region he had gone,
To search for thee, divine Endymion!

He was a Poet, sure a lover too,
Who stood on Latmus' top,[6] what time there blew
Soft breezes from the myrtle vale below;
And brought in faintness solemn, sweet, and slow
A hymn from Dian's temple; while upswelling,
The incense went to her own starry dwelling.
But though her face was clear as infant's eyes,
Though she stood smiling o'er the sacrifice,   200
The Poet wept at her so piteous fate,
Wept that such beauty should be desolate:

---

[4] See Shelley's *Hymn of Pan*, p. 918.
[5] Narcissus died despairing of love for his own reflection, and was turned into a flower.
[6] Latmus was the mountain in Asia Minor where Endymion was first visited by Cynthia, the moon. See *Endymion*, p. 1026.

So in fine wrath some golden sounds he won,
And gave meek Cynthia her Endymion.

Queen of the wide air; thou most lovely queen
Of all the brightness that mine eyes have seen!
As thou exceedest all things in thy shine,
So every tale, does this sweet tale of thine.
O for three words of honey, that I might
Tell but one wonder of thy bridal night!   210

Where distant ships do seem to show their keels,
Phoebus awhile delayed his mighty wheels,
And turned to smile upon thy bashful eyes,
Ere he his unseen pomp would solemnize.
The evening weather was so bright, and clear,
That men of health were of unusual cheer;
Stepping like Homer at the trumpet's call,
Or young Apollo on the pedestal:
And lovely women were as fair and warm,
As Venus looking sideways in alarm.   220
The breezes were ethereal, and pure,
And crept through half closed lattices to cure
The languid sick; it cool'd their fever'd sleep,
And soothed them into slumbers full and deep.
Soon they awoke clear eyed: nor burnt with thirsting,
Nor with hot fingers, nor with temples bursting:
And springing up, they met the wond'ring sight
Of their dear friends, nigh foolish with delight;
Who feel their arms, and breasts, and kiss and stare,
And on their placid foreheads part the hair.   230
Young men, and maidens at each other gaz'd
With hands held back, and motionless, amaz'd
To see the brightness in each other's eyes;
And so they stood, fill'd with a sweet surprise,
Until their tongues were loos'd in poesy.
Therefore no lover did of anguish die:
But the soft numbers, in that moment spoken,
Made silken ties, that never may be broken.
Cynthia! I cannot tell the greater blisses,   239
That follow'd thine, and thy dear shepherd's kisses:
Was there a Poet born?—but now no more,
My wand'ring spirit must no further soar.—

[1816]   [1817]

[Sonnet]
"After dark vapours . . ."

AFTER dark vapours have oppress'd our plains
    For a long dreary season, comes a day
    Born of the gentle South, and clears away
From the sick heavens all unseemly stains.

The anxious month, relieved of its pains,
　　Takes as a long-lost right the feel of May,
　　The eyelids with the passing coolness play,
Like rose leaves with the drip of summer rains.
The calmest thoughts come round us—as of leaves
　　Budding,—fruit ripening in stillness,—autumn
　　　　suns　　　　　　　　　　　　　　　　10
Smiling at eve upon the quiet sheaves,—
Sweet Sappho's cheek, ¹—a sleeping infant's breath,—
　　The gradual sand that through an hour-glass
　　　　runs,—
A woodland rivulet,—a Poet's death. ²

[1817]　　　　　　　　　　　　　　　　[1817]

[Sonnet]
ON RECEIVING A LAUREL CROWN
FROM LEIGH HUNT

MINUTES are flying swiftly, and as yet
　　Nothing unearthly has enticed my brain
　　Into a delphic Labyrinth—I would fain
Catch an immortal thought to pay the debt
I owe to the kind Poet who has set
　　Upon my ambitious head a glorious gain.
　　Two bending laurel Sprigs—'tis nearly pain
To be conscious of such a Coronet.
Still time is fleeting, and no dream arises
　　Gorgeous as I would have it—only I see　　10
A Trampling down of what the world most prizes,
　　Turbans and Crowns, and blank regality;
And then I run into most wild surmises
　　Of all the many glories that may be.

[1817]　　　　　　　　　　　　　　　　[1914]

[Sonnet]
TO THE LADIES WHO
SAW ME CROWN'D

WHAT is there in the universal Earth
　　More lovely than a Wreath from the bay tree?
　　Haply a Halo round the Moon—a glee
Circling from three sweet pair of Lips in Mirth;

And haply you will say the dewy birth
　　Or morning Roses—riplings tenderly
　　Spread by the Halcyon's ³ breast upon the Sea—
But these Comparisons are nothing worth—
Then is there nothing in the world so fair?
　　The silvery tears of April?—youth of May?　　10
Or June that breaths out life for butterflies?
　　No—none of these can from my favourite bear
Away the Palm—yet shall it ever pay
　　Due Reverence to your most sovereign eyes.

[1817]　　　　　　　　　　　　　　　　[1914]

HYMN TO APOLLO

GOD of the golden bow,
　　And of the golden lyre,
　　And of the golden hair,
　　　　And of the golden fire,
　　　　　　Charioteer
　　　　　　Of the patient year,
　　　　Where—where slept thine ire,
When like a blank idiot I put on thy wreath,
　　　　Thy laurel, thy glory,
　　　　The light of thy story,　　　　　　10
Or was I a worm—too low crawling for death?
　　　　O Delphic Apollo!

The Thunderer grasp'd and grasp'd, ¹
　　　　The Thunderer frown'd and frown'd;
　　The eagle's feathery mane
　　　　For wrath became stiffen'd—the sound
　　　　　　Of breeding thunder
　　　　　　Went drowsily under,
　　　　Muttering to be unbound.
O why didst thou pity, and beg for a worm?　　20
　　　　Why touch thy soft lute
　　　　Till the thunder was mute,
Why was I not crush'd—such a pitiful germ?
　　　　O Delphic Apollo!

The Pleiades were up, ²
　　　　Watching the silent air;
　　The seeds and roots in Earth
　　　　Were swelling for summer fare;
　　　　　　The Ocean, its neighbour,
　　　　　　Was at his old labour,　　　　30
　　　　When, who—who did dare

---

³ The kingfisher, supposed to be able to calm the surface of the winter sea and build a nest on it.
　¹ I.e., Jupiter and his thunderbolt. The eagle was his emblem. See also Shelley's *Prometheus Unbound*, p. 852.
　² Constellation rising in early spring (in England).

---

¹ See *Sleep and Poetry*, ll. 381–84, p. 1020, n. 17.
² Chatterton, perhaps. See *To Chatterton*, p. 1000, and letter to J. H. Reynolds, September 21, 1819, p. 117.

To tie for a moment thy plant round his brow,
    And grin and look proudly,
    And blaspheme so loudly,
And live for that honour, to stoop to thee now?
    O Delphic Apollo!

[1817]   [1836]

Oh! what a power hath white simplicity!
    What mighty power has this gentle story!   10
    I that for ever feel athirst for glory
Could at this moment be content to lie
    Meekly upon the grass, as those whose sobbings
    Were heard of none beside the mournful robins.

[1817]   [1817]

[Sonnet]
DEDICATION
[of *Poems* 1817]

To LEIGH HUNT, Esq.

GLORY and loveliness have passed away;
    For if we wander out in early morn,
    No wreathed incense do we see upborne
Into the east, to meet the smiling day:
No crowd of nymphs soft voic'd and young, and gay,
    In woven baskets bringing ears of corn,
    Roses, and pinks, and violets, to adorn
The shrine of Flora in her early May.
But there are left delights as high as these,
    And I shall ever bless my destiny,   10
That in a time, when under pleasant trees
    Pan is no longer sought, I feel a free
A leafy luxury, seeing I could please
    With these poor offerings, a man like thee.

[1817]   [1817]

[Sonnet]
ON SEEING THE ELGIN MARBLES

MY spirit is too weak—mortality
    Weighs heavily on me like unwilling sleep,
    And each imagin'd pinnacle and steep
Of godlike hardship tells me I must die
Like a sick Eagle looking at the sky.
    Yet 'tis a gentle luxury to weep
    That I have not the cloudy winds to keep
Fresh for the opening of the morning's eye.
Such dim-conceived glories of the brain
    Bring round the heart an undescribable feud;   10
So do these wonders a most dizzy pain,
    That mingles Grecian grandeur with the rude
Wasting of old Time—with a billowy main—
    A sun—a shadow of a magnitude.

[1817]   [1817]

The medieval verse allegory The Floure and the Leafe, *which was erroneously attributed to Chaucer in Keats's time, contains a situation analogous to that Keats describes in the* Ode to a Nightingale (*where he also echoes the language of Dryden's translation of this tale*).

[Sonnet]
[Written on a Blank Space at the End of Chaucer's Tale 'The Floure and the Lefe']

THIS pleasant tale is like a little copse:
    The honied lines do freshly interlace
    To keep the reader in so sweet a place,
So that he here and there full-hearted stops;
And oftentimes he feels the dewy drops
    Come cool and suddenly against his face,
    And by the wandering melody may trace
Which way the tender-legged linnet hops.

[Sonnet]
TO B. R. HAYDON,
WITH THE FOREGOING SONNET
ON THE ELGIN MARBLES[1]

HAYDON! forgive me that I cannot speak
    Definitively on these mighty things;
    Forgive me that I have not Eagle's wings—
That what I want I know not where to seek:
And think that I would not be over-meek
    In rolling out upfollow'd thunderings,
    Even to the steep of Heliconian[2] springs,
Were I of ample strength for such a freak—
Think too, that all those numbers should be thine;
    Whose else? In this who touch thy vesture's hem?
For when men star'd at what was most divine   11
    With browless idiotism—o'erwise phlegm—
Thou hadst beheld the Hesperean shine
    Of their star in the East, and gone to worship them.

[1817]   [1817]

---

[1] See headnote to *Addressed to Haydon* [*I*], p. 1014.
[2] See *To Charles Cowden Clark*, note 1, p. 1012.

ON A LEANDER GEM

Small paste reproductions of classical scenes were very popular.
The one referred to in the following poem apparently represented
Leander's swim across the Hellespont to meet Hero.

[Sonnet]
ON A LEANDER GEM WHICH MISS REYNOLDS, MY KIND FRIEND, GAVE ME

COME hither all sweet maidens soberly,
   Down-looking—ay, and with a chastened light,
   Hid in the fringes of your eyelids white,
And meekly let your fair hands joined be,
Are ye so gentle that ye could not see,
   Untouch'd, a victim of your beauty bright—
   Sinking away to his young spirit's night,
Sinking bewilder'd 'mid the dreary sea:
'Tis young Leander toiling to his death.
   Nigh swooning, he doth purse his weary lips   10
      For Hero's cheek, and smiles against her smile.
   O horrid dream! see how his body dips
      Dead-heavy; arms and shoulders gleam awhile:
He's gone: up bubbles all his amorous breath!

[1817]   [1829]

[Sonnet]
ON "THE STORY OF RIMINI"
[by Leigh Hunt]

WHO loves to peer up at the morning sun,
   With half-shut eyes and comfortable cheek,
   Let him, with this sweet tale, full often seek
For meadows where the little rivers run;
Who loves to linger with that brightest one
   Of Heaven—Hesperus—let him lowly speak
   These numbers to the night, and starlight meek,
Or moon, if that her hunting be begun.
He who knows these delights, and too is prone
   To moralise upon a smile or tear,   10
Will find at once a region of his own,
   A bower for his spirit, and will steer
To alleys, where the fir-tree drops its cone,
   Where robins hop, and fallen leaves are sear.

[1817]   [1848]

[Sonnet]
ON THE SEA

IT keeps eternal whisperings around
   Desolate shores, and with its mighty swell
   Gluts twice ten thousand caverns, till the spell
Of Hecate[1] leaves them their old shadowy sound.
Often 'tis in such gentle temper found,
   That scarcely will the very smallest shell
   Be moved for days from where it sometime fell,
When last the winds of heaven were unbound.
Oh ye! who have your eye-balls vexed and tired,
   Feast them upon the wideness of the Sea;   10
      Oh ye! whose ears are dinn'd with uproar rude,
   Or fed too much with cloying melody,—
      Sit ye near some old cavern's mouth and brood
Until ye start, as if the sea-nymphs quired!

[1817]   [1817]

---

[1] Goddess of the moon, the earth and the underworld.

ENDYMION

If Keats undertook Endymion *partly as a test of his ability to create and make real to himself an imaginative world adequate to his visionary expectations—a task similar to that of Endymion himself—his four thousand lines are a personal triumph. But it was also a test he could not expect a reader to find equal interest in, which may explain his public disparagement of the poem, beginning with the Preface.*

In the three books that succeed the one reprinted here, Endymion pursues his search for his mysterious goddess under the land and sea, witnesses the fulfillment of sexual love in the seasonal reunion of Venus and Adonis, meets Glaucus and discovers he is the one destined to restore youth to Scylla and redeem the bodies of all drowned lovers by a love dedicated to the service of humanity, and finally is united with Cynthia. But in discovering his dream, he also meets a forlorn Indian maid, for whom he feels human (rather than idealized or humanitarian) love, but who is forbidden to accept him. In the rather abrupt ending, he is about to escape his dilemma by becoming a hermit when the Indian maid is revealed as Cynthia. Apparently Endymion's search has been protracted because he had sought to achieve his ideal directly, rather than through the medium of human feeling and human experience.

The epigraph is from Shakespeare's Sonnet 17; see also To Chatterton, p. 1000.

F R O M

ENDYMION

A POETIC ROMANCE

"The stretched metre of an antique song"

———❦———

INSCRIBED
TO THE MEMORY
OF
THOMAS CHATTERTON

———❦———

PREFACE

Knowing within myself the manner in which this Poem has been produced, it is not without a feeling of regret that I make it public.

What manner I mean, will be quite clear to the reader, who must soon perceive great inexperience, immaturity, and every error denoting a feverish attempt, rather than a deed accomplished. The two first books, and indeed the two last, I feel sensible are not of such completion as to warrant their passing the press; nor should they if I thought a year's castigation would do them any good;—it will not: the foundations are too sandy. It is just that this youngster should die away: a sad thought for me, if I had not

some hope that while it is dwindling I may be plotting, and fitting myself for verses fit to live.

This may be speaking too presumptuously, and may deserve a punishment: but no feeling man will be forward to inflict it: he will leave me alone, with the conviction that there is not a fiercer hell than the failure in a great object. This is not written with the least atom of purpose to forestall criticisms of course, but from the desire I have to conciliate men who are competent to look, and who do look with a zealous eye, to the honour of English literature.

The imagination of a boy is healthy, and the mature imagination of a man is healthy; but there is a space of life between, in which the soul is in a ferment, the character undecided, the way of life uncertain, the ambition thick-sighted: thence proceeds mawkishness, and all the thousand bitters which those men I speak of must necessarily taste in going over the following pages.

I hope I have not in too late a day touched the beautiful mythology of Greece, and dulled its brightness: for I wish to try once more, before I bid it farewel.

Teignmouth, April 10, 1818

———❦———

BOOK I

A THING of beauty is a joy for ever:
Its loveliness increases; it will never
Pass into nothingness; but still will keep
A bower quiet for us, and a sleep
Full of sweet dreams, and health, and quiet breathing.
Therefore, on every morrow, are we wreathing
A flowery band to bind us to the earth,
Spite of despondence, of the inhuman dearth
Of noble natures, of the gloomy days,
Of all the unhealthy and o'er-darkened ways   10
Made for our searching: yes, in spite of all,
Some shape of beauty moves away the pall
From our dark spirits. Such the sun, the moon,
Trees old, and young sprouting a shady boon
For simple sheep; and such are daffodils
With the green world they live in; and clear rills
That for themselves a cooling covert make
'Gainst the hot season; the mid forest brake,
Rich with a sprinkling of fair musk-rose blooms:
And such too is the grandeur of the dooms[1]   20

———————

[1] Here meaning fate or destiny.

We have imagined for the mighty dead;
All lovely tales that we have heard or read:
An endless fountain of immortal drink,
Pouring unto us from the heaven's brink.

Nor do we merely feel these essences
For one short hour; no, even as the trees
That whisper round a temple become soon
Dear as the temple's self, so does the moon,
The passion poesy, glories infinite,
Haunt us till they become a cheering light   30
Unto our souls, and bound to us so fast,
That, whether there be shine, or gloom o'ercast,
They alway must be with us, or we die.

Therefore, 'tis with full happiness that I
Will trace the story of Endymion.
The very music of the name has gone
Into my being, and each pleasant scene
Is growing fresh before me as the green
Of our own vallies: so I will begin
Now while I cannot hear the city's din;   40
Now while the early budders are just new,
And run in mazes of the youngest hue
About old forests; while the willow trails
Its delicate amber; and the dairy pails
Bring home increase of milk. And, as the year
Grows lush in juicy stalks, I'll smoothly steer
My little boat, for many quiet hours,
With streams that deepen freshly into bowers.
Many and many a verse I hope to write,
Before the daisies, vermeil [2] rimm'd and white,   50
Hide in deep herbage; and ere yet the bees
Hum about globes of clover and sweet peas,
I must be near the middle of my story.
O may no wintry season, bare and hoary,
See it half finished: but let Autumn bold,
With universal tinge of sober gold,
Be all about me when I make an end.
And now at once, adventuresome, I send
My herald thought into a wilderness:
There let its trumpet blow, and quickly dress   60
My uncertain path with green, that I may speed
Easily onward, thorough flowers and weed.

Upon the sides of Latmos [3] was outspread
A mighty forest; for the moist earth fed
So plenteously all weed-hidden roots
Into o'er-hanging boughs, and precious fruits.
And it had gloomy shades, sequestered deep,
Where no man went; and if from shepherd's keep

A lamb strayed far a-down those inmost glens,
Never again saw he the happy pens   70
Whither his brethren, bleating with content,
Over the hills at every nightfall went.
Among the shepherds, 'twas believed ever,
That not one fleecy lamb which thus did sever
From the white flock, but pass'd unworried
By angry wolf, or pard [4] with prying head,
Until it came to some unfooted plains
Where fed the herds of Pan: ay great his gains
Who thus one lamb did lose. Paths there were many,
Winding through palmy fern, and rushes fenny,   80
And ivy banks; all leading pleasantly
To a wide lawn, whence one could only see
Stems thronging all around between the swell
Of turf and slanting branches: who could tell
The freshness of the space of heaven above,
Edg'd round with dark tree tops? through which a
    dove
Would often beat its wings, and often too
A little cloud would move across the blue.

Full in the middle of this pleasantness
There stood a marble altar, with a tress   90
Of flowers budded newly; and the dew
Had taken fairy phantasies to strew
Daisies upon the sacred sward last eve,
And so the dawned light in pomp receive.
For 'twas the morn: Apollo's upward fire
Made every eastern cloud a silvery pyre
Of brightness so unsullied, that therein
A melancholy spirit well might win
Oblivion, and melt out his essence fine
Into the winds: rain-scented eglantine   100
Gave temperate sweets to that well-wooing sun;
The lark was lost in him; cold springs had run
To warm their chilliest bubbles in the grass;
Man's voice was on the mountains; and the mass
Of nature's lives and wonders puls'd tenfold,
To feel this sun-rise and its glories old.

Now while the silent workings of the dawn
Were busiest, into that self-same lawn
All suddenly, with joyful cries, there sped
A troop of little children garlanded;   110
Who gathering round the altar, seemed to pry
Earnestly round as wishing to espy
Some folk of holiday: nor had they waited
For many moments, ere their ears were sated
With a faint breath of music, which ev'n then
Fill'd out its voice, and died away again.

---

[2] Crimson.
[3] Mountain in Asia Minor traditionally associated with the Endymion legend.

[4] Leopard.

Within a little space again it gave
Its airy swellings, with a gentle wave,
To light-hung leaves, in smoothest echoes breaking
Through copse-clad vallies,—ere their death,
    o'ertaking   120
The surgy murmurs of the lonely sea.

   And now, as deep into the wood as we
Might mark a lynx's eye, there glimmered light
Fair faces and a rush of garments white,
Plainer and plainer shewing, till at last
Into the widest alley they all past,
Making directly for the woodland altar,
O kindly muse! let not my weak tongue faulter
In telling of this goodly company,
Of their old piety, and of their glee: 130
But let a portion of ethereal dew
Fall on my head, and presently unmew[5]
My soul; that I may dare, in wayfaring,
To stammer where old Chaucer used to sing.

   Leading the way, young damsels danced along,
Bearing the burden of a shepherd song;
Each having a white wicker over brimm'd
With April's tender younglings: next, well trimm'd,
A crown of shepherds with as sunburnt looks
As may be read of in Arcadian books;[6]   140
Such as sat listening round Apollo's pipe,
When the great diety, for earth too ripe,
Let his divinity o'er-flowing die
In music, through the vales of Thessaly:[7]
Some idly trailed their sheep-hooks on the ground,
And some kept up a shrilly mellow sound
With ebon-tipped flutes: close after these,
Now coming from beneath the forest trees,
A venerable priest full soberly,
Begirt with ministring looks: alway his eye   150
Stedfast upon the matted turf he kept,
And after him his sacred vestments swept.
From his right hand there swung a vase, milk-white,
Of mingled wine, out-sparkling generous light;
And in his left he held a basket full
Of all sweet herbs that searching eye could cull:
Wild thyme, and valley-lilies whiter still
Than Leda's love,[8] and cresses from the rill.
His aged head, crowned with beechen wreath,
Seem'd like a poll of ivy in the teeth   160
Of winter hoar. Then came another crowd
Of shepherds, lifting in due time aloud

Their share of the ditty. After them appear'd,
Up-followed by a multitude that rear'd
Their voices to the clouds, a fair wrought car,
Easily rolling so as scarce to mar
The freedom of three steeds of dapple brown:
Who stood therein did seem of great renown
Among the throng. His youth was fully blown,
Shewing like Ganymede[9] to manhood grown;   170
And, for those simple times, his garments were
A chieftain king's: beneath his breast, half bare,
Was hung a silver bugle, and between
His nervy knees there lay a boar-spear keen.
A smile was on his countenance; he seem'd,
To common lookers on, like one who dream'd
Of idleness in groves Elysian:[10]
But there were some who feelingly could scan
A lurking trouble in his nether lip,
And see that oftentimes the reins would slip   180
Through his forgotten hands: then would they sigh,
And think of yellow leaves, of owlet's cry,
Of logs piled solemnly.—Ah, well-a-day,
Why should our young Endymion pine away!

   Soon the assembly, in a circle rang'd,
Stood silent round the shrine: each look was chang'd
To sudden veneration: women meek
Beckon'd their sons to silence; while each cheek
Of virgin bloom paled gently for slight fear.
Endymion too, without a forest peer,   190
Stood, wan, and pale, and with an awed face,
Among his brothers of the mountain chase,
In midst of all, the venerable priest
Eyed them with joy from greatest to the least,
And, after lifting up his aged hands,
Thus spake he: 'Men of Latmos! shepherd bands!
Whose care it is to guard a thousand flocks:
Whether descended from beneath the rocks
That overtop your mountains; whether come
From vallies where the pipe is never dumb;   200
Or from your swelling downs, where sweet air stirs
Blue hare-bells lightly, and where prickly furze
Buds lavish gold; or ye, whose precious charge
Nibble their fill at ocean's very marge,
Whose mellow reeds are touch'd with sounds forlorn
By the dim echoes of old Triton's horn:
Mothers and wives! who day by day prepare
The scrip, with needments, for the mountain air;
And all ye gentle girls who foster up
Udderless lambs, and in a little cup   210
Will put choice honey for a favoured youth:
Yea, every one attend! for in good truth

---

[5] Release.
[6] Pastoral poetry.
[7] Apollo was sent into exile in Thessaly as a shepherd.
[8] Jupiter, who assumed the shape of a swan to make love to Leda.

[9] Cup-bearer of the gods.
[10] In Greek mythology, the area of the underworld reserved for the virtuous.

Our vows are wanting to our great god Pan.
Are not our lowing heifers sleeker than
Night-swollen mushrooms? Are not our wide plains
Speckled with countless fleeces? Have not rains
Green'd over April's lap? No howling sad
Sickens our fearful ewes; and we have had
Great bounty from Endymion our lord.
The earth is glad: the merry lark has pour'd   220
His early song against yon breezy sky,
That spreads so clear o'er our solemnity.'

    Thus ending, on the shrine he heap'd a spire
Of teeming sweets, enkindling sacred fire;
Anon he stain'd the thick and spongy sod
With wine, in honour of the shepherd-god.
Now while the earth was drinking it, and while
Bay leaves were crackling in the fragrant pile,
And gummy frankincense was sparkling bright
'Neath smothering parsley, and a hazy light   230
Spread greyly eastward, thus a chorus sang:

    'O THOU, whose mighty palace roof doth hang
From jagged trunks, and overshadoweth
Eternal whispers, glooms, the birth, life, death
Of unseen flowers in heavy peacefulness;
Who lov'st to see the hamadryads [11] dress
Their ruffled locks where meeting hazels darken;
And through whole solemn hours dost sit, and hearken
The dreary melody of bedded reeds—
In desolate places, where dank moisture breeds   240
The pipy hemlock to strange overgrowth;
Bethinking thee, how melancholy loth
Thou wast to lose fair Syrinx [12]—do thou now,
By thy love's milky brow!
By all the trembling mazes that she ran,
Hear us, great Pan!

    'O thou, for whose soul-soothing quiet, turtles [13]
Passion their voices cooingly 'mong myrtles,
What time thou wanderest at eventide
Through sunny meadows, that outskirt the side   250
Of thine enmossed realms: O thou, to whom
Broad leaved fig trees even now foredoom
Their ripen'd fruitage; yellow girted bees
Their golden honeycombs; our village leas
Their fairest blossom'd beans and poppied corn;
The chuckling linnet its five young unborn,
To sing for thee; low creeping strawberries
Their summer coolness; pent up butterflies

Their freckled wings; yea, the fresh budding year
All its completions—be quickly near,   260
By every wind that nods the mountain pine,
O forester divine!

    'Thou, to whom every faun and satyr flies
For willing service; whether to surprise
The squatted hare while in half sleeping fit;
Or upward ragged precipices to flit
To save poor lambkins from the eagle's maw;
Or by mysterious enticement draw
Bewildered shepherds to their path again;
Or to tread breathless round the frothy main,   270
And gather up all fancifullest shells
For thee to tumble into Naiad's cells,
And, being hidden, laugh at their out-peeping;
Or to delight thee with fantastic leaping,
The while they pelt each other on the crown
With silvery oak apples, and fir cones brown—
By all the echoes that about thee ring,
Hear us, O satyr king!

    'O Hearkener to the loud clapping shears,
While ever and anon to his shorn peers   280
A ram goes bleating: Winder of the horn,
When snouted wild-boars routing tender corn
Anger our huntsmen: Breather round our farms,
To keep off mildews, and all weather harms:
Strange ministrant of undescribed sounds,
That come a swooning over hollow grounds,
And wither drearily on barren moors;
Dread opener of the mysterious doors
Leading to universal knowledge—see,
Great son of Dryope, [14]   290
The many that are come to pay their vows
With leaves about their brows!

    'Be still the unimaginable lodge
For solitary thinkings; such as dodge
Conception to the very bourne of heaven,
Then leave the naked brain: be still the leaven,
That spreading in this dull and clodded earth
Gives it a touch ethereal—a new birth:
Be still a symbol of immensity;
A firmament reflected in a sea;   300
An element filling the space between;
An unknown—but no more: we humbly screen
With uplift hands our foreheads, lowly bending,
And giving out a shout most heaven rending,
Conjure thee to receive our humble Pæan,
Upon thy Mount Lycean! [15]

---

[11] Tree nymphs.
[12] See Shelley's *Hymn of Pan*, p. 918.
[13] Turtledoves.

---

[14] Pan—the All—was the son of Dryope and Hermes.
[15] Mountain sacred to Jupiter and to Pan.

Even while they brought the burden to a close,
A shout from the whole multitude arose,
That lingered in the air like dying rolls
Of abrupt thunder, when Ionian shoals   310
Of dolphins bob their noses through the brine.
Meantime, on shady levels, mossy fine,
Young companies nimbly began dancing
To the swift treble pipe, and humming string.
Aye, those fair living forms swam heavenly
To tunes forgotten—out of memory:
Fair creatures! whose young children's children bred
Thermopylæ [16] its heroes—not yet dead,
But in old marbles ever beautiful.
High genitors, unconscious did they cull   320
Time's sweet first-fruits—they danc'd to weariness,
And then in quiet circles did they press
The hillock turf, and caught the latter end
Of some strange history, potent to send
A young mind from its bodily tenement.
Or they might watch the quoit-pitchers, intent
On either side; pitying the sad death
Of Hyacinthus, when the cruel breath
Of Zephyr slew him,—Zephyr penitent,
Who now, ere Phœbus mounts the firmament,   330
Fondles the flower amid the sobbing rain.
The archers too, upon a wider plain,
Beside the feathery whizzing of the shaft,
And the dull twanging bowstring, and the raft
Branch down sweeping from a tall ash top,
Call'd up a thousand thoughts to envelope
Those who would watch. Perhaps, the trembling knee
And frantic gape of lonely Niobe, [17]
Poor, lonely Niobe! when her lovely young
Were dead and gone, and her caressing tongue   340
Lay a lost thing upon her paly lip,
And very, very deadliness did nip
Her motherly cheeks. Arous'd from this sad mood
By one, who at a distance loud halloo'd,
Uplifting his strong bow into the air,
Many might after brighter visions stare:
After the Argonauts, in blind amaze
Tossing about on Neptune's restless ways, [18]
Until, from the horizon's vaulted side,
There shot a golden splendour far and wide,   350
Spangling those million poutings of the brine
With quivering ore: 'twas even an awful shine
From the exaltation of Apollo's bow;
A heavenly beacon in their dreary woe.

Who thus were ripe for high contemplating,
Might turn their steps towards the sober ring
Where sat Endymion and the aged priest
'Mong shepherds gone in eld, [19] whose looks increas'd
The silvery setting of their mortal star.
There they discours'd upon the fragile bar   360
That keeps us from our homes ethereal;
And what our duties there: to nightly call
Vesper, the beauty-crest of summer weather;
To summon all the downiest clouds together
For the sun's purple couch; to emulate
In ministring the potent rule of fate
With speed of fire-tailed exhalations; [20]
To tint her pallid cheek with bloom, who cons
Sweet poesy by moonlight: beside these,
A world of other unguess'd offices.   370
Anon they wander'd, by divine converse,
Into Elysium; vieing to rehearse
Each one his own anticipated bliss.
One felt heart-certain that he could not miss
His quick gone love, among fair blossom'd boughs,
Where every zephyr-sigh pouts, and endows
Her lips with music for the welcoming.
Another wish'd, mid that eternal spring,
To meet his rosy child, with feathery sails,
Sweeping, eye-earnestly, through almond vales: 380
Who, suddenly, should stoop through the smooth
        wind,
And with the balmiest leaves his temples bind;
And, ever after, through those regions be
His messenger, his little Mercury.
Some were athirst in soul to see again
Their fellow huntsmen o'er the wide champaign [21]
In times long past; to sit with them, and talk
Of all the chances in their earthly walk;
Comparing, joyfully, their plenteous stores
Of happiness, to when upon the moors,   390
Benighted, close they huddled from the cold,
And shar'd their famish'd scrips. Thus all out-told
Their fond imaginations,—saving him
Whose eyelids curtain'd up their jewels dim,
Endymion: yet hourly had he striven
To hide the cankering venom, that had riven
His fainting recollections. Now indeed
His senses had swoon'd off: he did not heed
The sudden silence, or the whispers low,
Or the old eyes dissolving at his woe,   400
Or anxious calls, or close of trembling palms,
Or maiden's sigh, that grief itself embalms:

---

[16] Spartan city defended against the Romans.
[17] Changed into stone after her children were killed by Apollo.
[18] The Argonauts sailed with Jason in the *Argo*, in quest of the Golden Fleece.

---

[19] Age.
[20] Comets.
[21] Open country.

But in the self-same fixed trance he kept,
Like one who on the earth had never stept.
Aye, even as dead-still as a marble man,
Frozen in that old tale Arabian.[22]

Who whispers him so pantingly and close?
Peona, his sweet sister:[23] of all those,
His friends, the dearest. Hushing signs she made,
And breath'd a sister's sorrow to persuade   410
A yielding up, a cradling on her care.
Her eloquence did breathe away the curse:
She led him, like some midnight spirit nurse
Of happy changes in emphatic dreams,
Along a path between two little streams,—
Guarding his forehead, with her round elbow,
From low-grown branches, and his footsteps slow
From stumbling over stumps and hillocks small;
Until they came to where these streamlets fall,
With mingled bubblings and a gentle rush,   420
Into a river, clear, brimful, and flush
With crystal mocking of the trees and sky.
A little shallop,[24] floating there hard by,
Pointed its beak over the fringed bank;
And soon it lightly dipt, and rose, and sank,
And dipt again, with the young couple's weight,—
Peona guiding, through the water straight,
Towards a bowery island opposite;
Which gaining presently, she steered light
Into a shady, fresh, and ripply cove,   430
Where nested was an arbour, overwove
By many a summer's silent fingering;
To whose cool bosom she was used to bring
Her playmates, with their needle broidery,
And minstrel memories of times gone by.

So she was gently glad to see him laid
Under her favourite bower's quiet shade,
On her own couch, new made of flower leaves,
Dried carefully on the cooler side of sheaves
When last the sun his autumn tresses shook,   440
And the tann'd harvesters rich armfuls took.
Soon was he quieted to slumbrous rest:
But, ere it crept upon him, he had prest
Peona's busy hand against his lips,
And still, a sleeping, held her finger-tips
In tender pressure. And as a willow keeps
A patient watch over the stream that creeps
Windingly by it, so the quiet maid
Held her in peace: so that a whispering blade

Of grass, a wailful gnat, a bee bustling   450
Down in the blue-bells, or a wren light rustling
Among sere leaves and twigs, might all be heard.

O magic sleep! O comfortable bird
That broodest o'er the troubled sea of the mind
Till it is hush'd and smooth![25] O unconfin'd
Restraint! imprisoned liberty! great key
To golden palaces, strange minstrelsy,
Fountains grotesque, new trees, bespangled caves,
Echoing grottos, full of tumbling waves
And moonlight; aye, to all the mazy world   460
Of silvery enchantment!—who, upfurl'd
Beneath thy drowsy wing a triple hour,
But renovates and lives?—Thus, in the bower,
Endymion was calm'd to life again
Opening his eyelids with a healthier brain,
He said: 'I feel this thine endearing love
All through my bosom: thou art as a dove
Trembling its closed eyes and sleeked wings
About me; and the pearliest dew not brings
Such morning incense from the fields of May,   470
As do those brighter drops that twinkling stray
From those kind eyes,—the very home and haunt
Of sisterly affection. Can I want
Aught else, aught nearer heaven, than such tears?
Yet dry them up, in bidding hence all fears
That, any longer, I will pass my days
Alone and sad. No, I will once more raise
My voice upon the mountain-heights; once more
Make my horn parley from their foreheads hoar:
Again my trooping hounds their tongues shall loll 480
Around the breathed boar: again I'll poll
The fair-grown yew tree, for a chosen bow:
And, when the pleasant sun is getting low,
Again I'll linger in a sloping mead
To hear the speckled thrushes, and see feed
Our idle sheep. So be thou cheered, sweet,
And, if thy lute is here, softly intreat
My soul to keep in its resolved course.'

Hereat Peona, in their silver source,
Shut her pure sorrow drops with glad exclaim,   490
And took a lute, from which there pulsing came
A lively prelude, fashioning the way
In which her voice should wander. 'Twas a lay
More subtle cadenced, more forest wild
Than Dryope's lone lulling of her child;[26]
And nothing since has floated in the air
So mournful strange. Surely some influence rare

---

[22] In *The Arabian Nights* a man who was black marble from the waist down.

[23] Keats's invention.

[24] Light, open boat.

[25] Halcyon, that favorite poetic bird.

[26] Probably not the mother of Pan, but the Dryope who was changed into a tree while nursing her child.

Went, spiritual, through the damsel's hand;
For still, with Delphic emphasis, she spann'd
The quick invisible strings, even though she saw   500
Endymion's spirit melt away and thaw
Before the deep intoxication.
But soon she came, with sudden burst, upon
Her self-possession—swung the lute aside,
And earnestly said: 'Brother, 'tis vain to hide
That thou dost know of things mysterious,
Immortal, starry; such alone could thus
Weigh down thy nature. Hast thou sinn'd in aught
Offensive to the heavenly powers? Caught
A Paphian dove²⁷ upon a message sent?   510
Thy deathful bow against some deer-head bent,
Sacred to Dian? Haply, thou hast seen
Her naked limbs among the alders green;
And that, alas! is death.²⁸ No, I can trace
Something more high-perplexing in thy face!'

Endymion look'd at her, and press'd her hand,
And said, 'Art thou so pale, who wast so bland
And merry in our meadows? How is this?
Tell me thine ailment: tell me all amiss!—
Ah! thou has been unhappy at the change   520
Wrought suddenly in me. What indeed more strange?
Or more complete to overwhelm surmise?
Ambition is no sluggard: 'tis no prize,
That toiling years would put within my grasp,
That I have sigh'd for: with so deadly gasp
No man e'er panted for a mortal love.
So all have set my heavier grief above
These things which happen. Rightly have they done:
I, who still saw the horizontal sun
Heave his broad shoulder o'er the edge of the world,
Out-facing Lucifer,²⁹ and then had hurl'd   531
My spear aloft, as signal for the chace—
I, who, for very sport of heart, would race
With my own steed from Araby; pluck down
A vulture from his towery perching; frown
A lion into growling, loth retire—
To lose, at once, all my toil breeding fire,
And sink thus low! but I will ease my breast
Of secret grief, here in this bowery nest.

'This river does not see the naked sky,   540
Till it begins to progress silverly
Around the western border of the wood,
Whence, from a certain spot, its winding flood
Seems at the distance like a crescent moon:
And in that nook, the very pride of June,

Had I been used to pass my weary eves;
The rather for the sun unwilling leaves
So dear a picture of his sovereign power,
And I could witness his most kingly hour,
When he doth tighten up the golden reins,   550
And paces leisurely down amber plains
His snorting four. Now when his chariot last
Its beams against the zodiac-lion cast,³⁰
There blossom'd suddenly a magic bed
Of sacred ditamy, and poppies red:
At which I wondered greatly, knowing well
That but one night had wrought this flowery spell;
And, sitting down close by, began to muse
What it might mean. Perhaps, thought I, Morpheus,
In passing here, his owlet pinions shook;   560
Or, it may be, ere matron Night uptook
Her ebon urn, young Mercury, by stealth,
Had dipt his rod in it: such garland wealth
Came not by common growth. Thus on I thought,
Until my head was dizzy and distraught.
Moreover, through the dancing poppies stole
A breeze, most softly lulling to my soul;
And shaping visions all about my sight
Of colours, wings, and bursts of spangly light;
The which became more strange, and strange, and dim,
And then were gulph'd in a tumultuous swim: 570
And then I fell asleep. Ah, can I tell
The enchantment that afterwards befel?
Yet it was but a dream: yet such a dream
That never tongue, although it overteem
With mellow utterance, like a cavern spring,
Could figure out and to conception bring
All I beheld and felt. Methought I lay
Watching the zenith, where the milky way
Among the stars in virgin splendour pours;   580
And travelling my eye, until the doors
Of heaven appear'd to open for my flight,
I became loth and fearful to alight
From such high soaring by a downward glance:
So kept me stedfast in that airy trance,
Spreading imaginary pinions wide.
When, presently, the stars began to glide,
And faint away, before my eager view:
At which I sigh'd that I could not pursue,
And dropt my vision to the horizon's verge;   590
And lo! from the opening clouds, I saw emerge
The loveliest moon, that ever silver'd o'er
A shell for Neptune's goblet: she did soar
So passionately bright, my dazzled soul
Commingling with her argent spheres³¹ did roll

---

²⁷ From Venus's temple in Paphos.
²⁸ Acteon, who in punishment for seeing Diana bathing was turned into a stag and torn to pieces by his own dogs.
²⁹ The morning star.

³⁰ Leo.
³¹ Each planet, in ancient astronomy, was assumed to have its own hollow globe surrounding it.

Through clear and cloudy, even when she went
At last into a dark and vapoury tent—
Whereat, methought, the lidless-eyed train
Of planets all were in the blue again.
To commune with those orbs, once more I rais'd   600
My sight right upward: but it was quite dazed
By a bright something, sailing down apace,
Making me quickly veil my eyes and face:
Again I look'd, and, O ye deities,
Who from Olympus watch our destinies!
Whence that completed form of all completeness?
Whence came that high perfection of all sweetness?
Speak, stubborn earth, and tell me where, O where
Hast thou a symbol of her golden hair?
Not oat-sheaves drooping in the western sun;   610
Not—thy soft hand, fair sister! let me shun
Such follying before thee—yet she had,
Indeed, locks bright enough to make me mad;
And they were simply gordian'd 32 up and braided,
Leaving, in naked comeliness, unshaded,
Her pearl round ears, white neck, and orbed brow;
The which were blended in, I know not how,
With such a paradise of lips and eyes,
Blush-tinted cheeks, half smiles, and faintest sighs,
That, when I think thereon, my spirit clings   620
And plays about its fancy, till the stings
Of human neighbourhood envenom all.
Unto what awful power shall I call?
To what high fane?—Ah! see her hovering feet,
More bluely vein'd, more soft, more whitely sweet
Than those of sea-born Venus, when she rose
From out her cradle shell. The wind out-blows
Her scarf into a fluttering pavilion;
'Tis blue, and over-spangled with a million
Of little eyes, as though thou wert to shed,   630
Over the darkest, lushest blue-bell bed,
Handfuls of daisies.'—'Endymion, how strange!
Dream within dream!'—'She took an airy range,
And then, towards me, like a very maid,
Came blushing, waning, willing, and afraid,
And press'd me by the hand: Ah! 'twas too much;
Methought I fainted at the charmed touch,
Yet held my recollection, even as one
Who dives three fathoms where the waters run
Gurgling in beds of coral: for anon,   640
I felt upmounted in that region
Where falling stars dart their artillery forth,
And eagles struggle with the buffeting north
That balances the heavy meteor-stone;—
Felt too, I was not fearful, nor alone,

But lapp'd and lull'd along the dangerous sky.
Soon, as it seem'd, we left our journeying high,
And straightway into frightful eddies swoop'd;
Such as aye muster where grey time has scoop'd
Huge dens and caverns in a mountain's side: 650
There hollow sounds arous'd me, and I sigh'd
To faint once more by looking on my bliss—
I was distracted; madly did I kiss
The wooing arms which held me, and did give
My eyes at once to death: but 'twas to live,
To take in draughts of life from the gold fount
Of kind and passionate looks; to count, and count
The moments, by some greedy help that seem'd
A second self, that each might be redeem'd
And plunder'd of its load of blessedness.   660
Ah, desperate mortal! I ev'n dar'd to press
Her very cheek against my crowned lip,
And, at that moment, felt my body dip
Into a warmer air: a moment more
Our feet were soft in flowers. There was store
Of newest joys upon that alp. Sometimes
A scent of violets, and blossoming limes,
Loiter'd around us; then of honey cells,
Made delicate from all white-flower bells;
And once, above the edges of our nest,   670
An arch face peep'd,—an Oread 33 as I guess'd.

   'Why did I dream that sleep o'er-power'd me
In midst of all this heaven? Why not see,
Far off, the shadows of his pinions dark,
And stare them from me? But no, like a spark
That needs must die, although its little beam
Reflects upon a diamond, my sweet dream
Fell into nothing—into stupid sleep.
And so it was, until a gentle creep,
A careful moving caught my waking ears,   680
And up I started: Ah! my sighs, my tears,
My clenched hands; for lo! the poppies hung
Dew-dabbled on their stalks, the ouzel 34 sung
A heavy ditty, and the sullen day
Had chidden herald Hesperus away,
With leaden looks: the solitary breeze
Bluster'd, and slept, and its wild self did teaze
With wayward melancholy; and I thought,
Mark me, Peona! that sometimes it brought
Faint fare-thee-wells, and sigh-shrilled adieus!—   690
Away I wander'd—all the pleasant hues
Of heaven and earth had faded; deepest shades
Were deepest dungeons; heaths and sunny glades
Were full of pestilent light; our taintless rills
Seem'd sooty, and o'er-spread with upturn'd gills

32 Knotted, in the manner of that knot tied by King Gordius of Phrygia—the Gordian Knot that only Alexander the Great undid, by cutting it apart.

33 Mountain nymph.
34 The European blackbird.

Of dying fish; the vermeil rose had blown
In frightful scarlet, and its thorns out-grown
Like spiked aloe. If an innocent bird
Before my heedless footsteps stirr'd, and stirr'd
In little journeys, I beheld in it   700
A disguis'd demon, missioned to knit
My soul with under darkness; to entice
My stumblings down some monstrous precipice:
Therefore I eager followed, and did curse
The disappointment. Time, that aged nurse,
Rock'd me to patience. Now, thank gentle heaven!
These things, with all their comfortings, are given
To my down-sunken hours, and with thee,
Sweet sister, help to stem the ebbing sea
Of weary life.'

            Thus ended he, and both   710
Sat silent: for the maid was very loth
To answer; feeling well that breathed words
Would all be lost, unheard, and vain as swords
Against the enchased crocodile, or leaps
Of grasshoppers against the sun. She weeps,
And wonders; struggles to devise some blame;
To put on such a look as would say, *Shame
On this poor weakness!* but, for all her strife,
She could as soon have crush'd away the life
From a sick dove. At length, to break the pause,   720
She said with trembling chance: 'Is this the cause?
This all? Yet it is strange, and sad, alas!
That one who through this middle earth [35] should pass
Most like a sojourning demi-god, and leave
His name upon the harp-string, should achieve
No higher bard than simple maidenhood,
Singing alone, and fearfully,—how the blood
Left his young cheek; and how he used to stray
He knew not where; and how he would say, *nay*,
If any said 'twas love: and yet 'twas love;   730
What could it be but love? How a ring-dove
Let fall a sprig of yew tree in his path;
And how he died: and then, that love doth scathe
The gentle heart, as northern blasts do roses;
And then the ballad of his sad life closes
With sighs, and an alas!—Endymion!
Be rather in the trumpet's mouth,—anon
Among the winds at large—that all may hearken!
Although, before the crystal heavens darken,
I watch and dote upon the silver lakes   740
Pictur'd in western cloudiness, that takes
The semblance of gold rocks and bright gold sands,
Islands, and creeks, and amber-fretted strands
With horses prancing o'er them, palaces
And towers of amethyst,—would I so tease

My pleasant days, because I could not mount
Into those regions? The Morphean fount
Of that fine element that visions, dreams,
And fitful whims of sleep are made of, streams
Into its airy channels with so subtle,   750
So thin a breathing, not the spider's shuttle,
Circled a million times within the space
Of a swallow's nest-door, could delay a trace,
A tinting of its quality: how light
Must dreams themselves be; seeing they're more
            slight
Than the mere nothing that engenders them!
Then wherefore sully the entrusted gem
Of high and noble life with thoughts so sick?
Why pierce high-fronted honour to the quick
For nothing but a dream?' Hereat the youth   760
Look'd up: a conflicting of shame and ruth
Was in his plaited brow: yet, his eyelids
Widened a little, as when Zephyr bids
A little breeze to creep between the fans
Of careless butterflies: amid his pains
He seem'd to taste a drop of manna-dew, [36]
Full palatable; and a colour grew
Upon his cheek, while thus he lifeful spake.

'Peona! ever have I long'd to slake
My thirst for the world's praises: nothing base,   770
No merely slumberous phantasm, could unlace
The stubborn canvas for my voyage prepar'd—
Though now 'tis tatter'd; leaving my bark bar'd
And sullenly drifting: yet my higher hope
Is of too wide, too rainbow-large a scope,
To fret at myriads of earthly wrecks.
Wherein lies happiness? In that which becks
Our ready minds to fellowship divine,
A fellowship with essence; till we shine,
Full alchemiz'd, and free of space. Behold   780
The clear religion of heaven! Fold
A rose leaf round thy finger's taperness,
And soothe thy lips: hist, when the airy stress
Of music's kiss impregnates the free winds,
And with a sympathetic touch unbinds
Eolian magic from their lucid wombs:
Then old songs waken from enclouded tombs;
Old ditties sigh above their father's grave;
Ghosts of melodious prophecyings rave
Round every spot where trod Apollo's foot;   790
Bronze clarions awake, and faintly bruit,
Where long ago a Giant Battle was;
And, from the turf, a lullaby doth pass

---

[35] Midway between heaven and the underworld.

[36] Miraculous substance on which the Israelites subsisted in the wilderness.

In every place where infant Orpheus slept.
Feel we these things?—that moment have we stept
Into a sort of oneness, and our state
Is like a floating spirit's. But there are
Richer entanglements, enthralments far
More self-destroying, leading, by degrees,
To the chief intensity: the crown of these   800
Is made of love and friendship, and sits high
Upon the forehead of humanity.
All its more ponderous and bulky worth
Is friendship, whence there ever issues forth
A steady splendour; but at the tip-top,
There hangs by unseen film, an orbed drop
Of light, and that is love: its influence,
Thrown in our eyes, genders a novel sense,
At which we start and fret; till in the end,
Melting into its radiance, we blend,   810
Mingle, and so become a part of it,—
Nor with aught else can our souls interknit
So wingedly: when we combine therewith,
Life's self is nourish'd by its proper pith,
And we are nurtured like a pelican brood.[37]
Aye, so delicious is the unsating food,
That men, who might have tower'd in the van
Of all the congregated world, to fan
And winnow from the coming step of time
All chaff of custom, wipe away all slime   820
Left by men-slugs and human serpentry,
Have been content to let occasion die,
Whilst they did sleep in love's elysium.
And, truly, I would rather be struck dumb,
Than speak against this ardent listlessness:
For I have ever thought that it might bless
The world with benefits unknowingly;
As does the nightingale, upperched high,
And cloister'd among cool and bunched leaves—
She sings but to her love, nor e'er conceives   830
How tiptoe Night holds back her dark-grey hood.
Just so may love, although 'tis understood
The mere commingling of passionate breath,
Produce more than our searching witnesseth:
What I know not: but who, of men, can tell
That flowers would bloom, or that green fruit would
          swell
To melting pulp, that fish would have bright mail,
The earth its dower of river, wood, and vale,
The meadows runnels, runnels pebble-stones,
The seed its harvest, or the lute its tones,   840
Tones ravishment, or ravishment its sweet,
If human souls did never kiss and greet?

'Now, if this earthly love has power to make
Men's being mortal, immortal; to shake
Ambition from their memories, and brim
Their measure of content; what merest whim,
Seems all this poor endeavour after fame,
To one, who keeps within his stedfast aim
A love immortal, an immortal too.
Look not so wilder'd; for these things are true,   850
And never can be born of atomies
That buzz about our slumbers, like brain-flies,
Leaving us fancy-sick. No, no, I'm sure,
My restless spirit never could endure
To brood so long upon one luxury,
Unless it did, though fearfully, espy
A hope beyond the shadow of a dream.
My sayings will the less obscured seem,
When I have told thee how my waking sight
Has made me scruple whether that same night   860
Was pass'd in dreaming. Hearken, sweet Peona!
Beyond the matron-temple of Latona,[38]
Which we should see but for these darkening boughs,
Lies a deep hollow, from whose ragged brows
Bushes and trees do lean all round athwart,
And meet so nearly, that with wings outraught,
And spreaded tail, a vulture could not glide
Past them, but he must brush on every side.
Some moulder'd steps lead into this cool cell,
Far as the slabbed margin of a well,   870
Whose patient level peeps its crystal eye
Right upward, through the bushes, to the sky.
Oft have I brought thee flowers, on their stalks set
Like vestal primroses, but dark velvet
Edges them round, and they have golden pits:
'Twas there I got them, from the gaps and slits
In a mossy stone, that sometimes was my seat,
When all above was faint with mid-day heat.
And there in strife no burning thoughts to heed,
I'd bubble up the water through a reed;   880
So reaching back to boy-hood: make me ships
Of moulted feathers, touchwood, alder chips,
With leaves stuck in them; and the Neptune be
Of their petty ocean. Oftener, heavily,
When love-lorn hours had left me less a child,
I sat contemplating the figures wild
Of o'er-head clouds melting the mirror through.
Upon a day, while thus I watch'd, by flew
A cloudy Cupid, with his bow and quiver;
So plainly character'd, no breeze would shiver   890
The happy chance; so happy, I was fain
To follow it upon the open plain,
And, therefore, was just going; when, behold!
A wonder, fair as any I have told—

---

[37] Pelicans supposedly fed their young by picking at their own breasts.

[38] Latona was the mother of Cynthia and Apollo.

The same bright face I tasted in my sleep,
Smiling in the clear well. My heart did leap
Through the cool depth.—It moved as if to flee—
I started up, when lo! refreshfully,
There came upon my face, in plenteous showers,
Dew-drops, and dewy buds, and leaves, and flowers,
Wrapping all objects from my smothered sight,　901
Bathing my spirit in a new delight.
Aye, such a breathless honey-feel of bliss
Alone preserved me from the drear abyss
Of death, for the fair form had gone again.
Pleasure is oft a visitant; but pain
Clings cruelly to us, like the gnawing sloth 39
On the deer's tender haunches: late, and loth,
'Tis scar'd away by slow returning pleasure.
How sickening, how dark the dreadful leisure　910
Of weary days, made deeper exquisite,
By a fore-knowledge of unslumbrous night!
Like sorrow came upon me, heavier still,
Than when I wander'd from the poppy hill:
And a whole age of lingering moments crept
Sluggishly by, ere more contentment swept
Away at once the deadly yellow spleen.
Yes, thrice have I this fair enchantment seen;
Once more been tortured with renewed life.
When last the wintry gusts gave over strife　920
With the conquering sun of spring, and left the skies
Warm and serene, but yet with moistened eyes
In pity of the shatter'd infant buds,—
That time thou didst adorn, with amber studs,
My hunting cap, because I laugh'd and smil'd,
Chatted with thee, and many days exil'd
All torment from my breast;—'twas even then,
Straying about, yet, coop'd up in the den
Of helpless discontent,—hurling my lance
From place to place, and following at chance,　930
At last, by hap, through some young trees it struck,
And, plashing among bedded pebbles, stuck
In the middle of a brook,—whose silver ramble
Down twenty little falls, through reeds and bramble,
Tracing along, it brought me to a cave,
Whence it ran brightly forth, and white did lave
The nether sides of mossy stones and rock,—
'Mong which it gurgled blythe adieus, to mock
Its own sweet grief at parting. Overhead,　939
Hung a lush screne of drooping weeds, and spread
Thick, as to curtain up some wood-nymph's home.
"Ah! impious mortal, whither do I roam?"
Said I, low voic'd: "Ah, whither! 'Tis the grot
"Of Proserpine,40 when Hell, obscure and hot,

"Doth her resign; and where her tender hands
"She dabbles, on the cool and sluicy sands:
"Or 'tis the cell of Echo, where she sits,
"And babbles thorough silence, till her wits
"Are gone in tender madness, and anon,
"Faints into sleep, with many a dying tone　950
"Of sadness. O that she would take my vows,
"And breathe them sighingly among the boughs,
"To sue her gentle ears for whose fair head,
"Daily, I pluck sweet flowerets from their bed,
"And weave them dyingly—send honey-whispers
"Round every leaf, that all those gentle lispers
"May sigh my love unto her pitying!
"O charitable Echo! hear, and sing
"This ditty to her!—tell her"—so I stay'd
My foolish tongue, and listening, half afraid,　960
Stood stupefied with my own empty folly,
And blushing for the freaks of melancholy.
Salt tears were coming, when I heard my name
Most fondly lipp'd, and then these accents came:
"Endymion! the cave is secreter
Than the isle of Delos.41 Echo hence shall stir
No sighs but sigh-warm kisses, or light noise
Of thy combing hand, the while it travelling cloys
And trembles through my labyrinthine hair."
At that oppress'd I hurried in.—Ah! where　970
Are those swift moments? Whither are they fled?
I'll smile no more, Peona; nor will wed
Sorrow the way to death; but patiently
Bear up against it: so farewel, sad sigh;
And come instead demurest meditation,
To occupy me wholly, and to fashion
My pilgrimage for the world's dusky brink.
No more will I count over, link by link,
My chain of grief: no longer strive to find
A half-forgetfulness in mountain wind　980
Blustering about my ears: aye, thou shalt see,
Dearest of sisters, what my life shall be;
What a calm round of hours shall make my days.
There is a paly flame of hope that plays
Where'er l look: but yet, I'll say 'tis naught—
And here I bid it die. Have not I caught,
Already, a more healthy countenance?
By this the sun is setting; we may chance
Meet some of our near-dwellers with my car.'

This said, he rose, faint-smiling like a star　990
Through autumn mists, and took Peona's hand:
They stept into the boat, and launch'd from land.

[1817]　　　　　　　　　　　　　　　　　[1818]

---

39 Actually sloths are herbivorous—feeding entirely on
leaves, shoots, and fruits.
40 Daughter of Ceres and Jupiter, who was carried away by
Pluto to be queen of the underworld.

41 Celebrated as the birthplace of Cynthia and Apollo.

LINES RHYMED IN A LETTER RECEIVED FROM OXFORD

I

THE Gothic looks solemn,
The plain Doric column
Supports an old Bishop and Crosier;
The mouldering arch,
Shaded o'er by a larch
Stands next door to Wilson the Hosier.

II

Vice—that is, by turns,—
O'er pale visages mourns
The black tassell trencher or common hat;[1]
The Chantry boy sings,   10
The Steeple-bell rings,
And as for the Chancellor—*dominat.*[2]

III

There are plenty of trees,
And plenty of ease,
And plenty of fat deer for Parsons;
And when it is venison,
Short is the benison,—
Then each on a leg or thigh fastens.

[1817]   [1883]

LINES
["Unfelt, unheard, unseen"]

UNFELT, unheard, unseen,
I've left my little queen,
Her languid arms in silver slumber lying:
Ah! through their nestling touch,
Who—who could tell how much
There is for madness—cruel, or complying?

Those faery lids how sleek!
Those lips how moist!—they speak,
In ripest quiet, shadows of sweet sounds:
Into my fancy's ear   10
Melting a burden dear,
How 'Love doth know no fullness nor no bounds.'

True!—tender monitors!
I bend unto your laws:
This sweetest day for dalliance was born!
So, without more ado,
I'll feel my heaven anew,[1]
For all the blushing of the hasty morn.

[1817]   [1848]

STANZAS
["You say you love . . ."]

I

YOU say you love; but with a voice
    Chaster than a nun's, who singeth
The soft Vespers to herself
    While the chime-bell ringeth—
    O love me truly!

II

You say you love; but then you smile
    Cold as sunrise in September,
As you were Saint Cupid's nun,
    And kept his weeks of Ember.[2]
    O love me truly!

III

You say you love—but then your lips
    Coral tinted teach no blisses,
More than coral in the sea—
    They never pout for kisses—
    O love me truly!

IV

You say you love; but then your hand
    No soft squeeze for squeeze returneth,
It is like a statue's, dead,—
    While mine to passion burneth—
    O love me truly!

V

O breathe a word or two of fire!
    Smile, as if those words should burn me,
Squeeze as lovers should!—O kiss
    And in thy heart inurn me!
    O love me truly!

[1817]   [1914]

---

[1] Mortarboards were worn by commoners.
[2] "He rules."

[1] To "feel one's heaven" was contemporary slang for sexual caressing. See Gittings (1968).
[2] Periods of abstinence and fasting.

STANZAS
["In a drear-nighted December"]

I

In a drear-nighted December,
   Too happy, happy tree,
Thy branches ne'er remember
   Their green felicity:
The north cannot undo them,
With a sleety whistle through them;
Nor frozen thawings glue them
   From budding at the prime.

II

In a drear-nighted December,
   Too happy, happy brook,   10
Thy bubblings ne'er remember
   Apollo's summer look;
But with a sweet forgetting,
They stay their crystal fretting,
Never, never petting [1]
   About the frozen time.

III

Ah! would 'twere so with many
   A gentle girl and boy!
But were there ever any
   Writh'd not at passed joy?   20
To know the change and feel it,
When there is none to heal it,
Nor numbed sense to steel it,
   Was never said in rhyme.

[1817]   [1829]

[Sonnet]
TO MRS. REYNOLDS'S CAT

CAT! who hast past thy Grand Climacteric,[2]
   How many mice and Rats hast in thy days
   Destroy'd?—how many tit bits stolen? Gaze
With those bright languid segments green and prick
Those velvet ears—but pr'ythee do not stick
   Thy latent talons in me—and upraise
   Thy gentle mew—and tell me all thy frays
Of Fish and Mice, and Rats and tender chick.

---

[1] Complaining.
[2] In a man, sixty-three years. The equivalent age in a cat is
nine or ten years. The tone parodies Miltonic invocation.

Nay look not down, nor lick thy dainty wrists—
   For all the weezy Asthma,—and for all   10
Thy tail's tip is nicked off—and though the fists
   Of many a Maid have given thee many a maul,
Still is that fur as soft as when the lists
   In youth thou enter'dst on glass-bottled wall.

[1818]   [1830]

LINES ON SEEING A
LOCK OF MILTON'S HAIR

CHIEF of organic [1] numbers!
   Old Scholar of the Spheres!
Thy spirit never slumbers,
   But rolls about our ears,
For ever, and for ever!
O what a mad endeavour
   Worketh he,
Who to thy sacred and ennobled hearse
Would offer a burnt sacrifice of verse
   And melody.   10

How heavenward thou soundest,
   Live Temple of sweet noise,
And Discord unconfoundest,
   Giving Delight new joys,
And Pleasure nobler pinions!
O, where are thy dominions?
   Lend thine ear
To a young Delian [2] oath,—aye, by thy soul,
By all that from thy mortal lips did roll,
And by the kernel of thine earthly love,   20
Beauty, in things on earth, and things above
   [I swear!]

When every childish fashion
   Has vanish'd from my rhyme,
Will I, grey-gone in passion,
   Leave to an after-time
   Hymning and harmony
Of thee, and of thy works, and of thy life;
But vain is now the burning and the strife,
Pangs are in vain, until I grow high-rife   30
   With old Philosophy,
And mad with glimpses of futurity!

---

[1] Organlike.
[2] Reference to Delos, where Apollo was born.

For many years my offerings must be hush'd;
  When I do speak, I'll think upon this hour,
Because I feel my forehead hot and flush'd,
  Even at the simplest vassal of thy power,—
    A lock of thy bright hair,—
    Sudden it came,
And I was startled, when I caught thy name
    Coupled so unaware;   40
  Yet, at the moment, temperate was my blood.
I thought I had beheld it from the flood.

[1818]   [1838]

[Sonnet]
ON SITTING DOWN TO
READ KING LEAR ONCE AGAIN

O GOLDEN tongued Romance, with serene lute!
  Fair plumed Syren, Queen of far-away!
  Leave melodizing in this wintry day,
Shut up thine olden pages, and be mute:
Adieu! for, once again, the fierce dispute
  Betwixt damnation and impassion'd clay
  Must I burn through; once more humbly assay
The bitter-sweet of this Shakespearian fruit:
Chief Poet! and ye clouds of Albion,
  Begetters of our deep eternal theme!   10
When through the old oak Forest I am gone,
  Let me not wander in a barren dream,
But, when I am consumed in the fire
Give me new Phœnix wings to fly at my desire.

[1818]   [1838]

[Sonnet]
"When I have fears . . ."

WHEN I have fears that I may cease to be
  Before my pen has glean'd my teeming brain,
Before high-piled books, in charact'ry,
  Hold like rich garners the full-ripen'd grain;
When I behold, upon the night's starr'd face,
  Huge cloudy symbols of a high romance,
And think that I may never live to trace
  Their shadows, with the magic hand of chance;
And when I feel, fair creature of an hour!
  That I shall never look upon thee more,   10
Never have relish in the faery power
  Of unreflecting love!—then on the shore
Of the wide world I stand alone, and think
Till love and fame to nothingness do sink.

[1818]   [1848]

SONG
["O blush not so! . . ."]

I

O BLUSH not so! O blush not so!
  Or I shall think ye knowing;
And if you smile the blushing while,
  Then maidenheads are going.

II

There's a blush for won't, and a blush for shan't,
  And a blush for having done it:
There's a blush for thought and a blush for naught,
  And a blush for just begun it.

III

O say not so! O say not so!
  For it sounds of Eve's sweet pippin;   10
By these loosen'd hips you have tasted the pips
  And fought in an amorous nipping.

IV

Will you play once more at nice-cut-core,
  For it only will last our youth out,
And we have the prime of our kissing time,
  We have not one sweet tooth out.

V

There's a sigh for aye, and a sigh for nay,
  And a sigh for I can't bear it!
O what can be done, shall we stay or run?
  O cut the sweet apple and share it!   20

[1818]   [1883]

SONG
["Hence Burgundy . . ."]

HENCE Burgundy, Claret, and Port,
  Away with old Hock and Madeira,
Too couthly ye are for my sport;
  There's a beverage brighter and clearer.
Instead of a pitiful rummer,[1]
My wine overbrims a whole summer;
  My bowl is the sky,
  And I drink at my eye,
Till I feel in the brain
  A Delphian pain—   10

---

[1] Large drinking glass.

Then follow, my Caius![2] then follow:
  On the green of the hill
  We will drink our fill
  Of golden sunshine,
  Till our brains intertwine
With the glory and grace of Apollo!

God of the Meridian,
   And of the East and West,
To thee my soul is flown
   And my body is earthward press'd.
It is an awful mission,
A terrible division;
And leaves a gulph austere
To be fill'd with worldly fear.
Aye, when the soul is fled
To high above our head,   10
Affrighted do we gaze
After its airy maze,
As doth a mother wild,
When her young infant child
Is in an eagle's claws—
And is not this the cause
Of madness?—God of Song,
Thou bearest me along
Through sights I scarce can bear:
O let me, let me share   20
With the hot lyre and thee,
The staid Philosophy.
Temper my lonely hours,
And let me see thy bowers
More unalarm'd!

[1818]   [1848]

LINES ON THE MERMAID TAVERN

SOULS of Poets dead and gone,
What Elysium have ye known,
Happy field or mossy cavern,
Choicer than the Mermaid Tavern?[3]
Have ye tippled drink more fine
Than mine host's Canary wine?
Or are fruits of Paradise
Sweeter than those dainty pies
Of venison? O generous food!
Drest as though bold Robin Hood   10
Would, with his maid Marian,
Sup and bowse from horn and can.

---

[2] Reynolds sometimes used this as a pen name.
[3] Traditional gathering place of Elizabethan writers.

I have heard that on a day
Mine host's sign-board flew away,
Nobody knew whither, till
An astrologer's old quill
To a sheepskin gave the story,
Said he saw you in your glory,
Underneath a new-old sign
Sipping beverage divine,   20
And pledging with contented smack
The Mermaid in the Zodiac.

Souls of Poets dead and gone,
What Elysium have ye known,
Happy field or mossy cavern,
Choicer than the Mermaid Tavern?

[1818]   [1820]

ROBIN HOOD
TO A FRIEND

No! those days are gone away,
And their hours are old and gray,
And their minutes buried all
Under the down-trodden pall
Of the leaves of many years:
Many times have winter's shears,
Frozen North, and chilling East,
Sounded tempests to the feast
Of the forest's whispering fleeces,
Since men knew nor rent nor leases.   10

No, the bugle sounds no more,
And the twanging bow no more;
Silent is the ivory shrill
Past the heath and up the hill;
There is no mid-forest laugh,
Where lone Echo gives the half
To some wight, amaz'd to hear
Jesting, deep in forest drear.

On the fairest time of June
You may go, with sun or moon,   20
Or the seven stars to light you,
Or the polar ray to right you;
But you never may behold
Little John, or Robin bold;
Never one, of all the clan,
Thrumming on an empty can
Some old hunting ditty, while
He doth his green way beguile
To fair hostess Merriment,
Down beside the pasture Trent;   30

For he left the merry tale
Messenger for spicy ale.

Gone, the merry morris din;
Gone, the song of Gamelyn,[1]
Gone, the tough-belted outlaw
Idling in the 'grenè shawe;'
All are gone away and past!
And if Robin should be cast
Sudden from his turfed grave,
And if Marian should have
Once again her forest days,   40
She would weep, and he would craze:
He would swear, for all his oaks,
Fall'n beneath the dockyard strokes,
Have rotted on the briny seas;
She would weep that her wild bees
Sang not to her—strange! that honey
Can't be got without hard money!

So it is: ye let us sing,
Honour to the old bow-string!
Honour to the bugle-horn!   50
Honour to the woods unshorn!
Honour to the Lincoln green!
Honour to the archer keen!
Honour to tight little John,
And the horse he rode upon!
Honour to bold Robin Hood,
Sleeping in the underwood!
Honour to maid Marian,
And to all the Sherwood-clan!   60
Though their days have hurried by
Let us two a burden try.

[1818]   [1820]

[Sonnet]
TO ——— [2]
["Time's sea hath been . . ."]

TIME'S sea hath been five years at its slow ebb;
    Long hours have to and fro let creep the sand;
Since I was tangled in thy beauty's web,
    And snared by the ungloving of thine hand.
And yet I never look on midnight sky,
    But I behold thine eyes' well memoried light;
I cannot look upon the rose's dye,
    But to thy cheek my soul doth take its flight;

I cannot look on any budding flower,
    But my fond ear, in fancy at thy lips,   10
And harkening for a love-sound, doth devour
    Its sweets in the wrong sense:—Thou dost eclipse
Every delight with sweet remembering,
And grief unto my darling joys dost bring.

[1818]   [1844]

[Sonnet]
TO THE NILE

SON of the old moon-mountains African![1]
    Chief of the Pyramid and Crocodile!
    We call thee fruitful, and, that very while,
A desert fills our seeing's inward span;
Nurse of swart nations since the world began,
    Art thou so fruitful? or dost thou beguile
    Such men to honour thee, who, worn with toil,
Rest them a space 'twixt Cairo and Decan?[2]
O may dark fancies err! they surely do;
    'Tis ignorance that makes a barren waste   10
Of all beyond itself. Thou dost bedew
    Green rushes like our rivers, and dost taste
The pleasant sun-rise. Green isles hast thou too,
    And to the sea as happily dost haste.

[1818]   [1838]

[Sonnet]
"Spenser! a jealous honourer . . ."

SPENSER! a jealous honourer of thine,[3]
    A forester deep in thy midmost trees,
Did last eve ask my promise to refine
    Some English that might strive thine ear to please.
But Elfin Poet 'tis impossible
    For an inhabitant of wintry earth
To rise like Phœbus with a golden quell
    Fire-wing'd and make a morning in his mirth.
It is impossible to escape from toil
    O' the sudden and receive thy spiriting: 10
The flower must drink the nature of the soil
    Before it can put forth its blossoming:
Be with me in the summer days and I
Will for thine honour and his pleasure try.

[1818]   [1848]

---

[1] Fourteenth-century verse romance.
[2] The Lady he saw for some few moments at Vauxhall. [Note in one of the contemporary transcripts.]

[1] Mountains of the Moon, believed then to be the source of the Nile.
[2] Englishmen on their way to India landed at Alexandria, sailed up the Nile to Cairo, went overland to the Red Sea.
[3] J. H. Reynolds.

[Sonnet]
ANSWER TO A SONNET
ENDING THUS:

'Dark eyes are dearer far
Than those that mock the hyacinthine bell;'
By J. H. REYNOLDS.

BLUE! 'Tis the life of heaven,—the domain
    Of Cynthia,—the wide palace of the sun,—
The tent of Hesperus, and all his train,—
    The bosomer of clouds, gold, grey and dun.
Blue! 'Tis the life of waters—ocean
    And all its vassal streams: pools numberless
May rage, and foam, and fret, but never can
    Subside, if not to dark-blue nativeness.
Blue! Gentle cousin of the forest-green,
    Married to green in all the sweetest flowers,—   10
Forget-me-not,—the blue bell,—and, that queen
    Of secrecy, the violet: what strange powers
Hast thou, as a mere shadow! But how great,
When in an Eye thou art alive with fate!

[1818]   [1848]

"O THOU WHOSE FACE"
*Written in a letter to J. H. Reynolds, postmarked 19 February
1818. The sentence leading into the poem reads, "I had no idea
but of the morning, and the thrush said I was right—seeming to
say,*

"O thou whose face . . ."

O THOU whose face hath felt the Winter's wind,
    Whose eye has seen the snow-clouds hung in mist,
    And the black elm tops 'mong the freezing stars,
To thee the spring will be a harvest-time.
O thou, whose only book has been the light
    Of supreme darkness which thou feddest on
Night after night when Phœbus was away,
    To thee the Spring shall be a triple morn.
O fret not after knowledge—I have none,
    And yet my song comes native with the warmth.   10
O fret not after knowledge—I have none,
    And yet the Evening listens. He who saddens
At thought of idleness cannot be idle,
And he's awake who thinks himself asleep.

[1818]   [1848]

[Sonnet]
"Four seasons fill the measure . . ."

FOUR seasons fill the measure of the year;
    There are four seasons in the mind of man:
He has his lusty Spring, when fancy clear
    Takes in all beauty with an easy span:
He has his Summer, when luxuriously
    Spring's honied cud of youthful thought he loves
To ruminate, and by such dreaming nigh
    His nearest unto heaven: quiet coves
His soul has in its Autumn, when his wings
    He furleth close; contented so to look   10
On mists in idleness—to let fair things
    Pass by unheeded as a threshold brook.
He has his Winter too of pale misfeature,
Or else he would forego his mortal nature.

[1818]   [1819]

"Where be ye going . . ."

I

WHERE be ye going, you Devon Maid?
    And what have ye there in the Basket?
Ye tight little fairy just fresh from the dairy,
    Will ye give me some cream if I ask it?

II

I love your Meads, and I love your flowers,
    And I love your junkets mainly,
But 'hind the door I love kissing more,
    O look not so disdainly.

III

I love your hills, and I love your dales,
    And I love your flocks a-bleating—   10
But O, on the heather to lie together,
    With both our hearts a-beating!

IV

I'll put your Basket all safe in a nook,
    Your shawl I hang up on the willow,
And we will sigh in the daisy's eye
    And kiss on a grass-green pillow.

[1818]   [1848, 1883]

"Over the hill and over the dale"

Over the hill and over the dale,
And over the bourn to Dawlish [1]—
Where Gingerbread Wives have a scanty sale
And gingerbre[a]d nuts are smallish.

Rantipole [2] Betty she ran down a hill
 And ki[c]k'd up her pettic[o]ats fairly
Says I I'll be Jack if you will be Gill.
 So she sat on the Grass debonnairly.

Here's somebody coming, here's som[e]body coming!
 Say I 'tis the Wind at a parley   10
So without any fuss any hawing and humming
 She lay on the grass debonnai[r]ly.

Here's somebody here and here's somebody there!
 Say's I hold your tongue you young Gipsey.
So she held her tongue and lay plump and fair
 And dead as a venus tipsy.

O who would'nt hie to Dawlish fair
 O who would'nt stop in a Meadow
O [who] would not rumple the daisies there
 And make the wild fern for a bed do. 20

[1818]   [1848, 1925]

John Hamilton Reynolds (1794–1852)—solicitor, minor poet, essayist—wished his tombstone to say only "The Friend of Keats." The painting referred to is The Enchanted Castle *by Claude.*

TO J. H. REYNOLDS, ESQ.

Dear Reynolds, as last night I lay in bed,
There came before my eyes that wonted thread
Of Shapes, and Shadows and Remembrances,
That every other minute vex and please:
Things all disjointed come from North and south,
Two witch's eyes above a cherub's mouth,
Voltaire with casque and shield and Habergeon,
And Alexander with his night-cap on—
Old Socrates a tying his cravat;
And Hazlitt playing with Miss Edgeworth's cat; [3] 10

[1] Bourn = river; Dawlish is near Teignmouth on the river Exe in Devon.
[2] Wild; disorderly.
[3] Maria Edgeworth (1767–1849), moralistic novelist; Hazlitt (in *On the English Comic Writers*, 1819) dismissed her.

And Junius Brutus pretty well so, so,
Making the best of's way towards Soho.
 Few are there who escape these visitings—
P'erhaps one or two, whose lives have pat[i]ent wings;
And through whose curtains peeps no hellish nose,
No wild boar tushes, [4] and no Mermaid's toes:
But flowers bursting out with lusty pride;
And young Æolian harps personified,
Some, Titian colours touch'd into real life.—
The sacrifice goes on; the pontiff knife 20
Gleams in the sun, the milk-white heifer lows,
The pipes go shrilly, the libation flows:
A white sail shews above the green-head cliff
Moves round the point, and throws her anchor stiff.
The Mariners join hymn with those on land.—
You know the Enchanted Castle it doth stand
Upon a Rock on the Border of a Lake
Nested in Trees, which all do seem to shake
From some old Magic like Urganda's [5] sword.
O Phœbus that I had thy sacred word 30
To shew this Castle in fair dreaming wise
Unto my friend, while sick and ill he lies.
 You know it well enough, where it doth seem
A mossy place, a Merlin's Hall, a dream.
You know the clear Lake, and the little Isles,
The Mountains blue, and cold near neighbour rills—
All which elsewhere are but half animate
Here do they look alive to love and hate;
To smiles and frowns; they seem a lifted mound
Above some giant, pulsing underground. 40
 Part of the building was a chosen See
Built by a banish'd santon [6] of Chaldee:
The other part two thousand years from him
Was built by Cuthbert de Saint Aldebrim; [7]
Then there's a little wing, far from the Sun,
Built by a Lapland Witch turn'd maudlin [8] nun—
And many other juts of aged stone
Founded with many a mason-devil's [9] groan.
 The doors all look as if they oped themselves,
The windows as if latch'd by fays & elves— 50
And from them comes a silver flash of light
As from the Westward of a summer's night;
Or like a beauteous woman's large blue eyes
Gone mad through olden songs and Poesies—
 See what is coming from the distance dim!
A golden galley all in silken trim!

[4] Tusks.
[5] Urganda the Unknown, a sorceress in *Amadis of Gaul* (a fifteenth-century romance).
[6] Moslem holy man.
[7] An invented name, with a pun perhaps on "brim" = whore.
[8] From Mary Magdalene, traditionally, though falsely, identified with the reformed prostitute.
[9] A mason's assistant; though possibly with a pun on meas-ondue (*Maison Dieu*), a poorhouse.

Three rows of oars are lightening moment-whiles
Into the verdurous bosoms of those Isles.
Towards the shade under the Castle Wall
It comes in silence—now tis hidden all.   60
The clarion sounds; and from a postern grate
An echo of sweet music doth create
A fear in the poor herdsman who doth bring
His beasts to trouble the enchanted spring:
He tells of the sweet music and the spot
To all his friends, and they believe him not.

   O that our dreamings all of sleep or wake
Would all their colours from the sunset take:
From something of material sublime,
Rather than shadow our own Soul's daytime   70
In the dark void of Night. For in the world
We jostle—but my flag is not unfurl'd
On the Admiral staff—and to philosophize
I dare not yet!—Oh never will the prize,
High reason, and the lore of good and ill
Be my award. Things cannot to the will
Be settled, but they tease us out of thought.
Or is it that Imagination brought
Beyond its proper bound, yet still confined,—
Lost in a sort of Purgatory blind,   80
Cannot refer to any standard law
Of either earth or heaven?—It is a flaw
In happiness to see beyond our bourn—
It forces us in Summer skies to mourn:
It spoils the singing of the Nightingale.

   Dear Reynolds, I have a mysterious tale
And cannot speak it. The first page I read
Upon a Lampit [10] Rock of green sea weed
Among the breakers—'Twas a quiet Eve;
The rocks were silent—the wide sea did weave   90
An untumultuous fringe of silver foam
Along the flat brown sand. I was at home,
And should have been most happy—but I saw
Too far into the sea; where every maw
The greater on the less feeds evermore:—
But I saw too distinct into the core
Of an eternal fierce destruction,
And so from Happiness I far was gone.
Still am I sick of it: and though to-day
I've gathered young spring-leaves, and flowers gay
Of Periwinkle and wild strawberry,   101
Still do I that most fierce destruction see,
The shark at savage prey—the hawk at pounce,
The gentle Robin, like a pard or ounce,
Ravening a worm—Away ye horrid moods,
Moods of one's mind! You know I hate them well,
You know I'd sooner be a clapping bell

To some Kamschatkan missionary church,
Than with these horrid moods be left in lurch—
Do you get health—and Tom the same—I'll dance,
And from detested moods in new Romance [11]   III
Take refuge—Of bad lines a Centaine dose [12]
Is sure enough—and so 'here follows prose'.—

[1818]   [1848]

ISABELLA

*In February 1818 Keats probably heard William Hazlitt, in a
lecture, recommend translations from Boccaccio—especially this
one from the fifth novel, the fourth day of the* Decameron—as
*likely to prove very "successful." Keats did not in fact translate
it—he used a 1620 English translation—but set it in verse.*

ISABELLA

OR,

THE POT OF BASIL

I

FAIR Isabel, poor simple Isabel!
   Lorenzo, a young palmer in Love's eye! [1]
They could not in the self-same mansion dwell
   Without some stir of heart, some malady;
They could not sit at meals but feel how well
   It soothed each to be the other by;
They could not, sure, beneath the same roof sleep
But to each other dream, and nightly weep.

II

With every morn their love grew tenderer,
   With every eve deeper and tenderer still;   10
He might not in house, field, or garden stir,
   But her full shape would all his seeing fill;
And his continual voice was pleasanter
   To her, than noise of trees or hidden rill;
Her lute-string gave an echo of his name,
She spoilt her half-done broidery with the same.

III

He knew whose gentle hand was at the latch,
   Before the door had given her to his eyes;
And from her chamber-window he would catch
   Her beauty farther than the falcon spies;   20
And constant as her vespers would he watch,
   Because her face was turn'd to the same skies;
And with sick longing all the night outwear,
To hear her morning-step upon the stair.

---

[10] Limpet.

[11] I.e., *Isabella*, below.
[12] One hundred.
[1] Pilgrim seeking love.

IV

A whole long month of May in this sad plight
   Made their cheeks paler by the break of June:
'To-morrow will I bow to my delight,
   'To-morrow will I ask my lady's boon.'—
'O may I never see another night,
   'Lorenzo, if thy lips breathe not love's tune.'—   30
So spake they to their pillows; but, alas,
Honeyless days and days did he let pass;

V

Until sweet Isabella's untouch'd cheek
   Fell sick within the rose's just domain,
Fell thin as a young mother's, who doth seek
   By every lull to cool her infant's pain:
'How ill she is,' said he, 'I may not speak,
   'And yet I will, and tell my love all plain:
'If looks speak love-laws, I will drink her tears,
'And at the least 'twill startle off her cares.'   40

VI

So said he one fair morning, and all day
   His heart beat awfully against his side;
And to his heart he inwardly did pray
   For power to speak; but still the ruddy tide
Stifled his voice, and puls'd resolve away—
   Fever'd his high conceit of such a bride,
Yet brought him to the meekness of a child:
Alas! when passion is both meek and wild!

VII

So once more he had wak'd and anguished
   A dreary night of love and misery,   50
If Isabel's quick eye had not been wed
   To every symbol on his forehead high;
She saw it waxing very pale and dead,
   And straight all flush'd; so, lisped tenderly,
'Lorenzo!'—here she ceas'd her timid quest,
But in her tone and look he read the rest.

VIII

'O Isabella, I can half perceive
   'That I may speak my grief into thine ear;
'If thou didst ever any thing believe,
   'Believe how I love thee, believe how near   60
'My soul is to its doom: I would not grieve
   'Thy hand by unwelcome pressing, would not fear
'Thine eyes by gazing; but I cannot live
'Another night, and not my passion shrive.

IX

'Love! thou art leading me from wintry cold,
   'Lady! thou leadest me to summer clime,
'And I must taste the blossoms that unfold
   'In its ripe warmth this gracious morning time.'
So said, his erewhile timid lips grew bold,
   And poesied with hers in dewy rhyme: 70
Great bliss was with them, and great happiness
Grew, like a lusty flower in June's caress.

X

Parting they seem'd to tread upon the air,
   Twin roses by the zephyr blown apart
Only to meet again more close, and share
   The inward fragrance of each other's heart.
She, to her chamber gone, a ditty fair
   Sang, of delicious love and honey'd dart;
He with light steps went up a western hill,
And made the sun farewell, and joy'd his fill.   80

XI

All close they met again, before the dusk
   Had taken from the stars its pleasant veil,
All close they met, all eves, before the dusk
   Had taken from the stars its pleasant veil,
Close in a bower of hyacinth and musk,
   Unknown of any, free from whispering tale.
Ah! better had it been for ever so,
Than idle ears should pleasure in their woe.

XII

Were they unhappy then?—It cannot be—
   Too many tears for lovers have been shed,   90
Too many sighs give we to them in fee,
   Too much of pity after they are dead,
Too many doleful stories do we see,
   Whose matter in bright gold were best be read;
Except in such a page where Theseus' spouse [2]
Over the pathless waves towards him bows.

XIII

But, for the general award of love,
   The little sweet doth kill much bitterness;
Though Dido silent is in under-grove,
   And Isabella's was a great distress,   100
Though young Lorenzo in warm Indian clove
   Was not embalm'd, this truth is not the less
Even bees, the little almsmen [3] of spring-bowers,
Know there is richest juice in poison-flowers.

---

[2] Ariadne. See *Sleep and Poetry*, ll. 335–6, p. 1019.
[3] Because the bees' murmuring sounds like the prayers of those hired to pray for others.

XIV

With her two brothers this fair lady dwelt,
  Enriched from ancestral merchandize,
And for them many a weary hand did swelt
  In torched mines and noisy factories,
And many once proud-quiver'd loins did melt
  In blood from stinging whip;—with hollow eyes
Many all day in dazzling river stood,   111
To take the rich-ored driftings of the flood.

XV

For them the Ceylon diver held his breath,
  And went all naked to the hungry shark;
For them his ears gush'd blood; for them in death
  The seal on the cold ice with piteous bark
Lay full of darts; for them alone did seethe
  A thousand men in troubles wide and dark:
Half-ignorant, they turn'd an easy wheel,
That set sharp racks at work, to pinch and peel.[4]   120

XVI

Why were they proud? Because their marble founts
  Gush'd with more pride than do a wretch's tears?—
Why were they proud? Because fair orange-mounts
  Were of more soft ascent than lazar stairs?[5]—
Why were they proud? Because red-lin'd accounts
  Were richer than the songs of Grecian years?—
Why were they proud? again we ask aloud,
Why in the name of Glory were they proud?

XVII

Yet were these Florentines as self-retired
  In hungry pride and gainful cowardice,   130
As two close Hebrews in that land inspired,[6]
  Paled in and vineyarded from beggar-spies
The hawks of ship-mast forests—the untired
  And pannier'd mules for ducats and old lies—
Quick cat's-paws on the generous stray-away,—
Great wits in Spanish, Tuscan, and Malay.

XVIII

How was it these same ledger-men could spy
  Fair Isabella in her downy nest?
How could they find out in Lorenzo's eye
  A straying from his toil? Hot Egypt's pest[7]   140
Into their vision covetous and sly!
  How could these money-bags see east and west?—
Yet so they did—and every dealer fair
Must see behind, as doth the hunted hare.

---

4 See Dryden's *Annus Mirabilis* (1667).
5 Stairs in a house for lepers.
6 Palestine.
7 Plague visited on Egypt; see Exod. 10:21-3.

XIX

O eloquent and famed Boccaccio!
  Of thee we now should ask forgiving boon,
And of thy spicy myrtles as they blow,
  And of thy roses amorous of the moon,
And of thy lilies, that do paler grow
  Now they can no more hear thy ghittern's tune,[8]
For venturing syllables that ill beseem   151
The quiet glooms of such a piteous theme.

XX

Grant thou a pardon here, and then the tale
  Shall move on soberly, as it is meet;
There is no other crime, no mad assail
  To make old prose in modern rhyme more sweet:
But it is done—succeed the verse or fail—
  To honour thee, and thy gone spirit greet;
To stead thee as a verse in English tongue,
An echo of thee in the north-wind sung.   160

XXI

These brethren having found by many signs
  What love Lorenzo for their sister had,
And how she lov'd him too, each unconfines
  His bitter thoughts to other, well nigh mad
That he, the servant of their trade designs,
  Should in their sister's love be blithe and glad,
When 'twas their plan to coax her by degrees
To some high noble and his olive-trees.

XXII

And many a jealous conference had they,
  And many times they bit their lips alone,   170
Before they fix'd upon a surest way
  To make the youngster for his crime atone;
And at the last, these men of cruel clay
  Cut Mercy with a sharp knife to the bone;
For they resolved in some forest dim
To kill Lorenzo, and there bury him.

XXIII

So on a pleasant morning, as he leant
  Into the sun-rise, o'er the balustrade
Of the garden-terrace, towards him they bent
  Their footing through the dews; and to him said,
'You seem there in the quiet of content,   181
  'Lorenzo, and we are most loth to invade
'Calm speculation; but if you are wise,
'Bestride your steed while cold is in the skies.

---

8 Form of guitar.

XXIV

'To-day we purpose, ay, this hour we mount
  'To spur three leagues towards the Apennine;
'Come down, we pray thee, ere the hot sun count
  'His dewy rosary on the eglantine.'
Lorenzo, courteously as he was wont,
  Bow'd a fair greeting to these serpents' whine;   190
And went in haste, to get in readiness,
With belt, and spur, and bracing huntsman's dress.

XXV

And as he too the court-yard pass'd along,
  Each third step did he pause, and listen'd oft
If he could hear his lady's matin-song,
  Or the light whisper of her footstep soft;
And as he thus over his passion hung,
  He heard a laugh full musical aloft;
When, looking up, he saw her features bright
Smile through an in-door lattice, all delight.   200

XXVI

'Love, Isabel!' said he, 'I was in pain
  'Lest I should miss to bid thee a good morrow
'Ah! what if I should lose thee, when so fain
  'I am to stifle all the heavy sorrow
'Of a poor three hours' absence? but we'll gain
  'Out of the amorous dark what day doth borrow.
'Good bye! I'll soon be back.'—'Good bye!' said
      she:—
And as he went she chanted merrily.

XXVII

So the two brothers and their murder'd man   209
  Rode past fair Florence, to where Arno's stream
Gurgles through straiten'd banks, and still doth fan
  Itself with dancing bulrush, and the bream
Keeps head against the freshets. Sick and wan
  The brothers' faces in the ford did seem,
Lorenzo's flush with love.—They pass'd the water
Into a forest quiet for the slaughter.

XXVIII

There was Lorenzo slain and buried in,
  There in that forest did his great love cease;
Ah! when a soul doth thus its freedom win,
  It aches in loneliness—is ill at peace   220
As the break-covert blood-hounds of such sin:
  They dipp'd their swords in the water, and did
      tease
Their horses homeward, with convulsed spur,
Each richer by his being a murderer.

XXIX

They told their sister how, with sudden speed,
  Lorenzo had ta'en ship for foreign lands,
Because of some great urgency and need
  In their affairs, requiring trusty hands.
Poor Girl! put on thy stifling widow's weed,
  And 'scape at once from Hope's accursed bands;
To-day thou wilt not see him, nor to-morrow,   231
And the next day will be a day of sorrow.

XXX

She weeps alone for pleasures not to be;
  Sorely she wept until the night came on,
And then, instead of love, O misery!
  She brooded o'er the luxury alone:
His image in the dusk she seem'd to see,
  And to the silence made a gentle moan,
Spreading her perfect arms upon the air,   239
And on her couch low murmuring 'Where? O where?'

XXXI

But Selfishness, Love's cousin, held not long
  Its fiery vigil in her single breast;
She fretted for the golden hour, and hung
  Upon the time with feverish unrest—
Not long—for soon into her heart a throng
  Of higher occupants, a richer zest,
Came tragic; passion not to be subdued,
And sorrow for her love in travels rude.

XXXII

In the mid days of autumn, on their eves,
  The breath of Winter comes from far away,   250
And the sick west continually bereaves
  Of some gold tinge, and plays a roundelay
Of death among the bushes and the leaves
  To make all bare before he dares to stray
From his north cavern. So sweet Isabel
By gradual decay from beauty fell,

XXXIII

Because Lorenzo came not. Oftentimes
  She ask'd her brothers, with an eye all pale,
Striving to be itself, what dungeon climes
  Could keep him off so long? They spake a tale   260
Time after time, to quiet her. Their crimes
  Came on them, like a smoke from Hinnom's vale;[9]
And every night in dreams they groan'd aloud,
To see their sister in her snowy shroud.

---

[9] Where the Ammonites sacrificed their children to Moloch.

XXXIV

And she had died in drowsy ignorance,
   But for a thing more deadly dark than all;
It came like a fierce potion, drunk by chance,
   Which saves a sick man from the feather'd pall [10]
For some few gasping moments; like a lance,
   Waking an Indian from his cloudy hall   270
With cruel pierce, and bringing him again
Sense of the gnawing fire at heart and brain.

XXXV

It was a vision.—In the drowsy gloom,
   The dull of midnight, at her couch's foot
Lorenzo stood, and wept: the forest tomb
   Had marr'd his glossy hair which once could shoot
Lustre into the sun, and put cold doom
   Upon his lips, and taken the soft lute
From his lorn voice, and past his loamed ears
Had made a miry channel for his tears.   280

XXXVI

Strange sound it was, when the pale shadow spake;
   For there was striving, in its piteous tongue,
To speak as when on earth it was awake,
   And Isabella on its music hung:
Languor there was in it, and tremulous shake,
   As in a palsied Druid's harp unstrung;
And through it moan'd a ghostly under-song,
Like hoarse night-gusts sepulchral briars among.

XXXVII

Its eyes, though wild, were still at dewy bright
   With love, and kept all phantom fear aloof   290
From the poor girl by magic of their light,
   The while it did unthread the horrid woof
Of the late darken'd time,—the murderous spite
   Of pride and avarice,—the dark pine roof
In the forest,—and the sodden turfed dell,
Where, without any word, from stabs he fell.

XXXVIII

Saying moreover, 'Isabel, my sweet!
   'Red whortle-berries droop above my head,
'And a large flint-stone weighs upon my feet;
   'Around me beeches and high chestnuts shed   300
'Their leaves and prickly nuts; a sheep-fold bleat
   'Comes from beyond the river to my bed:
'Go, shed one tear upon my heather-bloom,
'And it shall comfort me within the tomb.

XXXIX

'I am a shadow now, alas! alas!
   'Upon the skirts of human-nature dwelling
'Alone: I chant alone the holy mass,
   'While little sounds of life are round me knelling,
'And glossy bees at noon do fieldward pass,
   'And many a chapel bell the hour is telling,   310
'Paining me through: those sounds grow strange to
     me.
'And thou art distant in Humanity.

XL

'I know what was, I feel full well what is,
   'And I should rage, if spirits could go mad;
'Though I forget the taste of earthly bliss,
   'That paleness warms my grave, as though I had
'A Seraph chosen from the bright abyss
   'To be my spouse: thy paleness makes me glad;
'Thy beauty grows upon me, and I feel
'A greater love through all my essence steal.'   320

XLI

The Spirit mourn'd 'Adieu!'—dissolv'd, and left
   The atom darkness in a slow turmoil;
As when of healthful midnight sleep bereft,
   Thinking on rugged hours and fruitless toil,
We put our eyes into a pillowy cleft,
   And see the spangly gloom froth up and boil:
It made sad Isabella's eyelids ache,
And in the dawn she started up awake;

XLII

'Ha! ha!' said she, 'I knew not this hard life,
   'I thought the worst was simple misery;   330
'I thought some Fate with pleasure or with strife
   'Portion'd us—happy days, or else to die;
'But there is crime—a brother's bloody knife!
   'Sweet Spirit, thou hast school'd my infancy:
'I'll visit thee for this, and kiss thine eyes,
'And greet thee morn and even in the skies.'

XLIII

When the full morning came, she had devised
   How she might secret to the forest hie;
How she might find the clay, so dearly prized,
   And sing to it one latest lullaby;   340
How her short absence might be unsurmised,
   While she the inmost of the dream would try.
Resolv'd, she took with her an aged nurse,
And went into that dismal forest-hearse.

XLIV

See, as they creep along the river side,
    How she doth whisper to that aged Dame,
And, after looking round the champaign wide,
    Shows her a knife.—'What feverous hectic flame
'Burns in thee, child?—What good can thee betide,
    'That thou should'st smile again?'—The evening
        came,   350
And they had found Lorenzo's earthy bed;
The flint was there, the berries at his head.

XLV

Who hath not loiter'd in a green church-yard,
    And let his spirit, like a demon-mole,
Work through the clayey soil and gravel hard,
    To see scull, coffin'd bones, and funeral stole;
Pitying each form that hungry Death hath marr'd,
    And filling it once more with human soul?
Ah! this is holiday to what was felt
When Isabella by Lorenzo knelt.   360

XLVI

She gaz'd into the fresh-thrown mould, as though
    One glance did fully all its secrets tell;
Clearly she saw, as other eyes would know
    Pale limbs at bottom of a crystal well;
Upon the murderous spot she seem'd to grow,
    Like to a native lily of the dell:
Then with her knife, all sudden, she began
To dig more fervently than misers can.

XLVII

Soon she turn'd up a soiled glove, whereon
    Her silk had play'd in purple phantasies,   370
She kiss'd it with a lip more chill than stone,
    And put it in her bosom, where it dries
And freezes utterly unto the bone
    Those dainties made to still an infant's cries:
Then 'gan she work again; nor stay'd her care,
But to throw back at times her veiling hair.

XLVIII

That old nurse stood beside her wondering,
    Until her heart felt pity to the core
At sight of such a dismal labouring,
    And so she kneeled, with her locks all hoar,   380
And put her lean hands to the horrid thing:
    Three hours they labour'd at this travail sore;
At last they felt the kernel of the grave,
And Isabella did not stamp and rave.

XLIX

Ah! wherefore all this wormy circumstance?
    Why linger at the yawning tomb so long?
O for the gentleness of old Romance,
    The simple plaining of a minstrel's song!
Fair reader, at the old tale take a glance,
    For here, in truth, it doth not well belong   390
To speak:—O turn thee to the very tale,
And taste the music of that vision pale.

L

With duller steel than the Perséan sword [11]
    They cut away no formless monster's head,
But one, whose gentleness did well accord
    With death, as life. The ancient harps have said,
Love never dies, but lives, immortal Lord:
    If Love impersonate was ever dead,
Pale Isabella kiss'd it, and low moan'd.   399
'Twas love; cold,—dead indeed, but not dethroned.

LI

In anxious secrecy they took it home,
    And then the prize was all for Isabel:
She calm'd its wild hair with a golden comb,
    And all around each eye's sepulchral cell
Pointed each fringed lash; the smeared loam
    With tears, as chilly as a dripping well,
She drench'd away:—and still she comb'd, and kept
Sighing all day—and still she kiss'd, and wept.

LII

Then in a silken scarf,—sweet with the dews
    Of precious flowers pluck'd in Araby,   410
And divine liquids come with odorous ooze
    Through the cold serpent-pipe refreshfully,—
She wrapp'd it up; and for its tomb did choose
    A garden-pot, wherein she laid it by,
And cover'd it with mould, and o'er it set
Sweet basil, which her tears kept ever wet.

LIII

And she forgot the stars, the moon, and sun,
    And she forgot the blue above the trees,
And she forgot the dells where waters run,
    And she forgot the chilly autumn breeze;   420
She had no knowledge when the day was done,
    And the new morn she saw not: but in peace
Hung over her sweet basil evermore,
And moisten'd it with tears unto the core.

[11] The sword with which Perseus cut off the Gorgon's head.

LIV

And so she ever fed it with thin tears,
  Whence thick, and green, and beautiful it grew,
So that it smelt more balmy than its peers
  Of basil-tufts in Florence; for it drew
Nurture besides, and life, from human fears,
  From the fast mouldering head there shut from
    view: 430
So that the jewel, safely casketed,
Came forth, and in perfumed leafits spread.

LV

O Melancholy, linger here awhile!
  O Music, Music, breathe despondingly!
O Echo, Echo, from some sombre isle,
  Unknown, Lethean,[12] sigh to us—O sigh!
Spirits in grief, lift up your heads, and smile;
  Lift up your heads, sweet Spirits, heavily,
And make a pale light in your cypress glooms,
Tinting with silver wan your marble tombs.   440

LVI

Moan hither, all ye syllables of woe,
  From the deep throat of sad Melpomene![13]
Through bronzed lyre in tragic order go,
  And touch the strings into a mystery;
Sound mournfully upon the winds and low;
  For simple Isabel is soon to be
Among the dead: She withers, like a palm
Cut by an Indian for its juicy balm.

LVII

O leave the palm to wither by itself;
  Let not quick Winter chill its dying hour!—   450
It may not be—those Baälites[14] of pelf,
  Her brethren, noted the continual shower
From her dead eyes; and many a curious elf,
  Among her kindred, wonder'd that such dower
Of youth and beauty should be thrown aside
By one mark'd out to be a Noble's bride.

LVIII

And, furthermore, her brethren wonder'd much
  Why she sat drooping by the basil green,
And why it flourish'd, as by magic touch;
  Greatly they wonder'd what the thing might mean:
They could not surely give belief, that such   461
  A very nothing would have power to wean
Her from her own fair youth, and pleasures gay,
And even remembrance of her love's delay.

12 Lethe is the river of forgetfulness in Hades.
13 The Muse of tragedy.
14 Worshippers of false gods.

LIX

Therefore they watch'd a time when they might sift
  This hidden whim; and long they watch'd in vain;
For seldom did she go to chapel-shrift,
  And seldom felt she any hunger-pain;
And when she left, she hurried back, as swift
  As bird on wing to breast its eggs again;   470
And, patient as a hen-bird, sat her there
Beside her basil, weeping through her hair.

LX

Yet they contriv'd to steal the basil-pot,
  And to examine it in secret place:
The thing was vile with green and livid spot,
  And yet they knew it was Lorenzo's face:
The guerdon of their murder they had got,
  And so left Florence in a moment's space,
Never to turn again.—Away they went,
With blood upon their heads, to banishment.   480

LXI

O Melancholy, turn thine eyes away!
  O Music, Music, breathe despondingly!
O Echo, Echo, on some other day,
  From isles Lethean, sigh to us—O sigh!
Spirits of grief, sing not you 'Well-a-way!'
  For Isabel, sweet Isabel, will die;
Will die a death too lone and incomplete,
Now they have ta'en away her basil sweet.

LXII

Piteous she look'd on dead and senseless things,
  Asking for her lost basil amorously;   490
And with melodious chuckle in the strings
  Of her lorn voice, she oftentimes would cry
After the Pilgrim in his wanderings,
  To ask him where her basil was; and why
Twas hid from her: 'For cruel 'tis,' said she,
'To steal my basil-pot away from me.'

LXIII

And so she pined, and so she died forlorn,
  Imploring for her basil to the last.
No heart was there in Florence but did mourn
  In pity of her love, so overcast.   500
And a sad ditty of this story born
  From mouth to mouth through all the country
    pass'd:
Still is the burthen sung—'O cruelty,
'To steal my basil-pot away from me!'

[1818]   [1820]

[Sonnet]
TO HOMER

STANDING aloof in giant ignorance,[1]
 Of thee I hear and of the Cyclades,[2]
As one who sits ashore and longs perchance
 To visit dolphin-coral in deep seas.
So thou wast blind!—but then the veil was rent,
 For Jove uncertain'd Heaven to let thee live,
And Neptune made for thee a spumy tent,
 And Pan made sing for thee his forest-hive;
Aye, on the shores of darkness there is light,
 And precipices show untrodden green;   10
There is a budding morrow in midnight;
 There is a triple sight in blindness keen;
Such seeing hadst thou, as it once befel
To Dian, Queen of Earth, and Heaven, and Hell.[3]

[1818]   [1848]

ODE TO MAY. FRAGMENT

MOTHER of Hermes![4] and still youthful Maia!
     May I sing to thee
As thou wast hymned on the shores of Baiæ?[5]
     Or may I woo thee
In earlier Sicilian? or thy smiles
Seek as they once were sought, in Grecian isles,
 By bards who died content on pleasant sward,
 Leaving great verse unto a little clan?
O, give me their old vigour, and unheard
 Save of the quiet Primrose, and the span   10
     Of heaven and few ears,
Rounded by thee, my song should die away
     Content as theirs,
Rich in the simple worship of a day.

[1818]   [1848]

ACROSTIC

OF MY SISTER'S[1] NAME

GIVE me your patience Sister while I frame
Exact in Capitals your golden name
Or sue the fair Apollo and he will
Rouse from his heavy slumber and instill

<hr/>

[1] Keats knew no Greek; Homer (line 5) was blind.
[2] Greek island group in the southern Aegean.
[3] The moon had three names—Phoebe, Diana, Hecate—
indicating her rule over heaven, earth, and the underworld.
[4] Maia, daughter of Atlas, was Mercury's (Hermes') mother
by Jupiter.
[5] Bay of Naples. See Shelley's *Ode to the West Wind*, p. 903.
[1] His sister-in-law Georgiana Augusta Wylie, married to
George Keats. The initial letters of each line spell her name.

Great love in me for thee and Poesy.
Imagine not that greatest mastery
And Kingdom over all the Realms of verse
Nears more to Heaven in aught than when we nurse
And surety give to love and Brotherhood.

Anthropophagi in Othello's mood;   10
Ulysses stormed, and his enchanted belt
Glow[ed] with the Muse, but they are never felt
Unbosom'd so and so eternal made,
Such tender incense in their Laurel shade,
To all the regent sisters of the Nine
As this poor offering to you, sister mine.

Kind sister! aye, this third name says you are;
Enchanted has it been the Lord knows where.
And may it taste to you like good old wine,
Take you to real happiness and give   20
Sons, daughters and a home like honied hive.

[1818]   [1877]

"Sweet, sweet is the greeting . . ."

SWEET, sweet is the greeting of eyes,
 And sweet is the voice in its greeting,
When Adieux have grown old and goodbyes
 Fade away where old Time is retreating.

Warm the nerve of a welcoming hand,
 And earnest a Kiss on the Brow,
When we meet over sea and o'er Land
 Where furrows are new to the Plough.

[1818]   [1925]

<hr/>

ON VISITING THE TOMB OF BURNS
*Robert Burns was buried in St. Michael's Church, Dumfries,
Scotland. The text and punctuation of this poem are very un-
certain in the only manuscript, an imperfect transcript. The
editing here accepts the arguments of Miriam Allott in* The Poems
of Keats *(1970).*

<hr/>

[Sonnet]
ON VISITING THE TOMB OF BURNS

The Town, the churchyard, and the setting sun,
 The clouds, the trees, the rounded hills all seem,
 Though beautiful, cold—strange—as in a dream,
I dreamed long ago. Now new begun
The short-liv'd, paly Summer is but won
 From Winter's ague, for one hour's gleam.
 Through sapphire-warm, their stars do never beam;
All is cold Beauty; pain is never done

For who has mind to relish, Minos ¹-wise,
  The real of Beauty, free from that dead hue   10
    Sickly imagination and sick pride
  Cast wan upon it! Burns! with honour due
    I have oft honour'd thee. Great shadow, hide
Thy face; I sin against thy native skies.

[1818]   [1848]

[Old Meg]

  OLD MEG she was a Gipsey,
    And liv'd upon the Moors;
  Her bed it was the brown heath turf,
    And her house was out of doors.

  Her apples were swart blackberries,
    Her currants, pods o' broom;
  Her wine was dew of the wild white rose,
    Her book a churchyard tomb.

  Her Brothers were the craggy hills,
    Her Sisters larchen trees;   10
  Alone with her great family
    She liv'd as she did please.

  No breakfast had she many a morn,
    No dinner many a noon,
  And, 'stead of supper, she would stare
    Full hard against the Moon.

  But every morn, of woodbine fresh
    She made her garlanding,
  And, every night, the dark glen Yew
    She wove, and she would sing.   20

  And with her fingers, old and brown,
    She plaited Mats o' Rushes,
  And gave them to the Cottagers
    She met among the Bushes.

  Old Meg was brave as Margaret Queen ²
    And tall as Amazon;
  An old red blanket cloak she wore,
    A chip hat had she on.
  God rest her aged bones somewhere!
    She died full long agone!   30

[1818]   [1838]

<hr>

  ¹ Judge of the underworld.
  ² Perhaps Margaret, daughter of Henry VII, wife of James IV
of Scotland.

[Song About Myself]

  THERE was a naughty Boy,
    A naughty boy was he,
  He would not stop at home,
    He could not quiet be—
      He took
      In his Knapsack
      A Book
      Full of vowels
      And a shirt
      With some towels—   10
      A slight cap
      For night cap—
      A hair brush,
      Comb ditto,
      New Stockings
      Fold old ones
      Would split O!
      This Knapsack
      Tight at's back
      He rivetted close   20
    And followéd his Nose
      To the North,
      To the North,
    And follow'd his nose
      To the North.

  There was a naughty boy
    And a naughty boy was he,
  For nothing would he do
    But scribble poetry—
      He took   30
      An ink stand
      In his hand
      And a Pen
      Big as ten
      In the other.
      And away
      In a Pother
      He ran
      To the mountains
      And fountains   40
      And ghostes
      And Postes
      And witches
      And ditches
      And wrote
      In his coat
      When the weather
      Was cool,
      Fear of gout,
      And without   50

When the we[a]ther
Was warm—
Och the charm
When we choose
To follow one's nose
To the north,
To the north,
To follow one's nose to the north!

There was a naughty boy
  And a naughty boy was he,   60
He kept little fishes
  In washing tubs three
    In spite
    Of the might
    Of the Maid
    Nor affraid
    Of his Granny-good—
    He often would
    Hurly burly
    Get up early   70
    And go
    By hook or crook
    To the brook
    And bring home
    Miller's thumb,[1]
    Tittlebat
    Not over fat,
    Minnows small
    As the stall
    Of a glove,   80
    Not above
    The size
    Of a nice
    Little Baby's
    Little finger—
    O he made
    'Twas his trade
    Of Fish a pretty Kettle
    A Kettle—A Kettle
    Of Fish a pretty Kettle   90
    A Kettle!

There was a naughty Boy,
  And a naughty Boy was he,
He ran away to Scotland
  The people for to see—
    There he found
    That the ground
    Was as hard,
    That a yard

Was as long,   100
That a song
Was as merry,
That a cherry
Was as red—
That lead
Was as weighty,
That fourscore
Was as eighty,
That a door
Was as wooden   110
As in England—
So he stood in
  His shoes and he wonder'd,
  He wonder'd,
He stood in his
  Shoes and he wonder'd.

[1818]   [1883]

[Sonnet]
TO AILSA ROCK

HEARKEN, thou craggy ocean pyramid!
  Give answer from thy voice, the sea-fowls' screams!
  When were thy shoulders mantled in huge streams?
When from the sun was thy broad forehead hid?
How long is't since the mighty Power bid
  Thee heave to airy sleep from fathom dreams?
  Sleep in the lap of thunder or sunbeams,
Or when grey clouds are thy cold coverlid?
Thou answer'st not; for thou art dead asleep;
  Thy life is but two dead eternities—   10
The last in air, the former in the deep;
  First with the whales, last with the eagle-skies—
Drown'd wast thou till an earthquake made thee steep,
  Another cannot wake thy giant size.

[1818]   [1819]

[Sonnet Written in the
Cottage Where Burns Was Born]

THIS mortal body of a thousand days
  Now fills, O Burns, a space in thine own room,
Where thou didst dream alone on budded bays,[1]
  Happy and thoughtless of thy day of doom!

---

[1] Small fish.

[1] Poetic laurels.

My pulse is warm with thine own Barley-bree,[2]
   My head is light with pledging a great soul,
My eyes are wandering, and I cannot see,
   Fancy is dead and drunken at its goal;
Yet can I stamp my foot upon thy floor,
   Yet can I ope thy window-sash to find   10
The meadow thou hast tramped o'er and o'er,—
   Yet can I think of thee till thought is blind,—
Yet can I gulp a bumper to thy name,—
   O smile among the shades, for this is fame!

[1818]   [1848]

[The Gadfly]

ALL gentle folks who owe a grudge
   To any living thing
Open your ears and stay your t[r]udge
   Whilst I in dudgeon sing—

The gadfly he hath stung me sore
   O may he ne'er sting you!
But we have many a horrid bore
   He may sting black and blue.

Has any here an old grey Mare
   With three Legs all her store   10
O put it to her Buttocks bare
   And Straight she'll run on four

Has any here a Lawyer suit
   Of 17, 43[1]
Take Lawyer's nose and put it to 't
   And you the end will see.

Is there a Man in Parliament
   Dum[b] founder'd in his speech
O let his neighbour make a rent
   And put one in his breech   20

O Lowther[2] how much better thou
   Hadst figur'd to'ther day
When to the folks thou madst a bow
   And hadst no more to say

If lucky Gadfly had but ta'en
   His seat upon thine A—e
And put thee to a little pain
   To save thee from a worse.

Better than Southey[3] it had been
   Better than Mr. D——   30
Better than Wordsworth too I ween
   Better than Mr. V——

Forgive me pray good people all
   For deviating so
In spirit sure I had a call—
   And now I on will go—

Has any here a daughter fair
   Too fond of reading novels
Too apt to fall in love with care
   And charming Mister Lovels[4]   40

O put a gadfly to that thing
   She keeps so white and pert
I mean the finger for the ring
   And it will breed a Wert—

Has any here a pious spouse
   Who seven times a day
Scolds as King David pray'd; to chouse
   And have her holy way—

O let a Gadfly's litt[l]e sting
   Persuade her sacred tongue   50
That noises are a common thing
   But that her bell has rung

And as this is the summum bo
   Num of all conquering
I leave withouten wordes mo'
   The Gadfly's little sting[5]

[1818]   [1883]

LINES WRITTEN
IN THE HIGHLANDS
AFTER A VISIT
TO BURNS'S COUNTRY

THERE is a charm in footing slow across a silent plain,
Where patriot battle has been fought, when glory had
   the gain;
There is a pleasure on the heath where Druids old
   have been,
Where mantles grey have rustled by and swept the
   nettles green;

---

[2] Ale.
[1] A lawsuit begun in 1743.
[2] William Lowther, Earl of Lonsdale (1787–1872), Tory M.P. for Westmorland, helped Wordsworth get his post as Distributor of tax stamps.

[3] Robert Southey, poet laureate. See Byron's *A Vision of Judgment*, etc. The missing names below have not been clearly identified.
[4] Hero of Scott's *The Antiquary*.
[5] This poem is printed as it appears in Keats' letter of 18 July, 1818.

There is a joy in every spot made known by times of old,
New to the feet, although each tale a hundred times be
    told;
There is a deeper joy than all, more solemn in the
    heart,
More parching to the tongue than all, of more divine
    a smart,
When weary steps forget themselves upon a pleasant
    turf,   9
Upon hot sand, or flinty road, or sea-shore iron scurf,
Toward the castle or the cot, where long ago was born
One who was great through mortal days, and died of
    fame unshorn:
Light heather-bells may tremble then, but they are far
    away;
Wood-lark may sing from sandy fern,—the Sun may
    hear his lay;
Runnels may kiss the grass on shelves and shallows
    clear,
But their low voices are not heard, though come on
    travels drear;
Blood-red the Sun may set behind black mountain
    peaks;
Blue tides may sluice and drench their time in caves
    and weedy creeks;
Eagles may seem to sleep wing-wide upon the air;
Ring-doves may fly convuls'd across to some
    high-cedar'd lair;   20
But the forgotten eye is still fast lidded to the ground,
As Palmer's, that with weariness, mid-desert shrine
    hath found
At such a time the soul's a child, in childhood is the
    brain;
Forgotten is the worldly heart—alone, it beats in
    vain.—
Aye, if a madman could have leave to pass a healthful
    day
To tell his forehead's swoon and faint when first
    began decay,
He might make tremble many a one whose spirit had
    gone forth
To find a Bard's low cradle-place about the silent
    North!
Scanty the hour and few the steps beyond the bourn
    of care,
Beyond the sweet and bitter world,—beyond it
    unaware!   30
Scanty the hour and few the steps, because a longer
    stay
Would bar return, and make a man forget his mortal
    way:
O horrible! to lose the sight of well remembere'd face,
Of Brother's eyes, of Sister's brow—constant to every
    place;

Filling the air, as on we move, with portraiture
    intense;
More warm than those heroic tints that pain a
    painter's sense,
When shapes of old come striding by, and visages of
    old,
Locks shining black, hair scanty grey, and passions
    manifold.
No, no, that horror cannot be, for at the cable's length
Man feels the gentle anchor pull and gladdens in its
    strength:—   40
One hour, half-idiot, he stands by mossy waterfall,
But in the very next he reads his soul's memorial:—
He reads it on the mountain's height, where chance he
    may sit down
Upon rough marble diadem—that hill's eternal crown.
Yet be his anchor e'er so fast, room is there for a
    prayer
That man may never lose his mind on mountains
    black and bare;
That he may stray league after league some great
    birthplace to find
And keep his vision clear from speck, his inward sight
    unblind.

[1818]   [1822]

ON VISITING STAFFA

*The tiny island of Staffa, near the Isle of Mull off the west coast
of Scotland, contains Fingal's Cave which, as Keats notes with
regret, was becoming a fashionable tourist attraction.*

ON VISITING STAFFA

NOT Aladdin magian[1]
Ever such a work began;
Not the wizard of the Dee[2]
Ever such a dream could see;
Not St. John, in Patmos' Isle,[3]
In the passion of his toil,
When he saw the churches seven,
Golden aisl'd, built up in heaven,
Gaz'd at such a rugged wonder.
As I stood its roofing under,   10
Lo! I saw one sleeping there,
On the marble cold and bare.
While the surges wash'd his feet,
And his garments white did beat

---

[1] Magical.
[2] Merlin.
[3] St. John is said to have written his Revelation there.

Drench'd about the sombre rocks,
On his neck his well-grown locks,
Lifted dry above the main,
Were upon the curl again.
'What is this? and what art thou?'
Whisper'd I, and touch'd his brow;   20
'What art thou? and what is this?'
Whisper'd I, and strove to kiss
The spirit's hand, to wake his eyes;
Up he started in a trice:
'I am Lycidas,' said he,
'Fam'd in funeral minstrelsy!⁴
This was architected thus
By the great Oceanus!⁵—
Here his mighty waters play
Hollow organs all the day;   30
Here by turns his dolphins all,
Finny palmers great and small,
Come to pay devotion due—
Each a mouth of pearls must strew.
Many a mortal of these days,
Dares to pass our sacred ways,
Dares to touch audaciously
This Cathedral of the Sea!
I have been the pontiff-priest
Where the waters never rest,   40
Where a fledgy sea-bird choir
Soars for ever; holy fire
I have hid from mortal man;
Proteus⁶ is my Sacristan.
But the stupid eye of mortal
Hath pass'd beyond the rocky portal;
So for ever will I leave
Such a taint, and soon unweave
All the magic of the place.'
'Tis now free to stupid face,   50
To cutters, and to Fashion boats,
To cravats and to petticoats:—
The great sea shall war it down,
For its fame shall not be blown
At each farthing Quadrille⁷ dance.
So saying, with a Spirit's glance
He dived!

[1818]   [1838]

[Sonnet Written Upon Ben Nevis]

READ me a lesson, Muse, and speak it loud
    Upon the top of Nevis, blind in mist!
I look into the chasms, and a shroud
    Vaporous doth hide them,—just so much I wist
Mankind do know of hell; I look o'erhead,
    And there is sullen mist,—even so much
Mankind can tell of heaven; mist is spread
    Before the earth, beneath me,—even such,
Even so vague is man's sight of himself!
    Here are the craggy stones beneath my feet,—   10
Thus much I know that, a poor witless elf,
    I tread on them,—that all my eye doth meet
Is mist and crag, not only on this height,
But in the world of thought and mental might!

[1818]   [1838]

"'TIS THE WITCHING TIME..."

Like many of the poems composed during Keats's northern tour in the summer of 1818, this was sent in a letter to his brother George and his sister-in-law Georgiana in America. The prophecy made here is for their child.

"'Tis the witching time . . ."

'TIS 'the witching time of night,'
    Orbed is the Moon and bright
And the Stars they glisten, glisten,
Seeming with bright eyes to listen
    For what listen they?
For a song and for a cha[r]m
See they glisten in alarm
And the Moon is waxing warm
    To hear what I shall say.
Moon keep wide thy golden ears   10
Hearken Stars, and hearken Spheres
Hearken thou eternal Sky
I sing an infant's lullaby,
    A pretty Lullaby!
Listen, Listen, listen, listen,
Glisten, glisten, glisten, glisten
    And hear my lullaby?
Though the Rushes that will make
Its cradle still are in the lake:
Though the linnen then that will be   20
Its swathe is on the cotton tree;
Though the wollen that will keep
It wa[r]m, is on the silly sheep;
Listen, Star's light, listen, listen,
Glisten, Glisten, glisten, glisten
And hear my lullaby!

⁴ A reference to Milton's *Lycidas*, the elegy for Edward King.
⁵ One of the Titans.
⁶ A minor sea god, who could change his shape; a sacristan is a sexton, a caretaker of a church.
⁷ The name both of a popular card game and a dance.

Child! I see thee! Child I've found thee
Midst of the quiet all around thee!
Child I see thee! Ch[i]ld I spy thee
And thy mother sweet is nigh thee!　　　　　　30
Child I know thee! Child no more
But a Poet *ever*more.
See, See the Lyre, the Lyre
In a flame of fire
Upon the little cradle's top
Flaring, flaring, flaring.
Past the eyesight's bearing—
Awake it from its sleep
And see if it can keep
Its eyes upon the blaze.　　　　　　　　　　40
Amaze, Amaze!
It stares, it stares, it stares,
It dares what no one dares!
It lifts its little hand into the flame
Unharm'd, and on the strings
Paddles a little tune and sings,
With dumb endeavour sweetly!
Bard art thou completely!
Little Child
O' the western wild　　　　　　　　　　　50
Bard art thou completely!—
Sweetly, with dumb endeavour.—
A Poet now or never!
Litt[l]e Child
O' the western wild
A Poet now or never![1]

[1818]　　　　　　　　　　　　　　　[1848]

[Modern Love]

AND what is love? It is a doll dress'd up
For idleness to cosset, nurse, and dandle;
A thing of soft misnomers, so divine
That silly youth doth think to make itself
Divine by loving, and so goes on
Yawning and doting a whole summer long,
Till Miss's comb is made a pearl tiara,
And common Wellingtons[2] turn Romeo boots;
Till Cleopatra lives at number seven,
And Antony resides in Brunswick Square.　　　10
Fools! if some passions high have warm'd the world,
If Queens and Soldiers have play'd deep for hearts,
It is no reason why such agonies

Should be more common than the growth of weeds.
Fools! make me whole again that weighty pearl
The Queen of Egypt melted,[3] and I'll say
That ye may love in spite of beaver hats.

[1818]　　　　　　　　　　　　　　　[1848]

FRAGMENT
["Welcome joy ..."]

> 'Under the flag
> Of each his faction, they to battle bring
> Their embryon atoms.'—MILTON.[1]

WELCOME joy, and welcome sorrow,
　Lethe's weed and Hermes' feather;
Come to-day, and come to-morrow,
　I do love you both together!
　I love to mark sad faces in fair weather;
And hear a merry laugh amid the thunder;
　Fair and foul I love together.
Meadows sweet where flames burn under,
And a giggle at a wonder;
Visage sage at pantomime;　　　　　　　　10
Funeral, and steeple-chime;
Infant playing with a skull;
Morning fair, and stormwreck'd hull;
Nightshade with the woodbine kissing;
Serpents in red roses hissing;
Cleopatra regal-dress'd
With the aspic at her breast;
Dancing music, music sad,
Both together, sane and mad;
Muses bright and muses pale;　　　　　　　　20
Sombre Saturn, Momus hale;—
Laugh and sigh, and laugh again;
Oh the sweetness of the pain!
Muses bright, and muses pale,
Bare your faces of the veil;
Let me see; and let me write
Of the day, and of the night—
Both together:—let me slake
All my thirst for sweet heart-ache!
Let my bower be of yew,　　　　　　　　　30
Interwreath'd with myrtles new;
Pines and lime-trees full in bloom,
And my couch a low grass tomb

[1818]　　　　　　　　　　　　　　　[1848]

---

[1] This poem is printed exactly as it appears in Keats' journal-letter of 14–31 October 1818.
[2] Short boots named for the Duke of Wellington, the hero of Waterloo (1815).

---

[3] Cleopatra was said to have dissolved a pearl and drunk it in a toast to Antony.
[1] Misquoted from *Paradise Lost*, II, 898ff.

FRAGMENT
[" Where's the Poet? . . ."]

WHERE'S the Poet? show him! show him,
Muses nine! that I may know him!
'Tis the man who with a man
   Is an equal, be he King,
Or poorest of the beggar-clan,
   Or any other wondrous thing
A man may be 'twixt ape and Plato;
   'Tis the man who with a bird,
Wren or Eagle, finds his way to
   All its instincts; he hath heard   10
The Lion's roaring, and can tell
   What his horny throat expresseth,
And to him the Tiger's yell
   Comes articulate and presseth
On his ear like mother-tongue; . . .

[1818]   [1848]

FANCY

EVER let the Fancy roam,
Pleasure never is at home:
At a touch sweet Pleasure melteth,
Like to bubbles when rain pelteth;
Then let winged Fancy wander
Through the thought still spread beyond her:
Open wide the mind's cage-door,
She'll dart forth, and cloudward soar.
O sweet Fancy! let her loose;
Summer's joys are spoilt by use,   10
And the enjoying of the Spring
Fades as does its blossoming;
Autumn's red-lipp'd fruitage too,
Blushing through the mist and dew,
Cloys with tasting: What do then?
Sit thee by the ingle, when
The sear faggot blazes bright,
Spirit of a winter's night;
When the soundless earth is muffled,
And the caked snow is shuffled   20
From the ploughboy's heavy shoon;
When the Night doth meet the Noon
In a dark conspiracy
To banish Even from her sky.
Sit thee there, and send abroad,
With a mind self-overaw'd,
Fancy, high-commission'd:—send her!
She has vassals to attend her:

She will bring, in spite of frost,
Beauties that the earth hath lost;   30
She will bring thee, all together,
All delights of summer weather;
All the buds and bells of May,
From dewy sward or thorny spray
All the heaped Autumn's wealth,
With a still, mysterious stealth:
She will mix these pleasures up
Like three fit wines in a cup,
And thou shalt quaff it:—thou shalt hear
Distant harvest-carols clear;   40
Rustle of the reaped corn;
Sweet birds antheming the morn:
And, in the same moment—hark!
'Tis the early April lark,
Or the rooks, with busy caw,
Foraging for sticks and straw.
Thou shalt, at one glance, behold
The daisy and the marigold;
White-plum'd lilies, and the first
Hedge-grown primrose that hath burst;   50
Shaded hyacinth, alway
Sapphire queen of the mid-May;
And every leaf, and every flower
Pearled with the self-same shower.
Thou shalt see the field-mouse peep
Meagre from its celled sleep;
And the snake all winter-thin
Cast on sunny bank its skin;
Freckled nest-eggs thou shalt see
Hatching in the hawthorn-tree,   60
When the hen-bird's wing doth rest
Quiet on her mossy nest;
Then the hurry and alarm
When the bee-hive casts its swarm;
Acorns ripe down-pattering,
While the autumn breezes sing.

Oh, sweet Fancy! let her loose;
Every thing is spoilt by use:
Where's the cheek that doth not fade,
Too much gaz'd at? Where's the maid   70
Whose lip mature is ever new?
Where's the eye, however blue,
Doth not weary? Where's the face
One would meet in every place?
Where's the voice, however soft,
One would hear so very oft?
At a touch sweet Pleasure melteth
Like to bubbles when rain pelteth.
Let, then, winged Fancy find
Thee a mistress to thy mind: 80

Dulcet-eyed as Ceres' daughter,[1]
Ere the God of Torment taught her
How to frown and how to chide;
With a waist and with a side
White as Hebe's,[2] when her zone
Slipt its golden clasp, and down
Fell her kirtle to her feet,
While she held the goblet sweet,
And Jove grew languid.—Break the mesh
Of the Fancy's silken leash;   90
Quickly break her prison-string
And such joys as these she'll bring.—
Let the winged Fancy roam
Pleasure never is at home.

[1818-19]   [1820]

Here, your earth-born souls still speak
To mortals, of their little week;   30
Of their sorrows and delights;
Of their passions and their spites;
Of their glory and their shame;
What does strengthen and what maim.
Thus ye teach us, every day,
Wisdom, though fled far away.

    Bards of Passion and of Mirth,
    Ye have left your souls on earth!
    Ye have souls in heaven too,
    Double-lived in regions new!   40

[1819]   [1820]

ODE
["Bards of Passion . . ."]

BARDS of Passion and of Mirth,
Ye ha e left your souls on earth!
Have ye souls in heaven too,
Double-lived in regions new?
Yes, and those of heaven commune
With the spheres of sun and moon;
With the noise of fountains wond'rous,
And the parle[3] of voices thund'rous;
With the whisper of heaven's trees
And one another, in soft ease   10
Seated on Elysian lawns
Brows'd by none but Dian's fawns
Underneath large blue-bells tented,
Where the daisies are rose-scented,
And the rose herself has got
Perfume which on earth is not;
Where the nightingale doth sing
Not a senseless, tranced thing,
But divine melodious truth;
Philosophic numbers smooth;   20
Tales and golden histories
Of heaven and its mysteries.

    Thus ye live on high, and then
On the earth ye live again;
And the souls ye left behind you
Teach us, here, the way to find you,
Where your other souls are joying,
Never slumber'd, never cloying.

SONG

*Robert Gittings (see Bibliography) argues that this poem com-
memorates the consummation of an affair between Keats and a
Mrs. Isabella Jones, whom he met at Hastings in 1816 and who
later urged him to write* The Eve of St. Agnes. *See also the
letter to George and Georgiana Keats, October 24, 1818.*

SONG
["Hush, hush! . . ."]

I

HUSH, hush! tread softly! hush, hush, my dear!
    All the house is asleep, but we know very well
That the jealous, the jealous old bald-pate may hear,
    Tho' you've padded his night-cap—O sweet Isabel:
        Tho' your feet are more light than a Faery's feet,
        Who dances on bubbles where brooklets meet.—
Hush, hush! soft tiptoe! hush, hush, my dear!
For less than a nothing the jealous can hear.

II

No leaf doth tremble, no ripple is there   9
    On the river,—all's still, and the night's sleepy eye
Closes up, and forgets all its Lethean care,
    Charm'd to death by the drone of the humming
        May-fly;
        And the moon, whether prudish or complaisant,
        Has fled to her bower, well knowing I want
No light in the dusk, no torch in the gloom,
But my Isabel's eyes, and her lips pulp'd with bloom.

III

Lift the latch! ah gently! ah tenderly—sweet!
    We are dead if that latchet gives one little clink!
Well done—now those lips, and a flowery seat— 19
    The old man may sleep, and the planets may wink;

---

¹ Proserpine, who was carried away by Pluto (the God of
Torment) to be queen of the underworld.
² Goddess of youth, and a cup-bearer.
³ Speech.

The shut rose shall dream of our loves and awake
Full-blown, and such warmth for the morning's
       take,
The stock-dove shall hatch her soft brace and shall
       coo,
While I kiss to the melody, aching all through!

[1819]   [1845]

HYPERION

In the volume in which Hyperion *first appeared, the publishers
prefixed the following notice:*

ADVERTISEMENT

IF any apology be thought necessary for the appearance
of the unfinished poem of HYPERION, the publishers beg
to state that they alone are responsible, as it was printed
at their particular request, and contrary to the wish of the
author. The poem was intended to have been of equal
length with ENDYMION, but the reception given to that
work discouraged the author from proceeding.

Fleet-Street, June 26, 1820.

*And one manuscript of the poem includes an even more extensive
statement, later canceled:*

ADVERTISEMENT

The Publishers think it right to state that it was not the
wish of the Author that the ensuing fragment should meet
the public eye. He commenced the Poem just before the
Publication of his Endymion; and he abandoned the
intention of proceeding with it, in consequence of the
reception that work experienced from some of the
reviews.—The fragment remains therefore in the same
state in which it was originally written; and the Author's
health is not at present such as to enable him to make any
corrections. The Publishers have however prevailed upon
him to allow of its forming a part of this volume: and
they are content to take upon themselves whatever blame
may attach to its publication.

*The poem begins at that point in mythological history when the
Olympians have defeated all the Titans except Hyperion, and
Apollo is to become his successor and the destined god of the arts
and imagination as well as the sun. The wars of the Titans are
confusingly described by a variety of authors, ancient and
modern, and Keats's version cannot be ascribed to any one source.*

HYPERION

A FRAGMENT

BOOK I

DEEP in the shady sadness of a vale
Far sunken from the healthy breath of morn,
Far from the fiery noon, and eve's one star,
Sat gray-hair'd Saturn[1] quiet as a stone,

---

[1] Hyperion's brother, Jupiter's father, leader of the Titans.

Still as the silence round about his lair;
Forest on forest hung above his head
Like cloud on cloud. No stir of air was there,
Not so much life as on a summer's day
Robs not one light seed from the feather'd grass,
But where the dead leaf fell, there did it rest.   10
A stream went voiceless by, still deadened more
By reason of his fallen divinity
Spreading a shade: the Naiad[2] mid her reeds
Press'd her cold finger closer to her lips.

Along the margin-sand large foot-marks went,
No further than to where his feet had stray'd,
And slept there since. Upon the sodden ground
His old right hand lay nerveless, listless, dead,
Unsceptred; and his realmless eyes were closed;
While his bow'd head seem'd list'ning to the Earth,
His ancient mother, for some comfort yet.   21

It seem'd no force could wake him from his place;
But there came one, who with a kindred hand
Touch'd his wide shoulders, after bending low
With reverence, though to one who knew it not.
She was a Goddess of the infant world;[3]
By her in stature the tall Amazon
Had stood a pigmy's height: she would have ta'en
Achilles by the hair and bent his neck;
Or with a finger stay'd Ixion's wheel.[4]   30
Her face was large as that of Memphian sphinx,
Pedestal'd haply in a palace court,
When sages look'd to Egypt for their lore.
But oh! how unlike marble was that face:
How beautiful, if sorrow had not made
Sorrow more beautiful than Beauty's self.
There was a listening fear in her regard,
As if calamity had but begun;
As if the vanward clouds of evil days
Had spent their malice, and the sullen rear   40
Was with its stored thunder labouring up.
One hand she press'd upon that aching spot
Where beats the human heart, as if just there,
Though an immortal, she felt cruel pain:
The other upon Saturn's bended neck
She laid, and to the level of his ear
Leaning with parted lips, some words she spake
In solemn tenour and deep organ tone:
Some mourning words, which in our feeble tongue
Would come in these like accents; O how frail   50
To that large utterance of the early Gods!
'Saturn, look up!—though wherefore, poor old King?

---

[2] River nymph.
[3] Thea, Hyperion's wife.
[4] The constantly turning wheel to which Ixion was chained by
Zeus for seeking Hera's love.

'I have no comfort for thee, no not one:
'I cannot say, "O wherefore sleepest thou?"
'For heaven is parted from thee, and the earth
'Knows thee not, thus afflicted, for a God;
'And ocean too, with all its solemn noise,
'Has from thy sceptre pass'd; and all the air
'Is emptied of thine hoary majesty.
'Thy thunder, conscious of the new command,⁵   60
'Rumbles reluctant o'er our fallen house;
'And thy sharp lightning in unpractised hands
'Scorches and burns our once serene domain.
'O aching time! O moments big as years!
'All as ye pass swell out the monstrous truth,
'And press it so upon our weary griefs
'That unbelief has not a space to breathe.
'Saturn, sleep on:—O thoughtless, why did I
'Thus violate thy slumbrous solitude?
'Why should I ope thy melancholy eyes?   70
'Saturn, sleep on! while at thy feet I weep.'

    As when, upon a tranced summer-night,
Those green-rob'd senators of mighty woods,
Tall oaks, branch-charmed by the earnest stars,
Dream, and so dream all night without a stir,
Save from one gradual solitary gust
Which comes upon the silence, and dies off,
As if the ebbing air had but one wave;
So came these words and went; the while in tears
She touch'd her fair large forehead to the ground,   80
Just where her fallen hair might be outspread
A soft and silken mat for Saturn's feet.
One moon, with alteration slow, had shed
Her silver seasons four upon the night,
And still these two were postured motionless,
Like natural sculpture in cathedral cavern;
The frozen God still couchant on the earth,
And the sad Goddess weeping at his feet:
Until at length old Saturn lifted up
His faded eyes, and saw his kingdom gone,   90
And all the gloom and sorrow of the place,
And that fair kneeling Goddess; and then spake,
As with a palsied tongue, and while his beard
Shook horrid with such aspen-malady:
'O tender spouse of gold Hyperion,
'Thea, I feel thee ere I see thy face;
'Look up, and let me see our doom in it;
'Look up, and tell me if this feeble shape
'Is Saturn's; tell me, if thou hear'st the voice
'Of Saturn; tell me, if this wrinkling brow,   100
'Naked and bare of its great diadem,
'Peers like the front of Saturn. Who had power
'To make me desolate? whence came the strength?

'How was it nurtur'd to such bursting forth,
'While Fate seem'd strangled in my nervous grasp?
'But it is so; and I am smother'd up,
'And buried from all godlike exercise
'Of influence benign on planets pale,
'Of admonitions to the winds and seas,
'Of peaceful sway above man's harvesting,   110
'And all those acts which Deity supreme
'Doth ease its heart of love in.⁶—I am gone
'Away from my own bosom: I have left
'My strong identity, my real self,
'Somewhere between the throne, and where I sit
'Here on this spot of earth.⁷ Search, Thea, search!
'Open thine eyes eterne, and sphere them round
'Upon all space: space starr'd, and lorn of light;
'Space region'd with life-air; and barren void;
'Spaces of fire, and all the yawn of hell.—   120
'Search, Thea, search! and tell me, if thou seest
'A certain shape or shadow, making way
'With wings or chariot fierce to repossess
'A heaven he lost erewhile: it must—it must
'Be of ripe progress—Saturn must be King.
'Yes, there must be a golden victory;
'There must be Gods thrown down, and trumpets
        blown
'Of triumph calm, and hymns of festival
'Upon the gold clouds metropolitan,
'Voices of soft proclaim, and silver stir   130
'Of strings in hollow shells; and there shall be
'Beautiful things made new, for the surprise
'Of the sky-children; I will give command:
'Thea! Thea! Thea! where is Saturn?'

    This passion lifted him upon his feet,
And made his hands to struggle in the air,
His Druid locks to shake and ooze with sweat,
His eyes to fever out, his voice to cease.
He stood, and heard not Thea's sobbing deep;
A little time, and then again he snatch'd   140
Utterance thus.—'But cannot I create?
'Cannot I form? Cannot I fashion forth
'Another world, another universe,
'To overbear and crumble this to nought?
'Where is another Chaos? Where?'—That word
Found way unto Olympus, and made quake
The rebel three.⁸—Thea was startled up,
And in her bearing was a sort of hope,
As thus she quick-voic'd spake, yet full of awe.

---

⁵ Jupiter, the Thunderer, now rules the gods.

⁶ After Saturn's banishment, he is said to have gone to Italy
to share Janus' rule, and there inaugurated the Golden Age.
⁷ The Titans, unlike their successors the Olympians (like
Apollo), are men of power rather than imagination.
⁸ Jupiter, Neptune, Pluto—the three sons of Saturn, who take
over the heavens, the sea, and the underworld.

'This cheers our fallen house: come to our friends,
'O Saturn! come away, and give them heart;   151
'I know the covert, for thence came I hither.'
Thus brief; then with beseeching eyes she went
With backward footing through the shade a space:
He follow'd, and she turn'd to lead the way
Through aged boughs, that yielded like the mist
Which eagles cleave upmounting from their nest.

Meanwhile in other realms big tears were shed,
More sorrow like to this, and such like woe,
Too huge for mortal tongue or pen of scribe: 160
The Titans fierce, self-hid, or prison-bound,
Groan'd for the old allegiance once more,
And listen'd in sharp pain for Saturn's voice.
But one of the whole mammoth-brood still kept
His sov'reignty, and rule, and majesty;—
Blazing Hyperion on his orbed fire
Still sat, still snuff'd the incense, teeming up
From Man to the sun's God; yet unsecure:
For as among us mortals omens drear
Fright and perplex, so also shuddered he—   170
Not at dog's howl, or gloom-bird's hated screech,
Or the familiar visiting of one
Upon the first toll of his passing-bell,[9]
Or prophesyings of the midnight lamp;
But horrors, portion'd to a giant nerve,
Oft made Hyperion ache. His palace bright
Bastion'd with pyramids of glowing gold,
And touch'd with shade of bronzed obelisks,
Glar'd a blood-red through all its thousand courts,
Arches, and domes, and fiery galleries;   180
And all its curtains of Aurorian[10] clouds
Flush'd angrily: while sometimes eagle's wings,
Unseen before by Gods or wondering men,
Darken'd the place; and neighing steeds were heard,
Not heard before by Gods or wondering men.
Also, when he would taste the spicy wreaths
Of incense, breath'd aloft from sacred hills,
Instead of sweets, his ample palate took
Savour of poisonous brass and metal sick:
And so, when harbour'd in the sleepy west,   190
After the full completion of fair day,—
For rest divine upon exalted couch
And slumber in the arms of melody,
He pac'd away the pleasant hours of ease
With stride colossal, on from hall to hall;
While far within each aisle and deep recess,
His winged minions in close clusters stood,
Amaz'd and full of fear; like anxious men
Who on wide plains gather in panting troops,

When earthquakes jar their battlements and towers.
Even now, while Saturn, rous'd from icy trance,   201
Went step for step with Thea through the woods,
Hyperion, leaving twilight in the rear,
Came slope upon the threshold of the west;
Then, as was wont, his palace-door flew ope
In smoothest silence, save what solemn tubes,
Blown by the serious Zephyrs, gave of sweet
And wandering sounds, slow-breathed melodies;
And like a rose in vermeil tint and shape,
In fragrance soft, and coolness to the eye,   210
That inlet to severe magnificence
Stood full blown, for the God to enter in.

He enter'd, but he enter'd full of wrath;
His flaming robes stream'd out beyond his heels,
And gave a roar, as if of earthly fire,
That scar'd away the meek ethereal Hours
And made their dove-wings tremble. On he flared,
From stately nave to nave, from vault to vault,
Through bowers of fragrant and enwreathed light,
And diamond-paved lustrous long arcades,   220
Until he reach'd the great main cupola;
There standing fierce beneath, he stampt his foot,
And from the basements deep to the high towers
Jarr'd his own golden region; and before
The quavering thunder thereupon had ceas'd,
His voice leapt out, despite of godlike curb,
To this result: 'O dreams of day and night!
'O monstrous forms! O effigies of pain!
'O spectres busy in a cold, cold gloom!
'O lank-eared Phantoms of black-weeded pools!   230
'Why do I know ye? why have I seen ye? why
'Is my eternal essence thus distraught
'To see and to behold these horrors new?
'Saturn is fallen, am I too to fall?
'Am I to leave this haven of my rest,
'This cradle of my glory, this soft clime,
'This calm luxuriance of blissful light,
'These crystalline pavilions, and pure fanes,
'Of all my lucent empire? It is left
'Deserted, void, nor any haunt of mine.   240
'The blaze, the splendor, and the symmetry
'I cannot see—but darkness, death and darkness.
'Even here, into my centre of repose,
'The shady visions come to domineer,
'Insult, and blind, and stifle up my pomp.—
'Fall!—No, by Tellus[11] and her briny robes!
'Over the fiery frontier of my realms
'I will advance a terrible right arm
'Shall scare that infant Thunderer, rebel Jove,
'And bid old Saturn take his throne again.'—   250

---

[9] The appeal for prayers for someone dying.
[10] Dawnlike; rose-colored.

[11] Mother of Cybele, Saturn's wife.

He spake, and ceas'd, the while a heavier threat
Held struggle with his throat but came not forth;
For as in theatres of crowded men
Hubbub increases more they call out 'Hush!'
So at Hyperion's words the Phantoms pale
Bestirr'd themselves, thrice horrible and cold;
And from the mirror'd level where he stood
A mist arose, as from a scummy marsh.
At this, through all his bulk an agony
Crept gradual, from the feet unto the crown,   260
Like a lithe serpent vast and muscular
Making slow way, with head and neck convuls'd
From over-strained might. Releas'd, he fled
To the eastern gates, and full six dewy hours
Before the dawn in season due should blush,
He breath'd fierce breath against the sleepy portals,
Clear'd them of heavy vapours, burst them wide
Suddenly on the ocean's chilly streams.
The planet orb of fire, whereon he rode
Each day from east to west the heavens through,   270
Spun round in sable curtaining of clouds;
Not therefore veiled quite, blindfold, and hid,
But ever and anon the glancing spheres,
Circles, and arcs, and broad-belting colure,[12]
Glow'd through, and wrought upon the muffling dark
Sweet-shaped lightnings from the nadir deep
Up to the zenith,—hieroglyphics old,[13]
Which sages and keen-eyed astrologers
Then living on the earth, with labouring thought
Won from the gaze of many centuries: 280
Now lost, save what we find on remnants huge
Of stone, or marble swart; their import gone,
Their wisdom long since fled.—Two wings this orb
Possess'd for glory, two fair argent wings,
Ever exalted at the God's approach
And now, from forth the gloom their plumes immense
Rose, one by one, till all outspreaded were;
While still the dazzling globe maintain'd eclipse,
Awaiting for Hyperion's command.
Fain would he have commanded, fain took throne   290
And bid the day begin, if but for change.
He might not:—No, though a primeval God:
The sacred seasons might not be disturb'd.
Therefore the operations of the dawn
Stay'd in their birth, even as here 'tis told.
Those silver wings expanded sisterly,
Eager to sail their orb; the porches wide
Open'd upon the dusk demesnes of night
And the bright Titan, phrenzied with new woes,
Unus'd to bend, by hard compulsion bent   300
His spirit to the sorrow of the time;

And all along a dismal rack of clouds,
Upon the boundaries of day and night,
He stretch'd himself in grief and radiance faint.
There as he lay, the Heaven with its stars
Look'd down on him with pity, and the voice
Of Cœlus,[14] from the universal space,
Thus whisper'd low and solemn in his ear.
'O brightest of my children dear, earth-born
'And sky-engendered, Son of Mysteries   310
'All unrevealed even to the powers
'Which met at thy creating; at whose joys
'And palpitations sweet, and pleasures soft,
'I, Cœlus, wonder, how they came and whence;
'And at the fruits thereof what shapes they be,
'Distinct, and visible; symbols divine,
'Manifestations of that beauteous life
'Diffus'd unseen throughout eternal space:
'Of these new-form'd art thou, oh brightest child!
'Of these, thy brethren and the Goddesses!   320
'There is sad feud among ye, and rebellion
'Of son against his sire. I saw him fall,
'I saw my first-born[15] tumbled from his throne!
'To me his arms were spread, to me his voice
'Found way from forth the thunders round his head!
'Pale wox I, and in vapours hid my face.
'Art thou, too, near such doom? vague fear there is:
'For I have seen my sons most unlike Gods.
'Divine ye were created, and divine
'In sad demeanour, solemn, undisturb'd,   330
'Unruffled, like high Gods, ye liv'd and ruled:
'Now I behold in you fear, hope, and wrath;
'Actions of rage and passion; even as
'I see them, on the mortal world beneath,
'In men who die.—This is the grief, O Son!
'Sad sign of ruin, sudden dismay, and fall!
'Yet do thou strive; as thou art capable,
'As thou canst move about, an evident God;
'And canst oppose to each malignant hour
'Ethereal presence:—I am but a voice;   340
'My life is but the life of winds and tides,
'No more than winds and tides can I avail:—
'But thou canst.—Be thou therefore in the van
'Of Circumstance; yea, seize the arrow's barb
'Before the tense string murmur.—To the earth!
'For there thou wilt find Saturn, and his woes.
'Meantime I will keep watch on thy bright sun,
'And of thy seasons be a careful nurse.'—
Ere half this region-whisper had come down,
Hyperion arose, and on the stars   350
Lifted his curved lids, and kept them wide
Until it ceas'd; and still he kept them wide:

---

12 Technical term from astronomy.
13 The signs of the zodiac.

14 Father of Hyperion.
15 Saturn.

And still they were the same bright, patient stars.
Then with a slow incline of his broad breast,
Like to a diver in the pearly seas,
Forward he stoop'd over the airy shore,
And plung'd all noiseless into the deep night.

BOOK II

JUST at the self-same beat of Time's wide wings
Hyperion slid into the rustled air,
And Saturn gain'd with Thea that sad place
Where Cybele and the bruised Titans mourn'd.
It was a den where no insulting light
Could glimmer on their tears; where their own groans
They felt, but heard not, for the solid roar
Of thunderous waterfalls and torrents hoarse,
Pouring a constant bulk, uncertain where.
Crag jutting forth to crag, and rocks that seem'd　　10
Ever as if just rising from a sleep,
Forehead to forehead held their monstrous horns;
And thus in thousand hugest phantasies
Made a fit roofing to this nest of woe.
Instead of thrones, hard flint they sat upon,
Couches of rugged stone, and slaty ridge
Stubborn'd with iron. All were not assembled:
Some chain'd in torture, and some wandering.
Cœus, and Gyges, and Briareüs,
Typhon, and Dolor, and Porphyrion,[16]　　20
With many more, the brawniest in assault,
Were pent in regions of laborious breath;
Dungeon'd in opaque element, to keep
Their clenched teeth still clench'd, and all their limbs
Lock'd up like veins of metal, crampt and screw'd;
Without a motion, save of their big hearts
Heaving in pain, and horribly convuls'd
With sanguine feverous boiling gurge of pulse.
Mnemosyne[17] was straying in the world;
Far from her moon had Phœbe wandered;　　30
And many else were free to roam abroad,
But for the main, here found they covert drear.
Scarce images of life, one here, one there,
Lay vast and edgeways; like a dismal cirque
Of Druid stones, upon a forlorn moor,
When the chill rain begins at shut of eve,
In dull November, and their chancel vault,
The Heaven itself, is blinded throughout night.
Each one kept shroud, nor to his neighbour gave
Or word, or look, or action of despair.　　40
Creüs was one; his ponderous iron mace

Lay by him, and a shatter'd rib of rock
Told of his rage, ere he thus sank and pined.
Iäpetus another; in his grasp,
A serpent's plashy neck; its barbed tongue
Squeez'd from the gorge, and all its uncurl'd length
Dead; and because the creature could not spit
Its poison in the eyes of conquering Jove.
Next Cottus: prone he lay, chin uppermost,
As though in pain; for still upon the flint　　50
He ground severe his skull, with open mouth
And eyes at horrid working. Nearest him
Asia, born of most enormous Caf,[18]
Who cost her mother Tellus keener pangs,
Though feminine, than any of her sons:
More thought than woe was in her dusky face,
For she was prophesying of her glory;
And in her wide imagination stood
Palm-shaded temples, and high rival fanes,
By Oxus or in Ganges' sacred isles.　　60
Even as Hope upon her anchor leans,
So leant she, not so fair, upon a tusk
Shed from the broadest of her elephants.
Above her, on a crag's uneasy shelve,
Upon his elbow rais'd, all prostrate else,
Shadow'd Enceladus,[19] once tame and mild
As grazing ox unworried in the meads;
Now tiger-passion'd, lion-thoughted, wroth,
He meditated, plotted, and even now
Was hurling mountains in that second war,　　70
Not long delay'd, that scar'd the younger Gods
To hide themselves in forms of beast and bird.
Not far hence Atlas; and beside him prone
Phorcus, the sire of Gorgons.[20] Neighbour'd close
Oceanus, and Tethys, in whose lap
Sobb'd Clymene among her tangled hair.
In midst of all lay Themis, at the feet
Of Ops the queen; all clouded round from sight,
No shape distinguishable, more than when
Thick night confounds the pine-tops with the clouds:
And many else whose names may not be told.　　81
For when the Muse's wings are air-ward spread,
Who shall delay her flight? And she must chaunt
Of Saturn, and his guide, who now had climb'd
With damp and slippery footing from a depth
More horrid still. Above a sombre cliff
Their heads appear'd, and up their stature grew
Till on the level height their steps found ease:
Then Thea spread abroad her trembling arms
Upon the precincts of this nest of pain,　　90

---

16 These are all Titans, the names and number of which are
uncertain in Greek mythology.
17 Mnemosyne (Memory), the mother of the Muses by
Jupiter, who is seeking Apollo.

18 Keats invents Asia's history. Caf is a huge mountain.
19 Another Titan, the strongest of the conspirators against
Jupiter.
20 Atlas is a Titan; Phorcus a sea-deity, who fathered the
Gorgons with his sister Ceto.

And sidelong fix'd her eye on Saturn's face:
There saw she direst strife; the supreme God
At war with all the frailty of grief,
Of rage, of fear, anxiety, revenge,
Remorse, spleen, hope, but most of all despair.
Against these plagues he strove in vain; for Fate
Had pour'd a mortal oil upon his head,
A disanointing poison: so that Thea,
Affrighted, kept her still, and let him pass
First onwards in, among the fallen tribe.   100

    As with us mortal men, the laden heart
Is persecuted more, and fever'd more,
When it is nighing to the mournful house
Where other hearts are sick of the same bruise;
So Saturn, as he walk'd into the midst,
Felt faint, and would have sunk among the rest,
But that he met Enceladus's eye,
Whose mightiness, and awe of him, at once
Came like an inspiration; and he shouted,
'Titans, behold your God!' at which some groan'd;
Some started on their feet; some also shouted;   111
Some wept, some wail'd, all bow'd with reverence;
And Ops, uplifting her black folded veil,
Show'd her pale cheeks, and all her forehead wan,
Her eye-brows thin and jet, and hollow eyes.
There is a roaring in the bleak-grown pines
When Winter lifts his voice; there is a noise
Among immortals when a God gives sign,
With hushing finger, how he means to load
His tongue with the full weight of utterless thought,
With thunder, and with music, and with pomp: 121
Such noise is like the roar of bleak-grown pines;
Which, when it ceases in this mountain'd world,
No other sound succeeds; but ceasing here,
Among these fallen, Saturn's voice therefrom
Grew up like organ, that begins anew
Its strain, when other harmonies, stopt short,
Leave the dinn'd air vibrating silverly.
Thus grew it up—'Not in my own sad breast,
'Which is its own great judge and searcher out,   130
'Can I find reason why ye should be thus:
'Not in the legends of the first of days,
'Studied from that old spirit-leaved book
'Which starry Uranus with finger bright
'Sav'd from the shores of darkness, when the waves
'Low-ebb'd still hid it up in shallow gloom;—
'And the which book ye know I ever kept
'For my firm-based footstool:—Ah, infirm!
'Not there, nor in sign, symbol, or portent
'Of element, earth, water, air, and fire,—   140
'At war, at peace, or inter-quarreling
'One against one, or two, or three, or all
'Each several one against the other three,

'As fire with air loud warring when rain-floods
'Drown both, and press them both against earth's
        face.
'Where, finding sulphur, a quadruple wrath
'Unhinges the poor world;—not in that strife,
'Wherefrom I take strange lore, and read it deep,
'Can I find reason why ye should be thus:
'No, no-where can unriddle, though I search,   150
'And pore on Nature's universal scroll
'Even to swooning, why ye, Divinities,
'The first-born of all shap'd and palpable Gods,
'Should cower beneath what, in comparison,
'Is untremendous might. Yet ye are here,
'O'erwhelm'd, and spurn'd, and batter'd, ye are here!
'O Titans, shall I say "Arise!"—Ye groan:
'Shall I say "Crouch!"—Ye groan. What can I then?
'O Heaven wide! O unseen parent dear!
'What can I? Tell me, all ye brethren Gods,   160
'How we can war, how engine our great wrath!
'O speak your counsel now, for Saturn's ear
'Is all a-hunger'd. Thou, Oceanus,
'Ponderest high and deep; and in thy face
'I see, astonied, that severe content
'Which comes of thought and musing: give us help!'

    So ended Saturn; and the God of the Sea,
Sophist and sage, from no Athenian grove,
But cogitation in his watery shades,
Arose, with locks not oozy, and began,   170
In murmurs, which his first-endeavouring tongue
Caught infant-like from the far-foamed sands.
'O ye, whom wrath consumes! who, passion-stung,
'Writhe at defeat, and nurse your agonies!
'Shut up your senses, stifle up your ears,
'My voice is not a bellows unto ire.
'Yet listen, ye who will, whilst I bring proof
'How ye, perforce, must be content to stoop:
'And in the proof much comfort will I give,
'If ye will take that comfort in its truth.   180
'We fall by course of Nature's law, not force
'Of thunder, or of Jove. Great Saturn, thou
'Hast sifted well the atom-universe;
'But for this reason, that thou art the King,
'And only blind from sheer supremacy,
'One avenue was shaded from thine eyes,
'Through which I wandered to eternal truth.
'And first, as thou wast not the first of powers,
'So art thou not the last; it cannot be:
'Thou art not the beginning nor the end.   190
'From Chaos and parental Darkness came
'Light, the first fruits of that intestine broil,
'That sullen ferment, which for wondrous ends
'Was ripening in itself. The ripe hour came,
'And with it Light, and Light, engendering

'Upon its own producer, forthwith touch'd
'The whole enormous matter into Life.
'Upon that very hour, our parentage,
'The Heavens and the Earth, were manifest:
'Then thou first born, and we the giant race,   200
'Found ourselves ruling new and beauteous realms.
'Now comes the pain of truth, to whom 'tis pain;
'O folly! for to bear all naked truths,
'And to envisage circumstance, all calm,
'That is the top of sovereignty. Mark well!
'As Heaven and Earth are fairer, fairer far
'Than Chaos and blank Darkness, though once chiefs;
'And as we show beyond that Heaven and Earth
'In form and shape compact and beautiful,
'In will, in action free, companionship,   210
'And thousand other signs of purer life;
'So on our heels a fresh perfection treads,
'A power more strong in beauty, born of us
'And fated to excel us, as we pass
'In glory that old Darkness: nor are we
'Thereby more conquer'd, than by us the rule
'Of shapeless Chaos. Say, doth the dull soil
'Quarrel with the proud forests it hath fed,
'And feedeth still, more comely than itself?
'Can it deny the chiefdom of green groves?   220
'Or shall the tree be envious of the dove
'Because it cooeth, and hath snowy wings
'To wander wherewithal and find its joys?
'We are such forest-trees, and our fair boughs
'Have bred forth, not pale solitary doves,
'But eagles golden-feather'd, who do tower
'Above us in their beauty, and must reign
'In right thereof; for 'tis the eternal law
'That first in beauty should be first in might:
'Yea, by that law, another race may drive   230
'Our conquerors to mourn as we do now.
'Have ye beheld the young God of the Seas,[21]
'My dispossessor? Have ye seen his face?
'Have ye beheld his chariot, foam'd along
'By noble winged creatures he hath made?
'I saw him on the calmed waters scud,
'With such a glow of beauty in his eyes,
'That it enforc'd me to bid sad farewell
'To all my empire: farewell sad I took,
'And hither came, to see how dolorous fate   240
'Had wrought upon ye; and how I might best
'Give consolation in this woe extreme.
'Receive the truth, and let it be your balm.'

    Whether through pos'd conviction, or disdain,
They guarded silence, when Oceanus

[21] Neptune.

Left murmuring, what deepest thought can tell?
But so it was, none answer'd for a space,
Save one whom none regarded, Clymene;
And yet she answer'd not, only complain'd,
With hectic lips, and eyes up-looking mild,   250
Thus wording timidly among the fierce:
'O Father, I am here the simplest voice,
'And all my knowledge is that joy is gone,
'And this thing woe crept in among our hearts,
'There to remain for ever, as I fear:
'I would not bode of evil, if I thought
'So weak a creature could turn off the help
'Which by just right should come of mighty Gods;
'Yet let me tell my sorrow, let me tell
'Of what I heard, and how it made me weep,   260
'And know that we had parted from all hope.
'I stood upon a shore, a pleasant shore,
'Where a sweet clime was breathed from a land
'Of fragrance, quietness, and trees, and flowers.
'Full of calm joy it was, as I of grief;
'Too full of joy and soft delicious warmth;
'So that I felt a movement in my heart
'To chide, and to reproach that solitude
'With songs of misery, music of our woes;
'And sat me down, and took a mouthed shell   270
'And murmur'd into it, and made melody—
'O melody no more! for while I sang,
'And with poor skill let pass into the breeze
'The dull shell's echo, from a bowery strand
'Just opposite, an island of the sea,
'There came enchantment with the shifting wind,
'That did both drown and keep alive my ears.
'I threw my shell away upon the sand,
'And a wave fill'd it, as my sense was fill'd
'With that new blissful golden melody.   280
'A living death was in each gush of sounds,
'Each family of rapturous hurried notes,
'That fell, one after one, yet all at once,
'Like pearl beads dropping sudden from their string:
'And then another, then another strain,
'Each like a dove leaving its olive perch,
'With music wing'd instead of silent plumes,
'To hover round my head, and make me sick
'Of joy and grief at once. Grief overcame,
'And I was stopping up my frantic ears,   290
'When, past all hindrance of my trembling hands,
'A voice came sweeter, sweeter than all tune,
'And still it cried, "Apollo! young Apollo!
'"The morning-bright Apollo! young Apollo!"
'I fled, it follow'd me, and cried "Apollo!"
'O Father, and O Brethren, had ye felt
'Those pains of mine; O Saturn, hadst thou felt,
'Ye would not call this too indulged tongue
'Presumptuous, in thus venturing to be heard.'

So far her voice flow'd on, like timorous brook 300
That, lingering along a pebbled coast,
Doth fear to meet the sea: but sea it met,
And shudder'd; for the overwhelming voice
Of huge Enceladus swallow'd it in wrath:
The ponderous syllables, like sullen waves
In the half-glutted hollows of reef-rocks,
Came booming thus, while still upon his arm
He lean'd; not rising, from supreme contempt.
'Or shall we listen to the over-wise,
'Or to the over-foolish, Giant-Gods? 310
'Not thunderbolt on thunderbolt, till all
'That rebel Jove's whole armoury were spent,
'Not world on world upon these shoulders piled,
'Could agonize me more than baby-words
'In midst of this dethronement horrible.
'Speak! roar! shout! yell! ye sleepy Titans all.
'Do ye forget the blows, the buffets vile?
'Are ye not smitten by a youngling arm?
'Dost thou forget, sham Monarch of the Waves,
'Thy scalding in the seas? What, have I rous'd 320
'Your spleens with so few simple words as these?
'O joy! for now I see ye are not lost:
'O joy! for now I see a thousand eyes
'Wide-glaring for revenge!'—As this he said,
He lifted up his stature vast, and stood,
Still without intermission speaking thus:
'Now ye are flames, I'll tell you how to burn,
'And purge the ether of our enemies;
'How to feed fierce the crooked stings of fire,
'And singe away the swollen clouds of Jove, 330
'Stifling that puny essence in its tent.
'O let him feel the evil he hath done;
'For though I scorn Oceanus's lore,
'Much pain have I for more than loss of realms:
'The days of peace and slumberous calm are fled;
'Those days, all innocent of scathing war,
'When all the fair Existences of heaven
'Came open-eyed to guess what we would speak:—
'That was before our brows were taught to frown,
'Before our lips knew else but solemn sounds; 340
'That was before we knew the winged thing,
'Victory, might be lost, or might be won.
'And be ye mindful that Hyperion,
'Our brightest brother, still is undisgraced—
'Hyperion, lo! his radiance is here!'

All eyes were on Enceladus's face,
And they beheld, while still Hyperion's name
Flew from his lips up to the vaulted rocks,
A pallid gleam across his features stern:
Not savage, for he saw full many a God 350
Wroth as himself. He look'd upon them all,
And in each face he saw a gleam of light,

But splendider in Saturn's, whose hoar locks
Shone like the bubbling foam about a keel
When the prow sweeps into a midnight cove.
In pale and silver silence they remain'd,
Till suddenly a splendour, like the morn,
Pervaded all the beetling gloomy steeps,
All the sad spaces of oblivion,
And every gulf, and every chasm old, 360
And every height, and every sullen depth,
Voiceless, or hoarse with loud tormented streams:
And all the everlasting cataracts,
And all the headlong torrents far and near,
Mantled before in darkness and huge shade,
Now saw the light and made it terrible.
It was Hyperion:—a granite peak
His bright feet touch'd, and there he stay'd to view
The misery his brilliance had betray'd
To the most hateful seeing of itself. 370
Golden his hair of short Numidian curl,[22]
Regal his shape majestic, a vast shade
In midst of his own brightness, like the bulk
Of Memnon's image at the set of sun
To one who travels from the dusking East:
Sighs, too, as mournful as that Memnon's harp[23]
He utter'd, while his hands contemplative
He press'd together, and in silence stood.
Despondence seiz'd again the fallen Gods
At sight of the dejected King of Day, 380
And many hid their faces from the light:
But fierce Enceladus sent forth his eyes
Among the brotherhood; and, at their glare,
Uprose Iäpetus, and Creüs too,
And Phorcus, sea-born, and together strode
To where he towered on his eminence.
There those four shouted forth old Saturn's name;
Hyperion from the peak loud answered, 'Saturn!'
Saturn sat near the Mother of the Gods,
In whose face was no joy, though all the Gods 390
Gave from their hollow throats the name of 'Saturn!'

Book III

Thus in alternate uproar and sad peace,
Amazed were those Titans utterly.
O leave them, Muse! O leave them to their woes;
For thou art weak to sing such tumults dire:
A solitary sorrow best befits
Thy lips, and antheming a lonely grief.
Leave them, O Muse! for thou anon wilt find

---

[22] Like a lion's mane.
[23] An Egyptian statue, said to make a sound like the snapping of a harp string when struck by the rising or setting sun.

Many a fallen old Divinity
Wandering in vain about bewildered shores.
Meantime touch piously the Delphic harp,   10
And not a wind of heaven but will breathe
In aid soft warble from the Dorian flute;
For lo! 'tis for the Father of all verse.
Flush every thing that hath a vermeil hue,
Let the rose glow intense and warm the air,
And let the clouds of even and of morn
Float in voluptuous fleeces o'er the hills;
Let the red wine within the goblet boil,
Cold as a bubbling well; let faint-lipp'd shells,
On sands, or in great deeps, vermillion turn   20
Through all their labyrinths; and let the maid
Blush keenly, as with some warm kiss surpris'd.
Chief isle of the embowered Cyclades,
Rejoice, O Delos,[24] with thine olives green,
And poplars, and lawn-shading palms, and beech,
In which the Zephyr breathes the loudest song,
And hazels thick, dark-stemm'd beneath the shade:
Apollo is once more the golden theme!
Where was he, when the Giant of the Sun [25]
Stood bright, amid the sorrow of his peers?   30
Together had he left his mother fair
And his twin-sister sleeping in their bower,[26]
And in the morning twilight wandered forth
Beside the osiers of a rivulet,
Full ankle-deep in lilies of the vale.
The nightingale had ceas'd, and a few stars
Were lingering in the heavens, while the thrush
Began calm-throated. Throughout all the isle
There was no covert, no retired cave
Unhaunted by the murmurous noise of waves,   40
Though scarcely heard in many a green recess.
He listened, and he wept, and his bright tears
Went trickling down the golden bow he held.
Thus with half-shut suffused eyes he stood,
While from beneath some cumbrous boughs hard by
With solemn step an awful Goddess [27] came,
And there was purport in her looks for him,
Which he with eager guess began to read
Perplex'd, the while melodiously he said:
'How cam'st thou over the unfooted sea?   50
'Or hath that antique mien and robed form
'Mov'd in these vales invisible till now?
'Sure I have heard those vestments sweeping o'er
'The fallen leaves, when I have sat alone
'In cool mid-forest. Surely I have traced
'The rustle of those ample skirts about
'These grassy solitudes, and seen the flowers

[24] Where Apollo was born.
[25] Hyperion.
[26] Latona and Diana.
[27] Mnemosyne, mother of the Muses.

'Lift up their heads, as still the whisper pass'd.
'Goddess! I have beheld those eyes before,
'And their eternal calm, and all that face,   60
'Or I have dream'd.'—'Yes,' said the supreme shape,
'Thou hast dream'd of me; and awaking up
'Didst find a lyre all golden by thy side,
'Whose strings touch'd by thy fingers, all the vast
'Unwearied ear of the whole universe
'Listen'd in pain and pleasure at the birth
'Of such new tuneful wonder. Is't not strange
'That thou shouldst weep, so gifted? Tell me, youth,
'What sorrow thou canst feel; for I am sad
'When thou dost shed a tear: explain thy griefs   70
'To one who in this lonely isle hath been
'The watcher of thy sleep and hours of life,
'From the young day when first thy infant hand
'Pluck'd witless the weak flowers, till thine arm
'Could bend that bow heroic to all times.
'Show thy heart's secret to an ancient Power
'Who hath forsaken old and sacred thrones
'For prophecies of thee, and for the sake
'Of loveliness new born.'—Apollo then,
With sudden scrutiny and gloomless eyes,   80
Thus answer'd, while his white melodious throat
Throbb'd with the syllables.—'Mnemosyne!
'Thy name is on my tongue, I know not how;
'Why should I tell thee what thou so well seest?
'Why should I strive to show what from thy lips
'Would come no mystery? For me, dark, dark,
'And painful vile oblivion seals my eyes:
'I strive to search wherefore I am so sad,
'Until a melancholy numbs my limbs:
'And then upon the grass I sit, and moan,   90
'Like one who once had wings.—O why should I
'Feel curs'd and thwarted, when the liegeless air
'Yields to my step aspirant? why should I
'Spurn the green turf as hateful to my feet?
'Goddess benign, point forth some unknown thing:
'Are there not other regions than this isle?
'What are the stars? There is the sun, the sun!
'And the most patient brilliance of the moon!
'And stars by thousands! Point me out the way
'To any one particular beauteous star,   100
'And I will flit into it with my lyre,
'And make its silvery splendour pant with bliss.
'I have heard the cloudy thunder: Where is power?
'Whose hand, whose essence, what divinity
'Makes this alarum in the elements,
'While I here idle listen on the shores
'In fearless yet in aching ignorance?
'O tell me, lonely Goddess, by thy harp,
'That waileth every morn and eventide,
'Tell me why thus I rave, about these groves!   110
'Mute thou remainest—Mute! yet I can read

'A wondrous lesson in thy silent face:
'Knowledge enormous makes a God of me.
'Names, deeds, gray legends, dire events, rebellions,
'Majesties, sovran voices, agonies,
'Creations and destroyings, all at once
'Pour into the wide hollows of my brain,
'And deify me, as if some blithe wine
'Or bright elixir peerless I had drunk,
'And so become immortal.'—Thus the God,   120
While his enkindled eyes, with level glance
Beneath his white soft temples, stedfast kept
Trembling with light upon Mnemosyne.
Soon wild commotions shook him, and made flush
All the immortal fairness of his limbs;
Most like the struggle at the gate of death;
Or liker still to one who should take leave
Of pale immortal death, and with a pang
As hot as death's is chill, with fierce convulse
Die into life: so young Apollo anguish'd: 130
His very hair, his golden tresses famed
Kept undulation round his eager neck.
During the pain Mnemosyne upheld
Her arms as one who prophesied.—At length
Apollo shriek'd;—and lo! from all his limbs
Celestial   *   *   *   *   *   *

  *   *   *   *   *   *   *   *

THE END

[1818-19]   [1820]

THE EVE OF ST. AGNES

Burton's Anatomy of Melancholy, *which Keats read diligently, alludes to the superstition that a maiden may, by fasting on St. Agnes' Eve (January 20), expect to dream of her husband or first lover. He apparently derived many of the details of the ritual from John Brand's* Popular Antiquities *(1777).*

THE EVE OF ST. AGNES

I

St. Agnes' Eve—Ah, bitter chill it was!
The owl, for all his feathers, was a-cold;
The hare limp'd trembling through the frozen grass,
And silent was the flock in woolly fold:
Numb were the Beadsman's fingers, while he told
His rosary, and while his frosted breath,
Like pious incense from a censer old,
Seem'd taking flight for heaven, without a death,
Past the sweet Virgin's picture, while his prayer he
   saith.

II

His prayer he saith, this patient, holy man;   10
Then takes his lamp, and riseth from his knees,
And back returneth, meagre, barefoot, wan,
Along the chapel aisle by slow degrees:
The sculptur'd dead, on each side, seem to freeze,
Emprison'd in black, purgatorial rails:
Knights, ladies, praying in dumb orat'ries,
He passeth by; and his weak spirit fails
To think how they may ache in icy hoods and mails.

III

Northward he turneth through a little door,
And scarce three steps, ere Music's golden tongue
Flatter'd to tears this aged man and poor;   21
But no—already had his deathbell rung;
The joys of all his life were said and sung:
His was harsh penance on St. Agnes' Eve:
Another way he went, and soon among
Rough ashes sat he for his soul's reprieve,
And all night kept awake, for sinners' sake to grieve.

IV

That ancient Beadsman heard the prelude soft;
And so it chanc'd, for many a door was wide,
From hurry to and fro. Soon, up aloft,   30
The silver, snarling trumpets 'gan to chide:
The level chambers, ready with their pride,
Were glowing to receive a thousand guests:
The carved angels, ever eager-eyed,
Star'd, where upon their heads the cornice rests,
With hair blown back, and wings put cross-wise on
   their breasts.

V

At length burst in the argent revelry,
With plume, tiara, and all rich array,
Numerous as shadows haunting fairily
The brain, new stuff'd, in youth, with triumphs gay
Of old romance. These let us wish away,   41
And turn, sole-thoughted, to one Lady there,
Whose heart had brooded, all that wintry day,
On love, and wing'd St. Agnes' saintly care,
As she had heard old dames full many times declare.

VI

They told her how, upon St. Agnes' Eve,
Young virgins might have visions of delight,
And soft adorings from their loves receive
Upon the honey'd middle of the night,
If ceremonies due they did aright;   50
As, supperless to bed they must retire,
And couch supine their beauties, lily white;
Nor look behind, nor sideways, but require
Of Heaven with upward eyes for all that they desire.

VII

Full of this whim was thoughtful Madeline:
The music, yearning like a God in pain,
She scarcely heard: her maiden eyes divine,
Fix'd on the floor, saw many a sweeping train
Pass by—she heeded not at all: in vain
Came many a tiptoe, amorous cavalier,   60
And back retir'd; not cool'd by high disdain,
But she saw not: her heart was otherwhere:
She sigh'd for Agnes' dreams, the sweetest of the year.

VIII

She danc'd along with vague, regardless eyes,
Anxious her lips, her breathing quick and short:
The hallow'd hour was near at hand: she sighs
Amid the timbrels, and the throng'd resort
Of whisperers in anger, or in sport;
'Mid looks of love, defiance, hate, and scorn,
Hoodwink'd with faery fancy; all amort,   70
Save to St. Agnes and her lambs unshorn,
And all the bliss to be before to-morrow morn.

IX

So, purposing each moment to retire,
She linger'd still. Meantime, across the moors,
Had come young Porphyro,[1] with heart on fire
For Madeline. Beside the portal doors,
Buttress'd from moonlight, stands he, and implores
All saints to give him sight of Madeline,
But for one moment in the tedious hours,
That he might gaze and worship all unseen;   80
Perchance speak, kneel, touch, kiss—in sooth such
        things have been.

X

He ventures in: let not buzz'd whisper tell:
All eyes be muffled, or a hundred swords
Will storm his heart, Love's fev'rous citadel:
For him, those chambers held barbarian hordes,
Hyena foemen, and hot-blooded lords,
Whose very dogs would execrations howl
Against his lineage: not one breast affords
Him any mercy, in that mansion foul,
Save one old beldame,[2] weak in body and in soul.   90

XI

Ah, happy chance! the aged creature came,
Shuffling along with ivory-headed wand,
To where he stood, hid from the torch's flame,
Behind a broad hall-pillar, far beyond

The sound of merriment and chorus bland:
He startled her; but soon she knew his face,
And grasp'd his fingers in her palsied hand,
Saying, 'Mercy, Porphyro! hie thee from this place;
'Thy are all here to-night, the whole blood-thirsty
        race!

XII

'Get hence! get hence! there's dwarfish Hildebrand;
'He had a fever late, and in the fit   101
'He cursed thee and thine, both house and land:
'Then there's that old Lord Maurice, not a whit
'More tame for his gray hairs—Alas me! flit!
'Flit like a ghost away.'—'Ah, Gossip dear,
'We're safe enough; here in this arm-chair sit,
'And tell me how'—'Good Saints! not here, not
'Follow me, child, or else these stones will be   [here;
        thy bier.'

XIII

He follow'd through a lowly arched way,
Brushing the cobwebs with his lofty plume,   110
And as she mutter'd 'Well-a—well-a-day!'
He found him in a little moonlight room,
Pale, lattic'd, chill, and silent as a tomb.
'Now tell me where is Madeline,' said he,
'O tell me, Angela, by the holy loom
'Which none but secret sisterhood may see,
When they St. Agnes' wool are weaving piously.'

XIV

'St. Agnes! Ah! it is St. Agnes' Eve—
'Yet men will murder upon holy days:
'Thou must hold water in a witch's sieve,   120
'And be liege-lord of all the Elves and Fays,
'To venture so: it fills me with amaze
'To see thee, Porphyro!—St. Agnes' Eve!
'God's help! my lady fair the conjuror plays
'This very night: good angels her deceive!
'But let me laugh awhile, I've mickle time to grieve.'

XV

Feebly she laugheth in the languid moon,
While Porphyro upon her face doth look,
Like puzzled urchin on an aged crone
Who keepeth clos'd a wond'rous riddle-book,   130
As spectacled she sits in chimney nook.
But soon his eyes grew brilliant, when she told
His lady's purpose; and he scarce could brook
Tears, at the thought of those enchantments cold
And Madeline asleep in lap of legends old.

XVI

Sudden a thought came like a full-blown rose,
Flushing his brow, and in his pained heart
Made purple riot: then doth he propose
A stratagem, that makes the beldame start:

---

[1] The name, perhaps from Burton, means "nobly born."
[2] Conventional sixteenth-century term for a nurse.

'A cruel man and impious thou art: 140
'Sweet lady, let her pray, and sleep, and dream
'Alone with her good angels, far apart
'From wicked men like thee. Go, go!—I deem
'Thou canst not surely be the same that thou didst
        seem.'

XVII

'I will not harm her, by all saints I swear,'
Quoth Porphyro: 'O may I ne'er find grace
'When my weak voice shall whisper its last prayer,
'If one of her soft ringlets I displace,
'Or look with ruffian passion in her face:
'Good Angela, believe me by these tears;   150
'Or I will, even in a moment's space,
'Awake, with horrid shout, my foemen's ears,
'And beard them, though they be more fang'd than
        wolves and bears.'

XVIII

'Ah! why wilt thou affright a feeble soul?
'A poor, weak, palsy-stricken, churchyard thing,
'Whose passing-bell may ere the midnight toll;
'Whose prayers for thee, each morn and evening,
'Were never miss'd.'—Thus plaining, doth she
A gentler speech from burning Porphyro;   [bring
So woful, and of such deep sorrowing,   160
That Angela gives promise she will do
Whatever he shall wish, betide her weal or woe.

XIX

Which was, to lead him, in close secrecy,
Even to Madeline's chamber, and there hide
Him in a closet, of such privacy
That he might see her beauty unespied,
And win perhaps that night a peerless bride,
While legion'd fairies pac'd the coverlet,
And pale enchantment held her sleepy-eyed.
Never on such a night have lovers met,   170
Since Merlin paid his Demon all the monstrous debt.

XX

'It shall be as thou wishest,' said the Dame:
'All cates and dainties shall be stored there
'Quickly on this feast-night: by the tambour frame [3]
'Her own lute thou wilt see: no time to spare,
'For I am slow and feeble, and scarce dare
'On such a catering trust my dizzy head.
'Wait here, my child, with patience; kneel in prayer
'The while: Ah! thou must needs the lady wed,
'Or may I never leave my grave among the dead.' 180

‹◇◇◇◇◇◇◇◇◇◇◇◇◇◇◇◇◇◇◇◇◇◇◇◇◇›
[3] For embroidery.

XXI

So saying, she hobbled off with busy fear.
The lover's endless minutes slowly pass'd;
The dame return'd, and whisper'd in his ear
To follow her; with aged eyes aghast
From fright of dim espial. Safe at last,
Through many a dusky gallery, they gain
The maiden's chamber, silken, hush'd, and chaste;
Where Porphyro took covert, pleas'd amain.
His poor guide hurried back with agues in her brain.

XXII

Her falt'ring hand upon the balustrade,   190
Old Angela was feeling for the stair,
When Madeline, St. Agnes' charmed maid,
Rose, like a mission'd spirit, unaware:
With silver taper's light, and pious care,
She turn'd, and down the aged gossip led
To a safe level matting. Now prepare,
Young Porphyro, for gazing on that bed;
She comes, she comes again, like ring-dove fray'd and
        fled.

XXIII

Out went the taper as she hurried in;
Its little smoke, in pallid moonshine, died: 200
She clos'd the door, she panted, all akin
To spirits of the air, and visions wide:
No uttered syllable, or, woe betide!
But to her heart, her heart was voluble,
Paining with eloquence her balmy side;
As though a tongueless nightingale should swell
Her throat in vain, and die, heart-stifled, in her dell.

XXIV

A casement high and triple-arch'd there was,
All garlanded with carven imag'ries
Of fruits, and flowers, and bunches of knot-grass,
And diamonded with panes of quaint device,   211
Innumerable of stains and splendid dyes,
As are the tiger-moth's deep-damask'd wings;
And in the midst, 'mong thousand heraldries,
And twilight saints, and dim emblazonings,
A shielded scutcheon blush'd with blood of queens
        and kings.

XXV

Full on this casement shone the wintry moon,
And threw warm gules on Madeline's fair breast,
As down she knelt for heaven's grace and boon;
Rose-bloom fell on her hands, together prest,   220
And on her silver cross soft amethyst,
And on her hair a glory, like a saint:
She seem'd a splendid angel, newly drest,
Save wings, for heaven:—Porphyro grew faint:
She knelt, so pure a thing, so free from mortal taint.

XXVI

Anon his heart revives: her vespers done,
Of all its wreathed pearls her hair she frees;
Unclasps her warmed jewels one by one;
Loosens her fragrant boddice; by degrees
Her rich attire creeps rustling to her knees: 230
Half-hidden, like a mermaid in sea-weed,
Pensive awhile she dreams awake, and sees,
In fancy, fair St. Agnes in her bed,
But dares not look behind, or all the charm is fled.

XXVII

Soon, trembling in her soft and chilly nest,
In sort of wakeful swoon, perplex'd she lay,
Until the poppied warmth of sleep oppress'd
Her soothed limbs, and soul fatigued away;
Flown, like a thought, until the morrow-day;
Blissfully haven'd both from joy and pain;   240
Clasp'd like a missal where swart Paynims pray; [4]
Blinded alike from sunshine and from rain,
As though a rose should shut, and be a bud again.

XXVIII

Stol'n to this paradise, and so entranced,
Porphyro gazed upon her empty dress,
And listen'd to her breathing, if it chanced
To wake into a slumberous tenderness;
Which when he heard, that minute did he bless,
And breath'd himself: then from the closet crept,
Noiseless as fear in a wide wilderness,   250
And over the hush'd carpet, silent, stept,
And 'tween the curtains peep'd, where, lo!—how fast
    she slept.

XXIX

Then by the bed-side, where the faded moon
Made a dim, silver twilight, soft he set
A table, and, half anguish'd, threw thereon
A cloth of woven crimson, gold, and jet:—
O for some drowsy Morphean amulet!
The boisterous, midnight, festive clarion,
The kettle-drum, and far-heard clarionet,
Affray his ears, though but in dying tone:—   260
The hall door shuts again, and all the noise is gone.

XXX

And still she slept an azure-lidded sleep,
In blanched linen, smooth, and lavender'd,
While he from forth the closet brought a heap
Of candied apple, quince, and plum, and gourd
With jellies soother than the creamy curd,

---

[4] A paynim is a pagan, but the term has often been used to refer to a Moslem. "Clasp'd," then, may mean shut and not used, or held protectively.

And lucent syrops, tinct with cinnamon;
Manna and dates, in argosy transferr'd
From Fez; and spiced dainties, every one,
From silken Samarcand to cedar'd Lebanon.   270

XXXI

These delicates he heap'd with glowing hand
On golden dishes and in baskets bright
Of wreathed silver: sumptuous they stand
In the retired quiet of the night,
Filling the chilly room with perfume light.—
'And now, my love, my seraph fair, awake!
'Thou art my heaven, and I thine eremite:
'Open thine eyes, for meek St. Agnes' sake,
'Or I shall drowse beside thee, so my soul doth ache.'

XXXII

Thus whispering, his warm, unnerved arm   280
Sank in her pillow. Shaded was her dream
By the dusk curtains:—'twas a midnight charm
Impossible to melt as iced stream:
The lustrous salvers in the moonlight gleam;
Broad golden fringe upon the carpet lies:
It seem'd he never, never could redeem
From such a stedfast spell his lady's eyes;
So mus'd awhile, entoil'd in woofed phantasies.

XXXIII

Awakening up, he took her hollow lute,—
Tumultuous,—and, in chords that tenderest be,
He play'd an ancient ditty, long since mute,   291
In Provence call'd, 'La belle dame sans mercy:'
Close to her ear touching the melody;—
Wherewith disturb'd, she utter'd a soft moan:
He ceased—she panted quick—and suddenly
Her blue affrayed eyes wide open shone:
Upon his knees he sank, pale as smooth-sculptured
    stone.

XXXIV

Her eyes were open, but she still beheld,
Now wide awake, the vision of her sleep:
There was a painful change, that nigh expell'd   300
The blisses of her dream so pure and deep
At which fair Madeline began to weep,
And moan forth witless words with many a sigh;
While still her gaze on Porphyro would keep;
Who knelt, with joined hands and piteous eye,
Fearing to move or speak, she look'd so dreamingly.

XXXV

'Ah, Porphyro!' said she, 'but even now
'Thy voice was at sweet tremble in mine ear,
'Made tuneable with every sweetest vow;   310
'And those sad eyes were spiritual and clear:

'How chang'd thou art! how pallid, chill, and drear!
'Give me that voice again, my Porphyro,
'Those looks immortal, those complainings dear!
'Oh leave me not in this eternal woe,
'For if thou diest, my Love, I know not where to go.'⁵

XXXVI

Beyond a mortal man impassion'd far
At these voluptuous accents, he arose,
Ethereal, flush'd, and like a throbbing star
Seen mid the sapphire heaven's deep repose
Into her dream he melted, as the rose   320
Blendeth its odour with the violet,—
Solution sweet: meantime the frost-wind blows
Like Love's alarum pattering the sharp sleet
Against the window-panes; St. Agnes' moon hath set.

XXXVII

'Tis dark: quick pattereth the flaw-blown sleet:
'This is no dream, my bride, my Madeline!'
'Tis dark: the iced gusts still rave and beat:
'No dream, alas! alas! and woe is mine!
'Porphyro will leave me here to fade and pine.—
'Cruel! what traitor could thee hither bring?   330
'I curse not, for my heart is lost in thine
'Though thou forsakest a deceived thing;—
'A dove forlorn and lost with sick unpruned wing.'

XXXVIII

'My Madeline! sweet dreamer! lovely bride!
'Say, may I be for aye thy vassal blest?
'Thy beauty's shield, heart-shap'd and vermeil
'Ah, silver shrine, here will I take my rest   [dyed?
'After so many hours of toil and quest,
'A famish'd pilgrim,—saved by miracle.
'Though I have found, I will not rob thy nest   340
'Saving of thy sweet self; if thou think'st well
'To trust, fair Madeline, to no rude infidel.'

XXXIX

'Hark! 'tis an elfin-storm from faery land,
'Of haggard seeming, but a boon indeed:
'Arise—arise! the morning is at hand;—
'The bloated wassaillers will never heed:—
'Let us away, my love, with happy speed;
'There are no ears to hear, or eyes to see,—
'Drown'd all in Rhenish and the sleepy mead:
'Awake! arise! my love, and fearless be,   350
'For o'er the southern moors I have a home for thee.'

⁵ The last two lines of this stanza, removed as too expicitly sexual, once read:

So while she speaks his arms encroaching slow
  Have zon'd her, heart to heart—loud the dark winds blow.—

XL

She hurried at his words, beset with fears,
For there were sleeping dragons all around,
At glaring watch, perhaps, with ready spears—
Down the wide stairs a darkling way they found.—
In all the house was heard no human sound.
A chain-droop'd lamp was flickering by each door;
The arras, rich with horseman, hawk, and hound,
Flutter'd in the besieging wind's uproar;
And the long carpets rose along the gusty floor.   360

XLI

They glide, like phantoms, into the wide hall;
Like phantoms, to the iron porch, they glide;
Where lay the Porter, in uneasy sprawl,
With a huge empty flaggon by his side:
The wakeful bloodhound rose, and shook his hide,
But his sagacious eye an inmate owns:
By one, and one, the bolts full easy slide:—
The chains lie silent on the footworn stones;—
The key turns, and the door upon its hinges groans.

XLII

And they are gone: ay, ages long ago   370
These lovers fled away into the storm.
That night the Baron dreamt of many a woe,
And all his warrior-guests, with shade and form
Of witch, and demon, and large coffin-worm,
Were long be-nightmar'd. Angela the old
Died palsy-twitch'd, with meagre face deform;
The Beadsman, after thousand aves told,
For aye unsought for slept among his ashes cold.

[1819]   [1820]

THE EVE OF SAINT MARK

*A superstition similar to that for St. Agnes's Eve held that a
person standing near the church door at twilight on April 24
would have a vision indicating which members of the parish
would be ill during the following year, and which of these would
survive.*

THE EVE OF SAINT MARK

UPON a Sabbath-day it fell;
Twice holy was the Sabbath-bell,
That call'd the folk to evening prayer;
The city streets were clean and fair
From wholesome drench of April rains;
And, on the western window panes,
The chilly sunset faintly told
Of unmatured green vallies cold,

Of the green thorny bloomless hedge,
Of rivers new with spring-tide sedge, 10
Of primroses by shelter'd rills,
And daisies on the aguish hills.
Twice holy was the Sabbath-bell:
The silent streets were crowded well
With staid and pious companies,
Warm from their fire-side orat'ries;
And moving, with demurest air,
To even-song, and vesper prayer.
Each arched porch, and entry low,
Was fill'd with patient folk and slow, 20
With whispers hush, and shuffling feet,
While play'd the organ loud and sweet.

The bells had ceased, the prayers begun,
And Bertha had not yet half done
A curious volume, patch'd and torn,
That all day long, from earliest morn,
Had taken captive her two eyes,
Among its golden broideries;
Perplex'd her with a thousand things,—
The stars of Heaven, and angels' wings, 30
Martyrs in a fiery blaze,
Azure saints in silver rays,
Aaron's breastplate, and the seven
Candlesticks John saw in Heaven,
The winged Lion of Saint Mark,
And the Covenantal Ark,
With its many mysteries,
Cherubim and golden mice.[1]

Bertha was a maiden fair,
Dwelling in the old Minster-square; 40
From her fire-side she could see,
Sidelong, its rich antiquity,
Far as the Bishop's garden-wall;
Where sycamores and elm-trees tall,
Full-leaved, the forest had outstript,
By no sharp north-wind ever nipt,
So shelter'd by the mighty pile.
Bertha arose, and read awhile,
With forehead 'gainst the window-pane.
Again she tried, and then again, 50
Until the dusk eve left her dark
Upon the legend of St. Mark.
From plaited lawn-frill, fine and thin,
She lifted up her soft warm chin,
With aching neck and swimming eyes,
And dazed with saintly imag'ries.

All was gloom, and silent all,
Save now and then the still foot-fall
Of one returning homewards late,
Past the echoing minster-gate. 60

The clamorous daws, that all the day
Above tree-tops and towers play,
Pair by pair had gone to rest,
Each in its ancient belfry-nest,
Where asleep they fall betimes,
To music of the drowsy chimes.

All was silent, all was gloom,
Abroad and in the homely room:
Down she sat, poor cheated soul!
And struck a lamp from the dismal coal; 70
Leaned forward, with bright drooping hair
And slant book, full against the glare.
Her shadow, in uneasy guise,
Hover'd about, a giant size,
On ceiling-beam and old oak chair,
The parrot's cage, and panel square;
And the warm angled winter screen,
On which were many monsters seen,
Call'd doves of Siam, Lima mice,
And legless birds of Paradise, 80
Macaw, and tender Av'davat,[2]
And silken-furr'd Angora cat.
Untired she read, her shadow still
Glower'd about, as it would fill
The room with wildest forms and shades,
As though some ghostly queen of spades[3]
Had come to mock behind her back,
And dance, and ruffle her garments black.
Untired she read the legend page,
Of holy Mark, from youth to age, 90
On land, on sea, in pagan chains,
Rejoicing for his many pains.
Sometimes the learned eremite,
With golden star, or dagger bright,[4]
Referr'd to pious poesies
Written in smallest crow-quill size
Beneath the text; and thus the rhyme
Was parcell'd out from time to time:

'Gif ye wol stonden hardie wight—
Amiddes of the blacke night— 100
Righte in the churche porch, pardie
Ye wol behold a companie
Approchen thee full dolourouse
For sooth to sain from everich house

---

[1] The biblical passages alluded to in these lines include Lev. 8:8 (Aaron's breastplate); Rev. 1:20 and 4:6–9 (the candlesticks and the lion); Heb. 9:1–5 (the ark of the covenant); and I Sam., 6:4 (the five golden mice).

[2] Indian songbird.
[3] The traditional death card in fortune-telling.
[4] Signs for footnotes, as used for author's notes in this text.

Be it in City or village
Wol come the Phantom and image
Of ilka gent and ilka carle
Whom coldè Deathè hath in parle
And wol some day that very year
Touchen with foulè venìme spear   110
And sadly do them all to die—
Hem all shalt thou see verilie—
And everichon shall be the(e) pass
All who must die that year Alas
——Als writith he of swevenis,
Men han beforne they wake in bliss,
Whanne that hir friendes thinke hem bound
In crimpede shroude farre under grounde;
And how a litling child mote be
A saint er its nativitie,   120
Gif that the modre (God her blesse!)
Kepen in solitarinesse,
And kissen devoute the holy croce,
Of Goddes love, and Sathan's force—
He writith; and thinges many mo:
Of swiche thinges I may not show.
Bot I must tellen verilie
Somdel of Saintè Cicilie,
And cheiflie what he auctorethe
Of Saintè Markis life and dethe:'   130

At length her constant eyelids come
Upon the fervent martyrdom;
Then lastly to his holy shrine,
Exalt amid the tapers' shine
At Venice,—

[1819]   [1848; 1926]

[Sonnet]
"Why did I laugh tonight? . . ."

WHY did I laugh to-night? No voice will tell:
  No God, no Demon of severe response,
Deigns to reply from Heaven or from Hell.
  Then to my human heart I turn at once.
Heart! Thou and I are here sad and alone;
  Say, wherefore did I laugh? O mortal pain!
O Darkness! Darkness! ever must I moan,
  To question Heaven and Hell and Heart in vain.
Why did I laugh? I know this Being's lease,
  My fancy to its utmost blisses spreads;   10
Yet could I on this very midnight cease,
  And the world's gaudy ensigns see in shreds;
Verse, Fame, and Beauty are intense indeed,
But Death's intenser—Death is Life's high meed.

[1819]   [1848]

Charles Brown (1787–1842), merchant, then playwright and man of letters, was closely associated with Keats from 1817 until Keats left for Rome. Brown accompanied him on the Scottish walking tour in 1818; the two lived together at Wentworth Place, Hampstead, and collaborated in the writing of Otho the Great.
  The poem is deliberately written "in the manner of Spenser." See also Wordsworth's Stanzas Written in My Pocket-copy of Thomson's "Castle of Indolence," *p. 265.*

CHARACTER OF CHARLES BROWN

I

HE is to weet a melancholy carle.[1]
Thin in the waist, with bushy head of hair,
As hath the seeded thistle when in parle[2]
It holds the Zephyr, ere it sendeth fair
Its light balloons into the summer air;
Thereto his beard had not begun to bloom,
No brush had touch'd his chin or razor sheer;
No care had touch'd his cheek with mortal doom,
But new he was and bright as scarf from Persian loom.

II

Ne cared he for wine, or half-and-half;   10
Ne cared he for fish or flesh or fowl,
And sauces held he worthless as the chaff;
He's deigned the swine-head at the wassail-bowl;
Ne with lewd ribbalds sat he cheek by jowl;
Ne with sly lemans[3] in the scorner's chair;
But after water-brooks this Pilgrim's soul
Panted, and all his food was woodland air
Though he would oft-times feast on gilliflowers rare.

III

The slang of cities in no wise he knew,
Tipping the wink to him was heathen Greek;   20
He sipp'd no olden Tom or ruin blue,[4]
Or nantz[5] or cheery-brandy drank full meek
By many a damsel hoarse and rouge of cheek;
Nor did he know each aged watchman's beat,
Nor in obscured purlieus would he seek
For curled Jewesses, with ankles neat,
Who as they walk abroad make tinkling with their feet.

[1819]   [1848]

---

[1] Knave.
[2] Discourse.
[3] Lovers.
[4] Types of gin.
[5] Brandy from Nantes.

LA BELLE DAME SANS MERCI

*A later version of this poem, perhaps revised with the help of
Leigh Hunt, appeared in the* Indicator *in May 1820. It is
generally considered inferior to the original version.*

LA BELLE DAME SANS MERCI
A BALLAD

I

O WHAT can ail thee, knight-at-arms,
   Alone and palely loitering?
The sedge has wither'd from the lake,
   And no birds sing.

II

O what can ail thee, knight-at-arms,
   So haggard and so woe-begone?
The squirrel's granary is full,
   And the harvest's done.

III

I see a lilly on thy brow,
   With anguish moist and fever dew,   10
And on thy cheeks a fading rose
   Fast withereth too.

IV

I met a lady in the meads,
   Full beautiful—a faery's child,
Her hair was long, her foot was light,
   And her eyes were wild.

V

I made a garland for her head,
   And bracelets too, and fragrant zone;[1]
She look'd at me as she did love,
   And made sweet moan.   20

VI

I set her on my pacing steed,
   And nothing else saw all day long,
For sidelong would she bend, and sing
   A faery's song.

VII

She found me roots of relish sweet,
   And honey wild, and manna dew,
And sure in language strange she said—
   'I love thee true'.

VIII

She took me to her elfin grot,
   And there she wept, and sigh'd full sore,   30
And there I shut her wild wild eyes
   With kisses four.

IX

And there she lulled me asleep,
   And there I dream'd—Ah! woe betide!
The latest dream I ever dream'd
   On the cold hill side.

X

I saw pale kings and princes too,
   Pale warriors, death-pale were they all;
They cried—'La Belle Dame sans Merci
   Hath thee in thrall!'   40

XI

I saw their starved lips in the gloam,
   With horrid warning gaped wide,
And I awoke and found me here,
   On the cold hill's side.

XII

And this is why I sojourn here,
   Alone and palely loitering,
Though the sedge is wither'd from the lake,
   And no birds sing.

[1819]   [1820; 1848]

[Sonnet]
TO SLEEP

O SOFT embalmer of the still midnight,
   Shutting, with careful fingers and benign,
Our gloom-pleas'd eyes, embower'd from the light,
   Enshaded in forgetfulness divine;
O soothest Sleep! if so it please thee, close,
   In midst of this thine hymn, my willing eyes,
Or wait the amen, ere thy poppy throws
   Around my bed its lulling charities;
Then save me, or the passed day will shine
Upon my pillow, breeding many woes;   10
   Save me from curious conscience, that still hoards
Its strength for darkness, burrowing like a mole;
   Turn the key deftly in the oiled wards,
And seal the hushed casket of my soul.

[1819]   [1838]

---

[1] I.e., girdle of flowers.

[Sonnet]
ON FAME [I]

FAME, like a wayward girl, will still be coy
  To those who woo her with too slavish knees,
But makes surrender to some thoughtless boy,
  And dotes the more upon a heart at ease;
She is a Gipsey, will not speak to those
  Who have not learnt to be content without her;
A Jilt, whose ear was never whisper'd close,
  Who thinks they scandal her who talk about her;
A very Gipsey is she, Nilus-born,[1]
  Sister-in-law to jealous Potiphar;   10
Ye love-sick Bards! repay her scorn for scorn;
  Ye lovelorn Artists! madmen that ye are!
Make your best bow to her and bid adieu,
Then, if she likes it, she will follow you.

[1819]   [1837]

[Sonnet]
ON FAME [II]

'You cannot eat your cake and have it too.'—*Proverb*.

HOW fever'd is the man, who cannot look
  Upon his mortal days with temperate blood,
Who vexes all the leaves of his life's book,
  And robs his fair name of its maidenhood;
It is as if the rose should pluck herself,
  Or the ripe plum finger its misty bloom,
As if a Naiad, like a meddling elf,
  Should darken her pure grot with muddy gloom:
But the rose leaves herself upon the briar,
  For winds to kiss and grateful bees to feed,   10
And the ripe plum still wears its dim attire,
  The undisturbed lake has crystal space;
Why then should man, teasing the world for grace,
Spoil his salvation for a fierce miscreed?

[1819]   [1848]

[Sonnet]
[On the Sonnet]

IF by dull rhymes our English must be chain'd,
And, like Andromeda,[2] the Sonnet sweet
Fetter'd, in spite of pained loveliness;
Let us find out, if we must be constrain'd,

---

[1] Gypsies were thought to have come from Egypt; Potiphar was jealous of Joseph because his wife was attracted to him: Gen. 39.
[2] She was chained to a rock for praising her own beauty.

Sandals more interwoven and complete
To fit the naked foot of poesy:
Let us inspect the lyre, and weigh the stress
Of every chord, and see what may be gain'd
By ear industrious, and attention meet;
Misers of sound and syllable, no less   10
Than Midas[3] of his coinage, let us be
Jealous of dead leaves in the bay wreath crown;
So, if we may not let the Muse be free,
She will be bound with garlands of her own.

[1819]   [1848]

ODE TO PSYCHE
Psyche is the personification of the human soul, usually represented as a butterfly, who is loved by Eros and pursued by him, and united with him, in a variety of ways, in several legends.

ODE TO PSYCHE

O GODDESS! hear these tuneless numbers, wrung
  By sweet enforcement and remembrance dear,
And pardon that thy secrets should be sung
  Even into thine own soft-conched ear:
Surely I dreamt to-day, or did I see
  The winged Psyche with awaken'd eyes?
I wander'd in a forest thoughtlessly,
  And, on the sudden, fainting with surprise,
Saw two fair creatures, couched side by side
  In deepest grass, beneath the whisp'ring roof   10
Of leaves and trembled blossoms, where there ran
    A brooklet, scarce espied:
'Mid hush'd, cool-rooted flowers, fragrant-eyed,
  Blue, silver-white, and budded Tyrian,
They lay calm-breathing on the bedded grass;
  Their arms embraced, and their pinions too;
  Their lips touch'd not, but had not bid adieu,
As if disjoined by soft-handed slumber,
And ready still past kisses to outnumber
  At tender eye-dawn of aurorean love: 20
    The winged boy I knew;
But who wast thou, O happy, happy dove?
    His Psyche true!

O latest born and loveliest vision far
  Of all Olympus' faded hierarchy!
Fairer than Phœbe's sapphire-region'd star,
  Or Vesper, amorous glow-worm of the sky;

---

[3] The king to whom Bacchus gave the power of turning all he touched to gold.

Fairer than these, though temple thou hast none,
    Nor altar heap'd with flowers;
Nor virgin-choir to make delicious moan   30
    Upon the midnight hours;
No voice, no lute, no pipe, no incense sweet
    From chain-swung censer teeming;
No shrine, no grove, no oracle, no heat
    Of pale-mouth'd prophet dreaming.

O brightest! though too late for antique vows,
    Too, too late for the fond believing lyre,
When holy were the haunted forest boughs,
    Holy the air, the water, and the fire;
Yet even in these days so far retir'd   40
    From happy pieties, thy lucent fans,[1]
    Fluttering among the faint Olympians,
I see, and sing, by my own eyes inspired.
So let me be thy choir, and make a moan
    Upon the midnight hours;
Thy voice, thy lute, thy pipe, thy incense sweet
    From swinged censer teeming;
Thy shrine, thy grove, thy oracle, thy heat
    Of pale-mouth'd prophet dreaming.

Yes, I will be thy priest, and build a fane   50
    In some untrodden region of my mind,
Where branched thoughts, new grown with pleasant
        pain,
    Instead of pines shall murmur in the wind:
Far, far around shall those dark-cluster'd trees
    Fledge the wild-ridged mountains steep by steep;
And there by zephyrs, streams, and birds, and bees,
    The moss-lain Dryads shall be lull'd to sleep;
And in the midst of this wide quietness
A rosy sanctuary will I dress
With the wreath'd trellis of a working brain,   60
    With buds, and bells, and stars without a name,
With all the gardener Fancy e'er could feign,
    Who breeding flowers, will never breed the same:
And there shall be for thee all soft delight
    That shadowy thought can win,
A bright torch, and a casement ope at night,[2]
    To let the warm Love in!

[1819]   [1820]

ODE TO A NIGHTINGALE

1

MY heart aches, and a drowsy numbness pains
    My sense, as though of hemlock I had drunk,
Or emptied some dull opiate to the drains
    One minute past, and Lethe-wards had sunk:
'Tis not through envy of thy happy lot,
    But being too happy in thine happiness,—
        That thou, light-winged Dryad of the trees,
            In some melodious plot
Of beechen green, and shadows numberless,
    Singest of summer in full-throated ease.   10

2

O, for a draught of vintage! that hath been
    Cool'd a long age in the deep-delved earth,
Tasting of Flora and the country green,
    Dance, and Provençal song, and sunburnt mirth!
O for a beaker full of the warm South,
    Full of the true, the blushful Hippocrene,[1]
        With beaded bubbles winking at the brim,
            And purple-stained mouth;
That I might drink, and leave the world unseen,
    And with thee fade away into the forest dim: 20

3

Fade far away, dissolve, and quite forget
    What thou among the leaves hast never known,
The weariness, the fever, and the fret
    Here, where men sit and hear each other groan;
Where palsy shakes a few, sad, last gray hairs,
    Where youth grows pale, and spectre-thin, and dies;
        Where but to think is to be full of sorrow
            And leaden-eyed despairs,
Where Beauty cannot keep her lustrous eyes,
    Or new Love pine at them beyond to-morrow.   30

4

Away! away! for I will fly to thee,
    Not charioted by Bacchus and his pards,[2]
But on the viewless[3] wings of Poesy,
    Though the dull brain perplexes and retards:

---

  [1] Shining wings.
  [2] In the legend, Cupid was forced to meet Psyche in the dark
to conceal his identity.

---

  [1] The spring on Mt. Helicon sacred to the Muses.
  [2] Titian's painting of Bacchus and Ariadne. See *Sleep and
Poetry*, lines 335-6, p. 1019, above. "Pards" are leopards, who
draw the chariot.
  [3] Invisible.

Already with thee! tender is the night,
  And haply [4] the Queen-Moon is on her throne,
    Cluster'd around by all her starry Fays;
      But here there is no light,
  Save what from heaven is with the breezes blown
    Through verdurous glooms and winding mossy
          ways.   40

5

I cannot see what flowers are at my feet,
  Nor what soft incense hangs upon the boughs,
But, in embalmed darkness, guess each sweet
  Wherewith the seasonable month endows
The grass, the thicket, and the fruit-tree wild;
  White hawthorn, and the pastoral eglantine;
    Fast fading violets cover'd up in leaves;
      And mid-May's eldest child,
  The coming musk-rose, full of dewy wine,   49
    The murmurous haunt of flies on summer eves.

6

Darkling I listen; and, for many a time
  I have been half in love with easeful Death,
Call'd him soft names in many a mused rhyme,
  To take into the air my quiet breath;
Now more than ever seems it rich to die,
  To cease upon the midnight with no pain,
    While thou art pouring forth thy soul abroad
      In such an ecstasy!
  Still wouldst thou sing, and I have ears in vain—
    To thy high requiem become a sod.   60

7

Thou wast not born for death, immortal Bird!
  No hungry generations tread thee down;
The voice I hear this passing night was heard
  In ancient days by emperor and clown:
Perhaps the self-same song that found a path
  Through the sad heart of Ruth, when, sick for home,
    She stood in tears amid the alien corn; [5]
      The same that oft-times hath
  Charm'd magic casements, opening on the foam
    Of perilous seas, in faery lands forlorn.   70

8

Forlorn! the very word is like a bell
  To toll me back from thee to my sole self!
Adieu! the fancy cannot cheat so well
  As she is fam'd to do, deceiving elf.

Adieu! adieu! thy plaintive anthem fades
  Past the near meadows, over the still stream,
    Up the hill-side; and now 'tis buried deep
      In the next valley-glades:
  Was it a vision, or a waking dream?
    Fled is that music:—Do I wake or sleep?   80

[1819]   [1819]

ODE ON A GRECIAN URN

1

THOU still unravish'd bride of quietness,
  Thou foster-child of silence and slow time,
Sylvan historian, who canst thus express
  A flowery tale more sweetly than our rhyme:
What leaf-fring'd legend haunts about thy shape
  Of deities or mortals, or of both,
    In Tempe or the dales of Arcady? [1]
What men or gods are these? What maidens loth?
  What mad pursuit? What struggle to escape?
    What pipes and timbrels? What wild ecstasy?   10

2

Heard melodies are sweet, but those unheard
  Are sweeter; therefore, ye soft pipes, play on;
Not to the sensual ear, but, more endear'd,
  Pipe to the spirit ditties of no tone:
Fair youth, beneath the trees, thou canst not leave
  Thy song, nor ever can those trees be bare;
    Bold Lover, never, never canst thou kiss,
Though winning near the goal—yet, do not grieve;
  She cannot fade, though thou hast not thy bliss,
    For ever wilt thou love, and she be fair!   20

3

Ah, happy, happy boughs! that cannot shed
  Your leaves, nor ever bid the Spring adieu;
And, happy melodist, unwearied,
  For ever piping songs for ever new;
More happy love! more happy, happy love!
  For ever warm and still to be enjoy'd,
    For ever panting, and for ever young;
All breathing human passion far above,
  That leaves a heart high-sorrowful and cloy'd,
    A burning forehead, and a parching tongue.   30

---

4 Perhaps.
5 Ruth had to leave home and work for her kinsman Boaz because of a famine. See Ruth 2:3.

---

1 Both the Vale of Tempe in Thessaly and Arcadia were noted for their pastoral beauty.

4

Who are these coming to the sacrifice?
  To what green altar, O mysterious priest,
Lead'st thou that heifer lowing at the skies,
  And all her silken flanks with garlands drest?
What little town by river or sea shore,
  Or mountain-built with peaceful citadel,
    Is emptied of this folk, this pious morn?
And, little town, thy streets for evermore
  Will silent be; and not a soul to tell
    Why thou art desolate, can e'er return.   40

5

O Attic shape! Fair attitude! with brede [2]
Of marble men and maidens overwrought,
With forest branches and the trodden weed;
  Thou, silent form, dost tease us out of thought
As doth eternity: Cold Pastoral!
  When old age shall this generation waste,
    Thou shalt remain, in midst of other woe
Than ours, a friend to man, to whom thou say'st,
  Beauty is truth, truth beauty, [3]—that is all
    Ye know on earth, and all ye need to know.   50

[1819]   [1820]

ODE ON MELANCHOLY

1

No, no, go not to Lethe, [4] neither twist
  Wolf's-bane, [5] tight-rooted, for its poisonous wine;
Nor suffer thy pale forehead to be kiss'd
  By nightshade, ruby grape of Proserpine; [6]
Make not your rosary of yew-berries,
  Nor let the beetle, nor the death-moth be
    Your mournful Psyche, [7] nor the downy owl
A partner in your sorrow's mysteries;
  For shade to shade will come too drowsily,
    And drown the wakeful anguish of the soul.   10

2

But when the melancholy fit shall fall
  Sudden from heaven like a weeping cloud,
That fosters the droop-headed flowers all,
  And hides the green hill in an April shroud;

Then glut thy sorrow on a morning rose,
  Or on the rainbow of the salt sand-wave,
    Or on the wealth of globed peonies;
Or if thy mistress some rich anger shows,
  Emprison her soft hand, and let her rave,
    And feed deep, deep upon her peerless eyes.   20

3

She dwells with Beauty—Beauty that must die;
  And Joy, whose hand is ever at his lips
Bidding adieu; and aching Pleasure nigh,
  Turning to poison while the bee-mouth sips:
Ay, in the very temple of Delight
  Veil'd Melancholy has her sovran shrine,
    Though seen of none save him whose strenuous
      tongue
Can burst Joy's grape against his palate fine;
  His soul shall taste the sadness of her might,
    And be among her cloudy trophies hung.   30

[1819]   [1820]

CANCELLED STANZA

The relation of the cancelled stanza to the completed poem is uncertain. There may have been other canceled stanzas, now lost. Garrod (see Bibliography) suggests that whether *(line 9) may be a miswriting of* weather.

[Cancelled Stanza of the Ode on Melancholy]

THOUGH you should build a bark of dead men's
    bones,
  And rear a phantom gibbet for a mast,
Stitch creeds together for a sail, with groans
  To fill it out, blood-stained and aghast;
Although your rudder be a dragon's tail
  Long sever'd, yet still hard with agony,
    Your cordage large uprootings from the skull
      Of bald Medusa, certes you would fail
      To find the Melancholy—whether she
        Dreameth in any isle of Lethe dull.   10

[1819]   [1848]

---

  [2] Anything woven or interlaced.
  [3] As printed in *Lamia* [&c.] . . . *and Other Poems* (1820), this phrase appears in quotation marks, but they do not occur in the autograph or the first printed text (in a periodical, Jan. 1820).
  [4] The underworld river of obliviousness.
  [5] Aconite, a poisonous root sometimes used to reduce pain or fever.
  [6] Queen of the underworld.
  [7] See *Ode to Psyche*, p. 1077.

ODE ON INDOLENCE

'They toil not, neither do they spin.'[1]

I

ONE morn before me were three figures seen,
  With bowed necks, and joined hands, side-faced;
And one behind the other stepp'd serene,
  In placid sandals, and in white robes graced;
They pass'd, like figures on a marble urn,
  When shifted round to see the other side;
    They came again; as when the urn once more
Is shifted round, the first seen shades return;
  And they were strange to me, as may betide
    With vases, to one deep in Phidian[2] lore.   10

II

How is it, Shadows! that I knew ye not?
  How came ye muffled in so hush a masque?
Was it a silent deep-disguised plot
  To steal away, and leave without a task
My idle days? Ripe was the drowsy hour;
  The blissful cloud of summer-indolence
    Benumb'd my eyes; my pulse grew less and less;
Pain had no sting, and pleasure's wreath no flower:
  O, why did ye not melt, and leave my sense
    Unhaunted quite of all but—nothingness?   20

III

A third time came they by;—alas! wherefore?[3]
  My sleep had been embroider'd with dim dreams;
My soul had been a lawn besprinkled o'er
  With flowers, and stirring shades, and baffled
      beams:
The morn was clouded, but no shower fell,
  Tho' in her lids hung the sweet tears of May;
    The open casement press'd a new-leav'd vine,
Let in the budding warmth and throstle's lay;
  O Shadows! 'twas a time to bid farewell!
    Upon your skirts had fallen no tears of mine.   30

IV

A third time pass'd they by, and, passing, turn'd
  Each one the face a moment whiles to me;
Then faded, and to follow them I burn'd
  And ached for wings because I knew the three;

The first was a fair Maid, and Love her name;
  The second was Ambition, pale of cheek,
    And ever watchful with fatigued eye;
The last, whom I love more, the more of blame
  Is heap'd upon her, maiden most unmeek,—
    I knew to be my demon Poesy.   40

V

They faded, and, forsooth! I wanted wings:
  O folly! What is Love! and where is it?
And for that poor Ambition—it springs
  From a man's little heart's short fever-fit;
For Poesy!—no,—she has not a joy,—
  At least for me,—so sweet as drowsy noons,
    And evenings steep'd in honied indolence;
O, for an age so shelter'd from annoy,
  That I may never know how change the moons,
    Or hear the voice of busy common-sense!   50

VI

So, ye three Ghosts, adieu! Ye cannot raise
  My head cool-bedded in the flowery grass;
For I would not be dieted with praise,
  A pet-lamb in a sentimental farce!
Fade softly from my eyes, and be once more
  In masque-like figures on the dreamy urn;
    Farewell! I yet have visions for the night,
And for the day faint visions there is store;
  Vanish, ye Phantoms! from my idle spright,
    Into the clouds, and never more return!   60

[1819]   [1848]

---

  [1] Matt. 6:28.
  [2] Phidias was the sculptor of the Elgin Marbles. See Keats's
sonnets to B. R. Haydon, p. 1014.
  [3] Different editors using different manuscripts order these
stanzas differently. This order is that of Garrod. Other orders
are: 1, 2, 4, 5, 3, 6 and 1, 2, 3, 6, 5, 4.

LAMIA

At the conclusion of this poem in the 1820 edition Keats quoted the following story from Burton's Anatomy of Melancholy:

Philostratus, in his fourth book *de Vita Apollonii*, hath a memorable instance in this kind, which I may not omit, of one Menippus Lycius, a young man twenty-five years of age, that going betwixt Cenchreas and Corinth, met such a phantasm in the habit of a fair gentlewoman, which taking him by the hand, carried him home to her house, in the suburbs of Corinth, and told him she was a Phœnician by birth, and if he would tarry with her, he should hear her sing and play, and drink such wine as never any drank, and no man should molest him; but she, being fair and lovely, would live and die with him, that was fair and lovely to behold. The young man, a philosopher, otherwise staid and discreet, able to moderate his passions, though not this of love, tarried with her a while to his great content, and at last married her, to whose wedding, amongst other guests, came Apollonius; who, by some probable conjectures, found her out to be a serpent, a lamia; and that all her furniture was, like Tantalus' gold, described by Homer, no substance but mere illusions. When she saw herself descried, she wept, and desired Apollonius to be silent, but he would not be moved, and thereupon she, plate, house, and all that was in it, vanished in an instant: many thousands took notice of this fact, for it was done in the midst of Greece.

Burton's *"Anatomy of Melancholy."* Part *3.* Sect. *2.*
Memb. *1.* Subs. *1.*

LAMIA

PART I

UPON a time, before the faery broods
Drove Nymph and Satyr from the prosperous woods,
Before King Oberon's bright diadem,
Sceptre, and mantle, clasp'd with dewy gem,
Frighted away the Dryads and the Fauns
From rushes green, and brakes, and cowslip'd lawns,
The every-smitten Hermes [1] empty left
His golden throne, bent warm on amorous theft:
From high Olympus had he stolen light,
On this side of Jove's clouds, to escape the sight   10
Of his great summoner, and made retreat
Into a forest on the shores of Crete.
For somewhere in that sacred island [2] dwelt
A nymph, to whom all hoofed Satyrs knelt;
At whose white feet the languid Tritons poured
Pearls, while on land they wither'd and adored.
Fast by the springs where she to bathe was wont,
And in those meads where sometime she might haunt,
Were strewn rich gifts, unknown to any Muse,
Though Fancy's casket were unlock'd to choose.   20

---

[1] Hermes (Mercury) was known for his love affairs.
[2] Mt. Ida, in Crete, where Jupiter was educated.

Ah, what a world of love was at her feet!
So Hermes thought, and a celestial heat
Burnt from his winged heels to either ear,
That from a whiteness, as the lily clear,
Blush'd into roses 'mid his golden hair,
Fallen in jealous curls about his shoulders bare.
From vale to vale, from wood to wood, he flew,
Breathing upon the flowers his passion new,
And wound with many a river to its head,
To find where this sweet nymph prepar'd her secret
          bed: 30
In vain; the sweet nymph might nowhere be found,
And so he rested, on the lonely ground,
Pensive, and full of painful jealousies
Of the Wood-Gods, and even the very trees.
There as he stood, he heard a mournful voice,
Such as once heard, in gentle heart, destroys
All pain but pity: thus the lone voice spake:
'When from this wreathed tomb shall I awake!
'When move in a sweet body fit for life,
'And love, and pleasure, and the ruddy strife   40
'Of hearts and lips! Ah, miserable me!'
The God, dove-footed, glided silently
Round bush and tree, soft-brushing, in his speed,
The taller grasses and full-flowering weed,
Until he found a palpitating snake,
Bright, and cirque-couchant [3] in a dusky brake.

She was a gordian [4] shape of dazzling hue,
Vermilion-spotted, golden, green, and blue;
Striped like a zebra, freckled like a pard,
Eyed like a peacock, and all crimson barr'd;   50
And full of silver moons, that, as she breathed,
Dissolv'd, or brighter shone, or interwreathed
Their lustres with the gloomier tapestries—
So rainbow-sided, touch'd with miseries,
She seem'd, at once, some penanced lady elf,
Some demon's mistress, or the demon's self.
Upon her crest she wore a wannish fire
Sprinkled with stars, like Ariadne's tiar:
Her head was serpent, but ah, bitter-sweet!
She had a woman's mouth with all its pearls complete:
And for her eyes: what could such eyes do there   61
But weep, and weep, that they were born so fair?
As Proserpine still weeps for her Sicilian air. [5]
Her throat was serpent, but the words she spake
Came, as through bubbling honey, for Love's sake,
And thus; while Hermes on his pinions lay,
Like a stoop'd [6] falcon ere he takes his prey.

---

[3] Lying in circular coils.
[4] Intricately knotted.
[5] From which she was abducted by Pluto.
[6] Preparing to dive.

'Fair Hermes, crown'd with feathers, fluttering
    light,
'I had a splendid dream of thee last night:
'I saw thee sitting, on a throne of gold,   70
'Among the Gods, upon Olympus old,
'The only sad one; for thou didst not hear
'The soft, lute-finger'd Muses chaunting clear,
'Nor even Apollo when he sang alone,
'Deaf to his throbbing throat's long, long melodious
    moan.
'I dreamt I saw thee, robed in purple flakes,
'Break amorous through the clouds, as morning
    breaks,
'And swiftly as a bright Phœbean dart,[7]
'Strike for the Cretan isle; and here thou art!
'Too gentle Hermes, hast thou found the maid?'   80
Whereat the star of Lethe[8] not delay'd
His rosy eloquence, and thus inquired:
'Thou smooth-lipp'd serpent, surely high inspired!
'Thou beauteous wreath, with melancholy eyes,
'Possess whatever bliss thou canst devise,
'Telling me only where my nymph is fled,—
'Where she doth breathe!' 'Bright planet, thou hast
    said,'
Return'd the snake, 'but seal with oaths, fair God!'
'I swear,' said Hermes, 'by my serpent rod,
'And by thine eyes, and by thy starry crown!'   90
Light flew his earnest words, among the blossoms
    blown.
Then thus again the brilliance feminine:
'Too frail of heart! for this lost nymph of thine,
'Free as the air, invisibly, she strays
'About these thornless wilds; her pleasant days
'She tastes unseen; unseen her nimble feet
'Leave traces in the grass and flowers sweet;
'From weary tendrils, and bow'd branches green,
'She plucks the fruit unseen, she bathes unseen:
'And by my power is her beauty veil'd   100
'To keep it unaffronted, unassail'd
'By the love-glances of unlovely eyes,
'Of Satyrs, Fauns, and blear'd Silenus' sighs.
'Pale grew her immortality, for woe
'Of all these lovers, and she grieved so
'I took compassion on her, bade her steep
'Her hair in weïrd syrops, that would keep
'Her loveliness invisible, yet free
'To wander as she loves, in liberty.
'Thou shalt behold her, Hermes, thou alone,   110
'If thou wilt, as thou swearest, grant my boon!'
Then, once again, the charmed God began
An oath, and through the serpent's ears it ran

Warm, tremulous, devout, psalterian.[9]
Ravish'd, she lifted her Circean[10] head,
Blush'd a live damask, and swift-lisping said,
'I was a woman, let me have once more
'A woman's shape, and charming as before.
'I love a youth of Corinth—O the bliss!   119
'Give me my woman's form, and place me where he is.
'Stoop, Hermes, let me breathe upon thy brow,
'And thou shalt see thy sweet nymph even now.'
The God on half-shut feathers sank serene,
She breath'd upon his eyes, and swift was seen
Of both the guarded nymph near-smiling on the
    green.
It was no dream; or say a dream it was,
Real are the dreams of Gods, and smoothly pass
Their pleasures in a long immortal dream.
One warm, flush'd moment, hovering, it might seem
Dash'd by the wood-nymph's beauty, so he burn'd;
Then, lighting on the printless verdure, turn'd   131
To the swoon'd serpent, and with languid arm,
Delicate, put to proof the lythe Caducean[11] charm.
So done, upon the nymph his eyes he bent
Full of adoring tears and blandishment,
And towards her stept: she, like a moon in wane,
Faded before him, cower'd, nor could restrain
Her fearful sobs, self-folding like a flower
That faints into itself at evening hour:
But the God fostering her chilled hand,   140
She felt the warmth, her eyelids open'd bland,
And, like new flowers at morning song of bees,
Bloom'd, and gave up her honey to the lees.
Into the green-recessed woods they flew;
Nor grew they pale, as mortal lovers do.

Left to herself, the serpent now began
To change; her elfin blood in madness ran,
Her mouth foam'd, and the grass, therewith besprent,
Wither'd at dew so sweet and virulent;
Her eyes in torture fix'd, and anguish drear,   150
Hot, glaz'd, and wide, with lid-lashes all sear,
Flash'd phosphor and sharp sparks, without one
    cooling tear.
The colours all inflam'd throughout her train,
She writh'd about, convuls'd with scarlet pain:
A deep volcanian yellow took the place
Of all her milder-mooned body's grace;
And, as the lava ravishes the mead,
Spoilt all her silver mail, and golden brede,[12]
Made gloom of all her frecklings, streaks and bars,
Eclips'd her crescents, and lick'd up her stars: 160

---

[7] I.e., ray of sunshine.
[8] Hermes as conductor of dead souls.
[9] A psaltery is an ancient stringed instrument.
[10] Like Circe, the seductress who turned men into swine.
[11] Like the snakes on Hermes' staff (the Caduceus).
[12] Embroidery.

So that, in moments few, she was undrest
Of all her sapphires, greens, and amethyst,
And rubious-argent:[13] of all these bereft,
Nothing but pain and ugliness were left.
Still shone her crown; that vanish'd, also she
Melted and disappear'd as suddenly;
And in the air, her new voice luting soft,
Cried, 'Lycius! gentle Lycius!'—Borne aloft
With the bright mists about the mountains hoar   169
These words dissolv'd: Crete's forests heard no more.

Whither fled Lamia, now a lady bright,
A full-born beauty new and exquisite?
She fled into that valley they pass o'er
Who go to Corinth from Cenchreas'[14] shore;
And rested at the foot of those wild hills,
The rugged founts of the Peræan rills,
And of that other ridge whose barren back
Stretches, with all its mist and cloudy rack,
South-westward to Cleone.[15] There she stood
About a young bird's flutter from a wood,   180
Fair, on a sloping green of mossy tread,
By a clear pool, wherein she passioned
To see herself escap'd from so sore ills,
While her robes flaunted with the daffodils.

Ah, happy Lycius!—for she was a maid
More beautiful than ever twisted braid,
Or sigh'd, or blush'd, or on spring-flowered lea
Spread a green kirtle to the minstrelsy:
A virgin purest lipp'd, yet in the lore
Of love deep learned to the red heart's core: 190
Not one hour old, yet of sciential brain
To unperplex bliss from its neighbour pain;
Define their pettish limits, and estrange
Their points of contact, and swift counterchange;
Intrigue with the specious chaos, and dispart
Its most ambiguous atoms with sure art;
As though in Cupid's college she had spent
Sweet days a lovely graduate, still unshent,
And kept his rosy terms in idle languishment.

Why this fair creature chose so fairily   200
By the wayside to linger, we shall see;
But first 'tis fit to tell how she could muse
And dream, when in the serpent prison-house,
Of all she list, strange or magnificent:
How, ever, where she will'd, her spirit went;
Whether to faint Elysium, or where
Down through tress-lifting waves the Nereids fair

Wind into Thetis' bower by many a pearly stair;
Or where God Bacchus drains his cups divine,
Stretch'd out, at ease, beneath a glutinous pine;   210
Or where in Pluto's gardens palatine[16]
Mulciber's columns gleam in far piazzian line.
And sometimes into cities she would send
Her dream, with feast and rioting to blend;
And once, while among mortals dreaming thus,
She saw the young Corinthian Lycius
Charioting foremost in the envious race,
Like a young Jove with calm uneager face,
And fell into a swooning love of him.
Now on the moth-time of that evening dim   220
He would return that way, as well she knew,
To Corinth from the shore; for freshly blew
The eastern soft wind, and his galley now
Grated the quaystones with her brazen prow
In port Cenchreas, from Egina isle
Fresh anchor'd; whither he had been awhile
To sacrifice to Jove, whose temple there
Waits with high marble doors for blood and incense
        rare.
Jove heard his vows, and better'd his desire;
For by some freakful chance he made retire   230
From his companions, and set forth to walk,
Perhaps grown wearied of their Corinth talk:
Over the solitary hills he fared,
Thoughtless at first, but ere eve's star appeared
His phantasy was lost, where reason fades,
In the calm'd twilight of Platonic shades.
Lamia beheld him coming, near, more near—
Close to her passing, in indifference drear,
His silent sandals swept the mossy green;
So neighbour'd to him, and yet so unseen   240
She stood: he pass'd, shut up in mysteries,
His mind wrapp'd like his mantle, while her eyes
Follow'd his steps, and her neck regal white
Turn'd—syllabling thus, 'Ah, Lycius bright,
'And will you leave me on the hills alone?
'Lycius, look back! and be some pity shown.'
He did; not with cold wonder fearingly,
But Orpheus-like at an Eurydice;[17]
For so delicious were the words she sung,
It seem'd he had lov'd them a whole summer long:
And soon his eyes had drunk her beauty up,   251
Leaving no drop in the bewildering cup,
And still the cup was full,—while he, afraid
Lest she should vanish ere his lip had paid
Due adoration, thus began to adore;
Her soft look growing coy, she saw his chain so sure:

---

13 Silver with red highlights.
14 The port of Corinth.
15 Village on the road from Corinth to Argus.

16 Pluto's palace gardens in the underworld. Mulciber (Vulcan) builds Pandemonium in Book I of *Paradise Lost*.
17 As Orpheus looked back at Eurydice (thus causing her eternal confinement in Hades).

'Leave thee alone! Look back! Ah, Goddess, see
'Whether my eyes can ever turn from thee!
'For pity do not this sad heart belie—
'Even as thou vanishest so I shall die.   260
'Stay! though a Naiad of the rivers, stay!
'To thy far wishes will thy streams obey:
'Stay! though the greenest woods be thy domain,
'Alone they can drink up the morning rain:
'Though a descended Pleiad,[18] will not one
'Of thine harmonious sisters keep in tune
'Thy spheres, and as thy silver proxy shine?
'So sweetly to these ravish'd ears of mine
'Came thy sweet greeting, that if thou shouldst fade
'Thy memory will waste me to a shade:—   270
'For pity do not melt!'—'If I should stay,'
Said Lamia, 'here, upon this floor of clay,
'And pain my steps upon these flowers too rough,
'What canst thou say or do of charm enough
'To dull the nice remembrance of my home?
'Thou canst not ask me with thee here to roam
'Over these hills and vales, where no joy is,—
'Empty of immortality and bliss!
'Thou art a scholar, Lycius, and must know
'That finer spirits cannot breathe below   280
'In human climes, and live: Alas! poor youth,
'What taste of purer air hast thou to soothe
'My essence? What serener palaces,
'Where I may all my many senses please,
'And by mysterious sleights a hundred thirsts
      appease?
'It cannot be—Adieu!' So said, she rose
Tiptoe with white arms spread. He, sick to lose
The amorous promise of her lone complain,
Swoon'd, murmuring of love, and pale with pain.
The cruel lady, without any show   290
Of sorrow for her tender favourite's woe,
But rather, if her eyes could brighter be,
With brighter eyes and slow amenity,
Put her new lips to his, and gave afresh
The life she had so tangled in her mesh:
And as he from one trance was wakening
Into another, she began to sing,
Happy in beauty, life, and love, and every thing,
A song of love, too sweet for earthly lyres,
While, like held breath, the stars drew in their
      panting fires.   300
And then she whisper'd in such trembling tone,
As those who, safe together met alone
For the first time through many anguish'd days,
Use other speech than looks; bidding him raise
His drooping head, and clear his soul of doubt,
For that she was a woman, and without

Any more subtle fluid in her veins
Than throbbing blood, and that the self-same pains
Inhabited her frail-strung heart as his.
And next she wonder'd how his eyes could miss   310
Her face so long in Corinth, where, she said,
She dwelt but half retir'd, and there had led
Days happy as the gold coin could invent
Without the aid of love; yet in content
Till she saw him, as once she pass'd him by,
Where 'gainst a column he leant thoughtfully
At Venus' temple porch, 'mid baskets heap'd
Of amorous herbs and flowers, newly reap'd
Late on that eve, as 'twas the night before
The Adonian feast;[19] whereof she saw no more,   320
But wept alone those days, for why should she adore?
Lycius from death awoke into amaze,
To see her still, and singing so sweet lays;
Then from amaze into delight he fell
To hear her whisper woman's lore so well;
And every word she spake entic'd him on
To unperplex'd delight and pleasure known.
Let the mad poets say whate'er they please
Of the sweets of Fairies, Peris,[20] Goddesses,
There is not such a treat among them all,   330
Haunters of cavern, lake, and waterfall,
As a real woman, lineal indeed
From Pyrrha's pebbles[21] or old Adam's seed.
Thus gentle Lamia judg'd, and judg'd aright,
That Lycius could not love in half a fright,
So threw the goddess off, and won his heart
More pleasantly by playing woman's part,
With no more awe than what her beauty gave,
That, while it smote, still guaranteed to save.
Lycius to all made eloquent reply,   340
Marrying to every word a twinborn sigh;
And last, pointing to Corinth, ask'd her sweet,
If 'twas too far that night for her soft feet.
The way was short, for Lamia's eagerness
Made, by a spell, the triple league decrease
To a few paces; not at all surmised
By blinded Lycius, so in her comprized.
They pass'd the city gates, he knew not how,
So noiseless, and he never thought to know.

As men talk in a dream, so Corinth all,   350
Throughout her palaces imperial,
And all her populous streets and temples lewd,
Mutter'd, like tempest in the distance brew'd,

[18] One of the constellations of seven stars, daughters of Atlas.

[19] The feast of Adonis—a fertility rite—commemorating his death and seasonal rebirth.
[20] Persian name for fairies.
[21] After the flood Zeus had brought about to punish mankind, Deucalian and Pyrrha, who alone were saved in a sort of ark, repopulated the earth by throwing stones behind them which became men and women.

To the wide-spreaded night above her towers.
Men, women, rich and poor, in the cool hours,
Shuffled their sandals o'er the pavement white,
Companion'd or alone; while many a light
Flared, here and there, from wealthy festivals,
And threw their moving shadows on the walls,
Or found them cluster'd in the corniced shade   360
Of some arch'd temple door, or dusky colonnade.

Muffling his face, of greeting friends in fear,
Her fingers he press'd hard, as one came near
With curl'd gray beard, sharp eyes, and smooth bald
    crown,
Slow-stepp'd, and robed in philosophic gown:
Lycius shrank closer, as they met and past,
Into his mantle, adding wings to haste,
While hurried Lamia trembled: 'Ah,' said he,
'Why do you shudder, love, so ruefully?
'Why does your tender palm dissolve in dew?'—   370
'I'm wearied,' said fair Lamia: 'tell me who
'Is that old man? I cannot bring to mind
'His features:—Lycius! wherefore did you blind
'Yourself from his quick eyes?' Lycius replied,
''Tis Apollonius²² sage, my trusty guide
'And good instructor; but to-night he seems
'The ghost of folly haunting my sweet dreams.'

While yet he spake they had arrived before
A pillar'd porch, with lofty portal door,
Where hung a silver lamp, whose phosphor glow   380
Reflected in the slabbed steps below,
Mild as a star in water; for so new,
And so unsullied was the marble hue,
So through the crystal polish, liquid fine,
Ran the dark veins, that none but feet divine
Could e'er have touch'd there. Sounds Æolian²³
Breath'd from the hinges, as the ample span
Of the wide doors disclos'd a place unknown
Some time to any, but those two alone,
And a few Persian mutes, who that same year   390
Were seen about the markets: none knew where
They could inhabit; the most curious
Were foil'd, who watch'd to trace them to their house:
And but the flitter-wingèd verse must tell
For truth's sake, what woe afterwards befel,
'Twould humour many a heart to leave them thus,
Shut from the busy world, of more incredulous.

---

²² Philosopher, magician, and reformer of the first century
of the Christian era.
²³ As from an Aeolian harp; see p. 441.

PART II

LOVE in a hut, with water and a crust,
Is—Love, forgive us!—cinders, ashes, dust;
Love in a palace is perhaps at last
More grievous torment than a hermit's fast:—
That is a doubtful tale from faery land,
Hard for the non-elect to understand.
Had Lycius liv'd to hand his story down,
He might have given the moral a fresh frown,
Or clench'd it quite: but too short was their bliss
To breed distrust and hate, that make the soft voice
    hiss.   10
Besides, there, nightly, with terrific glare,
Love, jealous grown of so complete a pair,
Hover'd and buzz'd his wings, with fearful roar,
Above the lintel of their chamber door,
And down the passage cast a glow upon the floor.

For all this came a ruin: side by side
They were enthroned, in the even tide,
Upon a couch, near to a curtaining
Whose airy texture, from a golden string,
Floated into the room, and let appear   20
Unveil'd the summer heaven, blue and clear,
Betwixt two marble shafts:—there they reposed,
Where use had made it sweet, with eyelids closed,
Saving a tythe which love still open kept,
That they might see each other while they almost
    slept;
When from the slope side of a suburb hill,
Deafening the swallow's twitter, came a thrill
Of trumpets—Lycius started—the sounds fled,
But left a thought a-buzzing in his head.
For the first time, since first he harbour'd in   30
That purple-lined palace of sweet sin,
His spirit pass'd beyond its golden bourn
Into the noisy world almost forsworn.
The lady, ever watchful, penetrant,
Saw this with pain, so arguing a want
Of something more, more than her empery
Of joys; and she began to moan and sigh
Because he mused beyond her, knowing well
That but a moment's thought is passion's passing bell.
'Why do you sigh, fair creature?' whisper'd he: 40
'Why do you think?' return'd she tenderly:
'You have deserted me;—where am I now?
'Not in your heart while care weighs on your brow:
'No, no, you have dismiss'd me; and I go
'From your breast houseless: ay, it must be so.'
He answer'd, bending to her open eyes,
Where he was mirror'd small in paradise,
'My silver planet, both of eve and morn!
'Why will you plead yourself so sad forlorn,

'While I am striving how to fill my heart   50
'With deeper crimson, and a double smart?
'How to entangle, trammel up and snare
'Your soul in mine, and labyrinth you there
'Like the hid scent in an unbudded rose?
'Ay, a sweet kiss—you see your mighty woes.
'My thoughts! shall I unveil them? Listen then!
'What mortal hath a prize, that other men
'May be confounded and abash'd withal,
'But lets it sometimes pace abroad majestical,
'And triumphs, as in thee I should rejoice   60
'Amid the hoarse alarm of Corinth's voice.
'Let my foes choke, and my friends shout afar,
'While through the thronged streets your bridal car
'Wheels round its dazzling spokes.'—The lady's
          cheek
Trembled; she nothing said, but, pale and meek,
Arose and knelt before him, wept a rain
Of sorrows at his words; at last with pain
Beseeching him, the while his hand she wrung,
To change his purpose. He thereat was stung,
Perverse, with stronger fancy to reclaim   70
Her wild and timid nature to his aim:
Besides, for all his love, in self despite
Against his better self, he took delight
Luxurious in her sorrows, soft and new.
His passion, cruel grown, took on a hue
Fierce and sanguineous as 'twas possible
In one whose brow had no dark veins to swell.
Fine was the mitigated fury, like
Apollo's presence when in act to strike
The serpent [24]—Ha, the serpent! certes, she   80
Was none. She burnt, she lov'd the tyranny,
And, all subdued, consented to the hour
When to the bridal he should lead his paramour.
Whispering in midnight silence, said the youth,
'Sure some sweet name thou hast, though, by my
          truth,
'I have not ask'd it, ever thinking thee
'Not mortal, but of heavenly progeny,
'As still I do. Hast any mortal name,
'Fit appellation for this dazzling frame?
'Or friends or kinsfolk on the citied earth,   90
'To share our marriage feast and nuptial mirth?'
'I have no friends,' said Lamia, 'no, not one;
'My presence in wide Corinth hardly known:
'My parents' bones are in their dusty urns
'Sepulchred, where no kindled incense burns,
'Seeing all their luckless race are dead, save me,
'And I neglect the holy rite for thee.
'Even as you list invite your many guests;
'But if, as now it seems, your vision rests

'With any pleasure on me, do not bid   100
'Old Apollonius—from him keep me hid.'
Lycius, perplex'd at words so blind and blank,
Made close inquiry; from whose touch she shrank,
Feigning a sleep; and he to the dull shade
Of deep sleep in a moment was betray'd.

    It was the custom then to bring away
The bride from home at blushing shut of day,
Veil'd, in a chariot, heralded along
By strewn flowers, torches, and a marriage song,
With other pageants: but this fair unknown   110
Had not a friend. So being left alone,
(Lycius was gone to summon all his kin)
And knowing surely she could never win
His foolish heart from its mad pompousness,
She set herself, high-thoughted, how to dress
The misery in fit magnificence.
She did so, but 'tis doubtful how and whence
Came, and who were her subtle servitors.
About the halls, and to and from the doors,
There was a noise of wings, till in short space   120
The glowing banquet-room shone with wide-arched
          grace.
A haunting music, sole perhaps and lone
Supportress of the faery-roof, made moan
Throughout, as fearful the whole charm might
          fade.
Fresh carved cedar, mimicking a glade
Of palm and plantain, met from either side,
High in the midst, in honour of the bride:
Two palms and then two plantains, and so on,
From either side their stems branch'd one to one
All down the aisled place; and beneath all   130
There ran a stream of lamps straight on from wall to
          wall.
So canopied, lay an untasted feast
Teeming with odours. Lamia, regal drest,
Silently paced about, and as she went,
In pale contented sort of discontent,
Mission'd her viewless servants to enrich
The fretted splendour of each nook and niche.
Between the tree-stems, marbled plain at first,
Came jasper pannels; then, anon, there burst
Forth creeping imagery of slighter trees,   140
And with the larger wove in small intricacies.
Approving all, she faded at self-will,
And shut the chamber up, close, hush'd and still.
Complete and ready for the revels rude,
When dreadful guests would come to spoil her
          solitude.

    The day appear'd, and all the gossip rout.
O senseless Lycius! Madman! wherefore flout

The silent-blessing fate, warm cloister'd hours,
And show to common eyes these secret bowers?
The herd approach'd; each guest, with busy brain,
Arriving at the portal, gaz'd amain,   151
And enter'd marveling: for they knew the street,
Remembered it from childhood all complete
Without a gap, yet ne'er before had seen
That royal porch, that high-built fair demesne;
So in they hurried all, maz'd, curious and keen:
Save one, who look'd thereon with eye severe,
And with calm-planted steps walk'd in austere;
'Twas Apollonius: something too he laugh'd,
As though some knotty problem, that had daft   160
His patient thought, had now begun to thaw,
And solve and melt:—'twas just as he foresaw.

He met within the murmurous vestibule
His young disciple. ''Tis no common rule,
'Lycius,' said he, 'for uninvited guest
'To force himself upon you, and infest
'With an unbidden presence the bright throng
'Of younger friends; yet must I do this wrong,
'And you forgive me.' Lycius blush'd, and led
The old man through the inner doors broad-spread;
With reconciling words and courteous mien   171
Turning into sweet milk the sophist's spleen.

Of wealthy lustre was the banquet-room,
Fill'd with pervading brilliance and perfume:
Before each lucid pannel fuming stood
A censer fed with myrrh and spiced wood,
Each by a sacred tripod held aloft,
Whose slender feet wide-swerv'd upon the soft
Wool-woofed carpets: fifty wreaths of smoke
From fifty censers their light voyage took   180
To the high roof, still mimick'd as they rose
Along the mirror'd walls by twin-clouds odorous.
Twelve sphered tables, by silk seats insphered,
High as the level of a man's breast rear'd
On libbard's [25] paws, upheld the heavy gold
Of cups and goblets, and the store thrice told
Of Ceres' horn, and, in huge vessels, wine
Come from the gloomy tun with merry shine.
Thus loaded with a feast the tables stood,
Each shrining in the midst the image of a God.   190

When in an antichamber every guest
Had felt the cold full sponge to pleasure press'd,
By minist'ring slaves, upon his hands and feet,
And fragrant oils with ceremony meet
Pour'd on his hair, they all mov'd to the feast
In white robes, and themselves in order placed

Around the silken couches, wondering
Whence all this mighty cost and blaze of wealth could
    spring.

Soft went the music the soft air along,
While fluent Greek a vowel'd undersong   200
Kept up among the guests, discoursing low
At first, for scarcely was the wine at flow;
But when the happy vintage touch'd their brains,
Louder they talk, and louder come the strains
Of powerful instruments:—the gorgeous dyes,
The space, the splendour of the draperies,
The roof of awful richness, nectarous cheer,
Beautiful slaves, and Lamia's self, appear,
Now, when the wine has done its rosy deed,
And every soul from human trammels freed,   210
No more so strange; for merry wine, sweet wine,
Will make Elysian shades not too fair, too divine.
Soon was God Bacchus at meridian height;
Flush'd were their cheeks, and bright eyes double
    bright:
Garlands of every green, and every scent
From vales deflower'd, or forest-trees branch-rent,
In baskets of bright osier'd gold were brought
High as the handles heap'd, to suit the thought
Of every guest; that each, as he did please,   219
Might fancy-fit his brows, silk-pillow'd at his ease.

What wreath for Lamia? What for Lycius?
What for the sage, old Apollonius?
Upon her aching forehead be there hung
The leaves of willow and of adder's tongue; [26]
And for the youth, quick, let us strip for him
The thyrsus, [27] that his watching eyes may swim
Into forgetfulness; and, for the sage,
Let spear-grass and the spiteful thistle wage
War on his temples. Do not all charms fly
At the mere touch of cold philosophy?   230
There was an awful rainbow once in heaven:
We know her woof, her texture; she is given
In the dull catalogue of common things.
Philosophy will clip an Angel's wings,
Conquer all mysteries by rule and line,
Empty the haunted air, and gnomed mine—
Unweave a rainbow, as it erewhile made
The tender-person'd Lamia melt into a shade.

By her glad Lycius sitting, in chief place,
Scarce saw in all the room another face,   240
Till, checking his love trance, a cup he took
Full brimm'd, and opposite sent forth a look

---

[25] Leopard's.

[26] Plants emblematic of grief and sorrow.
[27] Bacchus's staff, wound with ivy.

'Cross the broad table, to beseech a glance
From his old teacher's wrinkled countenance,
And pledge him. The bald-head philosopher
Had fix'd his eye, without a twinkle or stir
Full on the alarmed beauty of the bride,
Brow-beating her fair form, and troubling her sweet
    pride.
Lycius then press'd her hand, with devout touch,
As pale it lay upon the rosy couch: 250
'Twas icy, and the cold ran through his veins;
Then sudden it grew hot, and all the pains
Of an unnatural heat shot to his heart.
'Lamia, what means this? Wherefore dost thou
    start?
'Know'st thou that man?' Poor Lamia answer'd not.
He gaz'd into her eyes, and not a jot
Own'd they the lovelorn pietous appeal:
More, more he gaz'd: his human senses reel:
Some hungry spell that loveliness absorbs;
There was no recognition in those orbs.   260
'Lamia!' he cried—and no soft-toned reply.
The many heard, and the loud revelry
Grew hush; the stately music no more breathes;
The myrtle sicken'd in a thousand wreaths.
By faint degrees, voice, lute, and pleasure ceased;
A deadly silence step by step increased,
Until it seem'd a horrid presence there,
And not a man but felt the terror in his hair.
'Lamia!' he shriek'd; and nothing but the shriek
With its sad echo did the silence break.   270
'Begone, foul dream!' he cried, gazing again
In the bride's face, where now no azure vein
Wander'd on fair-spaced temples; no soft bloom
Misted the cheek; no passion to illume
The deep-recessed vision:—all was blight;
Lamia, no longer fair, there sat a deadly white.
'Shut, shut those juggling eyes, thou ruthless man!
'Turn them aside, wretch! or the righteous ban
'Of all the Gods, whose dreadful images
'Here represent their shadowy presences,   280
'May pierce them on the sudden with the thorn
'Of painful blindness; leaving thee forlorn,
'In trembling dotage to the feeblest fright
'Of conscience, for their long offended might,
'For all thine impious proud-heart sophistries,
'Unlawful magic, and enticing lies.
'Corinthians! look upon that gray-beard wretch!
'Mark how, possess'd, his lashless eyelids stretch
'Around his demon eyes! Corinthians, see!
'My sweet bride withers at their potency.'   290
'Fool!' said the sophist, in an under-tone
Gruff with contempt; which a death-nighing moan
From Lycius answer'd, as heart-struck and lost,
He sank supine beside the aching ghost.

'Fool! Fool!' repeated he, while his eyes still
Relented not, nor mov'd; 'from every ill
'Of life have I preserv'd thee to this day,
'And shall I see thee made a serpent's prey?'
Then Lamia breath'd death breath; the sophist's eye,
Like a sharp spear, went through her utterly,   300
Keen, cruel, perceant, stinging: she, as well
As her weak hand could any meaning tell,
Motion'd him to be silent; vainly so,
He look'd and look'd again a level—No!
'A Serpent!' echoed he; no sooner said,
Than with a frightful scream she vanished:
And Lycius' arms were empty of delight,
As were his limbs of life, from that same night.
On the high couch he lay!—his friends came round—
Supported him—no pulse, or breath they found,   310
And, in its marriage robe, the heavy body wound.

[1819]   [1820]

                "Pensive they sit . . ."

PENSIVE they sit, and roll their languid eyes,
Nibble their toasts and cool their tea with sighs;
Or else forget the purpose of the night,
Forget their tea, forget their appetite.
See, with cross'd arms they sit—Ah! hapless crew,
The fire is going out and no one rings
For coals, and therefore no coals Betty brings.
A fly is in the milk-pot. Must he die
Circled by a humane Society?[1]
No, no; there, Mr. Werter[2] takes his spoon,   10
Inverts it, dips the handle, and lo! soon
The little struggler, sav'd from perils dark,
Across the teaboard draws a long wet mark.

    Romeo! Arise! take snuffers by the handle,
There's a large cauliflower in each candle.
A winding sheet[3]—ah, me! I must away
To No. 7, just beyond the Circus gay.
'Alas, my friend, your coat sits very well;
Where may your Taylor live?' 'I may not tell—
O pardon me—I'm absent: now and then.   20
Where *might* my Taylor live? I say again
I cannot tell, let me no more be teas'd;
He lives in Wapping, *might* live where he pleas'd'.

[1819]   [1877]

[1] The Royal Humane Society, to prevent drowning, was
founded in 1774.
[2] Goethe's *The Sorrows of Werther.* Werther worries about his
inadvertent killing of insects, etc. See Blake's *An Island in the
Moon,* p. 151.
[3] When it takes the form of a folded sheet, the wax on the
side of a candle is an omen of death.

TO AUTUMN

1

SEASON of mists and mellow fruitfulness,
    Close bosom-friend of the maturing sun;
Conspiring with him how to load and bless
    With fruit the vines that round the thatch-eves run;
To bend with apples the moss'd cottage-trees,
    And fill all fruit with ripeness to the core;
        To swell the gourd, and plump the hazel shells
With a sweet kernel; to set budding more,
    And still more, later flowers for the bees,
    Until they think warm days will never cease,   10
        For Summer has o'er-brimm'd their clammy
           cells.

2

Who hath not seen thee oft amid thy store?
    Sometimes whoever seeks abroad may find
Thee sitting careless on a granary floor,
    Thy hair soft-lifted by the winnowing wind;
Or on a half-reap'd furrow sound asleep,
    Drows'd with the fume of poppies, while thy hook
        Spares the next swath and all its twined flowers:
And sometimes like a gleaner thou dost keep
    Steady thy laden head across a brook;   20
    Or by a cyder-press, with patient look,
        Thou watchest the last oozings hours by hours.

3

Where are the songs of Spring? Ay, where are they?
    Think not of them, thou hast thy music too,—
While barred clouds bloom the soft-dying day,
    And touch the stubble-plains with rosy hue;
Then in a wailful choir the small gnats mourn
    Among the river sallows, borne aloft
        Or sinking as the light wind lives or dies;
And full-grown lambs loud bleat from hilly bourn;   30
    Hedge-crickets sing; and now with treble soft
The red-breast whistles from a garden-croft;
    And gathering swallows twitter in the skies.

[1819]   [1820]

THE FALL OF HYPERION
The changes herein from the first Hyperion *make this an entirely
different poem, not a revision. It too, however, is unfinished. See
Keats's letter to Reynolds of September 21, 1819, p. 1118.*

THE FALL OF HYPERION

A DREAM

CANTO 1

FANATICS have their dreams, wherewith they weave
A paradise for a sect; the savage too
From forth the loftiest fashion of his sleep
Guesses at Heaven: pity these have not
Trac'd upon vellum or wild indian leaf
The shadows of melodious utterance.
But bare of laurel they live, dream and die;
For Poesy alone can tell her dreams,
With the fine spell of words alone can save
Imagination from the sable charm   10
And dumb enchantment. Who alive can say
'Thou art no Poet; mayst not tell thy dreams'?
Since every man whose soul is not a clod
Hath visions, and would speak, if he had lov'd
And been well nurtured in his mother tongue.
Whether the dream now purposed to rehearse
Be Poet's or Fanatic's will be known
When this warm scribe my hand is in the grave.

    Methought I stood where trees of every clime,
Palm, myrtle, oak, and sycamore, and beech,   20
With Plantane, and spice blossoms, made a screen;
In neighbourhood of fountains, by the noise
Soft-showering in mine ears; and, by the touch
Of scent, not far from roses. Turning round,
I saw an arbour with a drooping roof
Of trellis vines, and bells, and larger blooms,
Like floral censers swinging light in air;
Before its wreathed doorway, on a mound
Of moss, was spread a feast of summer fruits,
Which nearer seen, seem'd refuse of a meal   30
By Angel tasted, or our Mother Eve;
For empty shells were scattered on the grass,
And grape stalks but half bare, and remnants more,
Sweet smelling, whose pure kinds I could not know.
Still was more plenty that the fabled horn [1]
Thrice emptied could pour forth, at banqueting
For Proserpine return'd to her own fields,
Where the white heifers low. And appetite
More yearning than on earth I ever felt

◇◇◇◇◇◇◇◇◇◇◇◇◇◇◇◇◇◇◇◇◇◇◇◇◇◇◇◇◇◇◇◇◇◇◇◇◇
[1] The horn of plenty of Ceres, Proserpine's daughter.

Growing within, I ate deliciously;   40
And, after not long, thirsted, for thereby
Stood a cool vessel of transparent juice,
Sipp'd by the wander'd bee, the which I took,
And, pledging all the Mortals of the world,
And all the dead whose names are in our lips,
Drank. That full draught is parent of my theme.
No Asian poppy, nor Elixir fine
Of the soon fading jealous Caliphat;[2]
No poison gender'd in close monkish cell
To thin the scarlet conclave of old men,[3]   50
Could so have rapt unwilling life away.
Amongst the fragrant husks and berries crush'd,
Upon the grass I struggled hard against
The domineering potion; but in vain:
The cloudy swoon came on, and down I sunk
Like a Silenus[4] on an antique vase.
How long I slumber'd 'tis a chance to guess.
When sense of life return'd, I started up
As if with wings; but the fair trees were gone,
The mossy mound and arbour were no more;   60
I look'd around upon the carved sides
Of an old sanctuary with roof august,
Builded so high, it seem'd that filmed clouds
Might spread beneath, as o'er the stars of heaven;
So old the place was, I remembered none
The like upon the earth: what I had seen
Of grey Cathedrals, buttress'd walls, rent towers,
The superannuations of sunk realms,
Or Nature's Rocks toil'd hard in waves and winds,
Seem'd but the faulture[5] of decrepit things   70
To that eternal domed monument.
Upon the marble at my feet there lay
Store of strange vessels, and large draperies,
Which needs had been of dyed asbestos wove,
Or in that place the moth could not corrupt,[6]
So white the linen; so, in some, distinct
Ran imageries from a sombre loom.
All in a mingled heap confus'd there lay
Robes, golden tongs, censer, and chafing dish,
Girdles, and chains, and holy jewelries—   80
    Turning from these with awe, once more I rais'd
My eyes to fathom the space every way;
The embossed roof, the silent massy range
Of columns north and south, ending in mist
Of nothing; then to Eastward, where black gates
Were shut against the sunrise evermore.
Then to the west I look'd, and saw far off

An Image,[7] huge of feature as a cloud,
At level of whose feet an altar slept,
To be approach'd on either side by steps,   90
And marble balustrade, and patient travail
To count with toil the innumerable degrees.
Towards the altar sober-pac'd I went,
Repressing haste, as too unholy there;
And, coming nearer, saw beside the shrine
One minist'ring;[8] and there arose a flame.
When in mid-May the sickening East Wind
Shifts sudden to the South, the small warm rain
Melts out the frozen incense from all flowers,
And fills the air with so much pleasant health   100
That even the dying man forgets his shroud;
Even so that lofty sacrificial fire,
Sending forth maian incense, spread around
Forgetfulness of everything but bliss,
And clouded all the altar with soft smoke,
From whose white fragrant curtains thus I heard
Language pronounc'd. 'If thou canst not ascend
These steps, die on that marble where thou art.
Thy flesh, near cousin to the common dust,
Will parch for lack of nutriment—thy bones   110
Will wither in few years, and vanish so
That not the quickest eye could find a grain
Of what thou now art on that pavement cold.
The sands of thy short life are spent this hour,
And no hand in the universe can turn
Thy hour glass, if these gummed leaves be burnt
Ere thou canst mount up these immortal steps.'
I heard, I look'd: two senses both at once
So fine, so subtle, felt the tyranny
Of that fierce threat, and the hard task proposed.   120
Prodigious seem'd the toil, the leaves were yet
Burning,—when suddenly a palsied chill
Struck from the paved level up my limbs,
And was ascending quick to put cold grasp
Upon those streams that pulse beside the throat:
I shriek'd; and the sharp anguish of my shriek
Stung my own ears—I strove hard to escape
The numbness; strove to gain the lowest step.
Slow, heavy, deadly was my pace: the cold
Grew stifling, suffocating, at the heart;   130
And when I clasp'd my hands I felt them not.
One minute before death, my iced foot touch'd
The lowest stair; and as it touch'd, life seem'd
To pour in at the toes: I mounted up,

---

[2] Alluding to the story in *The Arabian Nights* of a poison that rendered its victim unconscious.
[3] The College of Cardinals, who elect a new pope.
[4] One of the followers of Bacchus.
[5] Failure.
[6] Matt. 6:19–20.

[7] Saturn.
[8] Moneta, priestess of the temple and narrator of the vision. Some temples of Juno were dedicated to Juno Moneta (the "admonisher"), and in one of these, coins were made (hence, the word "money"). But Keats apparently uses her as equivalent to Mnemosyne, mother of the Muses.

As once fair Angels on a ladder flew.[9]
From the green turf to heaven.—'Holy Power,'
Cried I, approaching near the horned shrine,
'What am I that should so be sav'd from death?
What am I that another death come not
To choak my utterance sacrilegious here?'   140
Then said the veiled shadow—'Thou hast felt
What 'tis to die and live again before
Thy fated hour. That thou hadst power to do so
Is thy own safety; thou hast dated on
Thy doom.' 'High Prophetess,' said I, 'purge off
Benign, if so it please thee, my mind's film—'
'None can usurp this height,' returned that shade,
'But those to whom the miseries of the world
Are misery, and will not let them rest.
All else who find a haven in the world,   150
Where they may thoughtless sleep away their days,
If by a chance into this fane they come,
Rot on the pavement where thou rotted'st half.—'
'Are there not thousands in the world,' said I,
Encourag'd by the sooth voice of the shade,
'Who love their fellows even to the death;
Who feel the giant agony of the world;
And more, like slaves to poor humanity,
Labour for mortal good? I sure should see
Other men here: but I am here alone.'   160
'They whom thou spak'st of are no vision'ries,'
Rejoin'd that voice—'they are no dreamers weak,
They seek no wonder but the human face;
No music but a happy-noted voice—
They come not here, they have no thought to come—
And thou art here, for thou art less than they—
What benefit canst thou do, or all thy tribe,
To the great world? Thou art a dreaming thing;
A fever of thyself—think of the Earth;
What bliss even in hope is there for thee?   170
What haven? every creature hath its home;
Every sole man hath days of joy and pain,
Whether his labours be sublime or low—
The pain alone; the joy alone; distinct:
Only the dreamer venoms all his days,
Bearing more woe than all his sins deserve.
Therefore, that happiness be somewhat shar'd,
Such things as thou art are admitted oft
Into like gardens thou didst pass erewhile,
And suffer'd in these Temples; for that cause   180
Thou standest safe beneath this statue's knees.'
'That I am favored for unworthiness,
By such propitious parley medicin'd
In sickness not ignoble, I rejoice,
Aye, and could weep for love of such award.'
So answer'd I, continuing, 'If it please,

Majestic shadow, tell me: sure not all
Those melodies sung into the world's ear
Are useless: sure a poet is a sage;
A humanist, Physician to all men.   190
That I am none I feel, as Vultures feel
They are no birds when Eagles are abroad.
What am I then? Thou spakest of my tribe:
What tribe?'—The tall shade veil'd in drooping
      white
Then spake, so much more earnest, that the breath
Mov'd the thin linen folds that drooping hung
About a golden censer from the hand
Pendent.—'Art thou not of the dreamer tribe?
The poet and the dreamer are distinct,
Diverse, sheer opposite, antipodes.   200
The one pours out a balm upon the world,
The other vexes it.' Then shouted I
Spite of myself, and with a Pythia's[10] spleen,
'Apollo! faded, farflown Apollo!
Where is thy misty pestilence to creep
Into the dwellings, thro' the door crannies,
Of all mock lyrists, large self-worshipers,
And careless Hectorers in proud bad verse.
Tho' I breathe death with them it will be life
To see them sprawl before me into graves.   210
Majestic shadow, tell me where I am,
Whose altar this; for whom this incense curls:
What Image this, whose face I cannot see,
For the broad marble knees; and who thou art,
Of accent feminine, so courteous.'
Then the tall shade, in drooping linens veil'd,
Spake out, so much more earnest, that her breath
Stirr'd the thin folds of gauze that drooping hung
About a golden censer from her hand
Pendent; and by her voice I knew she shed   220
Long-treasured tears. 'This temple sad and lone
Is all spar'd from the thunder of a war
Foughten long since by Giant Hierarchy[11]
Against rebellion: this old Image here,
Whose carved features wrinkled as he fell,
Is Saturn's; I, Moneta, left supreme
Sole priestess of his desolation.'—
I had no words to answer; for my tongue,
Useless, could find about its roofed home
No syllable of a fit majesty   230
To make rejoinder to Moneta's mourn.
There was a silence while the altar's blaze
Was fainting for sweet food: I look'd thereon,
And on the paved floor, where nigh were pil'd
Faggots of cinnamon, and many heaps

---

[9] Jacob's ladder—Gen. 28:12.

[10] She delivered the oracles of Apollo at Delphi in a sort of frenzy or trance.
[11] The war of the Titans against the rebelling Olympians.

Of other crisped spicewood—then again
I look'd upon the altar and its horns
Whiten'd with ashes, and its lang'rous flame,
And then upon the offerings again;
And so by turns—till sad Moneta cried,   240
'The sacrifice is done, but not the less,
Will I be kind to thee for thy goodwill.
My power, which to me is still a curse,
Shall be to thee a wonder; for the scenes
Still swooning vivid through my globed brain
With an electral changing misery
Thou shalt with those dull mortal eyes behold,
Free from all pain, if wonder pain thee not.'
As near as an immortal's sphered words
Could to a mother's soften, were these last: 250
But yet I had a terror of her robes,
And chiefly of the veils, that from her brow
Hung pale, and curtain'd her in mysteries
That made my heart too small to hold its blood.
This saw that Goddess, and with sacred hand
Parted the veils. Then saw I a wan face,
Not pin'd by human sorrows, but bright blanch'd
By an immortal sickness which kills not;
It works a constant change, which happy death
Can put no end to; deathwards progressing   260
To no death was that visage; it had pass'd
The lily and the snow; and beyond these
I must not think now, though I saw that face—
But for her eyes I should have fled away.
They held me back, with a benignant light,
Soft-mitigated by divinest lids
Half closed, and visionless entire they seem'd
Of all external things—they saw me not,
But in blank splendor beam'd like the mild moon,
Who comforts those she sees not, who knows not   270
What eyes are upward cast. As I had found
A grain of gold upon a mountain's side,
And twing'd with avarice strain'd out my eyes
To search its sullen entrails rich with ore,
So at the view of sad Moneta's brow,
I ached to see what things the hollow brain
Behind enwombed: what high tragedy
In the dark secret Chambers of her skull
Was acting, that could give so dread a stress
To her cold lips, and fill with such a light   280
Her planetary eyes; and touch her voice
With such a sorrow—'Shade of Memory!' [12]
Cried I, with act adorant at her feet,
'By all the gloom hung round thy fallen house,
By this last Temple, by the golden age,
By great Apollo, thy dear foster child,
And by thyself, forlorn divinity,

The pale Omega of a wither'd race, [13]
Let me behold, according as thou said'st,
What in thy brain so ferments to and fro.'—   290
No sooner had this conjuration pass'd
My devout lips; than side by side we stood,
(Like a stunt bramble by a solemn Pine)
Deep in the shady sadness of a vale,
Far sunken from the healthy breath of morn,
Far from the fiery noon and Eve's one star.
Onward I look'd beneath the gloomy boughs,
And saw, what first I thought an Image huge,
Like to the Image pedastal'd so high
In Saturn's Temple. Then Moneta's voice   300
Came brief upon mine ear,—'So Saturn sat
When he had lost his realms'—Whereon there grew
A power within me of enormous ken,
To see as a God sees, and take the depth
Of things as nimbly as the outward eye
Can size and shape pervade. The lofty theme
At those few words hung vast before my mind,
With half unravel'd web. I set myself
Upon an Eagle's watch, that I might see,
And seeing ne'er forget. No stir of life   310
Was in this shrouded vale, not so much air
As in the zoning of a summer's day
Robs not one light seed from the feather'd grass,
But where the dead leaf fell there did it rest.
A stream went voiceless by, still deaden'd more
By reason of the fallen Divinity
Spreading more shade: the Naiad 'mid her reeds
Press'd her cold finger closer to her lips.
Along the margin sand large footmarks went
No farther than to where old Saturn's feet   320
Had rested, and there slept, how long a sleep!
Degraded, cold, upon the sodden ground
His old right hand lay nerveless, listless, dead,
Unsceptred; and his realmless eyes were clos'd,
While his bow'd head seem'd listening to the Earth,
His antient mother, for some comfort yet.
    It seem'd no force could wake him from his place;
But there came one who with a kindred hand
Touch'd his wide shoulders, after bending low
With reverence, though to one who knew it not.   330
Then came the griev'd voice of Mnemosyne,
And griev'd I hearken'd. 'That divinity
Whom thou saw'st step from yon forlornest wood,
And with slow pace approach our fallen King,
Is Thea, [14] softest-natur'd of our Brood.'
I mark'd the goddess in fair statuary
Surpassing wan Moneta by the head,

---

[12] Mnemosyne (Moneta) also represents Memory.

[13] She is the last (Omega, the last letter in the Greek alphabet) of the Titans.
[14] Wife of Hyperion. See *Hyperion*, I, 31–51, p. 1060.

And in her sorrow nearer woman's tears.
There was a listening fear in her regard,
As if calamity had but begun;   340
As if the vanward clouds of evil days
Had spent their malice, and the sullen rear
Was with its stored thunder labouring up.
One hand she press'd upon that aching spot
Where beats the human heart; as if just there
Though an immortal, she felt cruel pain;
The other upon Saturn's bended neck
She laid, and to the level of his hollow ear
Leaning, with parted lips, some words she spoke
In solemn tenor and deep organ tune;   350
Some mourning words, which in our feeble tongue
Would come in this-like accenting; how frail
To that large utterance of the early Gods!—
'Saturn! look up—and for what, poor lost king?
I have no comfort for thee, no—not one;
I cannot cry, *Wherefore thus sleepest thou*:
For heaven is parted from thee, and the earth
Knows thee not, so afflicted, for a God;
The Ocean too, with all its solemn noise,
Has from thy sceptre pass'd; and all the air   360
Is emptied of thine hoary Majesty.
Thy thunder, captious at the new command,
Rumbles reluctant o'er our fallen house;
And thy sharp lightning in unpracticed hands
Scorches and burns our once serene domain.
With such remorseless speed still come new woes
That unbelief has not a space to breathe.
Saturn, sleep on: Me thoughtless, why should I
Thus violate thy slumbrous solitude?
Why should I ope thy melancholy eyes?   370
Saturn, sleep on, while at thy feet I weep.'—
    As when, upon a tranced summer-night,
Forests, branch-charmed by the earnest stars,
Dream, and so dream all night, without a noise,
Save from one gradual solitary gust,
Swelling upon the silence; dying off;
As if the ebbing air had but one wave;
So came these words, and went; the while in tears
She press'd her fair large forehead to the earth,
Just where her fallen hair might spread in curls,   380
A soft and silken mat for Saturn's feet.
Long, long, those two were postured motionless,
Like sculpture builded up upon the grave
Of their own power. A long awful time
I look'd upon them; still they were the same;
The frozen God still bending to the Earth,
And the sad Goddess weeping at his feet.
Moneta silent. Without stay or prop
But my own weak mortality, I bore
The load of this eternal quietude,   390
The unchanging gloom, and the three fixed shapes

Ponderous upon my senses a whole moon.
For by my burning brain I measured sure
Her silver seasons shedded on the night
And ever day by day methought I grew
More gaunt and ghostly—Oftentimes I pray'd
Intense, that Death would take me from the vale
And all its burthens—Gasping with despair
Of change, hour after hour I curs'd myself:
Until old Saturn rais'd his faded eyes,   400
And look'd around and saw his kingdom gone,
And all the gloom and sorrow of the place,
And that fair kneeling Goddess at his feet.
As the moist scent of flowers, and grass, and leaves
Fills forest dells with a pervading air,
Known to the woodland nostril, so the words
Of Saturn fill'd the mossy glooms around,
Even to the hollows of time-eaten oaks,
And to the winding in the foxes' holes,
With sad low tones, while thus he spake, and sent   410
Strange musings to the solitary Pan.[15]
'Moan, brethren, moan; for we are swallow'd up
And buried from all godlike exercise
Of influence benign on planets pale,
And peaceful sway above man's harvesting,
And all those acts which Deity supreme
Doth ease its heart of love in. Moan and wail.
Moan, brethren, moan; for lo! the rebel spheres
Spin round, the stars their antient courses keep,
Clouds still with shadowy moisture haunt the earth,
Still suck their fill of light from sun and moon,   421
Still buds the tree, and still the sea-shores murmur.
There is no death in all the universe
No smell of Death—there shall be death—moan,
        moan,
Moan, Cybele,[16] moan, for thy pernicious babes
Have chang'd a God into a shaking Palsy.
Moan, brethren, moan, for I have no strength left,
Weak as the reed—weak—feeble as my voice—
O, O, the pain, the pain of feebleness.
Moan, moan; for still I thaw—or give me help: 430
Throw down those Imps,[17] and give me victory.
Let me hear other groans; and trumpets blown
Of triumph calm, and hymns of festival
From the gold peaks of heaven's high piled clouds;
Voices of soft proclaim, and silver stir
Of strings in hollow shells; and let there be
Beautiful things made new, for the surprize
Of the sky-children'—So he feebly ceas'd,
With such a poor and sickly sounding pause,
Methought I heard some old man of the earth   440

---

[15] After the passing of the Golden Age, Pan is alone.
[16] Rhea, mother of the Olympian gods (Zeus, Hades, etc.).
[17] The sons of Satan.

Bewailing earthly loss; nor could my eyes
And ears act with that pleasant unison of sense
Which marries sweet sound with the grace of form,
And dolourous accent from a tragic harp
With large-limb'd visions. More I scrutinized:
Still fix'd he sat beneath the sable trees,
Whose arms spread straggling in wild serpent forms,
With leaves all hush'd: his awful presence there
(Now all was silent) gave a deadly lie
To what I erewhile heard: only his lips   450
Trembled amid the white curls of his beard.
They told the truth, though, round, the snowy locks
Hung nobly, as upon the face of heaven
A midday fleece of clouds. Thea arose,
And stretch'd her white arm through the hollow dark,
Pointing some whither: whereat he too rose
Like a vast giant seen by men at sea
To grow pale from the waves at dull midnight.
They melted from my sight into the woods:
Ere I could turn, Moneta cried—'These twain   460
Are speeding to the families of grief,[18]
Where roof'd in by black rocks they waste in pain
And darkness for no hope.'—And she spake on,
As ye may read who can unwearied pass
Onward from the Antichamber of this dream,
Where even at the open doors awhile
I must delay, and glean my memory
Of her high phrase:—perhaps no further dare.

Canto 2ᵈ

'MORTAL, that thou mayst understand aright,
I humanize my sayings to thine ear,
Making comparisons of earthly things;
Or thou might'st better listen to the wind,
Whose language is to thee a barren noise,
Though it blows legend-laden through the trees—
In melancholy realms big tears are shed,
More sorrow like to this, and suchlike woe,
Too huge for mortal tongue, or pen of scribe.
The Titans fierce, self-hid, or prison-bound,   10
Groan for the old allegiance once more,
Listening in their doom for Saturn's voice.
But one of our whole eagle-brood still keeps
His Sov'reignty, and Rule, and Majesty;
Blazing Hyperion on his orbed fire
Still sits, still snuffs the incense teeming up
From man to the sun's God: yet unsecure,
For as upon the Earth dire prodigies
Fright and perplex, so also shudders he:
Nor at dog's howl, or gloom-bird's Even screech,   20

---

[18] The other Titans who have fallen.

Or the familiar visitings of one
Upon the first toll of his passing bell:
But horrors, portion'd to a giant nerve,
Make great Hyperion ache. His palace bright,
Bastion'd with pyramids of glowing gold,
And touch'd with shade of bronzed obelisks,
Glares a blood red through all the thousand Courts,
Arches, and domes, and fiery galeries;
And all its curtains of Aurorian clouds
Flush angerly: when he would taste the wreaths   30
Of incense breath'd aloft from sacred hills,
Instead of sweets, his ample palate takes
Savour of poisonous brass and metals sick.
Wherefore when harbour'd in the sleepy West,
After the full completion of fair day,
For rest divine upon exalted couch
And slumber in the arms of melody,
He paces through the pleasant hours of ease,
With strides colossal, on from Hall to Hall;
While, far within each aisle and deep recess,   40
His winged minions in close clusters stand
Amaz'd, and full of fear; like anxious men
Who on a wide plain gather in sad troops,
When earthquakes jar their battlements and towers.
Even now, while Saturn, rous'd from icy trance
Goes, step for step, with Thea from yon woods,
Hyperion, leaving twilight in the rear,
Is sloping to the threshold of the west.—
Thither we tend.'—Now in clear light I stood,
Reliev'd from the dusk vale. Mnemosyne   50
Was sitting on a square edg'd polish'd stone,
That in its lucid depth reflected pure
Her priestess-garments. My quick eyes ran on
From stately nave to nave, from vault to vault,
Thro' bowers of fragrant and enwreathed light,
And diamond paved lustrous long arcades.
Anon rush'd by the bright Hyperion;
His flaming robes stream'd out beyond his heels,
And gave a roar, as if of earthly fire,
That scar'd away the meek ethereal hours   60
And made their dove-wings tremble: on he flared

*   *   *   *   *

[1819]   [1856]

[Sonnet]
"The day is gone . . ."

THE day is gone, and all its sweets are gone!
  Sweet voice, sweet lips, soft hand, and softer breast,
Warm breath, light whisper, tender semi-tone,
  Bright eyes, accomplish'd shape, and lang'rous
    waist!

Faded the flower and all its budded charms,
   Faded the sight of beauty from my eyes,
Faded the shape of beauty from my arms,
   Faded the voice, warmth, whiteness, paradise—
Vanish'd unseasonably at shut of eve,
   When the dusk holiday—or holinight   10
Of fragrant-curtain'd love begins to weave
   The woof of darkness thick, for hid delight;
But, as I've read love's missal through to-day,
He'll let me sleep, seeing I fast and pray.

[1819]   [1838]

KING STEPHEN

*After Keats and Charles Brown as collaborators finished the
verse play,* Otho the Great, *Keats began* King Stephen *on his
own. Ill health, or the actor Edmund Kean's trip to America, or
some dissatisfaction may have caused him to abandon it. The
action centers on Stephen's defeat by the Empress Maud at
Lincoln Castle in 1141—it was to have continued through the
death of Stephen's son Eustace and the accession of Henry.*

KING STEPHEN

A FRAGMENT OF A TRAGEDY

ACT I

SCENE I.—*Field of Battle*

Alarum. Enter King STEPHEN, *Knights,
and Soldiers.*

Stephen. If shame can on a soldier's vein-swoll'n
    front
Spread deeper crimson than the battle's toil,
Blush in your casing helmets! for see, see!
Yonder my chivalry, my pride of war,
Wrench'd with an iron hand from firm array,
Are routed loose about the plashy meads,
Of honour forfeit. O that my known voice
Could reach your dastard ears, and fright you more!
Fly, cowards, fly! Glocester is at your backs!
Throw your slack bridles o'er the flurried manes,   10
Ply well the rowel with faint trembling heels,
Scampering to death at last!
   First Knight.   The enemy
Bears his flaunt standard close upon their rear.
   Second Knight. Sure of a bloody prey, seeing the
    fens
Will swamp them girth-deep.
   Stephen.   Over head and ears,
No matter! 'Tis a gallant enemy;
How like a comet he goes streaming on.

But we must plague him in the flank,—hey, friends?
We are well breath'd,—follow!

   Enter Earl BALDWIN *and Soldiers, as defeated.*

   Stephen.   De Redvers!
What is the monstrous bugbear that can fright   20
Baldwin?
   Baldwin. No scare-crow, but the fortunate star
Of boisterous Chester, whose fell truncheon now
Points level to the goal of victory.
This way he comes, and if you would maintain .
Your person unaffronted by vile odds,
Take horse, my Lord.
   Stephen.   And which way spur for life?
Now I thank Heaven I am in the toils,
That soldiers may bear witness how my arm
Can burst the meshes. Not the eagle more
Loves to beat up against a tyrannous blast,   30
Than I to meet the torrent of my foes.
This is a brag,—be't so,—but if I fall,
Carve it upon my 'scutcheon'd sepulchre.
On, fellow soldiers! Earl of Redvers, back!
Not twenty Earls of Chester shall brow-beat
The diadem.   [*Exeunt. Alarum.*

SCENE II.—*Another part of the Field*

*Trumpets sounding a Victory.
Enter* GLOCESTER, *Knights, and Forces.*

   Glocester. Now may we lift our bruised visors up,
And take the flattering freshness of the air,
While the wide din of battle dies away
Into times past, yet to be echoed sure
In the silent pages of our chroniclers.
   First Knight. Will Stephen's death be mark'd
    there, my good Lord,
Or that we gave him lodging in yon towers?
   Glocester. Fain would I know the great usurper's
    fate.

   Enter two Captains severally.

   First Captain. My Lord!
   Second Captain. Most noble Earl!
   First Captain. The King—
   Second Captain.   The Empress greets—
   Glocester. What of the King?
   First Captain   He sole and lone maintains
A hopeless bustle mid our swarming arms,   11
And with a nimble savageness attacks,
Escapes, makes fiercer onset, then anew
Eludes death, giving death to most that dare
Trespass within the circuit of his sword!
He must by this have fallen. Baldwin is taken;
And for the Duke of Bretagne, like a stag

He flies, for the Welsh beagles to hunt down.
God save the Empress!
 Glocester.   Now our dreaded Queen:
What message from her Highness?
 Second Captain.   Royal Maud 20
From the throng'd towers of Lincoln hath look'd
 down,
Like Pallas from the walls of Ilion,[1]
And seen her enemies havock'd at her feet.
She greets most noble Gloster from her heart,
Intreating him, his captains, and brave knights,
To grace a banquet. The high city gates
Are envious which shall see your triumph pass;
The streets are full of music.

   Enter Second Knight.

 Glocester.   Whence come you?
 Second Knight. From Stephen, my good Prince,—
 Stephen! Stephen!
 Glocester. Why do you make such echoing of his
 name? 30
 Second Knight. Because I think, my lord, he is no
 man,
But a fierce demon, 'nointed safe from wounds,
And misbaptized with a Christian name.
 Glocester. A mighty soldier!—Does he still hold
 out?
 Second Knight. He shames our victory. His valour
 still
Keeps elbow-room amid our eager swords,
And holds our bladed falchions all aloof—
His gleaming battle-axe being slaughter-sick,
Smote on the morion[2] of a Flemish knight,
Broke short in his hand; upon the which he flung 40
The heft away with such a vengeful force,
It paunch'd the Earl of Chester's horse, who then
Spleen-hearted came in full career at him.
 Glocester. Did no one take him at a vantage then?
 Second Knight. Three then with tiger leap upon
 him flew,
Whom, with his sword swift-drawn and nimbly held,
He stung away again, and stood to breathe,
Smiling. Anon upon him rush'd once more
A throng of foes, and in this renew'd strife,
My sword met his and snapp'd off at the hilts. 50
 Glocester. Come, lead me to this Mars—and let us
 move
In silence, not insulting his sad doom
With clamorous trumpets. To the Empress bear
My salutation as befits the time.
    [*Exeunt* GLOCESTER *and Forces.*

---

[1] Pallas Athena aided the Greeks at Troy.
[2] Visorless helmet.

SCENE III.—*The Field of Battle.*

   Enter STEPHEN *unarmed*

 Stephen. Another sword! And what if I could seize
One from Bellona's[3] gleaming armoury,
Or choose the fairest of her sheaved spears!
Where are my enemies? Here, close at hand,
Here comes the testy brood. O, for a sword!
I'm faint—a biting sword! A noble sword!
A hedge-stake—or a ponderous stone to hurl
With brawny vengeance, like the labourer Cain.[4]
Come on! Farewell my kingdom, and all hail
Thou superb, plum'd, and helmeted renown, 10
All hail—I would not truck this brilliant day
To rule in Pylos with a Nestor's beard[5]—
Come on!

   Enter DE KAIMS *and Knights, &c.*

 De Kaims. Is't madness or a hunger after death
That makes thee thus unarm'd throw taunts at us?
Yield, Stephen, or my sword's point dip in
The gloomy current of a traitor's heart.
 Stephen. Do it, De Kaims, I will not budge an inch.
 De Kaims. Yes, of thy madness thou shalt take the
 meed.
 Stephen. Darest thou? 19
 De Kaims. How dare, against a man disarm'd?
 Stephen. What weapons has the lion but himself?
Come not near me, De Kaims, for by the price
Of all the glory I have won this day,
Being a king, I will not yield alive
To any but the second man of the realm,
Robert of Glocester.
 De Kaims. Thou shalt vail to me.
 Stephen. Shall I, when I have sworn against it, sir?
Thou think'st it brave to take a breathing king,
That, on a court-day bow'd to haughty Maud,
The awed presence-chamber may be bold 30
To whisper, there's the man who took alive
Stephen—me—prisoner. Certes, De Kaims,
The ambition is a noble one.
 De Kaims.   'Tis true,
And, Stephen, I must compass it.
 Stephen.   No, no,
Do not tempt me to throttle you on the gorge,
Or with my gauntlet crush your hollow breast,

---

[3] Roman goddess of war.
[4] Who murdered Abel.—Gen. 4:8.
[5] Nestor of Pylos was one of the most respected of the older Greek leaders. The identification of "sandy Pylos" and the location of Nestor's palace in 1939 by the late Carl Blegan was one of the triumphs of modern archaeology. The site yielded the first Linear B tablets found on the mainland, leading to the discovery that their language was Greek.

Just when your knighthood is grown ripe and full
For lordship.
    A Soldier. Is an honest yeoman's spear
Of no use at a need? Take that.
    Stephen.   Ah, dastard!
    De Kaims. What, you are vulnerable! my prisoner!
    Stephen. No, not yet. I disclaim it, and demand   41
Death as a sovereign right unto a king
Who 'sdains to yield to any but his peer,
If not in title, yet in noble deeds,
The Earl of Glocester. Stab to the hilts, De Kaims,
For I will never by mean hands be led
From this so famous field. Do ye hear! Be quick!
    [*Trumpets. Enter the Earl of* CHESTER *and Knights.*

SCENE IV.—*A Presence Chamber.* Queen MAUD *in
    a Chair of State, the Earls of* GLOCESTER *and*
    CHESTER, *Lords, Attendants.*

    Maud. Glocester, no more: I will behold that
      Boulogne:
Set him before me. Not for the poor sake
Of regal pomp and a vain-glorious hour,
As thou with wary speech, yet near enough,
Hast hinted.
    Glocester. Faithful counsel have I given;
If wary, for your Highness' benefit.
    Maud. The Heavens forbid that I should not think
      so,
For by thy valour have I won this realm,
Which by thy wisdom will I ever keep.
To sage advisers let me ever bend   10
A meek attentive ear, so that they treat
Of the wide kingdom's rule and government,
Not trenching on our actions personal.
Advis'd, not school'd, I would be; and henceforth
Spoken to in clear, plain, and open terms,
Not side-ways sermon'd at.
    Glocester.   Then, in plain terms,
Once more for the fallen king—
    Maud.   Your pardon, Brother,
I would no more of that; for, as I said,
'Tis not for worldly pomp I wish to see
The rebel, but as a dooming judge to give   20
A sentence something worthy of his guilt.
    Glocester. If't must be so, I'll bring him to your
      presence.
                    [*Exit* GLOCESTER.
    Maud. A meaner summoner might do as well—
My Lord of Chester, is't true what I hear
Of Stephen of Boulogne, our prisoner,
That he, as a fit penance for his crimes,
Eats wholesome, sweet, and palatable food

Off Glocester's golden dishes—drinks pure wine,
Lodges soft?
    Chester. More than that, my gracious Queen,
Has anger'd me. The noble Earl, methinks,   30
Full soldier as he is, and without peer
In counsel, dreams too much among his books.
It may read well, but sure 'tis out of date
To play the Alexander with Darius.
    Maud. Truth! I think so. By Heavens it shall not
      last!
    Chester. It would amaze your Highness now to
      mark
How Glocester overstrains his courtesy
To that crime-loving rebel, that Boulogne—
    Maud. That ingrate!
    Chester.   For whose vast ingratitude
To our late sovereign lord, your noble sire,   40
The generous Earl condoles in his mishaps,
And with a sort of lackeying friendliness,
Talks off the mighty frowning from his brow,
Woos him to hold a duet in a smile,
Or, if it please him, play an hour at chess—
    Maud. A perjured slave!
    Chester.   And for his perjury,
Glocester has fit rewards—nay, I believe,
He sets his bustling household's wits at work
For flatteries to ease this Stephen's hours,
And make a heaven of his purgatory;   50
Adorning bondage with the pleasant gloss
Of feasts and music, and all idle shows
Of indoor pageantry; while syren whispers,
Predestin'd for his ear, 'scape as half-check'd
From lips the courtliest and the rubiest
Of all the realm, admiring of his deeds.
    Maud. A frost upon his summer!
    Chester.   A queen's nod
Can make his June December. Here he comes.

[1819]   [1848]

TO ——
["What can I do . . ."]

WHAT can I do to drive away
Remembrance from my eyes? for they have seen,
Aye, an hour ago, my brilliant Queen!
Touch has a memory. O say, love, say,
What can I do to kill it and be free
In my old liberty?
When every fair one that I saw was fair,
Enough to catch me in but half a snare,
Not keep me there:
When, howe'er poor or particolour'd things,   10
My muse had wings,

And ever ready was to take her course
Whither I bent her force,
Unintellectual, yet divine to me;—
Divine, I say!—What sea-bird o'er the sea
Is a philosopher the while he goes
Winging along where the great water throes?

How shall I do
To get anew
Those moulted feathers, and so mount once more   20
Above, above
The reach of fluttering Love,
And make him cower lowly while I soar?
Shall I gulp wine? No, that is vulgarism,
A heresy and schism,
Foisted into the canon law of love;—
No,—wine is only sweet to happy men;
More dismal cares
Seize on me unawares,—
Where shall I learn to get my peace again?   30
To banish thoughts of that most hateful land,[1]
Dungeoner of my friends, that wicked strand
Where they were wreck'd and live a wrecked life;
That monstrous region, whose dull rivers pour,
Ever from their sordid urns unto the shore,
Unown'd of any weedy-haired gods;
Whose winds, all zephyrless, hold scourging rods,
Iced in the great lakes, to afflict mankind;
Whose rank-grown forests, frosted, black, and blind,
Would fright a Dryad; whose harsh herbag'd meads
Make lean and lank the starv'd ox while he feeds;   41
There bad flowers have no scent, birds no sweet song,
And great unerring Nature once seems wrong.

O, for some sunny spell
To dissipate the shadows of this hell!
Say they are gone,—with the new dawning light
Steps forth my lady bright!
O, let me once more rest
My soul upon that dazzling breast!
Let once again these aching arms be plac'd,   50
The tender gaolers of thy waist!
And let me feel that warm breath here and there
To spread a rapture in my very hair,—
O, the sweetness of the pain!
Give me those lips again!
Enough! Enough! it is enough for me
To dream of thee!

[1819]   [1848]

---

[1] The American frontier in Kentucky, where his brother George had been financially ruined, partly as a victim of unscrupulous advice. See note on p. 1118.

[BRIGHT STAR]

The date of the composition of this sonnet has been estimated as early as July 1819 and as late as the autumn of 1820 (when Keats did revise it as it appears below). In an earlier version it concludes:

> *No;—yet still stedfast, still unchangeable,*
> *Cheek-pillow'd on my Love's white breast,*
> *To touch, for ever, its warm sink and swell,*
> *Awake, for ever, in a sweet unrest;*
> *To hear, to feel her tender-taken breath,*
> *Half-passionless, and so swoon on to death.*

[Sonnet]
[Bright Star]

BRIGHT star! would I were steadfast as thou art—
  Not in lone splendour hung aloft the night
And watching, with eternal lids apart,
  Like nature's patient, sleepless Eremite,
The moving waters at their priestlike task
  Of pure ablution round earth's human shores,
Or gazing on the new soft fallen mask
  Of snow upon the mountains and the moors—
No—yet still steadfast, still unchangeable,
  Pillow'd upon my fair love's ripening breast,   10
To feel for ever its soft fall and swell,
  Awake for ever in a sweet unrest,
Still, still to hear her tender-taken breath,
And so live ever—or else swoon to death.

[1819?]   [1838]

[Sonnet]
"I cry your mercy . . ."

I CRY your mercy—pity—love!—aye, love!
  Merciful love that tantalises not,
One-thoughted, never-wandering, guileless love,
  Unmask'd, and being seen—without a blot!
O! let me have thee whole,—all—all—be mine!
  That shape, that fairness, that sweet minor zest
Of love, your kiss,—those hands, those eyes divine,
  That warm, white, lucent, million-pleasured
    breast,—
Yourself—your soul—in pity give me all,
  Withhold no atom's atom or I die,   10
Or living on perhaps, your wretched thrall,
  Forget, in the mist of idle misery,
Life's purposes,—the palate of my mind
Losing its gust, and my ambition blind!

[1819]   [1848]

"THIS LIVING HAND..."

*Although early readers and editors assumed this poem was
addressed to Fanny Brawne, manuscript evidence has convinced
most modern editors that it was a fragment of verse designed either
for a play or for a longer poem, and that its speaker is not
necessarily Keats.*

"This living hand . . ."

THIS living hand, now warm and capable
Of earnest grasping, would, if it were cold
And in the icy silence of the tomb,
So haunt thy days and chill thy dreaming nights
That thou wouldst wish thine own heart dry of blood
So in my veins red life might stream again,
And thou be conscience-calm'd—see here it is—
I hold it towards you.

[1819]   [1898]

ODE TO FANNY

I

PHYSICIAN Nature! let my spirit blood![1]
  O ease my heart of verse and let me rest;
Throw me upon thy Tripod,[2] till the flood
  Of stifling numbers ebbs from my full breast.
A theme! a theme! great Nature! give a theme;
    Let me begin my dream.
I come—I see thee, as thou standest there,
Beckon me out into the wintry air.

II

Ah! dearest love, sweet home of all my fears,
  And hopes, and joys, and panting miseries,—   10
To-night, if I may guess, thy beauty wears
    A smile of such delight,
    As brilliant and as bright,
As when with ravished, aching, vassal eyes,
    Lost in soft amaze,
    I gaze, I gaze!

III

Who now, with greedy looks, eats up my feast?
  What stare outfaces now my silver moon!
Ah! keep that hand unravished at the least;
    Let, let, the amorous burn—   20
    But, pr'ythee, do not turn
The current of your heart from me so soon.
    O! save, in charity,
    The quickest pulse for me.

IV

Save it for me, sweet love! though music breathe
  Voluptuous visions into the warm air;
Though swimming through the dance's dangerous
    wreath;
    Be like an April day,
    Smiling and cold and gay,
A temperate lily, temperate as fair;   30
    Then, Heaven! there will be
    A warmer June for me.

V

Why, this—you'll say, my Fanny! is not true:
  Put your soft hand upon your snowy side,
Where the heart beats: confess—'tis nothing new—
    Must not a woman be
    A feather on the sea,
Sway'd to and fro by every wind and tide?
    Of as uncertain speed
    As blow-ball[3] from the mead?   40

VI

I know it—and to know it is despair
  To one who loves you as I love, sweet Fanny!
Whose heart goes fluttering for you every where,
    Nor, when away you roam,
    Dare keep its wretched home,
Love, Love alone, has pains severe and many:
    Then, loveliest! keep me free
    From torturing jealousy.

VII

Ah! if you prize my subdued soul above
  The poor, the fading, brief, pride of an hour;   50
Let none profane my Holy See of love,
    Or with a rude hand break
    The sacramental cake:
Let none else touch the just new-budded flower;
    If not—may my eyes close,
    Love! on their last repose.

[1820?]   [1848]

---

[1] Bloodletting surgically and with leeches was still a common
medical practice and part of the treatment Keats was receiving.
[2] The three-legged seat of the Sybil when prophesying at
Delphi.

[3] The dandelion gone to seed.

PROSE

LETTERS

In the following letters, emendations made by the editor (Hyder Edward Rollins) are indicated as follows:

Brackets [ ] *indicate misspellings corrected or necessary words added.*

Braces { } *indicate words or letters added to replace those torn away or obliterated.*

Angle marks ⟨ ⟩ *enclose words or letters Keats himself wrote and then canceled.*

Many obvious errors and slips of the pen are not corrected.

TO B. R. HAYDON

Margate Saturday Eve
[10, 11 May 1817]

My dear Haydon,

Let Fame, which all hunt after in their Lives,
Live register'd upon our brazen tombs,
And so grace us in the disgrace of death:
When spite of cormorant devouring time
The endeavour of this pre⟨a⟩sent breath may buy
That Honor which shall bate his Scythe's keen edge
And make us heirs of all eternity.[1]

To think that I have no right to couple myself with you in this speech would be death to me so I have e'en written it—and I pray God that our brazen Tombs be nigh neighbors. It cannot be long first the endeavor of this present breath will soon be over—and yet it is as well to breathe freely during our sojourn—it is as well if you have not been teased with that Money affair—that bill-pestilence. However I must think that difficulties nerve the Spirit of a Man—they make our Prime Objects a Refuge as well as a Passion. The Trumpet of Fame is as a tower of Strength the ambitious bloweth it and is safe—I suppose by your telling me not to give way to forebodings George has mentioned to you what I have lately said in my Letters to him—truth is I have been in such a state of Mind as to read over my Lines and hate them. I am "one that gathers Samphire dreadful trade"[2] the Cliff of Poesy Towers above me—yet when, Tom who meets with some of Pope's Homer in Plutarch's Lives reads some of those to me they seem like Mice to mine. I read and write about eight hours a day. There is an old saying

well begun is half done"—'t is a bad one. I would use instead—Not begun at all 'till half done" so according to that I have not begun my Poem and consequently (a priori) can say nothing about it. Thank God! I do begin arduously where I leave off, notwithstanding occasional depressions: and I hope for the support of a High Power while I clime this little eminence and especially in my Years of more momentous Labor. I remember your saying that you had notions of a good Genius presiding over you—I have of late had the same thought. for things which [I] do half at Random are afterwards confirmed by my judgment in a dozen features of Propriety—Is it too daring to Fancy Shakspeare this Presider? When in the Isle of W⟨h⟩ight I met with a Shakspeare in the Passage of the House at which I lodged—it comes nearer to my idea of him than any I have seen—I was but there a Week yet the old Woman made me take it with me though I went off in a hurry—Do you not think this is ominous of good? I am glad you say every Man of great Views is at times tormented as I am—

Sunday Aft. This Morning I received a letter from George by which it appears that Money Troubles are to follow us up for some time to come perhaps for always—these vexations are a great hindrance to one—they are not like Envy and detraction stimulants to further exertion as being immediately relative and reflected on at the same time with the prime object—but rather like a nettle leaf or two in your bed. So now I revoke my Promise of finishing my Poem by the Autumn which I should have done had I gone on as I have done—but I cannot write while my spirit is fe⟨a⟩vered in a contrary direction and I am now sure of having plenty of it this Summer —At this moment I am in no enviable Situation—I feel that I am not in a Mood to write any to day; and it appears that the lo⟨o⟩ss of it is the beginning of all sorts of irregularities. I am extremely glad that a time must come when every thing will leave not a wrack behind. You tell me never to despair—I wish it was as easy for me to observe the saying—truth is I have a horrid Morbidity of Temperament which has shown itself at intervals—it is I have no doubt the greatest Enemy and stumbling block I have to fear—I may even say that it is likely to be the cause of my disappointment. How ever every ill has its share of good—this very bane would at any time enable me to look with an obstinate eye on the Devil Himself—ay to be as proud of being the lowest of the human race as Alfred could be in being of the highest.

---

[1] Shakespeare's *Love's Labor's Lost*, I, i, 1–7 (slightly misquoted).

[2] From Shakespeare's *King Lear*, IV, vi, 15.

I feel confident I should have been a rebel Angel had the opportunity been mine. I am very sure that you do love me as your own Brother—I have seen it in your continual anxiety for me—and I assure you that your wellfare and fame is and will be a chief pleasure to me all my Life. I know no one but you who can be fully sensible of the turmoil and anxiety, the sacrifice of all what is called comfort the readiness to Measure time by what is done and to die in 6 hours could plans be brought to conclusions.—the looking upon the Sun the Moon the Stars, the Earth and its contents as materials to form greater things— that is to say ethereal things——but here I am talking like a Madman greater things that our Creator himself made!! I wrote to Hunt yesterday— scar[c]ely know what I said in it—I could not talk about Poetry in the way I should have liked for I was not in humor with either his or mine. His self delusions are very lamentable they have inticed him into a Situation which I should be less eager after than that of a galley Slave—what you observe thereon is very true must be in time. Perhaps it is a self delusion to say so—but I think I could not be deceived in the Manner that Hunt is—may I die tomorrow if I am to be. There is no greater Sin after the 7 deadly than to flatter one-self into an idea of being a great Poet— or one of those beings who are privileged to wear out their Lives in the pursuit of Honor—how comfortable a feel it is that such a Crime must bring its heavy Penalty? That if one be a Selfdeluder accounts will be balanced? I am glad you are hard at Work—'t will now soon be done—I long to see Wordsworth's as well as to have mine in:[3] but I would rather not show my face in Town till the end of the Year—if that will be time enough—if not I shall be disappointed if you do not write for me even when you think best— I never quite despair and I read Shakspeare—indeed I shall I think never read any other Book much— Now this might lead me into a long Confab but I desist. I am very near Agreeing with Hazlit that Shakspeare is enough for us—. . . .'T is good too that the Duke of Wellington has a good Word or so in the Examiner.[4] A Man ought to have the Fame he deserves—and I begin to think that detracting from him as well as from Wordsworth is the same thing. I wish he had a little more taste—and did not in that respect "deal in Lieutenantry" You should have heard from me before this—but in the first place I did not like to do so before I had got a little way in the 1st Book and in the next as G. told me you

were going to write I delayed till I had hea[r]d from you—Give my Respects the next time you write to the North[5] and also to John Hunt[6]—Remember me to Reynolds and tell him to write, Ay, and when you sent Westward tell your Sister that I mentioned her in this—So now in the Name of Shakespeare Raphael and all our Saints I commend you to the care of heaven!

Your everlasting friend
John Keats—

Benjamin Bailey (1791–1853) was an Oxford student when Keats first knew him; later he became Bishop of Ceylon.

To Benjamin Bailey

Hamps[t]ead Oct[r] Wednesday
[8 October 1817]

My dear Bailey,

After a tolerable journey I went from Coach to Coach to as far as Hampstead where I found my Brothers—the next Morning finding myself tolerably well I went to Lambs Conduit Street and delivered your Parcel—Jane and Marianne[1] were greatly improved Marianne especially she has no unhealthy plumpness in the face—but she comes me healthy and angular to the Chin—I did not see John I was extrem{e}ly sorry to hear that poor Rice after having had capital Health During his tour, was very ill. I dare say you have heard from him. From No 19 I went to Hunt's and Haydon's who live now neighbours. Shelley was there—I know nothing about any thing in this part of the world—every Body seems at Logger-heads. There's Hunt infatuated—theres Haydon's Picture in statu quo. There's Hunt walks up and down his painting room criticising every head most unmercifully—There's Horace Smith tired of Hunt. The web of our Life is of mingled Yarn" Haydon having removed entirely from Marlborough street Crips must direct his Letter to Lisson Grove North Paddington. Yesterday Morning while I was at Brown's in came Reynolds—he was pretty bobbish we had a pleasant day—but he would walk home at night that cursed cold distance. Mrs Bentley's children are making a horrid row[2]—whereby I regret I cannot be transported to your Room to write to you. I am quite disgusted with literary Men and will

---

[3] Haydon's mammoth painting, *Christ's Entry into Jerusalem*, in which Keats and Wordsworth both appear.

[4] The journal that Leigh Hunt edited for thirteen years—until 1821.

[5] I.e., to Wordsworth.

[6] Leigh Hunt's brother John, publisher of the *Examiner*.

[1] The sisters of J. H. Reynolds.

[2] Keats and his brothers were living with Benjamin Bentley, a postman, in Hampstead.

never know another except Wordsworth—no not even Byron—Here is an instance of the friendships of such—Haydon and Hunt have known each other many years—now they live pour ainsi dire jealous Neighbours. Haydon says to me Keats dont show your Lines to Hunt on any account or he will have done half for you—so it appears Hunt wishes it to be thought. When he met Reynolds in the Theatre John told him that I was getting on to the completion of 4000 Lines. Ah! says Hunt, had it not been for me they would have been 7000! If he will say this to Reynolds what would he to other People? Haydon received a Letter a little while back on this subject from some Lady—which contains a caution to me through him on this subject—Now is not all this a most paultry thing to think about? You may see the whole of the case by the following extract from a Letter I wrote to George in the spring.[3] "As to "what you say about my being a Poet, I can retu[r]n "no answer but by saying that the high Idea I have "of poetical fame makes me think I see it towering to "high above me. At any rate I have no ⟨wi⟩ right "to talk until Endymion is finished—it will be a test, "a trial of my Powers of Imagination and chiefly "of my invention which is a rare thing indeed—by "which I must make 4000 Lines of one bare cir- "cumstance and fill them with Poetry; and when I "consider that this is a great task, and that when done "it will take me but a dozen paces towards the "Temple of Fame—it makes me say—God forbid "that I should be without such a task! I have heard "Hunt say and may be asked—why endeavour after "a long Poem? To which I should answer—Do not "the Lovers of Poetry like to have a little Region to "wander in where they may pick and choose, and in "which the images are so numerous that many are "forgotten and found new in a second Reading: "which may be food for a Week's stroll in the "Summer? Do not they like this better than what "they can read through before M[rs] Williams comes "down stairs? a Morning work at most. Besides a "long Poem is a test of Invention which I take to be "the Polar Star of Poetry, as Fancy is the Sails, and "Imagination the Rudder. Did our great Poets ever "write short Pieces? I mean in the shape of Tales— "This same invention seems i{n}deed of late Years to "have been forgotten as a Poetical excellence{.} "But enough of this, I put on no Laurels till I shall "have finished Endymion, and I hope Apollo is " {not} angered at my having made a Mockery at him at "Hunt's" You see Bailey how independant my writing has been—Hunts dissuasion was of no avail—

---

[3] This letter has disappeared.

I refused to visit Shelley, that I might have my own unfetterd scope—and after all I shall have the Reputation of Hunt's elevé—His corrections and amputations will by the knowing ones be trased in the Poem—This is to be sure the vexation of a day— nor would I say so many Words about it to any but those whom I know to have my wellfare and Reputation at Heart—Haydon promised to give directions for those Casts and you may expect to see them soon —with as many Letters You will soon hear the dinning of Bells—never mind you and Gleg will defy the foul fiend—But do not sacrifice your heal[t]h to Books do take it kindly and not so voraciously. I am certain if you are your own Physician your stomach will resume its proper strength and then what great Benefits will follow. My Sister wrote a Letter to me which I think must be at $\frac{e}{y}$ post office Ax Will to see. My Brothers kindest remembrances to you— we are going to dine at Brown's where I have some hopes of meeting Reynolds. The little Mercury I have taken has corrected the Poison and improved my Health—though I feel from my employment that I shall never be again secure in Robustness—would that you were as well as

> your sincere friend & brother
> John Keats

The Dilks are expected to day—

To Benjamin Bailey

[22 November 1817]

My dear Bailey,

I will get over the first part of this (*un*said) Letter as soon as possible for it relates to the affair of poor Crips—To a Man of your nature, such a Letter as Haydon's must have been extremely cutting—What occasions the greater part of the World's Quarrels? simply this, two Minds meet and do not understand each other time enough to p[r]aevent any shock or surprise at the conduct of either party—As soon as I had known Haydon three days I had got enough of his character not to have been surp[r]ised at such a Letter as he has hurt you with. Nor when I knew it was it a principle with me to drop his acquaintance although with you it would have been an imperious feeling. I wish you knew all that I think about Genius and the Heart—and yet I think you are thoroughly acquainted with my innermost breast in that respect or you could not have known me even thus long and still hold me worthy to be your dear friend. In passing however I must say of one thing that has pressed upon me lately and encreased my Humility

and capability of submission and that is this truth—
Men of Genius are great as certain ethereal Chemicals
operating on the Mass of neutral intellect—by they
have not any individuality, any determined Character.
I would call the top and head of those who have a
proper self Men of Power—

But I am running my head into a Subject which I
am certain I could not do justice to under five years
s[t]udy and 3 vols octavo—and moreover long to be
talking about the Imagination—so my dear Bailey
do not think of this unpleasant affair if possible—do
not—I defy any ha[r]m to come of it—I defy—I'll
shall write to Crips this Week and reque[s]t him to
tell me all his goings on from time to time by Letter
whereever I may be—it will all go on well—so dont
because you have suddenly discover'd a Coldness in
Haydon suffer yourself to be teased. Do not my dear
fellow. O I wish I was as certain of the end of all
your troubles as that of your momentary start about
the authenticity of the Imagination. I am certain of
nothing but of the holiness of the Heart's affections
and the truth of Imagination—What the imagination
seizes as Beauty must be truth[1]—whether it existed
before or not—for I have the same Idea of all our
Passions as of Love they are all in their sublime,
creative of essential Beauty—In a Word, you may
know my favorite Speculation by my first Book and
the little song I sent in my last—which is a representa-
tion from the fancy of the probable mode of operating
in these Matters—The Imagination may be compared
to Adam's dream[2]—he awoke and found it truth. I
am the more zealous in this affair, because I have
never yet been able to perceive how any thing can be
known for truth by consequitive reasoning—and yet
it must be—Can it be that even the greatest Philo-
sopher ever ⟨when⟩ arrived at his goal without
putting aside numerous objections—However it may
be, O for a Life of Sensations rather than of Thoughts!
It is 'a Vision in the form of Youth' a Shadow of
reality to come—and this consideration has further
conv[i]nced me for it has come as auxiliary to an-
other favorite Speculation of mine, that we shall
enjoy ourselves here after by having what we called
happiness on Earth repeated in a finer tone and so
repeated—And yet such a fate can only befall those
who delight in sensation rather than hunger as you
do after Truth—Adam's dream will do here and
seems to be a conviction that Imagination and its
empyreal reflection is the same as human Life and
its spiritual repetition. But as I was saying—the
simple imaginative Mind may have its rewards in the

repeti[ti]on of its own silent Working coming
continually on the spirit with a fine suddenness—to
compare great things with small—have you never by
being surprised with an old Melody—in a delicious
place—by a delicious voice, fe[l]t over again your
very speculations and surmises at the time it first
operated on your soul—do you not remember
forming to youself the singer's face more beautiful
that[3] it was possible and yet with the elevation of the
Moment you did not think so—even then you were
mounted on the Wings of Imagination so high—that
the Prototype must be here after—that delicious face
you will see—What a time! I am continually running
away from the subject—sure this cannot be exactly
the case with a complex Mind—one that is imagina-
tive and at the same time careful of its fruits—who
would exist partly on sensation partly on thought—to
whom it is necessary that years should bring the
philosophic Mind—such an one I consider your's
and therefore it is necessary to your eternal Happiness
that you not only ⟨have⟩ drink this old Wine of
Heaven which I shall call the redigestion of our most
ethereal Musings on Earth; but also increase in
knowledge and know all things. I am glad to hear
you are in a fair Way for Easter—you will soon get
through your unpleasant reading and then!—but
the world is full of troubles and I have not much
reason to think myself pesterd with many—I think
Jane or Marianne has a better opinion of me than I
deserve—for really and truly I do not think my
Brothers illness connected with mine—you know
more of the real Cause than they do[4]—nor have I any
chance of being rack'd as you have been—you perhaps
at one time thought there was such a thing as Worldly
Happiness to be arrived at, at certain periods of
time marked out—you have of necessity from your
disposition been thus led away—I scarcely remember
counting upon any Happiness—I look not for it if it
be not in the present hour—nothing startles me
beyond the Moment. The setting sun will always set
me to rights—or if a Sparrow come before my
Window I take part in its existince and pick about
the Gravel. The first thing that strikes me on hea[r]ing
a Misfortune having befalled another is this. 'Well
it cannot be helped.—he will have the pleasure of
trying the resourses of his spirit, and I beg now my
dear Bailey that hereafter should you observe any
thing cold in me not to but[5] it to the account of heart-

---

[1] See the last stanza of *Ode on a Grecian Urn*, p. 1080.
[2] *Paradise Lost*, Book VIII.

---

[3] than.
[4] This, and the references in the preceding letter to Bailey and
elsewhere to mercury, have led some biographers to speculate that
Keats was suffering from syphillis. There seems to be no way to
resolve this question.
[5] put.

lessness but abstraction—for I assure you I sometimes feel not the influence of a Passion or Affection during a whole week—and so long this sometimes continues I begin to suspect myself and the genuiness of my feelings at other times—thinking them a few barren Tragedy-tears—My Brother Tom is much improved —he is going to Devonshire—whither I shall follow him—at present I am just arrived at Dorking to change the Scene—change the Air and give me a spur to wind up my Poem, of which there are wanting 500 Lines.[6] I should have been here a day sooner but the Reynoldses persuaded me to spop in Town to meet your friend Christie—There were Rice and Martin—we talked about Ghosts—I will have some talk with Taylor and let you know—which please God I come down a[t] Christmas—I will find that Examiner if possible. My best regards to Gleig—My Brothers to you and Mrs Bentley.

Your affectionate friend
John Keats—

I want to say much more to you—a few hints will set me going Direct Burford Bridge near dorking

To George and Tom Keats

Hampstead Sunday
22 December 1818[1]
[21, 27(?) December 1817]

My Dear Brothers

I must crave your pardon for not having written ere this & & I saw Kean[2] return to the public in Richard III, & finely he did it, & at the request of Reynolds I went to criticise his Luke in Riches— the critique is in todays champion, which I send you with the Examiner in which you will find very proper lamentation on the obsoletion of christmas Gambols & pastimes: but it was mixed up with so much egotism of that drivelling nature that pleasure is entirely lost. Hone[3] the publisher's trial, you must find very amusing; & as Englishmen very ⟨amusing⟩ encouraging—his *Not Guilty* is a thing, which not to have been, would have dulled still more Liberty's Emblazoning—Lord Ellenborough has been paid in his own coin—Wooler & Hone have done us an essential service—I have had two very pleasant evenings with Dilke yesterday & today; & am at this moment just come from him & feel in the humour to go on with this, began in the morning, & from which he came to fetch me. I spent Friday evening with Wells[4] & went the next morning to see *Death on the Pale horse.*[5] It is a wonderful picture, when West's age is considered; But there is nothing to be intense upon; no women one feels mad to kiss; no face swelling into reality. the excellence of every Art is its intensity, capable of making all disagreeables evaporate, from their being in close relationship with Beauty & Truth—Examine King Lear & you will find this examplified throughout; but in this picture we have unpleasantness without any momentous depth of speculation excited, in which to bury its repulsiveness—The picture is larger than Christ rejected—I dined with Haydon the sunday after you left, & had a very pleasant day, I dined too (for I have been out too much lately) with Horace Smith & met his two Brothers with Hill & Kingston & one Du Bois, they only served to convince me, how superior humour is to wit in respect to enjoyment— These men say things which make one start, without making one feel, they are all alike; their manners are alike; they all know fashionables; they have a mannerism in their very eating & drinking, in their mere handling a Decanter—They talked of Kean & his low company—Would I were with that company instead of yours said I to myself! I know such like acquaintance will never do for me & yet I am going to Reynolds, on wednesday—Brown & Dilke walked with me & back from the Christmas pantomime. I had not a dispute but a disquisition with Dilke, on various subjects; several things dovetailed in my mind, & at once it struck me, what quality went to form a Man of Achievement especially in Literature & which Shakespeare posessed so enormously—I mean *Negative Capability*, that is when man is capable of being in uncertainties, Mysteries, doubts, without any irritable reaching after fact & reason—Coleridge, for instance, would let go by a fine isolated verisimilitude caught from the Penetralium of mystery, from being incapable of remaining content with half knowledge. This pursued through Volumes would perhaps take us no further than this, that with a great poet the sense of Beauty overcomes every other consideration, or rather obliterates all consideration.

Shelley's poem[6] is out & there are words about its being objected too, as much as Queen Mab was.

---

[6] *Endymion.*
[1] This letter survives only in an unreliable transcript, which is apparently dated in error.
[2] Edmund Kean (1787–1833), Shakespearean actor, for whom Keats later began *King Stephen*. Keats was also reviewing plays for the *Champion*.
[3] William Hone, a bookseller, had just been acquitted of libel. Lord Ellenborough, Lord Chief Justice, had sentenced Leigh Hunt to prison in 1813.

---

[4] Charles Wells—see *To a Friend who Sent Me Some Roses*, p. 1009.
[5] By Benjamin West (1738–1820), American painter living in England, president of the Royal Academy. He was then eighty.
[6] *The Revolt of Islam*, pp. 802 ff.

Poor Shelley I think he has his Quota of good qualities, in sooth la!! Write soon to your most sincere friend & affectionate Brother.

[Signed] John

Mess[rs] Keats
Teignmouth Devonshire

To J. H. REYNOLDS

Teignmouth May 3[d]
[3 May 1818]

My dear Reynolds.

What I complain of is that I have been in so an uneasy a state of Mind as not to be fit to write to an invalid. I cannot write to any length under a disguised feeling. I should have loaded you with an addition of gloom, which I am sure you do not want. I am now thank God in a humour to give you a good groats worth—for Tom, after a Night without a Wink of sleep, and overburdened with fever, has got up after a refreshing day sleep and is better than he has been for a long time; and you I trust have been again round the Common without any effect but refreshment.—As to the Matter I hope I can say with Sir Andrew "I have matter enough in my head" in your favor And now, in the second place, for I reckon that I have finished my Imprimis, I am glad you blow up the weather—all through your letter there is a leaning towards a climate-curse. and you know what a delicate satisfaction there is in having a vexation anathematized: one would think there has been growing up for these last four thousand years, a grandchild Scion of the old forbidden tree, and that some modern Eve had just violated it; and that there was come with double charge, "Notus and Afer black with thunderous clouds from ⟨Sera⟩ Sierra-leona"[1]—I shall breathe worsted stockings sooner than I thought for. Tom wants to be in Town—we will have some such days upon the heath like that of last summer and why not with the same book: or what say you to a black Letter Chaucer printed in 1596: aye I've got one huzza! I shall have it bounden gothique a nice sombre binding—it will go a little way to unmodernize. And also I see no reason, because I have been away this last month, why I should not have a peep at your Spencerian—notwithstanding you speak of your office, in my thought a little too early, for I do not see why a Mind like yours is not capable of harbouring and digesting the whole Mystery of Law as easily as Parson Hugh does Pepins[2]—which did not hinder him from his poetic

Canary[3]—Were I to study physic or rather Medicine again,—I feel it would not make the least difference in my Poetry; when the Mind is in its infancy a Bias ⟨in⟩ is in reality a Bias, but when we have acquired more strength, a Bias becomes no Bias. Every department of knowledge we see excellent and calculated towards a great whole. I am so convinced of this, that I am glad at not having given away my medical Books, which I shall again look over to keep alive the little I know thitherwards; and moreover intend through you and Rice to become a sort of Pip-civilian. An extensive knowledge is needful to thinking people—it takes away the heat and fever; and helps, by widening speculation, to ease the Burden of the Mystery[4]: a thing I begin to understand a little, and which weighed upon you in the most gloomy and true sentence in your Letter. The difference of high Sensations with and without knowledge appears to me this—in the latter case we are falling continually ten thousand fathoms deep and being blown up again without wings and with all [the] horror of a ⟨Case⟩ bare shoulderd Creature—in the former case, our shoulders are fledge⟨d⟩, and we go thro' the same ⟨Fir⟩ air and space without fear. This is running one's rigs on the score of abstracted benefit—when we come to human Life and the affections it is impossible how a parallel of breast and head can be drawn—(you will forgive me for thus privately ⟨heading⟩ treading out[5] my depth and take it for treading as schoolboys ⟨head⟩ tread the water⟨s⟩)—it is impossible to know how far knowledge will console ⟨as⟩ us for the death of a friend and the ill "that flesh is heir to⟨o⟩— . . .

You may be anxious to know for fact to what sentence in your Letter I allude. You say "I fear there is little chance of any thing else in this life." You seem by that to have been going through with a more painful and acute ⟨test⟩ zest the same labyrinth that I have—I have come to the same conclusion thus far. My Branchings out therefrom have been numerous: one of them is the consideration of Wordsworth's genius and as a help, in the manner of gold being the meridian Line of worldly wealth,—how he differs from Milton.—And here I have nothing but surmises, from an uncertainty whether Miltons apparently less anxiety for Humanity proceeds from his seeing further or no than Wordsworth: And whether Wordsworth has in truth epic passion⟨s⟩, and martyrs himself to the human

---

[1] *Paradise Lost*, X, 702.
[2] In Shakespeare's *The Merry Wives of Windsor*, I, ii, 11.

[3] "Canary" for "Quandary" is a joke in the same play.
[4] See Wordsworth's *Tintern Abbey*, p. 202, and its use later in this letter.
[5] I.e., out *of*.

heart, the main region of his song. In regard to his genius alone—we find what he says true as far as we have experienced and we can judge no further but by larger experience—for axioms in philosophy are not axioms until they are proved upon our pulses: We read fine——things but never feel them to thee full until we have gone the same steps as the Author.—I know this is not plain; you will know exactly my meaning when I say, that now I shall relish Hamlet more than I ever have done—Or, better—You are sensible no man can set down Venery as a bestial or joyless thing until he is sick of it and therefore all philosophizing on it would be mere wording. Until we are sick, we understand not;—in fine, as Byron says, "Knowledge is Sorrow";[6] and I go on to say that "Sorrow is Wisdom"—and further for aught we can know for certainty! "Wisdom is folly"—So you see how I have run away from Wordsworth, and Milton; and shall still run away from what was in my head, to observe, that some kind of letters are good squares others handsome ovals, and others some orbicular, others spheroid—and why should there not be another species with two rough edges like a Rat-trap? I hope you will find all my long letters of that species, and all will be well; for by merely touching the spring delicately and etherially, the rough edged will fly immediately into a proper compactness, and thus you may make a good wholesome loaf, with your own leven in it, of my fragments —If you cannot find this said Rat-trap sufficiently tractable—alas for me, it being an impossibility in grain for my ink to stain otherwise: If I scribble long letters I must play my vagaries. I must be too heavy, or too light, for whole pages—I must be quaint and free of Tropes and figures—I must play my draughts as I please, and for my advantage and your erudition, crown a white with a black, or a black with a white, and move into black or white, far and near as I please—I must go from Hazlitt to Patmore, and make Wordsworth and Coleman[7] play at leap-frog—or keep one of them down a whole half holiday at fly the garter—"From Gray to Gay, from Little to Shakespeare"—Also as a long cause requires two or more sittings of the Court, so a long letter will require two or more sittings of the Breech wherefore I shall resume after dinner.—

Have you not seen a Gull, an orc, a sea Mew, or any thing to bring this Line to a proper length, and also fill up this clear part; that like the Gull I may *dip*—I hope, not out of sight—and also, like a Gull, I hope to be lucky in a good sized fish—This cros-

sing[8] a letter is not without its association—for chequer work leads us naturally to a Milkmaid, a Milkmaid to Hogarth Hogarth to Shakespeare Shakespear to Hazlitt—Hazlitt to Shakespeare and thus by merely pulling an apron string we set a pretty peal of Chimes at work—Let them chime on while, with your patience,—I will return to Wordsworth—whether or no he has an extended vision or a circumscribed grandeur—whether he is an eagle in his nest, or on the wing—And to be more explicit and to show you how tall I stand by the giant, I will put down a simile of human life as far as I now perceive it; that is, to the point to which I say we both have arrived at—' Well—I compare human life to a large Mansion of Many Apartments, two of which I can only describe, the doors of the rest being as yet shut upon me—The first we step into we call the infant or thoughtless Chamber, in which we remain as long as we do not think—We remain there a long while, and notwithstanding the doors of the second Chamber remain wide open, showing a bright appearance, we care not to hasten to it; but are at length imperceptibly impelled by the awakening of the thinking principle—within us—we no sooner get into the second Chamber, which I shall call the Chamber of Maiden-Thought, than we become intoxicated with the light and the atmosphere, we see nothing but pleasant wonders, and think of delaying there for ever in delight: However among the effects this breathing is father of is that tremendous one of sharpening one's vision into the ⟨head⟩ heart and nature of Man—of convincing ones nerves that the World is full of Misery and Heartbreak, Pain, Sickness and oppression—whereby This Chamber of Maiden Thought becomes gradually darken'd and at the same time on all sides of it many doors are set open—but all dark—all leading to dark passages— We see not the ballance of good and evil. We are in a Mist—*We* are now in that state—We feel the "burden of the Mystery," To this point was Wordsworth come, as far as I can conceive when he wrote 'Tintern Abbey' and it seems to me that his Genius is explorative of those dark Passages. Now if we live, and go on thinking, we too shall explore them. he is a Genius and superior [to] us, in so far as he can, more than we, make discoveries, and shed a light in them—Here I must think Wordsworth is deeper than Milton— though I think it has depended more upon the general and gregarious advance of intellect, than individual greatness of Mind—From the Paradise

[6] See *Manfred*, I, i, 10, p. 603.
[7] George Coleman (1762–1836), minor playwright.

[8] In the days of expensive postage and paper, people frequently saved both by turning the paper 90° and writing across what they had just written.

Lost and the other Works of Milton, I hope it is not too presuming, even between ourselves to say, his Philosophy, human and divine, may be tolerably understood by one not much advanced in years, In his time englishmen were just emancipated from a great superstition—and Men had got hold of certain points and resting places in reasoning which were too newly born to be doubted, and too much ⟨oppressed⟩ opposed by the Mass of Europe not to be thought etherial and authentically divine—who could gainsay his ideas on virtue, vice, and Chastity in Comus, just at the time of the dismissal of Codpieces⁹ and a hundred other disgraces? who would not rest satisfied with his hintings at good and evil in the Paradise Lost, when just free from the inquisition and burning in Smithfield? The Reformation produced such immediate and great⟨s⟩ benefits, that Protestantism was considered under the immediate eye of heaven, and its own remaining Dogmas and superstitions, then, as it were, regenerated, constituted those resting places and seeming sure points of Reasoning—from that I have mentioned, Milton, whatever he may have thought in the sequel, appears to have been content with these by his writings—He did not think into the human heart, as Wordsworth has done—Yet Milton as a Philosop⟨h⟩er, had sure as great powers as Wordsworth—What is then to be inferr'd? O many things—It proves there is really a grand march of intellect—, It proves that a mighty providence subdues the mightiest Minds to the service of the time being, whether it be in human Knowledge or Religion—I have often pitied a Tutor who has to hear "Nomᵉ: Musa"¹⁰—so often dinn'd into his ears—I hope you may not have the same pain in this scribbling—I may have read these things before, but I never had even a thus dim perception of them; and moreover I like to say my lesson to one who will endure my tediousness for my own sake—After all there is certainly something real in the World—Moore's present to Hazlitt is real—I like that Moore, and am glad ⟨that⟩ I saw him at the Theatre just before I left Town. Tom had spit a leetle blood this afternoon, and that is rather a damper—but I know—the truth is there is something real in the World Your third Chamber of Life shall be a lucky and a gentle one—stored with the wine of love—and the Bread of Friendship—When you see George if he should not have recēd a letter from me tell him he will find one at home most likely—tell Bailey I hope soon to see him—Remember me to all The leaves have been out here, for MONY a

day—I have written to George for the first stanzas of my Isabel—I shall have them soon and will copy the whole out for you.
Your affectionate friend
John Keats.

Mʳ John H. Reynolds
        Little Britain
                Christs Hospital London.—

TO BENJAMIN BAILEY

Inverary July 18ᵗʰ
[18, 22 July 1818]

My dear Bailey,
    The only day I have had a chance of seeing you when you were last in London I took every advantage of—some devil led you out of the way—Now I have written to Reynolds to tell me where you will be in Cumberland—so that I cannot miss you—and when I see you the first thing I shall do will be to read that about Milton and Ceres and Proserpine ¹—for though I am not going after you to John o'Grotts ² it will be but poetical to say so. And here Bailey I will say a few words written in a sane and sober Mind, a very scarce thing with me, for they may her{eaf}ter save you a great deal of trouble about me, which you do not deserve, and for which I ought to be ba[s]tinadoed. I carry all matters to an extreme—so that when I have any little vexation it grows in five Minutes into a theme for Sophocles—then and in that temper if I write to any friend I have so little selfpossession that I give him matter for grieving at the very time perhaps when I am laughing at a Pun. Your last Letter made me blush for the pain I had given you—I know my own disposition so well that I am certain of writing many times hereafter in the same strain to you—now you know how far to believe in them—you must allow for imagination—I know I shall not be able to help it. I am sorry you are grieved at my not continuing my visits to little Britain—yet I think I have as far as a Man can do who has Books to read to³ subjects to think upon—for that reason I have been no where else except to Wentworth place so nigh at hand—moreover I have been too often in a state of health that made me think it prudent no[t] to hazard the night Air—Yet further I will confess to you that I cannot enjoy Society small or numerous—I am certain that our fair friends⁴ are glad I should come for the mere sake

⁹ Pouch in the crotch of close-fitting breeches; cod = scrotum.
¹⁰ I.e., the reciting of grammatical cases.

¹ *Paradise Lost*, IV, 268–272.
² John o'Groat's—northernmost point on mainland of Scotland.
³ and.
⁴ The Reynolds sisters.

of my coming; but I am certain I bring with me a Vexation they are better without—If I can possibly at any time feel my temper coming upon me I refrain even from a promised visit. I am certain I have not a right feeling towards Women—at this moment I am striving to be just to them but I cannot—Is it because they fall so far beneath my Boyish imagination? When I was a Schoolboy I though[t] a fair Woman a pure Goddess, my mind was a soft nest in which some one of them slept though she knew it not—I have no right to expect more than their reality. I thought them etherial above Men—I find then⁵ perhaps equal—great by comparison is very small—Insult may be inflicted in more ways than by Word or action—one who is tender of being insulted does not like to think an insult against another—I do not like to think insults in a Lady's Company—I commit a Crime with her which absence would have not known—Is it not extraordinary? When among Men I have no evil thoughts, no malice, no spleen—I feel free to speak or to be silent—I can listen and from every one I can learn—my hands are in my pockets I am free from all suspicion and comfortable. When I am among Women I have evil thoughts, malice spleen—I cannot speak or be silent—I am full of Suspicions and therefore listen to no thing—I am in a hurry to be done—You must be charitable and put all this perversity to my being disappointed since Boyhood—Yet with such feelings I am happier alone among Crowds of men, by myself or with a friend or two—With all this trust me Bailey I have not the least idea that Men of different feelings and inclinations are more short sighted than myself—I never rejoiced more than at my Brother's Marriage and shall do so at that of any of my friends—. I must absolutely get over this—but how? The only way is to find the root of evil, and so cure it "with backward mutters of disseevering Power".⁶ That is a difficult thing; for an obstinate Prejudice can seldom be produced but from a gordian complication of feelings, which must take time to unravell⟨ed⟩ and care to keep unravelled—I could say a good deal about this but I will leave it in hopes of better and more worthy dispositions—and also content that I am wronging no one, for after all I do think better of Womankind than to suppose they care whether Mister John Keats five feet hight likes them or not. You appeard to wish to avoid any words on this subject—don't think it a bore my dear fellow—it shall be my Amen—I should not have consented to myself these four Months tramping in the highlands but that I thought it would give me more experience, rub off

more Prejudice, use [me] to more hardship, identify finer scenes load me with grander Mountains, and strengthen more my reach in Poetry, than would stopping at home among Books even though I should reach Homer—By this time I am comparitively a a mountaineer—I have been among wilds and Mountains too much to break out much about the[i]r Grandeur. I have fed upon Oat cake—not long enough to be very much attached to it—The first Mountains I saw, though not so large as some I have since seen, weighed very solemnly upon me. The effect is wearing away—yet I like them mainely—We have come this evening with a Guide, for without was impossible, into the middle of the Isle of Mull, pursuing our cheap journey to Iona and perhaps staffa⁷—We would not follow the common and fashionable mode from the great imposition of expense. We have come over heath and rock and river and bog to what in England would be called a horrid place—yet it belongs to a Shepherd pretty well off perhaps—The family speak not a word but gælic and we have not yet seen their faces for the smoke which after visiting every cr{a}nny, (not excepting my eyes very much incommoded for writing), finds it way out at the {door.} I am more com{f}ortable than I could have imagined in such a place, and so is Brown—The People are all very kind. We lost our way a little yesterday and enquiring at a Cottage, a yound Woman without a word threw on her cloak and walked a Mile in a missling rain and splashy way to put us right again. I could not have had a greater pleasure in these parts than your mention of my Sister—She is very much prisoned from me—I am affraid it will be some time before I can take her to many places I wish—I trust we shall see you ere long in Cumberland—at least I hope I shall before my visit to America more than once I intend to pass a whole year with George if I live to the completion of the three next—My sisters well-fare and the hopes of such a stay in America will make me observe your advice—I shall be prudent and more careful of my health than I have beeen—I hope you will be about paying your first visit to Town after settling when we come into Cumberland—Cumberland however will be no distance to me after my present journey—I shall spin to you a minute—I begin to get rather a contempt for distances. I hope you will have a nice convenient room for a Library. Now you are so well in health do keep it up by never missing your dinner, by not reading hard and by taking proper exercise. You'll have a horse I suppose so you must make a point of sweating him. You say I must study Dante—well the only Books I have with me are those

---

⁵ them.
⁶ Milton's *Comus*.

⁷ See *On Visiting Staffa*, p. 1055.

three little Volumes. I read that fine passage you mention a few days ago. Your Letter followed me from Hampstead to Port Patrick and thence to Glasgow—you must think me by this time a very pretty fellow—One of the pleasantest bouts we have had was our walk to Burns's Cottage, over the Doon and past Kirk Alloway—I had determined to write a Sonnet in the Cottage. I did but lauk it was so wretched I destroyed it—howev^r in a few days afterwards I wrote some lines cousin-german to the Circumstance which I will transcribe or rather cross scribe in the front of this—Reynolds's illness has made him a new Man—he will be stronger than ever—before I left London he was really getting a fat face—Brown keeps on writing volumes of adventures to Dilke—when we get in of an evening and I have perhaps taken my rest on a couple of Chairs he affronts my indolence and Luxury by pulling out of his knapsack 1st his paper—2^{ndy} his pens and last his ink—Now I would not care if he would change about a little—I say now, why not Bailey take out his pens first sometimes—But I might as well tell a hen to hold up her head before she drinks instead of afterwards—Your affectionate friend

John Keats—

Richard Woodhouse (1788–1834) was legal advisor to Taylor & Hessey (Keats's publishers). He made careful transcripts of many of Keats's unpublished poems, some of which are now the only surviving texts.

TO RICHARD WOODHOUSE

[27 October 1818]

My dear Woodhouse,

Your Letter gave me a great satisfaction; more on account of its friendliness, than any relish of that matter in it which is accounted so acceptable in the 'genus irritabile' The best answer I can give you is in a clerklike manner to make some observations on two principle points, which seem to point like indices into the midst of the whole pro and con, about genius, and views and atchievements and ambition and cœtera. 1st As to the poetical Character itself, (I mean that sort of which, if I am any thing, I am a Member; that sort distinguished from the wordsworthian or egotistical sublime; which is a thing per se and stands alone) it is not itself—it has no self—it is every thing and nothing—It has no character—it enjoys light and shade; it lives in gusto, be it foul or fair, high or low, rich or poor, mean or elevated—It has as much delight in conceiving an Iago as an Imogen. What shocks the virtuous philosop[h]er, delights the camelion Poet. It

does no harm from its relish of the dark side of things any more than from its taste for the bright one; because they both end in speculation. A Poet is the most unpoetical of any thing in existence; because he has no Identity—he is continually in for—and filling some other Body—The Sun, the Moon, the Sea and Men and Women who are creatures of impulse are poetical and have about them an unchangeable attribute—the poet has none; no identity—he is certainly the most unpoetical of all God's Creatures. If then he has no self, and if I am a Poet, where is the Wonder that I should say I would ⟨right⟩ write no more? Might I not at that very instant [have] been cogitating on the Characters of saturn and Ops?[1] It is a wretched thing to confess; but is a very fact that not one word I ever utter can be taken for granted as an opinion growing out of my identical nature—how can it, when I have no nature? When I am in a room with People if I ever am free from speculating on creations of my own brain, then not myself goes home to myself: but the identity of every one in the room begins to to press upon me that, I am in a very little time anhilated—not only among Men; it would be the same in a Nursery of children: I know not whether I make myself wholly understood: I hope enough so to let you see that no dependence is to be placed on what I said that day.

In the second place I will speak of my views, and of the life I purpose to myself—I am ambitious of doing the world some good: if I should be spared that may be the work of maturer years—in the interval I will assay to reach to as high a summit in Poetry as the nerve bestowed upon me will suffer. The faint conceptions I have of Poems to come brings the blood frequently into my forehead—All I hope is that I may not lose all interest in human affairs—that the solitary indifference I feel for applause even from the finest Spirits, will not blunt any acuteness of vision I may have. I do not think it will—I feel assured I should write from the mere yearning and fondness I have for the Beautiful even if my night's labours should be burnt every morning and no eye ever shine upon them. But even now I am perhaps not speaking from myself; but from some character in whose soul I now live. I am sure however that this next sentence is from myself. I feel your anxiety, good opinion and friendliness in the highest degree, and am

Your's most sincerely
John Keats

---

[1] Characters in *Hyperion.*

TO GEORGE AND GEORGIANA KEATS

[14, 16, 21, 24, 31 October 1818]

My dear George; There was a part in your Letter which gave me a great deal of pain, that where you lament not receiving Letters from England—I intended to have written immediately on my return from Scotland (which was two Months earlier than I had intended on account of my own as well as Tom's health) but then I was told by ⟨Haslam⟩ Mʳˢ W——¹ that you had said you would not wish any one to write till we had heard from you. This I thought odd and now I see that it could not have been so; yet at the time I suffered my unreflecting head to be satisfied and went on in that sort of abstract careless and restless Life with which you are well acquainted. This sentence should it give you any uneasiness do not let it last for before I finish it will be explained away to your satisfaction—

I am g[r]ieved to say that I am not sorry you had not Letters at Philadelphia; you could have had no good news of Tom and I have been withheld on his account from beginning these many days; I could not bring myself to say the truth, that he is no better, but much worse—However it must be told, and you must my dear Brother and Sister take example frome me and bear up against any Calamity for my sake as I do for your's. Our's are ties which independent of their own Sentiment are sent us by providence to prevent the deleterious effects of one great, solitary grief. I have Fanny and I have you—three people whose Happiness to me is sacred—and it does annul that selfish sorrow which I should otherwise fall into, living as I do with poor Tom who looks upon me as his only comfort—the tears will come into your Eyes—let them—and embrace each other—thank heaven for what happiness you have and after thinking a moment or two that you suffer in common with all Mankind hold it not a sin to regain your cheerfulness—I will relieve you of one uneasiness of overleaf: I retu[r]ned I said on account of my health—I am now well from a bad sore throat which came of bog trotting in the Island of Mull—of which you shall hear by the coppies I shall make from my Scotch Letters—Your content in each other is a delight to me which I cannot express—the Moon is now shining full and brilliant —she is the same to me in Matter, what you are to me in Spirit—If you were here my dear Sister I could not pronounce the words which I can write to you from a distance: I have a tenderness for you, and an admiration which I feel to be as great and more

◇◇◇◇◇◇◇◇◇◇◇◇◇◇◇◇◇◇◇◇◇◇◇◇◇◇◇◇◇◇◇◇◇◇◇◇◇◇

¹ Mrs. Wylie, Georgiania Keats's mother.

chaste than I can have for any woman in the world. You will mention Fanny—her character is not formed; her identity does not press upon me as yours does. I hope from the bottom of my heart that I may one day feel as much for her as I do for you—I know not how it is, but I have never made any acquaintance of my own—nearly all through your medium my dear Brother—through you I know not only a Sister but a glorious human being—And now I am talking of those to whom you have made me known I cannot forbear mentioning Haslam as a most kind and obliging and constant friend—His behaviour to Tom during my absence and since my return has endeared him to me for ever—besides his anxiety about you. . . . I came by ship from Inverness and was nine days at Sea without being sick—a little Qualm now and then put me in mind of you—however as soon as you touch the thore all the horrors of sick[n]ess are soon forgotten; as was the case with a Lady on board who could not hold her head up all the way. We had not been in the Thames an hour before her tongue began to some tune; paying off as it was fit she should all old scores. I was the only Englishman on board. There was a downright Scotchman who hearing that there had been a bad crop of Potatoes in England had brought some triumphant Specimens from Scotland— these he exhibited with national pride to all the Lightermen, and Watermen from the Nore to the Bridge. I fed upon beef all the way; not being able to eat the thick Porridge which the Ladies managed to manage with large awkward horn spoones into the bargain. Severn has had a narrow escape of his Life from a Typhous fever: he is now gaining strength—Reynolds has returned from a six weeks enjoyment in Devonshire, he is well and persuades me to publish my pot of Basil as an answer to the attacks made on me in Blackwood's Magazine and the Quarterly Review. There have been two Letters in my defence in the Chronicle and one in the Examiner, coppied from the Alfred Exeter paper, and written by Reynolds—I do not know who wrote those in the ⟨Quarterly⟩ Chronicle—This is a mere matter of the moment—I think I shall be among the English Poets after my death. ⟨The⟩ Even as a Matter of present interest the attempt to crush me in the ⟨Chro⟩ Quarterly has only brought me more into notice and it is a common expression among book men "I wonder the Quarterly should cut its own throat.'

It does me not the least harm in Society to make me appear little and rediculous: I know when a Man is superior to me and give him all due respect—he will be the last to laugh at me and as for the rest I feel that I make an impression upon them which insures me personal respect ⟨whic⟩ while I am in sight whatever they may say when my back is turned. . . . The Miss Reynoldses are very kind to me—but they have lately displeased me much and in this way—Now I am coming the Richardson. On my return, the first day I called they were in a sort of taking or bustle about a Cousin of theirs[2] who having fallen out with her Grandpapa in a serious manner, was invited by M^rs R—— to take Asylum in her house—She is an east indian and ought to be her Grandfather's Heir. At the time I called Mrs R. was in conference with her up stairs and the young Ladies were warm in her praises down stairs calling her genteel, interresting and a thousand other pretty things to which I gave no heed, not being partial to 9 days wonders—Now all is completely changed—they hate her, and from what I hear she is not without faults—of a real kind: but she has othe[r]s which are more apt to make women of inferior charms hate her. She is not a Cleopatra; but she is at least a Charmian.[3] She has a rich eastern look; she has fine eyes and fine manners. When she comes into a room she makes an impression the same as the Beauty of a Leopardess. She is too fine and too conscious of her Self to repulse any Man who may address her—from habit she thinks that nothing *particular*. I always find myself more at ease with such a woman; the picture before me always gives me a life and animation which I cannot possibly feel with any thing inferiour—I am at such times too much occupied in admiring to be awkward or on a tremble. I forget myself entirely because I live in her. You will by this time think I am in love with her; so before I go any further I will tell you I am not—she kept me awake one Night as a tune of Mozart's might do—I speak of the thing as a passtime and an amuzement than which I can feel none deeper than a conversation with an imperial woman the very 'yes' and 'no' of whose Lips is to me a Banquet I dont cry to take the moon home with me in my Pocket not do I fret to leave her behind me. I like her and her like because one has no *sensations*—what we both are is taken for granted—You will suppose I have by this had much talk with her—no such thing—there are the Miss Reynoldses on the look out—They think I dont admire her because I did not stare at her—They call her a flirt to me—What a want of knowledge? she walks across a room in such a manner that a Man is drawn towards her with a magnetic Power. This they call flirting! they do not know things. They do not know what a Woman is. I believe tho' she has faults—the same as Charmian and Cleopatra might have had—

Yet she is a fine thing speaking in a worldly way: for there are two distinct tempers of mind in which we judge of things—the worldly, theatrical and panto-mimical; and the unearthly, spiritual and etherial—in the former Buonaparte, Lord Byron and this Charmian hold the first place in our Minds; in the latter John Howard, Bishop Hooker rocking his child's cradle and you my dear Sister are the conquering feelings. As a Man in the world I love the rich talk of a Chariman; as an eternal Being I love the thought of you. I should like her to ruin me, and I should like you to save me. Do not think my dear Brother from this that my Passions are head long or likely to be ever of any pain to you—no

" I am free from Men of Pleasure's cares
  By dint of feelings far more deep than theirs '

This is Lord Byron,[4] and is one of the finest things he has said. . . .

[24 October].

I called on Hunt yesterday—it has been always my fate to meet Ollier there—On thursday I walked with Hazlitt as far as covent Garden: he was going to play Rackets—I think Tom has been rather better these few last days —he has been less nervous. I expect Reynolds tomorrow Since I wrote thus far I have met with that same Lady again,[5] whom I saw at Hastings and whom I met when we were going to the English Opera. It was in a street which goes from Bedford Row to Lamb's Conduit Street—I passed her and turrned back—she seemed glad of it; glad to see me and not offended at my passing her before We walked on towards Islington where we called on a friend of her's who keeps a Boarding School. She has always been an enigma to me—she has ⟨new⟩ been in a Room with you and with Reynolds and wishes we should be acquainted without any of our common acquaintance knowing it. As we went along, some times through shabby, sometimes through decent Street[s] I had my guessing at work, not knowing what it would be and prepared to meet any surprise—First it ended at this Hou{s}e at Islington: on parting from which I pressed to attend her home. She consented and then again my thoughts were at work what it might lead to, tho' now they had received a sort of genteel hint from the Boarding

---

[2] Jane Cox, daughter of Mrs. Reynolds's only brother, who lived in India.

[3] See Shakespeare's *Antony and Cleopatra*.

[4] Actually Leigh Hunt, in *The Story of Rimini*, misquoted.

[5] Mrs. Isabella Jones, who was living under the "protection" of an elderly Irishman named Donat O'Callaghan, may have been the subject of "*Hush, hush, tread Softly*" and even *Bright Star*. She certainly suggested *The Eve of St. Agnes* to Keats. A sexual liason between them has been suggested but not proven (see Gittings).

School. Our Walk ended in 34 Gloucester Street Queen Square—not exactly so for we went up stairs into her sitting room—a very tasty sort of place with Books, Pictures a bronze statue of Buonaparte, Music, æolian Harp; a Parrot a Linnet— A Case of choice Liquers &c &c &. she behaved in the kindest manner —made me take home a Grouse for Tom's dinner— Asked for my address for the purpose of sending more game—As I had warmed with her before and kissed her—I though[t] it would be living backwards not to do so again—she had a better taste: she perceived how much a thing of course it was and shrunk from it —not in a prudish way but in as I say a good taste— She cont[r]ived to disappoint me in a way which made me feel more pleasure than a simple kiss could do— she said I should please her much more if I would only press her hand and go away. Whether she was in a different disposition when I saw her before—or whether I have in fancy wrong'd her I cannot tell—I expect to pass some pleasant hours with her now and then: in which I feel I shall be of service to her in matters of knowledge and taste: if I can I will—I have no libidinous thought about her—she and your George are the only women à peu près de mon age whom I would be content to know for their mind and friend-ship alone—I shall in a short time write you as far as I know how I intend to pass my Life—I cannot think of those things now Tom is so unwell and weak. Not-withstand your Happiness and your recommendation I hope I shall never marry. Though the most beautiful Creature were waiting for me at the end of a Journey or a Walk; though the carpet were of Silk, the Cur-tains of the morning Clouds; the chairs and Sofa stuffed with Cygnet's down; the food Manna, the Wine beyond Claret, the Window opening on Win-ander mere, I should not feel—or rather my Happiness would not be so fine, a⟨nd⟩s my Solitude is sublime. Then instead of what I have described, there is a Sublimity to welcome me home—The roaring of the wind is my wife and the Stars through the window pane are my Children. The mighty abstract Idea I have of Beauty in all things stifles the more divided and minute domestic happiness—an amiable wife and sweet Children I contemplate as a part of that Bea{u}ty. but I must have a thousand of those beauti-ful particles to fill up my heart. I feel more and more every day, as my imagination strengthens, that I do not live in this world alone but in a thousand worlds— No sooner am I alone than shapes of epic greatness are stationed around me, and serve my Spirit the office ⟨of⟩ which is equivalent to a king's body guard —then 'Tragedy, with scepter'd pall, comes sweeping by" According to my state of mind I am with Achilles shouting in the Trenches or with Theocritus in the Vales of Sicily. Or I thro⟨ugh⟩w my whole being into Triolus and repeating those lines, 'I wander, like a lost soul upon the stygian Banks staying for waftage,'[6] I melt into the air with a voluptuousness so delicate than I am content to be alone—These things com-bined with the opinion I have of the generality of women—who appear to me as children to whom I would rather give a Sugar Plum than my time, form a barrier against Matrimony which I rejoice in. I have written this that you might see I have my share of the highest pleasures and that thought I may choose to pass my days alone I shall be no Solitary. You see therre is nothing spleenical in all this. The only thing that can ever affect me personally for more than one short passing day, is any doubt about my powers for poetry—I seldom have any, and I look with hope to the nighing time when I shall have none. I am as happy as a Man can be—that is in myself I should be happy if Tom was well, and I knew you were passing pleasant days—Then I should be most enviable—with the yearning Passion I have for the beautiful, connected and made one with the ambition of my in-tellect. Th[i]nk of my Pleasure in Solitude, in com-parison of my commerce with the world—there I am a child—there they do not know me not even my most intimate acquaintance—I give into their feelings as though I were refraining from irritating {a} little child —Some think me middling, others silly, others foolish —every one thinks he sees my weak side against my will; when in truth it is with my will—I am content to be thought all this because I have in my own breast so great a resource. This is one great reason why they like me so; because they can all show to advantage in a room, and eclipse from a certain tact one is reckoned to be a good Poet—I hope I am not here playing tricks 'to make the angels weep': I think not: for I have not the least contempt for my species; and though it may sound paradoxical: my greatest eleva-tions of soul leave⟨s⟩ me every time more humbled— Enough of this—though in your Love for me you will not think it enough. Haslam has been here this morn-ing, and has taken all the Letter's except this sheet, which I shall send him by the Twopenny, as he will put the Parcel in the Boston post Bag by the advice of Capper and Hazlewood, who assure him of the safety and expedition that way—the Parcel will be forwarded to Warder and thence to you all the same. There will not be a Philadelphia Ship for these six weeks—by that time I shall have another Letter to you. Mind you I mark this Letter A. By the time you will receive this you will have I trust passed through the greatest of your fatigues. As it was with your Sea

---

[6] Shakespeare's *Troilus and Cressida*, III, ii, 9-11.

sickness I shall not hear of them till they are past. Do not set to your occupation with too great an a[n]xiety —take it calmly—and let your health be the prime consideration. I hope you will have a Son, and it is one of my first wishes to have him in my Arms—which I will do please God before he cuts one double tooth. Tom is rather more easy than he has been: but is still so nervous that I can not speak to him of these Matters —indeed it is the care I have had to keep his Mind aloof from feelings too acute that has made this Letter so short a one—I did not like to write before him a Letter he knew was to reach your hands—I cannot even now ask him for any Message—his heart speaks to you—Be as happy as you can. Think of me and for my sake be cheerful. Believe me my dear Brother and sister

Your anxious and affectionate Brother
John—

This day is my Birth day—
All our friends have been anxious in their enquiries and all send their rembrances

TO GEORGE AND GEORGIANA KEATS

Letter C—   sunday Morn Feby 14—
[14, 19 February, 3 (?), 12, 13, 17, 19 March,
15, 16, 21, 30 April, 3 May 1819]

My dear Brother & Sister—How is it we have not heard from you from the Settlement yet? The Letters must surely have miscarried—I am in expectation every day—Peachey wrote me a few days ago saying some more acquaintances of his were preparing to set out for Birkbeck—therefore I shall take the opportunity of sending you what I can muster in a sheet or two—I am still at Wentworth Place—indeed I have kept in doors lately, resolved if possible to rid myself of my sore throat—consequently i have not been to see your Mother since my return from Chichester— but my absence from her has been a great weight upon me—I say since my return from Chichester—I believe I told you I was going thither—I was nearly a fortnight at Mr John Snook's and a few days at old Mr Dilke's—Nothing worth speaking of happened at either place—I took down some of the thin paper and wrote on it a little Poem call'd 'St Agnes Eve'—which you shall have as it is when I have finished the blank part of the rest for you—I went out twice at Chichester to old Dowager card parties—I see very little now, and very few Persons—being almost tired of Men and things—Brown and Dilke are very kind and considerate towards me—The Miss Reynoldses have been stoppi[n]g next door lately—but all very dull—Miss Brawne

and I have every now and then a chat and a tiff—Brown and Dilke are walking round their Garden hands in Pockets making observations. The Literary world I know nothing about—There is a Poem from Rogers dead born—and another satire is expected from Byron call'd Don Giovanni [1]. . . .

[19 February]
. . . We lead verry quiet lives here—Dilke is at present in greek histories and antiquit[i]es—and talks of nothing but the electors of Westminster and the retreat of the ten-thousand—I never drink now above three glasses of wine—and never any spirits and water. Though by the bye the other day—Woodhouse took me to his coffee house—and ordered a Bottle of Claret —now I like Claret whenever I can have Claret I must drink it.—'t is the only palate affair that I am at all sensual in—Would it not be a good Speck to send you some vine roots—could I be done? I'll enquire—If you could make some wine like Claret to d[r]ink on summer evenings in an arbour! For really 't is so fine—it fills the mouth one's mouth with a gushing freshness—then goes down cool and feverless—then you do not feel it quarelling with your liver—no it is rather a Peace maker and lies as quiet as it did in the grape—then it is as fragrant as the Queen Bee; and the more ethereal Part of it mounts into the brain, not assaulting the cerebral apartments like a bully in a bad house looking for his trul and hurrying from door to door bouncing against the waistcoat; but rather walks like Aladin about his own enchanted palace so gently that you do not feel his step—Other wines of a heavy and spirituous nature transform a Man to a Silenus; this makes him a Hermes—and gives a Woman the soul and imortality of Ariadne for whom Bacchus always kept a good cellar of claret—and even of that he could never persuade her to take above two cups—I said this same Claret is the only palate-passion I have I forgot game I must plead guilty to the breast of a Partridge, the back of a hare, the backbone of a grouse, the wing and side of a Pheasant and a Woodcock passim Talking of game (I wish I could make it) the Lady whom I met at Hastings and of whom I said something in my last I think, has lately made me many presents of game, [2] and enabled me to make as many—She made me take home a Pheasant the other day which I gave to Mrs Dilke; on which, tomorrow, Rice, Reynolds and the Wentworthians will dine next door—The next I intend for your Mother. These moderate sheets of paper are much more pleasant to write upon than those

---

[1] Samuel Rogers, *Human Life*; the first two cantos of *Don Juan* were not published (even then anonymously) until July 1819.
[2] Isabella Jones. See previous letter.

large thin sheets which I hope you by this time have received—though that cant be now I think of it—I have not said in any Letter yet a word about my affairs —in a word I am in no despair about them—my poem has not at all succeeded—in the course of a year or so I think I shall try the public again—in a selfish point of view I should suffer my pride and my contempt of public opinion to hold me silent—but for your's and fanny's sake I will pluck up a spirit, and try again—I have no doubt of success in a course of years if I persevere—but it must be patience—for the Reviews have enervated and made indolent mens minds—few think for themselves—These Reviews too are getting more and more powerful and especially the Quarterly —They are like a superstition which the more it prostrates the Crowd and the longer it continues the more powerful it becomes just in proportion to their increasing weakness—I was in hopes that when people saw, as they must do now, all the trickery and iniquity of these Plagues they would scout them, but no they are like the spectators at the Westminster cock-pit— they like the battle and do not care who wins or who looses. . . .

—this may teach them that the man who rediicules romance is the most romantic of Men—that he who abuses women and slights them—loves them the most—that he who talks of roasting a Man alive would not do it when it came to the push—and above all that they are very shallow people who take every thing literal A Man's life of any worth is a continual allegory—and very few eyes can see the Mystery of his life—a life like the scriptures, figurative—which such people can no more make out than they can the hebrew Bible. Lord Byron cuts a figure—but he is not figurative—Shakspeare led a life of Allegory; his works are the comments on it. . . .

*Friday 19*th [March]

Yesterday I got a black eye—the first time I took a Cr{icket} bat—Brown who is always one's friend in a disaster {app}lied a lee{ch to} the eyelid, and there is no infla{mm}ation this morning though the ball hit me dir{ect}ly on the sight—'t was a white ball—I am glad it was not a clout—This is the second black eye I have had since leaving school—during all my {scho}ol days I never had one at all—we must e{a}t a peck before we die—This morning I am in a sort of temper indolent and supremely careless: I long after a stanza or two of Thomson's Castle of indolence— My passions are all asleep from my having slumbered till nearly eleven and weakened the animal fibre all over me to a delightful sensation about three degrees on this side of faintness—if I had teeth of pearl and the breath of lillies I should call it langour—but as I

am + I must call it Laziness—In this state of effeminacy the fibres of the brain are relaxed in common with the rest of the body, and to such a happy degree that pleasure has no show of enticement and pain no unbearable frown. Neither Poetry, nor Ambition, nor Love have any alertness of countenance as they pass by me: they seem rather like three figures on a greek vase—a Man and two women—whom no one but myself could distinguish in their disguisement.[3] This is the only happiness; and is a rare instance of advantage in the body overpowering the Mind. I have this moment received a note from Haslam in which he expects the death of his Father who has been for some time in a state of insensibility—his mother bears up he says very well—I shall go to twon tommorrow to see him. This is the world—thus we cannot expect to give way many hours to pleasure—Circumstances are like Clouds continually gathering and bursting—While we are laughing the seed of some trouble is put into ⟨he⟩ the wide arable land of events— while we are laughing it sprouts is grows and suddenly bears a poison fruit which we must pluck—Even so we have leisure to reason on the misfortunes of our friends; our own touch us too nearly for words. Very few men have ever arrived at a complete disinterestedness of Mind: very few have been influenced by a pure desire of the benefit of others—in the greater part of the Benefactors ⟨of⟩ & to Humanity some meretricious motive has sullied their greatness—some melodramatic scenery has fascinated them—From the manner in which I feel Haslam's misfortune I perceive how far I am from any humble standard of disinterestedness— Yet this feeling ought to be carried to its highest pitch, as there is no fear of its ever injuring society—which it would do I fear pushed to an extremity—For in wild nature the Hawk would loose his Breakfast of Robins and the Robin his of Worms The Lion must starve as well as the swallow—The greater part of Men make their way with the same instinctiveness, the same unwandering eye from their purposes, the same animal eagerness as the Hawk—The Hawk wants a Mate, so does the Man—look at them both they set about it and procure on{e} in the same manner— They want both a nest and they both set about one in the same manner—they get their food in the same manner—The noble animal Man for his amusement smokes his pipe—the Hawk balances about the Clouds —that is the only difference of their leisures. This it is that makes the Amusement of Life—to a speculative Mind. I go among the Feilds and catch a glimpse

+ especially as I have a black eye

3 See *Ode on Indolence*, p. 1081.

of a stoat or a fieldmouse peeping out of the withered grass—the creature hath a purpose and its eyes are bright with it—I go amongst the buildings of a city and I see a Man hurrying along—to what? The Creature has a purpose and his eyes are bright with it. But then as Wordsworth says, "we have all one human heart"[4]—there is an ellectric fire in human nature tending to purify—so that among these human creature{s} there is continually some birth of new heroism —The pity is that we must wonder at it: as we should at finding a pearl in rubbish—I have no doubt that thousands of people never heard of have had hearts comp{l}etely disinterested: I can remember but two— Socrates and Jesus—their Histories evince it—What I heard a little time ago, Taylor observe with respect to Socrates, may be said of Jesus—That he was so great a⟨s⟩ man that though he transmitted no writing of his own to posterity, we have his Mind and his sayings and his greatness handed to us by others. It is to be lamented that the history of the latter was written and revised by Men interested in the pious frauds of Religion. Yet through all this I see his splendour. Even here though I myself am pursueing the same instinctive course as the veriest human animal you can think of—I am however young writing at random—straining at particles of light in the midst of a great darkness —without knowing the bearing of any one assertion of any one opinion. Yet may I not in this be free from sin? May there not be superior beings amused with any graceful, though instinctive attitude my mind my fall into, as I am entertained with the alertness of a Stoat or the anxiety of a Deer? Though a quarrel in the streets is a thing to be hated, the energies displayed in it are fine; the commonest Man shows a grace in his quarrel—By a superior being our reasoning{s} may take the same tone—though erroneous they may be fine—This is the very thing in which consists poetry; and if so it is not so fine a thing as philosophy—For the same reason that an eagle is not so fine a thing as a truth—Give me this credit—Do you not think I strive—to know myself? Give me this credit—and you will not think that on my own accou[n]t I repeat Milton's lines

> "How charming is divine Philosophy
> Not harsh and crabbed as dull fools suppose
> But musical as is Apollo's lute"—

No—no for myself—feeling grateful as I do to have got into a state of mind to relish them properly— Nothing ever becomes real till it is experienced—Even a Proverb is no proverb to you till your Life has illus-

[4] In *The Old Cumberland Beggar*, p. 210.

trated it—I am ever affraid that your anxiety for me will lead you to fear for the violence of my temperament continually smothered down: for that reason I did not intend to have sent you the following sonnet— but look over the two last pages and ask yourselves whether I have not that in me which will well bear the buffets of the world.

[21 April]
... The whole appears to resolve into this—that Man is originally 'a poor forked creature' subject to the same mischances as the beasts of the forest, destined to hardships and disquietude of some kind or other. If he improves by degrees his bodily accomodations and comforts—at each stage, at each accent there are waiting for him a fresh set of annoyances—he is mortal and there is still a heaven with its Stars abov{e} his head. The most interesting question that can come before us is, How far by the persevering endeavours of a seldom appearing Socrates Mankind may be made happy—I can imagine such happiness carried to an extreme— but what must it end in?—Death—and who could in such a case bear with death—the whole troubles of life which are now frittered away in a series of years, would the{n} be accumulated for the last days of a being who instead of hailing its approach, would leave this world as Eve left Paradise—But in truth I do not at all believe in this sort of perfectibility—the nature of the world will not admit of it—the inhabitants of the world will correspond to itself—Let the fish philosophise the ice away from the Rivers in winter time and they shall be at continual play in the tepid delight of summer. Look at the Poles and at the sands of Africa, Whirlpools and volcanoes—Let men exterminate them and I will say that they may arrive at earthly Happiness—The point at which Man may arrive is as far as the paralel state in inanimate nature and no further—For instance suppose a rose to have sensation, it blooms on a beautiful morning it enjoys itself—but there comes a cold wind, a hot sun—it can not escape it, it cannot destroy its annoyances—they are as native to the world as itself: no more can man be happy in spite, the world{l}y elements will prey upon his nature—The common cognomen of this world among the misguided and superstitious is 'a vale of tears' from which we are to be redeemed by a certain arbitary interposition of God and taken to Heaven. What a little circumscribe[d] straightened notion! Call the world if you Please "'The vale of Soul-making'ˣ Then you will find out the use of the world (I am speaking now in the highest terms for human nature admitting it to be immortal which I will here take for granted for the purpose of showing

a thought which has struck me concerning it) I say 'Soul making' Soul as distinguished from an Intelligence—There may be intelligences or sparks of the divinity in millions—but they are not Souls ⟨the⟩ till they acquire identities, till each one is personally itself. I{n}telligences are atoms of perception—they know and they see and they are pure, in short they are God—how then are Souls to be made? How then are these sparks which are God to have identity given them—so as ever to possess a bliss peculiar to each ones individual existence? How, but by the medium of a world like this? This point I sincerely wish to consider because I think it a grander system of salvation than the chryst⟨e⟩ain religion—or rather it is a system of Spirit-creation—This is effected by three grand materials acting the one upon the other for a series of years—These three Materials are the *Intelligence*—the *human heart* (as distinguished from intelligence or Mind) and the *World* or *Elemental space* suited for the proper action of *Mind and Heart* on each other for the purpose of forming the *Soul* or *Intelligence destined to possess the sense of Identity.* I can scarcely express what I but dimly perceive—and yet I think I perceive it—that you may judge the more clearly I will put it in the most homely form possible —I will call the *world* a School instituted for the purpose of teaching little children to read—I will call the *human heart* the *horn Book* used in that School—and I will call the *Child able to read, the Soul* made from that *school* and its *hornbook.* Do you not see how necessary a World of Pains and troubles is to school an Intelligence and make it a soul? A Place where the heart must feel and suffer in a thousand diverse ways! Not merely is the Heart a Hornbook, It is the Minds Bible, it is the Minds experience, it is the teat from which the Mind or intelligence sucks its identity—As various as the Lives of Men are—so various become their souls, and thus does God make individual beings, Souls, Identical Souls of the sparks of his own essence —This appears to me a faint sketch of a system of Salvation which does not affront our reason and humanity—I am convinced that many difficulties which christians labour under would vanish before it —There is one wh[i]ch even now Strikes me—the Salvation of Children—In them the Spark or intelligence returns to God without any identity—it having had no time to learn of, and be altered by, the heart— or seat of the human Passions—It is pretty generally suspected that the chr[i]stian scheme has been coppied from the ancient persian and greek Philosophers. Why may they not have made this simple thing even more simple for common apprehension by introducing Mediators and Personages in the same manner as in the hethen mythology abstractions are personified—

Seriously I think it probable that this System of Soulmaking—may have been the Parent of all the more palpable and personal Schemes of Redemption, among the Zoroastrians the Christians and the Hindoos. For as one part of the human species must have their carved Jupiter; so another part must have the palpable and named Mediatior and saviour, their Christ their Oromanes and their Vishnu—If what I have said should not be plain enough, as I fear it may not be, I will but you in the place where I began in this series of thoughts—I mean, I began by seeing how man was formed by circumstances—and what are circumstances?—but touchstones of his heart—? and what are touch stones?—but proovings of his hearrt?—and what are proovings of his heart but fortifiers or alterers of his nature? and what is his altered nature but his soul?—and what was his soul before it came into the world and had These provings and alterations and perfectionings?—An intelligence⟨s⟩—without Identity—and how is this Identity to be made? Through the medium of the Heart? And how is the heart to become this Medium but in a world of Circumstances?—These now I think what with Poetry and Theology you may thank your Stars that my pen is not very long winded. . . .

God bless you my dear Brother & Sister
Your ever affectionate Brother
John Keats—

To J. H. Reynolds

Winchester. Tuesday
[21 September 1819]

My dear Reynolds,
. . . The side streets here are excessively maidenlady like: the door steps always fresh from the flannel. The knockers have a staid serious, nay almost awful quietness about them.—I never saw so ⟨many⟩ quiet a collection of Lions' & Rams' heads—The doors most part black, with a little brass handle just above the keyhole, so that in Winchester a man may very quietly shut himself out of his own house. How beautiful the season is now. How fine the air. A temperate sharpness about it. Really, without joking, chaste weather—Dian skies. I never lik'd stubble fields so much as now—Aye better than the chilly green of the spring. Somehow a stubble plain looks warm—in the same way that some pictures look warm—this struck me so much in my sunday's walk that I composed upon it.[1] I hope you are better

---

[1] See *To Autumn,* p. 1090.

employed than in gaping after weather. I have been at different times so happy as not to know what weather it was—No I will not copy a parcel of verses. I always somehow associate Chatterton with autumn. He is the purest writer in the English Language. He has no French idiom, or particles like Chaucer⟨s⟩—'tis genuine English Idiom in English words. I have given up Hyperion—there were too many Miltonic inversions in it—Miltonic verse cannot be written but in an artful or rather artist's humour. I wish to give myself up to other sensations. English ought to be kept up. . . . I would give a guinea to be a reasonable man—good sound sense—a says what he thinks, and does what he says man—and did not take snuff— They say men near death however mad they may have been, come to their senses—I hope I shall here in this letter—there is a decent space to be very sensible in—many a good proverb has been in less— Nay I have heard of the statutes at large being chang'd into the Statutes at Small and printed for a watch paper. Your sisters by this time must have got the Devonshire ees—short ees—you know 'em—they are the prettiest ees in the Language. O how I admire the middle siz'd delicate Devonshire girls of about 15. There was one at an Inn door holding a quartern of brandy—the very thought of her kept me warm a whole stage—and a 16 miler too—"You'll pardon me for being jocular."

Ever your affectionate friend
John Keats—

TO GEORGE AND GEORGIANA KEATS

Winchester Septr Friday—
[17, 18, 20, 21, 24, 25, 27 September 1819]

My dear George,

. . . We are certainly in a very low estate: I say we, for I am in such a situation that were it not for the assistance of Brown & Taylor, I must be as badly off as a Man can be. I could not raise any sum by the promise of any Poem—no, not by the mortgage of my intellect. We must wait a little while. I really have hopes of success. I have finish'd a Tragedy which if it succeeds will enable me to sell what I may have in manuscript to a good avantage. I have pass'd my time in reading, writing and fretting—the last I intend to give up and stick to the other two. They are the only chances of benefit to us. Your wants will be a fresh spur to me. I assure you you shall more than share what I can get, whilst I am still young—the time may come when age will make me more selfish.

I have not been well treated by the world—and yet I have capitally well—I do not know a Person to whom so many purse strings would fly open as to me—if I could possibly take advantage of them— which I cannot do for none of the owners of these purses are rich—Your present situation I will not suffer myself to dwell upon—when misfortunes are so real we are glad enough to escape them, and the thought of them. I cannot help thinking Mr Audubon a dishonest man[1]—Why did he make you believe that he was a Man of Property? How is it his circumstances have altered so suddenly? In truth I do not believe you fit to deal with the world; or at least the american worrld. . . .

Saturday—
[18 September]

With my inconstant disposition it is no wonder that this morning, amid all our bad times and misfortunes, I should feel so alert and well spirited. At this moment you are perhaps in a very different state of Mind. It is because my hopes are very paramount to my despair. I have been reading over a part of a short poem I have composed lately call'd 'Lamia'—and I am certain there is that sort of fire in it which must take hold of people in some way—give them either pleasant or unpleasant sensation. What they want is a sensation of some sort. I wish I could pitch the key of your spirits as high as mine is—but your organ loft is beyond the reach of my voice—I admire the exact admeasurement of my niece in your Mother's letter—O the little span long elf—I am not in the least judge of the proper weight and size of an infant. Never trouble yourselves about that: she is sure to be a fine woman—Let her have only delicate nails both on hands and feet and teeth as small as a May-fly's. who will live you his life on a square inch of oak-leaf. And nails she must have quite different from the market women here who plough into the butter and make a quatter pound taste of it. I intend to w[r]ite a letter to you Wifie and there I may say more on this little plump subject—I hope she's plump—'Still harping on my daughter'—This Winchester is a place tolerably well suited to me; there is a fine Cathedral, a College, a Roman-Catholic Chapel, a Methodist do, an independent do,—and there is not one loom or any thing like manufacturing

---

[1] The naturalist John James Audubon (1785–1857) persuaded George Keats to invest all his money in a boat to carry freight down the Ohio and Mississippi rivers. The boat had already sunk when George gave up his money, and he was convinced that Audubon had cheated him. Shortly thereafter Audubon declared himself bankrupt, and began making paintings of birds.

beyond bread & butter in the whole City. There are a number of rich Catholic[s] in the place. It is a respectable, ancient aristocratical place—and moreover it contains a nunnery.... When I left Mr Abbey on monday evening I walk'd up Cheapside but returned to put some letters in the Post and met him again in Bucklersbury: we walk'd together th[r]ough the Poultry as far as the hatter's shop he has some concern in—He spoke of it in such a way to me, I though[t] he wanted me to make an offer to assist him in it. I do believe if I could be a hatter I might be one. He seems anxious about me. He began blowing up Lord Byron while I was sitting with him, however Says he the fellow says true things now & then; at which he took up a Magasine and read me some extracts from Don Juan, (Lord Byron's last flash poem) and particularly one against literary ambition.[2] I do think I must be well spoken of among sets, for Hodgkinson is more than polite, and the coffee-german endeavour'd to be very close to me the other night at covent garden where I went at half-price before I tumbled into bed—Every one however distant an acquaintance behaves in the most conciliating manner to me—You will see I speak of this as a matter of interest. On the next Street I will give you a little politics. In every age there has been in England for some two or th[r]ee centuries subjects of great popular interest on the carpet: so that however great the uproar one can scarcely prophesy any material change in the government; for as loud disturbances have agitated this country many times. All civiled countries become gradually more enlighten'd and there should be a continual change for the better. Look at this Country at present and remember it when it was even though[t] impious to doubt the justice of a trial by Combat—From that time there has been a gradual change—Three great changes have been in progress—First for the better, next for the worse, and a third time for the better once more. The first was the gradual annihilation of the tyranny of the nobles. when kings found it their interest to conciliate the common people, elevate them and be just to them. Just when baronial Power ceased and before standing armies were so dangerous, Taxes were few. kings were lifted by the people over the heads of their nobles, and those people held a rod over kings. The change for the worse in Europe was again this. The obligation of kings to the Multitude began to be ˙ forgotten—Custom had made noblemen the humble servants of kings—Then kings turned to the Nobles as the adorners of the[i]r

power, the slaves of it, and from the people as creatures continually endeavouring to check them. Then in every kingdom therre was a long struggle of kings to destroy all popular privileges. The english were the only people in europe who made a grand kick at this. They were slaves to Henry 8th but were freemen under william 3rd at the time the french were abject slaves under Lewis 14th The example of England, and the liberal writers of france and england sowed the seed of opposition to this Tyranny—and it was swelling in the ground till it burst out in the french revolution—That has had an unlucky termination. It put a stop to the rapid progress of free sentiments in England; and gave our Court hopes of turning back to the despotism of the 16 century. They have made a handle of this event in every way to undermine our freedom. They spread a horrid superstition against all inovation and improvement —The present struggle in England of the people is to destroy this superstition.[3] What has rous'd them to do it is their distresses—Perhaps on this account the pres'ent distresses of this nation are a fortunate thing —tho so horrid in the[i]r experience. You will see I mean that the french Revolution put a temporry stop to this third change, the change for the better— Now it is in progress again and I thing in an effectual one. This is no contest beetween whig and tory—but between right and wrong. There is scarcely a grain of party spirit now in England—Right and Wrong considered by each man abstractedly is the fashion. I know very little of these things. I am convinced however that apparently small causes make great alterations. There are little signs wherby we may know how matters are going on—This makes the business about Carlisle the Bookseller of great moment in my mind. He has been selling deistical pamphlets, republished Tom Payne and many other works held in superstitious horror. He even has been selling for some time immense numbers of a work call 'The Deist' which comes out in weekly numbers—For this Conduct he I think has had above a dozen ⟨Prosecutions⟩ inditements issued against him; for which he has found Bail to the amount of many thousand Pounds—After all they are affraid to prosecute: they are affraid of his defence: it ⟨will⟩ would be published in all the papers all over the Empire: they shudder at this: the Trials would light a flame they could not extinguish. . . .

---

[2] Canto I, stanza 218.

[3] Keats has in mind, among other events, the Peterloo Massacre at Manchester which occurred just a month before, and is mentioned later in this letter. See Shelley's *The Mask of Anarchy*, p. 886.

[21 September]

... 'T is best to meet present misfortunes; not for a momentary good to sacrifice great benefits which one's own untramell'd and free industry may bring one in the end. In all this do never think of me as in any way unhappy: I shall not be so. I have a great pleasure in thinking of my responsibility to you and shall do myself the greatest luxury if I can succeed in any way so as to be of assistance to you. We shall look back upon these times—even before our eyes are at all dim—I am convinced of it. But be careful of those Americans—I could almost advise you to come whenever you have the sum of 500£ to England —Those Americans will I am affraid still fleece you— If ever you should think of such a thing you must bear in mind the very different state of society here— The immense difficulties of the times—The great sum required per annum to maintain yourself in any decency. In fact the whole is with Providence. I know now how to advise you but by advising you to advise with yourself. In your next tell me at large your thoughts, about america; what chance there is of succeeding there: for it appears to me you have as yet been somehow deceived. I cannot help thinking Mr Audubon has deceived you. I shall not like the sight of him—I shall endeavour to avoid seeing him— You see how puzzled I am—I have no meridian to fix you to—being the Slave of what is to happen. I think I may bid you finally remain in good hopes: and not teise yourself with my changes and variations of Mind—If I say nothing decisive in any one parti-cular part of my Letter. you may glean the truth from the whole pretty correctly—You may wonder why I had not put your affairs with Abbey in train on receiving your Letter before last, to which there will reach you a short answer dated from shanklin. I did write and speak to Abbey but to no purpose. You last, with the enclosed note has appealed home to him—He will not see the necessity of a thing till he is hit in the mouth. 'T will be effectual—I am sorry to mix up foolish and serious things together—but in writing so much I am obliged to do so—and I hope sincerely the tenor of your mind will maintain itself better. In the course of a few months I shall be as good an Italian Scholar as I am a french one—I am reading Ariosto at present: not manageing more than six or eight stanzas at a time. When I have done this language so as to be able to read it tolerably well—I shall set myself to get complete in latin and there my learning must stop. I do not think of venturing upon Greek. I would not go even so far if I were not per-suaded of the power the knowledge of any language gives one. the fact is I like to be acquainted with foreign languages. It is besides a nice way of filling up intervals &c Also the reading of Dante in well worth the while. And in latin there is a fund of curious literature of the middle ages—The Works of many great Men Aretine and Sanazarius and Machievel—I shall never become attach'd to a foreign idiom so as to put it into my writings. The Paradise lost though so fine in itself is a curruption of our Language—it should be kept as it is unique—a curiosity. a beautiful and grand Curiosity. The most remarkable Production of the world—A northern dialect accommodating itself to greek and latin inversions and intonations. The purest english I think—or what ought to be the purest—is Chatterton's—The Language had existed long enough to be entirely uncorrupted of Chaucer's gallicisms and still the old words are used—Chatter-ton's language is entirely northern—I prefer the native music of it to Milton's cut by feet I have but lately stood on my guard against Milton. Life to him would be death to me. Miltonic verse cannot be written but it the vein of art—I wish to devote myself to another sensation. . . .

     Believe me my dear Brother and Sister
       Your affectionate and anxious Brother

TO FANNY BRAWNE

Great Smith Street
Tuesday Morn
[19 October 1819]

My sweet Fanny,

     On awakening from my three days dream ("I cry to dream again")[1] I find one and another astonish'd at my idleness and thoughtlessness—I was miserable last night—the morning is always restorative—I must be busy, or try to be so. I have several things to speak to you of tomorrow morning. Mrs Dilke I should think will tell you that I purpose living at Hampstead—I must impose chains upon myself—I shall be able to do nothing—I shold like to cast the die for Love or death—I have no Patience with any thing else—if you ever intend to be cruel to me as you say in jest now but perhaps may sometimes be in earnest be so now—and I will—my mind is in a tremble, I cannot tell what I am writing.

Ever my love yours
John Keats

---

[1] *The Tempest*, III, ii, 151.

To Fanny Brawne

[March (?) 1820]

Sweetest Fanny,

You fear, sometimes, I do not love you so much as you wish? My dear Girl I love you ever and ever and without reserve. The more I have known you the more have I lov'd. In every way—even my jealousies have been agonies of Love, in the hottest fit I ever had I would have died for you. I have vex'd you too much. But for Love! Can I help it? You are always new. The last of your kisses was ever the sweetest; the last smile the brightest; the last movement the gracefullest. When you pass'd my window home yesterday, I was fill'd with as much admiration as if I had then seen you for the first time. You uttered a half complaint once that I only lov'd your Beauty. Have I nothing else then to love in you but that? Do not I see a heart naturally furnish'd with wings imprison itself with me? No ill prospect has been able to turn your thoughts a moment from me. This perhaps should be as much a subject of sorrow as joy—but I will not talk of that. Even if you did not love me I could not help an entire devotion to you: how much more deeply then must I feel for you knowing you love me. My Mind has been the most discontented and restless one that ever was put into a body too small for it. I never felt my Mind repose upon anything with complete and undistracted enjoyment—upon no person but you. When you are in the room my thoughts never fly out of window: you always concentrate my whole senses. The anxiety shown about our Loves in your last note is an immense pleasure to me: however you must not suffer such speculations to molest you any more: nor will I any more believe you can have the least pique against me. Brown is gone out—but here is Mrs. Wylie—when she is gone I shall be awake for you.—Remembrances to your Mother.

Your affectionate
J. Keats.

To Fanny Brawne

[March (?) 1820]

My dearest Girl,

In consequence of our company I suppose I shall not see you before tomorrow. I am much better to day—indeed all I have to complain of is want of strength and a little tightness in the Chest. I envied Sam's walk with you to day; which I will not do again as I may get very tired of envying. I imagine you now sitting in your new black dress which I like so much and if I were a little less selfish and more enthousiastic I should run round and surprise you with a knock at the door.[1] I fear I am too prudent for a dying kind of Lover.—Yet, there is a great difference between going off in warm blood like Romeo, and making one's exit like a frog in a frost—I had nothing particular to say to day, but not intending that there shall be any interruption to our correspondence (which at some future time. I propose offering to Murray)[2] I write something! God bless you my sweet Love! Illness is a long lane, but I see you at the end of it, and shall mend my pace as well as possible

J—K

To Fanny Brawne

Wednesday Morng.
[5 July (?) 1820]

My dearest Girl,

I have been a walk this morning with a book in my hand, but as usual I have been occupied with nothing but you: I wish I could say in an agreeable manner. I am tormented day and night. They talk of my going to Italy. 'Tis certain I shall never recover if I am to be so long separate from you: yet with all this devotion to you I cannot persuade myself into any confidence of you. Past experience connected with the fact of my long separation from you gives me agonies which are scarcely to be talked of. When your mother comes I shall be very sudden and expert in asking her whether you have been to Mrs. Dilke's, for she might say no to make me easy. I am literally worn to death, which seems my only recourse. I cannot forget what has pass'd. What? nothing with a man of the world, but to me deathful. I will get rid of this as much as possible. When you were in the habit of flirting with Brown you would have left off, could your own heart have felt one half of one pang mine did. Brown is a good sort of Man—he did not know he was doing me to death by inches. I feel the effect of every one of those hours in my side now; and for that cause, though he has done me many services, though I know his love and friendship for me, though at this moment I should be without pence were it not for his assistance, I will never see or speak to him until we are both old men, if we are to

---

[1] Fanny Brawne and her mother lived in the other half of the house in Hampstead.
[2] Byron's publisher.

be. I *will* resent my heart having been made a football. You will call this madness. I have heard you say that it was not unpleasant to wait a few years—you have amusements—your mind is away—you have not brooded over one idea as I have, and how should you? You are to me an object intensely desireable— the air I breathe in a room empty of you is unhealthy. I am not the same to you—no—you can wait—you have a thousand activities—you can be happy without me. Any party, any thing to fill up the day has been enough. How have you pass'd this month? Who have you smil'd with? All this may seem savage in me. You do not feel as I do—you do not know what it is to love—one day you may—your time is not come. Ask yourself how many unhappy hours Keats has caused you in Loneliness. For myself I have been a Martyr the whole time, and for this reason I speak; the confession is forc'd from me by the torture. I appeal to you by the blood of that Christ you believe in: Do not write to me if you have done anything this month which it would have pained me to have seen. You may have altered—if you have not—if you still behave in dancing rooms and other societies as I have seen you—I do not want to live—if you have done so I wish this coming night may be my last. I cannot live without you, and not only you but *chaste you; virtuous you.* The Sun rises and sets, the day passes, and you follow the bent of your inclination to a certain extent—you have no conception of the quantity of miserable feeling that passes through me in a day.—Be serious! Love is not a plaything—and again do not write unless you can do it with a crystal conscience. I would sooner die for want of you than—

Yours for ever
J. Keats.

To Fanny Brawne

[August (?) 1820]

I do not write this till the last, that no eye may catch it.

My dearest Girl,

I wish you could invent some means to make me at all happy without you. Every hour I am more and more concentrated in you; every thing else tastes like chaff in my Mouth. I feel it almost impossible to go to Italy—the fact is I cannot leave you, and shall never taste one minute's content until it pleases chance to let me live with you for good. But I will not go on at this rate. A person in health as you are can have no conception of the horrors that nerves and a temper like mine go through. What Island do your friends propose retiring to? I should be happy to go with you there alone, but in company I should object to it; the backbitings and jealousies of new colonists who have nothing else to amuse them selves, is unbearable. Mr Dilke came to see me yesterday, and gave me a very great deal more pain than pleasure. I shall never be able any more to endure to society of any of those who used to meet at Elm Cottage and Wentworth Place. The last two years taste like brass upon my Palate. If I cannot live with you I will live alone. I do not think my health will improve much while I am separated from you. For all this I am averse to seeing you—I cannot bear flashes of light and return into my glooms again. I am not so unhappy now as I should be if I had seen you yesterday. To be happy with you seems such an impossibility! it requires a luckier Star than mine! it will never be. I enclose a passage from one of your Letters which I want you to alter a little—I want (if you will have it so) the matter express'd less coldly to me. If my health would bear it, I could write a Poem[1] which I have in my head, which would be a consolation for people in such a situation as mine. I would show some one in Love as I am, with a person living in such Liberty as you do. Shakspeare always sums up matters in the most sovereign manner. Hamlet's heart was full of such Misery as mine is when he said to Ophelia "Go to a Nunnery, go go!" Indeed I should like to give up the matter at once—I should like to die. I am sickened at the brute world which you are smiling with. I hate men and women more. I see nothing but thorns for the future— wherever I may be next winter in Italy or nowhere Brown will be living near you with his indecencies—I see no prospect of any rest. Suppose me in Rome— well, I should there see you as in a magic glass going to and from town at all hours,

I wish you could infuse a little confidence in human nature into my heart. I cannot muster any— the world is too brutal for me—I am glad there is such a thing as the grave—I am sure I shall never have any rest till I get there At any rate I will indulge myself by never seeing any more Dilke or Brown or any of their Friends. I wish I was either in your a[r]ms full of faith or that a Thunder bolt would strike me.

God bless you—J. K—

---

[1] Perhaps the *Ode to Fanny*, p. 1100. This is probably Keats's last letter to Fanny.

TO PERCY BYSSHE SHELLEY

Hampstead August 16th [1820]

My dear Shelley,

I am very much gratified that you, in a foreign country, and with a mind almost over occupied, should write to me in the strain of the Letter beside me.[1] If I do not take advantage of your invitation it will be prevented by a circumstance I have very much at heart to prophesy—There is no doubt that an english winter would put an end to me, and do so in a lingering hateful manner, therefore I must either voyage or journey to Italy as a soldier marches up to a battery. My nerves at present are the worst part of me, yet they feel soothed when I think that come what extreme may, I shall not be destined to remain in one spot long enough to take a hatred of any four particular bed-posts. I am glad you take any pleasure in my poor Poem;—which I would willingly take the trouble to unwrite, if possible, did I care so much as I have done about Reputation. I received a copy of the Cenci, as from yourself from Hunt. There is only one part of it I am judge of; the Poetry, and dramatic effect, which by many spirits now a days is considered the mammon. A modern work it is said must have a purpose, which may be the God—*an artist* must serve Mammon—he must have "self concentration," selfishness perhaps. You I am sure will forgive me for sincerely remarking that you might curb your magnanimity and be more of an artist, and 'load every rift' of your subject with ore. The thought of such discipline must fall like cold chains upon you, who perhaps never sat with your wings furl'd for six Months together. And is not this extraordina[r]y talk for the writer of Endymion? whose mind was like a pack of scattered cards—I am pick'd up and sorted to a pip. My Imagination is a Monastry and I am its Monk—you must explain my metap[hysics] to yourself. I am in expectation of Prometheus every day. Could I have my own wish for its interest effected you would have it still in manuscript—or be but now putting an end to the second act. I remember you advising me not to publish my first-blights, on Hampstead heath—I am returning advice upon your hands. Most of the Poems in the volume I send you have been written above two years, and would never have been publish'd but from a hope of gain; so you see I am inclined enough to take your advice now. I must exp[r]ess once more my deep sense of your

kindness, adding my sincere thanks and respects for Mrs Shelley. In the hope of soon seeing you [I] remain

most sincerely yours
John Keats—

TO CHARLES BROWN

Rome. 30 November 1820.

My dear Brown,

'Tis the most difficult thing in the world ⟨for⟩ to me to write a letter. My stomach continues so bad, that I feel it worse on opening any book,—yet I am much better than I was in Quarantine. Then I am afraid to encounter the proing and conning of any thing interesting to me in England. I have an habitual feeling of my real life having past, and that I am leading a posthumous existence. God knows how it would have been—but it appears to me—however, I will not speak of that subject. I must have been at Bedhampton nearly at the time you were writing to me from Chichester—how unfortunate—and to pass on the river too! There was my star predominant! I cannot answer any thing in your letter, which followed me from Naples to Rome, because I am afraid to look it over again. I am so weak (in mind) that I cannot bear the sight of any hand writing of a friend I love so much as I do you. Yet I ride the little horse,—and, at my worst, even in Quarantine, summoned up more puns, in a sort of desperation, in one week than in any year of my life. There is one thought enough to kill me—I have been well, healthy, alert &c, walking with her—and now—the knowledge of contrast, feeling for light and shade, all that information (primitive sense) necessary for a poem are great enemies to the recovery of the stomach. There, you rogue, I put you to the torture,—but you must bring your philosophy to bear—as I do mine, really—or how should I be able to live? Dr Clarke is very attentive to me; he says, there is very little the matter with my lungs, but my stomach, he says, is very bad. I am well disappointed in hearing good news from George,—for it runs in my head we shall all die young. I have not written to X X X X X[1] yet, which he must think very neglectful; being anxious to send him a good account of my health, I have delayed it from week to week. If I recover, I will do all in my power to correct the mistakes made during sickness; and if I should not, all my faults will

---

[1] Shelley had written from Italy asking him to stay with the Shelleys, suggesting he avoid France ("not worth seeing"), praising *Endymion* moderately, and recommending his own *Prometheus Unbound* and *The Cenci*. Keats did not live to see Shelley in Italy.

[1] Since no manuscript copies of the letter exist, the names have never been discovered (Brown removed them in printing the letter in his *Life of Keats*).

be forgiven. I shall write to x x x to-morrow, or next day. I will write to x x x x x in the middle of next week. Severn is very well, though he leads so dull a life with me. Remember me to all friends, and tell x x x x I should not have left London without taking leave of him. but from being so low in body and mind. Write to George as soon as you receive this, and tell him how I am, as far as you can guess—and also a note to my sister—who walks about my imagination like a ghost—she is so like Tom. I can scarcely bid you good bye even in a letter. I always made an awkward bow.

God bless you!

John Keats.

GENERAL BIBLIOGRAPHY

Limited to works concerning more than one poet, or their period, published after 1950.

BIBLIOGRAPHICAL INFORMATION

The English Romantic Poets: A Review of Research, ed. T. G. Raysor (1956).
The English Romantic Poets and Essayists: A Review of Research and Criticism, ed. C. W. and
    L. H. Houtchens (1957; rev. 1966).
Romantic Poets and Prose Writers, ed. R. H. Fogle (1967).
Philological Quarterly: annual bibliography to 1964.
English Language Notes: annual bibliography since 1964.
New Cambridge Bibliography of English Literature, Vol. III (1969).

LITERARY, SOCIAL, OR POLITICAL HISTORY

M. H. ABRAMS, *The Mirror and the Lamp: Romantic Theory and the Critical Tradition*
    (1953).
R. ALTICK, *The English Common Reader* (1956).
P. M. BALL, *The Central Self: A Study in Romantic and Victorian Imagination* (1969).
G. BOAS, "The Romantic Self: An Historical Sketch," *Studies in Romanticism* (1964).
J. T. BOULTON, *The Language of Politics in the Age of Wilkes and Burke* (1963).
E. H. GOMBRICH, *Art and Illusion* (1956).
R. W. HARRIS, *Romanticism and the Social Order 1780–1830* (1969).
E. J. HOBSBAWM, *The Age of Revolution: Europe 1798–1848* (1962).
I. JACK, *English Literature 1815–1832* (1963).
M. NICOLSON, *Mountain Gloom and Mountain Glory: The Development of the Aesthetics of
    the Infinite* (1959).
P. QUENNELL, *Romantic England: Writing and Painting 1717–1851* (1970).
F. L. RENWICK, *English Literature 1789–1815* (1963).
E. P. THOMPSON, *The Making of the English Working Class* (1963).
L. M. TRAWICK, ed., *Backgrounds of Romanticism* (1967).
R. WILLIAMS, *Culture and Society: 1780–1950* (1958).
C. WOODRING, *Politics in English Romantic Poetry* (1971).

LITERARY CRITICISM

M. H. ABRAMS, ed., *English Romantic Poets: Modern Essays in Criticism* (1960).
——, *Natural Supernaturalism* (1971).
J. BENZIGER, *Images of Eternity* (1962).
H. BLOOM, *The Visionary Company: A Reading of English Romantic Poetry* (1961; rev. 1971).
——, ed., *Romanticism and Consciousness: Essays in Criticism* (1970).
E. E. BOSTETTER, *The Romantic Ventriloquists* (1963).
I. H. CHAYES, "Rhetoric as Drama: An Approach to the Romantic Ode," *PMLA* (1964).
H. S. DAVIES, *The Poets and Their Critics: II. Blake to Browning* (1962).
W. P. ELLEDGE and R. L. HOFFMAN, eds., *Romantic and Victorian: Studies in Memory
    of William H. Marshall* (1971).
G. ENSCOE, *Eros and the Romantics: Sexual Love as a Theme in Coleridge, Shelley and Keats*
    (1968).
R. A. FOAKES, *Romantic Criticism: 1800–1850* (1968).
N. FRYE, ed., *Romanticism Reconsidered: Selected Papers from the English Institute* (1963).
——, *Fables of Identity: Studies in Poetic Mythology* (1963).
——, *A Study of English Romanticism* (1968).
L. R. FURST, *Romanticism in Perspective* (1969).

A. S. GERARD, *English Romantic Poetry: Ethos, Structure and Symbol in Coleridge, Wordsworth, Shelley and Keats* (1968).

J. O. HAYDEN, *The Romantic Reviewers, 1802–1824* (1969).

A. HAYTER, *Opium and the Romantic Imagination* (1968).

F. W. HILLES and H. BLOOM, eds., *From Sensibility to Romanticism: Essays Presented to Frederick A. Pottle* (1965).

P. HODGART and T. REDPATH, eds., *Romantic Perspectives: The Work of Crabbe, Blake, Wordsworth, and Coleridge as Seen by Their Contemporaries and by Themselves* (1964).

K. KROEBER, *Romantic Narrative Art* (1960).

——, *The Artifice of Reality: Public Style in Wordsworth, Foscolo, Keats and Leopardi* (1964).

S. K. KUMAR, ed., *British Romantic Poets: Recent Revaluations* (1966).

J. V. LOGAN, J. E. JORDAN, and N. FRYE, eds., *Some British Romantics: A Collection of Essays* (1966).

D. PERKINS, *The Quest for Permanence: The Symbolism of Wordsworth, Shelley and Keats* (1959).

A. THORLBY, ed., *The Romantic Movement* (1967).

W. WALSH, *The Use of Imagination: Educational Thought and the Literary Mind* (1959).

E. WASSERMAN, *The Subtler Language* (1959).

——, "The English Romantics: The Grounds of Knowledge," *Studies in Romanticism* (1964).

B. WILKIE, *Romantic Poets and Epic Tradition* (1965).

INDEX OF TITLES

O

P

INDEX OF FIRST LINES

A

A bird who for his other sins, 500
A flower was offered to me, 56
A glorious people vibrated again, 913
A green and silent spot, amid the hills, 467
A hater he came and sat by a ditch, 809
A little black thing among the snow, 55
A lovely form there sate beside my bed, 502
A Sensitive Plant in a garden grew, 906
A simple child, dear brother Jim, 187
A slumber did my spirit seal, 227
A sworded man whose trade is blood, 495
A thing of beauty is a joy for ever, 1026
After dark vapours have oppress'd our plains, 1022
Ah Sun-flower! weary of time, 57
Ah! who can e'er forget so fair a being? 1002
All gentle folks who owe a grudge, 1054
All look and likeness caught from earth, 494
All Nature seems at work. Slugs leave their lair—, 500
All the night in woe, 55
All thoughts, all passions, all delights, 479
Amid the smoke of cities did you pass, 247
Among all lovely things my Love had been, 260
An old, mad, blind, despised, and dying king, 905
An Ox, long fed with musty hay, 475
And did those feet in ancient time, 88
And is this—Yarrow?—*This* the Stream, 389
And Los & Enitharmon builded Jerusalem weeping, 67
And Peter Bell, when he had been, 893
And thou wert sad—yet I was not with thee, 602
And what is love? It is a doll dress'd up, 1057
Are there two things, of all which men possess, 481
Arethusa arose, 916
ARIEL to *MIRANDA*: Take, 964
Art thou a Statist in the van, 230
Art thou pale for weariness, 943
As from the darkening gloom a silver dove, 1000
As from their ancestral oak, 905
As I lay asleep in Italy, 886
As late I lay in Slumber's shadowy vale, 434
As late I rambled in the happy fields, 1009
As the Liberty lads o'er the sea, 602
As when far off the warbled strains are heard, 434
At midnight by the stream I roved, 466
At the corner of Wood Street, when daylight appears, 209
Away! the moor is dark beneath the moon, 786
Away with your fictions of flimsy romance, 537

B

Bards of Passion and of Mirth, 1059
Before I see another day, 201
Before those cruel Twins, whom at one birth, 923
Behold her, single in the field, 361
Behold, within the leafy shade, 262
Beneath yon birch with silver bark, 473
Best and brightest, come away, 963
Blue! 'Tis the life of heaven,—the domain, 1042
Bob Southey! You're a poet—Poet-laureate, 651
Bright star! would I were steadfast as thou art—, 1099
Brothers! between you and me, 784
By Derwent's side my Father's cottage stood, 180
Byron! how sweetly sad thy melody! 1000

C

Can I see anothers woe, 22
Cat! who hast past thy Grand Climacteric, 1038
Chameleons feed on light and air, 910
Chief of organic numbers! 1038
Children of the future Age, 58
Clouds, lingering yet, extend in solid bars, 365
Come hither all sweet maidens soberly, 1025
Come hither my sparrows, 40
Cruelty has a Human Heart, 60

D

Darkness surrounds us; seeking, we are lost, 393
Dar'st thou amid the varied multitude, 781
Daughters of Beulah! Muses who inspire the Poets Song, 88
Dear Child of Nature, let them rail! 255
Dear Mother, dear Mother, the Church is cold, 57
Dear native Brook! wild Streamlet of the West, 431
Dear Reynolds, as last night I lay in bed, 1043
Death, where is thy victory! 782
Deep in the shady sadness of a vale, 1060
Does the Eagle know what is in the pit? 23
Doubtless, sweet Girl! the hissing lead, 536

E

Earth has not anything to show more fair, 267
Earth, ocean, air, belovèd brotherhood! 790
Earth raised up her head, 53

[1135]